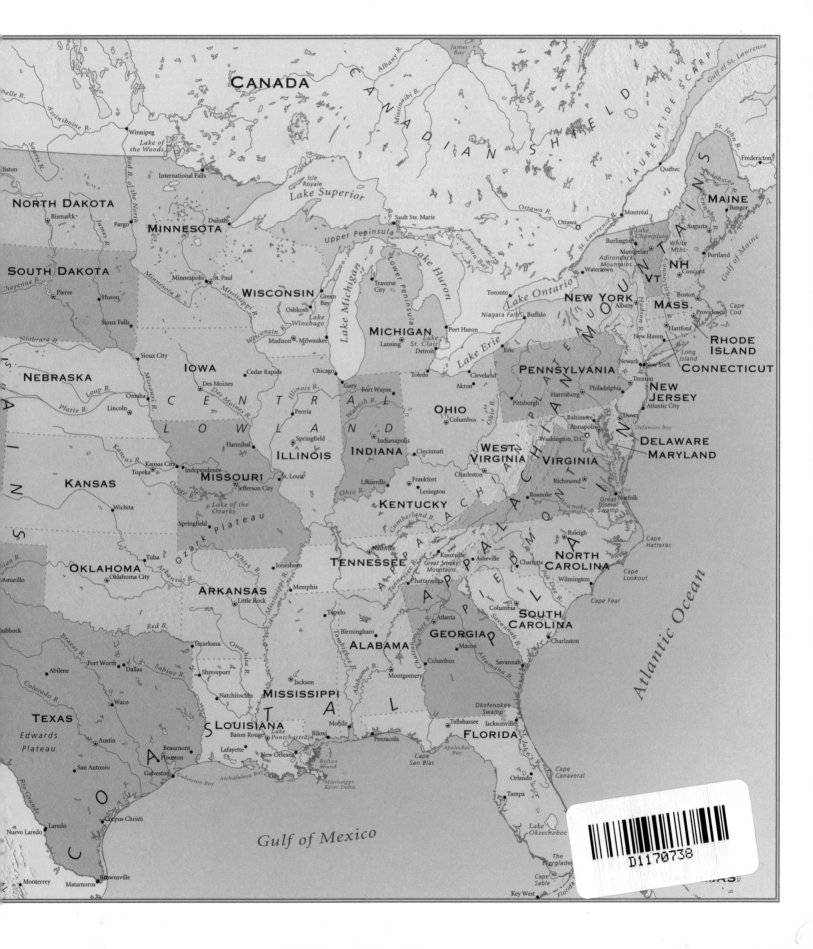

# INVENTING AMERICA

## SECOND EDITION

# Inventing America

## A HISTORY OF THE UNITED STATES

SECOND EDITION

PAULINE MAIER

MERRITT ROE SMITH

ALEXANDER KEYSSAR

DANIEL J. KEVLES

W. W. NORTON & COMPANY

NEW YORK  LONDON

W. W. Norton & Company has been independent since its founding in 1923, when William Warder Norton and Mary D. Herter Norton first published lectures delivered at the People's Institute, the adult education division of New York City's Cooper Union. The Nortons soon expanded their program beyond the Institute, publishing books by celebrated academics from America and abroad. By mid-century, the two major pillars of Norton's publishing program—trade books and college texts—were firmly established. In the 1950s, the Norton family transferred control of the company to its employees, and today—with a staff of four hundred and a comparable number of trade, college, and professional titles published each year—W. W. Norton & Company stands as the largest and oldest publishing house owned wholly by its employees.

Composition by GGS Book Services, Inc.
Cartography by maps.com
Manufacturing by R. R. Donnelley—Willard Division

Editor: Steve Forman
emedia editor: Steve Hoge
Project editor: Thomas Foley
Photo researcher: Stephanie Romeo
Editorial assistants: Sarah England and Rebecca Arata
Manuscript editor: Alice Vigliani
Manuscript editor for the First Edition: Susan Gaustad
First Edition book design by Joan Greenfield
Book design adapted for the Second Edition by Paul Lacy
Cover design: Andrew M. Newman Graphic Design

The Library of Congress has cataloged the one-volume edition as follows:

Inventing America: a history of the United States/Pauline Maier . . . [et al.].
   —2nd ed.
        p. cm.
   Includes bibliographical references and index.
   ISBN 0-393-92674-5
   1. United States—History. I. Maier, Pauline, 1938–

   E178.1.I58 2006
   973—dc22
                                                            2005054731
W. W. Norton & Company, Inc., 500 Fifth Avenue, New York, NY 10110
                    www.wwnorton.com

W. W. Norton & Company Ltd., Castle House, 75/76 Wells Street, London,
   W1T 3QT

2 3 4 5 6 7 8 9 0

*For Eleanor Smith Fox (1908–2001), mother, guiding light, friend.*—Merritt Roe Smith

*For Anne Kevles, who so much wanted to cast her vote in the next election;*
*Eric F. Goldman, who shepherded a young physicist into American history;*
*Bettyann, partner in all things; and Jonathan, Beth, David, and their children*
*here and to come, shapers of the new century.* — Daniel J. Kevles

*To the memory of my parents, Alexander and Grace Atkinson Keyssar, who*
*were buffeted by some of this history, but endured—to make*
*many things possible.* Alexander Keyssar

*For Corinne Maier, Alina Maier, and Dries Rooryck, who will help make the*
*history of the twenty-first century.* —Pauline Maier

# Contents

# CONTENTS

# CONTENTS

# CONTENTS

# CONTENTS

## CHAPTER 33
## INNOVATIONS AND DIVISIONS IN A GLOBALIZING SOCIETY:
### 1970–2000   945

## CHAPTER 34
## THE POLITICS OF DIVISION:
### 1993–2001   972

# CONTENTS

# Maps

# *Preface to the Second Edition*

*Inventing America* is a mainstream textbook with a difference: instead of an encyclopedic survey it is a text enhanced by a compelling theme. We were gratified when the initial response to the book's publication in 2003 confirmed the need for such a book in the U.S. survey course. There were excited adopters at hundreds of colleges and universities across the country, and even the popular press took notice of the book and its distinctive approach. We are grateful for the support that so many survey instructors have shown the book, and we have worked hard to incorporate their many good suggestions for revisions that, we hope, make the Second Edition even more effective as a teaching text.

*Inventing America* traces the theme of innovation in American life. Tocqueville articulated this theme well in this assessment of how Americans approach their affairs: "To escape from the spirit of system, from the yoke of habits, from family maxims, from class opinions . . . ; to take tradition only as information, and current facts only as a useful study for doing otherwise and better . . . to strive for a result without letting themselves be chained to the means . . . these are the principal features that characterize what I shall call the philosophic method of the Americans."

Examples of the willingness to *experiment in the face of changing needs and circumstances* range from the adaptations the colonists made to survive in an unfamiliar environment to the New Deal's try-anything response to the Depression; from the adoption of a radically redesigned corporation as a distinctive economic institution to the establishment of regulations intended to bind industry to the public interest; from the forging of an African-American culture by slaves to the resourceful efforts of women to find ways of combining family and career. And since the late nineteenth century, Americans have sought to remake their position in the world, mixing pragmatism with evangelism, drawing from the experience of failure as well as success.

In connection with the innovation theme *Inventing America* closely charts the material dimension of American history. Tracing the large transformations in the material life of Americans—housing, diet, health, childbearing, work, industrial growth, electrification, the rise of cities and suburbs, the automobile, consumerism, and so on—we explore the relationships among innovation, material development, and everyday life.

We are, of course, mindful of the important counterexamples to Tocqueville's generalization: many significant developments in American history cannot be considered innovative or the results of innovation, and these must be and are part of our story. And Americans are not uniquely innovative; as we show, many of the ideas and approaches applied here originated elsewhere. Nor do we count all of the new departures Americans have taken as positive: we explore a number of social, political, and economic initiatives that have brought unfortunate consequences, intended or unintended. The achievement of a powerful material civilization has come at significant cost to America's and the world's resources, especially in the twentieth century. And there have long been inequities in the distribution of the fruits of that civilization, underwritten by inequalities in rights ascribed to race, class, and gender. Even with these qualifications, however, we find the innovation theme to be a useful device for integrating the social and the political, the material and the cultural, in American life. However, Tocqueville's observation points to a belief Americans have long had about themselves, a historically operational fact in itself.

The innovation theme is a supple one. It allows us to draw into the mainstream historical areas central to American life but long neglected in American history survey textbooks—science and technology. Technological innovation has been a keynote in our history from early times, when in a remarkable feat of plant breeding pre-Columbian peoples cultivated primitive grains into maize. Our lives and those of our students are now thoroughly infused with technology and the products of scientific research. For most of our history these areas have been embedded in everyday lives and activities; only in relatively recent times have science and technology become areas of specialized knowledge based in separate

institutions. Another keen observer, Walter Lippmann, captured the broad significance of science for American life: "Science is the culture under which people can live forward in the midst of complexity, and treat life not as something given but as something to be shaped." In our text we aim to show students how integral science and technology have been to the American story.

To take a pivotal example, electrification is a key development that goes far beyond Edison and the light bulb: it is the story of a far-reaching technological system that transformed everyday life first in the city and eventually in the countryside. An important component of the social history of modern America, it also raised fundamental questions of ownership and distribution that have roiled politics and the courts since the late nineteenth century. And the electrical system was central to the modern economy that powered the United States to world prominence in the twentieth century. Our approach to science and technology then is not to isolate it from the mainstream history but to embed it in that history and show how it clarifies and enriches our understanding of the American past and present.

In this Second Edition of *Inventing America*, we have strengthened the theme of innovation in American history as it applies to politics, society, the economy, and culture. We have also pared the text of any excess detail in order to streamline the presentation for students. The result we hope is a tighter presentation that maintains the narrative appeal and the analytical insights of the original. At the same time we have kept the book abreast of the latest and best research in the field, a daunting task in itself.

The book is now organized into eight multi-chapter Parts, each one with an Introduction that sets out the broad themes that infuse the chapters. The Part Introductions also explore the applications of the innovation theme in the events and developments of the period.

In Part I (chapters 1–4), recent archeological work informs the discussion of early Virginia. There is a new discussion of the early printed literature of America and its relation to the prevailing cultural norms of Britain. We see the many adaptations made by Native Americans, the Spanish, French, and English, and by African slaves, to their mutual presence on the North American continent.

In Part II (chapters 5–9), the Second Edition extends the discussion of how the Revolution initiated a new regime of innovation that increasingly differentiated the United States from Europe. Americans created a new, republican government with written constitutions, and adopted laws that encouraged invention and redesigned the corporation so it better fit American society and culture. They forged new trade relationships, pursued new forms of domestic manufacturing and patenting, and undertook new departures in science and technology. And, aware of their growing differences from Europeans, Americans began to invent new collective identities for themselves in the arts and literature. They were indeed inventing America, or, at least, an America.

The first independent black nation in the Americas was created in the 1790s, and this new edition includes a fuller discussion of the Haitian Revolution and the powerful implications it had for the United States. It also expands the discussion of the Lewis and Clark expedition, especially Sacagawea's important role in the undertaking. It includes new material on the steamboat as an incremental invention. And this edition looks more closely at the different sources of power that fueled America's industrial growth. In this section we trace the transition from water power to steam power and how this shift facilitated the growth of small factories in the cities, spurring the rise of the mid-Atlantic manufacturing corridor.

Part III (chapters 10–13) carries the story beyond the War of 1812 to discuss the broad forces of economic, technological, and social change that were propelling the United States into a new, industrial era and, in the process, kindling divisive sectional tensions. It introduces the concept of the "market revolution" and explores its relationship to the industrial revolution and to the politics of the 1820s and 1830s. The discussion of slavery probes more deeply into slave culture, paying close attention to slave music and its impact on white music, especially through the minstrel show as a new form of popular entertainment. We also include new material on medicine, public health, and the environment during the "cholera years" from 1832 to 1860. We explore the Second Great Awakening as a source of innovation across American life. A new section highlights the advent of high-speed printing and its effect, through the mass circulation of newspapers and pamphlets, on reform movements, most notably abolitionism and anti-slavery. And we have expanded the discussion of the women's rights movement and its relationship to the larger abolitionist and temperance reform movements of which it was an integral part.

In Part IV (chapters 14–17), we provide a new discussion of the geological surveys conducted by the states and their significance for industrial development. A new section on the Perry Expedition to Japan gives us a snapshot of America's developing material power in the displays of wealth and technology the expedition carried to Yokohama harbor. We also see the significance of the expedition for the heated sectional politics of the 1850s. A new section explores the writers who contributed to a proslavery ideology in the 1850s. And we also recast the origins of the Republican Party around the emergence of a third-party system in American politics. A newly reorganized discussion of the Civil War more tightly integrates home-front developments with the progress of the war itself. We show that the war was notable not just for the horrific death tolls it produced—in good part the result of a revolution in armaments—but also because it was a new kind of conflict, one with profound implications for politics and society, business and technological development, especially in the postwar period.

Part V (chapters 18–21) charts the vast changes in politics, society, technology, and the economy following the Civil War, all of which contributed to the emergence of the United States as a world power by the end of the nineteenth century. The innovation theme finds strong expression in this period of big change. We incorporate new material on Southern politics after the Civil War, and on the conflicts over the voting rights of African Americans, immigrant workers, and women. We have brought new research to bear on the discussion of the evolution of American empire, including new perspectives on the Spanish-American War and U.S. involvement in Latin America, especially Nicaragua.

Part VI (chapters 22–25) embraces the Progressive era through the Great Depression and the New Deal. We present political reform in this period as a type of innovation that is tightly coupled to broad material change. The discussion of Progressivism includes new material on muckraking and progressivism in the South. Continuing our attention to developments in the West, here we also focus on two key resource issues—water and electrification. Both of these issues have been at the core of Western politics, economic development, and environmental protection in the twentieth century. In this section we have expanded the coverage of World War I and the 1920s and divided these subjects into two separate chapters. These chapters include an expanded discussion of the tumultuous year of 1919, with its deadly flu epidemic and intense racial, ethnic, and class tensions, evidenced (among other places) in the Seattle General Strike. We also give stronger coverage to the Harlem Renaissance and artistic innovation during the 1920s, as well as the social history of African Americans during World War I and the 1920s.

Part VII (chapters 26–30) has been reorganized to cover large events in a more self-contained way. The coverage of America's involvement in World War II, for instance, now falls entirely within one chapter. We include new discussions of Southern agriculture and industry during the 1950s, and the significant population movements in the region. We also extend our discussion of the West by looking at the ways in which economic development transformed the landscape. The construction of dams, for instance, turned rivers into

machines for the provision of electric power and water to cities, suburbs, and farms. This was a catalyst for the rapid expansion of "high-tech" industries and the growth of metropolitan areas in the West. In a new section we explore the importance of private business in developing the newly emergent electronics industry. The cultural invention of America continued apace in this period. We give fresh treatment to the arts in postwar America, most notably the film industry, graphic arts, and especially rock 'n' roll music—all of which quickly achieved a global impact through mass distribution networks and the expanding medium of television.

In Part VIII (Chapters 31–35) we see how the innovation theme applies to contemporary America. To amplify this theme we have created a new chapter (33) on the broad and important social and economic changes that occurred from the 1970s through the 1990s. This chapter can serve as a counterpart to others in the book that focus on major periods of innovation: Chapter 6 (on the changes spurred by the Revolution), Chapter 12 (on the changes in everyday life brought by industrialization), and Chapter 18 (on the vast changes brought by the rise of big business and cities in the late-nineteenth and early-twentieth centuries). We discuss the advent of new technologies that have spurred the economy and transformed our lives—the personal computer, the Internet, cell phones, iPods, and so on. We also address breakthroughs in biotechnology and the political debates that have surrounded genetic engineering and other innovative health and medical research. Globalization is another theme of this chapter, which features discussions of the economic and so-

cial issues raised by global integration, including the new wave of immigration to America from Asia, Latin America, and the Caribbean. And finally, Chapter 35 carries the story on through the summer of 2005.

Each of the coauthors took responsibility for drafting different sections of *Inventing America*: Maier, Chapters 1–8; Smith, Chapters 9–16; Keyssar, Chapters 17–25; Kevles, Chapters 26–35. However, all of us fully collaborated from the beginning of the project, jointly developing its themes and an outline of the book, and then reading and critiquing each other's chapters with the aim of achieving consistency in approach throughout.

## Pedagogy

We have concentrated on making the Second Edition of *Inventing America* a superior teaching text. In addition to tightening the presentation by paring detail, we have added pedagogical elements intended to help students extract and master the major points in each chapter. At the end of each chapter we have included **review pages** with lists of key terms (and the pages where they are discussed), chronologies, and summary questions. Instructors have commented on the usefulness of our **focus-question system**, which alerts students to the major theme in a section by running the relevant focus question at the top of each right-hand page. The new **Part Openers** emphasize the innovation theme and other broad themes that thread through a succession of chapters. There is a new **Glossary** of terms and events at the end of the book. And we have expanded the popular **American Journal** boxes, which now appear in every chapter. These present excerpts from primary documents that vividly show the impact of prevailing technologies on everyday life. All of these tools are meant to strengthen the students' hold on particulars and their vision of the whole.

## Student Website

The *Inventing America Digital History Center* (*www.ww norton.com/inventing*), authored by Karen Dunn-Haley (California State University, Monterey Bay), is an extensive resource for student review, test preparation, and research in a wealth of primary source materials. Hundreds of multimedia source materials expand on the innovation theme and examine America's material development. The site's resources include reproductions of primary documents, newspaper articles and journal entries, as well as archival images, audio passages, and video files. Helpful Media Analysis Worksheets direct student responses to the different media sources; students can transmit these worksheets to faculty via email or Norton's Gradebook. The website also includes interactive review materials and chapter summaries, quizzes, flashcard exercises, outlines, timelines, and chapter bibliographies. Norton iMaps allow students to explore historical maps interactively.

## eBook

The online e-book version of *Inventing America* offers the full content of the print book in a new, innovative e-book platform. The e-book enables students to highlight and search text, take marginal notes, print selections from the text, zoom in on art and maps, and more. The e-book is directly linked to the Digital History Center's resources and incorporates many of its interactive elements.

## Study Guide

The Study Guide, created by Kenneth J. Winkle (University of Nebraska) and Wendy Wall (Colgate University), contains chapter objectives and outlines, short-answer and essay questions, and chronologies that support students as they work through the text.

## Instructor Resources

Instructor's Manual and Test Bank by Amy Bix (Iowa State University), with supplementary test-item file questions by James Sargent (Virginia Western Community College). The Instructor's Manual contains chapter outlines, lecture ideas, discussion topics, and lists of audio-visual and Web resources. Available in print and electronic formats, the Test Bank, now

with more than 2700 questions, is an ample resource for test questions on *Inventing America*.

## Norton Media Library

This useful CD-ROM brings together a wealth of images and multimedia embedded in Powerpoint presentations with lecture outlines organized around the text. Sure to enliven classroom discussion, these presentations are easy to use and free to adopters.

## Norton Resource Library— wwnorton.com/nrl

The Norton Resource Library provides comprehensive instructor resources in one centralized online location. In the library, instructors can download ready-to-use, one-stop solutions for online courses, such as WebCT e-Packs and Blackboard Course Cartridges, or they can tailor these premade course packs to suit their own needs. The library's exceptional resources include: Powerpoint lecture slides, complete with artwork from the text; images, maps, and figures from the text for use on a course Web page; chapter overviews, summaries, and outlines; test banks, and glossaries.

## Norton Gradebook—wwnorton.com/college/nrl/gradebook

Norton Gradebook is an online application that allows instructors and students to store and track their online quiz results effectively. Student results from each quiz are uploaded to the password-protected Gradebook, where instructors can access and sort them by section, chapter, book, student name, and date. Students can also access the Gradebook to review their personal results and see how they perform in relation to the class, as well as to all classes using the Gradebook nationally. Registration for the gradebook is easy and no setup is required.

## Acetate Transparencies of all of the maps in the text

# Acknowledgments

In preparing revisions of *Inventing America* for this Second Edition, the authors have accrued many debts, and they take pleasure in thanking those who helped.

Pauline Maier is indebted to Meg Jacobs, Karen Ordahl Kupperman, Mary Beth Norton, and Harriet Ritvo for their generous, expert help on parts of her chapters. She would also like to thank Jim Sargent for his helpful suggestions for revisions in the Revolutionary War discussions. Both Maier and Merritt Roe Smith are happy to express their gratitude to Greg Clancey and Rob Martello for the research assistance they provided; Victor McElheny for his excellent substantive and stylistic comments; and to the students of their team-taught course on American history to 1865, whose responses to their draft chapters led to several improvements. Both greatly appreciate the support of the staff in the MIT Department of Science, Technology, and Society, especially Judy Spitzer.

Merritt Roe Smith is also grateful for help with research from Sean P. Adams, Ronald Rainger, Ron Radano, Karin Ellison, Greg Galer, Rebecca Herzig, Hannah Landecker, David Mindell, Jennifer Mnookin, Russell Olwell, and Tim Wolters. Special thanks are due Charles Dew, Richard John, and Jamie Pietruska for crucial input on Chapters 9–16.

Alexander Keyssar would like to thank Katherine Castles, D'arcy Brissman, Elisa Slattery, Eve Sterne, Nicole Perrygo, Andrew Neather, Noeleen McIlvenna, Daniel Levison Wilk, and especially Paul Husbands for their labors in gathering materials for this book. Robert Chisholm helped immensely in preparing the revisions for this edition. Keyssar is also grateful to the many undergraduates in his introductory U.S. history courses on whom he first tried out much of the material in his chapters. He would like to acknowledge the cheerful and essential support of the History Department staff at Duke University, especially Vivian Jackson, and the late Andrea Long, as well as his assistant at Harvard, Allyson Kelley.

Daniel J. Kevles is grateful to John L. Heilbron for helping to point the way to this book; to Ellen Chesler and James Hershberg for early advice; to William Deverell and Peter Westwick for comments on chapters; to Michelle Brattain, Richard Kim, and Peter Neushul for research on particular subjects; and to Helen Zoë Veit for reports on topics in the current edition. He is greatly indebted to Wendy Wall for her research during the project's startup phase and for her insights in a jointly taught course on recent America. His debt is immeasurable to Karen Dunn-Haley, who has lived with this project almost as long as he has, unflaggingly providing material and analyses, historiographical assessments, critical commentary, and encouragement for the first edition. She generously enlisted again in the effort for this edition by supplying material for various revisions, the last chapter, and several new entries for the "American Journal." Kevles is also grateful for the support of the Division of the Humanities and Social Sciences at the California Institute of Technology, especially John Ledyard, Susan Davis, Marion Lawrence, and Michelle Reinschmidt; and of the Department of History of Yale University, particularly Jon Butler and Paul Freedman, the chairs since his arrival there, and Jean Cherniavsky, Carolyn Fitzgerald, and Barbara McKay, whose helpfulness goes beyond the call of staff duty. And he wishes to thank the Andrew W. Mellon Foundation, whose support enabled him to spend more time on the writing.

The coauthors collectively are grateful for the critical comments provided by the readers of their manuscript:

For the First Edition:
Robert Angevine, George Mason University
James Axtell, College of William and Mary
Michael Barnhart, State University of New York at Stony Brook
Mark V. Barrow, Jr., Virginia Tech
Amy Bix, Iowa State University
Angela Boswell, Henderson State University
Anthony Carey, Auburn University
Paul G. E. Clemens, Rutgers University
Charles B. Dew, Williams College
Glen Gendzel, Tulane University
A. W. Giebelhaus, Georgia Institute of Technology
Larry Gragg, University of Missouri at Rolla
Michael G. Hall, University of Texas at Austin
Dwight Henderson, University of Texas at San Antonio
Richard R. John, University of Illinois at Chicago
Karen Ordahl Kupperman, New York University
Frank Lambert, Purdue University
Daniel Lewis, California Polytechnic State University, Pomona
Eric T. L. Love, University of Colorado, Boulder
David S. Lux, Bryant College

William M. McBride, United States Naval Academy
Robert M. S. McDonald, United States Military Academy
James Mohr, University of Oregon
Jerald E. Podair, Lawrence University
Chris Rasmussen, University of Nevada at Las Vegas
Jan Reiff, UCLA
Susan Rugh, Brigham Young University
Andrew Schocket, Bowling Green State University
Ron Schultz, University of Wyoming
Bryant Simon, University of Georgia
Robert Stoddard, University of British Columbia
David Tanenhaus, University of Nevada at Las Vegas
Stanley J. Underdal, San Jose State University
Helena M. Wall, Pomona College
Wendy Wall, Colgate University
Jessica Wang, UCLA
Kenneth Winkle, University of Nebraska


For the Second Edition:
David Tanenhaus, University of Nevada, Las Vegas
William F. King, Mt. San Antonio College
James Sargent, Virginia Western Community College
Justin Nordstrom, State University of New York at
   Brockport
Susan Rugh, Brigham Young University
Richard John, University of Illinois at Chicago
Michael Egan, Western Washington University
Shirley Wajda, Kent State University

Mansel Blackford, Ohio State University
Ronald Rainger, Texas Tech University
Bob Gomez, San Antonio College
Sylvia McGrath, Stephen F. Austin State University
Paul Gilmore, California State University, Fresno
Steven W. Usselman, Georgia Tech University
John Reda, University of Illinois, Chicago
Sarah Rose, University of Illinois, Chicago
Robert McDonald, United States Military Academy
Michael J. Connolly, Purdue University North Central
Elwood Jones, Trent University

The authors are deeply indebted for generous support of
the project to the Alfred P. Sloan Foundation, especially to
Arthur Singer for his decisive early interest, and Doron Weber
for his ongoing enthusiasm. They are very grateful to W. W.
Norton for the care it has taken in producing the book—in
particular, to Steve Forman, their editor, for his patience, advice, and critical readings; and to Alice Vigliani for her skilled
manuscript editing. At Norton they owe many thanks also to
Sarah England, Rebecca Arata, Marian Johnson, Thom Foley,
and Ben Reynolds for keeping this big project on the rails.
Stephanie Romeo did the splendid work reflected in the
book's fine illustration program. Karen Dunn-Haley conceived, researched, and captioned the rich digital materials
employed on the student website. The efforts of Steve Hoge at
Norton were critical in bringing the digital history component to fruition. Steve Dunn and Dan Jost helped introduce
this new edition to the survey market.

# About the Authors

PAULINE MAIER is William R. Kenan Jr. Professor of American History at the Massachusetts Institute of Technology. Her specialty is the period of the American Revolution, on which she has published extensively, including *From Resistance to Revolution: Colonial Radicals and the Development of American Opposition to Britain, 1765–1776* and *The Old Revolutionaries: Political Lives in the Age of Samuel Adams.* Her most recent book is *American Scripture: Making the Declaration of Independence.*

MERRITT ROE SMITH is Leverett and William Cutten Professor of the History of Technology at the Massachusetts Institute of Technology. His research focuses on the history of technological innovation and social change. His publications include *Harpers Ferry Armory and the New Technology* and *Military Enterprise and Technological Change.* He is a fellow of the American Academy of Arts and Sciences.

ALEXANDER KEYSSAR is Matthew W. Stirling Jr. Professor of History and Social Policy, John F. Kennedy School of Government, Harvard University. His specialty is the social and political history of the late nineteenth and twentieth centuries. His first book was *Out of Work: The First Century of Unemployment in Massachusetts.* His most recent book is *The Right to Vote: The Contested History of Democracy in the United States.*

DANIEL J. KEVLES is Stanley Woodward Professor of History at Yale University. He has published extensively on the history of science and the intersections of politics, science, and technology in the twentieth century. His works include *The Physicists: The History of a Scientific Community in Modern America* and *In the Name of Eugenics: Genetics and the Uses of Human Heredity.* His most recent book is *The Baltimore Case: A Trial of Politics, Science, and Character.*

# INVENTING AMERICA

## SECOND EDITION

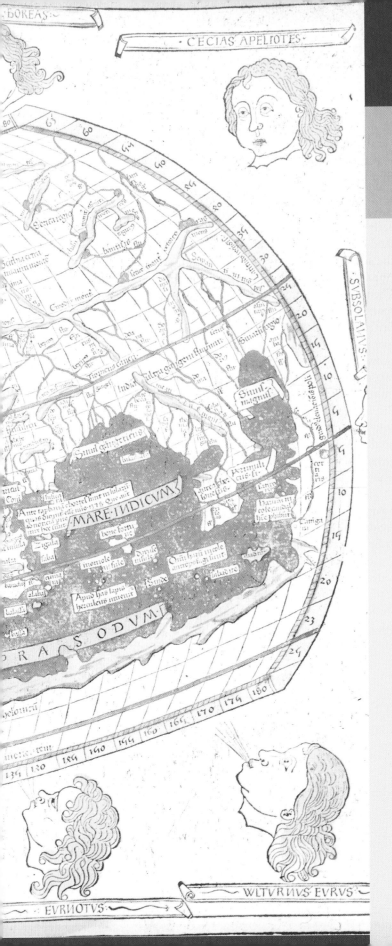

# Part 1

# EMPIRES

At first, survival was the issue. Since human life began elsewhere, the first Americans and many who followed them had to travel from somewhere else and learn to live in an unfamiliar land. The first to arrive were probably hunters from Asia who found a rich animal population to sustain them. But as human beings spread over what became North and South America, they adapted to dramatically different environments. A major shift in the world's climate and the disappearance of many large animals further tested their capacity for innovation. They became not just hunters and gatherers, but fishermen and farmers. Their inventiveness can be seen not just in the variety of cultures they created, but also in tools such as spear points, that changed form as the animal population changed; in trade goods manufactured from a wide range of materials; and in the development of corn, perhaps the most important product of human plant breeding of all time. The descendants of these first Americans created civilizations of great complexity and sophistication—in the Valley of Mexico, for example, and Peru.

Thousands of years later, Europeans sailed west across the great "ocean sea"—the Atlantic—to "discover" America. They drew upon innovations in ship design, navigational instruments, and mapping; in turn, the knowledge early European explorers brought back to Europe contributed to a dramatically new understanding of the world and its geography.

This reconstruction of the lost map that accompanied Ptolemy's *Geography* (which was discovered in the 15th century) shows a world divided, according to Ptolemy's system, into lines of latitude and longitude. There is no America, and parts of the world that were relatively remote, for the ancients, such as southern Africa and the Indian Ocean, are represented inaccurately. However, much of Europe, western Asia, and North Africa are shown with remarkable precision.

The Americas were not at first a welcome discovery: they posed a barrier between Europe and Asia that generation after generation of seamen tried to find a good way through or around. But the "New World" had its attractions—above all, the precious metals Europeans craved (and the Spanish got), lands that could produce sugar and other commercial crops for the European market, and native people who, it seemed, would make fine workers and perhaps also fine converts to the Christian religion. When the diseases Europeans brought killed vast numbers of Native Americans, causing a demographic catastrophe of staggering proportions, the Europeans imported other people—above all, Africans—to take their place. Meanwhile, American crops gradually spread across the globe, sustaining a population growth from which other immigrants would be drawn.

Survival in America was at first a challenge for Europeans, too. The death rates in some new colonial settlements were high, and illness, particularly in the period immediately after settlers first arrived, was common. With time, however, the populations of the European settlements stabilized and grew. European colonies differed dramatically in their economies, in the size and ethnic origins of their populations, in the relationships they maintained with the native peoples, and in their religions and political systems. By the late seventeenth century, Spain had colonies on mainland North America in New Mexico and Florida; the French were in Canada and the Mississippi Valley; and the British colonies—which had absorbed Dutch and Swedish settlements—ran along the Atlantic coast. These empires competed with each other, enlisting the support of Native Americans in a struggle for land and trade.

Finally, in 1763, the British won title to all the territory between the Mississippi and the Atlantic, expelling the French from mainland North America and the Spanish from Florida.

A vibrant growth rate characterized the British settlements, whose population doubled every generation. In the early- and mid-eighteenth century, British colonists seeking land pushed north into New Hampshire, settled Georgia in the south, and spread west into the mountain valleys in the Appalachian chain that roughly paralleled the Atlantic coast. Then they began to eye lands beyond the mountains—which sparked conflict with the French. Although the various British colonies were themselves different from each other in many ways—above all, in their economies and religious traditions—they still shared a pride in being British. Over time, prosperity and population growth allowed colonists to acquire more British goods, to build some larger houses after British models, and even to anticipate the emergence of a less equalitarian, more hierarchical social structure like that of England. And they celebrated the fact that their provincial governments were structured like "the British constitution," which Enlightenment writers everywhere celebrated.

To be sure, life in America demanded adjustments and innovations—above all, at first, when the relatively primitive conditions of colonial life made it most unlike life "at home" in Britain. But colonial culture was more self-consciously imitative than innovative: Americans wanted to approximate England in style, in culture, and, above all, in government. In 1763, they saw their future and that of North America as increasingly British. That was exactly what they wanted. There was little reason to think their fate might take another turn.

# Chapter 1

# "MEN PRONE TO WONDER":

## AMERICA BEFORE 1600

Sailors navigating by the stars with a sea full of monsters, from a woodcut of 1575.

## The Peoples of Ancient America

**Focus QUESTIONS**

■ **Where did the peoples of ancient America come from, and how did they live?**

■ **Why did Europeans first go to America?**

■ **How did the Spanish Conquistadors win control of the American mainland?**

■ **What was the "Columbian exchange" and how significant was it?**

It was a strange sight—"a very lion to our seeming, in shape, hair, and colour," swimming in the sea not by moving its feet like other beasts, "but rather sliding upon the water with his whole body (excepting the legs) in sight," not diving and then rising above the water like whales or porpoises, but "confidently shewing himselfe above water without hiding." As the creature passed between the ship of watching Englishmen and the shore, "turning his head to and fro, yawning and gaping wide, with ougly demonstration of long teeth, and glaring eies," he "sent forth a horrible voyce, roaring or bellowing as doeth a lion, which spectacle wee all beheld . . . as men prone to wonder at every strange thing, as this doubtlesse was, to see a lion in the Ocean sea, or fish in the shape of a lion."

The story appeared in an account of English navigator Sir Humphrey Gilbert's return voyage from America in 1583. What the sailors saw in the cold waters of the North Atlantic was not a lion but something altogether new and unknown to them. How full of strange things, this "America," this place so long unknown to Europeans and so full of unfamiliar creatures that could only be described with language from another place that did not quite fit what stood before the observers' eyes ("a very lion to our seeming"). How could European readers distinguish truth from myth, reality from the fables of popular books such as *The Travels of Sir John Mandeville, Knight* (1356), which told of "men . . . without heads" who had "eyes in either shoulder" and mouths that were "round shaped like a horseshoe, y-midst their breasts"? In 1557, a French visitor to Brazil confessed "that since I have been in this land of America, . . . everything to be seen—the way of life of its inhabitants, the form of the animals, what the earth produces—is so unlike what we have in Europe, Asia, and Africa that it may very well be called a 'New World' with respect to us."

Were the people who lived in this "New World" equally struck by the peculiarities of Europeans? One of the first accounts of a meeting between the two cultures, in the logbook of the explorer Christopher Columbus for December 18, 1492, reports the reactions of a native "king" and his "councilors" (more European words of approximation) on the island of Tortuga when Columbus described Spain's king and queen, who "commanded and ruled over all the best part of the world," and displayed colorful banners with the royal arms or the holy cross emblazoned upon them. "I saw well," Columbus wrote, "that they took everything as a great wonder." But did the Tortugans wonder at the Spanish king and queen and their banners, or at Columbus's babbling in a language they could not understand? For both sides in the scene, there was cause enough for awe, amazement, and reflections on the disparity between the known and the newly encountered.

Those first confrontations of Europeans and Indians remain a cause of wonder today because of the epic stories that lay behind them, and because of their vast consequences. The meetings of strangers in the northern reaches of the western Atlantic or on beaches in the West Indies brought the descendants of migrants from Asia who had moved south and east over the American continents through thousands of years face-to-face with men who heralded a new migration to America, this time westward from Europe. There were no human occupants of these "new" lands when the first migrants arrived, so all Americans without exception were, are, and always will be immigrants or the children of immigrants from every part of the earth. And however inauspicious the first encounters of Indians and Europeans might have seemed, with their handful of scruffy participants, the effects—on the lives of the first Americans and those who joined them; on power relationships; on the cultures and economies of both America and Europe; on the movements of plants, animals, people, and diseases across space; on European understandings of humans and the natural world—were monumental. Some of the most horrific consequences showed themselves with remarkable speed. Others came more slowly but in time penetrated all parts of the globe, provoking or sustaining changes that everywhere deepened the chasm between the Old World of the past and the New World of the future.

## The Peoples of Ancient America

The stories of the "Indians" (a word based on the mistaken belief of Columbus, who first encountered them, that he had reached the East Indian islands of Asia) are different from those of Europeans for a reason of enduring importance. The Indians, who had mastered techniques for surviving in America that Europeans would only painfully acquire, never developed a technology of writing. (There are exceptions, however: the Mayan people of central America, or "Mesoamerica," for example, did have a system of writing.) All the nations of Europe, by contrast, had written languages; and by the time Europeans arrived in America, the printing press had also become part of their lives. As a result, the first extant descriptions of the earliest Americans were written by Europeans whose accounts often tell as much or more about the writers than they do about the peoples observed.

These bizarre, headless creatures appeared in a 1599 book by the Nürnberg writer and printer Levinus Hulsius, that promised to give a "marvelous description of the gold-rich kingdom of Guiana" in the northeastern part of South America. Distinguishing the real from the imaginary in accounts of America was not always easy.

The work of modern anthropologists, archaeologists, and demographers, who analyze physical remains, quantifiable data (population size, for example), and other forms of evidence, can also help reconstruct the lost worlds of ancient America. Even geneticists and linguists contribute to the debate over the earliest occupants of the Americas. What they can tell about the past is often different from what written sources reveal. The questions they ask, however, are often the same that fifteenth-century Europeans asked: Who, to begin, were these Indian peoples, and where did they come from?

### CREATION AND MIGRATION

Christians and Jews knew where they came from. The Bible told of the first human being, Adam, and how God formed a woman, Eve, from Adam's rib so that Adam would not be lonely. They lived in a paradise until God drove them out because, after being tempted by a serpent, they ate the fruit of a forbidden tree. All living persons descended from that first human couple. The Bible also told how God, angered by the

sins of humankind, once destroyed the world with a great flood, saving only one good man, Noah, his family, and the animals he gathered together, two by two, on a great ark.

Indians had their own creation stories, passed on not through books but orally, told and retold from generation to generation. Sometimes, as with the Arapaho people of North America's Great Plains, priests related a story to a few chosen elders for fear that errors would creep in with uncontrolled retellings. Those stories frequently described an earlier life unlike that of the present and a benevolent Great Spirit or god who set rules for the people. Sometimes they told of ancestors who were driven from underworlds as a punishment for disobeying their god or gods; sometimes they described the emergence of earth from a watery world. Some tales included "trickster" figures in the shape of animals—a coyote, for example, or a raven—whose influence, like the Bible's serpent, accounted for pain and illness, strife and death. These stories gave the people a sense of common origin and purpose, accounted for evil, provided a basis for rules that

7

sustained order, and sometimes promised a return of harmony in an afterlife.

Modern scientific accounts of the Indians' origins are also wonderful in their way. Today's humans, they say, evolved from apelike ancestors in Africa and appeared (as Cro-Magnon Man) in Europe some 40,000 years ago. From the first, human beings showed a marked penchant for travel: before they appeared in Europe, some early humans apparently managed to make their way from Africa to Australia, which means they had learned to build and operate boats. Others pushed overland into Asia. And eventually human beings began to migrate from Asia to America. Some experts think these migrations began about 15,000 to 20,000 years ago. Perhaps they occurred earlier: archaeological evidence from a site in Canada's northern Yukon Territory indicates that people lived in Arctic regions of America as early as 27,000 or 29,000 years ago. The issue remains unsettled.

The earliest migrants, hunters in search of prey, probably traveled over a subcontinent, now known as Beringia, that linked today's Siberia and Alaska at the site of the Bering Strait and extended as much as a thousand miles from north to south. That soggy, treeless landmass existed because great glaciers had sucked up so much water that the world's oceans sank some 300 feet. The ice age that produced these glaciers, known as the Pleistocene, began some 2.5 million years ago, but its frigid climate waxed and waned, with periods of intense cold giving way at times to temperatures like those of today. One particularly severe stretch lasted from about 80,000 to 9,000 or 10,000 years ago, time enough for migratory hunters to make their moves. Then the ice began to melt, again submerging lands and whatever physical evidence they held of their human inhabitants deep below the ocean's surface. Even then the distance between Asia and America at the Bering Strait—about fifty-six miles, with islands breaking the gap—was not so great as to prevent people with wooden dugout or skin boats from crossing to the other side.

Not all early migrants, however, crossed there. Skeletal remains suggest that a people distinct from modern American Indians, Caucasoid people whose biological features indicate that they might have come from southern parts of Asia or perhaps even Europe, once lived on the North American continent. They could have traveled east from Asia over the Aleutian Islands, or west from Europe through the North Atlantic, which offered a long but feasible route over ice and land during the Pleistocene. Perhaps several distinct migrations occurred at different times from different places.

Once the migrants had arrived in North America, they found wonderful prey for hunting: giant, elephant-like mastodons; mammoths, some of which are the largest elephants ever known (a full fourteen feet tall), and others with thick, woolly coats and long, upward-turning tusks; and enormous, shaggy bison, saber-toothed tigers, and a variety of game birds. There were also native horses and camel-like creatures, fearsome wolves, and giant ground sloths. Much of the land, however, was anything but hospitable: a thick sheet of ice extended from what is now western Alaska and the Yukon River drainage area in central Alaska, which remained unglaciated, eastward across the North American continent to Long Island (New York) and down to where the Ohio and Mississippi rivers now join. Tundra, great treeless plains, stretched below the ice from the Great Plains eastward into Pennsylvania and New Jersey; farther south, forests covered places such as Virginia, while the lower elevations of what is now the western United States and Mexico were filled with grasslands.

The end of the ice age (9,000 or 10,000 years ago) transformed the land and its climate. The melting of the glaciers caused the sea to rise and probably brought massive flooding throughout the world—which might explain why many Indian folktales tell, like the Old Testament, of a great deluge deep in the past. As the glaciers receded, they left deposits of topsoil scraped from the north in the Missouri and Ohio valleys and mixed stones and rocks with the soil of what is now New England. Everywhere temperatures moderated; wet places gradually became dry; deciduous forests appeared and spread across North America but later gave way in some places, like the Great Plains, to perennial grasslands with occasional stands of trees in streambeds and wherever else their roots could find water.

These changes challenged both animals and humans. Many of the largest animals probably found adaptation impossible and gradually died out. (Some scholars argue, alternatively, that they were wiped out by Indian hunters, who reduced their numbers beyond the point of recovery.) Again, Indian tales sometimes associated great floods with the end of a time when monsters ruled the earth. Roughly three dozen categories (or genera) of plant-eating mammals disappeared, among them mammoths and mastodons, the massive sloths, camels, and horses. Later, many carnivorous animals, including American cheetahs, lions, tigers, the dire wolf, and a short-faced bear, followed them into extinction. Smaller creatures like birds found it easier to survive, often by changing habitat.

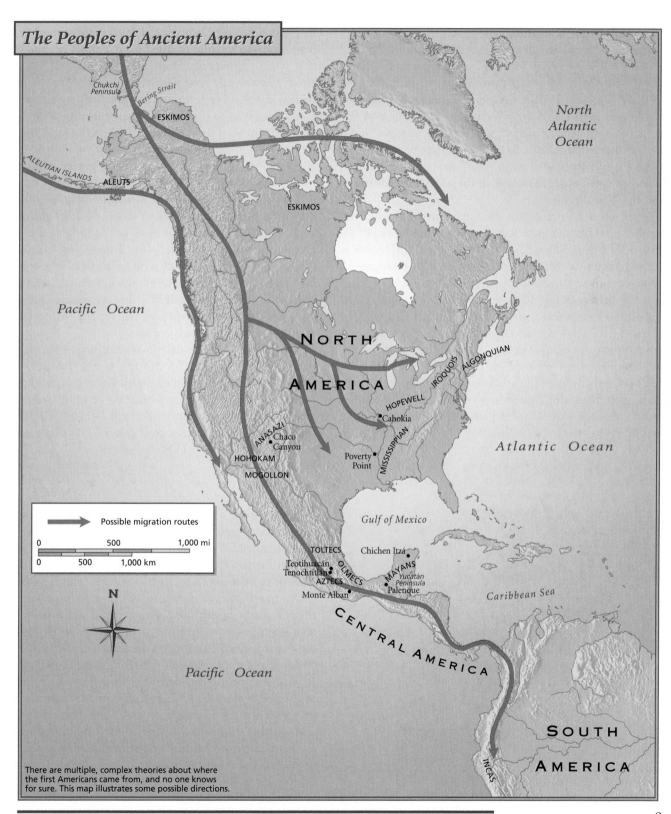

## The Peoples of Ancient America

Chukchi Peninsula

Bering Strait

ESKIMOS

ALEUTIAN ISLANDS

ALEUTS

ESKIMOS

*North Atlantic Ocean*

*Pacific Ocean*

NORTH

AMERICA

IROQUOIS

ALGONQUIAN

HOPEWELL

Cahokia

ANASAZI

Chaco Canyon

HOHOKAM

MOGOLLON

Poverty Point

MISSISSIPPIAN

*Atlantic Ocean*

Possible migration routes

| 0 | 500 | 1,000 mi |
|---|-----|----------|
| 0 | 500 | 1,000 km |

*Gulf of Mexico*

TOLTECS

Chichen Itzá

Teotihuacán
Tenochtitlán
AZTECS
OLMECS
MAYANS
*Yucatán Peninsula*
Palenque

Monte Alban

*Caribbean Sea*

N

CENTRAL AMERICA

*Pacific Ocean*

SOUTH

AMERICA

INCAS

There are multiple, complex theories about where the first Americans came from, and no one knows for sure. This map illustrates some possible directions.

This map indicates the routes by which the first Americans probably arrived and dispersed through the Americas. However, their places of origin and times of arrival remain subjects of debate.

Humans did the same thing. The penchant of early peoples for migration seems to have continued almost nonstop once they arrived in America. Some moved across the northern edge of the North American continent to Greenland in the North Atlantic—or did they get there by some route from the east? Others fanned out over North America or pushed farther south, into Mexico and beyond. Charcoal samples found in Brazil indicate that humans lived there long before the end of the ice age. By 10,000 B.C.E., these irrepressible travelers walked or sailed along the coast all the way to the southernmost tip of South America.

People came to occupy all the unglaciated parts of both continents with remarkable rapidity. They had no doubt always lived by gathering seeds, nuts, berries, and other foods as well as by hunting. Now, as the largest animals disappeared, people continued to gather food from the wild while replacing the flesh of mammoths and the like with fish, poultry, and relatively small mammals such as rabbits and deer or—on the plains—bison. They also developed ingenious devices to help them survive in environments of an astounding variety. Hunters used spears with chiseled stone points to kill their prey, and they invented the atlatl (spear-thrower), essentially a long stick from which spears were thrown to increase their thrust. Even so, it wasn't easy to penetrate the tough hide of a bison, so hunters stampeded herds of bison over cliffs. They then butchered the carcasses and dried strips of meat or made pemmican—a mixture of dried meat, animal fat, and berries that, when properly stored in containers made of hide, could be kept as a winter food source. In dry areas, people created basins or wells to collect rainwater and took advantage of the cactus's capacity to store liquid. Acorns became a dietary staple. The Miwok, who lived in the foothills of North America's Sierra Nevada, developed ways not only to store, shell, and grind acorns but also to leach out the bitter-tasting tannin from acorn meal.

The first peoples of ancient America probably spoke a variety of languages. Once in America, cut off from their homelands and faced with the necessity of adapting to a variety of new environments, the differences among them became even greater. Without a system of writing to stabilize speech, base languages splintered into hundreds of related tongues that became mutually unintelligible. And as people spread over the land, particular groups claimed specific territories separated by imprecise, porous borders.

These early American peoples traded goods with each other across great distances. Sometimes, as the palisades (stake fences) that often surrounded their villages suggest, they went to war. Perhaps they even wondered at other groups' languages, customs, and accomplishments. And in time, there developed in central Mexico a great cultural homeland for many inhabitants of Central and North America.

### MEXICO

About 9,000 years ago, people in the Tehuacán Valley, on a high plateau in the south-central part of today's Mexico, began to cultivate a wild grass called "teosinte." They carefully selected mutant forms of that primitive grain—which had only two rows of small seeds (kernels) and no cob or husks—that displayed more desirable characteristics, planted them, again used the best plants as seed stock, and continued the process season after season, generation after generation. The result was maize, which Americans call "corn," a cultivated food so unlike its wild ancestor, and so adaptable to different growing conditions, that its creation was perhaps the most important plant-breeding achievement of all time. These early agriculturists also began growing crops such as avocados, chili peppers, grain amaranth, and squash. Different people to their north and east were growing pumpkins and gourds. Soon beans and cotton joined the list of staples. These New World developments took place perhaps 1,000 years after people in Southeast Asia began growing wheat

An Indian cultivating corn with a digging stick.

and barley. It is likely that both areas independently developed agriculture as a means of survival in the post–ice age world.

The invention of agriculture had similar effects wherever it occurred. It made people less dependent on nature's chance bounty, facilitated the gathering of plant foods, and made possible the survival of larger and more concentrated human populations with more complex social structures than those that arose where hunting and the seasonal gathering of non-cultivated foods were the only means of sustenance. At first, it seems, people grew food to supplement the hunt. Then, as growing populations pushed hunters toward the territory of other peoples, agriculture became a way of slowing or stopping physical expansion, of providing food without invading neighbors' lands and incurring the risk of war. As people found ways to dry and store crops such as corn, they became sedentary—a change that often coincided with the making of pottery, which is too fragile to keep hauling from place to place. None of these changes happened overnight: the first pottery seems to have appeared in Mexico several millennia after the beginnings of agriculture. In the meantime, the population continued to grow. And some of the greatest concentrations of people and the most complex cultures in the Americas developed in areas of Mesoamerica, where the climate allowed the cultivation of crops year-round and agriculture became an established way of supporting life.

Villages appeared in the Tehuacán Valley about 5,000 years ago. At first, their populations grew more slowly than that of the neighboring Olmecs, who lived on lowlands along the Gulf of Mexico near the modern city of Veracruz. The Olmecs supported themselves in part by commerce, trading jade and obsidian, a form of hard volcanic glass that could be made into tools with extraordinarily sharp edges. They also produced great sculptures and buildings, the first of note in the region's history. After a time, however, the Tehuacán highlanders outpaced their coastal rivals; they extended their cultivated lands, compensating for a lack of regular rainfall by establishing systems of terracing and irrigation. Perhaps they also learned to create *chinampas,* incredibly fertile raised beds of land formed by cutting canals in swampy areas along Lake Texcoco and fertilized with pond weeds and mud.

There, in the high mountain plateau of central Mexico, the great city of Teotihuacán, the most powerful of pre-Columbian America, emerged some 2,000 years ago. The city was a religious as well as a trading center, with massive pyramidal temples along a broad central street, all built by slaves who had to move great slabs of stone without the help of large work animals or wheeled vehicles. The elite lived in stone buildings where windowless private rooms, some with elaborately painted walls, opened onto courts or patios, while artisans huddled in warrens of tiny rooms along the city's back streets. Teotihuacán was the home of workshops where specialized craftsmen made knives, spear points, scrapers for cleaning animal hides, and other tools from obsidian; it also was a mecca for merchants from other parts of Mesoamerica, who brought their goods to exchange for other exotic items. Estimates of the city's population vary. Some say it reached 45,000 in the second century C.E., others that it was that large much earlier. At its height, in about C.E. 650, it numbered at least 125,000 people and might have been twice that size. No city of contemporary Europe could compare.

Elsewhere, too, urban centers appeared with great temples and also ball courts of stone, with tiered bleachers from which spectators could watch ball games. These contests may have been as much religious or civic ritual as sport, since at their end one set of players was put to death. Monte Alban, a city in the mountains near the trading town of Oaxaco, resembled Teotihuacán in its design, in its practice of an intensive agriculture supported by terracing and irrigation, and in the presence of both massive religious structures and housing for its people. On the Yucatán peninsula, in the midst of jungle-like forests, and sweeping south and west through parts of modern-day southern Mexico and into Guatemala, the Mayan people also created impressive ceremonial centers—over a hundred of them after about C.E. 300, many of which remain hidden today beneath tangled tropical growth.

The Mayans possessed an advanced knowledge of astronomy and mathematics, a complex calendar more accurate than the Julian calendar of contemporary Europe, and a written language composed of both ideographs (pictures that represent ideas) and phonetic components. They used this language to make illustrated manuscripts or books of bark paper, long inscriptions on funerary vases, and stone engravings. The Mayan written language proved difficult for modern scholars to decipher, although the inscriptions seem to provide dynastic histories of the Mayan rulers. The lands the Mayans occupied were often unsuited for intensive agriculture, particularly at a time when people farmed with "digging sticks," not plows, and without oxen or work horses. Perhaps for that reason, they lived in scattered clusters. Their greatest cities, such as Chichen Itza in the Yucatán or Palenque in Chiapas, boasted massive temples, public buildings, and great plazas that remain stunning testaments to the engineering

This map, from the early sixteenth century, shows the Aztec capital, Tenochtitlán, which was on an island connected to the mainland by causeways.

capacities and ability of their creators to command massive human labor. Still, the Mayan cities never approached the population of Teotihuacán.

The great centers of Mesoamerica in its classic period (between C.E. 300 and 600–900), a time that saw the creation of massive architectural monuments, came to a mysterious end. Teotihuacán was abandoned and burned sometime around 700. The Mayans left one ceremonial center after another in the decades before and after 800, and Monte Alban suffered the same fate a century later. Because there are virtually no written records, the cause or causes of the catastrophe remain unknown. Did natural calamities precipitate the decline of the great cities? Did the ancient cities outgrow their capacity to sustain themselves? Did peasants, pushed to desperation by the demands of their urban masters, revolt? Or did attacks from outside, perhaps by the Toltec people from the north, lead to the abandonment of these cities and religious centers?

Hundreds of years later, beginning in the thirteenth century, the Mexica, or Aztecs, a people from the north who claimed descent from the Toltecs, would sweep down into the Valley of Mexico, found a new great city, Tenochtitlán, on an island in Lake Texcoco, and conquer the neighboring people. But the arrival of the Aztecs, whose empire was in place by the mid-fifteenth century, cannot explain the earlier disappearance of Teotihuacán and other centers of classic Mesoamerica.

The results of that disappearance are only slightly easier to trace. Some lesser population centers managed to survive and even grow, particularly in the high valley of central Mexico; but overall the period after the abandonment of Teotihuacán seems to have been one of war, instability, and population decline in one part of the region after another.

### NORTH AMERICA

Human beings occupied North America from at least the end of the ice age. Some if not all of the first settlers of what became the continent's temperate regions swept south from Alaska to the eastern side of the Sierra Nevada, then spread east and south over the continent. Certain Indians today, including the Cherokees, Choctaws, and Chickasaws, recall old stories of long marches from west to east. The Creeks say that their ancestors traveled in search of the land of the rising sun until they arrived at a great ocean; then they stopped, making a home in what is today the southeastern United States. The Delawares tell a similar migration story, but with a twist: they say that the first Algonquian-speaking peoples stopped to settle the middle of the continent before some moved on to the east coast.

According to many of these often-told tales, the Indian peoples did not choose their homelands by chance or simply because they had arrived at the land's end. Instead, they received a sign of where they should stop—for example, a sacred pole that pointed in the direction the migrants should go became still when they had arrived at their destination. Their lands, then, had been chosen for them by the Great Spirit. Because land bonded many Indians' with their ancestors and the gods, it had spiritual as well as practical meaning. Yet many Indian peoples moved to new parts of the continent because of war, climatic changes, or other compelling reasons. Their history is one of migrations long and short, and sometimes of deadly conflicts after groups crossed the zigzagged frontier zones that divided the lands and cultures of North America's peoples and transformed the continent into a oversized jigsaw puzzle.

## WAYS OF LIFE

Although some coastal Indians subsisted on fish, most of the earliest Americans were hunters. Large, fluted, Clovis stone spear points (named after a site near the town of Clovis, New Mexico, where they were first found), which were mounted on wooden staves and used to hunt the huge animals of the ice age, have been discovered in every part of the mainland United States. Their use seems to have ended about 9200 B.C.E. Their successor, the artfully fluted Folsom spear points (also discovered in New Mexico), were smaller and better suited for the smaller prey of the post-ice age hunt.

The bow and arrow was a far more accurate and powerful weapon, but, like much American technology of later times, it first appeared in Europe or Asia: wooden arrow shafts dating back to 9000 B.C.E. have been found in northern Germany. The bow and arrow moved via Asia to the Arctic region of North America by 3000 B.C.E., which suggests that some contact between the continents continued after the ice age had ended. The weapon spread eastward, then slowly to the south, reaching the Great Plains about C.E. 200. The proud peoples of Mesoamerica, however, refused to adopt it. Did they consider the bow and arrow a weapon of the "barbarians" to their north?

The peoples of ancient North America were capable of amazing creations. At Poverty Point, in today's Louisiana, they built sometime between 1800 and 500 B.C.E., a peculiar set of earthworks—three mounds and six concentric groups of parallel ridges formed in a semicircle, like an amphitheater, that extended over two-thirds of a mile. How they moved so much earth remains unknown, except that it had to involve the labor of people with only modest tools. The site held materials from far-flung places—copper from the Great Lakes region, lead from Missouri, stone from Kentucky, Indiana, and Ohio. Trade networks, it seems, were already in place. And the community at Poverty Point included craftsmen who made jewelry, polished stone figurines, tools, and clay objects that were probably heated in a fire, then thrown into watertight baskets to make water boil. Poverty Point's influence can be seen at another hundred sites as far away as Florida and Missouri.

Farther north, in the Ohio Valley, other peoples of a later time built more earthworks, sometimes in the shapes of animals: one 1,254-foot slithering snake was raised four or five feet from the ground. The tradition of mound building continued among the Hopewell people, named after a site in southern Ohio (100 B.C.E.–C.E. 400), who built enormous burial mounds in geometric shapes. Beneath the mounds lay extraordinarily beautiful artifacts: for example, the profile in mica of a long-fingered human hand; pipes, sometimes inlaid with pearls and bone, in the form of animals; a falcon made of cold-hammered copper. The materials used came from hundreds of miles away in all directions. The Hopewell grew some of their food, including squash, pumpkins, and sunflowers, and they made pottery. Did agriculture in the Ohio Valley begin independently, rather than through contact with the by-then-experienced farmers of Mesoamerica? It's possible, since the Hopewell do not seem to have grown corn.

An oversized human hand, made of mica by Hopewell Indians; excavated from an Indian gravesite in Ohio.

The peoples of the far north, Eskimos and Aleuts, adapted to the conditions of their environment with great ingenuity, building homes and fishing shelters of ice, creating clothes of fur and feathers to ward off the cold, developing fish traps, kayaks, and harpoons for hunting seals and whales. Others who lived along the Pacific Northwest and the California coast exploited the bounty of the sea so successfully that they became relatively sedentary without inventing or adopting agriculture. But perhaps the most distinctive cultures of subarctic North America were in the Southwest, adjacent to Mesoamerica. There, in a region that included parts of modern-day Utah, Colorado, Arizona, New Mexico, and northern Mexico, people were growing corn and other food some 3,500 years ago, long before agriculture appeared elsewhere in North America.

By C.E. 500, the Southwest contained three separate but similar cultures, each with its own language or languages. The

13

Ruins of Anasazi cliff dwellings at Mesa Verde, Colorado.

New Mexico, which the Anasazi developed around 900, included nine towns, many of whose buildings formed a semicircle that opened to the south to maximize solar heat. Some structures were huge: Pueblo Bonito ("beautiful town" in Spanish) was four or five stories high and could house 800 to 1,000 people. Chaco Canyon also had hundreds of miles of unpaved roads, some 30 feet wide—which is strange for a people with no draft animals or wheeled vehicles. A farming people who lived in an arid region, the Anasazi developed elaborate water systems with terraces, dams, reservoirs, and irrigation ditches. All of these North American accomplishments resembled similar developments in the great Mesoamerican cultural centers, yet each was different; each achievement—whether in architecture, town planning, or ceramic design—carried the distinctive mark of the people who created it.

Further east, a very different society developed at Cahokia, an enormous site four miles east of the Mississippi River and across from modern St. Louis. A trading center with perhaps 20,000 people at its height, Cahokia was the largest city in North America. It covered some 200 acres divided into plazas and gardens, all surrounded by a palisade that required 20,000 logs. Its most prominent landmark was a massive pyramid, 100 feet tall, made of earth, not stone, but otherwise reminiscent of Mexican structures. The Mississippian people of Cahokia also began to grow maize (corn) with large cobs, like those painstakingly developed over several centuries by Mesoamericans. Corn culture soon spread between the Mississippi River and the Atlantic, where Cahokia's influence was strongest.

Corn cultivation also spread up the Mississippi and to lands north of the Ohio River, then east to the Atlantic seaboard. There Algonquian and Iroquoian people adopted the easily grown plant. Not all of these incipient farmers became sedentary; many cultivated crops only to supplement the hunt. Nuts, berries, and other products of the wild also remained important food sources for the Indians of the East and North, many of whom burned the forests' underbrush every year to encourage the growth of wild strawberries and

Hohokam people probably migrated from the south and took up lands in today's Arizona, where they demonstrated their Mexican heritage by building hundreds of miles of canals to irrigate their crops and constructing ball courts reminiscent of those found throughout Mesoamerica. Like their neighbors, the Hohokam were traders and craftsmen whose products included graceful ceramic jars with red geometric designs painted on a buff background. Farther east and south, the Mogollon people, ancestors of the Zuni, settled in forests and upland meadows in Arizona and northern Mexico. There they lived year-round in houses dug into the earth and grouped in villages near their farmlands. They also created ceramic pottery, some of which dates as early as C.E. 750–1000, which they painted in intricate black and white patterns.

To the north of the Hohokam and Mogollon, the Anasazi, ancestors of the Pueblos, also lived in pit houses and produced handsome ceramics painted in gray or black on white. But between C.E. 700 and 1000, they began constructing large aboveground housing complexes. Chaco Canyon in northwestern

other natural food crops, reduce the population of pests such as rodents and mosquitoes, and encourage deer and other game to move nearer the forests' edge. But agricultural products, particularly corn, became a continuing part of the Indian diet because they could be stored for winter consumption—or, as the Iroquian-speaking Hurons of the Great Lakes area would discover, used as trade goods with other peoples who lived too far north to grow corn.

Then, around 1140, one or more disasters struck. The Anasazi abandoned Chaco Canyon, and the Hohokam left many of their population centers. Even Cahokia's population began to drop around 1300. By 1500, the city was in ruins. Elsewhere, too, there were signs of trouble: in about 1450, for example, large villages on the Queen Charlotte Islands of the Pacific Northwest were abandoned. Why? In the Southwest, drought might explain the crisis. But the answer is nowhere certain. It seems likely, however, that the population of pre-Columbian North America—a disputed figure, with estimates ranging from 1 million to 18 million—peaked at about 1,200, then began to decline.

At almost every point, uncertainty surrounds the Indians' earliest history. Their story is told in terms of spear points and pottery fragments—in terms of what they made, not what they said. It's a story in which millennia pass like months in the histories of cultures with written records, a story for the most part without heroes or villains. Even the names of Indian peoples and places are often inventions of a later time: "Anasazi" means "enemy ancestors" in the language of the Navajo people who arrived in the Southwest after 1700; "Cahokia" is the name given the city by Indians who arrived after it had been abandoned. The original names have been lost.

We know enough, however, to recognize that mobility, diversity, and inventiveness were American characteristics long before the first Europeans arrived.

## European Discovery and Conquest

Like their Indian predecessors, the earliest European arrivals seem to have stumbled on America. Beginning in the eighth century, Norsemen, or Vikings, who had been pushed from their homes in Scandinavia by wars and population growth, settled the Faeroe, Shetland, and Orkney Islands in the eastern North Atlantic. Then they moved farther west, first to Iceland in about 874 and later, under the leadership of Erik the Red, to

Greenland. In about 986, a ship blown off course on its way to Greenland sighted the North American coast, which Leif Erikson, the son of Erik the Red, and other members of his family explored. The Norse founded at least one camp there at L'Anse aux Meadows in northern Newfoundland, where in the 1960s archaeologists discovered remains that date back to about C.E. 1000. Aside from that evidence, the tale of the Viking explorations is known mainly through Norse sagas written down long after the events they describe. In any case, the Newfoundland settlement failed, perhaps because of

A ceramic vase or urn, one of a very few artifacts found at the Cahokia site (in today's Missouri).

encounters with hostile Indians whom the sagas call "skraelings." By the thirteenth century, Iceland and Greenland had also entered a period of decline, so little came of that beginning, knowledge of which remained confined to Scandinavia.

The results were different in 1492, when Christopher Columbus set eyes on lands in the western Atlantic. News of his discovery spread and led to further explorations, and then to efforts at conquering and controlling the newly discovered lands and their peoples. The European discovery of America has long been considered a central event of the Renaissance, a period roughly from the mid-fourteenth through mid-sixteenth century in which Europe saw a "rebirth" of learning that was increasingly focused on humans and the world. In truth, Europeans ventured out to discover new lands for economic as well as intellectual reasons. The religious mindset of Europe's medieval past also shaped those people of the Renaissance who enlarged Europe's understanding of the world, leading them to try to serve the cause of God while enriching themselves and advancing their own places in the world.

### FROM THE MEDITERRANEAN TO THE ATLANTIC

The process that ultimately brought Europeans to America began with expeditions that headed not west but east. Beginning in the late eleventh century, European Christians undertook a series of Crusades to win control of the Holy Land from its Islamic rulers. After a first flush of success, the Crusaders failed in the face of powerful resurgent Muslim forces, and by the late thirteenth century, they had been forced back to Europe. But militant Western Christianity persisted, above all in Spain, where Christians spent hundreds of years attempting to rid the land of Muslims who had arrived there in 711, an effort known as the *reconquista* ("reconquest"). By the fifteenth century, the Muslims, or Moors, were confined to the kingdom of Granada, which bordered the Mediterranean Sea in the southern side of the Iberian peninsula. Granada fell to Spanish Christians in 1492, ending the *reconquista;* but there were other places where crusading Christians could exercise their zeal on people who might be more open to conversion than the Islamic followers of the prophet Mohammed. The Spanish carried to America both institutions and attitudes that had been formed over the centuries of the *reconquista.*

Although Western Christians' efforts to conquer the Holy Land failed, that experience increased their knowledge of the Mediterranean, a region whose technology was at the time superior to that of western Europe. There, too, Europeans encountered writings of the ancient world that had been lost in Europe and acquired a taste for new foods and flavors. In the fifteenth century, the Mediterranean was a vigorous trading area. That great water highway carried to Europe items produced along its shore, such as grain and salt for preserving fish, as well as a vast array of luxury goods from Asia. Among imports from the East were Chinese silks, Indian cotton, precious stones, and above all, spices—a category that included drugs, cosmetics, dyes, perfumes, even glue and sugar. Pepper, cinnamon, cloves, and other condiments, used for flavoring and preserving food, proved a welcome addition to the bland diets of Europe.

Certain Italian city-states, particularly Genoa and Venice, controlled the trade between the Mediterranean and western Europe. They used their monopoly to raise the prices of goods, which would have been high in any case since the items were often brought overland from Asia to ports on the eastern Mediterranean. High prices led purchasers to seek other suppliers and caused potential suppliers to find new routes to Asia.

Portugal led the way. Situated on the far western side of the Iberian peninsula, with a long Atlantic coastline, the country was well positioned to extend its influence into the Atlantic and down to Africa. Old histories sing the praises of Dom Henrique, the son of Portugal's King John I (r. 1385–1433), who became known among English scholars as Prince Henry the Navigator. He was probably more an anti-Muslim militant anxious to support his followers than the intellectual of myth, anxious to learn about things "hidden from other men, and secret." Prince Henry nonetheless supported Portugal's capture of Ceuta in Muslim North Africa (1415) and sponsored voyages that, through the early fifteenth century, pushed ever farther down the West African coast, through waters once considered impenetrable, to destinations previously unknown to Europeans. By the time of his death in 1460, Portuguese sailors had traveled as far south as Sierra Leone, well below the point where, according to legend, a Sea of Darkness consumed those foolhardy enough to venture into its waters. Then, after a pause, Portugal's King John II (r. 1481–1495) resumed explorations of the African coast. Under John II, Bartholomeu Dias finally sailed all the way to the southernmost point of Africa and around the Cape of Good Hope, in 1487–88. From there, the Portuguese could sail up the east coast of Africa to India, which Vasco da Gama did in 1497–99.

Explorations of Africa had several profitable by-products. Portuguese ships blown off course first discovered Madeira, an island in the Atlantic that the Portuguese claimed (1418–19), colonized, and made into a profitable source of sugar (a commercial product of rapidly growing popularity)

Prince Henry the Navigator as he appeared in a religious painting of the late fifteenth century, by the Portuguese Renaissance artist Nuno Goncalves.

and wine. They developed the Cape Verde Islands (1445) and attempted unsuccessfully to take the Canary Islands, which became instead a possession of Spain. The Portuguese also acquired the Azores (1431–54), which stretched a thousand miles into the Atlantic from western Portugal, about a third of the way to America, and islands along the African coast farther south, including São Tomé. West Africa, aside from providing a route to Asia, produced a number of valuable trade products, including ivory, fur and oil from seals, black pepper, some gold dust, and a supply of "black gold"—dark-skinned slaves who were first used as domestic servants, artisans, and market or transportation workers in Lisbon or Seville, and later as laborers on sugar plantations in the Atlantic islands.

To reach West African or island locations and return home raised challenges beyond any faced by European sailors at the time of the First Crusade. As a result, the Portuguese (and other Europeans) began using and developing navigational devices, many of which were of Arab origin, and building better ships for the needs of explorers and traders who sailed not the Mediterranean, an inland sea, but the open ocean.

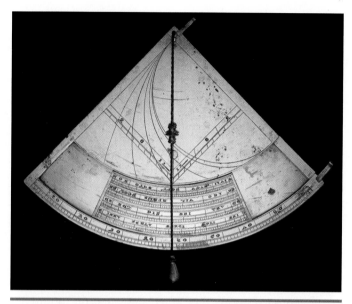

A fourteenth-century English quadrant, used to determine latitude at sea. Mariners aligned sights on the right with the polestar, then noted where the plumb line hit the scale on the rounded edge. Accurate readings were difficult on a turbulent sea.

## FIFTEENTH-CENTURY NAVIGATION

The Norse sailed the North Atlantic on small, single-decked and single-masted ships with a square sail. Their route to Greenland included a stretch on the open sea of over 1,000 nautical miles; otherwise, most of their voyages remained within sight of land. The Greenland crossing was daunting, however, and the Vikings made it regularly over several centuries without the benefit of any known charts or instruments, except perhaps for a lead that could be dropped to determine depth and the nature of the sea's floor. The Vikings gauged the distance they had traveled mainly by dead reckoning, estimating their speed and so their distance from their point of departure. Like other sailors of early times, they took into account sounds and smells, the presence of birds or other animals, of ice or fog, or the color of the sea to determine their location. It could even be that when Norse seamen were beyond sight of land, they studied the height of the sun at midday or, at night, the polestar (North Star), by which they could determine at least roughly on which latitude they were sailing. How they made those measurements remains a mystery, but by knowing their latitude and the latitude of their destination, the Vikings could keep on course in the open sea. Unfortunately, clouds or fog often prevented celestial observations. Norse sagas testify

that the seamen often lost all sense of direction or landed at the wrong place.

Most fifteenth-century European sailors were not much better off. Dead reckoning remained the usual way of determining location. Seamen did have use of the compass, an instrument of Chinese origin. It consisted of a magnetized iron wire or needle mounted on a pin so it could move freely; the pin itself was mounted on a base, or "card," that marked off directions. The needle pointed to the north, but not exactly; in fact, the extent to which magnetic north deviated from true north at different points on the globe (as a result of mineral deposits in the earth) was understood and charted only in the sixteenth century. Within confined sea spaces, such as the Mediterranean, the compass was the standard instrument for keeping ships on course. But the deviation of magnetic from true north made the compass of only limited use for navigation over substantial distances across several degrees of latitude. On the open ocean, European seamen instead followed the technique of "running down the latitude": once they knew the latitude of their destination, they would sail north or south to that degree of latitude, then turn east or west until they caught sight of land. At first, they determined latitude by observing celestial bodies; but by the late fifteenth century, two instruments existed to make that job easier: the quadrant and the astrolabe.

The quadrant was an instrument in the shape of a quarter circle with 90 degrees marked off on the outer, circular edge, and with a plumb line (a line with a weight at one end) that hung down from the apex (the circle's center) toward the edge. Pinhole sights along one of the straight sides were aligned with the polestar. By noting where the plumb line hit the scale, mariners could determine their latitudes with reasonable accuracy. However, this procedure required a relatively calm sea; otherwise the plumb line would bob around, making useful readings impossible.

As a result, seamen came to prefer other devices, such as the mariners' astrolabe, which was a simplified version of a complex instrument used by astronomers since the Middle Ages. It consisted of a disk, usually six to ten inches wide, with degrees marked along the outer edge, and an alidade, or indicator, mounted across the center and pointing toward the edge. The astrolabe was usually hung at a place onboard convenient for taking readings, since it needed to be perpendicular (again, a problem on a heaving deck); then a seaman would move the alidade until it pointed to the polestar. Later, in the sixteenth century, a cheaper, wooden handheld device, the cross staff, emerged to measure latitude. A seaman aimed the instrument at a star much as a crossbowman would take aim (thus "shooting" the star), then adjusted a sliding crosspiece so that it indicated the distance between the horizon and the star. He could then read the star's altitude from a scale marked along the central rod. Accurate readings, however, required great skill, and mistakes were common.

The quadrant and astrolabe depended on readings based on the polestar—which gradually disappeared from sight as ships, such those of Portugal exploring the African coast, slipped below the equator. As a result, Portugal's King John II commissioned a set of mathematicians to devise a method of determining latitude by observing the sun. From their work emerged the first European navigation manual, which was published in 1509 but probably circulated in manuscript before then. The book included a list of latitudes for locations from Lisbon to the equator, a table of the sun's declinations, and instructions on determining latitude with reference to either the sun or the North Star. The manual was the most advanced statement of fifteenth-century navigation. It became the basis for navigators' training in Portugal and Spain after 1500, and these navigators spread its influence beyond the Iberian peninsula. To decide how far a ship had traveled,

however, sailors remained dependent on dead reckoning, because the determination of longitude was much more complex than that of latitude. No practical means of finding longitude at sea emerged until the late eighteenth century.

The Portuguese also developed ships that were exceptionally maneuverable and well suited for open-ocean sailing. Most European ships at the beginning of the fifteenth century were designed for carrying cargoes along coasts over relatively short distances. They were short and broad, and powered by a single mainsail that worked well when the wind was behind it. On other occasions, they depended on galleys of oarsmen to keep the boat moving. Soon designers in Portugal and southern Spain began building ships longer and narrower than the usual merchant ships—the caravels, which became the main vessels of the explorers—and equipped them with triangular lateen sails, borrowed from Arab predecessors, that allowed a ship to sail with winds blowing not just from behind but from either side. Ships gradually became longer and larger, higher in the water with more decks and more space for cargoes and crews (necessary on voyages that could last several months), and equipped with a complex combination of sails. By late in the fifteenth century, ships with two large square sails and a lateen auxiliary sail, allowing both speed and maneuverability, became common on oceangoing vessels.

Mapping, too, underwent substantial development. The Renaissance brought new means of conveying proportions and distance in drawings and paintings, and a similar effort to make maps that accurately portrayed the earth's geography. First, expert mapmakers in Venice, Genoa, and Majorca (or, later, Barcelona and Lisbon) expanded the "portolan," or sea chart, which existed mainly for the Mediterranean in the late Middle Ages, to incorporate islands in the Atlantic and the West African coast. These navigation charts, which showed distances and bearings according to the compass between given locations, included remarkably accurate sketches of coastlines on single large sheets of vellum, with the names of ports written perpendicular to the coasts. They specified offshore hazards such as rocks or shoals but gave no information on currents, tides, or sea depths. Later marine charts included the western Atlantic and sometimes indicated the degree of latitude at which ports were located and the deviation between true and magnetic north.

World maps were different. Created in the Middle Ages for devotional purposes or to express cosmological beliefs, not as aids to navigation, they characteristically showed a single large landmass surrounded by water with Jerusalem at or near the center. In the fifteenth century, they, too, changed—in response first to the rediscovery of ancient learning, including the *Geography* of Claudius Ptolemy (long known to the Arabs but first translated into Latin in 1406), and later to firsthand information brought back by explorers and traders. Ptolemy, an Egyptian who lived in the second century C.E., attempted to summarize all the geographical knowledge of his time. He not only understood that the earth was round (as did others before him and most knowledgeable Europeans of the fifteenth century) but also proposed a system of dividing the sphere into 360 degrees of latitude and longitude. Although the use of such coordinates to locate places on the globe was not entirely unknown in medieval Europe, Ptolemy's use of them seemed revolutionary when his *Geography* reappeared there in the fifteenth century. The system he used as a basis for constructing maps had the effect of reducing a world filled with mystery to a predictable geometric order. However, Ptolemy underestimated the size of the earth by about a quarter, and his depiction of lands and bodies of water outside the Mediterranean world was more imaginative than accurate. He nonetheless became the leading source of geographical information for Renaissance scholars. His errors would be corrected by the observations of sailors who often understood the utility of sailing by latitude without knowing the term or understanding the mathematics behind the use of celestial observations.

Maps were not simply artistically presented records of known facts. They also had a political function: they designated those parts of the world that specific European countries claimed as their own, erasing in the process the claims of native peoples. Moreover, printing, which allowed maps to be replicated and widely distributed, increased their imperial influence. Yet the very incompleteness of the information maps conveyed provoked curiosity and inspired further explorations.

What exactly lay in the waters west of Europe and east of Asia? One theory proposed the existence of antipodes, countervailing masses of land on opposite sides of the earth, which implied that there was one or more vast continents somewhere out in the "Ocean Sea" to balance Eurasia and Africa. Another theory held that the world's surface was mainly covered by land, most of which was known, and that the Ocean Sea was not as wide as many people thought. One prominent cosmographer estimated the distance from the Canary Islands to China as 5,000 miles. That was not quite navigable in the fifteenth century, but the journey could be

Christopher Columbus as painted by Sebastiano del Piombo in 1519, after Columbus's death. There is no known portrait of Columbus made from life.

broken at Japan and other islands that were known or hypothesized.

Fifteenth-century world-map makers included in the waters west of Europe not only newly discovered or rediscovered islands such as the Azores and Canaries, but others as yet unseen with names such as Antillia or Isle of Brasil. Were they real, like the "lion in the Ocean sea" that Sir Humphrey Gilbert's crew would observe in 1583, or a figment of someone's imagination? The only way to know for sure was to go and have a look.

## CHRISTOPHER COLUMBUS

The man who most wanted to go was Christopher Columbus, the red-haired, ruddy-faced son of a Genoese weaver and textile merchant. Born in 1451, Columbus became a merchant seaman and made several voyages in the Mediterranean and along the eastern Atlantic coast. In 1476, he is said to have joined a Genoese fleet bound for England that the French attacked off the Portuguese coast. He was rescued from the wreckage and went to Lisbon, where his brother Bartholomew was a map and chart maker. At some point in the mid-1470s, still working as a merchant seaman, he probably sailed to England, Iceland, and Ireland, which would have increased his knowledge of the Atlantic. Columbus eventually became the captain of his own ship. In 1479, he married a Portuguese woman whose father collected maps and writings on the Atlantic, and they spent a few years in the Madeira Islands. After his wife's death in 1484, he returned to Lisbon with a son, Diego, and in 1485 moved again, this time to the Spanish city of Seville, another lively maritime center.

By then, Columbus was convinced that it was possible to reach Asia by sailing west from Europe. He had little formal education but was fluent in several languages, including Portuguese, and kept up with contemporary cartography, geography, and cosmology as best he could. He was also a devout Christian who decided that the Garden of Eden was on the side of the earth exactly opposite Jerusalem, such that each provided the center for different, antipodal hemispheres. His idea of sailing westward to Asia was, however, based more firmly on a set of mutually reinforcing geographical and mathematical errors. Columbus owned a copy of Cardinal Pierre d'Ailly's *Imago Mundi*, written about 1410. He read and reread the book, filling its margins with handwritten comments, and seems to have accepted virtually everything

The earliest depiction of Columbus's landing in the New World, from Giuliano Dati's *Narrative of Columbus*, 1493.

d'Ailly said, including his estimate of the width of Asia—which was far too large. Columbus also knew Ptolemy's estimate of the circumference of the globe—which was far too small. Together, these two mistakes had the effect of moving the eastern edge of Asia closer to Europe (without, of course, taking account of the fact that America lay between them). How great was the gap between Europe and Asia? Florentine cosmographer Paolo Toscanelli argued that some 5,000 miles separated the Canary Islands and the Chinese city of Quinsay (Hangzhou), whose riches the thirteenth-century traveler Marco Polo had described. But Columbus figured the voyage was only about 3,500 miles. He also figured the distance to Japan was even less—maybe by as much as 1,500 miles if Japan was that far from the Asian coast, as Marco Polo claimed (incorrectly)—and so technically possible to reach by sailing westward.

When Columbus presented his proposal to Portugal's King John II, the king was uninterested. Not only did his advisers question Columbus's reasoning, but after Dias had rounded the Cape of Good Hope in 1487–88, Portugal had no need for another route to Asia. Columbus then tried unsuccessfully to interest England, France, and Spain in his scheme. Finally, in 1492, Queen Isabel of Castile agreed to sponsor his voyage. Expansion within the Iberian peninsula was a prerequisite for external expansion, and in that year Spain finally defeated the Moors in Granada. Isabel then promptly expelled the Jews from Spain (the name for the kingdoms joined as a result of her marriage, in 1469, to Ferdinand of Aragon). With the Spanish Crown's power at home reasonably secure, it could use its experience in conquering internal enemies to facilitate conquest elsewhere. In 1492, Spain—or, more exactly, Isabel—was ready to turn outward.

In April, the contract was signed: Columbus would be admiral and become governor of any lands he discovered, with a claim to one-tenth of all the trade or treasure from those newly discovered territories. The promises made to Columbus were in the tradition of the *adelantados*, men licensed by the Crown to win territory from the Moors. In return, they were given governing powers and a share in the spoils. The *adelantados* were normally self-financed, but the Crown ordered the port of Palos to supply the newly appointed "Admiral of the Ocean Sea" with three ships. They included two 60-ton caravels, the *Niña* and the *Pinta*, and, as the flagship, a cumbersome, 120-ton merchant vessel, probably built to carry wine and not particularly well suited for Columbus's purpose, which he renamed the *Santa María*.

The small fleet sailed first to the Canaries and then, on September 6, 1492, set to sea, heading first south to the 28th parallel, then due west, "riding the latitude" with a good wind. A little over a month later, on October 12, a crew member on the *Pinta* caught sight of land (perhaps Watling Island in the Bahamas), where the Spaniards first landed. Columbus named the island San Salvador ("holy savior"), then went on to explore the Bahamas as well as Cuba and what he called Hispaniola ("Spanish island," now Haiti and the Dominican Republic). There, after the *Santa María* was wrecked on Christmas Day, he founded a post called La Navidad ("the Nativity"), the first European settlement in the Americas since the time of the Vikings. He left thirty-five men on Hispaniola when he set sail for Spain in January 1493. With him he brought a few Arawak Indians, parrots, and some gold jewelry bartered from the natives, but no news of gold mines despite his prayer, "Our Lord in his pity guide me that I may find gold." The inhabitants of the islands, Columbus assured Queen Isabel, were friendly and generous, and would make fit converts to Christianity. As for the land and the animals and plants of this island world, he reported that they were sometimes much like those of Spain but at other times strange. The fish were a particular surprise, "so *different* from ours," with such beautiful colors "that everyone marvels . . . and takes great delight in them." The birds, too, were "of so many sorts and so different from ours, that one is left marveling." Even the foods were different: Cuba grew vegetables that were "like carrots" but tasted "like chestnuts" (probably potatoes) and beans "very different from ours."

News of Columbus's discoveries preceded his return: a letter he sent a supporter on February 15, 1493, while still off the Canaries on the return trip, was printed at Barcelona, then reprinted another eight times that year. As the news spread, questions arose over just what lands he had "discovered" and who owned them. The pope confirmed Spain's claim in two bulls (official papal pronouncements) entitled *Inter Caetera* (1493) that also said that all future discoveries west of a north-south line 100 leagues west of the Azores and Cape Verde Islands would belong to Spain. Portugal's John II protested; and by the Treaty of Tordesillas (1494), Portugal and Spain agreed to move the dividing line to 370 leagues west of the Cape Verde Islands, with Portugal holding title to lands discovered to its east. In that way, Portugal won what became Brazil on the eastward bulge of South America, which Pedro Álvares Cabral discovered in 1500.

Columbus lived to make three more voyages to America. The second (1493–96) was the greatest: he set off from Cadiz with seventeen ships and some 1,200 men. After claiming Dominica, Antigua, Guadeloupe, and Puerto Rico for Spain, the expedition arrived at Hispaniola to discover that La Navidad had been totally destroyed. That led to brutal reprisals against the natives, whom the Spanish enslaved and used to seek gold and to work the land. Columbus left his brothers in charge of a new settlement called Isabela, but—in a pattern that would be repeated again and again—the settlers broke into bitter factions, food supplies failed, and disease wasted away the weakened population. Columbus's third voyage (1498–1500) was smaller and ended disastrously when the new Spanish governor of Hispaniola charged the admiral and his brothers with having grievously misgoverned the colony and sent them home in chains. The fourth and final voyage (1502–04) was no more successful. Although Columbus explored the coast of Central America, which he came to think was a new part of Asia that no one had previously mapped, all four ships of the expedition were lost, and he returned to Spain only after being rescued from Jamaica, where he had been marooned for a year.

Columbus's death in 1506 went almost unnoticed, and his reputation since has experienced ups and downs as extreme as those of his lifetime. He clearly was no administrator, and he proved perfectly willing to take the lands and enslave the Arawak people of the West Indies, who, like the native people of the Canary Islands, were wiped out by imported diseases within a century of the Spaniards' arrival. His own inclination, however, was to establish trading factories in the lands he discovered, like those of Portugal on the west coast of Africa, rather than colonies that displaced older inhabitants. His vision was more mystical than scientific—especially by the time of his third voyage, when he thought of himself as chosen by God for some great Christian mission—and he never knew exactly what he had found.

But it was Columbus who announced to Europe the existence of lands in the western Atlantic that were previously unknown to them. And he was without dispute one of the greatest navigators of all time, a man who was not just remarkably lucky (after all, the Caribbean islands lay about where he expected to find Japan, and the American mainland where China should have been), but who quickly found the best and shortest routes in the middle latitudes to and from America. In 1492, he set out west from the Canaries near the 28th parallel with the northeast trade winds behind him, and

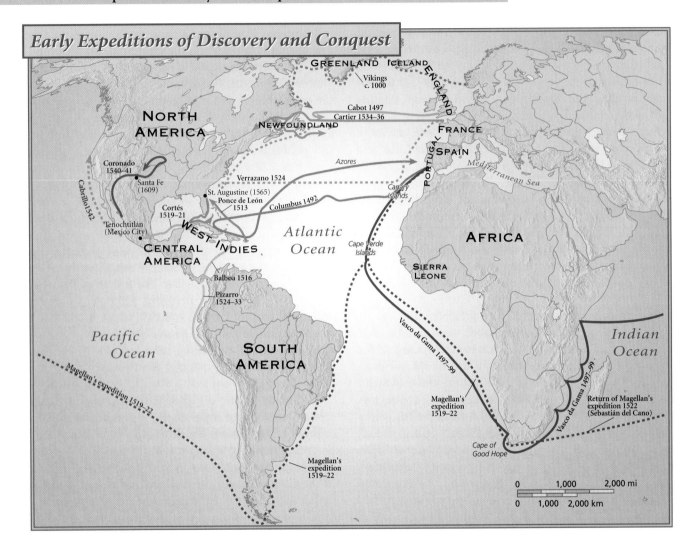

Early Expeditions of Discovery and Conquest

on his return he struck north looking for a westerly wind, which he quickly found on the latitude of Bermuda. On his second voyage, he made some slight improvements in the route, which became standard for later Spanish voyages. For a man who lived in an age of navigation, that alone was a claim to distinction.

FURTHER EXPLORATIONS

Not everyone agreed with Columbus that the lands he discovered were parts of Asia. Peter Martyr, another Italian who, like Columbus, settled in Spain, and author of the popular *De Orbe Novo*, remarked in 1494 that "when treating of this country one must speak of a new world, so distant is it and so devoid of civ-

ilization and religion." In the next century, more and more observers came to share Martyr's conclusion. The truth, however, could only be established by further observations.

Two years after Peter Martyr made his pronouncement, King Henry VII of England commissioned John Cabot to explore the North Atlantic for a passage to the Orient. Cabot (Giovanni Cabato) was an Italian, probably from Genoa like Columbus, but he became a citizen of Venice. After studying navigation in Spain, he made his home in Bristol, an English port on the Atlantic. In 1497, Cabot went to sea in a small ship, the *Matthew*, with a crew of only eighteen or twenty men. The ship swung out beyond Ireland and turned north and then west, riding the latitude without, it seems, benefit of either astrolabe or quadrant (some seasoned seamen disdained the use of those tools). They made a landfall in what the English would later call "New Found Land," which Cabot claimed for England. Members of the Cabot expedition saw no people on these lands, though they observed signs of human habitation. The coastal waters, they noted, were so alive with fish that they could be caught with baskets.

Cabot became a hero after reporting his findings, and English merchants eager to find a northwest passage to China helped finance a larger expedition in 1498. It ended badly: all four of Cabot's ships were lost, and he with them. Later, in 1504 and 1508–09, Sebastian Cabot, John's son, made additional voyages into northern waters, perhaps reaching the Hudson Bay, but he failed to find a northwest passage. By then, fishermen had brought cargoes of fish, especially cod, to Bristol from the North Atlantic fisheries. English ships soon began sailing every spring to Newfoundland, returning with their catch in the fall. The Cabot voyage of 1497 gave England a claim to North America, and the annual pilgrimages of fishermen added to the country's knowledge of the North Atlantic. Portuguese, French, and, from the 1520s, Spanish fishermen also visited Newfoundland, making the town of St. John's an international meeting place where fishermen from many countries gathered and swapped navigational information. It was from Newfoundland that Sir Humphrey Gilbert sailed in 1583, when his men sighted the curious "lion" swimming in the sea.

Other voyages added to European knowledge of North America. In 1524, King Francis I of France sent Giovanni de Verrazano, a Florentine, to find a route through North America to Asia. He failed, but in the course of his search Verrazano explored the Atlantic coast from the Carolinas up as far as Nova Scotia. And between 1534 and 1536, Jacques Cartier, who came from Normandy in northern France, explored the waters west of Newfoundland for Francis I. Cartier sailed up the St. Lawrence River to Quebec and then, in smaller boats, to Montreal. True to form, he claimed the land for France, although the climate proved dishearteningly cold and the land gave little evidence of the gold and other riches Cartier sought.

Spain and Portugal—or Italians sailing under those flags—explored the lands farther south. Amerigo Vespucci, a wealthy and well-connected Florentine businessman who took an interest in geography and navigation, participated in three or four of these voyages—first from Spain between 1497 and 1499, and then two more after he moved to Portugal. Vespucci commanded no voyage of exploration; he traveled, as one source said, as a person "who knew cosmography and matters pertaining to the sea." Later he wrote accounts of his voyages—or, more likely, someone else fabricated reports based on a handful of his letters—that proved very popular. Vespucci, it seems, doubted from the first that the lands Columbus found were part of Asia. After seeing Brazil, he concluded, like Peter Martyr before him, that the explorers had discovered a "new land," a continent that was, in effect, a barrier between Europe and Asia.

At about the time Vespucci's travel account was published, a set of scholars assembled at the Cathedral of St. Die in today's Alsace-Lorraine to create a new edition of Ptolemy's world atlas that would include the discoveries of Portugal and Spain. In 1507, they published an *Introduction to Cosmography . . . to which are added The Four Voyages of Amerigo Vespucci. . . .* The atlas proposed that the "fourth part of the earth"—beyond Europe, Asia, and Africa—that "Amerigo discovered" should be called "Amerige, the land of Amerigo . . . or America." Accordingly, a set of maps by Martin Waldseemüller that were published with the book labeled the western landmass "America." Other cartographers copied the map, so the name "America" caught on—although Spain continued to refer to its discoveries as "Las Indias" or "the Indies."

On Waldseemüller's map, America appears as a long, thin strip of land with no geographical features on its western side. Thereafter, explorers gradually accumulated more information on the geography of America and what lay beyond it. In 1513, Juan Ponce de León explored the coast of Florida; three years later, Vasco Nuñez de Balboa arrived at Panama and caught sight of another great body of water, the Pacific Ocean, on the other side. The ocean's dimensions, however, remained unknown until Fernando Magellan, a Portuguese navigator sailing for Spain, circumnavigated the globe (1519–22) on a voyage that was perhaps the age's most spectacular navigational achievement. Magellan did not live to see the trip completed; he and several crew members were killed in the Philippine Islands in 1521. Juan Sebastián del Cano, who assumed command, continued on to the Spice Islands (now the Molucca Islands of Indonesia), down around the east coast of Africa, and up the Atlantic to Spain. The voyage disproved Ptolemy's estimate of the world's size: the distance west from Europe to Asia was enormous, and two continents, North and South America, blocked the route. Vast regions remained to be explored and mapped, and the search for a passage through or over the Americas continued. But in less than a century, knowledge of world geography had been transformed.

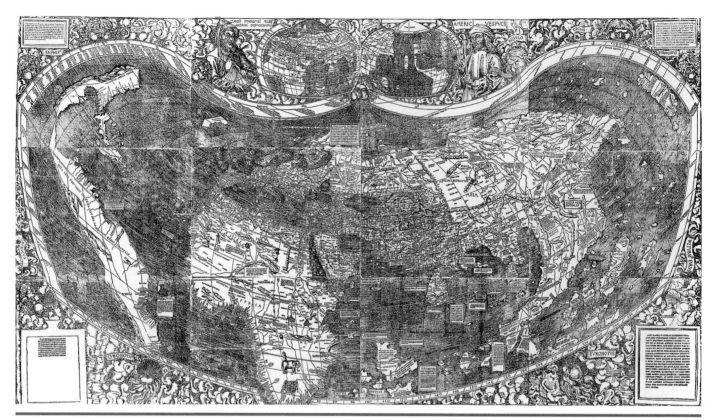

The famous Waldseemüller map of the world, first published in 1507, gave America its name. Note the figures of Ptolemy and Amerigo Vespucci at the top.

### THE CONQUEST OF MEXICO

For a quarter century after Columbus's first voyage, Spain concentrated its attention on the islands in the western Atlantic. In 1496, the Spanish began building the city of Santo Domingo, their first governmental center in the Americas. Then they began the conquest of Puerto Rico, Jamaica, the Bahamas, and, in 1511, Cuba. The settlers clustered in cities, as they had in Spain, forcing the natives to supply gold and food and to work on sugar plantations founded on the model of Madeira. In the late 1490s, royal officials formally granted groups of Indians to specific settlers in reward for service. Those grants were known as *encomiendas*. The recipient of an *encomienda*, an *encomendero*, formally assumed responsibility for the protection and Christianization of the Indians entrusted to him, and in return he received from them tribute in the form of goods and labor. In fact, however, the *encomienda* led to the virtual enslavement of the Indians.

Some clergymen questioned the Spaniards' right to rule and exploit native peoples, but defenders of the system insisted that in 1493 the pope had granted Spaniards dominion over "pagans" whom they were to convert. On encountering new groups of native peoples, the Spanish formally read a *requerimiento*, or notice, written in Spanish, demanding that the natives accept Spanish rule and Christianity or their lands would be seized and they would be killed or enslaved. Soon, however, the Indian population began to decline: the native people of Hispaniola, who numbered as many as a million in 1492, all but disappeared by the middle of the next century as a result of imported illnesses as well as Spanish cruelty and exploitation. The supply of gold also began to run out. So the Spaniards looked for other places to supply the wealth and labor that the Caribbean islands lacked.

In 1517, an expedition that explored Yucatán and the Gulf of Mexico reported the existence of civilizations on the mainland that were richer and more populous than any in the Caribbean. Two years later, the Spanish governor in Havana commissioned the thirty-four-year-old Hernando Cortés, a headstrong and ambitious *encomendero* who had helped conquer Cuba, to make contact with the Indian empire in Mexico. Cortés set sail with eleven ships and over 500 men, including Bernal Días del Castillo, who later wrote a detailed history of the conquest of Mexico.

The invaders landed near the modern town of Veracruz on the Gulf of Mexico. Upon learning that the center of power and wealth lay inland, they began a march to the Valley of Mexico, collecting thousands of Indian allies along the way. The Aztec rulers of Mexico had established their power only within the previous century, and their yoke was not light. They collected heavy tribute, or taxes, enslaved defeated peoples, and seized their lands. The Aztecs also herded thousands of subject people to temples where executioners cut out their hearts and offered the still-throbbing organs to a god who, the Aztecs believed, demanded human sacrifices to make the sun rise and the world continue. Cortés had little difficulty winning support from Indian peoples anxious to break loose from the Aztecs' hold. After thousands of the powerful Tlaxcalans joined the Spanish forces, the Aztec ruler, Montezuma II, decided to invite Cortés to enter his capital, Tenochtitlán, peacefully. The Spaniards were amazed as they wound through the mountains and looked down at the cities and villages below, some on dry land, another—Tenochtitlán—located in the midst of a great lake and connected to the land by causeways, with temples and other stone buildings "arising from the water . . . like an enchanted vision." Indeed, Bernal Días recalled, "some of our soldiers asked whether it was not all a dream. . . . It was all so wonderful that I do not know how to describe this first glimpse of things never heard of, seen or dreamed before." Tenochtitlán, which the Spaniards entered on November 8, 1519, held some 300,000 people—far more than any city in Spain. The market to its north at Tlatelolco, where every day thousands of people bought a vast array of goods including foods, jewelry, feathers, birds, utensils, building materials, and slaves, was also like nothing they had ever seen. And the Spaniards found Tenochtitlán's bloodstained temples and, even more, the Aztecs' consumption of human flesh both surprising and profoundly repugnant. To be sure, the Spanish were themselves capable of vicious cruelty, but cannibalism was not in their repertoire.

Montezuma fed the Spaniards' greed with gold and other gifts. But, distrusting his intentions, they seized and held him

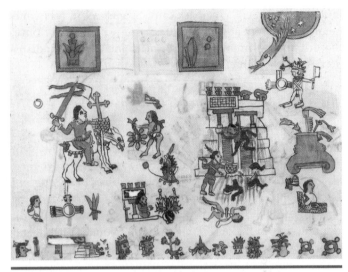

Cortés arriving at the Aztec capital, Tenochtitlán (later Mexico City), by an unknown Aztec artist, 1519–22.

captive until he was killed in the midst of a massive uprising against the invaders. On the night of June 30–July 1, 1520—La Noche Triste ("sorrowful night")—Aztec insurgents forced the Spaniards to flee the city, losing the riches they had collected as well as a third of their men. But over the next year, Cortés reorganized his followers, mobilized his Indian allies, and built thirteen brigantines—twin-masted, square-rigged vessels—that he equipped with firearms and used to control the causeways and block supplies from entering the island city. Finally, on August 21, 1521, the Spanish retook Tenochtitlán, destroying many of its buildings and people in the process.

There, on the ruins of the Aztec capital, Cortés began to build Mexico City, a center of Spanish colonial power over what became New Spain. The metropolis would be, Cortés decided, a New World creation more beautiful than even the city of Venice, with which it was frequently compared. The building of Mexico City exceeded any European project of the Renaissance. In the spring of 1523, according to contemporary reports, some 400,000 Mexican Indians were working "with such fervor that the labourers sang, and the songs and voices scarcely ceased at night." Forced labor was nothing new to the common people of Mesoamerica, but under the Spanish, unlike under all previous rulers, workers had access to an array of European building tools such as nails, screws, pulleys, wheelbarrows, and wheeled carts with, equally astonishing, mules to pull them. The Mexicans, Spanish observers commented, were "friends of novelties." And why not? For once, those European imports served not to increase the Indians' burdens but to lighten them.

### THE SPREAD OF SPANISH POWER

With the defeat of the Aztecs, the *conquistadores,* or conquerors—tough, avaricious Spaniards, generally of low birth or the younger sons of noble families, eager to improve their place in life—set out in search of other peoples to subdue and despoil. Between 1524 and 1533, Spaniards under Francisco Pizarro defeated the Inca peoples of Peru's Andean highlands, accumulating in the process thousands of pounds of gold and silver. Like Cortés, Pizarro used divisions among the Incas to his advantage. The hierarchical structure of Incan society, like

that of the Aztecs, also made conquest easier; by putting themselves at the apex of power in place of the old Incan rulers, the Spanish assumed command of the whole. However, factional disputes among the Spaniards delayed final consolidation of their power until the 1570s. The campaign against the Mayan people of the Yucatán peninsula and Guatemala, who lacked a central government, began in 1527; eighteen years passed before the Spanish established control.

From Peru, expeditions of discovery and conquest extended out to Chile and Colombia. Other Spaniards from Mexico City journeyed to parts of Central America unclaimed by Europeans and then to the north. Francisco Vásquez de Coronado marched into New Mexico and ventured as far north as modern-day Kansas in 1540 and 1541, and Juan Rodriguez Cabrillo sailed up the California coast and claimed that land for Spain in 1542. When neither these

---

*American Journal*

## *Where Do You Go Shopping?*

*Bernal Díaz Del Castillo, who accompanied Cortés during his conquest of Mexico, provided several descriptions of Indian life in his "History of the Conquest of New Spain." Among them is an account of the market at Tlatelolco, which was not only a place to buy and sell, but an immense spectacle as well, not least for the visiting Spaniards.*

Cortes and his men "were astounded at the great number of people and the quantities of merchandise, and at the orderliness and good arrangements that prevailed, for we had never seen such a thing before . . . Let us begin with the dealers in gold, silver, and precious stones, feathers, cloaks, and embroidered goods, and male and female slaves who are also sold there. They bring as many slaves to be sold in that market as the Portugese bring Negroes from Guinea. . . . Next there were those who sold coarser cloth, and cotton goods and fabrics made of twisted thread, and there were chocolate merchants. . . . In this way you could see every kind of merchandise to be found anywhere in New Spain, laid out in the same way as goods are laid out in my own district of Medina del Campo, a centre for fairs, where each line of stalls has its own

particular sort. So it was in this great market. There were those who sold sisal cloth and ropes and the sandals they wear on their feet, which are made from the same plant. . . . in another part [of the market] were skins of tigers and lions, otters, jackals, and deer, badgers, mountain cats, and other wild animals, some tanned and some untanned. . . . There were sellers of kidney-beans and sage and other vegetables and herbs in another place, and in yet another they were selling fowls, . . . also rabbits, hares, deer, young ducks, little dogs, and other such creatures. Then there were the fruiterers; and the woman who sold cooked food, flour and honey cake. . . . Then came pottery of all kinds. . . . Elsewhere they sold timber too, boards, cradles, beams, blocks and benches. . . . I must also mention, with all apologies, that they sold many canoe-loads of human excrement, which they kept in creeks near the market. This was for the manufacture of salt and the curing of skins, which they say cannot be done without it. . . .

"But why waste so many words on the goods in their great market? If I describe everything in detail I shall never be done."

explorers nor their successors found new empires rich in gold and silver, interest in North America declined.

In 1565, the Spanish founded a post at St. Augustine in Florida—the first permanent European settlement in North America—mainly to protect the route of the treasure ships that carried vast cargoes of precious metals from Peru and Mexico to Spain. That outpost was originally part of an elaborate scheme by the *adelantado* Pedro Menéndez de Avilés to establish a settlement in Florida from which the Spanish could control the eastern coast of North America. By 1600, only St. Augustine remained as a monument to Menéndez's failed dreams. A military outpost with some 500 people, mostly men who lived on government salaries, St. Augustine was sufficiently costly and its continued strategic value so questionable that the Crown decided to abandon it in 1606. Only the pleas of Franciscan missionaries that converted Indians needed access to the sacraments and that the missions needed military protection changed the mind of Spain's "most Christian King." As a result, that isolated Spanish base survived and then slowly grew, so that by 1700 St. Augustine held perhaps 1,500 people, including black slaves and Hispanized Indians.

The story of New Mexico was much the same. The *adelantado* there was Juan de Oñate, a wealthy, Mexican-born man from a high-ranking family, who formally took possession of New Mexico in 1598. Oñate dreamed of rich mines, abundant Indian laborers, and an easy passageway to the Atlantic or the Pacific, both of which he believed were so near that New Mexico could be supplied by sea. But within a year, his dreams began to go sour: hungry soldiers threatened mutiny; Spanish abuse provoked a revolt by the pueblo of Acoma, which Oñate's soldiers brutally repressed; and many colonists, fearing starvation, fled to Mexico. Bankrupt and charged with mismanagement, Oñate lost his commission in 1606, and the settlement of what a Spanish official called that "worthless land," hundreds of miles beyond the nearest settlements in northern Mexico, was nearly abandoned. Again the pleas of Franciscan missionaries secured the colony's survival. Through most of the seventeenth century, the Villa Real de Santa Fe (1610) was New Mexico's only municipality, though another community grew up after 1659 at El Paso del Norte (today Ciudad Juárez). Meanwhile, Hispanic settlers spread out along the Rio Grande to take advantage of Indian labor. The Spanish waited until late in the eighteenth century to establish frontier garrisons (*presidios*) and missions in California at San Diego (1769), Monterey (1770), and San Francisco (1776).

Charles V (r. 1516–56) was the embodiment of Spanish power in this period.

In short, the Spanish found what they sought in Central and South America: sources of wealth greater even than what Portugal gained from trade with Asia. The Crown would have trouble enough establishing its authority over that mainland empire given the independent, ambitious men who had taken possession of the Indians and their lands. As for the relatively barren territory to Mexico's north that Spain also claimed, there was no reason to pay the cost of consolidating the Crown's hold on it. In effect, most of North America was left to the Indian peoples who already lived there. In time, that terrain would provide bases for European nations who joined the contest for America relatively late and had to take whatever lands they could get.

### IMPERIAL GOVERNMENT

In the early sixteenth century, the Spanish Crown established an imperial governing structure in which ultimate power over its American possessions rested, in theory and often in fact, in its hands. At the apex of that structure stood the Council of the Indies, an institution created in 1524 out of the Council of Castile, the closest royal advisers. The Council of the Indies, which remained in Spain, drafted and issued laws for Spain's American territories and served as an appellate judicial court for civil cases that arose in the colonies. It also nominated both religious and secular officers and actively monitored their conduct in America, replacing those who were inept, corrupt, or in any way disloyal to the Crown.

Viceroys were the highest Spanish imperial officials in America. They were almost always born in Spain—*peninsulares,* not Creoles, or persons of Spanish blood born in America—and held office at the queen's or king's pleasure. Viceroys were responsible for executing the Council of the Indies' edicts, maintaining civil and military order, and overseeing the collection of revenues, the administration of justice, and Indian welfare—in short, for all aspects of Spanish rule in the colonies.

*Audiencias,* advisory and judicial bodies that could also do some provisional legislating for the territory under their supervision, were a step lower on the imperial hierarchy. There were more of them in America than there were viceroyalties, which they often predated, and they answered directly to the Council of the Indies.

The Crown and its advisers worked to undercut contrary interests and competing sources of power. For example, they excluded "heretics" from the colonies. No religious cleavages would divide the Spanish population of the New World, nor would there be communities of colonists at odds with the Crown's militant Catholicism.

The Spanish Crown also selected as colonial officials only persons highly likely to remain its loyal servants. That was the point of appointing viceroys who were almost always Spanish-born. Creoles were generally considered only for lower positions—and not in the regions where they were born, to which they might feel an affiliation that would compromise their loyalty to the Crown. Viceroys' conduct was also monitored through *visitas,* special commissions that visited incumbents to examine their enforcement of critical laws, and *residencias,* formal hearings held at the end of their terms. Retired viceroys could be punished severely for deviations from strict loyalty to the Crown while they were in office.

To be sure, the system was more perfect on paper than in reality. The communications system of the sixteenth and seventeenth centuries, which required months if not years for reports of problems to arrive in Spain and the appropriate orders to be conveyed back to America, limited the Crown's capacity to control its empire. Official inaction frequently greeted unpopular laws or edicts, and little could be done to make the system more responsive. "If death came from Madrid," one Spanish official commented, "we should all live to be very old men." The greatest threat to the Crown's dominance came, however, in the persons of the *encomenderos,* local strongmen who had received grants of rights over groups of Indians. Not only was their exploitation of the natives at odds with the Crown's religious sense of responsibility for the Indians' well-being, but the *encomenderos* became a locus of power potentially at odds with the Crown.

In one way after another, Spain attempted to stem the power of the *encomenderos.* It forbade the granting of more *encomiendas,* then declared that those in existence could not be passed on to *encomenderos'* heirs. When that edict proved unenforceable, the Crown attempted to limit the number of generations that could receive an *encomienda* by right of inheritance. These edicts more than any others tested the effectiveness of the Crown in maintaining its dominance. In the end, it won out over the *encomenderos* not so much because of its power to force compliance but because of a development that it by no means desired. A massive decline in the Indian population gradually undercut the power of the *encomenderos.* And so the pyramidal structure of Spanish imperial governance remained in place, providing both a model and a point of contrast for subsequent European regimes in the Americas.

## The Columbian Exchange

What allowed Cortés and a few hundred Spaniards to defeat the Aztecs, who vastly outnumbered them? His recruitment of allies among Indians discontented with Aztec rule reduced the imbalance of numbers. And Cortés, like Columbus, was lucky: he arrived in the first year of a fifty-two-year cycle in the Aztec calendar, just when, according to prophecy, the god Quetzalcoatl ("feathered serpent") would return from the East. Perhaps Montezuma thought Cortés was the returning god, which would help explain why he welcomed the Spaniard to Tenochtitlán.

Or did European technology explain the Spanish conquest? Cortés and other *conquistadores* carried gunpowder, which Europe had received from China. And the Spaniards' cannons and muskets provoked terror and panic among the Indians, who had no previous acquaintance with firearms. The Indians were also terrified by the horses the Spaniards rode, and by their mastiffs, huge dogs that could rip men apart. Nevertheless, the Aztecs recovered sufficiently to force the Spaniards from Tenochtitlán, raising the very real prospect that the conquest would be short-lived. Then Spanish technical advantages really came into play as they built, in effect, a navy, which helped them to reclaim the water bound city.

Spaniards on horses as depicted in a wall painting at Canyon de Chelly, in Arizona.

The Spanish also possessed a deadly, unseen ally: smallpox. After Cortés and his men had been driven from the city, according to an Indian account, "there came amongst us a great sickness. . . . It raged amongst us, killing vast numbers of people. It covered many all over with sores: on the face, on the head, on the chest, everywhere." Many died of the disease and others of starvation because "there was no one left alive to care for them." The pestilence lasted for "sixty days of horror," then diminished. "And when this had happened, the Spaniards returned." Smallpox seems also to have claimed the ruler of the Incas, which led to a division between claimants for his office that Pizarro used to great effect.

Diseases brought from Europe devastated the populations of the Americas. They were, however, only part of the "Columbian exchange"—a vast, complex intercontinental transfer of goods, plants, animals, and diseases that occurred after 1492. The results were more far-reaching than anyone anticipated.

## DISEASE AND DEMOGRAPHY

When Columbus arrived, most and perhaps all the peoples of the Americas had been isolated from other parts of the world for thousands of years. They were probably also descended from healthy ancestors. The weak and the sick were unlikely to join those parties of long-distance hunters who made their way across Beringia or the islands to its south, and any who died in the cold lands of the north were left there, with whatever infectious agents had caused their illnesses. Later, after Europeans had arrived, Indians could look back on earlier times with longing. "There was then no sickness," recalled a Mayan from Mexico's Yucatán peninsula, "they had no aching bones; they had then no high fever; . . . they had no burning chest" or "abdominal pain" or "consumption" or "headache," and "the course of humanity was orderly. The foreigners made it otherwise when they arrived here." In truth, however, the pre-Columbian peoples of America were far from disease-free. Ancient skeletons and deposits of human waste yield evidence that Indians suffered from dietary deficiencies, intestinal parasites of one sort or another, tuberculosis, and syphilis. The earliest Americans probably also suffered from various bacterial or viral infections whose presence defies detection after so long a passage of time.

But the Indians had had no exposure and so developed no resistance to many illnesses of fifteenth-century Europe. Those diseases, which were often contracted from airborne bacteria or viruses, proved to be even more deadly in the New World than they were in the Old. Smallpox appeared on Hispaniola in 1519 and then spread to the mainland, wiping out large numbers of native people. Individuals who survived smallpox might succumb to measles, influenza, mumps, typhus, diphtheria, or plague, which swept through the islands and then the mainland's population in waves after 1493.

This Aztec drawing shows some victims of a smallpox epidemic in shrouds (center), while two others, covered with pox, are dying (on the right).

What percentage of the native population died in the immediate aftermath of the European arrival? To answer requires knowing the population of the Americas in 1492, and on that there is no consensus. Estimates range from just over 8 million to 100 million. (By contrast, the population of Spain was under 7 million in 1492, and in 1500 the population of all Europe, east as well as west, was about 70 million.) One study of the Valley of Mexico estimates the population there at about 25 million in 1519, when Cortés arrived, and 1 million in 1600—a decline of 96 percent. Even if the original population was substantially lower, say 10 million, then dropped to 2 million, the decline was still on the order of 80 percent.

No doubt acts of Spanish brutality, which the Spanish colonist and priest Bartolomé de Las Casas carefully described in his *Brief Account of the Destruction of the Indies,* a report submitted to the Hapsburg emperor Charles V in 1540, contributed to the problem. If Las Casas and other observers were correct, the Indians not only suffered from overwork but were so demoralized that they frequently chose not to bear children. However, steep population declines occurred even among the scattered peoples of North America who re-mained free of subjection to the Spanish or any other European power. Disease and depopulation, in fact, often preceded the arrival of Europeans. That was true, for example, in sixteenth-century Peru and again in seventeenth-century New England, where Indians "died in heaps" during a severe epidemic before the English colonists arrived. It did not require a European to transmit European diseases: that could be done very effectively by contagious Indians who traveled from place to place infecting others after even brief contacts with European explorers or fishermen.

Nor were Europeans untouched by illness. The influenza that arrived in Hispaniola with Columbus's second voyage in late 1493 struck down settlers as well as Indians. By 1495, the combined effects of hunger and illness had reduced the newly arrived Spanish population by two-thirds. Columbus himself became deathly ill on several voyages, and in 1500 a missionary reported that all his fellow friars were in bad health and that "here one finds oneself always somewhat ill." But Spaniards and other Europeans who had contracted diseases such as smallpox, measles, or mumps as children were immune for life, which meant they could sometimes sleep in the same cabin with dying Indians without suffering any ill effects. Europeans were, however, vulnerable to syphilis, a disease that appeared in a new and severe form in Europe soon after Columbus first returned; it probably (though not certainly) came from America. Syphilis has devastating effects, particularly when it first appears in a population, but it spreads more slowly than diseases like smallpox since it is transmitted sexually. Its impact on the European population was nowhere near that of European diseases on America.

Whatever the percentage decline in the Indian population, the results were catastrophic, and hardly pleasing to the Spanish, who were counting on the Indians to be their labor force. In the Caribbean, where the native people disappeared altogether, the Spanish soon began importing African slaves to take their places. On the mainland, where the base populations were greater, the decline stopped short of extinction, and eventually the Indian population began to recover. By then, however, European hegemony was firmly established and complete cultural recovery was impossible. Massive death broke the lines of transmission by which the old told stories they had heard as children to the young and enjoined them to carry on the ways of their ancestors. Not even cultures whose past was recorded escaped: afraid that the written books or codices of the Aztecs perpetuated idolatry and superstition, the Spanish destroyed as many of them as they could. The presence of the Spaniards and the plants, animals, religious practices, and ways of doing things they brought with them altered the Indians' world in such far-reaching ways that survival itself required that they adapt to circumstances different from anything their ancestors had known.

## PLANTS AND ANIMALS

While the human populations of the Americas declined, the populations of animals imported from Europe multiplied. The Spaniards wanted meat and imported pigs—not the docile, slothful animals of modern farms, nor wild boars, but lean, mean animals that could survive on their own in the wild. And more than survive: one account claimed that two dozen hogs shipped to Cuba in 1498 had grown to 30,000 within sixteen years. Explorers customarily left sets of pigs on uninhabited islands as a ready source of food for the future. They also brought sheep, goats, and above all cattle, which also quickly multiplied—and caused immense distress by invading Indians' unfenced fields and consuming their crops. In the short run, the importation of European animals contributed to the Indians' malnutrition and susceptibility to disease; in the long run, however, it added to the food supply because cattle transformed grass into meat. Cattle also provided hides for leather, which itself became a major export as well as an important new product for domestic consumption, and tallow for making candles—one of the most important devices the Spanish added to Indian life, a relatively safe way to banish the dark of night.

Chickens (and so eggs, another welcome addition to the Indians' diets), rats, and cats were also imports, as were mules and oxen, the first draft animals many Indians saw. Horses, too, came on Spanish ships back to America, where their ancestors began. Horses were critical to Spanish rule, since they allowed the rapid movement of orders, information, and soldiers across great distances. In effect, the horse served as one of the first American communications systems. Moreover, once horses escaped into great grasslands like those in northern Mexico and the North American plains, they formed enormous herds with mounts for any person who could capture them. Only then did formerly settled, agricultural Indians such as the Sioux and Comanches become hunters and horsemen whose riding and shooting skills would slow down European invasions of their lands.

The Spanish also imported plants such as olive trees for oil and grapevines for wine, but those crops did not thrive every-where in America. Spaniards preferred wheat to corn, and by the mid-sixteenth century Mexico was producing enough wheat that it could export grain to the Caribbean. Rice (originally from Southeast Asia) and bananas (from Africa) did well in wet lowlands where not much else would grow. The Spanish imported some other plants inadvertently. Grass and weed seeds, hidden in dirt or dung or in the cuffs of clothing, soon spread on fields overgrazed by the prolific new livestock, gradually replacing native ground cover. Kentucky bluegrass, daisies, and dandelions were among these imports.

The most portentous imported plant was sugarcane. Spain's Muslim population originally taught Spanish Christians how to grind sugarcanes to extract their juice and then boil the juice down to produce sugar. Northern Europeans developed a taste for the sweet stuff at the time of the Crusades, when they came into contact with Mediterranean Muslims. By the fifteenth century, the European demand for sugar was strong and on the rise. Portugal began growing sugar profitably on Madeira and Spain in the Canaries and then, beginning in 1493, in the Caribbean, where it thrived. From there, the crop spread to those extensive parts of the American mainland that had adequate sun and rain. The Spanish cultivated sugarcane from the Gulf of Mexico down into South America, but within a century Portuguese Brazil became an even greater producer, with hundreds of mills turning out thousands of tons of sugar for European markets. High profits from sugar sales allowed planters to continue purchasing African slaves wherever Indian sources of labor declined or disappeared. Indeed, sugar production was a major reason for the importation of some 9.5 million African slaves to the Americas between 1505 and the late nineteenth century. In the Caribbean, blacks soon outnumbered all other peoples.

Animals and plants moved not just from east to west, but also in the reverse direction. American animals rarely became more than curiosities in Europe, but American plants were something else again. Explorers quickly noted the unfamiliarity of many American trees and other plants and brought seeds or specimens home, where they were absorbed into newly founded botanical gardens so quickly and thoroughly that even the experts lost track of what came from where. Agricultural plants produced the greatest impact. America gave Italy the tomato, France the string bean, and Ireland the potato—to say nothing of chocolate and raspberries, its gifts to humankind. Tobacco also traveled from America to Europe, where it was welcomed at first as a means of preventing or curing illnesses.

The Columbian Exchange

This illustration from 1595 by the celebrated engraver Theodor de Bry shows black slaves helping to make sugar on the Spanish island of Hispaniola. As the native American workforce died away, the Spanish brought Africans to take their places on plantations in the Caribbean.

People outside the Americas adopted these new crops very slowly, so it took time before the impact of American crops became observable. After 1650, the world's population began to grow dramatically, more than quadrupling in the next 300 years, with that of Europe (including Russia) increasing more than fivefold. The reasons it rose so rapidly are open to debate, but the introduction of American crops surely enabled the earth to sustain the population growth in Europe, Asia, and even Africa. Many people from those continents would later migrate to America, voluntarily or involuntarily, filling the places of those who had died from the diseases Europeans had carried there.

## WAYS OF THOUGHT

From the beginning, Columbus and other explorers noted that they were discovering facts about the world "unknown to the ancients," whose learning Renaissance Europe had rediscovered. In fact, Europeans of the fifteenth and sixteenth centuries identified error after error in ancient writings about the world. Finally, in the 1570s, the Antwerp geographer Gerhardus Mercator declared that Ptolemy's *Geography* was no longer useful and that henceforth geographical information should be conveyed in new ways, as did the atlases of his time, great books of maps that presented modern knowledge of the world both artistically and accurately, area by area. To be sure, Mercator's famous "projection"—the mathematically derived lines that governed his depictions of the earth's surface—was built on Ptolemy's own system for defining locations on the earth. But the *Geography*, Mercator maintained, had become so out-of-date that it remained only of historic interest.

More important, the spread of American crops increased the earth's capacity to feed ever larger numbers of people by allowing a more efficient and productive use of the land. Maize (corn) is the best example: it prospers in soils too dry for rice and too wet for wheat, requires a relatively short growing season, and can feed both humans and cattle. Its caloric yield per unit of land is double that of wheat. The potato grows, like wheat, in temperate climates, but it produces more food per unit of land than wheat does, and farmers can cultivate it productively on small plots, even at high elevations (as did the Incas in Peru). The sweet potato, another crop native to America, produces high yields even in bad soils and is resistant to drought. And the thick roots of manioc, or tapioca, a shrub grown in frost-free climates, can be processed into a flour widely used in tropical parts of the world where wheat cannot grow.

The accumulation of new information was not confined to geography. Take botany: in the mid-sixteenth century, German and English herbalists, who studied plants and their uses, particularly those of medicinal significance, listed about 500 different plants. That was roughly the number known to the ancient world. In the early seventeenth century, a Swiss professor of anatomy and botany described some 6,000 distinct plants; and at the end of that century, an English botanist could catalogue almost 12,000—a twenty-four-fold increase in a century and a half. Many of the new listings came from the Middle East, Africa, and Asia, but soon American specimens added to the total. How could naturalists make sense of their sprawling subject matter? At first, they tried to reconcile new observations with inherited works, suggesting that some new plant might be the same as another known to the ancients, but that was a losing game. The proliferation of known plants strained traditional ways of cataloguing and led ultimately to the creation of a new unit of taxonomy, the genus, by which the plant world was organized into a more manageable 600 groups.

Beyond these specific developments lay a more basic one: gradually Europeans were becoming less dependent on inherited authority and more inclined to base their knowledge of the world on empirical observations, defining general principles on the basis of known facts. This transformation led in time to what the world would call "science." The conventional event marking the birth of modern science is the London publication of Sir Francis Bacon's *Instauratio Magna* (Great Instauration, or restoration) in 1620. The cover of that work showed a great ship, with square and lateen sails, moving from the Mediterranean past the Pillars of Hercules—the high rocks beside the Straits of Gibraltor—into the Atlantic Ocean. The voyages of discovery, by which European explorers found the Americas, had become a metaphor for all human quests for new knowledge.

None of these changes happened quickly. The great age of botanical and biological classification, for example, came some 250 to 300 years after Columbus first commented on the novelty of American plants and animals. Ancient texts did not immediately loosen their grip on people's minds; indeed, the authority of the Bible retained its power long after the rise of modern science. Moreover, older ways of making sense of experience persisted, particularly that which explained events as the results not of natural forces but as specific, purposeful interventions of God in human affairs. From that perspective, the massive deaths of Indians was itself a "wonder" in a now-archaic sense—an extraordinary event that revealed God's will for the world. As one seventeenth-century Protestant clergyman concluded, God sent epidemics to clear New England of "those pernicious creatures," the Indians, "to make room for better growth." At times, the Spanish exhibited a

The cover of Sir Francis Bacon's *Instauratio Magna* (London, 1620), whose publication is often taken as the starting point of modern science. Here, a great ship of exploration sails from the Mediterranean past the Pillars of Hercules, the western entrance to the Strait of Gibraltar, into the Atlantic Ocean. By 1620, the voyages of exploration had become a metaphor for all of mankind's search for new knowledge.

similar way of thought: in the battle for Tenochtitlán, when "the Christians were exhausted from war," a follower of Cortés recalled, "God saw fit to send the Indians smallpox."

Could there be any greater testimony to the Europeans' superiority—and that of the Christian God over Indian gods—than their survival and, indeed, the multiplication of the European population as the Indians' numbers declined? How could the Europeans explain the marvelous events that left them in control of so many parts of the New World except as an act of God and perhaps as a reward for their efforts to repress heathenism in America?

Like the plants and beasts that populated the earth, groups of people were different from one another and therefore subject to classification; and the categories Europeans used reflected their assumptions of superiority. By their nakedness, their "idolatrous" religions, their frequent lack of skills such as writing, the Indians—particularly those who lived, as observers put it, "without magistrates or republic," were nomadic, or lived in caves like wild beasts—were "barbarians" or "savages" and distinctly backward when compared with the "civilized" people of contemporary Europe. The arrival of Europeans did not therefore simply add to an American mosaic of peoples that had been thousands of years in the making. There could be no middle way between idolatry and Christianity, barbarism and civilization, no celebration of diversity. Europeans knew that their ways and beliefs were superior and would triumph over those of their rivals.

Vast numbers of Indians remained, assisting or resisting the newcomers. In remote parts of America, some continued traditional patterns of life as if little had changed. But Indians who rode on horseback or cooked their meals in iron pots already lived in a world different from that of their ancestors, a world in many ways as new to the Americas' oldest residents as it was for its most recent immigrants. That strange new world would put the Indians' historic skill at adaptation to its most severe test.

## Suggested Reading

James Axtell, *Beyond 1492: Encounters in Colonial North America* (1992)

Michael Coe, Michael Dean Snow, and Elizabeth Benson, *Atlas of Ancient America* (1986)

Alfred W. Crosby, *The Columbian Exchange: Biological and Cultural Consequences of 1941* (1972)

Felipe Fernández-Armesto, *Before Columbus: Exploration and Colonisation from the Mediterranean to the Atlantic, 1229–1492* (1991)

Charles Gibson, *Spain in America* (1966)

Stephen Greenblatt, *Marvelous Possessions: The Wonder of the New World* (1991)

Frederick E. Hoxie, *Encyclopedia of North American Indians* (1996)

Karen Ordahl Kupperman, ed., *America in European Consciousness, 1493–1750* (1995)

J. H. Parry, *The Age of Reconnaissance* (1964)

David J. Weber, *The Spanish Frontier in North America* (1992)

# Chapter Review

## Summary
### QUESTIONS

■ How can scholars learn about the lives of people who left no written records?

■ In what ways was pre-Columbian native society especially well developed in the Valley of Mexico?

■ How did technology and disease help Cortés and a handful of Spaniards defeat the powerful Aztecs, who vastly outnumbered them?

■ In what sense can people accurately use the term "New World" for the Americas?

■ Which of the "Columbian Exchanges" had the greatest impact?

## Chronology

| | |
|---|---|
| **986** | Norse settlement at L'Anse aux Meadows in Newfoundland. |
| **1487–88** | Bartholomeu Días sails around Cape of Good Hope. |
| **1492** | Christopher Columbus lands in the Bahamas. |
| **1497** | John Cabot claims Newfoundland for England. |
| **1497–99** | Vasco da Gama sails to India. |
| **1513** | Juan Ponce de León explores the Florida coast. |
| **1519** | Hernando Cortés arrives on the American mainland |
| **1519–22** | Fernando Magellan sails around the world. |
| **1521** | Cortés takes Tenochtitlán from the Aztecs. |
| **1533** | Francisco Pizarro defeats the Incas of Peru. |
| **1540–41** | Francisco Vásquez de Coronado marches into North America, going as far north as Kansas. |
| **1542** | Juan Rodriguez Cabrillo sails up the California coast and claims California for Spain. |
| **1565** | The Spanish found St. Augustine in Florida. |
| **1598** | Juan de Oñate formally takes possession of New Mexico. |

## Key Terms

Mesoamerica (p. 7)

The Anasazi (p. 14)

New Spain (p. 25)

*Conquistadores* (p. 26)

Columbian Exchange (p. 29)

# Chapter 2

# THE EUROPEAN SETTLEMENT OF NORTH AMERICA:

## THE ATLANTIC COAST TO 1660

A watercolor of Indian fishing techniques by John White, whom Sir Walter Raleigh sent to Roanoke in 1585 and then again in 1587. The Indians speared fish and also used weirs or traps (the fence-like devices at left).

QUESTIONS

■ **What developments in Europe led the French and English to explore and claim land in North America?**

■ **How were the early French, Dutch, and Swedish colonies different from one another?**

■ **How did colonial Virginians learn to survive in America?**

■ **What distinguished New England from British colonies in the Chesapeake?**

In 1600, the Spanish had established only two bases in the lands north of Mexico: a two-year-old settlement in the Southwest, where Juan de Oñate's dream of a New Mexico more glorious than the old was already going bad; and the small, shabby community of soldiers and settlers on the Florida coast at St. Augustine, whose future remained far from secure. Aside from the seasonal visits of fishermen to Newfoundland, those fledgling settlements constituted the European presence in North America, tenuous beachheads on a continent still securely possessed by Indians who had lived there since time immemorial.

Spain, however, could no longer depend on an exclusive claim to North America based on a papal grant. The pope's jurisdiction, France's King Francis I told the Spanish ambassador in 1540, was spiritual and did not extend to dividing the world's lands among kings. Title to territory in America, as the king saw it, depended on exploration, conquest, and, above all, colonization.

That was easier said than done. Both France and England had tried but failed to establish settlements in North America before 1600. Success required sending groups of people to the New World who could survive while performing or getting others to perform activities that enriched the parent state. On that standard, Spain had been conspicuously successful in Mexico and lands farther south, but its example was not of much use—and could even be positively misleading—in North America, which had a colder climate, different resources, and fewer native people.

In the first half of the seventeenth century, several northern European nations did found lasting settlements along the St. Lawrence River and on the eastern shore of North America. Their colonies differed from one another in their economies, religious traditions, cultures, even their relationships with Indians. Some of those distinctions faded away with time; others set patterns whose influence, for better or worse, would be felt far into the future.

## False Starts

Two dreams first attracted France and England to North America: (1) finding a water route to Asia, and (2) discovering kingdoms rich in silver and gold, as the Spanish had done in Mexico and Peru. Europeans were also propelled into North America by national rivalries that developed during the sixteenth century.

### EARLY FRENCH INITIATIVES

Giovanni de Verrazano's voyage of 1524 demonstrated that there was no "northwest passage" below Nova Scotia. A decade later, the French explorer Jacques Cartier headed farther north and sailed up the St. Lawrence. That river, he learned, drained a great landmass, and rapids barred all but skilled canoemen from proceeding beyond the Indian village that later became Montreal. In short, the St. Lawrence provided no passageway to China.

After spending the winter of 1535 at Quebec, Cartier and what remained of his crew returned to France. They took along a set of kidnapped Indians who told vague stories of a fantastically rich kingdom just a little farther west of where

Cartier had gone. And so the French returned in 1541, but they found no more gold-rich nations than did an expedition by the Spaniard Francisco de Coronado in the Southwest that year. A second taste of a Canadian winter, moreover, snuffed out for the rest of the century France's desire to found a settlement in that "savage" north country, "uninhabitable" through half the year.

If the French couldn't find gold and silver, perhaps they could seize it—which was one reason they founded Fort Caroline on the Florida coast, near the homeward route of the Spanish treasure ships. Spain had sat back while the French pushed up the St. Lawrence, but this new affront it could not tolerate. Pedro Menéndez de Aviles brutally massacred Fort Caroline's men in 1565, when France and Spain were at peace. The attack provoked France's protests, but not much more. One reason was that Fort Caroline was a project of Huguenots, French Protestants who had broken away from the Catholic Church. The French Crown, however, remained Catholic.

**LEFT:** Martin Luther, whose criticisms of church practices led to a splintering of the Christian community, by Lucan Cranach the Elder, 1520.

**RIGHT:** John Calvin (in a portrait possibly by Hans Holbein), who developed the doctrine of predestination, which called into question the efficacy of good works.

On August 24, 1572, a powerful faction of France's Catholic nobility attempted to suppress religious divisions within France by slaughtering Huguenot leaders who had gathered in Paris. That event, the St. Bartholomew's Day Massacre, triggered two decades of civil wars, which prevented further French activity in North America. Many of France's most knowledgeable proponents of overseas expansion were Huguenots, and those who survived the massacre shared their rich knowledge of the New World with explorers and colonizers from Protestant countries. In that and many other ways, the great sixteenth-century split in Western Christianity known as the Reformation had a powerful impact on America's future.

### THE REFORMATION

In 1492, when Columbus first sailed west, all Christian Europeans acknowledged the spiritual leadership of the pope in Rome. Then, in 1517, Martin Luther, a German monk, nailed a list of ninety-five theses, or propositions for public debate, on the door of a church in the town of Wittenberg. Luther questioned the Church's sale of indulgences, credits against time in purgatory that could be bought and stored up by the faithful. He also doubted whether good works could earn salvation. Some of his arguments had been raised by earlier reformers who also wanted to rid the Church of corruption and

return to the simpler piety of early Christianity, but Luther went further. He founded his own church based on the Bible alone. He rejected saints, fast days, a celibate clergy, transubstantiation (the belief that in the mass, bread and wine are literally transformed into the body and blood of Christ), and all but two sacraments—baptism and holy communion—because he could find no scriptural basis for them. Luther had the Bible translated from Latin into German and encouraged his followers to read it. He also made sermons, presented in the vernacular, and the singing of hymns by the congregation important parts of religious services.

The splintering of the Christian community did not end with Luther. In Germany, a variety of Protestant sects emerged. They included pacifists and radical egalitarians who wore plain clothes, refused to respect worldly rank or to take oaths, and rejected infant baptism. Reformers sometimes went in the other direction. In Geneva, Switzerland, for example, John Calvin—an exiled French Lutheran (the term for French Protestants until the mid-sixteenth century, when they began to be called Huguenots)—founded a tightly governed community under God's "saints," that is, those He knew would be saved and so were predestined for salvation. The Calvinists, as determined believers in predestination, denied that people could in any way earn salvation by acts of will. They firmly believed their fates were wholly in the hands of God, who could give or withhold saving grace for reasons beyond human understanding or control. However, most Protestants shared Luther's emphasis on the Bible and his rejection of saints, indulgences, transubstantiation, and many other practices of the Catholic Church, including its insistence on a celibate clergy and submission to the pope's authority. Soon Europeans divided into two camps, Catholic and Protestant, whose convictions seemed to dictate that they fight each other to the death.

England at first remained Catholic. King Henry VIII (r. 1509–47) denounced Luther's teachings by writing a tract in *Defense of the Seven Sacraments,* for which the pope bestowed on him the title "Defender of the Faith" (which British monarchs still claim). Then, in 1533, after a twenty-

Queen Elizabeth I gained the throne at age twenty-five and became one of England's most powerful monarchs (Portrait by Marcus Gheeraerts the Younger).

year marriage that produced only one daughter, Henry decided to divorce his Spanish wife, Catherine of Aragon, and marry Anne Boleyn. When the pope refused to give his permission, Henry cut the link between England and Rome. He also dissolved England's monasteries and seized church lands, but changed little else, essentially putting himself in the pope's place as head of the Church of England and leaving the rest in place.

Under the brief reign of Henry's son Edward VI (r. 1547–53), reformers pushed for greater changes in the Church of England. But on Edward's death, his older sister, Mary, the Catholic daughter of Henry and Catherine of Aragon, inherited the throne. She returned England to the pope and tried to purge her realm of Protestants, burning hundreds of them at the stake for their "heretical" beliefs. Many others fled to the Continent, including Calvin's Geneva. After Mary's death in 1558, those "Marian exiles" returned home, anxious to bring English Protestantism nearer in line with the more extensive reforms of continental Europe.

The new queen, Elizabeth I, was securely Protestant; because she was the daughter of Anne Boleyn, her birth and claim to the throne were illegitimate in the eyes of the Catholic Church. Elizabeth's reign was long, from 1558 to 1603. During that time, England laid the foundations for subsequent overseas expansion.

### THE FOUNDATIONS OF ENGLISH EXPANSION

While Portugal and Spain were establishing their American empires, several considerations kept England from following in their footsteps. During the sixteenth century, however, each of those constraints disappeared or shifted in ways that encouraged England to claim territory outside the British Isles.

*Diplomatic Change.* Until the mid-sixteenth century, deference to Spain, an ally, helped keep England from claiming land in America. After Elizabeth I became queen, however, England and Spain inevitably became enemies. Spain supported the claim to the English throne of Mary, Queen of Scots, a Catholic, over that of Elizabeth, which did not please the woman who was one of England's all-time toughest monarchs. Hostility between the two countries increased after 1566–67, when Spain's King Philip II decided to put down a revolt in the Spanish Netherlands, which started an eighty-year war with Dutch Protestants. Finally, in 1585, England and Spain also went to war.

*Religious Change.* The conflict between Protestants and Catholics within Europe naturally expanded into a contest in the New World for souls as well as territory, as each side aspired to teach the Indians "true religion" and save them from Catholic or Protestant "heresy." Moreover, Henry VIII's dissolution of England's monasteries freed for overseas expansion young gentlemen who in earlier times might have spent their days cloistered from the world.

*Economic Development.* The English Reformation (which began with Henry VIII's split from the Catholic Church) coincided with a major transformation in England's economy. In the early sixteenth century, England's commerce focused on selling woolen cloth at a great international market in Antwerp (in Belgium), where English traders received in exchange a wide range of imported merchandise. But the Antwerp

The Spanish Armada, 130 ships and 30,000 men strong, was devastated by storms and English forces in the summer of 1588. This depiction was painted by the English school, 16th century.

market collapsed in the mid-sixteenth century, forcing the English had to find new ways of selling their exports. For that purpose, they founded great trading companies such as the Muscovy Company (1555), the Levant Company (1581), and the East India Company (1600), which developed trade routes to Russia, the eastern Mediterranean, and India.

Individual entrepreneurs also joined the search for new sources of profit. In 1562, Sir John Hawkins began a series of voyages to sell slaves from West Africa to colonists in the Caribbean, where Spanish traders had a monopoly. In 1568, the viceroy of Mexico mounted a devastating attack on his fleet, during which Hawkins managed to save only 100 of his 400 men and two of his six ships. After that "outrage," English seamen, like their Huguenot mentors, took to plundering Spanish ships and territory. Sir Francis Drake, who was with Hawkins on the 1568 expedition, became one of the greatest English raiders, a man who was for all practical purposes a pirate, except that, as he noted later in life, the word "pirate" applied only to those who undertook risk "for small things," not for "millions." In 1572, Drake seized Spanish treasure being carried across the Isthmus of Panama;

in 1585–86, he plundered Spanish settlements at Santo Domingo and Cartagena; then, for good measure, he burned the Spanish garrison at St. Augustine, Florida, on his way home.

In the course of these events, England became a seafaring nation—a prerequisite for colonizing North America. Despite her island location, England had been a nation of landlubbers in Columbus's day. Even her sixteenth-century trade with Antwerp depended on foreign ships to carry goods across the English Channel. But then King Henry VIII began the task of building a royal navy, and in 1577 Queen Elizabeth I appointed Sir John Hawkins as treasurer of the navy and asked him to restore and expand her father's fleet. Eleven years later, England boasted some twenty-five large or midsized ships and eighteen oceangoing pinnaces (ships with both oars and sails), a formidable force for the time. Trading companies and freewheelers such as Drake, who circumnavigated the globe in 1580, also added to England's stock of ships and skilled seamen. These developments explain why English expeditions to find a northwest passage to Asia or to search for gold in North America during Elizabeth's reign were led not by Italians like John Cabot but by natural-born Englishmen such as Martin Frobisher (three voyages, 1576–78) and John Davis (another three, 1585–87). England's historic defeat of the Spanish fleet, the Armada, in 1588 finally announced her arrival among the maritime powers of the world.

The sixteenth century also saw major changes in English mining and metal processing. In 1540, the English introduced the blast furnace, in which iron ore was melted down to liquid with a fluxing agent that separated iron from other elements in the ore. The country's annual output of iron rose almost five times in the next century, but it still failed to satisfy the demand for items such as skillets, trivets, nails, andirons, locks, and keys. Similar advances in glassmaking and textile production added to the list of newly available consumer items that were quickly absorbed into the middle-class's standard of living.

England's ready supplies of coal, lead, and iron ore sustained this early industrial development. But iron mills and glass producers absorbed prodigious amounts of timber. So did shipbuilding (it took over 2,000 large oak trees to build a warship) and the concurrent "great rebuilding" of rural England, as increasingly prosperous landowners built, expanded, and refurnished their homes. By the early seventeenth century, England was in the midst of a timber crisis, with the price of firewood doubling and tripling. That predicament turned English eyes westward, to the densely wooded lands of North America.

*Political Consolidation.* Overseas expansion required internal territorial and political integrity. But during the fifteenth century, as Spain and Portugal moved into the Atlantic, the British Isles contained several kingdoms whose people spoke a variety of languages. Gradually they fell under English rule—Wales, to England's west, when Elizabeth's grandfather became King Henry VII, in 1485; Cornwall and Devon in the island's southwest after the Crown crushed uprisings there in the sixteenth century. Scotland remained outside the realm until the accession of James I, the son of Mary, Queen of Scots, in 1603. By then, much of Ireland was also under English control. In this process of expansion, England became the seat of Great Britain, a nation consisting of what once had been separate peoples, and a nation ready to continue extending its dominion outside the British Isles. The English conquest of Ireland, moreover, shaped England's colonization of

America, much as Spain's campaign against the Moors produced institutions and attitudes that the Spanish carried to the New World.

### THE ENGLISH AND IRELAND

Early seventeenth-century Englishmen spoke not of colonizing America but of "planting," or founding plantations, there. A plantation was a segment of England "transplanted" abroad so it could take root, grow, and mature into a place much like England itself. The English had developed the concept of planting in Ireland, which during the sixteenth century became England's first (to use the more modern word) colony.

England's claims to Ireland went back to the twelfth century, when Anglo-Norman conquerors invaded Ireland. But by 1485, when Henry VII became king, English control of Ireland was limited to the English Pale, a narrow strip on the island's east coast that extended from a few miles south of the English capital at Dublin north to Dundalk. The rest of Ireland ("beyond the Pale") consisted of fifty or sixty little kingdoms ruled by chieftains who were either of native Irish descent or "Old English"—that is, the descendants of Normans who had become in name, manners, and even language almost indistinguishable from the native Irish.

Ireland was important to England because it lay sufficiently near England's west coast to serve as a center of intrigue for factions within England and for her enemies on the European Continent. Its location also made Ireland a potential threat to England's expanding trade. In the early sixteenth century, the English Crown tried to secure greater control over Ireland by negotiating agreements with Irish chieftains. When that failed, it decided to pacify and Anglicize Ireland by repopulating it with people from England.

The first plantations were in the Midlands, from which the "wild Irish" could mount raids on the Pale, and the next at Munster in the southwest of Ireland. During the early seventeenth century, the English founded another plantation to the north in Ulster, where the native Irish were deeply entrenched. After suppressing an insurrection there, the English declared the land forfeit, expelled the former owners, and made plans for resettling Ulster with emigrants from England and also Scotland. As in earlier plantations, many Irish actually stayed on their old lands as tenants. Others fled into the woods and made occasional plundering expeditions on the plantations, which became military outposts. The "planters" concluded that there could be no living with the native Irish unless they somehow consented to adopt English "civilitie."

The English carried that conclusion to America, where the English told of Indians wearing "large mantels of deare skins not much differing in fashion from the Irish mantels" and compared Indians' leggings with "Irish trousers." The Indians' way of building houses also seemed "much like the wild Irish." And both people fought in similarly "savage" ways, letting out "horrible shouts and screeches" at the start of battles like "infernall hellhounds." Moreover, many of the people involved in planting Ireland later helped plant America. They included Sir Francis Drake and Sir Humphrey Gilbert (who was knighted for service in Ireland) as well as Gilbert's half-brother Sir Walter Raleigh, who made the first efforts to found English settlements in North America.

## ENGLAND'S VISION OF AMERICA

America was less critical to England's security and trade than Ireland. Why found plantations there? Richard Hakluyt the younger, an English geographer, historian, and enthusiast for overseas expansion, provided some answers in his *Discourse of Western Planting* (1584), a treatise written as part of an unsuccessful effort to persuade Queen Elizabeth to finance English colonization of America.

English plantations, Hakluyt argued, would advance the Protestant religion, and if the English acted quickly they would keep "the spanishe kinge from flowinge over all the face of . . . America." The Indians, Hakluyt said, would "revolte cleane from the Spaniarde" and voluntarily "yield themselves" to Elizabeth's rule once they saw that the English treated them with "humanitie, curtesie, and freedome." North America would also provide a fine market for English wool and a source of goods that England otherwise had to buy from other European nations. America could supply the Royal Navy with masts, pitch, tar, and hemp. Since merchants would not venture across the Atlantic except with ships of "greate burden," trade with America would serve to increase England's naval strength.

Hakluyt assumed that England's American plantations would provide a refuge for Protestants "from all partes of the worlde." But foreign immigrants would, of course, adopt English ways and rule. Who among the English people would migrate? Soldiers too unruly to be absorbed at home once wars ended, young men ruined by debt or who "by some folly of

youthe . . . are not able to live in England," the children of wandering beggars, unemployed seamen, indeed the unemployed of all types "hurtfull and burdensome to this Realme." Such troublesome folk could be "unladen" in America, where they would magically become a productive people serving England and "their own more happy state."

Hakluyt's vision of migration and personal transformation reflected a sense of social crisis that pervaded England in the 1580s. The population of England and Wales was expanding rapidly: between 1500 and 1650, it grew from less than 3 million to over 5 million people. At the time Hakluyt wrote, moreover, landlords were enclosing their lands—fencing off open fields, which were then used for intensive agriculture or, more often, for pasture—and evicting tenants. An extraordinary rise in the price of rents as well as of other basic goods, including cereals, meat, and wood and other building materials, made survival in the countryside increasingly difficult for those who did not own or hold secure leases on land. Some took up marginal plots on the outer edges of England's settled areas. More often, people migrated to towns and ports such as York, Bristol, Newcastle, or Norwich, whose populations doubled and tripled in the century between 1550 and 1650, or to London, which grew almost tenfold, from a city of 60,000 in 1500 to one of 550,000 people in 1700. There, in the urban centers, England's "excess" people were highly visible and hard to ignore.

But would the people England wanted to get rid of make good colonists? Hakluyt did not ask that question. For him and his countrymen, interest in America rested not only on a pull, a desire to reap predictable gains, but also on a powerful push, to relieve the home country of a real and growing burden. "If Englande crie oute and affirme that there is so many in all trades that one cannot live for another as in all places they do," Hakluyt said, then a colony in North America "offreth the remedie."

## GILBERT AND RALEIGH

Sir Humphrey Gilbert, a soldier and courtier from the southwest part of England ("the West Country"), first picked up the idea of colonizing North America from Huguenots who had tried to establish bases in Carolina and Florida during the 1560s. In 1578, after he had spent time in the Munster plantation, where he acquired a reputation for brutality against the Irish, the queen gave him license to found a settlement in an uninhabited part of North America. Gilbert spent five years

The 1590 edition of Thomas Hariot's *A Briefe and True Report of the New Found Land of Virginia* included a series of engravings by Theodore de Bry based on John White's paintings and drawings of the Indians. This example shows the Indians' "verye wonderfull" way of making boats by burning out the center of a log and scraping away the destroyed wood with shells.

planning his new colony and selling some lands there to finance the venture, then set out to have a look at the place. He claimed Newfoundland for the English Crown as John Cabot had once done, and he studied the coast for possible sources of precious metals. But his ship went down in a storm off the Azores on its homeward trip. Gilbert was last seen, the story goes, with a book in his hands, shouting out, "We are as near heaven by sea as by land."

Queen Elizabeth granted Gilbert's half-brother Sir Walter Raleigh an extension of Gilbert's patent. Raleigh's attention shifted toward the area south of the Chesapeake Bay. In April 1585, Raleigh sent Sir Richard Grenville (a buddy from Ireland) to Roanoke Island off North Carolina with seven vessels carrying 108 settlers. Early reports said the place was a paradise with a pleasing climate and fertile soil, and that the local "savages" were "most corteous, and very desirous to have clothes." But the English proved unwilling and perhaps incapable of doing anything to feed themselves except demand food from the native people, who had no great excess to give away. And when the Indians tried to get rid of their rapacious, uninvited guests, the English governor, Ralph Lane (who also had been involved in planting Ireland), killed the chief and his advisers. Then the hungry settlers hitched a ride to England with Sir Francis Drake, who had stopped at Roanoke after torching St. Augustine.

Grenville, who had sailed to England for supplies, returned to find the Roanoke colony deserted. When he left again, fifteen men remained on the island. Indians killed some; the rest tried to sail away, then disappeared altogether. Not content to leave bad enough alone, Raleigh sent another 117 men, women, and children to America in 1587 under the leadership of John White, an artist who had joined the earlier expedition to sketch the plants, animals, and people of the New World. Although Raleigh wanted this new expedition to settle farther north in the Chesapeake Bay area, it ended up back on Roanoke, with predictable results. When, after a trip to England, White returned to Roanoke in 1590, he found the settlement deserted, his books in ruins, the armor he had carefully brought to America turning to rust. "Croatoan," the name of a nearby island, had been carved on a post. But no trace of the settlers was ever found.

England remained without a base on the North American continent. Raleigh's expeditions produced, however, one enduring document: *A Briefe and True Report of the New Found Land of Virginia* (1588), by Thomas Hariot, a mathematician who joined the first expedition to observe the country's natural resources. Hariot, who tried to learn the Indians' language before going to America, gave a detailed, sympathetic account of the native people. A 1690 edition of Hariot's book included engravings by Theodore De Bry based on John White's drawings of the Indians. These pictorial images introduced Europeans to a dignified Indian people who lived in ordered villages surrounded by carefully cultivated fields and who exercised considerable ingenuity—for example, by burning away parts of logs to help shape them into boats. De Bry's Indians even looked remarkably like the "barbarian" ancestors of contemporary Englishmen, whom the book also portrayed. Apparently no intrinsic inferiority distinguished "savage" Americans from "civilized" Europeans, and so, with time, the former could become like the latter. Indeed, a people so inventive in building communities and boats or creating ingenious devices for fishing, as another engraving indicated, were already partway there. Hariot's text and De Bry's prints suggested that North America might not replay the history of Ireland.

Hariot was all for trying to found another settlement. However, the sad fate of Raleigh's colony along with England's war with Spain, which continued until 1604, ended English colonizing efforts for the rest of the sixteenth century.

# True Beginnings

By the time the English began planting again, they had neighbors. France, and later the Netherlands and Sweden, successfully established settlements along the Atlantic coast in the early seventeenth century.

## NEW FRANCE

Cartier's sixteenth-century explorations did not find rich and populous empires to conquer like those of the Aztecs and Incas, but the French eventually discovered another reason for maintaining a presence in North America. Beaver pelts, bought from the Indians, found a profitable market in Europe, where they were made into fashionable felt hats. French fishermen along the northern coast began that trade. While drying their catch for shipment home, fishermen dawdled on shore, which gave them a chance to trade with the local Indians. Fish paid for the voyages, and pelts obtained from the Indians added profits that eventually became an attraction in themselves.

In 1606, a company of merchants to whom the French Crown granted a monopoly of trade established a year-round base at Port Royal on the Bay of Fundy (now Annapolis Royal, Nova Scotia). Two years later, the company began another at Quebec under the leadership of Samuel de Champlain. Because the St. Lawrence River narrowed at Quebec, it was an ideal site for preventing interlopers from traveling further inland. Since the Iroquois who once lived near Quebec had died or left, the new settlers could begin growing food, ending their dependence on unreliable supply ships from Europe, without displacing Indians from the land. The Quebec settlement existed, however, not to grow crops for export but to trade furs. That required good relations with the Indians in surrounding areas, as did the other great activity that brought the French to Canada: the harvesting of souls. Franciscan missionaries first performed that work; then, after 1625, Jesuits took over. The Jesuits were willing to go to the Indians and share their ways of life, risking their own lives in the process, and did not insist that the Indians entirely conform to French "civilization."

After joining an Indian war party, Champlain became acquainted with the water route that linked the St. Lawrence to the Hudson River. He also established trade relations with the Hurons, who lived between Lakes Huron and Ontario and became trading middlemen, exchanging furs from more north-ern Indians for European goods. Indians taught the French to make birchbark canoes, graceful and wonderfully light boats that could carry men and heavy loads of trading goods over inland rivers. The French gradually came to know the Great Lakes region, which would one day be part of France's North American empire. They had, in fact, claimed the foremost water route to the interior of the continent. In 1642, they strengthened their control of that route by establishing a post, Montréal, at the falls of the St. Lawrence.

The French hold on Canada remained weak in the late 1620s, when King Louis XIII's first minister, Cardinal Richelieu, oversaw the creation of the Company of New France to develop the settlements and foster missionary work. The Crown granted it a monopoly on everything but fishing. In return, the company had to settle at least 4,000 French Catholics in North America within fifteen years. No Huguenots could go: religious dissension would divide the colony and compromise its Catholic missionary work.

The first contingent of 400 new immigrants arrived in 1628, when Quebec had only sixty to eighty colonists, a handful of buildings, and maybe twenty acres of farmland. To encourage migration, the Company of New France tried granting long, narrow plots of land along the St. Lawrence to *seigneurs,* who then imported more settlers at their own cost. The Catholic Church also bought land and prepared it for settlement. Support came from wealthy, pious Catholics who were perhaps inspired by the *Jesuit Relations,* an account of Jesuit activities that was published annually from 1632 to 1673 and circulated among educated people. Despite these efforts, however, the colony grew very slowly. By 1650, New France's population stood at about 2,000, and its future remained uncertain.

## NEW NETHERLAND

The story was much the same to the south along the Hudson River, where the Dutch West India Company established a colony, New Netherland, on lands Henry Hudson described after 1609 when he sailed the ship *Half Moon* up the river that now carries his name. Fifteen years later, the first major contingent of settlers, mainly French-speaking Walloons from what today is Belgium, arrived in New Netherland and established bases on the Delaware and Connecticut rivers and at the site of an older trading post, which became Fort Orange, on the Hudson River where Albany now stands. Since large ships could navigate the Hudson for some 150 miles inland,

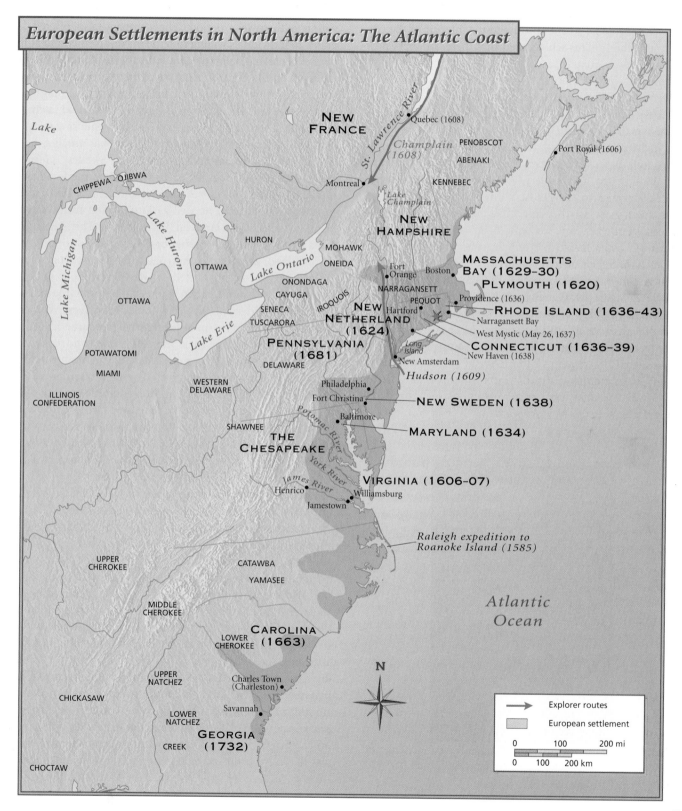

## European Settlements in North America: The Atlantic Coast

*Lake*

**NEW FRANCE**

Quebec (1608)

*St. Lawrence River*

PENOBSCOT

Port Royal (1606)

*Champlain (1608)*

ABENAKI

Montreal •

*Lake Champlain*

KENNEBEC

CHIPPEWA - OJIBWA

HURON

MOHAWK

**NEW HAMPSHIRE**

*Lake Huron*

OTTAWA

*Lake Ontario*

ONEIDA

Fort Orange

Boston •

**MASSACHUSETTS BAY (1629–30)**

*Lake Michigan*

ONONDAGA

NARRAGANSETT

**PLYMOUTH (1620)**

OTTAWA

CAYUGA

Hartford

Providence (1636)

**RHODE ISLAND (1636–43)**

SENECA

IROQUOIS

PEQUOT

Narragansett Bay

*Lake Erie*

TUSCARORA

**NEW NETHERLAND (1624)**

West Mystic (May 26, 1637)

**CONNECTICUT (1636–39)**

POTAWATOMI

**PENNSYLVANIA (1681)**

*Long Island*

New Haven (1638)

MIAMI

DELAWARE

New Amsterdam

*Hudson (1609)*

ILLINOIS CONFEDERATION

WESTERN DELAWARE

Philadelphia •

**NEW SWEDEN (1638)**

Fort Christina •

SHAWNEE

*Potomac River*

Baltimore •

**MARYLAND (1634)**

**THE CHESAPEAKE**

*York River*

*James River*

**VIRGINIA (1606–07)**

Henrico •

Williamsburg •

Jamestown •

*Raleigh expedition to Roanoke Island (1585)*

UPPER CHEROKEE

CATAWBA

**Atlantic Ocean**

YAMASEE

MIDDLE CHEROKEE

**CAROLINA (1663)**

LOWER CHEROKEE

**N**

UPPER NATCHEZ

Charles Town (Charleston) •

CHICKASAW

Savannah •

LOWER NATCHEZ

→ Explorer routes

**GEORGIA (1732)**

CREEK

European settlement

CHOCTAW

| 0 | 100 | 200 mi |
| 0 | 100 | 200 km |

the river provided a splendid route to the interior of the continent and the Indians who traded furs there. In 1626, however, the Dutch abandoned their dispersed, hard-to-defend settlements—only temporarily in the case of Fort Orange—and brought settlers together at the southern tip of Manhattan Island. There they built the city of New Amsterdam.

Like New France, the Dutch colony was primarily a trading post, not a plantation. Still, the Dutch West India Company needed to found a stable settlement to establish its claim to the land. It supplied the settlers at New Amsterdam—which guarded entrance to the Hudson River—with farming tools, plants, and livestock so they could, like their trade rivals at Quebec, feed themselves. New Netherland, however, soon proved to be relatively unprofitable and remained far less important for the Dutch than their outposts in Africa, the West Indies, South America, and Batavia (Indonesia). Indeed, after 1624 when it captured Bahia in Brazil, the Dutch West India Company concentrated its resources and attention on developing sugar plantations there to supply the expanding European market. But rather than abandon New Netherland, the company found ways to pass the cost of settlement to others. In 1629, it offered patroonships, substantial grants of land for a manorial estate, to persons who brought sixty other settlers to New Netherland (thirty if they went to New Amsterdam) at their own expense

Peter Stuyvesant, the director-general of New Netherland from 1647 until 1664.

within a three-year period. The company also offered land grants to individuals willing to settle in New Netherland at their own expense. These grants led to the development of Rensselaerwyck on the Hudson near Fort Orange, which became not just a private estate but a thriving community that engaged in the fur trade and also had a brickyard, tanneries, and sawmills.

Despite these attractions, few Dutch people saw reason to leave the Netherlands for America. Perhaps as much as half of the colony's population consisted of Swedes, Germans, Frenchmen, and Danes, some of whom had made homes in the Netherlands, whose religious tolerance attracted refugees from all over Europe, as well as Englishmen from New England who took up land on Long Island. The Dutch West India Company began importing African slaves to remedy its chronic labor shortage in the 1620s; forty years later, persons of African descent constituted between 7 and 9 percent of the colony's population. By then, some had become free and were themselves holders of property, including slaves. Women in New Netherland also had substantial freedom: like Dutch wives, they often kept their maiden names and could own property apart from their husbands. Still, a colony so diverse in its peoples, and with relatively few Dutch settlers, was no "New Netherland" in anything but name. Peter Stuyvesant, the colony's most able director, saw New Netherland's population, created as it was from "the scrapings of all sorts of nationalities," as a potential cause of disunity and so a serious disadvantage to a colony surrounded by European rivals and Indians who were sometimes hostile.

Since the company existed primarily to trade, its relationship with the Indians should have been amicable, like that of the French. The company also respected Indian titles and bought the lands it wanted, occasionally for bargain prices. Its purchase of Manhattan for sixty guilders of trade goods, a mere trifle, might well be the world's greatest real estate coup. In fact, Dutch relations with the Iroquois who were their trading partners were far better than with the Algonquian-speaking Indians who lived along the lower Hudson. There, between 1641 and 1645, the settlers fought a devastating war caused in part by the belligerent policies of the colony's current governor, William Kieff. A spurt in the colony's growth probably also excited the Indians' hostility. After 1639, the company increased the amount of land offered to immigrants and allowed settlers to engage in trade. The population doubled within five years, which meant colonists were moving onto still more territory that had once belonged to Algonqians. Close contact between Europeans and Indians itself caused friction: Indians' dogs

New Amsterdam, the main settlement of the New Netherland colony, detail from a map by Jansson Visscher, 1660.

(which were still much like wolves) ate Europeans' cattle and chickens; Europeans' livestock trampled Indians' fields, and so on. In 1655, an apparently trivial conflict in an orchard led to an Indian attack on Manhattan that spread to distant settlements. Fifty colonists and sixty Indians died, twenty-eight houses burned, and large numbers of farm animals died or disappeared before the so-called Peach War ended.

The colony's main settlement, New Amsterdam, developed slowly, like the colony itself. In the 1620s, it consisted of a fort, some thirty primitive houses, a market, a two-story mill, and a few canals and streets. The company maintained farms, or "bouweries," north of the settled area. An appointed director and council, whose members were given to quarreling with each other and with the director, ruled through most of New Netherland's existence with no input from the settlers. When the strong-willed Stuyvesant became director in 1647, he found the place dilapidated and the occupants notable mainly for their persistent drunkenness, which was facilitated by the presence of no less than seventeen tap houses. Stuyvesant limited tavern hours, repaired New Amsterdam's streets and buildings, completed a church on which work had languished, and started a school. He also gave the city a government. At first its officers were appointed, but after 1653, when the Dutch States General granted New Amsterdam a charter, they were elected. The officials met together as a court once a week in the Stat Huis, or State House, a converted tavern, and exercised both civil and criminal jurisdiction.

## NEW SWEDEN

Stuyvesant also took over New Sweden, a colony on the Delaware River founded by the Swedish West India Company in 1638. That first and only Swedish colony in the Americas claimed territory by right of Indian purchase from what is today Trenton, New Jersey, south to Cape Henlopen at the mouth of the Delaware Bay. Its major base lay on a small river (Christina Kill) that flowed into the Delaware Bay, where the city of Wilmington stands today. There the New Sweden Company built Fort Christina, named after the Swedish queen, and later established a village, Christinahamn, beside it. The colony monopolized the fur trade in the Delaware Valley, establishing subsidiary forts at several locations to reinforce its control. In 1655, the Dutch West India Company sent Stuyvesant and 300 men to recapture a Dutch fort at New Castle, Delaware, that the Swedish governor had seized. Stuyvesant went on to capture Fort Christina and, with it, New Sweden.

The Swedish colony's impact persisted, however, thanks to some Finnish settlers who were already experienced frontiersmen when they arrived in America. Their ancestors had made their way by 1600 from their homelands near the Russian border to interior Sweden. In the course of their migrations through the woodlands of northern Europe, they developed skills and techniques appropriate to other forested frontiers: they became expert axemen who could build crude structures with readily available materials, hunters who also raised hogs and cattle, and farmers who cut and burned brush and other growths to prepare fields for planting. Their ways of life were so well suited to the American frontier that subsequent generations of American frontiersmen carried them on. Of particular importance were the Finns' way of making log cabins with a distinctive V notch at corners, where the logs locked into each other; their three-sided hunter's shanty, built with the open side toward the fire, whose heat the shanty's pitched roof reflected downward in a remarkably efficient way; and their way of making "worm," or "snake," fences consisting of whole or split logs placed at an angle to each other in panels six or seven rails high. New Sweden's Finnish settlers introduced these structures to the Delaware Valley, and they persisted in a similar form on later North American frontiers.

In 1655, New Netherland absorbed New Sweden's roughly 700 people, of whom 40 to 50 percent were Finns. Throughout the next decade, a healthy flow of immigrants further increased the Dutch colony's population, which reached 8,000 to 9,000 in the mid-1660s. By then, however, the British colonies of North America held about 90,000 settlers. It was, in fact, primarily the British who "peopled" European North America. They established thriving plantations first along the Chesapeake Bay and then in New England. Two more different places are difficult to imagine.

## The Chesapeake

The Virginia colony, founded in 1607, and its northern neighbor Maryland, begun a quarter-century later, had so much in common that they are often together referred to as "the Chesapeake." It was in Virginia, though, that the British discovered by trial and error—mostly error—what it took to succeed at planting the New World. The first problem they confronted was basic: how would they pay the costs?

### THE COMPANY AS COLONIZER

The failed colonial efforts of Gilbert and Raleigh made clear that planting a colony cost more than any one private person could afford. Since the Crown was unwilling to foot the bills, private investors would have to pool their capital to finance overseas expansion. The English, like the French, Dutch, and Swedes, did this through companies formed primarily to carry on trade. The demands of trade and colonization, however, were different, and company sponsorship was not necessarily well fitted for setting up anything but modest and reliably profitable trading posts.

A similar need to finance costly operations had inspired the creation of Britain's great trading companies, such as the East India Company. Those that were formally incorporated received a charter from the Crown that defined their governing structure and, to make the start-up costs worthwhile, gave them an exclusive right to carry on trade with a stated market, such as Russia. Sometimes companies financed ventures from a "joint stock," a fund collected from many investors who later divided any profits in proportion to the amount they had invested or, which was the same thing, the number of shares they had purchased. The joint stock device allowed not only merchants to invest, but others, including large landholders, whose wealth increased substantially as England's population and rents swung upward. Merchants characteristically favored companies that paid solid profits. Members of the landholding gentry were often also attracted by projects that could enhance the power and glory of England or serve a religious purpose. They were therefore good investors for colonial projects, which seldom provided quick returns and often produced none at all. In the course of Virginia's troubled history, the balance of investors shifted from merchants to gentry.

### FOUNDING VIRGINIA

In 1606, the British Crown granted a charter to two separate groups of investors for the settlement of Virginia, which then included all of North America along the Atlantic Ocean between the 34th and 45th degrees of north latitude (that is, between a point in Maine just north of modern Bangor and North Carolina's Cape Fear River). The Virginia Company of Plymouth received permission to establish its "first seat," or settlement, in the northern reaches of the grant. The Virginia Company of London was to found its base farther south. The land between the Potomac River and today's New York City was open to both companies, but neither could start a settlement within a hundred miles of one established by the other. A royal Council of Virginia, appointed by the Crown and resident in England, oversaw two subsidiary councils that managed the affairs of the Plymouth and London companies. The 1606 charter promised English colonists all the "liberties, franchises, and immunities" of their countrymen in the British Isles.

In the summer of 1607, the Virginia Company of Plymouth sent forty-four men to a place the Indians called Sagadahoc at the mouth of the Kennebec River on the Maine coast. Beset by what reports called "childish factions," unstable leadership, and an unusually cold winter, most of the settlers returned to England after a year. Before long, the colony collapsed entirely, and investors saw no reason to throw good money after bad. The Virginia Company of London was richer and more successful. In December 1606, it sent to sea three small ships, the

*Susan Constant, Godspeed,* and *Discovery,* under the command of Captain Christopher Newport, an experienced sailor who had once worked for the Muscovy Company. The ships carried 144 men and boys, all employees of the Virginia Company of London, to found an outpost near the Chesapeake Bay. After four months, they arrived at what was for them a "land unknown" since no Englishman had ever explored or mapped the Chesapeake. By then, about 40 passengers had died or disappeared. A few weeks later, the 100 or so survivors began building a base they called Jamestown, from which, despite a plague of difficulties, emerged Virginia, the first British colony of seventeenth-century America.

The Virginia Company of London tried to avoid the mistakes of earlier English and French settlements. It instructed Captain Newport to locate a river suitable for western exploration and to seat the first settlement upstream to shield it from attacks by other European powers, such as the one that had destroyed an earlier Huguenot base in Florida. An upstream location would also be convenient for trading with Indians. The company told Newport to avoid marshlands, but the site chosen for Jamestown, on a peninsula about sixty miles up the James River (named, like Jamestown, after King James I), was swampy. Still, there was a good view up and down the river, and the site seemed easy to defend from attacks by sea or by land.

After the Jamestown site had been chosen, the company instructed the men to form three groups to explore the area. They were to look for a water passage to the Pacific (some bad ideas die hard) and for promising sources of minerals; build a storehouse and fortifications, as the Portuguese did in their West African trading posts; and plant grains and root vegetables. Newport explored the James River and the colonists built a fort, but they didn't plant food crops. Not that the colonists had enough to eat—while at sea they had consumed most of the provisions they brought from England. Now each settler's daily ration of food consisted of a half-pint of wheat and a half-pint of barley "boiled with water," and the barley, according to Captain John Smith, a colonist and future leader of the colony, had "fried" in the ships' holds and contained "as many worms as grain." The settlers apparently did not know how to fish or hunt. "Though there be fish in the sea, fowls in the water, and beasts in the woods," Smith reported, "their bounds are so large, they so wild, and we so weak and ignorant, we cannot much trouble them." The colonists assumed that if supplies from England ran out, the Indians would feed them. And in those "desperate" circumstances of 1607, Smith wrote,

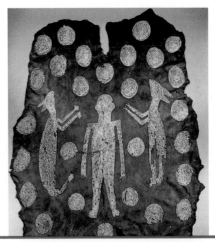

A mantle made of a deer skin sent by Powhatan to King James I through Captain Christopher Newport. Powhatan was the leader of the Algonquian Indians in the vicinity of Jamestown.

God "so changed the hearts of the savages, that they brought such plenty of their fruits, and provision, as no man wanted."

However, relying on the Indians for food made the English dependent on them. And if the English purchased or seized too much of the Indians' food, they risked becoming an insupportable burden—with results like those at Roanoke. Virginia's Indians outnumbered the English many times over: Smith estimated the nearby Indian population at about 5,000, and he probably understated its size. Moreover, Indians in the vicinity of Jamestown were members of a confederacy under the Algonquian chief Powhatan, whose subjects were not abused like those of Montezuma. That confederacy enhanced the Indians' capacity to get rid of annoying intruders.

The London company's well-intentioned efforts to make the colony succeed also sometimes made its survival more difficult. At great expense, the company sent new contingents of settlers to the colony, but without adequate supplies. Many early settlers were gentlemen unaccustomed to taking orders from others or performing manual labor. And some of the craftsmen the company recruited had skills that proved useless in Virginia. One group of settlers included, for example, a jeweler, refiners, goldsmiths, and even a perfumer. What the colony needed, Smith understood, were carpenters, masons, "husbandsmen" (farmers), fishermen, and "diggers up of trees" and "roots"—common laborers willing to work. The company financed each of the first shipments of supplies with a separate joint stock, which is why one 1608 supply ship

An Indian town called Secoton in a watercolor by John White.

brought an order that the colonists send back £2,000 worth of goods to repay investors for their expenses. The settlers tried to produce commodities for sale in England such as pitch and tar, glass, "soap ashes," and clapboards. But they could produce none of them efficiently or economically. "In over-toiling our weak and unskillful bodies, to satisfy this desire of present profit," Smith said, "we can scarce[ly] ever recover ourselves from one supply to another."

The settlers' worst enemies, however, were themselves. The best way "to prosper and to Obtain Good Success," the company's 1606 instructions counseled them, "is to make yourselves all of one mind for the Good of your Country and your own and to serve and fear God," since "every Plantation which our heavenly father hath not planted shall be rooted out." Nonetheless, as in one New World settlement after another, the men of Virginia quarreled, stole supplies from the common store for their own consumption or to trade with the Indians for their personal profit, and became at times so obsessed with gold that other, life-sustaining activities ceased. By January 1608, only 38 persons remained alive of the original 144 who had set to sea thirteen months earlier.

### CAPTAIN JOHN SMITH

At first, Virginia had no government capable of forcing the errant settlers to behave. Authority rested in a council appointed by the Virginia Company of London and a president whom the councilors elected and could overrule. John Smith, a twenty-seven-year-old soldier and adventurer with the capacity to knock the motley crew of Anglo-Virginians into shape, was among those named to the first council, but his colleagues expelled him because he had supposedly participated in a mutiny at sea. They also threw out their president only a few months after electing him.

The situation improved after September 1608, when the council reinstated Smith and, in recognition of his ability to obtain corn from the Indians, gave him complete authority over the colony. The bright son of an English farmer, Smith had served as a soldier of fortune in the Netherlands and also Hungary, where he was captured and taken to Turkey as a slave. Those experiences taught him critical survival skills. In America, Smith spent time exploring, sketched a detailed map of Virginia, and gathered material he would later use in his landmark *Generall Historie of Virginia, New England, and the Summer Isles* (1624). He was given to a kind of tall-tale bragging that later became a stock-in-trade in the American West: for example, he made the Indians stand "amazed with admiration" (as would we) at the astronomical phenomena he could demonstrate with the use of a compass; Indian women found him irresistible; and his guns never missed their mark. With just one shot, he could make Virginia's "naked devils" tumble "one over another," and the Indians hated fighting with him, he wrote, "almost as ill as hanging, such fear they had of bad success."

Smith also had a keen eye for the plants and peculiar animals that thrived in Virginia, which he knew were of interest in England, and made careful observations of the Indians and the way they lived. He saw himself as a Cortés-like figure and thought the Indians should work for the English, much as the peoples of Mexico worked for the Spanish. But he admired the natives' agricultural skills and praised Indian corn as more productive per seed planted than European wheat. Smith noted how the Indians built their warm, snug houses (with young trees, which were "bowed and tied," then covered with mats or the bark of trees, leaving a hole at the top to allow smoke from

Captain John Smith, the historian and first successful leader of the Virginia colony, who mapped the New England coast during a voyage in 1614. The portrait is from the map of the area that appeared in Smith's *General Historie of Virginie, New England, and the Summer Isles* (1624).

their fires to escape), and how they made the boats, nets, hooks, and bows and arrows with which they fished and hunted. At certain times of the year, he observed, the Indians left their "habitations" and divided their people into "companies" that traveled inland to the heads of rivers, where there was "plenty of game." In short, despite the sense of superiority he shared with other Englishmen, Smith was able to learn from the Indians.

Once in charge of the colony, he divided settlers into groups and forced them to work, declaring, "He that will not worke, shall not eate (except by sicknesse he be disabled)." He also moved the settlers out of Jamestown, where they had become sick, especially in July and August. In those months, the spring discharge of water from the mountains ceased, the river's level dropped, its salt level rose, and the water the settlers drank became contaminated, as a contemporary account put it, with "slime and filth." The colonists probably suffered from dysentery, typhoid, and also salt poisoning, which explains in part their "swellings," lassitude, and irritability as well as their tendency to die. By scattering colonists in the countryside, like the Indians, moving them toward freshwater springs and away from the James estuary, Smith lowered the death rate substantially. Between the fall of 1608 and the summer of 1609, at most 21 of 130 persons died, and 11 of those drowned.

## THE CHARTERS OF 1609 AND 1612

In 1609, when its "first seat" seemed firmly established, the Virginia Company of London received a new charter from the Crown that extended the colony's boundaries 200 miles north and south from Old Point Comfort at the base of the Chesapeake Bay and "from sea to sea, north and northwest." That was an enormous grant, far greater than anyone actually understood since Europeans, who still could not measure longi-

tude, had no idea just how far the Pacific lay from the eastern coast of North America. The charter of 1609 also made the London company a joint-stock company, able to sell shares to the public, and gave it greater control over the colony. Effective power rested in the company's treasurer, Sir Thomas Smith, whose rule was as autocratic as John Smith's in Virginia. Still, the change was significant. The British Crown did not centralize colonial power in its hands, as the Spanish Crown had done, but granted major responsibility for its first North American colony to a private concern.

In 1612, the Crown granted the company another charter that extended the colony's boundaries far enough out to sea to include Bermuda, or Somers Island, which had been discovered in 1609. The charter also gave the company a seven-year exemption from paying English customs duties and allowed it to run national lotteries to raise money for Virginia. Finally, the charter ended the old royal council and gave responsibility for company affairs to its stockholders. All members of the company would meet as a "great court" four times a year to decide matters of general policy. "Ordinary courts," which only twenty shareholders had to attend, would meet weekly with the company's treasurer to discuss more immediate issues. Perhaps investors would be more willing to support a company over whose affairs they had greater influence. Of course, profits were the greatest inducement to investment—and of those, the company had seen precious little. But hope springs eternal.

## DEVELOPING VIRGINIA

In 1609, with its new charter in hand, the Virginia Company of London mounted a national campaign to recruit investors and settlers. It offered shares in the company not just for money (from "adventurers," or investors) but as a reward for migration (by "planters"). For seven years, settlers would be company employees, drawing food and supplies from a common storehouse. Then, in 1616, shareholders would divide the company's wealth, and each of them, planters and adventurers alike, would receive at least 100 acres of land. By the spring of 1609, some 600 men, women, and children climbed on board the nine ships of a "great fleet" that the London company sent to Virginia.

The company also revised the government in Virginia. Henceforth, a governor would have "full power and authority" over both military and civil affairs. In the next few years, the colony's strong governors imposed a quasi-military regime under a set of harsh laws remembered as the "Laws Divine, Moral and Martial." Those laws organized settlers into work

The cover of a brochure advertising the splendors of living in Virginia. Published in London during 1609, its aim was to lure settlers to the struggling colony.

gangs, as Smith had done, and they required "everie man and woman" to attend religious services twice a day or face severe punishments. They prescribed the death penalty for a wide range of crimes—sodomy, rape, adultery; stealing from the general store or from other colonists, even taking grapes or "any ears of corne" from public or private gardens; and, what seemed to evoke the most extreme concern, attempting to leave the colony, whether by sea or by fleeing to the Indians. Even under these laws, however, colonists worked only five to eight hours a day in summer, three to six in winter.

The worst times for the colony occurred when there was no governor or deputy governor. One particularly hard period, Virginia's "starving time," came in the winter of 1609–10, after Smith suffered a gunshot wound and set sail for England but before the new governor or deputy had arrived. One contemporary account said that of 500 colonists alive when Smith left, many recently recruited by the London company, there remained six months later "not past sixtie men, women, and children," all "miserable and poore creatures" who had survived by consuming "roots, herbes, acornes, walnuts, berries, now and then a little fish." A modern study argues that slightly fewer

than 200 colonists actually spent the winter of 1609–10 in Virginia, and of them 100 survived, 15 were killed by Indians, and 80 died of other causes. That was bad enough. By spring, the survivors decided to abandon Virginia and were sailing down the James when the new governor arrived and convinced them to turn back. Again in 1611, two months after one governor left and before his replacement arrived, the people could be found "at their daily and usual work bowling in the streets."

Still, Virginia survived and even expanded geographically as many people left sickly Jamestown to live in fortified settlements between the mouth of the James River and the new town of Henrico (now Richmond) at the fall line, where water drops from the mountains in falls or rapids that block upriver navigation. A modest allocation of land to some settlers in 1614 made the colony something beyond a company camp. These new landowners assumed more responsibility for feeding themselves and for contributing corn to the company store, which newcomers drew upon. The colonists remained dependent on the Indians for much of their food, but that didn't keep them from treating the Indians with contempt. In fact, they had a nasty habit of murdering Indians with a nonchalant brutality and then, stranger still, destroying their fields of corn.

The colony also found, finally, something it could sell profitably. John Rolfe, a settler who had married Powhatan's daughter Pocahantas, began experimenting with tobacco seed from the West Indies in about 1612. That seed produced a plant whose leaves were milder and more pleasant for Europeans to smoke than the variety of tobacco grown by Virginia's Indians, and in 1617 Virginia sent a cargo of this tobacco to England. It sold for three shillings a pound—less than tobacco from the West Indies, but more than anything else the Virginians produced.

But could a colony be founded on tobacco? Europeans first welcomed tobacco for its supposed medical benefits, but soon they smoked it simply for pleasure. Sure, it was addictive, and smoking rapidly became less than entirely respectable. Tobacco provided, however, a beginning, a way of making the colony solvent. Then perhaps it could produce other goods of more basic importance to England.

### THE GREAT CHARTER

Something about Virginia fostered dreams despite its way of making them go sour. The dream that took over the Virginia Company of London in 1619 belonged to Sir Edwin Sandys, leader of a contingent of stockholders who elected him trea-

Pocahontas, the daughter of Powhatan and the wife of Virginia colonist John Rolfe, in a painting based on a 1616 engraving by Simon Van de Passe.

surer. Sandys proposed to develop and invigorate the colony by means of an ambitious plan. He would build up the population by giving land to immigrants. Anyone who paid his own way to Virginia or the passageway of others would receive a "headright" of fifty acres per person. Sandys encouraged groups to migrate by offering them adjacent grants of land in separate communities known as "particular plantations." And he offered to bring impoverished people to the colony at the company's expense if they would then work company lands for seven years on a sharecropping basis, keeping half their earnings. After their term of indenture (the contract by which they agreed to work a set number of years) was over, they, too, would receive fifty acres. Undeveloped land in Virginia was of little value to the company; it might as well give land away, then charge landowners a modest quitrent (tax on land) of a shilling a year per fifty acres held.

Sandys saw no reason Englishmen would travel to a place where they had far less freedom than at home, so he ended the old "Laws Divine, Moral and Martial." From now on, the colony's government would include an assembly consisting of an appointed governor's council and an elected House of Burgesses. The assembly could make laws for the colony, although the laws required the company's approval before going into effect. Colonists welcomed the instructions Sandys gave Virginia's new governor, which included these changes, as their "great charter" because they established "English liberty" in Vir-

ginia, much as the Magna Carta (1215) had done for England itself. The new assembly met on June 30, 1619. It was the first representative assembly in British America—but not the last.

As if to gild the lily, Sandys promised to "ease all the Inhabitants of Virginia forever of all taxes and public burthens" to the extent possible, and so to remove "all occasion of oppression and corruption." Officials would be paid from the proceeds of lands worked by company tenants. Sandys also tried to develop new exports. He sent Germans to build sawmills that would cut timber into boards for export; skilled Italians to create a glassworks; and an experienced English iron maker to oversee the construction of a well-equipped ironworks at a place called Fallen Creek. In and near Jamestown, archaeological evidence suggests that glass blowers, potters, brewers, distillers, apothecaries, pipemakers, and wine growers were busily at work in the late 1710s and 1720s. Sandys proposed to Anglicize the local Indians so Anglo-Virginians could live with them in peace. Some Indian families would reside within the English settlements; others would be educated at a new Indian college built at Henrico and supported by a grant of 10,000 acres of land that would be worked by company tenants. The colonists could only conclude that they were destined to become "the most happy people in the world."

## FAILURE

It didn't work. Over a three-year period, Sandys recruited over 3,500 people to join the 700 already in Virginia. Most of them died, some quickly of disease, especially when, weakened by long voyages at sea, they arrived to find no shelter and little if any food. By March 22, 1622, the colony's population stood at only 1,240; about 3,000 people had already disappeared. Then another 347 died in a massive Indian attack mounted by Opechancanough, Powhatan's warlike brother and successor, in an all-out effort to stop, once and for all, the colonists' expansion onto Indian lands.

The attack took the colonists by complete surprise. Indians had moved easily through the settlements, trading, eating, and even sleeping at homes of colonists who, it seems, felt no sense of danger. On the morning of the massacre, Smith reported, some Indians "sat downe at breakfast with our people, whom immediately with their owne tools they slew most barbarously, not sparing either age or sex, man woman or childe." Indians familiar with colonists' work patterns also found it easy to kill men in the fields. Among the casualties were the man appointed to develop the Indian college and the ironmaster. The Indians also burned the buildings at Fallen Creek and tossed the workmen's expensive imported tools into the water. The English then decided that "wee must drive them, or they us out of the country," but that was no easy thing given the colony's reduced manpower and the Indians' preference for surprise attacks over open battles.

The Indians actually killed far fewer Virginians than those company officials who shipped large numbers of settlers without making sufficient provision for their needs on arrival, or the greedy men who held power in the colony and ruthlessly exploited newcomers to produce tobacco for their own personal profit. After a brief dip, tobacco prices rose back to three shillings a pound, enough to make a man rich if he could produce the leaf in quantity. But tobacco was a highly labor-intensive crop: seedlings had to be planted in a sheltered place in early spring and transplanted to prepared fields sometime in April, and then, during the growing season, the top growth bud had to be carefully picked off so the plants branched out, producing more leaves. Plants also needed to be inspected regularly and insects picked off and destroyed. Once harvested, tobacco was hung to dry in shaded places or, later, sheds. Then, after about six weeks, leaves could be removed from the branches and packed in barrels for shipment abroad. To produce a lot of tobacco, and so to make a fortune during the "boom" of the 1620s, required therefore not just land but a lot of workers. Labor, which in England seemed to be in excess supply, was the key to wealth in Virginia.

Who would fill the demand for workers? Not the handful of African slaves brought to Virginia by a Dutch ship in 1619. There were not enough of them; they were too expensive, and there was not much incentive to buy a lifetime of slave labor when life was short. Nor could Indians fill the need. Before the massacre of 1622, they sometimes did odd jobs around the colony for pay. But among the Indians, agriculture was women's work, and Indian women were busy growing their own crops. To capture Indians and force them to work for the colonists would, in any case, only have increased resentments and sparked reprisals. That left Englishmen, who were not great workers, but they would have to do.

So the avaricious henchmen of early Virginia—no longer the gentlemen of the colony's opening years, who had long since died or returned home, but men of humbler birth who fought to better themselves in this new land and who maneuvered themselves onto the governor's council or into other colonial offices—took control of the colony's new immigrants. They purchased the labor of some indentured servants and then stole others, tricking freemen into becoming tenants or making company servants work on their private lands. Often they treated white indentured servants more like things than like fellow men. "I thought no head . . . able to hold so much water as hath and doth dailie flow from my eyes," a young English servant, Richard Freethorne, wrote his "loveing and kind" parents in 1623. He was cold, having few clothes, and hungry. Since arriving, he'd consumed nothing but peas, "loblollie" (a thin mixture of cereal and water), a bit of beef, and a few mouthfuls of bread. "I have eaten more in a day at home" than in an entire week in Virginia, he said. Day and night, he claimed, the people cried out, "Oh that they were in England," even if they had to sacrifice an arm or leg to get back and were required to spend the rest of their lives begging from door to door. Such boys rarely lived long enough to realize the dreams that had brought them to Virginia.

### A ROYAL COLONY

In 1624, after a special investigative commission confirmed rumors of extreme mismanagement, the Crown cancelled Virginia's charter. The next year, Charles I became king and announced that the colony's government would henceforth "depend upon ourself, and not be committed to any company or corporation." So Virginia became a royal colony. The downward trajectory of power was, it seems, reversed; now the English Crown, like its Spanish counterpart, would rule its overseas possessions.

But royal governors soon found that to govern Virginia, they needed the help of local planters who knew the colony well and had established positions of power within its developing society. Governors appointed such men to their council—but at times it wasn't altogether clear who governed whom. In 1635, when councilors disagreed with Governor John Harvey over Indian policy and the colony's stand toward the new colony of Maryland, they "thrust him out." That is, the councilors seized Harvey, put him under armed guard, sent him back to England, and chose one of their number to serve as governor in his place. The king reappointed Harvey but later replaced him with a governor more acceptable to the Virginians.

When the new governor arrived in 1639, he announced that the colony's assembly would be reinstated. In fact, the elected House of Burgesses, which was dear to the Virginians, had never completely disappeared. It met on scattered occasions after 1624, and in 1634 it took the monumental step of organizing local governments in the form of county courts. By then, the colony's population had spread along both sides of the James River up to the falls that divided the tidewater from the hill country, or piedmont, farther inland. Virginians had also moved north, claiming land between the James and York rivers, settled the York's northern shore, and crossed the Chesapeake to take up lands on the Eastern Shore (the large peninsula that separates the Chesapeake Bay from the Atlantic).

As the population spread out, trips to the capital, Jamestown, to register land titles and wills or to perform similar tasks became increasingly inconvenient. Officials in Jamestown also found executing those routine jobs for the entire colony more onerous as Virginia's population grew, which it did in great jumps after the mid-1630s. Under the new system, each of eight large counties (whose number later increased) established courts made up of justices of the peace who heard minor criminal and civil cases and carried out various administrative tasks. Each county also had a sheriff, a clerk, and a variety of other officers. Over time, the assembly gave them responsibility for one job after another until the counties became the colony's most important administrative centers.

The governor appointed county officials in the name of the Crown. But it soon became customary in Virginia for governors to appoint county officeholders from residents nominated by the county courts. Local officials in the British colonies had local interests, local loyalties. Although the political system centered in the Crown, it incorporated colonists in the making of laws, and in many cases it depended on them to execute these laws. This was an empire with a difference.

## MARYLAND

In 1632, Charles I granted the new colony of Maryland to his friend George Calvert, Lord Baltimore, a Catholic who wanted to found a refuge for English Catholics. The original charter gave Calvert land west from the Delaware Bay along the 40th parallel down to the southern bank of the Potomac River and inland to that river's "first fountain" (waterfall). The Potomac turned more sharply to the northwest than anyone suspected, but what Calvert lost in land he gained in power. He was the absolute owner and lord of Maryland. He held the land in his own name and could establish and conduct its government by himself, although the colonists had to give their advice and consent to laws. And Calvert could pass the colony on to his heirs. Since he died before the charter was sealed, Maryland became the possession of his son Cecelius Calvert, who shared his father's ambition. Maryland

Charles Calvert, the 3rd Lord Baltimore, became Maryland's governor in 1661. A Catholic, he was frequently at odds with the Protestant assembly. This portrait is by the German painter Johann Closterman.

thus became a "proprietary" colony under the Calverts, who were its proprietors. The colonies Britain founded in the West Indies at about the same time—St. Christopher (1624), Barbados (1627), Nevis (1628), Montserrat and Antigua (about 1632)—were also begun as proprietary colonies. By then, the Virginia Company of London's lamentable record had brought the use of commercial companies for founding colonies into some disrepute. However, by giving land to settlers who paid their own way to America and provided their own supplies, the old Virginia Company of London had hit upon a way to pass many of the costs of founding settlements to the colonists themselves. Later colonies followed suit. Calvert, for example, offered settlers liberal land grants. Most of those who went to Maryland (beginning in 1634) were Protestants, and that led to persistent conflicts between the proprietor and colonists, who used the elected assembly to oppose Calvert, his governor, laws, and religion.

Although different issues arose in the politics of Maryland and Virginia, their systems of government were similar. In Maryland, the proprietor appointed the governor, which the Crown did in Virginia; but both colonies elected assemblies, and, as its population spread, Maryland established a county court system much like Virginia's. The two colonies experienced much the same climate, and both of their economies depended on tobacco. In part for those reasons, the Chesapeake colonies developed societies that distinguished them not only from other parts of British North America but from England itself.

### A PLACE LIKE ENGLAND?

The idea of overseas plantations implied that colonies would replicate their mother country. In some ways, Virginia and Maryland did that. Their language, values, and habits all reflected their English origin. The settlers' devotion to elected assemblies and to local government also had roots in England, as did their sense of what kinds of work were appropriate for men and for women.

But there were differences, too. For one thing, any settled society has a roughly equal number of men and women. The first settlers of Virginia, however, were usually single men in their twenties. They had traveled from hundreds of places in the west and south of England to ports such as Bristol or London and, finding no work or perhaps hoping for adventure and opportunity, signed on for America. Since only a handful of women migrated, men vastly outnumbered women. In Virginia's second decade, there were about four or five men for every woman, so it was impossible for the population to grow substantially by natural increase.

The colony's labor system made the problem worse. Young women who arrived as indentured servants—virtually all of them—could not marry until their terms of service were over, which chopped from four to seven years off their prime childbearing time. If a girl bore a "bastard" child (one born out of wedlock) before her indenture had expired, she had to work an additional year or two to repay her master for labor lost and the "trouble of his house." Probably few immigrant women married before age twenty-five, which meant that, assuming they nursed infants, which affected birth intervals, they bore at most four or five babies. In Maryland, at least a quarter of all children died within their first year and 40 to 55 percent before age twenty. And so through most of the seventeenth century, Virginia's and Maryland's populations grew less from births than from immigration.

Life was short in the early Chesapeake. In one Virginia county, which was much like many others, women generally died in their late thirties. Probably many suffered from malaria, a mosquito-borne disease especially dangerous to the young, the old, and pregnant women. If they made it past their childbearing years, women could expect to live longer than men of the same age. But most men died in their forties, about a decade earlier than Englishmen "at home." Since women typically married older men, they frequently survived their husbands—and then remarried quickly. Women of virtually all sorts were in demand since there were so few of them, but in Virginia, at least, widows with inherited wealth became the prize catches. They brought their "dower right" to a third of their dead husband's estate and frequently served as executors of their children's inherited property—a role their new husbands generally took over. And wives were useful: they raised vegetables, milked cows, made cheese and butter, cooked, washed, and took care of children. Sometimes in the seventeenth century, especially if a family lacked servants, they even worked in the fields, though women shed fieldwork when better times arrived. The records suggest that these women of early Virginia were a tough bunch. They had more power than their English sisters, and they felt no compunction about expressing their convictions and desires in what some might have considered unbecoming ways.

With so many adults dying in their childbearing years, Virginia produced crop after crop of orphans. Almost a quarter of all children had lost one or both parents by the time they were five years of age, and over half by the time they turned thirty. Sometimes orphans found themselves in families with no natural parent—living, for example, in the household of their dead mother's second (or later) husband and his "now wife," as the phrase went. Such children had to grow up fast, if only to protect their inheritances from dishonest stepfathers. There the government helped them. In Virginia, guardians had to present their accounts for auditing every year at special "orphans' courts." Children could request a new guardian when they reached their fourteenth year. Under the circumstances, with death lurking at the door, communities of people formed to take care of each other: networks of blood relatives and quasi-kin—godparents, relatives by marriage, or just caring neighbors—stepped in to protect stranded children.

The early Virginians' attitudes toward work had roots in England, where laws attempted to pass work around so that everyone had a little and discouraged go-getters who selfishly tried to hold two jobs at once. Of course, some people in the Chesapeake were able to live relatively easy lives because they forced others to work for them. The Virginia gentry's treatment of servants, whom they bought, sold, and even gambled away like pieces of property, established patterns for the future—as one servant suggested when he complained that his master treated him like a "slave." It also reinforced an old English dislike of working for others in any capacity, even for wages. Independence was highly esteemed in Virginia, where men aspired to work for themselves so they didn't have to take orders and could do as they chose. Dependence was for women, children, and servants of one sort or another. A commitment to individualism in that sense and to personal freedom became an enduring part of Virginia's culture.

Virginia and Maryland were similar in some ways to British West Indian colonies such as Barbados, which in the 1620s and 1630s grew tobacco on farms with white indentured servants and had high mortality rates and few women. Even more, the Chesapeake resembled what later generations knew as the American West. In 1607, Jamestown was Europe's Far West. The resemblance was clearest in Virginia's early years, when its rivers were full of floating taverns where lonely men gathered to gamble and drink their misery away. Death was a constant presence on the western frontiers of European settlement, and women were rare—but unusually strong. And what frontiersmen showed respect for Indians or absentee owners or anyone else who interfered with their ambitions?

By the 1630s, however, Virginians began to have more settled lives. Tobacco prices fell; then planters began growing more corn, and they found ways to protect their hogs and cattle from wolves and wandering Indians. Feeding themselves ceased to be a problem. Throughout the seventeenth century, Virginians lived in hut-like houses of one or two rooms and made of split logs attached to vertical supports that were simply stuck in the ground. Those structures were remarkably ephemeral compared with the stone houses of England. The Virginians' farms were not clustered together but spread out along rivers and navigable streams, the highways of their time, so tobacco could be more easily loaded onto boats and shipped to markets far away. Still, the increased incidence of families and of communities in which people traveled fair distances to visit each other, talk, dance, play games, and help each other in times of trouble marked the emergence of something more than a frontier outpost. So did the establishment of county governments. Virginia and soon also Maryland were becoming societies of a type different in many ways from both England and other North American colonies. The Chesapeake's distinctiveness becomes all the more clear when it is compared with its sister colonies in the North.

## New England

Portrait of Elizabeth Freake and her baby, Mary, painted in New England during the 1670s by a local painter. The flat, primitive image was characteristic of most American art at that time.

About 100 Englishmen crossed the Atlantic in 1620 on the *Mayflower* and founded a colony at Plymouth in New England. Soon thereafter, others made homes or started fishing posts at scattered places along the northern Atlantic coast. But what posterity has remembered as the "Great Migration" to New England began in 1630 when a fleet of eleven ships carried some 700 men, women, and children as well as livestock and other supplies to a new colony in the Massachusetts Bay, north of Plymouth. By the time the Great Migration ended twelve years later, about 20,000 English people had gone to New England. That region would eventually include several colonies: Massachusetts, Connecticut, Rhode Island, and New Hampshire, as well as Plymouth and New Haven, which remained separate colonies in the early seventeenth century.

New England was dramatically different from the Chesapeake in many ways. For one thing, Englishmen began to settle it several decades after Virginia had been founded, and their leaders tried to avoid Virginia's mistakes. Since New England could not grow a single staple crop such as tobacco for sale in Britain, it developed a more varied economy than the Chesapeake. Most early New England settlers came, moreover, not from the south and west of England, which sent many settlers to the Chesapeake, but from the east ("East Anglia"). They traveled not alone but in groups that included entire families, and then made their homes in towns, not isolated plantations. Immigration to Virginia continued throughout the seventeenth century, but that to New England slowed to a trickle after 1642, when the outbreak of civil war in England prompted potential settlers to stay home. New England's population nonetheless grew rapidly by natural increase, since sex ratios there were relatively even, couples bore many children, infant mortality was low, and adults lived long lives.

Some of these distinctions can be explained by the accidents of place and time. Others, however, stemmed from the fact that most of those who settled New England were Puritans, members of a particular radical strain in English Protestantism whose beliefs shaped the region's society and culture.

## PURITANISM

"Puritan" began as a derogatory term for English Calvinists of the sixteenth and seventeenth centuries who wanted to purify the Church of England by eliminating still more remnants of the pre-Reformation Catholic past. Puritans compiled long lists of "unscriptural" practices that the Church of England

John Winthrop, the first governor of the Massachusetts Bay Colony.

retained—various liturgies and set prayers (they described the Book of Common Prayer, for example, as "culled and picked out of that popish dung-hill, the mass book," and thus "full of abominations"); the rituals in baptism, communion, marriages, and burials; clerical vestments; tithes, canon law, bishops' courts, and so on. These reformers wanted a simpler church with no central bureaucracy, a church that would emphasize the essence of religion—piety and Bible reading—over outward show.

At the core of Puritanism, however, lay a concept of the church not as a building, or a vast structure of clergymen and believers, but as a community of covenanted "saints." Like other Calvinists, the Puritans believed in predestination: God knew who was destined to spend eternity with Him (His saints) and who was damned even before those people were born. The Puritans believed that God's church on earth (the church visible) should approximate the church destined to exist in heaven (the church invisible) by consisting, to the extent possible, only of the saved. These saints had to form voluntary agreements—covenants—by which they pledged to help each other live according to God's will. That belief rested on a passage from the Book of Psalms (50:5) in the Old Testament: "Gather my saints together unto me; those that have made a covenant with me by sacrifice."

The main problem with the Church of England, Puritans said, was that it was formed not by covenant but by the state. Moreover, it excluded nobody—everyone born in England was automatically a member—and therefore lacked "discipline," a capacity to admonish and ultimately expel serious sinners. Some Puritans, known as Separatists, thought that those failures so corrupted the established church that God's people had no choice but to leave it and form their own separate churches. One group of such Separatists went into exile in Leiden, Holland. Later, some members of that congregation, fearing that their children were becoming Dutch, moved on to America, where they founded the Plymouth Colony in 1620. Other Puritans saw within the Church of England a core of saints sufficient to legitimize it in God's eyes. The founders of the Massachusetts Bay Colony (1630) were of that sort. The first governor of Massachusetts, John Winthrop, even condemned the Separatists for the "spiritual pride" that led them to abandon those "weak Christians" within the Church of England who were in need of "tender care." Once in New England, however, the Massachusetts Bay colonists organized their own covenanted churches and gradually became much like their Separatist brethren.

Puritanism's appeal lay precisely in traits that most modern people find distasteful: its tight communities of "mutually watchful" people who were always prying into each other's affairs, noting moral lapses, admonishing sinners, and encouraging them to live according to God's word. Individual privacy had no place in Puritanism. But in an England where old bonds were disappearing—where tenant families were being forced off the land, young people moving about in search of work, and new forms of commerce and manufacturing pulling workers to places far from their ancestral homes—the involvement of individuals with each other was appealing. Puritanism offered a way of belonging, of connecting with others, in a lonely world. The Puritan assurance of salvation to God's chosen "saints" and of His "providence" (special care) for His people was also comforting at a time when death was always near and little in life could be called secure. The doctrines and group orientation of Puritanism also made it extraordinarily well suited to master the challenges of colonization.

## THE CROWN AND THE COLONY

Why did the Puritans leave England? Most of those who went to Massachusetts were people with some property, and they were more than ready to exploit what opportunities for profits America offered. But considering that their Great Migration occurred in a relatively short period of time, it seems likely that most left England not for economic opportunity so much as to flee oppression and for a chance to practice their religious beliefs freely.

Under James I (r. 1603–25), who was no friend of Puritanism, many Puritans found ways of making do within the Church of England. They might, for example, subsidize ministries and so win the right to appoint a sympathetic clergyman, or they might pay special lecturers who preached to Puritan-minded worshipers after regular Anglican church services. But making do became increasingly impossible under Charles I (r. 1625–49). After the king's ardent supporter William Laud became bishop of London and then archbishop of Canterbury, the Church of England seemed to be galloping toward Catholicism. Committed to restore the "beauty of holiness," Laud and other high-church clergy, with the king's support, restored traditional ceremonies and sacraments as well as altar rails, vestments, crosses, and an array of other devices that the Puritans found profoundly offensive. Charles I, moreover, seemed determined to rule autocrati-

cally. In 1629, he dissolved Parliament, which did not meet again for eleven years. Then, with a free hand, the king and Laud burned and banned Puritan writings, and fired or repressed increasing numbers of Puritan ministers and lecturers. John Winthrop complained about the "suspension and silencing" of learned clergymen for their refusal to conform to directives from the church hierarchy, and their replacement with "scandalous and dumb ministers."

If the Puritans went to Massachusetts Bay to practice their religious beliefs freely, they had to make sure that the problems they faced in England didn't follow them. The leaders of this migration were more prosperous and powerful than those from Leiden who had founded Plymouth, and they used their money and connections to give the colony substantial independence. They began working with older companies organized under patents or grants from the Council for New England, a reorganized form of the 1606 Virginia Company of Plymouth. But that left the settlement at the mercy of whoever controlled the parent company in England. And so the Puritan leaders secured a charter from the Crown for their own joint-stock company, the Massachusetts Bay Company, in March 1629. Not even a charter provided enough protection, though, since charters could be rescinded, as the dissolution of the Virginia Company of London five years earlier had demonstrated.

Gradually a group of Puritans from the eastern counties of England took over the Massachusetts Bay Company. They decided in late August 1629 to emigrate and to take "the whole government together with the patent for the said plantation" with them to New England. Within a matter of weeks, they elected their own candidates as company officials. As a result, leaders of the first settlers were good Puritans such as Winthrop, a respected member of the gentry who gave up his manorial home and all the comforts it offered to lead this exodus to the New World.

Once in America, the company government outlined in the charter became a civil government. A governor and his assistants took charge of the colony, and the assistants met with the colony's inhabitants (or, beginning in 1634, their elected representatives) in a General Court, which was originally a stockholders' meeting. In that way, the colony avoided splitting authority between a company in England and a settlement in America, which, some contemporary authorities claimed, had contributed to Virginia's problems. The Massachusetts Bay Colony was no ill-considered venture: its leaders invested their minds as well as their pocketbooks and, indeed, put their lives on the line. They would make this plantation work.

Virginia's leaders also demanded and received—or seized—considerable power over colonial affairs, as their "thrusting out" of Governor Harvey demonstrated. But in New England, the quest for autonomy was ideological and rigid. And the leaders' precautions proved wise. Before long, the Crown became aware of their activities and in 1634 began legal proceedings against the Massachusetts Bay Company's charter. In response, the colonists proceeded to fortify their harbor, train troops, and gather arms. Meanwhile, the old Council for New England yielded its charter to the Crown, which put a royal commission under Laud in charge of its territories. That action, Governor Winthrop testified, "occasioned the magistrates and deputies to hasten our fortifications." None of their military preparations proved necessary, since troubles nearer home absorbed King Charles's attention. First a war with Scotland, then an intensifying struggle with Parliament and religious dissenters, which culminated in civil war, preoccupied the king between 1642 and 1649. Finally, in 1649, Parliament tried Charles I for his crimes. He was convicted and beheaded.

During the next decade, the Puritan-dominated Parliament ruled an England without king or lords under a Commonwealth (1649–53) and then the Protectorate of Oliver Cromwell and, after his death, Richard Cromwell.

During England's time of troubles, the Massachusetts Bay Colony became a self-governing commonwealth. So, in effect, did Virginia; but there the colonists' loyalty remained with the Crown, while the New Englanders favored Parliament, whose followers included the mass of English Puritans. In many other ways, too, Puritanism made New England strikingly different from the Chesapeake colonies.

## MAINTAINING ORDER

New England had no need for the rigid, militaristic laws of early Virginia. It set out to follow another kind of rule. In 1630, en route to Massachusetts Bay on board the *Arbella*, Governor John Winthrop explained to the first settlers the mission God had given them. As fellow Christians, the

---

*American Journal*

## What's for Dinner?

*Along with grains boiled or baked with milk or water, which were the mainstays of most English farmers' meals, meat and fish seem to have been on New Englanders' tables from the first. In bad times, when there was no bread or, worse yet, beer, people drank water, and they sometimes had to make do with lobster.*

*Plymouth Colony, September 1621:*

"They begane now to gather in y$^e$ small harvest they had, and to fitte up their houses and dwellings against winter, being all well recovered in health & strength, and had all things in good plenty; for as some were imployed in affairs abroad, others were excersised in fishing, aboute codd, & bass, & other fish, of which y$^{ey}$ tooke good store, of which every family had their portion. All y$^e$ somer ther was no wante. And now begane to come in store of foule, as winter aproached, of which this place did abound when they came first (but afterward decreased by degrees). And besids water foule, ther was great store of wild Turkies, of which they tooke many, besids venison, &c.

Besids they had aboute a peck a meale a weeke to a person, or now since harvest, Indean corne to y$^t$ proportion. Which made many afterwards write so largly of their plenty hear to their freinds in England, which were not fained [feigned], but true reports."

*And in April 1623, when times were harder:*

"The best dish they could presente their freinds with was a lobster, or a peece of fish, without bread or any thing els but a cupp of fair spring water. And y$^e$ long continuance of this diate, and their labours abroad, had something abated y$^e$ freshnes of their former complexion. But God gave them health and strength in a good measure; and shewed them by experience y$^e$ truth of y$^t$ word, Deut. 8. 3, Yt man liveth not by bread only, but by every word y$^t$ proceedeth out of y$^e$ mouth of y$^e$ Lord doth a man live."

Governor William Bradford, *Bradford's History "Of Plymouth Plantation." From the Original Manuscript . . . By Order of the General Court*

colonists "ought to account our selves knitt together" into one body by a "bond of love." That meant "wee must bear one another's burthens, wee must not looke only on our own things, but allso on the things of our brethren." The settlers had "entered into Covenant with [God] for this work," which demanded that they treat each other with "meekness, gentleness, patience and liberality, . . . delight in each other, make others' Condicions our own," and "keepe the unitie of the spirit in the bond of peace." Then "men shall say of succeeding plantacions: the lord make it like that of New England: for wee must Consider that wee shall be as a Citty upon a Hill, the eies of all people are uppon us." But if the colonists selfishly embraced "carnall intencions, seeking greate things for our selves and our posterity," the Lord would "breake out in wrathe against us."

If fear of God's wrath was not enough, the Puritans had in the covenant a means of avoiding the social fragmentation so deadly to many an early settlement. Take, for example, the experience of the Pilgrims who settled Plymouth. They embarked for America as part of a commercial venture to found a particular plantation in Virginia. Many of the 102 passengers on the *Mayflower,* which carried them across the Atlantic, were not Puritans but persons from London or Southampton, England, who had been hired by the merchant sponsors of the expedition. When it became clear that the ship would land outside the Virginia patent, some declared that no one had authority over them now and threatened to go off by themselves. Then, on November 11, 1620, a group of 41 people signed a compact, or covenant. It said,

> We whose names are underwritten, do . . . solemnly and mutually in the Presence of God and one another, covenant and combine ourselves together into a civil body politic for our better ordering and preservation, . . . and by virtue hereof do enact, constitute, and frame, such just and equal Laws, Ordinances, Acts, Constitutions, and Offices, from Time to time, as should be thought most meet and convenient for the general good of the Colony; unto which we promise all due Submission and Obedience.

The Mayflower Compact was, in effect, an extension of the church covenant to civil circumstances. Since the Plymouth Colony never succeeded in obtaining a charter from the Crown, the compact provided a basis for its government. The "saints" from Leiden made up a majority of the signers and so were able to elect the colony's first governor, John Carver, as well as his successor, William Bradford, a gentle man but a firm leader and a scholar (Bradford's history *Of Plymouth*

*Plantation* remains a classic of American literature) whose leadership ended only with his death in 1657.

Elsewhere in New England, the Puritan covenant served the same function of providing a means of maintaining order. The founders of a Massachusetts town sometimes bound themselves together in both a church covenant and a separate town covenant designed to prevent discord. For example, those who signed the town covenant of Dedham, Massachusetts, in 1636 agreed "to profess and practice one truth according to that most perfect rule, the foundation whereof is everlasting love," and to "keep off from us all such as are contrary minded." Any differences that arose would be referred for settlement to "some one, two, or three others of our said society to be fully accorded and determined without any further delay." All who took up land in the town agreed to obey all "orders and constitutions" of the town, and anyone who arrived later would be asked to sign the covenant on behalf of himself "and his successors . . . for ever."

The emergence of separate towns in New England seemed to some a violation of the settlers' obligation to be "knitt together" as in one body. The first settlers probably expected to live together in a place they planned to call Boston, but sickness and the threat of an attack by the French sent the first arrivals scattering into what became seven towns on or near the Massachusetts Bay. The settlement on the Shawmut peninsula, a hilly piece of land that jutted into the bay, became Boston—the colony's capital—in part because it was readily accessible by water for colonists who lived elsewhere (indeed, the Indian word "Shawmut" meant "where there is a going by boat"). But neither Boston nor the nearby towns could absorb the wave after wave of new refugees who arrived during the 1630s. The number of towns in Massachusetts began to multiply, and the population spread out in a way the original leaders had not anticipated.

Puritans quickly formed tight communities within their towns. The covenants they formed were partly responsible; so were land-distribution policies. Often the male heads of a town's first households received town lots, where they built their houses, and also woodlots, planting lots, pastures, and meadowland more distant from the town center. After a time, families became more dispersed as their need for land, particularly to pasture their livestock, pulled them from the center. Some towns, in fact, scattered farms over the landscape from the first, although their people gathered regularly to worship or consult on public affairs. New Englanders didn't have to arrange themselves along rivers and streams, as the Virginians did to facilitate shipping tobacco to market, and their religious beliefs counteracted the tendency toward isolation. After all, Puritans were supposed to watch over and support each other in the struggle to live according to God's word. New Englanders obviously marched to a different tune than settlers in the Chesapeake.

## POPULATION GROWTH

Seldom did Puritans journey to New England alone. Mature men came with wives, children, and sometimes other relatives. Immigrants therefore came from all age groups: only people over age sixty were less numerous than in England. Family migration also meant that from the start New England had far more women than the Chesapeake. One study of emigrants to New England found that women and girls made up about half the total. Even if the overall ratio was three men to two women, it moved toward parity in the next generation, which was native-born. People could, moreover, marry earlier in life since there were far fewer indentured servants in New England than in the Chesapeake. New England's rural economy depended primarily on a system of family labor, by which children worked for and with their parents or, sometimes, for neighbors to offset debts.

The consequences were dramatic. New Englanders followed the biblical injunction to increase and multiply: married couples brought six to eight children into the world, and the population grew by leaps and bounds. The Great Migration to New England stopped abruptly in 1642 as Puritans chose to remain in England and join the fight against the Crown. Some New Englanders even returned home to help the Puritan forces. Nonetheless, the population kept growing. In the next half century, although New England saw very little additional immigration, its population seems to have risen by 45 percent *each decade,* reaching 87,000 in 1690. The contrast with the Chesapeake is striking. In 1700, Massachusetts alone had 56,000 people, mostly third-generation Americans, and Virginia had about 42,000, many of whom were still immigrants.

New England was a healthy place, and that contributed to its growth rate. Between 75 and 90 percent of all children survived to age twenty-one, after which they could look forward to a long life. In one inland town, men of the first generation lived into their seventies, and their sons into their sixties, which was amazing in the seventeenth century. Despite the perils of childbirth, their wives often lived almost as long—so there were far fewer second or third marriages than in the Chesapeake. Chil-

dren were more likely to know their grandparents in New England than anywhere else in the world. Did that add to the children's sense of security? Did it give them a greater sense of tradition than their counterparts in the Chesapeake? It probably meant they were less independent since their parents were around to watch over them. Some parents seem to have delayed giving their sons legal title to family land until late in life and in other ways contrived to keep their children near them. Perhaps they worried about who would care for them in old age.

## EDUCATION

Since the Puritans were required to read the Bible, they placed a high premium on literacy. There, as in other areas, responsibility rested first and foremost with the family, the primary social institution, which they saw as a "little commonwealth." In 1642, the Massachusetts General Court ordered town selectmen "to take account . . . of all parents and masters, and of their children, especially of their ability to read and understand the principles of religion and the capital laws of this country." And in 1647, Massachusetts, anxious to outfox "that old deluder, Satan," who tried hard "to keep men from the knowledge of the Scriptures," required all towns of fifty households to appoint a schoolmaster to teach children to read and write. When they grew to a hundred households, the towns had to organize grammar schools whose masters prepared able boys to attend college.

By then, Massachusetts Bay had a college, the British colonies' first. Although founded in 1636, Harvard College began to function well only in the 1640s, when its president, Henry Dunster, established a four-year program that was taught entirely by Dunster until a few capable graduates came to his aid. He modeled the curriculum on that of Emanuel College of Cambridge University in England, from which he and several other Puritans had graduated. Students studied the natural sciences as well as rhetoric, logic, philosophy, Latin, and Greek.

Puritans established Harvard because they wanted educated clergymen, but only about half the men it graduated in its first half century went into the ministry. As a result, the ripple effects of the college, and indeed of the colony's general willingness to invest resources in developing human capacities, reached far beyond the church. The migrants came from a sophisticated culture; in America, they continued to read not just the Bible but works by men such as the English Puritan poet John Milton or the beloved *Pilgrim's Progress* by John Bunyan. And they themselves kept journals to trace the workings of God in their lives.

During the late 1630s, the first press in North America began operating in Cambridge, Massachusetts. Its first publications were modest—copies of an oath for freemen (voters in colony-wide elections), an almanac, a book of psalms. Later New Englanders eagerly bought locally published sermons as well as autobiographies and biographies, including "captivity narratives" that described the experiences of colonists captured by Indians such as *A Narrative of the Captivity, Sufferings, and Removes of Mrs. Mary Rowlandson* (1682). The great majority of titles published in the British colonies came from New England, which continued thereafter to exert an influence on American thought and letters out of proportion to the number of people who first settled that area. But many of New Englanders' most memorable writings, such as the Reverend Edward Johnson's *The Wonder-Working Providence of Sion's Saviour in New England* (1654) or the Reverend Cotton Mather's gargantuan history of New England, *Magnalia Christi Americana* (1702), were published in England. So was the moving poetry of Anne Bradstreet, a Puritan woman who arrived with Winthrop on the *Arabella*: it first appeared in London as *The Tenth Muse Lately Sprung Up in America* (1650). Similarly, the early "histories" of Captain John Smith and Robert Beverly's *The History and Present State of Virginia* (1705) were printed in England. Colonists remained Englishmen, and the audience they most wanted to inform and impress was "at home."

In terms of its commitment to education and the printed word, however, the seventeenth-century Chesapeake was different from New England. "I thank God, there are no free schools nor printing" in Virginia, wrote that colony's royal governor, William Berkeley, in 1671; "and I hope we shall not have these hundred years; for learning has brought disobedience, and heresy, and sects into the world, and printing has divulged them, and libels against the best government. God keep us from both!"

## WORK, WORK, WORK

New Englanders knew how to work. Soon after Governor Winthrop landed in Massachusetts in 1630, according to one account, he perceived "what misery was like[ly] to ensue through idleness," and so "fell to work with his own hands and thereby so encouraged the rest . . . that there was not an idle person to be found in the whole plantation." Within a decade, the settlers prepared 12,000 acres for planting crops.

An English cartoon of 1653 that shows a Puritan, on the left, telling Father Christmas to "keep out." The cartoon ridiculed the Puritans' hostility toward Christmas as a "popish" holiday.

The Puritans celebrated industriousness as a godly virtue and understood work as a religious obligation. God, they believed, gave everyone a "calling" in life, and all callings—whether to the ministry or the farm, the shop or the countinghouse—were honorable in His eyes. Although He expected His people to work hard at their callings, they were not to work for profit alone. What wealth they collected was held "in trust" from God, who expected them to use it, as Governor Winthrop explained in his speech on the *Arbella*, "for the glory of his Creator and the good of the Creature, Man."

If some people lost their way and became greedy, both the church and the state were there to set them right. In the 1630s, when the rapid increase in population caused runaway inflation, Massachusetts tried to force merchants to ask no more for an item than a "just price," which was the price people would normally pay for it, and to prevent money lenders from charging "usurious," or exorbitant, rates. Before long, however, the government essentially abandoned its effort to regulate the market. Puritans nonetheless continued to stress people's Christian obligation to help neighbors in need, not profit from their distress. As Winthrop said, a righteous man had a duty to give to a needy neighbor "according to his necessity," even if the neighbor's capacity to repay his benefactor was in doubt. Persons who honored their obligations in that way and still prospered could interpret their wealth as a sign of God's blessing—which was itself a powerful reason to work hard.

Puritans had another stimulus to work: they did not recognize a large number of "popish" holidays like Christmas that, in England, were occasions for closing up shop. Once sabbaths and holy days were deducted from the total, England was left with about 220 workdays per year, while New England had over 300.

### DISSENSION

Did the Puritans' way of life make New England a peaceful haven? Maybe at first, and in some places for a generation or more. But soon the region was wracked by controversy over what the colonists cared about most: religion.

Massachusetts was not designed to accommodate persons of different religious views. Puritans tolerated only adherents of their own beliefs. Others had, as one writer put it, complete freedom to go somewhere else. After 1631, the colony declared that only church members could be freemen. Clergymen could not participate in the government (the settlers had had enough of that with Archbishop Laud), but the state supported and sustained the church, which in theory performed a civic function by teaching morals. But how wide a range of views were acceptably orthodox? That question emerged quickly because the flood of committed, contentious Puritans who arrived in the colony during the 1630s included both trained theologians and articulate laypersons whose views were not always compatible with each other or with those of the colony's rulers.

Take Roger Williams, a likable enough fellow who had studied at Cambridge University before coming to Massachusetts in 1631. His views proved more Separatist than those of the colony: he refused an invitation to serve the Boston church as its minister unless it repudiated all ties with the Church of England. When the Boston church held firm, he went off to Plymouth—but even Plymouth's Separatism wasn't up to Williams's standards. Soon he began raising one "dangerous" argument after another. Williams didn't like the way Massachusetts ministers met to consult each other, which looked to him like the beginning of a disgusting church hierarchy; he questioned the legitimacy of the colony's charter because, he said, the king had no right to give away lands that belonged to the Indians; and he wanted the state to have nothing whatsoever to do with religion. He argued that officials should not administer oaths to "unregenerate," or unsaved, people, and

that regenerate people should not pray with the unregenerate even if they were family members. Williams's extreme form of Puritanism threatened the colony's civil and social structure. After his fellow ministers failed to persuade him that his views were in error, the General Court expelled him from Massachusetts. Rather than return to Archbishop Laud's England, Williams fled south in early 1636 to what became Rhode Island, a new colony that provided a home for those whose views were too far out for the Bay Colony.

The controversy around Anne Hutchinson was even more divisive. Hutchinson and her family followed her minister in England, the Reverend John Cotton, to Massachusetts. Cotton, who became minister at the Boston church, emphasized that grace alone, not good behavior, identified God's saints, and he instituted a change in the requirements for church membership. Living a moral life was enough to qualify for membership in English Puritan churches, but in Boston—and then elsewhere in the colony—prospective church members had to explain how and when they first experienced God's grace. That reduced the number of people who became church members. Hutchinson then took Cotton's teachings to even greater extremes.

Sometime in 1635, she began holding meetings of women in her home, where she commented on recent sermons. Soon men began attending. Before long, Hutchinson criticized local ministers for teaching that by living a good life people could prepare themselves for God's grace. People could do nothing to affect God, she insisted; He was omnipotent and inscrutable to humans, bestowed His grace freely, and could save even the most wicked human devil if He so chose. Opponents characterized Hutchinson and her followers as Antinomians—literally, people "against law"—because their teachings undermined all attempts to live according to God's laws. Hutchinson also attacked the colony's ministers, all of whom except Cotton and her brother-in-law, John Wheelwright, were "without grace" in her opinion and so unqualified to preach God's word. She and her followers soon started heckling the "unregenerate" ministers or marching from meetinghouses when they began to speak. The controversy ripped apart a community that was supposed to be "knitt together"—but so what? Christ came, Wheelwright proclaimed, to send fire upon the earth. Others disagreed. That a woman led the Antinomians only made things worse. Women were supposed to be meek and submissive; public controversies and intellectual argument were outside their proper sphere.

After a public fast day failed to restore peace, leading ministers attempted but failed to convince the Hutchinsonians of their errors. Finally, the General Court tried and banished the sectaries—first the men, including Wheelwright, whom it convicted of "contempt and sedition" for kindling bitterness in the colony. Then the court tried Hutchinson, who did a fine job of parrying questions put to her by Governor Winthrop until, finally, she announced that God revealed Himself to her directly. That was heretical: orthodox Puritans believed that God revealed Himself only through the Bible. As a result, the General Court banished Hutchinson from the colony, and even the Boston congregation, which was once full of her supporters, excommunicated her. She went, of course, to Rhode Island—although Wheelwright and about twenty families of his own followers moved instead to New Hampshire, where they founded the town of Exeter. Before long, Winthrop recorded, the divisions within Boston declined, "all breaches were made up, and the church was saved from ruin."

### NEW COLONIES

Except for Plymouth, the various colonies of New England were settled primarily by migrants from Massachusetts. In 1636, a group from Watertown, Dorchester, and Newtown (later Cambridge) moved to the Connecticut Valley, where they founded the towns of Wethersfield, Windsor, and Hartford. The settlers of Connecticut sought more and better lands than were available near the Massachusetts Bay, but theological considerations probably also prompted their move. Their leader, the Reverend Thomas Hooker, favored less demanding standards for church membership than John Cotton, whose views dominated Massachusetts Bay churches. Rhode Island, which was settled by religious refugees from Massachusetts, was still less restrictive; there, tolerance extended to almost any form of religion. But the people of New Haven, a separate colony founded by a group of London Puritans who left Boston in March 1638, were religious conservatives. New Haven's churches closely regulated the lives of their members and were quick to censure or even excommunicate those who did not conform. In time, the New Haven Colony included the towns of Milford, Guilford, and later Stamford and Greenwich, as well as several on Long Island (in today's New York). Similarly, Plymouth became the center of settlements that stretched from Cape Cod west to the Narragansett Bay.

In all of these colonies, the town became the basic unit of government. The Massachusetts General Court delegated one task after another to the towns, which became responsible for defense, education, tax collection, and a host of other public activities. After 1634, delegates to the Massachusetts general assembly were elected by town meetings. The Fundamental Orders of Connecticut (1639), the basic instrument of government in Connecticut, brought the separate towns of Hartford, Windsor, and Wethersfield together in a federation. Similarly, the colony of "Rhode Island and Providence Plantations," which received a charter from Parliament in 1644, confederated the towns of Providence, Portsmouth, Newport, and Warwick. The colony's assembly, which met four times a year, moved from town to town, with no home base.

The importance of town government in New England was much like that of counties in the Chesapeake. Indeed, the vitality of local government became a distinction of the English colonies—and provided a grounding in self-government lacking in many other colonial empires.

### THE COST OF EXPANSION

Puritans' first encounters with Indians near their settlements were relatively peaceful because there were very few native people there. An epidemic between 1616 and 1619 had left much of the area near Plymouth and the Massachusetts Bay unpopulated. To the colonies' south, however, the Pequots (who lived in what would become eastern Connecticut) and the Narragansetts (whose territory ringed the Narragansett Bay in what became Rhode Island) had avoided the epidemic's ravages. Those two tribes were rivals for the fur trade down the Connecticut River, which the Pequots dominated. The establishment of trading posts on the river by the Plymouth colonists and the Dutch threatened the Pequots' hegemony and led to violent clashes. At first, those incidents were between traders and Indians, but they spread. After Indians attacked Wethersfield, Connecticut, the colonies of Massachusetts Bay and Connecticut undertook "an offensive warr ag't the Pequoitt."

The decisive action took place at an Indian fort in what is now West Mystic, Connecticut, in the early morning of May 26, 1637. With their Narragansett and Mohegan allies encircling the fort, the English forced their way inside, where they discovered a large number of wigwams—which they decided to burn, using gunpowder to build a fire that "blazed most terribly." Those who tried to flee the conflagration were cut down by Indians or English soldiers outside. In about half an hour, some 400 Pequots died, most of them old men, women,

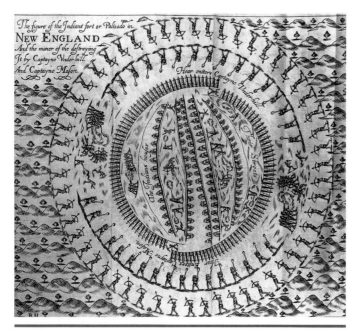

A seventeenth-century engraving depicting the battle at what is now West Mystic, Connecticut, on May 26, 1637. At the center is the Pequot village, with its burning houses inside a palisade fence with two openings where, the engraving indicates, the colonists entered. Settlers are shown firing guns at Indians armed with bows and arrows. Outside the palisade fence are more colonial soldiers and, behind them, their Mohegan and Narragansett allies. This image first appeared in Capt. John Underhill's *Newes from America . . .* (London, 1638).

and children. In the following weeks, the English and their allies chased the terrified Pequots into the woods, slaughtering many and selling others into slavery. Within two months, about 700 Pequots had died or been captured, although the English lost fewer than 100. In 1638, the Treaty of Hartford put an end to the Pequots as a people, taking away their name as well as their lands.

The violence at West Mystic shocked even the Narragansetts, whose mode of warfare, like that of most other Indians, was more ceremonial than deadly. Once the massacre ended, an English officer reported, the Narragansetts cried, "*Mach it, mach it; that is, it is naught, it is naught, because it is too furious, and slaies too many men.*" The English had learned their deadly way of war in Ireland and earlier wars in the Netherlands. But Indians, too, could learn to burn homes and massacre enemies' families.

The English took pride in their weaponry. In an earlier maneuver on nearby Block Island, one Englishman rejoiced that only a single volley showed the Indians that "our bullets . . . out-reach their arrows." But volleys were about all the English could shoot. They used old-fashioned matchlock muskets that were fine for formal battles in good weather on open fields, where, as in Europe, each side began by shooting volleys at the other side. Those muskets couldn't be aimed; in fact, they had no sights. They were so heavy that a brace was necessary to support the barrel, and unless the match—a rope of combustible material—could be kept lit, a gunman had no way of detonating his gunpowder and making the gun fire. Such weapons were unsuited for forest warfare or for so wet a climate as New England's. Nor were they hunting weapons—but then, New England's settlers were no more hunters than those who founded Virginia. Hunting in England was a sport for the upper class. Sometimes the colonists might shoot at a thick flock of birds and hit something, anything, but that was about it. Most of the meat the colonists ate came from farm animals. Occasionally they feasted on deer or waterfowl, but they usually bought those foods from Indians, who knew how to hunt.

Indians were from the first interested in acquiring guns, but not the matchlock muskets that most colonists owned. The Indians insisted on the more modern and expensive flintlock muskets, which dispensed with the match and used flint to create a spark that detonated gunpowder more reliably. Flintlock muskets were also lighter, and the Indians preferred relatively short barrels because they were more convenient for hunting in the woods. Accustomed to hitting targets with bows and arrows, they quickly became expert marksmen. They probably also shot several small balls ("swan shot") rather than the customary European musket balls, which increased the hunters' chances of hitting their prey.

One colony after another tried to prevent the sale of guns to Indians, but there was always some trader somewhere, often from New Netherland, who was willing to give the Indians what they wanted in return for the furs that they alone could supply. Indians, moreover, spent enough time working in the settlements that they soon learned to repair their weapons and even cast bullets. They proved, in fact, to be a technologically adaptable people who, for example, melted down swords (which are pretty useless in a forest) and kettles to make metal arrowheads, fitting European materials to their own needs and culture.

A soldier with an old matchlock musket, which required the use of a brace before firing. Although in Europe the weapon was commonly used on the battlefield, it was ill-suited to frontier uses, such as hunting.

In short, the Indians learned from the Europeans a more devastating form of warfare than they had known and acquired firearms that allowed them to practice war with a vengeance. Before long, the English settlers had reason to regret being such good teachers. Their only recourse was to become students themselves: to obtain better guns, learn to aim them, and pick up Indian ways of war—ambushes and surprise attacks, which settlers had first condemned as an unmanly "skulking way of war" compared with the formal battlefield encounters they considered more civilized. The results would be deadly.

## A PLACE LIKE ENGLAND?

New England was in many ways true to its name: the region meant to become a new and better version of the mother country, not its replication. Certainly New England's narrow religious character distinguished it even from the England of the 1650s, which was also ruled by Puritans. There the need for civil peace in a nation filled with persons of different religious convictions prompted Oliver Cromwell and the English Puritans to adopt a system of religious toleration, which most New Englanders considered a sinful concession to error. Righteous and proud of their church establishment and laws requiring religious uniformity, Massachusetts Bay and the colonies closest to it pulled away from England; only Roger Williams was at home with Oliver Cromwell. New England's economy, however, had much more in common with the mother country than with that of the tobacco colonies. It developed a genuine mixed economy, one that was primarily agricultural but included a commercial sector and even some manufacturing.

The middle-class immigrants to Massachusetts did not expect to reduce their standard of living substantially by coming to America. That standard required textiles, metal tools and utensils, and other items that were generally imported from England. During the 1630s, paying for these imported items was no problem. The masses of arriving immigrants brought with them money earned by selling their homes and businesses in England. On arrival, they bought what they needed to get settled—homes or the materials to build them, food, and livestock. Merchants then used the money they received to pay for imports. But when the flood of arrivals stopped, the New England economy went into crisis: the price of cattle, for example, fell by as much as 75 to 80 percent in a year. How to pay for imports became a real problem.

What could New England trade for the goods it needed? The region's climate was so much like England's that it could produce few products that England lacked. The greater part of New England's people were farmers who set out to grow the grains they knew in England—particularly wheat, barley, and also rye for making beer—using traditional farming techniques and tools. Unlike Plymouth in its opening years, the Massachusetts Bay Colony had plows—thirty-seven of them by 1637, each of which served many farms—and also oxen to pull the plows. But familiar grains did not always do well in American soil. Indian corn did much better and soon became a popular crop. However, it was even less likely to find a market in Europe than grains that the English were growing in sufficient quantities for themselves. Similarly, the colony's expanding stock of cattle, pigs, and poultry allowed it to feed its people but did not provide an easy way to pay for manufactured imports. And although New Englanders did collect beaver pelts from the Connecticut Valley and northeastern New England for shipment abroad, the supply of pelts from those areas soon dried up, and the Dutch controlled trade with Indians west of the Hudson.

One way to deal with the problem was to reduce imports, which the Massachusetts General Court tried to do by encouraging domestic cloth production. But, except in remote areas where there was no alternative to homespun, New Englanders continued to use imported cloth. Their need for iron, however, led to one of the most technologically advanced industrial projects in seventeenth-century America: the Hammersmith Iron Works on the Saugus River in Lynn, Massachusetts.

John Winthrop Jr., the gregarious, enterprising son of Massachusetts's grave first governor, put together the set of English investors who funded the enterprise. He then surveyed possible locations and finally settled on the Saugus site, which had a good supply of bog iron. After the General Court agreed to give the enterprise free land, tax exemption, freedom from militia duty for employees, and a twenty-one-year monopoly on iron making, the organizers constructed an ironworks that was large and technologically advanced even by English standards.

The Hammersmith Iron Works included an enormous blast furnace, some twenty-five feet tall, whose fire was fed by a huge leather bellows opened with power from a waterwheel and closed by counterweights. Iron ore was melted in the furnace with charcoal and gabbro rock, a fluxing agent (a material that combined chemically with waste products to separate them from iron) readily available in the area. Then skilled workmen drained off the waste (or slag) and ran the molten iron into a sand mold that resembled a sow nursing piglets. The resulting product, called "pig iron," could be cast in clay forms to make pots and similar iron products. But it still contained too many impurities to withstand stress. So the Hammersmith Works also maintained a three-hearth forge. There skilled ironworkers reheated the pig iron, stirring it to burn off excess carbon, let it solidify, and then, to remove more impurities, worked the red-hot iron with an enormous hammer powered by one of the forge's four waterwheels. The result was wrought iron, which local blacksmiths formed into horseshoes or tools such as axes, hoes, spades, and mattocks to peel back sod and open fields for planting. Hammersmith even had a water-powered rolling and slitting mill, where iron was formed into long sheets, then cut into strips that could easily be made into nails.

Hammersmith generated a great amount of iron—but no profits. The investors cried mismanagement and dismissed one director after another. The real problem, however, was the high cost of wages and supplies. By the 1650s, the investors refused to throw more good resources after bad, creditors panicked, and the company collapsed amid a flurry of lawsuits. Although a group of local merchants tried to start it up again, high costs finally forced Hammersmith to close in 1676. A number of less ambitious furnaces, or "bloomeries," continued, however, at several other sites. At a bloomery, an ironmaster melted a small quantity of iron over a charcoal fire on a stone hearth, fanning the flames with bellows to increase the temperature and so to separate out most of the slag. He then hammered the iron as it cooled to break up remaining lumps of waste products. The resulting bar iron could be heated and hammered into various shapes, which answered most colonial needs. Some of these bloomeries lasted into the nineteenth century.

A local supply of iron was invaluable, but it remained relatively expensive and left unanswered the big question of how

A modern reconstruction of the seventeenth-century Hammersmith Iron Works in Massachusetts, showing an "undershot" waterwheel, with which the water hit the wheel at its bottom.

New England would pay for its imports. Selling fish was one possibility. When troubles in Britain kept English fishermen from American waters in the 1640s, the colonists moved right in. At first, they supplied fish to local consumers; then New England fish merchants paired up with London merchants in an arrangement that brought American fish—often dried cod—to Spain or the Wine Islands (the Azores, Madeira, the Canaries) for credits that paid for shipments of manufactured goods from Britain.

After a while, New Englanders were able to make voyages to southern Europe on their own. And they discovered a new market in the Caribbean islands, where, after growing tobacco and then briefly cotton with limited success, planters began in the 1640s, with the encouragement and instruction of Dutch traders, to produce sugar instead. On Barbados, planters were so busy making sugar, a correspondent wrote Governor John Winthrop in 1647, that they would "rather buy foode at very deare rates than produce it by labour, so infinite is the profitt of sugar workes after once accomplished." In the Caribbean, New Englanders could sell "refuse" fish—dried cod that was broken, oversalted, or damaged and so could not be sold in southern Europe—to feed the slaves that sugar planters bought in place of indentured servants. Caribbean planters also needed horses and livestock, grain and timber. And they wanted more slaves. One New England voyage of 1644 brought fish to the Canary Islands and picked up slaves, which the crew then sold in Barbados. That opened an entirely new line of trade. Soon New England became a major source of supplies for the West Indies, where again it received credits from British merchant houses with which to pay for imports.

## MILLS AND THE BUILDING OF NEW ENGLAND

A key device in New Englanders' changing ways of life was the mill, an ancient machine that harnessed some source of power to turn a wheel, which could be used to perform tasks otherwise done by human labor. In the West Indies, treadmills often ground sugarcane, a step in the refinement of sugar. There the power often came from horses that trod in endless circles—which helps explain why New England shipped so many horses to the Caribbean. Barbados also built windmills, as did New Amsterdam (which used them to grind grain) and some Massachusetts towns. Watermills were, however, the most advanced form of mechanical power in the early seventeenth century, and New Englanders built them almost everywhere they could. Although disgruntled English workers were known to burn down mills that replaced human labor, in America the scarcity of workers made labor-saving devices like watermills popular. New England could also count on a wealth of rivers, streams, and waterfalls to turn the wheels. And the region's long coastline allowed the construction of tide mills, which captured water in a special pond or cove at high tide, then slowly released it through a sluice, where it nicely turned a wheel while making its way back into the sea.

Sometimes the mechanisms were simple. Horizontal mills, for example, consisted of a wheel, often of wood, attached to a horizontal millstone by means of a central rod. The wheel was so positioned that a stream of water turned it, rotating the millstone above. Millers ground grain between that top stone and another just beneath it. These devices were cheap and popular: people would walk miles to have their grain

This photograph shows the heavy timber framing and massive central chimney of a house built in New Ipswich, Massachusetts, in 1698. The house was originally covered with clapboards. It is now at the National Museum of American History in Washington, D.C.

ground in a gristmill rather than eat the coarse bread produced by grinding grain in a mortar or a hand-worked set of grinding stones.

Other New England mills, like those at Hammersmith, were more elaborate. They had great wheels immersed perpendicular to moving water, which ran below them (undershot wheels), dropped down from above (overshot), or hit them at some point midway ("pitchback," or "breastshot"). Then by a series of cranks and gears, usually fashioned of wood, the power could be used to perform a large number of tasks such as opening bellows, working trip-hammers—or sawing wood.

Without a sawmill, timber had to be either split into rough boards, as the Virginians did, or sawed into planks by hand, often by pit sawing, where one man worked down in a hole or pit and another man worked above, pulling or pushing a long saw blade up and down through a log held in a frame. That was hard work and especially nasty for the guy on the bottom. How much better to have waterpower work the blade or blades up and down (circular saws remained two centuries away) and, sometimes, move a log against the blade. By the end of the seventeenth century, virtually every Massachusetts township had at least one sawmill, which produced boards mainly for local consumption. Sawmills also made possible large-scale commercial production for export—which was the primary purpose of a string of sawmills first built in the 1630s along the Piscataqua River in New Hampshire. In the 1640s, Boston merchants who recognized the mills' commercial possibilities began to take them over, and then built more there and in Maine (which remained part of Massachusetts). The first patent issued in Massachusetts—and perhaps anywhere in the mainland colonies—went in 1646 to an ironmaster, Joseph Jencks, "for the making of Engines for mills to goe with water for the more speedy dispatch of worke . . . with a new Invented Saw-Mill, that things may be afforded cheaper than formerly." By contrast, as late as 1649, Virginia, with its rich supplies of timber and iron, had no sawmills whatsoever. Later, however, it would possess abundant grist and sawmills, though mainly to supply local demand.

The demand for boards and other timber products was almost unremitting in a country being built anew. And nothing made of wood lasted forever: Boston, for example, suffered devastating fires no less than nine times in its first 130 years, so it had to be rebuilt again and again. A good part of the homes and plantation structures in the British West Indies were made of wood that generally came, like Boston's, from northern New England. The ready availability of sawn boards also opened other opportunities. They could be used, for example, to build furniture—or at least to provide the crude backs and drawer bottoms for pieces otherwise made of hand-processed wood.

More important, the availability of relatively cheap sawn boards made the work of constructing houses easier. House frames in New England were usually made of oak logs shaped into a square with a broadaxe. If the shaped logs were visible, their sides were evened out with an adze, a hoe-like tool whose blade was curved and sharp, but which nonetheless left the telltale clefts still observable today on the exposed beams of historic houses. Wooden pegs (tenons) inserted through holes (mortises) held together the carefully shaped parts of "mortise and tenon" joints in the frame, but colonists tried to keep the need for such "joinery" to a minimum. It helped a lot when colonists could enclose their houses by nailing mill-sawn pine boards to vertical posts or fastening them on beams to make floors. Roofs, which were at first covered with bundles of rush or straw, were later sheathed with boards and then covered with shingles—which colonists split from logs and then shaped by hand with a drawknife, a two-handled tool for shaving wood.

Sawn boards also allowed the development of shipbuilding. As New England's commerce grew, merchants needed ships, and it made sense to build them in America. England lacked the wood; indeed, she became a major purchaser of ships made in shipyards at Salem, Boston, and other points along the New England coast. Ships also required iron for bolts, braces, and anchors, and those needs provided more incentive to develop a domestic iron industry. To build a ship was a complex task that, in a major shipyard, involved many skilled workers: shipwrights to oversee the work, ship smiths to do ironwork, sawyers to produce irregular structural pieces of wood that could not be milled, carpenters, joiners, and caulkers. And some products, particularly cordage and sailcloth, had to be imported.

Shipyards, like mercantile voyages, sawmills, forges, and wharves and docks, were usually financed by sets of investors who pooled their capital and divided the profits—another example of New England's penchant for group efforts. Creative finance and mercantile initiative contributed to New England's early economic growth, but the most important factor was the capacity of one activity to inspire other "linkages"—fishing and trade, for example, brought a need for ships, which increased the demand for sawn boards and iron fittings, and so for building more sawmills and forges. The high cost of labor as well as the widespread demand for iron tools and utensils and for high-quality milled grain encouraged the development of water-driven technology. And literacy equipped people to recognize opportunities and figure out how to implement them. Enterprises sometimes failed, mainly because of high labor costs, but not for lack of effort. New Englanders' godly industriousness saw to that.

## SUCCESS OR FAILURE?

By 1660, New England was a bustling, prosperous place. Most of its people were farmers who worked their own land or that of their fathers, but even inland towns produced some live-stock and food for export. Boston had become the preeminent colonial port, leaving behind New Haven and other would-be rivals along the Atlantic coast. It was a very different town from the Boston of Anne Hutchinson, and its changes paralleled those throughout the region. Young John Winthrop Jr. seemed to typify his generation. Less obsessed with theology than science, especially chemistry and metallurgy, Winthrop became the first American member of the Royal Society, England's premier scientific organization. He was also an entrepreneur who moved easily between England and America and was welcome in both crazy Rhode Island and rigid New Haven. The Puritans' work ethic, group orientation, and attention to the education of the young had helped produce a people far more prosperous than anyone familiar with the rocky, thin soil of cold New England would have predicted, and more worldly than the founders had hoped.

Had New England lost its way, giving in to those "carnall intencions" of which Winthrop's father had warned on the *Arbella* thirty years earlier? Surely it had to make compromises along the way. The fishermen who worked the waters off the Massachusetts and Maine coasts were seldom Puritans: most had arrived after 1640, when the Great Migration was over, and were often west-country fishermen who wandered down from Newfoundland when the fishing season ended. Like the first Virginians, they were young, single, and poor, and they had a penchant for drinking and brawling. The imported ironworkers were much the same. These were not the kind of folk John Winthrop Sr. had expected to people his "City upon a Hill."

Had the colony given up too much of its original vision in pursuing economic success? Or did its prosperity witness God's pleasure in His New World chosen people? Whatever the answer, there could be no doubt that by 1660 the New England and Chesapeake colonies were firmly planted on a land where no stable European settlements had existed only sixty years earlier. In only a few decades, settlers had established cultural, economic, and political patterns whose influence would last for centuries.

Before long, the prosperity of these colonies attracted the attention of England's newly restored Crown. Then their independence would pass, and they would be become, happy or not, part of an empire.

## *Suggested Reading*

Virginia DeJohn Anderson, *New England's Generation: The Great Migration and the Formation of Society and Culture in the Seventeenth Century* (1991)

James Axtell, *Natives and Newcomers: The Cultural Origins of North America* (2001)

Carol E. Hoffecker et al., eds., *New Sweden in America* (1995)

Stephen Innes, *Creating the Commonwealth: The Economic Culture of Puritan New England* (1995)

Peter C. Mancall, *Envisioning America: English Plans for the Colonization of North America, 1580–1640* (1995)

Edmund S. Morgan, *American Slavery, American Freedom: The Ordeal of Colonial Virginia* (1975)

David Quinn, *The Elizabethans and the Irish* (1966)

Oliver A. Rink, *Holland on the Hudson: An Economic and Social History of Dutch New York* (1986)

Thad W. Tate and David Ammerman, eds., *The Chesapeake in the Seventeenth Century: Essays on Anglo-American Society* (1979)

Daniel Vickers, *Farmers & Fishermen: Two Centuries of Work in Essex County, Massachusetts, 1630–1850* (1994)

# Chapter Review

## Summary QUESTIONS

- What prompted nations other than Spain and Portugal to explore and seek territory in America?

- How did the English experience in Ireland affect the English colonization of America?

- Why did several early European efforts to found colonies in North America fail?

- What distinguished New Netherland from the English colonies in Virginia and Massachusetts?

- How did the religious differences affect the demographic differences between Virginia and Massachusetts?

## Chronology

| | |
|---|---|
| 1517 | Martin Luther's 95 theses usher in the Protestant Reformation. |
| 1585–87 | Sir Walter Raleigh sends settlers to Roanoke Island. |
| 1606–7 | The Virginia colony is founded at Jamestown. |
| 1608 | Samuel de Champlain founds Quebec. |
| 1620 | Pilgrims found colony at Plymouth. |
| 1624 | The Dutch found New Netherland. |
| 1629–30 | Puritan settlers found the Massachusetts Bay Colony. |
| 1632 | Charles I grants proprietary colony of Maryland to George Calvert, Lord Baltimore. |
| 1636 | Roger Williams founds Rhode Island. |
| | Harvard College is established. |
| 1638 | New Sweden is founded. |
| 1655 | New Netherland takes over New Sweden. |

## Key Terms

Plantation (p. 41)

New France (p. 44)

The Virginia Company (p. 48)

Puritanism (p. 58)

The Pequots (p. 65)

**Access the *Inventing America* StudySpace at wwnorton.com/studyspace**

PERSONAL PLAN ■ REVIEW MATERIALS ■ RESEARCH AIDS ■ MULTIMEDIA

# EMPIRES:

## 1660-1702

*William Penn's Treaty with the Indians*, by Benjamin West (1771). This eighteenth-century painting depicts William Penn's legendary treaty of 1682 with the Delaware chief, Tamanend. The French philosopher Voltaire once said that treaty was "never sworn to and never broken," at least half of which was untrue. West's image of a peaceful, Quaker-dominated Pennsylvania nonetheless had a powerful impact.

*Focus*
QUESTIONS

■ *How did England's colonies in America become part of a British empire?*

■ *How did New France expand as part of the French empire?*

■ *How did the Iroquois respond to European imperial conflicts in this period?*

■ *Why did the Pueblos rise up against Spanish rule in 1680?*

■ *What connected the Salem witchcraft crisis with Indian wars on the New England frontier?*

Rebecca Nurse did not seem like a witch. The wife of a prosperous farmer in Salem Village, Massachusetts, a covenanted member of the church in Salem Town, a beloved mother and grandmother, she was to all appearances a model Christian. But in late March 1692, she stood accused of mysteriously torturing another villager, Ann Putnam; her daughter, also named Ann; and a young neighbor, Abigail Williams. Then another Salem Villager, Henry Kenny, testified "that since this Nurse came into his house he was seizd twise with an amazd condition."

"What do you say" to these accusers? the magistrates asked. "Oh Lord help me," the old woman cried, "& spread out her hands"—at which the accusers seemed "grievously vexed." How could she explain the sufferings of those who charged her? Rebecca agreed they were "bewitcht," but not by her. That they saw a ghostly "apparition" of her proved nothing, since "the Devil may appear in my shape." And if Rebecca Nurse said so, who could doubt that Satan was on the loose in Massachusetts, urging people to "sign his book" and join his empire in its epic struggle against the rule of God?

Satan was apparently one of several powers trying to enlarge their dominion in North America during the late 1600s. Great Britain, France, Spain, and nearby Indians engaged more tangibly in an all-out effort to extend or reestablish their hold on the continent; and the French, Spanish, and Indians often seemed like the devil incarnate to the British settlers. Those imperial struggles affected not only people involved in the Salem witchcraft crisis, but all American colonists through much of the next century.

## Great Britain

Oliver Cromwell, England's Protector and leader of the Puritan forces that had executed King Charles I, died in 1658. His son and heir, Richard Cromwell, could not control the army or the territory his father had governed. Exhausted by disorder, the English Parliament finally called the son of Charles I back from exile. The new king, Charles II, was an easygoing chap interested above all in his mistresses and the pleasant pastimes of court life. By the time of his death in 1685, he had produced no legitimate heir. As a result, the crown passed to his brother James, the Duke of York, who spent most of his short reign alienating his subjects.

King James II tried to rule without Parliament but with the help of the army, and he made no effort to conceal his Catholicism. When his Catholic wife gave birth to a son who would be raised Catholic and would become first in line to inherit the throne, his Protestant subjects had had enough. They rallied behind the king's Protestant son-in-law, William of Orange, who invaded in November 1688 and forced James II and his son into exile. In 1689, the English called to the throne William and his wife, Mary, James's Protestant daughter by an earlier marriage.

At first glance, that story seems as filled with stops and starts as the complex previous history of seventeenth-century England, with its civil wars and turns from monarchy to Commonwealth to Protectorate. During that earlier time of troubles, the British colonies in the Chesapeake and New England had become virtually independent. But not now:

Britain's hold over North America increased in a more or less continuous way between the Restoration of Charles II in 1660 and 1702, when Anne, a second Protestant daughter of James II, inherited the throne from the childless William and Mary.

## FILLING IN THE COAST

During the reigns of Charles II and James II, the British acquired lands that linked and extended their previous holdings on the eastern coast of North America. There they established what eventually became six new British mainland colonies: North and South Carolina; New Jersey and New York; Pennsylvania and Delaware.

*Carolina.* In 1663, Charles II rewarded eight of his supporters by giving them a proprietary title to all the land between Florida and the southern border of Virginia and westward "sea to sea." He also granted them considerable power over this new colony of Carolina: like the proprietors of Maryland, they received all "Rights, Jurisdictions, Privileges, Prerogatives . . . and Franchises of what kind soever . . . in as ample man-

ner as any Bishop of Durham, in our Kingdom of England" had ever exercised. Like the lands of the bishops of Durham, which lay on England's border with Scotland, Maryland and Carolina were frontier regions whose proprietors would need, it seemed, substantial authority to defend their territory against hostile neighbors.

By the 1660s, the sense that England contained a surplus of people was gone. The country had work enough for its people and was anxious to keep them at home. New colonies would have to be peopled from older ones or from other sources. Barbados was one promising source of settlers. Over the previous two decades, wealthy planters there had expanded their landholdings so they could produce more sugar, an extremely profitable commodity. Those former planters who were squeezed out would surely go to Carolina in return for generous grants of land as "headrights" for themselves and the servants and slaves they brought with them. Virginia's governor, William Berkeley, thought some Virginians would also move to Carolina since all the land in Virginia's Tidewater section was already claimed. Migrants from New England and Bermuda, both of which were well populated, might also settle there. Then, without incurring the loss of much except the empty territory they had used to lure settlers, the proprietors could make good money by charging annual "quitrents" on land.

Virginians did indeed cross their southern border and settle the more northerly regions of the Carolina grant along Albemarle Sound. And settlers from Barbados went farther south, bringing their slaves along. As a result, what later became South Carolina was the first British mainland colony that began with a labor system based on black chattel slavery. Under this system, persons of African origin or descent were bound to work not for a set number of years, like white indentured servants, but for life; their children were also born into a life of perpetual servitude, and they stood in law as the property, or chattel, of their masters. (On the development of slave labor in America, see Chapter 4.)

Plans for the colony took the form of a written document, the Fundamental Constitutions of Carolina of 1669, which provided for dividing the colony into provinces, counties, seigniories, baronies, and still-smaller colonies. Two-thirds of the land would be held by hereditary nobles with exotic titles such as "landgrave" and "cacique," the rest by manorial lords and ordinary landowners. The Fundamental Constitutions decreed that no one could "disturb, molest or persecute another for his . . . opinions in Religion or his way of Worship," which made Carolina attractive to dissenters, but allowed

Charles II, here receiving a pineapple, a symbol of hospitality, from the colony of Barbados.

state support for the established church to avoid alienating potential Anglican settlers. It also gave masters absolute control over their slaves. The document provided for a governor and a Grand Council, which would serve as both a court and a plural executive, and for a parliament, or assembly, elected by men who needed only fifty acres to qualify for the vote and would have the benefit of a secret ballot.

The Fundamental Constitutions of Carolina, in short, was a curious blend of provisions inspired by an older European feudal world, which were ill suited to a thinly settled frontier territory, and the more advanced policies adopted to attract immigrants such as religious toleration and broad political participation. The document never went entirely into effect, but it made a lasting impact on the colony both for what it did and what it neglected to do. It did not, for example, provide for local government, which failed to develop in Carolina as it had in the Chesapeake and New England.

Carolina grew slowly at first because of internal divisions and conflicts with Indians and the Spanish. The proprietors' dream of easy riches never materialized: they were forced to contribute heavily to the colony and to forgo quitrents during its first decades. For those sacrifices they received little in return.

In 1680, settlers founded the city of Charles Town (which became Charleston a century later) on land adjoining a harbor with good ocean access at the confluence of the Cooper and Ashley rivers. Carefully laid out with streets at right angles to each other, it was the first planned city of British North America. Over the next two years, the colony's population doubled, reaching 2,200 in 1682. It continued to grow with new influxes of French Huguenots, English dissenters, and Scots. After experimenting with a variety of warm-climate crops including cotton and indigo, the colonists developed a profitable trade in timber products, livestock, and later rice. Both the open-range cattle farming practiced in South Carolina and the rice culture depended heavily on the skills of African slaves. By 1708, a majority of South Carolina's 9,000–10,000 people were black.

A very different society emerged in the Albemarle province, or North Carolina, as it was called after 1691. Although there, too, livestock and timber products provided good sources of income, planters also grew substantial amounts of tobacco. Dense forests and unpassable swamps separated the Albemarle settlers from Virginia, yet they shared many characteristics with people in the Chesapeake region. Slaves, for example, represented a far smaller percentage of the 4,000–5,000 North Carolinians in 1700 than they did of the more prosperous Carolinians to their south. The two Carolinas maintained little contact with each other and had separate governments, although they were formally split only in 1729, when England's Parliament bought out the proprietors. At that time, the Crown, to the colonists' delight, assumed responsibility for governing the two colonies.

*New York and New Jersey.* A year after the Carolina grant, Charles II gave his brother James, the Duke of York, the territory between the Connecticut and Delaware rivers, including the Hudson Valley and Long Island. That stretch of land later became the colonies of New Jersey and New York. It also included a good chunk of Connecticut. In fact, the duke's grant took in lands in Maine, the islands of Nantucket and Martha's Vineyard, and the entire Dutch colony of New Netherland. Negotiations might settle conflicts of title between the Duke of York and other Englishmen, but James sent commissioners and a fleet to establish his power over the Dutch colony, which he proposed to reduce to "an entyre submission and obedience." The fleet arrived at New Amsterdam in August 1664. A few days after its arrival, Governor Peter Stuyvesant, who commanded too few soldiers and supplies to hold out against the invaders, surrendered. Before long, Dutch outposts on the Hudson and the Delaware followed suit, and New Netherland fell under the English Crown and the proprietorship of the Duke of York. The Dutch managed to reconquer the area in 1673, but they lost it for good a year later.

James's charter from the Crown did not require him to call an elected assembly, and he was not inclined to do so on his own. As he wrote to one of his governors, assemblies showed an "aptness . . . to assume to themselves many priviledges w[hi]ch prove destructive to . . . the peace of the governm[en]t." Nevertheless, his need for money and the resistance of many colonists to paying taxes imposed without their consent convinced the duke to call an assembly in 1683—but it came to an end four years later, when James became king.

Within months of first receiving his proprietary grant, James gave the area between the Hudson and Delaware rivers, which became New Jersey, to a couple of followers, Sir George Carteret and John, Lord Berkeley (brother of the Virginia governor, William Berkeley), without informing his governor in New York. Meanwhile the governor gave out land in New Jersey, some to groups of testy New England Puritans, on generous terms different in critical details from those of Carteret and Berkeley. Is it any wonder that much of New Jersey's colonial history consists of fights over land claims and what political rights they conferred?

*Pennsylvania.* By 1681, when the Crown granted William Penn title to the last of Britain's seventeenth-century North American colonies, it was already turning against private colonial jurisdictions. But Penn was a friend of the Duke of York, and his father, Admiral William Penn, held a large claim on the royal treasury at the time of his death for loans and service in the Royal Navy.

After briefly attending Oxford University, studying law, and managing his father's Irish estates, the younger Penn, to his father's dismay, joined the ranks of Quakers, a not-yet-respectable religious movement. The Quakers (a derogatory term, like "Puritan," that somehow stuck), or Friends (because they were members of the Society of Friends), believed that God's spirit was in all people equally and without exception, which made it hard to say one person was better than another by virtue of birth or any other distinction. They saw no need of priests or ministers—people could discover God simply by attending to their "Inner Light"—or of ceremonies or religious artifacts. They despised rank and outward show, dressed in plain clothes, and addressed each other as "thee" and "thou." Quakers refused to kneel or bow to anyone, they wouldn't even tip their hats to men that the world considered of high rank. They also refused to take oaths, to fight wars, or to engage in any acts of violence, all of which they thought violated God's rule of love. To many in Restoration England, the

A Quaker meeting by an unidentified British artist c. 1735–40, in which women participated equally with men.

Quakers were ridiculous fanatics—and, it should be said, some early Quakers had acted in pretty outrageous ways, disrupting church services, for example, or appearing naked in public places to show how God would strip men down to essentials. They were also considered threats to the standing order and safest locked up in jail. Penn, who was himself imprisoned four times for publicly professing his beliefs, dreamed of founding a refuge for Quakers and other persecuted religious dissenters. In return for a colonial grant to lands west of the Delaware between New York and Maryland, where he hoped to set up that refuge, Penn was willing to forget the Crown's debt to his father.

In 1681, after nine months of bureaucratic scrutiny, Charles II granted Penn's petition. The king liked Penn personally, and having the lands Penn wanted settled with Englishmen would be very much to Britain's advantage. It's possible that Charles II also looked with pleasure on the prospect of shipping a fair number of annoying Quakers off to a part of the world far from England. Penn's patent to what became Pennsylvania took effect in March, when it received the "great seal" from England's lord chancellor. At the time, William Penn was thirty-six years old. He would live another thirty-seven, dying in 1718.

Penn's lands were extensive: they stretched from New York to Maryland, and west through five degrees of longitude. His charter described some of the province's borders, particularly that to the south, only vaguely or in ways that made no sense given the geography of the area. As a result, Penn spent much of his life trying to settle Pennsylvania's border with Maryland—a feat that was not finally accomplished until the 1760s, long after his death, when the current proprietors of the two colonies engaged Charles Mason and Jeremiah Dixon to survey what became known as the Mason-Dixon line.

Penn held extensive powers over the new colony. In the ordinary course of affairs, however, he needed the advice and consent of an elected assembly in promulgating laws. Penn also had to honor and respect the laws of Parliament regulating trade, and to keep an agent in England to answer charges of dereliction in that regard. The Crown explicitly required him to allow customs officials in his province, permit appeals to the Crown from the decisions of Pennsylvania courts, and send to England for review transcripts of all laws within five years of their enactment. No earlier proprietary charter included that last provision, which was a sign of changing times. Penn's charter also protected the place of Anglicans within the colony. But it did nothing to bar his intention of opening the colony to people of dissenting views.

William Penn, the founder of Pennsylvania, in a portrait by Francis Place, 1696.

And so Penn set out to found a "holy experiment," a colony that would serve God's "truth and people" and provide "an example . . . to the nations." But unlike the example to others that John Winthrop once hoped Massachusetts would become, Penn's experiment would show how people of different religious convictions, Quakers and non-Quakers alike, could live together with complete freedom to worship God as they chose. To advertise his colony, Penn wrote two pamphlets that circulated widely within England, Wales, and Ireland, and, once they were translated into Dutch and German, through northern Europe. From the beginning, Pennsylvania's population included Swedes and Finns, Dutchmen and Germans, along with English, Welsh, and Irish settlers. They came for the liberty Penn offered and for land: "fifty acres shall be allowed," he said, "to the Master for every Head [brought into the colony], and Fifty Acres to every Servant when their time is expired." Penn also purchased from the Duke of York another three counties farther south on the Delaware River (later the separate colony of Delaware) to ensure that the new port of Philadelphia would have secure access to the sea.

The Frame of Government that Penn designed for the colony in 1682 provided for an elected council and an assembly. As proprietor, he or, in his absence, a deputy governor would act with the council to propose laws (which the assembly could approve or reject), create courts and appoint judges, manage the treasury, and in general see that the colony was well governed. To the Frame of Government he attached forty laws. The first—which the colony's first assembly con-firmed on December 4, 1682—provided freedom of religion for all who believed in God.

Even the port city of Philadelphia, located at the confluence of the Delaware and Schuylkill rivers, attracted Penn's careful attention. He wanted it to be "a green country town, which will never be burnt" as London had been in a horrible fire during 1666, "and always be wholesome." After late October 1682, Penn worked with the province's surveyor general to create a plan by which the city's streets formed a rectangular grid whose longest sides ran east and west between the rivers. Five square, symmetrically arranged open areas broke the pattern's monotony. Four were meant for recreation, but the plan dedicated the largest, a central area of ten acres, to "Houses for Public Affairs." None of the public buildings built there dominated the city, which remained spread out, decentralized. Streets were at first named after people, but within a few years that form of human vanity yielded to simple numbers, descriptive names such as "Front," "High," and "Broad" Street, and other nonpersonal designations such as "Walnut," "Chestnut," and "Mulberry" Street. Penn allowed wealthy purchasers choice river locations, particularly along the Delaware. Still, the city plan, with its grid of identically sized blocks formed by cross-cutting streets, had a certain consonance with Quaker ideals. It was simple and orderly, and it suggested a society where people were free and equal, not tucked under the superior authority of some powerful family or institution.

These provisions failed to make everyone happy. Some settlers, including large investors whom Penn had favored, resented the locations assigned them and the fact that Penn's plans were foisted on the people without consultation. The settlers expressed their dissatisfaction in a "Humble Remonstrance & address" they presented to the proprietor. Meanwhile members of the assembly complained about their inability to initiate laws, and the mutterings grew louder after Penn—who, unlike most proprietors, actually lived for a time in his colony—returned to England to defend his land titles in 1684 and ended up staying there until 1701. Colonists bickered with a deputy governor named John Blackwell so persistently that Penn confessed deep personal sorrow over their fighting and urged them by mail "for the love of God, me and the poor country be not so governmentish, so noisy, and open in your dissatisfaction." Blackwell rejoiced when, finally, Penn revoked his appointment. Of the Pennsylvania Quakers, Blackwell observed that "each prays for his neighbor on First Days and then preys upon him the other six."

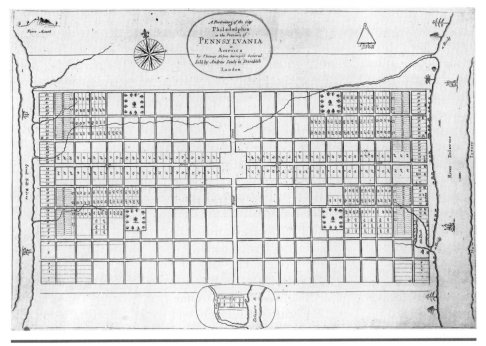

William Penn's 1681 plan of Philadelphia. Penn wanted an open city, with streets arranged on a grid plan like that of other late seventeenth-century American cities, but with parks that broke the checkerboard pattern.

## WAR AND REBELLION

So dramatic an expansion of English settlement caused a new wave of conflicts with Indians. Englishmen often considered their cultivation of what were once Indian lands as a sign of civilization's victory over barbarism and savagery. Roger Williams—who disagreed with other Puritans on this as on many other issues—recalled New Englanders' calling Indians "Heathen Dogges" who should be "all cut off" so the colonists would be "no more troubled with them" and the land opened for settlement by Christians. The colonists' successful displacement of Indians seemed to them a sign of God's providence for His chosen people, much as He had provided for the Jews when He settled them in Israel. The Indians and a handful of New Englanders such as Williams saw things differently.

So did William Penn. Indians, the Quakers believed, were entitled to respect like all other people. Perhaps, as Penn said, they remained "under a dark Night" with regard to Christian truth, "yet they believe in a God and Immortality, without the help of Metaphysicks." Penn even suspected that the Indians descended from the Old Testament Jews—a nice switch on New Englanders' self-serving use of the Bible. He insisted on purchasing from the natives those lands the king had granted him. He also told the Indians that he hoped to avoid "the unkindness and injustice that hath been too much exercised toward you by the people of these parts of the world." In realizing that ambition, it helped that only the southeastern and western reaches of Pennsylvania were still home to substantial numbers of Indians. Even there, however, the Quakers' pacifism kept Pennsylvania's early history free of those egregious acts of violence against Indians that marked Virginia's and New England's early history.

At the time of Pennsylvania's settlement, moreover, the wisdom of maintaining peaceful relations with the Indians was undeniable. New England had just suffered an Indian war that came close to totally destroying the settlements there. At almost the same time, a conflict with Indians in the backcountry

In 1701, Penn approved a "charter of liberties" that restructured the colony's government in a way that lasted for another 75 years. It eliminated the council and gave the assembly complete control over legislation. Not even that concession, which created a unicameral legislature, brought peace between the proprietor and an assembly dominated by an entrenched group of not-very-peaceful Quakers. Soon the three lower counties on the Delaware River, which contained few Quakers, organized their own legislature and became, for all practical purposes, a separate colony. However, that colony, later called Delaware, shared a governor with Pennsylvania.

These protracted conflicts were not what Penn had envisioned. His experiment was hardly the first and surely not the last effort by Europeans to create in America a model society that would fulfill God's will and improve the state of mankind. None worked out as their projectors dreamed. But considered against those other experiments, Pennsylvania's actually turned out pretty well. In a time when people were still being killed for their religious beliefs, the colony established a system of religious toleration that remained a monument to freedom on into a later, more enlightened time.

of Virginia sparked a devastating civil war between two groups of Englishmen that left the colony's capital in ruins.

*King Philip's War.* New England's troubles began in Plymouth Colony. There a peace treaty negotiated with Massasoit, the chief, or sachem, of the nearby Wampanoag Indians, in 1621 brought peace through Massasoit's lifetime and that of his son, Wamsutta (or Alexander), who died in 1662. The new sachem, Wamsutta's brother Metacom, or King Philip, as he was also called, accepted a new agreement that formally acknowledged his people's subjection to the English Crown. But thirteen years later, Philip turned against the English settlements. Was he angered by fines that were levied on him by Plymouth courts, by the colonists' seemingly unending quest for land on which to pasture their cattle, and by their cultural and political imperialism, which threatened to extinguish the Indians' identity altogether? Or was he pushed into hostilities by younger warriors, who in turn were angered by the colonists' hanging of three Indians convicted of murder? Rumors that King Philip was planning war circulated long before an English settler shot and killed an Indian who was looting abandoned homes in the Ply-

King Philip, or Metacom, sachem of New England's Wampanoag Indians, who turned against the settlers and so helped begin the bloody conflict remembered as King Philip's War, 1675–76.

mouth Colony town of Swansea. In retaliation, Indians attacked the town on June 20, 1675—and the war was on.

It did not remain confined to Plymouth Colony. The litany of towns attacked or destroyed by Indians hopped across the map of New England, utterly oblivious of the lines that separated colony from colony. Terrified for their lives, colonists flocked toward the coast until, by April 1676, the town of Sudbury, only seventeen miles west of Boston, had become a frontier town. Some twenty-five New England towns, over half the total, were severely damaged or destroyed. Estimates of deaths among the colonists vary, but perhaps a tenth of the region's men were killed along with another 1,500 women and children. And the war's cost must also include the cattle taken off or killed and the hay, corn, and other crops destroyed.

Southern New England's Indians were no longer fighting the quasi-ceremonial wars of times past and sparing noncombatants. They had learned the English style of war at places like West Mystic, Connecticut, nearly forty years earlier. Now they used torches and special "fire arrows" (arrows wrapped with rags sometimes containing brimstone) to set colonists' houses in flames, and at one point they even employed a wheel-borne device carrying burning materials to attack a colonial garrison under siege. However, rather than adopt the traditional English preference for open-field battles, the Indians continued to mount ambushes and surprise attacks on towns and militia companies—with extraordinary success. Their skillful marksmanship with flintlock muskets, acquired at first for hunting, added to the death tolls.

The war was not, however, a simple fight of Indians against Europeans. The Wampanoags found allies among the Narragansetts, who also lived near the Narragansett Bay, and the more northerly inland Nipmuc and Pocumtuck Indians. But some Indians remained neutral, and others sided with the colonists. The English could also draw on resident communities of "praying" Indians, who had been converted to Christianity by devoted missionaries such as the Reverend John Eliot, the famous "apostle to the Indians." There were probably over 2,000 of them on the eve of the war, but in Massachusetts they—and other friendly Indians—attracted so much suspicion that the Bay Colony sent some 500 Christian Indians to Deer Island in Boston Harbor, where as many as half died during their internment due to inadequate food and shelter.

After the colonists had suffered extensive losses, however, some militia officers began enlisting Indians first as scouts (a job at which colonists seemed particularly inept) and then as soldiers. With the help of Indian allies, companies of Massachusetts and Plymouth soldiers began pushing back the Indian offensive. A change in tactics also helped. Prejudices in favor of European-style warfare continued, but gradually colonists stopped condemning what they had once called the Indians' "skulking way of war" and came to appreciate the military value of stealth, sudden raids, and good marksmanship. At long last, they even abandoned matchlock for flintlock muskets, as had the Indians long before. The man who finally shot King Philip on August 12, 1676, was an Indian who fought in a unit of both Indians and Englishmen under Plymouth's Captain Benjamin Church, who advocated the colonists' adoption of Indian raiding tactics and practiced what he preached. A century later, those tactics would not be Indian, but American.

The colonists' victory—indeed, their survival—depended, in short, on divisions among the region's Indians and on the settlers' adoption of Indian tactics. But for New England's Indians, friend and foe alike, King Philip's War was a massive defeat. In the six months before Philip's death, the colonial forces killed or captured thousands of enemy Indians. The victors executed some prisoners and sent others, including Philip's wife and child, to the West Indies, where they were sold as slaves. Indian losses represented a greater part of their shrunken population than did those of the settlers against their own increasing numbers. Surviving Indians sometimes fled to New York or Canada and were absorbed into other tribes. Indian allies also suffered, since close contact with colonists, John Eliot testified, taught many "to love strong drink," which "proved a horrible snare." Thereafter, New England's Indian population—ally and enemy, Christian and "heathen"—continued to decline from disease until, by the middle of the next century, only a few thousand remained.

Colonists welcomed news of King Philip's death as if it meant the war had ended. But fighting soon began on the Maine frontier, where the Abenaki Indians continued to attack English settlements. An incident at the seaport town of Marblehead, Massachusetts, in July 1677 suggests the extraordinary hatred these wars provoked: there a crowd of women attacked and killed two captured Indians, leaving the bodies "with their heads off and gone, and their flesh in a manner pulled from the bones." Elsewhere the enormous task of rebuilding began, absorbing New England's energy and resources and reducing its capacity to defend its independence against further threats.

***Bacon's Rebellion.*** The situation in Virginia was different. After mounting a deadly but unsuccessful uprising in 1644 (in which some 500 colonists died), the descendants of Powhatan moved inland. But by 1660, most land along the Tidewater had been claimed, so new immigrants—one thousand of whom were arriving every year—and newly-freed servants who wanted land in Virginia had to go upriver. There they again encountered Indians. The situation was ripe for trouble, and in July 1675 an Indian raid on a frontier plantation set off a series of bloody raids and counter-raids. News of King Philip's War increased the frontiersmen's fear: they decided that Indians all along the Atlantic coast had joined a "Generall Combinacion" to exterminate white settlers.

Violence also occurred between two groups of white Virginians who differed, among other things, on how to respond to the frontier crisis. On one side was Governor William Berkeley, an Englishman of wit and sophistication, then in his seventies, who had been reappointed as Virginia's governor (a job he first held in the 1640s) by Charles II. Berkeley had some serious enemies in Virginia because of his favoritism to a handful of followers and his refusal for some fifteen years to allow a new assembly election. As the governor and his faction centralized authority, the power of local governments declined. That left discontented frontiersmen few peaceful, legal ways to defend themselves and their interests.

In early 1676, rather than march against the Indians, Berkley decided to build a series of forts along the heads of rivers and man them with generously paid soldiers from the Tidewater counties and some friendly Indians. The frontiersmen said that hostile Indians would sneak through the forest between Berkeley's forts, whose costs would be paid from their taxes and go to the same people whose pockets Berkeley always lined. Moreover, to the frontiersmen, all Indians were bad: even if they weren't cutting settlers' throats, they were holding lands Englishmen could put to better use. So the frontiersmen took matters into their own hands. They recruited as their leader Nathaniel Bacon, the twenty-nine-year-old son of a good English family whose overseer had been killed by Indians and who had some private grievances against Berkeley.

Then the story got truly complicated. Berkeley declared Bacon and his followers rebels and finally called a new assembly election. When Bacon appeared to take a seat in the new assembly, Berkley had him arrested. After Bacon apologized, Berkeley pardoned him and promised to give him a commission to march against the Indians. But once the assembly dissolved, the governor again declared Bacon and his followers rebels against the king. At that point, Bacon moved his troops—he had raised some 1,300 volunteers—not west, against the Indians, but east, against Berkeley, who promptly fled Jamestown for Virginia's eastern shore.

Bacon's Rebellion was not a simple war of the have-nots against the haves. To be sure, Bacon's followers on the frontier had little love for the land-rich, selfish planters of the Tidewater. But Bacon had no objection to elite rule in principle; he just thought Berkeley's followers were unqualified for the power and privileges they enjoyed. Let us examine their origins, he once proposed, and see whether their "extractions and Education" were not "vile." For three months, while Bacon fought the Indians, some of his and Berkeley's followers went around pillaging the estates of men on the opposite side. The result was a redistribution of property not so much from rich to poor, in the manner of Robin Hood, as from one group of rich people to others who figured they should be richer. Little property was destroyed until late September 1676, when Bacon burned Jamestown to the ground so the governor could not return there. Bacon remained in control another month, but after his sudden death on October 26, the rebellion collapsed like a pricked balloon.

Charles II sent a fleet of ships and 1,000 men to put down Bacon's Rebellion. He also appointed a three-man commission to investigate the settlers' grievances and ensure that insurgents were treated fairly. One of the commissioners was supposed to replace Berkeley as governor, but the elderly governor would have none of it. He proceeded to execute rebels right and left and to confiscate their property. Then he set out for England, where he died before he had a chance to justify his actions.

Is Bacon's Rebellion a story worthy of Shakespeare's art or a slapstick comedy? Surely it included moments of high theater. Consider the governor's speech to one of Bacon's fallen followers: "Mr. Drummond, you are welcome. I am more glad to see you than any man in Virginia. Mr. Drummond, you shall be hanged in half an hour." Like King Philip's War in New England, Bacon's Rebellion augured the end of the game for nearby Indians, whom settlers soon pushed beyond the mountains. The nastiness between groups of white Virginians during 1675–76, however, soon faded away. Before long, the descendants of Bacon's and Berkeley's rather indelicate followers began to intermarry and produce what magically became, by the middle of the next century, the very classy and powerful "first families of Virginia" (or FFVs).

Charles II's forceful response signaled another portentous change. Virginia would no longer be left to do more or less

what it wanted; it had become too valuable to the Crown. The reason lay in England's new laws regulating trade and taxing imports, including tobacco.

## DEFINING THE EMPIRE: TRADE

Mid-seventeenth-century Englishmen knew that trade was the route to wealth and power. The most powerful trading country of the time was the Netherlands: Dutch ships sailed everywhere—to the Baltic and the North Sea, to Asia and the South Pacific, to other European ports, and west to North and South America. Their ships and navigational equipment were superior to those of their competitors; their cargoes were more capacious; their pricing and credit policies more advantageous. During those years when England remained preoccupied with domestic affairs and unable to protect her commercial interests abroad, the Dutch moved in, trading freely with both royalist Virginia and Puritan New England.

During the 1650s Parliament tried to stop the Dutch from reaping the economic benefits of Britain's empire. Its efforts were largely unsuccessful, and they lapsed entirely in 1660, when Charles II regained the throne. The idea of squeezing the Dutch out of Anglo-American trade nonetheless persisted since the king and his advisers were anxious to encourage British merchants. Soon Parliament passed a series of new trade laws that were far more effective than their predecessors. Those laws defined the economic relationship of Britain with her American colonies for the next century.

*The Navigation Acts.* The basic Navigation Act of 1660 required that all goods shipped into or out of British territory (which included Ireland and the American colonies) had to be carried in ships of British manufacture with British masters and crews that were 75 percent British. It also required that certain "enumerated commodities" (goods that were explicitly mentioned in the act) be sent only to British territory. Most of the enumerated commodities, such as sugar, cotton, ginger, indigo, and various other dyewoods, came from the West Indies; the only major item from the North American mainland was tobacco. Colonial governors had to take oaths that they would enforce the act within their provinces, and shippers carrying enumerated goods had to post a bond at their port of departure guaranteeing that they would carry those goods to another British port.

Subsequent laws extended the system and tightened its enforcement. Where the Navigation Act of 1660 concerned ex-

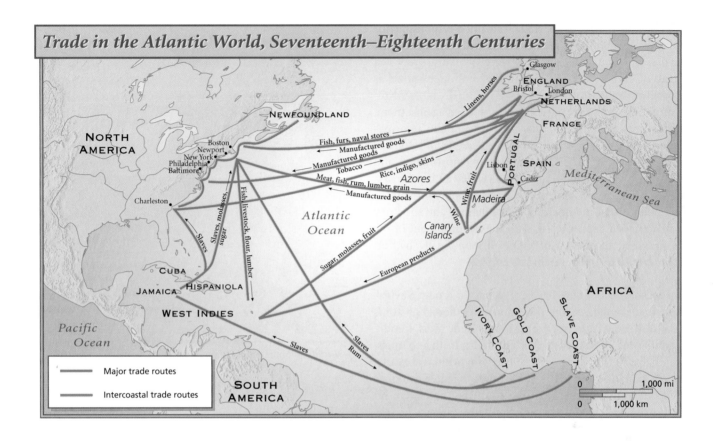

## Trade in the Atlantic World, Seventeenth–Eighteenth Centuries

ports from British territories, the Staple Act of 1663 regulated imports. Any goods sent from Europe to the British colonies, it said, had first to go through Britain, where they would be unloaded (and any duties on them collected), then reloaded for reshipment on British ships. There were some exceptions: salt for the New England fisheries (though not for the Southern colonies), wine from the Azores, and horses as well as servants and various provisions from Ireland could be shipped to the colonies directly. The Staple Act gave British merchants a monopoly on the export trade and, since British import taxes often raised the price of goods from foreign countries, provided British manufacturers of similar goods with a competitive advantage in colonial markets.

Massachusetts got off easily. It had no products on the 1660 enumerated list and benefited greatly from the provision that allowed it to import salt directly from places such as Portugal's Cape Verde Islands. But where the laws interfered with their interests, Massachusetts shippers found ways of getting around them. They (and some shippers from other colonies) would take on goods, including enumerated prod-

ucts such as sugar and tobacco, go to another colonial port where they'd get their bond refunded, then dart off to Amsterdam or another European port where they could often get a far higher price for their cargoes than in Britain. Moreover, the goods they smuggled home could often be sold for less than British imports.

The Plantation Duty Act of 1663 tried to end such illegal trade by making shippers pay duties on enumerated goods *at the port of embarkation,* not on arrival in Britain. That required establishing customs agents to collect duties within the colonies. The agents whom the Crown appointed and stationed in America were everywhere a physical manifestation of the king's power—and in many places the first and only personal representatives of the Crown colonists had ever seen. And they served under a new, permanent Board of Customs Commissioners in London.

***The Lords of Trade and the Board of Trade.*** In 1674, King Charles II appointed certain members of his Privy Council to serve as a standing Committee for Trade and Plantations. That body, known as the Lords of Trade, remained responsible for encouraging England's trade and oversaw the administration of her plantations until 1696, when King William III replaced the Lords of Trade with another, similar committee known as the Board of Trade. Those advisory committees received reports on the colonies and any complaints lodged against them, and sometimes appointed special boards to obtain information they wanted. They also recommended persons for appointment as royal officials, oversaw their performance, and played a central role in setting colonial policy. Other departments of the king's government bore responsibility for administering policies that the Board of Trade defined and the Privy Council approved. Nonetheless, with the establishment of the Lords and then the Board of Trade, Britain finally had an agency responsible for overseeing its empire.

*Later Legislation.* In 1696, Parliament passed a new Navigation Act that regularized the procedures of colonial customs agents throughout the king's dominions and, most important, established special courts of admiralty in the colonies. Before then, customs cases were tried in ordinary courts, where colonial juries had a way of acquitting fellow colonists accused of wrongdoing. In admiralty courts, there were no juries. Instead, judges trained in the specialized law of the seas decided cases. Those judges would be more likely than local juries to crack down on colonial scofflaws.

The commercial structure of England's empire was then more or less complete. Its development had continued, almost seamlessly, despite changes in regime. Later modifications of the system added new products to the enumerated list such as rice and naval stores (masts, pitch, tar, and other products, usually produced from pine trees in places such as North Carolina or northern New England). Other acts restricted specific colonial manufactures: the Wool Act of 1699 outlawed the exportation of both wool and woollen cloth from Ireland and the colonies, the Hat Act of 1732 prevented colonists from exporting hats, and the Iron Act of 1750 made illegal the construction of new iron mills to make finished iron goods (although it also allowed colonial pig and bar iron to enter England tax-free). Finally, the Molasses Act of 1733 placed a high duty on molasses imported into the colonies from the non-British West Indies. All these measures were designed to make sure that each colony contributed to the growth and prosperity of England and the other English colonies, not to that of the Dutch or other commercial rivals of Britain.

A Virginia planter smokes a pipe while a slave cultivates tobacco and another moves a cask (for shipping tobacco). The illustration comes from an English tobacco label of about 1730.

*Effects of the Trade Laws.* At first, Britain's navigation regulations devastated the economy of the Chesapeake. Planters could no longer sell their tobacco to whatever shipper offered the best price. They had to send tobacco on British ships to Britain, where it was either consumed or reexported by British merchants to purchasers elsewhere. In the early 1660s, British merchants could not handle all the tobacco from the Chesapeake, so supply exceeded demand and tobacco prices fell precipitously. The Royal Treasury, however, came out fine. It received 2 pence (or cents) on every pound of tobacco imported—which was more, and often a lot more, than the planters who grew the tobacco got for their trouble. Tobacco prices dropped to 0.5 pence a pound in 1666 and rarely rose above 1.2 pence before 1700. But duties on tobacco from Virginia and Maryland produced a quarter of all England's customs revenue during the 1660s and made up perhaps a twentieth of the government's total income. That amount exceeded returns from duties on sugar or any other import. As the fleet sent to put down Bacon's Rebellion demonstrated, Charles II was not about to tolerate any threat to the well-being of that golden egg.

New England's economy was affected far less by the regulations. Not only did the Navigation Acts rest more lightly on New England than on the Chesapeake, but in 1662 and 1663 the king granted Connecticut and Rhode Island new charters that allowed them powers of self-government like those of Massachusetts and left their religious establishments virtually untouched. He also offered to renew the Massachusetts charter so its people could "enjoy all their privileges and liberties." The king did demand that oaths of allegiance be taken and justice dispensed in his name, that Anglicans enjoy freedom of worship, and that qualifications for the vote depend on property rather than church membership. But considering what he might have demanded from colonists who had been so disloyal to his father, that wasn't much.

Massachusetts was not grateful. The colony refused Charles's offer, denied the authority of a commission the king sent there in 1664, and insisted that its charter of 1629 gave the colony's government complete and exclusive authority over its internal affairs. Meanwhile local merchants and shippers did what they could to circumvent those provisions of the Navigation Acts that did cause them trouble. Edward Randolph, whom the Lords of Trade sent on a mission to the Bay Colony and who later became Boston's collector of customs, complained about the colonists' disregard for royal authority almost from the moment he arrived in 1676.

Randolph was a splendid example of the royal bureaucrats who were suddenly appearing throughout King Charles's dominions. Ambitious, hungry for the fees and other material benefits they expected from their offices in America, they interpreted all resistance to them as opposition to the Crown and sent letter after letter to England urging their superiors to show the colonists who was boss. Randolph, who came from a wealthy English family that had fallen on hard times, looked down on the government of Massachusetts as run by "inconsiderable Mechanicks." He claimed that the colony's disregard for the laws of trade cost the Crown £100,000 a year—a vast exaggeration—and urged the king to send out the navy to force Massachusetts into line. Royal authority could be established easily, he said, because King Philip's War had reduced the colonists' capacity to resist.

Massachusetts was not the only colony that tried to get around the new trade laws. In Maryland, Lord Baltimore's deputy governor actually killed a royal customs collector. But Massachusetts's strident opposition to any infringements of its independence finally convinced the Crown that enforce-ment of the trade laws required more than sending customs agents to America. It required taking control of the colonies' internal governments.

## TIGHTENING THE CROWN'S HOLD

At the time of the Restoration (1660), Virginia was the only colony in North America ruled directly by the Crown. In 1679, New Hampshire became the second. The patent given William Penn in 1681 placed restrictions on his government that had not been imposed on earlier proprietors, but such restrictions soon seemed insufficient. In 1683, the king's government formally decided against granting any new private jurisdictions, and then it started canceling old ones. The Crown filed charges against Massachusetts for exercising a long list of unlawful powers, and in 1684 it revoked the Bay Colony's old charter. Next the Crown turned against Rhode Island and Connecticut; then the proprietary government of New Jersey came on the block.

With the accession of James II to the throne in 1685, this centralizing trend took a new turn. James and his ministers decided to group colonies in administrative units similar to the viceroyalties of the Spanish empire. First they combined New Hampshire, Massachusetts, Plymouth, Rhode Island, and Connecticut into a new government called the Dominion of New England, with a governor and council appointed by the Crown but no elected assembly. Sir Edmund Andros, a former military man who had served as governor of New York, became governor of the Dominion and took up residence in Boston late in 1686. Two years later, the Crown added New York and New Jersey to the Dominion, which then stretched all the way from Maine to the Delaware River.

## THE "GLORIOUS REVOLUTION"

King James's policies in America were of a piece with those in England, where he tried to rule without Parliament, canceled the charters of independent towns or boroughs, and also appointed Catholics to political and military offices. To justify those appointments, James proclaimed a policy of toleration, which implied that he could, by royal prerogative, overrule a 1673 act of Parliament, the Test Act, that required all officeholders to take communion in the Church of England. That alienated both the liberal Whigs, who supported Parliament, and the conservative Tories, who normally defended the Crown but

William and Mary, joint rulers of England from 1689 (Mary died in 1694, William in 1702). Portrait by Sir Godfrey Kneller, c.1690.

were deeply committed to the established Church of England. In fact, James II found that he had so little support in November 1688, when William of Orange invaded, that he fled to France.

In February 1689, members of the House of Lords and House of Commons issued a Declaration of Rights proclaiming that "the late King James the Second" had endeavored to "Subvert and Extirpate the Protestant Religion, and the Laws and Liberties of this Kingdom." It listed the acts by which he did so and noted that he had "Abdicated the Government," leaving the throne "vacant." The Declaration of Rights then stated in positive terms the rights that James had violated (for example, it said "That levying . . . Money for . . . the Use of the Crown . . . without Grant of Parliament . . . is illegal"). Finally, it offered the Crown to James's daughter Mary and her husband, William of Orange, with "intire Confidence" that they would preserve the people "from the violation of their Rights, which they have here asserted, and from all other Attempts upon their Religion, Rights, and Liberties." In later times, the British would call this series of events and the constitutional changes they brought their "Glorious Revolution."

As if to prove their British and Protestant identity, the American colonies followed suit, throwing off the oppressive hand of James and his henchmen—and adding to the internal disorder that was becoming a way of life in late seventeenth-century America.

*Massachusetts.* Massachusetts led the way. There, Governor Andros had managed to alienate virtually all the colonists, including Anglican merchants who initially rallied to his support. He at first appointed such men to his council but ignored their advice, turning instead to a handful of recently arrived royal appointees whom the colonists called "strangers." Many people still resented the loss of their elected assembly, and after Andros tried to raise taxes, several towns declared that Englishmen could not be taxed without their consent or that of their elected representatives. Andros promptly arrested several protesters, some of whom were punished after being convicted by juries said to be "packt." He also forbade towns from meeting more than once a year to elect local officers and demanded that landholders petition for royal patents to their lands. Petitioners had to pay fees to the king's officials for "regularizing" titles to their inherited lands (indeed, the king's men had a way of charging "extraordinary fees" for one "service" after another) and then pay annual quitrents to the Crown. The new royal government also tried to take over the ungranted lands, fields, and woods that the towns used for timber or pasture or as reserves for future generations.

Religious concerns added to the colonists' discontent. Andros ended public support for the Congregationalist (Puritan) Church and seized part of a public burying ground on which to build King's Chapel, Boston's first Anglican church (indeed, its first non-Puritan church of any sort). Were old-time Puritans going to be forced to attend Anglican services? Worse yet, was Andros perhaps not Anglican but, like his king, Catholic? Did he plan to turn the province over to Catholic France? When Indians friendly to the French attacked frontier settlements in Maine, the governor marched against them with both royal and provincial troops. In doing so, his critics charged, he left Boston vulnerable to French attack.

Early in the morning of April 18, 1689, armed mobs gathered in Boston's streets, where they were soon joined by militia companies. Around noon, a group of prominent local leaders took charge of the insurrection. Soon armed countrymen began flooding into Boston and nearby Charlestown. By nightfall on April 19, British soldiers stationed on Fort Hill and a royal ship in the harbor had surrendered, and royal officials including Andros and Edward Randolph were under arrest. Massachusetts once again lay in the hands of men who were mostly of Puritan descent. They justified the overthrow of the Dominion of New England as an effort like that of William of Orange to save Great Britain from "Popery and

Slavery." In fact, Boston would not receive confirmation of the Glorious Revolution in England until more than a month had passed. In the meantime, the province resumed government under its old charter, although many people questioned the charter's authority. Until a clearly legitimate government emerged, order and stability in Massachusetts would remain a dream.

*New York: Leisler's Rebellion.* Elsewhere events mirrored those in Massachusetts, though with differences that reflected local circumstances. In New York, where Andros's lieutenant governor, Francis Nicholson, and a set of local councillors exercised authority under the Dominion of New England, some colonists resented the elimination of an elected assembly. And almost everyone hated the fees exacted by the new royal officials and the monopolies and other privileges the officials granted to a few favorites, including themselves. The presence of Catholics among local royal officials provoked fear of a plot to deliver the colony to France, and those fears increased when Nicholson (a "pretended Protestant," some said) failed to announce the fall of James II and proclaim the new king and queen.

Finally, on May 31, 1689, local militias in New York City seized the city's fort. After a few days, a leader emerged among the militiamen, Captain Jacob Leisler, a German immigrant and New York merchant. An elected Committee of Safety confirmed Leisler's leadership in early June, and a few days later Nicholson fled to England. In an address to William and Mary, the New York militiamen expressed "exceeding joy" at England's "deliverance from popery tyranny and slavery" and explained they had risen up against "bitter papists" to keep New York from being "betrayed to any forraigne Enemy." The insurgents proclaimed the new king and queen on June 22, and they insisted that their "taking & securing of the fort" was "singely & Solely for their ma[jes]ties service."

Regaining control of the colony was, however, no easy matter. Parts of the countryside and the city of Albany on the Hudson were ready to accept William and Mary, but not Leisler's leadership. Nor were remaining members of Nicholson's council willing to agree that they were traitorous papists. The Leislerians, two old councillors charged, were "all men of meane birth sordid Education and desperate Fortunes" and therefore unqualified to govern. And so New York, like Massachusetts, remained in an uncertain state as it awaited news from England of William and Mary's "disposing of our government," as the militiamen put it.

*Maryland.* Maryland wasn't even part of the Dominion of New England. Nonetheless, like colonists elsewhere, Marylanders suffered from low tobacco prices, rising taxes, and oppressive fees, and they resented the doling out of lucrative privileges to a few favored insiders. Maryland Protestants also suffered fears of a Catholic plot much like Protestants in Massachusetts and New York. The Calvert family had founded Maryland as a refuge for Catholics, but by the 1680s some 95 percent of Maryland's 25,000 people were Protestant. Antiproprietary insurrections occurred there in 1659, 1676, and 1681; indeed, Maryland was in such persistent "torment," one observer informed the Lords of Trade, that it was "in very great danger of falling in pieces."

These discontents peaked after the messenger Lord Baltimore sent to order the proclamation of William and Mary died before leaving England. By June 1689, when the new king and queen had been proclaimed almost everywhere except Maryland, colonists began organizing "An Association in arms for the defense of the Protestant religion and for asserting the right of King William and Queen Mary to the Province of Maryland and all the English dominions." In July, the association overthrew Lord Baltimore's supporters and helped form a revolutionary government that finally declared William and Mary king and queen with enormous fanfare. Soon explanations and declarations, memorials and antimemorials with long lists of signatures arrived in England from Maryland. Whether the colony would be Baltimore's again was an issue for the new king and queen to decide.

## THE REVOLUTIONARY SETTLEMENT

In England, the Glorious Revolution firmly established the power of the House of Commons. No king could henceforth set aside laws that Parliament had approved or raise taxes or maintain an army ("the purse and the sword") without the consent of the House of Commons. A new Triennial Act required the Crown to call a new election every three years. That interval was later changed to seven years, but the point remained the same: no members of the House of Commons could remain in office without regular reaffirmation of support from the country. Sovereign power in Britain lay not in the Crown alone but also in Parliament, that is, in the king, House of Lords, and House of Commons acting together.

The power of Parliament was even more firmly established in the next century. After 1707, the Crown in effect lost its right to veto acts the Lords and Commons had approved. In that sharing of power by King, the House of Lords, and the House of Commons, each part of the government supposedly checked the others, preventing abuses of power. There lay the glory of what eighteenth-century writers described as the "British constitution," which was not a written document but a system of government. The British constitution, its admirers said, was so constructed that it protected the liberty of the people more reliably than the constitution of any other nation.

In America, too, the Glorious Revolution established elected assemblies as an essential part of colonial government. It also ended once and for all efforts to combine colonies into units like the Dominion of New England. Henceforth the colonies returned to their separate, historic identities. King William was not, however, far different from James II in his desire to centralize the government of Britain's colonies and establish Britain's power over its dominions—as the Navigation Act of 1696 and the establishment of the Board of Trade suggest. He also, like James II, tended to appoint military men as royal governors. The administration of the colonies remained first and foremost a Crown responsibility, and evidence suggests that by the beginning of the eighteenth century the colonists had reconciled themselves to that situation.

The immediate outcome of the 1689 insurrections differed, however, from place to place. The postrevolutionary "settlement" was least settling in New York. Leisler, still afraid of a Catholic plot, hesitated to accept the credentials of the emissary sent by the colony's new royal governor. Once in power, that governor restored many of Nicholson's former councillors to power and had Leisler and his son-in-law tried and convicted of treason. They were condemned to be "hanged by the Neck and being Alive their bodies be Cutt Down to the Earth that their Bowells be taken out and they being Alive burnt before their faces that their heads shall be struck off and their Bodys Cutt in four parts." For the next quarter century, the colony remained torn by bitter factionalism between Leislerians, who deeply resented the injustice done to men profoundly loyal to the Protestant cause, and anti-Leislerians, who thought no punishment too harsh for upstart revolutionaries.

Maryland and Massachusetts avoided that fate. Maryland became a royal colony in which onetime insurgents became part of the ruling order (although a subsequent Lord Baltimore, who was raised a Protestant, regained title to the province, but with less extensive powers than under the original grant). Massachusetts received a new charter in 1691 that gave the Crown more power over internal government than it had exercised under the colony's original charter of 1629. Henceforth, Massachusetts

would have a governor appointed by the Crown and an elected assembly (though property, not membership in the established church, determined who could vote). Its council, which advised the governor and also served as an upper house of the legislature, was not appointed by the Crown, as in other royal colonies, but elected by the assembly, although the royal governor could veto the assembly's choices. Under the Massachusetts charter of 1691, Plymouth lost its separate existence and became part of the Bay Colony, as did Maine to the north. But Rhode Island and Connecticut (which absorbed the New Haven colony) succeeded in getting their old charters back.

Despite such variety, the power of England over its colonies was clearly on a continuing ascent. In 1660, there had been only one royal colony, Virginia, but by 1730, New Hampshire, New York, New Jersey, North Carolina, and South Carolina—altogether a full half of the colonies at the time—fell into that category. Of the others, three were charter colonies: the essentially self-governing Connecticut and Rhode Island, as well as Massachusetts, whose government was a hybrid with aspects of both a charter and a royal colony. By 1730, Maryland had again become a proprietary colony, as had Pennsylvania and also Delaware. Except for Pennsylvania and Delaware, all of the colonies had bicameral legislatures; and their governors, whether elected or appointed by either the Crown or a proprietor, were answerable to the Crown. The British imperial system was perhaps imperfect, including as it did various administrative inconsistencies. But by the early eighteenth century, the colonies were undeniably part of a British empire.

## Competitors for a Continent

In the background of each 1689 colonial insurrection lay the rumble of frontier wars with Indians who acted, the settlers feared, as agents of Catholic France. Soon those conflicts expanded as European and native American powers mounted major campaigns for trade, land, people, and political dominion, adding to the astonishing instability of late seventeenth-century North America.

### FRANCE

The small northern colony of New France had all it could do to survive in the mid-seventeenth century. It existed to trade furs and convert Indians to Catholicism, and the Huron

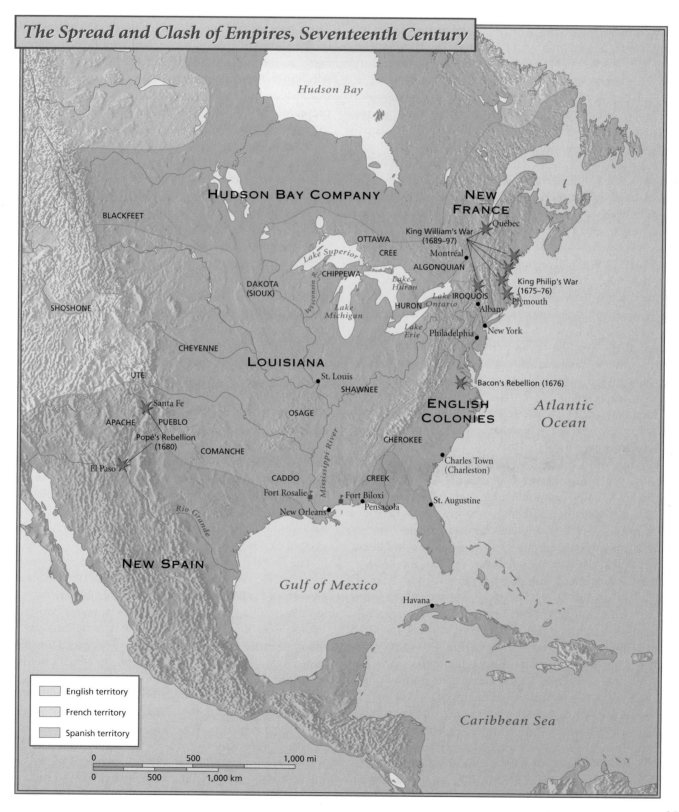

## The Spread and Clash of Empires, Seventeenth Century

*Hudson Bay*

HUDSON BAY COMPANY

NEW FRANCE

BLACKFEET

OTTAWA
CREE

King William's War
(1689–97) — Québec

Montréal

*Lake Superior*

ALGONQUIAN

CHIPPEWA

*Lake Huron*

DAKOTA
(SIOUX)

*Lake Michigan*

IROQUOIS

*Lake Ontario*

Albany

HURON

*Lake Erie*

King Philip's War
(1675–76)
Plymouth

SHOSHONE

CHEYENNE

Philadelphia

New York

UTE

LOUISIANA

St. Louis

Bacon's Rebellion (1676)

SHAWNEE

ENGLISH
COLONIES

*Atlantic
Ocean*

Santa Fe

APACHE

PUEBLO

Popé's Rebellion
(1680)

COMANCHE

OSAGE

*Mississippi River*

CHEROKEE

Charles Town
(Charleston)

El Paso

CADDO

Fort Rosalie

Fort Biloxi
Pensacola

CREEK

St. Augustine

*Rio Grande*

New Orleans

NEW SPAIN

*Gulf of Mexico*

Havana

**Legend:**
- English territory
- French territory
- Spanish territory

0    500    1,000 mi
0    500    1,000 km

*Caribbean Sea*

nation of the Georgian Bay area, north and west of Lake Ontario, was critical to both of those activities. The Hurons, who had been a trading people since long before Europeans arrived in America, collected furs from Algonquian tribes to their north and west, then exchanged them for goods from the French. Jesuits had established several missions among them but found it difficult to convert the Hurons to Christianity—until 1635–40, when baptisms rose dramatically just as a lethal disease swept through the Huron villages, reducing the population (estimated at about 18,000) by half. Then the Iroquois, relatives of the Hurons with whom they had long been estranged, began a devastating attack on the weakened Huron nation, initiating the deadly Beaver Wars.

*The Beaver Wars.* The Iroquois Five Nations—the Mohawks to the east, the Senecas to the west, and the Oneidas, Onondagas, and Cayugas between them—lived south of what is now Lake Ontario in the area between the Mohawk and Genesee river valleys. Until the 1630s, their inland location apparently shielded them from European germs, but once the Dutch, English, and French moved onto the margins of their homelands, the Iroquois suffered one epidemic after another. By tradition, the Iroquois adopted war captives to replace lost warriors; now, with population losses on an unprecedented scale, they again embarked on what was in part a "mourning war" to replace their dead.

The Iroquois also needed furs to trade for European goods, on which they had become dependent. Since beavers were no longer to be had on their lands, they hijacked canoes loaded with pelts gathered farther north and west at the junction of rivers. Now they went even further, turning viciously against the Hurons, trying at once to seize captives and to put themselves in the Hurons' place as middlemen between northern hunters and European purchasers. The Iroquois traded, however, not with the French but with their Dutch (and later English) rivals at Fort Orange (or Albany). By 1649, the Iroquois had massacred hundreds of Hurons, martyred French missionaries, and burned their missions. They adopted some of the survivors and forced others to flee their old homes and seek refuge with other Indian groups—whom the Iroquois then also attacked and destroyed.

On the basis of nonmilitary criteria, the Iroquois' victories were not entirely successful. Without the Hurons to block them, resourceful French fur traders themselves pushed west from Montreal, a new settlement on an island at the confluence of the Ottawa and St. Lawrence rivers, into the interior.

There they secured furs directly from the Ottawas who lived on the shores of Lake Superior, and later French *coureurs de bois* ("runners of the woods," a term for inland traders and adventurers) ventured all the way north to the Hudson Bay, establishing trade with Indians there. In that way, the French prevented the Iroquois from replacing the Hurons as middlemen and kept the northern and western fur trade for France.

Still, the continual threat of Iroquois attack strained New France, whose future required that the Iroquois threat be somehow stopped. The old Company of New France was nearly bankrupt and so unable to defend the colony. An effort by the colonists to take over also proved unequal to the challenge. Finally, a savior appeared in the form of the French Crown.

*Colbert's Reforms.* In 1663, King Louis XIV took direct control of New France, making it a royal province and delegating its direction to Jean-Baptiste Colbert, his imaginative and energetic minister. Colbert wanted the colony to supply France and her island colonies with materials that they would otherwise have to buy from non-French sources. Like the British, Colbert tried to end the colony's trade with the Dutch; and by the mid-1670s, he succeeded in giving French merchants a monopoly of trade with both the French West Indies and New France. He encouraged the colonists to become self-sufficient in all essentials and to export foodstuffs and timber to the West Indies. For a time, the Crown subsidized the transportation of immigrants and livestock to New France. Colbert wanted to establish in Canada a diversified economy, one that would exploit mineral deposits and develop forest industries. His vision was not altogether unrealistic: the economy he projected for New France closely resembled that of neighboring New England.

The government Colbert provided was, however, strikingly different from New England's. The internal administration of New France was divided between a governor-general and an intendant. The governor-general was always a professional soldier who held responsibility for maintaining law and order, defense, and Indian relations. The intendant, often a lawyer, was responsible for everything else—in effect, for civil government, including the administration of justice and finance. The Crown appointed both officials, and both oversaw subordinate officers within the colony. There was no elected assembly, but high-ranking officials developed other ways of receiving information from the colonists—through militia companies, for example, or ad hoc assemblies of the people that the governor-general and intendant occasionally gath-

The city of Quebec, which looked down on the St. Lawrence River, was protected from waterborne enemies by high bluffs. All other enemies would have to contend with the high walls that encircled the city. This view was painted by Richard Short in 1761.

ered to advise them on specific issues or problems. The government of New France was centralized and autocratic, but not arbitrary. Colonists rarely complained about the system, although they did occasionally express discontent with particular officeholders.

Most important, the Crown took on the colony's defense and dispatched a regiment of some 1,500 men to Canada. After the French mounted two campaigns against the Mohawks, the Five Nations negotiated a peace at Quebec. It lasted until the 1680s, some twenty years, which gave Colbert time to get his policies in place. During these years, the colony began to expand. Immigration increased while royal subsidies lasted; and soldiers sent to the colony were encouraged to remain when their military campaigns were over. Then the population continued to grow by natural increase. Canadian women married on average at age twenty-two, two or three years younger than in France, and Canadian families had five to six children compared with four to five in France—not that much of a difference. However, the survival rate of children was so much higher in America that the Canadian population doubled in every generation while that of France grew hardly at all. By the time of Colbert's death in 1683, the population of New France, thanks to both immigration and births, had grown to over 10,000—a fourfold increase since 1650.

The colony's economy also grew, stimulated in part by supplies bought by the Crown to support the king's regiment. Colonists gradually cleared and settled the forested lands along the St. Lawrence River between Quebec and Montreal, and the production of wheat increased substantially. But no extensive trade in timber or masts emerged. The cost of preparing and shipping them to France proved too high, and ships built in New France cost twice those built in the mother country. Nor did trade with the French West Indies thrive, despite a great increase in sugar production and the islands' subsequent capacity to purchase goods. In truth, the Canadians were not very interested in these forms of enterprise; they preferred farming and trading furs for quick profits. If the economy of Canada did not fulfill Colbert's ambitions, it nonetheless allowed ordinary settlers—the *habitants*—lives that were notably more comfortable than those of their counterparts in rural Europe, which was apparently good enough for them.

*French Expansion.* Colbert wanted the French to build a strong, defensible trading base along the St. Lawrence, not to spread throughout the vast interior. But he could not control the *coureurs de bois;* nor, for that matter, could he contain the expansionism of the colony's powerful governor-general, Louis de Buade de Frontenac, an egotistical, strong-willed man who arrived in 1672 and governed New France for the next decade as if it were his feudal domain. In spite of Colbert's directions, the governor-general established Fort Frontenac on Lake Ontario in 1673, then additional trading posts at Niagara (between Lakes Erie and Ontario) and at Michilimackinac (between Lakes Huron and Michigan), all of which stamped the Great Lakes as French trading territory. Tightening France's hold had become increasingly important after the British Hudson Bay Company (1670) established posts along the bay and took over much of the French trade with the nearby Cree Indians. Henceforth, the French and British were in competition for trade in the far north and the Great Lakes region.

## Competitors for a Continent

The greatest expansion of France lay, however, in the Mississippi Valley. After hearing Indian reports of a great river that flowed to the Gulf of Mexico or perhaps to California, providing the long-sought passageway to the Pacific, Frontenac dispatched two men to explore the Mississippi—Louis Joliet, a priest turned fur trader, and Jacques Marquette, a Jesuit who knew several Indian languages. Setting out in May 1673 from Green Bay on Lake Michigan, they paddled down the Wisconsin River to the Mississippi and into a world that filled them with wonder. They saw vast prairies, animals like none they'd seen before (catfish that could overturn a canoe, huge cougars), and the rough waters of the Missouri River ("I have seen none more dreadful," Marquette reported). The two men made it to the Arkansas River before local Indians convinced them that the river did not flow into the Pacific and that particularly fierce Indians lived farther south.

War in Europe kept the French from following up on Joliet's and Marquette's discoveries, but the project caught the attention of René-Robert Cavelier, the Sieur de La Salle, who had settled in Canada in the 1660s and, as a fur trader, became familiar with the continent's northern interior. La Salle returned to France in 1677 and convinced Colbert that he should secure the Mississippi Valley for France. After building a series of posts in the north, La Salle began moving down the Mississippi. He arrived at the river's mouth in 1682 and claimed "all the nations, peoples, provinces, cities, towns, villages, mines, minerals, fisheries, streams and rivers" that fed into the Mississippi for France. He named that vast territory Louisiana, after his king.

The claim was brazen, and in the short run nothing came of it. After reporting his discovery in France, La Salle sailed back in 1685, but he was unable to locate the mouth of the Mississippi from the Gulf of Mexico. He had, like so many others, made an erroneous reading with his astrolabe and, looking for a landfall at the wrong degree of latitude, ended up in Texas. There, in circumstances that remain clouded in mystery, he died at the hands of his own men.

Another decade passed before France began to make good on La Salle's claims. It established a base at Fort Biloxi on the Gulf of Mexico in 1699, then at Mobile and at Fort Rosalie (Natchez), and finally founded New Orleans as the administrative center of Louisiana in 1722. Peopling the colony was a challenge, even after the Crown abandoned its restrictions on the migration of non-Catholics and of French vagrants, prisoners, and other social undesirables to Louisiana. It also recruited German and Swiss settlers, even though many of them were Lutherans. But the migrants often died en route or soon after arriving, which made recruiting voluntary settlers still more difficult. In the end, Louisiana, unlike New France, came to depend on the labor of African slaves.

The purpose of Louisiana was imperial: France claimed it first and foremost to edge out the Spanish and, even more, the British, whose traders were already moving west from the Carolinas. By claiming a great arc of land from the mouth of the St. Lawrence to the west and south all the way to the Gulf of Mexico, a stretch of territory so vast that its hold was necessarily loose, France seemed to invite conflict with other powers. Its claims to the Illinois Country provoked the first such conflict—with the Seneca Indians, part of the Iroquois Five Nations, who considered that territory to be their own.

"New Biloxi" (in an engraving by John Law) was still a primitive camp in 1720, when it served as a stopping point for settlers waiting for small boats to take them up the Mississippi. It had only one permanent structure, a large warehouse.

An Iroquois longhouse, showing smoke emerging from the roof. Most longhouses were about 120 feet long, but some could be as much as 400 feet in length. Several families occupied a longhouse, and groups of them shared meals cooked over fires built at intervals along a central corridor.

## THE "IMPERIAL IROQUOIS"

The people known to us as the Iroquois were, in fact, only called that by the French in the seventeenth century. The Dutch and British referred to them as the Five Nations (or, in the early 1700s, when the Tuscaroras migrated from the Carolinas and joined up, the Six Nations). Sometimes they used the name "Seneca" or "Mohawk" for all members of the Iroquois league. The Iroquois identified themselves with words that meant "extended house," or "longhouse," the dwelling that characterized their culture. Through most of the colonial period, they probably included fewer than 10,000 people, but they have long been described as an imperial power virtually without parallel among the Indian peoples of eastern North America, "the Romans of the Western World." It now seems, however, that the notion of the "imperial Iroquois" is a good example of the errors that come from seeing Indians through European eyes. Although the Iroquois did not found a state, much less aspire to an empire like those of Europe, they were nonetheless a force to be reckoned with. They played a critical role in the struggle among Europeans for economic and political control of North America.

The Iroquois were an agricultural people whose women, like other Indian women, grew corn, beans, and squash while the men hunted and fished. They spoke a language distinct from that of neighboring Algonquian peoples. And they were communal: the Iroquois lived in towns or adjacent hamlets whose population density of 200 per acre was greater than that of any other part of the Northeast, European or Indian. They built palisades around their towns, and within them constructed, in parallel rows, longhouses some 20 feet wide and up to 400 feet long. First the Iroquois dug saplings into the ground, side by side in long lines, then bent them over to form a rounded roof that they later covered with bark, leaving holes roughly every 20 feet to let out smoke from fires spaced along a central corridor. The interior walls held compartments with sleeping and storage space for individual families, who shared a fire and the food cooked over it—generally a soup of vegetables with meat or fish—with those on the opposite side. Reciprocity was at the center of life in the longhouses, where people huddled together through the cold winters, eating from one pot. Families did have property of their own, but it was distributed according to need and use rather than abstract title. And property was valuable, aside from its immediate practical uses, mainly because it could be given away, forming bonds of obligation that extended and reinforced the ties that made up Iroquoian societies.

Women held substantial authority among the Iroquois. There is some evidence that Iroquoian customs were matrilocal—that is, men generally went to live in their wives' villages, and lineages were traced through the female line. The elder women chose and advised the men who headed their villages, and it was the women who called for mourning wars to replace dead family members and so to replenish the family's strength. They also decided whether to adopt or execute the captives warriors brought home. The Iroquois adopted so many people taken from other groups that eventually those among them who could claim pure Iroquois blood became a minority. Rejected prisoners, however, were tied to a stake and burned from feet to head with firebrands or similar instruments held by villagers (including women and children), then were scalped, had hot sand thrown on their bare skulls, and were finally killed with a knife or hatchet, disemboweled, and chopped into pieces, which were then tossed into the soup pots, cooked, and consumed.

*The Great League of Peace and the Iroquois Confederation.* Since they valued the lives of family members so highly, the Iroquois tried to fight in ways that avoided fatalities among their men. They favored surprise raids and ambushes over open-field confrontations, and they fled when clearly outnumbered. They also worked hard to maintain peace among

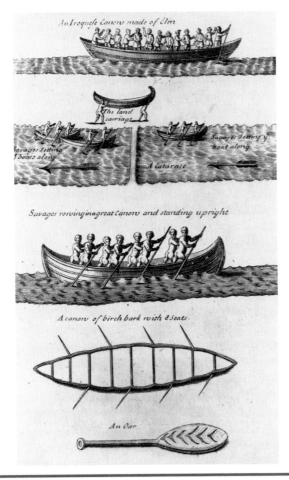

The Iroquois were masters at canoe transport. This early English illustration by Louis-Armand de Lom d'Arce de Lahontan, 1703, shows, from the top, an Iroquois canoe made of elm, the process of portage (carrying) and navigation in rough waters, Indians paddling while standing upright, and, at bottom, the scheme of a birchbark canoe with eight seats and an Iroquois oar.

maintaining peace, not of setting policy. It had no governing authority.

An Iroquois confederation of village leaders with something akin to political authority emerged only in the 1600s as a result of the first Beaver Wars. Its members were diplomats, men who negotiated peace with the French between 1665 and 1667. One such leader was the Onondaga Garakontié, a skilled orator with a peculiar capacity to understand Europeans. The leaders adapted the internal peacekeeping rituals of the Great League of Peace, including protracted speeches and extended gift-giving, to a new purpose: negotiating the Iroquois' relationships with European powers. By the 1660s, it seems, leaders from the four western Iroquois nations—the Mohawks came in only later—met occasionally to discuss issues of common concern, forming a loose confederation separate and distinct from the Great League of Peace. The confederation was emphatically not a single nation like those of Europe, but instead an alliance whose members retained autonomous power. At times, whether for convenience or from misunderstanding, the British and French regarded the confederation as if it could speak and negotiate with authority for its member nations. In the 1660s, however, each group made peace with the French separately.

That peace opened the way for Jesuit missionaries to enter Iroquoian villages, which in turn provoked conflicts among three factions of Iroquois—Catholics sympathetic to the French, others more attracted to the British (who had by then taken control of New York and the formerly Dutch trading post at Albany), and those Iroquois who saw wisdom in staying clear of European conflicts altogether. In the 1670s, those who sided with the British won out. The governor of New York negotiated an alliance, or "Covenant Chain," with the Five Nations, whose headmen joined the British in elaborate rituals at Albany that echoed those of the Iroquois' Great League of Peace. Gradually the Iroquois forced the Jesuits out of their villages, and Catholic Indians moved to New France.

With the stabilization of their relationship with the British, the Iroquois began once again to lash out against French "intruders" and other enemies. In 1687, after treacherously seizing Iroquois ambassadors who had gone to Fort Frontenac to negotiate peace at the French governor-general's invitation, the French sent a force of some 800 men against the Senecas, destroying their villages and food supplies. The Iroquois retaliated with a series of devastating raids on New France. And so the Beaver Wars reopened, but with a twist. Now they were entangled in European politics.

themselves. Sometime in the fifteenth and sixteenth centuries, after a period of incessant wars, the Iroquois peoples negotiated a series of alliances and established a Great League of Peace. Each year thereafter, a Grand Council of some fifty headmen, or sachems, from the various towns of the Five Nations met, registered complaints, and exchanged gifts, reinforcing the bonds that preserved peace. When one of the sachems died, he was ceremonially "requickened," or reincarnated, in a kinsman chosen by the older women of his clan, so the league continued over time. But the Great League of Peace was not a state, much less an empire. It provided a means of

*King William's War.* After the Glorious Revolution, King William brought Britain into a war with France. As a result, the early battles between the Iroquois and New France became part of a larger imperial confrontation known in Europe as the War of the League of Augsburg (1689–97) and in British America as King William's War. In that war, the Iroquois fought as allies of the British, and their attacks on towns and isolated farms along the St. Lawrence soon left New France near to collapse. The French king then recalled the seventy-year-old Count Frontenac for a second term as governor-general. He quickly rallied the militias of New France and their Indian allies and in 1690 organized a three-pronged attack to the south. The first sought nothing less than to capture New York, which would give France an ice-free route to the Atlantic via Lake Champlain and the Hudson River. Frontenac also hoped that his show of force would rupture the Iroquois-English alliance. His expedition chose to attack the small palisaded village of Schenectady some thirteen miles to the north and west of Albany. It was an easy target: the sleeping villagers had left the town's gates open, guarded only by a couple of snowmen. The attackers killed about sixty people and took another twenty-seven captives, then returned to Canada.

Frontenac's other targets were in northern New England. There the Abenaki peoples of the area had formed a confederation to drive the English out of the north country. British settlements in Maine were mostly small, poor, desolate frontier outposts, dedicated to fishing and subsistence farming or, farther south, particularly along the Piscataqua River where

the colonists had built dozens of sawmills, to producing timber products for export. Homes were not clustered as in the early Massachusetts towns, but scattered across the landscape, which made them particularly vulnerable to attack. Defense strategy rested on a series of garrison houses made of thick, squared logs and built specifically to withstand Indian attacks, where neighboring settlers gathered in times of trouble. However, carelessness at the garrison house in Dover, New Hampshire, led to a devastating attack in June 1689. Visiting "friendly" squaws who were allowed to spend the night inside waited until the others were asleep, then opened the doors to warriors. The Indians killed, tortured, and captured settlers, and left their homes and mills plundered and burned. Additional attacks in August prompted the British to abandon all their settlements north of Casco (Falmouth), Maine.

In the late winter of 1689–90, Frontenac's armies joined the Abenaki attack on New England—first at Salmon Falls, a small milling village near the ill-fated Dover, which a company of French and Indians destroyed on March 18, 1690. Two months later, a larger Franco-Indian force took Casco, Maine, and Fort Loyal at nearby Portland. The Indians slaughtered or took captive colonists who had surrendered after being promised safe passage to another English settlement, killed livestock, and both sacked and burned what buildings remained in what was becoming a painfully repetitious story. In 1690, a New England army under Sir William Phips failed to end the attacks. In fact, the war in northern New England continued another two years after the European war ended with the Peace of Ryswick (1697). Among the casualties were the towns of York, Maine, so thoroughly destroyed in 1692 that it seemed unlikely ever to be rebuilt, and Durham, New Hampshire, which the Indians destroyed in 1694. They also attacked Wells, Maine, and the Massachusetts towns of Groton, Haverhill, and Andover, all within forty miles of Boston. The wars were devastating as well to the Abenakis, whose numbers were seriously depleted by 1699, when, finally, they negotiated peace.

In the meantime, the French turned directly against the Five Nations: in 1696, they ruined Onondaga and Oneida villages, destroying their crops and opening a real prospect of famine. New York provided the Iroquois with some military supplies, but not as much as the Indians needed nor what they could reasonably expect from an ally. By the end of the war, the Five Nations had lost a quarter to a half of their fighting men, and perhaps 2,000 of their 8,600 people. There is little mystery why, in treaties negotiated at Montreal and

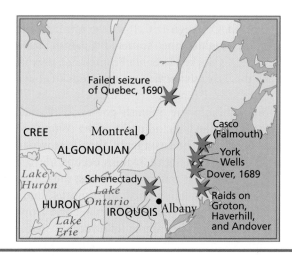

King William's War

Albany in 1701, the Iroquois agreed to remain neutral in European wars, or why over the next decades—in which the European powers again went to war—they became increasingly united on a policy of neutrality.

## SPAIN

The Spanish carefully monitored the expansion of other European powers within North America. In 1685, they learned of La Salle's designs on the "Mischipipi," which would pose a threat to Spanish shipping on the Gulf of Mexico and perhaps to its mines in Mexico. They mounted several expeditions to find La Salle, and it was Spaniards who finally discovered the ruins of his camp in Texas and learned the story of his death from Indians and a few survivors of the French expedition. Spain still maintained its old post at St. Augustine on the Atlantic. In November 1698, it began building another small fort at Pensacola to strengthen its hold on the gulf. In November 1700, however, the (Spanish) Hapsburg emperor Carlos II died after naming as his heir Phillipe d'Anjou, the grandson of France's King Louis XIV. That decision put the rivalry of France and Spain on hold.

*New Mexico.* Spain's greater efforts at the time were concentrated in New Mexico. However, the number of Spaniards there was never large, and the settlement remained dependent on coerced Indian labor. Even the Franciscan missions in the area were built by Indians who worked the missions' fields, raised their livestock, and carried the surpluses to market, sometimes voluntarily and maybe even "with pleasure," as one friar insisted, but often unwillingly. The tributes exacted by local *encomenderos* increased Indian resentment. So did the Spaniards' patently illegal—because it violated a royal edict—practice of selling Indians into slavery.

The Indians of New Mexico rebelled on a fairly regular basis, destroying property and killing Spaniards, including missionaries. The insurgents had numbers on their side. There were about 17,000 Pueblos living in about two dozen separate towns, far fewer than the 60,000 in New Mexico earlier in the century but still more than the roughly 3,000 Spaniards there. However, the Pueblos were spread over several hundred miles and spoke a variety of often mutually unintelligible languages. As a result, their revolts tended to be local, limited, and relatively easy for the Spanish to repress.

Pueblo discontent increased after a serious drought reduced their food crops. Then neighboring Navajo and Apache

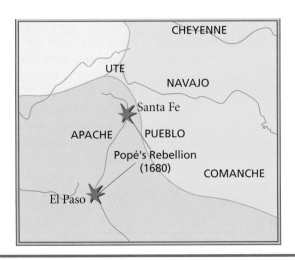

Locations of Popé's Rebellion

Indians made repeated raids on the Pueblos' fields and farms, increasing the shortages. The distressed Pueblos could only wonder why, if the friars' God was real, He provided for them so poorly, and they turned back to their traditional gods. The Spaniards, however, could not tolerate such a retreat to paganism. In 1675, they hanged three Pueblo priests and whipped another forty-three Indian participants in the native religious revival, among whom was a man named Popé. Five years later, shortly after King Philip's War ended in New England, the Pueblos and some Apaches united behind Popé. Within a few weeks, they mounted the most successful Indian revolt in North American history, a massive uprising that destroyed the New Mexico colony.

*Popé's Rebellion.* On August 10, 1680, the revolt erupted with massive force against the scattered Spanish farms and ranches. Refugees flocked to Santa Fe, then fled down the Rio Grande to the Spanish settlement at El Paso (now Ciudad Juárez) some 300 miles away.

The toll was high: the Spanish governor estimated that over 400 colonists died, including 21 of the colony's 33 Franciscan missionaries. The insurgents also destroyed or ransacked the physical remains of Spanish occupation, including the churches. The revolt was, in fact, against the Christian religion as well as exploitation and other injuries, and against Spanish culture, including Spanish language and crops. Popé, according to one account, ordered followers to "break up and burn the images of the holy Christ, the Virgin Mary and the other saints," even to throw the holy water and oils into the river and then plunge in and wash off themselves the "holy sacraments," including baptism.

The revolt didn't stop there. All along the northern edge of New Spain, or Mexico, an array of Indian peoples shed Spanish rule and destroyed missions and settlements. For the next fourteen years, New Mexico remained in Indian hands. The Spanish returned in the 1690s under the leadership of Diego de Vargas, who by diplomacy and force secured the allegiance of several Pueblo communities. However, Spain's hold on the territory remained insecure. Vargas retook Santa Fe in 1694 and then subdued other Pueblos—who mounted another massive uprising two years later. With the help of Indian allies, Vargas suppressed the rebellion, but he failed to win the total subordination of the region's Indian peoples. For them, the struggle for autonomy was costly, reducing the population from 17,000 to 14,000, which itself caused a reshuffling of people and places. Nonetheless, there were some positive results. The Spanish were henceforth less intolerant of native religions, less exploitative, less oblivious of royal edicts issued for the protection of Indians.

Not that the Spanish took responsibility for provoking the revolt. They explained the event as a form of divine punishment for otherwise unacknowledged sins. If not the work of God, they added, the Indian uprising was surely the work of the devil. That way of thinking was by no means confined to the Catholic Spanish. It was shared, in fact, with the most anti-Catholic European settlers in America: the Puritans of New England.

## Satan Joins the Fight

How could New Englanders make sense of the calamities that hit their New World promised land? Troubles had rained down on the region like the trials of Job. First customsmen and other royal emissaries threatened New England's autonomy; then Massachusetts lost the charter it had proudly held for over a half century; and before long, Governor Andros and other servants of James II invented new ways to harass the colonists. Moreover, a plague of Indians almost destroyed the settlements in the 1670s and, in 1690, seemed to be at it again, this time with the help of the Catholic French.

Long before, on board the *Arbella* as it sailed westward across the Atlantic, John Winthrop told the first settlers that their covenant with God required them to be "knitt together" with an unselfish "bond of love." He also warned that if the

The Reverend Cotton Mather (1663–1728), minister of Boston's Old North church, a prolific writer, and a true believer in witchcraft. This portrait was done by Peter Pelham in 1727.

colonists' commitment to each other failed and they embraced "carnall intencions, seeking great things" for themselves and their posterity, the Lord would "break out in wrathe against us." Were the colonists now feeling God's wrath?

So it seemed to the acting governor and General Court of the Massachusetts Bay Colony. They issued a proclamation in March 1690 stating that New England's "long Series of Afflictions and Calamities" showed "the anger of the righteous God." The edict called for a rigorous campaign against *Provoking Evils* such as blasphemy, Sabbath-breaking, idleness, drunkenness, and "Uncleanness." Only by reform could the colonists ward off the "imminent danger of perishing."

The Reverend Cotton Mather agreed. In a 1689 sermon entitled *The Present State of New England Considered,* written, as its published title revealed, *Upon the News of an Invasion by bloody Indians & French-men begun upon Us,* Mather said that New England was in danger of being delivered to its "old Land-Lord, *Satan,*" who had ruled the region before Christians arrived, when it remained in the possession of Indians. The reason lay in that "most *Bewitching* thing," a love of the world. Mather, one of the colony's most erudite clergymen, knew that "the Divils have a great hand in Exciting and Supporting" New England's enemies, which he learned from "the mouth of a possessed child." The devil appeared, however, not only on the northern frontier in the guise of French and Indian armies, but also in Salem, Massachusetts, where he seemed to take possession of more than a single child.

## SALEM WITCHCRAFT

Even now, after more than three centuries and despite shelves of books on the subject, it remains hard to know precisely what happened at Salem in 1692. The records are incomplete, and the guesses of earlier historians have taken their place in standard histories as if they were established facts. What does seem clear is that the event began not in Salem Town, a prosperous seaport, but in Salem Village, a poorer, inland agricultural community that remained legally part of Salem Town but had its own church. There in the early months of 1692, Betty Parris, the young daughter of the Reverend Samuel Parris, contracted a strange illness, and a physician suggested her ailment was of supernatural origin. Soon a group of Betty's friends accused three women of causing her illness. The accused were older women whose morals or personal circumstances made them obvious suspects—Sarah Good, a poor, pipe-smoking, contentious hag given to begging; Sarah Osborne, who had lived with a man before marrying him; and Tituba, an Indian slave in the Parris household. In late Febru-

An English print published with a 1589 pamphlet that told the story of three women who were convicted of practicing witchcraft and hanged. On the lower right, an animal seems to suckle from a woman's face. At Salem in 1692, authorities again sought evidence of strange growths on an accused witch's body, assuming that "familiars," strange beasts that were considered to be devils, would suck there.

ary, the state issued warrants for their arrest, and two members of the provincial council held a public examination of the accused witches in the Salem Village meetinghouse. The event could have ended there, but Tituba confessed, implicating Good and Osborne at the same time. The villagers' worst fears were confirmed: the devil was at work in Salem.

Soon the number of accused people began to multiply, taking in women and men who would ordinarily have seemed above criticism, such as Rebecca Nurse. The number of accusers also grew as women like the elder Ann Putnam joined in, and others, male and female, readily offered testimony against one or another of the accused. The examinations became public spectacles where the "victims" screamed out as their bodies twisted into hideous contortions whenever the accused witches came in sight—but then they were cured when touched by the "witches," supposedly because the demons possessing them returned to the oppressors' bodies. Within weeks, the jails—nasty, unhealthy places—became packed with would-be witches. Under Massachusetts law, witchcraft was a capital offense, but the accused were not tried until May, when the new Massachusetts charter arrived along with the colony's new royal governor, William Phips.

Within a few days of his arrival, Phips created a special Court of Oyer and Terminer—a type of court meant for instances where a short-term incident produced many cases to be heard—to pass judgment on the accused witches. The first session was held on June 2, and on June 10 the first convicted witch was hanged. The court clearly sought, and won, convictions: when a jury declared Rebecca Nurse innocent, Lieutenant Governor William Stoughton, the presiding chief justice, sent it back to deliberate further. That was a violation of the established practice in England, where no judge could interfere with a jury's decision to acquit. By early October, twenty-six people had been convicted of witchcraft, and nineteen of them were already executed. At least another two of the accused had died in jail, and a twenty-second victim, Giles Cory, was pressed to death with heavy stones in an effort to make him enter a plea and so recognize the authority of the court, which he refused to do. Another fifty of the accused had confessed, and the jails were still full of people awaiting trial.

There were many reasons to question the proceedings, but the most troubling concerned the evidence admitted in court. Confessions were considered particularly convincing. Those who confessed were not executed—perhaps because their testimony against other accused witches was so useful. After all,

American Journal

## What If You Get Sick?

*The first step in any treatment program is diagnosis, and in the seventeenth century, explanations for illness included supernatural as well as natural considerations. Note that this passage from the Reverend Cotton Mather's diary was written in 1693, when the Salem witchcraft crisis was over, and Mather apparently participated in a dissection to discover the cause of his child's death. "Scientific" investigations of the body clearly existed side by side with what would today be regarded as superstition.*

"On March 28 [,1693]. Tuesday, between 4 and 5 A.M. God gave to my Wife, a safe Deliverance of a Son. It was a child of a most comely and hearty Look, and all my Friends entertained his Birth, with very singular Expressions of Satisfaction. But the Child was attended with a very strange Disaster; for it had such an obstruction in the Bowels, as utterly hindred the Passage of its Ordure from it. Wee used all the Methods that could bee devised for its Ease; but nothing wee did, could save the Child from Death. . . .

"When the Body of the Child was opened, wee found, that the lower End of the Rectum Intestinum, instead of being Musculous, as it should have been, was Membranous, and altogether closed up. I had great Reason to suspect a Witchcraft, in this praeternatural Accident; because my Wife, a few weeks before her Deliverance, was affrighted with an horrible Spectre, in our Porch, which Fright caused her Bowels to turn within her; and the Spectres which both before and after, tormented a young Woman in our Neighbourhood, brag'd of their giving my Wife that Fright, in hopes, they said, of doing Mischief unto her Infant at least, if not unto the Mother; and besides all this, the Child was no sooner born, but a suspected Woman sent unto my Father, a Letter full of railing against myself, wherein shee told him, Hee little knew, what might quickly befall some of his Posterity."

*From the Diary of Cotton Mather, 1681–1708*

---

dead witches could tell no tales. The court also looked for evidence of peculiar growths on witches' bodies, which could serve as "tits" for nursing "familiars" (little demons); of instances where people suffered some misfortune after provoking the accused person's anger; and of superhuman capacities of one sort or another. In case after case, however, the court also admitted "spectral evidence," that is, evidence in the form of testimony by accusers that they had seen ghostly images of the accused afflicting them. Following the advice of Cotton Mather, the judges concluded that Satan could not assume a person's shape without the person's permission. If so, the appearance of a specter was proof that the accused had made a pact with the devil. But what if, as Rebecca Nurse asserted, the devil could take the shape of an innocent person? The Bible told of his doing that on occasion.

On October 3, 1692, the Reverend Increase Mather, Cotton Mather's father, preached a sermon to a meeting of ministers in Cambridge that contested the validity of spectral evidence. It was better, he said, that ten witches escape than that one innocent person be condemned. His sermon was published later in the month as *Cases of Conscience Concerning Evil Spirits Personating Men* with the endorsement of several noted clergymen. That helped break the bubble. By then, too, the accusers had begun implicating persons whose rank or status put them beyond suspicion—high members of the provincial government, the wife of a minister who had supported the trials, maybe even Lady Mary Spencer Phips, the governor's wife. Soon Governor Phips announced that there would be no further imprisonments or trials for witchcraft and, supported by a vote of 33 to 29 in the General Court, dissolved the Court of Oyer and Terminer. In early 1693, the state's new Superior Court of Judicature tried the remaining cases. Although Stoughton remained that court's presiding judge, it acquitted forty-nine people and convicted only three, whom Phips immediately reprieved. In April, the governor dismissed all remaining prisoners and issued a general pardon.

The witchcraft crisis defies all simple explanations. Deep factional conflicts within Salem Village and between Salem

Village and Salem Town contributed to the crisis, at least in its early stages. Those who accused others of being witches tended to be supporters of the church in Salem Village and of its minister, the Reverend Mr. Parris, and several were members of the Putnam family. The accused were often Salem Villagers who were not members of the village church and opposed Parris; often, too, they lived in or had some close association with Salem Town and its thriving commercial economy and with the town's prominent Proctor family. However, accusations extended well beyond the borders of Salem Village and Salem Town.

The Indian wars help explain why the crisis spread. The witchcraft proceedings began about the time news arrived of the Indian massacre at York, Maine. Essex County, which includes Salem and borders the coast of northeast Massachusetts, had received many refugees from New Hampshire and Maine during 1677–78, and it maintained close ties with the communities that were attacked and often destroyed during King William's War. Some of the accusers were themselves refugees who had lost parents and other family members to Indian violence and now supported themselves as servants in Salem Village households. What mixture of resentments and desperate fears fed into their conduct is hard to assess, but young people who had witnessed inhuman violence on the frontier knew evil firsthand and were no doubt ready to war against the devil themselves. As the frontier pushed down toward Essex County, the notion that the devil stalked the land and had, as witnesses often said, "tawny" skin like the Indians, became all too believable. In 1692, an accused witch in the town of Billerica—which would suffer an Indian attack three years later—confessed that she had made a pact with the devil while "under great discontentedness & troubled w[ith] feare" in return for a promise that "if she would serve him she would be safe from the Indians."

If the executed Salem witches were in some measure war casualties, the number of victims was modest: far fewer died in Salem than in those obscure, vicious, forgotten Indian attacks on Salmon Falls, Maine, and Dover, New Hampshire. Salem lives on in memory because its victims were cut down not by wartime enemies but by neighbors, persons who set in place a classic witch hunt in which the accused could save their lives only by confessing and implicating others, and so extended the net of accusations until, finally, they crossed the line of credibility. The fascination of the Salem episode also lies in the vivid example it provides of people's capacity to turn against fellow humans, however innocent. That so extreme an example of cruelty occurred in a community that first set out to realize Christian charity is especially disheartening. Observers can still argue over whether or not a personal Satan exists and was at work in Salem. But that evil walked the town's dusty roads is beyond controversy.

### WITCHCRAFT AND THE RISE OF MODERN SCIENCE

In Europe, witchcraft crises had often coincided with major wars. They reached a peak there between 1450 and 1650 and were particularly severe in areas torn by chaos during the Thirty Years' War (1618–48). In America, too, accusations of witchcraft tended to coincide with wars or war scares. Today, however, charges of witchcraft seem archaic, an expression of superstitions utterly out of keeping with modern scientific thought.

The seventeenth century saw the birth of a modern science based on objective experimentation and observation. In England, it was the age of Sir Isaac Newton, whose *Mathematical Principles of Natural Philosophy* (1687) demonstrated that all motion conformed to mathematical laws; of Sir Robert Boyle, a founder of modern chemistry; and of William Harvey, who on the basis of observations first described the circulation of blood, and whose revolutionary studies of anatomy and physiology eventually gave rise to scientific medicine. The discovery of mechanical rules of motion were particularly significant since they suggested a world that went on without the ad hoc interventions of God (or Satan). But in America as in Europe, some enthusiasts for the new science such as Cotton Mather were also ready to defend the existence of witchcraft. If God governed the world by discoverable laws, the study of those laws was a way to know God; but who could doubt that an all-powerful God could, on occasion, act outside the laws He had enacted? Even those who came to regret their roles in Salem sometimes affirmed the existence of occult forces and divine intervention in human life. Samuel Sewall, for example, publicly apologized for his role as a judge in the witchcraft trials after his family suffered several afflictions, which he saw as punishments for some horrible sin. After 1700, however, skepticism about the irregular intervention of supernatural forces in human affairs increased among educated people in both Europe and America, and witchcraft prosecutions gradually disappeared.

War, however, did not. The heritage of the seventeenth century in North America lay in a hardening of imperial systems and territorial claims that continued to produce armed conflicts thereafter. The primary European contenders remained France, whose claims in 1700 included lands from the mouth of the St. Lawrence west to the lake country and south through the Mississippi Valley; Spain, whose empire centered in Mexico, but which also held territory in Florida and New Mexico; and Great Britain, whose major mainland colonies stood between the Appalachians and the Atlantic coast in a long but now continuous strip from Maine to the Carolinas.

Indian peoples lived in scattered communities throughout these territories. On occasion, as in New Mexico or New England, they tried with considerable success to push European settlers from their ancestral lands. The Indians, though, were not one people but many who were often at odds with each other and as anxious to win European support in those rivalries as the Europeans were for Indian support in their own. And the Indians, who had become dependent on imported trade goods, were often more interested in establishing stable relationships with Europeans than in reclaiming the continent for themselves alone. Both sets of peoples had been changed by the other. The Indians had become Europeanized in their use of foreign textiles, metals, and foods, and sometimes in their religions. Even Popé's Rebellion in New Mexico, the century's greatest effort to reclaim Indian culture, failed to convince the Pueblos to give up the comfort of wool clothing or to abandon various crops or livestock introduced by the Spanish. For their part, the Europeans had become Indianized in their cultivation of corn and, above all, in their ways of war.

The outcome of all these changes was unlikely to depend exclusively on alliances and wealth, or on political and technical competence. The future also turned on those peculiar and somewhat mysterious forces that allowed one people to multiply while others watched their children die, or had none to watch. And was God's will irrelevant? For European contenders, the contest for America represented in good measure a war of religion between the Protestant British and the "Catholic Powers." Both sides thought God was on their side, and only time could tell if either was right.

## Suggested Reading

Charles McLean Andrews, *The Colonial Period of American History,* vol. 3: *The Settlements* (1937)

Paul Boyer and Stephen Nissenbaum, *Salem Possessed: The Social Origins of Witchcraft* (1974)

W. J. Eccles, *France in America* (1972)

Jill Lepore, *The Name of War: King Philip's War and the Origins of American Identity* (1998)

Patrick Malone, *The Skulking Way of War: Technology and Tactics among the New England Indians* (1991)

Mary Beth Norton, *In the Devil's Snare: The Salem Witchcraft Crisis of 1692* (2002)

Daniel K. Richter, *The Ordeal of the Longhouse: The Peoples of the Iroquois League in the Era of European Colonization* (1992)

Carl Ubbelohde, *The American Colonies and the British Empire, 1607–1763* (1975)

Richard White, *The Middle Ground: Indians, Empires, and Republics in the Great Lakes Region, 1650–1815* (1991)

# Chapter Review

## Summary
### QUESTIONS

- Why did Britain tighten its hold on its American colonies after 1660?

- Why were there uprisings not only in England but also in Massachusetts, New York, and Maryland during the late 1780s? What impact did those uprisings have?

- What role did the Beaver Wars play in the history of North America?

- Were the Iroquois an imperial people?

- How was the Salem witch crisis related to French and Indian attacks on communities in northern New England?

## Chronology

| | |
|---|---|
| **1618–48** | The Thirty Years' War in Europe. |
| **1660** | Parliament passes the first Navigation Act. |
| **1675–76** | King Philip's War (Indian war in New England). |
| | Bacon's Rebellion in Virginia. |
| **1680** | Popé's Rebellion against Spanish rule in New Mexico. |
| **1681** | William Penn founds Pennsylvania. |
| **1682** | The Sieur de La Salle claims Louisiana for France. |
| **1689** | Glorious Revolution in England. |
| **1689–97** | King William's War (in Europe, War of the League of Augsburg). |
| **1692** | Witchcraft trials begin in Salem, Massachusetts. |

## Key Terms

King Philip's War (p. 80)

The Glorious Revolution (p. 86)

The Iroquois (p. 93)

Popé's Rebellion (p. 96)

Witchcraft crisis (pp. 99–100)

**Access the *Inventing America* StudySpace at wwnorton.com/studyspace**

PERSONAL PLAN ■ REVIEW MATERIALS ■ RESEARCH AIDS ■ MULTIMEDIA

# Chapter 4

# BENJAMIN FRANKLIN'S WORLD:

## COLONIAL NORTH AMERICA, 1702–1763

A portrait of Benjamin Franklin painted by Robert Feke in about 1748. His clothes, wig, and posture mark him as a man who aspired to be an English gentleman.

QUESTIONS

■ *What caused rapid population growth in the British North American colonies?*

■ *How did American slavery change as the slave population grew?*

■ *In what ways did American society and culture grow more refined in the eighteenth century?*

■ *How did the colonists forge a stronger common identity as both Britons and Americans in the eighteenth century?*

"Your kind present of an electrical tube, with directions for using it, has put several of us on making electrical experiments, in which we have observed some particular phaenomena that we look on to be new." So a little-known Philadelphia printer named Benjamin Franklin wrote Peter Collinson, a London merchant who had sent scientific apparatus to the Library Company of Philadelphia for the use of its patrons. The year was 1747, and Philadelphians knew full well that they did not live at the center of civilization. What we've discovered, Franklin said apologetically, "may not be new to you, as among the numbers daily employed in those experiments, on your side the water, 'tis probable some one or other has hit on the same observations." At least Collinson would know that his electrical tube was not lying around unused.

Collinson was a member of the preeminent institution for the promotion of experimental science of its day, the Royal Society of London. First formed in 1660 and chartered by King Charles II in 1662, the society turned its attention to a stunning range of subjects. It drew no line between the investigation of nature's basic principles (science in the modern sense) and their practical applications (technology); indeed, its charter committed the society to promote "by the authority of experiments" both "the sciences of natural things" and "of useful arts." The structure of plants and animals was of as much interest to members as astronomy, the nature of electricity, medicine, or "Mechanical Inventions" like the "Engin fit to strike the Whales with more ease and surnesse, and at a greater distance," whose possible development the society discussed in 1663.

Even before receiving its royal charter, the Royal Society appointed a Committee for Foreign Correspondence to establish contact with like-minded people in distant parts of the world, including the American colonies. Moreover, the society—or individual members, like Collinson—requested information from its correspondents, and sometimes supplied data-gathering instruments such as thermometers (first devised in 1606 by Galileo), barometers, telescopes, and even, it seems, an occasional electrical tube. The information gathered was often read to the society and sometimes later published in its *Philosophical Transactions,* which by the mid-eighteenth century had become the world's foremost scientific publication.

From the first, moreover, the Royal Society included colonists as members. John Winthrop Jr., the promoter of the Hammersmith Iron Works and governor of Connecticut, was one of the original members. Between 1663 and 1783, the society elected another sixteen American colonists as a result of their interest in and contributions to science. Their presence on the membership list indicates how far the colonies had come since their early years. At first, as Winthrop wrote in 1668, settlers had "work enough" and "difficulties sufficient to settle a comfortable way of subsistence" by breaking ground, clearing land, planting orchards, and constructing buildings, fences, and fortifications "as in beginning of the world." But by the eighteenth century, the physically absorbing job of planting colonies had, for the most part, been done, and there was time for study and reflection. With a little help from the Royal Society, men of science within America found each other, exchanged letters and papers across colonial borders, and bound themselves together in what the society itself once referred to as an international "Republic" of men attempting "to Promote & advance Science and usefull knowledge."

The British North American colonies grew spectacularly in population and prosperity during the early eighteenth century. That growth allowed a new refinement of life in one area after another. Colonists rebuilt their homes in ways inspired by English models and filled them with new "comforts"—consumer goods, many of which were imported from the mother country. Such improvements, like the colonists' connections with the Royal Society, reinforced their identity as Britons, as did their provincial politics and their participation in Britain's recurrent wars against France and Spain. By the 1760s, the colonists were self-consciously British to an extent unequaled at any earlier period. At the same time, the old sectarian hostilities that separated them from one another started to give way, and the colonists began to assume a common identity as Americans.

## Population Growth

Benjamin Franklin was a dabbler in science, as were many people of his time; it was for them a pastime, not a profession. Born at Boston in 1706, the youngest son in a large family (he remembered thirteen children sitting at dinner) of a Boston candle and soap maker, Franklin received only a few years of formal education. His father removed him from grammar school at age ten to assist him in his business, Franklin later recalled in his autobiography. When young Benjamin didn't take to making candles, his father sought an alternative trade that would better suit the boy, and ended up apprenticing him to Benjamin's brother James, a printer. Under the terms of his indenture, Benjamin—then twelve years old—"put himself apprentice to his brother to learn his art, and with him, after the manner of an apprentice, to serve" until he was twenty-one.

It was a fortunate choice. James soon began publishing his own newspaper, the *New England Courant,* which, with Boston's two other newspapers, heralded a new era. Newspapers were the first mass medium, and print would remain the only way of reaching a broad public for another two centuries. Benjamin Franklin was in at the beginning, setting type and, like other printers at the time, writing some of the texts he printed. He had always been a reader; he later claimed that he could not remember a time he could not read. He began with works of divinity in his father's library (and later regretted the time he "wasted" with them), then turned to more secular writings. Now, as he worked at perfecting his prose style, he took as models contemporary English publications, such as the stylish *Spectator*. The fruit of his efforts was a series of letters to the editor of the *New England Courant* from one "Silence Dogood"; the fourth letter alone—a satire on Harvard College published in May 1722, when Franklin was sixteen years old—would do credit to an essayist many times his age.

"Prose writing," Franklin later pronounced, "has been of great use to me . . . and was a principal means of my advancement." His ability to describe his electrical work clearly and logically, in language accessible to any intelligent reader, would contribute to his reputation as a scientist. In the short run, however, his celebrity as an author created a strained relationship with his brother. At age seventeen, Franklin ran away to Philadelphia, leaving his apprenticeship behind. There he eventually published his own newspaper and, in time, became an investor in several papers. That allowed him to retire from active printing in the 1740s and devote his time to electrical experiments and a variety of other pursuits. One of the subjects that attracted his attention was demography.

### OBSERVATIONS CONCERNING THE INCREASE OF MANKIND

Franklin took up the subject of demography in an essay attacking the Iron Act of 1750, by which Parliament prohibited the establishment of new mills and forges for processing iron in the American colonies. There was no real danger of competition with British manufactures, Franklin asserted; the American demand for British goods was increasing so rapidly that it would soon be "beyond her Power of supplying." As a result, Britain should not restrain colonial manufactures. "A wise and good Mother will not do it. To distress, is to weaken, and weakening the Children, weakens the whole Family."

Clearly he thought of the Americans as part and parcel of the British family. But his argument depended in good part on his analysis of population dynamics distinct to America. Population theories based on "fully settled old Countries," Franklin wrote in his *Observations Concerning the Increase of Mankind* (1754), do not suit "new Countries, as America." A population increases, he argued, in proportion to the number of marriages, and marriages grow in proportion "to the ease and Convenience of supporting a Family." Where families are easily supported, "more Persons marry, and earlier in Life." In crowded cities and in "Countries full settled," people delay marriages until late in life or avoid marrying altogether, and that, he suggested, was generally true in Europe. In America, however, land was plentiful, and laboring men who understood "Husbandry" could "in a short Time save Money enough to purchase a Piece of new Land" sufficient to support a family. As a result, "marriages in America are more general, and more generally early, than in Europe":

> If it is reckoned there, that there is but one Marriage per Annum among 100 Persons, perhaps we may here reckon two; and if in Europe they have but 4 Births to a Marriage (many of their Marriages being late) we may here reckon 8, of which if one half grow up, and our Marriages are made, reckoning one with another at 20 Years of Age, our People must at least be doubled every 20 Years.

The situation was destined to continue because the vast territory of North America "will require many Ages to settle . . . fully." In the interim, colonial labor would remain expensive, since men agreed to work for others only temporarily and for high rates of pay; then they went off to work for themselves on their own land, had children, and sent the population spiraling. The original 80,000 English immigrants to America, Franklin said, had multiplied until by the mid-eighteenth century the American population stood at about a million. If in the next century that population doubled "but once in 25 years," its progeny would constitute "more than the People of England, and the greatest Number of Englishmen will be on this Side the Water. What an Accession of Power to the British Empire," he exclaimed, "by Sea as well as Land!"

Although Franklin's figures were estimates, not measurements, no generalization about the colonies was repeated more often by Americans after mid-century than his claims on demographic growth. Every colonist seemed to know that the population of British North America was doubling every twenty to twenty-five years, which was taken as a sign of vitality and a source of enormous pride.

Was Franklin's estimate correct? Not for all colonies in all periods. The Chesapeake, for example, got off to a rocky start. By 1700, however, sex ratios among white Virginians and Marylanders approached balance, indentured servitude (which delayed marriage) declined, native-born women married at relatively young ages (twenty-two or twenty-three by the mid-eighteenth century), and longevity increased. A marriage produced on average seven or eight children in the eighteenth century, and five or six were likely to reach adulthood. As a result, the population began to grow by natural increase, as it had in New England long before. Modern efforts to define population levels (which were not directly measured by decennial censuses until 1790) indicate that Franklin's estimates were close to the mark. The total population of the mainland

A register for the family of Massachusetts resident Samuel Colton. His first wife, Flavia, died childless at the age of twenty-two. Samuel remarried two and a half years later. He and his second wife, Lucy, had seven children, four of whom survived to adulthood. Note the number of children and their lifespans, and also the lifespans of the parents.

British colonies stood at about 250,000 in 1700; by 1775, it had reached 2.5 million That was already over a third the population of England and Wales combined, and the rate of growth in America was substantially higher than that "at home." At some point in the future, more English people would live in America than in Britain itself—as Franklin predicted.

### SOURCES OF GROWTH

Why was the British North American population growing so fast? The base cause was, as Franklin surmised, a high birth rate. By the eighteenth century, colonial women married from four to five years earlier than their counterparts in Europe, which in a precontraceptive society translated into more births. The colonial population was also healthier, probably because it had more reliable access to food, particularly meat. Not only did better nutrition lead to higher survival rates among infants and longer lives, but it explains why by the 1770s men from the continental North American colonies averaged 3 to 3.5 inches taller than their British counterparts.

If births accounted for 80 percent of the new population, immigration made up the other 20 percent. And it was particularly important in the middle colonies, including Franklin's Pennsylvania, where in the eighteenth century immigration helped push the annual population growth rate to about 3.4 percent, substantially higher than New England's 2.4 percent or the Chesapeake's 2.7 percent.

Franklin didn't talk about immigration, particularly that from non-British sources, perhaps because he didn't like it. There was no need for foreign immigrants, he argued; left alone, the British would readily fill the land by "natural generation." He drew an analogy with plants, any type of which ("for Instance, . . . Fennel") would take over vacant lands where they had no need to compete with other plants for the "Means of Subsistence." So, too, a land "empty of other Inhabitants . . . might in a few Ages be replenish'd from one Nation only . . . for Instance, with Englishmen," whom he preferred especially over the "Spaniards, Italians, French, Russians and Swedes," all of whom he described as having a "swarthy Complexion." So did the Germans, as Franklin saw it, except for the Saxons, ancestors of the English, whom he was willing to include among "White People."

Most colonists remained of British origin. But immigration not only increased the size but also changed the character of colonial society, making it more ethnically diverse—despite Franklin's preferences.

## IMMIGRATION

In the late seventeenth century, the British government began restricting emigration, particularly of craftsmen (although many made their way to America despite these restrictions). The one exception was criminals, who after 1718 could accept "transportation" to the colonies as an alternative to punishment in England. Most of the estimated 50,000 convicted felons Britain sent to North America went as servants to the Chesapeake. Franklin, as usual, had something to say on the subject. In a newspaper essay of 1751, he noted that the British government

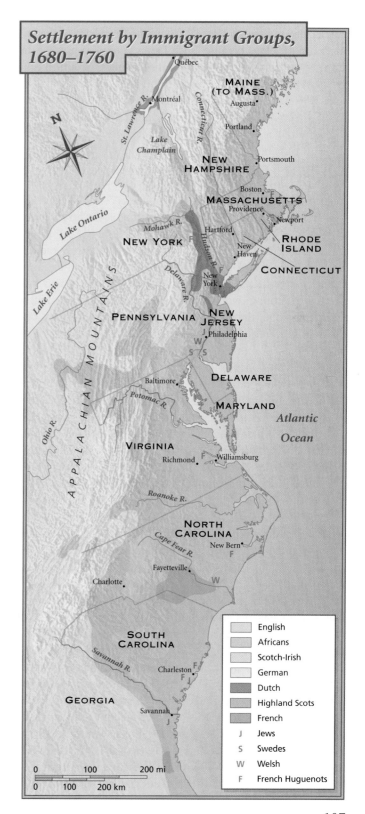

**Settlement by Immigrant Groups, 1680–1760**

Legend:
- English
- Africans
- Scotch-Irish
- German
- Dutch
- Highland Scots
- French
- J  Jews
- S  Swedes
- W  Welsh
- F  French Huguenots

### The Development of American Slavery

had decided to prevent colonial assemblies from barring the immigration of felons because "such Laws . . . tend to prevent the IMPROVEMENT and WELL PEOPLING of the Colonies." So kind a concern, he said, deserved a return favor. He proposed sending to England American rattlesnakes, which were as likely as felons to change their nature with a change of climate. The snakes, he proposed, should be *"transported"* to Britain and released in "Places of Pleasure about London; in the Gardens of all the Nobility and Gentry . . . but particularly in the Gardens of the *Prime Ministers,* the *Lords of Trade* and *Members of Parliament,* " to whom the colonists were *"most particularly* obliged."

French Huguenots—Protestants from a Catholic country—were a more respectable and welcome set of immigrants. Between 2,500 and 5,000 of them, a relatively modest number, arrived in America sometime after 1685, when Louis XIV revoked the Edict of Nantes, which since 1592 had granted freedom of worship to French Protestants. Most went to New England, the rest to New York or South Carolina. The Huguenots were for the most part an enterprising, middle-class people who fit readily into colonial society.

A small component of Jews, mostly of Portuguese or Spanish origin who came from refugee communities in the Caribbean, also appeared in Newport, New York City, Philadelphia, and Charleston. There were altogether only about 250 Jewish families in the mainland colonies by the 1770s. The Jews were generally merchants or tradesmen. They had their own synagogues, charitable organizations, and schools; and unlike the Huguenots, they remained for the most part a people apart.

There were also Scottish immigrants—often Jacobite supporters of the exiled James II and his son, Bonnie Prince Charlie, who came from the highlands of Scotland. Catholic, clannish, and given to speaking Gaelic rather than English, they settled in isolated places such as the Mohawk Valley of New York or the western reaches of North Carolina, and were again less integrated into the old population than the Huguenots. The first contingents arrived after a failed Scottish uprising of 1715, but another migration including perhaps 40,000 Scots arrived between 1763 and 1775, when Parliament outlawed further emigration from Scotland. Smaller numbers of more cosmopolitan Scots from cities like Glasgow also went to the Chesapeake as "factors," or agents, to manage the tobacco trade.

Some Catholics from the south of Ireland also came. By the 1760s, there were about 6,000 in Pennsylvania and 10,000 in Maryland. Catholics found little welcome in the militantly Protestant American colonies of the eighteenth century. In Maryland, provincial statutes forced "Papists" to worship in private (1704) and then, in 1715 and 1718, excluded them from office and denied them the vote, even in local elections, unless they took oaths that proclaimed their allegiance to the British king and denied the doctrine of transubstantiation (that bread and wine were turned into the body and blood of Christ at consecration in a Catholic mass). And in 1756, Maryland's provincial assembly, which had to raise revenue for Britain's war with Catholic France, taxed their land at double the rate paid by Protestant neighbors. Even so, Maryland Catholics were probably better off than their counterparts in England or Ireland, where the law restricted their purchase, lease, and inheritance of property.

A far larger flow of immigrants came from the north of Ireland—the old seventeenth-century plantation of Ulster—and were Protestant dissenters from the Church of England, usually Presbyterians. In the American context, these people were identified as Scotch-Irish, although their ancestors might have come from England as well as the lowlands of Scotland before crossing the Irish Sea to help plant Ireland. After 1715, they left Ireland in droves, moving westward like their predecessors, this time across the Atlantic to establish new homes in North America; by 1770, there were perhaps 200,000 of them in the colonies. As dissenters from the Anglican Church, the Scotch-Irish suffered legal discrimination in Ireland, but by 1717–18, when the first great waves of migration from Ulster began, their reasons for leaving were probably economic. They suffered from a series of bad harvests and a wave of "rent racking": as the long-term leases on their land expired, English landlords racked up the rents by two or three times to levels the Scotch-Irish settlers could not pay and still maintain what was to them an acceptable standard of living. A depression in the linen industry led to another immigration spurt later in the eighteenth century.

The Scotch-Irish first tried settling in northern New England, but, finding a less than cordial welcome there, in the mid-1720s they began going to western Pennsylvania. From there, they moved into the Great Valley of the Appalachians, then steadily south until they made up a conspicuous part of the population in the western reaches of Maryland, Virginia, the Carolinas, and also the new state of Georgia. The Scotch-Irish were quintessential frontiersmen, carving farms from the wilderness, ignoring the land claims of both Indians and eastern speculators, and so, from the perspective of some older colonists, causing more than their share of trouble.

Another substantial addition to the colonial population came from German-speaking parts of northern Europe and,

A Conestoga wagon, or covered wagon, which was first made in western Pennsylvania during the mid–eighteenth century. The wagon, set over broad wheels and pulled by a team of horses, was designed to carry heavy loads over rugged terrain. Unlike the "covered wagons" of the nineteenth century, its ends were higher than the middle to keep goods from spilling out on inclines. The name comes from Pennsylvania's Conestoga Valley.

again, was Protestant. The Germans were an enormously diverse group both in their place of origin (they came from parts of what is today Germany, Luxembourg, and Switzerland) and, more dramatic, in their religious convictions. Many were members of Protestant pacifist sects—Mennonites, Amish, Dunkers, Schwenkfelders, and the like—who wanted to live simple lives in isolated communities where they could worship God as they chose without interference. Another sizable group of Moravians, or United Brethren, espoused a similar lifestyle except that they were less committed to isolation and were not pacifists. Most of the German immigrants, however, were mainline Lutherans and Reformed Protestants, whose reasons for migration were more economic than religious.

German immigration began, slowly, in the 1720s, but a half century later perhaps 125,000 Germans had arrived. Many paid their own way; others contracted to work for periods of time, usually three or four years, as "redemptioners," a variety of indentured servitude. (Redemptioners borrowed money for their passage and provisions from shippers; then, once in America, they indentured themselves to farmers or merchants who redeemed the loans.) There were German settlers all along the colonies' western frontier, but the greater part of them settled in Pennsylvania, where they made up a

third of the population by the 1770s. These were the Pennsylvania Dutch, or, more accurately, the Pennsylvania Deutsch (the German word for "German"). The settlers' tendency to "Germanize" his beloved Pennsylvania distressed Franklin, who exchanged letters with Collinson on how to induce the Germans to abandon their native tongue and speak English.

Immigrants came as the result of both a push—religious oppression or economic misfortunes—and a pull, the prospect of religious freedom and economic opportunity, which lay for most in the availability of freehold land. They came, too, with the encouragement of the British government, which from the late seventeenth century lured immigrants from rival nations to its colonies with promises of liberty, economic advancement, land, and the "rights of Englishmen." And so America became a land of opportunity. However, the largest group of eighteenth-century immigrants—one that included some 250,000 people—did not cross the Atlantic voluntarily or in pursuit of a better life. They were African slaves. Their arrival exerted an impact not just on the colonies' labor system and economy but on their society and politics—on attitudes toward race and toward freedom—that was nothing less than revolutionary.

## The Development of American Slavery

The Spanish had long since brought African slaves to their colonies, and English seamen tried to break into the slave trade even before their countrymen began planting the New World. But since the English did not own slaves, English law did not recognize the institution. It did, however, recognize other forms of unfreedom. For example, men and women who indentured themselves as apprentices to learn a craft or to work as servants were not free during the term of their indenture. When slaves first arrived in the mainland British colonies early in the seventeenth century, they were treated much like other unfree persons.

The conditions of their lives changed dramatically, however, in the late seventeenth and early eighteenth centuries. It was only then that great numbers of slaves arrived in North America and many colonies passed from being, as the historian Ira Berlin put it, "societies with slaves" to "slave societies."

### SEVENTEENTH-CENTURY BEGINNINGS

The first slaves arrived at Jamestown on a Dutch ship—not a "slaver" but a "man-o'-war" that happened to stop there—in

1619. "Twenty Negars" were sold on that occasion to John Rolfe, a large number for the time. Most slaves arrived in small lots of ten or less brought in by privateers or pirates, or as the leftover portion of cargoes that went unsold in the prime slave markets of the West Indies, where by the mid-seventeenth century sugar plantations seemed to consume an unending stream of slaves. Rarely did whole ships of slaves sail to the mainland, and rarely did the slaves that arrived come directly from Africa. These "Atlantic Creole" people, as Berlin calls them, were part of a polyglot society that had emerged on the coast of Africa, in Europe, and in the West Indies. There, along the wide rim of the Atlantic Ocean, Africans, Europeans, and sometimes native Americans met each other, interbred, learned each other's languages, became acquainted with and sometimes adopted new religions, and acquired skills necessary in their peculiar world at the interstices of several cultures. Those black Creoles who survived their initial contact with other peoples had or perhaps developed a resistance or immunity to the diseases that produced high death rates at slave factories on the African coast.

Once in North America, slaves often worked side by side with indentured servants and free whites, even on occasion with their owners. They were usually expected to support themselves and received in return the right to any excess food or livestock they produced and the profits from its sale—which eventually allowed some enterprising slaves to purchase their freedom. Some former slaves even acquired servants and slaves of their own.

Since Chesapeake planters had to make do with slaves who could not be sold in the West Indies, where planters strongly preferred male slaves, the slaves sold on the mainland included women. Consequently, through most of the seventeenth century the ratio of men to women among the Chesapeake's black population was probably more equal than among whites. That allowed blacks to marry and have families. Since they were also relatively healthy, their numbers grew by natural increase long before the white population could even replace itself. Those who were free founded communities, notably on the eastern shore of Virginia and Maryland, where members of leading black families sometimes took white spouses without, it seems, imposing any stigma on the white partner. Like other colonists,

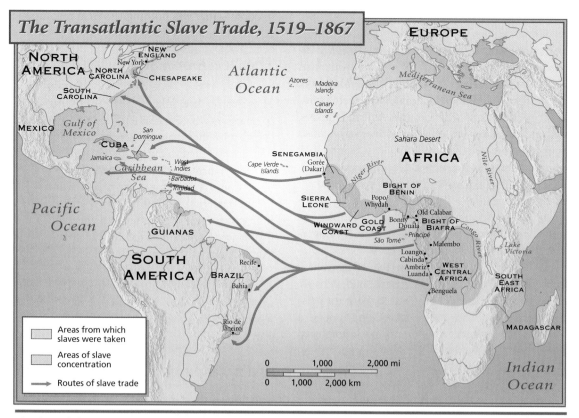

**The Transatlantic Slave Trade, 1519–1867**

Areas from which slaves were taken

Areas of slave concentration

Routes of slave trade

The data of this map was based on studies conducted by the historians David Eltis and Ira Berlin

## Volume of Transatlantic Slave Arrivals (in thousands)

| | to British Mainland North America | | to British Mainland North America |
|---|---|---|---|
| 1519–1600 | | 1776–1800 | 24.4 |
| 1601–1650 | 1.4 | 1801–1825 | 73.2 |
| 1651–1675 | 0.9 | 1826–1850 | |
| 1676–1700 | 9.8 | 1851–1867 | 0.3 |
| 1701–1725 | 37.4 | All Years | 361.1 |
| 1726–1750 | 96.8 | Share of Total | |
| 1751–1775 | 116.9 | Transatlantic Slave Trade | 3.8% |

The above data on slave imports to the British North American Mainland are drawn from a study by the historian David Eltis, published in the *William and Mary Quarterly* (January 2001). Note the growth in slave imports after 1701, the peak in 1751–1775, and the precipitous drop after 1776, followed by a resurgence in 1801–1825.

these freedmen wanted to own land, and they took care to register land titles and debts and have their wills notarized in the county courthouse. They could sue and be sued in the courts like other colonists. To be sure, free blacks were a minority: most blacks remained slaves. But in the early seventeenth-century Chesapeake, where personal freedom, property holding, and family conferred status and blacks shared in all those blessings, and where the overall population included only a tiny percentage of black people, race was neither an automatic sign of inferiority nor an obstacle to membership in the larger society.

Nor was slavery confined to the plantation colonies. Some of the largest concentrations of slaves were in New York, since the Dutch had drawn on African as well as European sources to people New Netherland. About 30 percent of New Amsterdam's population was slave in 1638, and 20 percent in 1664, when the English took over. By then, slaves constituted about 5 percent of New Netherland's overall population—about the same as in the contemporary Chesapeake. Although the Dutch made manumission (emancipation) difficult, one in five slaves had become free. As in the Chesapeake, blacks owned land, could sue in Dutch courts, sometimes married and baptized their children in the Dutch Reformed Church, and even participated in the Dutch militia. Rhode Island also

had a substantial number of slaves; and they were present in smaller concentrations throughout New England and the middle colonies. Slaves, in short, were ubiquitous.

Like other colonists, most slaves worked on farms or else in rural tanneries, mines, or iron furnaces. Urban slaves could be found on the docks or in homes, where they served as domestic servants. Those slaves or their ancestors had generally arrived singly or in small groups from the West Indies and almost never directly from Africa. They were familiar citizens of the Atlantic world who might or might not be of mixed blood, spoke English and perhaps a few other languages as well, and adjusted readily to the routines of provincial life. Such slaves fit right in to a society that wove various forms of unfreedom into the fabric of life. But as their numbers rose, they increasingly became a people apart.

## TOWARD A SLAVE SOCIETY

In the late seventeenth and early eighteenth centuries, slaves began arriving in North America by the shipload, not odd lots, and they increasingly came straight from Africa. Soon colonial legislators adopted statutes that defined the American institution of black chattel slavery. Slavery, those laws declared, meant servitude for life; it was a condition confined to blacks (and sometimes Indians); and the children of slave mothers were also slaves. New laws, like one adopted by the Virginia General Assembly in 1691, also outlawed interracial marriages. In the next half-century, Chesapeake lawmakers prohibited free blacks from employing white servants, voting or holding office, serving on juries, or bearing arms. Blacks were also forbidden or discouraged from practicing various crafts or engaging in trade. The details of such laws and the extent to which they were enforced varied from colony to colony, but everywhere slavery became a distinct, racially defined, lawful institution.

Why the change? It coincided with a decline in the supply of English indentured servants, who originally came to America because they could not find work in England. By the last decades of the seventeenth century, as the English population stabilized, more jobs opened up and real wages increased in England, so noncriminals who had a choice often stayed home. Parliament also began to discourage English migration to America. The opening of new colonies on the Hudson and Delaware rivers, moreover, gave white immigrants alternative destinations that offered greater opportunities to the poor than the southern colonies, which absorbed the greater part of the new slave population.

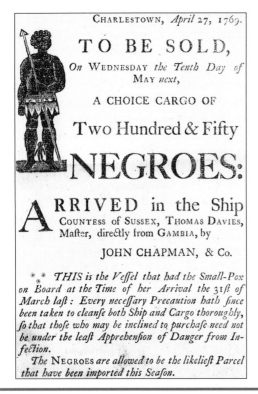

CHARLESTOWN, *April 27, 1769.*

TO BE SOLD,

On WEDNESDAY *the Tenth Day of* MAY *next,*

A CHOICE CARGO OF

Two Hundred & Fifty

NEGROES:

ARRIVED in the Ship
COUNTESS of SUSSEX, THOMAS DAVIES, Mafter, directly from GAMBIA, by

JOHN CHAPMAN, & Co.

\*\*\* *THIS is the Veffel that had the Small-Pox on Board at the Time of her Arrival the 31ft of March laft : Every neceffary Precaution hath fince been taken to cleanfe both Ship and Cargo thoroughly, fo that thofe who may be inclined to purchafe need not be under the leaft Apprehenfion of Danger from Infection.*
*The NEGROES are allowed to be the likelieft Parcel that have been imported this Seafon.*

Advertisement for the sale of 250 slaves, probably by auction, at Charlestown (Charleston, South Carolina) on May 10, 1769. Note the statement at the bottom. Smallpox was a deadly disease, and colonists took great precautions to prevent its spread. The ship *Countess of Sussex* arrived on March 31 and was probably kept in isolation away from the community until it and its slaves could be safely brought into the town.

Indentured servitude also had disadvantages that were fresh in the minds of Virginia's leading planters in the late 1670s: servants not only eventually became free, forcing their masters to find new workers, but discontented former servants could be very dangerous, as Bacon's Rebellion proved. As life expectancy increased in the Chesapeake, it began to make economic sense to pay the extra money to buy a lifetime of labor and the labor of slaves' children rather than a few years of work from a servant. The turning point probably occurred around 1660, when Virginia adopted its first slave laws, but low tobacco prices caused by the Navigation Acts prevented planters from buying slaves in quantity at that time.

By the end of the century, however, the supply of available slaves increased. Dutch traders who dominated the slave trade at mid-century had rarely ventured to North America: there

was business enough in Brazil and other markets nearer Africa than the North American mainland. Similarly, the Royal African Company, which displaced the Dutch as supplier of slaves to the British colonies, did most of its business in the West Indies. But the company could neither fill the colonies' demand for slaves nor protect its lawful monopoly, which it lost altogether in 1698. Private traders moved in, happily supplying slaves to Chesapeake purchasers who by 1700 were able to pay prices that more than compensated for the longer voyage. By then, in fact, the profitability of tobacco compared well with that of the West Indies' sugar, the price of which had dropped substantially over the previous decades.

As Virginia and Maryland planters bought more and more slaves, the Chesapeake passed from being a society with slaves to a slave society in which slaves were not incidental but a fundamental component of the social fabric that transformed all other parts. The impact of increased slave importations differed, however, from one part of the colonies to another.

*The Chesapeake.* The change to a slave society happened rapidly in the Chesapeake. In 1668, there were more than five white servants for every slave in one Virginia county, which was much like the rest of the Chesapeake. But by 1700, black slaves outnumbered white servants. During the intervening decades, slave imports began to soar: planters bought more slaves between 1695 and 1700 than in the previous twenty years. One Virginian out of twenty was a slave in the mid-1660s; by 1720, slaves constituted one out of four. Twenty years later, 40 percent of all Virginians were slaves.

The new slaves came increasingly not from communities along the West African coast but from the interior of the continent, where marauding bands of African slave traders captured people for the express purpose of selling them. Slaves from coastal regions had come from distinct communities: those from the north, for example, might be Ashantis and Yorubas, and those from the south Ibos or Mbundus. Slaves from the interior of Africa similarly belonged to hundreds of different "nations," some small, others extending over great distances, each distinguished from the others by language, religion, and leadership. These people knew themselves not as "Africans" but as Akan, Igbo, Mande, or some other specific association. And for them, no process of cultural homogenization, such as distinguished the Atlantic Creoles of the early seventeenth century, had occurred. They rarely spoke a European language or a "pidgin," or creole, language that would allow communication, and they had no acquaintance with Eu-

Slaves packed together in the hold of a Spanish ship seized by a British warship as it sailed from Africa to the West Indies. Watercolor by Lt. Francis Meynell, artist for the British Royal Navy.

ropean religions, work routines, or culture. To govern such a people seemed to require force; and provincial laws allowed owners far greater leeway in disciplining slaves than they had with white servants. Slavery became more brutal than it had been, and also more demeaning. In the seventeenth century, Chesapeake slaves generally had names that suggested their rich cultural history and a certain dignity, such as "Antonio Johnson," "Domingo Mathews," or "John Francisco." Thereafter owners gave slaves, like animals, single names like "Joe" or mocked them with names like "Julius Caesar" or "Cato."

The slaves arrived in a weakened condition, having spent some six months from capture marching toward the coast and confined in dungeons or open pens at the slave "factories," where they were sold to European slave merchants. Perhaps half of all slave deaths occurred in Africa. The survivors were crammed into tight spaces on slave ships for an additional two months with inadequate food and sanitation facilities. On average, 10 to 20 percent of the slaves (and many white crewmen as well) died on the "Middle Passage"—the middle leg of the slavers' transit from England to Africa to America and back to England. Not all slaves submitted passively: one out of ten slave voyages experienced rebellions, and it seems that insurrections were most likely on ships carrying a relatively high number of female slaves. More slaves expired soon after their arrival when exposed to European childhood diseases such as measles and whooping cough. On the other hand, because they came from

places where yellow fever was endemic, slaves had often acquired an immunity to that disease. The high incidence among Africans of the sickle-cell trait, a malformation in blood cells that can be life-threatening but provides some resistance to malaria, also made them peculiarly attractive to planters in the malaria-prone southern lowlands. Resistance to malaria became all the more valuable after 1680, when a common, mild form of the disease gave way to a far more virulent and lethal type.

Survivors of those dangers faced a life different from the ones their seventeenth-century slave predecessors had known. Opportunities for earning an independent income and using it to buy freedom were virtually gone. Indeed, the Chesapeake's old communities of free blacks disappeared as their members fled, managed to pass as white, or in some cases were re-enslaved. The social and working relationships with whites that characterized the lives of the Atlantic Creoles also disappeared. Even ties with other blacks, particularly family ties, were difficult to establish in the Chesapeake, where much of the slave population lived in small groups on scattered, remote plantations. Owners eventually grasped the economic advantage in possessing "breeding negroes": "a woman who brings a child every two years [is] more profitable than the best man on the farm," the Virginia planter Thomas Jefferson wrote in his *Farm Book,* since "what she produces is an addition to the capital, while his labor disappears in mere consumption." But it took time before owners came to that understanding, purchased women as well as men, and were willing to reduce the workloads of pregnant female slaves. Meanwhile, planters bought young males—and the black population's sex ratios became unbalanced as those of whites became balanced. Decades passed before a small, native-born black population emerged and, approaching the mid-eighteenth century, began to grow.

These blacks produced a culture unlike that of the relatively assimilated Atlantic Creoles. Theirs was a separate African American culture that carried elements of the African past and borrowed only selectively from white cultures. The gradual acceptance of an African identity by people who had thought of themselves as Mande, Bambara, Igbo, or Akan was a phenomenon not unlike that of the Wurtembergers, Alsatians, Palatines, and Swiss who found themselves grouped together as Germans, an identity they had never known in Europe.

At the same time, the relationships among the Chesapeake's white people changed. In earlier days, slaves and servants readily associated with each other; in fact, their liaisons, not those of masters and slaves, were probably responsible for

### The Development of American Slavery

The survival of African culture among American slaves is evident in this late eighteenth-century painting of a South Carolina plantation. The musical instruments, pottery, and clothing are of African origin, probably Yoruba. This painting was found undated and unsigned in Columbia, South Carolina, but the paper confirms that it is from the late-eighteenth century.

*South Carolina.* The story elsewhere resembled the situation in the Chesapeake, with some variations. Many of South Carolina's first settlers were slaves brought by their masters from Barbados. In the early pioneer years of the colony, slave and master could be found working together side by side, and slaves received a certain amount of autonomy (and respect) as guides, cattle herders, even militiamen. But the extent and character of the colony's slave system shifted with the development of rice culture in the 1790s and the production of indigo (a blue dye) a half-century later.

The presence of black laborers facilitated the development of rice culture. The English had no experience growing that crop. Rice had, however, been grown for centuries in West Africa, and the methods adopted in South Carolina showed a striking similarity to those used in Africa. Gangs of barefoot black workers planted the crop, pressing seeds into the ground with their heels, as in Africa. Then they flooded the fields until the seeds sprouted, drained and hoed the fields, and repeated the whole process, working in muddy soil under a scorching sun with swarms of insects adding to their discomfort. After the harvest, slaves (often women) beat the rice in a mortar, then winnowed it, using woven instruments like those used in Africa to separate grain and chaff. The massive earthworks that directed water to the fields needed constant repair. Growing rice was backbreaking, disagreeable work that whites saw as "only fit for slaves."

Processing indigo was no better. South Carolinians turned to producing the dye when King George's War (1739–48) caused a dramatic drop in rice prices. The teenaged Eliza Lucas (later Eliza Lucas Pinckney) began experimenting with indigo as manager of her father's plantations near Charleston. She sold her first crop in 1744. From the planters' perspective, indigo held great advantages: it grew on soil too dry for rice, required attention when rice did not (allowing a more efficient use of slave laborers), and could still be sold profitably when the market for rice fell. Slaves cultivated the crop and then, after the plants leafed out in July (and again in August and maybe also

the greatest number of mulatto children born in the colonies during the early parts of the seventeenth century. But as slavery became an increasingly demeaning status reserved for blacks, even the whites lowest on the social scale pulled away, making skin color a powerful social distinction. In the past, rich planters and poor freemen had stood against each other, as during Bacon's Rebellion; now they bonded together. The great planters expected a certain deference from those not of their status. But they also welcomed smaller landowners to their homes, helped them get their tobacco to market, and cultivated a common identity among free white Virginians.

Was Virginia's ruling class consciously using the color line to divide onetime servants and black slaves, who in 1676 had joined Bacon's army in roughly equal numbers? Whatever they meant to do, that was the effect: divisions in Virginia became more of race than of class. White Virginians shared, above all, a profound pride in the freedom they enjoyed regardless of their wealth. They knew the value of liberty because they witnessed on a daily basis the degradation of people who lacked it.

This detail, from a 1773 map by John Lodge, of a low-country county in South Carolina shows the process of preparing indigo. Note the slaves carrying leaves for processing, and the racks for drying blocks of indigo on the right.

September), carefully pruned them and placed the leaves in great tubs. There, as the leaves fermented, they gave off an increasingly disgusting smell and attracted clouds of flies. Finally, slaves picked out the leaves, drained the liquid into other vats, and beat it with paddles until the brew was ready to be set with lime. This process produced a mud-like blue sediment, which, after the liquid was again drained off, could be dried and cut into blocks for sale to textile producers abroad. The work was arduous and often unpleasant. It required great skill to make indigo cakes of the right color and consistency, and also to construct the necessary vats and other equipment. All that was done by slaves.

Rice and indigo made coastal Carolina home to the greatest concentration of wealth in North America. Planters used the profits from selling those slave products to purchase more slaves. Before 1710, about 300 slaves entered the colony each year; in the 1720s, the annual arrivals exceeded 2,000. Slave imports dropped after 1739, when some 60 "Angolan" slaves rose up at Stono, South Carolina, and murdered about 20 whites. But soon planters overcame their fears, and the slave trade recovered. In the 1770s, about 4,000 slaves arrived in South Carolina each year. Blacks constituted a majority of South Carolina's population by 1708, and they outnumbered whites two to one in 1720. One visitor commented that the colony looked "like a negro country." Nowhere else on the mainland was the concentration of slaves so high. The closest equivalent lay in the sugar islands of the West Indies, where the population was often 80 percent black. And, as on the islands, only continued importations kept the slave population from falling. South

Carolina's black population began to grow from natural increase only in the 1760s, several decades later than in the Chesapeake.

Most of the slave population of South Carolina was clustered on large plantations. In 1720, three-quarters lived on plantations with at least ten slaves, and by 1750 about one-third lived on plantations with fifty or more slaves. Owners were often absent, spending seasons that were uncomfortable and unhealthy in more salubrious places like Charleston or Newport, Rhode Island. That gave slaves a certain autonomy. So did the colony's task system of labor. Slaves had to complete a set amount of work per day—for example, planting or weeding a quarter acre. After that, their time was their own to tend private gardens, raise livestock, weave baskets, or do anything else they chose. If slaves sold surpluses of their own production, the proceeds were theirs; as a result, slaves became big-time peddlers in South Carolina, even though buying freedom was no longer a likely outcome. The harder they worked at their task, the more quickly they could turn to their own thing. The task system provided an ingenious way to build incentive into a nonwage economy and so to keep slaves at work without close supervision or persistent discipline.

In part because there were large numbers of Africans nearby, slaves on South Carolina's plantations sometimes found it possible to continue religious rituals and social traditions from their past. They even lived in quarters that they built using traditional African methods. To allow communication among people whose native tongues were often mutually unintelligible, they developed a new common language, Gullah, which contained elements from both English and African languages. And once the unbalanced sex ratios and high mortality that afflicted the first generations of African immigrants subsided, the physical proximity of plantation slaves facilitated family life: South Carolina's slaves seldom had to travel miles to visit a spouse, unlike slaves scattered on the small farms and plantations of the Chesapeake.

When the slave system became particularly harsh, slaves resisted. They could feign ignorance and an incapacity to learn jobs assigned them, or break tools—which reduced demands for sustained hard work but reinforced stereotypes of blacks as fecklessly childlike "Sambos." Arson and poison, crimes whose perpetrators were difficult to trace, also held a place in the slaves' repertoire. And they could run away. After 1700, few places to hide remained in the Chesapeake, but "maroon societies" of runaways proliferated in the tangled, swampy lowlands of Carolina and on its upland frontier, where pioneer farmers often felt little sympathy for the wealthy, slaveholding planters near the coast. The governor of Spanish Florida provided another refuge when he founded a black settlement north of St. Augustine, Gracia Real de Santa Teresa de Mose, as a home for runaway slaves from the North. The slaves who participated in South Carolina's Stono Rebellion of 1739 planned to go to "Mose."

But not all of South Carolina's slaves lived on plantations, and those in Charleston or Beaufort led radically different lives and had far less reason to escape than their rural relatives. Through most of the eighteenth century, those city slaves lived in a world dominated by whites. They picked up English quickly and, like the earlier Atlantic Creoles, learned the ways and adopted the styles of the prevailing white culture. Many became artisans (or mechanics, in the language of the day), working as coopers (who made barrels for shipping products abroad), carpenters, blacksmiths, seamstresses, and the like. Sometimes they were allowed to hire themselves out, compensating their owners from their earnings and renting their own independent quarters. Surrounded by planter wealth and a profusion of consumer goods, they sometimes flaunted their own prosperity, riding about in fancy clothes on handsome horses—which raised eyebrows and provoked largely unsuccessful efforts to exclude blacks from various economic activities. A greater contrast with plantation slaves, planting rice seeds in steaming, fly-ridden mudflats, is hard to imagine.

*The North.* The northern colonies never became slave societies like the Chesapeake and South Carolina, but there, too, the slave population increased, and legislatures adopted new laws that defined the institution and established rules and procedures specially for slaves. New England was the least affected: there farmers remained true to their traditional system of family labor. But in Boston, as in Newport, New York, and Philadelphia, slaves became standard fixtures in the households of wealthy merchants and common even in the homes of middle-class people such as the Franklins. They also worked at the docks and in trades connected with shipping such as rope making, sail making, and shipbuilding. Everywhere in the North, slave imports rose when conditions such as war kept white workers in Europe. Once the supply of white immigrants increased, slave imports dropped. The flow was therefore uneven, but the net yield remained significant. Newport's population was 10 percent slave in 1750, twice what it had been thirty years

## A LAW
### For Regulating Negroes and Slaves in the Night Time.

BE It Ordained by the Mayor, Recorder, Aldermen and Affiftants of the City of New-York, convened in Common-Council, and it is hereby Ordained by the Authority of the fame, That from hence-forth no Negro, Mulatto or Indian Slave, above the Age of Fourteen Years, do prefume to be or appear in any of the Streets of this City, on the South-fide of the Frefh-Water, in the Night time, above an hour after Sun-fet; And that if any fuch Negro, Mulatto or Indian Slave or Slaves, as aforefaid, fhall be found in any of the Streets of this City, or in any other Place, on the South fide of the Frefh-Water, in the Night-time, above one hour after Sun-fet, without a Lanthorn and lighted Candle in it, fo as the light thereof may be plainly feen (and not in company with his, her or their Mafter or Miftrefs, or fome White Perfon or White Servant belonging to the Family whofe Slave he or fhe is, or in whofe Service he or fhe then are) That then and in fuch cafe it fhall and may be lawful for any of his Majefty's Subjects within the faid City to apprehend fuch Slave or Slaves, not having fuch Lanthorn and Candle, and forth-with carry him, her or them before the Mayor or Recorder, or any one of the Aldermen of the faid City (if at a feafonable hour) and if at an unfeafonable hour, to the Watch-houfe, thereto be confined until the next Morning) who are hereby authorized, upon Proof of the Offence, to commit fuch Slave or Slaves to the common Goal, for fuch his, her or their Contempt, and there to remain until the Mafter, Miftrefs or Owner of every fuch Slave or Slaves, fhall pay to the Perfon or Perfons who apprehended and committed every fuch Slave or Slaves, the Sum of *Four Shillings* current Money of *New-York*, for his, her or their pains and Trouble therein, with

This New York City statute of 1731 was one of several northern ordinances that regulated the activities of minorities, prohibiting black, mulatto, and Indian slaves from appearing on the city's streets after sunset without a lantern and candle. Those who violated the law could be jailed and whipped if their masters agreed.

earlier. And New York City's population was 14 percent black—part new, part native born, and mostly slave—by the 1760s.

South of New England, moreover, slaves became increasingly prominent in the rural workforce. In fact, it was not altogether easy after the mid-eighteenth century to define a clear line between the economy of the Chesapeake and that of the middle colonies. Planters in Maryland and northern Virginia began switching from tobacco to grain, which found a profitable market in Europe, while Pennsylvania farmers, who had long grown grain, began buying slaves. Along the Hudson Valley and on Long Island in New York, or in parts of northern New Jersey, farmers switched to slave labor in even higher proportions.

Legislatures responded quickly to the new situation. To avoid having the white nonslaveholding population bear the burden of indigent former slaves (freed, for example, because of age), one legislature after another restricted manumissions or forced owners to support former slaves who became dependent on charity. Other laws restricted or prohibited blacks' voting, serving in militias, testifying in court, or holding property. In both North and South, legislatures periodically combined ad hoc regulations into comprehensive slave codes that bore strong similarities wherever they were passed.

From a modern perspective, the lack of opposition to slavery seems as striking as its rapid spread. In 1700, Samuel Sewall, the onetime judge in Salem's witch trials, wrote a tract entitled "The Selling of Joseph" that attacked slavery on religious grounds. "It is most certain," he said, "that all Men, as they are the Sons of Adam, are Coheirs; and have equal Right unto Liberty, and all other outward Comforts of Life." Some Quakers also publicly opposed slavery. But theirs were voices crying in the wilderness. Slavery, it seems, struck most seventeenth- and eighteenth-century white colonists as an alternative to indentured servitude, with one form of service no more immoral than the other. They also argued that slaves were "cut out for hard Labour and Fatigue" and that their situation was better in America than in Africa. It took another time, and a major change in principles and sensitivities, before Americans were ready to condemn the institution of slavery.

## Expansion, Prosperity, and Refinement

The growth of the colonies and an increasing prosperity, which the expansion of slavery both reflected and enhanced, transformed American life. Population spread; life among many persons of European origin became less harsh, with more material comforts; and white colonists increasingly engaged in fashionable forms of study and reflection. Life became, in the language of the time, refined.

### THE FOUNDING OF GEORGIA

In 1700, colonists remained clustered in separate settlements that were rarely far from the Atlantic or the major rivers that fed into it. A half-century later, the British colonial population stretched almost continuously along the coast and perhaps 150 miles inland. In the North, settlers claimed lands in upstate New York (including what became Vermont), Maine, New Hampshire, and Nova Scotia; in the West, farmers moved into the Great Valley of the Appalachians, beginning often in Pennsylvania but arriving by the 1750s in the western regions of the

Carolinas. And in the South, the eighteenth century saw the founding of Georgia, the last of the original thirteen colonies.

In a sense, Georgia was there waiting to be founded in the lands between Florida and South Carolina. To the British, that territory was part of Carolina; to the Spanish, it was Florida. The local Indians' sympathy for Spain made the British even more anxious to tighten their hold on the contested territory. South Carolinians, moreover, hoped that its settlement would plug the hole through which their slaves escaped to St. Augustine. The Board of Trade took up a suggestion by General James Oglethorpe, an old, militantly anti-Spanish soldier, who proposed stemming the Spaniards' ambitions by settling Georgia—a colony he named after Britain's King George—with England's poor.

The Crown, more protective of its power than it had been a century earlier, granted a charter in 1732 to a set of trustees who would hold Georgia in trust for twenty-one years, after which it would revert to the Crown. The new colony ran between the Savannah and Altamaha rivers and from "sea to sea." To believe the literature, Georgia was heaven on earth, a fertile field where exotic crops would thrive and the most depressed people in England would be magically transformed into productive subjects of the king. The trustees (a third of whom were fellows of the Royal Society) planned the new colony carefully. They would appoint a president and the members of a Common Council, who would govern the

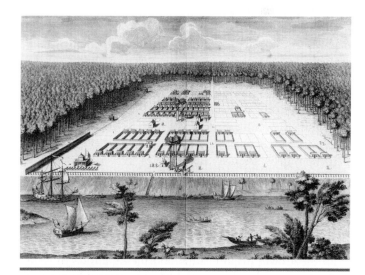

This engraving of Savannah, Georgia (c. 1735), was based on a drawing by Peter Gordon, the town's first bailiff. The engraving was shown in England to encourage emigration to Georgia.

colony without an elected assembly. Individuals could own no more than 500 acres, so the settlement would be more concentrated and easier to defend. Georgians could leave their lands only to male heirs, who could shoulder a gun against enemies; if a planter had no sons, title to his land went back to the trustees when he died. Slavery was illegal, since slaves (whose loyalty to their masters remained suspect) would weaken the colony militarily. The trustees allowed no "rum, brandies, spirits or strong waters" in the colony and would not let just any poor people migrate there. Only those who were "virtuous and industrious" could pass muster with the Georgia trustees and their agents.

Oglethorpe set out in the fall of 1732 with 32 families and founded the city of Savannah. Before long, however, it became clear that the venture wasn't working. By 1740, about 3,000 people had gone there, but many had already left. The trustees had to make the place more attractive, which they did by destroying their vision, point by point. They allowed women to inherit land, lowered quitrents, and permitted settlers to own up to 2,000 acres. The ban on alcohol and slaves fell along with restrictions on buying and selling land. Still the settlers objected: why didn't they have a voice in their government like other colonists? The trustees allowed them an assembly, but only to voice grievances, not to make laws. With such a forum and no constructive role to perform, the colonists complained up a storm. Finally, sick of it all, the trustees turned control of the colony over to the Crown in June 1751, two years before their trusteeship expired.

"It is clear as light itself," a pamphlet of 1743 insisted, "that negroes are as essentially necessary to the cultivation of Georgia, as axes, hoes, or any other utensil of agriculture." As if to prove the point, once the trustees' restraining hand disappeared, Georgia quickly came to look like another South Carolina. The planters were "stark Mad after Negroes" and bought them in volume until coastal Georgia had a black majority whose members were busily growing rice, and Savannah sprouted planter mansions much like those of Charleston. Georgia became a slave society almost overnight. There was, it seemed, no other way the colony could prosper.

### THE DISTRIBUTION OF WEALTH

With the growth of population and the expansion of settlement, the development of rice, indigo, and grain exports, and the establishment of a slave labor system, the British colonies prospered. The rewards went disproportionately to planters who possessed enough assets to purchase slaves and to merchants who could tap into the profits of overseas trade. There were also poor white people in the colonies, including victims of war, new immigrants, and young persons who had not yet inherited land or whose families' lands had been divided over so many generations that their own shares were meager. Compared with Europe, however, the American population included relatively few poor people, while the middle class—composed of individuals with sufficient means to support themselves with some independence—was extraordinarily large. The size of the middle class was, in fact, the most distinctive characteristic of British North American society by the 1760s and 1770s.

The rich were easy to find by the mid-eighteenth century: they lived in the great plantation houses of the Chesapeake or the lower South, in fine urban mansions at Savannah or Charleston, or in the spacious homes of merchants in northern cities. Like their British ancestors and generations of later Americans, they used their new wealth to improve their living conditions. The benefits of prosperity were not, however, confined to the rich. Colonists of "middling" rank also remodeled their homes or built new ones and added new possessions that ameliorated their onetime hardscrabble lives. The growth of a consumer economy encouraged the growth of domestic manufactures, which remained, however, a relatively small part of the overall economy.

### LIFE AT HOME

Forget the spanking clean, neat, freshly painted houses in "colonial villages" constructed for modern tourists. Most seventeenth- and eighteenth-century colonial homes looked nothing like them. For one thing, few were painted on the outside. Most were made of split or sawed boards that, like modern wooden garden benches, faded into a gray that blended into the landscape. And they were small affairs, often consisting of a single room measuring perhaps eighteen by twenty feet on the inside with a chimney at the end. Sometimes there were two rooms with a chimney at the center. Upstairs there might be a loft reached by a ladder or ladder-like stairway. New Englanders occasionally added a lean-to on the back of a house, giving it a characteristic saltbox shape. "Earthfast" or "puncheon" houses, crude structures consisting of rough exterior walls nailed to corner posts that were simply punched into the ground, were by no means confined to early Virginia. Early colonial houses often lacked masonry foundations, although some contained cellars

**LEFT:** Large fireplaces such as this one, in the Paul Revere House, Boston, were used for cooking as well as heating. Note the chains and hooks for hanging pots and the oven to the right. Red-hot coals would be shoveled into the oven to heat it, then pushed aside when baking bread, pies, and other foods. Large fireplaces were inefficient sources of heat for a house.

**RIGHT:** A new-style small fireplace, which was more successful than the large old fireplaces in heating a room. Such small fireplaces demanded that cooking be relegated to another part of the house. This fireplace, which dates from 1750, is in the Seth Wetmore House in Middletown, Connecticut. Note also the wood paneling and classical pilasters on either side of the fireplace, characteristic of eighteenth-century home improvements.

There were no indoor bathrooms: the great outdoors was the place to go—most of the time. Even in the *late* eighteenth century, according to a French traveler, American men were given to urinating through the holes in broken windowpanes. The traveler followed their example, and when he encountered an inn where the windows were too high, his host kindly provided a cooking pot to stand on! Add that practice to the presence of manure, a by-product of the preferred transportation system, horses, as well as of various other animals wandering around, and it's hard to avoid the conclusion that early America had a characteristically earthy smell.

In the eighteenth century, colonists often divided single-room houses or added a second room, separating the old, all-purpose hall from a parlor used for entertaining guests. A new second story sometimes provided additional sleeping space with more privacy than was possible when an entire family (including servants) crowded into one room. Cooking, too, was gradually relegated to separate buildings in the southern colonies or the lean-to tacked onto New England homes. This differentiation of space was a fundamental characteristic of home improvements, eighteenth-century style.

Most of the great colonial mansions of Virginia, as elsewhere, were built between 1720 and 1760. Until then, perhaps 80 percent of Virginia's wealthy planters still lived, like their neighbors, in one- or two-room houses that were one or one and a half stories high. In building their great houses, wealthy colonists imitated not the homes of English aristocrats, which remained well beyond reach, but those of middle-class Englishmen. Like their English prototypes, colonial America's Georgian mansions displayed balanced facades embellished with classical details such as pilasters beside doorways or at corners. Inside, a spectacular central staircase divided the house into sections that allowed abundant space for entertaining visitors. Many of the new houses were made of brick, which surely stood out from the mass of dull gray houses nearby. So did those clapboard houses that were increasingly painted after the middle of the eighteenth century—and, the

in which boards held back the earthen walls. Occasionally they had whitewashed interior walls; otherwise, inside rooms went unfinished. Easily built, most houses didn't last long.

These modest houses were everywhere in the early years of settlement and, indeed, could be found on into the nineteenth century. They were not comfortable. Their air conditioning was of the natural, earth-friendly variety that works best in winter. Cracks between exterior boards might be filled with mud or some other material, but the walls generally lacked insulation. Windows consisted of small openings covered with oiled cloth or wooden shutters and only rarely with expensive glass. Heat came from vast fireplaces whose drafts pulled cold air into a house through cracks and other openings until a person was, as Franklin once noted, "scorch'd before while he's froze behind." Ink was known to freeze in inkwells, even in heated rooms. And since fireplaces were used for cooking as well as warmth, they continued to pump heat into houses in summer when outside temperatures soared.

Water for cooking or cleaning came from streams or had to be hoisted from wells with buckets and carried inside.

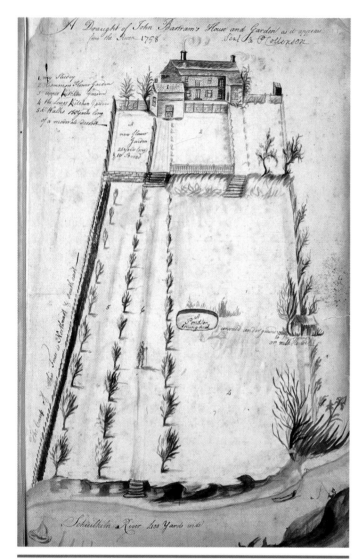

The house and garden of Pennsylvania naturalist John Bartram in 1758. Franklin and Washington were frequent visitors to the house and grounds of this great naturalist.

to appear in the North American colonies in the late 1600s, and they were almost mandatory for elegant homes by the 1720s.

The new styles sometimes arrived in the colonies through fashion setters such as Governor Francis Nicholson, who moved Virginia's capitol from Jamestown to Williamsburg, then built a governor's mansion there in the style of the English architect Christopher Wren that was unlike any other house in early eighteenth-century Virginia. Buildings such as the Virginia governor's mansion or, in New England, the house merchant Thomas Hancock built on Boston's Beacon Hill between 1737 and 1740 served as models that others could imitate. To build such houses required, of course, substantial wealth, but that was not enough. They also awaited the availability of carpenters, plasterers, and other craftsmen who had learned to execute fashionable designs in London, then moved to the English provinces or to America—where they arrived in substantial numbers during the early eighteenth century along with English guidebooks for realizing the new styles.

Before long, the aesthetic influence of the great houses trickled down to less affluent households. More than a few substantial farmhouses, for example, sprouted carved wooden pilasters beside their south-facing doors and added staircases and rooms for specialized functions, including parlors for receiving visitors. Gradually, too, houses of both rich and middling colonists became more comfortable. Enclosing windows with glass brought more light into homes while making them more weather-tight—which meant more windows could be added, further brightening interiors. Inefficient large fireplaces disappeared from major interior rooms once cooking moved elsewhere. Openings of two or three feet, it turned out, improved the draft and produced more heat. Adding an iron stove was better yet, although the famous "Franklin stoves" are misnamed. The design Franklin proposed in a 1744 tract, *An Account of the New Invented Pennsylvanian Fire-Places,* employed contemporary scientific principles to increase heat while siphoning smoke down through a duct and then out through the chimney of an extant fireplace. Franklin hoped to see his "Pennsylvania Fire-Place" mass-produced and sold for a price ordinary people could pay. Unfortunately, his stove didn't work: smoke would not siphon down through the masonry duct unless it was uniformly hot. Later, other inventors modified Franklin's design, usually adding a smoke outlet on the top like those on other stoves already in use. Franklin's attempt to improve life for the common man as well as the rich was, however, a sign of the time.

evidence suggests, in strong shades of red, brown, green, or blue, not soft pastels or pusillanimous white.

Ornamental gardens, too, came into style. The fashion began in England during the seventeenth century as travelers to Italy or France began attempting to replicate the gardens they had seen on the Continent. Most were formal, with straight paths, sometimes filled with gravel or sand, dividing square or rectangular beds that might include exotic plants collected from distant parts of the earth. Such gardens first began

*Consumer "Comforts."* The acquisitions of the colonial rich are familiar: graceful Chippendale furniture, sets of imported dishes and silver flatwear, "turkey" rugs, mirrors, and the velvet waistcoats or satin dresses so conspicuous in portraits by eighteenth-century painters such as Boston's John Singleton Copley. Unlike today, textiles were the premier article of conspicuous consumption: the rich displayed them draped over tables or beds, hanging over windows, or fashioned into the clothes they wore. These were the appurtenances of the genteel life that provided a standard for others to emulate.

Articles accumulated by less affluent people were less likely to survive. But accumulate them they did, beginning in the late seventeenth century and continuing in increased volume in the eighteenth. The middle classes added to the spare furnishings of earlier times, which generally consisted of stools, benches, an occasional chair, small chests for storage and sitting, and beds (mats or mattresses). Tables were often planks on trestles that, like the beds, could be moved aside when not used. Now even ordinary families began to acquire bedsteads (essentially frames, with or without headboards, that allowed them to lift bedding off the floor) and more chairs. No longer did people eat from shared cups and bowls that they passed around or trenchers (platters) from which they scooped up food with spoons or, sometimes, their hands. Individual knives and forks appeared along with individual ceramic dishes.

Franklin chronicled the first arrival of such "luxuries" into his household when he was still a working printer living with great frugality. For breakfast, he recalled, he usually ate "Bread & Milk (no Tea,) . . . out of a twopenny earthen Porringer with a Pewter Spoon." Then one morning, Franklin found his meal "in a China Bowl with a Spoon of Silver . . . bought for me without my Knowledge by my Wife" for the "enormous Sum of three and twenty Shillings," since "she thought her Husband deserv'd a Silver Spoon & China Bowl as well as any of the Neighbours." Later, he noted, "as our Wealth encreas'd," they added to their china and silver until it was worth "several Hundred Pounds."

What people ate and drank also changed. Sugar was one of Europe's first luxury goods, tobacco another. Tea, the favored drink of colonists as well as the English, soon joined the list. Early in the eighteenth century, the gentry adopted the drink along with elaborate devices for its ritual service—tea pots, cups, strainers, sugar tongs, and the like. By mid-century,

---

*American Journal*

## What Do You Do For Fun?

"Rode down to the Iron Works Landing to see a Vessell launched," then "went to smoke a Pipe, at Ben. Thayers, where the Rabble filled the House. Every Room, kitchen, Chamber was crowded with People. Negroes with a fiddle. Young fellows and Girls dancing in the Chamber as if they would kick the floor thro. Zab Hayward, not finding admittance to the Chamber, gathered a Circle round him in the lower Room. There He began to shew his Tricks and Postures, and Activity. He has had the Reputation, for at least fifteen Years, of the best Dancer in the World in these Towns. Several attempted, but none could equal him, in nimbleness of heels. But he has no Conception of the Grace, the Air nor the Regularity of dancing. . . . He caught a Girl and danced a Gigg with her, and then led her to one side of the Ring and said, 'Stand there, I call for you by and by.' This was spoke comically enough, and raised a loud laugh.

He caught another Girl, . . . and held her by the Hand while he sung a song, describing her as he said. This tickled the Girls Vanity, for the song . . . described a very fine Girl indeed. . . . Thus, in dancing, singing songs, drinking flip, running after one Girl, and married Woman and another, and making these affected, humorous Speeches, he spent the whole Afternoon.—And Zab and I were foolish enough to spend the whole afternoon in gazing and listening. . . .

"Fiddling and dancing, in a Chamber full of young fellows and Girls, a wild Rable of both sexes, and all Ages, in the lower Room, singing, dancing, fiddling, drinking flip and Toddy, and drams.—This is the Riot and Revelling of Taverns And of Thayers frolicks."

John Adams's diary for November 25, 1760

everyone, including the inmates of Philadelphia's poorhouse, was drinking tea—not from china cups with silver spoons, but perhaps from ceramic cups made in the English midlands. The diet of the rich became more varied as English cookbooks began to appear in the eighteenth century, necessitating still more elaborate tableware and varied cooking utensils. How long would ordinary folk remain content with the once-standard yeoman's midday meal of boiled meat, beans or porridge, bread, cheese, and beer or milk?

*The Family.* Changes in houses and their furnishings signaled changes in family life among white colonists. The provision of separate sleeping quarters for adults and children allowed a privacy impossible in the crowded houses of the seventeenth century. And as houses became more comfortable, they became places where family members might choose to linger, not just take shelter from the elements. Meals, once utilitarian events that interrupted labor, became occasions where people might break up their day with pleasure, and perhaps engage in discussions like those Franklin recalled from the family meals of his childhood. Tea provided another occasion for sociability.

Even marriage seemed to be changing. In seventeenth-century New England, marriages were in good part property arrangements negotiated by parents for their children. Couples needed to be emotionally compatible, but affection did not decide the bargain. In the eighteenth century, couples increasingly chose their own spouses, even without parental permission (as indicated by a surge in premarital pregnancies), and affection became an expected part of the relationship. (Of course, this kind of union sometimes failed, as a rise in Massachusetts divorce petitions after 1764 indicated; and court records confirm that domestic abuse is not a modern invention.) Children, whom seventeenth-century Puritans regarded as natural sinners whose will had to be broken so they would be subject to their godly parents, came to be understood as needing nurture as much as discipline. In the Chesapeake, too, parents gave evidence aplenty that they took delight in their children. To some extent, these developments were heralded among Pennsylvania Quakers, who had long since seen children as innocent "tender plants" and allowed them, when older, to choose their own spouses. In short, as houses became homes, families were increasingly defined by emotional bonds.

The family also became more private. Above all in seventeenth-century New England, families had been primarily responsible for tasks such as housing nonrelatives who were poor or indigent and educating their children; now such responsibilities were sometimes delegated to institutions such as almshouses or schools. The family remained a unit of production in which men and women had defined roles. And women's roles—which emphasized indoor activities—in some ways increased in importance as the home became more of a haven, the meal more of an event, and the parlor a place where friends and neighbors gathered. Visiting and being visited was at the core of colonial social life, particularly in rural areas; and women, as mistresses of their houses, were essential to a process by which disparate people were woven into a new and largely voluntary community.

## DOMESTIC MANUFACTURES

The greater part of the goods colonists collected came from abroad. Some were supplied by colonial craftsmen, although high labor costs prevented the development of extensive manufacturing. Where wood was the material of choice, as in furniture manufacturing, American craftsmen sometimes held an advantage over English competitors. By the late colonial period, major colonial cities boasted skilled artisans who created highly finished chests and chairs and tables, perhaps taking into account guidebooks like Thomas Chippendale's *Gentleman and Cabinet-Maker's Directory* (1754), but incorporating into their furniture distinctive design elements of their own. The mass of colonial-made furniture was, however, simpler, for a less elite domestic market or for export to the West Indies. Bulky items like sledges and sleighs, wagons and carts, and most of the coaches and carriages owned by colonists were made on this side of the Atlantic. Most of these were no doubt inelegant vehicles suitable mainly for farm use. The colonies were, however, the prime source for one luxury item, spermaceti candles—which were notably superior to tallow or wax candles—once whale hunting took off in the North Atlantic after about 1715.

It's also worth noting that some 26 colonial refineries satisfied a full three-quarters of the domestic demand for sugar by the late colonial period, and that mainland colonists consumed 60 percent of the 8.5 million gallons of rum distilled from imported molasses in British North American distilleries. The iron industry was even more impressive: by the mid-1770s, the colonies maintained 82 charcoal-fueled furnaces, 175 forges, and a large number of bloomeries whose total product was greater than that of England and Wales. Indeed, it amounted to about one-seventh of the world's iron production overall. Again, a good part of that iron was used to make items for domestic consumption.

The extent of American manufacturing can easily be exaggerated. The colonies' primary products remained agricultural, and most were produced with traditional, even ancient, methods. In fact, farmers who worked at nonfarming tasks in off seasons, whether on a piecework system or at facilities near home, contributed substantially to America's manufacturing output. Nonetheless, many manufactures, including some of the most refined, came out of artisan shops in a handful of colonial cities. Those cities were critical not only to the economy of colonial America but to its culture as well.

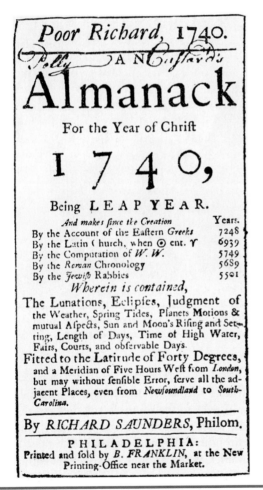

The cover of Benjamin Franklin's popular almanac, known as *Poor Richard's Almanac*, for 1740. It was supposedly written by one Richard Saunders, whose aphorisms helped guide readers to wisdom, prosperity, and contentment. Equally practical was the information provided on tides, weather, length of days at various times of the year, fairs, courts, and so on.

## CITIES

Colonial cities grew dramatically with the increase in trade and general economic expansion: New York's population rose from 5,000 to 21,000 between 1700 and the 1770s, while Philadelphia's grew to almost 22,000, which made it the largest city in British North America. Charleston and Newport, although about half the size of those larger ports, experienced similar rates of change. Only the population of Boston, which was hard hit by deaths in King George's War (in the 1740s) and the need to support veterans' widows and children, stalled along the way. It had risen from about 6,700 in 1700 to over 16,000 in the early 1640s, but declined to 15,600 before 1760.

Overall, the urban population of the British North American colonies (defined as those who lived in communities of 2,500 or more) accounted for only 5 to 8 percent of the total population. The colonial cities were nothing like Paris, which already had a half million people in 1700, or London, whose population in 1750 had reached 575,000 and was still growing at a quick pace. In feeling, they were small towns, as a London-born Philadelphia woman recognized. "We hardly dare tell one another our thoughts," she wrote her father, "lest it should spread all over town; so, if anybody asks you how we like Philadelphia, you must say very well."

The impact of cities on colonial life was, however, out of all proportion to their size and population share. The major cities were busy ports in the Atlantic trade and provincial capitals where governors resided and assemblies met. There merchants gathered in coffeehouses or taverns to talk and exchange information; there artisan shops lined the streets, making everything from barrels or hats to articles of silver or gold. In cities, one could find booksellers and lending libraries, such as the Library Company of Philadelphia, which Franklin helped organize in 1731. The lending libraries spread to other cities in the 1740s, then doubled in number each decade through the rest of the century.

In the colonial cities, printers published the newspapers that provided the only public way of transmitting news besides word of mouth. The first, the *Boston News Letter*, appeared in 1704, and the vast majority of all colonial publications—pamphlets, almanacs, books—also came out of New England. Other newspapers followed—the *New England Courant, New York Journal, Newport Mercury*, the Pennsylvania, Virginia, and South Carolina *Gazettes*: some thirty-seven were being published by the mid-1770s. Most were weekly papers of four pages that presented news in columns headed with the names of places such as Glasgow or London or Philadelphia, then listed by date news items that were taken out of late-arriving newspapers from those places. Colonial newspapers also included letters, essays, and a variety of merchants' ads.

Like colonists' homes, cities changed in appearance between the late seventeenth and eighteenth centuries. Those built earlier lacked any prescribed order or plan. Even today, the oldest sections of Boston remain, like the seventeenth-century city, a maze of twisting streets. The streets of late seventeenth-century cities, however, were laid out in straight lines and at right angles to each other, forming grids in which grand avenues, large public buildings, and open spaces broke the monotony. That was true not only of Philadelphia (1682) but also of Charleston (1672) as well as towns founded later, such as Annapolis and Williamsburg, both of which were developed in the 1690s by that trendsetting governor, Francis Nicholson. And so gradually colonial cities gave up their old ramshackle quality and took on a more ordered and refined appearance.

## NATURAL HISTORY

The study of science, particularly of plants and animals ("natural history"), became more widespread and influential in the developing culture of the eighteenth-century colonies. From the very beginning, the flora and fauna of the New World attracted intense interest among Englishmen. One of the first papers John Winthrop Jr. presented to the Royal Society was "On Maiz," or Indian corn. He carefully described the plant, its uses, and its cultivation, apparently to the members' great satisfaction. By 1662, Winthrop explained, the English settlers fertilized their land with fish ("as the Indians had done") or cow dung, and, "loading the Ground with as much as it will beare," planted beans, squash, and pumpkins in the same fields as corn, again following the Indians' example. The settlers also threw turnip seeds on the soil late in the season and so enjoyed yet another bountiful "crop of turneps in the same Field."

European interest in American plants first came from herbalists who studied them for their medicinal uses. Later, the growing fashion among gentlemen in building gardens and collecting exotic plants added to the interest in American flora. As the number of known plants multiplied, old systems of classification proved inadequate and new systems emerged, among which the systems of Carolus Linnaeus, a Swedish botanist, published in 1758, became widely accepted. As a result, much of eighteenth-century American "science"—a word that then denoted all sorts of systematic knowledge, not just that of the

A charming buffalo painted by Mark Catesby. His *Natural History* was considered a great work of science and of art.

material world—was botanical. The Royal Society, or, more often, individual members, occasionally subsidized botanical expeditions, usually to the southern colonies and the West Indian islands, whose natural life was especially unfamiliar to northern Europeans. The most successful naturalist they sponsored was Mark Catesby, a young English plant enthusiast.

Catesby first went to Virginia to visit a sister in 1712. Once there, he began collecting seeds. He also helped wealthy planters develop botanical gardens on their estates. Catesby traveled extensively in Bermuda and Jamaica as well as Virginia, and he regularly sent carefully collected plant specimens to England. Finally, in 1720, Sir Francis Nicholson, now the newly appointed royal governor of South Carolina, granted Catesby an annual pension "to Observe the Rarities of that Country for the uses and purposes of the [Royal] Society." Soon other English patrons joined Nicholson, as did the planter elite once Catesby arrived in South Carolina. In return, the naturalist supplied them with specimens for their private gardens.

During the three years he remained in America, 1722–25, Catesby traveled to different regions, always taking extensive notes, making drawings and watercolors of the plants and animals he saw, and collecting specimens. After returning to England, he worked in nurseries that specialized in American plants while preparing his masterpiece, *The Natural History of Carolina, Florida, and the Bahama Islands* (1731–43). The book was the first fully illustrated guide to American plants and animals. It became an important reference work both for naturalists in the field and for persons debating classification systems. Even in its time, Catesby's book was understood—like the great maps of the Renaissance—as a work both of science and of art.

People born in America also became caught up in the task of collecting and classifying American plants, which was international in character. Individuals with the same interests knew each other, corresponded, and exchanged writings, drawings, and specimens, whether they lived in Britain, the Netherlands, Sweden, or America. For colonists, however, the critical link to that small world was in England, and more specifically in the circle of people associated with the Royal Society of London. For example, Peter Collinson, Franklin's benefactor, not only encouraged Americans interested in science to make their work known to the Royal Society, he also introduced them to each other and to persons of note in Europe.

Take the case of John Bartram (1699–1777), a largely self-educated Quaker who started out with modest means but managed to buy a farm on the Schuylkill River about three miles outside Philadelphia, where he developed a five-acre botanic garden. His interest in botany recommended him to other Pennsylvanians who not only exchanged plants with him but lent him books and, best of all, put him in contact with Collinson. Bartram corresponded with Collinson, who was himself an avid gardener, from the 1730s until Collinson's death in 1768. During that period, Collinson sent Bartram supplies, seeds, plants, even clothes. He also recruited other patrons for Bartram's extensive collecting expeditions, told him whom to contact in other colonies, and introduced him to men of similar interests abroad, including Catesby and Linnaeus, who once called Bartram "the greatest natural botanist in the world." Collinson even got Bartram appointed royal botanist in 1765.

By modern standards, what a peculiar scientific community these men made up! Most participants were amateurs: the study of plants required little specialized knowledge. Field naturalists, persons caught up in the gardening craze, and men such as Linnaeus, who were attempting to define the taxonomic relationships within the realms of plants and animals, all found much to say to each other. The fact that building gardens with exotic plants was a genteel pastime, a way of marking off the members of a social elite, drew wealthy patrons into the group. But the community's borders readily stepped over social boundaries: talented men of no particular social distinction such as John Bartram—or Benjamin Franklin—were warmly embraced. In fact, many tradesmen and other "common men" flocked to scientific lectures, which became vastly popular in America and Europe during the eighteenth century. Gender proved a more formidable obstacle to membership than class, although Cadwallader Colden, a New Yorker of wide-ranging scientific interests, trained his bookish daughter Jane in botany. She became an informed and creative naturalist. Both Collinson and Linnaeus admired her drawings.

## SCIENCE AND SUPERSTITION

If a fascination with plants and, to a lesser extent, animals bound together many eighteenth-century American men of science, their interests usually spilled over into other subjects. For example, the Reverend Cotton Mather, an early colonial member of the Royal Society, sent the society a vast collection of *Curiosa Americana,* "facts" and observations that touched on astronomy, botany, zoology, geology, mathematics, anthropology, and medicine. Some of his submissions—on the existence of monsters, for example—seem today, as they did to members of the Royal Society, unsubstantiated and of questionable relevance to experimental science.

The line between science and superstition was not always easy to draw. Mather's greatest achievement lay in his advocacy of inoculation to avoid smallpox, one of a handful of advances in eighteenth-century medicine, a form of science that lagged behind others. Inoculation, according to one authority, was "the chief American contribution to medicine prior to the nineteenth century." Mather read about inoculation in the Royal Society's *Philosophical Transactions* and received confirmation of its efficacy from his slave Onesimus, who was familiar with its use in Africa. In short, liquid taken from a smallpox pustule on a stricken person's body was injected into slashes or with pinpricks on the arms of people undergoing the procedure. Inoculated people then came down with a mild form of smallpox (which, however, they could pass on in the natural way to others, who would get it in full force) and were henceforth immune.

When Mather and a local doctor began inoculating people after a smallpox epidemic hit Boston in 1721, they were greeted with outrage from, among others, the city's one university-trained medical doctor. It turned out, however, that while the mortality rate among noninoculated people who contracted the disease was 15 percent, the rate among the inoculated was about 2 percent (and those who died, Mather speculated, could have contracted smallpox or some other lethal disease before being inoculated). Those results were duly reported to the Royal Society. But before the results were in, it was not irrational to consider the injection of smallpox "juice" into healthy people an irresponsible act akin to the techniques used to identify witches.

A more compelling antidote to the mindset of times past lay in astronomy, a field in which, like botany, data from America was of compelling interest to Europeans. John Winthrop (1714–1779), a great-grandnephew of John Winthrop Jr., the first American fellow of the Royal Society, was for some forty years Harvard's Hollis Professor of Mathematics and Natural Philosophy (the contemporary term essentially for the physical sciences). One of the few professional scientists in the British colonies, Winthrop introduced several generations of Harvard students to modern science and mathematics, collected scientific instruments for the study of physical phenomena, submitted various papers based on his own celestial observations to the Royal Society, and also prepared lectures and articles of a scientific nature for the interested public. In 1755, he explained earthquakes, which were traditionally understood as manifestations of God's displeasure, in physical terms, noting their wave-like character.

Winthrop wrote about meteors and comets, which again were once understood as "wonders" by which God sent special messages to humans. He also participated in an extensive international effort to collect data on Venus's transit between sun and earth in 1761 and 1769, on the basis of which astronomers hoped to calculate the distances between the sun, earth, and other planets.

The most significant contributions to scientific understanding that emerged from the colonies were, however, Franklin's theories, confirmed by experiment, on the nature of electricity.

An eighteenth-century print depicting Franklin's kite experiment.

### FLYING KITES

Even as a young man, Benjamin Franklin knew who was who in science: on a visit to London in 1725, when he was not yet twenty years old, he wanted to meet Sir Isaac Newton and Sir Hans Sloane, both prominent members of the Royal Society. Franklin lacked the mathematical preparation to read Newton's *Principia* (1687), but he carefully studied Newton's *Optics* (1704), which was written in plain English and included scientific propositions with a "proof by experiments" provided for each. Soon he set out to do some experimenting himself.

When Franklin and a handful of fellow Philadelphians began studying electricity in the mid-1740s, it was a relatively new subject. English and French observers had made certain basic observations—that electricity spread from one area to another, and that some materials conducted electricity and others did not. A French investigator had also observed the existence of two kinds of electricity, which were created by rubbing different materials against each other. Franklin, who knew so little of

European scientific writings that he had no idea how much of what he said was new, also argued that electricity (or "electric fire," in the language of the day) behaved like a fluid and, moreover, was a distinct natural element made up of minute particles that could penetrate other types of matter. Rubbing materials against each other, Franklin said, transferred electrical matter out of one body (making it what Franklin called "negative") to another (which therefore became "positive"). Negatively charged bodies attracted and were attracted by positively charged ones. Electrical discharges, moreover, brought together negative and positive electrical charges without destroying electrical matter (this is now designated the principle of conservation of charge). Franklin's letters to Collinson described in detail experiments that suggested or confirmed his theories.

European experimenters of the time wondered at the workings of the Leyden jar, a device capable of storing electricity. Franklin believed that the jar's outside was negatively charged, the inside positively. He tried coating the sides of a plate of glass with metal foil and found it worked as well as a jar. One could, he reasoned, link a series of glass plates into an "electrical-battery" and so increase the electricity stored. Franklin also hypothesized that lightning was an electrical event that brought together and neutralized positive and negative charges in different clouds or between clouds and the earth. Lightning and electricity, he wrote, had many common characteristics: they gave off light of the same color, moved quickly, made cracks or noises, and could kill animals and melt metals. That suggested they were the same, but were they? "Let the experiment be made."

The experiment Franklin first proposed required the construction on some high tower or steeple of a sentry box large enough to hold a man and an electrical stand. An iron rod with a pointed top—which he said attracted electricity more effectively than blunt tops—should extend out the door of the sentry box and upward another twenty or thirty feet. The experimenter, whom Franklin instructed to keep his feet on the dry floor or on an insulated stool, should hold a loop of wire by a wax handle (which would act as an insulator). If, as Franklin hypothesized, the rod pulled electricity down from the clouds, it would produce sparks when the wire came near it. The sentry box experiment was successfully performed in France during 1752, after a French translation appeared of Franklin's *Experiments and Observations on Electricity.*

Then Franklin had another idea. Forget the sentry box: send a kite up during a thunderstorm, and that could pull electricity down from the clouds just as well. The kite, he said, should have a foot-long pointed wire attached to its upper end. At the other end of the twine, near the person flying the kite (who was to remain in a shelter, keeping the end of the string dry so it would not conduct electricity), a key should hang from a ribbon. When the kite and twine became wet by rain, they would "conduct the electric fire freely" and emit sparks when brought near the key. The electricity derived from that source could be used to "perform all the . . . Experiments which are usually done by rubbing a Glass Globe or Tube," which demonstrated "the Sameness of the Electric matter with that of Lightning." Whether Franklin in fact tried the experiment remains a subject of controversy. In any case, he did not write to Collinson on the subject until October, the same month a full account of his "Electrical Kite" experiment appeared in the *Pennsylvania Gazette.* By then, he had learned about the successful sentry box experiments in France.

Collinson published Franklin's *Experiments and Observations on Electricity, Made at Philadelphia in America* (first edition, 1751), a compendium of his letters on electricity, and presented it to the Royal Society. Two years later, the society awarded Franklin its prestigious Copley Medal, the highest distinction it could bestow, for his "Curious Experiments and Observations on Electricity." And in 1756, it elected him to membership, allowing him to add the prestigious letters F.R.S. (Fellow of the Royal Society) to his name.

Franklin's achievement was outstanding by any measure; his contributions to the basic understanding of electricity were of such significance that contemporaries compared him with Newton. Franklin did not, however, stop at the theoretical level; he also probed the practical applications of his discoveries. In 1753, he published instructions on "How to Secure Houses, etc., from Lightning" by use of pointed lightning rods, which could safely conduct strokes of lightning into the ground. Franklin regularly used scientific principles in inventing useful items—not just lightning rods but bifocals, the "Pennsylvania stove," and a musical instrument called the "armonica." Even his foray into demographic theory had, or so he argued, practical implications for British policymakers. Later in life, he conducted research on the Gulf Stream, an investigation into oceanography that he knew had important implications for navigation.

When Franklin began conducting experiments with his fellow Philadelphians, they in turn conferred with colonists elsewhere. By 1743, he appreciated the utility of these contacts sufficiently to propose forming an American Philosophical Society that would bring together "virtuosi or ingenious men residing in the several colonies." Members would "maintain a constant correspondence" on a long list of topics, from

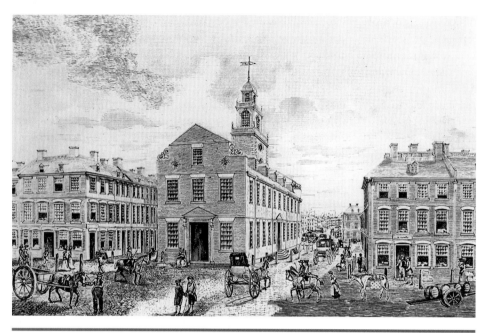

The Boston State House, built in 1713. The colony's General Court (its legislature) met there.

"new-discovered plants, herbs, trees, etc." and their uses to new ways of treating diseases, "new and useful improvements in any branch of mathematics" or chemistry, and "new mechanical inventions for saving labor, of improving the breed of animals, in planting or gardening, etc." Franklin's Philosophical Society would, in short, foster inventiveness among Americans for their own advantage and that "of mankind in general." And it would keep up a correspondence with the Royal Society of London and a similar group in Dublin that was "already begun by some intended members."

The suggestion came too early. It took another generation before "The American Philosophical Society . . . for Promoting Useful Knowledge" was successfully launched in Philadelphia. By then, Franklin had left behind the most fertile period in his scientific work, from 1743 to 1752, and embarked on another career—in politics.

## Being British, Becoming American

It was no accident that Franklin wrote about the "American" population, grouping the colonies together, or proposed an American Philosophical Society, not an organization for Penn-

sylvania alone. A sense of common identity was slowly developing among many people of British North America, one that involved an intense common identification with the mother country and also an understanding that they were members of the British family with certain marked distinctions.

The imitation of British styles in all the colonies and the increased contact among colonists with an interest in science helped bind together what were once separate and distinctive communities. But the most powerful forces working to break down colonial particularisms and forge a common identity as British and American during the eighteenth century were politics, religion, and war.

### KING AND COMMONS, COLONIAL STYLE

Each colony's politics possessed unique characteristics, but the politics of all the colonies—with the possible exception of Connecticut and Rhode Island, where all officials were elected—had a lot in common. Colonists thought of their governments as versions of the much-praised British constitution, under which the king (or governor), the House of Lords (or council), and the House of Commons (or colonial assembly) shared power. In Britain, it was said, those powers were balanced after the Glorious Revolution, allowing a stability in government that also protected liberty by preventing any one power from oppressing the people. That was not, in fact, how government worked in Britain: the king usually found ways to influence members of the increasingly powerful Commons so they could work together. In America, however, governors and assemblies often squared off against each other. Such squabbles resembled English politics of the previous century, when Parliament, and particularly the House of Commons, grappled for power with formidable kings. The reason for the difference lay in the contrasting impacts of the Glorious Revolution in England and in America.

The post-1688 revolutionary settlement curtailed monarchical power in England but imposed no similar checks on the power of royal governors. As a result, royal governors wielded some powers that even the king could not claim. In England, for example, the king lost his right to veto acts of Parliament early in the eighteenth century. Royal governors could, however, veto acts of assembly and in fact were required by their instructions from the king to veto certain kinds of laws and to suspend the operation of others until the Crown could review them. A governor could also dissolve or prorogue an assembly: he could, that is, bring it to an end and call a new election, or else tell the representatives to go home until he felt like calling them back into session. Although governors could keep particularly congenial assemblies in place indefinitely, the king had to call an election at least every three, and later every seven, years. Governors could appoint judges, who, beginning in the 1750s, held office at the king's pleasure, which meant they could be removed from office if the king (or his representative, the governor) didn't like the way they operated. English judges, by contrast, held office for life on good behavior. And while the king had to contend with a House of Lords made up in part of nobles who inherited their offices, governors worked with councils whose members were, like the governors, appointed by the king—which meant they should have been, and generally were, on the governor's side in any controversies. In all these ways, the governors were, within their colonies, even more powerful than the king.

Not that the royal governors (or, with some variations, the governors in the proprietary colonies of Pennsylvania, Delaware, and Maryland) had it easy. A governor was usually dependent on the assembly for his salary, which gave the assembly quite a bit of leverage over him. Governors were always instructed to secure a permanent salary, but the assemblies (with the exception of Virginia, which after Bacon's Rebellion levied a tax on tobacco to pay its governor) refused. Nor did governors enjoy the patronage power—the power to appoint people to various offices—that helped the king influence the House of Commons to support him and his policies. What patronage the governors once exercised was, in the course of the eighteenth century, whittled away by either the Crown or the assembly. Nor did they have much flexibility in establishing working relationships with the assemblies since their instructions and also their commissions (formal public documents that laid out the government of a colony) constrained their freedom of action in one way after another. Finally, because governors were appointed through the British patronage system, they were

vulnerable once they left for America: others could play the same game they had played, and force them out of office. The average tenure of an eighteenth-century royal governor was only about five years—not enough time to build up much power.

The assemblies not only commanded greater stability than governors (some members might lose an election, but rarely if ever were all delegates replaced) but held a strong sense of their importance as the provincial equivalent of Britain's House of Commons. The assemblies demanded privileges enjoyed by the Commons, such as the exclusive right to initiate money bills. Then they claimed powers the Commons did not have: they insisted, for example, on extraordinary powers over the colonies' finances and on appointing the colonies' treasurers. The assemblies were usually the only organ of provincial government chosen by the people, which added to their sense of importance. The people, in turn, were represented by a relatively wide electorate for the time, consisting of white Protestant adult males who could fulfill a property qualification such as fifty acres of land, which was often pretty easy to acquire. Nonlandholding urban craftsmen could also often vote. (It should be said, however, that large numbers of qualified colonists chose not to vote.)

As the elected assemblies rose in strength, the powers of appointed councils gradually declined. As a result, provincial

The seventeenth-century political philosopher John Locke, in a portrait by John Greenhill, c.1672–76.

politics often led to knock-down, drag-out, two-sided fights between the governors and assemblies, or more exactly between groups within the assembly that supported one side or the other. Conflict of that sort was not yet considered altogether legitimate: the day when struggles for power were "just politics" with no suggestion of sedition remained at least a century away. Contenders could justify their opposition to the king's governor by claiming that he was attempting to usurp authority beyond his allotted share and to violate the liberty of the people. That was what the opponents of Charles I and James II had argued in the seventeenth century. And so the colonists lapped up late seventeenth-century Whig writings such as Algernon Sidney's *Discourses Concerning Government* and John Locke's *Second Treatise of Government,* which were written to justify opposition to James II, or eighteenth-century writings that drew on those and similar sources, such as John Trenchard and Thomas Gordon's popular newspaper essays, "Cato's Letters." Colonists also read French political writings, including Montesquieu's *Spirit of the Laws,* which discussed the British constitution.

In general, writers in the English revolutionary tradition saw political officials as trustees for the people, who had first set up government to protect their freedom. Should officials exercise powers the people had not given them or fail to protect popular freedom, the people could remove them from office and, if they chose, reconstitute government so it would better serve their interests. To be sure, revolution was not to be indulged in casually. Liberty required a stable rule of law; it could not thrive in the midst of anarchy, so writers articulated a series of conditions to be met before the people could resist or replace their rulers. Their grievances had to be so significant that "the body of the people" recognized their danger, and all the peaceful means of resistance had to be tried before force became acceptable. Then no more force could be used than was necessary. By the mid-eighteenth century, resistance was also limited by a rule of prudence. Unless they had a good chance of winning, the people should not rise up against their rulers because if they lost they'd be even worse off.

Colonists did not need to read Sidney or Locke or Trenchard and Gordon to learn these "revolution principles": they encountered them in a score of other writers, in newspapers and sermons, even in a book like Sir William Blackstone's *Commentaries on the Laws of England,* first published in the 1760s, which treated Locke as an authority on the Glorious Revolution of 1689. The colonists had good reason, then, to assume that their political ideology was nothing less than orthodox English thought. "The people" were, moreover, an active force in eighteenth-century American communities. "The people" acted as militia or posse members to enforce the law and, sometimes, as mobs to defend the public interest extra-legally where the established government did not or could not act.

To the powers that governed Britain, however, the idea that the people had a real and practical power to judge their rulers was part of a past that had to be buried so Britain could enjoy its eighteenth-century stability. Parliament—king, Lords, and Commons acting together—was sovereign: that is, it exercised ultimate power that was over and beyond the people "out of doors." From that perspective, the truculence of colonial assemblies and other popular institutions (town meetings and juries, for example) constituted a violation of good order; and from mid-century, British officials proposed several different plans for reorganizing colonial governments to reinforce the power of the mother country and its appointed colonial officials. Once Britain tried to implement those plans, however, the results were predictable. The colonists would resist, citing perfectly fine, seventeenth-century English principles to justify their opposition.

## THE RECONSTRUCTION OF AMERICAN RELIGION

Religion more than anything else made the first British colonists turn their backs on each other. Few who lived in seventeenth-century Massachusetts had anything good to say about Quakers, and Virginians were not altogether welcoming toward Puritans. By the 1760s, however, hostility between different Protestant groups had declined considerably. One reason was a wave of mid-eighteenth-century religious revivals remembered as the "Great Awakening."

The revivals answered a decline in religious fervor that was apparent in a reduced incidence of "conversion experiences" among second- and third-generation New Englanders. The children of church members, these people had been baptized as infants, but unless they later gave evidence of receiving grace they could not become full members of their Congregational (or Puritan) churches. Then could their children be baptized? Ministers, dismayed as they watched church membership decline precipitously, met in 1657 and came up with a makeshift solution known as the Half-Way covenant: the children of church members who lived upright lives but had not experienced God's grace could become "halfway" members of the church, distinguished from full members only in that they could not take communion or vote on church matters. They

The Methodist evangelist George Whitefield, as painted by John Wollaston, soon after Whitefield's famous 1739–41 tour of colonies that sparked revivals everywhere.

could also have their children baptized. That was a big step back from the rigor of first-generation Puritanism, and the back-stepping continued thereafter. The difference between full and halfway church members gradually faded away, and membership came to turn not on the willingness of an inscrutable God to save depraved sinners but on human reason and will. "Try whether you can't give . . . consent" to God's will, Cotton Mather urged his listeners; "if you *can*, 'tis done." Church membership, nevertheless, continued to decline.

Much the same process had occurred outside New England by the eighteenth century—until the revivals instituted an about-face. They began among the Dutch Reformed congregations in New Jersey after the Reverend Theodore Frelinghuysen arrived from Holland in 1719, preached moving sermons that stressed piety over good works, and within a decade had waves of people "awakening" to religion. Soon the revivals spread to the nearby Presbyterian congregation of the Reverend Gilbert Tennent; then they began to appear farther north, in Connecticut. In 1734–35, the Reverend Jonathan Edwards set a revival going in Northampton, Massachusetts, that spread throughout the Connecticut Valley. Suddenly, Edwards recalled, "all the talk in companies . . . was upon the

things of religion, and no other talk was anywhere relished," and "the spirit of God went on in His saving influences . . . in a truly wonderful and astonishing manner."

The flood tide of the revivals came, however, with the arrival of George Whitefield, a twenty-four-year-old English evangelist, in 1739 at Philadelphia. In only nine days, Whitefield effected a wonderful change in the ways of Philadelphians who had been "thoughtless or indifferent about religion." Suddenly, Benjamin Franklin recalled, "one could not walk thro' town in an evening without hearing psalms sung in different families of every street." Whitefield traveled through New Jersey, New York, and New England, with similar results everywhere; the audience for his farewell sermon in Boston was estimated at over 23,000, more than the town's total population. Later he toured the South, then revisited the middle colonies and New England before returning to England in 1741. Waves of religious awakenings continued to break out here and there over the next few decades—among Virginia's Presbyterians in 1748, and later among Methodists—but they never reached the high pitch of 1739–41.

It's possible to dismiss the revivals' appeal as an exercise of theatricality in a society starved for entertainment. The preachers were nothing if not moving speakers: even Franklin, who remained untouched by Whitefield's message, admired his oratory (though he seems to have spent his time during one outdoor sermon conducting experiments to see how far the evangelist's voice carried). That cannot explain, however, why an ordinary farmer like Nathan Cole in Connecticut dropped everything when he heard Whitefield was going to preach at a nearby town and found himself "in a trembling fear" even before the evangelist opened his mouth. Or why, after realizing that his "righteousness would not save" him, Cole became obsessed with "hell fire" and his own sinfulness until he was, like Puritans of old, reborn with the grace of God. Whitefield and other revivalist preachers, unlike most of their counterparts in Europe, were distinctly Calvinistic: they stressed the distance between man and God, and they shouted out—like Tennent—that men were "damned, damned, damned." Did audiences perhaps sense that the pleasures eighteenth-century prosperity brought, and the efforts that people invested in a struggle for material things, were deviations from God's way, and find some relief in confronting their sinfulness? Or is it best to explain the Great Awakening, as Jonathan Edwards did, simply as an amazing work of God?

The results were no less amazing. The Awakening led to the founding of a host of new colleges, including today's

Brown, Princeton, Dartmouth, Rutgers, and the University of Pennsylvania. Revivalists were clearly not anti-intellectual; they founded educational institutions to train American-born ministers who could carry on their religious traditions.

More important, the revivals redrew the map of American religion. Not everyone was swept in by the Awakening: old-line conservatives who found the revivalists offensive or dangerous refused to let them preach in their churches, forcing itinerant ministers to preach to crowds in public halls or outdoors in open fields. But then the revivalists lashed back at the conservatives, condemning them as an "unconverted ministry," in Tennent's words, or a body of "dead men" to God, in Whitefield's. Communities split between conservative "old lights" and revivalist "new lights" (or the "new side" among Presbyterians) who left their local parishes and joined congregations gathered by choice and conviction, not by place of residence. The Presbyterian Church split into two synods, adding to the religious diversity that new immigrant groups brought to Pennsylvania and the southern backcountry. Even the orthodox Congregationalist colonies of New England were transformed. Some conservatives gravitated toward the Anglican Church, going all the way in their search for order and stability, while dissenters distributed themselves among hundreds of religious congregations, many of which eventually became Baptist. The dozen or so American Baptist churches in 1740 had increased to some 500 by 1775, and they were spread throughout the colonies from New England into the South.

So dramatic a transformation necessarily brought pressure on the established churches—churches that provincial governments endorsed and supported—that existed in all the colonies except Pennsylvania, Delaware, and Rhode Island. The Baptists in particular resented requirements that they contribute to another church or suffer civil disabilities as a result of their convictions. Eventually, Baptists opposed any interference whatsoever by civil government in people's religious beliefs and practices. Moreover, despite the bickering that the revivals first provoked, the multiplication of religious groups ultimately led to a new acceptance of religious differences. What once had been sects arrayed against each other became denominations, groups within American Protestantism distinguished by the convictions of their members, which others could respect even if they did not share those convictions.

Colonial Catholics were left out of that development. They remained, in the opinion of their Protestant neighbors, outsiders, advocates of a false and dangerous religion. Despite the splintering of churches under the influence of the Awakening, most British colonists developed a common identity as militant Protestants in the course of the eighteenth century as a result of the long series of wars that they and the British government were fighting against the Catholic powers, France and Spain.

## THE COLONIAL WARS

Most of America's eighteenth-century wars were spillovers from struggles that centered in Europe. The war known in America as King William's War (1689–97), and in Europe as the War of the League of Augsburg, had scarcely ended when Queen Anne's War (1702–13), known in Europe as the War of the Spanish Succession, began. After a generation of peace came King George's War (1739–48), also known as the War of Jenkins's Ear (after a smuggler who said he lost an ear to the Spanish in an encounter off the coast of Florida) and then as the War of the Austrian Succession once France entered the conflict.

In the colonies, these wars retraced well-trod tracks over and over with few permanent effects. The British won Newfoundland and Nova Scotia from France in the Treaty of Utrecht (1713), which ended Queen Anne's War. The French then built a fort at Louisbourg to protect the entrance to the St. Lawrence River, and it became a place where privateers (private ships licensed to attack enemy ships) found harbor and so a thorn in the side of New England. Massachusetts mounted a major attack on the fort at enormous expense in 1745 and managed to take it. But the British returned it to France under the Treaty of Aix-la-Chapelle (1748). Expeditions against St. Augustine in the South had no more lasting results.

Military action brought some people—contractors, for example—enormous profits, but the most enduring results of the early colonial wars were death and instability. Mortality rates for soldiers were appalling, though more from disease than combat. Only about 600 of the 3,600 colonists who joined a 1741 campaign against Porto Bello and Cartagena (both Spanish mainland bases in the Caribbean) returned home; Massachusetts alone lost 90 percent of its 500 volunteers to yellow fever, dysentery, or starvation because of extreme mismanagement. During the 1745 siege of Louisbourg, only about 150 of almost 4,000 soldiers died—but later, while militiamen did garrison duty there, dysentery killed about half of the survivors "like rotten sheep," according to one witness. The loss of so many men had enormous ripple effects. Even before the Louisbourg operation, almost a third of Boston's adult women were widows and, in many cases, dependents on public charity. That pushed taxes upward, driving those who had a choice to other

The young George Washington in uniform, painted in 1772 by Charles Willson Peale.

communities. The problems of war, moreover, had a way of persisting after the treaties were signed. Indian attacks continued between wars, and privateers often became pirates in peacetime, posing a recurrent threat to merchant shippers. These were problems the colonists could live without.

Given relative rates of population growth, a major conflict seemed likely between Britain and its rivals for North America. The Hispanic population of Florida reached only about 3,000 by 1760. French Louisiana also grew haltingly in its early years: in 1731, there were only about 2,000 Europeans there—and they were a polyglot group, including soldiers, convicts, and a variety of other immigrants—plus an additional 3,800 black slaves. Three decades later, Louisiana's white population had doubled, to 4,000, with another 5,000 slaves. New France, or Canada, was larger, with about 55,000 whites in the mid-eighteenth century. But by then, the British mainland colonies' population was 1.2 million and growing rapidly. Could it possibly remain strung out on a long, wide strip of land along the Atlantic seaboard? The Board of Trade encouraged the British population to expand into contested territory, which in 1721 it pronounced "one of the most effectual means to prevent the growing power of the French" in the West. The Crown later

approved the creation of Georgia specifically to block Spanish possession of the land south of the Carolinas.

There remained, of course, a substantial number of Indians with long-standing claims to lands contested among Europeans. Colonial negotiators tried to settle those claims in a series of treaties that they generally interpreted more generously than the Indians. For example, under the Treaty of Lancaster (1744), negotiated on the Pennsylvania frontier by the Iroquois and representatives of Maryland, Virginia, and Pennsylvania, the Indians gave up those lands that lay within Virginia's charter. On that basis, Virginia expansionists claimed title to territory along the Ohio River and the Great Lakes, which the Indians surely did not mean to give up. In 1747, one of the negotiators at Lancaster helped organize the Ohio Company of Virginia, which two years later received from the Crown a grant of 200,000 acres beyond the mountains and the Monongahela River with a promise of 300,000 more if they settled 2,000 people on that land within the next seven years. Soon other companies organized to get in on the bonanza. The ingredients were in place for an explosive confrontation.

It began in the Ohio Country. In 1749, the French sent an emissary there to warn British traders to leave, impress the Indians, and plant along the Allegheny and Ohio rivers lead plates stating that the territory belonged to France. Then the French destroyed a major post where Indians and Pennsylvanians traded, and began building forts to confirm their possession. Virginia's governor demanded that the French leave "the King of Great Britain's territories." In the winter of 1754, he sent a company of about fifty Virginia militiamen to build a fort at the juncture of the Allegheny and Monongahela rivers, where Pittsburgh now stands. The site was important: from there, the Ohio River flows down to the Mississippi. But in April, a French army forced the Virginians out and proceeded to build its own Fort Duquesne.

Meanwhile, another Virginia militia company under a twenty-two-year-old officer named George Washington made its way through the woods to support Virginia's fort builders, unaware that they'd been displaced. Washington was a minimally educated surveyor and planter of no distinction, anxious to join the ranks of the colony's genteel leaders. He had little military experience. Upon learning that a French company was near his camp at Great Meadows, he decided to attack. The details of the engagement are murky; but in the end, a dozen or more Frenchmen were dead, including their commander, who had been horribly murdered by an Indian allied to the British.

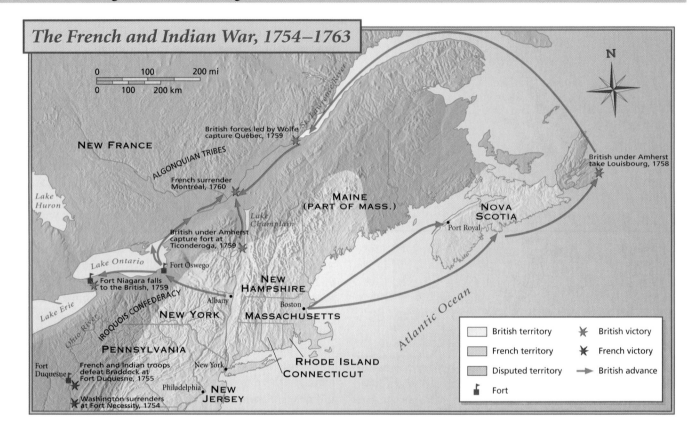

### The French and Indian War, 1754–1763

Washington turned back toward home. Chased by the French, he hastily constructed a camp aptly named Fort Necessity. There, after suffering a humiliating defeat in a driving rain that kept the Virginians' muskets from firing, he signed terms of capitulation that, given the conditions, he could hardly read. These terms not only committed the Virginians to leave the Ohio Valley and not return for a year but also placed responsibility for the French commander's "assassination" squarely on Washington. That was no way to begin a glorious military career. Young Washington's blundering in 1754 set off the last and greatest of the colonial wars, the French and Indian War, known in Europe, with its later start, as the Seven Years' War (1756–63), a conflict of massive proportions that brought actions in Africa, India, and the Philippines as well as America and Europe.

### THE FRENCH AND INDIAN WAR

The French did well in the war's opening years. The civilian population of New France might have been relatively low, but the colony included a strong component of soldier-settlers under one strong government. By contrast, the British were scattered in thirteen separate colonies more given to bickering than cooperating with each other. To counteract that problem, the British Board of Trade called a conference of colonial delegates to meet at Albany in 1754. Seven delegations appeared, but neither the colonial legislatures nor the Crown showed much enthusiasm for a plan of union, largely drafted by Franklin, that the delegates proposed. It called for "one general government" with a governor-general and a representative Grand Council to manage Indian affairs and defense and to raise taxes for those purposes. "Everyone cries, a union is necessary," Franklin wrote, "but when they come to the manner and form of the union, their weak noodles are perfectly distracted." Negotiations with the 150 Indian delegates who appeared were equally ineffectual. The Iroquois held tight to their neutrality.

The British nonetheless decided to answer the events of 1754 with a complex military campaign to check French advances. They sent General Edward Braddock to command the operation, which came to a bad end. Braddock set out in 1755 with an army of 2,500 men to take Fort Duquesne, which at the time held about 250 French regulars and Canadian militiamen. In desperation, the French persuaded their Indian allies to ambush the advancing British column, which they did. Braddock's lead soldiers retreated under fire, causing chaos among the troops behind them. In the end, some 900 men died, including Braddock. Young Washington was among the survivors.

The war didn't turn around until the great war minister William Pitt came into power in 1758 and decided not to concentrate on the war that had broken out in Europe two years earlier, but to put Britain's main effort into taking Canada. Pitt promised to compensate colonists for their expenses in the war, which had a magical effect on the assemblies' willingness to cooperate, and sent Britain's best commanders to march against French strongholds. In 1758, the British suffered a serious defeat at Ticonderoga, a French fort on Lake Champlain, but an army under General Jeffrey Amherst took Louisbourg. Then the French abandoned Fort Duquesne as British troops came near and their Indian allies defected. For the British, it was a good beginning.

The next year went even better. Pitt planned an ambitious campaign. First he would take Fort Niagara, between Lakes Ontario and Erie, and cut off French access to the lakes further west. Then a two-pronged attack would move against Quebec and Montreal. The first, under Amherst, would come up from New York along the water route from the Hudson River through Lakes George and Champlain to the Richelieu River and the St. Lawrence. The second, under General James Wolfe, would travel up the St. Lawrence from Louisbourg.

The scheme worked, but not exactly as planned. A combined British, American, and Indian force took Fort Niagara on July 25; and the expedition under Amherst captured Ticonderoga in 1759 but could get no farther than Lake Champlain before winter set in. The taking of Quebec was then left to Wolfe, who faced a ticking clock—he had to be out of the St. Lawrence before the water froze. Wolfe put Quebec under siege, but the French commander, the Marquis de Montcalm, refused to engage, waiting for winter to save his day. Finally, in September, Wolfe found a way to float ships down the river at night to a spot from which his troops could scurry up a hill to a flatland, the "Plains of Abraham," outside the city. When morning broke on September 13, Montcalm looked out on Wolfe's army in formation. He engaged; in the resulting battle, both Wolfe and Montcalm were killed, but when the shooting stopped, the British held Quebec. The next year, they easily took Montreal, and for all practical purposes the war was over in America although it lingered on abroad.

The Peace of Paris (1763), which finally ended the war, redrew the map of North America. All of Canada and Louisiana east of the Mississippi, with the exception of New Orleans, went to Britain. Spain, an ally of France, gave Florida to Britain—although by a secret protocol, France gave Spain those portions of Louisiana west of the Mississippi. Except for two islands in the Gulf of St. Lawrence, which were to be used by fishermen, and the sugar islands of Guadeloupe and Martinique, the French had lost their American empire.

## TAKING PRIDE

The British victory was great, and the colonists, above all those who had fought in the war along with British regulars, shared in the glory. To be sure, they had been confined in separate units

A romanticized painting of the death of General James Wolfe during the battle at Quebec in September 1759. The American painter Benjamin West created this, his most famous work, in 1770.

## Being British, Becoming American

Benjamin Franklin printed this "Join, or Die" cartoon just before the Albany Congress convened in 1754. Franklin was a strong advocate of colonial unity then and in later times.

and consigned much of the slug work of war. New England soldiers in particular had looked on the regulars and their willingness to hold the field under fire with a kind of amazement: imagine just standing there when you could hide behind a tree. The neatly ordered British camps, with tents arranged according to rank and sanitary facilities removed from eating and sleeping areas, must also have awakened awe. The provincials' camps were so different, made up of a wild assortment of huts and shacks and sometimes framed houses arranged willy-nilly; and the farm-boy soldiers were hard to restrain from relieving themselves anywhere near at hand, much as they did at home. Their armies, too, were different, made up of like people commanded by local dignitaries who were often kinsmen, and who tried to persuade their men to do the right thing rather than order them around.

And what sense could the colonists make of the cruel British discipline, the horrible floggings of soldiers with cats-o'-nine-tails, sometimes for hundreds of lashes until a man's back had no more skin? Or the executions for what sometimes seemed minor infractions of rules? The British soldiers' proclivity for "cussing" and lewd women, and their disregard for the Sabbath, also seemed alien and morally repulsive. If the British found the New Englanders to be bad soldiers, the provincials found the redcoats to be sinful men.

How important were these differences? The colonists were not a people apart but a people among, a denominated group within the British family with certain distinctions, but no more than differentiated the Scots from the English or the Welsh. Americans' differences from fellow Britons "at home" were far less in the eighteenth century than they had been in the seventeenth, when poverty and the task of surviving kept them from imitating English ways and fashions. Colonists had no intention of following the morals of the king's armies, but in other ways they expected to be more, not less, like the British as time went on. What most colonists wanted was to approximate the ways of the mother country, their model of achievement and fashion.

Benjamin Franklin was no longer in America when the peace came. He had traveled to London to persuade the Crown to displace the proprietors and govern Pennsylvania directly. Once there, he formalized his membership in the Royal Society and attended meetings regularly, presenting letters and papers, joining in discussions, making it his "club." How wonderful to have such esteemed intellectual colleagues close at hand, and to be able to talk and argue and speculate together almost at will. In that company, the American master of electricity commanded a certain respect: in 1760, Franklin became an elected member of the Royal Society's governing council; the next year, he helped select papers for the *Philosophical Transactions*. He was living the good life. Best of all, there was no reason it should ever end.

## Suggested Reading

Fred Anderson, *A People's Army: Massachusetts Soldiers in the Seven Years' War* (1984), and *The Crucible of War: The Seven Years' War and the Fate of Empire in British North America, 1754–1766* (2000)

Bernard Bailyn, *The Origin of American Politics* (1967)

Bernard Bailyn and Philip D. Morgan, eds., *Strangers within the Realm: Cultural Margins of the First British Empire* (1991)

Ira Berlin, *Many Thousands Gone: The First Two Centuries of Slavery in North America* (1998)

Richard L. Bushman, *The Refinement of America: Persons, Houses, Cities* (1992)

Cary Carson, Ronald Hoffman, and Peter J. Albert, eds., *Of Consuming Interests: The Style of Life in the Eighteenth Century* (1994)

I. Bernard Cohen, *Benjamin Franklin's Science* (1990)

Philip D. Morgan, *Slave Counterpoint: Black Culture in the Eighteenth-Century Chesapeake and Lowcountry* (1998)

Raymond Phineas Stearns, *Science in the British Colonies of America* (1970)

New Perspectives on the Transatlantic Slave Trade, *William and Mary Quarterly*, 3d Series, LVIII (January, 2001)

# Chapter Review

## Summary QUESTIONS

- Why did slaves first become a substantial part of the population in North American colonies during the late seventeenth and early eighteenth centuries?

- How did slave society differ between the Chesapeake and South Carolina?

- Which parts of the "Old World" provided large numbers of immigrants to eighteenth-century British North America?

- What explains the prosperity of the colonies in the eighteenth century?

- How could colonists of the mid-eighteenth century think of themselves both as British and, increasingly, as Americans?

## Chronology

| | |
|---|---|
| **1619** | First African slaves arrive at Jamestown. |
| **1702–13** | Queen Anne's War (in Europe, War of the Spanish Succession). |
| **1704** | The first colonial newspaper, the *Boston News Letter,* appears. |
| **1722–25** | Mark Catesby's travels result in the first guide to American plants and animals. |
| **1732** | Georgia is founded. |
| **1739** | Stono Rebellion, slave uprising in South Carolina. |
| **1739–41** | High point of the Great Awakening. |
| **1739–48** | King George's War (in Europe, War of the Austrian Succession). |
| **1745** | Siege of Louisbourg, on the St. Lawrence River. |
| **1752** | Benjamin Franklin devises "Electrical Kite" experiment. |
| **1754–63** | The French and Indian War (in Europe, beginning 1756, the Seven Years' War). |

## Key Terms

Indentured servitude (p. 109)

Slave society (p. 112)

Consumer goods (p. 122)

Provincial politics (p. 129–130)

Great Awakening (p. 130)

**Access the *Inventing America* StudySpace at wwnorton.com/studyspace**

PERSONAL PLAN ■ REVIEW MATERIALS ■ RESEARCH AIDS ■ MULTIMEDIA

# Part 2

## A NEW REPUBLIC

THE TROUBLE BETWEEN GREAT BRITAIN and its North American colonies began in the mid-1760s with a fight over taxes. The colonists insisted that the British Parliament could not tax them without their consent. In response, Parliament asserted its right to bind the colonists "in all cases whatsoever." Since Parliament would not back down from this stance, the colonists gradually came to see their situation as a conflict between an imperial authority determined to exercise absolute power and a people threatened with "slavery." The Americans resisted exercises of "unconstitutional" authority while pleading for redress of their grievances. But, when those hopes failed—and after Britain hired German soldiers to help put down the colonists' "rebellion"—the Second Continental Congress finally renounced the rule of George III and claimed a "free and equal place" among the "powers of the earth."

The Declaration of Independence carefully stated that the Americans proposed to "alter" not to "expunge" their former systems of government. Some aspects of the British system seemed worth keeping—elected assemblies and trial by jury, for example—but the British system of monarchy and hereditary power had to be excised. In 1776, the Americans founded a republic, which they defined as a government where all power came directly or indirectly from the people. All such governments, in the past, had failed. So once again, survival would be the primary challenge of the new American republic. The establishment of a republic made the American cause something more than a colonial rebellion. It became a revolution; and one that Thomas Paine argued, was of importance to all mankind.

The revolution could not succeed without a victory in the war with Britain. Yet victory seemed anything but certain

*American Commissioners of the Preliminary Peace Negotiations with Great Britain* , an unfinished painting by Benjamin West (1782). From left, John Jay, John Adams, Benjamin Franklin, Henry Laurens, and Franklin's grandson William Temple Franklin.

when the fighting began on April 19, 1775, in the Massachusetts towns of Concord and Lexington. But eventually, in October 1781, the Continental Army won a decisive victory at Yorktown, Virginia—thanks in no small part to the help of the French army and navy. The final peace treaty, the Peace of Paris (1783), granted the United States title to all the land south of Canada and north of Florida between the Atlantic seaboard and the Mississippi River. It also won British recognition of American independence.

In the meantime, the establishment of a republic led to other transformations. Under Congress's instructions, the states designed and adopted the world's first written constitutions. Social changes followed as well. Republics were traditionally associated with equality, which the Americans tried to realize at first just among white men. Soon, however, Americans began asking what other groups—religious dissenters? blacks? women?—were affected by the doctrine that all men are "born" or "created equal" with a God-given right to "life, liberty, and the pursuit of happiness." State legislatures began to dismantle the old church establishments that gave preference to the members of one church over others, and passed laws that brought an end to the institution of slavery, either gradually or immediately, in many northern states. The steps toward racial and gender equality were, however, modest at best.

State legislatures also sought to make the United States economically independent of Britain. They encouraged new ventures by issuing patent and copyright laws. They created corporations in a redesigned form to avoid the taint of privilege, which had long discredited corporate entities. Newly established American corporations built roads and bridges and improved river transportation to facilitate internal trade. Those early corporations included the country's first commercial banks, which provided a way of mobilizing money for the use of entrepreneurs. No longer was American culture primarily imitative, as it had been before 1776. It had become innovative.

The most important innovation of all was perhaps the drafting and ratification of the federal constitution. By replacing the nearly bankrupt Confederation, the reformers of 1787 and 1788 tried once again to establish what George Washington once called "a respectable nation." However, much remained for the new federal Congress to do. Under the leadership of Secretary of the Treasury Alexander Hamilton, it approved measures that put the United States on a firm financial basis, it rounded out the judiciary, and it sent to the states for ratification a "bill of rights" to be appended to the Constitution. The 1790s saw an immense surge in prosperity as wars in Europe opened new opportunities for American merchants. While at home, divisions within the political realm fostered the emergence of a two-party system not anticipated by the founders. Later, in 1803, the Louisiana Purchase would dramatically expand the size of the new nation encouraging exploration and expansion.

Divisions over a trade embargo championed by President Thomas Jefferson—like the divisions over the Alien and Sedition Acts a decade earlier— threatened to tear the new nation apart in the early part of the century. It then suffered repeated humiliations during its second war with Britain, the War of 1812, which, however, also allowed the growth of a domestic manufacturing sector. Later, in 1819, sectional conflict reappeared, when Missouri applied for admission to the Union as a slave state. But tensions declined the year after as Congress adopted a compromise that not only settled the current problem but also decided which states, yet to be carved from the Louisiana territory, could be organized as slave states and which could not. Perhaps, it seemed, that divisive issue had finally been settled for good.

As a result, the United States approached 1826 and the 50th anniversary of independence with a strong sense of pride and patriotism. The founders' work seemed over and a new generation had come into power determined to build on their achievements. The republic had survived and, for the moment, its future looked good.

# TOWARD INDEPENDENCE:
## 1764–1783

This engraving of the events at Lexington and Concord, by Amos Doolittle, shows British soldiers marching through "the South Part of Lexington" while being shot at by colonists on April 19, 1775. At the time, Doolittle was a member of the New Haven militia, which arrived in Massachusetts soon after the battles were fought. Doolittle therefore did not witness the events he portrayed, but claimed to work "from original paintings taken on the spot," apparently by someone else. His engravings, which he sold to the public, present the American side of the story. They prominently display, for example, private homes set on fire by the king's soldiers.

141

■ **What were the main points of dispute between the American colonists and Britain in the 1760s and 1770s?**

■ **How did the Americans gradually assume authority over their own affairs in the period before independence?**

■ **How did the United States manage to defeat Britain in the War for Independence?**

Never were the American colonists more proud of being British than at the end of the French and Indian War. Britain's heroes—above all the great war minister William Pitt and his generals, Sir Jeffrey Amherst and James Wolfe—were American heroes. In every colony, Americans expressed the deepest affection for King George III, who was only twenty-two years old in 1760 when he inherited the throne from his grandfather.

By all signs, Britain's victory and the Peace of Paris (1763) marked a watershed in American history. With all of French and Spanish North America east of the Mississippi except for the city of New Orleans under the British flag, the persistent wars that had dogged colonial life for a century and more were, it seemed, finally over. Moreover, once the free government of Protestant Britain replaced what the colonists described as the "absolutism" of Catholic France and Spain, an unparalleled era of growth and prosperity seemed sure to follow. Celebratory sermons by New England clergymen told the story: by bringing about "the downfall of New France, the North American Babylon," one preacher explained to his congregation, God had transplanted "British liberty to where till now it was unknown." With the colonists' "peaceful and undisturbed enjoyment of this good land, and the blessings of our gracious God with it," he foresaw "towns enlarged, settlements increased, and this howling wilderness become a fruitful field which the Lord hath blessed." Another Congregationalist pastor went so far as to predict that the population of America, now that it was thrown open to British colonization, would grow to 60 million in a century and a half—a figure that understated by over 30 million the population of the United States alone in 1910.

Nowhere in the victory celebrations of the early 1760s was there even a hint of the greater historical watershed to come, the event remembered as the American Revolution. Yet thirteen years after the Peace of Paris established Britain's hege-mony on the North American continent, the people of the original thirteen British colonies declared their independence, threw off not just the rule of George III but of kings and all other hereditary rulers, and reinvented themselves as a new nation "separate and equal" among the "powers of the earth." Independence was not what either the Americans or the British wanted; each side, in its way, struggled to prevent it for over a decade. And yet it came. The question is why.

## "No Taxation Without Representation," 1764–1774

There was one problem with the colonists' expansive vision of their future at the end of the French and Indian War. The lands between the British settlements and the Mississippi River were already inhabited, and the Indians' presence was likely to interfere with British-Americans' "peaceful and undisturbed enjoyment of this good land."

In 1763, the British tried to pacify the frontier by issuing a proclamation that forbade colonial settlements west of a line that ran through the Appalachians, an inland chain of mountains that extended from New England into the Carolinas. The proclamation dismayed Americans who dreamed of westward expansion.

Britain also decided to retain French posts in the trans-Appalachian West. General Jeffrey Amherst, the British commander in chief, abruptly ended the French practice of giving Indians substantial presents, which had sustained the chiefs' influence over more restive young warriors. Amherst arrogantly expected the Indians to obey the peremptory orders he issued. Instead, in the spring of 1763, the Ottawa leader Pontiac attacked Detroit. Other Indians followed his example, bringing chaos and death to British forts and settlements from the Great Lakes to the western reaches of Pennsylvania. The king replaced Amherst with General Thomas Gage, who managed to undo much of the damage. Pontiac's Rebellion nonetheless suggested that, if only to retain the lands it had won in the West, Britain needed to keep an army in America.

Who would pay for it? The war left the British government with a debt of almost £130 million, an enormous sum by contemporary standards. Responsibility for the budget lay with a stern and rigid minister, George Grenville, who since April 1763 had been first lord of the treasury and chancellor of the exchequer and so oversaw government finances. It seemed obvious to him that the colonists, as major beneficiaries of the British victory, should help shoulder the burden not perhaps of paying off old debts, but at least of keeping a British army in postwar America. Estimates put that cost at about £250,000 a year, and other expenses added another £100,000 to the projected new annual expenditures stemming from Britain's enlarged North American empire.

And so the division between Britain and America began with an argument over taxes. From there, it grew into a larger conflict over authority and subjection not unlike that between Amherst and the western Indians—and with similar consequences.

### ROUND ONE: THE SUGAR AND STAMP ACTS

Customs duties were one way to begin raising money. Britain had regulated American trade for a century, but the customs establishment in America brought in substantially less revenue than its cost to the Crown. That was not as strange as it might seem, since British trade laws were designed primarily to shape the course of trade. The British used devices such as duties and bounties to encourage Americans to trade only with other British possessions and to produce goods that the mother country would otherwise have to purchase from foreign suppliers. Britain's gains were indirect, in the profits of her shippers and manufacturers or in the prosperity of colonists in the West Indies, which ultimately increased the tax revenues flowing into the king's treasury. But now, desperate for new sources of income, the king's government decided to make the colonial customs service a paying proposition.

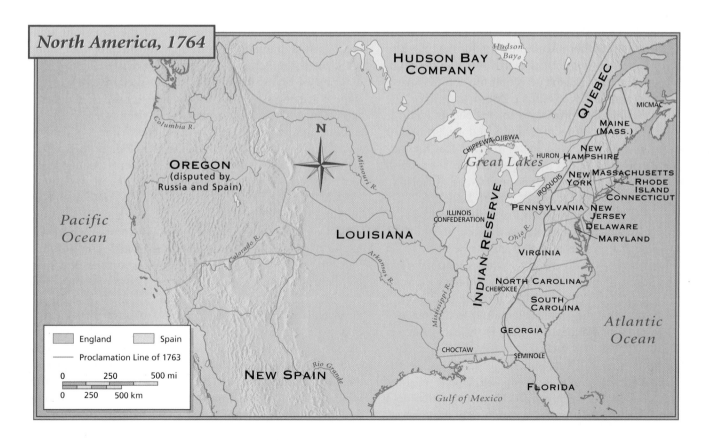

**North America, 1764**

On March 9, 1764, Grenville proposed that Parliament level new duties on a series of articles imported into the colonies. Among them was molasses, a by-product of sugar refining that the colonists used as a sweetener or, more often, distilled into rum, which they then exchanged for imports such as slaves or sold locally in enormous quantities. Parliament subsequently approved the Revenue Act of 1764, known as the Sugar Act. It imposed a duty of "3d" per gallon (three pennies, or pence, written "d" for the old Roman denarius coin) on molasses imported from the non-British West Indies, which was half the duty set by an earlier law, the Molasses Act of 1733. That older, heavier duty had not prevented colonists from importing molasses from the "foreign," particularly the French, West Indies, where it was plentifully available (the French preferred brandy to rum, and so had less use for molasses) and also cheaper than in the British islands. Colonial shippers did not always pay the duty; instead, they smuggled foreign molasses into the colonies, bribing customs agents to look the other way. There was, in fact, a set rate for bribing agents that varied from port to port, but it was always substantially less than six pence per gallon.

Grenville assumed that colonists could easily pay the new, reduced duty. And now the king's government intended to enforce the law. It had, in fact, already begun reforming the customs service to make it more efficient and responsible; and in 1763, Parliament authorized the peacetime use of British naval vessels in American waters to enforce British trade laws. The Sugar Act itself included provisions to facilitate its enforcement, demanding elaborate procedures and paperwork of colonists trading with the West Indies to prove that the molasses they carried came from the British islands. The act also changed the rules for prosecuting persons accused of violating the law in ways that stacked the cards against them.

The Sugar Act looked superficially like earlier trade laws, but it was more than an effort to regulate commerce: "it is just and necessary," read the preamble, "that a revenue be raised . . . in America for defraying the expense of defending, protecting, and securing the same." In other words, it was meant to raise money from the colonists. The only problem from the government's point of view was that the act seemed unlikely to raise enough money: the ministry estimated that it would bring in £40,000–£50,000 per year, a small part of the Crown's projected postwar costs in America. As a result, the parliamentary resolutions that initiated the Sugar Act proposed another measure to help fill the budgetary gap, a direct excise tax, similar to a modern sales tax, in the form of a stamp duty—that is, tax

stamps would be required on specified items sold in the colonies, like taxes on whiskey and some other alcoholic beverages today. Never before had Parliament imposed a tax on the colonists. Implementation of that measure was, however, delayed a year so that the Americans could be consulted. Grenville suggested that the colonists might propose a better way of raising revenue and perhaps assume responsibility for collecting it themselves. But he made no serious effort to let the colonists tax themselves, and he never so much as answered inquiries about the amount they would need to raise. What he really wanted was the colonies' prior consent to a Stamp Act, and that he did not get.

The colonists' arguments against the Sugar Act were often economic. A three-pence duty on a gallon of molasses was no less prohibitive than one of six pence, they claimed. If enforced, it would choke off trade, wiping out the income colonists used to purchase imports from the mother country, which had increased so substantially in recent years that they exceeded British exports to the British West Indies. As molasses imports into the American mainland fell, Britain would lose not only the expected revenue from the new duty but also the profits from selling those goods to the colonists. In short, *British* interests would suffer, not just those of the Americans.

Both the substance and the tone of the American argument shifted dramatically once news of the proposed stamp tax crossed the Atlantic. Thereafter, colonists employed the language of rights. Parliament, they insisted, had no right to impose a stamp tax or, for that matter, to raise revenue from the colonists in any way whatsoever. Within the British system, taxes were a "free gift of the people" and so could be levied only with the consent of the people or of their representatives, which protected their property from rulers' avarice. Freedom from taxation without consent was a basic right of Englishmen that the colonists in no way gave up by migrating to America: the original settlers and their descendants were "free-born subjects, justly and naturally entitled to all the rights and advantages of the British constitution." Since the colonists elected representatives to their provincial legislatures and not to the House of Commons, only their provincial legislatures could tax them.

Several colonies petitioned against passage of Grenville's Stamp Act. Parliament refused even to receive the petitions because they denied its right to tax colonists; indeed, colonial opposition strengthened Parliament's support for the Stamp Act, which it finally approved in March 1765. That measure, which was to take effect on the first of November following, laid direct taxes on a number of articles sold in the American

One of the stamps prepared for sale in the colonies under the Stamp Act of 1765.

colonies including pamphlets, almanacs, newspapers and newspaper advertisements, playing cards and dice, as well as a wide range of legal and commercial documents. The taxes would have to be paid in gold and silver, which were hard to come by in the colonies. Some of the taxes were quite high: for example, a tax of two shillings sterling on newspaper ads plus a half-penny tax on the newspaper itself were substantial compared with the basic price of the newspaper and, moreover, put pressure on printers, the colonies' leading opinion makers. By taxing legal documents, the Stamp Act also stepped on the toes of lawyers, who were among the most articulate and politically active Americans. Persons accused of violating the Stamp Act would be tried in admiralty courts, whose usual jurisdiction covered cases that arose on the high seas, and which had no juries. Parliament assumed that the colonists would simply obey its orders.

Colonists condemned the provision for trying cases under the Stamp Act in admiralty courts as an effort to circumvent their right to trial by jury—which it was, since colonial juries had a way of acquitting fellow colonists. But the colonists' opposition to the Stamp Act remained firmly centered on the principle of "no taxation without representation." In response, British spokesmen insisted that Americans were "virtually" represented in Parliament. Members of the House of Commons, they explained, spoke not only for the interests of those who voted for them but also for the good of all the British people everywhere—those who had the right to vote and those who did not; those in the British Isles and those in distant British colonies.

The concept of virtual representation was an ingenious effort to make sense of what the House of Commons had become: a collection of some 558 members selected, for reasons buried deep in the past, by a peculiar set of constituencies that bore no relation to population levels or contemporary importance. The Universities of Oxford and Cambridge sent representatives to the House of Commons, as Scotland had done since 1707; but most members were chosen from English counties, which contained relatively broad electorates, or from English boroughs where the right to name a member of Parliament was sometimes attached to a few parcels of land. At the same time, populous new manufacturing centers such as Manchester and Birmingham could send no representatives at all.

Virtual representation made no sense to Americans, who lived in a new country, unencumbered by mysterious ancient privileges, where representation was roughly tied to population. Their experience was with "real," or "attorneyship," representation, by which delegates spoke for those who elected them—or risked losing their seat in the next election. How could anyone seriously claim, one newspaper essayist asked, that the Americans were represented by "members whom we never chose? If we are not their constituents, they are not our representatives." In a widely circulated pamphlet of 1765—one of the first carried by ship or horse from colony to colony, and welcomed everywhere as presenting the American position—Daniel Dulany of Maryland conceded that virtual representation might make some sense in England. There representatives, voters, and nonvoters were all affected by whatever laws and taxes Parliament passed. But virtual representation could not cross the Atlantic, he argued, since the interests of colonists and the British people "at home" were not the same, but directly opposed: if Parliament taxed the Americans, it would thereby spare its own members and all other taxpayers in the British Isles from that burden. Then, logically, taxes on Americans would gradually increase until the colonists were crushed under the burden.

In 1766, Virginia's Richard Bland went further. Virtual representation, he argued, made no sense anywhere. "I cannot comprehend how Men who are excluded from voting at the Election of Members of Parliament can be represented in that Assembly," he wrote, "or how those who are elected do not sit in the House as Representatives of their Constituents." If, as some said, nine-tenths of the people of Britain lacked the right to vote for members of Parliament, then that "great Defect in the present Constitution" of Britain should be repaired and the constitution returned to "its original Purity" to "prevent any 'Order or Rank of the Subjects from imposing upon or binding the rest without their Consent.'" Bland's pamphlet was less widely distributed than Dulany's, but significant nonetheless. Within a few years, the controversy over taxes had allowed colonists to understand that they were different from Britons in the mother country in ways they had never suspected, and to see American practices not as provincial and thus inferior, but as superior.

The British, on the other hand, saw a far greater issue at stake than the nature of representation. Parliamentary supremacy—that is, the right of Parliament, consisting of the king, House of Lords, and House of Commons acting together, to do anything it chose to do—was for them a fundamental political principle. The basic rights of Englishmen asserted in historic documents such as the Magna Carta (1215) and the Petition of Rights (1628) were limitations on the power of the king, who had historically posed the greatest threat to English liberty. Finally, in 1689, the king had been forced to work with the Lords and Commons, above all in laying taxes and raising or maintaining the army ("the purse and the sword"). In that way, the British had established a "constitution," or system of government, that was the envy of liberty-loving people everywhere. Its strength lay in investing sovereignty, or ultimate authority—which, according to eighteenth-century political wisdom, had to be concentrated in some one place or civil war and chaos would follow—not in a single person but in Parliament, which represented all the "estates" or social segments of the realm. Because the king, Lords, and Commons shared power, no one of them could become so powerful as to threaten the freedom of Britons. From that perspective, anyone who denied that Parliament held ultimate authority either was a supporter of royal absolutism or did not understand British government at all. The best way to deal with such silliness, Britain's rulers concluded, was to hold firm and let time win converts to wisdom and truth as London understood them.

### RESISTANCE AND REPEAL

Opposition to the Stamp Act took many forms. On May 30, 1765, Virginia's House of Burgesses passed a set of resolutions asserting that Virginians possessed the same liberties, privi-

leges, and immunities as natural-born Englishmen living in England. Taxation with the consent of the people or of persons they chose to represent them, "who can only know what taxes the people are able to bear, or the easiest method of raising them, and must themselves be affected by every tax laid on the people," the Burgesses declared, "is the only security against a burthensome taxation, and the distinguishing characteristic of British freedom." The "Virginia Resolves" were, however, better known for two provisions that the House of Burgesses rejected but that were nonetheless published in newspapers elsewhere in America as if they had been passed. One said that Virginians were not bound to obey tax laws that had not been approved by their provincial assembly. The other denounced as public enemies all supporters of taxes not approved by the assembly.

The colonies also protested collectively. In October 1765, delegates from nine colonies (all but New Hampshire, Virginia, North Carolina, and Georgia) met as a Stamp Act Congress at New York and approved a set of resolutions drafted largely by a Pennsylvania delegate named John Dickinson, a lawyer deeply proud of being British who would become one of the most respected writers on behalf of the American cause. The resolutions asserted again that the colonists held all the rights of the king's subjects within the kingdom of Great Britain, including "the undoubted right of Englishmen, that no taxes be imposed on them but with their own consent," and added that the colonists were not, "and from their local circumstances cannot be, represented in the House of Commons in Great Britain." Only provincial legislatures could therefore tax the colonists. The Stamp Act Congress also affirmed the colonists' right to trial by jury, and it condemned "the duties imposed by several late Acts of Parliament" as "extremely burthensome and grievous." Petitions including these resolutions were promptly sent to the king and both houses of Parliament in the hope of securing repeal of the Stamp Act and the objectionable restrictions on trade enacted in 1764.

The town of Boston hit upon a more effective way to fight the Stamp Act. On the morning of August 14, 1765, an effigy of Andrew Oliver, who had been appointed stamp distributor for the Massachusetts Bay Colony, appeared hanging from a tree in Boston's South End. All day it remained on display, dutifully "stamping" goods brought into the town for sale. That evening, a crowd took down the effigy, which it paraded through the streets and then down to the docks. There the crowd destroyed a small office Oliver had recently built, perhaps to carry out his duties as stamp officer, and finally burned the effigy in a great bonfire. A contingent of the crowd went on, against the orders

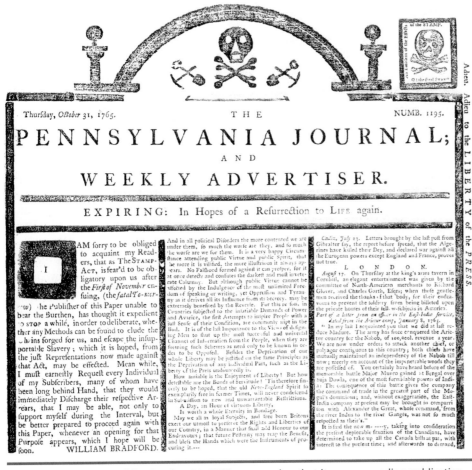

The Pennsylvania Journal for October 31, 1765, announcing that it was suspending publication rather than submit to the Stamp Act, which imposed a stamp tax on newspapers. Before long, however, many papers resumed publication even though they could not get the required stamps. Since the Stamp Act was "unconstitutional," the argument went, colonists had no obligation to obey it.

brief period. Elsewhere, on November 1, newspapers ceased to publish, and many courts and offices closed for lack of the required stamps.

In late 1765 and early 1766, after the Stamp Act had been nullified, local resistance movements with a variety of names merged into a new, intercolonial organization, linked through correspondence networks, called the Sons of Liberty. Its purpose was to block any new efforts to implement the Stamp Act and to maintain order in areas unaffected by the Act (see pages 153–54). The Sons of Liberty also assumed leadership of an effort to resume business as usual: since the Stamp Act was unconstitutional, the argument went, colonists need not obey it. Gradually newspapers began publishing again, courts reopened, and customs officers—sometimes after visits from the Sons of Liberty—began issuing unstamped clearances for ships. By the spring of 1766, many colonists were going about their daily lives as if the Stamp act had never been passed. For good measure, colonial merchants formed nonimportation agreements that cut off purchases of certain imports such as mourning clothes and the gloves customarily given out at funerals. They hoped to disrupt specific sectors of British manufacturing and so to provoke pressure for a repeal of the Stamp Act within England. As a result, colonial imports from Britain dropped by 13 or 14 percent between 1764 and 1765, and those Britons facing ruin because of the shrinking American market did not suffer in silence.

Parliament had little choice but to give in. That was easier because George Grenville had been forced from office in July 1765 by the king, who objected not to Grenville's policies but to the minister's way of lecturing him in a protracted and querulous manner. Grenville's successor, Charles Watson-Wentworth, the Marquis of Rockingham, had opposed the Stamp Act and was unwilling to enforce it. As a result, in March 1766, Parliament repealed the Stamp Act. But first it approved a Declaratory Act

of its leaders, to attack Oliver's home. The next day, amid rumors of further violence, Oliver promised to give up the stamp distributorship. And if no one distributed the stamps, the Stamp Act could not go into effect. The Stamp Act had been nullified in Massachusetts with no loss of blood and relatively little property damage.

The technique was so compelling that in one colony after another stamp officers resigned their offices either voluntarily, to avoid Oliver's fate, or under the immediate threat of mob violence. Only in the distant and thinly populated colony of Georgia did the stamp distributor avoid having to resign his office, and only there did the Stamp Act take effect for even a

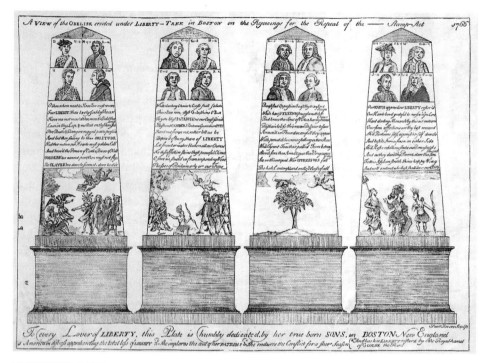

Paul Revere helped prepare an obelisk for Boston's celebration of the Stamp Act's repeal. Made of oiled paper on a wooden frame and lit from inside by candles, the display caught fire and was destroyed. Revere, however, produced this engraving of its design and inscription, which celebrated the support colonists had received from British "patriots" such as William Pitt and affirmed the Americans' loyalty to Britain. "No disaffection stains these peaceful Climes," it read. "The foes of Britain only are our Foes."

that affirmed the right of Parliament to make laws and statutes that bound the colonies and people of America "in all cases whatsoever." In short, it abandoned the Stamp Act, but not the principle of parliamentary supremacy.

### ROUND TWO: THE TOWNSHEND CRISIS

Many colonists regarded the Declaratory Act as a face-saving device upon which Parliament would never act. However, a handful of Americans anticipated more trouble. "What could not be brought to pass by an undisguised and open attack upon our liberties," predicted a patriot in Providence, would be attempted again "by secret machinations, by artifice and cunning." Boston's Samuel Adams, who was emerging as a leading defender of colonial rights, privately suggested that Parliament's next attempt to raise revenue from the colonies would come in the form of a trade law—like the Sugar Act, which seemed su-

perficially familiar and had attracted less opposition than the Stamp Act.

Rockingham fell from power after only fourteen months in office. Charles Townshend, the chancellor of the exchequer, dominated the new government and did exactly what Adams had predicted. In 1766, Parliament had reduced the duty on molasses from three to one pence per gallon and levied it on molasses from the British as well as the "foreign" West Indies. All pretense of using the duty to regulate trade—that is, to encourage mainland colonists to confine their trade to the British islands—was abandoned. The duty on molasses was designed simply to raise revenue for the Crown; it was therefore a tax. Nonetheless, Townshend noted, the colonists paid it. If the colonists preferred to enrich the royal treasury through levies on trade rather than other kinds of taxes, he reasoned, why not let them have their way?

In 1767, the chancellor brought into Parliament a series of measures known as the Townshend Revenue Acts. The most significant of them imposed new duties on colonial imports of glass, lead, paint, paper, and tea. The colonists were already required to purchase those articles from Britain, so the law obviously was not meant to regulate trade in the interest of the British community as a whole. Indeed, the colonists could avoid the duties only by manufacturing the articles themselves, which was directly contrary to the mother country's economic interests. Not only did the Townshend duties undermine the provincial assemblies' exclusive right to tax colonists, but the funds raised would be used "for defraying the charge of administration of justice, and the support of civil government in such provinces where it shall be found necessary" as well as to meet the expenses of "defending, protecting, and securing the said dominions." At the time, colonial assemblies were responsible for paying the salaries of royal governors, judges, and other Crown appointees, and they had used their role as paymaster to make the king's officers more amenable to colonial interests.

Townshend was determined to end once and for all the colonial assemblies' self-proclaimed right to exercise powers like those of the House of Commons, as he made absolutely clear in his heavy-handed treatment of the New York legislature. The problem there began in 1765 when Grenville ushered a Quartering Act through Parliament. Under its terms, colonial assemblies were required to house British troops stationed within their territory in public barracks or uninhabited houses and to supply them with a specified list of items, including firewood, candles, bedding, vinegar, salt, cooking vessels, and a prescribed amount of beer, cider, or grog (rum mixed with water at a ratio of one to four). The New York assembly balked. The Quartering Act, it argued, was nothing but a tax law whose levies were collected in goods instead of money, and it was therefore as objectionable as the Stamp Act. When, finally, the assembly agreed to supply British troops, it pretended to do so on its own initiative, without mentioning the Quartering Act or complying with its terms exactly. It supplied firewood, candles, and cooking utensils but not salt, vinegar, cider, beer, or grog, and so avoided any acknowledgment of Parliament's right to tax Americans. In retaliation, Townshend persuaded Parliament to pass the New York Suspending Act, restraining the New York assembly from passing any laws until it complied completely with the Quartering Act of 1765.

In the event that any colonists had failed to notice the drift of British policy, they were awakened in December 1767 by twelve newspaper essays that began to appear in the *Pennsylvania Chronicle*. The essays were quickly reprinted in other colonial newspapers and then, when the series was complete, as a pamphlet published not only in America but in London, Dublin, and (translated into French) Amsterdam. John Dickinson's "Letters from a Farmer in Pennsylvania" began by attacking the New York Suspending Act: if the New York assembly could be deprived of the "privilege of legislation" for refusing to submit to parliamentary taxation, "why may they not, with equal reason, be deprived of every other privilege?" And if Parliament could deprive New York of its rights, it could do the same to the other colonies. Nothing, the "Farmer" argued, would so encourage such attempts as the colonies' inattention to the interests of each other, "for the cause of *one* is the cause of *all*."

The main target of the "Farmer's Letters," however, was the Townsend duties. A tax, Dickinson said, was "an imposition on the subject, for the sole purpose of levying money," and under that definition the Townshend duties were taxes that demanded opposition every bit as much as had the Stamp Act. Colonists should unite against them. But caution was necessary to avoid anger producing anger until the quarrel turned into "an incurable rage." Like virtually every other American, but perhaps more ardently than most, Dickinson wanted to avoid independence. If once the colonies were separated from their mother country, he asked, "what new form of government shall we adopt, or where shall we find another Britain to supply our loss? Torn from the body, to which we are united by religion, liberty, laws, affections, relation, language and commerce, we must bleed at every vein." He recommended "the constitutional modes of obtaining relief," particularly petitions from colonial assemblies "to the powers that can afford us relief." He thought the chances were good that they would do the job. "We have an excellent prince, in whose good dispositions . . . we may confide," he wrote, and "a generous, sensible, and humane nation, to whom we may apply." But if petitions to king and Parliament proved ineffectual, he recommended "withholding from Great Britain all the advantages she has been used to receive from us"—that is, another boycott on imports.

Accordingly, once their petitions for repeal of the Townshend Revenue Acts failed, the colonists organized nonimportation associations. Specific provisions varied from colony to colony, but

Samuel Adams, as painted by John Singleton Copley in 1770, when Adams was Boston's leading opponent of British infringements on American rights.

overall the associations led to dramatic reductions in imports: in New York and Philadelphia, for example, imports fell to less than half of previous levels. The associations' impact on Britain was offset by an expanding European market. Nonetheless, by 1770, the king's new first minister, Frederick, Lord North, who would remain in office for twelve years and bring some welcome stability to the king's government, was ready to repeal the Townshend Acts. He abandoned all of Townshend's duties "on commercial principles," except for the tax on tea. That he kept to demonstrate Parliament's continuing right to tax Americans.

When news of the Townshend Acts' partial repeal arrived in America, first Newport, then New York, then one port after another abandoned their nonimportation agreements. Some colonists, however, continued to boycott tea—except for tea imported from Holland by "patriotic" smugglers.

## A "QUIET PERIOD"?

On March 5, 1770, the day the House of Commons approved the partial repeal of the Townshend Revenue Acts, British troops shot into a hostile crowd in Boston, wounding eleven and killing five in what would soon be called the Boston Massacre. The troops had been sent to Boston in the fall of 1768 to strengthen the king's government and keep the peace. The Bostonians were not pleased. Like all Britons, they disliked peacetime armies and governments that depended on military force to buttress their authority. Free men, they said, were not governed at the point of a gun. The soldiers' fondness for whores and coarse language, their disregard for the Sabbath, and their willingness to work for wages below the norm also led to repeated clashes with local people. Now, with blood spilled on King Street, the town demanded that the soldiers be sent to Castle William, a fort on an island in Boston Harbor. The acting governor, Thomas Hutchinson, complied. But the trials of soldiers indicted for murder were put off until the fall, when the anger that greeted the massacre would have cooled. Then, finally, a welcome but uneasy peace arrived in Boston.

Elsewhere, too, the early years of the 1770s were a "quiet period" in which the struggles between colonists and mother country ceased. Still, the imperial relationship remained more troubled than a decade before: the conflict between Parliament's claim to an absolute and universal authority and the colonists' insistence that its powers were limited remained unresolved. Early in the dispute, colonists assumed that Parliament's effort to tax them was a mistake that would easily be corrected; but their optimism dimmed as king, Lords, and Commons violated

Paul Revere's engraving of the Boston Massacre, March 5, 1770. Revere—who copied with only modest changes a painting by the Boston artist Henry Pelham—shows soldiers lined up, purposefully shooting civilians. In the background, gunsmoke comes from a window in the Customs House, which suggests that the hated British customsmen were involved in that doleful event. The engraving gives no indication that Bostonians had helped provoke violence by taunting the soldiers, throwing snowballs (some with rocks inside) at them, and even calling out "Fire! Fire!"

American rights, as they saw it, with one measure after another. Moreover, the British government seemed to be following similar policies in England, Ireland, and elsewhere.

Who was responsible? The king's ministers and also the members of Parliament fell under suspicion; by 1770, even King George, a dogged defender of parliamentary right, was occasionally accused of complicity in the sowing of grievances. Enthusiasm for the future of British North America, so high after the French and Indian War, was gone, and in place of their old British heroes Americans now had at least two of their own—Daniel Dulany, the brave Marylander who had refuted to his countrymen's satisfaction the ridiculous notion that colonists were virtually represented in Parliament, and the eloquent "Pennsylvania Farmer," John Dickinson.

What the Anglo-American world experienced in the early 1770s was, then, not so much peace as, in Samuel Adams's

An engraving depicting "Indians" throwing tea into the harbor during the Boston Tea Party from W. D. Cooper's *History of North America* (London: 1789).

with the old duty in place, the ministry thought that East India Company tea, freed of English internal taxes and middlemen's profits, could undersell smuggled tea. For the colonists, however, cheap East India Tea was a sugar-coated bitter pill: if they swallowed it, they admitted that Parliament could lay taxes on them. Other taxes would almost certainly follow. Since the Tea Act gave the East India Company a monopoly on the sale of tea in the colonies, it also threatened the livelihoods of all independent American tea merchants, including those patriotic smugglers who had allowed colonists to drink tea without compromising their political principles. Then, to make a bad situation worse, the East India Company decided to appoint as consignees men whose politics were suspect from the American perspective, including two sons and a nephew of Thomas Hutchinson, who had become royal governor of Massachusetts. Governor Hutchinson publicly defended parliamentary supremacy. Moreover, a series of his letters to England, which Benjamin Franklin had sent to Massachusetts, seemed to prove that he had recommended policies that violated American liberty.

In September 1773, the East India Company decided to send a half million pounds of tea to Boston, New York, Philadelphia, and Charleston. In the last three of those ports, opponents of the Tea Act succeeded in persuading the consignees to resign. New York and Philadelphia also persuaded the captains of tea ships to turn around before they had formally entered the harbor and to return their cargoes to England. Charleston's tea ship entered the harbor and sat there, with its tea still on board, until a twenty-day waiting period expired. At that point, the king's customs agents seized the "noisome leaf" and stored it in the basement of the customs house, where it remained, with the duties unpaid. In Boston, however, the tea ship slipped into the harbor. And there the consignees fled to the protection of British guns at Castle William and adamantly refused to resign their commissions. For a full twenty days, Bostonians tried to find a way for the tea ships to leave the harbor and take their cargoes back to England with the duties unpaid. However, the customs agents, and then Governor Hutchinson, refused to

phrase, a "sullen silence" among contenders who lacked for the moment a pressing issue over which they could fight. The quiet could have persisted, allowing suspicions to dissipate and differences to be worked out over time. The Americans still wanted to remain under the British Crown as desperately as the Crown sought to preserve the empire. But the British government had not learned to let sleeping dogs lie.

## TEA AGAIN

The calm ended with Parliament's adoption of a Tea Act in May 1773, a measure meant to help the East India Company, then near bankruptcy, recover financially by selling in America the 17 million pounds of tea it had on hand. Under that act, Parliament agreed to refund all taxes levied within England on tea that the company later reexported to the colonies. That would lower the company's costs and so the price it had to charge colonial purchasers. Henceforth, moreover, the East India Company could sell tea in America through its own agents, or "consignees." Previously the company had to sell its tea at public auction to middlemen who then tacked their own profits onto the price. The company asked that the old Townshend duty on tea also be removed, but the government refused, holding tight to that one remaining assertion of parliamentary supremacy. Even

grant clearances so the ships could legally leave the harbor. Since the British navy was guarding the sea lanes, no uncleared vessel could make an escape. If the tea remained on board and the customs agents seized it (as the law allowed) twenty days after the arrival of the first tea ship, the *Dartmouth*, on November 28, there was little doubt that the consignees would pay the duty.

Finally, on the evening of December 16, 1773, the night before the *Dartmouth*'s cargo became subject to seizure and after Hutchinson had refused a final appeal for clearances, Samuel Adams told a mass meeting that the people there could do nothing more to save their country. With a whoop, a crowd of men from Boston and surrounding towns, some disguised as Indians, swept down to the ships and threw into the sea some 90,000 pounds of tea from the *Dartmouth* and two other tea ships that had arrived more recently. Despite the noise with which it began, the "Boston Tea Party" (a name it acquired much later) was a carefully ordered event. Observers reported that the night was interrupted only by the sound of axes breaking open the tea chests and of tea being dumped into the water. A young lawyer from Braintree named John Adams, a country cousin of Boston's better-known Samuel Adams, found the event "magnificent." The destruction of the tea, he said, was "so bold, so daring, so firm, intrepid, & inflexible, and it must have so important Consequences and so lasting, that I cannot but consider it as an Epocha in History."

## THE COERCIVE ACTS

The British government's reaction confirmed Adams's prophesy. It had had enough. Now, with the full cooperation of Parliament, the Crown set out to bring the colonists to heel, starting with those annoying Bostonians. On the government's initiative, Parliament passed a series of four Coercive Acts in the spring of 1774.

- The *Boston Port Act* prohibited the loading or unloading of ships in the port of Boston after June 1 and until the town had paid the East India Company and the customs service for losses stemming from the Tea Party. All whose livelihoods depended on the port, from merchants through humble porters, were suddenly unemployed; even food and fuel could be brought into the town only under escort and with the permission of customs officers, who were relocated to Salem, a smaller port north of Boston.

- The *Massachusetts Government Act* annulled Massachusetts's charter of 1691 and revised its government to cut back popular participation and enhance the power of the Crown. The colony's council, or upper house, which had been elected by the assembly (the lower house), would henceforth be appointed by the Crown and hold office at the king's pleasure. Juries would be summoned by the sheriffs, who were royal appointees, not, as before, elected by the towns, and the colonists' beloved democratic town meetings could henceforth meet only once a year unless they received the prior consent of the governor.

- The *Administration of Justice Act* allowed Crown officers in Massachusetts who were accused of committing a capital offense while putting down a riot or executing the revenue acts to be tried in Britain. The colonists, who called that law the "Murder Act," predicted that it would encourage royal officials to kill colonists, knowing they would be acquitted in England. The suggestion that officials could not receive a fair trial in Massachusetts was particularly resented since soldiers involved in the Boston Massacre had been defended by two lawyers who were also ardent defenders of the American cause, John Adams and Josiah Quincy Jr. Four soldiers and their captain were acquitted, and two guardsmen were found guilty only of manslaughter, a remarkable outcome given the widespread anger that followed the event.

- A final measure, a new *Quartering Act,* which permitted British troops to be quartered within towns, applied not just to Massachusetts but to all colonies. Its force, however, was first felt in Massachusetts, where a heavy contingent of troops were brought back into Boston, and General Thomas Gage, still the commander of the British army in North America, replaced Hutchinson as governor of the colony. In effect, Massachusetts was put under military rule.

The king's ministers hoped that these measures would divide the colonies, punishing Massachusetts while warning others to accept Parliament's superintending power and so avoid the Bay Colony's fate. Instead, the Coercive Acts drew the colonies together. Americans labeled them the "Intolerable Acts" and often included in the list a fifth new law, the *Quebec Act,* by which Parliament finally defined a permanent civil government for Quebec, the Canadian colony Britain had acquired from France. The act extended Quebec's boundaries to include all the territory west of the Appalachians and north of the Ohio River, an enormous grant of land that effectively undercut several colonies' claims to the West based on their original grants from the Crown. The new government of Quebec would include no elected assembly; instead, a council appointed by the Crown would make laws, and Parliament explicitly reserved the right to impose taxes. Civil cases would be tried without juries. Moreover, Catholics were given religious toleration and their church confirmed in privileges held under French rule. That was as damning a provision as any for colonists who thought Catholicism and absolutism, like Protestantism and liberty, went hand in hand. The dark purposes of British policy now seemed, as the Virginian George Washington put it on July 4, 1774, "as clear as the sun in its meridian brightness."

To let the British pick the colonies off, one by one, would have been madness. So the other colonies sent aid to help Bostonians impoverished by the Port Act. Meanwhile, inter-colonial committees of correspondence, which had been organized on the initiative of Virginia's House of Burgesses in 1773 and early 1774, arranged the meeting of a Continental Congress to coordinate opposition efforts in the various colonies.

## The Transfer of Authority, 1765–1776

The series of disputes with Britain that began in the 1760s brought a gradual transfer of power from the king's government to the colonists. The extent of change was limited at first, and almost inadvert, as colonial leaders sought not to arrogate prerogatives of the Crown but to contain resistance within acceptable bounds. With each new crisis, however, the authority of the resistance movement expanded until, by the time Americans decided to sever their ties with Great Britain and its king, they were already largely self-governing.

### KEEPING THE PEACE AND REGULATING TRADE

The first efforts to force stamp distributors to resign were the work of isolated local groups who knew what occurred in other colonies mainly through newspaper accounts. They soon discovered that violence tended to spread if grievances unrelated to the Stamp Act became confused with opposition to parliamentary taxation. For example, on August 26, 1765, twelve days after the first Stamp Act uprising in Boston, a mob destroyed the home of Lieutenant Governor Thomas Hutchinson and attacked court and customs officials, probably because they had been involved in taking depositions against local smugglers. On the next day, a demonstration against the Stamp Act in Newport, Rhode Island, led to several days of uncontrolled rioting.

The cascading disorder was frightening and politically counterproductive since it alienated potential supporters. It also vio-

lated standards for resistance and revolution that the colonists had learned from seventeenth-century English defenders of the right of revolution such as John Locke and Algernon Sidney, or other writers who continued that tradition in the eighteenth century. Resistance, those writers insisted, should answer only major threats to liberty, those so prominent that "the body of the people," not just a minority, recognized the danger. Force, moreover, was legitimate only after all the peaceful means of redress had failed, and then no more should be used than absolutely necessary. A ruler who acted against law "ceases in that to be a Magistrate," Locke said, and, "acting without Authority," could be opposed like anyone else "who by force invades the Right of another." In effect, while resisting unlawful acts of their rulers, the people reassumed the authority those rulers had surrendered and were obliged to exercise that authority, as colonial newspapers asserted in late 1765, with the same care expected of regularly constituted officials, taking steps to ensure "that they do no Injustice, or suffer it to be done by others." Some eighteenth-century writers added still another rule of thumb for

"The Bostonians Paying the Excise Man, or Tarring and Feathering." With the Boston Tea Party in the background and a noose hanging from the Liberty Tree, this British cartoon shows American colonists abusing a British tax official. Printed by Robt. Sayer & J. Bennett, Map and Printseller, 1774.

those who would oppose oppressive rulers: resistance should be attempted only if there was a good chance of success, since a failed effort would worsen the plight of the people.

After the violence at Boston and Newport, colonial leaders took extraordinary steps to confine extra-legal action to resisting the Stamp Act and to ensure that no "mischievous Extravagancies" accompanied it. When a crowd forced the Connecticut stamp officer to resign on September 18, 1765, it marched in military formation; leaders, identified by their distinctive clothing, kept the crowd in order. At Philadelphia in October, a large mass meeting sent a delegation of seven men to confer with the colony's stamp distributor, so he did not confront the crowd directly. Increasingly, too, social and economic boycotts replaced threats of violence. For example, in late October, the freemen of Essex County, New Jersey, declared that they would have "no Communication" on "any Occasion" with anyone who supported the Stamp Act, "unless it be to inform them of their Vileness."

An intercolonial association called the Sons of Liberty institutionalized these ad hoc efforts to maintain order. The organization was first formed in late 1765 and early 1766, to raise and coordinate military resistance if the Crown used its army to enforce the Stamp Act in New York. Its leaders were drawn from the middle and upper classes, but they tried to extend membership throughout the white adult male population in order to speak for the "body of the people" as understood at the time. Once fear that Britain would use its army against the colonists had passed, the Sons of Liberty worked to maintain peace and preserve civil government where it remained unaffected by the Stamp Act. Sometimes they established elaborate procedures for that purpose. In Albany, New York, the Sons of Liberty adopted careful rules forbidding acts that disturbed the public tranquility or the private peace of any person "under colour or pretense of the cause of LIBERTY" without the advice and consent of an elected committee of thirteen members. Resolutions adopted by the Sons of Liberty always stressed their loyalty to the Crown and desire to maintain the British constitution, which, they said, demanded opposing the "unconstitutional" Stamp Act. The organization disbanded after the Stamp Act was repealed, and, indeed, often organized celebrations of that event. But at the height of their power, the Sons had, in effect, taken on responsibility for maintaining the peace, a primary function of government, which left royal officials feeling defenseless and devoid of power. As Hutchinson complained in March 1766, "the authority of every colony is in the hands of the sons of liberty."

The transfer of authority progressed further between 1767 and 1770 under the nonimportation associations that answered the Townshend Revenue Acts. Committees responsible for enforcing the associations investigated complaints against alleged violators of the agreements and then, if the accused were found guilty, imposed sanctions, generally in the form of boycotts. Occasionally the committees also attempted to regulate prices so merchants could not make windfall profits on old inventories at the cost of the public. Even the committees' language suggested that within the sphere of power defined by the nonimportation agreements, they, not the king's customs establishment, exercised authority: goods imported against the associations were sometimes called "contraband," and tea smuggled from Holland could be "lawfully sold," but it was a "high crime" to sell goods from England.

## THE FIRST CONTINENTAL CONGRESS

Once Parliament approved the Coercive Acts, the transfer of effective authority from the king's government to organizations whose power came from popular consent proceeded at an accelerated rate. In 1774, when royal governors refused to convene colonial assemblies or dissolved them to prevent the election of delegates to a continental congress, the assemblies met as extra-legal congresses or conventions to choose their representatives and, increasingly as the crisis deepened, to perform other acts of government. Twelve colonies, all but Georgia, sent delegates to the First Continental Congress, which opened at Philadelphia on September 5, 1774, and continued in session until October 26. The First Continental Congress was not a revolutionary body; its purpose was to coordinate the colonies' opposition to the Coercive Acts and, above all, to decide whether to inaugurate a new nonimportation movement and, if so, to set its terms so they would be the same everywhere. By a firm and united resistance, it sought redress and reconciliation.

Soon after the Congress convened, news arrived that the British fleet had bombarded Boston for an entire night. The report proved false, but not before several groups of men throughout New England and the middle colonies set out to join in the defense of Boston. Then, on September 16, Paul Revere, an express rider from Massachusetts, arrived in Philadelphia with a set of resolves adopted by a convention of towns in Suffolk County. The resolutions called on the people to disobey the Coercive Acts, refuse to pay taxes to the royal government, elect militia officers, and learn the art of war. Congress endorsed these "Suffolk Resolves." Massachusetts should act only on the defensive, it later declared, but if an attempt was made to execute Parliament's recent laws by force, "all America ought to support" the colony in fighting the British army. Those decisions tipped the Congress toward the politics of its more radical members. It yielded to radicals again when it defeated and then expunged from its records all mention of a "Plan of Union" proposed by Pennsylvania's Joseph Galloway. Galloway's plan affirmed the supremacy of Parliament and called for the creation of an American Grand Council—essentially a congress of colonial delegates—that would remain subordinate to Parliament but whose consent would be necessary before any act of Parliament bound the Americans. Suspicions of Parliament and arguments against its claims to power over the colonies had gone too far by 1774 for Americans to affirm, as Galloway proposed, that Parliament held ultimate authority over their lives.

Before dissolving, the First Continental Congress adopted a colonial bill of rights. It reasserted that Americans had all the rights and privileges of the king's subjects born within Great Britain, denied that Parliament could bind the Americans in any way—even through trade regulations—without their consent, and listed several specific acts of Parliament that violated American rights. The Congress also adopted an elaborate plan of economic coercion, the Continental Association, which it hoped would build support within Britain for redressing America's grievances. The association included a nonimportation agreement that called for ending the importation of goods from England and Ireland; several products, including molasses, from the West Indies; as well as tea and slaves from anywhere in the world after December 1, 1774. A companion nonconsumption agreement would go into effect on March 1, 1775. Implementation of a nonexportation agreement was, however, delayed until September 10, 1775, and would then take effect only if Parliament had not repealed a number of objectionable laws, which were named. Committees elected in "every county, city, and town" by those qualified to vote for members of their provincial assemblies would enforce the association.

The provision on enforcement was a particularly important part of the Continental Association. It brought into being an elaborate network of local extra-legal committees, hundreds of them, whose responsibilities multiplied as Britain's authority

**LEFT:** General Thomas Gage, head of the British army in America and military governor of Massachusetts in 1774–75, in a portrait by John Singleton Copley.

**RIGHT:** Margaret Kemble Gage, the American-born wife of General Gage, as painted in 1771 by John Singleton Copley. She might well have sent Massachusetts patriots information that Gage planned an expedition to Lexington and Concord on April 18–19, 1775.

dissolved. In some colonies, the committees quickly took charge of acquiring arms and finding ways to pay for them; sometimes, too, they became a police force that made colonists who were uncertain about their allegiance choose between casting their lot with the Americans or seeking a safe haven under the protection of the king's troops. In colonies such as Virginia, where county government had been entrusted to Crown appointees, the investment of responsibility in elected committees was itself a revolutionary change, and a sign of what—as some conservatives came to fear—the future would hold.

In October 1774, however, the First Continental Congress still believed that the Anglo-American conflict could be settled. It sent petitions for redress to the king and people of Great Britain and called for the assembling of a successor Congress at Philadelphia on May 10, 1775, only if the Americans' grievances had not already been redressed.

### BEGINNING A WAR

Neither King George nor his ministers nor Parliament was inclined to retreat. The Crown submitted Congress's petition to Parliament buried in a pile of other American papers; and when colonial agents requested permission to speak on its behalf, the House of Commons refused by a resounding vote of 218 to 68. Petitions from within England demanding reconciliation for economic reasons received no more serious consideration. The king and his ministers understood how important the colonies and their trade were to Britain's prosperity, and, like Parliament, they had no intention of risking their loss by treating troublemakers with respect. Instead, the "unruly children" would have to learn obedience.

So far, however, harsh measures had failed miserably. The Coercive Acts, which were supposed to divide the colonists, brought them together. And one, the Massachusetts Government Act, designed to reinforce royal authority, caused its total collapse. News of that act arrived in the Bay Colony on August 6, 1774. Within a month, Governor Gage reported that the countryside was in arms, with mobs closing the king's courts and forcing members appointed to the colony's new council to resign their offices or to flee and put themselves under the protection of British troops.

The Crown, however, could not leave bad enough alone: failures led to further efforts at punishment and reprisal. In February 1775, Parliament—on the suggestion of Lord North, still the king's leading minister—declared that Massachusetts was in a state of rebellion and was supported by other colonies. It asked the king to take whatever measures were necessary to "enforce due obedience to the laws and authority of the Supreme Legislature." Then it approved a New England Restraining Act that excluded the New England colonies from the North Atlantic fisheries and barred them from all trade except with the mother country or the British West Indies. Later Parliament extended those commercial restraints to Pennsylvania, New Jersey, Maryland, Virginia, and South Carolina. If the colonies refused to trade with Britain, then Britain would prevent their trading with anyone else. And so the Crown forced those members of the colonial merchant community who were hesitant about the Continental Association into the arms of their more politically extreme neighbors.

George III—an unimaginative man, disinclined to think through the complex constitutional arguments raised in the controversy, and determined to maintain Britain's authority—had already decided that only arms could hold the empire together. "The New England Governments," he wrote Lord North on November 18, 1774, "are in a state of rebellion," and "blows must decide whether they are to be subject to this country or independent." With most members of the British ruling class, he believed that military force would eas-ily decide the contest in the mother country's favor. Amateur colonial soldiers, they assumed, could never hold out against the trained regular soldiers of the British army.

General Gage once shared that conviction, but by early 1775 he had changed his mind. The colonial forces were not a "Boston rabble," he reported from Massachusetts, but "the freeholders and farmers of the country" who were both numerous and in a "fury." They could not easily be put down, certainly not with the 3,000 men he had on hand, but there was hope if the mother country would increase his army to 20,000. Alternatively, Britain could suspend the Coercive Acts and find some way of allowing colonists representation in Parliament. The king responded by trying to replace Gage, who seemed to have lost his hold on reality, with Amherst, whom Gage had replaced a decade before, and whose stubborn demands for obedience had apparently regained their charm. When Amherst declined, the government simply ordered Gage to arrest the province's leaders and to take the offensive against what Lord Dartmouth, the king's minister for American affairs, described as a "rude rabble without plan, without concert, and without conduct." Gage received a copy of Dartmouth's letter on April 14, 1775. Four days later, he sent a contingent of 600 to 700 men to seize colonial arms stored at the town of Concord, some twenty miles west and north of Boston.

The Americans managed to see Dartmouth's letter before Gage did and also received intelligence of the march before it set out—perhaps from the general's American-born wife. When Gage's troops arrived at Lexington on April 19, the local militia had already lined up on the "Green," a piece of open land at the town's center. The militiamen, who meant more to make a statement than to fight a battle, had begun to disperse when a shot of unknown origin rang out. Immediately the British soldiers emptied their muskets into the fleeing men, killing eight and wounding ten. Then the king's army marched on to Concord. Most of the arms stored there had been moved to neighboring towns or hidden: some weapons, for example, were buried in the freshly dug furrows of a nearby field. The soldiers broke or destroyed what they could find—a few cannons, some wooden carriage wheels, and "500 pounds of ball," which they threw in a pond (from which the colonists later rescued it). The British regulars fought a company of local militiamen at Concord's North Bridge, and around noon they began a seventeen- or eighteen-mile march back to Boston.

Along the route, thousands of militiamen from nearby towns had gathered. Now they shot from all sides at the marching

British regulars, who would probably never have made it back to camp had Gage not sent out another 900 men as reinforcements. In all, 73 British soldiers and 49 provincials were killed. Another 192 of Gage's men (and 39 colonials) were wounded, and 22 were captured by the Americans. After the battle, moreover, angry colonial militiamen confined the British army to Boston, which lay on a peninsula linked to the mainland by a narrow neck of easily guarded land. There the king's troops would remain, held effectively under siege by Lord Dartmouth's "rude rabble," for almost a year.

The bloodshed at Lexington and Concord led to other military confrontations. On May 10, a contingent of troops from western Massachusetts under Colonel Benedict Arnold and Connecticut soldiers under Ethan Allen seized the British fort at Ticonderoga on Lake Champlain. Two days later, they took the British stronghold at Crown Point, farther north. In capturing Ticonderoga, the provincials won not only a store of cannons that they sorely needed but substantial control of a strategically critical water route from the St. Lawrence River in Canada south via the Richelieu River to Lake Champlain, Lake George, the Hudson River, and ultimately New York City.

On June 17, provincials again engaged British forces at the Battle of Bunker Hill, where British regulars tried to seize a colonial entrenchment on the highlands of Charlestown, a site north and east of Boston from which the Americans could command Boston and its harbor. The provincials held their stronghold through two frontal assaults by the regulars, then fled when their ammunition ran out. Technically the British won the day, but at the cost of some 1,054 casualties (both dead and wounded) as opposed to just under 400 on the American side. By then it was clear that the "magic" of regular soldiers no longer worked, if it ever had, and that it would be much harder to force the Americans into obedience than King George and his advisers assumed.

## THE SECOND CONTINENTAL CONGRESS

When the Second Continental Congress assembled at Philadelphia on May 10, 1775, news of Lexington and Concord had spread throughout the colonies. The outbreak of war meant that this Congress would not be, like its predecessor, a mere ad hoc consultative body. It became, in effect, the first government of the United States.

The Second Continental Congress had no more than assembled when questions began pouring in for the delegates to decide. New York asked how it should react to the imminent arrival of British troops on Manhattan Island. Then, once the Congress learned that American soldiers had captured Ticonderoga and Crown Point, it had to decide how to keep that triumph from poisoning the prospects for reconciliation with Britain. First it justified the seizure of those strongholds as a defensive act by people afraid that an invasion from Canada would use the arms stored there against them. But in late June, after hearing pleas from Arnold and Allen, Congress authorized an American invasion of Canada that the British understandably saw as an offensive act.

In the meantime, Congress received a request from Massachusetts that it

A view of the Battle of Bunker Hill by an unknown artist, showing British ships in the water between Boston and a peninsula to the north where the battle occurred, with the town of Charlestown in flames.

assume responsibility for the army assembled in Cambridge, across the Charles River from Boston. Soon Congress began purchasing supplies and arranging medical services for the "Continental army." It defined the army's structure and then began appointing its officers, making one of its members, George Washington (who wore his buff-blue Virginia military uniform to sessions of Congress), the army's commander in chief. Congress did not, however, simply leave the war in Washington's hands, but continued to appoint officers, called up men and decided where they should go, and regularly sent military orders to the commander in chief.

Nonmilitary problems also came tumbling onto the agenda. As royal governments collapsed, provincial congresses and conventions asked Congress how they should proceed. In early June, Congress told Massachusetts to return to its charter of 1691 and act as if the royal governor were absent; later in the year, it advised New Hampshire, South Carolina, and Virginia to set up new governments, based on a "full and free representation of the people," that would remain in place until the conflict with Britain was settled. Congress also took charge of Indian affairs, the continental post office, and the regulation of trade (modifying the Continental Association to allow the importation of war supplies), and attempted to resolve disputes between the colonies. It could not levy taxes, but it could borrow money, and in 1775 it devised another independent if unstable source of revenue by issuing paper money.

The Second Continental Congress was poorly structured to handle so many duties. Like the First Congress, it consisted of a simple representative assembly in which each colony had one vote regardless of size or population or the number of delegates it sent. Congress itself exercised all power—legislative, executive, and even on occasion judicial—with the help of only a few clerks hired after it decided to issue currency. Special committees of delegates exercised responsibility for specific tasks, and sometimes all the delegates together met as a Committee of the Whole to discuss major topics freely, since no official records of committees' deliberations were kept on such occasions. In the end, however, all decisions, great or trivial, were made by Congress itself. The workload was so heavy that Congress normally convened six days a week, Monday through Saturday, from morning through late afternoon, with committees meeting earlier in the morning and later in the evening.

Congress's powers were determined by the instructions each colony gave its delegates. In short, it could do only what a majority of delegates were authorized to approve. Most delegates held instructions "to concert, agree upon, direct and order" whatever Congress thought best to obtain a redress of grievances and restore harmony between the mother country and her colonies. Such instructions allowed military resistance, Congress assumed, since there would be no hope for redress and reconciliation if the British army overran the colonies.

In more direct compliance with its constituents' desire for reconciliation, Congress sent another petition to the king, drafted in the most courteous and respectful terms by none other than John Dickinson, in July 1775. But George III refused to receive the petition on the throne or to answer it, and a few days after it arrived—on August 23—he issued a proclamation stating that the Americans were engaged in an "open and avowed rebellion." Two months later, on October 26, 1775, the king declared in an address to Parliament that the American rebellion was "manifestly carried on for the purpose of establishing an independent Empire" and that the colonists' professions of loyalty were meant "only to amuse" while they

King George III, as portrayed by the studio of Allan Ramsay in the early 1760s, soon after he ascended to the throne. Although he was at first wildly popular among the Americans, George III's unwillingness to consider seriously American petitions for redress ultimately convinced the colonists that they had no viable alternative to independence.

prepared for a "general revolt." Finally, in December, the king approved a Prohibitory Act, which forbade all trade with the thirteen North American colonies; made colonial vessels and their cargoes, whether in port or at sea, forfeit to the Crown as if they were the property of open enemies; and allowed the impressment of those vessels' crews into the Royal Navy.

Meanwhile, the royal governor of Virginia, Lord Dunmore, declared his colony under martial law, began collecting a Loyalist army, and, on November 17, promised freedom to slaves who left their masters and joined the king's cause. Nothing could have alienated the planter elite of the southern colonies more. Americans had earlier complained that the British were attempting to turn Indian "savages" against them; now it seemed that slaves, too, were being encouraged to cut their masters' throats. Reconciliation seemed increasingly remote.

News of the king's October speech arrived at Philadelphia in early January 1776 with reports that the British had burned Norfolk, Virginia, much as they had burned Charlestown, Massachusetts, and Falmouth (Portland), Maine. Suddenly Congress's position changed. When one of the delegates suggested that they deny the king's charge that Congress sought independence—as they had done a month before, after receiving news of his August proclamation—Congess hesitated. Then, on January 9, the first copies of *Common Sense* appeared in Philadelphia and rapidly spread throughout the colonies. The work of Thomas Paine, a little-known Englishman who had arrived in America only in late 1774, that pamphlet argued for independence with colorful, hard-hitting language that appealed to ordinary people. Paine spoke to people's fears; he spoke to their dreams; he enlisted one argument after another, letting them tumble over each other with more passion than order. Above all, Paine argued, American freedom could never be secure under British rule because the British constitution—the British system of government—was flawed, and the main flaws consisted of monarchy and hereditary rule. Only by eliminating claims to power by right of birth and making all officials dependent on popular choice— that is, by founding a republic—could Americans hope to enjoy a free and peaceful future.

Events reinforced Paine's arguments. In February, news arrived of the Prohibitory Act, which seemed to John Adams like an "Act of Independence" because, by putting the colonies outside the king's protection, it released them from the obligation of obedience. The final blow came in the spring, when colonists learned that the king had hired German soldiers to help put down the American "rebellion." To hold out, the colonists needed the help of another country, such as France, but to get such help they would have to declare their independence. After all, France's interest lay in reducing the British empire, not helping put it back together again.

By spring, too, the problem of government had become too general for the temporary solutions Congress proposed the previous year for Massachusetts, South Carolina, New Hampshire, and Virginia. Where royal governors remained, colonists questioned whether they should be obeyed, while sheriffs and some other colonial officeholders, including judges, hesitated to take the standard oath of allegiance to the Crown. Finally, on May 10, 1776, Congress approved a resolution calling on all colonies "where no government sufficient to the exigencies of their affairs have been hitherto established" to adopt new governments. Five days later, Congress added a radical preface explaining that, given recent acts of the king, Lords, and Commons of Great Britain, it had become "necessary that every kind of authority under the said Crown should be totally suppressed" and that new governments be established "under the authority of the people."

On the very same day, May 15, the Virginia Convention instructed its congressional delegates to propose that Congress declare the United Colonies independent of Great Britain. And so on June 7, a Virginia delegate, Richard Henry Lee, moved "that these United Colonies are, and of right ought to be, free and independent States, that they are absolved from all allegiance to the British Crown, and that all political connection between them and the State of Great Britain is, and ought to be, totally dissolved."

Congress, meeting as a Committee of the Whole, debated the resolution on Saturday, June 8, and again on Monday the 10th. Delegates agreed that independence had become unavoidable. They debated whether it should be adopted then or later, after an agreement had been reached with France on the terms of an alliance. Those arguing for delay also noted that several colonies, including Maryland, Delaware, New Jersey, Pennsylvania, and New York, had precluded their delegates from approving independence. Postponement would give those colonies time to reconsider their position. Finally, the delegates agreed to delay the decision until the beginning of July. But on June 11, Congress appointed a committee of five to draft a declaration of independence. Its chairman was Thomas Jefferson. The other members were John Adams, Robert R. Livingston of New York, Roger Sherman of Connecticut, and Benjamin Franklin, who had returned from London with convictions about British rule far different from those of a decade earlier.

## FRANKLIN'S POLITICAL ODYSSEY

No one had wanted to remain in the empire more than Benjamin Franklin. He loved living in London, mixing with men of science and letters who held him in high esteem. He therefore watched with alarm Britain's increasingly severe policies toward the colonies and the colonists' growing disaffection for Britain. In late 1772, while still in London, he sent to Boston a packet of letters written by the Massachusetts governor, Thomas Hutchinson, that, he thought, proved that Hutchinson had provoked Britain's repressive colonial policies, including its decision to use soldiers against civilians. When Massachusetts' leaders read the letters, they would no longer regard Britain "as a harsh unkind Mother" and put "the blame where it ought to lay," on Hutchinson. And that, he hoped, would open the way to reconciliation.

The plan misfired. The colonists became enraged at Hutchinson; but in the controversy that followed, Franklin—who felt compelled to acknowledge that he had sent the letters to America—found himself accused of fomenting sedition. On January 29, 1774, at a meeting of the king's Privy Council to consider a petition from Massachusetts that Hutchinson be removed from office, the solicitor general, Alexander Wedderburn, mounted an hour-long, bitter attack on him. Franklin had stolen the letters, Wedderburn charged; and he was the "true incendiary" behind colonial unrest. On the advice of his counsel, Franklin stood silent while Wedderburn spoke. The hall was crowded with dignitaries who came to see the spectacle. The humiliation was not something Franklin would forget.

He nonetheless remained in England, watching the government take ever harsher steps against the colonists, until finally he set sail in March 1775. Even then he thought he might return to England the next fall. But on May 6, the day after he landed in Philadelphia, Pennsylvania elected him a delegate to the Second Continental Congress, and he was soon fully absorbed in American affairs. Reconciliation became for Franklin, as for other colonists, an impossible dream; and by June

Benjamin Franklin was portrayed as an unpretentious American in a simple fur hat and spectacles in this French print. The French idolized Franklin, who served as an American diplomat in Paris during the late 1770s and early 1780s.

1776, he was ready for independence. Alexander Wedderburn had done the Americans a great service by helping to ensure that in any imperial division Franklin would side with the colonists. Franklin's services were an enormous asset to the American cause.

## LOYALISM

Some colonists continued to hold back from independence. Loyalists—American opponents of independence—constituted, by modern estimates, a fifth of the total population. They were a miscellaneous lot, including artisans and common farmers along with wealthy merchants whose income depended on trade with England and British officeholders who supported the Crown almost instinctively. Some were tenants whose landlords sided with the Revolution; others lived in the backcountry and opposed independence because of long-standing resentments toward the "patriots" who ruled in the East or because they had never heard about the events that gradually undermined other Americans' affection for Britain. The supporters of independence had devised methods of spreading news, such as the committees of correspondence Boston established in 1772 to inform and politicize particularly those colonists in remote towns. Still, the arrival of news on the distant frontier remained uneven at a time when newspapers and letters, carried from place to place on ships or horseback, were the major means of internal communications.

Many Loyalists, however, had good reason for opposing independence. Some came from ethnic or religious minorities, such as the Anglicans in Connecticut, who thought their liberty would be more secure under the Crown than in a system of majority rule. Slaves, too, could well see their greatest prospect of freedom in supporting the king. Still other Loyalists were recent British immigrants who could not take sides against the country in which they had been born and raised. And even informed, white, American-born colonists could decide against independence out of fear. Despite the assurances of *Common Sense*, they said, the colonists had no chance of holding out against the power of Great Britain, and a severe repression would surely follow military defeat. But by the summer of 1776, most colonists seem to have concluded that they could avoid destruction by the king and his German "mercenaries" only if they declared independence and sought outside help. Self-preservation made independence necessary, they said; there really was no choice.

## TOWARD INDEPENDENCE

Meanwhile, the war entered a crisis that seemed to support the predictions of doom. The Canadian campaign had begun slowly and then gone from bad to worse: American forces put Quebec under siege, then attacked the city on December 30, 1775. The result was disastrous. General Richard Montgomery was killed; the second-in-command, Colonel Benedict Arnold, was wounded; and the Americans suffered 60 casualties and lost another 400 men who were taken prisoner. A lack of supplies and the ravages of smallpox weakened the remnants of the invading army until, with the arrival of British reinforcements in May 1776, the Continental army retreated in total chaos. A second offensive in June ended in similar disarray, leaving the northern frontier open to incursions by Canadians and their Indian allies.

The Continental army was more successful in Massachusetts. With cannons and other heavy supplies heroically floated down the Hudson, then dragged with sleds, wagons, and oxen some 300 miles from Ticonderoga, the Americans succeeded in fortifying Dorchester Heights to Boston's south. That made the British position untenable. General William Howe, who had replaced Thomas Gage as commander of the British North American army, evacuated the town on March 17, 1776, and sailed his men to Halifax, Nova Scotia. There he gathered forces for a major offensive somewhere along the Atlantic coast. In late June, hundreds of British ships began to arrive, sails aloft, at the entrance to New York's harbor.

On July 1, the Second Continental Congress resolved itself once again into a Committee of the Whole. The debates on Richard Henry Lee's resolutions recapitulated earlier discussions and culminated with a divided vote of 9 to 4 in favor of independence. The next day, with some abstentions from the Pennsylvania delegation, the arrival of Caesar Rodney, who swung the Delaware delegation into line, and a change of position by South Carolina, Congress approved independence with the support of twelve colonies. Only New York held out. A week later, it, too, finally instructed its delegates to consent, and independence became a unanimous decision of all the colonies, or, as they had become, states. The British government's decision to force the Americans into obedience had, in effect, brought the loss it most feared.

Once Congress approved independence, it again resolved itself into a Committee of the Whole to consider the Declaration of Independence proposed by the committee it had appointed on June 11. The draft was, as Josiah Bartlett of New Hampshire commented, "a pretty good one," written by Thomas Jefferson under guidelines from the drafting committee. Parts of the manuscript were musical, others overstated and in need of a good editing, which the delegates gave it, changing phrases, rewriting passages, and cutting out about a quarter of the proposed text. Finally, on July 4, 1776, Congress approved the Declaration and arranged for it to be "authenticated and printed" and sent to "the several assemblies, conventions and committees, or councils of safety, and to the several commanding officers of the continental troops" so it could be "proclaimed in each of the United States, and at the head of the army." As John Hancock, the president of

This painting by John Trumbull, often labeled *The Signing of the Declaration of Independence*, actually shows the drafting committee presenting its draft declaration to Congress on June 28, 1776. Trumbull painted the scene several decades after it occurred, and he exaggerated the number of men in attendance.

Congress, explained, it was important "that the People may be universally informed" that they had, as the document stated, assumed a "separate station" among the "powers of the earth."

And so the Declaration of Independence wound through the country and was publicly read in both major port cities and small towns or villages, always with abundant "huzzahs." In place after place, crowds seized the occasion to tear down statues, paintings, or other symbols of the king and British monarchy, often trampling them underfoot or burning them in great bonfires. It was not one "unfeeling" king, as Paine had called George III, that they rejected, but all kings. This was not a simple colonial rebellion but a revolution, an effort to create a different form of government from Britain's, a republic in which the people would rule. But first they would have to establish the independence they proclaimed—on the battlefield.

## A War for Independence

Only a gambler who liked betting against high odds would have put his money on the Americans. Britain had a long military tradition; its army was organized, trained, and equipped, and had just won a major world victory, as the Peace of Paris (1763) affirmed. Britain also boasted a powerful navy, with some eighty-two "ships of the line"—the largest naval vessels—at sea or ready to be armed in June 1776. Congress had no navy to speak of, and the Continental army was a motley collection of volunteers who shocked General Washington when he first laid eyes on them at Cambridge. The men were willing to fight, he said, but they lacked all discipline. When he tried to impose order, the men had a way of not reenlisting. And when the army left Massachusetts, many New Englanders were unwilling to go with it.

To win the war, Washington argued, the Americans needed regular soldiers who enlisted for three years or the duration of the war and officers paid well enough that "men of quality" would take on the job. That proposal ran smack into an old Anglo-American suspicion of "standing armies"—that is, regular, paid, professional military forces, which were regarded as dangerous instruments with which ambitious rulers could enforce obedience and "enslave" the people. Congress therefore hesitated. Navies were more difficult to turn against the governed, and so less feared. Early in the war, Congress tried to build a Continental navy, and American shipbuilders—who had never before built a warship—managed by Herculean effort to produce thirteen frigates (medium-sized warships). By 1779, the British had captured or destroyed most of them. The navy was also crippled by sailors' preference for sailing on privateers, private ships that attacked British vessels with the permission of Congress for a share of the spoils. The privateers performed a substantial service for the American cause, bringing the war even into British home waters. Theirs was, however, a rather scattershot operation, directed by private initiatives, not central command.

The British understood their advantages. They had also learned in 1775 that victory would be harder to gain than they originally thought. The police action they attempted to carry out in Massachusetts was insufficient: they could not simply capture a few leaders

*Die Zerstörung der Königlichen Bild Säule zu Neu Yorck | La Destruction de la Statue royale a Nouvelle Yorck*

This engraving illustrates the destruction of a statue of King George in New York City, in July 1776.

and expect the rebellion to collapse. The British had a war on their hands, and wars they knew how to win. And so, in the summer of 1776, they gathered outside New York City one of the strongest armies and fleets ever seen in North America to that time. By August, General William Howe and his brother, Admiral Lord Richard Howe, had under their command some 45,000 experienced soldiers and sailors—against Washington's 28,000, of whom only 19,000 were at all fit for duty and none were seasoned military men. Manhattan Island, surrounded by water, was an ideal place for the British: with their powerful fleet, they could easily move troops from place to place, outflanking the Continentals almost at will.

## THE CAMPAIGN OF 1776

Washington's situation was impossible, but he did his best. First he divided his troops, sending some to defend Brooklyn Heights on Long Island, which he had to control in order to defend New York City. But when the British took the offensive there on August 27, 1776, the American lines collapsed and Washington's forces suffered 1,500 casualties to the enemy's 400. Fortunately, General Howe did not advance after his victory, and on the night of the August 29, under cover of a heavy fog and with the help of some expert mariners from Marblehead, Massachusetts, Washington managed to transfer the rest of his battered troops across the East River—which the British navy had failed to secure—to Manhattan.

The retreat from Long Island was the first of many American retreats in the campaign of 1776. On September 12, Washington moved his troops to northern Manhattan; he built fortifications at Harlem Heights, then, after Howe sailed up the East River and made a landing to the north, moved to White Plains in Westchester County on the mainland. There he fought a battle with Howe on October 28, then slipped away again while Howe waited for reinforcements. But on November 16, Howe took the American garrison Washington had left behind at Fort Washington on the western side of Manhattan, capturing its 2,800 men. Two days later, a contingent of redcoats under Charles, Lord Cornwallis, captured Fort Lee, on the opposite shore of the Hudson River, and with it a substantial store of military supplies. Washington then retreated down through New Jersey, where people were busily signing oaths of loyalty to the Crown to avoid being punished as traitors after the imminent collapse of the American cause.

Even Washington was near despair. He managed to bring his troops across the Delaware River into Pennsylvania on December 11. The next day, Congress, fearing a British attack, fled Philadelphia for Baltimore. But then Washington broke the string of defeats on December 26 when, after recrossing the Delaware River on Christmas Day, he surprised a British garrison at Trenton, New Jersey, taking 918 prisoners and killing 30 of the king's soldiers while the Americans suffered only five casualties. Then, on January 3, he won another stunning victory at Princeton. The battles of Trenton and Princeton were among the most important of the war. They restored morale and allowed Washington to take his troops into winter camp (war in the eighteenth century was a summer and fall sport, since the guns of the day fired poorly in cold weather) at Morristown, New Jersey. That meant the Continental army would be around to fight again in 1777.

The victories also secured Washington's leadership. With the fall of Forts Washington and Lee, dissatisfaction with the commander in chief had mounted, and some saw an alternative leader in General Charles Lee, an erratic Englishman who had joined the American forces and become the darling of several members of Congress. Lee differed from Washington in his concept of how the war should be fought: he proposed an "irregular" war fought by citizen soldiers on a variety of fronts. If the militia were trained and ready to engage whenever the British entered their territory, the king's troops, Lee reasoned, would find themselves simply overwhelmed and incapable of putting down the "rebellion." Washington preferred to fight a more conventional war, with a regular army of trained soldiers and respectable officers who agreed to serve for the duration of the war in return for good pay and other benefits. He put no faith in the militia except, perhaps, in the opening stages of a war, when passions ran high. To expect inexperienced, untrained men "just dragged from the tender Scenes of domestic life" to fight a protracted war against the British army was, he told Congress, totally unrealistic. Lee's strategy lost in part because Lee's ambitions got the best of him: he dawdled in following orders to join forces with Washington in late 1776, perhaps hoping that if Washington failed to reverse his pathetic record, Congress would fire him and put Lee in command. But the British captured Lee in a New Jersey tavern, which effectively removed him from contention for the army's top job.

In the dark days of 1776, Congress finally agreed to expand the Continental Army and to recruit men willing to join for at least three-year terms in return for a bounty payment of $20 (which would later be increased), a yearly clothing issue, and the promise of 100 acres of land if they served until the end of

## What's for Dinner?

*"As to provision of victuals, ... When we [soldiers in the Continental army] engaged in the service we were promised the following articles for a ration: one pound of good and wholesome fresh or salt beef, or three fourths of a pound of good salt pork, a pound of good flour, soft or hard bread, a quart of salt to every hundred pounds of fresh beef, a quart of vinegar to a hundred rations, a gill of rum, brandy, or whiskey per day, some little soap and candles. . . But we never received what was allowed us. Oftentimes have I gone one, two, three, and even four days without a morsel, unless the fields or forests might chance to afford enough to prevent absolutte starvation. . . .*

*"If we had got our full allowance regularly, what was it? . . . The beef that we got in the army was, generally, not many degrees above carrion; it was much like the old Negro's rabbit, it had not much fat upon it and but a very little lean. When we drew flour, which was much of the time we were in the field or on marches, it was of small value, being eaten half-cooked besides a deal of it being unavoidably wasted in the cookery. . . .*

*"When General Washington told Congress, 'The soldiers eat every kind of horse fodder but hay,' he might have gone a little farther and told them that they eat considerable hog's fodder and not a trifle of dog's—when they could get it to eat."*

Joseph Plumb Martin, *Private Yankee Doodle; Being a Narrative of Some of the Adventures, Dangers and Sufferings of a Revolutionary Soldier*

the war. It also gave Washington, on his request, total military control. Henceforth the war would be fought in his way—by a regular army, with militias relegated to a supporting role. Unfortunately, Congress proved unable to recruit men in sufficient numbers, so Washington was forced to fight more defensively than he preferred. Soldiers in the Continental Army were usually drawn from the poorest and most marginal members of society, including African Americans. Like their officers, soldiers joined in good part for the material incentives Congress offered, not from selfless patriotism. To be sure, the soldiers often went unpaid or were given paper certificates that rapidly depreciated in value, and schemes for rewarding officers fared no better. Nonetheless, despite traditional fears of professional soldiers, the Americans depended upon a "standing army" to win their independence, and, under Washington's leadership, they defended their Revolution with a decidedly conservative military strategy.

Washington's leadership was critical. His most conspicuous qualification for command was his height: at over six feet tall, and with a robust, athletic build, he looked like a commander. But, as he readily admitted, his military credentials were weak.

He had essentially no successful combat experience when he first took control of the Continental Army. But no American had better qualifications, and Washington learned from his mistakes: at the battle of Princeton in January 1777, he demonstrated a skill in military tactics that stood in sharp contrast with his blunderings of the previous year. Above all, however, Washington believed in the Revolution. He told Congress in 1776 that he held no lust for personal power and more than any American dreamed of "turning the Sword into a ploughshare." When Congress's incompetence provoked discontent, Washington suppressed an effort by some officers to give him dictatorial political power. At the end of the war, he resigned his commission and went home once again to take up farming. By then, Washington had become, for good reason, an American hero like no other before or since.

### ARMS

The arms on which Washington's army depended were as traditional as his strategy. In truth, Americans were more innovative in their use of weaponry at the beginning than at the end

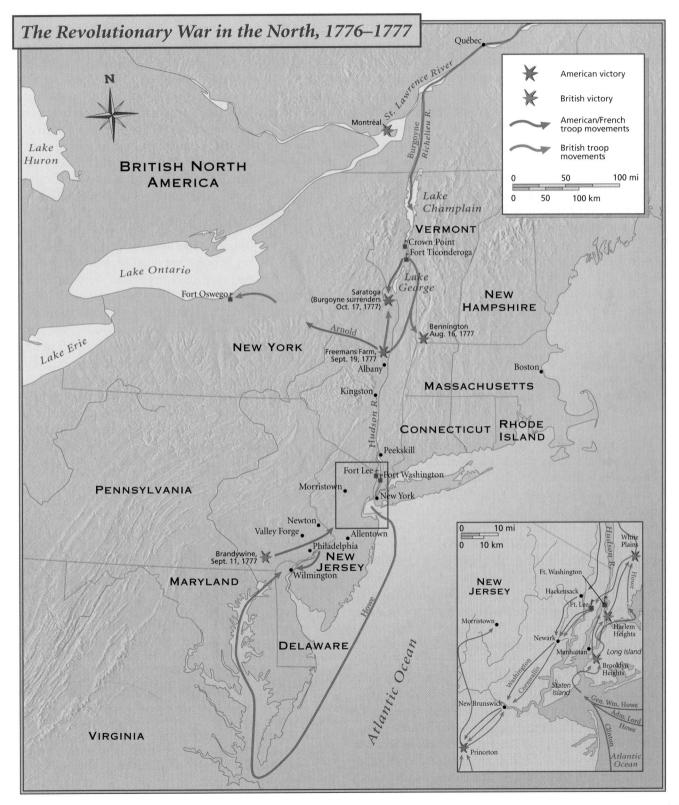

## The Revolutionary War in the North, 1776–1777

| | |
|---|---|
| ★ | American victory |
| ✦ | British victory |
| ⤳ | American/French troop movements |
| ⤳ | British troop movements |

0    50    100 mi
0    50    100 km

Québec

*St. Lawrence River*

Montréal

*Burgoyne*
*Richelieu R.*

Lake Huron

BRITISH NORTH AMERICA

Lake Ontario

*Lake Champlain*

VERMONT
Crown Point
Fort Ticonderoga

Fort Oswego

Saratoga
(Burgoyne surrenders
Oct. 17, 1777)

*Lake George*

NEW HAMPSHIRE

Lake Erie

*Arnold*

NEW YORK

Bennington
Aug. 16, 1777

Freemans Farm,
Sept. 19, 1777
Albany

Boston

Kingston

MASSACHUSETTS

*Hudson R.*

CONNECTICUT    RHODE ISLAND

Peekskill

Fort Lee    Fort Washington

Morristown    New York

PENNSYLVANIA

Newton
Valley Forge    Allentown

Philadelphia

Brandywine,
Sept. 11, 1777    NEW JERSEY

Wilmington

MARYLAND

*Howe*

DELAWARE

VIRGINIA

*Atlantic Ocean*

### Inset (New Jersey):

0    10 mi
0    10 km

NEW JERSEY

Morristown

Newark

*Washington*

*Cornwallis*

New Brunswick

Princeton

*Hudson R.*

White Plains

Ft. Washington

Hackensack

Ft. Lee

Harlem Heights

Manhattan

*Howe*

Long Island

Brooklyn Heights

Staten Island

*Gen. Wm. Howe*

*Adm. Lord Howe*

*Clinton*

*Atlantic Ocean*

165

of the war. In 1775, Washington expected great things from the "six companies of expert riflemen," which were soon increased to nine, that the Second Continental Congress had ordered raised in Pennsylvania, Maryland, and Virginia and sent to the front at Boston. "They are the finest marksmen in the world," claimed John Hancock, and could "do execution of their Rifle Guns at an amazing distance." That was possible because rifles, unlike the more common muskets, contained spiraled grooves in the interior of their barrels, and the grooves made bullets spin, facilitating their projection through the air. A capable rifleman could hit a target at least twice the distance possible for soldiers armed with smoothbore muskets, whose range of effectiveness was no more than 75–100 yards.

The rifle was first developed in central Europe and brought by German immigrants to Pennsylvania, where gunsmiths gradually adapted its design to American needs. The "Pennsylvania rifle," a strikingly handsome gun of brass, iron, and wood, was manufactured in shops from western New York down into Georgia by the time of the Revolution. Since each gun was custom-made for its purchaser, no two were exactly alike. In general, however, American rifles had a longer barrel than their European counterparts, which improved their balance and accuracy. They were also lighter, with a smaller caliber and narrower exterior dimensions, which fitted the needs of men who used rifles not for stationary sports, as in Europe, but on the move, for hunting and Indian warfare. No doubt riflemen could also help pick off redcoats. And so Washington welcomed the riflemen who arrived in 1775 with their distinctive frontier attire—buckskin breeches, hunting shirts, moccasins trimmed with porcupine quills, toting tomahawks and hunting knives—and gave them special quarters. Clearly he regarded them as an elite force.

But experience didn't match expectations. The independent-minded riflemen found little to do during the siege of Boston, and they proved so unruly that even Washington came to regret their presence. In most battle situations, moreover, the riflemen turned out to be useless or worse. Their capacity for hitting distant targets was no help in the miserable street fighting at Quebec in December 1775, and they were essentially defenseless while reloading their weapons, which was a relatively slow process. Muskets, which could be loaded faster than rifles and, unlike rifles, had bayonets attached to their barrels, were preferable in close combat. They could also be fired with coarser powder than rifles, and during the Revolutionary War having any powder whatsoever was something of a triumph. Just getting enough muskets was a big problem. Not all militiamen owned

guns at the war's beginning, and those they had were often obsolete or broken and so different from one another that a militia company sometimes needed as many as seven different kinds of ammunition. To acquire large numbers of Pennsylvania rifles would have been an impossible task since those rifles were crafted in American shops, required far more hand tooling, and were therefore significantly more expensive than muskets.

Congress did what it could to encourage the domestic production of arms, calling on the states in 1775 to keep their gunsmiths at work and specifying standard dimensions (guns should have "a good bridle lock, ¾ of an inch bore," and be "of good substance in the breech," with a barrel 3 feet 8 inches long and an 18-inch bayonet). Congress also encouraged the establishment of gunpowder mills, and pamphlets like *Essays Upon the Making of Salt-Petre and Gunpowder,* published by Pennsylvania congressman Henry Wiser, provided directions. Gunpowder mills appeared along streams in almost every colony, and by 1780 Americans had produced some 200,000 pounds of gunpowder—a small fraction of the amount needed, most of which came from abroad, but still an impressive achievement. The presence of German immigrants acquainted with the art of making gunpowder helped, as did the colonists' familiarity with watermills. Many gunpowder mills were converted gristmills—which resumed grinding grain when the war was over, assuming they hadn't blown up in the interim, as many did.

A contemporary drawing that shows an American soldier from the frontier, carrying a rifle and dressed in buckskin with a tomahawk stuck in his belt. Note the black British soldier on the left; both he and the soldier beside him are carrying muskets with bayonets attached.

The colonies' impressive prerevolutionary production of iron was also a distinct asset. In the course of the war, American furnaces and forges, many of which were located in Maryland and western Pennsylvania, produced musket barrels, cannons, cannon and musket balls, and other military supplies. Among their products was an enormous iron chain, 500 yards long, with heavy links 2 to 3½ feet in length, that Americans stretched across a narrow point in the Hudson in April 1778 to keep enemy ships from sailing up the river. Most manufacturing of war supplies was done by hand, but in the largest gun manufactures waterwheels powered triphammers, grinding wheels, and boring machines. The Americans remained nonetheless dependent on European suppliers for most firearms as well as gunpowder and saltpeter for domestic gunpowder mills. The challenge of gathering an adequate volume of any weapons that required skilled craftsmanship was so great that at one point Benjamin Franklin, the very symbol of American inventiveness, suggested that pikes (pointed stakes) and bows and arrows should become the standard American weapons. The way a nation fights reflects its state of economic and managerial development, and the United States in 1776 was a decidedly undeveloped nation.

By late 1776, the high hopes that first greeted the riflemen at Cambridge had passed, and the army began phasing them out in favor of musketmen. To use musketmen most effectively required training so they could shoot volleys of fire in disciplined formation. But careful training made little sense unless men would remain in the army from one campaign to another. That was, of course, what Washington wanted—a trained, regular army.

## 1777: A REVERSAL OF FORTUNE

The British planned a major military campaign again in 1777. General John Burgoyne would lead an expedition from Canada down to the Hudson, where he would meet an up-river campaign under Howe. Then, with control of the same western water route that Benedict Arnold and Ethan Allen had tried to secure for the Americans in 1775, the British could seal radical New England off from the rest of the country. The British ministry also approved a proposal by Howe that he take Philadelphia, which it assumed could be done quickly, freeing Howe for his rally with Burgoyne.

In the campaign of 1777, the British learned that they, too, faced some powerful disadvantages. In earlier wars, they were able to depend on the colonists for food and vehicles such as carts and wagons. Now the army's supplies had to be shipped from England across the Atlantic, where vessels were frequently picked off by privateers or blown off course to the West Indies. Administrative inefficiency also took its toll: various snafus in England delayed the arrival of supplies for the 1777 campaign until late in the fighting season. Then Howe, suddenly wary of Washington's troops, decided that, rather than risk attacks on a marching army, he would sail to Philadelphia. He set out from Manhattan on July 23 with 15,000 men (leaving another 7,300 there under the command of General Henry Clinton), sailed down the Atlantic past the Delaware Bay, then turned up the Chesapeake. He finally landed on August 25 some 50 miles southwest of Philadelphia, which was about 100 miles from where he began. Given prevailing winds, Howe had traveled the equivalent of 1,000 miles, losing precious time in the process. On September 11, however, he defeated the Continentals at Brandywine Creek, where Washington tried to block British access to Philadelphia. Once again the Second Continental Congress, which had returned to Philadelphia in March, fled its capital, this time to Lancaster and then to York, Pennsylvania.

The British took Philadelphia on September 26 and put down an American counteroffensive at Germantown on October 4. They remained in Philadelphia through the winter of 1777–78, dancing, feasting, and enjoying a fine social season, since it was much too late to get back for their appointment with General Burgoyne on the Hudson. Howe, it seems, was never all that anxious to make that rendezvous. Did he fear enhancing the record of a potential rival within the British officer corps? After the Battle of Brooklyn Heights, and again later in 1776, when Washington was dragging his way down New Jersey, Howe had failed to attack the vulnerable Continentals. The Crown had commissioned the Howe brothers as peace negotiators—a role Congress gave them little chance to exercise—as well as military commanders. Did they think that a vigorous execution of the war would make peace even less likely? They might also have felt some lingering affection for the Americans, who had paid great honor to their elder brother, a British officer beloved by the colonists who had died in the French and Indian War. Or perhaps Howe was simply protecting his army since its men and virtually all their supplies had to be supplied from England at enormous cost. Whatever the reason, Howe's inaction might well have prevented a British victory in 1776 and 1777, when their chances of putting down the American "rebellion" were far better than in the years to come.

A War of Independence

General John ("Gentleman Johnny") Burgoyne, as portrayed by Sir Joshua Reynolds eleven years before Burgoyne surrendered to the Americans at Saratoga, New York, in October 1777.

Meanwhile, poor John Burgoyne was learning the hard way that Britain's military advantages nosedived once they moved inland, away from the sea and other major water routes. In mid-June, the general set out from Canada with about 7,700 men. Burgoyne did not travel light: with his troops came some 2,000 women and children as well as 1,500 horses, many of which were needed to pull a baggage train that included 30 wagons for the personal necessities of "Gentleman Johnny"—silver service, various changes of uniform, cases of his preferred champagne. The contingent at first moved south by boat, taking Fort Ticonderoga with its large store of gunpowder and supplies in early July. Then, after fighting off a group of Americans at Hubbardston, Vermont, he took nearby Skenesborough. After a three-week lull, Burgoyne decided not to return north to Ticonderoga and sail down Lake George, but to advance by a land route that required hacking his way through thick woods, building bridges, even constructing an extensive wooden causeway. Americans toppled trees across Burgoyne's path, slowing him to a snail's pace.

The general's Indian allies made things even worse. In late July, they shot, stripped, and scalped the fiancée of a Loyalist soldier. That news alarmed Americans, who feared for the safety of their own families, particularly after Burgoyne failed to punish the murderers. He had, in fact, rigidly forbidden the Indians to engage in atrocities, but he feared that reprisals would alienate his Indian allies. American newspapers made the most of the incident, and local militiamen rushed to join the fight in defense of home and hearth, multiplying the number of men Burgoyne faced. As the balance of forces shifted, Burgoyne's Indians, who were no fools, gradually chose discretion over valor and slipped away from the British camp, turning the odds even more radically against the king's forces.

Burgoyne's first military setback came at Bennington, Vermont, where in mid-August American troops, mostly miliamen, killed or captured the greater part of a contingent of soldiers sent to seize some badly needed supplies. Burgoyne then crossed to the western side of the Hudson and tried to move south toward Albany, but he found his route blocked by American entrenchments at Bemis Heights, New York. Help from New York failed to reach him: General Clinton had started up the Hudson with 3,000 men on October 3 but returned to New York for reinforcements before pushing beyond Esopus (now Kingston, New York). Meanwhile, Burgoyne advanced on the Americans but was thrown back when Arnold, who had been relieved of his command by General Horatio Gates, his jealous superior officer, nonetheless rushed forward, leading an American charge that saved the day. At that moment, Arnold, who suffered a serious leg wound in the engagement, seemed destined to become one of the great military heroes of the American war.

Burgoyne retreated seven miles north to Saratoga, New York. But his cause had become hopeless: the Americans already outnumbered his men by 3 to 1, and day by day their forces grew while his dwindled. Finally, on October 17, Burgoyne surrendered. His remaining 5,700 men laid down their arms. Under the terms Burgoyne negotiated, they would be sent back to England and take no further part in the war.

The American triumph at Saratoga transformed the war because it led directly to an American alliance with France. The French court, determined to weaken its traditional enemy, Great Britain, had sent secret aid to the Americans even before they declared their independence. However, France hesitated to conclude a formal alliance in 1776, when a succession of military defeats brought the survival of the American cause into question. France also needed time to build up its navy. But in December 1777, after news of Saratoga arrived, French officials told the American commissioners in Paris—Silas Deane, Arthur Lee, and Franklin—that France had decided to recognize American independence.

Negotiations began in January, and on February 6, 1778, French and American representatives in Paris signed three agreements. By the first, a treaty of amity and commerce, France recognized American independence, and in return the Americans granted France certain trading privileges. By the second, a treaty of alliance, France agreed to fight with the Americans in "common cause" if and when war broke out between France and Britain and to continue engaged until American independence was ensured. The United States was left free to conquer Canada and Bermuda. France could seize the British West Indies but promised to take no territory on the North American mainland. Both countries agreed not to conclude peace with Britain without the other's consent, and the alliance would continue "forever." The third agreement, which was secret, allowed Spain to enter the alliance. At the signing ceremony, Franklin wore the same, now somewhat faded suit of Manchester velvet he had worn the day Alexander Wedderburne publicly humiliated him. He wanted to "give it a little revenge," Franklin told Deane.

In April 1778, in a desperate effort to forestall American ratification of the treaties, the British ministry introduced into Parliament a series of measures designed to provide the basis for reconciliation, then appointed the Earl of Carlisle to head a peace commission authorized, as earlier efforts were not, to negotiate with Congress. The terms—repeal of the Tea and Coercive Acts, a promise by Parliament not to tax the Americans, the possibility of suspending all other objectionable laws passed since 1763—might have worked a few years earlier. On June 17, however, Congress notified the Carlisle Commission that it would consider only an agreement for the withdrawal of British troops from America and British recognition of American independence. Meanwhile, an engagement between French and British ships off the coast of Brittany led to war, so France joined with the Americans in their struggle for independence. Another year would pass before Spain entered the war; but Spain, anxious about her own colonial possessions, refused to recognize American independence. In fact, Spanish participation in the war was less significant than that of France, which made all the difference for the American cause.

The Franco-American alliance dramatically reduced British chances of victory in America. No longer could the British concentrate their forces there, as they had done at New York in 1776; they now had an enemy nearer home and also had to defend Bermuda and British colonies in the Caribbean. Moreover, the enlistment of the now powerful French navy on the American side robbed Britain of what had been a considerable military advantage. In the past, the British, with virtually un-contested control of the American Atlantic coast, had little trouble holding American ports—in the course of the war, they held every major American port at one time or another—but experienced great difficulty controlling territory in the interior. If that situation had continued, the war would probably have ended with a negotiated peace by which, in one way or another, the Americans would return under Crown rule. The French navy made possible an American victory that would confirm independence and allow a continuation of the republican political revolution that accompanied it.

## THE ROAD TO YORKTOWN

In 1778, the British government assessed the changed situation and adopted a third plan of war, one distinctly different from those of 1775 and 1776. It decided to cut its commitments in the North, evacuating Philadelphia and using its bases at New York and Newport to mount attacks at various points along the Atlantic coast to break the will of the "rebels." The Crown also encouraged its Indian allies to mount deadly raids on the western frontier.

In 1776, the Declaration of Independence had accused the king of having "endeavoured to bring on the inhabitants of our frontiers, the merciless Indian Savages, whose known rule of warfare, is an undistinguished destruction of all ages, sexes and conditions." Now frontier regions from New York south suffered devastating violence in which both sides were guilty of the "undistinguished destruction of all ages, sexes, and conditions." George Rogers Clark, an Indian-hating Kentuckian whom the Virginia legislature sent west in 1778 to defend its frontier, imitated the Indians he fought, dressing in a hunting shirt and breech cloth, blackening his face, and inspiring his men by shouting out a war whoop. Clark demonstrated his ruthlessness by publicly tomahawking to death Indian prisoners within sight of the British garrison under siege at Vincennes in the Illinois Country. Raids in western New York under General John Sullivan destroyed Indian crops, cut down fruit trees, and burned towns, forcing thousands of hungry Iroquois to seek refuge during the winter of 1777–78 with the British at Fort Niagara. Not all Indians sided with the British, but American frontier fighters found it hard to distinguish one Indian from another: in 1782, for example, militiamen murdered ninety-six Indian men, women, and children at the Delawares' town of Gnadenhuetten, all of whom were Moravian Christians and determinedly neutral in the Anglo-American war. Indian raiders were no kinder.

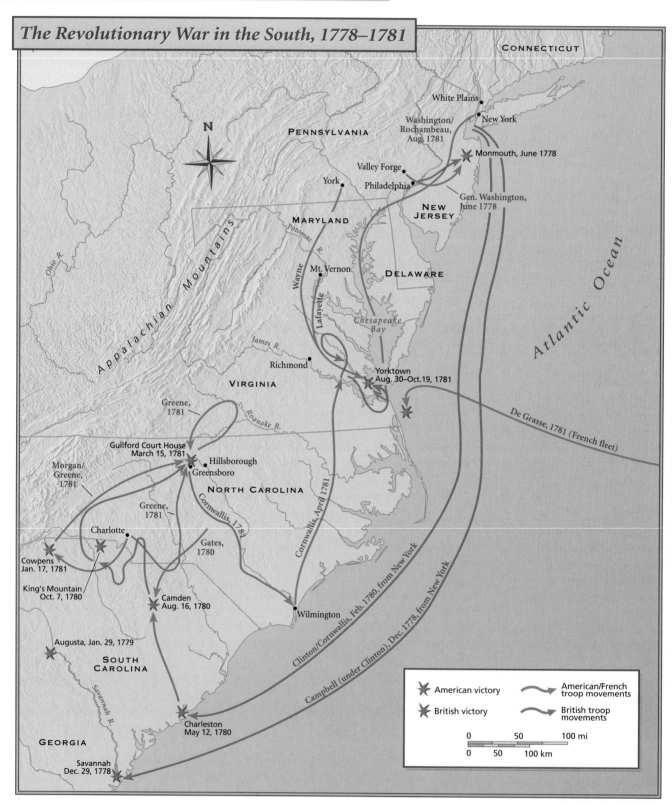

## The Revolutionary War in the South, 1778–1781

CONNECTICUT

White Plains

New York

Washington/Rochambeau, Aug. 1781

PENNSYLVANIA

Monmouth, June 1778

Valley Forge

York

Philadelphia

NEW JERSEY

Gen. Washington, June 1778

Wayne

MARYLAND

Mt. Vernon

DELAWARE

Potomac R.

Lafayette

Chesapeake Bay

Atlantic Ocean

James R.

Richmond

Yorktown
Aug. 30–Oct.19, 1781

VIRGINIA

De Grasse, 1781 (French fleet)

Greene, 1781

Roanoke R.

Guilford Court House
March 15, 1781

Hillsborough

Greensboro

Morgan/Greene, 1781

NORTH CAROLINA

Cornwallis, 1781

Greene, 1781

Cornwallis, April 1781

Charlotte

Gates, 1780

Cowpens
Jan. 17, 1781

King's Mountain
Oct. 7, 1780

Camden
Aug. 16, 1780

Wilmington

Clinton/Cornwallis, Feb. 1780, from New York

Campbell (under Clinton), Dec. 1778, from New York

Augusta, Jan. 29, 1779

SOUTH CAROLINA

Savannah R.

Charleston
May 12, 1780

GEORGIA

Savannah
Dec. 29, 1778

Ohio R.

Appalachian Mountains

N

### Legend

✹ American victory

✷ British victory

American/French troop movements

British troop movements

0    50    100 mi
0    50    100 km

Neither side held a monopoly on savagery; neither sought anything short of the enemy's total destruction.

The main British objective after 1778 was, however, not the West but the South, where it expected substantial Loyalist support. The South seemed the most vulnerable part of the United States, divided as it was into slave and free, and with white colonists along the Tidewater often at odds with those in the interior. The British also tried to apply a lesson they had learned during earlier campaigns in the North. Victory in this war required more than defeating the enemy on the battlefield and taking nominal control of territory. It demanded winning and holding the allegiance of the people.

King George marked the change in strategy by replacing William Howe as head of the British forces in America with Sir Henry Clinton, the third general to hold that position since the war began. By contrast, the American army still remained under its first commander, George Washington. His bedraggled 11,000 soldiers—2,000 of them without shoes— spent the cold and snowy winter of 1777–78 at Valley Forge, eighteen miles northwest of Philadelphia, where Howe was waiting out the season in comfort. A breakdown of the American supply system left men at Valley Forge without adequate food or clothing, huddling in what the twenty-year-old Marquis de Lafayette, one of an important set of Europeans who joined the American fight, described as "little shanties." Perhaps a quarter left or died in the course of that winter; but those who stayed and survived were better prepared for combat as a result of their rigorous drilling under the command of "Baron" Frederick von Steuben, a Prussian and onetime aide-de-camp of Frederick the Great, who arrived at the camp in February.

Von Steuben's impact became clear in June 1778, when Washington broke camp to pursue Clinton, who evacuated Philadelphia on June 18 and began marching across New Jersey toward New York City. General Charles Lee, who had been freed in exchange for British prisoners and returned to military service in May, attacked the British at Monmouth (New Jersey) Court House on June 28, then strangely ordered a retreat, for which he was subsequently court-martialed. Washington was able to rally the men, who then stood their ground through repeated attacks. In the end, Clinton escaped, but the Continental soldiers' performance had given the commander reason for satisfaction.

Not much else went right. An effort to retake Newport by a coordinated action of Continental troops and the French fleet, which absorbed most of the summer of 1778, failed. The

following December, Clinton took Savannah and, a month later, Augusta, Georgia. In May 1780, he seized Charleston along with a 5,400-man American garrison under General Benjamin Lincoln. Then Clinton returned north, leaving behind 8,000 British troops under Lord Cornwallis, confident that Georgia and South Carolina had essentially been rewon and that Cornwallis would easily take the upper South.

As Cornwallis seized new territory, the British organized Loyalist militia companies to ensure continued submission to British rule. But once the British army left an area, supporters of the Revolution crawled out from the swamps and other hiding places and turned the war in the South into a bitter, nasty civil war, in which the lines of division sometimes echoed nothing more than long-standing local rivalries. Meanwhile, the British incapacity to control plundering and terrorism at the hands of British officers drove throngs of previously uncommitted persons into the American camp, which went far to undo Clinton's triumph.

In June 1780, Congress commissioned General Horatio Gates to lead a new American army in the South. But Gates's leadership (and army) soon came to an end at Camden, South Carolina, where in mid-August he lost almost 2,000 men; he personally fled all the way to Hillsboro, North Carolina, 160 miles away, his military career in tatters. Again there was no Continental army in the South, but the war continued. Meanwhile, Congress appointed General Nathaniel Greene to succeed Gates, and in December 1780 Greene began piecing together a third American army in the South.

Lacking the men to attack Cornwallis, Greene used what resources he had to nibble away at the enemy. The American general Daniel Morgan cleverly employed "unreliable" militiamen at a battle near Cowpens, South Carolina, in January 1781, sending those "irregular" troops against Tarleton, then bringing up regulars to the redcoats' surprise as they chased the retreating militiamen. By spring, reinforcements enlarged Greene's army to 4,400. He technically lost the battle at Guilford Court House on March 15, where he applied a battle plan much like Morgan's at Cowpens, but Cornwallis's 500 casualties were so costly that he retreated to Wilmington, North Carolina, and then in April to Virginia, seeking reinforcements. There Cornwallis could join forces with, strangely enough, Benedict Arnold. The previous fall, Arnold had conspired to deliver the American post at West Point, New York, to the British, but the plot was dramatically discovered in September 1780. Arnold escaped capture, made it to British lines, and thereafter fought for the king. Moved by resentments of real

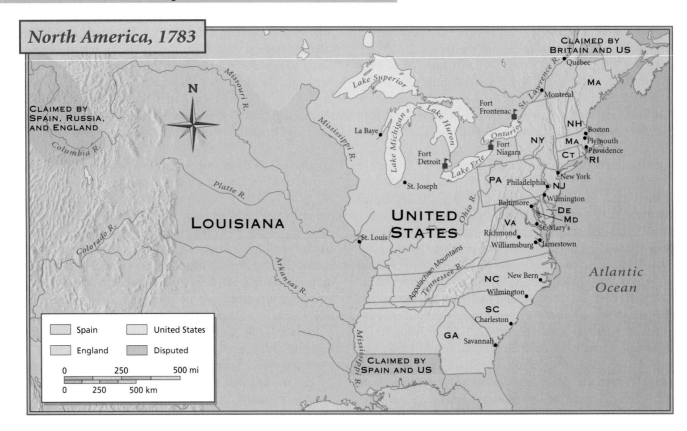

**North America, 1783**

CLAIMED BY
BRITAIN AND US

CLAIMED BY
SPAIN, RUSSIA,
AND ENGLAND

*Lake Superior*

*St. Lawrence R.*

Québec

MA

Montréal

N

*Missouri R.*

Fort
Frontenac

NH
Boston

La Baye

*Lake Michigan*

*Lake Huron*

*Mississippi R.*

*L. Ontario*

Fort
Niagara

NY

MA

Boston
Plymouth
Providence

*Columbia R.*

Fort
Detroit

*Lake Erie*

CT

RI

St. Joseph

*Platte R.*

*Ohio R.*

PA

Philadelphia

New York

NJ

LOUISIANA

UNITED
STATES

Baltimore

Wilmington

DE
MD

*Colorado R.*

St. Louis

VA

St. Mary's

Richmond

Williamsburg

Jamestown

*Arkansas R.*

*Appalachian Mountains*

*Tennessee R.*

NC

New Bern

*Atlantic
Ocean*

Wilmington

SC

Charleston

GA

Savannah

*Mississippi R.*

CLAIMED BY
SPAIN AND US

| | | |
|---|---|---|
| Spain | | United States |
| England | | Disputed |

0        250        500 mi

0    250    500 km

---

and imagined injustices, a man who had once seemed destined to become a great American military hero became instead the new nation's foremost traitor.

While Greene and a set of skillful subordinate officers gradually reclaimed most of South Carolina, Cornwallis swept through Virginia, almost capturing Governor Thomas Jefferson and the Virginia legislature at Charlottesville in June 1781. Finally, seeking a place where he could receive reinforcements from Clinton in New York, Cornwallis settled in at Yorktown on the southern shore of the York River near the Chesapeake Bay.

When Washington learned that a French fleet under the Marquis de Grasse would be available for action in the Chesapeake between August and October, he saw his chance. With French ships in the bay preventing Clinton from sending support, Washington could move his forces to Cornwallis's rear, enclosing him in a trap. By early September 1781, de Grasse controlled the Chesapeake, and Washington and the Compte de Rochambeau, who commanded a French army of 5,000, moved rapidly to Virginia and began siege operations. By mid-October, Cornwallis's position at Yorktown was hopeless,

and he surrendered. On October nineteenth, the 8,000 captured British soldiers laid down their arms.

### THE PEACE

There was no military reason for the war to end at Yorktown. The British still held Savannah, Charleston, and New York. But when news of Yorktown reached London on November 25, 1781, the king's minister, Lord North, exclaimed, "Oh God, it is all over." A restive Parliament and a nation tired of paying ever-increasing taxes to sustain an increasingly pointless war made it impossible to replace Cornwallis's army. In March 1782, North resigned his office, and his successor, Lord Rockingham—the same man who had orchestrated the repeal of the Stamp Act—opened peace negotiations. On Rockingham's death four months later, that responsibility fell to a ministry under the Earl of Shelburne, who had defended the Americans in Parliament during the 1760s and 1770s.

The politics of peace were different from those of war. With Britain's empire effectively dismembered, the main French war

General George Washington and his generals at Yorktown. The American artist Charles Willson Peale did the painting in 1781 soon after the decisive Battle of Yorktown.

1784. The the United States could finally take up that "separate and equal station" among the "powers of the earth" that it had claimed on July 4, 1776.

The trans-Appalachian West, whose delivery to "British liberty" New England's clergymen celebrated some twenty years earlier, was now part of the United States. Would American rule lead, at last, to an era of unprecedented growth, with "towns enlarged, settlements increased, and this howling wilderness become a fruitful field which the Lord hath blessed"? The havoc left in the West by a war far more brutal than tradition recalls made fulfillment of that expansionist dream more likely. The once-powerful Iroquois confederation, long an obstacle to the westward movement, was now split, with a Loyalist segment in Ontario and another in the state of New York. Elsewhere, too, devastation destroyed old ruling structures and scattered Indian peoples far from their familiar homelands, with ripple effects that extended all the way to the lands of the Comanches and Apaches far to the southwest. The great losers in the American war for independence were not the British, who went on to build another empire, but the Indians, who had nowhere else to go.

objective had been realized. The Comte de Vergennes, the French minister who had negotiated the Franco-American alliance and now participated in negotiating the peace, had no interest in the creation of a strong American republic with capacious western lands. France, moreover, was obliged by an agreement with Spain to continue fighting until Spain won Gibralter. The United States had no particular obligations to Spain, and no interest whatsoever in delaying peace. But Congress had instructed its peace commissioners to agree to no terms without France's prior consent, as the alliance treaty specified.

The commissioners—now John Adams, John Jay, and Benjamin Franklin, who were later joined by Henry Laurens—assessed the situation and decided to ignore those instructions. They signed preliminary articles of peace with Britain on November 30, 1782, then presented the terms to Vergennes as a fait accompli. In that way, they won British recognition of American independence and a generous territorial settlement by which the postwar United States extended south to the 31st parallel (the northern border of Florida), which reverted from British to Spanish control, and west to the Mississippi, except for New Orleans, which remained in Spanish hands. Congress promised to recommend that the states treat Loyalists fairly and to honor its debts; Britain agreed to withdraw its land and sea forces "with all convenient speed." The final peace treaty was signed at Paris on September 3, 1783, and ratified by Congress on January 14,

## Suggested Reading

John Richard Alden, *The American Revolution, 1775–1783* (1954)

Bernard Bailyn, *Ideological Origins of the American Revolution* (1992)

M. L. Brown, *Firearms in Colonial America: The Impact on History and Technology, 1492–1792* (1980)

David Hackett Fischer, *Washington's Crossing* (2004)

Merrill Jensen, *The Founding of a Nation: A History of the American Revolution, 1763–1776* (1968)

Pauline Maier, *From Resistance to Revolution: American Radicals and the Development of Intercolonial Opposition to Britain, 1765–1776* (1972), and *American Scripture: Making the Declaration of Independence* (1997)

Jerilyn Greene Marston, *King and Congress: The Transfer of Political Legitimacy, 1774–1776* (1987)

Jack N. Rakove, *The Beginnings of National Politics: An Interpretive History of the Continental Congress* (1979)

Charles R. Ritcheson, *British Politics and the American Revolution* (1964)

John Shy, *A People Numerous and Armed: Reflections on the Military Struggle for American Independence* (1976/1990)

# Chapter Review

## Summary QUESTIONS

- How did the Anglo-American conflict change after the Coercive Acts?
- Why did the British refuse to compromise with the Americans in the Revolutionary era?
- How did the colonists gradually assume the powers of self-government between 1765 and 1776?
- What strategy did General Washington use in fighting the British army?
- Why did the American War for Independence end with the battle of Yorktown?

## Chronology

| | |
|---|---|
| 1765 | Parliament passes the Stamp Act (repealed March 1766). |
| 1767 | The Townshend Revenue Acts (partially repealed in 1770). |
| 1773 | Tea Act. |
| December 16, 1773 | The Boston Tea Party. |
| 1774 | Parliament passes the Coercive, or "Intolerable," Acts. |
| September 5, 1774 | The First Continental Congress convenes in Philadelphia. |
| April 19, 1775 | The Revolutionary War begins with the Battles of Lexington and Concord. |
| May 10, 1775 | The Second Continental Congress convenes. |
| July 4, 1776 | Congress approves the Declaration of Independence. |
| October 17, 1777 | Burgoyne surrenders at Saratoga. |
| February 6, 1778 | France sides with the colonies against Britain. |
| October 18, 1781 | Cornwallis surrenders at Yorktown. |
| 1783 | Treaty of Paris: British recognize American independence, and trans-Appalachian West becomes part of United States. |

## Key Terms

Virtual representation (p. 145)

Sons of Liberty (pp. 147, 154)

Second Continental Congress (p. 157)

Declaration of Independence (pp. 159, 161)

Yorktown (p. 172)

Access the *Inventing America* StudySpace at wwnorton.com/studyspace

PERSONAL PLAN ■ REVIEW MATERIALS ■ RESEARCH AIDS ■ MULTIMEDIA

# Chapter 6

# INVENTING THE AMERICAN REPUBLIC:

## THE STATES, 1776-1790

A view of the Old State House in Boston (painted by James Brown Marston in 1801), where both houses of the Massachusetts legislature met and the governor maintained his office until 1798.

QUESTIONS

■ *In what ways were the first state constitutions innovative?*

■ *What impact did the Revolution have on American society?*

■ *What important economic innovations occurred in the 1780s?*

The Anglo-American war was not itself revolutionary. Except for the attacks on British soldiers as they marched from Concord to Boston on April 19, 1775, and the irregular fighting later in the South and the West, the Americans fought in the traditional way that General Washington preferred, depending primarily on a regular army. And they finally won, at Yorktown, with a conventional siege operation.

Not that there was a lack of interest in innovative military techniques or devices. In 1777, the Second Continental Congress asked the states to forward information on any "discoveries and improvements in the arts of war." David Bushnell of Connecticut, a farm boy and Yale graduate given to tinkering, devised an ingenious "Turtle," a primitive submarine propelled by foot-driven paddles, with which he planned to fire torpedoes—which he also developed—into the bottoms of British ships. But nothing came of the idea, or, it seems, of other clever proposals, except perhaps for the great chain and other obstacles employed to block British ships from American rivers. Even standard military tasks such as designing forts and breastworks or river defense systems were challenging for the Americans because they lacked military engineers. With the arrival in 1777 of European engineers such as Thaddeus Kosciuszko, that problem was partially overcome. Their coming coincided with Baron von Steuben's effort to teach Continental soldiers drill routines adapted from Prussian precedents. In one way after another, Americans struggled to approximate European military standards. Improving on those standards lay well beyond their capacity.

Meanwhile, Americans' emerging strength in science stalled. Earlier promising trends peaked in 1768 with the establishment of the American Philosophical Society in Philadelphia. The first volume of the society's *Transactions* (1771), which reported Americans' remarkably accurate observations of the 1769 transit of Venus across the sun, won extensive acclaim in Europe. Later, John Adams proposed the founding of a sister society in Boston. The American Acad-emy of Arts and Sciences, chartered by the Massachusetts legislature in 1780, published the first volume of its *Memoirs*—the French-inspired name was a sign of the times—three years later. In the meantime, however, the American Philosophical Society, and American science in general, had sunk into a certain lassitude. The problem lay partly in the deaths of prominent figures such as John Bartram (1777) and Harvard professor John Winthrop (1779). A handful of others, including Charleston's Alexander Garden and one of the most promising members of the next generation, Benjamin Thompson, from Rumford (now Concord), New Hampshire, became Loyalist exiles; Thompson—later Count Rumford—did virtually all of his scientific work, including pioneering studies on the nature of heat, abroad. However, several distinguished American scientists became absorbed in activities on behalf of the American cause. They included Pennsylvania's David Rittenhouse, a clock maker and self-taught Newtonian remembered mainly for the orreries (mechanical devices that accurately represent the motion of planets around the sun) he constructed in the 1770s, and Benjamin Franklin, the dean of American scientists. When Franklin wasn't representing the United States abroad, he sat in the Second Continental Congress, presided over the convention that designed Pennsylvania's constitution of 1776 (which Rittenhouse also attended), and later, after returning from France, participated in the federal Constitutional Convention. Franklin also found time to continue his scientific studies—for example, measuring water temperature while at sea in an effort to chart the Gulf Stream. But the main work of his life had become political.

The creation of a workable republic became, in fact, the most fascinating challenge of the age, a form of innovation that outdistanced all others. "You and I, dear friend," John Adams wrote the Virginian George Wythe in 1776, "have been sent into life at a time when the greatest lawgivers of antiquity would have wished to live. How few of the human race have ever enjoyed an opportunity of making an election of government, more than of air, soil, or climate, for themselves or their children! When, before the present epoch, had three millions of people full power and a fair opportunity to form and establish the wisest and happiest government that human wisdom can contrive?" His friend Thomas Jefferson agreed. The creation of a good government was, Jefferson said, "the whole object of the present controversy," and a task so interesting that every individual would want to have a say in it.

In the end, Americans' contributions to the science of government transformed the independence movement into a revolution. Years later, in *The Rights of Man* (1791–92), Thomas Paine concluded that "the independence of America, considered merely as a separation from England, would have been a matter of but little importance." The Americans' struggle with Britain acquired broad historical significance only because it was "accompanied by a revolution in the principles and practise of governments." The Revolution also set in motion social and economic transformations whose effects would be felt far into the future. In those ways, too, the American Revolution became a revolution in the modern sense of the word, not an occurrence that moved a people back along a cyclical path like the revolution of the sun or the moon, which the word previously implied, but a traumatic event that shifted the course of history in a radically new direction.

The greatest effects were felt at home. In short, the Revolution transformed a colonial culture of imitation, which sought to approximate ever more faithfully British models of achievement, into a national culture that fostered innovations. The first steps toward revolutionary change—institutional, social, and economic—occurred within the several states, since it was there that power rested once Americans cut loose from Britain.

## The First State Constitutions, 1776–1780

The process of redesigning government began with the very short constitution New Hampshire enacted in January 1776 and the more elaborate document South Carolina adopted the following March. Both of those states' new governments were emergency measures, created to preserve "peace and good order" and provide for the people's security until, as the New Hampshire constitution put it, the "present unhappy and unnatural contest with Great Britain" was settled.

In the meantime, colonists there and in other states where royal authority collapsed discovered that self-government had unexpected charms. No longer were Americans forbidden to trade in markets or to manufacture goods when they competed with the mother country. And no longer did they have to endure royal governors who were ignorant of their laws and interests, answerable to the Crown alone, and against whom redress was impossible, as South Carolina's chief justice, William Henry Drayton, put it in April 1776, "by any peaceable means." In South Carolina, the people could choose officials from among themselves and raise "the poorest man" to the highest office if he had "virtue and merit." Even the makeshift government that Congress suggested for Massachusetts back in June 1775, with an assembly and council organized according to its charter of 1691 but no royal governor, a government entirely under the control of the people, seemed by early 1776 "more free and happy" than the government of their ancestors. Suddenly, and surprisingly, the colonists discovered that the persons best qualified to govern them were themselves.

That was, of course, the message of Thomas Paine's *Common Sense* (1776; see Chapter 5). Until the colonists shook off monarchy and hereditary rule and placed power in republican institutions that depended on popular choice, Paine argued, they would find no lasting peace or freedom. Republics, however, were by no means problem-free. By reputation, they

An 1800 portrait (artist unknown) of Thomas Paine, author of *Common Sense*.

were prone to "tumult and riot" (if the people rule, who will be ruled?) and had a nasty habit of giving way to despotism as people embraced strong leaders to end the disorder. None of the great republics of the past—those of Rome or Athens or England's own Commonwealth of the 1650s—had survived, which gave reason for pause. But as the war persisted, grievances mounted, and reconciliation came to seem an impossible dream, it became increasingly difficult to maintain civil authority under the makeshift, part-legal, part-revolutionary governments in place. That was why, in its resolutions of May 10 and 15, 1776, the Second Continental Congress recommended that colonies in which "no government sufficient to the exigencies of their affairs has been hitherto established" break with the past and "adopt such government as shall, in the opinion of the representatives of the people, best conduce to the happiness and safety of their constituents in particular and America in general." In the months that followed, the people of one state after another began designing new governments for themselves and their children.

On May 15, 1776, the same day that Congress finally approved its resolutions on government, the Virginia convention (the state's revolutionary legislature) authorized the preparation of a Declaration of Rights and "a plan of government . . . to maintain peace and order in this Colony, and secure substantial and equal liberty to the people." George Mason drafted the declaration, which the convention revised and then adopted on June 12. Finally, on June 29, the convention enacted a constitution that, unlike its predecessors in New Hampshire and South Carolina, was permanent (that is, it was to continue indefinitely, until the people chose to replace it). In fact, the preamble to the Virginia constitution, written by Thomas Jefferson, formally declared the state independent of Britain, which gave Virginia a short jump on Congress.

Before the "United States in Congress Assembled" finally declared independence, New Jersey also produced a new constitution, and other states followed. In the course of 1776, all but three states either wrote new constitutions or, in the cases of Connecticut and Rhode Island, adjusted their colonial charters to fit more exactly an independent republic. Then, in 1777, New York and Georgia adopted new constitutions. So did Vermont, which was trying to break off from New York and become the fourteenth state—an ambition it would not realize until fourteen years later. Finally, in 1780, Massachusetts enacted the last of the first state constitutions, which many observers considered the best of the lot, in part because Massachusetts could learn from others' mistakes. Before long,

This portrait of John Adams was done by Benjamin Blythe at Salem in 1766, when Adams was at the start of his long political career. It is the earliest known portrait of Adams.

states began replacing their first, flawed efforts: South Carolina, for example, replaced its constitution of 1776 in 1778, New Hampshire in 1784, Pennsylvania in 1789.

The fact that men were creating the governments that would bind them was, as John Adams noted, itself remarkable. The details of how they executed that task are even more fascinating. The first constitutions included an array of peculiar devices: electoral colleges, vetoes that could be overridden, limits on terms in office, councils of one sort or another. In the course of a few short years, the variety declined; patterns emerged, and certain solutions to nagging institutional problems won an enduring place in American government. The states served as a laboratory for the nation as a whole: in 1787, a federal constitution would be built in good part from state precedents. But the governments established for the states remained important in themselves, since the states were by far the more powerful agencies of government. It was they who made most of the decisions that shaped and regulated Americans' daily lives. And so it would remain on into the twentieth century.

## THE PROBLEM OF DESIGN: SIMPLE OR COMPLEX?

The first problem confronted by state constitution writers was one of basic design: should governments be simple or complex, with constituent parts that were separated and balanced against one another? Britain's unwritten constitution distributed power among the king, House of Lords, and House of Commons, each of which represented a component of British society—the monarch, aristocracy, and people. On critical issues, such as collecting taxes or maintaining an army, no one part of government could act without the consent of the others, which explained, according to the wisdom of the time, why liberty survived in the British world.

Thomas Paine disagreed. "The Constitution of England is so exceedingly complex," he wrote in *Common Sense,* "that the nation may suffer for years without being able to discover in which part the fault lies." His concept of good government came from what he described as "a principle in nature which no art can overturn, viz. that the more simple any thing is, the less liable it is to be disordered, and the easier repaired when disordered." There Paine, an enthusiast of popular science who would later claim fame for designing an iron bridge, revealed the technical bent of his mind: the rule he stated remains today a basic principle of engineering known as the "kiss" rule ("Keep it simple, stupid"). Two of the three parts of the British constitution—the king and Lords—represented for him "*constitutional errors*" that contributed nothing but trouble to British freedom. What liberty Britons had, he said, was due to the republican part of their constitution, the elected House of Commons. The "Constitution of England" was "sickly" because the Crown had corrupted and now controlled the Commons, as it always would if it got the chance. It was best, then, to get rid of monarchy and, for good measure, any equivalent of the House of Lords, and to build anew on a republican, or popular, base. Paine's proposal for state government was simple in the extreme: it consisted of an annually elected assembly with a "president only" (that is, a presiding officer). He added that representation in the assemblies should be equal, their business "wholly domestic" (that is, confined to matters internal to the state), and that they should be subject to the authority of a Continental Congress.

John Adams was appalled. By its "crude, ignorant Notion of a Government by one assembly," he lamented, *Common Sense* would "do more Mischief . . . than all the Tory Writings together"; Paine was a powerful writer, but he remained "very ignorant of the Science of Government." Adams explained his own position in *Thoughts on Government* (1776). He agreed that there was "no good government but what is republican," but Adams believed that a single, all-powerful assembly such as Paine proposed would make, execute, and enforce laws arbitrarily. In time, it would vote itself perpetual and "not scruple to exempt itself from the burdens which it will lay without compunction on its constituents." Moreover, Adams felt, no single body was competent to exercise all the powers of government. An assembly couldn't be an effective executive because it was too cumbersome and open; it couldn't be a judiciary because it was "too numerous, too slow, and too unskilled in the laws." The powers of a republic had to be more carefully arranged to ensure "an impartial and exact execution of the laws."

Under the scheme of government Adams proposed, the people would annually elect a lower house of assembly, which should be "in miniature an exact portrait of the people at large." The assembly would then choose an upper house, or council. Those two parts of the legislature would together elect a governor, also annually, who would be able to act on his "free and independent" judgment. The governor could nominate and appoint other government officials including judges, and he could veto acts of the legislature, although his implementation of those powers might require the advice and consent of a "privy council" of advisers. To ensure that the judiciary remained independent, Adams insisted that judges be given fixed salaries and hold office during good behavior—that is, indefinitely.

The rough plans of government that Paine and Adams threw out for discussion in 1776 provided stark alternatives that had rough counterparts in the state constitutions actually adopted. At first, the simple "Paineite" model won out, which made sense given Americans' experience. In most colonies, the governors had represented an alien power, answerable to the king. Although there were some popular royal governors, the likes of Virginia's Lord Dunmore or Thomas Hutchinson of Massachusetts came more quickly to mind in the mid-1770s, so it seemed best to eliminate powerful, independent executives. The Crown also appointed the members of most colonial upper houses, which meant that the lower houses of assembly were the only institution of provincial government elected by and responsible to the people. Moreover, in the immediate past, after royal governments had collapsed, many states were governed with reasonable success by assemblies or congresses or conventions that consisted of an elected body of delegates with a presiding officer. As a result, although no state simply enacted Paine's model government, the constitutions that the states adopted in 1776 tended to entrust power to elected assemblies and either to eliminate separate executives or to hamstring their power.

That was the case even where constitutions established an apparently complex set of institutions not so different from those of Adams's plan. Take the Virginia constitution of 1776. Under its terms, the people elected annually a House of Delegates from the resident freeholders of counties and towns. The people also elected an upper house, or "senate"—a word borrowed from the American republic's Roman ancestor—from the resident freeholders of twenty-four special districts. Senators had to be twenty-five years of age or older and, unlike members of the House of Delegates, held office for four years. The House of Delegates and senate together were called the General Assembly, which the constitution described as a "complete Legislature." The governor was elected by the General Assembly, as were almost all other executive officers as well as the judges of various state courts.

Virginia's governor was kept on a short leash: he had to be reelected each year, and after three years in office he was disqualified for four years. The purpose of that practice, known as rotation in office, was, as the Virginia Declaration of Rights explained, to restrain public officials from oppression by returning them for fixed periods to a "private station," where they would share "the burdens of the people." The governor's powers were also severely limited. He could not prorogue or dissolve the assembly, nor could he make appointments as royal governors had done. To exercise what executive powers he possessed required the consent of a Council of State whose eight members were, again, chosen by the General Assembly and could hold office for no more than three years out of six. With all those restrictions, it's hard to see the governor as a threat to anything. But just in case, the constitution gave the assembly power to impeach him. It could also impeach judges accused of "mal-administration, corruption," or other acts "by which the safety of the State may be endangered."

The Virginia constitution placed so much power in the General Assembly that it was subject to the same objections Adams had raised to Paine's plan of government. Thomas Jefferson complained that in Virginia "all the powers of government, legislative, executive, and judiciary," were invested in the legislature, which was "precisely the definition of despotic government." And despotism, Jefferson said, would be as oppressive in the hands of 173 men—the number of Virginians in the General Assembly—as in those of one.

Portrait of Thomas Jefferson by Charles Willson Peale (c. 1791).

Pennsylvania offered an even clearer example of an unbalanced government. The Continental Congress's resolutions of May 10 and 15 were designed specifically to bring down the old elitist, proprietary government of Pennsylvania, which stood determinedly against independence, and to enfranchise the Philadelphia artisans and backcountry farmers who were ardent opponents of Britain. The resolutions succeeded: the old government fell; Pennsylvania voted for independence and began the process of writing a new, republican state constitution, which it adopted in September 1776. That "radical" constitution placed power firmly in a unicameral (single-chamber) legislature like that Paine had prescribed—but since Pennsylvania had a unicameral legislature through most of the eighteenth century, that was less of a change than it might seem. Members of the new assembly were annually elected by an unusually broad electorate consisting of male taxpayers resident in the state for at least one year. The assembly then chose a council, which was the closest Pennsylvania came to an executive power. No plural executive can act with the effectiveness of a single person, and the Pennsylvania Council was so weak that it couldn't even elect its own presiding officer without the assembly joining in the decision.

The only real check on the Pennsylvania assembly was the people—and their countervailing force was extraordinarily powerful. Assemblymen came up for reelection every year and could serve only four years out of seven. All votes were public, and the assembly's sessions were normally open to the public. The assembly, moreover, could not enact laws in a single session: an election had to intervene between their introduction and enactment so the people could have their say. Pennsylvania, in short, gave the assembly what power it was willing to entrust to government, but its constitution of 1776 came close to creating a direct democracy (rule directly by the people).

It took time to unlearn the experience of the past—to realize that the people could rule through institutions other than assemblies, that governors in a republic need not be as dangerous as those appointed by a king, that there were ways of separating and balancing powers that did not simply mimic Britain. After a time, Americans turned toward more complex governments in which power was, as Jefferson (and Adams) advocated, "so divided and balanced among several bodies of magistracy, as that no one could transcend their legal limits without being effectually checked and restrained by the others." The New York constitution of 1777, for example, set up an assembly and senate, which together (as in Virginia) constituted the colony's legislature, and also a governor. Because the people directly elected all three units of government, each had an independent base of power. Assemblymen came up for election every year, but senators had four-year terms, and the governor held office for three years before facing the electorate again. New York's governor wielded far more power than his counterpart in Virginia: he could command the state's armed forces, convene the legislature and also prorogue it for limited periods, and recommend acts of legislation. He could also veto laws "inconsistent with the spirit of this constitution, or with the public good"—acting there in conjunction with a Council of Revision—although his vetoes could be overridden by a two-thirds vote of the legislature. With a Council of Appointment, he could make appointments, including that of judges to the state supreme court. The existence of those pesky councils indicated that confidence in executive power was not entirely restored. Still, New York went a long way toward building countervailing forces, or checks on power, into its government.

Massachusetts traveled farther down the same road. John Adams wrote the first draft of the Massachusetts constitution of 1780, which was the last of the first state constitutions, and it suggests how his thinking had developed since 1776. The form itself indicated a certain documentary maturity: where Penn-

sylvania's "Plan or Frame of Government" consisted of forty-eight numbered provisions, and Virginia's constitution of unnumbered provisions that were simply listed one after another, the Massachusetts constitution was divided into chapters and sections and articles. Chapter I covered the legislative power, Chapter II the executive, Chapter III the judiciary, Chapter IV delegates to Congress. Two additional chapters provided for Harvard College, the "U. Mass." of its time, and various other issues. The constitution invested power in an assembly elected by the towns, a senate elected from special districts set up according to the proportion of public taxes paid by residents, and a governor—all elected annually. The governor had to act in conjunction with a council of eight members chosen from the cohort of forty senators by joint ballot of the senators and assemblymen sitting "in one room." Once elected to the council, however, an individual could no longer serve in the senate. The governor had the power to adjourn and prorogue the General Court—a term for both houses of the legislature that was carried over from Massachusetts's colonial charters—and could appoint judges as well as a large number of other officeholders. He could also veto acts of the General Court, although a two-thirds vote of the legislature could override that veto. The governor was commander in chief of the state's armed forces and received "an honorable stated salary, of a fixed and permanent value," which, in times past, the legislature had absolutely refused to grant the colony's royal governor.

When other states revised their original constitutions, they often took the Massachusetts constitution as their model. The New Hampshire constitution of 1784 was clearly based on that of Massachusetts, although the state's chief executive was called not governor but president. Already in 1784, the word "president," which originally designated a weak executive, a person who presided over meetings of delegates, was being used for a strong, elected executive with independent power, capable of checking even the legislatures, which were deeply established in the affections of the American people.

## MIXED GOVERNMENT OR SEPARATION OF FUNCTIONS?

The first state constitutions moved from simple and unbalanced to complex and balanced, but what exactly did they separate and balance? The British system of mixed government pitted against each other king, Lords, and Commons, which represented different social groups. There were some efforts to follow that model in early American state governments, using devices such as property qualifications for office or differential voting qualifications to make assemblies, senates, and governors speak for different social groups. Under the New York constitution, for example, persons qualified to vote for senators had to satisfy a freehold (or real estate) qualification five times greater than that for persons qualified to vote for assemblymen. And in Massachusetts, governors were required to have at least a £1,000 freehold and be residents of the state for seven years; senators needed a £300 freehold or a total estate (which included personal as well as real property) of £600 and to be five-year residents; while members of the assembly were required to have a freehold of only £100 or a total estate of £200 and could be residents of the state for as little as a year. But were those requirements appropriate in a republic? Didn't they create social divisions among citizens who should have been equal before the law? Differential property requirements for officeholding surely undercut the capacity of meritorious poor people to hold the highest offices of the state.

American governments gradually dropped differential property requirements and other remnants of mixed government except for age or residency requirements, which excluded no one from even the highest offices on a permanent basis and could be understood as indications of experience and knowledge—that is, of merit. As the fixation with balancing social groups waned, attention turned increasingly toward separating and balancing governmental functions.

The constituent elements in the separation of functions—which, again, had roots in the English past—were not the two houses of the legislature and the king or governor, but the legislative, executive, and judiciary. Those were the divisions separated out in the first three articles of the Massachusetts constitution of 1780. Four years earlier, in fact, the Virginia Declaration of Rights had proclaimed "that the legislative and executive powers of the State should be separate and distinct from the judiciary." The Virginia constitution, however, seemed to violate the separation of powers right and left, particularly in giving the General Assembly so much control over the executive branch.

What, then, did separation of functions mean? For one thing, it meant that the same person could not hold offices in more than one division of government—that is, there could be no plural officeholding. A governor could not also serve in the legislature or the judiciary; a legislator could not serve in the executive or judiciary; a judge could not serve in the executive or legislative branches. That system differentiated American postrevolutionary governments from those of the past. In colonial Massachusetts, for example, Thomas Hutchinson had served simultaneously as lieutenant governor, a member of the upper house of legislature, and a judge of the supreme court, which annoyed ambitious young men like John Adams who would have liked to hold at least one of those offices. The rule also durably distinguished American from British government, where cabinet members were also (and still are—indeed, must be) members of Parliament.

Separation of functions provided a way of checking the all-powerful legislatures created by many of the first state constitutions. Those legislators, it

The Pennsylvania State House, where the Pennsylvania assembly met, in an engraving by Wm. Birch & Son from 1799.

turned out, had a way of riding roughshod over restraints—even those in the state constitutions, which legislatures seemed to honor or disregard almost at will. The assemblies sometimes also passed stay laws, which delayed the collection of debts, and tender laws, which forced creditors to accept depreciated paper currency even for debts contracted in hard money. Such measures did more damage to property rights than any action the British had taken before 1776, complained creditors such as Maryland's outspoken Charles Carroll of Annapolis (father of Charles Carroll of Carrollton, who signed the Declaration of Independence). State legislatures violated the rights of unpopular minorities such as Loyalists, and religious minorities also seemed vulnerable to abuse. In short, to some observers the unbridled power of elected legislatures raised the unanticipated specter of majoritarian tyranny.

What could be done? Revive the power of governors, as was done in New York and Massachusetts; give them independent power bases and the veto power so they could check legislative wrongdoing. And establish a judiciary independent of both the legislative and the executive branches. The independence of the judiciary was an English tradition that the Crown had violated in America by forcing judges to hold office on the king's pleasure. Now most states gave judges their offices on good behavior and provided that they receive, as the Virginia constitution put it, "fixed and adequate salaries," which shielded them from manipulation by legislative paymasters. But other provisions made judges dependent on legislative support: the Massachusetts constitution, for example, said that the governor, "with consent of the council," could remove judges from office "upon the address of both houses of the legislature." And in some states, the legislatures chose judges for a set term of years and then decided whether or not to renew their commissions. Tenure in office seemed like a form of life peerage, a throwback to the aristocratic past, and awoke suspicion. Until the republican character of the judiciary was more firmly founded, it would remain less independent and notably weaker than the executive or legislative parts of American government.

## THE PROBLEM OF AUTHORITY

Another problem faced by the creators of the first American constitutions was more basic than the overall design of government. It concerned nothing less than the nature of a constitution's authority. What exactly was a constitution? What was the source of its power? And how could it be made different from ordinary laws?

The concept of a constitution in American minds was unlike anything that existed in Great Britain—which had caused no end of confusion before 1776, when colonists condemned acts of Parliament as "unconstitutional." The British constitution was nothing more than a term for the way British government was constituted, that is, for the set of institutions, laws, and customs by which Britain was governed, a system whose principles of organization were not laid out on paper. How then, the British wondered, could an act of Parliament be unconstitutional?

For Americans, however, a constitution was written. A constitution was also a statement of fundamental law, which was different from the ordinary laws that governed, say, traffic or trade or liquor sales. A constitution underpinned the legitimacy of ordinary laws by granting specific powers to government and defining the way those powers were to be exercised. The colonists' concept of a constitution drew on their experience with charters and instructions to governors: after all, such documents were written, and they defined the structure of colonial government and limited the powers exercised by various officials. To ideas based on the past, however, the Americans added another: for them, constitutions corresponded to the original compact by which individuals in a state of nature formed a society and government, a process that had been described in John Locke's *Second Treatise of Government* and a host of other writings of the seventeenth and eighteenth centuries. To say an act of government was unconstitutional meant, then, that it violated those basic rules of the state that the people had made a condition of their allegiance. An unconstitutional act therefore had no legitimate binding force. By mid-1776, the Americans were beyond trying to explain to the British what they meant by "constitutional." Instead, they had to create constitutions that realized in fact the somewhat odd notions in their minds. How could they do that?

Some states held special elections before their legislatures drew up a constitution, so the legislators received authorization from the people for executing that task. Delaware declared that certain "fundamental rules" in its constitution could not be changed, while others could be altered only with the consent of five-sevenths of the assembly and all seven members of its legislative council, considerably more than for ordinary legislation. That was as far as the states went toward differentiating constitutional provisions from other laws. None of the state constitutions written in 1776 and 1777 were, for example, submitted to the people for approval. All were drafted and then enacted by elected legislatures. And what the assemblies created, they could change (or, more worrisome, simply ignore).

The problem, then, was how to write a constitution that bound the legislators. The answer came not so much from prominent leaders like John Adams as from ordinary people who were also thinking through the most challenging issues of their time. Massachusetts towns such as Concord and, above all, Pittsfield in the remote western reaches of the state insisted that the process had to begin at the bottom, with the people themselves, who would elect delegates to a special convention whose sole purpose would be to write a "Constitution of Government." The draft constitution the convention produced would then be submitted back to the people, who could reject or ratify it. A constitution enacted in that way would be different from other laws; it would be a direct act of legislation by the people, a way by which they created, charged, and limited the government that would henceforth order their lives.

In 1778, the people of Massachusetts rejected a proposed constitution in part because it had been drafted by the General Court. The constitution submitted for their approval two years later was the work of a constitutional convention—another invention of the revolutionary era—elected by the people in town meetings. Later, the people again met in town meetings to ratify the document proposed by the convention. Finally, theory and practice went hand in hand. "The body politic," explained the constitution's preamble, "is formed by a voluntary association of individuals: it is a social compact, by which the whole people covenants with each citizen, and each citizen with the whole people, that all shall be governed by certain laws for the common good." The critical enacting clause of the constitution followed from that theory: "We . . . the people of Massachusetts," it read, ". . . do agree upon, ordain, and establish, the following *Declaration of Rights, and Frame of Government,* as the CONSTITUTION OF THE COMMONWEALTH OF MASSACHUSETTS."

An elected legislature could violate such a document only at its peril. It would have to face the people and, as it happened, the judiciary. Written constitutions had the advantage of being enforceable in the courts. And so the creation of constitutions by the sovereign people gave the judiciary a popular function. Someone, after all, had to watch over a constitution, making certain that its provisions were honored. In 1776, the Pennsylvania constitution had established a Council of Censors—another of those odd devices in the early constitutions—to meet every seven years and perform precisely that task. In Massachusetts, the regular courts took on

that function, ensuring that constitutional provisions were honored by all who were bound by them. Judges became, in short, protectors of the will of the sovereign people as stated in constitutions that the people had proposed and ratified.

### DECLARATIONS OF RIGHTS

Several states also adopted declarations or bills of rights either as separate enactments or as integral parts of their constitutions. What was their function? Whom did they bind? And what was the source of their power?

The American declarations or bills of rights took their name from an English ancestor. In February 1689, the Lords and Commons, acting as a convention (which at that time indicated that Parliament was imperfect or incomplete because James II had fled the country), adopted a Declaration of Rights that included three parts. The first formally ended the reign of James II, who, it charged, had endeavored to subvert the established Protestant religion "and the Lawes and Liberties of this Kingdome." The second part stated in positive terms the "undoubted Rights and Liberties" that the king had supposedly violated. And the final part declared that William of Orange and his wife, Mary, the Protestant eldest daughter of James II, who would preserve the British people "from the violation of their rights which they have here asserted and from other attempts upon their Religion Rights and Liberties," should be "declared King and Queen of England." Once William and Mary were established on the throne, Parliament revised and reenacted the declaration as England's Bill of Rights.

The American declarations or bills of rights corresponded to the second section of the British document. Indeed, the 1776 Virginia Declaration of Rights repeated some phrases from the British declaration, such as its clause against cruel and unusual punishments, almost word for word. Since the states generally adopted their declarations of rights before enacting constitutions or made them an opening part of the constitutions, their declarations of rights were, as in 1689, a statement of rights that the new regime created by the constitution was supposed to protect more faithfully than the regime that preceded it.

Beyond those apparent similarities, however, lay some critical differences. William and Mary were bound by the English Declaration of Rights because they had agreed to its terms in accepting the Crown. In effect, the declaration stated the terms of a contract between them and the nation represented by the House of Lords and House of Commons. All the great British constitutional documents such as the Magna Carta and the

WILLIAMSBURG, June 1.

Gwin's Island, which contains 2300 acres of land, with about 500 head of cattle, 1000 sheep, &c. situate at the mouth of Piankatank river, is now possessed by the enemy. Lord Dunmore landed 800 men there on Monday last, who have thrown up an entrenchment on the land side, which is guarded chiefly by the black regiment. The Gloucester militia were assembled on the opposite shore, and on Tuesday had one man mortally wounded by a swivel ball; but as the ships of war had taken care to secure the pass, and our men having no cannon, it was utterly impossible to interrupt them.

By express from Maryland, we are informed that Governor Eden has obtained a pass to go to England, and begs he may not be molested.

*The following Declaration was reported to the Convention by the Committee appointed to prepare the same, and referred to the consideration of a Committee of the whole Convention; and, in the mean time, is ordered to be printed for the perusal of the members.*

*A DECLARATION of RIGHTS made by the Representatives of the good people of Virginia, assembled in full and free Convention; which rights do pertain to us and our posterity, as the basis and foundation of government.*

1  THAT all men are born equally free and independant, and have certain inherent natural rights, of which they cannot, by any compact, deprive or divest their posterity; among which are the enjoyment of life and liberty, with the means of acquiring and possessing property, and pursuing and obtaining happiness and safety.

2. That all power is vested in, and consequently derived from the people; that magistrates are their trustees and servants, and at all times amenable to them.

3. That government is, or ought to be, instituted for the common benefit, protection, and security of the people, nation or community. Of all the various modes and forms of government, that is best, which is capable of producing the greatest degree of happiness and safety, and is most effectually secured against the danger of maladministration; and that, whenever any government shall be found inadequate or contrary to these purposes, a majority of the community hath an indubitable, unalienable and indefeasible right to reform, alter or abolish it, in such manner as shall be judged most conducive to the public weal.

A copy of the Virginia Declaration of Rights, as published in the Pennsylvania Gazette on June 12, 1776.

1628 Petition of Rights were the same: they were agreements between the king and representatives of the nation, and their provisions limited what the king could do. The Americans, however, had no king, and their declarations of rights were not the texts of agreements between officeholders and the people since there were no officeholders in place when those declarations were adopted. What, then, gave those documents authority? Ratification by state assemblies? If so, were the declarations of rights ordinary or fundamental law? They bound, it seemed, the government; but their wording sometimes made their demands sound less than mandatory. For example, the Virginia Declaration of Rights stipulated, like the English one, "that excessive bail ought not to be required" and also that in certain legal cases "the ancient trial by jury is preferable to any other, and ought to be held sacred." The Pennsylvania Declaration of Rights even said that elections "ought to be free" and that freedom of the press "ought not to be restrained." Were those provisions suggestions or requirements? And what if governors or legislators chose to ignore them?

To add to the complications, several American declarations of rights asserted a series of basic political principles that went unmentioned in British antecedents. There they followed the example of the Virginia Declaration of Rights, which many American newspapers printed in a form that emerged from the convention's drafting committee without the modifications that the Virginia assembly later made. As a result, that draft—written by George Mason, one of the most underappreciated members of the founding generation—exerted a far greater influence than the official Virginia Declaration of Rights. According to the draft, "all men are born equally free and independant [sic], and have certain inherent natural rights, of which they cannot, by any compact, deprive or divest their posterity; among which are the enjoyment of life and liberty, with the means of acquiring and possessing property, and pursuing and obtaining happiness and safety." The words seem familiar today because Thomas Jefferson adapted them in drafting the second paragraph of the Declaration of Independence. More important, however, they made their way, with minor variations, into several state bills of rights, including those of Pennsylvania and Massachusetts, as well as Vermont (1777), and New Hampshire (1784). Did such rights get their force from the law of nature or because the states enacted them? Perhaps the rights to life, liberty, "the means of acquiring and possessing property, and pursuing and obtaining happiness and safety" could be understood as natural rights. But what about the assurances in the Pennsylvania Declaration of Rights that a person accused of crimes "had a right to be heard by himself and his council, to demand the cause and nature of his accusation, to be confronted with the witnesses," and to have "a speedy public trial, by an impartial jury of the country"? Those rights emerged, it would seem, not from nature but from English legal tradition.

The foundations of the first American bills of rights were, in fact, a confused jumble of conflicting possibilities. In practice, however, those documents gradually assumed an authority essentially like that of the constitutions. In Massachusetts, both the Declaration of Rights and the constitution were formally agreed upon, ordained, and established by the people, which made them statements of fundamental law. And since declarations of rights were written, they, too, could be enforced by the courts. It took time before their legally binding character was everywhere established. But when that happened, the fact that they could be enforced in the courts served not only to provide a strong undergirding for an American tradition of rights but also to give the judiciary an honored, republican function as the guardian of the people's rights and liberties. In short, the institutional implementation of ideas about basic rights served again to shore up the weakest of the three parts of American government, making not just the separation but the balance of functions more substantive.

## RELIGIOUS FREEDOM

Aside from the recognition of bills of rights as a common part of states' fundamental laws, the revolutionary era brought substantial progress in the definition and establishment of specific individual rights, particularly freedom of religion. That transformation occurred at the state level. In the seventeenth and eighteenth centuries, most colonies had established religions, which in New England (except for Rhode Island) meant that people were required to attend and contribute to the Congregational Church, and in the South to the Church of England. Religious freedom took the form of religious toleration, by which certain sects were granted exceptions to the rules: dissenters—the adherents of churches other than the established church—might, for example, be allowed to support their own teachers and preachers rather than those of the established church, or to vote and exercise other civil functions despite their unorthodox religious affiliations.

Toleration, however, was not a right but a privilege, one granted only to religious groups that, in the opinion of secular authorities, taught good morals and in general were "regular enough" to be granted exemptions from the standing religious laws. Catholics, for example, were denied toleration: they could not vote, hold office, or practice law, and even in Maryland,

originally founded as a Catholic refuge, they could attend mass or give their children religious instruction only in the most private and unobtrusive circumstances. Some Protestant groups, such as Baptists in Massachusetts, were also denied the privilege and so had to help support the Congregational Church.

During the course of the Revolution, some states moved toward implementing a new and more radical religious freedom by separating church and state. One force for change lay among Baptists and other "irregular" religious groups whose membership had multiplied during the religious ferment of the mid-eighteenth century and who found it outrageous that they had to request exemption from standing religious laws and have their practices judged by secular authorities. These dissenters found a powerful spokesman in the Baptist leader Isaac Backus, who skillfully played on the rhetoric of the Revolution, charging with hypocrisy those who were "filling the nation with the cry of LIBERTY and against *oppressors*," because they themselves were "violating that dearest of all rights, LIBERTY OF CONSCIENCE." Year after year, Baptists and other religious minorities were "taxed without their consent" to "uphold a worship which they conscientiously dissent from." According to Backus, the state had no claim to judge religious beliefs since church and state were by nature different: the state was governed by majority rule, but God said that only "a *few* find the narrow way, while *many* go in the broad way." During the Revolutionary War, Baptists in several Massachusetts communities refused to pay taxes to support a church whose teachings they opposed, creating divisions at a time

An engraving of a baptism from Morgan Edwards's *Materials Towards A History of the American Baptists* (Philadelphia, 1770). The Baptists were among the religious groups who pushed for formal recognition of religious freedom.

when colonial unity against Britain seemed essential. Even between colonies, religion could cause painful divisions—as the Massachusetts delegates to the First Continental Congress discovered when they were taken to task by a set of Quakers for the colony's oppressive religious establishment. The question necessarily arose whether the benefits of religious establishments were worth their cost.

The front line of change was not, however, Massachusetts but Virginia, where religious dissenters joined hands with Thomas Jefferson and James Madison, men of the Enlightenment who saw religion as a matter of opinion that, like all forms of thought, should be free of legal restraint. Their first victory came with the Virginia Declaration of Rights (1776), which proclaimed that "religion, or the duty which we owe to our Creator, and the manner of discharging it, can be directed only by religion and conviction, not by force or violence," and that therefore "all men are equally entitled to the free exercise of religion, according to dictates of conscience." No longer would the Anglican Church receive exclusive state support. But could Virginia levy a "general assessment" and use the funds it collected to sustain a variety of religious groups? Since a republic depended on the morals of the people, argued Patrick Henry and others like him, the Revolution made the moral instruction of religion more important than ever. From that perspective, to end state support for so essential a service seemed mad.

Madison and Jefferson would have none of it. Finally, in January 1786, with the support of many religious dissenters, they successfully secured passage of the Virginia Statute of Religious Freedom. "Almighty God hath created the mind free," the statute declared, and all attempts to influence it by punishments or civil incapacities bred only "hypocrisy and meanness." The statute ended clearly and forcefully all laws that compelled individuals to support a religion or ministry or punished them in any way because of their religious beliefs, and it provided that "all men shall be free to profess, and by argument to maintain, their opinion in matters of religion" with no effect on their civil capacities. The act also stated that the rights it declared were "of the natural rights of mankind," so any future legislative effort to repeal or narrow its provisions would be "an infringement of natural right."

Virginia showed the way to the future, but the future didn't arrive all at once. Even Pennsylvania, long the center of American religious liberalism, whose Declaration of Rights ensured that citizens' civil rights could not be denied or abridged on the basis of their religious beliefs or "peculiar mode of religious worship," confined that protection to men who ac-

knowledged "the being of a God." Atheists need not apply. Then the Pennsylvania constitution required members of the assembly to take an oath of office that not only acknowledged their belief in God but also proclaimed both the Old and New Testaments to be the work of "Divine inspiration." That provision effectively excluded Jews from the assembly despite the Declaration of Rights—which one set of Philadelphia Jews protested, not because they "perticularly" wanted to hold office but because exclusion from office made them less than equal citizens of the republic.

Similarly, the Massachusetts Declaration of Rights (1780) protected individuals' right to worship God according to the dictates of conscience so long as they did not "disturb the public peace, or obstruct others in their religious worship." But it also authorized towns to provide for public worship and "public Protestant teachers of piety, religion, and morality" and to require attendance at the instructions of such "public teachers," although, as before, some religious groups were allowed to support their own teachers instead. It required at least another half-century before church and state were finally severed in Massachusetts.

Patrick Henry, one of the most eloquent orators in revolutionary America, first made his name opposing the Stamp Act. By the mid-1780s, he had become an advocate of state support for religion, although not for any one church or sect. Without religion, he feared, the morals of the people would decline, and that would inevitably bring down the American Republic. This portrait by Thomas Sully (1851) was after a miniature done from life.

Few of the Revolution's innovations were, in fact, accomplished in a minute. They happened over time, gradually effecting transformations that few if any foresaw when the first cries went up against parliamentary taxation, and with which some of the most ardent defenders of colonial rights—Patrick Henry, for example—were not entirely happy. Even the "improvements" in the science of government worked out between 1776 and 1780 were implemented only gradually, since many states kept their first state constitutions, warts and all, for substantial periods of time. New York retained its constitution of 1777 for forty-five years. Virginia clung to its first constitution for fifty-four years, Maryland for sixty-five, New Jersey for sixty-eight, North Carolina for seventy-five. The Massachusetts constitution of 1780, although heavily amended, is still in effect, making it the oldest still-functioning written constitution in the world. Now many countries have written constitutions, and all those countries have, in that way at least, been touched by the American Revolution.

## Society: The Meanings of Equality

Innovations in government were part of a broader story of change that penetrated virtually every aspect of life. The rules that governed society were among the first to come under question. Colonial Americans had expected that over time America would come to look more and more like Britain, and even produce its own aristocracy. Then, almost overnight, "aristocrat" became a derogatory term. In 1776, Americans rejected social ranks determined by birth—indeed, all "artificial" or man-made distinctions. Only those "distinctions of nature" or "of heaven," as Paine put it in *Common Sense*, were worthy of respect. The result was a more "equalitarian" society. But what exactly did that imply?

The Declaration of Independence proclaimed that "all men are created equal." That phrase, like Mason's "all men are born equally free and independent," referred originally to the state of nature, before governments were established. It meant that neither God nor nature had granted some people authority to rule others; all persons were equal in that they were, in effect, self-governing in the state of nature. All legitimate authority was founded, as the Declaration also said, on the consent of the governed.

What, then, about American society once it had an established government? Equality was traditionally considered necessary for a republic, and many Americans thought that the absence of great disparities of wealth as well as of fixed social ranks made their society peculiarly well suited for a republican government. Widespread ownership of freehold property, moreover, gave Americans an independence, a freedom from manipulation by others, that was essential for a self-governing people. But could economic equality be sustained in the future? Respect for property rights ruled out any simple redistribution of property. Instead, hopes for an egalitarian society came to rest on a system of "partible" inheritances by which even the greatest fortunes would be divided in equal parts among a deceased person's children, causing a "revolution" in property holding with the passing of each generation.

Republican equality also had a more immediate meaning for the supporters of independence, as one public body after another testified in the spring and early summer of 1776. The Virginia convention, for example, specified that the state's new constitution should "secure substantial and equal liberty to the people." Grand juries in South Carolina took delight in establishing a new government whose benefits extended "generally, equally, and indiscriminately to all" and under which "the rights and happiness of the whole, the poor and the rich, are equally secured." And, as noted earlier, South Carolina's Judge William Henry Drayton took pride in the fact that his state's new, republican government allowed voters to raise even "the poorest man" to the "highest dignity" if he had "virtue and merit."

None of these statements suggested that individuals would be alike in all ways or that society would be without ranks of any kind. But they insisted that government treat everyone alike and that status reflect merit, not privilege. Eighteenth-century Americans were not, in fact, alike in all regards; an array of distinctions—regional, religious, and racial, as well as of wealth, occupation, education, and sex—marked one group off from another and sometimes designated lines of power and subordination. Just how important would those differences be in the new equalitarian social order? And which traits gave evidence of the "virtue and merit" that appropriately distinguished one person from another in a republic?

### THE EQUALITY OF ADULT WHITE MEN

The first order of business was to determine what distinctions were legitimate among adult white men, who constituted the political community and thus "the people" as that term was generally used in the late eighteenth century. It was there that some of the greatest battles were won, some so successfully that they hardly seem victories any longer. Religious divisions, for example, marked powerful social cleavages in colonial America, as indeed they do today in many parts of the world. To be sure, the extreme conflict between Quakers and Congregationalists, or Puritans and Anglicans, of the seventeenth century became muted after the 1680s, as different Protestant groups linked arms against the "Catholic powers" in one war after another. The division between Protestants and Catholics remained, however, deep and impassioned. The independence movement was itself militantly Protestant. That it opened the way for a new order in which Catholics such as the younger Charles Carroll of Maryland could hold office was one mark of its revolutionary impact.

In a republic, rank rewarded merit, or ability, and also virtue, which often implied to Americans little more than conforming to the standard rules of Christian morality. Some suggested that wealth provided a rough index of ability, which justified the differential property qualifications for office in the first state constitutions, but wealth soon came into dispute as a measure of merit. Virtue and rectitude could be found, as even some conservative spokesmen observed, in men "destitute of property." A wealthy man might be less likely to act dishonestly out of need than a poor one, but wealth fostered an "aristocratic" idleness and luxury, and it could lead to unbecoming vices such as avarice. Benjamin Franklin once volunteered that "some of the greatest rogues" he had known were "the richest rogues." If so, to prefer men of wealth simply because they were wealthy made no sense. To give them legal recognition or privileges was even worse: that would create a European-type class system and so move away from the republican ideal. Ending legal privileges based on property did not, however, end the Americans' wild scrambling for wealth, which not only continued to distinguish man from man but had immediate personal benefits as well.

If rank in a republic depended on merit and virtue, it was within reach of large numbers of ambitious young men. What equality meant for a substantial part of the population was, in short, opportunity—a chance to raise their personal, economic, and social status, and to build better lives for themselves and their children. The shattering of class ceilings meant that every honor, every attainment worth having, lay within reach for the able. The result was a great outpouring of energy fired by personal ambition and often by a confidence that private quests for betterment contributed to the nation's development.

The end of British rule, moreover, increased the opportunities available to America's new and ambitious men, who frequently sought to acquire traditional signs of status. The possession of land, for example, had always conferred respectability. And since the American victory ended British efforts to contain westward expansion, with the end of the war settlers poured into the once-bloody fields of Kentucky and what would become the state of Tennessee. The white population of the area immediately to the south of the Ohio River soared from 12,000 in 1783 to over 100,000 by 1790. Indian

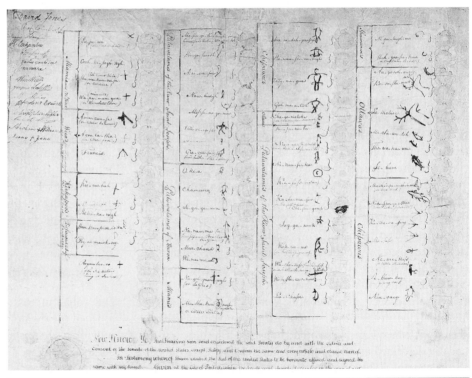

The Treaty of Greenville took eight months to negotiate and was signed on August 3, 1795, "to put an end to a destructive war, to settle all controversies, and to restore harmony and friendly intercourse." Note the drawings that represent the signatures of the delegates of the twelve Indian tribes.

resistance still blocked expansion north of the Ohio until 1795, when, after the Battle of Fallen Timbers, the Treaty of Greenville (Ohio) defined boundaries between the territories of the Indians and those of the United States. Then a new group of settlers left New England for richer lands in the West, often ignoring those hard-won and carefully negotiated borders. The societies the migrants founded were different from those in the East. The West could boast no established families or confining traditions and fewer persons of great wealth. There, a talented man of modest means could make his mark far more easily than, say, in Virginia, New York, or Massachusetts.

Holding public office was also considered an honor; and there opportunities for upward mobility expanded even in the eastern states because of an increase in the number of offices filled by election and the departure of Loyalists. Among the roughly 100,000 white Americans who went into exile during the War for Independence (some to England, others to the West Indies or Canada), men who had held appointed offices under the Crown were represented far out of proportion to their incidence in the population as a whole. They included everyone from justices of the peace to judges, members of the upper houses of legislature, and governors. The departure of so many experienced officeholders created openings for others. And as men who would once have spent their lives as legislators moved to higher positions, the legislatures were filled with others from a notch or two down the social scale in terms of wealth, education, and other marks of traditional respectability.

Such opportunities were reinforced, moreover, by reforms that brought a fuller and fairer representation of the people, including those in remote towns and counties where the richest men were at best of middling status by the standards of communities along the Atlantic seaboard. The bottom of society did not rise to the top; nothing so radical happened. Nevertheless, the social requisites of power broadened. Legislatures that were once filled by "gentlemen" became, in a word, democratized, which in turn brought a raucous, interest-based politics on a scale unknown in colonial America.

If future leaders of the Republic were to be drawn from the best qualified in the population at large—and the size of the pool from which republics could choose their leaders was frequently described as one of their greatest strengths—the people in general would need to be better educated. In the late eighteenth century, tracts, proposed laws, even provisions in state constitutions called for a broad dissemination of knowledge. Schools could at once prepare talented boys for public office, teach them how to manage their affairs and contribute to economic development, and inculcate morals that sustained public order. Schemes for comprehensive systems of public education nonetheless came to little. The revolutionary era did, however, bring a dramatic increase in private academies and in colleges and universities; indeed, more institutions of higher education were founded in the last two decades of the eighteenth century than during the entire colonial period.

Newspapers were perhaps a more effective way of educating the public. The Massachusetts printer Isaiah Thomas calculated that there were 37 weekly newspapers in the American colonies on the eve of independence; by June 1810, their number had grown to 360, and many were published daily. The same period saw a change in the papers' contents, as an emphasis on news gave way to informative essays on topics ranging from politics to literature and science. The press became, as Thomas observed, a way "of conveying, to every class in society, innumerable scraps of knowledge." That development was all the more impressive because it was market-driven, supported by hundreds of thousands of ordinary Americans ready to spend their pennies and time to increase their knowledge and improve their minds.

Such people were unlikely to yield to others who might have had greater wealth, better-established families, even university degrees, but whose arguments were unpersuasive. And that, with the opportunities afforded by a more fluid social system, was what republican equality implied for white men—an end to the deference, the instinctual yielding of "inferiors" to their "betters," that had been part of America's British past, and a chance to become themselves a bit better than others in an equalitarian America where rank remained but was always up for grabs. The Revolution changed the conditions of their lives, and the energy they invested in taking advantage of the new reign of opportunity created ripple effects that, in turn, further transformed American life in one way after another.

## THE FIRST EMANCIPATION

Did equality cross the color line? Certainly the Revolution touched the lives of African Americans, awakening hopes and providing circumstances in which they, too, might become free. Some 50,000 slaves, or 10 percent of the total slave population, fled their masters during the course of the Revolutionary War. Many of them, particularly in the South, headed for British lines. Sometimes they were recaptured; sometimes the need for food and shelter forced them to return to their former homes. Many who did reach the "protection" of the British army succumbed to the diseases that haunted eighteenth-century army camps, or were forced to work as laborers in ways that resembled slavery but lacked the self-interested, paternalist protection that was one of slavery's meager comforts. At Yorktown, for example, General Cornwallis used former slaves to build his fortifications but then, as the siege continued and his food supplies dwindled, drove the blacks out of the camp, forcing them, as one German officer noted, "with fear and trembling . . . to face the reward of their cruel masters." Only about 20,000 former slaves left with the British at the war's end, finding new homes in places such as Jamaica, London, or, ultimately, Sierra Leone, the colony Britain founded for former slaves. There, on Africa's western coast, they reenacted the "dying times" of America's own early colonies.

For blacks who stayed in North America, freedom was a more realistic immediate goal than racial equality. It was difficult to deny the legitimacy of blacks' striving for freedom in a country that had, after all, made liberty its cause. Those whites who ignored the inconsistency of slaveholders opposing British political "slavery" were reminded of their hypocrisy by the slaves themselves as well as by American Loyalists and British observers such as the writer Samuel Johnson, who wondered why the greatest "yelpers" for freedom were drivers of slaves. The assertions in the Declaration of Independence and many state bills of rights that men were created or born equal and that all legitimate authority derived from consent also undermined a slave system in which status was inherited and mastership had no foundation in consent. That's why the Virginia convention modified George Mason's draft Declaration of Rights to say that men were not "born equally free and independent" but were "by nature equally free and independent" and possessed inherent rights of which they could not deprive their posterity "when they enter into a state of society." The revised text did not deny that slaves were men or that they had inherent rights. But it freed the commonwealth of Virginia from an obligation to protect those rights since, as everyone in the convention agreed, slaves had never entered Virginia's all-white society.

Elsewhere, however, many Americans decided instead to resolve the inconsistency between principle and practice. As a result, the Revolution brought the first widespread effort to dismantle the American system of black chattel slavery, which was then still a young institution, having begun to take legal form in isolated acts of provincial legislation during the late seventeenth century. The first assault was on the slave trade, which, in fact, several colonies had tried to discourage before independence, but found their efforts blocked by royal vetoes. The Continental Association established a ban on slave imports that several states later incorporated into their laws or constitutions: the Delaware constitution of 1776, for example, declared that no person brought into the state from Africa "ought to be held in slavery under any pretense whatever; and no Negro, Indian, or mulatto slave

This 1792 painting by Samuel Jennings of *Liberty Displaying the Arts and Sciences* shows Liberty as a woman with a "liberty cap" on a stick, sitting beside a table with books on philosophy and agriculture while African Americans look on with awe. Chains—shackles—lie at Liberty's feet. Learning would thrive in a free country, the artist assumed, and the truth would make blacks as well as whites free.

ought to be brought into this State, for sale, from any part of the world."

Next the assault turned against slavery itself. The Pennsylvania legislature adopted a gradual emancipation act in 1780, and soon thereafter some Massachusetts slaves successfully won their freedom in the state courts by arguing that slavery was inconsistent with a provision in the state's Declaration of Rights that said all men were "born free and equal." Then several other northern states passed gradual emancipation laws—Connecticut and Rhode Island (1784), New York (1799), then New Jersey (1804). It is no surprise that emancipation came most easily in northern New England, where there were few slaves. It met greater resistance and took a more grudging form in states with substantial slave populations that performed basic economic functions, such as New York, New Jersey, and also Pennsylvania (whose gradual emancipation acts freed no slaves until far in the future). Emancipation laws provided that all slaves born after a certain date (March 1, 1780, in Pennsylvania; July 4, 1800, in New York) would become free when they reached a certain age (in New York, twenty-eight for men, twenty-five for women). Any children they had borne by then remained enslaved, however. Slaves born before the magic date also remained enslaved unless they or, more often, networks of family members purchased their freedom.

Slaves could also run away, as many—particularly young males—did not only during but also after the war. Perhaps a half to three-quarters of Philadelphia's young slave men escaped during the 1780s. If recaptured, they ran away again; or perhaps they retaliated against their oppressors by setting the waves of fires that northerners generally attributed to blacks and that indicated how costly to white security it would be to maintain slavery. What freedom blacks gained was, moreover, often incomplete since whites could and did require blacks to sign long-term work contracts as a condition of manumission or employment.

Meanwhile, white indentured servitude gave way to wage labor, and apprenticeships to other forms of training, so legal forms of unfreedom for white adult men (except convicted criminals) gradually disappeared. That made restrictions on black freedom all the more invidious. Nonetheless, by 1804 all northern states had accepted some scheme of emancipation. There, at least, the slave system's end was in sight.

## What's for Dinner?

*American Journal*

January 20, 1779:

"It is the poor negroes who alone work hard, and I am sorry to say, fare hard . . . "They are called up at day break, and seldom allowed to swallow a mouthful of homminy, or hoe cake, but are drawn out into the field immediately, where they continue at hard labour, without intermission, till noon, when they go to their dinners, and are seldom allowed an hour for that purpose; their meals consist of homminy and salt, and if their master is a man of humanity, touched by the finer feelings of love and sensibility, he allows them twice a week a little fat skimmed milk, rusty bacon, or salt herring, to relish this miserable and scanty fare. The man at this plantation [the Jones plantation, near Charlottesville, Virginia], in lieu of these, grants his negroes an acre of ground, and all Saturday afternoon to raise grain and poultry for themselves. After they have dined, they return to labor in the field, until dusk in the evening . . .

"As I have several times mentioned homminy and hoe-cake, it may not be amiss to explain them: the former is made of Indian corn, which is coarsely broke, and boiled with a few French beans, till it is almost a pulp. Hoe-cake is Indian corn ground into meal, kneaded into a dough, and baked before a fire, but as the negroes bake theirs on the hoes that they work with, they have the appellation of hoe-cakes. These are in common use among the inhabitants, I cannot say they are palateable, for as to flavor, one made of sawdust would be equally good, and not unlike it in appearance, but they are certainly a very strong and hearty food."

Thomas Anbury, "Lieutenant in the Army of General Burgoyne," in *Travels Through the Interior Parts of America*.

In the South, the story was different. Virginia and Maryland passed laws that facilitated private emancipations, but they reversed that modest step well before the last of New York's or New Jersey's slaves became free. The problem was not that whites in the Chesapeake particularly liked their slave system or thought it consistent with the principles of the Revolution. But, since their states included far more slaves than most northern states, emancipation would leave them with a higher number of free blacks, which they did not want. Whites in the upper South were therefore open to arguments for emancipation only when coupled with plans for the "colonization," or deportation, of former slaves. And in the lower South, not even colonization found many supporters. Having lost a large portion of their slave workforce during the desperate fighting in the last stages of the Revolutionary War and unable to imagine a plantation economy without slaves, planters in Georgia and South Carolina were desperate for more slaves, not fewer. Before long, their spokesmen would begin defending the slave system; then, early in the nineteenth century, Georgia and South Carolina would again begin importing African slaves. And so, gradually, as emancipation spread in the North, slavery became what it had never been before: a distinctively southern institution.

One of the most important results of revolutionary emancipation was the emergence of a free black community within the United States. In 1790, that community included some 60,000 people, many of whom were in the Chesapeake, and it grew to over 108,000 within the next decade. Everywhere, however, the presence of free black Americans raised questions about their status and rights. Inequality ruled: in the North, free blacks were seldom offered good jobs; they could not purchase properties in certain neighborhoods; they did not serve on juries or (except for a brief, exceptional period in New Jersey) vote. At first they found shelter in the households of whites who employed them as domestic servants; later they clustered in their own neighborhoods and founded their own clubs, schools, and charities. Emancipation, in short, brought the beginning of segregation.

It also brought the beginnings of racism in the sense of a systematic, quasi-scientific assertion of whites' natural superiority over blacks. The future was forecast by Thomas Jefferson, who found himself, in *Notes on the State of Virginia* (written in 1781, published in 1785), trying to explain his proposal that Virginia free its slaves, send them to Africa, and import Europeans to do their work. Why not just keep the freed slaves and pay them for their labor? Because of old resentments, Jefferson said, and because of the "real distinctions which nature has made" between blacks and whites, distinctions that were hardly confined to skin color and, he suggested, affected intellectual capacities as well. He asserted, for example, that no blacks were capable of "tracing and comprehending the investigations of Euclid" or writing poetry (although he conceded that they had an exceptional talent for music).

In the next century, American "scientists" worked hard to confirm what Jefferson advanced as a suspicion. Their research was of particular interest to a nation that had rejected all artificial social distinctions but accepted and indeed reaffirmed those decreed by nature. If race involved differences that went beyond superficial skin color, it could become an acceptable mark of rank and subordination, a way of explaining why free blacks were beneath whites as much as the slaves were subordinate to their masters. In time, in fact, the "natural" category of race would prove far more confining and

Benjamin Banneker, a free black surveyor and mathematician, produced his own almanac. His accomplishments, he argued, disproved Thomas Jefferson's suggestion in his *Notes on the State of Virginia* (1785) that blacks were incapable of doing mathematics.

demeaning a designation than those class categories that the Revolution made "un-American."

Among the most outspoken opponents of the emergent racism were the free blacks. In 1791, Benjamin Banneker, a free black surveyor and mathematician, sent Thomas Jefferson a copy of an almanac that included astronomical calculations he had made and that would have seemed to answer Jefferson's suspicion that mathematics lay beyond black capacities. Others would later join in the attack on Jefferson's statement, which became a powerful symbol of all that black (and white) advocates of racial equality opposed. Free blacks were also among the most active advocates of a complete emancipation of slaves and of black rights. Like Isaac Backus, they made good use of revolutionary rhetoric on behalf of their cause. The existence of a free black community was, after all, itself a product of the Revolution, an event whose heritage was, by later lights, a mixed bag—bringing at once the beginnings of emancipation, segregation, and an explicit racism, but which shaped the future of American politics and society nonetheless.

This stunning portrait of Abigail Adams was done by Benjamin Blythe in 1766, when Blythe painted a companion portrait of John Adams. She became her husband's most loyal political supporter and adviser.

## WOMEN'S PLACE

If nature determined rank in the American republic, not just "inferior races" but also the "weaker sex" faced a future of permanent subordination. Age, too, helped determine who wielded power, but childhood was at least impermanent. Race, sex, age: those were the biological, or natural, differences that readily came to mind, and the last two seemed the least problematic. Only when women and children were left out, John Adams once observed, could individuals in a state of nature be described as "equal, free, and independent of each other." If the subordination of women and children was firmly established in the law of nature, how could they be anything but subordinate under formal governments?

The best-known effort by a woman to mobilize revolutionary rhetoric on behalf of her sex is Abigail Adams's letter asking her husband, John, to "remember the ladies" in drafting laws for the new Republic and to take from husbands the "unlimited power" they had over their wives. At the time, married women did not have a legal existence apart from their husbands and so had little protection against men's attempts to use them "with cruelty and indignity." Her plea for ending men's "absolute power over Wives" seems modest enough in retrospect, although there was the hint of a larger agenda in her statement that women would not "hold ourselves bound by any Laws in which we have no voice, or Representation."

Some women, like free blacks, contested the significance of superficial biological differences. Judith Sargeant Murray, the daughter of a wealthy merchant from Gloucester, Massachusetts, and the wife of John Murray, a Universalist minister, drafted an essay, "On the Equality of the Sexes," as early as 1779, although it was published only in 1790. The apparent difference in the minds of men and women, she wrote, came from differences in their education—from nurture, not nature. If they received the same opportunities as men, women would be equally accomplished, as had been proven by those women in history who "towered above the various discouragements by which they have been so heavily oppressed." Women should not be educated as if their whole purpose lay in becoming wives, she argued; they should be taught skills that allowed them to be independent.

Such arguments for women's equality had little effect. Far more influential were the insights of Benjamin Rush, whose "Thoughts on Female Education" (1787) argued that the women of the American Republic should be so educated that they could instruct their sons "in the principles of liberty and government." The Revolution did, in fact, bring expanded educational opportunities for the girls who would become "republican mothers." In 1789, Massachusetts required that towns provide elementary education for girls as well as boys.

The late eighteenth century also saw the founding of many private academies for girls, particularly in New England, where young women studied not just needlework but subjects such as history and mathematics. The middle-class female graduates of the academies were prominent among those nineteenth-century feminists who demanded a more substantive equality than was possible for women confined to the domestic sphere.

What didn't happen is, in retrospect, as striking as what did. Women had done a lot to support the American cause: they wore clothes made from homespun yarn and drank herbal concoctions rather than tea during the time of the non-importation agreements; they managed the farms when their husbands went off to fight; and some even tramped behind the army, doing laundry, taking care of the wounded, preparing food. But the Revolution had little immediate impact on women's subordinate status. Men's "absolute power over Wives" remained as much in place after the Revolution as before. Even small steps toward requiring women's consent to the laws that governed them proved ephemeral. In 1790, New Jersey adopted an electoral law that referred to voters explicitly as "he" or "she" with no restriction on race, enfranchising women and free blacks. But seventeen years later, the state reversed course and once again confined the vote to white men.

At most, educational reforms effected after 1776 led toward transformations realized later, when the equality among men made women's dependency particularly invidious and humiliating. Did legal equality for women imply a transformation of private relationships more disturbing to the country's male republican legislators than black emancipation? Few of the social transformations the Revolution brought about were anticipated when the event began, and most took time to work out. But women's emancipation, it seems, went beyond what seemed compatible, if not with justice and ideological consistency, then with social order.

## THE ARTS AND SCIENCES

The transforming influence of the Revolution on American culture—"arts and sciences" in the language of the day—was no greater than its influence on the status of women. Five years before independence, two young American writers, Hugh Henry Brackenridge and Philip Freneau, composed an epic poem, "The Rising Glory of America," which they read at their commencement at the College of New Jersey (Princeton). A new age of artistic achievement, they predicted, was

about to begin in America, "where freedom holds the standard high." That didn't happen. Why not?

The experience of two of the most accomplished American painters, John Singleton Copley and Benjamin West, suggests an answer. Both chose to work in London. Compared to the English, Copley explained, Americans were "not half removed from a state of nature." And in fact, the market for sumptuous portraits of would-be aristocrats like those Copley once painted in pre-revolutionary Boston all but died after independence. Not only did aristocratic pretensions become outmoded, but art itself came to seem to many people a form of anti-republican decadence.

Consider, for example, the career of Charles Willson Peale, a onetime Maryland saddler who became an artist and actually studied under West in London before 1769. A committed patriot, active in the miltia and on revolutionary committees, Peale painted portraits, of which the best known are of George Washington. In the 1780s, however, he had difficulty getting sufficient commissions to support his large family: "the state

Charles Willson Peale painted this view of himself in his museum in 1822.

of the Arts in America is not very favorable at present," he wrote West. Later he ingeniously staged public exhibits in Philadelphia for which he charged admission fees. Finally he founded a museum that displayed a great variety of stuffed animals and other artifacts, arranged, he claimed, according to Linnean classifications, along with portraits of leading eighteenth-century Americans. He also staged musical events and "magic lantern" shows with mock thunderstorms and the like to bring crowds to his museum. Clearly an artist needed to be innovative and entrepreneurial to survive in the new republic.

Writers were no more successful. After graduating from college, Brackenridge, as ardent a supporter of the Revolution as Peale, became a journalist and lawyer. His wartime writings— two plays, a few short pieces of prose—were little more than propaganda. He worked as a judge while composing his masterpiece, *Modern Chivalry* (published in several volumes between 1792 and 1815), a long, rambling tale that predicted a decline in the quality of American leadership with the rise of democracy. By the end of his life, even Brackenridge knew his writings would not endure. His colleague Freneau became an accomplished poet, although he is remembered more often as a partisan newspaper editor of the 1790s.

Often Americans were on the defensive in discussions of their land and culture. Take Thomas Jefferson's efforts to refute the theories of Georges de Buffon, a leading French naturalist who claimed that all natural life degenerated in America. In his *Notes on the State of Virginia,* Jefferson spent several pages defending the capacities, sexual and other, of American Indians and arguing that indigenous animals were no smaller than those in other parts of the world. He put great stock in the bones of what he called an American "mastodon," a massive creature that he thought still roamed the land in the West. Later, when serving as a diplomat in France, Jefferson had carcasses of American elk shipped to him and put on display. Buffon had a look but left the smelly spectacle unconvinced.

Jefferson was no more successful in refuting a 1774 assertion by the Abbé Raynal, a French historian and philosopher, that America had not yet produced "a good poet, an able mathematician, a man of genius in a single art or a single science." In war, Jefferson noted, the country had produced George Washington, in physics Benjamin Franklin, and in astronomy David Rittenhouse. With regard to poetry, however, Jefferson commented that Raynal's question would remain unfair until the Americans had "existed as a people as long as the Greeks did before they produced a Homer, the Romans a Virgil, the French a Racine and Voltaire, the English a Shakespeare and Milton." American artistic accomplishments, Jefferson seemed to confess, were still in the future.

## The Economy: Adversity and Innovation

By all appearances, the American Revolution was an economic disaster so severe that, by one modern estimate, the per capita gross national product declined by almost half between 1774 and 1790. The reasons are not hard to find. The war was long—longer than any other in American history until the Vietnam War—and was fought on American soil. The implications for future productivity were especially great in the South, where property lost or destroyed included a substantial part of the region's labor force—the thousands of slaves who fled to the British or otherwise disappeared in the course of the war. Commercial restrictions by the Continental Congress and Parliament prevented the sale of American goods abroad in the early years of the war; thereafter, the presence of the British navy and its attempt to blockade major American ports made even coastal trade perilous. Independence, moreover, ended the bounties that had supported the production of goods such as indigo and naval stores; and after the peace, the British excluded Americans from their old and familiar markets in Britain and the West Indies.

Paper money at first made economic transactions easier and so encouraged a specialization that was all but impossible with the modified forms of barter common in colonial America. But the advantage was short-lived, since Continental currency rapidly lost value: the amount of hundredweight units of flour that £100 in paper currency could buy in Pennsylvania dropped from 143.3 in 1776 to 0.71 in 1781. Barter, by which useful products were exchanged for other useful products, seemed attractive compared with exchanges for money whose usefulness declined almost by the minute. In March 1780, the state of Virginia even imposed a "specific tax" payable in grain, hemp, or tobacco!

To make matters worse, after 1783 British and other foreign suppliers rushed to sell Americans the consumer goods they had so long gone without, offering liberal credit terms. Imports shot up to about three times the level of exports, since Britain also refused to buy many American products. Making up the difference drained the country of the hard currency it had collected from wartime European sources and left an additional debt that most merchants were unable to repay when the boom ended. The result was a mass of bankruptcies and a general economic contraction from which the country took several years to recover.

## NEW DEPARTURES

The story of the American economy in the 1780s is not, however, one of unrelieved bleakness. Adversity is what people make of it, and Americans made it the occasion for a series of innovations, some of which laid the foundation for an explosive future expansion. In the upper Chesapeake, planters continued to shift from tobacco to wheat as a primary crop. Wheat could be grown economically with a smaller labor force; moreover, because of poor crops in Europe, it could be sold abroad at a good profit. The wealthiest of eighteenth-century colonial planters, it should be said, had seldom confined themselves to farming: they also invested in western land and other potentially profitable ventures such as iron foundries. In the 1780s, planters again found investment opportunities in western land and in other projects, including those designed to ease western trade by improving river transportation. George Washington, for example, played a key role during 1784 and 1785 in organizing the Potowmack Company, which was formed to facilitate trade from points as far away as Ohio in the West to Alexandria, Virginia, and Georgetown, Maryland, in the East by building a series of canals around rapids in the Potomac River. Planters did not, however, step in to replace those agents of Scottish mercantile companies who had handled the colonial tobacco trade. Instead, merchants from Philadelphia and other northern ports took over, and thereafter northern shippers continued to handle the transoceanic sale of southern agricultural products—which in the 1790s helped turn the balance of payments with Europe decidedly in the Americans' favor.

Wartime and postwar necessity, in fact, led northern merchants to seize one opportunity after another. With old trade routes blocked, merchants sought new ones, most dramatically in China and India, where Americans brazenly competed head-on with the British East India Company. For example, on February 22, 1784, the 300-ton *Empress of China* left New York for Canton, a thirteen-gun salute accompanying its departure: nationalism and economic adventure went hand in hand. The ship had been built in Baltimore; its voyage was financed by mercantile firms in Philadelphia and New York whose on-board agent (or "supercargo") came from Boston. The *Empress* returned thirteen months later with a cargo of tea and cotton cloth that earned investors a 25 percent profit, inspiring more northern merchants to enter the China trade and to try other nontraditional routes, sometimes with stunning success. One cargo of pepper from the East Indies to Salem, Massachusetts, was sold at a profit of 700 percent. Gains at that level were, of course, unusual, and the China trade made up only a small part of American shipping. It was extremely risky and also expensive, requiring investments many times greater than the colonists' former jaunts to the West Indies, and it tied up capital for a year or more rather than a few months. As a result, syndicates of sometimes a dozen or more mercantile firms financed voyages to the Orient. Those syndicates were themselves a novelty in America, and they suggested an openness to creative financing of a sort that might support other ambitious forms of enterprise.

Expanding settlements in the West provided another market for inventories that piled up, unsold, in the East. Philadelphia merchants, for example, sent dry goods by wagon and riverboat to Kentucky, exchanged them for furs or flour or tobacco, and then packed those products on riverboats that sailed down the Mississippi to the Spanish settlement at New Orleans. There, finally, goods could be sold for gold or silver, or packed on ships for sale elsewhere. Inland trade, however, was difficult, in part because rivers too often ran the wrong way and roads were primitive at best, which made overland transportation rates very high. And Spain controlled the lower reaches of the Mississippi, which it closed to American shipping in 1784.

Land speculation was a good investment opportunity, one built on a certain nationalistic confidence that the territory claimed by the United States would soon be settled. But the mania for land soon got out of hand, as investors bought on credit huge tracts in remote places about which they knew little.

This nineteenth-century engraving shows a spinning jenny, designed by James Hargreaves, from 1767.

Unable to sell the land to settlers or European investors fast enough to meet payments, prominent speculators went under. Even Philadelphia's Robert Morris, a consummate entrepreneur and perhaps the greatest financial wizard of his time, ended up in debtor's prison because of land speculations gone bad.

The immediate postwar period also saw a new interest in manufacturing. The problems there were well known from the colonial past, when many manufacturing initiatives failed because of the high cost of labor and a scarcity of capital. Now ways of overcoming those obstacles emerged. The American Revolution coincided with the beginning in England of an industrial revolution that substituted power-driven machines for hand labor in manufacturing textiles. If machines could replace human labor, then perhaps the United States could develop a manufacturing sector sufficient to end its dependence on Europe for articles such as cloth, which constituted a substantial portion of American eighteenth-century imports. The new nation had ready access to raw materials and also an array of craftsmen skilled in working wood and iron who could build machines—with which, it seems, one American after another became fascinated in the 1780s.

But Americans needed designs for textile machinery, and the British government did everything possible to keep these from leaving Great Britain, whether on paper or in the heads of emigrants. Nonetheless, as early as 1774–75, two spinning jennies, devices for spinning thread from fiber, were constructed in Philadelphia. Both jennies improved on the design patented in England by James Hargreaves only five years earlier, in 1770. Machines for carding raw cotton and wool—passing them through thin wire teeth to remove dirt and arrange fibers in parallel lines for spinning—also attracted the attention of American inventors, and it seems that a carding engine was smuggled into Philadelphia as early as 1783.

Several state governments actively encouraged the development of manufacturing. Massachusetts even acquired and set on display carding, roving (twisting carded fibers in preparation for spinning), and spinning mechanisms made under the direction of two Scottish immigrants, who were in turn sponsored by Hugh Orr, the owner of a cannon foundry in the town of East Bridgewater. By May 1787, when the Massachusetts "State Models" first went on view, another immigrant had arrived in the Bay State with descriptions and models of English carding and spinning machines. After some trials, again sponsored by Orr, those designs were implemented by the Beverly Cotton Manufactory, a company that the Massachusetts legislature incorporated in 1789.

One of the people who went to see the Massachusetts state models was a merchant from Providence, Rhode Island, named Moses Brown. With his partner, William Almy, Brown went on to found spinning mills based on English machinery at Providence in the spring of 1789 and, later that year, at Pawtucket, Rhode Island. Brown and Almy had trouble getting the mills to operate successfully, but a solution appeared on December 2, 1789, when a twenty-one-year-old immigrant, who had served an apprenticeship in English mills at Darbyshire and thoroughly understood England's most advanced textile machinery, wrote Brown offering to help. Samuel Slater's arrival in Rhode Island marked a new departure in American manufacturing, one that would lead, finally, to profits (see Chapter 8).

PATENTS AND COPYRIGHT

During the 1780s, the states also began adopting legal tools, often again based on British models, to encourage inventiveness and facilitate entrepreneurship. The flurry of interest in British machines during the 1770s and 1780s accompanied a substantial development in American patent law, which before 1776 had attracted interest in only a handful of colonies among which South Carolina was preeminent. As before, patents were usually granted to individual inventors, such as Henry Guest, who received from the legislatures of New Jersey (1779), Pennsylvania (1780), and New York (1780) an exclusive right for a limited time to make a form of oil and blubber for tanning leather by a process he had developed.

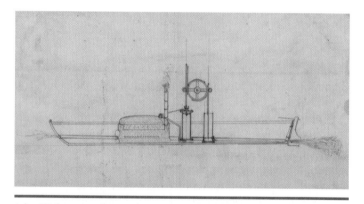

John Fitch was a pioneer in steam navigation and one of the early users of patents to protect inventions. He made this sketch of a steamboat in 1787, the year he was successful in launching and operating a steam-powered vessel on the Delaware River.

The Pennsylvania law required Guest to print an account "in English and German of the said materials by him discovered or invented" so no one would "unknowingly" violate his patent and also so others could "prosecute the said manufactures to their own advantage" after his patent expired. The purpose, in short, was to promote "useful manufactories" that benefited the state, not to grant a monopolistic privilege. In January 1787, when Maryland issued a patent to one Robert Lemmon for spinning and carding machines he had created, the grant explicitly stated the assembly's desire not only to encourage "useful inventions" but also to "promote the manufacture of cotton and wool within this state."

The patents of the 1780s witness, in fact, the imaginative efforts of both states and individual Americans to overcome obstacles to economic development on several different fronts. States granted patents, for example, for an angle-measuring device designed to solve trigonometry problems associated with the surveying of land, and for a steam engine "more powerful in its operation, and more simple . . . than any hitherto in use." Others were granted to John Fitch and James Rumsey, who both attempted to develop steam navigation (which, of course, would improve inland upstream river transportation), and to Oliver Evans, one of the most productive inventors of his time, for several mechanisms, including some that would perform basic tasks in flour mills "without the assistance of manual labor." Although most of these patents came to nothing, Evans went on to establish flour mills that represent the first instance of fully automated production in any form of processing or manufacturing whatsoever.

The number of patents granted by the several states increased dramatically in the late 1780s, when the worst of the postwar economic depression had passed, and in 1784 South Carolina gave "the Inventors of useful machines" exclusive rights over their creations for fourteen years. That patent clause appeared almost as an afterthought in "An Act for the Encouragement of Arts and Sciences" designed primarily to protect authors' rights over their written work. Copyright law was, in fact, another area where the states took enormous strides forward in the 1780s, although before independence only one colony—Massachusetts in 1672—had granted legal protection to authors. Noah Webster, a teacher in Goshen, New York, who wrote *A Grammatical Institute of the English Language,* a textbook for spelling, reading, and grammar, was the most vocal advocate of copyright legislation. (He eventually earned enough from his book to finance work on an American dictionary that made him famous.)

The copyright movement built, too, on a desire to promote American literature and so prove, as the Pennsylvania writer Hugh Henry Brackenridge once put it, that Americans were not "so many Ouran[g]-Outans of the wood." Connecticut led the way by passing a general "Act for the Encouragement of Literature and Genius" in January 1783, and within the next two years one state after another followed suit. Only Delaware failed to act, which meant that the laws of Maryland and Pennsylvania died on the vine since they were to become effective only when all the other states acted.

The preface to the Massachusetts copyright law included an eloquent assertion that people's security in "the Fruits of their Study and Industry" was "one of the natural Rights of Men, there being no Property more peculiarly a Man's own than that which is produced by the Labour of his Mind." Similar references to writings as intellectual property thread through contemporary discussions of copyright law. However, since copyrights that held in one state but could be violated elsewhere were not especially useful, uniform state action was critical. Many states included in their copyright statutes a provision that extended protection to nonresident authors only if their home states had passed similar laws. The protections of state copyright laws were also characteristically confined to citizens of the United States. As a result, they posed no problems for American printers who in the 1780s were busily reproducing pirated versions of English novels, and thereby exploiting another economic opportunity that independence brought. If security in intellectual property was a natural right, principle and practice were again at odds among such printers. But the circumstances of the 1780s made it hard to renounce profits of any kind, and certainly those gained at the cost of Great Britain, who, after all, had helped bring on the Americans' postwar economic blues.

### THE AMERICAN CORPORATION

The invention of the American corporation was the legal innovation of the 1780s that, along with the creation of government under a written constitution, had the most far-reaching implication for the future economic development of the United States. And corporations, unlike patents and copyright, would long remain primarily under the control of the states.

A corporation was an organization formally created by a state-granted act or charter of incorporation that gave the members of a group the right to make binding laws for their institutional self-government and to act in law as a single person, with the right to hold property, to sue and be sued, and to persist after the lifetimes of its founding members. Charters of incorporation sometimes included other benefits; indeed, the advantages of incorporation have changed substantially over time.

In England, corporations had often been given monopolistic grants or other special advantages: the Virginia Company of London, for example, received an exclusive right to colonize a defined part of North America. As a result, corporations came under attack as privileged institutions, an accusation that should have made them anathema in revolutionary America. "No man, or set of men, are entitled to exclusive or separate emoluments or privileges from the community, but in consideration of public services," the Virginia Declaration of Rights proclaimed; and one state after another repeated the principle. By the time of the Revolution, in fact, the British, who sustained a strong antimonopolistic tradition, had ceased to develop the corporation for profit-seeking ventures and would not revive that institution until well into the nineteenth century. In Britain, the partnership became the characteristic legal form of business during the early industrial era. But not in the United States. Here corporations began to multiply in the 1780s, and the trend continued thereafter, as one nineteenth-century jurist put it, almost incurably, as if Americans lacked a "moral means to resist it."

Most corporations in the 1780s were *not* formed for business purposes. Those created by the Massachusetts General Court, which led the nation in the development of corporations, generally incorporated towns, districts, or other units of local government, religious groups, educational institutions, or charities and similar nonprofit organizations. The basic advantages of incorporation—a defined structure, the capacity to protect assets in the courts, persistence through time—were as important for those types of organizations as for profit-seeking companies. At the time, no distinction was drawn between public and private corporations. In the eighteenth century (and, indeed, the nineteenth), no organization could be incorporated unless it served a public purpose, which many acts of incorporation carefully specified. In chartering the Potowmack Company, for example,

the Virginia legislature stated that "the extension of the navigation of the Potowmack river, from tide water to the highest place practicable . . . , will be of great public utility." The Maryland legislature also chartered the Potowmack Company, and Virginia and Maryland each purchased 50 shares of its stock, which together accounted for a fifth of all outstanding shares. Although private investors bought the remaining 400 shares (which sold for $440 each), the Potowmack Company remained a quasi-public enterprise. Indeed, all corporations were quasi-public bodies whose creation allowed money-strapped state legislatures to enlist private individuals in carrying out work that governments themselves might otherwise do—building roads, improving rivers, constructing bridges, founding schools, and sponsoring projects for the economic development of the state.

Efforts to incorporate cities such as Boston, or to reincorporate Philadelphia, which had been a chartered city before independence, inspired some of the most divisive controversies of the time. Opponents attacked incorporated cities as bastions of privilege and impediments to economic growth because they entrusted power to a favored few "freemen" and had historically imposed restrictions on who could trade and practice crafts within their boundaries. Moreover, because corporate charters could not be breached by legislatures, corporations were condemned as *imperia in imperio*—that is, as governments within the government—and as institutions

The magnificent Charles River Bridge made travel between Cambridge and Boston much easier. It was built by the Charles River Bridge Company (1785), one of Massachusetts's first postrevolutionary for-profit corporations.

whose creation reduced the power of the sovereign people as embodied in the legislatures.

But the proponents of corporations, inspired by the creativity recently invested in state constitutions, insisted that there was no reason America's incorporated cities had to be like those of times past. The corporations they designed allowed for elected officials who held office for limited terms and often broad electorates. Moreover, city charters, like state constitutions, set up increasingly complex governments with bicameral legislatures separate from the executive and judiciary. Cities were incorporated for only limited terms: they regularly had to return to the state legislature for renewals, which kept them firmly under legislative control. By the late 1780s, the fourteen incorporated cities of colonial America had grown to thirty-four. The redesigning of city charters pioneered in the 1780s so successfully reshaped American urban government that by the nineteenth century they came to seem the least objectionable of any type of corporation.

The handful of immediate postwar incorporations for profit-seeking ventures included the Potowmack Company (1784), Massachusetts's Charles River Bridge Company (1785), the Beverly (Massachusetts) Cotton Manufactory (1789), and banks, including the Bank of North America (1782), the Massachusetts Bank (1784), and the Bank of New York (organized in 1784, chartered in 1791). These were relatively large-scale efforts, requiring capital beyond the means of individual Americans. Incorporation allowed such companies to be financed by a large number of investors, who became members of the corporation by buying shares in a public subscription. Later any profits would be divided on a per-share basis. Such a way of massing capital was well suited to the United States, where wealth was relatively broadly distributed and even the greatest fortunes were modest compared with those of Europe. Investors also probably felt more comfortable committing their assets to organizations with defined governing structures and firm, written rules of procedure. In short, the corporation provided a way of addressing Americans' need for capital just as machines gave hope of addressing their perennial labor scarcity.

In truth, many profit-seeking corporations were modest in scale, and not all states proved equally at home with the institution. Even for mining and manufacturing, some states, particularly Pennsylvania, preferred individually owned companies or proprietorships. Almost everywhere, however, the great bulk of profit-seeking corporations were formed to improve internal transportation. River-improvement projects were among the earliest examples. Later, states incorporated

Robert Morris, in a portrait by Robert Edge Pine, c. 1785. The Continental Congress's Superintendent of Finance, he organized the Bank of North America, the country's first commercial bank.

vast numbers of companies to build bridges, turnpikes, and the like. Occasionally states developed such projects themselves. Nonetheless, the transportation infrastructure that made possible the creation of a broad domestic market was in good part the work of corporations.

Everywhere incorporation was critical to the early development of banks, which, by increasing the flexibility and sophistication of financial transactions, had a powerful impact on economic development. In 1781, Robert Morris organized the first major American commercial bank, the Bank of North America (BNA), as a way of rebuilding the finances of the United States, for which it served as a creditor and a bank of deposit. At the time, Americans had little if any experience with commercial banks. Thomas Willing, a former Philadelphia merchant who directed the BNA's daily operations, described the undertaking as like entering a "pathless wilderness" for which there were no books of directions to follow; only accident, he suggested, led the bank to replicate English precedents. The purchase of shares gave the bank its initial assets. It also received deposits, on which depositors could write checks—then a novelty in America—and it issued banknotes, redeemable at the bank in specie (gold or silver), which served as a circulating medium. With that capital, the BNA provided merchants with short-term loans, which were relatively safe, but which merchants needed so desperately that the bank was able to declare a 8.74 percent dividend in 1782, its first year of operation. The BNA's usefulness and profitability soon inspired imitators elsewhere.

The creation of business corporations was often controversial. And, as with incorporated cities, criticism led to the development of charters that answered critics' objections. Widespread hostility toward privilege guaranteed, for example, that early charters allowed corporations no privileges that individual entrepreneurs lacked, such as limited liability, which limited shareholders' responsibility for corporate debts. Charters often included complex voting requirements to limit the power of large shareholders and enhance that of smaller investors. They also defined exactly what corporations could lawfully do, limited the amount of real and movable property corporations could hold, and either remained valid for only a limited term of years or explicitly reserved the legislature's right to amend or repeal the charters they granted. Even the most famous battles, such as one that took place over the Bank of North America and culminated with the Pennsylvania legislature's canceling its charter in 1785, were fought over specific provisions in charters. Pennsylvania reincorporated the BNA in 1787, but its new charter included several constraints on the bank's duration, activities, and holdings that together "new modeled" the bank so it would better "harmonize with the government of this country," as one contemporary writer put it.

Charters and constitutions were, in fact, similar: both described the governing structure and set the basic rules of organizations that had been formed by a mutual agreement (or compact) among a set of people. Where corporations participated in activities beyond those specified in their charters, their acts could be declared null and void in the courts, much as acts of government could be declared unconstitutional. The familiarity of their structure probably contributed to the popularity of corporations. To work within carefully constructed organizations, whose management structures and rules of procedure were defined in a written founding document, came to be an American way of doing business of any kind, whether for profit or not.

The emergence of corporations therefore had a powerful effect on the form as well as the development of American society. The Revolution did not produce a nation of independent individuals acting alone, as myth would have it. Individuals soon learned that effectiveness required joining forces with others; and if the associations they created were, as became increasingly common, legally incorporated, they were clearly placed under the control and supervision of the state legislatures. In that way, the associations avoided the frequent contemporary charge of being "self-created," free-floating mini-governments that exercised prerogatives belonging more properly to the people as a whole or to the state. And so American society gradually became a web of organizations, all formed voluntarily from below, that penetrated the most local day-to-day activities; it became a series of corporations bound together in a federal system.

The newly independent states had moved rapidly, establishing not only the world's first republican governments organized under written constitutions but also reforms that ranged from religious freedom and emancipation through a reorganization of cities and business associations. They did what they could to channel the energies released by the Revolution and the relatively small caches of American capital into activities that would sustain a dramatic economic expansion in the future. Here and there—with patents and copyrights in particular—the states acted in areas that demanded regulation on a national scale. But in early 1787, the federal system of organizations that the states were constructing step by step lacked a capstone, a national government that might serve as what one contemporary called a "great corporation, comprehending all others." That deficiency would, however, soon be remedied.

## Suggested Reading

Ira Berlin, *Many Thousands Gone: The First Two Centuries of Slavery in North America* (1998)

Bruce W. Bugbee, *Genesis of American Patent and Copyright Law* (1967)

Joseph J. Ellis, *After the Revolution: Profiles of Early American Culture* (1979).

Brooke Hindle, *The Pursuit of Science in Revolutionary America, 1735–1789* (1956)

David J. Jeremy, *Transatlantic Industrial Revolution: The Diffusion of Textile Technologies Between Britain and America, 1790–1830s* (1981)

Linda Kerber, *Women of the Republic: Intellect and Ideology in Revolutionary America* (1986)

Pauline Maier, "The Revolutionary Origins of the American Corporation," *William and Mary Quarterly*, 3d series, 50 (1993): 51–84

Mary Beth Norton, *Liberty's Daughters: The Revolutionary Experience of American Women* (1980)

Gordon S. Wood, *The Creation of the American Republic, 1766–1787* (1969)

# Chapter Review

## Summary

### QUESTIONS

■ How were the New York and Massachusetts constitutions different from those written in 1776?

■ What did equality mean at the time of the Revolution?

■ What held back the advancement of "the arts" in the early republic?

■ How did state legislatures in the 1780s attempt to foster innovation and lay a foundation for economic growth?

## Chronology

| | |
|---|---|
| **1776** | Thomas Paine's *Common Sense* and John Adams's *Thoughts on Government* published. |
| **May 10, 15, 1776** | Second Continental Congress calls for the creation of new state governments under popular control. |
| **June 1776** | Virginia Declaration of Rights. |
| **1776–1780** | The thirteen states adopt new, written constitutions or modify their colonial charters. |
| **1780** | Pennsylvania adopts a gradual emancipation law. |
| **1782** | Bank of North America established. |
| **January 1786** | The Virginia Statute of Religious Freedom. |
| **1789** | Massachusetts requires elementary education for girls as well as boys. Brown and Almy found spinning mills in Rhode Island. |

## Key Terms

Separation of functions (pp. 182–183)

Declarations of rights (pp. 184–186)

Emancipation (p. 192)

Racism (p. 193)

The corporation (pp. 199–200)

# Chapter 7

# INVENTING THE AMERICAN REPUBLIC:

## THE NATION, 1776–1788

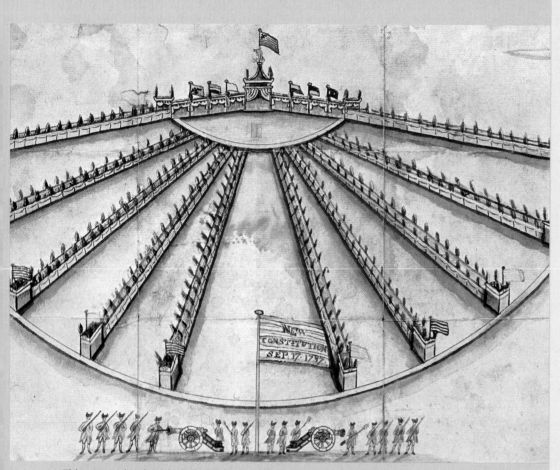

This watercolor done by David Grim in 1788 shows the banquet pavilion where New York City celebrated ratification of the federal Constitution on July 23 of that year. The pavilion was designed by Major Pierre-Charles L'Enfant, who later helped design Washington, D.C. Ten tables representing the states that had by then ratified the Constitution (New York would become the eleventh three days later) were arranged in a semicircle, suggesting a rising sun. Some 5,000 marchers participated in the day's Federal Procession and then attended the banquet. The flag at the bottom recalls the day the Constitutional Convention adjourned.

QUESTIONS

■ *What were the achievements and failures of the Confederation government?*

■ *Why did some people advocate replacing the Articles of Confederation and creating a dramatically different national government?*

■ *How did members of the Constitutional Convention resolve the issues that divided them ?*

■ *How did Federalists get the Constitution ratified?*

■ *What did the Antifederalists fear?*

In the best of summers, Philadelphia is an uncomfortable city, and the summer of 1787 was, some said, the worst in forty years. In May, before the sweltering weather settled in, delegates to a convention called to repair the Americans' national government began to arrive from one state after another. In the end, all but Rhode Island sent representatives.

The convention members were a living *Who's Who* of revolutionary America. The Virginia delegation included George Washington, already first in the hearts of his countrymen; George Mason, author of the state's constitution and much-imitated Declaration of Rights; Governor Edmund Randolph; the esteemed jurist George Wythe; and the young James Madison. South Carolina sent John Rutledge and two Pinckneys (who, as if to confound later generations, were named Charles and Charles Cotesworth). Benjamin Franklin came from Pennsylvania; John Dickinson, the beloved "Pennsylvania Farmer" of two decades earlier, now represented Delaware; and Washington's former aide-de-camp, Alexander Hamilton, sat for New York. Most of these distinguished men—fifty-five in all—remained through the summer, when, according to a French visitor, the heat and humidity made breathing a challenge and "the slightest movement" painful. The delegates had a mission. They were going to save the American Revolution from imminent failure.

The task they undertook—to strengthen the national government—was among the most difficult of the revolutionary era. In 1776, Americans were understandably unwilling to re-create a central authority like that of Britain or to grant a central government powers they had denied to Parliament, such as the power to tax and to regulate commerce. In 1776, moreover, Americans had relatively little experience with a domestic national govern-

ment. The several colonies had begun coordinating political action only in the 1760s, and the Continental Congress first became a national government in 1775, after Lexington and Concord. That inexperience made initiatives toward the creation of a new national government relatively tentative. The political systems of the states, by contrast, had been established as far back as the early seventeenth century; there Americans knew what worked and what didn't and so could begin redesigning their state governments with some confidence.

Americans well read in history and the emerging science of politics saw still another problem. Republics were traditionally considered appropriate only over small areas, such as Athens or Sparta in ancient Greece. Large republics, so the common wisdom went, included so many different interests that agreement upon the common good became all but impossible. Persistent internal conflict eventually led to the rise of a strong ruler and the death of the republic. It seemed, then, much better to keep power firmly on the state level. This theoretical consideration went hand in hand with a final, practical obstacle to the creation of a strong nation: in 1776, the states, having recently acquired unprecedented power, were unwilling to give away much more than they already had conceded to the Second Continental Congress.

The first "permanent" central government, under the Articles of Confederation (ratified in 1781), was the best Americans could agree upon at the time. In many ways, it made substantial improvements over the Second Continental Congress, its predecessor. By the late 1780s, however, the weakness of the Confederation and a conviction that some further checks on the states' exercise of power had become necessary leading to calls for a new and stronger national government.

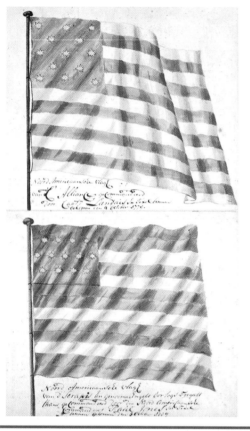

A 1779 watercolor sketch of American flags by an unknown artist. Although the flag had not yet taken on a standardized form, each of these flags included thirteen stars and stripes to represent the number of states in the Union at that time.

The Philadelphia Convention of 1787 wrote a constitution to fill that need. But old questions came up again: Was the constitution the convention proposed a step forward in the science of politics or a throwback to the form of government Americans had rejected in 1776? Could a republican government survive over so extensive a nation? As a result, ratification of the Constitution was itself an extraordinary political accomplishment—a victory, against the odds, over deep, articulate, and widespread opposition.

## From Confederation to Constitution

In the spring of 1776, the job of writing and ratifying a plan of government for the United States probably seemed no more challenging than many others before the Continental Congress. In fact, the task proved surprisingly difficult, and it absorbed more time than any individual state required to perform the same task.

The resolutions Richard Henry Lee moved on June 7, 1776, which called on Congress to declare independence, also asked it to have "a plan of Confederation . . . prepared and transmitted to the respective Colonies for their consideration and approbation." A committee appointed to draft a plan of union then submitted for Congress's consideration a document written mainly by John Dickinson. Although Congress was able to consider, revise, and adopt the Declaration of Independence in two days, it took over a year to agree on the Articles of Confederation. Finally, on November 15, 1777, it approved a much-revised version of the Dickinson draft and asked the states to act quickly (by March 10, 1778), since ratification was "essential to our very existence as a free people." But the states did not finally ratify the Articles of Confederation for three and a half years, during which time the old Second Continental Congress continued to act as the nation's government. The Articles finally went into effect in March 1781, less than eight months before the war's end. By then, the government they established was, in the eyes of some informed critics, already outmoded.

### THE CONFEDERATION

Why did the Articles of Confederation remain so long in Congress? Distractions caused by the war in 1776 and 1777 played a part. The Articles also raised substantive issues that were destined to recur in future debates on national government, such as representation. The Dickinson draft continued the old Congress's system of giving each state one vote. But populous states such as Virginia wanted representation in Congress proportioned to population, especially since the Dickinson draft also specified that state contributions to the Confederation would be "in Proportion to the Number of Inhabitants of every Age, Sex and Quality, except Indians not paying Taxes." The large states lost on representation but succeeded in getting requisitions (state contributions to the national treasury) proportioned according to the lands surveyed and granted within a state, which provided a measure of how much land was economically productive, and taking into consideration buildings and other improvements. That provision, however, was so difficult to implement that the Confederation ended up proportioning levies among the states roughly according to population.

Then there was the issue of western land, which six states claimed on the basis of "sea to sea" clauses in their original grants from the Crown. New York made a similar claim on the basis of concessions it had received from the Iroquois. Another six states, however, had defined western borders. The latter, especially Pennsylvania and Maryland, wanted the western territory to belong to the United States as a whole, for which the Dickinson draft provided. Instead, the final Articles of Confederation said that "no State shall be deprived of territory for the benefit of the United States." Then Maryland refused to ratify, which kept the Articles from going into effect since ratification had to be unanimous. Congress tried to resolve the impasse in September 1780 by recommending that the states give up their claims to unappropriated lands, as New York had done earlier that year. After Virginia began the process of ceding to Congress its lands north and west of the Ohio River, Maryland finally ratified the Articles in March 1781.

The Articles of Confederation made no pretense of constituting a fundamental law: they created "a firm league of friendship" among states. None of their authority came directly from the sovereign people. The government of the Confederation, like the Second Continental Congress, was entrusted to a body of delegates elected annually by the states; there was no separate executive or judiciary. In fact, it resembled the legislature-heavy governments formed by so many states in 1776. Five years later, the design of state government had advanced significantly, which was one reason the announcement of the Articles' ratification coincided with calls for their replacement.

## THE ARTICLES AND NATIONAL GOVERNMENT

The Articles of Confederation nonetheless nudged the development of national government forward a few paces. The very fact that the states formally committed themselves to an American Confederation and "Perpetual Union" under a written document went well beyond the situation under the Second Continental Congress, an ad hoc, jerry-built body whose powers changed with the instructions delegates received from their home governments. And the Articles included new and important provisions, such as that "the free inhabitants of each of these states . . . shall be entitled to all privileges and immunities of free citizens in the several states," with "free ingress and regress to and from any other State, and shall enjoy therein all the privileges of trade and commerce, subject to the same duties, impositions, and restrictions, as the inhabitants thereof." That provision was basic to the creation of a na-

tional market: there would be no customs houses between New York and New Jersey or between any other states. The Articles also made a solid first stab at defining the division of authority between the nation and the state, giving Congress, for example, "sole and exclusive power" to determine peace and war or conduct foreign relations, and making it "the last resort on appeal in all disputes . . . between two or more states."

Progress continued once the Articles were ratified. When the original system of government-by-committee became clearly inadequate, Congress created executive departments for war, foreign affairs, and finance, entrusting each to an official who was not a member of Congress. In addition, Congress organized a national post office and set up commissions to bring order to the national debt, which at the war's end was in chaos, having been contracted by hundreds of purchasers and borrowers in as many places. The commissions did a heroic job of sorting out who owed what to whom, which was a necessary preliminary to paying off the debt.

Although Congress could not tax, by the late 1780s it had found an independent source of income in the sale of western lands ceded to it by the states. An Ordinance of 1785 provided for the division of the West into "townships of six miles square" that would in turn be divided into 36 lots of 640 acres each, one of which was to be set aside for the support of public schools. Then sales could begin, with one lot the minimum purchase and the price $1 per acre.

## THE NORTHWEST ORDINANCE

How would the West be governed? In resolutions adopted on October 10, 1780, Congress promised that the western lands would be "formed into distinct republican States" that would "become members of the federal Union and have the same rights of sovereignty freedom and independence as the other states." Then, in early 1784, after ratifying the 1783 Treaty of Paris, which confirmed American possession of the trans-Appalachian West, Congress appointed a committee "to Prepare a Plan for the Temporary Government of the Western Territory." The committee and its chairman, Thomas Jefferson, proposed a plan for dividing the territory into states (not colonies, as some previous documents called them) and suggested names for ten of them—Sylvania, Michigania, Cherronesus, Assenisipia, Metropotamia, Illinoia, Saratoga, Washington, Polypotamia, and Pelisipia. The plan stated that settlers should be allowed to adopt the constitutions of any already established state as the basis for their temporary governments and then,

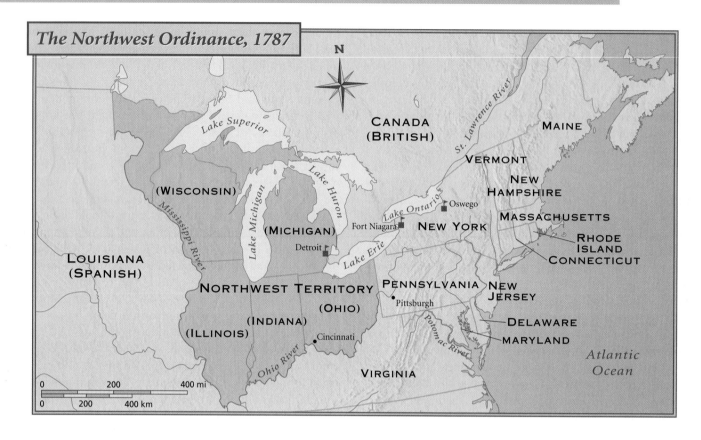

The Northwest Ordinance, 1787

when a state contained 20,000 "free inhabitants," Congress could authorize it to call a convention and adopt a permanent constitution. States could then become full members of the federal Union—subject, however, to certain restrictions. They could not, for example, leave the Union, and the committee draft declared that "after the year 1800 . . . there shall be neither slavery nor involuntary servitude in any of the said states," except as punishment for crimes of which an individual was "duly convicted." Congress revised the proposed resolutions before adopting them in April 1784, eliminating the names suggested for the new states and also the restriction on slavery.

The Land Resolutions of 1784 never went into effect. Three years later, Congress replaced them with the Northwest Ordinance, which provided for the organization of three to five states—eventually Ohio, Indiana, Illinois, Michigan, and Wisconsin—from the territory north of the Ohio River and west to the Mississippi. That meant there would be fewer states larger in size than Jefferson preferred. In an initial "territorial" stage, those future states would be governed by officials appointed by Congress, and not entirely self-governing,

as under the earlier resolutions. This change reflected the conviction of several influential observers, including George Washington, that westerners were ignorant, semisavage "banditti" who honored the laws of neither God nor man and had no respect for Indian titles. Settlers of that sort would have to be taken firmly in hand or they would involve the United States in one Indian war after another. When the population of a territory included 5,000 free adult men, according to the ordinance, resident freeholders could elect representatives to an assembly, which in turn would nominate ten men from whom Congress would choose five as an upper house. The governor, whom Congress appointed, would have an absolute veto over legislation. However, when the free population reached 60,000, the territory could establish a republican government under institutions like those of the original states and apply for admission to the Union.

The Northwest Ordinance solved the old problem of how to make the people of colonial settlements free and equal with those in the "mother country" by abandoning altogether old ideas of imperial organization. There would be no dependent colonies, and no difference among the peoples of the United States that depended on where they lived, since all new states would enter the Union "on an equal footing with the original states in all respects whatsoever." The ordinance also included provisions that assured the residents of a territory of basic civil rights, including freedom of religion and trial by jury, provided that the "said Territory" and the states formed therein "shall forever remain a part of . . . the United States of America." Unlike Congress's earlier Land Resolutions, the ordinance declared that "there shall be neither slavery nor involuntary servitude in the said territory, otherwise than in the punishment of crimes whereof the party shall have been duly convicted."

The ordinance applied only to the Northwest Territory, and its binding power ceased once that area was organized into states. However, it provided a model and precedent for organizing all future states, particularly by ensuring that they would be free and equal members of the Union. For that reason, it is one of the most important pieces of legislation in the entire history of the United States.

## THE CASE FOR CHANGE

Why was it necessary to replace the Articles of Confederation? Because the Confederation was so strapped for money, and so incapacitated by structural problems, that it could not exercise even the powers clearly assigned to it. Some nationalists also wanted to strengthen the national government to check abuses of power by the states. At first, the Continental Congress paid for the Revolutionary War by issuing currency, but by the time the Articles were ratified its money had so depreciated that the currency was virtually without value. Congress then asked the states to raise on its behalf set amounts of money (requisitions). Several states struggled to comply, but they never contributed enough to pay Congress's bills. Congress then borrowed money from Americans (including soldiers and military suppliers, who received certificates for their services or goods) and from foreign countries, but it still needed money to pay interest and retire its debts. Congress asked the states in 1781 and again in 1783 to "vest a power in Congress" to impose duties on imports specifically to service the war debt. If it had that power, Congress could also retaliate against Britain and other countries that put up barriers against American trade. But because amendments to the Articles required unanimous consent, the refusal of a single state to ratify—and Rhode Island rejected the first "impost" amendment, New York the second—prevented that modest change. Eventually, Congress

would get funds from the sale of western lands, but that was in the future and its bills were falling due immediately.

The Confederation could not act effectively in foreign affairs. It was unable to persuade Great Britain to leave its posts in the West because, the British said, the American states had not respected Loyalist rights under the Treaty of Paris. It could neither retaliate against nor buy off pirates on the Barbary Coast of North Africa, who attacked American ships and sold their crews as slaves. And it could do nothing when Spain refused to recognize the 31st parallel as the southern border of the United States and, in 1784, closed the Mississippi to American traders. Negotiations between John Jay and the Spanish minister, Don Diego de Gardoqui, broke down in 1786 when, after a bitter debate, Congress barely authorized Jay to "forbear" American navigation rights on the Mississippi for twenty-five years in return for a favorable commercial treaty. Seven states voted in favor of Jay's proposal, and five opposed it. Under the Articles of Confederation, nine affirmative votes were necessary to ratify treaties, so the vote doomed Jay's efforts.

By coming so close to giving up navigation of the Mississippi, Congress alienated settlers of the trans-Appalachian West, whose future development required free access to the

John Jay of New York, secretary of foreign affairs from 1784 to 1790. His 1785 attempt to negotiate an agreement with Spain that would have barred American trade on the Mississippi for twenty-five years provoked massive opposition in the West. This portrait by Gilbert Stuart was begun in 1784 and not completed until 1818.

river. Could the United States hold the West? Would Kentucky leave the United States and join Spain? Would Vermont, over which New York was unwilling to release its claims, join British Canada? Indeed, could the Confederation even bind the old states together when peace made union less imperative than it had been during the Revolutionary War?

In December 1783, when the Continental army disbanded, even Jefferson thought Congress should cease meeting constantly. Instead he proposed that after holding brief meetings to discuss whatever issues arose, it should leave the Confederation's limited business in the hands of a committee of states and so "destroy the strange idea of their being a permanent body, which has unaccountably taken possession of the heads of their constituents." By the late 1780s, Congress was frequently incapable of doing any significant business because fewer than nine states had delegations present. Under the Articles of Confederation, it needed the approval of nine states to exercise its most important powers. For all other business except adjourning from day to day it needed the approval of seven states, and even that was difficult to get because of conflicting state interests. Moreover, if a state's two delegates—the minimum required under the Articles—disagreed with each other, their state essentially lost its vote, making it all the harder for Congress to get the requisite nine or seven state votes.

Meanwhile, many states simply stopped paying their requisitions to Congress. Sometimes they instead took over that part of the federal debt owed to their citizens by converting federal securities into state bonds. To men like Alexander Hamilton, a national debt was a national bond, a common obligation that held a people together. By that reasoning, for the Confederation to lose responsibility for paying off its debts was nothing less than a blow to the union. Moreover, without any steady source of income, Congress was unable to service the country's foreign debt, which remained its responsibility. The United States defaulted on an interest payment owed to France in 1785, and it seemed unlikely to pay off a chunk of the principal due for payment in 1787. To people such as Washington, that was a national disgrace. It was also dangerous: at the time, nations usually negotiated loans to finance wars. Without good credit, the United States would be incapable of borrowing funds in a national emergency, which would undermine its ability to defend itself.

Hamilton was one of the most active supporters of a stronger central government. Born in 1757 on Nevis, one of the Leeward Islands in the West Indies, he was the illegitimate child of a Scottish merchant of aristocratic descent and the daughter of a French Huguenot doctor and planter. His parents had separated before his mother died in 1768, leaving him essentially an orphan. Four years later, at age fifteen, Hamilton came to North America, alone, after some generous supporters recognized his extraordinary intelligence and arranged for him to attend King's (Columbia) College in New York. Before long, he began writing pamphlets on behalf of the American cause, and later he joined the Continental army, becoming an adjutant to General Washington. Ambitious and self-confident to the point of arrogance, Hamilton had a way of rubbing people the wrong way. But there were few native-born Americans who invested so much effort and intellect on behalf of their country. He was also one of a handful of Americans who understood national finance.

Hamilton's loyalties were not to a state but to the nation. That was common enough among certain immigrants—including Thomas Paine—who joined the revolutionary movement soon after arriving, and so developed a primary dedication to the United States rather than to a state. It was also common among the officers of the Continental army who had suffered from Congress's incapacity to provide adequate supplies or regular pay. One of Hamilton's strongest allies in the struggle for a more viable nation was, however, a native-born Virginian who never served in the Continental army.

James Madison attended the College of New Jersey (now Princeton), which perhaps gave him a less provincial perspective than that of many Virginians, and he first entered politics with the Revolution. Shy and physically unimposing, Madison was less assertive than Hamilton, and he would have been an easy man to overlook except for the power of his mind. Madison approached the problems of American government from the broadest perspective, studying historical precedents to understand the nature of confederations as well as analyzing the problems experienced under the institutional arrangements of the 1780s. He became an astute observer of American constitutional development and, in effect, a practicing political scientist with few peers in any other time or place. Intelligence and a shared commitment to a vigorous national government brought Madison and Hamilton together. While the partnership lasted, it exerted a formidable influence on the course of history.

For Madison, the conduct of the states in the 1780s was as much a cause of concern as the Confederation's weakness. In a memorandum composed in April 1787 on the "Vices of the Political System of the United States," he listed one lamentable example of state conduct after another. The states had encroached on federal authority, made treaties with Indians and with each other, and refused to honor the terms of treaties negotiated by Congress, including the 1783 Treaty of Paris. They had also trespassed on each other's rights, restricting commercial exchanges, passing laws that favored their own ships or manufactures over those of other states, or creating paper money and interfering with the collection of debts, which affected the rights of creditors in other states as well as those in their own.

The state legislatures seemed, in fact, to be in the midst of an orgy of lawmaking. The "short period of independency," Madison observed, had filled as many pages in state lawbooks "as the century which preceded it," and that "luxuriancy of legislation" had become a nuisance, a pestilence, because the legislatures often changed or replaced laws "before any trial can be made of their merits" and before remote parts of the state even knew of their existence. Many new laws were, in his view, unjust, the work of triumphant majorities promoting "base and selfish" interests while pretending to support the public good. Such "irregularities" seemed almost unavoidable under the state governments of

his time, considering the lowly "sphere of life" from which so many members of their powerful legislatures were drawn.

The Confederation could do nothing to remedy the situation. It had no power of coercion, no sanction that could enforce even straightforward provisions in the Articles. Nor could it protect the states against insurrections by seditious, propertyless minorities. Indeed, the Confederation was not a government as the Americans had come to understand it, only a league of states, since the Articles of Confederation had not been ratified by the people. The Confederation was also incapable of serving the national welfare by providing uniform national legislation where it was needed—and here Madison mentioned not just naturalization and education, but also copyright and "grants of incorporation for national purposes, for canals and other works of general utility."

Above all, however, Madison saw a need to contain the energetic, ambitious, dangerously democratic governments of the states. For him, the primary advantage of a federal

*American Journal*

## How Do You "Call" Home?

*Delegates to the Continental Congress who left families behind—like New Hampshire's Dr. Josiah Bartlett—often lived with considerable anxiety. To get news from home required having some persons carry a letter by ship, carriage, or horseback from one place to another, which took more time than for a child to get sick and die in an age of fevers. Bartlett peppered his wife with questions about the family and their farm, and mentioned politics only occasionally. Sometimes he worried his children would forget him.*

Josiah to Mary Bartlett, Philadelphia:
Saturday, September 16, 1775

"I Arrived yesterday at this place about noon, after a pretty agreeable Jorney. . . . I hope & trust that you & my family are well as nothing will give me So much Uneasiness as to hear any of you are Dangerously Sick in my absence. . . ."

Philadelphia, October 2, 1775

"I am pleased to hear . . . that Ezra is Better . . . I have been Concerned about that poor Child . . . you will See in the newspaper all the publick news: I

want to be informed of Sundry things from you . . . whither Levi has been to School . . . whither we are like to have a Gramer School . . . whether the womans School Goes on . . . whether you are like to Settle a minister . . . whither Judkins has finished Glazing the House . . . Remember my Love to all the Children in particular and let them Know that I Dayly think of them and hope when I Return I Shall have the pleasure to hear of their Good Behavior. . . ."

Philadelphia, November 6, 1775

"I have been now above 2 months from home & had but 2 Letters from you Tho I have wrote you 7 or 8 before this I hope you and the family are all in Good health . . ."

Philadelphia, December 25, 1775

"am sorry to inform you that I Cannot return to you at present. So much Business lays before the Congress; I fear it wont rise for Some time, when it Does rise, one Delegate from Each Colony must tarry to transact the Publick Business in the recess, So that I think I Shall not be able to return till towards Spring."

government capable of protecting its sphere of authority was that such a government would constitute another check on the states and their dangerously democratic legislatures. The power of the central government could be enhanced safely, Madison concluded, because in all previous confederate governments power had descended, as if determined by a natural law like that of gravity, from their central institutions to their constituent members. Fear of despotism in federated governments was therefore unfounded; indeed, the American experience of state power run wild was perfectly in keeping with the experience of previous confederations as Madison understood it. The challenge for America's political engineers was to reverse the flow—to create a central government powerful enough to hold its own against the states.

Other nationalists, however, were less concerned with the wrongdoings of the states than with the pathetic debility of Congress. They wanted to create a "respectable nation," one that paid its debts, and so maintained its credit, and one that had a "coercive power" by which it could force compliance with lawful exercises of its constitutional powers and protect the interests and welfare of the American people. They wanted, in short, a United States that could hold, as the Declaration of Independence put it, a "separate and equal station" among the "powers of the earth."

## TOWARD THE CONSTITUTION

The nationalists made their move at Annapolis, Maryland. Nine states agreed to meet there in September 1786 to discuss interstate commercial problems at the invitation of Virginia (an invitation prompted by Madison), but only five state delegations had arrived when the convention met on September 11, hardly enough to solve the problems of domestic trade. Rather than simply adjourn, however, on September 14 the convention adopted a report drafted by Hamilton. It asked the states to send representatives to another convention, which would meet at Philadelphia on the second Monday of May 1787 to discuss *all* matters necessary "to render the constitution of the Federal Government adequate to the exigencies of the Union."

The call for a new convention went out to the states. It also went to the Continental Congress, which had discussed changes to the Articles of Confederation earlier in 1786 but abandoned the effort since it seemed impossible to achieve the required unanimous consent to amend the Articles. Was this initiative any more hopeful? Not even the firmest nationalists agreed on that. But the proposed convention started to look like an event

worth taking seriously after December 1786, when Virginia appointed a delegation with George Washington, the country's number one hero, at its head. Finally, on February 21, 1787, Congress endorsed the proposal, saying it was "expedient" that a convention meet "for the sole and express purpose of revising the Articles of Confederation." By then, seven states had already elected delegates—Virginia, Pennsylvania, New Jersey, North Carolina, New Hampshire, Delaware, and Georgia.

### SHAYS'S REBELLION

Meanwhile, events in Massachusetts increased interest in the convention. Massachusetts was anything but soft on debtors. The state had levied heavy taxes since the early 1780s to meet the current costs of government, pay congressional requisitions, and retire its war debts, which it hoped to do within the decade. As much as 30 or 40 percent of those taxes were levied on polls, that is, on men over the age of sixteen regardless of their ability to pay. To make matters worse, in 1780–81 the General Court passed a series of laws that made only gold and silver legal tender; debts therefore had to be paid in hard currency. Then the trade crisis of 1784–86 reduced the supply of hard money even in Boston, where residents complained that "such a scarcity of money . . . was never known amongst them," causing the value of that which remained to soar (that is, causing deflation). Pressed by British creditors to pay up, merchants called for the payment of debts owed by their customers—debts that would have to be repaid with dollars or pounds worth more than what had been originally borrowed, if hard money could be found to pay them at all. Legal actions over debts multiplied in the mid-1780s and in some western counties involved almost a third of the adult men. Their situation was perilous: defaulting debtors could be locked up in the cold, miserable jails of the time for even small debts of six shillings, or they might see their property—the cattle and land that supported their families—auctioned off for what seemed a fraction of their value.

Desperation led to resistance, first peaceful, then forceful. Many towns petitioned the General Court for redress either separately or through county conventions like those of a decade earlier. They requested paper money to provide a circulating medium and counteract deflation, laws allowing debts to be paid in goods fairly assessed, a reduction in the costs of government, taxes more keyed to people's ability to pay, and the appointment of arbitration panels to handle debt cases rather than the courts. The petitioners also proposed moving the capital inland (as many states agreed to do during the revolutionary era) so it would be less influenced by rich eastern mercantile interests. In the late summer and fall of 1786, mobs closed down the courts in several rural communities to hold off foreclosures until the General Court could act.

But the legislature chose repression over relief: forms of resistance appropriate against British tyranny were inappropriate, it seemed, against a republican government, where redress could be won through the ballot box. The General Court passed a severe sedition act and set about raising troops, which proved difficult since people were hesitant to march against neighbors and countrymen. In the end, a set of volunteer soldiers, mostly from eastern parts of the state, financed by loans from wealthy merchants and led by General Benjamin Lincoln, put down the rebellion in the western part of the state. Lincoln's troops dispersed insurgents under Captain Daniel Shays as they attempted to storm a Confederation arsenal at Springfield, Massachusetts, in late January 1787, and then pursued the fleeing rebels all the way to Petersham, New Hampshire, where they were defeated again on February 4. That was, for all practical purposes, the end of an event remembered as Shays's Rebellion.

In fact, the insurgents were not traitors but hard-pressed farmers who were often, like Captain Shays, veterans of the Continental army. Only a handful of the disaffected were willing to take up arms against the state. In the end, help came through the ballot box: the elections of May 1787 so altered the composition of the Massachusetts General Court that it finally allowed debtors some relief.

An eighteenth-century woodcut by an unknown artist depicting Daniel Shays, the leader of Shays's Rebellion, and Job Shattuck, one of his top supporters.

The legislature's change of heart did not reassure people horrified by the rebellion in Massachusetts, which seemed too much of a piece with developments in other states where restive popular forces, whether in or out of their legislatures, seemed to threaten the rights of property as well as justice and good order. In October 1786, before the worst of Shays's Rebellion, George Washington expressed fear that the "commotions and temper of numerous bodies in the eastern states" seemed to confirm what America's enemies maintained: that men "are unfit for their own government." Such fears multiplied in the following months. That explains why a profound sense of mission drew so many distinguished delegates to Philadelphia in May 1787, when the Constitutional Convention opened. The fate of the republic, and so of the American Revolution, seemed to rest in their hands.

## The Philadelphia Convention

The delegates knew firsthand the strengths and weaknesses of America's revolutionary governments. Eight had served in the constitutional conventions of their states, seven had been governors, and thirty-nine—over 70 percent—had served in the Continental Congress. A full third had also served in the Continental army, that breeding ground of nationalism. The delegates' average age was forty-two, but some of the most ardent were younger: Hamilton was only thirty, Madison thirty-six. At age eighty-one, Benjamin Franklin was by far the oldest. Neither Thomas Jefferson nor John Adams participated since they were representing the United States in France and in England. When Jefferson heard about the convention's membership, he described it as an "assembly of demi-gods."

That such men attended the convention raised suspicions in observers like Patrick Henry that more was involved than an effort to revise the Articles of Confederation. Their suspicions increased when, in its opening days, the convention decided to keep its deliberations secret.

### ELECTING OFFICERS, DEFINING THE RULES

The Constitutional Convention did not convene on the second Monday in May, as the call from Annapolis specified; not until the 25th had enough state delegations arrived for the delegates to get down to business. They met in the east room of the Pennsylvania State House, where the Continental Congress had signed the Declaration of Independence. Delegates sat grouped in threes and fours at tables covered with green cloth, facing the presiding officer's high-backed chair and the gray paneled east wall. Tall windows on the north and south sides let in light, while their slatted blinds cut the sun's force. Outside, gravel spread on the streets reduced the noise from traffic.

The convention devoted its opening days to electing officers, Washington as president and William Jackson as secretary, and defining the rules of procedure. Each state, the delegates agreed, would vote as a unit, with seven states constituting a quorum. Moreover, issues on which a vote had been taken could nonetheless be raised again at a later time. As a result, the convention's course of debate was not linear, with one problem after another taken up and resolved in logical order; it was more circular, since the convention regularly reconsidered previous decisions as later developments cast them in another light.

The convention also decided that "nothing spoken" in the convention would "be printed, or otherwise published or communicated without leave," and that the votes on specific provisions would not be recorded. Did the delegates decide to keep their proceedings secret so they could plot to undermine the Articles of Confederation without causing a public outcry? Many delegates were convinced that the Articles had to be replaced and understood that a proposal to establish a more powerful national government would provoke angry opposition. However, they seem to have had another purpose in mind when they adopted the rule of secrecy: only in that way could these experienced, informed leaders debate freely, changing positions as they were persuaded by others in what became in part an intense and productive working seminar on the cutting issue of their time, the architecture of a free government.

The official journals of the convention reflect the delegates' decision on secrecy: they are succinct to a fault, at least from the vantage of historians who want to know what happened. Fortunately, some delegates made their own notes on parts of the proceedings, and James Madison laboriously kept an extraordinarily complete set of "Notes" on the debates. He took a seat in front of Washington and carefully recorded not just what the convention discussed day by day but what individual delegates argued—even copying the full texts of speeches when he could—and how the state delegations voted. Madison, however, refused to allow publication of his "Notes" while any member of the convention remained alive. He also thought the "Notes" should not be made public until the Constitution was "well settled by practice, and till a knowledge of the controver-

James Madison, as portrayed by Charles Willson Peale in 1783, when Madison was one of Virginia's representatives in the Continental Congress.

sial part of the proceedings of its framers can be turned to no improper account." Finally, in his last will and testament, concluded about a year before his death on June 28, 1836, he authorized his widow, Dolley, to oversee their publication.

Why did Madison keep so copious a record? No doubt it was of help to him personally both during the convention and later, in fighting for the Constitution's ratification. He also understood that the Philadelphia Convention of 1787 was historically important. Madison had learned from history, which provided the data bank for his political science; so, he believed, would posterity—if it had the materials from which to construct an "unbiased" account of the past. By the time of his death, it seems, Madison thought his record of the federal convention would teach younger Americans that political divisions were nothing new. By fighting their way through disagreements as severe as those of later times, the "founding fathers" produced the federal Constitution. Americans of the 1830s had come to consider that document as a work more of God than of men—and certainly not of men who had interests to defend and who had to argue, compromise, and sometimes justify results they didn't entirely like.

## THE VIRGINIA AND NEW JERSEY PLANS

From Madison's "Notes," we know that on May 29, after the convention had concluded its preliminary business, Virginia's governor, Edmund Randolph, took the floor. It was essential to save the republic, Randolph began, and the Articles of Confederation, although the best that could be achieved eleven years earlier "in the then infancy of the science of constitutions, and of confederacies," would no longer do. Much, he implied, had been learned in the interim, particularly by the experiments and experience with constitutions within the states. As a result, the delegates should not try to patch up the Articles but should start over from scratch. Randolph then presented a plan that the Virginia delegation had drawn up in the week after May 17, when all its members were present in Philadelphia waiting for the convention to convene. Madison certainly played a role in defining its contents, but not even he could dictate to a delegation that included such formidable members as Randolph, George Mason, George Wythe, and last but not least, George Washington.

The Virginia Plan was not a draft constitution but a set of fifteen rough resolutions, some with blanks still to be filled in. The new government, according to the Virginia proposal, should have a bicameral legislature with power to pass laws that affected the nation as a whole as well as a separate executive and judiciary; and it should be not an alliance of sovereign states but a true government, with powers granted by the people through special state constitutional conventions. The Virginia Plan described the powers of Congress in general terms, proposing that it act "in all cases to which the separate States are incompetent, or in which the harmony of the United States may be interrupted by the exercise of individual [state] legislation." However, a Council of Revision (like that of New York) consisting of the executive and "a convenient number of the National Judiciary" would review acts of Congress and could veto them. Other provisions revealed nationalists' horror at what state legislatures were doing: the national legislature would have power to veto state laws that in its opinion violated the articles of union and could even bring force against states that failed to fulfill their duties under those articles.

For two weeks, the convention discussed, revised, and expanded the Virginia Plan. Then, on June 15, William Paterson of New Jersey rose and presented an alternative proposal. It, too, envisioned a radically stronger national government with separate legislative, executive, and judicial branches. The legislature under the New Jersey Plan would be a unicameral body like the old Confederation Congress, but it could exercise critical powers that its predecessor lacked. The New Jersey Plan did not, like the Virginia Plan, describe Congress's authority in general terms, but instead stated explicitly that it would have the power to tax by duties on imports and by a stamp (or excise) tax, and to regulate trade and commerce both between the states and with foreign nations. The New Jersey Plan also proposed that the laws and treaties of the United States "shall be the supreme law of the respective states," enforceable in state as well as federal courts. And, like the Virginia Plan, it authorized the federal executive to use force against states where necessary to enforce obedience to the laws and treaties of the United States.

The New Jersey Plan, however, took the form of revisions to the Articles of Confederation. The delegates met, Paterson said, to create not the best government possible but "such a one as our constituents have authorized us to prepare, and as they will approve." But to propose amendments to the Articles was to fail: amendments still required unanimous consent, and Rhode Island had not even bothered to send delegates to Philadelphia. And so, on June 19, the convention voted 7 to 3 to proceed on the basis of the Virginia Plan—which meant that the delegates were abandoning the Articles altogether and setting out to propose the best government they could devise.

## REPRESENTATION

One remaining issue provoked divisions so severe that the very survival of the convention came into question. The Virginia Plan made a state's representation in both houses of the legislature proportional to either the taxes it paid or its free population. The New Jersey Plan instead gave each state a single vote, as under the Confederation, regardless of its population, and delegates from the small states continued to insist on equal representation even after the New Jersey Plan was voted down. Naturally, delegates from states with large populations such as Virginia or those that expected to grow dramatically in the near future disagreed. In a republic, they argued, representation should be proportioned to population so that each person had roughly equal power. That principle had been "improperly violated" in the Articles of Confederation, and they could not accept any new plan of government that did not repair the defect. "Are not the Citizens of Pen[nsylvania] equal to those of N[ew] Jersey?" Pennsylvania's James Wilson asked; "does it require 150 of the former to balance 50 of the latter?" Delegates from small states insisted that they were bound by their instructions to reject any plan that did not give the states equal voting power. The large states were just as unyielding. If a separation of the states "must take place," Wilson declared, "it could never happen on better grounds" than "the just principles of representation."

The debates began on June 20, and by July 2 the convention was deadlocked. "We are now at a full stop," Connecticut's Roger Sherman noted. Would the delegates "break up" without accomplishing anything? "Something must be done," pleaded Elbridge Gerry of Massachusetts, "or we shall disappoint not only America, but the whole world." If the convention failed, he suggested, so would the Union, and then the country would "be without an Umpire to decide controversies and must be at the mercy of events. What too is to become of our treaties—what of our foreign debts, what of our domestic? We must make concessions on both sides." Unwilling to accept failure, the convention finally appointed a committee with one member from each state "to devise and report some compromise" on the issue of representation.

The committee met on July 3, took time out to celebrate the Fourth of July with other delegates, and issued its report the next day. Each state, it proposed, would have equal power in the Senate; but representation in the House of Representatives would be proportioned to the number of free persons, including servants, and three-fifths "of all other Persons" except "Indians not taxed." Direct taxes would be apportioned according to the same formula, which came from an amendment to the Articles of Confederation proposed in 1783. To further reassure the large states, the committee suggested that all revenue bills should originate in the House of Representatives and not be "altered or amended" by the Senate.

"Other persons" meant slaves, and the three-fifths provision therefore served to increase the power of southern states. The formula did not imply that a slave was three-fifths of a person. To have counted 100 percent of the slave population would have given still more power to their masters, not reaffirmed the slaves' humanity. The question was whether slaves should be counted at all in apportioning representation and direct taxes. If slaves were property, why shouldn't other forms of property—New England's cows for example—be counted? Obviously, the provision was less than entirely satisfactory. In fact, the compromise itself was wholly satisfactory to nobody, not even to the members of the committee, who proposed it without enthusiasm. But finally, on July 16, the delegates accepted the compromise proposal because the only alternative seemed to be closing up shop and going home.

Once that point was settled, an underlying fundamental agreement on what had to be done—which could be seen in the radical changes that both the Virginia and New Jersey Plans proposed—allowed the convention to proceed more smoothly. It probably helped that some delegates who opposed the direction the convention was taking, including two of the three New York delegates, left for home in early July. Henceforth, the problem was not to overcome hardened divisions but to design a new, national government that would have real power and provide a check on the states, yet pose no threat to the liberties of the people.

## FROM THE VIRGINIA PLAN TO A CONSTITUTION

The convention proceeded to expand and revise the resolutions Randolph had introduced. After a brief recess between July 26 and August 6, while a Committee of Detail created a draft constitution from those propositions on which the convention had agreed, the debates resumed. Then a Committee of Style met between September 8 and 12 to incorporate into the document changes made in the previous month and produce a more finished version of the Constitution. Its report looked a lot like the Massachusetts constitution, with a preamble and opening articles on the legislative, executive, and judicial powers. Again the convention reconsidered one provision or another until September 17, when it dissolved.

On point after point, the convention revised and improved the Virginia Plan. Rather than have the upper house elected by the House of Representatives from candidates nominated by state legislatures, as the Virginia Plan proposed, the convention let the state legislatures elect senators. That made the Senate a more effective check on the House—but tied it more closely to the states. Later the convention gave senators six-year terms and allowed them to vote individually, which freed them somewhat from state control. The House would be popularly elected to ensure, as Madison said, a "necessary sympathy" between the people and the government.

What powers would fall to Congress? The convention, following the proposal of its Committee of Style, chose to be specific. The list of congressional powers in the Articles of Confederation was a beginning, but Congress also received power "to lay and collect taxes," "to regulate commerce," and to make all laws "necessary and proper" for carrying out the powers the federal government received under the Constitution. "To promote the progress of science and useful arts,"

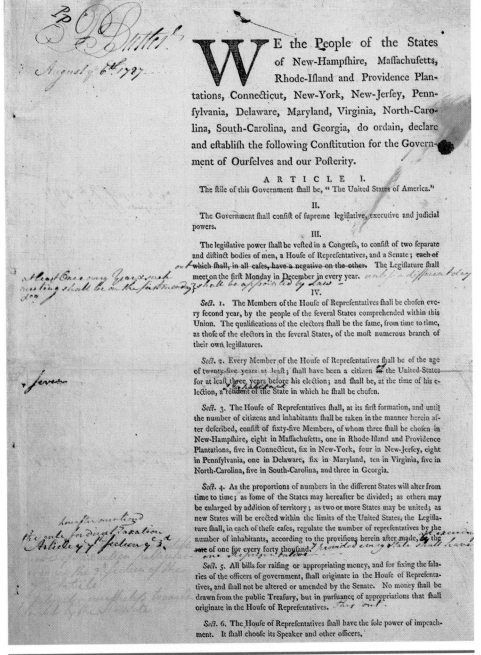

This first version of the Constitution was the work of a Committee of Detail that met between July 26 and August 6. The committee used the twenty-three propositions on which the convention had agreed as well as the New Jersey Plan and a proposal by Charles Pinckney of South Carolina. After the committee submitted its report, the convention began amending the draft, which was printed for delegates' consideration with wide margins in which they could mark changes agreed on by the convention. The notes and changes on this printing were made by South Carolina delegate Pierce Butler.

Congress received the power to grant authors and inventors "the exclusive right to their respective writings and discoveries" for a limited time. The convention did not give Congress power to grant charters of incorporation, which Madison proposed in order to facilitate the chartering of interstate canals or roads; controversies over the Bank of North America and the Bank of New York suggested that such a provision would increase opposition to the Constitution, whose ratification was no sure thing. The states, however, were explicitly denied the right to "coin Money; emit Bills of Credit," or "make anything but gold and silver Coin" legal tender. Nor could they pass laws "impairing the Obligation of Contracts" (Article I, Section 10). The property of creditors would be more secure with than without the new Constitution.

Should Congress also have power to prohibit or discourage the importation of slaves? That issue provoked divisions comparable only to those over representation. One of the most ardent opponents of the slave trade was a Virginian, George Mason, who said that slavery was "inconsistent with the principles of the revolution and dishonorable to the American character." Delegates from South Carolina and Georgia, however, insisted that they needed more slaves and could not approve a constitution that outlawed the slave trade, although a modest tax on slaves, as on other imports, seemed reasonable. Some northerners thought the issue was best left to the states and assumed that, in any case, the number of slaves was sure to decline over time. As the population grew, poor laborers would so multiply, Connecticut's Oliver Ellsworth said, "as to render slaves useless. Slavery in time will not be a speck in our Country." Perhaps for that reason, the Constitution, which was designed for the ages, does not include the words "slave" or "slavery." Its provision on the slave trade, for example, says that "the migration or importation of such persons as any of the states now existing shall think proper to admit" could not be prohibited by Congress before 1808, although a "a tax or duty" could be imposed on those imports "not exceeding 10 dollars for each person" (Article I, Section 9).

The Virginia Plan proposed only that "a National Executive be instituted," without offering more detail on its structure. The convention chose to entrust the executive power to one person—a president—over the objections of Governor Randolph, who thought the office should go to a committee, as in Pennsylvania. Gradually, the convention gave the president substantial powers. He would become commander in chief of the army and navy and of the state militias. He could also veto acts of Congress—and alone, not as a member of a Council of Revision, as the Virginia Plan had proposed. But his veto could then be overturned by a two-thirds vote of Congress, which followed state precedents. He could appoint judges, ambassadors, and other officers of the United States, and also make treaties—but only with the "advice and consent" of the Senate.

This powerful new executive was not an "elective Monarchy," as some charged, since the president, unlike a king, held office for a limited period. The president could, like the vice-president and other civil officers, also be impeached (that is, indicted) by a majority vote of the House of Representatives for "treason, bribery, or other high crimes and misdemeanors." An impeached president would then be tried for those offenses by the Senate, where conviction required a two-thirds vote. Punishment could not go beyond removal from office and disqualification from holding "any office of honour, trust or profit under the United States," although he or she remained subject to later prosecutions in the courts.

As the list of presidential powers grew, it became clear that the president should not hold office for seven years and then be ineligible for reelection, as the convention had provisionally decided in early June. The convention reduced that term to four years and put no limit on eligibility for re-election. But who would the electors be? That, according to James Wilson, a lawyer of Scottish birth who played a persistent and powerful role in the convention's debates, was the most difficult question the convention had to decide. It did not want to enhance Congress's power by letting it elect the president. Direct election by the people was for some

delegates an ideal solution, but it seemed unlikely that the people would know much about candidates from states other than their own. Moreover, since more people could vote in the northern than the southern states, particularly those with substantial slave populations, direct popular election would disadvantage the South. As a result, the convention enlisted an indirect method of election similar to one used to elect state senators under the Maryland constitution of 1776.

Each state would elect, according to a method determined by its legislature, a number of presidential electors equal to the number of senators and representatives it sent to Congress. The persons chosen would meet within their state, like those within other states, on a date Congress determined. That decentralization of the electoral process seemed to make it less prone to corruption. Each elector would cast ballots for two different candidates, at least one of whom came from another state. The list of results would be signed, certified, and sent to the president of the United States Senate, who would bear responsibility

James Wilson, a Pennsylvania delegate to the Constitutional Convention and a man who, more than any other, laid the intellectual foundations of American Federalism by locating sovereignty firmly in the people. This watercolor on artist board is by J. B. Longacre, after J. P. H. Elouis (c.1825).

218

for opening the returns "in the presence of the Senate and the House of Representatives." The person with the greatest number of votes, so long as those votes equaled a majority of electors, would become president, and the person with the next-highest total would become vice-president. The convention expected votes to be scattered, so a candidate would receive the requisite number of electoral votes to become president only on rare occasions. It was also possible, since the president and vice-president were elected by the same ballot, that two people could be tied, each with votes that equaled a majority of electors. In case of a tie or the lack of a majority, the election of the president would be thrown to the House of Representatives, where, for this purpose, each state delegation would have one vote. The system seemed a reasonable if cumbersome solution to the problems anticipated by the delegates. The convention finally accepted it in early September, when the clock was running down.

The convention also decided that there would be one Supreme Court and such inferior courts as Congress chose to establish. The judges would hold office "on good behavior," and their salaries could not be reduced while they remained on the bench. They could be removed from office only through the difficult process of impeachment. Equally important, the delegates carefully described the extensive jurisdiction of federal courts, and they added to the Constitution a phrase suggested by the New Jersey Plan: the Constitution as well as the laws and treaties of the United States would be "the supreme Law of the Land" and binding on all judges, including those of the states, regardless of what their state laws and constitutions said. That seemed to eliminate the need for a congressional veto on state laws—although on that point Madison remained unconvinced. In the future, state laws that contravened the Constitution would be set aside by the courts. And there would be no provision for the nation using force to bring the states in line. Even Madison came to understand that such a provision would institutionalize civil war.

Finally, the convention specified, like the Virginia Plan, that the proposed new Constitution would be submitted to special conventions elected by the people. That procedure justified the opening lines, adapted from the Massachusetts constitution of 1780: "We the People of the United States . . . do ordain and establish this Constitution for the United States." The authority of the Constitution came from the people of the various states, not from the state governments, and would be enforced on individuals (although state officials were also bound to comply with that "supreme Law of the Land"). Moreover, the Constitution would take effect when nine states, not all thirteen, had voted to ratify. Those provisions made it more likely that the Constitution would be ratified. They circumvented the state legislatures, which had the most to lose but could hardly deny the people's right to consider the proposed Constitution through specially elected conventions. Nor could one state, or four, block ratification. And once nine states had ratified, the others would have to decide not whether they loved the Constitution, but whether they would remain parts of the American Union or go their separate ways. That stacked the deck for ratification.

## A RISING SUN?

In the final days of the convention, Elbridge Gerry of Massachusetts moved that a committee be appointed to prepare a bill of rights. George Mason seconded the motion. Such a document could easily be prepared in a few hours, he said, using the state declarations of rights as models, and it would "give great quiet to the people." He was right, but not one state supported the proposal. In the end, Mason's fear that the powers granted to the federal government were too great got the best of him. Like Gerry and his colleague Edmund Randolph, Mason remained at the convention to the end but refused to sign the finished Constitution.

In fact, few if any of the thirty-nine delegates who signed the document agreed with everything it said. Madison himself thought the Constitution included several fatal errors, starting with its violation of proportional representation in the Senate. He also thought the convention's unwillingness to give Congress a veto on state laws was a big mistake. In a moment of despair in early September 1787, Madison even wrote Jefferson that he feared the new Constitution would "neither effectually answer its national object nor prevent the local mischiefs which every where excite disgusts ag[ain]st the state government[s]."

Madison and most delegates, however, chose to follow the advice of Franklin, which was conveyed in a final speech that James Wilson read for him. There were parts of the Constitution about which he, too, had doubts, Franklin confessed. But "the older I grow, the more apt I am to doubt my own judgment, and to pay more respect to the judgment of others." And so "I agree to this Constitution with all its faults, if they are such," because "I think a general Government necessary for us," and "doubt whether any other Convention . . . may be able to make a better Constitution." In fact, Franklin was astonished at how near the Constitution approached perfection, "and I think it will astonish our enemies, who are waiting with confidence to hear that our councils are confounded like those of the Builders of Babel; and that our States are on the point of separation, only to meet hereafter for the purpose of cutting each other's throats." Thus he consented to the Constitution "because I expect no better, and . . . am not sure, that it is not the best. The opinions I have had of its errors, I sacrifice to the public good." Franklin urged the other delegates in a similar manner to "doubt a little" their "own infallibility" and to work "heartily and unanimously" for the Constitution's ratification.

George Washington presides while delegates to the Philadelphia Convention sign the final Constitution on September 17, 1787, as the artist Thomas Prichard Rossiter pictured that event some fifty years later.

Even then the delegates returned to discussing the Constitution. At issue was a provision in Article I that "the Number of Representatives shall not exceed one for every forty Thousand," which a Massachusetts delegate suggested be changed to "one for every thirty Thousand" in the interest of "lessening objections to the Constitution" by providing a fuller representation of the people. Then, for the first time, George Washington intervened in the debates. The "smallness of the proportion of Representatives" seemed to many delegates, he said, "insufficient security for the rights & interests of the people," and, since it was desirable that objections to the Constitution be reduced to the extent possible, he hoped the suggestion would be adopted. And it was, unanimously.

Finally, after agreeing to affirm that the Constitution had been adopted "by the unanimous consent of the States present" on September 17, 1787, and to entrust its journals to Washington rather than to destroy them, the delegates came forward to sign the document. Meanwhile, as Madison related in his "Notes," Franklin called to the attention of a few nearby delegates the chair of the president, which had a sun painted on its back. Artists, he noted, had trouble distinguishing a rising from a setting sun, and often in the course of the convention's debates he had stared at the president's chair, wondering which it depicted. "But now at length I have the happiness to know that it is a rising and not a setting Sun."

## Ratification

The finished Constitution went first to the Confederation Congress, which, after some deliberation, voted that it should be sent to the state legislatures "to be submitted to a Convention of Delegates chosen in each state by the people thereof." The race was on.

### THE STATE RATIFYING CONVENTIONS

Pennsylvania wanted to be the first to ratify—hopeful, some said, that Philadelphia would then become the nation's capital. There the Federalists, who advocated ratification, used strong-arm tactics, literally dragging dissenting members into the Pennsylvania assembly so it had the quorum necessary to call a convention. The Pennsylvania convention met on November 21, 1787, and, after vigorous and sometimes acrimonious debate, on December 12 ratified the Constitution by a 2-to-1 vote. By then, however, Delaware had already ratified (December 7). New Jersey followed after only a week of discussion (December 18), and Georgia—which sought federal help against Indians—consented unanimously (as had Delaware and New Jersey) on January 2, 1788. Seven days later, the Connecticut convention voted 128 to 40 in favor. That made five, and from then on the struggle got harder.

Massachusetts was next. Town meetings there had repeatedly discussed constitutional documents of one sort or another, and drawing on that experience, many confidently decided that the proposed Constitution was no good and expected their convention delegates to vote against ratification. But the Federalists, who were on the whole more educated and articulate than their opponents, refuted one objection after another. An effort to cut off debate, reject the Constitution quickly, and dissolve the convention before the Federalists could spin their magic failed when Samuel Adams intervened. His first impulse had been against ratification, but he believed in deliberative democracy. Finally, Adams and Governor John Hancock cooked up a proposal that Massachusetts ratify but suggest the adoption of several amendments. That gave delegates a way of explaining to the folks back home why they had voted in favor. And so, on February 7, 1788, the convention voted to ratify, 187 to 168. Thereafter, several states followed suit and linked ratification with a list of recommended amendments to "remove the fears & quiet the apprehensions" of many people and, as Massachusetts put it, "more effectually guard against an undue administration of the Federal Government." Without that device, it's doubtful that the Constitution would have been adopted.

A handful of Antifederalists, as the Constitution's critics were called, spoke to an audience of confident Federalists in the Maryland convention, which voted on April 28 to ratify—and without suggesting amendments—by a lopsided vote, 63 to 11; then, on May 23, South Carolina decided in favor by a 2-to-1 vote. Finally, on June 21, New Hampshire became the ninth state to ratify: the Constitution would become law. However, Virginia and New York had not yet decided, and a nation without those states would have been most peculiar.

The debates in the Virginia convention were at once deeply probing and highly emotional. The old firebrand Patrick Henry took the floor repeatedly, arguing passionately against ratification in long, rambling speeches. Madison and other Virginians younger than Henry such as Edmund Pendleton—and eventually also Edmund Randolph—answered him. On June 26, Virginia voted in favor, 89 to 79. The convention not only recommended amendments but also declared ominously that

"The Looking Glass for 1787," a political cartoon printed at New Haven, Connecticut, in 1787, depicts divisions in Connecticut politics over the proposed Constitution. The Federalists, with whom the cartoonist sympathized, represent the trading and commercial interests, while Antifederalists utter phrases such as "Tax Luxary" and "Success to Shays," suggesting they were uneducated, rabble-rousing incendiaries.

the powers granted by the people to the new federal government "may be resumed by them whensoever the same shall be perverted to their injury or oppression." Still, Virginia would remain in the Union.

A special messenger brought the news to the New York convention, meeting in Poughkeepsie. Even so, the deliberations there continued for another four weeks. Finally, after proposing no fewer than thirty-two amendments to the Constitution, the convention voted to ratify by 30 to 27, a very close vote. Rhode Island still held out (no surprise), as did North Carolina. But the new government could be organized without them.

### THE GREAT NATIONAL DEBATE

What objections were raised against the Constitution? For one thing, Antifederalists argued, the United States was far too large for a substantive republican government, and under the new Constitution it would certainly revert to monarchy or aristocracy. The Constitution was a step backward, they claimed; it re-created all that the colonies had rejected in 1776 by giving Congress powers that the colonists had denied to Parliament and by entrusting vast executive power to a single person. Richard Henry Lee, who had moved independence in the Second Continental Congress, found it "really astonishing that the same people, who have just emerged from a long and cruel war in defense of liberty, should agree to fix an elective despotism upon themselves and posterity!" The Constitution, Patrick Henry added, "squints toward monarchy."

More specifically, some Antifederalists, George Mason among them, complained that the Constitution lacked a bill of rights. Such a document, they assumed, would protect the right to trial by jury in both civil and criminal cases, along with a series of other rights that went unmentioned or seemed imperiled by the Constitution. One right that worried many Antifederalists was the right to "no taxation without representation," which had been central to the Americans' case against Parliament before 1776. The Antifederalists said the Constitution's provision that the number of representatives in Congress "shall not exceed one for every thirty thousand"—which, of course, had been even worse (one for every forty thousand) before the convention's final day—was insufficient to provide a full and free representation of the people. (The Massachusetts constitution, by contrast, allowed towns an additional representative whenever their population grew by 250 adult white men.) That was especially worrisome given Congress's broad taxing power. Several states requested an amendment that would prevent Congress from laying direct taxes—which included poll and property taxes—without first requisitioning the states to provide their share of the general levy "in such way and manner as the Legislatures of the respective States shall judge best." With the threat of congressional taxation hanging overhead, the states would certainly honor requisitions, despite their previous bad record on that score. There would then be no taxation without a level of representation possible only at the state level.

The Constitution, Antifederalists insisted, created a "consolidated government" inconsistent with the persistence of the states, a government that would assume all powers of legislation and whose laws would be "supreme and controul the whole." The checks and balances built in to the Constitution were inadequate in the Antifederalists' eyes: the government's powers would soon be grotesquely expanded at the cost of liberty. Congress's right to change the places of elections for members of the House of Representatives (Article I, Section 4) would allow it to "say that the election for all the states might be had in New York." Congress's exclusive jurisdiction over the new nation's capital (Article I, Section 8) would give it the freedom to hang "any who shall act contrary to their commands" and offer asylum to would-be tyrants and others who oppressed the people. And the lack of religious qualifications for office meant that "Papists and Pagans might be introduced into office; and that Popery and the Inquisition may be established in America."

The debate raged not only on the convention floor but in pamphlets and newspapers. The well-known *Federalist Papers* by Madison, Hamilton, and John Jay of New York, a series of eighty-five essays first published in New York City newspapers between October 1787 and the following spring, offered a particularly thorough analysis and defense of the Constitution, but not the only one. Both sides produced a torrent of essays, speeches, and manifestos during the ratification contest, and both sides advanced compelling arguments. If the Federalists had no monopoly on wisdom, they did enjoy certain other distinct advantages. Most newspaper printers favored the Constitution, and the cities and rural areas served by navigable rivers tended to fall in their camp. The people in those regions not only were involved in trade, which the Constitution would bene-

This banner of the Society of Pewterers was carried in the Federal Procession in New York, which celebrated ratification of the Constitution on July 23, 1788. In general, artisans such as the pewterers favored ratification. They believed that a stronger federal government would bring an expansion of trade and an economic prosperity from which they, and the country in general, would benefit.

fit, but often were better educated than their rural peers. Antifederalists tended to be from more remote places, which (like the "Shaysite" interior sections of Massachusetts) sometimes had good reason to fear that a strong central power would be used against them.

The most prominent Antifederalist spokesmen—men like Lee or Henry—had been leaders of the independence movement, which is probably why they so readily saw the ghost of British tyranny in the Constitution. Fear, sometimes exaggerated to outlandish dimensions, dominated their arguments. However, Antifederalists often admitted that the Articles of Confederation had failed. Many of them were, in fact, ready to support the Constitution if it was amended in ways that clarified ambiguous provisions, modified dangerous powers, explicitly protected certain rights, and in general made the new government less of a threat to American freedom as they understood it. They saw no good reason why, as the Federalists insisted, they had to accept the Constitution as a whole or reject it altogether. Shouldn't "we the people" be able to fine-tune the document before putting it into effect?

Some veterans of 1776 such as Franklin and Washington supported the Constitution, but the core of Federalist leadership lay with a younger generation possessed less with fear than with hope for the future. Born in the late 1740s and 1750s, those young men of the revolution had entered politics with the elected extra-legal governments of the 1770s, not under the old regime, and by 1787 had mastered tricks of democratic politics in ways that alarmed their opponents as much as the Constitution itself. The Federalists pushed for a rapid ratification of the Constitution as written, with no modifications whatsoever, even if large minorities were left behind. That was dramatically different from the independence movement, which unfolded slowly and sought unanimity.

Having less of the old regime to unlearn, the young Federalists could also push the radical insights of 1776 further, advancing the science of politics beyond what the previous generation had accomplished. British imperial and American federal government, they insisted, were different, and fears appropriate for a monarchical government an ocean away were inappropriate in a government of elected persons chosen from among the people and who held office for limited terms. James Wilson responded to charges that the Constitution created a consolidated government by providing an intellectual foundation for American Federalism. In the United States, he said, the people were sovereign (that is, held ultimate power), and from that pool of power they could create two levels of government to perform distinct tasks on their behalf. There was no more reason those governments should conflict than that parallel lines would meet. And James Madison took on the old chestnut about republics working only in small areas. He argued in the tenth *Federalist Paper* that small democracies were particularly subject to the violence of majoritarian tyranny and so to turbulence and contention. The solution lay in greater size. "Extend the sphere and you take in a greater variety of parties and interests" and make it less likely that "a majority of the whole will have a common motive to invade the rights of other citizens." Moreover, in large republics, the people's voice fed into legislation not directly but filtered through representatives who had to speak for several sets of interests at once. The substantial populations of large republics also made it more likely that persons capable of performing that task could be found.

In the end, however, the Antifederalists shared much with the Federalists. Both wanted the Revolution and the Republic it founded to succeed; both recognized the inadequacies of the Articles of Confederation; both thought the Constitution less than perfect; both put a high value on American liberty. If the flaws in the Constitution proved to be as grave as its critics predicted, the Federalists argued, they could be repaired by a peaceful process of amendment that was now in the realm of the possible since amendments no longer required unanimous consent. And if the Constitution proved thoroughly inadequate, it could be replaced, as some states had already done with their first constitutions. But before repairs could be made, before a better design could be drawn, the Constitution of 1787 needed to be tried and its weaknesses confirmed by actual experience.

And so, once the Constitution was ratified, the Antifederalists took not to the swamps, as southern guerrillas had done in the last days of the Revolutionary War, but to the polling places and legislative halls, lending their hands to make the new government work. That willingness, with their insistence on amendments designed to protect Americans' rights, was perhaps the greatest of their contributions. It meant that the new government could be organized and given a fair try, that the experiment would be run.

## Suggested Reading

Christopher and James Lincoln Collier, *Decision in Philadelphia: The Constitutional Convention of 1787* (1986)

MAX M. Edling, *A Revolution in Favor of Government: Origins of the U.S. Constitution and the Making of the American State* (2003)

Max Farrand, *The Framing of the Constitution of the United States* (1913)

David C. Hendrickson, Peace Pact: The Lost World of the American Founding *(2003)*

*Merrill Jensen,* The Articles of Confederation *(1966), and* The New Nation: A History of the United States During the Confederation, 1781–1789 *(1950)*

*Cecelia M. Kenyon, ed.,* The Antifederalists *(1966, 1985)*

*James Madison,* Notes of Debates in the Federal Convention of 1787, *ed. Adrienne Koch (1966)*

*Jackson Turner Main,* The Antifederalists: Critics of the Constitution, 1781–1788 *(1961, 1974)*

*Jack Rakove,* James Madison and the Creation of the American Republic *(1990)*

*Robert Allan Rutland,* The Ordeal of the Constitution: The Antifederalists and the Ratification Struggle of 1787–1788 *(1966)*

*Gordon S. Wood,* The Creation of the American Republic, 1766–1787 *(1969)*

# Chapter Review

## Summary
### QUESTIONS

■ In what ways did the Articles of Confederation mark an advance over the Second Continental Congress?

■ Why did the Annapolis Convention call a constitutional convention?

■ What issues divided the Constitutional convention?

■ How did the delegates overcome those divisions?

■ How did the Constitution proposed by the convention differ from the Virginia plan?

■ What distinguished Antifederalists and Federalists in the debates over ratification of the federal Constitution?

## Chronology

| | |
|---|---|
| March 1781 | Articles of Confederation ratified. |
| September 1786 | Annapolis convention calls a Constitutional convention. |
| 1786–87 | Shays's Rebellion. |
| February 1786 | Continental Congress calls a convention to amend Articles of Confederation. |
| May 25, 1787 | The Constitutional Convention convenes in Philadelphia. |
| May 29, 1787 | Edmund Randolph presents the Virginia Plan. |
| September 17, 1787 | The Constitutional convention adjourns. |
| September 28, 1787 | The Continental Congress forwards the Constitution to the states. |
| October 1787 | Federalist Papers begin to appear in New York newspapers. |
| June 21, 1788 | The Constitution becomes law when New Hampshire is the ninth state to ratify. |

## Key Terms

Articles of Confederation (p. 205)

The Northwest Ordinance (p. 208)

Shay's Rebellion (p. 213)

The Virginia and New Jersey Plans (p. 215)

Ratification process (pp. 220–222)

---

**Access the *Inventing America* StudySpace at wwnorton.com/studyspace**

PERSONAL PLAN ■ REVIEW MATERIALS ■ RESEARCH AIDS ■ MULTIMEDIA

# Chapter 8

# ESTABLISHING THE NEW NATION:

## 1789–1800

Tontine Coffee House, c. 1797, by Francis Guy.

QUESTIONS

- *How did the new president and Congress begin to flesh-out the Constitution?*

- *What caused the surge of American prosperity in the 1790s?*

- *What were the major political divisions that marked the 1790s?*

Once New Hampshire cast the deciding vote for ratification, the Continental Congress could begin making arrangements for setting the new government in motion. The First Federal Congress, it decided, would meet on March 4, 1789, at New York, "the present seat of Congress." New York's city council, hoping to enhance its bid to become the permanent capital, promptly began remodeling the old City Hall at Nassau and Wall Streets into Federal Hall, an elegant meeting place for Congress.

Bells, flying flags, and cannon fire welcomed the day appointed for the delegates to assemble. Unfortunately, only thirteen representatives out of fifty-nine from the eleven states then in the Union had arrived, and only eight of the twenty-two senators. Old habits, it seemed, die hard. Not until April 1—April Fools' Day, a bad sign—did the House have a quorum of members present. Five days later, the Senate also had a quorum, so it could finally count the presidential electoral votes that had been cast the previous February. George Washington, with sixty-nine votes, became the unanimous choice for president, as expected; and John Adams, with the next highest number of votes, thirty-four, became his vice-president.

And so began one of the most formative and also tumultuous decades in American history. The new president and Congress had to put flesh on the bare bones of the Constitution—to transform the institutional structure outlined at Philadelphia in 1787 into a working government. Whether the federal government acted in foreign or domestic affairs, however, it fomented fears and divisions that threatened at times to bring the Americans' experiment with substantive central government to a quick end. In fact, the greatest achievement of the federal government in its opening years was the simplest of all: it survived.

## Getting Started

If the new Congress's slow start recalled the old Continental Congress and its waning attendance, a burst of activity soon made clear that this was, indeed, a new game. Most senators

and representatives were experienced in public service, had favored ratification of the Constitution, and were now ready to organize the new government and set it on a solid foundation. But the past kept haunting their proceedings: in one way after another, the new American government seemed to recall British imperial rule, which rekindled old fears and hostilities.

### POLITICAL RITUAL

Nowhere was the problem more apparent than in the realm of ritual, the ceremonies and procedures that signaled the relationship of one part of the government with another. Since the Constitution said little about how intragovernmental affairs should be conducted, the political rituals of the American Republic had to be invented. But were they to be modeled on British precedents or created anew in ways more appropriate to a republic? The distinction wasn't always obvious. The only way some loyal Americans could imagine executing certain acts was in the way the British did them, so the conflict began almost immediately.

Because Washington was a firm republican, he wanted his eight-day journey from Virginia to New York free of monarchical ostentation. But in towns all along the way, people came out to pay honor to the new president. They fired cannons, rang bells, shouted out acclamations. On the last leg of the journey, as Washington crossed Newark Bay and, exhausted, made his way toward his living quarters on Manhattan's Cherry Street, young girls tossed flowers in his path while the strains of "God Save the King" drifted through the air.

Already some began to suspect that such ceremonies predicted the transformation of the president into an elected monarch. The presidential inauguration on April 30, 1789, did nothing to calm their anxiety. Robert R. Livingston, chancellor of the State of New York, administered the oath of office to Washington—who wore for the occasion a relatively simple, American-made brown suit—from an open portico at Federal Hall. Then Livingston turned to the assembled

A print showing the triumphal arches erected near Philadelphia to welcome George Washington on his way to New York and his inauguration as first president of the United States, April 1789; from *Columbian Magazine*.

the southern Indians. The procedure seemed awkward and, in the end, proved unsatisfactory to both sides. Some senators sensed that they were being coerced into rubber-stamping proposals determined by the executive branch, and Washington found disconcerting the Senate's hesitation simply to give its consent on the spot. He never again sought the Senate's consent in person, and later he abandoned even written communications before negotiating a treaty. Instead, he submitted finished documents for the senators' consideration. In that way, the Senate became less of an executive body, advisory to the president, and the president became less like a prime minister who executed the will of the Senate and more of an independent executive.

crowd outside on Wall Street and cried out, "Long live George Washington, President of the United States!"—just as the British shouted, "Long live the king!"

The Senate, according to one member's notes, discussed at length British precedents in deciding issues such as how to receive the president on Inauguration Day and how to communicate with the House of Representatives. Some senators advocated bestowing titles on high-ranking officials. Only the objections of the House of Representatives undercut a Senate committee's recommendation that the president be addressed as "His Highness the President of the United States of America, and Protector of their Liberties." In the interest of congressional harmony, the Senate finally agreed that the proper address would be " 'the President of the United States,' without addition of title." In this matter, at least, the view prevailed that British practice was irrelevant to the American Republic.

In some areas, questions of ritual and procedure had long-term consequences for the relationships of national institutions. Consider the constitutional provision that the president could make treaties "with the Advice and Consent of the Senate": did that imply that the president had to consult the Senate before concluding treaties, perhaps visiting its chamber in person? Washington thought it did, and in August 1789 he went to the Senate to consult on a treaty he hoped to negotiate with

## THE EXECUTIVE BRANCH

In other areas, the First Federal Congress resolved institutional issues in a more direct manner. Article II, Section 2, of the Constitution referred to "executive Departments," each under a "principal Officer," but said nothing about the number or responsibilities of those departments. The Constitution focused on the president and vice-president, leaving Congress the task of fleshing out the executive branch. Soon after convening, Congress passed laws creating three separate departments for foreign affairs, war, and the treasury. Washington appointed Thomas Jefferson to head the first of those departments, but until Jefferson took office six months later, John Jay continued to supervise the nation's foreign affairs. Washington selected Henry Knox, a veteran officer from the Revolutionary War, to head the War Department, as he had under Confederation, and Alexander Hamilton as secretary of the treasury. Soon Washington began treating department heads as a board of advisers, or "cabinet."

Some advocated the establishment of a fourth executive department for domestic affairs with responsibility for encouraging scientific and technological advances and internal improvements as well as more standard functions such as taking the constitutionally mandated census, conducting relations with Indians, and keeping federal records. Instead, in September

1789, Congress changed the Department of Foreign Affairs into a State Department and entrusted it with several of those duties.

The supervision of federal patents and copyrights was among the new tasks assigned to the renamed State Department. The Constitution explicitly granted Congress power "to promote the Progress of Science and the useful Arts, by securing for limited Times to Authors and Inventors the exclusive Right to their respective Writings and Discoveries." Congress had no more than met when it began receiving petitions from writers and inventors who understood that federal patent and copyright laws would make unnecessary multiple applications to the states (whose number, moreover, would soon begin to multiply as the West was settled and organized politically). In 1790, Congress enacted and, on April 10, the president signed a federal patent law that gave inventors "sole and exclusive right and liberty" for a period "not exceeding fourteen years" to make and sell inventions under a federal patent. On May 31, Washington signed a similar measure "for the encouragement of learning" by securing federal copyright to the authors or creators of "maps, charts, and books." Both measures underwent subsequent revisions, but the advantage of a single national patent or copyright was so obvious that the system itself remained firmly in place. For a time, Jefferson, who had an interest in technical devices, personally scrutinized patent applications submitted to the State Department, and he testified that the patent law gave "a spring to invention beyond my conception." Many proposals were "trifling," but some described inventions "of great consequence which have been proved by practice, and others which if they stand the same proof will produce great effect."

While Congress was at work establishing the first three executive departments, James Madison, a member of the House of Representatives, raised another important issue: the president needed the Senate's consent in appointing department heads, but Madison proposed that Congress explicitly grant the chief executive power to remove department heads without consulting the Senate. Some representatives argued that there was no need to grant the president the power of removal since the Constitution gave him an implied authority to do so, a position that Madison eventually adopted. As a result, the first House bill creating an executive department said nothing about the power of removal, which prompted intense debate in the Senate. In the end, the Senate's vote was tied—but then Vice-President Adams cast his vote in favor of the president's power to fire officials without the Senate's consent. Congress established the other executive departments in the same way, with no provision on the removal of their

heads from office. The result, again, was to enhance the power of the president and to make the executive branch more independent of the Senate than it might otherwise have been.

The creation of executive departments led to the establishment of a federal bureaucracy. The president thereby received powers of appointment that, along with the power of granting contracts and financial favors, had helped the British king secure followers in the House of Commons and so, as the Americans saw it, to undermine what checks on power had been built into the British constitution. The prospect of similar "corruption" haunted certain members of the First Federal Congress.

Congressional actions affected regional as well as personal interests, which further complicated the houses' decisions. Legislation for a federal postal system, for example, foundered because of squabbling over the location of post roads, which were likely to become economic arteries and would therefore affect the fates of communities they passed through as well as those they bypassed. The mail nonetheless was delivered since Congress renewed for short periods of time the old postal service of the Confederation.

Finally, in 1792, Congress enacted a Post Office Act that was worth waiting for, a law justly described as an agent of

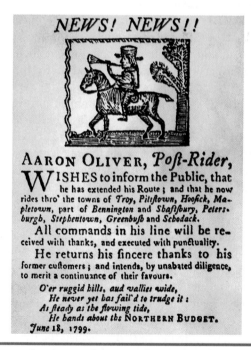

A newspaper advertisement for Aaron Oliver, in the Northern Budget, 1799, offering his services as a post rider in the vicinity of Troy, New York.

change rivaled by few others of the time. It prohibited public officials from using their power over the mail as a surveillance technique, which protected American freedom. Equally important, the act permitted newspapers to travel through the mail on extremely favorable terms and established procedures that encouraged the expansion of mail routes from the Atlantic seaboard into the trans-Appalachian West. That privilege fed the already explosive growth of newspapers and allowed the news to penetrate remote parts of the nation. Four decades later, a French visitor discovered that a farmer in the Michigan Territory enjoyed more access to nonlocal information than did the inhabitants of more densely populated sections of metropolitan France. The Post Office Act undercut local isolation, supported commercial development, and allowed informed, popular political participation on a scale unanticipated by any of the wise men who had gathered at the Philadelphia Convention in the summer of 1787.

## THE JUDICIARY

The Constitution vested federal judicial power "in one Supreme Court, and in such inferior courts as the Congress may from time to time ordain and establish." That left many blanks for Congress to fill in. Early in its first session, the First Federal Congress set up a committee with one member from each state to prepare a judiciary bill. The proposed bill was then printed, and members of Congress sent copies to their constituents, particularly lawyers and judges, for comment.

After further debates and amendments, the Federal Judiciary Act of 1789 specified that the Supreme Court would consist of a chief justice and five associate justices. The act also set up a system of federal district courts and circuit courts (which met in different places). State courts were granted original jurisdiction in most civil cases involving federal questions, although the decisions of the highest state courts could be appealed to the Supreme Court. Section 25 of the act was especially important. It allowed the Supreme Court final say in all cases that involved constitutional issues; indeed, the Supreme Court could overturn state laws and court rulings if they conflicted with the Constitution, federal laws, or treaties of the United States. Southerners immediately took alarm, realizing that federal courts could force them to pay debts owed to British creditors, as the 1783 Treaty of Paris specified. In general, however, the Judiciary Act defined the jurisdiction of federal courts more narrowly than the Constitution allowed. By giving state courts concurrent jurisdiction, the Judiciary

Act saved the cost of establishing and maintaining an extensive federal court system while undercutting fears that an expanding federal judicial leviathan would destroy state courts.

The Judiciary Act provided for the appointment of an attorney general who would serve as a legal adviser to the president and the heads of executive departments and "prosecute and conduct all suits in the supreme Court in which the United States shall be concerned." Edmund Randolph of Virginia accepted that position, and John Jay became the first chief justice of the Supreme Court. The First Federal Congress also adopted a Punishment of Crimes Act, which defined as federal crimes treason, counterfeiting federal records, and murder, disfigurement, and robbery if committed within a federal jurisdiction or on the high seas. The act authorized judges to sentence convicted murderers to be dissected after being executed for purposes of medical research, and it even defined punishments for persons attempting to "rescue" bodies from dissection. Scientific advance, it seems, was a congressional objective from the beginning—even, in this case, against intense popular opposition to the practice of dissection.

## A BILL OF RIGHTS

What sometimes seems to latter-day Americans the most important accomplishment of the First Federal Congress—the federal Bill of Rights—had trouble just getting on Congress's agenda. To most congressmen of 1789, that proposal seemed far less pressing than a host of other issues that commanded their immediate attention. Even the measure's most vocal advocate, James Madison, became its champion more from political necessity than from profound conviction. Madison's observations of state conduct in the 1780s had convinced him that "parchment barriers" to power such as the state bills or declarations of rights were ineffectual; only institutional checks and balances, like those built in to the new federal Constitution, provided reliable protection for the people's liberty.

Thomas Jefferson, however, offered some powerful reasons for a bill of rights in private letters to Madison after the Philadelphia Convention had ended. Jefferson pointed out, for example, that a bill of rights could be enforced in the courts. Equally important, during the ratification controversy the Antifederalists had criticized the Constitution because it lacked a bill of rights and proposed literally hundreds of amendments for the new Congress to consider. Antifederal sentiment ran high in Virginia, and some Antifederalists, including Patrick Henry, blocked Madison's election to the Senate and threatened to prevent his election to the House of Representatives, too. Had he not promised to support constitutional amendments, Madison might well have sat at home through the first years of the new government in whose design and ratification he had played so important a role. It occurred to him, moreover, that the enactment of a few provisions protecting those basic liberties on which everyone agreed would undercut Antifederalist fears and perhaps prevent passage of the more destructive amendments they proposed, amendments that cut into substantive federal powers including the power to impose direct taxes.

As a result, in June 1789 Madison moved in the House of Representatives that a "declaration" be "prefixed to the constitution" as several states had done, and that it assert some familiar principles:

> That all power is originally vested in, and consequently derived from the people.
>
> That Government is instituted, and ought to be exercised for the benefit of the people; which consists in the enjoyment of life and liberty, with the right of acquiring and using property, and generally of pursuing and obtaining happiness and safety.
>
> That the people have an indubitable, unalienable, and indefeasible right to reform or change their government, whenever it be found adverse or inadequate to the purposes of its institution.

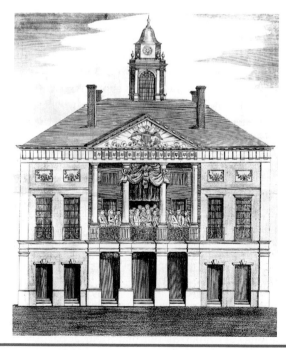

Federal Hall in New York City, where the First Federal Congress met in April 1789, sketch by Amos Doolittle.

Those lines were essentially a watered-down version of the Virginia Declaration of Rights that lacked any statement of men's original equality, their possession of inherent natural rights, or their right to abolish (as opposed to reform or change) their government. The changes were perhaps meant in part to offset the hostility of slaveholders, who by 1789 understood clearly that assertions of men's equality and inherent rights were at odds with the institution of slavery. Madison also proposed other changes in the body of the Constitution: he wanted to insert provisions protecting several basic civil rights among the restrictions on Congress in Article I, Section 9, and add to the next section a statement that "no state shall violate the equal rights of conscience, or the freedom of the press, or the trial by jury in criminal cases."

Madison's proposals were too much for his congressional colleagues. After all, hadn't the people demonstrated that they liked the Constitution as it was by electing so many Federalists to the Senate and House? Congressmen were also hesitant to fiddle with the Constitution's wording, which, after all, had been ratified by the people. They eliminated Madison's "prefix" and, in September 1789, sent to the states twelve proposed amendments to the Constitution, which were to be listed at its end like the afterthoughts they were. Of those twelve, the states ratified ten, which became part of the Constitution on December 15, 1791. That Bill of Rights was another bare-bones legal document, a lawyer's list of basic civil and judicial rights, one of which (the Ninth Amendment) declared that the rights enumerated did not "deny or disparage others retained by the people," and another (the Tenth) that reserved powers "not delegated to the United States by the Constitution, nor prohibited by it to the States, . . . to the States respectively, or to the people." The rejected amendments would have changed the wording of the Constitution's provision on representation and limited congressmen's ability to increase their pay. Had they passed, the set of amendments would not have looked very much like a bill of rights, and even without them the amendments bore little resemblance to the states' bills of rights. Indeed, in the early nineteenth century some members of the federal judiciary did not think the federal Constitution included a bill of rights!

Because neither the federal Constitution nor the first ten amendments (or Bill of Rights) included any statement about men's fundamental equality or possession of inherent rights, persons who found those old revolutionary ideas relevant to some cause in national politics turned to the Declaration of Independence. By 1789, that document was remembered mainly for its association with independence. Soon, however, the Declaration took on new life not as a revolutionary manifesto but as a statement of principles for the guidance of an established nation. As that happened, attention began to turn from the document's last paragraph, which declared independence, toward the second. It said: "We hold these truths to be self-evident; that all men are created equal; that they are endowed by their Creator with certain inalienable rights; that among these are life, liberty, and the pursuit of happiness; that to secure these rights, governments are instituted among men, deriving their just powers from the consent of the governed. . . ."

In its original form, that single, long sentence went on to say that "whenever any form of government becomes destructive of these ends" (the protection of rights), the people had a right "to alter or abolish it" and to substitute a new government "as to them shall seem more likely to effect their safety and happiness." It asserted, in short, the right of revolution, which the people were exercising in 1776. After being chopped off in the middle, however, the sentence became a statement of the government's fundamental obligation to secure the people's "inalienable rights," of which "life, liberty, and the pursuit of happiness" were only a few examples. In this form, the sentence operated like a bill of rights, proclaiming the government's obligation to honor and protect certain rights. Once it assumed that function, the Declaration of Independence seemed to become part of the nation's basic constitutional order.

More immediately, Congress's adoption of a Bill of Rights encouraged North Carolina (November 21, 1789) and Rhode Island (May 29, 1790) to ratify the Constitution and rejoin the Union. For the short run, that was benefit enough; and before the eighteenth century was over, Vermont (1791), Kentucky (1792), and Tennessee (1796) expanded the Union from thirteen states to sixteen. In the long run, the Bill of Rights, that half-hearted act of the First Federal Congress, would assume an importance beyond anything its unenthusiastic creators had imagined. But it took about a century and a half for its significance to be felt. In the meantime, the document's relative unimportance fully justified Madison's original low expectations.

## A SYSTEM OF FINANCE

Achieving financial integrity was among Congress's primary objectives, and one of the first tasks to which it turned in its opening session. With relatively little squabbling, Congress approved a tariff of 5 percent on all imported goods except those on a special list, which were subject to specific duties. It also approved a Tonnage Bill that levied charges on ships entering American ports according to their carrying capacities as measured in tons. The charges were less on American-built and -owned ships than on "all other ships." That was a welcome encouragement to American shippers, who suffered from the discriminating regulations of other nations but had previously watched ships from those countries sail freely into American ports.

Other acts of 1789 established ports of entry where federal customs officials, with the power of search and seizure, would set up shop, much as their unpopular British predecessors had done. The United States also assumed ownership and responsibility for the lighthouses, buoys, and beacons that the states had established to facilitate coastal navigation, which ruffled some feathers. All these acts made a powerful point: the new federal government was going to be a presence in people's lives, particularly people who lived along major waterways.

The government would also be fiscally responsible. The Federal Appropriations Act for 1789 consisted of a single paragraph authorizing the expenditure of $639,000 to cover the current cost of the federal government. The sum was based on reports from the treasury that listed all the recipients of federal moneys and the sums owed them, down to the penny.

Fiscal responsibility also required paying the country's revolutionary debts. Article VI of the Constitution specified that "All Debts contracted and Engagements entered into, before the Adoption of this Constitution, shall be as valid against the United States under this Constitution, as under the Confederation." But how exactly should the debt be retired? The problem was sufficiently vexing that on September 21, 1789, ten days after Hamilton became secretary of the treasury, the House of Representatives asked him to prepare a plan for supporting the public credit. The following January, Hamilton submitted his first report on the public credit, one of four epic reports he prepared for Congress. A second report focused on the creation of a national bank (December 1790), a third on the establishment of a mint (January 1791), and the fourth on American manufactures (December 1791). Together, they provided a comprehensive plan for a national financial system and the economic development of the United States.

Hamilton's approach to the debt issue was characteristically ambitious. He proposed not only that the United States pay in full the principal and accrued interest on the debt owed to foreign nations ($11,710,378), but that it pay at par (the original face value) the nation's domestic debt ($44,414,085 with arrears of interest) and, moreover, assume responsibility for pay-

Alexander Hamilton, in a portrait painted by the American artist John Trumbull in 1792, when Hamilton was secretary of the treasury.

ing off the remaining Revolutionary War debt of the states (estimated at about $25 million). Holders of debt certificates would turn them in and receive in return new, interest-paying federal government bonds for the principal and 4 percent interest for the period since the original certificate was issued. Hamilton anticipated meeting interest payments from indirect taxes, especially import duties, while deferring payment of the principal indefinitely. If public creditors needed cash, they could sell their bonds to other investors—and for a much better price than in the late 1780s, when the United States was essentially bankrupt. As a result of these changes, wealthy people would be more willing to lend money to the government in the future, which was a major purpose of "securing public credit."

Hamilton's proposal that the United States pay its debt to foreign nations raised no dispute. However, his proposal to pay the nation's domestic debt at par (face value) was controversial because most of the original holders of that debt—soldiers or suppliers of the Continental Army—had sold the certificates they had received in return for services or goods at substantially less than par value. Moreover, once word of Hamilton's proposal got out, speculators began buying up all the certificates of government indebtedness they could lay their hands on, expecting to make a handsome profit when the government paid for them at par. Madison, who found that offensive,

proposed that the government pay current holders of the debt "the highest price which has prevailed in the market" and distribute the difference between that price and the (higher) par value to the "original sufferers." The idea won sympathy but was soundly rejected because it undercut the goal of demonstrating that the government would faithfully support its creditors. Executing Madison's proposal was probably also beyond the capacity of the Treasury Department, which lacked the manpower and the records necessary to identify and locate the original owners of all notes of federal indebtedness. It didn't hurt that many members of Congress had themselves scrambled to buy shares of the federal debt and so stood to profit from government funding at par so long as the return went entirely to those who actually held debt certificates.

The assumption of state war debts was the most controversial of all the Hamilton proposals. States whose debts were small (Georgia, North Carolina, Maryland) or that had already paid off much of their debts and expected to extinguish them entirely in the near future (Virginia) resented the prospect of having to help retire the unpaid debts of other states, which in some cases (Massachusetts, New Jersey, New York, South Carolina) remained substantial. With passions high, Congress came to an impasse so severe that all legislative business nearly stopped. Positions tended to follow sectional lines, with most southern states opposing assumption and northern states favoring the measure. Southern rancor increased when northern congressmen proved willing to consider petitions against slavery and the slave trade submitted by Quakers in early 1790. After a searing debate, the House of Representatives declared that Congress not only lacked the power to ban the slave trade before 1808 but also had no authority whatsoever to emancipate or regulate the treatment of slaves within the states. In effect, that vote in the spring of 1790 put debate over the institution of southern slavery off Congress's agenda. Still, the strain was so intense that some observers predicted that the Union itself would split, then collapse in civil war.

Another compromise averted that dire fate and also settled an issue that had bedeviled Congress: where the new government would permanently reside. Under that agreement, which was worked out through a complex set of maneuvers by Hamilton, Jefferson, Madison, and Pennsylvania's Robert Morris, southerners (Madison in particular) agreed to accept the assumption of state debts in return for locating the nation's permanent capital on the shores of the Potomac River. Morris threw in his support in return for a promise that the temporary capital would be moved from New York to

Philadelphia—where, he hoped, it would somehow remain after 1800, when the new federal capital was supposed to be occupied. The votes in Congress were nonetheless close, turning on the changed position of a few critical senators and congressmen. But the measures passed, one after another. And so in December 1790, the First Federal Congress met in Philadelphia, and planning for the new capital replaced fears of secession.

Hamilton's proposal for a national bank passed Congress with large majorities despite Madison's insistence that Congress had no constitutional right to charter a bank or, for that matter, to create any corporation. That was an important turnabout for Madison, who as recently as 1789, during discussions of the president's power to dismiss cabinet members, had accepted the constitutional legitimacy of implied powers. His objection bothered Washington, who consulted his secretary of state and his attorney general, Jefferson and Randolph. Both, like Madison, believed a national bank was unconstitutional because the Constitution did not explicitly give Congress the power to charter a bank. Then Washington turned to Hamilton, who had the advantage of seeing Jefferson's and Randolph's opinions before composing his own. Hamilton asserted that the bank *was* constitutional under the provision

The Bank of the United States, which opened for business in Philadelphia during 1791, in an engraving by William Birch & Son, 1799. Hamilton's proposal for a national bank had provoked strong opposition since the Constitution did not explicitly give Congress power to establish a bank.

authorizing Congress to make laws "necessary and proper" for executing its other powers, such as the collection of taxes and regulation of trade. Moreover, no provision precluded Congress from chartering banks. Although it seems that Washington was not fully persuaded, he sided with Hamilton because the issue came within Hamilton's sphere of responsibility. The president signed the Bank Bill and so averted a confrontation with Congress that would surely have followed had he—for the first time—exercised his veto power.

In April 1792, Congress adopted the proposals in Hamilton's report on the mint, a technical document concerned with the weight and value of American coinage, with little opposition. His report on manufactures fared less well. Hamilton provided an economically sophisticated case for the development of a mixed economy, with vital manufacturing and commercial sectors. Such an economy, he argued, would increase American prosperity and make the United States less dependent on foreign nations for critical products. The report did not disparage agriculture, which, the report said, had "intrinsically a strong claim to pre-eminence over every other kind of industry" and would itself benefit from greater economic diversity. Traditional barriers to the development of manufacturing, Hamilton argued, could be overcome by mobilizing machines, immigrants, women, and children to offset the high cost of adult male labor, and using banks, foreign investment, and a funded debt as sources of capital.

References to banks and the funded debt pointed up the interconnectedness of Hamilton's reports, each of which supported his ambitious vision for the American future. The last report also surveyed the current state of American manufactures and listed policies that would encourage their further development. Some of those policies, particularly federal patents, were already in place. However, Congress was not ready to adopt protective duties and bounties. By discouraging imports, high tariffs would lower the revenue from customs fees, which provided a major part of the federal government's income. Spokesmen for agricultural interests also feared that protective tariffs would spur retaliatory measures abroad and so reduce foreign purchases of American agricultural products. As a result, the federal government failed to take an activist role in encouraging manufacturing, a role that states such as Massachusetts had already enthusiastically assumed (see Chapter 6). The report remains therefore a repository of information on the state of American manufactures at the time and a reflection of Hamilton's thought rather than the beginning of a major change in federal policy.

## THE PROBLEM WITH DREAMS:
## THE PASSAIC AND THE POTOMAC

Hamilton found a more direct way to realize his dreams of development through the Society for Establishing Useful Manufactures (SUM), which set out to establish a large manufacturing complex along the Passaic River at the present site of Paterson, New Jersey. The SUM won a charter from the New Jersey legislature in the fall of 1791, just before Hamilton issued his report on manufactures. Hamilton was neither an officer nor a shareholder in the society, although he was among its most enthusiastic supporters.

The scheme for the complex was grand: the SUM purchased 700 acres on which it planned to found a town with lodgings for employees. It also began to acquire machinery to manufacture a vast variety of goods, including several types of cloth, paper, clothing, pottery, and metal wire. The planned complex would even include "a brewery for the supply of the manufacturers." The charter authorized the company to issue $500,000 in stock, which could later be expanded to $1 million. The first stock issue of $100,000 sold out within days.

But beginning in 1792, things started to go wrong. Investors began selling shares for profits once their price started to rise, preferring quick gain to long-term growth. Even some of the original directors were so anxious for a quick buck that they not only sold their own shares but also embezzled company funds. The machinery the company purchased was poorly designed and unreliable; and the laborers recruited from abroad—because too few Americans with appropriate skills were available—turned out to be, according to some reports, lazy, ignorant louts. Most important, an enterprise on the scale Hamilton and his associates hoped to create was far beyond the management skills of Americans at that time, so the SUM lacked effective, capable leaders who could mold the operation into an effective means for generating profits. Some manufacturing processes nonetheless continued until 1796, when the di-

rectors decided to close them down to prevent further losses. The SUM then took on another life as a real estate operation. At least there, in the management and sale of land, Americans of the 1790s were something more than rank amateurs.

The other great dream of the time, a dazzling new American capital on the shores of the Potomac, fared much the same. Its location was chosen to satisfy Virginians, for whom it was convenient—as it was not for many others—and who believed the Potomac was destined to become a major water route to the West. The idea of erecting the city of Washington in the District of Columbia on boglands carved from Maryland and Virginia was, however, impractical in the extreme, and plans for its execution compounded the problem.

Jefferson envisioned an impressive federal capital. His dream was taken to still greater lengths by a French engineer, Major Pierre-Charles L'Enfant, who in August 1791 presented a plan for the capital every bit as ambitious as the proposals for the SUM. L'Enfant envisioned 160-foot-wide "transverse avenues" that would cut across a more simple grid of streets,

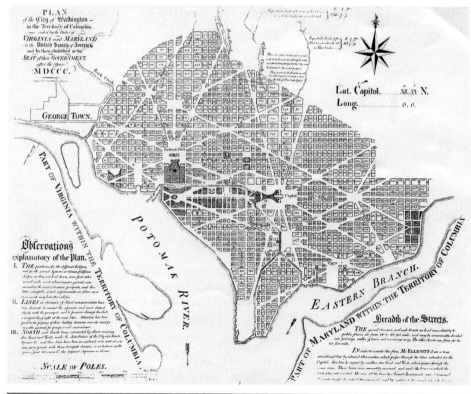

A plan of Washington, D.C., in 1800 that shows the grid pattern of streets with cross-hatched "transverse avenues" proposed by Major Pierre-Charles L'Enfant.

30-foot-wide walkways, great public squares, and massive public buildings connected by long vistas across carefully cultivated parklands. His plan recalled Versailles, the French town where he had lived as a child and which King Louis XIV once hoped to make the capital of France. Jefferson and Washington liked L'Enfant's plans, but they were wildly inappropriate for the capital of a republic that was to be built on an almost uninhabited stretch of land. Moreover, because New York's Hudson River provided a better link with the West than the Potomac, the city of Washington was unlikely to develop a commercial life capable of attracting and sustaining a substantial population.

How, then, would the development of the capital be financed? Virginia and Maryland together contributed $192,000, hardly more than a beginning. The rest, Jefferson insisted, had to come from land sales in the federal district itself; President Washington could not ask for congressional appropriations, or the whole location issue might be reopened. But land auctions failed to draw buyers, and in 1796—when the SUM ended manufacturing operations—the president finally had to ask Congress for authority to borrow $500,000. Congress promised to "make good the deficiency" if the sale of lands pledged as collateral proved insufficient to repay the loan, which they almost certainly would. The president's language so understated the problems that it did little to sustain the honor of "honest George." In the meantime, financial troubles contributed to conflicts that, in turn, led to L'Enfant's dismissal in early 1792, less than a year after he began working on the new capital. His successors suffered similar fates.

There was a real question, in fact, whether the Americans were capable of executing so ambitious a scheme as L'Enfant had proposed. Take the problem of designing the Capitol, for which competitors were asked to submit designs. The prize went to a Dr. William Thornton, who had no expertise in architecture and whose plan, based on classical models, turned out to include major technical deficiencies when, finally, a person who knew something about architecture examined it. Too bad we didn't know that earlier, Washington commented; but some plan, any plan, had to be adopted and, "good or bad, it must be entered upon." The Capitol's cornerstone was laid before the building plans were complete; several supervising architects in succession lost their jobs; and it took seventy-one years before the Capitol was completed. By then, the country could boast architects and engineers of its own, as well as manufacturing enterprises that fulfilled visions not so different from that of a great industrial complex on the banks of the

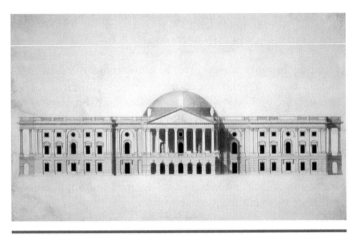

A watercolor of the U.S. Capitol painted in the mid-1790s by William Thornton, who won the prize for its design. What Thornton painted was a dream: it took seventy-one years for the Capitol to be built.

Passaic. Rome wasn't built in a day, nor was the United States, and all the wishes of its most ardent supporters could not make up for the broad-based managerial and technological inadequacies that held back development on several fronts.

The failure of the SUM and the pathetic beginnings of the national capital reflected a larger truth. The United States began as a nation of amateurs; that was a source of its energy and remains part of the early Republic's charm. Sometimes amateurs are capable of astounding innovations. The eighteenth century was kind to men like Benjamin Franklin, who turned his attention from one field of interest to another, making significant contributions in several; and the early nineteenth would also offer opportunities aplenty to ingenious amateurs. But already in the 1790s, the realization of many grander ambitions required specialized skills. Until Americans could acquire them, the fulfillment of those dreams was necessarily postponed into the future.

## Prosperity

The bleak scenes on the banks of the Passaic and Potomac were not repeated everywhere. Consider, for example, the story of Boston, a town that had once been the leading port of British North America but lost considerable ground through much of the eighteenth century. First the heavy death toll among men who helped fight Britain's wars with France checked the town's population growth, then it suffered severely from Britain's exclusion in 1783 of American ships from markets in the British West Indies. Boston's merchants tried desperately to open new trade routes, and, although trade with Portugal increased, initiatives in the Mediterranean came to a halt once the Barbary pirates of North Africa turned loose on American ships. But on August 9, 1790, almost three years after leaving Boston, the *Columbia* under Captain Robert Gray became the first American ship to circumnavigate the globe, bringing the prospect of a profitable trade among the Pacific Northwest, China, and the United States. The tariffs and other legislation enacted by the First Federal Congress also gave Bostonians hope since they allowed American ships distinct advantages in both transoceanic and coastal trade. Even so, progress was slow: only in 1792 did Boston's per capita exports exceed those of the mid-1770s.

Then, suddenly, the port sprang to life. Between 1790 and 1800, Boston's population grew from just over 18,000 to almost 25,000—an increase of about 40 percent—and most of the increase came after 1793. In 1790, the town looked much as it had forty years earlier, but now it underwent a major physical transformation. Banks and insurance companies started to cluster along State Street, and striking new buildings appeared, some designed by Charles Bulfinch, a native Bostonian and 1781 Harvard graduate. Bulfinch studied architecture in France and England, then returned home in 1787, just in time to become an investor in the *Columbia*'s voyage. He built an elegant string of brick townhouses—the Tontine Crescent—along a curved street at Franklin Place, and massive Georgian houses with bowed fronts on Boston's Beacon Hill. The Boston State House, built in 1795 with a distinctive gilded dome, was perhaps the most eloquent early sign of Boston's new prosperity. Soon the town would literally outgrow its colonial boundaries, filling in coves and straightening out the harbor front, beginning a process of expansion that allowed a seventeenth-century peninsula to become home to a modern city.

In most Atlantic ports, the story was much the same. In fact, other towns and cities along the East Coast outstripped Boston's population growth both in percentage gain and in absolute numerical growth: Baltimore almost doubled in size between 1790 and 1800, to a population of 26,000, and Philadelphia, still the largest American city, grew by over 50 percent to 69,500—and that despite a devastating outbreak of yellow fever in 1793 that claimed thousands of lives. New

York's expansion was even more impressive. From 1790, when it held just over 33,000 people, New York added 27,000 more within a decade, reaching a population of 60,500 by 1800, and it was still growing. With access via the Hudson River to a rich backcountry as well as a fine ocean harbor, New York saw its imports and exports exceed those of Philadelphia in 1797, although it took a bit longer for New York to become the nation's most populous city. In each case, as in Boston, population growth accompanied physical expansion, new construction, and other signs of prosperity. That sudden, explosive growth began a process of urbanization that would continue in the next centuries.

What explained these transformations? Not a major departure from old activities, but a revival of what merchants in Boston and other ports had long been good at: commerce and trade. "The harbor of Boston is . . . crowded with vessels," one observer reported in late 1794. "Eighty-four sail have been counted lying at two of the wharves only," and "it is reckoned that not less than four hundred and fifty sail of ships, brigs, schooners, sloops and small craft are now in this port." That was quite a change from ten years earlier, when American trade had languished under the force of British restrictions. The reason for the difference was simple: in 1793, the major powers of Europe were at war over events stemming from the French Revolution. That war opened a major opportunity for the carriers of neutral nations such as the United States, one that American shippers—now with the support of a viable national government—were prepared to exploit as much as possible.

## EXPORTS AND THE "CARRYING TRADE"

The United States stood to profit from Europe's war in two ways. Belligerents needed products the Americans could supply, including wheat and other foodstuffs. They also needed the services of neutral shippers to carry goods from their colonies and other parts of the world since ships flying the flags of warring nations faced attack by their enemies. France saw the situation clearly and in February 1793 formally opened its colonial empire to American ships. Spain did not follow suit until 1797, and, although Britain continued to exclude American ships from her West Indian colonies, that restriction often went unenforced as the war in Europe strained the capacities of the Royal Navy. As an early nineteenth-century American observer explained, the European war "created a demand for our exports, and invited our shipping for the carrying trade of a very considerable portion of Europe; we not only carried the colonial productions to the several parent states, but we also became the purchasers of them in the French, Spanish and Dutch colonies." Such goods—sugar, for example, or coffee and cocoa—were brought into the United States, then reexported to Europe, where "the demand . . . for foreign merchandise . . . secured to all these cargoes a ready sale, with a great profit." On the return voyage, ships carried goods of European origin to the United States, from which many were again reexported to markets in the Caribbean or other parts of the Americas.

The percentage growth of reexports during the period was truly spectacular. They went from $300 million in 1790 to $1.7 million three years later and in 1801 reached $46.6 million, which was only slightly less than the value of domestic exports, although they, too, were growing rapidly. Between 1793 and 1801, the sum total of American exports (including both domestic products sold abroad and reexports) went up about three and a half times, from $26.1 million to $94.1 million. American consumption of imported goods—often finished manufactured products—more than doubled in those years, from $30.8 million in 1793 to $66.7 million in 1801, but, unlike during the 1780s, the sale of American goods and services more than offset their cost. The result was an explosive increase in wealth, which lay behind the fine homes and public buildings that appeared in one port city after another.

In the 1790s, trade offered enticements enough for profit. If, however, a European peace undercut the opportunities filling merchants' pockets through international commerce, they might well invest their new wealth in less traditional activities such as industrial manufacturing.

### RIPPLE EFFECTS

The beneficiaries of the dramatic expansion in trade were not confined to merchants or to port cities. As more and more vessels put to sea, the demand for seamen rose, and there is evidence of a resulting rise in wages. For instance, ordinary Boston seamen who signed on for the *Columbia*'s first voyage to China in 1787 were paid $5 a month, and skilled seamen $7 a month. By 1799, some merchants were paying boys $8–$10, ordinary seamen $14–$17, and skilled seamen $18 a month. (For purposes of comparison, a contemporary army private received $3 a month.)

The demand for ships also rose. Before the Revolution, Americans—particularly in New England—had manufactured a substantial volume of ships, but shipbuilding foundered in the 1780s, when the British government and British insurance rates discouraged the purchase and use of American-made vessels. Once commerce revived, however, so did shipbuilding, since now the purchasers were often Americans. Ships were built on the Delaware River near Philadelphia and at towns along the Atlantic coast both south and north of Boston. Shipbuilding facilities in Maine and New Hampshire, which contained huge lumber reserves and an abundance of sawmills, also hummed with activity, bringing increased prosperity and, again, population growth to that for-

Philadelphia's Delaware River front in the 1790s, full of ships at dock, with their masts down; painted by Thomas Birch.

merly remote region. Ships needed not just wood but ropes and sails, spurring increased business and income among suppliers and their employees, some of whom were farmers looking for work in the agricultural off-season.

Similarly, the expansion of seaborne trade promoted the development of ancillary services such as docks and warehouses, insurance companies and banks. The growing urban populations, drawn to ports by the opportunities they offered, also had to be fed, which required moving foodstuffs from the countryside into towns and cities. That explains in part the 1790s enthusiasm for turnpikes, which were characteristically built on a wagon-wheel pattern, like spokes protruding from a hub out into the hinterland, along which crops traveled into urban centers. River improvements, bridges, early canals, and similar projects also aided transportation. Those improvements accelerated the spread of a market economy (that is, of the area within which people buy and sell with each other frequently) whose development was already under way during the 1780s. And since a market economy serves to guide resources "to their most productive uses," its spread encouraged further economic development.

### THE NEW AMERICAN PRACTICAL NAVIGATOR

Navigation itself was open to improvement in this age of sailing ships, when skill and chance—or the blessing of God—contributed as much as science to a voyage's success. Knowing a ship's location was a big help, especially when it sailed not just on familiar jaunts along the coast or to the West Indies, but around the world.

By the 1790s, the problem of fixing location by determining longitude had been solved—by John Harrison, a self-taught English clockmaker who constructed a series of innovative "sea clocks," or chronometers, that could keep accurate time despite variations in conditions at sea. A navigator could determine local time at sea by setting his ship's clock to twelve when the sun reached its midday height; then, with another accurate clock that told him the time at his point of departure, he could compare the two. Since the earth takes twenty-four hours to turn 360 degrees, each hour of difference amounted to 15 degrees of longitude. (What that meant in terms of distance traveled varied with latitude: a degree of longitude translates to sixty-eight miles at the equator, but almost nothing at the North or South Pole. However, once a mariner knew both his latitude and longitude, he could calculate the distance he'd come.)

This marine chronometer was created in 1759 by John Harrison (1693–1776), who invented the device to help determine longitude at sea.

There was, however, a problem with Harrison's invention: chronometers were extremely expensive. As a result, in the 1790s few American vessels carried them. The available chronometers of the day were also frail and, unlike Harrison's amazing creations, so unreliable that even in later times, when their use became more common, ships sometimes carried three chronometers to avoid misreadings. But there was an alternative method of calculating longitude that had been favored by Harrison's critics: for a relatively modest price, navigators could acquire a reflecting quadrant, an invention of 1731 that made use of paired mirrors to enable navigators to measure the angular distance between the moon and some visible fixed star, even on a bobbing ship. They could then compare the results with tables in Greenwich time (the time at the Royal Observatory in Greenwich, England) to determine local time and, using that figure, calculate their location. The method became fairly common after the publication of lunar tables in the *Nautical Almanac* (1767). Reading "lunars" required care, since an error of even one minute (that is, one-sixtieth of a degree) would cause a thirty-mile miscalculation of location. To make matters worse, the published tables included many errors.

A solution to that problem came from Salem, Massachusetts, in 1790 the sixth largest town in the United States. Nathaniel Bowditch was born there in 1773 to the family of a local sailor and barrel maker who had trouble supporting his family. Although his unusual talent for mathematics appeared early, Bowditch's formal education ended at age ten, when he went to work with his father and later as a ship chandler, or supplier. Meanwhile, he educated himself, making good use of a local Philosophical Library that included not just the *Transactions of the Royal Society of London* and the works of such towering British scientists as Robert Boyle and Isaac Newton, but scientific and mathematical treatises in German and French. Anxious to unlock their secrets, young Bowditch learned the languages necessary to read those works of European science.

Then, in 1795, he went to sea on the first of five voyages to China and the East Indies, during the course of which he rose from clerk to captain. On dull days, Bowditch studied mathematics. He also checked the available charts and tables of navigation against his own observations and, later, against the manuscript records of the East India Marine Society at the East India Museum in Salem, which included logs kept by its members. He found some 8,000 errors in the standard tables, many

Nathaniel Bowditch, as painted by Charles Osgood in 1835, when Bowditch had become a prosperous businessman.

of which could lead to shipwrecks. Fortunately, Bowditch caught the attention of a publisher in another Massachusetts coastal town, Newburyport. Together, they published an improved version of an English text, John Hamilton Moore's *The New Practical Navigator,* in 1799, informing readers only that the changes had been made by "a skillful mathematician and navigator." A second edition appeared in 1800.

In 1802, the first edition of Bowditch's own book, *The New American Practical Navigator,* appeared simultaneously in England and the United States. It included twenty-nine tables as well as hundreds of pages of text that explained the uses of geometry and trigonometry, various mathematical calculations critical to navigation, as well as navigational tools such as the compass, quadrant, and sextant. It also included a glossary of terms related to the sea and information on business devices such as bills of exchange and marine insurance. The book was, in short, a complete handbook of navigation, and it became the seaman's bible as it went through one edition after another.

*The New American Practical Navigator* was not a scientific achievement on the order of Benjamin Franklin's work with electricity, but Bowditch resembled Franklin in being self-educated and in his commitment to using science for practical purposes. His book saved ships and cargoes as well as lives, and so made commerce more profitable. Bowditch's approach also fed the rage for self-education that followed the Revolution and made American crews, who were known to spend their downtime studying Bowditch, more technically sophisticated navigators. Bowditch himself demonstrated the utility of scientifically informed navigation when, on the last voyage of his seafaring career, he guided the 260-ton ship *Putnam* safely into port through a dense snowstorm. He glimpsed one landmark to confirm his position but otherwise depended entirely on "scientific navigation."

Then, at just over thirty years of age, Bowditch took up another career—as president of the Essex Fire and Marine Insurance Company, one of the new corporations chartered in postrevolutionary Massachusetts. During his twenty years in that office, while he continued his studies of mathematics and astronomy, the firm paid average annual dividends of 10 or 12 percent. Nathaniel Bowditch was a man of his time.

## COTTON

In 1790, the United States included some 3.9 million people, including 700,000 slaves. About 200,000 Americans lived in the trans-Appalachian West, and their numbers almost doubled by 1800. The westerners knew that their future depended on their ability to get goods to market, which is why they tended to settle near rivers. The great bulk of the population, however, remained east of the mountains, with roughly half in the North and half in the plantation South.

Except for Baltimore, which assumed importance with the growth of trade in grains, southern cities did not share in the urban growth spurred by trade. Charleston, for example, grew at a much slower rate than ports to its north (indeed, at a rate lower than that of overall American population growth). Charleston did not reap substantial benefits from the reexport trade because it lacked a substantial merchant community. Merchants from elsewhere carried most of South Carolina's products to market, and its exports were not thriving. Rice once had made South Carolinians rich, but rice exports actually declined between the 1770s and 1790s. States in the Chesapeake, whose tobacco—which had accounted for as much as a third of all exports from the British North American colonies—could no longer be shipped to Britain, faced a similar dilemma, which many planters solved by growing wheat instead. But wheat did not grow well in the warmer regions of the South. What, then, could they produce?

Cotton was the answer. It could be successfully grown anywhere south of the 37th degree north latitude (which crosses Virginia from a point just north of Norfolk), and the ecology of the region farther south was ideally suited for its cultivation. That region had the 200–210 frostless days and 20–25 inches of annual rainfall that cotton requires. In the South, moreover, rain tended to fall more in the spring and midsummer than later in the season, an ideal situation that could be replicated in few other places before the use of artificial irrigation. The sea islands off the coast of Georgia and South Carolina already produced a form of long-staple cotton (cotton with a long fiber), but another variety, with a short staple, could be grown inland, even in upland regions. Moreover, although cotton could be grown on small family farms, it could also be cultivated profitably in large units, allowing southern plantation owners to use the slave labor force that accounted for a substantial part of their wealth.

To whom would the cotton be sold? To American cotton manufacturers? Applications for incorporation from companies such as the Beverly Cotton Manufactory in Massachusetts stressed that they would use American raw materials, but the textile industry had barely begun in the United States during the 1790s, and its beginning was full of failures. For example, a "very Compleat" carding and spinning mill built in 1795 on the Brandywine River north of Wilmington, Delaware, burned to the ground in 1797—a victim, some charged, of British arson.

The one apparent success, a factory Samuel Slater constructed for the firm of Almy and Brown in Pawtucket, Rhode Island, in 1793—a signal year for the American economy—was essentially a spinning mill with, at first, only 100 spindles. A labor force of women and children produced cotton thread that Almy and Brown sold to weavers and knitters who worked elsewhere. In the period 1793–1803, the operation managed to make a profit of $18,000. That, like the first voyage of the

The first cotton mill in America, established by Samuel Slater (1768–1835) at Pawtucket, Rhode Island, on the Blackstone River.

*Columbia* (which actually made no profit at all), was promising. Two-thirds of the mill's $100,000 in expenditures had gone for raw cotton, but such a sum was hardly enough to encourage an expansion of southern production. Moreover, the firm preferred to buy West Indian long-staple cotton because it was cleaner than the American product. In the southern states, Moses Brown wrote in 1791, "the present production in the mixed manner in which it is Brought to Market does not answer good purpose," so he bought imported cotton despite "the Discouragement of the Impost." By the late 1790s, Almy and Brown had begun using cotton from Georgia, but the cost of raw cotton remained high. Clearly it would take time, an advance in quality, and perhaps also a reduction in cotton prices before American production would absorb a substantial volume of domestic raw cotton.

But cotton, recently a luxury product imported from India or Egypt, had a future. Cotton cloth was more comfortable than wool in warm weather and could be more easily laundered; indeed, the appearance of cotton clothing signaled a revolution in personal hygiene and comfort. By 1801, Almy and Brown were receiving orders for their cotton thread faster than the firm could fill them. And by then, the cotton industry was already well established in Britain. Since theirs was not a climate in which cotton could be grown, the British had to import the raw material they processed. In 1780, Britain imported less than 7 million pounds of cotton, but then, owing to a series of technological innovations (which the Americans were trying to imitate), both production and imports rose meteorically. Britain imported 22 million pounds of cotton in 1787; fifty years later, the United Kingdom (including both Great Britain and Ireland) would import 407 million pounds. That market was a star worth catching.

But there was one problem: the long-staple cotton that could only be grown in limited areas along the southeastern coast of the United States was much easier to clean than the short-staple cotton of the inland South. Bolls of long-staple cotton could simply be passed through two grooved rollers turned by a crank, as on old-fashioned mechanical clothes wringers. The smooth black seeds caught in the rollers' grooves and fell out. But the short-staple, green-seeded cotton that could be grown over most areas of the South had fuzzy fibers that clung tenaciously to the seeds. If short-staple cotton was put through rollers, the seeds held tight and came out the other side or, worse, broke into pieces that scattered through the fiber. Once successfully cleaned, however, upland cotton was a high-quality product, strong and smooth.

Some technical device was needed to solve the problem of separating seeds from fibers. Tradition ascribes the invention of that device to Eli Whitney, a New Englander who happened to be in Georgia when the need for a new cotton "gin" (short for "engine") was the stuff of common conversation. Whitney, who was born in 1765, taught school for a time, then attended Yale College. After graduating in 1792, he went South, expecting to take a job as tutor to the children of a family in South Carolina. His ship sailed from New York to Georgia, where he visited Mulberry Grove, the home of General Nathanael Greene's widow, near Savannah. There, he later wrote his father, when "involuntarily . . . thinking on the subject," he came up with "a plan of a Machine." Then, "in about ten days," he said, "I made a little model, for which I was offered, if I would give up the right and title to it, a Hun-

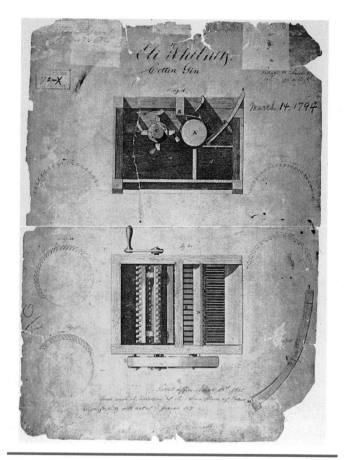

The drawing of a cotton gin that Eli Whitney included in his original application for a federal patent on March 14, 1794.

dred Guineas." So rather than continuing on to South Carolina, he remained in Georgia, "perfecting the Machine." By April 1793, he had built a functioning "Cotton Gin" for which he secured a patent in 1794.

Whitney's machine used wire teeth arranged on a cylinder within a box-like container to tear cotton fiber from the seeds. The wire teeth picked up raw cotton and pulled it through slots on an iron bar that were too narrow for the seeds to pass through. As the seeds dropped into a box, brushes on smaller cylinders, which moved in the direction opposite that of the major cylinder, pulled the fiber off the teeth. This was not a high-tech device that required mathematical or scientific sophistication; it was a relatively simple machine operated by belts that were turned by a crank, such as any reasonably skilled mechanic with access to shop tools and common building materials could construct. And it was easy to operate. One man could turn the crank of the prototype machine, Whitney explained to his father, and clean ten times as much cotton—and clean it much better—than could be done by any earlier process.

But Whitney's wasn't the only "cotton gin," or necessarily the best. In the time he was constructing his patent model, several other men devised machines for cleaning short-stable cotton, mostly improved versions of the old roller model that had some advantages over Whitney's "gin." Whitney's device, users complained, not only broke the cotton's fibers but left a large number of small knots in the ginned cotton that were almost impossible to remove. Roller gins did not have that problem, so they rose in popularity. Meanwhile, some southern mechanics improved Whitney's design by substituting a series of circular saws separated by "spacers" for Whitney's cylinder with metal teeth. Whitney's business partner filed several suits for patent infringement, with mixed results.

In any case, the use of cotton gins revolutionized southern agriculture in a remarkably short period. The United States exported only 488,000 pounds of cotton in 1793; in 1794, the amount more than tripled, to 1.6 million pounds, and by 1801 reached almost 21 million pounds. Within a generation, the American South became the world's predominant producer of raw cotton.

In later years, southerners might have asked whether cotton was a blessing or a curse. It shackled the region to slave labor, and it changed the relationships among white southerners in ways that would have unforeseen consequences. Since cotton soon far outdistanced the production of grains, rice, and sugar, it also transformed the South from a producer of many raw materials to a region that grew essentially one crop for export.

However, the dangerous economic consequences of that change became apparent only in the future. For the moment, faced with lagging markets and a workforce of black slaves who, it seemed, could neither be freed without unacceptable social consequences nor profitably employed, prominent white southerners harbored few misgivings about rushing into a cotton economy. Cotton for them was a great and welcome blessing.

## A New Party System?

In retrospect, Congress was divided from its opening days. The disputes over titles and in general between men who thought certain British practices should be continued and those who scoffed at the idea, seem to mark the first appearance of two political groups that became, over the course of the 1790s, reasonably settled and even organized. Whatever those differences represented, the groups (or parties) did not simply continue previous divisions over ratification of the Constitution. Most members of the First Federal Congress had been Federalists in 1787 and 1788, and the two most active organizers of the ratification movement, Hamilton and Madison, became leaders of opposing groups in the politics of the later 1790s. The emergent divisions were over new issues, new situations, new antagonisms.

The parties of the 1790s were not, however, the same as those of forty or fifty years later. By then, politics had become a great national game between two "teams," each with a devoted electoral following that it carried to the polls year after year, sometimes winning, sometimes losing, and never suffering a sense that victory or defeat had an effect more lasting than the distance between one election and the next. Such a political system lay in an inconceivable future. The ethics of the 1790s demanded that patriotic men devote themselves to the public good, upon which every rational, informed person not "corrupted" by a desire to serve his immediate self-interest would agree. To solicit votes was not a respectable practice: voters were supposed to support candidates because of their qualifications, not because the voters' had been courted. And to organize a following with the intention of seizing power from a standing government, even through the ballot box, was regarded as a form of sedition.

So long as these convictions held, there could be no simple formation of a party system. Each stage in the development of political divisions during the 1790s brought denials that any such thing was happening. The parties that did emerge, moreover, could not serve the beneficial function that two-party systems usually perform—regularizing and moderating opposition as contenders move toward the center in a struggle to win the middle ground. The parties of the 1790s, in fact, were more like those of the 1770s than those of later times. The "Republicans," on the one hand, modeled themselves on the revolutionary movement and resisted government policies that, in their opinion, echoed those Great Britain had adopted between 1765 and 1776; the "Federalists," on the other hand, struggled to uphold the government born of the Revolution against internal subversion. Both saw themselves as fighting to save the Republic; each questioned the other's motives and denied its legitimacy. The conflict between those parties often seemed as real a threat to the future of the United States as the threat Americans had posed to British rule a generation earlier.

## BEGINNINGS

The record of congressional voting tells the story: divisions in the First Federal Congress were irregular, with alliances shifting from issue to issue. Hamilton and Jefferson both served as department heads in Washington's administration and remained on good terms for several years. Madison, meanwhile, supported the administration from his place in the House. But gradually Jefferson—and Madison—developed deep suspicions of Hamilton and all he stood for. Meanwhile, voting patterns in Congress showed two groups, later called Federalists and Republicans, taking different stands more consistently. The two sides also began trying to increase their strength by intervening in state elections and by appealing to the public through the press. John Fenno's *Gazette of the United States* defended the Federalist, pro-administration position; then, in October 1791, those who opposed the direction taken by the Washington administration established a paper that presented their position—the *National Gazette*, edited by the poet Philip Freneau, an admirer of Jefferson.

Those who shared Jefferson's and Freneau's views called themselves Republicans because they were defending the Republic against men who, they claimed, were trying to subvert the American Revolution. The local groups that formed to support Republican views and candidates for office, known as "democratic" or "republican" clubs or societies, modeled themselves on the Sons of Liberty, who had resisted British policies before independence. From the vantage point of people who remembered well the provocations that had led to independence, the Washington administration gave persistent cause for worry.

Consider its use of military power. In May 1792, Congress passed a Militia Act that authorized the states to organize men between the ages of eighteen and twenty-four into militia units. The troops were later used against farmers in western Pennsylvania who opposed an excise tax on whiskey passed by Congress in 1791 to supplement federal revenues from tariffs. Excise taxes—taxes levied on the manufacture, purchase, or possession of certain consumer goods—were never popular in either England or America; and this particular excise tax posed a particular hardship on farmers west of the Appalachians, who transported and sold their grain to eastern customers in the more portable form of whiskey. Rather than pay the tax and cut into their already meager profits, the

A late eighteenth-century painting, by an unknown artist, depicting General George Washington setting out to repress the Whiskey Rebellion.

farmers resisted, first peacefully, then with violence—for example, by tarring and feathering tax collectors, which itself recalled revolutionary opposition to Britain. In September 1794, Washington finally ordered the repression of the so-called Whiskey Rebellion. With Hamilton at his side, he personally led 15,000 militiamen into western Pennsylvania. Resistance had crumbled by the time the troops arrived, and Washington pardoned the two main insurgents after they were convicted of treason.

For people who remembered old adages against standing armies, it was disquieting to see the United States sending troops against its own people. Just as resistance to the whiskey tax recalled opposition to the Stamp Act (another excise tax), Washington's use of troops recalled British efforts to suppress civilian opposition in Boston before the Boston Massacre and again beginning in 1774.

Political divisions first emerged over domestic issues but deepened during a series of crises over foreign policy that reopened the nagging issue of America's relationship with Great Britain. Domestic and foreign policy were, however, never entirely separate since decisions in one area frequently carried implications for the other.

## FOREIGN AFFAIRS UNDER WASHINGTON

Hamilton saw much to admire in Britain. He modeled his financial policies in part on those of William Pitt the younger, a great British minister who took office in 1783. The success of Hamilton's financial program, moreover, depended on smooth relations with Britain: duties on imports provided a major source of federal revenue, and most American imports came from Britain. Hamilton by no means advocated returning the Americans to British rule; he had, after all, fought for independence as an officer of the Continental army. Nor did he seek to establish a monarchy in the United States. But he thought an amicable relationship with the onetime mother country would best serve American interests.

Jefferson remained deeply hostile to Britain, and his Anglophobia fed his growing antagonism toward Hamilton. The treasury secretary's method of finance, with a bank and large funded debt, seemed—as in part it was—based on a British model, one that Jefferson considered dangerous because it allowed abundant opportunities for corruption. Nor did Jefferson regard with pleasure an American future with large industrial manufacturing complexes like that planned for Paterson, New Jersey. Americans' independence and "virtue" depended for Jefferson on the fact that so many of them were farmers who worked for themselves, not for others. "Dependance," he wrote in *Notes on the State of Virginia,* "begets subservience and venality, suffocates the germ of virtue, and prepares fit tools for the designs of ambition." Better, he thought, to let our workshops remain in Europe than to risk losing those essential strengths.

Jefferson was also deeply loyal to France, the Americans' old ally in the War for Independence. While serving as minister to France during the 1780s, he had witnessed the beginnings of the French Revolution—which in his opinion only tightened the bond between France and America, whose Revolution, he thought, had inspired the French. Most Americans shared his enthusiasm for the French Revolution until it took a turn unlike anything the American Revolution brought, with escalating popular violence, the execution of King Louis XVI (1793) and the establishment not of regular constitutional government but the arbitrary violence of Maximilien Robespierre and the Terror. Events in France horrified Hamilton, who argued that the Franco-American Treaty of 1778 was with the French king and so ceased once he died. Jefferson justified the violence and declared that the treaty was with the French nation, and so still binding.

In fact, there were limits to even the Jeffersonians' enthusiasm for revolution. They confronted those limits in Saint-Domingue, a wealthy French colony in the Caribbean where in 1791 a slave uprising started a thirteen-year struggle that culminated in 1804 with the creation of Haiti, the first independent Latin American republic and the first independent black nation in the Americas. Slaves intent on vengeance as well as freedom burned plantations and massacred whites; then violence broadened as the insurrection became at once a war for independence from France and a bloody civil war fought among and between the colony's 32,000 whites, 28,000 free blacks, and 500,000 slaves, many of whom had been born in Africa (figures for 1790). Efforts to supress the revolution by Britain, Spain, and France only added to the carnage. By 1804, some 100,000 islanders had died along with another 70,000 European soldiers and seaman. Saint Domingue's old white planter class had vanished from the island, its plantations were in ruins, and its exports had fallen to a trickle.

Jeffersonians, who included large numbers of southern slaveholders, did not cheer when revolutionary France abolished slavery in Saint-Domingue (1793) and then in all its colonies (1794) and also declared all French citizens equal regardless of race. Their discomfort increased when the success of Haiti's black revolutionaries inspired unrest among enslaved blacks in the American South, the Caribbean beyond Haiti, and South

A nineteenth-century engraving of the slave revolt on Saint Domingue, which later became Haiti in 1804.

America. The revolutions Jeffersonians celebrated were of whites, left a meritocratically defined upper class in charge, and minimized the loss of life and property. As thousands of refugees from Saint-Domingue flocked to the United States telling stories of rapes and murders, southern states began to discourage manumissions and cut back the privileges of free blacks, encouraging them to go elsewhere. In his *Notes on the State of Virginia*, Jefferson had argued that whites and emancipated slaves could not coexist peacefully; Saint-Domingue seemed to prove him right. Curiously, the Federalists—whose base of power was in the North—provided more support for the Haitian Revolution than the Jeffersonians, mainly because they wanted to maintain Americans' lucrative trade with the island.

As issues in foreign policy came to dominate Washington's administration, the differences between Federalists and Antifederalists widened. Gradually, they extended from the cabinet and Congress down into the electorate and shaped responses even to events such as Philadelphia's yellow fever epidemic. Republican doctors, including Dr. Benjamin Rush, the leading physician of his day, traced the disease to unhealthy local conditions such as swamps or unsanitary docks. Their Federalist and nonpartisan counterparts said it was imported, perhaps by a French privateer or French-speaking refugees from Saint-Domingue. (In fact, both were right: yellow fever is carried from infected persons—perhaps refugees—to healthy ones by mosquitoes bred locally, but nobody knew that until 1901.) Republicans led the relief work, sometimes following Rush's prescription of draining large amounts of blood from victims. Federalists, who believed in contagion, fled the city.

Within the government, differences over foreign policy began in the early 1790s, when Britain seemed likely to go to war first with Spain and then with France. Jefferson argued that Britain's situation gave the United States an opportunity to secure concessions in return for American neutrality; and several issues stemming from the 1783 Treaty of Paris needed settling. The British had never evacuated their posts in the Northwest, and westerners suspected the British of using those bases to provoke Indian attacks on the American frontier. The United States also sought compensation for slaves the British had carried off during the Revolutionary War, and hoped to persuade Britain to open its West Indian islands to American traders. But on April 22, 1793, Washington—influenced by Hamilton, who desperately wanted to avoid any altercation with Britain—issued a proclamation that essentially announced American neutrality without even trying to secure any concessions in return. A few months later, Jefferson submitted his resignation as secretary of state, which took effect at the end of the year.

He was still in office, however, when a new French minister, Edmond Genet, arrived in the United States—and tried to build on American enthusiasm for the French Revolution by hiring American privateers to sail under the French flag against British ships in the North Atlantic and raising a military expedition against Spain. Jefferson tried to stop Genet's violations of American sovereignty but could do little with that "hothead" who talked "of appeals . . . from [the president] to Congress, from them to the people, urging the most unreasonable and groundless propositions, & in the most dictatorial style &c. &c. &c." Finally, on July 12, 1793, Washington's cabinet requested Genet's recall. Because the Jacobins under Robespierre had taken power in France, Genet instead remained in the United States, married the daughter of New York's governor, became a citizen, and devoted his life to agriculture, raising a family and conceiving schemes for public improvements such as canals. He became, in short, much like many other Americans of his time.

Meanwhile, American relations with Britain moved into a state of crisis over trade. New British Orders in Council (regulations issued by the Crown) undercut the old rule that "free ships make free goods," which had allowed American traders to carry goods to and from the ports of European belligerent powers. Instead, the British invoked the Rule of 1756, by which no neutral nation could engage in trade during war from which it was excluded during peacetime. Then, in December 1793, the British suddenly and without warning began seizing American ships in the West Indies. A cry went up for reprisals, such as severe restrictions on British trade, and if that should lead to war, some Americans were ready. Mobs harassed British seamen, and volunteer corps began organizing for a possible rerun of the Revolutionary War.

Wiser counsels prevailed. For one thing, in January 1794, the British decided to allow neutral vessels to buy goods in enemy colonies provided they carried them to the ports of a neutral country. Thereafter, American ships simply picked up goods in, for example, Saint-Domingue, touched base at a port within the United States, paid duties on the goods (most of which were subsequently refunded if they were reexported), then turned around and set sail for France. This procedure, American merchants said, was legal under Britain's new policy, and the British agreed. And that's why reexports played so large a part in America's new prosperity.

Seeking a more stable settlement, Washington sent a special mission to Britain headed by John Jay, whose nomination the Senate confirmed in April 1794. Finally it looked as though the United States might secure concessions in return for remaining neutral in Europe's war. Soon after Jay's departure, the United States received an invitation from Sweden and Denmark to join an alliance of neutrals. On Hamilton's advice, Washington rejected the offer; and Hamilton, ever anxious to placate Britain, told the news to the British minister, George Hammond. In truth, the British understood that since the United States was not a naval power, her participation in the League of Armed Neutrality would make little difference. Jay therefore had little to trade for British concessions, and he received almost none.

Under the draft treaty Jay negotiated, Britain promised to surrender its posts in the Northwest by July 1, 1796, but the United States would have to let British fur traders remain there. The British offered compensation for the ships seized in the West Indies in late 1793, but the United States had to compensate British creditors for prerevolutionary debts that remained unpaid. Moreover, the United States had to give up its view of the rights of neutral ships during the current war

A view of Detroit by an unknown British officer in 1794, a year before Jay's Treaty finally brought to an end British occupation of its former posts in the West.

and for two years after the war's conclusion. Britain made no promise to cease impressing American seamen into the Royal Navy or to grant compensation for slaves seized during the Revolutionary War. The draft treaty did support the right of American and British ships to free navigation on the Mississippi, and it opened the West Indian trade to some American vessels—provided the ships carried to the rest of the world no molasses, sugar, coffee, cocoa, or cotton from the West Indies or, which was extraordinary, from the United States itself. That last provision would have ended the reexport trade, the lifeblood of the urban Northeast's new prosperity.

A treaty that asked so much of the United States and gave so little provoked widespread hostility in a country that, in any case, harbored few kindly feelings toward Britain. The Senate struck out the provision on the West Indies trade but accepted the rest of Jay's Treaty. Despite an uproar in the press and large popular meetings in several cities, Washington approved the treaty, which was finally signed on November 19, 1795. The opposition proceeded to carry the battle into the House of Representatives, which, under the leadership of James Madison, asserted its right to examine treaties before granting funds for their implementation. Washington refused House demands for the government's correspondence with Jay, which he saw as a violation of the executive branch's prerogatives. That decision set another important precedent. In the end, even the House granted the appropriations necessary to execute the treaty (on April 30, 1796). It knew the United States could not afford a war with Britain.

If Jay's Treaty was a mixed blessing, the Washington administration soon scored a few less ambiguous triumphs. One was over the Indians, although it took some doing. Efforts to make Indians recognize the territorial claims of the United States under the 1783 Treaty of Paris had failed: not surprisingly, the Indians insisted that they were unaffected by Europeans' treaties. Washington at first tried to follow a policy, proposed by Secretary of War Knox, of recognizing Indian claims and restraining white expansion except on lands the Indians sold voluntarily. That would work, Knox thought, because as farms spread westward the population of wild animals that sustained Indian life would decline, and then the Indians would willingly give up large tracts of land.

Knox was wrong. The administration was able to buy Indian title to lands in Kentucky and part of Ten-

nessee, but north of the Ohio River members of the Miami Confederation (which encompassed eight western tribes) resisted the spread of settlements that threatened their hunting grounds. To protect frontier settlers and gain title to the Northwest, the administration gradually went back to using force against the Indians. At first, that effort failed miserably: in 1790, Indians crushed an invasion of the Ohio Territory by some 1,400 U.S. troops, and the next year destroyed an even larger army on the banks of the Wabash River. Finally, in an effort to "pacify" the West, Congress authorized the creation of a 5,000-man regular army, which General Anthony Wayne rigorously trained before leading it into Indian territory. On August 20, 1794, Wayne soundly beat the Indian forces at the Battle of Fallen Timbers on the Maumee River, just south of what is today Toledo, Ohio. Under the Treaty of Greenville (August 3, 1795), the Indians ceded title to the southeastern corner of the Northwest Territory and a few enclaves farther inland (including the sites of Detroit and Chicago) and agreed to receive annual payments of about $10,000 in return. That agreement and news of Jay's Treaty, under which the British, who had encouraged Indian resistance, would finally leave their western posts, led to a new surge of western settlement. Within four years, some 45,000 people had moved into what became, in 1803, the state of Ohio.

This painting depicts General Anthony Wayne and his officers at the signing of the Indian Treaty of Greenville, which was penned in 1794 after they had defeated the Potawatomi Indians. The Treaty ceded to the United States a large tract of Indian land, including the site that would later become Chicago.

Soon the Treaty of San Lorenzo, sometimes called Pinckney's Treaty after the American negotiator, Thomas Pinckney, settled American problems with Spain. Under its terms, Spain accepted the Mississippi River and the 31st parallel as the western and southern borders of the United States and allowed Americans to deposit goods at New Orleans (where they would be loaded on oceangoing ships) for three years and at some other point thereafter. Both nations agreed to prevent Indians in their territory from invading the other's lands. The treaty was signed at Madrid on October 27, 1795. It remained a major accomplishment of the Washington administration, which, through a time of unprecedented turmoil, succeeded in securing both British and Spanish recognition of American sovereignty over the vast stretch of land it had received in 1783 under the Treaty of Paris.

## THE ELECTION OF 1796

The presidential election of 1792 was a near nonevent. Washington ran unopposed. Three electors abstained, but Washington received all of the remaining 132 electoral votes. John Adams won reelection as vice-president by a healthy margin. The election of 1796 promised to be far less predictable, particularly if Washington chose to retire, as many observers anticipated. But no announcement confirmed their speculation until, finally, on September 19, 1796, Philadelphia's *Daily American Advertiser* carried the text of the president's "Farewell Address," dated September 17.

That address, which Washington never presented orally, had long been in the works: Madison contributed to a draft in 1792, when Washington first contemplated retiring from the presidency. Hamilton made more recent textual changes. It was a moving statement, beginning with expressions of the sixty-four-year-old Washington's gratitude to his "beloved country" for the honors and confidence it had invested in him and a reference to "the increasing weight of years" that admonished him "more and more, that the shade of retirement is as necessary to me as it is welcome." Then the president offered advice, based on "much reflection," that might "contribute to the permanency of your felicity as a People." He urged his countrymen to support the public credit, to "observe good faith and justice towards all Nations" while avoiding permanent alliances with any, and to disdain "overgrown Military establishments," which were always "inauspicious to liberty." But the thrust of his message concerned the country's political divisions.

Washington considered any opposition to an established republican government seditious. He saw himself as the head not of a ruling party but of the government, and he considered all organized opposition to the government a threat to the rule of law. In a message to Congress of November 1794, he had referred to the "democratic-republican" clubs—organizations that worked peacefully on behalf of Republican policies—as "self-created societies" whose support contributed to the violence in western Pennsylvania and which were as objectionable as actual insurrections. After Washington's condemnation, the societies dissolved, but Thomas Jefferson was furious. Not only had Washington (under the influence of Hamilton, "the servile copyist of Mr. Pitt") used a "military force for civil purposes," Jefferson said, but in attacking the democratic societies he had violated the freedom "of association, of conversation and of the press" in a way not even England, though "advancing to the establishment of an absolute monarchy, has yet been bold enough to attempt."

Now, in his Farewell Address, Washington offered a full-force attack on political parties: the "alternate domination of one faction over another" was itself "a frightful despotism" and led to a more "formal and permanent despotism" by allowing "cunning, ambitious, and unprincipled men . . . to subvert the Power of the People and to usurp for themselves the reins of Government." To Washington, in short, the "baneful spirit of Party" was a real and present threat to the future of the American Republic.

The election of 1796 was nonetheless shaped by partisan politics. Adams ran for president as Washington's successor, but Hamilton tried to get Thomas Pinckney—who had just successfully negotiated the Treaty of San Lorenzo—elected instead. Under the procedures stated in the Constitution, each elector cast two votes without specifying which was for president and which for vice-president. The person who won the highest number of votes became president, and the candidate with next-highest number became vice-president. Hamilton attempted to persuade southern Republicans, who favored Thomas Jefferson, to cast their second vote for Pinckney. Then, with a full share of the Federalists' votes, Pinckney would outrank Adams.

Hamilton's scheme failed: Adams's supporters in the North anticipated the danger and scattered their second votes among several vice-presidential candidates. In the end, Adams became president with 71 votes, 3 more than Jefferson; Jefferson in turn received 9 more than Pinckney and so became Adams's vice-president.

## THE ADAMS ADMINISTRATION

It seems strange in retrospect, this administration with a president from one party (Federalist) and vice-president from another (Republican). But Adams and Jefferson had been allies in the struggle for independence and, in the 1780s, had deepened their bonds while serving together as diplomats in Europe. Adams's attitude toward Hamilton was not so different from Jefferson's. Adams, too, had reservations on aspects of Hamilton's financial policies, such as the national bank, and continued to distrust the use of military force against civilians. After Hamilton's maneuverings in the election of 1796, Adams had more reason to distrust and resent the one-time secretary of the treasury—and no one harbored resentments more powerfully than John Adams. Jefferson, moreover, respected Adams and even instructed his followers that if the 1796 electoral vote for president was tied, they should vote for Adams because "he has always been my senior." Or did Jefferson realize that, given the deteriorating situation in Europe, the incoming administration was likely to face challenges that would better be left to someone else?

John Adams, second president of the United States (1797–1801). This portrait was probably begun by Gilbert Stuart in 1798, during Adams's presidency, but finished later, after Adams's death in 1826, by Jane Stuart.

At first, it looked as though old party differences might disappear. Adams and Jefferson even moved into the same Philadelphia boarding house. In his inaugural address, Adams held out an olive branch to the Republicans by emphasizing his hostility to monarchy and aristocracy as well as his esteem for France, where he had lived as a diplomat for several years. He even suggested making Jefferson's friend James Madison a special envoy to France, whose relationship with the United States had become troubled after the United States signed Jay's Treaty. But Madison was uninterested, and Adams withdrew the nomination after his cabinet, whose members had first taken office under Washington, expressed its determined opposition.

Keeping his predecessor's cabinet was a mistake that future presidents would not repeat. Not only was the cabinet's loyalty to Adams in doubt, but its most prominent members—Timothy Pickering, secretary of state; James McHenry, secretary of war; and Oliver Wolcott Jr., secretary of the treasury—were a far cut below the brilliance of Washington's first cabinet. That became a significant problem since Adams spent a good part of his presidency at home in Quincy, Massachusetts, at first because his wife, Abigail, was in poor health, and later under the illusion that he could perform his job as well there as in Philadelphia. While the president was absent, the cabinet exercised considerable power.

Problems with France remained pressing. After getting news of Jay's Treaty, the French began seizing American ships bound for England, would not recognize the neutral rights of American ships, and in December 1796 refused to accept the new American minister to France, Charles Cotesworth Pinckney of South Carolina (a cousin of Charles Pinckney). Finally, in May 1797, President Adams appointed a commission to France consisting of two Federalists, Pinckney and John Marshall of Virginia, as well as a Republican, Elbridge Gerry of Massachusetts. In announcing the mission to Congress, Adams also called for defensive military preparations, which the Republicans objected to, believing militarization would further antagonize France. That ended the honeymoon. Henceforth, foreign affairs frayed the relationship between Adams and Jefferson and rekindled old political divisions.

## THE XYZ AFFAIR

The French minister, Charles-Maurice de Talleyrand, refused for several weeks to receive the American commissioners.

Then, to their surprise, three agents of Talleyrand (identified subsequently only as X, Y, and Z) visited the commissioners and demanded an American loan to France and a bribe for Talleyrand of $250,000. "Not a sixpence," Pinckney was said to have replied; and he and Marshall set out for home, leaving Gerry to represent the United States.

Outrage greeted Adams's announcement of the demand. Republicans in Congress asked to see the diplomatic papers, which Adams—unlike Washington after Jay's Treaty—supplied; after all, they fully supported his administration's position. Congress repealed the 1778 treaty with France and took additional steps to increase American military strength, which triggered Republican fears.

Meanwhile, Adams and Secretary of State Pickering, in an effort to support American commerce and strike at French power in the Americas, sent a consul general to Saint-Domingue with instructions to establish relations with the revolutionaries and their leader, Toussaint L'ouverture. American trade provided the Haitian revolutionaries with arms and food and also a market for their products. And so the Federalists, whom the Jeffersonians condemned as counter-revolutionaries, provided critical support for perhaps the most radical revolution of the time.

The results of strengthening the military were also sometimes far different from what the Republicans expected.

## GUNS AND SHIPS

The Federalists used military contracting during the war scare with France to encourage innovations in armaments manufacturing. Consider the contract that Secretary of the Treasury Wolcott signed in 1798 with Eli Whitney, who promised to deliver 10,000 muskets to the government in a little over two years. That rate of production was unknown among contemporary arms makers, who carefully crafted each gun by hand. Whitney, however, promised to use "machinery moved by water" to reduce labor input and facilitate the manufacturing process. Later, when arguing for contract extensions, he also promised to make guns with parts that could be inter-changed, so the army could fix broken guns with parts from others. Whitney, however, had no experience making guns. He had desperately needed government funds to keep his business from going into bankruptcy (having spent a fortune protecting his cotton-gin patent), but he failed to deliver the promised muskets on time. And those muskets did not have interchangeable parts: that advance would be made later by other arms makers.

The Adams administration was more successful at encouraging military innovations through its new Department of the Navy, under the leadership of Benjamin Stoddert, a Revolutionary War veteran and the successful owner of a commercial shipping firm. Stoddert became the first cabinet officer who owed his appointment to Adams, and he served the president well.

When Stoddert took office in June 1798, the United States had only one ship at sea, but more were on the way. In 1794, in an effort to check the attacks of the Barbary pirates on American shipping, Congress had authorized the construction of six new frigates—ships that were smaller than the "ships of the line," the largest and most powerful ships in the great navies of the era, but faster and more maneuverable. Part of the order was canceled the next year when the United States signed a

This 1797 cartoon, in which a five-headed monster (France) demands "Money, Money, Money!!," was inspired by the XYZ Affair. The three American representatives on the left respond, "We will not give you six pence."

peace treaty with Algeria, but three ships remained in production. They were built according to technologically innovative plans that are generally attributed to Philadelphia master shipbuilder Joshua Humphreys, although others contributed to the designs. Humphreys conceived of a ship that combined heavy firepower, approaching that of ships of the line, with the speed of a frigate, characteristics thought to be mutually exclusive. These "super frigates" would have distinctively long, sleek hulls and towering sail rigs to enhance speed, and they would carry an unusually large number of heavy guns mounted on two decks. According to Humphreys, that design would make the American ships "superior to any European frigate" and allow them to avoid action except "on their own terms."

However, by increasing the length and armament (and therefore the weight) of the ships and by providing sleek hulls, the new designs made the ships especially susceptible to a bending of the keel (the lowest part of the ship's bottom, or hull) known as "hogging" because the keel's curvature resembled the arch of a hog's back. Hogging at first slows a vessel's speed, and it can eventually cause the keel to crack, sinking the ship. The phenomenon was a well-known problem in wooden ship design and the reason why speed and heavy armament were considered incompatible. Hogging occurs because upward water pressure is greatest at the center of a ship, where the hull is widest. Moreover, the ship's heavy, gun-laden desks brought downward pressure on its outer ends. These forces—up at the center, down at the ends—increase with the length of a ship because length has a leveraging effect. The frigate's designers found a way to mitigate the problem—an integrated system of interlocking beams and immense internal braces with diagonal "riders" made of live oak, a particularly dense wood, that carried the guns' weight down to the most vulnerable part of the keel and so counteracted the stress that led to hogging.

The builders also constructed unusual, three-layered hulls with cross planks of white oak, another extremely dense, rot-resistant wood. At points, the hulls of the new ships were as much as twenty-five inches thick, which made them virtually impervious to enemy fire. Their construction, a massive project carried out by shipbuilders in three different ports for political reasons, with sawyers (some of whom were slaves) in Georgia cutting and shipping timber and Humphreys overseeing the whole operation, was like nothing Americans had accomplished before. With projects like this, Americans began to develop the management skills that were so conspicuously and disastrously absent on the banks of the Passaic.

The new super frigates—USS *United States,* USS *Constellation,* and USS *Constitution* (later dubbed "Old Ironsides" after a sailor watched enemy cannonballs bounce from its surface and shouted, "Huzzah! Her sides are made of iron!")—were launched in 1797. They provided a fine beginning for the new U.S. Navy. Stoddert worked to acquire an additional six frigates as well as some forty smaller ships. He encouraged the development in America of techniques for rolling copper to sheath the ships' bottoms (a challenge that was finally met by Boston's Paul Revere); the domestic manufacture of carronades, short-range guns for splintering wood; and the creation of American sources of hemp, canvas, and other articles needed by the navy. Stoddert also built, virtually from scratch, a respectable naval officers corps and established a program for the recruitment and training of promising young midshipmen. Within a relatively short period, the United States possessed a navy capable of providing American merchant ships substantial protection and offsetting wildcat fears of a French invasion, mounted from the West Indies, of the American southern seaboard. All this Stoddert accomplished during a trying two-year period, from 1798 to 1800, while American and French ships engaged in an undeclared war on the seas that threatened continually to blossom into a regular, declared war.

The gun deck of the USS *Constitution*. The heavy cannons on the ship brought great pressure down on its keel. Without countervailing measures, the pressure would have helped cause a misshaping of the keel known as "hogging."

## THE ALIEN AND SEDITION ACTS

As the war fever grew, Adams fell into Washington's way of thinking, regarding critics of his government as seditious people who put their confidence in France rather than their own government. Federalists in Congress went further, passing a series of laws for the suppression of the Republicans and the Republican press. Three Alien Acts, passed in June and July 1798, moved against immigrants, who were often members of the Republican Party. An Alien Enemies Act, which allowed the president to arrest or banish enemy aliens, would take effect only if war was declared. Another Alien Act allowed the president to deport any foreigners he considered dangerous to the public peace and safety, and a Naturalization Act increased the time of residence before immigrants could become citizens—and thus acquire voting rights—from five to fourteen years. Finally, a Sedition Act provided punishments including imprisonment for persons who combined "to oppose any measure or measures of the government of the United States" or who wrote, printed, spoke, or published "any false, scandalous, and malicious writing or writings against the government of the United States, or the President of the United States, . . . to defame . . . or to bring them . . . into contempt or disrepute." That law would expire on March 3, 1801, when the next presidential administration took power.

The Sedition Act was a reformed version of earlier English sedition laws: it allowed truth as a defense, and it specified limited, not open-ended, punishments. But the act was administered in a violently partisan way. Among the victims were Matthew Lyon, an outspoken Republican congressman from Vermont remembered for a raucous fight on the floor of Congress with Federalist Roger Griswold, who was up for reelection. Lyon's attacks on Federalist policies won him a four-month jail sentence (during which he was reelected) and a $1,000 fine. The editors of Republican newspapers, who spent their lives trying to make the Adams administration and its policies objects of contempt, were also attacked and forced to cease publication, even to go into hiding.

## THE VIRGINIA AND KENTUCKY RESOLUTIONS

The Alien and Sedition Acts alarmed Thomas Jefferson and James Madison. They seemed to disprove Madison's old theory that there was no danger in placing power at the center of a confederated government. Neither the checks and balances built in to the Constitution nor the "parchment barriers" in the Bill of Rights had kept the Federalists from violating the basic freedoms of assembly, speech, and the press.

Jefferson anonymously drafted a set of resolutions that the Kentucky legislature adopted on November 16, 1798, asserting that "as in all other cases of compact among parties having no common Judge, each party has an equal right to judge for itself" when the compact was violated and to determine the appropriate "mode and measure of redress." On that basis, Kentucky proceeded to declare several acts of Congress, including the Alien and Sedition Acts, unconstitutional and therefore "void and of no force." The Kentucky legislature sent its resolutions to the state's U.S. senators and representatives with a request that they work to repeal "the [aforesaid] unconstitutional and obnoxious acts." It also sent copies of the resolutions to the other states, asking that they similarly declare the specified acts "void and of no force" and request their repeal. The laws in question, Kentucky maintained, amounted to an "undisguised declaration" that the federal government intended to assume power to bind the states "in all cases whatsoever"—a clear reference to the British Declaratory Act of 1766. Unless arrested, that effort could "drive this state into revolution" and strengthen those enemies of the Republic who believed "that man cannot be governed but by a rod of iron."

Madison drafted another set of resolves that the Virginia legislature adopted on December 24, 1798. They, too, condemned the Alien and Sedition Acts as "alarming infractions" of the Constitution and saw in congressional legislation an effort to "consolidate" the states by degrees and "transform the present republican system of the United States into an absolute, or, at best, a mixed monarchy." Virginia asserted that in the case "of a deliberate, palpable, and dangerous exercise" of unconstitutional powers by the federal government, the states as parties to the federal compact "have the right and are in duty bound to interpose for arresting the progress of the evil."

Both the Kentucky and the Virginia Resolutions failed. The state legislatures that replied—essentially all those from Maryland north—disavowed Kentucky's and Virginia's constitutional arguments. Some, like Rhode Island, argued that the power of judging the constitutionality of acts of Congress was vested exclusively in the Supreme Court of the United States, not in state legislatures. Kentucky, however, stuck to its guns and passed another set of resolutions on February 22, 1799, that restated its previous position and added that a "nullification" by the states of all acts of Congress unauthorized by the Constitution was the

## *What if You Get Sick?*

American Journal

"On Thursday Decr 12th [1799] the General [George Washington] rode out to his farms . . . Soon after he went out, the weather became very bad . . . A heavy fall of snow took place on friday, which prevented the General from riding out as usual. He had taken cold (undoubtedly from being so much exposed the day before) and complained of having a sore throat . . .

"About two or three o'clk Saturday Morning he awoke Mrs Washington & told her he was very unwell, and had had an ague [fever]. She observed that he could scarcely speak. . . . As soon as the day appeared . . . he desired that Mr Rawlins, one of the Overseers who was used to bleeding the people, might be sent for to bleed him before the doctors could arrive. . . . I found him breathing with difficulty—and hardly able to utter a word intelligibly . . . A mixture of Molasses, Vinegar & butter was prepared, to try its effect in the throat; but he could not swallow a drop . . . Mr. Rawlins came in soon after sun rise—and prepared to bleed him. When the Arm was ready—the General, observing that Rawlins appeared to be agitated, said, as well as he could speak, 'don't be afraid,' and after the incision was made, he observed 'the oriface is not large enough.' . . . Mrs. W being . . . uneasy lest too much blood should be taken, it was stop'd after about half a pint was taken from him. Finding that no relief was obtain'd . . . I

proposed bathing the throat externally with Salvalaltita. . . . A piece of flannel was then put round his neck His feet were also soaked in warm water. This, however, gave no relief."

In the meantime, several doctors arrived. They "put a blister of cantharides on the throat & took more blood . . . and had some Vinegar & hot water put into a Teapot, for the General to draw in steam from the nozel." They also gave him "sage tea and Vinegar to be mixed for a Gargle," but when the general "held back his head to let it run down [his throat], it put him into great distress and almost produced suffocation." In the afternoon, he was "bled again, and the blood ran slowly . . . and did not produce any symptoms of fainting." They also administered "calomil & tarter em." but "without any effect." Around 6 P.M., the general told his physicians, "'I feel myself going . . . let me go off quietly; I cannot last long.'" Two hours later, the doctors "applied blisters to his legs, but went out without a ray of hope." About 10, with great difficulty, Washington said, "'I am just going. Have me decently buried, and do not let my body be put into the Vault in less than two days after I am dead.' I bowed assent." A little while later, "he expired without a struggle or a Sigh!"

Tobias Lear's journal entry on the death of George Washington at Mount Vernon, December 15, 1799

"rightful remedy" while promising to oppose violations of the Constitution "in a constitutional manner."

Virginia took another approach. Madison drafted a "Report" that reexamined the constitutional issues under debate. The problem, he said, was that the word "states" had several meanings. The power to judge the constitutionality of federal laws lay in the states not as territories nor as governments, but as "the people composing those political societies, in their highest sovereign capacity," because it was the people—not the legislatures—who had ratified the federal Constitution. The Supreme Court's power was not superior to that of the people, since the courts were the people's cre-

ation. Like other branches of the government, the judiciary could violate the Constitution and so must remain subject to scrutiny. Moreover, the "Report" continued, "the authority of constitutions over governments, and of the sovereignty of the people over constitutions, are truths . . . at no time, perhaps, more necessary than at present." But since the people exercised their sovereign power through conventions, not legislatures, the resolutions adopted by the Virginia legislature were just a statement of opinion, not an effort to nullify federal laws. That was a clever but theoretically sophisticated effort to answer those who accused the legislature of acting improperly.

Still, the basic powers of government had not been the subject of such searching debate since the time of the Revolution. That precedent was not reassuring.

## PEACE

John Adams ended the crisis. He fought off demands from ardent Federalists for a declaration of war, and he listened instead to a stream of reports from Europe suggesting that France had become more open to conciliation. In February 1799, without consulting his cabinet, Adams nominated William Vans Murray as minister to France. That alone eased tensions by offering a prospect of peace. Murray did not set out until October, when he was accompanied by two other commissioners. When they arrived, Napoleon Bonaparte had seized power and was ready to repair France's relationship with the United States. Napoleon was unwilling to compensate the Americans for past losses, but he agreed to respect the rights of neutral ships in the future and ended France's campaign against American ships. The scare was over.

Adams's appointment of Murray was an act of courage that drew on the skills and instincts he had developed earlier as a diplomat. But it alienated a substantial part of his Federalist supporters and cast into doubt his reelection as president. In May 1800, Adams finally dismissed McHenry and Pickering from his cabinet and took control of his administration. It was too late. So was news of the peace agreement, which arrived only after the election.

## THE ELECTION OF 1800

Republicans organized for the election as no political group had done before, with local and state committees directed by a caucus of Republican congressmen in Philadelphia. Meanwhile, Republican newspapers attacked the government for its violations of basic liberties, its creation of a navy and army, and the taxes levied to support them. Their own candidate for president was Jefferson, and for vice-president, Aaron Burr. Charles Cotesworth Pinckney was Adams's running mate. Once again Alexander Hamilton tried, as in 1796, to manipulate the vote so that Pinckney outranked Adams, and once again he failed. Considering the circumstances, Adams did well, winning 65 electoral votes—only 6 fewer than in 1796—and Pinckney 64. But both Jefferson and Burr received 73 votes, and it took thirty-six ballots in the House of Representatives, in which each state had for this purpose one vote, to break the tie. Jefferson finally won, ironically, with the help of Hamilton, who urged Burr's supporters to cast blank ballots. Compared with Burr, Hamilton concluded, Jefferson was the lesser evil.

## THE END OF A CENTURY

Jefferson's inaugural, on March 4, 1801, was the first to take place in the nation's new capital on the Potomac. If Washington, D.C., was a symbol of the nation's future, or even the future of the federal government, the prospects looked grim indeed. It showed no sign of the prosperity that touched the government's previous homes in New York and Philadelphia: Washington was a backwater, a "city" with unpaved streets that turned to dust in the dry days of summer and into mud streams when it rained. The executive residence, first occupied by the Adamses, remained, like the Capitol, unfinished. What was built had been constructed so poorly that chunks of ceiling fell and pillars split within a few years of their installation. There were no streetlights, no street signs; grand avenues became cow paths. The city was home to flies and mosquitoes, frogs and also hogs, who happily gobbled up garbage in the roadways. An uninformed visitor witnessing the scene could only wonder whether some disaster had occurred. Was Washington half built, or half destroyed?

This campaign banner of 1800 reads, "T. Jefferson, President of the United States" and also, "John Adams no more."

The new president nonetheless looked to the future with confidence. He thought of his election as the "Revolution of 1800" because it brought to an end the repressive policies of the Federalists. Through the ballot box, Americans had averted the potentially bloody revolution that the Kentucky Resolutions seemed to predict. Now that constitutional government had been reestablished, the new president suggested, the threats to freedom and republicanism that he saw in the policies of the Federalists and also the political divisions that answered them would, along with the eighteenth century, disappear forever. He reminded his listeners that "every difference of opinion is not a difference of principle. We have called by different names brethren of the same principle. We are all Federalists; we are all Republicans." Anyone who wished to dissolve the Union or end the Republic should henceforth "stand undisturbed as monuments of the safety with which error of opinion may be tolerated where reason is left free to combat it."

The new president spoke of "a rising nation, spread over a wide and fruitful land," crossing the seas "with the rich productions of their industry," conducting commerce with foreign nations and "advancing rapidly to destinies beyond the reach of mortal eye." Would an honest patriot, "in the full tide of successful experiment, abandon a government which has so far kept us free and firm"? Some said "that man cannot be trusted with the government of himself. Can he, then, be trusted with the government of others? Or have we found angels in the forms of kings to govern him? Let history answer this question."

Jefferson had no doubt of history's answer. The election showed that men could be trusted with their own self-government. The Republic would survive.

## Suggested Reading

Charlene Bangs Bickford and Kenneth R. Bowling, *Birth of the Nation: The First Federal Congress, 1789–1791* (1989)

Laurent Dubois, *Avengers of the New World: The Story of the Haitian Revolution* (2004)

Stanley Elkins and Eric McKitrick, *The Age of Federalism* (1993)

Joseph J. Ellis, *Founding Brothers: The Revolutionary Generation* (2000)

David P. Geggus, ed., *The Impact of the Haitian Revolution in the Atlantic World* (2001)

David J. Jeremy, *Transatlantic Industrial Revolution: The Diffusion of Textile Technologies Between Britain and America, 1790–1830s* (1981)

Richard R. John, *Spreading the News: the American Postal System from Franklin to Morse* (1995)

Angela Lakwete, *Inventing the Cotton Gin: Machine and Myth in Antebellum America* (2003)

Douglass C. North, Terry L. Anderson, and Peter J. Hill, *Growth and Welfare in the American Past: A New Economic History* (1983)

Michael A. Palmer, *Stoddert's War: Naval Operations During the Quasi-War with France, 1798–1801* (1987)

Martin S. Pernick, "Politics, Parties, and Pestilence: Epidemic Yellow Fever in Philadelphia and the Rise of the First Party System," *William and Mary Quarterly*, 3d Series, XXIX (1972), 559–86.

Merritt Roe Smith, "Eli Whitney and the American System of Manufacturing," in Carroll W. Pursell Jr., ed., *Technology in America: A History of Individuals and Ideas,* 2nd ed. (1990)

Dava Sobel, *Longitude: The True Story of a Lone Genius Who Solved the Greatest Scientific Problem of His Time* (1996)

Dirk J. Struik, *Yankee Science in the Making* (1948)

Helen E. Veit et al., eds., *Creating the Bill of Rights: The Documentary Record from the First Federal Congress* (1991)

Gavin Wright, *The Political Economy of the Cotton South: Households, Markets, and Wealth in the Nineteenth Century* (1978)

James Sterling Young, *The Washington Community, 1800–1828* (1966)

# Chapter Review

## Summary

### QUESTIONS

- How did Alexander Hamilton's policies put the United States on a solid financial basis?

- Why did Congress agree to put the national capital on virtually uninhabited boglands near the Potomac River?

- How did cotton solve the economic problems of the American South in the 1790s?

- What advice did George Washington give Americans in his "Farewell Address"?

- Why did Jefferson call the election of 1800 "the revolution of 1800"?

## Key Terms

The Bill of Rights (p. 231)

Hamilton's reports (p. 232)

The re-export trade (p. 238)

Cotton gin (p. 242)

The Alien & Sedition Acts (p. 253)

## Chronology

| | |
|---|---|
| April 1789 | First Federal Congress meets in New York; George Washington elected president |
| June 1789 | Beginning of the French Revolution |
| April–May 1790 | Federal patent and copyright laws passed. |
| 1790–91 | Hamilton submits plans for financial system and economic development. |
| 1791 | Slave uprising in the French Caribbean colony of Saint-Domingue marks the beginning of the Haitian Revolution |
| December 15, 1791 | The Bill of Rights added to the Constitution. |
| 1792 | The Post Office Act. Washington re-elected President |
| April 1793 | Eli Whitney invents cotton gin. |
| 1794 | Whiskey Rebellion. |
| 1796 | John Adams elected President |
| 1798 | The XYZ Affair. |
| June–July 1798 | The Alien and Sedition Acts. |
| November/ December 1798 | The Kentucky/Virginia Resolutions. |
| 1800 | Thomas Jefferson elected president |
| 1802 | Nathaniel Bowditch's The New American Practical Navigator appears. |

*Chapter 9*

# THE FABRIC OF CHANGE:

## 1800–1815

View of the Boston Manufacturing Company mills at Waltham, Massachusetts, c.1825. As the rural scenery indicates, the city of Waltham grew around textile manufacturing and, also, later, the production of world-famous "Waltham" pocket watches and clocks.

**Focus QUESTIONS**

■ **How did the nation move in major new directions during Jefferson's first term?**

■ **How did the embargo spur new developments in the economy?**

■ **How did the War of 1812 arise, and what were its major events?**

■ **What significant economic developments resulted from the War of 1812?**

Thomas Jefferson took office at the dawn of a new century amidst a sense of change and anticipation. One indicator came from the Census Office, which announced in 1801 that the population of the United States stood at 5.3 million, a 35 percent increase since 1790. The Republic's population would continue its steep increase, nearly doubling by 1820 and more than doubling again by 1840. This meant a growth rate of more than 33 percent each decade over a fifty-year period, far exceeding that for any country in Europe. The rapid growth was powered mainly by an unprecedented commercial and geographic expansion, the leading edge of which emanated from the bustling cities of New York, Philadelphia, Boston, and Baltimore. Seaborne trade built the wealth of these port cities and the resources to invest in new ventures like textile manufacturing.

With a population of 70,000, Philadelphia was America's largest city in 1800, second in the world only to London in the value and volume of trade that passed through its harbor. Ten years later, New York City would eclipse Philadelphia in population and trade, and by 1821 New York would attract 37 percent of all imports entering the United States. In 1820, there were twelve U.S. cities with populations exceeding 10,000, only two of which, New York and Philadelphia, had more than 100,000 people. Forty years later, 101 cities (most of them located in the Northeast and Midwest) boasted populations of more than 10,000, with eight surpassing 100,000. By then, New York was in a league of its own with over 1 million inhabitants.

Despite the rapid growth of New York and other seaboard cities, the United States remained overwhelmingly agricultural and rural in 1800. Most Americans, 75 percent, lived in the countryside and made their living from farming, while only 5 percent lived in cities. The remaining 20 percent lived in towns and villages that serviced the rural population. Be-

neath the surface, however, even the agrarian economy was changing. People were on the move: with the increasing scarcity of good farmland in the East, the distribution of bounty lands to veterans of the American Revolution, the opening of Ohio to white settlement, and the speculative activities of numerous land companies, Americans were heading westward, eventually crossing the Appalachians into the Ohio and Mississippi River valleys. Kentucky (1792) and Tennessee (1796) had already entered the Union as states, soon to be followed by Ohio in 1803. As western migrations continued, the demographic center of the United States would move from a point twenty-three miles east of Baltimore in 1800 to a point twenty miles south of Chillicothe, Ohio, by 1860. This change reflected not only a geographic shift in population but the gathering momentum of an industrial economy.

The lure of the West was unmistakable in other ways as well. As the region's population grew, a western market emerged as the largely agrarian population looked eastward for manufactured goods and other hard-to-obtain supplies. Northeastern merchants, aware of escalating tensions in Europe and their potential threat to overseas trade, began to cultivate trade with western outposts from Lake Erie to Memphis. But this alternative posed its own problems, the most serious of which was transportation. In 1800, the best trade route to the American West was by water along the Atlantic coast into the Gulf of Mexico and up the Mississippi River to New Orleans. The problem was that the Spanish controlled the port of New Orleans and, through it, all trade that passed up and down the Mississippi from Tennessee, Kentucky, Ohio, western Virginia, and western Pennsylvania. Given the uneasy situation in Europe, this route could be closed to American traffic at any time.

The other option, to ship goods westward via a series of connecting roads, rivers, and canals, was still unformed in

1800. No canal system connected the East Coast with the so-called western waters. Roads became little more than rutted paths after fifty or sixty miles, virtually impassable during mud seasons and always excruciatingly slow and bumpy to travel even in good weather. Stagecoaches, the fastest land conveyances of the day, rarely did better than four or five miles an hour. Larger and heavier freight wagons moved at an even slower pace, often taking weeks to cover 100 miles. Inland transportation throughout the country was not only slow but prohibitively expensive. The lack of well-maintained roads and canals choked commercial development by hindering western farmers from sending their surplus goods to eastern cities and eastern merchants from tapping western markets. Both groups expressed frustration, while rumors spread that the states and territories of the trans-Appalachian West might abandon the Union, form their own republic, and align themselves with the Spanish at New Orleans.

## Setting a Course

Such was the state of affairs when Jefferson became president in March 1801. Well educated, the fifty-seven-year-old Virginian was a lawyer by training, with a distinguished political and diplomatic record. He was also a respected amateur sci-

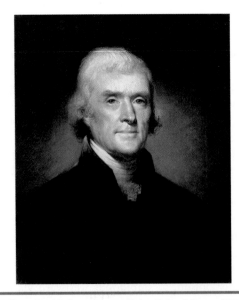

Thomas Jefferson, third president of the United States (1801–09).

entist who counted among his friends some of the world's leading authorities on natural history (encompassing botany and zoology), geology, geography, meteorology, and astronomy. "Science is my passion, politics my duty," he explained to a correspondent in later life. His "fondness for philosophical studies," however, did not prevent him from engaging in practical pursuits. Always interested in agricultural improvements, he had used his mathematical and mechanical skills in 1788 to design a moldboard for turning soil that improved the efficiency of the common plow. As the American ambassador to France (1784–89), he had informed the United States about the latest European innovations in textile machinery, firearms with interchangeable parts, steam engines, and other technological improvements of the age. "I am not afraid of new inventions or improvements," Jefferson later wrote the artist-inventor Robert Fulton. "Where a new invention is supported by well-known principles, and promises to be useful, it ought to be tried."

### JEFFERSON'S SOCIAL VISION

What Jefferson did fear were cities. His reading of classical history suggested that the early republics of Greece and Rome had succumbed to despotism when propertyless people crowded into cities. During his diplomatic stay in Europe, he had witnessed the grinding poverty of Paris and London. Like Benjamin Franklin, Jefferson believed that "manufactures are founded in poverty." It was the poor without land who had to "work for others at low wages or starve." Since most of Europe's manufacturing operations were located in cities, he took a dim view of both. "While we have land to labor," he cautioned, "let us never see our citizens occupied at the workbench. . . . Let our work-shops remain in Europe. . . . The mobs of great cities add just so much to the support of pure government as sores do to the strength of the human body."

The key element in Jefferson's social theory was freehold agriculture. He maintained that the "cultivators of the earth are the most valuable citizens . . . the most independent, the most virtuous, and they are tied to their country and wedded to its liberty and interest by the most lasting bonds." So long as people owned their own farms and worked hard to provide the basic necessities of life, the Republic would survive, even flourish. In order to ensure that sufficient land would be available for freeholders to occupy, Jefferson envisioned the United States expanding relentlessly across the continent. Like other American leaders, he considered it America's God-given destiny. As early as 1792, he proposed an expedition to map the vast territories west of the Mississippi River. Indeed, mapping the country and expanding what he termed "the empire of liberty" would not only preoccupy him as president but remain a goal to his dying day.

Agriculture and expansion constituted the essence of Jefferson's vision for the young Republic. Yet despite his stature as the primary author of the Declaration of Independence and spokesman for democracy in America, his vision had limits. Native Americans, blacks, and other people of color were excluded. Although he frequently decried slavery and called for the gradual emancipation and recolonization of slaves back to Africa, he himself owned as many as 223 slaves and, according to recent DNA and circumstantial evidence, is very likely to have fathered at least one child by a slave concubine, Sally Hemmings. As for machine-based manufacturing, Jefferson was enough of a realist to recognize that it had to be developed to lessen America's dependency on foreign goods and to establish a dynamic domestic economy. But he continued to cast a wary eye on factory enterprises that employed large labor forces. His politics thus reflected a conservative social philosophy that would increasingly conflict with the economic and social currents of the times. Moreover, as president, he became an agent of changes that would fundamentally alter the course of the Republic and set the terms for political debate for at least two generations.

View of Ezekiel Derby's farm near Salem, Massachusetts, c. 1800, by Michele Felice Corne. The orderly appearance of the farm, especially its whitewashed fences, large house, and numerous barns and outbuildings, indicates that the Derbys were prosperous. Most farmers were not as well off.

## Jeffersonian Economy

Jefferson entered office determined to undo the centralizing program of the Federalists and to return governing power to the states. Public finance assumed a high priority, because Jeffersonians believed that the Federalists had enacted protective tariffs and excise taxes that favored eastern merchants and discriminated against their main base of support, farmers and planters. In 1801, most of the nation's $112 million debt accrued from the federal government's assumption of state debts. Jefferson deeply regretted "the dinner table bargain" struck with Alexander Hamilton some ten years earlier that had led to the federal government's assumption of state debts in exchange for locating the national capital on the banks of the Potomac. Whereas Hamilton considered the assumption of debts a national blessing that tied the states closer to the federal government, Jefferson viewed it as a burden and a corrupting influence on government at all levels.

When Jefferson asked Secretary of the Treasury Albert Gallatin to develop a plan for retiring the debt, Gallatin responded by proposing an austerity program that earmarked $7 million a year toward total payment of the debt by 1816. Since the federal government's annual income hovered around $9 million, this left about $2 million for its annual expenses. To stay within such a lean budget, Gallatin proposed making drastic cuts in the

Albert Gallatin, secretary of the treasury in the Jefferson and Madison administrations (1802–14). Painting by Thomas Worthington Whittredge (after Gilbert Stuart).

number of federal employees, particularly those in the military. The intended reductions sought to kill two birds with one stone. Not only would they lower the national debt, but they would also diminish the size of the federal government—something Jefferson considered essential if the United States was to recapture the pristine, states-oriented republicanism of its revolutionary past. "We are hunting out and abolishing multitudes of useless offices," the president wrote with satisfaction to his son-in-law, "striking off jobs, lopping them down silently."

Since Jefferson and Gallatin considered the navy the largest drain on the treasury, they slashed its budget by more than half, intending to leave only one frigate and several smaller gunboats in active service. The army fared better during the Jefferson administration because of its value to American expansion into Indian territory. The president was particularly sensitive to this issue, since some of his strongest support came from western and southern states, where land hunger and expansionism tended to drive politics. Jefferson nonetheless reduced the size of the regular army to 3,350 officers and enlisted men and stationed them either along the western frontier or at East Coast forts remote from large cities. As long as the army remained isolated and out of sight, its existence seemed less troubling to Jeffersonians, who distrusted standing armies as a threat to liberty.

## THE COURT SYSTEM

In the highly partisan environment following the election of 1800, one of the most vexing questions facing the Jefferson administration was the judiciary. Republicans controlled both houses of Congress, but Federalists held the vast majority of federal judgeships, and in the eyes of Jeffersonians virtually all of them were arrogant, undemocratic, and opposed to anything that smacked of republicanism. To make matters worse, the passage of the Judiciary Act early in 1801 created sixteen new circuit court judgeships, allowing the lame-duck president John Adams to pack them with Federalists shortly before he left office. In addition to allowing for these "midnight appointments," the Judiciary Act reduced the number of Supreme Court justices from six to five, threatening to delay and perhaps even prevent Jefferson from appointing anyone to the Court. And when Oliver Ellsworth resigned as chief justice, Adams nominated and the Senate approved Secretary of State John Marshall—a bitter Jefferson enemy—to the post. Jefferson never forgave Adams for these affronts, nor could he tolerate them. Jefferson backed a bill introduced in the Senate in January 1802 to repeal the Judiciary Act and thus do away with the midnight judges and restore the number of Supreme Court justices to six. The bill squeaked through by only one vote, passed the House, and was quickly signed into law by the president.

While the Jeffersonian Republicans succeeded in halting the Federalist effort to expand control over the federal court, the repeal of the Judiciary Act did nothing to check Federalist judges who held earlier appointments. Jefferson and his supporters in Congress decided to use impeachment to remove the most troublesome of these judges from office. Their first victim, a federal district judge from New Hampshire named John Pickering, a chronic alcoholic with serious mental problems, made a relatively easy target. The Republican-dominated House of Representatives moved the case for impeachment, and the Senate convicted and removed him from office in March 1804.

The same day that the House issued its verdict against Judge Pickering, it initiated another major impeachment proceeding. This time, the intended victim was Associate Justice Samuel Chase of the Supreme Court. Well known as a signer of the Declaration of Independence, Chase was an arch-Federalist who, in the view of many Jeffersonians, had exhibited "oppressive and disgusting" partisanship on the bench. Although the case for impeachment was made in the House of Representatives,

Republicans failed to muster the necessary two-thirds majority in the Senate to convict Chase. Federalists hailed the acquittal as a great victory, while most Republicans reacted bitterly to the verdict. Chase returned to his place on the Supreme Court and continued to vilify his Republican opponents until his death in 1811. Although the Supreme Court remained intact with a five-to-one Federalist majority, Jefferson would nonetheless have the opportunity to appoint three Republicans to the bench before he left office.

The most irksome of Adams's appointments, in Jefferson's opinion, was that of John Marshall as chief justice of the Supreme Court. Although distant cousins, Jefferson and Marshall genuinely disliked each other, and over time their mutual dislike grew into open hatred. The tall, thin, black-eyed Marshall was an avowed Federalist who possessed an uncanny ability to construct elaborate arguments that sounded impartial but invariably turned back on his opponents. This quality, coupled with his "lax lounging manners" and "profound hypocrisy," made Jefferson extremely wary of him. "When conversing with Marshall," he confided, "I never admit anything. . . . So great is his sophistry you must never give him an affirmative answer or you will be forced to grant his conclusion. Why if he were to ask me if it were daylight or not, I'd reply, 'Sir, I don't know, I can't tell.' "

John Marshall, chief justice of the U.S. Supreme Court (1801–35). Portrait by James Reid Lambdin (after Henry Inman).

Marshall showed his genius for subtlety in the 1803 case of *Marbury v. Madison.* William Marbury was a minor figure who had been named a justice of the peace in the District of Columbia by President Adams. However, Marbury's letter of appointment had not been delivered to him before Adams left office, and upon Jefferson's inauguration, Secretary of State James Madison refused to deliver it. Marbury hired a lawyer who went to the Supreme Court to compel Madison to perform his "duty."

The resulting decision, written by Marshall, made two points. On the one hand, it asserted that Marbury had a right to his commission and publicly chided the Jefferson administration for refusing to deliver it. However, after chastising the president, the decision stated, on the other hand, that the Court had no authority to order Madison to deliver Marbury's commission, because the congressional legislation that had granted that authority under the Judiciary Act of 1789 exceeded the constitutionally defined powers of the judiciary and was therefore null and void.

The decision revealed Marshall's genius at its maddening best. On the surface, the Supreme Court appeared to hand the president a victory by refusing to force Madison to deliver Marbury's commission. At a deeper level, however, the Marshall Court, while seemingly constricting its authority, was actually expanding it. In *Marbury v. Madison,* the Court relinquished a relatively minor power regarding the delivery of commissions in order to assert a much greater power in nullifying an act of Congress as unconstitutional. In doing so, it established not only the precedent for judicial review but also the Supreme Court's right to interpret the meaning of the Constitution.

### THE LOUISIANA PURCHASE

As America's population grew and increasing numbers of white settlers looked westward for affordable land, events were unfolding that would dramatically change the map of America and influence the nation's political, economic, and social development for much of the nineteenth century. At issue was the so-called Louisiana Territory, a vast area that stretched from the Mississippi River in the East to the Rocky Mountains in the West and north to Canada. Like many Americans, Jefferson harbored the belief that Louisiana would some day belong to the United States. It was thought that control of Louisiana, long considered a natural extension of the United States, loomed critical in defending the country's expanding frontier against Indian raids and foreign adventurers as well as serving

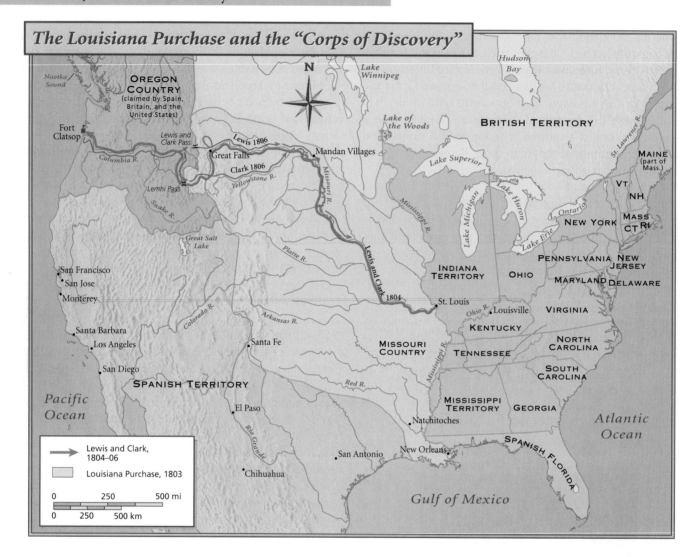

The Louisiana Purchase and the "Corps of Discovery"

as a valuable source of raw materials—most notably the lucrative western fur trade. Most important, in Jefferson's view, the Louisiana Territory would be America's safety valve: a seemingly limitless territory to which Indians could be removed ahead of white settlement and, above all, a place where landless immigrants from the East might move to carry on the American agrarian tradition that he deemed so essential to the well-being of the Republic.

Controlled for most of the colonial period by the French, Louisiana had been ceded to Spain in 1763, following France's defeat in the Seven Years' War. So long as Spain, now the "sick man of Europe," held Louisiana, Jefferson was content to wait for the inevitable day when American settlers would sweep

into the trans-Mississippi West and take it by default. Contentment turned to concern, however, when news reached Washington in May 1801 that Spain, with its colonial empire in shambles, had secretly ceded the Louisiana Territory as well as the city of New Orleans back to France. Spanish control of the Louisiana region was one thing; French control was quite another—especially because Napoleon Bonaparte had recently come to power and had designs on reestablishing a French empire in North America. Jefferson learned in the fall of 1802 that officials in charge of New Orleans had suddenly closed its port as well as the entire lower Mississippi to American commerce. Outraged westerners, who shipped their products to eastern markets through New Orleans and numbered among Jefferson's strongest supporters, began to call for military action against the French. Jefferson responded by urging Congress to appropriate funds for possible military action against New Orleans. In the meantime, he instructed the American ambassador to France, Robert Livingston, to approach Napoleon about selling New Orleans to the United States and sent his old friend and ally Governor James Monroe of Virginia to join the negotiations.

That mission had a surprising outcome, one directly related to the success of black revolutionaries on the island of Saint Domingue (Haiti). Thanks in part to the Federalists' efforts to maintain trade with Saint Domingue, the black leader Toussaint Louverture could get the supplies he needed to defeat the efforts of France and other European countries to put down the Haitian revolution. Jefferson had opposed trade with Saint Domingue for fear it would allow the spirit of black insurrection to spread from there to the American South. He also refused to recognize the independent republic of Haiti after it was founded in 1804. There he had the support of others from the slave South, who would do nothing that might seem to legitimate the Haitians' revolution. (Indeed, the United States did not recognize Haiti until 1862, when Southern states had left the union.) And yet the islands' success in holding off France along with Napoleon's need to finance a renewed war with Britain led him to make Jefferson an offer that became one of the greatest achievements of Jefferson's presidency. Napoleon offered to sell not only New Orleans, but all of Louisiana to the United States for $15 million (80 million francs). Presented with the prospect of nearly doubling the area of the United States at the price of three cents an acre, Livingston and Monroe moved quickly to seal the bargain before Napoleon could change his mind. They decided to proceed without Jefferson's formal approval and signed an agreement with the French government on April 30, 1803.

Once the official documents reached Washington, Jefferson, though pleased with the deal, faced a dilemma. As someone who believed in a strict interpretation of the Constitution, he knew that the nation's governing document contained nothing about the acquisition of new territory. The proper procedure would have been to amend the Constitution before making the purchase, but time was of the essence. With overwhelming public approval and the urging of his closest advisers, Jefferson decided to send the treaty forward to Congress for approval. After all, he had the power to make treaties, and by doing so in this instance he was avoiding war. Although Louisiana's $15 million price tag amounted to about twice the government's annual revenue, Congress quickly sanctioned the treaty and appropriated the money. Even leading Federalists like John Adams, Alexander Hamilton, and John Marshall approved of the action. For his part, Jefferson never held that the purchase was constitutional. He would later observe that "it is incumbent on those who accept great charges to risk themselves on great occasions," adding that "to lose our country by a scrupulous adherence to written laws, would be to lose the law itself." Jefferson was willing to take the risk, even if it meant compromising his principles. On December 20, 1803, Spanish officials at St. Louis turned over control of the Louisiana Territory to an American delegation.

The timing of the Louisiana Purchase could not have been better, for Jefferson had already decided to send a "Corps of Discovery" across the continent in search of a northwest passage to the Pacific Ocean. To carry out this mission, he selected Meriwether Lewis, a young Virginian who had served with General Anthony Wayne in the Old Northwest (the area including the present-day Ohio, Indiana, Illinois, Michigan, and Wisconsin) and most recently as his private secretary. Lewis's "talent for observation" coupled with his army service and knowledge of the "Western country" (including its plants and animals) made him the perfect candidate for the job. Lewis, in turn, asked that an old Army friend, William Clark, join him as joint commander of the enterprise, and Jefferson approved.

## LEWIS AND CLARK

Secrecy surrounded the expedition until news of the Louisiana Purchase became public. In the meantime, Jefferson gave Lewis access to his large personal library of scientific works and tutored him in meteorology, geography, surveying, and paleontology (fossil study). He also sent Lewis to Lancaster and Philadelphia, Pennsylvania, for an intensive two-month period of more formal training with prominent natural scientists. In addition to studying botany, paleontology, medicine, mathematics, and navigational astronomy, Lewis learned how to use sextants and other scientific instruments necessary for making observations and plotting the course of the Corps of Discovery. Before leaving Philadelphia in late June 1803, he purchased navigational instruments (including a $250 chronometer, the most expensive item carried on the expedition) and standard reference books on astronomy, mineralogy, botany, and other subjects as well as a supply of medicines for the journey. Provided with an order from the secretary of war, he also acquired rifles and muskets as well as an iron boat frame from the

## Jeffersonian Economy

### American Journal

### What's for Dinner?

*As Lewis and Clark made their way up the Missouri River during the fall of 1804, they encountered numerous tribes with whom they sought to establish friendly relations. One group was the Teton Sioux, whom the expedition met at the mouth of the Bad River near present-day Pierre, South Dakota. Although their four-day stay (September 24–28) began and ended with tense moments, the intervening two days were spent feasting and dancing, as Lewis and Clark described in their diaries.*

"September 26th. Captains Lewis and Clark, who went on shore one after the other, were met on landing by ten well-dressed young men, who took them up in a robe highly decorated and carried them to a large council-house, where they were placed on a dressed buffalo-skin by the side of the grand chief. The hall or council-room was in the shape of three-quarters of a circle, covered at the top and sides with skins well dressed and sewed together. Under this shelter sat about 70 men, forming a circle round the chief, before whom were placed a Spanish flag and the one we had given them yesterday. This left a vacant circle of about six feet diameter, in which the pipe of peace was raised on two forked sticks, about six or eight inches from the ground, and under it the down of the swan was scattered. A large fire, in which they were cooking provisions, stood near, and in the center about 400 pounds of buffalo meat as a present for us. As soon as we were seated, an old man got up, and after approving what we had done, begged us take pity on their unfortunate situation. To this we replied with assurances of protection. After he had ceased, the great chief rose and delivered a harangue to the same effect; then with great solemnity he took some of the most delicate parts of the dog which was cooked for the festival, and held it to the flag by way of sacrifice; this done, he held up the pipe of peace, and first pointed it toward the heavens, then to the four quarters of the globe, then to the earth, made a short speech, lighted the pipe, and presented it to us. We smoked, and he again harangued his people, after which the repast was served up to us. It consisted of the dog which they had just been cooking, this being a great dish among the Sioux, used on all festivals; to which were added [pemmican], a dish made of buffalo-meat, dried or jerked and then pounded and mixed raw with grease; and a kind of ground potato, dressed like the preparation of Indian corn called hominy, to which it is little inferior. Of all these luxuries, which were placed before us in platters, with horn spoons, we took the [pemmican] and the potato, which we found good, but we could as yet partake but sparingly of the dog. We eat and smoked for an hour, when it became dark. Everything was then cleared away for the dance, a large fire being made in the center of the house, giving at once light and warmth to the ballroom."

Elliott Coues, ed., *History of the Expedition under the Command of Lewis and Clark*

Harpers Ferry National Armory. All told, Lewis assembled over 2,300 pounds of supplies and equipment, enough to fill two large Conestoga wagons for the difficult overland journey to Pittsburgh and, from there, by keelboat down the Ohio River toward the Missouri Country.

On July 5, 1803, the day after news reached the capital that France had formally agreed to sell the Louisiana Territory to the United States, Lewis quietly departed Washington on the first leg of his western journey; he subsequently rendezvoused with Clark at Louisville, Kentucky, in November. Then the two set off for their winter encampment about eighteen miles north of St. Louis, near the entrance to the Missouri River. In May 1804, the Corps of Discovery, comprising twenty-nine carefully selected men, boarded their keelboat and proceeded to row, pole, and pull their way up the Missouri.

It was a treacherous and dangerous journey. Several of their original calculations proved wrong. Having planned to cross the continent primarily by water, Lewis and Clark assumed they would have to carry their boats only a short distance from the headwaters of the Missouri River to the headwaters of the Columbia River and believed that the whole trip would take from eighteen months to two years. They had no idea that the terrain would be so difficult or that they would have to forage off the land in order to avoid starvation. The available technology of 1803–06 did not allow for any single mode of transportation to be used by such a large party: they started with boats, then switched to horses, then back again to boats. Besides foraging for food, the men depended on trade with local Indian tribes, not all of whom were friendly.

The party slowly ascended the Missouri River, taking over five months to reach their winter quarters with the Mandan people about sixty miles above the present-day site of Bismarck, North Dakota. Here they enlisted a French Canadian trapper named Charbonneau and his fifteen-year-old Shoshone Indian wife, Sacagawea, as interpreters and guides. Described by Lewis as a woman of "fortitude and resolution," Sacagawea played a critical role as an interpreter to the native peoples the party encountered and as a provider of wild artichokes and other foods that supplemented the group's diet of buffalo and elk meat. Equally important, her presence with the Corps of Discovery, in Clark's words, "reconciles all the Indians, as to our friendly intentions," because "a woman with a party of men is a token of peace."

Upon leaving the Mandans in April 1805, the party pushed up the Missouri River and around the falls at present-day Great Falls, Montana, where they encountered their first grizzly bear. Then they moved into the Rocky and Cascade Mountains, desperately looking for a passage through the mountains and down the Snake and Columbia rivers to the Pacific Ocean. Even with the help of Sacagawea's people, who provided them with horses and information about the mountainous terrain, it was a difficult passage that brought near starvation before they reached the Columbia. Moving downriver, in November 1805, they reached the Pacific, where they built a fort named "Clatsop" after a local Indian tribe and settled in for a long rainy winter.

The following March the Corps began its trek homeward, going up the Columbia and recrossing the mountains, where the group divided into two parties to explore parts of present-day Montana. They rejoined at the junction of the Yellowstone and Missouri rivers, excited about the prospect of returning home and not realizing that many at home had given them up for lost. The party moved quickly down the Missouri, sometimes covering seventy to eighty miles a day, until they reached St. Louis on September 21, 1806, nearly two and a half years after setting out. A triumphant reception

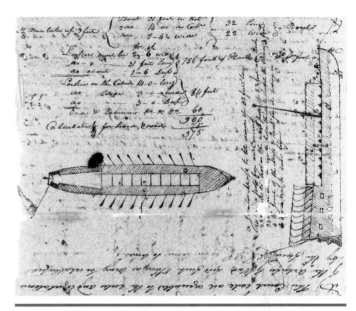

William Clark's sketch of the fifty-five-foot keelboat made at Pittsburgh for the expedition. Capable of carrying twenty-two men and twelve tons of supplies and equipment, the boat proved difficult to manage in the rapidly flowing currents of the Missouri River.

awaited them in St. Louis. As shots rang out, nearly all of the town's 1,000 residents lined the riverfront to greet them with shouts and cheers.

Throughout their travels, Lewis and Clark followed Jefferson's detailed instructions to the letter, making daily observations of climatic conditions, collecting hundreds of specimens, and keeping detailed journals that recorded not only the plants, minerals, and wildlife of the regions visited but also ethnographic information about the native peoples they encountered. They also noted the topographical "face of the country" and took "observations of latitude & longitude, at all remarkable points" during their journey. Above all, they heeded the president's injunction to make their observations "with great pains & accuracy" so that they would be of use "for others" as well as themselves.

Newspapers from Kentucky to New York hailed the return of Lewis and Clark, emphasizing their bravery and pointing to the national benefits of the expedition. Although Jefferson had initially characterized the expedition as a "literary" venture, its real purpose was to locate "the most direct and practicable water communication across this continent for the purposes of commerce" and to solidify American claims not only to the Rocky Mountain region but also to the Oregon

Country beyond. The most immediate beneficiaries of the expedition's discoveries were the fur companies, who straightaway used the knowledge accumulated by Lewis and Clark to extend their network of trading posts deep into the upper reaches of the Missouri River. In the process, they would trap beaver to near extinction.

But Jefferson had more in mind than the fur trade. In his view, the maps Lewis and Clark prepared would also serve to guide white settlers into these areas and thus extend the "empire of liberty." For him, the West represented America's future. Even before Lewis and Clark returned home, three other federally sponsored expeditions (two military, one civilian) had headed up the Red River to explore the still-disputed southern boundary of the newly acquired Louisiana Territory. And there would be many more, owing primarily to Lewis and Clark's resounding success. In effect, they created a model for army exploration of the American West that would continue throughout the nineteenth century.

Lewis and Clark also established themselves as pioneering naturalists by contributing to a better scientific understanding of the regions they explored. Along the way, they collected botanical, mineral, and animal specimens as well as Indian artifacts, which they transported in crates back to the president in Washington. Jefferson kept some of these materials for his personal collection at Monticello, his Virginia plantation, but most of them ended up in Philadelphia, adorning the collections of the American Philosophical Society, the Academy of Natural Sciences, and painter Charles Willson Peale's well-known museum of natural history. Among the more notable specimens were the hides and skeletal remains of a bighorn sheep, a pronghorn antelope, several elk, and a grizzly bear. There were also numerous bird skins, and 216 sheets of dried, pressed plants representing 173 different species, 70 to 75 of which were completely new to the world of science.

Largely as a result of Lewis and Clark's collecting activities, Philadelphia became the leading center in America for the study of natural history. Before the arrival of these specimens, the trans-Mississippi West was a remote area "of rumor, guess, and fantasy." But Lewis and Clark's artifacts and specimens began to put a face on the West, greatly stimulating public interest. Aspiring artists, explorers, and scientists began making plans to visit the "high country" in order to collect, record, and make discoveries of their own. Leading them all were units of the United States Army, whose wagon roads, topographical surveys, maps, and fortified settlements paved the way for the many "crossings" that would follow.

## Troubled Times

With his party's popularity at an all-time high, Thomas Jefferson easily won reelection in 1804: he carried every state but two (Connecticut and Delaware) and overwhelmed his Federalist opponent, Charles Cotesworth Pinckney of South Carolina, by 162 electoral votes to 14. The election not only signaled the decline of the Federalist Party, but it also revealed how personal ambition and extremist political maneuvering continually threatened the fragile Republic. Already in turmoil, the Federalist Party suffered a crushing blow before the election when Vice-President Aaron Burr shot and killed Alexander Hamilton in a July 1804 duel at Weehawken, New Jersey. Burr, always a political schemer, had long since parted ways with Jefferson over the 1800 election deadlock, and he was dumped from the Republican ticket long before the 1804 election. He became involved with an extremist Federalist faction (known as the "Essex Junto") that advocated the establishment of a separate nation called the "Northern Confederacy," consisting of the New England states as well as New York and New Jersey. Urged on by separatist friends in the Federalist Party, Burr ran for governor in New York in February 1804 and was denounced by Hamilton as a traitor and a "despicable" character. Burr lost. He blamed his defeat on Hamilton, and the deadly duel was the result.

With Hamilton's death, the Federalist Party deteriorated, and Burr became a political outcast. Forced to flee to avoid prosecution for murder, he became involved in another political intrigue that involved capturing Mexico, separating part of the newly acquired Louisiana Territory from the United States, and establishing a western empire under his rule. Although Jefferson knew of Burr's activities, he did not take action until word reached him in November 1806 that Burr and a group of armed supporters were heading down the Ohio River to attack New Orleans. Jefferson ordered Burr's arrest for treason and had him returned to Richmond, Virginia, for trial. When a jury presided over by Chief Justice Marshall acquitted Burr, an irate Jefferson had him rearrested on other charges and sought to move the trial to a friendlier court in Ohio. Before he could do that, however, the wily Marshall

### The Knell.

At New-York, on Thursday last, of a wound received the morning previous, in a duel with Col. Burr, Gen. ALEXANDER HAMILTON. We are not enabled to add particulars, nor are we disposed to offer any reflections on this melancholy event, at present. In some future number, we shall endeavor to evince our respect for this truly great man.

The gentlemen of the bar, who were attending the Circuit at Claverack, on hearing the confirmation of the above intelligence, unanimously agreed to wear a crape on the left arm for one month, as a token of their regard for Gen. Hamilton.

Alexander Hamilton's obituary as it appeared in *The Balance and Columbian Repository* of Hudson, New York.

freed Burr on bond and the former vice-president escaped to Europe, his career in shambles.

## WINDS OF WAR

The same escalating tensions in Europe that had initially benefited the United States with Napoleon's decision to sell Louisiana soon led to a quagmire in foreign affairs. American overseas trade had prospered since the mid-1790s. Owing to their status as neutral carriers, Yankee shippers enjoyed a lucrative trade with Great Britain and the British West Indies as well as a rapidly growing reexport trade in tropical produce (coffee, sugar, indigo, leather hides, etc.) with French and Spanish colonies in the East and West Indies, Latin America, and the Philippine Islands. America's merchant marine was rapidly becoming the largest in the Atlantic, something that did not go unnoticed by British merchants, who longed to tap into the markets of Spain's vast but weakening Latin American empire. Conditions began to change in 1803, however, when the perennial enemies France and England went to war for the fourth time in fifty years. This time, hostilities would not cease until the defeated Napoleon was permanently banished to the island of St. Helena in 1815.

During the first two years of the so-called Napoleonic Wars, world prices for farm goods (like cotton and wheat) rose, and the American carrying trade boomed as England and France clashed on land and at sea. By 1805, the two powers had become virtually stalemated, with England in command of the sea and France firmly in control of the European Continent. At that point, the two belligerents began to supplement direct military action with indirect economic warfare. Britain acted first by issuing a series of Orders in Council that, in effect, sought to blockade Napoleonic Europe by ordering all vessels going there to stop first in English ports, submit to inspections of their cargoes, pay certain fees, and obtain clearance papers to proceed. Not to be outdone, Napoleon responded with a series of decrees that threatened the seizure of any vessel that complied with the British blockade.

The United States repeatedly protested the warring countries' violations of America's rights as a neutral nation, but to no avail. Of the two, Britain posed the greater threat to American commerce because its navy controlled the sea lanes and could pounce on merchant ships almost at will. Much to America's consternation, British forces frequently halted American ships within sight of the U.S. coastline as well as on the high seas. Moreover, the British seized not just contraband cargoes but also seamen who were suspected of either deserting from the British navy or being British subjects and therefore liable to impressment (forcible enlistment) in the British navy. Yet despite continued harassment by England and France, American seaborne trade experienced a healthy 12.5 percent increase between 1805 and 1807. Even in the midst of wartime prohibitions and seizures, merchants stood to make considerable profits if only one ship in three evaded its pursuers.

Of all the depredations committed on American commerce, the most controversial were the British navy's impressment procedures. Between 1793 and 1811, nearly 1,000 seamen were forcibly removed from American vessels and pressed into British service. Although estimates vary, foreigners (many of whom were Englishmen) constituted between one-third and one-half of the labor force in the American merchant marine. Desperately short of manpower, officers of the Royal Navy paid little attention to naturalization papers that claimed American citizenship and took anyone they suspected of being British. On at least two occasions between 1798 and 1805, British warships even stopped vessels of the United States Navy and took off suspected deserters. Such actions aroused public indignation. In the spring of 1806, for example, a riot broke out in New York after an American seaman died when hit by a shot fired from the British HMS *Leander*. Although Thomas Jefferson retaliated by ordering the arrest of the *Leander*'s captain and banning it and its sister ship from taking on water and provisions in American ports, British searches and seizures continued unabated.

### THE EMBARGO OF 1807

The crisis came in the summer of 1807, when news arrived from Norfolk, Virginia, that the British ship *Leopard* had fired on the American frigate *Chesapeake* and inflicted twenty-one casualties before British officers boarded the American vessel and hauled off four suspected deserters. The country pulsed

A patriotic American cartoon published during the war, showing the American snapping turtle "Ograbme" ("embargo" spelled backward) attacking a British merchant.

with anger as reports of the *Chesapeake* affair filled the newspapers. "Never since the battle of Lexington have I seen the country in such a state of exasperation," Jefferson noted. With a majority in Congress behind him, he probably could have secured an immediate declaration of war. But recognizing that the United States was ill prepared for conflict with a major European power, he instead closed all American ports to the Royal Navy and instructed the American ambassador in England to demand reparations as well as a complete renunciation of British impressment. Although Prime Minister George Canning agreed to recall the officer responsible for firing on the *Chesapeake*, return three of the four captured sailors (one had already been hanged for desertion), compensate the families of those killed or wounded in the incident, and promise not to board American navy vessels in the future, he reasserted his government's right to use force in retrieving deserters from the Royal Navy.

Rebuffed yet again, Jefferson had three options. He could call for a declaration of war, do nothing, or impose trade sanctions on Great Britain. In the Non-Importation Act of 1806, Congress had already authorized him to prohibit the importation of certain products from the British empire. But Jefferson had come to believe that even stronger measures were needed. He therefore called on Congress to pass a bill that would impose a total trade embargo not only on England and France but on all nations. In effect, the United States would wall itself off from the rest of the world; no ships would leave the country, and none would enter. Convinced that neither England nor France—but especially England, since the United States absorbed nearly 45 percent of its exports—could do without American trade, Jefferson expected that both countries would abandon their seizure policies. Although merchants strongly protested the measure and Secretary of the Treasury Gallatin remained skeptical that economic coercion would bring favorable results, the Republican Congress nonetheless passed the Embargo Act, and Jefferson signed it into law on December 22, 1807.

The embargo represented an eighteenth-century response to a nineteenth-century crisis. Remembering the various boycotts and nonimportation agreements employed during the revolutionary era, Jefferson and the Republican Congress turned to them again in the hope that they would force Britain and France to recognize American rights as neutral traders. However, much had changed since the Revolution. During the quarter century since 1781, the United States had assembled one of the largest merchant marines in the world—one that operated on a global scale. The trade that flowed from it put hard cash in the pockets of easterners and brought unprecedented prosperity not only to the Eastern Seaboard but also to inland areas that participated in its larger mercantile network. By imposing a complete trade embargo on the nation, Jefferson and his Republican colleagues seemed out of step with the times and unable to recognize the larger economic implications of their political actions. In this respect, the embargo represented a mismatch between the expanding economy and the eighteenth-century ideas that informed the Jeffersonian approach to political economy.

The Embargo Act brought almost immediate economic disaster. In 1808 alone, trade plummeted by more than 80 percent, and prices for leading farm exports like cotton and wheat fell by 23 percent. America's mercantile sector, a primary source of national income and economic growth, stood in shambles. Moreover, although Jefferson had anticipated that the embargo would be painful for merchants, he had no idea that it would hit farmers hard as well. Wheat prices fell from a high of two dollars a bushel to less than ten cents, and tobacco was practically worthless. Once-prosperous planters and farmers found themselves saddled with debt and declining property values. Yet, bad as things were, Jefferson clung tenaciously to the hope that England and France would eventually yield and recognize America's rights as a neutral country. In the meantime, he prepared for the worst.

As the depression worsened, evasions of the embargo multiplied. From Maine through upstate New York and all along the Canadian border, smuggling operations rapidly expanded. Even greater evasions took place along the Atlantic Seaboard as ships slipped out to sea and headed for foreign ports under the pretense of engaging in coastal trade with other American cities. By August 1808, Gallatin had become convinced that the embargo was a failure. "The embargo is now defeated," he wrote gloomily to the president, "by open violations, by vessels sailing without any clearances whatever." Still, Jefferson persisted in the belief that England and France would relent.

Willing to use "all means . . . by force of arms or otherwise" to suppress popular resistance to the embargo, Jefferson came dangerously close to subverting civil liberties in the interest of enforcing the law. Indeed, there was much that seemed distinctly Hamiltonian in his policies by the end of his second term. He seemed unconcerned that the embargo contradicted Republican principles by concentrating unprecedented power in the hands of the chief executive and by allowing him to deploy the army and navy against civilians

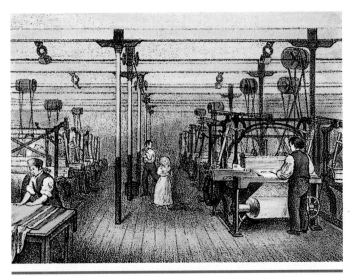

A weave room in an early New England cotton textile mill. Women and children as well as men worked in the mills.

for purposes of enforcement. Nor did he overly concern himself with the protections against unreasonable searches and seizures granted by the Fourth Amendment.

*The Emerging Factory System.* With the embargo, Jefferson, the apostle of agrarianism, unwittingly opened the door to a fundamental change in the American economy. Adventuresome entrepreneurs seized on unexpected advantages that the embargo dropped into their laps. With overseas commerce at a virtual standstill and British products cut off from American markets, entrepreneurs shifted their capital into machine-based manufacturing and, in some cases, expanded earlier operations. Such was the case with Samuel Slater of Pawtucket, Rhode Island. Having established a pioneering cotton-spinning mill with two Providence merchants (Almy and Brown) in 1790, Slater struck out on his own in 1799 and expanded his holdings to three different textile mills by 1811. He would become involved with at least a dozen other businesses related to textile manufacturing before he died in 1835.

Nor was Slater an exception. Between 1807 and 1810, the number of textile mills in the United States jumped from fifteen to eighty-seven. All along the Atlantic Seaboard, new manufacturing ventures in textiles and other consumer products took up the slack created by the exclusion of British manufactures. The significance of this new market was unmistakable not only to budding entrepreneurs like Slater but also to seasoned merchants. They had made a lot of money in international trade between 1793 and 1807 and now looked to manufacturing.

The sudden onset of what one of Slater's partners called "cotton mill fever" had yet another important economic implication. It partially substituted for the losses sustained by southern planters when the bottom dropped out of the lucrative cotton-export market with the embargo. In 1807, the total volume of American cotton exports to foreign countries approached 70 million pounds. After plummeting to around 15 million pounds in 1808, the market rebounded to reach an all-time high of 90 million in 1810, as prospects for peace brightened briefly, only to tumble again with the outbreak of the War of 1812. Yet even in the midst of lower prices and cordoned export markets, the decrease in total cotton production in the South was not dramatic. Established as well as prospective planters, eyeing cotton as a lucrative cash crop, continued to place new lands under cultivation. The demand for slave labor intensified, and pressure increased on Indian tribes in Georgia, Alabama, and Mississippi to relinquish their ancestral lands in the face of white expansion.

*A New Role for Government.* In addition to its impact on cotton markets and the textile industry, the embargo had two other significant and unforeseen consequences. One had to do with building a national transportation system; the other, with the manufacture of firearms for military purposes.

The population growth and westward movement of this period fed a groundswell in favor of a publicly supported system of roads and canals. These appeals found a sympathetic listener in Secretary of the Treasury Gallatin, a resident of western Pennsylvania who owned several manufacturing ventures. His "Report on Roads and Canals," issued in 1808, called for a ten-year program of federal aid to private development projects amounting to $20 million or more. Gallatin justified this aggressive proposal for federal intervention into the economy by arguing that a national system of roads and canals "will shorten distances, facilitate commercial and personal intercourse, and unite, by a still more intimate community of interests, the most remote quarters of the United States," thus "strengthen[ing] the bonds of union." Above all, he maintained that strong federal support for such "internal improvements" would "stimulate the spirit of enterprise so conspicuous in the American character." Once such enterprises were stable, the government would withdraw its support and allow them to operate on their own.

Gallatin's proposal cast the federal government in a new, even unique, role as a venture capitalist. At the same time, he inadvertently advanced a novel thesis concerning national economic development: government in/government out. The federal government should intervene in the marketplace to reduce the risks associated with the early stages of industrial and technological innovation, and then withdraw once these enterprises became profitable. Gallatin's strategy surpassed Alexander Hamilton's famous 1791 "Report on Manufactures" in boldness and vision. His report would subsequently be looked upon as a great planning document, a model of its kind.

Little came of Gallatin's proposal at first. The embargo slashed tariff revenues, and the anticipated surplus of government funds intended to pay for the program vanished. Nevertheless, one project, begun before his report was issued, survived. This was the so-called Cumberland, or National, Road, the first federally funded highway in

The Fairview Inn on the busy Cumberland/National Road near Baltimore, painted by Thomas Coke Ruckle, 1814. Note the Conestoga freight wagons (often used by settlers moving west) on the lower right, drovers taking a herd of cattle to market (lower left), and the stagecoach (left center).

America. Although sanctioned by Congress in 1806, actual construction of the road (which ran from Baltimore westward through Cumberland, Maryland; Wheeling, Virginia [now West Virginia]; and Columbus, Ohio; to Vandalia, Illinois) did not begin until after the War of 1812. Even then, Jeffersonian Republicans questioned the constitutionality of using federal funds to construct and maintain it. Only after intensive lobbying by western congressmen did the road get built. In the end, it took forty-four years for the National Road to reach Vandalia, some sixty-five miles short of its projected destination at St. Louis. Clearly, the bonds that would eventually link the Republic together were tied slowly and with great political difficulty.

While Gallatin fashioned his report on roads and canals, Congress in 1808 passed an Act for Arming and Equipping the Militia that provided an annual appropriation of $200,000 to buy small arms and other military equipment. The legislation was part of an ongoing effort to bring more uniformity to what federal authorities considered undisciplined and ineffectual state-controlled militia units. Nineteen manufacturers—most of them small ventures with fewer than twenty or thirty employees, located in either New England's Connecticut Valley or the Philadelphia area—signed contracts with the War Department. Of the 85,200 smoothbore muskets contracted for, slightly less than half were actually delivered.

Although the effort to equip the militia produced, at best, mixed results, the act of 1808 established an important precedent by indirectly subsidizing the development of a firearms industry. During the next twenty years, several dozen small start-up firms received federal contracts to manufacture swords, muskets, pistols, and rifles for distribution to state governments. As Eli Whitney had in 1798, some of these contractors received monetary advances from the federal government that helped them set up their businesses. They were viewed as supplementing the output of the national armories at Springfield, Massachusetts, and Harpers Ferry, Virginia. Chronic problems persisted over the quality of arms delivered to the government, and many contractors continued to default on their contracts. Yet despite these shortcomings, the so-called contract system subsidized a half-dozen inventive arms makers who, over the years, would play a key role in the development of interchangeable manufacturing methods and, more broadly, the establishment of the American machine tool industry. Foremost among them was Simeon North, a blacksmith-turned-arms-maker from Middletown,

Connecticut, who, in addition to becoming a highly skilled artisan, first introduced the modern milling machine around 1817. As "machines that made machines," milling machines and other such tools proved fundamentally important to the advent of the industrial revolution in America.

## A FATEFUL SPIRAL

Faced with a failed embargo, a country in economic and political turmoil, and wavering support within Congress and his own cabinet, Thomas Jefferson had no desire to seek a third term in the election of 1808. He thus felt relieved when his old friend and ally James Madison received the Republican nomination for president.

Madison handily won the election, but not by the resounding majority that had reelected Jefferson four years earlier. The Federalist candidate, again Charles Cotesworth Pinckney, made a much stronger showing this time, and his party gained twenty-four seats in Congress, even though Republicans continued to control both houses. The election campaign revealed the extent of division the embargo had left behind. Although Jefferson continued to defend the measure, he recognized that it had failed to serve its purpose. A few days before leaving office, he supported a congressional motion to repeal the embargo and replace it with the Non-Intercourse Act, which reopened trade with all nations except Great Britain and France. Convinced that war would soon follow, Jefferson spent his last days in Washington taking care of personal affairs and awaiting Madison's inauguration.

War *would* follow, but not as quickly as Jefferson had anticipated. In 1810, when the Non-Intercourse Act expired, Congress replaced it with Macon's Bill Number Two. This law restored commerce with both Britain and France while promising that if one of them repealed its restrictions against American commerce, the United States would immediately cease trading with the other. Seeing an opportunity to turn America against England, Napoleon announced that France would revoke its decrees against neutral shipping, adding shrewdly, "it being understood that the English are to revoke their orders in council." Although John Quincy Adams, son of the former president and the American ambassador to Russia, cautioned Madison that Napoleon was setting a trap "to catch us in a war with England," the president took the bait and announced that nonintercourse would be reinstated against Great Britain.

Much to Madison's chagrin, Napoleon showed promptly that he had no intention of living up to the bargain. During the next two years, the French continued to seize American merchant vessels, while relations between Britain and the United States deteriorated to the point of all-out war. Ironically, two days before Congress formally approved a declaration of war in June 1812, the British government, under pressure at home, suspended its orders in council against American shipping. But this news, brought by sailing vessel, came too late to Washington. By then, other events had occurred to hasten the conflict.

## Mr. Madison's War

The first shots in the War of 1812 were fired not on the high seas but rather along America's trans-Appalachian frontier. There the continuing incursions of white settlers and the aggressive behavior of their political leaders brought conflict with Indians from the Great Lakes to the Gulf of Mexico. Indian tribes east of the Mississippi River had long-standing grievances against whites. Beginning in 1783 with the Treaty of Paris, Great Britain had abandoned its Indian allies by failing to reserve any tracts of land for them and instead granted to the United States all the territory from the Atlantic coast to the Mississippi. Thereafter, many tribes had been pressured or even forced at gunpoint to relinquish huge tracts to the federal government. During the administrations of Jefferson and Madison, for example, fifty-three treaties of cession were signed with various Indian leaders, through which the United States obtained millions of acres of land in return for annual payments and promises not to intrude further into their hunting grounds. But treaties signed were almost always broken, as white settlement continued to spread during the early decades of the nineteenth century. In Indiana alone, the white population surged from 5,600 in 1800 to 24,500 in 1810 and to over 147,000 by 1820. Similar trends could be found throughout the Old Northwest as well as farther south in the Mississippi Territory, where the influx of white settlers and their slaves, attracted by lands suited for raising cotton, soon outnumbered the native inhabitants.

As far as the U.S. government was concerned, nothing was allowed to stand in the way of territorial expansion. Even Jefferson, who wrote with admiration about Native Americans and greeted their leaders with respect, frankly acknowledged in a letter to the governor of Ohio that "our settlements will gradually circumscribe and approach the Indians and they will in time either incorporate with us as citizens of the United States or remove beyond the Mississippi. . . . They must see that we have only to shut our hand to crush them, and that all our liberalities to them proceed from motives of pure humanity only." These remarks capture not only Jefferson's personal attitude but also his policy as president. In his view, Native Americans were doomed regardless of whether they abandoned their nomadic, hunting-oriented ways and assimilated into white culture or were driven by force beyond the Mississippi. Eventually, their history would be terminated by the inexorable march of white civilization. Although Jefferson denied that he had ordained this fate, he felt no compunction about implementing strategies that would bring it about.

Other than the use of force, federal officials—Jefferson among them—devised sophisticated schemes for securing land from various Indian groups. One of the most effective ways was to establish government trading posts on or near Indian lands. At these outposts, blankets, cloth, ammunition, and iron tools were exchanged for beeswax, deerskins, and other animal pelts. But the trading posts also existed to extend credit to tribal leaders and draw them into debt. Although he didn't invent this strategy, Jefferson encouraged it. The essential idea was to get tribes to turn over land in payment for their debts. By entangling Indians in a chronic cycle of indebtedness, the federal government, often working with

Tecumseh, the Shawnee war chief and champion of an Indian confederacy, wanted to stop American settlement in the Midwest. The artist and date of the portrait are unknown.

Tenskwatawa "The Prophet," brother of Tecumseh and leader against American expansion in the Midwest, in a portrait by George Catlin, 1830.

private trading companies and land speculators, acquired vast tracts at a pittance.

## THE PROPHET AND TECUMSEH

Given the ongoing tensions between white settlers and Native Americans, it was only a matter of time before the Indians' festering resentments hardened into widespread resistance. During the summer of 1805, a Shawnee holy man named Tenskwatawa ("the open door"), having fallen into a trance and experienced a spiritual awakening, began to call on his people to reject the evil influences of white civilization and return to their traditional ways. Among other things, Tenskwatawa—who became known as "the Shawnee Prophet"—instructed his followers to cease all contact with whites and stop using any clothing, tools, or food produced by white people. The only exception to this rule was of firearms, which the Prophet permitted for self-defense but not for hunting. All game had to be taken by bow and arrow

or other traditional methods. The Prophet promised that if his people followed these precepts and kept themselves pure, "the Master of Life" would restore them to happiness and prosperity.

As Tenskwatawa's message spread to other tribes, hundreds of Indians journeyed to his village on the Tippecanoe River in the Indiana Territory, called, appropriately, Prophetstown. There they met the Shawnee mystic and heard his elder brother Tecumseh speak of forming an Indian confederacy aimed at stopping white expansion and even regaining lands that had already been lost. Arguing that the land "belongs to all," Tecumseh condemned previous treaties as fraudulent because they had been validated by a few corrupted village chiefs and not by all the people. At the same time, the Prophet castigated white Americans as children of a "Great Serpent" that "grew from the scum of the great water when it was troubled by the Evil Spirit." Convinced that all whites were devils, converts from the Delaware tribe returned to their villages and initiated a witch hunt that resulted in the deaths by burning of four kinsmen who had converted to Christianity and adopted white ways. Alarmed by news of these excesses as well as an upsurge of Indian raids on white settlements, Governor William Henry Harrison of the Indiana Territory decided to call out the militia and march on Prophetstown to disperse the Prophet's followers and end Tecumseh's fledgling confederacy.

What became known as the Battle of Tippecanoe occurred on November 7, 1811, at Prophetstown, while the warrior chief Tecumseh was in the South recruiting allies among the Creek, Chickasaw, and Choctaw nations. The Prophet made the mistake of telling his warriors that they would be invulnerable to the white men's bullets and would easily secure a victory. When the promise of victory turned to defeat, the Prophet's influence quickly dissipated, and along with it went Tecumseh's vision of a dominant Indian confederacy. Upon returning to Indiana early in 1812, Tecumseh found Prophetstown burned to the ground, its provisions destroyed, and his allies scattered. He would spend the next two years trying to rebuild his shattered confederacy and fighting the hated Americans. In the meantime, warfare continued along the frontier from Michigan to Mississippi as warriors from numerous tribes, still eager for combat, wreaked havoc on white settlements and terrified their inhabitants. In the Old Northwest, William Henry Harrison emerged as a popular hero widely known as "Old Tippecanoe." His military victory propelled his political career, culminating in 1840 with his election to the presidency.

## Mr. Madison's War

News of Harrison's victory at Prophetstown reached Washington not long after the Twelfth Congress had assembled for its first session in November 1811. Among its members were a number of younger congressmen led by the new Speaker of the House and master political tactician, Henry Clay of Kentucky, and the equally talented John C. Calhoun of South Carolina. Like Clay, many members came from the western sections of the country and had lost family members and friends in the Indian wars. They seemed unable to recognize that the aggressiveness of their constituents had anything to do with ongoing violence on the frontier; in their view, Great Britain was the culprit. Upon learning that English-made firearms had been found on the battlefield at Tippecanoe, they became all the more convinced that British agents were inciting Indians against the United States and that something had to be done to eliminate their suspected base of operations in Canada.

That was not all. Clay, Calhoun, and their colleagues—collectively known as the "War Hawks"—were fed up with Britain's belligerent and condescending treatment of the United States as well as President Madison's seemingly endless attempts to find a diplomatic solution. Angry at Britain's continued assaults on the high seas and arrogance at the bargaining table, they were determined to take a stand even if it meant going to war.

### THE CLASH

By May 1812, even Madison had concluded that further diplomatic efforts were useless, and he began to draft a war message to Congress. In it, he claimed that Britain was already in "a state of war against the United States," citing the continuing impressment of sailors, violations of neutral rights, the presence of British warships in American waters, the incitement of Indians, and the refusal to negotiate. Although Congress approved the measure, its vote was divided, with the strongest opposition coming from the commercially oriented Federalist strongholds of Connecticut, Massachusetts, and New York. On June 18, Madison signed the bill declaring war against Great Britain. To his Federalist opponents, the conflict would become known as "Mr. Madison's War," and they made the most of it in the presidential election of 1812. Although Madison soundly defeated the "peace party" candidate and Republicans retained control of both houses of Congress, a persistent antiwar clamor—fanned by merchants angry about the loss of overseas trade—continued in New England and New York.

The War of 1812 lasted two and a half years and took place primarily in three regions of the country: along the Canadian-American border from Lake Erie in the West to the St. Lawrence River valley and Lake Champlain in the East; in the deep South from the Mississippi Territory along the Florida panhandle to New Orleans; and in the Chesapeake Bay area. From the outset, weak executive leadership and poor preparations plagued the war effort. The Madison administration, particularly its inept leaders at the War Department, had no clearly defined strategy other than striking at Canada—the one British possession that American troops could reach—and attacking Britain's Indian allies, most notably the rebellious Tecumseh. Since a majority of people in upper Canada (today the province of Ontario) originally came from the United States, many Americans concluded that it could be easily taken—"a mere matter of marching," as Thomas Jefferson put it. They soon found out otherwise.

After two years of vicious fighting along the Canadian border and numerous failed attempts to invade one another's territory, American and British forces remained stalemated in virtually the same positions they had occupied at the outset of the war. One significant event in the border war occurred in October 1813, when an American army commanded by General William Henry "Old Tippecanoe" Harrison invaded upper Canada east of Detroit and defeated a combined British and Indian force at Moraviantown on the Thames River. Reported among the dead was the Shawnee leader, Tecumseh, although his body was never found. Tecumseh's death brought an abrupt end to his Indian confederacy, delivered a crushing blow to hopes for an independent Indian territory in the Great Lakes region, and secured the Old Northwest for the final stage of white settlement.

In the South, hostilities began with an Indian war and ended with a belated American victory at New Orleans. Thanks in large part to Tecumseh's influence, Indian resistance to continued white expansion into the Mississippi Territory grew dramatically after 1811. By 1813, civil war had broken out among the Creek Indians as militant tribesmen in the northern part of the territory called "Red Sticks" clashed with those "Lower Creeks" who had become more assimilated into white culture as planters and slave owners. The so-called Creek War came to a head in August 1813, when the Red Sticks, in retaliation for a previous attack by a joint force of white militia and their Lower Creek allies, assaulted Fort Mims and killed 250 men, women, and children. In response, an army consisting of 1,400 whites,

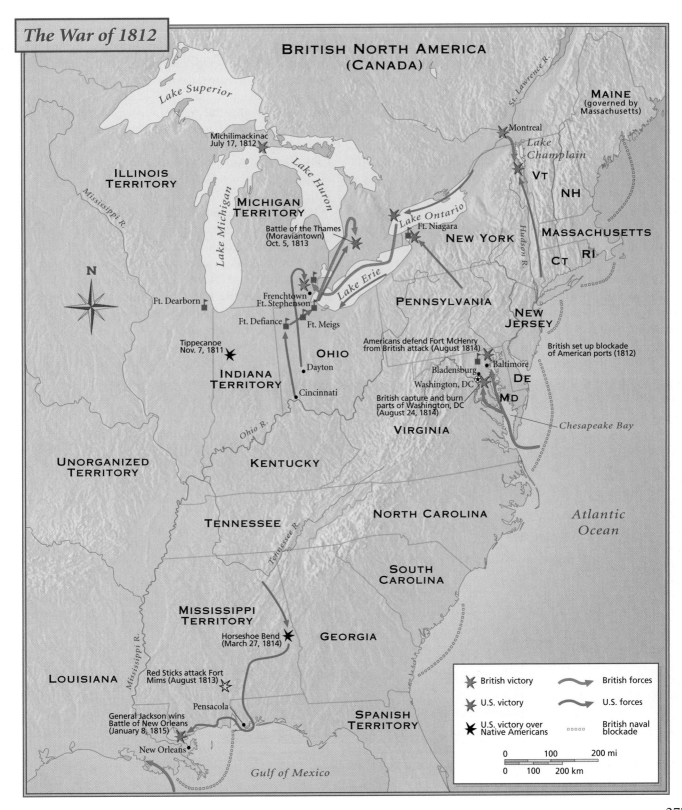

The War of 1812

BRITISH NORTH AMERICA
(CANADA)

*Lake Superior*

*Lake Michigan*

*Lake Huron*

Michilimackinac
July 17, 1812

ILLINOIS
TERRITORY

MICHIGAN
TERRITORY

*St. Lawrence R.*

MAINE
(governed by
Massachusetts)

Montreal

*Lake Champlain*

VT

NH

N

Ft. Dearborn

Battle of the Thames
(Moraviantown)
Oct. 5, 1813

*Lake Ontario*
Ft. Niagara

NEW YORK

MASSACHUSETTS

CT   RI

*Lake Erie*

*Hudson R.*

Frenchtown
Ft. Stephenson

Ft. Defiance   Ft. Meigs

PENNSYLVANIA

NEW
JERSEY

Tippecanoe
Nov. 7, 1811

OHIO

Dayton

INDIANA
TERRITORY

Cincinnati

Americans defend Fort McHenry
from British attack (August 1814)

British set up blockade
of American ports (1812)

Bladensburg   Baltimore

Washington, DC

DE

MD

*Mississippi R.*

*Ohio R.*

UNORGANIZED
TERRITORY

KENTUCKY

British capture and burn
parts of Washington, DC
(August 24, 1814)

VIRGINIA

*Chesapeake Bay*

TENNESSEE

*Tennessee R.*

NORTH CAROLINA

*Atlantic
Ocean*

SOUTH
CAROLINA

MISSISSIPPI
TERRITORY

Horseshoe Bend
(March 27, 1814)

GEORGIA

*Mississippi R.*

Red Sticks attack Fort
Mims (August 1813)

LOUISIANA

Pensacola

SPANISH
TERRITORY

General Jackson wins
Battle of New Orleans
(January 8, 1815)

New Orleans

*Gulf of Mexico*

| ✷ British victory | ⟿ British forces |
| ✷ U.S. victory | ⟿ U.S. forces |
| ✦ U.S. victory over Native Americans | ⸱⸱⸱⸱⸱ British naval blockade |

0        100      200 mi

0    100   200 km

500 Cherokees, and 100 Lower Creeks under the command of Andrew Jackson pursued the Red Sticks and ultimately defeated them at the Battle of Horseshoe Bend on March 27, 1814. Over 800 Red Sticks died at Horseshoe Bend. The few who survived escaped to Spanish Florida, where they joined runaway slaves and Seminole tribesmen in raiding ever-expanding American settlements.

Andrew Jackson, a Tennessee planter and land speculator as well as a military leader, ignored the support he had been given by friendly Creeks and proceeded to impose a treaty on the Creek nation that exacted 14 million acres of land from them—over two-thirds of their territory and more than half of the present state of Alabama. Jackson's military subjugation of the Creeks boded ill for other Indian tribes in the South and east of the Mississippi River. The Creeks not only lost huge chunks of land but also were systematically squeezed into ever smaller enclaves. The same fate awaited other tribes like the Choctaws, Chickasaws, Cherokees, and Seminoles. By the late 1830s, all of them would be forcibly "removed" to lands beyond the Mississippi.

"The Taking of the City of Washington in America," wood engraving published by G. Thompson, 1814.

While Jackson's army moved on to secure Mobile and a portion of western Florida from Britain's ally Spain before converging on New Orleans, events in the Chesapeake Bay area went far less well. With the defeat and (temporary) exile of Napoleon to the island of Elba in 1814, Britain was free to focus the full force of its military power on the United States, which was no match for the Royal Navy in an all-out sea war. When a large British flotilla appeared in the Chesapeake in August 1814 and disgorged an army of 4,500 combat-proven veterans, American commanders could do little but adopt a delaying action and hope for the best. When it became apparent that the invaders were heading for Washington, a feeble attempt to stop them at Bladensburg, Maryland, resulted in a rout. Critics of the debacle accused Madison and his cabinet of cowardice in the face of the enemy. On August 24, the British army entered Washington and set fire to the Capitol building and the presidential mansion (which, when subsequently repainted, became known as the White House).

Having humiliated the Madison administration and the Congress, the British forces next set their sights on Baltimore. Encountering a spirited resistance there, they assaulted Fort McHenry at the entrance to the harbor with a bombardment of incendiary and case-shot rockets and cannon shells. Although the British failed to capture Baltimore, the assault threw a scare into the city's inhabitants. Having personally witnessed the night-long bombardment of Fort McHenry, with "the rockets' red glare" and "the bombs bursting in air," a lawyer named Francis Scott Key composed the verses that subsequently became known as "The Star-Spangled Banner."

At the very time that British forces were wreaking havoc on Washington and Baltimore, peace negotiations had already begun in the Flemish city of Ghent. The British delegation initially made heavy demands, insisting on control of the Great Lakes, the cession of a substantial portion of Maine, and the establishment of a neutral Indian state to serve as a buffer zone between the United States and Canada. However, when news arrived that the British had failed to take Baltimore and another invading army had been repelled by the Americans at Plattsburgh, New York (on the western shore of Lake Champlain), the British government instructed its envoys to move toward compromise. Great Britain had been at war for more than two decades and had suffered an enormous loss of lives as well as a spiraling national debt. Moreover, Europe remained restive as rumors spread that Napoleon was about to return from his exile at Elba and attempt to reestablish his lost European empire. After months of negotiating, the British and American commissioners signed the Treaty of Ghent on Christmas Eve 1814.

On paper, the accord amounted to little more than an armistice, leaving matters about as they had stood before the war. Although the United States retained the section of western Florida it had seized from Spain, no other significant territorial cessions were made, nor did the treaty mention impressment, neutral rights, or the Indian menace, grievances for which the Americans had originally gone to war. But to war-weary Americans, that did not seem to matter. By and large, the public greeted the news of peace with bonfires, ringing bells, and a great sense of relief that the conflict had ended.

## POLITICAL AFTERMATHS

Although generally viewed as a diplomatic and military draw, the War of 1812 had significant political consequences. It greatly weakened the military and political power of Native Americans from the Appalachians to the Mississippi and opened the floodgates for further white incursions into unsettled territory. The war also made heroes of William Henry Harrison and Andrew Jackson, the two military leaders most responsible for subduing the Indian resistance, and propelled their political careers. Finally, the war and its immediate aftermath sounded the death knell of the Federalist Party and led to a period of realignment when American politics was dominated by a single but amorphous political party.

On January 8, 1815, two weeks after the Treaty of Ghent was signed, Andrew Jackson inflicted a devastating defeat on a large British army at the Battle of New Orleans. While ensuring Britain's ratification of the peace accords, news of Jackson's triumph provided a tremendous boost to the Madison administration and excited patriotic fervor throughout the country. Just as William Henry Harrison's name had become associated with Tippecanoe, Jackson's became associated with New Orleans. Despite the fact that he, like Harrison, was a man of wealth and a Tennessee politician, admiring publicists and political allies depicted him as a frontier farmer/freedom fighter fresh from the plough and committed above all else to defending the nation's honor against British tyranny. Such characterizations pleased Jackson, and he did his best to cultivate them.

While Jackson's political prospects soared at war's end, those of the Federalist Party came crashing down. The great stronghold of Federalism lay in the northeastern seaboard states, especially New England. Leading businessmen and clergy of the region had long criticized the domestic and foreign policies of Jefferson and Madison as being anticommercial and biased toward the French. When the war came, Federalists not only denounced it but also tried to embarrass the Madison administration by refusing to make loans to the U.S. government, opposing call-ups of state militias, and defying wartime restrictions by openly trading with the enemy. Some even talked of seceding from the Union.

Convinced that Republican blundering during the war would soon return their party to power, New England Federalists convened at Hartford, Connecticut, in the fall of 1814 to plot their strategy. Although a few extremists continued to call for secession, the majority of delegates settled on a plan aimed at curbing the power of republicanism in the South and West. They endorsed a series of amendments to the Constitution that, among other things, would eliminate the three-fifths method of counting slaves for the apportionment of seats in the House of Representatives, prevent the president from serving more than one term, and require a two-thirds majority in Congress for the admission of new states to the Union, embargoes on trade, and declarations of war.

Whatever hope members of the Hartford convention had for the future were dashed, however, when news of Jackson's victory at New Orleans and the Treaty of Ghent arrived almost simultaneously. Already angered by Federalist obstructionism during the war, Republicans accused their opponents of conspiracy, sedition, and outright treason. The Federalist Party quickly became the object of public scorn. Although the party would linger on into the 1820s, the election of 1816, which swept James Monroe into the presidency, revealed that the Federalists were no longer a viable force in

An early view of Fulton's *Clermont* steaming up the Hudson River from New York to Albany, c. 1810, in a French lithograph by an unknown artist. Note the vessel's resemblance to traditional sailing ships of the day.

## STEAM POWER

The application of steam power to transportation marked one of the entering wedges of the industrial revolution in America. The best known of the inventors of the steamboat was Robert Fulton. Although not the first person to apply steam power to the propulsion of water craft, he was the most successful. Fulton launched his "*North River* steamboat" (later renamed the *Clermont*) at New York City in August 1807. An unorthodox-looking vessel, the boat measured 150 feet long and 13 feet wide, with straight sides and a flat bottom that drew only 18 inches of water. It had two masts fore and aft for carrying square sails. What was new and noteworthy, however, was the *North River*'s source of power—a large, vertically standing, low-pressure, English-built steam engine situated beneath the deck and attached through a diamond-shaped crank to 15-foot paddle wheels on each side of the boat

American politics. Monroe was Madison's handpicked successor and the fourth Virginian to hold the nation's highest office since 1789. The presidency was becoming known as the "Virginia Dynasty."

## Toward a New Mechanical Age

The War of 1812, like other major conflicts, brought with it far-reaching economic, technological, and social changes. The war and its aftermath began a major shift in the economy from an agrarian base toward an increasingly industrial one, characterized by the widespread adoption of machinery. There were a number of precedents for this change. One, already noted, was the innovative work of Samuel Slater and other talented English immigrants in establishing the American textile industry. Another was the introduction of the steamboat, arguably America's first significant contribution to world technology.

amidship. A boat that belched smoke, hissed steam, and thudded from the motion of its crankshaft and piston! It presented a strange sight to the crowds that gathered along the shore to watch its first run up the Hudson River. A few spectators ran away as the boat approached, but many others "waved their handkerchiefs and hurrahed for Fulton" and his invention. Although he heard some sarcastic remarks about "Fulton's folly" before the *North River* got under way, Fulton was cheered by the result. "I overtook many sloops and schooners to the windward and parted with them as if they had been at anchor," he wrote triumphantly to a friend. "The power of propelling boats by steam is now fully proved."

The invention proved to be so popular and profitable that Fulton and his partners proceeded to build more vessels and, for a time, monopolized the steamboating business in New York waters and on the lower Mississippi. Once successfully deployed in and around these port cities, steamboating—especially passenger and, to a lesser degree, mail packet service—spread quickly to other rivers as well as to the Great Lakes region. By 1817, 17 steamboats were operating on western rivers. Thereafter, the number of steam-powered vessels plying the Ohio, Mississippi, and their tributaries grew steadily from 69 in 1820 to 187 in 1830 and 536 in 1850. The rivers became the capillaries of a vast system of water-based transportation.

Over time, a distinctive steamboat type emerged on western rivers. Characterized by barge-like flat bottoms capable of navigating in shallow water, outfitted with one or two passenger decks above the main deck, and powered by high-pressure steam engines located on the main deck (and not in the hold, as was customary with eastern steamboats), the western steamer became not only a workhorse on the Mississippi and its tributaries but also an American icon celebrated in art and popular writing of the period. Although Robert Fulton and his associates made important contributions to the new design, others did too. Among them were Henry Miller Shreve, a famous riverboat captain (after whom Shreveport,

The steamboat *Ouishita* on the Mississippi River at St. Louis, in a painting by George Catlin c. 1832. By the 1810s, steamboats operating on western rivers had taken on a different appearance from their eastern counterparts. In addition to using more compact, American-made, "high pressure" steam engines, western river steamers were built with flatter bottoms, which allowed them to navigate in as little as three feet of water.

Louisiana, is named), and Daniel French, an engine-builder from Brownsville, Pennsylvania, near Pittsburgh. All told, the western steamboat was the result of incremental changes over several decades after 1811. It was the product of many inventive minds—some famous, others anonymous—as often is the case with new technologies that have major consequences.

The great advantage of the steamboat over older craft was its speed, especially when moving upstream. Whereas early steamboats averaged around 50 miles a day, keelboats and other handpoled and pulled vessels could do no better than 20 miles a day and substantially less under adverse conditions. Equipped with more powerful engines and improved hulls, steamboats were capable of averaging 100 miles a day by the mid-1820s. Neither keelboats nor wagons could come close to managing those speeds even under the best of conditions. More than any other conveyance, the steamboat hastened the movement of white settlers into Indian territory and, as such, served as a vehicle of conquest as well as economic change. As one American journalist put it in 1841, "Steam navigation colonized the West."

Steam power and steam engineering proved to be particularly important to the developing economy of the Ohio Valley. In a region richly endowed with timberlands and coal deposits but with few good water-power sites, steam engines quickly found applications in manufacturing as well as river transportation. Owing mostly to the construction of steamboats, the manufacture of steam engines became one of the earliest and most important industrial products of Pittsburgh, Wheeling, Cincinnati, and Louisville. The remarkable assemblage of skilled machinists, ironworkers, and carpenters initially attracted to these cities by the steamboat business helps to explain their emergence before the Civil War as centers of transportation and industry.

Because finished engines were so expensive, early builders felt lucky if they received three or four orders a year. This meant that they had to supplement their income by executing less ambitious work, such as hand tools and decorative ironwork, for smaller customers. European visitors often commented on the versatility of American machine shops, noting that their lack of specialization exposed them to a

View of waterpowered paper mills on the Brandywine Creek, c. 1830, by John Rubens Smith. Similar mills existed on the Brandywine and elsewhere for manufacturing cotton and woolen cloth and making gunpowder.

white-lead works for making paint, flour and lumber mills, a barrel factory, glassworks, and furniture shops. Elsewhere around the country during the war, hundreds of mill hamlets and small manufacturing villages sprang up along the fall lines of rivers and streams. The war also stimulated a variety of manufacturing activities ranging from small blacksmith and machine shops that served the needs of local manufacturers to larger mills for making everything from flour to gunpowder.

The corridor spanning New York City through Trenton, Philadelphia, and Wilmington as far south as Baltimore quickly emerged as a manufacturing region that rivaled New England's pioneer armories and mills. Both regions acquired reputations for particular products and manufacturing technologies. Whereas New England became best known for its cheap cotton textiles, precision-made firearms, and light machine-tools, the mid-Atlantic corridor soon acquired a reputation for high-end textiles (fine woolens, for example), steam engines, and heavy machinery for making everything from boiler plate to ships' bottoms. As the industrial revolution took root throughout the country, different regions developed different products and different technological styles of making things.

The character of industrial expansion depended on the types of energy resources available in each region. In rural enclaves like the Brandywine Valley in Delaware, water rather than steam provided the driving force behind industry. Manufacturing centers in outlying areas of rural America like the Brandywine Valley initially outpaced industrial development in larger cities like New York and Philadelphia, with their smaller, shop-oriented "metropolitan" forms of industrialization. Cities such as these boasted good harbors and strategic locations, but without access to waterfalls they had to turn to steam to power their manufacturing ventures. This urban reliance on steam power created a lucrative market for wood and coal fuel sources and played a central role in stimulating a large anthracite mining industry in eastern Pennsylvania. But the reliance on steam power initially impeded the growth

wider variety of technical problems and, as a result, greater opportunities for innovation. Moreover, early steam-engine works served an educational purpose. Long before the first engineering schools came into being, these shops trained a cadre of steam engineers and mechanics who went on to build ever larger machine shops and foundries. "Graduates" of these shops played a pivotal role in introducing the next generation of steam engines, railway locomotives, and other types of heavy industrial machinery in America.

The appearance of steamboats on America's rivers provided the most visible evidence of the new mechanical age ushered in by the war years. But the textile and firearms industries also grew rapidly in this period, following a similar trend toward mechanization. From Boston in the North to Richmond in the South and Pittsburgh and Cincinnati in the West, the war spurred a surge of manufacturing activity to meet the demand caused by wartime shortages of British manufactures. Cincinnati, little more than a frontier village of 750 people in 1800, nearly quadrupled its population by 1810 and grew into a small city of almost 10,000 by 1820. When the War of 1812 ended, this "Queen City" had four cotton mills, a woolen factory, a

of large-scale manufacturing in eastern cities. Compared with waterwheels and water turbines, steam engines were expensive to build and operate. A much older technology, waterwheels were better understood by factory masters and could readily be constructed along rural fall lines to produce usable power. So it was in the countryside, not the city, where the factory system experienced its fastest growth. Mechanization transformed the rural landscape even as it spurred the growth of cities.

## THE BOSTON MANUFACTURING COMPANY

The most important factory to appear during the War of 1812 was the Boston Manufacturing Company in rural Waltham, Massachusetts. The enterprise began when a group of twelve Boston merchants, headed by Francis Cabot Lowell, diverted a portion of their capital from shipping to manufacturing after the British blockade of American ports had virtually halted overseas trade. Lowell and his associates focused on cotton cloth production because they had previous trade experience with cotton and believed that a lucrative market existed in North America. Moreover, Lowell's visits to British mills between 1810 and 1812 fed his vision of what might be accomplished in America.

Historians would later refer to Lowell's initial group of merchant investors as the "Boston Associates." They were a tight-knit group, some related by marriage or connected through previous business relationships. Early in 1813, Lowell and his closest associate and brother-in-law, Patrick Tracy Jackson, decided to go forward with the cotton venture. They obtained a charter from the Massachusetts legislature incorporating the Boston Manufacturing Company and raised the unparalleled sum of $100,000 (soon to grow to $300,000, then $600,000) in initial stock subscriptions from their mercantile associates. They then acquired a mill site on the Charles River some eight miles west of Boston in the village of Waltham, where they built the first of two large water-powered factories for the production of a plain, multipurpose cloth called "sheeting."

Lowell hired an able and well-connected master mechanic named Paul Moody to superintend the operation. Between his arrival at Waltham in 1813 and the beginning of production two years later, Moody devoted most of his time to equipping the mill with machinery for producing cotton cloth. Using a model provided by Lowell and assisted by workers from the company's newly established machine shop,

Moody succeeded in the fall of 1814 in building a full-scale power loom for weaving. Lowell was thrilled with the result. Years later, merchant Nathan Appleton, one of the original Boston Associates, recollected "the state of admiration and satisfaction with which we sat by the hour, watching the beautiful movement of this new and wonderful machine, destined as it evidently was, to change the character of all textile industry."

The power loom was the rock on which the Boston Manufacturing Company built its business strategy. Elsewhere in the United States, weaving was conducted separately from spinning. But Lowell and his partners aimed at making the entire product under one roof. Building an integrated manufacturing facility was a risky move, completely novel in the textile industry. In effect, it meant that raw cotton would enter the mill at one end and come out the other as finished cloth. In between, a series of machines attended by young female workers (of whom more will be said in Chapter 12) took the raw material, cleaned and carded (combed) it, spun it into thread, and wound the thread onto bobbins, which fed banks of power looms that wove it into cloth. To Lowell and Moody, the power loom provided the missing link in the manufacturing process. By bringing power weaving into their mill rather than sending thread out to local weavers, they achieved control over the entire manufacturing process. This gave them a decided advantage over other textile manufacturers, and allowed their enterprise unlimited possibilities for growth.

In a continuous manufacturing operation such as this, one mechanical process depended on the smooth execution of another, and success depended on having threads spun to virtually uniform sizes. Any irregularities in a machine-based system of production could cause managerial nightmares, especially when economic efficiencies and, ultimately, profit depended on consistently making a product with uniform weights and dimensions. Early manufacturers like Moody and Lowell became single-minded in their pursuit of uniformity and control over every aspect of production. As we shall see, this compulsion had a significant impact on those who worked on the shop floor.

The Boston Manufacturing Company's decisions on the types of cloth to produce were influenced by market considerations, but also by labor policy. From their visits to textile mills in England and the United States, Lowell and Moody learned that skilled workers—particularly mule spinners (workers who tended large spinning machines called "mules") and handloom weavers—could be independent, troublesome employees. Moody therefore did everything he could to avoid the use of skilled labor by breaking cloth production down to its simplest elements, assigning only one element to each worker, and devising "stop motions" that would automatically disengage machines if something went wrong. Given the state of textile technology in 1814–15, only coarse goods—such as garments for slaves—lent themselves to such a specialized degree of mechanization, and these became the focus of production at Waltham.

The decision to produce cheap fabrics at Waltham proved to be a stroke of genius. While scores of small mills producing finer goods faltered and often failed in the face of renewed British competition after the War of 1812, the Boston Manufacturing Company prospered. The Waltham mill began to turn out its first cotton sheeting in a piecemeal way in 1814, and production began to hit stride two years later, after a number of mechanical kinks and bottlenecks had been worked out. Once under way, annual sales skyrocketed from about $34,000 in 1817 to nearly $350,000 in 1822. By then, the Boston Associates had added a second mill to its Waltham complex and had increased its investment in the property to $771,000. With their mills churning out three miles of cloth a day and their Boston marketing house selling every yard of it with calls for more, stockholders enjoyed extremely good returns on their investments. In 1817, the company paid its first dividend of 20 percent. During the next decade, annual dividends maintained this remarkable rate and sometimes exceeded it. Lowell and his partners had expected to make a profit, but not even in their wildest dreams had they imagined that it would be so great.

## REGIONAL SPECIALIZATION

Rather than following one route to industrialization, the United States followed many. Textiles, flour milling, and gun making were among the earliest and most important, but there were others. Shoe making evolved from a small craft-based enterprise into a mass production industry by mid-century. Iron forges and machine shops grew at a rapid pace, supplying the needs of all sorts of engineering ventures. And in urban areas, printing and sewing trades combined with the construction of steam engines and railway locomotives to form a particular "metropolitan" brand of industrialization, characterized by highly skilled as well as highly "sweated" labor. Among the latter were women seamstresses—often im-

migrants—who worked under poor conditions at low wages for the emerging ready-made clothing industry in cities from New York to Cincinnati.

As machine-based manufacturing began to take hold in the Northeast, cotton became the South's most valuable commodity. In 1810, plantations located mainly in South Carolina and Georgia had produced 178,000 bales of cotton for markets primarily in the British Isles. Although production flagged during the war years, the coming of peace and the reopening of European trade prompted a great surge in cotton cultivation and, with it, the expansion of slavery. In 1815, planters sent 209,000 bales—each weighing generally from 500 to 600 pounds—to market. As the world textile industry expanded and the price of raw cotton increased, more and more planters got into the business. This growth, in turn, set off what became known as "Alabama fever": hundreds of white settlers and their slaves streamed into the Mississippi Territory (comprising mainly the present states of Alabama and Mississippi), intent on making their fortunes and, in the process, displacing the region's Indians. By late 1817, the year the state of Mississippi entered the Union, cotton production approached 272,000 bales. Two years later, when Alabama came into the Union, it stood at 349,000 bales. By the 1820s, the South had become the world's foremost supplier of cotton, and southern politics began to reflect the dominant economic influence of "King Cotton."

Compared with the cotton culture of the deep South, a more diversified economy developed in the area west of the Appalachian Mountains that comprised the Old Northwest Territory and parts of the upper South bordering the Ohio and Mississippi rivers. There agriculture was also the dominant occupation. But owing to differences in climate and the length of the growing season, farms focused mainly on the production of wheat, corn, and livestock products. These were shipped downriver to New Orleans for distribution to southern buyers as well as markets located in the Northeast and, later, Europe. As with the spread of cotton cultivation in the deep South, rising prices for agricultural goods induced mass migrations of white settlers into the rich lands of Ohio, Indiana, Illinois, Michigan, Iowa, Wisconsin, and Missouri after the War of 1812. In 1816, Indiana entered the Union, followed by Illinois in 1818 and Missouri three years later. Thereafter, the region developed rapidly. And as fast as the white population grew, Native American culture declined.

Given the long-standing reliance of western farmers on the Ohio and Mississippi rivers to get goods to market, the

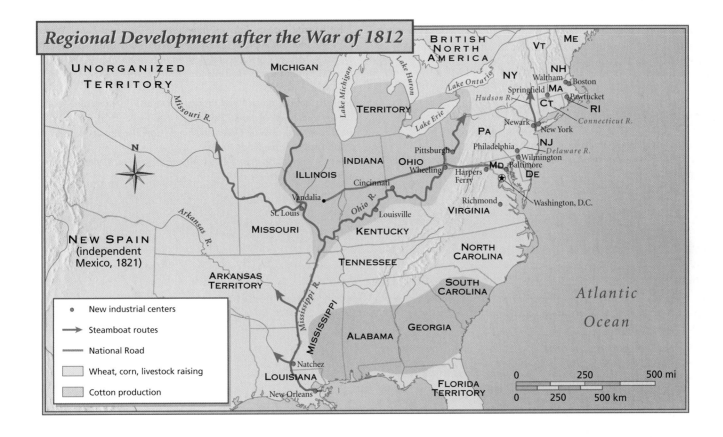

**Regional Development after the War of 1812**

region's commerce moved mostly southward. But with the opening of the National Road after the War of 1812 and especially with the advent of an east-west network of canals and railroads several decades later, western trade became more directly connected with growing markets in the Northeast. The east-west trade received further impetus when the discovery of rich deposits of lead in Missouri, copper in Michigan, and coal and iron ore in western Pennsylvania, southern Ohio, and northern Kentucky attracted eastern capital to the region. Cities such as Cincinnati, Louisville, St. Louis, and Pittsburgh experienced rapid growth after the war. In the South, by contrast, only New Orleans was a fast-growing city.

As the West became more diversified after the War of 1812, the economy of the Northeast—like that of the South—became more specialized. But as the Northeast's economy developed increasingly toward manufacturing and heavy industry, older pursuits like shipping, the mercantile trade, and even agriculture continued to play important roles. Although the number of city and town dwellers grew in proportion to

farmers, farming continued to be a leading occupation. Farm families adjusted to the growth of urban-industrial markets and the influx of nonperishable western foodstuffs by supplying perishable items such as milk, butter, eggs, fruit, and vegetables. They also supplemented their farming income by making palm-leaf hats, weaving cloth, and doing other "outwork" for local merchants and manufacturers during the winter months.

It is ironic that Thomas Jefferson, the apostle of agrarianism, and his party presided over a fundamental shift in the American economy toward an urban-industrial future. Steamboats, factories, and regional specialization—these innovations indicated that Jefferson's cherished social vision of America as a nation of farmers was breaking down. Life as he had known it would never be the same. Jefferson's vision would remain a powerful influence in American politics and culture for generations to come, but it no longer represented the driving force of American life. The United States was experiencing the initial stages of an industrial revolution, and like all fundamental changes, this one brought tensions that soon manifested themselves not only in business and labor relations but also in sectional strife. In all of this, the War of 1812 stood as a watershed.

## Suggested Reading

Thomas C. Cochran, *Frontiers of Change* (1979)

Joseph Ellis, *American Sphinx: The Character of Thomas Jefferson* (1997)

Donald R. Hickey, *The War of 1812* (1989)

Louis C. Hunter, *Steamboats on Western Rivers* (1949)

John Lauritz Larson, *Internal Improvement: National Public Works and the Promise of Popular Government in the Early United States* (2001)

David R. Meyer, *The Roots of American Industrialization* (2003)

Gary E. Moulton, ed., *The Lewis and Clark Journals: An American Epic of Discovery* (2003)

John R. Nelson, *Liberty and Property: Political Economy and Policymaking in the New Nation, 1789–1812* (1987)

Paul E. Rivard, *A New Order of Things: How the Textile Industry Transformed New England* (2002)

James P. Ronda, *Lewis and Clark Among the Indians* (1998)

John Sugden, *Tecumseh* (1997)

# Chapter Review

## Summary
### QUESTIONS

- What were Thomas Jefferson's economic policies and how did they fit with his political philosophy?
- What is the significance of the Lewis and Clark expedition?
- What impact did the War of 1812 have on the American economy?
- How did the invention of the steamboat contribute to America's society and economy?
- Thomas Jefferson once declared that both science (his "passion") and politics (his "duty") were fundamental elements of his personal vision and experience. How did his vision for the republic integrate science and politics?

## Key Terms

The Louisiana Purchase (pp. 263–265)

The Embargo of 1807 (p. 270)

Tecumseh (p. 275)

Steam power (p. 280)

The Boston Manufacturing Company (p. 283)

## Chronology

| | |
|---|---|
| 1803 | *Marbury vs. Madison.* |
| | Napoleonic Wars begin. |
| December 20, 1803 | The Louisiana Purchase. |
| May 1804–September 21, 1806 | Lewis and Clark's Corps of Discovery. |
| August 1807 | Robert Fulton launches the first steamboat. |
| December 22, 1807 | Embargo Act signed into law. |
| November 7, 1811 | Battle of Tippecanoe. |
| June 18, 1812 | War declared against Britain. |
| 1813 | Boston Manufacturing Company founded in Waltham, Massachusetts. |
| December 24, 1814 | Treaty of Ghent ends War of 1812. |
| January 8, 1815 | Battle of New Orleans. |
| 1817 | Milling machine introduced. |

SITUATION OF AMERI

# Part 3

# A CULTURE OF IMPROVEMENT

THE UNITED STATES HAS EXPERIENCED a number of defining moments in its history, but none more telling than the War of 1812. Commonly referred to as "the Second War for Independence," the war and its aftermath marked America's coming of age as an independent republic—and its final separation from Great Britain and its sprawling empire. Thereafter, a gradual rapprochement took place between the two nations as the United States sought to insure its political independence by achieving economic independence through the establishment of home-grown industrial enterprises and expanded trade networks. To that end, the war prompted a number of novel technological and economic changes that propelled the United States in a new and different direction. Supported by federal and state government policies that encouraged economic development, postwar America witnessed the construction of road, canal, and railroad systems as well as the widespread introduction of novel machine-based factory manufacturing operations. These innovations stimulated trade and helped knit the country together as a national market economy. Altogether these changes signified the onset of a market revolution that by mid-century would make the U.S. economy the second largest in the world.

Largely as a consequence of these shifts, American society was becoming more open and engaged. It was a time of expansive optimism, a time when people believed that the "rising glory of America" had no bounds. One indicator was the expansion of the electorate in which white males who formerly did not have the right to vote acquired full rights as citizens. Another was the invention of modern political parties that catered to the new popular electorate and, thanks to the advent of novel printing technologies, spread their platforms and proposals far and wide through the medium of newspa-

The *Situation of America, 1848,* an oil on wood panel painting created by an unknown artist in New York, 1848. From the Collection American Folk Art Museum, New York—Promised gift of Ralph Esmerian. (p1.2001.58—34 x 57 x 1⅜").

pers and the U.S. postal delivery system. Indeed, politics itself became more intense after the closely contested presidential election of 1824. All these changes, and more, bespoke of a widespread belief in progress, especially the idea that the United States was on a path that one day would make it "the greatest nation of the earth."

Progress in the mechanical arts, politics, and the economy paralleled important developments in religion and society. Beginning early in the century and continuing into the 1840s, a major religious revival known as "the Second Great Awakening" swept across America. Led by evangelical protestant denominations—especially Methodists and Baptists—it sent hundreds of circuit-riding preachers into the countryside in search of converts to Christianity. While their primary objective was individual conversions, they also sought, as one writer put it, "to dispel ignorance, check vice, and create a pure public opinion, favorable to sound morals and true religion." They were joined in this quest by other religious sects—notably the Shakers, Mormons, and Oneida Perfectionists—who proved extremely creative in their efforts to meld everyday living with their overarching interest in perfecting their spiritual lives and achieving salvation. The search for perfection—the ultimate form of progress in a culture of improvement—also manifested itself in secular utopian communities that spread across the nation during the 1830s and 1840s.

Although the great revival aimed primarily at reforming the individual, it was but a short step to reforming society at large. During the postwar years reform groups affiliated with evangelical churches, anxious to achieve a total Christian environment that would "purify" America, organized reform movements and established tract societies for the mass distribution of literature that promoted everything from Bible-reading and Sabbath-keeping to temperance and free public schools. The most famous, and certainly most controversial, of these reforms was the antislavery movement, particularly its most radical wing—abolitionism. Given its controversial objective, abolition quickly became politicized and divided the nation along sectional lines. The ultimate outcome would be a deadly Civil War.

As much as the idea of progress prevailed in post-War of 1812 America, the reform movement had limits while eco-

nomic advance came at certain costs. Sectional tensions over the extension of slavery into new territories beyond the Old South emerged in 1819 over the admission of Missouri to the Union as a slave state. At the same time, attitudes toward race, class, gender, and ethnicity grew more pronounced in protestant America with the appearance of factory towns and the expansion of industry. While generally enthusiastic about invention, white Americans from older working families nonetheless expressed ambivalence about the new technology and the possible threats it posed to their earning power and status. They resented having to compete in the job market with growing numbers of free blacks and immigrants. As women and children entered the labor force, men found fewer employment opportunities at good wages and the pressures of industrial work grew more intense. Life itself became more stratified, something that became readily apparent in the contrast between the stately mansions of merchants and mill owners and the plain dormitories and tenements of factory hands. With stratification came social tensions that manifested themselves in strikes, riots, and radical political movements—all in their way expressing certain doubts about the course of technological change. The old world of craftsmanship was being replaced by a new world of machinery. A "mechanical age," driven by massive waterwheels and steam engines, was at hand.

Mechanization fostered even more fundamental cultural changes. As the market revolution gained momentum, the need for timely work schedules and timely deliveries grew in importance. These demands, in turn, reinforced old protestant values that emphasized time saving, thrift, and hard work—values that employers from factory masters to slave owners sought to enforce through the imposition of work rules, rigid schedules, and the use of clocks to measure time. Indeed, clocks with their relentlessly ticking pendulums and moving minute hands became a master symbol of the new mechanical age and its market-driven processes. Thanks to the new regimen and the mass production of cheap clocks, virtually every household in America became time-conscious by the 1840s. Time was more than an abstract concept. In the hands of factory masters and entrepreneurs, it became a powerful tool that shaped the workings of the new industrial order.

# A NEW EPOCH:

## 1815–1828

In September 1848, photographers Charles Fontayne and William S. Porter set up their camera on a rooftop along the Ohio River in Newport Kentucky, to get a panoramic shot of Cincinnati. They panned their camera across Cincinnati's waterfront, capturing separate segments of the growing city's skyline. The resulting images from that day, eight whole-plate daguerreotypes, are known as *The Cincinnati Panorama*. By this time, Cincinnati was well known for its steamboat-building and meatpacking enterprises. The latter proved so important that Cincinnati also became known as "Porkopolis.

*Focus*
QUESTIONS

■ How was the American population changing in this period?

■ How did the Madisonian Platform represent a new vision of the federal government as a catalyst of change?

■ What developments were strengthening the forces of sectionalism in this period?

■ How did American foreign policy become more assertive in this period?

■ How were the tides of American politics shifting after the election of 1824?

"We stand at this moment," an observer in New York declared in 1821, "on the brink of fate, on the very edge of the precipice. . . . We are no longer to remain plain and simple republics of farmers, like New-England colonists, or the Dutch settlements on the Hudson. We are fast becoming a great nation, with great commerce, manufactures, population, wealth, luxuries, and with the vices and miseries that they engender." Speaker of the House Henry Clay of Kentucky agreed, declaring, "A new epoch has arisen." Political leaders of Clay's generation knew that this new epoch was closely related to the mechanical technologies on the rise around them.

The three most debated political issues of the day—banks, tariffs, and internal improvements—were all tied to the new mechanical age. Four of the five leading political figures of the time—Clay, John C. Calhoun, John Quincy Adams, and Daniel Webster—took up the cause of "industry and improvement." Even the fifth, Andrew Jackson, stood for the expansion and progress of American industry, although his views on the role of the federal government in the economic arena often put him at loggerheads with the others. Like most Americans, all five leaders had emerged from the war with strong nationalist and patriotic feelings. But as the pace of change quickened during the postwar period, they repeatedly found themselves challenged by constituents who feared the central government, placed regional economic and social interests ahead of national interests, and, accordingly, held different views about the relationship of individual states to the nation. The emerging tension between national and sectional interests would alter the structure of American politics and infuse it with a dangerous divisiveness.

## Population Growth

In 1815, the United States counted roughly 8.4 million inhabitants, up 58 percent since 1800. Overwhelmingly white, agrarian, and Protestant, nearly three-quarters of the population came from an English, Scottish, or Scotch-Irish background. The remainder of the white population were primarily German, Irish Catholic, French, Spanish, or Dutch. Next in numbers came involuntary immigrants, namely African slaves, and free blacks. In 1790, blacks constituted nearly 20 percent of the population, but their numbers were declining in proportion to whites. By 1840, the total black population numbered around 2.9 million souls, but its percentage of the total population had fallen to 17 percent. In the next decade, it would decline to 16 percent.

People of Native American ancestry were not even listed on the census returns, a clear indicator of their irrelevance to the U.S. government. One estimate for 1790 placed them at roughly half a million, spread thinly around the country. Relatively few Indians remained in the Northeast. In New England, the once-mighty Abenakis, Pequots, Mohegans, Penobscots, Narragansetts, Passamaquoddies, and Wampanoags had been reduced to hundreds. While they retained their ancient languages and continued to practice some of their impressive crafts, they nonetheless became increasingly absorbed into a part of the dominant white culture that, according to one observer, "resemble[s] that of the lower orders in our cities." The same fate awaited other native peoples in other parts of the country as land-hungry white Americans used political trickery and, often, military force to remove them from their lands.

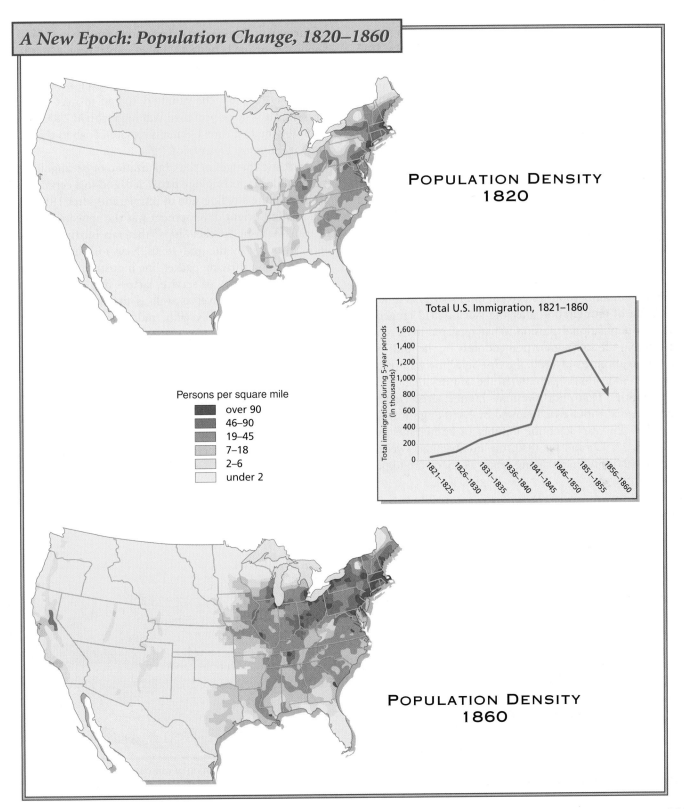

**A New Epoch: Population Change, 1820–1860**

POPULATION DENSITY
1820

Persons per square mile

- over 90
- 46–90
- 19–45
- 7–18
- 2–6
- under 2

Total U.S. Immigration, 1821–1860

Total immigration during 5-year periods (in thousands)

1,600
1,400
1,200
1,000
800
600
400
200
0

1821–1825
1826–1830
1831–1835
1836–1840
1841–1845
1846–1850
1851–1855
1856–1860

POPULATION DENSITY
1860

## The Madisonian Platform

A striking feature of the census data is the changing regional distribution of the population over time. In 1815, nearly 50 percent lived in the northeastern part of the United States comprising the New England states, New York, New Jersey, Pennsylvania, Delaware, and Maryland. A little more than one-third lived in the southern states of Virginia, North Carolina, South Carolina, Georgia, Louisiana, and the future states of Florida, Alabama, Mississippi, Arkansas, and Texas. The fastest-growing region was the trans-Appalachian West, consisting of Kentucky, Tennessee, Ohio, and the future states of Indiana, Illinois, Missouri, Michigan, Iowa, and Wisconsin. Growth was nothing less than spectacular in the five states—Ohio, Indiana, Illinois, Michigan, and Wisconsin—that once made up the Old Northwest Territory. In 1800, about 51,000 white people, or 1 percent of the nation's total population, inhabited the Old Northwest. By 1850, that number would balloon to 4.5 million, about 20 percent of the national total.

A burst of immigration after the War of 1812 ignited the country's population explosion. What appeared to be a modest influx in the 1820s grew tremendously by the mid-1840s. The national census of 1820, the first since the war, revealed that 8,385 individuals had entered the country that year, the vast majority from northwestern Europe. Irish migrants headed the list with 3,614, followed by 2,410 English and 968 Germans. Ten years later, the number of immigrants nearly tripled to 23,322, and by 1840, the number had swelled to over 84,000, more than tripling again. Then, owing to political turmoil in Europe and a devastating famine in Ireland, the floodgates opened. In 1848, for example, over 226,000 foreigners entered the country. Again, Irish, German, and English immigrants headed the lists. During the next six years, from 1849 to 1854, the numbers soared to over 2 million, reaching an all-time pre–Civil War high with 427,833 in 1854, when for the first time Germans replaced Irish as the leading immigrant group in America.

Dramatic changes in the organization of oceangoing commerce and ship technology paralleled, and to a certain degree prompted, the swelling tide of immigrants after 1815. A particularly important development was the appearance in 1818 of trans-Atlantic "packet ships" that ran on fixed schedules between ports. By the mid-1820s, New York had emerged as the center of a thriving packet-line industry that emphasized speed and regularity of service, factors that significantly improved passenger travel as well as the delivery of overseas mail. Operating initially with traditional sailing vessels, the packets introduced regular steamship service in 1838. Already linked to the west by the Erie Canal and excellent steamboat lines on the Hudson River, New York became, with the introduction of packet ships, America's leading commercial center and port of entry for European immigrants.

All told, more than 5 million people came to the United States between 1819 and 1860—over half of them during the 1840s and 1850s. Observers who were aware of these dizzying numbers had trouble comprehending fully what they meant.

View of the Miami Canal at Dayton, Ohio, 1831–32, by Thomas Kelah Wharton, 1831. Before the coming of railroads, canals served briefly as the primary carriers of people, raw materials, and commercial goods from the East Coast to the Midwest.

To some, they bespoke progress, expansion, and optimism about the future. To others, they signaled the breakup of old ways, the threat of alien religions and undue foreign influences, and apprehension about the future. One thing seemed clear to all: the rapid population growth was bringing considerable change to all sectors of American society.

## The Madisonian Platform

When the War of 1812 ended, James Madison was nearing the end of his second and final term as president of the United States. Although criticism of his wartime leadership had taken its toll, he entered the postwar period uplifted by widespread nationalistic feeling. Madison was intent on redeeming his tarnished reputation and charting a course for the country that would secure the prosperity everyone so eagerly hoped for.

After consulting with congressional leaders and reviewing proposals that had been set aside during the war years, Madison unveiled his plan on December 5, 1815, in his Seventh Annual Message to Congress. In it, he urged legislative action on five fronts: military affairs, banking and currency, protective tariffs, internal improvements (particularly roads and canals), and a national university. Altogether, the agenda became known as the "Madisonian Platform," a coherent program of political action that constituted nothing less than a blueprint for national economic development. Implicit in the message was the idea of moving the federal government from periphery to center stage as a catalyst of change—something that challenged the very core of Jeffersonian beliefs.

### MILITARY REFORM: THE UNIFORMITY SYSTEM

The Madisonian agenda began with the military. Despite the widespread popular belief that the United States had won the War of 1812, insiders knew that the conflict had been a logistical and strategic nightmare. Even before the war ended, Congress, at the president's urging, passed legislation aimed at improving the organization of the regular army and its relationship to state militia units. In February 1815, for example, Congress enacted a law that placed the national armories at Harpers Ferry, Virginia, and Springfield, Massachusetts, as well as all private arms contractors under the direct supervision of the U.S. Army Ordnance Department. Influenced by former French officers in the American army, the chief of ordnance (arms and munitions) and his assistants had long been calling for greater "system and uniformity" in the manufacture of firearms. With the passage of the "Act for the better regulation of the Ordnance Department," they quickly announced a program to establish standardized patterns for all small arms supplied to the U.S. government and eventually to manufacture weapons with interchangeable parts that could easily be repaired on the battlefield.

As it turned out, interchangeable manufacturing methods developed incrementally over thirty years, not dramatically and fast. Scores of talented machinists, army ordnance officers, and private entrepreneurs cooperated in developing the new technology. An important benchmark occurred around 1816, when Simeon North, a private arms contractor to the federal government from Middletown, Connecticut, succeeded in making the lock, or firing mechanism, of horsemen's pistols with interchangeable parts. Another important stage was reached ten years later when John H. Hall, a New Englander working at the Harpers Ferry National Armory, was able to produce a patented breech-loading rifle (bearing his name) with interchangeable parts. By 1831, Hall and North reached another plateau when, after considerable difficulty, they successfully (and separately) made Hall rifles at Harpers Ferry and Middletown (some 400 miles apart) whose parts would interchange. The final stage took place at the Springfield National Armory, where, during the early 1840s, the government's workshops were retooled with the latest gauges and machinery to produce 20,000 to 30,000 muskets annually with interchangeable parts. Springfield would again demonstrate its prowess during the Civil War when, in 1864, it reached the unprecedented production level of 276,000 rifle-muskets a year. Such manufacturing capability would not be surpassed until Henry Ford introduced the mass-production assembly line for making Model T automobiles at Highland Park, Michigan, in 1913.

Openness and accessibility proved to be one of the earmarks of the small arms industry as it developed and refined methods that became known abroad as "the American system" of manufacturing. By the mid-1840s, novel manufacturing methods pulled together at the national armories began to spread to all sorts of factories and machine shops turning out metal products. Helping to push this change were former ordnance officers who left the army and assumed managerial posts with privately owned firearms businesses, foundries, and railroads. But skilled workers counted for more than managers. "Armory practice," as it came to be called, was usually transmitted by skilled workers who received their early training at one of the public or private armories and then moved on to new positions as master machinists and production supervisors at other manufacturing establishments. Countless firms, large and small, followed this pattern, thereby acquiring the latest armory know-how—faster and cheaper than they could by learning it all over by themselves.

More often than not, those who borrowed the new technology had to adapt it to different uses, leading to further refinements and inventions. By the 1850s, armory methods could be found in factories making sewing machines, pocket watches, padlocks, railway equipment, shoes, wagons, and hand tools. And the key transmitters of these methods were New England machine-tool firms closely connected with the Connecticut Valley arms industry, especially the Springfield National Armory.

The Upper Water Shops of the Springfield Armory, 1830. Here, iron components of muskets and pistols were forged before being transported by wagon to another set of shops about a mile away to be machined for assembly. By the 1840s, Springfield had become a leading center of interchangeable manufacturing and machine-tool building in America.

### UNIFORMITY AT WEST POINT AND THE POST OFFICE

The person who presided over the early stages of the army's uniformity project was South Carolina's John C. Calhoun. An avid nationalist, Calhoun possessed a first-class mind, enormous energy, and driving intensity. During the War of 1812, he had been an outspoken critic of the Madison administration's management of the war effort, accusing the president and his cabinet of incompetence. Although Madison recognized Calhoun's talents, he also knew that the South Carolinian had ruffled too many feathers to serve in his cabinet. But after Madison retired in 1817, his successor, James Monroe, asked Calhoun to take over the War Department.

Leaving the House of Representatives in November 1817, Calhoun entered his new office determined to reorganize the military and eradicate the mismanagement he had denounced. Early on, he endorsed the Ordnance Department's budding uniformity program and emphasized the need for discipline and systematic control over everything in the army, from the training of cadets at the U.S. Military Academy at West Point, New York, to more mundane matters such as record keeping and accounting practices. Above all, Calhoun envisioned the army as something more than a fighting force. At a time when people eyed standing armies with suspicion, he felt that the U.S. Army could and should be used for constructive civil purposes.

One of Calhoun's first actions as secretary of war was to appoint Captain Sylvanus Thayer as superintendent of the academy at West Point. Thayer's mission was to reinvigorate the academy, which had been established by Congress in 1802 but had recently fallen on hard times. His model became the innovative French École Polytechnique in Paris with its emphasis on strong training in mathematics, science, and engineering in addition to traditional military subjects. Analytical rigor and discipline became the focus of Thayer's program. His goal was to produce not just competent soldiers but "soldier-technologists" who could build roads and canals (and later, railroads) as well as fortifications. Under Thayer's leadership, West Point would emerge as the nation's top engineering school, rivaled before the Civil War only by the Rensselaer Polytechnic Institute at Troy, New York (established in 1824). The academy's best graduates went into the elite army

*American Journal*

## How Do You Get the News?

The largest and arguably the most popular government agency in America, the U.S. Post Office grew exponentially during the early years of the republic. In 1790, only 75 post offices existed in the United States. The number jumped to 903, by 1800, then to 3000 by 1815, and to nearly 4000 four years later. "In point of public utility," a newspaper editor noted in 1810, "it holds a rank but little inferior to printing." "Copies may be multiplied at the [newspaper] press, but, without this establishment," he continued, "how limited must be their distribution."

The following excerpt, from an Albany, New York publication entitled THE AMERICAN PLOUGH BOY (1820), captures the importance that Americans assigned to the postal system in these years. Among other things, the writer considers the Post Office a critical catalyst of America's westward expansion.

"Among the many conveniences which we at the present day enjoy, there is none that ranks higher and deservedly so, than the general distribution of Post offices throughout our country. There is scarcely a village in these United States so obscure, but what is weekly gladdened with the welcome appearance of the POST. To say nothing of the pleasure which we receive from obtaining FRESH NEWS, pamphlets, magazines, and reviews on a calculated day, and at a moderate expense: to say nothing of the facility of doing business by mail, which has undoubtedly increased wealth to a very great extent by giving early advice of the state of the market: there are two consequences arising from an universal distribution of Post offices . . .

1st–They tend to increase the contentment and happiness of the people.

2d.–They are no small cause of the rapid settlement of our western world; a rapidity of settlement without a parallel. . .

See the tide of emigration rolling far towards the setting sun. See the sons of the east now approximating in their settlements to the strong mountains. The cause is the certainty which we now enjoy of receiving stated and speedy information from any quarter you please. A few days carries a communication with mathematical certainty from one point of the Union to the other. Distance is thus reduced almost to contiguity; and the ink is scarcely dry, or the wax cold on the paper, before we find in our hands, even at a distance of hundreds of miles, a transcript of our dearest friends' mind. . .

These thoughts were suggested by observing that several petitions were before Congress, for the extension of post roads. If we consider the beneficial effects arising from them, we must always feel a pleasure when new ones are established, for they certainly cause pleasure to some, and pain to none. (signed) A COUNTRY CURATE."

*The American Plough Boy, and Journal of the board of Agriculture* [Albany, N.Y.], II (No. 31; Saturday, December 30, 1820).

corps of engineers, ordnance, and artillery intent on bringing greater system and uniformity not just to the manufacture of firearms but to every aspect of military affairs. Low-ranking graduates were assigned to army posts located mainly on the western frontier, their hopes for advancement about as remote as their assignments.

While Thayer revamped West Point's curriculum, Calhoun reorganized the War Department, issuing in 1821 a set of regulations that established clear lines of authority from his office to every branch of the army. The earmarks of Calhoun's new approach—accountability, precision, control—were the same as Thayer's at West Point. Moreover, both schemes meshed with the emphasis that the Ordnance Department placed on uniformity in the sphere of manufacturing. Under the new rules, every army unit (from infantry regiments in the West to the national armories in the East) was required to prepare monthly, quarterly, and annual reports that detailed what they were doing, the condition of their equipment, and how they

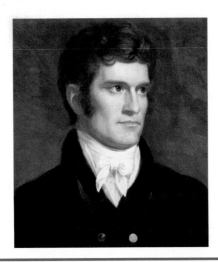

John C. Calhoun, James Monroe's secretary of war (1817–25).

had spent funds allocated to them. Secretary Calhoun and his staff used these reports not only to account for expenditures, but also to compare the performances of individual officers, army units, and army installations, including the national armories. Above all, the new regulations allowed the War Department to exercise greater control over the army's far-flung, multiunit operations. In effect, the War Department under Calhoun's leadership created a bureaucratic management structure that would become a model not only for other government institutions but also for private enterprise.

An early beneficiary of Calhoun's innovations was the U.S. Post Office. In operation since 1775, the postal system had grown as the population grew. By 1816, the system employed more than 3,000 postal officers, 69 percent of the entire federal civilian workforce. By 1828, the United States had 74 post offices for every 100,000 people, and the U.S. Post Office served an area spread over 116,000 square miles, delivering nearly 14 million letters and 16 million newspapers annually. More than any other branch of the federal government, it had the most frequent contact with the general public and their everyday lives. "For the vast majority of Americans," one writer observes, "the postal system *was* the central government."

The person who presided over the expansion of the Post Office during the 1820s was John McLean, a politically ambitious lawyer-politician from Ohio. A friend and protégé of Calhoun, McLean drew on Calhoun's experience as secretary of war in bringing greater system and efficiency to the operations of the

Post Office. Like Calhoun, McLean distributed a detailed set of regulations that covered everything from accounting and inventory methods to the sorting and distribution of mail. He and his competent staff oversaw the scheduling of mail deliveries around the country and negotiated contracts with privately owned postrider, stagecoach, and steamboat lines for carrying the mail.

Of all these conveyances, stagecoaches were the most important until railroads superseded them during the 1840s. In 1828, McLean estimated that the Post Office had under its direct control 17,584 horses, 2,879 carriages, and 243 smaller wagons. As Calhoun had at the War Department, he strongly supported the construction of roads, bridges, and other internal improvements and sponsored the production and distribution of maps that hung in virtually every post office in the United States, reminding the public how important good roads were to the prompt delivery of the mail. Because he headed the country's largest organization and controlled more jobs—public or private—than any other individual in America, McLean was a formidable force in American politics and a perennial contender for the presidency.

The organizational innovations introduced by Calhoun and McLean helped power the expansion of the American economy. These new methods traveled with former army officers (many of them West Point graduates) and postal officials who, after serving the U.S. government, entered private business as consultants, engineers, plant superintendents, and company presidents. With them went the skills, habits of mind, and penchant for system, control, and accountability that characterized the emerging industrial economy and the modern technological age.

### BANKING REFORM

The most pressing domestic problem facing the federal government in 1815—and the second major item on the Madisonian Platform—was the chaotic state of the country's money and banking system. Although the U.S. Mint had issued a limited number of gold, silver, and copper coins each year, the United States had no national currency. Whatever paper money existed came from state-chartered banks. Before the War of 1812, the First Bank of the United States had served as an effective brake on unregulated state banks that issued worthless paper currency by collecting and returning suspect bills and demanding that they be redeemed in gold or silver coin. With the failure of Congress to renew the bank's charter in 1811, that brake was removed, and it did not take long for unbacked paper money to flood the market and prompt runaway inflation.

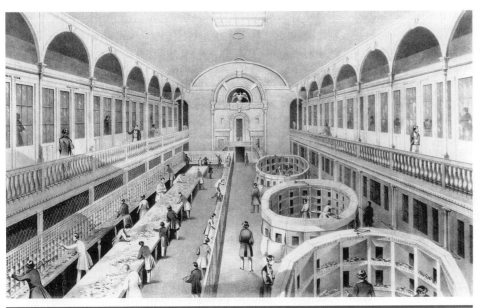

Interior view of the U.S. Post Office at New York (1844), showing the uniform system used for sorting letters, newspapers, and packages for distribution to all parts of the United States and abroad.

bill. The bank bill subsequently passed the House by a healthy margin and, with certain amendments—the most important of which mandated that all government debts be collected in legal U.S. currency (gold or silver) or in banknotes redeemable, on demand, in specie—moved through the Senate to become law on April 10, 1816.

In its final form, the new law provided the Second Bank of the United States with a twenty-year charter and established it as a semiprivate corporation with a capital stock of $35 million. The bill also stipulated that, like its predecessor, the Second Bank's headquarters would be in Philadelphia, with branch banks located throughout the country. Equally important, the bank was obligated to pay the U.S. government a fee, or "bonus," of $1.5 million in three installments over the first four years of its operation. This last point, the so-called Bonus Bill, would soon become a bone of contention when Congress turned to the subject of internal improvements.

Wary of currency presented to them from banks whose credit ratings they knew nothing about, merchants and manufacturers either refused to accept such money or, more often, discounted its value by as much as 30 or 40 percent.

The situation had grown so bad by 1814 that the U.S. Treasury stood on the verge of bankruptcy. Since people invariably chose to pay the government in depreciated paper money rather than hard specie, the treasury became a dumping ground for state banknotes of suspicious worth. Federal officials consequently experienced considerable difficulty using funds collected in one part of the country to pay debts owed elsewhere. The government moved to correct the problem by chartering a Second Bank of the United States. Finding themselves in a situation reminiscent of Jefferson's when debating the constitutionality of the Louisiana Purchase, James Madison and other leading members of the Republican Party quietly set aside questions about the constitutionality of the bank in the interest of solving the currency crisis and placing the treasury on firm financial footing at a time of rapid national expansion.

In January 1816, the House Committee on National Currency introduced a bill calling for the establishment of the Second Bank of the United States. In dramatic fashion, House Speaker Henry Clay, who had strenuously opposed rechartering the First Bank in 1811 on constitutional grounds, stepped down from his podium to admit his mistake and endorse the

Compared with the hundreds of state-chartered banks throughout the country, the Second Bank of the United States was an extraordinarily powerful institution. Simply put, they were small and it was big—very big. In addition to its capital stock of $35 million, the Second Bank became the repository of all federal monies. The paper currency it issued and the loans it made had the full weight of the federal treasury behind them. The bank could also wield considerable influence over interest rates throughout the country. With branches in every important commercial city, it could do exactly what it was chartered to do—namely, act as a stabilizing influence on a rapidly growing economy.

But stability came at a price. The Second Bank of the United States sometimes used its power to stop certain state-chartered banks from issuing paper currency of questionable worth, thereby reducing their ability to make loans. With state banks facing such competitive disadvantages, it did not take long for them to level charges against the Second Bank as an unconstitutional monopoly that favored eastern monied interests. Although the bank survived such accusations throughout the 1810s and 1820s, a political boiling point would come

Headquarters of the Second Bank of the United States in Philadelphia, a prime example of what became known as Greek Revival architecture. The building still stands near Independence Hall in Philadelphia and currently serves as an art museum.

in 1832 with the reelection campaign of President Andrew Jackson. Ironically, the bank's very economic strength became the source of its greatest political vulnerability.

## PROTECTING AMERICAN MANUFACTURERS

As soon as the War of 1812 ended, British manufacturers, eager to undermine U.S. manufacturing and tap the expanding North American trade, began dumping goods in New York and other eastern ports at low prices that threatened to damage, if not destroy, the infant industries that had taken root in the United States during the embargo and war years. In response to calls for government protection from manufacturers centered in Pennsylvania but supported by kindred groups in New England, Ohio, and Kentucky, the Madison administration proposed a tariff bill that offered moderate protection to American manufacturers but fell short of the virtually complete protection of the war years. On imports of cotton and woolen textiles, for example, Madison's secretary of the treasury recommended taxes of 33½ percent and 28 percent, respectively, on the value of goods being imported. When the bill reached the House Ways and Means Committee, however, the rates for both products were slashed to 20 percent, even though the same committee (which had a large southern contingent) ratcheted up the duty on imported sugar to a whopping 56 percent. The setting of tariff rates clearly involved sectional economic interests and, accordingly,

sectional politics. In 1816, after considerable debate, Congress settled on a tariff that levied duties of 30 percent on textile imports for two years, followed by 25 percent for two more years, and finally leveling off in the fifth year at 20 percent.

The idea of scaling down rates over a five-year period came from Daniel Webster, a representative from New Hampshire and an opponent of the protective tariff. Webster, as well as many others in Congress, believed that five years of protection should be enough to place American manufactures on an equal footing with foreign competitors. House Speaker Clay, however, felt differently. His unstinting efforts on behalf of high protective tariffs for all American products made him a hero to many manufacturers. The Delaware gunpowder maker and outspoken protectionist E. I. du Pont became a close friend of Clay's at this time and a staunch supporter of the Kentuckian's subsequent races for the presidency. So, too, did other budding industrialists.

When Madison stepped down from the presidency in March 1817, it seemed a foregone conclusion that Clay would emerge as the foremost spokesman for the Madisonian Platform. In fact, by the mid-1820s, the platform would become better known as Clay's "American System." Whatever the label, they stood for the same thing: protective tariffs, internal improvements, and a strong national bank, all of which assumed an activist role on the part of the federal government as a catalyst of economic growth in advance of free-market forces. Viewed in this light, the Tariff of 1816 served as a critical inducement for industrial development.

Considerable maneuvering went on behind the scenes as the tariff bill took shape. No one proved more effective a lobbyist than the Boston Manufacturing Company's Francis Cabot Lowell. He advocated a tariff that would afford greater protection to cheap cotton goods made by his company than to goods of finer quality from places like Pawtucket, Rhode Island, or Philadelphia. Moreover, Lowell helped persuade Calhoun and other representatives from the cotton-growing regions of the South to support the measure because, he maintained, it protected growers as well as manufacturers from cheap cottons from India that were beginning to compete with American goods.

Calhoun supported the tariff primarily for patriotic rather than economic reasons. National defense and national unity were his primary concerns, but he also realized that economic barriers had to be erected if the United States was to achieve economic independence from Britain. Other southern politicians felt the same; with little or no interest in manufacturing, they voted in favor of protectionism out of an avid nationalism. But that attitude would soon change. While the North veered increasingly toward an industrial economy, the South remained steadfastly agrarian. Cotton was its primary cash crop, and it was dependent on foreign trade for the export of cotton, tobacco, and other raw materials and the import of European manufactured goods. On strictly economic grounds, its leaders recognized that the new tariff threatened foreign trade while increasing the prices southerners had to pay for European imports. With the North and South developing in different directions, it was only a matter of time before their economic differences became manifest in increasingly bitter political clashes.

## INTERNAL IMPROVEMENTS

The most ambitious part of the Madisonian Platform—and the keystone of Clay's American System—concerned internal improvements. Scarcely 100 miles of canals existed in the United States in 1816. Roads in most parts of the country were little more than rutted wagon paths that often became impassable during wet weather. Well-maintained turnpikes and toll roads existed in eastern Pennsylvania, New Jersey, New York, and southern New England, but they often proved prohibitively expensive for the transportation of commercial goods. The National Road, the one federally funded project that sought to link the East with the West, had not yet reached Wheeling on the Ohio River. Every well-informed person recognized that an interconnecting system of roads, canals, steamboat lines, and (later) railroads was essential to economic and geographic expansion. Three questions, however, stood foremost in their minds: Who would be in charge of building such a system? Where would the projects be placed? Who would benefit most from them? At issue was the economic survival of some communities and regions over others.

Although Madison initiated the idea of internal improvements and Clay vigorously supported it, Calhoun took the lead in pressing the issue before Congress. Early in 1817, before he became secretary of war, he sponsored a bill that proposed using the $1.5 million bonus and the dividends from the government's stock in the Second Bank of the United States for the construction of roads and canals. In doing so, he sidestepped the tricky constitutional issues raised by the Bonus Bill by pointing to the military significance of internal improvements and appealing to nationalist sentiments. "Let it never be forgotten," he argued in one of his most impassioned speeches, "that the extent of the republic exposes us to the greatest of calamities—*disunion*. . . . Whatever impedes the intercourse of the extremes with this, the centre of the republic, weakens the union. . . . Let us, then, bind the republic together with a perfect system of roads and canals. Let us conquer space."

When New England Federalists and old-line Jeffersonian strict constructionists questioned the constitutionality of the Bonus Bill, Calhoun replied that the "general welfare" clause made it constitutional. When they continued their opposition, Calhoun appealed to practicality and common sense. "If we are restricted in the use of our money to the enumerated powers [stated in the Constitution], on what principles can the purchase of Louisiana be justified?" he asked. For Calhoun, as well as for other nationalists in Congress, a national transportation system was essential—"the condition of our greatness," as he put it.

Despite Calhoun's eloquence, the Bonus Bill encountered rough sledding: after squeaking through Congress, Madison vetoed the bill on constitutional grounds. Indeed, Madison's veto delivered a blow to postwar nationalism and signaled the abandonment of his expansive economic platform. As much as he tried, even the dynamic Clay could not resurrect the Bonus Bill. President Monroe stood firm in his opposition to using the bonus and dividends from the Second Bank of the United States to create a permanent fund for internal improvements.

All was not lost, however. After declining to sign a bill to extend the National Road into Ohio in 1822, President Monroe issued a lengthy paper entitled "Views of the President of the United States on the Subject of Internal Improvements," in which he admitted that Congress had "the unlimited power to raise money" and appropriate it "to the purposes of common defense and of general, not local, national, not State benefit." This gave congressional nationalists the opening they needed, and they moved quickly to test the president by passing an appropriations bill to repair the National Road—which, cast in the appropriate language of national defense, Monroe signed.

Calhoun kept pressing his views on Monroe about the strategic importance of roads and canals for national defense. Intent on making the War Department the locus of an internal improvements empire, he recommended that the Army Corps of Engineers conduct surveys for roads and canals throughout the nation and, when finished, be placed in charge of their construction. With Calhoun at the peak of his popularity and Clay steering the legislation as Speaker of the House, it did not take long for the first phase of Calhoun's plan to materialize in the General Survey Act of 1824. The bill's emphasis on national defense again enabled President Monroe to sign it into law.

The General Survey Act served an important purpose. The legislation permitted the president to assign army engineers to privately owned transportation companies for the purpose of conducting land surveys of possible routes, estimating costs, and actually supervising construction. Between 1824 and 1828, members of the Army Corps of Engineers worked on ninety-six different projects, most of which were surveys of either state or privately owned roads and canals. After 1828, railroad surveys began to claim an increasing proportion of the engineers' work. One of the earliest and most important was the Baltimore and Ohio Railroad, which originated in the eastern seaport of Baltimore in 1828 and branched westward across the Appalachians into the Ohio Valley at Wheeling and from there on to Cincinnati and St. Louis. By the time the Corps of Engineers wrapped up its work under the General Survey Act in 1840, nearly fifty new railroads had been surveyed—a remarkable accomplishment. As with the development of interchangeable manufacturing, the silent workings of the federal government exercised an enormous influence on industrial development while fostering private enterprise.

The *John Bull*, an early steam locomotive built in England by railroad pioneer Robert Stephenson and shipped to the United States for use on the Camden and Amboy Railroad (New Jersey) in 1831. Once in use, *John Bull's* owners added several important innovations—most notably a pair of pilot wheels (in front) to give the locomotive greater stability and a cowcatcher to move obstructions off the rails.

## Toward Sectionalism

At a time when the future of the United States seemed boundless, two events cast a pall over the nation and shifted the tide from nationalism to sectional interests and bitter political debate.

### THE PANIC OF 1819

While Republican Party leaders struggled over implementing the Madison-Clay platform, the country experienced its first economic depression since the 1780s. Instability set in when the Napoleonic Wars precipitated a spiraling European demand for American farm products. As prices for corn, cotton, flour, beef, and pork soared, an immense speculation in land took place as enterprising Americans scrambled to take advantage of the opportunities for gain presented by Europe's woes.

Cotton proved to be the most volatile commodity. In January 1815, the price of ginned cotton stood at less than 20 cents a pound. By June 1816, it had jumped to the unheard-of level of 30 cents a pound, reaching an all-time high of 33.5 cents a pound in January 1818. The boom was on. As planters and farmers rushed to buy and cultivate more land, the production of agricultural goods—led by cotton—rose accordingly. Since the best opportunities for land acquisition existed in the trans-Appalachian West, the greatest speculations occurred there. Encouraged by policies that allowed the purchase of land on credit, banks—including, for a time, the Second Bank of the United States—jumped into the burgeoning market, making loans to buyers with little or no money down and often no collateral.

What American speculators did not count on was the resilience of the overseas economies. As European agriculture began to recover and as British textile manufacturers turned to India for cheaper cotton, prices for cotton and other staples began to fall. In November 1818, the bubble burst as prices for all goods plummeted. By July 1819, the price of raw cotton stood at less than 15 cents a pound, exactly half the price for the same month a year earlier. Farmers who had bought tracts of land expecting that prices would at least stay the same found themselves deep in debt. Lending banks, which had often issued paper currency far in excess of their specie holdings to support the boom, now teetered on the brink of disaster as the value of their assets dried up with falling prices. When the Second Bank of the United States, which had been lax in its oversight of the currency system, finally began in 1819 to present these banks with their notes and demand payments in hard cash, a full-scale panic ensued. Hundreds of banks, unable to redeem their notes, failed, and thousands of speculators lost their property to foreclosures.

The Panic of 1819 depressed the American economy for nearly six years, with farmers and planters in the Midwest and Southwest particularly hard hit. Once under way, the panic also caught merchants, manufacturers, and working people in its spiraling fall. One response was a widespread call for "stay laws" aimed at protecting debtors in danger of losing their property to creditors. Ten states, including Maryland, Pennsylvania, and Vermont, passed stay laws. Another response was the appearance of trade unions that protested deteriorating working conditions and called for the abolition of imprisonment for debt, an end to fraudulent payments in paper money worth less than its stated value, prohibitions on government-licensed monopolies, and other workplace and social reforms. Within ten years, the union movement would gather momentum, coalesce into the Working Men's Party, and run candidates in the presidential election of 1828. But more broadly, and especially in the West, people blamed the panic and resulting depression on the Second Bank of the United States and wanted it dismantled.

The bank had been badly mismanaged before 1819, but it could hardly be held responsible for the global economic readjustments that followed the Napoleonic Wars and the speculative greed they sparked in America. Western critics nonetheless believed that the bank had caused the depression because it had tightened credit at the wrong time, setting the downturn in motion. As property values fell and bankruptcies mounted, western cities from Pittsburgh to New Orleans suffered immensely. The Second Bank found itself the owner of all sorts of defaulted property and, in the words of Thomas Hart Benton, became "the engrossing proprietor of whole towns." In the minds of westerners like Benton, the Philadelphia-based bank had become a "Monster" because its strict money policy favored eastern creditors who devoured everything in sight. The Panic of 1819 exacerbated sectional divisions within the Republican Party and made the Second Bank of the United States a burning political issue during the next decade.

## THE MISSOURI COMPROMISE

In the midst of the panic, a second crisis traumatized the nation. Late in 1819, the territory of Missouri applied for admission to the Union as a slave state; this move would spark a bitter debate in both houses of Congress between December 1819 and March 1820 over the expansion of slavery and Missouri's admission to the Union.

Before the Missouri controversy, an implicit understanding between the North and South had allowed new states to enter the Union generally in pairs, so that an equal balance between free and slave states could be maintained in the Senate. In 1820, the United States consisted of twenty-two states, evenly divided between free and slave. Missouri's request for admission ignited controversy because, as the first state other than Louisiana (1812) to be carved out of the immense Louisiana Purchase, it was viewed as setting a precedent concerning the future of slavery in other newly admitted states. Politicians from the North and East had never been happy with the "three-fifths" compromise made in the Constitutional Convention of 1787 (which counted nonvoting slaves in apportioning the seats in the House of Representatives), because it gave slave states a voting advantage over free states. They therefore expressed strong feelings about extending such apportionment schemes beyond the Mississippi into places like Missouri. Power politics, it seems, was as much at play during the Missouri debates as any humanitarian concern with the future of slavery in the territories.

Thanks to some skillful maneuvering by Clay, the deadlocked Congress worked out a compromise. The agreement had three components. First, Missouri came into the Union as a slave state. Second, Maine, formerly a part of Massachusetts, was admitted as a free state, thereby preserving the balance between free- and slave-state votes in the Senate. Finally, slavery was thereafter prohibited in all territories north of latitude 36°–30′, the southern boundary of Missouri. With the approval of both houses, President Monroe signed the Missouri Enabling Bill into law on March 6, 1820.

The Missouri Compromise, as it came to be called, received mixed reactions. Nationalists in the North and South hailed the agreement and lauded Henry Clay for his statesmanship as the great "Pacificator." Northern enemies of slavery, however, condemned the compromise because it served southern interests by allowing slavery in Louisiana Purchase territories south of 36°–30′. While generally applauding the compromise, pro-slavery southerners nonetheless felt uncomfortable because it established the precedent that Congress might, in the future, enact laws regarding slavery. They also viewed the Tallmadge Amendment and subsequent attempts to restrict slavery in Missouri as a plot on the part of northern politicians to disrupt the Virginia-led "Republican Ascendancy" fashioned by Thomas Jefferson and his successors and to build a new northern party on its ruins. In such ways, sectional allegiances were becoming a source of divisive feelings. For his part, the elderly Jefferson viewed the Missouri controversy as "a firebell in the night" that threatened to sound "the knell of the Union." "We have the wolf by the ears," he wrote pessimistically to a friend, "and we can neither safely hold him, nor safely let him go." In Jefferson's mind, the Missouri Compromise may have temporarily banked the fires of sectionalism, but it did not put them out. Events would prove him right.

## Adams's Nationalist Foreign Policy

The Panic of 1819 and the Missouri controversy revealed the clashing interests that divided North from South, East from West. But national expansion remained the major theme of the Monroe administration's foreign policy. Between 1817 and 1824, the United States adopted a bold posture in foreign affairs under the leadership of Monroe's secretary of state, John Quincy Adams. Rarely was American diplomacy pursued with greater bravado than during Adams's eight years at the State Department.

As the eldest son of President John Adams, John Quincy Adams was raised in the corridors of power. He had spent most of his distinguished career in the diplomatic service representing the United States in Britain, Russia, the Netherlands, and Prussia before becoming secretary of state in 1817. Possessed of a sharp tongue and even sharper mind, Adams shared a number of traits with his equally talented colleague at the War Department, John C. Calhoun. Both were well educated, highly

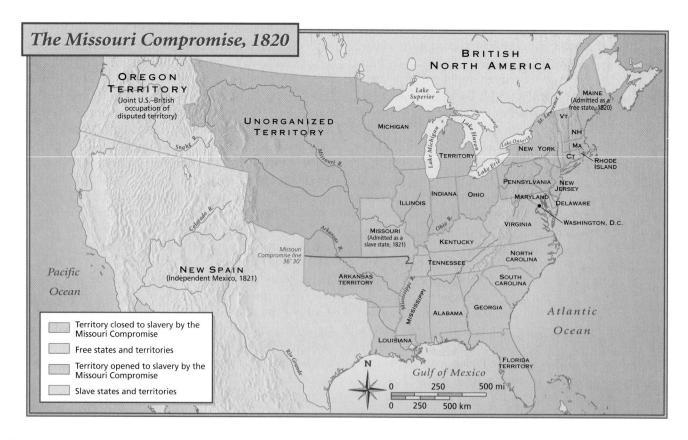

*The Missouri Compromise, 1820*

disciplined, and intense individuals. Both could be cold and austere. Both embraced the Madisonian Platform, believing that the federal government should play an activist role in advancing science, technology, and economic growth. Above all, both were outspoken nationalists who believed that America had a God-given destiny to establish, as Adams put it, "our proper dominion . . . [over] the continent of North America."

Four interrelated concerns defined Adams's foreign policy strategy. First and foremost was his determination to expand American territory. Second was the realization that Spain's Latin American empire was crumbling in the wake of the Napoleonic Wars and that newly independent states like Colombia and Mexico were seeking both diplomatic recognition and trade relationships with other nations. Third was Adams's conviction that Great Britain, through its possession of Canada, its powerful navy, and its interest in dominating trade in both North and South America, posed the greatest economic as well as military threat to the United States. British ambitions therefore needed to be contained if the United States was to realize its desire for expansion in the Americas. Fourth was Adams's view that, with the rapid growth of American manufactures and the loss of privileged access to British West Indian markets, trade with Latin American republics was becoming increasingly important to the United States. If the British could be kept at bay, the United States stood to dominate the Latin American trade and profit enormously.

Adams's commitment to American expansion became explicit in the treaties he negotiated. A case in point is the Anglo-American Convention of 1818, in which he succeeded in establishing perpetual fishing rights for American vessels off the shores of Newfoundland and designating the 49th parallel as the boundary between the United States and Canada from the Lake-of-Woods (in northern Minnesota) to the Rocky Mountains. The latter agreement proved to be particularly important because it brought British recognition of the Louisiana Purchase and all U.S. territorial claims that went with it, including American control over the present states of North Dakota, Montana, and Idaho. The convention also declared that the "Northwest Country" of Oregon beyond the Rockies would remain "free and open" to the subjects of both the United States and Britain for ten years. While this proved to be less than what he wanted, Adams felt confident that in ten years American settlers would pour into the Oregon Country and eventually secure it peacefully for the United States.

Adams's greatest diplomatic coup proved to be the so-called Transcontinental Treaty (also known as the Adams-Onís Treaty) with Spain in 1819. For years, Americans had coveted the Spanish province of Florida. At the time of the Louisiana Purchase, the region included not only the present state of Florida but also the southern portions of Alabama and Mississippi. Exactly what Adams predicted for Oregon had already occurred in Florida. In 1810, American settlers who lived in the region seized the westernmost part of the Florida panhandle. During the War of 1812, American forces took another chunk, including the strategically important port of Mobile. For Adams and many other Americans, it was only a matter of time before the United States would gather in all of Florida.

A turning point came in December 1817, when President Monroe ordered forces under General Andrew Jackson to the Florida border to suppress the activities of Seminole Indians who were raiding American settlements and providing a haven to escaped slaves. When the Spanish and French governments subsequently protested Jackson's punitive expedition into Florida (where he seized two Spanish forts, burned Seminole villages, and executed two British citizens suspected of inciting the Seminole raiders), Adams responded with a threat of his own. If Spain could not control its territory, the United States would; either relinquish Florida immediately, Adams declared, or "Spain would not have the possession of Florida to give us."

Faced with Adams's ultimatum and knowing that it could not control its border with the United States, Spain came to terms. On February 22, 1819, a date that Adams purposely chose to commemorate Washington's birthday, the Transcontinental Treaty was signed. Spain ceded all of Florida to the United States and relinquished all claims to territories north of the 42$^{nd}$ parallel, including the Oregon Country. The United States, in turn, acknowledged Spanish ownership of Texas and agreed to assume all claims made by American merchants against Spain for damages suffered during the Napoleonic Wars, to an amount not exceeding $5 million.

## SPANISH CLAIMS AND THE BIRTH OF LOWELL

All told, the Transcontinental Treaty represented a landmark in America's territorial expansion and one of the great triumphs of John Quincy Adams's long diplomatic career. To carry out the monetary settlements stipulated by the agreement, Congress established a Spanish Claims Commission in 1821 to compensate those with claims against the Spanish government. In effect, the money doled out by the commission during the next three years represented the purchase price of Florida. As a strong proponent of the Madison-Clay

View of Lowell, Massachusetts, America's most famous textile-manufacturing center, c. 1825.

platform and a native of Massachusetts, Adams found further satisfaction when a sizable chunk of the Spanish claims moneys ended up going to his home state and helping to build what, by the 1840s, would become the most extensive manufacturing town in America.

The person who secured the Spanish claims funds for Massachusetts industry was Daniel Webster. A native of New Hampshire and an avowed Federalist, Webster was already well known as a friend of business and a gifted orator. At a time when conflict of interest had little meaning in American society, Webster served simultaneously as a U.S. congressman (and later senator from Massachusetts) and as the chief lobbyist and legal representative of the Boston Associates in Washington. With careful coaching from Francis Cabot Lowell and others, he had played an important role, beginning in 1816, in preparing tariff and patent legislation that favored the interests of the associates but not necessarily all textile manufacturers. Of all his work on behalf of the associates, however, none proved more impressive than his involvement with the Spanish Claims Commission.

Since the bulk of American claims against Spain involved vessels and cargoes lost by merchants during the Napoleonic Wars, a number of Boston Associates as well as several marine insurance companies owned by them became eligible to seek reimbursement. They consequently engaged Webster to represent them before the Spanish Claims Commission, paying him a commission of 5 percent on every dollar they were awarded. Webster proceeded to win over $1 million for them, fully 20 percent of the total claims disbursements.

But that's only part of the story. Webster presented his claims to the commission between 1821 and 1824, the very time that the Boston Associates decided to expand their textile operations beyond Waltham by acquiring a site some twenty-five miles to the north, where the Merrimack River fell thirty-five feet in the space of one mile and had the capability of generating over 9,000 horsepower. After naming the new center after the recently deceased Francis Cabot Lowell, the associates incorporated the Merrimack Manufacturing Company in 1822 and the Hamilton Manufacturing Company in 1825 at a total cost of $1.2 million—almost exactly the same amount that came to them from the Spanish Claims Commission. While it can't be proved that the claim funds were applied directly to the construction of Lowell's early mills, at the very least they had the effect of freeing up venture capital for investment there. Moreover, Webster was rewarded for his services by being allowed to purchase four shares in the highly profitable Merrimack Manufacturing Company, an opportunity usually reserved for those in the associates' innermost circle. The price of these shares came close to the commissions he received from his Spanish claims work. In 1831, Webster won additional payments for the Boston Associates from a French Claims Commission, which corresponded with a second wave of mill building that took place at Lowell between 1832 and 1837.

In just seventeen years (1822–39), Lowell grew from a quiet agricultural village of 200 people into a thriving industrial city of over 18,000. By 1839, America's "city of spindles" had outdistanced the famous mills of Manchester, England, to become the world's leading producer of textiles. The city's nine textile corporations employed over 8,500 workers, three-quarters of whom were young women between the ages of eighteen and twenty-five. Each week its twenty-nine mills churned out over 1 million yards of cloth while consuming 890 bales of cotton. In 1830, in order to satisfy the mills' voracious appetite for cotton, the Boston Associates built one of America's earliest railroads (the Boston and Lowell Railroad) to move the raw material more expeditiously inland from the port of Boston. Businesses from machine shops to dry-goods stores sprang up in Lowell to serve the daily needs of the textile corporations and their employees. But above all, there was the city's primary product: cheap and sturdy cotton cloth. Lucrative markets beckoned not only in the United States but also in Asia and especially in Central and South America. To that end, the Boston Associates strongly supported an aggressive foreign policy that thrust open the doors to markets around the world.

### THE MONROE DOCTRINE

Trade and territorial expansion were central to American foreign policy. This was especially so in the declaration that became known as the Monroe Doctrine. Two developments keyed President Monroe's declaration. One was the potential threat of the so-called Holy Alliance—among Russia, Prussia, and Austria—to restore Spain's lost American colonies. The other was an imperial decree in 1821 by Czar Alexander I of Russia, who ruled Alaska, asserting that all lands in the Pacific Northwest above the 51st parallel belonged to Russia and that no foreign vessels would be permitted within 100 miles of its coastline. In effect, the Russian announcement denied the rights to the Oregon Country that the United States had recently obtained from Spain in the Transcontinental Treaty, as well as the right of American merchants to trade in the area. Of course, Great Britain and the United States protested the action.

In the fall of 1823, British prime minister George Canning proposed that Great Britain and the United States issue a joint declaration against European intervention in Latin America. President Monroe seemed to favor the idea, especially when former presidents Jefferson and Madison recommended it. But not so John Quincy Adams. Canning's proposal offended Adams's nationalist sensibilities and aroused his suspicions. Since the British navy would see to it that other European nations stayed out of Latin America anyway, said Adams, what purpose would a joint declaration serve other than to forestall America's future interests in the region? Instead, he recommended that the United States issue a unilateral declaration, thereby asserting its independence from Europe and maintaining complete freedom of action in the Western Hemisphere.

Adams's argument again won the day. On December 2, 1823, in his annual address to Congress, the president issued the doctrine that became associated with his name. The message established three basic principles: noncolonization, isolation, and nonintervention. Concerning the first, Monroe forthrightly stated that "the American continents ... are henceforth not to be considered as subjects for future colonization by any European powers." As for the second, "in the wars of the European powers," Monroe declared, "we have never taken part, nor does it comport with our policy to do so." Finally, he warned Europe about intervening in American affairs. "We should consider any attempt ... to extend their system to any portion of this hemisphere as dangerous to our peace and safety," he concluded. America was for Americans; Europeans were to keep their hands off.

The language of the declaration came from Monroe, but the crucial ideas behind the message originated with John Quincy Adams. In the short run, the Monroe Doctrine had little immediate effect because the Holy Alliance, in the face of British opposition, had already abandoned any intention of intervening in Latin America. Moreover, Adams's repeated protests had induced the czar to renounce his claims to all territory south of 54°–40′ in the Pacific Northwest. Nonetheless, the Monroe Doctrine made Americans feel as if they were standing up to European bullies and asserting themselves in hemispheric politics. And in the long run, the Monroe Doctrine, along with Washington's Farewell Address, became the foundation on which American foreign policy rested for over a century.

As it turned out, the principles enunciated in the doctrine proved more of a challenge to the industrial, seaward-oriented British, whose merchant marine controlled a substantial portion of the Latin American trade, than to any other European power. But England nonetheless continued to pursue its com-

James Monroe, fifth president of the United States (1817–25), and the last of the so-called Virginia Dynasty of presidents.

mercial interests in the Americas as if nothing had happened. A race was on to see who would control the commerce, if not the territory, of the Pacific Northwest and all of Latin America, and this time the key players were Britain and the United States, the most rapidly industrializing nations in the world.

## The Election of 1824

The sectional divisions generated by the Missouri crisis and the Panic of 1819 set the stage for the presidential election of 1824. The Virginia Dynasty was coming to an end, and the Republican program for national economic development was dissipating into bitterly contested personal and sectional agendas. In previous administrations, the office of secretary of state had served as a stepping-stone to the White House. Thomas Jefferson's secretary of state had been James Madison, and Madison's secretary of state had been James Monroe. John Quincy Adams therefore seemed the logical choice to succeed Monroe, and he certainly wanted the job. But others did, too: two of them were Monroe's secretary of war, John C. Calhoun, and secretary of the treasury, William Crawford of Georgia. Calhoun quickly dropped out of the race to run successfully for the vice-presidency. He was only forty-two years old in 1824, and he could afford to be patient. Crawford, a giant of a man and an early favorite to win, won the endorsement of Jefferson and stayed in the race even though he

was gravely ill. The two most serious challengers, to Adams, however, were Henry Clay and Andrew Jackson.

The dynamic and resourceful Clay lusted for the presidency. As Speaker of the House, he was well known to Washington insiders. Unlike the other candidates, he offered a clearly defined program in his American System of internal improvements, protective tariffs, and a strong national bank. The trouble was that sectional interests were becoming so strong that virtually no region embraced the whole system. The Kentuckian's stand on internal improvements, for example, won little support in New York and New England, while his position on high tariffs won him even less support in the cotton South. Clay's strongest backing came from the border states and the Midwest. But even there his stand on the national bank encountered stiff opposition from supporters of Andrew Jackson in neighboring Tennessee.

Of all the candidates, the volcanic Jackson, a military hero known as "Old Hickory," enjoyed the greatest popularity. His personal appearance, especially his tall build and strong features, proved to be another attraction; he *looked* presidential. As early as February 1823, a popular convention of Jackson supporters meeting in Harrisburg, Pennsylvania, chose him as their candidate to succeed Monroe. Unlike Clay, Jackson had no clear program of action. Even though he had served in the House of Representatives and the Senate, he remained a Washington outsider. In Congress, he had voted in favor of the General Survey Act and a new protective tariff. As a slaveholder, he also opposed federal efforts to restrict slavery. But first and foremost, he was a military man and a nationalist, and this made him attractive to a growing number of voters, particularly in the expanding West and South.

When the results of the election came in, Jackson won nearly as many popular votes as Adams and Clay put together. However, he failed to win a majority in the electoral college, which meant that, for a second time, the election was thrown into the House of Representatives. Under the Twelfth Amendment, only the three top electoral vote getters remained eligible. Clay was eliminated from the contest, but as Speaker of the House and victor in the states of Kentucky, Missouri, and Ohio, he was, ironically, placed in the position of kingmaker. He threw his support to Adams.

Clay's choice seemed logical enough. Apart from their natural rivalry as the West's leading political figures, Clay and Jackson had been bitter enemies ever since Clay had condemned Jackson's invasion of Florida in 1818. William Crawford, for his part, was seriously ill and, in any event, was an outspoken states' rights opponent of Clay's beloved American System. By a process of elimination, only Adams remained. Although the freewheeling Clay and the somber Adams had little in common personally, both were avid nationalists who saw eye to eye on the need for the American System. Thus Clay, in total disregard of Jackson's popular vote as well as the Kentucky legislature's instructions to support Old Hickory, used his considerable power as House Speaker to see to it that Adams was elected on the first ballot.

At this point, Adams made an honest but costly mistake. Soon after his election, he announced Clay's appointment as his secretary of state and, it appeared, heir apparent. Howls of protest immediately erupted from Jackson's camp to the effect that Adams and Clay had struck a "Corrupt Bargain." Jackson excoriated Clay as "the Judas of the West" and asserted that "corruption and intrigues at Washington . . . defeated the will of the people." Others, like the irascible Jeffersonian John Randolph of Virginia, sneered at the unholy alliance between "the Puritan [Adams] and the black-leg [Clay]." "It was impossible [for Jackson] to win the game," he claimed, because "the cards were packed." An outraged Clay subsequently challenged Ran-

dolph to a duel over these remarks. Although three shots were fired, neither man was injured. But the political damage had been done.

## DISRUPTION OF THE AMERICAN SYSTEM

For the next four years, Adams labored under the shadow of the election of 1824. Hard as he tried, he could not neutralize the criticism that came from the Jacksonian camp and its growing league of supporters. Nor could he deflect the country from a decided turn away from postwar nationalism toward states' rights and sectionalism. In his inaugural address, Adams emphasized that "the spirit of improvement is abroad upon the earth" and summoned the country to a full-blown program of federally sponsored public works. Among other things, he recommended the founding of a national university, the construction of an astronomical observatory, the establishment of a uniform standard of weights and measures, the reform of the patent system, the creation of a new Department of the Interior, the exploration of western territories, and the construction of a vast system of roads, canals, and harbor facilities that would accelerate the growth of commerce. Even Clay seemed taken aback by the president's ambitious vision. In fact, of all of Adams's cabinet members, only Secretary of the Treasury Richard Rush approved of "near the whole."

Jacksonians seized on Adams's inaugural address to criticize his administration. His concluding remark admonishing Congress not "to slumber in indolence" or be "palsied by the will of our constituents" allowed them to resurrect the old accusation that "all Adamses are monarchists" and to argue that this Adams, in particular, cared not at all about the will of the people. Tarred first by the brush of corruption and now with the brush of antidemocracy, the president seemed at a loss as to how to explain himself.

Years later, an embittered Adams reflected on the cause of his stillborn presidency. "The great effort of my administration," he wrote a friend in 1837,

> was . . . the application of all the superfluous revenue of the Union into internal improvement which . . . would have afforded high wages and constant employment to hundreds of thousands of laborers, and in which every dollar expended would have repaid itself fourfold. . . . With this system . . . the surface of the whole Union would have been checkered over with railroads and canals. . . . When I came to the Presidency the principle of internal improvement was swelling the tide

John Quincy Adams, son of former president John Adams and sixth president of the United States (1825–29).

*of public prosperity, till the Sable Genius of the South saw the signs of his own inevitable downfall in the unparalleled progress of the general welfare in the North, and fell to cursing the tariff and internal improvement, and raised the standard of free trade, nullification, and state rights. I fell and with me fell, I fear, never to rise again in my day, the system of internal improvement by means of national energies.*

Adams's grand plan fell victim to more than the accusations of Jacksonians and "the Sable Genius of the South," a reference to slavery. Deepening sectional divisions throughout the country had already dampened the prospects for his federally centered program. First Virginians (including Thomas Jefferson), then other southerners objected to the idea of a national university and an astronomical observatory as a scandalous waste of money. How were such institutions to be financed? By higher tariffs? To southerners, such proposals meant the expansion of the federal government and its encroachment on the states. They warned that if the central government could build canals, schools, and observatories, it could interfere with slavery. Did Adams's "federative fraternity," one of them pointedly asked, include "a system of emancipation"? Many thought so.

Equally worrisome to Jacksonians from all parts of the country was the growing size of the central government and the patronage power of officials who oversaw large bureaucracies like the Post Office, the Second Bank of the United States, and internal improvement projects. Since Jackson was the only major candidate who lacked access to such patronage in the election of 1824, Jacksonians railed against it. Although Adams refused to use patronage appointments to reward supporters, plenty of others did.

But these were not the only complaints. Adams's commitment to use the sale of public lands as a source of revenue for internal improvements alienated many who lived west of the Appalachians. They feared that this would mean higher land prices, which in turn would slow western settlement. James K. Polk of Tennessee ably conveyed westerners' sense of alarm and the social as well as sectional antagonisms it generated. "The policy," he argued before Congress in 1830, "is, to sell your lands high, [and] prevent thereby the inducements to emigration, retain a population of paupers in the East, who may, of necessity, be driven into manufactories to labor at low wages for their daily bread." In Polk's mind, Adams and his northern cronies were conspiring not just against western farmers but against working people everywhere. Such a policy showed Adams for what he was: an elitist puppet of eastern monied interests. Again, sectional politics was rearing its disruptive head.

Adams's demeanor as president did little to defuse these attacks. Part of the problem rested with his flinty personality; part stemmed from his inability to surround himself with trusted and able cabinet members; and part arose from his unwillingness to use the spoils system to reward loyal supporters. His supporters consequently drifted away, and with them went any semblance of a strong party organization capable of defending and advancing his political agenda.

All these factors worked against Adams's form of federalism and in favor of states' rights. The latter, in turn, quickly became identified with grassroots democratic reform under the banner of Andrew Jackson. Old Hickory's managers shrewdly cultivated his image as a heroic military commander while proclaiming him "a uniform and consistent democrat." He was a man of the people leading a revolt against not only political corruption but also corrupt politicians' control of politics. Most important, he would return power to where it rightfully belonged: the states and, through them, the people.

Adams lacked such management. Despite his intellectual ability and impressive national vision, he lacked the political skill to be an effective president. His personal failings, however, were only part of the story. Fundamental changes were taking place in the structure of American politics, changes that placed new demands on presidential leadership. Politics was being reconfigured in response to the increasing regional specialization of the economy. The unfolding of these changes marked the arrival of an expansive but also tension-filled era in American history.

## Suggested Reading

Robert G. Angevine, *The Railroad and the State* (2004)

Maurice G. Baxter, *Henry Clay and the American System* (1995)

Daniel Feller, *The Jacksonian Promise: America, 1815–1840* (1995)

Forest G. Hill, *Roads, Rails, and Waterways: The Army Engineers and Early Transportation* (1957)

Richard R. John, *Spreading the News* (1996).

Merrill D. Peterson, *The Great Triumvirate: Webster, Clay, and Calhoun* (1987)

Charles G. Sellers, Jr., *The Market Revolution: Jacksonian America, 1815–1846* (1991)

C. Edward Skeen, *1816 America Rising* (2003)

Merritt Roe Smith, *Harpers Ferry Armory and the New Technology* (1977)

George R. Taylor, *The Transportation Revolution, 1815–1860* (1951)

# Chapter Review

## Summary

### QUESTIONS

■ What were the most pressing problems facing the United States after the War of 1812? How would you prioritize them?

■ What role did John C. Calhoun and John McLean play in defining the "New Epoch"? What vision did they share in common?

■ What was Henry Clay's "American System"? How did it relate to the "American system" of manufacturing? Why were both important to the long term growth of the Untied States?

■ What was the Missouri Compromise? Why was it significant?

■ Who best represented America's vision for the future in 1824, John Quincy Adams or Andrew Jackson?

## Key Terms

The Madisonian Platform (p. 295)

The Panic of 1819 (p. 303)

The Missouri Compromise (p. 303)

The Transcontinental Treaty (p. 305)

The Monroe Doctrine (p. 307)

## Chronology

| | |
|---|---|
| December 5, 1815 | The Madisonian Platform introduced. |
| 1816 | Tariff of 1816. |
| April 10, 1816 | Second Bank of the United States chartered. |
| December 1817 | Andrew Jackson attacks Seminoles in Florida. |
| 1819 | Panic leads to six-year depression. |
| February 22, 1819 | Transcontinental Treaty (Adams-Onis Treaty) signed with Spain. |
| March 6, 1820 | The Missouri Compromise. |
| 1822 | Textile mills established at Lowell, Massachusetts. |
| December 2, 1823 | Monroe Doctrine issued. |
| 1824 | General Survey Act. |
| 1827 | Baltimore & Ohio Railroad chartered (construction begins in 1828). |
| 1831 | Hall and North produce rifles with interchangeable parts. |

# Chapter 11

# POLITICAL INNOVATION IN A MECHANICAL AGE:

## 1828–1840

*Stump Speaking*, painted by George Caleb Bingham, c. 1856.

- **How did sectional interests affect the alignment of parties in the 1820s?**

- **What were the main political and social innovations of the Jacksonian period?**

- **How did the issue of state vs. federal authority emerge under Jackson?**

- **What were the central issues in the controversy over the Bank of the United States?**

- **How was the legal basis for commercial expansion established in this period?**

- **How did the policy of Indian removal come about?**

- **How did a new party system emerge in the 1830s?**

The thirteen years from the controversial presidential contest of 1824 through Andrew Jackson's two terms as president was a time of vast economic and political ferment in America. New technologies speeded up the pace of life while spurring westward expansion. Some viewed these great changes with hope, while others regretted the loss of an older world with its valued traditions. The deaths of John Adams and Thomas Jefferson on the same day—July 4, 1826, the fiftieth anniversary of the Declaration of Independence—seemed to symbolize this passing.

Between 1824 and 1837, the United States experienced the onset of a transportation revolution, the expansion of a factory system incorporating new manufacturing methods, and the explosive growth of urban centers such as New York and Baltimore. With each new technology came greater occupational specialization. Cash wages began to supplant older barter arrangements and other sorts of non-monetary exchanges so common in the past. The demand for store-bought goods, formerly expensive and in short supply, now escalated. People from all sections of the country yearned for larger arenas in which to buy and sell. As roads, canals, and railroads penetrated the countryside, eventually crossing the Appalachian Mountains into the Ohio and Mississippi river valleys, an identifiable national economy began to emerge.

Together, these changes signaled the beginning of a "market revolution"—a change that would transform the United States from a nation of farmers into a nation of city dwellers and industrial employees. The transformation would continue into the twentieth century, but its basic earmarks—an industrial economy oriented toward national and international markets—were becoming apparent by the 1830s. The changing structure of the American economy raised issues that changed the structure of American politics as well. In place of the well-educated and urbane Jefferson and Adams, the rough-hewn and aggressive Andrew Jackson came to symbolize the new age.

Although politics remained essentially local, national issues dominated debate during the 1830s. The three great issues—tariffs, internal improvements, and the national bank—were spawned by the market revolution with its new manufacturing and transportation systems. Prompted by the Madisonian Platform, politicians like John Quincy Adams and Henry Clay had sought to jump-start the American economy by using the federal government, especially its executive departments, in planning and executing the American System. But Andrew Jackson bolted from their ranks, especially after the "Corrupt Bargain" of 1824. Concerned about the growing power of the federal government and fearful about the potential threat it posed to slavery in America, he tried to turn back the clock to Jeffersonian times by constraining federalism. In the process, Jackson and his supporters would create a new institution—the Democratic Party, a permanent organization that relied on the spoils system to reward loyal party workers with federal government jobs. One of the great political innovations of the nineteenth century, the Democratic Party was the first mass party in America. Like the Jeffersonian dogma on which it was based, it stood for states' rights and limited government while at the same time championing democracy (for white males) and perpetuating the institution of slavery through aggressive territorial expansion—especially into Indian territory. Although Jackson and his party would succeed in reducing the power of the federal government, they could not stop the gathering momentum of the market revolution. Nor did they wish to. Rather, they turned it into a different channel, one dominated by market forces and private enterprise rather than by federally centered initiatives.

## Jacksonian Democrats

For nearly a decade after the War of 1812, the United States had only one major political party. The demise of the Federalists left the Jeffersonian Republican Party as the dominant force in politics. Yet rather than being a highly centralized organization with a clear chain of command, the Jeffersonian Republicans consisted of numerous factions dominated by local personalities who operated primarily at the state level, with little interest in a coordinated national organization. The party's fragility became apparent during the bitter political

skirmishes that occurred during and after the election of 1824. After the election, followers of John Quincy Adams and Henry Clay formed the National Republican Party, and in 1834 its successor, the Whig Party, while those who favored Andrew Jackson coalesced into the Democratic Party. Both parties were driven more by a thirst for office than by high-minded political principles. Of the two parties, the Jacksonian Democrats put together the most formidable national organization. Critical to its success were party-sponsored newspapers that attacked the opposition, promulgated party positions, kept the membership together, and organized campaigns. Newspaper editors accordingly served as party managers and often as local party leaders.

Atop the Democratic Party leadership stood Andrew Jackson. During the 1820s, he had gone from being a nationalist who quietly supported higher tariffs and internal improvements to a presidential candidate who increasingly adopted a states' rights platform and questioned the constitutionality of federally funded internal improvements and, most of all, the federally chartered Second Bank of the United States. Jackson found an important ally in New York's Senator Martin Van Buren. A talented political organizer, Van Buren viewed himself as a disciple of Thomas Jefferson. He steadfastly opposed a strong central government. This also meant that he opposed Henry Clay's American System as well as John Quincy Adams's expanded version of it. Like Jackson, he believed that the foundation of a free society rested on "good old jeffersonian Democratic republican principles." More than anyone else, Van Buren was responsible for assembling the coalition of eastern, southern, and western interest groups that, in the late 1820s and early 1830s, resulted in the Democratic Party.

### THE SOUTH CAROLINA EXPOSITION AND PROTEST

One person Van Buren recruited to Jackson's cause was John C. Calhoun. No one had been more blatantly nationalistic during and immediately after the War of 1812 than Calhoun. Yet between 1824 and 1828, he adopted an increasingly vehement states' rights po-

Andrew Jackson speaking to a crowd of well-wishers.

sition in domestic matters while continuing as a nationalist in military and foreign affairs.

Calhoun's retreat from economic nationalism stemmed from his frustrated ambitions for the presidency as well as the changing political circumstances in his home state of South Carolina. He could not abide the election of John Quincy Adams, because he believed that "bargain and corruption" had tainted the process. In the support South Carolina had given Jackson, Calhoun recognized a shift away from his brand of economic nationalism. This became evident in 1825, when states' righters in the South Carolina legislature—irked by higher tariff rates on European imports at a time of falling cotton prices—passed resolutions declaring the protective tariff (passed in 1824) and internal improvements unconstitutional and accused Calhoun of being a party to both measures. With cotton prices continuing to fall and planters blaming their misfortunes on the protective tariff, Calhoun began to draw back from economic nationalism and turn toward states' rights in an effort to salvage his political career.

Knowing of Calhoun's alienation from the Adams administration and his political difficulties at home, Van Buren courted the South Carolinian throughout 1826. At this time, Calhoun openly broke with Adams and Clay over the American System as well as their conciliatory policy toward slave revolts that were erupting in Latin America. Underlying these conflicts were long-standing personal animosities between Clay and Calhoun. The final break came in 1826 when Van Buren and Calhoun agreed that Calhoun would join forces with Jackson and become his vice-presidential running mate in the election of 1828.

As the election approached, Calhoun became increasingly drawn into the tariff debate. As president of the Senate, he had already revealed his opposition to protective tariffs in 1827, when he cast the deciding vote against a bill strongly supported by northern farmers that would have raised duties on imported woolen goods. However, a far more serious challenge occurred the following year when Congress, largely at Van Buren's instigation, passed and President Adams signed a new tariff bill that jacked up duties on foreign imports to the highest levels since the War of 1812. Van Buren pushed for the new Tariff of 1828 because he wanted to garner support for Jackson from the Northeast and Midwest in the upcoming election. But in doing so, he touched off a storm of protest from southern politicians, including Calhoun, who felt that they had been duped by the wily "Red Fox of Kinderhook."

Throughout the South, the Tariff of 1828 became known as the "Tariff of Abominations." South Carolina took the lead

in condemning the law when a special committee of the state legislature asked Calhoun to prepare a document setting forth the wrongs done by the federal government and how they could be remedied. He agreed to undertake the task.

The product of his labors was entitled *The South Carolina Exposition and Protest.* In it, he argued that the Tariff of 1828 levied an unjust tax on the South because its high rates not only helped northern manufacturers but also invited retaliatory measures by European countries—particularly Great Britain—that exported manufactured goods to the United States. Since cotton was America's leading export and since southerners benefited economically from access to cheaper European imports, the higher tariff meant that they were saddled with a double burden: already low prices for cotton and now higher prices for manufactured goods. A constitutional remedy for such an intolerable law had to be found, and Calhoun discovered it in what he referred to as the "compact" theory of government. Since the Constitution represented a compact between the original thirteen states, it followed that sovereignty ultimately rested with the people of the individual states, not the federal government. Calhoun therefore reasoned that a state had the right to nullify any federal law that operated against its best interests until three-fourths of all the states decided the question in a special convention. If the federal government persisted in enforcing the law within the nullifying state or used force against it, that state in turn had the right to secede from the Union.

The *Exposition and Protest* struck forcefully at federal power and placed state sovereignty at the center of the American political system. Calhoun admitted that he had crafted a harsh solution to the sectional problem. But he saw it as something of a compromise. He loved the Union, but he feared for his state. He believed that a strongly worded statement on nullification would offset the demands of radical "fire-eaters" within his state who were calling for immediate secession, bring all parties to their senses, and, in effect, save the Union.

In the short run, South Carolina's nullification movement had little impact because no other state joined the protest. But the publication of the *Exposition and Protest,* after the 1828 election, put Calhoun on a collision course with Jackson. Nor would southerners forget the document. Calhoun had made his point brilliantly, and his ideas would become a rallying point for those who would eventually break from the Union in 1861.

A good deal more was at stake than tariffs, however. By the late 1820s, many South Carolinians had grown fearful of the rise of antislavery groups in the North and blamed them for slave unrest like the alleged 1822 conspiracy of Denmark Vesey, a free black in Charleston who supposedly plotted to seize ships and take off for Santo Domingo. They used every opportunity to excoriate the activities of radical abolitionist groups as well as the more conservative American Colonization Society, founded in 1816 and dedicated to the removal of free blacks from the United States to Africa. As much as protective tariffs galled southerners, they represented "the occasion rather than the real cause" of southern discontent.

Calhoun put the issue succinctly. If the northern majority who controlled Congress could use "the right of laying duties, not only to raise revenue, but to regulate the industry of the country," what was to prevent it from acting on "any purpose that the majority think to be for the general welfare"? The answer seemed perfectly obvious to South Carolina fire-eaters like Judge William Harper. "In contending against the Tariff," he observed in 1831, "I have always felt that we were combating the symptom instead of the disease. [Federal] Consolidation is the disease.... Tomorrow may witness ... [an attempt] to relieve ... your free negroes, first; and afterwards, your slaves." The vulnerability felt by slaveholders in 1828 would soon become the source of bitter divisions in American politics.

### THE ELECTION OF 1828

As early as December 1827, John Quincy Adams privately acknowledged that he would probably not be reelected to a second term. Having lost majorities in both houses of Congress the previous fall, his political future looked grim. Nonetheless, Adams determined not to go down without a fight. His chief opponent was Andrew Jackson, whose managers depicted him as a Washington outsider who stood for the common man against privileged elitists like Adams.

While he did indicate an antipathy toward the Second Bank of the United States, Jackson was vague about issues like the tariff and internal improvements. Like Adams, he remained silent about the provision of free public schools, the abolition of imprisonment for debt, the establishment of a ten-hour workday, and other egalitarian reforms. Instead, the campaign degenerated into mud slinging and personal invective.

When the election results came in, Jackson won a convincing but not overwhelming victory. Adams captured 44 percent of the popular vote and carried all of New England, as well as Delaware, New Jersey, and most of Maryland. New York divided between the candidates, but Jackson carried

everything else, including Henry Clay's home state of Kentucky. The victory meant that for the first time a westerner would occupy the White House and two slaveholders—Jackson and Calhoun—would hold the top positions in the federal government.

The election also signified a transfer of power from the East to the West. Recognizing this, northerners and southerners vied to strengthen their economic and political ties to the West. With the new president a southerner by birth, southern politicians looked to Jackson to protect their section's vital interests, most notably slavery. They also counted on the support of his vice-president, Calhoun, who in 1828 considered Jackson an ally and fully expected to succeed him.

Among the most important questions of the day was who would control the burgeoning trade west of the Appalachians. New York, with the Erie Canal and excellent steamboat service down the Hudson River to the sea, held a decided advantage, but other states from Massachusetts and Pennsylvania in the North to Maryland, Virginia, and South Carolina in the South hurried to challenge New York's lead. Efforts to secure economic connections with the West also meant building South-West and North-West political alliances. The resulting maneuvering over national legislation pertaining to tariffs, banks, roads, rails, and waterways brought sectional differences to the very center of American politics.

## Jackson and the Expansion of Democracy

Andrew Jackson's inauguration on March 4, 1829, was unlike anything Washington had ever seen. Thousands of supporters converged on the Capitol to see the "old hero" sworn in. Amid thunderous applause, Jackson moved to the podium, bowed to the "majesty of the people," and delivered a brief speech in which he promised to protect states' rights, pay off the national debt, and adopt "judicious" policies concerning tariffs and internal improvements. He also promised to return power to the people by reforming the civil service and correcting "those abuses that have brought the patronage of the Federal Government into conflict with the freedom of elections, and ... have placed or continued power in unfaithful or incompetent hands." Although Jackson did not mention the Adams administration by name, few listeners missed the meaning of his remarks. Daniel Webster saw the situation differently: it was not "the people" but office seekers who flooded Washington for Jackson's inaugural. "*They really seem*

A satirical view of Jackson's inaugural celebration entitled "The President's Levee, or All Creation Going to the White House." The artist, no Jackson supporter, clearly wished to portray the mob-like behavior of the throngs that attended the party.

Although he did not coin the phrase, Jackson believed in the dictum "To the victors belong the spoils." His oft-stated objective was to reduce, if not totally eliminate, a growing "class" of government bureaucrats who, in his view, seemed to think that they should hold their offices for life. During his first eighteen months in office, he removed 919 federal appointees, virtually all of whom held well-paid supervisory positions. In the largest bureaucracy—the U.S. Post Office—the housecleaning began at the top when Jackson replaced the postmaster general, his chief clerk, and the first and second postmasters general, followed by over 400 postmasters. Those dismissed tended to be the highest paid, and most came from those parts of the country—New England, the mid-Atlantic, and Midwest—where the Jacksonian party was weakest. There were relatively few dismissals in the South and Southwest, where the Jacksonian movement was strongest.

In short, the Jacksonians used patronage positions to install people loyal to the party and to consolidate their political base in areas where it needed strengthening. By removing competent people from office, the spoils system challenged the meritocratic government agencies that Calhoun and John McLean had presided over during the 1820s. Its impact would become even more widespread as Jackson's successors expanded it during the next thirty years.

### VOTING RIGHTS

How much did Andrew Jackson influence the expansion of democracy in America? Although his new political party would become known during the 1830s as the Democratic Party, and as much as he touted "the sovereignty of the people," called for majoritarian rule, and cultivated his image as a "man of the people," Jackson was more of a symptom than a cause of democracy in America. Before he became a candidate for president, democratic impulses were already sweeping the country, and they came from all corners of the Republic. The War of 1812 was an important benchmark.

Before the conflict, most state constitutions restricted the right to vote to free adult white males who either owned property or paid taxes in their communities. But when it came to actually voting, enforcement of the rules varied from state to state and often from one community to another within the same state, depending on who oversaw elections. In numerous

*to think that the country is rescued from some dreadful danger,"* he noted sarcastically.

While anti-Jacksonian critics like Supreme Court justice Joseph Story roundly condemned the noisy celebration as "the reign of KING MOB," Jackson supporters relished the scene for what it symbolized. "It was a proud day for the people," a western newspaper reported. "General Jackson is *their own* President . . . [and] he was greeted by them with an enthusiasm which bespoke him the Hero of a popular triumph."

If any single principle informed Jackson's politics, it was his commitment to democratic majority rule. He repeatedly declared that "the people are the government, administering it by their agents; they are the Government, the sovereign power." To Jackson, the people included free adult white males but not blacks, Indians, or women. Nonetheless, for its time, his conception of democracy marked a significant departure from the ideas of his predecessors in the White House. Jackson believed that key government officials should be directly elected "by the people," not indirectly elected by state legislatures (as were U.S. senators) or appointed (as were federal judges). He advocated an end to elitism and special privilege in government, and he demanded "a general extension of the law which limits [all government] appointments to four years." The system should be changed through "rotation of office."

communities, legally ineligible males voted. The prevailing rule seemed to be that so long as you were a white male and a recognized member of the community, you could vote.

It was only a matter of time before property-oriented restrictions gave way to broader voting rights. The new state of Ohio, upon being admitted to the Union in 1802, pointed the way when it adopted a constitution that extended the franchise to all white males who either paid taxes or worked them off by devoting a certain amount of time each year to building and maintaining public roads. The movement toward universal white male suffrage gathered further momentum after the War of 1812, when five new states—Indiana, Illinois, Alabama, Missouri, and Maine—adopted constitutions that opened up the franchise. Soon Connecticut, Massachusetts, and New York jettisoned all property qualifications for voting and adopted minimal tax-payment standards. By the 1850s, virtually all white males could vote, although restrictions continued to be imposed on free blacks and other minorities.

The right to vote expanded so dramatically after the war because of changes in America's social structure brought on by a rapid population growth and the onset of industrialization. Between 1820 and 1850, the population of the United States more than doubled to over 20 million people, cities grew, and vast new territories came under the American flag. As machine-based manufacturing spread, a growing proportion of the population owned little or no property at all. From these artisans, mechanics, small shopkeepers, tenant farmers, and laborers came grassroots pressure to expand the franchise in the form of petitions to state legislatures and state constitutional conventions. A Louisianan aptly captured the spirit of the age when he observed, "If a man can *think* without property, he can *vote* without property." Clearly, political values were inclining in the direction of democracy.

Economic and political self-interest also played a role in expanding the electorate. In sparsely populated regions of the country, voters supported white male suffrage because they believed that doing so would encourage settlement, raise property values, and stimulate economic development. In the highly partisan ferment of the 1820s and 1830s, politicians supported the expansion of the franchise because it gave them the opportunity to win new voters and gain an edge over opponents. Even employers tended to support the new democracy because it allowed them to influence the outcome of local elections by swaying their employees.

In industrial communities, not only did workers seek to vote, but factory masters urged them to go to the polls. Near Wilmington, Delaware, for example, the gunpowder manufacturer E. I. du Pont and his sons regularly closed their Brandywine works on election day and gave their men the day off with pay. On several election days during the 1810s and 1820s, the du Ponts, along with other local manufacturers, actually gathered their workers together (many of whom were foreign-born Irish who had yet to become citizens) and paraded them en masse to the polls at a nearby tavern, where they were treated to free drinks after voting.

Political adversaries frequently accused the du Ponts of illegally interfering with elections by encouraging their employees to vote and even handing them ballots for favorite candidates as they entered the polling place. The voting took place in the open, and with different political parties using different-colored ballots, it was easy to see what candidates a person supported. No evidence exists that the Du Pont Company fired anyone for voting the wrong ticket, although evidence from other communities suggests

George Caleb Bingham's painting *County Election* reveals the public culture of elections in early America. Election days were often festive occasions, a time when businesses closed and voters were treated to drinks by their employers. Voters, as Bingham's piece suggests, were exclusively male.

that such retaliations did occur. More than likely, the need rarely arose: Du Pont workers, as much out of self-interest as self-preservation, probably voted the way their employers did. Not until the widespread adoption of the secret ballot in the 1880s and 1890s would voter intimidation cease to be a factor in American politics.

## INNOVATIONS IN TRANSPORTATION

Although he had indicated his desire to limit the scope of the federal government and return power to the people at state and local levels, no one knew exactly where Jackson stood on the American System at the time of his election. As a U.S. senator, he had supported the General Survey Act and the higher Tariff of 1824, but he became suspiciously elusive about both subjects as a presidential candidate. The first clear sign of his different course occurred in May 1830, when he vetoed a bill that would have provided partial federal support for the construction of a turnpike from Lexington to Maysville, Kentucky.

With its northern terminus located just across the Ohio River from Cincinnati, the so-called Maysville Road was intended to link up with the National Road in Ohio and extend it southward through Kentucky and Tennessee to the Gulf of Mexico. Unlike the ill-cared-for dirt roads that passed for highways in most parts of the country, this was to be a well-constructed macadam road consisting of tar and crushed stone compressed on a graded and drained gravel bed. Such a cost-effective, lower-maintenance technology of road building promised to speed the flow of horse-drawn wagons and place inland towns like Lexington in closer contact and competition with the prosperous trade of the Ohio River valley.

Given the road's interstate connections and national scope, nearly everyone expected approval. But Jackson thought otherwise. In his veto message, he specifically questioned the national character of the road: the funds being appropriated were intended to connect two points within the same state. Like Madison and Monroe before him, he believed that federal aid to such intrastate projects was not sanctioned by the Constitution. What's more, he voiced general opposition to any federal funding of internal improvements within the United States.

Jackson's message stunned Congress and angered many of its members, including the president's archenemy, Henry Clay of Kentucky. After all, there was genuine popular support for internal improvements. Clay felt certain that Jackson had intended to punish his state out of personal enmity. He became even more convinced when he learned that Jackson had left unsigned (thereby exercising what became known as the "pocket veto" for the first time in American history) two other internal improvement bills, one of which was for a canal around the falls of the Ohio River near Louisville, Kentucky. But the real picture was more complicated. Standing behind Jackson, and urging him on was Secretary of State Martin Van Buren, a staunch opponent of federally supported internal improvements.

Even though Jackson ended up endorsing more internal improvement bills than any of his predecessors, on the whole he opposed federal involvement in the building of roads, canals, railroads, and waterways. In 1831, for instance, he announced that he was ending the army's participation in internal improvement projects under the General Survey Act. Two years later, he made a similar decision to turn over completed sections of the National Road to the states through which it passed. His support mainly went to projects that lay either outside or at the borders of state jurisdictions, such as the dredging of rivers and harbors or the building of wagon roads in territories that had yet to become states. Jackson thus did not completely reject the American System, but he recast its guiding principles, although with little logic or consistency.

The Maysville Road controversy took place during a period of innovation in the transportation of people and goods. It began during the Jefferson administration, when construction started on the great National Road project and steamboats began operating on eastern and western rivers. It hit full stride with the completion of New York's state-financed Erie Canal in 1825, and would culminate during the 1850s with the completion of several large "trunk line" railroads, so called because they originated in Eastern Seaboard cities and connected with various branch lines as they moved westward.

Of all these developments, the Erie Canal had the greatest immediate impact because it provided the first all-water route directly connecting the Great Lakes and the rapidly growing Midwest to the major eastern seaport at New York City. The Erie Canal poured "a river of gold" into New York, making it the center of commerce that it is today. The canal also inspired cities and states from Virginia to Illinois to emulate New York's example by tapping into the rich trade that flowed to and from the Midwest.

The Erie Canal not only carried manufactured goods westward and transported western produce eastward; it also became the passageway for thousands of native-born white Americans and European immigrants into the upper reaches

This view of the Erie Canal at Lockport, New York, shows workers (center) operating gates that controlled the flow of water from one elevation to another, thus allowing canal boats to ascend and descend elevations along the route. At Lockport, the Erie Canal dropped over sixty feet, requiring a series of five locks to raise and lower boats.

of New York and Pennsylvania and, beyond that, into the burgeoning midwestern states of Ohio, Indiana, Illinois, and Michigan. Along its course, boomtowns like Utica, Syracuse, and Rochester, New York, sprang up to supply the great migration and take advantage of the growing trade that flowed back and forth. As New York's success invited emulation, members of Congress and the Jackson administration were besieged with requests for federal funding to help build roads, canals, and railroads in other parts of the country. Most of these requests were turned down with the reminder that New York had constructed its canal system with its own state funds, not federal money.

The canal craze slowed appreciably by the late 1830s. Canals were costly to build ($20,000–$30,000 per mile and upward) and maintain. Both winter weather and recurrent flood damage interrupted the flow of traffic. Revenues were inadequate. Most significant, steam-powered railroads appeared just a few years after the canals. When boom times ended with the Panic of 1837 (see p. 337), followed by six years of economic depression, Pennsylvania and Indiana stood virtually bankrupt, while states like Ohio found themselves in financial difficulty because of their overextended investments in canal building. The canal boom halted around 1840, by which time the United States had built 3,326 miles of canals at a cost of roughly $125 million, or $37,580 per mile. Railroad construction, by contrast, had already reached 3,328 miles at an average cost of $17,000 per mile. Although most lines existed in the Northeast, railroads could be found in all parts of the country by the 1840s, and no end was in sight. By then, no one questioned that the "iron horse" represented the wave of the future.

In addition to costing less to build, rail lines could serve areas that could not be reached by boats and barges in either the drought of summer or the freezing of winter. And although canals and steamboats could ship goods more cheaply, railroads provided much faster service. Whereas horse- and mule-drawn freight wagons and canal boats averaged around two miles an hour, freight trains and steamboats averaged around twelve. More important, because railroads, unlike steamboats and canals, could be built more directly from one geographic point to another, they saved even more time than their traveling speeds suggest. During the 1850s, for example, a trip from Cincinnati to New York City by freight wagon could take forty to fifty days or more, depending on weather conditions. The same goods shipped downriver by steamboat to New Orleans and then by packet ship to New York required twenty-eight days, while those shipped on the Ohio canal system across Lake Erie to the Erie Canal and down the Hudson took eighteen. Railroads, by contrast, required only six to eight days, thus cutting the time by more than half that of their closest water-borne competitors.

Railroads were the high technology of their day. The sight and sound of a steam locomotive pulling a train of cars across varied landscapes made deep impressions on the public, as numerous works of art and poetry attest. The imposing size of the "iron horse," the powerful chugging of its steam engine, the rhythmic clickity-clack of its cars moving over segmented rails, the shrill shrieks produced when iron wheels engaged iron rails in sharp curves, the high, lonesome sound of the lo-

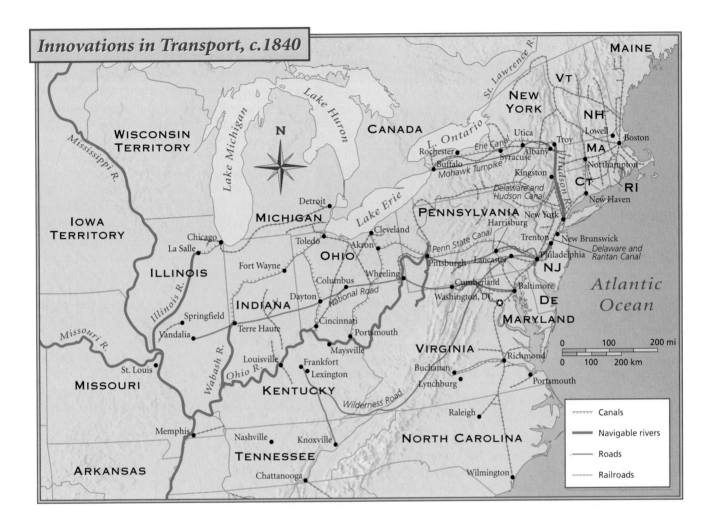

**Innovations in Transport, c.1840**

comotive's whistle as it passed over hill and dale—such images helped make the railroad the primary symbol of the nation's technological progress in nineteenth-century America.

Although the railway system would experience its greatest growth after the Civil War, many of its defining features appeared during the Jacksonian era. Of these, the most important were the management practices introduced by West Point–trained engineers. From the outset, these "soldier technologists" recognized that large-scale enterprises like railroads required systematic management. Accountability and control proved all the more important on single-track railways that had several trains running daily in different directions as well as scores of stations along the way selling tickets, shipping freight, and collecting revenues. In addition to engineering and overseeing the construction of railroads, the engineer-managers set up rules for their operations. Like the

army regulations on which they were based, these rules established clear lines of authority from top to bottom, codified everyday operating procedures and accounting practices, determined train schedules, and spelled out practices for employees at every level.

The engineers based their rules on an accumulated fund of experience that went back to their early training at West Point and included working under the military model introduced at the War Department during the early 1820s by Secretary Calhoun. All told, more than 120 West Pointers worked on American railroads before the Civil War, almost always as supervisors or consultants. As the industry grew during the 1830s and 1840s, more and more young men learned their engineering by working, in apprentice fashion, on canals and railroads. Such was the case for Benjamin Henry Latrobe, chief engineer of the Baltimore and Ohio; Daniel C. McCallum,

This lithograph by the New York firm of Currier and Ives (c. 1849–50) indicates how railroad carriage and locomotive designs had changed during the previous decade. Instead of resembling stagecoaches, the passenger cars had become larger and more rectangular. Likewise, the steam locomotive had evolved from a smaller British design into what became known as the "American" type, with four drive wheels, a four-wheel "lead truck" to help negotiate sharp corners, and a "cow catcher" in front to move obstructions off the rails.

general superintendent of the New York and Erie Railroad; and J. Edgar Thompson, president of the Pennsylvania Railroad. All three refined and extended the West Point paradigm by creating increasingly sophisticated administrative structures to operate their railroads. By the late nineteenth century, these railroads would number among the largest and most powerful corporations in America.

## Personal Tensions and Sectional Politics

By the time Jackson issued his Maysville Road veto in May 1830, he was already facing a serious crisis within his cabinet. The problem was his growing alienation from Vice-President Calhoun.

The crisis had three sources. One was a growing tension between Calhoun and Martin Van Buren over who would be Jackson's designated successor if, as many anticipated, he decided to serve only one term. A second and related source was the old information, brought to Jackson's attention by Van Buren, that Calhoun had been among those members of Monroe's cabinet who sought to discipline and punish the

general for invading Florida and attacking the Seminole Indians back in 1818.

Jackson may have gotten over the Seminole affair had it not been for another run-in with Calhoun. This time the problem centered on Peggy O'Neale, an attractive young widow who married Jackson's close friend and Secretary of War, John H. Eaton, in 1828. When rumors spread that the Eatons had been having an affair long before Peggy's first husband died, several cabinet families—led by Mrs. Floride Calhoun—snubbed them. Jackson, whose late wife had been similarly slandered during the 1828 campaign, came to Mrs. Eaton's defense and insisted that his cabinet members include the Eatons in their social gatherings.

When the Calhouns as well as three other cabinet families refused, an enraged Jackson stopped holding official cabinet meetings and began to rely almost exclusively on a "kitchen cabinet" of informal advisers that included his closest allies—among them Van Buren, who sided with him in the Eaton affair. With the executive branch hopelessly divided, the entire cabinet resigned in April 1831. By now, Calhoun had reached a point of no return. Banished from the inner circles of the Jackson administration and with his chances for the presidency growing ever dimmer, he withdrew further into the cocoon of states' rights.

### THE WEBSTER-HAYNE DEBATE

Just as the Eaton affair was coming to a boil, Calhoun became involved in one of the most memorable debates in American history. The confrontation began in the Senate when Connecticut's Samuel A. Foote, in a routine economizing measure, introduced a motion in January 1830 that would temporarily suspend the sale of any new public lands in the West until the federal government had disposed of some 72 million acres already on the market. Foote's resolution elicited an immediate reaction from Senator Thomas Hart Benton of Missouri, who angrily accused Foote and his New England colleagues of seeking to check the growth of the West in order to prevent the migration of workers that eastern manufacturers needed at home for factories and mills. In Benton's view, Foote's resolution, coupled with an already high protective tariff that benefited northern manufacturers, amounted to a giant eastern conspiracy, and Benton called on his southern colleagues to join him in defeating it.

At this point, South Carolina's senior senator, Robert Y. Hayne, came forward to support Benton. Assailing the Foote resolution as nothing more than an adjunct of the American System, he leveled a withering attack on its eastern proponents as unprincipled tyrants who sought to subjugate not only their workers but also the rest of the country, so they could reap huge profits.

Daniel Webster, who happened to stroll into the Senate chamber in the midst of Hayne's speech, could hardly believe his ears. Hayne was attacking the very people Webster represented, and Webster asked to be heard. "The East!" he began, "the obnoxious, the rebuked, the always reproached East! . . . Sir, I rise to defend the East." And defend he did—so vigorously that the original resolution that had ignited the debate receded into the background. The two men confronted each other over two different philosophies of government: Hayne defended "the Carolina doctrine" of state sovereignty and nullification, while Webster defended national power, which he captured in the famous phrase "Liberty *and* Union, now and forever, one and inseparable!"

The Webster-Hayne debate unfolded over a period of eight days in early 1830 and attracted large crowds to the Senate chamber. It came as no surprise that both sides claimed victory. Webster's brilliant oratory catapulted him into national prominence and made him an instant, though unlikely, candidate for the presidential election of 1832. Although Calhoun did not participate directly in the oratorical clash, he nonethe-

less carefully coached Hayne. The debate, after all, was as much about Calhoun and his doctrine of nullification as anything else.

What remained to be seen was how Jackson would react to the debate. That moment came on April 13, 1830, at a dinner organized by Benton, Hayne, and their supporters in honor of Thomas Jefferson's birthday. Hayne gave the keynote address, in which he sought to link Jefferson's role in the Virginia and Kentucky resolutions of 1798 with South Carolina's nullifiers. Warned ahead of time by Van Buren about Hayne's speech, Jackson came to the dinner prepared. When asked to propose a toast, he rose from his chair, looked directly at Vice-President Calhoun, and declared, "Our *Federal* Union—*It must be preserved.*" Calhoun came next. Upset by the president's toast, his hand trembled as he held up his glass and replied, "The Union: Next to our Liberty the most dear."

The die was cast. From there the relationship between the president and vice-president completely unraveled. In 1831, Jackson denounced Calhoun as "fit for any act of human depravity" and unceremoniously read him out of the Democratic Party.

## NULLIFICATION AND THE TARIFF OF 1832

Sectional tensions worsened during the presidential election campaign of 1832. At issue was tariff protection for northern manufacturers versus southern concern over the tariff's effects on the South's economy and the future of slavery there. With Clay challenging Jackson for the White House under the banner of National Republicanism, Congress passed a compromise tariff bill that modified but did not significantly reduce the high rates of the 1828 Tariff of Abominations. Calhoun pinned his hopes for a presidential veto on Jackson's states' rights leanings and earlier campaign promise to support a "judicious" tariff. But Jackson signed the bill, and the Tariff of 1832 became law.

For Calhoun, this was the last straw. Having been drummed out of the party and lost the opportunity to be Jackson's designated successor, he resigned the vice-presidency, ran for the U.S. Senate in South Carolina, and proceeded to put his theory of nullification into practice. At his urging, South Carolina's governor called a special session of the state legislature, which in turn took the grave step of calling for an election of delegates to a state convention that would take action on the new tariff. Secessionist sentiments ran high as the convention met on November 19, 1832, at the state capitol and, within a matter of

Legendary orator Senator Daniel Webster replying to Senator Robert Hayne, 1830.

days, passed an Ordinance of Nullification by an overwhelming margin. Declaring the Tariffs of 1828 and 1832 null and void in South Carolina, the ordinance also warned that if the federal government tried to force the collection of duties, South Carolina would secede from the Union.

Fresh from a hard-fought victory over Clay and the National Republican Party at the polls, President Jackson responded to the South Carolina ordinance by issuing a "Proclamation to the People of South Carolina" in which he scorned the idea of nullification and denied that any state had the right to secede from the Union. "The laws of the United States must be executed," he warned. "My duty is emphatically pronounced in the Constitution. Those who told you that you might peaceably prevent their execution deceived you. Their object is disunion. But be not deceived.... Disunion by armed force is *treason*."

To show that he meant business, Jackson placed a naval squadron on alert, ordered several thousand troops to the South Carolina border, sent ammunition to Forts Moultrie and Pinckney in Charleston Harbor, and notified commanders there to prepare for hostilities. He then sent a message to Congress on January 16, 1833, asking for quick passage of a Force Bill authorizing the use of military force against the rebellious South Carolinians.

Jackson's proclamation, followed by passage of the Force Bill, as well as the president's personal threats to hang Calhoun, came like claps of thunder before a dangerous storm. They surprised many northerners and sobered South Carolinians, the most radical of whom called for immediate secession from the Union. The nullifiers had seriously misjudged Old Hickory's commitment to states' rights as an equally strong commitment to state sovereignty. If anyone had doubted Jackson's nationalism, they had no cause to doubt it now. Much as he sought to shift domestic affairs from the federal to the state level, he was unmistakably committed to the Constitution as the supreme law of the land.

While nationalists like Daniel Webster hailed the president's stand, his closest advisers—particularly his new vice-president, Martin Van Buren—feared that it might destroy the Democratic Party. But considerable support existed for some sort of compromise. Henry Clay advanced a plan to lower the Tariff of 1832 over a period of ten years until all duties reached a moderate rate of 20 percent on the value of imported goods. Calhoun would have preferred more radical cuts over a shorter period of time, but he realized that it was either this deal or none. Continuing to balance his love for

the Union with his sectional loyalty and desirous to head off a confrontation, Calhoun agreed to the compromise. Jackson signed the compromise tariff into law on March 2, 1833. The South Carolina convention reconvened and repealed its Ordinance of Nullification, but in a final act of defiance it enacted another ordinance declaring the Force Bill null and void. This time, Jackson did not respond. Satisfied with the outcome, he declared that "nullification is dead." "The next pretext," he ominously predicted, "will be the negro, or slavery question."

## The Bank War

Of all the issues that heightened political tensions during the 1830s, none had greater long-term economic implications than the so-called Bank War of 1832–33. At the core of the controversy was the Second Bank of the United States (BUS). Established by act of Congress in 1816 and a centerpiece of the Madisonian Platform, the bank was headquartered in Philadelphia with branch banks scattered around the country. Although it made short-term loans to other banks and businesses, its primary purpose was to maintain monetary stability in the economy by controlling the amount of credit state-chartered banks could extend. Not surprisingly, state bankers took a dim view of the BUS's regulatory power and frequently accused it of discriminatory practices. Complaints about the bank tended to divide along an east-west axis, with capital-starved westerners the most vehement critics.

As a westerner who blamed the BUS for causing the Panic of 1819, Andrew Jackson had indicated after his election in 1828 that he intended to oppose renewing the bank's charter. The BUS represented everything he disliked about the eastern monied establishment. This elitist institution, with its access to all government funds, had far too much power over the economy to suit Jackson. Moreover, he was convinced that the bank had contributed money to his opponents and actively campaigned against him in the election of 1828. In fact, the bank's president, Nicholas Biddle of Philadelphia, had voted for Jackson in 1828 and would do so again in 1832.

The spark that ignited the Bank War, though, came not from Jackson but rather from his opponent in the 1832 election, Henry Clay. Convinced that the pressure of an upcoming election might push Jackson to change his mind and support the BUS, Clay persuaded Biddle to seek an early renewal of the bank's charter. Biddle knew that every member of Jackson's cabinet except Attorney General Roger Taney was pro-BUS and that both houses of Congress were well disposed toward it as well. The time seemed right to go forward.

## "KING ANDREW'S" VETO

As expected, the recharter bill moved through Congress and arrived on President Jackson's desk around the Fourth of July 1832. Without blinking, Jackson vetoed it. In a blistering message to Congress, he assailed the bank as an unconstitutional monopoly that favored eastern monied interests over less affluent westerners, corrupted the political process, and served "to make the rich richer and the potent more powerful" at the expense of "the humble members of society—the farmers, mechanics, and laborers—who have neither the time nor the means of securing like favors to themselves." The federal government, he concluded, must provide "equal protection" under the law to all segments of society. Friends of the BUS—especially those in Congress—railed at the imperious tone of the message. Biddle castigated it as a "manifesto of anarchy," while Clay denounced it as "a perversion of the veto power." Webster got to the heart of the matter when he accused Jackson of claiming "for the President, not the power of approval, but the primary power of originating laws."

What really shocked Jackson's adversaries, however, was his frontal assault on the Supreme Court. In the 1819 case of *McCullough v. Maryland,* the Court under Chief Justice John Marshall had ruled in favor of the bank's constitutionality. Jackson disagreed. In his veto message, he asserted that the chief executive and Congress "must each be guided by its own opinion of the Constitution."

The implications were clear. As the directly elected representative of the people, Jackson believed that the president should exercise legislative as well as judicial authority. He was taking a position radically different from that of previous presidents. "We have arrived at a new epoch," Webster exclaimed in disgust. "We are entering on experiments with the government and the Constitution, hitherto untried, and of fearful and appalling aspect." Clay and Calhoun, in an uncommon union of sentiments, agreed. All three expressed concern over "the rapid strides of Executive power," as Clay put it, and Calhoun warned of "the approach of despotic power." Opposition cartoonists began to depict Jackson as "King Andrew" the imperial president, wearing a crown, decked out in ermine robes, carrying a scepter, and trampling on the Constitution.

Buffeted by criticism from political opponents and members of his own party alike, Jackson fought back. He persuaded a majority of voters that the "Monster Bank" deserved to be scorned and exterminated. His reelection victory in 1832 was decisive. Clay carried only five states and part of another. All others except Vermont, which voted for a third-party candidate, went to Old Hickory and his Democratic Party.

## THE END OF THE BANK OF THE UNITED STATES

Bolstered by the election results, Jackson informed his cabinet in November 1832 that he intended to kill the "hydra-headed monster" by withdrawing all federal funds from the BUS and withholding any further deposits. Fearing that such action would shake public confidence and cause a financial panic, two successive secretaries of the treasury refused to remove the funds and were immediately fired by Jackson. These were the first dismissals of cabinet officers by a president, and they

"King Andrew the First," c. 1832.

led to further howls of protest from congressional critics like Clay and Webster. Jackson's third choice for the treasury, the outspoken anti-BUS attorney general, Roger Taney, promptly executed the president's order by withdrawing government funds from the bank and depositing all incoming funds in privately owned, state-chartered "pet banks" around the country. When its federal charter expired in 1836, the BUS was incorporated as a state bank under the name United States Bank of Pennsylvania. The institution eventually went bankrupt and closed its doors in 1841.

Jackson's fight against the bank unleashed a torrent of consequences he neither expected nor sought. The shifting of federal funds to pet banks led to a flood of paper money from unregulated state banks and fostered a speculative boom not unlike the one that had helped trigger the Panic of 1819. Recognizing this, Jackson sought to slow down the overheated economy by issuing a Specie Circular in July 1836, which required gold and silver coin in payment for the sale of public lands. Rather than slowing the inflationary spiral, however, Jackson's well-intentioned order had the opposite effect. Land purchases became more difficult for people of limited means, while wealthy land speculators continued to buy. In the process, speculators drained specie from eastern banks to make their purchases in the West.

Jackson also agreed to a bill sponsored by Henry Clay calling for the distribution of the federal surplus to the states in proportion to their representation in Congress. Although the legislation called these distributions "loans," no one expected them to be paid back, and the recipients quickly spent the funds, mainly for the construction of roads, canals, and railroads. While playing an important role in expanding America's transportation system, the so-called Distribution Act also contributed to growing inflation. As specie drained out of the pet banks, the banks began to tighten credit, raise interest rates, and call in loans. Like the Specie Circular, the Distribution Act tended to exacerbate rather than lessen a serious economic problem.

In the long run, the Jackson administration's fiscal policies, particularly the destruction of the Second Bank of the United States, ended efforts to introduce a central banking system and caused considerable economic instability. More than twenty-five years would elapse before the Legal Tender Act (1862) and the National Banking Act (1863) would seek to take up where the BUS had left off. In the meantime, the rapidly expanding country suffered from the absence of federal regulation, a sound credit policy, and a uniform currency. Economic disaster loomed on the horizon.

"The Downfall of Mother Bank," a pro-Jackson cartoon showing the bank crumbling and Jackson's opponents in flight in response to his removal of government deposits.

## Industry and the Law

At no time in its history has the United States had a laissez-faire economy—that is, completely free from government intervention. At the national level, the government supported industrial development through tariff, patent, and banking legislation and periodic subsidies to build roads, canals, and railways. Under the auspices of the U.S. Army, the federal government not only spurred the development of interchangeable manufacturing methods but also provided engineers and managers to guide the early stages of the transportation revolution. But that's only part of the story. States and local communities provided significant monetary support for developing industries. And courts as well as legislatures enthusiastically promoted industry and business. Public opinion after the War of 1812 agreed that America needed to establish once and for all its economic independence from Europe.

## STATE CHARTERS

The number of chartered corporations in the United States began to rise in the 1780s and then multiplied beyond all precedent in the early nineteenth century. The advantages of incorporation remained in the 1830s much the same as they had been a half-century earlier: a charter made a group into a "body politic," an artificial legal person, that could regulate its internal affairs, protect its assets in court, and persist over time.

Corporate charters were mini-constitutions that defined not only the form of a company's internal government but also the activities in which it could engage, the extent of its property, how stockholders voted, and even the distribution of dividends. Charters were usually granted for a limited period of time or gave legislatures the right to amend or repeal them; but given their enthusiasm for growth, legislatures were less likely to crack down on corporations that violated restrictions in their charters than to encourage promising companies with reduced taxes or rights to public lands. If the weakness of regulation gave the United States the appearance of having a laissez-faire economy, the government's active support of development made clear that it did not.

The most consistent supporter of federal intervention in the economy was the National Republican Party of Henry Clay and John Quincy Adams. But Jacksonian Democrats often pushed for federal aid to pet projects as well. Even leading states' rights advocates from South Carolina sought federal aid for the construction of a railroad at the height of the nullification crisis. Political principles mattered, but sometimes successful politicians had to bend to the wishes of their constituents, who often called for government intervention to improve economic conditions.

State and community governments went to considerable lengths to support industrial development. The Erie Canal, representing an investment of more than $7 million, was wholly owned by the state of New York. Other major canal systems in Pennsylvania, Ohio, Indiana, and Illinois were also state-owned. Ohio's Loan Law of 1837 provided matching funds to any internal improvement company (canal, turnpike, or railroad) that satisfied certain specifications. Although the Loan Law was repealed five years later, Ohio's legislature nonetheless passed more than 100 special laws between 1836 and 1850 authorizing loans to railroads within the state.

## THE SUPREME COURT AND THE OBLIGATION OF CONTRACTS

In the great government-stimulated rush toward mechanization and economic expansion after the War of 1812, disputes about contracts and property rights proliferated. The responsibility for sorting them out fell to the nation's judicial system. While most litigations came under the jurisdiction of state and local courts, those involving larger constitutional issues ended up before either the Supreme Court or one of the sixteen U.S. circuit courts. Under Chief Justice John Marshall, the Supreme Court boldly asserted its prerogatives and, by extension, those of the federal government over the states. A disproportionate number of precedent-setting cases bore directly on business and economic affairs. Four in particular deserve attention.

In *Fletcher v. Peck* (1810), the Court struck down a Georgia statute that sought to reclaim state lands along the Yazoo River from land speculators who had bribed members of the state legislature. Since the speculators had already sold a large part of the Yazoo tract to unsuspecting buyers who evidently were unaware of the fraud, the Marshall Court ruled in favor of the buyers (and against the state) because they had acted in good faith and, in the Court's view, had valid sale contracts. For Marshall and his colleagues, the key issue in the *Fletcher* case was the constitutional provision (Article I, Section 10) that prohibited states from "impairing the Obligation of Contracts." In two 1819 cases, *Dartmouth College v. Woodward* and *Sturgis v. Crowenshield,* the Court likewise invalidated state laws that impaired the obligation-of-contracts clause and ruled in favor of those who held prior contracts.

For all its aggressiveness in expanding federal power at the expense of the states, the Marshall Court's emphasis on established property rights and the sanctity of contracts revealed a fundamentally conservative political philosophy. The Court stood behind commercial development, but it did so with the conviction that real economic growth could only take place in a stable, orderly political and business environment. Given this philosophy, the Court proved hostile to state-sponsored bankruptcy and stay laws enacted during depressions and

327

Roger Brooke Taney, chief justice of the U.S. Supreme Court (1835–64).

*The Charles River Bridge Case.* The Court's "federalist era" ended with John Marshall's death in 1835. His successor as chief justice was Roger B. Taney of Maryland, a strong believer in free competition who soon took the Court in a different direction. The extent of the shift away from Marshallian principles was revealed in the 1837 case of *Charles River Bridge Company v. Warren Bridge Company.*

As the sole bridge connecting Boston and Cambridge, Massachusetts, the Charles River Bridge Company had long enjoyed monopolistic privileges. In response to a public outcry against the company's high toll charges, the Massachusetts legislature granted a corporate charter to the Warren Bridge Company with the stipulation that its bridge over the Charles River would eventually become public once the builder paid for its construction costs and made a modest profit. Having failed to win its suit against the Warren charter before Massachusetts tribunals, the Charles River Bridge Company, represented by Senator Daniel Webster, appealed to the Supreme Court, claiming that the Massachusetts law that established the Warren Bridge Company violated the obligation-of-contracts clause of the Constitution.

John Marshall would doubtless have sided with the Charles River Bridge Company. But not Roger Taney. A firm believer in equal rights (at least for adult white males), Taney had little tolerance for monopolies and special privileges that, under the old federalist system, had been an essential part of the business world. "While the rights of private property are sacredly guarded," he wrote in the Court's majority opinion, "we must not forget that the community also have rights." To deny the Warren Bridge Company its charter, he reasoned, would be tantamount to denying the Boston community its rights. Taney also thought that a decision in favor of the Charles River Bridge Company's monopoly would encourage other monopolies, which in the long run could stifle the country's economic development.

To Marshall, the obligation of contracts was a stabilizing influence on the economy; to Taney, it was a means of blocking competition and, therefore, economic prosperity. By 1837, the Marshallian idea of stability had given way to a more powerful concept—the idea of progress. The Taney Court agreed with the larger public that industrial and technological progress was an essential engine of democracy. More and more goods and services were becoming available to more and more people. Nothing—not even the obligation of contracts—should stand in the way.

business downswings that, in effect, protected debtors at the expense of their creditors. Such laws, in the Court's view, struck at the heart of the obligation of contracts. What's more, they fostered a free-for-all competitive atmosphere that threatened not only to disrupt the economy but undo the Republic. That was intolerable to the Marshall Court.

The Court's positions drew praise from business groups and their representatives, such as the Boston Associates and Daniel Webster, but to the state governments—whose rights were often being challenged—they were high-handed, undemocratic, and unconstitutional. The last of the Marshall Court's major decisions was handed down in 1824. In *Gibbons v. Ogden,* a case concerning steamboat travel in New York Harbor, the court decisively established federal over state power in the regulation of interstate commerce. Thereafter, an antifederalist reaction set in. With the disputed presidential election in 1824, the political winds began to shift as a growing number of voters embraced the egalitarian, states' rights philosophy of Andrew Jackson and the newly emerging Democratic Party. Marshall's influence began to recede even before Jackson's election, when the composition of the Supreme Court changed and it began to soften its stance on the obligation of contracts and sustain state bankruptcy laws.

## THE COURTS AND BUSINESS

The Supreme Court under both Marshall (1801–35) and Taney (1836–64) was consistently friendly toward business. Marshall's Court helped bring stability to the economy when it was buffeted by war, embargo, and a severe panic. Taney's Court, on the other hand, sought to provide greater flexibility within the law, and thus more opportunity for capitalists, during a period of dynamic growth. Although Taney and a majority of his colleagues embraced a states' rights view of the law, they followed their predecessors in developing a reasonable approach to commercial law that could be uniformly enforced throughout the nation.

Federal circuit courts also played an important role in the country's economic development. At one level, they opened their chambers to distant parties so that citizens of one state or region could settle business differences with citizens of others. At another, more mundane level, they served as arbitrators in local disputes over property rights. Inventors, for example, frequently turned to federal courts to protect their patent rights against infringers. The same courts likewise played a significant role in settling disputes between mill owners over rights to water power. The disputes often hinged on technological details. At Woonsocket, Rhode Island, in 1836, for instance, after a flurry of suits and countersuits, a circuit court judge appointed a local engineer to take measurements and establish dam levels for all to see so that water power on the Blackstone River could be equitably distributed to ninety-six mill sites in the neighborhood. In cases such as these, the courts relied heavily on the expertise of hydraulic engineers in determining a policy of "reasonable use." Even the law, it seems, could not escape the growing momentum of technological change. Legal innovation was the result.

## Trails of Tears

Whether measured in terms of industrial output, population growth, or new territory, expansion became a dominant theme in early nineteenth-century America. And nowhere was the country's expansionist impulse more evident than along its western borders. Between the 1790s and 1830s, thousands of white migrants streamed across the Appalachians to settle in the Ohio and Mississippi valleys and beyond. By 1812, Kentucky, Tennessee, Ohio, and Louisiana had already entered the Union. During the next twenty-five years, seven out of the eight new states came from the trans-Appalachian West. For many, rapid territorial expansion meant progress; but for Indians, it was a different matter.

Of all the politicians who supported national expansion, none was more determined than Andrew Jackson. Long before he became president, Jackson had advocated removing all Indians who lived between the Appalachians and the Mississippi River, forcefully if necessary, to lands west of the great river. His reasoning was bound by the racial assumptions and political concerns of the time. First, he considered the continued presence of native peoples in these areas a threat to the security of the United States. Memories of trouble-making by the British and their Indian allies during and after the War of 1812 weighed heavily on Jackson, and he was determined not to let them wreak havoc on white settlers again. Second, he rejected the territorial claims of various tribes from a legal standpoint. Just because Indians claimed certain lands as their hunting grounds did not give them right of ownership, he argued, because "they have neither dwelt nor made improvements" on them.

Finally, Jackson cited humanitarian reasons for removal. Noting that "some of the tribes have become extinct and others have left but remnants [of their culture] to preserve," he believed that the same fate awaited all native peoples who came in contact with the forces of white civilization. Having been raised in a society that justified slavery on grounds of racial inferiority, Jackson, like many of his contemporaries, also thought that Indians could never be fully "civilized." He believed they possessed certain racial "deficiencies" that could not be altered through education or cultural assimilation. For him, race determined culture, not the other way around. So the humane thing to do so was to remove the Indians to an isolated territory beyond the Mississippi where they would be free to follow their own traditions and not be "surrounded by the whites" with their alien technologies and institutions.

Jackson also took issue with a long-standing federal policy of recognizing native peoples as separate nations with their own governments. In Jackson's view, all Indians were subjects of the United States, and Congress therefore had the right not only to "legislate their boundaries" but also to seize their lands and make them part of the public domain. The Indians had only two choices: they could "emigrate beyond the Mississippi or submit to the laws of those States."

Trails of Tears

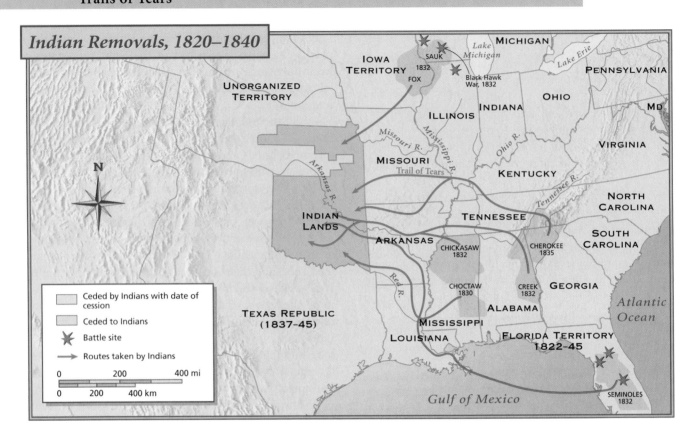

Indian Removals, 1820–1840

THE INDIAN REMOVAL ACT

By the time Jackson assumed the presidency, Indian removal had become a hot political issue in the South, where Georgia and the Cherokee people contested a large expanse of territory within the state's northwestern boundary. The Cherokees, who numbered around 20,000, claimed that they were a separate nation independent of the state of Georgia. In 1827, they acted in an innovative manner by adopting a written constitution that provided for a bicameral legislature, a judiciary, and an elected executive, John Ross, who became known as "the principal chief." Contrary to Jackson's thinking, many Cherokees had adopted the trappings of white civilization by becoming successful farmers, businessmen, and plantation owners. Some of the wealthiest Cherokees had even acquired African American slaves and lived in mansions that rivaled those of the wealthiest whites in the region. This doubtless fostered resentment on the part of many less affluent white Americans. The already tense situation worsened

during the 1820s, when gold was discovered on Cherokee lands.

Georgia claimed that its colonial charter as well as a compact signed with the U.S. government in 1802 gave it sole authority over the Cherokee people as well as their lands. To make its position clear, the Georgia legislature passed a resolution in 1827 stating "that the Indians are tenants at [Georgia's] will, and [Georgia] may at any time she pleases, determine that tenancy by taking possession of the premises." The legislature put the Cherokees on notice that if they continued "to turn a deaf ear to the voice of reason," harsh consequences would follow. "The lands in question *belong* to Georgia," the resolution concluded. "She *must* and she *will* have them."

Jackson's public statements on the subject encouraged the legislature to take further action against the Cherokees. Between 1828 and 1831, it passed a series of laws that divided Cherokee territory into five counties and placed them directly under Georgia's governance, invalidated all laws passed by the

Cherokee legislature, forbade it to meet, and created a "Georgia Guard" police force to make sure its directives were executed. In the meantime, Jackson urged federal legislation to establish a formal mechanism for removing Indians to the West. The bill passed, but only after a bitter debate during which anti-Jacksonian congressmen from the Northeast accused the bill's sponsors of instrumenting a land grab.

The Indian Removal Act of May 1830 established a specially designated Indian Territory in the present state of Oklahoma and provided $500,000 for negotiating with Indian tribes, paying them for any improvements (houses, mills, businesses, etc.) made on lands they currently occupied, and relocating them in the West. The act also guaranteed that each tribe would receive an amount of land in the new Indian Territory equivalent to what they had surrendered in the East. During the first year in the West, they would be given food, tools, and the protection of federal troops in order to help them get settled. Each tribe would function independently in its new terrain without interference from the United States.

Faced with pressure from the Georgia legislature and the Jackson administration to cede their lands and move west, Cherokee leaders sought to protect their rights by turning to the Supreme Court. They knew that Chief Justice Marshall was no friend of Jackson, and so they might have a reasonable

John Ross, the principal Cherokee chief who adamantly opposed removal to the Oklahoma Territory.

chance of success. The Court initially issued an ambiguous ruling in *Cherokee Nation v. Georgia* (1831), but a year later, in *Worcester v. Georgia,* it clearly recognized Cherokee independence by declaring that Georgia had no right to legislate for the Cherokees because they were a separate sovereign nation.

The Cherokee victory proved fleeting, though. Upon learning of the Supreme Court's verdict, Jackson is said to have retorted: "Well, John Marshall has made his decision: *now, let him enforce it!*" Recognizing that the Court could do nothing without the president's support, Georgia defied the ruling and continued making preparations for a state lottery that would distribute Cherokee lands to its white citizens.

### THE TREATY PARTY

While some 4,000 Cherokees had moved west before 1832, the vast majority refused to abandon their ancestral lands and bitterly resented those who did. But Cherokee solidarity began to fracture in the aftermath of the *Worcester* decision. Several prominent Cherokee leaders, depressed by the growing hopelessness of their situation, changed their minds and began to support the idea of removal. In December 1835, they signed the Treaty of New Echota with the U.S. government, ceding all Cherokee lands in return for $5 million, an equivalent amount of land in the new Indian Territory, transportation to the West, and the promise of food and tools for one year. The Cherokees would have two years to prepare for their departure, after which they would be forcibly removed from their lands. Although the Cherokee Nation's legitimate leaders vehemently protested the treaty as fraudulent, the U.S. Senate nonetheless ratified it in the spring of 1836, whereupon it went into effect.

Confusion and disbelief reigned among the Cherokee people as the fateful deadline approached. When federal troops under the command of General Winfield Scott began to arrive in May 1838 to enforce the treaty, few were prepared for what followed. In mid-June, the troops, assisted by Georgia militia, began to round up thousands of Cherokees and herd them into hot, crowded stockades to await deportation to the West. Writing from one of the deportation camps, a Baptist missionary reported, "The Cherokees are nearly all prisoners. . . . They have been dragged from their houses . . . [and] were allowed no time to take any thing with them, except the clothes they had on. . . . Many of the Cherokees, who, a few days ago, were in comfortable circumstances, are now victims of abject poverty. Some, who have been allowed to return home, under passport, to inquire after their property, have found their cattle, horses, swine, farming-tools, and house-furniture all gone." Years later a Georgia militiaman recollected, "I fought through the Civil War and have seen men shot to pieces and slaughtered by the thousands, but the Cherokee removal was the cruelest I ever saw."

Thus began what became known among the Cherokees as the "Trail of Tears," a grueling 1,000-mile journey—mostly on foot—that lasted more than five months. Some 16,000 persons began the trek; fewer than 12,000 survived it. To make matters worse, a bloody civil war broke out among the Cherokees as "Old Settlers" who had moved west before 1838 insisted that the newcomers live under their government and as the embittered newcomers, in turn, exacted revenge on the Treaty Party by killing three of its most prominent leaders. Nearly seven years elapsed before peace came to the fractured Cherokee nation.

### THE BLACK HAWK WAR

The Cherokees were only one of many tribes that faced removal beyond the Mississippi during the 1830s. Some went peacefully; others resisted. In Florida, for example, efforts to remove the Seminole people provoked a conflict that lasted seven years and cost thousands of lives. Farther north in Illinois, an embittered Sauk chief named Black Hawk led a short-lived effort in 1832 to take back lands that had been lost to white settlers as a result of a questionable treaty signed years earlier that

Black Hawk, Sauk war chief and Indian leader of the war that assumed his name.

had ceded 50 million acres to the United States for a pittance. The so-called Black Hawk War lasted less than four months and resulted in a devastating defeat for Black Hawk and his outnumbered group of Sauk and Fox warriors. Although he managed to evade capture after an army of federal troops and Illinois militia (one of whom was a young Abraham Lincoln) decimated his band, he was eventually betrayed to federal authorities by a group of neighboring Winnebagos with whom he had sought refuge. The reward was twenty horses and $100.

Black Hawk spent the next year in a federal prison near Washington, D.C. Upon his release, Andrew Jackson paraded him throughout the Northeast so people could see the rebellious "savage" and so Black Hawk could "see the strength of the white people." Black Hawk finally returned in disgrace to what remained of his people in the remote reaches of present-day Iowa. Thus ended the last impediment to white settlement in the Old Northwest.

Before Jackson left office in 1837, over 45,000 Indians had been removed to the trans-Mississippi West, and many others had died. In the process, they relinquished about 100 million acres of land to the United States in return for 32 million acres of western land and $68 million in payments and subsidies. As one congressman who supported the removals put it, "What is history but the obituary of nations?" Should the United States, he continued, "check the course of human happiness—obstruct the march of science—stay the works of art, and stop the arm of industry, because they will efface in their progress the wigwam of the red hunter, and put out forever the council fires of his tribe?" To Jacksonians and a majority of white Americans in 1837, the answer was clear.

## The Jacksonian Legacy

The U.S. Senate ratified the Treaty of New Echota, making the Cherokee removal a political reality, near the end of Jackson's second term as president. Jackson's presidency was largely focused on domestic issues, especially those called forth by America's economic development and expansion. His attacks on internal improvements and the Bank of the United States were designed to redistribute power in domestic economic affairs from federal to state levels. But Jackson established a clear demarcation between states' rights, which he supported, and state sovereignty, which he rebuffed during the South Carolina nullification crisis. His appointees to the Supreme Court, notably of Roger Taney as chief justice in 1836, steered the Court away from the federalist positions of John Marshall. Yet despite his desire to hold the power of the federal government in check, Jackson enhanced the power and prestige of the presidency. He imprinted his strong personal character on the office—a feisty, direct, no-nonsense style allied to nationalism and a commitment to American territorial expansion.

Some challenges Jackson avoided. He detested the rapidly growing antislavery movement but ducked the whole question of slavery and its expansion into new territories. When American settlers in Texas revolted against Mexico in 1836 and sought their independence as a slave-holding republic, Jackson moved cautiously. He feared igniting controversy in a critical election year that saw his longtime ally and heir apparent, Martin Van Buren, running for the presidency. Despite his close friendship with the Texas revolutionary leader, Sam Houston, he delayed recognizing the new republic until a few days before he left office.

Osceola, famed Muskogee Seminole war leader who engineered major victories over American troops during the Second Seminole War in Florida. Captured under a flag of truce in 1837, he died of malaria in a South Carolina prison the following year. The Second Seminole War (1835–42) proved to be the longest and costliest Indian war in U.S. history.

## THE MODERN POLITICAL PARTY

It was during the Jacksonian period that the modern political party came into existence, complete with new organizational methods for selecting candidates and conducting campaigns. These campaigns became lively contests that involved open-air rallies, torchlight parades, candidate debates, periodic violence, and a broader level of participation on the part of not only white male voters but also nonvoting female lobbyists and activists.

Such political innovation paralleled important social, institutional, and technological changes during the 1820s and 1830s. As the white population grew exponentially, the geographic expanse of the nation widened, and industrialization began to take off, American society became increasingly infused with immigrants from different ethnic and religious backgrounds, many of whom voted. Politicians soon recognized that ethno-cultural and class distinctions could be used for cultivating new constituencies. To spread their political messages, party leaders took advantage of a rapidly expanding communications network fostered by the U.S. Post Office, distributing millions of party newspapers, campaign documents, and other sources of political propaganda to all corners of the country.

The new politics fed off new technologies. For example, high-speed printing innovations served as enabling agents for

the invention of the modern political party. Prior to the 1830s, newspapers and other party documents could not be widely distributed because they were still being laboriously produced on hand-operated wooden printing presses. The situation changed, however, between 1833 and 1835 with the introduction of much larger steam-driven printing presses with industrial capacities that quadrupled output while slashing the price of newspapers from six cents to a penny a copy. New York City, with its established machine shops for producing steam engines and heavy equipment, became the center of this "print revolution." New York newspapers were the first to introduce the penny press, with its emphasis on cheap mass circulation of the latest news and politics. Already avid readers with high literacy rates among the adult white population, Americans flocked to buy newspapers, books, magazines, and other materials that flowed from the city's publishing houses. As new print technologies and paper-making methods continued to speed production while reducing costs during the 1830s and 1840s, newspapers and publishing houses proliferated across the country. And political organizers took notice.

Influenced by the new technologies of the age, political activists began during the 1830s to use machines and factories as metaphors to describe their new organizations. To control public opinion in an increasingly pluralistic society, they were forced to build political coalitions, ultimately forming the first fully institutionalized political parties that placed party loyalty ahead of ideology. All this depended on having the institutions and technology that could disseminate information on a massive national scale.

Newspapers proved particularly important in building party organizations and shaping public opinion. Between 1790 and 1828, the number of newspapers published in the United States went from 92 to 861, and by 1840 had jumped to over 1,400—a phenomenon that reflected the introduction of high-speed printing technologies. Editors and publishers became the field marshals of their parties and played prominent roles in selecting candidates and devising electoral strategies in their states. They also influenced who received patronage jobs in local post offices and other government agencies after successful elections. Nothing was more important than the distribution of political patronage. It was the glue that held parties together and a defining feature of the new party system that emerged during the 1830s and 1840s.

The chief architect of the Democratic Party was New York's Martin Van Buren. After putting together a strong party organization in his home state after the War of 1812, he went on to join Andrew Jackson in the presidential campaign of 1828. From the outset, he maintained that political partisanship enhanced democracy by allowing issues to be openly debated and challenging voters to make important choices. Rejecting the views of Thomas Jefferson, George Washington, and other "founding fathers," "Little Van" believed that division and conflict were constructive and should become a permanent feature of American politics.

### WHIGS VERSUS DEMOCRATS

The new Democratic Party soon had a rival in the Whig Party, which conducted its first campaign in the congressional elections of 1834. Formed by leaders such as Henry Clay and Daniel Webster, and composed of old-line Federalists, National Republicans, moral zealots, and social reformers, the Whigs were slower to assemble a national organization owing to their heterogeneous origins. What initially united them was their determined opposition to Jackson and especially what they perceived to be his high-handed manner in waging the Bank War and in undermining Supreme Court decisions he disagreed with.

Genuine philosophical differences separated the Whigs and Democrats. The Whigs, like their Federalist and National Republican predecessors, emphasized national issues and supported a strong federal government. By contrast, the Democrats, like the Jeffersonian Republicans, emphasized state issues and the need for limited government and local autonomy. While the Whigs believed in a hierarchical society that promoted a general "harmony of interests" and supported trickle-down economic policies aimed at achieving prosperity as well as social order, the Democrats generally touted the "common man" and distrusted "the aristocratic wealthy," who, they believed, often profited at the expense of the majority.

Although Whig politicians were more pro-bank and pro-tariff than their Democratic counterparts, little separated the two parties concerning internal improvements. When it came to the construction of canals, turnpikes, and railroads, voting patterns tended to reflect local interests as Whigs and Democrats from the same district often joined forces in supporting or opposing such legislation. The two parties disagreed more on issues pertaining to social and economic reform. Whigs tended to be more interested in humanitarian reform. A higher percentage of Whigs supported public education than Democrats. Likewise, a much higher percentage of Whigs than Democrats supported the antislavery movement. Yet more Democrats than Whigs favored an end to imprisonment for debt. Here, as elsewhere, Whigs and Democrats differed fundamentally on the proper role of government. Whigs generally favored an activist government that would foster reform, while Democrats viewed most humanitarian reform efforts as "meddlesome interferences."

Why did men vote the way they did? In many areas, ethnic and religious tensions divided the electorate. Catholic immigrants often tended to vote Democratic, while free blacks, Protestant immigrants, and native-born evangelical Christians supported Whig candidates. At the same time, the wealthiest citizens frequently split their vote between Democratic and Whig candidates. For all concerned, personal rivalries and friendships as well as kinship connections made a difference, as did class interests and moral considerations such as one's views on slavery.

Besides the Democrats and Whigs, fraternal groups like the Working Men's Party became a political force during the late 1820s, a result of the country's turn to industrialization. The most important third party to emerge, however, was the Anti-Mason Party, a movement that originated in western New York state and quickly spread to other parts of the country

The press room of a Boston publishing house, c. 1852. Note the women workers operating the long line of steam-powered printing presses.

personal preferences, and came to believe that a strong organization held the key to electoral success. "ORGANIZE, ORGANIZE," the editor of the Seneca Falls (New York) *Democrat* exhorted his readers in 1842. "Parties in our republic . . . may be compared to contending armies," another Democratic editor observed five years later; "there must be system, discipline, order, regularity, union, and concert of action." In fact, party organization was taking on the trappings of industrial organization.

The new party system that emerged during the 1830s redefined American politics and changed the very meaning of the word "party." In the Federalist-Republican era, "party" carried the negative connotation of "faction." By the late 1830s, a party was thought to be an organization rather than a zealous attitude. The new approach was characterized by well-organized national parties that disseminated information on a massive scale and used the spoils system to reward loyal party workers. This represented a new era in which parties dominated politics as they never had before.

during the late 1820s in response to the mysterious disappearance of a former Freemason who threatened to expose the secret practices of the fraternal order. Convinced that the Masons had conspired to cover up his murder, the Anti-Mason Party set out to undermine the Masonic Order by opposing any Mason who ran for office.

As it turned out, the Whig Party profited greatly from the anti-Masonic frenzy. Since Jackson and Van Buren were Masons, the Democratic Party quickly became tainted by anti-Masonic attacks, even though prominent Whigs like Henry Clay also had Masonic ties. Whig Party leaders deftly implied that their Democratic opponents were conspiratorial and anti-democratic. As the 1830s went on, the Whig Party forged alliances with the Anti-Mason Party in local and national elections and eventually absorbed it. But the Anti-Masons permanently influenced both Whigs and Democrats by pioneering such novel practices as open-nominating conventions and the publication of party platforms.

The essence of the new party system, which historians now refer to as "the second party system," was open and unrepentant partisanship. Party leaders emphasized the need for discipline and unity in supporting the party ticket, regardless of

## Panic and Depression

In the midst of these political realignments came the election of 1836. Since Jackson had long since indicated his desire to see Van Buren succeed him as president, it came as no surprise when the Democratic national convention meeting in Baltimore quickly nominated the New Yorker as the party's standard bearer. The interesting question was, who would contest Van Buren for the presidency?

Meanwhile, distrust and ill feeling swirled within the ranks of the newly formed Whig Party as its leaders sought a presidential nominee. Henry Clay wanted the nomination, but his loss to Jackson four years earlier made him an unlikely choice. It soon became evident that the Whigs had neither the organization nor the party unity to match the Democrats. While they agreed on the need to expand federal power and

*American Journal*

## How Do You Get the News?

*Americans were avid readers who, thanks to the advent of high-speed steam-powered printing presses and cheap postal rates, had access to all sorts of mass-produced reading materials by the 1830s. Among the most popular were the Bible and newspapers. The following selection by a British writer indicates just how widespread keeping up with the news actually was.*

"In no other country in the world, perhaps, is the newspaper press so powerful an engine as in the United States. Nowhere else is it so omnipresent in its action, so omnipotent in its influence. . . . In the northern states especially, the ability to read and write is universal. In a state of society which converts every man into an active politician . . . the constant yearning for political intelligence is incredible. . . . The newspaper offices may be said to be, to the Americans generally, what the gin-palaces are to a section of the London population—the grand source whence they derive the pabulum of excitement. Such being the case, it is no wonder that journals should multiply amongst them. Almost every shade of opinion, political, social, or religious, has now its representative organ or organs. The press in America speaks to every one and of every one. Its voice is heard in every cabin in the land; its representatives are found thickly scattered over every settlement; its power is irresistible . . . making itself felt in every public department, and at the same time exercising a tremendous influence over private life.

In England, the daily papers are confined to the metropolis. In America, the daily press may be said to be the rule . . . The newspaper is an essential feature in almost every American village. Towns, such as in England would have no newspaper of their own, have in America their daily journals. It is seldom that a population as low as two thousand is to be found without them. . . .

If there be one thing . . . which marks an American newspaper, it is the violence of its political disquisitions. . . . Into the political vortex they are all drawn . . . in the strife of party, they are all ranged. On the eve of an election, their political complexion is discerned at a glance by the 'ticket' which heads their editorial columns, the 'ticket' consisting of the names, in large type, of the candidates whose election they advocate. . . . The asperity with which they conduct the political battle under their respective ensigns is a great blemish on their character. They take and they give no quarter . . . and yet, in the main, the business of polling in America is a very peaceable affair . . . The wrath of the people effervesces in their party organs; and that bitterness and vituperation which are the creations of their printing presses, seldom lead to any desperate personal collision. The worst feature of the journals is, unquestionably, their gross and disgusting personality. To serve a party purpose, they invade, without scruple, the sanctity of private life. . . . The exultation of the successful party is unbounded; and they like to try the temper of their crest-fallen opponents, by making it as ostentatious as possible. They celebrate their victory by illuminating their houses, while their organs illuminate their pages. Sometimes a cock is perched at the head of the editorial columns, and being in the attitude of crowing, there can be no mistake of the object for which he is thus placed. In 1838 and 1840, when the Whigs triumphed in New York, a leading journal in Albany, the capital of the state, devoted one whole side to an enormous eagle, which was represented with outstretched wings flying over the country with the 'glorious intelligence.'"

"The American Newspaper Press," *The Living Age* 4 (Issue 45; March 22, 1845): 730–33 (as reprinted from Chambers Journal, a British publication)

revitalize the American System, Whigs often differed over the details and spent more time bickering among themselves than challenging their Jacksonian opponents. When it became apparent that they could not agree on a single candidate, they ended up nominating three—General William Henry Harrison of Ohio, Senator Daniel Webster of Massachusetts, and Hugh Lawson White of Tennessee. The Whigs hoped that each candidate might draw enough votes from each of their respective sections of the country to deny Van Buren a majority and throw the election into the House of Representatives, where they stood a better chance of success.

As it turned out, the Whig strategy nearly worked. Although Van Buren won a convincing majority in the electoral college, the popular vote proved to be much closer, with Van Buren winning by a margin of less than 2 percent. Although he had been one of the primary organizers of the Democratic Party and possessed considerable personal charm, Van Buren lacked Old Hickory's charisma. He was too much of a political insider, too much an organization man. Without Jackson's strong endorsement, he might have lost. His base of support in the South and Southwest was shaky. Van Buren thus emerged from the election victorious but lacking momentum. The new Democratic Party was vulnerable in the new two-party system that had emerged.

Less than two weeks after the inauguration, the financial crisis that Jackson had sought to avert broke with a fury on his successor. The causes of the Panic of 1837—speculation in western lands, overextensions of credit, and mountains of debt backed by inadequate specie and too much paper money—were similar to those that had precipitated the economic crash some eighteen years earlier. Bad went to worse as prices fell, speculators defaulted on their loans, banks closed, and thousands of small farmers, beset by crop failures, lost their land to foreclosures. By the fall of 1837, unemployment lines lengthened as hundreds of shops and factories, unable to sell their products, closed their doors, never to reopen again. In many parts of the country, the shake-out left property values at a fraction of their original value. The United States teetered at the edge of total financial collapse.

From the outset, the Van Buren administration seemed helpless in the face of the panic and ensuing six-year depression. Adhering to the Jeffersonian adage that that government governs best which governs least, Van Buren warned citizens not to look to the federal government for relief. Relief must come from the states and local communities, where, to his way of thinking, essential power resided. He limited himself

This lithograph, entitled "Politics in an Oyster House," shows two citizens, one grasping a newspaper, engaged in discussion. Foreign visitors frequently commented on the American addiction to newspapers and politics.

to proposals for protecting the federal government's holdings. In a reversal of Jacksonian policies, he urged that distributions of the federal surplus to the states be postponed and that all federal monies be transferred from pet banks to federal treasury vaults (an independent treasury).

Van Buren's two proposals encountered bitter criticism from Whig politicians, who argued that both measures would take federal funds out of public circulation at the very time they were most needed. Although the postponement bill quickly moved through both houses of the Democratic Congress and became law, the Independent Treasury Act faced much tougher sledding as Whigs and maverick Democrats in the House of Representatives refused to support the measure. After a second wave of bank closings occurred in 1839, enough votes shifted to pass the Independent Treasury Act in June 1840. But, as Whig opponents had predicted, it did nothing to ease the depression. Serving only as the government's strongbox for keeping and disbursing funds, the independent treasury played no real regulatory role. The banking business remained completely decentralized and unregulated for more than two decades.

337

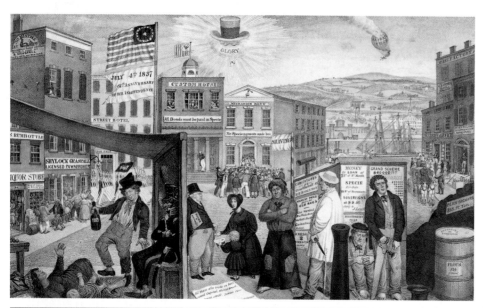

An anti-Jacksonian cartoon depicting the effects of the depression of 1837: a bank panic and beggars in the street.

too hard for a national bank. Even more remarkable, he appeared to abandon his main plank by admitting that federal sponsorship of internal improvements no longer remained a great national issue. That the chief spokesman of the American System would retreat from the statist policies he had so vigorously championed for more than twenty years speaks volumes about the larger impact of the Jacksonian political economy and the market revolution of which it was a part. Younger up-and-coming politicians, like Abraham Lincoln of Illinois, would not forget the essential ingredients of Clay's vision. But for the time being, the American System had receded from the public's eye. By the late 1830s, other issues pressed for attention.

The economic disaster was a political disaster for Van Buren, who had virtually no chance for reelection in 1840. Yet he was no political failure. More than anyone other than Andrew Jackson, Van Buren was the architect of the Democratic Party. He was a master political organizer who saw the value to a democracy of having a vigorous two-party system. As one of Jackson's closest advisers, he played a key role in formulating the party's states' rights philosophy and putting in place policies that shifted power away from the federalist agenda of Henry Clay and John Quincy Adams. By 1837–38, this shift had become so pervasive that even Clay—the foremost spokesman of the American System—began to relax his position. He had already accepted a lower tariff as part of the compromise of 1832. As he sought to win southern support in making yet another bid for the presidency in 1840, Clay reiterated his flexibility on the tariff while agreeing not to press

## Suggested Reading

Michael Les Benedict, *The Blessings of Liberty* (1996)

Colleen A. Dunlavy, *Politics and Industrialization: Early Railroads in the Untied States and Prussia* (1994)

Daniel Feller, *The Jacksonian Promise: America, 1815–1840* (1995)

William W. Freehling, *Prelude to Civil War: The Nullification Controversy in South Carolina* (1966)

Albert Hurtado and Peter Iverson, eds., *Major Problems in American Indian History* (1994)

Alexander Keyssar, *The Right to Vote* (2000)

Edward Pessen, *Jacksonian America: Society, Personality, and Politics* (1978)

Robert V. Remini, *Andrew Jackson*, 3 vols. (1977–84)

Carol Sheriff, *The Artificial River: The Erie Canal and the Paradox of Progress* (1996)

Anthony F. C. Wallace, *The Long, Bitter Trail: Andrew Jackson and the Indians* (1990)

# Chapter Review

## Summary

### QUESTIONS

- Why did the Second Bank of the United States become such a controversial political issue? Why did Andrew Jackson object so strenuously to the Bank? To what extent, if any, was the dismantling of the Bank responsible for the Panic of 1837?

- Who was responsible for the Indian "removals" of the 1830s? Were they justified?

- How did the relationship between technology and politics change during the Jacksonian era? What is the Erie Canal's significance?

- How did the government regulate economic, legal, and social changes in the United States? How did the Supreme Court rulings of John Marshall and Roger Taney differ in this respect? (Compare John Marshall's contributions to jurisprudence with those of Roger Taney.)

- Who invented the modern political party? Why? Why did new party organizations appear during the 1830s?

## Chronology

| | |
|---|---|
| 1825 | The Erie Canal completed. |
| 1828 | Calhoun's *The South Carolina Exposition and Protest* published. |
| | "Tariff of Abominations." |
| March 1829 | Andrew Jackson inaugurated |
| January 1830 | Webster-Hayne debate. |
| May 1830 | Indian Removal Act. |
| 1832 | Black Hawk War. |
| November 1832 | South Carolina's Ordinance of Nullification. |
| 1832–33 | Bank War. |
| 1837 | *Charles River Bridge Company v. Warren Bridge Company.* |
| | Financial panic. |
| June 1838 | Cherokees' "Trail of Tears." |

## Key Terms

Jacksonian Democracy (p. 314, 316–317)

Nullification (p. 315, 323–324)

The Erie Canal (pp. 319–320)

The Bank War (p. 324)

Trail of Tears (p. 332)

*Chapter 12*

# WORKER WORLDS IN ANTEBELLUM AMERICA

Edward Hicks, *An Indian Summer View of the Farm and Stock of James C. Cornell of Northampton, Bucks County, Pennsylvania* (1948). Mr. Cornell, like most farmers who could afford to have their properties rendered by an artist, was making a statement about his status as a leading citizen of Bucks County. Here he displays his prized animals and property to admiring friends. Note the uniform, geometric pattern of Cornell's farm and the resemblance it bears to the uniformity and system found in factory operations.

- **How was farm life changing in the antebellum North?**
- **What were the main features of the slave system in the antebellum South?**
- **What were the main features of the factory system in the antebellum period?**
- **How did the widespread use of clock time affect work in this period?**

Before the Civil War, most Americans still lived on small, family-owned farms and followed the agrarian lifestyle idealized by Thomas Jefferson. But other types of labor were becoming more visible and more controversial. As cotton became America's primary export to Europe, plantation agriculture spread slavery across the South and subjected slaves and their masters to a strange and cruel way of life. At the same time, mechanized factories and large mill complexes emerged as an alternative to farming while fanning the development of mass transportation systems and the growth of urban areas. The new employment opportunities attracted a growing proportion of European immigrants entering the United States. Particularly in the northeastern states, industrial capitalism had begun, and with it dawned the modern age.

Whether on the farm, on the factory floor, or under the tyrannical bonds of slavery, the world of work experienced major changes. And some of these changes—mechanization, increased regimentation, and adherence to clock time—eventually reconfigured the face of politics, society, and the economy.

## A Nation of Farmers

In one of his most frequently quoted statements, Thomas Jefferson proclaimed that "those who labour in the earth are the chosen people of God, if ever he had a chosen people." Over the years, Jefferson continued to believe that agriculture and the agrarian way of life were not only central to America's special character but essential to the survival of the Republic. In his view, those who led a country life were more honest and industrious, independent and responsible, than city people. Because land ownership gave individuals a propertied stake in society, Jefferson considered landholders "the most precious part of a state." "I think our governments will re-

main virtuous for many centuries as long as they are chiefly agricultural," he wrote, adding that "this will be as long as there shall be vacant lands in any part of America." "When [people] get piled up upon one another in large cities, as in Europe," he warned, "they will become corrupt as in Europe."

Jefferson's outspoken agrarianism fit with his times. In 1800, the year of his election as president, rural people outnumbered city people by more than 15 to 1. Although the ratio would narrow to 5.5 to 1 in 1850 and 4 to 1 in 1860, family farms were still common in all parts of the United States. Artists of the time captured the grandeur of America's natural environment in their paintings. Asher B. Durand's panoramic view of *Dover Plains, Dutchess County, New York* (1848), for instance, conveys a sense of the beauty, peacefulness, and wholesomeness of rural life. By the 1850s, New York firms like Currier and Ives began to mass-produce such views as color lithographs and made them available at affordable prices. Extremely popular, the lithographs did much to romanticize the agrarian tradition long after it ceased to be the primary influence on American life and politics.

### FARM LIFE

Farms varied in size and orientation depending on their geographic location and time of settlement, and the interests, ambition, and good fortune of their owners. In sparsely settled areas along the frontier, the main objective was to build a cabin, clear the land, and plant enough basic crops (like corn) so that the farmer could "get by." Later he might plant various vegetables, fruit trees, and grain crops as well as raise cattle, horses, hogs, sheep, turkeys, chickens, and geese. Clearing the land required back-breaking labor. Since heavy rocks and stumps had to be removed and brush piled and burned to create a field, neighboring farmers often relied on one another for help. They also lent each other tools and sometimes even small amounts of money.

Asher B. Durand, *Dover Plains, Dutchess County, New York* (1848).

Most farms in the antebellum (pre–Civil War) period generally raised the same types of crops and livestock. Virtually all farms had "milch" cows, for example. Whereas dairy farmers might own a herd of sixteen to forty milkers, other farmers—whether they raised cash crops or remained at a subsistence level—kept a cow or two to feed their families. Most farmers raised hay, oats, corn, grain, potatoes, garden vegetables, fruits, chickens, hogs, and cattle, and they all owned oxen or horses for fieldwork and basic transportation. Farms differed in emphasis and the proportion of their crops and livestock, not in their methods.

Everyone in farm households had certain responsibilities, divided up along gender lines. Men's work included plowing, seeding, and cultivating the fields, clearing the land and hauling rocks, building and repairing fences, chopping wood, and caring for larger livestock such as horses, oxen, cattle, and sheep. Women, in addition to keeping house, preparing meals, and caring for children, did the milking, tended gardens, raised chickens, spun woolen yarn and wove homespun cloth, and made soap and candles as well as butter, cheese, and other dairy products. Cheese making required considerable skill, and in some households it became an important source of income, as did surpluses of grain, livestock, eggs, and butter. During the winter months, northern farm women often supplemented the family income by making palm-leaf hats and other items for local merchants who supplied them with the raw material and paid them either in cash or, more likely, credit at their general stores.

Given the many tasks that farming entailed, farm couples often had large families. Beginning at the age of six or seven—sometimes earlier—both boys and girls were expected to feed the chickens, gather eggs, slop the hogs, weed plants, sweep the house, and keep wood boxes full. As children reached puberty, they began to take on gender-related chores: young men joined their fathers in the field, and young women helped their mothers in the house. Depending on the size of the farm and the ages of children, farm families frequently employed live-in "hired hands" to lighten their toils. Sometimes these workers were relatives who stayed for the season; sometimes they were unmarried aunts or uncles who resided permanently with the family.

Farm life required a considerable degree of flexibility. Men helped out with the milking, gardening, and feeding of livestock, while women and their daughters often joined the men in the field during the haying, harvesting, and butchering seasons, when time was of the essence to prevent spoilage. During such periods of intense labor, neighbors and kinfolk assisted one another. The sheer drudgery of stacking hay in one-hundred-degree barn lofts or the trauma of hearing hogs frantically squeal as their throats were being cut during the late-fall slaughter suggests that farming could be a hard life. To be sure, it had its compensations in the form of land ownership, personal independence, a generally healthy work environment, close-knit neighborly acts of helping and sharing, and communal activities such as barn dances and quilting bees. But for those who worked hard to keep up and perhaps even get ahead, it was a demanding life.

As the larger economy became more market oriented, farmers established deepening business relationships with local merchants who owned general stores and dealt in a range of goods. There they exchanged home-grown produce for both essential goods and "fancy goods" like fine woolens, brass buttons, and ladies' hats. Relatively little cash changed hands in these barter-type relationships. Instead, farmers and merchants "settled up" periodically, paying what they owed in hard cash.

As the transportation revolution broadened trade networks, farming became more cash oriented and commercialized. As early as the late 1820s, agents from business firms in the cities traveled the countryside buying livestock, grain, cheese, and other farm commodities. If an exchange of goods took place on the spot, the farmer or his wife usually received an immediate cash payment. If a contractual agreement was drawn up, the farmer received a cash advance on signing the contract and full payment either on delivery or soon thereafter. In either case, both farm families and merchants were pulled into market relationships of increasing complexity.

Old ways persisted, however. Farmers tended to be conservative people who felt uneasy about establishing business relationships with distant companies whose owners they neither knew nor fully trusted. They generally steered a middle course between the rising, impersonal market economy and the more traditional "moral economy" with its face-to-face relationships and long-standing personal business associations. A German immigrant living in Illinois conveyed a sense of the shifting moral economy in rural America when he wrote in 1851 that "the Americans living around us are thoroughly good neighbors, ready and willing to be of help. But in business they are just as crafty as all their countrymen. When doing business they have no conscience at all."

## PLOWS AND REAPERS

Just as the manufacturing economy moved increasingly toward more standardized products for growing markets, so too did agriculture—though more slowly. The shift from subsistence to more commercially oriented farming first occurred in areas that were experiencing industrial development and urban growth. In New York, for example, the completion of the Erie Canal in 1825 and the attendant growth of manufacturing centers along its path from Troy to Utica, Syracuse, Rochester, and Buffalo stimulated the rise of dairy farming throughout the region. Rather than focusing on wheat as a cash crop (as they previously had), New York farmers turned increasingly to the production of milk, butter, and cheese for the growing city trade in the Northeast. These products were initially processed on the farm by women, but the demand grew, so that factory production eventually replaced home production, and, in the process, men took over the industry. With the coming of railroads during the 1850s, the dairy zone spread beyond New York, New

England, and Pennsylvania into northern Ohio and Indiana and eventually into large expanses of the Midwest, notably Wisconsin, Illinois, Minnesota, and Iowa. By 1880, dairy farming would become, in the words of a prominent spokesman, "the greatest single agricultural interest in America." Each shift marked the spreading influence of the market revolution.

Compared with the rapid spread of mechanization in industry, farmers adopted new technologies slowly. Before the 1850s, milking, planting, cultivating, and harvesting were largely done by hand. The symbol of agriculture in popular iconography, the plow, provides a good example of the pace of change in farm technology.

Although plows had been used for centuries, the process of plowing remained one of the most physically demanding and skilled jobs on a farm. The common plow of the 1820s consisted of a wooden moldboard and a wrought-iron plowshare attached to a simple wooden beam with handles that the farmer grasped as he shouted commands to a team of oxen or horses pulling the device. By the 1830s, the wrought-iron plows made by local blacksmiths began to give way to cast-iron plows with standardized parts. Although simple, cheap, and easily repaired, cast-iron plows nonetheless had shortcomings. Cutting a straight furrow proved difficult under any circumstances. Worse, plowmen had to stop constantly and back up in order to scrape away sod that stuck to the iron blade and wooden moldboard. Made from a relatively brittle metal, cast-iron plowshares (the cutting part) frequently broke in tough soils, and they proved all but unusable on the heavy, damp prairie soils of the Midwest.

Inventors sought to develop improved plows, but not until the late 1830s did one appear that made a significant difference. First introduced in Illinois by John Deere and several competitors, the new plow consisted of a wrought-iron moldboard with a hardened steel cutting edge. It became known as the "singing plow" because it made an audible vibration as it cut through (or scoured) the soil and delivered the furrow without any need to clean the blade. With this new steel plow, an average farmer could go from plowing eight acres a season to plowing as many as eighty. The new problem was how to increase the speed and capacity for harvesting crops.

The 1830s and 1840s witnessed other advances in the mechanization of farming, the most notable being the development of horse-drawn reaping machines for harvesting grain. Although all the elements of a successful mechanical reaper for cutting and bundling wheat existed in England by 1820, more than two decades elapsed before two Americans—

Unlike most early manufacturers, Cyrus H. McCormick excelled at marketing his product. Here, a company advertisement re-creates McCormick's first demonstration of his horse-drawn reaper in 1831.

Cyrus H. McCormick and Obed Hussey—working independently of each other, came up with competing reaper designs that actually worked. Of the two inventors, McCormick achieved more commercial success, primarily because he continued to improve his machine and developed an innovative marketing strategy. In 1848, McCormick chose to build his factory in Chicago because it was not only located in the midst of the American wheat belt but it was also emerging as a key railroad hub that served as one of the gateways to the West. Like John Deere, McCormick prospered, and both companies went on to rank among the largest and most successful agricultural equipment makers in the world.

As important as the innovations of Deere and McCormick were, the mechanization of American farming nonetheless proved to be a long-term process. Before the Civil War, most farmers simply could not afford to buy expensive farm equipment other than the all-essential plow and perhaps a harrow for breaking up freshly plowed soil. That would change during the war years as labor shortages and higher prices for farm products prompted more farmers to acquire reapers, mowers, and other labor-saving equipment. Yet even then, the vast majority of small farmers continued to plant, cultivate, and harvest their crops primarily by hand, and would do so well into the twentieth century.

### THE PROCESSING OF FOOD

Like the mechanization of farming, the application of scientific knowledge to agriculture also proceeded slowly. In the eighteenth century, a number of "gentlemen farmers" like George Washington and Thomas Jefferson kept abreast of developments in Europe by joining agricultural societies and corresponding with leading agricultural reformers. They also experimented with new seed varieties, practiced crop rotation, and imported purebred animals, such as Merino sheep. But such farmers were a small minority. By and large, farmers remained ignorant of "scientific agriculture," even though important discoveries in soil chemistry during the 1840s pointed to the importance of using fertilizers and rotating crops.

Food processing picked up speed before the Civil War. The fully automated mills that Oliver Evans had developed during the mid-1780s for grinding grains into flour (see Chapter 6) evolved into large commercial mills that could be found throughout the United States in the 1820s. Rice milling developed along similar lines, with enterprising South Carolina planters, anxious to reduce losses caused by erratic hand-processing methods, adapting Evans's automated methods to the shelling, cleaning, polishing, and packing of rice.

In most parts of the country prior to the Civil War, long before refrigeration, the meat trade centered on small, locally owned slaughterhouses that served local customers with fresh, smoked, pickled, and salted pork, mutton, and beef. The one major exception was Cincinnati, which emerged during the 1830s as the largest pork-packing center in North America. Two factors established Cincinnati's reputation as "Porkopolis." One was its location on the Ohio River, with access both upstream and down to large markets and plentiful sources of hogs. The other was the development of an ingenious disassembly system of butchering. The process began with the dead hogs hung face down from hooks attached to a large rotating horizontal wheel suspended from the ceiling of the plant. Apprentice butchers then cleaned, gutted, and delivered the carcasses to adjacent tables, where master butchers severed the heads and feet and cut up the remains into hams, shoulders, and sides. These were further divided into smaller cuts and graded before being taken to the packing rooms to be smoked, pickled, and salted before shipment.

Over the years, Cincinnati's meat packers also became proficient in making use of what had formerly been considered waste products. Procter and Gamble, the internationally known twentieth-century company, originated in Cincinnati when William Procter, a candle maker, and James Gamble, a soap maker, formed a partnership in 1837 to manufacture Neat's foot oil from pigs' feet and soap from the vast quantities

A slaughterhouse "disassembly" line c. 1873. By the 1860s, meatpackers in Cincinnati and Chicago were hanging gutted pigs from hooks attached to pulleys running on overhead rails, so that the carcasses could be moved systematically from one butcher to another for the removal of various body parts. Such disassembly procedures would later influence Henry Ford's development of the moving assembly line for automobiles.

of lard that came from local slaughterhouses. The factory system had come to agriculture.

Even small farmers felt the effects of the factory system. Farmers who contracted with large processing firms to deliver livestock, grain, fruits, vegetables, and raw milk became enmeshed in a time- (and profit-) oriented system as they pressed to meet schedules and avoid late-delivery penalties. Farm machinery was introduced not only to save labor but also to bring greater regularity and uniformity to planting, cultivating, and harvesting. Agricultural reformers who called for the adoption of purebred animals did so primarily because they sought to achieve higher yields and better standards of quality. By the 1850s, American agriculture was being significantly influenced by the policies of the rapidly growing manufacturing and transportation industries, especially the railroads. Although no one realized it at the time, the stage was being set for the scaling up and ultimately the incorporation of agriculture. In the long run, the new agricultural regime would spell the end of the small family farm.

## The Peculiar Institution

In the antebellum years, no region of the United States was more oriented toward agriculture than the South. Indeed, agriculture thrived there almost to the exclusion of everything else.

Other than New Orleans, the South had no large cities to compare with those in the North. And relatively little mechanized manufacturing existed in the region. Most southern manufacturing and agricultural processing firms relied largely on New England, mid-Atlantic, and Ohio Valley machine shops for their basic operating equipment. The same was true of southern railroads. Although cotton textile factories could be found throughout the South, their size paled in comparison with those in the North. Massachusetts alone possessed more cotton mills in 1860 than did all eleven southern states that eventually formed the Confederacy.

Yet owing primarily to the soaring industrial demand for raw cotton, the southern economy prospered during the antebellum period. The region's per capita income ranked fourth in the world in 1860, behind only Australia, England, and the northern United States. The cotton crop had exploded eightfold from 335,000 bales in 1820 to 2,799,000 bales in 1850, and then nearly doubled to an all-time pre–Civil War high of 5,387,000 bales in 1859. Throughout the antebellum period, cotton not only represented America's largest single foreign export, it also dwarfed all other exports in dollar value. As many white southerners proclaimed, "Cotton is King!"

Southern prosperity rested on the backs of black slaves. By the mid–nineteenth century, the emancipation movement that began in the North during the revolutionary period had eliminated black chattel slavery altogether above the Mason-Dixon line, making slavery a southern phenomenon. Known among southerners as the "peculiar institution," slavery expanded rapidly during the early nineteenth century as the cotton culture pressed in from the Atlantic coast first to inland South Carolina and Georgia, and then to new states farther west and south. In 1790, the national census reported just under 700,000 slaves in the United States, the vast majority of whom lived in the South. By 1810, their numbers had increased by more than 70 percent to almost 1.2 million, and by 1860 they had more than tripled again to nearly 4 million. New arrivals accounted for only a tiny part of that number: in 1808, Congress passed legislation to outlaw further imports of slaves, although international slave traders continued to smuggle small numbers of

A cotton plantation, probably in Louisiana, c. 1850–65.

Large plantations made up the third and most visible type of southern agriculture. Varying in size from hundreds to tens of thousands of acres and owned by a small but politically powerful planter elite (some 10,000 families), they commanded fifty or more slaves. The largest plantations were located in the deep South, and most, though not all, grew cotton. Of the eighty-eight planters who owned more than 300 slaves in 1860, for example, twenty-nine grew rice, among them the one individual in the South who owned more than 1,000 slaves. Altogether a quarter of the slave population lived on large estates consisting of 50 or more slaves; half lived on medium-size plantations of 10–49 slaves; and the remainder lived on farms of 1–9 slaves. Most slaves lived on moderately sized estates that grew cotton as a cash crop. Slave ownership not only represented an enormous capital investment but also indicated social status in the white community. As one southerner put it, "A Man's merit in this Country, is estimated according to the number of Negroes he works in the field."

### MASTERS AND SLAVES

On some coastal plantations, masters would sometimes absent themselves from the premises and might even leave slaves in charge of the operation. There the old task system of colonial days survived for a time: slaves, who were often highly skilled, had to perform a set amount of work per day, and then their time was their own. That system gave slaves an incentive to perform their assigned tasks even in the absence of white supervision. By contrast, owners generally lived on the new upland plantations that grew cotton, and so could supervise and discipline slaves. There a gang system of labor took hold that allowed slaves little free time, a source of considerable tension in the master-slave relationship.

The system of gang labor functioned in various ways. On farms and plantations with fewer than ten slaves, owners tended to work alongside their slaves and to supervise them directly. On those with more than ten but less than thirty slaves, masters seldom worked in the fields except at harvest

slaves into the South. The rapid expansion of the slave population came, for the most part, from natural increase.

In 1860, slaves constituted roughly one-third of the South's 12.3 million population. The fastest-growing segment of slavery was concentrated in the deep South because that's where cotton, rice, and sugar were grown. As the demand for slaves grew in response to the expansion of cotton cultivation, older states like Virginia became important sources of supply for the prospering domestic slave trade. Slave trading became one of Virginia's largest income producers after the War of 1812.

While slaves could be found in such occupations as domestic servants, skilled craftsmen, and industrial workers, the majority worked as field hands. Three types of farmers existed in the antebellum South. Most numerous were small farmers who were too poor to own slaves and lived off the land primarily to support themselves. Next came middle-class farmers who owned larger spreads and often grew cotton as a cash crop to supplement the usual run of corn, oats, hogs, and livestock. Depending on the extent of their holdings, members of this group might own anywhere from one or two to forty or fifty slaves. However, not all of them grew cotton. In Kentucky, for example, farmers employed slaves to grow hemp as a cash crop, while their counterparts in Virginia and North Carolina focused mainly on tobacco. In the great Valley of Virginia, moreover, wheat became a favored cash crop, while some enterprising slaveholders combined farming with the production of iron for commercial sale.

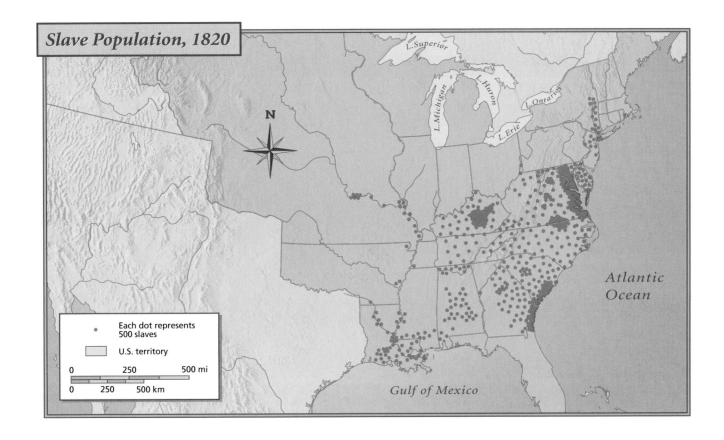

**Slave Population, 1820**

Each dot represents 500 slaves

U.S. territory

0   250   500 mi

0   250   500 km

L. Superior
L. Michigan
L. Huron
L. Ontario
L. Erie

Atlantic Ocean

Gulf of Mexico

time. In both cases, however, owners knew their slaves by name and interacted with them personally. Slaves on such modest-sized plantations were rarely specialized: they had several different work assignments and experienced relatively little regimentation. Still, their workday lasted from sunrise to sunset and included few sanctioned breaks.

On large plantations with fifty or more slaves, conditions were more rigid. Masters might periodically inspect the fields, but they rarely if ever supervised or directly participated in the work. Instead, they hired white overseers to take charge of the plantation workforce. The overseer, in turn, divided the slaves into gangs, each headed by a "driver" who supervised work in the fields and, more often than not, was an older slave in whom the overseer placed some modicum of trust.

In the summer of 1854, a traveler in Mississippi described a slave gang as it returned from the field after a day's labor. "First came, led by an old driver carrying a whip, forty of the largest and strongest women I ever saw together; they were all in a simple uniform dress of a bluish check stuff, the skirts reaching little below the knee; their legs and feet were bare;

they carried themselves loftily, each having a hoe over the shoulder, and walking with a free, powerful swing, like chasseurs [light infantry] on the march." Next came plow hands leading their mules, "the cavalry, thirty strong, mostly men, but a few of them women. . . . A lean and vigilant white overseer, on a brisk pony, brought up the rear."

This description conveys the degree of organization and specialization that characterized slave labor forces on large plantations. A sense of military regimentation in the description of the women in uniform dress with hoes slung over their shoulders was telling: plantation masters and agricultural writers throughout the South frequently used military and factory metaphors to describe the ideal type of plantation that owners sought to run. "Every thing," one writer noted, "moves on systematically, and with the discipline of a regular trained army." Indeed, the chain of command from master to overseer to drivers to field hands closely resembled the system found in both the military and private industry.

Few, if any, plantations actually ran with clockwork precision. The real world of chattel slavery rested on a regimen of forced

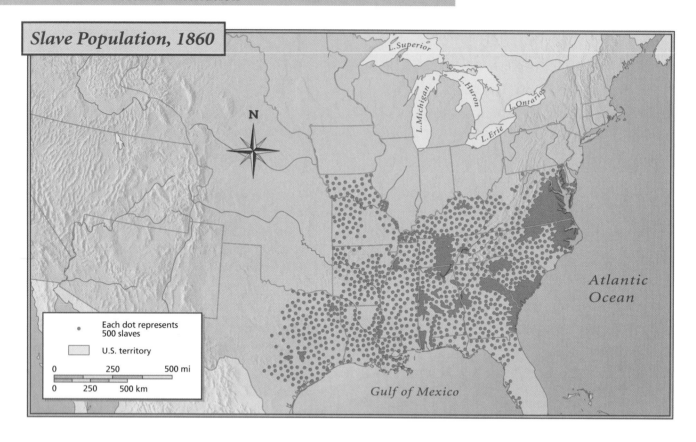

*Slave Population, 1860*

Each dot represents 500 slaves

U.S. territory

labor that revealed all sorts of tensions, evasions, compromises, and confrontations. To be sure, many masters sought to encourage their slaves by rewarding them for work well done. Incentives included garden plots (from which they could keep or sell what produce they raised), permission to raise chickens and, occasionally, hogs or a cow, extra holidays, and special privileges such as passes that allowed them to travel to nearby plantations and towns to visit friends and relatives. Some masters established work quotas for their labor gangs; anything done beyond the required amount resulted in either cash payments or, more often, credit at the plantation store. Others went so far as to establish profit-sharing agreements, such as the Louisiana sugar planter who paid his slaves a dollar for each hogshead (large barrel) of sugar they prepared. In one instance, a Virginia ironmaster even permitted his most valued slave to open a savings account at a local bank for the astonishing amount of $100. Such practices, another Virginian noted, served as "a powerful lever . . . to enforce obedience and fidelity."

But behind the carrot always loomed the stick. Every aspect of a slave's life was circumscribed by rules that dictated when to get up in the morning, when to eat, when to go to work, how to do the work, when to take breaks, when to quit, and when to go to bed. Rules also governed activities that lay beyond the immediate realm of work, such as hunting, fishing, keeping garden plots, obtaining permission to get married, selling or trading goods, and leaving the plantation premises for any reason. Such rules, which were enforced according to the whims of the masters, supplemented state laws that prohibited slaves from learning to read or write, conducting public assemblies of any sort, possessing liquor or firearms, hiring themselves out, or moving about without a pass from their owner. Like plantation rules, state "slave codes" aimed at subordinating slaves to white authority, although they tended to be inconsistently enforced.

Slaves who transgressed rules could expect to be punished. Some masters refused to discipline them with physical force. If slaves broke the rules, they were denied certain privileges. If they persisted in unruly behavior, the ultimate—though reluctantly reached—solution was to turn them over to a slave trader to be sold. Most slaveholders, however, did not agree with this "persuasion doctrine," nor did they believe in unrestrained brutality. Instead, they adopted a paternalistic approach that viewed slaves as children who needed the threat as well as the occasional application of disciplinary measures in order to ensure good order and correct behavior.

Depending on the temperament of the owner and the seriousness of the offense, slave punishments could entail public humiliations (like making men wear women's clothing and do women's work) or confiscating garden crops and livestock and reducing their rations. Slaves could be put in stocks, confined with iron-pronged collars on their necks, or branded and mutilated. The most-used method of punishment proved to be the whip, the ultimate symbol of the master's power.

Floggings, more often than not, were communal affairs intended to intimidate those who witnessed the event as well as punish the person being whipped. The severity of punishment depended on the type of whip being used. Slaveholders who wished to make an impression but not seriously injure the person used a "stout flexible stalk" covered with leather that had a thin "buckskin cracker" attached to it; this whip, according to one observer, made "a very loud report, and stings, or 'burns' the skin smartly, but does not bruise it." Slaveholders ordinarily avoided the use of shorter and thicker rawhide whips because they severely lacerated the skin, which besides being life threatening left disfiguring scars that lowered a slave's market value. Still, many slaves—both men and women—could be found with "large raised scars or whelks" four to six inches in length on their shoulders, buttocks, and lower backs. After flogging a slave, particularly brutal masters and overseers would pour brine on the wounds to increase the painful effects. Whether or not they were on the receiving end of a whip, people who witnessed a flogging never forgot its excruciating physical and psychological effects.

Slaves also lived in perpetual fear of being sold and separated from their families and friends. Any number of circumstances—personal pique, financial need, the settlement of an estate after a master's death—could result in a slave's being sold. During the half-century before the Civil War, hundreds of thousands of slaves from the upper South were sold "down river" to cotton-producing states in the deep South. "All the time we would see 'nigger traders' coming through the country," a former slave recalled. "I have seen men and women cuffed to 60-foot chains being took to Lynchburg, Va., to the block to be sold." "On New Year's day we all were scared," another remembered. "That was the time for selling, buying, and trading slaves. We did not know who was to go or come."

Masters interfered with the lives of their slaves in many other ways. Some insisted on naming slave children. Others,

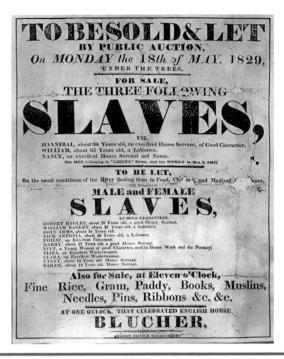

An 1829 broadside announcing the auction of three slaves and the rental of eleven others (five females, six males), along with the sale of "that celebrated English horse Blucher."

who considered religion a stabilizing force, would assemble their slaves for Bible readings and to hear white preachers, yet forbade them to conduct their own religious services. Still others demanded that slave couples secure their permission before getting married and punished those who sought a divorce or engaged in extramarital affairs. Yet often the very masters who demanded moral rectitude of their slaves forced themselves on slave women. "How many have fallen before this temptation!" a Virginian wrote in disgust. "So many that it has almost ceased to be a temptation to fall!"

### SLAVE RELIGION AND MUSIC

The slave quarter was far enough away from the "big house" that slaves were able to find some measure of privacy and interact with one another more or less on their own terms. There people did everything from eating and sleeping to fighting, praying, and making love. Two activities in particular—religion and family life—proved especially important in shaping the slave's inner world. Most masters approved of them because they saw them as stabilizing influences on the slave population.

## The Peculiar Institution

Although some of the largest plantations retained white preachers on their staffs, most slaves "got religion" by hearing the Christian gospels read to them by their masters, responding to calls from itinerant white missionaries, and attending Sunday services at white churches with white congregations. Slaves gravitated more to the evangelical, and often highly emotional, services of Baptists and Methodists than to the more reserved Episcopalians and Presbyterians. Even then, slaves remained leery about sermons they heard from white ministers that emphasized the virtue of obedience. "Dat ole white preacher," a former slave recalled, "jest was telling us slaves to be good to our masters. We ain't keer'd a bit 'bout dat stuff he was talling us 'cause we wanted to sing, pray, and serve God in our own way."

The desire to serve God in their own way led to the development of a new religious tradition in the slave community that blended elements of white evangelical Christianity and African culture. What ultimately emerged was a distinctive African American style of Christianity that took evangelical religion to a new level of intensity while substituting themes of oppression and deliverance for the slaveholder's theology of obedience and trust. Subtle expressions of protest against enslavement were embedded in the sermons of self-styled (and mostly illiterate) black preachers and in the songs that slave congregations sang. The Old Testament story of Moses delivering his people from bondage proved particularly meaningful, as did deeply moving spirituals like "Nobody Knows the Trouble I've Seen" and "Lord Keep Me from Sinking Down."

This African American dance was drawn by artist Lewis Miller during a trip to Virginia in 1853. The banjo and bones are African instruments, while the fiddle is European.

Whether sermons and songs expressed lament at the slave's deplorable condition or joy in the knowledge that salvation awaited every person, the new religion provided slaves with a spiritual life that transcended the drudgery and pain of their daily toils and gave hope that better times were coming.

As much as slave music helped to sustain hope and preserve African cultural traditions, its distinctive, innovative style had a formative impact on American music. It took a long time for black spirituals to reach white audiences, but when they did—thanks to the preservation efforts of Northerners who went south during the Civil War and especially the moving performances of postwar black choirs like Fisk University's celebrated Jubilee Singers—their impact was enormous. By the 1870s, songs like "Deep River" and "Swing Low, Sweet Chariot" had become part of America's larger musical repertoire and a source of inspiration for churchgoers of all colors and persuasions.

Black music influenced even larger audiences with the introduction, in the 1840s, of the minstrel show—a combination of song, dance, and often raucous humor that poked fun at everything from politicians to upper-class pretensions. Performed by white musicians in blackface, minstrel shows proved enormously popular with white audiences throughout the country and continued into the twentieth century. One of the most talented composers of the era, Stephen C. Foster, became famous by borrowing from black music to produce major minstrel hits like "De Camptown Races" and "Oh! Susanna."

Through high-speed printing, hard-driving, toe-tapping melodies like "Oh! Susanna" and "Old Dan Tucker" were mass-produced and sold cheaply as sheet music for use in American homes. Once printing houses grasped the enormous economic potential of sheet music, a substantial business in popular music emerged in the United States. Building on the surging demand for what became known as "parlor music," piano and pipe organ makers like Jonas Chickering of Boston began to shift their manufacturing methods from one-of-a-kind hand craftsmanship for selective clients to mass production for mass buyers. By the 1850s, for the first time, music and music making were becoming a big business in America.

As important as blackface minstrelsy was to the rise of popular music and mass entertainment, the new venue had a deplorable downside. While borrowing shamelessly from indigenous black music and dance, minstrel performers constructed their acts to comport with prevailing racist sentiments that stereotyped blacks as ignorant and uncouth, thus playing into the hands of those who defended slavery as a natural condition in society. Among the most famous stereotypes were "Sambo," "Jim Crow," and "Zip Coon," characters that portrayed blacks as obsequious buffoons or cunning ne'er-do-wells. Such characterizations would become hated reminders of white racism and black subordination in America. To add injury to insult, black innovators never received a nickel in compensation when minstrel performers adapted their music and dance routines to the white stage.

## SLAVE FAMILY LIFE

If religion and music provided hope and consolation, family life proved a fragile buffer against the daily abuses of slavery. Although masters encouraged their slaves to marry and have children, slave marriages had no legal standing because these people were property, not citizens. Married slaves faced the constant threat of being separated either by sale or, if the couple were owned by different masters, by a move. Other intrusions, particularly the unwanted sexual advances of white masters and overseers, further complicated slave marriages. Yet family life persisted and even flourished.

Slave housing was crude by any standard. The usual family accommodation consisted of a one-room log structure measuring sixteen by eighteen feet with an unfinished interior. On prosperous plantations, better units housed single families of three to seven people and had stone chimneys and plank floors. On poorer plantations, however, living conditions could be far more spartan and crowded. Many cabins had no chimneys and rested on dirt floors.

With their husbands often owned by other masters and residing elsewhere, women shouldered the task of nurturing and raising children. Always eager to increase the number of slaves they owned, white masters expected slave women to have plenty of children—the more the better. Motherhood conferred status within the slave community and heightened a woman's monetary value to the master. Barren women were disparaged, made to work harder, and often sold off. Compared with male slaves, whose value fell with age and declining physical stamina, women generally maintained their value into their elderly years by working as house servants, cooks, midwives, seamstresses, or weavers. By and large, slave women led trying lives that saw their husbands and children mistreated and degraded before their eyes, and themselves victimized by hard work, physical violence, and sexual exploitation.

Although far from excellent by twentieth-century standards, the typical slave diet was relatively healthy. In addition to their usual rations of cornmeal and pork (or bacon), slaves supple-

"Jim Crow," the mythical happy-go-lucky black slave stereotype created and fostered by slave owners and other white Americans prior to the Civil War. After the war discriminatory state and local legislation against black Americans became known as "Jim Crow laws."

mented their diets with vegetables and chickens grown in their garden patches and wildlife taken by fishing, trapping, or hunting. Luxury items such as sugar, salt, and coffee were sometimes distributed by owners and sometimes obtained at the plantation store in exchange for produce. There is evidence that the general health of adult slaves was probably no worse than that of many southern whites. The death rate among slaves was slightly higher than for whites. Infant mortality rates among slaves proved much higher, however, mainly because slave women were forced to work up to the moment of giving birth and forced back to work too soon afterward. Slaves succumbed to the same diseases as whites, although, owing to the sickle-cell trait, they suffered less from malaria. On the other hand, they suffered more from pulmonary disease, cholera, tetanus, and other common diseases. Because they were considered valuable investments, they received more medical attention than did most southern whites, who rarely if ever visited a physician.

351

*American Journal*

## What's for Dinner?

*The escaped slave and abolitionist leader Frederick Douglass published several autobiographical accounts of his experience as a slave on the plantation of Colonel Edward Lloyd in eastern Maryland. The following describes the slave diet, which consisted mainly of ground corn, pork scraps, and locally caught fish, like herring. Elsewhere in his writings, Douglass noted that slaves supplemented this sparse diet by fishing, hunting, and tending small garden plots whenever time allowed.*

"As a general rule, slaves do not come to the quarters for either breakfast or dinner, but take their 'ash cake' with them, and eat it in the field. This was so on the home plantation; probably, because the distance from the quarter to the field, was sometimes two, and even three miles.

"The dinner of the slaves consisted of a huge piece of ash cake, and a small piece of pork, or two salt herrings. Not having ovens, nor any suitable cooking utensils, the slaves mixed their meal with a little water, to such thickness that a spoon would stand erect in it; and, after the wood had burned away to coals and ashes, they would place the dough between oak leaves and lay it carefully in the ashes, completely covering it; hence, the bread is called ash cake. The surface of this peculiar bread is covered with ashes, to the depth of a sixteenth part of an inch, and the ashes, certainly, do not make it very grateful to the teeth, nor render it very palatable. The bran, or course part of the meal, is baked with the fine, and bright scales run through the bread. This bread, with its ashes and bran, would disgust and choke a northern man, but it is quite liked by the slaves. They eat it with avidity, and are more concerned about the quantity than about the quality. They are far too scantily provided for, and are worked too steadily, to be much concerned for the quality of their food. The few minutes allowed them at dinner time, after partaking of their coarse repast, are variously spent. Some lie down on the 'turning row,' and go to sleep; others draw together, and talk; and others are at work with needle and thread, mending their tattered garments. Sometimes you may hear a wild, hoarse laugh arise from a circle, and often a song. Soon, however, the overseer comes dashing through the field. *'Tumble up! Tumble up,* and *to work, work,'* is the cry; and, now, from twelve o'clock (mid-day) till dark, the human cattle are in motion, wielding their clumsy hoes; hurried on by no hope of reward, no sense of gratitude, no love of children, no prospect of bettering their condition; nothing, save the dread and terror of the slave-driver's lash. So goes one day, and so comes and goes another."

Frederick Douglass, *My Bondage and My Freedom*

---

Given the primitive state of medical knowledge before the Civil War, though, that may have been more of a disadvantage.

### SLAVE RESISTANCE

As slave parents struggled to endure, they did the best they could to raise their children in a loving environment and to pass on certain customs and values that would serve them well in later life. Since the vast majority of slaves could not read or write, children learned mainly through verbal instruction. Storytelling and songs proved important not only in conveying moral values and religious beliefs but also in describing the outside world and offering practical advice about how to interact with whites. So-called trickster tales, like the story of "Br'er Rabbit," were filled with charming characters and great humor yet at the same time conveyed lessons about the need for quickwittedness, wariness, and even deceit when dealing with whites. Such tales often parodied white society, holding its double standards, hypocrisy, and injustices up to ridicule. They revealed a spirit of protest that often eluded the white community and, in doing so, gave slaves a degree of satisfaction.

In addition to trickster tales, plaintive songs, and other forms of passive protest, slaves found more assertive ways to resist their masters. The most common included everyday acts of noncooperation and "silent sabotage" such as pretending to misunderstand orders, working carelessly or at a slow pace, "accidentally" breaking tools, feigning illness, stealing, mistreating animals, and, in extreme cases, setting buildings on fire. While some slaveholders attributed such acts to inherent laziness and stupidity, others considered them nothing but sheer "rascality." A northerner observing a gang of slaves on a South Carolina plantation noted that the overseer was "constantly directing and encouraging them, but . . . as often as he visited one end of the line of operations, the hands at the other end would discontinue their labor, until he turned to ride towards them again." "Hands won't work unless I am in sight," a Virginia planter wrote in anger and exasperation. "I left the Field at 12 [with] all going well, but very little done after."

Running away and outright resistance constituted more direct challenges to the slave master's authority, and resistance occurred far more frequently than most slave owners wished to admit. Although premeditated murders and other acts of slave violence sometimes took place, most confrontations involved spur-of-the-moment blowups in which an angry slave reacted to some intolerable situation such as persistent brow-beating or repeated whippings. Because harsh words and blows were often exchanged, slaves who confronted masters or overseers often took flight immediately afterward in order to avoid punishments administered in a fit of rage. More often than not, they returned on their own after a day or so once tempers had cooled and the likelihood of brutal retaliation had diminished.

The decision to run away permanently took some serious planning. More men than women ran away, and more from the upper South than the deep South, which was hundreds of miles from free territory. The journey from slavery to freedom required resourcefulness and a great deal of luck. Most fugitives made their way north on their own. Once they reached the border areas between free and slave states, sympathetic blacks and whites sometimes fed and sheltered them and conducted them to other safe havens. Such individuals became collectively known as the "Underground Railroad," but their operations were much less systematic than the railroad analogy suggests. Even with the help of antislavery sympathizers, a fugitive's likelihood of success remained slim. In addition to paid slave catchers hired by owners, white "slave patrols" roamed every southern state pursuing runaways and stopping suspicious blacks and demanding to see their owner-issued travel permits. Capture by a slave patrol was one of the worst things that could happen to a fugitive, because, unlike the owner or paid slave catcher who had a fi-

Photo of a crawl space behind sliding shelves made in 1810 by the Reverend Alexander Dobbin of Gettysburg, Pennsylvania. Such hiding places sheltered runaway slaves throughout the northern states and were a critical part of the Underground Railroad.

nancial stake in the slave's condition, the patrol couldn't care less whether they returned the subject dead or alive.

With shorter distances to travel, runaway slaves from border areas like Maryland or Kentucky stood a better chance of success. Still, escaped slaves had to be constantly on guard for fear of being betrayed in exchange for a slave catcher's reward. Such concerns extended to fellow blacks, for, as one escaped slave put it, "twenty-one years in slavery had taught me that there were traitors even among colored people." And once a fugitive entered free territory, there were no guarantees of work. Racism was rampant throughout the North as well as the South. Former slaves were sometimes even driven out of town. Yet even against these daunting odds, tens of thousands of slaves sought to break their bonds and achieve freedom during the pre–Civil War years. Only about 1,000 a year succeeded.

Slavery, with its environment of suspicion and fear, was the foundation of antebellum southern society. Slaves lived in constant fear of their masters' godlike authority to interfere in every aspect of their lives. Masters, in turn, feared slave recalcitrance, random acts of violence, and the loss of runaways. Even the nearly three-quarters of the South's white population who did not own slaves were touched by the peculiar institution. Slavery was the scaffold of their social status and economic well-being. The desire to keep blacks in their place thus became the cement that held together an otherwise segmented society in the South. "I reckon the majority would be right glad if we could get rid of the niggers," a poor white informed a northern traveler. "But it wouldn't never do to free 'em and leave 'em here. I don't know anybody, hardly, in favor of that. Make 'em free and leave 'em here and they'd steal every thing we made. Nobody couldn't live here then." "From childhood," the same northerner concluded, "the one thing . . . which has made life valuable to the mass of whites has been that the niggers are yet their inferiors." "It is African slavery that makes every white man in some sense a lord," a southern editor asserted, adding, "Color gives caste."

Southern whites' greatest fear was of a massive slave rebellion. Reports of slave conspiracies circulated throughout the South, but few actually materialized. In 1800, a plot by Gabriel Prosser, a Richmond blacksmith, and his brother Martin, a slave preacher, was thwarted before it could begin. Two decades later, in 1822, Denmark Vesey, a free resident of Charleston, South Carolina, and a leader in the city's black church, planned an armed attack on the city only to be betrayed, arrested, and executed. Only one revolt resulted in widespread violence in the three decades before the Civil War.

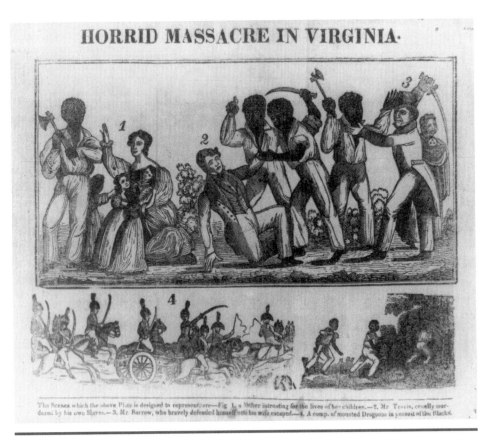

It occurred in August 1831 and was led by Nat Turner, a slave preacher from Southampton County in southeastern Virginia, who claimed that God had called him to strike down the "Serpent" that held his people in bondage. Convinced that "the first should be last and the last should be first," Turner gathered a small force and initiated his crusade by killing his master as well as the master's family. The rebellion lasted two days and embraced a twenty-mile area of Southampton County. During that time, his seventy-some followers killed fifty-nine whites—men, women, and children—before being routed by a better-armed white force consisting of local guards and state militia. In the days that followed, the white community took its vengeance. "Many negroes are killed every day," a local minister wrote, "the exact number will never be known." Although Turner initially eluded his pursuers, he was eventually captured, tried, and hanged. In the end, over one hundred blacks died in Southampton's reign of terror.

Long after Nat Turner went to his grave, the governor of Virginia remained "fully convinced that every black preacher in the whole country east of the Blue Ridge . . . was in" on Turner's

This woodcut engraving, entitled "Horrid Massacre in Virginia," depicts four scenes from the Nat Turner rebellion. The first panel (1) shows a mother pleading for the lives of her children; the second (2) shows a slave owner being "cruelly murdered by his own slaves"; the third (3) shows a Mr. Barron defending himself while his wife and infant child escape; and the fourth (4) shows Army Dragoons chasing down Turner and his men. Interestingly, nothing is said about what happened to the rebel slaves once they were captured.

"secret." Fear of further uprisings lingered as well. Another Virginian was more explicit. "These insurrections have alarmed my wife so as really to endanger her health," he lamented to an associate in Ohio. "I have not slept without anxiety in three months. . . . There has been and there still is *panic* in all this country. . . . There is no principle of life. Death is autocrat of slave regions." These words suggest, as well as any can, the degree to which southern whites, having constructed the machinery of slavery, had become caught in its very works.

Slave uprisings, wherever they occurred, brought tension and anxiety. A case in point is the Amistad affair. In 1840–41, the U.S. Supreme Court infuriated the VanBuren administration and the slaveholding South when it released 36 illegally imported Africans who had risen up against their Spanish captors on the slave ship *L'Amistad* and killed everyone on board except for two Spaniards named Montez and Ruiz (their purported owners) and a Cuban-born slave cabin boy. Because the non-English speaking Africans received highly visible support from Northern abolitionist lawyers who not only defended them in court but also raised funds for their return to their African homeland, the Amistad case drew widespread attention to the abolitionist movement and the plight of slavery. But among pro-slavery advocates, the Amistad affair constituted yet one more instance that "Yankee" radicals were conspiring against the South's "peculiar institution."

## Industrial Labor and the Factory System

Compared with farming, industry represented an altogether new type of labor in early nineteenth-century America. Two characteristics distinguished the factory system as it evolved in the United States: one was its sheer extent, and the other its presence in the countryside. European observers frequently commented on the widespread adoption of machinery in the United States. Unlike England, where steam power was widely used by the late eighteenth century, the United States possessed thousands of streams with falls of water capable of driving machinery. Many nineteenth-century factories stood on spots formerly occupied by colonial grist-, fulling, and sawmills. Steamboats and steam railroads carried the great bulk of passengers and freight in early industrial America, but waterwheels drove its factory system. American industry relied on waterpower well into the 1860s. Not until the Civil War did steam power begin to gain ascendancy.

Most small waterpowered mills in early nineteenth-century America generated no more than a few horsepower and were owned, operated, and often built by local farmers with the assistance of a local carpenter or millwright. Most processed grain and lumber for local customers. Larger mills, numbering in the thousands, focused on manufacturing goods for regional and national markets. Often both types of mill evolved out of local agricultural pursuits. A case in point is E. I. Du Pont de Nemours and Company, a gunpowder manufacturer established on the family farm near Wilmington, Delaware, in 1803. During the nineteenth and early twentieth centuries, it grew into one of the nation's largest corporations.

Rural mills were also the seedbeds of villages and larger communities. The presence of a gristmill might cause an original farmstead to expand into a small village with several houses, a general store, blacksmithy, church, and post office. Larger mill complexes often attracted other businesses and, before long, grew into towns. Some, like Lowell, Massachusetts, developed into flourishing industrial cities. Although mill communities concentrated in New England and the Middle Atlantic states, the pattern spread across the United States.

More often than not, a mill was a community's largest employer, and mill owners frequently had other business investments in the neighborhood such as general stores, real estate, and residential properties. They helped found and direct local banks. In local politics, mill owners often urged their employees to support candidates who favored their business interests. In the establishment of local churches and public schools, they served not only as benefactors but also as deacons, vestrymen, and trustees. Most were well aware, as the Lowell textile magnate Patrick Tracy Jackson put it, that "the village steeple is the unfailing companion of the waterwheel." They firmly believed, as did most people, that churches and schools fostered values of virtue, honesty, and thrift that carried over into the workplace. Early factories even looked like churches.

Although their backgrounds varied, mill owners and factory masters were almost exclusively male. One exception was Rebecca Lukens (1794–1854) of Coatesville, Pennsylvania. The daughter of a Quaker forge master, the thirty-one-year-old mother of three young daughters suddenly found herself thrust into the business when her physician husband, who managed the family's Brandywine Iron Works, died unexpectedly in 1825. Although friends urged her to dispose of the financially strapped enterprise, Mrs. Lukens, with the help of two brothers-in-law, ran the operation for the next twenty-two years and

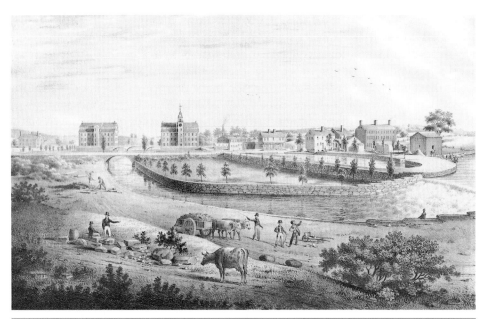

This lithographic rendering of the Crown and Eagle cotton mills at North Uxbridge, Massachusetts, provides a panoramic view of a small factory village c. 1830, with its worker housing, company store, and requisite mill stream for waterpower. A fine example of the Rhode Island system of small- and medium-size mills influenced by Samuel Slater, the Crown and Eagle contrasts with the much larger mills built by the Boston Associates at Waltham, Lowell, and other northern New England sites.

itable product—and this objective presented the most formidable challenge to manufacturers, for on it rested the success of the other two. A successful work environment involved not only building and equipping mills and hiring workers, but also establishing the divisions of labor and the rules of conduct governing the employees. To handle their most vexing daily issue, the organization and control of workers, manufacturers resorted to traditional paternalistic practices.

In the context of early American industry, the controlling idea behind paternalism was that workers should show proper deference to their employers and unhesitatingly comply with their commands. There was no room for democracy on the factory floor. Indeed, early factory masters resembled southern plantation owners in the lofty social positions they occupied. Along with impressive property holdings and high social standing, they often held political offices and headed local militia units. A wide circle of people depended on them for jobs, housing, loans, and business patronage. Yet despite these dependencies, life and labor in early industrial communities revealed subtle patterns of reciprocal social relationships.

turned it into a highly profitable operation. When she relinquished the business to her sons-in-law in 1847, the waterpowered Lukens mill employed two dozen workers, had been completely rebuilt, and was producing some of the finest iron for steam-engine boilers in America. Under her leadership, the mill had gone from making nails and barrel hoop iron for local customers to making much heavier pieces of rolled iron for a growing national market. As an entrepreneur in an age of change, Rebecca Lukens proved more than able.

## PROFITS AND PATERNALISM

Early American factories were a varied lot. They ranged from Lowell's mass-production textile mill complexes with their all-female workers to more modest enterprises like Rebecca Lukens's Brandywine Iron Works. All shared the same fundamental objectives. One was a straightforward economic interest in making a profit. Another was to manufacture a product that would find and hold a niche in the market. A third was to create an environment that would encourage the making of a prof-

*The Brandywine Iron Works.* Members of the Lukens family well understood the nature of paternalism. "Kindness with firmness" became their guiding principle, yet they realized that business success depended on cultivating loyalty and trust among their employees. In effect, this meant that an informal code based on certain "understandings" governed life and labor at the Brandywine Iron Works. It was understood, for instance, that a forge worker could occasionally ask a comrade to fill in for him and leave work early without incurring the owner's wrath. It also was understood that furnace and forge crews did not have to work on days of excessive summer heat. While the Lukens family frowned on the use of alcohol, workers knew that they would not be fired for occasional drunkenness or misconduct. There seemed to be no stated rule about how many times a person might transgress the owner's authority before he was disciplined or dismissed. Although these under-

Rebecca Pennock Lukens, a successful ironmaster at a time when women rarely became involved in the business world.

standings remained vague, they seemed to function well. There is no evidence that the owners ever suddenly fired a worker.

The Lukens brand of paternalism extended workers a safety net as well. Mill workers knew that they would keep their jobs and company-owned housing even during hard times. In fact, before the Civil War the Lukens family sometimes ran their rolling mill at no profit during economic downturns in order to keep their workers employed and avoid losing them. If the mill closed temporarily, mill hands were put to work on the family farm. They also received food, fuel, and other provisions "on account" at reduced prices from the company store. In these and other ways, a safety net existed under the Lukens family's benevolent brand of paternalism.

*Women Workers at Lowell.* Paternalism wore a different face at Lowell, Massachusetts. There the Boston Associates sought to govern their mills through more stringently enforced rules and regulations. Lowell specialized in the manufacture of cotton cloth rather than boilerplate, and its mills were much larger than those of the Lukens family. In 1836, Lowell boasted twenty mills with 6,000 workers, while the Lukens operation consisted of one rolling mill with approximately 20 workers. Even more striking was the social makeup of the two communities' working populations. In contrast with Lukens's male workers, 85 percent of Lowell's labor force consisted of single women between the ages of fifteen and twenty-nine. Whereas most of the Lukens workers lived with their families in company-owned housing, Lowell's female workers lived apart from their families in dormitories.

From the outset at Lowell, the Boston Associates continued the policy they had established at Waltham, Massachusetts, during the War of 1812: they equipped their factories with self-acting machinery that took little skill to operate. This allowed them to hire cheap female labor rather than skilled but more expensive and potentially troublesome male workers. To attract a workforce, they had to reassure young women and their families that Lowell was a good place to work—not, in the words of a New York mill owner, "sinks of vice and immorality," but, on the contrary, nurseries of morality, industry, and intelligence." To the associates, Lowell and its mills were more than a place of labor and production; they constituted a great social experiment, moral gymnasiums where employees would not only earn wages—sometimes saved for dowries— but also experience moral and spiritual growth.

Besides their factory work rules, Lowell's textile corporations sought to weave other threads into the moral fiber of their female labor force. Company regulations circumscribed the workers' world with prohibitions against the use of "ardent spirits," Sabbath-breaking, foul language, "dissolute manners," and the like. Moreover, strict evening curfews were imposed by the company boardinghouses in the interest of "moral deportment and mutual good will." Former mill girls frequently reminisced about the "pleasant life" they had experienced while working in Lowell, but they also acknowledged that the powerful corporations could be oppressive.

Despite its awesome economic success, Lowell's tight social fabric began to fray by the mid-1830s, when feverish expansion gripped the textile industry. In the Northeast alone, hundreds of firms sprang up hoping to capture lucrative markets for cotton goods in the South, the West, the Caribbean, and various U.S. cities. As competition increased and technological improvements expanded the capacity of textile machinery, prices and profits began to fall. Caught in a competitive spiral, Lowell companies and others like them in New Hampshire, Maine, and Massachusetts began to adopt cost-cutting measures, the brunt of which fell on their workers. The managers at Lowell installed new and faster machinery, speeded up the pace of machinery, stretched out workloads by assigning additional machines to mill girls, and lowered the piece rates (rates paid for work done by the piece). Within a few years, output per worker nearly doubled, while wages increased only slightly. But pressures mounted.

## Industrial Labor and the Factory System

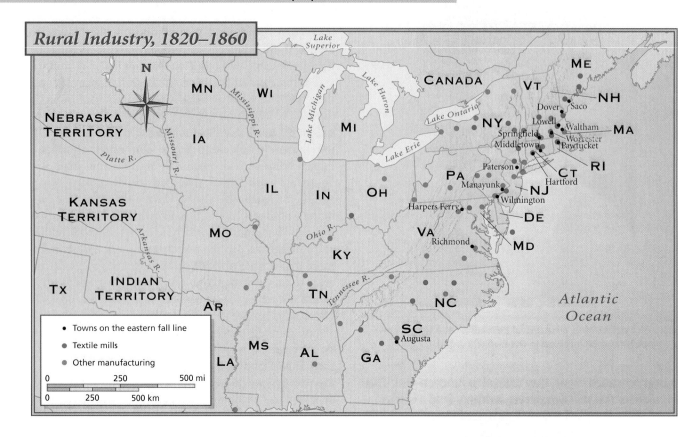

Rural Industry, 1820–1860

The first sign of trouble at Lowell occurred in February 1834, when 800 women walked off their jobs to protest a 12.5 percent wage reduction. Although the strikers represented less than one-sixth of Lowell's labor force and the incident lasted only a few days, emotions ran high. Reflecting tensions of gender and power in the community, male factory agents condemned the protest as an "amizonian [sic] display," arguing that the strikers were both unfeminine and ungrateful. The female workers, on the other hand, felt wronged by the mill owners' high-handed treatment as well as by the "unjust and unreasonable" cut in their wages. In the end, the strike failed, but the workers found some solace in the fact that they had reminded the "purse proud ARISTOCRATS" that they were equal in birthright if not in economic power.

Another strike took place in 1836, this time in response to mill owners' raising of the price for room and board at boardinghouses. This action involved more workers (some 1,500 to 2,000) than the earlier strike and succeeded in getting the companies to rescind their charges. The victory nonetheless proved fleeting. In 1837 and again in 1840, Lowell's mill women experienced further wage cuts. With the United States in the midst

of a serious depression, they had little choice but to accede. In the meantime, speedups and stretch-outs continued to take their toll on both the earnings and nerves of the workers.

Confronted by relentless pressure to increase their productivity and aware that their earlier methods had been less than successful, Lowell's women workers adopted a different strategy during the 1840s. In December 1844, they founded the Lowell Female Labor Reform Association with the intent of mitigating the ill effects of factory work through political action. They also joined other labor and reform groups to organize a massive but ultimately unsuccessful petition campaign to get the Massachusetts legislature to limit factory work to ten hours a day (they normally worked twelve to fourteen hours a day). In the months that followed, leaders of the association testified at hearings about the polluted air in cotton mills and the unreasonably short periods they were allowed for meals. A ten-hour limit on daily labor would, they maintained, improve their health and enhance their "intellectual, moral and religious habits."

Taking advantage of the recently introduced steam-powered printing press, the Lowell Female Labor Reform Association also began to publish three-to-six-page pamphlets in which reform leaders described themselves as "wage slaves" and repeatedly referred to the Declaration of Independence and the revolutionary republicanism of their ancestors to articulate their position against the repressiveness of factory masters. Writing in the first issue of the association's publication "Factory Tracts," a worker using the pen name of Amelia asserted that "we will soon show these *drivelling* cotton lords, this mushroom aristocracy of New England who so arrogantly aspire to lord it over God's heritage, that our rights cannot be trampled upon with impunity; that we will no longer submit to that arbitrary power which has for the last ten years been so abundantly exercised over us."

Amelia's acerbic essay did not represent the feelings of all of Lowell's workers, however. During the 1840s, another group of mill women published a company-sponsored journal called *The Lowell Offering*, which was more favorably disposed toward mill owners and less inclined toward reform. Nevertheless, Amelia's language indicates the degree to which class and gender feelings revealed themselves in Lowell by the mid-1840s. Native-born Yankee women began leaving, and the mill owners replaced them with what they hoped were more tractable Irish immigrants. With this change, the community's formative period ended.

*Beyond Paternalism.* Lowell would continue to be one of the nation's leading textile-manufacturing centers well into the twentieth century, but the original paternalism of the Boston Associates had, by the mid-1840s, turned into crass commercialism and social neglect. One big difference was that Irish Catholic immigrants, fleeing the Potato Famine in their homeland, began to replace Yankee girls in the mills. As more and more Irish immigrants arrived in Lowell, crowded slums began to replace the once beautifully kept, company-owned boardinghouses. As the founders of Lowell began to retire and their shares passed into other hands, the social vision that had constituted much of Lowell's original genius faded away. Under the new regime, workers were viewed not as the objects of a special stewardship that emphasized moral and intellectual improvement, but as commodities whose services could be bought and sold. In the mid-1840s, a mill superintendent reflected a growing sentiment among manufacturers when he stated, "I regard my work people just as I regard my machinery. So long as they can do my work for what I choose to pay them, I keep them, getting out of them all I can."

Lowell's textile mills and the Lukens family's Brandywine Iron Works represent dramatically different responses to the process of industrialization. Lowell was a large company town consisting of thousands of workers; Brandywine was a small

The cover of the *Lowell Offering*, one of the first American periodicals to be written exclusively by women. Note the well-dressed mill girl with book in hand (indicating her literacy), surrounded by garden greenery, the mill and church steeple in the background, and a beehive (symbol of hard work).

countryside enclave with a handful of workers. Lowell's mills were owned by joint-stock corporations, Brandywine by a single family. Absentee owners governed Lowell at a distance, while the Lukens family resided on the spot. Owners did not know workers at Lowell. At Brandywine, the owners often worked alongside their employees and knew them and their families on a first-name basis. In the views of most contemporary writers, the industrial future lay with Lowell.

Paternalism would give way to profit calculation in the factory, yet the clash of interests between owners and workers did not erupt into open conflict. Ethnic and racial tensions proved to be far more divisive than class feelings in antebellum America. Moreover, the day-to-day interactions between managers and workers on the shop floor lubricated the social gears. Workers blended deference with defiance, which took the form

Many small factories, like J&R Fisher's Bloomingdale Flint Glass Works of New York (1837), were timber-framed structures with shingle siding and a cupola with a weathervane on the roof. What distinguished them from large "saltbox" houses of the period was the adjoining building and smoke stack, which indicates that the Fisher factory was probably powered by a steam engine.

Workers in these trades had little recourse other than to turn to radical forms of protest. A prime example is the Working Men's Movement, which appeared in the late 1820s from Philadelphia to Boston and spread as far west as Zanesville, Ohio. Skilled craftsmen and small shop masters who felt increasingly pressed by the expanding business system, often led by well-educated radical reformers, organized under the banner of the Working Men's Party and, among other things, campaigned for free public schools, shorter working hours, better working conditions, improved housing, and an end to imprisonment for debt. Although short-lived, the movement foreshadowed the emergence of labor unions and demonstrated that even in an optimistic age of enterprise, a segment of the population was dissatisfied with its condition and receptive to calls for radical reform.

## BEYOND THE FACTORY GATE

In the early industrial period before the Civil War, workers sometimes left the factory—despite rules to the contrary—to hunt and fish, drink and carouse, visit friends and relatives, farm, tend gardens, or do household chores. Employers tended to interpret such breaks as evidence of unreliability, laziness, dishonesty, and ungratefulness, but this was not necessarily the case. Hunting, fishing, gardening, and farming, for example, continued to be necessary activities for workers to provide food for their families, and helped them accommodate the new industrial order while trying to preserve older ways they valued.

Religion also gave workers an anchor that was beyond the boss's grasp. Consider the Irish Catholics who labored at the risk-laden Du Pont gunpowder mills near Wilmington, Delaware. Early on, the company's founder, E. I. du Pont, established the Brandywine Manufacturers' Sunday School near the powder works. The Sunday school had two objectives. One was to instruct the children of the largely immigrant workforce to be "good and enlightened citizens" by exposing them to the "first rudiments of knowledge," reading and writing. The other was to

of subtle shop-floor practices. One such practice was pacing (also known as "soldiering" among nineteenth-century factory masters), or controlling the pace of their work. Examples of pacing included working to certain "stints," or output quotas; taking unauthorized breaks; looking for "missing" tools; sharpening and repairing other tools; and reading newspapers while at work. Such strategies enabled workers to counter the threat of wage cuts or stretch-outs posed by speedier, more efficient new technologies. Most factory masters forbade these practices in their work rules, but enforcement proved difficult.

Pacing was critical in the nineteenth-century workers' world, and may help to explain why workers in some trades tended to resort to political protest more readily than others. Skilled machinists, like those at the Springfield Armory, were militant about their rights and privileges, but since they could negotiate work conditions, they rarely exhibited radical political tendencies. By contrast, in "sweated" trades like shoemaking, ready-made clothing, and anthracite mining, piece rates and ruthless competition pressed wages and workers to the breaking point.

promote "good and orderly behavior" and prevent the students from "spending the Sabbath in idleness and contracting habits of vice and immorality," words that bear a striking resemblance to early factory regulations. But the Irish Catholic workers chafed at exposing their children to the Protestant beliefs of their employers and eventually established a Catholic school in nearby St. Joseph's parish, thereby reminding the du Ponts that even though their workers earned a living at the mills, those workers did not necessarily orient their lives around them. The same held true for working communities throughout the United States.

Churches, general stores, and taverns were the focal points of culture in early nineteenth-century communities. Taverns existed everywhere—in towns, cities, the countryside, and especially, by the 1820s, near working populations. Besides selling alcoholic beverages, many doubled as post offices, courtrooms, and even polling places. Taverns and saloons were considered male domains. Relatively few women frequented them; those who did soon acquired reputations as "women of easy virtue" or worse. Men went there to drink, gamble, share stories, complain about bosses, and dream the impossible dream. In some communities, taverns served as meeting places where workers organized over workplace issues. But to employers, Protestant clergymen, and female temperance reformers, they were often looked upon as "the devil's playground."

During the early years of industrial development, factory masters followed the time-honored practice of allowing workers to drink during working hours. Canal diggers, ironworkers, and others who labored at heavy tasks often received rations of rum and whiskey as part of their monthly wages. Some masters owned local taverns, while others sold whiskey at their company stores. At his gunpowder mills near Wilmington, du Pont strictly forbade the use of tobacco products and "spirituous liquors" during working hours. Yet he sold both at his company store and continued to do so even after several deadly explosions had taken place. Du Pont also occasionally treated his workforce to drinks at a nearby tavern. However, his children proved less tolerant and repeatedly tried to crack down on their employees' drinking and "frolicking" at local taverns. Judging from the flourishing bar trade that persisted in the neighborhood throughout the nineteenth century, the du Ponts failed to curb this aspect of the workers' world. Despite the existence of a strong temperance movement during the antebellum period, the same proved true of other industrial communities.

Extended networks of kinship and friendship formed the heart of early industrial communities. These special bonds defined a community's inner life and governed its social dynamics. Women played a particularly important role. While thousands found work in factories, most stayed home to raise families, take in boarders, do outwork for merchant-manufacturers, and perform other chores such as cooking, keeping gardens, and raising small livestock. Their steady presence in the local neighborhoods and churches made them bulwarks of the community. Through a "porch culture" of visiting and gossip, they kept abreast of what was going on with neighbors. When relatives or neighbors became ill and could not work, or were otherwise in need, women stepped in to care for them and their children. When someone died, they prepared the body for burial, kept vigil, and provided the grieving family with food. Such neighborly acts did as much as anything to strengthen bonds in working communities. The customs Thomas Jefferson associated with agrarian America thus penetrated early industrial communities and became an integral part of working-class culture.

## ILLNESSES AND INJURIES

The combination of high-speed machinery and the use of steam engines in industrial settings greatly increased the number of work-related accidents in nineteenth-century America. Female workers in Lowell's massive textile mills frequently wrote home about colleagues who had lost fingers, limbs, and sometimes even their lives by becoming entangled in the gears and moving parts of textile machinery. At metalworking factories, machine shops, and foundries as well as on the railroads, accidents such as lost fingers and broken bones happened so frequently that only the most serious were reported in the press. No health insurance existed. Employers commonly provided short-term assistance for injured employees, but not necessarily long-term compensation. When serious injury or death occurred, workers themselves often took up a collection and presented a "purse" to the injured party or to family members.

Although workers could petition employers to compensate them for injuries suffered on the job, the decision to do so was up to the employer. Sometimes workers received a cash settlement, sometimes nothing. Textile mills and mining companies were notorious for blaming workers for accidents. Other manufacturers, however, were more responsible. As early as 1815, for example, E. I. du Pont initiated a policy of caring for injured workers and compensating the widows of those killed by explosions and other on-the-job accidents at his gunpowder mills. Benefits to the injured included free medical care and, in the cases of several permanently disabled employees, annual pensions. Death benefits included funeral expenses, a yearly pension of $100 to the widow, rent-free housing so long as the widow remained single, and the guarantee of work for immediate family members. By nineteenth-century standards, these were extremely generous benefits.

Industrial employment also gave rise to a number of heretofore unknown occupational diseases, many of them silent killers. Early on, for example, metalworkers at cutlery and firearms factories discovered that grinding machines operating at high speeds could be a "deadly business." In addition to being blinded by chips and splinters of hot metal flying off the machines, workers succumbed to lung disease from breathing the minute metal shavings and dust-contaminated air that permeated grinding shops. Similar illnesses afflicted textile workers, especially those who labored in the carding and spinning rooms of mills. "Fly," consisting of loose cotton fibers and dust, filled the air. After working in a noisy mill for several months, workers frequently complained of headaches, sinus infections, and breathing problems. Little did they or their employers know that prolonged exposure to fly could lead to more serious complications, one of which was byssinosis, or brown lung disease, an often fatal affliction.

The accidents and illnesses associated with factory work often escaped public notice; not so with public transportation. Between 1816 and 1848, 233 steamboat boiler explosions occurred in the United States, with the loss of over 2,500 lives and nearly 3,000 injuries. The human carnage mounted as steamboats grew larger and pressed for faster travel times. Congress finally passed a steamboat-inspection law in 1852 that had some teeth, and over the next eight years fatalities from steamboat explosions fell by 65 percent.

The 1852 legislation established an important precedent. For the first time, the federal government sought to regulate the affairs of private enterprise in the interest of public safety. This action foreshadowed such powerful regulatory agencies as the Interstate Commerce Commission, the U.S. Food and Drug Administration, the Civil Aeronautics Board, and, more recently, the Environmental Protection Agency. We can see one of the roots of the regulatory state in this direct response to an unanticipated consequence of technological change—steamboat boiler explosions.

## The Cholera Years

Surrounded by natural abundance and imbued with the biblical injunction to "fill the earth and subdue it," Americans were not environmentally conscious. Especially in frontier areas, nature was viewed as harsh and unforgiving, an enemy to be conquered. The quicker rivers could be tamed, marauding animals exterminated, and forests leveled, the better.

The market revolution—with its rapidly expanding factory and transportation systems, banks of machinery, chemical works, smoke-belching steam engines, worker tenements, and urban congestion—reinforced these attitudes. Unaware of the implications of their actions for personal or public health, virtually everyone dumped garbage wherever it was convenient; placed privies and cesspools near wells and other sources of drinking water; and kept hogs, chickens, and other animals

This view of the steamboat *Medora* reveals how devastating steam boiler explosions could be. The newly-built *Medora* blew up on her maiden voyage in Baltimore Harbor on April 14, 1842, resulting in 28 dead and 40 wounded. Such disasters resulted in public clamor for more rigorous inspections of steam boilers, especially those on steamboats.

penned up in backyards and basements, often allowing them to roam the streets to forage in the garbage. The absence of street cleaning services meant that garbage, horse dung, and dead animals remained in the streets over long periods of time, attracting disease-carrying vermin. To make matters worse, manufacturers dumped inorganic as well as organic wastes into rivers, streams, and canals, often close to places where people drew their drinking water. These practices exacted a heavy price.

For years, people experienced "sick seasons" in the late summer and early fall when business came to a halt and entire communities sought to escape to the countryside until the blight passed. At Harpers Ferry, Virginia, for example, a mysterious illness called "bilious fever" struck almost annually from the 1810s through the 1820s, leaving scores of victims in its wake. Other epidemics such as typhoid fever and dysentery, as well as yellow fever and smallpox, decimated communities. Although local doctors suspected that contaminated water supplies had something to do with the onset of sick seasons, they had no way of knowing with certainty because the science of bacteriology had yet to emerge. The upshot was that pollution-borne illness and disease plagued Americans through most of the nineteenth century. Indeed, untrustworthy water supplies may help to explain why Americans were such heavy consumers of alcohol. According to one estimate, annual consumption in 1830 reached an all-time high of four gallons per person, with roughly two-thirds (some 60 million gallons) being imbibed by adult males.

Of all the diseases and fevers that struck early industrial America, the most devastating was Asiatic cholera. When cholera struck, as it did between 1832 and 1834, a high percentage of those infected died. In New York City, for example, the epidemic peaked in the summer of 1832 and, by the end of the year, claimed over 5,000 lives. In New Orleans, a city of some 50,000 people, between 4,500 and 5,000 lives were lost. In smaller cities like Cincinnati, St. Louis, Sandusky, and Wheeling, the death rates were even higher, often exceeding 10 percent of the total population. Cholera knew no boundaries, striking small towns and farming areas as hard as it did cities.

Cholera was a fearsome disease because its onset was so abrupt and the chances of survival, at least during the 1830s and 1840s, so remote. A victim could be hale and hearty one morning and dead the next day. Moreover, cholera was a particularly violent disease that literally squeezed the life out of people through painful cramps, acute vomiting, and severe diarrhea. Anyone who saw the corpse of a cholera victim did not soon forget the agonizing image of death that it conveyed.

Physicians and public health officials were at first at a loss as to what to do in response to an outbreak of cholera because they possessed no scientific knowledge about the disease's causes or its possible treatment. Prevailing medical theory posited the origin of the disease as something in the local environment. But what? One school of thought held that the disease spread through human contact; another maintained that cholera, yellow fever, and other diseases arose from contact with dirt and filth. Not until 1849, owing mainly to medical research in Europe, did empirical evidence become available pointing to water contaminated by the excreta and vomit of cholera victims as a primary carrier of the disease. Even then, the news arrived too late to be of much use in halting the spread of a second major cholera epidemic that year.

Another forty years would elapse before European researchers popularized the germ theory of disease. Such knowledge had little impact on the ongoing degradation of the natural environment. Americans continued to cut down forests, kill wild animals, contaminate water supplies, and pollute the environment with reckless abandon.

## Clock Time

Life and labor were all affected to different degrees by the most subtle yet far-reaching technological change of this period: reckoning time. Mechanical clocks and watches had existed since the earliest settlements in North America, but few people owned them. Timepieces were expensive and were considered forms of adornment and personal status rather than useful devices for conducting business. Colonial Americans responded to the church bells that called them to worship and the horns that sounded the arrival of ships or stagecoaches. Yet, lacking clocks themselves, most gauged the passage of time by reckoning the position of the sun during daytime and the moon and stars at night. People normally started their days at sunrise and ended them at sunset, and most businesses adopted sunup-to-sundown work schedules. Even early factory operations paid their employees by the day or by the piece rather than by the clocked hour. Farmers likewise counted time in terms of days, fortnights (two weeks), moons, and seasons, as did travelers. Natural rhythms rather than ticking clocks governed the lives of most Americans well into the nineteenth century. But with the advent of clock time, all this changed.

An early example of mass production, this inexpensive wooden "box clock" was made by Eli Terry of Bristol, Connecticut. By the 1830s, clocks with interchangeable parts made of stamped brass began to replace clocks with wooden parts. In 1853, a British visitor reported that Connecticut's largest clock maker was turning out 600 brass clocks a day and selling them for as little as $2.

A growing consciousness of time was an integral part of the market revolution in America. Emphasizing the order and uniformity essential to the smooth running of a machine-based economy, time consciousness incorporated the values of punctuality, thrift, and hard work that were central tenets of America's Protestant tradition. The image of the clock soon became a powerful cultural symbol of a modernizing America because it melded together, as no other symbol did, the moral and utilitarian components of a diverse society focused on getting ahead.

Two factors hastened the spread of time consciousness in the United States: cheap clocks, and railroads. Beginning in 1816, just as the uniformity system of manufacturing began to take shape in the nation's armories, a Connecticut clockmaker named Eli Terry began to produce a simple, wooden-geared box clock, made with interchangeable parts. By 1825, Terry had refined his design and was producing some 9,000 shelf clocks a year, which he sold for as little as $10 apiece. By then, other Connecticut manufacturers had begun to emulate Terry's methods and were churning out thousands of cheap but well-made wooden shelf clocks for markets as far west as Cincinnati and St. Louis and as far south as New Orleans. To reach these distant markets, Connecticut clockmakers dispatched a small army of traveling salesmen. These "Yankee peddlers" soon peppered the countryside with weight-driven, hour-striking clocks that most anyone could afford. "In Kentucky, Indiana, Illinois, Missouri, and here in every dell of Arkansas and in every cabin where there was not a chair to sit on," an English traveler recorded in 1834–35, "there was sure to be a Connecticut clock." By the early 1840s, New England clockmakers were mass-producing hundreds of thousands of rugged "Ogee" shelf clocks with brass working parts for as little as $1.50 each. By 1850, three-quarters of the white population owned some sort of timepiece.

The railroad also played an important role in making Americans more time conscious. One way it did this was by delivering the mail. As early as the 1790s, the U.S. Post Office had sought to speed and regularize the delivery of mail. Although stagecoaches and ocean-going ships performed reasonably well in meeting weekly delivery schedules, service improved noticeably during the 1830s and 1840s, when the postal service began to award mail contracts to newly built railroads. "The advantages of the railways, over all other means of conveyance," a convention of North Carolina businessmen concluded in 1839, "is the saving of time, the annihilation of space. *Time is money,* and the attainment of greater speed and certainty, amounts, in effect, to a reduction of expense." "We may add, truly," another southerner affirmed, "that the railroad is the great apostle of progress."

The earliest railroads ran on single tracks, with daily traffic moving in both directions. To avoid accidents, it was necessary to schedule precise arrival and departure times. Despite the best efforts of railroad managers, however, a number of head-on collisions occurred during the 1830s and 1840s, causing serious injuries and deaths. Not until the widespread introduction of the electric telegraph during the 1860s did the problem begin to subside. Telegraphy enabled station masters to signal each other instantaneously about the location of oncoming trains and move one of them to a siding in order to allow the other to pass. Railroads also began adopting standard schedules that stipulated arrival and departure times by the minute rather than the hour or half hour. These developments, along with postal contracts that imposed severe monetary penalties for late pickups and deliveries, placed a high premium on punctuality. Anyone who received mail or shipped goods or traveled by train quickly became acquainted with railroad schedules and, accordingly, railway time. Indeed, the railroad soon became the primary arbiter of time in America.

The railroads had important allies in fostering time consciousness in antebellum America. As early as the 1790s, factory masters began to install clocks and bells in their mills, as a way of establishing standard hours of labor. Tardy employees were reprimanded and often fined; repeat offenders eventually lost their jobs. By the early 1830s, the Springfield Armory had begun to time employees at their jobs in an effort to gauge their efficiency and establish standard piece rates for work performed. Southern plantation owners adopted similar strategies. Eagerly heeding calls by agricultural reformers for "a strict observance of a well-timed system of economy," some planters ventured northward to visit the great mill towns of Waltham and Lowell in search of "hints," as one put it, that would prove useful in managing their plantations and preparing their cotton for market. Like the northern factories, southern plantations had their clocks, bells, work rules, job timings, and detailed accounting procedures. The main difference between the two lay in the North's reliance on free wage labor and mechanized production and the South's reliance on slave labor and hand methods. "Bells and horns!" a former slave exclaimed in disgust. "Bells for this and horns for that! All we knowed was go and come by the bells and horns!"

Neither slaves nor factory workers were thrilled by the time discipline that their masters sought to impose, and they often resisted through slowdowns, absenteeism, and forms of sabotage. In 1842, workers at the Harpers Ferry Armory in Virginia walked off their jobs in protest when the superintendent installed a clock and insisted that they relinquish their loosely structured work habits for a rigidly enforced ten-hour day. But as much as workers resented clock time, they nonetheless got used to it, as did farmers, townspeople, and city dwellers throughout the country. Clock time increasingly penetrated the web of business and social relationships that connected most everyone. Owing largely to the market revolution, Americans were becoming a time-oriented society.

In early nineteenth-century America, life and labor on the farm, the slave plantation, and the factory floor described three distinct paths of development for the country and became bases for sectional antagonisms that were gathering strength in national politics. While white northerners and southerners generally supported national expansion in the interest of acquiring more territory, they differed over the type of labor systems best suited to meet their needs. Northerners stood for free labor, while southerners supported slave as well as free labor. Such differences, as much as anything else, accounted for the era's intensified sectional feelings.

Further complicating matters, mechanization gave rise to a new class of workers who labored for wages in the expanding network of factories, workshops, canals, and railroads. Largely renters rather than property owners, they periodically protested to their employers about being made "slaves of machines" while asserting their rights as free-born citizens. Reflecting the racism of the times, they also had little tolerance for free blacks who competed with them for jobs in the open market and cared little about the scourge of slavery in the South. Apologists for southern slavery sowed the seeds of class antagonism by accusing northern industrialists of fostering a kind of "wage slavery" that prevented workers from becoming landowners and improving their status in life.

As workers sought to improve their condition and southerners became increasingly defensive about their peculiar institution, the United States experienced a religious awakening that, among other things, prompted a tenacious abolitionist crusade against slavery. Sectional antagonisms deepened as antislavery feeling grew in the North and southern resistance to criticism stiffened. By the 1840s, the future of slavery dominated American politics and, in 1861, would disrupt the Union. During the four years of civil war that followed, worker worlds would be dramatically altered, if not turned completely upside down.

## Suggested Reading

Ira Berlin, *Generations of Captivity: A History of African-American Slaves* (2004)

Richard Crawford, *America's Musical Life: A History* (2001)

Charles B. Dew, *Bond of Iron: Master and Slave at Buffalo Forge* (1994)

Thomas Dublin, *Women at Work: The Transformation of Work and Community in Lowell, Massachusetts, 1826–1860* (1979)

Charles E. Rosenberg, *The Cholera Years* (1987)

Mark Smith, *Mastered by the Clock: Time, Slavery, and Freedom in the American South* (1997)

Merritt Roe Smith, *Harpers Ferry Armory and the New Technology* (1977)

Theodore Steinberg, *Nature Incorporated: Industrialization and the Waters of New England* (1991)

Carlene Stephens, *On Time: How America Has Learned to Live by the Clock* (2002)

Anthony F. C. Wallace, *Rockdale* (1978)

# Chapter Review

## Summary QUESTIONS

■ What impact did mechanization and the market revolution have on the "workers world" prior to the Civil War?

■ To what extent did the market revolution deepen the entrenchment of slavery in the South?

■ How did slaves and industrial workers attempt to control, or resist, the changing conditions of their labor? To what extent were they innovators?

■ How important were environmental factors in the lives of farmers, slaves, and factory workers?

■ Why did clocks and time-consciousness become so commonplace in early nineteenth-century America? What does increased time-keeping and time-consciousness reveal about the types of values that prevailed in American society?

## Key Terms

Market Revolution (pp. 342–343)

Antebellum Slavery (pp. 345–355)

Paternalism (p. 356)

The Lowell Mills (p. 357)

Clock Time (pp. 363–365)

## Chronology

| | |
|---|---|
| 1815 | Du Pont establishes benefits policy for workers at gunpowder mills. |
| 1825 | Eli Terry mass-produces shelf clocks. |
| August 1831 | Nat Turner's Rebellion. |
| 1834, 1836 | Workers (mostly women) walk off the job at Lowell mills. |
| 1837 | William Proctor and James Gamble form partnership to manufacture soap and foot oil. |
| December 1844 | Lowell Female Labor Reform Association founded. |
| 1848 | McCormick reaper factory built in Chicago. |
| 1852 | Congress passes stringent steamboat-inspection law. |
| 1860 | Slave population reaches 4 million, nearly one-third the population of the South. |

**Access the *Inventing America* StudySpace at wwnorton.com/studyspace**

PERSONAL PLAN ■ REVIEW MATERIALS ■ RESEARCH AIDS ■ MULTIMEDIA

# Chapter 13

# THE AGE OF IMPROVEMENT:

## RELIGION AND REFORM, 1825–1846

Perhaps the most famous railroad painting in American art, George Inness's *The Lackawanna Valley* (c. 1855) shows a train loaded with anthracite coal pulling out of Scranton, Pennsylvania. The juxtaposition of the locomotive with the pastoral landscape leaves open whether the painting is meant to celebrate the new technology and industrialization or lament the vanishing of the wilderness.

- ■ **How did American culture register the new technologies of the 1820–1840s?**

- ■ **What were the connections between religious reform and broader social and economic change in this period?**

- ■ **How did religious reform influence the movement to abolish slavery?**

- ■ **What were the main characteristics of political abolitionism?**

- ■ **What were the limits to reform in the antebellum period?**

## "The Progress of the Age"

On November 17, 1847, Senator Daniel Webster returned to his native New Hampshire to deliver a speech at the opening of a railroad. "It is an extraordinary era in which we live," he observed. "It is altogether new. The world has seen nothing like it before. . . . We see the ocean navigated and the solid land traversed by steam power, and intelligence communicated by electricity. Truly this is almost a miraculous era. What is before us no one can say, what is upon us no one can hardly realize. The progress of the age has almost outstripped human belief; the future is known only to Omniscience."

Webster's speech captured a widespread popular feeling. If any single concept had seized the hearts and minds of Americans in the decades following the War of 1812, it was the idea of progress and its ready association with new technologies. People were fascinated by machines that could weave yards of cloth in a matter of minutes, cut and shape metals to dimensions of one-thousandth of an inch, and travel hundreds of miles over land and water in a fraction of the time it had taken older conveyances. Above all, Americans were captivated by "that mighty agent," the steam-powered railroad.

Emily Dickinson expressed the feelings of many when she composed a short poem to "The Railway Train."

*I like to see it lap the miles,*
*And lick the valleys up,*
*And stop to feed itself at tanks;*
*And then, prodigious, step*
*Around a pile of mountains,*

. . .

*Complaining all the while*

*In horrid, hooting stanza;*
*Then chase itself down hill*
*And neigh like Boanerges;*
*Then, punctual as a star,*
*Stop—docile and omnipotent—*
*At its own stable door.*

Like Dickinson, Americans generally viewed the "iron horse" with a sense of awe as well as trepidation. Like Webster, they also believed that the new technologies were wrenching the country out of an isolated rural age and catapulting it into a different epoch. Hardly anything—politics, family life, religion, the economy—remained untouched by technological change. Many writers felt certain that "life was being made over new."

Because railroads were the most visible proof of "the progress of the age," they became associated with progress in other realms of life, as revealed in Currier and Ives's 1868 lithograph entitled *Across the Continent: Westward the Course of Empire Takes Its Way.* Although published after the Civil War, the print nonetheless expressed a common viewpoint that dated back to the Jacksonian era. In the center foreground, the locomotive and its train of cars chug away from a small village at the edge of civilization. The linear angle of the tracks, the telegraph lines, and the locomotive itself suggest the progressive character of the new technology as an engine of change. The artists' message is clear. The railroad is more than an engine of technological progress; it is the driving force of American civilization. Wherever it goes also go village agriculture, commerce, industry, public education, Christian religion, republican values, and, yes, even the extermination of the Indian.

Currier and Ives, *Across the Continent: Westward the Course of Empire Takes Its Way* (1868).

## TECHNOLOGY AND DEMOCRACY

Of all the great social ideas with which technological progress became associated, none proved more important than democracy. For many writers, the increasing availability, quality, and affordability of machine-made products was evidence of a democratizing influence. Horace Greeley, the ebullient editor of the *New York Tribune,* put it best. "We have *universalized* all the beautiful and glorious results of industry and skill," he wrote on viewing the mechanical wonders on display at New York's Crystal Palace Exhibition in 1853. "We have made them a common possession of the people.... We have democratized the means and appliances of a higher life."

In the opinion of the French observer Alexis de Tocqueville, the affinity between democracy and technology was a defining feature of American culture. Among the questions Tocqueville sought to address while visiting the United States in the 1830s was "Why the Americans Are More Addicted to Practical Than to Theoretical Science." His answer seemed disarmingly simple. "Those who cultivate the sciences amongst a democratic people," he argued, "are always afraid of losing their way in visionary speculation. They mistrust systems; they adhere closely to facts and the study of facts with their own senses.... To minds thus predisposed, every new method which leads by a shorter road to wealth, every machine which spares labour, every instrument which diminishes the cost of production, every discovery which facilitates pleasures or augments them, seems to be the grandest effort of the human intellect." In conclusion, "You may be sure that the more a nation is democratic, enlightened, and free, the greater will be the number of those interested promoters of scientific genius, and the more will discoveries immediately applicable to productive industry confer gain, fame, and even power to their authors."

Americans were experimenting and breaking new ground. In the process, they were seeking new identities and missions, not only for themselves as individuals but also for the larger society in which they lived. The discovery of the "American self" thus had many dimensions. At the individual level, it involved personal concerns with self-identity, self-reliance, and especially

Currier and Ives's lithograph encapsulated more than a generation of public thought about the influence of the new machine technology on society. Many people believed that technological progress led inevitably to social progress. In addition to steam locomotion, they pointed to the availability of cheap manufactured goods, inexpensive newspapers and books, a greater variety of agricultural products, and improved sanitary practices as examples of "the progress of the age."

Such society-shaping innovations led others to make even larger claims about the impact of the new technology. "The mechanician not the magician is now the master of life," Governor Edward Everett of Massachusetts confidently asserted in 1837. "The inventors of machinery," a New Yorker declared the same year, "have caused a greater revolution in the habits, opinions, and morals of mankind, than all the efforts of legislation." If machinery could be brought to such a state of perfection, observers asked, why not society? As a Massachusetts clergyman put it in 1844, "No reform is now deemed impossible, no enterprise for human betterment unpracticable. Everything must be made better." The small minority of critics who warned that the new technology had the capacity to exploit, even enslave, labor and defile the natural environment were more often than not dismissed as "croakers ... who see misery and ruin close at hand."

self-improvement. At the societal level, it involved the construction of an idealized view of America, a vision of what its mission could and should be. Both constructions were fundamental to how the United States would be seen in the eyes of its citizens and as well as the world. Both were integral to what would become known as the "age of improvement."

### THE HUDSON RIVER SCHOOL

The construction of the American self was even more apparent in the art and literature of the period. In contrast to eighteenth-century artists and writers, who tended to look to Europe for inspiration, nineteenth-century American artists sought to liberate themselves by turning to American subjects. In the fine arts, this new spirit could be seen in the work of painters like George Caleb Bingham, who sought to capture on canvas the home-grown democratic impulses of the period, and George Catlin, who set out to portray native Americans and their cultures before they fell victim to white civilization.

The most sophisticated and best known art of antebellum America came from a group located in and around New York City known as the "Hudson River school," founded by English immigrant Thomas Cole. Captivated by the idea of America's uniqueness as "Nature's Nation," Cole and his associates set out to portray the grandeur and essential purity of the country's natural environment at the very time that it was being transformed by the new machine technology. A number of Cole's early paintings focused on wilderness scenes like *The Falls of Kaaterskill* (1826), located in the Catskill Mountains near his home. But by the mid-1830s, his work had shifted from purely natural landscapes to pastoral scenes that depicted a harmonious middle ground between raw nature and industrial civilization.

The fact that Cole included waterpowered mills in at least four of his landscapes indicates his willingness to incorporate elements of the mechanical age into his pastoral art. At one point in his personal notes, Cole even refers to mills and factories as "the Castles of the United States" that "tell the tale of the enterprise and industry of the present generation."

In addition to mills, artists of the Hudson River school often incorporated steam railroads into their paintings. Although Cole bitterly condemned a railroad built near his home for desecrating the natural environment, he nonetheless included one in an 1843 painting entitled *River in the Catskills*. There, he blends the locomotive and the bridge it's crossing into the natural landscape in a way that excites no fear or unease. Instead of blackening and fouling the air, the gentle wisp of smoke from the engine seems to dissipate before the viewer's eyes. Yet the somewhat denuded and faded look of the landscape suggests that Cole was warning of what might happen if industrial civilization was allowed to despoil nature in the name of material progress. Such concern gives *River in the Catskills* an ambivalent quality that can also be seen in the work of other Hudson River artists.

Thomas Cole, *River in the Catskills* (1843). Note the partially obscured railroad locomotive and its train of cars crossing the bridge over the river in the distance (left center).

### LITERATURE

American literature, like art, flowered during the antebellum period, and it, too, expressed a sense of ambivalence about the machine age. Influenced by artistic trends in Europe, American writers sought to emulate their romantic impulses while focusing on American subjects and celebrating the uniqueness of the New World environment. A nostalgia for a simpler life closer to nature and therefore to God runs throughout much of the literature. We see it, for instance, in the wilderness novels of James Fenimore Cooper, especially his five enormously popular "Leatherstocking" tales, beginning with *The Pioneers* in 1823 and ending with *The Deerslayer* in 1841. We also see it in Washington Irving's "Rip Van Winkle," "The Legend of Sleepy Hollow," and other tales about life and folklore in long-settled regions of the Hudson Valley. Both writers eventually grew embittered about America's turn toward industrial capitalism and, worst of all, the crass, money-grubbing materialism that seemed to grip more and more of their countrymen. In 1842, Irving confessed that he "would like nothing more" than to "blow up all the cotton mills . . . and make picturesque ruins of them." "If the Garden of Eden were now on earth," he groused six years later, "they would not hesitate to run a railroad through it."

The romantic conception of nature, individualism, and national feeling was shared by other prominent writers. One group centered at Concord, Massachusetts, near Boston, referred to themselves as Transcendentalists, because they sought to go beyond, or transcend, the purely rational thought and "cold calculation" associated with technology and industry to discover new "truths" through spiritual growth and close communication with nature. Ralph Waldo Emerson, a leading writer and poet who lived in Concord and was often

identified as the founder of the Transcendentalist movement, best caught its mystical spirit in his 1836 essay "Nature." Conceiving nature as "a remoter and inferior incarnation of God," he observed that "in the woods, we return to reason and faith. There I feel that nothing can befall me in life. . . . Standing on the bare ground, —my head bathed by the blithe air, and uplifted into infinite space, —all mean egotism vanishes. I become a transparent eyeball; I am nothing; I see all; the currents of the Universal Being circulate through me; I am part or parcel of God." To be a Transcendentalist meant being partly a mystic, partly a worshiper of nature, and, most of all, a believer in one's ability to penetrate the inner essence of things.

Emerson initially believed that "Machinery & Transcendentalism agree well," that technological progress might lead to human progress. But like many other intellectuals, Emerson became ambivalent about the changes taking place, at times hailing the "mechanic arts" as a great liberating force for mankind and on other occasions expressing concern about their negative implications. He seemed, moreover, to grow more pessimistic with the passage of time. "What have these arts done for the character, for the worth of mankind?" he asked in 1857. "Are men better?" The answer seemed clear. "Tis too plain," he concluded, "that with the material power the moral progress has not kept pace."

Similarly, in *Walden* (1854), Emerson's Transcendentalist student and friend Henry David Thoreau denigrated his neighbors in Concord for leading "lives of quiet desperation" connected with trade and factory work. "Men have become tools of their tools," he lamented. He also characterized the railroad that passed by Walden Pond on its way from Boston to Concord as "that devilish Iron Horse," noting at one point that "we do not ride upon the railroad; it rides upon us." Yet on another occasion, even as the whistle of the locomotive penetrated his woodland retreat "like the scream of a hawk," he admitted that "I feel refreshed and expanded when the freight train rattles past me."

Such ambiguities lie at the heart of Thoreau's Walden experience. For him as well as for other writers, the problem was not the technology, but the uses to which it was being put. This question runs through Nathaniel Hawthorne's allegorical short story "The Celestial Railroad" (1846), in which a steam locomotive and its cars are depicted as a satanic instrument following a path straight to hell, and Herman Melville's *Moby Dick* (1851), the story of Captain Ahab's relentless pursuit of a great white whale, and one of the great American novels.

Ralph Waldo Emerson, transcendentalism's leading light.

Henry David Thoreau.

Unlike the nation's leading artists and writers, newspaper editors, journalists, and other popular writers openly celebrated the advent of the machine age and the "inventive genius" that made it possible. Whether in eulogistic biographies or shorter sketches in journals, writers sought to enshrine inventors with the nation's leading military and political heroes. Just as George Washington became known as "the father of his country," so famous inventors like Eli Whitney, Robert Fulton, and Oliver Evans were considered "artists of their country." At a time when the word "technology" was rarely used, people associated invention with the "mechanical arts" and placed inventors on the same plane as the country's other artists—its writers and painters. And many inventors considered themselves key players in the ongoing effort to reform society. Indeed, the expression "Yankee ingenuity" gained currency at this time, indicating the extent to which invention and technology were bound up with the idea of shaping the American self.

## The Second Great Awakening

The spread of democratic and technological change took place at a time of tremendous religious ferment. The "Second Great Awakening," a religious revival that began in the 1790s, reached a crescendo during the 1820s and continued well into the 1840s. Drawing particularly on the evangelical methods of the rapidly expanding Baptist and Methodist denominations, the Second Great Awakening had two points of origin: in the Northeast, where Yale College president Timothy Dwight and his students sparked revivals both on campus and throughout New England and New York; and in the Old Southwest—especially Kentucky and Tennessee—where preachers like James McGready attracted hundreds of anxious souls to outdoor "camp meetings" to hear the word of God and be "born again." The most famous outdoor revivals occurred at Cane Ridge, Kentucky (near present-day Lexington), in August 1801, where more than 10,000 people gathered to listen to heart-stirring evangelists and pray that they might "see the light."

The Second Great Awakening launched bold, even radical, religious innovations. Among its most important features was an optimistic and democratic theology that appealed to common people. In contrast to the older Calvinist viewpoint that people were predestined to heaven or hell and could be saved only if God had "elected" them, the new evangelical theology emphasized individual free will and, most important, the idea that everyone was equal in the eyes of God. It followed that each individual could gain salvation by "seeing the light," by choosing heaven over hell. Rather than embracing a stern God of judgment as many "old light" Calvinists did, adherents of the Second Great Awakening believed in a "new light" God of love and free, saving grace for all. Many of them were affiliated with denominations that exercised local governance, elected their own ministers, and believed in "a priesthood of all believers." These democratic religious ideas helped to advance political democracy in America.

Important organizational innovations accompanied the democratic theology. Under Methodist bishop Frances Asbury, thousands of itinerant preachers—called "circuit riders"—scoured the country in search of converts. Asbury himself averaged some 5,000 miles a year on trips (primarily on horseback) that took him across the Allegheny Mountains sixty-two times. Following him was a small army of Methodist and Baptist itinerants who "took the Word" to every corner of the country. Commitment and devotion brought success. The Methodists would become the largest Protestant denomination in the United States by 1865, followed by the Baptists, who would surpass them in numbers later in the century. To this day, the presence of hundreds of "little white churches" in rural areas across the country mark the sites where circuit riders once visited and, in the process, established lasting communities of believers.

Revivalism was another key feature of the Awakening. When an evangelist arrived in a small town, local business often came to a standstill for days. A significant social event, exciting and personally intense, a revival could touch virtually everyone in the community. Surviving records reveal the emotional swings that people experienced as they underwent conversion. Such experiences, called "exercises," included everything from blackouts and fainting spells to trances and visions, uncontrollable laughing, jerking, barking, and rolling on the ground. Congregationalist and Presbyterian ministers, however, often frowned on these physical exercises and the mass hysteria they generated. Yet even the most controlled preachers frequently filled their sermons with references to hellfire and brimstone and, as one critic put it, threatened their listeners with "*instant and eternal damnation . . . unless they repent forthwith.*"

The emotional intensity of evangelical revivals underscored the importance of two other innovations: a new style of preaching and new forms of music. Gone were the stylized texts formally delivered by highly educated ministers that had characterized eighteenth-century sermons. In their place were free-form sermons delivered with great energy by unschooled lay preachers. They used the language of the common folk to tell stories, instill hope, and make no-holds-barred threats and appeals to sway their listeners.

The same was true of the new folk-based music that accompanied the Second Great Awakening. Purposely intended "to excite the passions" and encourage congregations to clap their hands, shout, and jump, the new gospel music drew on call-and-response patterns commonly found in black religious music as well as well-known folk tunes of the period. The catchy melodies were easy to remember, and could be sung at work and play as well as at prayer.

"Old light" conservatives often condemned such exuberant preaching and singing as ungodly. But the more they complained, the more popular the "new measures" became. By the 1820s publishers were rushing out popular hymnbooks, tracts, and Bibles to meet the burgeoning demand. Just as politicians of the period took advantage of new high-speed technologies to print newspapers and broadsides, religious groups did the same. By 1830 a weekly Methodist newspaper had 25,000 subscribers—among the largest in the world—while the American Bible Society had installed sixteen steam-powered presses and was printing over one million Bibles annually. Evangelical leaders understood the power of the printed word. "The PULPIT AND THE PRESS are inseparably connected," one of them proclaimed in 1823. "The press must be supported or the pulpit falls."

Most evangelicals associated with the Awakening were millennialists and perfectionists. They believed that God had chosen America to lead the world into the final thousand years of peace and prosperity before the Second Coming of Christ, and that American culture needed to be unified under evangelical Protestantism and cleansed of evil before the day of final judgment—in effect, perfected. Such ideas had important political implications. They reinforced the old Puritan belief that America was "the New Jerusalem," destined to occupy a special place in world history. This theme had justified American territorial expansion in the past, and it would soon reappear in a more virulent form under the banner of Manifest Destiny. Furthermore, evangelical Protestants advocated moral reforms aimed at ridding society of such sinful practices as drunkenness, idleness, Sabbath-breaking, prostitution, war, and (in the North) slavery, each one a subject of political controversy. Moral progress melded nicely with the technological progress of the age; in millennialist thought, both provided clear evidence of America's redemptive world mission.

The Second Great Awakening gathered momentum just as Congregationalism was disestablished in Connecticut (in 1818) and Massachusetts (in 1833), marking the end of

This early nineteenth-century view of a camp meeting shows well-dressed listeners, mostly women, experiencing conversion "exercises" in response to the preacher's powerful exhortations.

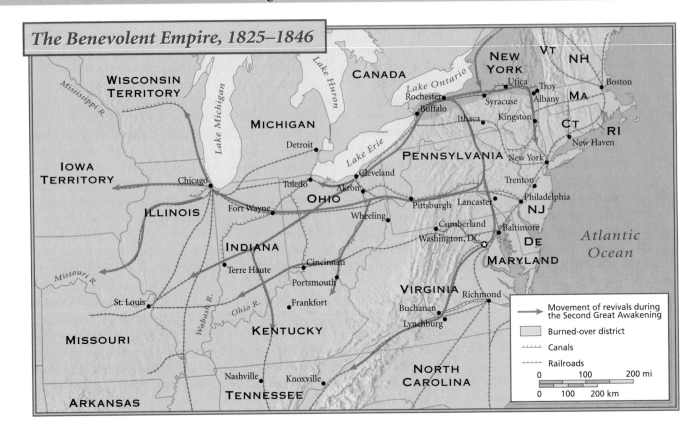

The Benevolent Empire, 1825–1846

Movement of revivals during
the Second Great Awakening

Burned-over district

Canals

Railroads

state-supported religions in America and the final separation of church and state in public affairs. As religious sects multiplied, denominationalism (the phenomenon of many religious groups competing with one another for members) imprinted itself on American culture in unprecedented ways. This was most apparent in upstate New York, where the Erie Canal and the rapid industrial transformation that accompanied it helped to kindle one of the most momentous religious revivals in all of American history. There, the fires of religion burned with such intensity that the region became known as "the burned-over district."

Along the towpaths and boomtowns of the Erie Canal could be found all the kinds of people that white evangelical Protestants most feared and wanted to "reform": Catholics, immigrants, paupers, and other "heathens," and sometimes even the primary agents of material progress, merchants and manufacturers. Then, as the transportation revolution spread westward into Ohio, Kentucky, Indiana, Illinois, and beyond, the agencies of Protestant religion and moral reform, collectively known as the "Benevolent Empire," moved with it. The geographies of religion, reform, and the market economy were part of the same westward-expanding process. Industrialization and reform were closely aligned with the new technologies of the era, especially what Daniel Webster referred to as "that mighty agent, steam." Both impulses carried with them the older civil and cultural institutions of the East into new territories and laid the foundations for new states that, they hoped, would further harmonize material and moral progress and ultimately achieve a more perfect society.

FINNEY'S REVIVALS

The person best known for kindling the fires of revivalism in the burned-over district as well as elsewhere in the Northeast and Midwest was Charles Grandison Finney. A lawyer whose religious conversion in 1821 resulted in his becoming a Presbyterian minister, Finney became the most sought-after preacher in America. Like other "new light" evangelists, he held that everyone had the God-given ability to achieve salvation if they would only repent, believe in Jesus Christ, and strive to perfect their lives in accordance with Christian precepts.

Finney believed that revival preaching had to be lively and exciting, even theatrical, so he carefully organized and orchestrated his services to excite the senses and attract potential converts. In an effort to enliven the expression of faith and get away from the dirge-like hymns that filled more traditional Presbyterian and Congregational services, he supported choir singing and encouraged his assistants to introduce more inspiring music into the services. One of them, Thomas Hastings of Utica, New York, composed the melody for "Rock of Ages," one of the greatest of all nineteenth-century hymns.

Between 1825 and 1837, Finney conducted revivals in factory towns and villages throughout the burned-over district and, once his reputation was established, moved on to preach to large assemblies in the seaboard cities of Wilmington, Philadelphia, Boston, and New York. One of his most successful revivals took place between September 1830 and March 1831 in the Erie Canal boomtown of Rochester, New York. Called there by local ministers and businessmen concerned about the "ungodly gain," "general backsliding," and "degeneracy" that accompanied the town's spectacular economic growth, Finney conducted a six-month crusade aimed not only at gaining converts but also at purging the community of its sinfulness, particularly drunkenness.

The results of Finney's Rochester crusade were impressive. During the 1830s, hundreds joined local churches and, in the process, adopted their perfectionist sentiments. Conversion bred piety, and piety bred self-restraint. Indeed, workers as well as their employers became more sober and serious about living godly lives. News of the Rochester revival spread Finney's fame far and wide. Invitations to conduct revivals came from all parts of the country as well as from Europe, and he led two major ones, in Boston and New York, before moving permanently to Oberlin College near Cleveland, Ohio, in 1835.

Finney's greatest impact was felt in the manufacturing districts of America, where the response was as enthusiastic as it had been at Rochester. Thousands of families responded to his call in the late 1820s and 1830s, during which years church attendance rose to an all-time high. Whereas one in twenty adults maintained some sort of church affiliation in the 1790s, three out of four did so by 1835. Moreover, through his support of theological schools in upstate New York, Ohio, and Illinois, Finney came into contact with young men training for the evangelical ministry who were receptive to his emphasis on Christian perfectionism, and to his message that believers "should . . . aim at being useful in the highest degree possible." Being useful meant leading a Christian life, diligently conducting revivals, and seeking not only to save individual souls but to reform all of society. This last goal, Finney's students believed, would perfect humanity and set the stage for a thousand years of peace.

### VISIONS OF UTOPIA

Joining Charles Finney's "holy band" in its mission to refashion society were the founders of so-called utopian communities. One-hundred communitarian experiments were initiated in the United States during the first half of the nineteenth century—an unprecedented number. Extraordinarily diverse, some were deeply religious, others were secular; some were well integrated into their surrounding cultural landscapes, while others remained isolated and in constant tension with their neighbors. Virtually all of them, however, held the common American belief that people could achieve a perfect society given the correct set of guiding principles, and had faith that science (and what would soon be identified as technology) could propel them toward this society. To utopian perfectionists, history was neither static nor cyclical

The "Finney Tent," erected at Oberlin College to house the large crowds that came to hear Finney preach and to experience conversion.

375

but progressive in character. The starting point lay in the establishment of experimental pilot projects that, they hoped, would grow into even larger communities and ultimately change the face of America.

*Robert Owen and New Harmony.* One of the best-known utopian communities was Robert Owen's settlement at New Harmony, Indiana. A native of Wales who set out for London at age ten to "seek his fortune," Owen moved through the ranks of the working class to become one of the most successful textile manufacturers in England. Having personally experienced the injustices of the British factory system, he committed himself to finding ways of ensuring that machinery would benefit workers rather than exploit them. For him, "the momentous question" of the age was "whether this vast gift of labour-saving machinery is to result in mitigation of the toil and melioration of the condition of the millions who have acquired it."

After successfully introducing labor and educational reforms at his cotton mill in New Lanark, Scotland, Owen sought a larger arena for his communitarian endeavors. He arrived in America late in November 1824 to great fanfare. "Make a man happy and you make him virtuous—this is the whole of my system," he told packed audiences that included President James Monroe and other government officials. "I am come to this country to introduce an entire new state of society; to change it from the ignorant, selfish system, to an enlightened, social system." Until the "selfish system," based on private property and the pursuit of profit, was replaced by communal property ownership, Owen saw little hope for "permanent improvement in the condition of the human race."

The New Harmony experiment initially attracted more than 800 individuals, ranging in background from prominent intellectuals to working-class families. Among the most prominent was William Maclure, a distinguished geologist, who persuaded several other natural scientists to join him at New Harmony in establishing a school that combined manual labor with hands-on scholarly instruction in "useful knowledge," particularly science. From the outset, however, there was little harmony at New Harmony. Disputes arose almost immediately over property rights, work assignments, levels of compensation, and how the backwoods utopia should be governed. Owen, who was frequently absent from New Harmony, proved incapable of reconciling the divergent personalities that splintered the community. His indecisive leadership coupled with the community's growing financial problems, as well as public criticism of his unorthodox ideas about private property, organized religion, and even marriage, brought about the dissolution of New Harmony in 1828. After disposing of the financially encumbered property, Owen returned to Britain with less than one-fifth of his original fortune. Although more than twenty smaller Owenite communities elsewhere in North America and Great Britain survived the failure of New Harmony, they, too, encountered internal problems and eventually disappeared.

*Brook Farm and the North American Phalanx.* Just as the Owenite movement was fading, another group had begun to capture the utopian imagination. Based on the writings of the French socialist Charles Fourier, the new movement held out the promise of a perfect new world by establishing communities called "phalanxes" (or "phalanges"), in which the participants held stock and found personal fulfillment by selecting occupations that best suited them. Twenty-eight Fourierist phalanxes were set up in the United States between 1841 and 1858, ranging as far west as Iowa and as far south as Texas. Two of the best known were Brook Farm at West Roxbury, Massachusetts, and the North American Phalanx near Red Bank, New Jersey. Founded by a former Unitarian minister in 1841, Brook Farm attracted a star-studded cast of Transcendentalist luminaries, including Ralph Waldo Emerson, Margaret Fuller, Nathaniel Hawthorne, and Henry David Thoreau. But, despite its laudable goal to build "a city of God" and "redeem society as well as the individual from all sin," Brook Farm quickly ran into financial difficulty and, after limping along for several years, was eventually sold at public auction in 1849.

The North American Phalanx, by contrast, experienced greater success. Founded in 1843, the phalanx comprised ninety residents who engaged primarily in agriculture, with each person choosing work that seemed the most satisfying. Despite difficulties in getting members to do all the tasks that needed to be done, the North American Phalanx by and large succeeded. It received considerable publicity through one of its benefactors, Horace Greeley, the reform-minded owner of the *New York Tribune*. Visitors to the phalanx often noted its friendly atmosphere and wholesomeness. Yet when a fire destroyed the gristmill in 1854, the members voted to dissolve the community rather than rebuild it, even though they had the resources to do so. After ten years, the novelty of the experiment in "plain living" and "high thinking" had worn off.

An improved Shaker washing machine designed particularly for hospitals, hotels, and laundries. This machine, patented in 1858, displays the Shakers technical ingenuity and craftsmanship. Art supplied by the Shaker Museum & Library, Chatham, New York.

*The Shakers.* Of the hundred or more communitarian societies established in America between the Revolution and the Civil War, the greatest success financially and socially was the Shakers. Unlike the secular Owenites and phalangists, the Shakers drew inspiration from their religious beliefs. The sect's founder, Mother Ann Lee, came from a poor, working-class family in Manchester, England. As a child she labored in a cotton mill; as a young woman she claimed to have experienced "religious impressions" that gave her "great light and conviction concerning the sinfulness and depravity of human nature, and especially concerning the lusts of the flesh." These mystical visions, coupled with her association with a radical group of Quaker dissenters, led her to claim that the millennium was at hand and that God had ordained her to be the Christ spirit that would initiate the "new dispensation," or Second Coming, on earth. Because Mother Ann's message attracted few believers in England, she decided to carry the gospel to America, where, she hoped, the ground for conversions would be more fertile.

"Ann the Word" and a small contingent of believers arrived in America in 1774. The sect grew steadily, reaching a high point during the 1850s with some eighteen communities (called "societies") spread across the country from Maine to Kentucky. The name "Shaker" derived from a contemporary reference to "Shaking Quakers" and the physical intensity of their services, especially their dancing, the purpose of which was to "shake sin from the body through the fingertips." Admirers considered their sacred songs and dances highly synchronized and beautiful, though others were appalled by what they saw.

The Shakers believed in universal salvation, practiced celibacy, and sought to live apart from the world in order to achieve Christian perfection. But they did not divorce themselves from worldly economic activities, which they often described as "consecrated industry." Shakers developed thriving businesses in the sale of garden seeds, medicinal herbs, tanned goods, brooms and brushes, leather whips, baskets, straw and palm leaf hats and bonnets, and all sorts of kitchen products—from apple butter and maple syrup to relishes and sauces.

Their best-known products, which came from their woodworking shops, met very high standards for quality and workmanship. Shaker-made furniture—slat-back chairs, cabinets, tables, clock cases, and the like—reveal a lightness and simplicity of design that is unmatched in the annals of American craftsmanship. Ornamentation and other "superfluities" were considered sinful because they revealed "the pride and vanity of man." "The beautiful," one elder stated, "has no business with us." Yet in Shaker hands, simplicity exemplified elegance and beauty.

Upon visiting a Shaker village in 1849, a British writer commented on the sect's technical creativity, noting that "here machinery of every kind is always among their greatest blessings." Shaker artisans readily availed themselves of the latest mechanical know-how, even visiting places like the Springfield Armory to acquire it. After making forays into the outside world to examine machinery and manufacturing methods, they tended to replicate what they saw in-house rather than make outright purchases. Their most important innovations included a washing machine (reflecting a rare concern for lessening women's labor), a circular saw that was widely adopted throughout the country, and machines for planing and machining boards. In Shaker communities, technology was a natural ally of religion.

*Oneida Perfectionists.* A later group, the Oneida Perfectionists, were far more radical than the Shakers. Founded during the 1830s by a college-educated lawyer and evangelical clergyman, John Humphrey Noyes, the sect originated in Putney, Vermont, and in 1847 moved to Oneida, New York—the heart of the "burned-over district." Noyes and his followers believed that a person achieved perfection through a conversion experience, after which the believer was no longer capable of sinning. From this theology flowed a number of practices considered extreme in nineteenth-century America, most notably the idea of "complex marriage," whereby a sanctified man and a sanctified woman could have sexual relations regardless of their marital status. Perfectionism also extended to eugenics. In an effort to produce superior offspring, Noyes singled out the most spiritually advanced and physically fit members of the community to copulate and have children. Forty-five "stirpiculture" babies were born at Oneida—nine of them fathered by Noyes. No surprise, such practices prompted a host of critics to condemn Noyes as a false prophet and Oneida as his den of iniquity.

Accused of adultery and pursued by the law on numerous occasions, Noyes persisted in following the dictates of Christian perfectionism and speaking his mind on public issues. He endorsed temperance, pacifism, and the immediate abolition of slavery. Especially critical of the country's harsh treatment of slaves and Indians, in 1837 he renounced "all allegiance to the government of the United States" while asserting "the title of Jesus Christ to the throne of the world." In Noyes's world, religion trumped politics.

Despite the hostility that Oneida's political radicalism and unorthodox sexual practices aroused, the community prospered. Like the Shakers, the Perfectionists combined manufacturing with farming in order to generate income. After reaping large profits from the manufacture of steel traps in the mid-1850s, the Perfectionists turned to manufacturing silk thread, canned fruit, and silver tableware. This tableware, their one lasting material legacy, can be found in stores today as "Oneida silver plate."

In the end, the Shakers and Oneida Perfectionists met similar fates in spite of their economic success. After experiencing a period of spiritual growth and vitality, both eventually disappeared. Escalating problems over Noyes's controversial leadership and a falling away from religious ideals led to the decline of the Oneida community. Celibacy proved to be the undoing of the Shakers. With no offspring to carry on the founders' traditions, the sect declined in numbers and gradually died out. The significance of these communities lies in their pursuit of human perfection through separatist religious practices, and in their eager embrace of new machine technology as a way of lightening their daily chores so that they could devote more time to spiritual fulfillment. Both groups reflected the larger society's growing commitment to social progress and to technology and innovation as a means of achieving that progress.

### THE MORMONS

The largest and most successful new denomination to emerge in New York's "burned-over district" was the Church of Jesus Christ of Latter-Day Saints, also known as the Mormons. The new faith originally came together around a charismatic leader, Joseph Smith, and a sacred book. While living in upstate New York, Smith had a series of visions, the most important of which occurred in 1823, when the angel Moroni appeared and told him about a set of gold tablets hidden on a nearby hillside that detailed the ancient history of the Americas. Published in 1830 as *The Book of Mormon,* Smith's translation of the tablets was not meant to replace the Bible, but rather made the Western Hemisphere an additional source of revelation by identifying the American Indians as descendants of the ancient Israelites. While this "biblical" account proved satisfying to converts, it appeared blasphemous to other Christians, who hounded the Mormons from one settlement after another. When an anti-Mormon mob in Illinois lynched Smith and his brother in 1844, Mormon leaders prepared to move to the far West, beyond the reach of their enemies.

The exodus from Illinois, led by Joseph Smith's elected successor, Brigham Young, was a feat of careful planning and organization. Aided by army maps that pointed them in the direction of the Great Salt Lake Basin, the lead party, consisting of 540 wagons and some 1,500 refugees, set out on the treacherous journey in February 1846. By June, their 540

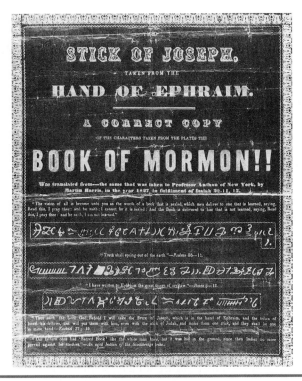

A flyer advertising Joseph Smith's translation of *The Book of Mormon*.

wagons had reached the Missouri River near Council Bluffs, Iowa. Following them were another 2,500 wagons divided into five or six companies and organized in pyramidal groups of tens, fifties, and hundreds of families. Each group had its own leaders and armed guards. All followed detailed regulations on the rigors of overland travel and the proper use of essential foodstuffs and other provisions as they made their way across the continent.

As the lead group blazed a wagon road along the northern side of the Platte River across Nebraska into eastern Wyoming and, from there, into the rugged high country that led through the South Pass to the Great Salt Lake Basin, they established way stations and planted crops for those following them. Despite these preparations, though, life on what became known as the Overland Trail was difficult. Wagons broke down, animals became lame, food supplies ran short, and people fell ill; some 200 died along the treacherous route. But under the determined leadership of Brigham Young and his circle of advisers, the Mormon exo-

dus continued, with the first contingent of settlers arriving in the Salt Lake region in July 1847. By the following fall, nearly 3,000 Mormon settlers had entered the Salt Lake region. Within two years they would establish the Provisional Government of the State of Deseret, the theocratic Mormon domain in the West. By 1850, the Mormon population in Utah approached 12,000, and reached 40,000 a decade later.

The Mormons were vilified more than any other utopian community of the period. *The Book of Mormon* was considered inflammatory in a society molded by evangelical Christianity, as was the Mormon practice of polygamy. But non-Mormon "gentiles" came to view the Mormons as dangerous outsiders as much because of their political economy as because of their religious or social doctrines. From the beginning, the "Saints," as they called themselves, not only lived apart from their neighbors but also preferred to trade among themselves. In local politics they tended to vote as a block, undermining democratic government and the separation of church and state in the eyes of critics. Moreover, many Mormon converts were poor, and they maintained generally friendly relations with native Americans, whom they attempted to convert to the faith. In the border state of Missouri, rumors spread that they were attempting to convert black slaves.

The Mormons were one of the first groups of white Americans to live in the radically different ecology of the Rocky Mountain West. The difficulties of surviving as agriculturalists in an arid land without the familiar resources of water, wood, or machine-made goods severely tested their faith and resilience as a community. For a time, Mormons endured preindustrial conditions, wearing woolen homespun and getting by with only a few machine-made tools. They succeeded in setting up local gristmills, sawmills, tanneries, and light industries for making soap, brooms, hats, and the like. But more ambitious plans to re-create the mines, ironworks, and factories of the East largely failed owing to the scarcity of capital, skilled labor, and equipment.

The defining technology of Mormon Utah became elaborate irrigation systems, which supported eastern-style farming. With arable land scarce, Mormon settlers learned early on how to convey water from distant mountain streams by building canals and tapping them with sluice gates and ditches that distributed water by gravity flow to farms and home lots. Everything depended on having adequate water for cultivation. Without it, green fields soon wilted, and the landscape returned to sagebrush. The Mormons' survival in the desert owed much to Brigham Young and other church elders—especially their ability to manage and distribute scarce water resources to the rapidly growing community. Only with the coming of the transcontinental railroad—which Young welcomed and even invested in—would the farming culture of the Mormons begin to integrate with the larger national economy, and parts of Utah take on the character of an industrial landscape.

Sarah M. Grimké.    Angelina M. Grimké.

## Evangelical Roots of Abolitionism

One of the striking features of the Second Great Awakening was a belief in religious equality, the ability of every soul to attain salvation. But as the evangelical movement spread to the South, it bumped up against the greatest example of inequality the nation could offer—slavery. The resulting tension between religious equality and slavery soon fed older antagonisms between the North and South to inflame the nation's most divisive issue.

### THEODORE DWIGHT WELD

The potential for conflict was high in Cincinnati, the rapidly growing city in southwestern Ohio. With its strategic location on the Ohio River, adjacent to slaveholding Kentucky, and its stature as a meatpacking center and leading builder of steamboats, the city maintained strong trade and social contacts with farmers, planters, and businessmen in the South. In 1833, a group of young men assembled at the Lane Theological Seminary in Cincinnati under the leadership of Theodore Dwight Weld, a Finney convert from western New York.

Already well known as an advocate of temperance, Sabbath-keeping, and the advanced education of women, Weld also opposed slavery. Before going to Ohio, he had supported the idea of gradual emancipation and had even sympathized with the American Colonization Society, which favored shipping all blacks, slave or free, back to Africa. Yet the colonization scheme never fully satisfied him: its assumption that blacks were inferior to whites and could not prosper in America ran against his belief that all people, regardless of race, were equal in God's eyes. In the

end, this conviction, coupled with an introduction to the writings of the Boston newspaper editor William Lloyd Garrison, made an abolitionist of Weld. His call for an immediate end to slavery and the granting of equal rights to freedmen caused considerable turmoil at the Lane Seminary and shocked local white society. Rather than submit to disciplinary action at the seminary, Weld and seventy-five of his comrades, called the "Lane Rebels," left in October 1834, many embarking on careers devoted to abolitionism. Weld, for example, rejected an offer from Finney to teach at Oberlin College and became an agent for the newly established Ohio Antislavery Society. During the next two years he traveled throughout much of Ohio as well as parts of western Pennsylvania, impressing audiences with his magnificent oratory and helping to establish local abolitionist societies.

Others followed similar paths to the abolitionist cause. Among them were Weld's long-time friend and fellow Lane rebel Henry B. Stanton and his wife, Elizabeth Cady Stanton—soon to achieve renown as a leader in the emerging women's rights movement. Like the Stantons, many of these reformers came from middle-class backgrounds in the Northeast, especially New England and the burned-over district of upstate New York. But not all. James G. Birney, one of the movement's most courageous leaders, was a prominent lawyer-politician and former slave owner from Alabama and Kentucky. Of equal stature were Sarah and Angelina Grimké, daughters of a wealthy, conservative slaveholding family in Charleston, South Carolina, who became outspoken abolitionists and controversial advocates of women playing roles usually reserved for men. In 1838, Angelina Grimké married Theodore Weld.

## WILLIAM LLOYD GARRISON

As much as Weld, Birney, the Stantons, the Grimké sisters, and countless others energized the abolitionist movement, its best-known leader—indeed, its animating force—was Boston's William Lloyd Garrison. A Baptist by conviction and a printer by trade, Garrison was working in Baltimore when his Quaker employer, Benjamin Lundy, and members of the city's free black community converted him to "the cause of the slave." Militant in his demands for the immediate emancipation of slaves, Garrison set out to break the "conspiracy of silence" that surrounded slavery. After being jailed in Baltimore for libel, he returned to his native New England and, with the financial support of New York merchants Arthur and Lewis Tappan, published the first issue of *The Liberator* in January 1831. In it, he announced that "I will be as harsh as truth, and as uncompromising as justice. On this subject, I do not wish to think, to speak, or write, with moderation. . . . I am in earnest—I will not equivocate—I will not excuse—I will not retreat a single inch—AND I WILL BE HEARD."

*The Liberator* never achieved a large circulation in the North, nor did its message attract many adherents there. Published as a weekly newspaper, it had only 50 white subscribers

William Lloyd Garrison.

in its first year and no more than 400 two years later. Most of those who read it were already true believers. But the publication found an enthusiastic audience among free blacks and fugitive slaves in the North, who in 1833 constituted over 60 percent of its readership. The escaped slave Frederick Douglass became one of its most ardent champions and, in 1848, went on to publish his own abolitionist newspaper, *North Star,* at Rochester, New York, in the burned-over district. Only a handful of southerners actually read *The Liberator,* but southerners heard plenty about it through commentary in their own press. And what they heard infuriated them. Many blamed the Bostonian for the bloody slave revolt led by Nat Turner in Southampton County in southeastern Virginia, shortly after *The Liberator* first appeared. Garrison never represented the whole of abolitionism, a diverse and decentralized movement. In fact, most northerners considered him a fanatic.

## THE AMERICAN ANTI-SLAVERY SOCIETY

Three factors—commitment, organization, and technology—propelled the abolitionist movement to the forefront of American society during the mid-1830s. In most cases, commitment to this cause came after a conversion experience not unlike those of religious revivals—a period of intense soul-searching and eventual acceptance of the doctrine that slavery was morally wrong. Then, like good evangelicals, abolitionists worked ceaselessly to convert others to the cause.

In 1833, the American Anti-Slavery Society, the first national organization of its kind in the United States, was established. William Lloyd Garrison composed the society's governing "Declaration of Sentiments," an ingenious document that drew on the precedents of the American Revolution to demand immediate emancipation and to argue that "our fathers were never slaves—never bought and sold like cattle—never shut out from the light of knowledge and religion—never subjected to the lash of brutal taskmasters." The declaration went on to condemn slavery as a sin "unequalled by any other on the face of the earth" and to attack the idea of deporting blacks to Africa. All those who signed the Declaration of Sentiments pledged to oppose racial prejudice in all its guises and to "secure to the colored population . . . all the rights and privileges that belong to them as men and as Americans." The signers also agreed that the method of achieving these ends should be through the old revivalist mode of "moral suasion" rather than the use of

**Political Abolitionism**

violence. To this end, they pledged themselves to organize antislavery societies in every city, town, and hamlet and to circulate pamphlets and broadsides (large sheets printed in bold letters) throughout the country to win over public opinion. In almost every instance, evangelical ministers and their churches became the organizing agencies of abolitionism at the local level.

Since most funding for the American Anti-Slavery Society came from wealthy New York merchants like the Tappan brothers, its main office was located in New York City. Weld and other agents working throughout the country received their instructions, literature, and paychecks from New York. The society also took advantage of the city's position as the center of the publishing trade. With important innovations occurring in high-volume printing, the leaders of the society were able to take advantage of this new technology when they decided in 1835 to mount a national campaign of moral suasion.

Called "the great postal campaign," the project aimed at peppering the country, especially the South, with abolition-ist literature. The recent development of steam-driven rotary presses (aptly called the "Lightning" machine) speeded the printing process. In 1833, for example, the average New York newspaper, using hand presses, could print around 200 impressions an hour; with the introduction of steam-driven rotary presses in 1835, output jumped to 5,500 copies an hour. Printing costs fell so much that the American Anti-Slavery Society went from distributing 122,000 pieces of literature in 1834 to 1.1 million pieces the following year. Other reform groups—notably the American Temperance Union, religious tract societies, and state and local abolitionist associations—had resorted to pamphleteering before 1835, but none of them achieved the massive distribution of the great postal campaign. The new printing technology strengthened the abolitionist cause by making mass distribution possible. In effect, technological innovation fostered social innovation.

Although the great postal campaign had an immediate and lasting impact, public reaction took a different turn than expected. Instead of recognizing the sinfulness of slavery and repenting, as abolitionists had anticipated, southerners exploded in rage and tried to suppress the mailings. On July 29, 1835, for instance, a crowd descended on the Charleston, South Carolina, post office and seized mailbags containing abolitionist literature. The next evening, the mob reappeared to burn effigies of William Lloyd Garrison and Arthur Tappan, using as fuel the material they had seized a day earlier. Elsewhere in the South, community leaders, prompted by large-plantation owners, established vigilance committees to seize any incoming mail that contained "incendiary literature." President Andrew Jackson, himself a slave owner, encouraged these actions by publicly denouncing the postal campaign and urging Congress to pass legislation aimed at banning abolitionist literature from the mails. Although nothing came of it, southerners redoubled their efforts to snuff out dissent against the "peculiar institution." And

This lithographic print was issued by Boston abolitionists after the 1835 raid on the Charleston, South Carolina Post Office. Sarcastically entitled "A New Method of Assorting the Mail," it sought to show the lengths to which slave-owning southerners would go to quell opposition to their "peculiar institution." Note the $20,000 reward posted on the wall of the post office for the capture of Arthur Tappan, a leading financial supporter of the abolitionist postal campaign.

they were supported by northern merchants and manufacturers who enjoyed lucrative trade relationships in the South. In the end, only Connecticut—a leading manufacturing state—responded with a law banning abolitionist speakers.

But the opposition to abolitionism continued. Many northern whites were unable to support the movement because it challenged the common belief in white supremacy. From New England to Ohio, "gentlemen of property and standing" took the lead in mounting attacks on abolitionist leaders while tapping deep veins of racism within the white community. In Cincinnati, irate antiabolitionists repeatedly attacked a print shop owned by James G. Birney, while in Boston another mob seized Garrison and dragged him through the streets at the end of a rope. The violence frequently spilled over against communities of free blacks. One abolitionist agent reported that he faced mobs on more than seventy occasions while working in Ohio and Pennsylvania. In the southern Illinois town of Alton on November 7, 1837, a mob set fire to a building where the abolitionist editor Elijah Lovejoy was guarding his press and murdered him as he ran, pistol in hand, into the street. The cause had its first martyr.

The American Anti-Slavery Society responded by mounting yet another major campaign, this time in the form of petitions to Congress. The idea of petitioning Congress to introduce legislation or redress grievances was not new. Evangelical reform groups in the North had mounted mass petition campaigns against Sabbath-breaking and the sale and consumption of alcohol, especially "demon rum." Petitions protesting slavery had begun in the eighteenth century and continued sporadically into the 1830s. The volume grew so drastically, however (by 1835 there were over 30,000), that in May 1836 the House of Representatives adopted a "gag resolution" that immediately tabled all antislavery petitions before they could reach the House floor for debate. Despite this effort to silence debate on slavery, the American Anti-Slavery Society decided the following year to increase pressure on Congress by conducting a petition campaign the likes of which had never been seen before. Some petitions aimed at ending slavery in the District of Columbia; others called for outlawing interstate trade in slaves; and still others sought to prevent new slave states from entering the Union. Women such as Elizabeth Cady (soon to be Elizabeth Cady Stanton), Angelina Grimké, Lucretia Mott, and Susan B. Anthony assumed key roles in organizing the campaign and gathering signatures. Grimké's involvement in the effort led her to observe that "the investigation of the rights of the slave has led me to a better understanding of my own." Indeed, the antislavery movement helped kindle debate over the right of women to participate in politics. After a year of intensive effort, the American Anti-Slavery Society announced that 415,000 petitions had been sent to Washington. Over half of the petitions contained the signatures of women.

Unlike the great postal campaign, which targeted newspaper editors, politicians, and civic leaders throughout the South, the petition campaign of 1837–38 was more of a grassroots operation that focused exclusively on the North. Still, it elicited angry responses from militant slave owners and "Northern men with Southern principles." And the more the "slave power" sought to silence abolitionists through gag rules, illegal mail searches, and mob violence, the more it drew attention to the movement while raising concerns over the safety of America's civil liberties. To many northerners with little sympathy for the antislavery cause, it seemed that essential rights of free speech, free assembly, and free press were being trampled by slave masters and their allies. "Our opposers are doing everything to help us," an elated supporter wrote to Garrison. Nothing had been "ever so much talked about as slavery is everywhere."

## Political Abolitionism

### ADAMS AND THE 1836 GAG RULE

By 1838, a growing number of abolitionist leaders openly acknowledged that their strategy of moral suasion was taking a new direction. The pamphleteering effort and the violent opposition it elicited was moving abolitionism away from its evangelical base toward a more ideological and political orientation. This shift became apparent in the controversy that rocked the House of Representatives over the 1836 gag resolution.

In the eye of the storm was former president John Quincy Adams, who had been elected to the House in 1830. Adams had never supported the abolitionist movement. Content to tolerate slavery wherever it existed, he had even confided to his diary his belief "that the general treatment of slaves is mild and moderate." He nonetheless harbored deep resentments toward southern slaveholders who, he believed,

## Political Abolitionism

had been instrumental in preventing his reelection in 1828. When the southern-controlled House of Representatives adopted the gag rule in 1836, Adams saw an opportunity to stand for a fundamental principle of free government—the right of petition—and to skewer old enemies. He therefore drew on his considerable skill as a parliamentarian to present petitions in defiance of the gag rule and to attack slavery as "a sin before the sight of God" during House floor debates. By the late 1830s, most southerners would have agreed with a Virginia congressman's remark that Adams had become "the acutest, the astutest, the archest enemy of Southern slavery that ever existed." After eight years of unstinting effort, Adams would finally see the gag rule repealed in 1844.

Several new congressmen joined Adams in opposing slavery, the gag rule, and the values of the planter class. Like Adams, they came from hotbeds of antisouthern and antislavery feeling that stretched from Boston westward into the Berkshire Mountains and along the Erie Canal into northern Ohio, northern Indiana, and southern Michigan. They had a mandate from their constituents to challenge the institution of slavery, even if it meant bolting against party discipline.

As the political storm over slavery gathered force, the American Anti-Slavery Society began to fracture. Personalities clashed while members differed over future tactics. Frustrated with the public opposition to the society's efforts at moral suasion, Garrison blasted away at religious and political leaders in *The Liberator*. He also began to attack the federal government itself, damning the U.S. Constitution and urging his followers not to vote or in any way become involved with an institution that supported human bondage and maintained it by force. Garrison would eventually call for even more drastic measures, including outright disunion. The only way the North could cleanse itself of the sin of slavery, he came to believe, was to expel the slave states from the Union. But such ideas were too radical for many other members of the American Anti-Slavery Society.

### ABOLITIONISM AND WOMEN

Another source of conflict among abolitionists centered on the place of women in the movement. Some younger women, active in the 1837–38 petition campaign, had openly defied their "appointed female sphere" by speaking before audiences that included men as well as women. Such "promiscuous" behavior appalled older, more straight-laced members of the American Anti-Slavery Society, such as James G. Birney and the Tappan brothers. When Angelina and Sarah Grimké undertook a lecture tour of New England in 1837, they encountered as much abuse from within the society as they did from antiabolitionists. Congregationalist ministers circulated a *Pastoral Letter* denouncing the sisters for speaking in public and admonishing them to obey men, not lecture to them.

William Lloyd Garrison sympathized with the Grimké sisters' growing realization that black slavery and male domination over women had much in common. When they and

A cartoon satirizing the gag rule in the House of Representatives. On the ground cowering over a pile of abolitionist petitions is John Quincy Adams. Standing above him behind a barrel is Congressman Waddy Thompson Jr., a Whig defender of slavery from South Carolina. Crouched next to Thompson are two slaves, one of whom whispers, "Abolition is down flat!"

other women abolitionists began to push for gender equality within the American Anti-Slavery Society, Garrison wholeheartedly supported them. In his view, they had done as much as, if not more than, male members to advance the cause during the 1830s. They therefore deserved not only recognition and thanks but also the right to vote, hold office, and participate fully in the society's affairs. Other society members, however—including a number of women—took a dim view of the "open platform" that extended full rights to all regardless of race or sex. Such beliefs became associated with Garrison's name, so much so that the term "Garrisonian" came to stand for everything ultra in the way of reform.

The differences that festered within the abolitionist ranks erupted at the society's annual meeting in July 1840, when Garrison and his supporters succeeded in getting an outspoken feminist named Abby Kelly elected to the executive committee. Upset with the result and Garrison's leadership, his opponents left the American Anti-Slavery Society, never to return. Some of the dissenters immediately joined with Lewis Tappan to form the American and Foreign Anti-Slavery Society in an attempt to redirect the abolitionist movement back to its more conservative evangelical roots. Always a maverick, Theodore Weld condemned both societies as morally bankrupt and self-serving, refused to join either one, and instead assisted John Quincy Adams in his fight against the gag rule. Others likewise abandoned both national organizations and devoted themselves to abolitionist activities at the local level. Still others joined James G. Birney and Henry B. Stanton in organizing the Liberty Party as an alternative to the Democratic and Whig presidential tickets in the election of 1840.

### THE LIBERTY PARTY

Third parties rarely win elections, but they can significantly influence the political process either by forcing major parties to modify their positions on key issues or by drawing votes away from major candidates. So it was with the Liberty Party, which grew directly out of the abolitionist movement and sought to call attention to the "slave power" conspiracy that dominated American politics. In 1840, James G. Birney received the party's nomination and ran on an "immediatist" platform that emphasized ending slavery in the District of Columbia, outlawing the interstate and coastal trade in slaves, and prohibiting the admission of new slave states to the Union. Urging citizens to "vote as you pray and pray as you vote," Birney and his supporters (called "Liberty men") conducted a campaign that resembled an old-fashioned religious crusade. When the results came in, the Whig party candidate, General William Henry Harrison, defeated the Democratic incumbent, Martin Van Buren, and Birney received fewer than 7,000 votes. But Liberty Party pressure on Whig and Democratic congressional candidates in Ohio, Pennsylvania, New York, and Massachusetts forced them to harden their positions against slavery. It proved to be a small but significant victory.

By pointing to the inherent contradiction between slavery and one of the most fundamental of American values—personal freedom—the Liberty Party forced people to confront not only the morality of slavery but also its ideological implications. The dichotomies of freedom/slavery and union/disunion increasingly polarized the North and South after 1840. These sectional tensions had surged to the forefront during the Missouri debates of 1820, the South Carolina nullification crisis of 1832, and the abolitionist postal and petition campaigns of the mid-1830s, but now they divided the Whig and Democratic Parties themselves. The American political system was faced with the supreme test of resolving the problem of slavery and maintaining the Union.

Cover to "I'll Be No Submissive Wife," a feminist ballad of 1835. Sample lyrics: "Should a humdrum husband say / That at home I ought to stay, / Do you think that I'll obey? / No no no, not I."

*American Journal*

## Where Do You Live?

*In nineteenth-century America, a common painting material was called "whitewash." Applied to everything from fences and the exteriors of buildings to the interiors of barns and houses, whitewash was popular because it was cheap, readily available, and easy to apply. In 1841, Catherine Beecher (the sister of abolitionist Harriet Beecher Stowe), believing that "cleanliness was next to godliness," published two handy recipes.*

"There is nothing which so much improves the appearance of a house and the premises, as painting or whitewashing the tenements and fences. The following receipts for whitewashing, have been found, by experience, to answer the same purpose for wood, brick, and stone, as oil-paint, and are much cheaper. The first is the receipt used for the President's house at Washington, improved by further experiments. The second, is a simpler and cheaper one, which the Writer has known to succeed, in a variety of cases, lasting as long, and looking as well, as white oil-paint.

*Receipt.*

"Take half a bushel of unslacked lime, and slack it with boiling water, covering it during the process. Strain it, and add a peck of salt, dissolved in warm water; three pounds of ground rice, boiled to a thin paste, put in boiling hot; half a pound of powdered Spanish whiting; and a pound of clear glue, dissolved in warm water. Mix, and let it stand several days. Then keep it in a kettle, on a portable furnace, and put it on as hot as possible, with a painter's or whitewash brush.

*Another.*

"Make whitewash, in the usual way, except that the water used should have two double-handfuls of salt dissolved in each pailful of the hot water used. Then stir in a double-handful of fine sand, to make it thick like cream. This is better to be put on hot. Coloring matter can be added to both, making a light stone color, a cream color, or a light buff, which are most suitable for buildings."

Catherine Beecher, *Treatise on Domestic Economy*

## The Limits of Antebellum Reform

Antebellum reformers came largely from white, middle-class, Protestant backgrounds. They thought of themselves not as social reformers but rather as Christian soldiers engaged in a war to uphold Protestant morality, republican principles, and technological progress against the forces of sin and barbarism. Their causes ranged from abolitionism, pacifism, and women's rights to temperance, public education, and prison reform. Their method of operation owed much to the evangelical religious movement, from which most of them came. They believed initially that reform would come about as a result of moral suasion, individual repentance, and voluntary action rather than through coercive government action. Yet as much as they committed themselves to moral and social improvement, they nonetheless harbored biases that reflected the culture in which they lived.

### BLACK ABOLITIONISTS

From the outset, free blacks and escaped slaves committed themselves wholeheartedly to the cause of immediate emancipation. They set up their own national society—the National Negro Convention Movement—in 1830, organized support groups within black churches, established voluntary associations aimed at educating blacks, and published newspapers devoted to abolitionism. From 1835 to 1843, they worked assiduously for the American Anti-Slavery Society.

Abolitionism even provided a forum for some African American women, a group rendered voiceless in most areas of public life. The abolitionist Sojourner Truth was born a slave in upstate New York in 1797. After slavery ended in New York in 1827, the thirty-year-old Truth, then named Isabella, became one of a small number of African American women preachers at Methodist camp meetings during the

Sojourner Truth.

Frederick Douglass.

told by a white colleague, "Better have a little of the plantation speech than not; it is not best that you seem too learned."

The son of a slave woman and white man, Douglass grew up in bondage in Maryland. After working at plantation jobs and as a ship's caulker in Baltimore, he escaped to freedom in 1838 and went on to achieve international fame as an abolitionist, orator, newspaper editor, and writer. His eloquent indictments of slavery soon made him America's most important black leader and a voice of hope for his people.

Douglass and other black reformers had long been among Garrison's strongest supporters and felt obligated to him for bringing them into the movement. But as Garrison's tactics changed during the late 1830s to embrace women's rights, pacifism, and nonresistance, they found themselves increasingly estranged from their white colleagues. Douglass finally broke with Garrison in 1847, mainly because of his old mentor's attempts to control what he said and the way he acted. Thereafter, black abolitionists blazed a path of their own.

## WOMEN'S RIGHTS

Their involvement in the antislavery movement prompted some middle-class women to protest their second-class status in society. The prevailing view of "true womanhood" held that a woman's proper place was in the home taking care of her husband and children. The assumption was that women were happy serving their families, but a growing number sought more.

The laws and customs of antebellum America kept women subordinate to men. Unable to enter business, make contracts, sue, or execute a will, married women had no economic rights at all. By law, all property belonged to their husbands, including any wages they earned outside the home. Women were excluded from the professions of law and medicine because colleges would not admit them. Most significant, they were denied the most basic of rights—the right to vote. No wonder women who took up the abolitionist cause felt a special bond with slaves. They were oppressed as well.

Elizabeth Cady Stanton felt this oppression keenly. A tireless organizer of women's abolition and temperance associations, with experience voting in their enclaves, raising money, circulating petitions, and distributing propaganda, Stanton discovered the meaning of citizenship in fighting for reform. In 1840, on her honeymoon, she was denied admission as a delegate to the World Antislavery Convention in London.

Second Great Awakening. She subsequently worked with New York prostitutes at an institution supported by the Tappan brothers and lived in two different utopian communities, the second of which—the Northampton Association in western Massachusetts—was overseen by William Lloyd Garrison's brother-in-law. It was at Northampton that Truth became involved with the antislavery movement. In the late 1840s, she joined the abolitionist circuit as a forceful speaker for the humanity of slaves and free blacks, including black women. Sharing lecture halls with Frederick Douglass and members of the British Parliament, Truth never shied away from taking issue with male antagonists. According to author Harriet Beecher Stowe, no one "had more of that silent and subtle power which we call personal presence than this woman."

By the late 1840s, many black abolitionists had become exasperated by their white colleagues' refusal to admit them to the highest levels of the movement. Not only were blacks excluded from leadership positions in the American Anti-Slavery Society, they also experienced condescending treatment. White abolitionists frequently denigrated black culture and urged African Americans to absorb their own "superior" precepts of piety, hard work, and the like. But the path of assimilation did not necessarily lead to equality. Black abolitionists like Douglass and Truth were prized for their effectiveness as public speakers, but even Douglass was once

387

Stanton and her friend, Lucretia Mott, indignant, "resolved to hold a convention . . . and form a society to advocate the rights of women."

In July 1848, Stanton and Mott organized the world's first women's rights convention. Held, appropriately, at Seneca Falls in New York's burned-over district, the convention attracted some 300 participants. The resulting document, entitled a "Declaration of Sentiments," was modeled after the Declaration of Independence and became the defining charter for the feminist movement in America. "We hold these truths to be self-evident," the Declaration began, "that all men and women are created equal." Next came a list of some fifteen grievances, the most telling of which pointed to "repeated injuries and usurpations on the part of man toward woman, having a direct object the establishment of a tyranny over her." Among the worst was being "compelled . . . to submit to laws, in the formation of which she had no voice."

The Declaration of Sentiments concluded with a series of twelve resolutions, all of which were unanimously adopted by the convention, except one—the "sacred right to the elective franchise." Stanton considered the right to vote "the cornerstone" of the movement and insisted on its inclusion in the final document. Although the resolution passed by a narrow margin, only one-third of the delegates ended up signing the Declaration. Clearly, a woman's right to vote was a divisive issue, even among reformers.

Once launched, the women's rights movement continued to organize and meet annually (except for 1857) until the Civil War period. One of the most active participants was Susan B. Anthony, recruited to the movement by Stanton in 1851. Anthony was instrumental in persuading New York's legislature to grant wives the same property rights as their husbands in 1860. But change came slowly.

## WORKERS

In contrast with their opposition to slave labor, antebellum reformers showed little interest in the condition of white workers. When labor-management discord erupted during the late 1820s and early 1830s and white artisans sought to protect their rights by organizing trade unions and running political candidates in local elections, they received limited support from the evangelical reform groups. In this instance, differences of class, religious belief, and ethnicity proved critical. Protestant reformers condemned strikes and other public displays by labor groups as a threat to good order. They deplored the extent to which workers drank and "frollicked" and denounced the labor movement as antagonistic to religion. The only issue on which workers and reformers agreed was the need for free public schools, and even then they did so for different reasons. From the tradesmen's perspective, public schools gave their children an opportunity for education and advancement. For Protestant reformers, schools were places where the "correct" values of honesty, thrift, hard work, and godliness could be instilled.

Even when the working women of Lowell, Massachusetts, organized the Female Labor Reform Association in 1844 and drew on the language of the Declaration of Independence to assert their "rights and privileges" as the "daughters of freemen," they were virtually ignored by women's rights advocates. The oppression that middle-class women like Angelina Grimké, Elizabeth Cady Stanton, and Lucretia Mott experienced in their own lives did not sensitize them to the plight of Lowell's "mill girls." Although bound by common Protestant values, these women came from different social classes and lived in different social worlds, one governed by the factory system, the other by a "cult of domesticity" that held that a woman's place was in the home. The middle-class reformers seemed unable to recognize that the inequities working people complained of had the same paternalistic roots as their own oppression.

## IMMIGRANTS

Protestant social reformers displayed even more insensitivity toward another group of Americans: non-Protestant immigrants. Up through the end of the War of 1812, most foreigners who entered the United States were white Anglo-Saxon Protestants. After the war, that trend began to change, dramatically by the mid-1840s.

The vast majority of immigrants in this period were Roman Catholics from Ireland and Germany. Often destitute, the Irish tended to settle in northeastern cities like Boston, New York, and Philadelphia. Germans also settled in the Northeast—particularly in New York, New Jersey, and Pennsylvania—but many more made their way inland either to buy farms in the Midwest or to settle in thriving German

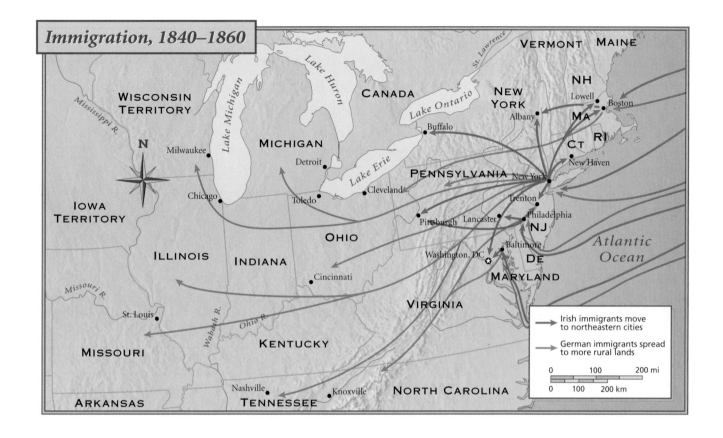

**Immigration, 1840–1860**

Legend:
→ Irish immigrants move to northeastern cities
→ German immigrants spread to more rural lands

communities at Cincinnati, St. Louis, and Milwaukee. Between 1840 and 1860, some 4 million people, among them 1.7 million Irish and 1.3 million Germans, entered the United States. Their arrival signaled a dramatic demographic shift especially noticeable in eastern cities like Boston and New York, where, by the 1850s, the number of foreign-born residents climbed to more than 50 percent of the total population.

The large influx of Irish Catholic immigrants, which began in the mid-1840s, stemmed mainly from a disastrous potato famine that struck Ireland in the fall of 1845. To make matters worse, the failure of the potato crop, the staple of the Irish peasantry, occurred in the midst of ongoing land enclosures and tenant evictions by largely Protestant British landlords. The displacement of thousands of peasants off the land led to widespread starvation and, ultimately, 1.5 million dead. The massive Irish emigration to America was an act of survival, although in some years as many as 20 percent died in passage or shortly after they arrived in the new land. Destitute Irish farmers who poured into eastern ports of the United States and Canada were generally condemned to a new kind of hardscrabble existence in urban slums. Men who once tilled the soil had to settle for ill-paid jobs digging ditches, foundations, and canals, while women became factory workers and servants in middle-class American homes. In a pattern that would hold through the next century, Irish immigrants were pitted against other immigrant groups and against African Americans in competing for jobs, housing, and status, by a business system increasingly aware of its ability to manipulate difference.

Public reaction to the tidal wave of immigration that began in the 1840s was varied. Manufacturers, construction contractors, and other industrial employers looked favorably on the influx of foreigners because they lowered labor costs. Native-born workers resented the competition that came from immigrants. The language and lifestyles of the newcomers annoyed virtually all segments of the Anglo

389

population. Most irksome of all, though, was the growing presence of Roman Catholicism. German and Irish Catholics were often characterized as an ignorant and superstitious lot who too easily fell under the "spiritual despotism" of Rome's papal hierarchy. The Irish in particular became caricatured as drunken and dishonest ne'er-do-wells whose growing political influence threatened to destroy the Republic and undo the fabric that bound Protestant America together.

The most vehement anti-Catholic attacks came from Protestant ministers in New England, New York, Pennsylvania, and Ohio. Evangelical stalwarts like Charles Grandison Finney and Lyman Beecher considered the new immigrants a serious threat and frequently spoke out against a "papist" conspiracy in America. In the early 1830s, Beecher delivered a series of blistering anti-Catholic sermons in Boston that inflamed public animosity. Catholic churches were burned, priests assaulted, and people driven from their homes from Philadelphia to Bangor, Maine. Beecher's involvement in organizing the American Temperance Society in 1826 owed much to his growing concern over the disruptive influence of "Romanists and Infidels." Throughout the antebellum period, in fact, the temperance movement engaged as much in nativist hostility as moral reform. The American Temperance Society's activities illustrate the odd mixture of humanitarianism, intolerance, progressivism, and self-righteousness that pervaded most aspects of reform.

Bigotry aside, temperance advocates were attacking a major social problem—one that posed special hazards to women and children. Americans were heavy drinkers, with annual per capita alcohol consumption in the 1820s at four gallons—triple what it is today. Filled with the same evangelical fervor that energized the abolitionist movement, temperance crusaders flooded the country with literature, conducted petition campaigns calling for legal restrictions on the manufacture and sale of "ardent spirits," and held public meetings urging people to "take the pledge" against their use. The immediate impact of the campaign was impressive. In less than a decade, consumption fell by 50 percent. At the same time, temperance reformers, sensing that tainted water supplies led people to strong drink, pressed city officials to provide "pure water" to their constituents through the establishment of urban water systems. An early success was New York's Croton Aqueduct, a project com-

The caption to this anti-Irish political cartoon notes sarcastically, "The balance of trade with Great Britain seems to be still against us. 630 paupers arrived in Boston in the steamship *Nestoria* . . . from Galway, Ireland, shipped by the British Government." Often overcrowded and disease-ridden, such transports became known as "coffin ships."

pleted in 1842 to convey drinking water some forty miles to the city.

## PUBLIC EDUCATION

Protestant reformers sought to Americanize immigrants by teaching them Protestant values. To this end, organizations such as the American Bible Society, the American Tract Society, and the American Sunday School Union distributed millions of booklets and essays. Another goal was free, tax-supported public education. In the mid-1830s, leading public school advocates like Horace Mann of Massachusetts denounced the intemperance, profanity, violence, and ignorance of the "dangerous classes" as vehemently as any Protestant preacher. Not only would public schools teach the three R's, Mann believed, they would also "inculcate all Christian morals," encourage good behavior, and serve as a "preventive and antidote" to the dangerous classes. In fact, Mann argued that free public education "does better than disarm the poor of their hostility toward the rich; it prevents being poor." It would thus become "the great equalizer of the condition of men."

Mann abandoned a successful law career to serve as secretary of the Massachusetts Board of Education, and thanks largely to his efforts the state legislature more than doubled its appropriations for public schools, substantially increased teachers' salaries, and established the first state college (called a "normal school") for the training of teachers. By the time Mann resigned his position in 1848 to run for John Quincy Adams's seat in Congress as an antislavery Whig, he had turned public education into one of the most popular reforms of the era. A proponent of "the glorious sphere of Benevolence," he also became a strong ally of other educational reformers. Among them was Boston's Dorothea Dix, whose tireless lobbying activities before state legislatures resulted in the establishment of prison educational facilities and state hospitals for the mentally ill.

Like other reform efforts, the public school movement had a bright side and a dark side. During the antebellum period, a growing number of northern states established public school systems that provided a basic education to millions who otherwise couldn't afford it. But reformers shaped curricula to reflect the interests of Protestant America. The Boston School Committee, for instance, described its mission among the city's Irish Catholic population as "taking children at random from a great city, undisciplined, uninstructed, often with inveterate forwardness and obstinacy, and with inherited stupidity of centuries of ignorant ancestors" and "forming them from animals into intellectual beings, and . . . from intellectual beings into Spiritual beings." Concerned about such challenges to their cultural and religious autonomy, Catholics responded with a nationwide network of parochial schools, hospitals, voluntary associations, and, eventually, colleges. These institutions were staffed by Catholic clergy intent on ensuring that health, education, and welfare comported with church doctrine.

From the 1820s to the 1850s, reform-minded Americans organized numerous movements to address new causes. A thriving market economy boosted many people into the

A typical view of a classroom c. 1850—in this instance the Emerson School for Girls in Boston, Massachusetts. Note the clock on the wall in the background and the bell on the teacher's desk. In schools, private or public, students not only learned reading, writing, and arithmetic, but also how to be punctual, time-oriented citizens.

middle class or higher, and this new prosperity allowed them to devote their energies to what they perceived as progressive causes. Just as important as economic prosperity was the widespread belief that the nation's good fortune would continue. The concept of America as a land of opportunity destined for greatness captured the popular imagination and paved the way for new utopian and charitable projects. Even though prejudice and racism pervaded society, unprecedented numbers of prosperous Americans sought to share their success, redeem the less fortunate, and reshape them in accordance with traditional Anglo-American values.

The reform movement also benefited from the telegraphs, newspapers, postal service, canals, steamboats, and railroads

## The Limits of Antebellum Reform

that allowed like-minded individuals to coordinate their ideas and actions over vast distances. Indeed, transportation and communication technologies were essential to the movement's success. But, even as the new technologies helped to create unity of action, other forces acted in the opposite direction. Sectional divisions that had long simmered at the surface of political life would soon boil over and absorb all of America in an escalating controversy that would shake the country to its very core. By the 1840s, slavery had become the great issue that divided the United States. And it would not go away.

## Suggested Reading

Robert H. Abzug, *Cosmos, Crumbling: American Reform and the Religious Imagination* (1994)

Jon Butler, et al., *Religion in American Life* (2003)

Sterling F. Delano, *Brook Farm: The Dark Side of Utopia* (2004)

Julie Roy Jeffrey, *The Great Silent Army of Abolitionism: Ordinary Women in the Antislavery Movement* (1998)

Carl F. Kaestle, *Pillars of the Republic: Common Schools and American Society, 1780–1860* (1983)

John F. Kasson, *Civilizing the Machine* (1976)

William S. McFeely, *Frederick Douglas* (1991)

David P. Nord, *Faith in Reading: Religious Publishing and the Birth of Mass Media in America* (2004)

Jan Shipps, *Mormonism: The Story of a New Religious Tradition* (1985)

Stephen J. Stein, *The Shaker Experience in America* (1992)

James Brewer Stewart, *Holy Warriors: The Abolitionists and American Slavery* (1996)

Judith Wellman, *The Road to Senaca Falls: Elizabeth Cady Stanton and the First Woman's Rights Convention* (2004)

# Chapter Review

## Summary

### QUESTIONS

- What is the significance of the Second Great Awakening? In what sense was it a force for innovations in America?

- Describe the most important Utopian movements of this period.

- What were the major beliefs and positions of the abolitionists?

- How did the women's rights movement emerge in this period?

- In what ways was social reform limited in this period?

## Key Terms

Hudson River School (p. 370)

Second Great Awakening (p. 372)

Abolitionism (p. 380)

Seneca Falls Convention (p. 388)

Temperence Movement (p. 390)

## Chronology

| | |
|---|---|
| 1824 | Robert Owen founds New Harmony. |
| 1826 | American Temperance Society established. |
| January 1831 | William Lloyd Garrison publishes first issue of *The Liberator.* |
| 1833 | American Anti-Slavery Society established. |
| 1835 | Anti-Slavery Society mounts "great postal campaign." |
| May 1836 | House of Representatives' gag resolution tables all antislavery petitions. |
| 1845 | Irish potato famine. |
| July 1847 | Mormon settlers reach the Great Salt Lake Basin. |
| 1854 | Henry David Thoreau publishes *Walden.* |

# Part 4

# THE DISRUPTION OF AMERICAN DEMOCRACY

HISTORY IS FULL OF IRONY AND CONTRA-DICTIONS, perhaps none more so than the two decades that preceded the outbreak of the Civil War. The great irony of that time was the juxtaposition of nationalism and section-alism—how intense nationalistic desires to extend the boundaries and thereby strengthen the United States coin-cided with equally intense sectional conflicts over the future of slavery in newly acquired territories. By the 1840s, a large majority of the population subscribed to the idea of Amer-ica's "Manifest Destiny" and applauded the territorial gains that came with the annexation of Texas, the settlement of Oregon, and the huge land cessions (among them, California) resulting from the Mexican War. Almost immediately, how-ever, disputes arose over whether these new territories should come into the Union as slave or free states. The country avoided disaster, thanks to the Compromise of 1850. But the truce did not last long, owing primarily to the South's intran-sigence on slavery and the refusal of Northerners to honor a key part of the compromise—the Fugitive Slave Act of 1851. Thereafter the United States faced one crisis after another, each of which stoked the fires of sectional antagonism. The final breaking point came in 1860 with the election of Abra-ham Lincoln as the sixteenth president of the United States. Unfairly viewed by many Southerners as a "Black Republican" and antislavery abolitionist, Lincoln's election prompted seven states—led by South Carolina—to secede from the Union and form the Confederate States of America in Febru-ary 1861. Within two months, Civil War erupted.

In the midst of these sectional clashes, the American econ-omy was growing at a torrid pace. Thanks primarily to the coming of railroads and the connections they made between far-flung regions of the United States, new nodes of economic

*The Battle of Antietam, a painting of a Union advance by Captain James Hope of the Second Vermont Volunteers. Over 4,000 men died on September 17, 1862, when the Battle of Antietam was fought.*

395

activity sprang up in the upper Midwest (wheat, corn, hog farming), the Great Lakes (lumber and mining), the Mountain West (mining and ranching), and the South (cotton, rice, sugar) that formed a dynamic link with manufacturing, agricultural processing, and mining enterprises in the East and Old Northwest (lower Midwest). Indeed, the growth of commodity output in agriculture, mining, manufacturing, and construction between 1839 and 1859 was an amazing 57% per decade, the highest of the nineteenth century. The extent of American growth became readily apparent to the rest of the world in 1851, when entries from the United States walked off with a surprising number of prizes and special recognitions at the London Crystal Palace Exhibition. Clearly the driver of American prosperity, in European eyes, was its rapid industrial progress and the inventive technologies that bolstered it. The fact that the U.S. Patent Office stood second only to the national capitol as the largest and most ornate building in Washington spoke volumes about America's love affair with the machine.

The Civil War proved just how powerful that machine had become. For four grueling years the opposing sides produced a harvest of death and destruction unparalleled in American history. Owing much to the technological innovations that preceded it, the war prompted an outpouring of weapons, food, and equipment on a massive scale in the North. It also witnessed the first large-scale use of railroads and telegraphy in warfare—the former for the movement of troops and supplies; the latter for the instantaneous communication of messages and the coordination of strategic movements over long distances. Professions like medicine were exposed to the winds of war and responded brilliantly by introducing numerous innovations in first-aid treatment, surgery, hospital care, and sanitation. The war also yielded lessons in the coordination and control of large organizations—lessons that would be put to use in the postwar business world. These and other changes clearly establish the American Civil War as the world's first industrially-based conflict. To the extent that it involved the massive deployment of all sorts of goods and services and involved large numbers of civilian as well as military participants, it also prefigured the advent of modern warfare.

With the defeat of the Confederacy, great hope existed in the North for peace and prosperity. The Union had been preserved and slavery abolished under the 13th Amendment (1865). Yet, while the North's industrial economy boomed in the immediate postwar years, the sullen South lay in shambles. Efforts to "reconstruct" the benighted Cotton Kingdom proved extremely difficult as President Andrew Johnson and the Republican Congress quarreled over what strategies to pursue. Johnson, a prewar Democrat from Tennessee, favored a lenient policy toward the South while his Radical Republican opponents pushed for more punitive and restrictive measures. At length, their differences led to the impeachment of Johnson—the first presidential impeachment in American history.

Although the Republican-dominated Congress succeeded in pushing through the 14th and 15th Amendments granting formal civil and political rights to former slaves, white Southerners vehemently resisted Reconstruction. Determined to pick up where they left off before the war, they tried to emasculate the new amendments by creating the Klu Klux Klan, resurrecting "Black Codes," and enacting other state and local laws aimed at restoring white supremacy and restricting the economic and civil rights of the freedmen. Such resistance, coupled with the onset of a serious depression in 1873 and political scandals in the administration of Johnson's successor, Ulysses Grant, drew Northern attention away from the South. Interest faded and Reconstruction ended after the disputed election of 1876, a disappointing failure that left most ex-slaves not only in poverty but without basic rights—an outcome that had serious long-term repercussions for race relations in the United States.

# Chapter 14

# NATIONAL EXPANSION, SECTIONAL DIVISION:

## 1839–1850

This post–Civil War painting, *American Progress*, by John Gast, shows the goddess "Liberty" (symbol of the United States) moving westward across the continent while stringing telegraph wire. Accompanying her are symbols of American progress—miners, pioneer farm families, stagecoaches, telegraph lines, and steam railroads—and fleeing from these forces are Indians, buffalo, wild horses, and a snarling bear.

397

- **How did Texas and Oregon become objects of American expansion?**

- **What were the major political issues raised by territorial expansion?**

- **How were American forces able to prevail in the Mexican War?**

- **How was the future of slavery becoming a political issue in this period?**

- **What was the significance of the California gold rush?**

- **How did the Compromise of 1850 address the issue of slavery in the territories?**

## Manifest Destiny

In 1839, editor John L. O'Sullivan published an article in his New York *Democratic Review* declaring that "our country is destined to be the great nation of futurity." Six years later, O'Sullivan coined the term "Manifest Destiny" to summarize his belief that the United States had "the right . . . to overspread and to possess the whole of the [American] continent which Providence has given us for the development of the great experiment of liberty and federated self-government entrusted to us." The expression quickly caught on among proponents of territorial expansion, but the basic idea was not new. From the early days of the Republic through the presidency of Andrew Jackson, political leaders had repeatedly stated that, as one Democratic congressman put it, "this continent was intended by Providence as a vast theatre on which to work out the grand experiment of Republican government, under the auspices of the Anglo-Saxon race."

O'Sullivan's phrase captured the essence of this view and brought Jefferson's "Empire for Liberty" and Jackson's desire to extend "the area of freedom" into a new era. But this period, in which Manifest Destiny reached its highest pitch, also brought the strains of sectionalism to a new level of tension. The counterpoint of national expansion and sectional division increasingly demanded political attention. And if the first principle of Manifest Destiny was Anglo-Saxon expansion, the lesson was that other people—Native Americans, Mexicans—would have to give way.

### THE TEXAS REVOLUTION

While Americans cast covetous eyes on the Southwest and Oregon during the 1820s and 1830s, the primary object of their attention by 1838 was Texas. Eighteen years earlier, a bankrupt lead-mine owner from Missouri named Moses Austin had secured permission from Spain to act as an *empresario,* or colonization agent, in settling 300 families from the United States in Texas. When Austin died in 1821, his son Stephen succeeded him. Stephen's plans were delayed, however, when the overthrow of Spanish rule in Mexico (1821) forced him to renegotiate his father's colonization agreement with the newly independent Mexican government.

Between 1824 and 1835, Austin brought more than 8,000 Americans into Texas, more than any of the forty other *empresarios* who had negotiated colonization agreements with the Mexican government. By 1835, the Anglo-American population in Texas reached 35,000, outnumbering the Mexican population there by 7 to 1. As Texas quickly became Americanized, tensions with Mexico increased. Cultural differences between the *norteamericanos* and Mexicans lay at the heart of the problem. American settlers had originally promised to become Mexican citizens, and to convert to Mexico's state religion of Roman Catholicism. But they remained strongly attached to the United States and continued to hold Protestant Sunday services, violating Mexican law.

A serious confrontation occurred in 1829, when Mexico's president abolished slavery throughout the country. Some 90 percent of Anglo Texans were American southerners who either owned slaves or expected to do so in the future, and they

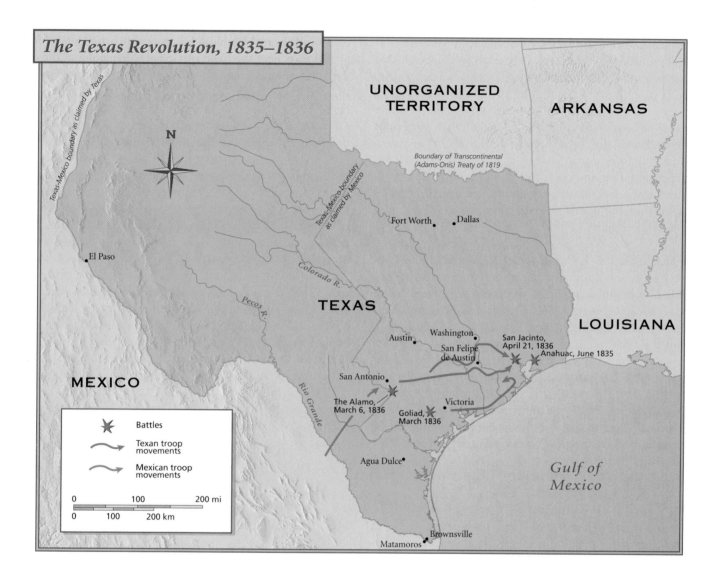

**The Texas Revolution, 1835–1836**

resisted abolition. Although angry protests induced the Mexican government to exempt Texas from its antislavery ruling, bitterness and distrust lingered. There were continual land disputes and Anglo complaints that they lacked a voice in Mexico's government. Mexican laws prohibited further American colonization and limited all labor contracts to ten years, which, in effect, meant a gradual end to slavery. Most threatening of all, Mexico began to garrison troops in Texas communities. With each passing year, the gulf between the American community and the Mexican government grew wider. So, too, did separatist sentiment on the part of the Americans.

Discontent soon turned to open resistance. Word reached Texas late in 1834 that the recently self-proclaimed Mexican dictator, General Antonio Lopez de Santa Anna, had decided to send an army to Texas to clamp down on the Americans. It was rumored that Santa Anna intended to disenfranchise them, abolish their local governments, and send them packing back to the United States. Aiming to preempt Santa Anna, a separatist "war party" of forty armed men led by William B. Travis seized a Mexican garrison at Anahuac on Galveston Bay in June 1835. Learning of the attack, Santa Anna resolved to launch an all-out military campaign to crush the rebels and teach all of Texas a lesson.

As Santa Anna's army moved north, it encountered increasing armed resistance. Yet as late as November 1835, a convention (called a "consultation") with representatives from a dozen American communities in Texas voted against declaring independence from Mexico. Instead, the delegates issued a Declaration of Causes for taking up arms, condemning Santa Anna's dictatorial regime while pledging loyalty to the Mexican government "so long as that nation is governed by the constitution and laws." But the convention also established a provisional government and named Sam Houston as the commander of its army. Slowly but surely, a Texas revolution was taking shape.

***The Alamo, Goliad, and San Jacinto.*** Angered and embarrassed by a series of military defeats, Santa Anna left Mexico City to take personal command of his army. Arriving at San Antonio late in February 1836, he struck his first blow against a contingent of Americans who had barricaded themselves behind the adobe walls of an abandoned mission called the Alamo. After ten days of fierce fighting during which his troops suffered heavy losses, Santa Anna's forces finally took the Alamo on March 6. Of the 187 Texan defenders of the Alamo, all but one died—the only survivor was a slave named Joe who belonged to Colonel Travis, the commander of the rebel garrison. Less than two weeks later, Santa Anna delivered another crushing blow. His troops surprised a rebel force of 350 men near the town of Goliad. After holding the captives for a week, Santa Anna's men marched them to a wooded area outside the town and shot them down in cold blood. Santa Anna, it was thought, ordered the massacre.

The Alamo and Goliad massacres united Texans as nothing had before. "Remember the Alamo," "Remember Goliad" became rallying cries that energized their revolution. Even while the Alamo was under siege, a convention of Texans issued a formal declaration of independence modeled on the American document of 1776 and formed the republic of Texas. As news of the escalating conflict filtered back to the United States, hundreds of volunteers crossed the border to join Sam Houston's army. To the consternation of the American population in Texas, Houston's outnumbered and ill-equipped forces retreated before Santa Anna's army for more than seven weeks. But all this time, Houston was drilling his troops and waiting for the right moment to strike a decisive blow. That moment arrived on April 21, when his rebel force surprised a segment of Santa Anna's army in a wooded area near the San Jacinto River. After fifteen minutes of vicious fighting, 630 of Santa Anna's soldiers lay dead on the battlefield, many of them killed out of vengeance; 730 more were taken prisoner. Texan casualties numbered 9 dead and 30 wounded. A day later, Santa Anna was captured trying to escape in the uniform of a common soldier.

***The Republic of Texas.*** The Battle of San Jacinto effectively ended the Texas revolution. Santa Anna was taken to the new government's temporary headquarters at Velasco and forced to sign two treaties: one recognizing the independence of Texas, the other pledging his support to the new republic and acknowledging the Rio Grande as its southern boundary.

Later that year, Houston was elected first president of the republic of Texas. Of the 6,000 persons who voted, 99 percent favored immediate annexation to the United States. Upon entering office in October 1836, Houston, pledged to fulfilling that task, dispatched a special agent to Washington with instructions to "make every exertion to effect annexation with the least possible delay."

The Mexican army assaulting the Alamo, 1836.

General Sam Houston, hero of San Jacinto and first president of the republic of Texas (1836–38).

By the time President Houston's emissary reached Washington, Andrew Jackson was in the final months of his presidency. His hand-picked successor, Martin Van Buren, had just won a convincing victory over several Whig opponents, yet Jackson seemed uneasy. Houston was a longtime friend and political ally, and Jackson would have liked nothing better than to annex Texas. But the abolitionist movement had gained considerable political momentum during the past year, and its leaders were bound to stir up a hornet's nest if debate over the annexation of slaveholding Texas reached Congress. Jackson was also aware that Mexico refused to recognize Texas's independence and that annexation would in all likelihood lead to war. Moreover, President-elect Van Buren, himself no friend of slavery, seemed cool to the idea of annexation. All these considerations, along with signs that the economy was about to enter a downward spiral, caused Jackson to back away from annexation. But on March 2, 1837, two days before he left office, he signed a document officially recognizing the republic of Texas as a sovereign state. Texas was not in the Union, but half a loaf was better than none.

## THE OREGON COUNTRY

While Texans stewed over annexation, American expansionism gathered momentum in the far West. At issue was the Oregon Country, half a million square miles that lay between the Pacific Ocean and the continental divide. Oregon em-braced not only the present states of Oregon, Idaho, and Washington and parts of Montana and Wyoming, but also almost half of the Canadian province of British Columbia, as far north as 54°–40′ latitude.

Before 1840, Oregon was primarily the domain of Indians, trappers, and fur-trading companies. While both Great Britain and the United States claimed the region, they had agreed in an 1818 treaty to a joint occupation of the sprawling territory. So long as settlement remained sparse and the fur trade prospered, the agreement worked reasonably well, with the British tending to stay north of the Columbia River and Americans to the south. The situation began to change, however, during the early 1840s. An increasing number of midwestern farm families down on their luck from the depression of 1837–41 sold what remained of their holdings and trekked along the Oregon Trail. A tortuous three-month journey across the continent and through the Rocky Mountains brought the farmers into the fertile Willamette Valley south of the Columbia River near Portland.

The American community in Oregon numbered less than 2,000 in 1843. Yet, to the chagrin of the British, it formed a

This cartoon about the Oregon boundary dispute shows a pugnacious "America" squaring off against his somewhat bemused and larger opponent, "England."

401

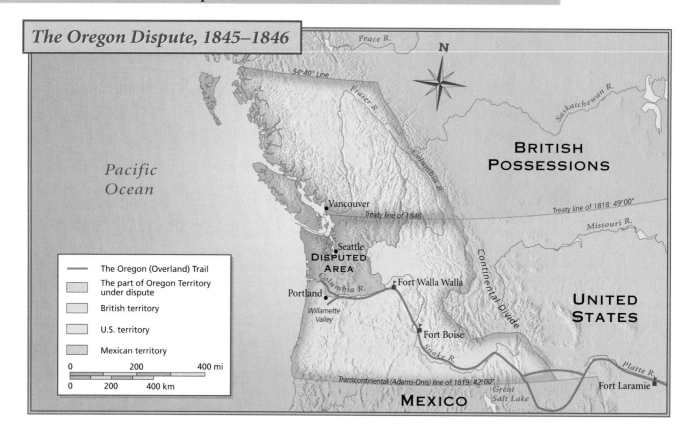

**The Oregon Dispute, 1845–1846**

Legend:
- The Oregon (Overland) Trail
- The part of Oregon Territory under dispute
- British territory
- U.S. territory
- Mexican territory

territorial government with the explicit intent that "the United States of America extend their jurisdiction over us." By 1845, the American population had more than doubled to 5,000. As "Oregon fever" spread, midwestern expansionists began to petition the federal government to end its joint occupation agreement with Britain and claim all of Oregon for the United States. Their slogan became "54–40 or fight."

## The Politics of Expansion

### THE ELECTION OF 1844

American voters not only chose a president in 1844; they also decided the question of territorial expansion. The electoral outcome was widely viewed as a national referendum on the politics of Manifest Destiny.

Of the four candidates in the field, the most visible was President John Tyler, a former Democrat turned Whig who ascended to the office in 1841 when William Henry Harrison

died suddenly of pneumonia after only a month in office. Next came Henry Clay of Kentucky, the economic nationalist and perennial Whig Party favorite who twice before—in 1824 and 1832—had run for the presidency, only to fail. Clay's Democratic counterpart was former president Martin Van Buren of New York, a staunch Jacksonian and party architect, who had been defeated in 1840 by Harrison. Last came Kentucky's James G. Birney, the candidate of the small but outspoken abolitionist Liberty Party. Of the four, only Clay and Birney would survive the nomination process.

President Tyler's chances of survival seemed remote by 1844. Democrats considered him a political renegade, and he had been drummed out of the Whig Party for vetoing several key pieces of legislation. As a politician without a party, Tyler needed a political miracle to retain his office and eventually withdrew from the race. Meantime, the Whig convention in Baltimore unanimously nominated Clay as its standard bearer. Fearful that "annexation and war with Mexico are identical," Clay opposed the annexation of Texas and called for "union, peace, and patience." In making no reference whatsoever either to expansion or to Texas, the Whig platform sidestepped the issue of slavery altogether.

Not so the Democrats. Although Van Buren was the early favorite, the Democratic convention ended up nominating James K. Polk. A former congressman, speaker of the House, and governor of Tennessee, Polk was a longtime supporter of Andrew Jackson, a stalwart Democrat, and an outspoken expansionist. Long before the convention met, he had indicated that he favored the immediate annexation of Texas. The Democratic Party's platform went even further, boldly declaring that "the re-occupation of Oregon and the re-annexation of Texas at the earliest possible period are great American measures." By adopting such an aggressive stance, the Democrats sought not only to attract both northern and southern expansionist votes but also to clearly demarcate themselves from the Whigs.

The election itself featured invective and mudslinging from all sides. Long-standing economic differences between Whigs and Democrats over tariffs, banking and currency, and revenue distribution paled in comparison with the Texas question and the larger issue of territorial expansion. Although Clay softened his stance on Texas annexation as the campaign wore on, his waffling probably cost him as many votes among Whigs as he won. Polk's expansionist views on foreign policy, on the other hand, attracted strong support in the Midwest and deep South. When the election returns came in, "Young Hickory" emerged victorious, but only by about 38,000 votes. Indeed, Clay might have won the election if he

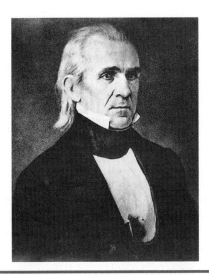

James K. Polk, eleventh president of the United States (1845–49).

had carried New York; but Birney's Liberty Party syphoned off just enough antislavery Whig support to give Polk a 5,106-vote edge and all of New York's electoral ballots. In this election, as in others, the presence of a third party made an enormous political difference.

### THE INTERNATIONAL DIMENSION

Despite his narrow victory, Polk claimed a popular mandate to fulfill America's Manifest Destiny. Convinced of the same, the outgoing President Tyler again pushed for the immediate annexation of Texas and, through some clever legislative maneuvering, succeeded at length in winning congressional approval. On March 1, 1845, three days before he left office, Tyler signed the resolution, and the congress of the Lone Star Republic voted unanimously for annexation on June 16. With President Polk's wholehearted approval, Texas entered the Union in December as the twenty-eighth state. The government of Mexico immediately severed diplomatic relations with the United States.

In the midst of the crisis with Mexico, Polk turned his attention to the Oregon boundary question. At least four times before, the United States had approached Great Britain about settling the boundary at the 49th parallel, only to be rebuffed. Bolstered by Democratic campaign slogans like "All of Oregon or none" and "54–40 or fight," Polk warned the British in his inaugural address in March 1845 that "our title to the country of the Oregon is 'clear and unquestionable.'" With threats of war rumbling on both sides of the Atlantic, the new president quietly informed the British minister to Washington that he would settle for the 49th parallel even though the United States had a rightful claim to all of Oregon. When the minister flatly refused the offer, Polk reasserted his original demand for all of Oregon, even if it meant war with England. In his message to Congress in December 1845, he even reintroduced the Monroe Doctrine to warn the British that "no future European colony or dominion shall with our consent be planted or established on any part of the North American continent."

The United States and Great Britain came dangerously close to war during the spring of 1846. Determined to follow "a bold & firm course," Polk notified the British in May of his intention to end the joint occupation of Oregon. Equally determined not to relinquish all of Oregon to America, Britain began to outfit thirty warships for action against the United States. But serious political problems at home caused the

British to alter their position and offer to settle the boundary at the 49th parallel. Reluctant at first to accept the deal but aware that war with Mexico was imminent, Polk submitted the treaty to the Senate. Although a few radical expansionists protested his "surrender" to the British and demanded "every foot or not an inch" of Oregon, the Senate ratified the agreement on June 15, 1846.

By the time the Oregon Treaty was signed, the United States had already declared war on Mexico, which refused to recognize Texas's independence and its subsequent annexation by the United States. Texas, in turn, insisted that its southern border lay along the Rio Grande rather than its original Mexican boundary at the Nueces River. And with expansionist sentiment widespread, Americans now sought to acquire the Mexican province of California.

American merchants and sea captains involved in the fur, whaling, and China trades had long known about the scenic beauty and commercial potential of California. But political leaders did not notice the area until a navy expedition under Captain Charles Wilkes sailed into San Francisco Bay in 1838 and subsequently reported that "Upper California may boast one of the finest, if not the very best harbour in the world." The publication of Wilkes's report in 1845 heightened the American appetite for California. Reflecting the business interests that some of his most important Massachusetts constituents had in the "Pacific trade," Senator Daniel Webster declared that "the port of San Francisco would be twenty times as valuable to us as all Texas." Although he differed with Webster on Texas, President Polk nonetheless recognized the value of California. Convinced that the British had designs on the region, he confided to a friend that "in reasserting Mr. Monroe's doctrine I had California and the fine bay of San Francisco as much in view as Oregon." Polk wanted California. It was the richest prize yet in North America.

### OUTBREAK OF WAR

The spark that ignited the war with Mexico came not from California, however, but from Texas. In June 1845, Polk ordered General Zachary Taylor and a small army of 1,500 men to move into Texas and occupy the disputed territory between the Nueces River and the Rio Grande, claimed by both Mexico and Texas. By July 25, Taylor had reached Corpus Christi on the Gulf Coast but decided not to move closer to the Rio Grande for fear of provoking war. While Taylor encamped on the south side of the Nueces near Corpus Christi, Polk re-

General Zachary Taylor, whose exploits during the Mexican War resulted in his election as twelfth president of the United States (1849–50).

ceived word that the Mexican government was willing to discuss the boundary question. He dispatched John Slidell of New Orleans to Mexico City with instructions not only to resolve the disputed boundary, but also to offer Mexico $25 million for California and another $5 million for the territory of New Mexico, plus the cancellation of $6 million in claims by American citizens against Mexico for the loss of property suffered during its many political upheavals.

When Slidell arrived in Mexico City in December 1845, the Mexican government refused to receive him, ostensibly because his appointment had not been officially confirmed by the U.S. Senate. By the time Slidell's Senate confirmation reached the Mexican capital, a new government had come to power that refused either to negotiate the Texas boundary or to receive Slidell. When news of Slidell's treatment reached Washington, Polk readied for war by ordering General Taylor and his enlarged force of 4,000 to move farther south to the banks of the Rio Grande. Taylor reached the north side of the river just across from the Mexican town of Matamoros on March 26, 1846. With each side suspiciously eyeing the other, the inevitable clash occurred two weeks later. "*War has commenced,*" an American soldier wrote excitedly in his diary, "and we look for a conflict within a few days."

News of the clash near Matamoros arrived the day after a disgusted John Slidell had returned to Washington and counseled the president that "nothing is to be done with those people, until they have been chastised." Convinced that he had no alternative, Polk sent a war message to Congress on May 10 in which he claimed that despite "every effort at reconciliation," Mexico "has passed the boundary of the United States, has invaded our territory, and shed American blood upon the American soil." Although both houses responded by passing war resolutions by large majorities, there was considerable dissent. Abolitionist and antislavery Whigs denounced Polk's actions, claiming that he had purposely provoked the Mexicans into hostile action in order to satisfy the interests of "Land Jobbers and Slave-Jobbers." At the same time, an obscure Whig congressman from Illinois named Abraham Lincoln challenged the Polk administration to point to the exact "spot" on American soil where American blood had been shed. Implicit in young Lincoln's "spot resolution" was the denial that Texas's boundary extended as far south as the Rio Grande as well as the charge that President Polk had maneuvered the United States into a war.

## THE WILMOT PROVISO

The Democratic Party was also divided over the war and its implications. A large majority of Democrats had initially supported Polk's expansionist policies, but they soon split over the future of slavery in the new territories. The flash point came when David Wilmot, a freshman representative from Towanda, Pennsylvania, introduced an amendment to an appropriations bill in August 1846 that excluded slavery from

Representative David Wilmot, author of the highly controversial proviso that prohibited slavery in any territory acquired from Mexico.

any territory that might be acquired from Mexico. Wilmot's "Proviso" shocked the Polk administration. Wilmot had consistently supported the president's legislative agenda, including the annexation of Texas, but he now pointed the way for "free-soil" Democrats who opposed the expansion of slavery into new territories. Free-soilers did not necessarily sympathize with blacks or support abolition. To the contrary, Wilmot himself viewed the West as a white man's preserve where "the sons of toil, of my own race and own color" could establish new roots without having to compete against either slave or free black labor.

Wilmot's amendment, which passed in the House but failed in the Senate, nevertheless had momentous consequences. By focusing public attention on the future of slavery in new territories, it pulled politics away from issues of national expansion toward the widening sectional differences between the North and the South. The issue of slavery in the territories would be debated and voted on repeatedly over the next fifteen years. And as slavery increasingly dominated the political agenda, sectional antagonisms grew more intense.

## "Jimmy Polk's War"

The Mexican War was fought mainly on three fronts: from the Rio Grande southwest toward Monterrey and Buena Vista; in California and the inner reaches of New Mexico; and from the coastal city of Vera Cruz westward to Mexico City.

### THE MAJOR CAMPAIGNS

From the outset, President Polk played a direct role in coordinating U.S. forces. Sending Zachary Taylor to secure Texas's southern boundary on the Rio Grande, he ordered a naval blockade of Mexico's eastern coast, hoping that it would force the Mexican government to accede to his territorial demands. Although the blockade succeeded militarily, it failed to bring Mexico to the bargaining table. If anything, it hardened Mexican determination not to yield to the bullying of the United States. Convinced that their army was stronger than the largely volunteer American force, that their country's rugged terrain would create logistical nightmares for the invaders, and that European nations—particularly England and France—would come to their aid, Mexican leaders brimmed with confidence.

But they soon had cause for doubt. At the Battles of Palo Alto and Resaca de la Palma in May 1846, Taylor's smaller army

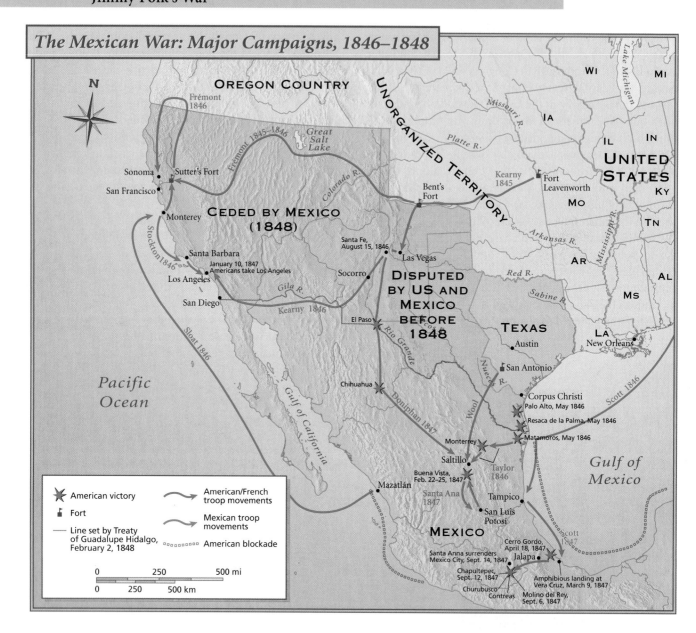

**The Mexican War: Major Campaigns, 1846–1848**

inflicted heavy casualties, forcing their Mexican opponents to retreat across the Rio Grande. Pressing the advantage, Taylor's troops crossed the Rio Grande, slowly moving inland toward the heavily fortified regional capital of Monterrey. Despite being outnumbered and outgunned, the Americans penetrated the city's outer walls and, after two days of intense fighting, took Monterrey on September 24, 1846. Continuing to penetrate deeper into Mexico's heartland, the Americans occupied Saltillo on November 16. There the invasion stopped because

Taylor was convinced that going farther into the heartland of Mexico would stretch his supply lines to the breaking point.

While Taylor's army rested at Saltillo, a much larger force of 15,000 men under the command of General Santa Anna marched northward to confront it. The two clashed just south of Satillo at Buena Vista, where Taylor's smaller army of 4,500, supplied with rifled firearms and light but mobile artillery, had taken up defensive positions in a battle formation that presaged what would become increasingly common during the Civil War. When two days of repeated assaults failed to dislodge the Americans, Santa Anna retreated—in effect ending the war in northern Mexico. Taylor remained with his army until October 1847, when he returned to New Orleans to a tumultuous welcome. A national hero, he began to contemplate a run for the presidency in the upcoming election of 1848.

Elsewhere, American forces were attempting to establish U.S. control over California and New Mexico. As in Oregon, several thousand Americans arrived in California during the early 1840s, most of them settling in the Sacramento Valley near a place called Sutter's Fort. Even before they learned that war with Mexico had been officially declared, a group of Americans revolted against local Mexican authorities in June 1846 and set about establishing an independent republic at Sonoma, replete with their own flag that carried one star and the symbol of a grizzly bear. Soon thereafter, a contingent of U.S. soldiers under Captain John C. Frémont arrived in the area to support the rebels while a U.S. naval squadron under Commodore John D. Sloat seized Monterey on the California coast and established control over the San Francisco, Sonoma, and Sutter's Fort areas. On August 17, Sloat's successor, Commodore Robert F. Stockton, announced the annexation of California to the United States with himself as governor and Captain Frémont as commander of "the California Battalion of United States troops."

While Stockton and Frémont sought to extend American control over all of California, a 1,400-man army under Colonel Stephen Watts Kearny marched westward from Fort Leavenworth (in present-day Kansas) with orders from President Polk to seize New Mexico and then move on to assist in the annexation of California. After easily taking Santa Fe on August 15, 1846, a small contingent under Kearney set out on a grueling march to southern California, arriving just in time to help Stockton and Frémont quell Mexican forces in the Los Angeles area. With the fall of Los Angeles on January 10, 1847, and all of California under American control, Polk's fondest desire was realized.

The third major American campaign began in October 1846. Polk and his advisers decided to attack Mexico's most important port at Vera Cruz and, from there, move an American army inland against Mexico City. The president turned to General Winfield Scott, an experienced senior officer and a superb organizer, to lead the invasion. Yet Polk was uneasy because he knew that Scott, like Zachary Taylor, had ties to the Whig Party and would probably use his military exploits as political capital once the war ended.

Calling for an amphibious landing of 15,000 troops, Scott ordered the attack on Vera Cruz in early spring before the deadly yellow fever season began. Much to Taylor's consternation, Scott also transferred more than half of Taylor's battle-tested veterans to the Vera Cruz expedition—a decision that prompted Santa Anna's ill-fated attack on Buena Vista in February 1847. Scott's strategy was to land American forces south of heavily fortified Vera Cruz, envelop it with artillery, and lay siege to it. The amphibious landing—the first of its type in American history—took place on March 9, 1847, when 10,000 troops went ashore in specially designed "surf-boats" requisitioned by Scott. Since the Mexican commander chose to remain behind the walls of Vera Cruz, the Americans experienced virtually no opposition. Blockaded by sea and cut off by land, the city surrendered less than three weeks later.

With Vera Cruz secured, the way inland lay open for Scott's army. The most challenging phase of the invasion began early in August, when Scott set out with more than 10,000 men on the final push toward Mexico City. At this point, he made a bold decision. Convinced that he did not have the manpower to maintain a supply and communication line to Vera Cruz, he decided "to render my little army a *self-sustaining machine*" by foraging off the land. In this, European observers

Scott's troops assaulting the fortress of Chapultepec, which led to the capture of Mexico City on September 14, 1847.

were convinced that Scott had committed a fatal error. "Scott is lost," the Duke of Wellington—perhaps the most famous soldier of the age—concluded. "He can't take the city, and he can't fall back upon his base."

But superb planning and leadership helped Scott's little army to endure and triumph. By August 20, 1847, the American forces had reached the outskirts of Mexico City. Outnumbered by more than three to one, Scott wisely decided not to attack the Mexican army under Santa Anna head-on. Relying on the advice of young engineering officers like Captain Robert E. Lee and Lieutenant P. G. T. Beauregard, he instead resorted to diversionary tactics and flanking movements to secure hard-fought victories at Contreas, Churubusco, Molino del Ray, and Chapultepec. On September 12, the first American troops entered Mexico City. The following day, Scott's 7,000-man army marched in. Santa Anna surrendered unconditionally on September 14.

### THE TREATY OF GUADALUPE HIDALGO

Although Scott's troops occupied Mexico City, a peace accord did not come immediately. Guerrillas posed a serious threat to the American invaders, and the Mexican government refused to negotiate. The war's cost in blood and treasure mounted, as did opposition to the conflict at home. A frustrated President Polk increased his territorial demands from Mexico, while ardent expansionists within the Democratic Party began calling for "All Mexico." Adding to Polk's irritation was his belief that a state department official named Nicholas P. Trist, sent the previous spring to open negotiations with the Mexican government, had botched the job and, even worse, had become a political ally of General Scott. Polk recalled him. Trist ignored Polk's order, however, and continued to represent himself as the official diplomatic agent of the U.S. government in Mexico City. Ultimately, on February 2, 1848, he signed the Treaty of Guadalupe Hidalgo, in which he committed the United States to pay Mexico $15 million and assume $3.25 million in claims of American citizens against Mexico—in return for the cession of California and New Mexico and the recognition of the Rio Grande as the southern boundary of Texas.

Although Polk was exasperated by Trist's conduct, the terms of the treaty largely fulfilled his original goals. He therefore decided to submit the document to the Senate for approval rather than heighten tensions festering within his party between southern "All Mexico" proponents and northern advocates of the Wilmot Proviso. Ratification came quickly. Although he would have liked more from Mexico, Polk seemed satisfied with the outcome. California and New Mexico, he told Congress in July 1848, "constitute of themselves a country large enough for a great empire." The United States now spread from the Atlantic to the Pacific. For the time being, America's Manifest Destiny had been satisfied.

### THE TECHNOLOGY OF WAR

A key to the U.S. victory lay in military leadership and superior technology. Although he lacked organizational ability and tactical sophistication, Zachary Taylor earned his battlefield nickname of "Old Rough and Ready" through sheer determination and coolness under fire. Winfield Scott, on the other hand, was a prickly and proper individual, as his nickname "Old Fuss and Feathers" suggested. Yet he proved to be a master planner and, in the Mexico City campaign, a brilliant field

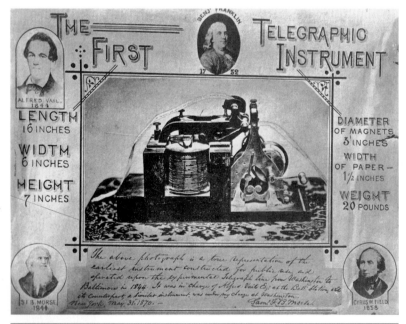

According to its inventor, Samuel F. B. Morse, this telegraph set was "the earliest instrument constructed for public use and operated upon the experimental telegraph line from Washington to Baltimore in 1844." Once successfully demonstrated, the new technology spread rapidly throughout the U.S.

*American Journal*

## How Do You Communicate?

*With few exceptions, American's hailed the introduction of the electric telegraph in 1844. The following excerpt from the 1851 edition of THE AMERICAN WHIG REVIEW exemplifies the popular enthusiasm that greeted "the Lightning Genius of the Ages," even comparing its potential with the exploits of the mythic Greek hero, Hercules. Note how the article exudes nationalist confidence and expansionist feeling while gliding over the sectional animosities that existed at the time. What areas of life does the writer expect telegraphy to affect? What does his essay reveal about the philosophy and purpose of the American Whig Party?*

"We find Electricity exercising and promising to exercise upon our times an influence not less than those of printing and the discovery of America in the days that have gone by. Steam seems feeble compared with it, and is, in fact, likely to be supplanted by it. Electricity is now doing a great many things, simultaneously—opening wonderful vistas into the coming time. It is still in its infancy; but, like Hercules, it is performing prodigies in its cradle . . . What its 'twelve labors' are yet to be, the most sanguine minds cannot venture of prophesy.

Of all countries, this is the most suitable for the Telegraph. Here the giant has amplest room to grow to full stature and stretch out his arms on every side. The telegraph is not succeeding in England as a trading speculation. The island is too circumscribed for that whose name and nature imply wide spaces. . . . In Germany . . . in France and other countries of Europe, where the telegraph is established, it is too much under the control of despots to be the beneficial agent it is designed and destined to be.

In conclusion, we must not omit to note one inevitable achievement of the electric telegraph,—the finest and most propitious of all! It tends to maintain the integrity of the Union; to bind the 'rods of empire' together in one magnificent fasces for Freedom to strike the tyrannies of the world with, or at least over-awe them. . . . To the arguments of those who anticipate separation on account of distance and extent of territory, the Telegraph replies by diminishing space and time in such a way that, in less than twenty years, all North America, from the Lakes to the Gulf, and from one ocean to the other, will be as compact to all intents and purposes as England was twenty years ago. Electric wires will bring the thoughts of the most distant States together in a few hours; and electric motors will cheaply bring the people of them together in a few days. And so, the Genius of the Great Republic—from Washington's Monument on the Potomac . . .—continue to extend her lightning fingers to all the extremest points of her continental dominion, and around an enlightened and happy brotherhood. 'Rivet the electric chain wherewith we are closely bound.' "

"Touching the Lightning Genius of the Ages," *The American Whig Review* 14 (no. 81; September 1851).

commander. Both men surrounded themselves with capable subordinates. In addition to Scott's Captain Lee and Lieutenant Beauregard, dozens of West Point graduates served in the Mexican War, many of them in the elite engineering, artillery, ordnance, and topographical engineering corps. Among them were Braxton Bragg, Ulysses S. Grant, Henry W. Halleck, Joseph E. Johnston, James Longstreet, George B. McClellan, George G. Meade, William T. Sherman, and George H. Thomas—all of whom would become renowned commanders some fifteen years later during the Civil War. The Mexican War thus served as an important training ground for the subsequent conflict.

The war previewed a number of new technologies that gave American forces a distinct advantage over their Mexican adversaries. By 1846, the United States stood second only to Great Britain as the leading industrial nation of the world.

Railroads and steamboats, two prominent technologies of the industrial era, were used to transport troops and supplies to the battlefront. Even the electric telegraph, only two years old in 1846, helped to facilitate the communication of military and diplomatic messages from Washington, D.C., to American outposts in Mexico. The experience gained with all three technologies served as a useful prelude to their massive deployment during the Civil War.

Of more immediate importance were the weapons used by American forces. By 1846, American armories were producing some of the most sophisticated small arms in the world. Regular infantry troops carried percussion muskets that were not only faster to load and more reliable than the older flintlock models used mainly by Mexican soldiers but also more easily repaired in the field, thanks to their interchangeable parts. Some troops, like Colonel Jefferson Davis's First Mississippi Volunteer Regiment, were armed with highly accurate (and interchangeable) rifles, while others carried the new six-shot revolving pistols invented by Samuel Colt of Hartford, Connecticut. Owing largely to their use during the Texas revolution and the Mexican War, Colt's six-shooters quickly became popular sidearms throughout the American West. All of these weapons traced their origins to the uniformity system of interchangeable manufacturing developed after the War of 1812 in America's armories.

In addition to the excellence of American small arms, the outcome of many important battles fought during the Mexican War hinged on the effective use of artillery. Thanks to design and manufacturing improvements introduced before the war, American artillery units were equal to any in the world. Although the American arsenal included howitzers and mortars for siege purposes, the basic weapon for use in battle was a "six-pounder gun," so-called because it fired a standard projectile weighing six pounds. Often referred to as "light" or "flying" artillery because of its impressive mobility, the six-pounder had greater range (1,500 yards) and fired a larger variety of pro-

jectiles than comparable Mexican guns. Gun crews could load and fire the piece in less than a minute, often three to eight times faster than their Mexican opponents. Under the supervision of West Point–trained officers, the flying artillery proved highly effective against numerically superior Mexican forces. Altogether, the success of American arms during the Mexican War verified the capability of the uniformity system of manufacturing introduced by the U.S. Army Ordnance Department at armories and arsenals before the war.

## The Election of 1848

The euphoria of victory could not dispel the tensions of a divisive war and a developing sectionalism. With the 1848 presidential election looming, President Polk, owing to declining health, chose not to seek a second term. Both major parties experienced the turbulence caused by the Wilmot

An 1848 election cartoon pointing to the difficulties Free Soil candidate Martin Van Buren faced in building an effective coalition between antislavery "conscience" Whigs, Liberty Party abolitionists, and "Barnburner" Democrats. On the far right, Lewis Cass waits for Van Buren to fall into the Salt River; on the left, abolitionists led by Horace Greeley and Abby Folsom beckon to the unsteady candidate while a concerned Charles Francis Adams (Van Buren's running mate) and William Lloyd Garrison look on.

Proviso and its sanctions against the spread of slavery into new territories. In New York state, for example, the Democratic Party had split into two hostile camps. The Barnburners, led by former president Martin Van Buren, supported the Wilmot Proviso. Their name came from their opponents, who charged that like the proverbial farmer who burned his barn to get rid of the rats, they were destroying the party in order to keep slavery out of new territories. The opposing Hunkers were conservative Democrats who "hunkered down," putting office-seeking ahead of political principle and taking a pro-South stand on the expansion of slavery.

Similar divisions also beset the Whig Party, with antislavery "conscience" Whigs squaring off against conservative "cotton" Whigs who did not want to rock the boat concerning slavery. Whigs and Democrats from the South often joined together in defending slavery, and their northern counterparts also acted together. These divisions and realignments beset Congress, where bitter feelings and at least one challenge to a duel fueled debate over a bill organizing a territorial government for Oregon. A bill excluding slavery from the Oregon Territory passed in August 1848, but only after nine months of debate and over the vehement protests of southern congressmen who believed that masters should be allowed to take their slaves into any new territory. All sense of decorum seemed to ebb away during the Oregon debates. As positions hardened over the expansion of slavery, Congress became a battle arena that pitted sectional antagonists against each other rather than a meeting place for working out common problems that faced the nation.

Tensions ran high in the presidential election campaign of 1848. Meeting in Baltimore, the Democrats nominated Senator Lewis Cass of Michigan. As ardent an expansionist as Polk, Cass strongly opposed the Wilmot Proviso, proposing instead that the inhabitants of each territory determine whether or not they would allow slavery—a formula that would become well known during the 1850s as "popular sovereignty." He also accepted the Democratic platform, which denounced abolitionism and evaded discussion of the great political issue of the day—slavery in the territories. In the view of Horace Greeley, the reform-minded editor of the *New York Tribune,* Cass's acceptance of the platform made him "the servile pimp of Slavery."

Although Henry Clay wanted the nomination, the Whig Party turned instead to "Old Rough and Ready" Zachary Tay-lor, the Mexican War hero. By his own admission, Taylor was apolitical. He had never joined the Whig Party; indeed, he had never voted. Even when supporters advanced his name as a possible presidential nominee, he maintained silence not only about slavery but also about other traditional Whig concerns such as the protective tariff and internal improvements. But as a Louisiana planter who owned more than 100 slaves, he seemed "safe" on the slavery question and therefore enjoyed strong southern support at the convention. Content to campaign solely on Taylor's war record, the Whigs adjourned without adopting a platform. As a sop to the disappointed Clay, the vice-presidential spot went to his friend and supporter Millard Fillmore of Buffalo, New York.

The evasive positions of the Whigs and Democrats concerning slavery failed to satisfy party members who supported the Wilmot Proviso or in other ways harbored antislavery sentiments. Such disenchantment burst into the open when Van Buren's Barnburner faction walked out of the Democratic convention in protest and, at its own convention at Utica, New York, nominated Van Buren as its presidential candidate. The Barnburner revolt within New York's Democratic Party set the stage for a much larger national gathering of pro–Wilmot Proviso Democrats, "conscience" Whigs, and Liberty Party leaders at Buffalo, New York, on August 9, 1848. Calling for a new third party based on antislavery principles to challenge the Whig and Democratic nominees, the delegates established the Free Soil Party with Van Buren for president and a platform that called for "No more Slave States and No more Slave Territory." "We inscribe on our banner, 'FREE SOIL, FREE SPEECH, FREE LABOR, AND FREE MEN,' " the platform declared, "and under it we will fight on, and fight ever."

Zachary Taylor won the election with 1,360,000 popular votes to 1,200,000 for Lewis Cass, a margin of less than 5 percent. Although Van Buren ran a distant third with slightly more than 291,000 votes (or 10.1 percent of the total ballots cast), he attracted enough dissident Democratic and Whig votes in the northern states to establish the Free Soil Party as a serious political force. The election demonstrated that the old issues—banks, tariffs, internal improvements—that had dominated American politics since the 1820s no longer held center stage. The future of slavery now dominated the discussion. What remained to be seen was how Taylor, a politically inexperienced military hero and slaveholder, would respond to the political instabilities he had inadvertently helped to create.

San Francisco, gateway to the California gold fields, was little more than a small town in 1849, with as many tents and shacks as houses. Telegraph Hill is in the background, as are dozens of ships bringing miners and supplies to the boomtown.

## California Gold

The one subject that attracted more attention than sectional politics was the discovery of gold in California. On January 24, 1848—less than two weeks before the end of the Mexican War—a worker employed by trader-entrepreneur John Sutter to build a sawmill on the American River some forty miles northeast of Sutter's Fort (soon to become the city of Sacramento) noticed a shiny golden particle in the flow of water from the mill's waterwheel. The worker reported his finding to Sutter, who tried to keep the news secret; still, word of the discovery inevitably spread through the local district and westward to San Francisco, San Jose, and Monterey. By the summer of 1848, hundreds of native "Californios" as well as recent American émigrés were rushing into the western foothills of the Sierra Nevada beyond Sacramento, hoping to strike it rich. Entire crews jumped ship upon anchoring in San Francisco Bay; soldiers deserted the army in droves; stores, sawmills, and brickyards closed; newspapers suspended publication for lack of workers; and commerce came to a standstill as merchants, lawyers, ranchers, and public officials abandoned their positions for the gold fields. In less than a month, San Francisco's population fell from several hundred to only a handful. The first phase of the California gold rush was on.

Although news of California's "gold mania" filtered back to the East Coast during the fall of 1848, it initially aroused little public interest. It wasn't until President Polk acknowledged in his annual message to Congress on December 5 that "mines of the precious metals existed to a considerable extent in California" that early skepticism gave way to enthusiasm. Groups of four to twenty pooled their resources and made ready for the arduous trip to California. From Maine to Florida and from New Orleans along the Texas coast to Corpus Christi and northward up the Mississippi to St. Louis, Louisville, Cincinnati, Pittsburgh, and the inner reaches of the Ohio, Missouri, and Tennessee Valleys, the reaction was the same. Thousands of men—young and old—from all walks of life departed by land and sea for the golden West in one of the greatest mass migrations in American history. Gold seekers also came from around the world, making the rush an international event. In little more than a year, the lure of gold swelled California's population from 13,000 to well over 100,000 by the end of 1849.

### THE MINING LIFE

The so-called "argonauts" who stampeded into California's gold district soon discovered that a miner's life could be difficult and disappointing. They worked ten to twelve hours a

412

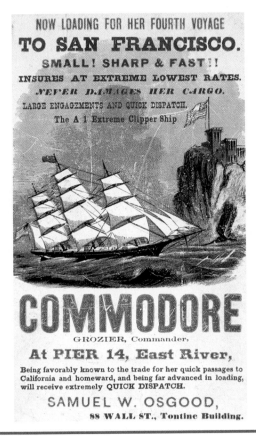

NOW LOADING FOR HER FOURTH VOYAGE
## TO SAN FRANCISCO.
### SMALL! SHARP & FAST!!
INSURES AT EXTREME LOWEST RATES.
*NEVER DAMAGES HER CARGO.*
LARGE ENGAGEMENTS AND QUICK DISPATCH.
The A 1 Extreme Clipper Ship

# COMMODORE
GROZIER, Commander,
## At PIER 14, East River,
Being favorably known to the trade for her quick passages to
California and homeward, and being far advanced in loading,
will receive extremely QUICK DISPATCH.
### SAMUEL W. OSGOOD,
88 WALL ST., Tontine Building.

Broadside offering passage to San Francisco on the clipper ship *Commodore.* Such postings could be found in virtually every American seaport during the late 1840s and early 1850s.

California's gold rush proved the adage about the early bird getting the worm. Gold seekers who arrived at the mines in 1848 and 1849 enjoyed considerable success. Some of them made even larger fortunes by moving into other occupations after they accumulated $1,000 or $2,000 in gold. Entertainers, merchants, doctors, and lawyers did especially well. Upon making $3,300 in less than two weeks after arriving in Sacramento, a young lawyer wrote to his parents in the East, "You have no idea of the extent of litigation in this city or the size of fees." Those who arrived at the mines after 1850 did less well. Although the annual production of gold in California soared from $10,151,360 in 1849 to an all-time high of $81,294,700 in 1852, per capita income among miners actually fell in that period. As more and more miners poured into California after 1850, they found that most of the best mining sites had already been taken up, subdivided into smaller plots, and begun to "play out."

## THE TECHNOLOGY OF MINING

The earliest miners found gold mainly by washing ore-bearing gravel dug from gulches and old streambeds in large tin pans. The heavier gold settled in the bottom of the pan as a miner swirled the water, gravel, and sand over the pan's lip. In order to increase their yields, miners working in teams, or "clubs," of four to six built downward-sloping wooden boxes set on top of rockers and open at the lower end. Called "rockers," or "cradles," because they resembled rocking chairs and baby cradles in their motion, such devices followed the same principle of washing and sifting gravel employed in panning. The advantage was that rockers processed a larger volume of gravel and hence yielded more gold. The gold settled in the bottom of the rocker during the washing process and accumulated against a series of raised wooden cleats positioned there. But the cleats did not catch everything, so many smaller gold particles were lost in the process.

So long as gold remained plentiful, rockers and the similar but larger "long toms" served miners reasonably well. Men working rich deposits on northern California rivers in 1848–49 typically earned $25 a day and, on rare occasions, as much as $500 to $5,000. Compared with the $1 wage that day laborers in the East commanded, these were fantastic earnings, even if the work was extremely difficult. But these profitable days did not last for long. During the early 1850s, new washing technologies, consisting primarily of extended lines of sluice boxes, were introduced to rework old deposits and capture fine particles of gold that had escaped the cleats of

day up to their knees in the icy waters of rushing mountain streams while shoveling gravel and panning for gold. Since few women were drawn to the mining camps, the men also had to assume domestic chores such as cooking, washing, and housekeeping. Given the physical intensity of mining and their inexperience with domestic work, most forty-niners not only ate poorly but also lived under primitive, unsanitary conditions. Many suffered from chronic illnesses such as scurvy or, worse, killer diseases such as cholera, smallpox, and dysentery. Those who could afford to eat at local boarding-houses or roadside kitchens frequently noted that a single meal cost as much in gold as they made in an entire day. On the East Coast, you could have a hearty breakfast for 25 cents; in the mining fields of California, the same meal might cost as much as $20. At a time when miners expected to earn from $20 to $50 a day, such prices became a fact of life.

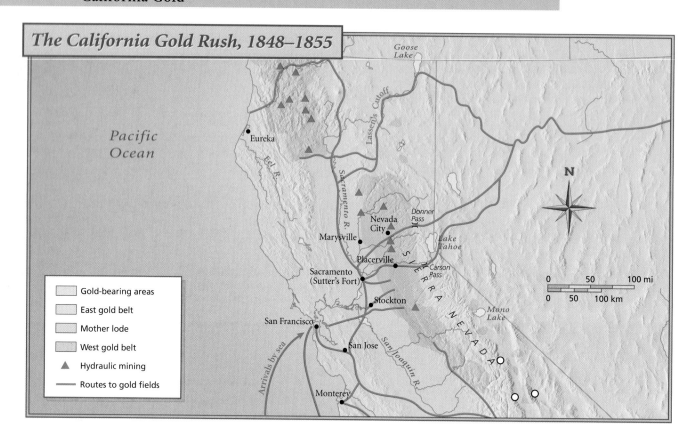

**The California Gold Rush, 1848–1855**

Legend:
- Gold-bearing areas
- East gold belt
- Mother lode
- West gold belt
- ▲ Hydraulic mining
- — Routes to gold fields

rockers. Miners also employed the age-old method of using mercury (commonly called "quicksilver") to absorb gold embedded in sands that had escaped their washing apparatus, then heating the amalgam in a vessel to burn off the mercury. They did not realize that the escaping mercury vapors would have toxic effects on themselves as well as on the surrounding environment.

By 1850, miners who had risked all to go to California were writing home that they could barely make ends meet. "I am perfectly astounded to see so few doing well," a store owner reported from the mining village of Placerville in 1850. "The real truth," a San Francisco newspaper subsequently reported, "there is gold still in those banks, but they will never yield as they have yielded. The cream . . . has . . . been taken off. We now have the river bottoms and the quartz veins; but to get the gold from them, we must employ gold. The man who lives upon his labor from day to day, must hereafter be employed by the man who has in his possession accumulated labor, or money."

The implication was clear: miners without money to invest in new technologies stood little chance of success. The day of

the small, independent miner working his own claim was passing. Taking his place were highly capitalized companies, often owned by absentee investors as far away as Boston. Such companies could afford the equipment and labor costs necessary to sink shafts deep into the earth in search of gold embedded in hard quartz rock, or build canals that would convey huge volumes of water under pressure to wash tons of earth from surrounding hillsides and deliver gold-bearing gravel to sluice boxes that sequentially washed and retrieved the precious metal. The latter method, called "hydraulicking," resulted in the construction of over 4,000 miles of canals and ditches in the Sierra foothills by 1857 at a cost approaching $11.9 million. The volume processed was enormous, as was the erosion that scarred the landscape.

As gold mining became increasingly industrialized, capital intensity replaced labor intensity, and miners who formerly worked their own claims became company employees. Although the resulting deforestation, erosion, and indiscriminate dumping of everything from mine tailings to personal garbage ravaged the landscape, no one seemed to mind so long as the mining operations yielded a profit. Whether owner, worker, or local merchant, the prevailing motto seemed to be "Get in, get rich, get out."

## POPULATION BOOM AND ETHNIC TENSIONS

The California gold rush had ripple effects throughout North America. California gold stimulated unprecedented economic growth by pumping over half a billion dollars into the American economy during the 1850s. Such wealth changed the face of northern California from a sparsely populated agricultural hinterland into a diverse economy that attracted not only miners and mine companies but also hundreds of businesses that catered to their needs. At the same time, mining camps sprouted into towns and towns into cities. San Francisco, for example, was little more than a trading outpost at the time gold was discovered at Sutter's mill in 1848. Within two years its population would boom to 25,000, and it more than doubled again by the end of the decade. Blessed with a great harbor, the city quickly became the West Coast's leading financial and commercial center as well as the location of foundries and machine shops that supplied the mining districts with everything from hand tools to steam engines. Similar developments occurred in Sacramento, Stockton, and leading mining towns like Marysville, although on a smaller scale. Serving as a gateway to the northern mines, Sacramento gained another advantage: it became the state capital in 1854.

California's growing population was dominated by men between the ages of twenty and forty. Unlike miners elsewhere, the forty-niners rarely brought their wives and children to California. It was too expensive, and the miners expected to get in and get out fast. In 1850, the mining town of Nevada City had a population of 2,683—97 percent male. In the nearby mining village of Grass Valley, men constituted 94 percent of the population. Although these figures would fall slightly during the next decade, men continued to outnumber women by a significant margin in California long after gold ceased to be its primary product.

Ethnic diversity was an early characteristic of the gold rush. Among the first to head for the gold fields were Hispanic Californios, though they were soon outnumbered by Americans. As the gold rush gathered momentum, miners arrived from all over the world—from Great Britain, Ireland, and Germany, and smaller numbers from Canada, China, Chile, Mexico, and France. Early on, this diversity brought lit-

Chinese and American miners pose next to a long tom.

tle social tension because there appeared to be plenty of gold for everyone. But as the tide of immigrants swelled, white Americans began to complain about foreigners taking jobs and claims that the Americans felt should rightfully belong to them. One proponent of this view protested that "nothing can be more unjust and immeasurable than for persons not citizens of the United States . . . to dig the gold found in California, on lands belonging to the American Government." Such ideas became popular among the American inhabitants of California and soon resulted in actions, both legal and extralegal, that aimed at reducing foreign influence.

Feelings of nationalism and racial superiority drove the exclusionist movement as much as the desire for economic gain. Lacking well-organized law enforcement agencies and courts to mete out justice, American-dominated communities organized vigilante committees during the early 1850s to curb lawlessness and root out undesirable elements. Since "undesirable" tended to conflate people of foreign birth with murderers, thieves, and prostitutes, the brunt of vigilante action most often fell on groups who were neither white nor Protestant.

California Indians and Spanish-speaking people became the first targets. The former, already small in number and weakened by over a century of European intrusions into their territories, were quickly dispersed and reduced to a condition of dependence. The latter, consisting mainly of Californios, Mexicans, and Chileans but indiscriminately

415

This San Francisco saloon, with its mix of Spanish, Mexican, Chinese, and Anglo patrons, might have been derogatively referred to as a "Spanish House."

law until officials suddenly rode into their camps, seized their property, and auctioned it off to satisfy their debts to the state.

A year later, the California legislature reenacted the foreign miners' tax but added a new wrinkle: although the law lowered the tax rate to three dollars a month, it excluded those who intended to become American citizens. But since a federal law of 1790 prohibited all but whites from becoming citizens, Chinese and other "colored" miners had no other option than to pay the tax. "It is strange that Americans are not willing to give foreigners an equal chance, when there is so much labor required to secure the uncertain gains which fall to the lot of the laborer here," an American missionary sympathetic to the plight of the Chinese observed. In mid-nineteenth-century America, religion, skin color, and cultural tradition mattered, in every section of the country.

## The Compromise of 1850

California's gold rush did not deflect national attention away from the growing controversy over slavery for long. California itself became enmeshed in sectional tensions in January 1850, when, at President Taylor's urging, its officials applied for immediate admission to the Union as a free state.

Angered by what they perceived to be the president's betrayal (Taylor, after all, was a Louisiana slave owner), southern politicians vowed to stop the process. In their eyes, the issue was critical because California's admission threatened to upset the equilibrium that currently existed between the fifteen free and fifteen slave states in the Senate. Since the North's population had long since outstripped that of the South, no such balance existed in the House of Representatives; nor did anyone expect the balance to be restored. All of the Oregon Territory as well as the upper part of the Louisiana Territory lay north of the Missouri Compromise line of 36°–30′. The best southerners could hope for was an extension of the Missouri Compromise line all the way to the Pacific, with the eventual establishment of slave states from the parts of California and New Mexico that lay below the line. California's admission as a free state would dash those hopes and thrust the South into the status of a permanent political minority. A growing number of white southerners became convinced by 1850 that antislavery forces in the North intended "to make war," as John C. Calhoun put it, "on a domestic institution upon which are staked our property,

called "Spanish" by white Americans, were viewed as posing the greatest threat to American control. Nativist agitators condemned their Catholicism and depicted them as the dregs of society who "dabble their hands in human gore as a pastime" and kill "with fiendish delight." Moreover, nativists used the terms "Spanish woman" or "señorita" almost always to refer to a prostitute, while "Spanish house" stood for the most depraved places of entertainment, regardless of the owner's nationality. Vigilante groups raided the mining camps of Hispanics and seized their property in a spate of actions that resulted in numerous deaths, arrests, and summary executions.

Although nativists aimed their attacks at all foreign groups during the early 1850s, they did so selectively and with varying intensity. European immigrants, for instance, suffered less abuse than Chinese and "other colored races." The selectiveness of American xenophobia became particularly apparent in April 1850, when the newly organized California state legislature enacted a law that levied a tax of twenty dollars a month on all foreign miners but then proceeded to collect the tax more consistently from Chinese and "Spanish" miners than others. Faced with loud protests, the legislature repealed the tax in March 1851, but not before it had worked enormous hardships. The levy hit Chinese miners especially hard. Because they tended to live apart from the rest of the mining community and could neither read nor write English, they remained unaware of the

Henry Clay presenting his California compromise resolutions to the U.S. Senate.

nally, every state legislature in the North except one had adopted resolutions calling for the prohibition of slavery in the territories. These grievances, and the attendant sense of crisis that gripped their districts, roused southern politicians to block the admission of California. Even moderate southerners were beginning to speak of secession. An unprecedented crisis was at hand.

### CLAY'S OMNIBUS BILL

Into this angry impasse stepped Senator Henry Clay of Kentucky, the "Great Pacificator" whose name had long been associated with the Missouri Compromise of 1820 and the resolution of the nullification crisis in 1833. Clay was seventy-two years old and in failing health, but his devotion to the Union was as strong as ever. Convinced that the Taylor administration was unequal to the task of solving the sectional crisis, Clay conferred with other Unionist stalwarts like Senator Daniel Webster of Massachusetts, and urged friends and fellow politicians to organize Unionist meetings to counter secessionist sentiments being spread by radical southern politicians called "fire-eaters."

On January 29, 1850, Clay entered the Senate chamber and asked to submit what he called "an amicable arrangement of all questions in controversy between the free and slave states, growing out of the subject of slavery." Clay then proceeded to count off the eight resolutions in his proposal:

our social organization and our peace and safety." Their only choice, as they saw it, was either to secure their position by getting the federal government to guarantee the future of slavery or to secede from the Union before it was too late.

Other issues were also exciting sectional tensions. President Taylor was urging New Mexicans to apply for statehood as soon as possible and to decide for themselves on the future of slavery—a position southerners found troubling given the president's stance on California. A bitter boundary dispute between New Mexico and Texas threatened to degenerate into an all-out border war. And having relinquished all their customs houses to the United States, and with them their primary source of revenue, Texans were upset that the federal government refused to assume the state's $10 million war debt. Southerners, moreover, deeply resented stepped-up efforts on the part of antislavery groups in the North to abolish slavery in the District of Columbia. They found even more galling the passage in northern states of "personal liberty" laws that prohibited local courts and law enforcement agencies from helping slave catchers return runaways from northern havens to their owners. Having lost thousands of slaves over the years, southerners were insisting on a more stringent federal fugitive slave law that would punish anyone who assisted runaways. Fi-

- the admission of California as a free state;

- the establishment of territorial governments for the remainder of the Mexican Cession (encompassing all of present-day New Mexico and Utah and parts of Colorado, Arizona, and Nevada) without any restrictions on slavery (which meant, in effect, that the territories themselves would decide on the future of slavery within their bounds);

- the settlement of the New Mexico–Texas boundary dispute at roughly the present limits;

- the federal government's assumption of Texas's pre-annexation debt as compensation for accepting an unfavorable boundary settlement with New Mexico;

- the promise that slavery would not be abolished in the District of Columbia without the consent of its citizens as well as those in neighboring Maryland;

- the abolition of the slave trade in the District of Columbia;

- assurance from Congress that it would not interfere with the domestic slave trade elsewhere in the South;

- and the passage of a new Fugitive Slave Act that would penalize anyone who attempted to interfere with the recovery of runaway slaves.

No sooner had Clay presented his "Omnibus Bill" than a number of Senate colleagues insisted on speaking against it. Southerners like Jefferson Davis of Mississippi felt that the South was getting the short end of the stick, while antislavery senators from the North, led by William Seward of New York, opposed the plan because they felt that it was too soft on slavery. A six-month debate ensued, beginning with a dramatic speech by Clay on February 5 and 6 that discussed each resolution in detail, warned southern disunionists that "war and dissolution of the Union are identical and inevitable," and ended with an emotional appeal to his Senate colleagues to draw back from the abyss and preserve the Republic as a shining example to the rest of the world.

The gravity of the situation drew crowds to Capitol Hill to hear Clay's speech and the others that followed. Among the most eagerly awaited was South Carolina's senior senator, John C. Calhoun, the most prominent southern politician and the acknowledged intellectual force behind the ideas of nullification and secession. Like Clay, Calhoun was not well at the time of the debates and, in fact, would not survive them. Bedridden, he dictated his speech to an assistant and on the appointed day had to be helped to his desk in the Senate chamber, where he sat in a slumped position, weak and emaciated, as a Senate colleague read the prepared text.

It was a solemn, even gloomy speech, filled with ominous references to how the constant "agitation of the slavery question" had snapped "some of the most important cords" that bound the Union together and "greatly weakened all the others." Once the last of these cords broke, Calhoun argued, only force could maintain the Union. At the same time, the speech displayed contempt for the Taylor administration's territorial policy and Clay's compromise. Although the South Carolinian offered no solution to save the Union, his warning about the South's discontent and the imminent danger that confronted the Union persuaded many listeners, including southern colleagues, of the need for compromise.

Three days after his speech, Calhoun left his sickbed and returned to the Senate to hear Daniel Webster's views. Because Webster was considered a free-soiler by many yet also known to support Clay's resolution, no one knew exactly what the "God-like Daniel" was going to say. But the crowds packed the Senate chamber to find out. "Mr. President," Webster intoned in his deep, resonant voice, "I wish to speak today not as a Massachusetts man, nor as a Northern man, but as an American, and a member of the Senate of the United States. . . . I speak for the preservation of the Union." He then spoke for more than three hours in favor of the compromise while urging his colleagues not to taunt the South with the Wilmot Proviso or reproach it about the extension of slavery into the territories when everyone knew that environmental conditions in those areas would exclude slavery in any case. Peace and conciliation lay at the heart of his message.

As soon as Webster sat down, reporters rushed to the nearest telegraph office to flash their reports back home. Across the country, partisan newspapers known for their criticism of Webster now hailed him as a great statesman and patriot. "He has this day exhibited a higher degree of moral courage than ever graced a great captain on the battle field," declared the Baltimore *Sun*. Even in the deep South, newspapers praised Webster for making "emphatically a great speech." In his home state of Massachusetts, however—supposedly friendly territory—the reviews were decidedly mixed. While some Whig newspapers supported him, others damned him as a traitor to the cause of free soil. Leading abolitionists were particularly upset. "He has walked for years among the gods, to descend from the empyrean heights and mingle . . . in a masquerade full of harlots and leeches," the educational reformer Horace Mann wrote in disgust. "'Liberty! liberty!' Pho!," Ralph Waldo Emerson confided to his journal. "The word *liberty* in the mouth of Mr. Webster sounds like the word *love* in the mouth of a courtezan."

In the weeks that followed, one senator after another mounted the podium to express his views on Clay's proposal. While speaking against the compromise on March 11 as "radically wrong and essentially vicious," William H. Seward of New York referred to "a higher law than the Constitution," a moral obligation that took precedence when it came to slavery. While the American Anti-Slavery Society printed 10,000 copies of Seward's speech for immediate distribution, southerners condemned the New Yorker's comments as inflammatory and irresponsible. As the debate rolled on and the hot, humid Washington summer approached, Clay and his supporters thought they had enough votes among southern Whigs and northern Democrats to pass the Omnibus Bill. But no one was certain.

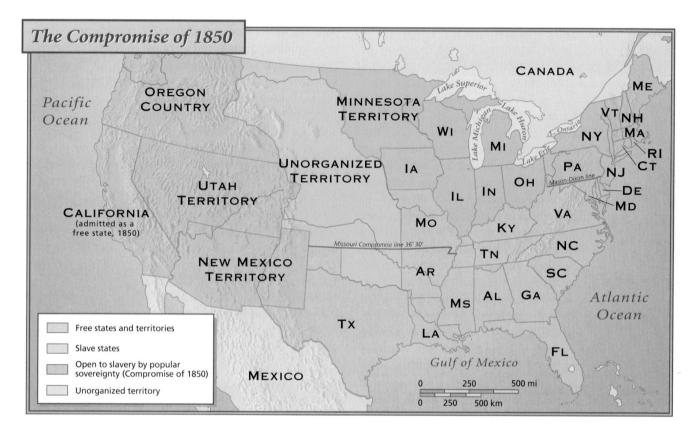

**The Compromise of 1850**

OREGON COUNTRY

Pacific Ocean

CANADA

MINNESOTA TERRITORY

UTAH TERRITORY

UNORGANIZED TERRITORY

CALIFORNIA (admitted as a free state, 1850)

NEW MEXICO TERRITORY

MEXICO

Missouri Compromise line 36° 30'

Mason-Dixon line

Gulf of Mexico

Atlantic Ocean

Lake Superior · Lake Michigan · Lake Huron · Lake Ontario · Lake Erie

ME · VT · NH · MA · NY · RI · CT · PA · NJ · DE · MD · WI · MI · IA · IL · IN · OH · VA · MO · KY · NC · TN · SC · AR · MS · AL · GA · TX · LA · FL

- Free states and territories
- Slave states
- Open to slavery by popular sovereignty (Compromise of 1850)
- Unorganized territory

0    250    500 mi
0    250    500 km

Southern "ultraists" continued to press for an extension of the Missouri Compromise line to the Pacific, and northern free-soilers attempted to insert the Wilmot Proviso into Clay's Omnibus Bill. Then, as the political skies seemed darkest, news arrived that President Taylor had suddenly taken ill on July 4. Five days later he was dead. Thrust into the limelight, his successor, Millard Fillmore of New York, made it known that he supported the Omnibus Bill. Yet when the bill came to a vote in the Senate on July 31, it collapsed under a rain of amendments that dismantled the compromise piece by piece. Shocked and exhausted, Clay sat at his desk with a blank stare, then silently left the Senate building.

Two days later Clay left Washington for some rest, but not before he pleaded with senators to pass the compromise measures as "separate and distinct" bills. Now the initiative passed to Stephen A. Douglas, an ambitious, thirty-seven-year-old first-term Democratic senator from Illinois whom an adversary described as a "steam engine in britches." Following Clay's call, Douglas broke up the Omnibus Bill into separate pieces and presented them to the Senate one at a time. This time the strategy succeeded. By the time Clay returned to Washington on August 27, the Senate had approved all but one of the measures. Three weeks later, both houses of Congress sanctioned the measures, and President Fillmore signed them into law.

## A GENERATION PASSES

The Compromise of 1850 represented a great political victory for Douglas, Webster, Fillmore, and, not least of all, Clay. All of Washington seemed to breathe a sigh of relief knowing that Congress had successfully passed through one of its most tumultuous sessions and that, for the first time in six years, it could meet without immediately getting embroiled in clashes over slavery. In the weeks that followed, crowds gathered in the streets to celebrate the accord, while great parties took place on Capitol Hill.

But not everyone shared these sentiments. "The question of slavery in the territories," abolitionist senator Salmon Chase of Ohio warned, "has been avoided. It has not been settled." Chase had a point. There were fundamental ambiguities in the Compromise of 1850, not least of which was the disposition of slavery in the territories. So long as northern congressmen could tell their constituents that the people of each territory could decide for themselves on the future of slavery while, at the same time, southern congressmen could report that the Wilmot Proviso was dead and that slave owners had the right to take their slaves into any territory, this key question remained unanswered. Moreover, it was not clear whether northern states would stand for a new Fugitive Slave Act that demanded that local bystanders assist slave catchers, denied fugitives the right to a trial by jury and to testify on their own behalf, and subjected anyone who either concealed or prevented the capture of an escaped slave to a fine of $1,000 and up to six months in prison. In these respects, the compromise measures represented more of a truce than a final settlement of the slavery question. But for the moment, many people chose to celebrate the occasion and hope for the best.

The debates leading to the Compromise of 1850 marked the last time that "the great triumvirate" of Daniel Webster, Henry Clay, and John C. Calhoun would appear together in the public arena. For nearly forty years, they had occupied center stage in American politics and had played key roles in the triumphs and failures of the era. Calhoun died in March 1850, before the debates had ended, and Clay and Webster would follow him to the grave within two years. Their passing signified a changing of the guard. From a generation who knew the founders of the Republic, experienced first-hand the threats to the new nation's survival during the War of 1812, and appreciated the expediency of compromise in the interest of preserving the Union, leadership passed to a younger, less patient generation of politicians raised in the party battles of the Jacksonian era and exposed to a new, more powerful

America in the throes of industrialization, economic growth, geographic expansion, and sectional conflict. The new generation included not only Stephen Douglas, Salmon Chase, and William Seward but also Jefferson Davis of Mississippi, Robert Barnwell Rhett of South Carolina, Abraham Lincoln of Illinois, and Charles Sumner of Massachusetts. It remained to be seen how well they would navigate the uncharted political waters of the 1850s and, most important, whether they could maintain the fragile bonds of the Union.

## Suggested Reading

William J. Cooper, *The South and the Politics of Slavery, 1828–1856* (1978)

Donald S. Frazier, ed., *The United States and Mexico at War* (1998)

William W. Freehling, *The Road to Disunion* (1990)

Michael F. Holt, *The Rise and Fall of the American Whig Party* (1999)

J. S. Holliday, *Rush for Riches: Gold Fever and the Making of California* (1999)

Robert W. Johannsen, *To the Halls of the Montesumas: The Mexican War in the American Imagination* (1985)

Susan Lee Johnson, *Roaring Camp: The Social World of the California Gold Rush* (2000)

Frederick Merk, *Manifest Destiny and Mission in American History* (1963)

Allan Nevins, *Ordeal of the Union, Vol. 1: Fruits of Manifest Destiny* (1947)

Rodman W. Paul, *California Gold: The Beginning of Mining in the Far West* (1947)

John C. Waugh, *On the Brink of Civil War: The Compromise of 1850 and How It Changed the Course of American History* (2003)

David J. Weber, *The Mexican Frontier, 1821–1846* (1982)

# Chapter Review

## Summary

### QUESTIONS

- What beliefs were attached to the slogan "Manifest Destiny?"
- What was the "Wilmot Proviso" and what was its significance?
- Why did the United States go to war with Mexico?
- What advantages did the United States possess in its war with Mexico? What disadvantages?
- What was the Compromise of 1850 and why did it fail?

## Key Terms

Manifest Destiny (p. 398)

Wilmot Proviso (p. 405)

The Mexican War (p. 405)

The Gold Rush (p. 412)

The Compromise of 1850 (pp. 416–419)

## Chronology

| | |
|---|---|
| March 6, 1836 | Fall of the Alamo |
| April 21, 1836 | Battle of San Jacinto ends Texas revolution. |
| December 1845 | Texas joins the Union. |
| April 25, 1846 | Mexican War begins at the Rio Grande. |
| June 15, 1846 | Oregon Treaty ratified. |
| August 1846 | The Wilmot Proviso introduced. |
| August 15, 1846 | United States takes New Mexico. |
| January 10, 1847 | United States takes California. |
| September 14, 1847 | Santa Anna surrenders. |
| January 24, 1848 | Gold first spotted in California. |
| February 2, 1848 | Treaty of Guadalupe Hidalgo. |
| September 1850 | The Compromise of 1850 (including the Fugitive Slave Act) signed into law. |

# Chapter 15

# A HOUSE DIVIDING:

## 1851–1860

American displays at the Crystal Palace.

- **How were technology and nationalism intertwined in the 1850s?**
- **How did an American science develop from explorations of the continent?**
- **What kept the slavery issue so divisive in the early 1850s?**
- **How did the debate over a transcontinental railroad heighten sectional divisions?**
- **How did the chances for sectional compromise diminish in the late 1850s?**
- **What was the significance of the 1860 election?**

## The Crystal Palace: Technology and Empire

As Americans celebrated the Compromise of 1850 and California gold poured into the nation's coffers, an event was being planned in London that would propel the United States in a new direction. Formally called "The Great Exhibition of the Works of Industry of All Nations," it quickly became known as the Crystal Palace, after the massive, iron-framed exhibit building whose plate-glass exterior sparkled like a crystal. The great exhibition ostensibly sought to celebrate peace and good will among nations while emphasizing the benefits of free trade. But it was more than that. The first of numerous world fairs to be held during the next fifty years, the Crystal Palace celebrated the technological progress of the age, and the political and military might that flowed from it. Technology as an engine of economic growth and colonial expansion was the unstated but central theme of the fair.

The exhibition opened to the public on May 1, 1851, with no less than 14,000 exhibitors—almost half of them foreigners, including many from France—mounting displays in the twenty-two-acre hall. While Austria, Belgium, and Russia sent finely crafted luxury objects embellished with jewels and precious metals, the Americans emphasized practical items such as soap and India rubber boots, as well as agricultural goods like "Henrico County" tobacco and South Carolina cotton. Upon visiting the Crystal Palace, Queen Victoria dismissed the American exhibits as "certainly not very interesting." The British humor magazine *Punch* went further: "We could not help . . . being struck by the glaring contrast between large pretension and little performance, as exemplified in the dreary

and empty aspect of the large space claimed by and alloted (*sic*) to America. . . . For a calculating people, our friends the Americans are thus far terribly out in their calculations." Although the New York editor Horace Greeley railed against such "meanly invidious and undeserved . . . slurs," even he had to admit that "the show from the United States disappoints." The *Richmond Enquirer* was more philosophical. "We often talk as if we were the only civilized nation on earth," its editor observed. "It is time that the conceit was taken out of us."

But British opinion of the American exhibits began to change once various juries started to examine the "Yankee notions" and submit them to competitive tests. The event that initially caught people's attention was a field trial in which two American-made reaping machines—one by Cyrus Hall McCormick of Chicago, the other by Obed Hussey of Baltimore—did extremely well. An English observer noted, "These reapers will cut from twelve to twenty acres of wheat in a day." McCormick's reaper won a coveted gold Council Medal from the jury on agricultural implements.

Other American entries received prestigious Council Medals as well, among them Charles Goodyear's patented India rubber garments and life rafts and Gail Borden Jr.'s "patent meat biscuits," used by the U.S. Army. Altogether, American exhibitors won 159 awards at the Crystal Palace exhibition—far fewer than the British and the French but nonetheless a very respectable showing.

The ultimate Yankee victory came on August 28, when the yacht *America* defeated the British *Titania* in a race off the coast at Cowes to win what later became known as the America's Cup. Unlike the competition for medals, where judgments could be subjective and open to national bias, the yacht race was an open competition decided solely by the skill of the participants and the quality of their vessels. The *America*'s rout of its British rivals came as a stunning blow to English pride. The *Liverpool Times* declared, "The Yankees are no longer to be ridiculed, much less despised. The new world is bursting into greatness—walking past the old world, as the Americans did to the yachts at Cowes. . . . America, in her own phrase, is 'going ahead' and will assuredly pass us unless we accelerate our speed."

### THE COLT PISTOL AND NATIONALIST EXPANSION

Nowhere was American ambition more evident at the Crystal Palace than in the activities of Samuel Colt. The inventor of a fast-firing six-shot pistol bearing his name, Colt went to London intent on drumming up international business for his factory in Hartford, Connecticut. With a workforce of 300 men and an annual output of 55,000 pistols, Colt's armory was already the largest and soon to be the most technologically advanced in America. As much a showman as an entrepreneur, Colt displayed more than 500 "patent revolvers" along with a few experimental repeating rifles at his booth in the Crystal Palace. Hundreds of visitors flocked to the exhibit, where they examined the inventor's pistols and listened to his promotional stories.

One of Colt's favorite tales was how, in the summer of 1844, fifteen Texas Rangers armed with his revolvers drove off about eighty Comanche Indians by "boldly attacking them upon their own ground, killing & wounding about half their number." The implicit message that the Colt revolver had introduced a new calculus of warfare was not lost on British military officials, who were engaged in similar wars of colonial expansion and conquest. In their view, the Colt revolver represented Anglo-Saxon ingenuity at its best and the ultimate tool of empire. Like so many other mid-nineteenth-century Americans caught up in the cult of technological progress and nationalist expansion, Colt could not see its racist implications. For him, the "progress of the age" meant the triumph of the Anglo-Saxon race and its associated Protestant principles, repub-lican institutions, and business systems. "Barbarians" and "savages"—whether Indians, Mexicans, or black Americans—had to submit to the dominant white man's civilization or be annihilated. In Colt's mind, his revolver was a "peace maker," an instrument of civilization.

Colt's pistols drew interest in his manufacturing methods as well as his products. Impressed by his remarks on these methods, the British government appointed a three-man Committee on the Machinery of the United States of America, made up of ordnance and artillery specialists, to investigate what was increasingly being referred to in England as "the American system of manufactures." Before leaving the United States in August 1854, the committee purchased over $100,000 worth of machinery and tools from two machine shops connected with the Springfield Armory, one of them the Crystal Palace award–winning firm of rifle manufacturers Robbins and Lawrence of Windsor, Vermont.

Earmarked for use at the Royal Small Arms Manufactory at Enfield, England, this equipment represented the first large-scale transfer of American manufacturing technology to a foreign country. Before 1854, the flow of technology had been in the opposite direction, with the United States as the perpetual borrower. Now, with firms like Colt and Robbins and Lawrence pursuing global markets, American technology—particularly machine tools, firearms, sewing machines, and other products made by armory methods—began to be exported overseas on a regular basis. More than the textile mills of Lowell or the nation's railroad system, "armory practice"

In 1851, Samuel Colt's steam-powered factory in Hartford, Connecticut, was the largest and most advanced privately owned armory in the United States and a showplace of American industry. Note the factory's Russian-style cupola, reflective of Colt's recent visit to Russia.

was the technology Europeans considered most novel, wanted to learn about, and began to acquire on an increasing scale beginning in the mid-1850s. Although the American arms industry was small compared with the textile and railroad industries, its impact throughout the world soon became significant, because its machine-based methods could also be applied to such products as pocket watches, typewriters, bicycles, business machines, and eventually automobiles. To supply the growing demand for armory-spawned technologies, a specialized machine-tool industry emerged in the Connecticut Valley during the late 1850s. And the catalyst for all this activity had been the Crystal Palace exhibition in London.

## An American Science

Despite the European accolades for American engineers and manufacturers, the pursuit of science in America was looked on as an adjunct to European science. With the exception of Benjamin Franklin and possibly one or two lesser figures, Americans were considered amateurs. While Americans collected and classified natural materials, Europeans formulated grand theories. In Europe, science had long enjoyed royal patronage as well as high social prestige, but American culture emphasized utility over purely intellectual pursuits. What counted most in the United States was empirical research that yielded practical results.

Still, the United States could boast a few world-class scientists in 1851, who were determined to challenge Europe's scientific superiority. Chief among them was Joseph Henry, head of the recently established (1846) Smithsonian Institution, whose pathbreaking research on electromagnetism had led, in 1844, to Samuel F. B. Morse's invention of the electric telegraph. Joining Henry was Alexander Dallas Bache, a graduate of West Point and an expert in terrestrial magnetism (the earth's magnetic field), who headed the Washington-based U.S. Coast Survey and whose great-grandfather was Benjamin Franklin. Henry and Bache gathered around them an inner circle of a half-dozen leading scientists half jokingly referred to as the "Lazzaroni," an Italian word for "beggars." Their purpose was to campaign against sloppy scientific amateurism while emulating the professional manner in which the best European scientists worked. The Lazzaroni hoped eventually to overtake, even surpass, the Europeans in scientific productivity and sophistication. An important result of

Joseph Henry, America's leading scientist and first secretary of the recently established (1846) Smithsonian Institution in Washington, D.C.

their efforts was the establishment of the American Association for the Advancement of Science, which held its first meeting in 1848 and represented a new stage in the development of American science.

From the outset, a major problem facing the association was locating financial support for scientific research. Indeed, the support for science to be found in the universities of Germany, France, and Britain had no equivalent in the United States. American colleges in the 1850s emphasized teaching over research and, in any case, lacked the money to build laboratories and procure the necessary equipment for serious scientific investigation. Reformers thus looked to government institutions, both state and federal, to take the lead in supporting the "new science" in America.

### GEOLOGICAL SURVEYS

In the states, the first support for the projects of science came from geological surveys. Spawned by the internal improvement programs of the 1820s and 1830s, these surveys reported on mineral deposits, soil conditions, and other "objects of interest" to state legislatures. Above all, they played a significant role in developing the use of anthracite and bituminous coal as major energy sources in the United States. Often the surveys went beyond their immediate, practical purposes, an English geologist noted, to "collect facts and publish speculations which they deemed likely to illustrate the general principles of the science and lead to a sound theoretical conclusion." In Pennsylvania,

### An American Science

for example, a state geological survey, initiated in 1836 at the behest of owners of anthracite coal mines, advanced the scientific study of mountain systems while providing valuable geological information on the location of coal deposits to mining companies. Nonetheless, geologists often found themselves at loggerheads with state legislatures who wanted less scientific theorizing and more "practical and useful" knowledge from the projects they supported. Many geologists gained "practical" experience with mining on such state surveys that launched them into new careers as private consultants to the mining industry.

### FEDERAL SUPPORT FOR SCIENCE

At the federal level, four agencies—the Smithsonian Institution, the U.S. Coast Survey, the U.S. Naval Observatory, and the U.S. Army Topographical Engineers—were the primary catalysts of scientific research. Under Joseph Henry, the Smithsonian aspired to become the nation's leading scientific establishment. Henry, who had little use for amateurism in science, sought to fashion it into an elite institute for advanced study by providing peer-selected scientists with research grants and then publishing their findings. Doing so, he believed, would fulfill the Smithsonian's charter for increasing and diffusing knowledge. But other government officials had their own ideas about what the Smithsonian should be doing, with the result that Henry struggled throughout the 1850s to implement his vision of basic science while trying to satisfy calls for more "useful" services.

One such innovation was a meteorology program at the Smithsonian in which observers from around the country collected daily information about weather conditions and telegraphed it to Washington. There, the data were posted daily on a national "weather map" and made available to newspapers across the country. (Once it became linked with a nationwide telegraph system after the Civil War, the program led to the development of modern weather reporting.) Another innovation was the creation of a National Museum at the Smithsonian to house patent models and other "curiosities" from the U.S. Patent Office along with natural history specimens brought back to Washington by government-sponsored exploring expeditions. Under the curatorship of Henry's talented assistant, Spencer Baird, the National Museum soon became the Smithsonian's most important branch and a beehive of activity in zoology, botany, ornithology, and other areas of natural history. Baird not only collected and studied these materials, he also tutored and helped to equip a generation of army, navy, and civilian explorers who set out to probe the American continent and

the oceans that lay beyond. Even more than Henry, he gave the Smithsonian Institution its enduring character.

Baird's success as an institution builder and scientific impresario brought him lasting relationships with a wide circle of professional and amateur scientists. Foremost among the amateurs was George Perkins Marsh, a diplomat-politician from Vermont who coached Baird in the intricacies of Washington politics and played a key role in securing his appointment at the Smithsonian. At a time when few professional scientists paid attention to the environmental costs of the industrial age, Marsh, like his fellow New Englander Henry David Thoreau, concerned himself with changes in the land and warned that people were rapidly making the earth "an unfit home for its noblest inhabitants." After several decades of fieldwork, Marsh published *Man and Nature, or Physical Geography Modified by Human Action* (1864), an original, authoritative look at nature's interconnectedness. Contrary to most scientific thinking at the time, Marsh argued that even small disturbances of nature's equilibrium could accumulate to transform the land and its creatures. "Man is ever a disturbing agent," he declared. "Wherever he plants his foot, the harmonies of nature are turned to discords." Foreshadowing a basic dispute among environmentalists, Marsh and Thoreau differed on what to do about environmental deterioration. Marsh was a conservationist who believed in selective harvesting and replenishment, while Thoreau was a pure preservationist. Both are regarded as precursors of today's environmental movement.

As important as the Smithsonian Institution was in promoting science in mid-nineteenth-century America, it was not the federal government's largest scientific operation. The U.S. Coast Survey's annual appropriations dwarfed those of the Smithsonian and supported five times as many scientific projects. Mapping the shorelines of the United States, the Coast Survey existed primarily to serve maritime navigation.

Maritime navigation was also the focus of Lieutenant Matthew Fontaine Maury, a commander of the U.S. Naval Observatory in Washington. Maury's staff gathered astronomical information as well as entries from hundreds of ships' logs on winds, currents, and general oceanographic data. From this work emerged six series of *Wind and Current Charts*, accompanied by a frequently updated book of *Sailing Directions* that proved enormously useful not only to naval commanders but also to commercial seamen engaged in whaling or the flourishing China trade. Thanks largely to Maury's analyses, ships sailing from New York to San Francisco in 1855 reduced their passage time by 26 percent, from 180 to 133 days. The previous year, the Boston clipper ship *Flying Cloud* achieved a record passage time from Boston to San Francisco of 89 days and 8 hours.

## WILKES'S NAVAL EXPEDITION

Of all the scientific activities sponsored by the U.S. government, military expeditions to the "western country" yielded the largest quantity of data and, arguably, the most impressive results. After Lewis and Clark's Corps of Discovery during Thomas Jefferson's presidency, the most productive of these early missions was the navy's United States Exploring Expedition between 1838 and 1842. Commanded by Lieutenant Charles Wilkes, a flotilla of six small ships embarked from Hampton Roads, Virginia, on a voyage that took it around Cape Horn, along 1,500 miles of Antarctica's coastline, into the central Pacific islands of Fiji and Hawaii, and, most important, as far north as the Columbia River, the inland waters of the Oregon Territory, and the Strait of Juan de Fuca near present-day Seattle. In addition to Wilkes, who was selected to command the expedition because of his scientific background, nine other "scientifics" endured the long, often dangerous voyage.

By the time Wilkes and his crew returned home, the voyage had cost almost $1 million and generated an impressive collection of some 160,000 zoological, ornithological, botanical, and ethnographic specimens. On this expedition, however, as on others, discovery shaded into incursion. After natives on a Fijian island attacked and killed two of his officers, Wilkes retaliated by killing more than eighty Fijians in a bloody battle, laying waste to two of their villages and seizing some of their belongings for his collection. Wilkes's massive collection eventually made its way to the Smithsonian Institution's National Museum, forming the core of the museum's holdings.

## FRÉMONT'S WESTERN EXPEDITIONS

While Wilkes steered a course homeward during the spring of 1842, army lieutenant John C. Frémont departed St. Louis on the first of five expeditions that would take him to the far West during the next ten years. A member of the U.S. Army Topographical Engineers and well connected politically as the son-

Lieutenant Wilkes sketched this sophisticated Indian fishing weir on the Chehalis River in present-day Washington state, 1841.

in-law of Missouri's Senator Thomas H. Benton, Frémont became one of America's best-known agents of nationalist expansion. In 1846—shortly before he played a central role in the seizure of California from Mexico (see Chapter 14)—he prepared a series of annotated maps detailing the route he had taken along the Oregon Trail from present-day Kansas City, Missouri, to the junction of the Columbia and Walla Walla rivers in southeastern Washington. These maps, along with Frémont's report on California and the Northwest, provided detailed information about the terrain, the weather conditions, the availability of water and food, and friendly or hostile Indian tribes. The U.S. Senate had 10,000 copies of Frémont's report published and distributed to prospective western immigrants. One of them was the Mormon leader Brigham Young, who later credited Frémont's report for inspiring him to leave Illinois and lead his persecuted flock to the Great Salt Lake Basin.

Frémont's career bridged two distinct periods of American exploration. The first, which began with Lewis and Clark and ended with the Mexican War, was adventurous in style and open-ended in coverage and method. The second, between the Mexican War and the Civil War, was more specialized and systematic. Exploring the vast area acquired by the United States through the Louisiana Purchase was the primary goal of the first period. The goal of the second was economic development through western settlement and the building of roads and railroads. In both periods, the acquisition of information about the flora, fauna, minerals, and native inhabitants of the West was a priority—and science benefited enormously.

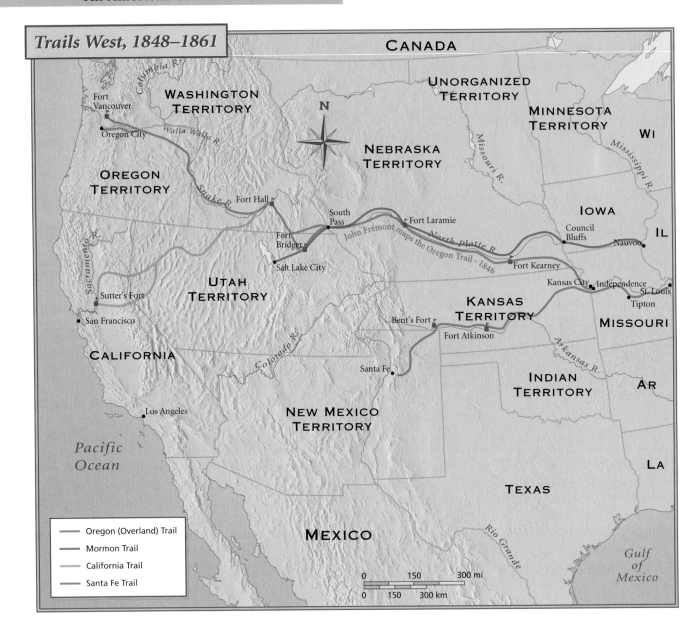

Trails West, 1848–1861

Legend:
— Oregon (Overland) Trail
— Mormon Trail
— California Trail
— Santa Fe Trail

## THE GREAT RECONNAISSANCE

Between 1848 and 1861, the federal government sent two dozen survey parties to the West, in what historians have come to call "The Great Reconnaissance." While some of these expeditions surveyed the Mexican-American border, searched for drinking water, and built wagon roads into the interior of the United States, the most ambitious and controversial assignments focused on a railroad route that would connect the East Coast with California. Six large survey teams went into the field between 1853 and 1854, each headed by an army topographical engineer in command of a military unit and accompanied by astronomers, meteorologists, botanists, geologists, physicians, naturalists, cartographers, and artists. Although the immediate results of the Pacific railroad survey proved inconclusive, the long-term scientific benefits were immense. In addition to providing detailed maps of western America, the survey teams

## Representing America in Japan

*Commodore Matthew Perry kept a journal of his
expedition to Japan in which he recorded
everything from the fascinating sites he saw to the
behavior of his crew in a new and exotic land
(including a black-face minstrel performance they
staged). Here is what he had to say about how his
Japanese hosts reacted to his two most important
gifts to the Emperor—a small-scale operating
steam railroad and an electric telegraph set—
technologies that the official report of his
expedition referred to as "those triumphs of
civilization."*

"For the first few days after our arrival at
Yokohama, Mr. Gay, the chief engineer assisted by
First Assistant Engineer Danby, was employed in
unpacking and putting in working order the
locomotive engine, whilst Messrs. Draper and
Williams were equally busy in preparing to erect
the telegraphic posts for the extension of the
magnetic lines. Dr. Morrow was also engaged in
unpacking and arranging the agricultural
implements, all intended for presentation to the
Emperor, after being first exhibited and explained.

The Japanese authorities offered every facility.
Sheds were prepared for sheltering the various
articles from the weather; a flat piece of ground was
assigned to the engineers for laying down the track
of the locomotive. Posts were brought and erected
as directed by Messrs. Draper and Williams, and
telegraphic wires of nearly a mile in a direct line
were soon extended in as perfect a manner as could
have been done in the United States. One end of the
wire was at the treaty house, the other at a building
allotted for the purpose, and communication was
soon opened between the two operators in the
English, Dutch, and Japanese languages, very much
to the amazement of the spectators.

Meanwhile the implements of husbandry had
been put together and exhibited, the track laid
down, and the beautiful little engine with its tiny
car set in motion. It could be seen from the ship,
flying round its circular path exciting the utmost
wonder in the minds of the Japanese. Although this
perfect piece of machinery was with its car finished
in the most tasteful manner, it was much smaller
than I had expected it would have been, the car
being incapable of admitting with any comfort even
a child of six years. The Japanese therefore who
rode upon it were seated upon the roof, whilst the
engineer placed himself upon the tender."

Matthew C. Perry, *The Japan Expedition 1852–54:
The Personal Journal of Commodore Matthew C.
Perry* (Smithsonian Institution Press, 1968).

brought back an enormous amount of data, drawings, and specimens that they deposited at the Smithsonian's National Museum. Much of this new knowledge was gathered in the thirteen-volume *Pacific Railroad Reports*. Published between 1855 and 1860 at a cost that exceeded the expense of the expeditions themselves, these richly illustrated volumes are considered the most valuable of the scientific reports to emerge from western exploration before the Civil War.

It is remarkable that the federal subsidy for the sciences in the 1840s and 1850s absorbed as much as one-third of the federal budget. All told, the federal government contributed more than all other agencies combined to the pursuit and professionalization of science in antebellum America. And this support came at a time when the usually parsimonious states' rights–oriented Democratic Party dominated the White House.

The reason for such strong federal support is clear: the United States was in an expansionist mode. "Manifest Destiny" was the rallying cry of the day. Beginning with the Louisiana Purchase and culminating with the military conquests of the Mexican War, the California gold rush, and the American triumphs at the Crystal Palace in London, the United States was becoming increasingly bound up in the quest for ever larger markets—both national and international. Science and its practical applications were universally viewed not only as the handmaidens of technological progress but also as the tools of American expansion.

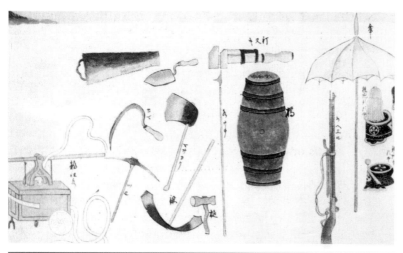

A selection of technological gifts brought to the Japanese by Commodore Perry's expedition.

### PERRY'S EXPEDITION TO JAPAN

Commodore Matthew C. Perry's expedition to Japan is a case in point. Closed to foreigners for more than two centuries (except for a small Dutch trading outpost at Nagasaki), Japan was an isolated feudal society ruled by a former warrior class known as samurai who were determined not to emulate Western civilization—particularly Christianity.

Japan took a dim view of foreigners landing on its shores and, according to several publicized reports, had treated shipwrecked American sailors harshly. Perry's mission was to initiate diplomatic relations with the Japanese government, seek humane treatment for shipwrecked Americans, open trade channels between the two nations, and, most important of all, establish stations where fuel-hungry U.S. Navy and commercial steamships could obtain coal at a reasonable price. "Our object is friendly commercial intercourse and nothing more," Secretary of the Navy William Graham emphasized to Perry prior to his departure.

Perry was well prepared for the mission. He was one of the U.S. Navy's most distinguished officers with a service record that dated back to the War of 1812. Prior to departing for Japan, he studied Japanese history, politics, manners, and customs. With the approval of his superiors, he also formulated a plan that began by making an imposing demonstration of America's military power to Japanese officials. His nine-ship fleet, with over 100 large guns, was the largest ever dispatched to the Pacific by the United States.

When Perry's flotilla dropped anchor near the feudal capital of Edo (now Tokyo) in 1854, his warships were loaded with gifts intended to impress the Japanese with America's technological prowess. The Commodore's Japanese translator described the cargo as it was being readied for the trip:

*"Machinery, farm implements, threshers, looms, mills to spin cotton, even a portable field oven . . . filled each ship's every corner. A railroad had been brought, disassembled. Unpacked and inspected now, there were the cutest little locomotive with tender, a fifty-person car tricked out in imperial finery, and several miles of rails. When the time would come to unload and parade in these many splendid things, we would create a nice, full-sized industrial exposition of our own."*

The demonstrations achieved their purpose. "The Japanese marveled most at the railroad," Perry's assistant wrote—a technology they soon emulated on full scale. They also expressed astonishment at an electric telegraph system set up to relay messages several miles as well as demonstrations of Colt pistols. Hall rifles, a daguerreotype camera, a copper surfboat, and scores of other artifacts new to Japanese eyes. But most impressive of all were the three "magnificent" steam-powered and heavily armed U.S. warships that sat in the harbor and fired awesome 13- to 17-gun salutes whenever Perry went ashore. Called "black ships" by the Japanese because they were painted black and belched black smoke from their steam boilers, they provided an intimidating platform for negotiations. To Japanese artists who depicted them, the black ships appeared demonic, even monstrous in nature. Their renditions captured the sense of trauma, fascination, and dread that the Japanese harbored toward the unwanted foreign "barbarians."

Perry's visit put Japanese officials in a difficult position. Undeveloped in industrial technology, Japan was confronted with the intimidating technological power of a determined American naval commander and the expansionist industrial nation that he represented. Convinced that it was useless to resist, the Japanese government reluctantly acceded to all of Perry's requests and opened the country's doors to a new world of advanced technology and foreign commerce.

## The Fugitive Slave Act and the Crisis of Union

Back home, Perry's expedition was hailed as a stunning triumph. The great poet Walt Whitman even composed a poem to "The New Empire" that was taking shape on the other side of the Pacific. Southerners, however, felt uneasy about the new empire because it seemed to exclude them. Perry's cargo told the story: virtually everything he presented to the Japanese was made in the North by northern manufacturers. Indeed, the future of the new empire seemed to rest with iron and steel, tools and machinery, firearms and steamboats, telegraphy and electricity—none of which played a central part in the South's economy. Cotton might still be king, but its reign was being challenged by new technologies and sources of power lodged in northern factories. As the triumph of "Yankee" technology and science abroad exposed the South's economic and political vulnerability, apprehensive southerners became all the more determined to defend their cherished "way of life," especially the institution of slavery. The one guarantee they had was the Compromise of 1850 and its most

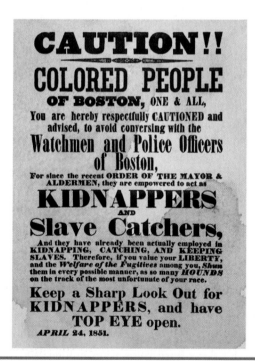

An abolitionist poster dated 1851, warning the "colored people of Boston" to "keep a sharp look out" for slave catchers in their midst.

important component, the Fugitive Slave Act. If that failed, everything else promised to unravel and send the nation careening toward a breakup.

The Fugitive Slave Act guaranteed controversy from the outset. Its provisions denied all fugitive slaves the right to a trial by jury and allowed newly appointed federal commissioners to hear cases instead of judges; moreover, each commissioner received a fee of $10 for every slave returned to his or her owner, as opposed to only $5 for every slave set free. The law also empowered federal marshals to enlist citizens in capturing suspected fugitives, or incur a $1,000 fine. Most significant of all, the Fugitive Slave Act applied to all runaway slaves, even those who had escaped from bondage many years before and had established new lives for themselves.

### *UNCLE TOM'S CABIN*

Enforcement of the Fugitive Slave Act caused a series of politically inflammatory spectacles in the North, of blacks being seized and led away in chains. One person whose anger over these episodes rang out was Harriet Beecher Stowe, the daughter of a nationally known evangelical Protestant minister and temperance reformer with close ties to the abolitionist community. In 1851, Stowe published a series of fictional articles in a Washington, D.C., newspaper depicting the evils of slavery. When the essays appeared the following year as a book entitled *Uncle Tom's Cabin,* readers around the country immediately gobbled up 300,000 copies. During the next decade, sales reached more than 2 million, and in the years that followed, 6.5 million worldwide, making *Uncle Tom's Cabin* one of the best sellers of all time.

Despite stereotyped characters and a sentimental plot, Stowe's novel made an indelible impression on readers. No one soon forgot the essential goodness of slaves like Uncle Tom and Eliza and their harsh treatment at the hands of evil slavemasters like Simon Legree. In fact, many in the North who had never seen a slave formed their impressions of slavery from *Uncle Tom's Cabin.* In the South, the book had an enormous political impact. Slaveholders denounced its "falsehoods" and "distortions" and tried unsuccessfully to have it banned from the region. Some measure of the effect of this book can be gained from a supposed remark by President Lincoln in 1862, during the Civil War, who greeted Stowe as the woman "who wrote the book that made this great war."

Poster advertising *Uncle Tom's Cabin*, c. 1859.

### THE SOUTHERN RESPONSE

*Uncle Tom's Cabin* infuriated proslavery Southerners. In their eyes, Stowe's novel not only libeled the South but also represented a new level of intensity in the "furious anti-slavery crusade" that had been building for more than twenty years. Instead of evoking feelings of guilt and persuading slave owners to abandon slavery, abolitionists like Mrs. Stowe provoked the opposite reaction: a concerted effort to justify and defend the peculiar institution. Led by evangelical Baptist, Methodist, and Presbyterian ministers, Southerners sought justifications for slavery in the Bible. They argued that Old Testament patriarchs had owned slaves and that in the New Testament the apostle Paul had urged a runaway to return to his master. Moreover, they cited Genesis 9:25, where Noah cursed his son, Ham, and all his descendents to lives of servitude. Because Ham was considered the ancestor of black Africans, Noah's curse was viewed as an explicit justification for black slavery and racial inequality. Proslavery apologists also emphasized that slavery made Christians of a race whose members otherwise would have been condemned to hell if they had remained in "heathen" Africa. Such assertions brought sectional divisions to the nation's religious organizations. In 1845, the Baptists and Methodists separated into distinct "northern" and "southern" contingents—among the latter, the Southern Baptist Convention.

One of the most aggressive defenders of slavery was the Virginian George Fitzhugh, whose books *Sociology for the South* (1854) and *Cannibals All!* (1857) as well as numerous essays condemned "the failure of free society" in the North, with its money-grubbing capitalists, greasy mechanics, and "moonstruck" theorists. In addition to maintaining that "slavery was morally right," Fitzhugh asserted that in "the slaveholding South all is peace, quiet, plenty, and contentment." In contrast to the North, with its hoards of poor and exploited immigrants and where "every man [is] for himself and the devil take the hindmost," Fitzhugh proudly asserted that "we have no mobs, no trades unions, no strikes for higher wages, no armed resistance to the law, [and] but little jealousy of the rich by the poor." Slaves were happy because they were well cared for by their masters. "We never saw one who did not like his slaves," he continued, "and rarely a slave who was not devoted to his master." As a result, Fitzhugh concluded, "we are the happiest, most contented and prosperous people on earth."

In addition to Fitzhugh and other proslavery polemicists, a group of natural scientists, known as the "American school of anthropology," added further fuel to the debate over slavery. They advanced the theory of "polygenesis," which held that each race was separate and distinct rather than part of the same species. Although rejected by religious fundamentalists as contrary to the teaching of the Bible (and later proven scientifically incorrect), polygenesis gave added support to the argument that whites were biologically superior to blacks and that servitude was a "natural condition" of inferior races.

These arguments inflamed the slavery controversy, spilled over into politics, and hardened positions on both sides. As events unfolded during the 1850s, each passing month brought a new crisis that compounded what had preceded it. With each crisis, compromise became more unattainable. Slowly but surely, the bonds of union were coming undone.

### PIERCE AND THE OSTEND MANIFESTO

*Uncle Tom's Cabin* was published in 1852, a presidential election year. President Millard Fillmore's efforts to enforce the Fugitive Slave Act had won support among southern Whigs but had alienated antislavery northern Whigs who viewed him as a lackey of the slaveocracy. Dissension among Whigs became particularly apparent in Fillmore's home state of New York, where William Seward opposed his nomination and supported the Mexican War hero, General Winfield Scott, for the presidency. After fifty-two tedious roll-call votes, Scott won the Whig Party nomination. Yet even though he agreed to "acquiesce in" the Compromise of 1850—including the enforcement of the Fugitive Slave Act—he failed to generate support among southern party members, many of whom condemned the ticket and shifted their allegiance to the Democratic Party.

The Democrats also went into their convention divided between sectional candidates, but they emerged after forty-eight ballots united around a dark horse, Franklin Pierce of New Hampshire. A former U.S. congressman and senator as well as a Mexican War veteran, Pierce was one Yankee trusted by southern politicians, who considered him "sound" on slavery and "as reliable as Calhoun himself." Even though the party endorsed a platform that stood firmly for the Compromise of 1850 (including strict enforcement of the Fugitive Slave Act) and pledged to keep slavery out of politics, it nonetheless succeeded in drawing Martin Van Buren and other free-soil Democrats back into its ranks. Such surprising unity boded well for Pierce, who carried twenty-seven out of thirty-one states in one of the most lopsided presidential victories since the War of 1812. Upon learning that Scott had garnered only 35 percent of the popular vote in the South and won majorities in only two of the fifteen slave states (Kentucky and Tennessee), a Georgia congressman ominously proclaimed that "the Whig Party is dead."

Among Pierce's strongest supporters was the ultranationalistic "Young America" movement, which called for the continued territorial expansion of the United States. Many of its most enthusiastic members were southerners who believed that, as one of them put it, "the safety of the South is to be found only in the extension of its peculiar institutions." While some Young Americans spoke of America's Manifest Destiny "over all Mexico, over South America, [and] over the West Indies," the most desirable prize of all was Spanish Cuba.

President Polk had indicated shortly after the war with Mexico had ended (1848) that he was "decidedly in favour of purchasing Cuba & making it one of the States of [the] Union." The idea of acquiring Cuba, with its potential for sugar, tobacco, and cotton cultivation, proved particularly attractive to southerners interested in expanding their political representation and power in the Congress. When Spain refused to sell Cuba, several privately funded expeditions attempted unsuccessfully to seize it. The final act came in October 1854, when the Pierce administration's minister to Spain, having failed to acquire Cuba for $120 million, joined with the American ministers to Britain and France in preparing a memorandum to the State Department known as the "Ostend Manifesto" (after the Belgian city where it was drafted). Having offered Spain a price "far beyond [Cuba's] present value" and "been refused," the ministers concluded that the United States "shall be justified in wresting it from Spain if we possess the power."

A proslavery lithograph from 1850 that favorably contrasts the easygoing life of southern plantation slaves with the harsh realities of "factory slavery" in England and, by implication, the northern United States.

433

The Ostend Manifesto was intended as a confidential government document, but details of the statement leaked out to the European press, and in November 1854 a New York newspaper published the story. Antislavery advocates branded the ministers' declaration a "Manifesto of Brigands"—yet another southern conspiracy to "grasp, to rob, to murder, to grow rich on the spoils of provinces and toils of slaves." In response to a subpoena from the House of Representatives, an embarrassed Pierce administration released the controversial Ostend correspondence and immediately jettisoned all further plans to obtain Cuba. By then, however, the damage had been done.

## Railroad Politics

Even the projected transcontinental railroad across the United States fell afoul of the widening sectional divide. As early as 1844, the New York merchant Asa Whitney had proposed constructing a railroad connecting the Atlantic with the Pacific. The federal government would finance the project through huge land grants to the builders, who in turn could sell smaller tracts to settlers. Nothing came of the proposal until after the war with Mexico, when competing groups from Chicago, St. Louis, Memphis, and New Orleans began vying to construct the railroad. Where would its eastern terminus be, in the North or the South? The stakes were high, with personal fortunes riding on the decision. Those communities through which the railroad, with its potentially vast western market, passed would enjoy a tremendous commercial boost.

Chief among the railroad politicians was Stephen A. Douglas of Illinois. Although he came from downstate, Chicago was Douglas's choice for the transcontinental terminus. He personally had real estate interests in the Chicago area and believed that the city, with its excellent harbor on Lake Michigan and connecting canal facilities to the south and west, was the ideal core of the nation's transportation lines.

Douglas was convinced that the chances of gaining the railroad for Chicago would be greatly enhanced if the vast area lying west of Iowa and Missouri could be formally organized into a territory so that a legislature could be established and land expropriated from its native inhabitants for white settlement. Early in 1853, Douglas and a House colleague from Illinois introduced bills to organize most of the remaining part of the Louisiana Purchase north of 36°–30′ as the Nebraska Territory. The House of Representatives promptly passed the bill, but a group of southern senators, led by David

R. Atchinson of Missouri, tabled the measure in the Senate. Their reasoning was simple: under the Missouri Compromise of 1820, the territory north of 36°–30′ outlawed slavery; hence they had no incentive to support the Douglas bill. Nor did the southerners want to give Chicago a commercial advantage over St. Louis, Memphis, Vicksburg (Mississippi), Natchez (Mississippi), or New Orleans. Knowing that Douglas needed his vote as well as those of several southern senators to pass the Nebraska bill, the proslavery Atchinson insisted that Douglas recast the bill to place "slaveholder and non-slaveholder upon terms of equality" in the new territory.

With the Nebraska legislation blocked and Douglas stewing over how to meet Senator Atchinson's challenge, Congress authorized $150,000 for the War Department to determine the best railroad route to California. Four major survey parties, each commanded by an army topographical engineer, set out for the West in the spring and summer of 1853, with four more taking the field the following fall and winter. But not even these engineers could devise an impartial solution to the politically loaded railroad question.

From a scientific standpoint the army surveys succeeded brilliantly, collecting an immense amount of specimens and data on the geology, botany, zoology, meteorology, and ethnology of the West. But from a political standpoint the surveys failed, revealing not one but several possible routes to the West Coast. This allowed war secretary Jefferson Davis of Mississippi to hold to his favored southern route, which roughly followed the 32nd parallel westward from Natchez to San Diego. He ignored at least two routes farther north that could have won over nearly all the contending parties for the transcontinental railroad, including Douglas. To secure the land needed for his southern route, Davis orchestrated the Gadsden Purchase in 1854, involving 19 million acres of Mexican land in what are now Arizona and New Mexico. Davis pushed the purchase through long before the army engineers had completed their surveys. In the end, sectional politics prevailed over science. Davis issued a report to President Pierce that recommended the southern route. However, rather than settling the question, the army surveys inadvertently stoked the fires of sectional controversy. And this time the conflagration could not be put out.

### DOUGLAS'S KANSAS-NEBRASKA ACT

While the topographical surveys were in progress, Douglas twice failed to fashion a Nebraska bill that would win the

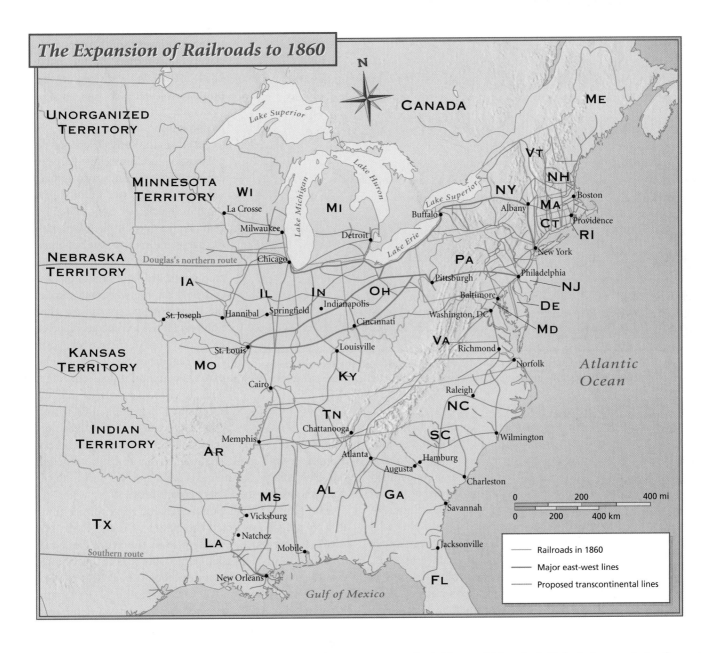

**The Expansion of Railroads to 1860**

N

CANADA

Legend:
— Railroads in 1860
— Major east-west lines
— Proposed transcontinental lines

votes of his southern colleagues. Finally he gave in, and on January 23, 1854, he introduced a new bill that created two territories—Kansas, west of Missouri, and Nebraska, west of Iowa and Minnesota. The bill conveyed an impression of balance, with Kansas likely to become a slave state and Nebraska free. The bill also stipulated that the people of each territory, not Congress, would decide on the future of slavery through the exercise of popular sovereignty. Since Kansas lay north of 36°–30′, this provision repealed the Missouri Compromise.

Douglas's Kansas-Nebraska bill fueled one of the fiercest congressional debates in American history. President Pierce initially balked at the legislation, because he considered the repeal of the time-tested Missouri Compromise line injudicious. But pressure from a delegation headed by Douglas and Jefferson Davis moved him to support the bill and make it "a test of party orthodoxy." It was a fateful decision.

Douglas's bill caught northern Whigs and Democrats by surprise, but the loudest opposition came from free-soilers who

The Pacific Railroad surveys produced a great fund of knowledge about the West, as well as some first-rate works of art. This lithographic view of a large buffalo herd near Lake Jessie in east-central North Dakota was done by the artist John Mix Stanley, c. 1853–54.

openly attacked the measure "as part and parcel of an atrocious plot" to make Kansas-Nebraska a "dreary region of despotism, inhabited by masters and slaves." Free-soilers also condemned Douglas for placing his presidential aspirations ahead of the national interest and accused him of serving as a henchman of "slavery despotism." As the debates heated up, anti-Nebraska groups sent petitions to Washington while ten state legislatures in the North either denounced the bill or refused their support. Every northern Whig in Congress opposed the bill.

But Douglas relentlessly pushed the Kansas-Nebraska Act, and it passed the Democratic-controlled Senate in March by a vote of 37 to 14. Only five free-state Democrats broke ranks to join the northern Whig and Free Soil opposition, indicating that the Pierce administration had indeed made the bill a test of party orthodoxy. Two months later, following more heated debates, the House of Representatives passed the bill by a margin of 13 votes. On May 30, 1854, President Pierce signed it into law.

### INNOVATIONS IN PARTY POLITICS

The Kansas-Nebraska Act was a deeply polarizing law. It killed the Whig Party by exciting already serious divisions between proslavery southerners and antislavery northerners in the party. By 1854, former Whigs were seeking new political affiliations that tied them closer to purely sectional rather than national interests.

Although the Kansas-Nebraska Act did not destroy the Democratic Party, its polarizing effects set the party on a narrowly sectional course. Evidence of the change came in the fall elections of 1854, when Democratic voters in the North deserted the party in droves to vote for other candidates. Going into the election, Democrats controlled both houses of Congress and held an overwhelming majority in the House of Representatives. The election cost House Democrats 72 percent of their seats from districts in the North and 13 percent from the South, leaving the party in a minority position. At the national level, the party lost its sectional balance as well. Beginning in 1855, southern Democrats outnumbered their northern counterparts in party councils, allowing them to steer the party in a proslavery direction. The balance that had once distinguished the "Democracy" of Andrew Jackson and Martin Van Buren was gone, and with it, the spirit of compromise.

The Thirty-fourth Congress, which met for the first time in March 1855, reflected the extent of the political realignments taking place. The demise of the Whig Party and the exodus of anti-Nebraska Democrats meant that the Democratic Party in the North now took a back seat to two new parties: the American, or "Know-Nothing," Party and the Republican Party. Although they emphasized different issues, these two parties often cooperated with each other, and eventually they would coalesce into a major party known as the Republicans. Their emergence signaled the third major shift in party politics since the founding of the Republic (the first being the Federalist/Jeffersonian split of the 1790s and the second, the Jacksonian Democrat/Whig realignment of the 1830s). This "third party system" contained the seeds of the two major political parties—Democrat and Republican—that we have today.

The American Party appeared in 1854 as an expression of long-standing antagonisms between predominantly Catholic

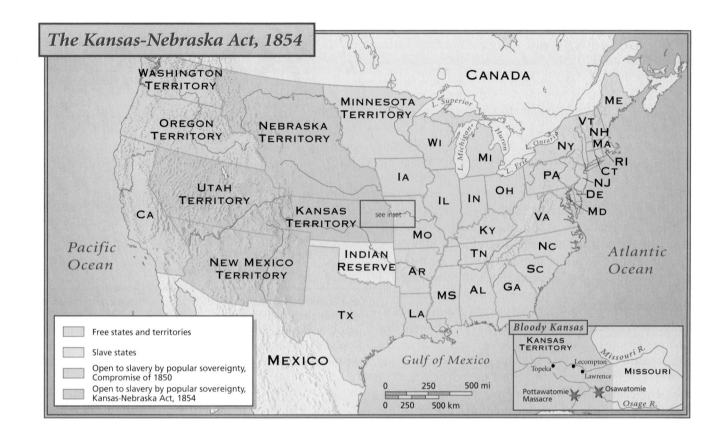

The Kansas-Nebraska Act, 1854

Free states and territories
Slave states
Open to slavery by popular sovereignty, Compromise of 1850
Open to slavery by popular sovereignty, Kansas-Nebraska Act, 1854

immigrant groups and the overwhelmingly Protestant native-born majority. Nativist tensions had escalated after 1845 when an unprecedented wave of immigration, led primarily by Irish Catholics fleeing the deadly Potato Famine, broke on U.S. shores. This pulse brought nearly 3 million immigrants—the largest number in American history—to the United States by 1854.

The nativist, anti-immigrant reaction followed the newcomers from their arrival in eastern port cities like Boston, New York, and Philadelphia to their inland destinations, such as Buffalo, Cincinnati, and Chicago. Since most of the new arrivals were impoverished peasant-laborers from Ireland and Germany, they were soon blamed for rising crime rates and public costs in urban areas. Nativists also noticed that by the early 1850s, more and more immigrants were beginning to vote. The percentage of foreign-born voters was growing much faster than that of native-born. Immigrant voters tended to support Democratic candidates and oppose temperance, antislavery, and other reform efforts, which put them on a collision course with

largely evangelical Protestants who headed these movements and, in the past, had voted Whig. The quarrel went beyond reform, however. Native-born white workers found themselves in competition with Irishmen and other recent immigrants for jobs. The growing resentment went both ways: the immigrants and their Catholic leaders attacked free-soilers, abolitionists, and Protestant reform groups while calling for tax-supported Catholic schools, where their children would not be exposed to the perceived heresies being taught in public schools.

Political nativism took form in secret fraternal societies such as the Order of United Americans and the Order of the Star-Spangled Banner. Their members pledged never to vote for Roman Catholics or other foreigners for public office, and supported efforts to pass temperance laws and raise the residency requirements for American citizenship to twenty-one years. When queried by outsiders about their political activities, they were instructed to reply, "I know nothing"—and so opponents derided them as "Know-Nothings." The Know-Nothing Party fielded its first slate of candidates in the congressional and state

437

elections of 1854, and it won impressive gains throughout the Northeast as well as in the border states and the deep South. "How people do hate Catholics," a Cincinnati editor exclaimed. The Congress that convened in March 1855 included at least fifty new House members who identified themselves as members of the American Party, and another seventy were elected with Know-Nothing support.

The Republican Party originated in the Midwest and gradually spread to former Whig strongholds in the Northeast. The party's primary concern was the expansion of slavery—especially, as Abraham Lincoln put it, the "moral wrong and injustice" of the Kansas-Nebraska Act in allowing slavery to expand into territory previously closed to it. Here it becomes clear that support for antislavery did not mean a belief in racial equality. Like other white Americans of the time, Republicans harbored racist ideas. Admitting that "he cared nothing for the 'nigger,'" a future Republican congressman from Pittsburgh declared that "it was not the mission of the Republican party to preach rebellion" but rather "deliverance to the white man." By this, he meant that Republicans opposed the extension of slavery into the territories as a hindrance to the ability of free white labor to earn a living wage there. This free-labor ideology could accommodate attacks on the "slave oligarchy" as well as support for legislation prohibiting free blacks from residing within certain states like Lincoln's Illinois. A hallmark of the Republican Party as it entered its first campaign in 1854, the ideology proved successful, at least in the North. Republican candidates made strong showings in state elections in the Midwest and Northeast, and they won approximately 105 House seats in 1854.

### BLOODY KANSAS

In the midst of these organizational innovations in American politics, the contest to determine whether Kansas would be slave or free began. It was a conflict that extended from the corridors of power in Washington to the rich soil of the Kansas Territory. New York's antislavery Whig (soon to be Republican) senator William H. Seward sounded the call to free-soilers. "We will engage in competition for the virgin soil of Kansas," he told his Senate colleagues, "and God give the victory to the side which is stronger in numbers as it is in right." Long before Seward made these remarks, a group of wealthy antislavery advocates headed by Amos Lawrence of Boston had raised $5 million and incorporated the Massachusetts Emigrant Aid Company "for the purpose of assisting emigrants to settle in the West." Although the incorporators originally thought that New Englanders

A mid-nineteenth-century nativist cartoon showing an Irish whiskey drinker and a German beer drinker carrying off a ballot box while other immigrants riot in front of an election polling place in the background. The message is clear: immigrants are a corrupt and disruptive influence on the Republic and its long-standing traditions.

would flock to Kansas, most of the company's support went to midwestern farmers who embraced the free-soil ideology. Slowly at first, but then in growing numbers, nonslaveholding settlers began to move into the Kansas Territory.

Determined not to be bested by Seward and his "free soil crowd," Senator David Atchinson of Missouri cautioned that "the game [for Kansas] must be played boldly." "If we win we carry slavery to the Pacific Ocean," he wrote a Senate colleague from Virginia, "if we fail we lose Missouri, Arkansas, Texas, and all the territories." When the newly appointed territorial governor called for the election of a legislature, Atchinson saw to it that supporters from Missouri flocked into Kansas to elect proslavery candidates. "There are eleven hundred men coming over from Platte County [Missouri] to vote," he boasted, "and if that ain't enough we can send five thousand—enough to kill every God-damned abolitionist in the Territory." In the legislature they elected, proslavery members outnumbered free-soilers thirty-six to three.

Appalled by the actions of Atchinson and his supporters, the territorial governor called for yet another election in certain districts where he was convinced that fraudulent voting had taken place. This time, free-soilers won most of the seats, but when they reported for duty in July 1855, they were turned away by the proslavery legislature seated at Lecompton. When the governor protested these actions in Washington, the Pierce administration removed him and appointed a successor thought to be more sympathetic with Senator Atchinson's views. In the meantime, the Lecompton legislature passed a series of laws that recognized the votes of nonresidents (thus validating the earlier elections), established strict slave codes, and imposed penalties on anyone who spoke out against slavery, assisted runaways, or in any way encouraged slave recalcitrance or revolts.

Free-soil Kansans, who now outnumbered their opponents, refused to recognize the legislature at Lecompton or obey its laws. Taking matters into their own hands, they called a convention in October 1855, drew up a free-state constitution, and elected their own governor and legislature, which they installed at Topeka. At this point, Kansas had two competing territorial governments: one representing free-soilers at Topeka, the other officially recognized by the Pierce administration and representing the proslavery constituency at Lecompton. Both sides were heavily armed and spoiling for a fight. That moment arrived in November 1855, when the murder of a free-soiler by a proslavery resident ignited a series of clashes along the Kansas-Missouri border. Only the intervention of Senator Atchinson, who urged his followers to bide their time, and the onset of a hard winter prevented a full-scale attack on the free-soil town of Lawrence by some 1,500 Missouri border raiders. But the following spring, the inevitable occurred when a large force of Missourians, purportedly armed with a warrant from a proslavery judge to arrest the leaders of the free-soil government for treason, rode into Lawrence, made several arrests, and burned and looted the town.

*The Sumner-Brooks Confrontation.* As civil war flared in Kansas, physical violence erupted on the floor of the U.S. Senate. There, on May 19–20, 1856, Charles Sumner of Massachusetts, one of the few outright abolitionists in Congress, delivered a blistering speech to packed galleries entitled "The Crime Against Kansas." Well known for his sharp tongue and condescending demeanor, Sumner referred in the speech to Senator Andrew P. Butler of South Carolina as a "Don Quixote who has chosen a mistress . . . the harlot, Slavery" and to Butler's home state for "its shameful imbecility from Slavery." As for that "noisome, squat, and nameless animal" Stephen A. Douglas, he was "the squire of Slavery, its very Sancho Panza, ready to do all its humiliating offices." Sumner ended his diatribe by calling for the immediate admission of Kansas to the Union as a free state.

As he had intended, Sumner's speech created a public furor. Although letters and telegrams from abolitionist supporters poured in to his office praising him for his "inspiring eloquence and lofty moral tone," Sumner's closest Senate colleagues thought that he had gone too far. To be sure, southerners thought so—especially Congressman Preston Brooks of South Carolina.

On May 22, two days after Sumner delivered his speech, Brooks waited until the Senate had concluded its business for the day, then entered the chamber and addressed Sumner, who was writing at his desk. "Mr. Sumner, I have read your speech twice over carefully. It is a libel on South Carolina, and Mr. Butler, who is a relative of mine." Before Sumner could rise from his chair, Brooks struck him on the head with his walking stick and continued to rain down blows until Sumner became "as senseless as a corpse . . . his head bleeding copiously from the frightful wounds, and the blood saturating his clothes." "I . . . gave him about thirty first rate stripes," Brooks later boasted. "I wore my cane out completely but saved the Head which is gold."

The attack made Brooks an instant hero in the South. On the other side, northerners condemned the attack as "brutal, murderous, and cowardly." Some vowed that they would vote Republican because they were appalled at the unrepentant "tone of the Southern Press, & the approbation . . . of the whole Southern People." Political observers predicted that the Democratic Party stood to lose 200,000 votes in the upcoming presidential election. The most ominous comment, however, came from the pen of the Transcendentalist writer Ralph Waldo Emerson: "I do

This cartoon, entitled "Southern Chivalry," shows South Carolina's Preston Brooks beating Charles Sumner, who is holding a copy of his speech, "The Crime Against Kansas," in his left hand.

not see how a barbarous community and a civilized community can constitute one state," he declared. "I think we must get rid of slavery, or we must get rid of freedom."

*The Pottawatomie Massacre.* The Sumner-Brooks confrontation brought sectional antagonisms to a boil throughout the United States, especially in Kansas. There, in the small, free-soil settlement of Osawatomie, a militant abolitionist and intensely religious individual named John Brown brooded over what he considered the miscarriage of justice by corrupt federal authorities as well as the atrocities committed by proslavery raiders from Missouri. Already upset about the sack of Lawrence, Brown, according to his son, "went crazy—*crazy*" when he heard about the Sumner beating. Determined to "fight fire with fire," he decided to "strike terror in the hearts of the proslavery people" by conducting a retaliation of his own. On May 24, 1856, Brown gathered a small force and rode into a proslavery settlement along Pottawatomie Creek, where in the dead of night they dragged five suspected proslavery agitators from their cabins and butchered them with broadswords specially sharpened for the purpose.

As news of the sack of Lawrence and the Pottawatomie massacre spread, southeastern Kansas became a bloody battleground. Chaos reigned during the summer and early fall of 1856. Fearing for their lives, families on both sides hastily packed their belongings and left the territory. Others joined guerrilla bands that marauded the countryside, shooting up towns, robbing stores and banks, burning settlers' homesteads, and running off their livestock. Among them was John Brown, described by a reporter from New York as "a strange, resolute, repulsive, iron-willed, inexorable old man" who quoted the Bible and believed that he was fighting a holy war against wickedness.

Owing largely to the resolute actions of Governor John W. Geary, appointed by the Pierce administration to pacify Kansas, guerrilla warfare slowly subsided during the fall of 1856. Geary disbanded the armed groups and used federal troops as a police force. He also convinced both sides that continued violence would hurt their causes in the upcoming presidential election. Some 200 people had died during the conflict, with property losses estimated at $2 million. Yet even though Geary put a stop to the worst of the fighting, his failure to get Kansans to agree on a state constitution, coupled with a falling out with the Pierce administration, led to his abrupt resignation in March 1857.

Sporadic fighting continued over the next three years as Geary's successors sought to hold fair elections and prepare a new constitution that would reflect the views of the territory's majority. The Democratic Party divided irretrievably over the slavery issue in Kansas, with President Pierce and his successor, James Buchanan, supporting the proslavery constitution drafted by the Lecompton legislature and Stephen A. Douglas denouncing it as a travesty of popular sovereignty. Free-soil Republicans eventually gained the upper hand in the territorial legislature and adopted a constitution that brought Kansas into the Union as a free state in January 1861, but by then renewed guerrilla warfare had cost hundreds of lives and more millions in destroyed property. As for the transcontinental railroad that had caused the Kansas imbroglio, it remained moribund—nothing more than a paper plan and a figment of Douglas's ambitious imagination.

## Buchanan and the Politics of Disunion

The turmoil in Kansas and the intense sectional hostility that flowed from it made 1856 a critical election year. Going into the race, leaders of the newly formed Republican Party realized that they had little chance of success unless they could attract Know-Nothing support. Playing on widespread prejudice against Catholics and immigrants, anger over the repeal of the Missouri Compromise, and support for temperance legislation as well as the ouster of corrupt politicians, the American Party had attracted thousands of former Whigs and Democrats to its nativist cause. But as formidable as it appeared, the party had failed to deliver on its promises to pass anti-immigrant and temperance legislation and to reform the political system. And it was proving vulnerable to opposition charges of bigotry, undemocratic secret practices, and gang violence during elections. Above all, the party was divided on the slavery question.

The American Party finally split in two at its national convention in February 1856. Fifty northern delegates walked out after southern delegates rejected a resolution calling for the repeal of the Kansas-Nebraska Act and the restoration of the Missouri Compromise. The division did not heal. "South Americans" nominated Millard Fillmore for president, and "North Americans" nominated Speaker of the House Nathaniel Banks. When Banks declined the nomination and threw his support to the Republican Party, thousands of Know-Nothings shifted their allegiance and cast Republican ballots in November. This critical realignment signaled the beginning of the end of the American Party while ensuring the future of the Republicans. In less than three years, they had grown from an obscure third party to a major player in the two-party system.

This 1856 campaign cartoon bitterly denounces the Democratic Party for the Kansas-Nebraska Act and the outbreak of civil war in Kansas. In the center is "Liberty" (the female symbol of the United States) imploring buckskin-clad President Franklin Pierce to "spare me gentlemen, spare me!" Pierce is surrounded by other Democratic Party leaders, notably Stephen A. Douglas (far right, who has just scalped a hapless farmer) and, next to him, the heavily armed Lewis Cass, who is licking his lips and scoffing, "Poor little Dear. We wouldn't hurt her for the world, would we Frank? ha! ha! ha!" On the left, James Buchanan is picking the pockets of another dead victim of the Kansas fighting, while Pierce's secretary of state, William Marcy (wearing the 50-cent trouser patch), assists him.

The Republicans still faced a tricky electoral task. Northern Know-Nothings shared Republicans' opposition to the Democratic Party, the Kansas-Nebraska Act, and what they considered the slave oligarchy of the South. But Republicans sought to downplay Know-Nothing issues of temperance and anti-immigrant policy, while still exploiting the hatred for Roman Catholics in the electorate. In some important state races, the Republicans supported Know-Nothing candidates in return for their support of the Republican presidential nominee, John C. Frémont.

Despite a lack of political experience, Frémont made an attractive candidate. He had gained national stature as "The Pathfinder," the country's most famous living explorer. He had also been a prominent advocate of California's admission to the Union as a free state, and he supported the same for Kansas. And Frémont was married to the daughter of Senator Thomas H. Benton, the sworn enemy of Missouri's proslavery Senator David Atchinson and his "border ruffians"; Benton's endorsement promised to attract significant support among former free-soil Democrats. The ambitious Frémont wanted the Republican nomination, and he got it on the first ballot.

The Democrats nominated James Buchanan, a long-time Jacksonian Democrat from Pennsylvania who was acceptable to the party's divided northern and southern factions. His initial support came from northern Democrats, but southerners quickly accepted his nomination, confident that he would support their interests in Kansas and oppose further agitation of the slavery question.

No two party platforms could have been more different, with the Republicans denouncing the Kansas-Nebraska Act and popular sovereignty, and the Democrats embracing them. The Democratic platform also supported states' rights and limited government while opposing federally funded internal improvements (other than the transcontinental railroad), high tariffs, and a national bank. Most important, the Democratic press identified Buchanan as the only legitimate candidate in the election, a factor that weighed heavily with Democrats and former Whigs who feared for the future of the Union. Buchanan emphatically pressed the point: "The Black Republicans must be . . . boldly assailed as disunionists, and this charge must be reiterated again and again," he asserted. "This race ought to be run on the question of Union or disunion."

Buchanan won the presidency and the Democrats recaptured both houses of Congress, but hardly by a landslide: Buchanan won 45 percent of the popular vote to Frémont's

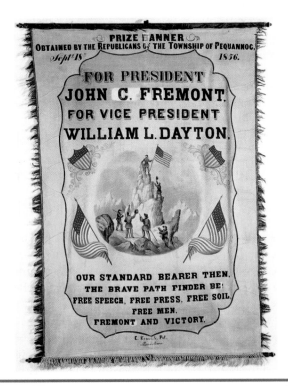

An 1856 presidential campaign banner touting the candidacy of John C. Frémont, the "brave path finder," and the Republican Party's principles of "free speech, free press, free soil, and free men."

33 percent and Fillmore's 22 percent. Although Fillmore did well in the South, the only state he carried was Maryland. With Buchanan winning all of the South and Frémont all of New England plus New York, Ohio, Michigan, Iowa, and Wisconsin, the crucial contests centered on the lower northern states of Illinois, Indiana, New Jersey, and especially Pennsylvania. Buchanan managed a narrow victory in Pennsylvania largely by warning voters that if elected, Frémont and the "Black Republicans" would cause the breakup of the Union and "turn loose . . . millions of negroes, to elbow you in the workshops, and compete with you in the fields of honest labor." Although they had lost the election, Republican Party leaders considered it a "victorious defeat." They realized that they could win the presidency in 1860 if they maintained their hold on the northern states already in their camp and added Pennsylvania and either Illinois or Indiana to the fold.

### THE *DRED SCOTT* DECISION

Buchanan launched his presidency on troubled political and economic waters. On March 6, 1857, two days after his inauguration, the Supreme Court exploded a judicial bombshell in the *Dred Scott* decision. Scott was an elderly Missouri slave whose master, an army surgeon, had taken him into Illinois and to Fort Snelling, in the northern part of the Louisiana Purchase (present-day Minnesota), for extended stays during the 1830s. Scott sued for his freedom on the grounds that Illinois was a free state and that Fort Snelling, under the provisions of the Missouri Compromise, was in free territory. Supported by a group of white abolitionists, Scott initially brought suit in the Missouri court system in 1846 and lost. But through a series of appeals and legal maneuvers, the case wound up before the Supreme Court in 1856.

Well aware of the case and its implications, President-elect Buchanan urged Chief Justice Roger Taney to render a decision that would effectively remove the slavery debate from Congress and quash the intensifying sectional conflict. The decision had three parts: first, the Court held that Scott was not a citizen by virtue of his African descent, and therefore had no right to sue in a federal court. At this point, the Court could have thrown out the case, but it went on to make two more pronouncements. One was that Scott's four-year residence in free territory did not make him free. The other was that Congress did not have the right to ban slavery north of 36°–30′ in the Missouri Compromise or, for that matter, anywhere else because such action conflicted with the Fifth Amendment, which guaranteed that no citizen could "be deprived of life, liberty, or property, without due process of law." Since, in the Court's view, slaves were property, they could be taken anywhere in the United States or its territories—despite what Congress or the territorial legislatures might legislate.

The *Dred Scott* decision pleased Buchanan and the slaveholding South. Democratic leaders throughout the country viewed it as "the funeral sermon of Black Republicanism." But events soon proved them wrong: *Dred Scott* invigorated the Republican movement. Outraged by the decision, Republican leaders attacked the Taney Court as part of a "slave power" conspiracy. Indeed, Senator William Seward of New York charged that Buchanan and Taney had conspired to render a decision favorable to the South. Although the president and chief justice denied the accusation, aroused Republicans vowed to make the case a political issue in the upcoming elections of 1858 and 1860 and, if victorious, to "reconstitute" the Supreme Court and overturn its "inhuman dicta, which denied the rights of citizenship not only to slaves, but also to free blacks in the United States." "The remedy," according to the Chicago *Tribune,* lay in "the ballot box." "Let the next President be Republican," its editor declared, "and 1860 will mark an era kindred to that of 1776."

## THE LINCOLN-DOUGLAS DEBATES

The sectional furor provoked by the *Dred Scott* decision, coupled with the ongoing crisis in Bloody Kansas, led to one of the most famous series of debates in American political history. In Illinois, Senator Stephen A. Douglas, the foremost proponent of popular sovereignty and a leading contender among northern Democrats for the presidency in 1860, was up for reelection in 1858. His adversary was Abraham Lincoln, a self-educated lawyer and former Whig who had emerged as a Republican leader in Illinois. Because he lacked Douglas's visibility and wanted to counter charges that he was a "Black Republican" whose abolitionist views would destroy the Union, Lincoln challenged Douglas to a series of seven debates to be held throughout the state during the late summer and early fall of 1858.

The Lincoln-Douglas debates attracted large crowds and, owing primarily to Douglas's national reputation, received widespread press coverage, including verbatim transcripts. The spectacle of the gangly and somewhat disheveled six-foot-four Lincoln trading verbal blows with the short and

Dred Scott.

stocky but impeccably attired Douglas was somewhat humorous. But once the debates began, there was nothing funny about the hard-hitting tactics of the two debaters, and their focus was on slavery and the fate of the Union.

From the outset, Lincoln accused Douglas of departing from the views of the founding fathers on slavery as expressed in the Declaration of Independence. By contrast, he said that Republicans, like the founders, "insist that [slavery] should . . . be treated as a [moral] wrong, and that it shall grow no more." Douglas, in turn, accused Lincoln of being an abolitionist whose "doctrine is revolutionary, and destructive of the existence of our government." In Douglas's view, including blacks among those "created equal" in the Declaration of Independence was a "monstrous heresy." "Are you in favor of conferring upon the negro the rights and privileges of citizenship?" he asked in the first debate. "No, no," responded the crowd. "Do you desire to strike out of our State Constitution that clause which keeps slaves and free negroes out of the State, and allow the free negroes to flow in . . . and cover your prairies with black settlements? Do you desire to turn this beautiful State into a free negro colony?" The crowd roared again, "No, no!" "If you desire negro citizenship . . . if you desire them to vote on an equality with yourselves," Douglas continued, "then support Mr. Lincoln and the Black Republican party. . . . For one, I am opposed to negro citizenship in any and every form. I believe this government . . . was made by white men, for the benefit of

443

## Buchanan and the Politics of Disunion

Abraham Lincoln at the time of the *Dred Scott* decision, 1857.

white men and their posterity for ever, and I am in favor of confining citizenship to white men . . . instead of conferring it upon negroes, Indians and other inferior races." The crowd cheered: "Good for you!" "Douglas forever!"

Douglas's racist barbs hit their mark. The more Lincoln tried to distance himself from abolitionism yet denounce slavery as a "moral and political wrong," the more Douglas hammered him about being a candidate of "the Abolition party" and the dire threat such "revolutionary principles" posed to white society. By the time of the fourth debate on September 18, Douglas had Lincoln on the defensive. "I am not, nor ever have been in favor of bringing about in any way the social and political equality of the white and black races," Lincoln insisted. "I am not, nor ever have been in favor of making voters or jurors of negroes, nor of qualifying them to hold office, nor to intermarry with white people. . . . There must be the position of superior and inferior, and I as much as any other man am in favor of the superior position being assigned to the white race."

Lincoln refused to leave the issue there, however. He coupled his comments on white superiority with a plea for fairness and the inclusion of blacks in the most basic tenets of American freedom—a clear indication of the direction in which he would move so dramatically in the years that lay just ahead. "I hold that . . . there is no reason in the world why the Negro is not entitled to all the natural rights enumerated in the Declaration of Independence, the right to life, liberty, and the pursuit of happiness," Lincoln told the crowd at Ottawa, Illinois. "I hold

that he is as much entitled to these as the white man. I agree with Judge Douglas that he is not my equal in many respects—certainly not in color, perhaps not in moral or intellectual endowment. But in the right to eat the bread, without leave of anybody else, which his own hand earns, *he is my equal and the equal of Judge Douglas, and the equal of every living man.*"

Even though these comments were greeted with "Great applause," according to a reporter present, it seems fair to say that, on balance, Douglas bested Lincoln on the race issue during their exchanges. If the debates revealed anything, it was the extent to which racism pervaded the culture of pre–Civil War Illinois and, by extension, all of America. Lincoln was part of this America, to be sure, but he was also capable, as he demonstrated during the debates, of rising above the cruder prejudices of his era and thinking of black men and women as human beings who deserved a chance to share in the promise of this country.

Lincoln also got in plenty of licks, none more telling than a question he posed during the second debate, held at Freeport on August 27. Suppose, Lincoln began, the people of Kansas adopted a state constitution that excluded slavery. But, he added, in the *Dred Scott* case the Supreme Court had decided that "states cannot exclude slavery from their limits." Whose position would Douglas support, that of the people of Kansas or that of the Supreme Court? Lincoln knew what Douglas's response would be: as the champion of popular sovereignty, he emphatically chose the people's position. "Whatever the Supreme Court may . . . decide as to the abstract question of slavery," Douglas insisted, "the people of a Territory have the lawful means to admit it or exclude it as they please, for the reason that slavery cannot exist a day or an hour anywhere unless supported by local police regulations . . . furnished by the local legislature." He concluded, "No matter what may be the decision of the Supreme Court on that abstract question, still the right of the people to make it a slave Territory or a free Territory is perfect and complete."

Douglas's response became known as the Freeport Doctrine. His ringing endorsement of popular sovereignty played well before his Illinois audiences and helped to get him reelected to the Senate, but it fatally damaged his standing with southern Democrats. Although Lincoln lost his senatorial bid, he emerged from the election as a Republican of national stature and a likely candidate for the presidency in 1860. Douglas likewise strengthened his position among northern Democrats and, much to the consternation of Buchanan, looked as if he would be the party's standard-bearer in 1860. Having clashed with the Buchanan administration over its support of

Cartoon depicting Stephen A. Douglas as a fearless gladiator fighting for popular sovereignty.

the proslavery Lecompton constitution and, in effect, denied the efficacy of the *Dred Scott* decision, Douglas with his victory struck a blow to Buchanan and his southern supporters.

THE PANIC OF 1857

The public uproar over *Dred Scott* and Bloody Kansas was joined by a financial panic that gripped the country during the fall of 1857. The crash came unexpectedly on August 24, when the New York office of an Ohio investment bank stopped making specie (gold and silver) payments on its notes and deposits because an employee had absconded with its funds. Thousands of depositors jammed their local banks intent on closing their accounts and being paid off in gold specie. Unable to meet the sudden surge of demand for specie, some 1,400 banks closed their doors while hundreds of investment houses and manufacturing firms declared bankruptcy. Before long, unemployed workers thronged the streets of northern cities shouting, "Bread or blood!" Some of the most serious incidents occurred in New York City, where hungry workers looted the shops of flour merchants and, on November 10, threatened to seize the U.S. Customs House (containing some $20 million) before they were dispersed by a contingent of marines and infantrymen.

Owing largely to continued infusions of California gold, the worst of the panic had subsided by December 1857, when New York bankers resumed specie payments and the stock market slowly began to recover. But the effects lingered for several years in northeastern and midwestern industrial communities. Although the Buchanan administration sympathized with the plight of those devastated by the crash, it did nothing to relieve their suffering. Instead, the president, in true Jacksonian fashion, blamed the panic on "the vicious system of paper currency" and "wild speculations and gamblings in stocks" and called for legislation that would punish banks and investment houses that acted recklessly. In Buchanan's view, rugged individualism, not government relief, was the answer. The economy would eventually right itself, he felt.

The Republican Party took a different tack. A number of Republican politicians, with backing from northern industrial leaders, attributed the depression to the Democratic Party's sponsorship of low tariffs. The tariff, Republicans argued, existed to protect American manufacturing from cheap European imports. Yet since the 1830s, the Democrats, led by southern cotton barons, had continually pushed the tariff downward until it no longer adequately protected American manufactures. According to the Republicans, the crisis point arrived in March 1857, when the new Buchanan administration, with strong southern support, sponsored legislation that cut the tariff to an all-time low, helping to trigger the panic and depression.

Right or wrong, the Republican argument made for good politics, especially in key states like Buchanan's Pennsylvania. In the 1858 congressional elections, Republican candidates received crucial support from workers who were dissatisfied with the Buchanan administration's laissez-faire economic policy. The promise of tariff-induced prosperity proved attractive, especially when coupled with new Republican proposals for free "homestead" land to farmers hit hard by the depression, agricultural and engineering colleges accessible at low cost to the children of farmers and workers, and the construction of the transcontinental railroad, which would put thousands to work. With their echoes of Henry Clay's American

445

Oil painting of New York City's *Wall Street, Half Past Two O'clock, October 13, 1857*. The Panic of 1857 put half of Wall Street's brokers out of business.

for their sins, he had decided to raise and equip an army, invade Virginia, and incite a slave rebellion that would spread throughout the South and eventually destroy its "evil institution."

Brown's target was the national armory at Harpers Ferry, Virginia, and its hoard of small arms. After months of planning and drilling, he made his move. In the early evening of Sunday, October 16, 1859, he gathered his twenty-one recruits (sixteen whites and five blacks), held a brief prayer meeting, and then ordered them to "get on your arms; we will proceed to the Ferry."

Everything went as planned at the start. But then gunshots rang out as the raiders stopped a midnight express train from Wheeling. Aroused by the gunfire, local residents gathered in the streets, where rumors of "slave insurrection" and "rapine and murder" quickly spread. But when it became apparent that the dreaded invasion force was nothing more than a handful of abolitionist fanatics, the crowd, joined by local militia units, surrounded the armory demanding revenge and firing at anything that moved. Although Brown's guerrillas had initiated the attack and killed five persons—four whites and one free black—they were not as wantonly brutal as the Virginians themselves. Over the next two days some raiders were shot, one of them dumped into the river to be used for target practice. On Tuesday, when a company of U.S. Marines under the command of Colonel Robert E. Lee finally captured Brown, he and his men were taunted, cursed, and spat upon as they lay wounded or dead in the armory yard.

System and the Whig Party platforms of the 1830s and 1840s, these proposals were not new. But repackaged with the Republican Party's antislavery platform, they took on a new life that appealed to a growing segment of the northern population.

### JOHN BROWN'S RAID

While controversy swirled around the Buchanan administration, and southerners—relatively untouched by the Panic of 1857—proclaimed the dominance of "King Cotton," the radical abolitionist John Brown was busy formulating a plan for an attack on the slave South that would turn its world upside down. With a price on his head after the 1856 Pottawatomie massacre in Kansas, Brown spent the next three years traveling throughout the North under assumed names, giving lectures and meeting with abolitionist groups in an effort to raise money for his "holy" cause. Convinced that southerners had to be punished

John Brown at the time of his ill-fated Harpers Ferry raid.

Harpers Ferry, Virginia (now West Virginia), 1857. The object of Brown's attack was the national armory at Harpers Ferry (center left) and its large arsenal of the latest military firearms.

fire-eaters encouraged the notion that all northerners were "Black Republicans" bent on inciting a slave war against the South. A joint committee of the Virginia legislature gave currency to such feelings when, on January 26, 1860, it reported "the existence, in a number of Northern States, of a widespread conspiracy, not merely against Virginia, but against the peace and security of all the Southern States." It was only ten years since the Compromise of 1850.

## The Election of 1860

There was little ground for compromise as the election of 1860 approached. Meeting in Charleston, South Carolina, in April 1860, the Democratic Party convention ended in shambles. Stephen A. Douglas came into the convention as the favorite of northern Democrats, but he had little support among southerners. The southern party members insisted that the Democratic platform include a call for a guarantee by the federal government that neither Congress nor any territorial legislature could, in the words of Jefferson Davis, "impair the constitutional right of any citizen of the United States to take his slave property into the common territories." When Douglas supporters refused to back the proposal because it went against their commitment to popular sovereignty, fifty delegates from the lower South walked out of the convention. Unable to agree on a candidate after fifty-seven acrimonious ballots, the convention adjourned with the understanding that it would reconvene at Baltimore in six weeks.

The hiatus did little to cool tempers or modify positions. The continuing impasse led virtually all of the southern delegates to walk out again and organize their own convention. They then nominated Vice-President John C. Breckinridge of Kentucky on a platform that called for the protection of slave property in the territories as well as the annexation of Cuba. Not to be outdone, the original Baltimore convention nominated Douglas on a platform that emphasized popular sovereignty and, as a sop to the South, strict enforcement of the Fugitive Slave Act.

During the six-week interval between Brown's capture on October 18 and his execution on December 2, sectional tensions reached new heights. All of Virginia and most of the South took on the appearance of an armed camp as militia units sprang to active duty and vigilante groups patrolled the countryside looking for suspicious persons of any color. Rumors persisted that armed bands of fugitive slaves were roaming the mountains and that an army of Yankee abolitionists was poised on the Pennsylvania border, ready to invade Virginia and free Brown. Northern admirers like Henry David Thoreau were already pronouncing Brown a martyr to the cause of freedom, and Brown seemed to want it that way. " *Let them hang me,*" he wrote to his brother. "I am worth inconceivably more to *hang* than for any other purpose." As he went to the gallows, he handed an attendant one last statement: "I John Brown am now quite *certain* that the crimes of this *guilty land : will* never be purged *away;* but with Blood."

Brown's spirited defense of his "invasion" and the ringing abolitionist eulogies that followed his execution sent a paroxysm of anger throughout the South. Despite a large body of northern opinion that castigated the raid, secession-minded

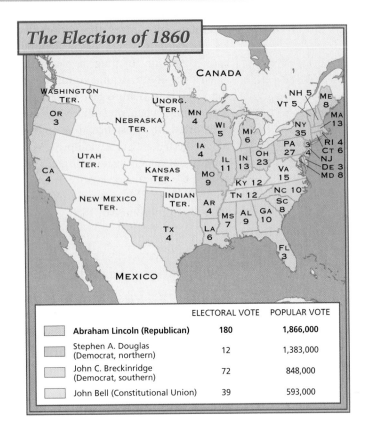

### The Election of 1860

| | ELECTORAL VOTE | POPULAR VOTE |
|---|---|---|
| **Abraham Lincoln (Republican)** | 180 | 1,866,000 |
| Stephen A. Douglas (Democrat, northern) | 12 | 1,383,000 |
| John C. Breckinridge (Democrat, southern) | 72 | 848,000 |
| John Bell (Constitutional Union) | 39 | 593,000 |

ery advocate who shocked listeners by pointing to "a higher law than the Constitution" and an "irrepressible conflict between freedom and slavery." At the same time, Abraham Lincoln was steadily gaining momentum among midwestern Republicans. Considered a quick-witted and resourceful politician, Lincoln did not have Seward's political baggage. He consequently won the nomination with the support of party leaders from key border states like Pennsylvania and Indiana, who considered him more electable.

While Douglas Democrats, Breckinridge Democrats, and the united Republicans mustered their forces, a fourth contending party appeared on the scene. Known as the Constitutional Union Party, it consisted mainly of old-line Whigs and former Know-Nothings who denounced the sectionalism that pervaded both major parties and, in the spirit of Henry Clay and Daniel Webster, appealed to the cause of the Union. Meeting in Baltimore in May 1860, these conservative nationalists refused to take a stand on the issues that divided the nation and instead adopted a platform that pledged "to recognize no political principle other than *the Constitution . . . the Union . . . and the Enforcement of the Laws.*" Well aware that they stood little chance of winning the election, party organizers hoped to carry several border states and draw enough votes away from Lincoln in key lower northern states to throw the election into the House of Representatives, where they might then exercise enough leverage to elect someone with strong unionist proclivities. Their candidate was John Bell of Tennessee, a life-long Whig and former secretary of war under William Henry Harrison. Although he owned slaves, Bell was not a fire-eater. Southern Democrats accused Bell and his party of trying to push the slavery question under the rug. "That issue," a southern editorial declared, "must be met and settled."

The election of 1860 surpassed all others to that point for tension, complexity, and excitement. Taking a page from their Whig predecessors' book, the Republicans organized a campaign that outdid their adversaries for enthusiasm and showmanship. They staged massive torchlight parades and organized "Wide Awake" clubs to provide local gatherings with plenty of vocal support. Party literature portrayed Lincoln as "Honest Old Abe," the rail splitter who was born in a log cabin and epitomized the common man. Leaders also emphasized that theirs was more than a one-issue party, a strategy that sought to moderate its radical antislavery image in order to attract voters from both slaveholding border states and lower northern states. Pennsylvania Republicans, for example, used the tariff issue to considerable effect; at the same

With the Democratic Party split down the middle, Republican leaders exulted in the knowledge that they had a good chance of winning the election. Although still limited primarily to the northern states, far more populous than the South, the Republican Party had matured since 1856. It was a stronger organization with a broad policy base that included antislavery, a strong protective tariff, a homestead act, a Pacific railroad, and internal improvements. The party now also extended a hand to foreign immigrants by favoring their "rights of citizenship." Moreover, party leaders like Senator William Seward of New York realized that they had to distance themselves from the radical abolitionist wing in order to win the election. "An Anti-Slavery man *per se* cannot be elected," Horace Greeley of the New York *Tribune* noted, "but a Tariff, River-and-Harbor, Pacific Railroad, Free-Homestead man *may* succeed *although* he is Anti-Slavery."

Seward loomed as the odds-on favorite going into the Republican convention at Chicago. As the former governor of New York and two-term senator, he was the most prominent member of the Republican Party. But he was also an antislav-

time, they pointed to the Buchanan administration's sorry record of corruption in making government contracts, distributing patronage, and bribing members of Congress. Since Douglas as well as Breckinridge Democrats were implicated in the scandals, Republican campaigners made great political capital by pointing to all Democrats as rascals associated with the immoral "slave power."

The stakes in the election were high, for the future of the Republic weighed in the balance. Southern politicians and editorialists warned that "the South will never submit to such humiliation and degradation as the inauguration of Abraham Lincoln." Despite these warnings, Republicans refused to believe that if they won, secession and war would follow. As early as 1856, Lincoln had declared that "all this talk about dissolution of the Union is humbug, nothing but folly." Four years later, he remained steadfast in the belief, noting that "the people of the South have too much good sense, and good temper, to attempt the ruin of the government." Even though Lincoln repeatedly promised not to interfere with slavery where it already existed, his image as a "Black Republican" and inveterate enemy of slavery not only persisted but grew among southerners.

The one candidate who viewed himself as a national candidate and refused to write off either section was Douglas. Although weakened by the hard living and hard drinking that would soon take his life, Douglas threw himself into the campaign like no one else. Unlike Lincoln, Breckinridge, and Bell, who followed tradition and stayed home while others campaigned for them, Douglas personally canvassed the country, vowing to prevent disunion. Even after he learned in early October that the Republicans had won crucial gubernatorial victories in Pennsylvania, Ohio, and Indiana, he continued on the campaign trail. "Mr. Lincoln is the next President," he told his friends. "We must try to save the Union." During the next month he conducted a whirlwind speaking tour that took him from Milwaukee to St. Louis, Memphis, Atlanta, Mobile, and other communities in the deep South. At each stop, the message was virtually the same: "not to ask for your votes . . . but to make an appeal to you on behalf of the Union." The "Little Giant" ended his odyssey on election day, an exhausted and dying man.

Lincoln won the election with 1.8 million votes, less than 40 percent of the total cast. With the exception of New Jersey (whose electoral votes he split with Douglas), he carried all eighteen free states, which gave him 180 electoral votes and a comfortable 27-vote margin of victory. That he won the election without even being on the ballot in ten southern states spoke to the skill of his organization, but it also indicated the degree of polarization that had occurred during the campaign. By contrast, Douglas polled well over 1.3 million votes spread across the country, but he carried only Missouri, which, coupled with New Jersey's split vote, gave him a disappointing fourth-place finish with 12 electoral votes. Breckinridge, who garnered fewer popular votes but won eleven southern states, came in second with 72 electoral votes, followed by Bell's 39 from Virginia, Kentucky, and Tennessee. For the first time in the country's seventy-two-year history, a party embracing principles hostile to slavery held the presidency. But even though the Republicans won the White House, they failed to win a majority in either house of Congress; nor did they control the Supreme Court.

It remained to be seen how the South would respond to the election. Both sides recognized that these were "revolutionary times" and that, for better or worse, a Republican would soon assume the most powerful position in the country. Forty years of sectional tension now were reaching a climax.

## Suggested Reading

Robert V. Bruce, *The Launching of Modern American Science, 1846–1876* (1987)

John P. Daly, *When Slavery was Called Freedom: Evangelicalism, Proslavery, and the Causes of the Civil War* (2002)

David H. Donald, *Lincoln* (1995)

Eric Foner, *Free Soil, Free Labor, Free Men: The Ideology of the Republican Party Before the Civil War* (2nd ed., 1995)

Stephen R. Haynes, *Noah's Curse: The Biblical Justification of American Slavery* (2002)

William Hosley, *Colt: The Making of an American Legend* (1996)

James L. Huston, *Calculating the Value of the Union: Slavery, Property Rights, and the Economic Origins of the Civil War* (2003)

Allan Nevins, *Ordeal of the Union. Vol. 2. A House Dividing, 1852–1857* (1947)

David M. Potter, *The Impending Crisis, 1848–1863* (1976)

Leonard L. Richards, *The Slave Power: The Free North and Southern Domination, 1780–1860* (2001)

John H. Schroeder, *Matthew Galbraith Perry* (2001)

# Chapter Review

## Summary
### QUESTIONS

- What was the "American system of manufactures" and how did it relate to earlier manufacturing developments in the United States?

- What did the London Crystal Palace Exhibition signify about the development of the American economy at mid-century?

- How did sectional tensions in the United States play out in political parties during the 1850s? How did electoral politics in 1856 and 1860 emerge from but also intensify sectional tensions?

- How did public perception of what was at stake in debates over slavery change during the 1850s? When did the United States reach a point of "no return" on the issue of slavery?

- Did Abraham Lincoln's election constitute an immediate menace to slavery?

## Chronology

| | |
|---|---|
| 1844 | Samuel F. B. Morse invents the telegraph. |
| 1846 | The Smithsonian Institution established. |
| | John C. Frémont maps the Oregon Trail. |
| May 1, 1851 | The Crystal Palace exhibition opens in London. |
| 1852 | Harriet Beecher Stowe publishes *Uncle Tom's Cabin*. |
| 1854 | The Gadsden Purchase. |
| | The Kansas-Nebraska Act. |
| November 1855 | Conflict breaks out in Kansas. |
| May 24, 1856 | The Pottawatomie Massacre. |
| 1857 | Financial panic. |
| March 6, 1857 | The *Dred Scott* decision. |
| October 16, 1859 | John Brown's raid at Harpers Ferry, Virginia. |

## Key Terms

The Great Reconnaissance (p. 428)

Kansas-Nebraska Act (pp. 434–437)

*Dred Scott* Decision (p. 442)

Lincoln-Douglas Debates (p. 443)

John Brown's Raid (p. 446)

# Chapter 16

# CIVIL WAR:

## 1861–1865

Artist's sketch of Confederate troops (right foreground) about to attack the Union line at Chickamauga Creek, September 19, 1863.

## QUESTIONS

**■ How did the Fort Sumter crisis end any chance of compromise?**

**■ What was the significance of the war at sea?**

**■ What were the military and political turning points in the course of the war?**

**■ To what extent is the Civil War the first modern war and what was its larger significance?**

**■ How did each side marshal its resources during the war?**

Secession was the first item on the agenda for South Carolina's legislature after the election of Lincoln. Gathering amid great fanfare on December 17, 1860, a specially elected state convention unanimously adopted an ordinance of secession three days later. Encouraged by South Carolina's bold action, Mississippi, Florida, Alabama, Georgia, Louisiana, and Texas soon followed suit. In early February 1861, representatives from all seven states met at Montgomery, Alabama, establishing the Confederate States of America and electing Jefferson Davis of Mississippi as president and Alexander H. Stephens of Georgia as vice-president. Asserting that Thomas Jefferson and the other founders had erred in the Declaration of Independence when they held that all men are created equal, Stephens emphasized that "our new government is founded upon exactly the opposite idea . . . that the negroe is not equal to the white man; that slavery . . . is his natural and normal condition." President Davis declared that he and his Confederate colleagues had left the Union "to save ourselves from a revolution" being perpetrated by Lincoln and his "Black Republican" allies. Secession was a bold step to forestall what Davis and his allies perceived as an imminent Yankee threat "to destroy their social system." Their foremost concern was the future of slavery, not states' rights. Little did they know that their actions would lead, swiftly and bloodily, to the end of slavery.

## Compromise Efforts

The seven states that formed the Confederacy now looked to the eight remaining slave states—Virginia, North Carolina, Tennessee, Arkansas, Kentucky, Maryland, Missouri,

and Delaware—to join them. The speed with which the Confederacy took shape disguised the presence of a significant minority in the lower South opposed to secession. In Alabama, for example, 39 percent of the delegates to the secession convention had voted against the measure; 30 percent of Georgia's delegates did the same. Unionist sentiment proved even stronger in the upper South and border states, which were more closely linked economically to the North than to the lower South, and had smaller slave populations. When voters in North Carolina and Kentucky refused to call secession conventions, and sitting conventions in Arkansas, Missouri, and Virginia rejected secession in the early spring of 1861, Unionists saw glimmers of hope. Still, the situation remained ominous. Tennessee's legislature expressed a pervasive view when it warned of resistance to any attempt to "coerce" the Confederate states or to invade "the soil of the South." Heeding these warnings, moderate Republicans such as William Seward urged President-elect Lincoln "to be conciliatory, forbearing and patient" and to "open the way for the rising of a Union Party in the seceding States which will bring them back into the Union."

But what compromise would satisfy both sides? With his cabinet rocked by scandals and himself accused of being in league with the secessionists, lame-duck President Buchanan worked behind the scenes to bring the divided parties together. His main hope rested with getting Lincoln to support a constitutional convention in which the North and South might iron out their differences. But Lincoln vacillated and then responded that he did "not desire any amendments to the Constitution." What little hope remained turned toward a compromise measure proposed by Senator John J. Crittenden, Henry Clay's successor from Kentucky.

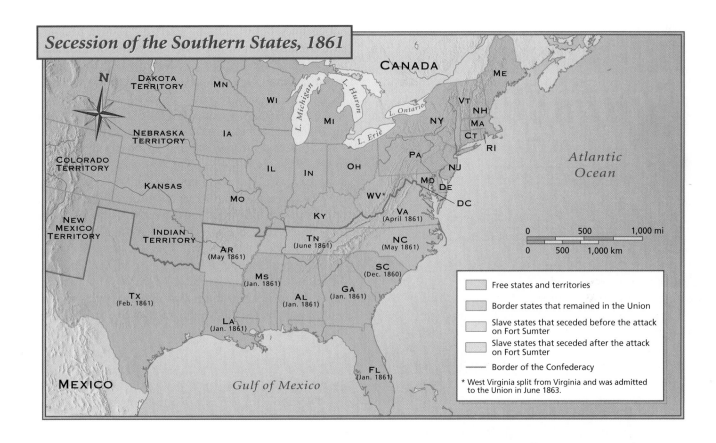

**Secession of the Southern States, 1861**

Free states and territories

Border states that remained in the Union

Slave states that seceded before the attack
on Fort Sumter

Slave states that seceded after the attack
on Fort Sumter

Border of the Confederacy

\* West Virginia split from Virginia and was admitted
to the Union in June 1863.

## CRITTENDEN'S COMPROMISE

Crittenden's compromise plan proposed to restore the Missouri Compromise line of 36°–30′ (breached by the Kansas-Nebraska Act) all the way to California and to guarantee that the national government would not interfere with slavery in states where it already existed. While Lincoln had no problem with the latter measure, as he would affirm in his inaugural address, he refused to entertain any compromise that involved "the *extension* of slavery." In December 1860, Lincoln had written to Alexander Stephens to assure him that his administration had no intention of disturbing slavery where it was. The only difference between North and South, he emphasized, was that "you think slavery is *right* and ought to be extended; while we think it is *wrong* and ought to be restricted." Since bringing back the Missouri Compromise would allow the extension of slavery south of 36°–30′, Lincoln warned Republican moderates who favored Crittenden's proposal that it "would lose us everything we gained by the election." Braced by these comments, the Republican members of the Senate committee that had initiated the Crittenden compromise ended up voting against it. So did two secessionist Democrats who reasoned that no compromise was possible without Republican support. In the end, Crittenden's bill was narrowly defeated on the floor of the now-reduced Senate, 25 to 23. All 25 nays came from Republicans.

## LINCOLN'S FIRST INAUGURAL ADDRESS

By the time Lincoln boarded a train in Illinois for his March 4 inauguration in Washington, he had already drafted a version of his inaugural address. Knowing that what he said could be taken as his first policy statement concerning the secession crisis, he chose his words carefully. The seven states of the new Confederacy had begun seizing federal forts, arsenals, customs houses, and treasury buildings that lay within their respective boundaries. Seven other states in the upper South and border-state areas were teetering on the brink of secession. Lincoln's first task in preserving the Union was to prevent further secessions. Then,

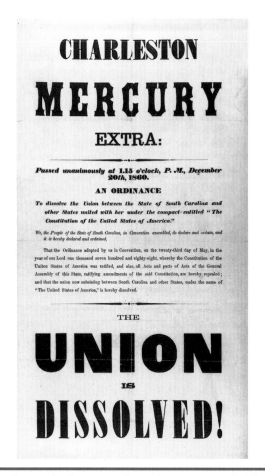

# CHARLESTON

# MERCURY

## EXTRA:

Passed unanimously at 1.15 o'clock, P. M., December
20th, 1860.

### AN ORDINANCE

To dissolve the Union between the State of South Carolina and
other States united with her under the compact entitled "The
Constitution of the United States of America."

We, the People of the State of South Carolina, in Convention assembled, do declare and ordain, and
it is hereby declared and ordained,

That the Ordinance adopted by us in Convention, on the twenty-third day of May, in the
year of our Lord one thousand seven hundred and eighty-eight, whereby the Constitution of the
United States of America was ratified, and also, all Acts and parts of Acts of the General
Assembly of this State, ratifying amendments of the said Constitution, are hereby repealed;
and that the union now subsisting between South Carolina and other States, under the name of
"The United States of America," is hereby dissolved.

# THE

# UNION

## IS

# DISSOLVED!

Headline from a Charleston, South Carolina newspaper boldly
proclaiming the dissolution and secession of South Carolina,
December 20, 1860.

perhaps, he could persuade the Confederate states to "reconstruct" themselves by returning to the Union.

In his inaugural address, Lincoln adopted a carrot-and-stick approach. The carrot was his oft-repeated promise not to interfere with slavery where it already existed and his assurance that the controversial Fugitive Slave Act would be strictly enforced. The stick was his determination to employ "all the powers at my disposal" to "reclaim the public property and places which have fallen; to hold, occupy, and possess these, and all other property and places belonging to the government, and to collect the duties on imports." Lincoln also assured the South that "the government will not assail *you*, unless you *first* assail *it*." He ended his address with an impassioned plea for the preservation of the Union. "We are

not enemies, but friends," he asserted. "Though passion may have strained, it must not break our bonds of affection." Yet behind these words stood a president who had just taken a "most solemn" oath to "preserve, protect and defend" the Union. Viewing the Union as "perpetual" and secession as the "essence of anarchy," he intended to see to it that "the laws of the Union be faithfully executed in all the States."

As expected, fellow Republicans generally hailed the speech as statesmanlike, while Southern secessionists denounced it as a "Declaration of War." In between were Northern Democrats and Southerners with Unionist sympathies—two groups that Lincoln most wanted to reach. Although some Northern Democrats criticized the speech as either waffling or bellicose, Stephen A. Douglas considered it a "peace offering" and announced that "I am with him." Similar comments came from the upper South, where Unionists felt bolstered by the "temperance and conservatism" of Lincoln's address and reasonably confident that they might yet stem the rising tide of secessionism.

## The Fall of Fort Sumter

Lincoln's biggest quandary upon entering office was what to do about federal properties that lay within the boundaries of the Confederacy. Most pressing was the status of Fort Sumter, a newly reconstructed fortification in the harbor of Charleston, South Carolina—the hotbed of secessionism and anti-Yankee feeling. Ever since South Carolina had seceded, its newly elected governor, Francis W. Pickens, had demanded the "immediate" surrender of not only Sumter but also Fort Moultrie and Castle Pinckney, two other coastal installations that guarded the entrance to Charleston. Although accused of complying with Southern demands, President Buchanan had, in fact, refused to relinquish any federal property in the South and warned Governor Pickens that "if South Carolina should attack any of these forts, she will then become the assailant in a war against the United States."

Despite Buchanan's warnings, pressure from South Carolinians continued to mount. The local Union army commander, Major Robert Anderson, expected an attack at any moment. To strengthen his position, Anderson disabled the guns at Fort Moultrie and, on the night of December 27, 1860, secretly moved his entire command to Fort Sumter. Outraged at Anderson's action, South Carolina responded the following day by seizing Fort Moultrie, Castle Pinckney, and the U.S. Customs House at Charleston. While Anderson waited in his offshore stronghold, South Carolina seized other federal facilities, closed the port of Charleston to all U.S. ships, and, at one point, fired on an unarmed vessel dispatched by the Buchanan administration with food for Anderson's beleaguered force.

The day after Lincoln took office, le learned that Major Anderson was running short of supplies and would need at least 20,000 troops to relieve Fort Sumter. At best, Anderson said, he could hold the fort six weeks before he and his men would be starved out and forced to capitulate. Secretary of State Seward and army commander General Winfield Scott recommended abandoning Sumter in the interest of avoiding an all-out war and reassuring Unionists throughout the South of the new administration's peaceful intentions. Although the president hesitated to make a final decision, the ambitious Seward, who viewed himself as Lincoln's premier and the real head of the government, began to spread the word that Sumter would soon be relinquished. However, Lincoln began to consider an effort to resupply Sumter. The plan was to send a fleet of warships to the outskirts of Charleston's harbor and, with smaller boats, transfer men and supplies to Fort Sumter under the cover of darkness. With the support of his cabinet, Lincoln gave the order to go ahead on April 4, 1861.

Once the relief fleet set sail for Charleston, the decision whether to allow the provisioning of Fort Sumter rested with the Confederacy's president and commander in chief, Jefferson Davis. Already under fire for not taking action against Sumter sooner and fearful that continued inaction might cost the Confederacy the support of the upper South, Davis came under pressure to "strike a blow." On April 9, Davis gave the order, and three days later General Pierre G. T. Beauregard's artillery opened fire. The Confederate bombardment lasted thirty-three hours, pummeling Anderson's outgunned force. Although the Union relief fleet arrived outside Charleston Harbor during the fighting, a storm prevented it from intervening. Anderson and his half-starved force surrendered to Beauregard on April 14.

The fall of Fort Sumter marked the onset of civil war. The day after Anderson's capitulation, Lincoln issued a proclamation calling on Northern governors for 75,000 militia troops to quell the rebellion. The president, confident that concerted action would end the insurrection, asked that the state troops be released for national service for a period of ninety days. To his surprise, the governors offered him twice the number of troops called for.

While an eruption of public enthusiasm swept over the North, the governors of six slave states still in the Union condemned the president's "unholy crusade." Kentucky's governor, expressing a common viewpoint, notified Washington that his state would "furnish no troops for the wicked purpose of subduing her sister Southern States." Elsewhere in the South, four more states—Virginia, Arkansas, North Carolina, and Tennessee—seceded and joined the Confederacy during the late spring of 1861. Although Southern speakers and editorialists made much of state sovereignty, regional honor, and resistance to coercion, the central issue for all of them centered on the

This photograph of the interior of Fort Sumter on the day of its surrender (April 14, 1861) shows the damage done by Confederate artillery. Note the bombed-out look of the barracks on the left as well as the damage inflicted on the fort's massive brick gun ramparts (upper right).

threat Lincoln and his "Black Republican" Party posed to the right of whites to own slaves and to take them anywhere they pleased.

PREPARING FOR WAR

Neither the Union nor the Confederacy was prepared for war, let alone a prolonged one. Few people, North or South, thought that the "rebellion" would last more than a couple of months. As the crisis deepened and hopes of a reconciliation disappeared, however, both sides sought to procure not only arms and munitions but everything from army blankets and tents to wagons, horses, and mules.

On paper, the North appeared to enjoy an overwhelming advantage in resources. Northern white males of fighting age outnumbered Southern whites by more than three to one. Equally daunting, the Northern states commanded over 90 percent of the country's manufacturing capacity. The census of 1860 clearly revealed the North's dominance in the production of firearms (97 percent), railway locomotives (96 percent), cloth (94 percent), pig iron (93 percent), boots and shoes (90 percent), and many other items. The same was true of mass transportation facilities, with the North possessing twice the railroad mileage of the South and several times the mileage in paved roads and canals. Only in food production did the South rival the North. Yet even then, the South's inferior railway system often prevented food and other supplies from reaching war zones.

Initially, at least, one Southern state appeared better prepared to wage war than others. In 1860, largely in response to John Brown's raid on Harpers Ferry, the Virginia legislature had appropriated money to rebuild the state's long-defunct "Manufactory of Arms," soon to be renamed the Richmond Armory. Moreover, on April 18, 1861—the day after the Virginia legislature voted for secession—a state militia seized the national armory at Harpers Ferry and dismantled its machinery for shipment to Richmond. All told, Virginia placed nearly two complete sets of arms-making machinery, thousands of tools, and tons of raw material at the disposal of the Confederate government. The Virginia militia also confiscated more than 4,000 finished firearms and enough components to assemble between 7,000 and 10,000 weapons of the latest design. The Harpers Ferry machinery eventually would be used to tool the two largest armories in the South, one at Richmond, the other at Fayetteville, North Carolina.

A poster calling for Irish volunteers to form a company in the Second Regiment of Baker's Brigade, Philadelphia, 1861.

The looting of the Harpers Ferry Armory dealt a serious blow to the Lincoln administration. Even with Harpers Ferry in production, the national armories did not have the capacity to arm 75,000 militia, to say nothing of the 400,000 extra troops Lincoln would call for in July 1861. The largest private armory in America—Samuel Colt's works at Hartford, Connecticut—could produce around 35,000 pistols a year, but needed time to retool to produce rifle-muskets, the standard infantry weapon of the period. War Department officials thus turned to foreign sources of supply for the small arms needed during the spring and summer of 1861.

During the first year of the conflict, War Department officials signed over thirty contracts with European and American arms brokers for the delivery of hundreds of thousands of foreign-made firearms. But the strategy worked poorly, as unscrupulous "speculators and 'middle men'" duped the government into signing loosely worded contracts that allowed them to substitute "guns of very inferior quality" for those promised. By the fall of 1862, most of the Union's needs for arms were being met by the Springfield Armory and twenty-four private contractors, who altogether delivered over 1,427,000 rifle-muskets during the war years—a remarkable feat of industrial production. New England armories accounted for 86 percent of these deliveries, the Springfield Armory topping all others with an output of more than 793,000.

Like the North, the Confederacy faced serious weapons shortages. Most of the 159,000 small arms seized from federal arsenals were obsolete or in need of repair, and gunpowder and ammunition were in short supply. Most serious of all, the Confederate states lacked the manufacturing capacity to produce such materials. To solve the problem, President Davis turned to Colonel Josiah Gorgas, a West Point graduate and head of the Confederate Ordnance Bureau. Gorgas devised a plan: to capture arms on the battlefield, build and equip arsenals in the South, and import arms and ammunition from Europe.

To get guns at once, Gorgas dispatched an army colleague to London. With letters of credit based on the sale of Southern cotton (known as "white gold") in England, the Confederacy procured two-thirds of its supply of weapons, plus "large quantities of saltpeter, lead, cartridges, percussion caps, flannel and paper for cartridges, leather, hardware, &C." By war's end, 600,000 small arms from Europe had reached Confederate armies, along with critical supplies of clothing, blankets, cloth, and shoes. Gorgas's skill as a planner coupled with the efforts of other West Point–trained supply officers helped build the Confederate armies into a formidable fighting force during the war.

## The War at Sea

Transporting the weapons and supplies acquired in Europe safely to ports in the South posed other problems. Within a week after the fall of Fort Sumter, Lincoln, heeding the advice of General Winfield Scott, imposed a blockade on the South that sought to cut off the Confederacy from all outside sources of supply. But with only forty-two ships available to patrol 189 harbors and over 3,000 miles of Southern coastline, the Union blockade was ineffective during the war's first year, with nine out of ten ships getting through. Lincoln's secretary of the navy, Gideon Welles, sought to acquire more warships and to provide them with fueling and repair bases by capturing key points along the southern coast. In August

1861, Cape Hatteras fell to a joint army-navy amphibious expedition. Shortly afterward, a navy flotilla captured Ship Island near Biloxi, Mississippi. During the next six months, four more successful assaults threatened to bottle up every major southern port east of the Mississippi River except Mobile (Alabama) and Wilmington (North Carolina). But even then, seven out of eight blockade runners successfully evaded Union patrols in 1862.

### THE *MONITOR* VERSUS THE *VIRGINIA*

Since the South had no navy to speak of, its efforts to break the blockade depended on the reconstruction of the *Merrimack,* a steam-powered, wooden-hulled frigate scuttled by Union forces in April 1861, when the state of Virginia seized the Norfolk Navy Yard. Newly outfitted with ten stationary guns and protected by four-inch-thick plates of laminated iron, the rechristened *Virginia* steamed out of Norfolk on March 8, 1862, and attacked the Union blockading squadron stationed at Hampton Roads, Virginia. With cannonballs bouncing harmlessly off its armor, the *Virginia* sank two Union warships, while three others ran aground trying to escape it. The action clearly demonstrated that traditional wooden vessels, no matter how many guns they carried, posed no threat to ironclads. President Lincoln and his advisers spent a sleepless night contemplating the *Virginia*'s next move, even though they realized that help was on its way to Hampton Roads in the form of a newly built ironclad called the *Monitor.* But would the smaller, two-gun *Monitor* check the larger *Virginia*?

When the *Virginia* left Norfolk on March 9 to finish off its grounded opponents, the *Monitor* was waiting. Hundreds of onlookers watched as the two vessels hammered each other for two hours at point-blank range. One cannonball after another struck armor and ricocheted into the sea. Neither ship was seriously damaged, but the *Virginia* eventually broke off the engagement and returned to Norfolk.

The contest ended in a tactical draw, but the North gained the strategic advantage. Stalemated by the *Monitor,* the *Virginia* was unable to do any more damage to the Union fleet, and Southern hopes for breaking the blockade dissipated.

The *Monitor* and the *Virginia* made an indelible impact on naval warfare. Not counting the *Monitor*'s two steam engines, screw propellers, and iron plating, the ship was said to contain fifty patentable inventions. Most noteworthy was the revolving turret, protected by eight inches of laminated iron all around, which housed two huge guns that could be aimed anywhere

The *USS Monitor* (right foreground) lent its name to other Union ironclad vessels during the Civil War. This painting depicts the battle with the Confederate ship *Virginia* on March 9, 1862.

fused to be drawn into a game of raider chasing.

Although Confederate blockade runners continued to get through, the Union blockade significantly reduced the total volume of Southern seaborne trade. Four years before the war, some 20,000 vessels entered and departed ports in the South; during the war, the number fell by 60 percent to 8,000. The smaller blockade runners had less cargo capacity than prewar merchantmen, and they frequently dumped their cargoes in order to gain speed when being pursued. Total trade volume shrank. The Union blockade forced the Confederacy to scramble to build a manufacturing base with which to produce guns, ships, uniforms, and other supplies. With its late start in industrial investment, the South never came close to rivaling the industrial colossus of the North. Nonetheless, the Confederacy, with the highest per capita wealth in North America and the fourth richest economy in the world produced and/or procured enough food, munitions, and equipment to keep its troops reasonably well provisioned until the last year of the conflict.

during an engagement without having to turn the ship. Such innovations, coupled with the *Monitor*'s impressive performance at Hampton Roads, convinced the Lincoln administration to concentrate on building ironclads, now also called monitors, for coastal and river service. Fifty-eight were in service by war's end and had become the mainstay of the Union fleet. The advent of the new technology presaged a major shift in ship design and naval warfare.

FIGHTING THE UNION BLOCKADE

Since its small navy would never seriously challenge Union forces on the high seas, the Confederate government turned to attacking merchant ships, hoping that such raids would disrupt the North's economy and force the Lincoln administration to divert warships from the blockade of ports in the South. Four Confederate cruisers built in England caused significant damage to the U.S. merchant marine. Nevertheless, commerce raiding did not have the intended effect. Northern merchants simply shifted their cargoes to foreign vessels, which enjoyed the status of neutral carriers. More important, the Union navy continued to focus on the blockade and re-

## The Land War

The blockade of ports in the South was part of a larger Union strategy devised by General Scott and supported by President Lincoln: to exert economic and political pressure on the South by sealing it off from the rest of the world along the coastline and up the Mississippi and slowly squeeze it into submission. Doing so, in Scott's view, would "bring them to terms with less bloodshed than by any other plan."

But while Lincoln hoped that the contest would not "degenerate into a violent and remorseless revolutionary struggle," he knew that some sort of large-scale invasion of Southern territory would be necessary. Even Scott admitted that the Union would have to "conquer the seceding states by invading armies." Nonetheless, he urged restraint. "Our patriotic and loyal Union friends," he cautioned, "urge instant and vigorous

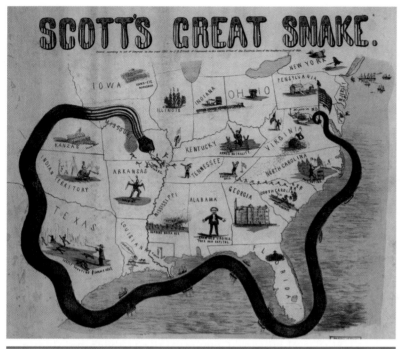

This lithograph reveals how General Winfield Scott's "Anaconda Plan" aimed at cutting off the South from outside supplies and internal trade by wrapping Union forces around the seceded states and economically squeezing them into submission.

action, regardless, I fear, of the consequences." Most outspoken were a group of radical Republican newspaper editors, led by the *New York Tribune*'s Horace Greeley, who ridiculed Scott's "Anaconda Plan" as too plodding and slow. Pressure for an invasion of the South mounted when news arrived that the Confederate Congress had transferred its capital to Richmond, Virginia, and would meet there for the first time on July 20, 1861. "FORWARD TO RICHMOND! FORWARD TO RICHMOND!" the *Tribune* headline demanded. "The Rebel Congress Must Not be Allowed to Meet There on the 20th of July."

### THE FIRST BATTLE OF MANASSAS (JULY 1861)

But meet they did, and just a day later the first major land battle of the Civil War occurred within twenty-five miles of Washington, near Manassas, Virginia (also called Bull Run). From a strategic standpoint, Manassas was important because it served as a railroad junction connecting Richmond with the rich farmlands and ironworks of the Shenandoah Valley. Lincoln knew that a large Confederate force under the command of General

Pierre G. T. Beauregard, of Sumter fame, guarded the railroads at Manassas Junction. If the Southerners could be defeated, the resulting panic and dispersal would lay open a direct path to Richmond. So the president ordered Union General Irvin McDowell to march against Beauregard. Although McDowell tried to postpone the action until his troops were better trained, Lincoln refused. "You are green, it is true," he wrote the general, "but they are green, also; you are all green alike."

Accompanied by reporters, congressmen, and curious civilians, McDowell's 35,000-man army began its march toward Manassas on July 11, 1861. It initially outnumbered Beauregard's force by 15,000, but it moved so slowly that 11,000 Confederate reinforcements under General Joseph E. Johnston were rushed over from the Shenandoah Valley by the Manassas Gap Railroad before the battle began. The maneuver was critical. It marked the first time railroads were used to rapidly deploy dispersed forces against an invading army.

The first major battle of the Civil War occurred on July 21, 1861. Although outnumbered and outgunned, the Confederates proved their mettle and sent the Union army stumbling back to Washington in disarray. Within a week after Manassas, a sobered President Lincoln signed two bills calling for the enlistment of 1 million three-year volunteers. Shaken in defeat, the Union war machine began gearing up at a massive scale during the summer and fall of 1861.

Death and destruction would revisit Virginia many times during the war. Harpers Ferry, with its key bridges over the Potomac and Shenandoah rivers and converging railway lines, shifted from Confederate to Union control and back again at least eleven times. However, Virginia was not the only state where key engagements occurred. A second major theater developed from the Mississippi Valley eastward to the Appalachian Mountains and through its passes into Georgia. In this "western" theater, Union strategists aimed at using the Mississippi River and its tributaries as invasion routes to penetrate the inner reaches of the Confederacy, thus isolating the Confederate heartland from its eastern neighbors. Critical supplies of food, horses, mules, and raw materials came from Tennessee and Arkansas, while Alabama, Mississippi, Louisiana, and Texas formed the heart of the cotton belt. Severing them from the eastern section of the Confederacy would deliver a devastating, if not fatal, blow.

As Christmas 1861 approached, spirits soared in Richmond, while a feeling of gloom descended on Washington. A string of Union naval successes along the Atlantic coast could not dispel the fact that Union armies had suffered serious defeats in Virginia and Missouri. To make matters worse, the Lincoln administration had become embroiled in a diplomatic crisis with Great Britain when a Union warship stopped the British mail steamer *Trent* on the high seas and forcibly removed two Confederate officials who were on their way to London and Paris to seek recognition and support for their government. For a time, it appeared that Britain and the United States might go to war as heated messages crossed the Atlantic. But in the end, the Lincoln administration issued an apology and released the two diplomats. "One war at a time," Lincoln wisely concluded.

Nonetheless, the so-called *Trent* Affair, in conjunction with military disappointments, put Congress in a foul mood. With Democrats criticizing the war and Republicans dissatisfied with its prosecution, the legislature established a Joint Committee on the Conduct of the War, a drastic challenge to Lincoln's leadership. Dominated by radical Republicans, the committee pressed Lincoln to adopt a more belligerent attitude toward the Confederacy and issue an emancipation proclamation that would free slaves held in the seceded states. It also conducted investigations into inefficiency in the army and sought to remove officers from command whom it suspected of being either inept or, worse, Democrats. "It is exceedingly discouraging," Lincoln wrote at the end of the year. "The people are impatient. . . . The bottom is out of the tub."

### SHILOH AND NEW ORLEANS

The political skies over Washington brightened early in February 1862 when news arrived that a joint army-navy expedition under the command of General Ulysses S. Grant had captured Forts Henry and Donelson in western Tennessee. Since Fort Henry guarded the Tennessee River and Fort Donelson guarded the Cumberland River, their surrender opened two invasion routes deep into Confederate territory. Within days, Nashville fell to Union troops, making it the first state capital within the Confederacy to be captured.

At the same time, Grant's army pursued the main Confederate force under General Albert Sidney Johnston southward along the Tennessee River. Johnston concentrated his army at the railway junction of Corinth in northeastern Mississippi, where he received reinforcements. Then he suddenly moved north and surprised Grant on April 6 at Shiloh, near Pittsburg Landing on the Tennessee River. Two days of vicious fighting produced frightful results with each side suffering more than 10,000 casualties, including 3,400 dead. One of them was the Confederate commander Johnston, who was shot in the leg and bled to death before he could receive medical treatment. As he rode by "piles of dead soldiers' mangled bodies . . . without heads and legs," General William Tecumseh Sherman wrote home that "the scenes on this field would have cured anybody of war." Yet despite the horror, the conflict only escalated. The bloody devastation at Shiloh, the first massive engagement of the Civil War, would become commonplace.

Better news—from New Orleans—soon flashed over the telegraph wires to Washington. On April 28, a fleet of warships and gunboats under the command of Admiral David G. Farragut and an accompanying army of 18,000 men under General Benjamin Butler blasted their way past Confederate forts guarding the gulf entrance to the Mississippi River. The next day, New Orleans and the mouth of the Mississippi were in Union hands. Farragut's fleet then pushed upriver to take Baton Rouge and Natchez. At the same time, a flotilla of ironclads under Captain Charles H. Davis steamed south from Island No. 10 on the Mississippi to take Memphis. A combined fleet under Farragut and Davis then tried to capture Vicksburg but failed. Nonetheless, the Union had achieved substantial results. Not only

General Ulysses S. Grant, the Union's most successful military commander.

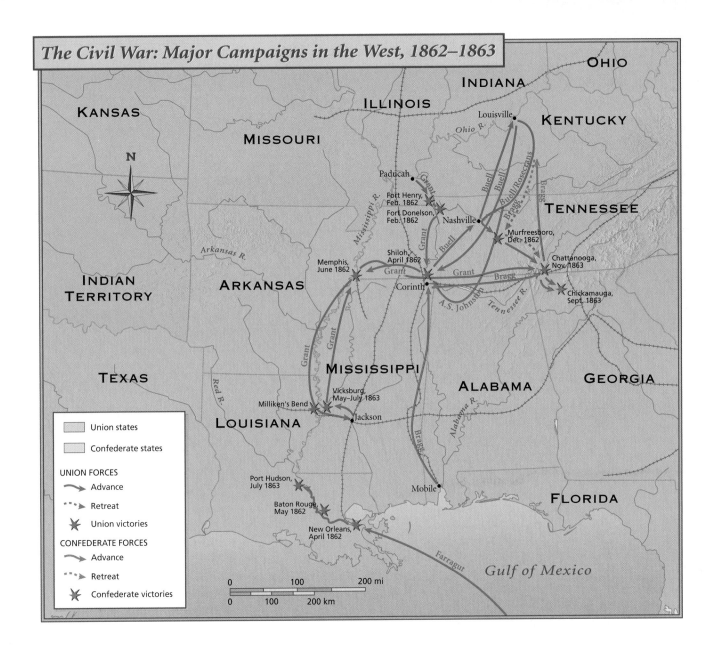

## The Civil War: Major Campaigns in the West, 1862–1863

Union states

Confederate states

UNION FORCES

Advance

Retreat

Union victories

CONFEDERATE FORCES

Advance

Retreat

Confederate victories

had the South lost control of almost all of the Mississippi River, it had also lost its largest city and one of its most important manufacturing centers.

### THE PENINSULA CAMPAIGN AND SECOND MANASSAS

The seesaw nature of the war became readily apparent during the early summer of 1862, when the North's momentum came to a crashing halt on the battlefields of Virginia and the tide turned in favor of the Confederacy. Most disconcerting was the failure of a seaborne invasion of Virginia's southeastern peninsula between the York and James rivers. Gobbling up precious time and resources, the so-called Peninsula Campaign resulted in embarrassing Union defeats outside Richmond and farther west in the Shenandoah Valley.

The culprit, in Lincoln's view, was General George McClellan, the overly cautious commander of the Army of the Potomac. McClellan repeatedly exaggerated the size of forces

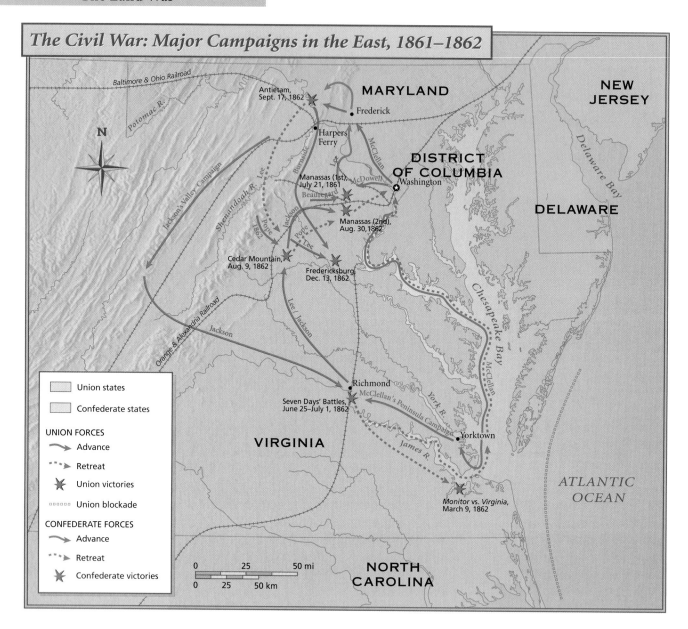

**The Civil War: Major Campaigns in the East, 1861–1862**

opposing him and moved hesitatingly against them. Opposite him was General Robert E. Lee, summoned to the field when his predecessor was wounded. An aggressive field commander, Lee led his 88,000 troops in seven days of battle during the Peninsula Campaign, hammering McClellan's army of 100,000 and driving it to retreat. Lee's success owed much to a brilliant diversionary campaign conducted in the Shenan-

doah Valley by General Thomas J. Jackson, who acquired the nickname "Stonewall" after his unstinting performance at the first Battle of Manassas in July 1861. Using deception, daring, and hard marching, Jackson's army of 17,000 kept three separate Union armies bottled up in the valley for over a month, thus preventing them from joining McClellan's invasion force on the peninsula.

Exasperated, Lincoln pulled the plug on the faltering Peninsula Campaign and fired McClellan, placing General John Pope in charge of the Union armies in Virginia. But Pope did not last long. Before he could combine his 50,000-man Army of Virginia with the remnants of McClellan's 100,000-man Army of the Potomac for an attack on Richmond from the north, Lee quickly moved his troops some sixty miles north by railroad to meet the challenge. Stonewall Jackson led the advance and won an imposing victory at Cedar Mountain on August 9, 1862. Then, after an amazing march that covered more than fifty miles in two days, Jackson's 24,000 troops circled behind Pope's army and sacked a Union supply depot at Manassas Junction, seizing much-needed shoes, uniforms, and ammunition. The raid soon precipitated the second Battle of Manassas (Bull Run) on August 29–30, in which Lee's lean, tough force of 55,000 smashed Pope's larger but disorganized army and sent it reeling back toward Washington. The Confederates suffered 10,000 casualties, an 18 percent rate, but Pope's force lost 16,000, or 25 percent. Lee had completely turned the tables on his Union adversaries. A month earlier, McClellan's army had gotten within five miles of Richmond. Now Lee's forces were within twenty miles of Washington.

## THE BATTLE OF ANTIETAM (SEPTEMBER 1862)

But the Confederacy, struggling against high odds, could not afford to rest on its laurels. Emboldened by his victory and sensing that the enemy was in disarray, Lee, in consultation with Jefferson Davis, decided to strike a decisive blow by invading the North. He intended to cut Washington's connections with the Midwest in two places—by severing the Baltimore and Ohio Railroad at Harpers Ferry, and by burning the Pennsylvania Railroad's mainline bridge over the Susquehanna River at Harrisburg. With an eye to the North's congressional election in November, Lee hoped that a successful invasion might persuade voters to throw Lincoln's Republican supporters out of office, replace them with "Peace Democrats," and "bring [the war] to a termination." Perhaps most important, Lee knew that diplomatic efforts were under way to gain British and French recognition of the Confederacy and, accordingly, their intervention in the war on the South's side. Britain and France waited for news of Lee's invasion before making the fateful decision. Much was at stake.

**LEFT:** Robert E. Lee, brilliant general in chief of the Confederate armies.

**RIGHT:** Lee's right arm: Thomas J. "Stonewall" Jackson.

Lee's invasion began on September 4, 1862, when the first of his troops crossed the Potomac River about forty miles above Washington. By then, Lincoln had fired Pope and called back McClellan to command the dispirited Army of the Potomac.

Two weeks later, on September 17, the two armies clashed along the banks of Antietam Creek just outside Sharpsburg, Maryland. The result was a veritable bloodbath—the deadliest single day of the entire war. As darkness fell on the battlefield, over 24,000 men lay dead or wounded, more than half of them Confederates. Lee had begun the campaign with roughly 45,000 soldiers under his command. After the Battle of Antietam ended, one-third of his army was dead or disabled. All told, the Union and Confederate armies sustained twice as many casualties in one day at Antietam as the United States lost altogether during the War of 1812, the Mexican War, and the Spanish-American War (at the end of the nineteenth century).

McClellan wired Lincoln that he had won a great victory at Antietam, but in fact it was a tactical draw. Bloodied but unbowed, Lee waited for McClellan to attack on September 18, but there was no attack. That evening, Lee gave the order to withdraw and, much to Lincoln's chagrin, escaped across the Potomac into Virginia. Exasperated by McClellan's "over-cautiousness" and "total inaction" in failing to pursue and destroy Lee's army, Lincoln eventually replaced him with General Ambrose Burnside. Antietam proved to be

## Casualties of War

*The face of battle elicited many expressions, none more heartrending than the thoughts of a dying Union sergeant named Jonathan Stowe, of Company G, Fifteenth Massachusetts Infantry Regiment. Seriously wounded at the Battle of Antietam on September 17, 1862, Sergeant Stowe remained on the battlefield nearly twenty-four hours before Confederate troops removed him to a local field hospital, where he waited another twenty-four hours to be treated. Through all this, Stowe managed to keep a diary as he watched comrades die and waited to hear from friends at home.*

*September 17 (Wesnesday)*—"Battle Oh horrid battle. What sights I have seen. I am wounded! . . . Am in severe pain. How the shells fly. I do sincerely hope I shall not be wounded again."

*September 18 (Thursday)*—"Misery acute, painful misery. How I suffered last night. . . . My leg must be broken for I cannot help myself scarcely any. I remember talking and groaning all night. Many died in calling for help. . . . Carried off the field at 10 a.m. by the Rebs who show much kindness but devote much time to plundering the dead bodies of our men. . . . Water very short. We suffer very much."

*September 19 (Friay)*—"Rebs retreat. Another painful night. . . . By and by our boys come along. . . . Dr. looks at my wound and calls it [a] doubtful case. Get me on ambulance at 3 p.m. but do not get to hospital till nearly dark. Plenty of water. . . . Nurses worn-out by fatigue. Placed on straw near the barn."

*September 20(Saturday)*—"Leg amputated about noon. What sensations—used chloroform hope to have no bad effects. There are some dozen or more [amputated] stumps near me."

*September 21 (Sunday)*—"Very weak and sore. . . . Hot weather by day cool at night. Hard to get nurses. . . . People come in from all parts of the country. Stare at us, but do not find time to do anything."

*September 22 (Monday)*—"Two men died last night. . . . How painful my stump is. I did not know I was capable of enduring so much pain. How very meager are accommodations—no chamber pots & nobody to find or rig up one. How ludicrous for 2 score amputated men to help themselves with diarrhea."

*September 23 (Tuesday)*—"Oh what long fearful horrid nights. What difficulties we have to content [with]. . . . Relief can hardly be found."

*September 24 (Wednesday)*—"One week today fought and wounded. Such a week. Suffering all around."

*September 25 (Thursday)*—"Such nights! Why they seem infinitely longer than days. The nervous pains are killing 2 or 3 every night. All sorts of groans & pleadings."

*September 26 (Friday)*—"Very cold last night. . . . This cold weather may all come for best, certainly maggots do not trouble so much and air is some purer."

*September 27 (Saturday)*—"Commence taking brandy none too soon. r. tells me I am dangerously ill and must take his prescription in order to change condition of blood."

*September 28 (Sunday)*—"Oh what lengths to the nights. The horrid smell from mortifying limbs is nearly as bad as the whole we have to content [with]."

*September 29 (Monday)*—"Slept a little more comfortable last night. Got nice soups and nice light biscuit and tart also nice butter from Mrs. Lee. . . . How the quinine keeps me parched for water and so sleepy and foolish. . . . I recd 4 letters from friends at home but am so boozy it takes the whole a.m. to read them. Mr. Dr. Kelsey dressed my stump admirably and am quite comfortable if the quinine does not choke me to death. It is far more quiet here but begins to rain."

On Wednesday, October 1, Sergeant Stowe died at Hoffman's Hospital near Sharpsburg, Maryland.

Robert E. Denney, *Civil War Medicine*

Lincoln visiting General McClellan and his staff at Sharpsburg, Maryland, after the Battle of Antietam, 1862.

McClellan's last campaign. Already an outspoken critic of Lincoln's war policies, he quickly became the darling of Northern Democrats who opposed the war and began to present himself as the one candidate who could defeat Lincoln in the election of 1864.

Despite this controversial outcome, the battle of Antietam ranks as one of the most decisive of the Civil War. As a result of Lee's failure to invade the North, Great Britain and France backed away from recognizing the Confederacy and, in effect, entering the war on its side—fateful decisions that might otherwise have led to a Southern victory.

## A New Warfare

The astounding casualty count at Antietam attested to a new and unfamiliar kind of warfare. For the first time in history, railroads and steamboats were moving tens of thousands of soldiers and tons of material over vast distances. Major battles were being fought for the control of steam transportation arteries. The electric telegraph was being used not only to keep Presidents Lincoln and Davis and their cabinets informed but also, in the case of the North, to coordinate and control the movement of supplies and armies themselves. Massive armies relying on mass-produced equipment were fighting an industrially based war that laid the foundations for modern warfare. The conflict witnessed the invention of the repeating rifles, submarines, mines, and machine guns. The massive deployment of rifled weapons, ironclad warships, railroads, telegraphy, and other new technologies altered the face of battle as well as supply logistics and, in doing so, forced changes in the strategy and structure of armed conflict. By 1863, for the first time, armies were not only attacking each other but also opposing civilian populations. General William Tecumseh Sherman put the new philosophy succinctly, "When one nation is at war with another, all the people of the one are the enemies of the other." Ordered "to destroy all depots of supplies of the rebel army, all manufactories (private or public) of guns, ammunition, equipment, and clothing for their use," Union armies decimated the Confederacy's capacity to feed, clothe, and arm itself. In effect, the Civil War became total war.

### THE NEW RIFLED FIREARMS

The Civil War was the first conflict to be fought largely with rifled firearms. From the outset, infantry on both sides were armed primarily with single-shot, muzzle-loading rifle-muskets (developed during the 1850s) that fired a hollowed-out bullet .58-inch in diameter known as the "Minie ball." Prior to that time, the standard infantry weapon of all nations had been the smoothbore musket, a muzzle-loading gun that fired a .69 inch (or caliber) single lead ball or, more often, a multiple load called "buck and ball" consisting of one large ball accompanied by three or four smaller balls. In the hands of common troops, a musket could rarely hit its target more than fifty or sixty yards away. Given their limited range, smoothbores proved most effective when equipped with

This 1864 photograph by Alexander Gardner shows a mobile telegraph unit in action. Note the telegrapher seated inside the covered wagon and the telegraph wires attached to it. Telegraphic messages greatly increased the speed of strategic information to and from the battlefield and proved enormously useful to both sides.

bayonets and used in frontal assaults; a charging soldier might get off two or three shots before closing in hand-to-hand combat.

The new rifled firearms changed all that. The spiral grooves cut into the barrels of these rifled weapons imparted a spinning motion to the bullets they fired, making them more accurate at longer distances. Standard single-shot rifle-muskets and breech-loading carbines were complemented by rapid-firing repeating rifles using self-contained paper and brass cartridges. These new guns fired hollowed-out, conically shaped bullets that had an effective killing range of over 200 yards—more than four times that of the traditional smoothbore musket. This change made attacking more difficult and defense more effective. It took military officials some time to figure out what was going on and to change their tactical manuals accordingly. In the meantime, defenders, dug in behind stone walls or other entrenchments, could mow down those who attempted to take their positions by frontal assault. The high losses on both sides testified to the deadly fire of defenders wielding rifled firearms.

Amputations accounted for 75 percent of the surgical procedures performed on soldiers. Since the large "Minie" bullets fired from rifles had a low muzzle velocity compared with modern rifles, they tended to flatten out when they hit human flesh and rarely exited the body. The resulting wounds destroyed vital organs, shattered and splintered bones, and chewed up the tissue surrounding them. If wounded soldiers were not treated on the spot, they could bleed to death or die of shock. Physicians could do very little for stomach and chest wounds other than probe for the bullet with forceps or their fingers, remove it, and hope for the best. Mortality rates for such wounds approached 100 percent. Wounds to the arms or legs presented greater hope. But lacking the facilities and knowledge to repair such wounds, surgeons more often than not resorted to amputation.

### TREATING THE WOUNDED

Most operations took place at temporary field hospitals hastily set up in houses or barns within a mile or two of the battlefront. There bare-armed doctors assisted by orderlies worked frantically to save the lives of the wounded. Using implements similar to those used in butcher shops, they were often unfairly accused of butchery and even resisted by patients at gunpoint. Chloroform and ether were commonly used to put patients under. When supplies of these anesthetics ran out, as they often did in the Confederate army, orderlies gave men whiskey to help dull the pain and prevent shock. Unaware of the need for antiseptic conditions, surgeons used the same unsterilized knives and saws on different patients, frequently wiping them as well as their bloody hands on their soiled aprons or whatever cloth was available. Although such surgeries generally succeeded from a technical standpoint, many patients subsequently died of gangrene, pyemia (blood poisoning), and other bacterial infections.

Once wounded soldiers received emergency treatment at field hospitals, they were taken by wagon to regimental hospitals and, from there, on to general hospitals to undergo further treatment and recuperate. Since few officials had anticipated a long war, neither side was prepared either to move the wounded from one hospital to another or to properly house them once they had arrived. Thanks largely to the lobbying efforts of a civilian volunteer organization known as the U.S. Sanitary Commission, established by Lincoln's executive order in June 1861, the surgeon general set up an ambulance corps staffed by specially uniformed and unarmed

This photograph shows a knife-wielding army surgeon about to amputate a soldier's leg at a field hospital near Gettysburg. The scene appears to be staged for the benefit of the photographer. Ordinarily, the surgeon and his assistants would be wearing aprons, the tent would not be decorated with a wreath, and there would not be so many other officers standing around.

mond, an enormous facility consisting of five separate hospitals with 8,000 beds in 150 newly constructed buildings. The North, for its part, built a hospital system that by the summer of 1863 consisted of 182 newly built hospitals with 84,000 beds; by the end of the war, the number had expanded to 204 hospitals with 136,894 beds.

By war's end, the United States had some of the best hospitals in the world. What's more, the war had served as a training ground for surgeons, anesthetists, epidemiologists, and general practitioners. One former Confederate medical officer observed that "the whole country is now furnished with a medical corps which the war has thoroughly educated and reliably trained." "I have lost much," another wrote, "but I have gained much, especially as a medical man. I return home a better surgeon, a better doctor." Yet much remained to be learned, especially in the operating room, where surgeons continued to probe for bullets with their bare fingers and used unsterilized bandages. Although a few practitioners were beginning to experiment with carbolic acid, iodine, chlorine, and other chemical agents in treating gangrenous wounds, the widespread adoption of antiseptic methods lay far in the future. Thousands who survived surgical procedures consequently died of bacterial infections.

## WOMEN AT WAR

Thousands of women, black and white, participated in the Civil War. Indeed, hundreds disguised themselves as men and served as soldiers in both armies, often seeing combat. Others engaged in espionage by gathering and transmitting information about troop movements and enemy fortifications to military officials. In July 1861, for example, a Washington, D.C., resident named Rose Greenhow rode ahead to alert General Pierre Beauregard about an impending Union army attack on Manassas, thus giving the Confederate army a significant advantage in the battle that followed. Greenhow, like many other female agents, was arrested, imprisoned, and eventually released, only to continue her surreptitious activities. Still, over the course of the war, not a single woman was executed for treasonous activities by either government.

Hundreds of women accompanied the Union and Confederate armies as laundresses, cooks, nurses, provisioners (also called "sutlers"), and "camp followers" (another name

soldiers who entered battle areas and removed the wounded. These "medics" proved so proficient that they served as a model for other nations as late as World War I.

In addition to supplying bandages, medicine, and volunteer nurses to army camps and hospitals, the U.S. Sanitary Commission instructed soldiers about proper cooking methods, the placement of drainage ditches and latrines, and personal hygiene. The commission's growing popularity with soldiers led Congress in April 1862 to give it the power to reform outdated army medical procedures. The result was such important innovations as the outfitting of hospital ships and specially designed railway cars, staffed by volunteer nurses, for transporting the wounded to army hospitals. These innovations help to explain why 4 percent fewer Union soldiers died of their wounds than did Confederates.

During the first two years of the war, everything from government buildings to factories and prisons were converted into hospital wards. The filthy conditions of these overcrowded hospitals were evidenced by sickening odors, unemptied bedpans, used dressings strewn about, clogged toilets and latrines, and contaminated water supplies. Gradually, such appalling conditions improved. The Confederate government led the way in 1862 with the Chimborazo complex in Rich-

### Financing the War

Women on both sides played important roles during the war. Not only did they serve as nurses, spies, and seamstresses, they also worked in the armaments industry. This engraving shows women workers at the Watertown Arsenal, in Massachusetts, making paper-wrapped rifle cartridges. Such labor required the utmost care because the main ingredient was gunpowder, which could explode at the slightest spark.

for prostitutes). Regardless of their primary calling, these army women tended to diversify their work as the war wore on. This was especially true of those who accompanied their husbands to the front lines and subsequently became known as "daughters of the regiment."

Most army women served as nurses in Union and Confederate hospitals. In a preprofessional era, none were professionally trained. Even in the hurricane of war, they frequently encountered opposition from army surgeons, who felt that the dreadful sights, coarse language, and exposure to male body parts made army hospitals "no place for a woman." The general superintendent of army nurses, Dorothea Dix, moved to disarm such criticisms and protect her nurses from charges of unwomanly behavior. Dix, already well known for her prewar reform work in insane asylums, emphasized "good conduct," "good character," and plain dress "without ornaments of any sort" for her nurses and demanded "habits of neatness, order, sobriety, and industry."

Some young women chafed under such factory-like rules. At the same time, they worked hard to see to their patients' comfort and considered their labor as much an act of Christian benevolence as patriotism. By war's end, they went home satisfied that they had helped to bring a "moral atmosphere" to the institutions they served while garnering respect in a world that had been an exclusive preserve of men. Thanks largely to their perseverance and good works, nursing and, to a lesser extent, medicine became increasingly professionalized and open to women after the Civil War.

### THE HOME FRONT

One of the great achievements of wartime productivity on both sides occurred in agriculture. The American population was still overwhelmingly rural in 1861; over 75 percent either farmed or lived in towns with populations under 2,500. Yet although hundreds of thousands (680,000 from the Midwest alone) of men left their farms to join the Union army, agricultural output expanded dramatically. Northern farms raised more wheat in 1862 and again in 1863 than the entire country had before the war. Indeed, the fall harvests of the early 1860s were so bountiful that the United States actually doubled its exports of wheat, corn, pork, and beef to famine-plagued Europe. No one doubted that the Union army was the best fed in the world.

Here women played another key role in the war. With so many menfolk away, farm women had no choice but to add men's work—plowing, planting, and harvesting—to the cooking, washing, milking, butter making, cleaning, sewing, and rearing of children and livestock that they had always done. Women who could not cope with these added tasks either sold out, went bankrupt, or abandoned farming until their husbands returned home. Those who stayed on, and could afford it, turned to new types of farm machinery.

*The New Farm Machinery.* Plenty of machinery existed. In the 1840s and 1850s, the agricultural machinery industry had emerged, led by the McCormick Harvester Company in Chicago and John Deere's plow works in Moline, Illinois. Now farm women equipped themselves with horse- or mule-drawn mowing machines and self-raking reapers. "So perfect is machinery," wrote an observer, "that men seem to be of less necessity. . . . We have seen, within the past few weeks, a stout matron whose sons are in the army, with her team cutting hay. . . . She cut seven acres with ease in a day, riding leisurely upon her cutter."

This image originally appeared printed on an envelope in the 1860s. Decorated envelopes, depicting patriotic themes like this, with the woman sewing representing the home front, were commonly used during and after the Civil War to send letters or as souvenirs.

But while farmers in the North hailed the new technology, few in the South did. Hampered by the lack of foundries and machine shops and constrained by mounting pressures for arms, wagons, and munitions, the South had scant resources to devote to manufacturing agricultural machinery. Even though the region's farmers converted thousands of acres from cotton to food crops, food shortages arose as early as 1862. A key factor was the loss of Tennessee—a major food-producing state—to Union forces early in the war. Then a lack of salt to preserve meat and a serious drought during the summer of 1862 drastically reduced the fall harvest. Equally serious, the region's railroads carried less and less from food-producing areas to troops in the field and cities that lay in harm's way. By the summer of 1862, railroads within Confederate war zones began to show significant wear and tear as armies crossed their paths, fought for their control, ripped up their rails, and destroyed their locomotives. Lacking adequate foundries and rolling mills to resupply what had been lost, the South's rail transport system deteriorated, as did the Confederacy's ability to feed and clothe itself.

By March 1863, conditions had grown so bad in Richmond that a Confederate War Department clerk recorded in his diary that "my wife and children are emaciated," and "the shadow of the gaunt of famine is upon us." Several weeks later, wives of workers in the Confederacy's largest cannon foundry and armory in Richmond marched on the governor's man-sion, demanding that the government release emergency food stocks being held in its warehouses. When the governor refused, a riot broke out as the mob, chanting "Bread or blood!," proceeded to smash windows and loot stores. Only after President Jefferson Davis appeared on the scene and threatened to order the local militia to fire on the crowd did it disperse.

## Financing the War

### THE CONFEDERACY AND ILLICIT TRADING

A particular hardship for Southerners was the failure of the Confederate government to pay its debts and guard against inflation. Strapped for hard money from the start, the Davis administration sought to pay for the war by selling interest-paying bonds. Subscribers eagerly bought up the first $15 million issued in April 1861, but subsequent efforts raised little money. Unwilling to levy taxes, short of cash, and burdened with rapidly escalating debt, the Confederate Congress in 1861 issued $119 million in unbacked paper currency. A year later, a second printing mounted to $400 million, with nowhere near enough gold or silver in the vaults to back the currency's worth. The best the government could do was to promise that these "treasury notes" would be redeemed in specie two years after the war ended. The only thing backing such "fiat money" was the faith of holders that the Confederacy would ultimately win the war.

Their faith was soon shaken by the effectiveness of the Union blockade, the deteriorating condition of railroads in the South, and the ups and downs of the land war. An inflationary spiral began. Millions in unbacked paper bills followed millions, and prices soared accordingly. The spiral accelerated after the double shock of Lee's defeat at Gettysburg and the fall of Vicksburg in July 1863. Within three months, prices skyrocketed 58 percent, and they continued to rise. In October 1863, a barrel of flour cost $70 in Richmond; four months later, it cost $250. Consequently, desertions from Confederate armies swelled as the war wore on. "Poor men have been compelled to leave the army to come home to provide for their families," a soldier absent without leave protested in December 1862. "We . . . are willing to defend our country but our families [come] first."

By the time the Confederate Congress realized it had no choice but to impose taxes on the citizenry, the Southern economy was already out of control. Faced with excise, property, and income taxes, people either evaded them or paid them in worthless Confederate currency. As prices shot up and scarcities mounted, people began to trade with the enemy even though both governments officially forbade it. The smuggling and black-market trading that had existed in border states since the beginning of the war swelled from 1862 as Union armies penetrated into Confederate territory. Southerners were desperately in need of salt, medicine, shoes, and clothing, and merchants in the North were equally desirous of acquiring raw cotton for textile manufacturing. While he viewed illicit trade as sapping the morale of Southerners, even

A Confederate $100 bill issued in December 1862. Note the portrait of John C. Calhoun in the lower left corner and slaves working in a field at the top.

Jefferson Davis had to concede that trading with the enemy "might be justified" in dire circumstances and "as a last resort." By 1864, the inflation-plagued Confederacy placed numerous mills and factories under government control by impressing their products at fixed prices and regulating their access to raw materials and labor. To states'-rights critics like the governor of North Carolina, such impressments not only smacked of "military despotism" but also denied the very principles for which the Confederacy was fighting.

## UNION EFFORTS IN FINANCE

In contrast with those of the increasingly desperate Confederacy, Union efforts to finance the war proved both innovative and successful. Like the South, the Union had three ways to pay for the war: taking out loans in the form of bond sales, levying taxes, and issuing paper currency called treasury notes. While the Confederate government opted primarily for the third way and experienced runaway inflation that by war's end exceeded 9,000 percent, the Lincoln administration combined all three measures and held inflation to 80 percent.

Such a remarkable performance owed much to the fiscal leadership of Secretary of the Treasury Salmon Chase of Ohio, who, with the assistance of Philadelphia banker Jay Cooke, conducted a massive advertising campaign aimed at selling war bonds throughout the North. Altogether, Cooke's firm marketed over $2.5 billion in bonds, financing two-thirds of the Union's war costs. Another 21 percent came from revenues realized from higher tariffs on imports, excise taxes, and the

first federal income tax in American history. The remaining 12 percent came from $750 million in non-interest-bearing treasury notes sanctioned by four congressional Legal Tender Acts. Issued in denominations from $1 to $1,000 and popularly known as "greenbacks" because their reverse sides were printed in green ink, they proved extremely popular even though they had no backing other than public faith in the federal government's promise to redeem them in the future. Their success, moreover, paved the way for the National Banking Act in 1863, which sought to create a uniform national currency by allowing banks to issue currency equal to 90 percent of their holdings in government war bonds. As its title suggests, the National Banking Act signaled the establishment of a national bank system and, eventually, the demise of state-chartered banks, whose erratic behavior had caused financial panics and seriously disrupted the American economy.

## THE REPUBLICAN BLUEPRINT

With Republicans dominating Congress, they were now in a position to enact a series of laws described by one historian as a "blueprint for modern America." That blueprint provided the legal framework for the emergence of the United States in the 1880s as the world's leading industrial power.

The first corner of the blueprint was the Homestead Act of May 20, 1862, which granted any citizen over the age of twenty-one 160 acres of free survey land if the settler lived on the land for five years and made improvements on it. Next came the Pacific Railroad Act, passed on July 1, 1862, authorizing the construction of a transcontinental railroad from Omaha, Nebraska, to San Francisco Bay. The cost was colossal, and only the U.S. government could finance it. In addition to lending the two companies (the Union Pacific and Central Pacific) that built the railroad $16,000 per mile on prairie land and $48,000 per mile for mountainous areas, the bill also made the generous provision of 6,400 acres of public land to the railroads for each mile completed. Even so, the railroads were desperate for money. Subsequent legislation, passed in 1864, doubled the land grants to 12,800 acres per mile and extended them to the construction of other transcontinental railroads. Altogether the federal government doled out 120 million acres to the transcontinentals during and after the Civil War, making them among the richest corporations in America.

The blueprint included boldly innovative designs for education. On July 2, 1862, President Lincoln signed the Morrill Act into law. Named after the Republican senator from Vermont who sponsored the legislation, the bill provided each state loyal to the Union with 30,000 acres of public land for each senator and representative then sitting in Congress. Each state could then sell the land to provide an endowment for at least one public college devoted to training in "agriculture and the mechanical arts." The long-term result was the establishment of sixty-nine "land-grant" institutions—from the University of Massachusetts (1862) and the University of Maine (1865) in the Northeast to the University of Illinois (1867) and Ohio State University (1870) in the Midwest, to the University of California at Berkeley (1868) in the West. These schools, owing their origins to the Morrill Act, form the backbone of America's public system of higher education today.

The impact of the Pacific Railroad and Morrill Acts was enormous. Beginning with the junction of the Union Pacific and Central Pacific Railroads and the driving of the famed "golden spike" at Promontory Point, Utah, in 1869, the transcontinental railroads carried thousands of settlers into the trans-Mississippi West. By 1864, over 1.2 million acres of land west of the Mississippi had been distributed by the federal government. The lion's share went to railroad companies and speculators, with less than 5 percent going to individuals under the Homestead Act. The Morrill Act, by contrast, vastly expanded educational opportunity and helped to populate the country with professional engineers, agriculturalists, doctors, lawyers, and schoolteachers. The only people who did not profit from these developments were those already on the land—Native Americans and people of Hispanic ancestry, who found themselves pushed aside by the "march of the

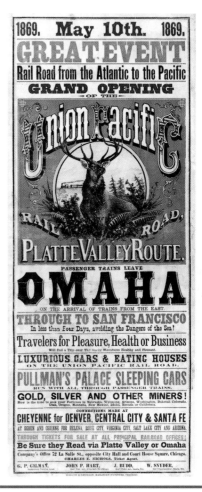

Poster announcing the opening of the nation's first transcontinental railroad in 1869.

white man's civilization" and condemned to second-class status in the aftermath of what some historians refer to as the "Second American Revolution."

## The War Intensifies

### MARSHALING MANPOWER

As casualties and losses from disease mounted during the winter and spring of 1862, the enthusiasm that had initially greeted the war quickly subsided. Having been overwhelmed by too many volunteers (and not enough weapons) early in

471

the conflict, both sides now faced serious manpower shortages. The Confederacy acted first. At the urging of Robert E. Lee, Jefferson Davis asked his Congress to enact a conscription law that would require current enlistees to serve an additional two years while subjecting all other able-bodied white males between the ages of eighteen and thirty-five to a draft of three years' service. The bill—the first of its kind in American history—passed in April 1862, shortly after the bloody Battle of Shiloh, but not without bitter debate. In addition to exempting a broad range of workers (from teachers and civil servants to telegraphers and miners), the law also allowed draftees to buy their way out of the army by hiring substitutes. Most controversial of all, owners and overseers of plantations with twenty or more slaves received automatic exemptions, thus giving rise to the phrase "A rich man's war but a poor man's fight."

Although the Confederate draft served its purpose in getting more men into the army (which increased by some 200,000 men in 1862), countless draftees evaded service by leaving their communities and moving to other areas. Others sold themselves as substitutes for as much as $300 in gold, only to desert from their units and sell themselves again to the highest bidder. Such practices became so prevalent that the Confederate Congress abolished substitutes in December 1863.

Although President Lincoln had no direct statutory power to institute a draft, he cited the authorization granted him under the Militia Act of July 1862 and ordered various state governors to supply 300,000 men between the ages of eighteen and forty-five for nine months' service. When some governors protested the order as an unconstitutional usurpation of states' rights and riots broke out in Pennsylvania and several midwestern states, Lincoln quietly rescinded the call. But not before federal troops had been sent to the trouble spots and several hundred draft resisters had been imprisoned without trial. On September 24, citing his executive war powers under the Constitution, Lincoln issued a proclamation suspending writs of habeas corpus (court orders that protected people against illegal imprisonment) throughout the country and ordering the arrest of anyone "guilty of any disloyal practice, affording aid and comfort to Rebels." This order, together with the release of the Emancipation Proclamation only two days earlier, elicited bitter denunciations on the part of Democrats opposed to the war. Delaware senator James A. Bayard asserted that Lincoln was "declaring himself a Dictator." To be sure, the suspension of habeas corpus and the effective declaration of martial law had a chilling effect on the administration's enemies. Fearful of arrest, Democratic editors began to tone down what they printed. Even private letter writers became careful about what they said.

*The Enrollment Act.* In the spring of 1863, at the height of Confederate military success and the depth of Union despair, Lincoln got what he wanted: a draft law called the Enrollment Act. While the new legislation did not allow occupational exemptions, it did permit the hiring of substitutes. What's more, the law allowed draftees to avoid service by paying a $300 "commutation fee" each time their names were drawn. Thaddeus Stevens, a radical Republican congressman from southeastern Pennsylvania, denounced the Enrollment Act as "a rich man's bill." Even more outspoken was Clement L. Vallandigham, a former congressman and Peace Democrat from Dayton, Ohio. Accusing Lincoln of abolitionist fanaticism and betraying the Union, Vallandigham made speeches pillorying the administration for "defeat, debt, taxation . . . the suspension of *habeas corpus* . . . of freedom of the press and of speech" and calling on his countrymen to "stop fighting. Make an armistice. . . . Withdraw your army from the seceded States."

With Vallandigham stumping around the country and Peace Democrats from Ohio to New York urging him on, it was only a matter of time before a reaction occurred. That moment arrived on May 5, 1863, when General Ambrose Burnside—the Union commander in charge of the military district bordering the Ohio River—had Vallandigham arrested at his Dayton home in the middle of the night and hauled off in chains to army headquarters in Cincinnati. Charged with making treasonous remarks, Vallandigham was quickly tried and convicted by a military court in Cincinnati and sentenced to two years in military prison.

Vallandigham's trial and conviction brought Lincoln a firestorm of criticism from outraged Democrats and anxious Republicans. Fearful that Vallandigham would become a political martyr for the cause of Peace Democrats and damage his chances for reelection in 1864, Lincoln commuted Vallandigham's sentence and banished him to the Confederacy. At the same time, he prepared a lengthy response to Democratic critics who accused him of ordering "arbitrary arrests" and abrogating civil liberties. In it, he pointed out that the Constitution provided for the suspension of these liberties "in cases of Rebellion or Invasion" and claimed that he had been "slow to adopt . . . strong measures" and did so only because the actions of Vallandigham and other protesters were "damaging the army, upon the existence . . . of which, the life of the nation depends." As for Vallandigham, the president took the moral high ground. "Must I shoot a simple-minded soldier boy who deserts, while I must not touch a hair of a wily agitator who induces him to desert?" he asked. "In such a case to silence the agitator, and save the boy is not only constitutional, but withal a great mercy."

Initially published in the *New York Tribune* and subsequently reprinted in pamphlet form, Lincoln's public letter was read by 10 million people. It did much to quiet criticism within the Republican Party and disarm his Democratic critics. But not completely. Army provost marshals had already begun enrolling draftees under the new conscription law and using warrantless searches to track down evaders. As a result of anger over the law as well as the army's strong-arm tactics, antidraft riots broke out in parts of the North, culminating in a week-long display of violence in New York City.

New York, with its large Irish Catholic population and powerful Democratic base, had never been Lincoln country. As much anti-Protestant as antiblack, Catholic leaders now hammered away at the rich man/poor man theme, warning also that the draft would force white workers to fight for black freedom only to see their jobs taken by blacks once the war had ended. When New York officials began drawing names of draftees on July 11, 1863, hundreds of angry Irishmen gathered at local pubs and churches, vowing that they would be damned before they would "go and carry on a war for the nigger." The next day the rioting began, with mobs setting fires to draft offices and singling out blacks for beatings and lynchings. As the violence escalated during the next four days, the rioters—two-thirds of whom were thought to be Irish—burned a black orphanage and, with chants of "Down with the rich," turned their wrath on the homes and businesses of leading Republicans and abolitionists. Police tried to quell the uprising, but only after July 16, when Lincoln's secretary of war dispatched federal troops, did the violence end. In the weeks that followed, 20,000 soldiers occupied New York as the draft process proceeded. Overall, the results of the July draft proved meager. Only 35,883 men throughout the North were actually inducted from the 292,441 names drawn, while another 52,288 paid commutation fees.

Lincoln would issue three more draft calls in 1863 and 1864. Although he did away with commutation fees in July 1864, the practice of hiring substitutes remained. In an effort to avoid the despised draft system, many Northern districts filled their quotas by offering monetary bonuses to men who volunteered for duty. As a result, only 6 percent of the more than 2.5 million men who served the Union during the war were draftees. Nonetheless, the Enrollment Act set an important precedent. In an age when the raising of armies had rested primarily with state governments, the new draft law fundamentally shifted the process of mobilization. In doing so, the federal government established the principle that it could call citizens to military service—something that would be repeated on a much larger scale and to greater effect by the selective service drafts of World Wars I and II.

## THE EMANCIPATION PROCLAMATION

The Civil War took a dramatic turn on September 22, 1862 when President Lincoln issued his preliminary Emancipation Proclamation, in which he warned the Confederate states that if they failed to put down their arms and return to the Union by January 1, 1863, all slaves within their boundaries "shall be then, henceforward, and forever free." Heeding the warnings of cabinet members that a blanket

The New York City draft riots aimed much of their ire at blacks living in the city. This scene depicts the lynching of James Costello, a free black shoemaker, on July 15, 1863. Note the burning building in the background.

proclamation might turn loyal slaveholding areas against the Union, Lincoln exempted Maryland, Kentucky, Missouri, Tennessee, and parts of Virginia and Louisiana from his order. He also indicated that once the Emancipation Proclamation took effect, freedmen would "be received into the armed service of the United States," a revolutionary pronouncement that struck at "the heart of the rebellion" and enraged Southerners.

That Lincoln understood the larger implications of his actions is clear from his correspondence during the fall of 1862. After January 1, "the character of the war will be changed," he acknowledged to an administration official. "It will be one of subjugation. . . . The South is to be destroyed and replaced by new propositions and ideas." Less than ten months earlier, he had hoped for victory with a minimal amount of bloodshed and decried a "remorseless revolutionary struggle." But as the fighting had escalated in scope and intensity, the limited conflict had expanded into a total war aimed at destroying the Confederacy. Lincoln had established a new agenda: unconditional surrender and the destruction of the South's peculiar institution. Abolitionists like William Lloyd Garrison hailed the new dispensation. Whether he wanted to or not, the president had joined their side.

## THE UNION IN CRISIS

With the Emancipation Proclamation, the winds of war shifted and the fighting became increasingly deadly during the summer and fall of 1862. While Lee's Army of Northern Virginia dominated its Union adversaries, Confederate forces west of the Appalachian Mountains launched a counteroffensive, with three aims: retaking lost ground in Tennessee, invading Kentucky, and preventing Ulysses Grant's Army of the Tennessee from capturing Vicksburg and controlling the entire length of the Mississippi River (see map on page 461). For a time, it appeared as if the strategy would succeed. Confederate cavalry under Generals Nathan B. Forrest and John Hunt Morgan wreaked havoc on Union supply lines by burning bridges, tearing up railroad tracks, and raiding supply depots. By September, an army of 30,000 under General Braxton Bragg had penetrated deeply into Kentucky and established a Confederate state government at Frankfort before being forced to withdraw through the Cumberland Gap back into Tennessee. Although the Union held, the year ended in a major disap-

pointment for the Lincoln administration: Grant's army failed to take Vicksburg. Although General William S. Rosecrans's Army of the Cumberland won a bloody contest at Murfreesboro/Stones River, Tennessee, it failed to crush Bragg's mangled forces.

Even worse news came from the East. Word arrived on December 13 that Lee's army had rebounded from Antietam to inflict a devastating defeat on the Army of the Potomac at Fredericksburg, Virginia (see map on page 462). Outnumbering Lee's forces by nearly 40,000, the Union army mounted thirteen brigade-level assaults on the dug-in Confederates only to be "swept from the field like chaff before the wind." The extent of the loss became apparent after the battlefield was cleared and medical units reported 12,600 Union casualties to the Confederate's 5,000. After reading the telegraph messages from Fredericksburg, a depressed Lincoln commented, "If there is a worse place than Hell, I am in it."

Events of the new year did nothing to boost Lincoln's confidence. Shaken by its defeat at Fredericksburg, the Army of the Potomac hit rock bottom in mid-January when it became bogged down on muddy roads and had to call off another attempt at capturing Richmond. At the same time, Grant's army experienced difficulties maneuvering into position for an assault on the "Gibraltar of the West" at Vicksburg. In one of the most ambitious engineering efforts of the war, the Union army made several valiant but unsuccessful attempts to divert the Mississippi River out of range of the heavy artillery that guarded the bluffs of Vicksburg and prevented gunboats and troop carriers from getting through. Indeed, everything seemed to be going wrong for the Union forces.

Amid these military failures, criticism hit the White House from all sides. Most controversial was the Emancipation Proclamation, which took effect on January 1, 1863. Enraged by the proclamation's freeing of slaves and its call for the enlistment of blacks in the Union army and navy, Confederate leaders threatened to execute any black captured in a Northern uniform. At the same time, Northern Democrats, known as Peace Democrats among fellow party members and Copperheads by their Republican adversaries, assailed Lincoln for issuing the "wicked, inhuman, and unholy" proclamation and repeated earlier warnings that such "Black Republican" policy would result in freed slaves flooding the North and competing with whites for jobs. Some Democrats even predicted that the freedmen would commit "rapine" and murder in the streets. The Republicans had experienced a net loss in the November 1862 elections of two governorships and thirty-four seats in the House of Representatives, largely in response to the Emancipation Proclamation. Republican leaders in Congress, still acting on the assumption that Lincoln was William Seward's puppet, called for a shake-up in Lincoln's cabinet and a more vigorous prosecution of the war. Through all these crises, the president, though experiencing bouts of depression, steered a steady, determined course.

In the spring of 1863, after months of effort, Grant's Army of the Tennessee succeeded in surrounding and laying siege to Vicksburg. But on May 6, Lee's outnumbered army of 60,000 (about half the size of the enemy) inflicted another embarrassing defeat on the Army of the Potomac at Chancellorsville, a country crossroads some nine miles west of Fredericksburg. The victory revealed Lee at his tactical best, but it exacted a serious toll. In addition to suffering 13,000 casualties amounting to 22 percent of his total force, Lee lost his most trusted associate, General Stonewall Jackson, who was mistakenly fired on by his own troops.

Jackson's death cast a shadow over the Army of Northern Virginia, but his death was nothing compared with the gloom that descended on Washington in the aftermath of Chancellorsville. "All is lost," Massachusetts abolitionist senator Charles Sumner exclaimed on hearing the news. In Richmond, the Confederate high command concluded that Chancellorsville presented a new opportunity to relieve pressure on the South and seek diplomatic recognition in Europe by again invading the North. Convinced that his army was invincible and that his troops would "go anywhere and do anything if properly led," Lee began reorganizing his army into an invasion force of 75,000.

## THE BATTLE OF GETTYSBURG (JULY 1863)

The Army of Northern Virginia's morale soared as it began its march down the Shenandoah Valley toward Pennsylvania early in June 1863. As with his first invasion of the North a year earlier, one of Lee's primary objectives was Harrisburg, the capital of Pennsylvania and an important railroad center that linked the East Coast with the Midwest. As it turned out, his army clashed with the Army of the Potomac at Gettysburg, a small town some thirty-nine miles south of Harrisburg. During the first three days of July, the opposing forces slugged it out in what became the largest and most important battle of the war. On the third day, July 3, the clash culminated with one of the most famous assaults in modern history, in which nine Confederate brigades marched across a mile-wide open expanse to attack the Union line in what became known as "Pickett's Charge." The result was a Confederate disaster, with nearly half of the 14,000 who went forward failing to return. All told, Lee lost more than one-third of his army at Gettysburg (3,903 killed, 24,000 wounded or missing), the Union more than one-quarter (3,155 killed, 20,000 wounded or missing). The Army of Northern Virginia would never be the same. Blaming himself for the defeat, Lee offered his resignation to Jefferson Davis, but Davis refused.

Once again, the Union forces did not close in for the kill. Rather than pursuing Lee's crippled army, the Union commander, General George Gordon Meade, allowed Lee to retreat southward across the Potomac River and back into Virginia. Lincoln expressed his frustration in a letter he drafted but did not send. "My dear general," he wrote on July 14, "I do not believe you appreciate the magnitude of the misfortune involved in Lee's escape. He was within your easy grasp, and to have closed upon him would, in connection with our other late successes, have ended the war. . . . Your golden opportunity is gone." The "other late successes" were the fall of Vicksburg on July 4 and the surrender of Port Hudson—the last remaining Confederate stronghold on the Mississippi River—five days later. Both victories owed much to the generalship of Ulysses S. Grant, whose reputation rose rapidly in Washington during the summer of 1863.

It is often said that Lee's retreat at Gettysburg, coupled with the fall of Vicksburg, marked the beginning of the end of the great rebellion. While there is some truth in the statement, the war was far from over in July 1863. Although a Confederate army under General Braxton Bragg evacuated Chattanooga, Tennessee—a key railroad town and an invasion gateway to Georgia—on September 8, it suddenly reversed the Yankee advance by winning a stunning victory at Chickamauga Creek less than two weeks later and threatened to retake Chattanooga. In need of an aggressive leader, Lincoln placed Ulysses Grant in command of all Union armies operating in the western theater and urged him to take the offensive. Grant sped to Chattanooga, where his armies won the Battles of Lookout Mountain and Missionary Ridge (November 23–25). Bragg's beaten army had no choice but to

## The War Intensifies

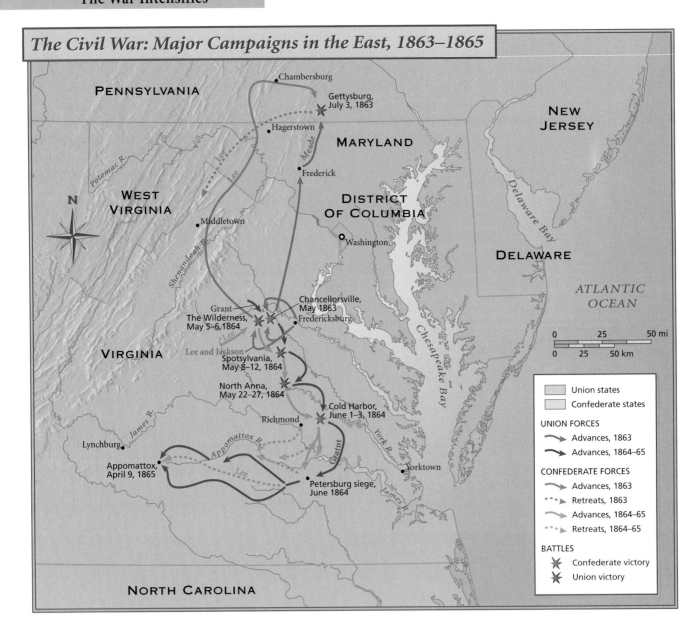

**The Civil War: Major Campaigns in the East, 1863–1865**

fall back along the tracks of the Western and Atlantic Railroad toward Atlanta. With Chattanooga secure, Grant spent the winter of 1863–64 rebuilding his railroad supply lines in Tennessee and Mississippi, resupplying his forces, and preparing for an all-out push on Atlanta the following spring. By the end of 1863, Southerners sensed that the Confederacy was in serious trouble. A Richmond diarist wrote that "gloom and unspoken despondency hang like a pall everywhere."

On November 18, Lincoln took a train to Gettysburg to participate in the dedication of a national military cemetery for those who had fallen in the great battle some four months earlier. Although Lincoln's speech took less than three minutes, it captured the political meaning of the war in words that soon became immortalized: "that all men are created equal . . . and that government of the people, by the people, for the people, shall not perish from the earth." Lincoln's

"Gettysburg Address" is widely recognized as the greatest speech ever made by an American politician.

## THE BRAVERY OF BLACKS

The enlistment of thousands of black troops in the Union army following the Emancipation Proclamation marked a crucial turning point in the Northern war effort. Originally considered fit only for garrison or fatigue duty, black soldiers pressed for the right to serve in combat and insisted that discriminatory practices—like lower pay and a smaller uniform allowance—be abolished. They eventually won all of these struggles. In July 1863, soldiers of the Fifty-fourth Massachusetts regiment stormed Fort Wagner near Charleston, South Carolina, in an engagement that was to reveal the courage of black troops in unmistakable terms. Their white commander, Colonel Robert Gould Shaw, son of a prominent Boston abolitionist family, died leading his men, and the regiment suffered heavy losses in the attack.

The lesson of Fort Wagner was clear—black soldiers were willing to lay down their lives for the country that promised freedom to their people. At Milliken's Bend near Vicksburg, at Port Hudson in Louisiana, and at the Battle of the Crater during the Petersburg campaign of 1864, black troops showed the same resolute qualities in battle that white Union soldiers displayed. By the end of the war, some 190,000 African Americans had served in the Union army and navy and had made a significant contribution to Northern victory.

## GRANT AND SHERMAN "PULLING TOGETHER" (1864)

With the urging of Congress, in March 1864 Lincoln promoted Grant to lieutenant general, the highest-ranking officer in the Union army, and summoned him to Washington. On the way, Grant met in Cincinnati with his friend and trusted subordinate General William Tecumseh Sherman, to devise a strategy for crippling the Confederacy and ending the war. Sherman would take command of the Union armies in the western theater, while, in accordance with Lincoln's wishes, Grant would make his headquarters with the Army of the Potomac. Knowing that the forces they commanded were much larger and better supplied than their adversaries, they decided to push simultaneous offensives against the two largest remaining Confederate armies in Georgia and Virginia, keeping in constant touch through telegraphy. No longer would they,

A Union volunteer corporal proudly holding his Model 1849 Colt revolver. This soldier's uniform, with its brass oval "U. S." belt, dark-blue woolen jacket, light-blue pants, and dark-blue "kepi" hat, illustrates what "standard issue" military garb looked like in the Union army by 1863. No such uniformity existed among units in the Confederate army.

as Grant put it, act "independently and without concert, like a balky team, no two ever pulling together." From now on, the pressure on the rebels would be relentless.

Grant began his part of the joint campaign early in May by moving against Confederate strongholds in Virginia. Some of the heaviest fighting of the war broke out, but now it was sustained. Once again the battle was joined in an area just west of Chancellorsville known as the Wilderness. True to form, Lee's 64,000-man Army of Northern Virginia halted the advance of the 115,000-strong Army of the Potomac. But Grant kept moving, refusing to admit defeat. Again and again, he attempted to outflank Lee's smaller army only to be met by spirited Confederate defenders who fought from behind an elaborate system of trenches and log fortifications. In quick succession, the Battles of Spotsylvania (May 8–12), North Anna (May 22–27), and Cold Harbor (June 1–3) exacted a terrible toll; the casualty lists shocked both North and South.

Finally, Grant's relentless counterclockwise movement took him southward across the James River to the outskirts of Petersburg, an important railroad and industrial center that supplied Richmond some twenty miles to the north. Now Lee's

## The War Intensifies

forces were held in what Lincoln called a "bulldog grip." Knowing that if he could take Petersburg, Richmond would inevitably fall, Grant ordered an attack on June 18. After four days of repeated assaults against the town's entrenched defenses, he decided to rest his exhausted troops, dig in, and lay siege to the beleaguered community. After seven weeks of fighting at a level of intensity never seen before, the Union and Confederate armies had become stalemated in trench warfare around Petersburg. Both sides were hurting. Indeed, the Army of the Potomac's 65,000 casualties exceeded the size of Lee's entire army at the outset of the campaign. Lee's casualty rates were equally grim. Between May and mid-June, he had lost at least 35,000 men, more than half of his army swept away. The psychological effects of such massive bloodletting got the best of even the more hardened soldiers. "For thirty days it has been one funeral procession past me," one of them cried, "and it has been too much!"

### The Fall of Atlanta.
While thousands of Union and Confederate soldiers were meeting their deaths in Virginia during the spring of 1864, General Sherman marched south from Chattanooga to capture Atlanta. His opponent, General Joseph E. Johnston, Braxton Bragg's successor, was a defensive specialist. His 60,000 men skillfully used the rugged Appalachian mountain terrain to oppose the advance of Sherman's larger 100,000-man army at Dalton, Resaca, Allatoona Pass, and New Hope Church, Georgia. Rather than confront Johnston's formidable defenses head-on, Sherman used his numerical superiority to outflank the Confederate army and repeatedly force it to fall back to new defensive positions. The one time Sherman attempted a frontal attack, at Kennesaw Mountain on June 27, his forces were thrown back with heavy losses (2,000 dead and wounded). From then on, he returned to the flanking maneuvers that had served him so well to force the Confederates off Kennesaw Mountain and push them southeast through Marietta, Smyrna, and across the Chattahoochee River to Atlanta.

Jefferson Davis, fearing that Johnston would abandon Atlanta without a fight, replaced him with the offensive-minded General John Bell Hood on July 17. Hood, not content to retreat while keeping his army intact, immediately threw the Army of the Tennessee against Sherman's invading forces at the Battles of Peachtree Creek (July 20), Atlanta (July 22), and Ezra Church (July 28). The cost was high: devastating defeats reduced his army by 15,000. Hood retreated within the formidable trenchworks that ringed

Atlanta and waited for Sherman's next move. For a time, it appeared that Sherman, like Grant before Petersburg, would be forced into a lengthy siege. But after a month of cat-and-mouse tactics, Sherman captured the last remaining railroad that supplied Atlanta and forced Hood to evacuate the city on September 1. The next day, the Union general telegraphed Washington that "Atlanta is ours, and fairly won."

### The Election of 1864.
No Union victory came at a more opportune time: 1864 was a presidential election year, and Lincoln faced the greatest challenge of his political career. Public frustration had mounted during the summer when great expectations for decisive victories in Virginia and Georgia failed

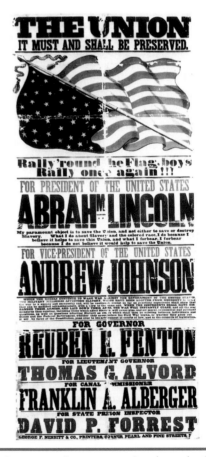

A Republican Party campaign poster urging the reelection of Abraham Lincoln, his vice-presidential running mate, Andrew Johnson of Tennessee, and Reuben Fenton, who subsequently became the Republican governor of New York.

to materialize. As Union casualty lists skyrocketed, Democratic politicians accused Grant of butchery and insensitivity and Lincoln of sending white men to their deaths in order "to allay" his "negro mania." Democratic newspaper editors taunted "Abe the Widowmaker" who "loves his country less, and the negroe more." "STOP THE WAR," they insisted, "all are tired of this damnable tragedy." Meeting in Chicago at the end of August, the Democratic Party nominated George B. McClellan for president on a platform that declared the war a failure and demanded "that immediate efforts be made for a cessation of hostilities." By then, even Lincoln admitted that "I am going to be beaten . . . and unless some great change takes place *badly* beaten."

The "great change" was the fall of Atlanta, the Confederacy's second-largest city and the symbolic center of the Confederate heartland. Three days after McClellan's nomination, the "glorious news" arrived. "The disaster at Atlanta," the Richmond *Examiner* observed, not only came "in the nick of time" to "save the party of Lincoln from irretrievable ruin,"

but also "diffuse[d] gloom over the South." Despair deepened during September and October as a Union army under the command of General Philip Sheridan laid waste to Virginia's beautiful Shenandoah Valley, the breadbasket of Lee's army, and in three successive battles virtually destroyed the Confederate opposition. With his army pinned down between Petersburg and Richmond, Lee realized that Grant was slowly closing the circle around him. If Davis could not provide more troops, he warned, "a great calamity will befall us."

Boosted by good news from the battlefields, Lincoln handily won the election with 55 percent of the popular vote and a 212-to-21 margin over McClellan in the electoral college. Nearly 74 percent of eligible males voted, many of them soldiers who either cast absentee ballots or returned home to vote. Of the 154,000 soldiers who voted, more than three-fourths favored Lincoln. The president won every state except Kentucky, Delaware, and New Jersey, and except for those three states, Republicans captured every governorship and state legislature in the North, including three-fourths of the

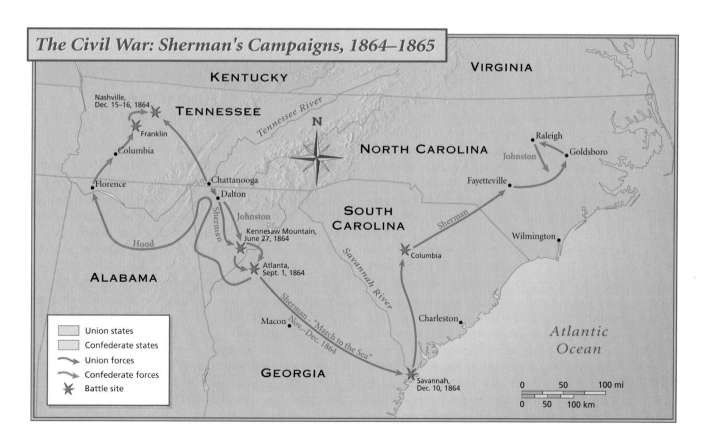

**The Civil War: Sherman's Campaigns, 1864–1865**

Although both sides engaged in the practice, this photo shows Union soldiers with Sherman's army destroying railroad tracks in Atlanta in 1864. After being removed from their beds, rails were piled on bonfires made from the wooden ties, brought to a red heat, and then bent around trees, forming what became known as "Sherman neckties."

rible and make them so sick of war that generations would pass away before they would again appeal to it." "I can make the march," he assured his superiors, "and make Georgia howl." Although Grant and Lincoln considered the proposal risky, they approved it.

On November 16, Sherman began his fabled "March to the Sea." Before leaving Atlanta, he sent 60,000 men under General George H. Thomas to pursue Hood's battered Confederate army into Tennessee while taking the remaining 62,000 on his advance through the Confederacy's heartland. Within two weeks, Thomas reported that his troops had beaten back a suicidal attack at Franklin, Tennessee. Two weeks later, on December 15–16, Thomas's forces attacked and virtually destroyed Hood's army at Nashville. Hood had evacuated Atlanta seven weeks earlier. After the Battle of Nashville, he was left with barely half his force, many of them barefoot and poorly armed. In the meantime, Sherman's army roared unopposed through Georgia and stood at the gates of Savannah on December 10. In a festive mood, the general telegraphed Lincoln: "I beg to present you, as a Christmas gift, the city of Savannah, with 150 heavy guns and about 25,000 bales of cotton." The same news sent a wave of despondency throughout the South. "One of the gloomiest [days] in our struggle," Confederate general Josiah Gorgas noted in his diary on December 19.

U.S. Congress. Political observers rightly interpreted the election as a triumph for Lincoln's war policy of abolition and unconditional surrender. "I am astonished," one of them wrote, at "the extent and depth of [the North's] determination to fight to the last." Jefferson Davis, however, remained as defiant as ever. "Nothing has changed," he told the Confederate Congress after the November elections. "We are fighting for existence; and by fighting alone can independence be gained."

*Sherman's "March to the Sea."* With the Confederacy down but not out, General Sherman proposed a bold plan. Instead of holding Atlanta and trying to maintain a vulnerable railway connection to Cincinnati through Chattanooga and Nashville as originally contemplated, he would cut his supply lines and strike out for Savannah and the Atlantic coast while living off the land and destroying everything that lay in his path. He understood that in order to win the war, he had to break the will of the civilian population as well as crush his military opponents. "We cannot change the hearts of those people of the South," he argued, "but we can make war so ter-

*Lee's Surrender at Appomattox (April 1865).* By January 1865, Lee's Army of Northern Virginia was the only major military force remaining in the Confederacy. With desertions mounting, supplies growing short, and Sherman's army moving rapidly through the Carolinas to join Grant at Petersburg, Lee's situation grew more desperate with each passing day. At one point, he even recommended arming slaves to fight in his army, a measure that ended up being defeated by one vote in the Confederate Senate. Nearly surrounded and outnumbered by more than two to one, with all avenues of escape cut off save one railroad, Lee knew that it was only a matter of time before he would have to abandon Petersburg and, with it, the cherished Confederate capital at Richmond. That day came on April 2, when Grant mounted a full-scale attack on Lee's thin gray line and forced it to retreat. The following day, Grant and Lincoln entered Petersburg, and the next day Lincoln, escorted by only ten sailors, walked the burned-out streets of Richmond and sat at Jefferson Davis's desk, less than forty hours after the Confederate president hastily left it.

A week later, on April 9, after several futile attempts to break through the Union lines and escape, Lee surrendered his starving army to Grant at Appomattox Court House. For all intents and purposes, the war was over. On April 11, a tired but greatly relieved Lincoln delivered a public address from the White House balcony calling for peace and national reconciliation. Among the throng of listeners was an actor and Confederate sympathizer named John Wilkes Booth. Upon hearing the president's remarks, Booth remarked angrily to a friend, "That means nigger citizenship. Now, by God, I'll put him through. That is the last speech he will ever make." True to his word, Booth shot Lincoln three days later as he and his wife, Mary, were attending a play at Ford's Theater in Washington. The following morning, the president was dead. The great American tragedy thus ended in yet another tragedy, with more to come.

## The Deadliest War

The Civil War was a deadly war—the deadliest in American history. A total of 620,000 soldiers—360,000 Federals, 260,000 Confederates—lost their lives; another 500,000 were wounded, and some 75,000 of them later died of their wounds. Indeed, more Americans died in one day at Antietam (4,800) than during the entire Revolutionary War (4,000). The three-day Battle of Gettysburg, in fact, claimed more lives than did the American Revolution and the War of 1812 put together. Adding some 50,000 Southern civilians who died as a direct result of the conflict, the loss of human life comes close to 750,000. The combined total of American deaths from all the other wars fought by the United States from 1776 to 1990 does not equal the carnage produced by the Civil War.

## Why the South Lost

No sooner had the war ended than participants as well as observers began to hypothesize about why the North won and the South lost. Robert E. Lee offered his view in his famous farewell to his troops at Appomattox, when he noted that "after four years of arduous service . . . the Army of Northern Virginia has been compelled to yield to over-whelming numbers and resources." In 1872, on the second anniversary of Lee's death, former Confederate corps commander Jubal A. Early asserted in a speech that "General Lee had not been conquered in battle, but surrendered because he had no longer an army with which to give battle. [It] had been . . . gradually worn down by the combined agencies of numbers, steam-power, railroads, mechanism, and all the resources of physical science." In the end, superior technology coupled with unlimited manpower forced Lee's submission.

Not everyone agreed with Early. Former Confederate generals Pierre Beauregard and Joseph E. Johnston castigated Jefferson Davis for his defensiveness, limited vision, and general failure of leadership, while others pointed to his disastrous financial policies as "the greatest single weakness of the Confederacy." Others criticized Davis and Lee for limiting their strategic vision to the Virginia theater and refusing to send troops to relieve Vicksburg during the critical summer of 1863. Davis was no match for Lincoln, later critics concluded, and only Lee rivaled Grant and Sherman as a great field commander.

Even so, historians characterized Grant and Sherman as being more "modern-minded" than Lee. Recognizing the inherent relationship between politics and war, Grant and Sherman developed the practice of total war and used it to great advantage during the last year of the conflict. Lee, by contrast, remained wedded to an older style of warfare that emphasized offensive strategy and tactics while neglecting to take into account the lethal effect that recently developed rifled firearms had brought to the battlefield. Although he achieved dazzling victories at Second Manassas (Bull Run), Fredericksburg, and Chancellorsville, his tendency to take the offensive whenever possible yielded casualty rates that the Army of Northern Virginia could not absorb. As a result, critics charged that Lee bled his army to death. A force of more than 70,000 at Gettysburg had been reduced to less than 30,000 by Appomattox. Indeed, Virginia's proud Stonewall Brigade, once consisting of five full regiments numbering 5,000 men, was left with only 210 "ragged survivors."

Other students of the Civil War maintain that the Confederacy's defeat owed less to failures of leadership than to tensions within Southern society. Citing the ongoing conflict over states' rights between certain governors and the Davis administration, resentments over a rich man's war and a poor man's fight, pockets of Unionist sympathy throughout the South, libertarian protests over increasingly centralized state

Confederate president Jefferson Davis of Mississippi.

policies, and the defection of tens of thousands of slaves to the Union cause, these analysts contend that loss of will rather than the lack of means led to the Confederacy's demise. Nevertheless, the most persuasive accounts of the war hold that the ultimate determinant of the Confederacy's collapse rested with events on the battlefield. Lincoln put it best in his second inaugural address when he referred to "the progress of our arms, upon which all else chiefly depends." Military events, not disillusionment at home, decided the outcome of the war.

Since the contest came down to military dominance, it is important to recall that the South was fighting for its independence, while the North was fighting to prevent it. In order to achieve its goal, the Confederacy did not necessarily have to invade and conquer the North or destroy its armies. The North, on the other hand, had to subjugate the South, which meant invading its territory and destroying its capacity to make war. Of the two, the Confederacy's task seemed more manageable. It needed to convince the North that a complete military victory was either unlikely or too costly in human and financial terms to be worth the price. The key to victory for both sides rested with breaking the other's will to fight, and that could only be accomplished through a string of military victories. In the end, the Confederacy failed to hold its territory against the Union juggernaut. By calling upon its vast human and material resources and bringing re-

lentless military pressure on the South, the North eventually won the war.

## A GREAT DIVIDE

The Civil War marks a great divide in American history. Before the war, most Americans lived in rural areas and followed agricultural pursuits. During the war, people learned how to mobilize and equip armies on a massive scale, lessons that would be applied often in the postwar period with the expansion of the factory system, the rise of big business, and the spread of mass transportation and communication networks. These were the ingredients of a new era, the beginning of the "modern age." They took root before the war, matured during the war, and predominated afterward. In the process, the United States was reconfigured—indeed, reinvented.

Equally important, Americans emerged from the war with an altered idea of what their country and government meant. The United States had survived as a nation. Instead of speaking of the United States as a pluralist "union" of states (as they had since the Revolution), people began to refer to it as a singular nation—"the United States is" rather than "the United States are." What's more, the locus of governmental power shifted from states' rights and local rule to a greater emphasis on central state authority. Through military drafts, wartime taxes, emergency confiscations, and pieces of legislation like the Homestead Act and National Banking Act, people experienced a more direct relationship with the federal government. This, too, demarcated the "old" America from the "new."

Above all, the war advanced democracy. In Lincoln's words, the country experienced "a new birth of freedom" so that "government of the people, by the people, for the people, shall not perish from the earth." Nowhere was this more evident than in the liberation of some 4 million slaves with the passage of the Thirteenth Amendment in 1865. Three years later, the Fourteenth Amendment would extend the boundary of freedom by guaranteeing citizenship and civil rights to "all persons born or naturalized in the United States." Finally, the Fifteenth Amendment (1870) granted the right to vote to all adult males regardless of "race, color, or previous condition of servitude." These legal guarantees marked great advances, to be sure, but would they be enforced? Would racism decline and justice prevail? Such questions remained unanswered as the new America faced the future.

## Suggested Reading

Gabor Boritt, ed., *Why the Confederacy Lost* (1992)

Robert E. Denney, *Civil War Medicine* (1994)

Charles B. Dew, *Apostles of Disunion: Southern Secession Commissioners and the Causes of the Civil War* (2001)

Drew Gilipin Faust, *Mothers of Invention* (1996)

Gary Gallagher, *The Confederate War* (1997)

Edward Hagerman, *The American Civil War and the Origins of Modern Warfare* (1988)

Earl J. Hess, *The Union Soldier in Battle* (1997)

Gerald E. Linderman, *Embattled Courage: The Experience of Combat in the American Civil War* (1987)

James M. McPherson, *For Cause and Comrade: Why Men Fought in the Civil War* (1997)

James M. McPherson, *Battle Cry of Freedom* (1988)

Brent Nosworthy, *The Bloody Crucible of Courage: Fighting Methods and Combat Experience in the Civil War* (2003)

Philip Paul Paludan, *"A People's Contest": The Union and the Civil War, 1861–1865* (1988)

Heather Cox Richardson, *The Greatest Nation of the Earth: Republican Economic Policies During the Civil War* (1997)

William H. Roberts, *Civil War Ironclads: The U.S. Navy and Industrial Mobilization* (2002)

Harold S. Wilson, *Confederate Industry: Manufactures and Quartermasters in the Civil War* (2002)

Stephen R. Wise, *Lifeline of the Confederacy: Blockade Running During the Civil War* (1988)

# Chapter Review

## Summary QUESTIONS

- Why could northerners and southerners compromise on the issue of slavery in 1820, 1832, and 1850, yet fail to do so in 1861?

- How did military and civilian perceptions of the conflict and its purposes change as the Civil War wore on?

- What was the significance of the Emancipation Proclamation?

- What role did new technologies play in the conduct of the war?

- Why did the North win the Civil War?

## Chronology

| | |
|---|---|
| February 1861 | The Confederate States of America established. |
| April 14, 1861 | Fort Sumter falls to the Confederates. |
| July 21, 1861 | First battle of Manassas. |
| March 9, 1862 | *Monitor* vs. *Virginia*. |
| May 20, 1862 | The Homestead Act. |
| July 2, 1862 | The Morrill (land-grant) Act. |
| August 29–30, 1862 | Second battle of Manassas. |
| September 17, 1862 | Battle of Antietam. |
| January 1, 1863 | Emancipation Proclamation takes effect. |
| July 3, 1863 | Battle of Gettysburg. |
| September 1, 1864 | Fall of Atlanta |
| April 9, 1865 | Lee surrenders at Appomattox. |

## Key Terms

Secession (p. 452)

Pacific Railroad Act (pp. 470–471)

Draft riots (p. 473)

Emancipation Proclamation (p. 473)

Gettysburg (p. 475)

Access the *Inventing America* StudySpace at wwnorton.com/studyspace

PERSONAL PLAN ■ REVIEW MATERIALS ■ RESEARCH AIDS ■ MULTIMEDIA

# Chapter 17

# RECONSTRUCTION:

## 1865–1877

Freedmen near a canal in Richmond, Virginia in 1865.

QUESTIONS

■ **What were the major issues at stake in the political Reconstruction of the United States?**

■ **How did blacks and whites piece together their lives in the postwar South?**

■ **Why did Reconstruction come to an end in the South?**

■ **What national and regional issues were resolved during Reconstruction?**

■ **What issues were resolved and which issues remained unresolved after the period of Reconstruction?**

"The trail of war," noted an English traveler to the Tennessee Valley in the late 1860s, "is visible throughout the valley in burnt up gin-houses, ruined bridges, mills, and factories . . . and in large tracts of once cultivated land stripped of every vestige of fencing." The city of Charleston, South Carolina, was "ruined"; "many fine mansions, long deserted, were fast mouldering into decay." Carl Schurz, a leading Republican and a general in the Union army, wrote that it was "difficult to imagine circumstances more unfavorable for the development of a calm and unprejudiced public opinion than those under which the southern people are at present laboring . . . When the rebellion was put down they found themselves not only conquered in a political and military sense, but economically ruined."

The North's military victory had settled two critical issues: the states of the Confederacy would remain part of the Union, and slavery would be abolished everywhere in the United States. But the end of military hostilities did not mean that the problems that had spawned the war had all been solved; moreover, the conquest of one region by another brought new issues to the fore. When would the rebellious states again participate in the national government? On what terms would these states be readmitted to the Union? How severely would the rebel leaders be punished? Most important, what would become of the South's black population, the former slaves—and, with them, of Southern society as a whole? What should Southern society look like after the war and after slavery?

The nation wrestled with these questions for more than a decade after the Civil War. Most white Southerners hoped to restore as much of the antebellum order as they could; the 4 million freed slaves, not surprisingly, had very different visions of the future. Northerners were divided over how harsh or magnanimous a peace to impose on the conquered South; they also disagreed about the degree to which Southern society would have to be transformed for the states of the Confederacy to regain power in the national government. The era of Reconstruction was tumultuous, filled with sharp partisan and regional conflict, bitter contests between Congress and the president, and recurrent outbreaks of violence in the South.

The changes wrought during this period, moreover, were not confined to the South. Reconstruction was national in scope, characterized everywhere by the growing economic prominence of industry and the political ascendancy of industrialists and financiers. Between 1865 and 1873, the nation's industrial output rose by nearly 75 percent, while more new miles of railroad track were laid than had existed before the Civil War. Manufacturing towns boomed in the Northeast. Chicago tripled its 1860 population and became a center of iron and steel production, meat packing, and the manufacture of agricultural machinery. Even more striking was the opening of the trans-Mississippi West through formal and informal—and sometimes downright shady—partnerships of government with railroad corporations and mining, lumber, and agricultural interests. Largely unsettled by Europeans in 1860, the West became the scene of rapid, helter-skelter development encouraged by the pro-business Republican Party.

## The Fate of the Union

### RECONSTRUCTION IN WARTIME

Even before the war ended, officials in Washington were taking steps to shape the contours of the postwar South and chart a course for its reintegration into the Union. The most fundamental issue on the agenda was slavery. Lincoln's 1863 Emancipation Proclamation clearly signaled the North's intention to bring an end to the peculiar institution. That intention was translated into law by the Thirteenth Amendment to the Constitution, approved by the Senate in 1864 and the House of Representatives in 1865: ratified by the states later in 1865, it permanently abolished slavery throughout the nation.

Lincoln, in 1863, also issued a Proclamation of Amnesty and Reconstruction, which spelled out the terms on which rebellious states could rejoin the Union. His action was based on the belief that Reconstruction was primarily an executive, rather than congressional, responsibility. The proclamation, commonly called the Ten-Percent Plan, reflected both his personal impulse to be magnanimous in victory and the hope that a generous Reconstruction policy might speed the end of the war. The plan offered a full pardon and the restoration of all property, except slaves, to all "persons" who took a loyalty oath and vowed to accept the abolition of slavery. Only a small number of high-ranking Confederate officials were deemed ineligible. When, in any state, such pledges numbered 10 percent of the number of votes cast in 1860, those who had vowed their loyalty could form a new state government. Once that government had determined to abolish slavery and provide for the education of black children, the state could be represented in Congress.

The Ten-Percent Plan was lenient in thrust and sketchy in details: it did not address the political or civil rights of freedmen, and it put few obstacles in the way of former rebels who might seek to regain control of their state governments. The plan, consequently, drew criticism from congressional Republicans who believed that the federal government ought to actively support the freedmen while promoting a transformation of social and political life in the South.

An alternative Republican plan, sponsored by Senator Benjamin Wade of Ohio and Representative Henry Davis of Maryland, offered a more punitive approach. The Wade-Davis Bill, which Congress approved in July 1864, permitted the states of the Confederacy to hold constitutional conventions and form new governments only after a majority of vot-ers had taken an "ironclad" loyalty oath. Confederate officials, as well as those who had borne arms "voluntarily," would not be permitted to vote for, or participate in, these conventions; and the new constitutions would have to ban slavery and repudiate all Confederate debts. Lincoln pocket-vetoed the Wade-Davis Bill (by not signing it), which angered his congressional critics and left the Ten-Percent Plan as the official, if vague, blueprint for Reconstruction.

Federal officials also found themselves confronted with another issue: Once freed, how would former slaves support themselves? Should the government help them to become economically independent of their former masters? Lincoln, intent on speedily restoring the Southern states to the Union, believed that federal intervention in the affairs of the South ought to be held to a minimum. (He hoped, in fact, that the "problem" of the former slaves would be solved by their emigration—a notion that was neither practical nor statesmanlike.) But many Radical Republicans, including Congressmen George Julian and Thaddeus Stevens, were convinced that the liberty of the freedmen would be illusory unless they owned property, landed property in particular. According to Julian, four million landless, impoverished black laborers would quickly be reduced to "a system of wages slavery . . . more galling than slavery itself."

Julian and other Radicals proposed to address the problem by confiscating Confederate lands and redistributing them to the freedmen. This idea came to the fore as early as 1862, when Congress passed the second Confiscation Act, which made all rebel property liable to confiscation. (A previous act applied only to property used in support of the rebellion.) At Lincoln's insistence, however, the second Confiscation Act limited any seizure of land to the lifetime of the owner, which effectively prohibited its permanent redistribution to freedmen. Moreover, the Ten-Percent Plan, by guaranteeing to return all property to rebels who took a loyalty oath, seemed to preclude the mass redistribution of land. Nonetheless, in 1864 and 1865, proconfiscation sentiment mounted in Congress, and both houses repealed the limiting clauses of the 1862 resolution: there was significant sentiment in favor of a program that would substantially alter the distribution of land, and economic power, in the South.

Meanwhile, in parts of the South that had been captured by Northern armies, military commanders found themselves dealing concretely, and urgently, with the same issues. On the South Carolina Sea Islands, in southern Louisiana, and eventually throughout the Mississippi Valley south of Vicksburg, victorious Northern armies ended up in possession of fertile lands temporarily abandoned by their owners; at the same time, they became responsible for the welfare of tens of thousands of impoverished freedmen, many of them refugees.

What ensued was a series of experiments in land and labor policy. Nearly everywhere, the freedmen displayed a preference for becoming self-supporting, for dividing the land into plots on which they could grow foodstuffs rather than cotton. In Davis Bend, Mississippi, a large group of slaves demonstrated they could also organize cotton production by themselves, as they took over and profitably ran plantations owned by Jefferson Davis and his brother. In most locales, however, Northern officials adopted more traditional arrangements: they leased the lands to white owners and mobilized the freedmen to work as agricultural laborers, for low wages and on year-long contracts enforced by the army. By the war's end, hundreds of thousands of former slaves were working on plantations that were superintended by the government.

It was against this backdrop that Congress, just before adjourning in March 1865, created the Bureau of Refugees, Freedmen, and Abandoned Lands, commonly called the Freedmen's Bureau. The bureau was charged with monitoring the condition of former slaves and delivering fuel, food, and clothing to the destitute, white and black alike. It also had the power to divide confiscated or abandoned lands into forty-acre parcels that could be rented, and eventually sold, to the freedmen. Although the bureau's powers were extraordinary—and set a precedent for public activism and intervention—Congress did not appropriate any funds for the bureau and anticipated that it would exist for only a year.

A depiction from *Harper's Weekly* of a freedmen's village, established under the auspices of the Freedmen's Bureau at Trent River, North Carolina, 1866.

### ANDREW JOHNSON AND PRESIDENTIAL RECONSTRUCTION

Six weeks after the Freedmen's Bureau was created, Abraham Lincoln was dead and Andrew Johnson had become the seventeenth president of the United States. Johnson, a pro-Union Democrat from Tennessee, had been nominated for the vice-presidency by the Republicans in 1864 to broaden their appeal in the border states. He seemed eminently qualified for the job. Born in humble circumstances in North Carolina, Johnson had served an apprenticeship as a tailor and then moved to the mountains of eastern Tennessee, where he married, learned to read and write, acquired a farm, and began a long career in politics. Elected first to the state legislature, he then served as governor, U.S. congressman, and U.S. senator. Johnson courageously stuck by his Unionist principles when Tennessee seceded, pre-

senting himself as a champion of the yeoman farmer and antagonist of the Southern plantation elite. "I will show the stuck-up aristocrats who is running the country," he once declared. "A cheap, purse-proud set they are, not half as good as the man who earns his bread by the sweat of his brow."

Experienced as he was, Johnson possessed personal traits that were not well suited to politics and that ill served him in the presidency. He was stubborn, intolerant of those who disagreed with him, reluctant to negotiate or compromise. "A slave to his passions and prejudices," as one contemporary noted, he was given to "unreasoning pugnacity." Indecisive and tactless, he lacked both close confidants and the suppleness of mind and vision so characteristic of his predecessor. A deeply insecure man, he also seemed to crave approval from the very aristocrats he claimed to despise.

Johnson's political beliefs, moreover, differed in key respects from those of Lincoln and other Republicans. A Democrat and not a Whig, as Lincoln had been, Johnson had a vision of the good society that was Jacksonian and agrarian, rather than industrial or urban; he was wary of Northern commercial interests and hostile to government intervention in the name of economic progress. Equally important, his racial views were conservative even by mid-nineteenth-century standards. Although Johnson fought the political dominance of aristocratic planters, he was not, until late in his career, an opponent of slavery. Indeed, he had bought some slaves himself and once voiced the peculiar wish "that every head of a family in the United States had one slave to take the drudgery and menial service off his family." In 1866, after a meeting with the orator and political leader Frederick Douglass, Johnson commented that Douglass was "just like any nigger . . . he would sooner cut a white man's throat than not."

Nonetheless, Johnson's accession to the presidency was initially welcomed by the Radical Republicans, who believed that the Tennesseean's vision of Reconstruction was closer to their own than Lincoln's had been. Senator Zechariah Chandler of Michigan even proclaimed that "the Almighty continued Mr. Lincoln in office as long as he was useful, and then substituted a better man to finish the work." In the wake of Lincoln's assassination, a punitive mood swept the North, and Johnson's public utterances implied that he would not be lenient in his treatment of the rebels. "Treason is a crime and must be made odious," he declared. "Traitors must be impoverished. . . . They must not only be punished, but their social power must be destroyed."

Johnson's first acts as president suggested that he would depart little from the course charted by his predecessor. Although Congress had adjourned in March 1865 and was not scheduled to meet again until December, Johnson declined to call a special session because he, like Lincoln, believed that Reconstruction was primarily an executive responsibility. In May and June, he issued a series of proclamations that replaced the Ten-Percent Plan. The first was a proclamation of amnesty and restitution that granted pardons and restored all property rights (except slave ownership) to everyone who took an oath avowing loyalty to the Union and support for emancipation. Confederate officials, as well as owners of taxable property valued at more than $20,000, were ineligible, although they could apply for amnesty individually to the president. (Johnson, true to his rhetoric, was taking aim at the rich as well as at political and military leaders.) Johnson then issued orders appointing provisional governors and instructing them to call state constitutional conventions; white men who had received amnesty would be eligible to vote for delegates to the conventions. In order to rejoin the Union, these conventions were expected to abolish slavery, nullify their acts of secession, and repudiate all Confederate debts.

Although most Radical Republicans were critical of Johnson's willingness to exclude blacks—including those who had served as soldiers—from the suffrage, his plan seemed, for a time, to be working. The provisional governors were generally pro-Union Democrats, and most delegates to the constitutional conventions were either Unionists or reluctant Confederates.

Andrew Johnson, seventeenth president of the United States (1865–69), shortly before his inauguration.

Former rebels took the loyalty oath en masse, while 15,000 members of the elite applied to Johnson personally for pardons.

But the white South—perhaps sensing the president's personal sympathies as a southerner as well as his hope of rebuilding a national Democratic Party that could carry him to reelection—grew defiant of its northern conquerors. The elected governor of Louisiana began to fire Unionist officeholders, replacing them with former Confederates. Mississippi and South Carolina refused to repudiate their Confederate debt; Texas and Mississippi chose not to ratify the Thirteenth Amendment; several states repealed without repudiating their secession ordinances. In the fall elections of 1865, large numbers of ex-Confederates were elected to office, particularly in the lower South; among them were twenty-five former Confederate leaders (including Alexander Stephens, previously vice-president of the Confederacy) who were elected to the U.S. Congress. Meanwhile, rebels whose lands had been seized were demanding their return, a demand that Johnson often bent over backward to satisfy.

Led by Mississippi and South Carolina, the new state governments also passed elaborate laws to govern the civil, social, and economic behavior of the freedmen. Some of this legislation, such as prohibitions on intermarriage or black jury service, also existed in the North. But the Black Codes, as these laws came to be called, went a great deal further, severely restricting the economic rights of the freedmen. In Mississippi, freedmen were required to sign year-long labor contracts that they could not break without forfeiting their wages and being subject to arrest; prospective employers could not offer a higher wage to a laborer already under contract; freedmen were prohibited from renting land in urban areas and could be arrested for vagrancy if they could not provide evidence of being employed. In South Carolina, African Americans had to obtain a license and pay a tax to perform any work other than farm labor or domestic service, while Louisiana and Texas tried to force black women to work by specifying that labor contracts had to include "all the members of the family able to work." Young blacks deemed to lack "adequate" parental support could be forcibly bound out as apprentices to their former masters. The Black Codes made clear that former slaves would be second-class citizens, at best.

By the time the Thirty-ninth Congress finally convened in December 1865, all of the Confederate states had formed new governments and elected representatives to Congress. President Johnson, acknowledging that Congress had the constitutional right to judge the qualifications of its own members, urged that these representatives be seated—which would effectively have brought an end to Reconstruction. Congress, however, declined to do so. Instead, expressing deep concern about conditions in the South, it formed a Joint Committee on Reconstruction to investigate the impact of Johnson's policies.

Despite this rebuff, the president was well positioned to carry out his Reconstruction policy or something close to it. Although Republicans dominated Congress, there were serious divisions within the party. Roughly half of all congressional Republicans (and more in the Senate) belonged to a loose coalition of moderates and conservatives. They sought more ample guarantees of black rights as well as legislation to protect freedmen and Unionists from violence, but they were not altogether dissatisfied with Johnson's approach, and they shared his desire to readmit the rebel states as expeditiously as possible. Standing in opposition to this coalition was the strong and ideologically coherent Radical wing of the party. Drawn primarily from New England and the northern states west of New England, the Radicals were moralists whose political views were forged by the struggle against slavery and by the successes of small-scale, competitive capitalism in the North. They sought to remake the South in the image of the North, a goal that demanded an active federal government, black suffrage, and land distribution. Committed and passionate as they were, most Radicals were nonetheless aware that they were out ahead of northern public

opinion (three northern states had rejected black suffrage in 1865) and that they themselves were outnumbered in Congress.

Soon after Congress convened, the Joint Committee on Reconstruction, chaired by the "moderate" senator William Fessenden of Maine, began extensive hearings, at which witnesses testified to the upsurge of violence, discrimination, and Confederate sentiment in the South. "It is of weekly, if not of daily, occurrence that freedmen are murdered" in Texas, reported General George Custer. In rural Alabama, "gangs of ruffians, mostly operating at night, hold individuals under a reign of terror," another general observed. A Confederate colonel was quoted as saying, "You have not subdued us; we will try you again."

In response, Republican moderates, led by the influential senator Lyman Trumbull of Illinois, drafted two pieces of legislation to protect the freedmen. The first extended the powers and life of the Freedmen's Bureau: the bill called for direct funding of the bureau, empowered it to build and support schools, and authorized bureau agents to assume legal jurisdiction over crimes involving blacks and over state officials who denied blacks their civil rights. The second measure, the Civil Rights Bill, defined blacks (indeed, all native-born persons except Indians) as U.S. citizens; it also specified the

Under the Black Code of Florida, any man fined for vagrancy and unable to pay the fine could have his services sold to the highest bidder. This engraving depicts a freedman's services sold at auction, 1867.

An 1866 cartoon by Thomas Nast depicting Andrew Johnson's veto of the Freedmen's Bureau bill.

rights inherent in citizenship, including the right to make contracts, own or rent property, and have access to the courts. No state could deprive any citizen of those rights; cases involving such violations would be heard in federal rather than state courts; and individuals who deprived a citizen of his rights would be subject to fine or imprisonment. Sweeping as the Civil Rights Bill was, it did not enfranchise blacks, permit them to sit on juries, or desegregate public accommodations.

To the shock of many, especially in moderate Republican circles, President Johnson vetoed both the Freedmen's Bureau and the Civil Rights bills in February and March 1866. In his veto messages, he insisted that the bills were illegal because they had been passed while the states of the South were unrepresented in Congress, a claim that completely denied Congress the right to formulate Reconstruction policy—or any policy, for that matter. Johnson attacked the Freedmen's Bureau as a fiscally unsound and constitutionally dubious agency, while maintaining that the Civil Rights Bill was an unconstitutional intrusion of the federal government into the affairs of states. His quarrel was not with the details of the bills but with the principles that lay behind them.

The president's vetoes were grounded in both conviction and political strategy. As a lifelong Democrat, Johnson believed in strong state governments and limited national power; he was also convinced that blacks were not the equals of whites and that government policies designed to promote equality could only have undesirable consequences. (He raised the specter of interracial marriage in one of his veto messages, for example.) Yet Johnson's actions were also aimed at dividing the Republican Party and isolating the Radicals. Doing so would leave a coalition of Democrats and moderate-to-conservative Republicans in control of Congress and boost his chances of being elected president in 1868.

Here Johnson miscalculated badly. Instead of dividing the Republican Party, his vetoes pushed the moderates toward more radical positions. While Democrats—both Northern and Southern—celebrated Johnson's actions, moderate and even conservative Republicans found themselves with a choice between allying with the Radicals or abandoning goals for which the war had been fought in the first place. In fact, they had no real choice, unless they were prepared to leave the freedmen at the mercy of the same Southerners who had enslaved them. Moderate and conservative Republicans broke with the president and sharply attacked his policies. "Those who formerly defended [Johnson] are now readiest in his condemnation," observed one Republican leader.

### THE FOURTEENTH AMENDMENT

The Republicans seized the initiative in the spring of 1866. In April, Congress overrode Johnson's veto of the Civil Rights Bill (marking the first time that a significant piece of legislation was passed over a presidential veto), and it then revised the Freedmen's Bureau Bill so that it, too, could be passed over a veto. In addition, the Joint Committee on Reconstruction worked throughout the spring to draft a constitutional amendment that would secure key objectives in a form that could not easily be reversed by presidential action or shifting legislative majorities. By the middle of June, the Fourteenth Amendment had received the necessary two-thirds majority from both houses of Congress and was sent to the states for ratification.

The Fourteenth Amendment contained three clauses that dealt with specific post–Civil War issues. One upheld the validity of the national (Union) debt while declaring that

A watercolor, *American Citizens (To the Polls),* commenting on the 1866 elections in which Southern blacks were permitted to vote.

neither the United States nor any individual state would repay debts incurred by the Confederacy during the rebellion. A second barred from public office anyone who, as an office-holder, had taken an oath to support the Constitution and then violated that oath by engaging in insurrection. A third mandated that a state that kept any adult male citizens from voting would have its representation in Congress reduced proportionately. This last clause was designed to prevent Southern states from increasing their representation as a result of the demise of slavery while still denying freedmen the right to vote. (A slave, in the original Constitution, had counted as three-fifths of a person for the purpose of representation.) It implicitly recognized the ability of the states to deny men the franchise because of their race, but it reduced any state's power in the national government if it did so. To the chagrin of women's suffrage advocates, the amendment, by using the word "male," tacitly recognized the right of states to deny women the vote without incurring any penalty.

The Fourteenth Amendment also articulated broad principles that over time would become key features of the constitutional landscape. Section 1 declared all native-born and naturalized persons to be citizens, thus nullifying the *Dred Scott* decision (1857), which had denied the citizenship of blacks. This formal definition of national citizenship was accompanied by a ban on any state's abridging the "privileges or immunities" of citizens. Section 1 also declared that no state could "deprive any person of life, liberty, or property, without due process of law"; nor could a state deny to any person "the equal protection of the laws." Although the precise meaning of these phrases would be debated by lawyers and judges for more than a century, their core intent was clear. The Fourteenth Amendment enshrined the principle of "equality before the law" in the Constitution while authorizing the federal government to actively defend equal rights when they were threatened by state governments. Written to protect African Americans in the post–Civil War South, the amendment articulated principles so significant and far-reaching that they would, over time, be applied to people and circumstances well removed from Reconstruction.

The Fourteenth Amendment became the platform of the Republican Party in the congressional elections of 1866, which were widely regarded as a referendum on Reconstruction. Opposing the Republicans was a new political grouping, the National Union Movement, organized by President Johnson as a coalition of conservatives from both parties. Johnson hoped that the movement could mobilize support for ending Reconstruction and readmitting the Southern states while avoiding the taint of treason that still clung to the Democrats.

The National Union was destined to defeat: the Northern electorate remained suspicious of Democrats, no matter what they called themselves, and incidents of mob violence against blacks in Memphis and New Orleans graphically underscored the need for the continued protection of black rights. Johnson himself antagonized voters with an ill-tempered campaign tour around the nation. "Why not hang Thad Stevens and Wendell Phillips?" he shouted to an audience in Cleveland. The Republicans won a far more lopsided victory than anyone had predicted, gaining ground in every state in the North and retaining large majorities in both houses of Congress.

### RADICAL RECONSTRUCTION AND THE IMPEACHMENT OF ANDREW JOHNSON

Despite the election results, neither Johnson nor the political leaders of the South seemed ready to capitulate, or even conciliate. Johnson defiantly predicted that his allies would win the next round of elections, while Southern legislatures, with Johnson's backing, emphatically rejected the Fourteenth Amendment. This intransigence led many moderate Republicans to overcome long-held reservations and embrace black suffrage as a central element in reordering the South. Only if armed with the franchise, it appeared, could blacks protect themselves against whites who would not accept them as equal citizens.

Working together, the moderates and the Radicals devised a Reconstruction Act that was passed in March 1867 over Johnson's veto. The act declared existing state governments to be merely provisional and reinstituted military authority everywhere in the former Confederacy except Tennessee, which had ratified the Fourteenth Amendment and been readmitted to the Union. The bill also outlined the steps that states would have to follow to regain full membership in the national government: holding new constitutional conventions (elected by adult males), ratifying the Fourteenth Amendment, and adopting constitutions that permitted blacks to vote. In the first months of 1867, Congress passed measures to limit the president's ability to obstruct Reconstruction. Among them was the Tenure of Office Act, which required the president to obtain the consent of the Senate before dismissing any official whose appointment required senatorial confirmation.

The Republicans were right to anticipate that Johnson would attempt to obstruct their program. Throughout 1867 and early 1868, he interfered in every way he could, appointing military commanders unsympathetic to the Republicans' goals, removing officials who seemed too sympathetic, insisting on interpretations of the Reconstruction Act that weakened its thrust, and encouraging the South to defy federal law. The skirmishing came to a head early in 1868 when Johnson removed Secretary of War Edwin Stanton, a Lincoln appointee and the one member of Johnson's cabinet who favored Radical Reconstruction. As secretary of war, Stanton occupied a critical place in the chain of command between Washington and the Union armies occupying the South. His removal, according to the Republicans, constituted a violation of the Tenure of Office Act.

Johnson's attempt to remove Stanton (who refused to turn in the keys to his office) prompted the House of Representatives to take the unprecedented step of impeaching the president. According to the Constitution, federal officials could be impeached for "treason, bribery, or other high crimes and misdemeanors," and many Radicals had talked of impeachment for more than a year, but it was the removal of Stanton that prompted some moderates to join their ranks. After two-thirds of the House had voted to impeach, the process moved to the Senate, where a two-thirds vote was necessary to convict the president and remove him from office.

The trial of Andrew Johnson in the Senate lasted from March 13 to May 26, 1868. Johnson's defenders maintained that what he had done was not an impeachable offense, that the president was merely testing the constitutionality of the Tenure of Office Act, and that the act didn't actually apply to Stanton anyway (because he had been appointed by Lincoln). Yet the legal arguments never did more than cloak the real issue: did Johnson's unceasing opposition to congressional Reconstruction, coupled with his apparent intention of restoring former Confederates to power and to the Union, constitute sufficient grounds to remove him from office? Most senators thought that they did. But a sizable minority did not—in part for legal reasons, in part because they feared setting a destabilizing precedent, and in part because they did not want Benjamin Wade, the Radical leader of the Senate, to ascend to the presidency. Johnson, who behaved with uncharacteristic decorum during the Senate proceedings, was acquitted by a margin of 1 vote. The final tally was 35 to 19 in favor of conviction, with 7 Republicans voting for acquittal.

Johnson's acquittal was not the only defeat suffered by the Radical Republicans in 1867 and 1868. In the state elections of 1867, black suffrage was rejected in Ohio, Minnesota, and Kansas, while the Democrats, who openly paraded their hostility to black rights, registered electoral gains in many states in the North.

A cartoon implying that President Johnson lacked the capacity to grasp the U.S. Constitution and was subsequently flattened by it.

## THE DEFEAT OF LAND REFORM

The Radical idea of confiscating Confederate lands and distributing them to the freedmen was never widely embraced in the Republican Party, but it had powerful supporters. Among them were Thaddeus Stevens of Pennsylvania, the leader of the Radicals in the House, and his counterpart in the Senate, Charles Sumner of Massachusetts. Stevens, the Republican floor leader of the House and the senior member of the Joint Committee on Reconstruction, was widely respected for his honesty and idealism while being feared for his sharp tongue and mastery of parliamentary tactics. Although frequently outvoted, Stevens saw himself as the leader of a righteous vanguard that would press forward the cause of social and racial justice against all opposition; even in death, he made a statement for racial equality by asking to be buried in a black cemetery. Sumner similarly was a man of principle, devoted to the notion that all individuals had to be equal before the law. An eloquent, charismatic figure, he had little patience for day-to-day politics, but he wielded enormous popular influence and was regarded by many African Americans as their most devoted champion in government.

The obstinacy of the white South lent support to the land-reform arguments of Stevens, Sumner, and others. Confiscation and redistribution, as Stevens pointed out, would simultaneously destroy the power of the plantation aristocracy and provide an economic foundation for black political and civil rights. "Strip a proud nobility of their bloated estates; reduce them to a level with plain republicans; send them forth to labor and teach their children to enter the workshops or handle the plow, and you will thus humble the proud traitors." Appealing as this vision may have been, however, the confiscation of land conflicted with basic Republican values: private property was to be protected, not seized, and free labor was to be rewarded with wages, not with free land from the government. *The Nation,* a respected Republican magazine, voiced the fear that the government giving freedmen land would imply "that there are other ways of securing comfort or riches than honest work." The *New York Tribune* proclaimed that "people who want farms work for them. The only class we know that takes other people's property because they want it is largely represented in Sing Sing." The Radical argument that blacks had already worked hard for this land, for two centuries, fell on few receptive ears.

This ideological resistance thwarted efforts at land redistribution in the mid-1860s. The issue came to a head in the spring and summer of 1867 when Stevens—gravely ill but fiercely committed to the cause—introduced a bill to give forty acres of confiscated land to each freedman. Stevens hoped that continued Southern defiance would finally prod exasperated moderates to accept confiscation, just as they had come to endorse civil rights and black suffrage. But his hopes were not fulfilled. Although the possibility of land reform captured the imagination of both the freedmen and the poor whites in the South, Northern Republicans were simply not prepared to go that far. Investment in the Southern economy was rumored to be frozen because of fears of confiscation, and moderate Republicans began to worry that confiscation would both hinder the growth of the party in the South and harm relations between labor and capital in the North. By the end of the summer of 1867, a congressional committee of Republicans issued a declaration that Reconstruction would not infringe property rights in the South. Land redistribution—the most radical approach to reconstructing the South—was a dead issue.

While these momentous events, and nonevents, were transpiring in Washington, the program of congressional Reconstruction was proceeding in the South. Under the supervision of the army, whites and blacks were registered to vote, with extraordinarily high black registration rates (over 90 percent in most states) bearing witness to the hunger of the freedmen for political rights. In the fall of 1867, elections were held for new constitutional conventions. Since many whites boycotted the elections, a large majority of the elected delegates were Republicans, roughly a third of whom were black, with another quarter consisting of recent migrants from the North.

Thaddeus Stevens.

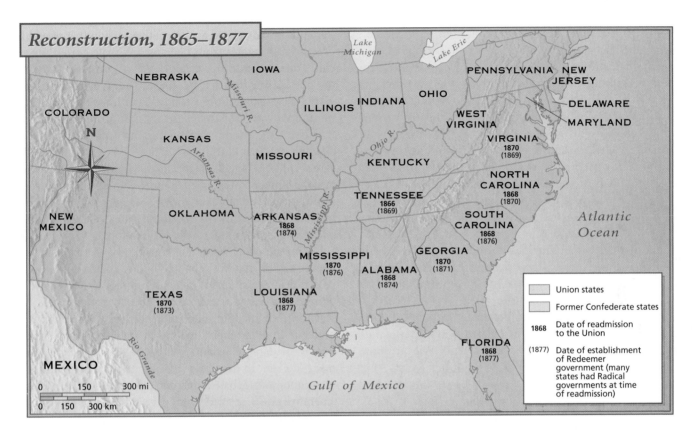

### Reconstruction, 1865–1877

Legend:
- Union states
- Former Confederate states
- **1868** Date of readmission to the Union
- (1868) Date of establishment of Redeemer government (many states had Radical governments at time of readmission)

State labels:
- VIRGINIA 1870 (1869)
- NORTH CAROLINA 1868 (1870)
- SOUTH CAROLINA 1868 (1876)
- TENNESSEE 1866 (1869)
- ARKANSAS 1868 (1874)
- GEORGIA 1870 (1871)
- MISSISSIPPI 1870 (1876)
- ALABAMA 1868 (1874)
- LOUISIANA 1868 (1877)
- TEXAS 1870 (1873)
- FLORIDA 1868 (1877)

Scale: 0 150 300 mi / 0 150 300 km

These delegates, derided by Southern conservatives as "ignorant Negroes cooperating with a gang of white adventurers," drew up impressively progressive constitutions. Not only did they institute male suffrage (often expressly repudiating financial and literacy requirements for voting), but they also created statewide public school systems for both whites and blacks and set up progressive tax systems that lightened the tax burden of small landowners. The constitutions were ratified, beginning in the spring of 1868, and Republican state governments began to be elected soon thereafter, thanks in good part to black voters. The Republican governments quickly approved the Fourteenth Amendment, which made their states eligible to be readmitted to full membership in the Union. In the summer of 1868, the representatives of seven states were seated in Congress (joining Tennessee); by 1870, Virginia, Mississippi, and Texas were also readmitted. In formal terms, at least, the Union was restored.

THE ELECTION OF 1868

Although the Republicans had failed to remove Andrew Johnson from office, they had high hopes of electing a new president in 1868. To carry the party's banner, they nominated Ulysses Grant, a West Point graduate, career military officer, and successful leader of the Union army. The forty-six-year-old Grant was a political moderate who had long opposed slavery and had endorsed congressional Reconstruction, thereby becoming a public adversary of Johnson. Grant was opposed by Democrat Horatio Seymour, a former governor of New York, and his overtly racist running mate, Frank Blair of Missouri. (Blair referred to the freedmen as "a semi-barbarous race of blacks who are worshippers of fetishes and poligamists.") In a heated campaign marred by outbreaks of violence in some states in the South, the Democrats threatened to roll back Reconstruction, while Grant presented himself as a peacemaker, promising to bring an end to the turmoil that had lasted for nearly a decade. Grant was elected by a large electoral college majority (214 to 80), although the popular vote was much closer. In all likelihood—and as a harbinger of things to come—a majority of white voters cast their ballots for Seymour and the Democrats.

Even before Grant took office, Congress was drafting what would become the Fifteenth Amendment, which declared that the right to vote "shall not be denied or abridged . . . on account of race, color, or previous condition of servitude." Support for such an amendment—which was outside the range of mainstream debate only a few years earlier—reflected the rapidly growing Republican conviction that the rights of freedmen would never be secure without the franchise: the amendment was designed to permanently guarantee the political rights of blacks by placing suffrage beyond the reach of state legislatures or state constitutional conventions. It would affect the North as well as the South; in 1868, blacks were unable to vote in eleven states in the North and all of the border states, a circumstance that undercut the moral authority of Northern advocates of black suffrage for the South. As the 1868 elections made clear, moreover, the Republicans had a partisan interest in the amendment: almost all blacks would vote Republican. The Fifteenth Amendment thus promised to enhance the fortunes of both the freedmen and the Republican Party.

Although pathbreaking, the amendment did not go as far as many members of Congress had hoped. Led by Massachusetts senator (and later vice-president) Henry Wilson, some

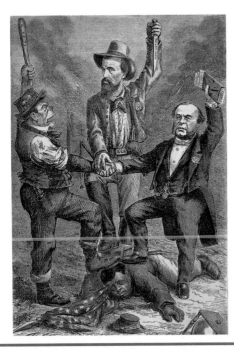

An 1868 cartoon by Thomas Nast criticizing the Democratic Party's opposition to Reconstruction. The three men standing represent the urban Irish of the North, unreconstructed southern Confederates, and northern capitalists.

Republicans advocated an alternative version that would have prevented the states from denying any male citizen the franchise "on account of race, color, nativity, property, education, or creed." Far broader in scope, the Wilson amendment would have brought universal male suffrage to the entire nation: in Wilson's words, it would carry out "logically the ideas that lie at the foundation of our institutions." The Wilson amendment, in addition, would have prevented the Southern states from disfranchising blacks through literacy tests or poll taxes. Many members of Congress, however, opposed this more inclusive language because they did not want to broaden the franchise in their own states, where literacy, tax, and nativity requirements were still in force.

After prolonged debate and considerable parliamentary maneuvering (during which each house of Congress actually passed the Wilson amendment), Congress approved a version that referred only to race, color, and "previous condition of servitude." Charles Sumner, among others, was so angry at this outcome that he refused to vote in favor of the amendment. But even without Sumner's support, the Fifteenth Amendment was sent to the states in the spring of 1869. After a year of acrimonious debate and some close votes in key states, the amendment was ratified in 1870, thanks in part to Republican dominance of most state legislatures.

## The Recovering South

The drama of Reconstruction was enacted on several stages. While grand matters of policy were being decided in Washington, the people of the South, white and black, were trying to rebuild their lives in a world shattered by four years of war and profoundly altered by Yankee victory.

Much of this world was physically scarred. Railroad lines were torn up nearly everywhere, roadbeds were destroyed, station houses burned, rolling stock gone. Bridges had been blown up, levees had collapsed from neglect, and roads were in poor repair. Through broad stretches of the countryside, the routines of rural life were stilled: Livestock was dead or scattered; fences were nowhere to be seen; fields were overgrown; houses, barns, and sheds stood empty. Some villages had simply vanished; indeed, a traveler noted that the site of a "once bustling town" was marked by a "single standing chimney." The cities—except, perhaps, for New Orleans—had suffered just as badly. Half of Atlanta had burned to the ground; the ware-

Lithograph showing a parade held in Baltimore in May 1870 to celebrate ratification of the Fifteenth Amendment, which prohibited states from denying men the vote because of their race, color, or previous condition of servitude. President Grant is at the upper left, Vice-President Colfax at the upper right; also pictured are Abraham Lincoln (lower left), John Brown (lower right), and, in the threesome at top, Frederick Douglass (middle) and Hiram Revels (right).

houses of Mobile had been destroyed by "the great explosion"; eighty blocks of Columbia, South Carolina, lay in ruins.

The South's economy had also collapsed. Agricultural output had plummeted; mines, mills, and factories were shuttered; and banks had virtually ceased to exist. The billions of dollars in capital that had been tied up in slaves had vanished, Confederate paper had become worthless, and nearly all insurance companies were bankrupt. In many areas, the transportation of goods had become impossible by rail, difficult and slow by river. Moreover, the war had claimed the lives of one-fifth of the region's adult white males as well as thousands of blacks. Poverty was widespread, destitution common. "In Alabama alone, two hundred thousand persons are in danger of extreme suffering, if not of actual starvation," reported *Harper's Weekly* in December 1865. "Women and children . . . begging for bread from door to door," noted a Freedmen's Bureau official, were an "everyday sight" in Randolph County. As late as 1870, per capita output was 39 percent lower than it had been in 1860; the total value of all

property (excluding slaves) had fallen by 30 percent.

## THE EXPERIENCE OF FREEDOM

For African Americans, Reconstruction was, above all, the experience of freedom. For some, this experience began before the end of war, with the arrival of Union troops and, often, the flight of their masters. For most, the first moments of freedom came in the spring of 1865.

First reactions to emancipation varied widely. One former slave in South Carolina recalled that "some were sorry, some hurt, but a few were silent and glad" when the master of their plantation called them together to announce that they were free. At another plantation, more than half the slaves were "gone" before the master had even finished speaking. Immediate displays of celebration were rare, but rapid changes in demeanor—from the deferential, compliant, cheerful slave to a more reserved, assertive, sometimes angry freedman—were not uncommon. Many plantation owners, particularly those who had abandoned their properties and returned after emancipation, were shocked by the lack of warmth displayed by their former slaves.

Perhaps the most common early response to emancipation was to move. Some men and women left their slave residences the instant their freedom was proclaimed; others waited a few days, weeks, or months before packing their meager possessions and departing. For most former slaves, feeling free meant leaving the place where they had lived in bondage, moving as they had not been permitted to move as slaves. As Richard Edwards, a black preacher in Florida, observed in 1865, "So long ez de shadder ob de gret house falls acrost you, you ain't gwine ter feel lake no free man, an' you ain't gwiner ter feel lak no free 'oman. You mus' all move—you mus' move clar away from de ole places what you knows, ter de new places what you don't know, whey you kin raise yore head douten no fear Marse Dis ur Marse Tudder."

Yet moving did not mean going far. Although there was a visible migration from the countryside to the city and, over time, a significant migration southward (to the belt of states stretching from Florida to Texas), most freedmen chose to remain in nearby rural areas. Their first post-emancipation homes were different spots in a familiar world.

They also began rebuilding that world, starting with their families. One of the most compelling goals of the freedmen was to reunite families that had been torn apart by slave sales: "in their eyes, the work of emancipation was incomplete until the families dispersed by slavery were reunited," observed a Freedmen's Bureau agent in South Carolina. "They had a passion for getting together. Every mother's son among them seemed to be in search of his mother; every mother in search of her children." Freedmen and women placed ads in newspapers in search of their loved ones and walked hundreds of miles to find them. Men and women also formalized relationships they had not been permitted to solemnize under slavery: mass weddings, with dozens of couples at a time, were frequent occurrences in the early months of emancipation. Family identities were further reinforced as the freedmen began to take last names, often selecting the name of someone known to them. "Precious few of 'em ever took that of their old masters," noted an overseer in Louisiana.

In addition to their families, the freedmen sought to build or rebuild two other institutions: churches and schools. De-nied equal footing in the biracial, yet white-dominated, churches that the South inherited from the antebellum era, African Americans withdrew from those congregations and created their own religious communities. In Charleston, the first new building erected after the war was a black church, and ten more had been constructed by 1866. Churches—sometimes makeshift, sometimes not—sprouted up across the countryside, serving both as places of worship and as centers for community social life.

Schools were built with even greater ardor. Since schooling had been denied to most slaves (90 percent of whom were illiterate in 1860), the freedmen greeted their emancipation as an opportunity to learn to read and write and to obtain education for their children. Helped by funding from the Freedmen's Bureau, Northern benevolent societies, and, later, the Republican state governments, the freedmen began operating schools everywhere—sometimes committing large portions of their own meager funds to keep schools running. Schools held sessions in churches, warehouses, storerooms, and stables; the Bryant Slave Mart was transformed into a school in Savannah, and in New Orleans a former slave pen was reborn as the Frederick Douglass School. In rural areas, freedmen negotiated labor contracts that included educational provisions for children; field hands in Selma, Alabama, demanded that their employer provide the materials to build a school, which they would construct and operate by themselves. Education was a source of independence and autonomy, second in importance only to the ownership of land.

Although the former slaves tacitly accepted racially separate churches and schools, they pressed for changes in the rules and conventions governing social interactions between blacks and whites. Particularly in urban areas, freedmen did not always stand when spoken to by whites or touch their hats or cede sidewalks to their "betters." They also began to question rules that either banned blacks or gave them inferior accommodations on railroads, streetcars, steamboats, or other public facilities. Grounded as much in custom as in law, these rules were sometimes challenged by freedmen through civil dis-

A freedmen's school on the James Plantation in North Carolina.

## How Was School?

The teacher in the third room was as great a contrast to the two we had just seen as was her school to theirs. She was smart, bright, looking for all the world like a Lowell factory girl of the better class; and her pupils, though by no means quiet as lambs, were in fine order. Their faces had evidently been washed systematically; long labors had forced upon their comprehension the advantages of clean aprons and pinafores; and they appeared attentive and noisily anxious to learn. This teacher seemed capable of giving an intelligent opinion as to the capacities of her scholars. She taught at the North, and she saw no difference in the rapidity with which whites and blacks learned to spell and read. There were dull scholars and bright scholars everywhere. Some here were as dull as any she ever saw; others were bright as the brightest. And she called out a little coal-black creature, who had been in school eight days, and was apparently not more than as many years old. The eyes of the little thing sparkled as she began to spell! Eight days ago she had not known her letters. From spelling she went to reading, and was soon found to have mastered every sentence on the charts hung about the walls.

Whitelaw Reid, "Among the Negro Schools,"
*After the war: A Tour of the Southern States,
1865–1866*

obedience, litigation, and appeals to Union army commanders. Occasionally the freedmen even won. A newspaper article in 1867 reported that in Charleston, "another streetcar difficulty occurred today. Two negroes got inside a streetcar, and, refusing to leave, were ejected by the police." In some states, the Republican governments of the late 1860s and early 1870s passed legislation outlawing discrimination in public facilities. Although rarely enforced, these civil rights laws did, at least briefly, help to diminish the strength of the color line.

To most whites, in contrast, the end of slavery only heightened the need for racial separation: "if we have social equality, we shall have intermarriage, and if we have intermarriage we shall degenerate," warned one anxious survivor of the war. Indeed, whites, too, were rebuilding their world during Reconstruction, socially as well as physically. In the sugar- and rice-growing regions of the coastal Carolinas, Georgia, and Louisiana, patterns of land ownership, wealth, and power changed substantially in the wake of the war—although that was not true where the economy was based on tobacco or cotton. Yet even where the social structure changed little, whites had to adjust to a post-emancipation social order that was un-settling. Former slaves could not be counted on to be deferential, to remain apart, to take orders, to stay in their "place." Whites often described the freedmen as "insolent" or "saucy."

White Southerners also found that they could not count on the coercive powers of the state to compel the freedmen to act "properly." In contrast to the antebellum world, state power, particularly after 1866, was wielded by Union army commanders and elected officials who were no longer committed to maintaining white control over blacks. In part for this reason, whites frequently began to take the law into their own hands, making this one of the most violent periods in the nation's history. Acts of violence against blacks, provoked by black "impudence" or "disrespect," were commonplace. In Greenville, South Carolina, a group of young white men stabbed a black man who had refused to step off a sidewalk when their paths crossed. Race riots, in which blacks were attacked and beaten by whites, erupted in Memphis, Charleston, New Orleans, Atlanta, Richmond, and Norfolk (Virginia): in the Memphis riot of 1866, white mobs killed forty-six African Americans.

Antiblack violence was also expressed in a more organized fashion, through vigilante, paramilitary groups such as the

## The Recovering South

This engraving depicts an incident that occurred in early May 1866, when whites assaulted blacks in Memphis, killing forty-six.

White Brotherhood and the Ku Klux Klan. By the late 1860s, the Klan had become a loose network of terrorist organizations dedicated to restoring full-blown white supremacy throughout the South. Klansmen—who came from all walks of life—roamed the countryside dressed in white sheets and assaulting, beating, and sometimes murdering freedmen, Northerners, Republicans, and wartime Unionists. Many Klan activists were angry veterans of the Confederate army, and they attacked black churches and schools as well as interracial couples, individuals who had been "impudent" or had financial disputes with whites, and freedmen who were outspoken politically or successful economically. Intent on destroying the Republican Party and preventing blacks from wielding political power, the Klan particularly targeted political leaders: at least 10 percent of the black members of the constitutional conventions of the late 1860s became victims of violence. Over time, moreover, the Klan's strategy worked as opposition voices were quieted and became fewer in number.

### LAND AND LABOR

Agriculture remained the heart of the South's economy, but just how it would be organized was sharply contested. Most freedmen wanted to own their own land; but within a year after the end of the war, almost all the land that had been distributed to blacks had been returned to its white owners, and the possibility of any significant governmental distribution of land soon became remote. It was, moreover, exceedingly difficult for former slaves to buy land even if they had the means

to do so: most whites would not, or were afraid to, sell land to freedmen. Consequently, the great majority of former slaves remained landless tillers of the soil; as late as 1880, only 20 percent of all black farm operatives owned land.

Whites, on the other hand, owned land but needed labor to make their property productive. In pursuit of inexpensive, hard-working labor, southern whites tried to attract immigrants or to import gangs of Chinese workers, but they had limited success. The agricultural labor force would have to be black, and in the eyes of many whites, it would therefore have to be coerced and closely supervised. "The nigger," commented one Alabama farmer, "*never* works except when he is compelled to." Becoming a cheap, disciplined plantation labor force was not, however, what the freedmen envisioned as their post-emancipation future, even if they failed to own land. They preferred to farm small plots of land as families rather than to work in closely overseen gangs reminiscent of slavery; they also wanted the freedom to move, change employers, and bargain over terms.

This clash of interests was played out in annual, sometimes daily, skirmishes between employers and employees—over the payment of wages, the terms of credit, the timing of payments, the rental of land, the selection of crops, the payment of debts. It was also expressed legally and politically. Landowners, often with the support of the Freedmen's Bureau and the Union army, tried to impose annual contracts on the freedmen, which were particularly stifling when the freedmen were paid only at year's end and were penalized for leaving early. The Black Codes passed by the Johnson government sought to limit the physical mobility of blacks (as did vagrancy laws aimed at discouraging urban migration) and restrict their job options. Landowners also sought to pass laws that would prevent employers from hiring someone else's employees—laws that would, in effect, prohibit the labor market from functioning as a market. When the Republican governments were in power, the tables were turned: laws restricting labor's rights were repealed, new measures helped to guarantee that workers would be paid when employers sold their property (including crops), and taxes on land were increased to encourage large landholders to sell portions of their property.

From this skirmishing and experimentation emerged the system of sharecropping that would dominate agriculture in the South for decades. Sharecropping was a fairly simple mode of organizing agriculture: the landowner provided land and tools, the sharecropper performed all the labor, and they split the crop (often fifty-fifty, but the terms varied widely). Or, stated differently, land was rented to tenants, with the

"Worse Than Slavery," an 1874 cartoon by Thomas Nast, depicts the plight of African Americans in the post–Civil War South.

rental payment being a share of the crop. This system appeared to have advantages for both blacks and whites. Blacks were able to work in individual household units, with some autonomy and independence; whites were assured that blacks had an incentive to work hard and produce a good crop. By 1880, more than half of all rural blacks worked on shares.

Alongside sharecropping, there developed another institution that proved to be just as durable but far more pernicious in its consequences: the crop-lien system. Farmers always needed credit—to purchase seed, supplies, fertilizer—and before the war, they had borrowed annually from "factors" or banks, pledging their land as collateral for loans that would be repaid once their crops were sold. After the war, however, the banking system was shattered, and the breakup of plantations into small farms operated by tenants (whether sharecroppers or cash tenants) meant that there were many more farmers who needed to borrow, most of whom did not own land that could serve as collateral.

Into this vacuum in the credit system stepped country merchants, many of whom were also landowners. These merchants advanced supplies to farmers, who secured the loans by giving the merchants a "lien" on their crops, which meant, in effect, that the merchant owned, or had the right to sell, the crop. The merchant, in addition, charged the farmer interest on the supplies advanced (often at exorbitant rates) and

sometimes was able to set the price at which the crop would be sold. In theory, this was a mutually beneficial set of transactions: a farmer who worked hard, had good weather, and sold his crop at a good price would pay off his debt to the merchant at the end of the year and pocket the difference.

But things rarely worked that simply. Most merchants had monopolies in their local areas and thus had the power to dictate the terms of the transaction, limiting a farmer's chances of actually profiting from his labors. Moreover, bad weather or declining prices would often leave the farmer in debt to the merchant at the end of the year; this generally obliged him to borrow from the merchant (and perhaps rent the merchant's land) again the following year. Most important, perhaps, merchants decided what crops the farmers would grow, and they commonly demanded that farmers grow *the* cash crop: cotton. Consequently, farmers grew more cotton and less food, which obliged them to buy foodstuffs from the merchants and increase their indebtedness. This practice also led to a sharp increase in cotton production, which lowered cotton prices—and thus the incomes of farmers—through much of the 1870s. In this way, small farmers became trapped in a system of "debt peonage," while the South's economy became excessively dependent on cotton.

Owing in part to declining cotton prices, agriculture in the South had difficulty recovering from the war. The region's per capita agricultural output remained below prewar levels for the remainder of the nineteenth century, while the per capita income of whites in the cotton states declined by one-third between the late 1850s and 1879. The income of blacks, of course, increased sharply in the first years after emancipation, but that trend was not sustained, and blacks continued to earn only half as much as whites.

Of equal importance, the stagnation of agriculture was accompanied by the region's failure to generate much industrial growth. In the eyes of many Republicans, both Northern and Southern, such growth was essential: railroad construction and industrial development, they believed, would stimulate urban growth and immigration, thereby enriching the region and reducing the power of landowning planters. State and local governments, particularly those dominated by the Republicans in the late 1860s, sought to encourage railroad construction and industrial growth. They offered railroad corporations financial inducements, including outright monetary grants, to get them to rebuild old lines and build new ones. To lure private enterprise, state legislatures passed laws to protect the property rights of corporations, to provide cheap labor in the form of

The Way They Live, a painting by Thomas Anshuntz depicting sharecroppers, 1879.

leased convicts, and to exempt many enterprises (including railroads, banks, and factories) from taxation.

These efforts failed. Although the railroad system was rebuilt and even extended to many interior towns, the overall growth was modest: 7,000 miles of new track were laid in the South between 1865 and 1879, compared with 45,000 miles in the North. The state governments had difficulty paying for the ambitious railroad projects they had launched, and they ended up both raising taxes and, later, cutting back on their commitments. The flow of funds between the public and private sectors, moreover, created fertile soil for corruption: bribery became commonplace in some states, and the Republican Party was tainted by publicly visible corruption. Despite the incentives offered to private enterprise, the politically unstable South had difficulty attracting investment from the North and from Europe, a problem that was compounded after 1873 by the economic depression that gripped the nation. The fruits of the Republican

dedication to the "gospel of prosperity" were limited, and the planting of new industries proceeded far too slowly to alter the overwhelmingly agricultural character of the region.

## The Road to Redemption

While the South was rebuilding, the North was booming. The economy grew rapidly, if unevenly, during the war; and, following a brief pause, the growth resumed after Appomattox. Between 1865 and 1873, industrial output soared, while 3 million immigrants poured into the country, most of them headed for the cities of the North and West. The North's victory was, in key respects, a victory of industrial capitalism over a more agrarian, paternalist social order, and the postwar years were a celebration of that triumph. Not only was the pro-industry Republican Party in power in Washington, but the first transcontinental railroad was completed, George Westinghouse invented air brakes for trains, and the Bessemer process for making steel (by blowing air through molten iron) was introduced into the United States. With fitting symbolism, the stock ticker was invented in 1872 by Thomas Alva Edison.

This unleashing of productive, and speculative, energies was felt throughout the North and in the West, which, with every issue of slavery resolved, was thrown wide open to new settlement. Businesses were built, fortunes were made, and new territories were inhabited. Yet the very ebullience of the economy, followed later by the shock of economic depression, had the effect of drawing attention away from Reconstruction, the South, and the issues that had led to war. By the mid-1870s, the eyes of the nation were more focused on the stock ticker than on the still-incomplete process of reconstructing the South.

### THE REPUBLICAN PARTY IN THE SOUTH

By the late 1860s, the fate of Reconstruction was closely tied to the fate of the Republican Party in the South. Yet the Republicans' hold on power in the region was tenuous, despite their electoral success in 1868. Support for the party came from upcountry whites (small farmers, many of whom had been Unionists), from low-country entrepreneurs who sympathized with the economic policies of the Republicans, and from immigrants from the North. But the great majority of Republican

**LEFT:** Joseph Rainey, U.S. representative from South Carolina, First District (1870–79).

**RIGHT:** Hiram Revels, U.S. senator from Mississippi (1870–71).

voters were black, a fact that worried the party's leaders. They feared that Republican prospects in both the North and the South, would be imperiled if the party failed to attract more white support and became identified as the "black" party.

Despite these concerns, the Republican Party made it possible for sizable numbers of African Americans to participate in electoral politics for the first time. Not only did freedmen vote, but they were also elected to office. Fourteen blacks, including some who were self-educated and others who were lawyers, were elected to Congress. Hiram Revels, a Methodist minister who had organized black regiments at the outset of the war, became one of Mississippi's senators, chosen by a predominantly Republican state legislature that had three dozen black members. In South Carolina, the home of secession, 55 percent of all state legislators in 1868 were African American men who only a few years earlier were not counted as citizens. In addition to the hundreds of black Republicans serving in Southern state legislatures, more than a thousand held local offices in towns and counties throughout the region. Turning the political order "bottomside up," as one Northern journalist put it, former slaves became active participants not only in politics but in governance, creating one of the most radical transformations of political life that the nation had ever witnessed.

The policies implemented by the Republican state governments were aimed at protecting the freedmen, modernizing Southern society, and constructing a more active state. They created public schools for both whites and blacks, revamped the judicial system, and built hospitals, penitentiaries, and asylums. In addition to rebuilding the infra-structure that had been destroyed during the war (roads, bridges, public buildings), the governments actively sought private investment in railroads and industry. Yet these projects cost money—which meant raising taxes and increasing the public debt by issuing bonds. Although not high by Northern standards, tax rates by 1870 were often triple or quadruple what they had been in 1860. Not surprisingly, such sharp increases in an era of economic stress spawned vehement opposition: in nearly every state, white landowners, who resented not only paying taxes but paying taxes that benefited freedmen and allegedly corrupt Republican officials, formed taxpayers' associations to demand reductions in state budgets.

High taxes and charges of corruption certainly fueled opposition to the Reconstruction governments, but the heart of that opposition remained what it always had been: the desire to restore white supremacy and to restrict the civil and economic rights of blacks. Although there briefly emerged a group of "New Departure" Democrats who spoke of accepting the changes wrought by Reconstruction, putting the Civil War behind them, and coexisting with Republicans, most Southern Democrats remained devoted to the goal of "Redemption": driving the Republicans out of power and restoring the South's traditional leadership. Democratic Redeemers began to win elections as early as 1869, and their electoral strength mounted in the early 1870s. So, too, did antiblack and anti-Republican violence, led by the Klan.

## THE GRANT ADMINISTRATION

Reconstruction was only occasionally on Washington's front burner after Ulysses Grant assumed the presidency in 1869. With Republican governments elected in the South and the region's congressional representation restored, both Congress and the new president turned their attention to other matters.

One such matter was civil service reform. The 1860s witnessed an eruption of criticism of the spoils system so prevalent in American politics: victorious politicians gave government jobs to the party faithful, who, in turn, contributed a percentage of their salaries to the party treasuries. Reformers, most of them well-educated Republicans from the Northeast, regarded such patronage practices as corrupt and inefficient, and they demanded that appointments be based on merit, certified by competitive examinations. President Grant endorsed these views but did not act on them very energetically. After a

503

presidential commission recommended both competitive exams and the prohibition of salary assessments, Grant did attempt to implement reforms through an executive order. But Congress refused to appropriate sufficient funds to enforce the regulations, and the spoils system lived on.

Much of the passion generated by this issue stemmed from a widespread concern about corruption in public life, an apprehension that public positions and institutions were being used to serve private ends. That the state, at all levels, was becoming larger only heightened these apprehensions. The Grant administration itself was subject to charges of nepotism and cronyism owing to the large number of appointees who were former army officers or relatives of the president's wife. Early in his administration, the president had to intervene to quash a scheme in which speculators were using "inside" government information to corner the gold market, a scheme from which Grant's sister and perhaps his wife stood to profit. In addition, several high officials in the administration, including the secretary of war, ended up leaving office in disgrace after being charged with accepting bribes. Although personally honest, Grant was both politically naive and altogether too trusting of his friends.

The most celebrated scandal of the era, the Credit Mobilier affair, involved congressmen rather than the White House. Credit Mobilier was a company created by the directors of the Union Pacific Railroad (who were also the directors of Credit Mobilier) to construct major new rail lines with financial assistance from the federal government. To keep Congress from taking any steps that might limit the profitability of the venture or peering too closely at the use of federal loans, shares in Credit Mobilier were given to a number of prominent congressmen in 1867 and 1868. Remarkably, when these transactions were finally exposed in 1872, only one member of Congress was formally censured, although the taint of involvement followed others.

Reconstruction moved back to center stage during the Grant administration only in 1870–71. In an attempt to undermine the Republican state governments, the Ku Klux Klan and other organizations ratcheted up the level of violence in 1870, killing hundreds of freedmen and causing local Republicans to plead for federal assistance. Congress responded with a series of Enforcement Acts making it a federal crime for state officials to deprive any individual of his civil and political rights or to discriminate against voters because of their race. The third such act, the Ku Klux Klan Act of April 1871, made it a federal crime for private individuals to conspire to

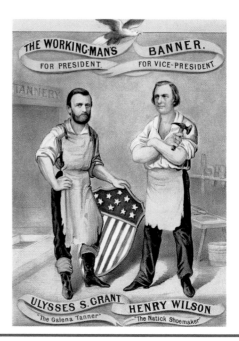

A campaign poster for the Republican ticket in the 1872 election, emphasizing both Grant's and Wilson's backgrounds as workingmen.

deprive others of their rights; it also authorized the president to use the army to enforce these laws and, if necessary, to suspend writs of habeas corpus (court-issued orders requiring that prisoners be brought to court to determine if they were lawfully imprisoned).

The Enforcement Acts were significant in two respects. First, they enlarged federal power: they gave the national government jurisdiction not only over state actions but also over certain categories of crimes committed by individuals. (The Democrats were so incensed over this expansion of the central government that twenty years later they repealed most provisions of these acts.) Second, the Enforcement Acts worked. The Justice Department, led by Attorney General Amos Akerman, born in New Hampshire but a longtime resident of Georgia, vigorously used its new powers to prosecute the Klan, while president Grant sent troops to, and suspended habeas corpus in, parts of South Carolina. Although the president, sensitive to charges of "military despotism," used his powers sparingly, the government's actions were energetic enough to cripple the Klan and dramatically lower the incidence of violence, thereby bolstering the morale of both the freedmen and the Southern Republicans.

## THE ELECTION OF 1872

Despite the success of some of Grant's policies, many Republicans lost faith in the president personally and in the party that he nominally headed but that seemed to hold him captive; in 1872, these disaffected Republicans joined some Democrats to form the Liberal Republican Party. Most Liberal Republicans were middle-class reformers who supported civil service reform, opposed high tariffs, and favored amnesty for former Confederates as well as the end of "bayonet rule" in the South. They were also convinced that the Republican Party, which some of them had helped to found, had lost its moral bearings and been taken over by unsavory professional politicians.

The Liberal Republicans met in convention in the spring of 1872 and, to the surprise of many, nominated journalist Horace Greeley as their presidential candidate. Greeley was a well-known figure with a track record of embracing quixotic, and sometimes contradictory, views; he was also not particularly interested in either civil service reform or lower tariffs. The centerpiece of his campaign quickly became sectional reconciliation and "home rule" by "the best people" of the South. Sensing the chance to beat Grant and to get a president sympathetic to their views, the Democrats also nominated Greeley, despite his having spent much of his career attacking the Democratic Party. But this fusion strategy backfired. Many Democrats could not bring themselves to support an old antagonist, and most Republicans feared that Greeley would deliver the South back to the Klan and former Confederates. Grant, despite a lackluster public image, was reelected with 56 percent of the popular vote, winning every state north of the Mason-Dixon line.

## RECONSTRUCTION IN RETREAT

Although Grant's reelection seemed to affirm the nation's commitment to Reconstruction, that commitment eroded rapidly for several reasons. The most important was the absence of any sign that conditions in the South were improving, that a stable political order was being established. In closely watched Louisiana, for example, disputes about the results of the 1872 elections led to the convening of two legislatures, the inauguration of two governors, and the arrival of federal troops. These episodes were followed, in 1873, by a clash between armed whites and black militiamen known as the Colfax massacre, which left roughly seventy blacks and two whites dead. Violence also enveloped the 1874 elections in Louisiana, setting off a chain of events that culminated in federal troops entering the state capitol building and evicting five Democrats before the Democrats could deny key legislative seats to Republicans.

Similar conflicts raged throughout the South, as splits emerged within the Republican Party and the Democrats grew emboldened by success. Redeemers, committed to white supremacy, low taxes, and home rule (which meant the removal of federal troops), captured the state governments in Arkansas, Alabama, and Texas, while making inroads in most other states. In 1875, Redeemers in Mississippi—a state with a black majority—put into action what became known as the "Mississippi Plan": a coordinated effort to force whites to abandon the Republican Party and then, through violence and intimidation, to prevent blacks from voting. "Carry the election peacefully if we can, forcibly if we must," declared Democratic newspapers. The plan worked, in part because the Grant administration declined to send troops to protect blacks and Republicans. Democrats in Mississippi gained power in an election in which unbelievably tiny Republican tallies (for example, 0, 2, and 4) were somehow recorded in counties with large black majorities.

Once in office, the Redeemers were not bashful about dismantling Reconstruction. They cut taxes, education spending (especially for blacks), and state funds for internal improvements. They altered the structure of local governments by making key offices appointive rather than elected, and they excluded blacks altogether from positions in law enforcement. The Redeemers also passed new vagrancy laws (designed to inhibit the movement of rural blacks and compel them to work for whites) as well as lien laws that gave landlords the first claim on crops grown by tenant farmers.

The successes of Redemption made clear that Reconstruction could be continued only with the prolonged, active, and military involvement of the federal government, a prospect that grew increasingly unpalatable in the North. As one Northern Republican acknowledged, "The truth is our people are tired out with this worn out cry of 'Southern outrages.'" Republican disillusion with Reconstruction was only deepened by the 1874 elections, in which Democrats scored major gains in all regions and won control of the House of Representatives for the first time in eighteen years.

The North's weariness with Reconstruction was also shaped by the severe economic depression that began in 1873. Precipitated by the collapse of the financial and railroad empire of Jay Cooke, the Panic of 1873 marked the end of the post–Civil War economic boom and the beginning of the longest uninter-

This Thomas Nast cartoon, published at the beginning of the Panic of 1873, suggests that the "bust up" on Wall Street was well deserved.

rupted business-cycle downturn of the nineteenth century (see Chapter 18). In the short run, the stock market closed, banks failed, and commercial houses and railroads went under; as the panic dragged on, farm prices declined, wages dropped sharply, and unemployment reached unprecedented levels. The Grant administration did little in response to the crisis, but this was not a failing peculiar to the president: the common wisdom throughout the late nineteenth century was that there was nothing much the federal government could do to alleviate a panic.

One critical upshot of the economic downturn was that the buoyant optimism of the late 1860s vanished. People worried about how to pay their rent, feed their families, pay their debts, and find work. In the South, the economic condition of the freedmen worsened because of falling cotton prices; in the Northeast, Midwest, and West, people were preoccupied with their own problems rather than those of African American freedmen in faraway states. Under the best of circumstances, distant political and social upheavals can hold the attention of a people only so long before being overridden by private concerns; and the mid-1870s were not the best of circumstances.

While the North's resolve was weakened by both politics and economics, the ability of the federal government to promote civil and political equality was diminished by the

Supreme Court. In what are known as the Slaughterhouse Cases, decided in 1873, the Court delivered a highly restrictive interpretation of the Fourteenth Amendment. Most pointedly, the Court concluded that the clause of the Fourteenth Amendment that declared that states could not "abridge the privileges or immunities of citizens of the United States" protected only the "privileges and immunities" of "national citizenship" (rather than "state citizenship"); these national privileges and immunities were of a very narrow sort—such as the right to use the nation's navigable waters. This interpretation clearly limited the reach of the Fourteenth Amendment as a weapon against discriminatory state laws; so, too, did the Court's insistence that the Fourteenth Amendment did not significantly alter the relationship between the states and the federal government and that the Court itself ought not to act as a "permanent censor" of state legislation.

Three years later, in *U.S. v. Cruikshank*, a case that arose out of the Louisiana Colfax massacre, the Court undercut the enforcement clause of the Fourteenth Amendment. Overturning the conviction of three men who had been charged with violating the civil rights of their victims, the Court argued that the postwar amendments gave the federal government power to prohibit rights violations by states but *not by individuals*. In the same year, in *U.S. v. Reese*, the Court ruled that the Fifteenth Amendment did not guarantee anyone the right to vote; it simply specified that certain reasons for denying someone the vote were unacceptable. In practice, *Cruikshank* meant that the enforcement of black rights now depended almost entirely on local officials, while the *Reese* decision set the stage for legally disfranchising blacks for ostensibly nonracial reasons.

### THE ELECTION OF 1876 AND THE COMPROMISE OF 1877

With the country in an economic depression, Reconstruction faltering, and the Republican Party stained by corruption scandals, the Democrats were well positioned for the 1876 elections. They chose for their standard-bearer the prominent reform governor of New York, Samuel J. Tilden, who was nationally known for having overthrown the Tweed ring (see Chapter 20). Tilden and the Democrats ran in opposition to the "corrupt centralism" of a Republican government, "which, after inflicting upon ten States the rapacities of carpet-bag tyrannies, has honeycombed . . . the Federal Government . . . with incapacity, waste, and fraud." To run against Tilden, the Republicans nominated Rutherford B. Hayes, a former Civil

War general and governor of Ohio who also had a reputation as a reformer. Although Hayes had been a moderate on Reconstruction and was noncommittal about the South during the campaign, the Republicans—outraged by new waves of violence aimed at intimidating Southern voters—waved the "bloody shirt" of the Civil War for months before the election.

Voters appear to have been more concerned about the economy than about party history. The Democrats ran well, in both the North and South, and Tilden garnered 250,000 more votes than Hayes, although this was partly because many intimidated Southern Republicans did not vote. In the electoral college, Tilden was 1 vote short of the 185 needed for victory, with the returns in three states (South Carolina, Louisiana, and Florida) in dispute. In all three, the accuracy of the final tally was challenged by charges of fraud and coercive violence. And in all three, Republican voting boards ended up certifying vote totals that made Hayes victorious, despite the ferocious protest of Democrats.

The result was an unprecedented political and constitutional crisis. The Republican voting boards were, without doubt, certifying returns in a partisan fashion, throwing out Democratic votes in order to guarantee a Republican victory. On the other hand, genuinely free elections, conducted without intimidation, would likely have produced Republican victories in Louisiana and South Carolina, and probably in Mississippi and North Carolina as well. It was thus not clear where the line ought to be drawn between legitimate and fraudulent voting results. It was also not clear who should decide, or how: the Constitution offered no guidelines.

After several months of confusion, investigation, and charges of corruption and dishonesty, Congress and President Grant created a commission to adjudicate the challenged returns. The commission consisted of five senators, five congressmen, and five Supreme Court justices, carefully selected to yield partisan balance. After that delicate balance was tilted slightly by the last-minute resignation and replacement of one member, the commission, by a series of 8-to-7 votes, certified all the returns in the Republicans' favor.

Meanwhile, some Hayes Republicans and Southern Democrats engaged in negotiations that helped pave the way toward a resolution of the crisis. Although no firm evidence exists that a formal "deal" was struck, informal understandings between key players were certainly reached. By the end of February 1877—just in time to permit the inauguration to proceed on schedule—most Democrats agreed not to mount a filibuster in the House of Representatives. Hayes was inaugurated on

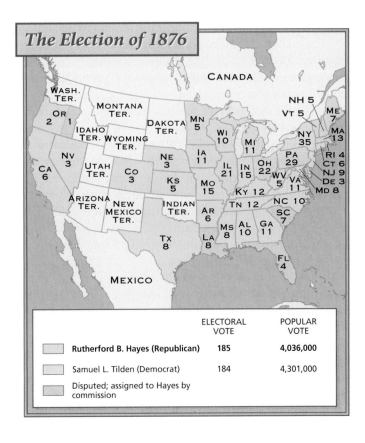

### The Election of 1876

| | ELECTORAL VOTE | POPULAR VOTE |
|---|---|---|
| **Rutherford B. Hayes (Republican)** | 185 | 4,036,000 |
| Samuel L. Tilden (Democrat) | 184 | 4,301,000 |
| Disputed; assigned to Hayes by commission | | |

March 4. His cabinet appointments included men well known for their conciliatory stance toward the former Confederacy, and his administration gave enthusiastic support to the federal funding of internal improvements in the South.

More important, in April 1877 Hayes withdrew federal troops from the capitals of South Carolina and Louisiana. This act led immediately to the collapse of Republican governments in those states and to the installation of Redeemer regimes in the only two states where the Republicans remained in power. The withdrawal of troops sent an unmistakable signal. A Republican may still have been in the White House, but Reconstruction was over.

## Legacies

The challenge faced by the men and women engaged in Reconstruction was daunting. As many Republicans understood, the task was not simply to restore the Confederate

507

states to the Union but to transform Southern society in order to make life in the region more consistent with the professed values of the Republic. To be successful, Reconstruction policies would have had to rebuild the South's economy while simultaneously reshaping both the social structure and the polity: the victors in the war would have had to satisfy the aspirations of 4 million newly freed, propertyless African Americans without provoking the deadly antagonism of white Southerners who owned all the region's property and were utterly dependent upon African American labor. The hatreds and mistrust bred by two centuries of slavery would have to be held in check long enough for more egalitarian patterns of interracial life to form and become commonplace. The task may not have been impossible, but it surely was Herculean and diplomatically delicate.

In retrospect, it is clear that there were positive achievements. The Union was restored, and once-rebellious states became full participants in the national government. Slavery was definitively abolished. Throughout the South, churches were built, as were schools for black children; families were reunited; hospitals, asylums, roads, and bridges were constructed. Thousands of freedmen even acquired their own farms. Perhaps most important, Congress and the states passed constitutional amendments that would ultimately protect a wide array of civil and political rights in the twentieth century. The Fourteenth and Fifteenth Amendments, although sometimes dormant, provided the legal framework for the equal-rights revolution of the mid–twentieth century. It is unlikely that these amendments would have been passed during any other period in the nation's history.

Yet the roster of successes was limited. For the most part, Reconstruction failed, and its failure had long-lasting consequences for the freedmen, for the South, for race relations, for the nation as a whole. The freedmen were granted formal political and civil rights but not the property or state support necessary to protect the exercise of those rights. The collapse of Reconstruction in the 1870s left a large majority of the 4 million former slaves as propertyless, agricultural workers in a society in which nearly all economic and political power was wielded by landowning whites. In such circumstances, it is hardly surprising that blacks were exploited, discriminated against, and eventually stripped of rights, such as voting, that they had formally obtained. Southern society became increasingly segregated in the wake of Reconstruction, and racial antagonisms became more pronounced.

Southern blacks and whites, moreover, inhabited a region economically damaged by war and hamstrung by the social and economic order that emerged after the war. It was in the 1860s that a large income and wealth gap opened up between the North and the South, a gap that did not start to narrow until after World War II. Postbellum society in the South was short of capital, ambivalent about industrialization, and reluctant to invest in institutions (such as schools) that might have accelerated development. The organization of agriculture spawned an overreliance on cotton; and cotton culture, with its high rates of farm tenancy, stimulated few agricultural innovations. Relatively unattractive and inhospitable to immigrants, the postwar South settled into decades of quasi-stagnation and high rates of poverty.

Reconstruction had political effects as well, some local, some national. The rout of the Republican Party in the South opened the way for the one-party system that came to dominate the region's political life for nearly a century, stifling dissent and depressing political participation. The existence of a conservative, one-party region in which most working people were excluded from politics pushed the national political spectrum toward the right, complicating or preventing reforms. The wording of the Fourteenth and Fifteenth Amendments, moreover, formalized the exclusion of women from electoral politics.

The era of Reconstruction came to an end without having set the nation on a course that could heal the wounds of slavery and promote greater racial harmony and social justice. Whether any other outcome was possible is difficult to judge; but the shortcomings of Reconstruction, without doubt, set the stage for the troubling history of race in modern America.

## Suggested Reading

R. H. Abbott, *The Republican Party and the South, 1855–1877: The First Southern Strategy* (1986)

Michael Les Benedict, *A Compromise of Principle: Congressional Republicans and Reconstruction, 1863–1869* (1974)

Walter L. Fleming, *Documentary History of Reconstruction* (1906)

Eric Foner, *Reconstruction: America's Unfinished Revolution* (1989)

Steven Hahn, *A Nation Under Our Feet: Black Political Struggles in the Rural South from Slavery to the Great Migration* (2003)

Leon Litwack, *Been in the Storm So Long: The Aftermath of Slavery* (1980)

Geoffrey Perret, *Ulysses S. Grant, Soldier and President* (1999)

Michael Perman, *Reunion Without Compromise* (1973)

# Chapter Review

## Summary
### QUESTIONS

- Why was there no land reform in the South in the aftermath of the Civil War?

- How did the Radical Republicans come to take control of Reconstruction policy?

- How did sharecropping and the lien system evolve out of the end of slavery?

- Why did Northerners not intervene more to stop the violence against African Americans in the South in the 1870s?

- Who were the opponents of black rights in the South?

## Chronology

| | |
|---|---|
| 1865 | Thirteenth Amendment ratified. |
| March 1865 | Freedmen's Bureau created. |
| 1866 | Congress passes Civil Rights Bill and Freedmen's Bureau Bill over President Johnson's veto. |
| | Ku Klux Klan founded in Tennessee. |
| March 1867 | Reconstruction Act passed. |
| 1868 | Fourteenth Amendment ratified. |
| May 26, 1868 | Johnson acquitted in impeachment trial. |
| 1870 | Last of the Confederate states readmitted to the Union. |
| | Fifteenth Amendment ratified. |
| 1872 | Thomas Edison invents the stock ticker. |
| 1873 | Panic sets off longest depression of the nineteenth century. |
| 1875 | Mississippi Plan prevents blacks from voting, allowing Democrats to gain power in that state. |

## Key Terms

Reconstruction Amendments (13th, 14th, 15th) (pp. 487, 491–492, 495–496)

Black Codes (pp. 489–490)

Radical Reconstruction (p. 493)

Sharecropping (p. 500)

Compromise of 1877 (pp. 506–507)

# Part 5

# ENGINES OF CHANGE

For Americans who lived through the last third of the nineteenth century, history seemed to be moving fast. The sectional crisis of the Civil War had barely come to an end when an extraordinary array of new challenges presented itself to the nation: the opening of the trans-Mississippi West; the proliferation of cities of a size and complexity unknown before 1860; the emergence of huge national corporations that wielded great economic and political power; flows of immigration larger and more diverse than ever before; swings of the business cycle that spiraled downward into "panics" once each decade; and dramatic strikes, involving thousands of workers, that shut down cities and sometimes escalated into violence. While all of this was happening, Americans were also trying to re-knit the relationship between the victorious North and a defeated South that included several million newly freed African Americans.

The rhythms of life and change in antebellum America seemed leisurely in comparison—and forever lost. Between the Civil War and the end of the nineteenth century, the United States hurtled forward into a full-blown industrial world where transportation was faster, communications were speedier, buildings were taller, and technological innovations piled on one another so quickly that new inventions themselves became routine. Meanwhile, the nation grew—greatly expanding its population, its settled land area, its economy, and even the territory it controlled.

The engines of change during this period were largely material—both economic and technological. Railroads and metal-hulled steamships expanded markets while breaking

---

*Cliff Dwellers*, a 1913 painting by George Bellows, depicts a crowded, lower-income, urban neighborhood.

511

down the isolation or autonomy of individual communities and regions. Large firms sought to exploit the new markets; but, to do so, they had to figure out how to manage themselves—how to structure, govern, and finance companies that could do business from New Jersey to Denver and beyond. Advances in science spawned new products and production processes, which in turn created new problems to solve. Fast-moving trains needed good brakes; the huge demand for steel meant that enormous quantities of iron ore had to be shipped safely and efficiently across the Great Lakes.

The men who conceived and carried out the most far-reaching innovations generally worked in the private sector: business owners, financiers, inventors, engineers, scientists, shop foremen, skilled machinists, and labor leaders. The big names of the era—admired or despised, but certainly known—were, by and large, not politicians or generals but railroad magnates like Jay Cooke, industrialists like Andrew Carnegie, or activists like Eugene V. Debs, the head of the American Railway Union. In ways large and small, such men (and a smaller number of women) were shaping the economic institutions and material underpinnings of an urban industrial society that was overwhelming the predominantly rural, agricultural world that had been America.

Innovators, of course, could be found in other arenas as well, including agriculture, social reform, political theory, the arts, and government at all levels—local, state, and federal. But these men and women were most often reacting rather than initiating, coping with rather than instigating the fundamental changes that were altering the contours of American life. Farmers and state officials were playing catch-up as they tried to devise methods of reining in the power of railroads. The rich explosion of political thought that marked the intellectual life of the era was at heart a response to the way in which growing corporate power threatened traditional democratic values and beliefs.

Especially near the end of this period, Americans also engaged in a redefinition of their nation's role in international affairs. Propelled by economic concerns as well as ideology, the United States relinquished its longstanding reluctance to actively participate in conflicts and disputes outside its continental borders. It fought a war, on two fronts, against Spain—a major, if declining European power—and seized territory in the nearby Caribbean and the distant Pacific. This was a new direction in public policy that flowed readily from the internal changes that were sweeping the nation; it also set the stage for the nation's role as a world power throughout the twentieth century.

# Chapter 18

# THE RISE OF BIG BUSINESS AND THE TRIUMPH OF INDUSTRY:

## 1870–1900

The manufacture of Bessemer steel at the Thomson Iron and Steel Works in Pittsburgh, PA 1886.

## An Industrial Economy

- **What were the key innovations that contributed to the triumph of industrialization between 1865 and 1900?**

- **What were the regional divisions in the nation's economy in the late nineteenth century?**

- **How did industrial development affect the class relations of this period?**

On May 10, 1876, President Ulysses Grant formally opened the Centennial Exhibition in Philadelphia. Long planned, the exhibition, which filled scores of buildings on a several-hundred-acre site in Fairmount Park, was the centerpiece of the nation's official celebration of its first 100 years of independence. Congress, when authorizing funds for the exhibition, had declared it to be "fitting that the completion of the first century of our national existence shall be commemorated by an exhibition of the natural resources of the country and their development, and of its progress in those arts which benefit mankind."

The opening ceremonies were filled with pomp, music, and dignitaries. The president was escorted by 4,000 troops, and he and Mrs. Grant were joined on the grandstand by Supreme Court justices, cabinet members, governors, senators, congressmen, high-ranking military officers, and a host of local officials. Once the president took his seat, an orchestra struck up the *Centennial Inauguration March,* composed for the occasion by German composer Richard Wagner; then a chorus sang the "Centennial Hymn," with words by poet John Greenleaf Whittier. After a brief speech by Grant declaring the exhibition officially open, 800 singers burst into the "Hallelujah Chorus" from Handel's *Messiah,* artillery on a nearby hillside fired a 100-gun salute, thirteen bells chimed, and the assembled notables, led by the president, marched to the main building, where they were joined by foreign guests and delegates.

The entire cortege then proceeded into Machinery Hall, where acres of motionless machinery surrounded a steam engine that rose more than forty feet above the ground. President Grant and Emperor Dom Pedro II of Brazil (the first reigning monarch ever to visit the United States) approached the engine and its builder, George H. Corliss, who showed them how to turn cranks that would start it. Once the cranks were turned, the cylinders and flywheel of the engine began to move; as they did, all the machinery in the hall, connected to the engine by thousands of feet of underground shafts and pulleys, sprang into motion. The spectators broke into a prolonged cheer. The largest steam engine in the world was providing power to machines that spun cotton, combed wool, printed newspapers, made shoes, pumped water, and performed hundreds of other tasks.

Machinery Hall became the main attraction of the enormously successful Centennial, and the Corliss engine became its celebrated symbol. Fittingly so. The nation's growth since independence had been closely linked to the rise of industry and the success of the steam engine. And the United States in 1876 stood on the threshold of an extraordinary period of economic growth and technological inventiveness. Two decades later, a writer in *Scientific American* would describe the years since the Civil War as "an epoch of invention and progress unique in the history of the world," and he was exaggerating only slightly. The number of patents issued more than doubled each year, and the list of prominent inventions included Alexander Graham Bell's telephone, Thomas Alva Edison's incandescent lamp and phonograph, the machine gun, the cable car, the electric streetlight, the Linotype machine, and a slew of significant advances in the use of electricity and electric motors.

Technological progress also seemed to be something for which Americans had particular gifts. As novelist William Dean Howells observed after a visit to the exhibition, "it is still in these things of iron and steel that the national genius most freely speaks; by and by the inspired marbles, the breathing canvases, the great literature; for the present America is voluble in the strong metals and their infinite uses." Howells marveled at the "thousand creations of American inventive genius" on display, yet he, like most visitors, was particularly awed by "the majesty of the great Corliss engine" with "its vast and almost silent grandeur." (The engine was "almost silent"

**LEFT:** The Corliss engine, the largest steam engine in the world, dominated Machinery Hall at the Centennial Exhibition in Philadelphia, 1876.

**RIGHT:** The arm and torch of the Statue of Liberty on display at the Centennial Exhibition.

falling wages were breaking out in one industry after another. (Relatively few workers attended the exhibition, both because there was an admission charge and because the exhibition was closed on Sundays, the only day off most workers had.) At the same time, antiblack violence was mounting in the South, Reconstruction was collapsing, and former Confederates were regaining control of Southern state governments. Most Southern states, in fact, refused to participate in the Centennial—which was hardly surprising, since their membership in the Union was involuntary.

The nation was also encountering some difficulties in the West, where Native Americans were resisting both modern technology and the encroachment of white civilization; in June 1876, the celebrated defeat of Colonel George Custer (who had gone to see the Centennial buildings before making what would be his final trip to the West; see Chapter 19) was a dramatic reminder that the Indian wars were not going well. Back in Washington, political scandals were erupting left and right, only to be overshadowed, late in the year, by a presidential election in which the candidate with the most votes lost. The Centennial Exhibition, in sum, told only half the story. Both the price and the fruits of progress had been shared unequally, creating new conflicts, new social divisions, new challenges. Some of the allure of the Corliss engine, perhaps, sprang from the hope that technology—writ large, towering above the ground—could offer solutions to the many problems, new and old, the nation needed to confront.

## An Industrial Economy

### AGRICULTURE AND INDUSTRY

Between the end of the Civil War and the turn of the century, almost everything connected with the American economy grew. The population rose from less than 40 million to more

because the boilers had been placed outside Machinery Hall.) Frédéric-Auguste Bartholdi, the creator of the not-yet-completed Statue of Liberty—the arm and torch of which were part of a Centennial sculpture exhibit—went a step further, finding beauty as well as power in the engine. "The lines are so grand and beautiful," he wrote, "the play of movement so skillfully arranged, and the whole machine was so harmoniously constructed, that it had the beauty and almost the grace of the human form."

The nation's centennial thus celebrated not just independence but also progress, not just liberty but technology: its past, its promise, its power, its capacity to generate wealth and improve people's lives. From the celebrations, one would hardly have known that the United States in 1876 was a nation deeply troubled and riddled with conflict. Outside the gates of the Centennial Exhibition, the country was in the midst of a severe economic depression; unemployed workers were demonstrating behind "blood-red banners," and strikes protesting

than 75 million; the total output of the economy, or gross national product (GNP), more than tripled; and GNP per capita (the quantity of goods and services produced per person) doubled.

Some of this growth was in agriculture, the traditional core of the American economy. The number of farms rose from 2 million in 1860 to 5.75 million in 1900; the number of improved acres of farmland rose similarly from 164 million to 416 million acres. Much of this expansion took place in the Midwest and West, with particularly rapid growth occurring in Missouri, Iowa, Kansas, Nebraska, Minnesota, the Dakotas, and the central valley of California. The 32 million people living on farms in 1900 were producing far more wheat, oats, rice, cotton, sugarcane, potatoes, pork, and beef than their predecessors had in the 1860s. This was so for three reasons: more land was under cultivation; some of the newly settled lands, particularly in the Midwest, were more fertile and easier to farm than land in the Northeast had been; and farmers were increasingly using new and improved technology.

This technology took many forms. The seed drill, or drill planter, conserved seed and made it easier to grow grains in easily tended, regular rows. Plows made with "chilled" iron (a hardening process patented in 1869) greatly facilitated plowing in the heavy, wet soil of the prairies. Hay balers, mowers, loaders, and forks reduced the labor cost of haymaking. The mechanical reaper, which had come into wide use in the

1850s, became sturdier and more efficient after the war, permitting more farmers to harvest more grain. (Since grains such as wheat had a harvest season of roughly two weeks, the quantity of grain a farmer could grow was always limited by the amount he could harvest in a brief, two-week interval.) Some of the innovative implements put to use after 1865 had been invented earlier, but their adoption was delayed until farms grew larger and machinery prices fell: between 1860 and 1900, the value of farm implements on the average midwestern farm more than doubled. Notably, no such change occurred in the South, where the enormous growth in the cotton crop was achieved almost entirely through increasing acreage rather than productivity.

New technology also came in the form of knowledge. Late nineteenth-century farmers learned about seed selection, soil conservation, the selective breeding of livestock, the matching of crop varieties to local conditions, and better methods of caring for livestock—all of which made their farms more productive. Farmers acquired this knowledge from diverse sources, including agricultural colleges funded in part through the Morrill Land Grant College Act (1862) and agricultural experiment stations created by the Hatch Act (1887). The federal government thus was a key source of agricultural innovation.

Vastly increased agricultural output led to declining prices, a trend reinforced by the internationalization of markets resulting from improved transportation. Corn that had sold for seventy cents a bushel in the early 1870s sold for half that fifteen years later; wheat prices fell nearly as much; cotton prices fell from sixteen cents a pound in 1869 to less than six cents a pound in 1898. Since this was a period in which the prices of most goods were falling, such drops were less calamitous for farmers than we might think. Still, falling prices was better news for consumers than for farmers, especially those farmers who had not increased their own productivity.

Significant as the growth of agriculture was, it paled in comparison with the growth of industry (see Table 18.1). Although the industrial revolution began long before the Civil War, it was between 1865 and 1900 that the United

A steam-powered wheat thresher on a farm near Fargo in the Dakota Territory, 1878.

### Table 18.1

**Changing Occupational Structure 1870–1900**

| Number of Persons Employed | 1870 | 1880 | 1890 | 1900 |
|---|---|---|---|---|
| Agriculture | 5,948,561 | 7,713,875 | 8,565,926 | 10,381,765 |
| Trade, Transportation, and Manufacturing | 3,922,148 | 5,656,229 | 9,004,590 | 11,852,273 |
| Steam Railroads | 154,027 | 236,058 | 462,213 | 582,150 |
| Mining | 165,696 | 249,397 | 387,248 | 563,406 |
| Iron and Steel Industry | 94,790 | 130,346 | 220,428 | 290,538 |
| Machinists | 54,755 | 101,130 | 186,828 | 283,145 |
| Boot and Shoe Manufacturing | 171,127 | 194,079 | 214,575 | 208,903 |
| Cotton Mills | 111,606 | 169,771 | 173,142 | 246,391 |

States became an industrial power. According to one index, manufacturing production increased nearly sixfold during these years. Manufacturing output began to exceed agricultural output in the 1880s, and by the turn of the century manufacturing, construction, and mining accounted for two-thirds of the economy. Similarly, by 1880, the number of non-farm workers topped the number of men and women working in agriculture. The United States—which had lagged behind Britain, Germany, and France as recently as 1860—was the world's leading manufacturing nation in 1900, producing 30 percent of its manufactured goods.

Two relatively new industries led this expansion. In 1860, the nation's largest industries had been cotton textiles and lumber milling; both remained important, but they were surpassed by the machinery and foundry industry and by iron and steel. The total quantity of raw steel produced—to cite one particularly vivid set of numbers—rose from 30,000 tons in 1868 to more than 11 million tons in 1900. During the same period, the production of bituminous coal (used to make steel) increased by 2,000 percent.

Clearly the nation's economic center of gravity shifted both to industry and to what William Dean Howells had called the "strong metals." It also moved geographically. During the Civil War, most manufacturing had been concentrated in New York, Philadelphia, and New England. But by 1880, the Midwest, too, had acquired an important industrial sector: Chicago had nearly 80,000 manufacturing workers, while Cincinnati had 59,000 and St. Louis more than 40,000. Industrialization, like the frontier, was moving west.

There were multiple reasons for the enormous expansion of the economy. Population growth, accelerated by immigration, enlarged the market for both foodstuffs and manufactured goods. At the same time, the railroads opened up distant markets for many businesses and farmers, as did improvements in shipping, both domestic and international. (The Great Lakes, for example, became one of the world's busiest waterways.) These enlarged markets created competition as well as opportunities; both helped to spawn technological advances that made industries more productive.

Growth was also fostered by the tariff policies of the federal government. The Republican Congress had increased tariffs (taxes on imported goods) during the Civil War, both to pay the expenses of the government and to satisfy northern industry's long-standing demand for protection against international competition. In the war's aftermath, high tariffs—often above 40 percent—remained the norm, although they occasionally declined during prosperous periods. How much impact these tariffs had is impossible to measure, but no doubt they stimulated some manufacturing industries and branches of agriculture, while having a negative impact both on consumers (who had to pay higher prices than they would have otherwise) and on exporters (who preferred free trade because they did not want to encounter high tariffs abroad).

### An Industrial Economy

A ceremony marking the completion of the first transcontinental railroad at Promontory Point, Utah, on May 10, 1869.

Dramatic as the growth of the economy may have been, it was hardly continuous or smooth. "Panics" (a term commonly used during this period) occurred every decade, bringing plunging stock prices, business and bank failures, and a temporary halt to economic growth. The Panic of 1873 precipitated a long depression that lasted until 1878; a more moderate downturn occurred in the mid-1880s; and a severe depression gripped the nation from 1893 through 1897. During each of these downturns, production, prices, and wages fell, while unemployment rose.

These widely felt depressions were themselves testimony to the increasing dominance of industrial capitalism. While agricultural economies are subject to the whims of nature, industrial capitalist economies have business cycles: periods of investment and expansion followed by periods of stagnation or decline, which, in turn, are followed by new periods of investment and expansion. It was between the Civil War and the turn of the century that the business cycle became a prominent feature of the economic landscape, broadly affecting the rhythms of economic life and transforming the language with new words such as "boom" and "unemployment." This was because the expansion of industry rendered an increasingly large proportion of the population directly vulnerable to business-cycle fluctuations. The men and women who lived through these episodes, moreover, did not have the comfort of believing they were riding the crests and troughs of a cycle; it was only in the second decade of the twentieth century that the concept of a business cycle was embraced by economists (whose field itself was something of a late nineteenth- and early twentieth-century invention). To citizens of the late nineteenth century, what happened in 1893 was not a cyclical downturn but a panic that had no guaranteed ending.

### RAILROADS

*I see over my own continent the Pacific railroad surmounting every barrier,*

*I see continual trains of cars winding along the Platte carrying freight and passengers,*

*I hear the locomotives rushing and roaring, and the shrill steamwhistle,*

*I hear the echoes reverberate through the grandest scenery in the world. . . .*

*I see the clear waters of lake Tahoe, I see forests of majestic pines,*

*Or crossing the great desert, the alkaline plains, I behold enchanting mirages of waters and meadows,*

*Marking through these and after all, in duplicate slender lines,*

*Bridging the three or four thousand miles of land travel,*

*Tying the Eastern to the Western sea,*

*The road between Europe and Asia. . . .*

—Walt Whitman, from "Passage to India," 1871

Railroads were at the heart of the economy. The enterprises that built and operated the railroads were the century's largest. They consumed immense amounts of capital, transported most of the nation's freight, and hired an enormous number of workers. The railroads also created a national economy out of what had been a loosely linked network of local and regional markets.

The most celebrated moment in the era's railway history occurred on May 10, 1869, at Promontory Point, Utah, when two teams of laborers, one Chinese and the other Irish, put down rails that linked the Central Pacific and Union Pacific railroads. Once the rails were aligned, a golden spike was hammered into place by Leland Stanford, the governor of California and president of the Central Pacific, and by T. C. Durant, the vice-president of the Union Pacific. With every blow of the sledgehammer transmitted by telegraph to a waiting nation, the first transcontinental railroad was completed.

This symbolic "tying" of "the Eastern to the Western sea" inaugurated a frantic wave of railroad construction. In 1865, the United States had 35,000 miles of railroad track; by 1900, it had nearly 200,000. By the 1890s, there were five transcontinental railroads, more than a dozen trans-Mississippi lines, and an immense web of track in the East providing multiple connections between all major (and even medium-sized) cities. At the end of the century, the railroads employed more than a million workers tending a system that had 1.4 million freight cars and 35,000 passenger cars in service. The capital to create this system (roughly $10 billion) came from private American sources, overseas investors, and the public sector; the federal government, as well as state and local governments, subsidized the roads through loans, land grants (totaling more than 150 million acres), and tax exemptions.

The rush to build railroads created its own instability. Overbuilt in many areas, railroads competed fiercely with one another, while business downturns periodically cut revenues and savaged stock prices. In 1876, 40 percent of all railroad bonds were in default; after the Panic of 1893, nearly 200 railroads were unable to pay their debts and were being operated under court supervision. Mark Twain reflected the views of many small investors when he noted that "this is the very road whose stock always goes down after you buy it, and always goes up again as soon as you sell it."

Nonetheless, great fortunes were made in railroading, from stock speculation, mergers, and construction-finance schemes as well as from the actual operation of the roads. The men who made these fortunes—including Jay Gould, Cornelius Vanderbilt, Collis P. Huntington, Thomas A. Scott, Leland Stanford, and James J. Hill—acquired a nationally visible wealth that was without precedent. In so doing, they became celebrated (occasionally reviled) figures who seemed to symbolize both the achievements and the excesses of the era.

New technology helped to spur the railroad boom. Steel rails lasted longer than iron, and once the price of Bessemer-produced steel dropped in the 1870s, railroads everywhere began to use the harder, more durable metal. Major gains in efficiency were also realized from the "compound" (two-cylindered) locomotive, which was more fuel efficient and powerful than its predecessor.

At the same time, two inventions made trains safer: air brakes and the automatic coupler. Braking was a problem for trains in the mid-nineteenth century because mechanical brakes had to be applied individually (by brakemen) to each car, which made for something less than smooth and reliable stops. Several inventors had developed devices (including the air brake) to solve this problem, but the railroads themselves were relatively uninterested until after the Civil War. Then, with both train speeds and the volume of traffic increasing, the railroads turned their attention to braking, just as the young George Westinghouse was receiving a patent on a brake system that used pressurized air to stop all cars simultaneously. Within a year after he had obtained his patent, Westinghouse's air brakes were being used on eight railroads. Once he had invented and perfected the triple valve (1873), a pressure-sensitive gauge that made the brakes virtually fail-safe, Westinghouse brakes, manufactured in Pittsburgh, became the industry standard.

Almost simultaneously, Eli Janney invented a coupling device that permitted cars to be coupled to or uncoupled from one another without brakemen having to step between them while they were moving, a process that had produced extraordinary carnage over the years (65,000 railroad men died on the job between 1870 and 1900). In 1893, one of the first pieces of safety legislation enacted by the federal government, the Railroad Safety Appliance Act, mandated the use of air brakes and Janney couplers on all interstate rail lines.

Other innovations also served the railroads and their customers. Bridge-building techniques improved substantially—particularly in the wake of several horrific accidents, including the well-known 1876 plunge of the Pacific Express into the Ashtabula (Ohio) River when a bridge came apart during a storm. (Train wrecks captured the public imagination in the late nineteenth century much as plane crashes do today.) Passenger comfort was significantly enhanced by the well-appointed, and sometimes luxurious, sleeping cars built by the Pullman Palace Car Company. An entire industry, meatpacking, was given an enormous boost by the development in the late 1870s of refrigerated freight cars that could transport meat without spoilage. The key innovation involved placing ice in overhead bins that allowed cool air to drop

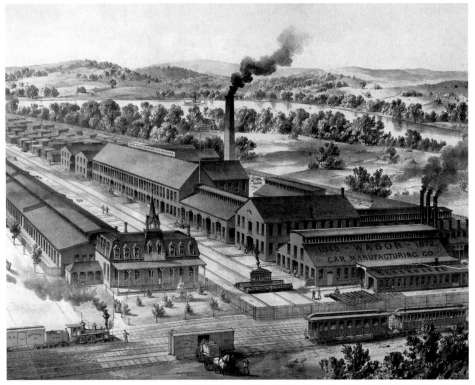

The Wason Manufacturing Company, Railway Car Builders, Springfield, MA 1872

and 1880s, about three-quarters of all Bessemer-produced steel ended up as railroad tracks. They spurred the growth of the telegraph industry by encouraging the erection of telegraph lines alongside the rails. The cattle and meatpacking industries were entirely dependent on the railroads, and farmers sold an increasing proportion of their crops in distant markets that could only be reached by rail. In 1890 (roughly the peak year), two-thirds of all freight in the United States traveled by rail.

Yet the railroads did not just stimulate the economy; they changed it. The 150,000 miles of track laid after the Civil War linked all the cities and most towns of the United States, making it possible for goods to be shipped easily and relatively cheaply from any one place to any other place. This network effectively nationalized the economy, opening markets and breaking down local and regional monopolies. Small entrepreneurs, skilled craftsmen, local factories—all faced new competition from

while keeping the ice from touching the meat (which discolored the meat and made it prone to spoil more rapidly).

Of equal importance were innovative managerial methods developed by railroad corporations and, later, imitated by much of American industry. Railroads were the nation's first big businesses, and because of their size, the physical distances they spanned, and the imperatives of coordination, they faced unprecedented managerial challenges. In response, the rail corporations replaced informal lines of authority with a formal, vertical chain of command that governed all divisions of the enterprise; to a considerable degree, management was separated from ownership, and managers themselves became quasi-professional. In addition, the railroads institutionalized long-run planning and developed modern accounting techniques. In fact, when the first graduate programs in business management appeared, just before World War I, their programs relied heavily on lessons learned from the railroads.

The impact of railroads on the nation's economy was immense. They provided a great stimulus to the iron and steel industry (and consequently to coal production): in the 1870s

outside, even as they simultaneously were able to broaden their own entrepreneurial horizons. Thanks to the railroads, the number of traveling salesmen quadrupled between 1870 and 1880, while mail-order houses like Montgomery Ward and Sears, Roebuck exploded into the forefront of retailing.

The impact of the railroads spilled over into countless other dimensions of American life. As both costs and travel times fell, hundreds of thousands of Easterners were able to see the West firsthand. Even a transcontinental trip could be made in less than ten days by 1880. Towns with good rail connections swelled into cities, while well-connected cities boomed: Chicago owed its status as a metropolis to its emergence as *the* railway hub linking the East to the West. Trains carried mail and newspapers everywhere; they brought the circus to small towns; long before radio or television, they encouraged the development of a national culture. They also encouraged people to wear watches—since even farmers whose daily rhythms were dictated by the sun had to abide by train schedules. The first sizable profits earned by Richard Warren Sears, the founder of Sears, Roebuck, came from selling watches in rural Minnesota.

Indeed, standard time zones in the United States were created by the railroads in 1883. Before then, every major city had its own local time, generally based on the position of the sun. This variability created havoc with rail schedules (among other things), but some cities steadfastly resisted any change: the proposition that Cincinnati should alter its clocks by twenty-two minutes "so as to harmonize with an imaginary line drawn through Pittsburgh," concluded a local newspaper,

"is simply preposterous. . . . let the people of Cincinnati stick to the truth as it is written by the sun, moon, and stars." But the railroads and their commercial allies prevailed, and on Sunday, November 18, 1883, the "Day of Two Noons," most American cities and towns adjusted their clocks to conform with four standard time zones.

The railways also loomed large in politics, spawning new government agencies and newly configured relationships

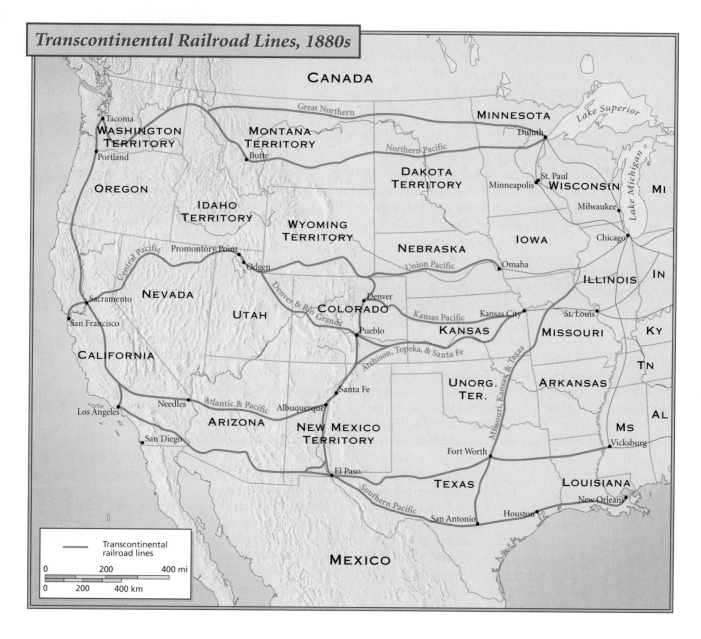

## Transcontinental Railroad Lines, 1880s

between private enterprise and the state. Although they were private corporations, the railroads performed a public function and commonly received governmental subsidies and charters. Consequently, states felt they had a right to oversee the behavior of the railroads. Even before the Civil War, four state railway commissions had been created; by 1897, the number had risen to twenty-eight. The earliest commissions served primarily to investigate and publicize concerns about railroad practices.

Public scrutiny of the railways intensified after the Civil War both because they were wielding increasing power over shippers and consumers and because competition was driving the railroads into pricing policies that seemed discriminatory. As more and more track was laid, railroads found themselves having to lower freight rates on lines where competition existed, while holding prices steady or even raising them on routes they monopolized. The result was a disparity between "short haul" and "long haul" freight rates: it was, for example, far more expensive to ship grain from Chicago to Pittsburgh than from Chicago to New York. Residents of small towns with only one rail line often had to pay much higher freight rates than shippers in nearby cities. At the same time, railroads began to give rebates or special contracts to preferred shippers—which meant that not everyone was paying the same price for the same service.

In response to these practices, a number of midwestern states passed in the 1870s what came to be known as the "Granger" laws because they were supported by farmers who belonged to an organization called the Grange. These laws created railway commissions, empowered them to set maximum or "reasonable" rates, and prohibited discrimination, long haul/short haul disparities, rebates, and other abuses. The laws constituted a pioneering effort on the part of public authorities to regulate the behavior of powerful private corporations.

In 1877, the Supreme Court, in *Munn v. Illinois,* upheld the constitutionality of the Granger laws, concluding that private property, when "affected with a public interest . . . must submit to be controlled by the public for the common good." Eight years later, however, the Court partially reversed itself, in *Wabash v. Illinois,* by striking down some state laws on the grounds that the federal government alone had the right to regulate commerce between the states. Since a great deal of freight traffic was interstate, the decision effectively gutted the Granger laws. Congress responded by passing the Interstate Commerce Act (ICA) in 1887, which prohibited discriminatory pricing policies, required published rate schedules, and

A cartoon attacking the railroad business headed by William H. Vanderbilt, son and successor to Cornelius Vanderbilt.

insisted that all railroad rates be "reasonable and just." Enforcement of the law was entrusted to an Interstate Commerce Commission (ICC) whose members were appointed by the president. Although much of the law was imprecisely worded and there was little agreement about what constituted "reasonable and just" rates, the ICA was a pathbreaking piece of legislation that established the right of the federal government to actively regulate some private enterprise.

Notably, federal regulation was not unwelcome to many railroad owners and managers. The rate wars of the 1870s and 1880s had threatened their profits, and private efforts to end "cutthroat competition" had repeatedly foundered. The most common such efforts involved establishing "pools," or "cartels," that would fix prices and divide up markets, but these anticompetitive agreements could not be enforced at law, and consequently they tended to collapse whenever a cartel member decided it was in his interest to break the agreement. Regulation therefore seemed to be necessary, and railroad owners agreed that one set of federal regulations was preferable to a bewildering array of state laws. Federal regulation also promised to standardize rules governing equipment, safety, and rights of way.

The passage of the ICA may also have facilitated the mergers that took place in the 1890s. In their efforts to stabilize the industry—which meant ending price wars, guaranteeing access to key trunk lines, and preventing new lines from sparking competitive chaos—the largest railroads began to reorganize themselves, merge with, or simply acquire their smaller rivals. With the help of investment bankers like J. P. Morgan, five huge rail systems were created that were large enough to stabilize prices and control a hefty proportion of the nation's freight. The mergers by which these systems were created took place after, not before, the ICC was established.

The great size and power of the railroads captured the imagination of Americans, leaving them fearful and fascinated by the "great monster, iron-hearted, relentless, infinitely powerful." In late nineteenth-century newspapers, magazines, novels, and paintings, the railroads loomed large, with the locomotive often symbolizing both the genius of invention and the potentially frightening qualities of mechanical, corporate, inhuman power.

## BIG BUSINESS

Railroads were not the only big businesses in 1900. In most industries, firms and plants became substantially larger between the Civil War and the turn of the century: the number of wage earners per establishment more than doubled, and the amount of capital invested rose even more rapidly. The degree of corporate concentration (the percentage of an industry controlled by its largest firms) also rose, sometimes dramatically; by the end of the century, Standard Oil refined 80 percent of the nation's oil, the Carnegie Company produced 30 percent of all finished steel, and two companies (General Electric and Westinghouse) had complete control of the electrical equipment industry. These were, of course, extraordinary enterprises, yet they symbolized the transformation of industry that occurred between Reconstruction and the beginning of the twentieth century. This was the era in which large corporations, with multiple plants, began to do business *nationally;* it was, indeed, the era that spawned the phrase "big business," an Americanism that made its first appearance in print in 1905 in *McClure's Magazine.*

Yet there was more to this transformation—and more to big business—than size. Firms did not simply acquire more workers and more capital; they also adopted a new institutional structure. This structure, which became the signature of the "modern business enterprise," had two key characteristics. The first was the presence of many distinct operating units, each with its own administration and accounts; in theory, each unit could function as an independent business. The second characteristic was management by a hierarchy of salaried executives.

All firms that became "big" businesses in the late nineteenth century developed or acquired these two structural characteristics, neither of which had appeared in any company before 1840. These features permitted firms by themselves to carry out steps that had once constituted market transactions between firms. Where grain, for example, had been sold from farmers to wholesale buyers to processors to a series of middlemen who shipped and distributed the processed product, the new multi-unit firms handled all the steps between the farmer and the local retailer. The "invisible hand" of the market, to use economist Adam Smith's famous phrase, was replaced by the visible hands of managers who coordinated the flow of materials, goods, and personnel among the different units of the enterprise.

The modern business enterprise appeared first among the railroads; its spread was linked to revolutionary changes in the ways that goods were distributed and produced. The changes in distribution came first, as wholesalers (who bought goods from producers and sold them to retailers) took advantage of the new speed of commerce to build regional firms that could move and sell goods quickly. They were joined by mass retailers who were capable of selling large quantities of diverse goods to consumers. Among the first mass retailers to appear in the 1870s were department stores, such as Marshall Field's, Macy's, Lord and Taylor, and Bloomingdale's, as well as Montgomery Ward, the first national mail-order house. Chain stores with branches in different cities (including the forerunners of A&P, Kroger, Grand Union, and Woolworth's) became prominent later in the century.

The transformation of manufacturing came a bit later and depended to a significant extent on new technology. Innovations in technique led to new and better products and more rapid production processes. This was particularly true in industries that depended on the application of heat to raw materials, such as oil refining and steel making. The average annual output of a blast furnace, for example, rose from 5,000 tons of steel to 65,000 tons between 1869 and 1899. Equally dramatic shifts occurred in some mechanical industries. In 1881, when a highly skilled cigarette maker could turn out

3,000 cigarettes a day, James Bonsack, a young man who later went into business with James Duke, patented a machine that could produce more than 70,000 in ten hours. Similar advances in speed were obtained by the first automatic canning factories, which led to the successes of Campbell's Soup, Heinz, and Borden's Milk.

Indeed, lured by the enormous markets opened up by the railroads, manufacturers in many industries strove to attain what would later be called "mass production." (The phrase itself became common only in the 1920s in the wake of a widely read, ghost-written article by Henry Ford.) Manufacturers introduced technological and organizational innovations to increase the efficiency of each department. Owners and engineers redesigned workplaces to accelerate the movement of materials from one place to another; they also introduced new statistical and accounting methods to measure the effects of their labors. They deployed electric motors (also new) to eliminate many of the cumbersome belts and shafts that conveyed steam power to operating machinery. And they designed goods—including farm machinery, sewing machines, and bicycles—with interchangeable parts that would make them easier to manufacture, market, use, and repair. Some manufacturers came closer to this mass-production goal than did others, but the goal was omnipresent.

The full-blown modern business enterprise appeared when mass production was integrated with mass distribution within a single firm. One route to this integration was taken in the 1880s by James B. Duke, a North Carolina tobacco

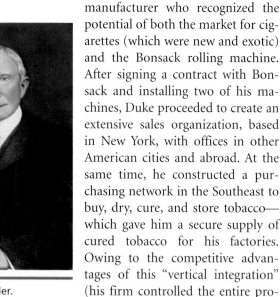

manufacturer who recognized the potential of both the market for cigarettes (which were new and exotic) and the Bonsack rolling machine. After signing a contract with Bonsack and installing two of his machines, Duke proceeded to create an extensive sales organization, based in New York, with offices in other American cities and abroad. At the same time, he constructed a purchasing network in the Southeast to buy, dry, cure, and store tobacco—which gave him a secure supply of cured tobacco for his factories. Owing to the competitive advantages of this "vertical integration" (his firm controlled the entire pro-

John D. Rockefeller.

duction process from raw materials to the consumer), Duke became the largest manufacturer in the industry and by 1890 was selling more than 800 million cigarettes a year.

An alternative path to bigness was through merger, or "horizontal integration," a path that became popular in the 1890s. John D. Rockefeller, for example, began his celebrated career as the owner of the Standard Oil Company, an oil refinery in Cleveland. He then bought a number of competitive refineries and formed an alliance with others to control output, keep prices up, negotiate shipping rates with the railroad, and (later) construct their own pipelines. This alliance had several different legal forms in the 1870s and 1880s, including a formal "trust" in which the shareholders of all member companies exchanged their stock for certificates in the Standard Oil Trust. In the mid-1880s, when the trust controlled more than three-quarters of the nation's refining capacity, Rockefeller and his allies moved into marketing, creating their own sales organization; later in the decade, Standard Oil began to buy oil fields and produce crude oil, controlling a third of the nation's supply by 1898.

The drive for bigness was only partially grounded in the imperatives of economic efficiency. In some cases, the impulse to construct large corporations was motivated primarily by the desire to increase profits by suppressing competition and maintaining prices. In the 1870s and 1880s, that impulse led many businessmen to form "pools," in which they agreed on prices and voluntarily divided up markets. When those voluntary pools failed (as they usually did because one member or another would decide that it was in his interest to break the agreement), businesses turned to trusts and holding companies; these were more effective because they held the stock of operating companies and could therefore coerce them into sticking to agreements. When trusts came under legal attack, mergers became the strategy of choice for businessmen intent on dominating markets and avoiding competition.

The formation of large enterprises was facilitated by changes in the laws governing corporations. Most business firms in the first two-thirds of the nineteenth century were sole proprietorships or partnerships, but the expansion of commerce was making corporate organization increasingly desirable: corporations could more easily attract investment because they could limit the liability of investors, and they were permanent legal entities that survived changes in leadership or personnel. Corporations, however, were still encumbered by restrictions put in place in earlier eras, when they were regarded as special franchises chartered by the state to serve public purposes. They were, for example, not permitted to own stock in other companies; nor could they dispose of their assets without the unanimous consent of shareholders. This collision of traditional law with growing economic imperatives was resolved by the emergence of a new legal conception of the corporation as a "natural entity" that required no special regulation by the state. New Jersey led the way, passing laws in 1889 and 1896 that legalized holding companies by permitting corporations to own stock in each other and also authorized corporations to dispose of their assets without a unanimous vote of shareholders. Not surprisingly, there was a vast migration of corporate headquarters to New Jersey after 1889.

The proliferation of large firms, mergers, and trusts was greeted with considerable alarm both within the business community and in the public at large. Owners of small enterprises complained that their larger rivals were monopolists who used illegitimate methods to gain competitive advantages; similar laments came from those who had to buy from or sell to powerful national corporations. Throughout the country, citizens expressed fear of the economic and political power of big business. "The outcry against the concentration of capital was furious," observed a character in Edward Bellamy's best-selling novel *Looking Backward* (1888). "Men believed that it threatened society with a form of tyranny." Firms like Standard Oil seemed to be destroying the competitive economic order from which they had sprung, while distant, faceless corporations could callously damage the livelihoods of millions of people. Big business, moreover, seemed increasingly able to control state legislatures: the phrase "to railroad" sprang from popular perceptions of the ways in which railroad corporations rammed laws through state legislatures.

Such sentiments spurred state governments to pass new laws to regulate competition and prevent corporate abuse. It also led a half dozen states in the 1880s to take legal action against holding companies. Big business fought such intervention, arguing that large enterprises were natural, inevitable, and beneficial. S. T. C. Dodd, Rockefeller's legal counsel, insisted that "you might as well endeavor to stay the formation of the clouds, the falling of the rains, or the flowing of the streams, as to attempt by any means or in any manner to prevent organization of industry, association of persons, and the aggregation of capital."

In 1890, the federal government responded to the mounting public concern about corporate power by passing the

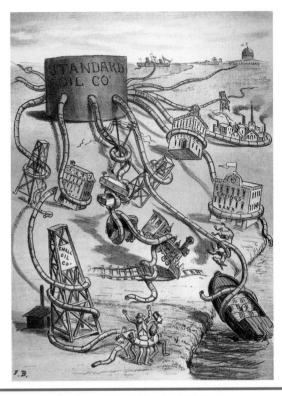

A cartoon depicting Rockefeller's Standard Oil Company as an octopus, a common metaphor for big business in the period.

Sherman Anti-Trust Act, which declared that "every contract, combination in the form of trust or otherwise, or conspiracy, in restraint of trade or commerce" was illegal. Similarly, it was unlawful for anyone to "monopolize or attempt to monopolize, or combine or conspire . . . to monopolize any part of the trade or commerce among the several states." The Sherman Act elevated long-standing common-law principles into federal law and offered significant rhetorical support for the virtues of a competitive economy.

Yet it had little impact on the conduct of business at the end of the century. Drafted almost entirely by conservative Republican lawyers, the language of the Sherman Act did not clearly distinguish between legal and illegal activities. What constituted "restraint of trade"? Just what was a monopoly? Such issues were left to the courts, and the courts in the 1890s were sympathetic to big business. In 1895, for example, the Supreme Court ruled that the Sugar Trust, which controlled 98 percent of the nation's sugar-refining capacity, did not violate the Sherman Act—and even if it had, it would have been guilty only of a misdemeanor. The act was not vigorously enforced and, in its early years, was deployed more often against labor unions than against corporations.

One ironic consequence of the Sherman Act may have been to accelerate corporate mergers. The wording of the act, as well as court decisions, suggested that holding companies and trusts were more vulnerable to legal attack than were outright consolidations. As a result, the years after 1895 witnessed the largest wave of mergers and consolidations in the nation's history. More than 1,800 independent firms disappeared into mergers between 1895 and 1904, and more than 70 of the resulting consolidations ended up controlling at least 40 percent of their industries. In many branches of manufacturing and commerce, oligopoly—the control of markets by a few companies—had come to stay. So had many of the giant firms that would dominate the economy for much of the twentieth century.

### INDUSTRY AND TECHNOLOGY

The spread of industry was accompanied by the arrival of a technologically modern world, a world we could recognize today. In key respects, including the prominence of science-based industries, the United States of 1900 more closely resembled the late twentieth-century nation than it did the antebellum world of 1860. The steel industry, for example, was in its infancy in the 1860s; by 1900, it was a giant. The same was true of the petroleum industry, which produced not only kerosene (and later gasoline) but by-products such as paraffin, petroleum jelly (Vaseline), and naphtha gas (used for lighting). Advances in chemistry also gave birth to the photographic industry and to celluloid, a precursor of plastic, used in diverse products ranging from dental plates to billiard balls to brushes. Even more prominent was the electrical industry. In 1882, there was only one electrical-power-generating plant in the United States; by 1902, there were 2,250, and two of the nation's largest firms, General Electric and Westinghouse, specialized in the design and manufacture of electrical goods.

Indeed, what transpired during these years was not simply the growth of new products and industries but the emergence of new *technological systems,* networks of interrelated products and devices that structured economic, social, and even political activity. People came to depend on these systems, to perceive them as indispensable to their own lives. The railroad network, for example, made long-distance transportation much faster and cheaper than it ever had been, and it shaped expectations accordingly. Not only were goods shipped over distances that

had been unimaginable a few decades earlier, but mail that had taken months to deliver now took weeks or even days. There were few towns in the late nineteenth century that did not see themselves as utterly dependent on their rail links to the rest of the world. Similarly, nearly a million miles of telegraph wires made rapid communication possible throughout the United States, as well as across the Atlantic. Newspapers relied on the telegraph to obtain information, as did participants in the booming financial and stock markets. By 1900, more than 80 million telegraph messages were transmitted annually.

The invention of the telephone launched another communications system. Alexander Graham Bell filed his patent for electromagnetic voice communication in 1876 and founded the Bell Telephone Company a year later. By the time Bell's patent expired in 1893, "long-distance" conversations were taking place (between New York and either Boston or Chicago) and more than 250,000 phones were in operation, most of them in businesses. Although some regarded the telephone as a "scientific toy" that could "never be a practical necessity," telephone use surged after 1894, when independent companies flocked into

Alexander Graham Bell at the New York end of the first long-distance call to Chicago, 1893.

the industry and promoted residential telephones, first in urban and then in rural areas. By 1920, there were 13 million telephones in the United States, and the ability of geographically separated individuals to hold conversations—something startling to nearly everyone in the 1870s—had become commonplace. "A fellow can now court his girl in China as well as in East Boston," reported one Massachusetts newspaper.

Both the telephone and the telegraph depended on electricity and thus were linked to the electrical system that transformed economic and social life. Many different inventors contributed to the electrical revolution of the late nineteenth century, but certainly Thomas Alva Edison stood in the forefront. A superb inventor and savvy entrepreneur, Edison was well aware that his inventions—such as the incandescent lightbulb, developed in the late 1870s—were not isolated creations but parts of a larger technological network.

> It was not only necessary that the lamps should give light and the dynamos generate current, but the lamps must be adapted to the current of the dynamos, and the dynamos must be constructed to give the character of current required by the lamps, and likewise all parts of the system must be constructed with reference to all other parts . . . The problem then that I undertook to solve was . . . the production of the multifarious apparatus, methods, and devices, each adapted for use with every other, and all forming a comprehensive system.

The electrical system thus included not only appliances but power generators, transmission lines, relay stations, and electromagnetic devices such as thermostats. In addition, electric motors provided power to streetcars and trolleys, made underground transportation (subways) feasible, and led to the redesign of workplaces and machinery in industries new and old. Particularly after direct current (which had a limited ability to travel distances) was replaced by alternating current in the late 1880s and 1890s, electricity became the preferred source of power for many industries, since it was relatively safe, cheap, and adaptable.

The technological innovations of the late nineteenth century were the offspring of advances in science, particularly chemistry and physics. Much of that scientific learning originated in Europe. The Bessemer process in steel manufacture was British (although it was almost simultaneously developed in the United States); and open-hearth furnaces, which displaced Bessemer converters late in the century, were first created in Germany and France. German chemists came up with such innovations as new dyes, fertilizers, synthetics, and brewing methods, which were imported to the United States.

The wireless telegraph was developed primarily by Guglielmo Marconi, based on discoveries in physics by Heinrich Hertz and James Maxwell.

Yet many technological advances were homegrown, made by independent inventors who were not affiliated with major corporations and who were choosing, by themselves, the problems on which they worked. Alexander Graham Bell was one such inventor; another was Nikola Tesla, who held a patent for an alternating current motor and made important discoveries in electricity. Orville and Wilbur Wright, who initiated the era of manned airflight in 1903, were also independent inventors, as was Hiram Maxim, the inventor of the machine gun.

But the most celebrated independent inventor was Edison. By the end of his life, Edison had acquired more than a thousand patents for an astonishingly diverse range of inventions and innovations: he made important contributions to the development of the telegraph, the telephone, the phonograph, electric light, electric power, magnetic ore separation, concrete construction, and motion pictures. He was also an extremely successful businessman, adept at finding investors for his projects and at creating companies to develop and market his innovations. In 1882, for example, backed by financier J. P. Morgan, Edison and the Edison Electric Illuminating Company installed an entire network of power generation and incandescent lighting in lower Manhattan. Less than a decade later, Morgan helped to merge the various Edison companies and several others into the General Electric Corporation.

Edison, moreover, developed a method of invention that symbolized the era's marriage of creativity to economic incentive. Possessing little formal education, he began his career as a Western Union operator, resigning in 1869 to devote himself full-time to invention. Backed by investors who hoped to profit from his improvements to telegraphic devices, Edison rented a building in Newark, New Jersey, equipped it with fine tools and machinery, and hired several talented machinist collaborators. After a half dozen years of success, he amassed enough capital to create what became known as his "invention factory" in rural Menlo Park, New Jersey. Situated between New York and Philadelphia, Menlo Park offered Edison and his collaborators a refuge from urban life, a self-contained country village where the task of invention could be pursued without interruption—in a locale easily accessible to major centers of finance and industry. At Menlo Park (and later at a larger installation in West Orange, New Jersey), he assembled a team of mechanics and craftsmen, as well as scientists and mathematicians who possessed learning that he himself lacked: "learned men, cranks,

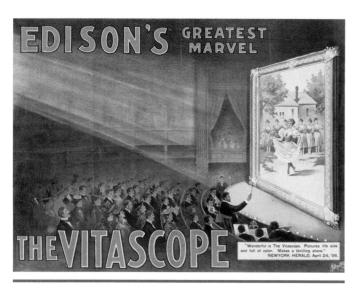

An 1896 poster celebrating another Edison invention, the motion picture. The vitascope, was a kind of projector.

enthusiasts, plain 'muckers,' and absolutely insane men," one member of the group later recalled. Edison also purchased the finest equipment that money could buy, as well as a large library. Although he cultivated the image of an eccentric genius, wearing stained shirts and sleeping on a cot in his laboratory, Edison was, in fact, creating a model of collaborative research, a way of institutionalizing the process of technological advance.

Edison's methods were widely emulated, although few inventors could match the creative or financial success of the "Wizard of Menlo Park." But the era of independent invention, though glorious, turned out to be brief. Technological research and innovation were increasingly carried out not by the independents but by industrial corporations. Firms had always tried to innovate, but by the end of the nineteenth century they were beginning to undertake systematic research. In 1900, the first formal research laboratory in American industry was founded—appropriately enough, at General Electric. The GE Laboratory had 8 staff members in 1901 and 102 by 1906. The Bell Telephone laboratories followed suit, with Westinghouse not far behind. Science-based industrial research was now being conducted by industry, which meant that industry was selecting the problems to be explored.

The consolidation of large corporations facilitated this trend and was reinforced by it. By the end of the century, firms like General Electric and Westinghouse had become sizable enough to afford full-blown research programs that would both develop new products and protect patents against the next wave of innovation. Moreover, by sponsoring research and controlling patents, they helped to perpetuate their own market supremacy: few small firms could compete with the research operations of giants like General Electric or AT&T.

These large corporations acquired the talents of an increasing number of college-trained engineers. Owing in part to the Morrill Act (1862), which offered federal land to states to establish colleges of "agriculture and mechanic arts," the nation had 85 engineering colleges by 1880, and thousands of students each year were earning engineering degrees. In contrast, there had been a mere 2,000 engineers recorded by the 1850 census and still only 7,000 in 1880. As a profession, engineering was a late nineteenth-century creation: professional societies like the American Society of Mechanical Engineers and the American Institute of Electrical Engineers were founded between 1870 and 1910. Most engineers became employees of big business, a vantage point from which they tended to identify the nation's progress with that of their firms.

## The Center and the Periphery

However integrated the emerging national economy may have been, significant regional differences persisted. Manufacturing had become predominant in the Northeast and Midwest, but elsewhere that was far less true. The South remained overwhelmingly agricultural, producing cash crops for shipment north and overseas. Meanwhile, the increasingly settled West became primarily an extractive economy, a place where natural resources such as copper and lumber were identified, removed from nature, and shipped away, often with little-noticed, long-term consequences for the environment. The southern and western economies, moreover, were not simply different; they were dependent on economic interests in the more metropolitan centers of the Northeast and the Midwest. In the language often applied to colonial relationships, the nation's northern manufacturing and financial belt constituted the economy's center, while the South and West were the periphery.

### THE SOUTHERN ECONOMY

Long after the end of Reconstruction, agriculture, particularly cotton, continued to dominate the economic life of the South.

As late as 1900, more than half of the region's labor force was engaged in farming, and the figure was above 60 percent in eight southern states. (In contrast, only 13 percent of the labor force worked in agriculture in the North Atlantic region, and there were only three states outside the South where the figure was above 50 percent.) The predominance of cotton was equally marked: in 1900, the cash value of cotton was roughly seven times that of tobacco, the second most important crop.

There was, to be sure, some industrial development. Advocates of a "New South" promoted not only railroads but manufacturing to lift the region out of its postbellum torpor and reduce its dependence on plantation agriculture. They had some success. Railroad mileage more than doubled in the 1880s alone, and in 1886 the South changed the gauge, or width, of its tracks to match the standard gauge in the rest of the nation. In the 1880s and 1890s, textile mills sprang up through the Piedmont region of the Carolinas and Georgia, while tobacco-processing plants revamped their methods and greatly expanded their output. At the same time, an iron and steel industry centered in Birmingham, Alabama, grew rapidly, and the lumber industry flourished, providing one-third of the nation's construction lumber. Still, the South continued to lag far behind the North, producing only one-tenth of the nation's manufactures (measured in dollars) in 1900. In most southern states, less than 15 percent of the labor force was engaged in manufacturing.

The South also remained poor. In 1880, the contrast between the South and the Northeast was similar to that between Russia (one of the poorest nations in Europe) and Germany (one of the wealthiest). In 1900, per capita wealth in the South was less than half the national average, and the disparity in incomes was comparable. Cotton prices remained low, and the new industries, such as textiles, typically generated low-wage jobs. On and off the farm, southern workers earned far less than their counterparts in the North.

Several factors contributed to this persistent poverty. In agriculture, the South had ensnared itself in a nasty cycle that greatly restricted incomes: relatively low cotton prices (and steady global demand) drove farmers to grow more cotton, which, in turn, lowered the price that farmers were paid—which meant that individual incomes increased hardly at all. The combination of sharecropping and the lien system, moreover, hindered the diversification of crops, while average farm size, contrary to the national pattern, was shrinking. In addition, the abundance of cheap labor (as well as the small size of farms) stood in the way of technological innovation.

This optimistic symbol of the New South arising from the ruin of the Civil War, from the Atlanta Exposition of 1895, shows her horn of plenty stuffed with steel, pig iron, and other products of the region.

Although patents for cotton-harvesting machinery were issued in the late nineteenth century, landowners had little incentive to develop or purchase new machinery.

The abundance of labor and the isolation of the labor force restrained development in other ways as well. Southern workers did not migrate to higher-wage areas (in part because of the fetters of the lien system), which helped to keep a lid on wages and to encourage the proliferation of low-wage industries. Moreover, in manufacturing as in agriculture, the availability of inexpensive labor discouraged technological advance. "Instead of installing machinery to do the work, we always undertook to do it putting in another cheap negro," commented one employer in the lumber business. Conditions in the South discouraged immigration and thereby kept the region from acquiring both skilled workers and the innovative ideas that often traveled with them.

The ability of southern industry to catch up with the North was further hampered by the region's late start, by the weakness of its infrastructure, by the northern ownership of many railroads and manufacturing plants, and by the absence of a local technological community, including a machine tools industry. These last two factors often reinforced one another: productive machinery tended to be imported, rather than developed in the South, and imported technology was not always effective in southern conditions. In the steel industry in Birmingham, for example, imported Bessemer converters did not work well because they were not designed to use local ores, which had a high phosphorous content.

The South's economy between Reconstruction and World War I had something of a colonial cast. Most workers were involved in growing or processing staple agricultural exports. Most industries were labor-intensive (with a high ratio of labor to capital) and paid low wages. To the extent that the region participated in more advanced industries, it did so with northern capital, on terms dictated by executives and investors in faraway cities. Not surprisingly, as late as 1919 the eleven states with the lowest per capita income were all southern.

## DEVELOPMENT OF THE WEST

According to the superintendent of the eleventh census, the American frontier disappeared sometime between 1880 and 1890. "Up to and including 1880, the country had a frontier of settlement," he wrote, "but at present the unsettled area has been so broken into by isolated bodies of settlement that there can hardly be said to be a frontier line."

The end of the Civil War and the completion of transcontinental railway lines had, in fact, greatly accelerated the development of the trans-Mississippi West. The population of the Pacific and mountain states almost doubled in the 1870s and again in the 1880s; growth in the "west central" states (stretching from Minnesota and North Dakota down to Texas and Louisiana) was even more rapid. By 1910, there were more than 25 million people living west of the Mississippi, 7 million in the Pacific and mountain states alone. At the turn of the century, all of the western territories except Oklahoma, New Mexico, and Arizona had been admitted to the Union as states.

Migrants to the West came from nearly everywhere. Large numbers of Scandinavians, Germans, Irish, and Canadians flocked to the farm states just west of the Mississippi. Mexican immigrants were numerous in the Southwest; California became home to tens of thousands of Chinese immigrants; and thousands of African Americans fled northwest, particularly to Kansas, to escape the repression of the post-Reconstruction

South. A majority of the westbound, however, were native-born whites drawn from the middling reaches of American society. Farmers, merchants, and professionals traveled in family units from east to west along the same latitude, often moving more than once. The railroads made their journeys briefer and less arduous than such treks had been before the Civil War.

Why were these people pouring into the West? For most, the answer was straightforward: they wanted land, to settle and to farm. Between 1862 and 1890, nearly 2 million people claimed free land under provisions of the Homestead Act. The typical westward migrant, however, *bought* land from a public land office, a speculator, or the railroads. To subsidize the construction of the railroads, the federal and state governments had given railroad corporations land equivalent in size to the state of Texas, adjacent to the railroad lines themselves. As a result, some of the most desirable land in the West (desirable because of its location) was removed from federal control and had to be purchased from the railroads. In part for this reason—but primarily because most urban workers lacked the capital and the knowledge to get started in farming, whether or not they had to buy land—the Homestead Act never did offer a realistic escape to impoverished, industrial workers.

Farming in the region offered new challenges to migrants from the East and Europe. As explorer, scientist, and surveyor John Wesley Powell warned in a report written in 1878, the most important natural fact about the West was its aridity: much of the nation west of the 100th meridian (a line stretching roughly from Bismark, North Dakota, to Abilene, Texas) did not receive enough rainfall to sustain conventional methods of farming. As one moved across the prairies of the west central states, annual rainfall totals steadily declined; precipitation in the Great Plains averaged only fifteen to twenty inches a year, less than half the norm in the Mississippi Valley. Farmers on the plains and beyond could not expect to grow wheat, corn, or other crops common in the more humid East.

Yet Powell's warnings were ignored. Encouraged by promoters, farmers flooded into the plains in the 1870s and 1880s. The flat, open grasslands were easy to clear and seemed well suited to new farm implements. Besides, most farmers believed that "rain follows the plow"—that cultivating the land and planting trees would stimulate rainfall. In the 1880s, that belief seemed well founded: the arrival of the farmers coincided with one of the periodic wet cycles on the plains, and crops, including wheat, were plentiful. But when the rains subsided, beginning in 1889, the results were devastating. Crops failed year after year; the earth turned dusty and hard.

A Colorado River canyon surveyed by John Wesley Powell, 1871–1874.

Some of the region's settlers stayed in place, awaiting the next wet cycle and eventually learning to "dry farm" with new crops and methods that required less moisture. But many left: some counties lost half of their population between 1890 and 1900. One Texas family explained its departure on a sign nailed to their abandoned cabin: "Two hundred miles to nearest post office, one hundred miles to wood, twenty miles to water, one mile to hell. God bless our home. Gone to live with the wife's folks."

Elsewhere in the West, especially in California, Oregon, and Washington, climatic conditions were more favorable, although water was rarely plentiful and control of the water supply was always a critical economic and political issue. The vastness of the territory, moreover, encouraged farming on a grand scale. In the Red River Valley of North Dakota and Minnesota, as well as in California's Central Valley, "bonanza farms" appeared in the 1870s and 1880s; these were corporate enterprises with absentee owners, fleets of machinery, hierarchical management, and hundreds of hired hands. Just west of Fargo, Oliver Dalrymple managed farms that employed 1,000 men for harvesting. Hugh Glenn of California, with 66,000 acres of land along the Sacramento River, may have been the single largest wheat grower in the world.

Bonanza farms, however, did not displace family farming. In fact, something close to the reverse happened in the 1890s: many of the enormous "factories in the fields" were subdivided and sold to family farmers. Why did the trend toward consolidation and big business not catch on in agriculture, as it certainly appeared it would in the 1880s? Two factors were important. First, the new technology that became widely available after the Civil War made it feasible for individual households to run reasonably large farms; there were no "economies of scale" that made bonanza farming more efficient than family farming. Second, family farmers were better able and more willing to weather bad years. When wheat prices fell in the late 1880s, farm households preserved their property and their way of life by working harder, cutting their expenses, and increasing their acreage. The absentee investors in bonanza farms, however, preferred to put their money elsewhere—which meant that many such farms simply went out of business.

Something similar happened in cattle ranching. The final slaughter of the already beleaguered buffalo in the 1870s (when the railroads and the market for buffalo hides led to the extermination of 5 million animals) created an ecological vacuum on the plains, which was quickly filled by cattle. With the railroads in place and a growing population in the East hungry for beef, cattle ranching became a booming industry: cattle could be fed on the open ranges and free grasslands of the plains and delivered to railroad depots in places like Abilene, Kansas. Eastern and European investors leapt into the industry, creating cattle companies and large corporate ranches. By the mid-1880s, there were 7.5 million head of cattle on the plains north of Texas and New Mexico.

Not surprisingly, the cattle ranching boom collided with the increased settlement of the plains, giving rise in the 1870s to yet another expression of American inventiveness: barbed wire. Farmers who wanted to protect their lands and crops from massive herds of cattle needed fences, but the conventional materials of fencing (wood and stone) were unavailable or prohibitively expensive. Wire twisted to produce painful barbs solved that problem. Farmers proceeded to enclose their fields with barbed wire, as did some large ranchers, in order to keep smaller herds out of their grazing lands; in Texas and elsewhere, "fence cutting" wars broke out between those who favored and opposed replacing the open range with a latticework of barbed wire.

Disaster struck the cattle ranching industry in the late 1880s. A combination of overgrazing, fencing, dry summers, and severe winters led to huge losses of livestock and the virtual disappearance of investors. What remained in the wake of this econo-ecological crisis were smaller ranches, often family owned (but still employing cowboys), different breeds of cattle, and heightened rancher responsibility for feeding cattle through the winter.

Despite the vicissitudes of business and weather, western agriculture grew rapidly: by 1910, the region grew 65 percent of the American wheat crop, contributing substantially to the nation's agricultural exports. Both in the plains and in parts of the Southwest, agriculture dominated the economy, occupying more than 40 percent of the labor force. Elsewhere in the region, mining, lumbering, and fishing were preeminent. Gold, silver, and copper mines could be found throughout the mountain states and California, while the forests of the Pacific Northwest provided lumber for the West and for export. Outside of California, there was relatively little manufacturing before 1900, particularly of finished goods.

Thanks to the railroads, the West, distant as it may have been, was integrated into a world economy even while remaining sparsely populated. (The railroads also determined the location of many towns and cities since, in the West, the railroads were built before most of the population arrived.) Much of what westerners produced was consumed elsewhere; most of what they consumed was produced elsewhere. The inhabitants of the West after the Civil War were not self-sufficient, but rather participants in an expansive capitalism. Extractive industries such as lumber, copper, and mining—and even ranching—required far more capital than the West itself could provide; consequently, promoters of the region frequently sought investment from the East and Europe. For better or worse, they were successful. Investment poured into the West, and outside of California—where San Francisco became a major center of capital, financing development throughout the state—lumber companies, copper mines, and ranches all came to be owned by nonwesterners or by large corporations with financial centers elsewhere. Early in the twentieth century, most of the privately held land in Nevada was owned by nonresident individuals or corporations; two-thirds of the state's industries had absentee owners. Nevada was an extreme case of a pattern that prevailed throughout the region.

While private citizens poured into the West in search of both land and riches, the federal government also stepped up its role in the region. In 1879, Congress passed legislation creating the United States Geological Survey; lodged in the Interior Department, the USGS was charged with the task of classifying the public lands and examining the geological structure and mineral resources of the nation. Led in its early years by Clarence King and by John Wesley Powell, the USGS engaged in extensive scientific research that served both to facilitate the exploitation of the West's resources and to buttress growing concerns about the preservation of the natural environment.

## Classes

The development of industrial capitalism meant much more than the replacement of farms by smokestacks, of small shops by large factories. It also deepened changes in the class structure that had been under way since the beginning of the industrial revolution early in the nineteenth century. One such change was the emergence of a national elite, an upper class that wielded economic (and sometimes political) power over large terrains and in multiple locales; these were men, and families, whose wealth gave them unprecedented nationwide prominence. Cornelius Vanderbilt, Andrew Carnegie, Henry Frick, John D. Rockefeller, Leland Stanford, James B. Duke, J. P. Morgan: the captains of late nineteenth-

Herding longhorn cattle aboard a freight train at Halleck, Nevada, to be shipped east, 1877.

century industry and finance, memorialized in institutions that still carry their names, had a visibility and influence far more substantial than regional business leaders had possessed before the Civil War.

More important was a widespread shift in the nature of the "middle class," a term that first came into use in the 1850s. The growth of industry and big business made it more difficult for people to be proprietors of any sort—farm owners, shopkeepers, artisans, manufacturers. Local manufacturers were bought out by national firms; retailers were driven out of business by Sears, Roebuck or Montgomery Ward. Since the population was rapidly growing, the *number* of persons who owned property on which they could earn a living did not actually decline, but the *percentage* did, as it had for much of the nineteenth century. By 1900, only one out of every four members of the labor force owned productive property; three-quarters of these were farmers.

At the same time, however, another segment of the middle class grew larger: salaried, white-collar employees. Big businesses created large numbers of managerial positions, clerical jobs, and openings for professionals, such as engineers. The men and women who held these jobs did not possess the independence or control over their working conditions that came with ownership, but they were educated, compensated decently, and reasonably secure in their positions. In the decades after the Civil War, this stratum more than quadrupled in size, increasing from roughly 5 percent of the labor force in 1870 to 11 percent (of a much larger labor force) in 1900.

Both the upper and middle classes flourished in the late nineteenth century. The economy was generating more and more wealth, and most of that wealth went to families in the higher echelons of the occupational structure. In 1870, the richest 1 percent of the population owned more than one-quarter of the nation's assets; the top 10 percent owned 70 percent. This highly skewed distribution of wealth did not become any more egalitarian between the 1870s and the beginning of World War I. If things changed at all, they moved in the opposite direction: according to some estimates, the richest 10 percent of the population held nearly 90 percent of the nation's wealth on the eve of World War I.

Incomes were also highly unequal. In 1880, for example, the general manager of the Chicago, Burlington and Quincy Railroad earned $15,000; the railroad's senior executives earned more than $4,000, while middle managers were paid between $1,500 and $4,000. At the same time, clerical workers in the railroad's Chicago office averaged about $800; carpenters,

blacksmiths, and other skilled workers were lucky if they made between $500 and $600; and unskilled laborers in Chicago were paid $1.32 a day (and they probably worked fewer than 250 days a year). These differences of income, like those of wealth, did not narrow discernibly before World War I.

Such inequalities underscore a critical feature of the late nineteenth-century social structure: the presence of an enormous industrial and agricultural working class. By 1870, more than two-thirds of all working Americans were *employees,* a figure that continued to rise in later decades. And most employees performed

J. P. Morgan, captain of industry and finance.

manual labor. Between 1870 and 1900, 60 to 70 percent of the nation's workforce consisted of wage earners who labored with their hands. By the turn of the century, the United States had more than 600,000 carpenters, 229,000 tailors and tailoresses, 563,000 miners, 246,000 cotton mill workers, 2.2 million day laborers, and 4.4 million agricultural laborers. The working class was nearly 18 million strong, and its particular circumstances—which had been diverging from those of the middle class throughout the nineteenth century—merit detailed inspection.

## JOBS AND INCOMES

The working class itself was a house of many mansions. It included skilled workers, such as machinists, carpenters, and iron puddlers (who stirred molten iron until it reached the right temperature and consistency), who possessed knowledge that took years to acquire and who often worked at a pace they set themselves, with little supervision. It also included semiskilled factory workers, men and women who tended machines and carried out one stage in a production process. At the bottom of the ladder were the unskilled, who held jobs that anyone could learn quickly: digging, lifting, hauling. One day laborer identified his trade by his rudimentary tools, calling himself a "pick and shovel man."

The most skilled could support their families in respectable circumstances, even owning a home and providing education for their children. The semiskilled were generally paid less, although better in some industries (such as furniture making)

Workers operating lathes in a New York City factory with little protection against accidents, 1900.

than in others (such as textiles). Daily wage rates for the unskilled were less than half those for skilled workers, and the unskilled also tended to work fewer days. Most semiskilled and unskilled men had difficulty supporting a family on their own incomes. Real wages (adjusted for changes in prices) rose more than 50 percent between 1870 and 1900, but a majority of the working class continued to live in, or not far from, poverty.

Most industrial workers were male. Although the number of women in the labor force reached 18 percent by 1900, women rarely worked outside their homes after they married and had children. (Married women, however, often provided critical supplements to household incomes by taking in boarders.) Single women frequently did join the paid labor force, where they tended to be concentrated in particular occupations, such as teaching, domestic service, and—later—clerical work. Even within large workplaces, they were restricted to specific, usually poorly paid, tasks: male and female cotton mill operatives, for example, generally did not tend the same machines in the same factories.

The contrast between working-class and middle-class lives, moreover, was not just a matter of income. Employees who labored with their hands usually worked six days a week, ten hours per day, under close supervision. In some industries, conditions were even more arduous: steelworkers routinely worked twelve-hour days, six days a week, and every Sunday half of all employees worked a "long turn" of twenty-four hours so that the day and night shifts could alternate while the blast furnaces kept running.

Dangers abounded. Between 1880 and 1900, 35,000 workers were killed on the job every year, while another half million were injured. Hundreds, often thousands, of miners died in accidents annually. In 1901, 1 out of every 137 trainmen was killed, 1 out of every 11 injured. The menace of accidents was accompanied by the threat of illness: black lung disease among miners, brown lung among textile operatives, tuberculosis in many trades. Being a worker was hazardous to one's health.

In addition, workers suffered from chronic job insecurity. The word "unemployment" first appeared in print in Massachusetts in 1887, announcing—a bit after the fact—the arrival of a new economic and social phenomenon: widespread, involuntary joblessness. Industrial capitalism had transformed the United States into a nation of employees whose ability to work was dependent on decisions made by employers. When the demand for goods slackened, workers did not have the option of slowing their labors; they were laid off with no pay. This occurred not only during depressions but year after year, sometimes seasonally and sometimes more episodically.

In an average year, between one-fifth and one-quarter of all workers experienced some unemployment, remaining jobless for an average of three months. During depressions, the figure soared: 35 to 40 percent of all workers were jobless during the worst years of the 1880s and 1890s, and they remained idle, on average, for nearly five months. While employers sought to maintain a "reserve army" of labor so that workers would always be available when they were needed, a distinctive characteristic of working-class life became the unsteadiness of jobs and the unpredictability of incomes.

This chronic uncertainty made workers wary of technological changes that could make jobs even more scarce. New machinery in woodworking, printing, metalworking, and cigar making (to cite just a few examples) permitted individuals to produce far more than they had been able to do previously, and the machinery consequently seemed to threaten people's jobs and livelihoods. In fact, the economy was growing so rapidly that relatively few people were suddenly driven out of their occupations because of new technology. The number of carpenters did not drop because turn-of-the-century woodworking machinery allowed, for example, bathtubs to be built in twenty minutes rather than several hours. Nor did typographers vanish overnight because of the invention in 1886 of the Linotype machine, an ingenious creation whose ninety-character keyboard permitted type to be set one line, rather than one character, at a time. But skilled workers did often encounter an eroding demand for their talents; their incomes slowly declined, while men and women who had fewer skills and understood less about the entire process of production joined their industry.

In some instances, this technologically induced "skill dilution" was a straightforward consequence of improvements in machinery and production techniques. In others, the process was more complex, grounded in conflict between workers and managers. The knowledge possessed by skilled workers often gave them substantial power, on the shop floor and in the labor market, and employers could undermine that power by introducing new machinery. In Fall River, Massachusetts, for example, textile mill owners decided to deploy new technology to rid themselves of skilled spinners who had a reputation for insisting on their autonomy. One Saturday, after the spinners had left, "we started right in and smashed a room full of [spinning machines] with sledge hammers," boasted one owner. When the spinners returned to work the following Monday, they found their machines destroyed, new technology in place, and semiskilled "girls" hired to do the spinning.

Similarly, production in iron and steel mills was often organized by skilled workers, who were paid by the ton, hired their own helpers, and negotiated tonnage rates with their employers. These knowledgeable, experienced workers possessed considerable power when bargaining with owners. The "manager's brains," as early twentieth-century labor leader Big Bill Haywood claimed, "were under the workman's cap." That fact, however, did not sit well with ambitious entrepreneurs like Andrew Carnegie and Henry Frick. In 1892, they responded to a dispute with their skilled workmen by locking the doors to their Homestead, Pennsylvania, steel plant and surrounding it with barbed-wire fences and armed guards. Frick and Carnegie then installed new technology that transformed most steel mill positions into semiskilled jobs.

Changes in workplace technology altered the structure of the labor force in ways that had mixed results for workers. The proportion of skilled workers declined, but so, too, did the proportion of unskilled workers who often performed backbreaking work for low wages. The major growth was in the percentage of men and women who held semiskilled jobs as machine tenders. New machinery permitted these operatives to produce more and earn more, although it also required them to work harder and faster. As the United States Industrial Commission reported in 1902, "In nearly all occupations an increasing strain and intensity of labor is required by modern methods of production. . . . The introduction of machinery and the division of labor have made it possible to increase greatly the speed of the individual workman." A cotton weaver confirmed that "anybody who works in the mills now knows it is not like what it was twenty-five or thirty years ago, because the speed of the machinery has been increased to such an extent." A superintendent at a Swift meat-packing plant offered the managerial view: "If you need to turn out a little more, you speed up the conveyors a little and the men speed up to keep pace."

## IMMIGRANTS AND MIGRANTS

In much of the country, the rapid growth of the working class—and thus the rapid growth of the economy—was made possible by immigration. More than 1 million immigrants entered the United States during every five-year period between the end of the Civil War and World War I. More than 9 million arrived between 1865 and 1890; another 16 million came between 1890 and 1915. (For immigration statistics, see the Appendix.)

Until the mid-1880s, the great majority of immigrants came, as they long had, from northern and western Europe: between 1876 and 1880, for example, Great Britain, Ireland, Scandinavia, Germany, and Canada accounted for more than 75 percent of all immigrants. During the final decades of the nineteenth century, however, immigration from these countries began to slow down, while new migratory streams flowed from southern and eastern Europe. Between 1906 and 1910, more than 1 million immigrants came

This 1880s drawing, from the humor magazine Puck, depicts the condition of workers as akin to those of slaves a few decades earlier.

from Italy alone, while another 2 million came from Russia, central Europe, and the Baltic states. To old-stock Americans, these "new" immigrants seemed more alien and less desirable than the "old" immigrants from western and northern Europe.

The story of immigration to the United States has often been told in romantic, even patriotic, terms: the "huddled masses" fled the Old World to seek the New; ambitious, if poor, Europeans escaping political, religious, and economic oppression set sail for the "Land of Freedom" to find liberty and prosperity. Such images contain a kernel of truth, yet they overemphasize the lure of America and pay too little attention to what was transpiring elsewhere. The millions of men and women who migrated to the United States were part of a broader global phenomenon. Throughout Europe and in many parts of Asia, the combination of population growth and economic change (often a restructuring of agriculture by landowners) pressured millions of people to leave their homes and try to make a living elsewhere. Some of these emigrants had property to sell and capital to bring; they became "settlers," intent on farming or establishing a business in a new province

or country. But most were not so lucky: they traveled with only their skills or their brawn, from Ireland to England, Canada, and the United States; from southern Italy to Milan, Buenos Aires, and New York; from Portugal to Brazil and Massachusetts; from China to the Philippines, Peru, and California.

There was, then, nothing uniquely American about immigration, except its size and diversity. The 25 million men and women who came to the United States between 1865 and World War I were a large part—but only a part—of a mass movement of labor that was a significant feature of modern world history. Freed from their moorings, migrants often journeyed to several cities or countries before settling down—a process facilitated both by the railroads and by steamships that made ocean travel relatively fast and cheap. A large proportion of the migrants who came to the United States, moreover, intended to return to their country of origin, and sooner or later many did. Only among the Irish and the Jews was the intention of permanent emigration almost universal.

The immigrants who came to the United States thus constituted a significant proportion of the nation's working class.

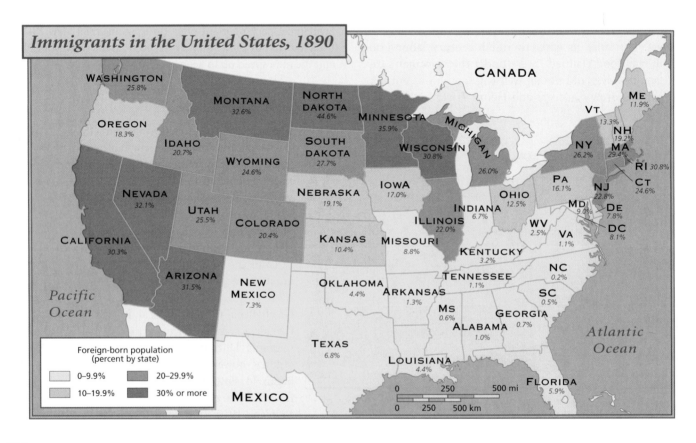

**Immigrants in the United States, 1890**

WASHINGTON 25.8%
OREGON 18.3%
MONTANA 32.6%
IDAHO 20.7%
WYOMING 24.6%
NEVADA 32.1%
UTAH 25.5%
CALIFORNIA 30.3%
ARIZONA 31.5%
NEW MEXICO 7.3%
COLORADO 20.4%
NORTH DAKOTA 44.6%
SOUTH DAKOTA 27.7%
NEBRASKA 19.1%
KANSAS 10.4%
OKLAHOMA 4.4%
TEXAS 6.8%
MINNESOTA 35.9%
WISCONSIN 30.8%
IOWA 17.0%
MISSOURI 8.8%
ARKANSAS 1.3%
LOUISIANA 4.4%
MICHIGAN 26.0%
ILLINOIS 22.0%
INDIANA 6.7%
KENTUCKY 3.2%
TENNESSEE 1.1%
MS 0.6%
ALABAMA 1.0%
GEORGIA 0.7%
OHIO 12.5%
WV 2.5%
VA 1.1%
NC 0.2%
SC 0.5%
FLORIDA 5.9%
ME 11.9%
VT 13.3%
NH 19.2%
MA 29.4%
RI 30.8%
NY 26.2%
PA 16.1%
NJ 22.8%
CT 24.6%
MD 9.0%
DE 7.8%
DC 8.1%

CANADA
MEXICO
Pacific Ocean
Atlantic Ocean

Foreign-born population (percent by state)
0–9.9%
10–19.9%
20–29.9%
30% or more

0    250    500 mi
0    250    500 km

*American Journal*

## What if You Get Sick?

*Young immigrant women hoping for a better life in America often ended up performing hard work for long hours—sometimes to the breaking point.*

"How many [*immigrant women*] give way under the strain of long hours, bad living conditions, and the confused excitement which comes with their new environment, few people realize. The tragedy of this physical breakdown was illustrated one summer when the services of the Immigrants' Protective League were asked on behalf of a young Polish girl. Although she seemed entirely well when she came and had been passed by the examining doctors at Ellis Island, she had developed tuberculosis after a few months of factory work in Chicago. She was taken to the County Hospital and soon learned that she had no chance of recovery. She was most wretchedly homesick when the visitor for the League saw her at the hospital. She had only a cousin in this country, who could not come to see her because it was the season of overtime work in his trade and the County Hospital was many miles away. She was unable to talk to those around her and found it impossible to eat the strange American food given her, and, worst of all, she realized that all her girlish plans to earn money, send for her mother, and marry well were to come to nothing. Polish food which we were able to procure for her did not comfort her, however, for she wanted only one thing–to be sent back home so that she might die with her mother. In this, too, she was disappointed, for although she improved somewhat when she learned that she was to be deported, she died alone at sea."

Grace Abbott, *The Immigrant and the Community*

In the North and West, factories, mines, and construction sites were peopled largely by immigrants. In 1900, 28 percent of the nation's day laborers, 44 percent of all miners, 36 percent of all steelworkers, and 38 percent of all cotton mill operatives were foreign-born. (Excluding the South, which had few immigrants, these percentages were even higher.) As early as 1880, in fact, most American workers were either immigrants, the children of immigrants, or African American. In forty of the fifty largest cities, at least 75 percent of all wage earners belonged to one of these three groups. Conversely, relatively few native whites, whose parents were also native-born, belonged to working-class occupations. Even in small midwestern cities like Dubuque, Iowa, and Joliet, Illinois, less than 20 percent of the working class (but more than 70 percent of the population) came from native white stock.

What this meant was that even before the turn of the century, class boundaries were coinciding with ethnic and racial boundaries. The middle class consisted overwhelmingly of white, native-born Protestants whose parents had also been born in the United States. The working class was predominantly African American in the South, and either foreign-born or of foreign parentage in the North. Workers were also more likely to be Catholic or Jewish. Within the working class, there was additional ethnic and racial stratification. In the South, some jobs and industries came to be viewed as "black," while others, such as textiles, were reserved for whites. In the West, the Chinese and other nonwhites were restricted to arduous, low-paying jobs, including railroad construction and domestic service. In the Northeast, the Italians, Irish, and Jews were similarly concentrated in particular occupations. The nation's labor markets were segmented not only by skill but also by gender, ethnicity, and race.

### SOCIAL MOBILITY

From the onset of industrialization, some Americans had worried that the nation's egalitarian promise would be undercut by the formation of a permanent working class. Such apprehensions were often eased by faith in the idea that the nation's bounty was great enough to give all Americans the opportunity

Recently arrived immigrants on a walkway at Ellis Island, ca. 1902. The large building in the background is the newly opened hospital.

chance of being hit by lightning than he did of becoming a company president. Most men who began their working lives as manual wage earners ended their careers as manual wage earners. In Boston and other well-studied cities, for example, three-quarters of all skilled and unskilled workers remained in the blue-collar ranks for their entire careers. Of equal importance, between 60 and 80 percent of the children of blue-collar workers were confined to the working class for their entire careers as well.

Yet there was social mobility in late nineteenth- and early twentieth-century America. Although Horatio Alger–type successes were rare, perhaps as many as one-quarter of all manual wage earners advanced into middle-class jobs; and between 20 and 40 percent of their children may also have experienced some upward mobility. To be sure, these figures did not apply to African Americans, who—North and South—encountered uniquely powerful obstacles to advancement. Nor were these figures similar for all immigrant and ethnic groups at all historical moments: in many cities, for example, Irish and Italian immigrants did not fare as well as English and Jewish migrants. Nonetheless, the possibility of advancement existed. Although it was highly unlikely that a day laborer would become rich, it was not unrealistic for a member of the working class to imagine advancing from rags to respectability. Class mattered; it shaped a person's life chances. But it was not a prison with unscalable walls.

to get ahead, to prosper. Inequality certainly existed in the United States, and the growth of manufactures may have made poverty more visible, but there was no cause for alarm; a poor boy who worked hard, studied hard, and saved his money could leave poverty behind.

This ideology received its most well-known nineteenth-century expression in the popular novels of Horatio Alger: the plot of these tales, published between the 1860s and 1890s, usually ended with the rise of a virtuous poor lad to a position of social respectability (and sometimes, through marriage, into the family of his employer). "In this free country poverty in early life is no bar to a man's advancement," declared one of Alger's characters. Of course, some hard-nosed contemporaries scoffed at such romantic visions: "If you tell a single concrete workingman on the B and O Railroad that he may yet be the president of the company," observed economist Richard Ely, "it is not demonstrable that you have told him what is not true, although it is within bounds to say that he is far more likely to be killed by a stroke of lightning." Despite the skepticism of men like Ely, there was widespread middle-class faith in the notion that men and women could exit the working class if they were willing to work hard and well.

In fact, both Ely and Alger captured elements of the truth. Ely was certainly correct that a railroad worker had a better

## Suggested Reading

Alfred D. Chandler, *The Visible Hand: The Managerial Revolution in American Business* (1977)

William Cronon, *Nature's Metropolis: Chicago and the Great West* (1991)

Herbert Gutman, *Work, Culture, and Society in Industrializing America: Essays in American Working-Class and Social History* (1977)

David A. Hounshell, *From the American System to Mass Production, 1800–1932: The Development of Manufacturing Technology in the United States* (1984)

Thomas Hughes, *American Genesis: A Century of Invention and Technological Enthusiasm, 1870–1970* (1989)

Thoms J. Misa, *A Nation of Steel: The Making of Modern America, 1865–1925* (1995)

Stephan Thernstrom, *The Other Bostonians: Poverty and Progress in the American Metropolis, 1880–1970* (1973)

C. Vann Woodward, *The Origins of the New South, 1877–1913* (1951)

## *Summary* QUESTIONS

■ How did the United States become the leading manufacturing nation in the world?

■ What were the different ways in which firms became "big" businesses?

■ What is a technological system? Describe one important system in this period.

■ In what ways were the West and the South like and unlike each other?

■ In what ways did the class composition of the United States change between 1870 and 1900?

## *Chronology*

| | |
|---|---|
| **May 10, 1869** | The Central Pacific and Union Pacific Railroads are linked at Promontory Point, Utah. |
| **1873** | Panic of 1873 precipitates a five-year depression. |
| **May 19, 1876** | President Grant opens the Centennial Exhibition in Philadelphia. |
| **1877** | Alexander Graham Bell founds the Bell Telephone Company. |
| **1882** | Thomas Edison and the Edison Electric Illuminating Company install electric lighting in lower Manhattan. |
| **November 18, 1883** | Four standard time zones adopted across the United States. |
| **1887** | The Interstate Commerce Act. |
| **1890** | The Sherman Anti-Trust Act. |
| **1893** | The Railroad Safety Appliance Act. |

## *Key Terms*

Transcontinental railroads (p. 519)

Big business (p. 523)

The electrical system (p. 527)

The New South (p. 529)

Bonanza farms (p. 531)

# AN INDUSTRIAL SOCIETY:

## 1870-1910

Lower Manhattan had become a business district by the 1890s, with electricity, telephone, and telegraph wires crisscrossing overhead.

- How was American society changing in this period?
- How did farm life change in the late nineteenth century?
- What developments contributed to the rise of the city?
- How did women's lives change in the industrial era?
- What were the main cultural expressions of the new industrial society?

The triumph of industrialization reverberated through nearly all dimensions of American life. Not only were work and workplaces transformed, but the very fabric of society was rewoven with a more industrial thread. People, things, and words moved faster, over unprecedented distances. Daily life on millions of farms was reconfigured by new technologies and new types of production. Millions of people poured into the nation's cities, living in more densely populated worlds than they had known; their presence transformed the physical environment, as well as the rhythms and contours of urban life. Gender roles, too, were affected, as workplaces became increasingly separated from homes, and as more and more women entered the labor force. Educational institutions revamped their curricula to match the needs of an industrial world; religions were challenged to respond to new moral and social problems; writers, artists, and scientists focused their attention on a social order that was challenging and unfamiliar.

These changes were experienced by a diverse people. The population included more than 4 million African Americans, as well as several hundred thousand Native Americans from different tribes. It included "old stock" white men and women of northern and western European descent, as well as more than a million Irish immigrants. In the North and West, the diversity was enhanced by "new" immigrants who seemed even more foreign to native eyes. Italians and eastern European Jews came in large numbers to the Eastern Seaboard; Czechs, Slovaks, Poles, and Hungarians arrived in many cities of the Midwest; Chinese and Japanese immigrants became a visible presence in the West.

Multiple languages were heard on city streets from the Atlantic to the Pacific. Catholics and Jews practiced their religion in locales that previously had been almost entirely Protestant. Ethnic neighborhoods, with distinctive cultures, sprouted up in New York, Chicago, Pittsburgh, San Francisco, Portland, and scores of other cities. The society that encountered the new industrialism was far more heterogenous than America had ever been before.

## Integration and Segmentation

Between Reconstruction and 1900, the ties that linked different regions and communities became stronger and more numerous. Free mail delivery came to communities of more than 10,000 people in 1887, and to rural areas in 1896. Trains carried millions of passengers each day, some of them hundreds of miles from home. Thanks to the telegraph, events in Washington were known hours, even minutes, later in Denver and San Francisco. The impact of decisions made by firms in the major cities rippled through the countryside.

At the same time, living patterns, as well as many artifacts of daily life—furniture, clothing, food, tools, machinery—became similar in communities far removed from one another. Standard time zones meant that men and women living hundreds of miles apart reported to work at the same time and attended church at the same hour on Sundays. Shoes manufactured in Lynn, Massachusetts, were worn from coast to coast; people everywhere bought identical watches from Sears, Roebuck; meat packed in Chicago found its way to dinner tables throughout the nation.

The integration of society was furthered by the extraordinary mobility of the population. In urban areas and rural counties, men and women were on the move. In Boston, only

60 percent of the city's residents in 1880 were still living there a decade later, and Boston's population was relatively stable compared with that of other locales. Indeed, men and women were moving in and out of the city at such a dizzying rate that the total number of people who lived in Boston at some point in the 1880s was three times as great as the city's total population at the end of the decade. This mobility was disproportionately concentrated in the working class, as blue-collar workers repeatedly relocated in response to unemployment and in the hope of finding better opportunities. But Americans of all classes were in motion—which meant that cities and towns were always filled with newcomers, many of whom would not remain long.

The flip side of national integration was the erosion of local communities as the center of people's lives. In 1870, most Americans lived in small communities that were the focal point of their social lives and identities. By 1900, those communities had grown larger, more internally divided, less distinctive, and less self-contained. People looked outward—for jobs, investments, consumer goods, even entertainment. The growth of national corporations made clear that power had shifted, that people's fates were no longer shaped primarily by local events. For many individuals, the town or city in which they lived ceased to be central to their aspirations or identities.

While the significance of geographic community declined, the importance of people's occupations rose. Men increasingly identified themselves by the work they performed, forging ties with those in similar pursuits in distant cities and states. Almost all professions formed national associations in the late nineteenth century—to distribute information, maintain standards, and defend professional interests. Workers attached their local labor organizations to national unions of men who belonged to the same trade. The nationalization of social life even extended to recreation. The United States Lawn Tennis Association, which held a national championship, was founded in 1881; the U.S. Golf Association followed suit the following decade; the first All-American college football team was selected in 1889.

This integration of American society was, however, accompanied by fragmentation along racial, ethnic, and class lines. Tensions deepened between dominant social groups—always white and generally Protestant—and "minorities" (who in some places constituted a numerical majority). African Americans, Native Americans, Asian immigrants, eastern and southern European immigrants all found themselves excluded from pursuits that were open to people of a different heritage. Although this was the era in which the Statue of Liberty was erected in New York Harbor, American society was not always eager to incorporate "others" into the mainstream of American life.

### THE JIM CROW SOUTH

The end of Reconstruction left the social standing of African Americans in limbo. Their rights were formally protected by constitutional amendments and by the Civil Rights Act of 1875, which made it illegal for blacks to be denied access to streetcars, trains, restaurants, hotels, and other public facilities. In addition, white southern leaders, hoping to reassure northern Republicans, proclaimed their intention of safeguarding the rights of freedmen. South Carolina governor Wade Hampton promised in 1877 to "secure to every citizen, the lowest as well as the highest, black as well as white, full and equal protection in the enjoyment of all his rights." Still, after the withdrawal of federal troops, blacks were at the mercy of those who had "redeemed" the South—men and women who believed that blacks were an inferior race and that close contact between blacks and whites would "pollute" white civilization. The vast majority of blacks, moreover, were enmeshed in a system of sharecropping and liens that left them economically dependent on white landowners and employers.

In the late 1870s and 1880s, racial lines were etched with increasing sharpness in the South, especially in cities. Al-

An African American classroom in Tuskegee, Alabama, ca. 1902.

though partially a carryover from antebellum practices, the movement toward segregation also reflected white apprehensions about controlling the behavior of free blacks, particularly in urban settings where social interactions were more common. Children went to racially separate schools almost everywhere, separate churches for blacks and whites were the rule, and blacks were compelled to find work in unskilled, poorly paid "black jobs." Although the extent of racial exclusion varied in different parts of the South (in some locales, race relations remained quite open and fluid), separation of the races became widespread in poorhouses, hospitals, courthouses, trains, hotels, theaters, and restaurants. Such segregation was often accomplished not by law but by custom and by individual enterprises, such as railroad corporations, restaurants, and saloons.

Legally mandated segregation, however, began not long after the end of Reconstruction. Antimiscegenation laws were passed everywhere by the early 1880s, reflecting a powerful white fear of sexual comingling. Indeed, the foremost targets of segregation were places where men and women, particularly black men and white women, might come into close contact. Between 1881 and 1891, nine states passed railway segregation laws that required separate cars for blacks and whites; and after 1890, "Jim Crow" legislation became universal and extensive. (Jim Crow was a stock character in minstrel shows, a happy, childlike rural black man.) Prompted in part by black resistance to informal, customary discrimination, municipal and state governments passed laws systematically separating the races. Not just trains, but railroad stations and ticket windows were segregated. So, too, were parks, playgrounds, swimming pools, streetcars, schoolbooks, and the Bibles on which people swore in court. The law formalized the status of African Americans as inferior, second-class citizens.

At the same time, lawlessness and violence against blacks were on the increase: more than a thousand black men were lynched in the 1890s, often by mobs that publicly tortured their victims before killing them. Lynchings, particularly in rural areas, served as instruments of social control and intimidation, commonly supported by white southerners of all classes. Although the incidence of lynching declined after 1900, more than a hundred blacks were lynched every decade through the 1930s.

The reaction of blacks to deepening segregation was mixed. Frequently, there was resistance, both individual and collective. A Richmond minister declared that "the negroes

Booker T. Washington in his office at the Tuskegee Institute, 1900.

must claim the right to sit with the whites in theaters, churches, and other public buildings, to ride with them on cars and to stay at the same hotels with them." African Americans challenged the rules by sitting in train cars and theaters that had become segregated. Streetcars were boycotted in nearly every city. Some blacks even went to court to try to enforce their rights—and occasionally won. Nonetheless, there was no mass opposition to Jim Crow. African Americans believed that segregated facilities were better than none (which often was the alternative). Others feared economic reprisals—or worse—if they protested, particularly after the outbreak of white race riots that occurred in Wilmington, North Carolina, in 1898, in which blacks were beaten and killed and their homes destroyed. Many acquiesced, making the best of a segregated world because there simply seemed to be no choice.

Perhaps the most well-known advocate of acquiescence was Booker T. Washington, the most celebrated black leader of the era. Born a slave in Virginia in 1856, Washington worked his way through school and in 1881 founded the Tuskegee Institute in Alabama, a vocational school for blacks. There he developed the view that for African Americans to progress, they ought to forgo battles for political and social rights and instead concentrate on learning skills, working hard, and acquiring property. In a famous speech to a mixed audience in Atlanta in 1895, he urged blacks to "glorify common labor" and insisted that economic advancement ought to be the primary item on the African American agenda. "Agitation of questions of racial equality," he declared, "is the extremest folly." Social segregation was not necessarily degrading to blacks and ought to be accepted. "In all things that are purely social we can be as separate as the fingers, yet one as the hand in all matters essential to mutual progress."

The Atlanta Compromise, as Washington's approach was called, was well received by whites, who were asked only to act fairly as employers and to lend a helping hand to their poorer fellow citizens. Whites in both North and South lionized Washington, who became a prominent national figure and an adviser to presidents. Many African Americans, however, regarded him as too accommodating, too willing to surrender equal rights. The most strenuous challenge to Washington came from well-educated northern blacks, such as William M. Trotter, editor of the *Boston Guardian,* and W. E. B. Du Bois, an elegant writer and rigorous scholar who was the first black man to earn a Ph.D. from Harvard. Du Bois became the primary spokesman for the Niagara movement, a group of northern blacks committed to the militant pursuit of legal, economic, and political equality. "We claim for ourselves every single right that belongs to a freeborn American, political, civil, and social; and until we get these rights we will never cease to protest and assail the ears of America," declared the Niagara Address in 1906. Du Bois and his colleagues envisioned progress spearheaded by the "Talented Tenth," the most cultivated and well-trained blacks, who could both set an example to whites and agitate to improve the conditions of less advantaged African Americans. In 1909, Du Bois and other members of the Niagara movement founded the National Association for the Advancement of Colored People (NAACP), which emphasized the use of legal strategies to end discrimination.

The implementation of segregation was achieved with the support of the Supreme Court, which, in a series of cases, stripped away the protection blacks seemed to have acquired through constitutional amendments and federal legislation. In 1883, the Court ruled that the Fourteenth Amendment outlawed discriminatory action by states but not by private citizens; at the same time, it declared that the Civil Rights Act had exceeded the authority granted to Congress and was not enforceable. Most important, the Court, in *Plessy v. Ferguson* (1896), embraced the doctrine of "separate but equal," legally sanctioning segregation. In 1892, Homer Plessy had boarded an East Louisiana Railway train and taken a seat in a white car in order to test an 1890 Louisiana law mandating separate cars for blacks and whites. The Court's decision maintained that "the underlying fallacy" of Plessy's complaint consisted "in the assumption that the enforced separation of the two races stamps the colored race with a badge of inferiority. If this be so, it is . . . solely because the colored race chooses to put that construction upon it." For the following half-century, segregation had the imprimatur of the American judiciary.

## REFORMING NATIVE AMERICANS

The federal government launched a new policy toward Native Americans in the late 1860s and early 1870s. Often called the "peace policy" (to distinguish it from the largely military approach taken in earlier decades), this initiative was the handiwork of northeastern reformers who prevailed on the government to emphasize honesty and fairness in dealing with the nation's 300,000 Indians. These reformers did not believe that Native Americans were an inferior race, but they did view Indian civilization as inferior; and they were convinced that in order to become the equal of whites, Indians needed to be civilized into the ways of Christian society. To achieve this end, reformers advocated the placement of all Indians on reservations where they could be instructed in agriculture and other skills; the reformers also convinced the government to transfer responsibility for Indian affairs from political appointees and the army to Protestant church groups.

Ironically, the first decade of the "peace policy" was marked by an upsurge of war, particularly on the Great Plains where Indians resisted the encroachments of white civilization as well as the government's efforts to confine them to reservations. Particularly fierce fighting broke out after an army expedition led by Colonel George Custer declared that it had discovered gold in the Black Hills of South Dakota, the heart of Sioux country. The government insisted that the Black Hills be either ceded or leased to whites; when the Indians refused, troops were sent in to protect the gold miners who were al-

W. E. B. Du Bois, leading spokesman for the Niagara movement and founder of the NAACP.

ready pouring into the region. The war began with several Sioux victories, including one at the Little Big Horn River in 1876 where Custer and all of his troops were killed. Yet the Sioux could not win a war against a large army that pursued them relentlessly, preventing them from acquiring food, supplies, and shelter. By 1877, most of the exhausted Sioux had surrendered. Similar strategies—of winter campaigns and in-

cessant pursuit—led to the defeat of the Cheyennes, Comanches, Kiowas, and Apaches.

In addition to these military campaigns, the Plains Indians were threatened by the destruction of the buffalo. A new tanning process made it possible for buffalo hides to be turned into cheap leather for straps and belts, while the railroads made it much easier to get the hides to market; herds

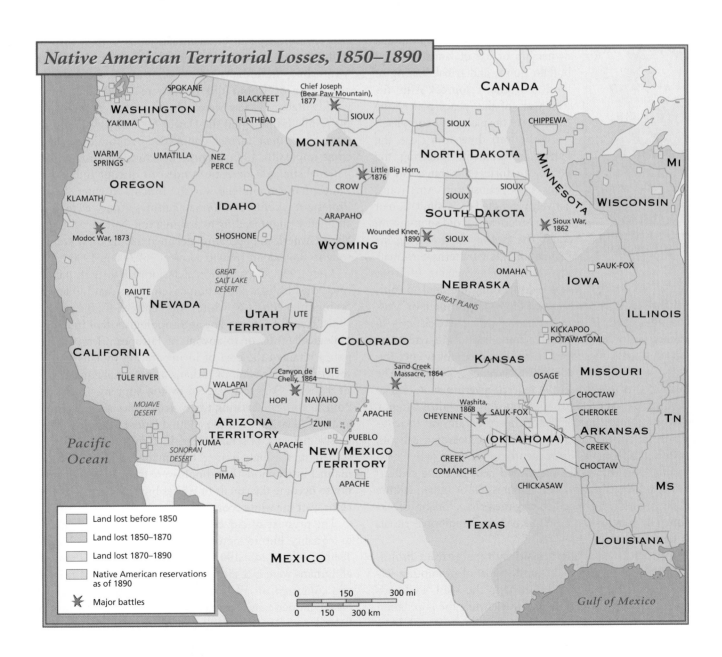

**Native American Territorial Losses, 1850–1890**

Land lost before 1850

Land lost 1850–1870

Land lost 1870–1890

Native American reservations as of 1890

✳ Major battles

### Integration and Segmentation

Sitting Bull, the leader of the Sioux tribe.

of buffalo were also a dangerous nuisance to trains. Responding to this opportunity, white hunters slaughtered millions of buffalo in the 1870s and 1880s; by the middle of the latter decade, the huge herds that had once roamed the plains had vanished. With them vanished the traditional economy of the Plains Indians and a way of life grounded in communal ownership or use of lands, seasonal buffalo hunts, and tribal sharing of food and other resources. After fifteen years of the "peace policy," the conquest of the plains was complete.

As the wars drew to a close, the federal government, reflecting the desire of reformers to transform Indians into mainstream Americans, actively promoted the assimilation of Native Americans. It did so in several ways. The first involved altering Indian landholding patterns, terminating communal ownership of lands and redistributing the land to individual families. The Severalty Act of 1887, sponsored by Massachusetts senator Henry L. Dawes, who had close ties to reformers, permitted Indians to acquire title to 160-acre reservation allotments after they had lived on them for twenty-five years; by so doing, they could also become U.S. citizens. The Dawes Act then permitted the federal government to sell to whites any reservation lands not allotted to individual families. The second element in the assimilation program was the education of Indian children—sometimes at boarding schools, away from their families—in order to imbue them with Christian values and with skills they would need in white civilization. The third element was the suppression of Indian culture and religion, which included cutting men's hair, forcibly breaking up religious ceremonies, and banning traditional rituals and marital practices.

The effort to assimilate Indians into mainstream Protestant society was inseparable from the goal of promoting settlement and economic development in the West. Railroads were crisscrossing the region with track, while the population of the West was skyrocketing, particularly in areas with large Indian reservations. Settlers, promoters, and the railroads all wanted access to Indian lands (which in 1880 still covered an area one and half times the size of California), and they supported assimilation because it seemed likely to serve their interests. As a senator from Kansas observed, "The time for bartering with the Indian for his land is passed. We have come to a time when under the operation of natural laws, we need all the land in this country for homes."

Indeed, settlers and railroad corporations benefited more from the assimilation policy than did Indians. Between 1880 and 1895, nearly half of all Indian lands were opened up to settlement or simply seized and given to the railroads. Meanwhile, the Indians—some of whom resisted the policy and some of whom did not—were caught between two worlds. Relatively few were able to convert themselves into the family farmers that the Dawes Act had envisioned; at the same time, their former communal economic life had become impossible to maintain. The education programs, both paternalistic and idealistic, tended to disrupt Indian society rather than smooth the way for Indians to enter the white, Protestant world. Traditional cultures, thus, were severely strained without leading to assimilation. Not surprisingly, the Native American population declined during these years from roughly 330,000 in 1860 to a low of 237,000 in 1900.

After 1900, the situation deteriorated further, partly because the idealistic conviction of reformers that Indians could become the equals of whites was replaced by the more pessimistic view, buttressed by anthropologists, that Indians were biologically inferior to anyone of European descent. Federal policy retained the goal of incorporating Indians into white society, but the vision of Indians as potential equals receded. As a result, Congress, backed by the Supreme Court, began both to abrogate existing treaty provisions and to control the affairs and lands (even the allotted lands) of Indians. The extensive network of schools remained in place, but their goals shifted: increasingly limited to providing only the most basic manual instruction, the schools were training Indian children not to become the equals of whites but to hold jobs at the periphery of the white economy.

The promise of citizenship for Indians, moreover, led not to equality but to new forms of second-class citizenship. Thanks in part to a 1901 act of Congress, more than half of all Indians were U.S. citizens by 1905, and in 1924 citizenship was conferred on all Native Americans. Yet citizens or not, Native Americans remained under the guardianship of federal agencies that could control their property and their personal affairs. In addition, states with significant Indian populations restricted their right to vote, disfranchising those who were "not taxed" or "not civilized." By the end of the first decades of the twentieth century, the hundreds of thousands of Indians who, a half-century earlier, had possessed their own cultures, governments, and patterns of social organization had been transformed into a minority group living at the margins of American society.

## STRANGERS IN THE LAND

The great waves of immigration that carried 20 million people to the United States in the late nineteenth and early twentieth centuries strained the social fabric and challenged the nation's receptivity to the foreign-born. A large majority of immigrants settled in urban, industrial areas, transforming the social landscape of the nation's cities. By 1910, more than half the population of most major cities consisted of immigrants and their children, which meant that the flavor of life in those cities was very different from what it had been forty years earlier. The reaction of native-born Americans to this influx was mixed. On the one hand, many industrialists believed that economic growth depended on immigrant labor, and most Americans took pride in their country's role as a refuge for those whom Emma Lazarus, in the poem inscribed on the Statute of Liberty, had called the "tired," the "poor," the "huddled masses yearning to breathe free." At the same time, workers increasingly feared immigrants as a threat to their jobs, while members of the middle and upper classes worried about the ways in which "foreigners" were transforming and even taking over "their" society.

The immigrants who faced the most virulent hostility were those who came to the United States from East Asia. Chinese immigrants, overwhelmingly male, began arriving on the West Coast in the 1850s, and by the 1880s the Chinese population peaked at more than 100,000. Most remained in the West, working on the railroads or in mining; later they fanned out into agriculture and light manufacturing and began to operate restaurants and laundries. From the outset, the Chinese encountered fierce antagonism and were periodically the

Shooting Buffalo on the line of the Kansas-Pacific Railroad, 1870s.

objects of mob violence. They were accused of undercutting white labor by working for starvation wages and were routinely described in language depicting them as subhuman—for example, as "groveling worms" or "more slavish and brutish than the beasts that roam the fields."

This hostility mounted in the 1870s, particularly in California, where incidents of violence were frequent and where the Workingmen's Party, led by Denis Kearny, mounted an all-out campaign to expel the Chinese and to end further immigration from China. This campaign bore fruit in 1882 when the federal government enacted legislation that halted Chinese immigration for ten years and declared that the Chinese were "aliens ineligible for citizenship." The suspension of immigration was later extended, leaving the Chinese unable to settle legally in the United States until 1943, when Congress passed a new law admitting roughly 100 Chinese immigrants per year. Numerous western states passed discriminatory laws that banned intermarriage, barred the Chinese from certain occupations, and prevented them from owning or leasing land. Several cities and towns, including Tacoma, Washington, and Truckee, California, expelled their Chinese residents; in San Francisco, popular prejudices made it impossible for the Chinese to find housing outside Chinatown.

An 1877 Edward Keller cartoon, "The First Blow at the Chinese Question," which depicts the tensions between recently-arrived Chinese immigrants and the mostly Irish members of the 'Workingmen's Party' in San Francisco.

After the 1880s, anti-Chinese fervor subsided, but it was succeeded by hostility aimed at Japanese immigrants who began arriving around the turn of the century. Fears of this new "Yellow Peril" mounted rapidly in the West, leading again to violence and to the passage of overtly discriminatory laws. In the Southwest, similar treatment was meted out to Mexican migrants, particularly those who were poor and had darker skins. Although never denied the right to become citizens, they were commonly limited to menial jobs, refused entry to public facilities, and compelled to attend segregated schools.

Discrimination against immigrants was not limited to the West or to men and women from Asia and Mexico. European immigrants—especially those from southern and eastern Europe and from Ireland—also inspired antagonism in many old-stock Americans. This nativism had several strands, all of which grew stronger under the pressure of rapid economic and social change. One strand, with roots in the antebellum era, was a middle-class anxiety that the immigrant population was rife with union organizers and dangerous radicals

who would destroy the American way of life. In the wake of the Haymarket affair in Chicago in 1886 (see Chapter 20), a notorious incident in which several policemen were killed by a bomb thrown at a meeting called by anarchists, one newspaper declared that the anarchists were "not Americans, but the very scum and offal of Europe." A second long-standing strand of nativism was aimed at Catholics, who were portrayed as adherents of superstition and despotism, breeders of corruption in municipal politics, and foot soldiers in a plot to undermine Protestant society. Secret anti-Catholic societies flourished in the 1880s and 1890s, particularly in the Midwest; the most prominent, the American Protective Association (APA), founded in Iowa in 1887, attracted hundreds of thousands of members and elected supporters to public office. Everyone who joined the APA was required to take an oath promising never to vote for a Catholic, never to hire a Catholic if a Protestant was available, and never to go on strike with Catholics.

Many old-stock Americans also came to believe that their own (superior) Anglo-Saxon "race" risked being debased or overwhelmed by the arrival of large numbers of non–Anglo Saxon immigrants. Such ideas were articulated, and given respectability, by prominent Protestant clergymen as well as by upper-class Bostonians such as Senator Henry Cabot Lodge. Pressing the distinction between "old" immigrants (from northern and western Europe) and "new" immigrants (from southern and eastern Europe), men like Lodge argued that the latter were inferior human specimens who could not be assimilated into American society.

Apprehensions about the "new" immigrants were heightened by social scientists who suggested that old-stock Americans were committing "race suicide" because their birthrates were far lower than those of eastern and southern Europeans. This racial strain of nativism was given further impetus after the turn of the century by eugenics, a collection of quasi-scientific ideas claiming that the human race could be uplifted by encouraging the breeding of the "best" while restricting the reproduction of the "worst." From the viewpoint of eugenics, the immigration of "degenerate breeding stock" was a threat to the well-being of the nation. Not only would genetic inferiors multiply, but interbreeding would debase the superior genetic stock. "The cross between any of the three European races and a Jew," wrote Madison Grant, one of the foremost advocates of racial purity, "is a Jew."

Many nativists sought federal legislation to restrict immigration. They were joined, particularly after the depression of the 1890s, by a growing number of trade unionists who feared that unrestricted immigration was creating unemployment and depressing wages. "We sympathize with the oppressed of the Old World," noted one union leader, but "[we are] an asylum whose dormitories are full." Despite such concerns, there were few modifications of the laws regulating non-Asian immigration before World War I. Some states, however, did pass laws that overtly discriminated against immigrants: in New York and Pennsylvania, for example, aliens (noncitizens) were barred from all employment on public works. Idaho even passed a law prohibiting private corporations from hiring aliens who had not yet declared their intention to become citizens.

But legal discrimination was the least of it. Throughout the nation, "new" immigrants were exposed to condescension, hostility, and sometimes violence. Anti-Semitic demonstrations and riots broke out periodically in the North and the South. Italians, stereotyped as violent and lawless, were occasionally assaulted and even lynched: in New Orleans in 1891, eleven Italian men, after being acquitted of murder, were lynched by a mob, to the approval of local newspapers. More routinely, "undesirable" immigrants were kept out of desirable occupations, denied entry to social events, compelled to live in their own neighborhoods, blamed for urban social problems. The "melting pot" was barely simmering.

## Life on the Farm

For the tens of millions of Americans who lived on farms, life changed, though not drastically, in the late nineteenth century. Railroads, refrigerator cars, and urban growth opened up new markets for almost all agricultural products. Nearly everywhere outside the South, technological innovations reduced the drudgery of farm work while increasing the productivity of farm labor. In the grain-growing regions of the Midwest, California, and the Great Plains, new plows, seed drills, threshing machines, harvesters, and combines permitted farmers to grow more with less backbreaking, repetitive toil (see Chapter 18). On dairy farms from New England to Minnesota, the centrifugal cream separator and cream tester made it easier for small farmers to sell their wares profitably to local creameries and butter factories. Progressive farmers were able to avoid waste and increase production by applying new scientific knowledge about breeding, care of the soil, and conservation.

Equally important, men and women who lived on farms began to have more contact with the urban world. Faster trains, running all night, brought mail to the hinterland in a matter of days; they also brought big-city newspapers crammed with photographs, tales of urban life, and pages of advertisements. By the 1890s, Chicago newspapers were available in small Illinois towns at seven A.M., not much later than when they hit the streets in the metropolis itself.

The most vivid, and perhaps influential, tissue connecting urban and rural societies consisted of the mail-order catalogs of retailers Montgomery Ward and Sears, Roebuck. "The Montgomery Ward catalog," declared a farm woman in Nebraska, "was a real link between us and civilization." Ward's catalog, only eight pages long when the business was launched, mushroomed to 540 pages, offering 24,000 items, by the 1880s; at the turn of the century, it was 1,200 pages, with 17,000 illustrations. The catalog offered farm families virtually every kind of product made in the United States: from gasoline stoves, bicycles, and batteries to dresses, underwear, and carriages, to toys, carpets, artworks, and pianos. By 1900, Ward, based in Chicago, was receiving more than 15,000 letters a day, some

A vision of plenty on the cover of the Sears, Roebuck catalog, 1899.

A pioneer family alongside their sod house near Coburg, Nebraska, 1887.

shucking the corn and hauling it off in wagons to the barn. The Gebbys rushed to complete the harvesting so that they could then plant their winter wheat crop as early in the fall as possible; harvesting the wheat was even more frenetic, since the entire crop had to be harvested within a two-week period.

In the 1880s and 1890s, the Gebbys purchased new farm machinery, but the seasonal pace of their efforts did not change. Within the farmhouse, too, seasonal rhythms predominated. The wood-burning stove was moved to the washhouse (where clothes were washed) each May and back into the house in early November. Handwoven rag carpets were put down each winter, cleaned and beaten each spring, and replaced by summer matting. Produce from the garden and the orchards was preserved late each summer and in the fall; windows were cleaned and washed every spring and fall, when the screens were put on and taken off.

Almost all the commercial operations of the farm were the domain of men. Jeremiah, his sons, and a hired hand plowed, planted, and harvested; they were also responsible for daily chores such as caring for the cattle and hogs and maintaining fences, tools, and machines. In addition, Jeremiah controlled the farm's finances: he decided when to sell the wheat crop and what livestock to buy; each year he also journeyed to Chicago, Cleveland, or Buffalo to sell cattle. Margaret, meanwhile, had full responsibility for child rearing and for maintaining the household: she did all the cooking and cleaning, baked bread, and preserved produce for the family's consumption. She made butter and collected eggs, some of which she sold at a local store (using the proceeds to buy spices, coffee, and tea), and she made most of her own clothes. (The men wore ready-made clothing.) Since the family was prosperous, she paid a neighbor to help with laundry, and by the 1890s some of her labors were lightened by the installation of indoor plumbing.

The Gebbys were settled and secure enough to enjoy a rich social life. They attended the Bellefontaine United Church each week and they belonged to a threshing ring, through which families took turns helping one another and socializ-

from towns as remote as Bywy, Mississippi. Farm families customarily sent their payments with their orders or paid at a local freight desk once their orders were received.

Thanks to the catalogs, farmers were able to acquire goods that had been rare or unknown in rural America: ready-made clothing, Aunt Jemima's Pancake Flour, hams, foodstuffs made by Heinz and Pillsbury, furniture, musical instruments, tools, and barbed wire so that they no longer had to build fences from hand-wrought rails. By giving farm families a glimpse of an urban style of living, the catalogs altered the tastes and reshaped the desires of many rural Americans.

Nonetheless, many aspects of farm life changed little. The rhythms of work and leisure continued to be molded by the seasons, by local climates, by the demands of individual crops. Similarly, the division of labor within farm households was shaped, as it long had been, by gender.

Margaret Dow Gebby and her husband, Jeremiah, for example, were relatively prosperous farmers in Bellefontaine, Ohio. They owned a 286-acre farm, raising corn and wheat and selling cattle to stockyards in Chicago and Buffalo. Each April, the Gebbys, with their sons and often a hired hand, worked feverishly to get corn planted, sometimes repeating their labors if the weather turned cold or wet and ruined the first planting. In September came the backbreaking work of harvesting corn: men walked the rows, slashing the stalks with one hand and gathering them up in the other, then

## Table 19.1

### Urban Population 1870–1910

| Number of Cities with Populations of: | 1870 | 1880 | 1890 | 1900 | 1910 |
|---|---|---|---|---|---|
| 25,000–100,000 | 38 | 57 | 97 | 123 | 179 |
| 100,000–250,000 | 8 | 13 | 17 | 23 | 31 |
| 250,000–500,000 | 6 | 4 | 7 | 9 | 11 |
| 500,000–1,000,000 | 2 | 3 | 1 | 3 | 5 |
| Over 1,000,000 | 0 | 1 | 3 | 3 | 3 |
| Total U.S. Population | 38,558,371 | 50,189,209 | 62,979,766 | 76,212,168 | 92,228,496 |

ing. Margaret could also draw on a kinship network of sisters, cousins, aunts, and nieces for assistance with dressmaking and sewing. Except in the busiest of seasons, the Gebbys visited frequently with family, friends, and neighbors. Margaret belonged to the local literary society, as well as the Women's Missionary Service, and the entire extended family usually gathered for a week in October to attend the county fair.

Although key contours of farm life were similar throughout the nation, these patterns were often bent by local conditions. The harsh environment of the Great Plains, for example—the cold, the wind, the capricious rainfall, the lack of wood for fuel or construction—made life far less comfortable than it was for the Gebbys in Ohio. Houses made of sod were easily penetrated by dirt, insects, and snakes; and harvest seasons were extremely short, compelling women and young children to work in the fields. The transience of the plains population—as waves of settlers poured in, stayed a few years, and then fled—made it difficult to replicate the social networks and institutions of the rural world farther east. Women, whose work did not require them to go to town, complained of the isolation, the lack of contact with friends. Luna Kellie, later an activist in the Populist Party, did not get to town at all in the first eighteen months she lived in Nebraska.

In the South, the poverty of the rural population, as well as its overdependence on a single cash crop, forced many women to work in the fields in addition to performing their regular tasks. "The women down this way," observed one sharecropper's wife, "got to the field 'bout as reg'lar as the men. Cotton will be openin' now in four weeks, and that'll be the last of the house except for cookin' and washin' and ironin' till its all picked." Kinship networks were highly developed in the rural South: even in the 1970s, the elderly Nate Shaw, who had been a sharecropper in Alabama, could recall the names and precise relationships of scores of family members from the turn of the century. But the combination of poverty, illiteracy, and poor roads severely limited the geographic and social horizons of most farmers.

Careful estimates suggest that between 1870 and 1900, more than 7 million people moved from rural to urban America, a migration comparable in scale to the movement west in the 1870s and 1880s. This migration had several sources: farm families had high fertility rates, which made it difficult for farmers to leave land to all their children; technological innovations lessened the demand for farm labor, while the cost of technology made it expensive for young people to start farms; and in the Northeast, farmers had trouble making a living in the face of competition from more fertile, larger farms farther west. Everywhere, moreover, men and women simply grew tired of the isolation and drudgery of life on a farm.

In addition to these "push" factors, there was a "pull" from the cities. Wages were higher in urban areas, jobs seemed more abundant, and there were opportunities for advancement into white-collar, managerial, or professional positions. In addition, the cities seemed more glamorous and exciting. There were amusements, stores overflowing with merchandise, thousands of strangers walking through the streets. As a character in a popular play declared, "Who wants to smell new-mown hay, if he can breathe gasoline on Fifth Avenue?"

During the 1880s, 40 percent of the nation's rural townships lost population; in parts of Ohio, Illinois, and New England, the

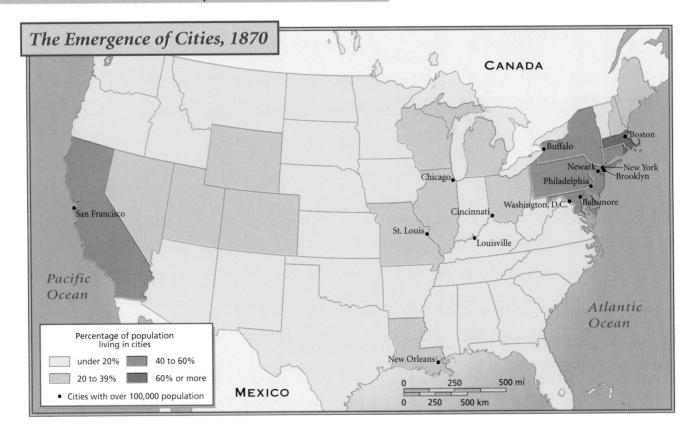

**The Emergence of Cities, 1870**

Percentage of population living in cities

- under 20%
- 20 to 39%
- 40 to 60%
- 60% or more
- Cities with over 100,000 population

figure was as high as 60 percent. Thousands of farms were simply abandoned in the Northeast. For the first time in the nation's history, there was a mass movement away from farming.

## The Rise of the City

### AN URBAN SOCIETY

No aspect of late nineteenth-century life was more important, or more dramatic, than the explosive growth of cities. In 1870, only New York and Philadelphia had populations greater than 500,000; by 1910, eight cities did, and three of these contained more than a million people. Smaller cities, too, multiplied in number. By 1910, 35 million people, or 39 percent of the population, lived in communities with more than 8,000 persons; in 1870, the figure had been 8 million. The growth of cities was fueled both by migrants from the countryside and by immigrants from Europe, Latin America, and Asia: in 1910, in all major cities north of Baltimore, most

of the population consisted of immigrants and their children.

The cities were of two types: metropolises and "specialist" cities. Most metropolises had sizable populations as early as 1870, and they were first and foremost commercial centers. Often situated where long-distance water transportation routes met railroad junctures, these were places where a region's products were brought for processing and shipping and where goods from outside the region arrived to be broken down and redistributed within the region. They were banking and financial hubs that, between 1870 and 1900, also became great manufacturing centers: New York, Chicago, and Philadelphia constituted the largest manufacturing clusters in the nation.

The smaller, specialist cities were themselves of two types. One provided financial and commercial services to the surrounding rural areas, while also processing and shipping local specialty goods that originated in the countryside. Richmond, for example, handled cigarettes, while Sacramento dealt in canned fruits and vegetables. In the Northeast and the Midwest, a second type of specialty city flourished: the mill city or manufacturing city. Fall River and New Bedford, Massachu-

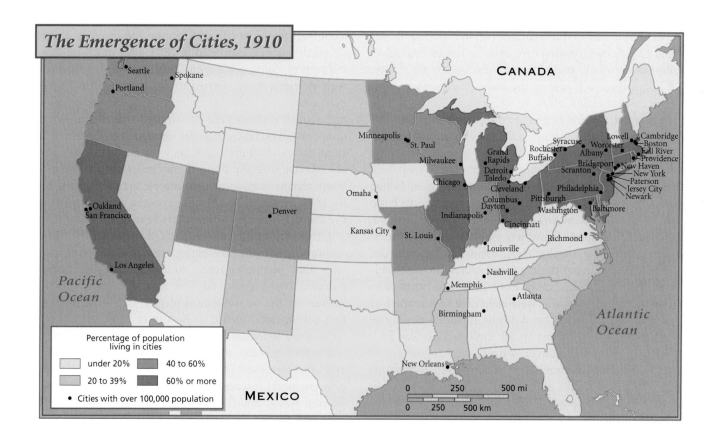

**The Emergence of Cities, 1910**

Percentage of population living in cities

under 20%
20 to 39%
40 to 60%
60% or more

• Cities with over 100,000 population

setts, made textiles; Lynn and Brockton, Massachusetts, made shoes; Dayton, Ohio, produced machine tools and cash registers; Columbus, Ohio, produced railroad cars. Taken together, these specialized cities formed two major manufacturing belts: one stretching along the Atlantic coast from Maine to Virginia, and the other extending from Buffalo west to St. Louis and Milwaukee. When linked to the larger, metropolitan centers by the railroads and the telegraph, these cities constituted a national urban market as well as a national urban society.

### EXPANDING URBAN SPACE

The dramatic growth of urban populations gave rise to both an expansion and a reconfiguration of urban space. The mid-nineteenth-century city was compact; its boundaries were set by the need of almost everyone to walk to work. The doubling or tripling of cities' populations placed irresistible pressures on those boundaries.

The expanding physical space of cities demanded new modes of transportation. Omnibuses (horse-drawn streetcars on wheels) had appeared in many places by mid-century, opening new areas to settlement, but they were slow, uncomfortable, and too expensive for anyone outside of the middle and upper classes. Similarly, commuter railroads permitted the wealthy to live in suburbs miles out of town, but they did not serve the majority of the population. Between 1850 and 1890, the most common form of public transportation became the horse-drawn streetcar on rails, an innovation made possible through a new technique of laying tracks flush on the pavement. These streetcars were larger, faster, and cheaper than omnibuses, and running on rails permitted them to have more predictable schedules. By 1887, 400 streetcar companies, in 300 communities, were conveying 175 million passengers a year.

Yet horse-drawn streetcars were dirty, crowded, and uncomfortable. "You can ride in a horse-car," wrote Mark Twain, "and stand-up for three-quarters of an hour, in the midst of a file of men that extends from front to rear . . . or you can take one of the platforms, if you please, but they are so crowded you will have to hang on by your eye-lashes and your toenails." Many riders were appalled at the spectacle of overworked horses straining to pull overcrowded cars, and the horses themselves contributed to urban pollution and disease. In the 1880s, 15,000 horses died each year on the streets of New York alone, with their carcasses often left to rot where they fell. The average droppings of a dray horse amounted to ten pounds a day.

Entrepreneurs and inventors came up with several alternatives to the horse-drawn streetcar. One was the elevated train, driven by steam power and run on tracks mounted on pillars. Elevated lines were constructed in several cities, including New York and Chicago, but they proved expensive to build and they were noisy, causing vibrations for blocks around, and they often dumped oil and hot ashes on unlucky pedestrians walking below. Another experiment was the cable car, pulled by a steam-driven underground cable. The first cable car line was built in San Francisco in 1873, and other cities gave them a try, but they also were expensive to construct, as well as prone to mechanical breakdowns. In addition, since all cars had to move at the same speed, there was no way for a cable car to ever "make up" any lost time.

The decisive breakthrough in transportation technology arose from the successful application of electricity to street railways. This became possible through a series of inventions in Europe and in the United States. In 1887, Frank Julian Sprague, who had once worked for Thomas Edison, accepted

A horse-drawn streetcar moves along rails on 23rd Street in New York City.

a contract from the city of Richmond to build an electrified streetcar system. Completed in 1888, after much on-the-spot innovation, Sprague's system used a central power source, with electric current carried to the streetcars through overhead cables. The cables were linked to the cars through wires and a small carriage called a "troller"—all such electric cars thus came to be called "trolleys." Sprague's trolleys were an instant success. Pollution-free, they traveled on tracks at variable speeds, reaching up to twenty miles per hour; they were faster, cheaper, and more comfortable than horse-drawn cars. By 1895, more than 800 trolley systems were in operation in the country, and horse-drawn cars were rapidly phased out.

Other innovations also facilitated the expansion of cities. Subways were made possible by newly designed electrical systems that permitted trains to run underground. (Steam-powered trains could not run any distance underground because of the accumulation of gas, smoke, and dirt.) The first subway was opened in Boston in 1897, with New York following a few years later. Equally important were improved techniques of bridge building, a critical endeavor in the many cities that were near rivers or harbors. In the 1870s, construction engineers learned to sink stable piers in deep, swiftly-flowing water, and 1883 witnessed the completion of the Brooklyn Bridge (linking Manhattan to Brooklyn), a strikingly beautiful, mile-long creation that became a symbol of American engineering prowess. Built by John Roebling and his son, Washington, the Brooklyn Bridge was the longest suspension bridge in the world, sturdy enough to carry two railroad lines, two double carriage lanes, and a footpath.

The enlargement of city space was aided by the widespread adoption of a new method of home construction: the "balloon frame" house, so called because its light, external frame replaced the heavy timber supporting walls that had dominated residential building for centuries. With machine-produced nails rather than complex joints, and with thin pieces of lumber set so that the stresses were spread throughout the structure, the balloon-frame house could be built inexpensively and rapidly. The result, in the 1870s and later, was the transformation of home building from a specialized craft into a large industry that saw hundreds of thousands of private residences erected in new neighborhoods opened by the streetcars.

The combination of streetcar systems and new modes of construction spawned the development of residential suburbs. On the outskirts of Boston, for example, the three suburbs of Roxbury, West Roxbury, and Dorchester swelled in population from 60,000 to 227,000 between 1870 and 1900. Outside Milwaukee, the village of Hart's Mill was transformed into the thriving suburb of Wauwatosa; near Norfolk, Virginia, a real estate company, relying on the streetcars, purchased a large tract of farmland and turned it into the exclusive suburb of Ghent. Nearly all residents of these suburbs were drawn from the middle and upper classes; they were seeking more living space, more community homogeneity, and an escape from the noise, pollution, and "foreignness" of the cities. Yet the suburbs themselves were also differentiated by class: the wealthy usually resided in areas farthest from the city, while middle-class citizens lived in more modest suburbs.

By 1900, the social geography of cities had been transformed. Whereas in 1850, in which residences and workplaces had been interspersed in a compact physical space, cities now had given way to large metropolises with functionally differentiated neighborhoods. City centers were occupied by office buildings, financial institutions, large retail stores, and cultural attractions; they were almost devoid of residences. Not far away were grimy factory districts, often adjacent to tenements inhabited by the working poor: recent immigrants, the unskilled, men and women who were unable to afford streetcar fares and compelled to live in the least desirable and most congested housing. Beyond this inner ring were more middle-class residential neighborhoods of apartments or single-family houses, and still farther out were suburbs. The new transportation networks tied different parts of the city together, permitting people to engage in activities in all parts of the city; yet at the same time, they encouraged the segregation of urban space by function and class. In 1890, journalist Jacob Riis published *How the Other Half Lives,* a classic description of life in New York's poor neighborhoods. What was notable about Riis's book was not only its content but the fact that it had to be written at all—that affluent New Yorkers had to turn to a book to find out how their fellow residents were living.

### THE IMMIGRANT CITY

The vast majority of immigrants lived in cities, and immigrants from the same country tended to cluster in particular residential areas. These immigrant neighborhoods had population densities two or three times the city average, with families and boarders crowded into tiny, dimly lit apartments. In Chicago's Packingtown district, near the stockyards, an average of twenty-eight people lived in the four small apartments that were typically carved out of a dilapidated two-story frame house. In New York, miserable, unsanitary conditions gave rise to an 1879 law requiring that all new tenements (the word originally referred to any multistory rental building housing more than three families) had to have a window in each room. The result was the "dumbbell" tenement, a design that spread rapidly throughout the country. The walls of dumbbell tenements had indentations on each side to permit the requisite number of windows; unfortunately, since the tenements were tightly packed against one another, most windows looked out onto noisy, dank air shafts that provided little light or ventilation.

Immigrant apartments typically housed two or three people per room: a married couple and their children, and often one or more boarders. Men commonly held blue-collar jobs, working unsteadily at low wages. Women contributed to the household economy by performing industrial piecework (such as finishing pants) in the home or, more often, by taking in boarders, usually single men. Children, too, were expected to contribute to the family income, either by working at home at jobs such as linking chains or by doing odd jobs in the streets.

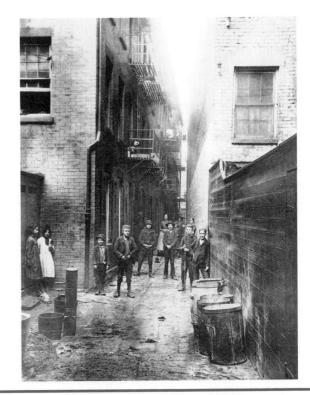

Street life in an immigrant neighborhood, 1888–89, as seen in a photograph by Jacob Riis.

Although life in these immigrant neighborhoods has sometimes been depicted with a romantic cast—colorful streets packed with pedestrians speaking a host of different languages, close-knit families struggling to get ahead, preserving parts of the Old World while learning the ropes in the New—hardships were commonplace. Living conditions offered few comforts and little privacy, and immigrants from southern Europe often found the cold intolerable. Diseases such as tuberculosis, bronchitis, and diphtheria were endemic, with death rates generally two or three times higher than they were in wealthier sections of the city. Work was unsteady, and food sometimes scarce.

Children, with no alternative places to play, risked accidents in the streets or on roofs.

Nonetheless, immigrants, most from peasant backgrounds, retained the hope that their lives and those of their children would improve, and they did their utmost to create communities in unfamiliar urban settings. They founded fraternal organizations, burial societies, cemeteries, ethnic clubs, and mutual aid societies; they also organized festivals, sporting events, and outings to parks and the beach. Everywhere they built churches and synagogues that became centers of community life. Catholics also built their own parochial schools.

*American Journal*

## What's for Dinner?

*When he was twenty-four, Jacob Riis, who had emigrated to the United States from Denmark three years earlier, became a police reporter in New York City. He was assigned to the Lower East Side, where he observed the hardships of tenement life. His book documenting these hardships,* How the Other Half Lives *(published in 1890), complete with photographs Riis had taken, outraged enough influential New Yorkers that legislation curbing tenement-house evils was soon passed. Following is a glimpse into the daily life of a Czech immigrant cigar maker and his large family. He was suffering from consumption (as a result of breathing in tobacco fumes) and no longer able to work.*

"In a house around the corner that is not a factory-tenement, lives now the cigarmaker I spoke of as suffering from consumption which the doctor said was due to the tobacco-fumes. Perhaps the lack of healthy exercise had as much to do with it. . . . Six children sit at his table. By trade a shoemaker, for thirteen years he helped his wife make cigars in the manufacturer's tenement. She was a very good hand, and until his health gave out two years ago they were able to make from $17 to $25 a week, by lengthening the day at both ends. Now that he can work no more, and the family under the doctor's orders has moved away from the smell of tobacco, the burden of its support has fallen upon her alone, for none of the children is old enough to help. She has work in the shop at eight dollars a week, and this must go round; it is all there is. Happily, this being a tenement for revenue only, unmixed with cigars, the rent is cheaper: seven dollars for two bright rooms on the top floor. No housekeeping is attempted. A woman in Seventy-second Street supplies their meals, which the wife and mother fetches in a basket, her husband being too weak. Breakfast of coffee and hard-tack, or black bread, at twenty cents for the whole eight; a good many, the little woman says with a brave, patient smile, and there is seldom anything to spare, but . . . The invalid is listening, and the sentence remains unfinished. What of dinner? One of the children brings it from the cook. Oh! it is a good dinner, meat, soup, greens and bread, all for thirty cents. It is the principal family meal. Does she come home for dinner? No; she cannot leave the shop, but gets a bite at her bench. The question: A bite of what? seems as merciless as the surgeon's knife, and she winces under it as one shrinks from physical pain. Bread, then. But at night they all have supper together—sausage and bread. For ten cents they can eat all they want."

Jacob Riis, *How the Other Half Lives: Studies Among the Tenements of New York*

Even more numerous than churches were saloons, which were centers of economic and social life for working-class men. Offering men free hot meals when they bought a beer or two, saloons were where immigrant men ate their lunches and relaxed in the evenings. The saloon keeper cashed checks, received mail, kept track of job opportunities, and gave people credit during hard times. The saloons hosted weddings and dances and served as meeting places for fraternal groups and labor unions. One survey of ten residential blocks in Chicago found an average of three saloons per block. Along "Whiskey Row," the streets that stretched from Packingtown to the factories, there were on average twenty-six saloons per block.

For women, patterns of sociability were markedly different. Traditional customs, as well as language barriers and the demands of running households, tended to confine women to their neighborhoods and often to their buildings. Yet in those buildings and neighborhoods, women developed important social ties. They taught newcomers where to shop, how to wash clothes, what kinds of kitchen utensils to buy. A resident of the Lower East Side in New York recalled that "if someone got sick, the neighbor took care of them. My mother went for an operation and the neighbor took the younger children. They would shop and cook. Neighbors gathered in the halls, brought out their chairs, and chatted."

With their parents occupied for long hours, children who were not working roamed the streets by themselves, sometimes getting into trouble. Others attended public schools where they learned English and absorbed the values of urban America; their numbers rose substantially by the end of the century owing to state laws requiring school attendance. Whether they attended school or not, the children of immigrants commonly found themselves torn between the traditions of their families and a new alluring society. Children quickly learned to speak English better than their parents, and they sought an independence that conflicted with parental expectations of obedience and family service. The tension between native-born children and foreign-born parents was an almost universal, if private, dimension of the immigrant experience.

## THE CITY OF LIGHTS

Not far from the congested immigrant quarters were altogether different urban environments—dazzling, new, vital, prosperous. Almost all major cities acquired new or rebuilt downtowns that served as centers of commerce, both local and national. One distinctive feature of these downtowns was tall buildings, in some cities tall enough to be called skyscrapers. Such buildings were made possible by Elisha Otis's invention of the elevator in the 1850s; by the 1880s, with the application of electric power, elevators became commonplace. At about the same time, a group of architects in Chicago developed a technique of using steel skeletons rather than thick, space-consuming supporting walls as building frames, permitting the construction of taller buildings. The perfection of plate glass allowed the new skyscrapers to have large windows, leading some buildings in New York and Chicago to be described as "towers of glass."

These skyscrapers were inhabited by large corporations, including the new headquarters of manufacturing firms that, thanks to the telephone, were able to separate their commercial and manufacturing operations. The internal organization of these buildings was itself innovative and hierarchical: different tasks were performed on different floors, with higher levels of management generally segregated from clerks, secretaries, and other white-collar employees. Hundreds, sometimes thousands, of people entered these buildings daily.

The other defining institution of the new downtown was the department store. First appearing in the 1870s, department stores could be found in hundreds of American cities by 1900, and some of them blossomed into urban palaces of consumption. Marshall Field's in Chicago was a small city in itself, selling enormously varied goods, employing as many as 90,000 workers, and equipped with fifty-three elevators, a medical dispensary, a post office, and the largest private telephone switchboard in the world. As distinctive as their size was the emphasis on luxury and the celebration of material abundance. This was achieved, in part, through the use of new technologies of glass, light, and color. Glass doors, shelves, and counters filled the interior spaces, while mirrors enhanced the illusion of endless space. Electric lights and prismatic light, which focused daylight into the stores, created the appearance of "refined Coney Islands," while the merchandise itself sported new colors, manufactured from chemical dyes, dazzling the eyes of shoppers. Some stores enhanced the theatricality by hosting plays and concerts; almost all built large, flood-lit display windows to give pedestrians an enticing glimpse of their wares. Department stores like Marshall Field's, Macy's, and Bloomingdale's in New York and Filene's in Boston were the vibrant nodes of an emerging culture of consumption that would endure throughout the twentieth century.

Crowds enjoy the Christmas windows of Macy's department store in New York City, 1884.

The prosperous, bustling metropolitan centers were undergirded and made more attractive by improvements in their physical infrastructure. Electric street lighting provided much brighter light than gas and kerosene lamps. Electric lighting also permitted businesses to work longer hours and entertainments, such as amusement parks, to remain open at night. In the 1890s, entrepreneur Samuel Insull developed two technologies that made possible the electrification of entire cities. One converted alternating current into direct current (and vice versa), which allowed electricity to be conveyed throughout a city at a reasonable cost. The second was a demand meter that measured not only a customer's energy consumption but also the timing and size of the customer's peak demand. Insull was thus able to apportion costs equitably while offering lower rates to those who used more kilowatts or who used them at off-peak hours. The result, early in the twentieth century, was the electrification of nearly all commercial buildings and a growing number of residences.

Between 1870 and 1900, most American cities also paved their streets. (Downtown streets were generally paved first, while politicians often jockeyed to get streets paved in their own neighborhoods.) Asphalt became the pavement of choice because it was inexpensive, quiet, durable, and clean; smooth asphalt streets made vehicular traffic more comfortable, while improving conditions for pedestrians, particularly in the rain. Underneath the streets, and on the outskirts of

large cities, even more prodigious engineering feats were under way: the construction of thousands of miles of water and sewer lines. To provide water to the skyrocketing population of New York, for example, a thirty-mile-long aqueduct was built; completed in 1893, it carried 300 million gallons of water to the city daily. Water was distributed over 660 miles of water lines and removed through 464 miles of sewers. Water systems such as these made the flush toilet and the bathtub standard equipment in the middle-class home; even many poor city residents could enjoy bathroom facilities familiar only to the elite in the nations of Europe.

## PUBLIC HEALTH AND THE CITY OF DISEASE

The new water and sewer systems were prompted in part by health concerns. Death rates rose from the early nineteenth century through the end of the Civil War, and they were particularly high for infants and young children. Many deaths resulted from infectious diseases that attacked densely populated cities: in addition to periodic epidemics of cholera, smallpox, and yellow fever, nineteenth-century Americans were vulnerable to pneumonia, influenza, whooping cough, scarlet fever, typhoid fever, dysentery, and—the biggest killer of all—tuberculosis. The medical profession at mid-century could do little to cure any of these diseases and accordingly was not held in very high repute; one prominent Boston physician even claimed that "more die of the practitioner than of the natural course of the disease."

In the first few decades after the Civil War, some progress was made by physicians, engineers, and others who constituted an emerging public health movement. Almost all of these men and women were "anticontagionists," or environmentalists, who were convinced that filth was the primary cause of disease and that the best way to improve health was to clean up the cities. With municipal officials, they worked to remove garbage, clear horse droppings from the streets, empty privies, inspect foods, and install water systems that would keep urban residents from having to drink water from contaminated wells and polluted rivers. They also promoted the construction of sewers and, somewhat later, tried to prevent sewage from being dumped in the rivers and lakes that supplied drinking water.

Perhaps the most influential anticontagionist was Colonel George E. Waring Jr., a Civil War veteran, agricultural and drainage engineer, and well-known scientific farmer. In the late 1860s and 1870s, Waring became interested in sanitary engineering and embraced the theory that most communicable diseases were caused by "sewer gas," which could originate in "the exhalations of decomposing matters in dung-heaps, pig-sties, privy vaults, cellars, cesspools, drains and sewers" and was often noticeable in the odors that arose from defective "water closets" (as early flush toilets were called). A prolific popularizer, Waring wrote numerous articles urging the universal adoption of the water closet, installed with proper plumbing to prevent sewer gas from leaking into homes. He also promoted the construction of new sewer systems, a cause that was given a dramatic boost in 1878 by a yellow fever epidemic in Memphis that killed 5,000 people and infected thousands more. Appointed by President Hayes to a special commission, Waring argued that the epidemic could be traced to the city's filth, and he convinced the National Board of Health to build a new sewage system for Memphis, a development that gave a strong impetus to sewer construction everywhere. In the 1890s, he was appointed commissioner of street cleaning for New York City, where he launched an aggressive campaign that transformed New York's streets from among the dirtiest to among the cleanest in the world.

Meanwhile, scientific discoveries in Europe were giving rise to new theories of disease, grounded in the notion that specific diseases were caused and transmitted by specific germs or bacteria. In the 1880s, the research of Louis Pasteur in France, as well as German discoveries of the bacteria that caused diphtheria and tuberculosis (the cause of roughly one out of every eight American deaths), constituted a serious challenge to the anticontagionists and launched a new era of scientific medicine, introduced to the United States in part by physicians who had studied in Europe. The bacteriological revolution did not immediately gain acceptance, but it spawned new laboratories designed to test the European theories and, if possible, to discover disease-causing organisms. By the early twentieth century, anticontagionist ideas were largely discredited: it was found that some forms of filth did contribute to the spread of disease, but the diseases themselves came not from vapors or sewer gas but from bacteria that could be identified, used diagnostically, and studied to develop both cures and methods of prevention.

This new, more scientific medicine did not immediately generate effective therapies, but it did have a significant impact on the practice of medicine and on popular conceptions of disease. Research scientists and physicians, few in number in the 1870s, became the elite of the profession while, cities created diagnostic laboratories to help physicians identify dis-

eases and limit contagion. Armed with new tools, the medical profession grew and gained credibility; and owing to new, strict sterilization procedures, hospitals became safer places for sick people. The number of hospitals in the nation grew from 178 in 1873 to more than 4,000 by 1909. In addition, the acceptance of bacteriological theories led the middle class to embrace public health measures; if diseases were caused by germs that could be carried by air, water, or insects, then the middle and upper classes, however good their plumbing, were vulnerable to the same maladies that afflicted the slums.

George Waring did not live to see his views discredited. In 1898, in the wake of the Spanish-American War, American army commanders in Cuba were alarmed by the prevalence of yellow fever and other diseases in Havana. Waring was appointed chairman of a commission that was sent to Havana to develop a plan for protecting the soldiers. Not surprisingly, Waring concluded that the elimination of yellow fever required the construction of a sewage system and paved roads as well as the introduction of water closets. Four days after Waring returned to the United States, he died of yellow fever. After his death, Havana was cleaned up, much as Waring had advocated, but yellow fever remained rampant. This led to the appointment of a new commission led by the more scientific- and laboratory-oriented Major Walter Reed. Reed's team determined that yellow fever did not spring from filth but was transmitted by a particular kind of mosquito, thus confirming a theory first developed by Cuban scientist, Carlos Juan Finlay. When the breeding places of these mosquitos were destroyed, yellow fever was eradicated.

## Women in Industrial Society

The economic and social changes that marked late nineteenth-century life opened up new opportunities for women, setting in motion trends that would become more visible in the twentieth century. The percentage of white women who graduated from high school, for example, rose from 15 percent in 1870 to 30 percent in 1900 to 60 percent in 1920; by the latter year, 25 percent of black women (compared with 5 percent in 1870) also graduated from high school. Throughout this period, a majority of all high school graduates were female. Post-secondary opportunities also expanded, thanks both to the founding of women's colleges such as Vassar, Smith, Wellesley, and Radcliffe, and to the creation of state universities (subsidized by the federal government's Morrill Act), many of which were coed. Although the percentage of women who attended college remained small, their numbers rose from 11,000 in 1870 to 85,000 in 1900.

Several factors contributed to this advance. Compulsory attendance laws in most states meant that more children went to school in the first place; boys were withdrawn from secondary school more often than girls so that they could help support their families; and there was an increase in the number of white-collar jobs (especially in teaching and clerical work) that required some education and were open to women. In addition, the notion that women would benefit from education was becoming more widespread: it could make them better wives and mothers, was intrinsically valuable, and would offer women a new range of opportunities. M. Cary Thomas, the president of Bryn Mawr, maintained that "the higher education of women" was "preparing the way for the coming economic independence of women."

The expansion of education was accompanied by a steady rise in women's participation in the paid labor force. While relatively few married women worked outside their homes, the number of young, single women who did so increased significantly, particularly among immigrants and African Americans. Women also began to enter, and even dominate, new occupations. In 1870, 70 percent of all working women

A female teacher leads a science class at a Washington, D. C., public school, 1899.

were domestic servants, but the changing economy created opportunities for women in semiskilled factory labor and in lower-echelon white-collar positions. Indeed, by World War I there were more female clerical workers than domestics, and women predominated in teaching and nursing, while also being widely employed in retail stores. Even black women, although generally relegated to menial jobs, made some gains, particularly in teaching.

What propelled women into the labor force? Households often needed multiple wage earners; employers welcomed women as low-cost employees; a declining marriage rate meant that there were more single women in the population; the educational backgrounds of middle-class women suited them well for jobs in rapidly expanding sectors; and college-educated women, in particular, sought work that was satisfying and fulfilling. Nonetheless, there was resistance to the idea of women working, particularly in middle-class families that upheld an ideal of domesticity and were not in dire need of the earnings that women could generate. Theodore Roosevelt gave voice to this view at the turn of the century, writing that "if the women do not recognize that the greatest thing for any woman is to be a good wife and mother, why, that nation has cause to be alarmed about its future." His widely shared vision helped to keep a lid on the employment of women, married women in particular. One remarkable sign of the tension between work and traditional gender roles was the fact that only a bare majority of female college graduates ever married.

The lives of most adult women, indeed, centered around their families. At the turn of the century, 90 percent of all women did marry, and child rearing, as well as household maintenance, remained a woman's domain. The number of children in each household, however, declined steadily, a trend that had begun in 1800. By 1900, the fertility rate among white women was about half what it had been a century earlier; among urban white native-born families, the drop was even sharper as many couples limited themselves to two children.

Notably, this drop in fertility took place despite legal changes that restricted access to abortion and birth-control devices. Until the mid-nineteenth century, first-trimester abortions were legal virtually everywhere and common among women of all classes. (Most women having abortions were married.) Then, pressed by an upsurge of public prudishness and a medical establishment seeking to professionalize itself, forty states passed anti-abortion laws between 1860 and 1890; by 1900, every state had banned abortion except in cases where the life of the mother was endangered. During the same period, an "anti-obscenity" campaign led by Anthony Comstock, a Connecticut dry-goods salesman devoted to combating sex in art, print, and private correspondence, succeeded in getting federal and state laws passed that drove birth-control information underground. The federal Comstock Law (1873), officially entitled "An Act for the Suppression of Trade in, and Circulation of Obscene Literature and Articles of Immoral Use," banned the importation, mailing, and interstate shipment of birth-control information and devices. The continuing drop in the fertility rate in the face of this legal onslaught suggests both that the laws were ineffective and that women were asserting their right to "voluntary motherhood" by limiting conjugal sex. In an interesting parallel, divorce rates also rose, albeit slowly, despite a tightening of divorce laws in most states.

Smaller families gave a different cast to the lives of women. Not only did they spend less time pregnant, but the burdens of raising children were lightened. Housewives' workload, however, was not lessened by new household technologies. Improved cooking equipment and washing machines, as well as the small electrical appliances that appeared between 1900 and 1920, had the effect not of giving homemakers free time but of raising the standards of housekeeping. Encouraged, in part, by a middle-class movement to ennoble homemaking by professionalizing it, women were expected to cook more diverse and nutritious meals, wash and iron clothes more frequently, keep houses tidier and cleaner, and even study child psychology.

Urban, industrial environments offered new social freedoms and a new range of activities to women. Young women working outside the home escaped parental supervision each day; many had the opportunity to socialize and enjoy commercial amusements at lunch or after work. Roughly a fifth of all working women, moreover, were economically independent, living in apartments and forming their own social networks and communities.

By the 1890s, many women were also embracing an ideal of the "New Woman." Generally from middle- or upper-class origins, better educated than most, and often single, the New Woman fused the values of Victorian womanhood with social activism and civic participation. These women were an important constituency for the women's clubs that began to appear after the Civil War and proliferated rapidly after 1890. The clubs included literary societies, mothers' clubs, alumnae associations, and reform groups; they reflected a desire for self-improvement, camaraderie, and social change. Although the club movement was dominated by middle-class white women, black women also formed clubs, often aiming not only to improve their own lives but to uplift their race as well.

The largest women's association of the era was the Women's Christian Temperance Union, founded in Chicago in 1873. Emerging from an Ohio-based movement that attempted to shut down saloons and control the alcoholic behavior of men, the WCTU, under the leadership of Frances Willard (president from 1879 to 1898), broadened its focus to attack the many evils for which men seemed to be responsible, including domestic violence, prostitution, the exploitation of labor, the abuse of prisoners, and political corruption. By 1890, the WCTU had 160,000 members nationwide and in Chicago alone was running two day nurseries, two Sunday schools, an industrial school, a free medical facility, and a shelter for 4,000 homeless or poor women. The WCTU played a key role in generating the public pressure that ultimately led to Prohibition; equally important, perhaps, it drew thousands of women into the association movement, often

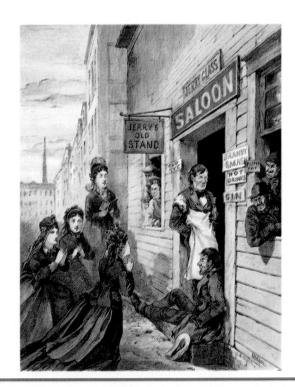

"The Temperance Crusade—Who Will Win?," a cartoon depicting women temperance advocates, 1874.

leading them into active campaigns for women's suffrage and other social reforms.

## Innovations in Social Thought

The social changes that swept across much of the United States between 1865 and 1900 echoed loudly in the nation's intellectual life. The innovators of the era were not all engineers, businessmen, and scientists; their ranks included novelists, poets, painters, scholars, clergymen, and judges. Living in a world both exciting and distressing, these men and women sought to understand the changes that were taking place—sometimes to accommodate to them, sometimes to resist. Such efforts at understanding led many intellectuals to cast aside hallowed traditions of belief, to invent new ideas and forms of expression, to develop different habits of thought. In so doing, social theorists like Henry George, novelists like William Dean Howells, and judges like Oliver Wendell Holmes were engaging in a process of innovation whose energy and imagination rivaled the more concrete and well-known achievements like those of Thomas Edison.

### EDUCATION

The growth of industrial society generated an enormous expansion of educational institutions. Free, public primary education was already well established in most states by the end of the Civil War, but it was after 1870 that most states adopted laws making school attendance mandatory for children between the ages of eight and fourteen. It was also during these years that the public high school became a central institution in American life. The number of public high schools rose from 500 in 1870 to more than 10,000 in 1910. In 1870, 57 percent of all children age five to seventeen attended public schools; fifty years later, the figure was 80 percent. This national trend was not matched in the still-rural South, where schooling did not become compulsory until the twentieth century and where educational opportunities remained limited, especially for African Americans. Well into the twentieth century, most black children did not even attend public elementary schools.

The same years witnessed the proliferation of kindergartens, which were often privately or philanthropically funded. The goal of kindergartens, as articulated by Elizabeth

Students saluting the flag in a New York City school, ca. 1900. The presence of flags in schools, as well as flag salutes, was new during this period.

Palmer Peabody, their foremost advocate, was to allow the young child "to take his place in the company of equals, to learn his place in their companionship, and still later to learn wider social relations and their involved duties." Implicitly, the kindergarten movement, as well as the movement for broadened public schooling in general, sought to have public institutions perform tasks that had once been entrusted to families. Schools were envisioned, in the words of John Dewey, the great educational philosopher of the period, as a "means for bringing people and their ideas and beliefs together, in such ways as will lessen friction and instability."

Both public schools and kindergartens were rooted in diverse, and sometimes contradictory, values. On the one hand, they stemmed from a democratic impulse to provide universal education and enhance the opportunities of all children, including those from immigrant and working-class families. Yet they also reflected industry's need for a disciplined labor force with appropriate skills, socialized into American and capitalist norms. This latter impulse became visible in the late nineteenth and early twentieth centuries as public schools developed vocational programs, offering different curricula to students from different class and ethnic backgrounds. Urban public schools thus disciplined students, inculcated them with American norms, and channeled them into different occupational tracks; at the same time, even poor students were empowered by their literacy, given skills with which they could criticize prevailing values, and offered some chance to compete for the better opportunities the economy had to offer. The tensions among these elements became an enduring hallmark of public education.

This was also the era when the American university acquired its modern form. Although the percentage of young adults obtaining college educations did not increase dramatically, the *number* did: undergraduate enrollment jumped from 50,000 in 1870 to 350,000 in 1910. Despite the skeptical views of some business leaders, a college degree became an important credential. In addition, a new, more secular generation of leaders in higher education was determined to build universities that would be on a par with the great institutions of Europe. Financed both by private benefactors, such as Ezra Cornell, Johns Hopkins, John D. Rockefeller, and Leland Stanford, and by federal and state funds (which turned the Universities of Michigan and Wisconsin, among others, into major academic institutions), universities rapidly became centers not only of higher education but of research. They developed specialized graduate programs in the professions and Ph.D. programs modeled on those in German universities, while placing new emphasis on the study of science and social science. In so doing, they transformed the professoriate into a profession, mandated both to teach and to conduct research within specialized disciplines.

One upshot of these changes was an educated and literate population that could comprehend, and participate in, the shifting intellectual currents of the day. The distinction between "highbrow" and "lowbrow" culture was never very marked in the nineteenth century, and the post–Civil War expansion of education meant that debates carried on among intellectuals were accessible to millions of citizens. Serious works of social thought, such as Edward Bellamy's novel *Looking Backward* (1888) and Henry George's *Progress and Poverty* (1879), a lengthy treatise on the sources of economic inequality, sold hundreds of thousands of copies and were devoured by a large reading public.

## SCIENCE AND SOCIETY

No single event had a more profound impact on intellectual life in this period than the publication of Charles Darwin's *Origin of Species* in 1859. Darwin's pathbreaking work, based on decades of research, offered a new, secular explanation of the diversity and character of life on earth. Casting aside the notion that a supreme being had simultaneously created the thousands of species of plants and animals on the planet, Darwin maintained that all living organisms were engaged in a competitive struggle for survival within their particular environments. Those that were most "fit"—the hardiest, most adaptable, or cleverest—lived to reproduce; over the long run, this process of "natural selection" led to the evolution of hardier and more fit species.

Darwin's theory of evolution challenged religious accounts of the creation and long-standing conceptions of the natural order as static and eternal. Equally important, it became a model, for scientists and other intellectuals, of an empirical approach to human knowledge, of painstaking, detailed research that could reveal the inner workings of nature and society. Indeed, as evidence accumulated to support Darwin's theory, and as advances in physics, chemistry, and bacteriology became increasingly visible (in part through the marvels of electricity), science itself acquired enhanced importance and prestige.

Darwinism, as developed and applied by Darwin's English contemporary Herbert Spencer, also offered a means of understanding and justifying the social changes wrought by industrial capitalism. By applying the principles of biological evolution to the study of society, Spencer suggested that humans, too, were engaged in a competitive struggle, in which the fittest prospered. One implication of this "social Darwinist," or Spencerian, idea was that nations and societies would become stronger only if unfettered competition were allowed to continue: governments, for example, should not interfere with the workings of the market is a capitalist economy. A second implication was that progress was necessarily slow, that society could improve only through a lengthy evolutionary process.

The foremost American advocate of social Darwinism was William Graham Sumner. Born into a working-class family, Sumner attended public schools, graduated with distinction from Yale, and entered the ministry. After serving as an Episcopal priest for several years, but increasingly drawn to secular, social issues, he accepted a newly created chair in political and social science at Yale in 1872. A prolific writer, Sumner spent three decades developing and promoting the Spencerian and social Darwinist ideas that first captured his attention in the 1870s. Denouncing government regulation of the economy, socialism, protectionism, and social reform, Sumner defended economic inequality by arguing that "millionaires are a product of natural selection" and that the poor, being less fit, deserved their fate. "Let every man be sober, industrious, prudent and wise," he wrote, "and poverty will be abolished in a few generations." He insisted that the only appropriate role of government was to defend "the property of men and the honor of women." Any other interference with the competitive struggle, including efforts to aid the poor, would only derail the process of natural selection and impede progress. Sumner's views were widely applauded by business leaders and political conservatives.

This conservative strain of social Darwinism set the terms of debate in political and social thought, but it did not go unchallenged. Among the most important dissenters was Frank Lester Ward, a Civil War veteran who worked his way through college and several graduate programs. Strongly interested in science and an ardent supporter of evolutionary theory, he was employed by the U.S. Geological Survey as a geologist and paleontologist in the 1880s and 1890s.

Yet Ward's interests transcended natural science, and he was most influential as a critic of social Darwinists and as a leader in the new field of sociology. In *Dynamic Sociology* (1883), Ward disputed the notion that the evolution of human societies followed or ought to follow the patterns of the natural world. Humans, unlike other organisms, had minds capable of transforming and controlling the world they inhabited. Informed with reason and guided by scientific investigation, humankind could best progress through invention and planning rather than unfettered and wasteful competition. Free-market economics, he argued, was not mandated by nature, and in fact undermined competition by permitting monopolies to arise. The regulation of economic affairs by democratic governments would serve the interests of society, while widespread educational opportunities would permit even the least talented citizens to improve themselves. "If nature progresses through the destruction of the weak, man progresses through the protection of the weak." Ward, in effect, accepted an evolutionary framework but argued that industrial society would best evolve through the application of human intelligence to economic and social problems.

Both Sumner and Ward were attempting to study society scientifically (an endeavor that gave rise to the field of sociology) in order to address issues raised by industrialization and the political unrest that accompanied it. They were not alone in this quest: many prominent intellectuals were attempting to address the same issues, and some of them attracted a considerable following. Edward Bellamy, writing in the 1880s and 1890s, believed that the abolition of private property was the key to restoring harmony and equality to the United States, and his ideas were so popular that hundreds of Bellamy, or Nationalist, Clubs were founded throughout the nation. Henry George struck an equally resonant note by advocating a "single tax" on land, which, he believed, would reduce inequality and prevent the formation of deep social cleavages. George's views were popular enough that he ran well in the New York mayoral election of 1886, besting Theodore Roosevelt. At the same time, economists such as Richard T. Ely, John R. Commons, and Thorstein Veblen broke with the classical notion that there were immutable laws governing economic behavior and promoted the detailed study of economic institutions.

Scientists also became involved in debates regarding gender and racial inequality. Darwin's argument that the abilities of men and women had diverged in evolutionary history (and that women had smaller brains) was deployed to oppose the advanced education of women, as were also ideas drawn from thermodynamics suggesting that if women spent their energies acquiring education, they would have less energy to carry out their reproductive functions. Other scientists argued that African Americans were less evolved than northern European whites and had lesser brain capacities; their social condition, thus, was the result of their biological inferiority. Given the growing prestige of scientific discourse, it became necessary for opponents of such views to conduct their own research and to present scientific arguments favoring equality.

## RELIGION

Although the era was an increasingly secular one, religion remained a potent force in intellectual and social life. The number of churchgoing Protestants, particularly Baptists and Methodists, increased significantly, while immigration brought millions of Catholics and hundreds of thousands of Jews to American cities. By 1900, there were nearly 150,000 Protestant churches in the nation, as well as more than 10,000 Catholic churches. The United States remained a religious and overwhelmingly Protestant nation, and clergymen continued to be among the most influential of Americans.

Organized religion had to confront two distinctive challenges in the late nineteenth century. The first came from science in general and Darwinism in particular: natural, or scientific, explanations of phenomena that had traditionally been understood in biblical terms. Among Protestants, the initial reaction to Darwin and to the growing eminence of science was hostile. Within a few decades, however, there emerged a liberal wing of Protestantism that tried to accommodate these new ideas. These "modernists" sought to bridge the gap between old faith and new science, between static and evolutionary views, even to reinterpret traditional biblical accounts in light of modern knowledge. New York's Henry Ward Beecher, the most influential Protestant cleric of the era, described himself as a "cordial, Christian evolutionist." Although Protestant conservatives continued to resist Darwinism as well as any tinkering with literal interpretations of the Bible, the more liberal, optimistic modernists captured the mainstream by the early twentieth century.

American Jews also felt a need to reconcile traditional beliefs with modern knowledge. Squarely facing this challenge, a convention of Reform Judaism (a movement that had emerged among German Jews in the United States) declared in 1885 that "the modern discoveries of scientific researches in the domains of nature and history are not antagonistic to the doctrines of Judaism." The impact of science was also visible in the most important new sect to emerge during this period: the Church of Christ, Scientist, founded by Mary Baker Eddy in 1879. Christian Scientists were devoted to the power of prayer, particularly for the sick. Eschewing modern medicine as well as tobacco, alcohol, and caffeine, they believed that illness could be cured through prayer and meditation, which brought one closer to God. Notably, however, they invoked the prestige of "science" in the very name of their denomination and regarded their methods of treating illness as scientific experiments that could be duplicated as proof of the existence of God's laws.

The second challenge to religion came from the vast inequalities spawned by industrial capitalism. While the middle and upper classes were thriving, the poor were growing more numerous, powerless, and desperate, and they were expressing their discontent in periodic strikes and riots. How should churches, which had long viewed themselves as the protectors of the weak, respond to these conditions? Among Protestants, two different reactions took shape: the Gospel of Wealth, and the Social Gospel movement.

Promoters of the Gospel of Wealth embraced laissez-faire capitalism and reassured the well-to-do that their prosperity was not only earned but a sign of divine approval. In a famous sermon, delivered an astonishing 6,000 times, Russell Conwell, a Baptist minister in Philadelphia, declared that everyone had "within their reach 'acres of diamonds,' opportunities to get largely wealthy." "I say that you ought to get rich, and it is your duty to get rich," he declared. "Because to make money honestly is to preach the gospel." Henry Ward Beecher, demonstrating that intellectual modernists could also be social conservatives, expressed little sympathy for striking workers in 1877. He declared that if a man did not smoke or drink, he could easily support a wife and six children on a dollar a day. "Is not a dollar a day enough to buy bread with? Water costs nothing; and a man who cannot live on bread alone is not fit to live." The notion that no one in America suffered from poverty "unless it be his sin" was welcomed by the prosperous.

In opposition to such views, other ministers organized what became known as the Social Gospel movement: they believed that the true task of Christianity was to rescue the poor, renew the social and economic order, and help bring about the Kingdom of God on earth. The two most well-known advocates of the Social Gospel were Washington Gladden and Walter Rauschenbusch, both of whom endorsed workers' rights and pressed Christians to rectify social injustices. Christianity, they argued, ought to be concerned not only with the behavior of individuals but with institutions that harmed men and women: salvation was not merely an individual matter but a question of constituting a just society.

Catholics and Jews had to confront these issues as well. The 1885 "Pittsburgh Platform" of Reform Judaism thus declared that it was in the spirit of Jewish law to "regulate the relation between rich and poor" and that "we deem it our duty to participate in the great task of modern times, to solve on the basis of justice and righteousness the problems presented by the contrasts and evils of the present organization of society." Within the relatively small Jewish community, there were few dissenters to such views. Among Catholics, however, a division emerged not unlike the split among Protestants. Although the Catholic Church devoted considerable resources to charity, most church leaders insisted that sin and vice, including intemperance, were personal deficiencies rather than social problems, that poverty was the will of God, and that the working poor would be saved by the church, not by legislation or political action. Such attitudes began to shift after Pope Leo XIII issued a famous encyclical, *Rerum novarum* (1891), in which he criticized the greed of capitalists, endorsed workers' right to unionize, and urged governments to

**Innovations in Social Thought**

care for the poor. But, except in scattered parishes led by progressive priests, change was slow in coming.

LAW, PHILOSOPHY, ART

The triumph of industry and the paradigm of evolutionary theory also had an impact on other realms of thought and culture. One was jurisprudence, where jurist Oliver Wendell Holmes spearheaded an attack on the long-standing notion that the fundamentals of law were unchanging principles that were to be logically and mechanically interpreted by judges. One of the great legal minds of the era, Holmes in 1881 published *The Common Law,* in which he argued that all laws developed in response to the "felt necessities of the time," including the needs of particular interest groups and changing historical conditions. "The life of the law has not been logic," he argued, "it has been experience." The decisions of judges, moreover, should be understood not as the results of impartial logic but rather as reflections of the values and beliefs of judges themselves. Holmes, who joined the Supreme Court in 1902 after twenty years as a justice in Massachusetts, maintained that law did and should evolve, just as economies and societies did. If the law were static and lagged behind social change, it would impede the course of evolutionary progress. Holmes's views did not spark an immediate change in judicial practices, but they became increasingly influential in the course of the twentieth century.

Similarly, philosophers William James and John Dewey, among others, challenged the long-accepted philosophical conviction that truth was fixed, abstract, and eternal, that the validity of ideas could be judged by their consistency with fundamental principles. The pragmatists, as Dewey, James, and their followers came to be called, argued that truth resided not in the abstract logic of ideas but in their practical consequences. Influenced both by the natural sciences and by evolutionary theory, they maintained that as the world changed, truths changed, that something was true not eternally but in particular circumstances; the value of an idea thus could be gauged through its application. For Dewey in particular, the appropriate method of truth-seeking was experimental, and the task of philosophers and other intellectuals was to help find positive solutions to real-world, contemporary problems.

Both painting and literature felt the impact of social change, veering toward realistic depictions of contemporary themes. One of the foremost painters of the era was Thomas Eakins, who studied in Europe in the 1860s and returned to

Thomas Eakin's *The Gross Clinic,* 1875.

Philadelphia to paint and teach. His paintings fused a meticulous attention to detail with the selection of boldly modern subjects. Some of his most well known, including *The Gross Clinic* (1875), depicted surgical operations, and *The Swimming Hole* (1883) displayed his mastery of the human form while also offering a raw depiction of male nakedness. As a portraitist, he was unsparing in his attention to realistic detail. Similarly, Winslow Homer, who began his career as a magazine illustrator during the Civil War, traveled through much of the United States and the Caribbean, painting lifelike scenes of farm life, of sailors and fishermen at work, and, with more romantic elements, seascapes.

Novelists in the 1880s and 1890s focused their attention on such social issues as corruption in business and politics, the miseries of life in the slums, and the mounting conflicts between labor and capital. The most influential realist was William Dean Howells, a fiction writer as well as editor of the *Atlantic Monthly* and then of *Harper's.* Both as a critic and as a novelist, Howells encouraged the realistic depiction of urban, industrial society. A realist, wrote Howells, "cannot look upon human life and declare this thing and that thing unworthy of notice, any more than a scientist can declare a fact of the material world beneath the dignity of his inquiry." In *The Rise of Silas Lapham* (1885) and *A Hazard of New Fortunes* (1890), Howells created finely grained descriptions of the interior dynamics of families, as well as the concrete meanings of social class.

Ironically, the movement toward realism in literature and art was accompanied by a trend that historian Lawrence Levine has called "the emergence of cultural hierarchy in America." During the early to mid-nineteenth century, there were no sharp boundaries separating "high culture" from works of mass popular appeal. The plays of Shakespeare were performed in cities and towns throughout the nation, by actors both professional and amateur, to mixed and sometimes rowdy audiences of social elites, middle-class families, and workers. Performances of opera and symphonic music were attended by men and women from all walks of life, seated—in different sections depending on the cost of tickets—in the same concert halls. Museums, containing eclectic collections of paintings and sculpture arrayed alongside mastodons and stuffed animals, attracted men, women, and children seeking amusement and edification.

All of this changed during the late nineteenth century. Prompted by the desire of the upper classes to claim "culture" as their own, by the professionalization of actors and musicians, and by a middle-class impulse to weed out audiences whose behavior seemed distracting, the traditionally great works of theater, music, and art became reserved to the middle and upper classes. Music and drama were performed by professionals (thereby increasing the cost of tickets); programs ceased to mix the classics with popular works; audiences were expected to be silent and reverential; aesthetic elevation was distinguished from mere entertainment. At the same time, museums converted themselves into temples of high culture, repositories of "great works" that were to be appreciated by the educated in silence and solemnity. In 1897, the Metropolitan Museum of Art in New York denied admission, on a weekday afternoon, to a plumber wearing overalls. The museum's director defended its action, saying that "we do not want, nor will we permit a person who has been digging in a filthy sewer or working among grease and oil to come in here, and by offensive odors . . . make the surroundings uncomfortable for others." The segmentation of industrial society made its mark even in the halls of culture.

## Suggested Reading

John Bodnar, *The Transplanted: A History of Immigrants in Urban America* (1985)

Richard Hofstadter, *Social Darwinism in American Thought* (1992)

Morton Horwitz, *The Transformation of American Law, 1870–1960: The Crisis of Legal Orthodoxy* 1992)

T. J. Jackson Lears, *No Place of Grace: Antimodernism and the Transformation of American Culture, 1880–1920* (1994)

Lawrence Levine, *Highbrow/Lowbrow: The Emergence of Culture Hierarchy in America* (1988)

Roy Rosenzweig and Elizabeth Blackmar, *The Park and the People: A History of Central Park* (1992)

Ronald Takaki, *Strangers from a Different Shore: A History of Asian Americans* (1989)

Richard White, *"It's Your Misfortune and None of My Own": A New History of the American West* (1991)

C. Vann Woodward, *The Strange Career of Jim Crow* (1955)

# Chapter Review

## Summary QUESTIONS

- What changes occurred in the legal and social condition of African Americans in the South and Native Americans in the West?

- How did changes in industry and technology affect the lives of farmers?

- What were the problems created by urbanization during this period, and how were they addressed?

- How did the lives of women change during these years?

- What was the impact of Darwin's theory of evolution on American ideas and beliefs?

## Chronology

| | |
|---|---|
| 1873 | Women's Christian Temperence Union founded in Chicago. |
| 1875 | Civil Rights Bill passed. |
| 1881 | Booker T. Washington founds the Tuskegee Institute in Alabama. |
| 1883 | The Brooklyn Bridge is completed. |
| 1887 | Free mail delivery starts in communities of more than 10,000 people. |
| | The first electric trolley cars were built. |
| 1896 | Supreme Court legally sanctions segregation in Plessy v. Ferguson. |
| 1897 | Boston opens subway line. |
| 1909 | W. E. B. Du Bois founds the National Association for the Advancement of Colored People. |

## Key Terms

Jim Crow (p. 543)

Immigration restriction (pp. 547–549)

Public health movement (p. 558)

The "New Woman" (p. 561)

Darwinism (p. 563)

# Chapter 20

# POLITICS AND THE STATE:

## 1876–1900

An 1892 parade in Chicago for the Democratic ticket of Cleveland and Stevenson.

- **What were the most distinctive characteristics of city politics in this period?**

- **In what ways were state governments the "laboratories of democracy"?**

- **What were the major insurgent political movements of the time?**

- **What were the major political issues at the national level?**

- **How did the courts respond to the tensions of the new industrial society?**

- **How did the political landscape change after the 1896 elections?**

Reflecting on the years between 1870 and the mid-1890s, historian and writer Henry Adams, the son and grandson of American presidents, wrote that "no period so thoroughly ordinary had been known in American politics since Christopher Columbus first disturbed the balance of American society." In many respects, Adams's judgment was correct. Particularly when viewed against the dramatic backdrop of the Civil War and the first years of Reconstruction, national politics had a humdrum flavor during the period that Mark Twain and Charles Dudley Warner dubbed "the Gilded Age." As students of American history have discovered year in and year out, few people remember exactly who the presidents were, or when exactly they served, between 1876 and 1900.

Yet far more was going on beneath the surface—and outside of Washington—than Adams suggested. The economic and social changes of the era offered complex challenges to public authorities: How should governments, at all levels, respond to the nationalization of the economy, the emergence of powerful private corporations, the rapid growth of an urban working class, the plight of farmers newly dependent on international markets and monopolized railways? Should authorities intervene to soften the impact of industrialization and urbanization? If so, should such intervention come from municipalities, from the states, or from the federal government? Answers were not easy to come by. The terrain was uncharted, and many competing interests were at stake.

Popular engagement in these problems, and in politics itself, was immense. Elections were closely contested, turnout was high, issues-based movements flourished, and new political parties sprouted up again and again. In cities, towns, and rural counties, men and women joined together to create new organizations, to learn from one another, and sometimes to take to the streets with their demands. Rallies and protests were commonplace, strikes periodically paralyzed parts of the country, and the depression of the 1890s spawned the first national march on the nation's capital, by unemployed workers seeking relief.

Still, as Henry Adams suggested, this was not an era of great political reform or statesmanship. Mainstream political life was characterized more by the evasion than the solution of problems, by corruption rather than idealism, by electoral battles contested more for patronage than for principles. The national political leadership, including the six men who occupied the presidency between 1877 and 1900, often seemed uninspired. The capacities of the state, inherited from a less industrial era and a less national economy, were limited, and the two major political parties, hampered by the courts, lacked the will or ability to transform those capacities. As a result, politics did seem rather ordinary, and the national government seemed oddly distant from the turbulence bubbling in the cities and countryside.

## Rule and Misrule in the Cities

In 1890, Andrew White, the president of Cornell University, declared that "the city governments of the United States are the worst in Christendom—the most expensive, the most inefficient, and the most corrupt." White's view was widely shared by his educated contemporaries, many of whom denounced urban governments as corrupt and wasteful models of misrule run by unprincipled political machines and milked by greedy private interests, such as utility companies. Yet the record of urban governments was more complex than these critics suggested. Cities were confronted with immense challenges as their populations skyrocketed: the demand for municipal services mounted, and the need to invest in expensive infrastructure—such as water and transportation systems— became irresistible. City governments met at least some of these challenges successfully; the often-infamous political machines, moreover, responded to the real needs of a significant portion of the urban population.

Between 1850 and 1900, almost all major cities, and many medium-size ones, did develop political machines, yet they were rarely as centralized or powerful as the label implied. ("Machine" was a term used by critics; participants referred simply to "the organization.") The pivotal figure in machine politics was the local ward leader in working-class, particularly immigrant, neighborhoods. The ward leader sometimes served as an alderman or a city council member and was often the proprietor of a local business, such as a saloon. He helped to procure city services for his neighborhood, jobs for faithful organization members, permits for street vendors, and access to the city government. In return, he expected his constituents to actively support the organization's candidates on election day. Citywide machines were generally unstable coalitions of ward leaders only periodically "ruled" by a single boss. The machines obtained funds for their operations by legally and illegally cutting deals with private businesses that stood to profit from contracts and franchises granted by the city. Most of these organizations were Democratic, although Republican machines flourished in Philadelphia, Pittsburgh, and Cincinnati.

## BOSS TWEED

Surely the most notorious machine politician of the era was William M. Tweed, who controlled the Tammany Hall organization in New York in the 1860s and early 1870s. Tweed, unlike many bosses, did not come from an impoverished background; he had studied bookkeeping and worked in his family's chair-making firm. Turning to politics, he then joined the Tammany organization, which had for decades been the executive arm of the Democratic Party in New York City. Tweed was elected first to the city council and then to Congress; by the late 1860s, he and his allies had gained control of Tammany, as well as much of the city government and portions of

THE "BRAINS"

THAT ACHIEVED THE TAMMANY VICTORY AT THE ROCHESTER DEMOCRATIC CONVENTION.

New York's Boss Tweed, portrayed as a money bag, in Harper's Weekly, 1871.

the state legislature. The Tweed ring was extraordinarily successful at winning elections, by mobilizing its supporters and, when necessary, by hiring "repeaters" to vote in multiple polling places and arranging to have election officials alter tally sheets. Tweed also allegedly paid $600,000 in bribes to get the legislature to change New York's charter so that his cronies could control appointments and the city's finances.

Tweed and his colleagues looted the public treasury, not just for the organization but for their own personal gain. Those who sought contracts from the city were obliged to kick funds back to the ring and were encouraged to pad their bills so that they could kick back even more. The epitome of these practices was reached in the construction of a new county courthouse that eventually cost more than the purchase price of Alaska. Tweed became a wealthy man, owning a Fifth Avenue mansion, an estate in Connecticut, a yacht, and a well-stocked stable of horses; he also distributed large sums of money to the poor and to the Catholic Church.

Tweed's downfall came in the 1870s when New York's more traditional establishment, alarmed at the overt corruption and the rapidly growing indebtedness of the city, mounted an investigation of the ring. This resulted in the indictment of numerous officials, including the mayor and eventually Tweed himself. Aided by the testimony of a disaffected sheriff, Tweed was convicted of 104 counts of bribery and fraud. The victim of his own excess and hubris, he died in jail in 1878.

Yet corrupt as Tweed and his cronies were, they did accomplish important things for the city. Circumventing the traditional slow mechanisms of urban administration, the Tweed regime succeeded in getting streets built, granting franchises to transit and utility companies, promoting the physical expansion of New York, and furthering the development of Central Park, one of the most impressive aesthetic achievements of urban America. The Tammany organization was also revered by poor and immigrant New Yorkers who knew that it was Tammany that delivered street cleaning, parks, and bathhouses to their neighborhoods and who turned to the organization for meals, cash, and fuel when they were in dire straits. The organization's popularity permitted Tammany to return to power after Tweed's fall, although his mildly chastened successors reduced the flagrancy of their graft.

DIVIDED RULE

Tweed's story was exceptionally dramatic and well publicized (owing in part to a crusading series in the *New York Times*), but the basic dynamics of machine politics were played out in cities across the country. Responding both to the increasing size and complexity of cities and to the needs of working-class immigrants and their children, machine politicians—who were among the nation's first full-time professional politicians—acted as brokers among different constituencies and as representatives of the city's poorer residents. That they felt entitled to profit from their services was an expression of the harsher side of machine politics. "I see my opportunity, and I take it," acknowledged Tammany's George Washington Plunkitt, as he carefully distinguished between "honest graft" (making money from contract letting or from insider knowledge of public construction plans) and "dishonest graft" (such as payoffs from vice establishments). Yet there was always a more positive side to the machines. As Martin Lomasney of Boston's South End put it, "There's got to be in every ward somebody that any bloke can come to—no matter what he's done—and get help. Help, you understand, none of your

law and justice, but help." In Lomasney's own neighborhood, he and his machine were the only significant source of aid for the unemployed in the early twentieth century.

Rarely did machines govern by themselves: they generally shared power with other political factions, constituencies, and officials. City councils, mayors, and independent commissions often contended with one another for power while possessing legal authority over different domains. Although the machines commonly wielded great influence in city councils, the councils themselves were generally losing power, owing to legal changes promoted by state governments. Meanwhile, mayors were gaining legal authority, including the ability to appoint department heads and veto city council measures. Big-city mayors, moreover, tended not to emerge from the world of ethnic, ward politics; they were usually successful businessmen, bankers, or lawyers, from old-stock, respectable Protestant families, wealthy enough to pay for their own electoral campaigns. Mayors held most of the reins of city government, furthering the interests of the downtown business community while negotiating deals and compromises with the ward-based machines.

There were also other centers of power, some elected, some appointed. Auditors and controllers were chosen to keep a close eye on financial matters; school officials, who controlled jobs and construction projects, were often elected on their own; independent commissions governed parks, water authorities, and health. Running a city increasingly demanded the employment of professionals and bureaucrats who, particularly after the passage of municipal civil service laws, remained in office for long periods and wielded substantial influence. Thanks to new technologies—in construction, transit, lighting, water, sewage, and health—experts, such as civil engineers, also became important figures in city administrations.

These governments, moreover, were not autonomous: by the second half of the nineteenth century, it was clearly established in law that cities were subservient to the states. State governments could revise city charters, and they frequently passed legislation dictating the policies of cities. Most often, these state laws were passed in cooperation with the cities, but that was not always the case: sometimes for partisan reasons and sometimes because of conflicts between urban and rural interests, state governments enacted legislation opposed by the city itself. Such legislative meddling ended up spawning a movement for the "home rule" of cities that was successful in a number of states, including Missouri and California, where cities acquired the right to draft their own charters. This enhanced autonomy was, however, accompanied by a trend that cut in the opposite direction: the creation of statewide commissions—dealing with water, sewage, health, and education—that imposed their own standards on city policies.

In the end, the record of late nineteenth-century city governments was mixed. They succeeded in expanding municipal services and in creating physical infrastructures that endured for decades; by international standards, American cities had impressively efficient transport, water, sewage, educational, utility, and public health systems. City governments also succeeded, by the end of the century, in streamlining their finances and reducing their debts—which were enormous in the 1870s and 1880s. Yet they were less successful in regulating private property and meeting the material needs of the poor. Housing conditions remained largely unregulated and were deplorable for many urban residents, while public welfare agencies, such as the overseers of the poor, lacked the resources to help the most needy urban residents. In fact, for reasons both fiscal and ideological, the task of caring for the poor was increasingly transferred to underfunded private charities that were less than sympathetic to the plight of men and women unable to support themselves.

With housing conditions largely unregulated, the urban poor often lived in deplorable conditions. This photo shows Italian immigrant families and their shacks in New York.

## Statehouses and Legislatures

State governments in the late nineteenth century were sometimes called the "laboratories of democracy." Decades before the federal government was pressed into action, governors and state legislators were challenged to devise solutions to the economic and social problems of the industrial era (see Chapter 6).

The nerve center of each state government was its legislature, comprised largely of part-time, amateur politicians who met for abbreviated sessions once or twice each year; legislators commonly had to broker conflicts between rural and urban constituents while also coping with a new breed of political actor, the professional lobbyist hired by a corporation. In addition to making state laws, legislators possessed the critical power of electing U.S. senators, who shaped national policies and controlled federal patronage.

One core issue faced by state governments was the regulation of large corporations in finance and transportation. Responding to popular pressure from farmers, small businessmen, and consumers who felt they were being gouged by "monopolies," states passed laws and created agencies to regulate railroads, banks, utilities, insurance companies, and grain-storage facilities; although such laws were often watered down through corporate influence, they were nonetheless pathbreaking interventions in economic affairs. State governments in the Midwest and the West also aided farmers by sponsoring irrigation projects and founding agricultural experiment stations, which began to be subsidized by the federal government in 1887. In addition, they passed laws to make public education compulsory, to promote public health regulations, and even to offer a modicum of protection to industrial workers by limiting the hours of women and children and compelling employers to pay wages in cash. Some state governments also dealt with the issue of alcohol consumption by adopting prohibition, while others enacted "local option" legislation.

Both the newness and the limits of state responses to industrialization were visible in the experience of Massachusetts with the problem of unemployment. Massachusetts, an innovator in social and economic policy, founded the nation's first Bureau of Labor Statistics in 1869; its second chief was Carroll D. Wright, who in the 1880s went on to become the first director of the U.S. Bureau of Labor Statistics. Under Wright's supervision, in 1878 the Massachusetts bureau attempted a systematic count of the unemployed for the first time in the nation's history. This initial effort was followed in 1885 by an exhaustive census survey of unemployment, the publication of which marked the first appearance in print of the word "unemployment." That survey was repeated in the 1890s and accompanied by a massive investigation of the "problem of the unemployed."

These studies of what was perhaps the most fundamental problem of an industrial, capitalist society were pioneering: in addition to recognizing the role of the state in addressing social ills, the surveys established that unemployment was a chronic, pervasive problem for workers. Wright and his successors discovered that in any year, 20 percent of all industrial workers experienced some joblessness; during depressions, the figure soared to 35 or 40 percent.

Yet despite these startling numbers, the state government did nothing to help. Although jobless workers demonstrated for months during the depression of the 1890s, the governor and the legislature—reluctant to expend state funds and suspecting that many of the unemployed were "idlers" who refused to work—took no action. The unemployed were left to fend for themselves or, if they arrived in the most dire straits, to obtain minuscule amounts of aid from municipal overseers of the poor and private charities. To make matters worse, the state toughened its vagrancy, or "tramp," laws, exposing jobless workers to the threat of arrest if they traveled from place to place searching for work.

State governments were also political battlegrounds, and many states, particularly in the Northeast, witnessed the emergence of strong party organizations led by a single powerful figure—who sometimes was also the speaker of the state assembly or the senior U.S. senator. The Republicans dominated state politics in New England and part of the Midwest, while the Democrats, despite remarkably durable opposition, controlled most of the South. Elsewhere—and even, at times, in these regional strongholds—elections were closely contested, with shifting majorities and victory margins so thin that considerable influence was wielded by third parties. High voter turnout was common, and for many citizens party allegiances were strongly felt, shaped by class and regional interests as well as by culture and religion. Men belonging to pietistic religions (such as Methodism, which emphasized a personal faith in God and personal behavior that would bring salvation) often voted Republican, while members of more liturgical faiths that emphasized doctrine rather than emotion (such as Catholicism) were more likely to support the Democrats.

The new departures in state activism were less substantial in the South than elsewhere. State regulation of the railroads tended to be weak in the South, while public health boards and education commissions were underfunded and unable to enforce statewide standards. Chastened by the indebtedness incurred during Reconstruction, states veered toward fiscal restraint, adopting low and regressive tax rates while sharply restricting expenditures.

Political life in the southern states was distinctive, thanks to the legacy of Reconstruction and to the persistence of race as a preeminent issue. Although the Democratic Redeemers who had captured the state governments in the 1870s remained in power, their reign was troubled. In most states, a majority of blacks continued to vote—and to vote Republican, through the 1880s—and they were often joined by independents and upcountry or mountain whites; at the same time, the Democratic Party itself split into factions, competing as much for office and patronage as for principle. Consequently, elections were fiercely contested, and Republicans, independents, and African Americans won local offices and seats in state legislatures. Elections also tended to be corrupt: all parties purchased votes outright, while blacks were sometimes paid not to vote at all.

In some states, most notably Mississippi, Democrats resorted to violence and intimidation to keep blacks from the polls. Beginning in the 1880s, they shifted their attention to legal techniques of circumventing the Fifteenth Amendment and disfranchising blacks. The first such effort was the written, secret ballot, which kept many illiterate men from voting. After 1890, the techniques became more varied: under the leadership of wealthy Democrats from black-belt counties (those fertile plantation regions that held large black populations), every state government in the South adopted laws and constitutional amendments designed to prevent blacks, and sometimes poor whites, from voting. Among the techniques of disfranchisement were literacy tests, poll taxes, cumulative poll taxes (requiring voters to pay a tax for each year since they had last voted), and primary elections restricted to whites. Such measures successfully disfranchised the vast majority of the black population; in Louisiana, for example, the number of registered black voters plummeted from 130,334 in 1896 to 1,342 in 1904. By removing African Americans from the polity, the Democrats secured control and placed the region under single-party rule. This critical development was facilitated by the federal government's decision in 1893 to terminate all remaining supervision of southern elections and by the stance of federal courts that tolerated restrictions on the franchise as long as those restrictions were not "facially" (explicitly) based on race.

## The Politics of Insurgency

A distinctive feature of political life during this period was the strength of insurgent, grassroots movements. Both in the cities and in the countryside, men and women responded to the stresses of economic and social change by forming new organizations to remedy problems and to promote a more just and democratic society. Millions of people held rallies and marches, went on strike, built alternative economic institutions, ran candidates for political office, pursued far-reaching reforms, and developed ideas that were disturbing, even threatening, to those who had traditionally wielded power. The politics of insurgency reached its peak in the 1890s, shifting the terms of mainstream politics while achieving a mixed record of successes and failures that set the stage for political life in the twentieth century.

### LABOR UNITING

Industrial workers first began organizing before the Civil War. They created reform organizations, unions, and workingmen's political parties, all of which tended to be locally based and short-lived. In the decades that followed the war, activist workers sought to build durable movements that would advance the interests of working people in an increasingly national economy. The organizations they built were both economic and political: unions to give workers more strength in bargaining with employers; political parties to promote far-reaching reforms; and hybrids that operated on both economic and political fronts. These organizations reflected workers' growing sense of exploitation and injustice, as did periodic outbursts of forceful protest and violence. Indeed, so deep was worker discontent that one of the central issues debated by working-class groups was whether their goal should be the abolition of the "wage system" or the pursuit of concrete gains within the structures of capitalism—or both.

*National Unions.* After the Civil War, it was clear to activists that local unions had little leverage in a national economy. By 1870, they had pieced together thirty-two national trade unions, the strongest of which were the iron molders, typographers, and shoemakers. In 1866, delegates from many of these unions, led by William Sylvis, the president of the Iron Molders' Union, met in Baltimore to found the National Labor Union. The NLU, which included reformers as well as unionists, sought to establish the eight-hour workday (and forty-eight-hour workweek), to reserve public lands for settlers rather than speculators, to create a federal Department of Labor, and to revamp the currency. The NLU succeeded in getting eight-hour laws passed in seven states, but most were weakly enforced and ineffective.

The NLU also advocated the development of consumers' and producers' cooperatives, so that workers could control their own means of production and avoid being exploited by "middlemen." Shoe workers, for example, banded together to sell the shoes they made directly to retailers (rather than wholesalers) and to buy clothing and food directly from producers. Idealistic in intent, the cooperatives nonetheless floundered because of an inability to obtain adequate credit. The NLU collapsed in the mid-1870s, as did the young national trade unions: jobless members were unable to pay dues, union treasuries shriveled, competition for jobs was fierce, and employers went on the offensive, driving wages down and compelling workers to choose between union membership and their jobs.

The return of prosperity revived the labor movement between 1878 and 1886. The organization leading the revival was the Noble and Holy Order of the Knights of Labor. Founded as a small secret organization in Philadelphia in 1869, the Knights went public in the late 1870s and welcomed as members not only skilled workers but "all producers," including unskilled workers, women, blacks (usually in segregated locals), and some members of the middle class. Only bankers, lawyers, liquor dealers, speculators, and stockbrokers were excluded. Headed by Terence V. Powderly, a former machinist, popular orator, and mayor of Scranton, Pennsylvania, the Knights advocated "a radical change in the existing industrial system." "The recent alarming development and aggression of aggregated wealth," declared its 1878 preamble, "render it imperative . . . that a check should be placed upon its power and upon unjust accumulation, and a system adopted which will secure to the laborer the fruits of his toil." Echoing some ideas of the NLU, the Knights sought an eight-hour day, the abolition of child and convict labor, equal pay for men and women who performed the same work, the development of cooperatives, and the establishment of bureaus of labor statistics; later they demanded public ownership of the communication, transportation, and banking industries.

To achieve their goals, the Knights undertook massive educational campaigns and political action. They lobbied at

This 1883 cartoon from the humor magazine *Puck* depicts the unequal contest between labor and monopoly (depicted as a railroad), with Jay Gould and others cheering in the stands.

statehouses and in Washington and eventually ran their own candidates for public (usually local) office. Many "assemblies" of the Knights also acted as unions, bargaining with employers over issues such as wages and hours as well as conducting strikes—despite the organization's official position that striking was to be used only as a last resort. The message of the Knights, as well as the diversity of their activities, struck a resonant chord: workers flocked to join the organization, especially after the Knights won a major strike against robber baron Jay Gould's southwestern rail empire (see Chapter 18). By 1886, there were local assemblies in nearly every city and midsized town; with 750,000 members, the Knights were the largest labor organization of the nineteenth century.

The Knights then stalled and fizzled. Absorbing vast numbers of new recruits stretched the organizational capacities of the union, and internal disputes emerged, particularly between those eager to pursue immediate economic gains and others, such as Powderly, who stressed a long-run vision of reform. Meanwhile, employers, including Jay Gould, counterattacked, defeating the Knights in one conflict after another. Most decisively, the Knights were undercut by competition from the resurgent national craft unions, whose leaders concluded that the economic interests of their members would best be served by national organizations consisting only of skilled workers belonging to the same trade. Long-term political goals—which even to many craft union leaders meant replacing capitalism with socialism—could then be pursued separately, through political parties. Immediate issues affecting labor as a whole, including those that required lobbying, could be addressed through an umbrella organization of trade unions, such as the one created in 1886, the American Federation of Labor (AFL).

As workers drifted away from the Knights, many moved toward the craft unions affiliated with the AFL. Comprised almost entirely of skilled white male workers, the national trade unions were designed to maximize the bargaining power of their members and to weather business depressions: it was no accident that its leaders were nearly all men who had personally experienced the collapse of organized labor in the depression of the 1870s. Members had to pay substantial dues; they received sickness, funeral, and (sometimes) jobless benefits; and union officers fought vigorously to maximize and protect the jobs available to their members. These unions generally did not include black workers, women, or semiskilled and unskilled workers with little market power. By 1892, forty trade unions, with roughly half a million members, had joined the AFL; the strongest were in the building trades and among skilled railway workers.

Although the national trade unions and the AFL were less inclusive and visionary than the Knights, neither their members nor their leaders abandoned politics or the desire for significant economic and social change. Many, if not most, adhered to a working-class political culture that resisted the dominant capitalist ethos. A hefty proportion of union members, including key leaders such as P. J. McGuire, president of the carpenters' union, were socialists: they believed that the economy would be better run and its rewards distributed more fairly if the people, through the government, owned the nation's major enterprises. The eight-hour movement, which became something of a crusade in the 1880s and 1890s, was fueled by the conviction that a shorter workday would eliminate unemployment and thus enhance the ability of workers to carry out profound social reforms. Even the AFL itself,

Samuel Gompers speaking in the 1880s, early in his career as a labor leader.

which later became more conservative, debated proposals for government ownership of all major industries.

The national trade unions, and the AFL, headed by former cigar maker Samuel Gompers, proved their organizational mettle by surviving the depression of the 1890s: almost all unions made it through the crisis, leaving the AFL with more than 400,000 affiliated members at the end of the business downturn in 1897. If the depression had deepened the conviction of many workers that the wage system had to be abolished, it had also underscored the need for lasting organizations that could protect workers against employers and economic adversity. The trade unions of the AFL grew rapidly with the return of prosperity: union membership nearly quintupled between 1897 and 1904, transforming craft unions of skilled workers into a durable feature of the institutional landscape.

*Politics and Strikes.* The insurgency of the working class was also expressed in electoral politics, particularly in the formation and growth of new parties. In the late 1870s, workers played an important role in the Greenback Labor Party, which

stressed expansion of the currency and the credit supply to restore power to workers and farmers. In 1878, the party (then calling itself the National Party) polled nearly a million votes nationwide, electing fifteen congressmen and scores of city and state officials. In the mid-1880s, candidates representing the Knights of Labor, as well as local workingmen's parties, ran for office (and sometimes won) on platforms advocating a graduated income tax, currency reform, an end to child labor, and government ownership of railroads and the telegraph. In New York in 1886, the United Labor Party was created to support the mayoral candidacy of author Henry George, who called for public ownership of all means of transportation and communication and for taxing any increases in the value of land—which George believed would discourage land speculation, limit monopolies, make it possible for workers to buy farms, and create a labor shortage that would raise wages and reduce inequality (see Chapter 19). Radical workers also created the Marxist Workingmen's Party of the United States, the Socialist Labor Party, and an anarchist movement that embraced "equal rights for all without distinction of sex or race" as well as direct workplace action to overthrow capitalism.

Working-class discontents further bubbled to the surface in militant strikes and demonstrations. Nearly every town with a population greater than 20,000 in the Northeast and Midwest witnessed a strike in the late 1880s or 1890s. Some were "sympathy" strikes in which workers walked off their jobs to express solidarity with other striking workers. Others erupted into major national events. In 1877, the announcement by the Baltimore and Ohio Railroad that it was, for the third time, cutting wages by 10 percent sparked a walkout in Martinsburg, West Virginia, that quickly spread to cities and towns throughout the North. Over the course of a month, tens of thousands of railway workers went on strike, dozens were killed by state militias and federal troops, and railroad property worth millions of dollars was destroyed by enraged strikers and mobs who had long felt oppressed by the powerful rail corporations. The Great Railroad Strike of 1877 raised the specter of insurrection in the minds of many middle-class Americans, prompting state governments to create national guard units to contain labor conflict. To house these volunteer units and their weapons, cities built massive stone armories—often in well-to-do neighborhoods—designed with gun loop-holes and towers to protect against what the mayor of New York called the "domestic peril of civil disorder."

In May 1886, these fears were fanned again when workers across the nation launched a general strike for the eight-hour day, marching in huge parades in Milwaukee, New York, San

An engraving depicting the Seventh Regiment Armory, Park Avenue, New York. Built between 1877–1880, the armory housed both ammunition and volunteer National Guardsmen in case of unrest or insurrection in the city (mostly due to labor disputes).

Francisco, and Chicago, among other cities. The protests were peaceful everywhere but in Chicago. There, on May 3, when eight-hour strikers joined an ongoing strike of iron molders, police fired into the crowd, killing and wounding several workers. The following day, a local anarchist group called for a protest meeting in Haymarket Square. The sparsely attended meeting was uneventful until the police, anticipating violence, attempted to break up the crowd. As they charged forward, a bomb was thrown that killed policemen as well as protesters. Convinced that a violent insurrection was in the offing, Chicago authorities arrested eight radicals for murder; after a blatantly rigged trial that offered little or no evidence, four were convicted and hanged, while another committed suicide in jail. In 1894, the courageous governor of Illinois, John Peter Altgeld, acknowledged that the trial had been a travesty of justice and pardoned the three surviving defendants. To this day, no one is sure whether the bomb was thrown by an anarchist, a police provocateur, or someone else.

No single event captured more elements of the conflict between labor and capital than the Pullman Strike of 1894.

The strike began among workers who manufactured Pullman cars, the comfortable sitting and sleeping quarters used by middle-class travelers on long rail trips. The company's employees all lived in the much celebrated, model company town of Pullman, just south of Chicago. The strike, undergirded by resentment of the Pullman company's paternalistic efforts to control workers' lives, was precipitated by the company's decision to reduce wages without reducing the rent that workers paid for company-owned housing. After the strike was launched, the Pullman employees asked for support from the fledgling American Railway Union (ARU), a bold new organization founded and led by Eugene V. Debs. Debs, former secretary-treasurer of the Brotherhood of Locomotive Firemen. He had concluded that it would be in the interest of all railway employees to replace the "brotherhoods" of skilled workers with a single industrial union that would include everyone—skilled and unskilled—who worked for the railroads. Workers by the thousands had signed up with the ARU, but in 1894 it was still a young and fragile organization.

Fearful that the ARU could not survive a major confrontation with the railroads, Debs opposed active support for the Pullman strikers, but the union nonetheless voted to instruct its members to refuse to work on trains carrying Pullman cars until the company agreed to bargain with its employees. Debs, bowing to a majority vote, declared that this act of solidarity was "the hope of civilization and the supreme glory of mankind." The railroad corporations then began firing em-

Eugene V. Debs, founder and leader of the American Railway Union. He was also a founder and leader of the Socialist Party and the Industrial Workers of the World.

ployees who refused to handle Pullman cars, which quickly led to strikes and boycotts that paralyzed train traffic throughout the Midwest.

At that point, the federal government stepped in on the side of the railroads. Attorney General Richard Olney, a former railway lawyer, hired 3,200 special deputies (paid for by the railroads) to keep the trains running, ostensibly to guarantee the flow of mail. At the same time, federal judges issued injunctions prohibiting the ARU and its members from continuing their boycott of trains carrying Pullman cars. One judge, William Howard Taft, later U.S. president and chief justice of the Supreme Court, wrote that things would not improve "until they have had much bloodletting. . . . They have killed only six of the mob as yet. This is hardly enough to make an impression." Over the objection of Governor Altgeld, President Cleveland authorized the use of federal troops to suppress the strike; their arrival in Chicago sparked violence that left dozens of strikers dead. When Debs and other leaders of the ARU refused to obey an injunction targeted at them, they were arrested, quickly convicted of contempt of court, and jailed. The government's posture, coupled with the fierce resistance of the railroads themselves, led to the defeat of the strike and the destruction of the ARU.

The Pullman strike had a far-reaching legacy. Debs's legal challenge to his arrest, spearheaded by attorney Clarence

National Guardsmen firing into the crowds in Chicago during the Pullman Strike, July 1894.

Darrow, produced the Supreme Court ruling *In re Debs,* which upheld Debs's conviction and sanctioned the use of blanket injunctions to prevent workers and unions from engaging in "conspiracies in restraint of trade" that might harm the interests of employers. Defeated in court, Debs was turned into a popular hero: when he left prison after a six-month term, he was met in Chicago by an admiring crowd of 100,000. Debs's own thinking about labor was also changed by the Pullman strike: he concluded that advancing working-class interests required broad-gauged political action rather than simple union organizing. As a result, he first joined the People's Party and several years later helped to organize the Socialist Party of America, which he led for decades.

## WOMEN'S SUFFRAGE

The movement for women's suffrage, begun before the Civil War, traveled a halting path during and after Reconstruction. Many suffragists, who had been abolitionists before the war, believed that the increasingly accepted notion that voting was a "right" belonging to all citizens would not only end racial discrimination but also open the polls to women. Elizabeth Cady Stanton, one of the pioneering leaders of the movement, declared that black suffrage would open the "constitutional door" and that women intended to "avail ourselves of the strong arm and blue uniform of the black soldier to walk in by his side."

But Reconstruction turned out to be a bitter disappointment for Stanton and her colleagues: rather than walking in the constitutional door, women found themselves more formally barred than ever before. The Fourteenth Amendment penalized states that deprived adult males of the right to vote, specifying a link between gender and suffrage for the first time. The Fifteenth Amendment, offering federal protection of the right to vote, made no reference to women; despite the efforts of suffragists to include a gender provision, it declared only that citizens could not be denied the right to vote "on account of race, color, or previous condition of servitude." The campaign to ratify the Fifteenth Amendment consequently split the suffrage movement and severed the close ties between suffragists and advocates of black voting rights. In addition, the Supreme Court ruled in *Minor v. Happersett* (1875) that the right to vote was not inherent in citizenship; the case had originated when Virginia Minor attempted to vote, claiming that she, as a citizen, was already enfranchised.

Disagreements over the Fifteenth Amendment led to the creation of two rival suffrage organizations. The more conservative

579

The Politics of Insurgency

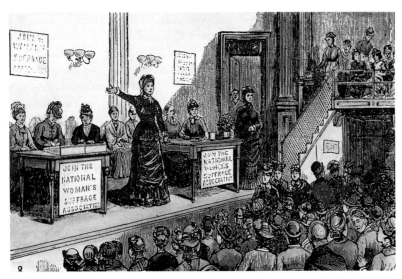

A meeting of the National Woman Suffrage Association in Chicago in 1880, with Elizabeth Cady Stanton speaking in the center of the platform.

even cause pregnant women to lose their babies and nursing mothers to lose their milk.

The other source of resistance was a declining faith in democracy itself. After the Civil War, in both the North and the South, sizable segments of the middle and upper classes began backing away from the notion that voting was a "right"; distrusting the ability of masses of people to make sound decisions, they resisted any expansion of the franchise. As a late nineteenth-century chronicler of woman suffrage wrote, "the opposition today seems not so much against women as against any more voters at all."

Partly in response to such ideas and partly because of the growing prominence of a new generation of more socially conservative suffragists, the arguments for enfranchising women tended to shift late in the century. Less emphasis was placed on voting as a right and on the equality of men and women, while more was given to claims that women had special virtues that would clean up politics and that politically engaged women would become better wives and mothers. More problematic, leaders of the movement argued that enfranchising women would help offset the menace represented by poor, immigrant, and black male voters. In the 1890s, for example, Stanton endorsed a literacy test as a qualification for voting, declaring that "the best interests of the nation demand that we outweigh this incoming pauperism, ignorance, and degradation, with the wealth, education, and refinement of

was the American Woman Suffrage Association (AWSA), founded by Lucy Stone and her husband, Henry Blackwell. The AWSA supported the Fifteenth Amendment, accepted male members, and focused exclusively on suffrage, which it attempted to obtain state by state. In contrast, the New York–based National Woman Suffrage Association, led by Stanton and Susan B. Anthony, was an exclusively women's organization that sought to obtain suffrage at the federal level, through a constitutional amendment; it also pursued such goals as equal pay for women and divorce law reform. Neither association had much success between 1870 and 1890, when the two reunited to form the National American Woman Suffrage Association. A constitutional amendment was introduced in Congress on several occasions, but it never received the approval of both houses, and most state referenda were rejected. By the turn of the century, only four sparsely populated western states (Wyoming, Colorado, Utah, and Idaho) had granted full suffrage to women. In some others, women did obtain more limited suffrage, such as the right to vote in school board elections.

Resistance to women's suffrage came from two sources. One was the belief that suffrage would be disruptive to family life and harmful to women themselves. Antisuffragists argued that enfranchisement would turn spouses against one another and corrupt women by bringing them into the impure world of politics. Voting would draw women into saloons and barbershops (which were common polling places) and could

An 1869 Currier and Ives lithograph suggesting that women's suffrage would disrupt family life.

580

the women of the republic." Belle Kearney, a prominent southern suffragist, claimed that "the enfranchisement of women would insure immediate and durable white supremacy, honestly attained."

The suffrage movement won few electoral victories and lacked a mass following during the late nineteenth century, but it did have an impact. In some states, pressure from the movement led to legal reforms, permitting married women to own property, keep their earnings, make contracts, and enjoy equal custody of their children. Nearly everywhere it compelled state legislators and constitutional conventions to think hard about the meaning and limits of democracy. The movement also energized large numbers of women who became active in public affairs and acquired political skills that would eventually contribute to their enfranchisement.

## FARMERS AND THEIR DISCONTENTS

In the South and West, men and women who worked on farms also took the path of political insurgency. They were angry about the high, and often discriminatory, rates railroads charged to transport their goods; they felt exploited by the middlemen who controlled grain elevators at key points in the transport system; they felt powerless in the face of fluctuating, and generally declining, agricultural prices in the world market; and they felt victimized by high credit costs and deflation, which increased the burden of their chronic and seasonal indebtedness. In the South, the lien system gave its own special twist to the dilemma of farmers.

Among the first collective responses to these conditions was the National Grange of the Patrons of Husbandry. Founded in 1867, the Grange became a large network of local associations, devoted to social and educational activities as well as to the development of cooperatives, owned collectively by groups of farmers, that could demand higher prices for farm products and buy supplies at volume discounts. In the 1870s, Grangers elected sympathetic legislators across the South and West, and they came to wield substantial political influence in Illinois, Iowa, Minnesota, and Wisconsin. In response, several midwestern states passed "Granger laws" regulating railroads and grain-storage elevators, as well as creating agricultural colleges and departments of agriculture. At its peak, the Grange had roughly 1.5 million members, almost all of whom were white. Black farmers created their own organizations, most notably the Agricultural Wheel in the lower Mississippi Valley. The Grange's influence began to wane in

the late 1870s, particularly as cooperatives failed in one state after another.

The Grange was succeeded by the more overtly political Farmers' Alliances. The Southern Farmers' Alliance was founded in Texas in 1877 and acquired a significant membership in the 1880s when it started sending "traveling lecturers" out through the countryside to talk about the problems afflicting farmers. Soon a Midwestern Alliance also formed, as did a Colored Alliance of black farmers. By 1889, the three groups claimed a membership of more than 4 million.

The Alliances maintained that railroads, bankers, and the entire credit system bore responsibility for the economic straits of farmers. Like the Grange, they advocated cooperatives, both as a solution to their problems and as a democratic form of economic organization. But the Alliances recognized the difficulty of building durable cooperatives in a world dominated by large corporations that controlled transportation and marketing networks and had little sympathy for the cooperative ideal. As a result, the Alliances turned quickly to politics, forming a coalition of "producers" with the Knights of

In "The Grange Awakening the Sleepers," a Granger alerts the public to the menace of the railroad monopoly, 1873.

Labor, and calling for the free and unlimited coinage of silver (see p. 589), the direct election of U.S. senators, government loans to farmers, and government control of communication and transportation. They also put forward the novel idea of creating government-sponsored "subtreasuries," or warehouses where farmers could store their nonperishable produce. The government would lend money (in effect, issuing new money) to farmers for up to 80 percent of the value of their stored products. The subtreasuries would thus provide farmers with easy, low-interest credit and permit them to keep their crops off the market until they chose to sell them; in so doing, the subtreasury system would create a flexible currency responsive to the actual output of the agricultural economy.

In 1890, the Alliances launched a remarkably successful political campaign, backing major-party candidates who agreed to support their platform. Their candidates won control of nearly a dozen state legislatures, captured numerous congressional seats, and became governors of several states. Most of their victories were in the South. This electoral success was accompanied by the flourishing of a culture in which masses of people collectively sought significant social change and embraced a vision of society as less hierarchical, less dominated by large corporations, more democratic, more experimental, and more humane. Hopeful as Alliance members were in the wake of the elections, they were nonetheless disappointed by the failure of candidates they supported to translate their platform into law. Consequently, they decided to abandon the strategy of supporting sympathetic major-party candidates and to create their own national party, the People's Party.

## The Nation State

While insurgent political movements were gathering steam, national electoral politics proceeded according to its own quadrennial rhythms, with both the major parties and the government in Washington seeming oddly distant from the discontents percolating around the nation. Although four of the five men to occupy the White House between 1876 and the mid-1890s were Republicans, electoral majorities were thin, and the Democratic candidates won more votes in four of the five elections. Control of Congress changed hands several times, and there were often Democratic majorities in the House while the Republicans controlled the Senate. Between 1875 and 1897, each party held both the presidency and a congressional majority for only a single two-year interval. Not surprisingly, the number of laws the federal government enacted was relatively modest.

### PARTIES AND ISSUES

The two major parties had different regional bases, somewhat different class constituencies, and different visions. Republican strength lay in the core of the industrial economy, the Northeast and the Midwest. The Republicans not only embraced industrial capitalism, they also advocated an active national state that could foster economic development. "One of the highest duties of Government," noted one Republican senator, "is the adoption of such economic policy as may encourage and develop every industry to which the soil and climate of the country are adapted." In the eyes of the Democrats, the Republican Party was the agent of "special interests," of business, particularly big business. Although that characterization tended to gloss over the close ties between many Democrats and powerful business interests, the most stable pillars of Democratic strength were white farmers in the South and parts of the West, as well as immigrant, particularly Catholic, workers in northern cities. The Democratic Party represented more of the nation's economic periphery, standing for states' rights, limited federal powers, and lower taxes.

*The Tariff.* The issue that most clearly distinguished the two parties, particularly in the 1880s and early 1890s, was the tariff—a tax on imported goods. Republicans supported protective tariffs, and Democrats opposed them or, at least, favored keeping them at modest levels. Tariffs were not particularly high in the 1870s, but in the following decade Republicans sponsored a series of bills raising them. By limiting competition from foreign producers, they believed, tariffs would allow domestic industries to prosper, leading to increased profits, more jobs, and higher wages. The Democrats regarded such arguments as fallacious, masking the greed of corporate interests. Tariffs increased the prices of protected goods such as sugar, iron, and textiles by as much as 50 to 100 percent, and higher prices for manufactured goods increased the cost of agricultural production—which made it harder for farmers to compete successfully in world markets. The Democrats also maintained, with some evidence, that workers gained little from tariff protection, that the main beneficiaries were businessmen who were pocketing large profits thanks to the government's interference with free trade.

Tariff policy was hotly debated because it pitted the interests of some individuals and regions against those of others. The tariff was also a powerfully resonant issue because in the late nineteenth century it was one of three key instruments of government intervention in the economy. (The other two were the money supply and, later, the regulation of business practices.) Tariffs had a broad impact on both producers and consumers, and they provided a high proportion (often more than 50 percent) of the federal government's total revenues.

Indeed, in the 1880s, increased tariffs swelled the government's coffers, so much that they generated a budget surplus that Republicans had to devise some way of spending. One way of doing so was expanding pension benefits for Civil War veterans and their families. This pension system, which had begun as a modest program to aid disabled soldiers, soon became a vast federal program, an odd hybrid of patronage and social welfare: some years, more than one-quarter of the federal budget went to the pension system, and by 1893 nearly a million former soldiers and their dependents were receiving pensions, consuming 42 percent of all federal revenues. Not surprisingly, the Civil War pension program provoked regional and partisan discontent. The Democrats opposed its enlargement both because of their opposition to high tariffs and because the program aided few of their constituents: the pensions were paid only to veterans of the Union army, few of whom either lived in the South or were immigrants.

*Civil Service Reform.* A far less partisan issue was civil service reform, which stood at the front of the national agenda in the late 1870s and early 1880s. It was put there by northeastern, liberal Republicans, many of them professionals and intellectuals, who were (at first derisively) called "Mugwumps" (after the Algonquian word for "chief"). Appalled by corruption and by the use of the expanding federal payroll as a source of party patronage, the Mugwumps led a vigorous campaign to make merit, rather than party affiliation, the basis of all federal employment. In so doing, they were implicitly advocating a shift in the financing of political parties, since it was customary for all holders of patronage jobs to give 2 percent of their salaries to the party that had appointed them. Among the reasons for embracing civil service reform was the extraordinary amount of time and energy that politicians had to expend on the distribution of patronage: President Benjamin Harrison estimated that during his first eighteen months in office, he spent four to six hours a day responding to requests for jobs.

By the early 1880s, both Democrats and Republicans were endorsing reform, and in 1883 Congress passed the Pendleton Act, creating a Civil Service Commission to supervise competitive examinations for about 10 percent of all federal jobs. The legislation also allowed the president to add positions to the civil service list and made it illegal for parties to require contributions from federal officeholders. One consequence of the latter provision was to make both parties more dependent on contributions from corporations.

The goal of civil service reform, beyond cleansing corruption and patronage from the federal government, was also to build a more efficient, modern administrative state, as required by a complex industrial society. The United States, unlike European nations, lacked a well-organized, central bureaucracy that could carry out the affairs of government and meet the needs of citizens and business for government services. In the industrial world of the late nineteenth century, there was a pressing need for efficient postal and customs services, for capable financial administration, for national standards of measurement. A bureaucracy based on merit, in which offices did not change hands with each election, seemed more likely to provide such services than a chaotically shifting patronage network.

*The Money Question.* One of the dominant issues of nineteenth-century politics was "the money question": deciding what was legal currency in the United States. The issue sounds perplexing to those of us living in the early twenty-first century, but to contemporaries it loomed as one of the most urgent matters of public policy. Between the Civil War and the end of the nineteenth century, the money question was always at or near the center of the political stage.

The issue had deep roots, stretching back to a decision made by the nation's first secretary of the treasury, Alexander Hamilton, who declared both gold and silver to be "legal tender" and thus payable for all public and private debts: Initially, their relative values were fixed at a ratio of 15:1, meaning that fifteen ounces of silver could be exchanged for one ounce of gold; however, the relative price of gold on the international market was slightly higher, so gold was hoarded and only silver circulated. But in 1834, the Treasury changed the ratio to 16:1, which had the opposite effect, later intensified by the discovery of gold in California: silver was hoarded, leaving gold in circulation. The only other currency in use before the Civil War consisted of notes issued by individual banks (not by the government) and backed by gold or silver specie. Since there were thousands of different notes in circulation, many of them counterfeit, bank notes tended to be accepted only at a discount, particularly outside the city in which they originated.

The federal government's need to finance the Civil War further complicated the situation. In 1862 and 1863, the government issued $450 million in paper money, roughly doubling the amount of currency in circulation. Although these "greenbacks" were declared to be legal tender, doubts about their long-term value led them to depreciate in comparison with gold; in 1864, for example, one could buy nearly three times as many goods with one gold dollar as with a greenback dollar. Of equal importance, issuing such a large quantity of money led to sharp price inflation.

All this set the stage for postbellum conflicts over the currency, grounded in economic self-interest, political beliefs, and passionately held, if often mistaken, ideas about money. The first matter to be addressed was what the government should do about the greenbacks. There were two opposing camps. On one side were those who favored removing the greenbacks from circulation and the "resumption" of an entirely bimetallic (gold and silver) or gold currency. Such a step, they believed, would replace inflation with deflation and benefit creditors, who were being repaid in inflated, or depreciated, paper dollars. Resumption was advocated by creditors, including bankers, and by intellectuals, businessmen, Protestant clergymen, and political leaders who were convinced that a sound currency had to be based on bullion, or specie. Many adherents of "hard money" were financial conservatives (usually Republicans) who opposed any government action that might disturb the natural laws of the free market, which was efficiently concentrating power in the hands of large, private financial institutions.

Arrayed in the opposing camp were "soft money" advocates who opposed resumption and wanted to keep the greenbacks in circulation. Among them were debtor businessmen as well as many chronically indebted farmers who did not want to repay debts in deflated, or more valuable, dollars. Soft money (not only greenbacks but any system that freed the money supply from the need to be backed by gold) was also advocated by entrepreneurs who wanted easier access to credit and by workers who believed that it would raise their incomes and stimulate the economy. Those who favored soft money—many of whom were Democrats—rejected the notion that currency had to be bullion-based and argued that it was the proper role of government to regulate the money

supply. Many also believed that a gold standard would concentrate economic power in the hands of the rich, breeding corruption, inequality, and exploitation, and that it was the duty of government to ensure equal opportunities for all citizens by preventing the formation of monopolies.

There was a great deal at stake in these debates. The federal government in the nineteenth century had few tools with which it could influence economic affairs, and its constitutional capacity to control the money supply was probably the most potent weapon in its small arsenal. How the government resolved the money question could affect the distribution of wealth, power, and incomes throughout the nation. To contemporaries, it loomed as a critical litmus test: would the state be responsive to the needs and beliefs of the "people" or to the demands and convictions of northeastern and midwestern bankers and capitalists?

In the aftermath of the Civil War, the federal government tried in a rather zigzaggy fashion to find compromises between the hard- and soft-money positions. Between 1866 and 1868, the government withdrew more than $40 million in

"The Silver Sun of Prosperity," an 1890 cartoon hailing the Sherman Silver Purchase Act as the key to prosperity.

greenbacks from circulation, but then stopped because of political opposition and fear of an economic contraction. After the panic of 1873, the government briefly reversed course and reissued $26 million worth of greenbacks. Then in 1875, Congress passed the Resumption Act, which declared that the government would begin redeeming greenbacks for gold in January 1879; the act was an attempt to return to a bullion-backed currency without causing a sharp drop in the money supply and prices. Its backers hoped that the knowledge that greenbacks could be redeemed would raise their value to par (the same value as gold) and thus eliminate any incentive for people to actually trade in their greenbacks; this was a critical gamble because, in fact, the treasury had less gold in reserve than the total outstanding issue of greenbacks. But the strategy worked, owing in part to favorable economic conditions. Few greenbacks were ever redeemed, and the nation returned to a gold standard without seriously deflating the currency.

"Opening the Floodgates," an 1890 cartoon showing the Republic being swept away by a flood of silver released by the Sherman Silver Purchase Act.

Meanwhile, silver was inching toward center stage. Since silver had dropped out of circulation after 1834, Congress, on the recommendation of the comptroller of the currency, passed the Coinage Act of 1873, which ended the minting of silver dollars. The act was little noticed when it was passed, but that changed quickly with the discovery of major new sources of silver in the western states. The growing supply of silver, coupled with diminishing worldwide demand (because many nations had turned to a gold rather than bimetallic currency), drove the market price of silver down; by 1874, the world price had dropped enough that the government would have been buying and minting silver under the rules that had applied before the Coinage Act. Silver mining interests, as well as advocates of an enlarged currency, were enraged, denouncing the Coinage Act as the "Crime of '73," engineered by banks to limit the currency, maintain a gold standard, and increase their own power. Although many soft-money advocates had been skeptical of silver, they now came to see it as a means of generating a large and flexible currency supply—the need for which seemed pressing as prices continued to drop from the 1870s until the late 1890s.

In response to pressure from the silver states, as well as soft-money interests, Congress in 1878 passed the Bland-Allison Act, which required the secretary of the treasury to purchase between $2 million and $4 million in silver each month; since the silver did not have to be put into circulation, the Bland-Allison Act was in some respects simply a subsidy for western silver producers. In 1890, Congress passed the Sherman Silver Purchase Act, which instructed the treasury to buy a larger quantity of silver each month and then to expand the currency by issuing treasury notes backed by the silver. The Sherman Act, too, was a compromise: it did not come close to meeting the demands of silver backers, and it also permitted the treasury to redeem notes in gold alone and thus to continue acting as though the nation were on a gold standard. The stage was set for the eruption of the silver issue into national politics in the 1890s.

*Regulating Business.* While the tariff and the money supply were two long-standing means through which the federal government intervened in the economy, the regulation of business practices was new to the late nineteenth century. As discussed in Chapter 18, this issue arose first with the railroads at the state level, as public officials attempted to deal with the concentration of economic power acquired by large corporations. After the courts had nullified state laws because of their impact on "interstate commerce" (which the Constitution considered the domain of the federal government), Congress passed the Interstate Commerce Act to regulate railroads in 1887; three years later, it passed the Sherman Anti-Trust Act, which outlawed monopolies that were in "restraint of trade." Although more Democrats than Republicans supported these laws, both parties were split, and the congressional votes tended to be more sectional than partisan, with opposition centered in the more business-dominated Northeast.

***The South and the Nation.*** One issue that sharply divided the two parties was whether or not the federal government should continue to oversee elections in the post-Reconstruction South. The Democrats opposed any continued federal involvement. The Republicans, however, were split on the issue. One faction, the Stalwarts, supported by strong Republican organizations in New York, Pennsylvania, and Illinois, believed that the party should stick to its Reconstruction-era strategy of securing a political base in the South by protecting the voting rights of African Americans. Their opponents (labeled "Half-breeds") thought it better to sacrifice the South to the Democrats than to risk weakening the party in the North with unpopular southern entanglements. In the late 1880s, this issue came to a head as the Democrats consolidated their hold on the South by preventing blacks from voting, which led to a series of contested congressional elections that had to be adjudicated by Congress.

In 1890, Representative Henry Cabot Lodge of Massachusetts, taking advantage of a brief moment when the Republicans controlled the presidency and both houses of Congress, introduced what came to be called the Lodge Force Bill. This measure provided for federally appointed election supervisors in any congressional district or city where 100 citizens requested their appointment; it also authorized the president to use military force, if necessary, to implement the law. Supporters believed that it would both protect black rights and generate enough Republican support in the South to help ensure the party's national dominance; as a happy by-product, it might also undermine the power of urban Democratic machines. The Democrats denounced the bill as an outrageous violation of states' rights, and some Republicans were unenthusiastic because they feared destabilizing a region in which northern firms had acquired financial interests. Consequently, the Lodge Bill was never passed, and in 1893 Congress repealed all laws authorizing federal supervision of elections, thus leaving the voting rights of African American

southerners in the hands of white state governments. Not until 1965, with the passage of the Voting Rights Act, would the federal government return to the South to enforce the Fifteenth Amendment (see Chapter 30).

## PRESIDENTIAL POLITICS, 1877–1892

National electoral campaigns were boisterous affairs. Both parties energized the faithful with parades, picnics, rallies, and bonfires, treating politics as recreation and entertainment. They also resorted heavily to sloganeering and emotion: the Republicans "waved the bloody shirt" to remind voters of the Democrats' ambivalence about the Civil War, while the Democrats charged the Republicans with being the corrupt handmaidens of big business. Both parties sent stump speakers crisscrossing the country to debate issues, and for the first time the mass distribution of pamphlets and tracts became commonplace. Yet the party positions on some key issues—such as business regulation and the money supply—were not very sharply differentiated, in part because both parties were internally split. Closely contested elections, moreover, led both Democrats and Republicans to avoid controversial issues, such as the prohibition of the sale of alcohol, and to gravitate toward centrist positions on others. Nonetheless, the two parties generally succeeded in bringing 80 to 90 percent of all eligible voters to the polls.

***Hayes, Garfield, and Arthur.*** The first post-Reconstruction president was Rutherford B. Hayes, who faced unusual handicaps when he assumed office in the spring of 1877. The circumstances of his election were so clouded that opponents called him "His Fraudulency." Hostile Democrats dominated Congress during most of his term; a long business depression, as well as the ordeal of Reconstruction, had soured the mood of the country; and a deeply entrenched patronage system hindered his ability to wield executive power. He had also announced in 1876 that he would serve only one term.

By all accounts, Hayes, a former congressman, governor of Ohio, and Union general, was an honest, intelligent man, a conciliator by temperament, a mainstream, pro-business Republican. Yet his achievements in office were few. He did strike several blows for civil service reform and against the patronage system, even antagonizing powerful New York senator Roscoe Conkling by removing Conkling's protégé, Chester A. Arthur, from his remunerative position as collector of customs in New York. Hayes also encouraged more humane policies toward Native Americans. Several policy decisions, however, damaged his reputation. In 1877, he sent troops to suppress the uprisings of workers flaring in many cities, leaving him open to the charge of being unsympathetic to working people. Moreover, by declining to send troops back to the South and doing little to protect southern blacks against the onslaught of "Redemption," he appeared to place a higher value on promoting national unity than on the rights of African Americans. After retiring from politics, Hayes became openly sympathetic to the needs of industrial workers and devoted considerable time to helping former slaves.

With Hayes out of the running, several prominent Republicans competed for the presidential nomination in 1880. One was John Sherman, secretary of the treasury and, before that, a congressman and senator from Ohio for more than twenty years. A second was James G. Blaine, Speaker of the House and a congressman since 1863, a charismatic figure depicted by his supporters as the "plumed knight" who threw "his shining lance full and fair against the brazen forehead of every traitor to his country." The third was Ulysses Grant, who, despite two uninspiring terms as president, was popular among professional politicians who had little use for either Blaine or Sherman.

When the Republican convention remained deadlocked after thirty-three ballots, delegates turned to a lesser-known Ohioan, Senator James A. Garfield, a nine-term congressman and Civil War hero. After Garfield's nomination, the convention, to placate Conkling and help the party win in New York, selected former customs collector Chester A. Arthur as his running mate. Meanwhile, the Democrats nominated General Winfield Scott Hancock, also a Civil War hero, to run with William H. English, a wealthy businessman and former congressman from Indiana. The campaign was hard-fought, with the Republicans abandoning the South to the Democrats and staking their hopes on Garfield's greater experience in government, his stand in favor of protective tariffs (which Hancock, incomprehensibly, labeled a "local issue"), and the taint of treason that still attached to the Democrats in the North. Garfield and Arthur gained a small plurality of the popular vote and were elected through a slim majority of 20,000 votes in New York.

In his first months in office, Garfield voiced a desire to reduce tariffs, institute civil service reform, and strengthen the country's economic ties to Latin America. He spent most of his time, however, trying to satisfy Republican leaders' demands for patronage positions. Day after day, he found himself dealing with what he called "disciplined office hunters" who drew papers "as highway men draw pistols." Exasperated with this ritual of presidential politics, Garfield earned popular support by squaring off against Conkling and refusing to bow to his demands for patronage. But Garfield's efforts were cut short when he was gunned down in early July by Charles Guiteau, an unsatisfied office seeker who had a messianic belief that he could save the Republican Party and the nation from destructive conflict by removing Garfield from office.

Garfield lived for nearly three months after he was shot. In September, when he died, Arthur, the very symbol of the spoilsman, became president. Despite the fears of reformers, Arthur served creditably in the presidency and even lent his support to the Pendleton Act, the passage of which seemed more urgent after Garfield's assassination. Arthur also supported federal regulation of the railroads and vetoed bills designed to benefit special corporate interests.

*Cleveland and Harrison.* Despite Arthur's unexpectedly sound performance, the Republicans did not nominate him in 1884, selecting James Blaine instead. A longtime power in the Republican Party, Blaine tried to make protective tariffs the centerpiece of the campaign, while also advocating continued civil service reform, a more energetic foreign policy, and an active federal government that would, among other things, develop the nation's waterways. Blaine's opponent was Grover Cleveland, the governor of New York. Cleveland ran

Grover Cleveland, twenty-second and twenty-fourth president of the United States (1885–89, 1893–97).

on his reputation as an honest, capable administrator, while defending states' rights and saying as little as possible about the tariff.

The parties' differences on issues were small enough to permit the 1884 campaign to degenerate into a carnival of mudslinging. The Democrats charged Blaine with corruption since he had several times used the power of his office to facilitate business deals from which he had secretly profited. As the details of these episodes became public, he was abandoned by the Mugwumps, as well as by traditionally Republican newspapers, while cartoons depicted him as a fawning ally of large corporations. Cleveland, too, turned out to have a personal vulnerability: it was reported that he had fathered an illegitimate child, a charge that he acknowledged was possibly true. Republicans then tried to damage Cleveland's reputation by relaying stories that he frequented brothels and by holding parades in which men pushed baby carriages, complete with dolls, chanting "Ma, ma, where's my Pa?" After all the mud had been slung, Cleveland won the election by the tiniest of margins, 48.5 percent of the popular vote, compared with Blaine's 48.3 percent. A switch of 550 votes in New York would have given the election to Blaine.

Although he was the first Democrat to gain the presidency since before the Civil War, Cleveland signaled his allegiance to the conservative, pro-business wing of his party through his cabinet appointments and by announcing his faith in "business principles" in his inaugural address. His administration, marked by a renewal of executive authority (he vetoed more than half the bills Congress passed) and a restoration of respectability for the Democratic Party, did not significantly depart from the policies of his predecessors. Among the more notable pieces of legislation passed between 1885 and 1888 were the Hatch Act, creating agricultural experiment stations; bills furthering Indian policy and civil service reform; and the Interstate Commerce Act, which was a congressional rather than presidential initiative (see Chapter 18). Cleveland's most serious setback was his inability to push tariff-cutting legislation through a Congress that was always partially under Republican control.

Cleveland was renominated in 1888, running against Senator Benjamin Harrison of Indiana, the grandson of President William Henry Harrison. Once more, the key issue in the campaign was the tariff: Cleveland maintained his stance in favor of lower tariffs, while Harrison depicted the Democrats as free-traders whose policies would cost American workers their jobs. Owing to the Republicans' superior organization

and the absence of intraparty discord, Harrison was elected in yet another extremely close election. Cleveland, who received overwhelming support in the South, actually won a majority of the popular vote, but Harrison eked out narrow victories in the crucial states of New York and Indiana, which gave him a decisive victory in the electoral college. The Republicans also won majorities in both houses of Congress, allowing them to control the executive and legislative branches for the first time in decades.

Harrison was a capable figure who appointed competent men to his administration while displaying a growing interest in foreign affairs. Yet he gave little active leadership to the nation and left a shallow imprint on its history. The two most important pieces of legislation enacted during his term were the Sherman Anti-Trust Act and the McKinley Tariff, which increased duties on many goods to unprecedented levels. In part because of popular resentment of these tariff increases, the Democrats gained control of the House of Representatives in the congressional elections of 1890, stymying any further presidential efforts to shape legislation with a free hand.

### THE PEOPLE'S PARTY AND THE ELECTION OF 1892

In 1892, Harrison and Cleveland squared off against each other again, the first time that two men with presidential experience had faced each other in an election. The campaign was dull, but relatively dignified. The leading issue was again the tariff, with Harrison defending protection while backing away from the extremes of the McKinley Tariff, and Cleveland favoring tariff reduction while eschewing the more decisive "tariff for revenue only" position of many fellow Democrats. The candidates also disagreed about the coinage of silver and, more sharply, about using the power of the federal government to support black voting rights in the South. Harrison was a supporter of the Lodge Force Bill, while Cleveland, anxious to retain the support of white southerners, opposed it.

Cleveland and the Democrats won a decisive victory. The Democrats also won sizable victories in the congressional elections and appeared to have become the nation's majority party.

The 1892 election also witnessed the appearance of the People's Party (or Populists), which brought the politics of insurgency into the national electoral arena. The party was formally launched on July 4, 1892, when 1,300 delegates from the Farmers' Alliances, the Knights of Labor, the American Federation of Labor, and a host of smaller organizations gath-

VOL. 20 NO. 503     JUNE 6 1891     PRICE 10 CENTS.

A PARTY OF PATCHES.
Grand Balloon Ascension—Cincinnati, May 20th, 1891.

A satirical and hostile view of the People's Party as "A Party of Patches," including the Farmers' Alliance, the Free Silver Party, and the Old Greenback Party, June 1891.

ered in Omaha and nominated candidates for that year's elections. They adopted a platform whose preamble announced the urgency of their mission.

> We meet in the midst of a nation brought to the verge of moral, political and material ruin. Corruption dominates the ballot box, the Legislatures, the Congress, and touches even the ermine of the Bench. The people are demoralized . . . the newspapers are largely subsidized or muzzled; public opinion silenced; business prostrated, our homes covered with mortgages, labor impoverished, and the land concentrating in the hands of the capitalists. . . . The fruits of the toil of millions are boldly stolen to build up colossal fortunes for a few.

The Omaha platform, steeped in the notion that "wealth belongs to him who creates it," called for reforms that farmer and labor groups had been demanding: government ownership of the railroads and telegraph; a graduated income tax; the reclamation of lands held by railroads and other corporate speculators; a flexible and inflated currency based on a subtreasury system as well as the free coinage of silver; postal

savings banks (to provide a secure place for working people to place their savings); the direct election of senators; immigration restriction; an eight-hour day for government jobs; and outlawing the use of Pinkertons (a private, rentable police force) against labor.

The central challenge facing the People's Party was to build a truly national organization that could bridge the divisions among its supporters. Doing so meant unifying farmers from the South and North, despite the legacy of the Civil War and differences in their ideas about currency reform: southern farmers tended to embrace the subtreasury plan developed by the Farmers' Alliances, while midwestern and western farmers favored the free coinage of silver. To succeed, the party also had to convince a heterogeneous working class to join with a farmer-dominated party and persuade voters everywhere to abandon previous party allegiances. Finally, the Populists had to resolve key conflicts about race: although there were prominent exceptions, such as Georgia's Tom Watson, most southern populists embraced white supremacy, which placed them at odds with black farmers and with many northern populists who rejected racial discrimination and even favored the Lodge Force Bill.

The Populists fared well in the 1892 elections. Their presidential candidate, General James B. Weaver, polled 8.5 percent of the vote, running strongly in the West and Southwest. They also elected three governors, five U.S. senators, ten congressmen, and nearly 1,500 local and state officials, despite substantial electoral fraud in the South that deprived them of hard-earned victories. But the party made few inroads among urban workers and had difficulty prying white southerners loose from the Democratic Party, which insisted that it alone could preserve white supremacy. Nonetheless, adherents of the People's Party were optimistic about its future and looked forward to the elections of 1894 and 1896.

### THE CRISIS OF THE 1890s

Soon after Grover Cleveland took office in 1893, the country plunged into the most severe depression it had ever experienced. Banks and businesses failed, millions of workers were unemployed, and farmers found themselves even more hard-pressed than they had been in the 1880s. The pessimistic vision of the Populists and labor radicals seemed to be vindicated. An economy controlled by large corporate monopolies could not meet the needs of the people; workers and farmers were suffering and angry. In the spring of 1894, thousands of unemployed

## The Nation State

A pro-Cleveland cartoon showing the president defying the hydra-headed free-silver movement.

workers from cities across the country began marching, on foot, to Washington to demand that the federal government launch public works programs to provide jobs for the unemployed. The most well known of these "armies" of protesters was led by Jacob Coxey, a colorful populist from Ohio. When "Coxey's Army" of 500 men reached Washington, it was harassed and disbanded by authorities; when Coxey himself tried to speak at the U.S. Capitol, he was arrested for walking on the grass.

Cleveland's response to the depression was no more deft than his government's reaction to Jacob Coxey. He attempted to fulfill his campaign promise of lowering tariffs to stimulate trade, but the new law that was passed, the Wilson-Gorman Tariff, contained so many amendments catering to special interests that it bore little resemblance to reform. In 1894, he authorized the use of federal troops to break the Pullman strike, which made him seem unsympathetic to labor. Most important, he joined Republicans in repealing the Sherman Silver Purchase Act: the nation's gold reserves were shrinking rapidly, and Cleveland believed, as did most bankers and big businessmen, that maintaining a gold standard was both a moral imperative and the key to economic recovery. Repealing the Sherman Act, however, had no impact on either the depression or the run on gold, which led Cleveland to shore up gold reserves by trading federal bonds for gold from a banking syndicate headed by financier J. P. Morgan. The transaction was immensely profitable to the bankers.

Cleveland's actions ignited a political storm. To many Americans, the depression seemed to call not for a return to the gold standard but rather for inflating the money supply in order to raise prices, stimulate production, and relieve the burden of debt. Cleveland's policies appeared to serve the interests of bankers and other creditors rather than farmers, workers, and small-business owners. The western, prosilver wing of his own party was enraged, and the Populists were heartened. The depression, moreover, bolstered support for the free coinage of silver among Democrats and previously skeptical Populists. One of the most popular publications of the 1890s was William H. "Coin" Harvey's *Coin's Financial School,* an illustrated pamphlet that pressed the cause of silver. A Mississippi congressman wrote to a member of Cleveland's cabinet that the book "is being sold on every railroad train by the newsboys and at every cigar store. It is being read by almost everybody."

The political damage to Cleveland and the Democrats was quickly apparent. In the 1894 congressional elections, many Democrats lost their seats. The Populist vote, centered in the West and South, was more than 40 percent greater

The cover of the bestselling *Coin's Financial School.*

than it had been in 1892, while the Republicans gained in the North. By the final year of his presidency, Cleveland was viewed as a conservative, pro-business politician who had failed to end a severe depression and whose monetary policies had shattered the Democratic Party.

### THE ELECTION OF 1896

As the 1896 election approached, insurgent political movements and the silver issue were both in the national spotlight. The nation was still sunk in depression, and the route out of economic crisis was far from clear. Proposals for radical political and social change were gaining audiences. Large constituencies believed that the free coinage of silver was essential to restoring prosperity, while others were equally convinced that only a full embrace of the gold standard would turn the trick. (Both groups, in fact, were mistaken, but, as is often true, beliefs were more important than realities in shaping economic policy.) Neither of the major parties, moreover, could ignore the threat of the Populists. Although the People's Party seemed unlikely to win the presidency, it seemed capable of drawing enough votes away from both parties to affect the outcome of the election and to become an important voice in Congress and in state governments.

The Republicans held their convention first, meeting in June to nominate William McKinley, a skillful, nationally prominent former congressman and governor from Ohio. McKinley, best known as a supporter of high tariffs, was the undisputed front-runner because of his popularity with business and with some labor groups who embraced the idea that high tariffs protected jobs. He was also the beneficiary of the assiduous preconvention campaigning orchestrated by his wealthy friend, retired businessman Marcus (Mark) Alonza Hanna. The Republican platform embraced protectionism, opposed the free coinage of silver, and insisted that "the gold standard must be maintained." When the platform was passed, a group of western silver Republicans, led by Senator Henry M. Teller of Colorado, walked out of the convention and left the Republican Party.

The Democratic convention, a month later, was less orderly, reflecting the splintering of the party that had occurred under Cleveland. The eastern, pro-gold Cleveland wing fought hard for its positions but was outnumbered by passionate delegates

William Jennings Bryan at the Democratic Convention of 1896.

from the South and West. The convention adopted a platform that repudiated much of what Cleveland had stood for, including the gold standard: it endorsed the unlimited coinage of silver as well as a federal income tax.

The dramatic highpoint of the platform debates occurred when former congressman William Jennings Bryan, a thirty-six-year-old Nebraskan well known for his oratorical skills, delivered a powerful speech on behalf of silver, farmers, and westerners. "I come to speak to you in defense of a cause as holy as the cause of liberty—the cause of humanity," he began. Drawing a divide between country and city, East and West, silver and gold, producers and capitalists, Bryan declared, "Burn down your cities and leave our farms, and your cities will spring up again as if by magic; but destroy our farms and the grass will grow in the streets of every city in the country." The stirring conclusion to his speech, both rebellious and religious, came to symbolize the tenor of the coming election campaign: "Having behind us the producing masses of the nation and the world, supported by the commercial interests, the laboring interests, and the toilers everywhere, we will answer their demand for a gold standard by saying to them: You shall not press down upon the brow of labor this crown of thorns. You shall not crucify mankind upon a cross of gold!" The speech so galvanized the convention that it nominated the young Nebraskan for the presidency on the fifth ballot, balancing the ticket with Arthur Sewall of Maine, a banker who also rejected the gold standard.

591

## The Nation State

The Democratic nomination of Bryan created a quandary for the Populists and exposed divisions within their ranks. Prosilver Populists, most from the West and the Midwest, advocated "fusion" with the Democrats and the nomination of Bryan by the People's Party. Others believed that the coinage of silver was a poor substitute for the subtreasury plan, that more broad-gauged reforms were needed in any case, and that nominating Bryan would destroy the party. Many southerners found fusion to be particularly distasteful because Populism in the South was, in critical respects, a rebellion against the Democratic Party, and they had already burned their bridges with the party of white supremacy.

The Populist delegates meeting in St. Louis were faced with a hard choice: they could either risk losing their political identity through fusion or virtually guarantee the election of McKinley by nominating their own candidate. After sharp debate, they chose to nominate Bryan and assert their independence by replacing vice-presidential candidate Arthur Sewall with Georgia's fiery antifusionist Tom Watson. In reaching this decision, they were influenced by assurances—which turned out to be false—that Bryan would ask Sewall to step aside and place Watson in the second spot on a fusion ticket. Bryan, however, refused to do so, leaving the Populists in the awkward position of supporting a presidential candidate who had repudiated their choice for vice-president.

The presidential campaign was a study in contrasting ideologies and political styles. Bryan barnstormed around the country, traveling 18,000 miles by train and giving more than 600 speeches. With eloquence and power, the young, energetic "Great Commoner" pressed the cause of silver at every stop, and spoke as well of railroad regulation and the need to halt the "operations of trusts, syndicates, and combines." Raised on a farm, a man of character and sincerity, Bryan conveyed a faith in the wisdom of the people, an evangelical vision of politics as inseparable from morality, and an optimistic conviction that his cause would eventually triumph. His charisma and message electrified the million or more people who heard him speak; for farmers, journalist William Allen White noted, "it was a fanaticism like the Crusades."

All of which struck fear in the hearts of many Republicans and eastern Democrats, a fear that the McKinley camp exploited. Mark Hanna realized early on that Bryan would be a forceful candidate. He also recognized the important role that corporate money could play in elections. Hanna solicited funds from banks, insurance companies, railroads, and other large corporations, raising an official total of $3.5 million,

A Republican Party placard shows the party candidate, McKinley, the symbol of "sound government, sound money, and prosperity," and labels his opponent, Bryan, a symbol of "bankruptcy and dishonor."

more than ten times the amount that Bryan had available. Standard Oil alone gave Hanna $250,000. Most reports suggest that the Republicans actually spent more than $7 million on the campaign, distributing millions of pieces of literature and funding more than a thousand speakers who were sent out to raise fears about Bryan and to sing McKinley's praises. With the help of special discounts from the railroads, Hanna also paid the expenses of 750,000 people who traveled, in carefully identified groups, to meet with McKinley at his home in Canton, Ohio. There each delegation attended a reception and listened to a short speech delivered from McKinley's front porch: this campaign technique permitted the Republican to meet with voters and repeatedly stress that his party was the vehicle of economic growth and the "full dinner pail" while not seeming to compete with Bryan's superior energy and oratorical skills. The press, overwhelmingly pro-McKinley, carried enthusiastic reports of these events while denouncing Bryan and caricaturing his ideas.

On election day, Bryan won more votes than any previous presidential candidate—nearly 800,000 more than Cleveland had garnered in 1892 and more than any Democrat would win for twenty years. Nonetheless, McKinley received a half million more votes than Bryan and won in the electoral col-

## How Do You Get the News: The Election of 1896

"The anxious crowd [in City Hall park] surged denser and more terrible in its ungovernable weight. Thousands stood craning their necks to the walls of the huge buildings before them, faintly outlined against the deep sky. Search-lights spun round the horizon, lighting up signal-kites floating aloft. On the screens appeared scenes shown by the cinematographe, which were received with alternate delight and derision. When the first returns were shown the crowd lost mastery of itself. The crowd broke against the wire fences, swept them down, and surged over the sacred enclosures. It could not help it. The laws of space and force were the only things that had not taken a night off for the election.

From the first moment of the arrival of returns, the direction of the stream was clearly apparent. New York City, where never before had a majority been given for a Republican President, was going steadily and surely for Mr. M'Kinley. One hundred districts, two hundred districts, three hundred districts, were heard from, and Mr. M'Kinley forged steadily ahead, till his majority in the city was certain to be at least 20,000. Then the serried masses began to open their lungs, and fierce yells and whoops and cheers crashed from side to side of the great square."

G. W. Steevens, *The Land of the Dollar* (Edinburgh and London, 1897)

*American Journal*

lege, 271 to 176. Bryan captured the South, the plains states, and the silver-producing Rocky Mountain states, but McKinley was victorious throughout the Northeast and the Midwest, as well as on the West Coast. The Republicans won every major city, increased their vote in rural areas of the Midwest, and retained control of both houses of Congress.

Bryan's defeat had several sources. One was that he was outspent and placed on the defensive by an unusually united Republican Party backed by nearly all major organs of public opinion. A second was that he failed to win majorities among urban—particularly ethnic—workers, which left him with little chance of making inroads in the Northeast and, more critically, in closely contested midwestern states such as Illinois and Ohio. Workers were intimidated by employers who stated that if Bryan won, "the whistle will not blow on Wednesday." Many workers also had some sympathy for McKinley's high tariff positions and found Bryan's evangelical style alien. Indeed, in 1896, there was a shift in the parties' ethnocultural appeals: it was the Democrats, not the Republicans, who were making a pietistic, cultural bid for votes. This attracted support among some

previously Republican voters (Methodists, for example), but it repelled segments of the traditionally Democratic Catholic working class.

The election of 1896 marked the end of the era of closely contested national elections and divided government: the Republicans were solidly in power, and they would remain in control of the national government for most of the next thirty-five years. McKinley's victory also signaled the end of the agrarian revolt against industrialism, the final chapter in the rebellion of small producers against corporate capitalism. After a century of uncertainty, wrote Henry Adams, "the majority at last declared itself . . . in favor of a capitalistic system with all its necessary machinery." The dynamics of the election left the People's Party mortally wounded: having lost both the election and its political identity, it did poorly in the 1898 elections and then virtually disappeared from the political stage. Despite the demise of the Populists, however, farmers did well economically after 1896: a year later, a sharp drop in European grain production increased the demand for American exports, and agricultural prices continued to rise well into the twentieth century. But never

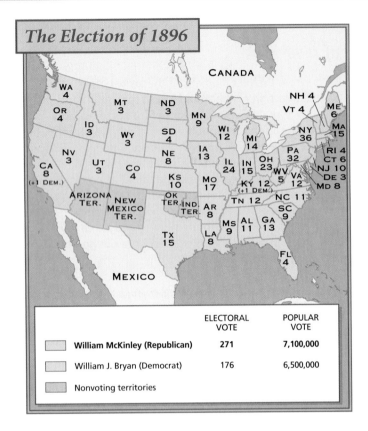

### The Election of 1896

| | ELECTORAL VOTE | POPULAR VOTE |
|---|---|---|
| William McKinley (Republican) | 271 | 7,100,000 |
| William J. Bryan (Democrat) | 176 | 6,500,000 |
| Nonvoting territories | | |

again would farmers be the powerful political force that they were in the years leading up to the 1896 election.

President McKinley and his fellow Republicans interpreted the election as a mandate to govern in the interest of the business community that had supported them. McKinley appointed bankers to head the Treasury and Interior Departments and a lumber baron as secretary of war. Congress, with the support of the president, passed the Dingley Tariff, which increased already high duties on imported goods to an average rate of 52 percent. In 1900, the Republicans pushed through the Gold Standard Act, which officially made gold the sole specie backing the money supply. Ironically, the discovery of gold in Alaska and South Africa, coupled with the development of new techniques of extracting gold from low-grade ore, led to an expansion of the currency and inflation—despite the defeat of the silver movement. Owing in part to these developments and in part to the return of prosperity at the end of the century, the formal adoption of a gold standard had no discernible impact on the economy.

## The Conservative Courts

Public policy in the United States has always been shaped by courts, as well as by legislators, governors, and presidents. In the late nineteenth century, the courts expanded their role, taking a more activist and ideological stance toward the "judicial review" of legislation. The federal judiciary was overwhelmingly Republican and consisted almost entirely of men drawn from well-to-do backgrounds. (State judges, many of whom were elected, were less uniform in their party affiliations and social origins, but they, too, tended to come from the upper reaches of society.) These men, responding to the transformations and tensions of the industrial world, came to see themselves as a critical bulwark in the defense of property rights. By the 1890s, they had come to fear the challenges to political and social order posed by working-class protest and insurgent political movements, and they saw the courts as defenders of property against the "excesses" of democracy.

This judicial posture spawned a new legal doctrine, often labeled "laissez-faire constitutionalism." Its consequences were most evident in two arenas: labor law, and the regulation of business practices by the government. In terms of labor law, the courts were increasingly hostile to any legislative efforts to intervene in the relationship between employers and employees. In 1885, for example, the New York Court of Appeals, in *In re Jacobs,* struck down an antisweatshop law that prohibited the manufacture of cigars in tenement houses, ruling that the law infringed on the "personal liberty" and freedom of contract of individual workers. For similar reasons, the courts voided an 1893 Illinois law that sought to protect women by limiting them to an eight-hour workday (six days per week). As important, federal judges, after the railroad strikes of 1877, repeatedly issued injunctions to end strikes and compel workers to return to their jobs. Originally these judges were following common law notions (derived from court decisions rather than statutes) that union-led strikes were conspiracies to violate the law and destroy the property of owners; but federal judges after 1890 frequently invoked the Sherman Anti-Trust Act to issue injunctions against striking unions because they constituted "conspiracies in restraint of trade." By the 1890s, injunctions to halt strikes were being issued by the hundreds, if not thousands, while new laws sought by labor were likely to be struck down by the courts.

Laissez-faire constitutionalism also had an impact on the ability of state and federal governments to regulate business

An 1888 cartoon criticizing the courts for crushing anarchy but sparing monopoly.

practices. In the 1870s (see Chapter 18), the Supreme Court had been tolerant of such regulation, ruling in *Munn v. Illinois* that the state of Illinois could regulate prices in grain-storage facilities in Chicago because such facilities were "clothed with a public interest" and because their regulation did not deprive their owners of property without due process of law. In the 1880s, however, business lawyers began to argue that the Fourteenth Amendment justified the judicial narrowing of regulatory laws: the amendment prohibited the states from abridging the "privileges and immunities" of citizens, from denying anyone "the equal protection of the laws," and from depriving "any person of life, liberty, or property without due process of law." Corporations, they argued, were "persons" under the amendment, and mere legislative enactment did not constitute "due process of law." This meant that the ability of government to regulate private enterprise was limited and would be defined not by legislatures, but by the courts.

The federal judiciary, and then the Supreme Court itself, came to embrace these arguments by the 1890s. In a series of cases, the courts overturned or narrowed state regulatory laws and imposed significant limits on the Interstate Commerce Commission. In 1895, the Supreme Court handed down three decisions that became pillars of the new constitutional order. In *U.S. v. E.C. Knight,* the Court ruled that the sugar trust, which refined 98 percent of the sugar in the United States, could not be declared a monopoly under the Sherman Anti-Trust Act because the act referred only to "commerce" and not to "manufacturing." The Court also decided in *In re Debs* that the Sherman Act was a legitimate basis for issuing an injunction against the American Railway Union to halt a sympathy strike against the railroads. Unions, it seemed, were more vulnerable to being declared "conspiracies in restraint of trade" than were manufacturers. Then, in *Pollock v. Farmers' Loan and Trust Co.,* the Court declared unconstitutional an 1894 federal law that would have imposed a 2 percent tax on all incomes over $4,000.

These decisions were opposed by labor organizations, reformers, progressive political figures, and even some lawyers and judges. Nonetheless, by the end of the decade, the federal courts had made clear that they would actively intervene to protect the rights of property and freedom of contract against legislative infringement and, more generally, to restrict the scope of government intervention in economic affairs. Many of the decisions handed down by the courts eviscerated popular legislation while establishing legal precedents that would endure for decades.

## The New Political Universe

After 1896, Americans found themselves participating in—or not participating in—what one political scientist has called a "new political universe." Not only did the Republicans gain control of the national government, but outside the sparsely populated West the nation was divided into two large, single-party regions. The South and some of the border states were dominated by the Democratic Party, while much of the North was controlled by the Republicans. This shift, under way before the election of 1896, reflected not simply the rebuff of agrarian radicalism but the Republicans' success in presenting themselves as the party of prosperity. By doing so, they were able to divide the politically rambunctious working class and win the support of skilled and unionized urban workers.

One characteristic of this new universe was a decline in electoral participation. In the South, the disfranchisement of

African Americans had lowered turnout even before 1896, but the trend became more pronounced thereafter: by 1908, turnout rates in the region had plummeted to 30 percent. In most northern states, turnout was between 80 and 95 percent in 1896, but it then began a gradual decline that would continue, with a few interruptions, through the twentieth century. Single-party dominance meant that parties no longer had to mobilize voters as they had done from the 1870s through the 1890s. Moreover, many citizens, particularly those near the bottom of the economic ladder, stopped going to the polls because they felt that electoral politics had little to offer them. Complex registration systems, literacy tests, and poll taxes in northern states also kept people, especially immigrant workers, from voting.

Linked to the drop in participation was the declining visibility of third parties. The politics of insurgency did not disappear after 1896, but the scale of activity was more limited. In most states, the chaotic, optimistic, rapidly changing multiparty world of the 1870s, '80s, and '90s gave way to a more solidly entrenched two-party or one-party system. The possibilities of insurgent victory, particularly given the complexities of the nation's federal structure of governance, seemed increasingly remote; the enthusiasm and energy so prominent in the late nineteenth century were dampened. The Democratic and Republican Parties, sustained by large organizations and nourished by corporate contributions, had a firm grip on both the institutions of governance and the apparatus of elections. Modern American politics had arrived.

## Suggested Reading

Henry Adams, *The Education of Henry Adams* (1907)

Edward L. Ayers, *Southern Crossing: A History of the American South 1877–1906* (1995)

Lawrence Goodwyn, *Democratic Promise: The Populist Movement in America* (1976)

Morton J. Horwitz, *The Transformation of American Law, 1870–1960* (1992)

Richard Oestreicher, *Solidarity and Fragmentation: Working People and Class Consciousness in Detroit, 1875–1900* (1986)

Gretchen Ritter, *Goldbugs and Greenbacks: The Antimonopoly Tradition and the Politics of Finance in America* (1997)

Nick Salvatore, *Eugene v. Debs: Citizen and Socialist* (1982)

Stephen Skowronek, *Building a New American State: The Expansion of National Administrative Capacities* (1982)

# Chapter Review

## Summary QUESTIONS

■ 1. What were the key challenges facing city governments and how successfully were they met?

■ 2. How central were state governments in solving the problems generated by industrialization?

■ 3. What were the primary concerns of industrial workers, and what steps did they take to cope with the problems confronting them?

■ 4. Why did the movement for women's suffrage make little headway during these years?

■ 5. Why was "the money question" such an urgent policy issue in this period?

## Chronology

| | |
|---|---|
| 1877 | The Great Railroad Strike. |
| | The Southern Farmers' Alliance founded in Texas. |
| 1886 | The American Federation of Labor founded. |
| May 4, 1886 | The Haymarket Affair. |
| 1892 | The People's Party founded. |
| 1893 | Panic begins severe depression. |
| | Congress repeals laws authorizing federal supervision of elections. |
| 1894 | The Pullman Strike. |
| 1900 | The Gold Standard Act passed. |

## Key Terms

Tammany Hall (p. 571)

Trade unions (p. 575)

The Pullman Strike (p. 578)

The suffrage movement (p. 579)

Soft money (p. 584)

Populism (p. 588)

---

**Access the *Inventing America* StudySpace at wwnorton.com/studyspace**

PERSONAL PLAN ■ REVIEW MATERIALS ■ RESEARCH AIDS ■ MULTIMEDIA

# Chapter 21

# A NEW PLACE IN THE WORLD:

## 1865–1914

A contemporary engraving that shows workers excavating the Panama Canal near Emperador.

■ **What were the main currents of foreign policy in the postbellum years?**

■ **What was the significance of the Spanish-American War?**

■ **Why did the United States become a world power in this period?**

■ **How did America wield its power overseas?**

In the immediate aftermath of the Civil War, the United States displayed little interest in events transpiring outside its continental boundaries. Preoccupied with sectional conflict and possessing a vast, sparsely settled West that could absorb its expansive energies for decades, the nation, unlike Britain and other European powers, seemed to have few imperial ambitions. In 1870, the only territory outside of North America that the United States officially controlled was a tiny, uninhabited Pacific atoll, and most Americans were content to keep it that way. "Our country," wrote *New York Tribune* editor Horace Greeley, "has already an ample area for the next century at least."

The country, moreover, had few of the tools necessary to influence affairs beyond its borders. The Department of State in Washington had roughly fifty employees. The army was shrinking in size daily, on its way to becoming a small force of 25,000 men, 15 percent of whom deserted each year. By 1890, the American army was half the size of Belgium's and slightly smaller than that of Bulgaria. Similarly, the post–Civil War navy consisted largely of small, aging wooden ships with little or no armor, powered by boilers so in need of repair that they could not travel at half their intended speed.

By 1914, the eve of World War I, all that had changed. American firms were trading and investing around the globe. American missionaries were spreading the gospel of Christianity and technological progress in Asia, the Middle East, and Latin America. The United States had taken formal possession of territory in the Caribbean and the Pacific, stretching from Puerto Rico and part of Cuba through Hawaii to the Philippines. It had fought its first overseas war, defeating a European empire and seizing some of its colonies. In diverse arenas, the nation had signaled to the imperial powers that it intended to be a major player on the international stage.

Meanwhile, the State Department had grown to include nearly 300 employees in Washington, with consular offices in more than 100 cities in 43 countries, while the Commerce Department had acquired a bureau devoted to promoting international trade. The army had 100,000 soldiers under its command, and the navy possessed more than 300 seaworthy ships, including 30 submarines and 35 armored battleships. Furthermore, the United States had exercised its might not only in an overseas war but by dispatching ships and soldiers to secure American interests, collect customs receipts, and police conflicts in locales that it did not legally control. For better or worse, the United States stood poised to become one of the foremost powers in the world.

## Postbellum Stirrings, 1865–1890

For twenty-five years after Appomattox, American foreign policy was shaped by two traditional yet contradictory impulses. One was expansive: throughout its history, the nation had grown in population and territory. Through purchases and conquest, the thirteen states hugging the Atlantic Seaboard had become a huge continental nation, and some Americans—particularly among the elite who molded foreign policy—believed that further expansion was both inevitable and desirable. Yet coexisting with this expansive urge was an inclination to steer clear of foreign entanglements, to enjoy the nation's geographic isolation from other powers. The United States could not easily be invaded; through the Monroe Doctrine, it had warned European nations to tread softly in the Western Hemisphere; and any involvement in European affairs seemed unnecessary. Moreover, as citizens of a republic that had once been a colony, many Americans (elite and otherwise) were opposed to the colonial domination of one people by another.

The most influential and prescient advocate of expansion was William Henry Seward, secretary of state under Presidents Lincoln and Johnson. Although once a supporter of the wholesale acquisition of new territories, including Canada and Mexico, Seward by the mid-1860s had begun to pursue a different vision—of commercial, rather than territorial, empire: the rapidly industrializing United States ought to establish naval bases in the Caribbean and the Pacific and erect a "highway" to Asia in order to gain access to foreign markets and expand its international trade. Eventually, Seward believed, the European colonial regimes would be supplanted by Americans who "value dollars more and dominion less."

In keeping with this vision, Seward signed a treaty purchasing Alaska from Russia in 1867. The secretary was convinced that the acquisition of Alaska, rich in natural resources, would enhance American power in the Pacific, check that of Britain, and nurture America's burgeoning friendship with Russia, which was eager to dispose of Alaska. Although many derided the idea as "Seward's folly" or "Seward's icebox," he eventually convinced the Senate to ratify the treaty and the House to appropriate $7.2 million for the purchase. Seward simultaneously persuaded Congress to annex the tiny, uninhabited Midway Islands to provide the United States with a base halfway between California and the Asian mainland. In May 1867, Seward penned an optimistic poem:

> Abroad our empire shall no limits know,
> But like the sea in boundless circles flow.

Seward's expansive ambitions were held in check by a Congress riven by internal conflicts, preoccupied with Reconstruction, and largely uninterested in acquiring overseas territories or bases. Indeed, in the late 1860s, the Senate blocked attempts to purchase the Virgin Islands, to gain exclusive rights to build a canal through the Colombian province of Panama, and to establish tariff reciprocity with Hawaii. In 1870, despite arm-twisting by President Grant, the Senate also voted down a treaty to annex the Dominican Republic, because senators were dubious about expansion and wary of adding to the nation's nonwhite population. As Seward himself acknowledged, there was little popular support in the United States for his "empire" with "no limits."

The industrial transformation of the United States, however, led more and more Americans to turn their gaze outward. Foreign trade increased dramatically after the Civil War, as did American investment overseas and European investment in the United States; between 1860 and 1897, imports doubled while exports more than tripled, (The positive balance of trade would last until the 1970s.) A rising proportion of U.S. exports, moreover, came from industry: not just the produce of America's fertile fields but steel, motors, kerosene, and even cigarettes were routinely shipped to distant corners of the globe. The well-being of Standard Oil, American Tobacco, and the Singer Manufacturing Company, as well as farmers in the South and West, thus seemed increasingly yoked to exports. Indeed, the rising productivity of American industry, coupled with the shock of periodic depressions, spawned a widespread belief that foreign markets were becoming essential to American prosperity, that the nation's productive capacity had outgrown its ability to consume.

Technological and ideological factors heightened American interest in developments abroad. Faster ships and railroads made foreign lands more accessible, while telegraph cables laid along the ocean floors (the first trans-Atlantic cable was completed in 1866) greatly speeded communication. Tropical territories also seemed more inviting once quinine, an extract from cinchona bark, was recognized as an effective prophylaxis against malaria, the mosquito-borne disease that had killed large numbers of European settlers and adventurers. Meanwhile, the "closing" of the frontier in the American West signaled the end of a long era of continental expansion, and social Darwinist notions of the "survival of the fittest" seemed readily applicable to the international arena. Although many social Darwinists were anti-expansionists, in part because they feared adding "inferior" races to American society, others argued that international conflict was inescapable and would surely lead to American economic, political, and cultural triumphs. In the widely read *Our Country* (1885), for example, Protestant minister Josiah Strong declared that Anglo-Saxons had a "genius for colonization" and that "God, with infinite wisdom and skill is training the Anglo-Saxon race for . . . the final competition of races."

Pressure for increased government involvement abroad sometimes came directly from Americans who lived and invested in foreign nations. In Costa Rica, for example, American Minor Keith gained control of both the railroads and banana production, becoming the dominant figure in the Costa Rican economy and forming the core of what would become the United Fruit Company (which Central Americans eventually would label "the octupus"). To protect his investments in a region troubled by political strife, Keith encouraged the U.S. government to signal its interest in stability with a show of force by the navy.

Similarly, the lush, strategically located islands of Hawaii hosted American planters and missionaries (the two were often indistinguishable) who came to own most of its sugar plantations. To gain access to the American market and tighten Hawaiian ties to the United States, these planters pressed Congress and the State Department for a treaty eliminating tariffs on Hawaiian sugar. Their success in 1875 spawned a dramatic increase in sugar production. When the treaty was renewed in 1887, it included an added provision granting the United States the right to use Pearl Harbor as a naval base. The place of the planters in Hawaiian society, however, remained precarious, thanks to deepening anti-American sentiment in the islands, as well as opposition to the tariff reductions by sugar producers in the United States. To solve these problems, one key group of planters began lobbying the United States to annex Hawaii outright.

Still, the makers of U.S. foreign policy remained ambivalent, and the government made few territorial acquisitions before the 1890s. Although several Republican secretaries of state, most notably James G. Blaine, who served under Presidents Garfield and Harrison, shared Seward's expansive vision, they were able to take only small steps toward transforming that vision into reality. In 1872, for example, the Senate agreed to lease the Samoan port of Pago Pago but rebuffed State Department efforts to turn Samoa into a protectorate. (Protectorates were diplomatic devices, generally governed by treaties, through which strong states agreed to protect vulnerable territories against third parties in return for specific favors and some control over the weaker territory's policies.) In 1889, Blaine also tried to interest Hawaii in becoming a U.S. protectorate, but the Hawaiians resisted. Several years later, pro-annexation whites, with some American support, seized power in a military coup and quickly signed an annexation treaty with Blaine and Harrison. But the treaty was repudiated by Harrison's successor, Grover Cleveland, who was less enthused about overseas acquisitions and wary of implementing an agreement that lacked the support of most Hawaiians. Even in Latin America, where the United States had long-standing interests, efforts to expand American influence and capture trade from the Europeans were more rhetorical than concrete.

## THE OLD ARMY AND THE NEW NAVY

A similarly halting pattern characterized efforts to build and modernize the armed forces. The army was small, with an oversized officer corps, dominated by Civil War veterans, that gave young men few chances to advance through the ranks. It was also slow to embrace new technology. Smokeless gunpowder (which kept guns cleaner and permitted soldiers to fire and remain hidden) was commonly used in Europe, but the army did not adopt a rifle that could use the new powder until 1892—although the widely used, smokeless "Krag" rifle was manufactured in the United States. Similarly, the army took years to recognize the potential of the first fully automatic machine gun, which was invented in 1885 by an American, Hiram Maxim.

The navy made more progress, perhaps because it seemed likely to play a larger role in future conflicts. By the early 1880s, the navy was antiquated and in disrepair: fewer than fifty ships were seaworthy, and none could contend with the more technologically advanced fleets of the European powers or even countries such as Chile and China. Prompted in part by a budget surplus that Republicans were eager to spend, Congress in 1890 authorized the construction of a series of

One of the new generation of U.S. Navy cruisers, c. 1890.

steel-armored ships, including three heavily armed battle-ships. Even that decision, however, was shaped by ambiva-lence about overseas involvement: Congress specified that these would be "sea-going, coast-line battleships," with a rela-tively short cruising range, designed primarily to defend the North American mainland.

Rebuilding the navy had important repercussions for indus-try and its ties to the government. Building armored ships de-manded expertise in the manufacture of high-quality structural steel, as well as specialized facilities for turning out armor and powerful guns. Since the United States lacked such expertise and facilities, the least expensive path was to buy key components abroad. Congress, however, led by Republicans, insisted that domestic sources of armaments be developed. The navy con-sequently built its own gun factory and subsidized the construc-tion of armor plants by Bethlehem Steel and Carnegie Steel. By the 1890s, when the decline in new railroad construction re-duced the demand for steel rails, steel manufacturers found themselves increasingly dependent on orders from the navy; not surprisingly, these firms often supported an aggressive foreign policy that would require a large navy. The United States also found itself drawn into an arms race with European powers, since larger guns required stronger, nickel-plated armor, which in turn created a demand for even more potent guns.

## Turning Point: The 1890s

During the final decade of the nineteenth century, the forces and actors favoring a more expansive foreign policy gained the upper hand. The United States asserted itself strongly against the European powers, particularly Britain. It con-ducted what Secretary of State John Hay called a "splendid little war" against Spain, as well as a less splendid, larger war against nationalist rebels in the Philippines. By 1900, the United States controlled bases, territories, and millions of people from the Caribbean to the western Pacific.

This surge in activity was spawned by a convergence of do-mestic and international developments. Abroad, the competi-tion for empire was becoming more heated: although the Spanish empire was losing strength, Britain and other Euro-pean powers were grabbing or consolidating colonies, bases, and foreign markets throughout Africa, Asia, and the Pacific; moreover, all of the contenders for empire were augmenting their military strength, especially their navies. At the same time, the subjects of imperial conquest, although unable to match European military technology, were becoming more re-bellious, threatening to create either instability or independent local governments, both of which were unwelcome to Western powers. For American policymakers, these movements on the international chessboard offered opportunities while height-ening pressure for a rapid entry onto the global stage.

Foremost among domestic developments was an increas-ingly turbulent economy. The depression of the 1890s, coming after two decades of sharp swings in the business cycle, ap-peared to validate the idea that the economy suffered from ex-cess capacity, or overproduction, and that the best cure was to sell more American goods abroad. As Secretary of State William R. Day wrote in 1898, "the output of the United States manufacturers, developed by the remarkable inventive genius and industrial skill of our people . . . has reached the point of large excess above the demands of home consumption. Under these circumstances it is not surprising that greater interest should be exhibited among our manufacturers, exporters, and economists in the enlargement of foreign markets for Ameri-can goods." Some labor groups rejected this analysis, arguing instead that the problem was not overproduction but under-consumption, which could be cured by increasing workers' wages. This may or may not have been true; what mattered was not "truth" per se but what influential people believed to be true about the economy. And in the 1890s, many business-men, intellectuals, and political leaders were convinced that the United States needed foreign markets and that it was in-cumbent on the government to help secure them.

The importance of the government's role in securing such markets was highlighted in one of the most influential books of the era, Alfred Thayer Mahan's *The Influence of Sea Power Upon History, 1660–1783*, published in 1890. Mahan, a Democrat and anti-imperialist until the mid-1880s, was a career naval officer and teacher at the Naval War College. His extensive reading of history, first about Rome and then about Britain, convinced him that the key to any nation's power was its dominance of the seas: "sea power is the centre around which other events move, not it around them." The growth and rising productivity of American industry, he believed, made it imperative for the nation to enlarge its foreign markets, yet this would heighten the possibility of international conflict and war. It was therefore essential that the United States develop a powerful naval fleet that could protect its commerce and defeat other navies in bat-tle. The only alternative, Mahan claimed, was to stimulate the domestic market through unacceptable "socialistic" measures.

Becoming a great naval power, however, required more than ships. The United States would also need coaling stations, communications centers, repair facilities (especially as ships became more technologically complex), and rest stops for the crews. For this reason, Mahan advocated the acquisition of permanent bases in the Caribbean and the Pacific; he even abandoned the Democratic Party in 1893 when President Cleveland refused to annex Hawaii. Mahan's arguments lent support not only to officials who sought to enlarge the navy, but to all who wanted to pursue a more expansionist foreign policy.

Other factors, less closely linked to the economy, contributed to the policy shifts of the 1890s. In addition to social Darwinism, deeply embedded convictions about American "specialness" lent support to efforts to implant the American way of life, and Protestant religion, in distant corners of the globe. In 1891 alone, 6,000 American students joined the ranks of Protestant missionaries fanning out to China, India, Japan, Egypt, and other countries to spread the gospel and promote Western values. Political leaders, moreover, were determined to make the United States one of the world's great powers, and in their vision of "greatness," economic, military, and political power were inseparable.

This did not mean that the entire country embraced expansionism in the 1890s. Independent Mugwumps such as Carl Schurz, *Nation* editor E. L. Godkin, and philosopher William James vigorously opposed expansion, as did numerous Republicans and Democrats, including William Jennings Bryan. The decade witnessed heated public debates about foreign policy, and no political party or social group, including the business community, was close to unanimous on the subject. Nor did the events of the 1890s constitute a sudden new departure in American foreign relations; the impulse toward expansionism had been gathering strength for decades. But what did happen in the 1890s was a decisive tilt in the balance of forces, the triumph of one tradition over another, the active embrace of a new international role that would endure for more than a century.

## BRITAIN, THE MONROE DOCTRINE, AND THE VENEZUELA CRISIS

Early in the 1890s, the United States began to flex its muscles in Latin America and to warn European powers, particularly Britain, that American interests would reign supreme in the Western Hemisphere. In 1891, the country squared off against Chile after two American sailors, on shore leave in Valparaiso, were killed by an anti-American mob. President Harrison de-

manded an apology and reparations; when the Chilean government responded hesitantly, Harrison sent a message to Congress that virtually invited a declaration of war. Chile quickly backed down, but the incident only heightened anti-Yankee sentiments. Two years later, American warships were dispatched to break a blockade of Rio de Janeiro's harbor organized by rebellious Brazilian naval officers, backed by Great Britain. At roughly the same time, the United States intervened to terminate a British protectorate in a strategically located region of eastern Nicaragua: Washington encouraged the Nicaraguan government to take formal control of the region, while declaring that the United States would protect the interests of both American and British investors.

These incidents paved the way for the Venezuela crisis of 1895, which marked a major turning point in hemispheric politics. The crisis had its origins in a fifty-year-old boundary dispute between Venezuela and the colony of British Guiana;

An 1895 cartoon critical of the Cleveland administration's inattention to British encroachments on the Monroe Doctrine.

at stake was an area rich in minerals (including gold) and encompassing the mouth of the commercially important Orinoco River. By the 1890s, Britain was acting as though it controlled the region, and it spurned Venezuelan efforts to negotiate the boundary. Venezuela then turned to the United States for help, even hiring an American lobbyist, former diplomat William L. Scruggs, to make its case in Washington.

Scruggs did an excellent job of presenting the Venezuelan viewpoint and tapping American fears of the British. Some Americans believed that Britain, having taken what it could in Africa and Asia, was turning its attention to Latin America, and that Britain's refusal to submit the boundary dispute to arbitration was evidence of its imperial designs. "If Great Britain can extend her territory in South America without remonstrances from us, every other European power can do the same," declared Senator Henry Cabot Lodge of Massachusetts. "We should then find ourselves with great powers to the south of us, and we should be forced to become at once a nation with a powerful army and navy, with difficulties and dangers surrounding us."

In February 1895, Congress unanimously passed a resolution calling on Britain to submit the dispute to arbitration; shortly thereafter, President Cleveland wrote to British prime minister Lord Salisbury reiterating the demand. The British, believing that their dispute with Venezuela was not the business of the United States, ignored the messages. The president then asked his new secretary of state, Richard Olney (who, as attorney general, had broken the Pullman strike and sent Eugene Debs to jail in 1894), to inform the British again how seriously the United States regarded the matter. Olney's extraordinary letter asserted American hegemony over the hemisphere more aggressively than ever before. Beyond invoking the Monroe Doctrine and other traditional arguments, Olney informed the British that "today the United States is practically sovereign on this continent, and its fiat is law upon the subjects to which it confines its interposition." Lest Britain fail to understand the sources of that sovereignty, Olney pointed out the "infinite resources" of the United States, "combined with its isolated position render it master of the situation and practically invulnerable as against any and all powers." Accepting arbitration, Olney maintained, was the only way Britain could establish that it was not engaged in an act of imperial aggression against Venezuela and the United States.

Four months later, Lord Salisbury replied to Olney and Cleveland, refusing arbitration and pointedly reemphasizing that Monroe Doctrine or no Monroe Doctrine, the United States had no jurisdiction in the matter. Cleveland responded by sending a message to Congress calling for a U.S. commission to determine the proper boundaries and warning Britain that the United States would "resist by any means within its power" Britain's seizure of territory that it did not rightfully possess. This veiled threat of war caught Britain's attention: recognizing that it had misunderstood the importance of the Monroe Doctrine to the American government, and concerned with more serious threats to its empire from France and Germany, Britain agreed to arbitration. The crisis ended immediately, and eventually an international commission recognized most of the British claims.

In the end, the most significant consequence of the crisis had little to do with the Orinoco or even with Venezuela, whose government was never consulted by the United States. By agreeing to arbitration, Britain had tacitly recognized American hegemony in the Western Hemisphere: the United States had faced off against the greatest power in the world, and it was Britain that had blinked.

### CUBA AND WAR WITH SPAIN

The United States had long kept a close eye on Cuba, ninety miles south of Florida. Before the Civil War, southerners, as well as some Cuban planters, had favored annexing the island

José Martí, writer and hero of the movement for Cuban independence.

to the United States as a slave state; and in 1868, when Cuban nationalists began a decade-long war for independence from Spain, most Americans regarded the rebel cause with sympathy. After the rebellion was defeated, the United States became home to thousands of Cuban emigrants and dissidents, including Jose Marti, a poet, man of letters, and political leader who would become the most revered figure in Cuban history.

Cuban discontent with Spanish rule continued through the 1870s and 1880s, while the island's economy became increasingly tied to that of the United States. Not only did Americans invest close to $50 million in Cuba's profitable sugar industry, but the United States was also the primary market for Cuban sugar and cigars. Then, in the 1890s, the Cuban economy was rocked, first by a worldwide decline in sugar prices and then, in 1894, by the Wilson-Gorman Tariff, which dramatically raised duties on sugar, cutting Cuban exports to the United States by 50 percent. The precipitous decline in the Cuban economy led to strikes; attacks on foreign-owned property, including cane fields; and a renewal of rebellion against Spain.

In response, Spain in 1896 sent 150,000 troops to Cuba. Led by General Valeriano Weyler, the Spanish army developed a strategy that would become a familiar means of suppressing guerrilla warfare in the twentieth century: he attempted to sever the contacts between rebel forces and the rural peoples who supported them by forcibly relocating large segments of the population into prison-like camps. Weyler's *reconcentrado* policy led to the deaths of more than 200,000 Cubans in overcrowded, filthy, and disease-ridden camps, earning him the nickname of "Butcher" in the American press.

The Cubans themselves were divided into several political factions. A small group favored continued Spanish rule. Some Creoles (born in Cuba but of Spanish ancestry) as well as many American planters and businessmen living in Cuba, preferred autonomy or "home rule" within the Spanish empire; as hostilities sharpened and that option appeared less feasible, they promoted annexation of the island to the United States. The vast majority of Cubans, however, wanted complete independence—a sentiment that was particularly strong among the poor and among black former slaves. (Slavery was abolished in Cuba only in the 1880s.) The leaders of the movement for Cuba Libre were accordingly wary of American interest in the island. Although they welcomed American diplomatic support, they feared that the United States might seek to replace Spanish with American rule. As Jose Marti famously asked, "Once the United States is in

Cuba, who will get her out?" Marti himself, probably the one leader who could bridge the class and racial divisions that permeated Cuban society, returned to Cuba in 1895, where he was killed by Spanish soldiers.

The conflict in Cuba in the 1890s was closely watched in the United States. Many members of Congress believed that the United States should intervene in Cuba, on humanitarian grounds or to protect American investments. Advocates of overseas expansion also saw the island's strategic location as an asset that could help Americans protect a future canal in Central America. Led by Democrats and Populists, Congress debated resolutions urging the government to take military action against the Spanish or to formally recognize the rebels as the legitimate

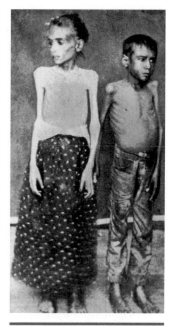

Cubans suffering from starvation during the Spanish-American War.

leaders of the island. But President Cleveland resisted such calls, preferring to exert diplomatic pressure on Spain to end the warfare and grant Cuba autonomy within the Spanish empire, a solution that would make Spain responsible for protecting American investments. Cleveland opposed any plan that would join the multiracial, class-torn island to the United States. He also feared that an independent, yet still unstable, Cuba might invite other European powers into the Caribbean.

When William McKinley became president in 1897, he shared Cleveland's reluctance to get too entangled in Cuba. Because he was taking office just as a severe depression seemed to be lifting, McKinley's overriding concern was promoting economic growth, and he feared that war would undermine the economy's recovery. A Civil War veteran, McKinley had a personal distaste for war: "I have been through one war; I have seen the dead piled up; and I do not want to see another," he told a friend. He also worried that the Constitution would not extend to any overseas territories that the United States acquired. Consequently, he, too, focused on diplomacy, urging Spain to grant Cuba autonomy and bring an end to Weyler's brutal *reconcentrado*.

McKinley's efforts seemed for a brief time to be working. In October 1897, Spain recalled General Weyler, promising to end the *reconcentrado* and to initiate reforms leading to autonomy within the empire. American cries for war subsided, and McKinley urged Congress to give Spain "a reasonable chance" to fulfill its commitments. But the Cuban movement for independence pressed forward, politically and militarily, and by early 1898 it was apparent to Cubans and Americans alike that Spain was losing its grip on the island.

American hopes for a diplomatic resolution were jarred by the *New York Journal*'s publication, in February 1898, of a purloined personal letter written by Enrique Dupuy de Lome, Spain's minister to Washington. De Lome suggested that Spain's promise of reform was largely cosmetic, and he derided McKinley as a "weak" man, "a bidder for the admiration of the crowd." De Lome resigned immediately, but his letter convinced many that Spain could not be trusted. A week later, the American battleship *Maine* exploded in Havana Harbor, killing 266 Americans. Although a modern study of the ship's remains concluded that the explosion was likely an accident, contemporaries immediately fixed blame on the Spanish—although the Spanish had much to lose by such an action. "Remember the *Maine*" became the battle cry of those demanding that the United States go to war.

By the end of February, the public clamor for war had grown intense. Sensationalist newspapers such as Joseph Pulitzer's *New York World* and William Randolph Hearst's *Jour-*

The wreckage of the battleship *Maine,* February 1898.

*nal* beat the drums loudly, and even some opponents of American intervention began to change their tune. President McKinley began to prepare for war, asking Congress for $50 million to ready the army and navy for action while reassuring business leaders that a war would not be too costly or damage the economic recovery. At the same time, he continued his diplomatic efforts, quietly seeking to purchase Cuba from Spain and then sending a series of demands to the Spanish government for brokering a resolution. By April, Spain had agreed to almost all of McKinley's demands, including the granting of an armistice, the permanent end to the *reconcentrado,* and the payment of reparations for the *Maine.* The Spanish government, however, refused to agree to McKinley's proposal that the United States mediate negotiations regarding Cuban sovereignty. And the Cuban rebels, meanwhile, rejected an immediate ceasefire, which would clearly have disadvantaged them militarily.

On April 11, McKinley sent a war message to Congress. Although war was a foregone conclusion, Congress spent days debating whether or not to recognize the Cuban revolutionary government; at stake was whether the goal of the war was to aid the rebels in achieving Cuban independence or, rather, to influence the shape of future Cuban regimes. McKinley opposed recognition; he pressed instead for intervention that would impose "hostile restraint" on both warring parties in order to guarantee peace and stability in Cuba. McKinley wanted to have as much freedom of action as possible, and he feared that the Cuban rebels might follow a path that would threaten American interests. After a week of political sparring, Congress agreed to McKinley's demand: the United States would not recognize the Cuban rebels and thus would not be intervening on their behalf. In turn, McKinley agreed to an amendment drafted by Senator Henry Teller of Colorado stating that "the United States hereby disclaims any disposition or intention to exercise sovereignty, jurisdiction, or control over said island except for the pacification thereof, and asserts its determination when that is accomplished to leave the government and control of the island to its people," On April 29, 1898, McKinley signed a congressionally approved declaration of war. What had been a Cuban war for independence had become the "Spanish-American" war.

### THE UNITED STATES AT WAR

The war in Cuba was swift and decisive. The American strategy at the outset was to impose a naval blockade, cutting the Spanish forces off from supplies and reinforcements while si-

Members of the U.S. Tenth Cavalry, an African American unit, on San Juan Hill in Cuba.

multaneously delivering supplies to the Cuban rebels. In so doing, the United States could buy time to raise and train ground troops. In late May, American warships, far superior to those of Spain, blockaded the Spanish fleet in the harbor of Santiago de Cuba. The navy quickly asked for ground troops to begin an attack on Santiago, and McKinley, shifting his strategy, chose to accelerate the ground war. Thanks to modern telegraph and telephone equipment and the creation of a command center at the White House, McKinley was the first president able to play an active role in military strategy.

Initiating a land war in Cuba meant rushing ill-equipped and barely trained soldiers into combat. Since the army was still a tiny force of 28,000 early in 1898, the United States had to rely on volunteers who, it turned out, were fast in coming: more than 200,000 men enlisted, including a "Silver Battalion" from Nebraska, organized by William Jennings Bryan, and the "Rough Riders" led by the combat-eager Theodore Roosevelt, who had resigned as assistant secretary of the navy in order to enlist. (Roosevelt had his uniforms custom-made by Brooks Brothers, a store catering to elite gentlemen.) Supplying, equipping, and training these volunteers, however, was a task that overwhelmed the weak administrative capacities of the army. Chaos and incompetence reigned at the over-populated training camp and staging area in Tampa. There were too few guns to go around, and the outdated rifles that were available still used black powder cartridges. Since no American factory produced tropical-weight khaki suitable for

uniforms, many soldiers had to wear their own clothes into battle; others were given heavy woolen army shirts designed to be worn in Alaska rather than in the suffocating heat of mid-summer Cuba. Sanitation facilities were grossly inadequate; rations sometimes included "knots of gristle, hunks of rope, and mummified maggots"; and diseases were rampant both in Tampa and in Cuba.

The Spanish nonetheless were quickly defeated: American forces tilted the balance in a war that Cubans were already waging with much success. On June 22, American soldiers arrived on the beaches east of Santiago, and, a week later, in the only major land battle of the war, army units broke through Spanish defenses and seized control of San Juan Hill. From the hilltops surrounding Santiago Harbor, they were able to train their artillery on the blockaded Spanish fleet. The Spaniards had little choice but to run the blockade; when they did, the faster and better-armed American warships opened fire, sinking or disabling every Spanish vessel within four hours, with the loss of only one American life. Demoralized and without any prospect of reinforcements or new supplies, the Spanish army capitulated on July 17. American troops, shunting aside the Cuban rebels, claimed control of the city. A few days later, American forces, firing few shots and losing only three men, also completed the occupation of the Spanish island of Puerto Rico.

## CONQUERING THE PHILIPPINES

The Caribbean was not the only theater of war. Beginning early in 1898, McKinley and his advisers had made plans to seize some or all of the Philippine islands in the event of a conflict with Spain. In the Philippines, consisting of thousands of islands 7,000 miles west of California, Spain was also battling a rebel insurgency, and the islands appeared to be an easy target for a foreign takeover. With the European powers, as well as Russia and Japan, jockeying for power in China, the Philippines held considerable strategic importance for the United States. Commercial interests wished to strengthen American access to Asian markets, and the Philippine port of Manila was perfectly located to serve as a base for the navy and commercial shipping. In February 1898, Assistant Naval Secretary Roosevelt sent a message to Admiral George Dewey of the Pacific fleet, instructing him to attack Manila if the United States declared war with Spain. From the outset, thus,

Celebratory cover of an American magazine, 1898.

the war to "save" Cuba was also a war for commercial and imperial advantage in the Pacific.

Hostilities began in the Philippines before a single American shot had been fired in Cuba. On April 30, Dewey's small squadron arrived undetected at the mouth of Manila Bay; the next day, it shelled the unprepared Spanish fleet for four hours, completely destroying it without losing an American life. Within a few days, the first American ground troops were dispatched to the Philippines, and by mid-August the American army, acting alongside—if not always with—the nationalist rebels, had defeated the Spanish and occupied Manila. Even before the last ground battles were fought (and unbeknown to troops in the field because of severed telegraph lines), Spain and the United States had signed an armistice.

President McKinley, meanwhile, took advantage of wartime conditions to accomplish a goal that he had long sought: the annexation of Hawaii. Convinced that the islands were critical to trade with Asia and concerned that European powers might be tempted to meddle, McKinley in 1897 had signed an annexation treaty with the white-dominated, pro-annexation

Hawaiian government. "We need Hawaii just as much and a good deal more than we did California," McKinley declared. "It is manifest destiny" (see Chapter 14). Congressional opponents stalled the treaty, arguing that protecting Hawaii would require an expensive navy, that annexation would lead the nation toward an unconstitutional colonialism, and that it would generate an unwelcome migration of cheap Asian labor to the West Coast. A year later, however, circumstances changed: Dewey was in Manila, and Hawaii was viewed as a vital coaling station and staging area for American troops. Since opposition remained strong, McKinley sent Congress a simple annexation resolution that would require only a majority vote of both houses, rather than the two-thirds vote of the Senate needed to ratify a treaty. The president also broke a House filibuster by threatening to use his war powers to seize the islands. Congress approved the resolution in July, and on August 12, 1898, Hawaii became a U.S. territory.

The acquisition of overseas lands continued in October, when delegates from Spain and the United States met in Paris to hammer out a peace treaty. (Notably, neither the Cuban nor Filipino rebels were invited to attend.) Since the United States held all the cards, the negotiations were one-sided: the Spanish government surrendered its sovereignty over Cuba and ceded Puerto Rico, Guam, and several small islands to the Americans. Spain also gave in to McKinley's demand that it turn over control not just of Manila but of the entire Philippines; to soften the blow, the Americans agreed to make a face-saving indemnity payment of $20 million to Spain. The treaty was signed in December, and McKinley submitted it to the Senate in January 1899.

Ratification, however, was not a sure thing, and the Senate's consideration of the treaty became the occasion for an impassioned national debate over the annexation of the Philippines and, more generally, the desirability of acquiring an overseas empire. Expansionists such as Senator Henry Cabot Lodge argued that the treaty served the nation's economic and diplomatic interests and that there was no feasible alternative to annexation, since an independent Philippines would soon be taken over by another European power. They also maintained that annexation would bring order to the islands, as well as Christianity and civilization to its people.

But some anti-imperialists, such as steel magnate Andrew Carnegie, disputed the claim that "trade followed the flag," arguing that the way to sell goods abroad was simply to make them better and cheaper. Carnegie, in fact, was so enraged that the United States seemed to be following in the imperial

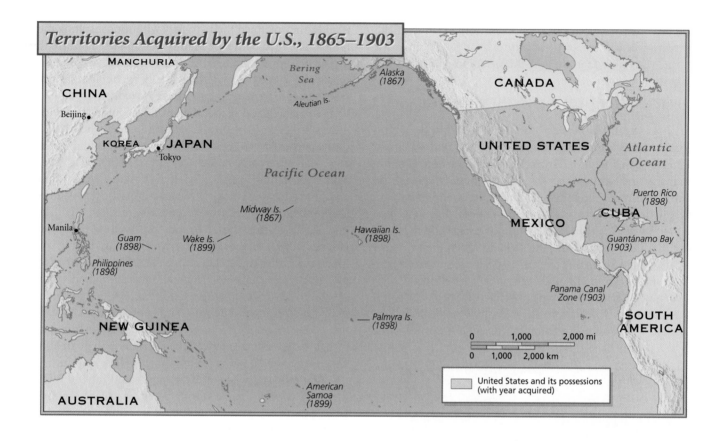

**Territories Acquired by the U.S., 1865–1903**

MANCHURIA

CHINA

Beijing

KOREA   JAPAN
        Tokyo

Manila

Guam
(1898)

Wake Is.
(1899)

Philippines
(1898)

NEW GUINEA

AUSTRALIA

Bering
Sea

Aleutian Is.

Pacific Ocean

Midway Is.
(1867)

Palmyra Is.
(1898)

American
Samoa
(1899)

Alaska
(1867)

CANADA

UNITED STATES

Hawaiian Is.
(1898)

MEXICO

Atlantic
Ocean

Puerto Rico
(1898)

CUBA

Guantánamo Bay
(1903)

Panama Canal
Zone (1903)

SOUTH
AMERICA

0      1,000      2,000 mi
0   1,000   2,000 km

United States and its possessions
(with year acquired)

footsteps of England that he offered to buy the Philippines for $20 million in order to grant the islands independence. Other anti-imperialists put forward constitutional and political arguments: the United States lacked the constitutional right to acquire colonies; the Constitution could not be applied to distant territories; and American democracy itself would be subverted by the undemocratic subjugation of other peoples. Senator George F. Hoar of Massachusetts voiced the fear that "we are to be transformed from a republic, founded on the Declaration of Independence . . . into a vulgar, commonplace empire, founded upon physical force." Anti-imperialists, who often shared the expansionists' view of Anglo-Saxon racial superiority, also believed that the possession of colonies would compound the nation's already difficult racial problems. As a senator from Missouri put it, "the idea of conferring American citizenship upon the half-civilized, piratical, muck-running inhabitants of two thousand islands seven thousand miles distant . . . is absurd and indefensible."

Above all, perhaps, the anti-imperialists believed that it was simply *wrong*, as well as un-American, to impose the will of the

United States by force on other people. As Senator Hoar argued, invoking the language of abolitionism, "No man was ever created good enough to own another. No nation was ever created good enough to own another." Between 1898 and 1900, the newly formed Anti-Imperialist League attracted thousands of members; centered in urban areas, especially in the Northeast, the ranks of the anti-imperialists included women who identified their own voteless condition with the oppression of colonized people, as well as public figures such as Mark Twain, Samuel Gompers, William Jennings Bryan, William Graham Sumner, and Grover Cleveland. Notably, the leadership of the movement consisted primarily of men in their sixties and seventies whose politics were shaped by the moral crusades of antislavery, equal rights, and civil service reform.

For a time, it appeared that the anti-imperialists might block ratification of the treaty with Spain. Early in February 1899, however, word reached Washington that gunfire had been exchanged between Filipino nationalists and American soldiers who were entering cities run by the Filipinos' provisional government. In circumstances in which a negative vote could be construed as lack of support for soldiers in the field, the treaty was ratified on February 6 by a 57–27 majority, only one vote more than the two-thirds required by law.

## SUPPRESSING REVOLUTION IN THE PHILIPPINES

That shots were fired between American troops and Filipino rebels was hardly surprising. The Filipinos were led by Emilio Aguinaldo, a well-educated former mayor and leader of a revolutionary organization that had fought bitterly against the Spanish. Aguinaldo initially welcomed American intervention, believing that the United States would act according to its own celebrated values and help the Filipinos realize the independence that they declared in June 1898. From the outset, however, the United States was reluctant to link itself too closely to the nationalist cause. Although Aguinaldo's army already controlled much of the Philippines outside of Manila, Admiral Dewey, following instructions from Washington, kept his distance, and when American ground troops finally arrived in the

General Emilio Aguinaldo, leader of the Filipino fight for independence and nationalism.

islands, they planned their strategy without consulting the Filipinos. The final battle for Manila was, in fact, a bizarre three-pronged event, as the Spanish fought hard to keep the feared rebels out of the city, while eventually encouraging American troops to enter and accept a Spanish surrender.

Even before the defeat of the Spanish, Aguinaldo and his followers had begun organizing a government; by the fall of 1898, they controlled numerous islands, including much of Luzon, the large island that contained the key city of Manila. The American consul general in Hong Kong described Aguinaldo as "dignified and just as the head of his government," and the revolutionary government as "apparently acceptable to the Filipinos." The nationalist rebels drew up a constitution for their nation and in January 1899 announced the creation of a republic of the Philippines, with Aguinaldo as president. But the United States, pursuing its own goals and convinced that the Filipinos were incapable of self-government, refused to recognize Aguinaldo's republic and began sending troops into areas he controlled. These incursions inevitably led to hostilities. By February, Aguinaldo, recognizing that the Americans had no intention of granting independence, declared war on the United States.

What followed was a war far longer and more costly than the conflict with Spain. During its initial phase, Aguinaldo's large, poorly equipped army fought set battles against American troops. When that strategy proved unsuccessful, his troops reverted to guerrilla war tactics, trying to make American rule costly through small-scale hit-and-run attacks on different islands; they forced the United States to fight a war of counterinsurgency, the first of many in the twentieth century. Subduing the nationalists required more than 120,000 American soldiers over a three-year period, and the nature of the warfare, which was tinged with racial and cultural antagonism, led to brutality on both sides. U.S. newspapers reported that American troops frequently used a form of water torture to compel captives to talk and that there were incidents of mass killing of unarmed civilians. One American officer justified the brutality to a reporter, claiming that "we must . . . have no scruples about exterminating this other race standing in the way of progress and enlightenment." Ironically, the United States even resorted to a policy of forcing civilians into camps, reminiscent of General Weyler's *reconcentrado* in Cuba.

Owing to superior weaponry, as well as a strategy of dogged pursuit designed by officers experienced in fighting Native Americans, the American forces did eventually prevail. Aguinaldo was captured in 1901, and most of his troops laid down their arms by the beginning of 1902. "Pacification" of the Philippines was facilitated by a shrewd American policy of granting amnesty to rebels who surrendered while building close ties with the Filipino elite, many of whom feared the nationalist rebels. The cost of victory, however, was high. More than 4,000 American soldiers died in the war, while thousands more were permanently disabled or weakened by tropical diseases and malnutrition. The carnage was far greater for the Filipinos: 15,000 rebels were killed in battle, and roughly 200,000 civilians lost their lives. Peace, moreover, was long in coming: insurgents continued to fight on some islands until 1913, and periodic rebellions against American power and influence would recur until late in the twentieth century.

## LEGACIES

"And so it has come to pass," reflected President McKinley privately in September 1899, "that in a few short months we have become a world power." His assessment was correct. The United States in a very short time had enlarged its influence in the Western Hemisphere, while acquiring strategic assets in the Pacific that permitted it to play an entirely new role in Asia. Yet the events of the 1890s also left the United States confronting a new question: what exactly would it do with the territories it possessed and the people it controlled? In the past, territorial acquisitions had always been accomplished through formal annexation, with an eye toward eventual statehood; but to most policymakers, these historical precedents did not seem applicable to the nation's new overseas lands.

Despite the Teller amendment, the fate of Cuba was undecided when the United States took formal possession of the island in January 1899. Although many Americans continued to support Cuban independence, others, including Leonard Wood, the military commander of Cuba, claimed that Cubans were incapable of self-government and that any elected Cuban government would be inimical to American interests. After months of debate, McKinley and his closest adviser, Secretary of War Elihu Root, opted for a cosmetic compromise. Because of its strategic importance and the scale of American investments, they sought to control Cuba, but they were sensitive to domestic opposition to annexation, reluctant to incorporate a nearby nonwhite nation into the United States, and concerned about provoking the Cubans into a new war for independence. As a result, they decided to grant Cuba formal independence, but with significant strings attached: Cuba could not become deeply indebted to any foreign power; it could not enter into any treaties that would

"impair" its independence; it was required to sell or lease lands, including Guantanamo Bay, to the United States to be used as naval bases; and the United States retained the right to intervene in Cuba "for the preservation of Cuban independence" and "the maintenance of a government adequate for the protection of life, property, and individual liberty."

These sweeping provisions, introduced in Congress in 1901 by Senator Orville Platt of Connecticut and later known as the Platt amendment, were attached to a formal treaty between the United States and Cuba. Secretary Root insisted that they also be incorporated into the new Cuban constitution. Not surprisingly, however, these severe limitations on Cuban sovereignty were not popular with the Cubans themselves. The island's first elections, managed and controlled by Americans, produced decisive victories for anti-American candidates, and Cuba's constitutional convention balked at including the Platt amendment in the new nation's constitution. Only after Root pointedly informed them that they had no choice if they wanted independence and access to American markets, did a narrow majority of Cuban delegates to the convention vote to accept the Platt provisions. The Platt amendment remained the cornerstone of American policy toward Cuba for decades, leading to periodic intervention by the United States and the long-enduring possession of a military base at Guantánamo Bay. For Cubans, the Platt amendment became a touchstone of rebellion and anti-American sentiments, proof that what their northern neighbors called a war against Spain was really fought to thwart Cuban independence. As Leonard Wood himself had commented, "There is, of course, little or no independence left Cuba under the Platt amendment." To make matters even worse, many Cuban farms, plantations, mines, and businesses were purchased by Americans, at depressed prices, early in the twentieth century.

The United States imposed a different policy on Puerto Rico, where it did not have to contend with rebellious forces. In 1900, prodded by McKinley and Root, Congress passed the Foraker Act (named after Senator Joseph Foraker of Ohio), which established Puerto Rico as an "unincorporated territory" of the United States, ruled by Congress and a governor appointed in Washington. Puerto Ricans were not made citizens until 1917, and no promise of statehood was ever offered. As a local newspaper noted in 1901, "We are and we are not a foreign country. We are and we are not citizens of the United States. The Constitution applies to us and does not apply to us." This ambiguity received legal sanction from the Supreme Court in 1901 in a series of landmark decisions that

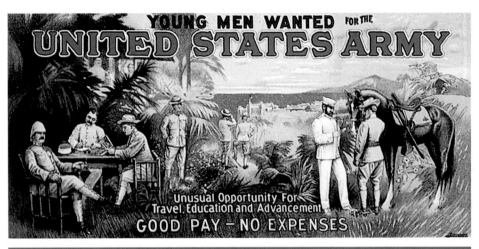

Recruiting poster for the U.S. Army, c. 1900.

came to be known as the "Insular Cases." The Court ruled that the people of unincorporated territories such as Puerto Rico possessed certain "fundamental rights" but not all the rights of Americans. The Constitution, in effect, did not "follow the flag." Or, as Elihu Root slyly noted in response to one of the Court's decisions, "As near as I can make out the Constitution follows the flag—but doesn't quite catch up with it."

The Constitution certainly did not follow the flag to the Philippines. After full-blown hostilities had ended, the Philippines were run by a governor-general appointed by the United States and supported by American troops and then by a U.S.–trained Filipino constabulary. Only Filipinos from the upper classes were allowed to participate in the government.

One other legacy of the Spanish-American War was a permanent shift in the size and mission of the American armed forces. In key respects, the war seemed to validate Alfred T. Mahan's theories about the significance of sea power. Accordingly, the United States continued to strengthen its navy, building a large fleet that included new, well-armed battleships. Since its overseas possessions had to be defended and because these technologically advanced ships demanded sophisticated repair and servicing centers, the country embarked on an ambitious program of naval-base construction, at Pearl Harbor and Cuba's Guantánamo Bay, among other places.

Changes in the army were even more dramatic. In the wake of the war, the United States jettisoned its long-standing ideological opposition to a large standing army: defending far-flung territories required a sizable, more professional force, ready to spring into action at short notice. Under the guidance of Secretary Root, the permanent size of the army increased four-fold, and its command structure was transformed. In addition, Congress passed the Dick Act in 1903 (named after Congressman Charles Dick of Ohio) which made the national guard accountable to the federal government as well as the states and designated the guard to be the backup for the army. One lesson of the war was that the armed forces needed to be nationalized and disciplined: local units of state militias had melded uneasily with career army officers. Meanwhile, money was poured into weapons development, leading to more powerful and accurate artillery, the adoption of the Model 1903 Springfield rifle (which remained in use for decades), and experiments with military aviation.

During the first decade of the twentieth century, the army also began to use motorized vehicles, while telephone, telegraph, and wireless networks were constructed in the Philippines, Alaska, and the Caribbean. (The Spanish-American War was the first in which telephones played a major role.) The army's Signal Corps, its most scientific and technological branch, was charged with developing the communications needed for overseas operations; the corps exploded in size from 8 officers, 52 soldiers, and an equipment budget of $800 to a dynamic unit of 1,300 within a few years. The United States, in effect, had joined an international arms and communication race: in the three years after the war, the overall military budget increased by more than 300 percent over the prewar level, while nonmilitary federal expenditures rose by less than 25 percent.

## The New Century

By the beginning of the twentieth century, the United States controlled what historians have called both "formal" and "informal" empires. Compared to Britain, France, Germany, and Portugal, its formal possessions—the Philippines, Hawaii, Puerto Rico, Guam, and Samoa—were few although they were critically located. Less formally, the United States wielded significant economic power and political influence in much of Central and Latin America. Between 1900 and the beginning of World War I, the country took further steps to strengthen its position and extend its influence. It did so with little domestic opposition: the anti-imperialist movement so visible at the end of the nineteenth century gradually faded, and most Americans appeared to accept their nation's growing role in world affairs.

## THE OPEN DOOR TO CHINA

Even before the new century began, the United States adopted a more active posture toward China. In the late 1890s, responding to China's military defeat by Japan and the weakening of its government, the European powers, led by Germany, began to carve out commercial spheres of influence in China, acquiring control over ports and railway connections. The United States feared that the Europeans and Japanese would gain enough dominance in China to block American exports, particularly of textiles, and close the potentially huge Chinese market to American trade. Whether the United States could forestall such developments was unclear. President McKinley had no desire to use force to pursue American interests, and he feared that aggressive steps in Asia would arouse the ire of anti-imperialists, jeopardizing his reelection in 1900. As Secretary of State John Hay wrote to McKinley, "We do not want to rob China ourselves, and our public opinion will not permit us to interfere, with an army, to prevent others from robbing her. Besides, we have no army." Hay consequently adopted a purely diplomatic strategy of stating American goals and trying to play the imperial powers off one another.

In September 1899, he sent what became known as the first "Open Door Note" to each of the powers involved in China (although notably not to the Chinese themselves). The note expressed a desire to encourage free trade and preserve Chinese territorial integrity. It asked each power to keep ports open to ships of all nations, to establish nondiscriminatory railroad rates within its sphere of influence, and to let the general Chinese tariff apply to all ports, with the tariffs to be collected by the Chinese. Although none of the imperial powers publicly agreed to Hay's terms, they tacitly assented, permitting Hay to declare in March 1900 that the Open Door had been accepted by all parties. The Open Door was a potential boon to American manufacturers, despite their government's relatively weak position in East Asia.

This 1900 cartoon shows Uncle Sam opening China to free trade while England (left) and Russia (right) look on.

The first Open Door Note was rapidly overtaken by events in China. In 1900, a militant, antiforeign group (who became known in the West as the Boxers, a loose translation of their Chinese name, referring to rituals carried out to protect themselves against the West's modern weapons) launched a rebellion against the imperialist presence in China. Supported by the empress of the crumbling Manchu dynasty, the Boxer rebels swept through northern China, destroying foreign property, killing foreigners, and eventually placing the foreign legations in Beijing under siege. The imperial powers responded by sealing off their areas of control and sending troops to lift the siege of Beijing in the summer of 1900. Among the expeditionary forces were 5,000 Americans whom President McKinley, in an unprecedented executive action, dispatched without consulting Congress or declaring war.

In the midst of the Boxer Rebellion, Secretary Hay, fearing an imperial splintering of China, issued his second Open Door Note, declaring that the United States respected Chinese "territorial and administrative integrity" and urging the other imperial powers to do the same. For reasons that had less to do with Hay's note than with their own preoccupations and fears, the secretary's wish was granted. In 1901, after the Boxers were suppressed, the imperialist powers withdrew all troops from Beijing, made no attempt to carve up China, and paid lip service to the principle of the Open Door. Behind the scenes, however, several European nations cut secret deals to retain their spheres of influence, leaving the door to China less than fully open.

The Open Door Notes did not achieve very much for the United States, beyond the symbolic assertion of its right to pursue trade opportunities in Asia. They did, however, help President McKinley win reelection against Democrat William Jennings Bryan in 1900. The apparent restraint of McKinley's China policy served to disarm the Democrats' anti-imperialist criticism. Although McKinley's new running mate, the pro-imperialist governor of New York, Theodore Roosevelt, barnstormed the country celebrating the use of force to subdue and eventually uplift "the barbarians," McKinley himself appeared as a careful, sober-minded defender of American economic interests abroad. He also challenged some of Bryan's positions, such as his advocacy of rights for Filipinos that his own party denied to African Americans in the South. With foreign policy issues politically neutralized, the economy booming, and the coinage of silver losing its appeal as an issue, McKinley won a decisive victory. Less than a year later, however, McKinley was dead, killed by an assassin, and the most ardently expansionist of American public figures was president.

## THE PANAMA CANAL

The most important foreign policy goal of Theodore Roosevelt's presidency (see Chapter 22) was the construction of a canal through Central America connecting the Atlantic and Pacific. The desirability of such a canal had long been evident: it would dramatically reduce shipping costs between the East and West Coasts, and potentially reinvigorate north-south trade routes through the nation's interior. The Spanish-American War and the acquisition of overseas territories added a military dimension to the case for a canal, because the capabilities of the navy would be substantially increased by shortening the transit time from the Atlantic to the Pacific. Roosevelt also viewed a canal, built and controlled by the United States, as a fitting symbol of America's new influence in world affairs.

In the year before his death, President McKinley had set the diplomatic wheels in motion for the building of a canal. Seizing an opportune moment when Britain was preoccupied with conflicts in South Africa, East Asia, and Europe, McKinley dispatched Secretary Hay to negotiate a termination of the 1850 Clayton-Bulwer Treaty, which had committed Britain

and the United States to joint construction and control of a canal. After several rounds of discussion, the two nations signed the Hay-Pauncefote Treaty in 1901, giving the United States the right to build a canal by itself, as long as British ships were charged the same tolls as American ships.

Attention then turned to the site of a canal. Nicaragua had long appeared to be the most promising location: although the route was relatively long, the presence of sea-level interior waterways promised to make construction easier than seemed likely in the Colombian province of Panama, where the French had failed in their effort to hack a canal through dense, disease-ridden terrain in the 1870s and 1880s. A new commission, however, concluded that the Panamanian route was preferable, especially if the United States could, at a reasonable price, buy the charter, some machinery, and property from the French company that had begun construction and still retained the exclusive right to build a canal in Panama. After much debate, Congress in 1902 authorized President Roosevelt to explore the Panama option, but to turn his attention to the Nicaraguan alternative if he could not quickly finalize an arrangement with Colombia.

Secretary Hay then negotiated a treaty with the foreign minister of Colombia, but the Colombian Senate rejected the treaty as too favorable to the United States and impinging on Colombian sovereignty. Roosevelt, who favored the Panama route, was enraged; denouncing the Colombians as "jackrabbits" and "foolish corruptionists," he refused to return to the negotiating table. Instead, he and his administration lent tacit support to a revolt organized by Philippe Bunau-Varilla, an engineer representing the French canal company and Panamanian investors who stood to lose $40 million if the canal project was abandoned or stalled. On November 1, 1903, Bunau-Varilla and his colleagues, in collaboration with Panamanian nationalists who had long sought freedom from Colombian rule, declared Panama to be an independent state. An American warship cruised offshore as the declaration was made, and a fleet arrived to show American support within days.

Bunau-Varilla, a French citizen who had never lived in Panama, then appointed himself foreign minister and immediately entered into negotiations with Secretary Hay. Before any Panamanians could arrive in Washington to join the negotiations, the Hay–Bunau-Varilla Treaty had been signed, on terms extremely favorable to the United States, including the granting of virtual sovereignty over the Canal Zone to the United States in perpetuity. Although Panamanian nationalists denounced the agreement as "the treaty no Panamanian

Cartoon showing death awaiting the builders of the Panama Canal, 1904.

signed," they accepted its terms, thanks to a mixture of American bribes and threats. The episode provoked a storm in the United States, with congressmen and newspapers attacking Roosevelt's dealings with Colombia as an "assault upon another republic over the shattered wreckage of international law." Even Roosevelt's inner circle expressed dismay. After the president had explained his actions at a cabinet meeting, he demanded to know if he had satisfactorily defended himself. "You certainly have," replied Secretary of War Elihu Root. "You have shown that you were accused of seduction and you have conclusively proved that you were guilty of rape." Despite such sentiments, the Senate ratified the Hay–Bunau-Varilla Treaty in February 1904.

The construction of the Panama Canal was an extraordinary feat of organization and engineering, made possible by late nineteenth-century innovations in management, technology, and science. For more than a year after the treaty was signed, the problems that had doomed the French stymied the Americans as well. Yellow fever, malaria, and pneumonia afflicted many of the Americans who went to Panama; others, fearing disease, fled; and the digging was impeded by breakdowns in

## What If You Get Sick?

"When called to a man (most of my work has been with men) who has had a chill some time during the previous night, has a pulse of 100 to 112, with temperature of 101.5° to 103°, headache (*cutting* across the forehead), backache running down into the thighs, *sore* muscles, skin hot if you hold your hand on it a while (hands and wrist not hot to gentle touch), anorexia, white tongue (may be a yellow center far back—the red edges and red diamond on tip will not show at once), suffused eyes, and notably or faintly purpled cheek bones with semipuffed upper lip, the hundred chances are you have a case of yellow fever.

Give three or four compound cathartic pills at once and as soon as possible give a hot foot bath (an all-over bath is better, but is not always possible), with or without mustard and salt. Mustard at this time is really a nonessential, but sometimes the patient thinks it is the proper thing; so with the table salt. As to the cathartic: calomel

at first is too slow and usually must be sent for, the pills contain enough of it and *are* in your vest pocket. Every yellow fever doctor should carry first doses of compound cathartic pills, compound acetanilide tablets, and such other pocket remedies as may be needed on emergency. A parade of a small medicine chest is not advised. Do not begin to make a reputation for wonderful medical skill now. Dwell on the dengue symptoms and the signs of malaria, and without great formality convince the patient that "it is not yellow," but do not say so. Keep back information about the actual temperature all the way through, but tell them about the height of the fever. No patient should ever hear that his fever went above 102° until after he gets well."

Surg. R. D. Murray, *The Treatment of Yellow Fever* (*Yellow Fever: Its Nature, Diagnosis, Treatment, and Prophylaxis,* 1898)

transportation and machinery. Things got on track only when President Roosevelt appointed John Stevens as chief engineer. Stevens was a construction engineer, with long experience in frontier settings, who had spent his career working for the railways. His first step on arriving in Panama in 1905 was to halt construction and to focus instead on creating an environment and an infrastructure that could support the largest construction operation in history.

Stevens had two main concerns. The first was minimizing the threat of disease so that manual workers and professionals would come to Panama. He hired Dr. William Gorgas, who had rid Havana of yellow fever, and asked him to clean up Panama City and Colón, the two major cities in the Canal Zone. Given top priority in obtaining workers and ordering supplies, Gorgas pursued his task relentlessly, fumigating the cities house by house. Mobilizing new scientific knowledge about the sources of infectious diseases, particularly water- and mosquito-borne diseases, Gorgas's Sanitation Department remained in action for a decade, disposing of garbage, digging drainage ditches, spraying oil on streams and swamps, and chasing down all possible sources of infection. Stevens meanwhile supplemented Gorgas's work by building housing for workers and by erecting a supply depot that included a cold storage plant capable of holding 94,000 cubic feet of food, a bakery, an ice cream factory, and a laundry.

Stevens's second concern was transportation—of people, supplies, equipment, and, most important, dirt. Stevens rec-ognized that the central engineering challenge of the project was figuring out how to move and where to put the 232 million cubic yards (338 million tons) of soil and rock that had to be dug from the canal site. To accomplish this task, he transformed the antiquated Panama Railroad, building nearly 300 miles of new track and ordering thousands of pieces of rolling stock, including 300 locomotives and 3,915 flatcars designed for earth removal. He also brought in new types of machinery, such as dirt spreaders, unloaders (to speed the task of getting dirt off the flatcars), and recently developed track shifters that permitted railway lines to be moved quickly so that dirt could be dumped in different spots. By 1907, the Panama Railroad, running 570 trains a day, was said to be the busiest railway in the world.

Stevens also played a critical role in the design of the canal itself. When he was appointed, no design had yet been approved in Washington, although it was presumed that a sea-level canal would be dug through the hilly terrain. Stevens, however, became convinced that a narrow sea-level canal, flanked by high walls, ran too high a risk of being obstructed

Dirt and rocks being loaded onto flatbed train cars in Panama by a 25-ton steam shovel.

Workers, digging by hand, during the construction of the Panama Canal.

by landslides, and that a "lock" canal could be built more cheaply and rapidly. By June 1906, he convinced the Canal Commission, the president, and Congress to follow his advice and adopt an engineering plan calling for the creation of an above-sea-level passageway, including the man-made Lake Gatun, connected to a network of locks that would raise and lower ships at each end of the canal. (The locks themselves were enormous concrete chambers that could be filled with or drained of water through a complex network of valves: ships entered the locks and were either raised or lowered 85 feet before proceeding on their journey.) When Stevens resigned as chief engineer in 1907, he left behind a coherent engineering plan, an efficient railroad, and an infrastructure that could support a labor force of thousands.

Stevens's successor was George W. Goethals, a career officer from the Army Corps of Engineers with abundant construction experience. Goethals, who remained on the job for seven years, created an effective managerial hierarchy and oversaw an international labor force that numbered as many as 50,000. A minority (called the "gold roll" because they were paid in gold-backed currency) consisted of skilled white males, mostly American, lured to Panama by high wages, free transportation, and free medical care. Their housing was comfortable, recreation and entertainment were provided, and the commissary did its best to provide these men and their families fresh meat, groceries, and at least some of the comforts of home. Most of the men who performed the physical labor of building the canal, however, were unskilled blacks from the Caribbean, joined by thousands of southern Europeans and roughly 1,000 Asians. These "silver" workers (paid in less valuable silver Panamanian currency) lived in cramped barracks, huts, or urban slums; they were poorly paid; they were compelled to use segregated hospitals, dining halls, and post offices; and they were denied rights (including the eight-hour day) that were legally mandated for government employees in the United States. The vast majority of workers who died in accidents or from disease were black.

For more than seven years, these workers, "gold" and "silver," dug their way 52 miles across the Isthmus of Panama. More than 61 million pounds of dynamite were exploded; 300 rock drills were continuously in operation; scores of steam shovels lifted dirt and rock from the site; hundreds of trains shuttled back and forth each day; millions of yards of concrete were poured to form the locks at the two ends of the canal. An ear-splitting cacophony of sound, day and night, the dramatic construction scene became a tourist attraction, with passenger trains ferrying the well-to-do to watch the canal being cut from the earth. Despite major landslides and the periodic buckling of the canal floor, the project was completed in 1913, almost a year ahead of schedule. Its final cost was around $350 million, with disease and accidents claiming the lives of 5,609 workers. The canal saw little traffic during its first years because of World War I, but by the 1920s more than 5,000 ships were passing through its locks each year. The time required for ships to pass from the Atlantic to the Pacific had been cut from weeks to twelve hours. An extraordinary and long-imagined feat of practical engineering had been completed; and the United States owned one of the most important waterways in the world.

## THE ROOSEVELT COROLLARY

In addition to superintending the construction of the Panama Canal, Theodore Roosevelt gave a new definition to American policy in the Western Hemisphere. This redefinition was precipitated by Venezuela's default on its debts to Great Britain and Germany. Tiring of unfulfilled promises of repayment, the two European nations, after notifying the United States, set up a naval blockade of the Venezuelan coast. Roosevelt, fearing the blockade might lead to war or German seizure of Venezuelan assets, pressured Britain and Germany to accept arbitration of their Venezuelan claims. Faced with the threat of American naval intervention, the two countries agreed to arbitration, and their claims were eventually settled by an international tribunal at The Hague in 1904.

The significance of the episode resided in the Europeans' recognition of American primacy in Latin America. It also brought to the fore broader issues: many Latin American and Caribbean regimes were economically and politically unstable, in part because of imperialist interventions, and that instability—characterized by revolutionary movements, violent changes of regime, and unreliable debt repayments—seemed likely to invite outside intervention. As Roosevelt saw the situation, this meant that the United States had to either tolerate European interference in Latin America or police the hemisphere itself. Encouraged by Britain and Germany, Roosevelt adopted the latter course. "In the Western hemisphere," he declared in an address to Congress in 1904, "the adherence of the United States to the Monroe Doctrine may force the United States, however reluctantly . . . to the exercise of an international police power."

617

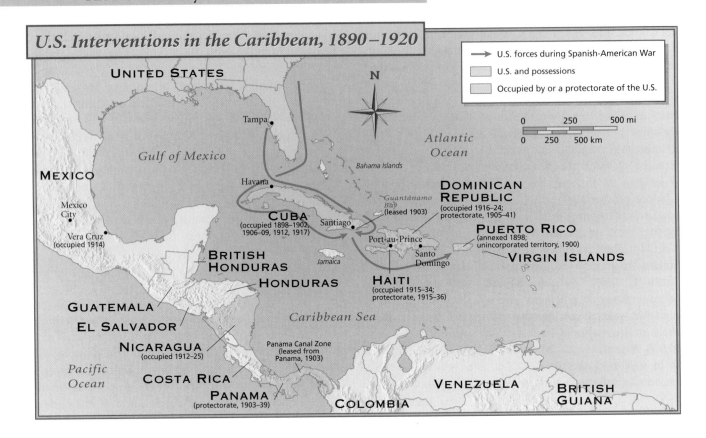

### U.S. Interventions in the Caribbean, 1890–1920

**Legend:**
→ U.S. forces during Spanish-American War
U.S. and possessions
Occupied by or a protectorate of the U.S.

0    250    500 mi
0    250    500 km

UNITED STATES

*Gulf of Mexico*

*Atlantic Ocean*

Tampa

MEXICO

Mexico City

Vera Cruz (occupied 1914)

Havana

*Bahama Islands*

CUBA (occupied 1898–1902, 1906–09, 1912, 1917)

Santiago

*Guantánamo Bay* (leased 1903)

DOMINICAN REPUBLIC (occupied 1916–24; protectorate, 1905–41)

PUERTO RICO (annexed 1898; unincorporated territory, 1900)

VIRGIN ISLANDS

*Jamaica*

Port-au-Prince

Santo Domingo

HAITI (occupied 1915–34; protectorate, 1915–36)

BRITISH HONDURAS

HONDURAS

GUATEMALA

EL SALVADOR

NICARAGUA (occupied 1912–25)

*Caribbean Sea*

*Pacific Ocean*

COSTA RICA

PANAMA (protectorate, 1903–39)

Panama Canal Zone (leased from Panama, 1903)

COLOMBIA

VENEZUELA

BRITISH GUIANA

Although couched as a mere amendment to the Monroe Doctrine, Roosevelt's corollary in fact announced a major shift in America's role. Monroe had warned European nations not to meddle in hemispheric affairs and to respect Latin American revolutions, as well as the independence of Latin American countries; Roosevelt, in contrast, was committing the United States to intervention to suppress revolutions and guarantee a "stability" that the United States alone would define.

Roosevelt soon had the opportunity to put his corollary into action. Between the late 1890s and 1903, social conflict spawned a series of military revolts in the Dominican Republic, leading to defaults on foreign loans. In 1903, the turmoil was so great that the United States and several European nations sent warships to Santo Domingo. To stabilize the situation, Roosevelt, in collaboration with Dominican president Carlos Morales, formulated a plan for the United States to take charge of Dominican customs collections and to oversee the repayment of the island nation's foreign debts. The rationale for taking control of customs was strategic and precise:

doing so would not only guarantee debt repayment, it would also give the United States de facto control of the national budget, since customs revenues were the government's primary source of income. Washington believed that it would reduce smuggling, graft, and the incentive for rebellion, permit a fractious army to be shrunk, and thus free up funds to stimulate economic development. Although Roosevelt denied any interest in annexing the Dominican Republic, his plan provoked a storm of opposition among Dominicans and in Congress. The arrangement was implemented nonetheless, and the United States remained in charge of Dominican finances until 1911.

Roosevelt's policy toward the Dominican Republic and other less developed nations was also shaped by ideological and cultural considerations. The president and the men around him saw the world as divided between "civilized" and "barbarian" peoples, and they believed that it was the responsibility of civilized white nations like the United States to train and uplift their less fortunate, usually nonwhite,

Cartoon of President Roosevelt, carrying a big stick and leading a fleet of war ships, striding through the Caribbean.

brethren. "It is a good thing for India," wrote Roosevelt to a friend, "that England should control it." Such cultural and racial condescension was widespread in American society. In 1898, a newspaper, after noting that Admiral Dewey had requisitioned 60,000 pounds of soap for the Philippines, observed that "soap and the Bible go hand in hand . . . in the development of the backward races." In 1904, the Louisiana Purchase Exposition in St. Louis included a display in which 1,200 Filipinos of various "types"—including "savages," "fierce followers of Mohammed," and the "more intelligent class"—lived in mock villages where they could be observed by American fair-goers.

Such views prevented Roosevelt and others from recognizing the aspirations of many foreign peoples and from understanding the dynamics of their societies. The desire of the Filipinos for independence could be dismissed because most Filipinos were "savages," incapable of self-government—at least until they were schooled by Americans. Similarly, a small country wracked by political divisions and economic inequalities was unlikely to achieve stability just because the United States controlled its finances for a few years. Five years after the United States turned the customs houses back to the Dominicans, Washington found itself sending troops to Santo

Domingo to quell rebellions and restore order. The troops would remain there for eight more years.

While Roosevelt was staking out a new role for the United States as the policeman of the Western Hemisphere, he was simultaneously trying to enhance American influence in Asia by acting as a mediator. In 1904, tensions between Russia and Japan over control of northern China and Korea erupted into war. Roosevelt shared a widespread American antipathy to tsarist Russia and quietly supported the Japanese, who had recently made positive overtures to the West. By mid-1905, the war had bogged down, with Japan lacking the resources for a lengthy conflict and the Russian government preoccupied with revolutionary upheaval in its own cities. Roosevelt embraced Japan's suggestion that he mediate the conflict. After rancorous negotiations in Portsmouth, New Hampshire, the two warring parties agreed to a settlement. Roosevelt won the Nobel Peace Prize for his efforts, although his diplomatic goals were soon thwarted by an agreement between Russia and Japan to carve up northern China and Manchuria. That agreement, coupled with a rising tide of antiforeign (including anti-American) sentiment in China, knocked the final props from under the Open Door policy.

The treaty Roosevelt had brokered between Japan and Russia also spawned anti-American anger among the Japanese, who blamed Roosevelt for robbing Japan of the fruits of military success. Tensions between the two nations were heightened by a domestic event. In response to a sharp increase in Japanese immigration that had begun in 1900, the San Francisco school board decided in 1906 to assign Japanese children to segregated classrooms—displaying once again the West Coast's antagonism to Asian immigrants. The Japanese government demanded that this insulting practice be halted. Roosevelt, who believed that the Japanese (unlike the Chinese) were "highly civilized people," resolved the conflict by negotiating a "Gentlemen's Agreement" in 1907 that called for an end to Japanese emigration to the United States in return for a commitment from San Francisco to stop segregating schoolchildren.

## DOLLAR DIPLOMACY AND WILSONIAN IDEALISM

The foreign policy course set by Presidents McKinley and Roosevelt was, in key respects, maintained by their successors,

William Howard Taft (1909–13) and Woodrow Wilson (1913–21). (See Chapter 22.) Taft, a lawyer by training, was more of a legalist than the rambunctiously nationalist Roosevelt, yet he, too, believed that foreign trade was essential to American well-being and that the government should play an active role in promoting international commerce. Having been the governor-general of the Philippines, Taft was also convinced that international peace was a prerequisite to prosperity and democracy.

Taft's conduct of foreign policy gave birth to the label "dollar diplomacy," a double-edged phrase suggesting both that the government was doing the bidding of Wall Street and that the administration wisely preferred using "dollars" rather than "bullets" to exert influence abroad. Both connotations were apt. Taft was notably cautious in using force, particularly in response to chaotic conditions on the Mexican border, but his preference for dollars did not mean renouncing the use of bullets. The war in the Philippines dragged on, soldiers were dispatched once again to Cuba, and Taft several times sent warships and troops to Nicaragua to install or preserve regimes friendly to American business interests.

Taft's successor, Woodrow Wilson, was a moralist in foreign affairs, as in other matters. He personally abhorred the imperialist exploitation of less developed nations, recognized that poverty and oppression bred revolutions, and believed deeply in democracy. Although Wilson, like his contemporaries, was convinced that international trade was vital to the nation's welfare, he was a scholar and a religious man who believed that Christian values and American political institutions should serve as a model for all nations. Wilson's was a missionary vision: the role of the United States was to assume leadership in world affairs, uplift other nations, discourage violent revolutions, and sponsor stable, gradual reform.

Wilson, however, became president just as Europe was hurtling into war and during a period when revolutionary movements in many parts of the globe were gathering steam. In those circumstances, despite—or perhaps because of—his idealist democratic convictions, he became one of the most interventionist presidents in American history. Not only did he lead the United States into World War I (see Chapter 23), he also sent troops into half a dozen Latin American nations as well as Russia.

Several of Wilson's interventions in the Caribbean and Central America followed precedents established during the first decade of the century. He kept marines in Nicaragua, eventually taking control of the nation's ports, railroads, and financial affairs. In 1916, Wilson insisted that elections be held to replace the American-friendly but unpopular President Adolfo Diaz; and, to no one's surprise, the candidate backed by the United States, Emiliano Chamorro, was elected president. Marines remained in Nicaragua until 1925.

The United States also sent soldiers to take charge of Haiti in 1915, after seven changes of regime in four years, most by assassination. Wilson, troubled by the tumult and by the growing influence of French and German economic interests, proposed an American takeover of Haitian customs offices. When the Haitians refused, the United States sent marines to seize funds from the Haitian treasury, precipitating a collapse of the government and an American military occupation that lasted until 1934. Although the United States did contribute to Haiti's development by sanitizing its cities and building roads and bridges, it also imposed a constitution favorable to American interests and permitting foreigners, for the first time, to own land. Many Haitians resisted the American occupation, and more than 3,000 died fighting the marines. Similar resistance surfaced in the Dominican Republic, where marines were once again sent in 1916. For eight years, the United States occupied the Dominican Republic, combating armed nationalists while establishing an impressive system of public education, controlling the nation's finances, and creating a national guard to maintain the American-enforced peace.

The United States also intervened in Mexico. In the late nineteenth and early twentieth centuries, during the long dictatorship of Porfirio Diaz, Americans had invested heavily in their southern neighbor. By 1910, the United States was the largest foreign investor in the country, and Americans controlled critical industries, including mining and railroads. Foreign investment helped transform Mexico's economic and social structure, which in turn led to a multipronged revolution that began to erupt in 1910. After Diaz was overthrown, the long border between the United States and Mexico became a hotbed of activity, as rebel groups and bandits moved back and forth across it, seeking supplies, arms, and shelter. Despite the threat to American lives and property, President Taft was cautious about intervention, although he did form a 20,000-man Maneuver Division to police the border.

Wilson, faced with different conditions, was less cautious. In 1913, conservative general Victoriano Huerta seized power in a coup, assassinating his predecessor, Francisco Madero. Wilson opposed Huerta's regime because of the violent way in which it had come to power and because of its ties to British oil interests.

Although Huerta's rule was subsequently legitimized by a reasonably free election, Wilson remained eager to seek his ouster. In 1914, the president took advantage of a minor incident in which American sailors were briefly arrested in Tampico to send the American fleet and occupation forces to the important Mexican city of Veracruz. A score of Americans and hundreds of Mexicans were killed in the battle for Veracruz, which led to an occupation of the city for seven months and eventually to Huerta's resignation.

Yet Huerta's successor, Venustiano Carranza, was also resistant to American influence. He advocated a more left-wing program, including agrarian reform, national ownership of all mineral rights, and restrictions on property holding by foreigners. When Carranza's regime was challenged by the forces of another revolutionary, Francisco "Pancho" Villa, Wilson threw his support to Villa, although he reversed himself in 1915 and recognized Carranza's government. Villa then launched a series of attacks across the Arizona and New Mexico borders, trying to demonstrate Carranza's lack of control of the country and to bait the United States into chasing Villa back into Mexico. The United States took the bait, sending a Punitive Expedition of 10,000 troops deep into Mexico in 1916 to capture Villa. The expedition ended up skirmishing not only with the "Villistas" but also with Carranza's troops before it was finally withdrawn in 1917. Although Villa was never captured and made occasional forays across the border for two years, Carranza remained in power.

Despite its failure to eliminate the Villistas, the Punitive Expedition did succeed in lessening conflict along the border. It also provided the United States with an opportunity to deploy new military technology. In Mexico, as in the Dominican Republic, the army introduced aircraft into military operations, which provided vital courier service to far-flung troops, taught important lessons to pilots and the army, and produced pioneering aerial photography. The army also used ten motorized truck companies to chase Pancho Villa, becoming less dependent on railways and more flexible in delivering supplies to combat units. In these respects at least, the Punitive Expedition proved to be America's first experiment with twentieth-century war.

American policies in the Caribbean and Latin America after 1900 clearly asserted U.S. dominance in the Western Hemisphere. Whatever interest European powers might have had in

Francisco "Pancho" Villa (center) and his fellow revolutionary Emilio Zapata (with sombrero on knee) in the Presidential Palace in Mexico City, 1914.

acquiring bases or colonies in the region was checked, as Presidents Roosevelt, Taft, and Wilson made clear that the United States would police the political and economic behavior of other states in the region. These policies protected American property and commerce and limited European involvement, but they had shortcomings. All too often, American intervention spawned rebellion and disorder rather than stability. It also created deep reservoirs of anti-American sentiment that would be tapped repeatedly in the course of the twentieth century.

## A New Empire

America's position in the world was transformed between the late 1860s and the beginning of World War I. Americans today often take as a given the global power and reach of the United States, as well as the significance of events abroad to American politics and business. But for much of the nineteenth century, America's relationship to international affairs was far different: rich in resources, devoted primarily to agriculture, and geographically protected from external threats, the United States played a small role in international politics and, aside from shifts in the global market for labor and agricultural goods, was little affected by events outside its borders. All of this changed in the late nineteenth and early twentieth centuries, setting the United States on a course to becoming a world power and, later, a superpower.

This change in the nation's global role was inextricably linked to the social and economic transformation of postbellum America. Power on the world stage was grounded in the success of American agriculture and industry. The felt need for foreign markets was magnified by the increasingly resonant dynamics of the business cycle. Racial conflict and ethnic tensions at home made many Americans reluctant to annex new territories and add to the nation's nonwhite population.

The country's impulse and capacity to reach outward were also shaped by science and technology. The productivity gains that led Americans to believe they were overproducing were rooted in the technological advances that transformed workplaces. The desirability of investment in some regions, as well as the feasibility of canal construction in Panama, was enhanced by medical knowledge that reduced the threat of infectious diseases. Advances in military technology strengthened the hand of all industrial nations in their relationships with less developed societies, while the telegraph, the telephone, faster ships, and then airplanes made it easier for men in Washington to monitor and influence events abroad.

What emerged during this period was not simply the American acquisition of "power," but a new structuring of American relationships with overseas nations. In its dealings with the European powers, as well as Russia and Japan, the United States established itself as an economic competitor, insisting on the right to trade and invest around the globe, capable of using military force to achieve its ends. (That this outward thrust was accompanied by the maintenance of high tariffs and a special sphere of influence in the Western Hemisphere testified to the malleability of principles when they conflicted with self-interest.) The United States acquired colonies during this era, but more commonly, it forged relationships that historian William Appleman Williams has aptly labeled "non-colonial imperialism." Outside of the Philippines, Hawaii, Puerto Rico, and a few other locales, the United States did not assert formal political or military control over overseas territories; nor did it dispatch colonists to live abroad, as Europeans did in Africa, India, and parts of South America.

What the United States did instead was to establish its dominance over other countries, such as Haiti and Nicaragua, while leaving them nominally independent. The rules governing financial and political affairs were made in Washington. The people who inhabited these countries were regarded as inferiors who were best controlled and tutored by Americans. Military power could be deployed to protect American interests and ensure that the rules were followed. Indeed, it was fitting that the most prominent exhibit at the 1893 World's Fair in Chicago was the "Great White Fleet," built by the United States Navy, a thirty-acre display that included full-sized replicas of the latest generation of American battleships.

## Suggested Reading

Akira Iriye, *The Cambridge History of American Foreign Relations, vol. 3: The Globalizing of America, 1913–45* (1993)

Walter LaFeber, *The New Empire: An Interpretation of American Expansion, 1860–1898* (1963)

David McCullough, *The Path Between the Seas: The Creation of the Panama Canal, 1870–1914* (1977)

Louis A. Perez, Jr., *Cuba and the United States: Ties of Singular Intimacy* (1990)

Emily Rosenberg, *Spreading the American Dream: American Economic and Cultural Expansion, 1890–1945* (1982)

Robert D. Schulzinger, *American Diplomacy in the Twentieth Century, 3rd ed.* (1994)

David Trask, *The War with Spain in 1898* (1981)

Russell F. Weigley, *History of the United States Army, enlarged ed.* (1984)

## Summary
### QUESTIONS

■ 1. What were the ways in which Congress expressed reluctance to engage in overseas expansion after the Civil War?

■ 2. What were the different sources (economic, political, ideological) of American expansion in the 1890s?

■ 3. How did the war over Cuba come to involve the Philippines?

■ 4. What were the challenges facing the United States in building the Panama Canal? Why did the U. S. succeed after France had failed?

■ 5. How did the Roosevelt corollary change the Monroe doctrine?

## Chronology

| | |
|---|---|
| 1866 | First trans-Atlantic cable completed. |
| 1867 | United States purchases Alaska from Russia. |
| 1895 | Crisis in Venezuela strengthens American power in the Western Hemisphere. |
| February 1898 | American battleship Maine explodes in Havana Harbor. |
| April–August 1898 | Spanish-American War. |
| August 12, 1898 | Hawaii becomes a U. S. territory. |
| December 1898 | Spain surrenders sovereignty over Cuba and the Philippines and cedes Puerto Rico and Guam to the United States. |
| September 1899 | John Hay sends Open Door Note to powers involved in China. |
| 1900 | Puerto Rico becomes unincorporated territory of the United States. |
| 1904 | Roosevelt's corollary to the Monroe Doctrine commits United States to policing the Western Hemisphere. |
| 1913 | Panama Canal completed. |

## Key Terms

*Reconcentrado* (p. 605)

Imperialism (pp. 608–609)

Platt Amendment (p. 611)

Open Door policy (p. 613)

Panama Canal (p. 614)

The Roosevelt Corollary (pp. 617–618)

# Part 6

# STATE AND SOCIETY IN A WORLD OF STRIFE

BETWEEN 1900 AND 1940, the United States took its place as a great power in a world that was being reconfigured by empire and made smaller by technology. Although Americans had sometimes chafed at their distance from cultural capitals such as Paris and London, they had long appreciated the security of living an ocean away from other powerful nations, from the wars that broke out periodically in Europe in the nineteenth century, from the populous countries of East Asia that seemed exotic yet difficult to understand. But the isolation of the United States was diminishing—due in part to the quickening of transportation and communication and in part to choices made by the American government. Early in the twentieth century, the United States acquired overseas territories, and stationed troops, as far away as the Philippines; and in 1917–18 it sent American soldiers across the Atlantic to intervene decisively in a European war.

Despite the nation's new and important global role, its energies and attention during these years remained focused primarily on domestic matters: taxes and tariffs, the regulation of business, the "labor question," the rights of women, the prices of agricultural products, immigration restriction, unemployment, and the revitalization of democratic institutions. All of these issues (and others) became the subject of prolonged, often complex, policy debates. A distinctive feature of this forty-year period was that more and more Americans were turning to the state—meaning public authorities at all levels—for help with the problems that concerned them.

*Changing West*, a panel from Thomas Hart Benton's 1930 mural, *America Today*. From the AXA Financial, Inc. collection.

625

The state, thus, became a critical locus of innovation, more important perhaps than it had been at any time since the writing of the federal constitution and the first state constitutions. Mayors and city councilors, governors and state legislators, cabinet officials, farmers, social reformers, labor activists: all sought to develop innovative public policies and programs to address problems that had begun rearing their heads in the late nineteenth century and persisted well into the twentieth. During the critical early decades of the twentieth century, most Americans were relinquishing the nineteenth-century belief that "the future will take care of itself." (The words were those of political thinker Herbert Croly in 1909.) They were seeking instead to safeguard the future by innovating: by changing laws, creating new governmental institutions and agencies, by experimenting with programs that had never been tried before.

One emblem of this shift could be found in the Constitution itself. This hallowed document, by design, was difficult to amend, and the political leaders of the nineteenth century were deeply reluctant to tinker with the work of the founding fathers. Between 1804 and 1912, only three constitutional amendments were approved by Congress and by the states, all of them passed between 1865 and 1870, all of them dealing with the repercussions of the Civil War. Between 1913 and 1933, however, six additional amendments were added to the Constitution, on subjects as varied as women's suffrage, taxation, and the consumption of alcohol. That this could occur reflected not a disregard or disrespect for the fundamental blueprint of government, but rather a new willingness to experiment in the public arena, to modernize the American state in order to cope with the problems of a modern society. That willingness was the hallmark of the era.

# Chapter 22

# THE PROGRESSIVE ERA:

## 1900-1916

New York City's Times Square at night, c. 1900.

A Growing Economy

**QUESTIONS**

■ **What were the economic underpinnings of Progressive reform?**

■ **How did developments in technology and science influence Progressivism?**

■ **What were the key elements of Progressive reform?**

■ **How did Progressivism address tensions of class, ethnicity, and race?**

■ **What were the experiences of women in Progressive reform?**

■ **How did Progressive reform influence national politics?**

"The Century is dead; long live the Century! Yesterday was the Nineteenth, today the Twentieth." So declared the *New York Times* on January 1, 1901. The citizens of New York marked the dawn of the twentieth century the night before, at a gala outdoor celebration in front of City Hall: the building was bedecked with 2,000 American flags, 2,000 red, white, and blue lightbulbs, and the words "WELCOME, 20TH CENTURY " in gigantic electrically lit letters.

An hour before midnight, city council president Randolph Guggenheimer addressed the crowd. "Tonight when the clock strikes 12, the present century will have come to an end. We look back upon it as a cycle of time within which the achievements in science and in civilization are not less than marvelous. The advance of the human race during the past 100 years has not been equaled by the progress of man within any of the preceding ages." Guggenheimer also expressed the "earnest wish" that "the crowning glory of the coming century shall be the lifting up of the burdens of the poor, the annihilation of all misery and wrong, and that the peace and goodwill which the angels proclaimed should rest on contending nations as the snowflakes upon the land."

A few moments before the clock struck twelve, the lights around City Hall were turned off, returning the crowd to the semidarkness that, until the 1890s, had been the norm of urban night. Then, at the stroke of midnight, lights were turned back on, new floodlights were illumined, and explosions of fireworks rained down from nearby skyscrapers. The whole city was filled with light, with "electric fountains and forests of fire," many of them red, white, or blue. "It was distinctly," as the *Times* observed, "an electric celebration."

Throughout the nation, Americans celebrated the arrival of a new century, with speakers marveling at the changes wrought during the nineteenth century and lauding the material, scientific, and technological advances that had transformed American society. Equally common was the sense of an unfinished agenda, the conviction that the social and political order had not kept pace with the material and the technological. The persistence of poverty and inequality seemed glaring in light of the nation's economic progress, and the absence of any true "brotherhood of man," as one newspaper put it, was all too evident.

The problems confronting American society early in the twentieth century were, indeed, much the same as they had been late in the nineteenth; so, too, were the economic and social forces shaping Americans' lives. Great wealth and economic power coexisted with broad swaths of poverty. New technologies transformed workplaces and the rhythms of daily life. Immigrants continued to pour into the rapidly growing cities, testing the limits of tolerance. Racial discrimination remained at the heart of southern social life and politics.

Yet the dawn of the new century marked the beginning of a more optimistic era. The seemingly uncontrollable roller-coaster ride of the late nineteenth century slowed a bit, and many Americans became more confident of their ability to meet the challenges they faced. The effort to grasp the "natural laws" governing economic and social life gave way to empirical investigations of specific issues; the Populist and often working-class cry for sweeping change devolved into a search for concrete, pragmatic reforms. In the words of the young Walter Lippmann, who would become one of the twentieth century's most influential political commentators, "drift" was replaced by "mastery."

The Electric Tower lit up at night at the Pan American Exposition, Buffalo, New York, 1901.

"We put intention where custom has reigned," he wrote in 1914. Reflecting a shift in middle-class attitudes, government became more active and forward-looking, while politicians from different parties scrambled to identify themselves as "progressive."

The first two decades of the twentieth century have, in fact, long been referred to by historians as the "Progressive Era." The period could as well be called the "era of electricity" or the "era of the automobile." There surely was a shift in temper in American public life, a surge of interest in social and political reform, but equally dramatic were the spread of electricity and the beginning of the nation's romance with the automobile. What distinguished these decades from their predecessors was not just the pace of reform but also the material and technological basis of daily life. These different domains were not unrelated to one another: the men and women who wrestled with social, economic, and political issues were influenced by the problem-solving mentality of the scientists and engineers who had wrought technological progress. If knowledge, ingenuity, and persistence could wipe out yellow fever and permit people to talk on the telephone, then surely they could also alleviate poverty, reduce inequality, and rein in the power of large corporations.

## A Growing Economy

Undergirding the optimistic temper of the era was a rapidly growing economy. Although the nation did experience two short panics, or recessions, in 1907–8 and 1913–14, growth was steadier than it had been in the late nineteenth century. While the nation's population rose from 76 million in 1900 to 106 million in 1920, gross national product nearly doubled, with the value of manufactured goods increasing sixfold. Although many Americans were troubled by the unusual problem of inflation— rising prices were a new experience for anyone born after the Civil War—middle-class incomes rose substantially, and real wages (adjusted for inflation) increased for most workers.

As was always true, the growth was uneven. Older industries, such as flour milling and textiles, grew modestly, while the steel industry spurted forward between 1900 and 1910 and then slowed considerably because of a dramatic decline in railroad growth. But new industries picked up the slack: the two stars of the era were automobiles and electrical machinery, joined during World War I by a booming shipbuilding industry. Manufacturing remained concentrated in the Northeast and the Midwest, although many textile plants migrated from New England to the Carolinas and Georgia in search of cheaper labor. The petroleum industry, originally centered in the Midwest, gravitated toward Texas, Oklahoma, and California.

Farmers did well, although agriculture was becoming a less common pursuit. Between 1900 and 1920, the farm population and the number of acres under cultivation rose only slightly, which meant that the percentage of Americans who were farmers declined. Farm incomes, however, increased substantially, thanks in part to a sustained rise in the prices of farm products. Although the collapse of the Populist movement after the election of 1896 marked a political defeat for farmers, many of their economic goals were achieved: even on the plains, farmers did well since rainfall was above average and wheat prices were high.

Farmers' fortunes were also enhanced by technological improvements, most notably steam-traction engines and then gasoline-powered tractors. (The word "tractor" was coined in 1905 to identify this new vehicle.) Powerful steam-traction engines were far more productive than horses or mules, but they were expensive and heavy (weighing ten to twenty-five tons) and consumed enormous amounts of fuel and water. Even at the peak of their popularity, between 1908 and 1915, only 5 percent

A steam-powered tractor pulls a plow, Chippewa County, Minnesota, c. 1914.

## Science, Technology, and Industry

Science-based industries, grounded primarily in chemistry and physics, flourished during the first two decades of the twentieth century. New scientific knowledge (much of which came from Europe) about atoms, molecules, gases, light, magnetism, and electricity lay at the heart of several industries while fostering innovation in others. In physics, for example, X-rays were discovered in 1895, radioactivity in 1896, and the electron in 1897. In 1900, German physicist Max Planck advanced the theory that radiation was emitted in quanta, discrete lumps of energy, rather than in a continuous wave. In 1905, Albert Einstein, then an employee in a Swiss patent office, published his theory of special relativity, with its remarkable implications that mass and energy were equivalent and that physical characteristics such as mass and time could vary depending on the relative movement of the observer.

of all farmers owned steam-traction vehicles. Recognizing the shortcomings of steam, inventors competed to develop sturdy, light, relatively inexpensive vehicles driven by gasoline-powered internal-combustion engines. Spurred on by labor shortages during World War I, manufacturers of these new tractors achieved some success: although the great majority of farmers continued to rely on animal power, more than 200,000 tractors—each capable of doing the work of three or more horses—were in use by 1920. Tractors reduced the number of hours of labor needed to produce crops, compensated for a growing scarcity of workers, and freed millions of acres for food production that had been used to support horses and mules.

Scientific gains also enhanced farm productivity. Advances in plant genetics led to crossbreeding that yielded improved variants of corn, wheat, and other crops. The new field of bacteriology generated methods of preventing devastating diseases, such as hog cholera. Chemists helped to produce fertilizers in addition to promoting the liming of farmland. These scientific advances were encouraged by the U.S. Department of Agriculture (USDA), an important center of scientific research, particularly in genetics and chemistry. It taught farmers about the latest advances in science at experiment stations and on demonstration farms; it also applied scientific knowledge to farm practices and the inspection of livestock. The efforts of the USDA were reinforced by the Smith-Lever Act of 1914 and the Smith-Hughes Act of 1917, which provided federal funds to support the teaching of new agricultural methods as well as agricultural extension programs at land-grant colleges.

Such discoveries launched waves of scientific research in the United States; they were also ripe with possibilities for practical application. The ability to manipulate electrons, for example, made it possible to amplify electrical signals, facilitating long-distance telephone calls and the transmission of radio signals. X-ray technology transformed the practice of orthopedics as well as some surgical specialties. Scientific investigation, in turn, was stimulated by the demands of industry and the search for profits. The industrial research facilities pioneered by General Electric and Bell Telephone (see Chapter 18) were joined by several hundred other industrial laboratories, including those of chemical firms such as Dow, Eastman Kodak, and Du Pont, which employed more than 1,200 chemists by the 1920s. Firms also began to promote scientific research in collaboration with universities such as MIT and the Drexel Institute; in Pittsburgh, the Mellon Institute funded graduate students and postdoctoral fellows to solve research problems submitted by industry.

These laboratories produced an array of new products for consumers and industry. Researchers at General Electric developed more precise X-ray machines and dramatically improved the quality of electric lighting by developing a tungsten filament and by filling bulbs with inert gas to prevent the blackening that occurred when filaments burned. Leo H. Baekeland, a Belgian-born chemist, invented a photographic paper that could be printed in artificial light (which he sold to Kodak), as well as "Bakelite," the first of a series of synthetic substances that had widespread use (in appliances, jewelry, and handles) as insulation against heat and electricity. Chemists developed improved acids and alkalis (such as caustic and bleaching powders), while scientific advances also spawned the first aluminum products, rayons, and high-speed carbon steel that remained hard at high temperatures and thus led to great improvements in machine-tool technology. Engineers and scientists trained in these laboratories fanned out into older industries, encouraging research and innovation.

In 1901, Congress created the National Bureau of Standards, authorizing the agency not only to establish and maintain standards of measure, such as units of electricity or light, but also to engage in any research necessary to do so. The physical sciences, declared Secretary of the Treasury Lyman Gage, were of great importance to the nation's well-being in part because the United States was competing in so many ways with the nations of Europe. Foreshadowing developments that would occur later in the twentieth century, the government also established, during World War I, laboratories designed to conduct research with military applications.

## TECHNOLOGICAL SYSTEMS

*Electricity.* As in the late nineteenth century, the fusion of scientific knowledge with entrepreneurial skill inspired not only individual products, such as photographic paper, but the development of large-scale, interconnected technological systems. The electrical system, created in the late nineteenth century but greatly enlarged during the first decades of the twentieth, had the most fundamental impact on society, particularly in cities. Electricity was the hallmark technology of the era, widely regarded as mysterious and all-powerful, capable of transforming every facet of American life. "God is the great electrician," proclaimed one celebrant, while the Sears, Roebuck catalogue in 1901 offered an electric belt that would allegedly restore men's sexual powers. The electrical system included several thousand utility companies by 1907, as well as firms that manufactured goods that ran on electric currents. By 1910, nearly all utilities were generating a standard alternating current, permitting power grids to be interconnected and electrical goods

to be produced to uniform specifications. By 1920, one-third of all homes were wired, almost all of which were in urban and suburban areas. Electricity had replaced gas, kerosene, and oils for lighting, and appliances such as electric fans, irons, and vacuum cleaners were becoming commonplace. Electricity also provided the power for urban and suburban rail systems. By 1920, there were more than 200,000 men who fit into the new census occupational category of "electrician."

The spread of electricity to workplaces was even more significant. A rarity in 1890, electricity became first the predominant source of light and then the predominant source of power in factories. The incandescent bulb was a great improvement over the gas lamp: it was brighter and steadier, did not raise temperatures or give off fumes, and was less likely to spark fires. It made precise, detailed work much easier; newspaper printers, who generally worked at night, were among the first to embrace electric lighting. Electric motors also had great advantages over those driven by steam or fossil fuels: they provided a steady source of power and light without generating much heat or consuming oxygen, and they could be regulated by electrically driven sensors and controls. Electricity made it easier to locate machinery in efficient sequences on the factory floor, while machine tools powered by electricity were faster, lighter, and more portable than their predecessors.

A General Electric Company exhibit inside the Electricity Building at the St. Louis Exposition of 1904.

631

Science, Technology, and Industry

Henry Ford with the first Ford automobile, 1896.

Electricity facilitated round-the-clock factory schedules, the use of cranes and lifts to carry heavy materials, and ventilation systems that made the air easier to breathe and kept machinery clean. The spread of electricity also meant that manufacturing operations could be located anywhere, since they no longer depended on a nearby source of waterpower or coal. This critical fact shaped the social geography of the West, where industry, developing in the twentieth century, was almost entirely concentrated in urban areas.

The contours of the electrical system were shaped not only by the requirements of science but also by social choices. In a broad-gauged public debate between 1890 and 1920, the vision of electricity as a public service contended with the notion that it ought to be treated as a private commodity. Should generating companies be publicly or privately owned? (Both forms of ownership existed in the 1890s.) Should there be many utility companies or just a few? Who should decide what locales or firms would get electrical service and at what cost? Gradually, the view of electricity as a private commodity controlled by private corporations won out. Although some public utilities endured and some rate regulations were put in place, the electrical supply became dominated by private enterprises, many of which were partially owned by the two giant manufacturers of electrical goods, Westinghouse and General Electric. One result was that electric power was used extensively for urban, commercial spectacles, such as adver-

tising and store window displays, while most of rural America remained without electricity at all—because it was not as profitable to extend service to sparsely populated areas. Even at the end of the 1920s, most farmers did not have electric lines running to their homes.

*The Automobile.* The other hallmark technological system of the era revolved around the automobile. Although the first autos were produced only in the 1890s, it was widely believed by the turn of the century that gasoline-powered vehicles would replace the horse-drawn carriage. Hundreds of entrepreneurs and inventors, many of them bicycle makers, machine-shop owners, or wagon manufacturers, rushed into this new industry, with impressive results. In 1899, 2,500 motor vehicles were produced in the United States; by 1907, the figure was 44,000; by 1916, it exceeded 1 million. The basic design was straightforward and durable: a four- or six-cylinder gasoline engine was mounted in the front of the vehicle, connecting through a gear box and propeller shaft to the rear axle. The first car buyers were wealthy sportsmen, businessmen, and professionals; in many towns and small cities, they included doctors who typically traveled to treat their patients.

By 1910, a shakeout was occurring in the industry, as successful large firms captured more of the market and drove their competitors out of business. The key survivors, including Ford and General Motors, were located in the Midwest, particularly in and around Detroit. Owing to its plentiful hardwood forests, the region contained a large group of carriage and wagon manufacturers, as well as producers of gasoline engines and an abundant supply of skilled, nonunion labor.

The central challenge confronting the automobile industry was economic as well as technological: how to build an automobile inexpensive enough so that people other than the wealthy could buy it. The man who most successfully tackled this problem was Henry Ford, a former machinist and mechanical engineer from Michigan, who built his first automobile in 1896 and in 1903 founded the Ford Motor Company. Like other manufacturers, Ford benefited from advances in the machine-tool industry, including the use of high-speed carbon steel and other alloys that allowed parts to be made with greater speed, precision, and interchangeability. Ford, however, went a critical step further, building a single car model that he improved from year to year, a strategy that greatly facilitated the use of standard parts and streamlined production processes. The Model T was first introduced in

1908. Eight years later, Ford produced more than half a million lighter, stronger, and less expensive units. By 1927, when production stopped, over 15 million Model Ts had been sold.

Ford achieved this success by improving the techniques of mass production, putting into practice what he called "the principles of power, accuracy, economy, system, continuity, and speed." Particularly in the pioneering plant he opened in Highland Park, Michigan, in 1910, he invested heavily in highly specialized machinery while subdividing labor on the shop floor. To augment continuity and speed, Ford in 1913 adopted the moving assembly line, a network of conveyor belts and overhead chains that carried all pieces of the automobile from one worker to the next. "Every piece of work in the shop moves," Ford observed a few years later. "There is no lifting or trucking of anything other than materials." The moving assembly line produced substantial savings, in part because employees were compelled to work more intensively, at a pre-set rhythm. Within a decade, the moving assembly line was adopted throughout the industry, hastening the disappearance of small manufacturers who could not afford to retool their plants.

Ford's assembly line and his production techniques in general were exemplars of "scientific management," a phrase and approach made popular by Philadelphia engineer and businessman Frederick Winslow Taylor. Taylor was one of the nation's first specialists in shop-floor management, and his short book *The Principles of Scientific Management* (1911) was the best-selling business book of the first half of the twentieth century. Taylor believed that workplaces could be made more efficient by training, inducing, and compelling

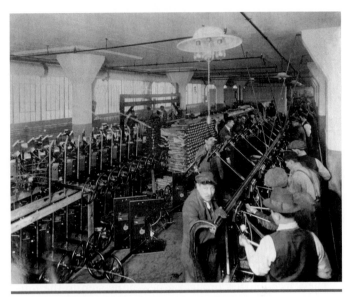

An early assembly line in auto manufacturing, c. 1910.

workers to labor more steadily and intensively. He conducted time and motion studies to analyze the tasks workers were expected to perform and then encouraged employers to reorganize work to minimize wasted motion and time. He also favored paying workers not by the hour but by the "piece" to compel employees, many of whom he described as "stupid," to work more quickly. "Faster work can be assured," wrote Taylor, "only through enforced standardization of methods, enforced adoption of the best implements . . . and enforced cooperation."

Not surprisingly, industrial workers resisted such schemes. One worker at the Ford Motor Company complained that "when the whistle blows he starts to jerk and when the whistle blows again he stops jerking." At Ford and elsewhere, a common response to the brutal intensification of work was absenteeism and high quit rates: in 1913, Ford's daily absentee rate was 10 percent, while annual turnover exceeded 350 percent. To reduce turnover, which was costly to the company, Ford doubled the daily wages of his most valued employees to five dollars a day. This strategy was successful in stabilizing the labor force and reducing operating costs.

The production of automobiles was only one component of an extensive technological system that would gradually replace the railroad network as the prime mover of the nation's economy (see Table 22.1). The system included manufacturers of rubber tires, car dealers, repair shops, thousands of

| Table 22.1 | | |
| --- | --- | --- |
| **MILES OF RAILROAD VS. SALES OF PASSENGER CARS, 1900–20** | | |
| | Miles of Railroad Built | Factory Sales of Passenger Cars |
| 1900 | 4,894 | 4,100 |
| 1905 | 4,388 | 24,200 |
| 1910 | 4,122 | 181,100 |
| 1915 | 833 | 895,900 |
| 1920 | 314 | 1,905,500 |

*Source: Historical Statistics of the United States: Colonial Times to 1970, Part I, Series Q 148, 152, 153, p. 716, and Series Q 329, p. 732.*

miles of newly paved roads, the financiers of car purchases, and networks of signals to regulate this new form of traffic. It also embraced the petroleum industry, greatly stimulating the demand for gasoline and giving birth to a new feature of the American landscape: the filling station.

By 1920, the major technological systems of the industrial era had entered the lives of almost all urban Americans and many who lived on farms as well. Homes and workplaces were lit by electricity. Food was processed by electrical machinery, transported by railroads or the first generation of trucks. Men and women communicated with one another through the telegraph or over the phone: by 1920, more than a third of all households had telephones (see Table 22.2). Americans traveled to work in vehicles powered by gasoline or electricity. Technologies and products that were exotic in 1900 were commonplace by 1920, transforming everyday life.

These technologies brought a new profession to the foreground of American life: engineering. As early as 1900, there were 45,000 engineers in the nation, making this profession second only to teaching. That number quintupled over the next thirty years, with the gains most pronounced in electrical and chemical engineering. Almost all engineers were men, and most, like Frederick W. Taylor, came from middle-class, Anglo-Saxon, Protestant families. Engineers in general, and electrical engineers in particular, were the point men of the new economy. They represented the fusion of scientific knowledge with industrial capitalism: most engineers were employed by large corporations, and it was their task to translate the principles of scientific knowledge into practical and profitable applications. As expert problem solvers and symbols of rationality, they were highly esteemed, while their successes stood as testimony to the value of applied science. "Science," wrote Walter Lippmann, "is the culture under which people can live forward in the midst of complexity, and treat life not as something given but as something to be shaped."

## Progressive Reform

"Reform" was the watchword of political life. Politicians of both major parties (and many smaller parties) called themselves reformers; and for some citizens reform became a vocation, even a profession. The impulse to reform, or to innovate in public policy, had multiple sources. These included an upper- and middle-class sense of responsibility for the welfare of society; religious beliefs that linked personal virtue to humanitarian action; the desire of some businessmen to make the economic environment more predictable; and pressure from labor and working-class groups eager to better their own lot. Reformers operated both within and outside the political arena, although all believed that the role of city and state governments, as well as Washington, ought to be expanded. At the heart of Progressivism was the conviction that public authorities should help solve the problems of an industrial society.

The desire for reform, however, did not yield a single Progressive "movement" or agenda. Some reformers focused on social issues, such as poverty, the assimilation of immigrants, public education, and child welfare. Others were more interested in what might be called the "political economy" of the era: they attempted to check the power of large corporations, revamp the banking system, and provide compensation for workers injured on the job. Still others devoted their energies to political reform, striving to eliminate corruption and make government officials more answerable to the public. In the West, in particular, reformers were deeply concerned about the natural environment, and throughout the nation reform campaigns sought to ban the sale of alcohol. The goals of Progressive reform were diverse, and they were backed by a varied and fluid set of political actors and coalitions.

What these reform efforts had in common was the conviction that, in Lippmann's words, life was "something to be shaped": American society could be improved through in-

### Table 22.2

#### TELEPHONE OWNERSHIP AND CALLS, 1900–20

|      | Number of Telephones[a] | Number per 1,000 Population | Average Daily Local Calls[a] | Average Daily Toll Calls[a] |
|------|-------------------------|------------------------------|------------------------------|------------------------------|
| 1900 | 1,356  | 17.6  | 4,773  | 149   |
| 1905 | 4,127  | 48.8  | 11,404 | 368   |
| 1910 | 7,635  | 82    | 18,256 | 602   |
| 1915 | 10,524 | 103.9 | 25,184 | 819   |
| 1920 | 13,273 | 123.4 | 31,836 | 1,327 |

[a]These figures are in the thousands.

*Source: Historical Statistics of the United States: Colonial Times to 1970, Part 1,* Series R 1–2, p. 783, and Series R 9–12, p. 783.

formed public policies. Progressives had less confidence than their predecessors that laissez-faire economics and Darwinian evolution (see Chapter 19) would inevitably erode the knotty problems of an urban, industrial nation. Progressive reformers believed that human intelligence could devise strategies for ameliorating poverty, limiting the power of big business, and sheltering workers against industrial accidents. "Progress" would come not by allowing natural laws to unfold but by seizing the reins of history. The "promise of American life," wrote Herbert Croly in 1909 in an influential re-

Scene of the destruction in Galveston, Texas, after the hurricane of 1900.

examination of American politics, could no longer be fulfilled "automatically" as it had been in the nineteenth century. It would require "official national action."

Whether the reforms of the era were genuinely "progressive" has been a matter of debate among historians. Some of the policies adopted clearly did help those in the lower reaches of the economic and social hierarchy. Others, however, shored up the power of large corporations, emphasizing efficiency at the expense of democracy, expertise rather than popular consent. This technocratic face of reform was bolstered by the problem-solving models of science and engineering, leading at times to an uneasy coexistence of technological and democratic approaches to complex social issues.

## URBAN PROBLEMS

The impulse to reform appeared first in the cities, surfacing during the economic crisis of the 1890s and persisting until after World War I. Three related issues were of paramount importance to urban reformers. The first was improving the delivery of basic services, such as transportation, water, and electricity. The second was elevating the living conditions of the working class and the poor, many of whom were immigrants. The third was transforming municipal governance to make cities run more efficiently and to reduce the power of political machines. All of these issues were publicized by a new breed of investigative journalists who came to be called "muckrakers." Prominent among them was Lincoln Steffens, whose magazine articles about urban life were collected into a widely read book, *The Shame of the Cities* (1906).

Several types of reformers pursued urban reforms. One group consisted of left-leaning Progressive politicians, such as Mayors Tom Johnson of Cleveland, Samuel "Golden Rule" Jones of Toledo, and Hazen Pingree of Detroit, who tried to eliminate political corruption and enhance the quality of urban life, particularly for working people and the poor. They built public parks, playgrounds, hospitals, and schools and even offered relief to the unemployed during depressions. They also fought against powerful private interests, such as utility and streetcar companies, to keep costs down and services widely distributed. Johnson, who was mayor of Cleveland from 1901 to 1909, led a prolonged fight to lower trolley fares while increasing the tax burden on utilities, railroads, and trolley companies. More than 100 cities ended up establishing municipally owned gas, water, electric, or transit companies.

Public ownership was particularly popular in western cities, including Los Angeles, San Francisco, and Seattle; this was so, in part, because westerners sought to reduce their dependence on private capital from the East. In Los Angeles, where a reliable water supply was essential to the city's growth, a badly managed private water system was replaced by a municipal department of Water and Power led by engineer William Mulholland from 1902 until 1928. Mulholland, with the support of federal officials, took control of the Owens Valley, on the eastern side of the Sierra Nevada, to secure water for the Los Angeles basin. The water flowing from the Owens Valley was then used to generate electricity, with the revenues to the city from the sale of electricity helping to underwrite the cost of the water project.

Other political figures, representing more middle-class and elite interests, focused on reforming the structure of city

635

governments. Convinced that machine politicians, partisan rivalries, and ward-based elections produced corrupt and inefficient regimes, these men sought to revamp city governance through several different mechanisms: replacing boards of aldermen and mayors with a small group of commissioners who combined legislative and executive functions; holding at-large, rather than ward-based, elections for city councils; making elections nonpartisan; and vesting executive authority in the hands of appointed city managers. These proposals were based on corporate models: in Dayton, Ohio, the president of the National Cash Register Company claimed that a city ought to be "a great business enterprise, whose stockholders are the people."

One of the first cities to change its structure was Galveston, Texas. In 1900, the city suffered the greatest natural disaster in American history, a hurricane and tidal wave that killed 8,000 of the city's 38,000 residents and left another 10,000 homeless. When the elected city council, already under fire because of sloppy financial practices, was unable to respond effectively to the emergency, it was dislodged by a coalition of bankers, businessmen, and property owners. The coalition drafted a new city charter, approved by the state legislature, that provided for the governor to appoint a five-man board to run the city. By 1920, hundreds of cities, particularly in the Midwest and the South, had similarly reconfigured their charters to adopt some version of commission or city-manager government. These innovations weakened the political influence of ethnic, working-class wards, although in most large cities political machines proved to be adaptable enough to weather the change in structure. Parallel measures were adopted for school boards, which became more centralized and depoliticized, with executive power vested in appointed professional superintendents. Such reforms were commonly sponsored by local elites, but in some locales they were backed also by labor and working-class groups.

Outside of electoral politics were reformers who worked directly with immigrants and the poor. The most well known were the women and men who lived in settlement houses, such as Jane Addams, the revered and influential founder of Chicago's Hull House in 1889. A college-educated woman from a well-to-do family, Addams and her colleagues spent decades building Hull House into a diverse community center where middle-class women developed a variety of services for working-class immigrant families. These included kindergartens, English lessons, and instruction in domestic skills and disease prevention, as well as employment information and training. Settlement-house residents like Addams learned firsthand about the lives of the poor, often served as unofficial lobbyists on their behalf, and came to believe that the key to social progress was to empower rather than "uplift" less advantaged citizens. Their efforts were complemented by other activists who focused on specific issues, such as improving public health and housing. Reformers also sought to improve public education by making schooling compulsory and creating vocational training programs for working-class children.

### STATE POLITICS

The impulse to innovate spread quickly from the cities to state governments, in part because many key issues could be addressed only by state legislatures and governors. A full-blown reform program appeared first in Wisconsin, owing to the pioneering efforts of Robert La Follette, governor from 1901 to 1909 and one of the first politicians to label himself "progressive." La Follette beefed up the regulation of railroads, imposed a graduated income tax as well as a tax on corporations, improved the civil service, banned direct corporate contributions to political parties, and instituted primary elections to reduce the power of party bosses. The Wisconsin program became a blueprint for other states, particularly after

Jane Addams, reformer and founder of Hull House.

1905, when scandals across the country revealed what many had long suspected: that corrupt relationships between business interests and state government officials were epidemic. In one state after another, Progressive politicians, often from dissident factions of the Republican Party, swept into office, promising to tame corporations and clean up political life.

State Progressives were acutely concerned with regulating vital industries. More than a dozen new railroad commissions were established, and the regulatory powers of others were strengthened to permit closer oversight of freight rates, illegal rebates to shippers, and safety. New state laws promoted mine safety, as well as the purity of food products. In addition, Progressive politicians promoted political reforms, such as recall elections, the use of initiatives and referenda (which permitted voters to decide policy questions through the ballot), and the direct election of U.S. senators. Responding to pressures from state reformers, popular election of senators was made mandatory by the Sixteenth Amendment, ratified in 1913.

Such democratizing efforts, however, were often accompanied by measures designed to reduce the size of the electorate. Elaborate registration systems, for example, winnowed the electorate in many states, while in the Midwest noncitizen aliens lost the right to vote. Although commonly touted as

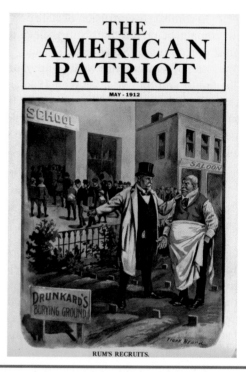

A 1912 editorial cartoon depicting the fear that brewers and saloon keepers were preying on the young.

A cartoon depicting the success of Governor Robert La Follette's reforms in freeing Wisconsin from the grip of the railroad "octopus."

anticorruption efforts, such laws served to limit the political power of urban workers; coupled with new regulations governing electoral procedures, they also reinforced the two-party system, making it more difficult for third parties to challenge the Democrats and Republicans.

Social reforms on the agenda of Progressive state officials ranged from mandatory smallpox vaccinations for children, to improved hospital and mental health facilities, to small "pensions" for mothers with young children. In addition, state governments became enmeshed in the drive to prohibit the sale of alcohol. Prohibition and temperance were largely cultural issues, pressed onto the political agenda by evangelical Protestants, mostly from rural areas, who found the drinking habits of urban-dwelling immigrants alien and immoral. Prohibition advocates maintained that drinking broke up families, lowered productivity, drove men and women into poorhouses and prisons, and corrupted politics. Support was particularly strong among women's groups who regarded alcohol as a source of marital abuse. Progressive politicians were not of one mind about Prohibition, with eastern Progressives joining ranks with their immigrant and Catholic constituencies to combat this intrusion of state power into a new domain of private life. Nonetheless, the prohibitionist forces mustered enough strength to prohibit the sale of alcohol in twenty-one states, many in the South and the West, between 1906 and 1917. Their national triumph came in 1919 with the ratification of the Eighteenth Amendment, which banned the manufacture, sale, and transportation of intoxicating liquors everywhere in the nation.

## Class, Ethnicity, and Race

Underlying many of the issues that came to the fore during the Progressive Era was the harsh reality of class differences. While the nation's elites were thriving and the middle class—the buyers of the Model T—was growing rapidly, most adults remained in the industrial and agricultural working class. The nation's 200,000 engineers were vastly outnumbered by the millions of men who were classified simply as "laborers" and millions more who were semiskilled factory operatives, migrant agricultural workers, or sharecroppers in the fields of the South. These men and women typically toiled for sixty hours or more per week, for low wages, in unhealthy or hazardous settings. Their incomes were gradually rising, but relatively few could support a family by themselves. Most workers, moreover, were immigrants, the children of immigrants, or black. Class boundaries, as was often true in American history, coincided substantially with ethnic and racial divides.

Whether these boundaries would harden or become more porous was one of the most critical questions facing Progressive Era society. Many social critics believed that the growth of industrial capitalism was widening the cleavages between social classes and limiting the ability for the poor to get ahead. Racial and ethnic divisions seemed to compound the problem, increasing the social distance between the haves and the have-nots, adding to the obstacles to mobility or assimilation.

The significance of this issue was apparent to most Americans, but it was not clear what, if anything, could be done about it. Workers, immigrants, and African Americans sought to better their conditions, both as individuals and through collective activities such as the formation of unions, immigrant self-help organizations, and political organizing. They also turned to state governments and to Washington for aid,

Textile strikers in Lawrence, Massachusetts, 1912.

often with the support of Progressive politicians. In the public arena, however, responses to class, ethnic, and racial problems were decidedly mixed. Most business interests opposed state intervention into the "labor question," while social prejudices shaped public responses to African Americans and foreigners. These were matters that did not readily succumb to the problem-solving mentality of engineers.

### UNIONS AND THE STATE

Trade unions flourished during the Progressive Era. Membership in the craft unions linked to the American Federation of Labor (AFL) grew steadily after the turn of the century and dramatically during World War I. The unions succeeded in increasing wages and improving working conditions, and by the end of World War I they had made the eight-hour workday the norm in industry. Yet the protective umbrella of unions covered primarily skilled workers like machinists, carpenters, railway engineers, and plumbers. Most semiskilled factory employees, as well as unskilled day laborers, were left out. This was so partly because less skilled workers were easy to replace and consequently more difficult to organize, and also because the unions of the AFL, buffeted by technological change and chronic unemployment, were determined to protect the jobs of their members, even at the expense of other workers. They negotiated contracts that guaranteed employment only to union members, while at the same time restricting access to unions themselves. The semiskilled and unskilled, including most blacks, immigrants, and women, were left to their own devices.

The vacuum left by the exclusive policies of the AFL was colorfully filled by a more radical organization, the Industrial Workers of the World (nicknamed the Wobblies), or IWW. Founded in 1905 at what was dubbed the "Continental Congress of the Working Class," the IWW sought to organize all workers—and especially the less skilled—in the hope of destroying capitalism and putting in its place a system of industry run and owned by workers. "The working class and the employing class have nothing in common," declared the provocative preamble to the IWW's founding document. Led by "Big" Bill Haywood, the charismatic former head of the western miners' union, the IWW first won support in the West, where state governments unabashedly protected property owners against the demands of miners, lumbermen, and agricultural workers. Between 1908 and 1912, the IWW led free-speech protests in western cities against ordinances that banned street meetings: in Spokane, Frank Little, a Wobbly organizer, was sentenced to thirty days in jail for reading the Declaration of Independence from a public platform. Within a few years, the IWW's militant determination to organize the unskilled also led thousands of immigrant factory workers in the East to join its ranks. In the textile capital of Lawrence, Massachusetts, in 1912, the IWW led a strike that gripped the attention of the nation: more than 10,000 immigrants from a dozen nations, both male and female, had joined together to protest a pay cut. It was "the first strike I ever saw which sang," noted one journalist.

While the IWW believed that capitalism would be overthrown through the "direct action" of workers who would lay down their tools and refuse to participate in private enterprise, other radicals adopted a different strategy: electing Socialists to public office. The Socialist Party, led by Eugene V. Debs, was a respected alternative party in cities and towns throughout the North and West. Socialists believed that the exploitation of workers would not end as long as industry was privately controlled and driven by the profit motive. They were also committed to using the machinery of electoral democracy to peaceably transform the nation's economy. This strategy had its successes. More than 300 cities and towns had Socialist officials in 1911; Milwaukee and Schenectady, New York, among others, had Socialist mayors. Victor Berger was elected to Congress from Wisconsin, the Socialist Party con-

trolled 25 percent of the vote in southern Oklahoma, and Eugene Debs himself polled 900,000 votes for president (6 percent of the total) in 1912. Although the Socialist Party never came close to wielding national power, its share of the vote was similar to that achieved in some European countries that in later decades developed strong socialist traditions.

Pressure from socialists, as well as progressive Republicans and Democrats, put working-class issues on the agenda of state governments. There they encountered resistance from conservatives who believed that public authorities should not intervene in the labor markets or in relations between employers and employees. In 1908, for example, a Massachusetts proposal to create a system of insurance payments for the unemployed was denounced by the governor as "not only a constitutional impossibility, but a logical absurdity." And Massachusetts was one of the most progressive states in the nation.

One of the few areas of legislative success involved workplace accidents, which killed and maimed hundreds of thousands of workers each year. Under existing law, a worker who was injured on the job (or his heirs) could receive compensation only by suing the company and proving that it was negligent—a difficult, expensive task that few accident victims could accomplish. In response to workers' complaints (as well as employers' fears of unpredictable jury awards), numerous states passed workmen's compensation laws that guaranteed accident victims modest payments, while limiting their right to sue. Although initially few workers were covered by the compensation laws, they nonetheless constituted a pioneering step in state supervision of workplace relationships. The same was true of factory and mine safety legislation passed during the period.

Progressives also had some success regulating child labor. In 1900, one out of every six children between the ages of ten and fifteen worked full time, and the figure was much higher in some southern states. Reformers regarded such figures as a scandalous indication that children were being exploited rather than educated. State legislatures (mostly in the North) consequently passed laws restricting the employment of children, but enforcement was lax, and state courts sometimes gutted the laws—although, over time, they became more sympathetic to state intervention on behalf of those too young to protect themselves. In 1916, partially in response to northern concerns that child labor in the South was depressing wage rates everywhere, Congress passed the Keating-Owen Child Labor Act, which prohibited the interstate shipment of goods manufactured or mined by children who

Group portrait of "breaker boys," young miners who sorted coal and picked slate; photo by Lewis Hine, 1910.

worked under dangerous conditions or for excessively long hours. The Supreme Court, however, declared the law unconstitutional in *Hammer v. Dagenhart* (1918), on the grounds that the federal government's power to regulate interstate commerce did not extend to the production of goods.

The Supreme Court also killed state efforts to regulate the hours of employment for male workers. Although state courts were growing more tolerant of laws mandating a maximum number of hours in the workday, the Supreme Court in 1905 invalidated a New York law that would have limited bakers to an eight-hour day and a forty-eight-hour week (*Lochner v. New York*). The justices concluded that the law interfered with the freedom of contract of bakers, which the states had no "compelling" interest in doing: baking, they observed, was not a "specially hurtful and unhealthy labor."

## IMMIGRATION RECONSIDERED

Outside the South, the "labor problem" was also an immigration problem. Between 1900 and World War I, the flows of immigration were larger than they ever had been: during the peak year of 1907 alone, more than 1.2 million immigrants arrived in the United States. Although this extraordinary migration spurred economic growth, it heightened competition for jobs and put downward pressure on wages. Most immigrants in this period came from eastern and southern Europe, and many viewed themselves as temporary migrants rather than perma-

nent settlers; their goal was to earn enough money in the New World to buy land or start a business in their own country. Although that goal sometimes shifted, more than a third of all migrants from parts of Europe and Asia eventually left the United States. Jewish immigrants, who had little desire to return to the oppression they faced in eastern Europe, were the most prominent exceptions, as the Irish had been in the nineteenth century.

The great majority of Progressive Era immigrants settled in cities; in so doing, they transformed the urban landscape. Ethnic neighborhoods of Italians, Slovaks, Poles, Jews, Greeks, Germans, the Irish, and Asians turned urban America into a checkerboard of cultural, religious, and linguistic diversity; workplaces often had a similar cast. The immigrant presence was felt also in politics, although many foreign-born residents did not vote either because they lacked citizenship or because they could not meet state suffrage requirements, such as literacy tests.

The ambivalence about immigration that native-born Americans had displayed for much of the nineteenth century intensified during the Progressive Era, in part because the "new" immigrants were more numerous and appeared more alien (see Chapter 19). While manufacturers continued to value immigrants as labor, a growing number of Americans feared that their cities were being "taken over" by foreigners. One response to this apprehension, favored by many reformers, was to "Americanize" immigrants: to teach them to speak

Young girl spinner in a Carolina cotton mill; by Lewis Hine, 1909.

Cartoon opposed to unrestricted immigration, 1890.

English, to send their children to school, and to have them adopt the mores of the host culture. A blend of humanitarian concern and condescension, these efforts were grounded in the hope of transforming southern and eastern Europeans into acceptable American citizens.

The period also witnessed growing efforts to discourage or restrict immigration. Acts of violence, particularly against Italians and Jews, were not uncommon; nor was social discrimination that kept new immigrants out of particular neighborhoods, schools, or occupations. The Immigration Restriction League, founded by elite New Englanders in 1894, lobbied Congress, with some success, to make it more difficult for immigrants to be naturalized and easier for them to be deported. Laws requiring prospective immigrants to be literate were passed by Congress in 1896, 1913, and 1915, but they succumbed to presidential vetoes.

The hostility to new immigrants was fed by scientific, or pseudoscientific, theories. Eugenicists, such as biologist Charles Davenport, believed that not only physical traits but some personality characteristics—such as "shiftlessness" or a predisposition to crime—were determined by genetics. People with these traits posed a threat to the hardy, virtuous

Nordic race that had made the United States great. The most popular statement of these views came in Madison Grant's widely read *The Passing of the Great Race* (1916), which maintained that Americans were committing "race suicide" by allowing millions of inferior men and women to immigrate, procreate, and intermingle with native-born Americans.

Such ideas, together with the stresses that immigration placed on urban living conditions, politics, and the labor market, led to growing support for restriction. In 1906, the American Federation of Labor, after a decade of ambivalence, called for restriction, and many business groups soon did likewise. The issue was then shelved during World War I, when immigration from Europe slowed to a trickle.

### RACE AND THE NATION

In the South, race remained the critical line of social cleavage. The region received few immigrants, but blacks accounted for a third or more of the population in eight states. African Americans, moreover, were not only a separate race but a working class critical to the region's agricultural and service sectors. Much of the white South was both dependent on black labor and committed to minimizing social interactions between blacks and whites.

The impulse to reform had little impact on race relations in the South. The region did have a Progressive movement, rooted in the rapid growth of numerous small cities (and thus of a middle class that was not directly dependent on black agricultural labor). Southern Progressives wanted to modernize their states, improve public education, rein in the power of railroads, and abolish the practice of leasing convicts to private employers. Governor Charles Aycock of North Carolina, for example, became known as the "educational governor," while his state's leading newspaper, the Raleigh *News and Observer,* campaigned tirelessly for railroad regulation. Southern Progressives also sought to promote political competition.

Yet political competition—and the Progressive moment itself—existed within the confines of single-party rule and increasingly rigid racial segregation. Jim Crow laws proliferated, particularly in the cities: by 1915, segregation (a term that became current only after 1900) was the norm not only in public conveyances and institutions but also in workplaces and residential neighborhoods. Despite the emergence of a small black middle class, consisting largely of shopkeepers, undertakers, and others who provided services to the black community, most African Americans remained trapped in rural isolation and poverty. Electricity, automobiles, and the telephone were not part of the southern black experience.

The oppression of African Americans was reinforced by a legal system that tolerated lynching while excluding blacks from juries and imprisoning them for petty offenses. (Many were then compelled to work as "convict laborers.") With the North turning a blind eye, southern states also completed the process of disfranchisement. The most efficient mechanism for doing so was the "white primary": one state after another ruled that only whites could participate in Democratic Party primary elections. Since there were no other viable parties in the South, victory in a Democratic primary was tantamount to election.

While some African Americans continued to struggle for equal rights, most were pessimistic about the possibility of reforming the institutionalized racism of the new South. An ever-growing number voted with their feet, migrating to the cities of the North. Between the 1890s and World War I, when the rate of migration accelerated dramatically, thousands of southern blacks traveled by boat to Philadelphia and New York or by rail to Chicago or western cities. Some were businessmen, intellectuals, and educated professionals like W. E. B. Du Bois and other founders of the northern-based NAACP (see Chapter 19). But most were uneducated and had few skills; nearly all were young, the children and grandchildren of former slaves.

In the North, they found "no crystal stair," as writer Langston Hughes put it. With manufacturing and white-collar jobs restricted to whites, black migrants generally worked as janitors, day laborers, barbers, and domestic servants. They were also obliged to live in predominantly black neighborhoods, a practice reinforced in some places by laws mandating racial segregation. In the largest cities of the North, including Chicago, New York, and Philadelphia, the swelling of the black population, coupled with the refusal of landlords to rent to blacks in most neighborhoods, led to the formation of black ghettoes. By 1920, for example, two-thirds of New York's rapidly growing black population (70,000 people) had migrated to Harlem. Located just north of New York's Central Park, Harlem had been a popular white, middle-class residential district until racial discrimination, real estate speculation, and the subdivision of large apartments transformed it into the overcrowded

Convict workers deployed to perform road work in Pitt County, North Carolina, autumn 1910. The inmates were quartered in wagons equipped with bunks and moved from place to place. The central figure in the picture is J.Z. McLawhon, county superintendent of chain gangs.

capital of black New York and the national capital of black culture. In many areas newly settled by blacks, outbreaks of racial violence, including lynching, reared their ugly head; in Abraham Lincoln's hometown of Springfield, Illinois, a race riot in 1908 drove 6,000 African Americans from their homes.

## Women and Reform

### JOBS AND RIGHTS

At the beginning of the twentieth century, Theodore Roosevelt declared that "the greatest thing for any woman is to be a good wife and mother." Most of his fellow citizens seemed to agree. Although women were having fewer children and were increasingly likely to enter the paid labor force, the ideal of domesticity remained pervasive. Ninety percent of American women did marry, and nearly all stopped working outside the home when they had children.

The lives of women were shaped also by their class, race, and ethnicity. Working-class women, whose fathers and husbands held low-paying, unsteady jobs, were more likely than their middle-class counterparts to work outside the home. Irish and black women commonly worked as domestic ser-

vants, while Italian women labored in seasonal manufacturing industries; more educated native-born women took jobs in the mushrooming clerical sector, where the primary tool of their trade became the typewriter, invented in 1868 and widely adopted by the early twentieth century. (Clerical work replaced domestic service during this period as the largest occupation for women.) The daily lives of farm women, white and black, were little different from what they had been in the late nineteenth century, although for some the burdens of rural isolation were lightened by advances in communication and transportation as well as by the increase in farm incomes.

The growth of the urban middle class led to a rise in educational opportunities for women: by 1920, 60 percent of white women were graduating from high school, and nearly 10 percent were enrolled in college. Most educated women, as long as they remained single, took jobs in traditional, sex-typed, white-collar occupations such as nursing, teaching, and library and secretarial work, all of which were rapidly growing. But a handful broke into male professions, including medicine, college teaching, and engineering, while others forged independent paths as intellectuals and social activists. One sign of the social strains on these pioneering women was that the marriage rate among college graduates was barely above 50 percent.

Women became more visible in public life than ever before. Barred from electoral politics in most states, women became particularly prominent as social reformers, focusing attention on the problems of poverty, alcoholism, child labor, prostitution, public health, and birth control. Women's clubs advocated protective legislation for women and children, reforms of the juvenile justice system, new housing codes, and separate facilities for women prisoners. The well-known founders of settlement houses, such as Jane Addams, were part of a broader movement of women who engaged in hands-on social reform while injecting social issues into political life. Ida B. Wells-Barnett, who had called international attention to the lynching of African Americans in the South in the 1890s, remained a highly audible voice against racial discrimination in Chicago, as well as the South. Late in the Progressive Era, Margaret Sanger pioneered efforts to make birth-control information available, in part to rescue working-class women from the burdens of having large numbers of children.

S. Josephine Baker was emblematic of these pioneers. Born to a wealthy Quaker family in 1873, Baker—whose mother had been in the first graduating class at Vassar—became a physician, graduating from the New York Infirmary for Women and Children in 1898. She began a private medical practice in New York but quickly discovered that distrust of women was so strong that she could not earn a living as a private physician. Accepting a position as an inspector with the New York City Health Department, Baker was appalled by the living conditions and ill health of the city's impoverished immigrants. Anguished by high rates of infant mortality, particularly in the heat of summer, Baker in 1908 sought out the family of every newborn in her district and offered help and instruction in the care of infants—which yielded a dramatic lowering of the infant mortality rate. This stunning success led to her appointment to the newly created post of chief of child hygiene in New York; in that role, she developed path-breaking programs in health education while providing vaccinations and uncontaminated milk to children throughout the city. In 1916, she began to lecture on child hygiene at the New York University Medical School; the following year, she received a doctoral degree in public health.

A suffragist and the author of five books, Baker was a self-conscious pioneer, never marrying and always aware that she was breeching the walls of all-male bastions. "I was young and active during the years when women began to be emancipated," she wrote years later in her autobiography. "Women were then making an effort to get out of the shadow-land

A Remington Typewriter Company employment office filled with female typists in the early 1900s.

S. Josephine Baker.

Gilman's vision of an egalitarian society was not achieved, but the women reformers of the era did win their share of victories. They were instrumental in securing passage of the Pure Food and Drug Act (1906), the Mann Act (prohibiting the transportation of prostitutes across state lines, 1910), and the Eighteenth Amendment (prohibiting the sale of alcohol, 1919), as well as the creation of a federal Children's Bureau (1912) that was instructed to "investigate and report . . . on all matters pertaining to the welfare of children and child life among all classes of our people." Women reformers also succeeded in persuading nineteen states to award "pensions" to needy divorced or widowed women with children. Although these "mothers' pensions" were rarely enough to support a household, they were an important step in the state's assumption of responsibility for meeting the needs of the poor.

The rationale for "mothers' pensions" was not a feminist one; it was, rather, that women, being more vulnerable and less self-sufficient than men, were entitled to greater protection from the state. A similar rationale was offered by the Supreme Court in the landmark case of *Muller v. Oregon* (1908), which upheld the constitutionality of an Oregon law that restricted the working hours for women; notably, the Court just three years earlier had struck down a similar New York law that applied to men. In explaining its unanimous decision in *Muller*, the Court maintained that it was legitimate for the state to intervene in the labor market to protect women because they were weaker than men and because their health and well-being would affect the vitality of their children. The Court's decision was based in part on a legal brief submitted by attorney Louis Brandeis (but largely written by his sister-in-law, Josephine Goldmark) that offered a detailed description of the lives of women workers.

## WINNING THE RIGHT TO VOTE

At the start of the twentieth century, the movement for women's suffrage was in the midst of a dispiriting period that came to be called "the doldrums." After winning the franchise in several western states in the 1880s and 1890s, the movement had lost momentum. Although women in numerous states were granted the right to vote in school board and other municipal elections, no states fully enfranchised women between 1896 and 1910.

Yet leaders of the suffrage cause showed no signs of giving up the campaign for political rights, and the movement was energized by steady infusions of educated middle-class women.

where they had dwelt for so long." Doing so had demanded personal accommodations. "If I was to be the only woman executive in the . . . department of health, I badly needed protective coloring. . . . My man-tailored suits and shirtwaists, and stiff collars and four-in-hand ties were a trifle expensive, but they more than paid their way as buffers . . . the last thing I wanted was to be conspicuously feminine when working with men."

The experiences of such women helped to generate a new wave of explicitly feminist thought. Indeed, the word "feminist" was coined in the 1910s to refer to someone favoring the full political, civil, and social equality of women. The foremost feminist thinker and writer of the era was Charlotte Perkins Gilman, author of *Women and Economics* (1898) and a member (as was Josephine Baker) of the first feminist organization, Heterodoxy, founded in 1912. Gilman argued that men and women were fundamentally similar, that apparent differences between them derived from disparate experiences and socialization. She believed that the core of gender inequality resided in the economic dependence of women on men, which over centuries had stunted the capacities of women by limiting their opportunities and confining them to the home. "Only as we live, think, feel and work outside the home," Gilman claimed, "do we become humanly developed, civilized, and socialized." She advocated child care and communal housekeeping to permit married women with children to work outside the home and realize themselves more fully.

Under the leadership of Carrie Chapman Catt and Harriet Stanton Blatch (the daughter of Elizabeth Cady Stanton), the National American Woman Suffrage Association (NAWSA) reorganized, raised funds, lobbied politicians, and launched door-to-door publicity drives. In 1906, the movement abandoned the position that the franchise should be limited to the educated (which had an anti-immigrant and anti-working-class tinge) and linked suffrage to broader issues of social reform. NAWSA sought the support of working-class women and tied the economic exploitation of women to their lack of political power. "Behind suffrage," labor organizer Leonora O'Reilly declared, "is the demand for equal pay for equal work."

A women's suffrage parade in New York, 1912.

NAWSA's organizational efforts were rewarded by victories in Washington, California, Arizona, Kansas, and Oregon between 1910 and 1912. Yet opposition remained strong, and suffrage referenda were defeated in midwestern and northeastern states between 1912 and 1914. Among the opponents were political machines, elite opponents of any further democratization, liquor interests, and some immigrant groups, particularly the Germans and Irish, who viewed the suffrage movement as protemperance. The movement was weakest in the South, where traditional gender views were reinforced by white fears of franchise expansion. Black women in the South formed their own suffrage organizations, arguing that they, perhaps more than anyone, needed political power; NAWSA, fearing a negative reaction, lent them little support.

In 1915, after a multi-year debate, NAWSA joined other organizations in a significant shift of strategy: instead of seeking changes in state laws, they would pursue an amendment to the federal Constitution. The text of the proposed Nineteenth Amendment was modeled on the Fifteenth:

*Section 1. The rights of citizens of the United States to vote shall not be denied or abridged by the United States or any State on account of sex.*

*Section 2. Congress shall have power, by appropriate legislation, to enforce the provisions of this article.*

The reasons for the shift were pragmatic. State campaigns were not only costly but nearly unwinnable in the South and in several northern states with particularly byzantine procedures for amending their constitutions. A federal amendment, in contrast, would demand only congressional approval by a two-thirds vote, followed by majority votes in the legislatures of three-quarters of the states. The major objection to a federal strategy came from advocates of states' rights, particularly in the South, but these objections were overridden, and Catt, the president of NAWSA, devised a "Winning Plan" to build support in the thirty-six states considered most likely to ratify a constitutional amendment.

What followed were several years of intensive grassroots organizing and protests (including daily pickets in front of the White House), coupled with a careful strategy of making women's suffrage an issue in state elections. Women could already vote in some states and could vote in some elections in many (see map); they could thus threaten to reward their allies and punish their opponents at the polls. By 1917, seven states had passed laws allowing women to vote in presidential elections; that same year, full suffrage was approved in New York, owing in part to an endorsement from the Tammany Hall organization.

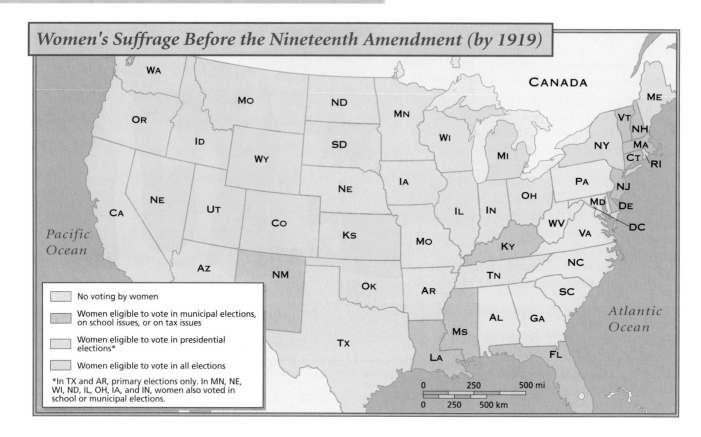

**Women's Suffrage Before the Nineteenth Amendment (by 1919)**

Legend:
- No voting by women
- Women eligible to vote in municipal elections, on school issues, or on tax issues
- Women eligible to vote in presidential elections*
- Women eligible to vote in all elections

*In TX and AR, primary elections only. In MN, NE, WI, ND, IL, OH, IA, and IN, women also voted in school or municipal elections.

The decisive turn came during World War I. To counter the traditional argument that women should not vote because they did not bear arms, suffrage groups mobilized in support of the war, selling bonds, knitting clothes, holding Americanization classes, and distributing gifts to soldiers and sailors. Such activities, coupled with unrelenting political pressure, finally led President Woodrow Wilson in January 1918 to announce his support of the Nineteenth Amendment. Wilson, who in 1916 had opposed the amendment because he, like most Democrats, regarded it as a state rather than federal matter, delivered an address to Congress in which he urged passage of the amendment "as a war measure." The House of Representatives voted in favor of the amendment the next day. The Senate, where antisuffrage southern Democrats constituted a larger bloc, took an additional year and a half to come aboard.

On August 18, 1920, after NAWSA had carefully executed its Winning Plan, Tennessee became the thirty-sixth state to ratify the Nineteenth Amendment. One of the longest political crusades in American history had come to an end, nearly doubling the size of the electorate.

## National Politics

The presidential election of 1900 was a rerun of the election of 1896. President McKinley was renominated by the Republicans, while the Democrats again selected William Jennings Bryan. Bryan put his oratorical talent and evangelical style on display across the nation. McKinley meanwhile remained in the White House, receiving carefully selected audiences. Bryan sought to place foreign affairs at the center of the contest, criticizing American imperialism and urging the withdrawal of American forces from the Philippines. Yet whatever misgivings Americans may have had about the Spanish-American War, the campaign was dominated by domestic concerns. The central issues once again were the currency and the tariff. Democrats continued to demand the coinage of silver to inflate the currency, a still-popular cause among debt-ridden farmers in the South and West. They also pressed hard for lower tariffs, which would benefit consumers; denounced the influence of big business; called for tougher antitrust regulation; and advocated inheritance and federal income taxes. In response, the Republicans presented themselves as defenders of the nation's business interests in an era of renewed prosperity: they insisted on the legitimacy of the gold standard (which would protect creditors and property owners) and promoted high tariffs to protect industry and the jobs of workers.

The Republicans had the winning formula: improving on their victory of 1896, they were victorious in all states in the Northeast and Midwest, as well as five western states that had supported Bryan four years earlier. The Democrats tightened their grip on the South, thanks in part to the disfranchisement of blacks, and they picked up some support from urban ethnic workers in the North. But the Republicans, aided by campaign coffers five to ten times larger than those of the Democrats, solidified their position as the nationally dominant party, a position they would retain until the 1930s. The regional dominance of each party also contributed to a decline in electoral turnout, a phenomenon that would continue through much of the twentieth century.

The 1900 election ushered a new political figure onto the national stage: the Republicans' vice-presidential candidate, Theodore Roosevelt. A flamboyant hero of the Spanish-American War, Roosevelt was the governor of New York and already a controversial figure. Immensely energetic and ambitious, Roosevelt drew large crowds wherever he campaigned, while creating some unease among party regulars: his nomination to the vice-presidency came about in part because New York's Republican leaders wanted to rid themselves of an unpredictable governor.

## THE ROOSEVELT ERA

Less than six months after President McKinley's second inauguration, he was assassinated in Buffalo, New York, by anarchist Leon Czolgosz. At age forty-two, Theodore Roosevelt became the youngest man ever to occupy the White House. He was also the first president whose personality dominated national public life and whose family received constant attention in the national press. An eastern aristocrat by birth and a western outdoorsman by temperament, Roosevelt was a restless man of action as well as an intellectual who had written ten books, including five serious works of history. Well read in literature, economics, and the natural sciences, he moved easily in the world of ideas and saw himself as the steward of the nation's destiny.

Roosevelt identified himself as an activist conservative who believed that the state had a positive role to play in a society stressed by rapid economic change. He had relatively little sympathy for the working class, fearing its potential inclination toward social revolution. Yet he had equally little patience for corporate greed and worried that the bourgeois life was undercutting the masculine virtues that had made the nation strong. A moralist at heart, he declared the presidency to be a "bully pulpit" from which he could exhort his fellow citizens to act virtuously. Roosevelt was also committed to strengthening the army and navy and to firming up the status of the United States as a great power (see Chapter 21).

During his first term in office, Roosevelt, lacking any personal mandate, acted cautiously and strove to fulfill promises made by his assassinated predecessor. Even his most celebrated action, which earned him the reputation of a "trust buster," had been set in motion by McKinley: this was the Justice Department's antitrust prosecution of the Northern Securities Company. The innocuous-sounding Northern Securities, put together by financier J. P. Morgan with railroad barons James J. Hill and E. H. Harriman, was a holding company (it held the stock of companies that actually operated enterprises) that controlled virtually all long-distance rail traffic between Chicago and the West Coast. Since the company was involved in interstate commerce, the Sherman Anti-Trust Act seemed applicable, although lawyers for Northern Securities argued that the act covered only carriers themselves rather than holding companies. The Supreme Court agreed with the government and ruled in 1904, in *Northern Securities Company v. U.S.,* that Northern Securities was in violation of the Sherman Act.

That same year, Roosevelt supported passage of the Elkins Act, which prohibited railroads from giving rebates to large shippers. He also promoted the creation of a new Department of Commerce that would include a Bureau of Corporations empowered to investigate the activities of companies engaged in interstate commerce. (Public support for such measures was heightened by the writing of another "muckraker," Ida Tarbell, who published in 1904 a damning *History of the Standard Oil Company.*) Both actions strengthened Roosevelt's trust-busting public image, not altogether deservedly. The Bureau of Corporations had relatively little power, and the Elkins Act was supported by the railroads themselves, which were happy to be rid of the pressure to kick back funds to their largest customers.

Roosevelt also seized the spotlight in 1902 when he successfully mediated a strike of anthracite coal miners. The

President Theodore Roosevelt speaks to a crowd in Willimantic, Connecticut in 1902.

president was shrewd in his choice of an occasion to display sympathy for workers: coal miners were known to work long days for low pay in extremely hazardous conditions, and their union was flexible in its demands. The mine owners, on the other hand, were stubborn and unpopular, none more so than George F. Baer, who had publicly observed that "God in His Infinite Wisdom has given control of the property interests of the country" to himself and his colleagues. Roosevelt's intervention—which resulted in better wages and working conditions but not recognition of the miners' union—suggested that the federal government, at long last, might be shading toward an even-handed, rather than promanagement, stance on labor disputes.

Only in one area did Roosevelt break any new ground in his first term: conservation. An outdoorsman and amateur naturalist himself, Roosevelt was repelled by the misuse of wilderness areas, particularly in the West. In 1902, despite opposition from within his own party, he fought hard for the Newlands Reclamation Act, which favored agricultural development while setting aside funds from the sale of public lands to promote irrigation and reclamation projects. Responding both to western environmentalists and to a broader national romance with the monumental scenery of the West, Roosevelt's government set aside large expanses of public land, including the Grand Canyon, as national parks or monuments. In addition, the president encouraged the activities of his friend Gifford Pinchot, who headed the nation's small Forest Bureau. With Roosevelt's support, Pinchot won congressional approval to transfer control of the nation's forest reserves to his bureau and to expand it into a new agency, the U.S. Forest Service. Pinchot also created the Forest Rangers to manage and protect the nation's undeveloped forests.

Roosevelt's initiatives were designed in part to help him gain control of the Republican Party, which included both traditional probusiness conservatives and Progressive insurgents like La Follette of Wisconsin and Congressman George W. Norris of Nebraska. In this endeavor, he was eminently successful, brushing aside concerns about his personality and thirst for power to gain, by acclamation, the Republican presidential nomination in 1904. In the campaign, Roosevelt proclaimed that he stood for a "Square Deal" for the American people, but he said little on specific issues. He was opposed by an almost equally conservative Democrat, Alton B. Parker of New York, who repudiated the silver issue and represented the northeastern, probusiness wing of the Democratic Party. The most hotly debated issue of the campaign was the tariff.

Roosevelt was elected in a landslide, winning thirty-two states and 57 percent of the popular vote. Parker won no state outside the South. The Democrats' shift to the right did not yield any gains in the business community, but it cost them support on their left flank: with Eugene V. Debs as its standard-bearer, the Socialist Party garnered 3 percent of the national vote (400,000 votes), while the Populists revived to win 100,000 votes in the South and West. Half a million fewer people voted in 1904 than in 1900.

Roosevelt's second term was more contentious and less productive. The economic and political power of big business became the center of policy debate in Washington, in part because key reformers such as Wisconsin's La Follette took seats in the Senate. The reformers, many of them Republicans from the Midwest, raised their voices against the trusts, demanded regulation, particularly of the railroads, and even began to question the virtues of high tariffs, which seemed to be protecting monopolies.

Roosevelt was of two minds on the monopoly question: he thought that big business was inevitable, even desirable, but that the power wielded by large corporations had to be restrained. As Mr. Dooley, the fictional bartender created by humorist Finley Peter Dunne, commented, "Th' trusts are heejoous monsthers built up be th'inlightened intherprise iv th' men that have done so much to advance progress in our beloved counthry. On wan hand I wud stamp thim underher fut; on th' other hand not so fast." Roosevelt accordingly opposed any broad, new antitrust measures while permitting his Justice Department to prosecute some of the worst abusers of corporate power under the Sherman Act.

The president, moreover, preferred administrative to legislative regulation, which led him to support the Hepburn Act, passed by Congress in 1906. This bill required rail corporations to adopt uniform bookkeeping practices and authorized the Interstate Commerce Commission to set maximum freight rates after investigating complaints from shippers. Although reformers such as La Follette regarded the bill as a watered-down measure that fell short of the rate regulation they sought, the Hepburn Act was one of the most significant bills of Roosevelt's presidency.

A similar achievement was the simultaneous passage of the Pure Food and Drug Act and the Meat Inspection Act in 1906. Reformers had repeatedly expressed concern about the purity of the nation's food supply and the misrepresentation of alleged "medicines," but efforts at regulation had been thwarted by conservatives and industry lobbyists. By 1906, however, several European countries, citing safety concerns, were threatening to stop importing American food and agricultural products. Roosevelt then intervened by mobilizing public opinion to overwhelm the conservative opposition. He received help from an unusual source—a novel, *The Jungle*, by Upton Sinclair, published in 1906. Sinclair's story, a moving portrait of the exploitation of Chicago's immigrant workers, included vivid descriptions of the horrific sanitary conditions in that city's meatpacking industry. The novel sparked "muckraking" magazine articles as well as a government investigation. The resulting Pure Food and Drug Act created the Food and Drug Administration (FDA), which was empowered to test and certify drugs before they went on sale; the Meat Inspection Act

## How Do You Make A Living?

*American Journal*

*The excerpt below is from one of the most widely known novels of the early twentieth century, Upton Sinclair's "The Jungle," first published in 1905. Jurgis Rudkus, the lead male character in the novel, was a Lithuanian immigrant living in Chicago, a man who had always tried to deal with adversity by working more and working harder. The passage expresses his reaction to what it was actually like to work on the floor of the stockyards in Chicago. Like most immigrants in the industrial centers of the United States, work was at the center of his life, and he spent sixty hours a week at the workplace.*

"This is the first time in his life that he had ever really worked, it seemed to Jurgis; it was the first time that he had ever had anything to do which took all he had in him. Jurgis had stood with the rest up in the gallery and watched the men on the killing beds, marveling at their speed and power as if they had been wonderful machines; it somehow never occurred to one to think of the flesh-and-blood side of it—that is, not until he actually got down into the pit and took off his coat. Then he saw things in a different light, he got at the inside of them. The pace they set here, it was one that called for every faculty of a man—from the instant the first steer fell till the sounding of the noon whistle, and again from half-past twelve till heaven only knew what hour in the late afternoon or evening, there was never one instant's rest for a man, for his hand or his eye or his brain. Jurgis saw how they managed it; there were portions of the work which determined the pace of the rest and for these they had picked men whom they paid high wages, and whom they changed frequently. You might easily pick out these pacemakers, for they worked under the eye of the bosses, and they worked like men possessed. This was called 'speeding up the gang,' and if any man could not keep up with the pace, there were hundreds outside begging to try."

authorized the Department of Agriculture to inspect and label meat. Ignored by Congress were the workers in the stockyards who were Sinclair's primary concern. "I aimed at the public's heart, and by accident I hit it in the stomach," the author reflected.

Despite this legislative achievement, 1907 marked the onset of political gridlock in Washington. Republican reformers, with some Democratic backing and often with the support of the president, pressed for laws that would further regulate business, restrict child labor, protect injured workers, lower the tariff, and tax the wealthy; all these measures were beaten back by the conservative Republicans who dominated Congress. The conservatives also clipped the wings of the increasingly controversial Gifford Pinchot and his Forest Service, although Roosevelt did manage to protect more than 15 million acres of western land from further development. To the president's chagrin, moreover, the Supreme Court continued to protect business interests threatened by regulatory reform. In his final address to Congress, Roosevelt observed that the justices, by interpreting laws, inescapably "enact into law parts of a system of social philosophy," and he criticized those justices who continued to adhere to "an outgrown philosophy which was itself the product of primitive economic conditions."

### THE SUCCESSOR: WILLIAM H. TAFT

When elected in 1904, Roosevelt had pledged not to run again in 1908; he had already served one almost-full term and respected the "wise custom" that limited presidents to eight years in office. The still-young and energetic president may have regretted that pledge, but in 1908 he prepared to leave the White House, announcing that he planned a lengthy safari to Africa. "Health to the lions," toasted his congressional adversaries.

Roosevelt retained enough clout to handpick his successor as the Republican candidate: his good friend and secretary of war, William Howard Taft. A distinguished lawyer from Ohio, Taft had served both as solicitor general of the United States and as administrator of the Philippines. A centrist within the Republican Party, Taft had strong antilabor credentials but was known to be leery of big business. Although supported by progressive Republicans, he ran on a platform written largely by the party's probusiness, conservative wing.

His Democratic opponent was the durable William Jennings Bryan, whose reform-minded supporters had regained control of the Democratic Party after the election debacle of 1904. Bryan again crisscrossed the country by train, giving eloquent speeches, attacking the Republicans as the handmaidens of large corporations, and promoting his campaign slogan, "Shall the People Rule?" The platform he ran on demanded lower tariffs, tougher regulation of business, an eight-hour day for government workers, and limitations on the use of injunctions against organized labor. The lines between the parties were drawn with such clarity that the American Federation of Labor abandoned its traditional nonpartisanship and endorsed Bryan's candidacy.

Yet the balance of power in national politics remained unchanged: the Democrats did better than they had in 1904, but Taft was victorious throughout the Northeast and Midwest and gained a few western states as well. Bryan won only seventeen states, most of them in the South; his defeat consigned him to the distinguished ranks of dominant political figures who never reached the White House. The election revealed clear ideological schisms within the electorate; taken together, Bryan (running on a very progressive platform) and Socialist Eugene Debs garnered 46 percent of the vote. But the Republicans remained the majority party.

Taft took office just as the crosscurrents of politics began to swirl with great force. A sharp, if brief, economic panic in 1907–8 infused reformers with a heightened sense of urgency, strengthening popular movements for women's suffrage, prohibition, immigration restriction, and labor reform. Insurgents in both parties, energized by these popular movements, forced new issues onto the national agenda, while sharpening their demand for more effective regulation of business. They also favored democratizing political life through the popular election of senators and changing congressional rules to diminish the power of the conservative old guard.

Taft, attempting to maintain Roosevelt's balancing act between reformers and conservatives, was able to oversee the passage of modest pieces of legislation. With his support, Congress strengthened the Interstate Commerce Commission, established the Federal Children's Bureau, created a system of postal savings banks, and gave the president the authority to lower tariffs as part of reciprocal trade agreements. With less support from Taft, Congress also passed the Sixteenth Amendment to the Constitution: ratified early in 1913, the amendment overruled a key Supreme Court decision of the 1890s and gave the federal government power to levy an income tax. On the antitrust front, Taft's administration was far more vigorous than Roosevelt's had been; it even secured the breakup of John D. Rockefeller's Standard Oil Company and the Duke family's American Tobacco Company.

But Taft could not hold the warring factions of his party together. Bitter fights broke out in Congress over the tariff and over the regulation of railroads, telephones, and the telegraph. Taft, at key junctures, sided with Republican conservatives, drawing him the enmity of the reformers. To make matters worse, a scandal erupted within the administration when Gifford Pinchot leaked to the press the news that Interior Secretary Richard Ballinger was being investigated for corruption. (The Interior Department and the Agriculture Department, where Pinchot's bureau was housed, were rivals for control of the nation's natural resources.) After several rounds of investigation and repeated accusations, Taft fired Pinchot, risking a break with Pinchot's patron, the absent yet ever-popular Theodore Roosevelt. Taft sought to shore up his position by campaigning for Republican conservatives in their primary contests against reformers in the 1910 elections. But he was swimming against the tide: in key states, including California and Wisconsin, the insurgents won sweeping victories. The Democrats, moreover, made unprecedented gains in that year's congressional elections, winning control of a branch of Congress for the first time in sixteen years.

A few months later, a group of reform-minded Republican senators and congressmen announced the formation of the Progressive Republican League. The group, acting within the Republican Party, criticized the corrupt ties between conservatives and business, demanded greater regulation of the railroads and all large corporations, and declared its opposition to Taft's renomination. Within Congress, the Progressives formed alliances with like-minded Democrats, while their leader, Wisconsin's Senator La Follette, became their standard-bearer and candidate for the presidency.

La Follette had little chance of unseating Taft, but he paved the way for Roosevelt's reentry into politics. Roosevelt had returned to the United States in the middle of 1910 and had kept some distance from the internecine warfare; he did, however, speak out often in favor of positions that Progressives had endorsed. In the winter of 1912, he announced that he, too, would seek the Republican nomination for president. Aware from the outset that the party's old guard would likely nominate Taft, Roosevelt was propelled both by a desire to join the fray and by the conviction that the historical moment called for a blend of "radical" reforms and conservative leadership, which only he could provide. Frustrated by the thought that he had been president at an inconclusive time, and unabashed at the prospect of elbowing La Follette aside, Roosevelt hoped to replicate the role of Lincoln, to lead a new political grouping—and, if necessary, a new party—that would save the Republic.

### THE ELECTION OF 1912

Roosevelt's prediction that his party would renominate Taft proved to be correct. When the Republicans met in convention in June 1912, the old guard rebuffed the insurgents, precipitating a walkout by pro-Roosevelt delegates. Two months later, Roosevelt and his followers formed the Progressive Party and launched a crusade to recapture the White House and revitalize American politics. In a fitting expression of their zeal (and perhaps their origins), the delegates to the Progressive convention sang "Onward, Christian Soldiers" and the Civil War–era "Battle Hymn of the Republic."

The Democratic Party, meanwhile, was enjoying a revival in national politics. Democrats had gained seats in the Senate, partly as a result of state laws authorizing the popular election of senators. (The selection of senators by state legislatures had favored the Republicans in the Northeast and Midwest, because cities were underrepresented in the legislatures.) They had won control of the House of Representatives, and the popular Champ Clark of Missouri had become Speaker of the House. Democrats had also emerged victorious in several key gubernatorial elections. Moreover, the positions they had been embracing for more than a decade—such as lower tariffs and tighter regulation of business—were gaining support. With the Republicans torn apart by conflict, the Democrats believed that they had an excellent chance of winning the White House in 1912.

One of the new Democratic governors was New Jersey's Woodrow Wilson. Born in the South, the son and grandson of Presbyterian ministers, Wilson had earned a doctorate in political science from Johns Hopkins University and taught at several universities. In 1902, he became the president of Princeton University, where he established a reputation as an educational reformer and an opponent of social privilege. A lifelong Democrat with long-standing interests in politics, Wilson drew the attention of the northeastern, anti-Bryan wing of the party, which endorsed him for governor in 1910. Once nominated, however, he made clear that his sympathies were more progressive than those of his political patrons. An articulate intellectual with an air of rectitude, Wilson was elected by a large majority and proceeded to implement a reform agenda that included the regulation of businesses, workplace safety, and limits on campaign spending.

## National Politics

Wilson emerged immediately as a leading candidate for the Democratic nomination for the presidency in 1912. He was a new face as well as a potential bridge between the southern and northeastern wings of the party. Yet Wilson was regarded with suspicion by Bryan supporters and faced formidable opposition from House Speaker Clark and southerner Oscar Underwood, the House majority leader. When the Democrats met in convention in June 1912, they deadlocked, with Clark leading the early balloting but unable to muster the necessary two-thirds majority. After forty-five inconclusive ballots, Bryan threw his support to Wilson, making the governor the Democratic nominee.

The campaign of 1912 was one of the most colorful and substantive of the twentieth century, combining charismatic personalities with an eloquent and sometimes profound debate about the role of the state in an industrial society. It also included the drama of Roosevelt being shot (but not badly wounded) in mid-campaign and the oddity of an incumbent remaining largely on the sidelines. Knowing he had little chance to win, Taft loomed as the pessimistic standard-bearer of high tariffs and conservative confidence in the business community. His former mentor, Roosevelt, barnstormed the country, articulating a vision of a conservative yet powerful central government that would lift the nation's moral tone while providing a counterweight to large business enterprises. Wilson was similarly energetic, positioning himself as the champion of opportunity in a more democratized society and economy.

The policy differences between Roosevelt and Wilson were not great. Both advocated political reforms such as direct primary elections, as well as social reforms including a minimum wage and maximum hours for workers and the abolition of child labor. Both opposed restrictions on immigration. Neither had much to say about the oppression of blacks in the South or about suffrage for women—which Roosevelt tepidly supported and Wilson dismissed as an issue for the states rather than for the national government. Foreign affairs were barely mentioned.

Even on the issue of the "trusts"—the centerpiece of the campaign—their differences were more of tone and rhetoric than substance. Roosevelt articulated a vision he called the "New Nationalism," accepting the permanence and value of many big businesses but insisting that the federal government should regulate large corporations to prevent them from unfairly wielding their economic power. Wilson's "New Freedom," in contrast, emphasized the desirability of preserving and restoring competition, by breaking up large businesses

Although Roosevelt did not win the 1912 presidential election, the Progressive, or Bull Moose, Party he started had become a powerful voting block. But when Roosevelt returned to the Republican party prior to the election of 1916, he left the Progressives without a presidential candidate. So both Wilson's Democrats and the Republicans, led by their new candidate Charles Evans Hughes, tried to win their allegiance and their votes.

and preventing mergers. Both men claimed that they did not oppose large corporations that had triumphed in fair economic competition; they criticized only those that had taken advantage of their size to stifle competition. Wilson thus was for "big business," but against the "trusts"; Roosevelt embraced "good trusts" while opposing "bad trusts." Both believed that "bad trusts" ought to be broken up and that even legitimate big businesses had to be subject to some government regulation. Although neither said so, both candidates were, in effect, agreeing with the Supreme Court's ruling in the Standard Oil case that only "unreasonable" restraints of trade—not restraints of trade per se—were illegal. That the line between reasonable and unreasonable restraints of trade was difficult to draw was little discussed.

The outcome of the election surprised no one: Taft and Roosevelt split the Republican vote, handing Wilson an easy victory. Fewer people (6.3 million) voted for Wilson than had voted for Bryan in 1908, but he carried forty states to gain an overwhelming advantage in the electoral college. Roosevelt came in second, with 4.1 million votes, while Taft polled 3.5 million. In part because of the continued disfranchisement of blacks in the South, turnout dropped once again. Eugene V. Debs, the Socialist Party candidate, won twice as many votes (900,000) as he had in 1908, and he ran particularly strongly in the West. Although Roosevelt and Wilson had both claimed to be "radicals," 6 percent of the electorate clearly believed that neither was radical enough.

## WILSON: THE SCHOLAR AS PRESIDENT

Wilson's first eighteen months in office were a stunning success. Reflecting his long-standing admiration for British parliamentary politics, Wilson worked closely with Democratic congressional leaders, including Champ Clark and Oscar Underwood, and shrewdly appointed William Jennings Bryan as his secretary of state. Breaking with tradition, he laid out a legislative program in his first inaugural address, held press conferences every week, and became the first president in more than a century personally to address Congress. He also gave speeches designed to educate the public about key issues.

Under Wilson's leadership, Congress passed three clusters of legislation—dealing with tariff revision, banking reform, and antitrust measures—that modernized the political economy of the United States. The first cluster involved tariff revision. By effectively painting the protectionist Republican old guard as the tool of corporate lobbyists, the Democrats, led by Underwood, overwhelmed the opposition and lowered most tariffs by about 25 percent. They thus lessened the government's protection of mature industries, potentially stimulating competition and moving the nation closer to free international trade. At the same time, the Democrats implemented a graduated income tax that applied primarily to the wealthy. In so doing, they reduced the government's financial reliance on tariffs and moved the nation toward a tax system grounded in the principle that those with greater resources should shoulder a larger share of the burden.

The second cluster of legislation involved banking reform. At stake were issues that had been prominent in politics for more than a century: the availability of credit outside of the major financial centers of the Northeast, control of the money supply (since issuing credit was a way of creating money), and the desirability of a national banking system that would impose some restrictions on individual banks and enhance financial stability. Pressures for reform were heightened by the Panic of 1907, yet there were major disagreements about the types of change that were necessary.

What emerged after months of debate was the Federal Reserve Act, passed in December 1913. A compromise among competing business interests, the act created a national bank-ing system that blended limited regional autonomy with a network of centralized controls. The regional autonomy was designed to promote the availability of credit outside the Northeast, while the controls were meant to promote stability by preventing banks from engaging in risky practices. The managers of the new banking system were to be selected by the federal government, but appointed for lengthy terms that would, in theory, insulate them from political pressures. In practice, the system was soon dominated by the powerful reserve bank of the nation's financial capital, New York, but the structure proved to be durable and flexible. A technocratic answer to questions that had long been politically prominent—who would control credit, the money supply, and the banking system; and whose interests would be served by any such system?—the Federal Reserve System effectively removed from the political arena issues that Americans had debated for decades.

After bank reform had been enacted, Wilson turned his attention to the problem of the trusts. His approach was two-pronged. The first was passage of the Clayton Act (1914), which fleshed out the skeleton that the 1890 Sherman Act had created, specifying business activities that constituted illegal restraints on trade as well as penalties for violations of the law. In keeping with Wilson's emphasis on preserving competition, it provided for the breakup of large corporations under some circumstances. To the delight of the American Federation of Labor, the Clayton Act further declared that trade unions were not "illegal combinations in restraint of trade" and thus were exempt from prosecution under the antitrust laws; the ability of federal courts to issue injunctions against unions was also limited. Long overdue in the eyes of workers, the Clayton Act provided a legal guarantee of the right to form labor unions.

The second prong of Wilson's antitrust policy was the creation in 1914 of the Federal Trade Commission (FTC), a new regulatory agency, modeled on the Interstate Commerce Commission, that was vested with the power to investigate alleged violations of the antitrust laws by any corporation engaged in interstate commerce. The FTC also had the authority to order companies to stop anticompetitive practices. As observers pointed out, the FTC seemed to be less in tune with Wilson's rhetoric than with Roosevelt's emphasis on the administrative regulation of big business. But to Wilson, as to Roosevelt, the problem of monopoly seemed complex enough to require ongoing supervision by a permanent agency staffed by antitrust experts. Critics of the FTC, including Roosevelt, charged Wilson with creating the form but not the substance of regulation, a criticism that was heightened when Wilson appointed industry representatives to the commission itself.

Although portrayed as efforts to rein in the excesses of corporate power, the Clayton Act and the Federal Trade Commission were welcomed by some business leaders. The new laws served to dampen widespread anticorporate sentiment by interposing an agency, and panels of experts, between the public and large corporations. They also clarified the rules of legal competition and thus made the business environment more predictable. Many businessmen further believed that one set of federal regulations was preferable to a bewildering array of (sometimes more stringent) state regulations. Both the Clayton Act and the act creating the FTC were written in close consultation with representatives of the business community.

Despite the successful passage of major legislation, the congressional coalition of liberal Democrats, Progressives, and progressive Republicans began to unravel. In 1914, conservative Republicans, aided by yet another business downturn, regained many of the governorships and congressional seats they had lost. Nonetheless, Wilson and his allies pressed forward with their reform program. They passed a law banning child labor (later overturned by the Supreme Court), and a federal loan program that freed farmers from dependence on banks and permitted them to sell their crops when market conditions were favorable. In 1916, Congress substantially increased the income tax and established an inheritance tax. To the delight of organized labor, it also passed the Adamson Act, which mandated an eight-hour workday on the railroads. Strongly supported by Wilson, who wanted to avoid a threatened national railroad strike, the Adamson Act helped to establish the eight-hour day as the norm in industry and transportation.

Wilson had one other key victory in 1916: his nomination of Louis Brandeis to the Supreme Court. Brandeis was a prominent attorney who had championed social reforms and antitrust litigation consistent with the ideals of the New Freedom. Brandeis was also the first Jew ever to be proposed for a seat on the High Court. Many well-known spokesmen for the legal community fiercely opposed the nomination on ideological grounds that were more than a little tinged with anti-Semitism. But congressional Democrats stood firm, and with the help of La Follette and other insurgents, the Senate approved Brandeis's appointment.

Wilson's achievements in office gave him a solid, progressive platform on which to run for reelection in 1916. With the Great War (renamed World War I only in the 1940s) raging in Europe, he also campaigned as the chief executive who had "kept us out of war." He faced a Republican Party that had regrouped with remarkable speed after the schism of 1912. Roosevelt had abandoned the Progressive Party and returned to the Republican fold, leaving the dismayed Progressives without a presidential candidate. The conservative Republican establishment, encouraged by its showing in the 1914 elections, nominated Charles Evans Hughes for president. A moderate former governor of New York, Hughes had the virtue of never having taken sides in the internecine warfare of 1912 because he was a justice of the Supreme Court, a position he resigned after being nominated for president. Although both parties debated foreign policy in general and avoidance of the European war in particular, the central issues of the campaign involved class and regional conflict. While Wilson cheerfully donned the mantle of reform, the Republicans denounced the Adamson Act as "class legislation" and criticized the graduated income tax as an appropriation of northeastern and midwestern wealth by the South and West.

Wilson won the closest election since the 1880s. He led Hughes in the popular vote by a margin of only 3 percent and won the electoral college because of an extremely narrow victory in California. Wilson was victorious throughout the

Louis D. Brandeis, lawyer, reformer, and later justice of the Supreme Court.

South and, with the backing of many former Progressives, in the West as well. Another key to his victory was the labor vote. Foreshadowing political changes that would be solidified in the 1930s, Wilson lured many urban, industrial workers away from the Republican Party—owing in good part to the Adamson Act. As a result, the Democratic vote rose throughout the Northeast and Midwest, and Wilson carried the traditionally Republican state of Ohio. Had Ohio followed the sectional pattern that had prevailed for decades, Charles Evans Hughes would have been president.

## THE LEGACY OF REFORM

Wilson, the reformer, had won a second term, but the Progressive Era was over. By the time of his second inaugural, in March 1917, the war in Europe had seized Wilson's attention, as well as the hopes and fears of the nation he led. With one key exception—the amendment granting suffrage to women—the wave of reform that had marked the first decade and a half of the twentieth century was spent.

The achievements of the Progressive Era at the national level seem relatively slender when matched against the political rhetoric of the period. The most prominent issue, the problem of the trusts, had been addressed, but large corporations continued to dominate the economic landscape. A new banking system had been created, but the centers of finance were unshaken. Workers gained some protection against workplace injuries, but they nonetheless remained vulnerable to most of the risks and uncertainties of industrial capitalism. Democratic rights had been extended in certain domains, such as the popular election of senators, the initiative and referendum, and the enfranchisement of many women. Yet African Americans throughout the South faced nearly insurmountable barriers to political participation, while immigrant workers in the North also faced discrimination. Moreover, administrative agencies, ranging from municipal utility agencies to the Federal Trade Commission, were removing key issues from direct popular control.

Yet what transpired during this era was not mere noise and bluster: in a piecemeal and halting fashion, reformers of different types erected much of the scaffolding of the modern American state. The national government became far more active than it ever had been in the past, and it assumed responsibility for regulating the rules of conduct and competition in the private sector. To carry out this multifaceted task, it created permanent agencies that could administer policies more flexibly and efficiently than could legislatures and courts alone. Reflecting widespread confidence in the models that emerged from science and technology, these agencies had a technocratic bent, emphasizing the role of experts and expertise in the solution of problems. Alongside these changes was a shift in the financial underpinnings of the federal government, away from tariffs and toward graduated income taxes. This shift altered the regional and class distribution of the tax burden, while tying the federal government's budget more directly to the growth of the economy.

This scaffolding was incomplete, particularly with respect to issues of poverty and inequality that were less amenable to technocratic approaches. But it marked a major advance from the final decades of the nineteenth century and provided institutions and models upon which later generations could build. The achievements of the Progressive Era also reflected a profound shift in the language of politics and public discourse. Roosevelt, Wilson, and others had identified themselves as "progressives," even as radicals. They embraced change as well as a vision of an activist state; in so doing, they legitimized the project of reform and carried into the social and political arena the belief in humanly controlled progress that had appeared to be the province of science and technology in the late nineteenth century.

## Suggested Reading

Herbert Croly, *The Promise of American Life* (1909)

Dewey W. Grantham, *Southern Progressivism: The Reconciliation of Progress and Tradition* (1983)

Richard Hofstadter, *The Age of Reform: From Bryan to F. D. R.* (1955)

David L. Lewis, *W. E. B. Du Bois: Biography of a Race, 1868–1919* (1993)

Arthur Link, *Woodrow Wilson and the Progressive Era, 1910–1917* (1954)

Walter Lippmann, *Drift and Mastery: An Attempt to Diagnose the Current Unrest* (1914)

Richard L. McCormick, *The Party Period and Public Policy: American Politics from the Age of Jackson to the Progressive Era* (1986)

David Montgomery, *The Fall of the House of Labor: The Workplace, the State, and the American Labor Activism, 1865–1925* (1987)

Theodore Rosengarten, *All God's Dangers: The Life of Nate Shaw* (1974)

# Chapter Review

## Summary QUESTIONS

■ In what ways did electricity and the automobile transform the lives of Americans?

■ What were the key city and state issues that concerned progressive reformers?

■ How were the lives of industrial workers improved during this period?

■ How and why were women able to gain the right to vote?

■ What were the key new steps taken with regard to government regulation of business, and do you regard them as "progressive"?

## Chronology

| | |
|---|---|
| 1901 | Congress creates the National Bureau of Standards. |
| 1906 | The Pure Food and Drug Act. |
| 1908 | Ford Motor Company introduces the Model T. |
| | Supreme Court, in Muller v. Oregon, upholds state laws restricting hours for female workers. |
| 1913 | Ford adopts the moving assembly line. |
| | Sixteenth and Seventeenth Amendments ratified. |
| December 1913 | The Federal Reserve Act creates a national banking system. |
| 1914 | Federal Trade Commission established. |
| 1919 | Eighteenth Amendment ratified. |
| August 1920 | Nineteenth Amendment ratified. |

## Key Terms

Progressivism (p. 634)

Women's suffrage (p. 645)

Conservation (p. 648)

New Freedom (p. 652)

Federal Reserve Act (p. 653)

Clayton Act (p. 653)

Adamson Act (p. 654)

# Chapter 23

# THE GREAT WAR:

## 1914–1918

James Montgomery Flagg's classic recruiting poster for the U.S. Army, 1918.

- **What drew the United States into World War I?**

- **How was American society affected by the war?**

- **What were the most important consequences of the war?**

In June 1914, in the beautiful, ancient Bosnian city of Sarajevo, a militant advocate of Slavic nationalism assassinated Archduke Franz Ferdinand, the heir to the throne of Austria-Hungary. Bosnia, a province of the Austro-Hungarian empire, was coveted by Serbia, an independent Slavic nation that sought to expand its borders in order to unite the Slavic peoples of eastern Europe (see map 23.1).

This single violent act, occurring thousands of miles from the borders of the United States, precipitated a war that quickly engulfed Europe and eventually led the American government to send hundreds of thousands of soldiers across the Atlantic. In late July, Austria-Hungary, backed by its ally, Germany, declared war against Serbia; Serbia, in turn, looked to its fellow Slavic state of Russia for support, and Russia turned to its ally, France. Within weeks, hostilities had been declared between two major alliances: the Central Powers (Germany, Austria-Hungary, and then Turkey) and the Allies (Britain, France, Russia, Japan, and Italy). Underlying the outbreak of war were tensions that had been brewing for decades over trade, borders, ethnicity, and imperial holdings.

Political and military leaders, on both sides, expected the war to end swiftly. They were wrong. After German armies swept through Belgium in 1914, their progress was stopped in northern France, leading to more than two years of bloody trench warfare along a front that barely moved. In the east, the Central Powers inflicted frightening casualties on the huge, but ill-equipped, Russian army, but the Russians did not buckle. By the beginning of 1917, five million soldiers had died, and the end of the war was nowhere in sight.

Few Americans regarded the war, or its combatants, with impartiality. Those of German descent, not surprisingly, favored the Central Powers, as did many of the Irish who were hostile to Britain as the enemy of Irish nationalism. Most Americans, however, felt far greater kinship with England and its allies: President Wilson was well known for his admiration

of British institutions, and he privately observed that a German victory would be destructive of "American ideals." Wilson nevertheless asked the American people to be "impartial in thought" as well as in deeds, and he feared that any American stance other than neutrality would lead "our mixed population" to "wage war on each other." He adopted a policy of formal neutrality toward the belligerents; most Americans agreed that the United States should remain detached from the conflict.

In his approach to foreign affairs, Wilson was more reserved than either Theodore Roosevelt or William Howard Taft. He appeared to be more principled, too—at times to the point of righteousness. But he was committed to protecting American interests. When Germany threatened American shipping, his insistence on maintaining freedom of the seas, long a vital American concern, brought the United States into the war on the side of the Allies.

The resulting mobilization accelerated many of the social, industrial, and technological developments under way since the turn of the century. It also brought a decisive end to the era of reform. When Hiram Johnson, the Progressive former governor of California, arrived in Washington as a freshman senator in the spring of 1917, he was appalled to discover how little interest there was in reform. "Everything here is war," he wrote to a friend. For a time, it was.

## The Road to War

### THE STRAINS OF NEUTRALITY

Despite the formal neutrality of the American government, it was difficult, if not impossible, for the United States to remain impartial in its actions. The Allies were major trading partners of the United States, and after the war began, British

**Europe Before WWI, 1914**

N

Norway
Sweden
Petrograd
Moscow
North Sea
Baltic Sea
Great Britain
Denmark
Netherlands
Russia
London
Berlin
Luxembourg
Belgium
Germany
Atlantic Ocean
Paris
Prague
France
Vienna
Switzerland
Austro-Hungarian Empire
Romania
Black Sea
Portugal
Italy
Sarajevo
Serbia
Spain
Montenegro
Bulgaria
Rome
Albania
Constantinople
Turkey (Ottoman Empire)
Greece
Sicily
Cyprus
Crete
Mediterranean Sea

Allied powers
Central powers
Neutral nations

orders for American goods—including arms—increased rapidly. During the first two years of the war, American exports to Britain and France nearly quadrupled, producing sizable profits for American industry and helping lift the United States out of a depression that had begun in 1914. Much of this trade, moreover, was financed by loans from American banks—which meant that the United States was, in effect, underwriting the Allied war effort and acquiring a financial interest in its outcome.

Meanwhile, American exports to the Central Powers plummeted, owing in part to the British navy's dominance of the seas and its determination to cripple the German economy. Britain blockaded German ports, seized allegedly war-related cargoes from neutral ships, and prevented most American ships from reaching Germany. President Wilson protested Britain's actions in 1914 and again in 1916, but his complaints yielded only minor concessions.

In response to these asymmetrical trading patterns, Germany declared in 1915 that all waters surrounding Britain constituted a war zone in which it would attempt to sink, without warning, any Allied merchant vessels. Germany further warned that neutral vessels, too, were at risk since the Allies frequently flew the flags of neutral countries on their own ships. This new policy, reflecting Germany's awareness of Allied dependence on American supplies, was made possible by a new instrument of warfare: the submarine (also known as the U-boat). The Germans relied on U-boats to patrol the Atlantic because at the time they were undetectable when running submerged, offsetting the British navy's heavy superiority in surface ships. In violation of conventions governing wartime interference with merchant vessels (conventions adopted prior to the development of submarines), German submarines typically attacked without warning, torpedoing ships and inducing heavy casualties. The Germans maintained that they had no other choice because a U-boat that surfaced to give a warning would be an easy target for British guns.

Americans were made dramatically aware of the impact of Germany's Atlantic strategy when, on May 7, 1915, a German submarine sank a British ocean liner, the *Lusitania,* causing the deaths of almost 1,200 people, including 128 Americans. Although the Germans had, in fact, published warnings in American newspapers that the *Lusitania* was a potential target because they believed it to be carrying munitions as well as passengers—a belief whose truth was confirmed many

years later—the attack outraged the American public. Wilson, however, reacted cautiously, demanding an apology and reparations from the German government, as well as a commitment to stop attacking passenger vessels. He insisted on trying to uphold the principle of neutral rights, declaring, "There is such a thing as a man being too proud to fight." In August 1915, in an effort to avoid American entry into the war, Germany ordered its submarines not to attack passenger ships.

### PEACE AND PREPAREDNESS

By the time the *Lusitania* sank, the American public was deeply divided about the war. Many progressives were morally opposed to war in general; they also feared that entry into the European conflagration would doom domestic reform.

As early as August 1914, more than 1,500 women, dressed in black, marched down Fifth Avenue in New York, carrying a white flag portraying a dove and an olive branch. Late in 1915, settlement house leaders Lillian Wald and Jane Addams, together with scores of other well-known progressive reformers, announced the formation of the American Union Against Militarism. (Financial support for the peace movement came from Andrew Carnegie and Henry Ford, among others.) Within the administration, Secretary of State William Jennings Bryan was a resolute voice against intervention in the war and a skeptic about the sincerity of Wilson's claims to neutrality: Bryan resigned his position to protest the one-sidedness of Wilson's sharp criticism of the Germans over the *Lusitania* incident while tolerating British violations of American neutrality and refusing to enact a ban on American travel in the ships of belligerents. It was not neutrality, Bryan claimed, for the United States to "insist that ammunition intended for one of the belligerents should be safeguarded in transit by the lives of American citizens."

The *New York Times* reporting the sinking of the British ocean liner *Lusitania* by a German submarine on May 7, 1915.

Other Americans, however, were convinced, even before the sinking of the *Lusitania,* that the United States

A cartoon from early 1917 that questions the American position of neutrality while extending loans and selling arms to Great Britain and its Allies.

ought to at least prepare for war against Germany. Popular sentiment was galvanized by news reports, many of them originating in British propaganda, that Germans were committing atrocities such as killing babies with bayonets. Anti-German opinion was further inflamed when German troops in 1915 sent thick clouds of chlorine gas rolling toward the French line on the Belgian front at Ypres, an introduction of chemical warfare that left hundreds of Allied soldiers choking, vomiting, and dying. Bankers and industrialists, including Cornelius Vanderbilt and Henry Frick, most of them from cities in the Northeast, mounted preparedness parades and formed a National Security League to lobby for universal military training as well as increases in the size of the army and the navy.

Wilson, his eyes at once on American interests and the election of 1916, threaded his way along the border between pacifism and preparedness, trying to keep the United States out of the war while acknowledging that such efforts might

be in vain. Hitherto, the government had rejected requests by major bankers such as J. P. Morgan to lend the Allies money, holding that such loans would violate the spirit of neutrality. In August 1915, however, members of Wilson's cabinet advised him that unless credit was extended to France and Britain, those countries would be unable to purchase goods in the United States, and the American economy as well as the Allied war effort would be weakened. In response, Wilson authorized loans to the Allies. By April 1917, American banks advanced up to $2.3 billion in credit to the Allies and only $27 million to Germany.

Late in 1915, Wilson asked Congress to increase military expenditures; at the same time, he sent a private emissary to Europe to try to negotiate an end to the bloodshed. But the negotiations failed, and in March 1916 a German U-boat torpedoed the *Sussex,* a French channel steamer, once again provoking a storm of protest. Wilson threatened to break diplomatic relations, and through the rest of the year the Germans (who claimed the *Sussex* attack was an error) generally refrained from making submarine attacks on passenger vessels.

Wilson owed his victory in the election of 1916 in part to his success in having kept the United States out of war. In a speech in January 1917, he eloquently envisioned a future based on "peace without victory" and called for the launch of an international organization that would promote "not a balance of power but a community of power."

### ENTRY INTO THE WAR

Wilson's hopes for peace were thwarted by a decisive change in German strategy. Early in 1917, the German command announced that its submarines would attack without warning all shipping headed for Allied ports. By taking this step, Germany gambled that it could cut off munitions and supplies to Britain and France and gain a military victory before the United States (which Germany fully expected to enter the war) could mobilize an effective army. In February and March 1917, German submarines sank more than a million tons of Allied shipping, jeopardizing the Allies' lifelines to the United States.

The sinking of merchant vessels galvanized public opinion against Germany. So, too, did the British interception of a telegram from the German foreign secretary, Arthur Zimmerman, to his envoy in Mexico: the telegram proposed an alliance with Mexico, in return for which Mexico would regain the lands it had lost in 1848—now the states of Texas, New Mexico, and Arizona. In early March, Wilson issued an executive order arming the merchant marine; two weeks later, he called up the national guard. Finally, on the evening of April 2, President Wilson asked Congress to declare war against the Central Powers. In an eloquent speech to a cheering Congress, Wilson reviewed his administration's efforts to stay out of the conflict while defending American rights at sea. Couching the decision to go to war in idealistic terms, he declared that "the world must be made safe for democracy." With "civilization itself seeming to be in the balance . . . right was more precious than peace." The United States, he concluded, was obliged to "fight for the things we have always carried nearest our hearts."

Support for going to war was not unanimous in Congress. In debates that lasted for days, critics pointed out that the idealism of some of the war's most ardent supporters was suspect, since they had long opposed democratic reforms at home. Other critics, including midwestern Progressives like George Norris and Robert La Follette, argued that the war would benefit only the wealthy who had business ties to Britain. Still others balked at the carnage that seemed in store for young American soldiers. But these opponents were swimming against the tide: in the end, only six senators and fifty representatives voted against the declaration of war.

## Prosecuting the War

The United States entered the war woefully unprepared. The army included 120,000 regulars and 80,000 newly federalized national guardsmen—altogether a tiny fraction of the Allied troops fighting in Europe. Most of what the U.S. military needed—including guns, munitions, uniforms, and airplanes—was in short supply. The army had no gas masks or industrial suppliers of poison gas. Its meager air service was unequipped with the machine guns or the flight instruments essential to combat operations. And the navy's best submarine detection apparatus could not even sense the presence, let alone determine the location, of a submerged U-boat cruising more than 200 yards away. To prosecute the war, the nation had to finance the mobilization, organize its economy for war production, raise an army, and equip its military services to fight in a conflict that, as a leading business executive remarked, combined the dreams of science fiction "with the horrors of Armageddon."

### FINANCING THE WAR

The war presented the Wilson administration with the largest problem of public finance that the nation had confronted since the Civil War. Although initial estimates were far lower (and were repeatedly revised upward), the direct cost of the war eventually came to $24 billion, more than twice the total budget of the U.S. government for the entire fifteen years that preceded the war. How to pay for the war was hotly debated. Many progressives argued that at least half the cost should be covered by increased taxes, particularly on businesses and on the wealthy who had benefited from the preparedness period and would also gain financially from the war itself. Key segments of the business community, however, preferred that the government borrow the funds for war—which would ease the short-run financial pain while heightening the risk of infla-

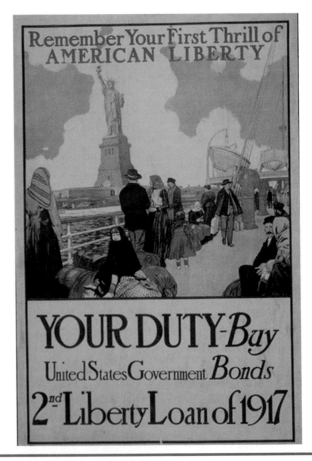

1917 poster urging Americans to buy government bonds to support the war.

tion. In the end, the administration financed about two-thirds of the cost of war by borrowing, mainly through a series of bonds called "Liberty Loans." The remaining one-third was paid for by higher excise and estate taxes, corporate income taxes, and sharply increased (but graduated) personal income taxes, made possible by the recent adoption of the Sixteenth Amendment. Neither income tax rates nor the size of the federal budget ever returned to their low prewar levels.

## WAR PRODUCTION

Mobilizing the nation for war meant mobilizing the economy to produce necessary military goods (materiel) while still meeting basic civilian needs. To carry out this enormous task, the government created a complex network of partnerships with business, particularly big business. Businessmen from major corporations flooded into Washington, taking only a dollar a year in pay while contributing their executive experience to the war effort. (Many of them continued to collect their corporate salaries, however.) In July 1917, after the failure of less formal mechanisms, the Wilson administration established a War Industries Board (WIB) to oversee producers of key raw materials and manufactures. It also established agencies to control trade, shipping, and railroad traffic; and, after passage in August of the Lever Food and Fuel Control Act, it created the Fuel Administration and the Food Administration. In all, nearly 5,000 agencies were established to manage the domestic wartime economy.

Mindful of the business community's long-standing opposition to government control, Wilson tried to mobilize the economy by relying on voluntarism. For example, the WIB at first was to act primarily as a coordinating agency for the nation's defense industries and to encourage production increases as well as the elimination of waste. But it quickly became evident that a largely voluntarist strategy was not succeeding in getting necessary goods produced and distributed. As a result, other measures were adopted to induce and coerce the cooperation of private business. Antitrust laws were suspended, minimum prices were established, and the government began to utilize "cost plus" contracts (according to which, companies would be paid for all of their production costs plus an agreed-upon profit) to guarantee substantial profits to participating firms. Ironically, given Wilson's ideological sympathy for small enterprises, big business got much bigger on his watch.

In some instances, government intervention became even more direct. Faced with extensive delays in railroad traffic at the end of 1917, for example, Wilson seized control of the railroads, and within months the government had forged thousands of miles of track owned by different companies into an integrated national transportation system. Early in 1918, to conserve fuel for heating and lighting, his fuel administrator introduced daylight saving time. In March, in the hope of inducing greater coordination and productivity in the industrial war effort, Wilson put more teeth into the WIB, appointing Bernard Baruch to head it and giving him the authority to do his job. Grown rich from speculating on Wall Street, Baruch possessed broad knowledge of the American economy. Using power and persuasion, he managed to shift a quarter of the economy from consumer to war production. The WIB reached into numerous niches in American economic life: its conservation division, for example, altered bicycle designs to save 2,000 tons of steel and captured enough metal for two warships by removing stays from corsets.

The agency that touched the lives of most Americans was the Food Administration, headed by Herbert Hoover. A wealthy mining engineer, Hoover had begun devoting himself to public service—most recently as the leader of humanitarian food relief in Belgium, which had faced catastrophic food shortages earlier in the war. Hoover sought to increase the domestic food supply by emphasizing both conservation and production—for example, in wheat, which was in short supply because part of the American harvest was going to U.S. soldiers and the Allies. Hoover urged consumers to practice wheatless Mondays and bake wheat-free breads, cakes, and cookies. Using the powers granted the food administrator in the Lever Act, he got farmers to plant more wheat by guaranteeing them a minimum price and establishing a grain corporation to buy their harvests. Hoover's policies led to increased wheat yields from 637 million to 921 million bushels in one year.

To further conserve grain, Congress passed a law limiting the production of alcoholic beverages. The measure boosted the long-standing efforts of moral reformers to outlaw alcohol consumption. In 1919, the states ratified the Eighteenth Amendment (which banned the importation or manufacture of intoxicating beverages); the following year, to enforce these strictures, Congress passed the Volstead Act, which prohibited the sale of any beverage containing more than 1 in 200 parts alcohol.

The combination of federal intervention and entrepreneurial energy succeeded in meeting the challenge of wartime mobilization: despite innumerable glitches and shortages (including a coal shortage during the severe winter of 1917–18), the output of the economy was far greater than ever before. In 1917, steel production was double its pre-war levels; the gross national production more than doubled between 1914 and 1920. Unprecedented in scale and scope, the government's intervention accelerated the organization of mass production while confirming progressive beliefs in the value of centralization, federal regulation, reliance on exports, and collaboration among business, government, and labor. Much of the machinery of intervention was dismantled after the war, but its effectiveness would be recalled when the nation faced the crisis of the Great Depression in the 1930s and when, in the 1940s, it needed to mobilize for war again.

### SCIENCE TO THE FRONT

Early in 1917, a leading scientist declared, "War must mean research." The government had taken steps to reduce the military's technological weakness in 1915 by creating the National Advisory Committee for Aeronautics, intended to foster aeronautical research, and in the following year by encouraging the National Academy of Sciences to establish an agency to help mobilize academic science for defense.

An American airplane equipped for combat in World War I.

After the country entered the war, the National Academy's agency spurred investigations into myriad techniques, devices, and substances for war. Chemists working on chemical weapons were incorporated into the army's new Chemical Warfare Service. Physicists developed submarine detectors that in 1918 allowed Allied ships and subchasers to find and sink submarines. Pyschologists helped screen draftees, adapting tests that purported to measure "I.Q." (intelligence quotient) to determine which recruits were most competent.

Most of the technological innovations that appeared during the war, however, originated not in the United States but in the European nations that had been fighting since 1914. These innovations included metal helmets for soldiers, flamethrowers, more lethal machine guns, new poison gases (as well as defenses against poison gases), and a first generation of armored tanks. Trucks and other motorized vehicles replaced horse-drawn vehicles in transporting men and materiel into combat. And aviation made its first significant appearance in war. Used at first strictly for reconnaissance, airplanes were later equipped with machine guns so that they could attack each other as well as observation balloons and troops on the ground. By the final year of the war, large squadrons of Allied airplanes, almost all of them built by the British and the French, were playing an important role in combat operations.

### INTO COMBAT

In Wilson's speech to Congress asking for a declaration of war, the president recommended raising an army through conscription or universal military service. The idea was controversial: Wilson himself had opposed universal service in 1916, leading to the resignation of his secretary of war. Opponents claimed that compulsory service would violate American ideals of freedom and voluntarism, militarize American society, and require racial integration of the armed services. Advocates of universal service, however, maintained that it would be more democratic and would serve as a "melting pot" that would "break down distinctions of race and class." In May 1917, Congress endorsed the president's view and enacted a Selective Service law that required all young men to register for possible military service. Draft boards peacefully registered more than 24 million men—only 1 to 2 percent of eligible males failed to register—and inducted about 2.8 million of them. Another 2 million volunteered, bringing the total serving in the war to about 4.8 million.

While the United States built its army, the war on the ground went poorly for the Allies. In November, in a battle in Belgium,

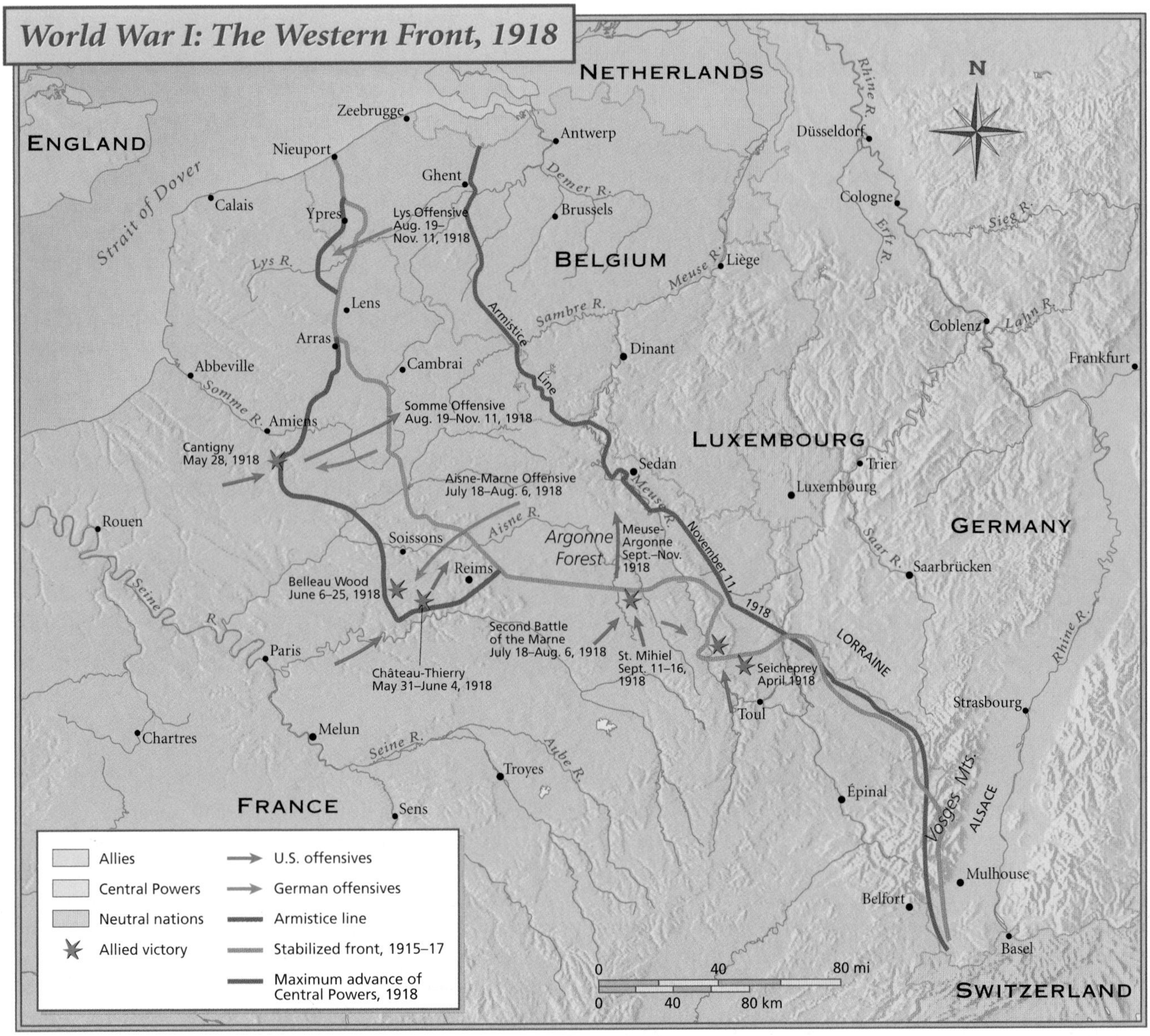
World War I: The Western Front, 1918
NETHERLANDS
ENGLAND
BELGIUM
LUXEMBOURG
GERMANY
FRANCE
SWITZERLAND
Strait of Dover
Zeebrugge
Nieuport
Antwerp
Ghent
Calais
Ypres
Brussels
Lys Offensive Aug. 19–Nov. 11, 1918
Lys R.
Demer R.
Lens
Arras
Cambrai
Abbeville
Somme R.
Amiens
Somme Offensive Aug. 19–Nov. 11, 1918
Cantigny May 28, 1918
Aisne-Marne Offensive July 18–Aug. 6, 1918
Rouen
Soissons
Aisne R.
Reims
Belleau Wood June 6–25, 1918
Argonne Forest
Meuse-Argonne Sept.–Nov. 1918
Second Battle of the Marne July 18–Aug. 6, 1918
Château-Thierry May 31–June 4, 1918
Paris
Seine R.
St. Mihiel Sept. 11–16, 1918
Seicheprey April 1918
Toul
Chartres
Melun
Troyes
Aube R.
Sens
Sambre R.
Meuse R.
Liège
Dinant
Armistice Line
Sedan
November 11 1918
LORRAINE
Düsseldorf
Rhine R.
Cologne
Erft R.
Sieg R.
Coblenz
Lahn R.
Frankfurt
Trier
Luxembourg
Saar R.
Saarbrücken
Strasbourg
Épinal
Vosges Mts.
ALSACE
Mulhouse
Belfort
Basel
N
Allies
Central Powers
Neutral nations
Allied victory
U.S. offensives
German offensives
Armistice line
Stabilized front, 1915–17
Maximum advance of Central Powers, 1918
0 40 80 mi
0 40 80 km

the British gained four miles at a cost of 400,000 casualties; in another near the Austrian border, the Italians suffered a catastrophic defeat. The Allies were further weakened that month by events in Russia. The previous March, a revolution had overthrown the brutal regime of Tsar Nicholas II, replacing it with a provisional democratic government under Alexander Kerensky. But on November 6, the Kerensky government succumbed to a revolution spearheaded by the revolutionary socialist Bolsheviks under the leadership of Vladimir Lenin and Leon Trotsky. The new Bolshevik government, propelled into power partly by the war-weariness of the Russian people, promptly signed an armistice with Germany at Brest Litovsk. Russia's withdrawal from the war allowed Germany to move thousands of soldiers from the eastern front to fight against the Allies.

## What Did You Do In the War?

*American Journal*

*July 14, 1918*
"I was on the board tonight when the battery was ordered to fire. The boys sure did raise Cain for a while. Things calmed down and at 10:30 I went to bed but at 11:30 I was awakened by terrific sounds, which showed that the big battle had commenced.

I never saw or heard anything so intense, the battle zone is alive with artillery and it is difficult to distinguish between the bursts of enemy shells and the roar of our guns.

As soon as I woke I ran down to the battery, the fourth gun had just blown up and Malcolm and Savio were lying on stretchers. Savio's right leg was practically off and his other badly emaciated. He was being attended to and I went to hold a blanket to shield Malcolm from the wind. The poor boy was unrecognizable. His face was emaciated and burned and he was holding up a stump of an arm. He said, 'Give em hell boys I guess I can't help any more.'

I spoke to him and held the arm putting my finger over the artery from which blood was squirting thus stopping the flow. He said thanks 'Doc' old boy. I'm not hurt very badly but it pains some. I only hope that when my time comes I am as game as this little eighteen year old boy.

The medic came soon and I helped him bandage Malcolm up and soon the ambulance came and both were taken to the hospital where they will have a hard fight for life.

Of course I was terribly sorry for him but I didn't have the least feeling of sickness because of the blood, which I thought I would have."

From *A Soldier in World War I: The Diary of Elmer W. Sherwood*

---

The Allies, of course, cheered American entry into the war. At the time, their prospects did not seem bright, particularly since shipping losses to German submarines in March and April were cutting heavily into supplies. Even before any American troops arrived, however, the Allies received a boost when an American admiral devised an effective means—the convoy—to protect merchant shipping against U-boat attacks. The ships would travel in groups screened on all sides by destroyers. If a submarine torpedoed one of them, it would place itself in dire jeopardy. In May 1917, shipping losses dropped one-third below the April high.

American troops began arriving in France within months of the declaration of war, although most did not reach the war zone until 1918. They served as members of the American Expeditionary Force (AEF) under General John J. Pershing, a tough, capable commander hardened by his leadership of the expedition against Pancho Villa in Mexico (see Chapter 21). By presidential order, the AEF was to fight in parallel with the Allies while remaining "distinct and separate" from them. Pershing, impatient with the trench-warfare mentality of the Allies, itched to engage in more aggressive combat. But in March 1918, when the Germans launched a massive spring offensive, the AEF was subordinated to a unified Allied command under the French general Ferdinand Foch. The AEF helped beat back the initial German assault. Then, in early June, when the Germans threatened Paris, the Americans helped significantly to halt the German advance in heavy fighting around the town of Château-Thierry and neighboring Belleau Wood. Near the cathedral city of Reims, they assisted in blocking a final German attempt to break through the Allied lines.

In mid-July 1918, the Allies and the AEF, now 1 million soldiers strong, mounted a major offensive against the Germans. In September, given his first independent command, Pershing led AEF troops against a German troop concentration around the town of St. Mihiel, about 150 miles east of

Paris on the Meuse River. The attack began at 1 A.M. on September 11, when, as one soldier wrote in his diary, in "one instant the entire front . . . was a sheet of flame, while the heavy artillery made the earth quake." Breaking from the seesaw of trench tactics, Pershing organized 500,000 American and 100,000 French troops into a war of movement that, aided by air cover from French and British squadrons, reduced the German concentration in four days. On September 26, 1.2 million American soldiers fought alongside the Allies to oust the Germans from the area of the Meuse River and the Argonne Forest. They clawed northward through the seemingly ubiquitous mud and against heavy German opposition, eventually gaining the city of Sedan and severing the major German rail supply route. It was the last major battle of the war.

Unlike the belligerents on the European continent, the United States suffered no physical damage from the war, and its casualty rate was far smaller—8 percent—than the 70 percent rate suffered by the Allies. Some 49,000 Americans fell in battle, with another 63,000 succumbing to disease. These were significant losses, but they paled in comparison to the millions of French, British, and Russian soldiers who lost their lives.

Most American soldiers, in fact, were either never in combat or not in combat for very long—facts that contributed to a popular cultural image of the war as a great "adventure" for young American men who otherwise would never have journeyed to Europe and enjoyed the pleasures of Paris. But the presence of millions of fresh American troops ended the stalemate of the great European war and determined its outcome. Those Americans who were in combat, moreover, were not spared the brutality of the war or the diverse ways in which technology had exacerbated the savagery of combat. For ground troops, the ordeal of battle was made worse than it had been in the past by machine-gunning aircraft and by long-range artillery fire. Some soldiers succumbed to "shell shock," a new syndrome or form of emotional breakdown, linked to the helpless vulnerability felt by soldiers on the ground faced with the sounds and destruction wrought by arriving munitions from distant and unseen guns.

## WARTIME SOCIETY

The war stimulated most sectors of the American economy, improving the lot of industrial labor and creating good times for agriculture. It also drew more women into the workforce and sharply accelerated the migration of blacks from the South to northern industrial cities. At the same time, an increasingly rigid emphasis on national unity led to the suppression of dissent, an intolerant stress on "Americanism," and a war against radicalism.

*A Booming Economy.* The demands of war added to the prosperity that war orders from Europe had begun generating in 1914. Between 1914 and 1918, overall factory output mushroomed by more than a third; automobile production quadrupled. Unemployment dropped to its lowest levels in decades (suggesting, once again, that the unemployed were indeed willing to work if jobs were available), with the predictable consequence that wages shot upward. For most workers and farmers, however, rising incomes were largely offset by inflation: owing both to market dynamics and to government policies (such as placing a floor under prices), the cost of living nationwide rose 77 percent. Food costs roughly doubled.

With labor scarce and prices rising, organized labor was primed to press for its own advantage, but its foremost leader, Samuel Gompers, the head of the American Federation of Labor (AFL), urged workers to refrain from striking during the war. He was convinced that unions and union members would gain more by cooperating with government

Allied troops await the enemy in one of the damp, vermin-infested trenches of World War I.

and business. Many workers, however, ignored his call: aware that corporate profits were extremely high and perhaps remembering that a railroad strike in 1916 had led to passage of the Adamson Act and an eight-hour day for all railway workers (see Chapter 22), employees throughout the nation went on strike in the six months after U.S. entry into the war.

In January 1918, the government appointed a War Labor Board to try to resolve disputes and avoid disruptions of production. The board issued rulings in 500 cases: it generally supported workers' right to organize unions but undercut that prolabor position by not requiring management to actually negotiate with labor organizations. Still, pressure from the board contributed to the eight-hour day becoming a norm in American industry, and union membership rose from 3 million in 1917 to 5 million in 1920. Federal agencies meanwhile pushed employers to honor a federal ban on child labor, allow safety and sanitation inspectors into their plants, raise wages, and offer other benefits to workers. In the interest of promoting efficiency and social stability, several states also enacted protections and benefits for industrial labor.

Business benefited more than labor from the war. Profits rose so rapidly that the government felt obliged to curtail them with an excess-profits tax that brought in $2.2 billion, more than three times as much as the personal income tax. In 1917, the net income of U.S. Steel reached $224 million, a level the company would not achieve again until 1954. And after the Department of Justice granted immunity against antitrust prosecutions to business combinations serving the public interest, the rate of corporate mergers climbed sharply.

*African Americans.* Between 1916 and 1918, some 450,000 blacks moved north, substantially increasing the African American population of Chicago, New York, and other cities in the industrial heartland. They were impelled out of the South by the ravages of floods and cotton-devouring boll weevils, as well as by the region's racially repressive social system. "A heap of families . . . was leavin going north," remembered Alabama sharecropper Nate Shaw. "They was dissatisfied with the way of life down here in the South." Ironically, some were able to leave because of inflation: rising cotton prices permitted them to pay off their debts under the lien system, leaving them free to seek employment elsewhere.

What beckoned them to the North was not simply a booming economy but (especially after U.S. entry into the war) labor shortages so pronounced that employers tore down the racial barricades that had surrounded blue-collar

jobs in industry. Earlier African American migrants to the North had been obliged to work in low-paying jobs in the service sector, but in the overheated economy of wartime, factory jobs became available; some northern employers even sent recruiters to the South to lure black workers, a practice that white southerners actively resisted out of fear that they would lose their semi-captive labor supply. These new opportunities launched a spirited black exodus from some areas of the South; and for a time, migrants did find jobs that paid far more than anything open to them in the South. "Nothing here but money, and it is not hard to get," wrote one new arrival in Chicago.

But the large-scale arrival of African Americans sparked conflicts, often with European immigrants, over housing, jobs, and political power. In 1917, rioting broke out in several cities, most notably in East St. Louis, Illinois, where whites brutally burned, beat, and stoned residents of a black neighborhood. Thousands of people then went on a rampage, burning, looting, and killing. After the riots in East St. Louis, blacks marched down New York's Fifth Avenue in silent protest, carrying banners that read: "Mr. President, Why Not Make America Safe for Democracy?"

Racial tensions were visible as well in the armed forces, which included some 260,000 blacks. They were assigned to

Soldiers of the African-American 369th Infantry Regiment, wearing the Croix de Guerre they earned in combat under French command.

segregated units that were, for the most part, commanded by whites. Sent mainly to training camps in the South, they suffered blatant racial abuse. In late August 1917, provoked by numerous racial incidents, including the beating of a black woman by a white policeman, hundreds of black soldiers of the Twenty-fourth Infantry Regiment stormed out of their Texas camp into the neighboring city of Houston and killed fifteen whites and Hispanics, among them five policemen. Of the sixty-four men tried in courts-martial, five were acquitted, nineteen were hanged, and the rest were sentenced to prison, a number of them for life.

About 50,000 black soldiers went to France. Most were given menial tasks, though some jobs, like unloading cargo from ships, were crucial to the war effort. The AEF allowed only one black regiment into combat in Europe: the Ninety-second, which had some of the few black officers trained during the war. However, four other black regiments fought under French command, and one was awarded the Croix de Guerre, the French honor for bravery under fire.

*Women.* In 1917, Florence Thorne of the AFL observed, "Out of . . . repression into opportunity is the meaning of the war to thousands of women." Secretary of the Navy Josephus Daniels brought women into his service, with the result that 11,000 of them worked in the navy as secretaries, nurses, and telephone operators. Women also found employment in new jobs such as running elevators, producing munitions, and delivering messages. Some were appointed to defense advisory boards. During the war, industry employed about 1 million women.

Inflation helped bring more married women into the paid workforce: "I used to go to work when my man was sick or couldn't get a job," said one wife, after prices had been rising for four years. "But this is the first time I ever had to go to work to get enough money to feed the kids, when he was working regular." Most working women were not new entrants to the labor force, but the war enabled many to move to better-paying jobs. Even so, they earned less than the men they replaced despite complaints from women and rulings to the contrary from the War Labor Board. And when the soldiers returned after the war, many women were edged out of the industrial labor force.

*Assaults on Civil Liberties.* The mobilization for war had a darker side: with American troops headed into battle, a natural emphasis on patriotism and unity devolved into attacks

Women machinists at work in a refrigerator plant during the war, 1917.

on dissent and civil liberties. Both public authorities and private citizens participated in these acts of repression, some of which were based in law and some of which were not. Their targets were clusters of distinct, yet overlapping, imagined enemies: ethnic groups suspected of supporting the Central Powers; pacifists and other critics of American participation in the war; and political radicals (mostly socialists or members of the Industrial Workers of the World) whose hostility to capitalism was readily depicted as un-American.

In April 1917, eager to mobilize public opinion behind the war, the Wilson administration created the Committee on Public Information (CPI), headed by the progressive journalist George Creel. With the aid of numerous well-known writers and opinion molders, the CPI set out to publicize and explain the reasons why the war was in the nation's interest; it also sought to hasten the Americanization of the huge number of immigrants who lived in the United States, effectively turning assimilation into a loyalty test. The CPI soon enlarged its role to include propagandizing and controlling public opinion, telling magazine readers, for example, that they should report to the Justice Department "the man who spreads pessimistic stories . . . cries for peace, or belittles our efforts to win the war."

These propaganda efforts were supplemented by changes in federal law. At the administration's urging, Congress in June 1917 passed the Espionage Act, which provided stiff fines and long prison terms for anyone convicted of obstructing the war effort by use of the mails or otherwise. In May 1918, Congress passed a new Sedition Act that threatened a twenty-year prison term to anyone who expressed a disloyal opinion or defamed the flag, the government, or the Constitution. The Supreme Court unanimously upheld the Espionage Act, signaling that the right to free speech under the First Amendment could be curtailed in wartime; with two dissenting votes, the Court also condoned the more vaguely worded Sedition Act.

The easiest targets of the drive for loyalty were German immigrants whose attachment to their heritage was interpreted as an absence of patriotism. State and local school districts banned the teaching of the German language; sauerkraut was renamed "liberty cabbage"; and Pittsburgh banned the performance of music composed by Ludwig von Beethoven. In a more ominous move, German Americans whose ideas were suspect were flogged or forced to kiss the American flag, and in one horrific incident near St. Louis a German immigrant (who, in fact, had tried to enlist in the American army) was wrapped in an American flag and lynched, for no crime other than his place of birth.

Popular and official wrath was also aimed at native-born opponents of American participation in the war—from settlement house worker Jane Addams to authors of antiwar articles to students circulating petitions. The most vehement repression, however, involved socialists and other left-wing activists who voiced opposition to the war as a savage conflict that would benefit business while costing the lives of working-class soldiers. Backed by conservatives who had long been eager to crack down on socialists (whose electoral strength had been growing), the government banned their publications from the mails and arrested their leaders. Roughly 2,000 people, most from the political left, were prosecuted under the Espionage and Sedition Acts, and 1,500 were convicted—including presidential candidate Eugene Debs, who was sentenced to ten years in prison for having given an antiwar speech. Victor Berger, a Socialist congressman from Wisconsin, was charged with violating the Espionage Act and not permitted to take his seat in Congress, despite having been elected by the citizens of his district.

Virtually the entire leadership of the Industrial Workers of the World was arrested and sent to prison, while many others were the victims of vigilante violence. In 1917, in Bisbee, Arizona, nearly 1,200 striking copper miners from the IWW were run out of town (and transported out of state) by a sheriff and 2,000 citizens armed and paid by the mine owners. That same summer, in Butte, Montana, Frank Little, an IWW organizer who had come to town to help striking copper miners (after a grisly mine fire that had killed dozens), was dragged from his bed and hung from a railroad trestle. Two months after his death, the Justice Department indicted him for conspiracy. The IWW, a colorful—if never mainstream—organization of unskilled and semiskilled workers, never rebounded from the repression of the war years.

## Retreat from Internationalism

Wilson had long hoped that the war would produce a more democratic world. He felt it imperative to articulate his vision of that goal after the new Bolshevik regime in Russia revealed that treaties signed by the European powers before 1914 included secret arrangements for parceling out territories among the victors. In a speech to Congress in January 1918, the president advanced a framework for the peace spelled out in what were quickly dubbed "the Fourteen Points." A majority of the points called for self-determination for the ethnic and national minorities under the domination of the Austro-Hungarian empire and the Turkish-led Ottoman empire, which controlled large areas of the Middle East. Most of the other points expressed a set of principles to govern relations among nations: absolute freedom of the seas, greater freedom of trade (meaning lower tariffs), open rather than secret agreements between countries, and the peaceful resolution of disputes by a "general association of nations" that came to be called the League of Nations.

In October 1918, after the failure of their last offensive, the Germans conveyed to Wilson that they would accept an armistice based on the Fourteen Points as a guide to a permanent peace settlement. The French and the British, at first reluctant, agreed to the terms after Wilson threatened to conclude a separate peace. Precisely at eleven A.M. on November 11, 1918, the guns in Europe fell silent. Crowds all over the United States cheered the end of the killing, and soon American troops began to sail home. Meanwhile, Wilson readied himself to personally lead the American delegation to Paris to negotiate the terms of the peace. The delegation

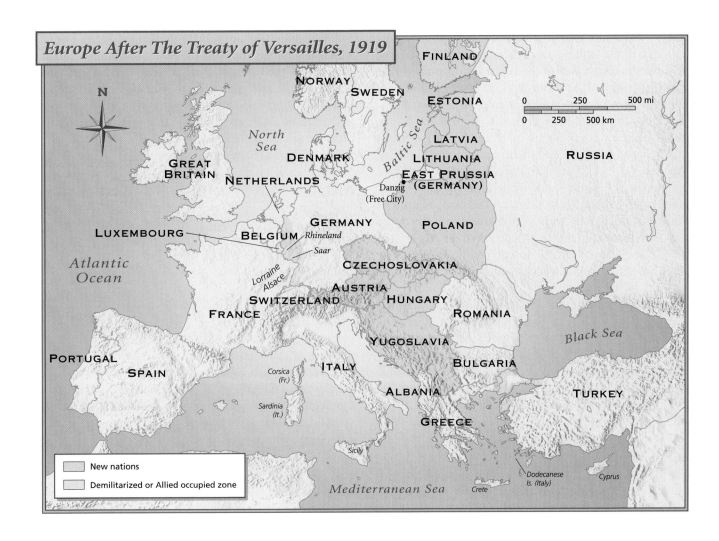

**Europe After The Treaty of Versailles, 1919**

New nations

Demilitarized or Allied occupied zone

sailed aboard the *George Washington* on December 4, 1918, making Wilson the first sitting president to cross the Atlantic.

### THE VERSAILLES PEACE CONFERENCE

Crowds greeted Wilson with great popular enthusiasm when he arrived in France, but the accolades masked the difficulty of the task before him. The leaders of the Allies—Georges Clemenceau of France, David Lloyd George of Britain, and Vittorio Orlando of Italy—were deeply skeptical about Wilson's program and more than a little put off by the righteous tone of the president's pronouncements. They did not share Wilson's antagonism to imperialism, and having suffered immense human and material losses during the war, they wanted retribution from Germany and its allies. The three

European members of the "Big Four" also regarded Wilson as a politically wounded leader who did not necessarily have the backing of his own government or people: the Republicans had handily won the congressional elections of 1918, and Wilson had formidable foes in congress. The cunning French leader, Clemenceau, commented, "God gave us the Ten Commandments and we broke them. Mr. Wilson has given us the Fourteen Points. We shall see."

What emerged from months of negotiation was the Treaty of Versailles, formally signed on June 28, 1919. The document was a compromise, containing elements of Wilson's idealism intermixed with a recognition of hard-knuckled political realities. Wilson's concern with self-determination was expressed in the acknowledgment of Poland as an independent nation and in the creation of two new nations—Czechoslavakia and

671

Yugoslavia—from the Austro-Hungarian and Ottoman empires. It was also present in the decision to strip Germany of its colonies, granting them to the Allies as trusteeships that were to lead eventually to independence. Wilson also succeeded in having a "covenant" to establish a League of Nations written into the peace treaty itself.

The agreement was harsh in its treatment of Germany, much as France and Britain had wished. In addition to seizing its colonies, the treaty gave parts of Germany to Belgium, Denmark, and Poland and returned to France the provinces of Alsace and Lorraine, which Germany had taken in 1871. It established a thirty-mile-wide demilitarized zone between France's eastern border and the Rhine River; strictly limited the size of the German armed forces; and awarded France control of the Saar Basin, Germany's rich source of coal, for fifteen years. Finally, it imposed on Germany the obligation to pay huge reparations, later fixed by an international commission at $33 billion. Satisfying as this punishment of Germany may have been to the war-battered Allies, the terms of the treaty were economically unworkable, as the British economist John Maynard Keynes argued in his powerful *Economic Consequences of the Peace* (1919). While Germany was required to pay huge reparations, it was denied much of the economic means—for example, the resources of the Saar Basin—to do so. As the world would soon learn, the punitive features of the treaty engendered a simmering resentment among many Germans.

In the separate Treaty of Sèvres, concluded with Turkey in 1920, the Allies liquidated the Ottoman empire, awarding the British a mandate to supervise Palestine and Iraq and the French similar responsibility in Syria and Lebanon. In 1917, the British foreign secretary, Arthur J. Balfour, had issued what would become known as the Balfour Declaration. Balfour had been one of Britain's leading Conservative politicians from the 1870s through World War I. He had spent many years in parliament and was currently serving three years (1916–1919) as the foreign secretary in the government headed by David Lloyd George. The Balfour Declaration was a letter written by Balfour on behalf of the British government to Lord Rothschild and the Zionist Federation. In the Declaration, Britain had pledged to help establish a Jewish "national home" in Palestine that would also give due regard to the rights of the Palestinians. They had promised to support the creation of independent Arab states—including, so the Arabs thought, one for the Palestinians, a commitment the British later denied they had made.

From mid-1918 until 1920, the United States joined the Allies in sending troops to the new Communist Russia, declaring that their purpose was to safeguard Allied war stores and protect Russian ports against German attack. But the Allied forces also supported anti-Bolshevik factions attempting to overthrow the new government (and denied the Russians a place at the peace negotiations). The seeds of distrust between the United States and the Soviets were then augmented by the refusal of the United States to recognize the Soviet regime.

## THE LEAGUE OF NATIONS

Wilson returned to the United States with his treaty, convinced that its most important feature was the charter of the League of Nations. The League was structured to contain a world court, an assembly of all independent nations, and a council led by five permanent members; it would provide an arena for the peaceful resolution of conflict, and its charter (adopted as part of the treaty) included a security provision that committed member nations to collectively oppose aggression and protect the territorial integrity of all countries. Pleased as he was with the charter, Wilson significantly underestimated the opposition it would arouse in Washington, particularly given his refusal to consult in advance with Republican leaders or with the Senate Foreign Relations Committee.

Many Republicans, including Henry Cabot Lodge, the head of the Foreign Relations Committee, refused to accept

A 1919 cartoon depicting Wilson's relationship to the League of Nations.

the League without formal, written reservations. They were particularly eager to guarantee that the United States maintain its autonomy on immigration and tariff issues; they also insisted that any measures taken by the League to police the peace would not undermine Congress's constitutional right to declare war. They were, in effect, wary of any collective agreements that could tie the hands of the United States. Other, more progressive senators, such as La Follette, criticized the League as preserving the special powers of imperialist nations. In July 1919, when the treaty reached the Senate for ratification, Lodge—a personal antagonist of Wilson—bottled it up in his committee.

Wilson, however, would not agree to any reservations, contending that trying to modify the covenant of the League would destroy the "whole vital structure" of the treaty. Furious at Lodge, in early September Wilson mounted an arduous speaking campaign in the West to rally public opinion behind the League. Three weeks, 9,000 miles, and thirty-seven speeches later, he collapsed and returned to Washington. On October 2, he suffered a severe stroke that left him an invalid, his mental and physical powers impaired. Thereafter, he was kept isolated by his wife, Edith Galt, who limited the information he received and the people he met.

On September 10, Lodge released the treaty to the Senate with amendments designed to satisfy the Republicans' reservations. Had Wilson been willing to compromise, the Senate might have ratified the treaty and put the United States into the League. But Wilson refused to accede to Lodge's terms. Lacking the necessary two-thirds Senate majority with or without reservations, the treaty died in November, and an attempt to revive it the following March failed utterly. To a significant extent, the Senate's action reflected attitudes toward the treaty in the country at large: despite Wilson's desperate speech-making tour, the idea of U.S. membership in the League enjoyed only limited popular support. Weary of war, many Americans preferred to avoid entangling alliances with the European powers. In October 1921, the United States ratified the Treaty of Berlin, which normalized its relations with Germany on the basis of the Versailles settlement without recognizing the League. Similar agreements soon followed with Austria and Hungary.

With its rejection of the League and the Treaty of Versailles, the United States pulled back from the active internationalism and idealism that had characterized its rhetoric and its policies when first entering the war. But the United States, in fact, was less isolated from other nations than at any time in its history. It was closely tied to Europe and to Latin Amer-

ica in trade and culture; technological advances, such as the radio and aircraft, promised to strengthen the links. The war years, moreover, had made the United States the world leader in international trade and had transformed it from a debtor to a creditor nation, becoming the globe's most important banker. The isolationist impulses that coursed through the body politic coexisted with this expanding network of international linkages. Moreover, the Wilsonian vision of a new world order shaped by a blend of democratic idealism, alliances, and enforcement was rebuffed but not extinguished. The League of Nations did exist, and the United States eventually participated in some of its discussions. Wilson's vision would continue to appeal to a number of Americans concerned with maintaining the security of the United States in an increasingly interdependent world.

## Coda: The Great Flu

If Americans in 1918 needed any further evidence of the frailty of human life and the interdependence of the world's peoples, it came in the form of the deadliest epidemic ever to strike modern societies. In the summer of that year, Americans

Officials inspecting Chicago street cleaners during the influenza outbreak, 1918.

began to be felled by a particularly virulent form of influenza: the first outbreaks had occurred earlier in the year around army camps in Kansas, and in July a second wave hit Boston at the same time that it struck cities in France and in Africa. Soldiers, crowded into training cramps in the South and East of the United States, quickly passed the disease to one another, with thousands falling ill simultaneously and many dying. Doctors and nurses succumbed in large numbers.

As the disease leapt from city to city across the United States and abroad, physicians, scientists, and public health officials desperately searched for a cure or a means of treatment. Although aware of viruses (too small to be seen by any technology then available), they focused their efforts instead on finding the bacillus or germ that caused the disease, as they had done successfully with yellow fever and other epidemics. But despite a prodigious scientific enterprise, in the United States and abroad, the search for a cure failed. It would not be until the 1940s, with the invention of the electron microscope, that viruses could be seen and distinguished from one another.

In the fall and winter of 1918–19, the epidemic ran its course. Across the globe, it killed between 20 and 50 million people, most of them in a three-month period in the fall of 1918. Among the dead were nearly 700,000 Americans, including more soldiers than had been killed in battle.

## Suggested Reading

John Keegan, *The First World War* (1998)

David M. Kennedy, *Over Here: The First World War and American Society* (1980)

Lloyd E. Ambrosius, *Wilsonian Statecraft: Theory and Practice of Liberal Internationalism during World War I* (1991)

Ellis Hawley, *The Great War and the Search for Modern Order: A History of the American People and Their Institutions, 1917–1933* (1979)

Arthur S. Link, *Woodrow Wilson: Revolution, War, and Peace* (1979)

## Summary
### QUESTIONS

- What were the key events or developments that led the United States into World War I?

- In what ways did the war draw the federal government into new types of activities and policies?

- How did the war affect the lives of Americans at home?

- What were the major terms of the Treaty of Versailles?

- Why did the United States not join the League of Nations?

## Chronology

| | |
|---|---|
| **August 1914** | World War I begins. |
| **May 7, 1915** | German submarine sinks the Lusitania. |
| **1916** | Margaret Sanger opens first birth-control clinic, in Brooklyn. |
| **April 6, 1917** | United States declares war against Germany. |
| **November 6, 1917** | Bolshevik revolution succeeds in Russia. |
| **January 1918** | President Wilson presents his Fourteen Points. |
| **September 1918** | Influenza epidemic strikes the United States. |

## Key Terms

Neutrality (p. 658)

Preparedness (pp. 660–661)

Inflation (pp. 662–663)

Fourteen Points (p. 670)

League of Nations (p. 672)

# A CONSERVATIVE INTERLUDE:

## THE 1920s

*Blues*, a 1929 painting by Archibald Motley, Jr., depicts one side of the 1920s: dance halls, jazz bands, and drinking despite the Prohibition.

- *What were the most significant political and social trends in America in the postwar years?*

- *What spurred the national economy in the 1920s?*

- *How did American culture and society change in the 1920s?*

- *What was Hoover's approach to government when he took office as president?*

The year 1919 was one of the most unsettled in the history of the Republic. While the great flu epidemic gradually ebbed and President Wilson pursued his dream of a League of Nations, the country made an uneasy transition from the excitement of war to the routines of peacetime. Soldiers—many of them changed forever by their experiences in uniform—were demobilized and sent home to search for jobs and housing; military contracts were cut back, forcing plants that had been refitted for war production to quickly shift gears. Prices kept soaring, straining many household budgets to the breaking point: by mid-1920, the cost of living was more than twice what it had been in 1914. Social tensions already visible during the war boiled over into an extraordinary wave of strikes, racial violence, and repression of political radicals and the foreign-born.

The 1920s, in contrast, would turn out to be a rather calm, uneventful decade in which most citizens turned away from politics and international affairs and focused their energies on private goals. Reflecting the dominant conservative mood, the Republican Party came to power in Washington (as well as in many states), intent on supporting the business community and diluting the governmental activism that had characterized the Progressive Era. Thanks in part to an economic boom that began in 1922 and lasted until 1929, the Republicans succeeded, for a time, in achieving those goals while presiding over a tranquil nation. But none of this seemed foreordained—or even likely—during the tumult of 1919.

## Red, White, and Black

### THE RED SCARE

The great strike wave of 1919 began on January 21 in Seattle when 35,000 shipyard workers walked off their jobs demanding better pay after two years of wage controls and rising prices. Several weeks later, the city's Central Labor Council, representing all unions in Seattle, declared a general strike in sympathy with the shipyard workers. For five days, 60,000 strikers brought the city to a standstill, paralyzing business and closing the schools. Seattle's mayor, Ole Hanson, denounced the strike's leaders as dangerous radicals who wanted to "take possession of our American government." He appointed thousands of deputies and asked for federal troops to help subdue the strike.

The Seattle strike lasted only a week, but for the remainder of the year, throughout the country, workers marched in picket lines to demand higher wages, shorter hours, and union recognition: in all, more than 3,500 separate strikes took place. In September, Boston police walked off their jobs to protest the firing of nineteen policemen simply for joining a union. Without police on the streets, violence and looting broke out, leading President Wilson to denounce the strike as a "crime against civilization." Shortly thereafter, 365,000 steel workers—many of whom were still laboring more than eighty hours a week—went on strike in response to the refusal of employers to recognize their union. With steel company executives denouncing the union's leaders as dangerous "reds," the strike was broken in two months. That same fall, nearly 400,000 bituminous coal miners walked out in a wage dispute; at the request of the mine owners, the federal government, invoking wartime powers granted by special legislation, issued an injunction to end the strike. The miners ignored the injunction, claiming that the powers had expired when the war ended. Only a sizable raise, coupled with an appeal from the president, brought the strike to an end.

This labor unrest conjured up images of a working-class uprising led by political radicals. Such images seemed to match events abroad: not only had a communist revolution succeeded in Russia, but as the war ended there were revolts in Hungary,

Bavaria, and Berlin. In March 1919, the Russian Communist Party even established the Comintern (or Third International), designed to agitate for communism around the globe. Meanwhile, the Socialist Party remained a presence—albeit a peaceful one—in the United States, and September 1919 witnessed the formation of two small American communist parties.

The nation's political temperature rose further owing to a series of bombings and attempted bombings that appeared to be tied to radical, or prolabor, political views. In the spring of 1919, a homemade bomb was delivered by mail to the office of Ole Hanson, Seattle's mayor. Within days, a similar bomb exploded at the home of a Georgia senator; postal inspectors then found more than a dozen bomb-containing packages addressed to John D. Rockefeller, the postmaster-general, and other prominent citizens. In early June, bombs exploded simultaneously in eight cities, killing two people and demolishing the entrance to the home of Attorney General A. Mitchell Palmer.

Bartolomeo Vanzetti (left) and Nicola Sacco leave jail at Dedham, Massachusetts, en route to the courthouse where they were sentenced by Judge Webster Thayer to die in the electric chair.

The combination of strikes and acts of violence ignited the "Red Scare," an outbreak of public and private repression aimed at political radicals (and especially foreign-born radicals). States passed severe sedition laws under which hundreds of accused subversives were imprisoned; others lost their jobs or fell victim to vigilante mobs who stormed radicals' headquarters and seized their literature or disrupted political demonstrations. The New York State Assembly expelled five duly elected Socialist members, and Attorney General Palmer told Congress that communists planned "to rise up and destroy the Government at one fell swoop." In late 1919 and early 1920, Palmer, aided by the head of the Justice Department's new anti-radical division, J. Edgar Hoover, mounted a series of raids (the "Palmer raids") on radical groups, often without either search or arrest warrants. His forces arrested over 6,000 people and found three pistols and no explosives. Most of those arrested were later exonerated, although the government deported some 556 persons of foreign birth.

The xenophobia (fear of foreigners) tapped by the Red Scare, moreover, spilled over onto immigrants who had nothing to do with radicalism. In 1920, a mob burned immigrants' homes in the southern Illinois mining town of West Frankfort; California passed a law forbidding Japanese ownership of land; and Henry Ford launched a newspaper campaign against Jews. The president-general of the Daughters of the American Revolution proclaimed that "nothing will save the life of this free Republic if these foreign leeches are not cut and cast out."

The Red Scare abated in 1920 as defenders of civil liberties criticized Palmer's actions and spokesmen for industries dependent on immigrant labor began attacking efforts to associate all foreigners with radicalism. In addition, Palmer himself lost credibility when his prediction of a widespread communist uprising on May 1, 1920 did not materialize. There was no panic about a conspiracy of radicals when, in September of that year, a powerful bomb went off outside J. P. Morgan's Wall Street office, killing thirty-eight people and injuring at least fifty-seven.

***The Sacco and Vanzetti Case.*** The most well-known single event of the Red Scare was the criminal case against Nicola Sacco and Bartolomeo Vanzetti, both Italian immigrants and political anarchists. In 1920, the two were tried and convicted of murdering the paymaster of a shoe factory in Braintree, Massachusetts. Both staunchly asserted their innocence, and their numerous defenders contended that they had been found guilty on the basis of little evidence and a mass of prejudice against radicals and immigrants. In response to widespread public criticism of the court, the Massachusetts governor appointed a blue-ribbon panel to reexamine the evidence and the trial transcript. The panel concluded that Sacco and Vanzetti had been rightly convicted, a verdict that still divides historians and that extended the bitter aftertaste of the Red Scare deep into the 1920s. On August 22, 1927, despite worldwide protests, the two men died in the electric chair.

*Race Riots.* The social tensions and violence that erupted in the postwar era also touched race relations, particularly in areas where returning soldiers found themselves competing for jobs with black migrants. Lynch mobs rampaged through parts of the South, and race riots broke out in twenty-five towns and cities, including Charleston and Washington, D.C., between April and October 1919. The bloodiest of these riots occurred in Chicago in the summer of 1919. It was set off when a black teenager, swimming in Lake Michigan, floated across the invisible line that divided black and white sections of the beach; the hostilities that erupted lasted for a week, leaving 38 people (including 23 blacks) dead, more than 500 injured, and 1,000 homeless. Two years later, Tulsa, Oklahoma, witnessed an equally devastating explosion of racial antagonism. A face-off at a court house, where armed African Americans (some of them veterans) had gathered to prevent the lynching of a young bootblack, led a heavily armed white mob to march on and destroy much of the thriving black community of Greenwood. At least 35 people were killed—some estimates ran much higher—and more than a thousand saw their homes destroyed.

## REPUBLICAN REIGN

The Red Scare, the attacks on organized labor, and the defeat of the Treaty of Versailles were all signs that the political mood of the nation was shifting to the right. Not surprisingly, then, the Republican Party in 1920 looked forward optimistically to taking the White House and retaining the control of Congress that it had won in 1918.

The Democratic convention nominated Governor James M. Cox of Ohio and Wilson's secretary of the navy, Franklin Delano Roosevelt of New York (a cousin of Theodore Roosevelt). They defended the League of Nations and Wilsonian idealism to an electorate predominantly sick of both. The Republicans, badly split by warring factions, finally chose their candidate in the smoke-filled room that spawned the phrase "smoke-filled room." The man the party's leaders selected was Warren G. Harding, an undistinguished but affable senator from Ohio. Harding said little about the League of Nations and promised the country "normalcy," by which he meant ending the Wilson administration's foreign and domestic activism. Eugene Debs, defiantly nominated for the presidency by the Socialist Party even though he was in jail, received 1 million votes. Still, the postwar swing to conservatism produced a landslide for Harding: he won 60 percent of the popular vote and 404 of the 531 electoral votes. For the first time in memory, the number of qualified voters who cast ballots fell below 50 percent, reflecting both fatigue with politics and relatively low turnout among newly enfranchised women voters.

Harding and his vice-president, Calvin Coolidge, replaced the progressivism and internationalism of the Wilson years with a probusiness conservatism. Yet while pursuing a formal isolationism, the government was attentive to national security and helped foster a variety of private initiatives abroad.

African-American men in Tulsa, walking to the convention hall after being "captured" by whites.

*Harding, Then Coolidge.* The Republicans took office just as the economy was sinking into a sharp cyclical downturn. Skyrocketing prices had led to the accumulation of excess inventories, and in the winter of 1920–21 the speculative wave crested—assisted by a tightening of credit by the Federal Reserve. Industrial output plummeted in 1921, and prices (to the relief of many consumers) fell even more sharply. As hundreds of thousands of farmers went bankrupt and millions of workers lost their jobs, pressure mounted on the administration to take action. (The unemployment rate probably reached 12–15 percent, but the government did not yet collect unemployment statistics.) In September 1921, Harding's highly esteemed secretary of commerce, Herbert Hoover, finally did respond, organizing the President's Conference on Unemployment—the first time that the federal government even tacitly accepted some responsibility for the problem of joblessness. After meeting for several weeks, however, the conference concluded that there was little for the federal government to do: "meeting the emergency of unemployment" was primarily the responsibility of local communities.

The Republicans' inaction did not cost them politically; the economy rebounded early in 1922, and it expanded fairly steadily until the end of the decade. The prosperity helped to make Harding an enormously popular president. A handsome man of limited talents, Harding surrounded himself with a bevy

Warren Harding (left), twenty-ninth president of the United States (1921–23), and Calvin Coolidge, thirtieth president (1923–29).

of political cronies from Ohio as well as highly respected cabinet officials, such as Hoover and Secretary of the Treasury Andrew Mellon. It was the former group—the Ohio gang, which held various offices in the administration—that got Harding in trouble; they engaged in a small orgy of corruption, much of it run from an illegal liquor establishment and brothel operated by a close confidant of the attorney general. The most celebrated incident involved Secretary of the Interior Albert Fall, who leased government oil reserves to private corporations, without competitive bidding, in return for satchels of cash delivered to his relatives. After the transactions were exposed, Fall became the first cabinet officer in American history to go to prison.

Harding himself, however, was spared most of the revelations and the taint of corruption: just as the scandals began to come to light, he died of a heart attack in August 1923. Harding was mourned as a beloved president by a public that did not yet know about most of the corruption. His successor, Calvin Coolidge, seemed the perfect antidote.

Stern, reserved, morally upright, and taciturn, the governor of Massachusetts at the time of the 1919 Boston police strike, Coolidge had won admiration then for telegraphing Samuel Gompers of the AFL: "There is no right to strike against the public safety by anybody, anytime, anywhere." Coolidge retained the notable and honest members of Harding's cabinet and prevented the corruption scandal from weakening the Republican Party. In 1924, Coolidge ran for election in his own right in a three-way race that pitted him against Senator Robert M. La Follette of Wisconsin, the candidate of the reconstructed Progressive Party, and the Democratic nominee, John W. Davis, a little-known corporate lawyer from New York. Coolidge won 54 percent of the popular vote, a decisive ratification of his conservative Republicanism.

The Harding and Coolidge administrations emphasized efficiency, limited government, and the encouragement of business. In 1921, at Harding's urging, Congress approved a Budget and Accounting Act that required the president to prepare an annual budget with the help of a new Bureau of the Budget and submit it to the House and Senate. In 1922, the administration obtained passage of the Fordney-McCumber Tariff, which raised general tariff rates to their highest levels in history—although it did make special provisions for those "most favored nations" that treated American exports generously. The tariff increases were designed both to protect some domestic businesses and to lessen the government's financial reliance on the income and corporate taxes that had been passed under Wilson. In keeping with his probusiness convictions, Treasury Secretary Mellon fought doggedly to lower taxes (over the opposition of a determined band of congressional progressives); he finally succeeded in 1926 and 1928 when Congress agreed to sharply cut inheritance taxes as well as personal income taxes, particularly for the wealthy.

Indeed, President Coolidge—who was more ideological than his predecessor—stated explicitly that he wanted his administration to be a "businessmen's government," and he went far toward achieving that goal. Regulatory agencies like the Federal Trade Commission did very little regulating, while other branches of the administration were openly hostile to organized labor. The Republicans actively supported scientific research on new, potentially profitable technologies, including those in the aeronautics industry; and the notoriously penny-pinching Coolidge agreed to the establishment in 1926 of a well-funded Aeronautics Branch in the Department of Commerce. Coolidge, however, offered only minimal help to farmers (see p. 686), and in 1927 and 1928 he stonewalled requests for federal assistance from victims, many of them black, of a catastrophic flood on the Mississippi River. The government, Coolidge noted, was not obligated to protect people "against the hazards of the elements." The *Wall Street*

---

*American Journal*

## What If Disaster Strikes?

*The passage that follows is taken from an article in the New York Times, May 1, 1927. The passage describes several of the different ways in which the swollen river overwhelmed or penetrated the levees on shore that were built to contain the Mississippi and to prevent floods.*

"The roar of the river's seething yellow waters may be heard for miles, filling the countryside with terror; great trees, which have been torn up by the roots, are drawn into minature maelstroms called "suck-holes" with reports like cannon shots: the current changes direction and a new channel is cut, usually where it will do the most damage: inland seas suddenly replace peaceful farms. . .

In the river, a familiar island vanishes as if dissolved by a magician, and half a mile further down, another to replace it appears with equal swiftness. Through broken levees the racing waters pour to their work of destruction, covering newly planted fields. Sweeping through houses and barns, they take along with them—tossing them about as if they were playthings—the bodies of animals and cherished household possessions. . .

The steady pressure of the flood forces some water through the levees; so long as this seepage remains clear, all is well, for the structure of the levee is holding. But let the seepage show muddy, and every one knows there is trouble ahead. . .

If the labor gangs who keep watch on the levee can sink sacks on the rive side of the embankment and thus check the leak, the menace will be quickly brought to an end. If a sand-boil appears, that is, a geyser-like formation behind the great revetment, it is ringed round at once with sacked earth and the water left free to spurt until pressure is equalized. . .

It is when a sand-boil gets away, though, that one of the most thrilling and unforgettable of all the many unusual sights and sounds that attend a Mississippi Valley flood may be seen and heard. . .

Then comes a crevasse. Crevasses are sometimes slow in arriving, but once begun they grow with terrifying swiftness. A tiny gash is made in a levee; it widens slowly for a few minutes as the beaten watchers continue their futile struggles, and then in a twinkling, the levee "goes out."

Chunks of earth, growing larger as the seconds pass, drop into the yellow flood, which leaps roaring past its barriers, and with a savage eagerness, races to its work of destruction. Frequently, the labor gangs are hard put to it to escape, so swiftly do the waters slash away the broken ends of the levee. Crevasses a mile or more in width are not uncommon; the area of the territory flooded through them depends only upon how far it is from the river to high ground."

From "Again the Old Dragon Mississippi Fumes" by Herschel Brickell, *New York Times*, May 1, 1927

A highway under water during the Mississippi River flood of 1927.

*Journal* observed approvingly that "never before has a government been so completely fused with business."

The Supreme Court, led by Chief Justice (and former president) William Howard Taft, deepened the conservative thrust. In 1922, the Court dispensed with protections that unions thought they had gained in the Clayton Act (1914) by permitting them to be sued under the antitrust laws. It overturned a federal law restricting child labor, and in 1923, in *Adkins v. Children's Hospital,* the Court reversed precedent and struck down a minimum wage law for women—claiming, among other things, that the achievement of suffrage by women had neutralized their right to special protection from the state.

The federal government under Harding and Coolidge, thus, halted or diluted Progressive Era reforms in key areas: the regulation of business; the distribution of tax burdens; and the protection of children, women, and labor. Only in the states and in individual cities did reformers achieve much success in the 1920s. Numerous states adopted (or enlarged) their workers' compensation systems; some sponsored innovative programs for the poor; and many cities streamlined their administrations while establishing zoning boards to limit chaotic, unbridled growth. Cities and states continued to be laboratories for experimentation in public policy, but their efforts were not replicated in Washington.

### FOREIGN AFFAIRS

Despite the nation's recoil from war and foreign entanglements, policymakers strengthened the military's capacity to deal with the increasingly high-technology character of defense. The Chemical Warfare Service became a permanent part of the army, while the armed services installed aeronautics facilities and a new naval laboratory on the banks of the Potomac.

Simultaneously, the government sought international agreements for arms control and against war. In 1921, responding to pressure from progressives in the Senate, the Harding administration convened delegates from nine countries for the Washington Arms Limitation Conference. Secretary of State Charles Evans Hughes, a former governor of New York and presidential candidate, surprised the gathering by calling for each nation to scrap a number of ships. The delegates then surprised the world by agreeing to the proposal in principle. By 1922, when it adjourned, the conference had agreed to nine treaties, including one that allowed the United States and Britain a fixed warship tonnage superior to that of Japan, France, and Italy while imposing a naval holiday by stopping all battleship construction for ten years. Britain, France, Japan, and the United States also agreed to respect each other's possessions in the Pacific. All nine nations pledged that they would honor Chinese sovereignty and the principle of the Open Door (see Chapter 21).

In 1928, Frank B. Kellogg, Hughes's successor as secretary of state, worked with the French foreign minister to develop the Kellogg-Briand Pact, a treaty outlawing war. The pact was ultimately signed by sixty-two nations, with the Senate ratifying it early in 1929 by a vote of 85 to 1. As a practical matter, the pact, which lacked any means of enforcement and allowed military actions for self-defense, had little weight. But the strong support it gained revealed that Americans across a wide spectrum wanted no more of war.

American policy toward Latin America was more ambivalent, reflecting a mix of interventionist reflexes and a new impulse to treat its southern neighbors with more respect. The United States ended military surveillance of Cuba's internal affairs and approved a treaty that compensated Colombia for its loss of Panama around the building of the Panama Canal (see Chapter 21). It also recognized Mexico's revolutionary government in return for an agreement to settle American claims and respect the oil rights granted to foreign companies before 1917. In 1923, Hughes signed a Pan-American treaty providing mechanisms for peaceful dispute resolution among the American nations. And in 1924, the United States withdrew the troops that Wilson had sent to the Dominican Republic—but only after creating and training a Dominican national guard, one of whose officers, Rafael Trujillo, quickly seized power and ruled over the nation until 1961.

In 1924, the United States was, in fact, still controlling the finances of ten Latin American nations, and the Coolidge administration, like its predecessors, felt entitled to intervene militarily to protect American interests. Coolidge sent troops to Honduras in 1924 to restore order in a small country dominated by the United Fruit Company; the American military was a presence in Haiti from 1915 to 1934. In 1925, Coolidge withdrew American soldiers from Nicaragua, where they had been maintaining a pro-American regime since 1912. Less than two years later, Coolidge sent them back, where they lent support to conservatives who were battling—among others—nationalist forces led by Cesar Augusto Sandino. Marines remained in Nicaragua until 1933, when they handed over the task of maintaining order to another American-trained national guard, headed by General Anastasio Somoza—whose allies murdered Sandino and whose family ended up imposing a corrupt dictatorship on Nicaragua until 1979.

*A Private Internationalism.* The government's quasi-isolationist policies in the 1920s masked a private internationalism—engagements abroad by private citizens, philanthropic organizations, and businesses. Scientists took advanced training in the great European centers of research and brought home the revolutionary new physics of the atom called "quantum mechanics." Civic leaders toured European cities, returning with ideas about urban planning and ways that private corporations might serve the greater public interest.

The U.S. government often encouraged this private internationalism and was itself involved with agencies of the League of Nations through unofficial observers and connections. From 1921 to 1923, Secretary of Commerce Herbert Hoover revived his wartime program of private famine relief to help feed approximately 10 million starving Russians—a humanitarian gesture he hoped would also thwart Bolshevik ends. American business, meanwhile, kept expanding its interests abroad, exporting more manufactured goods, agricultural products, and capital: thanks largely to the activities of American banks like J. P. Morgan and Company, total overseas American investment more than doubled between 1919 and 1930. This export of American capital was indeed essential to the postwar economic order. The United States had become a creditor nation (it was owed substantial sums by the Europeans), but high tariff barriers were preventing Eu-

ropean countries from obtaining dollars by selling goods in the United States. American loans and investments abroad, thus, supplied the dollars that Europeans needed to repay their debts from World War I and to purchase American goods.

In 1924, the United States intervened in Europe when Germany, its economy reeling from runaway inflation, began defaulting on its reparations payments to the Allies. Faced with a French and Belgian attempt to collect reparations by force, Hoover and Hughes suggested that a committee of private bankers headed by Charles G. Dawes negotiate the dispute. The resulting Dawes Plan adjusted reparations payments to levels consistent with German economic conditions and arranged for an injection of capital into the German economy. The capital, which came largely from American investors, helped restabilize the German currency and create a boom in the German economy. The United States, however, refused to restructure the $10 billion debt the Allies owed the U.S. Treasury.

## A Prosperous Nation

Undergirding the political popularity of the Republicans, as well as the nation's international influence, was remarkable economic growth. Gross domestic product rose roughly 50 percent between 1921 and 1929, prices were stable, and interest rates stayed relatively low. Thanks in part to the continued electrification of industry and to organizational lessons learned during the war, productivity soared in many industries, generating large profits for business while permitting millions of workers to earn higher real incomes.

### CONSTRUCTION

Between 1919 and 1926, a building boom produced new houses at a rate of almost 900,000 a year, more than twice that of previous decades. The expansion, centered around cities, made home-owning a real prospect for former renters. Even people without substantial incomes could purchase homes with "balloon mortgages," which required making only interest payments during the life of the loan while deferring repayment of the principal until the end of the loan. Most new houses included modern bathrooms with sinks and tubs, taps for hot and cold water, a toilet, and ceramic tile. Families replaced old coal or wood-fired stoves with gas or electric ranges, which left no ash residue to be cleaned away.

### THE AUTO INDUSTRY

Technological improvements helped inflame the American romance with the car. By the 1920s, automobiles could be started with an electric switch rather than by laborious hand-cranking. Their closed steel bodies and roll-down windows protected passengers against wind and road dust. And they were cheap, thanks in part to Henry Ford's assembly-line methods of manufacturing—the price of the Model T dropped to $294 in 1924, half of what it had been in 1912 (see Chapter 22).

The Ford Motor Company's dominant position in the industry began to erode in the face of competition from the new Chrysler Corporation and General Motors Corporation (GM). Ford, restrained in his approach to marketing, once quipped that Americans could have a Ford in any color they wanted so long as it was black. GM and Chrysler cut into Ford's market by introducing competitively priced cars in a variety of colors, optional equipment, model and styling changes, and, in the case of GM, the opportunity to buy cars on credit. Between 1921 and 1929, passenger car production more than tripled, reaching 4.8 million vehicles a year. The number of cars registered in the United States nearly tripled from 9 million to 26.5 million.

In 1916, pushed by constituents from both cities and farms, Congress had passed a Federal Road Bill that provided funds for states with highway departments; another was approved in 1921 designating 200,000 miles of roadway as eligible for a 50 percent federal subsidy. The 1921 act also set up a Bureau of Public Roads to plan a national highway system that, like the canals and railroads of earlier times, would stitch the country's cities and isolated rural communities into a more tightly knit nation.

Car production boosted the economy by stimulating the steel, paint, textile, electric, and tire industries. Car ownership also created a demand for oil, road construction, and assorted new

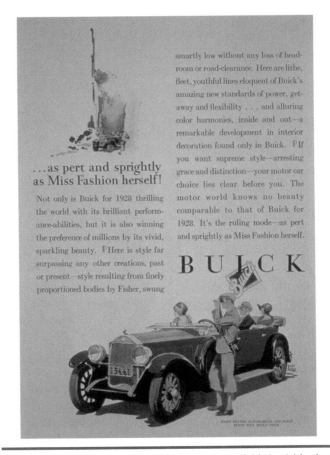

...as pert and sprightly as Miss Fashion herself!

Not only is Buick for 1928 thrilling the world with its brilliant performance-abilities, but it is also winning the preference of millions by its vivid, sparkling beauty. Here is style far surpassing any other creations, past or present—style resulting from finely proportioned bodies by Fisher, swung smartly low without any loss of head-room or road-clearance. Here are lithe, fleet, youthful lines eloquent of Buick's amazing new standards of power, get-away and flexibility . . . and alluring color harmonies, inside and out—a remarkable development in interior decoration found only in Buick. If you want supreme style—arresting grace and distinction—your motor car choice lies clear before you. The motor world knows no beauty comparable to that of Buick for 1928. It's the ruling mode—as pert and sprightly as Miss Fashion herself.

BUICK

An ad for the 1928 Buick, a General Motors car available in vivid colors.

A gas station designed to blend with the surrounding residential neighborhood in Macomb, Illinois, 1920s.

businesses—including car dealerships, gas stations, repair shops, parts-supply houses, roadside diners, motor hotels (soon contracted to "motels"), and the fast-food chains pioneered in 1926 by White Castle.

## APPLIANCES AND THE RADIO

The economic boom was further fueled by the ongoing electrification of the country. Ever more power lines crisscrossed the cities, lighting factories, homes, and streets, moving streetcars and assembly lines, driving drill presses and lathes. By the end of the decade, about 70 percent of American homes, including most in urban areas, were wired for electricity.

A new industry sprang up to meet the burgeoning demand for electric appliances such as irons, fans, vacuum cleaners, toasters, stoves, washing machines, sewing machines, and refrigerators. To encourage the purchase of these goods, retailers permitted people to buy on the installment plan, which created $2 billion to $3 billion in consumer debt. The small firms that initially constituted the appliance industry were often bought up by larger companies such as General Electric and Westinghouse, which then improved the products in research

The broadcast studio for station WDY in New Jersey, with drapes and towels used for acoustical control, 1921.

laboratories. By the 1920s, organized corporate research had become the standard in American industry, especially its high-technology branches; the number of industrial laboratories at least doubled over the decade, to more than a thousand. American industry was reported to be spending $133 million a year on research, twice as much as the federal government. "Science is not a thing apart," the *Saturday Evening Post* observed; "it is the bedrock of business."

The star product of the industrial laboratories was the radio, made possible by the invention of vacuum tubes early in the century. Consisting of a set of electrodes in a glass cylinder free of air, vacuum tubes could greatly amplify broadcast signals. Taking advantage of this technology, ham (amateur) radio operators around the country began to broadcast recorded music and local news. In 1920, Frank Conrad, a Westinghouse engineer and ham operator in Pittsburgh, began airing regularly scheduled music programs from his garage; he soon moved his transmitter to the top of the Westinghouse factory, obtained a federal license under the call letters KDKA, and proceeded to broadcast the results of the 1920 presidential election—thus transforming radio from two-way conversations into a medium of mass communication.

Radio stations soon proliferated across the country—500 began operating in 1922 alone—often interfering with each other by transmitting programs on the same or closely neighboring wavelengths. In 1927, Congress passed the Radio Act, which set up a Federal Radio Commission to work with the secretary of commerce in issuing licenses to radio stations and regulating stations' wavelengths and geographical range. Station transmitters grew far more powerful, able to cover at least 30,000 square miles. Meanwhile, the price of radios dropped; by 1930, almost half of American households owned radios.

Between 1923 and 1929, partly as a result of the explosive growth of the construction, auto, and radio industries, corporate income increased from $8.3 billion to $10.6 billion, while personal savings jumped from $19.7 billion to $28.4 billion. Now even working families could afford some of the products that technological innovation and mass production were making available.

## SHADOWS ON THE ECONOMIC LANDSCAPE

Despite the rosy overall picture, the prosperity of the 1920s was neither uniform nor evenly shared. Two of the mainstays of the industrial revolution, for example, the coal and textile industries, faltered significantly, as prices fell for much for the decade; New England textile communities were hit particularly hard as manufacturers fled to the South in search of cheaper labor. The railroads also did poorly, owing both to overcapacity and to competition from the young trucking industry.

*Agriculture.* The 1920s were also gloomy years for farmers. Although the prices of farm goods had soared during the war and remained high in 1919–20, they plummeted during the downturn of 1921, more sharply than did prices of manufactured goods. Agricultural prices, moreover, remained low for the entire decade: in 1929, for example, wheat, potatoes, and cotton were all selling for roughly half of what they had brought ten years earlier. The politically important parity ratio (an index comparing farm prices to the prices of goods farmers had to buy) rarely rose above 90 (compared to the figure of 100 for the good years of 1910–14).

Equally important, many farmers had incurred new debts during the wartime and postwar boom, as they bought land and machinery in the expectation of producing more at higher prices. When prices fell, paying off their loans became difficult, if not impossible, and many were obliged to declare bankruptcy or sell out. Small farmers were hit particularly hard, accentuating the renewed trend toward large-scale agricultural enterprises (later called "agribusiness"). In the 1920s, "farm factories" sprang up in the wheat-growing regions of Montana, North Dakota, and Kansas, in the fruit-growing areas of California, in the cotton belt of the deep South, and on livestock and poultry farms from Texas to Delaware. These enterprises sought to increase profits by adopting industrial methods of production and by exploiting research carried out by land-grant universities, the Department of Agriculture, and privately owned seed companies. Innovative techniques in farming increased the capital requirements and commonly led to further consolidations.

Throughout the 1920s, American farms produced more than the national market could absorb. President Coolidge signed into law several measures to assist farmers, including one to facilitate the cooperative buying and selling of their products. But he twice vetoed the popular McNary-Haugen Bill, which proposed that the government stabilize agricultural prices by buying up surplus production and selling it abroad. Coolidge argued that the bill sanctioned price fixing and would antagonize foreign producers.

Even on larger farms, men and women commonly lacked access to electricity and thus most electrical appliances. Men might ride a tractor, but women still did their washing with a scrub board, drew their water from a well with a hand-worked pump, and heated water on an old-fashioned stove. Family members trudged outside to use a privy even in the depths of winter. In the course of the decade, 6 million people left the land for the cities.

*Labor.* Even in the more urban, industrial sectors of the economy, the fruits of prosperity were not equally shared; the decade, in fact, witnessed a significant redistribution of wealth upward. As a result of Secretary Mellon's tax initiatives, people with annual incomes of $1 million paid less than one-third of the taxes they had paid at the beginning of the decade. Meanwhile, weak antitrust enforcement helped foster growing corporate concentration in numerous industries, including automobiles, films, coal mining, clothing, and grocers. By 1929, the 200 largest corporations controlled 20 percent of national wealth and 50 percent of corporate wealth. And despite the rapid economic growth, about one-third of families earned less than $2,000 a year, the minimum estimated for a decent standard of living; roughly one-fifth earned less than $1,000.

Organized labor, often defeated in the strikes of 1919, was further weakened by the economic downturn of 1921. Union membership fell from more than 5 million at the end of the war to 3.6 million in 1923, and it did not rise again until the late 1930s. This stagnation in union membership—unusual for a prosperous era—was due in part to the anti-union policies of the increasingly important large firms that relied on mass production, scientific management, and semiskilled labor. Managers of these firms used an array of different methods to keep unions at bay. Some would only hire workers if they signed "yellow-dog contracts" (affirming that a worker did not belong to a union and would be fired for joining one). Others instituted "welfare capitalism" programs that included company-sponsored (and -controlled) unions, life insurance benefits, profit sharing, and athletic teams. Paternalistic in thrust, these programs were designed to encourage loyalty, efficiency, and low turnover while not permitting workers' organizations to gain any independent power.

The conditions of assembly-line work in many mass production industries continued to exact heavy mental and physical tolls. Although Henry Ford had reduced the work week in his plants to 40 hours, many industrial workers continued to spend six 8-hour days on the job. A foreign journalist described what such work was like as he observed a riveter on the line at Ford's huge River Rouge complex near Detroit: "At

The auto assembly line at the Ford plant in Edgewater, New Jersey. Note the rails and chain by which the chassis was moved from worker to worker.

8 A.M. the worker takes his place at the side of a narrow platform down the center of which runs a great chain moving at the rate of a foot a minute. . . . The chain never stops. The pace never varies. The man is part of the chain, the feeder, and the slave of it."

## METROPOLITAN LIFE

In 1920, for the first time, more people lived in towns and cities than in rural areas, and the urbanizing trend continued until 1930. Urban growth occurred not just in the Northeast and the Midwest but also in parts of the South and especially in the West, where migrants poured into cities like Seattle, Portland, Denver, Dallas, and Houston. Los Angeles, which had a population of only 50,000 in 1890, held 1.2 million people by 1930. While urban growth in eastern and midwestern cities continued to inspire tall buildings (the art-deco Chrysler building in New York was the signature skyscraper of the decade), western growth tended more toward sprawl. Many Los Angelenos still lived in single-family homes.

*The Growth of Suburbia.* This movement of men and women into the cities was accompanied by a shift of population into the suburbs. Together, cities and suburbs formed swiftly expanding metropolitan areas—agglomerations of electric lights and streetcars, the clangor and jams of traffic, centers of communications, consumerism, and creativity. The expansion of suburbs, a process begun during the late nineteenth century with the building of electrified streetcar and commuter rail systems, was accelerated by the mass ownership of automobiles. The suburban population of the nation's ninety-six largest cities grew twice as fast as the cities themselves; Los Angelenos, for example, poured into the San Fernando Valley, which the city had annexed in 1915 but which had all of the social characteristics of a large suburb. Suburban residents often worked downtown, whisking to and from their homes on "expressways" with no cross streets or stop signs, like New York's handsome Bronx River Parkway, completed in 1923.

While most city dwellers did not own cars, the growing influx of suburban commuters caused severe urban congestion and (in many places, for the first time) parking problems. City officials responded by widening roads and building parkways, bridges, and tunnels to ease traffic flows; but the more they built, the more the problem grew. To make matters worse, motorized buses began to replace streetcars during the 1920s, something that General Motors (a leading bus manufacturer) encouraged by acquiring streetcar companies, tearing up their tracks, and closing them down. New York, a city that operated over 1,340 miles of trolley tracks in 1919, had only 337 miles remaining in 1939.

*Mass Media.* The new technologies of radio and motion pictures contributed to a nationalization of American culture. Radio brought listeners political conventions and prize fights, baseball and football games, comedies, and musical programs—including the crooning of Rudy Vallee and the twanging of "Grand Ole Opry," broadcast from WSM in Nashville, the emerging mecca of country music. In 1926, AT&T, General

Electric, Westinghouse, and the new Radio Corporation of America (RCA) jointly established the National Broadcasting Company (NBC), the country's first radio network, with sixteen member stations. NBC allowed local stations like Westinghouse's KDKA to develop programs tailored to their particular markets and to share programming with other affiliated stations. The network, centered in New York, could reach 54 percent of the American population. By 1930, it was also clear—after some debate about other models—that radio would depend on commercial advertising to pay the costs of broadcasting and program development.

Motion picture audiences grew dramatically during the decade, from an average of 40 million persons per week in 1920 to 100 million per week (out of a population of 123 million) in 1930. The advent of the "talkies" (motion pictures with sound) with *The Jazz Singer* in 1927 added to the appeal of an already popular medium. So did slapstick comedies with performers such as Charlie Chaplin and Harold Lloyd, Walt Disney's animated cartoons (Mickey Mouse was introduced in 1928), religious extravaganzas like *The Ten Commandments* (1923) and *The King of Kings* (1927), and sexually suggestive films that featured stars like Clara Bow or the matinee idol Rudolph Valentino. Among the first places to install the new air-conditioning systems—pioneered by the Carrier Engineering Corporation, among others—movie houses were especially popular in the summer.

Charlie Chaplin eating a shoe in "The Gold Rush," 1925.

Newspapers and magazines also helped to form a national culture. The number of daily newspapers declined in the 1920s—as papers with very specific constituencies or partisan viewpoints fell away—but the circulation of the surviving papers increased. Newspaper chains that owned papers in different cities also grew, standardizing the information and opinions disseminated to the 13 million people they served; and national news syndicates, often based in New York, provided the editors of member papers with news reports, editorials, and even advice columns. New large-circulation magazines such as *Time* (1923) and *The New Yorker* (1925) took their place on shelves alongside older publications such as the *Saturday Evening Post* and the *Ladies' Home Journal.* These publications penetrated the countryside as well as the cities, revealing to rural and small-town readers both the currents of thought and the material advances that were transforming middle-class urban life.

The print media also helped advance the increasing vogue of celebrity, devoting considerable attention to sports stars like George Herman "Babe" Ruth of the New York Yankees, who in 1927 set a towering record of sixty home runs; boxers Jack Dempsey and Gene Tunney, who in mid-decade twice slugged it out for the heavyweight title; and Gertrude Ederle, who in 1926 became the first woman to swim the English Channel. The media also drew the great German physicist Albert Einstein into the celebrity orbit, applauding him for his theory of relativity and its implication that huge stores of energy were locked in an atom, awaiting release.

Such individuals were appealing not only because of their glamour or wealth, the sheer human interest of their (sometimes scandalous) lives, or, in Einstein's case, his dreamy humility; but also because they left their mark as individuals in an increasingly organized and corporate world. When in 1927 the young pilot Charles A. Lindbergh flew solo across the Atlantic in his single-engine *Spirit of St. Louis,* he was given a ticker-tape parade back in New York and lionized in print, on the air, and in films. Prominent among the themes in the outpouring of bravos were his courage, character, and tenacity—proof that the individual could prevail against both the scoffers and the odds.

*Consumerism.* The 1920s witnessed a significant increase in the degree to which the identities of Americans—or middle-class Americans, at least—were linked to their powers and patterns of consumption rather than to their occupations or roles as producers. The opulent settings of many films created nationally available images of abundance, while radio and print

Babe Ruth lofting a home run into the right field upper deck at Yankee Stadium in 1927.

advertising hammered home the desirability of possessing material goods. These goods, moreover, were increasingly the same throughout the country, owing in part to the growing dominance of chain stores such as the A & P (for groceries) or Woolworth's, which had more than 1,500 stores by 1927.

Annual advertising budgets doubled during the decade, reaching more than $1.5 billion. Drawing on art, psychology, and sociology, advertisers presented products in ways that would stimulate consumer demand. They presented "a dream world," an observer noted, promising that what was displayed would bring idealized benefits, including "shining teeth, school girl complexions, cornless feet . . . odorless breath, [and] regularized bowels." Department stores commercialized the Christmas holiday season by inaugurating Thanksgiving Day parades and in-house Santas; and they hired special designers to create artistically staged show windows. The entrepreneurial genius Edward L. Bernays pioneered the field of public relations to develop a favorable climate for the sale of goods to a broad range of customers.

Advertisers sold brand names by invoking the authority of science and even religion, both talismans of the 1920s. One social observer remarked, "A sentence which begins with 'Science says' will generally be found to settle any argument in a social gathering or sell any article from tooth-paste to refrigerators." In *The Man Nobody Knows,* a portrait of Jesus Christ, the advertising executive Bruce Barton depicted Christ as a managerial genius for having "picked up twelve men from the bottom ranks of business and forged them into an organization that conquered the world."

Even if it had been permitted (which it was not), advertising was unnecessary to encourage the consumption of alcoholic beverages. Although many Americans were deeply convinced of the value of Prohibition, many others made moonshine in rural stills or imbibed liquor in city "speakeasies"; in fact, there were more illegal speakeasies operating in New York City than legal drinking establishments before Prohibition. By making illegal what people wanted to drink, Prohibition fostered a variety of criminal entrepreneurs, including bootleggers who smuggled alcohol into the country, gangs (like Al Capone's in Chicago) who had their fingers in virtually every part of the trade, and police who ignored the illegal commerce in exchange for bribes.

*Health, Public and Private.* Metropolitan life in the 1920s was becoming healthier, thanks to better sanitary facilities at home, regular trash collection on the streets, the purification of water supplies, and the inspection of milk. City residents also benefited from taking vitamins (discovered in 1915) and from vaccines and treatments that allowed doctors to cure, control, or prevent measles, diphtheria, diarrhea, tuberculosis, and syphilis. Nationwide, life expectancy rose from forty-nine to fifty-nine years during the first third of the century, while infant mortality rates fell sharply. Urban mothers, told to be concerned with the psychological as well as the physical development of their children, paid heed to the leading behaviorist, John B. Watson. He taught that with proper training, which included forcing children to eat on a rigid schedule (and not kissing them), any child could be made into a successful doctor, lawyer, or artist.

Many educated Americans also supported the popular doctrines of eugenics, which sought to exploit the new science of genetics for human biological improvement. Eugenicists claimed that "unfit human traits such as feeblemindedness, epilepsy, criminality, insanity, alcoholism, pauperism, and many others run in families and are inherited in exactly the same way

689

An exhibit promoting eugenics at the Kansas State Free Fair, Topeka, 1920.

as color in guinea pigs." Biologists, doctors, and psychologists warned that people with the genes for such traits were proliferating rapidly, and they urged that these people be prevented from having children. In pursuit of that goal, twenty-four states enacted eugenic sterilization laws during the 1920s, leading to 20,000 sterilizations by the mid-1930s. In 1927, in *Buck v. Bell*, the Supreme Court upheld the laws, with Justice Oliver Wendell Holmes Jr. explaining for the 8–1 majority: "It is better for all the world, if instead of waiting to execute degenerate offspring for crime, or to let them starve for their imbecility, society can prevent those who are manifestly unfit from continuing their kind."

## The Jazz Age

The famed novelist F. Scott Fitzgerald called the 1920s the "Jazz Age" after its signature music. Jazz had recently been brought to white northern audiences by black musicians from the South, and metropolitan America was marked by features that echoed the music's character: fast-paced creativity, cultural improvisation, breakaways from convention, and unabashed sexuality. The jazzy elements of the age bypassed many Americans, but those who embraced them produced innovations in art, self-expression, and identity with impacts that reached far beyond their own circles and period. This was a rich era in the evolution of a distinctively American art and literature.

### CULTURAL FERMENT

Many talented writers and artists found themselves alienated by the moralizing, self-satisfied America of business, Harding, and Coolidge. A number expatriated to Europe, and some turned their alienation into compelling art. Outlets for their work were provided by the mass-circulation magazines, adventurous new book-publishing houses, and innovative marketing methods such as the Book of the Month Club and the Literary Guild, both founded in 1926. The literary epicenter of the era was *The American Mercury,* a magazine founded in 1923 and edited by Baltimore journalist H. L. Mencken. Mencken was a discerning spotter of literary talent, as well as a forceful and iconoclastic social critic who wittily disparaged Republican politicians, sentimental reformers, pompous academics, Prohibition, patriotism, and Christian marriage. "Patriotism," Mencken once wrote, was "a favorite device of persons with something to sell." And a professional politician, in his view, had "to make so many compromises and submit to so many humiliations" that he became "indistinguishable from a streetwalker."

Sinclair Lewis, a native of Sauk Centre, Minnesota, helped inaugurate the literary decade with the novels *Main Street* (1920) and *Babbitt* (1922), both biting critiques of commercialism, hypocrisy, and conformity in small-town America. F. Scott Fitzgerald, a recent dropout from Princeton University, debuted simultaneously with *This Side of Paradise* (1920), a novel of lost and gilded youth drawn from the experience of his college years. Himself a paragon of the Jazz Age, Fitzgerald grew rich on royalties and partied on both sides of the Atlantic; but he cast a sharply critical, subtly moral eye on the corruptions of money and social climbing in his fiction, especially *The Great Gatsby* (1925). The next year, Ernest Hemingway, who had been living in Paris, published *The Sun Also Rises,* an exploration of how a loosely connected coterie of young Americans and their British counterparts wandering in Europe coped with the shattering personal impact of the war. A Red Cross volunteer who had been seriously wounded on the Italian front, Hemingway in 1929 published *A Farewell to Arms,* an influential antiwar novel that in direct, stiletto-sharp prose flayed the notions of "sacred, glorious, and sacrifice." A more overtly political critique of the war came in *Three Soldiers* (1921) by John Dos Passos, who had been an ambulance driver in wartime France. Four years later, Dos Passos published the widely read *Manhattan Transfer,* a portrait of life in New York in a stylistically innovative blend of news headlines, descriptive fragments, and stream-of-consciousness monologue.

The anonymity and separateness of urban life were also hauntingly captured in the paintings of Edward Hopper. In 1921, another artist, Stefan Hirsch, painted *New York, Lower Manhattan* to express, as he put it, his "recoil from the monstrosity that industrial life had become in megapolitania." Some artists commented obliquely on the straitlaced materialism of American society by embracing the sensual images and forms of African and Native American painting and sculpture.

## THE VITALITY OF SCIENCE

Some writers, poets, and social critics (calling themselves "humanists") believed that science and technology were distorting the values of American society while enhancing the odds of catastrophe if another war were to occur. Other artists and thinkers, however, were fascinated by the findings of science itself and by the material contours of a technologically modern world. The surrealist painter and photographer Man Ray drew inspiration from innovations such as X-rays. Georgia O'Keeffe refracted the dynamism and congestion of urban life in paintings that endowed steel and concrete with seemingly organic qualities, while Joseph Lozowick, a Ukrainian immigrant, depicted in his prints and oils the underlying order "in the verticals of [the American city's] smoke stacks, in the parallels of its car tracks, the squares of its streets, the cubes of its factories, the arc of its bridges, the cylinders of its gas tanks." Elsie Driggs, Charles Demuth, and Charles Sheeler,

among others, found beauty in the engineering exactitude of American technology, a theme that exemplified their "precisionist" artistic interests.

The humanist criticism of science was heatedly rebutted by the most famous American scientist of the era, Robert A. Millikan, who won the Nobel Prize early in the decade (for his work on electrons) and made the cover of *Time* near the end of it. Millikan insisted that the greatest threats to civilization were not science and its works but the "emotional, destructive, over-sexed" contents of modern literature and art. Scientists like Millikan advanced a conservative syllogism: science was good for business, business was good for America, and thus science was good for the nation's economic and spiritual well-being.

The probusiness climate was also good for university science, which was recognized as a key source of technological marvels and was consequently richly aided by gifts from philanthropic foundations, individual businessmen, and state legislatures. American science gained stature in key fields such as chemistry and physics, and it led the world in genetics. During the 1920s, Americans won three Nobel Prizes in science, and distinguished European scientists came to visit and sometimes to stay. When in 1932 Einstein announced that he would move from Europe to a research institute in Princeton, New Jersey, a French physicist observed that since "the Pope of physics" had moved, the United States would become "the center of the natural sciences."

## BLACKS IN THE CITIES

During the 1920s, more than 1.5 million African Americans migrated from rural to urban areas. Roughly a third moved to the growing cities of the South—to Atlanta and Houston and to numerous small cities like Mobile, Vicksburg, and Winston-Salem. In 1925, Durham, North Carolina, the home of the nation's three largest black-owned insurance companies, was called the "capital of the Black Middle Class." Jim Crow was alive and well in these southern cities, and blacks remained disfranchised, but there were, at least, jobs outside of agriculture as well as some of the amenities of urban life.

Most African American migrants headed north, to industrial centers large and small, and especially to Chicago and New York. Harlem—until 1910 a white, middle-class neighborhood—became a storied destination, the "Negro Mecca." The black population of Harlem was 73,000 in

1920, but 165,000 ten years later. Many African American migrants continued to work in service jobs, but the racial barriers in manufacturing that fell during World War I opened new jobs, by the scores of thousands, to blacks.

Three distinct political currents coursed through the black communities of the era. One was represented by the increasingly popular National Association for the Advancement of Colored People (NAACP), which stuck doggedly to a legal strategy aimed at enforcing the Fourteenth and Fifteenth Amendments as a means of ending both disfranchisement and segregation. The NAACP—whose most visible figure remained W. E. B. Du Bois—had substantial support among black professionals and business people. It was criticized, from the political left, by radicals like A. Philip Randolph, editor of the *Messenger*, who argued that the problem of race was largely a problem of economics, class, and capitalism. Randolph maintained that only by joining trade unions and through collective working-class political action could the condition of the black masses be improved.

Neither of these currents, however, attracted as much popular support as did the Universal Negro Improvement Association (UNIA), founded in 1914 by Marcus Garvey, a Jamaican who moved—with his organization—to New York in 1916. Garvey maintained that the liberation and development of the black community could be achieved only through migration from America to Africa. With religious zeal, he insisted that blacks were in all respects at least the equal of whites and that they ought to be proud of their race and of Africa's history. The UNIA organized chains of restaurants and grocery stores and urged blacks to patronize black-owned businesses. Although his back-to-Africa movement made little headway, Garvey's emphasis on black pride touched a responsive chord in the nation's ghettoes. The UNIA acquired a membership estimated at 80,000 and a far larger sympathetic following, perhaps numbering in the millions. The organization declined in the mid-1920s when Garvey's steamship line went bankrupt, and the government, unsettled by this new movement, prosecuted ten of the UNIA's leaders. Garvey himself was convicted of mail fraud and eventually was deported, but he had helped awaken the idea that, as an African American newspaper remarked, "black is beautiful."

That outlook permeated the work and thinking of the African Americans who gathered in Harlem in the 1920s to enlarge and renew black culture. As the poet Langston Hughes wrote, "We younger Negro artists now intend to ex-

Marcus Garvey, an advocate of black pride and leader of the Universal Negro Improvement Association.

press our individual dark-skinned selves without fear or shame. . . . We know we are beautiful." Hughes, Du Bois, novelist Zora Neale Hurston, Jean Toomer, Claude McKay, and others formed what became known as the "Harlem Renaissance." They sought an identity for blacks that was authentic and independent of white culture. A number of them contributed essays, stories, and poetry to *The New Negro,* a volume published by the philosopher Alain Locke in 1925 that served as a kind of manifesto for the movement.

What African Americans had to say about the "New Negro" caught the attention of whites less than did the jazz being played at nightclubs, especially in Harlem and Chicago. Jazz, which had its genesis in New Orleans at the turn of the century, moved northward during the war and quickly became popular across the country. Energetic and improvisational, jazz broke down the distinction between performer and audience, creating an emotional and aesthetic experience appealing to whites and blacks alike. White audiences flocked to popular spots such as the Cotton Club in Harlem to hear and dance to the music. Black artists such as Duke Ellington and Louis Armstrong—who introduced the extended solo as a new ingredient in jazz—reached national audiences through "race records" and radio broadcasts of their Harlem performances. Blacks not only gave the age its jazz but also infused American music with one of its most distinctive and enduring forms.

### WOMEN

After passage of the Nineteenth Amendment, Congress scrambled to please this mass of new voters, establishing a Women's Bureau in the Department of Labor (1920), granting women equal citizenship rights with men (the Cable Act, 1922), and sending to the states a constitutional amendment outlawing child labor (1924). Meanwhile, several states started allowing women to serve on juries; they also passed protective laws that set minimum standards for women's pay, limited women's working hours, or prohibited night work. In a more innovative move, women's groups convinced Congress to enter the field of health care. The Sheppard-Towner Act (1921) authorized the federal government to give states matching funds for clinics in which nurses instructed mothers on infant care and doctors provided preventive health checkups.

It soon became clear, however, that women did not vote as a block and, in fact, voted less often than men, which weakened legislators' desire to approve laws targeting women's interests. The states failed to ratify the child-labor amendment, while opposition defeated some efforts to get more women on juries. In 1929, urged on by the American Medical Association (AMA), which saw the publicly funded women's clinics as a threat to physicians' control of medical practice, Congress repealed the Sheppard-Towner Act.

Women themselves were divided over legislation that gave them special protections. Soon after achieving suffrage, Alice Paul and the National Women's Party (NWP) began arguing for an Equal Rights Amendment (ERA) to the Constitution: "men and women shall have equal rights throughout the United States and every place subject to its jurisdiction." This amendment would have rendered unconstitutional all laws that restricted women's right to make contracts, to control their personal property, to have equal guardianship rights over their children, and to serve on juries. The amendment also would have undermined all "protective" legislation, such as maximum hour laws, an outcome that Paul accepted because she believed that such laws, in fact, restricted women's opportunities. That this was a minority view became clear as the ERA failed to acquire much political traction. Most women's organizations opposed the ERA, which they considered "elitist" since it neglected the concrete problems faced by working women and catered instead to the ambitions of the more educated.

*Flappers, Birth Control, and Marriage.* To many young women of the 1920s, their elders' concern with suffrage and social reform seemed terribly dated. "Feminism," a journalist remarked, was a "term of opprobrium" to "flappers," as the chic young women of the era were dubbed. Flappers worked hard to look different from their Victorian predecessors: long curls gave way to short "bobs," skirts moved above the knee, and curves became outmoded. Women bound their breasts and dieted to reduce their hips and achieve a boyish shape; the bathroom scale made its appearance in the 1920s. Flappers wore makeup, which was once confined to prostitutes, took up smoking and drinking as signs of emancipation, and experimented sexually in the new privacy of automobiles.

Flappers did find common cause with reformers in the birth-control movement championed by Margaret Sanger. A

Two young women dressed in the style of flappers doing the Charleston on a rooftop ledge at Chicago's Sherman Hotel.

dedicated activist whose mother had died at age forty-nine after bearing eleven children, Sanger insisted that women would never be free or equal unless they could control their fecundity. Her early attempts to disseminate birth-control information and devices aroused strong opposition and led her to leave the country to avoid prosecution under the Comstock Law of 1873 (see Chapter 19). But in 1916, in a Brooklyn storefront, she opened the nation's first birth-control clinic, advertising the facility in handbills written in English, Yiddish, and Italian. By then, the courts were beginning to allow the distribution of contraceptives for the purpose of maintaining health, and five years later Sanger founded the American Birth Control League, a lobbying organization that became Planned Parenthood in 1942. Sanger sought to make birth control respectable by targeting married women and by insisting that diaphragms, the contraceptive she recommended, be fitted by doctors instead of obtained over the counter. She also appealed to eugenicists, arguing that the distribution of contraceptives to lower-income and immigrant groups would reduce their birthrates and thus improve the quality of the nation's population.

Despite their rejection of Victorian styles and morals, the young women of the era still believed in marriage, although that venerable institution was re-imagined to include sexual fulfillment and a limited number of children. The movies reinforced such images, dramatizing the single working woman's quest for escape from a boring life as a salesclerk or secretary through marriage to the right man, who was ideally rich and could buy her the "modern conveniences" that advertising hawked. But modern marriage did not always measure up to the movies. In 1920, 1 marriage in 7.5 ended in divorce; by 1929, the rate was 1 in 6 and in some cities had risen as high as 1 in 3.5.

Middle-class women who married in the 1920s faced somewhat different challenges from those their mothers had. They could buy, rather than make, clothing; they could purchase items like bread or butter that were once produced at home; they had the use of modern appliances to facilitate housework; and (in urban areas at least) they had fewer children to care for. But modern appliances were not automatic (washing machines, for example, required putting clothes through ringers several times and then hanging them outdoors to dry), and new standards of housekeeping were more demanding (underwear, for example, was now to be changed every day and sheets every week). Moreover, servants were far less common in the late 1920s than they had been earlier in the century, thanks to immigration restriction and the opening of other jobs to working-class women. Whether there was a net gain in the quality of life for middle-class women was unclear.

*Women in the Workforce.* The ideology of the era celebrated not only marriage but the possibility of fulfilling work for women. The media highlighted events that seemed to herald an explosion of new opportunities for women, such as the famed aviator Amelia Earhart's participation in a flight across the Atlantic in 1927, and the 1921 visit of Marie Curie, a French scientist and Nobel laureate, to the White House to receive from President Harding a gram of radium for cancer research.

The number of women college graduates doubled during the 1920s, as did the number in the professions. Those with doctorates, including 1,000 with Ph.D.s in science, quadrupled. Yet women who ventured into the professions still faced limited opportunities. Most professional women were confined to "nurturing" fields as teachers, librarians, or social workers. About half of American school systems forced teachers to resign once they married; and women academics had trouble getting jobs except at women's colleges. An authoritative survey of the academic world drew conclusions about women academics that could have been generalized to most working women: they were generally paid less, promoted more slowly, and treated with "a considerable degree of discrimination."

Overall, the percentage of women in the paid labor force increased modestly during the decade, to roughly 25 percent. The participation of married women who worked outside the home also rose (to 12 percent in 1930), but this seemed to have more to do with need than with glamorous new opportunities. Most married working women came from poorer households, and they took jobs outside the home in part because the traditional alternatives—keeping boarders or performing piecework at home—were becoming less available. More than one-quarter of married African American women in Detroit worked for wages, and more than 45 percent did so in New York. Although driven by necessity, some working women did also derive psychological benefits from their labors: the wife of an Indiana pipe-fitter, for example, reported that she used her wages from cleaning houses to purchase appliances like a "vacuum sweeper." She voiced pride that she no longer had to ask her husband's permission "because I buy these things with my money."

## BACKLASH

Despite the nation's prosperity and its reassuring geographic remove from the conflicts of Europe, there was anxiety in 1920s America, fear that the country was changing in unwelcome ways. For many white, Anglo-Saxon Protestants (WASPS), the nation's dominant social group, these anxieties centered on the cities with their flappers and speakeasies, Catholics and Jews, scientists and intellectuals who ridiculed life in small-town America. Most WASPS, indeed, continued to live in the small and medium-size towns of rural America, although many had themselves migrated to the cities and personally observed the excesses of urban life. Whether urban or rural, they lashed back at what they disliked about metropolitan America, insisting that the country remain alcohol-free ("dry") and launching cultural and political attacks against minority groups, immigrants, and the teaching of evolution.

*Revival of the Klan.* The resentments fueled the revival of the Ku Klux Klan (KKK) (see Chapter 17). Reorganized in Georgia in 1915, the Klan soon expanded its traditional zeal for upholding white supremacy against blacks to include the defense of "pure Americanism" against Jews, Catholics, and foreign influences. The KKK spread far beyond the South, gaining adherents across the country and establishing strongholds in places as diverse as Indiana, Colorado, Oklahoma, and southern Ohio. By 1924, the Klan reached an estimated membership of 4.5 million, and it wielded significant political power in numerous cities and states.

The Klan's white robes, elaborate rituals, and cross-burnings probably gave a psychological boost to ordinary Americans feeling marginalized by the dynamism of metropolitan society. Klansmen often resorted to threats, boycotts, and at times violence to intimidate deviants from traditional morals, punish violators of Prohibition, and keep blacks, Jews, Catholics, and "wayward" women in their place. The Klan abruptly faded after 1925, in part because of a scandal involving one of its Grand Dragons who was sent to prison for raping his young secretary and then refusing to call a doctor after she swallowed a lethal dose of poison. Nevertheless, bigotry against Catholics, Jews, and blacks remained pervasive: Jews, for example, were excluded from some residential neigh-

A Ku Klux Klan parade in Washington, D.C., September 17, 1926.

borhoods as well as resort hotels, and their access to private colleges, universities, and professional schools was severely restricted.

*Immigration Restriction.* White Protestant resentment of ethnic minorities fueled the long-standing drive for restrictions on immigration. World War I, of course, had brought trans-Atlantic immigration to a halt, but after the hostilities ceased, immigrants once again began to pour into the country in large numbers. Although many employers, alert to the ongoing need for cheap labor, argued against any limits on immigration, their views were opposed by a growing coalition of restriction advocates: union leaders who worried that immigration would adversely affect wages, staunch nativists who were convinced that foreign influences were adulterating American society, and businessmen who feared immigrants as infectious carriers of radicalism. In 1921, Congress passed an Emergency Quota Act to slow immigration down while the economy was reeling from a recession.

The more zealous restrictionists lobbied for a permanent law that would discriminate sharply against the most recent wave of immigrants from eastern and southern Europe. Adding "scientific authority" to the drive, eugenicists claimed that socially desirable traits were associated with the "races" of northern Europe, especially the Nordics, while the eastern and southern European races carried undesirable ones. Bowing to the clamor, the House and Senate in April 1924 passed with large majorities the National Origins Act, which permanently established restrictions on immigration. Biological and racial arguments figured prominently in the floor debates, with one congressman declaring that "the primary reason for the restriction of the alien stream . . . is the necessity for purifying and keeping pure the blood of America." The act reduced the annual quota for admission from any one country to 2 percent of the number of persons from that country who lived in the United States in 1890, when the population included few immigrants from eastern and southern Europe. It also banned all immigration from Japan. (The Chinese were already excluded.) The passage of this law brought the long chapter of open immigration in American history to an end.

The Scopes Trial drew large crowds and much media attention to the small tyown of Dayton, Tennessee in 1925.

Notably, the new law imposed no restrictions on immigration from Latin America or Canada, thus tacitly encouraging the migration of Mexicans, particularly to the Southwest. By 1930, the American population included more than a million people born in Mexico. Most of these migrants settled in the Southwest, working in agriculture, mining, or on the railroads, but thousands headed to the Midwest, particularly Chicago, where they found jobs in industry.

***The Scopes Trial.*** Many American Protestants felt acutely the challenges to religious faith raised by urban-associated science. Religious modernists, most of them centered in the cities, had found ways to reconcile Darwin's theory of evolution with their biblical beliefs, and in 1923 a dozen of the nation's leading scientists attested to their own support of a higher being. Nonetheless, numerous Protestants, particularly in the South, rejected the theory of evolution, embracing instead the doctrines of the recently emergent Fundamentalist movement, which insisted on the literal truth of every word in the Bible.

In the early 1920s, several southern states, under Fundamentalist influence, passed laws making it illegal to teach Darwin's theory of evolution in the public schools. Among them was Tennessee, which prohibited public school teachers from teaching any theory that denied the biblical creation story, such as the notion "that man has descended from a lower order of animals." Encouraged by the American Civil Liberties Union, John Thomas Scopes, a twenty-two-year-old biology teacher in Dayton, tested the law and was arrested. In 1925, he was convicted in a trial that drew nationwide attention as a clash between the city and the countryside, the South and the North, religion and science. The dramatic high point of the trial was the questioning by famed attorney Clarence Darrow of William Jennings Bryan, a staunch anti-evolutionist who had traveled to Dayton to join the prosecution. Darrow forced Bryan to affirm that he believed in the literal Bible, including its stories that Joshua had made the sun stand still and that Jonah had been swallowed by a whale. Bryan, however, admitted that he did not interpret the story of Genesis to mean that God had created the world in six days of regular length. The ridicule of Bryan's testimony convinced many people that anti-evolutionism had been defeated at Dayton. But the Tennessee law was upheld by the state supreme court, and anti-evolutionism, though remaining strong only in the South, worked a chilling, nationwide effect on high school biology texts. In 1930, an estimated 70 percent of public high schools did not teach evolution, a tacit censorship of the curriculum that continued into the 1950s.

## The Hoover Peak

The conservative backlash had lost some of its steam by the election season of 1928. Coolidge would likely have won re-election, but as the contest approached, he issued a character-istically terse pronouncement: "I do not choose to run for president in 1928." In his stead, the Republicans happily nom-inated Herbert Hoover, the forward-looking, scientifically adept, and much-admired secretary of commerce.

The Democrats also nominated an unusually able and re-spected candidate: the four-time governor of New York, Al-fred E. Smith. Growing up in a working-class family in Manhattan, Smith had climbed the ladder of New York poli-tics, earning a national reputation as an innovative manager and humanitarian reformer. In 1928, Smith overcame several southern rivals to win his party's nomination handily, but he was not leading a unified political party. Smith was a "wet" (meaning that he favored repeal of Prohibition), while many rural Democrats were "dry." Smith was also a Catholic, the

first non-Protestant to be nominated by a major party for the highest office in the land.

Since the two major parties were in substantial agreement about most policy issues (including tariffs and foreign af-fairs), the campaign ended up focusing on Prohibition and on personalities. Smith was widely slandered as a papal agent, "representative of an alien culture," and smeared as a traf-ficker in nuns and alcohol. Hoover, meanwhile, described Prohibition as a "great social and economic experiment" while presenting himself as an Iowa farm boy who had made good—the embodiment of traditional American values. Hoover also held the strong card of prosperity, for which the Republicans claimed complete responsibility.

Hoover won in a landslide, receiving 58 percent of the popular vote and 444 electoral votes to Smith's 87. Owing to southern concerns about Prohibition and Smith's Catholi-cism, Hoover even won seven states in the usually Democratic South. Smith's religion likely helped him in urban America: he won the twelve largest cities, all of which had voted Repub-lican in 1924, perhaps because of an outpouring of Catholic women voting for the first time. That urban vote was a signif-icant harbinger of things to come for the Democratic Party, but in 1929 it was Herbert Hoover who took office.

### THE "GREAT ENGINEER"

Herbert Hoover commanded enormous public confidence as a can-do figure devoted to the public interest. Orphaned at age ten, he had equipped himself with a degree in geology from Stanford University and then earned a fortune as a min-ing engineer and international businessman, ably applying scientific knowledge to the tasks of finding and processing raw materials for industrial use. Raised a Quaker, he retired at age forty in 1914 to devote himself to public service. People called Hoover a great humanitarian for his work as food ad-ministrator and in food relief during the war years. He repre-sented the moderate, internationalist wing within the Republican Party, speaking out for the League of Nations and against a rigid adherence to laissez-faire.

Hoover approached the affairs of government as the well-intentioned engineer he was. He believed that social and po-litical problems could be solved by fact-finding and expertise coupled with voluntarism and hard work. As secretary of commerce, he encouraged the formation of trade associa-tions to help industry reduce costs and stabilize employ-ment, strengthened the National Bureau of Standards as a

Herbert Hoover, the "Great Engineer," at the time of his inauguration in March 1929.

697

major scientific research laboratory, and mobilized local private relief agencies to create jobs. After his inauguration on March 4, 1929, a journalist remarked that Americans felt they "had summoned a great engineer to solve our problems for us."

### BRIGHT CALM

On receiving the Republican presidential nomination, Hoover predicted that the day was in sight "when poverty will be banished from this nation." When he took office in March 1929, he set out to pursue that vision and to carefully, incrementally, improve the well-being of the American people. His administration began collecting data on recent social trends and called a series of conferences on subjects such as child welfare, education, and public health. It took steps to raise efficiency in oil production, to reform the services offered under the Indian Bureau, to conserve national resources, and to enhance the federal government's effectiveness. Sensitive to the long-run difficulties of the nation's farmers, Hoover prevailed on Congress in June 1929 to approve a new Agricultural Marketing Act that would promote cooperatives to help stabilize prices; if the voluntary cooperatives failed, the government would purchase surplus crops.

This was business as usual, with an unusually knowledgeable and active president. But while Hoover was taking his well-prepared steps, the flaws in the American economy were deepening. After 1925, the prodigious growth rates of the early boom years began to drop in key sectors, notably residential construction and automobiles. Business inventories began to pile up in 1928, nearly quadrupling in value by midsummer of 1929. The signs were clearly pointing to a cyclical downturn. But the stock market ignored those signs, as investors indulged in what Hoover called "an orgy of mad speculation," driving glamour stocks like RCA through wild daily price changes.

The prosperity of the 1920s, in fact, was almost over when Hoover entered the White House. For nearly a decade, private enterprise had brought the nation rapid economic growth, solidified its standing as a world financial power, and accelerated its transformation into a resourceful metropolitan society with vibrant artistic and scientific centers. Government, by design, had played little role in these processes. But calamity was about to strike, and when it did, Americans would turn for hope and assistance to their government and to the accomplished engineer and humanitarian who stood at its helm.

## Suggested Reading

Lizabeth Cohen, *Making a New Deal: Industrial Workers in Chicago, 1919–1939* (1990)

Nancy F. Cott, *The Grounding of Modern Feminism* (1987)

Ruth Schwartz Cowan, *More Work for Mother: The Ironies of Household Technology from the Open Hearth to the Microwave* (1983)

Lynn Dumenil, *Modern Temper: American Culture and Society in the 1920s* (1995)

James Grossman, *Land of Hope: Chicago, Black Southerners, and the Great Migration* (1989)

Frederick Lewis Allen, *Only Yesterday: An Informal History of the 1920s* (1931)

John Higham, *Strangers in the Land: Patterns of American Nativism, 1860–1925* (1988)

Kenneth T. Jackson, *Crabgrass Frontier: The Suburbanization of the United States* (1985)

# Chapter Review

## Summary QUESTIONS

- What caused the Red Scare?
- What was American policy towards Latin America during the 1920s?
- Which industries did well in the 1920s and which did less well?
- What were the major new cultural trends of the 1920s?
- In what ways did the 19th Amendment alter the lives of women in the 1920s?

## Chronology

| | |
|---|---|
| 1919–20 | The Red Scare. |
| June 28, 1919 | Treaty of Versailles. |
| 1920 | Treaty of Sèvres liquidates the Ottoman Empire. |
| | Radios broadcast to wide audience for the first time. |
| 1923 | Death of Harding. |
| | Adkins Case. |
| 1925 | Scopes trial in Tennessee. |
| 1927 | Mississippi Flood. |

## Key Terms

The Red Scare (p. 678)

The Jazz Age (p. 690)

The Harlem Renaissance (pp. 691–692)

Flappers (p. 693)

Fundamentalism (p. 696)

# THE GREAT DEPRESSION AND THE NEW DEAL:

## 1929-1940

A food distribution center in St. Johns, Arizona, October 1940. Photograph by Russell Lee for the Farm Security Administration.

**QUESTIONS**

■ *What were the causes and consequences of the Great Depression?*

■ *What was Hoover's approach to the economic crisis?*

■ *What were the major successes and failures of FDR's first term?*

■ *What were the major social and cultural trends of the 1930s?*

■ *How successful was the New Deal overall?*

In 1929, the United States was the richest nation on earth, the richest nation the earth had ever seen. Although more than half of all households lived below contemporary standards of acceptable comfort, the first three decades of the twentieth century had witnessed remarkable economic growth. Salaries and wages in most occupations were well above late nineteenth-century levels, and the urban middle class was larger than ever. Renters had become home owners, adding new appliances to their domestic castles each year. Educational opportunities were expanding rapidly. Millions of Americans proudly drove the automobiles that were pouring off assembly lines in Detroit.

Optimism abounded—at least outside of agriculture and "sick" industries such as textile and coal. In December 1928, in his final State of the Union address, President Calvin Coolidge had observed that "no Congress of the United States ever assembled . . . has met with a more pleasing prospect than that which appears at the present time." Memories of past recessions—even the sharp downturn of 1920–21—had faded, and few experts detected clouds on the horizon. Andrew Mellon, the powerful secretary of the treasury and preeminent spokesman for the business community, had assured the nation that "the high tide of prosperity will continue." Safeguarding the future was the immensely capable Herbert Hoover, who was inaugurated as president in March 1929.

Nowhere was this optimism more palpable than in the stock market. Stock prices had risen significantly after 1921, with many stocks doubling in value by 1927. The climb had been interrupted periodically but had always recovered quickly, and with each recovery more Americans had turned their savings over to Wall Street. And why not? With corporations thriving and stock prices surging, it seemed only sensible for those with a bit of cash on hand to share in the profits of boundless prosperity. Only 3 percent of Americans actually owned stock, but a far larger number followed the market attentively, viewing it as a barometer of the nation's well-being.

Stock prices rose into the stratosphere in 1928 and continued soaring through the summer of 1929. At some unspecifiable moment in this giddy climb, the alchemy of boom times transformed optimism into outright speculation. Investors were no longer buying stocks because of the merits and profits of individual corporations but because they were convinced that stock prices, however high, would continue to climb higher. A share of General Electric stock that cost $128 in March 1928 was worth nearly $400 by September 1929; Anaconda Copper leapt from $54 to $131 in the same period.

This speculative impulse was encouraged by Wall Street, which permitted investors to buy stocks "on margin," putting up only 50 or 30 or even 10 percent of the purchase price. Using the shares as collateral, investors then borrowed the rest of the needed amount from their brokers, who in turn borrowed from banks and large corporations. These loans could be "called in" by brokers if stock prices dropped substantially, but that possibility seemed remote in the great bull market of 1928–29. As long as prices kept soaring, it seemed that a man with $30 could buy a $100 stock and sell it a year later for $130 or $150, pocketing a profit of 100 percent or more, minus a small interest charge for the loan. To many, the lure was irresistible.

But the bubble burst—as speculative bubbles always do. In early September, stock prices slid sharply, partially recovered, and then remained jittery for the next month. On October 23, the market plunged again, and the next day, "Black Thursday," pandemonium broke out on the floor of the New York Stock Exchange as prices plummeted in trading so heavy that the ticker lagged hours behind sales. The drop triggered margin calls that forced investors to sell their stocks to repay loans to brokers—which drove prices down even further. "Black

Cartoonist Rollin Kirby's portrayal of a response to "Black Thursday," October 24, 1929, when the stock market plunged.

Tuesday," October 29, was even worse than Black Thursday had been: panicked selling cut the prices of leading stocks by 10 to 20 percent, while the trading volume exceeded the previous record by 30 percent. The *New York Times* called it the "most disastrous" day in Wall Street's history.

The financial carnage did not end on Black Tuesday. By mid-November, the value of leading stocks was roughly half what it had been in early September. General Electric was down to $168; Anaconda Copper had sunk from $131 to $70. In a matter of weeks, great wealth had disappeared from the ledgers of companies and individuals; with it vanished what journalist Frederick Lewis Allen described as "the psychological climate" or "the state of mind" induced by the "Big Bull Market." Throughout the nation, Allen observed, there were men and women who experienced the stock market's fall as "the sudden and brutal shattering of hope."

The stock market crash was a spectacular event that left many of the rich feeling less rich and that wiped out the savings of hundreds of thousands of middle-class households. In so doing, it made Americans wary about investing in stocks in subsequent decades. Yet the debacle on Wall Street did not cause the economic catastrophe that came to be known as the Great Depression. The economy had begun a serious slowdown months before the stock market plummeted, and a downturn in the

business cycle was more than due. The crash accelerated that downturn in late 1929 and the first months of 1930, but it had little impact on the subsequent depth and length of the Depression. The bursting of the speculative bubble did not make inevitable the suffering and devastation that were to come.

## The Great Depression

### THE ECONOMY IN FREE-FALL

Indeed, even as the economy slowed in 1930, there were few expressions of alarm: the nation had experienced panics or depressions every decade since the 1870s, and there was no reason to think this one would be much different. In the spring of 1930, experts voiced the belief that the economy was starting to recover, and the stock market regained some of the ground it had lost. The *Baltimore Sun* described the crash as "a hangover" that followed "a spree" without affecting the "robust constitution" of the economy itself. Americans in 1930 believed that they were living through a routine undulation of the business cycle; the stumbling economy would soon right itself.

They were wrong. The downturn that began in 1929 proved to be of unprecedented depth, and it lasted for ten years. The economy plunged downward for the first four years of the Depression, and then recovered slowly and haltingly. The statistics are as dramatic as numerical evidence can be. The physical output of the economy dropped more than 30 percent between 1929 and 1933, rebounded slowly until 1937, and then plummeted once again (see Table 25.1). Prices also fell between 20 and 35 percent, which meant that the money value of the gross national product (combining the decline in output and the decline in prices) sank by nearly 50 percent between 1929 and 1933. The unemployment rate soared to almost 25 percent in 1933 and remained in double digits until 1941 (and even then the rate was 9.9 percent). Between 1931 and 1940, there were always between 7.7 million and 13 million persons unemployed, while millions more were working only part time (see Table 25.2).

The magnitude of these losses is difficult to grasp. One scholar has estimated that if the economy had grown at an average rate rather than sinking into a sustained depression, the difference in economic activity would have been enough to pay for more than 700,000 schools or 36 million homes or 3.6 million miles of highway. For nearly twelve years, the human and technological capacities of the economy were un-

Table 25.1

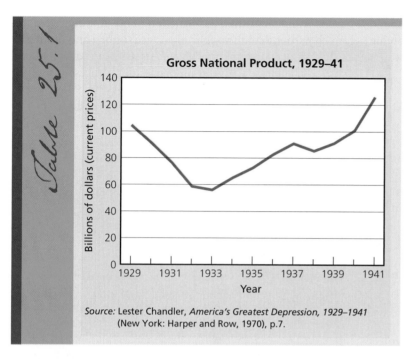

**Gross National Product, 1929–41**

*(Graph: Billions of dollars (current prices) vs. Year, 1929–1941)*

Source: Lester Chandler, *America's Greatest Depression, 1929–1941* (New York: Harper and Row, 1970), p.7.

Table 25.2

| UNEMPLOYMENT, 1929–41 | | |
|---|---|---|
| | Number of Persons Unemployed (in thousands) | Percentage of Labor Force Unemployed |
| 1929 | 1,550 | 3.2 |
| 1930 | 4,340 | 8.7 |
| 1931 | 8,020 | 15.9 |
| 1932 | 12,060 | 23.6 |
| 1933 | 12,830 | 24.9 |
| 1934 | 11,340 | 21.7 |
| 1935 | 10,610 | 20.1 |
| 1936 | 9,030 | 16.9 |
| 1937 | 7,700 | 14.3 |
| 1938 | 10,390 | 19 |
| 1939 | 9,480 | 17.2 |
| 1940 | 8,120 | 14.6 |
| 1941 | 5,560 | 9.9 |

Source: Chandler, *America's Great Depression*, p. 5.

derutilized, and the Depression came to an end only when the nation was gearing up for another war.

### THE SOURCES OF DISASTER

There was no single or simple cause of the Great Depression. Multiple factors, domestic and international, converged to transform a cyclical downturn into a prolonged catastrophe. One was the structural weakness of a banking system that had many independent units and few mechanisms for propping up banks that were in difficulty: in the early 1930s, the inability of borrowers to repay loans led to an epidemic of bank failures that erased savings accounts, reduced the credit supply, and accelerated the downward plunge of the economy. A second factor was the highly unequal distribution of wealth and income, which had been accentuated in the 1920s when the disposable income of the wealthiest 1 percent of Americans rose dramatically. This inequality reinforced the downturn by concentrating resources in the hands of the wealthy, who did not need to spend (or invest) the money they had available, rather than in the hands of average consumers, who typically spent nearly all their earnings. As a result, consumer spending that could have stimulated the economy was more limited than it might otherwise have been. Investment and the sale of luxury goods always plummeted in depressions much faster than the sale of necessities, such as food.

A third contributor, particularly to the length of the Depression, stemmed from a coincidence of timing. The cyclical downturn hit at a moment when the economy was shifting from a reliance on traditional industries, such as steel and textiles, to being propelled by newer industries, such as autos, processed foods, and tobacco. These new industries were heavily dependent on equity (stock) financing and thus were particularly hard hit after the collapse of the stock market. Although they rebounded quickly, they did not employ enough workers (or workers with the right skills) to make much of a dent in unemployment. Meanwhile, the older, more labor-intensive industries lacked the dynamism to recover at all before World War II.

As important as any of these structural factors was what economist John Kenneth Galbraith has called "the poor state of economic intelligence." The thinking of most government officials, bankers, and economists was shaped by inherited orthodoxies of economic thought and by past experiences that were no longer relevant to the conditions of the 1930s. These leaders brought to the crisis a mind-set, grounded as much in moral conviction as in evidence, that prevented them from adopting policies that might have significantly aided recovery; even worse, they frequently took steps that compounded the problem.

Throughout the nation, for example, public officials at all levels reacted to the downturn by trying to balance their budgets: the conventional wisdom was that such action would help restore the health of the economy. To achieve that goal, city and state governments (as well as the federal government, when it could) cut expenditures or raised taxes or did both. But the effect of these measures was counterproductive: they slowed the economy further by reducing the amount of money available to consumers to spend.

Even more important were failures of international economic policy: the Depression was international in scope and was caused in part by misguided policies adopted by both European governments and the United States. In response to falling production and rising unemployment, numerous governments, including that of the United States, instituted protectionist measures, such as high tariffs. Designed to protect domestic industries, these actions also slowed international trade. Since the United States was the leading creditor nation in the post–World War I financial order, European nations had to export goods to the United States in order to pay their debts. High tariffs made that difficult if not impossible.

In addition, Britain, the United States, and most other countries in Europe and Latin America insisted on clinging to the gold standard, which provided the framework for international financial relations. Each country's currency had a fixed value in relation to gold, and the precious metal itself flowed between nations in payment of debts. Every nation, moreover, was required to maintain a gold reserve to back its currency, which was convertible into gold on demand. Although ill understood at the time, the gold standard of the 1920s and 1930s operated in such a way as to pressure governments and central banks to slow down their economies. National leaders and central bankers firmly believed that the gold standard would restore economic health, but in fact it did the opposite, dragging one country after another deeper into depression. Most nations began to recover only after they belatedly and reluctantly abandoned the gold standard, but by then much of the damage had been done.

### PORTRAITS IN GRAY

The Depression penetrated the entire nation, but its impact on different cities and sectors of the economy was highly un-even. Manufacturing, construction, and mining were hit much harder than the public or service sectors; and industries that produced capital goods, such as steel and automobiles, suffered far more than did industries that processed food or other consumer products (see Table 25.3). By 1931, General Motors had laid off 100,000 of its 260,000 employees in Detroit; a year later, no one was working full time at U.S. Steel.

Table 25.3

| DECLINE IN INDUSTRIAL PRODUCTION, 1929–33 | |
| --- | --- |
| Industry | 1929–33 Percentage Decline |
| Shoes | 3.4 |
| Textiles | 6.4 |
| Cigarettes | 6.6 |
| Leather goods | 7.4 |
| Gasoline | 7.4 |
| Woolen and worsted cloth | 7.7 |
| Cotton | 11.4 |
| Tobacco products | 16.7 |
| Manufactured food | 17.8 |
| Cigars | 34.4 |
| Tires and tubes | 34.8 |
| Polished plate glass | 42.7 |
| Ships | 53.1 |
| Furniture | 55.6 |
| Nonferrous metals | 55.9 |
| Lumber | 57.9 |
| Iron and steel | 59.3 |
| Machinery | 61.6 |
| Cement | 63.1 |
| Nonferrous metals | 63.5 |
| Transportation equipment | 64.2 |
| Automobiles | 65.0 |
| Railroad cars | 73.6 |
| Copper | 78.9 |
| Common and face bricks | 83.3 |
| Locomotives | 86.4 |

Source: Chandler, America's Great Depression, p. 23.

More than half of all households experienced direct economic consequences of the Depression. Those who were relatively lucky continued working but at lower wages or for fewer hours, significantly reducing their families' incomes. They used up their savings, cut back on spending for recreation and clothing, bought less meat, gave up their life insurance policies, and sometimes moved to cheaper apartments or houses. Married women commonly attempted to make up for the decline in income with extra domestic labor, such as repairing worn-out clothing, washing their children's few respectable clothes each night, and cooking meals that could be stretched to offer more portions.

Such modest adjustments were only the beginning for the millions of men and women who lost their jobs altogether, many of whom remained out of work for a year or two or more—periods that were without precedent in their lives or in American history. The unemployed coped by eating little and poorly (milk for children became a luxury), shutting off their electricity, eliminating all expenditures for nonnecessities, forgoing visits to doctors, and barely heating their houses in winter. They exhausted what little savings they had, sent women and children into the labor force, borrowed from grocers and saloon keepers, and moved in with relatives.

They also searched relentlessly for work or for odd jobs—until they became so pessimistic that they stopped looking for employment altogether. When word spread that an employer might have a few jobs available, hundreds or even thousands of men and women showed up, desperately jockeying to become one of the chosen. Young men took to the roads (and rails), wandering the country in search of work. Every town and city had a street corner or spot where idled men simply stood, talked, and waited for nothing in particular, day after day. The emotional toll was severe. Helpless and cut off from their normal routines, the unemployed frequently sank into depression while traditional patterns of family life disintegrated.

Extreme deprivation was almost commonplace. Coal miners' families, evicted from company housing, lived in tents during the harsh West Virginia winters. In Oklahoma City, people searched through garbage pails for food, while one couple and their seven children inhabited a hole dug in the ground that they outfitted with chairs and beds. Homeless men found shelter in boxes, abandoned automobiles, and shantytowns on the outskirts of cities, under bridges, in railroad yards, or in municipal dumps. Diseases such as typhoid, diphtheria, and pellagra were rampant among the most impoverished. In New York, thousands of children suffered from malnutrition, and seven-year-olds were sent to soup lines in search of nourishment; in Utah and other states, hundreds stopped going to school because they had no clothes. "It's fairly common to see children entirely naked," reported one investigator.

Things weren't much better, although they were different, on the nation's farms. For farmers, the crisis of the 1930s came in the form of drastically reduced prices for their products. Those who owned or rented land could continue to grow crops, and they produced as much as ever. But they were selling their goods for 30, 40, or even 60 percent less than they had in the 1920s. Between 1929 and 1932, net farm income (figuring in the expenses of growing crops) dropped a staggering 70 percent. Although most farm families had shelter and enough to eat (attractions sufficient to draw many urban dwellers back to the countryside, reversing the migratory trends of previous decades), they had little disposable cash and were unable to buy new equipment or make needed repairs. With alarming frequency, farmers also began to default on their mortgages and lose their land. Their difficulties were deepened by the high rate of failure among rural banks: three-quarters of the banks that collapsed between 1930 and 1932 were in communities with populations of less than 2,500.

Most farmers lacked the amenities that had become standard in urban America: even in the mid-1930s, only 20 percent

Unemployed men waiting in line for bread and soup in Los Angeles, 1930.

of all farms had electricity, and only 10 percent had indoor toilets. And those who were poor became even poorer. In the rural South, tenant farmers and sharecroppers found their circumstances deteriorating, with food scarce, school systems barely functioning, health care inaccessible, and living conditions primitive. In Florida, California, and parts of the Midwest, migrant farm workers picked crops for pitifully low wages while living in shacks with no sanitation facilities or running water.

## THE DUST BOWL

In the plains states of Oklahoma, Texas, Kansas, and Colorado, nature made life even more difficult—and in some places, impossible. From 1930 to 1936, rainfall levels were abnormally low in much of the United States, and the drought that afflicted the plains turned farmlands into baked, cracked expanses of dry soil in which little could grow. Farming on the plains had grown rapidly during the first thirty years of the century, thanks in part to new technology: the tractor, harvester-thresher combine, and disk plow helped farmers conquer the difficult terrain and greatly increase the planting of wheat and cotton as cash crops. In doing so, however, farmers—much as John Wesley Powell had warned in the 1870s (see Chapter 18)—had undermined the fragile ecology of the plains, plowing excessively, allowing animals to overgraze, loosening the top layers of sod, and destroying the region's natural, if sparse, vegetation.

The result was disaster when the rains stopped. In 1932, dust storms began to afflict the region, and by 1934 they were reaching cataclysmic proportions. In May of that year, swirling winds blew the dry, loosened dust of the plains into gigantic dark clouds that turned day into night in one county after another; carried by the upper airstream, the storms deposited twelve tons of dirt on Chicago and sprinkled layers of dust on Boston, New York, and Atlanta. On the plains themselves, the dust blinded and suffocated animals, sanded the paint off houses, spawned epidemics of respiratory diseases, and filled houses with tiny particles of dirt. "The doors and

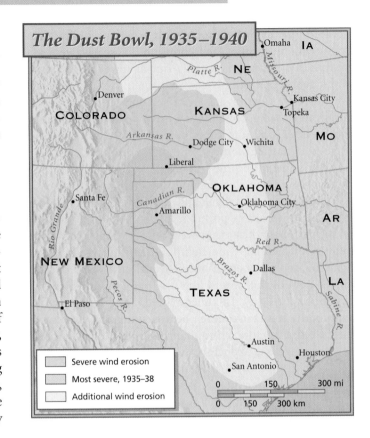

### The Dust Bowl, 1935–1940

Legend:
- Severe wind erosion
- Most severe, 1935–38
- Additional wind erosion

0    150    300 mi
0  150    300 km

A farmer and his children running through the winds of a dust storm in Cimarron County, Oklahoma, 1936.

windows were all shut tightly," reported one Kansas woman in 1935, but the dust "got into cupboards and clothes closets; our faces were as dirty as if we had rolled in the dirt; our hair was gray and stiff and we ground dirt between our teeth." In March 1935, one storm took more dirt from the plains than had been excavated during construction of the Panama Canal.

This "Dust Bowl" disaster sparked an exodus from the plains, with hundreds of thousands of families abandoning farms and rural towns. As songwriter Woody Guthrie put it, "We loaded our jalopies and piled our families in, / We rattled down the highway to never come back again." Labeled "Okies" or "exodusters," many of these desperate migrants headed to California, forming a unique migratory caravan of old cars and trucks, stuffed with people and household goods, chugging down Route 66 through New Mexico and Arizona. In California and elsewhere in the West, they often remained unemployed or found work as seasonal farm laborers. The migration of the Okies captured the nation's attention, particularly after its sympathetic portrayal in John Steinbeck's

1938 novel *The Grapes of Wrath,* as well as the 1939 movie based on the book, directed by John Ford.

### THE MIDDLE AND UPPER CLASSES

Not everyone who felt the sting of hard times was poor. One of the distinctive characteristics of the Great Depression was that it had a broad impact on the middle class as well as on workers and struggling farmers. For the first and only time in the twentieth century, large numbers of middle-class, white-collar employees suffered from prolonged unemployment. Laid off from their jobs and unable to find new ones, they experienced significant declines in their standard of living: their savings disappeared, their homes deteriorated, they gave up their cars as well as electrical and phone service, and they cut back on the educational plans for their children. Some, unable to meet mortgage payments, lost their houses. Similar fates befell middle-class owners of the many small businesses that failed.

Yet for many Americans the ordeal of the Great Depression was something that happened around them but not to them.

*American Journal*

## How Do You Get By?

"Joplin, Missouri, October 27, 1939
"Dear Mrs. Roosevelt,

"I am a 17 year old girl. I am writing to you for help in solving a very serious problem."

"My mother is very ill she may not live long. She has been sick for about 8 years. My step-dad is also sick. There is only my sister who is 15 years old and myself to take care of them. My step-dad is a World's War Veteran. He gets $100.00 a month. But that isn't enough to keep us on. It would be enough if we weren't in debt. We are in debt about $500. Everything we get we get on *Credit.* We have gotten in so deep in debt that we can't get out. We are desperate. We can't think of any way out. Me and my sister has given up trying to ever have a good time. We can't go to school because we are in debt. We can't do anything to have a good time because we have to stay at home to take care of mother. We don't even have decent clothes to wear. And with winter coming on we don't know what we're going to do for bed

clothes. Nothing we have is paid for. We do not own our own home. We rent. We don't have a nice modern home but we would be satisfied if what we do have was paid for. We are worse off than a W.P.A. worker. Collectors come every day wanting their money but we haven't got it. When pay day comes we have about 1/10 of what it takes to pay up. It is about to run me crazy. You can investigate us if you want to. We have no friends because of debt. I need glasses but I can't get them because I haven't any money. We didn't have any Christmas last year and I guess we won't this year.

"You have heard my story so please please please help us if you can because you don't know what it's like to be in debt.

"If you want a list of the people we owe I will send them.

"Respectively yours. N.C."

*From Dear Mrs. Roosevelt: Letters from Children of the Great Depression, ed. Robert Cohen.*

Millions never lost a day's work, and the rhythms of their lives were little different than they had been in the 1920s. Numerous investors took advantage of the economic decline to buy stocks at bargain prices or even to buy entire companies that were faltering. "We didn't know the depression was going on," reported one advertising executive whose business boomed as clients tried to combat the downturn by promoting their products more widely, especially on radio. Particularly for those solvent enough to weather the first storm of the stock market crash, there were fortunes to be made from the wreckage of the nation's economy.

## Herbert Hoover: The Engineer as President

President Hoover, like everyone else, viewed the downturn through the prism of recent experience, which suggested that the economy would rebound after a year or two. Yet he was far from passive after the jolt of the stock market crash. Bucking the advice of ardent conservatives such as his treasury secretary, Andrew Mellon, he actively intervened to prevent the stock market decline from leading to a general downturn. Hoover summoned bankers and other business leaders to the White House, eliciting promises from them not to cut wages or jobs so that workers' living standards and purchasing power could be maintained. He persuaded the Federal Reserve to ease credit and convinced railways and utility companies to accelerate planned construction projects. Hoover also encouraged Congress and state governments (whose collective budgets were larger than that of the federal government) to undertake public works projects.

Hoover thus took a more aggressive role in combating economic decline than any president ever had, but despite a slight (and temporary) improvement in production and employment early in 1930, his actions had little impact. Faced with declining revenues, business leaders soon found it impossible to honor their promises to maintain wage and employment levels; and as tax returns drooped, state and local governments had difficulty continuing planned construction projects, much less initiating new ones. Deficit financing—funding activities with loans—was not an acceptable countercyclical tool for administrators who believed in balanced budgets.

As the crisis worsened in 1930–31, Hoover's political standing began to falter, and he took a series of steps that proved to be counterproductive. In 1930, despite the warnings of many economists, he signed the Hawley-Smoot Tariff, a Republican measure that raised tariffs to their highest levels in history—and, in so doing, dampened international trade and fanned nationalist flames in Europe. Hoover also insisted on keeping the United States on the gold standard and in 1932 sponsored a tax increase to balance the federal budget. That same year, he responded to the collapse of many banks—and the demands of bankers—with a series of measures designed to shore up the banking system, facilitate lending, and reduce foreclosures on home mortgages. In the eyes of some critics, these measures amounted to "bank relief," an unprecedented federal intervention to rescue millionaires.

Such criticism was powerful because of Hoover's steadfast refusal to involve the federal government in relief of the unemployed. Hoover believed deeply that aid to the jobless should come from voluntary organizations and local governments, and he frequently reiterated the traditional conservative view that a federal "dole" would demoralize the unemployed. He took no steps to directly relieve the suffering of the jobless and opposed a Senate bill, introduced by liberal Democrats, calling for unemployment insurance. Meanwhile, business leaders like Henry Ford declined to take any responsibility for the jobless in their own communities, while others, such as the president of the National Association of Manufacturers, derided the needy for not practicing "the habits of thrift and conservation."

By the beginning of 1932, Hoover's political standing and personal popularity were sinking rapidly. The Republicans had lost seats in both houses of Congress in the 1930 elections, and, rightly or wrongly, the "Great Engineer" was increasingly blamed for the Depression. Hoover's expertise and managerial skill were no match for the forces driving the economy downward; his opposition to relief made him appear insensitive to the misery of millions; and he lacked the political and oratorical talents needed to assume the role of a compassionate leader struggling with difficult circumstances. Critics and cartoonists caricatured him as an aloof ideologue. Collections of makeshift shelters were renamed "Hoovervilles," while empty, pulled-out pants pockets came to be called "Hoover flags."

The president's unpopularity was reinforced in July 1932 when a "bonus army" of unemployed World War I veterans marched to Washington to demand early payment of a bonus they were scheduled to receive in 1945. The Senate refused to act on their request, but several thousand bonus marchers remained in Washington, squatting in buildings on Pennsylvania Avenue. Police efforts to remove the veterans led to violence and then to Hoover calling in federal troops. A cavalry unit, six tanks, and a column of infantry with fixed bayonets evicted the

Members of the "bonus army" encamped within sight of the Capitol in July 1932.

been widely heralded in the 1920s. This model was grounded in the presumption that the interests of all Americans were the same and that the problems generated by industrial capitalism could be solved by experts through rationality, knowledge, and good will. It was an approach to reform that relied heavily on top-down decision making and voluntary action rather than state policies. By the fall of 1932, most Americans believed that some other strategy was needed.

## Franklin D. Roosevelt: The First Term

Franklin Roosevelt was not an engineer but a politician. Born to a wealthy and prominent family in Hyde Park, New York, and educated at Groton and Harvard, Roosevelt, like his distant cousin Theodore, had a zeal for public service and the hurly-burly of political life. He served in the New York state legislature, was under-secretary of the navy under Woodrow Wilson, and became the Democratic vice-presidential candidate in 1920. The following year, at the age of thirty-nine, he was stricken with polio, which left him crippled for the remainder of his life, largely confined to a wheelchair, able to walk a few steps only with the aid of heavy steel leg braces. He spent much of the 1920s rebuilding his spirits and his body (acquiring a powerful torso and arms), while mapping a strategy for the pursuit of higher office. At Al Smith's urging, he ran for governor of New York in 1928 and was elected despite the defeat of the national Democratic ticket; having put together a powerful coalition of urban, ethnic voters, liberals, and upstate, more conservative Democrats, he was overwhelmingly reelected in 1930.

bonus army and burned down the shacks in Anacostia Flats, where the marchers had established a campsite. The federal government had responded to the pleas of jobless veterans by calling in the army to run them out of town.

Hoover had no chance of being reelected in 1932, and he knew it. His opponent, the popular Democratic governor of New York, Franklin D. Roosevelt, had little that was either concrete or innovative to say about the Depression, but the election was a referendum on Hoover and the Republicans, and its outcome was a foregone conclusion. Exhausted by nonstop work and wounded by barrages of criticism, the dispirited and pessimistic president campaigned listlessly and was defeated in a landslide. For Hoover personally, it was a bitter end to a stellar career: in four years he had gone from being the most admired man in America to being the most reviled. For the Republicans, the election of 1932 marked the end of a long period of national political dominance, as well as a repudiation of its celebratory identification of the interests of the nation with the interests of Wall Street and big business. Wall Street itself shared in the discredit, particularly as congressional hearings revealed that leading investment bankers and stock brokers had repeatedly violated the law and even profited from the distress of their clients.

In rejecting Hoover, the electorate was also registering a loss of confidence in a model of reform based on science and engineering that had emerged during the Progressive Era and

Roosevelt's skill at coalition building was critical to his successful pursuit of the presidency in 1932. As had been true since the late nineteenth century, the Democratic Party was split between a conservative, southern, prohibitionist wing and northern state parties that were commonly more liberal in economic matters, opposed to prohibition, and heavily populated by Catholic working-class voters. With both John Nance Garner of Texas and Al Smith also vying for the party's nomination, Roosevelt presented himself as a bridge candidate, capable of unifying the two regional branches. Once he had the nomination in hand (and Garner as his running mate), Roosevelt also reached out to progressive Republicans who had grown disillusioned with President Hoover and the Grand Old Party's domination by big business; although his victory in the general election was not in doubt, Roosevelt's broader political goal was to break the political dominance of the Republican Party by assembling a new coalition of progressive reformers, industrial workers, and the solidly Democratic South.

Roosevelt did not possess a very distinctive or clearly articulated political ideology although he did believe, more deeply than most, that the role of government was to serve ordinary people and to foster collaboration and mutuality rather than individualized competition. Alert to the changes that had transformed American society in his own lifetime, he sometimes displayed a sympathy for the disadvantaged that unnerved his more conservative backers. It was in this spirit that he declared, in accepting his party's nomination, "I pledge you, I pledge myself, to a new deal for the American people."

Still, the shape of that "new deal" remained vague during the campaign, and his opinions on key issues were mainstream. Like most Democrats, he favored lower tariffs, and he signaled the orthodoxy of his economic views by criticizing Hoover for incurring deficits in the federal budget. His most innovative stance was his support for government-sponsored unemployment insurance and old-age insurance, ideas that progressive reformers had begun to place on the agenda a decade and a half earlier.

Many political figures and analysts regarded Roosevelt as something of a lightweight: "He is a pleasant man," observed journalist Walter Lippmann, "who, without any important qualifications for the office, would very much like to be president." Although well educated, Roosevelt was not a reader and could rarely display the mastery of technical details so characteristic of his predecessor. Yet even skeptics were impressed by the extraordinary force of his personality, by his warmth, his restless energy, his cheery attentiveness, unshakable poise, and self-confidence—traits all the more remarkable in a man physically disabled. He has a "first-rate temperament" accompanying a "second-rate intellect," observed Justice Oliver Wendell Holmes.

That temperament, more than his past record or any systematic convictions, suggested an openness to innovation. "The country demands bold, persistent experimentation," Roosevelt had declared during the campaign. In the months between his election in November 1932 and his inauguration in March 1933, the need for such experimentation mounted. The misery of millions of jobless workers was deepening, rebellious farmers were mounting protest movements aimed at withholding food from the market, and bank failures were beginning to accelerate, leading one state after another to close its banks to prevent panicked citizens from withdrawing their remaining deposits. Roosevelt responded by consulting a steady stream of

This cartoon shows FDR leading his party, Congress, and the nation on a breakneck course toward emergency legislation, 1933.

political and business leaders, academics, and intellectuals to discuss the economic crisis in all its complexity. Peppering these men and women with questions, often seeming to agree with those holding contradictory views, displaying the full range of his charm and mental agility, the president-elect soaked in ideas and proposals like a sponge and assured his visitors that they had been heard. Even his closest advisers were not sure what Roosevelt would actually do when he took office.

### THE FIRST HUNDRED DAYS

The president's inaugural speech, on March 4, 1933, took clear aim at the country's mood of despair and anxiety. With the stock exchange and many banks closed, Roosevelt declared that the crisis was not due to any "failure of substance" but was rather the result of the "stubbornness" and "incompetence" of the "rulers of the exchange of mankind's goods." He promised to put people back to work, restore the health of agriculture, and regulate banking and investment. Insisting that "the only thing we have to fear is fear itself—nameless, unreasoning, unjustified terror," he announced that he was calling a special session of Congress to address these issues. If

Congress did not act, he would ask for emergency executive powers to "wage a war" against the Depression.

The speech was followed by an extraordinary wave of activity as Roosevelt and his aides delivered one piece of legislation after another to a receptive, even pliant, Congress. The first item on the agenda was the banking crisis. After closing all banks for four days to avoid further turmoil, the administration drew up a multipronged reform bill designed to enhance confidence in the banking system. Basically a conservative measure written to satisfy leading bankers, the Emergency Banking Act was approved by Congress within hours.

The night before the banks were to reopen, Roosevelt displayed his remarkable talent for mass communication as well as his mastery of the relatively new technology of radio. Holding the first of what were to be many nationally broadcast "Fireside Chats," the president explained what the banking reforms meant and assured his 60 million listeners that it was now safer to keep their money "in a reopened bank than under the mattress." The next day, deposits began to flow into, rather than out of, the nation's banks. Thanks to the radio, Roosevelt could speak directly to the people in his own voice, establishing what appeared to be an almost personal relationship; the number of letters written to the president from citizens throughout the nation was unprecedented.

The administration sounded another conservative note with the Economy Act, which cut the wages of federal employees and payments to veterans to balance the budget. Although many liberals opposed the bill, it passed easily. At the same time, Roosevelt proposed to increase revenues by immediately legalizing and taxing the sale of low-alcohol beer and wine. Even before Roosevelt had taken office, Congress had acted to repeal the Eighteenth Amendment, and the states, in less than a year, brought a complete end to the nation's embargo on the sale of alcohol. Roosevelt's euphemistically named Revenue Act meant that beer was sold legally on April 7, 1933, for the first time in more than a decade. Steam whistles and sirens sounded in the brewery city of St. Louis, while crowds filled the streets of Milwaukee to celebrate.

**The Agricultural Adjustment Act.** The president also acted quickly to bring relief to farmers, both because of the protest movements spreading through the countryside and because restoring the purchasing power of farmers might help boost the demand for manufactured goods. Led by Secretary of Agriculture Henry A. Wallace, a progressive Republican from Iowa and a highly respected authority on farming, the administration

drew up the Agricultural Adjustment Act (AAA), an omnibus bill that incorporated many reform ideas that had been circulating since the 1920s. The core of the measure was the provision of incentives to farmers to restrict their acreage so that output would be reduced and prices would rise; if they agreed to raise crops only on their "allotment" of land, farmers would be guaranteed a "parity" price for the goods by the government (parity representing a desirable ratio of farm prices to the prices of manufactured goods). The program was to be funded by a tax on the processing of farm products, paid for by processors—for example, those who milled the grain that farmers grew. The bill was a striking new departure in agricultural and economic policy, since its fundamental goal was to decrease the output of the nation's farms while having other sectors of the economy subsidize farmers who left some of their fields fallow.

**The Tennessee Valley Authority.** At the same time, Roosevelt launched an even more innovative program that was destined to help large numbers of farmers (among others) in the rural South. This was the Tennessee Valley Authority (TVA), a public corporation whose central goal was to generate electric power along the Tennessee River and to make and distribute nitrogen-based fertilizer from an already existing plant. The brainchild of Nebraska senator George Norris, the TVA was designed to bring electric power, new commerce, more productive farms, and modern industry to a large segment of the impoverished rural South, where most people were still living without the basic amenities that had become commonplace in the North. A stunning new use of federal power, the TVA was to have significant long-term effects on the development of seven states in the nation's most backward region.

**The Federal Deposit Insurance Corporation.** Nor was that all. The rush of activity that came to be called "the first hundred days" included bills that insulated home owners and farmers against foreclosures on their mortgages, a significant enhancement of personal security for millions. In addition, personal savings accounts were protected through the Federal Deposit Insurance Corporation (FDIC), which insured bank deposits: the FDIC was created as part of the Glass-Steagall Act, which separated investment banking from commercial banking in order to minimize the manipulation of financial institutions by bankers themselves.

**Aid for the Jobless: Initial Efforts.** Roosevelt also made efforts to help the unemployed. One modest program, which satisfied the president's long-standing interest in conservation, was the Civilian Conservation Corps (CCC), which put jobless young men to work in forestry and flood-control projects. Originally funded to enroll only 250,000 individuals, the CCC endured until the early 1940s, offering aid and new experiences to nearly 3 million men. A much larger and more controversial program, the Federal Emergency Relief Administration (FERA), involved the national government for the first time in the direct relief of the unemployed. Roosevelt, unlike his predecessor, recognized that such involvement, however ideologically undesirable, had become a necessity: millions were suffering, and neither private charities nor local or state governments possessed the resources to provide relief. Something had to be done, and the federal government alone was capable of acting. To administer the program, Roosevelt appointed one of his closest advisers from New York, Harry Hopkins, a crusty former social worker deeply influenced by the traditions of progressive reform.

*The National Recovery Administration.* Near the end of the first hundred days, the administration unveiled the centerpiece of its

efforts to revive the economy: the National Industrial Recovery Act (NIRA). Designed to stimulate production and inflate prices, the legislation authorized producers in each of the nation's industries to meet together to devise codes of fair competition, permitting them to set prices and divide markets much as cartels had sought to do before antitrust laws were enacted. These codes, however, had to be approved by the government-appointed National Recovery Administration (NRA), a step that gave the government enormous potential power over the conduct of economic affairs. In a significant gesture to labor, the act also provided for minimum wages and maximum hours, while affirming the right of workers to form unions and engage in collective bargaining. To help jump-start the economy, the legislation provided $3 billion for public works projects, to be developed by the Public Works Administration (PWA).

The NRA was a peculiar hybrid that sought to satisfy competing interests and accommodate different analyses of the causes of the Depression. To many businessmen who believed that the economy suffered from excessive capacity and competition, it promised release from the strictures of antitrust and an

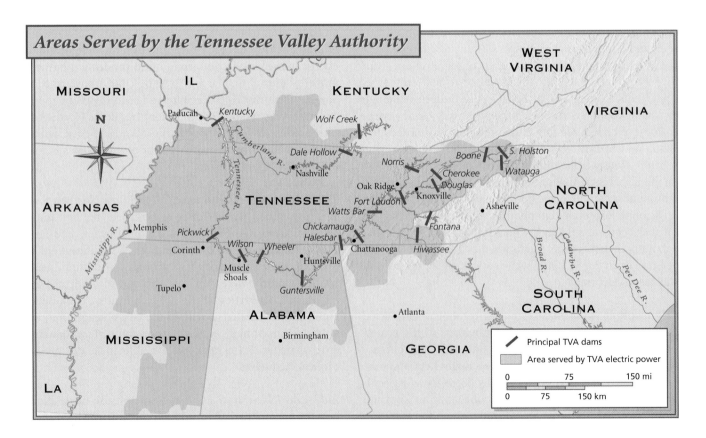

**Areas Served by the Tennessee Valley Authority**

end to the unfettered competition that had reduced profits. To some of the reformers in Roosevelt's administration, heirs to Theodore Roosevelt's "New Nationalism," the NRA offered a way for the government to step up the regulation of business, to replace the chaos of the market with rational economic planning. To labor and its liberal backers, it offered Washington's support for long-standing goals; John L. Lewis, head of the miners' union, likened the NRA to the Emancipation Proclamation. The NRA was thus a political compromise, grounded largely in the debate over monopolization and the trusts that had been so prominent between 1890 and 1915. Recovery would come from a restructuring of industry and an alteration of the relationship between the state and the economy.

By the middle of June 1933—the end of the first hundred days—Roosevelt and Congress had taken action on an extraordinary array of issues. They had brought an end to the banking crisis; created several programs to aid the unemployed; created a new legal and institutional framework for the conduct of business and agriculture; lessened the odds of Americans losing their homes, farms, and savings accounts; and initiated a major experiment in regional planning in the Tennessee River Valley. More a smorgasbord than a coherent reform package, the legislation was conservative in some respects, liberal in others, difficult to characterize in more than a few instances. Whatever its ideological coloration, the sheer pace of activity had broken the anxious gloom of the previous winter.

A CCC project in Lancaster, California, where 200 men from Ohio were building roads through the mountains to help fight forest fires.

*Leaving the Gold Standard.* There were few signs that the Depression was abating, and the president knew it. For this reason, Roosevelt in early July took one of the most controversial actions of his first term, issuing a message to a World Economic Conference in London that the United States would remain off the gold standard for the foreseeable future and would not participate in the conference's stated goal of fixing exchange rates among countries. The message was a bombshell in Europe and domestically: although the president had effectively taken the nation off the gold standard in the spring (by placing an embargo on the export of gold), it was widely believed that this was a temporary action that would be reversed at the London conference. But Roosevelt and many of his advisers had come to realize that their strategy of inflating prices was incompatible with a commitment to gold and fixed exchange rates. If the AAA and the NRA did succeed in raising the prices of domestically produced goods,

imports would increase, gold would have to flow out of the country to pay for the imports, and price deflation would return, dampening economic activity. Faced with that scenario, Roosevelt freed American policy from the fetters of the gold standard. His doing so led to the collapse of the London conference and to widespread denunciation of his administration. It also undermined international efforts to find a collective solution to the global economic slowdown and thereby stoked the already burning fires of nationalism in Europe and the Pacific.

## THE FIRST TWO YEARS

Despite the frenetic activity in Washington, the economy was slow to rebound. A few small spurts of growth spawned moments of optimism in 1933 and 1934, but each proved to be a false start on the road to recovery.

Some tangible signs of progress did appear in agriculture, owing in part to the AAA. Although the first attempts to restrict output, in the summer and fall of 1933, produced disturbing images of cotton fields plowed under and 6 million piglets slaughtered (while millions of humans remained hungry in the cities), the incentives offered by the AAA, coupled with the fortuitous arrival of drought in 1934, did limit farm production and spark an increase in prices. Most farmers

713

continued to demand compulsory output restriction, and militant members of the Midwestern Farmers Holiday Association went on "strike," dumping milk on highways and even blowing up dairies and creameries. In some areas, farm incomes rose enough in the mid-1930s to stem the tide of protest.

Yet the allotment program that was at the heart of the AAA had serious negative consequences for tenant farmers everywhere, most dramatically in the South. The payments to farmers for holding some of their acreage out of cultivation were paid to the owners of farmland. In theory, owners were to share those payments with their tenants, but often they did not. In the South, typically, white landowners pocketed their subsidies, evicting tenants or sharecroppers or simply preventing them from growing cash crops. Southern tenant farmers resisted such efforts, often militantly, but in the end many were driven off the land, leaving some of the nation's poorest citizens poorer than before.

The NRA was even less successful. It was launched with great ballyhoo by its colorful head, Hugh Johnson: supporters displayed the symbol of the NRA, a "Blue Eagle," on their storefronts and workplaces, and a quarter of a million people marched through the streets of New York celebrating the new program. Buoyed by popular support, Johnson convinced most industrial producers to agree to codes of fair practice and competition by the fall of 1933. But the codes did not seem to provide any stimulus to the economy. As important, different constituencies began to complain loudly that their interests were ill served. Small businesses, as well as progressive critics, claimed that the codes were buttressing monopolies; consumers objected that prices were increasing; big business resented the interference of the government; and labor leaders, lamenting that the prolabor clauses of the legislation were too weak, began to refer to the NRA as the National Run Around.

These conflicts within the NRA mirrored a broader problem that Roosevelt faced after his first few months in office. In the absence of any significant economic recovery, he found it increasingly difficult to hold together the broad coalition of business, labor, and farm interests that had supported him at the outset. The legislation of the first hundred days had included gestures toward diverse constituencies, but nearly all found things wanting, and their dissatisfactions deepened over time. Leaders of the business and financial community, even those who were Democrats, became suspicious of Roosevelt, even accusing him of being a dangerous radical: in addition to their disenchantment with the NRA, they were appalled by his departure from the gold standard and opposed his initiatives to regulate the stock exchange and the airwaves through the creation of the Securities and Exchange Commission and the Federal Communications Commission. As a vehicle for mobilizing their anti–New Deal sentiments, many of these big businessmen, led by the chairman of General Motors, founded the American Liberty League.

Progressives, too, were less than ecstatic with the early New Deal: they found the pace of reform slow and Roosevelt overly inclined to compromise with big business. Both within and outside the Democratic Party, self-identified progressives ran to Roosevelt's left in the midterm congressional elections of 1934, and they did exceedingly well, contributing significantly to unexpected Democratic gains. Reversing the longstanding pattern that parties in power lost ground during midterm elections, the Democrats emerged from the 1934 elections with sixty-nine Senate seats and a huge majority in the House. Nearly a dozen independents were also elected to Congress, and many more gained state and local offices.

One candidate who failed to win election in 1934 nonetheless gave a scare to mainstream politicians of both parties: Upton Sinclair, the aging novelist, socialist, and author of the famous muckraking novel of the Progressive Era, *The Jungle*. Sinclair lived in California, where he founded an organization

A 1932 Socialist Party campaign poster supporting Norman Thomas for president under the slogan "Repeal unemployment!"

called End Poverty in California (EPIC). EPIC's program called for the state to buy or rent uncultivated land and idle factories so that workers could grow their own food and manufacture necessities such as clothing and furniture. When Sinclair announced that he would seek the Democratic nomination for governor in 1934, his program struck a strong enough chord among voters that he won the Democratic primary. Squaring off in the general election against an arch-conservative Republican, he seemed to stand a good chance of being elected until conservative Democrats deserted the party in droves while Republicans launched a smear campaign against Sinclair, based on selective quotations from his early writings. With President Roosevelt standing on the sidelines, declining to endorse his own party's nominee, Sinclair went down to a decisive defeat in the general election.

## STIRRINGS ON THE LEFT

Sinclair's campaign in California was only one tip of an iceberg. Throughout the nation, the Depression gave birth or strength to political movements that challenged key features of traditional American political and economic life. Some questioned the viability of capitalism itself; others pressed for a wholesale redistribution of power and wealth within a free enterprise economy; still others focused on single issues. Despite the severity of the Depression, the nation never came near the brink of revolution; but for the first time since the late nineteenth century, radical and quasi-radical movements played a significant role in the nation's politics.

The Socialist Party, led by Norman Thomas after the death in the 1920s of Eugene Debs, experienced a resurgence of popularity, once again electing members to local offices in working-class cities such as Milwaukee and Bridgeport, Connecticut. Thomas himself polled nearly a million votes in the 1932 presidential election and was a widely respected voice for the view that the Depression clearly demonstrated the failure of capitalism. The Socialists were challenged on the left by the Communist Party of the United States, formed after World War I and committed to the overthrow of American capitalism and the political institutions that supported it. The Communist Party never had more than 100,000 members at any one time, but the number of persons who belonged to or sympathized with the party in the course of the 1930s was far greater. Its membership consisted largely of workers and intellectuals and was concentrated in a few key cities, including New York, Chicago, and Detroit. Members of

Police breaking up a labor gathering in San Francisco on the eve of the general strike in 1934.

the Communist Party—as well as several dissident communist groups, including followers of Leon Trotsky—were almost alone in organizing the unemployed in the early 1930s, staging demonstrations to demand adequate relief and resisting the eviction of jobless workers from their homes; they were also almost unique in promoting full equality for African Americans. Their militance and dedication gave them a prestige among workers that went beyond their numbers.

Both Socialists and Communists were active in a wave of labor unrest that swept parts of the country in 1934. Labor had been relatively quiet during the early years of the Depression, as union membership fell off and workers feared taking any action that could jeopardize their jobs. But stimulated in part by the hopes and disappointments generated by the NRA, workers in many cities engaged in strikes in 1934, some of them extremely militant and disruptive. Thousands of workers, for example, struck against the Electric Auto-Lite plant in Toledo, Ohio, precipitating a citywide conflict that one journalist characterized as a "civil war." Teamsters shut down Minneapolis, a longshoreman's job action led to a brief "general strike" of all workers in San Francisco, and textile workers walked off their jobs from Massachusetts to South Carolina in the largest strike in the nation's history. Blood flowed in many of these cities, as the police and private guards cracked down on workers and demonstrators: "a few hundred funerals," noted one textile industrial publication, "will have a quieting influence." Job security and wages were at issue in most of these conflicts, as was the right of workers to unionize; fueling the militance almost everywhere was something deeper—a profound sense of injustice, anger, and exploitation.

*Father Coughlin and Dr. Townsend.* A sense of injustice and grievance also infused other movements, several of which were spearheaded by individuals who became prominent political figures. One was Father Charles Coughlin, a parish priest in Royal Oak, Michigan. In the late 1920s, Coughlin began delivering sermons over the radio, at first locally and then, thanks to technological changes that strengthened the power of transmitters, to audiences in Chicago and Cincinnati. He was such a popular speaker that by 1930 CBS was broadcasting his talks over a new national network, allowing him to become the first exemplar of what would become an oddly familiar type: the man of the cloth who was also a media personality and political commentator. Coughlin's political views offered a blend of progressive Catholic doctrine, support for unions, hostility to bankers, and the conviction that inflating the currency through the coinage of silver was "the key to world prosperity." He initially supported Roosevelt, but then became an increasingly erratic critic of the New Deal, mixing dollups of anti-Semitism into his denunciations of a global conspiracy of bankers. Late in 1934, he founded the National Union for Social Justice, an organization that called for inflation and monetary reforms, the nationalization of important industries, and the protection of labor's rights. Coughlin's support was particularly strong among lower-middle-class Catholic immigrants, but his appeal was broader than that: his radio audience, the largest steady audience in the world, numbered upward of 30 million.

A much less controversial figure was Francis Townsend, an elderly physician from Long Beach, California, who rose to sudden prominence in the mid-1930s. In 1934, Townsend developed a scheme for "old age revolving pensions" that he believed would solve the problem of security for the elderly in the United States while simultaneously giving a major boost to the economy. Every person age sixty or older who retired from work would receive a check from the government for $200 each month, to be spent within a month of its issue: the retirements would make way for younger, unemployed workers; the elderly would have guaranteed incomes; and the spending would stimulate economic growth, enough to compensate for the 2 percent business tax required to fund the program. The Townsend plan was embraced by millions of citizens across the country, particularly older rural Protestants; its supporters

constituted the first organized appearance of "senior citizens" in the nation's political debates. Although critics ridiculed the plan's arithmetic, the Townsend program was endorsed by sixteen of California's twenty congressmen, among others. In some locales, belief that the plan would soon become law was so strong that elderly citizens tried to purchase goods with the promise to pay when their first Townsend checks arrived.

*Sharing the Wealth.* The most important new political leader to emerge during this period was Louisiana senator Huey P. Long. Brilliant, colorful, and shrewd, Long tapped a current of populist sentiment that had been underground since the 1890s. He rose to power in Louisiana in the 1920s by leading a revolt against the corrupt oligarchy of politicians and big businesses (including utility companies and Standard Oil) that had dominated the impoverished state for decades. As governor, he taxed the rich and business interests; built roads, schools, and hospitals; and constructed a political machine that became unchallengeable. With his election to the Senate in 1930 (for nearly two years he was both governor and senator), he entered the national political arena and was a key supporter of Roosevelt's nomination in 1932.

Long quickly became Roosevelt's most feared rival. Both publicly and privately, he criticized Roosevelt as being too tepid a reformer, and he positioned himself as the champion of the common man doing battle against an elite that included not only big business but also educated northeasterners such as Roosevelt and many of his advisers. In 1934, Long launched a national political organization with the slogan "Share Our Wealth" and the goal of redistributing the wealth of the richest Americans so that each family would own a home, a car, and a radio. He also favored a national minimum wage, a shorter work week, support for education, and huge spending on public works to provide jobs for the unemployed. By the spring of 1935, there were thousands of Share Our Wealth Clubs in the country, as well as a mailing list of millions of adherents. Long was transformed from a regional icon to a national figure, capable of drawing enormous crowds in locales as diverse as Iowa and Philadelphia. His meteoric rise and evident presidential ambitions were deeply worrisome to Roosevelt and his fellow New Dealers. Roosevelt's primary concern was that Long would run in 1936 as an independent and drain enough votes away from him to elect a Republican; others feared that the youthful Long would be a formidable candidate to succeed Roosevelt in 1940. Both possibilities were foreclosed in September 1935,

Senator Huey Long delivering a national radio address criticizing New Deal policies in March, 1935.

when Long was assassinated in Baton Rouge by the son-in-law of a judge whom Long was trying to remove from office.

The energy that poured into these diverse movements revealed both an impatience with the New Deal and the critical fact that the spectrum of political opinion had lurched sharply leftward between 1929 and the mid-1930s. The moderate liberalism of Roosevelt and his allies stood in contrast not only to the conservatism of Republicans and business Democrats but also to political beliefs that were more severely critical of capitalism itself. "I am not a liberal. I am a radical," declared Minnesota governor Floyd Olson, who advocated a "cooperative commonwealth" that would include government ownership of key industries. Intellectuals like John Dewey, the nation's leading philosopher, agreed. Dewey favored a moderate form of socialism that would place the state in control of the economy while also respecting and protecting individual liberties. Other intellectuals went further, embracing the more militant program of the Communist Party; among its well-known sympathizers were novelists John Dos Passos and Sherwood Anderson, literary critics Malcolm Cowley and Edmund Wilson, and African American poet Langston Hughes. To some, the Soviet Union (which was not experi-

encing a depression) stood as a model for Americans trying to build a more egalitarian society: scores of skilled American workers even went to the Soviet Union to work in its plants and catch a glimpse of the future. Such ideas were not beyond the pale in the midst of the Great Depression. "The country," observed Roosevelt's secretary of the interior, Harold Ickes, in his diary, "is much more radical than the Administration."

## THE SECOND HUNDRED DAYS

These stirrings throughout the country were not lost on the president. Roosevelt was nothing if not a masterful politician, with extraordinary antennae for shifting political winds. The nation's mood in the spring of 1935 seemed to demand renewed action and to create the opportunity for the president to promote legislation in which he deeply believed, particularly social insurance for the elderly and the unemployed. Consequently, Roosevelt and his advisers prepared a new set of measures to present to the more liberal Congress elected the previous November.

Roosevelt's determination was reinforced by a striking defeat for the New Deal at the hands of the Supreme Court. In May 1935, the Court unanimously ruled in *Schechter Poultry v. the U.S.* that the NRA was unconstitutional. The case arose when Schechter Poultry, a small Brooklyn firm, was found to be in violation of the NRA's Live Poultry Code. The Court found fault with the NRA because the agency's broad authority represented an excessive delegation of the legislative powers of Congress; more ominously, the Court also concluded that the federal government had no right to be imposing the poultry code in the first place because the Schechter firm was involved exclusively in intrastate commerce, while the Constitution gave Washington the right to regulate only interstate commerce. The decision was foreshadowed by Court rulings in several earlier cases, but it nonetheless jolted New Dealers. How could the federal government possibly contend with the economic crisis without having an impact on firms whose dealings remained within the boundaries of an individual state? The Court, according to the president, had embraced a "horse-and-buggy definition of interstate commerce." The demise of the increasingly unpopular NRA was not widely mourned (although Roosevelt himself remained attached to it), but the Court's objection could potentially be applied to nearly all major economic legislation.

Nonetheless, Roosevelt moved forward, with one eye on the Court and another on the movements building across the nation. The result was a series of measures, all passed in 1935,

717

A Works Progress Administration poster.

that are often described as the "Second Hundred Days" or the "Second New Deal."

***Aid for the Jobless.*** Relief for the unemployed remained a pressing issue: 8 million Americans were still jobless, for increasingly long stretches, and the initiatives launched in 1933 seemed inadequate. The PWA, administered by the cautious Harold Ickes, was slow in developing worthwhile construction projects, and its legal status was dubious after the *Schechter* decision because it was created as part of the NRA. Roosevelt had shut down the Civil Works Administration (CWA) in 1934 because he was concerned about its cost and because many of its jobs appeared to be "make work." Giving out money for "a few hours of weekly work cutting grass, raking leaves, or picking up papers in the public parks" seemed to him not much more than a "dole" that was "fundamentally destructive to the national fibre." The FERA continued to provide funds for direct relief to the jobless poor, but it paid only

a pittance and required applicants to make a demeaning declaration that they lacked the resources to support themselves.

What Roosevelt wanted—and what jobless Americans wanted—was a federal program that would relieve the urgent needs of the unemployed by paying them to perform meaningful work. In the eyes of the president and nearly all his contemporaries, work relief of some sort was preferable to paying people who remained idle. Yet the type of work that the jobless should perform was not obvious, since their abilities were diverse and it made little sense for them to engage in activities that would compete with private enterprise. Nor was it clear how pay scales could be set so that the unemployed could support themselves without earning more on work relief than they would earn in agriculture or industry.

The Emergency Relief Appropriations Act, which Congress approved in the spring of 1935, tried to address many of these issues: it was grounded in the presumption that unemployment was a durable problem and that the federal government ought to step in and give work to those the private sector could not absorb. The act increased support for the previously created CCC; it also re-funded the PWA to undertake large-scale public works projects that required advance planning. Although the PWA did not really begin pumping much money into the economy until 1938, the agency did leave an enduring legacy: it built schools, courthouses, city halls, and sewage plants all across the country, as well as such landmarks as New York's Triboro Bridge and Lincoln Tunnel and the bridge linking Florida's Key West to the mainland.

At the center of the initiative was a new and more innovative agency, the Works Progress Administration (later, Works Projects Administration), or WPA. The WPA, based on the largest appropriation in the nation's history, was designed to quickly create 3.5 million jobs without competing with private business. Its jobs would pay more than relief but less than prevailing local wages. The WPA was structured to take advantage of the diverse talents of the unemployed: it not only constructed hospitals, schools, and other public buildings but also hired artists, writers, historians, and actors (among others) to paint murals on public buildings, create and perform plays, interview former slaves, index historical records, and write guides to individual states and regions. The WPA was a magnet for criticism from conservatives, who were appalled by its cost and feared that it was supporting the "undeserving" poor or serving as a patronage base for the Democratic Party. It was also attacked by labor unions, who believed that the "security" wages paid would serve to depress wage rates, and by civil rights advocates, who were infuriated that southern blacks and Hispanic women in the West would receive lower wages than nearby whites. Nonetheless, the WPA had many enthusiastic supporters and by 1936 was employing a full 7 percent of American workers.

*The Wagner Act.* Workers with jobs also needed attention. Although section 7 (a) of the NIRA had promised workers the right to form unions and engage in collective bargaining, it lacked enforcement provisions and was generally ineffective. The *Schechter* decision gave prolabor legislators the opportunity to write a new law that would have more teeth. The driving force for such a bill was Senator Robert F. Wagner of New York, an educated, new-style Tammany Hall politician who had risen from humble, immigrant beginnings and become a powerful force for social welfare legislation. In 1935, with the somewhat less-than-enthusiastic backing of Roosevelt, Wagner successfully pressed the Democrat-dominated Congress to pass the National Labor Relations Act, often called the Wagner Act. The act gave federal protection to the right of workers to form unions and engage in collective bargaining. It also created the National Labor Relations Board (NLRB) to oversee the exercise of that right; the board was empowered to hold elections in which employees could democratically decide whether or not they wanted a union—and which union they wanted. Going further, the Wagner Act itemized actions that would constitute illegal "unfair labor practices" on the part of employers, including firing workers because of their union membership or pro-union activity, creating company-controlled organizations in lieu of independent unions, and refusing to bargain with a duly certified union. In so doing, the act deprived employers of some key weapons they had used to resist unionization.

Roosevelt was not a great fan of labor unions, but he understood that without them, workers were no match for large corporate employers. He also understood that industrial workers were a politically restive force as well as a critical constituency for the Democratic Party. The passage of the Wagner Act went a long way toward cementing the attachment of labor to the Democrats and, in so doing, helped to solidify the opposition to Roosevelt of many anti-union employers and employers' associations, such as the National Association of Manufacturers. Beyond partisan politics, the Wagner Act was significant both in serving as a charter for the unionization of American labor and in providing the basic framework of federal labor law for the remainder of the twentieth century.

*Social Security.* Roosevelt's heart was in the Social Security Act of 1935, a measure every bit as radical as the Wagner Act. In 1934, Roosevelt had entrusted the drafting of the legislation to a committee headed by Secretary of Labor Frances Perkins, the first woman ever to hold a cabinet position. Perkins, a Mt. Holyoke graduate schooled in social work at Jane Addams's Hull House, was a dedicated prolabor reformer who had led an official investigation of the horrific Triangle Shirtwaist Company fire (1911), which killed scores of young female workers, and had later served for years as an industrial commissioner in New York. She and Roosevelt agreed that the time had come for the United States to erect a system of social insurance that would prevent the widespread destitution they were witnessing in the mid-1930s; most industrialized countries had already adopted such systems.

A 1935 Social Security Board poster urging Americans to take advantage of the just-passed Social Security Act.

## Franklin D. Roosevelt: The First Term

The Social Security Act had three key provisions, each of which tempered Roosevelt's vision of a comprehensive insurance program with political, legal, and fiscal concerns. The first was a system of unemployment insurance that would provide automatic support to men and women who had lost their jobs; in 1935, such insurance existed only in the progressive state of Wisconsin. Because of fears that the courts might find a purely federal system to be unconstitutional, it was designed as a joint state-federal program, funded largely through state taxes that would be offset by federal monies. To the dismay of many longtime advocates, some of the nation's poorest (and minority) workers were not covered, and benefits in some states were utterly inadequate; but the legislation nonetheless established that workers had a right to public support when they were jobless.

As a second provision, the Social Security Act created pensions for the elderly. Bowing to what Perkins called American "prejudices," the pensions were financed by payroll taxes on employers and employees, establishing a contributory system that was a curious hybrid of insurance and compulsory savings. But Roosevelt shrewdly sensed that a contributory program would protect the pension system in the long run: since individuals were placing their own funds into social security accounts, "no damn politician can ever scrap my social security program." The act did not cover farm workers, domestic servants (many of whom were female and/or African American), or employees in small businesses, and it did not begin payments to anyone until 1940. Nonetheless, the legislation was a pathbreaking step in the public assumption of responsibility for the welfare of its citizens and in restructuring the very idea of retirement for most workers.

The third, more modest prong of the legislation provided for immediate grants to the states to provide relief to the elderly poor and to mothers of dependent children, many of whom had been abandoned by jobless fathers who hit the road in search of work. Although the funds allocated for such programs were small, the programs were an exception to the bias against a "dole" for the nonworking poor: over time, Aid to Dependent Children (later renamed Aid to Families with Dependent Children) became a critical element of the welfare state.

Roosevelt and his advisers wanted to include a system of national health care as part of a "cradle to grave" insurance system. The political obstacles, however, were so formidable that this goal was relinquished except for a few minor allocations for disabled people and some rural communities. In de-ciding not to press for a health care system in 1935, both the president and his advisers presumed that once the other ingredients of a social insurance system were in place, it would be soon be possible to add national health care to the mix.

*Rural Electrification.* For millions of farm-dwelling Americans, the creation of the Rural Electrification Administration (REA) in 1935 was a more significant event than the passage of the Wagner or Social Security Act. It reflected Roosevelt's personal belief that electricity was "no longer a luxury" but a "necessity." The goal of the REA, like that of the TVA, was to bring electricity to rural areas, something private enterprise had failed to do; unlike the TVA, the REA was national in its reach. After trying unsuccessfully to work with private utilities, the REA helped create local cooperatives to which it lent money for the construction of electric lines; it also offered engineering and legal assistance. The program was immediately successful, leading to the construction of electric transmission lines at 40 percent below the costs estimated by private utilities. Although a shortage of funds limited the breadth of the REA, its efforts brought electricity to more than 900,000 households by 1941.

For farmers across the nation, this meant that a half-century of electrical technology arrived in their homes all at once. Suddenly they had electric lights and radios; more than half of all new electric subscribers bought washing machines within a year, while more than a fourth bought refrigerators.

An electric milk-cooling tank which was far more efficient and less expensive than ice cooling methods.

On many farms electricity not only improved household conditions and lightened the burden of household labor, it also altered farm production itself. Keeping electric lights burning in chicken coops increased winter egg production; refrigeration preserved milk; and electric pumps helped to irrigate semiarid lands, particularly in the West. The REA, to be sure, did not reach most of the nation's poorest farmers, but it significantly advanced the spread of electrically based technology to rural America. In so doing, it helped to increase the efficiency of the nation's farms, contributing after 1940, ironically, to the renewed exodus of farmers from the land.

The REA and the TVA were two expressions of a larger New Deal vision of state-promoted economic development and technological diffusion. In addition to the many multipurpose dams built along the Tennessee River, the government launched other major dam projects, the most notable of which were the Grand Coulee Dam in central Washington and the Hoover Dam on the Colorado River at the border of northwestern Arizona and southeastern Nevada. Designed by engineers from the Department of Interior and the U.S. Army Corps of Engineers, these massive projects involved thousands of private contractors and tens of thousands of construction workers. The resulting structures were widely regarded as technological marvels. The huge turbine rooms and spillways of the Grand Coulee and Hoover dams attracted thousands of tourists and became symbols of the New Deal's faith in public power and public action. The western dams not only generated electricity but also irrigated semiarid farmlands and provided water to rapidly growing cities like Los Angeles.

Yet these great symbols of power and progress were not without their critics, who claimed that the chief beneficiaries were large landowners and corporations. Indeed, despite the government's stated desire to provide "electricity for all," nearly half the power generated by the TVA and the Grand Coulee Dam ended up being harnessed to large industrial users. Moreover, the many dams built along the Tennessee, Colorado, and Columbia rivers backed up water for miles, forming huge man-made lakes and forcing people to surrender their land and move. Native Americans saw their ancestral lands flooded and valued salmon runs destroyed. Advocates of the projects, however, remained convinced that the benefits far outweighed the costs. "When I think of the work which has been done" by the TVA, Senator George Norris mused in 1941, "it is too good to be true. It seems almost like a dream."

## THE ELECTION OF 1936

By 1936, Roosevelt had abandoned his effort to build a broad, multiclass coalition, and he shaped his political campaign, as he had shaped the Second New Deal, to fend off the challenge from the left in a country that was becoming increasingly radicalized. The decision was not his alone: the business community had begun turning against Roosevelt as early as 1934, and its hostility mounted with the Wagner Act, the Social Security Act, and a "soak the rich" tax proposal put forward in 1936. Business and financial leaders rallied behind the Republican nominee, Governor Alf Landon of Kansas, who criticized Roosevelt for excessive spending and for violating the Constitution; yet even Landon tacitly acknowledged Roosevelt's popularity by vowing to continue some New Deal programs.

Roosevelt happily ran against the Republicans and the "economic royalists" of the business community, sometimes savagely denouncing the "greed" and "autocracy" of "organized money." Most important, he succeeded in keeping most voters on the left from bolting to third parties. With Huey Long dead, the remnants of his Share Our Wealth movement joined with followers of Dr. Townsend and Father Coughlin to form the Union Party, which nominated William Lemke, a North Dakota congressman, for president. But the Social Security Act and the tax on the wealthy had taken the steam out of these movements. Similarly, Roosevelt's prolabor stances led some socialist union leaders to urge their members to forsake third-party movements and support the Democrats instead. In November, the president won a spectacular victory. Roosevelt received almost 28 million popular votes—61 percent of the total—to Landon's 16 million; the electoral college vote was 523–8, more lopsided than any split since Monroe's election in 1820. The Union Party polled less than 900,000 votes. The Democrats also increased their hold on Congress, winning 331 members of the House of Representatives compared with the Republicans' 89.

Building on trends that had first emerged in 1928, Roosevelt had reshaped the nation's politics and transformed the Democrats into the dominant national party. He carried sizable majorities in the country's industrial cities as well as among farmers in the South and West. Cracking the long-running hold of the Republican Party on African Americans, he even won majorities among the increasingly numerous blacks who had become enfranchised by migrating to the North. Most significant, he had enlarged the Democratic Party: his huge majority owed less to the conversion of voters from the Republican to the Democratic column than to the mass mobilization of new voters. Many were immigrants who had belatedly become American citizens (the years between 1928 and 1936 witnessed an extraordinarily high incidence of naturalization) or the children of immigrants who had reached voting age in the 1930s. Italian, Irish, Slovak, and Jewish industrial workers in Detroit, Pittsburgh, Cleveland, and New York—these men and women came out to the polls in unprecedented numbers and voiced boisterous approval of the New Deal.

## LABOR RISING

While Roosevelt's campaign for reelection was under way, so was another campaign that promised to reshape the economic and political landscape. This was the effort, led by rebellious union leaders from the American Federation of Labor (AFL), to organize workers in mass production industries, such as auto, steel, and rubber. Those workers, mostly semiskilled and unskilled, had remained outside the house of organized labor when unions were formed in earlier decades; as the Great Depression began, few belonged to unions, nearly all worked long hours for low wages, and most were either immigrants themselves or the children of immigrants. Their prospects of becoming union members seemed poor, since depressions had invariably witnessed a decline in union membership.

The leader of the effort to organize these men and women was the president of the United Mine Workers, John L. Lewis. The son of Welsh immigrants, Lewis, who grew up in the coal fields of Iowa, was a charismatic figure who became one of the most prominent—and, by some, feared—men in the United States from the 1930s to the 1950s. A large man with intense eyes and huge, bushy eyebrows, he was an eloquent speaker and a shrewd strategist. Lewis had concluded as early as the 1920s that the long-run protection of his own union depended on the organization of the steel industry (since steelmakers owned many mines and were key consumers of coal) and that the union movement itself could gain strength only if all men and women who labored in the same industry belonged to the same union.

Lewis spent much of 1933 and 1934 building up the membership of his own union and attempting to convince the leadership of the AFL (of which he was a vice-president) to begin an organizing drive in the mass-production industries. Despite the unfavorable economic conditions, Lewis believed that rank-and-file anger as well as the prolabor provisions of the

John L. Lewis, shown here addressing textile workers in Lawrence, Massachusetts, May 1937.

NRA had created an opening for action. The cautious, largely native-born leadership of the AFL appeared to agree but did little to support Lewis's efforts. At the AFL convention of 1935, Lewis reraised the issue, pointedly provoking a heated debate and a formal vote rejecting his proposal: after a dramatic moment in which he delivered a punch to the head of the carpenters' union, Lewis led a walk-out from the convention. With Sidney Hillman, the head of the Amalgamated Clothing Workers, and David Dubinsky, president of the International Ladies' Garment Workers' Union, Lewis then formed the Committee for Industrial Organization; it was renamed the Congress of Industrial Organizations (CIO) in 1938, two years after its leaders and their unions had been expelled from the AFL.

The CIO's first targets were the steel and auto industries. Encouraged by a temporarily improving economy, as well as the new legal protections contained in the Wagner Act, the CIO hired squads of organizers to fan out into the workplaces, recreation halls, bars, and fraternal associations of industrial America. The drive was funded largely by a war chest that Lewis and the mine workers had built up over several years. Although Lewis himself was not an ideological radical, many of the organizers the CIO deployed were Communists and Socialists who saw unionization as both a step toward social justice and a blow against capitalism. The Communists, in particular, were dedicated and skilled organizers, willing to suffer hardships and take risks for the cause.

*The CIO vs. General Motors.* The first major confrontation came in the auto industry, where a CIO-backed organizing committee squared off against General Motors, the world's largest corporation. GM was a vast, integrated network of parts manufacturing and assembly plants, centered in Detroit and the nearby city of Flint, Michigan; it employed more than 240,000 workers, only a skilled handful of whom belonged to unions. GM's workers, like those at Ford and Chrysler, suffered from annual layoffs, arbitrary hiring and firing practices, and sometimes brutally arduous working conditions. Organizers, including Socialist militant Walter Reuther, who had worked in a plant in the Soviet Union and would eventually become the president of the United Auto Workers, spent much of 1936 gathering supporters and developing a strategy to compel GM to recognize the union as the bargaining agent for all employees. Since GM was a staunchly anti-union firm that, like most other major corporations, spent a great deal of money trying to ward off unions and infiltrate organizing campaigns, a fierce strike was anticipated. The leadership of GM was also convinced that it had nothing to fear from the Wagner Act because it would soon be declared unconstitutional.

The conflict began dramatically in Flint in late December 1936, less than two months after Roosevelt's landslide reelection. In a bold strategic move, thousands of striking autoworkers, rather than leaving their jobs and forming picket lines outside, simply stopped the machinery and "sat down" inside several of GM's key plants. In doing so, they guaranteed that the company could not hire scabs (replacement workers) or take forceful action without risking damage to its machinery and facilities; by carefully selecting the sit-down targets, they hoped to prevent GM from producing cars at all, despite its large network of plants.

The action stunned GM and the public, not least because the sit-down loomed as a symbolic repudiation of private property rights. Within days, workers had seized other plants, and Flint became the center of national attention, with police guarding the plants, thousands of supporters forming picket lines outside, a "women's brigade" carrying food to the sit-down strikers, and reporters and camera crews circulating everywhere. GM denounced the strike as a Communist-inspired insurrection and demanded that the Democratic governor of Michigan, Frank Murphy, call out the national guard to evict the strikers. Murphy declined to do so, and public opinion, reflecting the era's broad political sympathy for the working class, remained on the side of the strikers. For more than six weeks, the strikers remained in the plants, care-

fully protecting the machinery from harm, doing calisthenics to remain in shape, and talking politics nonstop.

In mid-February 1937, GM surrendered, recognizing the United Auto Workers as the bargaining agent for the company's employees. The company did not immediately grant the pay raises or changes in working conditions that had been demanded, but it agreed to negotiate those issues with the union. The workers' victory gave an enormous shot of adrenaline to organizing efforts throughout the nation. So, too, did the announcement a few weeks later that U.S. Steel, the nation's largest steel producer and a notoriously anti-union firm, had given up without a fight: after secret discussions with Lewis, the corporation's president, Myron Taylor, declared that it would recognize the United Steel Workers as its workers' union. Many battles remained to be fought, and some of them, including those at Chrysler, Ford, and Republic Steel, produced violent encounters and bloodshed; in Chicago, on Memorial Day 1937, police opened fire at a demonstration near Republic Steel's plant, killing ten workers, most of them shot in the back.

But the bulwarks surrounding the mass production industries had been definitively breached. By the end of 1937, more than 200,000 autoworkers and 300,000 steelworkers had joined CIO-affiliated unions; the United Rubber Workers had won an eight-week strike against Firestone; and General Electric, as well as RCA, had recognized the United Electrical and Radio

General Motors workers at the sit-down strike in Flint, Michigan, January 9, 1937.

Workers. Total CIO membership numbered close to 4 million, as men and women in one industry after another rushed to join unions. The AFL also benefited from this surge in labor's strength and popularity, adding hundreds of thousands of new members. Some of these gains, for both the CIO and the AFL, proved short-lived, as employers counterattacked and the economy began to sink again in 1937 and 1938. Nonetheless, the union movement had acquired an institutional strength that it never had before, and it was well positioned to add millions more new members in 1941 and beyond, when wartime conditions created the tightest labor markets in decades.

The success of the CIO in the teeth of the worst depression in the nation's history would not have been easy to predict. That the organization achieved its goal of bringing the basic protections of unionization to millions of semiskilled and unskilled workers was, in part, the result of determined leadership, both nationally and in the hundreds of locals that sprang up in cities across the nation. The CIO's success also owed a great deal to the political climate established by the New Deal, a climate that led both the federal government and state officials like Frank Murphy to encourage unionization rather than weigh in on the side of anti-union corporations—as had often happened before.

In addition to these political factors, another process was at work: the development of a shared culture and sense of community among the millions of immigrant families, most of them eastern and southern European or Irish, who had come to the United States several decades earlier and who worked in its steel mills, rubber factories, and auto plants. No longer temporary sojourners in the land, these men and women had reasons to build new institutions in America; most of them, and all of their children, spoke English, and thanks to the radio and other forms of mass communication and entertainment, they possessed common frames of reference, whether their forebears hailed from Italy or Poland or County Cork. For such men and women in Flint, Pittsburgh, Chicago, Buffalo, and New York, the CIO was not simply an organization but a movement for dignity and self-improvement, in which and through which they could act together.

## Roosevelt's Second Term

Franklin Roosevelt's second inauguration, in January 1937—the anxious interregnum of 1933 had led Congress to permanently change inauguration day from March 4 to January 20—was a triumphant occasion for the president. Reelected by a record margin, Roosevelt enjoyed unprecedented popularity, and the economy, which had improved throughout 1936, continued to show signs of growth. Roosevelt could also point to an extraordinary string of achievements during his first term. Yet his inaugural address suggested that he would not rest on his record. "I see one-third of a nation ill-housed, ill-clad, ill-nourished," he declared. The president and his administration seemed prepared, politically and intellectually, to push the New Deal forward.

### TAKING AIM AT THE SUPREME COURT

The largest cloud on the New Deal's horizon was the Supreme Court. The Court's ruling against the NRA in 1935 was followed by a series of similarly conservative decisions: the Court destroyed the AAA by declaring its processing tax to be unconstitutional; threw out legislation designed to shore up the coal industry after the demise of the NRA; and even overturned a New York minimum wage statute on the grounds that it interfered with the freedom of individuals to make economic contracts. The implication of these decisions seemed to be that neither the federal government nor the states could do much at all to regulate economic affairs.

The Court's posture created uncertainty in the administration about how to promote economic recovery and design further social legislation, such as a federal wage and hours bill. As important, the Court's decisions suggested that it would uphold pending legal challenges to other landmark measures, including the Social Security Act and the Wagner Act, effectively nullifying the heart of the New Deal. Four of the nine justices appeared to be unshakably committed to an interpretation of the Constitution that would not permit the federal government to actively intervene in the economy or erect any system of social insurance; and the conservative four were generally able to corral at least one more vote (usually from Justice Owen Roberts) to gain a majority. The conservatives were judicial activists who had overturned legislation in the 1920s and 1930s at an unprecedented rate. Seven of the sitting justices had been appointed by Republican presidents, as had 80 percent of all federal judges in the lower courts. The average age of the Supreme Court's justices was seventy-one; Roosevelt himself had not yet appointed a single member.

Strategies for circumventing the Supreme Court had been discussed among New Dealers for several years, but Roosevelt finally acted in early February 1937, when he sent Congress a proposal that would permit him to appoint additional justices to the Court. Couched as a measure to speed up the process of judicial review and lighten the workload of aging judges, the "Court-packing" scheme would have allowed the president to appoint one additional justice (up to a total of six) for each member of the Court who had served for ten years and did not retire within six months after reaching his seventieth birthday. It also authorized the president to appoint several dozen new judges to lower federal courts. In a characteristically mischievous twist, Roosevelt made his plan public two days after hosting a White House dinner honoring the Supreme Court—and less than a week before the Court began hearing oral arguments on the Wagner Act.

The proposal provoked an uproar, in and out of Washington. The pretext that Roosevelt was concerned about the Court's efficiency was flimsy, and he was quickly denounced for trying to alter the balance of power among different branches of government. He was also attacked for disparaging the "capacities" of the elderly—by, among others, powerful

A 1937 cartoon showing Roosevelt attempting the impossible task of pulling his Supreme Court reform plan through the Senate.

politicians who had themselves reached the age of seventy. Since Roosevelt had not alerted congressional leaders or most members of his own cabinet that the proposal was forthcoming, he had few defenders, while Republicans, conservative Democrats uneasy about the administration's leftward drift, and editorial writers around the country heaped criticism upon him. Even his closest associates thought the scheme displayed "too much cleverness"; few thought it had much chance of getting through Congress.

The Court-packing scheme was widely regarded by contemporaries and historians as the most glaring mistake of Roosevelt's presidency, a rare moment when his political antennae failed him. Perhaps so: frustrated by the Court and riding a crest of personal popularity, Roosevelt may well have underestimated the opposition his proposal would provoke. Nonetheless, Roosevelt won the war, even if he eventually lost the battle for Court reform. In March 1937, seven weeks after the Court-packing plan had been unveiled, the Supreme Court, by a 5–4 vote, upheld a Washington state minimum wage law not unlike the New York law that had recently been nullified. Justice Roberts had changed his mind.

In early April, the Court convened to announce its decisions in a series of legal challenges to the Wagner Act, the most important of which was *National Labor Relations Board v. Jones and Laughlin Steel*. Chief Justice Charles Evans Hughes, a white-bearded, moderate Republican, often a swing vote himself, carefully read the decision aloud to a packed courtroom in what one contemporary described as tones "of infallibility which made the whole business sound like a rehearsal for the last judgment." To the delight of New Dealers and the astonishment of legal observers, the Court, by a 5–4 vote, upheld the Wagner Act. Deploying a circuitous logic, the majority held that unions served to maintain labor peace and prevent the disruption of interstate commerce; it was thus constitutional for the federal government to promote unionization through the mechanisms created in the Wagner Act. Justice Roberts, who had voted with the conservatives in overturning the NRA and the AAA, supported the majority decision, a change in position that came to be called "the switch in time that saved nine." Subsequent Court rulings continued in the same vein, upholding the Social Security Act and giving the federal government broad new latitude to intervene in economic affairs. Whether Roberts's shift was influenced by the pending threat of the Court-packing scheme is unclear, but there is no doubt that the Court had tacked in a new direction. Hugh Johnson, the former head of the NRA, wrote to Roosevelt that "I was taken for a ride on a chicken truck in Brooklyn two years ago and dumped out on a deserted highway and left for dead. It seems this was all a mistake."

The Supreme Court's shift took the wind out of the sails of the Court-packing scheme, preventing a confrontation between the executive and judicial branches. With the substantive war already won, Congress had little appetite for the controversial proposal, and by midsummer the president withdrew it. A month after the Court's decision on the NLRA, moreover, one of the conservative stalwarts, Justice Willis Van Devanter, announced his retirement, giving Roosevelt the opportunity to appoint liberal Alabama senator Hugo Black to the Court. By 1940, Roosevelt had appointed four additional justices, including Frank Murphy, the former governor of Michigan, and Felix Frankfurter, the highly respected protégé of retiring justice Louis Brandeis. The new justices were far more open to innovation and an expansion of federal power than their predecessors had been; discarding the adherence to laissez-faire that had been the Court's hallmark for half a century, the Roosevelt Court ushered in a new era in American jurisprudence, helping to build a powerful modern state while simultaneously protecting the civil liberties of minorities.

## THE EBBING OF REFORM

Roosevelt may have won the war over the Supreme Court, but the battles surrounding the Court-packing scheme left him politically weakened. Sensing the president's new vulnerability—something almost unthinkable immediately after the 1936 election—a powerful conservative opposition, including many Democrats, emerged in Congress. Its members issued a "Manifesto" in late 1937 that condemned the sit-down strikes, expressed fear that the Roosevelt administration was creating a class of people permanently dependent on government welfare, demanded lower taxes and a balanced budget, and affirmed support for states' rights and private enterprise.

Southern Democrats played a critical role in this resistance to the New Deal, because they feared that a powerful federal government committed to improving the lot of all Americans would inevitably interfere with the South's system of racial segregation and oppression. Although early New Deal programs had carefully tiptoed around matters of racial discrimination, those fears were not baseless. The president's wife, Eleanor—a niece of Theodore Roosevelt, who in the 1920s became an advocate of women's rights and an opponent of racial segregation—constantly pushed him toward more socially

Eleanor Roosevelt (speaking) alongside the black educator and activist Mary McLeod Bethune at a meeting on African American education, 1939.

radical steps. Partly for this reason, the New Deal not only provided poor blacks with jobs in programs such as the PWA and the WPA, but gave educated African Americans a record-breaking number of government appointments. Roosevelt appointed the first black federal judge, William Hastie, and made the black educator and activist Mary McLeod Bethune director of Negro Affairs in the National Youth Administration. Bethune hosted meetings of African Americans who served in the Roosevelt administration (sometimes called the "black cabinet") and used her friendship with Eleanor Roosevelt to promote African American causes. Eleanor Roosevelt, in short, formed ties with blacks that gave them unprecedented—if modest—access to the White House and helped win African American voters to the Democratic fold.

The president felt obliged to be more politically wary, as a conflict over a federal antilynching measure made grimly clear. The first years of the 1930s witnessed roughly 100 lynchings in which mobs, mostly in the South, not only killed but often tortured and mutilated blacks. In 1934, liberals in

Congress introduced a bill, drawn up by the NAACP, that would have initiated federal prosecution for lynching and prescribed penalties for local officials who refused to prosecute lynchers. The president, prodded by his wife, favored the bill but refused to put his full political weight behind it. By virtue of their secure electoral base in a one-party region, southern Democrats had considerable seniority in Congress and consequently headed critical committees. If he alienated them, Roosevelt explained, "they will block every bill I ask Congress to pass to keep America from collapsing." The anti-lynching bill was stalled by a filibuster in the Senate until it was finally withdrawn in February 1938.

Despite their victory, southern Democrats looked suspiciously on new initiatives from the Roosevelt administration. They were also aware that the climate of northern intellectual opinion about race was changing. Faith in eugenics, for example, was being supplanted by mounting evidence of the importance of cultural and social environments: Columbia University psychologist Otto Klineberg found that blacks living in the urban North scored higher on I.Q. tests than did some white rural southerners. Southerners knew too that some ardent New Dealers stood poised to meddle with the South's caste system; labor unions, among others, were already active in efforts to abolish the poll tax in southern elections.

The result was a legislative stalemate. The president called a special session of Congress in November 1937 to consider a series of measures, none of which were enacted. In 1938, the administration managed to get Congress's consent to only two important measures. One, a farm bill, reenacted (with some minor changes) provisions of the old Agricultural Adjustment Act, which the Supreme Court had struck down but which it now seemed likely to endorse. The bill authorized the federal government to compensate farmers for limiting acreage planted and to take other steps to keep market prices from dropping below a fixed parity price. The second measure, the Fair Labor Standards Act of 1938, prohibited child labor and required industrial employers to pay a minimum wage of 40 cents an hour and to honor a forty-hour work week. The act did not affect agricultural workers or domestic servants and consequently had a minimal impact on low-wage black workers.

But Roosevelt could not bring recovery and security to all Americans without addressing the situation in the South. *The Report on Economic Conditions in the South,* commissioned by the president and released in August 1938, highlighted the low living standards prevalent in the states of the old Confederacy and called for a national program to reduce the region's subordination to northern capital and integrate it into the national economy. Such a program—and perhaps all new programs—had no chance while southern conservatives remained in control of key congressional committees. As a result, Roosevelt actively intervened in the midterm elections of 1938, with disastrous consequences. The southern conservatives he opposed were triumphantly reelected; the liberals he supported lost. This personal defeat, combined with Republican gains in Congress, stripped Roosevelt of the mandate he had earned in 1936. The Fair Labor Standards Act turned out to be the last New Deal measure to get through Congress.

The economy added to the president's problems. After the halting expansion of 1933–37, the country suddenly suffered a contraction with ominous resemblances to that of the Hoover administration. The stock market crashed in the fall of 1937; then industrial production nosedived and unemployment surged. Some blamed Roosevelt's antibusiness campaign for undermining investors' confidence, while the president himself suggested that there was a conspiracy among his enemies to undermine the economy by cutting back capital investment—essentially a sit-down strike of the rich.

A group of committed young New Dealers had another view. Impressed by the theories of British economist John Maynard Keynes, whose book *The General Theory of Employment, Interest, and Money* appeared in 1936, they ascribed the contraction to the mistaken policies of the Roosevelt administration itself. Keynes taught that two long-standing pillars of economic thought were, in fact, inaccurate. The first was that savings were identical to investment, a notion that underlay the impulse to balance budgets and to economize in hard times. The second was that employment levels were closely tied to wages, an idea that justified wage cuts when unemployment was rising—because cheaper labor costs would stimulate production. Keynes maintained instead that employment levels were determined primarily by the size of aggregate demand in the economy, and that savings did not necessarily promote investment. One key implication of these ideas was that governments could effectively respond to downturns in the business cycle not by tightening their belts but by spending money (to increase "aggregate demand"), even if that meant temporarily running deficits. This idea was not altogether novel—even Hoover had considered some form of deficit spending—but Keynes's work gave it a powerful intellectual rationale that began to have a great impact on the thinking of economists in the late 1930s.

If Keynes was right, then the Roosevelt administration had made serious errors in late 1936 and 1937. After incurring significant deficits in 1936 to fund the PWA and WPA and to pay veterans' bonuses, the administration cut back its expenditures sharply in the hope of finally balancing the federal budget; meanwhile, Social Security taxes kicked in for the first time. Consequently, the federal budget developed a surplus, which served to reduce private expenditures and precipitate the contraction that began in the fall of 1937. According to this Keynesian reading, the solution was clear: more federal spending on a grand scale.

Roosevelt seemed to agree. But his administration was divided, with Secretary of the Treasury Henry Morgenthau publicly pledging to balance the federal budget and congressional conservatives firmly opposed to any more New Deal experiments. In the end, the spending initiatives the president took were far too small to make much difference, and the engine of New Deal reforms ground to a halt. The economy hobbled along for another two years until finally wartime expenditures (funded by enormous government deficits) brought an end to the depression.

## The Social Fabric

Not everything that happened in the 1930s was colored in depression gray. Despite the severity of the economic crisis and the often momentous conflicts taking place in Washington, life went on. Social patterns that had been taking shape for decades continued unaffected or with only small detours. Scientists remained in their laboratories and novelists at their desks; New York Yankees "iron man" Lou Gehrig stayed on the field until he was felled by the degenerative disease that came to bear his name.

The birthrate of the nation's population continued to decline, as it had been doing since the middle of the nineteenth century. So, too, did the death rate, owing in part to advances in medicine, such as the use of sulfa drugs, the development of a cure for pellagra (which afflicted many in the South), and the discovery of the importance of vitamins. Average life expectancy at birth rose from fifty-nine in 1930 to sixty-three in 1940.

The slowdown in immigration, begun in the teens, continued; indeed, immigration fell off sufficiently that many of the quotas established in 1924 were not filled, and there was more return migration to Europe than immigration to the United States between 1931 and 1936. In addition, many Mexican migrants returned to their homeland, some forced to do so by American officials who sought to lower the burden of relief-giving. The slower flows of immigration helped immigrants to become assimilated while easing social tensions among immigrant groups and between immigrants and natives. Perhaps the foremost symbol of this shift was the election of the half-Jewish, half-Italian Fiorello La Guardia as mayor of New York in 1934.

Americans also became more educated, a perhaps ironic consequence of the Depression. Although some school systems were badly hurt in the early 1930s and many teachers did not receive their full back pay until World War II, high school enrollments rose, partly because young people decided to remain in school since they couldn't get jobs anyway. Something similar happened in colleges and universities, where enrollments began to rise after a sharp dip early in the decade. By 1940, there were almost 1.5 million students on college campuses, most of them in less expensive, publicly supported schools. Not surprisingly, a growing number were studying the social sciences and history.

Cultural trends were shaped by the Depression, although not always in straightforward ways. National mass culture became increasingly significant, as families listened to their radios for 4.5 hours per day, went to movies as often as they could, and read tabloid newspapers, which tripled their circulation between 1930 and 1940. Many filmmakers, photographers, playwrights, and writers devoted their energies to searing, thoughtful, and sometimes funny depictions of social conditions: Charlie Chaplin's classic *Modern Times* (1935) was a stunning portrait of the plight of the factory worker ricocheting between spells of unemployment and the machine-driven dehumanization of work; Par Lorenz's documentary *The Plow That Broke the Plains* captured the role of farm technology and the profit motive in setting the stage for the Dust Bowl, while the photographs of Dorothea Lange powerfully portrayed the suffering and the courage of the migrants that the Dust Bowl spawned. Clifford Odets's immensely popular play *Waiting for Lefty*, first produced in 1935, explored the need for political solidarity within the working class. And Diego Rivera, a Mexican painter who had become famous in the 1920s, came to the United States in the early 1930s and painted an extraordinary mural on the walls of the Detroit Institute of Art, heroically depicting the automobile workers of that city. Rivera's work provided durable inspiration for public art in the United States, influencing, among others, the hundreds of painters who found work through the WPA.

A Martin M-130 in flight over San Francisco Bay, with the Golden Gate Bridge under construction below, mid-1930s.

terprises that would become commonplace after the war. Lawrence was awarded the Nobel Prize in physics in 1939.

The 1930s was the decade when commercial aviation came of age. Building on a series of engineering advances of the 1920s, the two major manufacturers of aircraft, Boeing and Douglas, introduced passenger planes that were faster, quieter, and more efficient than any previous aircraft. The Douglas DC-3, which carried twenty-one passengers, became particularly popular, accounting for 80 percent of domestic air travel by 1938. At the same time, the Martin M-130 and later the Boeing Clipper began regular flights to convey mail and passengers across the oceans. Passenger service from San Francisco to the Philippines began in 1936, and by 1939 Pan Am was offering biweekly flights from the United States to England and France. To enhance the attractiveness of air travel, the airlines, led by United in 1930, introduced "air hostesses" to bring "home-making instincts"

Yet much of popular culture was escapist, focusing on themes far removed from the realities of daily life. One of the most widely viewed films of the era was *Snow White and the Seven Dwarfs.* The publishing sensation of the decade was the bland, cheery *Reader's Digest,* which increased its circulation from 250,000 to nearly 7 million; the best-selling novel of the decade was *Gone with the Wind.*

Advances in science and technology marked the era. None was more important than the research of physicist Ernest O. Lawrence at the University of California at Berkeley. Funded by the federal government, the state of California, and private sources, Lawrence constructed a series of cyclotrons, or particle accelerators, that allowed him to investigate the nucleus of the atom; the cyclotron was also able to generate radioactive isotopes and neutrons that could be used for medical research and in cancer therapies. The knowledge of nuclear physics that resulted from this research helped to set the stage for the atomic bomb project in World War II. It was also a harbinger of the big science en-

into the cabins. The hostesses had to meet carefully drawn qualifications of age, height, weight, and appearance.

The increasingly crowded skies—passenger traffic increased tenfold between 1932 and 1941—led to more regulations and concerted efforts to improve the safety of air travel. The first air-traffic control center went into operation in Newark, New Jersey, in 1935 and was soon followed by others. In 1938, Congress created the Civil Aeronautics Authority (CAA), which supervised all of civil aviation and had special authority to investigate accidents and recommend preventive measures. The CAA certified the training of airport and airline personnel who made decisions about weather conditions in which aircraft could safely fly.

Engineering advances also improved travel on the ground. Cars and trucks became cheaper, more reliable, and faster; and thanks to local, state, and federal construction projects, roads were dramatically improved. In 1940, the Pennsylvania Turnpike was completed, the first lengthy four-lane "superhighway" with no intersections. At the same time, urban public transportation systems began a long-term decline in the quality and frequency of service.

Nowhere were technological changes more significant than on the nation's farms. Despite the Depression, the number of rubber-tired, gasoline-powered tractors in use doubled during the 1930s; they were particularly common in the corn belt and on large farms. Hybrid corn, developed through careful genetic selection in state agricultural experiment stations, became increasingly popular among midwestern farmers, in part because it facilitated the use of new corn-picking machines that worked best if the crop ripened all at once, stalks were strong and straight, and ears were at the same height off the ground. Hybrid corn was more resistant to disease and insects, and it produced higher yields per acre—which permitted farmers to reduce their acreage (as federal programs mandated) while growing more corn. The spread of hybrid corn, however, increased the capital costs of farming, because it had to be purchased from seed companies (it had to be produced annually through artificial pollination). These technological advances, while contributing to increased productivity, drove small farmers from the land.

A harbinger of the same pattern appeared in the South, where the first successful cotton picker was patented in 1928. Field trials of the mechanical cotton picker in the mid-1930s demonstrated that, despite the skepticism of numerous authorities (including the secretary of agriculture), a machine actually could pick cotton. In the later 1930s, large farmers in Texas and Oklahoma began to purchase these machines, setting the stage for the widespread mechanization of cotton picking in the postwar South.

President Franklin Delano Roosevelt speaking from the White House in one of his "Fireside Chats."

## Muddling Through

Few American presidents have been as loved or as hated as Franklin Roosevelt; and few periods have been as closely identified with a political leader, or with national politics, as were the years between 1933 and 1940. Roosevelt took office when the nation was crying out, almost desperately, for leadership, and he navigated the ship of state through some of the most troubled waters in the nation's history. The only man ever elected president four times, the charismatic and enigmatic Roosevelt—even his closest advisers often found him inscrutable—was the most important American politician of the twentieth century. Democratic successors from Harry Truman to John Kennedy to Lyndon Johnson claimed to be his heir; even the far more conservative Ronald Reagan kept a photograph of Roosevelt in his office.

Although Roosevelt did not succeed in ending the Great Depression—only World War II did that—the achievements of the New Deal were unquestionably substantial. To combat the Depression, Roosevelt presided over, indeed demanded, an immense increase in the size, authority, and influence of the federal government. With the nation watching (and listening on the radio), Washington assumed responsibility for the well-being of the economy and the welfare of the populace. The federal government became the employer of last resort to millions; it regulated financial institutions to steady the performance of banks and the stock market; it protected the owners of homes and farms; it stimulated economic and technological development in rural areas; it instituted a national minimum wage and a mandatory forty-hour work week. Inviting new constituencies into the halls of power, the government became less the representative of the business community (which it had been under long years of Republican rule) and more a "broker state" balancing the claims of diverse organized interest groups.

The New Deal also created institutions grounded in principles that reshaped the social compact linking the state to its citizenry. The Social Security Act, for example, certified the right of Americans to public support when they were jobless, when they were past their productive years, and if they were single mothers with dependent children. Through the Wagner Act, Americans were also guaranteed the right to form independent unions and not be punished for seeking to do so. Farmers meanwhile received federal aid to cope with a problem that had been building for decades: the overcapacity of agriculture. New Deal agricultural policy, although not exactly what the Populists of the 1890s had in mind, constituted a durable public commitment to intervene in the market to preserve the livelihoods of many farmers.

There were, to be sure, limits to the changes wrought by the New Deal, as both contemporaries and historians have

A 1937 poster for the Rural Electrification Administration, which aimed to bring electricity to rural areas around the country.

pointed out. Overwhelmingly focused on economic issues, the Roosevelt administration paid little attention to race and tolerated legal discrimination against blacks in the South, as well as against Hispanics and Asians. Although its concern for the disadvantaged produced enough gains for African Americans to draw them into the Democratic Party, the New Deal never challenged the racial boundaries drawn so starkly across the South; and its programs, responsive to the demands of southern white Democrats, often reinforced those boundaries. The outcry against the Supreme Court because of the 1935 *Schechter* decision had no parallel when the same Supreme Court, in the same year, upheld the constitutionality of the white primary in Texas.

Nor did the New Deal significantly diminish the power of large corporations. For all of Roosevelt's rhetoric against the greed of capitalists, the economic "royalists" clung to their ermine. Major banks continued to dominate the financial sector, and the extent of corporate concentration actually increased in the 1930s. The twenty largest oil companies, for example, increased their share of both crude oil production and refining capacity. By 1940, 48 percent of all employees in the nation worked for 1 percent of all employers. Similarly, in agriculture, the average size of farms increased, as did the percentage of farms that relied on hired workers. A "broker state" may well have been formed, but labor and agriculture remained junior partners in the joint venture. As important, the poorest and most vulnerable workers, in industry and on farms, were excluded from many of the protections the New Deal had to offer, including the Wagner Act and the Fair Labor Standards Act. For all of the hostility of conservatives, the New Deal did not much alter the sway of free enterprise or the distribution of economic power.

The New Deal was thus not nearly as revolutionary as many of its most ardent supporters and ferocious detractors claimed it to be. But in critical respects, that was precisely its point—and its goal. As the bleak years of the Depression wore on, analysts of American and European societies came to doubt the viability of either capitalism or democracy, and especially capitalist democracies. Fascist movements flourished in parts of Europe, socialist parties gained strength in many parts of the world, and the Soviet Union stood for some as a model of the future. Centrists and liberals alike experienced a loss of faith. In 1935, the liberal magazine *The New Republic,* founded during the Progressive Era by Walter Lippmann and Herbert Croly, observed that the choice facing the nation was between the "miseries of an essentially unregulated capitalisism" or "socialism": "there is no longer a middle course." The historic achievement of the New Deal was to demonstrate that there was indeed a middle course—that an active, innovative state, at least partially responsive to the demands of different social groups and centers of power, could preserve the basic institutions of capitalism and political democracy that Americans had erected over the course of a century and a half.

## Suggested Reading

Malcolm Cowley, *The Dream of the Golden Mountain: Remembering the 1930's* (1980)

Melvyn Dubofsky and Warren R. Van Tine, *An Oral History of the Great Depression* (1970)

Barry Eichengreen, *Golden Fetters: The Gold Standard and the Great Depression, 1919–1939* (1995)

Steve Fraser and Gary Gerstle, *The Rise and Fall of the New Deal Order* (1989)

David Kennedy, *Freedom from Fear: The American People in Depression and War, 1929–1945* (1999)

Donald Worster, *Dust Bowl: The Southern Plains in the 1930's* (1979)

## Summary QUESTIONS

- What was the relationship between the stock market crash and the Great Depression?

- What were the key policy initiatives adopted by President Roosevelt during the First Hundred Days?

- What was the significance of the movements led by Father Coughlin, Dr. Townsend, and Huey Long?

- What was the Second New Deal?

- Why did the New Deal appear to lose momentum in the late 1930s?

## Chronology

| | |
|---|---|
| October 1929 | Stock market crash. |
| 1930 | Smoot-Hawley Tariff. |
| 1933 | Agricultural Adjustment Act. |
| | Tennessee Valley Authority created. |
| | National Industrial Recovery Act. |
| | Federal Deposit Insurance Corporation. |
| 1935 | Schechter Poultry v. US declares NRA unconstitutional. |
| | Works Projects Administration. |
| | Wagner Act (NLRA). |
| | Social Security Act. |
| | Founding of the CIO. |
| 1936 | Re-election of FDR. |
| 1936–1937 | Sit-down strike of autoworkers at GM plant at Flint, Michigan. |
| February 1937 | FDR proposes the court-packing scheme. |
| April 1937 | Supreme Court, in NLRB v. Jones and Laughlin, upholds the Wagner Act. |
| 1938 | Fair Labor Standards Act. |
| | Pan Am begins biweekly flights from the U.S. to Europe. |

## Key Terms

The Dust Bowl (pp. 706–707)

First 100 Days (p. 711)

Share Our Wealth (p. 716)

Unemployment Insurance (p. 720)

Rural electrification (p. 720)

Unionization of the mass production industries (p. 722)

Court packing (p. 725)

---

**Access the *Inventing America* StudySpace at wwwnorton.com/studyspace**

PERSONAL PLAN ■ REVIEW MATERIALS ■ RESEARCH AIDS ■ MULTIMEDIA

# Part 7

# WORLD POWER

As war enveloped Europe and Asia in the 1930s, the United States sought to hew to the isolationism to which it had reverted after World War I. In the end, however, the nation could not escape the threat to its national security posed by the Axis powers—Germany, Italy, and Japan—in a world that technology, notably air power, was rendering ever smaller and more interdependent. Rising to the challenge of World War II, the United States invented organizations and methods to mobilize the nation's vast resources. It trained millions of men and women for the armed services and sent them across the globe to do battle in the name of freedom. It equipped them and aided its Allies, notably Britain and the Soviet Union, by exploiting its immense manufacturing capacity and mobilizing its scientific resources to an unprecedented degree. The Axis forces were overwhelmed by the allied troops, by the American production of a torrent of war goods, and by the superior military technologies that emerged from the laboratories, among them microwave radar and the atomic bomb.

After victory in 1945, the United States faced the challenge of maintaining its national security in a world of nuclear weapons, long-range bombers, and, as analysts were already predicting, intercontinental missiles. Breaking away from the longstanding tradition of peacetime isolationism, a bipartisan consensus formed around the belief that the United States had to help maintain a stable world order kept safe from armed aggression. The commitment to internationalism was intensified by the emergence of the Cold War, which was rooted in the transformation of the Soviet Union from an ally into an adversary, and by the establishment, in 1949, of a revolutionary Communist regime—the People's Republic—in China.

In the quarter century after World War II, the United States gave its new internationalism concrete meaning. It created a vibrant system of federally sponsored scientific research and training. It provided foreign aid to ease the poverty that fueled Communism and, in the developing world—the regions newly liberated from colonial rule that were then grouped as the Third World—to shape growth in the direction of democratic capitalism. The United States also established a far flung

Teenagers frequently gathered at drive-in restaurants like this one—Tiny Naylor's, in Los Angeles, 1959—which were hallmarks of the devotion to automobile culture and the disposable income of adolescents amid the prosperity of the postwar era.

system of military alliances whose aim was to prevent further Communist expansion. And it went to war to combat aggression, as when Communist North Korea invaded South Korea, in 1950, and in the 1960s, when forces supported by Communist North Vietnam waged a guerilla war against the pro-American regime in South Vietnam.

Some of the new departures, however, appeared to threaten the fabric of American democracy. At home, the defense against Communism led governments at all levels to impose loyalty and security requirements on their employees that rode roughshod over civil liberties, and in the country at large the fear of Communism fostered a climate of conformity intolerant of dissent. Abroad, the U.S. government at times resorted to covert subversion of regimes whose commitment to the West or to capitalism was in doubt and it cooperated with authoritarian governments so long as they were antiCommunist. By 1968, the end to the conflict in Vietnam was nowhere in sight and the country was bitterly divided over the war.

During World War II, the federal government had of necessity played a preponderant role in the nation's economy, but once peace came, Americans debated whether the innovations of New Deal government should remain in place. In the end, the debate resolved into a bipartisan consensus in favor of the government's continuing to take active responsibility for the general welfare, just as a consensus had formed in support of an internationalist foreign policy. Through the 1960s the bipartisan consensus brought about a steady expansion of the welfare state with measures intended, for example, to diminish poverty, provide medical care for the poor and the elderly, and strengthen education.

World War II stimulated an economic boom that was sustained during the first quarter of the Cold War by federal spending, a hefty portion of which went for defense. American business, drawing on and advancing the output of federally sponsored scientific research and training, produced a remarkable variety of technological innovations ranging from jet aircraft to antibiotics. They helped fuel the nation's prosperity and supplied the world's markets, further integrating the United States into the global economy. At the same time, enlightened business leaders, partly to stave off further federal intervention in the economy, pioneered the system of welfare capitalism, paying decent wages and providing medical insurance for their employees.

All the while, Americans were on the make and on the move, migrating from towns to cities, notably in the South, where federal spending was helping to promote manufacturing and urbanization, and to the rapidly developing West, where federally sponsored water and power projects made possible new settlement and economic development. In every region they moved in accelerating numbers to the suburbs, creating an ever-more metropolitan nation—and one that in the face of conformity was breaking new ground in the graphic arts, film, and popular music, especially with the birth of rock 'n roll.

Yet some features of the emerging metropolitan America were unsettling, particularly its ugly sprawl and pollution, byproducts of the technologies of prosperity. The more affluent the United States became, the more did many of its citizens call for environmental clean-up and protection. These initiatives were part of a new, broader movement for improvements in the quality of life—for example, promoting the arts, relieving the congestion of metropolitan living, preserving the architectural landmarks, and satisfying neighborhoods of cities. Such issues joined the traditional absorption with economic growth and opportunity as features of the national political agenda.

Perhaps the most vital innovation of the period was the widening movement for freedom and equality for minority groups and women. The movement was given leverage during World War II and the Cold War by the United States' defense of democratic rights. It was powerfully pioneered by courageous African Americans who mobilized to change their condition and who gained the help of sympathetic whites, key court decisions, and several new national laws. Other beleaguered groups, notably Hispanics and Native Americans, were inspired to launch their own civil rights movements, and so were women, who demanded not only equal opportunity in education and the workplace but also sexual liberation, access to contraception, and the right to opt for abortion. By the late 1960s, the civil rights movements were beginning to change the social texture of America.

Their growing success, however, aroused opposition among social conservatives. So did the antiwar protests and their association with the broad cultural rebellion that brought rock 'n roll and sexually graphic literature and films into the mainstream of American life. In the 1960s, the nation endured waves of violence, including assassinations, murders, beatings of civil rights activists in the South, and riots in the black ghettos of a number of northern cities. Late in the decade, the nation was troubled by anger on the right and on the left, and anxious apprehension in the middle that the country was coming apart.

# WHIRLPOOL OF WAR:

## 1932-1941

The enraged, bird-like monster in this painting of 1937, by the European artist Max Ernst, conveyed in surreally terrifying imagery the undeniably real menace of fascism on the continent.

**Focus QUESTIONS**

■ **Why was the United States isolationist early in the Roosevelt administration?**

■ **What were the initial American reactions to aggressions by Germany and Japan?**

■ **How was America drawn into the developing war in Europe and Asia?**

Shortly after noon on January 30, 1933, a little more than a month before Franklin Roosevelt's first inauguration, the president of Germany appointed Adolf Hitler chancellor of the national government. A onetime World War I army corporal, Hitler headed the Nazi Party (German shorthand for National Socialist German Workers' Party). He was a charismatic figure, a demagogic orator, ruthless politician, and self-styled revolutionary who hated Jews, Weimar democracy, and the Versailles Treaty (1919), which had demilitarized Germany and reconstructed the political map of the Continent. That night, tens of thousands of storm troopers celebrated Hitler's appointment in a torchlight parade, strutting in tight, jackbooted columns before cheering onlookers. The French ambassador remembered watching the procession: "The river of fire flowed past the French Embassy whence, with heavy heart and filled with foreboding, I watched its luminous wake."

Germany, its economy collapsing, was rife with fears and long-festering resentments, notably against the territorial losses and reparations forced upon it after World War I. Hitler, whom people called *Der Führer*—the leader—attributed Germany's suffering to the Allies, Communists, and Jews. He had won popular support by promising to restore Germany to its former glory and prosperity and by relying on the Nazi Party's storm troopers, a private army of bullies in brown shirts, to intimidate dissenters of all stripes. In March 1933, the Reichstag (the German national legislature) granted him dictatorial powers. With the aid of a secret political police known as the Gestapo, Hitler's regime terrorized Jews, destroyed civil liberties and civil rights, and crushed all opposition with a fearsome combination of law, intimidation, force, and torture.

Hitler called his Germany the "Third Reich"—meaning the third German empire, following the Holy Roman Empire and the empire established by Bismarck in 1871—and said that it would last a thousand years. He made no secret of his aim to regain the territory Germany had lost in Central Europe as a result of the post–World War I settlement. The Nazi government repudiated the Versailles Treaty, withdrew from the League of Nations, and initiated a program of accelerated rearmament. In 1936, Hitler sent the Wehrmacht, his nation's army, into the Rhineland, the German industrial region that bordered France and Belgium, nullifying its demilitarization under the Versailles Treaty.

The threat to peace posed by Hitler was enlarged by Benito Mussolini, the fascist dictator of Italy, and by militant nationalists in Japan. A onetime socialist who had come to power in 1922, Mussolini was a dynamic though pompous figure of grandiose pretensions. Under his regime, the state managed private property; suppressed Communists, Socialists, and even organized labor; and celebrated nationalism and imperialism. In 1935, Mussolini's troops struck from Italian Somalia into Ethiopia, an action of revenge that Mussolini had promised for the humiliating defeat they had suffered forty years before and that pitted bombers and fighters against villages and horsemen.

In Japan all the while, militant nationalists, including powerful members of the military, had increasingly challenged the legitimacy of the settlements following World War I, especially the terms of the treaties produced by the Washington Conference in 1922 and signed by, among other nations, the United States, Britain, and Japan. Taken together, the treaties established a Washington Conference system that kept British and American naval power superior to Japan's and sought to integrate China into the framework of international democratic capitalism and uphold that country's independence. The Japanese nationalists held that the system merely maintained Western imperial interests in Asia and prevented Japan from pursuing legitimate territorial and economic aims.

Hitler skillfully used mass media to promote his demagogic exploitation of German resentments.

The American people initially responded to the trends in Europe and Asia by intensifying their post-Versailles withdrawal from foreign affairs. As many of them saw it, the sacrifices of World War I had not made the world safe for democracy. If Europeans now wanted to start killing each other again, the United States had no obligation to stop them. The depth of their commitment to isolationism was made clear when in early 1935 the Senate defeated Roosevelt's proposal that the United States join the World Court, located at The Hague, in the Netherlands. In the heated debate on the measure, Senator Thomas D. Schall of Minnesota proclaimed, "To hell with Europe and the rest of those nations!"

During the 1930s, the power of isolationist sentiment handicapped Roosevelt's conduct of foreign policy. He was an internationalist, but he was compelled to walk a fine line between, on the one hand, protecting the interests of the United States and, on the other, doing so without defying domestic preferences. His capacity for leadership was increasingly taxed as events abroad bitterly divided Americans over the course for their country in a world marching toward war.

In China, the government of Jiang Jieshi (Chiang Kai-shek) progressively consolidated its power while tolerating the continuation of the special privileges to which the Western powers were long accustomed. Japan enjoyed similar arrangements, but the worldwide depression that began in 1929 intensified its hunger for the resources it might obtain in Manchuria, which already supplied major fractions of its pig iron and coal. In 1931, Japanese forces stationed in Manchuria had attacked the local Chinese troops and occupied the region, earning worldwide censure while establishing a puppet state called Manchukuo. In March 1933, Japan withdrew from the League of Nations, which had refused to recognize the new political entity. The next year, denouncing the limitations imposed by the Washington Naval Treaty of 1922 and its extension in the London Naval Treaty of 1930, Japan announced that it intended to abrogate the agreement.

In this American cartoon from 1931, the artist is pointing out the fact that Japan's seizure of Manchuria violated multiple international treaties and agreements.

739

# Encouraging Peace

### ROOSEVELT'S BRAND OF IDEALISM

Roosevelt was at heart a Wilsonian idealist, an enthusiast of the League of Nations who wished to use power in the service of achieving and maintaining a just international order. But in foreign as in domestic affairs, Roosevelt far more than Wilson tempered his ideals with pragmatism. In 1932, however, conceding to popular sentiment in the interest of winning the presidency, he publicly turned against American involvement in the League. He nevertheless appointed a fellow Wilsonian, Cordell Hull, as his secretary of state. And like his distant cousin Theodore Roosevelt, he appreciated the force of the big stick. His service as assistant secretary of the navy under President Wilson had sharpened his understanding of the realities of power. He was an innovator who refused to be bound by any single idea. He once wrote to Hull, "In pure theory, you and I think alike but every once in a while we have to modify principle to meet a hard and disagreeable fact!"

Roosevelt realized that the hard facts of the airplane and the submarine were undermining the ability of the United States to rely for its security on the protective moats of the Atlantic and the Pacific oceans. He believed that the United States continued to have a stake in a stable world order, that its security remained linked to the international configurations established by the Versailles Treaty and the Washington Conference system. He recognized that by contesting the postwar international arrangements, Germany, Italy, and Japan all threatened American interests and security.

### TRUSTING IN TRADE

Roosevelt's foreign policy early in his presidency melded concerns for national security with the principles of internationalism and the cause of economic recovery at home. Although he had torpedoed the London Economic Conference by refusing to participate in the stabilization of currencies, he recognized that the world's nations were interdependent; that the United States was intimately connected to many of them by ties of commerce, culture, and kinship; and that his country's economic well-being would ultimately be affected by the revival of their economies.

Shortly after entering the White House, Roosevelt began taking steps to grant recognition to the Soviet Union, hoping in part that the normalization of relations would facilitate renewed trade with the Soviets, which had plummeted since 1930. The president obtained Soviet promises to forgo subversive activities in the United States and to guarantee religious freedom to Americans in the Soviet Union. However, the formal recognition extended to Soviet Russia in 1933 proved to be what one historian has called "an event of monumental unimportance" because it did little to revive trade, halt Soviet efforts at internal subversion, or discourage Japanese militancy. More effective in encouraging trade was Roosevelt's backing of a bill, enacted in March 1934, that gave the president authority to negotiate reciprocal trade agreements, including tariff reductions that could be extended to any country that granted the United States most-favored-nation treatment or did not discriminate against it.

### THE GOOD NEIGHBOR POLICY

By 1933, trade with Latin America had fallen to roughly a quarter of the level of 1929. Roosevelt wanted to revive trade with the region and also to overcome long-standing suspicions that the United States was a bad neighbor. In one of the few references to foreign affairs in his inaugural address, he declared that he would "dedicate this Nation to the policy of the good neighbor"—an initiative that was apparently intended to apply to the world in general but that soon came to connote the administration's approach specifically to Latin America.

A major source of suspicion in Latin America was the United States' past interventions in the internal affairs of countries in the region; Cubans greatly resented the Platt amendment, which gave the United States the right to intervene in Cuba (see Chapter 21). The Hoover administration, repudiating Theodore Roosevelt's corollary to the Monroe Doctrine, had adopted a policy of nonintervention. It had also agreed to withdraw the marines that had been stationed in Haiti since 1915. On Pan American Day, in April 1933, Franklin Roosevelt declared that he respected the independence of the American republics and intended to deal with them on a basis of equality and cooperation.

Roosevelt's commitment to nonintervention was quickly tested in Cuba, where the dictator Gerardo Machado was forced out by rebels in August 1933 and his successor was quickly overthrown by an army coup. Roosevelt, refusing to send troops, emphasized to envoys from Mexico, Brazil, Chile, and Argentina that he had no desire to intervene in Cuba—marking the first time a president discussed U.S. policy for the hemisphere with Latin American diplomats. However, when in mid-September Cuban revolutionists formed another government, the United States declined to recognize it and adopted a wait-and-see attitude for its Cuban policy, including whether it would renegotiate the Platt amendment.

In December 1933, at the Seventh International Conference of American States meeting in Montevideo, Uruguay, the Roosevelt administration accepted, with only minor caveats, a declaration holding that no state had the right to intervene in another's "internal or external affairs." Roosevelt also endorsed a statement favoring the long-term liberalization of trade policy in the Americas. Secretary of State Hull told the president afterward that the conference had achieved a better state of good feeling toward the United States than any he had seen in a generation.

The United States soon showed that it took its Montevideo pledges seriously. When a more conservative government came to power in Cuba, the Roosevelt administration welcomed it with economic assistance, and in May 1934 the United States concluded a treaty that abrogated the Platt amendment, including its right to intervene in Cuba, but that allowed it to keep the American naval base at Guantánamo Bay. That summer, Roosevelt visited the Caribbean—a Good Neighbor trip, he called it—becoming the first sitting president to cross Panama or set foot in South America. During the next two years, the United States entered reciprocal trade agreements with five Latin states, opened trade negotiations with nine others, and concluded a new treaty with Panama that, modifying the agreement of 1903, rescinded American rights to intervene unilaterally and take control of Panamanian territory.

In 1936, Roosevelt initiated a meeting of the Latin American states in Buenos Aires to devise ways to safeguard peace among themselves. At home, he explained that his aim was to "isolate" America from war, noting that he had seen the blood and agony of armed conflict, and asserting, "I hate war." The president attended the conference himself, arriving to a tumultuously enthusiastic reception. Although the conference did not give Roosevelt all he wanted, it agreed to inter-American consultation in case the hemisphere was threatened.

## Avoiding the Disagreeable

### JAPANESE BELLIGERENCE

When the Japanese had occupied Manchuria in 1931, Hoover's secretary of state, Henry L. Stimson, declared that the United States would not recognize Japan's control of the region because its action violated international law. Roosevelt endorsed the so-called Stimson Doctrine, explaining that "American foreign policy must uphold the sanctity of international treaties." Yet he had reason to think that such moral condemnation alone was inadequate to halt aggression. In May 1933, the American ambassador in Tokyo wrote him that "Japan probably has the most . . . powerful fighting machine in the world today," adding that the Japanese armed forces considered the United States a "potential enemy" because it stood in the path of Japanese expansion.

To offset the increasing Japanese naval strength, in June 1933 Roosevelt directed that $238 million of funds appropriated for public works be used to construct cruisers and aircraft carriers. Added to a naval building program that Congress had already authorized, the order made for the largest peacetime naval construction program since before World War I. At the beginning of 1934, Roosevelt threw his support to a congressional bill that would authorize building the U.S. fleet up to the Washington Conference limits. While seeking peace, the president intended to bolster his country's ability to defend itself against aggression.

Still, Roosevelt did not want his naval construction program to alienate either Japan or the sizable pacifist movement in the United States. He insisted that in the end he hoped to achieve ongoing limitation of and possibly reductions in naval armaments in the renewed negotiations of the Washington and London Naval Treaties. Nevertheless, in January 1936, Japan ended its adherence to the naval treaties, walking out of the London Naval Conference after having been refused equivalent tonnage for its fleet with that of the major Western powers. That year, Japan also joined Hitler's Germany and Mussolini's Italy in a pact pledging the three countries to resist the efforts of the Communist International to incite revolutions.

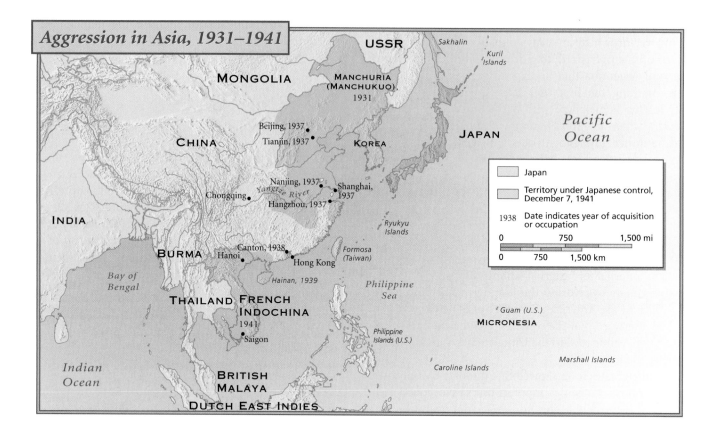

*Aggression in Asia, 1931–1941*

*War in China.* Japan soon dashed Roosevelt's dimming hopes for peace in Asia. In July 1937, Japan opened undeclared war on China, contending that given the Western imperial presence there, it deserved more land and resources as a matter of international justice. Striking southward, Japanese soldiers captured the key cities of Beijing, Tianjin, Shanghai, and Hangzhou as well as the national capital, Nanjing, on the Yangtze River, where they raped untold numbers of women and massacred some 200,000 civilians. In December, Japanese planes attacked British and American ships lying in the river, sinking the American gunboat *Panay*, which was evacuating American officials from the city. The Japanese government quickly apologized, explaining that the assault had been unauthorized, the responsible commander was being recalled, and indemnities would be forthcoming. But it also demanded that henceforth China subordinate itself politically and economically to Tokyo. In November 1938, Japan rejected the long-standing American-backed policy of the Open Door in China, announcing that it would create a "new order" in East Asia that would

knit Manchukuo, China, and Japan into a cooperative economic and cultural bloc.

The Chinese government of Jiang Jieshi (Chiang Kai-shek) refused to submit. After the Japanese occupied the eastern region of China in 1937, Jiang had moved his capital to Chongqing (Chungking), in the interior, and continued to fight the invaders in collaboration with the Communist forces led by Mao Zedong (Mao Tse-tung). Formerly antagonists of Jiang, the Chinese Communists allied themselves with him against the Japanese—partly because of the doctrine of the Popular Front, which called for Communists to join with other enemies of fascism, and partly because they bitterly resented the Japanese invasion of their territory.

## NAZI AGGRESSIONS

In the meantime, the course of events in Europe turned increasingly alarming. In July 1935, civil war broke out in Spain, pitting fascist rebel forces under General Francisco Franco against forces loyal to the country's democratic government. While the Soviet Union assisted the Loyalists with supplies and international brigades, Italy and Germany provided guns, tanks, planes, and some 60,000 troops to Franco, making the Spanish Civil War into a kind of testing ground for the newest weapons and techniques of warfare and for a contest of arms against fascist dictatorship.

In Germany, Hitler pressed to an extreme the kind of wrongheaded and racist biology that had undergirded the eugenics movement in the United States (see Chapters 19, 22, 24). By 1937, the Nazi government had sterilized more than 225,000 people found to suffer from allegedly hereditary diseases and disorders, including feeblemindedness, schizophrenia, epilepsy, blindness, drug or alcohol addiction, and physical deformities that interfered with locomotion or were grossly offensive. Nazi Germany celebrated the so-called Aryan race, people of northern European stock whose members, Nazis claimed, constituted the genuine German *Volk*. They castigated all others, especially Jews, holding that they were inferior to Aryans and were responsible, along with Communists, for Germany's economic breakdown.

In a set of laws enacted at Nuremberg in September 1935, the Nazis abolished citizenship for German Jews and, to the end of preventing "racial pollution," prohibited their intermarriage with non-Jews while making sexual relations between Aryans and Jews punishable by death. In November 1938, the Nazis barred Jews from theaters, concerts, high schools, and universities. In the darkness between November 9 and 10, 1938—a night people afterward called *Kristallnacht,* the "night of broken glass"—Nazi sympathizers throughout Germany and Austria burned synagogues, vandalized Jewish residences, and smashed Jewish shops and businesses.

Earlier that year, in March, Hitler had extended his racist dictatorship to the south, annexing Austria, and in September he plunged Europe into crisis by demanding the absorption into the Third Reich of the German-speaking portion of Czechoslovakia, the Sudetenland. As tensions mounted, the leaders of Europe convened in Munich. Anxious to avoid war, they appeased Hitler, allowing him the Sudetenland in return for his assurance that Germany had no further territorial ambitions. Returning to England, the British prime minister,

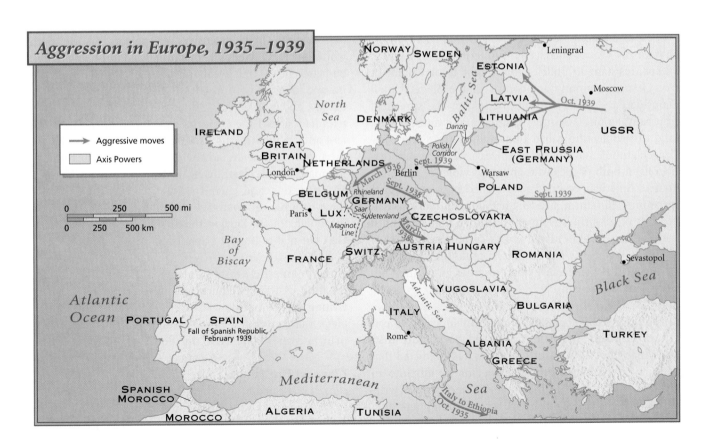

**Aggression in Europe, 1935–1939**

743

Neville Chamberlain, predicted that the Munich Conference would bring "peace for our time."

## THE INGREDIENTS OF ISOLATIONISM

Even as Hitler's dominion expanded, Japan assaulted China, and civil war ripped apart Spain, most Americans remained unwilling to confront the disagreeable facts so distant from their shores. In a speech in Chicago in October 1937, Roosevelt was prompted by Japan's recent march into China to warn that war was a dangerous "contagion" and that the world community would be warranted in imposing a "quarantine" against nations that spread the infection of violence. Isolationists denounced the quarantine idea, reminding Roosevelt of their political power and compelling him to shelve mention of interventionism for the time being.

The isolationists of the period constituted a coalition of disparate, often overlapping groups. They were strong in the Midwest, where many people tended to be suspicious of internationalists on the Eastern Seaboard. However, isolationist attitudes were prevalent in every region of the country and were well represented across the political spectrum. They were widespread among women, clerics, and students; among ethnic minority groups such as Irish Americans and German Americans, resistant to policies that might favor Britain or disfavor Germany; among antagonists of the Soviet Union who considered Germany a bulwark against the spread of Communism; among fascist sympathizers and anti-Semites, the kind of people who called Roosevelt's reforms the "Jew Deal"; even among many of the New Deal's warmest supporters, liberals in both parties who abhorred violence and worried that an American commitment to checking aggression in Europe would kill reform, just as it had done in World War I. Isolationists of all stripes were apprehensive that an activist internationalism would enlarge the discretionary powers of the president, raising the danger that he could tilt the country away from genuine neutrality and toward war, as they believed Wilson had done in 1917.

*Fear of Military Technologies.* To the large majority of Americans, the bloodbath of World War I had been more than enough. Since the 1920s, dozens of works had predicted that the advance of technology would make another war into an even worse conflagration. Military analysts and popular writers raised the specter of long-range aircraft bombing cities, including New York, Chicago, Detroit, Pittsburgh, and Wash-

Emperor Haile Selassie of Ethiopia savors a momentary triumph over an undetonated Italian bomb, one of the weapons that helped ultimately to defeat him.

ington, with high explosives or poison gas or, perhaps worse—if H. G. Wells's 1914 novel *The World Set Free* was to be believed—atomic weapons. To be sure, in the mid-1930s no one knew how to obtain the explosive release of atomic energy; and in 1925, the United States and forty other countries had signed the Geneva Protocol, condemning gas warfare and prohibiting its use. But Japan had refused to ratify the protocol, and so had the U.S. Senate, which found itself inundated with telegrams against the agreement from veterans, surgeons, and chemists. Italy, which had subscribed to the protocol, dropped 500-pound mustard-gas bombs on Ethiopian towns. During the Spanish Civil War, Italian and German planes bombed Spanish cities with high explosives, and the Japanese waged war from the air against Chinese cities. In an article in the widely read magazine *Life* in 1939, the humorist James Thurber deployed his signature irony in writing of a future war: "This time destruction was so complete, that nothing at all was left in the world, except one man, and one woman, and one flower."

*Claims of Past Mistakes.* Like Woodrow Wilson, many Americans in 1917 had judged that the United States had a genuine stake in maintaining what the kaiser's government threatened: freedom of the seas and a stable balance of power in

Europe. But while later generations tended to ratify their judgment, during the 1930s it was sharply challenged. Books and articles like the liberal journalist Walter Millis's *The Road to War,* a best-seller in 1935, argued that the country had been misled into World War I. According to this view, French and British propaganda had disposed the American public to favor the Allies by falsely portraying the Germans as monstrous, ready to burn libraries and kill innocent civilians on the high seas. American munitions makers and bankers were characterized as "merchants of death" who manipulated the American government to defend their financial interests in an Allied victory. Expanding on the idea that economic interests had led the United States into World War I, liberal analysts like the historian Charles Beard argued that the commitment to maintaining open markets for American goods in Europe and Asia inevitably threatened to draw the country into war. To be sure, the country did have a stake in open markets, and the Roosevelt administration regarded the expansion of exports as an important instrument of economic recovery. In actual fact, the United States' commercial relations with Japan far exceeded those with China; measured by economic interests, it had good reasons to remain friendly with Japan. But during the depression of the 1930s, when many of the country's troubles were attributed to greedy businessmen, arguments like Beard's version of international economic forces commanded a powerful following.

### LEGISLATING NEUTRALITY

In 1935, with the aim of avoiding the entanglements believed to have led the United States into war in 1917, Congress passed the first in a series of Neutrality Acts. As expanded in 1936, the legislation prohibited the sale to belligerents of implements of war as well as their transportation by American ships. It also forbade American loans and credits to belligerent nations and outlawed shipments of war materiel to either side in the Spanish Civil War. Roosevelt had wanted a discretionary arms embargo, but Congress made them mandatory, which blocked the president from tilting toward one side or the other in an armed conflict.

Critics pointed out that the neutrality laws were not, in their effects, genuinely neutral. They favored parties at war that were militarily strong and thus did not need to purchase war supplies abroad, and they disfavored parties that were militarily weak—for example, the Loyalists in Spain—and did need to purchase them. Renewing the Neutrality Act in 1937,

Congress added to the previous measures a mandate forbidding travel by Americans on the vessels of nations at war, but it also enacted so-called cash-and-carry provisions, which permitted the export to belligerents of certain nonmilitary goods so long as they were sold for cash and carried away in ships that did not sail under the American flag. Like the rigid neutrality measures, cash-and-carry was not strictly neutral in its consequences. It gave a boost to Britain, with its powerful navy and substantial cash reserves, but it also favored Japan, which enjoyed similar advantages, in its war against China—and thus heightened the threat to U.S. interests in Asia.

In the spring of 1938, a number of Americans were growing distressed by the declining fortunes of the Loyalists in Spain. Young volunteers went to Spain as members of the Abraham Lincoln Brigade to fight for the republican cause, and influential senators suggested that the Neutrality Act ought to be revised to lift the embargo on arms sales there. Roosevelt declined to support the move, mindful that the Loyalists had no money to buy arms and that it would cost the Democrats many Catholic votes in the upcoming congressional elections, since Franco enjoyed significant support among the American Catholic hierarchy.

### THE REFUGEE QUESTION

The plight of refugees from Hitler's Europe did little to diminish the insular nationalism at work in the United States. The Nazis had been encouraging the emigration of Jews, and Hitler began expelling them from Austria after annexing the country in March 1938, swelling the flood of refugees still further. Hitler's strongmen forced numerous Jewish scholars and scientists out of German universities and cultural institutions. Nazi officials justified the dismissals as a kind of purification. They maintained with Philipp Lenard, a German physicist, Nobel laureate, and supporter of the Nazis, that science "is racial and conditioned by blood"; that Einstein's physics was "Jewish physics" and as such "merely an illusion—a perversion of basic Aryan physics." Between 1933 and 1938, about 60,000 people fled Germany, Austria, and Italy for the United States. The immigrants included distinguished writers, artists, architects, musicians, scholars, and scientists, many of them aided in their flight by emergency assistance committees in Britain and the United States. Among them were the social psychologist Theodor W. Adorno, the political theorist Hannah Arendt, the psychoanalyst Karen Horney, the novelist Thomas Mann, the architect Walter

Among the refugees who fled fascist Europe in the 1930s (from left): harpsichordist Wanda Landowska, and physicist Enrico Fermi.

Gropius, the musician Wanda Landowska, the biologist Salvador Luria, the economist Oskar Morgenstern, the composer Igor Stravinsky, and the physicist Enrico Fermi, whose wife was Jewish.

Together, the refugee scholars and scientists greatly enriched American life—those in physics with the power of their mathematical techniques, experimental imagination, and frequently philosophical approach to the analysis of natural phenomena. For example, soon after arriving at Cornell University, Hans Bethe, a virtuoso in mathematical physics, produced a formidably comprehensive survey of nuclear physics that people called "Bethe's bible" and that was soon to be found on the desk of virtually every physicist in the United States.

Many other Europeans whose only distinction was a desire to live in freedom hoped to emigrate from Nazi-controlled areas, but the welcome extended to refugees was limited everywhere, including in the United States. American consular officials in Europe applied the rules of entry so strictly that even fewer refugees were being admitted than the restrictive immigration law of 1924 allowed. Congressman Emanuel Celler of Brooklyn snapped that the State Department had a "heartbeat muffled in protocol." However, the department only mirrored public sentiment: opinion polls showed strong resistance to any increase in immigration. The opposition arose partly from anti-Semitism, partly from worries on the part of some American Jews that more immigrants would provoke more anti-Semitism, and partly from the fear that newcomers would take jobs that Americans wanted for themselves.

Roosevelt was appalled by the Nazi persecutions, telling the press after *Kristallnacht,* "I myself could scarcely believe that such things could occur in a twentieth-century civilization." But judging it politically futile to attempt a change in the immigration laws, he sought instead to liberalize their administration. In 1936, he ordered American consulates to afford the refugees crowding their offices "the most humane treatment under the law." Trying to ensure that the German and Austrian quotas were fully used, he arranged for 15,000 German and Austrian refugees on visitors' permits to remain in the United States.

But Roosevelt's efforts on behalf of refugees were limited. In 1938, at his invitation, a conference convened at Evian-les-Bains, in France, to seek an international solution to their plight, but it produced nothing of consequence. Roosevelt himself, his eye evidently on public opinion at home, specified that "no country would be expected or asked to receive a greater number of emigrants than is permitted by existing legislation." In 1939, Congress blocked a change in the immigration quotas that would have allowed the entry of 20,000 German refugee children from Europe, many of whom were Jews. Local consulates and immigration offices were often unaccommodating. In June 1939, a shipload of 900 Jewish refugees was denied permission to land in Ft. Lauderdale, Florida, and was forced to return to an uncertain fate in Europe. Between 1938 and 1941, 150,000 refugees entered the United States, roughly 62,000 fewer than the law formally allowed.

### DEFENSE FOR THE AMERICAS

During the Munich crisis in September 1938, Roosevelt had privately urged Hitler to make peace, but within weeks of the settlement Hitler renewed his declarations of belligerency, and in response Roosevelt's foreign policy began to toughen. Early in 1939, he pointed out to the American people that "the world has grown so small and weapons of attack so swift" that war could no longer be contained, and "events of thunderous import have moved with lightning speed." The advance of technology had cut the time for response. "Survival cannot be guaranteed by arming after the attack begins."

Following that logic, Roosevelt held that in a world of well-armed aggressors the military preparedness of the United States had to be strengthened. In 1935, Congress had authorized an increase in the size of the enlisted army, whose active strength when Roosevelt took office was ranked seventeenth in the world, and in January 1938 it voted to expand the navy. But in the wake of Munich, Roosevelt was convinced that far more was needed, especially for the air forces.

*The Growth of Air Power.* A mixture of public and private initiatives had brought military aircraft a long way from the wood-and-cloth planes of World War I, with their limited range and speed. Following demonstrations in the early 1920s that aircraft could sink warships, the navy concluded that it needed better security for its battleships, which could be obtained with fighter aircraft launched from aircraft carriers. The navy constructed its first carrier—the USS *Langley*—in 1922 by converting a supply ship, superposing a flight deck onto its topside and transforming its large coal-carrying holds into a hangar deck. By 1927, two more carriers had been commissioned, and early in Roosevelt's administration, the keels of two more were laid. By then, naval doctrine recognized that aircraft launched from carriers could be used not just to protect battleships but also to strike offensively against an enemy fleet. The same technological advances that assisted civil aviation—for example, the creation of the DC-3 (see Chapter 25)—also contributed mightily to military aviation, making possible new long-range bombers such as the B-17, a four-engine "Flying Fortress" that flew for the first time in 1935 and that could deliver 4,000 pounds of bombs from 25,000 feet.

Despite the potency of American air power, Hitler's Luftwaffe was reported to be formidably superior—notably by Charles Lindbergh, who visited Nazi Germany several times and was warmly greeted by Nazi officials. Exaggerated estimates had it that Hitler commanded hundreds of long-range bombers capable of reaching the Americas from the western coast of Africa. In October 1938, Roosevelt called for vastly larger military expenditures—the sum was eventually set at $500 million—and at a White House conference the next month, he said he wanted an American air force of 10,000 planes and a capacity for producing 20,000 more a year.

*Only for the Neighborhood.* Roosevelt justified enhanced American air power as a deterrent to war and a measure of self-defense that would prevent the spread of a European war to the Americas. His air-power initiative won support from both liberals and conservatives, both finding it attractive to vote for new planes—for example, the B-17 bombers for the Army Air Corps—that were not for assaulting European cities but for attacking enemy troopships if they tried to sail west across the

Atlantic or east across the Pacific. The armed services argued in addition that coastal protection required long-range bombers that could fly between the East and West Coasts without refueling. To the end of defending the Eastern Seaboard, in January 1939 the navy formed an Atlantic Squadron.

The requirements of hemispheric defense reinforced the administration's commitment to the Good Neighbor policy. That policy had been severely strained when, in March 1938, Mexico announced the nationalization of its $400 million oil industry. Roosevelt resisted pressure to intervene and steered clear of an open break with the Mexican government. He encouraged a shift in military planning—from maintaining just U.S. national security to bolstering the security of the hemisphere. In December 1938, at the eighth Pan American Conference in Lima, Peru, Secretary of State Hull won a declaration that committed the Latin American states to joint defense against foreign threats.

In February 1939, the war in Spain ended with the victory of Franco's fascists. In March, Hitler's armies swallowed the rest of Czechoslovakia; in April, Italy invaded Albania. Roosevelt urged repeal of at least parts of the Neutrality Act, pointing out that their cash-and-carry provisions favored the Japanese equally with the British. But while Congress was willing to bolster the means of hemispheric defense, it was reluctant to modify the Europe- and Asia-oriented neutrality laws.

## A World at War

In Moscow on August 23, 1939, Germany and the Soviet Union signed a nonaggression pact, which included a secret agreement permitting Stalin to annex eastern Poland and the Baltic states in the event of a German-Polish war. The agreement stunned the world, since the two nations were sharp ideological antagonists, were ambitious for territory in eastern Europe, and seemed on the verge of war with each other. Both Hitler and Stalin, in fact, privately saw the pact as temporary, with advantages to each for the moment. Hitler, who was planning to move against Poland imminently, intended to protect his troops against Soviet intervention and discourage Britain and France from coming to Poland's aid. Stalin, pleased to have the territory in eastern Europe, aimed to buy time to prepare for the German assault on his country that he was convinced was sure to come.

"Next!" Cartoonist D.R. Fitzpatrick expresses the fear in August 1939 that Poland is in jeopardy of the mechanized might of Nazi aggression.

## THE OUTBREAK OF WORLD WAR II

Hitler invaded Poland on September 1, 1939, waging a blitzkrieg, or "lightning war," spearheaded by "Panzer" divisions—phalanxes of mechanized armor, especially tanks—protected on their flanks by German Stuka dive-bombers. Roosevelt got the news in a telephone call at three A.M. from his ambassador to France, William Bullitt. "Well, Bill," he said, "it has come at last. God help us all."

Two days later, Britain, which had signed a pact of mutual assistance with Poland, declared war on Germany, and so did France. On September 17, the Soviet Union, following the secret protocol in its pact with Hitler, marched into eastern Poland. Less than a week later, Poland capitulated, the victim of overwhelming power. In October, Stalin's troops occupied Latvia, Estonia, and Lithuania, and in late November they invaded Finland. After little more than a generation, a second European conflict, soon to become a world conflagration, had begun.

President Roosevelt issued a proclamation of neutrality and declared that he would expend every effort to keep war away from the United States, but he added that "even a neutral can-

not be asked to close his mind or conscience." He called a special session of Congress to revise the Neutrality Act, hoping to achieve a blanket repeal of the arms embargo. Many Americans were outraged by the Soviet actions, especially what Roosevelt called the "dreadful rape" of Finland. Polls showed that while less than a third of the country thought the United States should go to war to save Britain and France from defeat, a hefty majority supported every aid to the Allies short of war. But isolationists, including Charles Lindbergh, Herbert Hoover, and now, in the wake of the Nazi-Soviet Pact, the American Communist Party, remained unbending, opposing even the administration's program of cautious aid to the Finns. To their minds, a blanket repeal of the prohibition against arms sales to belligerents would put the country at risk of war. On November 4, 1939, forced to compromise, the president signed a Neutrality Act that permitted arms trade with belligerents but required that sales be made on a cash-and-carry basis.

During the winter of 1940, the European front appeared quiet, and in the United States people jeered at what an isolationist senator derided as "the phony war." Hitler, however, was merely waiting for the drying roads and clearing skies of spring. At dawn on April 9, 1940, in a renewal of the blitzkrieg, German troops struck to the north, occupying Denmark and rapidly vanquishing Norway. On May 10, turning westward, Hitler's armies invaded the Netherlands, Belgium, and Luxembourg, then advanced into France, sidestepping the main French army, which was arrayed along the Maginot Line—a string of heavy fortifications thought to be impregnable, named after the French minister who had directed its construction—by slashing around its northern end through the Ardennes Forest and toward the channel ports. The British Expeditionary Force, troops sent to France in the months following the invasion of Poland, retreated to the northern French coast, arriving at Dunkirk at the end of May with the Germans in close pursuit. A quarter-million British troops plus 110,000 French ones were evacuated to England over several days by heroic flotillas of British destroyers and small boats, many of them seagoing civilian vessels drafted from ports on the southern British coast.

On June 10, Italy, declaring war on the Allies, attacked France in the south, provoking President Roosevelt to comment, "The hand that held the dagger has struck it into the back of its neighbor." On June 22, just eleven weeks after the blitzkrieg began, France capitulated to Hitler, surrendering in the same railway car near Compiègne in which Germany had signed the armistice in November 1918. By the terms of the surrender, Germany occupied northern France, including

Paris; in the south, with its capital at Vichy, the French government under Marshal Pétain collaborated with the Nazis while remaining formally sovereign and maintaining control of French imperial possessions in Africa and Indochina.

Now, through the summer and fall of 1940, Hitler mounted a relentless air assault against Britain, targeting southern coast towns, air fields, and factories, shipping installations, and, ultimately, London. Eventually some 1,000 German planes crossed the channel each day, aiming to destroy Britain's lifelines of trade, shatter its productive capacity, and terrorize its people in preparation for a cross-channel invasion. In the course of the Battle of Britain, German bomber forces reduced the city of Coventry, including its famed cathedral, to rubble; blasted large parts of London; and killed or wounded tens of thousands of civilians.

The assaults only stiffened British resistance, especially that of Winston Churchill, a high-ranking member of the Conservative Party who had early recognized Hitler's threat to Britain. In 1938, Churchill had denounced the Munich agreement on the floor of the Parliament, calling it "a total and unmitigated defeat" and demanding that Britain stand up for freedom, but his admonitions had gone unheeded. Within days of the outbreak of the war, he was brought into

Londoners took shelter from German bombing attacks in the city's underground stations, where entertainers sometimes tried to keep up their spirits.

Chamberlain's cabinet and, in May 1940, in the face of the blitzkrieg, he succeeded Chamberlain as prime minister. In his mid-sixties, Churchill was indefatigable, eloquent, and unswerving in his resistance to the Nazis, calling on his people for the "blood, toil, tears, and sweat" essential to the uncompromising pursuit of victory.

The German bombers were met by hundreds of Royal Air Force (RAF) fighter craft, Spitfires and Hurricanes manned by young pilots who were guided to their targets by the new technology of radar (a term standing for "radio detection and ranging"), which had been developed independently in the United States, Britain, and Germany. Radar involved the process of sending out electromagnetic pulses, then detecting those reflected back by an object such as a ship or a plane. Beginning in 1937, the Air Ministry had established a line of fifty radar installations along Britain's Europe-facing coast. Called "Chain Home," the network detected incoming enemy bombers; determined their location, altitude, and flight paths; and gave Fighter Command fifteen to twenty minutes warning of their arrival, enough time to send its forces to intercept them. Some 2,500 pilots, about 20 percent of them volunteers from conquered European nations, rose against the German bombers and their swarms of protective fighters. More than 800 of England's fighter aircraft were destroyed, and for several weeks at a rate that exceeded production; but they downed some 600 German bombers and a comparable number of fighters, established control of the air over their country and the channel, and shattered Hitler's dream of an invasion. In August 1940, Churchill memorably said of the Battle of Britain, "Never in the field of human conflict was so much owed by so many to so few."

### THE AMERICAN RESPONSE

The swift success of Hitler's blitzkrieg stunned many Americans, but they were stirred by Churchill's resolve, the brave evacuation at Dunkirk, and the courage of both the RAF pilots and the British people. Through the 1930s, Americans had acquired graphic impressions of events abroad through the Movietone News shorts that preceded the main features in movie theaters and from live radio broadcasts at scenes of crisis. The dispatches from Munich about the threat of war had kept millions on tenterhooks. Now the CBS radio reporter Edward R. Murrow brought the Battle of Britain into American living

## Edward R. Murrow Broadcasts the Blitz

*American Journal*

*In 1937, at age 25, Edward R. Murrow went to Europe for CBS and soon established a corps of reporters who would convey to Americans at home the drama of the coming war and then the war itself. All of them, but especially Murrow, were fearless and dedicated journalists, and they would become prominent newscasters in the postwar United States. Millions of Americans listened to Murrow's broadcasts from London during the Nazi bombing of the city, conveying from the rooftops and the streets the impact of the blitz on the city and its people. Here, for example, is his radio report for September 25, 1940.*

"This is London, 3:45 in the morning. Tonight's attack against the central London area has not been as severe as last night; less noise, fewer bombs, and not so many fires. . . . I spent last night with a bomber pilot who had carried twenty-five loads of bombs over Germany. . . . When we left the studio we'd gone only a few blocks when we heard one coming down. As we lay on the sidewalk waiting for it to thump, he said, 'I'd feel better up there than down here.' . . .

Later we went out to see a fire. A block of cheap little working-class houses had been set alight by the firebombs. As we walked toward the blaze, gusts of hot air and sparks charged down the street. We began to meet women. One clutched a blanket, another carried a small baby in her arms, and another carried an aluminum cooking pot in her left hand. They were all looking back over their shoulders at that red glow that had driven them out into the streets. They were frightened . . . .

At dawn we saw Londoners come oozing up out of the ground, tired, red eyed, and sleepy. The fires were dying down. We saw them turn into their own street and look to see if their house was still standing. . . . Today I walked down a long street. The gutters were full of glass; the big red busses couldn't pull into the curb. There was the harsh, grating sound of glass being shoveled into trucks. In one window—or what used to be a window—was a sign. It read: SHATTERED—BUT NOT SHUTTERED. Near by was another shop displaying a crude lettered sign reading: KNOCKED BUT NOT LOCKED. They were both doing business in the open air. Halfway down the block there was a desk on the sidewalk; a man sat behind it with a pile of notes at his elbow. He was paying off the staff at the store—the store that stood there yesterday."

Edward R. Murrow, broadcast from London, Sept. 25, 1940, reprinted in *Reporting World War II, Part One: American Journalism 1938–1944* (2 vols; New York: The Library of America, 1995), vol. I, 98–100.

---

rooms, slowly intoning "This is London" over the airwaves across the Atlantic. He made graphic the human story of the blitz, telling of the long lines of people carrying blankets into the city's deep underground stations, where they would be safe from the night bombing. Sympathy for the British was especially strong on both coasts and in the South, in academic and intellectual circles, and among businessmen with an internationalist outlook. It also flourished among Jews, old-stock Anglophiles, and groups—Polish Americans, for example—with roots in countries Hitler had conquered. Pro-British sentiment was centered among Democrats, but it reached into the ranks of the GOP, too, with strong representation in the moderate, eastern wing of the party.

*The Mobilization of Science.* A strong desire to assist the British marked key sectors of American science. Like their countrymen, a number of scientists had been isolationists, but most, especially those connected to physics, had moved to a strong internationalism even before the fall of France. The nation's physics leadership, which included a number of Jews, knew from firsthand visits, correspondents abroad, or the refugees the virulence of Hitler's Germany. They also knew that the Third Reich still had scientists capable of developing new military technologies. They were especially concerned with what the Nazis might do with uranium fission. Discovered experimentally in Berlin in December 1938, this process released nuclear energy that conceivably could be concentrated into a bomb powerful enough to blow up a city like New York.

Albert Einstein, a pacifist before Hitler took power, had turned afterward into a staunch supporter of American rearmament and scientific involvement with the military. In August 1939, Einstein wrote a letter about nuclear fission to President Roosevelt that was to be delivered by an economist named Alexander Sachs. In October, having been delayed in obtaining an appointment by the press of business at the White House, Sachs brought the letter to a meeting with the president and succinctly explained the implications of fission, stressing that it might be used to produce explosives of unprecedented power. Roosevelt authorized action on the matter, with the result that a small uranium committee was established to link the government with the research of atomic physicists. However, it was given a budget of only $6,000 and had made little progress by the time of the blitzkrieg.

In May 1940, a small group of prominent scientists and engineers came together, all of them moderate Republicans and internationalists who felt that civilian scientific expertise had to be brought broadly to bear on national defense. They were led by Vannevar Bush, long an electrical engineer on the MIT faculty who was now involved with military aeronautics in Washington. Like his pro-preparedness scientific colleagues, Bush knew the practical side of science, the growing respect it commanded in high-technology businesses such as electronics and aircraft, and the difficulties its practitioners faced in getting the federal government, especially the military, to take it seriously. Both armed services had been committed to ongoing programs of research and development since World War I, but their budgets for this purpose had been kept to a pittance. They also maintained feeble connections with civilian science, partly because of the lack of funds, partly because the military thought civilian technical experts impractical.

Early in June 1940, Bush, sure that civilian science could have a far-reaching and decidedly practical impact on military technology, obtained President Roosevelt's approval for the creation of a National Defense Research Committee (NDRC). Chaired by Bush, the NDRC included the heads of Harvard, MIT, and the National Academy of Sciences. All agreed to use the nation's existing research establishment to the limit. The group took over control of nuclear research from the uranium committee, compiled a list of critical technical needs from the military, and soon began awarding research contracts—by December, 126 of them to thirty-two academic institutions and nineteen industrial laboratories.

**TIME**
THE WEEKLY NEWSMAGAZINE

VANNEVAR BUSH: GENERAL OF PHYSICS
In this war, Science is G-5.
(Science)

Vannevar Bush, a shrewd administrator and visionary leader, was key to the mobilization of scientists and engineers for national defense.

All the while, Roosevelt stressed to the public that it was in the national interest to help the Allies with material resources. Taking steps to make national defense a bipartisan issue, he encouraged the famed Kansas journalist William Allen White in May 1940 to form the broad-based Committee to Defend America by Aiding the Allies. In June, the president named two Republicans to his cabinet—Frank Knox, as secretary of the navy, and Henry L. Stimson, as secretary of war. In May, Roosevelt called on Congress to create an air force of 50,000 planes and an industrial capacity to produce at least 50,000 aircraft a year. Some of them he hoped could be sold to the Allies, a policy that opinion polls showed the public supported with an enthusiasm that mounted as the Nazis rolled across France. By the end of June, Congress had appropriated more than $3 billion for defense; by the end of October, $17 billion, including sufficient funds for a two-ocean navy.

## THE ELECTION OF 1940

The Republican Party remained isolationist at heart, but internationalist party members successfully won the presidential nomination for a dark-horse favorite, Wendell L. Willkie of Indiana. Willkie was likable, intelligent, and articulate, a utilities executive and foe of public power who was nevertheless sympathetic to many liberal goals. He believed that it was in the American interest to support Britain. In July, at the Democratic convention in Chicago, conservatives tried to persuade the convention against choosing Roosevelt, arguing that a third term was unprecedented and dangerous. However, anxiety about the war joined with Roosevelt's popularity to overwhelm fears and gain him the renomination. For vice-president, he chose Secretary of Agriculture Henry A. Wallace, a devoted liberal and staunch internationalist with strong credentials in the Midwest.

Desperate for votes and given contradictory counsel by his advisers, Willkie began hammering at Roosevelt's foreign policy, charging that the president was both soft on national defense and leading the country into war. With Willkie rapidly gaining on the president in the polls, Roosevelt went on the offensive in late October, declaring in Philadelphia, "I'm an old campaigner and I love a good fight." When he packed Madison Square Garden in New York, 40,000 people around the city watched the event on the fuzzy screens of the early television sets, the audience for the first televised political speech. In the heat of the campaign's closing days, Roosevelt told voters in Boston that "your boys are not going to be sent into any foreign wars."

On election day, Roosevelt won 27 million votes to Willkie's 22 million and trounced him in the electoral college by 449 to 82. But his popular majority had fallen 6 percentage points from 1936. The war and the New Deal had worked against him among German Americans, Irish Americans, and Italian Americans, and in the farms and country towns of the Midwest, yet they had both helped him enormously in the big cities, among lower-income and blue-collar groups, African Americans, Jews, and people with ties to Poland and Norway. The election revealed that much of the country remained happy with Roosevelt but divided and uncertain over the country's foreign course.

## BATTLE IN THE ATLANTIC

After the fall of France in June 1940, the sea war in Europe had reached north and west from the coasts of the British Isles, France, and Spain into the North Atlantic, with German U-boats slashing at Britain's lifeline in the convoy lanes out to Iceland. The German submarine fleet, which now enjoyed the use of French ports, soon began hunting in wolf packs, coordinated groups that stalked convoys for several days at a time. Churchill had been begging for destroyers, which were crucial to protecting

A 1940 campaign poster for FDR.

British shipping against Nazi submarines. Roosevelt, apprehensive about isolationist sentiment in Congress, responded to Churchill by executive action, announcing on September 3 that the United States would give fifty overage destroyers to Britain in exchange for ninety-nine-year leases of bases in the Caribbean and Newfoundland. Shrewdly packaged by Roosevelt, the arrangement offered the British more than the language of age implied: even though the vessels were four-funneled antiques from World War I, some of them barely seaworthy, they could be refitted for useful duty in the English Channel. And the transfer signaled the depth of the United States' commitment to the British cause. Willkie, setting aside partisanship, endorsed the deal. He also backed a proposal from the administration for conscription, the first such peacetime measure in the country's history. The Selective Service Act passed in September even though it aroused opposition across the political spectrum.

In the fall of 1940, Britain was running out of cash for arms purchases, but the U.S. Neutrality Act forbade providing any credit. In an eloquent Fireside Chat on December 29, 1940, Roosevelt declared that the United States had to serve as "the great arsenal of democracy," a resource for Britain's defense needs as well as its own. To that end, he said, the country had best forget the "silly, foolish old dollar sign." It could simply lend or lease war equipment to countries like Britain whose defense was vital to the United States on the understanding that the equipment would be returned, or returned in kind, after the war. Roosevelt likened the move to lending a garden hose to a neighbor whose house was on fire with the expectation of getting the hose back after the fire was put out. "Give us the tools and we will finish the job," Churchill pledged.

Passions on the issue ran high. When in January 1941 the president sent a lend-lease bill to Capitol Hill, congressional isolationists attacked it, with Senator Burton K. Wheeler of Montana likening lend-lease to the New Deal's farm policy, predicting that "it will plow under every fourth American boy." Roosevelt told reporters that Wheeler's statement was "the rottenest thing that has been said in public life in my generation." No matter: the president's Fireside Chat had won huge public approval, Wendell Willkie testified in favor of lend-lease legislation, and Congress passed it on March 11, 1941, appropriating some $7 billion for the purpose—more than four times the total outlays for national defense in 1940.

An English cartoonist welcomes America's lend-lease program, 1941.

By then, the Germans had increased the difficulty of getting goods to Britain by intensifying their U-boat attacks and stretching the Atlantic war zone farther west to Greenland and south to the lower end of Africa. During the spring of 1941, German submarines were sending merchant ships to the bottom at twice the rate they were being replaced. In April, with the agreement of the Danish government-in-exile, Roosevelt sent American troops to Greenland, a Danish possession, to help keep it out of Nazi hands. He also authorized American air and naval patrols to cover the Atlantic out to the rugged island. On May 27, 1941, five days after the sinking of an American merchant ship by a German submarine, he warned that the war in the Atlantic was "coming very close to home" and proclaimed the existence of a "national emergency" in the interest of strengthening American defense to the maximum.

*An Incipient Anglo-American Alliance.* Meanwhile, German-Soviet animosity had revived, partly as the result of friction between the two nations in the Balkans. Hitler, realizing that he could not invade Britain, wanted to eliminate the Soviet threat on Germany's eastern flank. On June 22, 1941, he sent 3 million troops to war against the Soviet Union (see map in Chapter 27). American Communists instantly flip-flopped, becoming passionate advocates of aid to the Allies. In contrast, many Americans could agree with the observation of Senator Harry S. Truman of Missouri: "Nazis are killing Communists, and Communists are killing Nazis. Let them bleed each other white." But Britain and the United States resolved to help Stalin battle the Nazis, their leaders holding, as Roosevelt put it, that to defeat Hitler, "I would hold hands with the Devil." In October, he made the Soviet Union eligible for lend-lease, and soon some American war materiel, though less than had been pledged, began making its way across the North Sea bound for Murmansk.

In August 1941, Roosevelt and Churchill rendezvoused on a warship off the coast of Newfoundland. The two men, having developed a personal relationship by letter and cable, had looked forward with pleasure to meeting each other. Roosevelt and Churchill each found the other greatly to his liking—self-confident, articulate, good-humored, and united in their eagerness for Hitler's defeat. At the conference, they cemented a working union that would persist until Roosevelt's death and overcome differences in policy that inevitably cropped up between them.

Roosevelt wanted to make clear to the public that even though he might hold hands with the Soviet devil and help imperial

Roosevelt (left) and Churchill in August 1941 aboard HMS *Prince of Wales*, where they issued the Atlantic Charter.

Britain, he was not compromising fundamental American beliefs. After several days, the two governments issued a declaration of principles that became known as the Atlantic Charter. The document opposed forced or undemocratic territorial changes; endorsed equal access to resources and trade ("with due respect for . . . existing obligations"); affirmed sovereignty and self-government as universal rights; and called in the postwar period for freedom from want and fear, the disarmament of aggressor nations, and, ultimately, a system of collective security.

Roosevelt also pledged to go beyond principle to further aid the British. According to what Churchill told his cabinet soon after the meeting, Roosevelt said "that he would wage war, but not declare it," that he would do "everything" to "force an incident . . . which would justify him in opening hostilities." In July, Roosevelt had extended the American defense zone to Iceland and sent troops to help protect it. After his meeting with Churchill, he authorized navy destroyers to escort British merchant shipping between the United States and Iceland, and he ordered the escorts to shoot any German submarine sighted anywhere in the defense zone.

On September 4, a German U-boat attacked the American destroyer *Greer,* firing its torpedoes after having been pursued by the *Greer* and depth-charged by a British plane. Roosevelt nevertheless told a national radio audience that the German submarine had "fired first" and without warning, initiating an act of "piracy." The president took advantage of the incident to announce his escort-to-Iceland policy and the order to shoot on sight, explaining, "When you see a rattlesnake poised to strike, you do not wait until he has struck before you crush him." He contended, in a slap at isolationists, that "it is time for all Americans . . . to stop being deluded by the romantic notion that the Americas can go on living happily and peacefully in a Nazi-dominated world."

In mid-October, Nazi torpedoes severely damaged one American destroyer and two weeks later sank another, the *Reuben James,* with the loss of 115 men. Following the *Greer* incident, the president had asked Congress to repeal the last key provisions of the Neutrality Act. In November 1941, acting on Roosevelt's request, both houses voted solidly to allow the arming of merchant ships and the transport of goods through the ocean war zones all the way to Britain and the Soviet Union. Now, as American escort crews braved the gale-force winds, bitter cold, and towering seas, Roosevelt waited for a hostile encounter in the North Atlantic that would force a declaration of war against Germany. Hitler, however, having run into stiff Soviet resistance in the East, ordered his U-boats to avoid confrontations with American vessels that might bring the United States into the war.

*Waging Undeclared War.* According to the polls, the nation overwhelmingly supported all aid to Britain, but on August 18 the Selective Service Act had been renewed in the House by a majority of just one vote. A large number of Americans were torn, hoping that the Nazis would be defeated but unwilling to wage war—especially war that sent American soldiers into battle—against them if they were not. Roosevelt himself hoped that the United States could help defeat the Nazis by using only air and naval forces, expressing a proclivity for relying more on technology than on troops that his countrymen shared.

Isolationist sentiment had been strengthened by the reduction of pressure on Britain that came with the German invasion of the Soviet Union. The America First Committee, formed by isolationists in September 1940 to contest what they saw as a trend toward war that was wholly wrong and unnecessary, insisted that American security would not be jeopardized by a Nazi victory. Charles Lindbergh, a passionate America Firster, held that the real enemy was to the east (meaning Russia and the Orient), which threatened to infiltrate the West with "inferior blood." The white race was in danger from a "pressing sea of Yellow, Black, and Brown," and Germany might save it. Most isolationists disavowed Lindberg's racism, but many worried about the broad discretionary powers that the president was acquiring by waging undeclared war.

All the while, Roosevelt kept stretching his authority to protect what he took to be the vital interests of the nation. In addition to misrepresenting the circumstances of the *Greer* incident, he authorized the FBI to investigate "subversive activities," which extended the agency's scope to include snooping into political groups. The bureau investigated organizations such as the Veterans of the Abraham Lincoln Brigade and people who expressed support for Lindbergh; it illegally intercepted and opened private correspondence with selected foreign countries and wiretapped without warrants. In July 1941, the president appointed William J. Donovan, a wealthy, energetic, and aggressive lawyer, to the new post of coordinator of information. On the face of it, Donovan's office was to obtain information relevant to national security, but he was secretly also given responsibility for "special operations," which meant covertly waging undeclared war against the Nazis in Europe. In defending the United States, Roosevelt thus misused some of its democratic institutions and set dangerous precedents, opening the door to later abuse of presidential power in the name of national security; but at the time, the heinousness of the Nazi threat made such measures seem justifiable.

## THE SEARING JAPANESE SUN

As Japan pursued its war against the Chinese, its aggressive presence in China became a touchstone of U.S. policy in Asia. China held a special, if somewhat self-contradictory, place in the hearts of many Americans. On the one hand, national law had long discriminated against the immigration and naturalization of people from China (see Chapter 19), and Chinese Americans continued to suffer from a variety of injustices. On the other, Protestant missionaries often devoted much of their lives to Christianizing the Chinese, and secular evangelists of Americanism took them to be a special target for conversion to democracy and capitalism. Now that the Chinese appeared to be fighting naked Japanese aggression, they earned mounting sympathy in America and Britain.

President Roosevelt admired the aspirations of the Chinese, but his support for China was also grounded in concern for the strategic interests of the United States. He wished to maintain the Open Door so that China could further develop in a democratic, capitalist direction and help block Japan's imperial ambitions. He was worried that Japan might threaten the Philippines and the supply of strategic materials that the Allies and the United States obtained from Southeast Asia—for example, the natural rubber that came from Indonesia. Roosevelt avoided activation of the Neutrality Acts against China and Japan, fearing that an arms embargo and the laws' cash-and-carry provisions would hurt China, which depended heavily on imports of war goods, far more than Japan. Thus the sale of goods to Japan continued, legally undergirded by the Japanese-American commercial treaty of 1911. In 1938, for example, American business supplied Japan with two-thirds of its oil and nine-tenths of its metal scrap.

In late 1938, polls showed that Americans were willing to take a stand on the war in China—far more so than they were on the war in Europe—particularly by prohibiting the sale of war supplies to Japan. However, President Roosevelt feared that such an embargo would weaken Japanese moderates and risk war. In July 1939, in response to congressional pressure, his administration told Tokyo that it intended to end the 1911 commercial treaty; but when it did, in January 1940, it declined to impose an embargo.

With the war in Europe now the primary concern, Roosevelt did not want a confrontation with Japan. Japanese expansionists,

D.R. Fitzpatrick depicts the savagery of the Nazis when a U-boat sank the *Reuben James* on November 1, 1941.

however, pressed for taking advantage of the war in Europe to break American and British economic power in Asia. In July 1940, a pro-expansionist government took office in Japan that was committed to incorporating British, French, and Dutch colonial possessions in Southeast Asia into the new Japanese order, which Japan later termed the Greater East Asia Co-Prosperity Sphere. With the aim of discouraging these ambitions, on July 31, 1940, the United States embargoed the shipment of aviation-grade gasoline to Japan, and on September 26 it extended the restriction to include shipments of iron and steel scrap. The next day, Japan joined Germany and Italy in a Tripartite Pact, pledging mutual assistance if any of the signatories was attacked by a nation with which it was currently at peace. At the end of November, the United States announced a $100 million loan and a gift of fifty fighter planes to China. The planes would be formed into a volunteer air force (later dubbed the Flying Tigers), and American citizens would be permitted to pilot them.

Japan, watchful of the Soviets in Siberia, did not immediately move into Southeast Asia, but once Hitler invaded Russia in June 1941, the Japanese government felt free to pursue its aims more aggressively. Japanese forces had already established themselves in the north of Indochina. At a conference in the presence of the emperor on July 2, the government resolved to move into the southern part of the region, and near the end of the month Japanese troops marched south, occupying several cities, including Saigon; this was a preparatory step toward takeovers of British Malaya and the Dutch East Indies, both rich in oil. At the end of the month, the Roosevelt administration, failing in an attempt to obtain a withdrawal, froze all Japanese assets in the United States and severely reduced oil shipments to Japan. Roosevelt hoped his actions would make Japan willing to bargain.

Civilians in the Japanese government wanted to try to resolve the conflict with the United States, but the military, anxious about Japan's declining oil supplies—it had only eighteen months of reserves under conditions of war—insisted that time was running out. At an Imperial Conference on September 6, Japan's leaders agreed that if by mid-October rapprochement with America appeared hopeless, the country would prepare for war against the United States, England, and Holland. Japan's conditions for peace included noninterference with its activities in China, the resumption of commercial relations, and a willingness to see its Co-Prosperity Sphere extended to Thailand and the Dutch East Indies. Roosevelt, with emphatic support from Churchill, who was anxious to keep open England's lifelines to its imperial possession, India, re-

fused to accept these demands, especially the abandonment of China.

In mid-October, the civilian prime minister of Japan resigned and was succeeded by General Hideki Tojo. Adamantly against compromise on China, Tojo opposed returning to any system in the western Pacific that was dominated by the United States. "Asia is the territory of the Asiatics," the Tokyo newspaper *Yomiuri* declared. Under the guise of attacking Western colonialism, however, Japan was manifestly pursuing an imperialism of its own that threatened Western security interests in the Pacific and that the United States would not accept.

*Pearl Harbor.* In November, the Japanese ambassador in Washington continued to negotiate. On November 26, with Roosevelt's approval, Secretary of State Cordell Hull reiterated to him that his country's forces must withdraw from China and Indochina, adding that once these conditions had been met, the United States would negotiate a liberal trade treaty with Japan. The Japanese, however, were all the while preparing for war. On November 25, a Japanese carrier force set out from the Kuril Islands, at the northeastern tip of Japan; its objective was a surprise attack on Pearl Harbor in Honolulu, where the American fleet was stationed.

Critics of Roosevelt later argued that the president deliberately maneuvered the United States into war—that he knew roughly when the attack would occur, was aware the target was Pearl Harbor, but nevertheless did nothing to prepare against it because he intended to use the Japanese deceit to break the isolationist deadlock at home. The charge is flatly contradicted by the evidence. At the level of grand strategy, Roosevelt considered Germany far more a threat to American security than Japan; he did not want to be distracted from the European war by a war in the Pacific.

True enough, the United States had broken the codes that the Japanese used in transmitting their military and diplomatic messages, but the coded Japanese traffic did not specifically identify the target. The consensus among American policymakers was that the Japanese would most likely strike southward, perhaps in the Philippines. On November 27, the navy sent a war warning to all its commands in the Pacific, ordering "appropriate defensive deployment"; the next day, the War Department sent a similar message, declaring "hostile action possible at any moment." In Hawaii, one of the several commands to which the war warning had been sent, the army and navy commanders expected only attempts at sabotage. They brought their defenses to high alert to defend against such action but not against an air attack.

Survivors on two burning battleships await rescue boats after the surprise attack on Pearl Harbor.

At seven A.M. on Sunday, December 7, 1941, two army operators at the radar station on the northern tip of Oahu, at Kahuku Point, detected what seemed to be as many as fifty planes some 132 miles to the northeast and headed for Hawaii. They telephoned their discovery to the Information Center, but the army command on Oahu had developed nothing like the British Chain Home system to act on radar intelligence. The officer on duty, thinking that the planes were a flight of B-17s arriving from the mainland, notified no one. Even if he had informed the proper authorities, the warning would have come too late to take significant defensive action. As a result of the focus on sabotage, none of the anti-aircraft batteries was manned and one-third of the fleet's ship captains as well as many of their officers were ashore. Approaching the Pearl Harbor naval base some minutes before eight A.M., a lead Japanese pilot radioed the carrier force, "Tora! Tora! Tora!"—a code signal that the U.S. fleet in the Pacific had been caught completely off guard.

Two waves of Japanese torpedo planes, dive-bombers, and fighters—the first comprising 9 aircraft, the second 20—struck the American ships, planes, and military installations at Pearl Harbor for almost two hours, killing 2,403 people and wounding another 1,178. Almost 1,000 of the dead perished when a single bomb struck the battleship *Arizona*, detonating its forward magazine and sinking the ship. The attack destroyed 188 planes and knocked out the bulk of the American battle fleet. But its aircraft carriers, which happened to be at sea, escaped, and since there was no follow-up attack, so did the fuel storage tanks and the dry dock facilities at the Pearl Harbor base.

The next day, in an address before a joint session of Congress that was broadcast to millions across the country, President Roosevelt denounced the surprise attack, calling December 7, 1941, "a day which will live in infamy." At Roosevelt's urging, Congress, with only one dissenting vote, enacted a declaration of war against Japan. The president, uncertain that he could obtain a similar declaration against Germany and Italy, waited to see what action they would take. On December 11, Hitler and Mussolini declared war on the United States, triggering the nation's formal entry into the battle that Roosevelt and, by now, millions of other Americans were convinced they had to fight.

## Suggested Reading

Robert Dallek, *Franklin D. Roosevelt and American Foreign Policy, 1932–1945*, rev. ed. (1995)

Akira Iriye, *The Origins of WWII in Asia and the Pacific* (1987)

Manfred Jonas, *Isolationism in America, 1935–1941* (1966)

Daniel J. Kevles, *The Physicists: The History of a Scientific Community in Modern America* (1995)

David Wyman, *Paper Walls: America and the Refugee Crisis, 1938–1941* (1968)

James McGregor Burns, *Roosevelt: The Soldier of Freedom* (1970)

Frank Freidel, *Franklin Roosevelt: A Rendezvous with Destiny* (1990)

Gordon W. Prange, *At Dawn We Slept: The Untold Story of Pearl Harbor* (1991)

# Chapter Review

## Summary QUESTIONS

- What was the Good Neighbor Policy?
- What fueled American isolationism in the 1930s?
- What role did technology play in breaking down American isolationism?
- What were the neutrality laws and how were they shaped by events?
- How did Franklin Roosevelt use the powers of the presidency to defend the United States and aid Great Britain before Pearl Harbor?

## Key Terms

Nazism (pp. 738, 743)

Isolationism (p. 744)

Neutrality Acts (p. 745)

The Atlantic Charter (p. 754)

Pearl Harbor attack (p. 757)

## Chronology

| | |
|---|---|
| January 30, 1933 | Adolf Hitler becomes chancellor of Germany. |
| July 1935–February 1939 | Spanish Civil War. |
| July 1937 | Japan goes to war with China. |
| March 1938 | Hitler annexes Austria. |
| November 9–10, 1938 | Kristallnacht throughout Germany and Austria. |
| September 1, 1939 | Hitler invades Poland, World War II begins. |
| Summer–Fall 1940 | Battle of Britain. |
| June 22, 1940 | France surrenders to Germany; German troops occupy northern France. |
| June 1941 | German forces invade Russia. |
| December 7, 1941 | Japan attacks Pearl Harbor. |

**Access the *Inventing America* StudySpace at wwnorton.com/studyspace**

PERSONAL PLAN ■ REVIEW MATERIALS ■ RESEARCH AIDS ■ MULTIMEDIA

# Chapter 27

# FIGHTING FOR FREEDOM:

## 1942-1945

Inspecting bomber turrets at Douglas Aircraft in Long Beach, California, 1944.

QUESTIONS

- ■ **What were the critical first steps America took after entering the war?**

- ■ **How did the United States mobilize for war?**

- ■ **What were the major effects of the war on American society?**

- ■ **What was the Allied strategy for victory in the Pacific?**

- ■ **What was the Allied strategy for victory in Europe?**

- ■ **Why did the United States drop atomic bombs on Hiroshima and Nagasaki?**

After Pearl Harbor, Adolf Hitler indulged in a verbal jig, telling his cronies, "I don't see much future for the Americans. It's a decayed country. And they have their racial problems, and the problem of social inequalities. . . . American society [is] half Judaized, and the other half Negrified. How can anyone expect a State like that to hold together—a country where everything is built on the dollar." Hitler's foreign minister knew better. He warned the Führer that if the Soviet Union's huge manpower was mobilized together with the United States' immense capacity for industrial production, the prospects for a victory by the Axis powers (Germany, Italy, and Japan) would be slim.

The foreign minister was right, but he might have added that the United States had the capacity to draw strength precisely from its diversity, from its growing willingness to mobilize against racism and inequality, and from the ideas that gave that mobilization voice. Unlike Woodrow Wilson, Roosevelt declined to call the country to battle to make the world safe for democracy. The disillusion attending the collapse of Wilson's program and now the renewal of war less than a generation after his "war to end all wars" had been fought—both made appeals to his vision untenable. The ideals promulgated by the Roosevelt administration emphasized preservation of the "American way of life" by protecting the country's security. Its enemies trampled on people's rights. The United States, in contrast, was fighting to safeguard the principles of freedom, especially the Four Freedoms that Roosevelt had articulated in a message to Congress in January 1941—freedom from fear, freedom from want, freedom of worship, and freedom of speech.

After Pearl Harbor, Roosevelt moved quickly to pursue the victory of ideas with the force of manpower and steel. At the opening of 1942, the United States and Great Britain joined with the Soviet Union and twenty-three other nations to form a Grand Alliance, pledging to commit their full resources to victory over the Axis Powers. To be sure, its three principal members were divided by important differences of outlook and national interest. Winston Churchill, a staunch imperialist, headed the world's leading colonial power. Joseph Stalin, dictator of the world's only Communist state, stood for the export of Soviet ideology around the world. Roosevelt, leader of a great capitalist nation and a himself a product of wealth, was a critic of colonialism and Communism. The men were united, however, by their ferocious opposition to Hitler, and they overrode their divisions in the interest of defeating Nazi Germany. Churchill no doubt spoke for all of them when he remarked, "There is only one thing worse than fighting with allies, and that is fighting without them."

The United States and Britain could not by themselves raise armies large enough to ensure victory by sheer numerical advantage. Their calculus of victory depended in part on the Soviet Union, with its armed forces of 8 million men and women, continuing to engage part of Hitler's Wehrmacht. It also hinged on their own achievement of overwhelming superiority in military technologies and the production of the goods of war. In the United States, the mobilization mounted in pursuit of that end greatly enlarged the federal government's powers and spending. It stimulated the economy to a blistering level of activity. It changed the lives of millions of Americans, including women and minority groups. And it transformed the relationship of the United States to the rest of the world.

## National Mobilization

### PRODUCTION FOR WAR

Among the Roosevelt administration's crucial tasks after Pearl Harbor was the conversion of American industry to a war footing, with the aim of accelerating the mass production of war goods. In January 1942, the president established the War Production Board (WPB) and gave it broad powers, including the authority to allocate supplies of raw materials to industry and curtail civilian production. When, in January 1942, the WPB shut down the civilian automobile industry, it not only turned the automakers' formidable manufacturing capabilities to the production of war items such as tanks and aircraft, but it also freed up for war purposes the resources the industry used in making cars—for example, 51 percent of the nation's malleable iron, 75 percent of its plate glass, 80 percent of its rubber, and more than 18 percent of its steel output. By 1943, war production totaled some $40 billion, ac-counting for 40 percent of the gross national product, some two and a half times as much as the proportion in 1941.

People were asked to conserve consumer items—for example, by turning in their used metal toothpaste tubes—but conservation was inadequate to meet the need for rubber, which figured significantly in the construction of military equipment such as battleships, bomber fuel tanks, and medical adhesive tape. Japan's control of Southeast Asia had cut off 98 percent of the United States' crude rubber supply; its remaining stock would suffice for only six months. A growing chorus of voices insisted that meeting wartime rubber needs would require drastic measures. In the late summer, a blue-ribbon committee spelled out the requirements: gasoline rationing and a national speed limit of thirty-five miles per hour to conserve the rubber on existing tires; and a major program to produce synthetic rubber. In September, on Roosevelt's orders, the WPB appointed a rubber czar who put the committee's recommendations into effect by shouldering through the construction of federally financed synthetic rubber factories and then leasing them to private corporations. In 1944, the new synthetic rubber industry turned out 750,000 tons of the material, enough to meet 90 percent of the nation's needs.

Under the guidance of the WPB, American industry achieved production miracles, turning out crucial war goods such as tanks, planes, and ships in far greater quantity than Britain, Germany, Japan, and the Soviet Union. In 1941, the Kaiser shipyards (in Portland, Oregon; Vancouver; Washington; and California, at Richmond and Los Angeles—all of them fed steel by a huge plant in Fontana, in southern California) produced the cargo-carrying vessel called a Liberty Ship in 355 days; in 1944, in fewer than 62 days. That year, the Boeing company's aircraft plants in Seattle, supplied by aluminum factories in Spokane and elsewhere, turned out 16 planes every 24 hours.

### CONTROLLING PRICES

Federal spending, pushed rapidly upward by the costs of war, amounted to more than $320 billion between 1940 and 1945, almost six times the total during Franklin Roosevelt's first two terms. The level of outlays made the federal government an unprecedentedly gigantic consumer, not only for weapons but also for items such as uniforms and shoes for the armed

The launch of a Liberty Ship from the Kaiser Shipyards in Richmond, California, a major feat of fast-paced production for the war effort.

761

forces. The government's enormous demand for goods and services put high pressure on prices, and so did wartime paychecks, since the diversion of material and productive capacity to war purposes created scarcities in civilian goods. For example, new cars and kitchen appliances were unavailable, and some foodstuffs like sugar were in acutely short supply. If the civilian economy had been allowed to operate under the rules of a purely free market, too much money would have been chasing too few products, with the result that prices would have skyrocketed, injuring many people, especially those in lower-income groups.

Roosevelt tried to deal with the problem by paying for as much of the war as possible through taxes. The wartime revenue acts raised rates in the highest brackets to 94 percent of net income. They also reduced the level of income exempt from taxes, compelling many more people to pay them. In 1941, only 7 million Americans filed income tax returns; in 1944, some 42 million did. In 1943, to facilitate its cash flow and ensure compliance, Congress enacted the system of with-

A poster urging the public to buy war bonds, 1942.

holding taxes from paychecks. Still, federal taxes paid for only about 41 percent of war spending. The rest came from loans, including $100 billion in war bonds that the government sold to its citizens. Increased taxes took some money out of the civilian economy, and so did war bond sales, but even both measures together were inadequate to deal with inflation.

In August 1941, to handle the matter, Roosevelt created the Office of Price Administration (OPA). The following April, the OPA announced a freeze on prices, enforcing it through thousands of local boards, which enlisted local volunteers, most of them women, to check whether merchants complied. The OPA, which administered the rationing of gasoline and tires, extended rationing to other necessities such as meat, sugar, shoes, coffee, and canned goods, and it issued books of coupons needed to purchase them. The manufacturers of Wrigley's gum and Coca-Cola, both heavy consumers of sugar, might have been devastated by the rationing, but both got around its restrictions by convincing the army and navy that American sailors and soldiers around the world craved their products.

Similarly, farmers successfully insisted on special treatment for agricultural prices, which drove up the cost of food, and labor in turn demanded compensatory increases in wages. When in July 1942 workers in several of the comparatively smaller firms in the steel industry demanded a wage increase of a dollar a day, the National War Labor Board, which had been created in January to manage labor practices and prevent strikes, devised the "Little Steel" formula. It capped wages for the duration of the war at their level of January 1, 1941, plus the 15 percent that the cost of living had risen since that date. The formula sapped the bargaining leverage of unions and, in the name of the war effort, denied them the right to seek a greater share of corporate income for their members. Still, prices began leveling off in mid-1943. Despite high-priced and illegal sales of some rationed goods in "black markets," the OPA managed to maintain overall price stability for the rest of the war. Between 1942 and 1945, after almost four years of war, consumer prices had risen only about 10 percent, compared with the increase of 62 percent during the year and a half of war that ended in November 1918.

### ECONOMIC BOOM

In the months after Pearl Harbor, as war contracts continued to energize the economy, unemployment virtually disappeared. Between 1940 and 1945, the gross national product

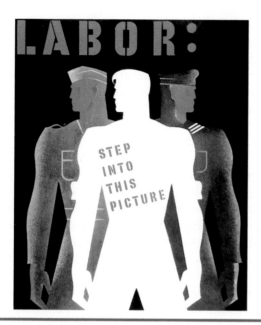

Labor is asked to do its part in the war effort.

more than doubled, reaching $211.9 billion. After-tax corporate profits climbed 70 percent; farm income doubled; and industrial wages shot up 50 percent even after adjustment for inflation. Partly because of higher taxes, the war economy somewhat reduced the gap between high- and low-income groups and generated a great surge in the size of the middle class.

The war mobilization also greatly affected the fortunes of labor and agriculture. Although the anti-inflation policy exemplified in the Little Steel formula limited wage increases, overtime pay helped drive up weekly earnings 70 percent on average. Under the circumstances, workers had little incentive to join unions, but by the end of the war organized labor had gained almost 6 million new members, largely because, in return for a no-strike pledge, the National War Labor Board insisted that unionized employers include a pro-union clause in their labor contracts. Getting around the cap on wages, a number of unions exercised the leverage they enjoyed amid the labor shortage to win their members unprecedented fringe benefits such as health and pension plans and paid vacations.

Although the no-strike pledge was widely observed at first, in 1943 some wildcat labor groups, discontented with the Little Steel formula, mounted short-lived work stoppages in shipyards and in factories making aircraft, leather, and steel.

During the spring, John L. Lewis led the United Mine Workers out on three strikes, and for a time the government took over the mines. Although polls showed that Lewis was the most hated man in America, some administration members believed that the mine workers had legitimate grievances. In November, after further confrontations, the government approved a settlement with the miners whereby they got an increase in wages, among other improvements.

The war blew away hard times for farmers. Demand for agricultural goods skyrocketed, not least because the millions of men and women serving in the military had to be fed. To reduce civilian demand, in 1942 Americans planted 6 million small plots for raising their own vegetables—they were called "victory gardens"—and in 1943, 20 million, harvesting 8 million tons of produce. Farmers bought new agricultural machinery, used better fertilizers, and increased production by 50 percent. At the end of the war, agricultural output of crops such as cotton, corn, wheat, and rice far exceeded that at the beginning. The government extended price-support policies to more commodities and roughly doubled the parity rate, a standard for farm prices. Agricultural income climbed steeply enough to put $11 billion into farmers' savings.

### REGIONAL CHANGES

The war mobilization accelerated regional development, especially in the South and West, but the dramatic change in economic activity was felt by cities and towns across the country. One woman remembered the transformation in Seneca, Illinois, a small town turned into a shipbuilding center: "The trucks began rolling in with great loads of material.... Then came the new people, cars and cars and cars.... You'd hear the *rat-a-tat-tat* of hammering all night long.... At the time we were only about a thousand people. One restaurant, an old hotel, that was all. All of a sudden Seneca and the surrounding area had about 27,000."

The South, which accounted for about a quarter of the country measured by land and population, housed more than two-thirds of domestic army and navy bases, including all but one of the army training camps, which poured money into local retail and service industries. Defense manufacturing contracts came to the region in abundance, stimulating the creation of high-wage enterprises for the production of aircraft and ships in communities such as Mobile (Alabama), Marietta (Georgia), and Pascagoula (Mississippi); of synthetic rubber in the oil-rich states of Texas and Louisiana; and of enriched

A worker burnishing the nose of a shell at a steel plant in Birmingham, Alabama, 1942.

uranium at an enormous plant that the atomic bomb project built for the purpose at Oak Ridge, Tennessee. The region's industrial plant doubled over what it had been in 1939, and industrial employment rose in comparable proportion. During the war, about a quarter of the southern population—some 4 million whites and blacks—left the farm, some for the North and West, most for the defense-boom areas in the South itself. It was said that for the first time since the Civil War, anyone who wanted a job in the South could get one.

Millions of people elsewhere were also on the move, migrating from farms to war production centers, from towns to cities, swelling the populations of Connecticut, Delaware, Florida, and Michigan, and especially of the far western states. Some 50,000 people worked for Boeing, and by 1945, shipyards in Washington and Oregon employed 150,000 people, including 100,000 at the Kaiser plants alone. During the war, migration into Oregon enlarged the state's population by almost 18 percent.

Comparable growth came in California, where, fueled by the state's flourishing war economy, the population grew by more than 14 percent. Roughly one out of eight defense con-

tracts, amounting to a total by 1945 of $70 billion, went to the state. War orders turned northern California into a huge center of shipbuilding and accelerated the growth of the aircraft industry in southern California, ensconcing the company names of Douglas, Lockheed, North American, and Hughes in the industrial firmament.

### THE ENLISTMENT OF SCIENCE

The emphasis given to war production was complemented by the high priority awarded to expertise. To a degree unprecedented in the country's wars, the government relied on myriad specialists, including mathematicians to decipher codes, psychologists and linguists to devise propaganda, and economists to help manage the supply and demand of goods. But no category of experts played a more decisive role in the war than scientists and engineers, especially physicists. American analysts knew that Hitler had technical talent at his disposal; they were supplying his forces with fast planes, formidable guns, and serviceable radar. Policymakers in the United States understood that the defeat of the Axis Powers required technological innovation fast-paced enough to keep the Allies ahead.

In June 1941, to facilitate the work of war research, President Roosevelt melded the initial agency of scientific mobilization into a new Office of Scientific Research and Development (OSRD) under the leadership of Vannevar Bush, the engineer who after the fall of France had called his attention to the importance of mobilizing science. The OSRD was given direct access to congressional appropriations, responsibility for research in military medicine, and the authority to develop promising new devices into prototypes ready for production. The office fulfilled its mission handsomely, generating military technologies and medical advances that contributed mightily to victory.

*Radar.* One of the most important of the OSRD's projects was at the Radiation Laboratory at MIT—the "Rad Lab," as it was called, which had a staff of almost 4,000, close to 500 of whom were physicists. The laboratory developed new radars based on a powerful vacuum tube called a "magnetron," which was a British invention. The magnetron generated "microwaves"—radio waves of ten to twenty times higher frequencies than the "long" waves employed in the existing army and navy radars; and it produced them with a thousand times greater energy than the most advanced American tube. Compared with long-wave radar, microwave radar detected ships and aircraft far more accurately and at longer distances.

Microwave radar from the Radiation Laboratory first contributed significantly to the war when in the spring of 1942 it was deployed against German U-boats that threatened cargo ships coming up the East Coast from Central and South America. Army B-18 bombers equipped with new air-to-surface-vessel (ASV) radar easily detected German submarines that surfaced to take in air. Together with navy destroyers and other aircraft equipped with long-wave search radar, the B-18s drove the enemy submarines 300 miles away from the coast by the end of 1942. The victory in the eastern sea lanes demonstrated that radar-equipped aircraft were much more effective at finding submarines in the vast expanse of the sea than were destroyers.

During the spring of 1943, losses to enemy submarines on the North Atlantic shipping routes suddenly reached critical proportions. At the urging of scientists and engineers, the navy shifted sharply from the prevailing antisubmarine strategy—defensive reliance on the convoy—to a new offensive strategy: searching for the German wolf packs in mid-ocean, using hunter-killer groups of long-range and carrier-based bombers fitted out with ASV radar. Shipping losses dropped from 245,000 tons in April to 18,000 tons in June. By early summer, Allied convoys were passing safely through lanes that had been perilous only a short time before. During the course of the war, the Radiation Laboratory developed a broad range of devices, including radar aids to bombing, fighter combat at night, and the navigation and ground control of aircraft. Microwave radar was also effectively coupled with new electronic systems that processed the information it provided about incoming aircraft and automatically aimed antiaircraft guns against them. Radiation Laboratory staff members would later say that the atom bomb only ended the war, that radar won it.

*A Physicists' War.* In August 1940, Vannevar Bush created an OSRD unit to provide the navy with a fuse for shells that would increase the chances of bringing down aircraft dive-bombing its ships. The likelihood of actually hitting an aircraft maneuvering evasively through the sky at some 300 miles an hour was low, and that of setting a time fuse—what the navy tended to rely on—so that a shell would detonate when it reached a plane was comparably small. The OSRD unit devised a fuse in the form of a rugged miniature radar that would trigger its carrier shell to explode when it reached a certain proximity to the attacking aircraft. On January 5, 1943, a Japanese plane zoomed toward the relatively unprotected fantail of the cruiser *Helena*. The ship's five-inch guns fired its shells armed with proximity fuses and destroyed their target on the second salvo. Naval officers promptly began demanding huge quantities of the fuses. At the peak of wartime output, five major plants spewed forth some 70,000 of them a day, and fuse production occupied a full 25 percent of the nation's entire electronics industry.

Early in the war, physicists and engineers at the California Institute of Technology began developing rockets. Rockets are propelled in opposite reaction to the hot gases they emit rather than by explosive force against a chamber, like a bullet or shell. Thus launched without recoil, they can arm small boats, airplanes, or even foot soldiers with firepower comparable to the five-inch guns on a battleship. Caltech rockets whooshed in ahead of the troops churning toward the beaches of North Africa in the autumn of 1942 and were used as standard naval ordnance in every subsequent landing in the Atlantic and Pacific theaters. By 1943, most of the nation's leading physicists had been mobilized for war research in radar, proximity fuses, rockets, the atom bomb, and numerous other OSRD projects. Long before the mushroom clouds rose over Hiroshima and Nagasaki, knowledgeable observers knew that in the way World War I had been a chemists' war, World War II was a war of physicists.

### THE MEDICAL WAR

OSRD medical scientists scored triumphs in saving lives on the battlefield and preventing the spread of infectious disease among the troops. During World War I, one of every seven or eight wounded soldiers treated in front-line hospitals died of infection; a powerful antibiotic would have saved many lives. In July 1941, a British biomedical scientist came to the United States in the hope of manufacturing such a pharmaceutical—a blue-green mold called "penicillium" that could combat bacterial infections in mice and humans. Penicillin—to use the name for the antibiotic that the British scientist and his colleagues hoped to make from the mold—would destroy them. An industrial penicillin program that produced the mold in quantity went into high gear in June 1943 following successful clinical tests on wounded soldiers. In 1945, penicillin production totaled enough to provide 21 million daily doses to soldiers suffering from wounds or infections such as venereal disease.

*Fighting Malaria.* In the Pacific and Middle Eastern theaters, malaria ranked second only to gonorrhea in producing casualties from infection. Malaria is caused by a parasite that is carried by the *Anopheles* mosquito, one of whose prime developmental environments is still, fresh water, the kind that occurs naturally in ponds or that accumulates in battlefield ruts and shell holes. When in 1942 American soldiers took the offensive at Guadalcanal, malaria caused five times as many casualties as combat, bringing down 100,000 personnel from all the armed services.

The long-standing drug for both prevention and treatment of malaria was quinine, which comes from the bark of a tree grown mainly in Indonesia. The Japanese now controlled some 90 percent of the world quinine supply. In late 1942, the military and the OSRD medical unit found a synthetic substitute for quinine—a drug called Atabrine, which the Germans had first developed. Despite several drawbacks such as turning skin and nails yellow, it proved to be the best synthetic antimalarial agent available during the war. By the summer of 1943, several companies were together turning out Atabrine at the rate of 1.2 billion tablets per year, and it was available to American troops in areas at high risk for malaria the world over.

Early in the war, the army opened a second front against malaria, aiming to suppress the *Anopheles* mosquito by spreading oil over water surfaces to prevent larval growth or to kill them by treating mosquito-infested areas with an insecticide. High hopes centered on DDT, which could be spread over large areas as a spray or dust, and was effective

American soldiers dust their clothing with DDT powder, the new protective against typhus, 1944.

not only against mosquitoes but against lice, which carry typhus, and fleas, which carry plague. In 1944, several American companies produced 10 million pounds of the insecticide. By 1945, aerial spraying with DDT was overtaking other antimosquito measures. According to several scientific studies, DDT in aerosol form did not pose a serious health hazard to human beings, but it did injure animals that ate it. It also threatened to upset the balance of nature where it was used, by, for example, killing off insects that were food for other species such as birds. Nevertheless, the military benefits of DDT were taken to be superior to its environmental costs, and it became a powerful weapon during the war in the fight against malaria and other insect-borne diseases.

*Replacing Blood.* Perhaps nothing was as indispensable to saving the lives of wounded soldiers, sailors, and fliers as blood—whole blood, or at least blood plasma, the principal fluid in blood. The speedy replacement of blood fluids is critically important for people suffering from hemorrhage, burns, and shock. The military established the industrial production of freeze-dried plasma and albumin, which draws fluid from tissues into the blood vessels, using blood donations gathered by the Red Cross. The donations were segregated into blood that came from whites and blood from blacks, a practice that honored racial prejudice but that was scientifically pointless, not to mention cruelly ironic. Blood plasma is easily subject to bacterial infection. The processes used to prevent such infection in the plasma supplies produced for the military were devised by Charles Drew, an African American physician. Scientists also devised methods to preserve fresh whole blood for twenty-one days, a fivefold increase over the prewar standard that made it practical for field-hospital use.

All told, the OSRD medical unit spent some $24 million—the cost of four hours of the war. Its principal projects more than repaid the investment. Blood substitutes administered on the battlefield saved thousands of soldiers who otherwise would simply have died from shock and hemorrhage. Thanks to penicillin, only about one out of thirty front-line soldiers died in field hospitals from infection, roughly a fourfold reduction from the rate in the first war. In Naples, Italy, in 1944, a typhus epidemic was halted completely after 1.3 million people were dusted with DDT. Although DDT would later earn censure as an environmental toxin, at the end of the war it was ranked with penicillin in the pantheon of biomedical miracles.

## The War and American Society

All the while, the administration sought to keep the nation's war aims—notably Roosevelt's Four Freedoms—before the American people, the overwhelming majority of whom told pollsters in 1942 that they did not have a clear idea what the war was about. The effort was advanced by the Office of Facts and Figures, which was replaced in the spring of 1942 with the Office of War Information (OWI). The information experts used all available media, including radio and films, to get their message across. Advertisers, with Roosevelt's encouragement, tied the benefits of liberty to the prospect of the good postwar life, predicting consumer marvels to come from wartime technical developments.

The OWI, which for a time had a Bureau of Motion Pictures, enlisted the Oscar-winning director Frank Capra to produce the *Why We Fight* series. The series tended to heavyhanded propagandizing, using enemy footage to contrast the pliant, oppressed citizens of Hitler's Germany or militaristic Japan with the resilient independence of Americans. Some filmmakers, left to their own devices, produced arresting documentary and fictional accounts of the war. Notable among them was the uncompromising documentary of the Battle of Midway made by John Ford, which won an Academy Award, and the classic *Casablanca*, in which the cynical owner of Rick's Café, played by Humphrey Bogart, gives the impression that he believes in nothing but assists his former lover in escaping so that her husband can carry on the fight for freedom.

The very dynamics of the war helped enlarge the meaning of freedom and equality. As Americans from diverse backgrounds were thrown together in factories, ships, planes, and ground-troop units, the war helped blur ethnic and religious divisions, breaking down barriers between Protestants, Catholics, and Jews. Margarita Salazar found herself mixing with Anglos—the term Hispanics tended to use for non-Hispanic whites—for the first time in her life in the war plants of Los Angeles. "We all blended in," she recalled, "men, women, Mexican, Italian." Hollywood helped acculturate moviegoers to the trend, producing a plethora of sentimental "platoon" films in which boys of Italian, Irish, Polish, Czech, and Anglo-Saxon backgrounds became friends, fought together, and wept when their buddies fell. The spread of equality benefited ethnic minority groups far more than other victims of discrimination, notably African Americans. But the rhetoric of war aims provided leverage for insisting that words like "freedom," "tolerance," and "equality" be taken seriously and heightened their place on the national agenda.

### WOMEN

During the war, more than 6 million women went to work, increasing the number who were already employed by almost 50 percent. By 1945, women accounted for a third of the paid workforce, even more in some defense industries. Married women came to outnumber single women in the workforce for the first time in the nation's history. Women took jobs traditionally identified with men, including work as lumberjacks, welders, miners, lathe and crane operators, machinists, taxi drivers, and even professional players in a women's baseball league. Suzie Secretary and Wendy Waitress turned into the popular wartime symbol of "Rosie the Riveter," depicted in cap and overalls, tools in hand.

The exigencies of war also opened opportunities for women in the new Women's Army Corps, commonly known as the WACs, the Navy Waves, and the Marine Corps Women's Reserve. Although initially opposed to the recruitment of women, military officers changed their minds once

"Rosie the Riveter" symbolized the capability of the nation's wartime women workers.

767

they realized that women could effectively fill a variety of noncombat positions ranging from clerks to chemists, mapmakers, and ferry pilots. Some 300,000 women eventually served in the armed services and affiliated organizations.

At home, women earned far more as factory hands than they did in their previous jobs. Four states enacted laws ensuring women equal pay for equal work, and some states prohibited job discrimination against women. Still, working women encountered reminders that they were not working men and could not expect male privileges; those at the Frigidaire plant in Dayton, Ohio, for example, angrily complained that they were paid less than men for comparable work and were denied equal seniority rights. Women in the workplace were expected to fill conventional stereotypes, to "bring glamour to the job," as a female federal official put it approvingly. Labor unions often stipulated that women would have to give up their jobs to men on their return from military service.

The forces pulling women back into the home remained powerful, especially for mothers with young children. "A mother's primary duty is to her home and children," the Children's Bureau in the Labor Department declared. Women with children under age fourteen made up only 32 percent of women in the workforce. Young mothers tended to stay home, partly because while child care facilities increased in number during the war, they served too few children. Critics who feared for the family pointed to the phenomenon of "latch-key children" (children who after school opened the door at home themselves because their parents were out working), sharp increases in the juvenile delinquency rate, and the jump in the divorce rate from 16 per 100 marriages in 1940 to 27 per 100 in 1944. Still, wartime experience taught millions of women the satisfactions of paid work and independence, and set many of them to thinking that rights to both, for all the practical problems of exercising them, were worth establishing in peacetime.

## AFRICAN AMERICANS

African Americans also made notable gains during the war. In the South, where the majority of blacks still lived and where they made up about a third of the population, planters and draft boards tried to keep as many as possible working on the land. Many African Americans nevertheless migrated from rural areas during the war, lured by the prospect of jobs in the thriving industrial plants. A number went to southern cities, but the majority—about 1,400,000, close to 16 percent of the blacks in the South—headed out of the region, roughly half to the North and half to the West, accelerating the Great Migration that had begun during World War I. In and out of the South, even those with high-demand skills, like welding, ran up against bald-faced discrimination. Craft unions in aircraft and shipping refused to accept African Americans, and white workers in some plants walked off their jobs to protest the hiring of blacks.

Blacks arrived in war-boom cities that were plagued by shortages in housing, social services, and police protection, and by increases in congestion, crime, and interracial tension. In 1943, several race-related riots erupted—the worst of them, a confrontation in June, in Detroit, where half a million people, including at least 60,000 blacks, had moved to work in war plants and formed a caldron of ethnic and racial resentments. Blacks and whites fought pitched battles while police shot looters and fired at rooftop snipers. An elderly black woman lamented the racial animosity that the riot had exposed: "There ain't no North no more. Everything now is South."

At the outset of the war, blacks fared in the military much as they did in American society. The prewar military had denied blacks eligibility for training as army officers or air corps pilots, confined them to jobs as mess stewards in the navy, and maintained strictly segregated forces. Although the Selective Service Act of 1940 banned discrimination in recruitment and training, African Americans were assigned to all-black army units. The new WACs, following tradition, also segregated whites and blacks. African American men in military training encountered segregated theaters, post exchanges, and canteens on the bases as well as racial prejudice—and, in the South, Jim Crow laws—beyond the camp gates.

African Americans grew more and more unwilling to put up with the indignities and barriers to advancement they encountered in defense industries, the armed services, and American life. During the war, about 1 million African Americans served in the armed forces, and more than half of them went overseas. There they tasted a freedom they did not enjoy at home. "The Europeans in our line of march had no racial hang-ups," a black master sergeant recalled, summarizing an experience that the return home would not erase. Black observers pointed out the patent contradiction between battling fascism and racism abroad while permitting racial discrimination and oppression to continue at home. Besides, they added, the United States' ongoing failures in race relations jeopardized its ability to court the good will of the rest of the world, the large majority of which comprised people of color.

In the spring of 1941, A. Philip Randolph, head of the Brotherhood of Sleeping Car Porters, called for 100,000 demonstrators to march in Washington to protest discrimination against blacks in the defense industries. In June, Roosevelt, eager to forestall the march, issued an executive order that banned racial discrimination in federal agencies and in companies with federal contracts. The order also established a Fair Employment Practices Commission (FEPC) to investigate the state of black defense employment. The FEPC exposed the ubiquity of discriminatory practices, which in turn led to efforts to increase black employment in aircraft companies, shipyards, and other defense installations. Many African Americans insisted on pursuing a "Double V" campaign—victory over both fascism abroad and racism at home. The rising aspirations of African Americans were supported by a growing number of white sympathizers. Eleanor Roosevelt lent the prestige of her position and the authority of her convictions to the African American cause, not least by participating in integrated social functions. The race riots drew the attention of white liberals to the gap between the rhetoric of freedom and the realities of the home front. Nazism, with its celebration of the master race, in effect made racism a dirty idea. And white politicos recognized the impact of the accelerating Great Migration northward. In 1940, the northern black vote had been larger than the majorities by which Roosevelt carried the four largest states, with 135 electoral votes—and northern politicians now felt the need to court it.

The military took steps to reform its racial practices, responding not only to protests from blacks and whites but also to the need to use as many able-bodied Americans as possible. Colonel Benjamin O. Davis, a soldier since the Spanish-American War, was promoted to general, becoming the first African American to hold that rank. The army ordered on-base facilities and certain schools, hospitals, and off-base services to operate without racial restrictions. In 1941, the army air corps established a training base for blacks at Tuskegee Institute in Alabama, and it created the first black air-combat unit. The navy opened its ranks to general black enlistments.

Overseas, commanders initially held that it would hurt morale and efficiency to put blacks into combat, but eventually, if only because whites did not see why blacks should be protected from the risks of war that they faced, black soldiers, sailors, and airmen were sent into fire—always under white command—in both Europe and the Pacific. When in October

African American pilots, members of a fighter squadron trained at Tuskegee Institute, are briefed for a combat mission at a base in Italy.

1944 an African American tank battalion arrived for duty with General George Patton's Third Army, Patton welcomed them heartily, saying they were "the first Negro tankers ever to fight in the American army. . . . I don't care what color you are, so long as you go up there and kill those Kraut sons-abitches." Eventually, black infantry were integrated into the combat army in Europe as platoons, and in 1944 the new secretary of the navy, James Forrestal, approved a program for integrating the crews of twenty-five combat vessels and later the whole auxiliary fleet.

Although early in the war both northern and southern soldiers favored segregation, most who served with blacks changed their minds. The captain of a black-crewed naval vessel noted in a letter to his parents that "there has been lot of bunk said about Negro crews," adding, "We can't see that they are different from others if treated the same. . . . They are anxious to make a name for themselves. They actually work harder." Blacks earned distinction wherever they served.

### NATIVE AMERICANS AND MEXICAN AMERICANS

The war brought tensions and a taste of new possibilities to both the Native American and the Hispanic communities, too. In Florida, the Seminoles declined to cooperate with the military draft, explaining that they were still technically at war with the United States; in the Southwest, the Hopis failed to appear for induction. Other Native Americans, however, saw

Navajo code talkers near the front in the Bougainville jungle, December 1943.

opportunity and even duty in the war. About 75,000 Native Americans left the Indian reservations for work in defense industries, and a number served in the armed forces. Some 400 Navajo constituted the Native American Code Talkers, a unit whose members did critically important duty with the Marine Corps in the Pacific by exploiting their language for secret communications and using it at the frontlines. The Navajo code baffled the Japanese, who were unable to crack it.

Hispanics in the United States were familiar with the kind of discrimination that African Americans endured. In 1940, 90 percent of Mexican Americans lived in Texas, California, Arizona, New Mexico, and Colorado. During the war, by agreement with the American and Mexican governments, tens of thousands more entered the country in response to the labor shortage, the majority as contract agricultural labor under the *bracero* (from the Spanish word for "arm") program, which had originated in World War I. Set apart by language and skin color, Mexican Americans were subjected to segregation (a sign outside a Texas church read "For Colored and Mexicans"), forced to live in filthy shanties, barred from good jobs, and paid less than whites even when they did essentially the same work. Jose Chavez, an Arizona native employed at the Phelps Dodge Company since 1936, noted that he trained Anglo workers who got $6.22 a day, $1.32 more than he did.

Many Mexican Americans left agricultural labor for the defense and garment industries in and around Los Angeles,

which was as crowded and beset by shortages as most wartime cities. Tensions with Anglos ran high. The newspapers talked of a Mexican American "crime wave," and the police cracked down on Hispanic youth clubs, making arrests for what seemed purely racial reasons. Young Mexican American men, seeking security and status, often joined gangs and took to wearing "zoot suits," originally a Harlem ensemble of broad-brimmed hat, long draped jacket, and high-waisted baggy trousers tight at the ankles, accompanied by a lengthy key chain and ducktailed hair. Early in June 1943, sailors from the Chavez Ravine Naval Base, hearing that servicemen had been attacked by zoot-suiters, invaded the barrios of Los Angeles and for four days, together with soldiers on leave, beat teenagers and stripped off their zoot suits. The street brawls spread to Pasadena, Long Beach, and even San Diego, soon turning into what, in the judgment of some historians, was a full-fledged race riot. Order was not restored until mid-June, after Los Angeles was declared off-limits to naval personnel.

Draft boards in the Southwest made extensive use of their lengthy lists of eligible Mexican Americans. Yet Hispanics volunteered for military service in numbers that were disproportionately high compared with their representation in the population. More than a third of a million of them served in the wartime military. Unlike African Americans, most Mexican American draftees were integrated as individuals into the infantry and saw considerable combat, some earning citations for distinguished service. All the while, Mexican American activists in Texas exploited the liberal rhetoric of the war and of the Good Neighbor policy to gain some ground against segregation in schools and other public facilities, improve the chance of getting higher-paying jobs, and win acknowledgment as full-fledged citizens.

## POLITICS AND THE LIMITS OF FREEDOM

*Japanese American Relocation.* The outbreak of the war threw a spotlight of prejudice on the 127,000 people of Japanese ancestry living in the United States. Most lived on the West Coast and about two-thirds were *nisei*—citizens born in the United States to the first generation of Japanese American immigrants. There was no evidence of espionage or sabotage by Americans of Japanese ancestry after Pearl Harbor, but many Americans on the West Coast were on edge enough to be acutely suspicious. Rumors abounded that the Japanese might attack. A California congressman declaimed in the House, "The only good Jap is a dead Jap."

Civic and military leaders on the West Coast, including liberals and moderates, clamored for the evacuation of all Japanese Americans and their internment in inland concentration camps. The primary stated reason was to forestall internal subversion. Army general John DeWitt, who originally opposed evacuation but who would command the operation, came to hold that it was impossible to distinguish between a loyal and a disloyal Japanese American. Following an inexplicable logic, DeWitt declared, "The very fact that no sabotage has taken place to date is a disturbing and confirming indication that such action will be taken." However, the demand for internment was partly energized by the ambitions of other Californians to obtain land, jobs, and businesses held by Japanese Americans.

In the spring of 1942, under the authority of an executive order from President Roosevelt, the U.S. government shipped the Japanese American populations of Washington, Oregon, and California—a total of 112,000 people—to relocation camps, most of them in bleak desert areas, where they were housed in barracks, one family to a room, and forced to lead regimented lives. (No such internment occurred in Hawaii,

Japanese Americans, their children bewildered, on the way to forced internment at a relocation center in 1942.

not least because the large size of the Japanese American community there—more than a third of the population—made it impractical.) Many of the internees lost their crops, farms, and bank accounts as well as insurance coverage and licenses to practice medicine or law. Roughly two-thirds of those interned were American citizens. Nevertheless, by and large the Japanese American community went along with the evacuation program without resistance, with some of its members seemingly considering their exile, as the Japanese-American Citizens League observed, a form of "our duty to our country."

Some Japanese Americans, however, angrily renounced their citizenship. At least a dozen openly resisted the evacuation order, including Fred Korematsu, who was arrested and whose case challenging the constitutionality of the evacuation policy made its way, along with several others, to the Supreme Court. In December 1944, in *Korematsu v. the United States*, the Court upheld the relocation policy by a majority of six to three, ruling that the action taken against Japanese Americans stemmed not from racial prejudice but from the requirements of military security. One of the dissenting justices castigated the removals program, declaring that it was based on an "erroneous assumption of racial guilt." (The government eventually came to agree with that view and in 1988 resolved to provide all Japanese Americans interned during the war with $20,000 in compensation.)

Despite the evacuations, some 33,000 Japanese Americans served in the armed forces, most of them as volunteers (Japanese Americans were ineligible for the draft from Pearl Harbor until January 1944). More than 6,000 served as linguists in the Pacific theater, accompanying troops into battle to interrogate Japanese prisoners and analyze letters, maps, and orders found on them and on the enemy dead. Several Japanese American units, including volunteers from the internment camps, served with distinction in North Africa and Italy, where the bravery and high casualty rate of one of the units won the attention of the press and the sobriquet "the Purple Heart Battalion."

Chinese Americans, Korean Americans, and Filipinos also went into the armed forces. They were eager to fight the Axis Powers, especially Japan, because it had warred against their ancestral nations. Many considered service in the U.S. military an opportunity and a privilege—a way, as one young Filipino immigrant put it, of "serving as an equal with American boys." Fair-employment regulations helped open new job opportunities for Asian Americans. In 1943, Congress repealed the Chinese Exclusion Act, responding to demands from Chinese Americans, whose cause was aided by Madame Jiang Jieshi (Chiang Kai-Shek) during a sojourn in the country.

***The United States and the Holocaust.*** In 1942, American newspapers reported that Nazi death squads were shooting thousands of Jews in occupied territories such as Poland and the Ukraine, and the German refugee novelist Thomas Mann told of the mass atrocities in broadcasts over the British airwaves. Early that year, at a conference in Wannsee, a suburb of Berlin, senior Nazi officials established coordinated plans for a "final solution" of what they called "the Jewish problem" in Europe. In the coming months, the German government established camps at places such as Auschwitz and Bergen-Belsen, where they systematically concentrated Jews by the thousands and murdered them in gas chambers. In 1942, word of German plans to kill Jews wholesale reached the State Department, and national magazine articles reported that the Nazis had embarked on a program to exterminate the Jews of Europe.

In response to the turn of events, a number of Americans began to think less about how to deal with Jews who had escaped from Europe and more about how to rescue from almost certain death those who remained under Hitler's control. As in the 1930s, the rescue movement ran into the obstacle of anti-Semitism. Jews, who constituted about 3 percent of the American population, were still barred from moving into certain neighborhoods, faced quotas at certain colleges and universities, and were unwelcome in many jobs. The rescue movement also was hampered by skepticism that the Nazis were really engaged in a program of mass extermination. To many critics, the enormity of the alleged Nazi crimes seemed akin to the reports of German atrocities that had been a feature of Allied propaganda during World War I.

The evidence and pressure for action nevertheless grew so overwhelming that in January 1944 President Roosevelt created the War Refugee Board, charging it to rescue victims of enemy oppression in imminent danger of death and especially to forestall "Nazi plans to exterminate all the Jews." The board smuggled refugees out of threatened areas such as Hungary, sponsored Red Cross relief packages to the concentration camps, and encouraged the creation of free ports to which refugees might be temporarily admitted. In the end, the board helped save approximately 200,000 Jews and at least 20,000 non-Jews.

The American rescue record was better than that of the other Allied nations, but to many people then and since, it was by no means good enough, especially weighed against the 6 million Jews killed in the Holocaust. Rescue advocates argued for additional measures—for example, bombing the railroads that brought Jews to the camps and their killing machinery. But the military did not want to divert air-force resources to nonmilitary objectives, and even some rescue advocates doubted that such actions would be effective given the speed with which the Germans were able to rebuild their factories and transportation systems. Still, the U.S. government might have done more, and sooner. The War Refugee Board enjoyed limited financial and administrative support within the government, and President Roosevelt dealt with the issue of mass exterminations in fits and starts, throwing neither the prestige nor the power of his office behind the board's work.

***A Shifting Political Agenda.*** Like Lincoln and Wilson before him, Roosevelt was willing to curtail civil rights and overlook atrocities in the interest of achieving military victory. Similar logic produced a rightward shift in the administration's economic policy. In 1943, Roosevelt himself remarked that "Dr. New Deal" had been succeeded by "Dr. Win the War." In order to supercharge industrial production, the government suspended antitrust prosecutions, permitted corporations tax write-offs, and guaranteed them profits by paying fixed fees above the costs they incurred in fulfilling war contracts. The system tended to benefit the largest corporations: 30 percent of defense-contract dollars went to the 10 biggest businesses. In 1940, the top 100 companies accounted for 30 percent of all manufacturing in the United States; in 1943, for 70 percent.

Wartime production and prosperity revived popular admiration for business while it diminished enthusiasm for liberal reform measures. Although working time lost to strikes during the war amounted to less than a tenth of a percent of the total, many people disliked labor unions because some, like John L. Lewis's miners, went out on strike. They also resented the intrusiveness of wartime government regulations, notably the reach of the Office of Price Administration seemingly into every crevice of the consumer economy. In response to managing the demands of the war, the number of federal employees more than tripled, to 3.8 million. In 1942, the military moved into the new Pentagon, then the largest building in the world, which housed some 35,000 personnel. The trends in bureaucratic growth irritated conservatives and even gave some liberals pause. Even once the country's totalitarian enemies were defeated, freedom, some warned, might be jeopardized in the United States by excessive state power that was homegrown, a specter that made an increasing number of Americans wary of further federal initiatives.

In the congressional elections of 1942, the Democrats lost eight seats in the Senate and fifty in the House, dramatically moving the balance of power on Capitol Hill in a conservative direction. Republicans and southern Democrats joined to block liberal attempts to extend the New Deal and to abolish some of its creations, including the Civilian Conservation Corps, the Works Progress Administration, and the National Youth Administration, all of which seemed superfluous in the full-employment economy. Congress also abolished the Rural Electrification Administration and passed the Smith-Connally Act, which was designed to curb the political and economic activities of trade unions partly by making it more difficult to strike and outlawing union contributions to political campaigns. In 1944, Congress rejected just about everything Roosevelt requested, including measures to deal with unemployment during reconversion from war to peace.

However, what Congress was unwilling to do for Americans in general, it showed itself more than willing to do for veterans when, in 1944, it unanimously enacted the Serviceman's Readjustment Act. Dubbed the "G.I. Bill of Rights" by the American Legion, one of its principal sponsors, the act provided both male and female veterans with numerous special benefits, among them low-interest loans to assist in the purchase of homes, businesses, and farms, and economic help in obtaining an education. The G.I. Bill would help defuse the threat of postwar recession and democratize access to home ownership, education, and business opportunity.

*The 1944 Election.* The Republican presidential nominee was Governor Thomas E. Dewey of New York, a forty-two-year-old moderate with internationalist inclinations who had vigorously prosecuted racketeers in New York City and had a reputation for administrative energy and efficiency. The Democrats, sensitive to Roosevelt's popularity and the need for stability in the middle of the war, refrained from disputing his candidacy for an unprecedented fourth term. But they fought heatedly over the choice of a vice-presidential nominee, eventually dumping Henry Wallace, the candidate of the liberal-labor wing of the party, in favor of Senator Harry S. Truman of Missouri, who had a down-the-line New Deal voting record and who, as a border-state politico, was acceptable to southerners.

Roosevelt struck observers as physically frail and lacking the spirit of his earlier White House days, but Dewey's harsh campaign attacks, including the charge that the Democratic

Party was being captured by "the forces of Communism," provoked the president to come out swinging. In a memorable nationwide radio address, he deftly ridiculed his opponents' charges by chiding them for attacking "my little dog Fala," declaring that he would not abide "libelous statements about my dog." Otherwise, the war and the postwar future dominated the election. Roosevelt, seeming once again to don the coat of Dr. New Deal, called for a future based on an economic bill of rights that he had proposed early in the year—a guarantee to Americans of an adequately paying job, decent farm income, sufficient medical care, decent housing, a good education, and "protection from the economic fears of old age, sickness, accident, and unemployment." He also stressed that the United States must not return to isolationism in the postwar period, that it had to remain involved in the world.

On November 7, Roosevelt defeated Dewey handily in the popular vote, 25.6 million to 22 million, and by a decisive margin of 432 to 99 in the electoral college. Democrats lost only one seat in the Senate while gaining twenty in the House. Northern black votes tipped eight states to Roosevelt. Despite the shift rightward, the large majority of Americans were unwilling to give up on the president who had carried them through the Depression and was now leading them in war.

## Fighting the War: The Pacific

Roosevelt took steps quickly after Pearl Harbor to facilitate both overt and covert war. He had formed a Joint Chiefs of Staff comprising representatives of the navy, army, and army air force, and at a meeting in Washington at the turn of 1942, he and Churchill formed a union of the American and the British military leadership. In June, Roosevelt established the Office of Strategic Services (OSS) for the centralized gathering and analysis of intelligence, and for the performance of such "special services"—they might include espionage, sabotage, and other secret operations—as the joint chiefs might direct.

Roosevelt and Churchill had agreed that their nations should give priority to the defeat of Hitler, then see to Japan, but the war in the Pacific compelled early attention. During the first week of January 1942, the Japanese occupied Manila, the Philippine capital. In March, on Roosevelt's orders, General Douglas MacArthur, the commander in the Philippines, left his forces for Australia to prepare a counteroffensive, grandiloquently announcing, "I shall return." In April and May, American and Philippine defense forces on the Bataan Peninsula and

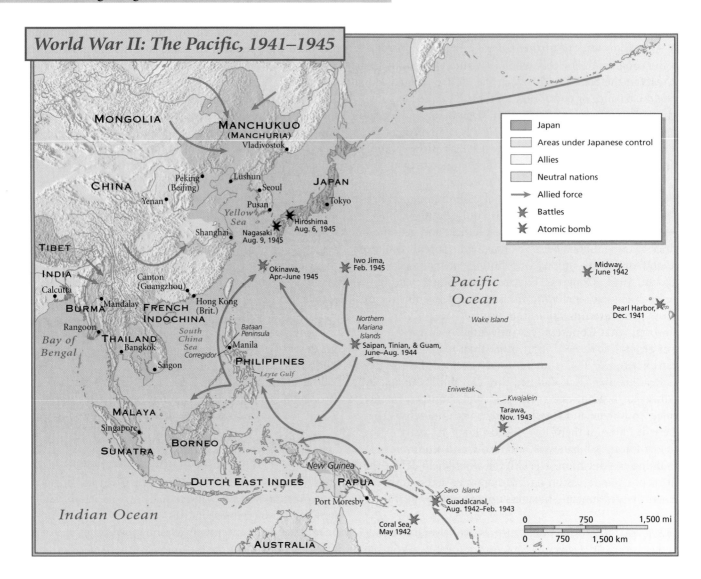

**World War II: The Pacific, 1941–1945**

Corregidor, at the entrance to Manila Bay, surrendered, unable to hold out any longer. The Japanese ordered the Bataan garrison of some 76,000 men, many of them exhausted and starving, to walk under a brutal sun sixty-five miles to a rail junction, where a train would take them to a prisoners' camp. Close to 1,000 Americans and several thousand Filipinos died or were murdered on what became known as the Bataan Death March. Another 6,000 men perished in the camp.

By mid-spring, the Japanese had also taken Wake Island, Guam, Sumatra, Java, Borneo, and the northern half of New Guinea. They had conquered Malaya, Thailand, and Burma, and had closed the Burma Road, the crucial overland route for transporting supplies to the forces of Jiang Jieshi (Chiang Kai-shek) in China. All told, they had overrun roughly 1 million square miles, much of it ocean, and 150 million people. Now they moved to take the rest of New Guinea and threaten Australia, which lay to the south across the Coral Sea.

The U.S. Navy, having broken Japan's naval code, was constantly monitoring its radio traffic in the Pacific. It knew where and approximately when the Japanese forces would strike. On May 7 and 8, 1942, an American naval task force that included two carriers beat back a Japanese force headed toward New Guinea in the Battle of the Coral Sea, thus blocking Japan's drive to the southeast. A few weeks earlier, sixteen

B-25 bombers under the command of Lieutenant Colonel James H. Doolittle had flown from the carrier *Hornet,* which had brought them within 700 miles of the Japanese mainland, to bomb Tokyo. While the action produced little damage and few casualties, it stirred the American public and showed the Japanese that the war would be brought home to them.

The Doolittle raid prompted Japanese naval forces to attempt a decisive blow against the Americans in the Pacific. They set their sights on Midway, the penultimate outpost of the Hawaiian Islands chain, less than 1,200 miles to the northwest of Oahu, hoping in the course of the action to draw out and destroy what remained of the U.S. Pacific Fleet. But the fleet commanders, with their ability to decipher Japanese radio traffic, knew once again where the attack was coming. At the Battle of Midway during the first week of June, a U.S. naval task force, although greatly outnumbered in ships and planes, destroyed almost half the Japanese aircraft and sent four carriers to the bottom.

The Battles of the Coral Sea and Midway ended Japan's naval offensive in the Pacific. Its naval forces would thereafter be placed on the defensive, retreating in the face of Allied assaults to the north and west. The outcomes of both battles depended on many ingredients, including the brilliance of the American commanders, the brave resolve of the carrier pilots, the acuity of the code breakers, and the technical advantage of radar. While the Japanese had no radar, several of the American ships and Midway itself were equipped with sets that the navy had developed and that gave early warning of oncoming Japanese aircraft. The two battles also signaled the arrival of a new era in naval warfare. The Japanese and the American surface ships never caught sight of each other. Apart from submarine attacks, all their offensive operations were carried out over long distances by carrier-based aircraft.

The Japanese nevertheless continued to threaten shipping to Australia and New Zealand from Guadalcanal, a volcanic island of tropical jungle in the Solomon Islands just 1,250 miles to the northeast of Queensland, Australia, and on which, according to intelligence reports, they were building an airfield. Early in August 1942, launching the first American ground offensive in the Pacific, marines landed on the island. They faced Japanese soldiers emerging from the jungle at night in wild, screaming suicide charges but fought to victory by early the following February.

These victories in the Pacific did not come cheaply. During the first half of 1942, the United States sent roughly quadruple the number of men and double the number of ships to the Pacific as it did to Europe. At Guadalcanal, the fighting on the ground was accompanied by several major battles at sea, as each side attempted to destroy the ability of the other to supply and support its troops. In a battle off Savo Island, near the landing beaches, the Japanese sank several ships and damaged another without suffering any losses themselves. Savo Island was a humiliating defeat for the U.S. Navy, perhaps the worst in its history, and it demonstrated that despite the reversal at Midway, the Japanese still possessed formidable naval strength.

### THE NAVY'S ADVANCE

Indeed, in 1942 the Pacific west of the Hawaiian Islands remained what the leading historian of the naval war once called "a Japanese lake." After Pearl Harbor, the Japanese had established an extensive defense perimeter, turning the islands and atolls of the Pacific into fortified barriers extending through much of the 2,000 miles that lay between the Japanese home islands and Hawaii as well as between Japan and Australia. To get at Japan itself, American military planners resolved on a two-pronged offensive, so that the Japanese could not concentrate

General Douglas MacArthur returns to the Philippines, 1944.

775

their forces against either line of action. One, under General MacArthur, would proceed via the large islands of the southwestern Pacific, starting with New Guinea and ultimately regaining the Philippines. The other, under Admiral Chester Nimitz, would approach Japan by taking the small islands and atolls of the central Pacific, many of them palm-treed tongues of sand and coral surrounding a lagoon.

The naval offensive began in November 1943 with the invasion of Tarawa and Makin, small atolls in the Gilbert Islands at the far end of the Japanese defense perimeter. Makin fell easily, but Tarawa was heavily defended by 5,000 Japanese troops, many of them dug into pillboxes and bunkers, some of which were twenty feet deep, built of coral and concrete, coconut logs and steel. These troops had to be forced out by flamethrowers, grenades, and mortars; and when it appeared they were losing, they fought ferociously, mounting a suicidal charge. Tarawa indicated that the brutal fighting the marines had first encountered at Guadalcanal would prove to be the rule in the Pacific. (The full, grim reality of the battle was revealed to the American public in the Oscar-winning Marine Corps documentary *With the Marines at Tarawa,* which unblinkingly—and for the first time in a war film—showed real American dead.)

Nimitz resolved simply to bypass the islands that were more strongly held, leaving them to atrophy by cutting off their lines of reinforcement and supply. His forces thus leapfrogged to the Marshall Islands, taking Eniwetok and Kwajalein, and by early 1944 they had gained control of both the Gilberts and the Marshalls. Wherever the marines landed, construction battalions—commonly called "Seabees," after the first letter in each of the two words—built a string of American military bases extending toward Japan.

Nimitz headed next for the islands of Saipan, Tinian, and Guam in the Marianas, the capture of which would bring Japan within reach of the new B-29 "Superfortresses." By now, 1944, American sea and air power in the Pacific, equipped with rockets and proximity fuses, was reaching formidable levels. On Saipan, the Japanese put up fierce resistance, but the island was secured within a month of the invasion. By mid-August, so were Tinian and Guam.

## MacArthur's Drive

By January 1943, MacArthur's troops had gained control of New Guinea in the area of Papua, at the southeastern end of the 1,500-mile-long island. Now MacArthur proceeded along the northern New Guinea coast, executing a brilliant series of amphibious landings that bypassed areas heavily defended by the Japanese, leaving them, as Nimitz was doing to the north, to wither on the vine. On October 20, 1944, MacArthur waded ashore at Leyte and, while standing in a monsoon rain, announced over a truck-mounted microphone, "This is the voice of freedom, General MacArthur speaking. People of the Philippines, 'I have returned.' "

The Japanese, who had more than a quarter million troops in the Philippines, were unprepared for the landing, but they put up stiff resistance on the ground and initiated the largest naval battle in history in Leyte Gulf. For the first time, some of the Japanese planes were devoted to kamikaze attacks. A tactic of desperation, kamikazes were suicide aircraft, each armed with one 550-pound bomb, their mission to crash and explode on carrier decks. (By the end of the war, they would sink or damage more than 300 U.S. ships and cause 15,000 casualties.) The ground fighting on Leyte, though heavy, ended in victory at the end of the year. MacArthur's forces moved on to the main Philippine island of Luzon and Manila, while Nimitz's proceeded through the Pacific, toward Japan.

By the winter of 1944–45, the war against Japan had turned relentlessly savage. Propaganda on both sides encouraged Americans and Japanese to think of each other as subhuman, akin to insects, reptiles, rats, or apes. A U.S. Army Air Force group under the command of thirty-eight-year-old General Curtis LeMay was bombing Japan from Saipan, Tinian, and Guam, in the Marianas, going after ports, aircraft factories, and other urban industrial targets with B-29 Superfortresses, which had a range of 4,200 miles and could carry ten tons of bombs. LeMay's forces blanket-bombed large urban areas in Japan with incendiaries and jellied gasoline, called "napalm," for the purpose of destroying dispersed industrial targets by igniting the wood-and-paper structures around them. On the night of March 9–10, 1945, a total of 334 B-29s fire-bombed Tokyo, killing at least 84,000 people and destroying some 16 square miles—roughly a quarter—of the city. By July, LeMay's crews had burned out 60 percent of Japan's sixty large cities and towns.

In February, to gain better home bases for bombing runs and a staging platform for the ultimate invasion of Japan, American forces invaded the small island of Iwo Jima, just 775 miles from one of the Japanese main islands, and in April they assaulted the much larger one of Okinawa, almost 80 miles long and just 350 miles from Tokyo. The Japanese fiercely defended both islands, fighting from networks of tunnels and caves, using their bayonets and, at times, their teeth when they ran out of ammunition. By the time victory came on Okinawa in mid-June, the battles for the two islands had cost the American forces their heaviest losses of the war in the Pacific—77,000 casualties, including almost 19,000 dead. But now Japan was handily within reach of American planes.

### FRUSTRATION IN CHINA

After Pearl Harbor, Washington was all the more eager to help China wage war against Japan, especially by supplying military equipment to the armies of Jiang Jieshi. Since the Japanese controlled most of Burma, including access to the Burma Road, the United States mounted an air supply operation, sending cargo-laden C-47 transports into China over the "hump" of the Himalayas.

However, the Nationalist regime, including its army, was weak, corrupt, and inefficient, and Jiang was far more interested in using his troops to check the advance of the Communist forces under Mao Zedong (Mao Tse-tung) than to battle the Japanese. In mid-June 1944, with Nimitz and MacArthur making great strides in the Pacific, the most Roosevelt expected from China was that Jiang's troops might keep a large number of Japanese troops diverted from the rest of the Pacific war. Although he remained eager to avoid the collapse of the Nationalist regime, he expected that it would eventually fall and that Jiang was to blame.

## The War in Europe

### STRATEGIC DIFFERENCES

In the months after Pearl Harbor, a debate quickly emerged between Roosevelt and Churchill over the strategy to pursue against Germany. Churchill, who linked military strategy to his country's geopolitical interests, preferred to focus first on the Mediterranean, where in central North Africa German armies were driving British forces eastward and by June were threatening Egypt. He wanted to ensure Britain's control of the Suez Canal, including its supply lines to India and the Far East, and he was fearful of repeating the slaughter of World War I by mounting a frontal assault against the German armies in France before the Allies could accumulate an overpowering invasion force. He contended that the Allies should take direct action against the Nazis by invading North

Africa—the plan was code-named "Operation Torch"—thus assisting the British in the battle they were waging to repel the Germans in Egypt.

General George C. Marshall, the U.S. Army chief of staff and a resolute public servant whose opinions Roosevelt respected highly, vigorously objected to Churchill's plan. The Germans were inflicting huge casualties on the Russians and had penetrated deep into Soviet territory, recently reaching the outskirts of Moscow and putting Leningrad under siege. Stalin was pressing Roosevelt and Churchill to open a second front against Hitler's forces in northern Europe at the earliest opportunity. Marshall, worried about Stalin's ability to hold out against Hitler, argued that the United States and Britain should build up a powerful military force in England, then invade the Continent in 1942, thus relieving the pressure on the Soviets as early as possible. Roosevelt himself had promised the Soviets that in 1942 a second front would be opened in the West.

Although Roosevelt tended to defer to Marshall's military judgment, he recognized the merits of Churchill's arguments against an early cross-channel invasion. With an eye on the public's morale and the 1942 elections, he also wanted to have American ground troops engage the Germans as soon as possible, in North Africa if necessary, even at the cost of disappointing Stalin. In July, to Marshall's distress, Roosevelt agreed to Churchill's plan for an invasion of North Africa in the autumn. But he also beefed up aid to the Soviets, wanting to ensure that they stayed in the war and would not negotiate a separate peace, as they had done in December 1917.

On November 8, 1942, an Anglo-American force of 100,000 men landed in Morocco and Algeria in an area nominally under the control of France's Vichy government. They gained the shore in flat-bottomed, diesel-powered craft known as "Higgins Boats," after their designer Andrew Higgins of New Orleans, that would prove indispensable in carrying fighting men from troop transports to the invasion beaches throughout the European and Pacific theaters. The commander was the American brigadier general Dwight D. Eisenhower, fifty-two years old and leanly handsome, who had impressed the British with his professional competence, unpretentious directness, sunny disposition, and ability to get the forces of his nation and theirs to cooperate. Local resistance to the invasion was weak and short-lived. On November 11, Eisenhower, with Roosevelt's approval, arranged an armistice with Admiral Jean Darlan, the commander of the Vichy armed forces, who happened to be in Algiers. In the

## World War II: Europe and Africa, 1940–1945

FINLAND

NORWAY

SWEDEN

ESTONIA

LATVIA

LITHUANIA

North
Sea

Baltic Sea

DENMARK

Danzig

EAST
PRUSSIA

Invasion of
Soviet Union,
June 22, 1941

SOVIET
UNION

IRELAND

Hamburg

Berlin

Warsaw

POLAND

GREAT
BRITAIN

Amsterdam

Battle of Britain
(Aug.–Oct., 1940)

London

NETHERLANDS

Dover

Elbe River

Dresden

Kiev

Atlantic
Ocean

Calais

BELGIUM

Prague

to Stalingrad
(Aug. 1942–Jan. 1943)

Cherbourg

Battle of the Bulge
(Dec., 1944)

GERMANY

BOHEMIA
MORAVIA

Malmédy

D day
(June 6, 1944)

Ardennes
Forest

LUX.

NORMANDY

Bastogne

Reims

SLOVAKIA

Paris

Munich

Vienna

HUNGARY

FRANCE

SWITZ.

AUSTRIA

ROMANIA

Belgrade

Bucharest

ITALY

Rimini

YUGOSLAVIA

Pisa

Florence

BULGARIA

Black
Sea

SPAIN

Corsica

Rome

Istanbul

Madrid

PORTUGAL

Salerno

ALBANIA

TURKEY

Sardinia

GREECE

Mediterranean

Sicily

Athens

SPANISH
MOROCCO

Oran

Sea

Casablanca

ALGERIA

MOROCCO

TUNISIA

Tripoli

LIBYA

EGYPT

### Legend

✳ Major battles

→ Allied forces

⇢ Heaviest Allied aerial bombing

→ Axis forces

--- Inside limit of German U-boat operations

Axis nations

Occupied by Axis

Allied nations

Neutral nations

0    200    400 mi

0    200    400 km

*"Remember that warm, soft mud last summer?"*

The resilient irony and iconoclasm of Bill Mauldin's Willy and Joe endeared them to troops and newspaper readers alike.

agreement, Darlan surrendered the French forces in return for being appointed governor general of French North Africa. Darlan was a prominent Nazi collaborator and exponent of the Vichy decrees against Jews, a living contradiction of the principles for which the Allies were fighting. The Darlan deal provoked a storm of protests in both Britain and the United States that ended only when a young French royalist assassinated Darlan on Christmas Eve 1942.

After the surrender of the Vichy French in North Africa, the Nazis had occupied the rest of France and Hitler had rushed troops and supplies to Tunisia, insisting, in what one of his generals later called an order of "unsurpassed madness," that his army fight to the death. Now Eisenhower's forces battled eastward across the sandy, featureless North African desert, driving into Tunisia while the British pressed westward from Tripoli. Caught between the British and American armies, the German forces faced crushing opposi-

tion. The war in North Africa ended on May 12, 1943, with the surrender of some 250,000 Axis troops.

## DELAY ON THE SECOND FRONT

In January 1943, Churchill and Roosevelt met in Casablanca, on the coast of Morocco, to debate the Allies' move into northern Europe. Stalin did not attend, explaining that he was needed at home because the Soviet army was locked in a savage and prolonged battle against the Wehrmacht at Stalingrad, deep in Russian territory on the Volga River. Despite his absence, Stalin's desire for a second front commanded Roosevelt's and Churchill's attention. But Churchill, eager to further secure the Mediterranean region, argued for using the troops already assembled in North Africa for an assault against Sicily that summer. Roosevelt and his military chiefs assented, not least because the United States had deployed such sizable forces in the Pacific—even more than were in North Africa and Britain—that an invasion of northern Europe in 1943 no longer seemed practical. At a press conference, Roosevelt announced that the war would end only with the unconditional surrender of the Axis Powers—a doctrine partly intended to convince Stalin of Western resolve, thus preventing another separate peace in the East.

By the spring of 1943, the Red Armies had broken out of Stalingrad; by the fall, they were on the offensive westward across a thousand-mile line. Stalin renewed his demand for the quick opening of a second front. However, Churchill prevailed upon Roosevelt to follow the capture of Sicily that summer with an invasion of Italy, holding that it would draw German troops down from northern Europe, but Roosevelt extracted an agreement from Churchill that after November the British and Americans would concentrate their troops in England for a cross-channel attack in May 1944.

## INTO ITALY

During the battle for Sicily, members of the Italian regime forced Mussolini's resignation, arrest, and imprisonment, with the formation of a new government under Marshal Pietro Badoglio. Although Badoglio was an enthusiastic fascist, official Rome recognized the deteriorating military situation for what it was and sued for peace with conditions. With Roosevelt's and Churchill's approval, Eisenhower negotiated a surrender that permitted Badoglio and his fascist associates to remain in power and eventually join the Allies as

779

## American Journal

### Bill Mauldin Recounts How GIs Lived on the Front Lines.

*Bill Mauldin, who turned 21 in 1942, was the most popular cartoonist of World War II. His work, which appeared in* Stars and Stripes, *the newspaper that GIs published for themselves, expressed the grubbiness, trials, and pretensions of rank that ordinary American soldiers, exemplified by his unshaved characters Willie and Joe, endured in their daily lives. His cartoons delighted GIs, sometimes infuriated officers, and won a Pulitzer Prize in 1945. In a book of text and gathered cartoons published that year, he recalled that the army was well fed behind the lines, but not always so at the front, especially in rough terrain that complicated the delivery of supplies. Here he describes how a company of infantry fared during the weeks they spent on a mountain in Italy, suffering mud, rain, snow, and freezing weather.*

During that entire period the dogfaces didn't have a hot meal. Sometimes they had little gasoline stoves and were able to heat packets of 'predigested' coffee, but most often they did it with matches—hundreds of matches, which barely took the chill off the brew. Soon the guys ran out of matches.

Because they were on K rations they had coffee only once a day. The dinner ration had synthetic lemonade—a mixture of carbolic acid and ersatz lemon power. Try drinking that in a muddy foxhole in freezing weather. The supper ration had a sort of bouillon soup, which was impossible. It takes a lot of water to make it, and a lot more to drown the salty thirst it causes. Usually there wasn't even enough water for the guys to brush their teeth because there weren't enough mules to haul it up. . . .

Since there is not much a cook can do while his company is in combat, his worth depends upon how many ration cases he can carry and not upon how flaky his corn break turns out. Occasionally a few cooks managed to get hot food up to their boys but this didn't happen very often.

Front-line troops got K and C rations because the bulky B units, which contain fruit juice, flour for pastries, and all the nice things a guy likes to eat, were too much for the mules, which had to carry everything else, including ammunition and water. The main trouble with K and C rations was their monotony. I suppose they had all the necessary calories and vitamins but they didn't fill your stomach and you got awfully tired of them.

It's a tragedy that all the advantages of being in the American army never get to those who need them most – the men at the front. It was the same with the Red Cross and movies and all of the rest of the better things. You just can't have variety shows and movie screens at the front.

Bill Mauldin, *Up Front* (Cleveland and New York: The World Publishing Co., 1945), pp. 168-172

---

co-belligerents. But Italy remained under the control of German forces.

Early in September 1943, the Allied forces landed in Italy, with the Americans striking at the coastal city of Salerno, on the western side of the Italian boot. The Germans promptly rescued Mussolini, reinforced their armies, and put up stiff resistance. During the succeeding months, British and American troops clawed up the Italian peninsula, spilling blood for every mile they gained against the German troops, who were dug into the craggy hills and rocky spurs that descended to the coast on both sides of Italy's mountainous central spine. When the Allied troops arrived in Rome, in June 1944, exu-

berant crowds, ecstatic at being rid of the Germans, bedecked their guns with flowers. But the German forces, although driven back to the north of Florence by August, dug in along a line from Pisa across Italy to Rimini and remained there, unmovable, until the last weeks of the war.

### BOMBING EUROPE

In the fall of 1942, in a major preparatory step for the cross-channel invasion, Britain and the United States initiated a combined round-the-clock bomber offensive against Germany, both to destroy its war production and, for the British,

The firestormed ruins of Hamburg after the Allied bombing in July 1943.

to break the morale of its civilian population. During four nights in July 1943, a British force bombed Hamburg, going after oil refineries, U-boat pens, docks, and dwellings with such relentlessness that the bombing precipitated a firestorm, burning 80 percent of the city's buildings and killing at least 30,000 civilians, including thousands of children.

The U.S. Eighth Air Force, based in Britain, made its mission precision daylight bombing of specific industrial and transportation targets. Bad weather rendered visual targeting virtually impossible much of the time, especially in the fall and winter; but after October 1943, the U.S. B-17 bombers were equipped with radar that peered through clouds and displayed a map of the terrain below on the round screen of an oscilloscope. A small contingent of civilian radar experts, most of them physicists, was established in the headquarters of the Eighth Air Force and became deeply involved in the planning and management of the air war. Despite being equiped with defensive armament and devices to fool enemy radars, the Eighth's B-17s flying into Germany suffered grievous losses, up to 10 percent on each mission. One flight surgeon saw to it that the crews got liquor rations after each mission—to help "relax them slightly from the horrors," he said.

In June 1944, Hitler opened a new era in the bombing of civilians by sending his new V-1 rockets—the V stood for "vengeance"—against London. Launched from Peenemünde, an offshore German island village in the Baltic, where they were designed and developed, the rockets were pilotless, radio-controlled missiles propelled by small engines that sped across the channel at 400 miles an hour; some 2,400 would strike London over several months, killing 6,000 people and wounding 40,000 more. They were a prelude to the V-2s—the first intermediate-range ballistic missiles—more than 1,000 of which were lofted from Peenemünde toward the British beginning September 8. On launch, the V-2s were powered by rockets along a 60-mile-high arc, then they fell toward England, accelerating as they descended to a speed of some 3,000 miles an hour. Many V-1s sent by the Nazis did not reach London because they were shot down by radar-guided fighters and antiaircraft guns firing proximity-fused shells, but the only defense the Allies had against the V-2s was to bomb and, ultimately, capture the launch sites.

Officially, it was U.S. Army Air Force policy in Europe not to engage in terror bombing. However, bombing by radar and even visually was highly inaccurate—B-17 crews dropped almost 90 percent of their bombs more than half a mile from the target—with the result that in practice American planes bombed civilian as well as military areas. Early in 1945, the British urged the American air forces to turn practice into overt policy by joining in the air campaign to break German morale. In February 1945, heeding British arguments, the U.S. air forces began to carpet-bomb cities, setting off a firestorm in Dresden that killed 35,000 people. In the end, the combined bomber offensive killed some 600,000 German civilians, injured 800,000 more, and devastated the manufacture of German fighter aircraft and aviation fuel. However, while it depressed German morale, it neither kept people from doing their jobs nor seriously dented most other war production. And it led influential members of the U.S. military to accept terror bombing as an instrument of warfare, and to consider the German V-1 and V-2 rockets as harbingers of the strategic future.

### THE INVASION OF FRANCE

To Stalin, the bombing offensive was no substitute for the second front in northern Europe. At Tehran, Iran, in November 1943, the fighting having turned in the Soviet Union, he met for the first time with Roosevelt and Churchill and successfully pressed his case for the cross-channel invasion. Roosevelt chose Dwight Eisenhower to command the action. Through the winter and spring of 1944, the Allied preparations for the invasion accelerated, producing a huge buildup of forces in England—thousands of guns, tanks, ships, and aircraft, and 3 million soldiers, sailors, and airmen.

The invasion began early in the gray dawn of June 6, D day, when thousands of ships appeared off the Normandy coast while thousands of planes thundered overhead, bombing the beach defenses ahead of the assault forces. The troops, disgorged from landing craft close to the shore, picked their way under heavy fire through obstacles planted by the Germans, dodging as they ran across the open sand for the shelter of the cliffs and pebbled banks. The first wave of Allied troops held on across the entire sixty-mile front, consolidated their positions on the invasion beaches, and then, followed by more waves of soldiers and guns and tanks and trucks, began the advance inland.

D day: American forces landing on a Normandy beach, June 6, 1944.

In the weeks after the Normandy landing, the Allied forces took northwestern France. Armored divisions under General George Patton, a gruff, aggressive commander brilliantly exploiting his tanks, turned east while to the north Anglo-Canadian divisions headed in the same direction, the two forces forming a great circle intended to entrap the main German army in Normandy. Patton wanted to complete the entrapment from the south at the town of Falaise, but in a decision that still excites controversy, the initiative was given to Montgomery's forces on the north. They were slow to close the circle, with the result that some 300,000 troops escaped through the Falaise gap.

Once through the gap, the Germans rapidly retreated, with the German commander in Paris, Dietrich von Choltitz, giving up the city in defiance of Hitler's order to burn it; and on August 25, troops of the free French marched triumphantly down the Champs-Elysées, followed by the U.S. Fourth Infantry Division. On August 15, an Allied force had landed in the south of France between Toulon and Cannes; it quickly proceeded up the valley of the Rhône and joined with part of the invasion forces in the north, thus establishing a continuous Allied line from Switzerland to the North Sea. In September, the Allies swept across France, but in the late fall the drive east slowed, beset by supply bottlenecks, stiffening German resistance, and the arrival of snowy weather.

The drive across Europe was costly. Soldiers relied for survival on each other and on the medics, one of whom was attached to every platoon. Wounded soldiers were ministered to and quickly transported back to field hospitals, where more than 85 percent of those who underwent emergency operations survived. Combat conditions took a heavy toll on the troops, even those who remained physically whole. During the winter of 1945, trench foot, which could lead to gangrene and amputation of toes or the feet, forced some 45,000 men (the equivalent of three infantry divisions) out of the front lines. The constant risk and reminders of death generated psychological and emotional strain. Combat efficiency fell after some ninety days at the front; after four to six months, almost everyone broke. The G.I.s nevertheless kept at their job, not out of any abstract commitment to war aims, later studies showed, but out of a desire to help each other, get the ordeal over with, and go home.

Eisenhower wanted to get it over with, too, and as quickly as possible with the V-2s descending on London, with the Soviet armies storming into Central Europe, and with who knew what progress the Germans were making toward the development of an atomic bomb. Despite the adversities of the late fall of 1944, he kept the Allied troops moving across a broad front toward Germany.

## BATTLE OF THE BULGE

On the morning of December 16, 1944, taking advantage of bad weather and the consequent absence of Allied air support for their troops, a quarter of a million Germans attacked Eisenhower's forces across a seventy-mile front in the thick forest of the Ardennes in Belgium and Luxembourg. By Christmas Day, the Germans had penetrated the Allied line in a bulge eighty miles long and fifty miles deep. However, despite the deep snow and subfreezing temperatures, small groups of G.I.s and even single soldiers fought back, courageously disrupting the German advance with an effectiveness far out of proportion to their numbers. Their tenacity may have been intensified by the report that on December 17, at Malmédy, Belgium, the Germans had murdered some eighty-six American prisoners of war. When the Germans invited an American force surrounded in Bastogne to surrender, their commander replied simply, "Nuts." Eisenhower, seeing that the German venture out of their defenses made them vulnerable, took the offensive as an opportunity rather than a disaster. The American forces were aided in the Battle of the Bulge by the proximity fuse, which, in its first deployment over land, was used to air-burst shells at a set height over German troops unsuspectingly massed under cover of fog and vulnerable to the hail of shrapnel from on high. In the battle, the goriest in American history, some 20,000 Americans were killed and 40,000 wounded. But by the end of January, it was over, and the Allies were once again pressing eastward, buoyed by the taste of impending victory.

## THE DEFEAT OF GERMANY

In March 1945, the Anglo-American armies in northern Europe crossed the Rhine and headed into Germany while the Russians moved into the Third Reich from the east. At the end of April, American and Russian troops met and celebrated at the Elbe River. In Italy, the Allied forces broke through the German line and headed into the northernmost regions of the country, driving toward the Alpine border with Austria and Switzerland.

As the American armies moved deeper into Germany, they encountered the concentration camps, with their gruesome evidence of the Nazis' barbarity. When in early April the Third Armored Division entered Nordhausen, the site of a slave

The gaunt figures of the living and the piled bodies of the dead shocked American troops when they liberated Nazi concentration camps like this one, at Mauthausen, Austria.

labor camp for the construction of V-2 rockets, its soldiers saw gaunt, skeletal creatures scarcely recognizable as human beings limping toward them. They came to what at first appeared to be piles of garbage and realized, when they saw part of a pile moving, that it contained enfeebled people. Eisenhower had been suspicious of the reports of such Nazi atrocities, but now he saw that they were not just propaganda. He promptly called on the Allied governments to send newsmen, photographers, and legislators to visit the camps and record firsthand what the Nazis had done. Following a visit to the concentration camp at Buchenwald, Edward R. Murrow broadcast what he had observed: "I pray you to believe what I have said about Buchenwald. . . . For most of it I have no words."

Hitler retreated into his bunker in Berlin and on April 30 killed himself. Two days later, the city was in Soviet hands. Shortly before three A.M. on May 7, 1945, the head of the German navy surrendered the Third Reich to Eisenhower at his headquarters in Reims, France.

## Clouded Victory

On April 12, 1945, less than a month before the defeat of Germany, the news flashed across the world from Warm Springs, Georgia: that afternoon, Franklin Roosevelt, thin and exhausted, had died of a cerebral hemorrhage. The next day, as his body was borne in a casket to the presidential train waiting to carry it north for burial at Hyde Park, New York, a black army musician stepped out from behind a portico and, tears streaming down his face, played the familiar Dvořák melody "Going Home." Millions of Americans shared his grief, producing a display of mourning not seen since the death of Lincoln. Roosevelt had filled their lives through depression and war for more than a dozen years, allaying their fears and giving them hope. Now he was gone, and the cheering that several weeks later greeted the victory in Europe was tempered by sorrow and uncertainty.

The new occupant of the Oval Office, Harry S. Truman, had to learn quickly how to deal with the Allies, manage the terrible atomic weapon that physicists were developing, and bring the war with Japan to a close. No wonder that the day after Roosevelt's death Truman remarked to reporters that he felt as though "the moon, the stars, and all the planets had fallen on me."

## ROOSEVELT'S POSTWAR ARRANGEMENTS

Truman had not been part of Roosevelt's inner circle and knew little about his wartime negotiations, agreements, projects, and plans. From 1943 onward, postwar arrangements had increasingly concerned the Big Three among the Allies—the United States, Britain, and the Soviet Union—both in their home governments and in their joint meetings. Roosevelt brought to these encounters an eagerness to establish in the peace a structure of international relations capable of preventing war, facilitating trade and economic stability, and maintaining national self-determination. While Churchill shared some of these goals, he also wanted to safeguard the British empire, including the routes to it through the eastern Mediterranean. Stalin, bent on protecting the Soviet Union from future Western attack, was determined to establish buffer zones of influence in Eastern Europe and to enfeeble Germany so that it could never wage war again. Some of these aims conflicted with Roosevelt's, but the president was, as he said after one of the wartime conferences, "a realist." To the end of sustaining the alliance and pursuing his postwar goals, he accommodated to what he could not alter, seeking to finesse the more difficult contradictions for the time being and work out differences through personal relationships with his Allied counterparts.

The Big Three first met together at a conference in Tehran in November 1943. Roosevelt, who appreciated Soviet eagerness for a buffer against Germany, told Stalin that he would

not oppose pro-Soviet governments in the Baltic countries, though he asked for a public commitment to elections, pointing out that American voters descended from Eastern European nationals wanted self-determination for their ancestral homelands. Stalin, on his part, promised that soon after the defeat of Germany he would join the war against Japan. Roosevelt also obtained Stalin's agreement to the establishment of a world-wide organization—what would become the United Nations—that would keep the peace in the postwar era. On his return to the United States, Roosevelt declared, "We are going to get along with him [Stalin] and the Russian people—very well indeed."

At a meeting in Moscow two months earlier, the Allied foreign ministers had committed their nations on paper to continued cooperation in the interest of postwar peace and security. In 1944, at a conference in Bretton Woods, New Hampshire, the Western powers established an International Monetary Fund, which was intended to stabilize the international value of national currencies. They also created the International Bank for Reconstruction and Development (later called the World Bank), which would lend money to countries devastated by the war and foster the revival of world trade.

The Big Three leaders convened for the last time in February 1945, at Yalta, in the Crimea, two months before Roosevelt's death. By then, the Red Armies occupied most of Eastern Europe and were establishing Communist regimes in the region. The month before, Stalin had recognized a Soviet puppet group as the sole government of Poland. Roosevelt and Churchill vigorously protested Stalin's action, insisting that the Polish government be broadly based and the product of free elections. Stalin agreed to diversify the Polish government and, possibly because he thought the Communists might win, to hold general elections as soon as possible.

The disposition of Germany after its defeat had been a key issue for the Big Three since Teheran. Stalin wanted to break it up permanently, but Churchill, suspicious of the Soviet Union, wanted Germany to be capable of maintaining a balance of power on the Continent. At Yalta, Stalin consented to its temporary division into four zones of occupation, including one for France. To gain Soviet help in the Pacific war, Roosevelt and Churchill promised Stalin concessions in Manchuria and the restoration to Russia of the territories it had lost in its war with Japan in 1904. In return, Stalin reiterated his pledge to declare war on Japan within two to three months of Germany's surrender—a crucial commitment in the minds of Roosevelt and Churchill, since, by invading

Churchill (left), Roosevelt (center), and Stalin at Yalta, February 1945.

Japanese-occupied Manchuria, Stalin's forces would pin down 1 million Japanese troops.

Conservative critics have long charged that Roosevelt and Churchill caved in to Stalin at Yalta, betraying Eastern Europe in a fruitless effort to appease the Soviet dictator. More recently, revisionist scholars have reversed this scenario, arguing that Stalin made most of the concessions and that the Anglo-Americans were mainly interested in keeping Eastern Europe and Asia safe for Western capitalism. However, the Red Army's presence in Eastern Europe left Roosevelt and Churchill little room for maneuver. They could only hope that Stalin would live up to his promise, made at Yalta, to consult on ways to help the peoples of Europe freely elect democratic governments. Consultation was, of course, far short of commitment. Still, contrary to the revisionists, while the Roosevelt administration strongly objected to left-wing totalitarian regimes in Eastern Europe, it was willing to accept social reformist governments friendly to the Soviet Union.

In all, Roosevelt thought, overconfidently, that he could handle Stalin with a combination of charm, personal cajolery, and economic measures. He doubted that Stalin would be ter-

ritorially aggressive and considered him more concerned with Soviet national interests than with the spread of Communism. However, soon after Yalta, Stalin violated his pledges to support political freedom in Romania and Poland. His behavior prompted Roosevelt to remark three weeks before his death, "We can't do business with Stalin. He has broken every one of the promises he made at Yalta." Still, Roosevelt declined to break with Stalin or even to push him hard, not least because he believed that the Allies needed the Soviets to conclude the war with Japan.

## THE ATOMIC BOMB

In the late spring of 1945, the Joint Chiefs of Staff completed plans for the invasion of the Japanese home islands, to begin the following autumn. They were convinced by the tenacity of Japanese resistance that the costs of an assault on Kyushu, the southernmost home island, which was to be invaded first, would be huge—at least 268,000 casualties if the planned invasion force suffered losses at the same rate as did the troops on Okinawa. Sizable additional losses would be incurred during the follow-up invasion of the main island of Honshu. Truman said he "hoped there was a possibility of preventing an Okinawa from one end of Japan to the other."

The key possibility was the atomic bomb, which Truman now knew about and which by the spring of 1945 seemed likely soon to become available. The bomb was the result of the effort, which had grown gigantic, that had originated with the discovery in December 1938 of nuclear fission—the splitting of the uranium atom, with the release of nuclear energy, upon its bombardment with neutrons. If many fissions occurred rapidly, the accumulated energy would create a powerful explosion. But scientists were at first unsure whether what was feasible in principle could be achieved in practice. Natural uranium occurs in two forms—U-235 and U-238—that are mixed together. Ways had to be found to separate the U-235, which fissions, from the far more abundant U-238, which does not.

In 1941, a young physical chemist at the University of California at Berkeley named Glenn T. Seaborg discovered that after bombardment with neutrons, U-238 eventually transforms itself into a new element. Seaborg christened it "plutonium." Plutonium was found to fission, just like U-235. Thus, if the abundant but nonfissioning U-238 could be fashioned into a controlled, chain-reacting pile, it could be transformed into enough fissionable plutonium to make an atomic explosive. In December 1941, encouraged by the progress to date, Vannevar

The fire-bombing of Tokyo on March 9-10, 1945, devastated one-quarter of the city.

lished on a mesa at Los Alamos, New Mexico, in March 1943 under the leadership of J. Robert Oppenheimer, a thirty-nine-year-old theoretical physicist. Soon hundreds of physicists, including some who had fled Hitler's Europe, were living and working at the isolated mesa, figuring out how to make workable atomic bombs from uranium and plutonium.

In early July 1945, the laboratory assembled a uranium bomb, code-named "Little Boy," for shipment to the 509th Composite Air Group, a specially trained B-29 unit in the South Pacific. Unsure of the plutonium weapon, they tested it—the exercise was code-named "Trinity"—just before dawn on July 16 in the desert near Alamogordo, New Mexico. A spot of light burst through the darkness, then boiled upward, exploding into a rainbow of fire that colored the desert wastes and lit up the mountain ranges in the distance. Moments later, the shock wave blasted through with the roar of 20,000 tons of TNT. After the first exhilarating cheers of success, there was an awesome silence. A line from the Hindu poem the *Bhagavad Gita* flashed through Oppenheimer's mind: "I am become Death, The shatterer of worlds."

Bush obtained a green light from President Roosevelt for a full-scale effort to build a bomb. Recognition that such a weapon was likely achieveable heightened the original fears that Germany might build an atomic weapon and in consequence added urgency to the project. During 1942, scientists working under the physicist Enrico Fermi designed and constructed an atomic pile in a doubles squash court under the stands of Stagg Field, the University of Chicago's unused football stadium, and, on December 2, achieved a controlled chain reaction, human civilization's first self-sustaining release of nuclear energy.

Recognizing that building an atomic bomb would require a huge industrial effort, Vannevar Bush helped arrange for the work to be assigned to a new Manhattan District of the Army Engineers. Commanded by General Leslie R. Groves, the Manhattan Project constructed a giant facility for producing uranium enriched in U-235 at Oak Ridge, Tennessee, and a nuclear reactor and processing works for the production of plutonium on the Columbia River at Hanford, Washington.

The apex of the Manhattan Project—a special laboratory for the design and development of nuclear weapons—was estab-

### THE END OF THE WAR

The news of the successful Trinity test reached Truman at Potsdam, a suburb of Berlin, where he was attending a meeting of the Big Three. In the preceding weeks, the Japanese had sent peace feelers to the Soviets, asking for mediation but with the caveat that unconditional surrender was unacceptable. The American government was aware of the Japanese approach from intercepted cables. James F. Byrnes, now Truman's close adviser and his designated secretary of state, warned that agreeing to this concession might be taken as a sign of weakness and lead to demands for others. The United States concluded that it should seek to end the war by warning the Japanese of the grave consequences of continuing it. On July 25, an order from Secretary of War Henry Stimson and General Marshall authorized the atomic bombing of Japan as soon after August 3 as

The physicist Robert Oppenheimer and General Leslie Groves view the remnants of the steel tower mount for the bomb that had been vaporized in the Trinity test at Alamogordo, New Mexico.

weather conditions permitted a visual attack. The next day, Truman and Clement Attlee, whom elections in Britain had just made prime minister in Churchill's place, issued a joint declaration warning Japan to surrender or suffer "prompt and utter destruction." Two days later, Japan rejected the Potsdam Declaration as "unworthy of reply." Truman, convinced by the rejection that delaying the use of the atomic bomb would be pointless, allowed the planned attack against Japan to proceed.

At 2:45 A.M. on August 6, 1945, three B-29s belonging to the 509th Composite Air Group rose from Tinian in the Marianas and headed for Japan, 1,500 miles to the north. In the belly of the lead plane, the *Enola Gay,* was Little Boy, the uranium bomb. The bombardier released Little Boy over Hiroshima, a large industrial city that was largely undamaged and included major military installations; and at 8:15 A.M., Japanese time, a great fireball incinerated the city, turning it into a wasteland of rubble covered with a huge column of smoke that rapidly swirled to 30,000 feet. Close to 80,000 people were killed in the attack, and tens of thousands more would die from burns and radiation poisoning.

The Japanese government, under the thumb of the military, nevertheless refused to surrender. Two days later, three months after the German capitulation, the Soviets declared war on Japan and invaded Manchuria. The next day, August 9, another B-29 dropped an implosive plutonium bomb, code-named "Fat Man," on Nagasaki, a major seaport, killing some 40,000 people. Still, it took the personal intervention of the emperor to counter the military's resistance to ending the war. On August 14, Japan agreed to surrender if the emperor was allowed to remain on his throne, a condition the Allies accepted on the understanding that he would be subordinated to the American commander of the occupation forces. On September 2, 1945, on the deck of the battleship *Missouri* in Tokyo Bay, Japanese officials and General Douglas MacArthur concluded the instruments of surrender.

## THE DECISION TO USE THE BOMB

At the time, editorial opinion and the polled American public overwhelmingly backed the atomic bombings of Japan because they brought the war to a speedy conclusion, but considerable debate has occurred since then over whether the instant destruction of two cities was truly necessary to end the conflict without an invasion. Dissenters from the bombings argue that surrender might have been achieved if the United States had told the Japanese before Hiroshima that they could keep their emperor, the condition the American government eventually accepted, or if it had demonstrated the bomb to the Japanese in an uninhabited area. The dissenters stress that in any case Japan, virtually defenseless before air attack and under effective blockade, was in fact already defeated and would have been forced to surrender by mid-autumn.

According to the dissenters, such alternatives were not given serious consideration for at least two reasons. Anti-Japanese racism and vengefulness pervaded the wartime United States. And Truman, Stimson, and Byrnes expected that ending the Pacific war quickly with the bomb would diminish Soviet claims at the peace table and signal that they had better keep their agreements and not act aggressively in the postwar era.

But, to turn to the other side of the debate, a high-level scientific panel, including Oppenheimer, advised Stimson that no technical demonstration would likely end the war and that it was too risky to try, not least because the bomb might be a dud. Indeed, some of Stimson's scientific advisers believed that the bomb would shock the Japanese into surrendering

The rising mushroom cloud from the atomic bombing of Nagasaki, August 9, 1945.

and frighten both the Soviets and the Americans into recognizing the need for international control of nuclear energy after the war. Whatever the ferocity of racist attitudes toward the Japanese, the United States would have dropped the atomic bomb on Germany had the weapon been ready soon enough. Even if the Japanese had been guaranteed their emperor, they might have asked for further concessions instead of surrendering. And while the Allies waited for surrender, thousands more lives would have been lost and the Soviets would have advanced further into Manchuria.

The news that the United States had a workable bomb certainly added steel to Truman's spine. At Potsdam after the Trinity test, he appeared to Churchill as "a changed man," telling "the Russians just where they got on and off." Truman merely went through the motions of informing Stalin about the bomb, casually mentioning to him at the end of a conference session that the United States had a new weapon. Stalin, who knew about the Manhattan Project from Soviet intelligence, replied merely that he hoped it would be used to good

effect against the Japanese. (Back in his headquarters afterward, he remarked that the Soviet A-bomb effort would have to be speeded up.)

Truman's expectation that the atomic bomb would make the Soviets more manageable may well have distracted him from pursuing alternative ways to end the conflict. Still, the alternative that loomed largest in his mind was an invasion, and no president able to order an atomic attack could have justified that action, with its cost of at least tens of thousands and possibly hundreds of thousands of American casualties. All things considered, the Hiroshima bomb was most likely dropped primarily to end the war promptly. So, probably, was the Nagasaki bomb, though with much less justification.

By now, the United States had been involved in the war more than twice as long—forty-five months—as it had in World War I. Fighting on a global scale, it had successfully raised an armed force of unprecedented size, around 15 million men and women, some seven times as many Americans as had served under Woodrow Wilson. The country had equipped them handsomely, mobilizing the economy and science, and had expanded the meaning of freedom and equality at home. It had joined in creating and sustaining a Grand Alliance that had achieved victory in Europe and the Pacific. But it had also created the most powerful weapon in history; and now that the weapon's destructiveness had been demonstrated, many American policymakers expected even more that it could be used to manage Stalin as the victors turned to the uncertainties of the postwar world.

## Suggested Reading

Nat Brandt, *Harlem at War: The Black Experience in WWII* (1996)

Alan Brinkley, *The End of Reform: New Deal Liberalism in Recession and War* (1995)

Robert Buderi, *The Invention That Changed the World: How a Small Group of Radar Pioneers Won the Second World War and Launched a Technological Revolution* (1996)

David M. Kennedy, *Freedom from Fear: The American People in Depression and War, 1929 – 1945* (1999)

Richard Rhodes, *The Making of the Atomic Bomb* (1986)

Harold Vatter, *The U.S. Economy in World War II* (1985)

Samuel J. Walker, *Prompt and Utter Destruction: Truman and the Use of Atomic Bombs Against Japan* (1997)

# Chapter Review

## Summary QUESTIONS

- What did the government do to mobilize the economy for the war?
- What advantages did science and technology provide America's military forces?
- How did the war affect women and members of racial and ethnic minority groups?
- How did the war shape the direction of American politics?
- What postwar goals did Roosevelt seek to achieve through his wartime diplomacy?

## Key Terms

War mobilization (p. 761)

Japanese-American internments (pp. 770–771)

The Holocaust (p. 772)

Second Front (p. 779)

Normandy invasion (p. 782)

Atomic bomb (p. 785)

## Chronology

| | |
|---|---|
| **June 1941** | Office of Scientific Research and Development established. |
| | Fair Employment Practices Commission created. |
| **1942** | Twenty-six-nation "Grand Alliance" formed. |
| **June 1942** | Battle of Midway. |
| **November 8, 1942** | English and American troops invade North Africa. |
| **1943** | Penicillin found to be an effective antibiotic. |
| **March 1943** | Bomb laboratory of the Manhattan Project established at Los Alamos, New Mexico. |
| **September 1943** | Allied forces land in Italy. |
| **1944** | The G.I. Bill of Rights. |
| | Western powers establish International Monetary Fund and World Bank at Bretton Woods, New Hampshire |
| **June 6, 1944** | Allied troops land at Normandy (D-Day) |
| **June/ September 1944** | Germans launch V-1/V-2 rockets toward England. |
| **December 1944** | Battle of the Bulge. |
| **February 1945** | Roosevelt, Churchill, and Stalin meet at Yalta. |
| **April 1945** | United Nations founded. |
| **May 7, 1945** | Germany surrenders. |
| **August 6/9, 1945** | Atomic bombs dropped on Hiroshima and Nagasaki, Japan. |
| **September 2, 1945** | Japan surrenders. |

**Access the *Inventing America* StudySpace at wwnorton.com/studyspace**

PERSONAL PLAN ■ REVIEW MATERIALS ■ RESEARCH AIDS ■ MULTIMEDIA

# A TROUBLED PEACE:

## 1945–1953

American auto companies like Chrysler advertised their products as symbols of familial prosperity in the postwar era.

QUESTIONS

■ **What were the major domestic challenges the Truman administration faced after the war?**

■ **What steps did the Truman administration take to contain the Soviet Union?**

■ **What were the important trends in postwar American society?**

■ **Why did fears of domestic subversion develop during the Cold War?**

■ **Why did the United States intervene in Korea?**

At the end of World War II, American power was unmatched anywhere else in the world. About 400,000 Americans had died in the conflict—291,000 in combat, the rest from accidents and disease—leaving shards of pain in every home displaying a gold star in the window, but losses in Europe had run much higher, reaching 20 million in the Soviet Union alone. The continental United States, unlike much of Europe and Britain, was physically undamaged, its industry and agriculture robust, its economy accounting for about half the world's gross annual product. The factories rapidly retooled for civilian production. With people now liberated from gas rationing and the thirty-five-mile-per-hour speed limit, General Motors boasted that it would convert "from tanks to Cadillacs in two months." Radar was heralded as a breakthrough means of guidance, navigation, and storm monitoring for air traffic and shipping, and its microwave technologies were said to enable a new era in voice and televised communications. And nuclear reactors were predicted to transform the country's economy of electrical power generation.

Improvements in health, safety, and convenience were in the offing, many of them spinoffs of war research. Antibiotics like penicillin promised to cure infectious disease, while DDT—no matter the reservations about its safety—was touted as a powerful tool against insect pests and the havoc they wreaked in human health, agriculture, and home gardens. Commercial companies appropriated surplus military technology for the dispersal of insecticides, including aerosol bombs, truck-mounted sprayers, crop-dusting aircraft, and fog generators. By 1950, at least 600 cities in 45 states were blanketing the streets with pesticide fogs. In 1949, *House Beautiful* declared, "the magic of dry DDT fog can wipe out flies and mosquitoes from the whole community for an entire year for only $2 to $5 a person" and was "harmless to you, your garden, and your house."

But the bright dawn of peace was suffused with trepidations and uncertainties. The nation's traditional pleasure in new technologies was offset by apprehensions about the destructiveness of some of them, especially nuclear weapons. Many Americans feared that the aftermath of World War II at home might resemble that of World War I, when the country slid into recession. By V-J ("victory over Japan") Day in August 1945, the armed services comprised 12 million Americans, including roughly two-thirds of all American men between ages eighteen and thirty-four. By mid-1947, more than 10 million of them had been mustered out, posing reentry problems of unprecedented magnitude for the veterans and their society. *The Best Years of Our Lives,* a film written by the playwright and former Roosevelt speechwriter Robert Sherwood, won multiple Academy Awards for its sensitive portrayal of the economic and emotional difficulties that many servicemen faced on their return home: finding a job; dissolving hasty wartime marriages (the divorce rate in 1945 zoomed to twice the prewar level); restoring family relationships after several years of separation; and for those who did not come back physically intact, coping with their disabilities and rebuilding a sense of self-worth.

Analysts questioned whether the economy could absorb the rapid return to civilian life of so many people. Their apprehensions were compounded by sharp cutbacks in defense spending—from slightly more than $93 billion in 1945 to about $55 billion in 1946—virtually all of it in defense. After V-J Day, the number of unemployed people doubled, jumping from half a million to a million. Americans wanted to revive the good times that had come with the mobilization for war, but they were divided over the role government should play in accomplishing that goal and, even more deeply, over whether the New Deal ought to be continued or curtailed.

## Conservatism, Prices, and Strikes

A serviceman returns home to his welcoming family after the war, 1945.

They were less divided over what their country's role should be in the postwar world. A broad constituency for internationalism had emerged in the United States, a development indicated by the huge success in 1943 of Wendell Willkie's book *One World*, which called for an end to military alliances and the creation of a postwar international organization that would ensure the peace while spreading democracy and democratic capitalism across the planet. In April 1954, in a sharp break with its historic isolationism, the United States joined forty-nine other countries in formally creating the United Nations. Its structure negotiated during the war, the U.N. included a General Assembly representing each member nation and a Security Council with five permanent members—the United States, Britain, the Soviet Union, France, and China (each of which could protect its vital interest by vetoing any action the council might recommend).

Most American policymakers believed that the United States could never again permit itself to fall into military weakness. They found a cause of World War II in the appease-

ment of Hitler at Munich—allowing him to take the Sudetenland in exchange merely for his word that he would seek no further territory; and they interpreted the outcome to mean that aggression had to be met with resistance, force with force. They held that the first line of America's defense lay far from its shores, that it was in the interest of national security to be involved in the world and shape it. Still, it was one thing to envision a strong national defense undergirding a postwar peace, quite another to bring about and maintain a stable international order in a world of political passions, conflicting national interests, and high-technology weapons.

In all, the post–World War II world posed a range of difficult challenges, a need for innovations in policies and actions to deal with a decidedly troubled peace. The nation had to reconvert the economy to a peacetime footing, sustain the prosperity the war had brought, and expand opportunities for all Americans that the fight for freedom implied. In foreign affairs, there was the need, in the face of the United States' chilling relations with the Soviet Union, to maintain the country's commitment to internationalism, prevent another conflagration, and establish a stable world order in which democracy and capitalism could flourish.

### THE NEW PRESIDENT

Under these combustible circumstances, Americans who knew something about Harry Truman (and not many did) doubted that he was up to the job of the presidency, let alone capable of filling Franklin Roosevelt's chair in the Oval Office. Truman had grown up in western Missouri helping to work his grandfather's farm and had seen combat as an artillery officer during World War I. After the war, he had failed at selling men's clothing but succeeded at politics as a protégé of the unsavory Kansas City machine, to which he owed his election to the Senate in 1934 and his squeak-through reelection in 1940. Truman loyally voted down the line with Roosevelt and the New Deal.

On becoming president, Truman disheartened observers by bringing political cronies into the White House, but he was doggedly honest, had read a lot of history, and had a straight-arrow concern for the public interest. He was scrappy, outspoken, and often courageous. He had contested the Ku Klux Klan in Missouri and declared during his reelection campaign that he believed in "not merely the brotherhood of white men, but the brotherhood of all men before the law." Remembering the profiteering during World War I, he volun-

President Truman holds his first press conference on April 17, 1945, a few days after succeeding FDR in the White House Oval Office.

teered to help prevent it this time, calling for the creation of a Senate investigative committee and chairing its probes with tenacity and evenhandedness.

Truman abhorred totalitarianism and was suspicious of the Soviets for their repression of freedom and dissent. When he entered the White House, he had limited experience in foreign affairs. Still, Truman was unafraid of responsibility—a sign on his presidential desk read, "The buck stops here"—and though he vacillated at times, he had the capacity for decisiveness. His tendency to cronyism was tempered by a regard for high-minded public servants like George Marshall and for politically minded ones like James F. Byrnes, both of whom he turned to as he worked to master Roosevelt's legacy and deal with the tempestuous issues of the peace.

## CONSERVATISM, PRICES, AND STRIKES

Eager to build on Roosevelt's achievements, in September 1945 Truman sent Congress a twenty-one-point package of New Deal–like legislation that included a call for national health insurance. Most of these initiatives languished in Congress, where the trend to conservatism continued. In lieu of national health insurance, which the American Medical Association (AMA) vigorously opposed, Congress passed the Hill-Burton Act, which provided federal funds for the construction of public and voluntary hospitals. The Full Employment Act of 1946, gutted by conservatives before its passage, gave the government the responsibility of achieving only "maximum" rather than "full" employment. To that end, it authorized tax cuts to stimulate investment, the promotion of government-business cooperation, and the creation of a Council of Economic Advisers.

A high postwar demand for goods brought about shortages and pressure for price increases in essentials such as cars, food, and housing. Congress ended price controls in mid-1946. The cost of consumer goods skyrocketed some 25 percent within two weeks, with the price of coffee jumping more than 50 percent and the price of meat climbing out of sight. Congress responded by reviving a mild version of price controls; but faced with the ire of farmers and meat producers, Truman lifted even those limp restraints shortly before the 1946 congressional elections. The rampant inflation made people angry, especially blue-collar workers, who were already reeling from the loss of wartime bonuses and overtime pay. Reports of high corporate profits and lavish executive salaries also provoked resentment.

Organized labor, which now accounted for more than a third of nonagricultural employment, flexed its considerable muscles, demanding a greater share of corporate profits even before the inflation became rampant. In November 1945, the United Auto Workers struck General Motors in Detroit, which was awash in record earnings. The UAW's leader was Walter Reuther, a hard-nosed idealist who believed that unions should use their power to advance more than their bread-and-butter interests. One UAW official declared that the strike opened an "era in which labor might break away from the bonds of business unionism, to wage an economic struggle planned to advance the welfare of the community as a whole." Besides demanding a 30 percent wage increase, the UAW insisted that G.M. open its books to public scrutiny and bring labor into its decisions so as to maximize production. The strike lasted 113 days and cost the company $90 million. G.M. boosted wages, but it refused to open its books or yield any of its managerial prerogatives. The settlement added up to a defeat for Reuther's larger vision—and signaled that social vision had a diminished place in union-management negotiations.

By mid-1946, more than 2 million workers—more than one out of every fourteen members of the labor force—had struck in a number of major industries, including steel, oil refining, and meatpacking. On April 1, John L. Lewis, relentless in his advocacy of coal miners' interests, threatened the vitals

Striking United Auto workers picket a General Motors plant, 1945.

of American society by calling 400,000 mine workers off their jobs. After forty days, President Truman ordered the army to seize the mines, but he also gave in to most of Lewis's demands, which he had earlier attacked as inflationary. A week later, the miners went back to work. In the spring of 1946, a railway workers strike completely shut down the nation's train system, which, in this era before superhighway travel and trucking, drastically reduced the movement of people and goods. Addressing Congress, Truman asked for government power to seize essential industries shut down by strikes, to draft strikers, and to put recalcitrant union leaders in jail. Interrupting his speech, he told the Congress that he had just been given news that the unions had just settled on terms he had proposed. The applause was thunderous, but it was deeply disturbing to many across the political spectrum that the president had recommended such means to halt the strike.

### POLITICAL EARTHQUAKE: 1946

By the fall of 1946, Truman had alienated labor, irritated millions by his waffling on prices, and made himself vulnerable to the worst form of attack an American politician can suffer—ridicule. "To err is Truman," people gibed. In the 1946 elections, the Republican Party won sweeping control of both houses of Congress for the first time since the election of Herbert Hoover in 1928.

The new, Eightieth Congress, controlled by a conservative-dominated Republican majority allied with southern Democrats, aimed not only to block extension of the New Deal but

to roll back as many of its advances as possible. During its first session, in 1947, Congress buried virtually every liberal initiative that came before it, enacted an income tax formula that reduced taxes on high incomes, and sought to curb the power of organized labor with the Taft-Hartley Act. The act's key provisions authorized the president to call for an eighty-day cooling-off period in nationally disruptive strikes, banned shops closed to nonunion members, and empowered the states to prohibit union shops by passing so-called right-to-work laws. The law provoked union outrage and a presidential veto that Congress promptly overrode. The actions of the Eightieth Congress seemed to place the future of the Roosevelt revolution in doubt.

## The Emergence of the Cold War

In foreign affairs, the immediate postwar years were marked by the beginnings of the Cold War, a costly, often tense face-off that would last more than a half century. When Truman entered the White House, relations between the Western Allies and the Soviet Union were already turning frosty. Stalin showed signs no signs of relinquishing control of Eastern Europe. In March 1946, Winston Churchill declared in an address at Westminster College of Fulton, Missouri, that "an iron curtain" had descended across that region.

Truman, privately declaring himself "tired of babying the Soviets," increasingly resisted their aggressive moves. Stalin, his eye on Iranian oil resources, kept Soviet troops in Iran after they were supposed to pull out in keeping with wartime agreements. They withdrew in May 1946 after the United States protested to the United Nations and made ready to confront the Soviets directly. In August, Stalin insisted to the Turkish government that the Soviet Union share equally in control of the Dardanelles, the straits providing an opening to the Mediterranean for ships from the Black Sea. The Soviets backed down after the United States, urging the Turks to refuse, showed support for Turkey by sending an aircraft carrier through the straits.

### DIVISION OVER THE ATOM

After Hiroshima and Nagasaki, Stalin had authorized a secret crash program to build a Soviet nuclear weapon, but amid the heightening tensions, Americans took comfort in the knowl-

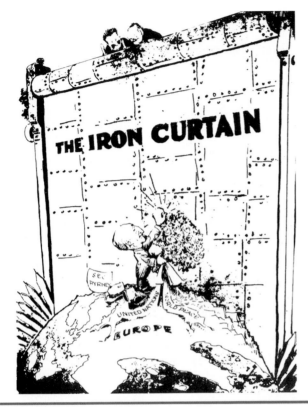

Cartoonist "Ding" Darling depicts the "iron curtain" that Winston Churchill, in his speech at Westminster College on March 5, 1946, accused the Soviets of drawing across Eastern Europe.

edge that the United States alone possessed the atomic bomb and, according to some predictions, would continue to be its sole possessor for a number of years. With demobilization rapidly proceeding—in 1947, the United States would have only 1.5 million people under arms, half the Soviet number—American policymakers like Secretary of State Byrnes saw the bomb as a means of countering Soviet superiority in conventional military forces in Eastern Europe. In 1946, the army air force established the Strategic Air Command, whose mission was to deliver nuclear bombs against the Soviet Union.

With the aim of further developing the American atomic arsenal, the administration had submitted to Congress a proposal to create an Atomic Energy Commission (AEC) to foster research and development in nuclear energy, especially its military uses. Many scientists protested the likely subjection of the agency to so much military influence. In July 1946, responding to the dissents, Congress established the AEC under

civilian control while giving the military a voice in shaping its program.

All the while, a number of atomic scientists had kept hoping that their Soviet brethren, aware that there could be no adequate defense against nuclear weapons, might help bring about an accord for international control of nuclear energy and make it work. To many Americans, some sort of agreement seemed imperative after the appearance, in 1946, of John Hersey's *Hiroshima*, a book that graphically portrayed the ghastly impact of the explosion on the city and its people. Macabre imaginings of what the United States might resemble after an atomic attack had begun to appear, exemplified by a drawing in *Life* magazine that showed the stone lions of the New York Public Library gazing over a sea of rubble as technicians crunched along testing radioactivity levels.

However, proposals for an international accord on atomic energy foundered on the United States' desire to maintain its nuclear monopoly and the Soviet determination to break it. The vast majority of the AEC's work came to be devoted to the development of weapons, with relatively little given to devising peaceful uses for nuclear energy.

## RESPONSIBILITY FOR THE COLD WAR

Deciding who was responsible for the beginnings of the Cold War—in many treatments the Soviet Union, in others the United States—has generated energetic historical debate. Truman's defenders point out that although, like Roosevelt, he was initially reluctant to antagonize the Soviet Union, he was rightly angered by the extension of Soviet totalitarianism to Eastern Europe. He was also concerned that Stalin's control of the region would deny American industry access to it, a closeout that would injure the economies of both Central Europe and the United States. Truman's critics indict him for his determination to maintain the American atomic monopoly, pointing to his expectation as early as Potsdam that nuclear weapons would help the United States keep the Russians in line. Critics fault him for failing to understand that the Soviet Union had legitimate national and security interests in Eastern Europe, seeing its as a first line of defense against another invasion from the West.

Misunderstandings on both sides undoubtedly contributed to the origins of the Cold War, but the United States and the Soviet Union were also divided by a genuine clash of political, economic, and ideological interests that Truman could hardly ignore either in principle or politically. Truman was mindful that conservatives were attacking the Yalta agreements as a "sellout" of

**Cold War Europe**

0 250 500 mi
0 250 500 km

- Members of the North Atlantic Treaty Organization (NATO)
- Members of the Warsaw Pact (Soviet counterpart to NATO)
- Nonaligned states
- Other Communist states

Eastern Europe and that the imposition of pro-Soviet regimes in the region outraged millions of Catholics and Americans of Eastern European origin, many of them Democratic voters.

### THE DOCTRINE OF CONTAINMENT

By 1946, some officials in the Truman administration had begun arguing for a coherent policy in Soviet relations that did not depend so heavily on nuclear weapons. It was already evident to them that the mere existence of the bomb would not affect Soviet actions in Eastern Europe and that it could not be used to force a change in the Polish government. The bomb only seemed to help heighten tensions with the Soviet Union.

Among the critics was George F. Kennan, the U.S. chief of mission in Moscow, a scholar-diplomat deeply steeped in Russian history. In February 1946, in an 8,000-word telegram to Washington, he argued that the Soviets were driven to aggressiveness by a "traditional and instinctive Russian sense of insecurity" arising from Russia's long-standing vulnerability to invasion from the West and its sense of the archaic inferi-

ority of its institutions. Soviet ambitions thus ought to be contained geographically and politically, Kennan maintained, with the expectation that over time the Soviet state would mellow or break up. In an article published two months later under the pseudonym "X," Kennan provided a summary of his arguments, calling the policy "containment." His analysis increasingly influenced the Truman administration's views about how to respond to the Soviets.

Truman first articulated the doctrine of containment early in 1947, in a policy initiative prompted by the situation in Greece, where the government was fighting a civil war against pro-Communist insurgents. Under Secretary of State Dean Acheson, a self-assured realist and a strong advocate of containment, advised Truman that a Communist takeover in Greece would make Turkey vulnerable to the Soviets and might open the Middle East and Africa as well as Italy and France to Soviet penetration. In mid-March, in a speech before a joint session of both houses of Congress, Truman went far beyond the immediate issues in the two countries, calling the battle in Greece part of a global struggle "between alternative ways of life" and warning that the "fall" of Greece would lead to losses to freedom elsewhere. "I believe that it must be the policy of the United States to support free peoples who are resisting attempted subjugation by armed minorities or by outside pressure," Truman declared, enunciating the commitment that came to be known as the Truman Doctrine. In mid-May, by substantial majorities in both houses, Congress appropriated $400 million, mainly for military aid, for Greece and Turkey over the succeeding fifteen months—thus authorizing U.S. intervention in a foreign civil conflict for the first time in the postwar era.

Conservatives questioned whether the policy of containment was practical or wise for the United States, thinking it economically costly and militarily risky. Critics on the left contested the policy as unnecessarily aggressive. Still others worried that containment, tied to the Truman Doctrine, would encourage Americans to see disputes with the Communist world primarily in military terms that would require military responses and ally the United States with undemocratic regimes only because they were anti-Communist. Kennan himself later said that what he meant by containment was primarily political and economic resistance to the Soviets. But the Truman Doctrine opened the way for future interventions abroad no matter whether essential U.S. interests were involved or whether Communist agitation was the primary reason for internal unrest.

### THE MARSHALL PLAN

In the spring of 1947, George C. Marshall, who had succeeded James Byrnes as secretary of state, was acutely worried about Europe, much of it impoverished and still rubble. The Communist parties in Italy and France were gaining significant support. Moreover, America's burgeoning prosperity depended in part on a huge export trade, largely with Europe, but Europe was running out of dollars to pay for its purchases. In a commencement address at Harvard in June, Marshall warned that if the United States did not help restore Europe's economy, "economic, social and political deterioration of a very grave character" would result. He called for extensive aid, a "cure rather than a palliative." Under the Marshall Plan, European governments would get grants of American goods that they could sell, using the proceeds to invest in their economies. Intended to stave off Communism by shoring up European democratic capitalism, the Marshall Plan amounted to the economic counterpart of the Truman Doctrine. Truman himself thought of the two programs as complementary, "two halves of the same walnut."

On Capitol Hill, conservatives in the Republican-dominated Congress derided the plan as a kind of international New Dealism. However, early in February 1948, Communists seized control of the government in Czechoslovakia, bringing that country into the orbit of Soviet control and sending shock waves through the West. Congress enacted the Marshall Plan before the end of the month, initially authorizing $4 billion and bringing the total to $17 billion in grants and loans by 1952. By 1951, the European recipients of the funds had increased their industrial output by 40 percent over that of the last prewar year.

### IN DEFENSE OF EUROPE

In 1947, the Soviet Union, moving to strengthen its hold on Eastern and Central Europe, announced an economic revitalization scheme of its own—the Molotov Plan, which it inaugurated with bilateral trade agreements with countries in the Eastern bloc. Stalin also set out to destroy political dissent in Eastern Europe, resorting to show trials, coerced confessions, and executions. In August, the Soviets forced out all left-wing

Soviet leader Joseph Stalin attempting to block the Marshall Plan's goal of a thriving free-market economy in Europe.

797

Berliners watch an American C-54 cargo plane arrive with supplies during the Soviet blockade of their city, July 1948.

anti-Communists from the Hungarian leadership and then rigged the elections to yield a pro-Soviet regime, initiatives that foreshadowed the Czech coup the following February.

The United States, Britain, and, with some reluctance, France increasingly saw the revival of the German economy as a key to fostering stability and resistance to the Soviets in Western Europe. In the spring of 1948, they pressed ahead with plans to unite the three Western zones of occupation into a West German state that would include the Western zone of Berlin and be integrated into the European economy. Defeating the Soviet determination to keep Germany weak, the effort would place the industrially rich Ruhr Valley permanently off-limits to the Soviets and foster a dynamic Western sector of Berlin deep in Soviet-held territory. In June, the Soviets cut off the flow of supplies by rail and truck from the Western zones of Germany into Berlin. Stalin's aim was to force the Western powers either to forgo the creation of a West German state or to abandon West Berlin.

Truman, determined to maintain West Berlin without violent confrontation, ordered an ongoing airlift of food and medical supplies into the city. American cargo planes began flying from the Western zones to Templehof Airport in West Berlin, landing about every three minutes around the clock and delivering 13,000 tons of goods a day. In July, Truman sent two groups of nuclear-capable B-29s to England, a veiled warning to the Soviets that they should not interfere with the Berlin-bound planes. The Soviets called off the Berlin blockade on May 12, 1949, 321 days after the airlift began. That month, the United States, Britain, and France ended the occupation of the Western zones and approved their union into the Federal Republic of Germany. The Soviets turned their zone into the German Democratic Republic, thus sealing the division of postwar Germany into East and West.

The blockade, which virtually transformed the image of Berlin in American eyes from that of Hitler's capital to a heroic outpost of freedom, generated substantially increased support for a policy of toughness toward Russia. The month it began, Congress revived the peacetime military draft. In April 1949, the United States joined in creating the North Atlantic Treaty Organization (NATO), an alliance of the North Atlantic nations, each of which pledged, in the language of the treaty's Article 5, to consider "an armed attack against one or more of them in Europe or North America . . . an attack against them all." For the United States, the formal commitment to the defense of Europe marked a historic break from its tradition of avoiding peacetime alliances.

### EAST ASIA

The Truman administration also enlisted Japan in the cause of containment. At the end of the war, General Douglas MacArthur had been appointed head of the occupation forces in Japan, with sole authority to reconstitute the Japanese system of government. In keeping with U.S. policy, he imposed on Japan a new democratic constitution that included a permanent renunciation of war. MacArthur called Japan "the western outpost of our defenses." The country loomed increasingly as a stable, anti-Communist power in the Pacific, one that could counter Soviet ambitions in the region (much as the United States hoped Germany would do in Europe). In 1947–48, as U.S.-Soviet relations worsened, the United States decided to rebuild Japanese industry, reversing its earlier postwar policy, and to expand its military bases in Japan.

## THE SINEWS OF NATIONAL SECURITY

Amid the emerging Cold War, national security commanded unprecedented peacetime attention. Even though defense appropriations kept falling, the defense budget in 1949 was roughly $14 billion, far higher even after adjustment for inflation than it had been in 1939. Pointing to the lessons of the war, policymakers held that the apparatus of national security needed to be better organized, more efficient, and well informed about developments elsewhere in the world. In 1947, Congress passed the National Security Act, which established an independent air force as a coequal branch of the military and unified all three armed services in a single military establishment soon named the Department of Defense (DOD). The act also created a National Security Council for better coordination between the military services and the State Department, and it established a Central Intelligence Agency (CIA) to coordinate foreign intelligence gathering.

*The CIA.* Although the CIA was initially limited to gathering and analyzing intelligence, after the Czech coup Truman allowed it to engage in covert operations abroad, and the Central Intelligence Act of 1949 authorized it to pursue such covert operations without accountability to Congress. That year, secret agency funds were used to establish the ostensibly private Radio Free Europe, which broadcast propaganda to Eastern Europe. The CIA also attempted to overthrow the Communist regime in Albania, inaugurating an era of peacetime political action hidden from public scrutiny.

*The Military and Technological Innovations.* The advent of the Cold War strengthened the belief that federal support of scientific research and development (R&D) constituted a key element in the nation's defense. Most of the money came from the military, and the bulk of its research support went to investigations into subjects closely related to the technologies of national security—for example, jet-powered aircraft, the newest innovation in flight. Defense agencies provided important support for the development of another technological innovation—electronic computers—that held great promise for a number of fields. Another product of the war, such computers had originated in the desire of some scientists and engineers to find a means to calculate artillery-firing tables (optimal aiming settings for guns under different conditions of wind and temperature) better than using hundreds of people to do the necessary arithmetic with hand-operated

J.W. Mauchly at work on the first electronic computer, ENIAC, February 1946.

adding machines. The first electronic computer, called ENIAC (for "electronic numerical integrator and computer") and completed near the end of 1945, was devised under a military contract at the University of Pennsylvania by J. Presper Eckert, a twenty-four-year-old electronics engineer, and John W. Mauchly, a young physicist. The computer used 18,000 vacuum tubes and could perform 5,000 operations per second. Immediately exploited to do a complicated nuclear-weapons calculation that would have taken one person 100 years at a desk calculator, it finished the job in six weeks.

ENIAC excited an interest in computers on the part of John von Neumann, a brilliant mathematical physicist and prewar refugee from Hungary. In June 1945, von Neumann had published a report laying out what came to be the basic constituents of an electronic computer (units for processing, program, input, and output). ENIAC lacked crucial elements in this design—for example, a capacious physical memory and an operating program—but during the next few years, several projects aimed to develop electronic computers containing all the von Neumann elements, thus laying the foundations of the American computer industry. All were spurred ahead by the engine of national security, through direct military support or military assistance to civilian sponsoring

799

agencies, or by the market created for computers by military contractors eager to employ them in R&D for aeronautics and rockets. The development of digital computers was part of the larger trend to what some analysts came to call "Pentagon Capitalism," the fueling of industrial growth, employment, and technological development through military expenditures.

Despite the emphasis on research in areas relevant to military technology, both civilian and defense policymakers recognized that maintaining military superiority in peacetime required vitality in every sector of the scientific enterprise, including basic research—that is, investigations of the fundamental laws and phenomena of nature without regard to their practical value. Thus, while emphasizing the development of nuclear weapons, the AEC sponsored research across a broad range of subjects, including high-energy particle physics, nuclear physics, nuclear medicine, and genetics. The United States increasingly led the world in science, partly because so many of the great centers of European research were devastated, partly because of its own richly developing capacities in the public and private sectors.

Electric washers, dryers, and refrigerators in abundance, staples of the buoyant postwar consumer economy.

## Prosperity and Tolerance

### A FLOURISHING ECONOMY

The high level of defense spending helped considerably to swell overall federal outlays and buoy the postwar economy. The federal budget, although falling after the war, turned around to reach $39 billion in 1950, more than four times what it had been in 1939. Now worries about a postwar economic downturn were stilled. A clear signal of optimism came from the birthrate. During the Depression, the number of live births per 1,000 Americans had averaged around 19. By 1947, it had risen 40 percent, to 26.6, the highest since 1921. (Marking the beginning of a baby boom, it would remain 24 or higher until the end of the 1950s.) Responding to demands for more schools and services, especially in the expanding suburbs, state and local spending shot up, more than doubling between 1945 and 1948 alone.

The United States led all other nations combined in the production of steel, oil, and automobiles, yielding its citizens far higher incomes on average than their counterparts elsewhere. People had money in the bank, the accumulated savings of the war years, and they proceeded to spend it on a cornucopia of products, among them electric clothes dryers, Polaroid cameras, and cars with automatic transmissions. The gross national product, $200 billion in 1946, climbed steadily, reaching $318 billion by 1950. Fewer veterans than expected immediately entered the labor market, since thousands of them—eventually almost half—availed themselves of the G.I. Bill to start businesses or get an education. Unemployment stayed down, hovering at slightly more than 4 percent.

### FACES AGAINST THE WINDOW

Americans by no means shared equally in the prosperity of the late 1940s. In 1947, only a minority of them owned their homes, while 30 percent of the nation's dwellings had no running water and 40 percent lacked flush toilets. By the standards of the era, some 30 percent of the population fell below the poverty level. A good many of the poor were African Americans in the South, where two out of three blacks still lived. In "Operation Dixie," the AFL and the CIO attempted in rival campaigns to organize southern textile and agricultural workers, but the drives failed. They were scuttled by the

NAACP staff with a poster recruiting people to join their battle against racial discrimination, 1940s.

Taft-Hartley law's discouragement of left-wing union organizing, by the relatively greater strength and power that white landowners enjoyed as a result of the New Deal's assistance to agriculture, and by warnings in the region that unionization would lead to desegregation.

At the end of the war, a CIO official, noting that "people have become accustomed to new conditions, new wage scales, new ways of being treated," had added, "Rosie the Riveter isn't going back to emptying slop jars." Indeed, a majority of working women had told pollsters they wanted to keep their jobs. But many people, including some in Congress, held that women ought to go home to open up space in the labor force for men returning from the war. By early 1946, more than 3 million women had left their jobs, many of them involuntarily. Some 200 women picketed the employment office at an auto plant holding signs that read, "Stop Discrimination Because of Sex" and "The Hand That Rocks the Cradle Can Build Tractors, Too."

For women who remained in the workforce, career opportunities were limited. They tended to hold lower-level jobs, far more so than during the war. Few received the same pay as men for the same work. The proportion of women in the professions kept declining. Those trying to become doctors faced medical-school admission quotas of 5 percent and refusals by most hospitals to accept them as interns. Still, by 1950, the

paid labor force included more than 18 million women, and 5 percent more women were working than in 1940. For the first time in the nation's history, more than half of working women were married, indicating that they were in the workforce for the long pull and not just biding time until the wedding day.

## A TURN AGAINST INTOLERANCE

Since the war, a number of middle-class women had been calling for an Equal Rights Amendment to the Constitution, but they ran into opposition from advocates of lower-income women who feared it would lead to the abolition of protective workplace regulations. President Truman called women's rights "a lot of hooey." In 1946, the amendment won a slim majority in the House, but it got nowhere in the Senate. The *New York Times* editorialized: "Motherhood cannot be amended, and we are glad the Senate didn't try it." The drive for the amendment nevertheless signified that the American agenda was being enlarged beyond bread-and-butter issues to embrace broader issues of rights. Although at the time women's rights receded into the background as a public issue, other groups, especially racial, religious, and ethnic minorities, were insisting on an end to the discriminations they suffered in American society. In the late 1940s, such minority groups knew brightening possibilities in achieving equal rights, but they also experienced disheartening, often bitter disappointments.

The war had done a good deal to discredit intolerance. Polls of G.I.s at the end of the war revealed that a majority placed above all other needs at home the necessity of eliminating racial and religious discrimination. A chaplain's remarks at a memorial service for the fallen of Iwo Jima expressed the increasingly common view that the living were obligated to ensure that all groups in America "enjoy the democracy for which all of them have paid the price."

The horrors of the Holocaust, publicized in graphic detail after the war, exposed the barbaric cruelties to which racism could lead. In November 1945, an Allied tribunal began trials of Nazi leaders at Nuremberg, Germany, charging them not only with responsibility for the war but with systematic murder and torture, especially at the concentration camps. Testimony revealed that Nazi doctors had used the inmates, the large majority of whom were Jews, as living subjects in a wide range of painful and even murderous experiments. By the end of the war, biologists and social scientists had arrived at a consensus on race that rebutted the vicious theories of the

Nazis and of racists in the United States. Summarized in a "Statement on Race" issued in 1950 by a branch of the United Nations, it held that there was no proof of innate differences in either mental characteristics or temperament among the groups of humankind.

The Cold War provided its own reasons for the repudiation of bigotry. "Americanism" came to be defined in contrast to Communism, as a commitment to freedom rather than in the nativist terms that had earlier disparaged immigrant ethnic minorities. The United States appeared hypocritical in preaching freedom abroad while it practiced discrimination at home, a contradiction that the Soviets did not fail to exploit. Thanks to immigration-restriction laws, only 8 percent of the population was now foreign-born, which diminished the social difficulty of assimilating foreigners. First-generation Catholics whose families had come from eastern or southern Europe reported that they now found fewer barriers to buying homes in upper-middle-class neighborhoods. The country's ability to absorb immigrants was celebrated as a sign of its commitment to "freedom," and its "Judeo-Christian" character was touted as distinguishing it from atheistic Communism.

In the postwar climate, popular magazines attacked prejudice in editorials, articles, and cartoons. Labor, educational, and women's groups joined Jewish and civil rights organizations in preaching tolerance through such devices as "Brotherhood Weeks." The trend reached into musical theater, expressing itself in a song from Richard Rodgers and Oscar Hammerstein's popular musical drama *South Pacific* that attacked prejudice ironically: "You've got to be taught to be afraid / Of people whose eyes are oddly made / and people whose skin is a different shade / You've got to be carefully taught."

Surveys showed that anti-Semitism in the United States was steadily declining in both private speech and political debate. To be sure, job advertisements continued to specify "gentiles only"; hardly any Jews were to be found in the executive suites of banking, heavy industry, communications, transportation, or public utilities companies; and Jews were barred from membership in two-thirds of men's business and social clubs. Still, in 1945, Bess Myerson was crowned "Miss America," the first Jew to win the title, and a growing number of resorts dropped their restrictions against Jews. In 1947, the Oscar-winning film *Gentleman's Agreement* dramatically attacked the anti-Semitic bigotry that permeated the restricted suburbs. Legislation and voluntary action began to end quotas limiting the admission of Jews to colleges, universities, and professional schools, while barriers to Jews in employment were also coming down.

## AFRICAN AMERICAN ASPIRATIONS

In 1947, the general manager of the Brooklyn Dodgers broke the major-league color barrier by signing Jackie Robinson. Jack Roosevelt Robinson had grown up in a slum in Pasadena, California, starred in multiple sports at UCLA, and commanded attention as a young standout in the Negro baseball leagues. While in the racially segregated wartime army, he successfully challenged the exclusion of blacks from Officers Candidate School and was court-martialed (and acquitted) for refusing to move to the back of a segregated military bus. Now, with the Dodgers, he was once again trying to shatter the status quo. In his first weeks on the team, he faced upturned spikes from opposition runners and cold shoulders even from some of his own teammates. But he prevailed with a combination of tight-lipped dignity and play dazzling enough to make him Rookie of the Year. Robinson's triumph, widely admired and publicized, helped expand tolerance toward African Americans in many walks of American life. Black musicians brought their recent innovation of bebop—jazz improvisations on the harmonic structures of familiar

Jackie Robinson, impressing fans and players alike with his strength of play and character, broke the color barrier in the major leagues.

tunes—to integrated clubs in downtown New York City. Black women were being hired as salesgirls in the swank department stores in the North; black blue-collar workers were taking on outspoken roles in labor grievance committees; and by 1946, more than two dozen blacks were serving in legislatures in every region outside the South.

Despite the tide toward tolerance, racial discrimination remained ubiquitous and often vicious. In the South, tufts of white cotton pinched onto screen doors, an indication of restriction to whites only, were emblematic of the racial segregation that remained the norm in schools, restaurants, hotels, restrooms, and even drinking fountains. Outside the South, the Federal Housing Administration encouraged the granting of mortgages so that "properties shall continue to be occupied by the same social and racial classes"—a policy that discouraged access to the burgeoning suburbs by blacks and other minorities. In the armed services, black soldiers traveled in Jim Crow railroad cars, lived in segregated barracks, shopped only at the Negro PX, and saw films in segregated post theaters.

In the postwar years, a growing number of African Americans refused to accept the status quo. Duke Ellington crafted musical critiques of segregation and injustice, notably his *Deep South Suite.* Many returning black veterans, having tasted freedom abroad, resolved that they would no longer put up with the lack of it at home. The logic of the Cold War provided opportunities. In 1947, the NAACP, in a petition to the United Nations that gained worldwide attention, declared, "It is not Russia that threatens the United States so much as Mississippi."

Lawsuits brought by blacks and whites persuaded the Supreme Court to begin weighing in on the side of equal treatment. In the late 1930s, the Court had begun to scrutinize laws that infringed on the protections provided by the Bill of Rights. Combined with the extension of the Bill of Rights to the states that had begun with the *Gitlow* case in the 1920s, the new standard established a doctrinal foundation for revolutionary change in civil rights law. Thus, in 1944, in *Smith v. Allwright,* the Supreme Court struck down white-only primary elections. In 1946, in *Morgan v. Virginia,* it held that segregation in public interstate travel was unconstitutional; and in 1950, in *Shelley v. Kraemer,* it found that restrictive covenants in housing—which prevented the sale of property to members of certain groups, in this case blacks—violated the Constitution.

In 1943, *Fortune* magazine had reported that in the South the "unity of whites against Negroes is not what it once was."

African Americans voting in the Democratic primary for the first time since 1890 in Jackson, Mississippi, 1946.

In the 1930s, reported lynchings of blacks happened on average a dozen times a year; between 1945 and 1950, the annual average fell to between two and three. In the larger southern cities, an increasing number of African Americans registered to vote so that the portion of blacks on the voting rolls jumped from 2 percent in 1940 to 12 percent by 1947, the year in which, for the first time, a black alderman was elected to the city council in Winston-Salem, North Carolina.

Still, the resistance to racial tolerance was pervasive, especially in the deep South, where advocates of racial change were often smeared as Communists. After the High Court's ruling on interstate travel, the biracial Congress of Racial Equality (CORE), which had been founded during the war, initiated "Journeys of Reconciliation," in which groups of blacks and whites would sit in the whites-only section of buses bound for the South. On a CORE journey to North Carolina, the riders were intimidated by the bus drivers, arrested by southern police, and sentenced to thirty-day jail terms. In September 1948, a black army veteran who boldly cast his ballot in Wrightsville, Georgia, was dead before sundown, and an all-white jury promptly acquitted the men accused of murdering him. Black suffrage was also blocked by a maze of harassments and economic intimidations, including loss of jobs, insurance policies, and lines of credit. In Alabama, the president of the state bar association spoke for numerous whites across the South when he declared, "No Negro is good enough and no Negro will ever be good enough to participate in making the law under which the white people in Alabama have to live."

## Truman Restored

### POLITICS AND MINORITY RIGHTS

The rising aspirations of minority groups inspired political strategists in the White House. In the view of most observers, Truman's chances to regain the presidency in 1948 were slim. In the judgment of the strategists, however, he might well keep the presidency by counting on the South, appealing to the West, and seeking the support of the coalition of groups that had returned Franklin Roosevelt to office, particularly labor, blacks, Jews, and other ethnic minorities. Truman's veto of the Taft-Hartley Act had renewed his backing among organized labor. His strategists recognized that an appeal to blacks would also be politically advantageous. In the presidential election of 1944, northern black votes had tipped the election to Roosevelt in eight states, including Michigan and Maryland, and in 1948 they could be similarly decisive in key northern states.

In February 1948, Truman endorsed to Congress the recommendations in *To Secure These Rights,* a report to the president from a committee of distinguished black and white citizens that called for an end to racial discrimination and segregation in areas ranging from housing and health care to suffrage and employment. He also announced that he would issue orders outlawing segregation in the armed services and the federal civil service. In June 1948, Truman became the first president to address a rally of the NAACP, telling a crowd of 10,000 from the steps of the Lincoln Memorial that the "serious gap between our ideals and some of our practices . . . must be closed."

In the spring of 1948, events in the Middle East presented an opportunity to strengthen his support among Jews. The Jews of Palestine intended to create a Jewish state—Israel—finding justification for the move in the Balfour Declaration of 1917, in which the British government had declared that it favored the creation of a home in Palestine for the Jewish people, so long as

it did not "prejudice the civil and religious rights of existing non-Jewish communities in Palestine."(Britain had recently invaded the Middle East to wage war against Germany's ally Turkey, with its Ottoman Empire; it hoped that the declaration would strengthen Jewish support for the war and would facilitate access to its colonial possessions in India and East Africa.) Most foreign policy officials opposed the creation of such a homeland, fearing that it would lead the Israelis into a losing war with Arabs, who greatly outnumbered them, and jeopardize the flow of oil to Europe and the United States. But Truman believed the case for a Jewish homeland was compelling on the merits and warranted on political grounds. "I have to answer to hundreds of thousands who are anxious for the success of Zionism. I do not have hundreds of thousands of Arabs among my constituents," he told the State Department. When on May 14, 1948, Israel declared statehood—prompting the predicted war with the Arabs, which Israel, to the surprise of many, won—the United States granted it recognition immediately. Truman's move enjoyed broad public support in the United States, partly because a Jewish homeland was thought to provide safe haven from another Holocaust.

### THE ELECTION OF 1948

An attempt by northern Democrats to dump Truman as their presidential nominee went nowhere, but southern Democrats, angry at the president's embrace of civil rights, were threatening to boycott the party's ticket. In response, after June, Truman backtracked on civil rights, sending no specific legislation on the subject to Capitol Hill and neglecting to issue the promised executive order on the armed services. When the Democratic National Convention met in July, he was willing to accept a weak civil rights plank in the party platform. However, Mayor Hubert H. Humphrey of Minneapolis insisted on amending the platform from the convention floor so that it called for abolition of the poll tax, a federal antilynching law, a permanent Fair Employment Practices Commission, and desegregation of the armed forces. The convention adopted the modified platform, whereupon thirty-five delegates from the deep South walked out waving the flags of the old Confederacy.

A. Philip Randolph (head of the Brotherhood of Sleeping Car Porters), chafing at Truman's failure to move against segregation in the armed services, warned that if the president did not act, he would mount a campaign of civil disobedience. In July, shortly after the convention, the president issued

A. Philip Randolph (left) leads demonstrators demanding a strong civil rights plank at the Democratic National Convention, July 1948.

executive orders banning discrimination in federal employment and establishing a committee to seek "equality of treatment and opportunity for all persons in the armed services without regard to race, color, religion or national origin." The services were slow to comply, but under pressure from the president all eventually accepted the policy of desegregation and began to inch toward making it a military reality.

The civil rights battle at the Democratic convention made Truman's reelection chances seem all the more bleak. The defectors joined with other southern segregationists to form the States' Rights Democratic Party, popularly known as the "Dixiecrats," which nominated Senator Strom Thurmond of South Carolina for the presidency. Dissidents on the Democratic left allied with Communists in a new Progressive Party that made Henry Wallace its standard-bearer and threatened to draw liberal votes from Truman in northern big-city states. The Republicans once again nominated Governor Thomas E. Dewey of New York, a moderate who, together with his running mate, Earl Warren, the popular governor of California, might appeal to Democrats and independents. Dewey, confident that Truman had no chance, mounted a dull, listless campaign, the effort of someone who appeared to believe that he was already president.

Truman, by contrast, ran a spirited race, whistle-stopping across the country with his wife and daughter, telling people from the rear of his train that a vote for Republicans was a vote to turn back the New Deal. He repeatedly attacked the "no-good, do-nothing" Eightieth Congress. He directed special attention to the groups his strategists had identified, attacking private electrical power interests in the Northwest, savaging the Republicans' indifference to farm-price supports in the Midwest, and speaking out for civil rights in Harlem in the East. Toward the end of the race, pollsters quit polling, predicting that a Dewey victory was a sure thing. But Truman was speaking to increasingly large and enthusiastic crowds yelling, "Give 'em hell, Harry." On election day, the voters gave him a stunning upset victory, with a margin over Dewey of 2.1 million popular votes and 114 votes in the electoral college.

Winning slightly less than 50 percent of the popular vote, Truman had run behind the Democratic ticket, which regained control of both houses of Congress. He had lost four deep South states to the Dixiecrats but only some strength in the normally Democratic Northeast to Wallace. With Truman earning kudos for the Berlin airlift, in progress during the campaign, the election tacitly endorsed the doctrine of containment. It also indicated that Americans did not want to turn back the social welfare clock. For the most part, the strategy of trying to hold together the Roosevelt coalition had succeeded triumphantly. Truman lost only Oregon out of the eleven states west of the plains. He carried Catholics, Jews, Americans of Eastern European background, and the overlapping constituency of organized labor. His majorities among blacks were enormous, with black votes proving decisive to his victory in the key states of Ohio, Illinois, and California. In January 1949, the black musicians Lionel Hampton and Lena Horne performed along with white stars at Truman's inauguration.

### THE FAIR DEAL

In early 1949, Truman proposed a long list of liberal measures to the new Congress, a package designed to provide a "fair deal" for the American people. But despite the Democratic victory in November, working control on Capitol Hill remained in the hands of southern Democrats and conservative Republicans. Congress hiked the minimum wage, provided for more public housing, and broadened Social Security. But it refused to act on civil rights and federal aid to education while declining to reform the tax structure, repeal

Taft-Hartley, or restructure the system of agricultural supports in ways that would benefit both small farmers and urban consumers. A renewed proposal to create an administration like the Tennessee Valley Authority for flood control and power generation in the Columbia Valley, in Washington State, went down to defeat in the face of charges that it would put "the entire United States under socialistic government-corporation rule." Another attempt at obtaining national health insurance failed utterly, losing partly because a well-financed advertising campaign by the American Medical Association warned that such a system would bring about "socialized medicine."

Amid the strongly conservative congressional climate, organized labor tended to seek broad gains for its workers less through governmental action than through innovative contractual agreements with employers. In the spring of 1948, Walter Reuther and General Motors negotiated a pioneering cost-of-living agreement that automatically adjusted the wage level of auto workers to rises in the consumer price index (a measure of the change in cost from the previous year of the goods and services purchased by a typical wage earner). During the late 1940s, industrial corporations increasingly provided their workers with benefits such as sick pay, paid vacations, and health coverage, a trend indicating the willingness of the private sector to provide social welfare, partly in decent recognition of workers' needs, partly to forestall an enlargement of governmental programs. By 1950, roughly half the civilian population had private insurance coverage for hospital costs, about a third for surgical costs.

## MEDICAL RESEARCH

Truman's first message to Congress on health care, in 1945, called for federal aid to medical research and education, a point in his package that conservatives as well as liberals were willing to support. The dramatic success of the wartime penicillin program pointed to the value of concerted attacks against disease. In 1948, Congress established the National Institutes of Health

---

*American Journal*

## What if You Get Sick?

*Infectious childhood diseases such as measles, mumps, chicken pox, diphtheria, and infantile paralysis were highly contagious before vaccines against them began to be developed in the 1950s. And before broadly effective antibiotics such as penicillin became available after World War II, children who came down with these diseases were often in for a rough time. In 1946, Dr. Benjamin Spock published* The Common Sense Book of Baby and Child Care, *a book that millions of parents would make their Bible and that in this first edition recommended the standard procedure for a family with a child ill with an infectious disease.*

"Quarantine. . . . This is first of all to prevent others—either adults or children—who have not had the disease from catching it unnecessarily. Another reason is that they will not be carrying the germs to others outside the home. . . .

"How do you maintain a good quarantine? You keep the child in one room and keep everyone else out except the one grownup who is taking care of him. She slips on a smock which is kept hanging in the room just for this purpose. This keeps her regular clothes from collecting germs. She takes it off every time she leaves the room. All the drinking and eating utensils that leave the room should be carried to the kitchen in a dishpan and boiled in it before being handled or washed or mixed with the utensils for the rest of the family.

"In the case of scarlet fever, diphtheria, and some other serious diseases, further precautions are required by some health departments. Sheets, pillow cases, night clothes may have to be soaked in antiseptic solution before being washed. The room may have to be stripped of rugs, curtains, bureau covers, etc., at the beginning of the disease. The health department may forbid anybody outside the family from entering the home. . . . "

Benjamin Spock, *The Common Sense Book of Baby and Child Care*

(NIH) as an umbrella for the National Cancer Institute and similar agencies. Soon the total number of such institutes reached eight, covering as many different diseases and disorders, and the NIH was on its way to forming a powerful complex for biomedical research and training. In the meantime, private philanthropy enlarged its support of biomedical research, giving special attention to the scourges of cancer and polio. Drawing on wartime research, biomedical scientists developed effective chemotherapies against childhood leukemias, while promising ones were found against Hodgkin's lymphoma.

## Setbacks, Loyalty, and Subversion

### THE "FALL" OF CHINA

In foreign affairs all the while, the Truman administration kept on with the policy of containment, but its aid to Jiang Jieshi (Chiang Kai-shek) in China—by 1949, $3 billion worth of loans and war surplus goods—seemed increasingly wasted.

Communist troops march through Beijing in June 1949, accompanied by trucks displaying propaganda and a large red star featuring a picture of Mao Zedong.

Mao Zedong's (Mao Tse-tung's) Communists had kept gaining ground, offering the peasantry reforms that Jiang's regime refused to entertain: an end to foreign dominance, agrarian overhaul, and emancipation from the Nationalist regime's corrupt and dictatorial character. American officials concluded that to keep Jiang in power would require extensive and ongoing U.S. economic and military intervention, an option the Truman administration rejected. By mid-1949, the Nationalists had been forced to abandon the major Chinese cities, and by the end of the year they had yielded mainland China to the Communists and left for the nearby island of Formosa (Taiwan).

Many Western nations granted recognition to the Communist regime. The American government expected to recognize it, too, hoping to encourage its independence from the Soviets. However, many American conservatives, bitter that the Truman administration had "lost" China, lobbied against recognition, and the Chinese declined to accept certain American conditions for obtaining it. The United States continued to recognize the Nationalist regime on Formosa as the legitimate government of China. Agitation from the "China lobby"—a loose alliance of individuals and groups, including many with missionary or business ties to Asia, the publisher of *Time,* and conservative Republicans from the Midwest and West—helped make recognition of the Communist regime almost unthinkable in mainstream public affairs.

### ESCALATION IN THE ARMS RACE

The Communist takeover in China shocked Americans, and so did Truman's announcement in late September 1949 that the Soviet Union had exploded an atomic bomb. While the news did not surprise most knowledgeable scientists—they had estimated that it would take the Soviets only five years or so to build their own bomb—it distressed millions of lay Americans, who, thinking the Soviets backward, had assumed it would take them much longer. Although the United States by now possessed a formidable and steadily expanding nuclear arsenal, a number of scientists and policymakers demanded that the nation embark on a crash program to build a thermonuclear weapon they called "the Super." Different from a fission bomb, it would work by fusing together nuclei of hydrogen, mimicking the reaction that fuels the sun. A hydrogen bomb would explode with the power of millions of tons of TNT in a blast a thousand times greater than the one that had destroyed Hiroshima. The H-bomb's most zealous advocate was Edward Teller, a theoretical physicist, refugee from Hungary, and hard-line anti-Communist, for whom the Super had become an obsession. He warned that if the Soviets beat the United States to a thermonuclear weapon, "our situation would be hopeless."

Opposed to a crash program to build an H-bomb was a distinguished complement of scientists and policymakers, J. Robert Oppenheimer among them. They considered such a weapon immoral, an instrument of genocide, and they hoped that American restraint would lead the Soviet Union to forgo its development, too. It also seemed highly likely that Teller's ideas for the hydrogen bomb would not work. However, Teller's advocacy of an H-bomb enjoyed powerful support. The Joint Chiefs of Staff judged it "foolhardy altruism" for the United States voluntarily to renounce such a super weapon, and Dean Acheson, now secretary of state, was unconvinced that a paranoid adversary could be persuaded to disarm by example. At the end of January 1950, President Truman authorized the crash program to build the weapon, even though no one knew how to build it.

The main problem was to find a way to initiate the fusion of the hydrogen fuel, a process that requires enormous energy. But at Los Alamos early in 1951, Teller and the physicist Stanislaw Ulam unexpectedly came up with a way to trigger hydrogen fusion using a uranium explosion. American physicists did not pose any moral objections to proceeding with the hydrogen bomb as they had in 1949, partly because they expected that if they could think of a method to ignite a hydrogen bomb, so could their Soviet counterparts. On November 1, 1952, the principle of the hydrogen bomb was demonstrated to work in a spectacularly successful test in the Pacific, code-named "Mike," that yielded a ten-megaton blast, 500 times the power unleashed at Hiroshima. The explosion produced a searing white fireball more than three miles across that swiftly darkened into a boiling cloud twenty-seven miles high atop a stem eight miles wide.

### A CLIMATE OF FEAR

A number of Americans tended to attribute Communist victories abroad to subversion at home, and the advent of the Soviet atomic bomb and the so-called fall of China to Communism heightened the tendency. Communists and Communist sympathizers were to be found in various walks of American life, including universities, science, government, entertainment, and the media. Many had embraced Communism during the 1930s, thinking it the answer to the Great Depression. Whatever their motives, they were automatically held to be subverting American democracy because the Communist Party usually followed the Soviet line. Communist affiliations did not in fact necessarily make someone disloyal to the United States or willing to pass secrets to Soviet agents. However, revelations of atomic espionage in Britain and Canada were enough to make not only Communists but non-Communists and even anti-Communists on the political left vulnerable to accusations of disloyalty. A number of Republicans red-baited their opponents in the 1946 congressional campaign, charging the Democrats, as a leader of the GOP said of Truman, with "appeasing the Russians abroad and . . . fostering Communism at home."

*The Truman Loyalty Program.* In March 1947, to counter Republican charges that he was soft on Communism, the president issued an executive order establishing a program to check the loyalty of the 2.5 million people who worked for the federal government. Among the criteria for suspicion of disloyalty would be past or present membership in allegedly totalitarian, fascist, or subversive organizations on a list to be drawn up by the attorney general. During the program's first year, the FBI checked out more than 2 million federal employees and conducted full investigations of over 6,000 of them. By 1952, several hundred workers would be dismissed and several thousand more would resign. No one was ever proved to have engaged in spying or sabotage.

The loyalty program made advocates of civil liberties shudder. J. Edgar Hoover, the director of the FBI, used his agency's powers to wage investigative war against alleged Communists, smearing them with rumor and innuendo. Vague suggestions by informants about past political associations often sufficed to force workers out of their jobs. Many people were called before loyalty boards because they were thought to be alcoholics, homosexuals, or debtors; and many were asked about the art on their walls or the recordings they owned. Truman privately wrote: "We want no Gestapo or Secret Police. FBI is tending in that direction. They are dabbling in sex life scandals and plain blackmail." In drawing up a list of subversive groups, the attorney general had no formal standard of subversiveness. Despite guarantees of due process in the proceedings, the departmental loyalty boards denied federal employees even the right to know the identity of their accusers, let alone the right to confront them.

The State Department withheld passports from left-leaning Americans, including celebrated singers, artists, and scientists. In 1950, overriding Truman's veto, Congress passed an Internal Security Act that compelled Communist organizations and their members to register with a new Subversive Activities Control Board and made members of such organizations ineligible for jobs in government or defense. The McCarran-Walter Immigration Act (1952), which Congress also passed over Truman's veto, facilitated FBI surveillance of suspect groups and the deportation of aliens suspected of subversiveness.

*The House Un-American Activities Committee.* Truman established the loyalty program partly because he wanted to forestall Republican attacks during the upcoming 1948 campaign that his administration was soft on Communism. He also said that he hoped the program would protect innocent federal workers from the extremes of the House Un-American Activities Committee (HUAC). The HUAC had been searching for subversives since its establishment in 1938, claiming to find Communist influence in labor unions, in government bureaus, and among African American dissidents. In the late 1940s, the HUAC's members included John Rankin of Mississippi, who later decried civil rights activists as "a part of the communist program, laid down by Stalin himself," adding, "Remember, communism is Yiddish."

The HUAC, undeterred from its inquisitions by the Truman administration's loyalty review program, hounded scientists, teachers, and film makers, among others. In 1947, for example, the HUAC called ten of the film industry's highly successful figures, most of them screenwriters, to testify about their politics and associations. Eight of them, including Dalton Trumbo, Hollywood's highest-paid screenwriter and a veteran of the Spanish Civil War, had Communist affiliations. All refused to answer the HUAC's queries, asserting that the committee had no right to inquire into their political beliefs and associations. They enjoyed the support of many prominent entertainers. The singer Frank Sinatra, who had been denounced before the HUAC as a "front" for Communists, protested, "If you make a pitch on a nationwide radio network for a square deal for the underdog, will they call you a Commie?"

At the hearings, the Hollywood Ten, as they came to be known, were cited for contempt. All were convicted and sent to prison, whereupon some of the outspoken stars, notably Humphrey Bogart, backed away from their criticism of the HUAC. In a meeting at the Waldorf Astoria Hotel in New York City, in November 1947, the major film producers announced

Screenwriter Dalton Trumbo, leaving the House Un-American Activities Committee's witness stand in 1947, angrily denounces its investigation of Hollywood as the start of an "American concentration camp."

that they were firing every one of the Hollywood Ten who was currently employed and vowed that they would not knowingly hire anyone who was a Communist. After the ten got out of prison, they found themselves blacklisted, unable to obtain work. Blacklisting quickly spread to the radio and television industries, too, which relied on private consulting firms to determine who was and who was not a subversive.

*The Case of Alger Hiss.* Many Americans were shocked by the testimony before the HUAC in August 1948 of Whittaker Chambers. A senior editor at *Time* magazine, Chambers had spied for Soviet military intelligence, breaking off his activity in 1938. He testified that during the 1930s he had received secret government documents from a State Department official named Alger Hiss. Hiss flatly denied the allegation, and many people, especially liberals, believed him. He had impeccable credentials, including a clerkship at the Supreme Court with Justice Oliver Wendell Holmes Jr. and membership in the American delegation at Yalta.

Chambers, however, showed reporters a hollowed-out pumpkin on his Maryland farm containing microfilms of documents that he claimed had been given him by Hiss. HUAC investigators eventually found that a typewriter once owned by Hiss had likely produced the typing on Chambers's documents. Since the statute of limitations had long since expired for Hiss's alleged treason, Hiss was indicted on charges of having perjured himself before the HUAC. He was tried and ultimately convicted in January 1950, serving forty-four months in prison. Hiss protested to his death in 1996 that he was innocent, although evidence from Russian sources published after the Cold War suggested that he had indeed been a Soviet agent. Whatever the case, in 1950 Hiss's conviction provoked widespread doubts that national security could be entrusted to the kind of New Deal/Fair Deal liberals, even those with credentials like Hiss's, who had populated the government for twenty years.

*The Effects of Fear.* The loyalty and security investigations actually uncovered few genuine subversives, while the fear of internal subversion severely damaged civil liberties in the United States. The powerful tendency to castigate and punish people not for what they did but for their political beliefs, associations, and declarations reached far beyond the hearing rooms of the administration's loyalty review program and the HUAC. In 1940, Congress had passed the Smith Act, which made it illegal merely to advocate the violent overthrow of the government. The act led to the trial and conviction of the leaders of the American Communist Party, who appealed their case to the Supreme Court. In 1951, in *Dennis v. the United States,* the Court upheld the constitutionality of the Smith Act, with the majority finding reason in the "gravity" of the Communist threat to depart from the doctrine that the right of free speech could be limited only if the exercise of it posed a "clear and present danger." Justices Hugo Black and William O. Douglas forcefully dissented, arguing that the majority opinion diluted the First Amendment to the point of protecting only "those 'safe' or orthodox views which rarely need its protection."

In 1949, the National Education Association, a body representing public school teachers, voted almost unanimously that Communists were "unfit" to teach in the schools; and a blue-ribbon panel headed by James B. Conant of Harvard and Dwight Eisenhower, now the president of Columbia University, announced that the same criterion should apply to university professors. Loyalty oaths were enacted by fifteen states—by 1953, the total would reach thirty-four, in addition to those by many local governments—requiring that public employees swear that they were not Communists and did not believe in the violent overthrow of the government. Drawing

national attention, the University of California fired some 10 percent of its faculty because they refused to sign a loyalty oath, and a similar fate befell professors at other universities who refused to cooperate with state and federal investigations into their political affiliations. In 1950, the Joint Committee on Atomic Energy required that all applicants for AEC fellowships obtain security clearances, whether they would be engaged in classified research or not. Albert Einstein complained to no avail that young scientists should not have to pay such a cost in "human dignity" to pursue research.

The climate of fear had a chilling effect on American culture and reform movements. It gave weight to the urging of Eric Johnston, the head of the Motion Picture Producers' Association, who wanted the film industry to make "no more *Grapes of Wrath . . .* no more *Tobacco Roads . . .* no more films that show the seamy side of American life . . . that deal with labor strikes . . . with the banker as villain." Community activists forced libraries and schools to remove social reformist books such as *The Grapes of Wrath* from their shelves. Labor unions purged Communists from their leadership, and civil rights groups similarly refused to cooperate with left-wing activists. Conservatives nevertheless charged that advocates of civil rights were Communists, a claim that Jackie Robinson denied when he testified before the HUAC, stressing, "Negroes were stirred up long before there was a Communist Party, and they'll stay stirred up long after the party has disappeared—unless Jim Crow has disappeared by then as well."

*McCarthyism.* The threat of internal subversion caught the attention of Senator Joseph McCarthy. During a speech in Wheeling, West Virginia, on February 9, 1950, McCarthy, then a little-known, first-term Republican from Wisconsin, waved a sheet of paper, declaring, "I have here in my hand a list of 205 [employees] known to the Secretary of State as being members of the Communist Party and who nevertheless are still working and shaping the policy of the State Department." The scrappy product of a farm family of nine children, McCarthy combined a grinning likeability with a no-holds-barred ambition and suspicions of the kind of people his friends called "Leftists." He won a circuit judgeship with a smear campaign and in office gained a reputation for sleazy dealings. Seemingly blind to the damage he did, he kept on shading the truth. Now he refused to release his "list" of Communists (which he eventually cut to 1), but amid the growing fear of internal subversion, his charges were earning

Joseph McCarthy (second from right) used the press to level reckless charges of Communist infiltration.

headlines. The term "McCarthyism," connoting smearing attacks on character and loyalty, quickly entered the American language.

McCarthy gained a major following in the United States, especially among conservative Republicans, midwesterners, ethnic minorities of Eastern European background, and anti-Communist Catholics. During the congressional elections of 1950, he was credited with helping to defeat four Democratic senators against whom he campaigned, including one who had called his accusations "a fraud and a hoax." (The Democratic advantage over Republicans in the Senate fell by a total of ten seats; in the House, by fifty-seven.) What bound McCarthy's supporters together was bitterness over the losses to Communism, especially in Eastern Europe and China, and a belief that privileged people like Alger Hiss, convicted of lying to Congress about his espionage, and even the resolute Cold Warrior Dean Acheson, whom McCarthy vilified as the "Red Dean," were responsible for it. A number of McCarthyites were also united by their ongoing anger at the New Deal. A conservative Republican from Nebraska sniped about Acheson, "I watch his smart aleck manner and his British clothes and that New Dealism, everlasting New Dealism in everything he says and does, and I want to shout, 'Get Out! Get Out! You stand for everything that has been wrong in the United States for years.'"

## Korea and Its Consequences

At mid-century, the United States was on tenterhooks, with the Cold War intensifying the flight from the reformism of the New Deal/Fair Deal and raising increasing apprehensions about the future of the nation's security. The president had asked a high-level committee for a review of defense policy in light of the Soviet acquisition of atomic weapons. In the spring of 1950, the committee produced National Security Council Memorandum Number 68 (NSC-68), which stated that the Soviet Union was a threat "not only to this Republic but to civilization itself" and that in a few years it would be capable of mounting a surprise atomic attack of potentially devastating proportions. NSC-68 urged that to deter such aggression the United States had to intensify intelligence operations, covertly encourage unrest in the Soviet satellite countries, and beef up research and development. It also had to proceed to full-scale rearmament, including the establishment of a substantial standing army and a quadrupling of the defense budget, if necessary at the sacrifice of domestic needs. But Truman was unwilling to go so far as to put the country on the virtual war footing recommended in NSC-68. In the spring of 1950, the administration sent Capitol Hill the lowest defense budget since V-J Day, and it sailed through Congress. But then war suddenly broke out in Korea and transformed the calculus of national security.

### WAR IN KOREA

Saturday, June 24, 1950: the news reached the State Department by cable at 9:26 P.M. Early that morning, military forces from Communist North Korea had crossed the 38th parallel into anti-Communist, pro-Western South Korea, initiating what appeared to be an all-out offensive. The head of North Korea had predicted to Stalin that the United States would not intervene to protect the South, perhaps because a speech that Secretary of State Dean Acheson had given in 1950 could be interpreted to mean that it was not within the American defense perimeter. Stalin promised North Korea supplies but little more. American officials were nevertheless sure that the invasion had been prompted by the Soviets. Truman told an aide, "There's no telling what they'll do, if we don't put up a fight right now." On Tuesday, June 27, the president committed air and naval forces to cover the South Korean troops. On Friday, General Douglas MacArthur, in Japan, warned that

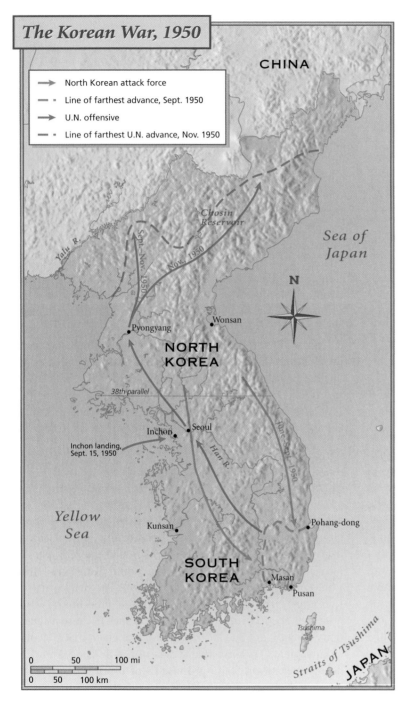

**The Korean War, 1950**

→ North Korean attack force
-- Line of farthest advance, Sept. 1950
→ U.N. offensive
-- Line of farthest U.N. advance, Nov. 1950

CHINA

Chosin Reservoir

Yalu R.

Sea of Japan

Pyongyang
Wonsan

NORTH KOREA

38th parallel

Inchon
Seoul

Inchon landing, Sept. 15, 1950

Han R.

Yellow Sea

Kunsan

Pohang-dong

SOUTH KOREA

Masan
Pusan

Tsushima

Straits of Tsushima

JAPAN

0    50    100 mi
0    50    100 km

the South Korean army would be overrun without help on the ground. Truman then authorized MacArthur to send American infantry under his command to Korea.

The United Nations, which at the moment the Soviets happened to be boycotting, had branded the North Koreans aggressors and adopted a resolution supporting armed assistance to South Korea. The willingness to put teeth into collective security heartened delegates from Western countries, giving them hope that the fledgling U.N. would not suffer the fate of the League of Nations. Truman had not consulted Congress, and there was no subsequent vote to authorize military action. Some members grumbled that nothing in the Constitution authorized the president to commit troops to combat on his own. Nevertheless, most Republicans and Democrats in Congress cheered Truman's action; even the grumblers supported it. Relief seemed to sweep through the Capitol that at long last the country was standing up to Communism.

At a press conference, Truman insisted that the United States was not at war, but was, in a reporter's phrase, in a "police action under the United Nations." (In fact, the U.S. forces in Korea, while formally an arm of the U.N., operated under the control of Washington.) The United States had entered a war that would continue for three years and in which it would provide 50 percent of the troops, with much of the rest supplied by South Korea. In July, Congress roared through a military increase of $10 billion, in support of the effort in Korea, inaugurating a huge enlargement in defense expenditures. In 1953, they would reach $52.8 billion, accounting for some $69 out of every $100 spent by the federal government.

### A SEESAW WAR

In the first weeks of the war, the North Koreans overwhelmed the U.N. forces—largely American and South Korean troops under MacArthur's command. The Americans were soft from occupation duty in Japan and, like the South Korean forces, inadequately equipped. Battling Soviet-made tanks with World War II bazookas, the U.N. armies frantically retreated until they managed to establish a defense perimeter some sixty-five

The see-saw war in Korea was made harsher by the bitter winters and the need to take and retake the same hills.

descending, in Truman's recollection—assured his commander in chief that the Chinese were unlikely to intervene and that if they did, they would be slaughtered. The president authorized American forces to cross the 38th parallel but not to antagonize China.

MacArthur directed his troops northward toward the Yalu River (the Chinese-Korean border), but in late November, marking a turning point in the war, huge waves of Chinese troops began pouring into North Korea. By January 1951, the U.N. troops had been driven back through bitter cold and hazardous passages deep into South Korea. Under General Matthew Ridgway, who had taken charge of the U.S. Eighth Army in December, the U.S. forces dug in, then doggedly counterattacked to the north. By late March, they had recaptured Seoul and most of the territory south of the 38th parallel. Now the war seesawed across the 38th parallel, stalemating both sides.

## THE SACKING OF MACARTHUR

The Truman administration said that the United States was fighting a "limited war" and that it wanted a diplomatic settlement, but MacArthur repeatedly and publicly insisted on taking the war to China—by, for example, bombing Chinese bases beyond the Yalu, in Manchuria. Thumbing his nose at Truman's authority as commander in chief, he disparaged the administration's Korean policies as tantamount to the "appeasement of Communism" and declared, "There is no substitute for victory." On April 11, 1951, Truman, backed by a unanimous recommendation from the Joint Chiefs of Staff, removed MacArthur from command, emphasizing that he could not tolerate such a challenge to presidential authority. Truman's action provoked widespread outrage, but by May the pro-MacArthur storm subsided. In congressional hearings, General Omar Bradley, speaking for the Joint Chiefs of Staff, persuasively argued that MacArthur's policies would have involved the United States in "the wrong war, at the wrong place, at the wrong time, and with the wrong enemy."

In June 1951, shortly before the hearings ended, the Russians intimated that they wanted a cease-fire in Korea. Peace negotiations began the next month, but they soon bogged down over the issue of repatriation of North Korean and Chinese prisoners of war, some 45,000 of whom did not want

miles north of Pusan, at the southeastern end of the Korean peninsula. But then, on September 15, 1950, in a brilliant gamble reminiscent of his tactics in World War II, MacArthur mounted a successful amphibious assault at Inchon, on the coast just west of Seoul, the South Korean capital. The U.N. troops, their casualties extremely light, soon took Seoul while other U.N. troops, breaking out of Pusan, moved northward. By the beginning of October, the area up to the 38th parallel was under U.N. control.

MacArthur insisted that the U.N. forces continue northward to North Korea's border with China, thus reuniting Korea under Western protection. American public opinion seemed to endorse the move, and so did the United Nations, which approved it in early October. However, China had warned that it would not tolerate American troops in the neighborhood of its border. (Unknown to American strategists, Stalin had encouraged Mao Zedong [Mao Tse-tung] to resist any American march northward, sending him huge shipments of guns and planes.) In mid-October, Truman, worried about the Chinese, flew to meet with MacArthur at Wake Island in the Pacific. MacArthur—arrogant and conto go home. The Truman administration insisted that repatriation had to be voluntary—a condition that the North Koreans and Chinese were still refusing to accept when Truman left office in January 1953, with the result that the fighting continued.

# They Liked Ike

## THE ELECTION OF 1952

As the conflict in Korea dragged on, many Americans grew angry and frustrated. In 1952, their frustration joined with the McCarthyite tide to raise Republican hopes in the coming presidential election. So did revelations of corruption in the Truman administration—notably, that payments had been made to several officials or their wives seemingly in exchange for favors such as federal loans. Truman, his standing in the polls abysmal, declined to run for reelection.

GOP conservatives, who were centered in the Midwest, pressed for the nomination of Robert Taft, their champion, a resolute foe of New Dealism and suspicious of American in-

Dwight D. Eisenhower runs for the presidency, Lawrence, Massachussetts, 1952.

volvements abroad. But the party's eastern wing of moderate internationalists found a powerful candidate in Dwight D. Eisenhower, the war hero and commander of the NATO forces. Although in 1948 Eisenhower had steered clear of presidential politics, he agreed to run now because he disliked Truman's tolerance for deficits and Taft's neo-isolationist leanings. Without campaigning, Eisenhower crushed Taft in the New Hampshire primary and went on to win the nomination. His running mate was thirty-nine-year-old Richard Nixon, a ferociously ambitious politico who had become a national figure by his pursuit of Alger Hiss while a member of the HUAC and by his election to the Senate from California two years earlier in a red-baiting campaign that earned him the nickname "Tricky Dick."

The Democrats awarded their nomination to Adlai Stevenson, a wealthy lawyer, the governor of Illinois, and a critic of McCarthyism. In the hope of keeping the South in the Democratic camp, they chose Senator John Sparkman of Alabama as his running mate, a choice consistent with Stevenson's willingness to tolerate racial segregation by leaving civil rights up to the states. During the campaign, Stevenson advanced a moderate middle-of-the-roadism in foreign and domestic affairs that was close to Eisenhower's, but he was drowned out by the Republican din over what their party strategists called $K_1C_2$—Korea, Communism, and Corruption.

In mid-campaign, it was revealed that Nixon had a private political fund donated by rich supporters in California. He responded with a sentimental, nationally televised speech that sidestepped the issue of the propriety of the fund, emphasizing instead his watch-the-pennies upbringing and his young family's modest circumstances, including his wife's wearing a "respectable Republican cloth coat." The speech not only saved his place on the ticket but also made the Republican Party, long identified as the party of the rich, look more like a haven for struggling, workaday Americans.

Eisenhower stayed on the high road, buoyed by his war-hero popularity and aided by the shrewd use of television in its presidential campaign debut. Staged TV advertisements brought Eisenhower's radiant smile and unpretentious forthrightness into millions of living rooms (roughly one-third of American households now had TVs), and many Americans sported campaign buttons declaring, "I like Ike." Late in the campaign, Eisenhower announced, "If elected, I shall go to Korea," a promise that stirred people even though he did not say what he would do there.

Eisenhower won in a landslide, gaining more than 55 percent of the popular vote and the overwhelming margin of 442 electoral votes against Stevenson's 89. The first Republican candidate since Herbert Hoover to break the Democratic hold on the South, he won in Florida, Texas, Virginia, and Tennessee. But the results added up more to a victory of the man rather than of the party. Although the Republicans won control of Congress, they enjoyed only a one-seat majority in the Senate and an eight-vote majority in the House.

## ENDING THE KOREAN WAR

Making good on his campaign pledge, Eisenhower went to Korea after the election, spending three days at the front. At the end of March, the Chinese indicated they might be willing to deal on the issue of repatriation. Although armistice talks resumed, Dulles, sensing resistance on the part of the Chinese, hinted through Indian diplomats that if the war continued, the United States might use atomic weapons. The Chinese and North Koreans, seeing that Eisenhower would offer no better terms than Truman, agreed to a cease-fire on July 27, 1953. The agreement reestablished the 38th parallel as the line of demarcation between North and South Korea and allowed Chinese and North Korean prisoners of war to decide for themselves whether they would return home; ultimately, 50,000 of them declined repatriation. The war had seen more than 33,000 Americans killed and 103,000 wounded and caused some 4 million total casualties, more than half of them civilians. It left Korea divided, with North Korea remaining a tyrannical member of the Communist bloc and South Korea developing into a prosperous, if often internally repressive, ally of the West.

## THE CONSEQUENCES OF KOREA

The seeming endlessness of the conflict in Korea had intensified the McCarthyite atmosphere, widening suspicions that pro-Communist subversion was at work in the United States. McCarthy himself had accused the Democrats of perpetrating "twenty years of treason." The war had deepened fears of Soviet aggression and accelerated the development of atomic and conventional defense technologies, including poison gases and intercontinental ballistic missiles. A high-ranking defense science advisor observed that at times the military "seem to be fanatics in their

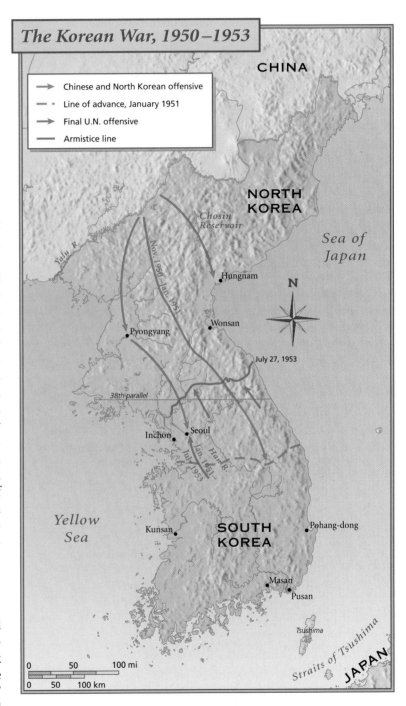

**The Korean War, 1950–1953**

→ Chinese and North Korean offensive
‑ ‑ Line of advance, January 1951
→ Final U.N. offensive
— Armistice line

CHINA

NORTH KOREA

*Chosin Reservoir*

*Yalu R.*

Nov. 1950–Jan. 1951

Hungnam

*Sea of Japan*

Pyongyang

Wonsan

July 27, 1953

*38th parallel*

Inchon   Seoul

*Han R.*

July 1953

Jan. 1951

*Yellow Sea*

Kunsan

SOUTH KOREA

Pohang-dong

Masan

Pusan

*Tsushima*

*Straits of Tsushima*

JAPAN

0   50   100 mi
0   50   100 km

belief of what the scientists and the technologists can do." The psychological sea change also made civilian scientists more enthusiastic about strengthening the nation's nuclear arsenal, some proposed, for example, to integrate nuclear weapons into conventional battle plans—and it helped defuse opposition to the hydrogen bomb.

*Extending Containment.* The Korean War had also encouraged policymakers to see the Soviet Union and Communist China as a monolithic bloc and stimulated the United States to globalize containment while reconfiguring its policies for European security. Turning its recent enemies into allies, America, in 1950, persuaded NATO to agree to the rearmament of Germany. In 1951, it entered pacts with Japan that restored Japanese sovereignty over the home islands and gave the United States the right to station American troops and planes on Japanese soil. The administration stationed the Seventh Fleet between China and Formosa (Taiwan), strengthened American commitments to counterrevolutionary forces in Southeast Asia, and, drawing a line against the Soviets in the Middle East, obtained military bases in Saudi Arabia and Morocco. By the beginning of the Eisenhower years, in the name of preventing the spread of Communism, the United States had extended its military presence across the globe and had made the military a worrisomely powerful force in peacetime life.

### TRUMAN'S LEGACY

At the time, Eisenhower's crushing victory over Stevenson was taken as a repudiation of Truman and his policies, but since then the Truman administration has gained consider-able retrospective respect. Despite its twists and turns, the administration carved out the essential elements of the nation's foreign and domestic policies in the postwar era. It successfully managed reconversion to a peacetime economy and despite the shift to the political right, advanced the Fair Deal version of the welfare state, explicitly placing minority rights, especially for African Americans, on the national agenda. Prompted by the technological shrinkage of the world and the emergence of the Cold War, Truman and the Congress committed the United States to continuing international engagement and to a variety of programs, research and development among them, to bolster national defense. The Truman administration had also made good on its commitment to collective security with the intervention in Korea, but the Korean War convinced many Americans that their country faced an era of acute danger. It produced consequences and Cold War attitudes that would significantly affect the nation long after the war itself ended.

## Suggested Reading

John Lewis Gaddis, *The United States and the Origins of the Cold War, 1941–1947* (1992)

Jon Halliday and Bruce Cumings, *Korea: The Unknown War* (1988)

Alonzo L. Hamby, *Man of the People: A Life of Harry S. Truman* (1995)

Susan M. Hartmann, *The Home Front and Beyond: American Women in the 1940s* (1982)

Arnold Rampersad, *Jackie Robinson: A Biography* (1997)

## Summary QUESTIONS

- What problems troubled the economy in the transition to peacetime?
- What was the doctrine of containment and what steps did the United States take in the late 1940s to put it into effect?
- What were the major trends in American politics in the postwar years?
- How did fear of communism affect civil liberties in the United States?
- Why did the United States intervene militarily in Korea yet decline to carry the war to China?

## Key Terms

The Cold War (p. 794)

The Truman Doctrine (pp. 796–797)

The Marshall Plan (p. 797)

The Fair Deal (p. 805)

HUAC (p. 809)

## Chronology

| | |
|---|---|
| 1946 | George Kennan outlines the policy of containment. |
| July 1946 | Atomic Energy Commission created. |
| 1947 | The Taft-Hartley Act. |
| | Jackie Robinson becomes the first African-American to play Major League Baseball. |
| 1948 | Berlin airlift. |
| | Scientists at Bell Laboratories invent the transistor. |
| February 1948 | The Marshall Plan initiated. |
| 1949 | Chinese Communists gain control of China. |
| April 1949 | NATO created. |
| June 1950-July 1953 | The Korean War. |
| 1952 | The McCarran-Walter Immigration Act. |
| November 1, 1952 | The United States explodes a hydrogen bomb in the Pacific. |

**Access the *Inventing America* StudySpace at wwnorton.com/studyspace**

PERSONAL PLAN ■ REVIEW MATERIALS ■ RESEARCH AIDS ■ MULTIMEDIA

# Chapter 29

# EISENHOWER, AFFLUENCE, AND CIVIL RIGHTS:

## 1954-1960

Levittown, New York, exemplified the affordability and sameness of tract housing in the expanding suburbs.

QUESTIONS

■ **What was the impact of McCarthyism on American society?**

■ **What was Eisenhower's strategy for protecting American security in the Cold War?**

■ **What drove the prosperity of the 1950s?**

■ **How did minority groups and women fare in the 1950s?**

■ **How did American culture break with prevailing conformity?**

■ **Why did the civil rights movement gain force in the 1950s?**

■ **What was the significance of the 1960 election?**

Corporal William Jensen, wounded in Korea, came home to Hastings, Nebraska, saw the stores on Second Street, and remarked with amazement, "Man, I never saw anything like it. This town is just one big boom." After the war, the boom roared on and the country found itself washed in a peacetime prosperity unseen since the 1920s. But while as a result of the New Deal and Fair Deal the prosperity was distributed more fairly than in the era of Harding, Coolidge, and Hoover, many Americans still suffered from poverty, intolerance, or both. And the pressures of the Cold War shadowed the good times. The climate of McCarthyism chilled dissent. The nuclear arms race accelerated, and the military acquired an unprecedented presence in peacetime American life. Many Americans feared, even as they savored their abundance, that Armageddon might be around the corner.

## Eisenhower the Centrist

To many Americans, Dwight Eisenhower, age sixty-two at his inaugural, was a reassuring president, publicly calm, affable, and seemingly above partisan politics, a man of sunny optimism, tested strength, and unquestionable devotion to public service. Having grown up in Abilene, Kansas, he had graduated from the U.S. Military Academy and spent his entire career in the army except for a brief stint as president of Columbia University during the late 1940s. He conducted his presidency in the manner of a general—relying on a hierarchy of aides, staff analysis, and the delegation of authority. He avoided taking the public lead on controversial issues, preferring to operate by the admonition in the Latin phrase on his desk plaque that meant "Gently in manner, strong in deed." Critics faulted him for the muddled syntax of his press conferences, but he used obfuscation as a political instrument. Advised once by his press secretary to say nothing about a controversial foreign policy issue, he replied, "Don't worry, Jim. If that question comes up, I'll just confuse them."

Eisenhower quietly but assiduously involved himself in policymaking for high-stakes matters, with special confidence in his abilities in foreign and military affairs. Staunchly anti-Communist, he held that the United States had to shoulder its responsibilities for collective security and should continue Truman's policy of extended global containment. His views were shared by his secretary of state, John Foster Dulles, a lawyer from New York City, the son of a Presbyterian minister, and a Wilsonian with extensive experience in diplomacy. Eisenhower worked closely with Dulles and permitted him to put a righteous face on the administration's approach to the world. Dulles's evangelical moralizing may have helped hold the right wing of the Republican Party in check, but it inflamed Soviet-American relations and raised expectations that the United States was ready to crusade against Communism everywhere. In practice, Eisenhower tempered Dulles's rhetoric with restraint.

## ACCOMMODATING TO THE WELFARE STATE

In domestic affairs, Eisenhower was a middle-of-the-roader, though he leaned to the probusiness right-center of the highway. Eisenhower wanted to limit federal power, return authority to the states, and balance the budget, even if that meant cutting agricultural price supports and reducing defense expenditures. The new administration opened all the national wildlife refuges to gas and oil leasing, and in its first budget doubled funds for the construction of access roads in national forests. While many Americans believed that oil drilled from tidelands belonged to the national government, Eisenhower signed legislation making it available to the states and private interests.

Nevertheless, Eisenhower's middle-of-the-roadism meant refusing the demands of the right for dismantling the New Deal/Fair Deal. Eisenhower was a political pragmatist, remarking that he would like to sell the Tennessee Valley Authority but figuring that "we can't go that far." And he understood that the welfare state met legitimate human needs. Although he declined to use deficit spending to stave off economic downturns, he supported extending Social Security to additional groups of workers and raising the minimum wage. While acting on behalf of business and industry, he accepted and somewhat extended the accomplishments of the New Deal/Fair Deal with the result that little changed in the size and scope of the federal government during his presidency. His acceptance of the welfare state, combined with his propensity for fiscal restraint and limited federal power, added up to a domestic policy that his enthusiasts cheered as Modern Republicanism.

## DEALING WITH MCCARTHYISM

Eisenhower considered Senator Joseph McCarthy's anti-Communism reckless, but he was willing to reckon politically with the climate of McCarthyism. Shortly after taking office, he issued an executive order that tightened loyalty requirements for federal employees at the cost of curtailing their civil liberties. Within a year under the new rules, some 2,200 personnel were ejected from the federal government, none of them a proved Communist. During the spring of 1953, Eisenhower was urged to commute the sentences of Julius and Ethel Rosenberg, who had

been convicted in 1951 of obtaining technical information about the atomic bomb during the war and passing it to the Soviets. (Soviet documents released after the Cold War indicated that he was probably guilty, she probably not.) Eisenhower refused to heed passionate public pleas on the Rosenbergs' behalf, and they were executed in June 1953. The next year, the government found J. Robert Oppenheimer, aside from Albert Einstein the most famous physicist in America, to be a security risk. Many Americans were shocked that not even Oppenheimer, with all he had done to develop the American nuclear arsenal, was immune from McCarthyism; they felt a chill descend on the free and open debate of controversial issues.

McCarthy himself, who headed his own investigative committee now that the Republicans controlled the Senate, hounded alleged subversives, trampling on civil liberties and even suggesting that Eisenhower's first year in office marked a twenty-first year of treason. Early in the spring of 1954, he took on the army, charging that it was infiltrated with Communists because it had promoted a left-wing dentist. But by now, he was running into courageous and influential criticism in the media. Once McCarthy went after the army, Eisenhower, who had been working against him privately, dis-

Senator Joseph McCarthy (standing) maps the location of Communists in the United States at the Army-McCarthy hearings in 1954. The army's chief counsel, Joseph Welch (seated to McCarthy's right), denounced him as a "cruelly reckless character assassin."

creetly encouraged the formation of a special Senate committee to investigate the attempt by McCarthy to obtain special privileges for an aide who had been drafted. The committee's hearings into the dispute between McCarthy and the army ran on TV for some five weeks. They revealed McCarthy's bullying tactics to an audience of millions, especially when he suggested that the law firm representing the army included a young lawyer who had once belonged to a Communist organization. Joseph Welch, a senior member of the firm and chief counsel for the army, rebuked McCarthy for the injury he had done the lawyer, declaring, "Until this moment, Senator, I think I had never gauged your cruelty or your recklessness. . . . Have you no sense of decency, sir, at long last? Have you left no sense of decency?" When Welch finished, the room burst into applause. In December, as a result of the hearings, the Republican-controlled Senate censured McCarthy by a vote of 67 to 22 for conduct "unbecoming" a member of the Senate. McCarthy's hunt for subversives had failed to expose a single spy. McCarthyism waned, and McCarthy himself died in 1957, a broken man.

### THE ELECTION OF 1956

While amid the good economic times many Americans were happy to say, "I like Ike," they liked him personally more than they cared for the Republican Party. In 1954, the Democrats recaptured both the House and the Senate, but in 1956 Eisenhower easily won reelection, trouncing Adlai Stevenson with more than 57 percent of the popular vote and 457 of the 530 votes in the electoral college. The Democrats kept control of Congress, even gaining a seat in each house—the first time since 1848 that a victorious presidential candidate had not carried at least one house on his coattails.

## Eisenhower, Arms, and the Soviets

In keeping with the president's fiscal conservatism and eagerness to achieve a balanced budget, the administration's defense policies continued to rely on high technology, especially nuclear weapons, to deter aggression. Republican policymakers counted nuclear arms cheaper than conventionally equipped manpower and maintained, as had their Democratic predecessors, that they posed a formidable counter to the Communists' overwhelming land forces, which the Free World preferred not to match in any case. In January 1954, Dulles announced the administration's

The launch of an Atlas intercontinental ballistic missile.

strategy for global security, which quickly came to be called the "New Look." The United States would rely on "massive retaliatory power" that could be deployed "instantly, by means and at places of our choosing." It would thus get "more basic security at less cost." To this end, during the 1950s the administration multiplied the country's nuclear arsenal fourfold, to about 6,000 weapons, and to deliver them brought to fruition the programs initiated during the Korean War to develop an intercontinental ballistic missile (ICBM), the Atlas.

### STAYING AHEAD OF THE SOVIETS

By the mid-1950s, the Soviets were known to possess hydrogen bombs and to be progressing toward the development of ICBMs, raising the possibility that they might become capable of launching a surprise attack against the United States. With the aim of deterring such an attack, the air force began developing a new generation of intercontinental missiles, including the solid-fueled Minuteman, which was cheaper than the Atlas, could carry hydrogen-bomb warheads, and—the feature that gave the missile its name—could be launched in retaliation

821

within sixty seconds of an alert, long before Soviet missiles would reach their targets. In 1960, the navy launched the first in a new class of nuclear submarines, built to carry sixteen of the navy's recently developed Polaris missiles. The ensemble of missile and ship would prove to be an essential element in the program of deterrence against surprise nuclear attack.

### ARMS CONTROL INITIATIVES

Eisenhower seemed at times to regard nuclear weapons casually, publicly declaring that he saw "no reason why they shouldn't be used just exactly as you would use a bullet or anything else." Yet shortly after taking office, he had worried to an aide, "We are in an armaments race. Where will it lead us? At worst to atomic warfare. At best, to robbing every people and nation on earth of the fruits of their own toil."

The death of Stalin shortly after Eisenhower took office raised hopes that East-West differences might be resolved through "peaceful negotiation," as the Soviets put it. At the end of 1953, Eisenhower proposed "Atoms for Peace"—a plan to divert fissionable materials for purposes such as electrical power generation—but the Soviets brushed it aside. In 1955, at a summit meeting in Geneva attended by the Soviet Union, Britain, France, and the United States, he called for a commitment to "Open Skies," a system of mutual aerial surveillance that would further diminish the likelihood of surprise nuclear attack. Nikita Khrushchev, an earthy, outspoken party boss who was emerging as the new Soviet leader, rejected the initiative, calling it a patent means of espionage. Still, Khrushchev kept the door open to negotiating areas of mutual interest, declaring in 1956, at the Twentieth Congress of the Communist Party, that war was not inevitable and that the United States and the Soviet Union could peacefully coexist.

### DEMAND FOR A TEST BAN

On March 1, 1954, the United States conducted a hydrogen bomb test, code-named "Bravo," in the Pacific. Within hours, a whitish ash—fallout from the blast—began speckling the *Lucky Dragon*, a Japanese fishing boat that had been some ninety miles from the site of the blast. The boat's crew arrived home suffering from radiation sickness, and by mid-March the world knew of their unlucky fate.

When the *Lucky Dragon* incident occurred, the issue of radioactive fallout was already simmering in the United States. In 1951, the Truman administration had begun testing

atomic weapons in Nevada, using a tract of land larger than the state of Rhode Island that was uninhabited and owned by the government. The Atomic Energy Commission repeatedly assured the public that it had nothing to fear from the radiation released by the test. Indeed, it suppressed or defused scientific information that fallout might in fact be hazardous to health. But complaints about radiation released by the tests came from people downwind from Nevada and Utah and from the residents of Troy, New York, where one evening in 1953 it rained nuclear debris from an atmospheric test in Nevada held just a couple of days earlier. The ill fate of the *Lucky Dragon* transformed their outcries into a national concern and stimulated an increasingly vociferous demand for a ban against the testing of nuclear weapons.

Biologists reported that radioactive substances from thermonuclear fallout were being detected in the soil and in foods (notably, milk), putting people, especially children, at higher risk for birth defects, leukemia, and monstrous mutations. Other scientists held that a test ban would halt further development of atomic weapons and might even encourage agreements to reduce nuclear arms. American sensitivity to the threat was no doubt heightened by a vogue of fear-provoking films that presented science-fictionalized consequences of atomic-induced genetic mutations, including giant ants (*Them!*) and a reptilian monster from the sea (*Godzilla*, an

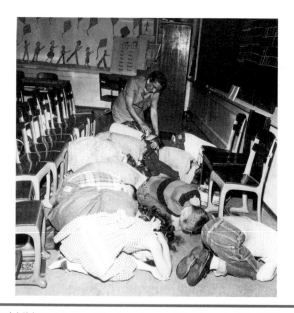

Schoolchildren practice "duck and cover" in a bomb drill, 1957.

import from Japan). Schools taught children nuclear fear by teaching them to "duck and cover"—that is, to crawl under their desks and cover their heads in the event of a nuclear attack. By 1957, polls revealed that Americans had come to support a test ban by almost two to one.

In 1958, Eisenhower initiated test-ban talks with the Soviets at Geneva. Anti-test-ban scientists worked against them, insisting that testing was indispensable for national security, especially for the development of compact warheads suitable for intercontinental missiles. They predicted that the Soviets would find a way to cheat, by testing weapons in huge underground caverns that would muffle the seismic shock waves and make them undetectable by instruments located in the West. Analysts concluded that not all underground tests might in fact be detectable, but that a limited test ban—one that prohibited tests in the atmosphere while allowing underground testing—might be workable. Underground testing would permit further development of nuclear weapons while the abolition of atmospheric tests would get rid of radioactive fallout, thus diminishes public fears of health risks. By the end of the Eisenhower administration, the goal of a limited nuclear test ban was high on the national agenda.

### THE SHOCK OF SPUTNIK

On October 5, 1957, Americans learned that the Soviet Union had launched the world's first artificial earth satellite, *Sputnik*. Twenty-nine days later, *Sputnik II* went up, packed with a maze of scientific instruments and signaling back the condition of a live dog named Laika. On December 6, the United States' attempt to launch its own satellite from Cape Canaveral fizzled in a cloud of brownish black smoke. The *Sputnik*s were taken to demonstrate that the Soviets possessed the rocket and guidance capability for intercontinental ballistic missiles and were well on the way toward putting a man into space.

The Soviet satellites stimulated calls for huge increases in defense spending. Eisenhower, avoiding panic, resisted them. He knew from secret intelligence that the United States was well ahead of the Soviets in intercontinental rocketry. Early in 1958, the U.S. military successfully launched a satellite, but the Soviet satellites prompted Eisenhower to strengthen policies for defense and space. Several weeks after *Sputnik*, he announced in a television address that he had brought

scientific expertise directly into the White House by appointing a presidential science adviser—the first in the nation's history—to assist him in national defense policymaking, with the aid of a President's Science Advisory Committee.

In 1958, the government established the National Aeronautics and Space Administration (NASA) to oversee and coordinate all nonmilitary activities in space research and development. Congress, resolute in its sense of Cold War competition and eager for federal contracts, pushed hard for the space program. Between 1957 and 1961, federal expenditures for research and development more than doubled to $9 billion annually, including a tripling in outlays for basic research to $827 million a year.

## Superpower Shift: The Developing World

In 1956, when Khrushchev affirmed the posture of peaceful coexistence at the Twentieth Party Congress, he also attacked Stalin as a tyrant and called for de-Stalinization of the Soviet Union and Eastern Europe. In the long perspective, Khrushchev's declarations opened a new era in Soviet history, but at the time his deeds contradicted his words. Later that year, taking him at face value, rioters in Poland successfully demanded

Hungarians burn the Soviet flag during their rebellion for freedom, 1956.

the appointment of an anti-Stalinist as head of state, and insurgents in Hungary mounted an outright rebellion against Soviet rule. Although the Hungarians called for American assistance, the administration refrained from providing any while Khrushchev crushed the Hungarian rebellion (in November) with tanks and troops. Policymakers recognized that intervention against Soviet power would risk a war that might escalate into a nuclear exchange. Despite wishing the contrary, modern Republicans, like their Democratic counterparts, were compelled to face the reality that the United States could not roll back the Soviets in Eastern Europe.

Partly for that reason, by the mid-1950s the focus of American attention in foreign affairs was beginning to shift away from Europe to what people then called the "developing world," now identified as the "third world" (denoting the fact that it was at a stage of development below that of the capitalist "first world" and the Communist "second world"). That world was emerging in the wake of nationalist revolts against colonial power and conservative monarchies in Africa, the Middle East, Latin America, and Southeast Asia. Americans expected that the nations liberated from monarchy or empire would want to follow the model of their own democratic and capitalist development. But in truth, many of these governments were weak or oppressive and could veer in any political or economic direction. Since almost all comprised nonwhite peoples, the racism still prevalent in the United States might discourage their friendliness to democratic capitalism. The Soviet Union was alert to these possibilities, and in the mid-1950s initiatives to gain the loyalties of third world countries became part of Cold War competition.

### SECURING THE THIRD WORLD

To protect its interests in these volatile regions, the United States gave economic aid to facilitate development along free-market lines and to create opportunities for American business. Partly for that reason, by the mid-1950s, the focus of American attention in foreign affairs was beginning to shift away from Europe to the developing world, then identified as the Third World (denoting the fact that it was at a stage of development below that of the capitalist First World and the Communist Second World). Several programs provided military aid to help local regimes in combating Communist threats from within as well as from without. The United States also relied on covert action mounted by the Central Intelligence Agency, often against nationalist regimes that were considered

pro-Communist simply because they tried to break the power of landed oligarchies and industrial elites. By 1957, the CIA had multiplied fivefold in the ten years since its founding, stationing 15,000 people throughout the world, and it devoted more than 80 percent of its budget to covert activities.

In the Philippines in 1953, the CIA helped a pro-American anti-Communist defeat a movement of Communist-leaning guerrillas and gain the presidency. In Iran that year, it fomented a successful coup that overthrew the country's independent prime minister, who had threatened the flow of oil to the West by nationalizing British petroleum interests, and installed in his place a successor controlled by the monarch Muhammad Reza Shah Pahlevi. The shah promptly gave the United States and Britain favorable oil concessions and provided the West a loyal ally at the southern edge of the Soviet Union. In 1954, the CIA set its sights on the elected government in Guatemala of Colonel Jacobo Arbenz Guzmán. A reformer with some Communist backing, Arbenz had appropriated more than 200,000 acres belonging to the American-owned United Fruit Company without compensating the company for as much as it claimed they were worth. The CIA drove him from power by arming and training a force of exiles and by providing air support for the invasion.

The United States often sided with dictators in Latin America, thinking they could be counted on as bulwarks against Communism, but the administration's posture fomented increasing anti-Yankee sentiment throughout the region.

### THE SUEZ CRISIS AND THE MIDDLE EAST

In 1954, power in Egypt was assumed by Gamal Abdel Nasser, an Arab nationalist eager to promote the industrialization of his country, partly by constructing the Aswan High Dam on the Upper Nile. In 1956, Nasser nationalized the Suez Canal, which was owned by foreigners, claiming that its revenues would finance the dam. At the end of October, in a joint action, Israeli, British, and French forces attacked Egyptian military installations with the aim of taking back the canal. Condemning the invasion, Eisenhower joined the Soviet Union in getting the United Nations to urge the three invading nations to withdraw. In early November, they pledged to depart and were gone within four months. Egypt retained control of the Suez Canal and eventually built the Aswan Dam.

Eisenhower won high praise at home and abroad for his temperate handling of the Suez crisis, but the episode provoked anti-western sentiment among the Arab nations, adding to the

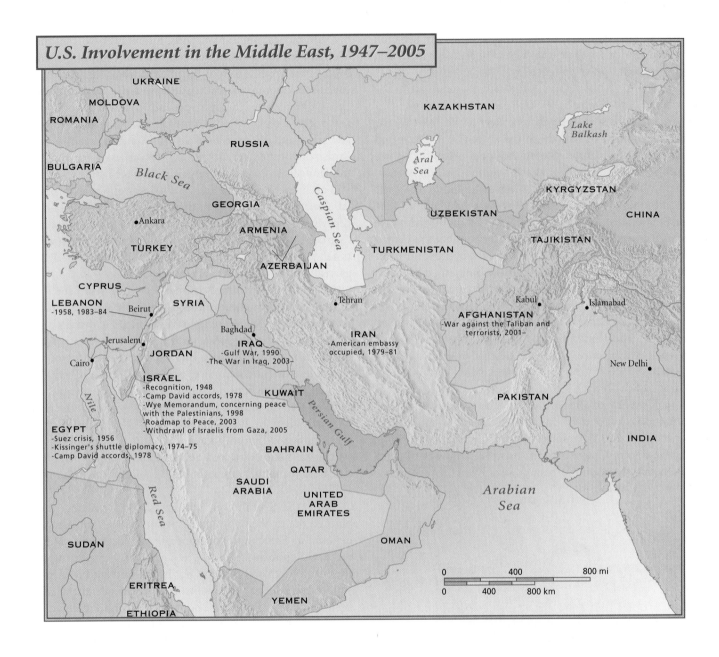

**U.S. Involvement in the Middle East, 1947–2005**

LEBANON
-1958, 1983–84

ISRAEL
-Recognition, 1948
-Camp David accords, 1978
-Wye Memorandum, concerning peace with the Palestinians, 1998
-Roadmap to Peace, 2003
-Withdrawl of Israelis from Gaza, 2005

EGYPT
-Suez crisis, 1956
-Kissinger's shuttle diplomacy, 1974–75
-Camp David accords, 1978

IRAQ
-Gulf War, 1990
-The War in Iraq, 2003–

IRAN
-American embassy occupied, 1979–81

AFGHANISTAN
-War against the Taliban and terrorists, 2001–

resentments they held against the United States for its speedy recognition of the State of Israel in 1948 and its aid to the new nation since. The crisis also greatly weakened the influence of Britain and France in the Middle East, thus leaving the United States as the principal bulwark against Russia and the guarantor of Western oil interests in the region. Eisenhower obtained approval from Congress for what became known as the Eisenhower Doctrine—a commitment to send military aid and, if required, troops to any nation in the Middle East that felt itself threatened by "international Communism."

In July 1958, Eisenhower was prompted to act on this doctrine after nationalists in Iraq overthrew the monarchy and installed an anti-Western regime, the first of many. The pro-Western government in Lebanon, fearing an overthrow there, requested American aid. Eisenhower, eager to show that the United States was ready to defend against further coups, dispatched 14,000 marines. The troops stayed in Lebanon only three months, withdrawing when it became evident that the government was not in jeopardy.

*Worries over Indochina.* In 1954, the Eisenhower administration faced a crisis in Indochina. After World War II, the French had sought to reestablish the authority in the region they had gained as imperialists in the late nineteenth century but had lost to the Japanese at the beginning of the war. In Vietnam, their neocolonial effort was contested by the Vietminh, a broad-based coalition led by Ho Chi Minh, a Communist nationalist. During the war, Ho had mobilized native resistance against the Japanese, and he hoped that the United States would side with his cause against the French. But after Mao Zedong's victory in China and the outbreak of the Korean War, the Truman administration had grown fearful of a potential Communist domination of Vietnam, which was part of Southeast Asia, with its abundant rice, natural rubber, tin, and oil. The United States began providing the French with military assistance, paying 75 percent of their war costs by 1954.

That year, the French found themselves encircled and facing a major defeat at Dien Bien Phu, a cluster of villages in a mountainous valley deep in rebel territory. A number of American officials, including Nixon, Dulles, and the chairman of the Joint Chiefs of Staff, urged Eisenhower to assist the French with ground forces and massive air strikes, possi-

bly with tactical nuclear weapons. Eisenhower worried that if Vietnam fell to Communists, countries surrounding it might become vulnerable. He put the issue in terms that came to be called the "domino theory": "You have a row of dominoes set up, you knock over the first one, and what will happen to the last one is a certainty that it will go over quickly." However, key army and congressional leaders, warning against a new Korea, opposed intervention. Eisenhower was wary of getting the United States bogged down in another land war in Asia and declined to help the French with conventional air strikes, let alone nuclear ones. "You boys must be crazy," he said angrily when shown a plan for nuclear weapons in Vietnam. "We can't use those awful things against Asians for the second time in less than ten years. My God!" In May 1954, the French garrison at Dien Bien Phu capitulated.

At the Geneva peace conference that year, the anti-Communist Vietnamese and the Vietminh agreed that Vietnam would be divided temporarily at the 17th parallel, with each sector under a separate government. The country was to be reunified in 1956 under a single government that would be freely elected. The Eisenhower administration disapproved of the Geneva settlement, fearing that the elections would produce a Vietnam unified under Ho Chi Minh, now the leader of North Vietnam. It countered Ho with Ngo Dinh Diem, the new premier of South Vietnam, a staunch anti-Communist, passionate nationalist, and devout Catholic, who had strong ties in the United States with the Catholic hierarchy and with Dulles.

With the Eisenhower administration's backing, Diem blocked South Vietnam's participation in the 1956 elections, deposed its French puppet emperor, and became president of the new Republic of South Vietnam. Diem sought to revive the South Vietnam economy, but he blocked land reform and suppressed political opponents. He increasingly alienated the predominantly Buddhist population, who resented his Catholicism as well as the corruption and arbitrariness of his regime. By 1958, with the assistance of North Vietnam, a National Liberation Front commonly known as the Viet Cong had formed and had begun waging guerrilla war against Diem.

*Security in Southeast Asia.* In 1954, the French defeat at Dien Bien Phu prompted Secretary of State Dulles to create the Southeast Asia Treaty Organization (SEATO) for the purposes of mutual defense. Unlike NATO, SEATO had no standing armed forces, but it seemed to some critics to involve the

Ho Chi Minh, president of the Democratic Republic of Vietnam, also known as North Vietnam, January 1955.

United States in too open-ended a commitment to resist Communist subversion in Southeast Asia. China continued to preoccupy policymakers, partly because of the Republican right wing's absorption with Asia, partly because the Eisenhower administration assumed, wrongly, that Mao Zedong's Communists must be responsible for the turmoil in Indochina. In January 1955, at Eisenhower's urging, Congress passed the Formosa Resolution, which gave the president blanket authority to use military force to protect Formosa (Taiwan) and the nearby Pescadores Islands, which Mao's forces had been shelling. Mao's saber-rattling coupled with the French defeat in Vietnam encouraged the United States to see the Communist world even more as an expansionist monolith and to extend still further its global commitments in defense of anti-Communist regimes.

## The Cold War, Technology, and the Economy

The economic boom of the 1950s was sparked in no small degree by the high defense spending of the period. Between the end of the Korean War and 1960, defense expenditures ranged between $40 billion and $47 billion annually, accounting for about half the federal budget, compared with a third in 1949. Defense agencies were huge consumers of goods and services (in 1953, the Atomic Energy Commission alone used 12 percent of all the electrical power generated in the United States). In effect, the United States embarked on a course of what has been called "military Keynesianism," after the general theories of the British economist John Maynard Keynes—in this case, stimulation of the economy by military spending—that contributed significantly to fueling innovation, employment, and overall economic growth.

High defense expenditures enjoyed powerful support from senators representing states in the South and the far West. Both regions had long displayed a strong commitment to national defense, but their historic devotion was now reinforced by the defense contracts flowing to states such as Washington, California, Georgia, and Texas. During the 1950s, the South's share of defense contracts more than doubled, rising to 15 percent of the total; California's also doubled, reaching a whopping 24 percent of the total by the beginning of the 1960s. Later studies concluded that during the 1950s defense spending was responsible for 10 percent of growth in the middle South and 21 percent in the Pacific region.

Apart from direct military spending, the rationale of national security helped justify federal expenditures that might otherwise have been more difficult to obtain. The most dramatic consequence of this tendency was the Interstate Highway Act of 1956, which provided $32 billion for 41,000 miles of high-speed roads throughout the country. The act was supported by and was enormously beneficial to the automobile, trucking, concrete, petroleum, and construction industries, among others, but it was also justified on the grounds that it would facilitate the transportation of military supplies and personnel in a national emergency. The measure further encouraged the American devotion to the automobile, enabling people even more than in the past to pile into cars and speed over long distances. It stimulated booms in motels, fast-food restaurants, and shopping centers. By 1960, Holiday Inn and McDonald's, both born in the 1950s, had turned into nationwide chains, harbingers of the trend to franchised businesses that produced H&R Block (tax return preparation), Cut & Curl (beauty salons), and AAMCO (auto repairs). By the end of the 1960s, franchise sales would total an estimated $190 billion.

### DEFENSE AND TECHNICAL COMPETITIVENESS

Policymakers and congressmen were determined that the United States remain ahead of the Soviet Union in all branches of science. Cold War competitiveness deepened the belief, born in World War II, that scientific research and training merited sustained federal encouragement. Both the AEC and partisans of atomic energy in Congress spoke of an "atomic power race" with the Soviets, considering it imperative that the United States beat the Soviet Union in bringing nuclear power to the third world. In 1954, the Republican Congress revised the Atomic Energy Act to permit private ownership of nuclear reactors and the leasing of nuclear materials to industry. The chairman of the AEC told the public that nuclear power would bring "energy too cheap to meter."

Defense agencies and defense-related ones like the AEC continued to provide between 80 and 90 percent of federal monies for research and development in physics, electronics, aeronautics, and computers. By 1960, federal dollars paid for 70 percent of the research and development (R&D) carried out in the electronics business, which now ranked fifth among American industries. During the 1950s, almost all the growth in electronics came from sales to the military services rather than from consumer products.

## The Cold War, Technology, and the Economy

**6 hours 55 minutes to Europe**

Jet passenger airliners speeded flight across oceans and continents, bringing the rest of the world closer for both vacationers and business travelers.

### INDUSTRY AND INNOVATION

The huge investments in military R&D spun off benefits to the civilian economy. For example, in 1959, signifying a leap forward in the aircraft industry, Pan American World Airways started flying passengers nonstop to Europe with jet-powered Boeing 707 planes, whose engines had been developed for the military, cutting the time for the journey from New York to Paris to 6 hours and 55 minutes, half the time of the fastest piston-engine plane. Taking advantage of the spinoffs, many small firms were founded with the aim of developing the knowledge and technologies into marketable products. They were fueled by the new and burgeoning venture capital industry, individuals and financial firms devoted to investing in pioneering companies.

All the while, many established industrial companies increased their spending on programs of scientific research and development. Those that had not previously invested significantly in R&D had been taught by the mobilization of science during World War II that organized research could produce profitable new technologies. An executive at the Ford Motor Company, which had previously invested little in science, told Henry Ford II that "Ford will not have many 'firsts' unless we get a few good thinkers and have a real research department." In mid-1951, Ford established a scientific laboratory in Dearborn, Michigan.

A number of firms, including those with established R&D programs, also saw in innovation a way to prosper without running afoul of the antitrust laws. The new products that might come from research could lead to company growth through diversification rather than through giantism in single areas of production and competition. This strategy prompted greater postwar investment in R&D at mainstay firms of American high technology, including Du Pont, General Electric, Kodak, AT&T, RCA, and IBM. In response to the creation of the Common Market in Europe in 1957 (a group of nations mutually free of tariff barriers), a number of American firms established research laboratories in Europe, thus laying part of the foundation for globalization.

The steel and automobile industries invested heavily in labor-saving technology, so that, for example, between 1945 and 1960 the number of hours required to produce a car dropped by half. During the same period, productivity in manufacturing on the whole increased by 52 percent. Drawing on technical advances that had begun in the 1930s and had been accelerated by military demands during World War II, the chemical industry increasingly found ways to turn petroleum and natural gas—they had replaced coal as its principal natural resource—into a variety of products. Different plastics increasingly replaced glass, leather, wood, steel, aluminum, and paper. New synthetic fibers—notably, polyester and acrylics—increasingly displaced natural cotton and wool in the textiles market, making available clothing that was easier to clean and resistant to shrinkage and wrinkling.

In 1948, a trio of scientists at the Bell Telephone Laboratories had devised the transistor, a technology that would revolutionize electronics (and earn the inventors a Nobel Prize). Picking up on radar-related work during World War II, they discovered that an arrangement of small wires and a semiconducting material could be made to control the flow of energy in electrical circuits. It would thus do the work of vacuum tubes, which were essential to every electronic device from radios to radar; but it was much smaller, consumed much less power, and promised to be more reliable. Although the invention of the transistor was accomplished with the Bell Laboratories' own funds, during the Korean War the military stepped in to speed up its development. By the end of the war, defense contracts had come to support fully half the work, and the military bought almost all the transistors first produced. However, transistors then began entering the commercial market, finding uses in hearing aids, portable radios, and, before long, computers.

## COMPUTERS

The Korean War had prompted a speedup in the development of high-speed digital computers, like Eckert and Mauchly's ENIAC (see Chapter 28), by both IBM and the Atomic Energy Commission. IBM soon brought out a reliable workhorse that defense contractors could use for scientific computing while other firms further developed computers, responding to demand for them in the government as well as in defense-related areas of the commercial market. In 1951, the Remington Rand Corporation delivered a machine to the Census Bureau called UNIVAC (an acronym for "universal automatic computer"), which fed its processors information via magnetic tape instead of punch cards. Early on election night in 1952, setting a precedent for election evenings, a UNIVAC computer at CBS forecast the Eisenhower landslide.

The air force, however, felt the need for a high-speed computer that would respond to inputs of information as they were being generated—that would operate, as computer experts liked to say, in "real time." As a result of the Soviet acquisition of the atomic bomb, the air force wanted to construct a national air warning and defense system across North America, with real-time computers that would detect a Soviet airborne nuclear attack against the United States over the North Pole. An effort to develop such a computer—it was called "Whirlwind"—was under way at MIT, and the air force stepped in with handsome support for it.

The project's prime mover was Jay Forrester, an electrical engineer in his early thirties who had gotten caught up with computers during the Korean War. Whirlwind needed a memory that was far more capacious and readily accessible than any yet devised. Forrester conceived the idea of forging the necessary memory from small magnetizable cores, each capable of rapidly storing and returning coded information. By 1953, the Whirlwind computer was operating successfully with a magnetic core memory, which eventually became an industry standard.

During the 1950s, defense contractors devised additional computer technologies for the early airborne warning system, including printed circuits (the forerunner of the microchip) and sophisticated software—notably, Fortran and Cobol, used for business analyses. Several companies exploited these technologies for the business market, but none so effectively as IBM, which achieved dramatic commercial success in 1953 with its first business-oriented mainframe computer. In 1955, IBM appropriated Forrester's innovation to produce the first commercial machine with magnetic core memory, a behemoth weighing 250 tons, firing 49,000 vacuum tubes, and, like all powerful computers of the day, occupying a large room. By 1960, some 5,000 computers had been delivered in the United States and another 2,000 elsewhere in the world, with IBM's products capturing an increasing share of the market. The company flourished partly because of its far-sightedness and know-how, but as the head of the firm later remarked, "It was the Cold War that helped IBM make itself the king of the computer business."

## AGRICULTURE

The long-running flight from the farm continued, aided and abetted by science and technology. In 1960, only some 8 percent of the employed workforce earned their living directly in agriculture, down sharply from about 12 percent in 1950 (and still more sharply from 20 percent in 1940). Yet that

An IBM office computer, c. 1955.

diminishing percentage produced enough to feed the United States and export a surplus to the rest of the world. The rise in productivity came from increasing mechanization but also from chemical herbicides and a diversifying arsenal of chemical insecticides. In 1958, one-sixth of the country's cultivated land was treated with 100 million gallons of liquid sprays and more than 800 million pounds of insecticide dusts, seeds, and fertilizers.

Larger, more richly capitalized farms were better able than small ones to exploit the tools of science and technology, with the result that the decline in agricultural population was accompanied by the consolidation of smaller, family-type farms into bigger ones. The trend toward agribusiness was further accelerated by federal policies that tied farm-subsidy payments proportionally to farm size and output and thus gave the advantage to more efficient, large-scale farms.

Dramatic shifts were taking place in southern agriculture. Machines for harvesting cotton, peanuts, and tobacco had started becoming available in the late 1940s. In an hour, a human being could pick up to 20 pounds of cotton; a mechanical picker from International Harvester could pick 1,000 pounds. In contrast to the past, southern growers now found several reasons to be interested in such innovation. The wartime migrations out of the region and from country to city within it had depleted the supply of unskilled labor to work the land. Continuing in the postwar years, these migrations created a demand for mechanical substitutes. Moreover, federal policies that sought to protect low-wage farm workers had the effect of encouraging large producers to replace their workers with machines. So did the increasing demands of blacks, including sharecroppers, for decent jobs, housing, education, and voting rights. The more whites perceived blacks as a troublesome presence, the more they welcomed mechanization as a means to drive blacks off the land and out of the region.

In 1950, only 5 percent of the southern cotton crop was harvested by machine; in 1960, 50 percent (and by the end of the 1960s, more than 90 percent). Such mechanization drastically reduced the population of white farm tenants between 1945 and 1959 by 67 percent, of black ones by 71 percent. The shift helped accelerate black migration out of the South into the cities of the North so that by 1970 barely half the American black population lived in the South, compared with 80 percent in 1940.

The mechanization of cotton farming also led to crop diversification. Small farmers had to cope with both competition from mechanized farms and reductions in federal cotton allotments (the number of acres a planter could use to raise cotton and still qualify for federal agricultural subsidies). They thus turned to raising soybeans, grains, peanuts, and livestock. Further diversification was stimulated by a rising national demand for frozen orange juice concentrate, a recent invention, and for poultry. After World War II, chickens, historically a small side business, became the most rapidly expanding element of southern agriculture. An Arkansas farmer marveled, "Who'd a thought that a dadburned chicken could scratch cotton off the land."

A mechanical cotton picker enabled one man to do what had been the work of many.

### "THE GOLDEN AGE IS NOW"

Yet the prosperity of the 1950s was also energized by federal socioeconomic programs, easy credit, population growth, and rising private investment. By 1960, monthly Social Security checks were being sent to 5.7 million families, almost five times more than the number receiving them in 1950. Federally subsidized loans permitted millions to buy homes, while private credit plans allowed them to buy goods such as cars, washing machines, and television sets. In 1960, some 33 million Americans owned homes, compared with about 23 million in 1950, and at least one television set was to be found in about 90 percent of American households, more than had running water or indoor plumbing. Buy-now, pay-later consumer habits were further stimulated by the arrival of the credit card, which Diner's Club introduced in 1950, and by commercial advertising, whose revenues more than doubled during the decade.

Between 1950 and 1960, the gross national product jumped from $295 billion to $526 billion, a 40 percent increase in dollars adjusted for inflation. The economy added almost 7 million jobs, reaching a total close to 66 million, the highest ever in the nation's history, while median family income rose 30 percent. Measured by their incomes, three out of five Americans came to enjoy middle-class standing, twice the proportion as in the 1920s. Some began investing in the stock market, long identified as a preserve only of the rich. In 1960, at least three-quarters of American families owned an automobile, while almost one in six owned two. Expressing the exuberant material prosperity of the era, advertising put a premium on cars that were big and flashy, heavy with chrome and tail fins. The annual inflation rate was less than 3 percent, and between 1955 and 1957 the unemployment rate hovered at just above 4 percent.

Americans took advantage of their prosperity in myriad ways. They had more children, continuing the baby boom and increasing the national population some 19 percent, to 181 million, the highest growth rate since the early century. The mushrooming number of young Americans stimulated the children's clothing and toy industries as well as home and school construction (10 million more children went to school in the 1950s than in the 1940s). The portion of Americans who had completed four years of high school rose from 33 percent in 1950 to 41 percent in 1960, which was more than double the percentage in 1930. Americans devoted one-seventh of the gross national product to entertainment. They bought boxloads of paperback books, and they attended college and professional basketball, baseball, and football games by the millions, creating a market for the new *Sports Illustrated*, which announced that "the golden age is now."

*Health.* The rising economic expectations were accompanied by expanding hopes for the improvement of health. The powerful antibiotic penicillin, developed during World War II, had opened a triumphal era in the battle against disease. In 1944, the American biologist Selman Waksman discovered streptomycin, an effective agent against tuberculosis as well as other diseases of microbial origin that became widely available in the postwar years (and earned Waksman a Nobel Prize). These two discoveries inspired American pharmaceutical manufacturers to increase their annual spending on research for new drugs more than sevenfold between 1949 and 1963. More than 300 prescription drugs were available in 1961 that had not been twenty years earlier, including antibiotics, antihistamines, cortisone, tranquilizers, and chemical therapies against cancer. Surgeons devised means to operate on the living human heart, replacing defective valves and installing pacemakers to regulate the beat. By 1960, the average life span had risen from sixty-three years in 1940 to almost seventy.

The arsenal of vaccines expanded to protect against whooping cough and diphtheria, but the most thrilling triumph was scored against polio. Parents dreaded the disease, since it tended to attack young children, especially in the warm weather of summer, killing some, and paralyzing many others. An epidemic in 1952 struck almost 58,000 children, leaving 1,400 of them dead. It was known from costly studies with monkeys that poliomyelitis was caused by an animal virus that attacked the cells of the nervous system. In Boston in 1949, a trio of scientists succeeded in growing poliovirus in laboratory cultures of human tissue, pointing the way to large-scale production of the coveted vaccine. Jonas Salk, at the University of Pittsburgh Medical School, exploited the new methods to develop a vaccine of dead polio virus. The vaccine was tested, in 1954, on thousands of 6- and 7-year-old children volunteered by their parents as Polio Pioneers.

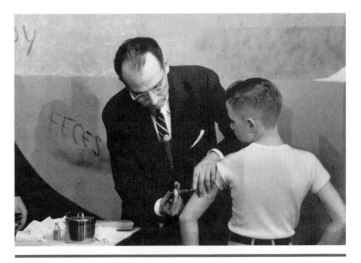

Dr. Jonas Salk administers his polio vaccine, 1955.

They got shots and lollipop rewards in school auditoriums, classrooms, and gyms (in Montgomery, Alabama, black children were inoculated on the open lawn of a white school because they were not allowed inside). On April 12, 1955, the tenth anniversary of the death of Franklin Roosevelt, church bells rang out across the country when Salk announced that the nationwide test program had proved effective. Polio vaccinations quickly became a standard feature of preventive medicine, and by 1962 only 910 cases of the disease occurred in the United States, compared with 58,000 in 1952.

*Labor.* The miracles of medicine were increasingly available to unionized labor, which continued to obtain medical benefits, cost-of-living adjustments, decent working conditions, and pensions. Save for a major battle in the steel industry in 1959, the number of strikes and lost worker-hours dropped significantly over the decade. Unions displayed little militancy, preferring the middle-of-the-road politics of the day. In 1955, the AFL and the CIO merged under the leadership of George Meany, an anti-Communist conservative who was disinclined to try to organize unskilled and semiskilled workers and gave up attempting to organize labor in the South.

Unions remained influential actors in American life and politics, but their power was diminishing. Many Americans

Teamsters president Jimmy Hoffa and supporters, 1958.

gained their impression of unions from *On the Waterfront,* the Academy Award–winning film of 1954 that exposed how mobsters and goons might dominate a longshoreman's union and how ordinary members had to battle to recapture the organization. Congressional hearings on corruption in unions such as the Teamsters, headed by Jimmy Hoffa, led to passage of the Landrum-Griffin Act in 1959, which allowed the federal government to oversee union affairs. The spread of automation in the coal, auto, and steel industries also cost unions members. Moreover, a mounting portion of the workforce—roughly half by the mid-1950s—were public employees, who were prohibited from striking, and white-collar workers (for example, people in sales, banking, advertising, management, research, and clerical occupations), who traditionally resisted unionization. In 1953, labor unions represented 36 percent of the workforce; in 1960, 31 percent.

*Women and Work.* Women were pressured from an array of cultural sources not to undertake careers in the paid workforce. Books, magazines, newspapers, and popular psychiatry all celebrated home, babies, and kitchen. Dr. Benjamin Spock's *Common Sense Book of Baby and Child Care* (1946), by far the dominant book in the field, emphasized that infants and children needed the devotion of full-time mothers, at least until they were three years old. Films replaced the forceful, self-reliant, professionally capable women of the 1940s with saccharine and submissive types. Television might show women as shrewd within their conventional roles—like Alice Kramden, Ralph's wife on Jackie Gleason's *The Honeymooners,* or Lucille Ball in *I Love Lucy,* effective for all her wackiness in seeking her ends; but popular programs such as *Father Knows Best, Ozzie and Harriet,* and *Leave It to Beaver* projected the stereotypical suburban wife: she cheerfully cleaned the house, chauffered the children, volunteered for school or church groups, deferred to her husband's judgment even if he was wrong, and worked for success in his job.

More women went to college, but in 1960 still far fewer than men. Compared with men, relatively few women entered graduate or professional school, many of which had quotas for women or would not admit them at all. In 1950, almost 60 percent of women between ages eighteen and twenty-four were married, compared with 42 percent in 1940. Eisenhower placed twenty-eight women in high government posts, but the appointments signified a continuing tokenism rather than a turn in policy or outlook.

Yet while many women professed to find the life of the stereotypical 1950s housewife fulfilling, others admitted to discontent. The obligations of domesticity left many college-educated women often feeling straitjacketed. Amid the conservative social standards of the day, women did not tend to take such discontent as warrant for divorce. Indeed, in the 1950s, divorce rates fell to a stable 10 per 1,000 married women from their peak—18 per 1,000—of the immediate postwar years. But out of either dissatisfaction with home-bound life or family need, or both, many women defied prevailing standards and went to work.

While women in the workforce had traditionally come from lower-income families, by 1960 a quarter of those whose husbands earned solidly middle-class incomes were employed outside the home, more than a threefold increase since 1950. Women from higher-income families worked to pay for children's education, the second car, or part of the bigger mortgage, or otherwise raise the family's standard of living. Whatever their family's social level, working women were paid less and promoted less frequently than their white male counterparts, although some—for example, those in the United Auto Workers and United Electrical Workers—managed to win better deals for themselves. Although the combination of home duties and outside work often proved stressful, it was turning into a virtually inexorable trend. By 1960, two out of every five women over age sixteen had jobs, double the portion in 1940. Still more striking, the proportion of married women in the workforce had also doubled, reaching 30 percent by 1960; and almost 40 percent of these women had children of school age.

## Migrations, Regions, and the Melting Pot

Roughly one out of five Americans changed domiciles each year. Many migrated across regions, a growing number of them turning south and west to the Sun Belt, the warm states that reached from the old Confederacy to California, still others to the Mountain States and the Pacific Northwest. The vast uprooting added to the popularity of country music, with its nostalgic radio programs and sad songs like those of Hank Williams, whose "Ramblin' Man" and "Lonesome Whistle" told of restless wandering and lost relationships.

Warm temperatures helped lure Americans to the Sun Belt and abundant land helped draw them to the West, but the common attraction in all these regions was their rapidly expanding economies, fueled by a mixture of federal stimulus, local initiative, and, in most places, attitudes favorable to business.

### DEVELOPMENT IN THE SOUTH

During World War II, nonfarm had exceeded farm employment for the first time in southern history, signaling that the South had entered a transitional phase—from a predominantly rural, agricultural economy to an urban, industrialized one like that of the rest of the United States. In the postwar period, the transition continued at an accelerating pace.

Southerners looked to further industrialization partly as a means to provide new employment opportunities for the labor—at least the white labor—that the mechanization of cotton farming was forcing off the plantations. To promote industrial growth, the states created incentives to entice business into the region, providing long-term tax exemptions for new manufacturing facilities, reductions in state corporate taxes, and loans as well as special services for new plants. They established several technological research centers such as the Research Triangle Park in North Carolina and formed industrial development corporations to recruit companies and personnel. They also advertised the region's advantages to corporate firms, often stressing the probusiness climate and relative absence of labor unions. (While about one in four members of the national labor force belonged to unions, the ratio was half that or less in much of the South.) One southern industrial promoter explained, "Hell, what we've been selling is peace and order, tellin' 'em that what we've got down here is stability—friendly politicians who are not going to gut a business with taxes, and workers who are grateful for a job and are not going to be stirring up trouble."

Southern boosters also avidly sought federal dollars, especially for defense. Southern congressmen, holding key committee chairmanships on Capitol Hill by virtue of the seniority system, directed defense appropriations into their districts. In the 1950s, the South's share of prime military contracts roughly doubled, rising to about 15 percent of the total (it would reach 25 percent in the 1970s, when more southerners would be working in defense-related industries than in textiles, synthetics, and apparel combined). Seven of the country's top ten defense contractors managed large facilities in the South, and defense was the single largest employer in four southern states. In 1956, the novelist and Mississippian William Faulkner noted, "Our economy is no longer agricultural. Our economy is the Federal Government."

Defense contracts were awarded to the South primarily for staples—notably, tobacco, food, and coal—rather than for high-technology products that yielded spinoffs into new civilian enterprises. Nevertheless, the combination of native promotionalism and federal spending significantly stimulated state and local economic development. The Lockheed aircraft company's Georgia branch, whose business was overwhelmingly in defense, was the largest industrial organization in the Southeast; it had employees in about a third of Georgia's counties, bought many of its materials from local suppliers, and paid several hundred million dollars a year in wages and salaries. The federal space program brought highly paid professional and skilled workers, increased income, supporting high-technology firms, and population growth to Huntsville, Alabama; Cape Canaveral, Florida; and Houston, Texas (the home of the Manned Spacecraft Center, later the Johnson Space Center).

Several national firms such as the International Harvester Corporation opened factories in the South for the production of agricultural machinery such as tractors and mechanical cotton pickers. Ford and General Motors built plants in Atlanta, Georgia, a gateway to the expanding market in Florida, encouraging businesses that produced tires and batteries to spring up nearby. A number of other national firms established branches in the South, bringing to the region insurance and retirement plans, national wage rates, and managerial know-how. By the end of the 1960s, the historic gap in manufacturing activity between the South and the rest of the country was virtually closed and southern industry, no longer dominated by its extractive sectors, was rapidly diversifying into chemicals, machinery, electronics, and transport equipment.

### THE TRANSFORMING WEST

Enormous growth occurred in the West, spurred by local ambition and by the embrace of Cold War imperatives, including the conviction that national security required dynamic economic development. Federal defense contracts poured into the region, promoting the expansion of existing industries, notably aircraft and ships; nurturing the development of incipient industries, particularly rockets and

electronics; and stimulating the creation of new ones. In Colorado, a defense-oriented chemical industry began to grow around federal installations for research in chemical warfare.

The growth was greatly enabled by federal water and power projects that had originated during the New Deal, proceeded through World War II, and in the peace became a staple of the regional economy. In Washington, the gargantuan Grand Coulee Dam on the Columbia River, completed in 1941, was joined by more than twenty-five more dams built on the river and its tributaries in the quarter century after the war. In California, the Shasta Dam on the Sacramento River, completed in 1944, was the first in a planned system of forty dams and twenty-eight hydroelectric plants. Similar projects were proposed for the Colorado River including the Glen Canyon Dam, in Arizona, which was completed in 1963 (see

The Grand Coulee Dam, on the Columbia River, part of the system that transformed water flow into the electrical power essential for the development of the West.

Chapter 30). The dams were coupled with an extensive network of ditches, reservoirs, and canals constructed to irrigate hitherto arid lands. As a result of federal reclamation projects, in the quarter century after 1945 the amount of irrigated land in the West nearly doubled, reaching almost 37 million acres.

The dam projects often damaged the environment and overrode Native American land rights (see Chapter 30), but, the electrical power they generated fueled the swift development of the region's industries, cities, and suburbs, as did the water pumped from their storage basins. While between 1940 and 1960 the national population increased by 36 percent, that in the arc of states from Texas to California and north through Utah and Nevada to Oregon and Washington jumped by 84 percent. The West was also becoming a region of metropolitan concentrations, including the sprawls centered on Seattle, Portland, Denver, Phoenix, Las Vegas, San Francisco, and Los Angeles. (By 1970, about five out of six people in the Mountain and Pacific Coast states would live in metropolitan areas.)

The new West was exemplified by California, whose economy grew in giant leaps, energized by the construction of waterways and roads, homes and schools, a multicampus university and college system, federal defense contracts, and the dollars generated by agricultural enterprise (the state's largest income producer). By 1960, California supplied the nation with one-third of its fruits and vegetables, while its farm production totaled $3 billion. In 1959, one in four prime military contracts went to California, where the economic importance of shipbuilding, aircraft, rocketry, and electronics now exceeded that of the traditional extractive industries such as mining and lumber. The strength and diversity of the state's economy was enlarged by the radio, film, and television industries centered in Los Angeles that also gave California a high national profile. California was a powerful magnet for migration, attracting the Brooklyn Dodgers to Los Angeles and the New York Giants to San Francisco in 1958. During the 1950s, California's population expanded by almost 49 percent, and by the early 1960s, it would rank as the most populous state.

## THE FLIGHT FROM DOWNTOWN

Within or across regions, people moved from farms to cities and, from cities to suburbs. Although this trend had been evident since early in the century, it now involved far greater numbers and represented

the social diversity of white ethnic America. The suburbs away from downtown were a powerful lure, with their greenery, better public schools, and chance to own a home. Cheap suburban housing was pioneered by the brothers William and Alfred Levitt, who used specialized teams, prefabricated modules such as plumbing systems, and assembly-line methods to erect family bungalows with lawns and yards and modern appliances at the rate of one every sixteen minutes. The houses were set down in planned Levittowns, the first of which opened on Long Island, New York, in October 1947. Suburban growth depended heavily on the construction of such tract housing. New suburban houses accounted for eleven out of every thirteen homes built during the 1950s.

The Federal Housing Administration helped the suburban expansion along, guaranteeing mortgages that required only a 5 percent down payment, and so did the Veterans Administration, which provided mortgages to veterans on even more favorable terms under the G.I. loan program. Suburban living was made easier by the federal, state, and local tax dollars that laid down freeways between suburban towns and urban workplaces. In the 1950s, more than 18 million people moved to the suburbs; in 1960, suburbs were home to almost one-quarter of the American population.

The Long Island Parkway in New York, 1952, an exemplar of the traffic congestion that was becoming a feature of suburban commuting.

835

The trend cost cities dearly. Their business tax bases such as downtown retail stores began to decline as more people spent their earnings in suburban shopping centers. The automobile drove out city public transit, whose share of passenger miles, 35 percent in 1945, would plummet to 5 percent by 1965. In 1949, the federal government began providing funds to cities for urban renewal. Neighborhoods designated as "slums" were razed to make way for office buildings and expressways so that suburbanites could more easily commute to and from the cities by car. By the 1960s, downtowns were turning increasingly into impersonal centers of business dominated by sleek, unornamented skyscrapers, modernist towers of flat glass facades exposing interior structural steel. They were inspired by the architect Mies van der Rohe, whose principal triumph, the Seagram Building (1958), soared above Park Avenue in New York, but many of them amounted to drab glass boxes, giving city centers an aura of facelessness, aloof from ordinary human concerns.

### SUBURBIA AND ASSIMILATION

During the 1950s, immigration subsided as an issue. The number of immigrants was small, averaging 250,000 a year. The percentage of foreign-born in the population, now one out of twenty, was at a low for the century, and so was the proportion of Americans born to at least one immigrant parent. To be sure, in both the suburbs and the cities ethnic loyalties remained powerful. Intermarriage between white minority group members—for example, between Poles and Irish, or Jews and non-Jews—occurred infrequently. However, the contacts—in schools, sports, PTAs, and community groups—of different European minority groups in the suburbs was beginning to break down ethnic differences, especially among the young. Similarly, the mass media provided experiences in common—televised baseball, for example—that spanned social divides.

Frictions between ethnic minority groups and the white, Anglo-Saxon, Protestant majority were also declining. The Cold War encouraged people to think of themselves as united in their Americanism and reinforced the eagerness of numerous immigrant descendants to assimilate to the American mainstream. Films both reflected and advanced the trend, showing Catholic priests, once identified as secretive and conspiratorial, as benign figures, towers of strength to their flocks. The Catholic community's passionate anti-Communism, including the support of many Catholics for Joseph McCarthy,

also commended its members to the Protestant majority. By now, few people thought of groups such as Irish Americans or Italian Americans as racially different. Genetics, anthropology, and psychology had destroyed the scientific underpinnings of that social belief. Ethnic minority group members perceived themselves as "white," and most other Americans saw them that way, too.

### ASIAN AMERICANS

Asian Americans, however, remained a group largely apart. The McCarran-Walter Act of 1952 had removed the long-standing considerations of "race" in eligibility for naturalization, thus permitting Asian immigrants to become citizens. A Japanese American remarked that "the bill established our parents as the legal equal of other Americans; it gave the Japanese equality with all other immigrants . . . a principle we had been struggling for." The act imposed low quotas on the number of people allowed to enter the United States annually from each Asian country, granting the largest quota—185—to Japan. However, laws authorizing the immigration of Asian war brides and political refugees allowed thousands of Chinese, Koreans, Japanese, and Filipinos to enter the United States outside the quotas. Between 1946 and 1965, the Chinese American population almost tripled, reaching 360,000. As a result of both natural increase and the arrival of women dependents, the historically huge imbalance between Chinese American men and women—a ratio of 7:1 in 1920—dropped to 1.3:1 in 1960.

Still, Asian Americans continued to face discrimination in American society. Japanese Americans in California were often unable to regain the property they had lost when they were sent to internment camps during World War II. Because of the Communist victory in China, many Chinese Americans were subjected to surveillance by the FBI and to deportation attempts by federal authorities on grounds that they were subversive. Among those driven out was Tsien Hsue-shen, a brilliant engineer at the California Institute of Technology, who was subjected to house arrest and then returned to mainland China, where he pioneered its missile program.

As with immigrant groups before them, the children embraced America's freewheeling culture, often breaking from the values of their parents, but the ties of culture and family remained powerful. Rather than melding into the suburbs, Asian Americans tended to remain concentrated in their own neighborhoods, especially on the West Coast, earning their living by running restaurants and other small businesses and dreaming of better lives for their children, especially through education.

## THE REVIVAL OF RELIGION

The growth of suburbs helped stimulate a renewal of religious activity. Churches provided places for belonging and identity in the rootlessness of the suburban environment. They were as much social centers as houses of worship. One church advertised, "Lots of acquaintances, not many friends? . . . Meet future friends in church next Sunday." Fortifying the suburban appeal, evangelists combined the old-time religion with new-time packaging, relying on mass mailings and television to spread the gospel. The evangelist Billy Graham called Americans to Christ through regular sermons on radio and television, a nationally syndicated newspaper column, and his Evangelistic Association, a huge operation that late in the 1950s received some 10,000 letters a week and contributions of $2 million a year. Graham's Roman Catholic counterpart was Bishop Fulton J. Sheen, who attracted enormous audiences for his prime-time television program, *Life Is Worth Living.*

In 1950, about one out of two Americans belonged to a church or synagogue; in 1959, about three out of five. Toward the end of the decade, all but 3 percent of Americans declared that they believed in God. Hollywood blockbusters reflected the trend, and so did popular music, with song titles like "I Believe" and "The Man Upstairs." In the *Power of Positive Thinking* (1952), a book that ran on the best-seller list for three years, the Reverend Norman Vincent Peale extolled the marvelous effectiveness of faith for individual self-improvement.

In 1954, Congress added the phrase "one nation under God" to the Pledge of Allegiance, and the next year it agreed to imprint "In God We Trust" on the nation's currency. Amid the climate of the Cold War, churchgoing helped unite Americans in their anti-Communism, a theme that rippled through the preachings of Billy Graham and the homilies of Bishop Sheen, and religion was celebrated as evidence of the superiority of the American way of life.

## OUTCASTS OF AFFLUENCE

Claims about the superiority of the American way of life ignored several plain facts. The prosperity of the day bypassed millions, and for some groups the blessings of liberty remained to be fully realized. Many senior citizens barely survived on low incomes without medical or hospital insurance.

While the portion of Americans who were impoverished declined by a third, more than a fifth—some 35 million people—still lived below the poverty line. Regionally, the poverty rate was highest in the South, and socially, it struck hardest at women heading households and at people of color.

*Hispanic Americans.* During the 1950s, the Hispanic population of the United States grew considerably. Puerto Ricans flocked to the mainland from their native island, drawn by the availability of jobs and low airfares to New York City. By 1960, about a million were living in the East Harlem section of New York, a fourfold increase since 1950. As people of color, they faced discrimination and indignities in housing, employment, schools, and police relations.

At the same time, Mexican Americans were entering the United States legally under the *bracero* program, expanded in the 1950s so that in 1960 these temporary workers made up about a quarter of migrant laborers. Many stayed on after their labor permits expired, joining the thousands of Hispanics who migrated across the southwestern border illegally. The Eisenhower administration, intensifying a program

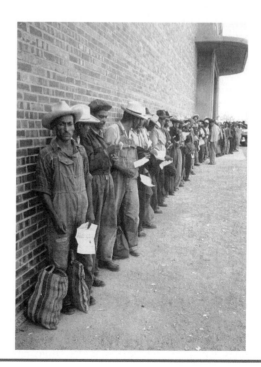

Mexican migrant workers lined up for work in the United States, 1951.

begun in 1950, deported the allegedly illegal immigrants, sending some 5 million back across the Rio Grande by the end of the decade. The roundups were often conducted without due-process protections, and even Mexican Americans in the country legally were often detained.

Although Hispanic organizations were powerless to stop the harassment, some did succeed in getting antidiscrimination laws passed in several southwestern cities. Many also opposed the flood of illegal migrants from the south, fearing that their arrival would undermine their own acceptance and depress wages. Ernesto Galarza, of the National Agricultural Workers' Union, tried to put an end to the *bracero* program and called on Congress to enact legislation guaranteeing farm workers decent wages, working conditions, housing, and health care, but the union's strikes were ineffective. By 1960, more than two-thirds of Mexican Americans lived in urban areas such as greater Los Angeles, leaving the jobs of agricultural labor to the recent arrivals. Hispanics began moving up the socioeconomic ladder and gaining political influence, but still a third lived below the poverty line.

*Native Americans.* Most Native Americans, a total of a half million people by 1960, lived on reservations and in poverty, but service in World War II had schooled some of them in the ways of the outside world and had encouraged them to claim the human rights for which they fought. Returning veterans found it outrageous that even though Native Americans were citizens of the United States, the state constitutions of Arizona and New Mexico still prohibited Indian suffrage in their state elections. One angry Navajo complained, "We went to Hell and back for what. For the people back home in America to tell us we can't vote!" In 1948, Arizona granted them suffrage; fourteen years later, New Mexico followed suit. In 1953, Congress enacted legislation permitting Native Americans to purchase guns and alcohol on and off the reservations, rights previously denied them by federal law.

That year, too, Congress endorsed a two-pronged program for Native Americans that had begun during the Truman years. One prong—"termination"—was aimed at ending their tribal status, the federal aid that went with it, and their standing as wards of the United States. Congress, which had made them citizens in 1924, would also grant them full citizens' rights. The other prong—"relocation"—was aimed at

abolishing the reservations and helping Indians to move to cities. Defenders of the program maintained that it would force Native Americans to care for themselves and to assimilate to the mainstream of society. Pressure for termination also came, however, from mining, agricultural, and lumber interests eager to obtain the remaining tribal lands. Between 1953 and 1960, armed by additional congressional legislation, the Eisenhower administration terminated more than 100 separate tribes or bands and relocated more than 60,000 Indians to urban areas.

Most Native Americans objected to termination. A Seminole petition to President Eisenhower declared, "We are not White Men but Indians, do not wish to become White Men but wish to remain Indians." Some Indians relocated to cities and succeeded; others endured low-paying jobs, inadequate schooling, and racial discrimination; about a third fled back to their tribes. For example, in Wisconsin the Menominees, having agreed to termination, suddenly found themselves subject to state and local taxes they could not pay. They often lost homes as well as tribal lands, and they were unable to afford the hospital and medical care the federal government had previously provided. The government found itself spending three times as much on welfare for the Menominees as it had provided in subsidies before termination. By 1958, the Eisenhower administration announced that no more tribes would be terminated without their consent. However, reloca-

Native Americans meet in the Southwest to consider a U.S. government relocation offer, 1950.

tion continued, and almost half of Native Americans were placed in urban areas by 1967.

*African Americans.* The Korean War had enormously speeded up racial integration of the armed services. After President Truman's 1948 order that they desegregate, the air force had quickly complied; the navy had said it would but dragged its feet; and the army, which included the largest percentage of blacks, had resisted. However, in response to the pressure for accelerating the process of military training, the color line soon disappeared from army bases across the country. In Korea itself, integration of troops was forced by battlefield emergencies. Whites took the situation in stride, and by 1953 nine out of every ten blacks were serving in integrated units.

Outside the military, however, blacks continued to suffer the debilitations of racial segregation and discrimination. The mechanization and consolidation that was transforming southern agriculture pushed African Americans out of farming, consigning them in rural areas to lives of poverty in housing with neither running water nor indoor toilets, and in urban areas to crowded, segregated neighborhoods, poorly paid jobs, or unemployment. Most blacks in the South continued to be barred from voting, and segregation continued to prevail in schools, restaurants, hotels, and most workplaces. Combined with the mechanization of agriculture,

such conditions led about 2 million blacks to migrate north and west. By the end of the 1950s, some 40 percent of blacks lived outside the South, compared with 23 percent in 1940.

While northern blacks could vote, their housing and job opportunities were decidedly limited. They crowded into the central cities, which, as whites moved to the suburbs, turned increasingly into black ghettos. Federal lending agencies discriminated against blacks, making it difficult for them to buy homes or open businesses. Urban renewal was supposed to produce new, low-cost housing, but in practice it turned into what critics termed "Negro removal," accompanied by racial segregation, including heavily black housing projects. Real estate practices and the prejudices of white residents closed most of the newly expanding suburbs to blacks. William Levitt, who refused to sell homes to African Americans in his Levittowns, explained, "I have come to know that if we sell one house to a Negro family, then 90 or 95 percent of our white customers will not buy into the community." When in 1957 a black family tried to move into Levittown, Pennsylvania, they were greeted with a barrage of rocks.

Most blacks could not afford to move into the suburbs anyway. Skilled trade unions—electrical, construction, sheet metal, plumbing—refused to admit them. Although they fared better in the United Auto Workers, an industrial union, they suffered humiliations on the shop floor and were denied a role in the union's leadership. North and South, racism continued to deny African Americans a decent material life as well as dignity and psychic comfort.

Florida segregation laws compelled African Americans to sit in the back of public vehicles like this Tampa bus, 1956.

## Breaking with Conformity

The Soviet triumph with *Sputnik* stimulated a spate of national soul-searching, not about poverty and discrimination but about the country's character and resolve. Sermons, editorials, and articles pronounced America chrome-plated and complacent, lax in educational standards, absorbed in materialism, and neglecting public services in favor of private indulgence. The Soviets, in contrast, were reported to be more disciplined and purposeful—educating their children more intensively, training twice as many scientists and engineers, and achieving a higher rate of economic growth. Many commentators contended with George Kennan, the architect of containment, that the country needed a greater "sense of national purpose" if it

Jasper Johns's *Three Flags*, 1958.

was to compete successfully with the Soviet Union for world leadership.

The post-*Sputnik* expressions of dissatisfaction with Eisenhower's United States were not new, only more intense. Through the decade, observers had been charging that much of affluent white America appeared beset by powerful pressures to conform. They dubbed its younger, college-educated members a "silent generation" in recognition of their lack of outspokenness on public issues and aversion to risk-taking. Yet in attacking conformity, these critics helped generate a culture of dissent from it, an embrace of individualism that permeated the arts and that was complemented by growing rebelliousness in social attitudes among younger Americans.

Even after the waning of McCarthyism, the climate of the Cold War had continued to chill social and political iconoclasm, but the culture of conformity was also fostered by the commercial and industrial ethos of the era. TV had expanded into a mass commercial medium, with annual advertising revenues close to $2 billion by 1961, more than a tenfold increase over the decade. In these pre-cable days, national broadcasting was dominated by three networks, which limited diversity in programming. Fear of alienating viewers and advertisers discouraged the airing of controversial matter. Critics found commercial televi-

sion willing to settle for lowest-common-denominator programming. It was less concerned with enlightenment than with mere entertainment, providing a potpourri of comedies and game shows, some of them unscrupulous. In 1958, it was revealed that two popular quiz shows, *Twenty-One* and *The $64,000 Question,* secretly provided some of their contestants with the answers to high-stakes questions.

Analysts contended that corporate life squashed individuality. The middle manager of a large corporation had become an "organization man," to use the title phrase of the sociologist William H. Whyte Jr.'s influential book of 1956—an employee compelled, in order to rise in the company, to get along with the group rather than assert his own convictions. A Monsanto Corporation training film showing men in white coats in a laboratory remarked, "No geniuses here; just a bunch of average Americans working together." In *The Lonely Crowd* (1950), influential in shaping social ideas through the 1950s, the sociologist David Riesman and his coauthors argued that the "old middle class" had been "inner directed," using an internal "psychological gyroscope" to make moral and personal decisions. By contrast, the "new middle class" was "other directed," seeking "approval and direction from others"—a habit deadly to individuality and independence.

### PERSONAL REBELLION AND LICENSE

Conformity and its consequences were probed critically by novelists and playwrights. In *The Man in the Gray Flannel Suit* (1955), Sloan Wilson suggested that corporate life forced men to give the demands of their jobs priority over their families. Men wept in their seats when they saw Arthur Miller's powerful *Death of a Salesman,* a play (first produced in 1949) that showed how the traveling salesman Willy Loman's hunger to be liked and successful made his life a hollow sham. For the most part, writers were apolitical: rather than argue for social change, their fiction explored individual character, spotlighting the tensions between personal authenticity and the conformist pressures of mass society. Jewish writers—notably Saul Bellow, Philip Roth, and Bernard Malamud—numbered among the most important new novelists of the period. Unlike Laura Hobson, whose *Gentleman's Agreement* (1947) focused on anti-Semitism, or the black novelist Richard Wright, whose *Native Son* (1940) indicted American society for its racism, they probed the conflicts imposed on individuals by upward mobility and materialism, treating them by turns intellectually, comically, or ironically.

American painters made New York City the world center of the graphic arts, forming what has been called an "academy of authenticity." Many of them pursued abstract expressionism, producing compositions of colors and forms that bore no obvious relationship to reality. Such works, using the unconscious and the primordial as rich sources of imagery, indicated a recoil from the socially engaged, politically oriented art characteristic of the 1930s. To be sure, several of these artists insisted on connecting with real objects. Jasper Johns, for example, painted oversize versions of the American flag, an ironic, ambiguous comment on what Americans of the 1950s made into a quasi-religious icon of anti-Communist patriotism. But most practitioners of what one observer called "action painting" seemed concerned with creating their identities in the very act of painting. One of the most famous was Jackson Pollock, whose sensuous canvases of splatters and drips mirrored the violent, rebellious intensity of his own life.

A small group of writers known as the "Beats" turned themselves into a living dissent from conformism. Famous among them was the novelist Jack Kerouac, author of *On the Road* (1957). Written in three weeks on a continuous roll of printer's paper, the book fictionalized the drug-and-sex-laden adventures of Kerouac and several friends as they traveled around the country indulging in spontaneous irresponsibility as they searched for love and meaning. Equally prominent was a friend of Kerouac's, the poet Allen Ginsberg, an open homosexual and political radical who wrote in his transfixing *Howl*, "I saw the best minds of my generation destroyed by madness / starving hysterical naked / dragging themselves through the negro streets at dawn looking for an angry fix." The Beats dressed in simple clothes and sneakers and grew beards; their celebrations of sexuality, alcohol, and drugs repudiated conformity and materialism while asserting the authenticity of individualism.

While Americans of the 1950s did not flaunt sexuality, many tolerated an increasing frankness about it. Popular novels such as the steamy *Peyton Place* (1956) graphically recounted sexual behavior in a New England town; the new magazine *Playboy* included centerfolds of voluptuous nude women and graphically erotic fiction; and among high-art works, Vladimir Nabokov's *Lolita* (1955) narrated the obsession of an older man for the nymphet of the title. The best-selling books by the scientist Alfred Kinsey—*Sexual Behavior in the Human Male* (1948) and *Sexual Behavior in the Human Female* (1953)—reported that both men and women were increasingly having sex earlier, outside of marriage, and in a variety of forms. According to Kinsey, some 10 percent of American males had engaged in homosexuality at some point in their lives; almost half the females in the country had indulged in premarital sex; and a quarter of them had committed adultery before the age of forty. Kinsey's results were controversial at the time, partly on moral grounds, and remain controversial now, mainly on scientific ones, but his extensive data revealed the generally incontrovertible fact that Americans were increasingly active sexually in a variety of ways that defied prevailing standards of middle-class morality.

## YOUNG AMERICA

One of the most popular writers of the 1950s was J. D. Salinger, whose adolescent protagonist in *Catcher in the Rye* (1951) considers the adult world phony and opts out of it by fantasizing a heroic life for himself. Moviegoers watched James Dean in *Rebel without a Cause* (1955) and Marlon Brando in *The Wild One* (1954) portray alienated middle-class youth journeying to the edge with motorcycles and fast cars. A car culture of risk—later memorialized in the film *American Graffiti* (1973)—was a staple of teenage suburban

Marlon Brando exemplified rebellious youth in *The Wild One*, 1954.

life, with its hot-rodding and drag racing, stag-like displays of horsepower arranged at drive-in malt shops. *Blackboard Jungle* (1955) unsparingly portrayed insolent, rebellious high school students in and out of the classroom. News reports made juvenile delinquency seem rampant and some schools and streets appear to be combat zones.

Teenagers found a rebellious culture of their own in music. Ballads remained popular, as did jazz, but what most captured the passionate attention of young Americans was the undisguisedly sexual rock and roll. Like jazz between the wars, rock was another American musical innovation that originated in the rhythm and blues of blacks, who faced barriers in performing it for white media and audiences. It was initially commercialized nationally by white musicians—notably, Bill Haley and the Comets, an all-white band that in 1955 introduced "Shake Rattle and Roll," then "Rock around the Clock," a huge hit with pounding drums and electric guitars. Sam Phillips, a white promoter who loved black music, reportedly said, "If I could find a white man with a Negro sound, I could make a billion dollars." He discovered precisely that man in Elvis Presley, a twenty-year-old native of Tupelo, Mississippi, who had grown up poor and a misfit in Memphis,

Tennessee, and who had an ear for white music, black music, and everything in between. Presley worshiped Brando and Dean. He affected their air of passive alienation, wore peg pants and pink shirts, and pomaded his thick black hair. He sang blues and country in a sultry voice and gyrated as his female fans screamed. Wags dubbed him "Elvis the Pelvis," a singer whose performances, one critic said, were "strip-teases with clothes on." In 1956, Presley's "Heartbreak Hotel" and "Hound Dog" sold millions of records. He drew an audience of some 54 million when he appeared on a national television variety show (with the cameras showing him from the waist up).

Like jazz before it, rock was soon being performed for white audiences by black stars, too, including Chuck Berry, Fats Domino, Little Richard, and Chubby Checker. Sung by blacks or whites, rock spread rapidly through American culture. In the late 1940s, inexpensive vinyl records that played at 45 rotations per minute (r.p.m.) had begun to appear, and with them inexpensive record players. Teenagers, their spending money from odd jobs and parental allowances giving them independent purchasing power, bought 10 million portable record players a year by the late 1950s and helped double the retail sales of records between 1954 and 1960. They also snapped up the new transistor radios, introduced in 1955, which gave them the freedom to listen to what they wanted, without relying on family radio sets. Electric guitars, becoming widely available during the 1950s, were appropriated by the first high school rock bands.

### CENSORSHIP AND THE LAW

Social conservatives deplored the uninhibited sensuality of rock, and they tried to suppress the circulation of sexually explicit writings by appealing to the law. A bookstore owner in San Francisco was prosecuted for selling Ginsberg's *Howl* on the grounds that it was obscene. Federal postal and customs regulations—some went back to the Comstock Act of 1873, which blocked the distribution of obscene materials through the mails—prevented the importation and circulation of controversial materials. So did state and local officials, with the result that Americans often had difficulty getting hold of books with sexual content, including even literary classics such as Henry Miller's *Tropic of Cancer* (1934) and D. H. Lawrence's *Lady Chatterley's Lover* (1932). The Hollywood Production Code continued to discourage the making of films that dealt with sex, drugs, and crime or that treated religion irreverently.

Elvis Presley rocking his teenage audience, 1956.

However, far greater license in expression developed during the 1950s, partly because of the expanding publication of sexually explicit materials, partly because the Supreme Court progressively tore down the legal sanction of censorship. Beginning in 1952, the Court ruled in a series of cases that movies were a form of expression protected by the First Amendment. Although in 1957 the Court held in *Roth v. United States* that obscenity was not constitutionally protected speech, it found in 1959 that a film of *Lady Chatterley's Lover* did not merit suppression for its content. And later that year, after lower federal courts held that a newly released, unexpurgated version of Lawrence's book was not obscene, the U.S. Post Office stopped trying to enforce the Comstock Act.

## Stirrings for Civil Rights

During the heyday of McCarthyism, the chilling of dissent in so many areas of American life likely discouraged African Americans from openly protesting their condition more than they did. Many, like the protagonist in *The Invisible Man*, Ralph Ellison's searing novel of 1952, appeared to cope with their circumstances by privately distinguishing between their authentic selves and the accommodating, often humiliating behavior that white society compelled of them in order to survive. But by the mid-1950s, a tendency to challenge the status quo was emerging in the black South. Returning black veterans brought back with them the experience of the integrated armed services. Television vividly displayed images of the better life. A growing black urban middle class had formed, some of its members educated at the region's black colleges. Accumulating economic power, they felt a mounting impatience with segregation, with the limitations it imposed on opportunity, dignity, and equality. In 1954, their conviction that it was grossly unjust was affirmed by the Supreme Court in its historic ruling against racially segregated education. And the next year, blacks in Montgomery, Alabama, moved to abolish segregation in their city's public transportation.

### BROWN V. BOARD OF EDUCATION

Since the late 1940s, civil rights lawyers had been setting their sights on the system of legally segregated public education. Virtually every student in the South attended a racially segregated school, and so did some students in ten states outside the region. Segregation continued to enjoy the sanction of the Supreme Court's decision in *Plessy v. Ferguson* (1896)—that the provision of racially separate but equal facilities for blacks and whites was constitutional. But primary and secondary schools for blacks and whites were often unequal. White schools in Mississippi, for example, received four and a half times as much money per pupil as did black schools.

The civil rights lawyers had successfully chipped away at *Plessy,* winning several rulings from the Supreme Court that where schools were unequal in facilities and staff, blacks had to be allowed access to the superior white ones. Now, in the early 1950s, they resolved to attack the doctrine of separate but equal head-on. The vanguard lawyer in the drive was Thurgood Marshall, chief counsel for the NAACP, who had been taught at Howard University Law School in the 1930s that the legal system could and should be used to advance the civil rights of African Americans and who had had traveled the South organizing blacks to fight for their rights.

In 1951, the NAACP sued the Board of Education of Topeka, Kansas, challenging the city's segregated public schools on behalf of several black families, including that of thirty-two-year-old Oliver Brown, a veteran, welder, and assistant pastor at his church. By 1952, *Brown v. Board of Education* had reached the Supreme Court. Marshall used the findings of the black social psychologist Kenneth B. Clark that segregation saddled blacks with "a permanent sense of inferiority" to contend that racially separate facilities were by their nature unequal.

The Court was now under the leadership of Chief Justice Earl Warren, a moderate Republican and three-term governor of California whom Eisenhower had appointed to the bench. While serving as attorney general of the state during World War II, Warren had been involved in the removal of Japanese Americans to internment camps, a chapter in his history he regretted deeply. On May 17, 1954, Warren delivered the unanimous decision of the Court: "We conclude that in the field of public education, the doctrine of 'separate but equal' has no place. Separate educational facilities are inherently unequal." On May 31, 1955, the Court gave practical force to its ruling, instructing the states to create public school systems free of racial discrimination with "all deliberate speed."

### WHITE RESISTANCE

Blacks and many whites were cautiously heartened by the Supreme Court's ruling, and some southern moderates

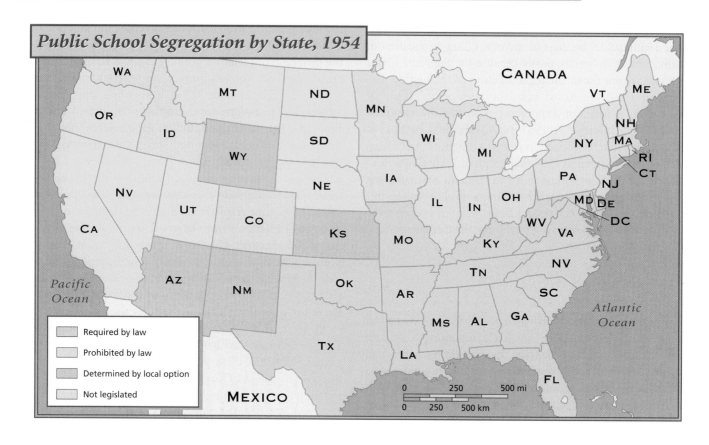

*Public School Segregation by State, 1954*

declared that they would comply with the decision, holding with Governor Jim Folsom of Alabama that "when the Supreme Court speaks, that's the law." By 1957, some 700 school districts, most of them in the border states, had desegregated their schools.

But elsewhere, especially in the deep South, segregationists denounced the ruling, pledging with Governor Herman Talmadge of Georgia to prevent the mixing of Negroes and whites with each other "socially or in our school systems." Waves of antiblack violence broke over the South, including the murder in 1955 of Emmett Till, age fourteen, in Tallahatchie County, Mississippi, because he had whistled at a white woman in a grocery store. His accused killers were arrested, tried, and freed by an all-white jury. The Klan went on the march again, and respectable people organized against the Supreme Court and desegregation by joining white Citizens Councils.

President Eisenhower dutifully desegregated federal installations and sought to integrate public schools and accommodations in Washington, D.C., a federal jurisdiction, but he

privately disapproved of the Supreme Court's ruling in *Brown*. He told reporters that while he accepted it, he would not endorse it, explaining, "I don't believe you can change the hearts of men with laws or decisions." Eisenhower now considered his appointment of Warren his "biggest damn fool mistake." When in 1956 the University of Alabama expelled its first black pupil in direct violation of a federal court order, the president refused to intervene. However, events in Little Rock, Arkansas, soon forced the president's hand.

*Little Rock.* In September 1957, school officials in Little Rock were ready as the result of a federal court order to desegregate Central High School, but Governor Orval Faubus tried to prevent them, using the excuse that integration would threaten public safety. When on the first day of school black children attempted to enroll at Central, a shrieking crowd surrounded them chanting, "Two, four, six, eight, we ain't gonna integrate." Television broadcast the proceedings to the nation, arousing dismay and anger at the vicious display of hatred. Eisenhower reluctantly federalized the Arkansas National Guard and sent 1,100 U.S. Army paratroops to protect the black students in the exercise of their legal right to attend the school.

The next academic year, Faubus, having handily won re-election, closed all the schools in Little Rock, attempting to lease them on a segregated basis to a private school corporation. More than 80 percent of the city's white students went to private schools or schools outside the city, while most black high school students did not attend school at all. Faubus's action helped inspire southerners elsewhere to resist school integration by devising strategies such as diverting public funds to private segregated schools. The Supreme Court soon ruled Faubus's evasive maneuver—and, by implication, others like it—unconstitutional, and in August 1959 the Little Rock public schools were reopened and integrated. Still, between 1958 and 1961, the number of southern school districts that embraced integration fell to only forty-nine, a decrease of some 93 percent from the previous three years. In 1959, Prince Edward County, Virginia, shut down its public schools rather than see them integrated.

## THE MONTGOMERY BUS BOYCOTT

Six months after the *Brown* decision, on December 1, 1955, Rosa Parks, a forty-five-year-old seamstress in Montgomery, Alabama, was seated toward the front of a bus on her way home. When more whites boarded, the driver yelled, "Niggers move back." Although Montgomery's black riders accounted

---

*American Journal*

*Marion Wright Edelman grew up during the 1950s in Bennetsville, South Carolina, a small rigidly segregated town that denied African Americans like herself access to essential public facilities, including the library, playgrounds, and the swimming pool. Defying such discouragements, she attended Spelman College, graduated from Yale Law School, worked for civil rights in Mississippi, and became one of the nation's leading advocates of children's welfare. She had been taught self-confidence, hard work, and social consciousness by her father, Reverend Arthur Wright, who was a minister in the town's Shiloh Baptist Church. Reverend Wright ministered to the social and economic as well as spiritual needs of his flock—for example, building a playground with a merry-go-round at the church so the children would feel their exclusion from the white facilities less keenly. As with many other African American churches in the South, Shiloh Baptist was a center of black-community life and a stimulant to dignity, self-respect, and social reformism among its parishioners.*

*Marion Wright Edelman later recalled the shaping influence of her parents and their church:*

"My belief that I and others could do more than complain, wring hands, or give in to despair at the wrongs rife in the world stems from my parents' examples. Daddy, a teacher-preacher who never raised his voice in the pulpit and who tried to educate our congregation's mind as well as touch its heart, taught that faith required action and that action could be sustained only by faith in the face of daily discouragement and injustice in our segregated society. Because the public playgrounds and many public services were closed to Black children, Mama and Daddy made our church a hub for children. Boy and Girl Scout troops, boxing, skating, ball games, and other physical activities provided outlets for pent-up boys' and girls' energy. Choirs, children's days, pageants, and vacation Bible school made church a welcoming haven rather than a boring chore. And the great preachers and role models invited to speak at Shiloh helped challenge our minds and widen our horizons and remind us of the sky above and of the rainbows in the clouds."

Marion Wright Edelman, *Lanterns: A Memoir of Mentors* (Harper Collins, 1999), pp. 8-9.

for more than three-quarters of bus passengers, they were supposed to surrender their seats to whites. Parks was mild-mannered, reasonable, a faithful member of her church; but she was also a member of the NAACP, and the previous summer she had attended a workshop on race relations where, as she later recalled, she gained the "strength to persevere in my work for freedom." Resentful of the bus company's policies, Parks stayed put in her seat. She was arrested, convicted, and, having refused to pay a $10 fine, was given a suspended jail sentence. Some of Montgomery's black leadership, long angry at the bus system, already had plans for a citywide bus boycott. Now that the respectable Parks had been arrested, they put those plans into effect.

The black churches, the fulcrum of spiritual and social life in the black community, supported the boycott and gave it an inspiring leader: the Reverend Martin Luther King Jr., an eloquent, twenty-six-year-old Baptist minister who had come to Montgomery the year before. Raised in comfort in Atlanta, King learned from his father, himself a prominent minister who had led black voter-registration drives, that racism was to be resisted. At Morehouse College and then at Boston University, King broke away from his father's fire-and-brimstone fundamentalism, embracing a modernist Protestantism committed to combating social inequality and injustice. He found a means to that end in the doctrine of nonviolent resistance to oppression, taking inspiration from the civil disobedience of Henry David Thoreau in the 1840s against the Mexican War and Mohandas Gandhi in the 1940s against British colonial rule in India. While a buttoned-down conservative in dress, King brought to the Montgomery bus boycott a socially transforming courage and vision. He shrewdly recognized that nonviolent tactics against injustice could arouse public opinion and stimulate sympathy for the black cause.

For more than ten months, black Montgomerians organized car pools, rode black-owned taxis whose drivers had agreed to carry passengers at lower fares, or simply walked. A journalist asked an old woman trudging along a road, "Aren't your feet tired?" She replied, "Yes, my feets is tired but my soul is rested." Membership in the white Citizens Council shot up; the Ku Klux Klan marched in the streets; King's house was bombed, and King, along with other leaders of the protest, was arrested, tried, and convicted of leading an illegal boycott. Still, Montgomery's blacks continued the boycott peacefully, persuaded by King that reacting with violence would undermine the righteousness and effectiveness of their cause.

Martin Luther King, Jr., after the Montgomery bus boycott, sits with a white man on one of the city's newly desegregated buses, December 1956.

In the meantime, the leaders of the boycott filed suit, challenging the constitutionality of bus segregation. In mid-November 1956, the Supreme Court held that the city ordinances governing bus seating violated the Fourteenth Amendment. The boycott had hurt Montgomery's businesses, and their leaders were eager to see the dispute settled. Shortly before Christmas 1956, thirteen months after the boycott began, Martin Luther King Jr. sat with a white man at the front of a bus.

The Montgomery bus boycott dramatically demonstrated that black Americans could press the issue of freedom by direct, nonviolent action. It also produced in Martin Luther King Jr. a new leader of protest. The boycott had been supported by black churches throughout the South. In January 1957, aware that their churches constituted an immeasurable resource in the battle for freedom and equality, black ministers from eleven states gathered in Atlanta and founded the Southern Christian Leadership Conference (SCLC), with King as its president.

## CIVIL RIGHTS: BECOMING A MOVEMENT

In the mid-1950s, the stirrings for civil rights were beginning to challenge the self-satisfied conservatism that had descended over the nation, raising questions about the merits of a golden age that excluded so many from its benefits. Amid the Cold War, a growing number of whites were coming to recognize that the United States could not tolerate racial bigotry while trying to sell democracy to a world of nonwhite peoples. Beyond that, the nascent movement for black civil rights aroused the conscience of white Americans, including influential clerics such as Billy Graham, who applauded King's nonviolent campaign for "setting an example of Christian love."

*Voting Rights.* In 1957, responding to the mounting agitation for black freedom, Congress passed the Civil Rights Act, which aimed primarily to protect the right to vote and was the first civil rights legislation since Reconstruction. Although lacking strong means of enforcement, the bill created a Civil Rights Commission and a Civil Rights Division in the Justice Department and empowered the attorney general to intervene on behalf of citizens prevented from voting. A second act in 1960 authorized the appointment of federal referees to protect voting rights. However, the Eisenhower administration did little to exploit the powers of the legislation. By 1961, the act had not added a single southern black to the voting rolls.

*Sit-Ins.* In Greensboro, North Carolina, late in the afternoon of February 1, 1960, four black freshmen from North Carolina Agricultural and Technical State University sat down at the whites-only lunch counter in the Woolworth's department store. The freshmen, aware of the Montgomery boycott, intended to desegregate Woolworth's lunch counter by using nonviolent tactics of resistance. No one served them, and the store closed early. The next day, they returned with twenty-three classmates, and by the end of the week 1,000 students, including some whites, had come to Greensboro.

Within two months, similar protests had erupted in fifty-four cities in nine states. The protesters were often attacked by local whites, including police, who blasted them with high-pressure fire hoses and put them in jail. The protesters nevertheless stuck to their nonviolent strategy and succeeded in desegregating several hundred lunch counters. A meeting of some 300 students over Easter weekend in 1960 led to the formation of the Student Non-Violent Coordinating Committee (SNCC), a protest organization independent of Martin Luther King's Southern Christian Leadership Conference that made sit-ins a major weapon in the battle for civil rights. By now, the agitation for civil rights was becoming a full-scale movement, demanding responses from the nation's conscience and government.

## Setbacks and the Election of 1960

At the end of the 1950s, the Eisenhower administration found itself in trouble. Domestically, its grudging response to the civil rights movement, a seeming abdication of moral and executive responsibility, disappointed many Americans. The national debt was approaching $300 billion, and a recession in 1957–58 produced an unemployment rate of almost 8 percent, the highest since the 1930s. And the administration's conduct of foreign affairs invited mounting criticism.

### THE DOCTRINE OF MASSIVE RETALIATION

Worries about nuclear war remained intense and were reinforced by stories such as Nevil Shute's *On the Beach* (1957), a bleak novel, made into a popular film two years later, that depicts the world after a nuclear war—everyone in the Northern Hemisphere dies from radiation, and the Southern Hemisphere awaits a similar fate. Strategic analysts argued that the threat of massive retaliation was not a realistic answer to Soviet challenges in the third world. Yet between 1953 and 1959, the emphasis on high-technology defense was accompanied by a cost-cutting reduction of the army by more than 40 percent. To the critics, the nation lacked the capacity to wage the kind of "limited wars" that might prove necessary to protect its interests in the third world. In an influential

Students from North Carolina Agricultural and Technical State University start the sit-in movement at Woolworth's in Greensboro, February 1960.

book titled *The Uncertain Trumpet* (1959), General Maxwell Taylor, a former army chief of staff, argued for the doctrine of "flexible response," the ability to fight "brushfire wars" using conventional weapons in remote regions of the world (a doctrine that helped lay the foundation for the later U.S. intervention in Vietnam; see Chapter 30).

### TROUBLE WITH THE SOVIETS

In the summer of 1959, Vice President Richard Nixon went to Moscow and fell into a spirited "kitchen debate" with Khrushchev—so called because it occurred at the kitchen display at the American National Exhibition—over the merits of the American and Soviet systems. While Khrushchev spoke with pride of the Soviet Union's productive women workers, Nixon extolled the merits and affordability of American consumer goods, emphasizing that the washing machines at the display were "designed to make things easier for our women." The next month, Khrushchev traveled to the United States, visiting Iowa cornfields and Camp David, the presidential retreat in Maryland, where he spent three days with Eisenhower. The two men agreed that they would meet together with the leaders of France and Great Britain at a summit in Paris in May 1960. Commentators celebrated the "spirit of Camp David," taking Khrushchev's earthy agreeableness as a sign of a possible thaw in the Cold War.

Hopes were dashed when two weeks before the summit, a Soviet missile brought down an American U-2, a plane that had been conducting overflight surveillance of the Soviet Union. The administration quickly said that the plane had been on a meteorological mission and had lost course. But then Khrushchev announced that the Soviets had the pilot, who, having parachuted to safety, had admitted that he was on a spy flight. Eisenhower now accepted full responsibility for the flight while administration spokesmen insisted that such flights were necessary to the security of the free world and would continue. At the summit, Khrushchev demanded an apology for the flights and the punishment of those responsible. Eisenhower refused, and Khrushchev walked out. The episode, dashing the spirit of Camp David, sent the temperature of the Cold War back down to freezing.

### CUBA

The most disturbing third world upheaval occurred on the American doorstep, in Cuba, which since 1952 had been

Fidel Castro (waving) leads his victorious rebel forces into Havana, Cuba, January 1959.

ruled by the pro-American dictator Fulgencio Batista. Although Vice-President Nixon had celebrated Batista as "Cuba's Abraham Lincoln," he was in fact a corrupt and repressive strongman. During the 1950s, an anti-Batista guerrilla movement under the leadership of Fidel Castro had steadily gathered strength, especially in the countryside; and in January 1959, Castro's forces succeeded in taking power. A young lawyer on the political left, Castro intended to reconstruct Cuba's oligarchic economy and society. When he visited the United States in April, many Americans welcomed him as a hero.

But Castro was already refusing to hold free elections and was jailing and executing opponents. He soon confiscated foreign property, including $1 billion worth of American investments. Announcing that he was a Communist, he allied Cuba with the Soviet Union and pledged support for leftist revolution in Latin America. In 1960, the United States cut off economic aid to Cuba and imposed a boycott on the island, prohibiting imports of Cuban sugar. The CIA began training exiles in Guatemala to invade the island and topple Castro. In a review of its Latin American policies, the Eisenhower administration concluded that more emphasis should be given to democracy, human rights, and economic development in the region, but the shift was too late to repair matters with Castro. In 1961, the United States severed diplomatic relations with Cuba, establishing a break that would last into the twenty-first century.

## THE ELECTION OF 1960

In the congressional elections of 1958, Democrats gained their largest majority in the House since 1936 and scored a sizable margin in the Senate. In 1960, since the Twenty-second Amendment to the Constitution barred Eisenhower from seeking a third term, Republicans pinned their hopes for retaining the White House on Vice-President Richard M. Nixon, who won his party's presidential nomination virtually uncontested and chose as his running mate Henry Cabot Lodge, a moderate Massachusetts Republican.

The leading contender for the Democratic nomination was John Fitzgerald Kennedy of Massachusetts, at age forty-three a young presidential candidate and the first Roman Catholic to make a serious run for the White House since Al Smith's failed attempt in 1928. The grandson of a Boston Irish politico, he was the son of Joseph P. Kennedy, a wealthy businessman who had been Franklin Roosevelt's ambassador to England and was ferociously ambitious to make Jack, the eldest surviving son among his nine children, president of the United States. Jack, often bedridden with a weak back, was a reader, somewhat detached and reflective. After graduating from Harvard, he enlisted in the navy and returned home a war hero for having saved the crew of his PT boat after it was sunk by a Japanese destroyer. Promptly elected to Congress and, in 1952, to the Senate, he initially embraced a hard-line anti-Communism, declined to speak out against Joseph McCarthy, and compiled a mixed record on civil rights measures. When he published *Profiles in Courage* (1956), a book about brave leaders in the American past—it was ghostwritten for him but nevertheless won a Pulitzer Prize—critics observed tartly that he had displayed little courage on key issues in his own time.

Kennedy's youth, meager accomplishments, and Roman Catholicism raised doubts among many Americans about his suitability for the White House. But his candidacy was greatly helped by his family's rich resources and an effective political organization. He met the issue of his Catholicism head-on in the primaries, (notably, in predominantly Protestant West Virginia), crushed his opponents, and won the nomination on the first convention ballot. Aiming for support in the South, he chose as his running mate one of his principal rivals for the nomination—Lyndon B. Johnson of Texas, the Senate majority leader.

Campaigning on the theme of the "New Frontier," Kennedy pledged to "get the country moving again," promising to close an alleged "missile gap" between the United States and the Soviets, accelerate the country's space efforts, boost economic growth rates, and support civil rights. Nixon differed little from Kennedy in age or on the main election issues, but he was somewhat disadvantaged by his red-baiting past. He was also unable to distance himself from the Eisenhower administration's weaknesses (notably, its misstep in the U-2 affair), or answer the charges of a missile gap, which actually did not exist, because proof that it did not was classified. Moreover, Kennedy was the bolder of the two campaigners and better exploited the power of television, by now an essential instrument of politics. In a televised speech to a group of Protestant ministers, he declared that he believed "in an America where the separation of church and state is absolute." In four precedent-setting televised debates that reached an audience of more than 70 million, Kennedy was tanned, confident, and dynamic, while Nixon, recently ill, appeared drawn, haggard, and hesitant. Although radio listeners judged the contest a draw, the TV audience gave the edge to Kennedy, who shot up irreversibly in the polls.

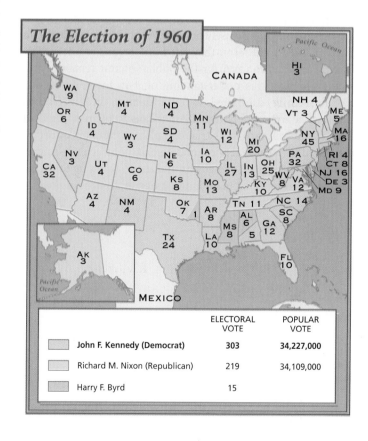

**The Election of 1960**

| | | ELECTORAL VOTE | POPULAR VOTE |
|---|---|---|---|
| | John F. Kennedy (Democrat) | 303 | 34,227,000 |
| | Richard M. Nixon (Republican) | 219 | 34,109,000 |
| | Harry F. Byrd | 15 | |

Still, the election was remarkably close, with Kennedy beating Nixon by only 119,000 votes, winning several key states by hair-thin margins and running behind his party, which maintained its solid congressional majorities even while losing twenty seats in the House. His Catholicism apparently hurt him among southern Protestants, although Johnson's presence on the ticket helped him carry much of the South, including the electoral prize of Texas. Kennedy ran strongly among blacks, and his religion aided him among Catholic voters in the Northeast and Midwest.

### THE EISENHOWER LEGACY

Eisenhower left the White House with a record of considerable accomplishment, at least during his first term. He had ended the war in Korea, kept the United States out of any other shooting conflicts, and sought cooperation with the Soviets. He had legitimized the New Deal/Fair Deal within the mainstream of the Republican Party, run his administration with quiet but effective force, and pursued policies that helped foster remarkable economic growth and technological innovation. Despite the foreign policy failures late in his administration, Eisenhower remained immensely popular. Although several scandals marred his second term, they left him personally untouched. His paramount concern for the public interest remained unquestioned, and his understanding of it in the realm of national security continued to be insightful. In his farewell address, he memorably urged Americans to guard against allowing the "military-industrial complex"—the interconnected system of the armed services and defense contractors—to gain unwarranted influence in government. And referring to the essential importance of maintaining popular control of government even in an era of nuclear weapons and intercontinental missiles, he warned that public policy must not "become the captive of a scientific-technological elite."

Yet to many of his contemporaries, Eisenhower's record was by no means unblemished. In the world at large, he tolerated an increasingly unbridled CIA and favored right-wing dictatorships over left-leaning governments, dealing heavy-handedly in particular with Vietnam and Cuba. Though he was deeply disturbed by the nuclear arms race, he had presided over its acceleration and permitted New Look cost-cutting to distort the nation's means of defense. Now, at the end of the Eisenhower years, some observers saw the country in a state of drift, vexed by urban blight and obligated to make right at long last the condition of African Americans. The old issues left unresolved and the new ones forming out of the 1950s—all were difficult, some were volatile. Together they constituted an emerging, insistent agenda for the United States and its new president.

## Suggested Reading

Stephen Ambrose, *Eisenhower, 2 vols* (1984)

Taylor Branch, *Parting the Waters: America in the King Years, 1954–1963* (1988)

Kenneth Jackson, *Crabgrass Frontier: The Suburbanization of the United States* (1985)

William McDougall, *The Heavens and the Earth: A Political History of the Space Age* (1985)

Elaine Tyler May, *Homeward Bound: American Families in the Cold War Era* (1988)

Ellen Schrecker, *The Age of McCarthyism: A Brief History with Documents* (1994)

Bruce J. Schulman, *From Cotton Belt to Sunbelt: Federal Policy, Economic Development, and the Transformation of the South, 1938–1980* (1994)

# Chapter Review

## Summary QUESTIONS

■ How did the United States seek to prevent Communism from making inroads in the Third World?

■ In what ways was Eisenhower a centrist in foreign and domestic policy?

■ What significant regional changes occurred in the 1950s?

■ What challenges arose to the culture of conformity?

■ What were the tactics and achievements of the emerging civil rights movement?

## Key Terms

McCarthyism (p. 820)

Sputnik (p. 823)

Third World (p. 824)

UNIVAC (p. 829)

Salk vaccine (p. 831)

*Brown v. Board of Education* (p. 843)

## Chronology

| | |
|---|---|
| **1954** | Army-McCarthy Senate hearings. |
| **May 17, 1954** | *Brown v. Board of Education.* |
| **April 1955** | Polio vaccine proves effective. |
| **December 1, 1955** | Rosa Parks arrested, leading to the year-long Montgomery (Alabama) bus boycott. |
| **October–November 1956** | Suez Canal crisis. |
| **November 1956** | Khrushchev crushes Hungarian rebellion. |
| **1957** | Soviets launch the first earth satellite, *Sputnik.* |
| **1958** | President Eisenhower initiates nuclear test-ban talks with Soviets in Geneva. |
| | National Aeronautics and Space Administration (NASA) established. |
| **1960** | Soviet missile brings down American U-2 plane. |
| | Sit-ins begin. |

**Access the *Inventing America* StudySpace at wwnorton.com/studyspace**

PERSONAL PLAN  ■  REVIEW MATERIALS  ■  RESEARCH AIDS  ■  MULTIMEDIA

# REFORM, RAGE, AND VIETNAM:

## 1960-1968

Thousands of Americans marched in cities around the country—as they did here in Washington, D.C. in 1969—to protest the Vietnam War.

## Focus QUESTIONS

- **What was the historical significance of the Cuban missile crisis?**

- **How and why did the civil rights movement change in the 1960s?**

- **What were the goals of the new environmental movement?**

- **What were the major initiatives of LBJ's Great Society program?**

- **What were the arguments for and against the War in Vietnam?**

- **How did the antiwar and countercultural movements affect American society?**

## Kennedy: Idealism without Illusions

Inauguration day 1961 was bright with promise, cold, crisp, the sky a clear blue, and the sun shimmering on newly fallen snow. John Kennedy declared in his address that the "torch has been passed to a new generation of Americans," and in a rejection of the indulgence of the 1950s, he summoned his country to new beginnings, memorably proclaiming: "Ask not what your country can do for you. Ask what you can do for your country. Ask not what America will do for you, but what together we can do for the freedom of man."

Kennedy was handsome and charming, gifted with a throwaway wit and effortless eloquence, the embodiment of action and intellect. Although in chronic pain and regularly medicated because of several ailments, including Addison's disease, a weakening disorder of the adrenal glands, he presented himself to the public as energetic and athletic. His presidency was further assisted by his wife, Jacqueline Bouvier Kennedy, a stylish and beautiful socialite who gave the administration a patina of cultivation and chic, and by news reports about their two small children, Caroline and John Jr. Years later, Americans would learn that Kennedy indulged in extramarital affairs, even while in the White House. But at the time, the press refrained from probing the intimate private lives of presidents. Kennedy was simply "exciting," a student at the University of Nebraska remembered. "You had a guy who had little kids and who liked to play football on his front lawn . . . [who talked] about pumping new life into the nation and steering it in new directions."

Unlike Eisenhower, with his penchant for orderly, decentralized, cabinet-oriented governance, Kennedy gathered power into the Oval Office and followed a freewheeling mode of decision-making intended to facilitate action. His administration included growth-oriented investment bankers, efficiency-minded management experts, and reformist professors and intellectuals. The president also found places for longtime aides from Boston concerned primarily with his political welfare. At his father's insistence, he appointed as attorney general his brother, thirty-six-year-old Robert F. Kennedy, who had entered public life as a staff member for Joseph McCarthy's Senate investigations. Robert had never tried a case in court, but he zealously pursued the administration's interests. The president gave his special assistant for national security, McGeorge Bundy, quick, tough-minded, and recently of Harvard, more authority in foreign affairs than his secretary of state, Dean Rusk, whom he found too cautious. He also permitted live television broadcasts of his press conferences, a first in American history and a practice that allowed him to shape opinion by speaking to the public directly.

As a member of the new generation, Kennedy held attitudes formed by the icy, restraining realities of the Cold War. He was, as his wife said of him, "an idealist without illusions." He was primarily concerned with foreign affairs, the subject to which he devoted most of his inaugural. "We shall pay any price, bear any burden, meet any hardship, support any friend, oppose any foe to assure the survival and success of liberty," he pledged.

## Kennedy: Idealism without Illusions

Kennedy commands one of his televised press conferences, 1962.

Kennedy's arrival in the White House opened an era of profound social transformation, accelerated in part by his clarion call for sacrifice. Thousands of young Americans worked for civil rights at home or signed up for the new Peace Corps, which offered the opportunity at low pay and poor living conditions to assist people in the third world. Yet the movement for change was also accompanied by resistance, turmoil, and often deadly violence.

### KENNEDY AND THE THIRD WORLD

In a speech released two days before Kennedy's inauguration, the Soviet premier, Nikita Khrushchev, contended that Communism would inevitably triumph, and to help it along he promised unreserved Soviet support for "wars of national liberation." Kennedy was eager to foster prodemocratic sympathies in third world countries by helping with their economic development, and he established warm relations with leaders in postcolonial Africa, including some who leaned toward socialism. But the administration was also determined to resist pro-Soviet uprisings while democracy took root. It extended the idea of "flexible response" to include fighting brushfire wars in undeveloped regions, organizing counterinsurgency forces such as the Green Berets, and increasing research in chemical and biological warfare.

*Latin America.* Kennedy regarded the presence of a Communist enclave in Cuba, just ninety miles from the Florida coast, as both an embarrassment and a threat, a potential exporter of revolution to the rest of Latin America. With Eisenhower's approval, the CIA had begun developing a scheme to train exiles from Cuba to invade their country and assassinate Fidel Castro. Despite moral and practical dissents among his advisers, Kennedy allowed the plan to proceed so long as it did not require any direct American intervention. On April 17, 1961, a team of 1,400 Cuban exiles landed at the Bahia de Cochinos (Bay of Pigs) expecting covert air support supplied by the United States, with planes that would take off from Nicaragua with Cuban pilots. But Kennedy, now fearing that the strike would openly implicate the United States, refused to provide the support. Within two days, the island's defenders had routed the invaders. Kennedy took full responsibility for the disaster, recognizing that the action had been poorly planned, incompetently executed, and shaped by a decision-making process that needed repair. But still hoping to get rid of Castro, the administration fostered covert CIA efforts to promote espionage, sabotage, and general mayhem on the island, including Castro's assassination.

Meanwhile, President Kennedy had resolved to blunt the appeal of Communism in Latin America by pressing for social reform in the region. In March 1961, he announced the inauguration of the Alliance for Progress, a $20 billion program of loans for economic development to which the hemispheric nations pledged adherence. Although the Alliance for Progress encouraged land reform and other democratic measures, during the 1960s some of the assistance went to counterinsurgency programs, including training and materiel for Latin American armed forces intent on maintaining internal security.

*Southeast Asia.* The disaster in Cuba made Kennedy cautious in dealing with the instabilities that kept cropping up in the former French Indochina. He refused to intervene militarily in Laos, where pro-Communist rebels were warring against the pro-Western government, believing that Laos was strategically unimportant to the United States. But Kennedy did consider it vital to American interests to defend the anti-Communist government of Ngo Dinh Diem in South Vietnam.

Assuming, like most Americans at the time, that the Soviets and Chinese were backing Ho Chi Minh's drive to "liberate" the South, Kennedy wanted to demonstrate the United States' readiness to resist the spread of Communism in the

## U.S. Involvement in Latin America, 1954–2005

**CUBA**
-Batista is overthrown and Castro assumes power, 1959
-U.S.-sponsored Bay of Pigs invasion, April 1961
-U.S. quarantine of Cuba during missile crisis, October 1962

**HAITI**
-Duvalier exiled, 1986
-Jean-Bertrand Aristide elected president, 1990

**GUATEMALA**
-U.S.-supported overthrow of Arbenz's government, 1954

**DOMINICAN REPUBLIC**
-Rebellion restores power to Bosch, 1965
-Occupation by U.S. military forces, 1965–66

**EL SALVADOR**
-U.S. military advisers support government during 12-year civil war, 1981
-Formal peace agreement, 1992

**GRENADA**
-Extremist coup topples government, Reagan orders invasion, and pro-Western government installed, 1983

**HONDURAS**
-U.S. supports Contra rebels from bases in Honduras, 1981

**NICARAGUA**
-Sandinistas overthrow dictator, 1979
-U.S. (secretly) aids Contra efforts to overthrow Sandinista government, 1981
-Congress forbids military aid to Contras, 1982
-Peace accord, 1989

**PANAMA**
-Start of talks on Canal Zone Treaty, 1964
-Canal Zone Treaty negotiated, 1978
-U.S. invades Panama; arrests Noriega for drug trafficking, 1989
-Control of canal returned to Panama, 1999

**CHILE**
-U.S. tries and fails to prevent election of socialist president Allende, 1970

Gulf of Mexico

Caribbean Sea

VENEZUELA

COLOMBIA

GUYANA

SURINAME

FRENCH GUIANA

ECUADOR

Amazon R.

PERU

BRAZIL

BOLIVIA

PARAGUAY

Atlantic Ocean

URUGUAY

ARGENTINA

Pacific Ocean

0 250 500 mi
0 250 500 km

---

third world. He dispatched a small advisory force of Green Berets to Vietnam and initiated limited clandestine actions against the North. Still, he was wary of American overcommitment in the war. When Diem's regime was threatened in the fall of 1961, Kennedy declined to send additional forces, remarking to an aide that he would eventually have to send more, adding, "It's like taking a drink. The effect wears off, and you have to take another." Yet after becoming convinced that the credibility of American resolve was at stake, he deployed additional troops—making a total of almost 17,000 by November 1963—for noncombat support of the South Vietnamese war effort.

Kennedy tried to persuade Diem to widen his popularity through economic and political reform, but Diem was authoritarian by nature and bolstered in his resistance to change by his brother Ngo Dinh Nhu, a repressive politico, and Nhu's acid-tongued, arrogant wife, Madame Nhu. In mid-June 1963, a Buddhist set himself on fire, the first of several such outcries

A monk sacrifices himself to protest the Diem regime's discrimination against Buddhists, Saigon, 1963.

against the Diem regime. On the face of it, the Buddhists were protesting religious discrimination by the dominantly Catholic authorities, but their uprising drew support from young anti-Western nationalists hostile to the French-speaking hierarchy in charge of the country. That summer, Diem and Nhu cracked down on the dissidents, jailing hundreds of them. A group of South Vietnamese military officers resolved to remove Diem from office, and the Kennedy administration assured them that the United States would accept a coup. The plotters took over on November 1, capturing and killing Diem and his brother. Although Kennedy was upset by the murders, which he had not expected, the United States quickly recognized the new government in Saigon.

### KENNEDY AND THE SOVIETS

In April 1961, the Russians launched Yury Gagarin into near-space orbit and brought him home. Although the United States sent a man into space three weeks later, the flight was only a fifteen-minute ride of less than one orbit from the launch site at Cape Canaveral, Florida. The Russian feat dealt a blow to the prestige of the United States and, by extension, to the image of the capitalist system in its competition with Soviet Communism among nations in the third world. Kennedy, sensitive to the setbacks from the Bay of Pigs and the Russian manned flight, searched for an initiative that

would put the United States ahead of the Russians, and he soon found it.

In late May 1961, in a special message to Congress, Kennedy called for the United States to "commit itself to achieving the goal, before this decade is out, of landing a man on the moon and returning him safely to earth." Pointing to "the battle" for the third world, he emphasized "the impact of this adventure on the minds of men everywhere, who are attempting to make a determination on which road they should take." Many scientists opposed the moon program, called Project Apollo, believing that the moon could be probed more cheaply and effectively with unmanned space vehicles; but their views were overridden by policymakers and other scientists who understood that international prestige—not to mention benefits to the aerospace industry—was at stake. During the 1960s, the United States would spend some $30 billion on Project Apollo—fifteen times more than it had invested in the Manhattan Project—a major feat of engineering that drew on the resources of engineers and scientists, universities, aerospace firms, and hundreds of subcontractors.

*Crisis over Berlin.* Kennedy, fearing that the Bay of Pigs had chilled U.S.-Soviet relations, was encouraged in May 1961 to learn that Khrushchev would welcome face-to-face discussions. In a meeting in Vienna the next month, Khrushchev, taking the measure of Kennedy, appeared to judge him easy to intimidate. Uppermost in Khrushchev's mind was the question of Germany, particularly Berlin, an island of Western capitalism deep in East Germany and an open gateway to the West for some 30,000 East German refugees from Communism a month. He told Kennedy that he intended to sign his own peace agreement with East Germany, which would likely end the West's access to Berlin and its occupation rights in the city. Kennedy replied that the United States would not tolerate such action.

Back in the United States, Kennedy, shaken by Khrushchev's bullying, declared the defense of West Berlin "the greatest testing place of Western courage and will." He tripled draft calls, mobilized 150,000 reservists, and requested an additional $3.2 billion in defense spending. Khrushchev likewise ordered major hikes in Russian defense spending. In mid-August, the East Germans cut off the refugee flow by building a wall of concrete and barbed wire along the line dividing East and West in Berlin. Amid the ensuing uproar, Kennedy avoided escalating the crisis but did send 1,500 troops to West Berlin, a signal that the United States would stand by the city. Through the fall,

The Berlin Wall, erected in August 1961, grimly symbolized the Cold War's separation of East and West.

the Berlin crisis eased, with Khrushchev backing down from his threat to sign a peace treaty with East Germany.

In September, however, the Soviet Union resumed nuclear testing in the atmosphere, breaking a de facto testing moratorium in place among the world's nuclear powers since 1958. Resolved to defend the United States' strategic interests, Kennedy ordered a building up of the nation's strategic arsenal, and in April 1962 a resumption of nuclear testing.

*The Cuban Missile Crisis.* In May, Khrushchev, who had privately called American nuclear behavior "particularly arrogant," sent to Cuba at least three dozen nuclear warheads, missiles capable of carrying them to most of the continental United States, and a contingent of Soviet commanders with independent authority to launch the weapons. He also supplied Castro with antiaircraft missiles and some 42,000 soldiers. Policymakers at the time, including Kennedy, wondered why Khrushchev chose to pursue such a risky course, and historians since then have similarly puzzled over his reasons. Khrushchev, who had inklings of the CIA's efforts against Castro, apparently wanted to bolster Cuba's defenses against a second invasion, which he feared Kennedy might mount, this time with American troops. Khrushchev considered Kennedy young and inexperienced, perhaps likely to let him get away

with an initiative that could also redress the Soviet disadvantage in strategic nuclear forces and offset missiles (called Jupiters) that the United States had begun installing in Turkey after *Sputnik.*

Even as the Soviets installed their offensive missiles, Khrushchev assured Kennedy that they were not doing so, but on October 16, 1962, surveillance data obtained from a U-2 overflight showed that he had lied. Kennedy and the highest-ranking members of his administration began deliberating immediately on how to respond, with the president secretly recording much of the debate on audio tape (transcripts of which became available in the 1990s). The president believed that he could not permit this unprecedented intrusion into the American sphere of interest. If left unanswered, it would encourage Khrushchev to further action, damage American credibility, and surely provoke a savage domestic political reaction. Kennedy was resolved to get the Soviet missiles out of Cuba, one way or another.

In tense meetings during the next six days, the president and his advisers debated how to do this. One faction, including the Joint Chiefs of Staff and, at the outset, Robert F. Kennedy, argued for an invasion or a surprise air strike against the missile bases. Another faction, including Secretary of Defense Robert S. McNamara and State Department officials, argued strongly against that course, one of its members contending that an air strike would be tantamount to inflicting a Pearl Harbor on a small country. The administration eventually resolved on a naval blockade that would prevent Soviet ships from bringing additional military shipments to Cuba, a policy that would demonstrate the U.S. refusal to tolerate the missiles and simultaneously give Khrushchev time to withdraw. On October 22, disclosing the crisis in a major television address, Kennedy announced that he was establishing a blockade and demanding the removal of the missiles and the destruction of their bases. He also warned Khrushchev that the United States would not tolerate any retaliation in Berlin or elsewhere and that a nuclear attack originating in Cuba would require "a full retaliatory response upon the Soviet Union."

Millions of Americans spent the succeeding days fearful that nuclear war might be imminent. American forces mobilized in Florida for an invasion. While the Soviets in Cuba rushed to complete the missile bases, their ships, some presumably carrying additional missiles, neared the island. Kennedy established the blockade line close to Cuba so as to maximize Khrushchev's time for reconsideration. On October 24, the Soviets signaled their ships to halt at sea. The next morning, the Soviet freighters turned around, while vessels without munitions agreed to be stopped and searched on the high seas. Dean Rusk remarked, with a relief that was widely shared, "We're eyeball to eyeball, and I think the other fellow just blinked."

Still, the missiles already in Cuba remained. After several more days of tense maneuvering, the Soviets agreed to remove them on the informal understanding that the United States would remove its Jupiters (which American policymakers had considered obsolete and had been planning to remove anyway) from Turkey. Khrushchev soon brought the missiles home and tore down their bases, although most of the 42,000 Soviet military personnel remained in Cuba. By the spring of 1963, the United States had removed the last of its Jupiters from Turkey, replacing them with the far more effective Polaris missiles carried on a submarine cruising the area. Americans praised Kennedy for his handling of the crisis.

*The Test-Ban Treaty.* Sobered by the face-off, Kennedy was all the more eager for a general nuclear test-ban treaty. He had learned about its advantages from the newly created White House Office of Science and Technology, staffed by scientists working on policy-related technical issues, mainly in national security. Apprised of the threat of nuclear proliferation and the danger of radioactive fallout from nuclear testing in the atmosphere, Kennedy urged in a June 1963 speech that the United States and the Soviet Union stop demonizing each other and join in pursuing their common interests.

That month, Kennedy and Khrushchev agreed to establish a "hot line" between their two countries to reduce the chance that a nuclear war might be ignited by miscalculation or misunderstanding. But the Joint Chiefs of Staff, backed by conservative scientists, insisted that a ban on underground nuclear tests was unpoliceable without more annual on-site inspections than the Soviets would accept. Kennedy compromised, obtaining an agreement with the Soviets and Britain for a test-ban treaty outlawing tests in the atmosphere, outer space, and under water. The Senate ratified the treaty by a vote of 80 to 19, subject to the proviso from the Joint Chiefs that underground testing would continue.

France, which had the bomb, and China, which wanted it, refused to sign the treaty. Moreover, the United States conducted many more tests, although underground, in the 1960s than it had in the 1950s. The Kennedy administration, having

The cartoonist Herblock's plea, May 1963, for Kennedy and Johnson (left) and Khrushchev (right) to put the nuclear genie back in the bottle by agreeing to a nuclear test-ban treaty.

already decided to add ten Polaris-armed submarines to the fleet and to double the Minuteman missile force, continued the buildup and pressed ahead with developing MIRVs—multiple warheads for installation on a single missile, each of them guidable to an independent target. Arms control efforts in the future would have to concern themselves with the systems that delivered nuclear explosives even more than with the explosives themselves. Yet if the treaty did not even slow the nuclear arms race, it did greatly reduce the hazards of radioactive fallout and signaled a thaw in the Cold War.

## Kennedy at Home

Kennedy placed economic growth—a major factor in getting the country moving again and reducing the 7 percent unemployment rate—at the center of his domestic agenda. He won passage of several economic stimulus measures—notably, an increase in the minimum wage (from $1.00 to $1.25 an hour), tax incentives for business, aid to depressed areas, and an expansion of Social Security to more groups of workers. In 1963, he proposed a broad-based tax cut that would stimulate the economy by leaving more money in the hands of consumers and business. Liberal critics faulted Kennedy, pointing out that a broad tax cut would favor business and the well-to-do. Kennedy argued that growth would improve conditions for everyone, including the poor.

However, he had come to recognize that the benefits of aggregate increases in national income tended to bypass many Americans. He learned from Michael Harrington's passionate *The Other America* (1962) that 40 to 50 million Americans, the large majority of them white, lived "at levels beneath those necessary for human decency." Experts found that the poor were marked by one or more of certain characteristics—over age sixty-five, nonwhite, or living in a household headed by a woman or in a little-educated family—and that a "culture of poverty" was transmitted from generation to generation. In the hope of helping both the white and black poor, Kennedy called on his advisers to draw up a plan emphasizing job training, education, nutrition, and direct aid to the poor.

The combination of the Apollo program and the defense buildup helped produce unbalanced budgets and with them the threat of inflation. Kennedy urged wage and price restraints on labor and business. In 1962, he persuaded the steelworkers' union to agree to a new contract with more moderate wage increases than it had obtained previously. He was infuriated when U.S. Steel and five other companies promptly announced price hikes. Declaring war on the industry, Kennedy forced the steel companies to back down.

Kennedy insisted that, having won the presidency by a mere 119,000 votes out of 68 million cast, he had no mandate for a program of sweeping change. Despite the hefty Democratic majorities on Capitol Hill, both houses were dominated by coalitions of Republicans and conservative Democrats, an obstacle to liberal legislation. He did submit several reform measures to Congress, including a federal health care program and federal aid to education, but they failed. Kennedy, never a Senate insider and caring less about domestic issues than about foreign affairs, was disinclined to pressure Congress. He made no headway on Capitol Hill with the broad tax cut, the main economic stimulus of his administration. Still, his spending on defense, a kind of military Keynesianism, helped boost economic growth, and so did the money that poured into the Apollo program, which by 1964 virtually quintupled the NASA budget. On the whole, Kennedy's policies helped initiate a new era of prosperity, marked by a leap in the yearly economic growth rate—between 1961 and 1963, the economy expanded by a robust 13 percent—a decline in unemployment, and an annual inflation rate of less than 2 percent.

## SCIENCE, TECHNOLOGY, AND THE ECONOMY

The economy also benefited from the new knowledge, technologies, and trained scientific manpower generated by public investment in scientific research. Defense and space took the lion's share of the federal R&D dollar, but people identified scientists and engineers as makers not only of bombs and rockets but also of the day's technological miracles—jet planes, computers, direct dial telephoning, transistor radios, stereophonic phonographs, color television, the videotaping that was transforming the coverage of news and sports, and the Xerox machines that were revolutionizing photocopying. Private firms were manufacturing nuclear reactors, spinoffs from the navy's reactors for submarines. Electric utilities, believing them reliable and competitive with fossil-fuel generators, were buying them—between 1963 and 1971, they would order 100 nuclear plants—and using them to power more than a million homes in the United States.

High-technology companies followed close on the heels of local Ph.D. programs—as on Route 128 outside of Boston, where the vitality of the area's remarkable electronic and computer firms was attributed to the scientific might of Cambridge's universities; or along the San Francisco Bay peninsula, where scientists and engineers trained at Stanford University and the University of California at Berkeley spawned a microelectronics industry and staked out the beginnings of Silicon Valley.

Federal funds for research and development continued to climb, reaching almost $15 billion by 1965, accounting for almost one-sixth of

The New Year's Day Rose Parade in 1954 in Pasadena, California, was the subject of the first national color-TV broadcast. Within a year color sets were being sold with larger screens and at lower prices.

the federal budget. The federal money drew many European scientists to the United States, enough to raise cries abroad of an alarming "brain drain."

During the 1960s, corporations increasingly sought growth through exploitation of science and technology (see Chapter 29). The resulting diversification into new products compelled many corporations to adopt a decentralized form of organization, one whose multiple parts could manufacture and distribute the firm's varied products. The move to decentralization intensified as more companies, moving to what came to be called "globalization," invested in overseas operations, either manufacturing or the acquisition of raw materials or both in less developed countries in Latin America, Africa, the Middle East, and East Asia. A central corporate office remained, but its job was to allocate resources among the firm's different parts and supervise their performance. Such tasks were greatly facilitated by computers, which enabled the maintenance of an efficient, decentralized structure spread over a large geographical area.

However, the heavy emphasis on defense R&D disadvantaged the civilian economy to an extent. The electronics industry, for example, increasingly devoted itself to improvements related to performance for military purposes rather than to products likely to appeal to civilian consumers. Defense-oriented firms tended to absorb a disproportionate number of talented scientists and engineers, diminishing the pool available to such basic industries as steel, automobiles, and oil. Some historians find in the emphasis on defense a cause of the United States' later loss of market leadership to foreign countries (notably, Japan) in fields such as consumer electronics and steel. For example, RCA had successfully pioneered the color television tube, and in 1964 American manufacturers commanded 94 percent of the American market for color sets. But RCA's own investment in R&D for consumer electronics steadily diminished in favor of ventures in other areas, including defense. By 1975, American companies' share of the color TV market had dropped to 67 percent in the face of strong competition from Japan and Europe. It would fall by 1987 to just under 17 percent.

## HORIZONS OF HEALTH

Affluence, the march of scientific medicine, and the rise in the number of older Americans all combined to raise the demands Americans placed on the health care system. One in six people over age sixty-five required hospital care, the price of which had doubled in the 1950s. By 1963, with Kennedy's endorsement, medical care for the elderly had won a place on the nation's legislative agenda. By 1967, Congress had also raised the health research budget to $1.4 billion, almost quadrupling the level in 1960.

By the early 1960s, Americans were recognizing that mental illness was a malady to be dealt with openly rather than hidden away in asylums. In 1963, President Kennedy, who had a mentally ill sister, signed the Mental Retardation Facilities and Community Mental Health Centers Act, which provided outpatient services for such problems as alcoholism, unwed motherhood, and delinquency. The law was part of a broader movement to deinstitutionalize the mentally disabled and return them to the community. Advocates of deinstitutionalization expected that, as Kennedy put it, "reliance on the cold mercy of custodial isolation will be supplanted by the open warmth of community concern and capability." Despite these good intentions, however, deficiencies in community support later relegated many of the released inmates to the ranks of the homeless.

## KENNEDY AND CIVIL RIGHTS

John Kennedy did not embrace the civil rights movement when he was in the Senate, and he kept his distance during the first two years of his presidency, finding it a distraction from foreign affairs. He feared that endorsing the movement would alienate southern Democrats (persistently a worry for Democratic presidents wanting to advance civil rights), jeopardize his legislative program, and risk the loss of the 1964 election. Kennedy nominated several hard-core segregationists to federal judgeships in the South and stalled for two years before fulfilling a campaign pledge to end segregation in federally assisted housing with a "stroke of the [presidential] pen."

However, black activism and white violence compelled the administration to act. In May 1961, the Congress of Racial Equality (CORE) launched Freedom Rides on buses into the deep South to spotlight the widespread violation of a recent Supreme Court order outlawing segregation in interstate bus stations. At a stop in Alabama, the Freedom Riders—more than half of them black, many of them students—were beaten with pipes, bicycle chains, and baseball bats; at another, they were mobbed, and the tires of one of their buses were slashed.

Attorney General Robert Kennedy, deciding that the Supreme Court's order had to be enforced, dispatched several

Federal marshals escort James Meredith at the University of Mississippi, 1962.

hundred federal marshals to quell the violence. At his request, the Interstate Commerce Commission prohibited the use of segregated facilities by interstate carriers. He brought Justice Department suits to protect voting rights in 145 counties and authorized department attorneys to appear as "friends of the court" in a broad spectrum of civil rights suits. Still, much to the disappointment of blacks, the attorney general tried to discourage direct action, urging reliance on the ballot and the courts, and refrained from intervening with federal force unless local law enforcement broke down.

Local law enforcement collapsed when, in October 1962, a federal court ordered the University of Mississippi to admit a black air force veteran, James Meredith, who wished to complete his education there. Governor Ross Barnett adamantly opposed the action, and at the university a riotous mob tried to prevent Meredith's enrollment, attacking his escort of federal marshals. Robert Kennedy dispatched 5,000 federal troops to restore order. Meredith went to school under the protection of federal guards, graduating in 1963.

***Birmingham and Beyond.*** The pressure kept mounting on the Kennedy administration to act on civil rights, as black activists, supported by increasing numbers of students and fed-up adults, challenged white racism in cities and towns across the South. Eager to force Kennedy's hand, Martin Luther King Jr. came to Birmingham, Alabama, a thriving business center dominated by rabid segregationists, to initiate demonstrations on Good Friday 1963. In early May, more than a thousand children joined him in a protest march only to be slammed by torrential streams from high-pressure water hoses that the police chief, Bull Connor, had ordered his force to turn on them. Americans were revolted to see television images of children blasted by water, shocked by electric cattle prods, and attacked by snarling dogs. The Kennedy administration quietly negotiated a settlement with Birmingham's anxious business establishment that halted the demonstrations in exchange for the desegregation of stores and lunch counters and the opening of clerical and sales jobs to blacks.

Civil rights protests swept through the South, and the Kennedy administration, worried that the movement might turn more militant, urged national business and civic organizations to pressure their local members to desegregate. The resistance of many white southerners was exemplified by Governor George Wallace of Alabama, who at his inauguration had pledged, "Segregation now . . . tomorrow . . . [and] forever!" and who, in June 1963, defied a federal court order compelling the University of Alabama to admit two black students. President Kennedy won their admission by sending federal troops to Tuscaloosa and enlisting the aid of Alabama's business leaders.

By now, the black revolution had engaged Kennedy's sense of right and wrong. In mid-June, in a passionate television address, he told the nation that civil rights was "a moral issue," at the heart of which was "the question . . . whether all Americans are to be afforded equal rights and equal opportunities." Within a week, Kennedy sent Congress a civil rights bill that aimed primarily at desegregating public accommodations and protecting voting rights.

Thousands of white Americans, many of them college students, had become civil rights activists or sympathizers, drawn to the movement by its moral purpose, the camaraderie of its marches, and its folk-rock music. The young Bob Dylan rapidly emerged in the early 1960s as a leading musical voice, a raspy, sardonic bard of protest who put Americans on notice that "The Times They Are a-Changin.'" Dylan's "Blowin' in the Wind," recorded in spirited harmony by Peter, Paul, and Mary, was the first protest song to make the Hit Parade. In late August 1963, some 250,000 people, including 50,000 whites, gathered in a march for freedom before the Lincoln Memorial, where, along with a rapt national

The huge crowd gathered in Washington for the freedom march filled the space between the Lincoln Memorial and the Washington Monument.

by his wife, Jackie, who redecorated the White House to showcase American art and history and guided the nation on a television tour of the results. The Kennedys hosted elegant evenings for artists, writers, musicians, and scientists. The president celebrated scientific and technological achievement for its own sake, embossing it with a kind of cultural pride.

The Kennedy rhetoric and images resonated with the new generation of Americans, better educated and more affluent than their predecessors, eager for material rewards but hungry for satisfactions beyond materialism for themselves and their children. In the 1960s, Americans grew increasingly concerned about their quality of life, including the vitality of the arts, the face of the urban landscape, and the health of the natural environment.

***Cultural Stirrings.*** The early 1960s marked the beginning of an explosion of high-cultural consumption. Many Americans tuned in to the growing number of FM radio stations, about a quarter of which were nonprofits devoted to broadcasting educational material and classical music. The growth of public television was encouraged by Newton Minow, the new chairman of the Federal Communications Commission, who in his first speech to broadcasters called TV a "vast wasteland." The number of public television stations burgeoned, reaching about 100 by mid-decade and providing a menu of serious music, debate, and drama. Philanthropic foundations—notably, the Ford Foundation, which became the largest patron of the arts in the country—helped vitalize operas, symphony orchestras, repertory theaters, and ballet companies in cities across the country.

Just as art was becoming a part of chic consumer culture, a new school of artists broke from abstract expressionism and began producing what was dubbed "pop art"—paintings, collage, and sculpture in the accessible idiom of the commonplace. One pioneer of the trend was Roy Lichtenstein, who painted canvases resembling comic-strip panels. Another was Andy Warhol, originally a commercial illustrator, who made

television audience, they heard the folksinger Joan Baez soar silver-toned through the movement's anthem, "We Shall Overcome," and Martin Luther King Jr. memorably sermonize, "I have a dream that my four little children will one day live in a nation where they will not be judged by the color of their skin but by the content of their character."

But much of the South was deaf to the impassioned calls for justice. In Jackson, Mississippi, late the same night of the president's speech in June, a sniper gunned down Medgar Evers, an activist in the local NAACP who had been organizing sit-ins in the downtown Woolworth's. In Birmingham, Alabama, less than three weeks after the March on Washington in August, a black church was bombed, killing four girls attending a Bible school class.

## THE QUALITY OF LIFE

By what he said and often by what he did, Kennedy celebrated admirable human endeavor for its own sake, beyond considerations of Cold War competition and economic stimulation. His natural inclinations in this direction were strengthened

*Campbell's Soup Can*, by the pop artist Andy Warhol, 1962.

art out of repetitive images of Campbell's Soup cans, traffic accidents, and faces of the movie stars Marlon Brando and Marilyn Monroe. Critics interpreted pop art as, variously, deadpan satire or celebrations of commercial culture, at once an acceptance of corporate dominance and an ironic commentary upon it. Whatever its intentions, pop art quickly won national attention and commanded skyrocketing prices.

*Architectural Preservation.* Even as the suburbs continued to grow, the architectural fate of the nation's cities began to capture the public's attention. Many objected to urban renewal because it was destroying neighborhoods and communities, often replacing them with modernist structures, tall, faceless piles of steel and glass that lacked human connection to the city life around them. Largely as a result of urban renewal, roughly a quarter of the country's historical pieces of architecture, most of them built before 1830, had been destroyed—at a cost, critics said, to the multiply textured, vibrant qualities of urban life.

The preservation of buildings, practiced in the United States since the nineteenth century, had long been energized by a desire to retain structures associated with important his-

torical figures—for example, George Washington's home in Mount Vernon, Virginia. Now urban Americans agitated to preserve older buildings as such, including the ornamental products of Victorian and Romanesque sensibilities that the modernists despised because of their scale and detail and their integral connection to their architectural surroundings. In the mid-1960s, cities began establishing landmark preservation agencies, and in 1966, Congress passed the National Historic Preservation Act, which stipulated that major historic works of architecture were to be preserved. Across the country, buildings that had outlived their initial purpose were saved by giving them new functions: in San Antonio, Texas, for example, the Lone Star Brewery building became an art museum; in San Francisco, an old chocolate factory was converted to the centerpiece of a retail complex called Ghirardelli Square.

*Environmental Protection.* The concern for quality in life included a renewed emphasis on the value of uncorrupted preserves of nature—forests, streams, deserts, and mountains. The constituency for preservation of nature had been growing since the late 1940s, becoming more democratized than before World War I. Indeed, the country's spreading affluence now gave people the time and means to become consumers of nature. Visiting the national parks, many Americans hoped to find in the unspoiled beauty of sights such as the Grand Teton Mountains relief from the sameness of suburbs, television, and fast-food restaurants.

In the developing West, the federal water and power projects had stimulated resentments. Irrigation tended to favor agribusiness over small farms and ranches. Dams inundated canyons and valleys, many of them belonging to Native Americans, and they angered people who cared about protecting western lands from human damage.

The resentments burst into full view during the early 1950s in the battle over Dinosaur National Monument in northwestern Colorado, near the Utah border. The monument covered hundreds of miles of wild, gorgeously colored canyons carved by the Green and Yampu rivers, part of the Upper Basin of the Colorado River. Since the Truman years, the federal government's plans for the basin included the construction of two dams in Dinosaur, one of them at Echo Park. Western advocates of the dams argued that they were badly needed for the electric power and irrigation that would bolster economic development and national security. Preservationists fought the dams partly to protect the national park system, but mainly to prevent the loss forever of the river canyons of Echo Park itself. In 1956, with the Dinosaur dams becoming a highly controversial environmental issue, Congress passed an omnibus bill authorizing the Upper Colorado Basin project without the two dams, substituting for them a dam at Glen Canyon in Arizona.

The Dinosaur battle united preservationists into a powerful coalition, including enthusiasts of white water, wildlife, and wilderness, and armed them with political, legal, and technical expertise. The victory encouraged them to go on the offensive, lobbying for a law of broad-gauged wilderness preservation to prevent any future Echo Park initiatives. Unlike Eisenhower, Kennedy supported the proposed act, which would pass in 1964. During the 1960s, membership in traditional environmental organizations skyrocketed, the Audubon Society's doubling, the Sierra Club's quintupling.

*Poisons and Pollutions.* Since the late 1950s, gardeners, scientists, conservationists, and state and local officials had been disparately crying out against the public and private spraying of insecticides. They warned that extensive use of the chemicals threatened birds, fish, animals, and human beings, who, as a state agency in Alabama declared, "may get the insecticides from vegetables, milk, or other everyday necessities of life."

The dissidents found a powerful, unifying voice when, in 1962, Rachel Carson, a biologist and gifted writer, published *Silent Spring,* an elegant dissection of the myriad ways that

Rachel Carson tells Congress of the need to curb the sale of chemical pesticides, a goal achieved by the new environmental movement.

herbicides and pesticides, particularly DDT, were poisoning humans and nature. Carson called the chemicals of weed and insect control "elixirs of death," explaining that they killed wildlife, especially birds, as they accumulated in the wild food chain, and that they threatened human health. "For the first time in the history of the world, every human being is now subjected to contact with dangerous chemicals, from the moment of conception until death," she wrote. Despite Carson's credentials, the book was greeted with a barrage of ridicule and denunciation from the chemical industry, parts of the food industry, academic scientists allied with both, and powerful sectors of the media. However, in a report published in May 1963, a special panel of Kennedy's Science Advisory Committee endorsed Carson's main conclusions, especially her view that pesticides, rather than being used until they were proved to be dangerous, should be demonstrated as safe before they were deployed. In 1972, the federal government banned the use of DDT, largely as a result of the outcry that Carson's book had raised.

In the meantime, *Silent Spring* captured enormous attention, prompting the environmental movement to embrace the goals of protecting nature and health against poisonous pollutants. Evidence of pollution seemed to be everywhere. Smog beclouded the cities, and in the countryside green algae and dead fish marked the pollution of streams, the seepage of chemicals and sewage into the soil and lakes. Expectations of good health and longer life spans were rising as conventional sanitation combined with antibiotics appeared to be wiping out infectious disease. There was a corresponding increase in the attribution of noninfectious diseases—notably, cancer—to environmental causes, and a comparable growth in eagerness to wipe the causes out.

## THE THOUSANDTH DAY

On November 22, 1963, John Kennedy and his wife were motorcading in an open car through cheering crowds in Dallas, Texas. Suddenly, around 12:30 P.M., the President crumpled, struck by an assassin's rifle fire in the head and neck. Secret Service men scrambled up over the trunk to shield him as the car sped to a nearby hospital, but he was clinically dead on arrival. The news of the president's death flashed across the country and around the globe. An outpouring of disbelieving sorrow flooded through the United States and the world. Television, aided since 1962 by communications satellites, broadcast the succeeding events in a series of unforgettable images: the capture of a prime suspect, Lee Harvey Oswald, an unstable Soviet sympathizer and champion of Castro; the murder of Oswald in a Dallas police station by Jack Ruby, the owner of a strip joint who said he had been overcome with grief for the slain president; the funeral cortege with its riderless black horse and the brave salute given it by the president's small son; and, finally, the burial at Arlington National Cemetery, where his grieving family lit an eternal flame.

Jackie Kennedy, in an interview that soon appeared in *Life* magazine, likened the Kennedy administration to King Arthur's Camelot, stating that it constituted "a magic moment in American history, when gallant men danced with beautiful women, when great deeds were done, when artists, writers, and poets met at the White House and the barbarians beyond the walls were held back." Perhaps John Kennedy, resistant to illusions, would have been the first to raise a skeptical brow to his widow's mythmaking. He had achieved the test-ban treaty, committed federal powers on behalf of the civil rights movement, gotten the economy moving again; but he had also presided over an escalation of the nuclear arms race, temporized on civil rights, and stimulated the economy with heavy expenditures on missiles and space. At the time of his death, key elements of his legislative program—the tax cut, the civil rights bill, and Medicare—were stalled in Congress.

How Kennedy would have dealt with Vietnam had he not been assassinated is beyond knowing. It is also highly disputed. The government of South Vietnam remained unstable and in danger of losing the war to Ho Chi Minh. Kennedy's defenders argue that in the fall of 1963 he had begun to talk privately of withdrawing American troops from Vietnam after the 1964 election and that he once said in a CBS television interview, "In the final analysis, it is their war. They are the ones who will have to win it or lose it." But he added in the interview that he did not believe the United States should withdraw. Invoking the domino theory, he equated the support of South Vietnam with the defense of Asia, declaring, "This is a very important struggle." Most of his close advisers agreed, and they would bring that view to his successor's administration.

Still, Kennedy's achievements were not inconsiderable for the limited time—the thousand-plus days—he had occupied the White House and for the conservative majorities he had faced on Capitol Hill. His bright wit, ironic humor, and zestful open-mindedness greatly advanced the breakaway from the solemn conformities of the Eisenhower years. He electrified the nation's youth, inspiring many of them to political

engagement; made irreverence fashionable once again; and put the quality of life, including culture and health, on the national agenda. During the months before his death, Kennedy himself appeared to be thinking anew about the fraught issues of war and peace, race and poverty. He was cut down before his contemporaries—or, for that matter, history—could know where he might have tried to lead the country.

## Lyndon Johnson: Taking Charge

Moments after Kennedy was shot, the Secret Service rushed Vice-President Lyndon Johnson to *Air Force One*, where shortly after 1 P.M., when Kennedy was pronounced dead, he was sworn in as the thirty-sixth president of the United States as his wife and Jackie Kennedy, her clothing spattered with blood, looked on. In the harrowing days that followed, Johnson reassured the American people and foreign leaders that the government of the United States was intact and shouldered his presidential duties with surefooted strength. To deal with the storm of questions swirling around the assassination, he promptly appointed an investigative commission under Chief Justice Earl Warren. It concluded in 1964 that the

Lyndon Johnson, with his wife on his right and Jackie Kennedy at his left, takes the presidential oath of office aboard *Air Force One*, November 22, 1963.

murder had in fact been committed by Lee Harvey Oswald and that he had acted alone. Critics then and later challenged these conclusions, claiming that Kennedy was the victim of one kind of conspiracy or another. But most scholars have found no credible evidence for any of these theories and have upheld the judgment of the commission.

Few politicos were as well prepared to take charge of the presidency as Lyndon Baines Johnson. Fifty-five years old, he had spent twenty-four years in Congress, half of them in the Senate, including his last six as majority leader. He began as an acolyte of Franklin Roosevelt and the New Deal—he liked to be called LBJ, just as Roosevelt was known as FDR—but he turned conservative after World War II, defending big corporations, especially those in Texas oil and gas, against big government. At the same time, he steered federal projects like the Manned Spacecraft Center into his state, growing rich himself with the help of his political connections and the shrewd business acumen of his wife, Claudia Taylor ("Ladybird") Johnson. As majority leader, he adopted flexible, middle-of-the-road positions, pursuing a politics of consensus to mobilize the Senate behind Eisenhower's internationalist foreign policy and moderate domestic programs.

Tall and physically imposing, Johnson built consensus with a formidable combination of persuasiveness, intelligence, and instinct for the jugular—what insiders called "the Johnson treatment." His detractors considered him a wheeler-dealer, often devious, cruel, and vindictive. Still, he was capable of generosity and compassion. Before turning to politics, he had taught briefly in a public school with many Hispanic children, and the experience had helped make him a passionate enemy of poverty and the illiteracy and disease that accompanied it. He knew that, as a southerner especially, he had to confront the issue of race, and he felt deeply that blacks suffered from historic wrongs that should be made right. Now he came to the presidency emancipated from the constraints of his southern base, saddened by how he had arrived in office but relishing the opportunity to use his considerable talents, experience, and knowledge of government in service of an expansive view of American possibilities.

### ENACTING THE KENNEDY PROGRAM

Johnson kept Kennedy's cabinet and urged Congress to memorialize the martyred president by moving quickly on his bills for a tax cut and for civil rights. Within four months of taking office, he won passage of a $10 billion tax reduction,

with the result that by 1966 the economy grew by almost another 25 percent, driving unemployment down to 4.5 percent and producing a budget surplus. The civil rights bill, passing the House with equal rapidity, ran into a southern filibuster in the Senate. LBJ intervened, applying the Johnson treatment to key Republicans who then led party centrists to join with northern Democrats to shut off the filibuster and pass the bill.

The most sweeping such legislation since Reconstruction, the Civil Rights Act of 1964 outlawed racial discrimination in public accommodations engaged in interstate commerce such as restaurants and hotels, empowered the attorney general to bring suits against school segregation, and strengthened federal protection of voting rights. The bill also prohibited discrimination in employment on the basis of race, color, religion, or national origin, and it established the Equal Employment Opportunity Commission to enforce the prohibition. In 1965, President Johnson issued an executive order requiring federal institutions and contractors to take affirmative action toward employing more nonwhites, an initiative that promised to enlarge opportunity in every region of the country, including the South, with its large number of federal contracts.

Drawing on the work that Kennedy had initiated, Johnson announced that it was time to declare "unconditional war on poverty in America" with an attack of unprecedented magnitude and scope. The Economic Opportunity Act, which Congress passed in mid-1964, authorized almost $1 billion for a variety of efforts, including Head Start for disadvantaged youngsters and the Community Action Program, whose purpose was to obtain "maximum feasible participation" of the poor in devising and running the antipoverty effort.

### LIBERTY, EQUALITY, AND THE SUPREME COURT

During the 1960s, a cascade of landmark decisions issued from the Warren Court that strengthened political equality and enlarged the scope of civil liberties. In *Baker v. Carr* (1962), the Court held unconstitutional the creation of state legislative districts that made one district grossly unequal in population to another, a malapportionment that gave rural districts in many states greater power than the more populous urban and suburban districts. In several follow-up cases in 1964, the Court laid down the standard of one person, one vote—which meant that every citizen was entitled to equal representation in the legislature. In *Engel v. Vitale* (1962), the Court ruled against officially sponsored prayer in the public schools. It also strengthened freedom of the press, holding in *Times v. Sullivan* (1964) that newspapers that published criticisms of public officials could not be held libelous unless they could be shown to have done so with "actual malice."

The justices ruled unanimously in *Gideon v. Wainwright* (1963) that an indigent defendant charged with a felony must be provided with an attorney at public expense. In a later case, they decided that suspects also had a right to a lawyer when under police interrogation. Dramatically extending these rulings in the case of *Miranda v. Arizona* (1966), the Warren Court found that police had to protect suspects against inadvertent self-incrimination by advising them when taken into custody that they had a right to an attorney and a right to remain silent. In *Griswold v. Connecticut* (1965), the Court struck down state bans on the use of contraceptives by married couples (it would do the same for single people in 1972), finding for the first time that the Constitution established a "zone of privacy" into which it would be "repulsive," as one justice observed, for the state to reach. In the late 1960s, the Court seemed likely to continue its bolstering of political equality and civil liberties, since it now included several Kennedy and Johnson appointees, including Thurgood Marshall, the first black justice.

## TOWARD THE GREAT SOCIETY

***The New Right and the Election of 1964.*** Lyndon Johnson, nominated in his own right for president at the Democratic convention, chose as his running mate Hubert Humphrey, a liberal senator from Minnesota and a spirited campaigner. Johnson ran on the theme of the Great Society, a vision for his domestic agenda that he had begun advancing in the spring. In conception, the Great Society melded the themes that ran through the president's initiatives against poverty and racism, the Supreme Court's enlargements of the meanings of liberty and equality, and the desire in the land for satisfactions beyond material abundance. The Great Society "is a place where the city of man serves not only the needs of the body and the demands of commerce but the desire for beauty and the hunger for community," Johnson said.

The Great Society flew against the tenets of a reenergized conservative movement that was seeking control of the Republican Party. Originating in the 1950s, the movement owed its revival in part to ideologues such as the journalist William F. Buckley, the son of a wealthy right-wing Catholic businessman and himself a fervent anti-Communist and founder of

the *National Review,* a journal devoted to the creation of a New Right. The movement spawned new activist groups such as the Young Americans for Freedom, which espoused views similar to Buckley's. It found adherents among Americans angry at the failure of the United States to roll back Communism, and among antagonists of big government, especially in the Southwest and West, who resented federal intrusions, taxation, and programs for lower-income and minority groups.

By the early 1960s, the New Right was also attracting many white southerners, furious at black gains and the federal role in fostering them. And it was appealing to a growing number of white blue-collar workers in the North, worried that the drive for racial equality would lead to the integration of their workplaces and neighborhoods. During the spring of 1964, these workers voted heavily for George Wallace in the Democratic primaries in Wisconsin, Indiana, and Maryland, helping him win between 30 and 45 percent of the vote in these states and revealing that white resentment against the civil rights movement was gaining political traction. North and South, the renewed conservatism was also stimulated by wrath against the Supreme Court's rulings on integration, censorship, and religion in the schools. Since the late 1950s, parts of the country had been dotted with billboards that read, "Impeach Earl Warren." A congressman from Alabama snapped that the Court had "put the Negroes in the schools and now they've driven God out."

At the Republican convention in July, a conservative coalition, wresting control of the proceedings from moderates, nominated Barry Goldwater, a likable but rigidly right-wing senator from Arizona. A champion of severely limited government, Goldwater wanted to abolish the progressive income tax, sell the Tennessee Valley Authority's steam-generating plants, and make Social Security voluntary. Although decidedly not a bigot, he had voted against the Civil Rights Act and opposed the War on Poverty. He criticized the Supreme Court for showing a lack of judicial restraint in its decisions on school integration, school prayer, and the rights of criminal defendants. Goldwater's candor and élan, his declaration that "extremism in the defense of liberty is no vice," stimulated his followers to passionate enthusiasm.

But many Americans were made apprehensive by his evident desire to turn back the clock to the kind of limited-government Republicanism that Herbert Hoover had exemplified. They were also frightened by Goldwater's shoot-from-the-hip approach to national security, particularly his seeming willingness to threaten the country's adversaries—

"Let Us Continue.."
—LYNDON B. JOHNSON

a Better Deal for You and America...

JOHNSON    HUMPHREY

ELECT Johnson AND Humphrey

VOTE LIBERAL COLUMN "C"

The Johnson-Humphrey ticket won a landslide victory in 1964.

notably, North Vietnam—with the use of nuclear weapons, an impression that the Democratic campaign encouraged. Goldwater faulted Johnson for failing to push for total victory in Vietnam. Johnson reassured the American people, "We are not going to send American boys nine or ten thousand miles from home to do what Asian boys ought to be doing for themselves."

President Johnson, perceived as a stable centrist compared with the extremists of the right, crushed Goldwater, winning 61 percent of the popular vote—breaking the previous twentieth-century record of Roosevelt's majority over Alf Landon in 1936 and losing only six states: Arizona and five in the deep South. Despite his defeat, Goldwater's inroads in the South and the white resentments manifest in the North sounded the early rumblings of a seismic political shift arising from the collision of black aspirations and white resistance. For the moment, however, what counted was the gain of thirty-seven northern Democratic seats in the House, which gave liberals a sufficient working majority to legislate Johnson's Great Society.

*Enacting the Great Society.* During Johnson's presidency, Congress produced a torrent of Great Society legislation, much of it in 1965, inviting comparison to the record legislative pace set during Franklin Roosevelt's first hundred days.

The huge Democratic majorities made the legislative juggernaut possible, but so did the tireless interventions of Lyndon Johnson, the consummate practitioner of consensus politics, who maneuvered the bills through roadblocks with a mixture of cajolery, threats, deal-making, and appeals to the national interest.

A number of measures addressed material issues: Congress established Medicare, a high priority for Johnson, which covered most medical and hospital costs for senior Americans, financing it through additional payments to Social Security; and Medicaid, which offered health care independent of age to the indigent, blind, and disabled. The minimum wage was increased from $1.25 to $1.60 and extended to more retail and service workers. Funds were allocated for the redevelopment of Appalachia, one of the country's most impoverished regions. Other measures provided the first federal scholarship program for undergraduates; authorized federal funds for distribution to schools, including parochial and private ones, on the basis of their numbers of needy children; encouraged the rehabilitation of slums; and financed the construction of low-income housing and rent supplements to low-income families.

Responding to the Great Society's attentiveness to the quality of life, Congress created National Endowments for the Arts and for the Humanities that would subsidize scholarships, museums, and the creative and performing arts and a program of federal support for public radio and television. It empowered the federal government to protect consumers against untruthful labeling and lending practices and to promote health and safety in the workplace. It set automobile safety standards, responding to the outcry stimulated by Ralph Nader's *Unsafe at Any Speed* (1965), a relentless indictment of the auto industry for putting looks and luxury ahead of survivability in a crash. Profoundly reforming immigration law, Congress abolished the preference given to people from northern Europe, opening the gates to all nationals on an equal basis. It established a Department of Transportation, a step toward dealing with metropolitan congestion, and a Department of Housing and Urban Development. The latter department was headed by Robert Weaver, the first African American to serve in the cabinet.

To protect the environment, Congress passed laws to clean up the nation's waters and air, the latter by giving the federal government power to set emissions standards for automobiles (scientists had learned that car exhausts were responsible for a sizable amount of smog). It enacted measures to preserve wild and scenic rivers, establish a national system of trails, and maintain endangered species. In response to a campaign by Ladybird Johnson, it also approved a law intended to reduce the number of highway billboards and get rid of highway junkyards.

*Voting Rights.* Black activists, their expectations heightened after the Civil Rights Act of 1964, wanted equal access to the voting booth in the South perhaps more than to restaurants. But blacks who tried to vote faced loss of jobs and credit, threats of violence, poll taxes they could not afford, and literacy tests administered to make them fail.

In 1964, the Student Non-Violent Coordinating Committee (SNCC) and CORE organized the Freedom Summer Project in Mississippi. The project brought volunteers, many of them white college students, into the state to set up "freedom schools" for black children, register black voters, and create the Mississippi Freedom Democratic Party (MFDP) to challenge the state's white-only regular party structure. The summer workers were arrested and beaten, drawing national attention to the battle for freedom in the state. The disappearance of three of them—Michael Schwerner and Andrew Goodman, both from New York, and James Chaney, a local African American—in June compelled a presidential dispatch of more than 200 federal personnel to search for them; in early August, the officials discovered that they had been murdered, then buried in an earthen dam. At the Democratic convention, the MFDP insisted that its delegates be seated in place of the regulars from Mississippi. Hubert Humphrey pushed through a compromise that gave the MFDP two at-large seats and barred from future conventions delegations from states that denied blacks the ballot. Although the compromise left the MFDP dissatisfied, it signaled a recognition by the national Democratic Party that voting rights loomed next on the agenda of civil rights.

The outcome accelerated a break that had been developing between the SNCC and Martin Luther King Jr.'s Southern Christian Leadership Conference (SCLC). The SNCC, encountering violence in the field and inadequate protection by federal law enforcement agencies, considered the SCLC, which was dominated by ministers, too conservative and ready to work with whites. The SNCC's leadership felt themselves, one observer put it, "the vanguard of a revolution which seeks to transform the system while King seems to be in the middle of an effort to reform it." The SNCC's increasing militancy, however, helped make King more active in pursuit of political and economic power for blacks.

In January 1965, King and the SCLC came to Selma, Alabama, a town of about 30,000 people, to join the SNCC in organizing mass protests that would dramatize the need for federal action on behalf of voting rights. Although blacks made up about 50 percent of the voting-age population, only 1 percent of them had managed to register to vote. The protesters were arrested when they marched to the Selma courthouse. When 600 of them, having resolved to petition Governor Wallace, strode across a bridge on the way to Montgomery, state troopers teargassed them, then clattered through the scattering crowd on horseback, whacking them with whips and clubs. The assault, televised nationally, outraged the nation. Within days, President Johnson, in an address to Congress, called for passage of a voting rights bill, declaring that the cause of the protesters "must be our cause,

Whites and blacks march for voting rights from Selma to Montgomery, Alabama, March 1965.

too" and bringing lumps to the throats of millions watching on television when he concluded, "We *shall* overcome."

The Voting Rights Act of 1965—signed by President Johnson in August 1965, in the same room in the Capitol where President Lincoln had signed the Emancipation Proclamation—abolished discriminatory literacy tests, provided federal officers to assist black voters to register, and authorized the Justice Department to suspend any test and to use federal examiners to register qualified black voters in counties where less than half the eligible black population was unregistered. The measure was complemented by the Twenty-fourth Amendment, ratified the year before, which abolished poll-tax requirements in federal elections, and by a Supreme Court decision in 1966 that outlawed poll taxes in all elections. By 1969, the percentage of black adults registered to vote in the South had jumped dramatically, reaching more than 60 percent in Alabama, Georgia, Louisiana, and Mississippi. The number of black voters across the South tripled, totaling 3.1 million. The black exercise of the ballot helped defeat segregationist officials and compelled white candidates to court black voters. Over time, it would have a transforming effect on southern politics and the realization of black aspirations.

***The Revival of Feminism.*** During the 1960s, the women's movement jolted back to life, winning gains under the Great Society and bringing about irreversible changes in what women expected of themselves and of their treatment. One source of the revival was the 1963 report of a Presidential Commission on the Status of Women. Addressing the issue from the orientation of labor, the report documented that women were paid less than men for the same work and were poorly represented in managerial or professional careers. Women, though roughly half the population, accounted for only 7 percent of the nation's doctors, fewer than 4 percent of its lawyers, and only a minuscule percentage of its scientists. The commission's findings reflected the fact that 36 percent of American women were working, and that an increasing number of those working had children—in 1960, 20 percent with youngsters under age six, 40 percent with children between ages six and seventeen. Its recommendations included paid maternity leaves, tax deductions for child care, and child care services for all income groups.

The feminist revival was also stimulated by the civil rights movement. Many young women involved in the movement were inspired by the strength, independence, and bravery of the black women of all ages who helped energize it. They took

to heart its claims to equality, acquired the self-confidence to pursue them, and learned the strategy and tactics of protest. Yet women in the movement found that they were expected to make the coffee but not to participate in decision-making. "The only position for women in SNCC is prone," Stokely Carmichael declared. Sexually exploited and relegated to second-class status, many women graduated from the civil rights effort convinced that the drive for equality had to be extended to gender.

The constituency for feminism was greatly increased by Betty Friedan's best-selling 1963 book *The Feminine Mystique.* Friedan, a suburbanite and mother with a background in labor journalism, described the mystique as a cluster of cultural assumptions—that women were by nature passive, subordinate, and nurturing, ideally suited to the domestic roles of making a home and raising children but unsuited for careers in business or the professions. Although millions of women led materially comfortable lives in the suburbs, Friedan argued, their conformity to the mystique left them with feelings of emptiness, suffering from "the problem that has no name." Friedan contended that women had to be free to pursue careers outside the home, embrace "goals that will permit them to find their own identity."

The feminine mystique was actually not so pervasive as Friedan believed, especially among lower-income and minority women, but her book electrified many middle-class, educated women. Beginning in the 1960s, thousands of women

Betty Friedan, the president of NOW, presents the case against sexual discrimination to a group of women in 1966. Many women later told Friedan that her ideas had changed their lives.

joined "consciousness-raising" groups, gathering to recount their experiences and explore their dissatisfactions. The groups cropped up in cities and on college campuses across the country and often led to efforts to create day care centers or women's health collectives. The group sessions taught women that "the personal is political," that many of their personal difficulties derived from social causes and had political remedies. Friedan's thesis, intensified in the consciousness-raising movement, transformed many women into supporters of a feminism that would break the bonds of their cultural imprisonment.

John Kennedy had initiated action on women's issues, ending separate federal job lists for men and women. In 1963, Congress passed the Equal Pay Act, which forbade employers to pay women less than men for the same work; and in 1964, at the behest of women labor activists, it incorporated into the civil rights bill of that year a provision—Title VII—that barred discrimination for reasons of sex. However, the new Equal Employment Opportunity Commission (EEOC) refused to enforce Title VII, its director calling the provision a "fluke conceived out of wedlock." In 1966, at a national meeting of state women's commissions, Betty Friedan moved to pressure the EEOC to enforce the law by helping to establish the National Organization for Women (NOW), its mission "to take the actions needed to bring women into the mainstream of American society, now, full equality for women, in fully equal partnership with men, NOW." In response to agitation by NOW, the EEOC began to enforce Title VII, beginning with the abolition of separate male and female help-wanted ads in the newspapers. And in 1967, by executive order, President Johnson required federal contractors to include "sex" in their nondiscrimination and affirmative action policies. By then, the new feminist movement was beginning to change the minds of many men, compelling them to recognize the barriers to women's ambitions and the merits of tearing them down.

## Lyndon Johnson: Reluctant Globalist

Unlike Kennedy, Lyndon Johnson preferred to devote his energies to reform at home. But the unruly world kept pressing in on him, compelling his attention in the Middle East, Latin America, and Asia, especially Vietnam. Johnson embraced the bipartisan consensus that had dominated American foreign policy since the end of World War II: that the United States had to play a major role in resisting aggression, preferably through collective security but if necessary alone. Johnson tended to see leftist or pro-Communist movements in the third world as instruments of a Soviet and Chinese drive for greater territorial domination—an outlook that was reinforced by his principal advisers in national security, Dean Rusk, Robert McNamara, and McGeorge Bundy, all of whom he had asked to remain at their posts after Kennedy's death and on whom he relied heavily.

Johnson avoided unnecessary provocations of the Soviet Union and China while seeking cooperation in matters of global mutual interest—notably, in slowing the arms race and quelling armed hostilities in the Middle East. But he was disposed to intervene where he judged that Communist advances jeopardized the United States' capacity to maintain world security and might also draw domestic criticism to his administration. He thus acted high-handedly toward Latin American countries, especially those he feared had been targeted by Fidel Castro for export of the Cuban revolution. And he vastly enlarged the United States' military role in Vietnam, committing the country to its longest and most divisive foreign war. The conflict provoked bitter dissent and helped destroy the prospects for achieving the Great Society. Together, the furies unleashed by the war and the social changes of the 1960s rendered Johnson's presidency untenable.

### THE MIDDLE EAST

The United States remained committed to Israel because of that country's pro-American posture, the strong support it enjoyed among American Jews, and the counter it provided to Soviet influence in the Middle East. On June 5, 1967, responding to threatening actions by Jordan, Syria, and Egypt, Israel launched a preemptive attack against all three, destroying the Jordanian and Syrian air forces, slashing through the Egyptian army, and heavily bloodying Jordan's. Johnson, worried that the Soviets might intervene, told the Israelis on June 10 that an immediate cease-fire was imperative. The next day the Six-Day War ended, with the Israelis having gained control of the Old City of Jerusalem, the West Bank of the Jordan River, the hills on its border with Syria called the Golan Heights, and the Sinai Peninsula, the expanse of desert on its border with Egypt.

In November, the United Nations Security Council passed Resolution 242, calling for Israel to withdraw from the territories it had recently occupied and, by implication, for the

Israeli troops occupying Syrian territory during the Six-Day War, June 1967.

Arab states to acknowledge Israel's sovereignty and independence. But the Arab states were still unwilling to recognize Israel, and Israeli forces remained in the captured territories.

## LATIN AMERICA

Johnson considered John Kennedy's Alliance for Progress a "thoroughgoing mess," judging that as a means of fostering economic growth and democratic development in the country's neighbors to the south, it was too antibusiness and unrealistic. He made his point man for Latin America Assistant Secretary of State Thomas Mann, a tough fellow-Texan and a hard-line anti-Communist eager to promote private investment in the area. Mann signaled a rightward shift in administration policy, telling American ambassadors to the region that the United States would no longer seek to punish military overthrows of elected governments and explaining that blocking Communism was more important than supporting constitutional norms.

The shift shaped the administration's response to civil unrest in Panama in 1964 against U.S. control of the Canal Zone. In January, the Panamanian president broke off diplomatic relations with the United States and, outraging many Americans, demanded a renegotiation of the 1903 treaty that had granted the United States rights in the zone. Johnson, along with Mann and his chief national security advisers, attributed the disturbances to pro-Castro sympathizers who threatened to establish another Cuba in Central America. Eager to keep the canal open, Johnson achieved a restoration of relations in April without ceding any control of it to Panama, agreeing instead to "review" rather than "negotiate" the differences dividing the two countries.

In the Dominican Republic a year later, a rebellion against the reigning military junta restored power to Juan Bosch, a left-leaning non-Communist. At the end of April 1965, Johnson sent 14,000 troops there—the number was soon increased to 22,000—explaining that the force was intended to protect American lives and to forestall a Communist takeover. Many observers believed that Johnson had grossly exaggerated the threats, and journalists began writing about the "credibility gap," a sign of emerging distrust of the administration's foreign policy.

## VIETNAM

On August 1, 1964, a North Vietnamese torpedo boat fired at the American destroyer *Maddox* in the Gulf of Tonkin. The *Maddox,* on patrol under a secret policy that President Johnson had initiated earlier in the year, was protecting South Vietnamese PT boats that were bombarding coastal bases in North Vietnam. Three days later, the *Maddox* and another American destroyer reported that they were both under attack. Although the reliability of the report was uncertain, Johnson promptly ordered air strikes against North Vietnam. He told the nation about the action that evening in a televised speech and asked Congress for support in resisting aggression against U.S. armed forces in the region. By the end of the evening, Congress had overwhelmingly passed the so-called Gulf of Tonkin Resolution, authorizing the president "to take all necessary measures to repel any armed attacks against the forces of the United States and to prevent further aggression in the area." Several senators had cautioned that such a resolution would grant the president a blank check to wage war against North Vietnam, but pro-Johnson senators assured their colleagues that the president had no such intention.

Whatever Johnson's intention may have been at the time, it is beyond dispute that he was convinced that the United States had to prevent the fall of South Vietnam to Communism. At

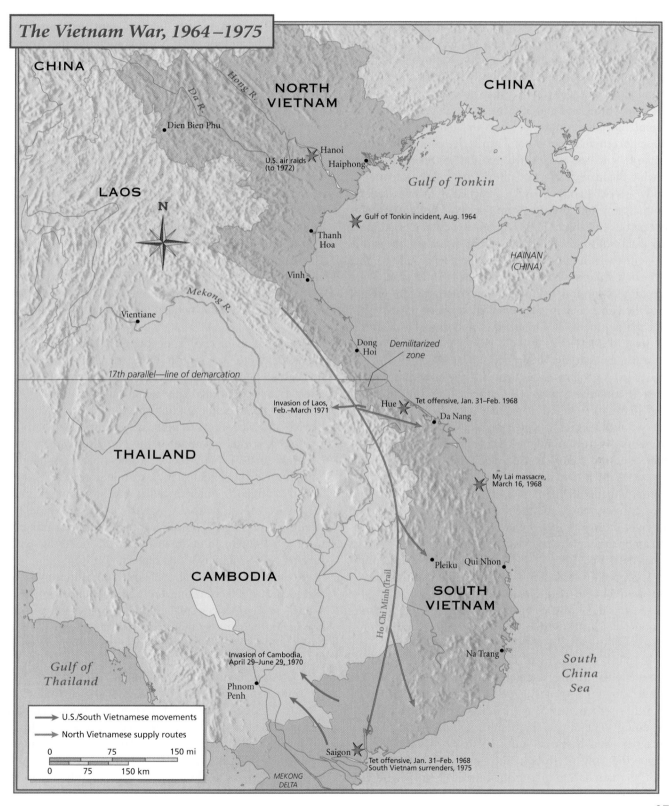

## The Vietnam War, 1964–1975

CHINA

LAOS

NORTH VIETNAM

CHINA

Da R.

Hong R.

Dien Bien Phu

U.S. air raids (to 1972)

Hanoi

Haiphong

*Gulf of Tonkin*

N

Gulf of Tonkin incident, Aug. 1964

*HAINAN (CHINA)*

Thanh Hoa

Vinh

*Mekong R.*

Vientiane

Dong Hoi

*Demilitarized zone*

17th parallel—line of demarcation

Invasion of Laos, Feb.–March 1971

Hue

Tet offensive, Jan. 31–Feb. 1968

Da Nang

THAILAND

My Lai massacre, March 16, 1968

Pleiku

Qui Nhon

CAMBODIA

Ho Chi Minh Trail

SOUTH VIETNAM

Na Trang

*South China Sea*

*Gulf of Thailand*

Invasion of Cambodia, April 29–June 29, 1970

Phnom Penh

Saigon

Tet offensive, Jan. 31–Feb. 1968
South Vietnam surrenders, 1975

U.S./South Vietnamese movements

North Vietnamese supply routes

| 0 | 75 | 150 mi |
| 0 | 75 | 150 km |

*MEKONG DELTA*

the time of his election victory in 1964, he worried that the situation in Vietnam was rapidly deteriorating. North Vietnam and the Viet Cong, the military arm of the National Liberation Front (NLF) in the South, had recently initiated an energetic political and military offensive. They now controlled roughly 40 percent of the land and 50 percent of the people in South Vietnam. Since the murder of Diem in 1963, the South Vietnamese government had become unstable, frequently changing hands, and lacked any real authority. During the year following the incident in the Gulf of Tonkin, Johnson and his key advisers debated their course of action. Johnson was anxious that he would lose the Great Society if he "got involved with that bitch of a war." He was at first reluctant to send more American troops—about 23,000 were in Vietnam at the end of 1964—into what might prove to be an endless ground conflict like the one in Korea. Wariness of the Soviet Union and China made him all the more skittish about enlarging the military role of the United States in the conflict.

Yet the president felt himself on the horns of a dilemma, confiding to McGeorge Bundy, "I don't think it's worth fightin' for," but adding, "I don't think we can get out." McNamara called Vietnam "a test case for the new Communist strategy": conquest by wars of national liberation. Johnson feared that if the United States failed to honor its commitment to South Vietnam, its pledges to defend freedom against Communist aggression might lose credibility. Echoing Eisenhower's domino theory, he told reporters, "We learned from Hitler at Munich that success only feeds the appetite of aggression." Abandon Vietnam, and "the battle would be renewed in one country and then in another country." Johnson held vivid in memory the bitter woes that had befallen Truman, among them McCarthyism, following the loss of China. He was determined not "to be the president who saw Southeast Asia go the way China went," apprehensive that such a defeat would boomerang against his own presidency.

Such considerations formed the background for Johnson's decision to escalate the war in February 1965, when South Vietnam was on the verge of defeat. In response to a Vietcong attack against an American military base at Pleiku, in the Central Highlands, the Pentagon launched Operation Rolling Thunder, an air campaign against North Vietnam that Johnson authorized because "doing nothing was more dangerous than doing something." The bombing, launched from naval air carriers and bases in South Vietnam, was intended to hamper the flow of troops and supplies southward from North Vietnam and to bolster the morale of the Saigon government. The next month, Johnson sent two battalions of marines to the air base at Da Nang, contending that American pilots had to be protected by American soldiers. He expected that, faced with the escalation of armed force, Ho Chi Minh would sooner or later "sober up and unload his pistol."

In the summer, as the situation of the South Vietnamese continued to deteriorate, Johnson ordered a review of U.S. policy. The chief opponent of escalation was Under Secretary of State George Ball, who had argued against the bombing campaign, predicting that it would not restore political stability in the South and would only heighten North Vietnam's resolve. Now Ball recommended abandoning South Vietnam altogether, expressing doubts that "an army of westerners can fight orientals in [an] Asian jungle and succeed." But he was a loner among White House policymakers. The debate ended in favor of the hawks, with Johnson authorizing a major increase in the American military commitment in Vietnam. By the end of 1965, fully 125,000 American soldiers were fighting there.

*"Where does it all end?"* The bombing and troop deployments failed to accomplish their immediate purpose—or their ultimate one, which was to force the North Vietnamese into peace negotiations. The military pressed Johnson to escalate further by sending ground forces against enemy sanctuaries in Laos and Cambodia; mining the harbor of Haiphong, a vital gateway for the North's supplies; and, as General Curtis LeMay, the air force chief of staff, urged, bombing North Vietnam "back to the Stone Age." Johnson, fearful of angering America's allies and provoking China and the Soviet Union, refused. Instead, he chose a middle way, steadily increasing the number of troops but confining them to South Vietnam and intensifying the bombing without striking North Vietnam's vital centers.

By early 1968, the number of American troops in Vietnam exceeded 500,000, counting both combat and support personnel, and American planes had dropped more tons of bombs on the country than the total let loose in all theaters during World War II. To the end of removing the enemy's ground cover, the United States released chemical defoliants such as Agent Orange over millions of acres, destroying half the timberlands in the South. Ground troops, authorized in 1965 to conduct "search and destroy" missions, demolished villages, killed civilians, and alienated the peasantry. In 1968, following the destruction of the village Ben Tre, an American major inadvertently expressed the growing illogic of the war, declaring, "We had to destroy the village in order to save it."

From time to time, Johnson halted the bombing in the hope of enticing Ho Chi Minh to the peace table, but the attempts repeatedly foundered on the administration's unwillingness to permit the negotiations to include the Viet Cong, the coalition in the South that had been waging war against the government with the North's support. Relative stability had returned to the South Vietnamese government when in mid-1965 General Nguyen Van Thieu won control of it together with his swashbuckling and bizarre prime minister, Nguyen Cao Ky (who considered Adolf Hitler a hero "because he pulled his country together"). The regime commanded diminishing support among the Vietnamese, especially in the countryside. Progress in the war was measured by "body counts"—estimates of the number of enemy troops killed. The number was in fact high—perhaps 220,000 by late 1967—but the estimates padded the toll by as much as 30 percent, stimulating misleading claims that the United States and the South Vietnamese were winning the war.

The North Vietnamese nevertheless fought on tenaciously despite the bombing of their cities, digging thousands of miles of tunnels to protect their citizens. They steadily replenished their troops and their Viet Cong allies in the South, sending men and supplies along the camouflaged routes through Laos of the Ho Chi Minh Trail. They infuriated American troops by their elusiveness, their ability to melt into the jungle and disappear into the local population. One American soldier wrote: "During the day they'll smile and take your money. At night they'll creep in and slit your throat." Some soldiers vented their anger, as at the My Lai massacre in 1968, by raping and murdering Vietnamese villagers.

Many of the American troops were confused by the war. On average, they were nineteen years old, seven years younger than their counterparts in World War II, less experienced in life and less clear about their country's war aims. They were supposedly risking their lives to defend democracy in South Vietnam, but antiwar protesters at home considered them criminals and the South Vietnamese often treated them with contempt. As the war dragged on, their watchword became survival rather than victory. Between 1966 and 1971, desertion rates quadrupled to almost 74 per 1,000—triple the worst rates of the Korean War. They took to assassinating officers—the process was called "fragging"—who ordered them into seemingly pointless battle. Many turned to the comfort of drugs, every variety of which was available cheaply and in abundance. In 1969, almost two out of three G.I.s were using marijuana, and one out of four had tried heroin.

A growing number of Johnson's advisers, notably Robert McNamara, knew that the war was not being won, that it was producing only killing and devastation, including, by late 1967, some 13,500 American dead. But Johnson was intolerant of the doubters, many of whom left the administration. Increasingly frustrated, like his troops in the field, Johnson was depressed by the lack of progress in the war and infuriated that "a little piss-ant country" should be so embarrassing the United States. In the spring of 1967, General William Westmoreland, the American commander in Vietnam, requested 95,000 more troops and said that another 100,000 would be needed the following year. Johnson gave him only 45,000. "Where does it all end?" he asked despairingly.

## Upheaval at Home

### THE ANTIWAR MOVEMENT

When the bombing campaign began, outspoken questioning of the war emerged almost immediately among the press and on the campuses. At the University of Michigan in March 1965, students and faculty introduced the teach-in—a gathering to question the merits of the intervention—and such

American troops probe a tunnel in search of North Vietnamese troops, 1968.

meetings quickly spread to other campuses. Many critics of the war held that Ho Chi Minh was a nationalist rather than an agent of either Soviet or Chinese hegemony, and that he had no interest in knocking over any dominoes in Southeast Asia. Some argued that the war was unwinnable, costly, and threatening to the Great Society. It was a civil war, the dissenters insisted. The United States had no vital interest at stake and thus had no business being in Vietnam.

For the first time, television brought a war into the nation's living rooms, the screens flickering with taped footage of battle and death. As troop commitments, casualties, and draft calls mounted, the questioning of the war turned into a full-scale movement against it. Newspaper columnists like Walter Lippmann attacked the country's involvement in Vietnam, and so did foreign policy experts such as George F. Kennan, civil rights leaders like Martin Luther King Jr., and the nation's leading baby doctor, Benjamin Spock. Although Congress regularly appropriated funds for the war, virtually without debate because its members felt obligated to support the troops in the field, opposition grew steadily on Capitol Hill. By 1967, in cities and towns across the land, people were marching in protest against the war, including 35,000 who in October demonstrated at the entrance to the Pentagon.

The antiwar movement was especially strong on the campuses of the leading universities, where students—and some faculty—occupied university buildings, disrupted the work of

Students gather at a teach-in on Vietnam at the University of California, Berkeley, May 21, 1965.

draft boards and army recruiters, and demonstrated with angry chants ("Hey, hey, LBJ, how many kids did you kill today?"). Protesting the Defense Department's pervasive influence in academic science, students occupied physics laboratories, demanded that universities divorce themselves from defense programs, and bombed several research facilities, including one at the University of Wisconsin, killing a postdoctoral scientist. Students made common cause with songs of protest that addressed the war in the sardonic vein of Country Joe and the Fish's "I Feel Like I'm Fixin' to Die Rag" ("What are we fightin' for / Don't ask me, I don't give a damn / Next stop is Vietnam. . . . So put down your books and pick up a gun / We're gonna have a whole lot of fun"). Seeing the war as an indictment of American society, students felt linked to protesters in European capitals such as Paris and Berlin who in 1968 battled police in the streets. A growing number were attracted to the New Left, a program of social radicalism expressed on campuses by the Students for a Democratic Society (SDS), which, along with denouncing the war as racist, called for a new emphasis on community and the achievement of social change through "participatory democracy."

Critics of the war also pointed out that the burdens of armed service were marked by glaring inequities. Student deferments kept many young middle-class men out of Vietnam, while the enlisted men and draftees sent there came disproportionately from low-income, working-class, and minority-group backgrounds. Draftees, who represented only a quarter of those who served in Vietnam, made up most of the infantry and accounted for between 50 and 70 percent of combat deaths. Black enlistees died in action at about twice the rate of enlisted men on the whole. Many draft-eligible young men ducked armed service by getting married, going to school, or joining the National Guard. Some fled to Canada or went underground.

Black activists attacked the selective service system, charging that most local draft boards were all white. The charismatic heavyweight boxing champion Muhammad Ali refused induction on grounds of his Muslim religion and conscientious objection to the war, declaring, "No Vietcong ever called me Nigger." (He was promptly relieved of his heavyweight title, excluded from boxing, and prosecuted for draft evasion.) Protesters burned their draft cards; some broke into draft boards to despoil their records. Bombings linked to radical groups targeted board offices, induction centers, and buildings housing the Reserve Officers Training Corps (ROTC).

Muhammad Ali, having refused induction into the army on religious grounds, was stripped of his heavyweight title and prosecuted for draft evasion in 1967.

Dissidents found oblique reflections of the seeming illogic of the Vietnam War machine in several popular novels about World War II. Joseph Heller's *Catch-22,* first published in 1961, brilliantly satirized the military for holding pompously to rules that made common sense into craziness and insanity into reason; and Kurt Vonnegut Jr.'s best-selling *Slaughterhouse-Five, or The Children's Crusade* (1969), a science fiction version of his World War II experiences in the firebombing of Dresden, indicted the war machine for producing madness and disintegration. The film industry, its memories of McCarthyism and the blacklist still fresh, declined to produce movies critical of the government's policy during Vietnam; but in 1970, *M\*A\*S\*H,* a subversive comedy about an army field hospital in the Korean conflict, indirectly spotlighted the war as an absurd waste of life.

## THE COUNTERCULTURAL REBELLION

Campus dissidents had early been inspired by Mario Savio, a mathematics graduate student at the University of California at Berkeley, who amid the free-speech movement there in 1964 likened the university to a machine and cried to a throng occupying the administration building: "It becomes odious, so we must put our bodies against the gears, against the wheels . . . and make the machine stop until we're free." On many campuses by the late 1960s, young Americans, products of the baby boom, were defying social norms of hard work, getting ahead, self-denial, and sexual restraint. Their numbers gave them strength. During the 1960s, the cohort between ages fifteen and twenty-four increased by almost 50 percent, accounting by 1970 for almost 18 percent of the population, a postwar high; a sizable number of them—half the eighteen-year-olds—were in college. They were active and vociferous enough to compel national attention as a youth-dominated "counterculture" who had opened a "generation gap" between themselves and their elders.

The counterculture, a kind of neoromanticism, expressed skepticism of science and reason and many of their institutionalized works, particularly corporate degradation of the environment and the military's high-technology destructiveness. Its devotees embraced psychedelic drugs, psychedelic art, acid rock, and sexual liberation. Many young Americans got high on marijuana and tried LSD or mescaline, embracing the instruction of Timothy Leary, formerly a Harvard psychologist and now an avid enthusiast of drug use, that everyone should "drop out, turn on, tune in." Some counterculturalists adopted "hippie" lifestyles—living in communes, sharing housing and property and often each other's bodies and beds. Wherever they lived, many displayed their contempt for consumerism by dressing in military fatigues, torn jeans, and tie-dyed T-shirts. The men often grew beards and long hair; some of the women went without bras.

The youth of the era had been "trained by music and linked by music," a critic in San Francisco remarked. Popular rock groups reached huge audiences—and often got rich—through radio and LP (long-playing) record albums, which had first been introduced in the late 1940s, and which permitted the popular music industry to sell multiple songs on a single record. Rock groups sang increasingly about sex, drugs, and personal freedom. The Beatles, the enormously popular group from Britain, exuded sexual energy in their mop-headed persons and mocking irreverence for everything adult in their music. Antiwar convictions were combined with celebrations of love, drugs, and sex in the exuberant musical *Hair,* which mixed attacks on the draft with frontal nudity and simulated orgies.

*American Journal*

## The College Scene

Before the 1960s, colleges acting in the place of parents (that is, *in loco parentis*) imposed a variety of rules on women undergraduates that were intended to inhibit sexual activity. In 1921, for example, Stanford University prohibited women both from "motoring" and from walking in the nearby hills "unchaperoned, after dark." Although by the 1950s many such restrictions had disappeared, most colleges required women students to be back in their dormitories by a certain hour—the times varied with class level—and men who brought their dates back late were expected to send them candy or flowers. By and large, women were not permitted to entertain men in their rooms, and where they were, the rules required that the door must remain open and at least three feet had to be kept on the floor. The sexual revolution that began in the 1960s virtually ended college governance of when, how, and where men and women students could get together. Indeed, by the 1980s, men and women students at many colleges were living in coed dorms and sharing bathrooms. A popular guide later addressed a feature of life under the new circumstances.

"Many young men worry about having an erection in . . . a coed bathroom. Surprising as it may seem, most of the women around you won't be staring at your crotch so you needn't be overly concerned. And the one good thing about a coed bathroom is if you do get an erection, you'll be in close proximity to a cold shower.

"College women can be certain that the men around them will be looking, but how much the men get to see is up to them. While it can be annoying to be under constant scrutiny, it also presents certain opportunities to attract the attention of Mr. Right."

Ruth K. Westheimer and Pierre Lehu, *Dr. Ruth's Guide to College Life: The Savvy Student's Handbook*

---

In August 1969, an estimated 400,000 young people attended the Woodstock Festival on a farm in upstate New York, a number of them indulging in drugs, nudity, and public sex, most of them listening through the din to the music of the day's rock and pop stars. That year, the popular film *Easy Rider* depicted the pleasures of drug highs and motorcycling on the open road.

By 1970, the counterculture was losing force, its image of love and gentleness shattered where its devotees tended to concentrate—notably, the Haight-Ashbury district in San Francisco and the East Village in New York City—by muggers, rapists, and drug dealers. In Los Angeles in 1969, the hippie Charles Manson and his communal "family" brutally murdered five people, including a pregnant actress.

But features of the counterculture had spread beyond the campuses and Haight-Ashbury to upper-middle-class suburbia. They left a legacy of changed fashions—in dress, hairstyles, and drug use—and modified attitudes toward sex roles and sexual behavior, especially for women. The cause of women's sexual liberty was advanced in the pages of middlebrow *Cosmopolitan* magazine by its editor, Helen Gurley Brown, and in books like Germaine Greer's *Female Eunuch* (1971), which urged women to take an assertive role in claiming their sexuality and sexual pleasure.

The spread of sexual permissiveness was aided by the new technologies of contraception. For several decades, advocates of planned parenthood and population control had been sponsoring research to develop chemical means of birth control. In 1960, in no small part as a result of this effort, contraceptive pills ("the pill") became commercially available. By 1970, some 12 million women were using them, drawn by their reliability even though they posed a small risk of adverse side effects. More women relied on the new IUD (intrauterine device), which was later prohibited as unsafe, or the longstanding mainstay, the diaphragm. Obtaining these devices required a doctor's prescription or insertion or fitting. Some states limited their distribution to married women until the Supreme Court struck down such restrictions in 1972; but in

A landmark celebration of peace and music: the Woodstock Festival in Bethel, New York, August 15-17, 1969.

the meantime, many doctors defied the law by providing them to single women.

The countercultural skepticism of science and technology also spread into mainstream culture. If people welcomed products of science such as the pill and stereos, they worried about technological threats, such as microelectronic bugging, and reminders of the fragility of technological civilization—notably, the 1965 power failure in New York that blacked out 80,000 square miles of the northeastern United States. Stanley Kubrick's widely admired film *2001: A Space Odyssey* (1968) was pervaded by a love-fear relationship with the computer Hal.

Bolstered by Supreme Court rulings that found unconstitutional most laws restricting sexually explicit materials, nudity and sex became commonplace in magazines, films, and theatrical productions. Pornographic theaters proliferated along downtown streets and highway strips, as did "adult"

bookstores and topless bars. By the early 1970s, the sexual revolution was ensconced in American life.

## MILITANCY AND BACKLASH

While the antiwar and countercultural movements gathered force, minority groups of color expressed their dissatisfactions with American society with greater militancy. Many were angered by the disproportionately large burden of the war that their young men were compelled to shoulder. Still more were made increasingly furious by the continuing inequalities they were forced to endure.

The fury was especially strong among blacks in the North. Although they could vote and, in principle, go where they pleased, the large majority remained segregated in slum housing, inadequate schools, and impoverished lives, and felt themselves constantly in peril of both crime and police brutality. The unemployment rate of sixteen- and seventeen-year-old black males in 1966 was almost 23 percent and rising (it would reach 39 percent in 1974). In 1960, some 3 million blacks, many of them high school dropouts, were on welfare (the total would reach 11 million in 1972). During the eight years after 1966, a period of soaring increase in the overall crime rate, the arrest rate for black males between ages thirteen and thirty-nine shot up almost 50 percent.

James Baldwin, a powerful writer and a black, noted, "To be a Negro in this country and to be relatively conscious is to be in a rage all the time." In 1963, Baldwin published *The Fire Next Time*, an eloquent warning of the explosive resentments simmering in the black community that took its pointed title from a line in a Negro spiritual, "God gave Noah the rainbow sign, No more water, The fire next time." The next year, Congressman Adam Clayton Powell Jr. of Harlem remarked that the southern phase of the "black revolution"—a middle-class movement with middle-class aims like equal rights before the

879

law—was ending. Now the northern, "proletarian," "rough" phase was imminent, raising the "gut issue of who gets the money." Powell added, "Watch out."

*The Fire Ignited.* One hot afternoon in July 1964, a white policeman shot and killed one of three black teenagers in an encounter in New York City. Angry blacks lashed out, rioting for five days in Harlem and Brooklyn. The next summer, in the Watts section of Los Angeles, a confrontation between white police and young blacks set off six days of looting, firebombings, and sniping at firefighters, police, and National Guard troops. The violence killed 34 people. In Detroit, a riot injured 1,000, left 43 dead, and destroyed $50 million worth of property. Almost forty such upheavals occurred in cities in 1966, more than 160 in 1967. All told, the riots between 1964 and 1968 killed some 200 people, injured 7,000, and destroyed almost $200 million worth of property.

In a report released in 1968, a National Advisory Commission on Civil Disorders, headed by Governor Otto Kerner of Illinois, laid responsibility for the riots at the door of "white racism," which had produced an "explosive mixture" of conditions in the northern black ghettos, and warned that "our nation is moving toward two societies, one black, one white—separate and unequal." Johnson declined to act on the commission's recommendations for additional programs of

In 1967, racial tensions burst into riots here in Detroit and in more than 160 other cities.

jobs, housing, and income subsidies, counting the estimated price tag of some $24 billion too expensive. He did, however, win passage of a federal open-housing law that would eventually eliminate discrimination in the sale and rental of 80 percent of the nation's housing, and of a safe-streets act that was intended to reduce urban crime but that authorized federal, state, and local law enforcement agencies to engage in wiretapping and bugging in particular situations.

*Black Power.* The urban rioting was accompanied by the growing embrace among northern blacks of the militant Nation of Islam, the Black Muslim religion led by Elijah Muhammad and articulated by Malcolm X. Eloquent and charismatic, Malcolm X repudiated integration and nonviolence, preaching instead black separatism from the "white devil," armed self-defense, and freedom by "any means necessary." A reformed petty criminal, he also emphasized self-reliance and black pride, telling African Americans to see themselves through their "own eyes, not the white man's." After falling out with the Muslims in 1964, Malcolm X began to speak of cooperation with integrationist civil rights leaders and with whites. The next year he was assassinated, allegedly by adherents of Elijah Muhammad resentful of his growing power. However, his compelling *Autobiography* (1965) became a Bible for young blacks intent on asserting their identity and gaining independence from the power of whites.

In 1966, Stokely Carmichael, then leader of the SNCC and an exemplar of its increasing militancy, exhorted, "The only way we gonna stop them white men from whippin' us is to take over. . . . What we gonna start saying now is Black Power!" In part, Black Power stood for the kind of racial self-respect that Malcolm X had called for and that the soul singer James Brown extolled in his line "Say it loud, I'm black and I'm proud." Yet for militants, it rippled with racial separatism, derision of whites as "honkies," and a slogan for the riots, "Burn, baby, burn."

Martin Luther King Jr. condemned the violence and separatism, declaring that "there is no salvation for the Negro through isolation." Surveys showed that most blacks continued to favor nonviolence, equality of opportunity, and integration. Black Power left its mark in expressions of cultural pride such as Afro hairstyles, soul food, and black studies programs in universities. It also added energy to the drive of African Americans for political power. They demanded local control of their schools and ran with

Malcolm X's charisma and preaching of black pride appealed to many African Americans, even if his message of black separatism did not.

increasing success for election to school boards and antipoverty boards. In 1967, for the first time in American history, black candidates won big-city mayoralties, in Gary, Indiana, and Cleveland, Ohio.

*Red Power, Chicano Power.* Amid the booming economy and reformist climate of the 1960s, Native Americans and Hispanics expressed rising expectations. The Kennedy administration emphasized tribal economic development for Native Americans, a policy dubbed the "New Trail." By 1963, with the authorization of the Area Redevelopment and Manpower-Training Acts, the policy had created public-works and job-training programs on reservations in twenty-one states. The next year, Native Americans demanded and received recognition in LBJ's War on Poverty, pointing out that they were more greatly disadvantaged than any other group. A special Indian "desk" was established in the Office of Economic Opportunity, and the government provided Indians with new housing, food assistance, rural electrification, health counseling, and jobs.

In the meantime, young Indian activists had been deriding "Uncle Tomahawks" the way black militants assailed "Uncle Toms." Demanding "Red Power," they insisted on the designation "Native Americans" and on greater control over federal programs for Indians. Under the War on Poverty's Community Action Programs, tribal councils came to administer federal grants for Native Americans. In 1968, in a remarkably strong speech, Johnson promised "a standard of living for the

Indian equal to that of the country as a whole" and freedom to choose whether to live in their homelands or in towns and cities. Within a few weeks, Congress passed the Indian Civil Rights Act, which sought both to strengthen constitutional protections for individual Native Americans and also, somewhat contradictorily, to exempt the tribes from having to respect those protections—for example, the right to civil and criminal trials in state courts.

The activists also called for compensation for the lands that had been taken from them in violation of federal laws and treaties. In 1964, the National Indian Youth Council held "fish-ins" to protest the state of Washington's depriving local tribes of treaty rights by arresting their members for fishing without licenses and out of season in the Columbia River and Puget Sound. Other fish-ins were staged across the Northwest with the participation of celebrities such as Marlon Brando and the comedian Dick Gregory. Federal court decisions upheld the tribal treaty rights in Washington, and the tribes developed long-term fish-conservation measures in cooperation with state agencies.

Mexican American activism was boosted by César Chavez, whose family had suffered exploitation as migrant agricultural workers in California. In 1962, he and Dolores Huerta, a community activist, organized the National Farm Workers' Association. The NFWA fought for union recognition, higher wages, and better working conditions with a strike that began in 1965 against the grape growers in Delano, in California's San Joaquin Valley. A devout Roman Catholic, Chavez spotlighted the merits of the cause of the agricultural workers and its commitment to nonviolence through personal fasts and by calling for a national boycott of California grapes (and later, lettuce) picked by nonunion labor. In 1970, the major grape growers in Delano signed a three-year contract with the NFWA.

By the 1960s, however, Mexican Americans had reason to be more concerned with urban than with rural issues. Of the 3.8 million Mexican Americans then living in the United States, close to 80 percent resided in metropolitan regions— 2 million lived in the barrios of Los Angeles alone—where they endured racism, discrimination, and poverty. Asserting "brown pride," young Mexican American activists, many of them educated, rejected assimilation, insisted on the designations "Chicano" and "Chicana," and raised the banner of "Chicano Power." They demanded bilingual education and college Chicano studies programs. Throughout the Southwest, Chicano activists organized for purposes such as defending against street crime or the police and delivering

Cesar Chavez, his hand raised, pleads with supporters to "be peaceful" when they picket strike-bound farms in California's Salinas Valley in 1970.

community services. In Texas, Jose Angel Gutierrez built the alternative political party La Raza Unida, which by the 1970s began to elect Mexican Americans to school boards and city councils. Some of the new Chicano action organizations would be short-lived, but the claims to rights and respect that they expressed would take root and continue to grow.

*Backlash.* The upheavals of the day fueled the New Right, enlarging its appeal considerably in what was often termed "Middle America"—middle- to lower-middle-class whites, many of them from recent immigrant backgrounds, in blue-collar occupations, and worshiping at Catholic or Protestant (including evangelical) churches. They adhered to traditional social values and cultural commitments, and they liked the resolute parents and obedient, fresh-faced children in the film *The Sound of Music* (1965), which enjoyed far more popularity than *Easy Rider.* Middle Americans were sufficiently antagonized not only by the sexual revolution but by the counterculture, the antiwar movement, feminist assertiveness, minority-group militancy, and urban riots to form a backlash against the trends of the 1960s.

Even though the women of Middle America were offended by sex discrimination, they challenged the disparagement by some feminists of raising children and the emphasis given by the women's movement to working outside the home. The discontents disliked the permissiveness and secularism of contemporary society. Worried about the rising incidence of crime, they assailed the Supreme Court for rulings on the rights of suspects that seemed to risk returning rapists and murderers to the streets. Their disapproval of ghetto riots and campus demonstrations catapulted the former screen actor Ronald Reagan into the governor's mansion of California in 1966 and helped elect other conservatives to office elsewhere in the nation. Reagan denounced radicals at the state university and quipped that a hippie was someone who "dresses like Tarzan, has hair like Jane, and smells like Cheetah."

The resentment of white Middle Americans against the civil rights revolution's turn to the North had intensified in response to court orders to open their neighborhoods and their occupations, often controlled by white craft unions, to blacks, and by court rulings compelling young children to be bused to integrated schools. Lower-income whites, unable to flee to the safe suburbs, were made apprehensive by the high crime rates in the nearby ghettos. Wherever they lived, many Middle American whites blamed rising rates of out-of-wedlock births among blacks for the high incidence of black delinquency, crime, and school dropouts and for the skyrocketing costs of welfare programs (which almost tripled in the 1960s) for single women with children. One city worker exclaimed, "These welfare people get as much as I do, and I work my ass off and come home dead tired. They get up late and can shack up all day long and watch the tube." In the fall of 1966, drawing on such resentments, Republicans regained enough seats in Congress to reestablish the conservative coalition that had blocked reform during Kennedy's administration and to slow considerably the Johnson legislative drive for the Great Society.

Although Lyndon Johnson's personal popularity had plummeted by late 1967, polls revealed that the war enjoyed wide bipartisan support, especially among Middle Americans. Many felt toward antiwar protesters like the construction worker who exploded, "Here were those kids, rich kids who could go to college, didn't have to fight. They are telling you your son died in vain. It makes you feel your whole life is shit, just nothing." The AFL-CIO convention rejected an antiwar resolution by a vote of 2,000 to 6, the head of the organization attesting, "I would rather fight the Communists in South Vietnam than fight them down here in the Chesapeake Bay."

Despite the protests on many campuses, the war commanded support among the overwhelming majority of college students, many of them working to get ahead in public and private schools (some of them religiously affiliated) and junior colleges operating outside the orbit of the elite universities. Middle Americans continued to hold the military in high regard. Robin Moore's *Green Berets* (1965), a book about the Special Forces in Vietnam, sold more than 1 million copies and was made into a movie starring John Wayne, the popular and politically conservative actor. The American commitment to winning was echoed in the famous remark of Vincent Lombardi, the coach of the powerhouse Green Bay Packers in the popular National Football League—whose games ABC began televising in 1970 on Monday nights—that "winning isn't everything; it's the only thing." Unlike most members of the antiwar movement, Middle Americans craved military victory in Vietnam.

## 1968: THE POLITICS OF PROTEST

Early in the morning of January 31, 1968—the first day of Tet, the Vietnamese New Year—a small corps of Vietcong burst into the guarded compound of the U.S. embassy in Saigon, inaugurating a wave of attacks by the North Vietnamese and the National Liberation Front that struck virtually every city, district capital, provincial capital, and significant hamlet in South Vietnam. The battles, which raged for three weeks, inflicted devastating losses on the NLF and North Vietnamese troops. For them, it was a major military defeat—but a political victory. The scope and daring of the Tet offensive jolted American public opinion, prompting many to conclude that despite the administration's optimistic reports of progress in the war, the enemy remained resiliently capable.

In the aftermath of the Tet offensive, polls showed that half the public believed that it had been a mistake for the United States to get involved in Vietnam. The number of Americans opposed to the war shot up—those from the antiwar left joined the ranks because Tet had intensified their moral objections; those from the prowar right because Tet had confirmed their conviction that the United States should withdraw if it was unwilling to take the hard steps to win the war. President Johnson's approval ratings plummeted to 35 percent, not much higher than Truman's rating at the time of the Korean stalemate.

In late 1967, Senator Eugene McCarthy, a Democrat from Minnesota, had announced that he would challenge Johnson for the presidential nomination as an antiwar candidate. A devout Catholic with a bent for poetry and phi-

losophy, McCarthy had long been raising moral objections to the war. Shortly after the Tet offensive, in the New Hampshire Democratic primary in February, he gained 42 percent of the vote to Johnson's 49 percent, a stunning showing against an incumbent president. In mid-March 1968, Robert Kennedy, who had turned against the war and who was now a senator from New York, also entered the presidential race. Although attacked as a political opportunist who was cynically attempting to steal McCarthy's thunder, he ran a rousing campaign, electrifying the poor, racial minorities, and white ethnic blue-collar groups, stirring the antiwar movement with calls for peace negotiations that would include the NLF, and inspiring devotees of Camelot to hope for a Kennedy restoration.

Within the administration, Tet, and a request by General Westmoreland for 200,000 more troops, prompted a wide-ranging review of war policy that was conducted by Clark Clifford, who had succeeded McNamara as secretary of defense. Doves warned that trying to press the war to victory would tear American society apart and alienate America's allies. Dean Acheson himself, an unimpeachable Cold Warrior, told Johnson that the Joint Chiefs of Staff "don't know what they're talking about." By now, Johnson was embittered, convinced that he had accomplished a great deal for his country, yet, as he told an aide, feeling "chased on all sides by a giant stampede coming at me from all directions."

On March 31, in a televised speech to the nation, Johnson announced a partial halt in the bombing of North Vietnam as well as a reduction in hostilities and invited the North Vietnamese to respond for peace. Then he declared that he wished to devote all his efforts to the quest for peace and, shocking even his closest advisers, concluded: "Accordingly, I shall not seek, and I will not accept, the nomination of my party for another term as your president." Two days later, trumpeting the coming close of Lyndon Johnson's presidency, McCarthy smashed the president in the Wisconsin primary.

*Death and Confrontation.* At the time of the Wisconsin primary, Martin Luther King Jr. was in Memphis, assisting sanitation workers who were striking for union recognition and better working conditions. On April 4, 1968, while standing on the balcony outside his motel room, he was shot and killed by James Earl Ray, a white convict escaped from prison. The crime devastated many whites, and angry blacks took to the

Mourners attend the funeral procession of Martin Luther King Jr. in Atlanta, April 9, 1968.

streets in 125 cities, some of which erupted in violence and flame. The rioting put almost 27,000 people in jail, injured more than 3,000, and left 46 dead.

By then, Hubert Humphrey, Johnson's vice-president, had joined McCarthy and Kennedy in the contest for the Democratic nomination. Although a longtime fighter for liberal causes who enjoyed strong support among party regulars, Humphrey was weakened by his close association with Johnson and the war. Kennedy beat both him and McCarthy in the California primary on June 4. But the following night, as he left his victory celebration in a Los Angeles hotel, he was assassinated by Sirhan Sirhan, a Palestinian immigrant who detested Kennedy's support of Israel. Kennedy's death, coming so soon after King's, was like a hammer blow to millions, black and white. Grieving throngs lined the railroad track awaiting the train that carried Kennedy's body from New York to Washington, where he was to be buried alongside his brother.

The killings of King and Kennedy led many Democrats to despair for the future of peace and racial justice. McCarthy continued to campaign, but he was cold, aloof, and uncomfortable with blacks—he said nothing when King was murdered; his candidacy failed to catch on beyond the issue of the war. When in August 1968 the Democratic National Convention convened in Chicago under the taut control of Mayor Richard J. Daley, the boss of the city's Democratic machine and a staunch Johnson loyalist, Humphrey's nomination was a foregone conclusion.

Taking matters into their own hands, around 5,000 demonstrators had come to the city—many to protest the administration's war policies; some, like Tom Hayden, to discredit the Democrats by provoking confrontations. Some marched outside the convention hall yelling obscenities. A few, calling themselves the Youth International Party ("Yippies"), intended to mock the system through, among other stunts, nominating a pig ("Pigasus") for the presidency. The police, on tenterhooks after the violence that had shaken the city following Martin Luther King's assassination, erupted in their own riot, clubbing demonstrators, hurling some of them through plate-glass windows, and assaulting the press. From the convention podium, Senator Abraham Ribicoff of Connecticut denounced "Gestapo tactics on the streets of Chicago."

Humphrey defended Mayor Daley and his police in the face of the extreme provocations they had faced, and polls revealed that a majority of Americans agreed with him. But the brutal uproar in Chicago damaged the ticket of Humphrey and his running mate, Senator Edmund Muskie of Maine, further tearing apart the Democratic Party. It propelled many of its adherents into the camps of Richard Nixon, whom the Republicans had nominated several weeks earlier, and George Wallace, who was running as the nominee of the new American Independent Party and whose hold on voters, only 11 percent in January, shot up to 21 percent in the month after the Chicago convention.

*Campaigning for Conservatism.* Wallace was a spoiler. With no chance to win the election, he hoped to capture enough votes in the South and the border states to throw it into the House of Representatives. Exploiting the backlash in the North and South, he attacked feminists, welfare mothers, hip-

Police tangle with demonstrators in the streets outside the Democratic convention in Chicago, August 28, 1968.

pies, radicals, school integrationists, antiwar demonstrators, and liberal intellectuals. "If any demonstrator ever lays [*sic*] down in front of my car, it'll be the *last* car he'll ever lay down in front of," he pledged. But he chose as his running mate General Curtis LeMay, who frightened people with statements about nuclear weapons reminiscent of the mad general in the film *Dr. Strangelove* (1964). Wallace steadily lost support to both Nixon and Humphrey.

Richard Nixon presented himself as a high-minded centrist; but with the aid of his running mate, Governor Spiro Agnew of Maryland, a onetime moderate who had turned rightward with the backlash, he also courted potential Wallace voters, appealing to blue-collar Catholics and white southerners. He also solicited Sun Belt suburbanites, whom he considered natural Republicans—comfortable beneficiaries of the new high-technology industries of plastics, electronics, aerospace, and chemicals that stretched from the Old South into Texas and California. Nixon stressed the need for a restoration of "law and order" and assailed the Supreme Court for expanding the rights of criminals and upholding the "forced busing" of schoolchildren to achieve integration. He proclaimed himself a spokesman for the "silent Americans," mute in the face of cacophonous protesters. Of Vietnam, he said only that he had a "secret plan" to end the war.

Humphrey, far behind Nixon at the beginning of the campaign, gained on him at the end of it, partly as a result of Johnson's announcement on October 31 of a complete bombing halt. Nixon nevertheless held on to score a narrow victory, winning 43.4 percent of the popular vote to Humphrey's 42.7 percent, distributed to translate into a margin of 301–191 in the electoral college. Wallace took 13.5 percent of the popular vote while gaining the 46 electoral votes of five deep South states. The Democrats retained control of the House, whose new members included Shirley Chisolm, from the Bedford-Stuyvesant section of Brooklyn, the first black woman ever elected to that body; and they kept control of the Senate, even though they lost seven seats. Humphrey won almost the entire black vote and a majority of blue-collar Catholics in the North.

Still, Nixon and Wallace together scored 57 percent of the vote, commanding not only the deep South but the upper South and the border region. Nixon also did exceptionally well in the West, where resentments of the distant federal bureaucracy ran high among natural-resource users like ranchers and oil companies, and where the backlash helped shape the white vote. Nationwide, Humphrey received fewer than 35 percent of white ballots.

## TRIUMPH AND TRANSITION

Lyndon Johnson, whose list of legislative achievements exceeded that of most presidents, broadly affected American life. By 1968, average family income had reached $8,000, double the amount of a decade earlier; the unemployment rate had fallen to 3.5 percent; and the poverty rate had been cut almost in half, dropping to 12 percent of the population. A good deal of the economic boom was attributable to Great Society programs—notably, the War on Poverty, expanded Social Security coverage, Medicare and Medicaid, housing subsidies, and aid to dependent children—that put cash and services in the hands of lower-income groups.

Blacks received a proportionately smaller share of the mushrooming prosperity than did whites, but some poverty programs—the Job Corps and Head Start, for example—significantly assisted minority groups. The civil rights acts of the Johnson years revolutionized blacks' access to both public amenities and the ballot box. Johnson's orders to federal contractors to practice nondiscrimination and affirmative action in hiring and promotion eventually yielded important benefits for women as well as minority groups, since federal contracts affected about a third of the labor force. In the mid-1960s, half of Americans over age sixty-five had no medical insurance; twenty years later, every senior citizen was covered.

The achievement of these gains rested in part on Johnson's ability to mobilize for a time the Roosevelt coalition—the alliance of labor, minority groups, and southerners that FDR had created and that had formed the backbone of welfare-state politics since the 1930s. But Johnson's conduct of the war in Vietnam had undermined his authority with the public, and many of his domestic achievements, especially those involving civil rights, had widened the cracks in the coalition signaled by the rise of the New Right. The election of 1968 hammered home the fact that American society, like the Roosevelt coalition, was badly driven by race, cultural conflict,

and war and that its commitment to the liberal welfare state was increasingly open to question.

## Suggested Reading

Robert Dallek, *Flawed Giant: Lyndon Johnson and His Times, 1961-1973* (1998)

Todd Gitlin, *The Sixties: Years of Hope, Days of Rage* (1987)

Robert Gottlieb, *Forcing the Spring: The Transformation of the American Environmental Movement* (1993)

George Hering, *America's Longest War*, 3rd ed. (1996)

Manning Marable, *Race, Reform, and Rebellion: The Second Reconstruction in Black America, 1945-1982*, 2nd ed. (1991)

Ernest May and Philip D. Zelikow, eds. *The Kennedy Tapes: Inside the White House during the Cuban Missile Crisis* (1997)

Richard Reeves, *President Kennedy: Profile of Power* (1963)

# Chapter Review

## Summary
### QUESTIONS

■ How did nuclear weapons and missiles figure in shaping the United States' relations with the U.S.S.R.?

■ Why did Americans become more concerned with the quality of life and what were the results of their concern?

■ What was the New Right and why did it gain strength during the 1960s?

■ What were the accomplishments of the civil rights movement and the women's movement?

■ Why did the Vietnam War so divide American society?

## Chronology

| | |
|---|---|
| 1960 | Contraceptive pill becomes widely available. |
| April 17, 1961 | Bay of Pigs invasion in Cuba. |
| May 1961 | Freedom Rides begin into deep South. |
| August 1961 | Berlin Wall built. |
| 1962 | Publication of Rachel Carson's *Silent Spring*. |
| October 1962 | Cuban missile crisis. |
| | James Meredith, a black student, enters the University of Mississippi. |
| July 1963 | Nuclear Test Ban Treaty. |
| August 1963 | March on Washington. |
| November 22, 1963 | President Kennedy assassinated. |
| 1964 | The Civil Rights Act. |
| August 1964 | Gulf of Tonkin Resolution. |
| 1965 | The Voting Rights Act. |
| 1966 | National Organization of Women established. |
| June 5–11, 1967 | Six-Day War in the Middle East. |
| January 31, 1968 | Tet offensive in Vietnam. |
| April 4, 1968 | Martin Luther King Jr. assassinated in Memphis. |
| June 5, 1968 | Robert Kennedy assassinated in Los Angeles. |

## Key Terms

Cuban Missile Crisis (p. 857)

Freedom Rides (p. 860)

The Great Society (p. 867)

Counterculture (p. 877)

Black Power (p. 880)

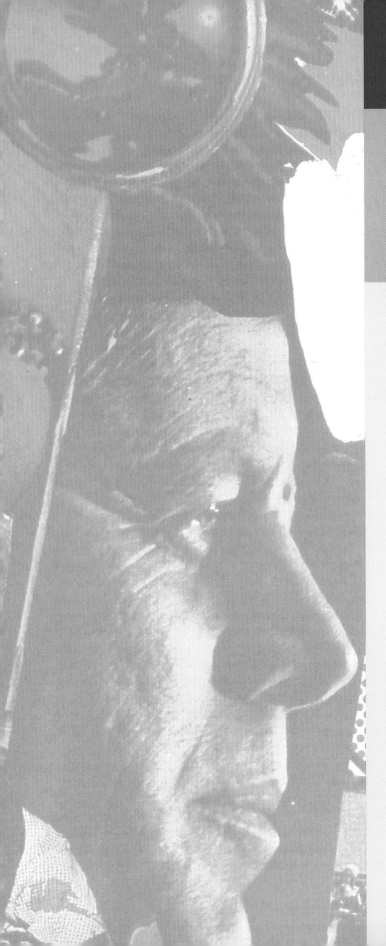

# Part 8

# OPPORTUNITIES AND LIMITS IN A GLOBALIZING WORLD

By 1973, American troops had been withdrawn from Vietnam, which diminished the civil antagonisms at home, but political divisions and suspicion of government persisted. They were accompanied during the Seventies by rampant inflation, stunted economic growth, and declining heavy industries, difficulties that were partly indigenous in origin, partly the result of the increasing interdependence of the world's markets, later called "globalization." Even more intensely than in the sixties, many Americans disliked the rise of sexual permissiveness, abortion rights, the advancing independence of women, and the insistence on civil rights for blacks, other minorities of color, and homosexuals. The resentments were compounded by a new wave of immigrants from Asia, the Middle East, and Latin America whose arrival in the United States strained the social fabric as well as state and local budgets.

Apprehensions about the economy joined with the social resentments to bring about a rightward realignment of attitudes, expectations, and politics. The shift was marked by a crumbling of the Roosevelt coalition—the alliance of labor, minority groups, and the white South that had sustained the liberal welfare state. Replacing it was a new alliance of fiscal conservatives committed to reduced government and social conservatives, including an energetic new religious right, eager for government to reverse what its members considered a decline in family and moral values. The alliance was an uneasy one, since many fiscal conservatives were social liberals, but it was sufficient to turn the South into Republican country, to give the religious right an influence in government that it had not enjoyed since the 1920s, and to exercise powerful influence in elections and policymaking into the early twenty-first century.

Beginning in the 1980s, activist executive leadership, long associated with liberals, was embraced by conservatives to curb inflation, deregulate the economy, and roll back the welfare

This collage by the artist Robert Rauschenberg vividly depicts the people, events, and turmoil of the 1960s, which would continue to affect American Society in the years that followed.

state. The economy moved into high gear once again, fueled by military spending, tax cuts, and international trade agreements that made the United States a partner in the globalizing market place. As in previous conservative eras, the dividends of the prosperity were distributed unevenly, producing a widening gap between the rich and everyone else. Many Americans lived without job security or health benefits, and homeless people wandered the streets of the major cities.

Paradoxically, the conservatism in government was accompanied by a dynamic ferment of economic and social change. The private sector bubbled with entrepreneurial creativity, drawing on the bank of federally sponsored research to produce the biotechnology and personal computer industries, cell phones, the Internet, and other innovations in medical technologies, communications, entertainment, and sports. An increasing portion of minority group members climbed into the middle class and moved to the suburbs, and the new immigrants enriched the nation's multiracial and multicultural character. Americans invented new arrangements for working, parenting, and shopping as a growing number of women entered the workforce.

Not long after the United States pulled out of Vietnam, the Saigon government fell to the rebels and the country was unified under the North's Communist leadership. The defeat of U.S. policy led Americans to curb the warmaking powers of the president and to grow wary of armed intervention against aggression, even Communist in origin, that did not incontestably threaten the United States' national security. American policymakers continued to see the hand of the Soviets behind left-leaning movements and regimes in the Third World, but the government for the most part refrained from armed intervention of its own, and when American troops were deployed they were withdrawn quickly. The United States preferred to work its will by resorting to covert action, some of it blatantly illegal.

But American foreign policy was also marked by major new departures, responses to the challenges and opportunities of the globalizing world. During the 1970s, in a breakaway from long-standing policy, the U.S. government recognized the People's Republic of China, a move that opened China's vast potential market to American goods. In a direct challenge to dictatorships everywhere, the United States placed human rights on the world political agenda. It also responded constructively to a change in Soviet leadership that at the end of the 1980s led to the replacement in Russia and its satellites of totalitarian institutions by democratic ones, the peaceful dismantling of the Soviet empire, and, soon, the end of the Cold War.

Through the 1990s the United States sought to establish a new world order, one that would protect American security, maintain a stable balance of power, and foster capitalism in post-Cold War Europe. However, stability was threatened by several rogue nations—North Korea, Iran, and Iraq—which seemed determined to acquire nuclear weapons, and by hostility between the Arab states and Israel, which after two brief wars had occupied territories heavily populated by Palestinians. The American government mounted repeated efforts to negotiate peace in the Middle East, not least because of U.S. dependence on its oil.

When in 1990 Iraq invaded oil-rich Kuwait to its South, the United States organized a multinational coalition that included a number of Arab states to wage the Gulf War, driving the Iraqis back across their border. Some Islamic fundamentalists, furious at the American intervention in the region, initiated a war of terror against the United States. In the wake of several attacks during the 1990s, the government increased its surveillance of potential terrorist activities, but the heightened guard proved inadequate against the conspirators of September 11, 2001.

The destruction and death the conspirators wrought that day constituted another turning point in the nation's history, one comparable to that brought about by the events at Pearl Harbor sixty years earlier. President George W. Bush declared war on terrorism, committing the United States to find and destroy its perpetrators and to retaliate against regimes that gave them safe haven. In a departure from the multilateralism that had characterized American foreign policy since 1940, the President made clear in several areas of policy that the United States would act unilaterally whenever the defense of its economic and military security required it. In a revival of the evangelism for democracy that had suffused American foreign policy through the nineteenth century, he proclaimed that the way to destroy terrorism was to bring democracy to the autocratic regions of the Islamic world that generated its support.

In pursuit of these ends, the Bush administration sent troops to Afghanistan and launched a war in Iraq. At home, it battled terrorism in ways that threatened civil liberties. Midway through the first decade of the twenty-first century, as the war against terrorism seemed likely to strech on indefinitely, it was evident that the events of September 11, 2001 had ushered the United States into an era fraught with uncertainty and peril.

# Chapter 31

## REVIVAL OF CONSERVATISM:

### 1969–1980

Anti-abortion protestors rally in front of the Capitol building in Washington, D.C. on January 22, 1979—the sixth anniversary of the *Roe v. Wade* decision.

891

## Focus QUESTIONS

■ *How successful was Nixon's policy of détente?*

■ *How did the Nixon administration deal with the major health and environmental issues in this period?*

■ *What series of events led to Nixon's resignation?*

■ *How did the Ford and Carter administrations deal with the energy crisis?*

■ *How did Carter's idealism affect his foreign and domestic policies?*

■ *What energized the emergence of the New Right during the 1970s?*

Richard Nixon faced a bitterly divided nation, a troublesome economy, and a draining war. The day after his election, he issued a victory statement inspired, he said, by a sign he saw a teenager carrying during the campaign: "We want to bridge the generation gap. We want to bridge the gap between the races. We want to bring America together." Not wanting "to end up like LBJ, holed up in the White House afraid to show my face on the street," he also intended "to stop that war. Fast." But Nixon's way of stopping the war made him unwelcome on many streets in America. He wound up dividing the country far more than he brought it together, and the social gaps that had opened in the 1960s over civil rights for women and minorities grew even wider.

## Nixon: World Strategist

Campaign commentators had spoken of a "new Nixon." The old Nixon, a product in part of the California of rampant developers, resentment of the East, and savage red-baiting, had a reputation for valuing no principle higher than the pursuit of political advantage. He was often distrustful, self-pitying, and suspicious, especially of the media. "You won't have Nixon to kick around anymore," he snapped at a press conference after losing the California gubernatorial race in 1962. During the next several years, Nixon resurrected himself politically, tirelessly helping Republican candidates for office and forging the new Nixon in the foreign and domestic fires of the mid-1960s.

The new Nixon, drawing on broad historical reading and reflection on contemporary geopolitical trends, envisioned himself a statesman. More judicious than before in his anti-Communism, he was a realist rather than a moralizer in world affairs. He was prepared to exploit the plain fact that the Communist world was no longer monolithic, if it ever had been, evident especially in a rift that was developing in Chinese-Soviet relations. While keeping the Soviet Union in check, he intended to pursue a strategy of détente—reducing tensions with the Communist world, slowing the nuclear arms race, and refraining from armed intervention where U.S. vital interests were not at risk. But his strategy depended first on ending the war in Vietnam, removing what one of his speechwriters called "a bone in the nation's throat."

In pursuit of these ends, Nixon concentrated control of foreign policy in the White House, relying heavily on his national security adviser, Henry Kissinger, who in 1973 became secretary of state. A refugee from Nazi Germany, a former Harvard professor, and a brilliant analyst of world nuclear politics, Kissinger was ambitious to be a foreign-policy maker in his own right. He admired the balance-of-power strategies of Prince Metternich, the Austrian statesman who had brought stability to Europe after the Napoleonic Wars; indeed, he seemed to rank stability ahead of democracy. His views of how to deal with the world dovetailed with Nixon's, and so did his penchant for intrigue and secretiveness in the conduct of foreign affairs.

### EXITING VIETNAM

While determined to bring American troops home from Vietnam, Nixon felt compelled to accomplish the withdrawal in an "honorable" way, which meant preserving an independent, pro-U.S. government in Saigon. In mid-1969, he announced what became known as the Nixon Doctrine: the United States would no longer act as a military protagonist in combating Communist subversion in the third world. Asian nations could count on America's moral and financial assistance; but if faced with armed challenges, they would have to defend themselves.

In Vietnam, the Nixon Doctrine translated into a huge increase in American aid that enabled the South Vietnamese forces to expand and, in a process called "Vietnamization," take over responsibility for most of the ground war. As they did, the number of American troops in Vietnam fell steadily, dropping from more than 500,000 in 1969 to some 30,000 by 1972. At Nixon's initiative, the draft was ended in 1973, twenty-five years after it was reestablished, with the United States henceforth to rely on an all-volunteer army. Nixon also sidestepped the obstacles to peace persistently raised by the South Vietnamese by sending Kissinger to negotiate secretly in Paris with the North Vietnamese foreign minister, Le Duc Tho. Meanwhile, in March 1969, he intensified the American bombing campaign against North Vietnam and secretly extended it to North Vietnamese bases and supply routes in neighboring Laos and Cambodia. Nixon told an aide, "I want the North Vietnamese to believe I've reached the point where I might do *anything* to stop the war."

*A Prolonged War.* Nixon's strategy failed to disrupt the North Vietnamese operations in Laos or Cambodia, where a civil war broke out between pro-Communist and pro-American forces. Nor did it persuade the North to plead for peace. In April 1970, Nixon ordered American and South Vietnamese troops to invade Cambodia, explaining to the country: "If when the chips are down the U.S. acts like a pitiful helpless giant, the forces of totalitarianism will threaten free nations and free institutions throughout the world." The venture proved indecisive militarily and stimulated the North Vietnamese to increase their support to the Cambodian Communist cadres (the Khmer Rouge), thus widening the war in Indochina. (After the Khmer Rouge triumphed, in 1976, it embarked on a savage policy of genocide that lasted until 1979, killing 2 million people.)

The invasion of Cambodia prompted widespread denunciations at home as well as abroad—some of Nixon's own staff resigned—and provoked a wave of nationwide protests reminiscent of 1968, many of them on college and university campuses. At Kent State University in Ohio, the governor called out the National Guard after rioting broke out downtown and the ROTC building was firebombed. On May 4, 1970, as students—some throwing stones but all unarmed—demonstrated against the governor's action, guardsmen on campus opened fire, killing four students and wounding eleven others. Ten days later, two students were killed at Jackson State University in Mississippi when police fired into a women's dormitory.

At Easter 1972, North Vietnam launched a major offensive, the largest since 1968. With the number of American troops in Vietnam now substantially reduced, Nixon responded with what the *New York Times* called "diplomacy through terror"—mining Haiphong Harbor and sending B-52s over North Vietnam's major cities. "The bastards have never been bombed like they are going to be bombed this time," he promised.

A horrified student at Kent State University kneels beside the body of one of the four demonstrators killed by National Guardsmen during antiwar protests on the campus, May 4, 1970.

*End of the American War.* All the while, Kissinger had continued his secret negotiations in Paris with Le Duc Tho, North Vietnam's negotiator. By the fall of 1972, the two men had arrived at a cease-fire agreement that required the withdrawal of all remaining American troops, arranged for the return of U.S. prisoners of war, and permitted North Vietnam to maintain troops in the South and the Vietcong to participate in a government of reconciliation. Kissinger returned home shortly before the upcoming presidential election, announcing that "peace is at hand." However, South Vietnam's President Thieu balked at the terms pertaining to the North Vietnamese troops and the Vietcong. Nixon tolerated Thieu's recalcitrance, but Le Duc Tho, angry at his obstinacy, pressed for still greater concessions. Nixon responded by ordering the most extensive bombing of North Vietnam yet during Christmas week 1972, with B-52s destroying factories, hospitals, houses, and transportation facilities in Hanoi and Haiphong. In Paris at the opening of 1973, the United States and North Vietnam agreed to a settlement much like the one Kissinger had negotiated in October, thus ending America's longest involvement in a war.

### DÉTENTE

The withdrawal from Vietnam enabled Nixon to pursue his grand strategy of détente, particularly to seek a transformation of the United States' relations with China. Following Mao Zedong's victory in 1949, the United States had refused to recognize the Communist regime, supporting instead the government on Taiwan as the legitimate China. It had vetoed the admission of the People's Republic to the United Nations and had cut off America's trade with the mainland regime while pressuring other Western nations to restrict theirs. But since the mid-1960s, China and the Soviet Union had been growing apart. Chinese leaders were made apprehensive when in 1968 Soviet troops suppressed a reformist government in Czechoslovakia and seemed to threaten Beijing by strengthening their forces along China's northern and western frontiers.

After Soviet tanks entered Prague, the Chinese signaled to the United States that they wanted to talk. Nixon and Kissinger welcomed the offer, seeing in China a counter to Soviet expansionism. Publicly indicating its new flexibility, China hosted a U.S. ping-pong team in Beijing in April 1971. Two months later, his way prepared in secret negotiations conducted by Kissinger, Nixon announced that he would visit the People's Republic "to seek normalization of relations."

On February 21, 1972, Nixon's plane touched down in China, making him the first sitting U.S. president to visit that country and initiating a media spectacle. Television cameras and news reporters sent daily reports to American homes of Nixon's triumphal tour, including the president beaming at the Great Wall and exchanging rice-liquor toasts with Mao Zedong and the Chinese premier, Jou En-lai (Chou En-lai), at the Great Hall of the People. Nixon agreed to the eventual withdrawal of American troops from Taiwan, the island off the Chinese mainland that remained under the control of the anti-Communist Chinese Nationalist government, and accepted Beijing's claim that Taiwan was part of China. His visit

President Nixon (second from right) meets with Mao Zedong (center), the leader of the People's Republic of China, in Beijing, February 21, 1972.

marked a historic turning point in the Cold War, opening the way to the restoration of full diplomatic relations with China, achieved in 1979. It also made the future of relations with the principal Communist powers what Kissinger called a "three-dimensional game," allowing the United States to play the Soviet Union and China off against each other.

*Missiles and the Soviets.* In May, achieving another presidential first, Nixon went to Moscow, returning with several agreements indicating that the United States' opening to China had made the Soviets eager to improve their relations with the West. The accords covered the sale of American grain to the Soviet Union, cooperation in the exploration of space, and a treaty on anti-ballistic missiles (ABMs) that had originated with the Johnson administration.

In 1964, the Chinese had exploded their first nuclear weapon, enlarging the potential nuclear threat, and soon the Russians started deploying a primitive ABM around Moscow. Partly to overwhelm the Soviet ABMs, the Johnson administration began installing MIRVs—multiple, independently targetable warheads—on single missiles. The American military and congressional Republicans began agitating for the establishment of an ABM system that would knock out incoming nuclear warheads, wherever they might come from. Despite the renewed nuclear bristling, the United States remained engaged with the Soviets on arms control, seeking agreements on both offensive and defensive missiles.

Building on the Johnson administration's efforts, the Nixon administration began serious strategic arms limitation talks (SALT) with the Soviets in 1969. At the time, Nixon proposed to deploy an antiballistic missile system to defend the country's offensive missile installations. In August 1969, in the face of protest rallies and warnings by distinguished scientists that the system would not work, Nixon's ABM program cleared the Senate by just one vote. Nixon, aware that the ABM system was vulnerable, authorized the United States' SALT negotiators to use it as a bargaining chip.

The SALT Treaty, signed in Moscow in 1972, allowed each country two ABM systems—one to protect its capital city, the other to defend a field of offensive missiles. A complementary agreement capped the number of offensive missiles allowed either side for five years to those already under construction or deployed. But the MIRV race continued, since the cap on the number of each side's missiles only encouraged each to pack their vehicles with as many warheads as possible. Still, the SALT Treaty, which the Senate ratified by an overwhelm-

ing majority, did dampen the ABM branch of the arms race, at least for the time being.

## THE THIRD WORLD

Outside of Europe, where relations between the two superpowers had stabilized, many regions were marked by instabilities that were seen to jeopardize American interests or make them ripe for the continued Soviet support of national liberation movements. Nixon and Kissinger, eager to thwart Communist advances in the third world without resorting to armed intervention, lent support to authoritarian right-wing governments and covertly sought to replace left-leaning regimes by staunchly anti-Communist ones.

*Anti-Communism by Other Means.* After the election of the Marxist Salvador Allende to the presidency of Chile in 1970, Kissinger declared, "I don't see why we need to stand by and watch a country go Communist due to the irresponsibility of its own people." Kissinger instructed the CIA to "destabilize" Allende's new government, and the United States terminated economic aid to Chile. Allende's government, which had been elected with only 36 percent of the vote and whose economic policies were questioned by many Chileans, might have lost power anyway. But in 1973, he was ousted and killed in a military coup in which the CIA was complicit. The new regime, a dictatorial military junta led by General Augusto Pinochet, aroused condemnation around the world for its practices of torture and oppression. Nixon nevertheless not only immediately recognized it but supplied it with generous economic aid.

In Africa, Nixon backed the Portuguese colonial authorities in Angola and supplied aid and comfort to the white regimes in Rhodesia and South Africa, both brutal in their treatment of black inhabitants. When Portugal quit Angola in 1975, the newly independent state was savaged by guerrilla warfare, one side supported by the Soviets, the other by the United States together with South Africa and China. With Kissinger's authorization, the CIA undertook covert armed intervention on behalf of the pro-American guerrillas, a move that the Soviets countered by importing 10,000 Cuban troops.

Kissinger ultimately endorsed black majority rule in Africa, convinced on grounds of realpolitik (realistic politics) that it was essential to gain the support of the vast majority of people living there. But throughout the third world, the Nixon-Kissinger policies intensified the impression that the

895

United States was less an inspiration to freedom than a bulwark of counterrevolution and right-wing authoritarianism.

*Israel, Arabs, and Oil.* Since the Six-Day War in 1967, Arab-Israeli tensions had mounted, exacerbated by the bitterness of the Palestinians who had been expelled from Israel. The Palestinians had formed the Palestine Liberation Organization, a political pressure group based in Jordan that sometimes resorted to terrorism. In Egypt, Anwar el-Sadat, a modernizing nationalist like his predecessor, Gamal Abdel Nasser, had come to power following Nasser's death in 1970. Faced with a steadily weakening economy, he decided to go to war against Israel in the hope of regaining control of the Suez Canal.

On October 6, 1973—Yom Kippur, the holiest day of the Jewish year—Egypt and Syria launched a full-scale attack against Israel. The United States pressed for a quick cease-fire and offered to mediate the conflict. However, the Israelis, caught off guard, facing advanced Soviet weapons and suffering high losses, sent Nixon a desperate plea for aid. The president announced that the United States would immediately send an airlift of arms to counter the Soviets' supply to Egypt. Pulling themselves together after ten days, the Israelis counterattacked, cutting off the Egyptian Third Army in the Sinai Peninsula. Although Israel, Egypt, and Syria accepted a U.N. call for a cease-fire, sporadic fighting continued. The Soviets, unwilling to let the Third Army be annihilated, threatened to intervene militarily. Then, on the night of October 24, Nixon took the unusual step of ordering American nuclear forces around the world onto an alert. At the same time, according to later claims by Israeli officials, the United States warned that it would abandon Israel unless Israel spared the Egyptian force and quit fighting. The next day, the cease-fire went fully into effect; six days later, the United States pulled back from the alert.

The American shipment of arms to Israel nevertheless angered the oil-producing Arab states. Acting through the Organi-

*American Journal*

## Impact of the Oil Crisis, 1973/74

*To cope with the oil crisis of 1973-1974, government regulators imposed measures such as Sunday shut-downs of gas stations and the allowance of gas purchases on alternate days to cars with license plates ending in odd or even numbers. The situation angered consumers waiting for the pumps, some of whom turned violent, and caused frustration as well as financial jeopardy for the service station owners. A New York Times reporter recorded the experiences of Norman Reichbach, the co-owner of a Getty service station just north of the city line between the Bronx and Yonkers, in New York.*

"Like the other day. I'm pumping gas and my wife drives up and gets on the end of the line. She's waiting maybe 15 minutes before I see her. So I wave her to the front of the line. She says she doesn't want to jump the line but I say it's O.K. Then this guy in front starts to complain. 'Look buddy,' I says, 'I sleep with her, not with you.'

"Gifts? You wouldn't believe it. Liquor. Ties. We got two propositions. I won't take money, but they offer.

"The gimmicks! This guy in a truck comes in for a grease job and oil change, and yeah, of course, gas; costs him three bucks for the lube and four bucks for four quarts. A week later he's back for another grease job and lube and gas. I says, 'Hell, no!' . . .

"Animals! People get to be animals for gas. The other day there's a long line at the pumps, right? A guy comes down the street and goes to make a right turn; he just wants to turn. Three guys think he's jumping the line and jump out of their cars to punch him in the mouth. Animals! . . .

"This can't last forever—we hope. Someday it's got to level off. . .

"Know how I feel now? My house faces the station. When I get up and go into the bathroom to brush my teeth I can see them lining up in their cars with their lunch and their thermoses, like they're going on an outing. And I get sick."

Ralph Blumenthal, "Manning the Pump is Like Manning a Battle Station," *The New York Times,* March 3, 1974.

This 1973 cartoon illustrates how the United States' foreign policy in the Middle East has been constrained by the country's reliance on Arab oil supplies.

zation of Petroleum Exporting Countries (OPEC), which they dominated, they embargoed all shipments of crude oil to the United States and Western Europe. The embargo, which lasted until March 1974, sent shock waves through the industrial world, quadrupling the price of a barrel of crude oil, precipitating acute fuel shortages, and driving a wedge in the Western alliance, whose European members along with Japan depended heavily on oil imported from the Middle East. In the United States, domestic oil was in short supply, and oil imports, much of it from the Middle East, jumped by almost a factor of two from 1970 to 1974. The price of gasoline at the pump shot up 40 percent, motorists waited in long lines to fill up, and many service stations simply ran out of gas. Since oil was essential for the transportation of both goods and people, the jump in oil prices threatened to affect the entire economy. To conserve oil, Nixon called for stepped-up licensing of nuclear power plants and a national speed limit of fifty miles per hour.

## Nixon at Home, Bright and Dark

Domestic affairs did not engage Richard Nixon as much as foreign policy. He had long thought the country "could run itself domestically without a President," relying only on "a competent cabinet." But bringing the country together was a presidential task and also good politics—or at least so Nixon thought during the early years of his administration. It dove-

tailed with his long-standing Eisenhower-like centrism in much of domestic affairs, which was reinforced by the urging of Daniel Patrick Moynihan, a Harvard sociologist and domestic adviser to Nixon, to maintain Johnson's antipoverty programs and pursue a moderate reformism. He was further pushed in a reformist direction by the inescapable political fact that both houses of Congress remained under Democratic control throughout his presidency.

To Nixon, moderate reformism meant dealing with social problems by relying less on direct action from the federal government and more on federal encouragement of reformist efforts by the states, private enterprise, and individuals. He launched several such initiatives, but most failed. The boldest was a proposal for scrapping the welfare system, whose clients, half of them children, had doubled between 1961 and 1972, and replacing it with a Family Assistance Plan that would guarantee direct annual incomes to the poor—for a family of four, $1,600 in cash and $800 in food stamps. The initiative passed the House but died in the Senate, caught in a political crossfire between liberals who considered the benefits too small and conservatives dead set against the concept of a guaranteed income.

Although Nixon vetoed legislation for national day care, he called for making child care expenses tax-deductible if both parents worked. He also recommended that the federal government share its revenues with the states in the form of earmarked block grants to spend as they wished, a plan that Congress did enact in 1972 and that the president hailed as the arrival of a "New Federalism."

Despite his moderate inclinations, Nixon remained suspicious, combative, and prone to anger, equating opposition to his policies with drives to bring him down personally. He frequently felt himself embattled, especially by the "eastern liberal establishment." Dissents from his policies brought out the darker angels of his nature. Drawing away from reconciliation, he turned toward confrontation, vengefulness, abuse of power, and, ultimately, the destruction of his presidency.

### STRUGGLING WITH THE ECONOMY

Nixon's presidency was vexed by increasingly acute economic problems. In fighting the Vietnam War, Lyndon Johnson had refused to scale back the programs of the Great Society or raise taxes, insisting that the United States could have both "guns and butter." The resulting federal deficits combined with high consumer spending to drive prices upward at an increasing rate. Between 1967 and 1970, the consumer price index rose some 16 percent, a major jump over the inflation rate that had prevailed since the mid-1950s. Nixon responded by encouraging the Federal Reserve Board to tighten the money supply and raise interest rates. Between January 1969 and mid-1971, these initiatives resulted in a recession, with unemployment rising to 6 percent, and still more inflation. Sensitive to the needs and political power of senior citizens, Nixon approved legislation that increased Social Security benefits while tying them to changes in the cost of living.

The rise in prices made American goods more expensive abroad, adversely affecting American exports. The recovered industries of Western Europe and Japan, many of their factories new and of superior efficiency, had already been increasing their share of the American market, notably in automobiles and consumer electronics. In 1971, Americans imported $3 billion more goods than they exported, the first deficit in the balance of trade since 1893. At the end of the year, Nixon formally devalued the dollar, which would discourage imports by making them more expensive for Americans and encourage exports by making American goods cheaper for foreigners. He also ended the dollar's convertibility into gold and allowed its price to rise and fall in response to the demand for it in foreign currencies, thus dissolving the international monetary system established at Bretton Woods (see Chapter 27).

Desperate to curb "stagflation"—the debilitating mixture of stagnation and inflation that was besetting the economy—Nixon declared himself a Keynesian. In 1970, he had announced that he would never impose wage and price controls in the interest of political expediency. Now, in August 1971, partly with an eye to the next year's election, he announced a ninety-day wage-price freeze—the first one since Truman took a similar action during the Korean War in 1951—and in early November he imposed wage and price controls. The inflation rate fell, but after his reelection Nixon substituted voluntary guidelines for controls. Prices then swiftly moved higher, inflating at a 10 percent annual rate by the end of 1973.

### SCIENCE AND THE ENVIRONMENT

Nixon displayed little active interest in the quality-of-life issues that had emerged in the 1960s—notably, culture, scientific achievement, and the environment. He did, however, react to political initiatives from the Democratic Congress and to the climate of opinion as it shifted in response to the beleaguered state of the economy and the inequities in society. The presi-

dent approved the creation of the Occupational Safety and Health Administration, which would oversee conditions in the workplace, and he endorsed enlarged funding for the National Endowments for the Arts and the Humanities. When *Apollo 11* landed on the moon in July 1969, Nixon joined millions of thrilled people around the world in listening to Neil Armstrong say, as his foot touched the lunar surface, "That's one small step for man; one giant leap for mankind." But Americans could also understand the reaction of a university student who, though "very proud," had to confess that he also "thought of all the people who live in the ghettos," adding, "The flag may be flying on the moon, but it is also flying in their neighborhoods, where there are poverty, disease, and rats."

Pollsters discovered that Americans ranked the space race far lower in importance as a national problem than water and air pollution or job training and poverty. The United States sent five more successful manned missions to the moon, the last of which occurred in 1972, by which time public interest in the Apollo Program had fallen sharply. By then, it was evident that the Soviets had given up the goal of sending their

Astronaut Edwin "Buzz" Aldrin on the moon, July 20, 1969. Neil Armstrong, commander of the *Apollo 11*, took the picture.

own crews to the moon and were more interested in cooperation rather than competition in space. In 1975, in the last manned mission of the decade, an American crew linked up with the orbiting Soviet *Soyuz 19* and jointly conducted experiments with its two cosmonauts.

Amid the declining interest in Apollo, hard times came to basic science. In 1967, the overall federal budget for research and development had turned downward for the first time since the Depression, falling 18 percent by 1973. Even so, physicists and their allies obtained authorization to construct a giant particle accelerator south of Chicago. Named the Fermi National Laboratory, after the refugee Nobel physicist Enrico Fermi, the accelerator enabled American scientists to carry out world-class work in high-energy physics during the rest of the century.

***Environmental Pollution.*** Before his presidency, Nixon had been indifferent to environmental matters. He favored job growth, especially in the auto industry, over strict environmental restrictions. But he was sensitive enough to the environmental movement's swelling political power—millions of people participated in the celebration of the first Earth Day in 1970—to want to be kept "out of trouble" in dealing with it, as he told his aide John Ehrlichman, a land-use lawyer sympathetic to environmental protection. During the Nixon years, a torrent of environmental measures cascaded through Congress and the White House. In January 1970, Nixon signed the National Environmental Policy Act, which opened the way to his establishment later that year of the Environmental Protection Agency (EPA), a body with sweeping regulatory powers. The act also directed all federal agencies to take into account the environmental impact of their activities, a requirement that gave ordinary citizens the opportunity to take these agencies to court if they did not. Congress cast a cold eye on new irrigation and dam projects in the West. It also enacted laws to clean up oil spills, improve air and water quality, and protect endangered species.

Scientific studies were beginning to link specific chemicals to human cancer. The studies were reinforced by tests of chemical carcinogenicity carried out on animals and by increasing knowledge of the genetic damage that chemicals caused. The data were overwhelming that the most significant environmental carcinogen was self-inflicted—smoke from tobacco. In 1970, the federal government toughened the law requiring warning labels on cigarette packages and banned advertisements for smoking from radio and television. The

A demonstration by environmentalists in New York City to help save the planet, one of many held around the country on Earth Day, April 22, 1970.

Nixon administration also prohibited the use of DDT and cyclamates, a sweetener said to cause cancer.

### APPEAL TO THE SILENT MAJORITY

Despite his stated eagerness to unite the country, Nixon turned confrontational as he devised a strategy for reelection. He resolved to mobilize what in 1969 he would call the "great silent majority," another term for Middle America, appealing in particular to whites in the South along with ethnic Catholics and blue-collar workers in the North. Convinced that people were "fed up with liberals," he aimed to solidify the conservative majority that appeared to be forming in the United States by exploiting the mounting resentment against inflation, crime, sexual permissiveness, demanding blacks, and domestic radicals.

***Covert War.*** Nixon himself had come to feel some of these resentments with venomous force. The domestic upheavals after Cambodia brought out his tendency, as an aide later wrote, to be "absolutely paranoid about criticism," and his attitudes shaped the outlook of his staff. Nixon mounted a largely secret war against liberal, dissident, and radical groups and individuals, using federal agencies to harass them with tax audits, spy on them with wiretapping, disrupt them by infiltration, and break them by prosecution. Previous presidents had indulged in one such tactic or another—most recently, John Kennedy and Lyndon Johnson in waging war against, respectively, organized crime and radical antiwar protesters. But Nixon's willingness to use such means was far more sweeping. He ordered the FBI and the CIA into the battle, even though the CIA was legally prohibited from engaging in domestic activities.

But in 1971, the *New York Times* published the Pentagon Papers, a documentary history of the United States' conduct of the Vietnam War through 1967 that the Defense Department had compiled and that Daniel Ellsberg, a former department analyst, had leaked to the newspaper. The documents covered only the Kennedy and Johnson years, but many of them were classified and their exposure jeopardized secret operations. Some revealed that the government then had not been straight with the American people about its actions, which implied that the government now might not be either. Nixon, furious, exploded to an aide, "Those sons of bitches are killing me. . . . We're up against an enemy, a conspiracy. They're using any means. We are going to use any means. Is that clear?" Nixon established a secret White House unit to stop such leaks—its members were known as the "plumbers"—using legal surveillance and illegal methods such as break-ins. In September 1971, in the first of a series of covert forays, the plumbers broke into the office of Ellsberg's psychiatrist in search of materials that might discredit him.

Nixon also constructed an "enemies list" made up of influential opponents of his policies whom he targeted for harassment. In 1973, he abolished the President's Science Advisory Committee, many of whose members doubted the wisdom of a missile defense. During the midterm election season of 1969–70, which coincided with the heated demonstrations against U.S. actions in Cambodia, Nixon unleashed Vice-President Agnew to attack the administration's enemies openly. Agnew, speaking to the resentments of the silent majority, disparaged antiwar protesters as "an effete corps of impudent snobs" and denounced the news media as "nattering nabobs of negativism." Nixon, hoping to exploit the widespread discontent with protests and violence,

stressed that the nation needed law and order. But many Democrats also embraced that theme. While, the Republicans gained two seats in the Senate, they lost nine in the House as well as eleven governorships.

*The Southern Strategy.* Nixon's moderate reformism extended to bread-and-butter issues for minorities. He created the Office of Minority Enterprises to promote black capitalism, and he approved subsidized housing for lower-income groups. In actions that affected corporations employing more than a third of the national labor force, he required that a fixed percentage of federal contracts be set aside for minority businesses and compelled federal contractors to create goals and timetables for the hiring and promotion of minorities. His Labor Department ordered unions across the country to enroll a specific number of blacks. However, Nixon was increasingly eager to woo whites—in the North, but especially the South—who felt threatened by the black drive for equality. He tried to block the protection of voting rights, impair the enforcement of fair housing, and halt the desegregation of public schools, especially through court-ordered busing.

Further in pursuit of his southern strategy, Nixon sought to reshape the Supreme Court by filling vacancies with appointees whose views were more congenial to his own. In 1969, he successfully nominated Warren Burger, a conservative federal judge, to succeed the retiring Earl Warren as chief justice. His nominees for the next open seat, both from the deep South, were rejected by the Senate—because of conflict of interest in the first case, intellectual mediocrity in the second. His next three appointees, all with strict-constructionist legal reputations, were approved. Contrary to expectations, however, the Burger Court hewed to a moderate course, retaining the essence of the *Miranda* rule and holding, in *Furman v. Georgia* (1972), against mandatory capital punishment. When the Nixon administration attempted to block publication of the Pentagon Papers, the Court decided, in *New York Times v. the United States* (1971), that the federal government did not have the power to prevent such material from being published. In 1971, in *Swann v. Charlotte-Mecklenburg Board of Education,* the Court upheld the constitutionality of busing to achieve school integration. Nixon, angry, went on national television to denounce the decision and call for Congress to enact a busing moratorium.

*The Election of 1972.* The Republicans renominated Nixon and Agnew. George Wallace, this time bringing his denunciations of integrationists and war protesters to the race for the Democratic nomination, piled up victories and strong showings in the South and Midwest, and on May 16 he won the primaries in Maryland and Michigan. But his candidacy was ended the day before, when he was shot and left paralyzed from the waist down. The Democrats chose George McGovern, a former history professor, now a liberal senator from South Dakota and a passionate opponent of the Vietnam War. McGovern's first-ballot victory was aided by new party rules requiring that every state delegation include young, minority, and female members in rough proportion to their presence in the population. An old-guard labor leader complained that the convention displayed "too much hair and not enough cigars," a crack that caught the convention's nationally televised image.

The image likely impaired McGovern's chances, but so did his withdrawal of support from his vice-presidential running mate, Senator Thomas Eagleton of Missouri, after it was revealed that Eagleton had undergone electric-shock therapy for depression. McGovern sounded like a radical, calling for immediate withdrawal of the American forces then still in Vietnam, the easing of penalties for marijuana use, and a program of income redistribution. Republicans, exploiting the resentments pervading Middle America, attacked him as a defender of "abortion, acid, and amnesty."

Nixon swept to an overwhelming victory, gaining nearly 61 percent of the popular vote, losing only Massachusetts and the District of Columbia, and dominating the electoral college 520 to 17. He appeared to have solidified the new conservative majority, winning solidly among blue-collar workers and Catholics in the North while carrying the entire South. However, the Democrats retained control of the House and increased their majority in the Senate by two seats, a sign that the New Deal coalition was not entirely shattered. While many Americans might have turned conservative on some issues, notably race, they remained moderate to liberal on others, especially the management of the economy.

## Watergate

Early in the election campaign, Nixon appointed Attorney General John Mitchell head of a new Committee to Reelect the President, later known as CREEP. Collecting millions in contributions, CREEP used some of the money to support a campaign of "dirty tricks" and espionage against Democrats. Possibly with Mitchell's approval, two of the White House plumbers planned a spying expedition to the Democratic National Committee Headquarters in the Watergate building in Washington. Early in the morning of June 17, 1972, a security guard caught five men breaking in to the headquarters with cameras and electronic surveillance devices in hand. Evidence found in their hotel rooms linked them to the White House, and one, James McCord, was quickly identified as working for CREEP.

Whether Nixon knew of the break-in beforehand or not, he was well aware of it within just a few days. Tapes produced by a voice-activated recording system that he had installed in the White House later revealed his response: cover up the crime. "Play it tough," he ordered H. R. Haldeman, one of his top aides. On June 23, Nixon ordered the CIA to tell the FBI that national security required a halt to the inquiry it had begun into the incident. The order, caught on tape, amounted to an obstruction of justice. The CIA refused to comply. Pursuing the cover-up, Nixon tried to buy silence from the burglars with some $400,000. He insisted publicly and privately that they had acted purely on their own, telling a press conference in July "categorically" that "no one in the White House staff, no one in this administration presently employed, was involved in this bizarre incident."

In January 1973, the five burglars together with the two plumbers came to trial before Judge John J. Sirica, in the U.S. District Court in Washington. In early February, not satisfied that his court had heard the full story, Sirica promised them stiff sentences unless they told the full truth. On March 23, McCord confessed that the defendants had perjured themselves and been pressured by the White House "to plead guilty and remain silent." In the meantime, Robert Woodward and Carl Bernstein, two young reporters on the *Washington Post*, began publishing revealing articles about CREEP's activities and the cover-up, drawing heavily on an anonymous knowledgeable source—he was revealed in 2005 as Mark Felt, the number two man at the F.B.I., in 1973—whom they called Deep Throat, a pseudonym borrowed from the title of a pornographic film of the day.

John Dean, the White House counsel, warned Nixon that "we have a cancer . . . close to the presidency, that's growing." In April, Nixon fired Dean, who, fearing that he would be saddled with the rap, decided to tell investigators what he knew. Later that month, Nixon announced that Haldeman and Ehrlichman had resigned and that he would clear up the spreading scandal. He appointed Secretary of Defense Elliot Richardson, a man of impeccable character, as his new attorney general. Under pressure from the Senate, Richardson appointed an independent special prosecutor for the spreading scandal of Watergate—Archibald Cox of the Harvard Law School, formerly Kennedy's solicitor general.

In May, a select Senate committee under Senator Sam Ervin of North Carolina began televised hearings into charges of corruption during the 1972 election. The proceedings held millions in thrall as Ervin, disarmingly casting himself as "a plain country lawyer," and his committee revealed the existence of Nixon's enemies list, his subjection of opponents to IRS audits, and his administration's responsiveness to illegal campaign contributions. Late in May, Nixon declared that his close aides, including Dean, had fashioned a cover-up without his knowledge. In June, Dean testified before the Ervin committee that the president had been fully involved in the cover-up. The question of Nixon's culpability pivoted on resolving the conflict between his word and Dean's, a seemingly impossible task.

But in July, the Ervin committee learned about the White House's voice-activated taping system. Cox and Ervin both sought access to the tapes. Nixon stonewalled, defending his action on grounds of executive privilege and national security. In October, as the result of a suit by Cox, a federal appeals court

Senator Sam Ervin of North Carolina, chair of the Senate Watergate committee, questions former presidential aide John Ehrlichman (back to camera).

ordered Nixon to turn over nine of the tapes to Judge Sirica. Nixon refused—and ordered Richardson to fire Cox. Richardson resigned rather than do so, and so did his deputy attorney general. The next ranking official in the Justice Department, Solicitor General Robert Bork, then did Nixon's bidding, carrying out what became known as the "Saturday night massacre." An avalanche of outrage swept across the nation and descended on the White House. In its face, Nixon relinquished the nine tapes to Sirica and appointed a new special prosecutor, Leon Jaworski, a conservative attorney from Houston.

### DOWNFALL

Nixon's troubles compounded when the U.S. district attorney in Maryland found that Vice-President Agnew had taken bribes while he was governor of Maryland and as vice-president. On October 10, 1973, Agnew resigned his office, pleading no contest to both the bribery counts and charges of income tax evasion. Following the procedures specified in the Twenty-fifth Amendment, which had been ratified in 1967, Nixon appointed the amiable Gerald R. Ford, the House minority leader, as his new vice-president.

Meanwhile, evidence surfaced that Nixon, in order to obtain a substantial tax deduction, had illegally backdated the gift of his vice-presidential papers and that the federal government had paid for improvements to his homes in San Clemente, California, and Key Biscayne, Florida. Nixon himself remained defiant, declaring at a nationally televised press session in November, "I am not a crook." The next month, the House Judiciary Committee began an impeachment inquiry. In March 1974, responding to evidence supplied by Jaworski, a grand jury recommended the indictment of seven Nixon aides including Haldeman, Ehrlichman, and Mitchell on grounds of perjury, obstruction of justice, and impeding the investigation of Watergate. Nixon was named as an unindicted "co-conspirator" because Jaworski believed he could not indict a sitting president.

That month, Jaworski and the House Judiciary Committee subpoenaed more tapes, particularly those of Nixon's conversations after the Watergate break-in. Nixon contested the subpoenas in court but, trying to wriggle out of the closing vise, did provide edited transcripts of the tapes. Dotted throughout with the bracketed phrase "expletive deleted," they revealed him as vindictive, bigoted, amoral, and foul-mouthed. Although they did not contain decisive evidence that he had obstructed justice—a smoking gun—they appalled even hard-line Republicans and intensified demands for his resignation.

In late July, the House Judiciary Committee adopted three articles of impeachment, accusing the president of obstructing justice in the Watergate investigation, abusing his power by exploiting agencies such as the CIA and the IRS for partisan purposes, and unconstitutionally resisting the committee's subpoenas. Of the twenty-one Republicans on the committee, six voted with the Democratic majority on the first charge, seven on the second, and two on the third.

At the same time, the Supreme Court, rejecting Nixon's claims of executive privilege, ruled that he had to give up the subpoenaed tapes. The unedited transcripts of the tapes finally provided the smoking gun, incontrovertible evidence that he had personally managed the cover-up, starting with his conversation with Haldeman six days after the break-in. Four anti-impeachment Republicans on the Judiciary Committee switched in favor of impeachment. A delegation of Re-

publicans led by Barry Goldwater told Nixon that he could count on no more than fifteen votes in the Senate against conviction. On August 9, 1974, Richard Nixon made history again, becoming the first president to resign. Gerald Ford, promptly sworn in as president, declared, "Our long national nightmare is over."

## COLD, GRAY MORNING

The nightmare may have ended, but it left consequences, and so, for both the better and the worse, did the explosive developments in foreign and domestic affairs that had transpired since Johnson's escalation of the war in Vietnam. With détente and the opening to China, Nixon had moved American foreign policy away from the post–World War II framework of a bipolar conflict between capitalism and Communism and adapted it to the reality—which the Vietnam War had demonstrated—that the Communist world comprised multiple centers only joined loosely if at all. The hard-line Cold Warrior had made the search for accommodations with Communism a legitimate goal for the United States. By ending the Vietnam War, he implicitly recognized that American power had limits. His enunciation of the Nixon Doctrine—marking a shift in foreign commitments that most Americans welcomed—declared, in effect, that the United States would no longer act as the world's military policeman, that in a world seething with postcolonial nationalist aspirations, there would be no more Vietnams.

Still, Nixon had wound down the Vietnam War in ways that threatened American democratic institutions. His highhandedness had been made possible by the steady accretion of presidential power, and the corresponding loss of congressional control, over national security since the beginning of the Cold War. In the War Powers Act of 1973, Congress attempted to restrict a president's power to make war indefinitely on his own while allowing him enough short-term autonomy to counter immediate threats to national security. Congressional investigations of the CIA and the FBI in 1975–76 revealed that both agencies grossly abused their power and provoked demands that they be reined in.

Since the 1930s, through World War II and much of the Cold War, Americans had tended to trust their government, especially the occupant of the White House. Now, both the Vietnam War and the Watergate scandal, with their lies and corruptions, encouraged distrust of the presidency, government in general, and

Richard Nixon flashes his signature salute on his departure from Washington after resigning the presidency, August 9, 1974.

indeed most authority in the United States. More than forty members of the Nixon administration were prosecuted for crimes. In 1974, aiming to reduce the incentive for politicos to sell favors, Congress provided for partial public financing of presidential campaigns and limitations on the role of private campaign contributions. Voter turnout had fallen from almost 64 percent in 1960 to just under 56 percent in 1972, an indication that Americans' expectations from government were steadily diminishing.

## Ford's Stewardship

"I am a Ford, not a Lincoln," the new president self-deprecatingly once said of himself. In 1974, Gerald R. Ford, age sixty-one, was a veteran Michigan congressman and right-of-center Republican, a dutiful party workhorse who had been rewarded with the House minority leadership before his elevation to the vice-presidency. The first chief executive not elected to either the presidency or the vice-presidency, Ford struck many Americans as less able than they liked their leaders to be. Still, he was unpretentious, affable, open, and honest, a refreshing change from Nixon. People were willing to allow him the benefit of the doubt, given the extraordinary circumstances of his ascent to the nation's highest office. Shortly after he entered the White House, Ford appointed, as his vice-president, Nelson Rockefeller, the former governor of New York, who was widely considered a sound choice.

But on September 8, a month after taking office, Ford stunned the country by fully and absolutely pardoning Nixon for "any and all crimes" he had committed against the United States during his presidency. While the aides who had done Nixon's bidding were punished, the pardon meant that his own offenses would never even be fully aired. Ford declared that his aim was "to heal the wounds throughout the United States," and in apparent keeping with that goal a week later he offered clemency to draft evaders during the Vietnam War in return for their taking an oath of allegiance and performing up to twenty-four months of alternate service. Nevertheless, millions of Americans were outraged by his pardoning of Nixon. Suspicions abounded that Ford had secretly agreed to the pardon in return for Nixon's appointing him vice-president. Whatever the truth of the matter, the deed greatly undermined Ford's credibility, heightening the nation's widespread distrust of its government.

### THE ECONOMY AND ENERGY

The continuing ripple effects of the OPEC price hikes drove up other prices, generating an inflation rate in 1974 of more than 12 percent. Ford responded with a program called Whip Inflation Now (WIN), which called for voluntary restraint in energy consumption and policy initiatives to slow the economy—notably, higher interest rates and reductions in federal spending. The inflation rate fell to slightly more than 9 percent the next year, but the price-cutting measures produced a severe recession. Between 1973 and 1975, the gross national product plunged 6 percent. In 1974, unemployment doubled to almost 9 percent, and the next year it climbed to 11 percent.

The economic troubles joined with resentments over Watergate in the 1974 congressional elections to produce a Democratic gain of forty-three seats in the House and three seats in the Senate. To stimulate the economy, Congress passed tax reductions in March and December 1975 that totaled $31 billion, but at Ford's insistence they were coupled to caps on spending. By 1976, the inflation rate had dropped to just under 5 percent, but at considerable cost in jobs.

In the landmark Energy Policy and Conservation Act of 1975, Congress established a 1-billion-barrel strategic petroleum reserve and required that domestic and imported automobiles meet average fuel efficiency standards—roughly doubling in ten years from 13 miles per gallon to 27.5 miles per gallon. The new standard promised to have a major impact on the oil supply, since at the time American cars and trucks burned one out of every seven barrels of oil used daily in the world.

### FOREIGN AFFAIRS

Ford kept Henry Kissinger on as secretary of state, reestablished a presidential science advisory apparatus, and continued Nixon's pursuit of détente with the Soviets. In a set of accords arrived at in Vladivostok, Siberia, in 1974, Ford and Brezhnev agreed to limit the number of strategic nuclear missiles on each side. In Helsinki the next year, Ford, Brezhnev, and the leaders of thirty-three other nations adopted another set of accords that formalized the post–World War II territorial boundaries and declared respect for human rights and greater freedom of travel. However, the Helsinki Accords were attacked by some Democrats as well as by the Republican right on grounds that they accepted the denial of freedom to the peoples of Eastern Europe. By 1976, Soviet oppression of

Jews and dissenters had aroused broad suspicion of détente in the United States.

*The Middle East.* The demonstrated vulnerability of Israel to concerted attack and of the United States to the oil embargo sent Kissinger to the Middle East to forge a political settlement. During much of 1974–75, he flew from one capital to another in what became known as "shuttle diplomacy." Kissinger kept the Soviets out of the peacemaking process so as to reduce their influence in the region. He achieved a pullback of forces along the Suez Canal, helped bring about an end to the oil embargo, and produced an Israeli-Syrian disengagement across the Golan Heights. Pressing Egypt and Israel to resolve their differences, he brought about a historic accord in the Sinai in September 1975 that provided for the withdrawal of Israeli troops from strategic parts of the peninsula and Egypt's opening of the Suez Canal to nonmilitary Israeli cargoes. Its way was greased by a U.S. commitment to supply advanced arms to Israel and a pledge not to deal with the Palestine Liberation Organization so long as it refused to recognize Israel's right to exist.

Egypt drew closer to the United States, gaining economic assistance but arousing enmity among other Arab states. Syria turned away from Egyptian president Sadat and adopted even a harder line against Israel. Nevertheless, Kissinger's tenacious shuttle diplomacy had added to Israel's security by neutralizing Egypt on its western flank and had improved the United States' own position in the Middle East.

*Asia.* Ford maintained the United States' distance from Vietnam, even after North Vietnam revived the war in 1974 and South Vietnam was threatened with defeat. In April 1975, Ford declared, "Today, America can regain the sense of pride that existed before Vietnam. But it cannot be achieved by refighting a war that is finished as far as America is concerned." The next month, Saigon fell to North Vietnamese troops and was immediately renamed Ho Chi Minh City. Television networks carried pictures of the desperate last exit of Americans, joined by South Vietnamese terrified of reprisals, from the helipad atop the U.S. embassy.

A few weeks later, the Khmer Rouge in Cambodia captured the American merchant ship *Mayaguez* in the Gulf of Siam. Ford got the crew back by ordering air strikes against Cambodia and sending the marines to the rescue. More American

South Vietnamese, desperate to reach the evacuation helicopters, crowd the walls of the U.S. embassy in Saigon as North Vietnamese forces take the city, April 29, 1975.

lives were lost in the operation (41) than the number of crew returned (39), but the venture, a small, momentary victory at a time of frustration over Southeast Asia, boosted Ford's popularity. The Vietnam War had cost the United States more than $150 billion and more than 360,000 casualties, including 58,000 dead, about 40 percent of whom were killed after Nixon took office. Some analysts consider the U.S. intervention in Vietnam as a necessary battle in the Cold War, but most historians consider it at best a tragic, costly error in policy, a misguided sacrifice of American blood and treasure.

## THE ELECTION OF 1976

Ford won the Republican nomination after fending off a strong challenge from Ronald Reagan, the onetime film actor, former governor of California, and champion of right-wing Republicans. He appeased conservatives by dumping Vice-President Nelson Rockefeller and designating Senator Robert Dole of Kansas as his running mate. James Earl Carter, a former governor of Georgia with virtually no standing in national affairs, emerged from among a crowded field of Democratic hopefuls to sweep the primaries and win his party's presidential nomination. A born-again Christian, he appealed to Americans disillusioned with Washington by styling himself as an unpretentious outsider, encouraging people to call him Jimmy, and promising that he would never lie. The Democratic vice-presidential nominee was Senator Walter Mondale, a liberal from Minnesota.

In the aftermath of Watergate, it seemed to many Democrats that, as one of them put it, "We could run an aardvark and win." Ford ran a lackluster campaign—and he astonished listeners in a debate with Carter by asserting, "There is no Soviet domination of Eastern Europe"—but Carter's campaign was also unimpressive. He promised little beyond honesty, decency, and goodness in government, appearing to believe that the high morality of his purpose would substitute for the murkiness of his proposals. By election day, Carter's sizable early lead in the polls had eroded. He squeaked to victory with only 51 percent of the popular vote but enough to gain him a margin of 297 to 240 in the electoral college. Apathy marked the election—only 53.3 percent of eligible voters cast ballots, down from 55.4 percent in 1972—an indication that Americans, disillusioned with government in the wake of Watergate, expected Washington to do little about the problems vexing the country at the opening of its third century since independence.

## Carter: A Presidency of Limits

On inauguration day in January 1977, Jimmy Carter forswore the traditional motorcade and formal dress to walk down Pennsylvania Avenue hand in hand with his wife, Rosalynn, wearing a standard business suit and overcoat. People appreciated the gesture of unpretentiousness, but they soon discovered that modest simplicity did not by itself make for an effective presidency. Carter's governmental experience had been confined to a stint in the Georgia legislature and one term as governor. He surrounded himself with a staff that was young, mainly from Georgia, and even less practiced than he was in national affairs. He dealt at a distance with Capitol Hill, declining to cultivate its leadership. As a result, "Carter couldn't get the Pledge of Allegiance through Congress," one politico noted.

Carter had campaigned as a kind of populist, yet, like the inauguration walk, his populism was more symbolic than substantive. He was an Annapolis graduate, a nuclear engineer, a successful farmer-businessman. Like Herbert Hoover, another engineer and businessman, he believed that complex issues would yield to careful rational analysis and that gov-

ernment would be more effective if it were made more efficient. Carter was highly intelligent and well intentioned; and though he lacked Woodrow Wilson's righteousness, his born-again Christianity added a touch of moral energy to his public purposes. In line with his gubernatorial record, he endorsed social progressivism, including civil rights for women and minorities. But Carter was not a liberal in the bread-and-butter manner of Lyndon Johnson. His commitment to progressive action was constrained by a reluctance to incur high federal costs. As his first budget director remarked, "He campaigns liberal, but he governs conservative."

### A TOUCH OF LIBERALISM

Making good on a campaign pledge to heal the wounds of Vietnam, Carter granted a full pardon to draft evaders the day after his inauguration. His action was applauded by liberals such as Senator Edward Kennedy, but it was denounced by conservatives, including the American Legion and the Republican national chairman, who declared it "a slap in the face to all those Americans and their families who did their duty." Sentiment on this issue reflected the ongoing division over the war itself. There had been neither celebratory parades for soldiers returning from Vietnam nor even national events of mourning for those who did not come back. But a few films debuted in the late 1970s—*The Deer Hunter* (1978), *Coming Home* (1978), and *Apocalypse Now* (1979)—that aroused sympathy for the men who fought in the war.

In 1980, Congress authorized the Vietnam Veterans Memorial on the National Mall in Washington. Maya Ying Lin, a twenty-one-year-old student of architecture at Yale University, produced the winning design, a simple wall of polished black granite inscribed with the names of the 57,661 American servicemen and women who had died in the war. Some veterans and conservatives attacked Lin's design as inappropriate or insulting, partly because, unlike conventional war memorials, it did not portray flags or soldiers, partly because she was of Asian extraction. Completed in 1982, the wall quickly became one of the nation's most revered war memorials, attracting millions of visitors, many of whom deposited flowers, flags, and tears at the site. Carter's pardon initiated a process whereby both supporters and opponents of the war began to find common, reconciling ground in concern for the Vietnam vets.

Carter instituted a wide-ranging reform of the civil service and otherwise advanced the liberal agenda through appoint-

The Vietnam Veterans Memorial, designed by Maya Lin (with a reflection of the Washington Monument), on the Mall in Washington, D.C.

ments and enforcement of civil rights laws. In addition to naming three women to his cabinet and a black as ambassador to the United Nations, he put more women, blacks, and Hispanic Americans into federal jobs, judgeships, and regulatory posts than had any previous president. He approved the congressional expansion of programs allocating federal work to minority contractors. He beefed up the Equal Employment Opportunity Commission, making it the lead agency in its area, and consolidated a confusing hodgepodge of activities into the renamed Office of Federal Contract Compliance and Programs. His administration fought racial and sexual discrimination by bringing class-action lawsuits against employers and called business to account for hiring methods such as employee tests that unfairly disadvantaged minority groups.

Carter's regulatory appointments reenergized the protection of consumers, the workplace, highway safety, and the environment. In December 1980, the president signed an environmental protection bill that preserved one-third of Alaska from development, thus doubling the entire area of the country's national parks and wildlife refuges. He also established an environmental superfund to clean up areas polluted with toxic wastes. Although he was deferential to the tobacco industry, his secretary of health, education, and welfare (HEW), Joseph Califano, was not. A reformed three-pack-a-day smoker, Califano labeled cigarettes "Public Health Enemy No. 1," called for smoking bans on all commercial flights, and urged Congress to increase federal cigarette taxes.

In 1979, fulfilling a long-standing desire of teachers and their allies, Carter persuaded Congress to split HEW into two new agencies: the Department of Health and Human Services and the Department of Education.

## A SHIFT TO ECONOMIC CONSERVATISM

Carter maintained that the country's economic robustness should come less from government than from voluntarism, private enterprise, and the free market. Federal regulatory agencies controlled the allocation of airline routes and the price of tickets, determined interstate trucking charges, decided banking interest rates and services, and regulated the rates of the nation's private telephone monopoly, AT&T. Economists increasingly agreed that such regulation was costly to businesses and to the public. The regulators too often collaborated with the regulated, maintaining artificially high prices and protecting inefficient corporations from market risks. The critics argued that the regulatory system stifled competition and slowed economic growth. By the mid-1970s, a bipartisan movement had emerged in Congress in favor of deregulating major industries.

Carter, eager, as he said, "to free the American people from the burden of over-regulation," collaborated with Congress to deregulate the airlines, the trucking industry, the railroads, and household movers; and he initiated the deregulation of the banking industry. Partly in the long-term interest of strengthening international competitiveness, he increased the overall budget for research and development. To stimulate the economy in the short term, he settled for modest public works programs and tax cuts, which hardly helped people earning too little to pay much in taxes. Federal spending on social programs peaked in 1976, then steadily declined.

## ENERGY AND INFLATION

Two weeks after his inauguration, Carter donned a cardigan sweater, sat down in an armchair in the White House library, and told a national television audience that "the energy shortage is permanent" but that the country could adjust to this new reality with individual and corporate conservation and "sacrifice." Carter did not mention foreign oil, but concern for U.S. dependence on it formed part of the background of his talk. American dependence on foreign oil had been rising steadily since World War II, with imports accounting for about 9 percent of consumption in

1950, 25 percent in 1970, and 46 percent in 1977. Although domestic oil prices had almost doubled since 1970, domestic production was falling.

In April, the president sent Congress an overarching energy plan intended to encourage both the conservation of energy and the development of new sources. He called his program the "moral equivalent of war"; its detractors preferred the acronym MEOW. Congress balked at the complexity of the proposals, and the president did little to press for their passage. Finally, in November 1978, a much-diminished version of the original plan cleared Capitol Hill, gutted of its most effective conservation features, notably a tax on gas-guzzling vehicles.

However, shortly after Carter signed the energy bill, the Iranian revolution (see next page) sent a second oil shock through the United States, causing fuel shortages, lengthy lines at gas stations, and a spike in prices from 30 cents to almost $1 a gallon. Hope rested with more fuel-efficient automobiles, which Detroit was developing under the goad of federal fuel standards. A doubling of the average miles per gallon—only fourteen in 1978—would by itself almost halve oil imports. Addressing the short term, in 1979–80 Carter decontrolled oil prices to encourage both conservation and the search for new oil fields. He obtained passage of a windfall profits tax on the resulting increase in oil-company income that would help pay for, among other things, mass transit. He encouraged the exploitation of solar energy through devices that convert sunlight to electricity or heat. And at his urging, Congress created a Synthetic Fuels Corporation to extract oil from tar sands, oil shale, and coal with the aim of producing more than 160 million barrels of oil a year by the early 1990s.

Between 1978 and 1980, U.S. oil consumption declined by 10 percent, but the sharp increase in oil prices escalated the inflation rate, which had begun creeping up after the 1974–75 recession, from 7.6 percent in 1977 to more than 11 percent in 1979. Carter had been exhorting business and labor to hold the line voluntarily on prices and wages. Now faced with such a staggering rise in prices, he appointed Paul Volcker, a devotee of monetary policy, to head the Federal Reserve Board (Fed). To tighten the money supply, the Fed hiked the interest rate it charged to major banks, helping to produce by 1980 exorbitantly high bank-interest rates of 20 percent and a recession accompanied by 7.8 percent unemployment. The inflation rate nevertheless moved higher, to more than 13 percent, which made for the worst year of stagflation yet.

## CARTER AND THE WORLD

Carter, inexperienced in foreign affairs when he entered the presidency, was inconsistent in his approach to the world. Breaking with the realpolitik of Nixon and Kissinger, he revived idealism in the stated aims of American foreign policy, but at times he jettisoned idealism, renewing covert action by the CIA and endorsing authoritarian regimes. He often appeared to waver in his approach to the Soviets, seeking accommodation on some matters, pursuing confrontation on others.

Carter declared in his inaugural address, "We can never be indifferent to the fate of freedom elsewhere. . . . Our commitment to human rights must be absolute." The president attempted to refuse aid to countries with poor human rights records, including, though with only gentle pressure, friends and allies. Critics attacked Carter's human rights efforts for jeopardizing détente and undercutting some of the nation's staunchest allies, such as South Korea. But Carter successfully put human rights on the world agenda; and by establishing a Human Rights Office in the State Department, he endowed it with an ongoing role in the making of American foreign policy.

Carter's signal achievement in Latin America was to bring to final fruition the efforts of presidents going back to Lyndon Johnson to resolve differences with the Panamanians over the Panama Canal. Carter submitted to the Senate two treaties transferring control of the Canal Zone to Panama by 1999. Conservatives, smarting over the loss in Vietnam and the OPEC oil crisis, opposed the treaties as another national humiliation. "We stole [Panama] fair and square," one senator said, expressing chauvinist indignation. But by lobbying hard for the agreement, Carter eked out one of his few congressional victories, obtaining ratification of the canal treaties in 1978 by only one vote. The outcome ended one of Latin America's long-standing grievances against the *Yanqui* colossus.

*The Middle East.* Carter may be remembered most for the peace accords that he facilitated between the president of Egypt, Anwar el-Sadat, and the prime minister of Israel, Menachem Begin. In November 1977, Sadat, his country's economy burdened by defense expenditures, announced that he was ready to go "to the ends of the earth" for peace. Invited to Jerusalem by Begin, he flew to Israel despite opposition from Arab recalcitrants, hoping to negotiate an end to the formal state of war that still existed between the two countries. In September 1978, building on Sadat's initiative, Carter brought the two leaders to Camp David, the presidential retreat in rural Maryland, for two

Egyptian president Anwar el-Sadat (left), President Carter, and Israeli prime minister Menachem Begin (right) sign the Camp David agreement, September 17, 1978.

weeks of difficult talks that produced a "framework" for peace. Carter pressed them to resolve their remaining differences, and at the White House the following March, Sadat and Begin signed a formal peace treaty that ended thirty years of war in exchange for Israel's returning the Sinai Peninsula to Egypt.

The Camp David accords provided that Israel would retain control of the West Bank and the Gaza Strip but that during a five-year transitional period the Palestinians there would be granted self-rule and "autonomy." At that point, the final status of the areas would be worked out by Israel, Egypt, Jordan, and—in a vague reference to the PLO—"representatives of the Palestinian people." The other Arab states, however, rejected the accords and ostracized Egypt, partly because the agreement left control of the territories in Israeli hands. Begin, bent on strengthening Israel's position in the territories, continued to expand Israeli settlements in the West Bank. In 1981, Sadat was assassinated by Islamic fundamentalists, punishment for having negotiated with Israel. Although his successor, Hosni Mubarak, continued Sadat's conciliatory policies, explosive tensions persisted between Israel on the one side and, on the other, the Palestinians and Arab irreconcilables led by Syria. The peace treaty nevertheless seemed a significant step toward a settlement in the region and a triumph for Carter.

The Middle East also provided Carter's most anguishing reverse. Like Nixon, Carter valued Shah Mohammad Reza Pahlavi of Iran, whom the United States had been supporting since 1953, when the CIA helped pave his way to power, as an

instrument of American interests in the Persian Gulf region. On a visit to Tehran in 1977, Carter complimented the shah on "the admiration and love which your people give to you." In fact, the shah had long been violating his subjects' human rights—his secret police, which had close ties to the CIA, had tortured and imprisoned some 50,000 people—and had been spending unprecedented amounts of Iranian wealth on arms from the United States instead of investing it in economic development. Opposition to his regime was bitter and widening, especially among the country's religious leaders, who strongly disliked the Westernizing trends the shah supported. In January 1979, a revolution led by Shiite fundamentalists forced the shah to flee to Europe. The new head of Iran was Ayatollah Ruhollah Khomeini, seventy-nine years old and a religious zealot. He rapidly turned the government into a theocracy that condemned modernization and preached hatred of the West.

In early November, Carter admitted the shah to the United States for cancer treatment, despite warnings that the action would jeopardize American diplomats in Iran. On November 4,

November 8, 1979: Crowds chant before a billboard taunting President Carter outside the U.S. embassy in Tehran, where militants held the American staff hostage for 444 days.

1979, armed students broke into the American embassy compound in Tehran and held fifty Americans hostage, opening a prolonged captivity and a chasm in U.S.-Iranian relations. The crisis increasingly frustrated and angered Americans as television carried nightly clips from Tehran of anti-American mobs demonstrating at the embassy and shouting "Death to America." Carter immediately froze Iranian assets in the United States and prohibited the importation of Iranian oil. An American mission to rescue the hostages in 1980 fell apart when a helicopter and a transport aircraft crashed into each other in the desert, killing eight servicemen. The episode added to the public's frustration over the hostage crisis and further undercut confidence in Carter's handling of it.

*The Soviets.* Carter was initially conciliatory toward the Soviets, hoping to diminish the chances of nuclear war. At a meeting in Vienna in June 1979, the United States and the Soviets, recognizing a mutual interest in arms control, signed the SALT II arms control agreement. The treaty called for equal limits on Soviet and American strategic forces. It nevertheless ran into trouble in the Senate, where critics insisted that it favored the Russians.

The trouble greatly intensified when, in December 1979, the Soviets invaded Afghanistan, where a pro-Moscow coup had brought a Marxist regime to power almost two years before. The Soviets were prompted to send the troops by the regime's inability to suppress the mujahideen—Muslims whose insurgency was supported by the CIA. Carter, declaring that the invasion had forced a "drastic change" in his opinion of Soviet goals, pronounced the action "a stepping stone to their possible control over much of the world's oil supplies." He tabled the SALT II Treaty, embargoed exports of high technology and grain to Russia, reinstituted registration for the draft, and banned American participation in the 1980 Summer Olympics in Moscow. He also promulgated the Carter Doctrine, declaring that the United States would repel any attempt to gain control of the Persian Gulf region "by any means necessary, including military force." Critics held that the president had misjudged Soviet intentions in the region and that the Carter Doctrine was unrealistic.

Carter had turned into a hard-liner. After his first two years in office, he had reversed the trend of reduced defense budgets and initiated the largest new-weapons program since before the Korean War. After the Soviet invasion of Afghanistan, Carter requested significant annual increases in military spending, with the aim of achieving military superiority over the Soviet Union. In July 1980, he signed a directive that called for sufficient arms to fight a prolonged nuclear war and to win it at every level of escalation. To critics, the directive, coupled with a move to a first-strike missile capability, threatened a dangerous escalation of the arms race.

## A Vexed Society

Although the nation's first centennial, in 1876, had occurred during one of its worst depressions, the celebrations had optimistically extolled the economic and technological future, powerfully symbolized in the exhibition at Machinery Hall (see Chapter 18) by George Corliss's giant steam engine. The festivals in the summer of 1976 were marked less by high expectations of marvelous tomorrows than by wistful nostalgia for a mythic past. Communities staged pie-eating contests and hog-calling competitions, while El Paso, Texas, enacted a Pony Express ride. A national television audience watched fireworks light up the sky over an armada of more than 200 tall sailing ships come from around the world to lie at anchor in New York Harbor.

The nostalgia bespoke discontent with the present and apprehension about the future. Americans were accustomed to expecting a better future for themselves and their children, but in the 1970s their confidence was eroding in the face of bedeviling difficulties. Abroad, the Soviet Union blew hot and cold in its commitment to peace, OPEC remained willful, and anti-Americanism flared in the Middle East. At home, major industries faced mounting international competition; the economy seemed stagnant; and the specter of energy shortages raised nagging doubts about the nation's economic future. The country remained divided over the claims of minority groups, women, and the culture of sexual freedom. Resentments lingered over the war in Vietnam. Ford had dealt ineffectually with most of the problems vexing the country. In the post-Nixon 1970s, the United States was suffused with a rare pessimism—a fear that it was now vulnerable, that it had lost the blessings of nature.

### THE FALTERING ECONOMY

The economy was suffering from deep and dispiriting structural problems. Between 1945 and 1965, industrial productivity, measured as output per man-hour, had climbed at an annual rate of 3 percent; now it was rising at a mere 1 percent per year, only a quarter of the rate in Germany and a fifth of that in Japan. The standard of living in the United States dropped to fifth in the world, below that of four European nations. Stagflation severely threatened the country's economic pillars, forcing federal bailouts of the Chrysler Corporation and of New York City just a year before the tall ships sailed into the harbor.

By the end of the decade, people had to pay twice as much as they did at the beginning for basic necessities and for an average single-family home. Real spending power for the average worker fell to its lowest point since 1961. Credit cards became consumer commonplaces, with people relying on them to buy goods in the present that they could pay for in the future. Private debt rose sharply. In California, many homeowners reeled under the skyrocketing property taxes generated by the sharp increase in property values. In 1978, angrily resorting to the initiative process, Californians passed Proposition 13, which slashed property taxes in half, capped the annual rate of possible increases, and inspired similar tax revolts in other states.

The economic weakness was especially acute in the nation's industrial heartland. During the 1960s, foreign-car imports had quadrupled their share of the American market; by 1980, their share had almost doubled again, to about 33 percent. Electronic goods from abroad captured a comparable

Abandoned factories like this one in Peekskill, New York exemplified the decline of the smokestack industries and the blue-collar unemployment arising from it.

portion of the market. At the end of World War II, the United States had produced almost two out of every three tons of the world's steel; by the opening of the 1970s, it accounted for only 15 percent. Japanese steel was better and cheaper than most of the American types, and the Japanese were selling more than 4 million tons of it a year in the United States. Foreign products gained a competitive advantage in part because of cheaper labor costs abroad, but domestic products suffered from shortsightedness among American industrial managers. Detroit's auto executives, for example, considered a preference for the smaller, more fuel-efficient cars coming from Europe and Asia "unpatriotic" and "un-American," as one of them put it. The captains of steel neglected to modernize their plants and invested only a paltry fraction of profits in research and development.

Since the end of World War II, job growth rates had been far higher in the clerical than in the blue-collar sector. Now the decline in the major manufacturing industries signaled that the United States was moving from a manufacturing to a service economy. The shift sent many workers downward on the economic and social ladder, especially in the region from Pennsylvania through upper Illinois and into Michigan, Wisconsin, and Minnesota, the centers of steel, auto, coal, and iron production. Once brawny and prosperous, the region was now a "rust belt," its smokestacks cold and factories closed. Like Aurora, in the iron range of Minnesota, many of its towns were dying, with their Main Street stores boarded up and "For Sale" signs on houses, cars, motorcycles, and campers.

Union membership continued to decline, accounting for only a quarter of the nonagricultural workforce, and unions faced intensifying efforts by management to weaken them. Some major corporations tried to meet the mounting foreign competition by demanding higher output from their workers. At the General Motors plant in Lordstown, Ohio, management sought to double its assembly-line output of cars by giving workers only thirty-six seconds to perform their tasks. The head of the United Auto Workers charged that business leaders had broken the fragile compact of cooperativeness that had prevailed during the good years in favor of conducting a "one-sided class war." In industries that continued to thrive, complicated manufacturing tasks were increasingly being taken over by robots and computers, a process that steadily eliminated skilled jobs. Unskilled jobs were being created in their place, many of them in the service sector, exemplified by the growth of fast-food restaurants like McDonald's and discount stores like Wal-Mart.

Signs of worker alienation appeared in rising absenteeism and drug addiction. The young rock star Bruce Springsteen caught the mood, rasping—in songs like "The River" and "Thunder Road"—of bleak, blue-collar towns short on work and long on losers, where "things that seemed so important" had "vanished right into the air." The film *Saturday Night Fever* (1977) showcased John Travolta escaping into the glittering world of the disco dance hall from the desperation of his otherwise no-exit blue-collar milieu.

In the mid-1970s, fewer than three out of five non-college-educated people thought that hard work would pay off, down from four out of five at the close of the 1960s. By 1979, most Americans came to think that inflation would be with them always, and they were convinced that the next year would be worse than the current one. They had it on the authority of the chairman of the Federal Reserve Board that "under [current economic] conditions the standard of living for the average American has got to decline."

## THE ENVIRONMENT AND PUBLIC HEALTH

American optimism had historically been grounded in no small part in the natural abundance of the continent and faith that technological change brought social progress. But now experts were predicting that the industrialized world, including the United States, was depleting the planet's natural resources at an accelerating rate, that the resources were finite, and that they were bound to run out.

Many environmentalists welcomed that dark prediction, seeing in it a solid reason for the United States to reject the exuberant consumerism that ravaged the land, air, and water. They made a cult classic of the 1973 book *Small Is Beautiful* by the economist E. F. Schumacher, an attack against unbridled material growth. In California, Governor Jerry Brown, an evangelist of the new age, proclaimed that the country had entered an era of limits and celebrated Schumacher's notion that "less is more." Many people embraced an ecological lifestyle that emphasized personal responsibility for the impact of daily living on the natural world. A number grew organic gardens, gave up gas-guzzling cars, and embraced recycling, composting, and natural fibers.

The new issues of poisons and pollution drew a new generation of activists into environmentalism. They responded to Paul Ehrlich's *Population Bomb* (1968) and Barry Commoner's *The Closing Circle* (1971), which warned against the threat to the vi-

ability of, respectively, an overpopulated and overexploited planet. In 1970, the new activists spearheaded Earth Day, a nationwide manifestation of antipollution protests and environmental cleanups. The new activists, eager to distance themselves from what they called "the birds and squirrels people," stood for a new agenda of environmental reform, especially the restoration of the land, air, and water to their unpolluted states.

To many environmentalists in the 1970s, technology seemed less a savior than a hazard. Their eagerness to curb its use threatened economic growth and thus pitted them against labor and lower-income groups. Whitney Young, the head of the Urban League, an organization of black moderates, had declared after the first Earth Day that "the war on pollution . . . should be waged after the war on poverty is won." Still, Americans of all classes and colors found worrisome the revelation that the soil under a housing development at Love Canal, near Buffalo, New York, was contaminated by chemical wastes that were believed to cause cancer and genetic defects among the

Fearful children protest the hazardous wastes dumped at the nearby Love Canal site in Niagara Falls, New York, August 1978.

residents. They were also worried about the danger to public health and safety that appeared to be posed by nuclear power.

*Nuclear Power.* The shortage of energy, the natural resource most crucial to American prosperity, divided the country, often bitterly. Many policymakers as well as environmentalists emphasized conservation, but some analysts held that the nation's energy supplies also needed to be increased—by finding new caches of oil and natural gas and by further developing nuclear power. But critics raised questions about the disposal of radioactive wastes produced by the power reactors; about the safety of reactors themselves, particularly their emergency core-cooling systems, which were designed to prevent overheating and meltdown; and about the impact of the heated water that reactors disgorged into rivers, lakes, and streams, endangering aquatic life.

Beginning in 1970, environmental groups brought suit against the Atomic Energy Commission (AEC) for approving the construction of a nuclear reactor some thirty miles from Washington, D.C. Analysts predicted that the reactor's discharged cooling water would likely thermally pollute the Chesapeake Bay. After a series of legal maneuvers, the judge in the case issued a strongly worded opinion that compelled the AEC to take into account all potential environmental hazards—as well as radiation issues—in the licensing of nuclear plants, on pain of incurring suits if it did not. In 1973,

convinced that AEC should not simultaneously promote and regulate nuclear power, Congress broke up the agency, awarding its regulatory functions to the brand-new Nuclear Regulatory Commission and its promotional ones to what, in 1977, became the Department of Energy.

In 1975, about 225 nuclear plants were ordered, under construction, or in operation. They would generate enough electrical power for some 100 million people, providing as much energy as six major oil fields. Utility companies reported that nuclear plants had already saved Americans more than $750 million on their 1974 electric bills. In 1976, addressing a widespread concern, a federal report concluded that with 1,000 reactors operating continuously, only one serious accident would occur in 10,000 years.

Such estimates were challenged by scientific experts who intervened in the process to license nuclear plants. The interventions helped double the time required to construct a nuclear plant to about ten years and, amid the climate of high interest rates, substantially increased the cost of building them. Experts' fears were substantiated in March 1979, when design flaws and errors committed by operators of the nuclear power plant at Three Mile Island, near Harrisburg, Pennsylvania, combined to cause a failure in the cooling system, a partial meltdown of the nuclear fuel, and the expulsion of some 800,000 gallons of radioactive steam into the air above the surrounding Susquehanna Valley. Coincidentally, the film *The China Syndrome,* a dramatic tale of an accident at a nuclear power plant, had just opened in the nation's theaters. The one-two punch of the real accident and the fictional one dealt the nuclear industry a setback that environmental activists by themselves might not have achieved. Utilities canceled orders for more than thirty nuclear plants, and no new orders were placed.

## A Surging Social Conservatism

Through the 1970s, people of color kept pressing their case for equal opportunity and treatment, especially in education, jobs, and housing, aided by the legislation and court decisions of the 1960s. The women's movement continued to agitate for its own interests, most of them symbolized by the Equal Rights Amendment (ERA), which prohibited the federal and

The cooling towers of the Metropolitan Edison Nuclear Power Plant at Three Mile Island, shut down after the accident in March 1979.

913

state governments from abridging a person's rights on account of sex. Passed by the Congress in March 1972, the ERA was quickly ratified by thirty states, leaving endorsement by only eight more to complete the process.

Gay men and lesbians sought to gain acceptance and establish rights for themselves. Features of the counterculture spread to parts of the middle and working classes. But these trends left many Americans groping for ways to deal with each other, their children, and even themselves. Amid the uncertainties, the resentments against the cultural transformations wrought during the 1960s gained strength, and so did the backlash against the drive by women and minority groups for greater equality.

Workers and students in New York demonstrate for affirmative action and against the Supreme Court's Bakke decision, June 1978.

### FAULT LINES: RACIAL, SEXUAL, AND CULTURAL

***Contesting Minority Gains.*** Court orders to desegregate the public schools by busing prompted whites who could afford it to send their children to private schools or to move to the predominantly white suburbs. The flight to the suburbs was further encouraged in 1974 by the case of *Milliken v. Bradley,* when a bare majority of the Supreme Court held that students could not be bused for the purpose of achieving racial integration between predominantly black cities and the largely white suburbs. To many whites remaining in the cities, such suburban insulation from the strains of school integration seemed arbitrary and unfair. Desegregation orders provoked angry confrontations in some cities, notably Louisville (Kentucky) and Boston, where people in white enclaves put up signs declaring, "We don't want any niggers in our school." A mother from a section of Boston vulnerable to busing complained to the judge who had ordered it, "How can it be the law of the land, as we are told, when you can move less than one mile away and be out from under this law?" In the late 1970s, pollsters found that 70 percent of whites strongly opposed "forced" busing, and that only 53 percent of blacks favored it.

Many whites considered affirmative action—particularly in hiring practices and college admissions—an indefensible replacement of equality of opportunity with equality of outcomes, and thus a violation of their constitutional right to equal protection under the law. Allan Bakke, a student, brought that view to court when he sued the Medical School of the University of California at Davis for refusing him admission because it regularly set aside 16 percent of its slots for minority students, many of whom were academically less qualified than he was. In 1978, in *Regents of University of California v. Bakke,* a sharply divided Supreme Court granted him victory, holding that a university could consider racial criteria as part of a competitive admissions process but that it could not rely on "fixed quotas" in determining its student body. In rulings during the next two years, however, the Court upheld a black hiring quota in the steel industry and a set-aside of 10 percent of federal funds for public works for minority contractors. The disparate nature of these rulings revealed that the Court was divided on the issue of affirmative action, but perhaps no more so than the country at large.

***Women.*** The cause of sexual freedom for women had become deeply embedded in American culture. In 1969, about three-quarters of American women believed premarital sex to be wrong; in 1973, only about a half did. Sexual liberty was reinforced by feminists' insistence that women ought to have the right to control their own bodies, in defiance of male or middle-class standards of propriety. The demand for women's autonomy made a commercial success of *Our Bodies, Ourselves* (1970), a book intended to provide women with greater control over their health. It also led to mounting agitation from both women and physicians for the legalization of abortion.

Between 1967 and 1970, a dozen states eased their antiabortion laws, making women eligible for the procedure who were the victims of rape or incest or whose lives were threatened by their pregnancies. In Texas, where abortion re-

Antiabortion demonstrators, carrying a sign with a symbolic fetus on top, protest outside the Capitol on the third anniversary of *Roe v. Wade*, January 22, 1976.

strictions were not eased, Norma McGorvey, using the name Jane Roe, sued for the right to abort her unwanted fetus. Deciding the case of *Roe v. Wade* on appeal in 1973, the Supreme Court drew on the right of privacy it had established to hold that the state could not interfere with a woman's right to abortion during the first three months of pregnancy; that during the next three months it could regulate that right in the interest of preserving maternal health; and that in the last three months it could bar abortions.

Despite such gains, women continued to feel aggrieved and threatened. Probably because so many more were employed and also had higher expectations, a growing number of women felt discriminated against in the workplace. Some feminists called attention to physical crimes against women and sought to deal with them by staffing rape-crisis centers and shelters for battered women. Many redoubled their efforts on behalf of the Equal Rights Amendment. But even though they won an extension of the deadline for ratification to June 30, 1982, the amendment failed to pass.

One reason for the defeat was that moderates in the women's movement, especially those in the unionized workforce, worried that complete legal equality might cost them the special dispensations—such as limits on the weight they could be asked to lift or a monthly sick day—they had fought so hard to achieve. But another reason for its defeat was the backlash against the women's movement that formed in the 1970s not only among men but among women themselves. Promoted by socially conservative women, it targeted both the ERA and abortion rights.

The chief enemy of the ERA was Phyllis Schlafly, a devout Catholic housewife, and mother of six children, who denounced the advocates of the ERA as "unkempt, lesbians, radicals, and socialists . . . women who had rejected womanhood—the God-given roles of wife and motherhood." Anti-ERA activists preyed on the fears of middle-class women that the amendment might lead to the end of alimony and maternal custody of children in divorces, the drafting of women, and the decriminalization of rape.

The Supreme Court's decision in *Roe v. Wade* provoked an antiabortion movement. Convinced that life was sacred from the moment of conception, its adherents claimed that abortion was murder. The movement drew leadership and support disproportionately from Catholics, fundamentalist Protestants, and women who had devoted themselves to being wives and mothers. Its advocates challenged the decision in court and protested at abortion clinics. A few resorted to violence, torching a Planned Parenthood facility in St. Paul, Minnesota, in 1973. The movement sought to pass state laws that would require parental or spousal consent before an abortion. In *Planned Parenthood of Central Missouri v. Danforth* (1976), the Supreme Court rejected such requirements, but in *H. L. v. Matheson* (1981), it upheld a parental notification rule for minors because parental consent is required before a minor can receive medical treatment. Antiabortionists won a victory in Congress in 1976 with the so-called Hyde Amendment, which prohibited the use of Medicaid funds for abortions except in cases of rape, incest, and endangerment of the woman's life, a restriction that the Court upheld.

*Gay Liberation.* For decades, gay men and lesbians had hidden their sexual preferences, fearing that to reveal them would cost them jobs or housing and make them vulnerable to blackmail or persecution, including physical assault. But now, adding to the broad-based insistence on sexual liberty, a growing number of gays and lesbians openly acknowledged

915

Activists demand gay liberation, New York City, April 1978.

their sexual orientation—that is, "came out of the closet." A number of prominent feminists publicly declared that they were lesbians—for example, Kate Millet, the author of *Sexual Politics* (1970), who earned national headlines when she told a Columbia University audience that she was bisexual. When in mid-1969 New York police descended on the Stonewall Inn, a gay men's bar in Greenwich Village, the patrons fought back, initiating five days of confrontation and arousing an assertive group consciousness among male homosexuals. By the early 1970s, hundreds of openly gay groups were battling the homophobia that pervaded American society. In 1973, the American Psychiatric Association removed homosexuality from its catalogue of mental disorders, emphasizing that gays and lesbians were by and large satisfied with their sexual orientation and exhibited no signs of psychopathology directly arising from it.

Many homosexuals migrated to New York and the even more tolerant environment of San Francisco, making it a gay mecca; the writer Armistead Maupin chronicled life there in a newspaper series, *Tales of the City,* that was later turned into a popular book and TV movie. Some gays turned New York and San Francisco into centers of an outlaw sexual culture that was defiant of the heterosexual majority's, marked by the practice of unprotected anal and oral sex with dozens to hundreds of partners, mainly in bathhouses, discos, and sex clubs. But apart from their sexual orientation, large numbers of homosexuals, male and female alike, were conventional in their overall attitudes and demanded only the right to pursue their lives free of harassment and discrimination. Together with various allies, homosexuals mounted initiatives for gay-rights ordinances in cities across the country.

Social conservatives, however, defeated the initiatives in St. Paul, Minnesota; Wichita, Kansas; Eugene, Oregon; and Dade County, Florida. Taking the offensive against gay liberation, state legislators in Oklahoma and Arkansas enacted measures that banned homosexuals from teaching in public schools and, in Arkansas, also denied them credentials as pediatricians and social workers. In California in 1978, liberals managed to defeat a statewide initiative mandating the firing of any schoolteacher who advocated homosexuality. But just a few weeks after the victory, the leader in the gay opposition to the initiative, San Francisco supervisor Harvey Milk, was gunned down in his office by Dan White, a former city official. When a predominantly blue-collar Catholic jury found White guilty only of voluntary manslaughter, riots broke out in the gay district of San Francisco.

*Searching for Self-Fulfillment.* Amid the social and cultural stresses of the 1970s, many Americans turned inward for insight, abandoning politics in favor of personal fulfillment. Millions tuned in to daytime radio and TV talk shows that featured discussions of hitherto taboo subjects such as pre-marital sex, adultery, and divorce and helped give rise to a confessional culture. Millions looked to pop music for entertainment and escape, providing enthusiastic audiences for a dizzying array of pop-music groups virtually none of which urged social change in the vein of Bob Dylan a decade earlier. Bruce Springsteen's songs, while they lamented rusting factories and blue-collar despair, often suggested that the modes of survival lay in flight or the magic of love. By the late 1970s, more than a third of young adults were using marijuana, and it became fashionable among well-to-do whites, including pop celebrities and young business executives, to indulge in cocaine.

Untold numbers of Americans sought to take control of their lives through faddish methods of self-realization. They participated, for example, in encounter groups, which aimed to reveal the authentic self and practiced transcendental meditation, taught at more than 200 centers. For millions, the quest for the sound spirit led through the healthy body. Middle-class Americans began taking themselves to tennis courts, racquet-ball clubs, swimming pools, jogging paths, and hiking and biking trails. People coupled their absorption with physical fitness to a concern for a healthy diet, limiting their intake of fat, sugar, and salt, eating less beef and more fish or chicken, preferring "natural" and organic foods to processed types.

As in other periods of stress, millions of Americans sought solace in religion. Unlike the religious revival of the 1950s, with its focus on suburban community and respectability, that of the 1970s was fueled in part by the drive for spiritual self-renewal, in part by the rise of Christian radio and TV programs. Surveys late in the decade revealed that 70 million Americans—more than one of every three adults—identified themselves as born-again Christians. The revival was intensified by charismatic leaders such as the Reverend Sun Myung Moon, a native of South Korea who touted himself as the new Messiah and whose Unification Church evangelized thousands of young Americans to a blend of Christian faith and anti-Communism. Eastern religions such as Zen Buddhism also gained adherents.

The commitment to achieving individual potential—whether through pop psychology, physical fitness, or religious renewal—prompted the writer Tom Wolfe to dub the 1970s the "me decade." In a book aptly titled *The Culture of Narcissism* (1979), the historian Christopher Lasch wrote, "To live for the moment is the prevailing passion—to live for yourself, not for your predecessors or posterity." In all, the cultural trends of the 1970s, coupled with the flight from public issues, helped lay the groundwork for a politics less concerned with an overarching public interest than with a self-absorbed individualism.

## Bid for Power

### THE CHRISTIAN RIGHT

The cultural trends of the day angered the Reverend Jerry Falwell, a fundamentalist Baptist based in Lynchburg, Virginia, who reached an estimated 15 million people weekly through his televised *Old Time Gospel Hour*. Falwell objected strongly to the rising rates of divorce and drug use, the women's movement, the ERA, and abortion on demand; the spread of pornography and homosexuality; and liberalism's invasion of the schools in the form of sex education, the prohibition

The Reverend Jerry Falwell exploited the mass media to promote the cause of the new religious right.

against school-sponsored prayer, and the teaching of biological evolution instead of biblical creationism. As other fundamentalist Protestants came to see the cultural trends of the 1970s the way Falwell did, in many parts of the country they tried to rid the schools of morally subversive books, protested sex education, and urged that biology courses include "scientific creationism"—natural evidence for the truth of the biblical Genesis. Fundamentalist dissidents increasingly sent their children to "Christian" private schools.

In 1979, Falwell founded the Moral Majority, a religious-oriented group that operated as a conservative political lobby and was welcomed by Washington-based political organizers intent on building a conservative coalition, the New Right. Falwell's organization effectively exploited television, computerized databases, and direct mail to raise money from millions of small contributors; it used the same means to mobilize them in support of right-wing candidates and legislative initiatives. At the movement's emotional core was a ferocious social conservatism that sought to rescue the United States from the libertine legacy of the 1960s.

## A CONSERVATIVE COALITION

The emergence of the New Right on social and cultural issues was accompanied by a shift rightward on economic issues that went far beyond calls for deregulation. The tax rebellion that began with the passage of Proposition 13 in California fueled attacks on government for taking money from people's pockets. In the mountain West, resentment of the environmental movement prompted the so-called Sagebrush Rebellion, whose participants demanded that restrictions on the exploitation of natural resources be lifted. Everywhere opponents of affirmative action demanded a reduction or elimination of the special dispensations granted to women and minorities of color.

The shift gained intellectual force from former liberals who had turned right in appalled response to the radicalism of the 1960s. Labeled "neoconservatives," they contributed articles to magazines such as *Commentary* and *Public Interest* warning against the dangers of excessive governmental controls at home and Soviet expansionism abroad. Conservatives sought to counter the liberal dominance of policy analysis by establishing their own think tanks such as the Heritage Foundation, funded by gifts and subscriptions from individuals and corporations. By and large, the economic conservatives were unsympathetic to the social conservatism of Falwell's Moral Majority and proposed instead to reduce the role of government. Falwell and his allies, generally indifferent to issues such as regulation and taxes, aimed to use government to restrict social behavior. Nevertheless, in the later 1970s the two conservative groups formed an alliance, albeit an uneasy one, of mounting influence against the liberal welfare state and the enlargement of personal liberties that had paralleled its growth.

## THE ELECTION OF 1980

In July 1979, in a nationally televised address that was quickly dubbed the "national malaise" speech, Carter attributed the difficulties in dealing with energy and inflation to "a crisis of the American spirit," declaring that the people had lost "confidence in the future." Critics countered that what the country had lost confidence in was its president. Jimmy Carter had brought honesty and integrity to the task of government. But while he had a good grasp of specific issues, he failed to articulate a larger vision in foreign or domestic affairs that moved either legislators or his fellow citizens. As a sitting president, Carter nevertheless gained support amid the crises in Afghanistan and Iran, and he and Mondale were renominated handily.

The Republicans nominated Ronald Reagan, the former movie actor, television host, two-term governor of California, and hero of the party's right wing. His vice-presidential choice was his principal primary opponent, George H.W. Bush of Texas, a moderate with a long career in public service, including a stint as a congressman and, most recently, as director of the CIA.

Reagan ran on a platform that favored tax cuts, a balanced budget, prayer in the schools, and a ban on abortions. He appealed to both economic and social conservatives, attracting support from the new religious right, tax-sensitive suburban Republicans, anxious blue-collar Democrats, and people simply out of patience with Carter's ineffectuality. Reagan spoke to the frustrations felt by many in foreign affairs, promising to bolster national defense and reassert American power in the world. He bested Carter in their single television debate, countering attacks with affable rejoinders and calling the sum of the unemployment rate and the inflation rate Carter's "misery index." "Are you better off than you were four years ago?" Reagan asked viewers. With the misery index, 14 in 1977, now at 20, the answer did not need to be spelled out. Reagan told campaign audiences, "A recession is when your neighbor loses his job. A depression is when you lose yours. And recovery is when Jimmy Carter loses his."

On election day, Reagan won 50.8 percent of the popular vote to Carter's 41 percent, with most of the remainder going to John Anderson, a liberal Republican congressman from Illinois who ran on an independent ticket. Turnout fell once again; almost 47 percent of eligible voters stayed home, which meant that Reagan was elected by only about a quarter of eligible voters. Still, he carried forty-four states, gaining 489 electoral votes to Carter's 49. Almost a quarter of previously Democratic voters voted for Reagan, the largest portion among them saying they switched because they resented government assistance to minority groups. The Republicans recaptured the Senate for the first time since 1952. Some liberal Democrats were defeated with the help of conservative televangelists and of the Moral Majority, which had registered more than 2 million new voters in 1979. Iran's humiliation of Carter also contributed to his loss. But after being invaded by

Iraq in September, the Ayatollah Khomeini's government decided it did not want to deal with two enemies at once. It released the hostages on Carter's last day in office, having held them for 444 days.

In 1978, *Time* magazine declared the 1970s "elusive, unfocused, a patchwork of dramatics awaiting a drama"—in all, a historical pause not "worth remembering." But history never halts, and in the 1970s it generated profound transformations. The drive to deregulate had begun a restructuring of the economy more along free-market lines while the resistance to minority aspirations, women's reproductive autonomy, and gay rights had fortified the reshaping of American politics that Nixon had sought to exploit. Now, with the energetic emergence of the new conservative coalition, the national political agenda shifted sharply to the right.

## Suggested Reading

William Chafe, *The Unfinished Journey: America since World War II* (2002)

Gary M. Fink and Hugh Davis Graham, eds., *The Carter Presidency: Policy Choices in the Post-New Deal Era* (1998)

John Robert Greene, *The Presidency of Gerald Ford* (1995)

Herbert Parmet, *Richard Nixon and His America* (1990)

Gaddis Smith, *Morality, Reason and Power: American Diplomacy in the Carter Years* (1986)

Daniel Yergin, *Prize: The Epic Quest for Oil, Money, and Power* (1991)

# Chapter Review

## Summary QUESTIONS

■ How did President Nixon achieve the withdrawal of U.S. forces from Vietnam?

■ What was American policy for the Middle East during this period?

■ Why were inflation and unemployment significant problems during this period, and how did the federal government deal with them?

■ What progress was made in environmental protection during the 1970s?

■ Why did a backlash develop against the movement for women's rights and what were its features?

## Chronology

| | |
|---|---|
| **July 1969** | *Apollo 11* lands on the moon. |
| **April 1970** | U.S. troops invade Cambodia. |
| | First Earth Day. |
| **June 17, 1972** | Watergate break-in. |
| **1973** | *Roe v. Wade*. |
| | U.S. completes withdrawal from Vietnam. |
| **1973–74** | OPEC oil embargo. |
| **August 9, 1974** | President Nixon resigns. |
| **1978** | Treaties transferring control of Canal Zone to Panama ratified. |
| **March 1979** | Egyptian president Sadat and Israeli prime minister Begin sign peace treaty. |
| | Accident at Three Mile Island nuclear plant. |
| **November 4, 1979** | Fifty Americans taken hostage in Iran. |

## Key Terms

Détente (p. 894)

ABM (Anti-Ballistic Missiles) (p. 895)

Silent Majority (p. 899)

Watergate (p. 901)

Deregulation (p. 907)

Iran Hostage Crisis (pp. 909–910)

Christian Right (p. 917)

**Access the *Inventing America* StudySpace at wwnorton.com/studyspace**

PERSONAL PLAN ■ REVIEW MATERIALS ■ RESEARCH AIDS ■ MULTIMEDIA

# "THE COLD WAR IS OVER":

## 1981–1992

President Reagan (right) and Soviet Premier Mikhail Gorbachev greet each other at their first summit, in 1985, a meeting that initiated the ending of the Cold War.

*Focus*

QUESTIONS

- ■ **What were the main elements and consequences of Reaganomics?**

- ■ **What was Reagan's stance on the Soviet Union and how did it affect his foreign policy?**

- ■ **What were Reagan's goals in Central America and how did his administration seek to achieve them?**

- ■ **What troubles arose in the greed-is-good culture?**

- ■ **How did President Bush seek to ensure stability in the post-Cold War world?**

- ■ **What was President Bush's approach to the slumping economy and other domestic issues?**

At the Reagan inaugural events, the guests poured out of limousines, the men in tuxedos, the women in designer dresses, their diamonds glittering in an unabashed display of opulence. The new president avidly expressed their credo, a conviction that the scope of government ought to be reduced and private enterprise unleashed. "Government is not the solution to our problem," he declared in his inaugural address. "Government *is* the problem."

Ronald Reagan had grown up far from wealth, in Dixon, Illinois, where his father suffered from alcoholism and his mother drew strength from her participation in an evangelical church. In his political youth, he was a devotee of Franklin Roosevelt and after World War II a leader of the screen actors' union, but the Cold War brought out in him a staunch anti-Communism, including a McCarthyite eagerness to root out reds in Hollywood. In the 1950s, leaving his waning acting career to become a corporate spokesman for General Electric, he increasingly identified with big business and turned sharply to the right.

Reagan entered politics as a supporter of Barry Goldwater's 1964 presidential campaign, and in 1966, with the help of a group of wealthy California Republicans, he was elected governor of the state. Yet his ideology was tempered by a political expediency that made him effective in the office. While denouncing campus antiwar protests and "welfare cheats," he compromised with the Democratic legislature to enact moderate programs, including strong budgets for the state university, welfare reform, and a liberalized abortion law. He embodied an easygoing, "aw, shucks" likeability that reinforced his praise of rugged individualism. People admired his courage and humor when as president in March 1981 he was seriously wounded in an assassination attempt by a lone gunman. "Honey, I forgot to duck," he told his wife, Nancy.

No one seemed to know Reagan well besides Nancy Reagan, a former actress whose father had helped initiate her husband's move to the right. A strong-minded, somewhat insensitive woman, she provoked criticism early in the administration, when the country was suffering double-digit inflation and high unemployment, for wearing a costly inauguration wardrobe and ordering (with private funds) expensive new china for the White House. She might rely on an astrologer to determine the dates of her husband's important public engagements, but she exercised a powerful influence in the White House, eventually prompting her husband to improve relations with the Soviets. Taking the lead in the administration's battle against drugs, she urged young people tempted by them to "Just say no."

Unlike Carter, Reagan was unconcerned with the details of policy, leaving them mainly to subordinates. His laissez-faire approach to administration made him seem detached from affairs of state. He sometimes told stories about purportedly real incidents that actually came from films. Critics considered him an ill-informed lightweight, a puppet whom others manipulated for their own ends. His seeming disengagement tended to insulate him from his administration's setbacks; a congresswoman tartly called him a "Teflon president," meaning that virtually nothing said against him stuck.

But Reagan knew a lot about the issues that interested him, and he took charge when he cared to. If indifferent to accuracy or details, he articulated major themes for his administration in simple, understandable terms—observers called him "The Great Communicator"—and he insisted that his subordinates operate within the broad framework of his conservative principles. Reagan sought to reconfigure the nation's agenda, deploying Rooseveltian activism and flexibility in pursuit of policies reminiscent of Calvin Coolidge, whose portrait he hung in the Cabinet Room. And although he was a hard-line Cold Warrior when he entered office, events both in the Soviet Union and at home led him to help bring an end to the Cold War.

## Reaganomics

Reagan proposed to halt inflation with high interest rates, stimulate the economy with tax reductions, and balance the budget through spending cuts while simultaneously raising defense appropriations—a contradictory agenda that George Bush had disparaged during the primaries as "voodoo economics." Conservative theorists argued that the necessary magic would be achieved by "supply-side economics": tax reductions, this theory had it, would generate enough new taxable economic activity to pay for both the reductions and necessary federal spending. In 1981, Congress slashed income taxes by 25 percent—5 percent in the first year and 10 percent in 1982 and 1983. The top rate was cut from 70 percent to 50 percent, a shift that made public policy out of the old trickle-down theory of conservatives—that investment encouraged at the top of society would eventually trickle down to benefit the bottom. Reagan's budget director conceded to a reporter that the administration's supply-side proposals were mainly intended as "a Trojan horse" to reduce the top tax rates.

Before the reductions had time to work their stimulating magic, the high interest rates the Federal Reserve Board was maintaining (and which Reagan privately supported) threw the economy into a severe recession. In 1982, unemployment shot up to almost 10 percent, almost 16 percent among industrial workers—the highest level of ongoing unemployment since the Depression of the 1930s. But by 1984, the steep interest rates had brought inflation down to 3.2 percent. Moreover, the economy had revived, partly because oil prices declined in response to the worldwide economic slump of the early 1980s, the development of new sources of non-OPEC oil in places such as Alaska and the North Sea, and reductions in oil use arising from conservation measures and technological innovations such as higher mileage-per-gallon cars. The revival was also a product of the Reagan tax cuts and large federal deficits, which in a Keynesian manner had increased the money available for the purchase of goods and services. Unemployment was down to 7.5 percent, and the gross national product (GNP) rose 6.8 percent, the largest annual increase since the Korean War.

Meanwhile, to balance the budget, Reagan took aim at federal spending. Social Security and Medicare, entitlements that accounted for almost half the federal budget, were politically untouchable. Interest on the national debt, another 10 percent of it, was legally so. Reagan's determination to increase defense spending left targetable for cuts only the 15 percent of federal outlays that included programs such as housing subsidies and Aid to Families with Dependent Children. The president pledged to maintain a "safety net" under the "truly needy." But 60 cents in every dollar of his 1981 spending cuts was hacked from the budget for social assistance—a total of $41 billion, including $2 billion from food stamps and $1 billion from school lunches.

Reagan sought to shrink the federal government further through the New Federalism, a policy of returning responsibility for welfare and regulatory programs to the states. It was an echo, but a hollow one, of Nixon's initiative to restore power to the states through revenue sharing. While state responsibilities were enlarged, however, the Reagan administration failed to provide enough funds to carry them out. During the 1980s, federal allocations to the states fell in constant dollars (dollars adjusted for inflation) almost 13 percent. Among the consequences of Reaganomics was a striking shortfall of investment in the nation's infrastructure such as roads, bridges, and air-traffic control systems. In this decade, capital outlays for basic public works fell to barely 1 percent of GNP, less than half the level in the 1960s.

Critics warned that education, an investment in human capital, was of such low quality as to threaten the national welfare. A blue-ribbon commission convened by Reagan's first secretary of education concluded in its 1983 report, "If an unfriendly foreign power had attempted to impose on America the mediocre educational performance that exists today, we might well have viewed it as an act of war." The commission's report prompted local efforts by primary and secondary schools to improve their quality, but it did not move Reagan to help them with federal aid, which fell in constant dollars during his presidency.

## DEFICITS

Reagan's budgetary slashes were substantially offset by his huge increases in military spending—$1.6 trillion was authorized over five years—and the tax-cut losses. The budgetary calculus was further distorted by high interest payments on the national debt and the additional revenue declines that accompanied the recession. Reaganomics, rather than achieving progress toward a balanced budget, led to deficits of unprecedented magnitude. The administration borrowed to meet the shortfall, nearly tripling the national debt by the time Reagan left office to $2.7 trillion. Interest payments on the debt moved up to the third rank in the national budget, behind only Social Security and national defense. "I'm not worried about the deficit," Reagan joked. "It's big enough to take care of itself."

Reagan's willingness to tolerate huge deficits was a sharp departure from the Republican Party's traditional dislike of deficit spending. A mirror shift occurred among Democrats, who now emerged as the deficit's principal critics. The reasons for this exchange of positions were the reasons for the mounting deficit: high defense spending, reduced social spending, and tax cuts that favored upper-income groups—a package that Republicans welcomed and Democrats did not.

GEORGE FISHER
Courtesy Arkansas Gazette

This 1984 cartoon pointedly illustrates the mushrooming budget deficit arising from the Reagan administration's combination of deep tax cuts and huge defense spending.

The deficits were all the more attractive to Reagan Republicans because the eventual need to deal with the accumulating debt would limit social spending far into the future. In another reversal, funding the escalating debt involved heavy borrowing from abroad, with the result that in 1985 the United States became a debtor nation for the first time since 1914, while Japan became the world's biggest creditor.

## DEREGULATION

Reagan greatly extended the deregulation process that Carter had initiated, expanding it in banking, the savings and loan industry, communications, and transportation. He also weakened federal controls by cutting regulatory budgets, staffing regulatory agencies with people hostile to their purposes, restraining enforcement, and scrapping regulations.

Deregulation, while fostering competition, brought consumers advantages as well as disadvantages. It permitted savings and loans institutions to extend credit for purposes other than home mortgages but allowed many of them to lend chancy ventures huge sums from federally insured deposits—a practice that, a federal official said, made the government a "full partner in a nationwide casino" and that ultimately cost taxpayers hundreds of billions of dollars in bailouts. Airline competition produced lower fares for travelers, but deregulation allowed the airlines to shut down service or charge much higher fares to out-of-the-way locations. By 1989, some 140 small towns no longer had air service.

Coincidentally, competition also entered the telephone industry when, in 1982, climaxing a long-developing antitrust action, a federal judge ordered AT&T, the regulated telephone monopoly, to be broken up into one long-distance company and twenty-two separate local telephone companies. The breakup inconvenienced many customers, who found themselves paying multiple monthly telephone bills. But new long-distance companies such as MCI and Sprint sprang into existence, driving down interstate calling rates; and new suppliers began providing innovative services and hardware, including answering machines, cordless phones, and cell phones.

Reaganite deregulation tended to favor private advantage over the public interest in areas of health, safety, and the environment. Regulations that compelled car and truck manufacturers to improve safety and reduce air pollution, that forced employers to maintain safe and healthy working conditions, and that protected people from hazardous food and drugs were all eased. As president, Reagan displayed his

had once provided. It would substitute an invulnerable technological shield for the distasteful and polluting task of dealing with the evil empire. It would render nuclear weapons, Reagan declared, "impotent and obsolete." In 1985, Congress endorsed SDI, authorizing $3 billion as the first installment on the necessary research and development. In the late 1980s, boosted by Star Wars appropriations, defense commanded about 70 percent of the federal R&D budget, a share approaching that of the 1950s.

## AFFIRMATION: THE ELECTION OF 1984

In the 1982 elections, the Republicans retained control of the Senate but lost twenty-five seats in the House, a signal of dissatisfaction with the high unemployment and tight money at that point of Reaganomics. But as the presidential election approached amid the renewal of prosperity, the Republicans cheered through the renomination of Reagan and Bush. The Reverend Jesse Jackson, a black advocate of the poor, won more than 20 percent of the vote in the Democratic primaries, but that party's nominations went to Walter Mondale, the former vice-president, and Congresswoman Geraldine Ferraro from New York City, the first woman ever nominated by a major party for the second-highest office. Mondale emphasized Reagan's seeming lack of substance, attacked the administration for increasing the gap between rich and poor, and warned that its rapidly accumulating deficit was dangerously mortgaging the country's future.

But Reagan deftly deflected Mondale's criticisms, disarmingly retorting in a television debate to Mondale's suggestion that he was too old for the presidency, "I won't hold my opponent's youth and inexperience against him." Reagan's television campaign theme drew on the renewing prosperity, declaring, "It's morning in America." Republicans derided Mondale as a "tax-and-spend liberal," an exemplar of the failures of the Carter years. Ferraro, who might have added electricity to the campaign, ran into trouble because of violations of campaign-spending laws and controversy surrounding her husband's business interests. On election day, Reagan won every state but Minnesota, smashing Mondale in the popular vote 59 percent to 41 percent and burying him in the electoral college with a majority of 525 to 13, a margin second only to Roosevelt's in 1936. He won or scored well in almost every major group except blacks and Jews, and continued to attract sizable numbers of blue-collar defectors from the Democrats. The Democrats retained control of the House, Republicans of the Senate.

## THE THIRD WORLD

In his second inaugural address, Reagan called for supporting anti-Communist "freedom fighters" throughout the third world. Soon dubbed the Reagan Doctrine, his declaration expressed an evangelical outlook that pervaded his foreign policy: it was the special mission of the United States not only to stand as a beacon of democracy and freedom but to help spread those blessings to the rest of the planet.

Reagan was ignorant of and indifferent to the indigenous forces in the third world that challenged pro-Western governments for their own reasons rather than Moscow's—for example, anger at economic exploitation or the suppression of political dissidents or both. He preferred to attribute such challenges to the Soviet Union, which, he insisted, "underlies all the unrest" in the world. His anti-Sovietism strongly shaped his approach to the Middle East and, especially, Central America.

*Stalemate and Terror: The Middle East.* Sure that Soviet machinations were responsible for the instability in the Middle East, Reagan hoped to bring moderate Arab states and Israel together into an anti-Soviet combination. But the prospective parties considered the future of the Palestinians far more important than any Soviet threat. Although, honoring the Camp David accords, Prime Minister Begin had returned the Sinai Peninsula to Egypt, he refrained from granting the Palestinians any autonomy in the West Bank and the Gaza Strip. Indeed, he expanded Israeli settlements with an evident eye toward future annexation of the territories. Reagan called for a freeze on settlements and independence for the West Bank "in association with Jordan," but Begin refused the proposal.

Palestinian guerrillas, on their part, mounted continual armed attacks against Israel from sanctuaries in southern Lebanon. In June 1982, Israel invaded Lebanon to drive out the guerrillas, but succeeded mainly in intensifying the civil war under way there among Muslims, Palestinians, and Christians and in heightening Arab-Israeli tensions. Secretary of State George Shultz recognized that the problems in the Middle East were specific to the region, not the result of Soviet ambitions. At his urging, Reagan proposed a comprehensive peace plan as a basis for negotiations between Israel and the moderate Arab states, but neither side accepted it. In 1983, in the hope of quelling the violence in Lebanon, the administration sent 2,000 marines there as part of a multi-

U.S. Marines carry a corpse from the rubble of the barracks destroyed by a truck bomb that killed 241 fellow marines, Beirut, October 1983.

national peacekeeping force. Seen as favoring the Israelis and the Christians, they were attacked by guerrillas and terrorists. In October, a suicide truck bomber killed 241 marines in a poorly guarded barracks in Beirut. The murders, a harbinger of terrorist attacks that would later increase in frequency, provoked grief and outrage at home, including a growing demand to pull the remaining marines out of Lebanon. In early 1984, Reagan reluctantly brought the troops home, his efforts toward a settlement in the Middle East scuttled by the intractability of the region's political rivalries and hatreds.

In December 1987, Palestinians living in occupied Gaza and the West Bank began an *intifada,* a civilian uprising against the Israeli authorities. Secretary Shultz attempted to work out an agreement for Palestinian autonomy among Israel, Jordan, and the Palestinians, led by Yasir Arafat, the head of the Palestine Liberation Organization; but his proposals dissatisfied the Palestinians, and the Israeli government refused to negotiate until the *intifada* ended. Unwilling to tolerate the uprising, Israeli forces repeatedly clashed with the Palestinian rebels, killing some 800 of them during the next three years. Despite opposition from the United States, Israel also continued to establish Jewish settlements on the West Bank.

In the meantime, terrorists brought the turbulence in the Middle East to the West, hijacking a TWA flight and an Italian cruise ship, killing an American aboard each; bombing a Berlin nightclub that American soldiers frequented;

and using a concealed bomb to down a Pan American jet flying over Lockerbie, Scotland, killing all 259 passengers and crew. Libya, headed by Colonel Muammar al-Gadhafi, was implicated in several of the incidents. Reagan retaliated, at one point bombing Tripoli, including Gadhafi's compound.

*Central America.* In Nicaragua in 1979, a popular insurrection threw out a right-wing dictatorship and installed a leftist government, the Sandinistas, which received support from Castro and the Soviet bloc. In El Salvador, where a right-wing government held sway, leftist guerrillas, encouraged by the Sandinista victory, fought to overturn the regime, drawing military assistance from Cuba and Nicaragua. Both Reagan and Haig held that Central America was threatened by "Communist aggression," ignoring the roots of political instability and resentment in poverty and repression.

In 1981, to deal with Nicaragua, Reagan directed the CIA to begin arming and organizing a guerrilla army—the Contras, many of them with ties to the deposed dictatorship—to wage war against the Sandinistas from bases in neighboring Honduras and Costa Rica. The next year, Congress responded with legislation forbidding the CIA or the Defense Department to provide any aid "for the purpose of overthrowing" the Nicaraguan regime. Despite the prohibition, the Reagan administration secretly continued to fund the Contras, obtaining support from private sources and foreign governments. (George Shultz, who in 1982 had succeeded Haig as secretary of state, warned Reagan that thus circumventing the Congress might constitute "an impeachable offense.") Reagan publicly celebrated the Contras as "the moral equivalent of our Founding Fathers." All the while, the administration tenaciously sought to bolster the regime in El Salvador, even though right-wing "death squads" were operating freely against members of the opposition.

The administration found an opportunity to strike more decisively against Communism in Grenada, a small Caribbean island where in October 1983 a Marxist government was overthrown by a more radical regime. On Reagan's orders, 2,000 marines invaded the island, partly to protect American students in medical school there. The marines drove out the new government and established a pro-American replacement. Most Americans hailed the invasion, as did the Grenadans and nearby Caribbean states. The action impelled the Nicaraguan Sandinistas to improve their behavior, at least for a time, and even to talk about negotiations.

*Scandal: Iran-Contra.* On November 3, 1986, a Beirut newspaper reported that the year before, the United States had sold antitank missiles to Iran in exchange for American hostages. The story was promptly confirmed by the Iranian prime minister, who said that in May Robert McFarlane, the president's national security adviser, had brought a small shipment of missile parts to Iran together with gifts, including a Bible inscribed by Reagan for the Ayatollah Khomeini and a cake decorated with a brass key for the mother of the principal Iranian go-between.

In the United States, outrage greeted the revelations that the administration had violated its own stated policy, and the government's long-standing one, against bargaining with terrorists. In fact, Reagan had privately deviated from that rule on several occasions. Now, in November 1986, he went on television to say that the United States had indeed shipped small caches of arms to Iran in an attempt to encourage a restoration of relations and assist Iran in its war with Iraq. He insisted that the charge that the arms had been sent in exchange for hostages was "utterly false." Later that month, the attorney general discovered and released to the public evidence of still worse activities: Lieutenant Colonel Oliver North, a staff member of the National Security Council (NSC) and a much-decorated Vietnam veteran, had diverted millions of dollars from the arms sales to provide the Contras in Nicaragua with military assistance. North's action, carried out with the knowledge of the head of the NSC, Admiral John Poindexter, was illegal, a defiance of the congressional mandate against military aid to the Contras. During the attorney general's investigation, North and his staff at the NSC purged computer files, shredded incriminating documents, and, together with the head of the CIA, William Casey, concocted cover-up stories about the affair.

By early December, Reagan's public approval rating had plummeted 21 points, to 46 percent, the sharpest one-month drop ever recorded for a president. At the end of February 1987, a bipartisan commission rapped Reagan for his lax "management style" and for trading arms for hostages; but it concluded that the president had not known "anything whatsoever" about the illegal payments to the Contras. In a televised address a few days later, Reagan conceded that while he had not thought he was trading arms for hostages, he had in fact mistakenly done so. In congressional hearings that summer, North, bemedaled in his uniform, defended all he had done as acts of selfless duty. While North suggested that Reagan had known everything, Poindexter testified that he had

*"AMERICANS SHOULD NOT BECOME OBSESSED WITH THE IRAN ARMS SCANDAL!"*

Reagan's evasion of responsibility for the Iran-Contra scandal reminded many Americans of Nixon's Watergate denials.

kept the diversion of funds to the Contras secret from the president. In 1988, in the course of a criminal trial, Poindexter repudiated his testimony in the hearings, declaring instead that Reagan had been fully aware of the diversion of funds to the Contras and had ordered the destruction of documents. In videotaped testimony, Reagan denied the allegation while seeming confused and claiming to be unable to recall most of the details of the scandal.

All the while, Reagan urged Congress to authorize military aid to the Contras, but Congress refused, insisting on a negotiated settlement in Nicaragua. A peace plan devised by President Oscar Arias of Costa Rica gained the support of the Central American governments and, by early 1988, of the Sandinistas. The Sandinistas entered into talks with the Contras, and a cease-fire was declared.

For a time, Reagan's complicity in Iran-Contra, whatever it was, gave rise to talk of impeachment. But the talk quickly subsided, not least because it seemed unsupportable to impeach a president for not knowing what his subordinates were doing.

*Flexibility: South Africa, the Philippines, and Haiti.* While Reagan revived John Foster Dulles's moralism in foreign affairs, he would go only so far in pursuit of higher purposes. He was guided by an overarching inclination to avoid committing American forces, especially on the ground, to sustained conflict. For Reagan, as for the American people in the aftermath of Vietnam, any armed intervention would have to be a short-term venture costing little in dollars or American lives: thus the compactness of the intervention in Grenada, the speediness of the withdrawal from Lebanon, and the mode of warring largely by proxy against the left in Nicaragua and El Salvador. Reagan was also capable of ignoring ideology to satisfy domestic political interests, defuse the objections of allies, and pursue practical geopolitics. The Reagan Doctrine was thus flexible, and responsive to events, notably in South Africa, the Philippines, and Haiti.

Throughout his first term, Reagan had adopted a policy of what a State Department official called "constructive engagement" in dealing with South Africa. The president called its harsh system of apartheid (racial segregation) "morally wrong and politically unacceptable," but while he urged the government to release its political prisoners and legalize black political movements such as the African National Congress (ANC), he was reluctant to back his rhetoric with coercive measures. Nevertheless, in September 1985, responding to nationwide demands for action, especially on the campuses, Reagan issued an executive order that prohibited computer sales, bank loans, and the export of nuclear technology to South Africa. The next year, Congress, overriding Reagan's veto, imposed still tougher economic sanctions on the regime, including a ban on all imports from South Africa, that could be lifted only after the country had made significant progress toward democratization.

In the Philippines, Reagan clung to the hope of saving the repressive regime of Ferdinand Marcos against the intensifying democratic protest movement led by Corazon Aquino, the widow of a murdered opposition leader. Reagan, who considered Aquino weak, feared Marcos's fall would lead to a Communist takeover. Shultz, however, successfully pressed Reagan to withdraw U.S. support from Marcos and provide him safe haven. In 1986, Marcos fled the country with his extensive entourage, and Corazon Aquino together with her followers joyfully established democratic government in the Philippines.

In Haiti, in mid-1985, the corrupt and dictatorial Jean-Claude ("Baby Doc") Duvalier got himself elected president for life with 99.9 percent of the vote. Dissent from the apparently rigged result soon turned into a tidal wave of protest that brought the country to the edge of chaos. The Reagan administration, seeing that Duvalier's government would topple, arranged for him to flee into exile. It then pressed policies of liberalization on the Haitian military, which took

control. The subsequent democratization led to the election in 1990 of a new president, Jean-Bertrand Aristide.

## SUMMITRY WITH THE SOVIETS

Although the Iran-Contra scandal impaired Reagan's authority, he recovered from the shadow it cast by contributing to a dramatic transformation in U.S.-Soviet relations during his second term. Brezhnev had died in 1982, and death had cut short the terms of the two men who succeeded him. (Asked why he was seemingly unwilling to meet with his Soviet counterparts, Reagan had quipped, "They keep dying on me.") But in November 1985, Reagan journeyed to Geneva for his first summit with a Soviet leader—Mikhail Gorbachev, who had become the new head of the Soviet Union in March. At age fifty-four, Gorbachev was vigorous, articulate, knowledgeable about the West, where he had traveled, and brimming with ideas for change. With his country beset by mounting economic difficulties, he intended to pursue a program of domestic reform. To this end, he wanted to ease Cold War tensions, cut expenditures on armaments, and, like Russian reformers before him, reach out to the West. After meeting him in London, Prime Minister Margaret Thatcher of Britain, Reagan's friend and fellow conservative, had remarked, "I like Mr. Gorbachev. We can do business together."

The Geneva summit made for a fresh start in U.S.-Soviet relations. Reagan and Gorbachev spent hours in candid conversation, often alone save for their interpreters. In public, Gorbachev conducted himself with flair, assiduously cultivating the media, as did his wife, Raisa. She was a sophisticated university graduate and something of a fashion plate, the first wife of a Soviet premier to capture the West's attention. Little substantive business was accomplished at Geneva, but at the end of the meeting Reagan and Gorbachev announced that they had agreed to hold two more summits. The striking news of the conference was the rapport that had developed between the two men. "[We] got very friendly," Reagan said.

During the next several years, Gorbachev sought arms agreements with the United States and boldly pursued an expanding program of domestic political and economic reform. An increasing number of analysts in the United States dared to hope that, with Reagan's help, the Cold War might actually be ending. But the Reagan administration initially responded to Gorbachev's efforts with suspicion, some of its hard-liners counting them as mere window dressing for continued Soviet oppression at home and imperialism abroad.

*Toward the End of the Cold War.* In October 1986, when Reagan and Gorbachev held their second summit, in Reykjavik, Iceland, the then-budding miracle had seemed to wilt. Gorbachev, who had proclaimed that it was imperative for the superpowers to reduce the threat of nuclear annihilation, arrived at the meeting with a sheaf of detailed proposals for arms control, including the elimination of all intermediate-range nuclear weapons in Europe. Reagan countered by proposing an agreement to destroy all nuclear weapons. To the surprise of many, Gorbachev agreed, on the condition that the United States continue to honor the ABM Treaty of 1972 by keeping its Star Wars research confined to the laboratory for ten years.

Reagan, his enthusiasm for Star Wars undiminished, rejected Gorbachev's condition, explaining later that it would have "killed our defensive shield." On the evening of October 12, he and Gorbachev emerged grim-faced from their final negotiating session, with neither an arms control agreement nor much good to say about each other. Secretary of State Shultz, one of the few in the administration who thought the Soviets were genuinely changing, had trouble concealing his distress. Gorbachev told reporters, "We have missed a historical chance. Never have our positions been so close."

In the months following the Reykjavik summit, Gorbachev reconsidered his view that arms control had to be accompanied by restraint on SDI. The Soviet physicist Andrei Sakharov, isolated in internal exile, urged that the two issues be decoupled, predicting that SDI would be costly to the United States and easily overwhelmed by the Soviets. At the end of 1986, by Gorbachev's personal order, Sakharov returned to Moscow and now pressed his case for arms control at the center of Soviet policymaking. In late February 1987, Gorbachev told the Reagan administration that he was willing to proceed with arms control negotiations without regard to SDI and wanted to conclude a treaty on intermediate-range nuclear weapons (INF) in Europe.

Gorbachev was simultaneously initiating profound changes inside the Soviet Union. In 1986, in order to bring pressure to bear on the Soviet bureaucracy, he had proclaimed *glasnost,* an opening of the Soviet system via greater freedom of expression and freedom of the press and the release of political prisoners. Now he was pushing ahead with *perestroika,* a restructuring of the Soviet economy to encourage private entrepreneurship as well as foreign trade and investment. In 1987, the Soviets announced that their troops would begin leaving Afghanistan within the next year.

Reagan, in deepening political trouble at home, speedily took up Gorbachev's offer for a meeting on the INF Treaty, expecting it to lead to a prestige-restoring summit before the end of the year. Anti-Soviet hard-liners were departing, leaving Shultz the key figure in a national security team disposed to think that the changes under way in the Soviet Union boded well for the United States and the world. In mid-June 1987, while in Berlin near the wall dividing the eastern and western zones of the city, Reagan called on Gorbachev to show unequivocally that the opening of Soviet society was more than a token gesture, declaring, "Mr. Gorbachev, tear down this wall."

At the summit, held in Washington in December, little of substance was accomplished beyond coming to a final agreement on the INF Treaty. When Reagan told Gorbachev that the United States would proceed with its research and development on SDI, Gorbachev responded flatly, "Mr. President, you do what you think you have to do. . . . I think you're wasting your money. I don't think it will work. But if that's what you want to do, go ahead." The INF Treaty—signed precisely at 1:45 P.M. on December 8 because Nancy Reagan's astrologer had advised her that this was the most propitious moment—eliminated about 1,280 Soviet warheads and about 429 American ones. Although the reduction constituted only about 4 percent of the combined Soviet and American nuclear arsenals, the agreement represented a significant step because it was the first to abolish an entire class of nuclear weapons and the first to provide for on-site verification that the Soviet missiles were being destroyed.

A cartoonist blames Reagan's Star Wars program for dashing arms-control hopes at the Reykjavik summit, October, 1986.

The achievement of the treaty was reinforced by the infectious good cheer that marked the summit. Expressing the "Gorbymania" that swept through the country, *Time* magazine designated Gorbachev its "Man of the Year," and—a first in Gallup polling—the general secretary of the Communist Party of the Soviet Union made the list of the ten most admired men in the United States. The following spring, Gorbachev initiated a restructuring of Soviet relations with its satellites and a transformation of the Soviet system into a political democracy, including an elected legislature and executive, an independent judiciary, and freedom of speech and assembly. In May, Reagan, acknowledging the momentous changes under way in the Soviet Union, remarked to "all those familiar with the postwar era, this is a cause for shaking the head in wonder."

## Reagan's America

Reagan's triumphal summitry abroad was accompanied by an exuberant prosperity at home. Between 1982 and 1988, the gross domestic product grew at an average annual rate of about 4 percent, generating more than 630,000 new businesses, 11 million jobs, and a drop in the unemployment rate from 7.4 percent to 5.5 percent. By 1988, mortgage rates had plummeted roughly 40 percent; by 1989, median family income corrected for inflation had shot up 12.5 percent. Corporate profits broke records, and so did the stock market. By 1989, the Dow Jones had more than doubled its level in 1982.

The rising economic tide lifted many boats, restoring the satisfactions of abundance across much of the social spectrum and permitting millions of Americans to avail themselves of the good life. The migration westward continued as people from virtually every social group sought economic opportunity—and for senior citizens, repose—in the sun-drenched states of the Southwest. The geographical migration was paralleled by the ongoing movement from cities to suburbs, with its satisfactions of space, greenery, fresh air, and home ownership. By 1990, suburbia was home to almost half the population, including a growing number of people of color.

Technology continued to ease and enrich people's lives. By the late 1980s, three out of four Americans cooked with microwave ovens; more than six out of ten watched and recorded videotapes on a VCR, and untold numbers listened to music on compact disc players, available since 1982. Cable television,

available in 20 million homes in 1980, reached some 53 million in 1990, providing programming for virtually every taste and interest, including twenty-four-hour news, old films, talk shows and sex shows, soap opera and classical opera, wildlife and nature, and professional as well as amateur sports.

But the good life in the 1980s was by no means free of troubles, some of them ongoing. The flight to suburbia reflected in part the long-standing desire for escape from urban problems such as crime, rundown neighborhoods, and declining urban schools. A number of Americans, eager for more protection than open living might provide, settled in gated communities, some 80,000 of which now dotted the suburban landscape, an eightyfold increase in just two decades. Similarly, senior citizens segregated themselves in communities restricted to older people, a number of them predominantly white, such as Leisure World in California and New Jersey.

Religious conservatism grew in the 1980s, gaining support from adherents of Orthodox Judaism and Orthodox Islam. A rabbi in St. Louis explained, "Fear motivates some of the drift to this old-time religion"—fear of moral dissolution and its impact on children, including drugs and violence in the schools and pornography everywhere. (In this decade, conservative Christians were joined in their war against pornography by several prominent feminists, who contended that pornography encouraged violence against women.)

### GREED IS GOOD

The Reagan years reminded some observers of the 1920s, not only in the ebullience of the prosperity but in the unevenness of it, and in the reckless materialism of the culture associated with it. Critics understandably disparaged Reaganomics as "welfare for the rich." Reagan's initial tax changes had channeled one dollar out of every twelve to Americans earning less than $15,000 a year, one in three to those with annual incomes greater than $50,000. His Tax Reform Act of 1986, a major overhaul of the tax system, closed numerous loopholes and removed nearly 6 million people from the tax rolls; but it also further slashed the top rate for individuals, from 50 percent to 28 percent. Then, too, increases in state taxes and in Social Security taxes, which were imposed to keep the system solvent, in effect nullified the Reagan tax cut for most working Americans, keeping their overall tax burden relatively unchanged. By the end of the decade, families earning under $10,000 wound up with a $95 net loss, while those making more than $200,000 gained more than $17,000. In 1988, the

*American Journal*

## What's for Dinner?

*In the mid-twentieth century, popular cookbooks featured traditional dishes—meat, fowl, potatoes, corn, green vegetables, and breads—that required time and labor to prepare. But in the 1950s, Americans, increasingly on the go, hungered for fast and cheap cooked food, and the new McDonald's restaurants, offering the menu at right, provided them with it. In the 1970s, the microwave oven began bringing the quick cooking of food into the home, with its mushrooming number of working wives. By the early 1990s, four out of five American homes had microwaves. By then, too, The Fannie Farmer Cookbook, an American standard, had added recipes that captured "the new ethnic flavors that have become a part of American cooking—such as some lively risottos, polentas, and pastas, and stir-frys." Many of these dishes could be bought ready for the microwave or ready to eat in chains like El Pollo Loco in southern California—an indication that most minority groups, busy like everyone else, had joined the fast-food revolution.*

### McDonald's
### Speedee Service

**MENU**

| | |
|---|---|
| **HAMBURGERS** | 15¢ |
| **CHEESEBURGERS** | 19¢ |
| **MALT SHAKES** | 20¢ |
| **FRENCH FRIES** | 10¢ |
| **ORANGE** | 10¢ |
| **ROOT BEER** | 10¢ |
| **COFFEE** | 10¢ |
| **COKE** | 10¢ |
| **MILK** | 10¢ |

richest 1 percent of Americans owned almost 15 percent of national wealth, almost twice the portion of 1980.

The decade produced a new group called "yuppies," a derisive acronym for "young urban professionals," upwardly mobile men and women with degrees in law or business, dressed for success and exuding the ambitions of an unrestrained materialism. Americans of all sorts became absorbed with celebrities—professional athletes, television newscasters, entertainers, clothing designers, even chefs, most of whom were admired for their professional skills but also for their opulent incomes. Among the heroes of Wall Street were manipulators of junk bonds, loans issued to finance the purchase of corporations for prices far higher than the corporations were worth. Some of the heroes were later exposed as crooked and went to jail.

Tom Wolfe's best-selling novel *Bonfire of the Vanities* (1987) relentlessly explored the culture of avarice, but reality outdid fiction. Amid the weakened oversight of Reaganite deregulation, a number of savings-and-loan institutions were looted by white-collar thieves, some of whom bought yachts and threw lavish entertainments. Ivan Boesky, one of the financial buccaneers of the decade—he later went to jail for fraudulent manipulations—proclaimed, "Greed is all right . . . everybody should be a little greedy," a sentiment that pervaded the popular film *Wall Street* (1987).

Some religious ministries combined evangelism with profiteering in ways reminiscent of *Elmer Gantry,* Sinclair Lewis's famed novel of the 1920s. Taking advantage of the rapid proliferation of cable TV, some 336 televangelists were broadcasting by 1989. One enjoyed an annual income of at least $1.6 million and owned six homes. He was later convicted on twenty-four counts of fraud and conspiracy, but the popularity of the televangelists remained undiminished. Some 33 million people subscribed to the Christian Broadcast Network's "700 Club," run by Marion G. "Pat" Robertson, and in 1987 the network, including its multiple enterprises, brought in $230 million.

Actor Michael Douglas as a greed-driven business executive, in the award-winning film Wall Street, 1987.

*The Challenger Disaster.* An attitude of success at all costs invaded even NASA's space shuttle program, which had been initiated in the 1970s as the agency's main successor to the moon shots. The shuttles were large, rocket-launched vehicles intended to fly for extended periods in near-earth orbit while their crews conducted scientific experiments and performed tasks—for example, launching or retrieving satellites—for military and commercial agencies. Since its beginnings, the shuttle program had been granted inadequate funding; during the Reagan administration, the budgetary cutbacks deepened while performance expectations remained high. Tragedy struck the program on January 28, 1986, when, as millions watched on television, the space shuttle *Challenger* exploded seventy-four seconds after liftoff, killing all seven astronauts aboard. In an investigation of the disaster, a presidential commission sharply criticized NASA and some of its contractors for subordinating safety to public relations. In order to keep to its announced shuttle-launch schedule, the agency had overworked its employees and allowed its contractors to take too many risks. The rockets bearing the *Challenger* had exploded because a small seal had cracked in the prelaunch cold air. Several engineers employed by the rocket manufacturer, aware of this possibility, had urged postponement of the launch, but, goaded by NASA managers, the company's executives had overridden their recommendation.

## STRESSES IN THE WORKFORCE

In the 1980s, a wave of mergers, takeovers, and restructurings—the most extensive in the nation's history—swept through corporate America. Encouraged by the administration's drive for deregulation, corporate raiders engineered hostile takeovers, often financing their conquests partly by selling some of the assets of the companies they acquired. Corporate directors resorted to restructuring to defend against takeover threats or respond to increased competition or both. Aimed at increasing a company's efficiency and reducing its vulnerability, restructuring tended to involve selling parts of the company unrelated to its main business and cutting the workforce. Many workers, including middle managers, thus found themselves laid off from jobs they had assumed would be theirs for life.

The smokestack industries, reeling still more from foreign competition in major sectors such as steel, automobiles, and electronics, continued to decline. The challenges from abroad were compounded by soaring imports and plummeting exports, which eliminated manufacturing jobs and more than tripled the trade deficit between 1981 and 1984, from $31 billion to $111 billion. Farmers also suffered setbacks. Between 1980 and 1986, crop prices dropped; in Iowa, the average value of farmland fell 55 percent. Farm foreclosures and bankruptcies climbed, reaching a post-Depression high. The downturn struck hard at related industries such as food processing and farm equipment and at small towns throughout the Midwest. In the later 1980s, a modicum of prosperity returned to the farms, the result of a rebound in agricultural exports, increased domestic demand, and a drought in 1988 that reduced supply. But foreign manufacturers remained strongly competitive against domestic producers—notably, in steel and automobiles.

By the mid-1980s, high-school-educated blue-collar workers earned $18,000 a year, a quarter less than they had fifteen years earlier. Faced with the rigors of competition, both old companies and new ones hired skilled workers at lower wages and benefits than those paid to senior, union-protected employees. The average compensation of truck drivers fell by a quarter, of pilots and flight attendants by as much as two-thirds. Many firms relied increasingly on part-time or temporary workers. Between 1982 and 1987, real hourly wages declined a half percent per year, making the period unique among those of economic boom since World War II. In his smash hit song "Born in the USA," Bruce Springsteen sang in

Hundreds demonstrated for jobs when President Reagan stopped in Philadelphia in 1982.

the bitter, ironic voice of a Vietnam veteran who could gain neither work nor help: "Down in the shadow of the penitentiary / Out by the gas fires of the refinery / I'm ten years burning down the road / Nowhere to run, ain't got nowhere to go."

Many middle-class Americans stayed even only by working additional hours, taking more than one job, or becoming two-earner couples. Employers, taking advantage of the high demand for work, expanded temporary jobs and cut back on full-time jobs with benefits. In 1984, the cash income of more than one in seven Americans fell below the poverty line, a sharp increase from one in nine in 1979, and the highest proportion since the beginning of Johnson's War on Poverty in 1965. The trend was especially sharp among people of color, many of whom were impoverished, degraded, and virtually hopeless. For the first time since the Depression, the streets and parks of the United States were speckled with homeless people, an estimated three-quarters of a million in 1988, some of them mentally disabled but many of them working poor, including more than a third who were families with children.

## Political Reckoning

Through the 1980s, an undercurrent of disquiet with the era's greed-is-good culture pervaded the country, as did dissatisfaction with the Reagan administration's approach to poverty, civil rights, and the environment, and with its high-handed subversion of the law in Iran-Contra. Signs of the uneasiness appeared in popular culture—not only in the songs of Bruce Springsteen but in benefit concerts mounted for farmers in the Midwest and the impoverished people of Africa.

The dissatisfaction expressed itself politically as well. In the 1986 elections, following the first revelations of Iran-Contra, the Democrats recaptured the Senate, winning a majority of ten seats. Now in control of both houses of Congress, they pressed for a more liberal legislative agenda, passing an $80 billion extension of the Clean Water Act over Reagan's veto, crushing a Republican attempt to cut back Medicare, and enacting a civil rights bill and a measure strengthening the bargaining power of labor. They also expanded the food stamp program, provided aid to the homeless and protection against catastrophic illness, and beefed up elementary and secondary education.

### THE ELECTION OF 1988

Expecting a victory over Reagan Republicanism, a number of Democrats sought their party's presidential nomination, but the field rapidly narrowed to Jesse Jackson, who emphasized the needs of the poor, and Michael Dukakis, the moderate governor of Massachusetts. After winning the primaries in major states, Dukakis took the nomination and chose for his vice-president Lloyd Bentsen, a right-of-center senator from Texas. Vice-President George Bush handily won the Republican nomination against Senator Robert Dole of Kansas. Bush then surprised his supporters by choosing as his running mate J. Danforth "Dan" Quayle, a young, hardworking, but undistinguished senator from Indiana whose gaffes during the campaign earned him widespread ridicule in the press.

Bush dissociated himself from the Iran-Contra scandal and moved toward the center by calling for "a kinder, gentler America." Otherwise, he embraced the Reagan record, stressing the restoration of prosperity, the reduction in inflation, and the dramatic turn for the better in Soviet-American relations. He campaigned on the pledge "Read my lips: no new taxes," the first phrase of which was borrowed from a tough-guy film. Bush's supporters, playing on the fears of crime and race, broadcast a television advertisement featuring a black man, a convicted killer who under a Massachusetts program had been furloughed from state prison only to commit rape and murder. Bush also attacked Dukakis for vetoing a bill that required students to recite the Pledge of Allegiance, a law that was likely unconstitutional, and, in a suggestive echo of McCarthyism, called Dukakis a "card-carrying member of the American Civil Liberties Union."

Dukakis, for his part, pointed to the failures of Reaganomics and stressed his gubernatorial accomplishments, but otherwise seemed wooden. In the November election, which produced the lowest turnout since 1924, Bush won 54 percent of the vote and carried forty states. The Democrats, however, kept control of both houses of Congress.

### THE REAGAN LEGACY

Ronald Reagan tamed inflation, revived the economy, and presided over a historic thawing of the Cold War. Conservatives came to assert that Reagan had prompted the stunning change in the Soviet Union with his military buildup and SDI. According to them, Gorbachev tried to compete with the United States in defense, realized that the Soviet economy was not up to the task, and concluded that change was imperative because the Soviet system was so inherently flawed. However, the claim is contradicted by the evidence. The Soviets neither responded to the Reagan administration's military buildup nor spent anything to create or counter SDI, especially since by 1987 Gorbachev was convinced that it would not work. What moved Gorbachev to his reforms was not any pressure from Reagan but his own recognition of the inherent weaknesses in the Soviet economy. What changed the Soviet Union was his desire to reconstruct it, and what Reagan contributed to the transformation of U.S.-Soviet relations was his willingness, person to person, to endorse Gorbachev's efforts.

A number of Reagan's accomplishments were won at a high price. He left the country with escalating trade deficits and a staggering debt. His laissez-faire policies helped American corporations restructure themselves to deal with mounting competition, especially from abroad; but his administration did little to assist the people whose jobs were lost or downgraded in the process. His tax reductions, government cutbacks, and resistance to civil rights exacerbated the inequalities in American society, a condition symbolized by the homeless wandering the big-city streets. Still, Reagan refurbished the image of American prowess and revived confidence in the nation's world pur-

pose. He left office with his popularity buoyed by the increasingly likely end of the Cold War. He had succeeded in shifting the center of American political culture away from the liberalism of the postwar decades. A combination of attrition and the creation of new seats in the federal courts had also permitted him to bolster the shift by appointing almost 400 federal judges, a majority of all those sitting in 1989. When Reagan left office, the middle of the political road ran through less regulation, lower taxes, more limited government. It remained to be seen whether such a restrained role for government would suffice to deal with the economic and security issues already evident in a globalizing, post–Cold War era.

## Bush Seeks a New Global Order

"The Cold War is over," Ronald Reagan remarked to a friend on leaving Washington at the end of his presidency. It was not quite over, but it soon would be, leaving Reagan's immediate successors in the White House with the enviable if difficult task of devising a new global order. Their principal challenge abroad was to protect American security while responding to the rising aspirations of peoples freed from Soviet control and to the growing problems of globalization. At home, in the near term, the challenge was to deal with the legacy of Reaganomics and an economic downturn that emerged in the wake of the Cold War. Prosperity returned in the early 1990s, inaugurating a record-setting economic expansion that was driven to a significant extent by technological innovations such as the Internet (see Chapter 33). But the United States remained divided over social and cultural issues such as race, immigration, abortion, and sexual behavior. And the nation encountered violence stoked by resentments of its power among extremists both at home and abroad.

George Herbert Walker Bush's inaugural celebration was twice as expensive as Reagan's, but the next day, in a gesture unseen since William Howard Taft had taken office, the new president and his wife threw open the doors of the White House, greeting some 4,000 people who had been waiting in line all night. The son of a U.S. senator from Connecticut, Bush was at once a product of privilege and a devotee of accomplishment. As a navy pilot during World War II, he won a Distinguished Flying Cross. After graduating from Yale in 1949, he moved to Texas, became a successful oilman, and in 1966 won election to the U.S. House of Representatives. Defeated for the Senate four years later, he served during the 1970s in a series of federal posts, including ambassador to the United Nations, head of the U.S. Liaison Office in China, and director of the CIA, before his election as Ronald Reagan's vice-president.

In all, Bush was a kind of regional and social hybrid, a Republican of the old internationalist Northeast and the new entrepreneurial Southwest, an embodiment of patrician obligation and business ambition. Closer to the domestic center than Reagan, he brought to the task of his presidency broad experience in government, in foreign affairs the attitudes of a hard-line but pragmatic Cold Warrior, and in domestic ones the convictions of a moderate conservative.

### THE END OF THE COLD WAR

When he entered the White House in 1989, George Bush was suspicious of the genuineness of Mikhail Gorbachev's commitment to *perestroika* and *glasnost*. But Bush's caution was overwhelmed by volcanic demands for freedom that redrew the political map of Central Europe with stunning speed. During the first year of his presidency, Hungary and Poland cast off most of their Communist leadership, and Estonia, Lithuania, and Latvia broke free of the Soviet Union. Upheaval followed in East Germany, where in early November, with Gorbachev having declared a hands-off policy, thou-

A man chisels a piece of the Berlin Wall for a souvenir, December 1989, a month after the East German regime was forced to open the gates to the West.

sands forced the regime to open the gates to the West and started tearing down the hated wall dividing Berlin. That winter, the Communist governments in Yugoslavia, Bulgaria, and Romania were overthrown, and a prodemocracy playwright became president of Czechoslovakia.

Bush navigated this tidal wave of change by trying to maintain a stable balance of power while fostering democratic capitalism in post–Cold War Europe. He was ably assisted by Secretary of State James Baker, a veteran of the Reagan administration and a long-standing ally. In East and West Germany, sentiment for reunification was mounting rapidly. Gorbachev, anxious about Russian security in the face of a united Germany and under pressure from hard-liners at home, resisted the union. But Bush opted for it, fearing otherwise an unpredictable instability in East Germany. In May 1990, during a summit in Washington, he granted Gorbachev a trade package to help shore him up against the hard-liners, and Gorbachev, in exchange, agreed to German reunification by 1994. In July 1991, at a summit in Moscow, Bush and Gorbachev signed the Strategic Arms Reduction Treaty (START I), an agreement to cut strategic nuclear weaponry ultimately by 30 to 40 percent.

The following month, however, Russian hard-liners attempted a coup against Gorbachev and his reforms. In defiance, hundreds of thousands of people protectively cordoned off the parliament, and Boris Yeltsin, the president of the Russian republic, rallied the crowd, courageously mounting a tank to denounce the plotters. Although the coup failed and Gorbachev retained power, he was increasingly overshadowed by Yeltsin and, in the end, overwhelmed by the liberalizing forces he had unleashed. In December 1991, the Soviet Union came to an end, replaced by a Commonwealth of Independent States comprising the eleven former Soviet republics. Gorbachev resigned, and Yeltsin reigned over Russia. In January 1993, Bush and Yeltsin signed START II, which called for a two-thirds reduction in long-range nuclear weapons within ten years and complete elimination of land-based missiles. The Cold War was now indisputably over.

### RIPPLES OF FREEDOM

The end of the Cold War produced ripple effects in world affairs far beyond the borders of what people for a time called "the former Soviet Union." The decline in Russian power permitted the United States to maneuver more freely in foreign affairs and to deal with regional issues more evenhandedly, taking demands for freedom on their merits rather than refracting them through fears of Soviet imperialism. The new conditions helped the United States resolve long-standing conflicts and tensions in South Africa and the third world, though China dishearteningly demonstrated that American leverage for freedom was far from limitless.

*South Africa.* Together with the winding down of the Cold War, the economic sanctions imposed on South Africa during the Reagan years yielded dramatic changes in the region. In 1988, a State Department official negotiated a de-escalation of the civil war in Angola, persuading Cuba and South Africa to withdraw their troops from the country and South Africa to withdraw its forces from neighboring Namibia, thereby granting it independence. In South Africa itself in 1990, a more moderate regime, come to power the year before, legalized the African National Congress and released its leader, Nelson Mandela, who had been in prison for twenty-seven years. President Bush ended the economic sanctions when in 1991 South Africa got rid of most of its apartheid laws. In 1992, white South Africans voted decisively to end apartheid, and negotiations were initiated to establish full democracy in the country.

*The Third World.* Secretary of State Baker acknowledged that Reagan's pro-Contra policy against the left-wing Sandinista government in Nicaragua had "basically failed." Changing course, Bush and the Congress devised an accord in 1989 that won the support of both the Sandinistas and the Contras. It provided for an end to the war, the release of political prisoners, enlarged freedom of the press, and national elections the next year—which produced the victory of an anti-Sandinista coalition. In El Salvador, where the United States had backed the right-wing government against leftist guerrillas, both sides concluded a peace agreement in 1992 that ended their twelve-year civil war and provided for a variety of reforms.

General Manuel Noriega, the dictator in Panama, had assisted the Reagan administration by helping to get arms to the Contras in Nicaragua, but he had imprisoned political opponents and grown personally wealthy by trafficking in drugs. In December 1989, with Noriega threatening American citizens in Panama, Bush launched Operation Just Cause, a military action that within twenty-four hours—and at the cost of 23 Americans dead and 394 wounded—freed the political opposition from prison and drove Noriega from power. Taken to the United States to stand trial, Noriega was convicted in April 1992 on multiple charges, including cocaine trafficking, money laundering, and racketeering, and sentenced to a U.S. prison.

*China.* The changes in the former Soviet Union emboldened advocates of liberalization in the People's Republic of China. During the spring of 1989, numerous young Chinese dissidents demonstrated for freedom. But while the Chinese government craved friendly relations and expanded trade, it was unwilling to tolerate the growing outspokenness of protesters. When several thousand of them occupied Tiananmen Square in Beijing, Deng Xiaoping, China's leader, labeled them "counterrevolutionaries," prompting the protesters to go on a hunger strike. On June 4, the army drove them out of the square, generating images on world television of unarmed youth defying tanks and machine guns. The crackdown killed 3,000 people, wounded 10,000 more, and thoroughly angered millions around the world.

Tiananmen Square in Beijing on May 4, 1989, where thousands of students demanding greater freedom were cleared out by troops and tanks.

Bush, eager to avoid a break with China, responded with sanctions such as delaying World Bank loans to Beijing; but, resisting pressure from Congress to impose harsher measures, he refrained from strongly condemning its actions. Instead, he sought to find common ground for further cooperation, urging, for example, that China release the dissidents arrested after the episode at Tiananmen Square. By the fall, the Beijing government had released some. In late May 1990, Bush renewed China's most-favored-nation trade status, and in the succeeding months he continued to press for improvement in Sino-American relations.

## THE GULF WAR

In the Middle East, the end of the Cold War provided militarily capable rogue states with greater latitude for aggression. The Soviet Union had at times exercised a stabilizing influence in the region, but it was now so weakened that the burden of maintaining order there fell more heavily on the United States.

In August 1990, Iraq invaded oil-rich Kuwait, its 140,000 troops rapidly overwhelming Kuwait's 16,000-man army. The action caught the United States as well as Egypt and Jordan by surprise, even though Iraqi troops had been observed moving toward the Kuwaiti border. Iraq, controlled by the dictator Saddam Hussein, was already a major oil power; the takeover of Kuwait added significantly to its leverage in the world oil market. The United States had supported Iraq in its war with Iran during the 1980s, but along with other governments it had worried about Iraq's growing programs for the production of chemical and nuclear weapons. The Bush administration considered the invasion an unacceptable violation of international law, a threat to regional stability, and a danger to American energy security.

In an address to the nation on August 8, the president declared "a line drawn in the sand" and insisted on the immediate withdrawal of all Iraqi forces from Kuwait. By then, eager to avoid Lyndon Johnson's errors during the Vietnam War, Bush, with the help of Secretary of Defense Dick Cheney, was building support for his policy both abroad and at home. He mobilized a thirty-nation coalition against Iraq, including the leading Arab states but not Israel, which he excluded so as not to antagonize the Arab allies. He also obtained a virtually unanimous resolution from the U.N. Security Council, including Russia, calling for a complete shutdown of trade with Iraq and authorizing nonmilitary measures to enforce the sanctions. Stepping up the pressure, the Bush administration sent 100,000 American troops to Saudi Arabia to protect that country and its oil against possible invasion and won pledges from Middle Eastern, European, and Asian nations for financial support of whatever actions might be necessary to force Saddam Hussein's troops out of Kuwait.

In early November, with Saddam's troops still in Kuwait, Bush announced an increase in the American forces in Saudi Arabia to 500,000, and at the end of the month the United Nations set a deadline of January 15, 1991, for Iraq to withdraw. Congress, with many Democrats in both houses dissenting, approved military action against Iraq. On January 16, one day after the U.N. deadline, the United States began attacking Iraq relentlessly from the air.

Americans had round-the-clock access to the war via the satellite television broadcasts of the Cable News Network (CNN), some of whose reporters spoke live and regularly from Baghdad even as it was under bombardment from American forces. But the Pentagon, mindful of how the relatively freewheeling press in Vietnam had affected public opinion of that conflict, heavily managed coverage of this one, refusing to allow filming of the gore of combat while exaggerating the effectiveness of the U.S. military's high-technology weapons. The practice would be repeated in future military engagements—notably, the Iraq War that began in 2003.

On February 23, a force of 200,000 troops, most of them American and the rest drawn from a coalition of countries joined with the United States against Saddam, moved against the Iraqi forces in Kuwait. In command was General Norman Schwarzkopf, a theatrical, self-confident, and much-decorated veteran of Vietnam. Just over four days after the invasion, Saddam agreed to a cease-fire that left him in power in Iraq. American casualties came to 148 dead and 458 wounded, compared with some tens of thousands of Iraqi dead. Bush, who won widespread approval for his handling of the conflict, proclaimed, "We went halfway around the world to do what is moral and just and right. . . . We're coming home now proud, confident, heads held high." Alluding to the recriminations and a self-doubt that had pervaded the country after its defeat in Southeast Asia, he added, "By God, we've kicked the Vietnam syndrome once and for all."

Still, although the armistice conditions subjected Iraq to trade embargoes and on-site inspections to prevent Saddam from rearming, the Bush administration was criticized for preventing General Schwarzkopf from advancing to Baghdad and ridding Iraq of its dictator. Bush responded that Kuwait had been freed and that he wanted to avoid further American losses. His advisers, concerned with the balance of power in

General Norman Schwarzkopf (right) chats with marines in Saudi Arabia before the start of the ground war against Iraq, February 1991.

the region, were also worried that deposing Saddam might so weaken Iraq as to enlarge the influence of Iran or Syria in the Middle East, an eventuality that would be adverse to American interests. However, Saddam's continuation in power forced the United States to be constantly on guard against him. Near the end of his presidency, Bush sent air strikes against Iraq when Saddam moved missiles into areas where the armistice prohibited them.

*Some Reasons for Hope.* Despite the persistence of the Iraqi threat, the United States' handling of the war had gained it good will among the principal Arab states. Bush, exploiting the advantage, revived efforts at achieving peace in the Middle East, an initiative that was supported by Syria, which was unable any longer to rely on the Soviets. In November 1991, talks began among Israel, the Palestinians, and several Arab countries. Progress was slowed by Palestinian violence against Jews and by the Israeli government's continued installation of Jewish settlements on the West Bank of the Jordan River. But the peace process nevertheless struggled forward, raising cautious hopes that eventually a settlement might be achieved.

## A Domestic Guardian

At home, Bush was frequently criticized for lacking "vision." Far less adept and engaged in domestic than in foreign affairs, he had no overarching legislative agenda. He conducted what

some historians have termed a "guardianship presidency." Bush aimed to consolidate the changes of the Reagan years, moderating some of their harsh impacts but on the whole hewing to policies of low taxes and limited government. But adverse economic trends compelled the president to find ways beyond guardianship and voluntarism. He had to deal with the ongoing failures in the savings and loan industry and the mounting annual federal deficit—$155 billion in 1988, $221 billion in 1990—both legacies of Reaganism. And he was forced to confront a severely slumping economy, a consequence largely of the end of the Cold War, along with the social strains accompanying the downturn.

### THE TROUBLED ECONOMY

When Bush took office, the failures of savings and loan institutions (S&Ls) were reaching crisis proportions. By 1989, as many as 350 S&Ls had gone bankrupt, the majority of them in New England and the Southwest; hundreds more bank failures were predicted. Deposits in these institutions were insured by the federal government, and bailout costs were estimated at up to $200 billion. In August 1989, responding to the crisis, Bush won passage of a measure that overhauled the federal regulatory structure for the S&Ls with the aim of making it more effective.

Polls showed that the federal deficit concerned Americans more than any other issue. Moreover, if the White House and Congress did not produce budgets that met the deficit-reduction targets in a 1987 law, federal spending would be automatically reduced, forcing a shutdown of certain government services. Faced with that possibility, Bush reneged on his campaign promise of no new taxes and angered many of his supporters by agreeing to the passage in 1990 of a combination of spending slashes and higher taxes intended to reduce the deficit over five years. Nevertheless, the annual deficit kept climbing, reaching $290 billion in 1992 and pushing the accumulated federal debt to more than $4 trillion.

*Recession.* With the end of the Cold War, defense spending fell between 1989 and 1992 by 12.6 percent in constant dollars. Industrial corporations, focusing more on their ability to compete in the international marketplace, intensified the restructuring that had begun in the 1970s. Taking advantage of the opportunities afforded by globalization, many companies laid off workers and shifted operations to countries where wages were lower than in the United States. A recession began in 1990. Followed by a weak recovery the next year, it set off a decline in consumer confidence, reductions in retail sales and housing starts, an increase in poverty, and a growth in unemployment to almost 7.8 percent in 1992.

Bush, seeing signs that the downturn might well affect his reelection chances, declared economic recovery his "No. 1 priority." In January 1992, he proposed to combat the recession with reduced taxes on gains from investments (capital gains) as well as tax incentives for business investment and for first-time home buyers. But although he had reached a compromise with Congress in 1991 that raised the minimum wage to $4.25, the president refrained from advancing any measures that would directly increase the spending power of lower-income groups. Democrats derided his proposals as too little and nothing more than political.

Bush held that the long-term strategy for the post–Cold War economy was economic growth, achieved in part by an expansion of international trade. Reagan had concluded a free-trade agreement with Canada in 1987, and Bush proposed to enlarge the free-trade zone to include Mexico. In 1991, he obtained authority from Congress to negotiate the North American Free Trade Agreement (NAFTA) on a fast track, despite opposition from some Democrats who feared that under NAFTA jobs would be lost to Mexico. He concluded the treaty in December 1992, but it awaited ratification at the end of his term. Earlier that year, he had led a trade mission to Japan, but he was unable to open the Japanese market more widely to American goods.

## CIVIL RIGHTS

Bush put the face of social diversity on his administration, choosing General Colin Powell as head of the Joint Chiefs of Staff, the first African American to hold that post, and for the first time appointing a Hispanic American to the cabinet. He also tapped a record-setting number of women for high federal posts, including secretary of labor, surgeon general, and, later in his administration, secretary of commerce.

Unlike Reagan, Bush was a friend of civil rights laws that protected minority groups against discrimination. In July 1990, he signed the Americans with Disabilities Act—a congressional study had shown that the vast majority of the 43 million Americans with disabilities suffered from segregation and discrimination—which prohibited employers from discriminating against people with disabilities who were otherwise qualified, required employers to provide physical access for disabled people, and expanded transportation services for them.

Workers at the White Furniture Company in Mebane, North Carolina, dejected and angry on being told that the factory will be closed in May 1993.

In April 1992, a riot erupted in the poor black area of South Central Los Angeles when a jury acquitted four policemen of assaulting an unarmed black man named Rodney King, even though a videotape that was repeatedly shown on national television plainly showed the officers beating him. In three days of looting and burning, more than 50 people died (the most in any race riot in the nation's history), some 4,000 were injured, and damage ran to more than one billion dollars. Bush flew to Los Angeles to see the destruction, and his Justice Department charged the officers with violations of federal civil rights laws. Two were ultimately convicted.

Like Reagan, Bush opposed affirmative action, and so, despite their social diversity, did key members of his administration. Moderate conservatives like himself, they represented a small but growing number of women and people of color in the United States who drew the line against racial and sexual preferences. In December 1989, the Department of Education, headed by a Hispanic American, ruled that scholarships set aside for minorities were illegal. The action provoked widespread outcries that prompted the resignation of the education secretary, but the administration continued to resist college aid linked to race.

### THE SUPREME COURT

After appointing Sandra Day O'Connor to the Supreme Court, Reagan had shifted it further to the right by filling vacancies with Antonin Scalia and Anthony Kennedy, both conservatives, and promoting William Rehnquist, another conservative, to chief justice. In 1990, Bush nominated David H. Souter, a respected centrist jurist from New Hampshire, to a vacancy on the Court, and he was confirmed without controversy. Then, in 1991, when Thurgood Marshall, the longtime champion of civil rights, retired from the high bench, Bush nominated Clarence Thomas, a conservative African American, to succeed him. Recently appointed to the U.S. Court of Appeals, Thomas was a graduate of Yale Law School, but he had only a brief and undistinguished record as a jurist; and though he had headed the Equal Employment Opportunity Commission (EEOC) in the Reagan years, he staunchly opposed affirmative action. Liberals charged that Bush was exploiting Thomas's race to place a conservative of mediocre talents on the Court.

Thomas nevertheless seemed headed for confirmation when in October 1991 Anita Hill, a black lawyer who had worked for Thomas at the EEOC, raised serious charges against him, first to the FBI and then in a dramatic hearing before the Senate Judiciary Committee. Hill claimed that Thomas had sexually harassed her, repeatedly asking her out and discussing pornographic films. Thomas flatly denied Hill's charges, calling the Senate hearing a "high-tech lynching." Members of the Senate committee, all of them male, tended to treat Hill's claims skeptically, while car bumper stickers declared, "We Believe You Anita." In the end, the Senate confirmed Thomas by the slim margin of 52 to 48.

The Hill-Thomas controversy raised the profile of sexual harassment as an issue in the United States, but Thomas's appointment added an unswervingly conservative vote to the Supreme Court, which had already been moving to the right. Since 1989, it had upheld laws limiting remedies available to women and minorities against employment discrimination and prohibiting the dissemination of information about abortion in federally funded clinics. In 1989, in *Webster v. Reproductive Health Services*, the Court upheld *Roe v. Wade* but also seemed to open the door to broad state regulation of abortion by permitting states to require medical tests to determine whether the fetus was yet viable or not. In 1992, by a majority of five to four in *Planned Parenthood of Southeastern Pennsylvania v. Casey*, the Court ruled explicitly that the state could impose certain restrictions on the exercise of reproductive choice, but it declared that *Roe v. Wade* had "established a rule of law and a component of liberty that the Court would not renounce."

Through the rest of the 1990s, the Court was neither consistently nor predictably conservative on any given case. It continued to resist school-sponsored prayer and restrictions on speech. But in several cases, it also bolstered the power of the states against federal authority, ruling, for example, that state employees could not sue in state courts for violations of federal labor laws. In all, as in the 1980s, the Court reflected the social and ideological divisions in the country at large.

### THE ELECTION OF 1992

Well into the second half of his term, the triumph of the Gulf War made Bush seem so strong a bet for reelection that few leading Democrats were willing to enter the presidential race. But William Jefferson (Bill) Clinton, the forty-six-year-old governor of Arkansas, resolved to defy the odds. After prevailing in an arduous round of primaries, Clinton won the party's nomination and chose as his running mate Albert Gore Jr., a liberal senator from Tennessee who had a serious interest in environmental protection. By then, George Bush's reelection appeared decidedly more problematic, largely because of the toll taken by the slumping economy.

The newly nominated Democratic candidates Bill Clinton (right) and Al Gore stop at a town meeting during their cross-country bus tour, July 1992.

Clinton brought to the campaign dashes of both the cool and the confessional, appearing on one TV show wearing dark glasses and playing the saxophone, revealing on another the type of underwear he wore ("Boxers or briefs?" the interviewer had asked). Rumors had long abounded that he indulged in sexual dalliances, but Clinton was capable of reinventing himself in the face of adversity. When the press reported an extramarital affair with a former nightclub singer, he appeared with his wife, Hillary Rodham Clinton, on the widely watched TV program *Sixty Minutes* and admitted that their marriage had encountered problems but insisted that it had emerged the stronger because of them. The Clinton campaign instructed its workers to remember "It's the economy, stupid," the main issue on the minds of the American people. Clinton promised to bring about economic recovery, welfare reform, national health coverage, and the development of new technologies.

Although statistics showed that the recession was ending—the economy had grown at a modest rate during the first two quarters of 1992—many Americans felt bruised by the downturn, the ongoing rise in health costs, and the impact of restructuring and reductions in corporate size. Bush was also undermined by attacks from the Republican right led by Patrick Buchanan, an economic isolationist and social conservative. Given the podium at the Republican convention, Buchanan and the evangelist Pat Robertson shocked moderates in and out of the party by savaging feminists, homosexuals, and advocates of reproductive choice. Bush, renominated with Dan Quayle, kept the party together, but his embrace of the right disturbed many voters. His campaign disparaged Clinton's devious (and successful) efforts to avoid the draft during the Vietnam War as well as his disingenuous admission that he had smoked marijuana but "had never inhaled." Late in the campaign, as polls showed Clinton pulling ahead, Bush derided Clinton and Gore as "crazies" and "bozos."

A challenge to both Bush and Clinton came from H. Ross Perot, a Texan who financed his own third-party campaign using some of the fortune he had made in the data-processing business. Outspoken and iconoclastic, Perot pilloried both Democrats and Republicans for absorbing themselves too much in party politics and too little in dealing with the recession and the deficit. For a time, he enjoyed strong support in the polls, an indication that many Americans were dissatisfied with the political status quo. But Perot was hypersensitive, willful, and volatile. He dropped out of the race in July, then at the beginning of October jumped back in, advancing his candidacy with millions of dollars' worth of television spots and in the presidential debates.

Clinton's political skills—commentators dubbed him "The Comeback Kid"—and the hangover of the recession combined to win him 43 percent of the vote to Bush's 38 percent. Perot gained 19 percent, the largest percentage ever won by a third-party candidate, taking probably far more of his share from Bush than from Clinton and helping to stimulate interest in the election. Voter turnout totaled 55 percent, up from 50 percent in 1988. Clinton won thirty-two states, carrying the Northeast and the Pacific Northwest, running strongly in the Midwest and the South, and accumulating 370 electoral votes compared with Bush's 168. Clinton attracted middle-income, blue-collar Democrats who had defected to Reagan. He also ran strongly among blacks, Hispanics, labor, and women, many of whom simmered with resentment against the treatment of Anita Hill and who helped elect six women (five of them fresh faces) to the Senate and forty-seven to the House. Colorado sent a Native American to the Senate. The number of African Americans in Congress almost doubled, reaching twenty-five; and the number of Hispanic Americans more than doubled, to seventeen. Democrats retained control in both houses.

Bush had managed the end of the Cold War shrewdly and energetically, encouraging democratic capitalism in former Communist countries and establishing a precedent for limited, multilateral military intervention against local aggression. But he dealt only fitfully with domestic concerns, courageously seeking to enlarge the North American free-trade zone yet responding to the nation's economic troubles with a peculiar lack of either empathy or effectiveness. Now, with the Cold War over, the focus of national attention turned inward and to the remarkable social, economic, and technological changes that, since the 1970s, had been reshaping American society.

## Suggested Reading

George Bush and Brent Scowcroft, *A World Transformed* (1998)

Frances Fitzgerald, *Way Out There in the Blue: Reagan, Star Wars and the End of the Cold War* (2000)

Haynes Johnson, *Sleepwalking through History: America in the Reagan Years* (1991)

Herbert Parment, *George Bush: The Life of a Lone Star Yankee* (1997)

Kevin Phillips, *The Politics of Rich and Poor: Wealth and the American Electorate in the Reagan Aftermath* (1990)

Michael Schaller, *Reckoning with Reagan: America and Its President in the 1980s* (1991)

# Chapter Review

## Summary
### QUESTIONS

- What policies did the United States pursue in Nicaragua and El Salvador, and how did those policies change?
- How and why did the Cold War end?
- What were the strengths and weaknesses of the American economy during the administrations of Reagan and Bush?
- Why did Bush initiate the Gulf War?
- What were the major developments in rights and opportunities for women and minority groups in the Reagan and Bush years?

## Chronology

| | |
|---|---|
| 1981 | Sadat assassinated. |
| 1981 | Sandra Day O'Connor appointed to the Supreme Court. |
| August 1981 | President Reagan fires two-thirds of air-traffic controllers' union. |
| March 1983 | Plans for Strategic Defense Initiative (Star Wars) announced. |
| October 1983 | 241 U.S. marines killed by suicide bomber in Beirut. |
| January 28, 1986 | Space shuttle *Challenger* explodes. |
| 1986 | Mikhail Gobrachev proclaims *glasnost* in Soviet Union. |
| Summer 1987 | Iran-Contra Senate hearings. |
| December 1987 | Reagan and Gorbachev sign INF Treaty. |
| December 1988 | Pan Am jet explodes over Lockerbie, Scotland, killing 259. |
| January–February 1991 | The Gulf War. |
| December 1991 | Soviet Union falls, replaced by the Commonwealth of Independent States. |
| 1992 | Apartheid ends in South Africa. |

## Key Terms

Reagonomics (p. 923)

Strategic Defense Initiative ("Star Wars") (p. 926)

Iran-Contra Scandal (p. 929)

Tiananman Square (p. 938)

The Gulf War (p. 939)

# Chapter 33

# INNOVATIONS AND DIVISIONS IN A GLOBALIZING SOCIETY:

## 1970-2000

In January 1983, *Time* celebrated the arrival of the personal computer in American life, an innovation that would create millions of jobs, transform the practices of business, and change the way people communicated, shopped, and learned about the world.

■ *How did national defense and private enterprise foster the emergence of the personal computer industry?*

■ *What were the major developments in biomedicine and health during the last quarter of the twentieth century?*

■ *What were the major environmental issues during the period?*

■ *How did women and minorities fare in American society during this period?*

Seen from the perspective of the Reagan and Bush presidencies, the shift to the political right in the 1970s initiated a sea change in American politics and government, the harbinger of a sustained departure from the commitment to federal activism that had characterized the period from the New Deal through the Great Society. More than that, during the last quarter of the century American society underwent broad transformations in its economic, social, and cultural character.

Even as conventional manufacturing declined, public and private initiatives in science and technology established innovative new industries. The United States found itself increasingly intertwined with a globalizing community, subject to intensifying foreign competition, widening opportunities in trade, and environmental trends that girdled the planet. American women came to know unprecedented opportunity and status in education and the workplace. An increasing number of minority-group members made their way in American society, attending college, obtaining better jobs, moving to better neighborhoods. Immigration once again began changing the face of the nation, adding to its talents, diversity, and multiple cultures. Yet these transformations intensified the social and economic resentments that had helped propel the shift to the right in the 1970s. And now, in the closing decades of the century, they kept the country uncomfortably divided.

## Innovation and the Economy

During the late 1970s, a general concern arose that the relative power of American innovation was falling. The downturn in public and corporate spending for research and development (R&D) that had begun in the late 1960s seemed to be adversely affecting not only the nation's military strength but also its economic vitality. The United States faced increasingly vigorous foreign competition, especially from Japan. The number of patents issued by the United States in 1978 was about the same—some 66,000—as it had been in 1966; the proportion issued to foreigners had almost doubled, from 20 percent to almost 40 percent. Throughout the decade, the United States' annual trade deficit in conventional manufactured goods doubled.

The loss was offset by a trade surplus in high-technology goods, which almost quadrupled. Partly in response to the global trend, both business and government renewed investment in R&D. They also devised new means of enlisting universities in the project of technological innovation—notably, the federal promotion of university research centers with industrial participation, some 1,100 of which had been created by the mid-1990s. With the aim of better penetrating markets in Europe and Asia, American firms also established or expanded existing laboratories in those regions of the world. Among the leading high-tech products of the 1970s were mainframe computers, semiconductors, chemicals, and pharmaceuticals. The new efforts at innovation focused on the leading prospects for the future—notably, biotechnology and personal computers.

### COMPUTERS FOR THE PEOPLE

Personal computers (PCs) sprang from several sources, primarily the military's patronage of microelectronics and the interests of hobbyists in democratizing the use of computers. An essential component of the PC was the integrated circuit, which formed all its electrical parts out of a flat piece of silicon, photoetching the connections between them. It was devised independently at Texas Instruments and at Fairchild Semiconductor Laboratories, in Palo Alto, California. Fairchild was an incubator for many of the engineers who would later develop the computing industry in what came to be known as Silicon Valley, the region heavy with computer firms on the peninsula south of San Francisco. Although integrated circuits were not developed with military patronage, the Defense Department and NASA provided a sizable portion of the early market for them. By the late 1960s, engineers in Silicon Valley were creating an integrated circuit on a small chip containing the calculating circuits equivalent to all those in a mainframe computer of the 1950s. In 1973, the Intel Corporation, founded by several veterans of Fairchild, announced that it had produced such a chip: the 8080.

Silicon Valley was home not only to many of the electronics graduates of nearby Stanford University and the University of California at Berkeley and the engineering experts of local firms such as Hewlett-Packard, but also to the community of hobbyists drawn to the use of time-sharing computers. Standard computing at the time required users to go to a central computer, put in their programs, and wait for them to be processed. Time-sharing connected users by wire from their offices to a central computer that automatically allocated processing time to different individuals; it gave users local access to their personal files and enabled them to use the central computer at any time for any purpose. Some computer hobbyists called for bringing computing power to the people by, for example, providing the public with free access to time-shared terminals. One enthusiast recalled the "strong feeling that we were subversives. We were subverting the way the giant corporations had run things."

In 1974, a small firm that three hobbyists had founded in Albuquerque, New Mexico, to sell radio transmitters for model airplanes went beyond the dream of universal terminal access to put computers themselves into everyone's hands. They started marketing a personal computer kit called the Altair. Selling for $397, the Altair ran on the Intel 8080 chip and was an instant hit with hobbyists, even though it had no keyboard or monitor. It spurred Bill Gates, a twenty-year-old Harvard student, and his high school friend Paul Allen, age twenty-two, to write a software program for it that they licensed to the Albuquerque firm. Gates dropped out of Harvard to develop the Microsoft Corporation, a software firm he and Allen founded in 1975 for the Altair venture. In 1976,

The Microsoft Albuquerque Group, December 1978. Top row: Steve Wood, Bob Wallace, Jim Lane. Middle row: Bob O'Rear, Bob Greenberg, Marc McDonald, Gordon Letwin. Front row: Bill Gates, Andrea Lewis, Marla Wood, Paul Allen.

Steve Wozniak, age twenty-five, and Steve Jobs, age twenty, began marketing a comparable personal computer, the Apple. Both were T-shirts-and-jeans devotees of the hobbyist electronics culture in Silicon Valley, where they had grown up; Jobs, with long hair and sandals, was an acolyte of vegetarianism, the Beatles, and transcendental meditation. They built the first Apples in the home garage of Jobs's parents.

Eager to expand the business, Jobs and Wozniak relinquished their T-shirts for suits, obtained venture capital (see Chapter 29), and in 1977 brought out the Apple II, which included a keyboard, a monitor, and a floppy-disk drive for storage. A later version, introduced in 1983, operated with a mouse and pull-down menus, both of which had been originally developed under contracts from the Defense Department and NASA. By this time, several other companies were selling personal computers. The software for them was initially confined to educational programs and games such as the wildly popular "Pacman," but in 1979 VisiCalc, a spreadsheet program, came on the market and demonstrated the value of the PC for business.

Bill Gates had already warned the hobbyists that he would consider free sharing of the software that Microsoft had produced for the Altair a form of piracy. By the late 1970s, personal computing was rapidly turning away from its countercultural origins into a lucrative for-profit enterprise. In 1981, IBM entered the PC market, enlisting Microsoft to provide the operating software for its machines. In response, Microsoft bought a software package that had been devised at Seattle Computer Products by Tim Paterson, a recent college graduate, and provided it to IBM as MS-DOS (short for "Microsoft Disk Operating System"). Gates sold IBM a license to use the system but maintained Microsoft's ownership, an arrangement that permitted the company eventually to earn billions of dollars by selling the right to use the system to other makers of personal computers. MS-DOS soon became an industry standard. The PC caught on so fast that two years later *Time* magazine designated the personal computer its "Man of the Year."

*Communications and the Internet.* Electronics continued to revolutionize communications, as they had done since World War II. By the mid-1990s, two-thirds of the country was wired for cable television. By 1995, 33 million Americans sub-scribed to cell phone services, which had arrived on the consumer scene in 1988, and thousands more were signing up every month. Satellites provided individual radio and TV stations with an increasingly diverse menu of programs, and the Telecommunications Act of 1996, the first major overhaul of policy in this area since the New Deal, sought to promote competition in the telecommunications sector by opening it up to multiple types of carriers, including cable and Internet companies. But the innovation with the most dramatic impact was the democratization and commercialization of the Internet into an electronics network that linked individual computers across the globe.

Like so many innovations that changed the way people lived, the Internet originated in the national defense program's patronage of science and technology. It was principally conceived in the late 1960s by a computer scientist at MIT named J. C. R. Licklider as a network that would preserve

## What Do You Do for Fun?

*American Journal*

*In 1975, video games burst into the Christmas market as a sell-out item, fetching prices of $100 and up. Products of the high-technology electronics industry, they worked by converting television sets into controllable fields of play. The consumer marketing director of the National Semiconductor Corporation noted happily, "The toy and game market is limited only by our imagination." Designers in the new personal computer industry were already dreaming up circuits to generate TV images that players could manipulate with the turn of a knob. Since then, computer games have become a huge industry. But to many parents and policymakers, their contents, like those of films and television, have seemed to encourage antisocial behavior, and the games thus helped fuel opposition to the libertine quality of American culture. The 1998 edition of Dr. Spock's Baby and Child Care, the most popular book in its field for half a century, advised parents that computers served many constructive educational purposes but that they had "a darker side."*

"I'm speaking about the majority of computer games. Most of these are variations on the theme of kill (shoot, laser, karate, kick, maim, beat up) the bad guys. These games are unimaginative carryovers of violent Saturday morning cartoons. The best that can be said of them is that they may help promote eye-hand coordination in children. The worst that can be said is that they sanction, and even promote, aggression and violent responses to conflict. But what can be said with much greater certainty is this: most computer games are a colossal waste of time. . . .

"Your job with regard to video games is much the same as it is with television viewing: to help pick the right video games and to set limits on how much time is to be spent playing them. Which video games are acceptable? Generally these are ones intended to teach, that convey information in an interactive and fun fashion. Others, while not primarily educational in intent, rely on intellectual skills (like deciphering clues) to achieve the goal."

Benjamin Spock and Steven J. Parker, *Dr. Spock's Baby and Child Care*, 7th ed.

communications in the event of nuclear attack. In the 1970s, scientists and engineers at different institutions developed the essential hardware and software that would permit different types of computers and networks to communicate with each other through an intermediate service provider. With the sponsorship of the Defense Department, a nationwide network rapidly developed among industrial and university scientists. It was used mainly for e-mail, which was pioneered in 1971 and which an authoritative 1978 report dubbed a "smashing success" that would "sweep the country."

Between the mid-1980s and the early 1990s, partly at the initiative of then-Senator Al Gore, the Internet was transferred to civilian control and then opened up to commercial use. In the meantime, scientists in Europe developed a program to retrieve information from any computer connected to the Internet by latching on to its standard address (a URL, for "universal resource locator"). They also devised a language (html, for "hypertext markup language") for presenting text and images, and protocols (http, for "hypertext transfer protocol") for transferring them from one computer to another. Programmers at a government computing facility in Illinois, having devised a browser, left in 1994 to develop a new, commercial version that they named Netscape. Together, these innovations led to the birth of the World Wide Web.

In the mid-1990s, Americans were operating some 96 million computers, an increasing percentage of them at home. Sales of information technologies by U.S. firms exceeded $280 billion. Revenues to computer and data-processing companies came to almost $150 billion, to domestic telecommunications services, $320 billion. Together, all sectors of the information technology industry employed more than 3.4 million people.

*Accommodating to the Digital Age.* After the mid-1990s, the Web spread with the freely accessible Internet across the globe. Its diffusion was accompanied by an avalanche of private companies founded to exploit it commercially, most of them with URLs that ended in the designation ".com" and were known accordingly as "dot-com" companies. By early 1999, about 74 million people, including two out of five adults, were accessing the Internet. They were aided by a variety of search engines such as Google to accomplish myriad purposes, including the purchase or auction of goods on line; checking local weather, entertainment, or sports listings; and surfing through a dizzying cornucopia of news and information (not all of it reliable) ranging from cooking recipes to es-

oteric trivia. In the mid-1990s, several companies introduced digital cameras, and soon software was available that enabled the downloading of images to personal computers, their incorporation into digitized documents, and their transmission over the Internet for uses ranging from family chitchat to business presentations.

Personal computers and work stations aided and abetted trends in the reorganization of the corporate workplace. They helped workers keep records, generate documents, and do accounting and data analysis. To the end of fostering creativity and innovation, many companies had diminished long-standing boss-to-worker managerial pyramids, flattening them to integrate those who planned and those who produced on a more coequal basis. Computers and the Internet enabled the members of such groups within the corporation and even those at a distance from it to interact and share information freely and efficiently. They also facilitated corporate decentralization, a trend that began in the 1960s with companies establishing branches across the United States and expanded in the 1980s when companies globalized into multinational operations.

But at the turn of the twenty-first century, the powers of digital electronics—the kind on which computers and the Internet relied—were proving to be a mixed blessing. E-mail inboxes were flooded with junk messages, commercial and otherwise, and hackers could spread destructive computer viruses across the world in a matter of hours. In December

Business associates at a lunch meeting with their laptops, which became an indispensable tool for financial and marketing analysis.

2003, Congress passed a law criminalizing deceptive or fraudulent e-mail practices, but it had little noticeable effect. In mid-2004, unwelcome messages, derogated as "Spam," constituted two-thirds of all e-mail, a greater amount than when the law was passed. The very openness of electronic networks rendered individuals vulnerable to invasions of privacy and jeopardized the security of government and business operations. The digitized construction of sound and images fostered artistic creativity—including, for example, the comic sort that inserted the character Forrest Gump in the 1994 film of that name into film footage of real historical events—but it also allowed for deceptive presentations and blurred the distinction between reality and illusion.

The ready availability of digitized sound and images also profoundly challenged traditional assumptions about the integrity of copyrighted material, a matter of no small interest to the producers of music and films. The most serious challenge to the music business came from a nineteen-year old nappy-haired college dropout named Shawn Fanning who in 1999 created a unique music search engine that he dubbed with his own school nickname, "Napster." Napster permitted one computer user to search all other computers connected to the service for a particular song in a digitized format called "MP3"; it would list all copies found, whereupon the user could download one of them to his or her own computer at no cost. According to one research survey, by the spring of 2000 three-quarters of college students were using Napster.

Defenders of the system considered the practice innocent file sharing, but music industry executives counted it a flagrant violation of copyrighted songs and, as such, a sharp threat to the recording industry. An estimated 14,000 MP3 downloads were occurring every minute, 90 percent of them copyrighted. In spring 2000, the heavy-metal band Metallica sued Napster for copyright infringement, opening a series of legal battles that pitted the music labels against the file-sharing service. In 2001, the federal courts ruled that Napster had to ensure that no copyrighted musical material was downloaded through its system. Napster decided it could not meet that standard and so shut down as a file-sharing service.

But the manifest demand for digitized music led Apple Computers in November 2001 to introduce its iPod, a sleek, shiny, hand-held device that could store and play up to 10,000 songs. Two years later, Apple opened a vast library of music through its Web-based iTunes music store to users of most types of computers. iTunes sold MP3 music files for 99 cents a song or $9.99 an album, at once satisfying both copyright holders, who received royalties, and avid downloaders. By early 2004, iPods were Apple's biggest seller by volume of units, valued by consumers as a pocket entertainment center and by the recording industry as a means of protecting property rights in the digital age.

## GENETICS AND BIOTECHNOLOGY

Biotechnology grew out of the advances in genetics that had begun in 1953, when the young American biologist James D. Watson and his British co-worker Francis Crick identified the structure of DNA (deoxyribonucleic acid), the molecule present in the nucleus of every cell that carries the inheritable essence of an organism—its genes—from one generation to the next. Using revealing X-rays of the molecule done by Rosalind Franklin, the researchers showed that DNA comprises a double helix joined at regular intervals across the distance between them by one or another of two pairs of chemicals. During the next decade, scientists in the United States and Europe found that the sequence in which these chemical pairs occur along the helix forms a genetic code that determines the physical characteristics of an organism.

James D. Watson (right) and Francis Crick, shortly after they discovered the structure of DNA in 1953.

*Hopes and Fears.* The working out of the genetic code gave rise to prospects of what was called "genetic engineering"—the manipulation of an organism's DNA to diagnose, treat, or cure genetic disease or to improve the organism itself, including human beings. Such prospects excited many biologists, journalists, and laypeople, but they also prompted a good deal of apprehension. The antinuclear and environmental movements had heightened sensitivity to the pitfalls of technological progress. Now critics charged that attempts to engineer the hereditary essence of living organisms, especially human beings, might endanger the balance of nature and threaten human dignity and freedom.

Americans had recently been reminded from the agricultural quarter of the hazards of attempting to subordinate vital nature to human will. Beginning in 1968, a disease known as southern corn leaf blight swept from the southeastern United States westward to Texas and northward to Wisconsin, destroying 15 percent of the 1970 corn crop at a cost to farmers of about $1 billion. The blight was eliminated within a year by breeding genes from other varieties of corn into the dominant hybrid strains, but the event called national attention to the susceptibility to disease of genetically homogeneous crops. Just six varieties accounted for nearly 40 percent of the country's wheat; four varieties for 65 percent of its rice; three for 76 percent of its snap beans; and only two for 96 percent of its peas. In 1972, the National Academy of Sciences declared in a widely quoted report, "Most major crops are impressively uniform genetically and impressively vulnerable."

Apprehensions about the manipulation of genetic material widened and intensified in the mid-1970s, when genetic engineering suddenly appeared on the verge of becoming an achievable reality. The breakthrough arose from a technique, invented by two biologists in the Bay Area in northern California, that permitted scientists to snip out a gene from the DNA of one organism and insert it into the DNA of another. This method of recombinant DNA opened the door to the transformation of organisms—plants, animals, and possibly even human beings—by changing their hereditary essence. Great benefits were predicted for science, medicine, and agriculture. Some biologists nevertheless worried that recombinant microorganisms carrying, for example, disease genes might threaten life or health or whole ecosystems. Others questioned the reconfiguring of life itself as an act of hubris that would lead to unpredictable and calamitous consequences.

In an unprecedented action, biologists in 1974 voluntarily agreed on a temporary moratorium on most research with recombinant DNA. After a review of its potential hazards in 1975, they renewed recombinant research under government-imposed guidelines for federally sponsored work using the new techniques. Public unease with recombinant research continued, however. Molecular biologists defeated further state and federal legislative threats to their research and gradually achieved an easing of the restrictions on investigations using recombinant DNA. But the skeptics remained suspicious that genetic engineering jeopardized public health and safety as well as the environment.

*War on Cancer.* Even as scientists were beating back the curtailment of their research, molecular genetics was advancing the understanding of cancer. Since the 1950s, accumulating research had implied to some biologists that viruses might be a major cause of tumors in human beings. Pressed by health activists and congressmen, President Nixon endorsed a national commitment to the goal of wiping out cancer, declaring in 1971 that "the time has come in America when the same kind of concentrated effort that split the atom and took man to the moon should be turned toward conquering this dread disease." At the end of the year, Congress and the president inaugurated a War on Cancer, which by mid-decade more than tripled the funds available for cancer research.

By the late 1970s, investigations thus supported led to a historic advance in understanding of the disease: most human cancers are not caused by viruses. Rather, they arise when normal genes involved in critical cellular functions go wrong. Their transformation into cancer-causing genes can arise spontaneously from mutations; it can also be provoked by interactions between genes and what people ingest, inhale, or encounter in the environment. These results did not yield cures or therapies for cancer immediately, but they pointed the way to more effective prevention of the disease and to its eventual treatment.

*The Birth of Biotechnology.* Along with the enlarged understanding of life processes that arose from recombinant molecular genetics came a drive to commercialize it. Herbert Boyer, one of the co-inventors of the technique of recombinant DNA, led the way, joining in 1976 with a venture capitalist to form the biotechnology firm Genentech—short for "genetic engineering technology." The company set out to produce human insulin, a protein in which diabetics are deficient and which was unavailable in large quantities. (Diabetics then relied on injections of insulin obtained from pigs.) In 1978, Genentech announced that its scientists had succeeded in producing the human protein by isolating the gene for it and then inserting the gene into bacteria, turning them into human insulin factories. Along with other newspapers and magazines, *Newsweek* heralded the achievement, proclaiming that "recombinant DNA technology can undoubtedly be used to make scores of other vital proteins, such as growth and thyroid hormones, as well as antibodies against specific diseases."

Commercialization was given a triple boost in 1980: the government ended most restrictions on recombinant research; Congress passed the Bayh-Dole Act, which encouraged universities to patent and privatize the results of federally sponsored research in high-technology; and the Supreme Court held in *Diamond v. Chakrabarty* that a patent could be issued on genetically modified bacteria, which established the legal doctrine that virtually any living organism could be patented. In 1985, the Patent and Trademark Office expanded patentability to include any kind of plant, and in 1987 it declared that patents were allowable on animals although not on human beings. The next year, it issued the world's first patent on an animal—a laboratory mouse that had been genetically engineered to be supersusceptible to cancer. In 1986, further to promote the commercialization of the practical results arising in federal research laboratories, Congress authorized governmental agencies to license patents on these results to private industry.

All the while, public and private investment in biomedical research mushroomed. Inspired by examples such as Genentech, new biotechnology companies sprang up to exploit the accumulating genetic knowledge. Together with major pharmaceutical firms as well as a number of oil and chemical giants, they formed a burgeoning biotechnology industry in the United States. It produced an increasing number of new agricultural products, drugs, and methods of medical diagnosis. It also provided the service of DNA fingerprinting, a means of identifying individuals that was widely used in criminal trials, on the battlefield, and at scenes of disaster. By the end of the century, the American biotechnology industry was valued at $350 billion and employed 174,000 people.

***The Human Genome Project.*** Human molecular genetics appeared so promising that in the late 1980s a number of geneticists urged the federal government to create a project in which they could learn all the details of the DNA in the "human genome," a term referring to all the genes contained

in human cells. Federal policymakers responded favorably, seeing in the project rich benefits for understanding and treating disease and for adding to the strength of the United States in the post–Cold War international economy. Begun in 1989, the project was soon producing a torrent of genetic information. In the late 1990s, a private company named Celera initiated its own effort to obtain the complete structure (the sequence of base pairs) of human DNA. The federal project and Celera both reached the goal simultaneously in June 2000, announcing that they had achieved a full draft of the sequence at a White House press conference in the company of President Clinton.

Building on the fears prompted by the uses of genetic engineering in the 1970s, many Americans watched these developments apprehensively. They feared that a new eugenics (state interference in human reproduction for the sake of biological "improvement") might occur, with all the social bias that had characterized the old eugenics (see Chapters 19, 22, 23), and that medical insurers or employers might use genetic information to deny applicants policies or jobs. Others worried that genetic manipulation of the natural world might run out of control, a theme that was chillingly explored in Steven Spielberg's popular film *Jurassic Park* (1993) and in the best-selling novel by Michael Crichton on

"*Genome*, Henderson! We're working on human *genome*!"

This cartoon character Henderson may have misunderstood the human genome project, but its promise for medicine, biotechnology, and the nation's competitiveness was clear to policymakers, entrepreneurs, and scientists alike.

which it was based. However, most people set aside their fears in favor of the hopes for treating disease that the genome project raised.

## Medicine and Health

By many measures, at the close of the century Americans on the whole were healthier than they had ever been. In 2003, infant mortality was down to an all-time low of 6.9 deaths per 1,000 live births. Life expectancy for children born that year was 77.6 years, an all-time high. Millions of Americans exercised regularly, while many consumed low-fat and low-calorie foods—for example, substituting frozen yogurt for ice cream—to reduce the risk of heart disease and stroke. Many Americans also sought to protect their health by eating only "organic" foods, agricultural products grown without potentially toxic products such as manufactured, chemical fertilizers or pesticides.

An arsenal of biomedical knowledge and technologies was available to prevent people from falling ill, to cure them if they got sick, and to assist their reproductive efforts. In vitro fertilization (IVF) enabled many infertile couples to bear children. Pioneered in England in the 1970s, IVF involved joining human sperm with human eggs in a shallow glass dish, then implanting the resulting fertilized eggs in a woman's womb. In some quarters, such efforts were at first morally condemned on grounds that making human embryos in the laboratory amounted to performing experiments on "potential human subjects" who might suffer birth defects because of the procedure but who could not give their consent. But after the first test-tube baby was born in England in 1978—a happy, healthy girl named Louise Brown—an increasing number of IVF clinics opened in the United States, and during the next two decades thousands of infertile women in the United States flocked to them in the hope of bearing children.

Heart, lung, and kidney transplants lengthened and improved lives. Lasers rendered surgery, dentistry, and ophthalmology more effective. New and powerful technologies came into use that could generate three-dimensional images of the interior of the body. When the would-be assassin who shot President Reagan in 1981 also wounded his press secretary, James Brady, in the head, doctors located a blood clot produced by a fragment of an exploding bullet that had entered Brady's brain using the CT-scan, which had recently been de-

veloped largely by the British and which used X-rays and computers to reveal objects and abnormalities in flesh and bone. Doctors then removed both the clot and the fragment with precision surgery, thus saving his life.

Physicians were also making increasing use of magnetic resonance imaging (MRI), a new, powerful technology that Americans helped devise. It exploited computers and the magnetic fields of molecules in the body to provide a detailed picture of soft tissue troubled by injury or disease. Together, CT-scans, MRI, and other imaging technologies, by revealing the interior condition of the body, produced a revolution in diagnostic medicine, not least because they greatly diminished the need for exploratory surgery. Similarly, the imaging technology of ultrasound was used to inspect the functions of organs such as the heart and to monitor fetal development. Increasingly for young couples, the first picture entered in the baby album was an ultrasound of their child in the womb.

Pharmaceutical companies produced not only antibiotics against infectious disease but also drugs for functional disorders, including high blood pressure, emotional distress, menopausal symptoms, and male sexual dysfunction. The relaxation of regulatory restrictions in the 1980s permitted drug companies to advertise their wares directly to consumers, with the result that ads urging people to ask their doctors for prescriptions to particular pharmaceuticals became commonplaces in the nation's print and broadcast media. In 1998, drug company revenues totaled $102 billion, 85 percent higher than just five years earlier. At the end of the century, public and private expenditures on health amounted to more than $1.2 trillion, representing about 13 percent of the gross domestic product and making health one of the nation's largest industries.

Still, the exhilarating expectations for the biomedical future were tempered by worrisome health issues. The miracle technologies, for example, intervened between doctors and patients, rendering the delivery of medical care more impersonal. The expense of technologies such as MRI were helping to drive up the cost of medical care, as were the costs of hospitalization and drugs. Americans with medical insurance were better protected against the trend than those without it. In 2003, about one in six Americans lacked medical insurance, including one in five blacks and one in three Hispanics. Life expectancy for black males at birth was 69.2 years, for black females, 76.1—respectively 6.2 years and 4.4 years lower than for whites.

In 1985, a panel convened by the National Institutes of Health concluded that obesity—an excess of weight in relationship to height—had become a national "killing disease," as demanding of medical attention as, for example, high blood pressure as a cause of serious illness and premature death. By 2003, the problem, attributed in part to overindulgence in foods high in fat and sugar, afflicted one-third of adults and—particularly worrisome—a growing number of children, a significant percentage of whose diets consisted of fast foods.

The miracles of medical technology could do little against destructive eating habits or the propensity of people to put themselves at risk from the damages of the deadly AIDS (acquired immune deficiency syndrome), smoking or drugs, and the ready availability of handguns.

### AIDS

Americans on all sides of the political spectrum grew increasingly worried about the mounting incidence of AIDS, which was recognized in 1981 as the root cause of several diseases—notably, pneumonia and certain cancers—that were breaking out among specific groups, most commonly homosexual men. In 1984, scientists in the United States and France determined that AIDS is caused by an infectious virus (HIV) that attacks the immune system, making people vulnerable to one or more of these wasting assaults. The virus enters the body mainly by transfusion with infected blood, intravenous drug injection with infected needles, or sexual intercourse with an infected person.

Blood-screening tests greatly diminished the risk of infection to people who depended on blood transfusions—notably, hemophiliacs. Analysts called for public distribution of clean needles to drug addicts, but the initiative failed in most places, since it ran into fierce opposition from conservatives and others fearful that it would encourage more drug use. In San Francisco, with its heavy concentration of homosexuals, public health authorities closed down the city's bathhouses and sex clubs in 1984 on grounds that the promiscuous gay sex they encouraged fostered disease and death. Other cities as well as gay activists waged public-information campaigns urging "safe sex" through condom use.

Although AIDS was initially concentrated among homosexuals and Haitian immigrants, who were heavy drug users, in the mid-1980s *Time* reported that "anxiety over AIDS is verging on hysteria in some parts of the country." Churchgoers feared infection from taking communion with a common cup; children shunned infected schoolmates; a number of employers and health providers turned away AIDS victims. According to a Gallup poll, more than two out of five Americans thought AIDS a punishment for moral decline. Television networks refused to carry announcements advocating the use of condoms, and the Reagan White House balked on moral grounds at endorsing condom messages.

But a growing number of Americans realized that moral condemnation would do little to retard the mounting incidence of the disease. Between 1981 and 1990, more than 157,000 people in the country were reported to have AIDS, and more than 98,000 of them died of it. The casualties included the Hollywood star Rock Hudson, whose death raised public awareness of the issue and also appeared to arouse Reagan's empathy for AIDS victims. In 1986, the president

The AIDS quilt, begun in 1987 and displayed on the Mall in Washington, D.C., in 1992, commemorated the deaths from the disease of more than 20,000 people.

called AIDS research a top priority, and in a report prepared at his request, the surgeon general urged Americans to halt the spread of AIDS with sexual abstinence, monogamy, and condoms. In the last years of the Reagan administration, federal funds for AIDS research almost doubled, reaching $655 million in 1988, and a presidential commission called for an end to discrimination against AIDS victims. Tolerance of AIDS victims was encouraged by the film *Philadelphia* (1993), in which Tom Hanks portrayed a lawyer who contracted the disease, was fired by his firm, and sued in response. In 1998, the Supreme Court ruled that the Americans with Disabilities Act applied to people with AIDS even if they showed no symptoms.

By 1996, 320,000 Americans had died of AIDS and another 650,000 to 900,000 were infected with HIV. But the incidence of new infections had fallen sharply since the 1980s, partly as a result of safer sex practices among homosexual males; and between 1993 and 1997, the incidence of AIDS itself in the United States declined by almost half, to 22 per 100,000 people. It continued to decline thereafter even among people infected with HIV because of the development of a cocktail of drugs devised from molecular biological studies that suppressed the virus's multiplication in the body.

Still, new strains resistant to drugs evolved constantly. Moreover, by the end of the decade, confidence in the cocktail was leading young gay men to revive the practice of promiscuous, unprotected sex, and public health officials were worried that the incidence of HIV infection might rise once again. Between 2000 and 2003, the number of cases of such infection increased by 5 percent among men while decreasing by 2 percent among women. Still, the incidence of AIDS had risen to an estimated 167 cases per 100,000 people, and the frequency of the disease was disproportionately high among Hispanics and blacks. For example, the incidence among blacks compared with whites was eight times higher for men and twenty-five times higher for women.

## SMOKING

In the 1980s, state and local governments passed antismoking laws, government agencies restricted smoking in the workplace, and many businesses banned it. The surgeon general himself, an avowed public enemy of smoking, called it as addictive as heroin or opium. Early in the 1990s, the federal government banned smoking on interstate buses and airline flights of six hours or less; in 1994, Amtrak followed suit for train trips of short and medium duration. The portion of adults who smoked continued to decline—falling to 26 percent by 1993, down from 42 percent in the late 1960s and 50 percent in 1950—but the portion of high-schoolers who took up tobacco, about one in four, remained high.

The war against smoking scored significant victories in suits against the tobacco companies by numerous states, all of them seeking compensation for the millions of dollars they spent through Medicaid for smokers' illnesses. By November 1998, all fifty states had reached a $206 billion settlement with the industry for the costs of caring for sick smokers. In 1997, the Clinton Administration declared tobacco an addictive drug subject to regulation by the FDA. In March 2000, the Supreme Court, in a 5-to-4 decision, ruled that the FDA lacked jurisdiction over tobacco; but the year before, Clinton's Justice Department, following the precedent set by the states, sued the tobacco industry to recover billions of federal dollars spent on smoking-related health care, accusing cigarette makers of a "coordinated campaign of fraud and deceit."

## DRUGS

The war against drugs won fewer victories. In the 1980s, the use of drugs was glamorized in the fiction of the young, hard-edged writers Bret Easton Ellis, Tama Janowitz, and Jay McInerney—the "Brat Pack," critics called them. In novels such as *Bright Lights, Big City* (McInerney), *Less than Zero* (Ellis), and *Slaves of New York* (Janowitz), they chronicled their gilded contemporaries, devotees of cocaine, damaged or destroyed by too much affluence and too few responsibilities. Experts reported that drug use actually declined in the 1980s among middle-class whites but that the popularity of cocaine and the more potent crack cocaine grew among the urban poor and people of color.

The inner cities were fraught with fierce competition for control of the drug trade that erupted in gang-related violence. There drug dealing and drug use were a growing industry; children apprenticing in the trade earned as much as $100 a day. Law enforcement officials estimated that perhaps one-half of all robberies, muggings, and burglaries were committed by drug addicts in need of money to pay for their habit. Drug offenders constituted the fastest-growing population sent to jail. At the end of the decade, more than half of Americans considered drugs a grave threat to the nation's well-being and security. The combined state, federal, and local bill for the war on drugs was $15 billion a year, three-quarters of which went to law enforcement and imprisonment.

Graffiti on a New York City wall, an attempt to inform inner city youths that drugs are lethal.

President George H. W. Bush declared a "War on Drugs" at both the domestic and the international levels, an initiative that helped justify his ousting of the dictator Manuel Noriega in Panama (see Chapter 32). Bush appointed a drug czar—former secretary of education William Bennett, a loquacious idol of the conservative right. Bennett moved to replace Nancy Reagan's pleas to "just say no" with more effective measures, including federal funds to expand the capacity of the criminal justice system to handle drug offenders, alternative sentencing programs for nonviolent drug offenders, and a strengthening of the interdiction of drug trafficking at the borders.

## The Metropolitan and Natural Environments

At the end of the century, the country's population comprised some 270 million people, a third higher than in 1970. Some 216 million Americans, 80 percent of the total, lived in 276 sprawling metropolitan areas—counties, small cities, towns, and villages tied to a central city. Economic recovery and then prosperity in the 1990s (see Chapter 34) enabled local governments to clean up the streets, improve transportation, and better protect public safety. As a result of civic, corporate, and philanthropic investment, many of the central cities offered people rich opportunities for entertainment and culture, including sports complexes, symphony halls, theaters, cineplexes, convention centers, museums, and striking sym-

phony spaces. Particularly breathtaking was the new Disney Hall in Los Angeles, a landmark designed by the architect Frank Gehry with the aid of computers. Completed in 2004 and bearing his telltale signature, it boldly fashioned curved metal surfaces into discrete sculptural shapes that were joined at sharp, angular edges to form an energetic ensemble expressing the haphazard accretions of urban life, especially in southern California, where Gehry resided.

Easing a long-standing fear in metropolitan America, the crime rate steadily declined between 1991 and 1998, with especially sharp drops in murder and robbery. Analysts found the reasons partly in the job-rich prosperity, which diminished desperation, and partly in the get-tough policies of state and local law enforcement. In mid-1998, the United States led the world in the size of its prison system, holding 1.8 million men and women behind bars—1 in every 150 Americans, a rate double that of the mid-1980s. In New York City, Mayor Rudolph Giuliani, elected in 1993 after pledging to crack down on criminals, strongly backed the police; crime in the city fell 44 percent in five years, while the murder rate dropped 48 percent.

### DOWNSIDES

For all their lure and excitement, the metropolitan areas knew many of the problems that had beset urban-suburban networks since at least the 1920s. They were sprawling, occupying 20 percent of the nation's land, twice the amount as in the 1970s. Some people found them impersonal and were prompted to seek out friendships on Internet dating services and to find companionship in local coffee shops such as those of the successful Starbucks chain, which quadrupled in number between 1991 and 1995. Despite the physical improvements for entertainment and culture, most metropolitan areas were marked by congested streets, clogged roads and freeways, deafening din, air pollution, and inadequate public services.

And while the streets grew safer, the schools appeared to grow dangerous. A series of deadly school shootings that began in 1997 took the lives of a number of teenagers. The worst such episode occurred at Columbine High School in the Denver suburb of Littleton, Colorado, where on April 20, 1999, two heavily armed students stalked through the school at lunchtime, spraying gunfire on their classmates and eventually turning their guns on themselves. Thirteen students and faculty died, while twenty-three were wounded. The two murderers, like most of their classmates the product of white, middle-class families, were said to be angry about being teased.

The father of a child killed at Columbine High School at a protest for gun control outside the National Rifle Association convention in Denver, April 1999.

Stunned by the school violence, Americans wondered whether safety could be found anywhere. In fact, the number of students killed in violent incidents across the country had not increased, but the shootings stimulated debate about dysfunctional families, school social environments, gun control, and the impact on teenage behavior of violence on television and in popular music.

The Columbine shootings helped intensify demands for gun control, including a "Million Mom March" on Washington, D.C., in May 2000. Together with congressional Democrats, President Clinton pushed for background checks on people who bought guns at gun shows, the one remaining major gun-sale venue that was completely unregulated. But gun-show promoters blocked the necessary legislation, arguing that such checks would put them out of business.

The threat of random violence, the impersonality, the sprawl, the gobbling up of land for housing and shopping malls—all appeared to fortify the traditional American yearning for a simpler, if mythological, rural life. During the 1990s, country music enjoyed the greatest popularity of any musical genre on the radio, capturing a weekly audience of almost 40 percent of adults and reaching an estimated 42 percent of households through its cable channel, Country Music Television. It was made appealing partly by stars such as Garth Brooks and the Dixie Chicks, who added edge to their performances by joining traditional broken-voiced renditions with rock-beat instrumental backups. But it also likely drew listeners because its lyrics often celebrated the satisfactions of an imagined rural life, as in songs like Tracy Byrd's "I'm from the Country," where "everybody knows everybody, everybody calls you friend / You don't need an invitation, kick off your shoes come on in."

## SUSTAINING THE ENVIRONMENT

Amid the ongoing spread of metropolitan sprawl, many Americans continued to relish the experience of nature and to sustain the movement for environmental protection, which, following its renewal in the 1960s, remained energetic through the rest of the century. Its advocates attended to ongoing local and national issues, but by the late 1980s, scientific experts were confronting them as well as policymakers with a new class of environmental hazards that were global in reach and threatening enough to warrant a place on the public agenda.

*Local and National Struggles.* The efforts of James Watt, Reagan's first secretary of the interior, to turn over as much of nature as possible to private developers angered many Americans, driving up membership in the Sierra Club as much as 25 percent. Attention to environmental degradation was also heightened by various events and findings—for example, when in March 1989 the oil tanker *Exxon Valdez* ran aground in Prince William Sound, Alaska, staining the surrounding beauty and jeopardizing its wildlife with a spill of more than 10 million gallons of crude oil; and when that summer the Environmental Protection Agency reported that air pollution in more than 100 cities exceeded federal standards. Grassroots activism for wilderness preservation, clean air and water, control of toxics, and shutting down nuclear power remained vigorous. The leadership included a disproportionately large number of women, many of whom were drawn to such activism by a concern over health risks that appeared to threaten themselves and their families.

Between the grassroots activists and the established groups, the environmental movement remained powerful enough to counter a number of Watts's initiatives. Congress blocked his attempt to turn strip-mining controls back to the states, and it expanded the National Park System over his opposition. When President George H. W. Bush took office in 1989, virtually no major industry or community had yet met the standards in the existing Clean Air Act. In 1990, at the president's initiative, Congress passed amendments to the act that would impose on all cities tightened controls on emissions from automobiles,

Cleaning up the huge oil spill from the Exxon Valdez tanker in Prince William Sound, Alaska, March 1989.

utilities, and industrial plants and that would use market incentives to encourage compliance. The Bush administration also began the huge task of ridding the areas around nuclear weapons facilities and nuclear power plants of the radioactive wastes that had been deposited during the Cold War. But Bush often gave development-oriented industrial corporations the edge in determinations of environmental policy; for example, he called for opening wilderness preserves in Alaska to oil exploration.

President Clinton provided funds to deal with more than 1,000 hazardous waste sites, including those at nuclear weapons facilities. He established or expanded several national monuments, one of which added 1 million acres to the Grand Canyon National Park. He also issued executive orders to protect from development more than 72 million acres of wildlife habitats, wetlands, and roadless forests, a total that placed him third behind only Jimmy Carter and Theodore Roosevelt in land protection. In 1996–97, at Clinton's urging, Congress enacted a bill to bolster the regulation of pesticides, and the administration put new air-quality standards in place to reduce the levels of soot and ozone on the ground.

*Global Jeopardies.* The most immediately pressing worldwide environmental issue was depletion of the ozone layer in the upper atmosphere. Since the ozone layer blocks the passage of

cancer-causing ultraviolet light from the sun, the depletion threatened human and animal life. The thinning of the layer had been found in the early 1970s by two American chemists, who later won a Nobel Prize for their achievement. The depletion arose from the growing commercial and industrial uses of chlorofluorocarbons (CFCs) in, for example, spray cans and air conditioners. The finding, though disputed for years, was gradually confirmed by scientists conducting computer simulations of the atmosphere and, most dramatically, by a British team who in 1985 detected an enormous depletion of the ozone layer over a huge region of Antarctica.

In 1987, the United States took the lead in negotiating the Montreal Protocol on Substances That Deplete the Ozone Layer. Designed to impose international controls on the release of CFCs into the atmosphere, the protocol called for cutting them to 50 percent of their 1986 levels by the end of the century. The agreement was ratified by twenty-nine nations and the Commission of the European Community, which together accounted for 83 percent of global consumption of CFCs and a related class of chemicals called "halons." In 1990, in response to evidence that the ozone layer was being depleted over heavily populated areas of the world, the Montreal Protocol was toughened by expanding the types of ozone-depleting chemicals it covered and speeding up the rate at which their use was to be reduced and phased out. Special assistance was also granted to third world countries so that they would not be hampered in raising their living standards.

Bush was reluctant to respond vigorously to what appeared to be another environmental threat—global warming. Scientific theory held that global warming was occurring as a result of concentrations in the atmosphere of certain gases, especially carbon dioxide ($CO_2$), which is a product of the burning of fossil fuels (coal, oil, and natural gas). The gases trap radiation reflected from the earth, creating a greenhouse effect that raises temperatures in the region close to the planet's surface. Analysts predicted dire consequences, including a tripling of the annual number of 90-degree days in cities of the mid-Atlantic region; a drying out of the great wheat baskets of the

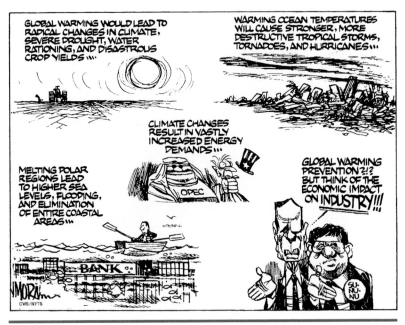

Despite the multiple threats of global warming, President Bush refused to take action because, as he explains here to a member of his cabinet, the cost of American industry would be too great.

world; and inundations of coastal areas arising from wholesale melting of polar ice. Yet save for nuclear power, a politically and economically unacceptable alternative since the late 1970s, there were no obvious substitutes for the fossil fuels that powered the engines of industrial civilization. The Bush administration stressed that the relationship of $CO_2$ emissions to global warming was too uncertain to warrant the economic dislocations that major restrictions on fossil-fuel burning would entail. Nevertheless, in 1992, at an Earth Summit of 200 nations in Rio de Janeiro, the American delegates did pledge to reduce the amount of greenhouse gases emitted. And at an international conference in Kyoto, Japan, in 1997, the Clinton administration, building on the Bush administration's pledge, pushed for a treaty that would reduce the emission of gases that contribute to global warming.

## Women and Minority Groups

In the 1970s and afterwards, the programs and protections deriving from the 1960s—the civil rights laws, affirmative action, and court decisions—helped improve the condition of a growing number of women and ethnic or racial minority group members. So did their new pride, their unleashed ambition, and a greater tolerance on the part of the white majority. In 1963, half of whites who were asked if they would object to a family member's bringing a black person home to dinner said yes; in 1982, fewer than a quarter did. About the same time, 80 percent of whites said they would support a well-qualified black candidate for president, a sharp reversal from the late 1950s, when two-thirds said they would not.

The prosperity of the 1980s and 1990s further propelled the growth of the middle class among African Americans, Hispanics, and Asians. But many were left behind, partly because of discrimination, partly because of the ongoing economic difficulties at the lower end of the skill and income scale. During the last quarter of the century, in greater or lesser degree, Americans of color grew increasingly divided among themselves between a burgeoning middle class and a deprived, impoverished lower one. The divide between people of color and the white majority also continued, exacerbated by the weakness of the low-end economy and by the ever-stiffening competitive pressures that American industry faced in a globalizing economy.

### WOMEN

Gendered stereotyping was in retreat. Title IX in the Educational Amendments Act of 1972 barred discrimination on the basis of gender in any educational program receiving federal assistance. The measure produced a dramatic impact in women's sports—for example, a threefold increase, to 25 percent, in the participation of girls in high school athletics. Universities launched women's studies programs, while television aired the popular *Mary Tyler Moore Show,* featuring a single career woman who was strongly interested in men but not desperate to get married. It was national news when, in February 1977, fifty secretaries in Chicago, Illinois, used their lunch hour to protest the firing of a legal secretary because she refused to make the office coffee, a task not included in her job description. The protest appeared to generate minor office revolutions across the country.

Early in the 1970s, after a state judge in Pennsylvania ruled that newspapers in Pittsburgh could no longer list jobs for

959

men and women separately, the practice vanished from the nationwide press. Toward the end of the decade, responding to court orders, New York City permitted women to apply for jobs as firefighters, the navy allowed them to serve on most of its regular vessels, and professional baseball—soon followed by basketball and football—opened its locker rooms to female journalists.

A growing number of women were also achieving positions of status and authority, both in reality and in popular culture. In 1976, Barbara Walters became the first woman to anchor a regular television newscast. Between 1975 and 1988, the number of women elected to Congress rose from nineteen to twenty-seven. And in 1996, in *United States v. Virginia*, the Supreme Court, deciding that the Virginia Military Institute could not refuse to admit women, implied that men-only admissions policies at state-supported colleges were unconstitutional. Meanwhile, entertainment media still provided traditional portraits of women, but mainstream culture took for granted women's sexual freedom and independence. In television and in film, female characters appeared as saucy, strong-minded, and sexually liberated, and in the workplace increasingly as coequals with men—tough, competent, sometimes cynical, faithless, or prone to violence, yet still feminine.

A number of women benefited from the drive for "comparable worth"—the claim by feminist labor advocates that women performing jobs comparable in difficulty and skills with those held by men should be paid the same for their work. By 1987, 40 states and 1,700 localities had enacted comparable-worth laws. Under these laws, women gained sizable wage increases—in some cases, up to 15 percent—over their previous rate of compensation. Further protecting women at work, in 1986 the Supreme Court ruled unanimously in *Meritor Savings Bank v. Vinson* that sexual harassment in the workplace, even if it does not result in job or promotion loss, violates Title VII of the Civil Rights Act.

By the mid-1990s, six in ten women were employed outside the home, including two-thirds of married women and more than half of women with children under age one. Among the ripple effects of so many women working during the day was a trend to stores remaining open in the evening. On average, women still earned less than men, but the gap had narrowed since the 1970s. By the end of the century, women owned more than a third of the nation's small businesses and accounted for about a quarter of all physicians, lawyers, and judges and a third of all professional athletes. In the mid-1990s, forty-eight women were serving in the House

Among the new opportunities open to women were careers in police work and, as for the woman here, in firefighting.

and eight in the Senate. Women represented about one in five state legislators and almost the same portion of mayors in all but the smallest cities.

*Feminism and the Family.* Yet women's issues remained a flash point in American society, in part because of the independence so many women were achieving. Many men resented women's advancement in the workforce, claiming that affirmative action was denying them jobs on the basis of their sex. Opposition on the part of many women as well as men to a woman's right to choose an abortion remained passionate. Social conservatives continued to consider feminism threatening to religion, traditional sexual standards, the dignity of homemakers, and the raising of children.

Beginning in the 1980s, many younger women distanced themselves from feminism. They had benefited from the women's movement but did not identify with it, even while endorsing the rights of sexual freedom and reproductive choice. The young pop stars Cyndi Lauper and Madonna posed a contrasting liberation to the buttoned-up young women working in business and law with songs such as "Girls Just Wanna Have Fun" and "Material Girl"; and they flaunted an unbuttoned sexuality in their self-presentation, wearing their underwear on the outside of their scanty clothes. A number of well-off young women left the workplace at least temporarily for home and children, many of them seeking to perfect their domestic lives with the help of Martha Stewart, who published guides to elegant entertaining and home decoration and built Martha Stewart Living, a powerful company worth a billion dollars.

Some feminists held that the women's movement was vulnerable to the social conservatives' family-oriented attacks against it. Betty Friedan, a bellwether among them, argued in her widely read *Second Stage* (1981) that feminists had to recognize that women wanted both careers *and* families and that "the real battle for equality" turned on the arrangements that would allow them to have both. Equal rights had to be undergirded by measures that would let women take advantage of them, including decent child care, child support, alimony, and maternity leave. Instead of taking men as the "enemy," Friedan contended, the women's movement had to challenge the structures and customs of corporate society with calls for flexible hours and family-friendly policies.

Various feminists, though, argued that Friedan's emphasis on family straitjacketed many women into unwanted roles and accepted the traditional view that women rightly shouldered the greater share of domestic and child-rearing responsibilities. The National Organization for Women (NOW) attacked a federal amendment to the Civil Rights Act in 1978 that compelled employers not to penalize women who took maternity leave; members feared that such leaves would discourage employers from hiring women at all. But in 1987, in *California Federal Savings and Loan v. Guerra*, the Supreme Court upheld the right of a state to mandate maternity leaves and, by implication, parental leaves for fathers. In the wake of the decision, feminists united behind the cause of the sex-neutral parental leave and placed the practicalities of family responsibilities high on the agenda of the women's movement.

## AFRICAN AMERICANS

By the late 1990s, four out of ten African Americans counted themselves members of the middle class and more than 1 million black families were affluent, double the portion twenty years before. One out of three blacks lived in suburbs, twice the representation as in the 1970s, and more than one out of three had attended college, more than triple the number in the 1970s. The statistical trend was reflected in the popular TV comedy *The Cosby Show,* which featured the adventures of a black middle-class family, the father a doctor and the mother a lawyer.

African Americans were gaining prominent roles in public life. More were in professional occupations such as law, jour-

**LEFT:** Television talk-show host Oprah Winfrey.
**RIGHT:** Golf champion Tiger Woods.

nalism, and engineering; more had been elected big-city mayors; and the House of Representatives included more than forty blacks, an eightfold increase over 1965. During roughly the same period, the number of black elected officials in the South shot up tenfold, with the trend producing a black mayor of Atlanta, one of the South's principal cities. Several blacks—notably, the talk-show host Oprah Winfrey, the comedian Whoopi Goldberg, and the actor Denzel Washington—commanded enormous power in the entertainment world. The young African American singer Michael Jackson won megastar status, admired not only for his dazzling performances but also for his wealth. Many blacks were a salient presence in professional sports, accounting for 80 percent of the players in the National Basketball Association, 66 percent of those in the National Football League, and 17 percent of those in major-league baseball. Several black sportsmen—the golfer Tiger Woods (who is also part Asian American), the basketball players Michael Jordan and Grant Hill—earned fortunes from lucrative advertising endorsements of special products, especially sports equipment.

*Discrimination and Poverty.* Still, racism and discrimination remained bitter realities. At the end of the 1990s, the median income of black families amounted to $28,000 a year, $16,000 less than that for white families. Blacks, even those in the suburbs, lived in largely segregated communities. Relatively few

961

films and TV shows starred blacks, and by most measures African Americans lagged behind whites in college attendance, occupational opportunity, socioeconomic status, and health. African Americans continued to encounter discrimination in ordinary commerce—for example, at food chains such as the International House of Pancakes or Denny's—and in corporate boardrooms such as that of the oil company Texaco, where some executives spoke of African American employees as "black jelly beans." Despite black protests, several southern states insisted on continuing to fly the Confederate flag over their capitols. And in June 1998, near Jasper, Texas, three white men chained a black man to a pickup truck and dragged him over the roads to his death.

Although the three men in Texas were ultimately convicted of murder (and two sentenced to death), African Americans had little confidence in law enforcement. Like Rodney King (see Chapter 32), they experienced police brutality. They were often subjected to racial profiling—being stopped on the highways, for example, simply because of the color of their skin, an offense that African Americans sarcastically dubbed "driving while black." Black males were especially vulnerable to discrimination and suspicion. The troubles that black women endured from white racism were sensitively explored in the novels of writers such as Toni Morrison, whose works—notably, *Beloved* (1987)—became popular in the 1990s and who in 1993 won the Nobel Prize for literature.

Poverty affected about one in four blacks, many of them in the inner cities. The causes included the restructuring of industry and the decline of its smokestack sector (see Chapter 32), which had a disproportionately high impact on unskilled labor; and the rising number of single mothers whose children were not supported by their fathers. The inner cities, cauldrons of crime and drugs, turned into battlegrounds for black gangs such as the Bloods and the Crips in Los Angeles, whose warfare took at least 400 lives. Black males were far more likely than white males to be murdered or spend time in prison. Throughout the period, many blacks endured slum housing, inadequate medical care, and dilapidated public schools.

*Anger and Accommodation.* Folk expressions of black discontent appeared in rap music, a kind of rhythmic rhyming spoken against an instrumental background known as hip-hop. Its more militant forms—notably, a West Coast product called "gangsta rap"—proclaimed hatred of women and advocated violence, with performers like Ice-T seeming to celebrate a cop killer and Public Enemy urging its audiences to

Across from Cabrini Green in Chicago, 1998, an alley view of the poverty that persisted amid plenty in the inner cities.

"fight the power." Some whites, including presidential candidate Bill Clinton in 1992, attacked rap for seeming to goad blacks into killing whites. But a good deal of rap was far more mainstream, recounting the dangers and glories of inner-city life. Beginning in the mid-1980s, rap was commercialized and brought to white audiences by Russell Simmons, himself experienced in the black street culture of New York, under the record label Def Jam.

Rap's rebelliousness appealed to young whites, who by the late 1990s bought 70 percent of its albums, including the gangsta rap variety. Rap entered mainstream culture, outselling country music, and became associated with a commercially lucrative style of teenage dress (oversize shirts, sneakers, loose jeans bunching down the buttocks, and baseball caps often worn backward). Its stars formed alliances with chic clothing manufacturers such as Calvin Klein. An executive at a black radio station in New York City remarked that rap was "not revolutionary," adding, "It's just 'Give me a piece of the action.'"

Black activists continued trying to mobilize against white racism and for social justice. In October 1995, minister Louis Farrakhan of the Nation of Islam, a kind of latter-day Malcolm X, led 400,000 black men on what was advertised as a "Million Man March" in Washington, D.C., where he called on them to accept greater responsibility for their families. But while Farrakhan preached self-help and racial pride, he also advocated black separatism and made anti-Semitic remarks, leaving an impression that alienated whites and many blacks. The Reverend Jesse Jackson persistently called for social justice, but his appeals made no headway against the prevailing devotion to the free market and limited government.

## NATIVE AMERICANS

The cause of Native Americans was advanced by Red Power advocates, many of them young, urban based, and college educated, who had turned more militant, organizing activist groups such as the American Indian Movement (AIM) and, beginning in 1969, occupying federal sites to call attention to Native American issues. In 1973, 200 armed men led by Russell Means and Dennis Banks of the AIM took control of Wounded Knee, a village on the Pine Ridge reservation where in 1890 some 300 Sioux had been massacred by U.S. soldiers, hoping to establish a type of tribal traditional governance free of federal

Leaders of the American Indian Movement march at Wounded Knee, South Dakota, during their confrontation with federal troops, March 1973.

control. Federal troops placed the occupiers under siege; gunfire killed two activists and paralyzed a federal marshal. The White House, however, declined to use sustained force against the occupiers, and the siege ended peacefully in May 1973, seventy-three days after it began, with the Nixon administration agreeing to discuss the treaty made with the Sioux in 1868.

During the Nixon administration, Native Americans obtained the creation of a cabinet-level Committee on Indian Affairs and more than a doubling of the budget of the Bureau of Indian Affairs. Tribal economic development was encouraged through federal loans, greater tribal control of natural resources, and the return to the tribes of thousands of acres of former Indian lands. The largest such cession, authorized by the Alaskan Native Claims Settlement Act in 1971, transferred 40 million acres, including mineral rights, to the Alaska Federation of Natives. With support from Nixon, who condemned the termination policies enacted in 1953 (see Chapter 29) as "morally and legally unacceptable," Congress soon passed the Menominee Restoration Act, which overturned the termination of that tribe. In 1974, Congress approved the landmark Indian Self-Determination and Education Assistance Act, which decisively ended termination and made the achievement of Indian self-determination an explicit federal goal.

From the 1970s onward, Native Americans gained increasing popular sympathy, aided by the success of entertainers such as the singer Buffy Sainte-Marie, a Cree. The film *Little Big Man* (1970), a sharp departure from the stereotypical arrows-and-rifles treatment, dealt with a survivor of the Indian wars of the late nineteenth century. Its director was inspired by the Vietnam War, and one of its supporting actors, Chief Dan George, a Squamish, won an Academy Award.

Following in Nixon's policy footsteps, President George H. W. Bush encouraged self-determination for Native Americans. During his presidency, the federal government relied more on Native Americans to run the programs of the Bureau of Indian Affairs and, giving them preference in hirings and promotions, increased their representation among the bureau's employees to 87 percent. In 1994, President Clinton, who had said he was one-eighth Native American, brought leaders from all the nation's tribes to the White House—a first in the nation's history—and signed a directive to safeguard Indian rights on tribal lands and to protect the use of eagle feathers for ceremonial purposes. In 2000, the Clinton administration returned

963

84,000 acres to the Ute tribe in northern Utah, the largest restoration of land in a century, and apologized for the federal government's treatment of Native Americans, including its "futile and destructive efforts to annihilate Indian cultures."

*Native American Rights.* In the late 1970s and early 1980s, the Supreme Court significantly enlarged the rights and powers of Indian tribes, holding that they could be governed by their traditional laws even if the laws conflicted with most constitutional rights. The Court also invigorated tribal rights guaranteed by past treaties, including the right of Native Americans to half the annual salmon harvest in the Pacific Northwest; the right to share water resources with the states; and the right to certain lands in the state of New York. In 1978, Congress added to the anti-assimilationist predilections of most tribes by passing the Indian Child Welfare Act, which discouraged the adoption of Indian children by non-Indians. But the enhancement of Indian civic pride and power did little by itself to ease the poverty, unemployment, alcoholism, and disease that continued to plague the reservations.

More promising was the entry of a growing number of Native Americans into business on the reservations. Exercising a right the federal government had provided in 1961 to use their lands for commercial or industrial purposes, Native Americans developed tourist attractions such as the White Mountain Apache ski resort, leased land for the construction of factories, and invested in commercial enterprises (for example, the Passamaquoddies and Penobscots bought the third-largest blueberry farm in Maine). In 1979, the Seminoles, in Florida, exploiting their tribal autonomy, opened a high-stakes bingo hall on their land. Although the state of Florida challenged the venture, a federal court upheld the Seminoles' right to pursue it. Netting $10 million a year from the games, the Seminoles provided a compelling moneymaking model for other Indian tribes to follow. The Bureau of Indian Affairs provided $64 million to finance casino construction. In 1986, the Mashantucket Pequot opened a bingo operation on their reservation in Connecticut that evolved by 1991 into the Foxwoods Gambling Casino, the most profitable casino outside of Las Vegas.

Indian reservations looked increasingly to gambling for revenues; by 1995, more than 100 had opened casinos, often against state opposition arising from fear of losing revenue from lotteries. The tribes used some of their revenues to address the long-standing social problems on their reservations, funding tribal colleges, community centers, and programs for treating alcoholism.

## A Nation of Nations

In the late twentieth century, the country was once again abrim with immigrants, recalling Walt Whitman's observation a century earlier that the United States was a "teeming nation of nations." In part a product of political and economic upheaval elsewhere in the world, the tide began in the 1970s and swelled through the rest of the century. Immigrants poured into the country at a rate not seen since the early twentieth century—an average of 450,000 a year in the 1970s, of 840,000 a year between 1980 and 1997, making a total of almost 19,000,000 newcomers over the period. In 2002, some 10 percent of Americans were foreign-born, more than twice the portion in 1970. Like the wave of immigrants at the beginning of the century, most spoke foreign languages and came with few job skills. But unlike the earlier immigrants, now the overwhelming majority originated outside Europe, in the Caribbean, Central and South America, and Asia.

Some 50,000 Sikhs marched in this religious parade, held in Yuba City, California in 2001, an annual event commemorating the anniversary of the holy book of Sikhism.

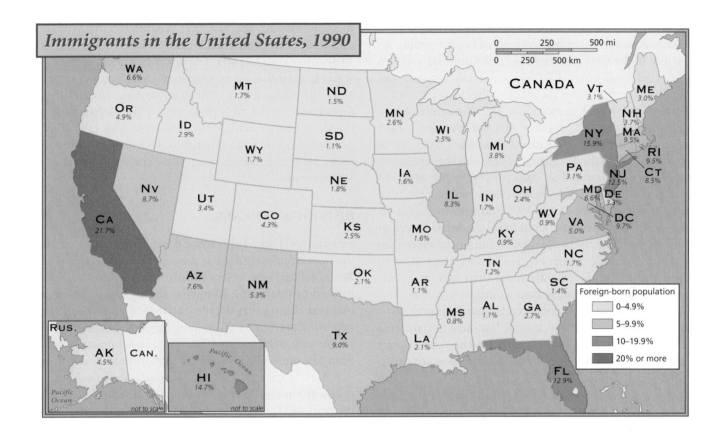

**Immigrants in the United States, 1990**

WA 6.6%
MT 1.7%
ND 1.5%
OR 4.9%
ID 2.9%
MN 2.6%
WI 2.5%
MI 3.8%
SD 1.1%
WY 1.7%
IA 1.6%
NE 1.8%
NV 8.7%
UT 3.4%
CO 4.3%
CA 21.7%
AZ 7.6%
NM 5.3%
KS 2.5%
OK 2.1%
MO 1.6%
IL 8.3%
IN 1.7%
OH 2.4%
PA 3.1%
NY 15.9%
VT 3.1%
ME 3.0%
NH 3.7%
MA 9.5%
RI 9.5%
CT 8.5%
NJ 12.5%
MD 6.6%
DE 3.3%
DC 9.7%
WV 0.9%
VA 5.0%
KY 0.9%
TN 1.2%
NC 1.7%
SC 1.4%
AR 1.1%
MS 0.8%
AL 1.1%
GA 2.7%
TX 9.0%
LA 2.1%
FL 12.9%
AK 4.5%
HI 14.7%
CANADA

Foreign-born population
0–4.9%
5–9.9%
10–19.9%
20% or more

Like the earlier wave of immigrants, the recent newcomers added diverse new threads to the nation's religious and cultural fabric. By the early twenty-first century, the United States included some 4 to 5 million Muslims, almost as many as the number of Jews and more than the number of Episcopalians. It also included as many as 4 million Buddhists, at least 1 million Hindus, and a quarter of a million Sikhs. While constituting altogether only about 3 percent of the population, the members of these religious groups were a salient presence in cities such as Los Angeles where the new immigrants tended to be concentrated.

## ASIAN AMERICANS

The influx from Asia was made possible by the Immigration Act of 1965, which allowed the admission of 170,000 immigrants annually from the Eastern Hemisphere and gave preference to specific categories of people, including family members of American citizens and permanent residents, pro-

fessional and technical workers, and refugees. Hundreds of thousands of Asians took advantage of the act to flee the persecution that targeted former American allies in Vietnam, Laos, and Cambodia; the authoritarianism in the Philippines and the People's Republic of China; and the instability in Korea, Taiwan, and Hong Kong. An additional stimulus to emigration was simply the economic hardship that characterized life in some of these countries, including, in Korea, India, and the Philippines, the underemployment or unemployment of many well-educated and professionally trained men and women.

Unlike the Asian migration of the nineteenth and early twentieth centuries, the new wave initially comprised a large number of urban, college-educated people, many of them doctors, scientists, engineers, and nurses. The influx of professional and technical workers diminished after the Immigration Act was amended in 1976 to tighten eligibility requirements for entry, and the national quotas were taken up increasingly by relatives of those already in the United

965

States. A growing number of Asian immigrants tended to be poor, uneducated, rural in background, and commanding little English. In the five years after the Communist takeovers in Southeast Asia, more than 400,000 Vietnamese, Laotians, and Cambodians came to America, many of them risking treacherous journeys by boat to escape. In 1980, Congress capped the annual quota for refugees at 50,000 and provided a more orderly system for their resettlement as well as a fixed period of economic and medical assistance. Even with the cap, immigration from Asia averaged 305,000 per year in the 1990s, 11 percent higher than the rate in the 1980s, bringing the total immigration from Asia between 1970 and 1997 to almost 6.5 million people. The new migration made the Asian American population far more diverse. In 1990, it comprised more than thirty distinct ethnic groups, with Chinese, Filipinos, and Japanese accounting for slightly more than half, and Vietnamese, Koreans, and Asian Indians a third.

The Asian immigrants tended to concentrate geographically—some in Texas, Louisiana, and Hawaii, but most in California and New York, especially in the greater metropolitan regions centered on Los Angeles, San Francisco, and New York City. They developed local cable TV stations broadcasting in Asian languages. Many Asian Americans attracted notice for their academic achievements, winning prizes in national science competitions and entering elite universities in disproportionately high numbers. A number of those with professional skills prospered rapidly, like the nurse from the Philippines who noted, "My one day's earning here in America is more than my one month's salary in Manila." But others, unable to find work that matched their qualifications, endured occupational downgrading that often left them frustrated and depressed. They earned their livings in blue-collar and service work or in family-operated small businesses such as dry cleaners, restaurants, and greengrocers. A Chinese immigrant trained in physics complained, "We are college graduates but are working in sewing or electronic factories. We all have taken a big step backwards in our profession or work."

While Asian Americans were regarded as "model minorities" because of their high-profile educational achievements, many, impoverished when they arrived, were handicapped by poor neighborhood schools, inadequate proficiency in English, and, for those from rural backgrounds, the difficulty of adjusting to American life. A recent arrival from Southeast Asia remarked, "We have been living in a jungle for a long time in Laos. This is another kind of jungle—a technological and bureaucratic jungle." Southeast Asians suffered white resentment, vandalism, and violence. "There's too many of them," one white fisherman on the Gulf Coast of Texas said of his Vietnamese counterparts. The attorney general of Massachusetts reported that often Southeast Asians "cannot even walk along the public streets without being physically attacked and threatened." In the mid-1980s, half of all Southeast Asians in the United States lived below the poverty line. Like other minorities of color, Asian Americans were divided within themselves between those who were advancing in society and those who were not.

## HISPANIC AMERICANS

Between 1971 and 1997, some 8.5 million Hispanics entered the United States legally, but they were accompanied by a huge flood of illegal newcomers, mainly from Mexico and Haiti, estimated to total some 10 million during the 1980s alone. In one year during that decade, the federal government apprehended more than 1.25 million illegal aliens, 95 percent of whom were Mexican. In 1986, with the administration's support, Congress passed the Immigration Reform and Control Act. Aiming to stem the flow of illegals while dealing practically with those already in the country, the act offered undocumented workers the right to become resident aliens—foreigners permitted to reside and work in the United States—or citizens and extended amnesty to all aliens who had entered the country illegally since January 1, 1982. It also imposed

Jose Luis Magallon in an aisle of his J & J Hardware store in the Echo Park district of Los Angeles, one of thousands of businesses in the rapidly expanding Hispanic communities in California.

fines on employers who hired undocumented workers in the future. By May 4, 1988, the deadline for amnesty, 1.4 million people had sought it, 71 percent of them from Mexico.

The amnesty did nothing to stanch the illegal flow. By 1999, Hispanics, their numbers enlarged by some 12 million more illegal immigrants, accounted for more than 31 million people, or slightly more than 11 percent of the population. Demographers predicted that they would soon likely outnumber African Americans and, by 2050, account for a quarter of the population.

About three-quarters of Hispanic immigrants lived in the band of southwestern states from Texas to California. Like many new Asian Americans, they made their way into unskilled jobs in manufacturing but even more so in the burgeoning service sector, finding employment as, for example, gardeners, domestics, care-givers, janitors, fast-food clerks, and agricultural laborers. A growing number opened small businesses that served their rapidly expanding communities, including groceries and restaurants that non-Hispanic whites also patronized. Hispanic newcomers continued to concentrate in the Southwest, especially California, where in 2000 Hispanics constituted about one-third of the population and held more than 4,000 public offices. Like Asian Americans, they tended to be marked by strong families, low crime rates, and rising wages. By 1998, the number of Latino and Asian-owned businesses in the Los Angeles metropolitan region had grown to 220,000, a threefold increase from the early 1980s.

But like minority groups of color, the Hispanic American population also included a growing urban underclass. As of 1989, only 61 percent of Hispanics in their late twenties had completed high school, compared with 82 percent of blacks and 86 percent of whites. In the late 1990s, more than a quarter of Hispanics lived in poverty, compared with the national average of about 9 percent, and about 8 percent had no jobs. Some 6 percent of all immigrants wound up on welfare, twice the percentage of people born in the United States who were on welfare.

Like Asian Americans, the expanding Hispanic community established a presence on cable TV through stations broadcasting in the Spanish language. Hispanic subjects were taken up in films, such as *El Norte* (1983), which dealt sensitively with the aspirations and pain of migrants from Central America desperately trying to overcome the obstacles to entering the United States.

Hispanics introduced new musical forms to the mainstream, including salsa, merengue, and Tejano, an energetic hybrid of rock, rhythm and blues, and rancheras melodies with a mixture of Spanish and English lyrics; "Macarena" earned the number 7 spot in the top ten hits of the 1990s, a decade whose most popular music was otherwise the hallmark of blandness. The rapidly expanding market for Spanish cultural products prompted *People* magazine to create a national Spanish-language edition, *People en Español,* which compiled record-breaking sales for a memorial issue devoted to the young Tejano singer Selena, who was murdered by a business associate.

## POLITICAL POWER AND CULTURAL RECOGNITION

The big-city machines that had served earlier immigrant groups were long gone, and many of the new Hispanic immigrants could not vote because they were not yet citizens or were in the country illegally. Nevertheless, they gained increasing access to the levers of power. As the result of a federal district court decision in 1971, Mexican Americans were deemed to constitute an identifiable minority group with rights to special federal assistance. The grant of official recognition encouraged Mexican American activists to greater organization and political effort as an ethnic group. In California in 1975, César Chavez's United Farm Workers (UFW) union was helped by the passage of a state labor-relations act that guaranteed such rights as elections for union officials by secret ballot and voting for migrant seasonal workers. That year, the UFW won a special victory, the outlawing of the short-handled hoe, which had forced field laborers to stoop or work on their knees. A revision of the Voting Rights Act in 1982 required the redrawing of congressional district lines to give designated minority populations a fair shot at winning elections if the configuration of an existing district in which they lived appeared to disadvantage them. Soon put into effect, the requirement helped increase the number of Hispanic congressional representatives to ten by 1990, twice the number at the end of the 1970s.

Hispanic cultural nationalism also made gains, particularly in Hispanics' demands for bilingual education. Organizations such as La Raza Unida maintained that bilingualism in the schools would facilitate the education of children who spoke Spanish at home and strengthen respect for Hispanic American culture. In 1974, the Supreme Court held that the San Francisco School Board was obligated to provide special accommodations in the public schools for children who did not speak English. The children in question were Chinese speakers; the issue was their right to be taught English; and bilingual education was only one of the remedies suggested by the Court. Nevertheless, the ruling was broadly taken as a warrant for bilingual instruction, and it had its broadest impact among Hispanics.

Minority-language students in the United States constituted 17 percent of the school-age population; most were in California, New York, and Texas; and in 1980, more than half of them spoke Spanish. In 1974, New York City, responding to Puerto Rican activists, established bilingual classes for some 200,000 students. By 1980, twenty-four states either mandated or permitted bilingual education. Federal spending on it jumped from $7.5 million in 1968 to $150 million in 1979. Such instruction also created a high demand for certified bilingual teachers. In 1975, the federal government, paralleling the educational trend, required that bilingual ballots be provided to all voters if more than 5 percent of them constituted a language minority.

By the late 1980s, advocates of bilingualism had become less ideological and more pragmatic. Areas inhabited by multiple ethnic minorities expressed a preference for English over the multilingual cacophony that might otherwise prevail in schools and government offices. For example, Monterey Park, California, where Asians made up more than a third of the population and Hispanics another third, passed a resolution that English be made the official language. Increasing numbers of immigrant parents, well aware of the economic advantages of fluency in English, wanted their children to have enriched instruction in the language. In 1988, responding to the demand, Congress amended the Bilingual Education Act and authorized funds for alternative programs.

*Multiculturalism.* The demand for bilingual education was complemented by a drive beginning in the late 1980s for what came to be dubbed "multiculturalism." Advocates of multiculturalism aimed to promote tolerance and respect for minority cultures and for women. Some went so far as to reject the goal of assimilation in American society, the standard for earlier waves of immigrants, in favor of promoting the maintenance of each ethnic or minority group's distinctive culture. Their metaphor for the United States was the salad bowl rather than the melting pot.

Multiculturalists found the principal means to their ends in reform of the curriculum, especially in literature and history, in the schools and colleges. The changes involved diversifying curricular content so that it attended far more to the lives, works, and values of women and minority groups and much less to those of white males from northern Europe.

Some multiculturalists seemed to claim that virtually the only subjects worthy of discussion in interpreting the development of the United States were race, class, and gender. Such impressions alienated many educators, cultural observers, and public officials who thought that students ought to learn about George Washington and Thomas Edison as well as Harriet Tubman and Rosa Parks.

Nevertheless, in the 1990s, multiculturalism gained a place in the schools, the colleges, and the culture at large. It succeeded partly because most of its advocates acknowledged the merit in the framework adopted for the history and social sciences in the California schools, which acknowledged that the United States had been a diverse people from the beginning but added: "Yet, even as our people have become increasingly diverse, there is broad recognition we are one people. Whatever our origins, we are all Americans." But multiculturalism also succeeded because it made too much sense to be rejected at a time when the United States was changing so dramatically—when women, minorities, immigrants, gays, and lesbians were barging through the door of equality; when greater critical scrutiny was being given to the relations of the United States to the world, especially its non-western sector; and when faith was eroding in the idea of progress and in science and technology as its instruments.

### RESENTMENTS

Immigration from the 1980s through the 1990s was comparable in magnitude to the newcomer total during the first two decades of the twentieth century, but the new wave did not provoke comparable fears and resentments. The earlier wave represented roughly 19 percent of the population in 1900; the later one, slightly more than 6 percent of the population in 1970. The new arrivals were thus far less disruptive to the arrangements of the country as a whole and, as a result, were far more tolerated nationally. Hispanics and Asians on their part embraced the most essential form of assimilation, increasingly marrying out of their respective groups at intermarriage rates (30 percent) approaching those of European ethnic groups.

However, the immigrant population jumped dramatically in some states—notably, California, where it reached almost 22 percent, largely as a result of the continuing concentration of Hispanics and Asians. In those regions, the newcomers encountered considerable resentment and discrimination. In Los Angeles, a white man complained, "No one speaks

The war against Affirmative Action prompted demonstrations in support of it, as here at the University of Michigan in 1998.

mentalist Christian denominations continued to grow. Attacks on abortion rights, feminism, affirmative action, and immigrants pervaded talk radio, Christian radio as well as TV stations, and, increasingly, the Internet. The Web, whose content was unregulated, provided a medium for some conservatives to billboard venomous, usually unfounded, disparagements of public figures and social trends. Radical anti-abortionists defaced or bombed abortion clinics. Outside an abortion clinic in Florida in 1995, one of them shot and killed a physician and his bodyguard; and at a clinic near Boston, another killed two and wounded five others.

Secularism, freewheeling behavior, and now violence in the public schools troubled many Americans, social conservatives especially. Many supported a voucher system that would permit them to send their children to private (including parochial) schools at public expense. Unhappy with the breakdown of what they called "family values," conservatives were also disquieted by the ongoing decline of the traditional nuclear family, in which a married couple live with their minor children under the same roof, and its replacement by a dizzying diversity of spousal, partnering, and parenting relationships. They contended that traditional views of American history and culture were being excluded from the classroom in favor of the emphasis on multiculturalism, women, and minority groups, a trend they disparaged as "politically correct" but intellectually distorted.

Conservatives of all stripes, including women and the growing number of people of color who counted themselves in the fold, found common ground in warring against affirmative action. In 1996, Californians passed Proposition 209, an initiative that ended racial preferences in college admissions. That year, too, a federal appeals court in Texas barred the use within its jurisdiction of race in university admissions. Universities devised ways to get around the prohibition—for example, by taking social and economic disadvantage into account in evaluating applicants—but like Proposition 209, the court's ruling set back efforts at achieving racial and cultural diversity in higher education. In 1995, in *Adarand Construction v. Pena*, the Supreme Court bolstered the turn away from broad programs of affirmative action. Deciding against the federal programs that gave preference to minority contractors, the Court indicated that affirmative action programs had to assist individual victims of past discrimination rather than simply benefit minorities.

By the 1990s, the divisions over social issues emergent in the 1960s and 1970s had been compounded by tensions

English, and it bothers me. I feel it's not my country anymore." During the 1980s, the backlash against bilingualism led voters in Arizona, Colorado, and Florida to pass English-only referenda.

In 1994, California voters approved an initiative that denied nonemergency welfare benefits and public-school access to the children of illegal immigrants; four years later, they passed another initiative that largely eliminated bilingual education in the state's public schools. In 1996, a federal welfare reform bill (see Chapter 34) restricted the access of legal immigrants to public assistance, and President Clinton signed immigration legislation that placed higher income requirements on sponsors and doubled the staffing of the border patrol. A poll found that more than two-thirds of respondents believed that Chinese Americans were "taking away too many jobs from Americans," "don't care what happens to anyone but their own kind," and "have too much power in the business world."

Through the 1990s, cultural resentments remained passionately in force. Membership in conservative and funda-

arising from the new immigration; the expanding claims for cultural, economic, and health equality; and the country's inescapable entanglement in the global community. At the same time, the new computer technologies and biotechnologies—along with the industries they created—were reshaping American society, establishing new economic opportunities and ways of work, transforming access to goods and information, and promising dramatic improvements in health care. All these boosts to national life buoyed the presidency of William Jefferson Clinton even while the social fissures escalated the difficulty of governance in the post–Cold War United States.

## Suggested Reading

Jane Abbate, *Inventing the Internet* (1999)

Elliott Robert Barkan, *And Still They Came: Immigrants and American Society, 1920 to the 1990s* (1996)

Paul E. Ceruzzi, *A History of Modern Computing* (1998)

Susan Faludi, *Backlash: The Undeclared War against American Women* (1991)

Ronald Formisano, *Boston against Busing: Race, Class and Ethnicity in the 1960s and 1970s* (1991)

Sheldon Krimsky, *Biotechnics and Society: The Rise of Industrial Genetics* (1991)

Bruce J. Schulman, *The Seventies: The Great Shift in American Culture, Society, and Politics* (2001)

# Chapter Review

## Summary QUESTIONS

■ How did the personal computer industry come into being and what was its impact on American life?

■ What were the origins of the biotechnology industry?

■ How did the United States deal with the threats to health of AIDS and smoking?

■ What social and economic advances and setbacks did women and members of minority groups experience during the last quarter of the twentieth century?

■ What were the major social divisions of the period?

## Chronology

| | |
|---|---|
| **1975** | Microsoft Corporation founded. |
| **1976** | Apple Computer founded. |
| **1978** | Louise Brown, the first test-tube baby, is born in England. |
| | Genetech announces the production of human insulin using the new techniques of biotechnology. |
| **1984** | French and American scientists identify the HIV virus. |
| **1986** | The Human Genome Project begins. |
| **March 1986** | *Exxon Valdez* oil spill in Prince William Sound, Alaska. |
| **1994** | Web browser Netscape created propelling the Internet into the Worldwide Web. |
| **October 1995** | "Million Man March" in Washington. |
| **1997** | Kyoto treaty. |
| **April 20, 1999** | Shooting at Columbine High School in Littleton, Colorado. |
| **2000** | The complete structure of human DNA is deciphered. |

## Key Terms

Personal computers (p. 946)

Genetic engineering (p. 951)

AIDS (p. 954)

Global warming (p. 958)

Ozone depletion (p. 958)

Multiculturalism (p. 968)

**Access the *Inventing America* StudySpace at wwnorton.com/studyspace**

PERSONAL PLAN  ■  REVIEW MATERIALS  ■  RESEARCH AIDS  ■  MULTIMEDIA

# Chapter 34

## THE POLITICS OF DIVISION:

### 1993–2001

Pro-Gore and pro-Bush supporters in the disputed election of 2000 make their preferences known at the U.S. Supreme Court on December 11, 2000, when it was hearing arguments on the Florida vote recount.

**QUESTIONS**

- *How did Clinton's move to the political center help advance his domestic agenda?*

- *What were the major social issues of the booming nineties?*

- *How was Clinton's impeachment viewed by most Americans in light of his domestic record?*

- *What strategies did the Clinton administration use to promote democracy in the post-Cold War world?*

- *What were the chief features of George W. Bush's domestic agenda?*

- *How did Bush's foreign policy depart from that followed by previous recent presidents?*

## The Clinton Presidency

William Jefferson Clinton, a Rhodes Scholar at Oxford University and a graduate of Yale Law School, was prodigiously intelligent, ambitious, and resilient, a politico of disarming charm and resourcefulness. He had been elected governor of Arkansas at age thirty-two and had spent most of his adult life in state public office. Aware that the national political center had moved to the right, he presented himself as a "New Democrat," a devotee of opportunity, equality, and economic growth achieved with fiscal restraint and encouragement of the private sector. Clinton courted the powerful, but he also possessed considerable empathy for the disadvantaged and dispossessed, a characteristic he attributed to having grown up in a small town where his friendships cut across lines of race and class and in a home where his abusive, alcoholic stepfather frequently troubled the family peace. "I feel your pain," he would often tell people suffering from adversity. Such empathy made for good politics amid the continuing demands for equality in the United States, especially by women and members of racial and immigrant minorities. Hillary Clinton, a fellow graduate of Yale Law School, was an ambitious, politically involved lawyer—she told a reporter that she had not "stayed home baking cookies"—and her husband promised that she would play an active role in his presidency, noting that voters would get two for the price of one.

Tolerant of diversity in lifestyles and attitudes, Bill Clinton was a staunch friend of affirmative action, abortion rights, and gay rights. He established a rainbow administration, appointing a woman as attorney general for the first time in the nation's history, and an African American, a Hispanic, and several other women to cabinet and subcabinet posts. He also successfully nominated Ruth Bader Ginsberg to the Supreme Court. He placed the issues of economic revival, the national debt, and health care high on his New Democrat agenda. Fascinated by the process of globalization, he followed Bush in making a major goal of his foreign policy the strengthening of American economic competitiveness in the post–Cold War world. In all, Clinton brought to the presidency a propensity for social liberalism combined with economic centrism, and an unembarrassed capacity to use personal revelation, hardball maneuver, tireless effort, or whatever else might be required to achieve his ends.

### THE ECONOMY AND FREE TRADE

A month after taking office, Clinton sent a tax-and-spending package to Capitol Hill that was intended to stimulate the economy and lower the debt. Congress rejected the proposal for stimulus spending, but in August 1993, despite outcries from Republicans, it raised taxes on high incomes, reduced them on low ones, and cut spending by $225 billion.

Clinton successfully politicked, persuaded, and cajoled to win approval of NAFTA, sure that the agreement would boost the American economy.

The Clinton administration regarded free trade as essential to a thriving economy but found itself in a battle royal when it sought congressional ratification of the expanded version of the North American Free Trade Agreement (NAFTA) that had been negotiated by the Bush administration and that would create the world's largest free-trade zone. The measure drew support and provoked dissent from both Democrats and Republicans, with advocates contending that it would create thousands of jobs and critics holding that it would result in the loss of thousands to Mexico, where goods would be produced free of the environmental and safety standards for manufacturing in the United States. In November 1993, with Clinton lobbying for the measure assiduously, NAFTA sailed through Congress by a comfortable margin.

Within a year, NAFTA was estimated to have cost some 12,000 people their jobs but to have created an additional 130,000 jobs by increasing exports to Mexico by some 23 percent. In December 1994, Clinton, with congressional support, signed an international trade agreement that abolished trade quotas, lowered tariffs worldwide by $744 billion—the largest such cut in history—and created a new international trade regime called the World Trade Organization.

By then, economic recovery was well under way. In October 1994, 3.5 million more Americans were employed than had been at the end of 1993; and by the close of the year, the unemployment rate had fallen to 5.4 percent, its lowest level since 1990. The deficit, down to $220 billion in 1994, was predicted to be lower still the next year. Consumer confidence was up, and retail sales were rising.

### SETBACKS: HEALTH CARE AND GAY RIGHTS

Shortly after taking office, Clinton appointed a task force headed by his wife to recommend a comprehensive system of health coverage. By then, Americans were spending more per capita on medical care than people in any other nation, and some 39 million lacked health insurance. After five months, the task force recommended an enormously complex hybrid of federal and private arrangements that would provide universal health coverage while employing market competition to keep costs down.

The plan drew a hailstorm of criticism. It was disparaged as a bureaucratic nightmare, an infringement on the freedom of both doctors and patients, and unacceptably expensive to employers, especially small businesses, and the government itself. By early 1994, despite Hillary Clinton's vigorous campaign on its behalf, the plan was dead. The effort, however, prompted the health care industry on its own to reorganize, expand its insurance coverage, and seek to control costs by using some of the mechanisms proposed by the Clinton commission. The Clinton administration, chastened by the defeat, henceforth took a small-step approach to health care—for example, obtaining legislation in 1996 that helped workers and their families keep their medical insurance if they changed or lost jobs.

In January 1993, Clinton announced that he intended to integrate homosexual men and women into all branches of the armed services—a departure from existing policy, which prohibited them in the military. Gays and lesbians were already serving in the military, but they had to keep their sexual orientation secret. Clinton's proposal outraged many conservatives, who felt that it implicitly legitimated homosexuality. It also generated considerable dissent from within the armed services on the grounds that the presence of overtly homosexual men and women in the ranks would

*American Journal*

## The Medically Uninsured

*In 2000, some 44 million Americans, a full 16 percent of the total population, had no medical insurance. Roughly four out of five of them were working families who earned too little to afford health insurance or whose employers didn't provide it, or who were between jobs. Many were too ill to get insurance but didn't qualify for a governmental health insurance program.*

*Among them was Jody Beal, who lived with his wife, Sandy, in Texas, where almost 25 percent of residents—one of the highest proportions in the nation—had no health insurance. Jody Beal had earned a decent middle-class income working in the oil fields in Texas and abroad. He had expected to retire at 65 in secure comfort, but at age 61, when he was momentarily between jobs and had no health insurance, he suffered congestive heart failure. He had two heart operations. Afterward, he couldn't work, and being without health insurance, he couldn't get the regular medical care required for his heart condition. In 2000, a year after Jody fell ill, the Beals, by then broke, discussed their plight with Hedrick Smith on a public television program about health care:*

> SANDY [opening bills]: "The first thing they ask you is, is are you insured. And then if you're not, well, you generally need to make some kind of down payment and—so that's basically where our money went...
>
> [reading from a bill]: "Our records indicate that payment arrangements extended to you on the above account have not been honored...
>
> "Well, they've turned it over to a collection agency as opposed to letting us work it out with them. That shoots any credit we had!..

"All the medical bills are about $125,000. That's with the two procedures and the emergency room visits and all that. The entire thing...

"I have got to get a job that's going to pay enough, that I can pay off the, the hospital, the doctors, and any future medical needs he has...

"Oh, at this stage in my life, I never anticipated anything like this; certainly not."

*NARRATOR:* "Desperate for work, Sandy Beal goes door to door selling funeral arrangements. . . . Working solely on commission, it takes Sandy three months to make just over $1,000...

Unable to work and saddled with a debt he can see no way to pay off, Jody now rarely goes out...

To save money, he checks his heartrate at a Wal Mart drugstore instead of having frequent checkups with his doctor."

*SANDY:* "Life is, is very difficult. It's just not fun when you can't go places and do things and you're constantly worried and concerned. When you feel that, that no matter what you do, it's possibly not going to be any better...it's just difficult to look to the future."

From the Transcript of *"Critical Condition: How Good Is Your Health Care?"* with Hedrick Smith, PBS. Part IV The Uninsured: 44 Million Forgotten Americans.

http://www.pbs.org/criticalcondition/program/uninsuredTrascript.htm

create tension among straights. In July, a compromise dubbed "Don't ask, don't tell" was adopted: the armed services would not inquire into the sexual orientation of recruits and would not discharge men or women suspected of being homosexuals. But gays and lesbians could not openly acknowledge their sexual preferences or engage in homosexual acts on or off military bases. The compromise dissatisfied Americans on both sides of the dispute, and later assessments revealed that it did little to make the military more tolerant of homosexuals.

The Clinton administration also stepped up the sexual integration of the armed services, with the result that women soon served aboard ships at sea, underwent basic training with men, and lived in sexually integrated barracks. By 1998, women accounted for one out of seven members of the armed services on active duty.

## ANGER ON THE RIGHT

The administration's stand on homosexuals in the military and the big-government flavor of its health care plan angered many conservatives, and so did increasing questions about the Clintons' character arising from their involvement during his gubernatorial years in questionable financial dealings and renewed allegations that Bill Clinton had engaged in sexual pecadillos. The Clintons denied all the charges, but the accusations received ongoing attention in the media. The couple's putative transgressions helped intensify continuing resentments over immigration, abortion, women's rights, pornography, sexual freedom, and the break away from "family values." Right-wing talk-show hosts such as the popular Rush Limbaugh held up the Clintons as exemplars of all that his listeners considered wrong with the country. In 1992, concern for the economy may have papered over the social and cultural resentments evident since the 1970s, but now, despite the surge in the economy and Clinton's victory with NAFTA, many Americans—especially those vulnerable to automation, corporate downsizing, and foreign competition—felt no better off economically.

*Violence on the Right.* A leading theme in the discontent was suspicion of government. Such wariness could be found across the political spectrum, but it was made especially acute on the far right by the government's own tragic actions.

At Ruby Ridge, Idaho, in 1992, a confrontation between an armed white separatist and dozens of law enforcement officers resulted in the deaths of the separatist's wife and thirteen-year-old son. Then in Waco, Texas, during February 1993, federal agents tried to search for illegal firearms at a fortified religious community occupied by the Branch Davidians and their apocalyptic leader, David Koresh. The Davidians opened fire, and in the ensuing gun battle people on both sides were killed and wounded. In April, federal agents acting under orders from Attorney General Janet Reno assaulted the compound. A fire broke out—whether Koresh or the agents ignited it is disputed—wiping out all seventy-six of the occupants, including women and children.

The episodes at Ruby Ridge and Waco galvanized the far right, stimulating the formation of more than 1,000 patriot groups and armed militias in thirty-six states. On the Internet, theories that the government was intent on wiping out white Christians were posted, along with information about how to construct bombs and other weapons. While such theories ranged ideologically from traditional conservatism to blatant racism, most viewed the federal government as an instrument of a conspiracy to impose a totalitarian regime on the United States. Such angry convictions led Timothy McVeigh, a decorated veteran of the Gulf War, and his ally, Terry Nichols, in April 1995 to truck-bomb the federal building in Oklahoma City, killing 168 people, including children in a day care nursery on the second floor, and injuring scores more. Tried and convicted of the crime, McVeigh was executed in 2001, and Nichols was sentenced to life in prison.

## ELECTIONS, 1994: A REPUBLICAN EARTHQUAKE

In 1994, responding to what polls revealed about voter concerns, the Clinton administration pressed for measures against crime and for welfare reform. Its anticrime bill banned assault weapons and provided $30 billion for drug treatment, prevention efforts, more prisons, and more police on the streets. Congress wrangled over the bill, then passed one similar to it. Clinton also introduced a bill intended to make good on his campaign pledge to "end welfare as we know it." The measure aimed especially to rein in the skyrocketing cost of Aid to Families with Dependent Children—it had jumped 31 percent since 1989—and to address the growing apprehension that the welfare system was encouraging many Americans into a condition of permanent dependency. In Congress, however, welfare reform took a back seat to the pending midterm elections.

*The "Contract with America."* Newt Gingrich, a Republican congressman from Georgia, sensed the resentments and in the summer of 1994 shrewdly capitalized on them by drawing up an election-year "Contract with America," a ten-point conservative plan that included middle-class tax cuts, welfare reform, congressional term limits, a tough anticrime measure, and a balanced-budget amendment. In a November landslide, the Republicans gained fifty-two seats in the House and eight in the Senate, recapturing Congress for the first time since 1954. They won eleven governorships, bringing their total to thirty and giving them command of a majority

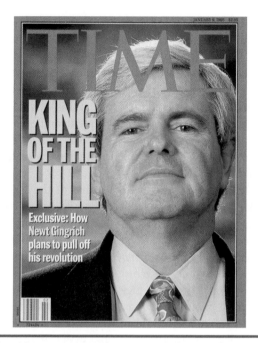

Newt Gingrich's "Contract with America" helped produce a Republican landslide in the 1994 congressional elections.

of statehouses for the first time since 1970; and they took control of seventeen more state legislative bodies. Republican leaders celebrated the landslide as a repudiation of big, activist government and the moral decline they claimed had come to plague the United States.

In January 1995, the 104th Congress arrived in Washington righteously ready, like the 80th Congress in 1947, to turn back the clock on the recent accomplishments of the New Deal / Fair Deal state. The House elected Gingrich its Speaker by acclamation—*Time* magazine declared him "King of the Hill"—and appointed Rush Limbaugh an "honorary member." The new members of Congress aimed to overhaul the welfare system, limit federal regulatory power, roll back gun control, beef up the defense budget, cut taxes, and reduce foreign aid. The House, afire with cultural as well as economic conservatism, sought to slash the budgets for several federal science agencies, the National Endowments for the Arts and Humanities, and the Public Broadcasting Corporation. Its efforts were tempered in the Senate, which also narrowly defeated a constitutional amendment for a balanced budget that the House had passed. The Republicans then attempted to enact a legislative program that would balance the budget in

seven years. But without reducing a number of social programs, it was impossible to balance the budget while simultaneously increasing defense spending and cutting taxes.

*Face-Off.* Clinton asserted that he would not tolerate hacking into the bone of social programs—notably, Medicare, Medicaid, and education. When the Republican Congress sent him spending bills that slashed appropriations for such programs, Clinton vetoed them, with the result that the federal government, temporarily having insufficient money to spend even for workers' paychecks, was partially shut down twice in the fall of 1995. The president also vetoed a bill to ban so-called partial-birth abortions, a late-term abortion usually done to safeguard the health of the mother that many conservatives nevertheless vehemently opposed.

Clinton had the better of the face-off, managing to blame Gingrich and his right-wing allies for the shutdown. The Republicans surrendered on the budget and voted an increase in the minimum wage to $5.15 an hour. They had been weakened by the consequences of the shutdown, including the laying off of thousands of federal workers near Christmastime. However, Clinton on his part recognized that the forces behind the Republican earthquake had to be reckoned with. His eye on the 1996 election, he moved closer to the political center of the day, which Reagan and now the Gingrich Republicans had drawn a good deal farther to the right from where it had been in, say, the Eisenhower years. Clinton embraced the Republican emphasis on budget balancing and debt reduction, basically vowing, as an aide recalled, "that he was never going to get caught in that big-government, big-this, big-that trap again."

The rightward shift helped prompt Clinton in August 1996 to sign a welfare reform act reversing policies that had prevailed since the New Deal. The law reduced spending on food stamps, but most important, it abolished the largest federal welfare program, Aid to Families with Dependent Children, thus scrapping a sixty-year federal commitment to children in poverty. Welfare was turned over to the states, which would be given federal block grants accompanied by stringent rules. Coverage for most welfare recipients was limited to two years at a stretch, with a lifetime total of five years, and the recipients were required to move from welfare to work.

Critics, including many Democrats, angrily attacked the law, warning that it would adversely affect mothers and children in the inner cities. But in September, the welfare rolls were down by some 2 million people from 1993, a result of

977

both the reform measure and the booming economy. Now with the presidential election just weeks away, Clinton focused like a laser beam on voters in the new political center.

### THE 1996 ELECTION

The Republican nominee was Senator Bob Dole, a seventy-three-old warhorse from Kansas, a pragmatic conservative with a dry wit. Dole faulted Clinton for lack of leadership, character, and trustworthiness. But he ran a dull campaign, was dogged by memories of the federal shutdown the previous fall, and was swamped by the wave of prosperity that was sweeping the country.

Economic abundance was proclaimed by every indicator. In the preceding five years, the principal stock market average had more than doubled, and in the preceding six, corporate profits had risen 70 percent, to $437 billion. The federal deficit was down by 60 percent, more than Clinton had promised. Even before the passage of the welfare reform act, the growth of the economy had shrunk welfare roles 37 percent since the last presidential election year. Clinton celebrated the creation of more than 10 million new jobs during his administration, an increase in family income of $1,600 after inflation, and the lowest unemployment rate (5.1 percent) in seven years as well as the biggest drop in poverty in twenty-seven years (from more than 15 percent to less than 14 percent of the population).

On election day, Clinton beat Dole handily in the electoral college, 379 to 159. He gained 49 percent of the popular vote to Dole's 41 percent, with most of the rest going to Ross Perot, who had mounted another independent candidacy (see Chapter 32). The Republicans lost ten seats in the House but maintained control of Congress. Voter turnout fell to 54.2 percent, an indicator that interest in the political system remained desultory.

## The Best and Worst of Times

During Clinton's second term, the economy boomed on. Unemployment fell steadily, reaching 4 percent in 2000, a thirty-year low. Between 1994 and 1998, the gross domestic product jumped by more than 14 percent, and during the first three months of 1999 it grew at an even faster annual pace. In 1997, three out of four homes had air-conditioning, four out of five

had washing machines, one out of two had automatic dishwashers and personal computers, and almost all had television sets. A growing number of Americans were watching films on DVDs, which would soon surpass VCRs as the home viewing technology of choice. In 1998, wages and benefits rose at twice the rate of inflation, which was only 1.7 percent. The poverty rate was down to 13.3 percent, and even a majority of the poor possessed amenities such as cars, TVs, and microwave ovens that most people in other parts of the world could only dream about.

Like the prosperity of the 1980s, that of the 1990s was a mixed story. The number of jobs in manufacturing continued to decline as corporations, in a process that came to be called "outsourcing," moved an increasing portion of their production activities to countries where labor was inexpensive. Domestically, meanwhile, franchised service businesses such as Kinko's copy centers and 7-Eleven convenience stores multiplied, offering owners new small-business opportunities and many immigrants a foothold in the job market. But while a record number of people held jobs, many of the new jobs were in the low end of the service sector, including telemarketing and sales, and custodial and domestic work. In mid-decade, more than one out of five Americans worked part time, with few or no benefits and no security or prospects of advancement. The unemployment rate among teenage job seekers ran to 16 percent in 1997, symptomatic of the growing requirement for skills—for example, with computers—and the deficiency of such skills among many young people. Just one out of seven workers belonged to a labor union, only 40 percent of the fraction in 1945, which meant that standards for wages, hours, and working conditions for all of labor were weakened.

Between 1989 and 1998, inflation-adjusted wages rose just 1 percent for the bottom fifth of workers but 16 percent for the top fifth. Adding to the disparity, the average chief executive earned 400 times more than his or her employees, a tenfold increase in that ratio since the 1960s. Many of the low-skilled people working in Silicon Valley could not afford the area's stratospheric housing prices and lived long commuting distances from their places of employment. Unlike the 1980s, the 1990s lacked naked celebrations of greed, but disquiet with some of the profit-maximizing practices of the marketplace were evident in the popularity of Scott Adams's cartoon strip *Dilbert,* which satirized corporate culture from the point of view of the hapless victims of restructuring and downsizing.

*Dilbert* was so popular because it comically exposed the frustrating features of corporate life familiar to millions of employees.

Democrats and Republicans disputed which party's policies were responsible for the robustness of the economy, but analysts at all points on the political spectrum agreed that a good deal of the economic miracle was attributable to technological innovation. Technology was steadily boosting worker productivity, yielding low unemployment without significant inflation. And according to a chorus of commentators, revolutions in biotechnology and communications were creating a "new economy" whose capacities were as unbounded as human ingenuity.

## THE BULL MARKET

The rapid growth, or expectations of such growth, of the new high-tech companies helped inflame the stock market. Between December 1990 and September 2000, the Dow Jones Industrial Average, a measure of the market's value, climbed more than 400 percent to over 11,000; and the index of the NASDAQ, a market heavy with stocks of high-tech companies, skyrocketed more than 1,000 percent, to over 4,000. America Online (AOL), the biggest Internet service provider, was valued at $26 billion, equaling the combined capital worth of the three major broadcasting networks. The inflation in stock values made billionaires of some of the men and women who pioneered the new-economy companies. The wealth of Bill Gates, one of the two founders of the Microsoft Corporation, mushroomed to more than $100 billion in 2000, which exceeded the combined assets of one-third of the American population.

Americans were tantalized by the prospect of quick stock market riches, an absorption that was reflected in the popularity during 1999 of the TV game show *Who Wants to Be a*

*Millionaire?* An unprecedented number of people began putting their money into stocks, aided by discount brokerage houses such as Charles Schwab and the wide availability of stock information on the Internet. By the end of the decade, stocks accounted for more than a quarter of the assets of American householders, a fifty-year peak. But the willingness to buy stocks at prices that were historically high compared with earnings reminded some observers of the 1920s. The chairman of the Federal Reserve Board remarked that the performance of the stock market expressed an "irrational exuberance" on the part of investors.

## A RESTRAINED DOMESTIC AGENDA

Riding the economic boom, Clinton continued the cautious and fiscally conservative strategy he had adopted after the Republican midterm victory in 1994. Mindful that Republicans still controlled Congress, he generally refrained from major legislative initiatives, preferring modest, at times tepid, proposals. But he did attend to issues that he knew his Democratic constituency and centrist Republicans cared about—notably, the environment, gun control, and tobacco (see Chapter 33).

Clinton paid no more than lip service to the cause of reforming campaign financing, an issue that had been stimulated by the increasingly large amounts of money that candidates and the major parties raised to pay for electioneering. In 1998, Senators John McCain, a Republican, and Russell Feingold, a Democrat, introduced a bill to curb reliance on large campaign contributions, but Republican senators blocked the measure, alleging that it was unconstitutional and did nothing to stop the advertisements by labor unions and other groups that tended to favor Democrats.

In 1997, Clinton signed a bill that provided some tax cuts and committed the federal government to achieving a balanced budget by 2002. By the opening of 1998, the combination of the government's fiscal restraint and the economic boom, which raised tax revenues, seemed likely to produce a balanced budget three years ahead of schedule. In his State of the Union address in January, Clinton predicted a small budgetary surplus for the next fiscal year, and the following January the Congressional Budget Office predicted that federal surpluses would total $2.6 trillion during the next decade. Although some Republicans wanted to bite into the surplus with tax cuts, Clinton successfully refused, insisting that most of it should go first to protecting Social Security, a position that enjoyed widespread support.

### SEX, LIES, AND IMPEACHMENT

From early 1998, Clinton's ability to advance even a modest domestic agenda was greatly undermined by the scandals that began tarring him and led to his impeachment the following year. The scandals came to light as a result of the work conducted by Kenneth Starr, who had been appointed a special prosecutor to look into several allegations of financial impropriety in the Clinton administration, including Whitewater. In January 1998, Starr received evidence that Monica Lewinsky, a young government intern, had been having an affair with the president that included her performing oral sex on him during visits to the Oval Office. Meanwhile, in late 1997, the attorneys for a woman who was pursuing a sexual harassment suit against the president had obtained a ruling from the Supreme Court requiring Clinton to answer their questions, establishing the precedent that a sitting president could be compelled to testify in a civil suit concerning actions that took place before his presidency. In January 1998, responding under oath to questions by the woman's lawyers, Clinton denied having a romantic relationship with Lewinsky. At Starr's request, Attorney General Janet Reno authorized him to expand his multiple investigations of Clinton into whether the president had lied in this testimony and had sought to obstruct justice by encouraging Lewinsky to cover up their affair.

*Tightening the Noose.* By now, January 1998, word of the relationship with Lewinsky was making headlines, an indicator that by the 1990s not even presidents were immune from scrutiny of their most personal lives. In a statement on national television at the end of month, Clinton emphatically declared, "I did not have sexual relations with that woman." Hillary Clinton blamed the array of investigations into the couple's activities on a "vast right-wing conspiracy." But in mid-August, aware that Lewinsky had given Starr physical evidence demonstrating a sexual encounter with him, Clinton conceded in videotaped testimony to Starr and a federal grand jury that his conduct with Lewinsky had been "wrong." He told the American people in a brief televised address that he had "misled" them and done injury to his family. Still, he defiantly insisted that he had not lied under oath nor asked anyone to lie for him.

On September 9, Starr gave Congress a videotape of Clinton's grand jury testimony and a 445-page report that listed eleven possible grounds for impeachment, some of which focused on charges that he had lied under oath. On October 8, the House voted to launch an impeachment inquiry by a solid majority of 258 to 176, with 31 Democrats joining most of the Republicans in support.

*Slipping Through.* The public had long thought Clinton was lying about his relationship with Lewinsky, but his numerous supporters now brushed off his conduct as sex between two consenting adults, covered up as anyone might conceal an illicit affair but by no means worthy of impeachment. "It's hard to get really excited," a waitress remarked. "What does the Clintons' sex life have to do with me?" Meanwhile, the public standing of Starr and the Republican Congress plummeted.

This cartoon comments on the belief of many Americans that the impeachment proceedings against President Clinton were driven solely by partisan politics.

In the congressional elections in November 1998, the Democrats gained five seats in the House while maintaining their number in the Senate and in state contests. Newt Gingrich, under fire himself for questionable financial dealings, announced that he would leave Congress.

All the same, on December 19, 1998, the House in a strongly partisan vote resolved to impeach Clinton on two articles—perjury and obstruction of justice—making him the second president (after Andrew Johnson) to be so treated. On January 27, 1999, the impeachment trial began in the Senate. After more than a month of partisan debate, the prosecutors failed to come near the two-thirds majority (67 votes) necessary for conviction on either article.

Pollsters found that Americans overwhelmingly believed Clinton guilty of the charges but that the vast majority did not want him removed from office. They cared much more about the booming economy, not to mention how to deal with the looming surplus, the solvency of Social Security, the increasing costs of medical care, and the emerging need to revitalize the military in the wake of post–Cold War budget reductions. Many had nodded vigorous assent when shortly before the impeachment trial began, Clinton delivered a confident State of the Union address exhorting the assembled Congress to deal with the people's business in "a spirit of civility and bipartisanship." Now that the ordeal of impeachment was over, they wanted their government to get on with their business.

## The Post–Cold War World

"Foreign policy is not what I came here to do," Clinton remarked several months after entering the White House. His heart in domestic affairs, he lacked an overarching vision for the post–Cold War world. Nevertheless, Clinton did bring a set of guiding principles to foreign policy. Foreshadowed by Bush and dubbed "democratic enlargement" by the Clinton White House, these principles aimed, as his staff laid them

Post–Cold War Europe

out, to "strengthen the community of market democracies, foster and consolidate new democracies and market economies where possible, and counter the aggression and support the liberalization of states hostile to democracy." A replacement of the Cold War policy of containment, democratic enlargement echoed Franklin Roosevelt's goal of promoting democratic capitalism in the world, but it gave far more attention to the demands of globalization than FDR could have dreamed of. Clinton told Congress in 1994, "We have put our economic competitiveness at the heart of our foreign policy."

Disparate problems abroad, some of them new, most ongoing, intruded on Clinton's presidency from the beginning. Some arose from the Soviet Union's collapse, others from the indirect consequences of its disappearance as a major player on the world stage, still others from indigenous antagonisms and conflicts. While the strategy of democratic enlargement helped resolve some of these disputes, several required military action.

### RUSSIA

American policymakers continued to fear instability in Russia, specifically the fragility of its new capitalist economy, the threat of political upheaval, and the uncertain control of its formidable nuclear arsenal. Between 1993 and 1996, Clinton produced $4.5 billion in bilateral assistance for President Boris Yeltsin's government, helping to curb inflation and stabilize the ruble. "The old rules have been turned upside down," observed one analyst. "Instead of containing the Russians, we now subsidize them." As a result, by 1996 more than 60 percent of Russia's gross domestic product was generated by its private sector, and foreign trade was up 65 percent compared with 1993. Clinton brought to fruition efforts begun by the Bush administration to arrange for the removal of nuclear stockpiles from the former Soviet satellites, now independent nations. Clinton also agreed with Yeltsin to detarget U.S. and Russian strategic missiles, so that for the first time since the early 1950s neither side would have missiles pointed at the other. Acting in accord with START I and START II (see Chapter 32), Clinton and Yeltsin reduced their countries' strategically deployed warheads from 20,000 to 7,000 by 1996, aiming eventually to bring the number down to 3,000.

### VIOLENCE IN THE FORMER YUGOSLAVIA

The lifting of Communist rule in Yugoslavia led in 1992 to the breakup of that country into five independent states, all of them divided against each other, and some within themselves, by ethnic and religious animosities. In 1991, one of them, Serbia, its people predominantly Orthodox Christian, attacked another, Croatia, whose population was largely Roman Catholic. In the spring of 1992, Serbs living in still another state, Bosnia (Bosnia and Herzegovina), mounted a war that combined conventional military means with rape, murder, and terror to "cleanse" the new country of its almost 2 million Muslims, about half the population. During the winter of 1993, the Bosnian Serbs laid siege to Srebrenica, a predominantly Muslim city and one of the richest in the Balkans (countries occupying the Balkan Peninsula), its people now starving and freezing. By 1993, the post–Cold War hostilities in the former Yugoslavia had left more than 100,000 people dead and produced 3.5 million refugees.

Print and television reports of the Serbian atrocities angered many Americans, but they were reluctant to commit troops to stop the fighting. While the Bush administration recognized Bosnia, it endorsed a U.N. embargo on arms shipments to all of the former Yugoslavia, a policy that in effect favored the Serbs, since they were much better equipped militarily than the Bosnian or Croatian forces. During the 1992 presidential campaign, Clinton had attacked Bush for "failing to stop the horror in Bosnia." Once in the White House, however, he was reluctant to send troops, fearing a lack of public support and jeopardy to his domestic program. He went no further than endorsing multinational peacekeeping efforts by the U.N., which were largely ineffective.

However, after sixty-five Bosnian civilians died in a mortar attack on Sarajevo in early February 1994, Clinton pledged to shelter the Bosnian Muslims in "safe havens." In July, the Serbs overwhelmed the safe havens of Srebrenica and Zepa, killing thousands of Muslim civilians and undercutting the credibility of NATO. The next month, Clinton, pressured by Congress, authorized NATO air strikes against Bosnian Serb air defenses.

In October, the administration obtained a cease-fire in Bosnia and in November brought the leaders of Croatia, Serbia, and Bosnia to Dayton, Ohio, for peace talks that resulted in mid-December in an agreement dubbed the "Dayton Accords." Bosnia would be a single nation divided into a Serb republic and a Muslim-Croat federation, both nominally loyal to a central national government. The peace would be ensured by a multinational Bosnian Implementation Force (IFOR). NATO would send 60,000 troops, 20,000 of them American. By now, NATO had been expanded to include

Poland, Hungary, and the Czech Republic, an enlargement that the Russians found threatening. To ease their fears, in a watershed move Clinton included Russian troops in the NATO peacekeeping forces.

Pollsters found that more than half of Americans opposed sending troops to Bosnia, but the Dayton Accords together with the IFOR halted the bloodshed in Bosnia and led to democratic elections in September 1998, arrangements for the return of refugees, and the prosecution for war crimes of certain Serbian leaders.

*Kosovo.* Violence in the former Yugoslavia was not over, however. In Kosovo, a province of Serbia on the Albanian border, ethnic Albanians were agitating for independence. In 1998, Slobodan Milosevic, the head of Serbia, set out to suppress what he called an "internal rebellion," sending in troops that resorted to impaling and decapitating residents and killing pregnant women. Secretary of State Madeleine Albright—the first woman to hold the office—warned, "We are not going to stand by and watch the Serbian authorities do in Kosovo what they can no longer get away with doing in Bosnia."

The Clinton administration, once again reluctant to intervene militarily, tried to bring about a negotiated settlement but failed. In March 1999, after more than a year of continued "ethnic cleansing" in Kosovo, NATO forces supported by some 31,000 American personnel began bombing military and communications targets in Serbia. The bombing ended in June, and, as in Bosnia, the United States, NATO, and the United Nations sent troops to maintain peace in Kosovo.

## CHINA AND THE PACIFIC RIM

In keeping with the economic emphasis of its foreign policy, the Clinton administration sought to create a huge free-trade zone in Asia, obtaining a pledge from the multinational Asia-Pacific Economic Cooperative forum in 1994 to develop a free-trading Pacific Rim by 2010. It also pressured Japan to open its domestic markets to American goods; renegotiating various market-access agreements, it achieved an increase in exports of 85 percent to Japan in sectors that the agreements covered. In February 1994, the Clinton administration lifted the U.S. trade embargo on Vietnam; the next year, it opened liaison offices there and normalized diplomatic relations.

China was rapidly emerging as a colossal market opportunity, but the Clinton administration's economic enthusiasm for China was offset by the Chinese government's capacity for

During his visit to China in 1998, Clinton, here with President Jiang Zemin in Tiananmen Square, failed to gain greater protection for human rights but did sustain the United States' expanding trade relationship with China.

high-handed behavior: China defied U.S. demands to halt sales of missile and nuclear technology to nations such as Pakistan and Libya; it continued to jail dissidents and cracked down on a movement for independence in Tibet; it also pirated American intellectual property, including films and compact discs, a rapidly growing portion of U.S. exports.

Clinton tried to persuade the Chinese government to behave differently by threatening trade sanctions and withholding shipments of high-tech goods such as communication satellites. During a visit to China in 1998, he engaged in a television debate, challenging Premier Jiang Zemin on China's human rights record (Jiang stubbornly defended the crackdown at Tiananmen Square) (see Chapter 32). But Clinton was willing to push the threats and punishments only so far. By the end of the 1990s, China was the United States' fifth-largest trading partner, a market for exports that accounted for approximately 170,000 American jobs and a beneficiary of tariff advantages that saved American consumers about $500 million a year on products such as shoes and clothing.

*North Korea.* North Korea, now the biggest supplier of missiles to Iran, Syria, and Pakistan, posed a nuclear hazard that spread far beyond its borders. In 1993, it withdrew from the nuclear nonproliferation treaty (an agreement banning the spread of nuclear weapons that was signed by more than sixty nations in 1969) and the following year refused to permit the International Atomic Energy Agency to inspect installations where it was suspected of producing plutonium. Clinton tried to establish closer ties to North Korea to dissuade it from pursuing its nuclear program, but in 1998 the country was found to be hollowing out an underground cavern—a possible nuclear test or production site—and that year it also test-fired a medium-range ballistic missile over Japan.

Tensions eased somewhat when in June 2000, just short of the fiftieth anniversary of the outbreak of the Korean War, the leaders of North and South Korea met in Pyongyang and signed an agreement allowing members of long-separated families from each country to visit each other. The Clinton administration subsequently announced that it would end economic sanctions against North Korea. But in negotiations with the United States, the North Koreans insisted on compensation for curtailing their export of missile technologies, a demand that Clinton rejected. At the end of Clinton's presidency, American policymakers remained suspicious of North Korea's intentions and worried that it might be developing nuclear-tipped missiles that could reach U.S. shores.

### PEACEMAKING IN HAITI AND NORTHERN IRELAND

In 1991, a year after Jean-Bertrand Aristide (see Chapter 32) was elected to head the Haitian government, he was ousted by a military junta. The junta imposed a reign of terror, driving thousands into exile, many of them fleeing in small boats across the sea for Florida. (Between 1991 and 1994, the Coast Guard rescued more than 68,000 such "boat people.") The Bush administration, fearing that admitting them would only encourage more to come and overload Florida's tolerance, began turning them back. Clinton, too, turned the boat people away. But in May 1994, responding to protests at home, he initiated economic sanctions against Haiti and obtained a U.N. Security Council resolution allowing a multinational force to oust the Haitian junta. Threatened with military intervention, the junta gave way. A multinational peacekeeping force, to which the United States contributed 21,000 troops, restored Aristide to power and enforced order in the country. The outflow of boat people dropped sharply. In elections at the end of 1995, Aristide was defeated by a former member of his government, René Préval, marking the first democratic transition of power in Haiti's history.

During his first year in office, Clinton made good on a campaign promise to try to bring about a settlement in Northern Ireland, long plagued by a declining economy and sectarian violence that pitted predominantly Catholic nationalists against predominantly Protestant loyalists to Britain. The president was convinced that renewed economic development would diminish the conflicts. In 1994, at a White House–sponsored economic summit in Ireland, Clinton won the British government's assent to an American role in its disarmament talks with the Irish Republican Army (IRA), which had long conducted a terrorist campaign against British rule in Northern Ireland. Chaired by former Senate majority leader George Mitchell, the talks developed so well that both Britain and Ireland invited Mitchell to preside over negotiations, which produced a comprehensive agreement in April 1998. The terms called for the IRA to lay down its arms and for the creation of a popularly elected assembly in Northern Ireland that would replace the British government as the local governing authority. In May, the agreement was ratified by voters in Northern Ireland and the Republic of Ireland. Initially a triumph for Clinton, it was jeopardized during the rest of his administration by the IRA's foot-dragging reluctance to honor the disarmament terms; but in October 2001, its leaders declared that they would begin turning in their weapons.

### FAILURE IN SOMALIA AND RWANDA

In December 1992, Bush had sent 25,000 troops to Somalia, in northeastern Africa, with the humanitarian aim of ending months of famine and anarchy. Soon the threat of starvation was over, and the view of Bush policymakers was that the incoming Clinton administration should accordingly end the mission. Clinton, however, decided to continue the intervention in the interest of nation building, expanding the famine-relief effort and assigning the troops the job of tracking down and arresting local warlords thought to be preying on the population. But on October 3, 1993, eighteen U.S. Army Rangers were ambushed and killed in a raid on a warlord's headquarters. Another twelve American soldiers died in other skirmishes, and by December 1993, responding to strong domestic pressure, Clinton had withdrawn all the American forces.

The failure in Somalia discouraged the United States and other Western nations from intervening in a devastating civil war that in 1994 broke out in Rwanda, a country already ravaged by AIDS. President Juvenal Habyarimana found his power increasingly threatened by dissenters among the Tutsi and even the Hutu, the ethnic group that dominated his government. He chose to mobilize support by turning the Hutu majority against the Tutsi, inciting an ethnic genocide that resulted in the slaughter of an estimated half a million Tutsi.

The Tutsi rebels retaliated, stimulating the flight of a tidal wave of Hutu refugees into neighboring Zaire. In 1998, on a visit to Rwanda, Clinton apologized for the United States' role in slavery, for its role in "crushing the aspirations" of Africa during the Cold War, and for the West's failure to halt the killing of so many Tutsis by Rwandan Hutu extremists.

## THE MIDDLE EAST AND THE SPREAD OF TERROR

As in Ireland, Clinton worked hard to bring the Israelis and Palestinians further along the road to peace. But his efforts were thwarted by outbreaks of violence on both sides, including terrorist attacks. Moreover, Iraq, where Saddam Hussein remained in power, continued to court conflict, and some of the hatreds that suffused the Middle East produced an increasing incidence of terrorism against the United States itself.

*The Palestinian-Israeli Conflict.* For a while during the Clinton administration, the Middle East seemed headed for peace. The Norwegians brokered an agreement—the Oslo Accords—between the Israelis and the Palestinian Liberation Organization (PLO) in which the Israelis gave the Palestinians self-government in the Gaza Strip and parts of the West Bank, while Yasir Arafat, the PLO chief, renounced terrorism and pledged to extend diplomatic recognition to Israel. At the request of the two parties, the agreement was formally signed in Washington, D.C., in September 1993 at a ceremony presided over by President Clinton, who prevailed on Arafat and the Israeli prime minister, Yitzhak Rabin, to shake hands.

In 1994, Clinton assisted Jordan and Israel in resolving their long-standing differences and concluding a formal peace treaty. The United States also persuaded Israel and Syria to agree in writing that they would provide security to civilians on both sides of the Israeli-Lebanese border and that Syria would stop attacks against Israelis by Hezbollah, a terrorist group that was Syria's client in the area. Otherwise, however, the Clinton administration made little headway toward a general peace between Syria and Israel. Moreover, in November 1995, a right-wing Israeli fanatic assassinated Rabin in retaliation for his peacemaking, and Benjamin Netanyahu, a hardline conservative, soon wrested the Israeli leadership from Rabin's party and put the peace process in cold storage.

In 1998, Clinton, determined, brought Netanyahu and Arafat to talks on the Wye River in Maryland and nudged them into an agreement called the "Wye Memorandum." The PLO pledged to rid its charter of language calling for the de-

Prompted by Clinton, Israeli prime minister Yitzhak Rabin (left) shakes hands with PLO leader Yasir Arafat after signing the Oslo Accords at the White House, September 1993.

struction of Israel and to exert tighter control over gun running. Israel committed itself to relinquish 14 percent of the West Bank to the Palestinians and release 750 of them from jail. But extremists on both sides remained adamantly opposed to compromise. In the summer of 2000, sustained violence erupted on the West Bank and the Gaza Strip, pitting Palestinians, often armed only with rocks, against Israeli troops, who often responded with gunfire. Anger on both sides increased as the casualties mounted. Clinton kept trying to mediate; but by the time he left office, the killing, amounting to a new intifada (see Chapter 32), was still going on and the peace process seemed moribund.

*Iraq.* Despite the allied victory in the Gulf War, Iraq remained a persistent source of tension in the Middle East. In the mid-1990s, Iraqi troops occasionally fired missiles against U.S. planes patrolling the no-fly zones that had been established over parts of the country. In retaliation, the allies used missiles to attack intelligence headquarters in Baghdad as well as Iraq's own missile and radar sites, and sent air, ground, and naval forces to the Persian Gulf region.

The allies maintained most of the economic sanctions they had imposed through the United Nations after the Gulf War of 1991, a policy that severely damaged the Iraqi economy.

985

They also insisted that Iraq open its facilities for potentially producing chemical, biological, or nuclear weapons to their inspection. In November 1997, Saddam Hussein, impatient with the sanctions, accused the U.N. inspectors of spying and ordered them to leave, opening a new round of disputes between Iraq on the one side and, on the other, the allies and the United Nations. In the following months, Saddam grew more defiant, trying to use the inspection issue to obtain a lifting of the sanctions. The allies, their suspicions of Saddam's intentions undiminished, refused. In mid-December, the United States and Britain launched sustained air strikes against Iraq's weapons-making program. In 2000, the sanctions remained in place, and Iraq seemed to be rebuilding its damaged military and industrial sites.

*Terrorism.* The sanctions against Iraq and the civilian suffering they generated, the presence of American troops on Saudi Arabian soil during and after the Gulf War, and the United States' support of Israel all angered a number of Muslims in the Middle East. They infuriated Osama bin Laden, a rich Saudi exile living in Afghanistan. Bin Laden hated the United States enough to finance a network of terror called "Al Qaeda," directed against the country. In February 1993, four

Osama bin Laden, financier and mastermind of the Al Qaeda terrorist network.

Muslim terrorists connected to bin Laden exploded a car bomb in the garage under one of the World Trade Center towers in New York City; although they failed in their ambition to topple the tower into its twin, they succeeding in killing 6 and injuring more than 1,000 people. In 1996, terrorists drove a truck bomb into an American army barracks in Saudi Arabia itself, killing 19 U.S. military service people. And in 1998, several other suicide truck bombers blew up an American embassy in Tanzania, killing 11, and another in Kenya, killing 213 Kenyan citizens and injuring thousands of civilians.

A few hours after the attacks in 1998, Clinton declared, "We will use all the means at our disposal to bring those responsible to justice, no matter what or how long it takes." In an operation code-named "Infinite Reach," U.S. planes attacked two targets believed to be associated with bin Laden—a pharmaceuticals plant in Sudan alleged to be a source of biochemical weapons, and a temporary base camp in Afghanistan labeled by Clinton "one of the most active terrorist bases in the world." (The owner of the plant denied that he had anything to do with bin Laden, and reporters visiting the site saw no evidence that he did.) During the trial of the organizers of the Africa bombings, testimony indicated that bin Laden and Al Qaeda had attempted to acquire weapons of mass destruction about five years earlier.

In 1996, the Taliban, a group of extreme Islamic fundamentalists, gained control of Afghanistan and extended their protection to bin Laden as a "guest." In October 1999, the U.N. Security Council, alarmed, resolved to impose limited sanctions against the Taliban in an effort to force them to turn over bin Laden immediately to a country where he could be brought to justice. The Taliban refused, and bin Laden and Al Qaeda grew bolder. A year later, terrorists linked to bin Laden attacked the USS *Cole* while it was anchored in the Yemeni port of Aden, killing seventeen of its crew and injuring forty-two.

Between 1990 and 1999, the FBI's counterterrorism budget more than tripled, and so did the CIA's. Still, in the wake of so many successful assaults, a number of analysts believed that the United States was inadequately on guard against the war of terrorism that was increasingly being waged against it. Some contended that it was only a matter of time before the terrorists would strike on American shores with far greater destructive effect than they had achieved in the 1993 bombing at the World Trade Center.

## THE CLINTON RECORD

So far as a large majority of Americans were concerned, Clinton had attended to their business very well. He had successfully pursued the post–Cold War work of resolving or controlling bitter antagonisms abroad and extending the global reach of democratic capitalism. Wrestling with a Congress that was often hostile, he had managed the economy through a record-breaking prosperity, reformed the welfare system, shored up Social Security, protected the environment, advanced the interests of minority groups and women, and made millions of people feel that he cared about them.

Democrats, savoring Clinton's victory and confident in his accomplishments, felt optimistic about keeping the presidency in the upcoming 2000 election. But a deep-seated ambivalence had emerged about the United States' role in the post–Cold War world; there were doubts among many—revealed, for example, by the lack of support for sending troops to Kosovo—that its military commitments ought to match its global economic engagements. And the glow of good times had been persistently blotched through the 1990s by the dark spots of social and cultural division. The differences had expressed themselves in the partisan divisions that had prevailed through most of Clinton's two terms. Clinton had managed to straddle them to a remarkable degree, but the revelations of shortcomings that led to his impeachment had given character and morality unusually high places on the election agenda. In 2000, despite their defeat on impeachment, Republicans optimistically geared up to battle for control of the White House.

## Election 2000

The Democratic nominee was Vice-President Al Gore, a native of Tennessee and a Harvard graduate, the son of a U.S. senator and himself the holder of national elective office since he won a House seat at age twenty-eight. Gore lacked Clinton's personal magnetism—people thought him wooden—but he was respected for his staunch environmentalism, enthusiasm for technological innovation, and detailed knowledge of public policy.

The Republican nomination went to George W. Bush of Texas, a son of the former president. A graduate of Yale and the Harvard Business School, Bush had compiled a reputation as a heavy drinker, mediocre businessman, and intellectual lightweight. But then, at age forty, he had become a teetotaler and born-again Christian. Affable and self-confident, he won election and then reelection to the Texas governorship, establishing a reputation for bipartisanship in the service of socially and economically conservative policies. He used his family name and contacts to accumulate a formidable presidential war chest. Bush's choice for vice-president, an attempt to offset his relative youth and inexperience in government, especially in foreign affairs, was Richard (Dick) Cheney, a Republican stalwart who had been former president Bush's secretary of defense during the Gulf War.

Gore distanced himself from Clinton the man, whose character the voters so disapproved of, while associating himself in a gingerly fashion with the Clinton economic record, which they so much admired. Gore promised to defend ordinary Americans against high prescription drug prices, inadequate education, and the Republican insistence on using the budget surplus to finance tax reductions that would mainly benefit the wealthy. Bush, on his part, campaigned for "compassionate conservatism"—by which he seemed to mean a government that was lean and limited but willing to care for those in need, especially by enlisting the private sector, including religious groups. He defended the Republican tax-cut proposals on grounds that the money in the surplus ought rightfully to be returned to the American people, and he insisted that the country deserved trustworthy leaders of character, a clear allusion to the scandals of the Clinton White House.

The field included two third-party candidates: Patrick Buchanan on the right and Ralph Nader on the left, both attacking the influence of big money on politics and the North American Free Trade Agreement. While Buchanan seemed no problem to Bush, it appeared that Nader might siphon enough votes from Gore to cost him more than one state. Pollsters predicted that the election would be close.

## DISPUTED OUTCOME

On election evening, November 7, the television networks followed their long-standing practice of calling the election state by state, using exit polls that asked people how they had voted. According to their projections, Bush had won most of the states from the Appalachian Mountains to the Rockies and from the Canadian border to the Gulf of Mexico. Gore had taken most of the West Coast and the Northeast as well as the industrial states in the upper Midwest. By late evening, it was evident that the next president would be the candidate

## The Bush Presidency: Beginnings

In its successive editions on the day after the 2000 presidential elections, the *Orlando Sentinel* expressed the uncertainty of the outcome.

who won Florida. The networks had earlier given the state to Gore, then decided it was too close to call, and finally, at 2:15 A.M., announced that it had gone for Bush.

By Florida law, the closeness of the vote triggered an automatic recount of the entire state, which gave the victory to Bush by 930 votes. Democrats suspected that the process had not been even-handed, since the governor of the state was Jeb Bush, a brother of the Republican candidate. They charged that the balloting had been distorted by irregularities, the most important involving the counting of punch-card ballots. In the punch-card method of voting, people registered their choices by poking out and removing a small indented rectangle (called a "chad"). A machine counted the votes by detecting the holes, but if the chads were not completely removed, the machine would likely not record the vote.

The election was contested for a month in a storm of press conferences, demonstrations, and, most important, lawsuits. In the crucial round of litigation, the Gore campaign, believing its candidate had really won the election, sought manual recounts of the punch cards in selected counties, while the Bush campaign, seeing victory in the status quo, fought to block any recounts. The Florida state supreme court, ruling in favor of the Gore campaign, authorized the manual recounts

and instructed the secretary of state to accept them after the date by which, according to state law, the counties had to submit their voting results. The recounts proceeded, and Bush's margin of victory steadily diminished.

Republicans cried foul, angrily contending that the Gore forces were attempting to steal the election. They said that the Democrats' insistence on manual recounts invited partisan vote counting, since deciding whether, for example, a partially removed chad was evidence of an intent to vote for Bush or Gore would be subjective. The Bush campaign appealed the Florida court decision to the Supreme Court, claiming that it denied their candidate equal protection of the laws.

The Court's decision in *Bush v. Gore*, handed down on December 12, consisted of two rulings. By 7 to 2, the Court halted the recounts ordered by the Florida court because, as Bush's lawyers had argued, they violated equal protection of the laws. But going further, a majority of only 5 to 4 held that no constitutionally acceptable recount procedure could be completed before the electoral college was to meet to cast its votes. The latter ruling effectively gave Florida to Bush, and Gore conceded in a gracious statement on nationwide television.

Many Americans considered the Court's decision blatantly partisan. Commentators quickly pointed out that the majority of five had all been appointed by Republicans and were the Court's most conservative members. They also noted that while the majority usually preferred to leave the states to govern their own affairs, in this case they had usurped Florida's right to manage its election procedures. In a blistering dissent, Justice John Paul Stevens observed: "Although we may never know with complete certainty the identity of the winner of this year's presidential election, the identity of the loser is perfectly clear. It is the nation's confidence in the judge as an impartial guardian of the rule of law."

The outrage was intensified by the fact that Gore had won the popular vote, beating Bush by a margin of 540,000. The election was the first since 1892, when Benjamin Harrison had gained the presidency, in which the loser in the popular vote won in the electoral vote. The outcome spotlighted the undemocratic nature of the electoral college, which awards voters in states with a small population far greater weight in presidential contests than it does voters in states with a large population. It also called attention to the variations in quality of vote-counting machines in different areas within states—and to the fact that the more error-prone machines tended to be used in counties with relatively large numbers of low-income and minority voters.

No matter the dispute: analysis of the nationwide vote revealed that Bush won because the prosperity of the 1990s had not helped Gore as much as good times historically tended to benefit the candidate of the incumbent party. Despite Gore's attempts to distance himself from Clinton, he suffered from his association with the scandals of the administration. He also lost significant support to Ralph Nader, who called for ridding politics of the corruptions of big money and who won 2.7 million votes, including almost 100,000 in Florida. Democrats won enough Senate races—including a victory for Hillary Rodham Clinton in New York—to produce a 50–50 tie in that chamber, and they narrowed the Republican margin of control in the House from nineteen to ten.

## The Bush Presidency: Beginnings

The night the Supreme Court ended the election, Bush promised the nation, "Whether you voted for me or not, I will do my best to serve your interests, and I will work to earn your respect." In his inaugural address, an eloquent reminder of the nation's principles, he adopted a conciliatory tone reminiscent of Jefferson's two centuries earlier, declaring, "America has never been united by blood or birth or soil. We are bound by ideals that move us beyond our backgrounds, lift us above our interests and teach us what it means to be citizens."

Bush appointed to his cabinet several women and African Americans, including Colin Powell as secretary of state, a Hispanic American, and two Asian Americans. But while some of his domestic appointees were moderates—for example, the head of the Environmental Protection Agency—his choices for the most powerful domestic posts were decidedly to the right of center. His head of Health and Human Services was a staunch opponent of abortion and, as governor of Wisconsin, had cut the state's welfare rolls by 90 percent by pushing through the nation's toughest welfare-to-work program. Bush's most controversial appointment was his nominee for attorney general, John Ashcroft, who had just been defeated for reelection to a Senate seat from Missouri. A devout fundamentalist Christian, Ashcroft had sought to criminalize abortion, fought desegregation of the St. Louis schools, and blocked the appointment of a black state jurist to a federal judgeship by grossly misrepresenting his record on the death penalty. Critics wondered how anyone with such right-wing convictions could fairly enforce the nation's laws, including those guaranteeing civil rights and a woman's right to choose. Ashcroft was nevertheless confirmed by his former Senate colleagues, some of whom said he was in fact highly ethical and fair-minded.

### GOVERNING FROM THE RIGHT

Bush's cabinet appointments revealed that, for all his attention to conciliation, he saw no reason in the closeness of the election to back away from his fundamentally conservative domestic agenda. Political circumstances augured well for getting what he wanted. For the first time since 1954, Republicans controlled the presidency, the House, and the Senate (the latter because Vice-President Cheney could vote when it split evenly on a measure). Bush asked Congress to enact a $1.6 trillion tax cut, an education bill that authorized school vouchers, and a measure (called a "faith-based initiative") authorizing religious organizations to give federal welfare assistance. He appointed a commission to look into the safeguarding of Social Security, choosing members who, observers predicted, were likely to recommend at least partial privatization of the system.

The tax cut loomed as Bush's highest priority, especially now that the economy might be heading toward recession. The downturn had begun suddenly at the end of 2000, revealing itself in the collapse of new-economy companies, the dot-coms that had seemed to defy the economic laws of gravity by operating at a loss while their stock prices soared. By early 2001, the NASDAQ stock index had plummeted some 60 percent from its high in March 2000, and the Dow Jones index had fallen about 10 percent. Corporations were cutting back on capital spending and production, consumer confidence was declining, and the unemployment rate was going up.

Bush now contended that the tax cut was needed to stimulate the economy. Democrats and some moderate Republicans objected that it largely favored the wealthy, would put little into the pockets of people who needed money, and would impact the economy too far in the future to avoid recession in the near term. Although the administration met critics of the bill partway, the bulk of the tax relief remained slated for upper-income taxpayers. The bill reduced income tax rates across all brackets, abolished the so-called marriage penalty, and provided for the eventual elimination of the estate tax. On May 26, a heavily Republican but bipartisan majority sent Bush for signature a $1.35 trillion tax cut—the largest since Reagan's in 1981—to be spread over ten years. Analysts estimated that the reduction in tax revenues promised to starve new spending programs far into the future, which made the

A cartoonist's view, in *The Louisville Courier-Journal*, that Bush's tax cut would be good medicine for the economy.

Bush tax cut a means to the Republican end of reducing the size and influence of the federal government.

## DIVISIONS IN CONGRESS

In the areas of energy and environment, Bush quickly reversed a regulatory rule that Clinton had issued to reduce the amount of the poison arsenic allowed where it occurred in drinking water and proposed to roll back Clinton's orders removing millions of acres of national forest from development. Sidestepping energy conservation, he emphasized policies to increase supplies. Bush issued an energy plan that called for a revived commitment to nuclear power, noting that nuclear plants already supplied about one-fifth of the nation's electricity "safely and without pollution," and he asked Congress for authority to open up the Arctic National Wildlife Preserve to drilling for gas and oil.

Bush's aggressive conservatism, however, aroused opposition, both among the public at large and within Congress, especially in the closely divided Senate. His action on arsenic provoked especially widespread criticism. His faith-based initiative was stalled, and his call for opening the wildlife preserve to drilling faced vigorous opposition in the Senate. Congress refused to endorse school vouchers. In December, though, after Bush agreed to leave that provision out, Congress passed—and the president signed—a bill that made schools accountable for higher standards of student achievement and provided federal funds to assist them in reaching that goal.

In May 2001, the prospects for Bush's conservative initiatives dimmed further when a Republican senator from Vermont declared himself an independent and voted to give control of the Senate to the Democrats. But that body remained one of the most closely divided in American history, and conservative Republicans continued to dominate the House. If moderates could block Bush's conservative programs, conservatives could foil moderate or liberal initiatives.

*Human Cloning and Stem-Cell Research.* The divisions in the Congress over social issues formed the background for Bush's policy toward the medically promising new field of human stem-cell research. Such research had been given a huge boost when in 1997 a British biotechnology firm announced that it had successfully cloned a sheep—its scientists named the lamb Dolly—from the udder cells of an adult ewe. Cloning an adult mammal involved the creation of an embryo genetically identical to it, then allowing the embryo to develop to birth in the womb of a female mammal of the same species. Many scientists had long believed such a feat technically impossible. Dolly's birth thus constituted a scientific milestone along the road of genetic engineering. In particular, it implied that the technology that produced her might be used to generate human embryonic clones for research and possibly for the creation of cloned human beings.

Using the technology to clone people—what came to be called "reproductive cloning"—was condemned by clerics, ethicists, and most scientists, including biotechnologists; but using it for research—this was dubbed "therapeutic cloning"—found strong support among biologists, groups eager for cures of particular diseases, the biotechnology industry, and many laypeople. The biologists were particularly concerned to use cloning to obtain human stem cells—that is, the nonspecialized cells present in very young embryos that possess the capacity to differentiate into the numerous specialized cells that constitute the developed functioning body. Once the cells were isolated, the embryos could be destroyed and the stem-cell lines could be studied in the laboratory. Such research promised to yield both greater understanding of human development and, perhaps, remedies for maladies such as Alzheimer's disease, damage to limbs and organs, and spinal cord injuries that cause paralysis.

On the advice of the government's National Bioethics Advisory Commission, President Clinton submitted a bill to Congress in 1997 that would ban human reproductive cloning but allow federal funds to be used for research in therapeutic human cloning so long as the embryos thus created were destroyed after at the most two weeks. Right-to-life groups had long successfully blocked federal support of research with human embryos; now they attacked Clinton's measure, holding that it was morally wrong to create human life only to destroy it. Congressional Republicans, refusing to support the proposal, introduced their own bill to ban all human cloning, not only for reproductive but even for therapeutic purposes. However, several key Senate Republicans, some of whose family members suffered from diseases that might ultimately be treatable as a result of stem-cell research, adamantly opposed a blanket ban on human cloning.

As a result, when President George Bush entered office, neither human reproductive nor therapeutic cloning had been banned, but neither had federal financial support for it been authorized. Many foreign countries had prohibited reproductive human cloning, but a number permitted research in therapeutic human cloning. In the United States, such research was also being vigorously pursued in the private sector, largely by several biotechnology companies, but their expenditures paled in comparison with the resources the federal government might invest in this research. The biomedical and biotechnology communities increasingly warned that the inability of the National Institutes of Health (NIH) to support research in human therapeutic cloning was threatening the globally competitive position of the United States in science and medicine.

On August 9, 2001, in the first televised address of his presidency, President Bush announced a resolution of the impasse in the form of an executive order. He authorized the NIH to support human stem-cell research that used any of the sixty-four human stem-cell lines that had already been obtained in private laboratories; but he also prohibited the NIH from funding stem-cell research that involved the creation of new human embryonic clones. Exquisitely crafted to satisfy the religious right and biomedical scientists and advocates, the order was nevertheless widely criticized—by Bush's right-to-life constituency because it acknowledged the sixty-four cell lines as legitimate subjects of federally funded research; by the biomedical science community because it limited such research to only those cell lines; and by patients' advocates because the limitations seemed certain to retard the development of therapies and cures for injury and disease.

## AMERICA FIRST

Bush's domestic conservatism was complemented by what many observers saw as a tendency to reduce the United States' engagement in the world, to adopt a go-it-alone posture toward the nation's friends and an antagonizing one toward others. On taking office, Bush treated the Russians coldly, delaying a meeting with their president, Vladimir V. Putin, expelling their diplomats for spying, and charging them with selling dangerous military technology to the Middle East. The administration scrapped an eight-year effort to achieve stronger international controls over chemical and biological weapons on grounds that the proposed agreement jeopardized the privacy of pharmaceutical laboratories and the secrecy of government programs. Bush also froze negotiations with North Korea that Clinton, partly to discourage that nation's development of a nuclear arsenal, had initiated.

Most important, Bush insisted that the United States would pursue the development of a National Missile Defense (NMD) even if it jeopardized relations with Russia. And he seemed to repudiate American participation in the international effort to combat global warming.

*National Missile Defense.* Since the end of the Cold War and the scrapping of Reagan's Strategic Defense Initiative, enthusiasts of missile defense had been calling for protection of the country against the relatively small number of warheads that might be launched either by accident or by design from a rogue state like North Korea or Iraq. On May 1, 2001, Bush announced that the United States intended to develop and deploy a National Missile Defense (NMD). The initiative meant scrapping the Anti-Ballistic Missile Defense (ABM) Treaty that the United States had concluded with the Soviet Union in 1972. It prompted a negative reaction from Putin, dissent from the nation's European allies, and vigorous criticism at home, where some observers assailed the president for withdrawing support from an agreement that had helped keep the world from nuclear war for thirty years.

In mid-December, Bush, rejecting compromise, formally notified Russia that the United States would withdraw from the ABM Treaty so that it could proceed with the development of the NMD. Putin called the withdrawal a "mistake" but said little else, an indication that, like Gorbachev before him, he expected that the Russian nuclear arsenal could likely overwhelm an NMD for at least the next quarter century.

*Global Warming.* In March 2001, Bush announced that the United States would not abide by the 1997 Kyoto Protocol to reduce the emission of greenhouse gases that cause global warming. An extension of the accord on climate that the first President Bush had signed at Rio de Janeiro in 1992, the

A demonstration against the Bush administration's environmental policies, in Washington, D.C., on April 30, 2001.

Kyoto agreement committed its signatories, including the United States, to reduce their greenhouse gas output to 5.2 percent below the level of 1990 within fifteen years. Bush withdrew from the protocol partly because it did not require reductions by China and India, developing nations that were major emitters of greenhouse gases. But his most important objection rested on his unwillingness to limit carbon dioxide emission when the U.S. economy was slowing. Bush explained to the chancellor of Germany, who was visiting the White House, "We will not do anything that harms our economy, because first things first are the people who live in America." Bush's decision infuriated European leaders. The United States was in effect asserting that it had the right to pervert the atmosphere covering every other nation: since the United States emitted fully one-quarter of the world's greenhouse gases, its withdrawal from the Kyoto agreement jeopardized the prospects of significantly reducing their presence in the atmosphere.

Before departing on a trip to Europe in June, Bush tried to soften the impression of his seeming indifference to the rest of the world by publicly acknowledging that temperatures were in fact rising because of human activities that involve the burning of fossil fuels (see Chapter 33). But while he insisted that the United States remained committed to join with other nations under the 1992 accord to reduce the threat of global warming, he did little more than appoint a committee to review the issue. In late July, 178 nations arrived at a final agreement for putting the Kyoto accords into effect. One European official, alluding to the nonparticipation of the United States, remarked, "I prefer an imperfect agreement that is living than a perfect agreement that doesn't exist."

### SUMMER 2001

Dissatisfaction with what many observers considered Bush's neoisolationism was widespread, matching in magnitude the dissent from his aggressive domestic conservatism. The United States remained in a sense two nations: the one secular, multiracial, and supportive of widening civil liberties; the other religious, predominantly white, and discontented with the consequences of broad social freedom. Unlike Clinton, Bush made few attempts—his policy on stem-cell-research was one of the few exceptions—to straddle the divide. Instead, he actively pressed the agenda of the social and economic right. Polls showed that two out of three Americans thought he cared more about protecting large corporate interests than about protecting ordinary working people. How effectively he could continue to govern from the right was open to question in the summer of 2001. But then, on September 11, terrorists struck New York City and Washington, D.C., shocking the world and blasting the United States, including its politics and government, into a new era.

## Suggested Reading

James MacGregor Burns and Georgia J. Sorenson, *Dead Center: Clinton-Gore Leadership and the Perils of Moderation* (1999)

Bill Clinton, *My Life* (2004)

Michael Lewis, *The New New Thing: A Silicon Valley Story* (2000)

Richard A. Posner, *An Affair of State: The Investigation, Impeachment, and Trial of President Clinton* (1999)

Stephen Thernstrom and Abigail Thernstrom, *America in Black and White: One Nation, Indivisible, Race in Modern America* (1997)

*Washington Post* political staff, *Deadlock: The Inside Story of America's Closest Election* (2001)

# Chapter Review

## Summary QUESTIONS

- What were Clinton's achievements in his domestic policy?
- In what ways were the 1990s prosperous and in what ways were they not?
- What were the main issues in American foreign policy during the 1990s?
- What role did the courts play in determining the outcome of the 2000 presidential election?
- What was conservative about Bush's domestic policy?

## Chronology

| | |
|---|---|
| **February 1993** | 1st attack on the World Trade Center in New York City. |
| **November 1993** | The North American Free Trade Agreement (NAFTA). |
| **April 1995** | Truck bomb kills 168 in federal building at Oklahoma City. |
| **November 1995** | Yitzhak Rabin assasinated. |
| **December 19, 1998** | House votes to impeach President Clinton. |
| **December 12, 2000** | In *Bush v. Gore*, the Supreme Court's ruling gave the state of Florida and therefore the 2000 election to George W. Bush. |
| **2001** | The United States withdraws from the Anti-Ballistic Missile Treaty of 1972. |
| **September 11, 2001** | Terrorists hijack four planes and attack the World Trade Center in New York City and the Pentagon in Washington, D.C. |

## Key Terms

Globalization (p. 973)

North American Free Trade Agreement (NAFTA) (p. 974)

"Don't ask, don't tell" (p. 975)

Contract with America (p. 976)

Dayton Accords (p. 982)

Human stem cells (p. 990)

National Missile Defense (p. 991)

Kyoto Protocol (p. 991)

# AT WAR AGAINST TERROR:

## SINCE 2001

Hurricane Katrina and the flooding it caused brought devastation to New Orleans and the Gulf Coast, and revealed the deep racial and economic fissures still disfiguring American society. Photography by James Nielsen, September 1, 2005.

QUESTIONS

- **What was the initial response of the U.S. to the attacks of September 11, 2001?**

- **What were the aims of the war in Iraq and the strategies employed to attain them?**

- **What were the other major foreign policy initiatives of the Bush administration?**

- **What tensions arose between the need for security and the preservation of civil liberties and human rights?**

- **What were the main social and economic issues in the Bush years?**

On Tuesday, September 11, 2001, America's world was suddenly and dramatically transformed. Within the space of an hour and a half that morning, two passenger airliners took off from Logan Airport in Boston, and two others took off from Newark Airport in New Jersey and Dulles Airport in Washington, D.C. All four, bound for California, were fully loaded with fuel. At some point not long after the planes were airborne, each was commandeered by four or five hijackers armed with box cutters and knives. "We have some planes," one of the hijackers was heard to say, mistakenly broadcasting a message he intended for the passengers. "Just stay quiet and you'll be OK. We are returning to the airport."

At 8:45 A.M., one of the planes from Boston crashed into the north tower of the 110-story World Trade Center in lower Manhattan, tearing a huge hole in the building and setting it ablaze. Eighteen minutes later, the second plane out of Boston struck the south tower and exploded. At 9:43, the plane from Dulles crashed into the Pentagon. Shortly after 10:00, the south tower of the World Trade Center, its reinforced concrete supports severely weakened by the intense heat of the jet-fuel fire, collapsed, showering a torrent of debris into the streets below. Just before 10:30, the north tower followed its twin into the dust, releasing a tremendous cloud of debris and smoke and severely damaging a nearby 47-story building—later in the day it, too, fell—and setting others in the area on fire. In Washington, in the meantime, the portion of the Pentagon that had been hit also collapsed.

Passengers on the fourth flight, in touch with relatives via cell phones, learned about the attacks on the Trade Center and the Pentagon; they concluded that their plane was being flown toward a target as well. Some decided to storm the cockpit, with the result that the plane crashed in a field southeast of Pittsburgh rather than into a building. (It was, in fact, headed toward the nation's capital.) All forty-four people on board were killed.

Within less than an hour of the first crash at the World Trade Center, the Federal Aviation Administration halted all flights at American airports for the first time in the nation's history and diverted to Canada all transatlantic aircraft bound for the United States. President Bush was in Florida, but the White House was evacuated and so were all other federal office buildings in the capital. Secret Service agents armed with automatic rifles were deployed opposite the White House in Lafayette Park. In New York, the stock exchanges and all state government offices were closed.

At a news conference in the mid-afternoon, New York's mayor, Rudolph Giuliani, when asked about the number killed, said, "I don't think we want to speculate about that—more than any of us can bear." That evening, the city reported that hundreds of its police officers and firefighters on the scene were dead or missing. In the weeks that followed, estimates of the deaths at the World Trade Center ran as high as 6,000; they were later reduced to 3,000. Some 200 people died in the crash at the Pentagon.

Less than an hour after the World Trade Center towers were hit, President Bush said that the country had suffered an "apparent terrorist attack." Later in the day, having been flown to an air force base in Louisiana for his protection, he assured the country that appropriate steps were being taken to protect American security, including the placement of the

The nation's shock and grief over the September 11th attacks are evident in this woman's face as she surveys the flowers, flags, and notices of the missing posted on a New York sidewalk.

U.S. military on high alert. By late afternoon, investigations had identified nineteen Middle Eastern men as the hijackers, and as the likely sponsor of the attack Osama bin Laden, who was still living in Afghanistan and running a network of terrorist training camps under the protection of the Taliban, the radical Islamic group that controlled the country (see Chapter 34). That evening, Bush addressed the nation from the White House, declaring that "thousands of lives were suddenly ended by evil" and promising to hunt down the responsible parties.

Foreigners had not attacked the mainland United States since the War of 1812. Americans watched the television broadcasts of September 11—the planes veering into the Trade Center towers, the towers collapsing—with disbelief. "This is impossible," an observer remarked, capturing the widespread reaction. Nothing in the nation's experience had prepared it for these events, particularly the dramatic demonstration that the marvelous technologies of contemporary civilization, from jet aircraft to the Internet, could be used to breach its defenses.

A commentator suggested that between the end of the Cold War and September 11, the United States had been on "a holiday from history"—a decade-long romp free of cares about the economy at home and threats from abroad. But now the holiday was over, suddenly ended by an attack that shattered the country's long-standing sense of domestic security.

## Combatting Terror

Following September 11, a wave of sympathy from abroad washed over the United States. The World Trade Center towers were a nerve center of the globalizing economy, and many nations had a stake in what they represented—both symbolically and in workaday practice. The tower victims included people from more than eighty nations, a feature of the destruction that was revealed by the names of lost spouses, parents, and children. Hundreds of posterboards appeared in city streets and parks pleading for information about people with names such as Schwartzstein, Henrique and Calderon, Kikuchihara and Tsoy, Cassino, Staub, and Egan. September 11 heightened every nation's sense of vulnerability to terrorist attack. The next day, the French newspaper *Le Monde* ran the headline "Nous sommes toutes les Américaines" (We are all Americans).

At home, September 11 prompted an outpouring of patriotism rarely seen since Pearl Harbor. American flags appeared in shop windows and on homes, buildings, cars and trucks, overpasses, and bridges. Millions of Americans pinned red, white, and blue streamers on their jackets. Across the country, people attended services for the victims, sent money to assist their families, and gave blood for the survivors. Commentators everywhere extolled the heroism of the firefighters and police who died in the line of duty at the World Trade Center. Thousands flocked to Ground Zero, the site where the World Trade Center's twin towers had stood, now hallowed ground, solemnly peering at the smoldering ruins and the workmen removing the debris. Many posted prayers and poems as well as notices of the missing on the protective chain-link fences at the site and on any available wall space around the city.

On one of the sheets of paper tacked up in New York's Grand Central Station, an anonymous poet expressed a sentiment that was widely held:

*Six thousand fallen heroes . . .*
*The six thousand angels, their trumpets blaring*
*Are calling us to arms,*
*Waking us up from our selfish slumber*
*To the truth of our lives, the evil in the world . . .*
*We must stop, turn, stand up together as one,*
*Arm in arm, pillars of strength.*

In the wake of September 11, Americans were united in resolve to respond to the threat of terrorism in whatever ways might be required—including military action.

## BUSH TAKES CHARGE

On Friday September 14, three days after the attacks, Bush visited Ground Zero, where rescue crews were frantically digging through the rubble in the hope of finding survivors. As the workers chanted "USA, USA," some people in the crowd shouted to Bush that they could not hear him. "I can hear you," he responded, stimulating roars from the crowd. "The rest of the world hears you. And the people who knocked these buildings down will hear all of us soon."

That same Friday, the Senate unanimously and the House by a margin of 420 to 1 voted to authorize the use of force against those responsible for the terrorist attacks, and Congress enacted a $40 billion emergency spending bill to combat terrorism and assist the recovery efforts in New York and Washington. Bush ordered the Defense Department to mobilize up to 50,000 reservists for "homeland defense." During the following two weeks, he issued an executive order authorizing the government to freeze whatever funds terrorists might have access to in the United States. He also visited

mosques, met with Muslim leaders, and strongly condemned reactionary violence and discrimination against Muslims. Islam was a religion of love, not hate, he said.

On the evening of September 20, in a somber address to a joint session of Congress, Bush announced the start of a "War on Terror." Certain that Osama bin Laden was responsible for the crimes of September 11, he demanded that the Taliban turn bin Laden and all the leaders of the Al Qaeda terrorist network over to the appropriate authorities and shut down all the terrorist training camps in the country. The Clinton administration had warned the Taliban that they would be held directly responsible for any attacks on Americans by bin Laden's terrorists so long as the Taliban provided them sanctuary. Now Bush declared, "These demands are not open to negotiation or discussion," warning that if the Taliban did not hand over the terrorists, they would "share in their fate." Bush added that the United States' humanitarian aid to the people of Afghanistan, a severely impoverished country, would increase. He stressed that America's war was with the terrorists, not with Muslims or Islam, whose texts and teachings did not

President Bush speaks to the crowd of firefighters, construction workers, and rescue crews at Ground Zero, three days after the attacks of September 11th.

sanction terror. But he pledged that the war would extend to terrorists everywhere and to the nations that harbored them; indeed, that it would "not end until every terrorist group of global reach has been found, stopped, and defeated."

The president announced that in a move to thwart terrorism at home, he was naming Pennsylvania governor Tom Ridge to the newly established post of director of homeland security. The government warned its citizens that terrorist attacks might occur again, a prediction that seemed to come true early in October, when it was reported that an employee at a tabloid newspaper in Florida had died of anthrax and that one of his co-workers had been infected with the deadly microbe. During the next several weeks, anthrax cropped up elsewhere, notably in the form of a white powder that arrived in an envelope mailed to the office of Tom Daschle of North Dakota, the Senate majority leader. An anthrax scare swept the country, prompting people to buy out local stocks of Cipro, the principal antibiotic against it. No one knew who was responsible for sending the anthrax, but President Bush said he would not be surprised if it was Osama bin Laden.

On October 26, in a climate of apprehension, Congress passed the USA Patriot Act, an administration measure that expanded the power of law enforcement agencies to pursue suspected terrorists. Without asking Congress, Attorney General John Ashcroft authorized eavesdropping on communications between detained suspects and their lawyers. And he announced that the government would try suspected terrorists who were not citizens in secret military tribunals, where the legal safeguards for fair proceedings and the standards for conviction were much weaker than in open civilian courts. The secrecy meant that a defendant could be charged, tried, and put to death without public knowledge. Many Americans across the political spectrum were outraged when Ashcroft, called to the Senate to explain these curtailments of civil liberties, admonished the critics: "Your tactics only aid terrorists, for they erode our national unity and diminish our resolve. They give ammunition to America's enemies and pause to America's friends."

Polls showed strong support for the administration's measures against terrorism. And Bush won high praise for the caution and deliberativeness with which he was handling the crisis, including his strong admonitions against intolerance toward Muslims. But some observers worried that the War on Terror would be endless, and they wondered just how the president would deal with the many nations that provided terrorists safe harbor. They were also apprehensive that war against terrorists abroad would lead to the deaths of many innocent people and that the search for them at home would threaten civil liberties.

## ACTION IN AFGHANISTAN

The overwhelming majority of Americans supported military intervention if the Taliban refused to comply with Bush's demands for dealing with terrorists camped within their borders. The Pakistanis tried to get them to comply but failed. Like his father in the period before the Gulf War, Bush built a coalition of support for action against the Taliban that included the nations of the former Soviet Union, particularly those bordering on Afghanistan, whose populations also included many Muslims, and Pakistan, which was predominantly Muslim. Hitherto tolerant of the Taliban and at loggerheads with the United States over its nuclear development program, Pakistan agreed to afford the United States assistance such as landing rights and intelligence; the United States soon lifted the economic sanctions it had imposed against Pakistan in 1998 in response to its nuclear tests and provided a generous package of economic aid.

The United Nations Security Council unanimously resolved to mount wide-ranging measures against terrorism, focusing especially on the financial support terrorists needed to carry out their acts. A key element in the work of persuasion was the increasingly convincing evidence that the United States compiled demonstrating Osama bin Laden's complicity in the September 11 attacks. The evidence was presented to the nation's European allies, and on October 4 Prime Minister Tony Blair of Britain detailed its contents in an address to Parliament that was broadcast to the world.

On October 7, the United States launched military operations against the Taliban. Since long before September 11, the U.S. armed forces had been undergoing a major transformation to equip themselves for the tasks they would face in the post–Cold War world. Designed to deal less with superpowers and more with enemies like the regime in Afghanistan, the changes at their core involved a departure from the deployment of overwhelming forces on the ground in favor of the combined use of small numbers of specially trained forces, air power, and high-technology precision weapons. The new technologies included robot aircraft that could perform high-risk surveillance and attack without putting American lives at risk, and instant distribution by e-mail of daily air orders that hitherto, in print form, were the size of telephone books that had to be delivered by plane to aircraft carriers. Bush's defense secretary, Donald Rumsfeld, was a strong advocate of the innovations in strategy and technology, and he saw Afghanistan as a theater for testing them.

In keeping with the new doctrine, the assault in Afghanistan began with air strikes against Al Qaeda terrorist camps and Taliban military installations, using improved versions of the laser-guided bombing employed in the Gulf War. The ultimate aim was to force the Taliban out of power, replace them with a broadly representative government, capture or kill bin Laden, and destroy the Al Qaeda terrorist network and its facilities. Most of the ground forces were supplied by the Northern Alliance, a collection of anti-Taliban factions, tribesmen, and warlords. They were soon joined by small contingents of American special forces trained to operate in Afghanistan's forbidding deserts and mountains, which in the south and east included warrens of caves where bin Laden and his forces were believed to be based.

The war progressed rapidly, with the Taliban abandoning Kabul, the capital city, in late November, leaving their southern stronghold of Kandahar several weeks later, then fleeing into the mountains. The progress was aided by the support of many Afghans, joyful at being released from the oppressive Taliban rule—from, for example, their prohibitions against music, games, television, and radios; their insistence that men not shave; and their consignment of women to virtual imprisonment in their homes. By January 2002, the Taliban were virtually defeated and an anti-Taliban Interim Authority was in place. In January 2004, the Authority's *loya jirga* (grand assembly) agreed on a constitution for the country.

Bin Laden remained at large, however—perhaps, some thought, somewhere in the caves in the rugged region on the Afghanistan-Pakistan border. And while the military victory had secured the cities, it had not brought the armed rural warlords under control or entirely subdued the Taliban, several thousand of whom continued to wage war in the rural areas of Afghanistan's south and east. Critics faulted the Rumsfeld doctrine: while it was effective in winning a war against a regime like the Taliban's, it seemed inadequate for securing the peace in a country that continued to be rife with fractious armed militias. While it reduced the number of American troops used to fight the war on the ground, it allocated inadequate personnel for the task of nation-building after the formal war had ended. And the United States was left largely alone for the postwar task in Afghanistan, with most of its allies in the war providing few troops and little financial aid.

The run-up to the first free elections in Afghanistan was marked by intimidating violence. Nevertheless, defying the Taliban's death threats, roughly 8 million of 10 million eligible Afghans registered to vote and made a success of the national elections in October 2004.

### THE BUSH DOCTRINE

The Bush administration recognized that September 11 had catapulted the United States into a new era and that the nation's long-term defense against terrorism required innovation in policy for national security. If during the Cold War arms and alliances had discouraged aggression by nation states, such means would not deter terrorists. They were not organized into states, and the threat of retaliation was useless against people willing to commit suicide to achieve their ends. Indeed, September 11 had shown that terrorists could wreak havoc with only a small expenditure of their own lives and money. The war in Afghanistan satisfied the need for an immediate response to bin Laden and his protectors, but it also was a tacit first step toward the development of the new policy, which the administration forged through 2002.

Eventually called the Bush Doctrine, the policy was grounded in the president's conviction that, as he put it, "the war on terror will not be won on the defensive," adding, "We must take the battle to the enemy, disrupt his plans, and confront the worst threats before they emerge." Thus the United States would not wait to be further attacked before taking action. Instead, it would seek out and destroy terrorists as well as the regimes that gave them haven or that might provide them with weapons of mass destruction.

Bush had displayed a propensity for unilateralism in his scrapping of the treaties on missile defense and global warming (see Chapter 34). The Bush Doctrine elevated unilateralism into a formal tenet of policy. While the United States would pursue international support for its actions, the president emphasized that the nation would "not hesitate to act alone, if necessary, to exercise our right of self-defense by acting preemptively against . . . terrorists." Bush contended that terrorism was fueled by frustration at the lack of democratic institutions in societies, many of them in the Islamic world. The United States thus aimed, the president said, to "extend the peace by encouraging free and open societies on every continent," including democratic institutions, free markets, and rights for women. And in service of all these ends, it had to possess military "strengths beyond challenge."

The Bush Doctrine mixed a number of themes in the history of American foreign policy. While the commitments to preemption and unilateralism constituted a sharp departure from the doctrines that had prevailed during World War II and the Cold War, they had precedents in nineteenth-century policy—for example, the wars against Mexico and Native Americans, and the promulgation of the Monroe Doctrine. The declarations for democracy called to mind Woodrow Wilson's evangelism for a world "safe for democracy." However, even though the Bush Doctrine's elements had antecedents, it represented a major innovation in policy for national security, one that in the name of defending civilization claimed the right to violate the sovereignty of states that were not themselves committing armed aggression but that could be charged with aiding and abetting terrorists.

## War in Iraq

In his State of the Union address in January 2002, Bush suggested that three nations—Iraq, Iran, and North Korea—were candidates for action under the Bush Doctrine. He declared: "States like these, and their terrorist allies, constitute an axis of evil, arming to threaten the peace of the world. By seeking weapons of mass destruction, these regimes pose a grave and growing danger. All nations should know: America will do what is necessary to ensure our nation's security. . . . I will not wait on events while dangers gather."

### A DISPUTED CASE FOR WAR

Iran and North Korea were attempting to develop nuclear weapons, but Iraq under Sadaam Hussein loomed most ominously in the administration's field of vision. Sadaam's brutal dictatorial regime was responsible for the deaths or imprisonment of tens of thousands of Iraqis. During the 1990s, Iraq's air defenses had fired on or threatened virtually every surveillance mission in the no-fly zone established following the Gulf War. Iraq had also offered cash rewards of $25,000 to the families of Palestinians who carried out suicide bombing attacks in Israel. In the late 1980s, it had possessed chemical and biological weapons and was interested in developing nuclear ones, too.

During the 1990s, weapons inspectors from the United Nations had been operating in Iraq to ensure that any stocks of such weapons that may have survived the Gulf War were destroyed and that no more were produced. In December 1998, they left the country, forced out by Sadaam and frustrated by his refusal to cooperate. That turn of events combined with subsequent intelligence gathering suggested to a number of policymakers that Sadaam was reviving his program for weapons of mass destruction. In 1998, the Clinton administration adopted a policy for Iraq of achieving the ouster of Sadaam. From the time Bush took office, a faction in his administration lobbied persistently for bringing about that change in regime soon by the use of American military force.

In October 2002, the CIA reported that Sadaam's arsenal definitely included chemical and biological weapons and that while it lacked nuclear weapons, it would likely include them, too, within five to seven years. In a televised speech on October 7, the president warned the nation that Iraq had produced 30,000 liters of anthrax and that it "gathers the most serious dangers of our age in one place." He stated: "Facing clear evidence of peril, we cannot wait for the final proof, the smoking gun, that could come in the form of a mushroom cloud". A few days later, the House and Senate voted by decisive majorities to authorize the president to use American armed forces in Iraq "as he deems to be necessary and appropriate." Many Americans empathized with the sentiments expressed in "Courtesy of the Red, White and Blue (The Angry American)," the country superstar Toby Keith's popular song with a clipped martial beat that warned all enemies: "And you'll be sorry that you messed with / The U.S. of A. / 'Cause we'll put a boot in your ass / It's the American way."

Many commentators and members of Congress had all the while been contending that any military intervention in Iraq should be multilateral and centered in the United Nations. Since the Gulf War, the U.N. had passed numerous resolutions insisting that Iraq destroy its weapons of mass destruction and implying that Iraq would face renewed military action if it did not, but the U.N. had done little to cow Sadaam other than to impose economic sanctions. In early November, under pressure from Bush, it demanded that Iraq report fully on its weapons programs and readmit the weapons inspectors. Sadaam allowed the inspectors to return, but they were hampered by lack of time, adequate staff, and clear information from the Iraqi government.

Bush sought support from the U.N. for war against Iraq, but while Britain sided strongly with him, France and Germany vigorously opposed military action and blocked the U.N. from sanctioning it. The German chancellor characterized Bush's drive to oust Sadaam as a military "adventure" that would undermine the war on international terrorism, destabilize the Middle East, and subject the West to retaliation by Arab and Islamic nations. At the end of January 2003, the chief U.N. arms inspector said that Sadaam had not yet genuinely accepted disarmament. Even so, the French and Germans held that the inspectors should be given more time, all that they needed to complete their job.

Bush, however, was running out of patience, and in his State of the Union address on January 27, 2003, he enlarged the case for war by strongly linking Sadaam to terrorism. According to British intelligence, Sadaam had "recently sought significant quantities of uranium from Africa." Multiple sources of evidence "reveal that Saddam Hussein aids and protects terrorists, including members of Al Qaeda," he said, seeming to imply that Iraq had been connected to the attacks of September 11. The president went on to warn that "secretly, and without fingerprints, he could provide one of his hidden weapons to terrorists, or help them develop their own."

To many Americans, Bush's move toward war with Iraq seemed highly questionable. The CIA was skeptical that Sadaam was trying to obtain uranium from Africa. If he was suspected of possessing weapons of mass destruction, why not let the inspectors continue their work? And if they failed, could he not be contained as other threatening nation states had been deterred from aggression? The evidence that he was aiding and abetting terrorists, especially Al Qaeda, was murky at best, and there was no credible evidence that he had had anything to do with September 11. (When asked on a television news program in the fall of 2001 whether Iraq was involved in the attacks, Vice President Cheney had said no.) To many critics, the Bush Doctrine seemed ill-conceived. Despite the administration's claims, Sadaam did not appear to pose an imminent threat to the Middle East or the United States. By claiming the right to wage preemptive unilateral war against him, the administration would encourage other nations—for example, Russia or Pakistan—to take similar action against troublesome countries on their borders.

Dissent had been building against Bush's Iraq policy both in the United States and abroad. Now, in mid-February, it burst into huge protest demonstrations, the largest since the Vietnam War, that drew several hundred thousand people in New York City, perhaps more in London, and an estimated 100 million people in cities around the globe. Speakers denounced Bush's rush to war and claimed that it had more to do with Iraq's oil than with dangerous weapons and tyranny.

Bush's policies had transformed perceptions of the United States in Europe from embattled victim to arrogant aggressor, and polls in Britain were split over whether the greater danger to peace was Sadaam Hussein or Bush himself.

Bush's seeming propensity for confrontation bothered many Americans, too, including several senior congressional Republicans. Senator Chuck Hagel, of Nebraska, complained that the administration was "seen as bullying people," adding, "You can't do that to democracies. You can't do that to partners and allies. It just isn't going to work."

Bush supplied his critics with plenty of ammunition, declaring at one point, for example, "I don't believe there's many shades of gray in this war. You're either with us or against us. You're either evil, or you're good." His division of the world into black and white gave many observers pause about the wisdom of his foreign policy. A respected political columnist wrote in *Time* magazine that "the world might have more confidence in the judgment of this President if he weren't always bathed in the blinding glare of his own certainty."

## "MISSION ACCOMPLISHED"

Bush, unperturbed, remained fixed on the goal of getting rid of Sadaam's dangerous regime, liberating the Iraqi people, ensuring the flow of Iraqi oil, and establishing a democracy in Iraq that would, by a process of contagion, topple reactionary governments elsewhere in the region. In the absence of U.N. support, the administration constructed what Bush called a "Coalition of the Willing," an alliance of some eighteen countries, including Spain, Italy, Slovakia, the Czech Republic, Japan, and South Korea. Key powers in the Middle East— Pakistan, Saudi Arabia, and Egypt—however, all declined to join the coalition, and so did Turkey, which refused the United States the use of its territory to attack Iraq from the north. Moreover, the members of the coalition provided only about one out of six of the troops for the war. The bulk of the armed forces were Americans.

On March 19, 2003, the United States bombed selected government targets in Baghdad, trying, unsuccessfully, to kill Sadaam, and the next day the coalition forces attacked, initiating the full-scale "Operation Iraqi Freedom." During the Gulf War, the alliance against Iraq had comprised some 500,000 troops. Now, in keeping with the new war doctrine, the coalition deployed only some 150,00 troops, 130,000 of them American men and women, relying on high-technology air power during the first few days of the conflict to "shock and awe"

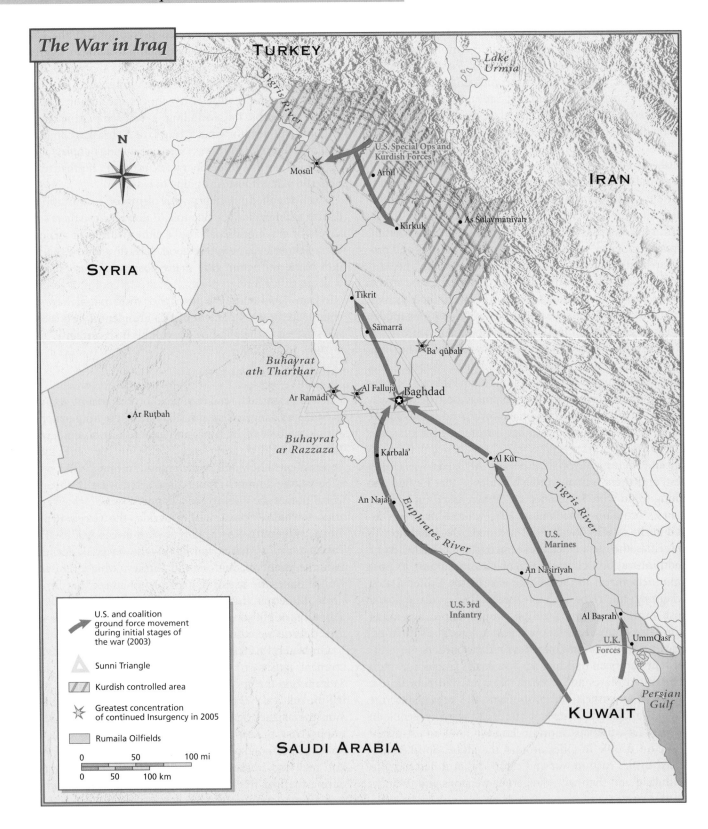

### The War in Iraq

TURKEY

*Lake Urmia*

SYRIA

IRAN

*Tigris River*

Mosul •

U.S. Special Ops and
Kurdish Forces

Arbil •

Kirkuk •

As Sulaymānīyah •

Tikrit •

Sāmarrā •

Ba' qūbah •

*Buhayrat ath Tharthar*

Al Fallujā •

• Baghdad

Ar Ramādī •

• Ar Ruṭbah

*Buhayrat ar Razzaza*

Karbalā' •

Al Kūt •

An Najaf •

*Euphrates River*

*Tigris River*

U.S.
Marines

An Nāṣirīyah •

U.S. 3rd
Infantry

Al Baṣrah •

UmmQaṣr •

U.K.
Forces

*Persian
Gulf*

KUWAIT

SAUDI ARABIA

**Legend:**

➤ U.S. and coalition
ground force movement
during initial stages of
the war (2003)

△ Sunni Triangle

▨ Kurdish controlled area

✴ Greatest concentration
of continued Insurgency in 2005

▢ Rumaila Oilfields

0    50    100 mi

0    50    100 km

Sadaam's troops into submission. Led by the United States, the forces launched several thousand precision-guided bombs and missiles against the nerve centers of his regime, including air defenses, communications facilities, political and military headquarters, and suspected chemical and biological weapons sites. Coalition troops simultaneously invaded from the south, crossing into Iraq from Kuwait and proceeding northward to secure the oil fields at Rumalia, then Basra, Iraq's second largest city, and moving ultimately toward Baghdad. The Iraqi forces, less than half the size they had been in 1991 at the time of the Gulf War, put up little opposition, many of them stripping off their uniforms and disappearing into the civilian population.

The coalition forces rolled into Baghdad in early April and took the city with ease. Many Iraqis were euphoric at their liberation, and on April 9, assisted by a contingent of marines, they pulled down a towering statue of Sadaam in one of the city's squares, a symbolic event that appeared repeatedly on television screens around the world. The coalition forces had suffered relatively few losses—122 Americans and 33 British dead. On May 1, 2003, President Bush landed in a fighter jet on the deck of the aircraft carrier USS *Abraham Lincoln,* at sea just off the coast of San Diego. Wearing a flight suit and backed by a banner proclaiming "Mission Accomplished," he addressed the nation, declaring, "Major combat operations in Iraq have ended."

At the outset of the war, Bush's handling of Iraq won strong approval. Responding to his suggestive assertions, many Americans associated Sadaam with the attacks of September 11 and embraced the war as the kind of retribution that the country singer Darryl Worley caught in his popular "Have You Forgotten?": "Some say this country's just out looking for a fight / After 9/11 man I'd have to say that's right." Cable television talk-show hosts often ridiculed dissenters from the war and the reasons for waging it. As the weeks went by, however, the coalition forces found no weapons of mass destruction or facilities for producing them. The administration insisted that they would eventually be located but added that even if they were not, the United States was right to have gone to war against Iraq because the world was a better place without Sadaam Hussein in power—a position with which, in May 2003, a bare majority of the public agreed.

## RECONSTRUCTION AND INSURGENCY

In mid-April 2003, the chief of the U.S. forces in Iraq told his commanders that he expected the large majority of combat forces to be withdrawn within sixty days, but, as Bush had remarked on the deck of the *Abraham Lincoln,* "We have difficult work to do in Iraq." The United States set about repairing the heavy physical damage from the war and restoring electrical power and water supplies, most of which were out of commission, having either deteriorated drastically under Sadaam or been destroyed during the conflict. In mid-May, the United States also established a Coalition Provisional Authority headed by Ambassador L. Paul Bremer III. The Authority worked with a Governing Council, created in July and comprising twenty-five prominent Iraqis from different ethnic and religious groups, to bring order to Iraq, revive its economy, and devise an interim Iraqi government that would eventually replace Bremer and the Authority and arrange for the election of a democratic regime.

Bringing order to Iraq, however, proved to be a good deal more difficult than the principal American war planners had anticipated. The victory of the coalition forces was followed by widespread looting. Far worse, at the end of May a suicide bomber attacked an American checkpoint outside the city of Najuf, initating a terrorist insurgency that gathered increasing force in succeeding months. Fueled by former members of Sadaam's regime, by nationalists angry at the American presence, and by foreign terrorists, some of them allied with Al Qaeda, the insurgency murdered and massacred coalition troops; recruits to the Iraqi police, military, and governing infrastructure; contract workers from abroad engaged in the effort of rebuilding; and Iraqi civilians. Some of the insurgents kidnapped journalists, aid staff, and contract workers, holding them for ransom or to force other nationals of the countries from which they came out of Iraq. Several of the victims were beheaded, with videos of the gruesome act posted on the Web sites of Islamic militants.

In the face of the insurgency, there was no significant withdrawal of American troops. They stayed to battle the terrorists, protect the reconstruction work, and help train an Iraqi police and military force capable of providing security on its own. They captured most of the officials in Sadaams's regime, killed his two sons in a raid in July, and, in mid-December 2003, captured Sadaam himself in a small cellar at a farmhouse near his hometown of Tikrit. "Ladies and gentlemen, we got him," Ambassador Bremer told journalists in Baghdad, to loud cheers from Iraqis in the audience. But Sadaam's capture did nothing to dampen the insurgency. It intensified in 2004, impairing the economic restoration of the country, the establishment of a democratic government, and the ability of the Iraqis to provide for their own security.

The U.S. government had effectively strategized the war but had failed to adequately plan for and manage the peace. On the eve of the invasion, in February 2003, the army chief of staff had warned that several hundred thousand troops would likely be required to maintain order and security after Sadaam's defeat, but he had been slapped down by Rumsfeld, one of whose aides called the estimate "wildly off the mark," and was forced into early retirement. The military's new doctrinal reliance on limited, specialized troops armed with high-precision technologies might work well in winning conventional battles, but as the experience in Afghanistan had suggested, it left too few troops in place to maintain order after the battles were over. Bremer later said that the United States never had enough troops in Iraq, either to secure the country's borders or to provide the stability needed for reconstruction.

The Bush administration was unable to persuade more countries to commit troops to Iraq, and by the spring of 2004 seveal participants in the Coalition of the Willing had withdrawn their forces in responses to the terrorist attacks, opposition to the war at home, or both. The United States was thus left with having to bear a still larger share of the job of maintaining order and security in Iraq. It met the demand in part by extending the tours of duty of some 10,000 troops beyond what they had signed up for, an action that demoralized them and their families. The troops were ill trained for some of their tasks, notably policing prisons such as Abu Ghraib, where captured Iraqi soldiers and insurgents were held (see pp. 1011–1012). And many troops complained that they were not adequately equipped to protect themselves against the assaults of the terrorist insurgency. When at a town meeting a soldier asked Rumsfeld why G.I.s had "to dig through local landfills for pieces of scrap metal and compromised ballistic glass to up-armor our vehicles," the secretary of defense could manage only a lame response: "You need time to catch up with demand. You go to war with the army you have."

The Iraqi army and national police force might have served to maintain order, but Bremer, eager to destroy all vestiges of Sadaam's power, disbanded both. His action consigned several hundred thousand young men to unemployment and discontent. Moreover, the CIA had failed to identify vast supplies of weapons hidden in mosques and schools. Unprotected, they provided an arsenal for the insurgents, including the hundreds of foreign terrorists who, prompted by anti-American animos-

ity in the Muslim world, flooded into Iraq across its unguarded borders. If before the invasion Sadaam had no significant ties with Al Qaeda, an intelligence analysis concluded that by early 2004 Iraq had replaced Afghanistan as a source of new recruits and a training ground for a new generation of terrorists.

## FORGING A DEMOCRACY

On June 1, 2004, Bremer and the Coalition Provisional Authority were succeeded by an interim Iraqi government led by interim Prime Minister Iyad Allawi. Among its major tasks was preparation for elections, scheduled to take place in January 2005, for a president and a national assembly that would form a transitional government and draft a constitution for Iraq. Faced with the rising intensity of the insurgency, the United States increased the number of troops in Iraq to reduce violence before and during the elections. Regulations required that a percentage of the candidates on slates be women, and women braved threats of assassination in order to run for office.

On election day, January 30, 2005, several polling places were struck by suicide bombings and mortar attacks that killed at least forty-four people, including the attackers. Nevertheless, some 60 percent of Iraq's 14 million eligible voters refused to be deterred. Some people walked miles to their polling places, and many waited in line for hours to vote. "We want the elections like the thirsty want water," a senior Iraqi told a reporter.

Iraqi women lining up to vote in elections for a transitional government, January 30, 2005.

The major victors in the elections were Shiite Muslims, religiously oriented and concentrated in the south, whom Sadaam had long persecuted, and Kurds in the north, against whom he had waged war in the 1980s. The losers were Sunni Muslims, many of whom boycotted the election. Concentrated in the areas in and around Baghdad, they had dominated the country politically under Sadaam. Sunni clerics and political leaders had urged them not to vote, and insurgents had threatened to kill anyone who did. Among the principal tasks for the new transitional government was to entice the Sunnis to participate in it, a condition essential for a stable, functioning democracy in Iraq. But the Sunnis tended to be secular in outlook while the Shiites tended to be religiously oriented. A number of Shiites were demanding that the constitution incorporate Islamic law into the state, particularly as it applied to family, marriage, and inheritance, all of which threatened to institutionalize the subordination of women.

The success of the election heartened many Americans, but no one expected that it would produce a reduction in the violence pervading Iraq. To the contrary, the terrorist insurgency intensified in its wake. American military and private contractors were making progress toward the restoration of electricity and water, and in the reconstruction of schools, hospitals, and other resources. But a growing portion of the funds for reconstruction had to be spent to maintain security, slowing the efforts to rebuild infrastructure and provide basic services. In early 2005, many Iraqi homes and businesses still had elecrical power only a few hours a day and raw sewage continued to flow into the Tigris River.

## COUNTING THE COSTS

As the war dragged on, it became increasingly clear that on the eve of the invasion Sadaam had had neither weapons of mass destruction nor a viable program for producing them. His military strength and capabilities had been declining. He had posed no real threat. The absence of weapons of mass destruction in Iraq led many people to wonder why the intelligence about them had been so faulty. It also provoked people to ask whether the Bush administration had used unreliable or exaggerated intelligence to persuade the country into the war.

In March 2005, a presidential commission concluded that the nation's intelligence agencies had been "dead wrong" in most of their judgments about Iraq's weapons of mass destruction, that they had promulgated a misleading case about

them in the media, and that their efforts constituted "a major intelligence failure." However, the report implicitly absolved the Bush administraton of manipulating intelligence to lead the country to war.

The United States was spending more than $1 billion a week in Iraq. As of mid-August 2005, more than 1,800 Americans had died there, another 13,000 had been wounded, and it was estimated that more than 25,000 Iraqi civilians had been killed. According to polls, 56 percent of Americans held that going to war in Iraq had been a mistake and 58 percent disapproved of Bush's handling of it.

## Peace and Proliferation

### A "ROAD MAP TO PEACE"

Early in his presidency, Bush dealt little with the ongoing conflict between Israel and the Palestinians, appearing to consider it intractable and to hold no hope that Yasir Arafat, the head of the Palestinians, could be counted on to end the suicidal attacks that had plagued Israel since the renewal of the intifada in September 2000 (see Ch. 34). But once the United States was committed to war against terrorism, his attention was drawn to the conflict as another theater of terrorist activity. He was also mindful that it was a festering source of antagonism between the West and the Muslim world, many of whose members resented the United States for its unswerving support of Israel. Pressured by several Arab leaders to take an active role in persuading Israel to withdraw from the Arab lands it had occupied after the war in 1967 (see Ch. 30), he was moved to act by an escalation of the violence in the region during the mid-spring of 2002, notably back-to-back suicide bombings against Israel.

In the month after September 11, Bush had become the first U.S. president since before the creation of Israel to suggest the idea of establishing a Palestinian state as part of an overall settlement. Now, in June 2002, he explicitly endorsed the creation of such a state on the condition that the Palestinians end their terrorism and freely elect new leadership "not compromised by terror," which meant implicitly getting rid of Arafat. The following April, a time when anti-American anger in the Muslim world was soaring in response to the invasions of Afghanistan and Iraq, the administration spelled out what it called a "road map to peace"—phased steps

An Israeli settler and his child are forced by Israeli soldiers to leave the Gaza Strip, summer 2005.

toward the creation of an independent, democratic, and viable Palestinian state living in peace and security with Israel and its neighbors. The key points included, on the Palestinian side, an unconditional renunciation of violence, the adoption of a democratic constitution, the holding of free elections, and an unequivocal recognition of Israel's right to exist; and on the Israeli side, a freeze on settlements in the occupied territories and eventually a withdrawal from all the occupied lands—in short, a trade of land for peace.

Israeli right-wingers strongly resisted the road map, but in May 2003, under pressure from the United States, the Israeli cabinet endorsed it, including the creation of a Palestinian state and a set of first steps toward an ultimate settlement, notably withdrawal from the lands occupied after the revival of the intifada in September 2000. Ariel Sharon, the Israeli prime minister and a longtime hardliner himself, told the dissidents on the right that Israel had to end its occupation of Palestinian lands. "It is not possible to continue holding three and a half million people under occupation. . . . This is a terrible thing for Israel, for the Palestinians and for the Israeli economy."

Early in June, Bush went to the Middle East to press the road map on both Arabs and the Israelis. Several Arab countries friendly to the United States, including Egypt, Saudi Arabia, and Jordan, declared support for it. Later in the month, Israeli and Palestinian negotiators agreed on the withdrawal of Israeli troops from the Gaza Strip and the West Bank town of Bethlehem. Militant Palestinian groups pledged to cease attacks against Israel, at least until they saw what would happen. The cease-fire failed to hold, but in succeeding months the United States pushed both sides back onto the road map. In October 2004, another milestone was achieved when the Israeli Parliament approved a withdrawal from the Gaza Strip. On the Palestinian side, the leadership issue was simplifed by the death of Arafat in November. The subsequent elections, held in January 2005, resulted in the victory of Mahmoud Abbas, the nominee of the Palestinian Liberation Organization, a pragmatist and a moderate who pledged to pursue peace negotiations with Israel.

In February, Israeli and Palestinian leaders declared simultaneous cease-fires, and Abbas said that the war with Israel was in effect over. In mid-August 2005, Israel withdrew its troops and its settlers from the Gaza Strip. Many left voluntarily, but Israeli soldiers had to remove several thousand by force.

With Sadaam's alleged weapons of mass destruction having become an empty justification for the war in Iraq, Bush had been increasingly emphasizing the leverage that the war would provide democracy in the Middle East. He hailed the Palestinian elections as indicative of democratic stirrings in the region that his policies had helped call into being. In November 2003, he had challenged Syria, Iran, and Egypt to heed the democratic claims of their peoples and had criticized Western nations for long accommodating the lack of democracy in the Middle East, saying it had done "nothing to make us safe because in the long run stability cannot be purchased at the expense of liberty." Now local elections had been initiated in Saudi Arabia, Egypt's president had proposed that his country's constitutiton be amended to permit other candidates to run against him, and Syria had withdrawn from Lebanon in the face of unprecedented popular protests against its presence.

### NUCLEAR PROLIFERATION

In late December 2003, Muammar al-Gadhafi, the head of Libya, announced that his country would abandon its efforts to develop nuclear weapons and would dismantle its nuclear facilities. Bush attributed Gadhafi's action to the ouster of Sadaam, declaring that the war in Iraq had unmistakably conveyed to Gadhafi the consequences of pursuing a nuclear weapons program.

Yet while the war may have to some degree impelled Gadhafi to relinquish weapons of mass destruction, the striking turnabout resulted from Libya's desire, expressed in diplomatic negotiations and compensatory concessions over several years, to overcome the renegade, isolated status to which the international community had relegated it after its involvement in the bombing of a Pan American airliner over Lockerbie, Scotland, in 1988 (see Chapter 32). The U.N. had progressively lifted its sanctions against Libya. Now, in exchange for its action on the nuclear front, including verifiable dismantling of its nuclear facilities, the U.N. sanctions were removed permanently.

Whatever the war in Iraq may have done to move Gadhafi, it had failed to dissuade North Korea and Iran, the two other nations on Bush's axis of evil, from developing the technological capacity to produce nuclear weapons. Both were signatories of the Nuclear Non-Proliferation Treaty, and both said their nuclear activities had peaceful purposes, which the treaty permitted subject to scrutiny by international observers. However, evidence was accumulating that both were secretly developing technology and facilities to enrich the uranium in reactor fuel rods to weapons-grade level or to extract from them the bomb-fuel plutonium. North Korea and Iran were both significantly assisted by rogue scientists from Pakistan. Preoccupied with the war in Iraq, the Bush administration debated the problem of nuclear proliferation in North Korea and Iran but made little headway against it.

*North Korea.* In October 2002, American officials accused North Korea of violating the Non-Proliferation Treaty, pointing to its secret enrichment of uranium, and they cut off free fuel-oil shipments to the country. Retaliating at the end of the year, North Korea withdrew from the treaty, evicted the international inspectors, and restarted a plutonium-based project that it had agreed to halt in 1994. The withdrawal—the first ever—stunned the world. Although at first taking a hard line with the North Koreans, the Bush administration joined four other nations—China, Japan, Russia, and South Korea—in talks with North Korea that began in Beijing in August 2003 and continued irregularly into 2005.

In February 2005, North Korea officially declared that it possessed nuclear weapons, confirming estimates the year before by U.S. intelligence. Under pressure from China among other nations, the Beijing talks resumed, but as of mid-2005 the Beijing negotiations remained at an impasse.

*Iran.* In 1995, the Russians contracted to complete a civilian reactor at Bushehr in Iran and to sell the Iranians the nuclear fuel necessary to power it, but Iran also built a secret uranium enrichment plant that could produce sufficient fuel for three to five bombs a year. Iran claimed that its nuclear facilities were intended for peaceful purposes only, but it conceded that it planned to build a reactor to generate plutonium, which could also fuel bombs. Russia remained committed to the Bushehr reactor because the project provided 20,000 jobs for its beleaguered nuclear industry. China, Pakistan, and North Korea were also assisting nuclear development in Iran.

Bush declared a nuclear-armed Iran unacceptable. While some hawks in the administration advocated fomenting regime change there, the White House preferred for the time being to rely on international inspections to ensure that Iran's nuclear program remained peaceful. However, Iran was reportedly engaged in clandestine weapons work, concealed from the inspectors. In 2004, at the urging of Britain, France, and Germany, Iran agreed to suspend activity at a uranium enrichment facility. In the spring of 2005, the European trio, with the backing of the United States, offered Iran a package of economic, political, technological, and security incentives in return for cooperation in ensuring the peacefulness of its nuclear program. In August, however, a newly elected hardline government rejected the proposal and restarted the enrichment plant.

Taking note of how North Korea and Iran had managed to advance their nuclear ambitions, the head of the International Atomic Energy Authority ruefully observed that while the United States was containing Iraq, the rest of the world had turned into a "Wal-Mart of private-sector proliferation"— where nuclear aspirants went shopping secretly at will. The worldwide free market in nuclear expertise and materials continued to be a serious threat.

## Intelligence, Security, and Human Rights

To many observers in the wake of September 11, the nation's intelligence agencies appeared to have failed at their job. The failure prompted a slew of questions essential to national security: How had the conspirators behind that terror-filled day managed to proceed with their purpose undetected? Why did their plot, once set in motion, succeed? What might be learned from that awful course of events to prevent a recurrence?

The families of the victims wanted answers, and sympathetic members of Congress sought to establish a commission of inquiry on the matter. The president resisted the effort, saying it would distract from the war on terrorism (the response prompted some to wonder whether the administration had something to hide). However, the White House and its allies in Congress had to reckon with the tenacity of four widows of the September 11 victims. One of them, whose husband had worked for a financial firm in the World Trade Center, later explained, "We simply wanted to know why our husbands were killed, why they went to work one day and didn't come back." The women crafted wooden signs, staged a rally that drew 300 people in the heat of the capital, pestered members of Congress, and finagled their way into the White House to make their case. In November 2002, Congress and the White House established the National Commission on Terrorist Attacks upon the United States, a bipartisan group of ten people commonly known as the 9/11 Commission.

Over the next year and a half, the Commission reviewed thousands of documents, conducted hundreds of interviews, and held twelve public hearings. In July 2004, it issued a 567-page report that was widely praised for its searching narrative of the conspiracy that produced the events of September 11, its insightful analysis of the failure to detect and prevent them, and its sober recommendations about how to strengthen the nation's defenses against terrorism.

The Commission unearthed a variety of unsettling facts. Both the FBI and the CIA each received reports over several years prior to September 11 revealing, for example, that some members of Al Qaeda were taking flying lessons and that Al Qaeda intended to use hijacked aircraft as bombs against American targets. But neither agency aggressively followed up on the reports, shared what it knew with the other, or brought such intelligence to the attention of high officials in the government. The military had no plan to attack or defeat Al Qaeda. Immigration authorities failed to detect travelers with false passports, and aviation security did not keep up to date its list of people to be excluded from flying or impose thorough screening of passengers.

Federal domestic agencies did not focus adequately on the threat of terrorist attacks at home, either in the Clinton administration or in the Bush administration. The president's daily briefing on August 6, 2001, was titled, "Bin Laden Determined to Strike Inside the United States," but since the briefing contained nothing specific as to the methods and targets of the attack, he took no special action. Richard A. Clarke, the chief counterterrorism officer in both administrations before Sep-

tember 11, testified to the Commission that he had told the Bush White House that terrorism was an urgent problem and had asked several times for a cabinet-level meeting on the threat of Al Qaeda, but was relegated with one exception to low-level hearings. Conveying his frustration in a letter to the president's national security advisor on September 4, 2001, he suggested that they "imagine a day after a terrorist attack, with hundreds of Americans dead at home or abroad, and ask themselves what they could have done." Yet even Clarke, whom the Commission counted as the most incisive expert on counterterrorism, doubted that action on his recommendations would have prevented the attacks on September 11.

The Commission found that on September 11 itself, extraordinary acts of heroism "saved lives and inspired a nation" but that federal, state, and local authorities were unprepared for the disaster and their response was often "improvised." To be sure, the Commission praised the nation's air traffic controllers for successfully grounding the entire national air fleet, some 4,500 aircraft, in less than three hours after the attacks, a rate of one every two seconds. But the controllers' tracking of the hijacked planes, which included losing the plane that struck the Pentagon for thirty-six minutes, left a good deal to be desired. The rescue efforts at the World Trade Center were plagued by inadequate communications between the New York City police and fire departments. Far more disturbing, confusion marked communications among the White House, the president, the military, and other federal agencies. Bush at one point had to rely on a cell phone to reach Vice President Cheney. Cheney authorized fighter jets to shoot down the hijacked planes, but the the order was not relayed to the fighter pilots.

The Commission observed that the United States was safer because of the offensive actions that it had taken against Al Qaeda, notably in Afghanistan. That said, it had to add, "But we are not safe." Its recommendations were designed to remedy to the greatest extent possible the deficiencies in the structure, policies, and management of the nation's defenses against terrorism. Among its principal recommendations was the creation of a cabinet-level director of national intelligence who would oversee and link the activities of all the government's intelligence agencies. In December 2004, Congress, with Bush's support, transformed a number of the Commission's recommendations into law, creating the new post of intelligence director as well as a National Counterterrorism Center to coordinate terrorism intelligence from everywhere in the government.

## SECURITY AT HOME

Despite these initiatives, Americans found good reason to remain apprehensive about terrorism. In December 2001, Richard Reid, an American who was a member of Al Qaeda, tried to ignite an explosive hidden in his shoes while on an American Airlines flight from Paris to Miami. Thwarted in the attempt, he was tried and convicted in October 2002, having disdainfully told the court, "Basically, yeah, I intended to damage the plane." That month, federal officials reported they had cracked a Portland, Oregon, terrorist cell made up of four American citizens who planned to join Al Qaeda and the Taliban in an anti-U.S. "jihad," or holy war.

In April 2003, federal agents arrested Iyman Faris, an American citizen born in Kashmir who had plotted with Al Qaeda to blow up the Brooklyn Bridge, an offense for which he was later convicted and sent to prison. Americans were reminded what might happen if terrorist efforts were not prevented when in Madrid, Spain, during one morning rush hour in March 2004, Islamic terrorists set off ten bombs in four commuter trains, killing dozens of people. In London, again during a morning commute in July 2005, terrorists blew up three subway trains and a double-decker bus, killing several dozen riders. (The attack in Madrid prompted the Spanish government to pull its troops from Iraq.) Analysts predicted that it was only a matter of time before similar assaults were mounted against the rail and bus systems in the United States, security for which had received much less funding and attention than had the air transport system.

The foiling of terrorist plots at home was in a sense another version of the policy of preemption, analogous to that of the Bush Doctrine abroad; it involved pursuing individuals and groups—like, for example, the cell in Oregon—on grounds that they might commit terrorist acts. The USA Patriot Act had been designed to facilitate such a purpose. It authorized federal agencies to search a broad range of records, including those bearing on a suspect's travel, video rentals, phone calls, Internet access, and even library usage, without a warrant and without the suspect's knowledge. It also permitted so-called sneak-and-peek warrants, searches of people's homes without their knowing they had been searched. And it allowed investigations of the records in financial institutions of anyone suspected of engaging in not only terrorist acts but also money laundering, a provision that enlarged the intrusive powers of government for purposes beyond terrorism to ordinary crime.

Advocates of civil liberties attacked these provisions of the USA Patriot Act, charging that they violated fundamental constitutional rights, notably the right to due process of law and protection against unreasonable search and seizure. Attorney General John Ashcroft responded that "we seek to secure liberty, not trade liberty for security," adding, "I have charged Department of Justice officials to think outside the box—but never outside the Constitution." The USA Patriot Act was set to expire in 2005. Bush called for its renewal, but a coalition of liberal Democrats and conservative Republicans, resentful of its invasion of privacy, intended to modify its egregiously intrusive provisions.

## DENIALS OF RIGHTS

The war against terror led to violations of human rights—some fostered under the authority of the act, others by order of the president, still others by military and intelligence officials. Immigrants from predominantly Muslim regions of the world, notably the Middle East, were singled out for heightened scrutiny, subjected to deportation hearings held in secret, and in some instances subjected to verbal and physical abuse.

Late in 2001, Bush, explaining that he could not let enemies of the United States "use the forums of liberty to destroy liberty itself," declared that people captured in the war against terrorism could be denied due-process rights if he found that they were "enemy combatants." A number of such designated combatants were at the American Camp Delta, at Guantánamo Bay, Cuba, which housed some 600 detainees, including some American citizens, most of them taken in Afghanistan. Many were detained indefinitely without a specification of charges or a hearing, and they were often held incommunicado, unable to speak to a lawyer or family members. According to the International Red Cross, some of the detainees were tortured.

*Abu Ghraib.* In late April and early May 2004, photographic evidence of cruel maltreatment of prisoners in U.S. custody at Abu Ghraib, near Baghdad, was published around the world. One of the pictures showed a naked man cowering against a wall before an unmuzzled, threatening dog; another, a hooded man standing on a box, arms out at an angle with wires attached to his fingers and toes (it was soon revealed that a wire also went to his penis and that he had been told he would be electrocuted if he fell off the box). The photos had been taken in November of the previous year, but according

One of the infamous photos—here the hooded man with wires attached to his body—depicting the abusive treatment of prisoners at Abu Ghraib that were published to the world.

to the International Red Cross the abuse had been going on for many months. "The elements we found were tantamount to torture," a Red Cross official said.

The practices at Abu Ghraib stunned many Americans, were condemned around the globe, and stimulated a sharp increase in anti-American sentiment in the Muslim world. Secretary of Defense Donald Rumsfeld felt compelled to apologize publicly for the treatment of the prisoners, calling what the photos revealed "blatantly sadistic, cruel and inhuman." In mid-May, in a report on the events at Abu Ghraib, a high-ranking army officer reported that the instances of abuse had been perpetrated by a half dozen or so military police in collaboration with several low-level military interrogators, including civilian contractors. Attorneys for several of the soldiers charged with the abuse said their clients had acted at the behest of military intelligence officials to soften up the prisoners for interrogation. The report found that the soldiers had acted "on their own volition," not on orders from senior officers. Asked by a senator what had gone wrong, the army's investigator said simply, "Failure in leadership, sir, from the brigade commander on down, lack of discipline, no training whatsoever, and no supervision."

However, in the wake of the scandal, Americans learned that Abu Ghraib, which housed as many as 7,000 Iraqis detained by

American forces, was only one of many worldwide detention centers, including the one at Guantánamo, operated by the U.S. military and the CIA as instruments of counterterrorism. Claiming to be outside the jurisdiction of the U.S. and international court systems, they were able to hold suspects without affording them access to conventional legal rights, including a lawyer and an impartial hearing, or protection from abuse.

At the beginning of June 2004, a Department of Justice memorandum on the treatment of prisoners came to public light. Prepared almost two years earlier, it appeared to establish a legal foundation for harsh treatment of suspected terrorists and leave ample room for the type of abuse visited upon prisoners at Abu Ghraib and Guantánamo. The document was widely denounced by human rights groups and in Congress, where one senator emphasized that the United States adhered to international conventions against abuse of prisoners "to protect my son in the military. . . . so when Americans are captured they are not tortured." The administration quickly disavowed the memo and pointed to an order in February 2002 by the president for the humane treatment of prisoners. At a meeting in the Oval Office, the president himself emphasized to reporters, "We do not condone torture. I have never ordered torture. I will never order torture."

Nevertheless, the administration appeared to have fostered a culture of local permissiveness for the treatment of prisoners in the war on terror. Official instructions as to what was permissible and what was not during interrogations were confusing and vague. Some of the abuse at Abu Ghraib had been carried out just for fun ("Just playing with him," the soldier who had wired the hooded man on the box explained), but a significant portion of it had been done as coercive measures during the course of interrogations.

### REDRESS IN THE COURTS

The administration's treatment of suspect immigrants, its pursuit of terrorist cells, and its indefinite holding of detainees were challenged in the courts. In 2002, a federal appeals court in Cincinnati, Ohio, held that the government had acted illegally by holding hundreds of deportation hearings in secret on the grounds that the people involved might be linked to terrorism. The decision questioned the Bush administration's commitment to an open democracy, with one of the judges writing reprovingly, "Democracies die behind closed doors."

By the spring of 2004, four detainee cases had made their way to the United States Supreme Court. The plaintiffs in all four cases had been held in government custody for months without being formally charged, given access to a lawyer, or provided an opportunity to contest their incarcerations. All were demanding that they be granted the elementary rights to due process that they had been denied.

The scandal at Abu Ghraib erupted just as the Court began its deliberations on the cases, and some observers speculated that the revelations of abuse might impact the Court's thinking. The rulings, which the Court issued late in June 2004, constituted a sharp rebuke to the Bush administration's claim to the suppression of due-process rights. In one case, the justices held that a U.S. citizen captured abroad while fighting for the enemy has a right to a lawyer and an impartial trial.

In two cases involving detainees at Guantánamo, the justices declared that while the president does have the power to capture and hold terrorists and their allies, including American citizens, all such detainees have the right to challenge their imprisonment in an American court. Writing for the majority, Justice Sandra Day O'Connor rejected the president's claim that he could designate people as enemy combatants without judicial oversight, observing that a process in which government claims are "simply presumed correct without any opportunity for the alleged combatant to demonstrate otherwise falls constitutionally short." She added, "We have long since made clear that a state of war is not a blank check for the president when it comes to the rights of the nation's citizens."

The government promptly granted its detainees hearings but still denied them legal representation, access to secret evidence, and the right to confront unnamed witnesses. In November 2004, a federal judge ruled that such denial of due process violated the Geneva Convention on prisoners of war and the standards of the American courts.

## The Economy, Health Care, and Gay Rights

The post–September 11 jitters worsened the economic slowdown. Many people refused to fly; stopped going to restaurants, theaters, or malls; and huddled close to home. War expenditures did not make up for the loss of commercial income. In December, taking further steps to stimulate the economy, the Federal Reserve Board reduced interest rates to their lowest levels since 1962. President Bush urged Americans to return to their normal pastimes, especially shopping, and pushed for a second round of tax reductions.

During 2001, consumer confidence continued to decline, manufacturing fell, and, as analysts had feared, the economy slipped into recession. State balance sheets, which had shown surpluses in 2000, went negative, forcing governments in the South and Midwest to cut their budgets for the first time in a decade. Economic indicators turned upward during 2002, but the recovery was sluggish and unsteady.

The economic weakness was attributed in part to the reluctance of Americans to invest and spend in the face of the threat of terrorism and, by the fall, the prospect of war with Iraq. Confidence in business was also shaken by the scandals sweeping through corporate America, notably the aftermath of the collapse of Enron, a multibillion-dollar energy conglomerate based in Texas whose operations were riven with fraud; the revelations in mid-2002 that the head of Tyco, one of the nation's major corporations, had, without authorization, spent millions of dollars of the company's funds on personal extravagances such as a yacht and a shower curtain that cost $6,000; and that Martha Stewart, the symbol of the successful businesswoman and a standard of behavior for the modern woman, had apparently illegally sold some stock in her personal portfolio. (She was later convicted of illegal stock dealing and lying to officials, which prompted one investor to remark, "The woman who told you how to be perfect failed to be perfect herself.")

*The Elections of 2002.* To many observers, the weakness in the economy, particularly the decline in the stock market and the persistently high unemployment rate, made it all the more likely that Republicans would lose ground in Congress, the normal mid-term trend for the party holding the White House. In the elections in November, however, Republicans gained ground, winning control of the Senate by one vote and increasing their majority in the House, a feat matched in recent times only by FDR in 1934 and Bill Clinton in 1998. Bush had campaigned intensively for Republican candidates in close races. His personal appeal appeared to have contributed to the GOP's triumph, but so did his toughness on national security, especially his focus on the war against terrorism and his insistence on confronting Iraq. Now, with Congress entirely under Republican control, he intended to press ahead with his economic and social agendas.

STRUGGLE FOR RECOVERY

With the aim of further stimulating economic recovery and growth, in January 2003 Bush proposed another round of tax cuts, almost $700 billion, to the new Congress. Critics charged that the proposed cuts were reckless. Factored into the budget that Bush submitted that month, they helped increase the projected deficit to more than $300 billion, a figure that did not include the impact of spending on the war in Iraq. It was unprecedented to cut taxes in the face of a war, and the cuts seemed unlikely to spur economic growth where it was needed. Congress, some of whose Republican as well as Democratic members were also worried about the deficit, agreed in May to reduce taxes by $318 billion over ten years, providing reductions in taxes on stock dividends, a two-year increase in the tax credit for children, and the speed-up in reductions for middle- and upper-income taxpayers authorized by the tax act in 2001.

In the succeeding months, the economy continued to grow, albeit slowly, at an annual rate between 3 and 4 percent, consumer confidence revived, and so did the stock market. Unemployment rose to 6.3 percent in June, but while the rate then began to fall, commentators spoke of a "jobless recovery." The nation lost jobs during much of 2003, and even when job growth resumed in September, the rate of improvement was weak. In 2003, the number people living in poverty increased for the third year in a row, reaching 35 million, or 12.5 percent of the population (compared with 11.7 percent in 2001). Among them were 12.9 million children, about 17.6 percent of the population under age eighteen.

The trouble on the job front was the manufacturing sector, where one in four jobs had disappeared since 1979, half of them—2.5 million—since Bush had taken office. A large number of them had gone overseas, where wages were lower, and no let-up in the loss seemed in the offing. The mismatch between recovery and jobs was also attributed to gains in productivity, which was growing at a high rate and enabling manufacturers to produce more with fewer workers. The Navistar truck plant in Springfield, Ohio, for example, employed 4,800 workers in the mid-1990s but only 1,100 in 2004. Three hundred of them had been involved in making the truck's cab; now, after automation, the task required only 44.

In the spring of 2004, the pace of job creation began to pick up, but it was erratic and the economic recovery remained far from robust. State budgets were still reeling, their revenues up to surplus level but their treasuries still too strapped to restore cuts in social services or roll back tax increases. Bush claimed that the surge in economic growth was the result of his tax cuts, but economists said it was partly the result of the Federal Reserve Board, which to help stimulate the economy had set interest rates at forty-year lows, and of the high level of military spending required by the war in Iraq. In January 2004, Bush submitted a budget that, without including the costs for the war, projected a deficit in the next fiscal year of $500 billion and at the same time called for making permanent the tax cuts passed in 2001. Congress, its eye on the deficit, declined to make the cuts permanent; but in September, its eye on the elections, it did extend the cuts scheduled to expire at the end of the year, including relief for married couples, the credit for families with children, and an expansion of the number of taxpayers in the lowest bracket.

HEALTH CARE

All the while, health care was forcing itself increasingly on the nation's agenda. Health care costs had been rising roughly 14 percent a year, four times as fast as most other consumer items. In 2003, more than 43 million people, about 15 percent of the population, had no health insurance. As in the past, many in the group, which included a disproportionately large number of Asians (18 percent), blacks (20 percent), and Hispanics (32 percent), were poor and unemployed, but now the rapidly rising costs of health insurance were cutting into coverage of the middle class. Many self-employed people—they represented one out of thirteen workers—found it too expensive, and many of those who worked for private companies found their employers eliminating or cutting back health benefits, forcing their employees to bear an increasing portion of the burden. Retirees were particularly hard hit. Many older Americans depended on their retirement health benefits as a supplement to Medicare, especially for assistance in purchasing prescription drugs, which Medicare did not provide.

*A Prescription Drug Benefit.* Senior citizens relied on an increasing variety of pharmaceuticals designed to deal with the illnesses and infirmities of age, but they were expensive. By 2003, widespread support had developed for adding a prescription drug benefit to Medicare, and in November, with Bush's support, Congress passed a bill for that purpose. It provided for sale to seniors of discount drug cards during 2004 and 2005, and it established, beginning in 2006, a direct Medicare drug benefit for which seniors would have to pay an annual premium as well as a share of the costs of the drugs they used. It offered subsidies to participants with low incomes and to private employers who continued to provide prescription drug benefits to their retirees.

When the discount drug cards became available in June 2004, far fewer seniors signed up to purchase them than the Bush administration had predicted. The card system was confusing to many, and in any case, rising drug prices had already nullifed the discount rates set the previous year. Some analysts predicted that when the drug benefit became available from Medicare in 2006, 3.5 million retirees would lose their company retirement packages and be forced to depend on Medicare's less comprehensive and more expensive prescription drug plan. Medicare had already been on shaky financial ground, and the new law worsened its prospects. Between the rapid rise in health costs and the increasing number of seniors, it was projected to run out of money in roughly a decade.

## GAY MARRIAGE

Early in the twenty-first century, some six million American men and women identified themselves as gay. According to reliable polls, about 7 out of 10 Americans knew a gay person, 40 percent more than in the mid-1980s, and 6 out of 10 counted themselves sympathetic to the gay community, a 50 percent increase over the same period. Most people supported equal rights for gays. As a sign of the shift, the antidiscrimination policy of Wal-Mart, the largest private employer in the country, now included sexual orientation.

Both reflecting and advancing the mainstream acceptance, many gays, singly or in couples, were bearing or adopting children, thus associating themselves with standard family concerns. Gay characters commonly appeared in films and prime-time television shows, including lesbian doctors on the popular *ER* and gay parents on *Queer as Folk.* In the spring of 2003, the U.S. Supreme Court took up the case of *Lawrence v. Texas,* which concerned the state's antisodomy law. At the time, such laws were on the books of thirteen states and were felt by gay men to be a brand of disapproval, one that was often invoked against them in disputes about jobs, child custody, and adoptions. In June, the Court found the Texas law an unconstitutional invasion of privacy that, in the words of the majority, "demeans the lives of homosexual persons."

Gays had also been gaining increasing legal sanction as well as social acceptance for civil unions and domestic partnerships. Such unions afforded gay couples the same rights as married couples with regard to, for example, parental responsibilities, the inheritance of estates, benefits from employers and insurers, and critical medical decisions. Many gays, however, had long contended that they should have the right to marry. Blocked by state laws that limited marriage to a man and a woman, they increasingly turned to the courts to obtain the right to same-sex marriage.

*Rights Granted.* In two rulings, the first in November 2003 and the second in February 2004, the Massachusetts Supreme Judicial Court held by 4 to 3 that legal equality for homosexuals required that they be permitted to marry in the state. In the majority's view, allowing civil unions but not legal marriage for gays amounted to "a demonstrable assigning of same-sex, largely homosexual, couples to second-class status." During the following year, 6,000 same-sex couples married in Massachusetts.

Similar rulings came down from lower courts in Washington state and San Francisco, where in February 2004 the mayor had already authorized the issuance of marriage licenses to same-sex couples. Inspired by the action in San Franciso, the mayors of New Paltz and Nyack, in New York state, began

The mayor of New Paltz, New York, Jason West, officiating at a public wedding ceremony for a gay couple in Spring 2005.

marrying gay couples, and in Portland, Oregon, county commissioners began issuing same-sex marriage licenses.

*Backlash.* Opposition to gay marriage in the United States had long been gathering force. In 1996, President Clinton had signed the Defense of Marriage Act, which Congress had passed by wide margins and which exempted states from having to recognize a marriage between partners of the same sex in another state. Now the ruling of the Massachusetts court produced a fiery backlash, starting with a vote in the Massachusetts legislature to ban same-sex marriage. Polls showed that two-thirds of Americans disapproved of legalizing it. As of August 2004, gay marriage was banned by laws or court rulings in forty-three states. Louisiana and Missouri passed constitutional amendments against it, and eleven states placed such amendments on the November ballot.

President Bush found alternative arrangements such as civil unions acceptable, but not same-sex marriage. Condemning the decision of the Massachusetts court, he called for a U.S. constitutional amendment to defend "the sanctity of marriage" as the union of a man and a woman against "activist judges" who would redefine the institution by court order. According to polls, support for a constitutional ban on gay marriage was widespread, endorsed even by many people who otherwise supported gay rights, but attempts to drive such an amendment through Congress in the summer of 2004 failed.

Commentators wondered what sanctified insitution of marriage Bush was referring to in the contemporary United States. In 2004, only roughly half of American adults were married, compared with 75 percent in the mid-1970s, and while at that time almost half conformed to the model of husband, wife, and offspring, only about a quarter did now. It may have been that precisely the decline in conventional marriage was helping to fuel the visceral energy in the movement against gay marriage. Religious values figured in the equation, too. The large majority of Americans who considered marriage a religious union, as distinct from a purely legal one, vigorously opposed same-sex marriages. Roman Catholic prelates attacked gay marriage as contrary to God's law, and leading Protestant churches splintered over the issue.

The cultural and religious dynamic suffusing the issue of gay marriage promised to give Bush an advantage in the upcoming presidential election. As a Republican congressional operative put it, Bush's support for the constitutional amendment would attract "Reagan Democrats, pro-life Democrats, churchgoing Democrats . . . a lot of Democrats who are not happy with Bush on economic policy."

## ELECTION 2004

Early in 2004, Democrats had high hopes of recapturing the White House in the upcoming presidential election. The war in Iraq was increasingly confounded by the insurgency, the United States' relations with its Continental allies remained troubled, the economy continued to lose jobs, the deficit was soaring, and Bush's approval ratings were falling steadily. By March, Senator John Kerry of Massachusetts had vanquished a crowded field of hopefuls in the Democratic primaries. He was nominated at the party's convention in July and chose as his running mate Senator John Edwards of North Carolina.

A son of privilege with a strong sense of duty, Kerry had gone to fight in Vietnam, where he earned decorations for valor as commander of a swift boat, and had come home to protest the war, testifying famously to Congress: "How do you ask a man to be the last man to die for a mistake?" A steadily moderate liberal in the Senate, he advanced a domestic agenda that differed from the president's. Like Bush, he opposed gay marriage but, unlike him, also a constitutional amendment banning it, and he held that gays should be permitted to serve openly in the military. He advocated a ten-year, $650 billion federal health insurance program that would cover amost all Americans, including children. And he called for tax policies that favored middle- and lower-income groups, emphasizing in September that the United States had some 900,000 fewer jobs than when Bush took office and that Bush would almost certainly be the first president since Herbert Hoover to preside over a net job loss during the course of his term.

In foreign policy, Kerry hammered Bush for the war in Iraq. Although he had voted to authorize military action against Sadaam, he strongly faulted the president for his embrace of unilateralism and preemption, particularly for rushing to attack Iraq when it did not pose an imminent threat and for fighting a war "without a plan to win the peace." He accused Bush of neglecting the real war on terrorism, the drive by Iran and North Korea to develop nuclear weapons, and the integration of China into the world economy. However, Kerry undercut his criticism of Bush's policy by appearing to reverse himself on the war issue—"I actually did vote for the $87 billion, before I voted against it," he said, referring to a bill to finance the war—and by proposing little different from Bush for what the United States should do in Iraq now that it was militarily engaged there.

Bush may have been faulted for alienating the allies, polarizing Congress, and singlemindedly taking the country into the war in Iraq; Republican campaign strategists turned such presidential characteristics to advantage by stressing that he was a tough, decisive leader in the war on terrorism and by portraying Kerry as untrustworthy and indecisive on the grave issues of national security. "You may not agree with me, but you know where I stand," Bush said repeatedly. Bush insisted that even though no weapons of mass destruction had been found in Iraq, getting rid of Sadaam had made the United States safer. "We are staying on the offensive—striking terrorists abroad—so we do not have to face them here at home," he declared.

On the domestic front, Bush pledged to press further his conservative agenda. He touted the creation of an "ownership society," calling for the establishment of private accounts in Social Security and health care and the expansion of home ownership. Bush campaiged against activist judges, reiterating his opposition to abortion and making clear his dissent from the rulings in favor of gay marriage.

The campaign was marked by innovations, including coverage by bloggers (short for "Web loggers"), and by the proliferation on both sides of advocacy groups independent of the campaigns themselves. The formation of the groups was stimulated by the passage in 2003 of a campaign finance reform law that prohibited contributions to political parties by labor unions and corporations while restricting those from individuals and political action committtees. Financed by thousands of contributions over the Internet or bankrolled by major party contributors, the advocacy groups tended to be partisan. Among the most influential was Swift Boat Veterans for Truth, an organization that was financed by a major Republican contributor and that sponsored television advertisements and a book charging, falsely, that John Kerry had not performed the heroic acts for which he had been decorated.

On election day, Bush won 51 percent of the popular vote to Kerry's 48 percent, thus becoming the first victorious candidate since 1988 to gain a majority of the popular vote. He captured thirty states spread across the South, the Great Plains, the Mountain West, and a large portion of the Midwest—enough to give him 286 votes in the electoral college to Kerry's 252. The Republican Party maintained control of the House and increased its majority in the Senate to 55.

Almost 60 percent of the voting age population cast ballots, the highest level since 1968, an indicator of the intensity of engagement in the contest.

According to pollsters, a majority of Americans considered the war in Iraq unjustified and Bush's policies hurtful to the economy. Many nevertheless voted for the president because they found him a bold, consistent leader and Kerry a flip-flopper on national security. Bush also received overwhelming support from social and religious conservatives, notably white evangelical Christians, whom his campaign had cultivated. In eleven states, many had been brought to vote by the presence on the ballot of the constitutional amendents banning same-sex marriage. The measures passed handily in all the states and Bush carried all but two of them, Oregon and Michigan.

## State of the Nation, 2005

Bush, having won election in his own right, emerged more confident and at ease than he had in 2001, when his ascent to the White House was surrounded by charges of political illegitimacy. Under cover of war, he intended to press on with his broad conservative agenda, hamstringing the federal government in what amounted to a repudiation of the welfare state that had originated in the 1970s and, given his enthusiasm for the privatization of Social Security, of many features of the social contract forged in the 1930s in the crucible of the New Deal and the Depression. His conservative supporters anticipated achieving something akin to a revolution by banning same-sex marriages, overturning *Roe v. Wade,* and blurring the line between religion and the state.

But the partisanship of recent years had left many voters in the middle worrying about the divisiveness in the country. Polls showed that the large majority of Americans continued to support the right of a pregnant woman to choose to abort her fetus. Even some conservatives in Congress broke ranks with Bush over maintaining the severe restrictions he had imposed on federally supported research with human stem cells, finding that the medical benefits they promised warranted an expansion of the program. Despite strong efforts by Bush early in his second term to promote the privatization of Social Security, the majority of Americans refused to go along with the scheme.

Hurricane Katrina was an event that dramatically exposed a number of the domestic divisions and inequities in the country. Katrina reached the Gulf of Mexico from the south on August 26th and struck the region centered on New Orleans on Monday, August 29th. Many residents had boarded up their homes, but the hurricane, by then a category-4 storm, with winds reaching 145 miles per hour, turned wooden structures into toothpicks, tore the roofs off concrete buildings, and destroyed thousands of dwellings and businesses. The city"s system of levees, overtaxed by the towering surge of water, gave way in several places, flooding about eighty percent of New Orleans from neighboring Lake Pontchartrain, submerging some areas under twenty feet of water.

The mayor had urged the city"s 500,000 residents to evacuate, but about 100,000 people did not own cars and did not have other means to get out. A sizable fraction of these people were poor and black, reflecting the high poverty rate in the city (28%) and the large number of the poor (84%) who were black. About 25,000 people took refuge in the Louisiana Superdome and another 20,000 were installed in the city"s convention center. Thousands more remained in their homes, climbing to the upper floors as the waters rose and then to the roofs if they could.

Before the hurricane struck, state and local officials had declared a state of emergency, and so had President Bush, who authorized the Federal Emergency Management Administration (FEMA) to provide aid. But virtually no aid came and thousands in New Orleans were left without food, water, or sanitation in the sweltering, humid heat of late summer. Conditions in the Superdome and the convention center, both reeking of garbage, urine, and human feces, were execrable. Dwight Williams, a 34-year-old truck driver who had been in the center for five days, complained, "Nobody tells us anything. They ignored us day after day. We had to survive completely on our own." Television broadcasts brought images of Katrina"s human costs to the world, much of it borne by blacks—dead bodies floating in the water and the people on rooftops waiting for help and rescue. Looting and violence broke out, partly an expression of criminality, partly the product of desperation for sustenance.

For several days after Katrina struck, President Bush gave no public evidence that he recognized either the magnitude of the devastation or the gross inadequacy of the administration"s response. Finally, on September 1, the White House turned active, increasing the number of guard troops in the city, invigorating FEMA's efforts, and calling for a Congressional appropriation of $10.5 billion in relief funds. The guard and FEMA brought food and water and accelerated evacuations to other cities. Initial estimates put the ultimate federal cost for relief at $100 billion or higher, and on September 7, Congress raised the appropriation for relief to $62 billion.

On September 13, Bush declared that he accepted responsibility for any failures by the federal government in dealing with the aftermath of Katrina and said that the disaster had exposed "serious problems" in the country's ability to respond to calamities such as a terrorist attack. In a speech in New Orleans two days later, the President noted that the Gulf Coast is marked by "deep, persistent poverty," adding that poverty "has roots in a history of racial discrimination, which has cut off generations from the opportunity of America." He pledged bold federal action to "rise above the legacy of inequality."

Postmortems of Katrina revealed that it was not only a natural disaster but a man-made disaster, too, a product in part of the conservative, anti-government attitudes that had come to dominate in Washington. Experts and officials had long known that New Orleans would be jeopardized by a category-4 storm. But funds requested by the Army Corps of Engineers to shore up the levees had been reduced. The Bush administration had installed officials at the top of FEMA who had no significant experience, if any, in disaster management. FEMA's staff and budget had been cut, and three quarters of its first-responder funds had been allocated to terrorism-related activities. Some scientists reported that powerful storms like Katrina were occurring more frequently because global warming was adding energy to the oceans, raising the surface temperature of the seas in tropical regions by nearly one degree Fahrenheit since the 1970s.

But the administration did not announce a review of its policies on global warming, and despite Bush's call for ending poverty and inequality, at least in New Orleans, his approach to relief was more conservative than bold, emphasizing, for example, measures such as tax relief and loans rather than direct aid. The President's policies for reconstruction included a waiver of the longstanding legal requirement that wages paid for with federal funds had to meet prevailing local standards. And conservative Republicans in Congress, wary of too much spending, insisted that the costs of Katrina had to be paid for by reductions in federal spending elsewhere, a position that Bush, too, embraced. The cuts most popular among conservatives were in Medicaid and food stamps, programs for the poor.

*American Journal*

## Surviving Katrina

*When Katrina struck New Orleans, Larry Bradshaw and Lorrie Beth Slonsky, emergency medical service workers from San Francisco, were staying at a hotel in the city's French Quarter while attending a conference. Located on high ground, the Quarter was not flooded, but by the fourth day the hotel guests in the area, some 500 people, were running short on food and water and adequate sanitation. They hired buses to take them to safety; the buses did not arrive. The hotel managers locked them out, telling them that they should find shelter in the Superdome or the city's convention center; both places were too full to accommodate them. All the while, they were unable to obtain water from any of the officials they encountered. A police commander advised them to walk down the Pontchartrain Expressway and cross the bridge to the West Bank of the Mississippi, saying they would find buses waiting to take them out of the city. At the bridge, they were met by armed sheriffs who fired over their heads, told them there were no buses, and blocked them from crossing, saying the West Bank was not going to become a haven for refugees. Their group retreated back along the expressway, where they established an encampment. Here Bradshaw and Slonsky recount the experience of the camp before the sheriffs broke it up.*

"All day long, we saw other families, individuals and groups make the same trip up the incline [of the Pontchartrain Expressway] in an attempt to cross the [Greater New Orleans] bridge, only to be turned away [by armed sheriffs]—some chased away with gunfire, others simply told no, others verbally berated and humiliated. Thousands of New Orleaners were prevented and prohibited from self-evacuating the city on foot. "Meanwhile, the only two city shelters sank further into squalor and disrepair. The only way across the bridge was by vehicle. We saw workers stealing trucks, buses, moving vans, semi-trucks and any car that could be hotwired. All were packed with people trying to escape the misery that New Orleans had become.

"Our little encampment [under a highway overpass] began to blossom. Someone stole a water delivery truck and brought it up to us. . . . A mile or so down the freeway, an Army truck lost a couple of pallets of C-rations on a tight turn. We ferried the food back to our camp in shopping carts.

"Now—secure with these two necessities, food and water—cooperation, community, and creativity followed. We organized a clean-up and hung garbage bags from the rebar poles. We made beds from wood pallets and cardboard. We designated a storm drain as the bathroom, and the kids built an elaborate enclosure for privacy out of plastic, broken umbrellas and other scraps. We even organized a food-recycling system where individuals could swap out parts of C-rations (applesauce for babies and candies for kids!).

"This was something we saw repeatedly in the aftermath of Katrina. When individuals had to fight to find food or water, it meant looking out for yourself. You had to do whatever it took to find water for your kids or food for your parents. But when these basic needs were met, people began to look out for each other, working together and constructing a community.

"If the relief organizations had saturated the city with food and water in the first two or three days, the desperation, frustration, and ugliness would not have set in."

Larry Bradshaw and Lorrie Beth Slonsky, in Counterpunch, 9/6/05

Still, whether the conservatives would prevail in their approach to the consequences of Katrina remained an open question, In the fall of 2005, Bush's popularity was down to 42 percent, the lowest level of his presidency, and a clear majority of Americans (57%) said they were dissatisfied by the government's response to Katrina. The hurricane had made clear to many Americans that they needed a government that was compassionate, caring, and competent not only in word but deed.

If Katrina helped reduce the President"s popularity, so did the ongoing war in Iraq. However confident the president might be, after more than three years of the war against terrorism the pursuit of the Bush Doctrine had raised a number of questions. Would preemption and unilateralism achieve the kind of bipartisan consensus support that collective security and multilateral engagement had enjoyed during the decades after Pearl Harbor? The war in Iraq had compelled Pentagon planners to query Rumsfeld's vision that the armed forces could win wars and keep the peace with small numbers of fast-moving, lightly armed troops. Many military analysts were coming to think that given the military's strained resources, the rhetoric of preemptive war was impractical for dealing with challenges like those posed by Iran and North Korea. What the nation needed was multilateral peacekeeping and the diplomatic assistance of allies.

Was it wise or practical to make democratization a paramount goal of American foreign policy? Perhaps it was, but September 11 appeared to expose a degree of anti-American animosity in parts of the Muslim world and the blood spilled in the attempt to democratize Iraq had turned the animosities in many quarters into hatred.

Some of the animosity derived from America's vanguard role in globalization. After the Cold War, Americans had trumpeted the spread through the world of global corporations and free markets, but the widening power of international capitalism prompted protests even in the West. Similar economic resentments festered in the third world, and they were compounded there by the intrusion of the social and cultural accompaniments of globalization—notably secularism and personal freedom, especially for women. The resentments helped fuel the growth of radical Islamic fundamentalism, including the militant-minority version invoked by Osama bin Laden.

The chances of war between any of the great powers was lower than it had been at any time in the twentieth century, but India and China were emerging as global economic powerhouses. The United States would need a good deal of wisdom and innovation to deal with the challenges they posed to the West's economic hegemony, technological superiority, and hunger for resources, especially oil. In the meantime, it had to figure out how to deal with the flight of manufacturing jobs abroad and the declining numbers of American students ambitious for careers in science and technology, the principal engine of material innovation.

Still, for all its problems, the United States remained strong and resourceful, and one of the poems posted at Grand Central Station after September 11 told the perpetrators of the attack why:

> Well, you hit the World Trade Center, but you missed America. . . .
> America isn't about a place, America isn't even about a bunch of
>     buildings,
> America is about an IDEA.

The idea, forged and enlarged through almost four centuries of struggle, had come to include many elements. The overarching ones—the Fourth of July standards of freedom, equality, democracy, and opportunity—continued to transcend the nation's diversity, bind it together, and at once invigorate and temper its response to the shadowy threats it was now compelled to confront.

## Suggested Reading

Richard A. Clarke, *Against All Enemies: Inside America's War on Terror* (2004)

Steve Coll, *Ghost Wars: The Secret History of the CIA, Afghanistan, and Bin Laden, From the Soviet Invasion to September 10, 2001* (2004)

John Lewis Gaddis, *Surprise, Security, and the American Experience* (2004)

Fred I. Greenstein, *The Bush Presidency: An Early Assessment* (2003)

Seymour Hersh, *Chain of Command: The Road from 9/11 to Abu Ghraib* (2004)

George Packer, *The Assassin's Gate: American In Iraq* (2005)

Ron Susskind, *The Price of Loyalty: George W. Bush, the White House, and the Education of Paul O'Neill* (2004)

Strobe Talbott and Nayan Chand, eds., *The Age of Terror: America and the World after September 11* (2001)

Bob Woodward, *Plan of Attack* (2004)

*The 9/11 Commission Report: Final Report of the National Commission on Terrorist Attacks upon the United States* (2004)

# Chapter Review

## Summary QUESTIONS

- What were the major components of the Bush doctrine and how were they implemented?
- What obstacles faced U.S. efforts to install democratic government in Iraq?
- How did efforts to strengthen security at home come in conflict with civil liberties?
- What role did differences over cultural issues play in the 2004 election?
- What were the political and social effects of the devastation brought by Hurricane Katrina?

## Chronology

| | |
|---|---|
| September 11, 2001 | Terrorist attacks on the World Trade Center buildings in New York City and the Pentagon building in Washington, D. C. |
| September 20, 2001 | Bush announces the start of a "War on Terror." |
| October 2001 | U. S. launches military operations in Afghanistan against Al Qaeda and the Taliban. |
| | Anthrax scare. |
| | USA Patriot Act passed by Congress. |
| March 2003 | U. S. initiates "Operation Iraqi Freedom" starting the War in Iraq. |
| May 1, 2003 | Bush announces the end of major combat operations in Iraq. |
| December 2003 | Sadaam Hussein captured. |
| | Bush administration announces the "Roadmap to Peace" policy for the Israeli/Palestinian problem. |
| April/May 2004 | Photos from Abu Ghraib released showing abuse of Iraqi prisoners by U. S. soldiers. |
| July 2004 | 9/11 commission report released. |
| August 2005 | Hurricane Katrina ravages New Orleans and the Gulf Coast. |

## Key Terms

The Bush Doctrine (p. 999)

War in Iraq (pp. 1000–1005)

Road map to peace (pp. 1005–1006)

9/11 Commission Report (p. 1008)

USA Patriot Act (p. 1009)

Hurricane Katrina (pp. 1015–1018)

**Agricultural Adjustment Act (1933)**   New Deal legislation that established the Agricultural Adjustment Administration (AAA) to improve agricultural prices by limiting market supplies; declared unconstitutional in *United States* v. *Butler* (1936).

**Alamo, Battle of the**   Siege in the Texas War for Independence, 1836, in which the San Antonio mission fell to the Mexicans, and Davy Crockett and Jim Bowie died.

***Alexander* v. *Holmes County Board of Education* (1969)**   Case fifteen years after the *Brown* decision in which the U.S. Supreme Court ordered an immediate end to segregation in public schools.

**Alien and Sedition Acts (1798)**   Four measures passed during the undeclared war with France that limited the freedoms of speech and press and restricted the liberty of noncitizens.

**America First Committee**   Largely midwestern isolationist organization supported by many prominent citizens, 1940–41.

**American Anti-Slavery Society**   National abolitionist organization founded in 1833 by New York philanthropists Arthur and Lewis Tappan, propagandist Theodore Dwight Weld, and others.

**American Colonization Society**   Organized in 1816 to encourage colonization of free blacks to Africa; West African nation of Liberia founded in 1822 to serve as a homeland for them.

**American Federation of Labor**   Founded in 1881 as a federation of trade unions, the AFL under president Samuel Gompers successfully pushed for the eight-hour workday.

**American Protective Association**   Nativist, anti-Catholic secret society founded in Iowa in 1887 and active until the end of the century.

**American System**   Program of internal improvements and protective tariffs promoted by Speaker of the House Henry Clay in his presidential campaign of 1824; his proposals formed the core of Whig ideology in the 1830s and 1840s.

**Antietam, Battle of (Battle of Sharpsburg)**   One of the bloodiest battles of the Civil War, fought to a standoff on September 17, 1862, in western Maryland.

**Antifederalists**   Forerunners of Thomas Jefferson's Democratic-Republican party; opposed the Constitution as a limitation on individual and states' rights, which led to the addition of a Bill of Rights to the document.

**Appomattox Court House, Virginia**   Site of the surrender of Confederate general Robert E. Lee to Union general Ulysses S. Grant on April 9, 1865, marking the end of the Civil War.

**Army-McCarthy hearings**   Televised U.S. Senate hearings in 1954 on Senator Joseph McCarthy's charges of disloyalty in the Army; his tactics contributed to his censure by the Senate.

**Atlanta Compromise**   Speech to the Cotton States and International Exposition in 1895 by educator Booker T. Washington, the leading black spokesman of the day; black scholar W. E. B. Du Bois gave the speech its derisive name and criticized Washington for encouraging blacks to accommodate segregation and disenfranchisement.

**Atlantic Charter**   Issued August 12, 1941, following meetings in Newfoundland between President Franklin D. Roosevelt and British prime minister Winston Churchill, the charter signaled the allies' cooperation and stated their war aims.

**Atomic Energy Commission**   Created in 1946 to supervise peacetime uses of atomic energy.

**Axis powers**   In World War II, the nations of Germany, Italy, and Japan.

**Aztec**   Mesoamerican people who were conquered by the Spanish under Hernando Cortés, 1519–28.

**Baby boom**   Markedly higher birth rate in the years following World War II; led to the biggest demographic "bubble" in American history.

**Bacon's Rebellion**   Unsuccessful 1676 revolt led by planter Nathaniel Bacon against Virginia governor William Berkeley's administration because it had failed to protect settlers from Indian raids.

***Bakke* v. *Board of Regents of California* (1978)**   Case in which the U.S. Supreme Court ruled against the California university system's use of racial quotas in admissions.

**Balance of trade**   Ratio of imports to exports.

**Bank of the United States**   Proposed by the first secretary of the treasury, Alexander Hamilton, the bank opened in 1791 and operated until 1811 to issue a uniform currency, make business loans, and collect tax monies. The Second Bank of the United States was chartered in 1816 but was not renewed by President Andrew Jackson twenty years later.

**Barbary pirates**   Plundering pirates off the Mediterranean coast of Africa; President Thomas Jefferson's refusal to pay them tribute to protect American ships sparked an undeclared naval war with North African nations, 1801–1805.

**Barbed wire**   First practical fencing material for the Great Plains was invented in 1873 and rapidly spelled the end of the open range.

**Battle of the Currents**   Conflict in the late 1880s between inventors Thomas Edison and George Westinghouse over direct versus alternating electric current; Westinghouse's alternating current (AC), the winner, allowed electricity to travel over long distances.

**Bay of Pigs Invasion**   Hoping to inspire a revolt against Fidel Castro, the CIA sent 1,500 Cuban exiles to invade their homeland on April 17, 1961, but the mission was a spectacular failure.

**Bill of Rights**   First ten amendments to the U.S. Constitution, adopted in 1791 to guarantee individual rights and to help secure ratification of the Constitution by the states.

**Black Codes (1865–66)**   Laws passed in southern states to restrict the rights of former slaves; to combat the codes, Congress passed the Civil Rights Act of 1866 and the Fourteenth Amendment and set up military governments in southern states that refused to ratify the amendment.

**Black Power**   Post-1966 rallying cry of a more militant civil rights movement.

**Bland-Allison Act (1878)**   Passed over President Rutherford B. Hayes's veto, the inflationary measure authorized the purchase each month of 2 to 4 million dollars' worth of silver for coinage.

**"Bleeding" Kansas**   Violence between pro- and antislavery settlers in the Kansas Territory, 1856.

**Bloody shirt, Waving the**   Republican references to Reconstruction-era violence in the South, used effectively in northern political campaigns against Democrats.

**Bonus Expeditionary Force**   Thousands of World War I veterans, who insisted on immediate payment of their bonus certificates, marched on Washington in 1932; violence ensued when President Herbert Hoover ordered their tent villages cleared.

**Boston Massacre**   Clash between British soldiers and a Boston mob, March 5, 1770, in which five colonists were killed.

**Boston Tea Party**   On December 16, 1773, the Sons of Liberty, dressed as Indians, dumped hundreds of chests of tea into Boston harbor to protest the Tea Act of 1773, under which the British exported to the colonies millions of pounds of cheap—but still taxed—tea, thereby undercutting the price of smuggled tea and forcing payment of the tea duty.

**Boxer Rebellion**   Chinese nationalist protest against Western commercial domination and cultural influence, 1900; a coalition of American, European, and Japanese forces put down the rebellion and reclaimed captured embassies in Peking (Beijing) within the year.

**Brain trust**   Group of advisers—many of them academics—that Franklin D. Roosevelt assembled to recommend New Deal policies during the early months of his presidency.

**Branch Davidians**   Religious cult that lived communally near Waco, Texas, and was involved in a fiery 1993 confrontation with federal authorities in which dozens of cult members died.

**Brook Farm**   Transcendentalist commune in West Roxbury, Massachusetts, populated from 1841 to 1847 principally by writers (Nathaniel Hawthorne, for one) and other intellectuals.

***Brown v. Board of Education of Topeka* (1954)**   U.S. Supreme Court decision that struck down racial segregation in public education and declared "separate but equal" unconstitutional.

**Budget and Accounting Act of 1921**   Created the Bureau of the Budget and the General Accounting Office.

**Bull Run, Battles of (First and Second Manassas)**   First land engagement of the Civil War took place on July 21, 1861, at Manassas Junction, Virginia, at which surprised Union troops quickly retreated; one year later, on August 29–30, Confederates captured the federal supply depot and forced Union troops back to Washington.

**Bunker Hill, Battle of**   First major battle of the Revolutionary War; it actually took place at nearby Breed's Hill, Massachusetts, on June 17, 1775.

**"Burned-Over District"**   Area of western New York strongly influenced by the revivalist fervor of the Second Great Awakening; Disciples of Christ and Mormons are among the many sects that trace their roots to the phenomenon.

**Burr conspiracy**   Scheme by Vice-President Aaron Burr to lead the secession of the Louisiana Territory from the United States; captured in 1807 and charged with treason, Burr was acquitted by the U.S. Supreme Court.

***Bush v. Gore* (2000)**   U.S. Supreme Court case that determined the winner of the disputed 2000 presidential election.

**Calhoun Resolutions**   In making the proslavery response to the Wilmot Proviso, Senator John C. Calhoun argued that barring slavery in Mexican acquisitions would violate the Fifth Amendment to the Constitution by depriving slave-holding settlers of their property.

**Calvinism**   Doctrine of predestination expounded by Swiss theologian John Calvin in 1536; influenced the Puritan, Presbyterian, German and Dutch Reformed, and Huguenot churches in the colonies.

**Camp David Accords**   Peace agreement between Israeli prime minister Menachem Begin and Egyptian president Anwar Sadat, brokered by President Jimmy Carter in 1978.

**Carpetbaggers**   Northern emigrants who participated in the Republican governments of the Reconstruction South.

**Chancellorsville, Battle of**   Confederate general Robert E. Lee won his last major victory and General "Stonewall" Jackson died in this Civil War battle in northern Virginia on May 1–4, 1863.

**Chattanooga, Battle of**   Union victory in eastern Tennessee on November 23–25, 1863; gave the North control of important rail lines and cleared the way for General William T. Sherman's march into Georgia.

**Chinese Exclusion Act (1882)**   Halted Chinese immigration to the United States.

**Civil Rights Act of 1866**   Along with the Fourteenth Amendment, guaranteed the rights of citizenship to freedmen.

**Civil Rights Act of 1957**   First federal civil rights law since Reconstruction; established the Civil Rights Commission and the Civil Rights Division of the Department of Justice.

**Civil Rights Act of 1964**   Outlawed discrimination in public accommodations and employment.

**Clipper ships**   Superior oceangoing sailing ships of the 1840s to 1860s that cut travel time in half; the clipper ship route around Cape Horn was the fastest way to travel between the coasts of the United States.

**Closed shop**   Hiring requirement that all workers in a business must be union members.

**Coercive Acts/Intolerable Acts (1774)**   Four parliamentary measures in reaction to the Boston Tea Party that forced payment for the tea, disallowed colonial trials of British soldiers, forced their quartering in private homes, and set up a military government.

**Cold war**   Term for tensions, 1945–89, between the Soviet Union and the United States, the two major world powers after World War II.

***Commonwealth v. Hunt* (1842)**   Landmark ruling of the Massachusetts supreme court establishing the legality of labor unions.

**Compromise of 1850**   Complex compromise mediated by Senator Henry Clay that headed off southern secession over California statehood; to appease the South it included a stronger fugitive slave law and delayed determination of the slave status of the New Mexico and Utah territories.

**Compromise of 1877**   Deal made by a special congressional commission on March 2, 1877, to resolve the disputed presidential election of 1876; Republican Rutherford B. Hayes, who had lost the popular vote, was declared the winner in exchange for the withdrawal of federal troops from the South, marking the end of Reconstruction.

**Congress of Industrial Organizations (CIO)**   Umbrella organization of semi-skilled industrial unions, formed in 1935 as the Committee for Industrial Organization and renamed in 1938.

**Congress of Racial Equality (CORE)**   Civil rights organization started in 1944 and best known for its "freedom rides," bus journeys challenging racial segregation in the South in 1961.

**Conspicuous consumption**   Phrase referring to extravagant spending to raise social standing, coined by Thorstein Veblen in *The Theory of the Leisure Class* (1899).

**Constitutional Convention**   Meeting in Philadelphia, May 25–September 17, 1787, of representatives from twelve colonies—excepting Rhode Island—to revise the existing Articles of Confederation; convention soon resolved to produce an entirely new constitution.

**Containment**   General U.S. strategy in the cold war that called for containing Soviet expansion; originally devised in 1947 by U.S. diplomat George F. Kennan.

**Continental Army**   Army authorized by the Continental Congress, 1775–84, to fight the British; commanded by General George Washington.

**Continental Congress**   Representatives of a loose confederation of colonies met first in Philadelphia in 1774 to formulate actions against British policies; the Second Continental Congress (1775–89) conducted the war and adopted the Declaration of Independence and the Articles of Confederation.

**Convict leasing**   System developed in the post–Civil War South that generated income for the states and satisfied planters' need for cheap labor by renting prisoners out; the convicts, however, were often treated poorly.

**Copperheads**   Northerners opposed to the Civil War.

**Coral Sea, Battle of the**   Fought on May 7–8, 1942, near the eastern coast of Australia, it was the first U.S. naval victory over Japan in World War II.

**Cotton gin**   Invented by Eli Whitney in 1793, the machine separated cotton seed from cotton fiber, speeding cotton processing and making profitable the cultivation of the more hardy, but difficult to clean, short-staple cotton; led directly to the dramatic nineteenth-century expansion of slavery in the South.

**Counterculture**   "Hippie" youth culture of the 1960s, which rejected the values of the dominant culture in favor of illicit drugs, communes, free sex, and rock music.

**Court-packing plan**   President Franklin D. Roosevelt's failed 1937 attempt to increase the number of U.S. Supreme Court justices from nine to fifteen in order to save his Second New Deal programs from constitutional challenges.

**Credit Mobilier scandal**   Millions of dollars in overcharges for building the Union Pacific Railroad were exposed; high officials of the Ulysses S. Grant administration were implicated but never charged.

**Cuban missile crisis**   Caused when the United States discovered Soviet offensive missile sites in Cuba in October 1962; the U.S.-Soviet confrontation was the cold war's closest brush with nuclear war.

**Crop-lien system**   Merchants extended credit to tenants based on their future crops, but high interest rates and the uncertainties of farming often led to inescapable debts (debt peonage).

**D-Day**   June 6, 1944, when an Allied amphibious assault landed on the Normandy coast and established a foothold in Europe from which Hitler's defenses could not recover.

***Dartmouth College v. Woodward* (1819)**   U.S. Supreme Court upheld the original charter of the college against New Hampshire's attempt to alter the board of trustees; set precedent of support of contracts against state interference.

**Declaration of Independence**   Document adopted on July 4, 1776, that made the break with Britain official; drafted by a committee of the Second Continental Congress including principal writer Thomas Jefferson.

**Deism**   Enlightenment thought applied to religion; emphasized reason, morality, and natural law.

**Department of Homeland Security**   Created to coordinate federal antiterrorist activity following the 2001 terrorist attacks on the World Trade Center and Pentagon.

**Depression of 1893**   Worst depression of the century, set off by a railroad failure, too much speculation on Wall Street, and low agricultural prices.

**Dixiecrats**   Deep South delegates who walked out of the 1948 Democratic National Convention in protest of the party's support for civil rights legislation and later formed the States' Rights (Dixiecrat) party, which nominated Strom Thurmond of South Carolina for president.

**Dominion of New England**   Consolidation into a single colony of the New England colonies—and later New York and New Jersey—by royal governor Edmund Andros in 1686; dominion reverted to individual colonial governments three years later.

**Donner Party**   Forty-seven surviving members of a group of migrants to California were forced to resort to cannibalism to survive a brutal winter trapped in the Sierra Nevadas, 1846–47; highest death toll of any group traveling the Overland Trail.

***Dred Scott v. Sandford* (1857)**   U.S. Supreme Court decision in which Chief Justice Roger B. Taney ruled that slaves could not sue for freedom and that Congress could not prohibit slavery in the territories, on the grounds that such a prohibition would violate the Fifth Amendment rights of slaveholders.

**Due-process clause** Clause in the Fifth and the Fourteenth amendments to the U.S. Constitution guaranteeing that states could not "deprive any person of life, liberty, or property, without due process of law."

**Dust Bowl** Great Plains counties where millions of tons of topsoil were blown away from parched farmland in the 1930s; massive migration of farm families followed.

**Eighteenth Amendment (1919)** Prohibition amendment that made illegal the manufacture, sale, or transportation of alcoholic beverages.

**Ellis Island** Reception center in New York Harbor through which most European immigrants to America were processed from 1892 to 1954.

**Emancipation Proclamation (1863)** President Abraham Lincoln issued a preliminary proclamation on September 22, 1862, freeing the slaves in the Confederate states as of January 1, 1863, the date of the final proclamation.

**Embargo Act of 1807** Attempt to exert economic pressure instead of waging war in reaction to continued British impressment of American sailors; smugglers easily circumvented the embargo, and it was repealed two years later.

**Emergency Banking Relief Act (1933)** First New Deal measure that provided for reopening the banks under strict conditions and took the United States off the gold standard.

**Emergency Immigration Act of 1921** Limited U.S. immigration to 3 percent of each foreign-born nationality in the 1910 census; three years later Congress restricted immigration even further.

**Encomienda** System under which officers of the Spanish conquistadores gained ownership of Indian land.

**ENIAC** Electronic Numerical Integrator and Computer, built in 1944, the early, cumbersome ancestor of the modern computer.

**Enlightenment** Revolution in thought begun in the seventeenth century that emphasized reason and science over the authority of traditional religion.

**Enola Gay** American B-29 bomber that dropped the atomic bomb on Hiroshima, Japan, on August 6, 1945.

**Environmental Protection Agency (EPA)** Created in 1970 during the first administration of President Richard M. Nixon to oversee federal pollution control efforts.

**Equal Rights Amendment** Amendment to guarantee equal rights for women, introduced in 1923 but not passed by Congress until 1972; it failed to be ratified by the states.

**Era of Good Feelings** Contemporary characterization of the administration of popular Democratic-Republican president James Monroe, 1817–25.

**Erie Canal** Most important and profitable of the barge canals of the 1820s and 1830s; stretched from Buffalo to Albany, New York, connecting the Great Lakes to the East Coast and making New York City the nation's largest port.

**Espionage and Sedition Acts (1917–18)** Limited criticism of government leaders and policies by imposing fines and prison terms on those who acted out in opposition to in the First World War; the most repressive measures passed up to that time.

**Fair Deal** Domestic reform proposals of the second Truman administration (1949–53); included civil rights legislation and repeal of the Taft-Hartley Act, but only extensions of some New Deal programs were enacted.

**Fair Employment Practices Commission** Created in 1941 by executive order, the FEPC sought to eliminate racial discrimination in jobs; it possessed little power but represented a step toward civil rights for African Americans.

**Family and Medical Leave Act (1993)** Allowed certain workers to take twelve weeks of unpaid leave each year for family health problems, including birth or adoption of a child.

**Farmers' Alliance** Two separate organizations (Northwestern and Southern) of the 1880s and 1890s that took the place of the Grange, worked for similar causes, and attracted landless, as well as landed, farmers to their membership.

**Federal Trade Commission Act (1914)** Established the Federal Trade Commission to enforce existing antitrust laws that prohibited business combinations in restraint of trade.

**The Federalist** Collection of eighty-five essays that appeared in the New York press in 1787–88 in support of the Constitution; written by Alexander Hamilton, James Madison, and John Jay but published under the pseudonym "Publius."

**Federalist party** One of the two first national political parties, it favored a strong central government.

**Fence-Cutters' War** Violent conflict in Texas, 1883–84, between large and small cattle ranchers over access to grazing land.

**"Fifty-four forty or fight"**   Democratic campaign slogan in the presidential election of 1844, urging that the northern border of Oregon be fixed at 54°40′ north latitude.

*Fletcher* v. *Peck* (1810)   U.S. Supreme Court decision in which Chief Justice John Marshall upheld the initial fraudulent sale contracts in the Yazoo Fraud cases; Congress paid $4.2 million to the original speculators in 1814.

**Fort Laramie Treaty (1851)**   Restricted the Plains Indians from using the Overland Trail and permitted the building of government forts.

**Fort McHenry**   Fort in Baltimore Harbor unsuccessfully bombarded by the British in September 1814; Francis Scott Key, a witness to the battle, was moved to write the words to "The Star-Spangled Banner."

**Fort Sumter**   First battle of the Civil War, in which the federal fort in Charleston (South Carolina) Harbor was captured by the Confederates on April 14, 1861, after two days of shelling.

**"Forty-niners"**   Speculators who went to northern California following the discovery of gold in 1848; the first of several years of large-scale migration was 1849.

**Fourteen Points**   President Woodrow Wilson's 1918 plan for peace after World War I; at the Versailles peace conference, however, he failed to incorporate all of the points into the treaty.

**Fourteenth Amendment (1868)**   Guaranteed rights of citizenship to former slaves, in words similar to those of the Civil Rights Act of 1866.

**Franchise**   The right to vote.

**"Free person of color"**   Negro or mulatto person not held in slavery; immediately before the Civil War, there were nearly a half million in the United States, split almost evenly between North and South.

**Free Soil party**   Formed in 1848 to oppose slavery in the territory acquired in the Mexican War; nominated Martin Van Buren for president in 1848, but by 1854 most of the party's members had joined the Republican party.

**Free Speech Movement**   Founded in 1964 at the University of California at Berkeley by student radicals protesting restrictions on their right to demonstrate.

**Freedmen's Bureau**   Reconstruction agency established in 1865 to protect the legal rights of former slaves and to assist with their education, jobs, health care, and landowning.

**French and Indian War**   Known in Europe as the Seven Years' War, the last (1755–63) of four colonial wars fought between England and France for control of North America east of the Mississippi River.

**Fugitive Slave Act of 1850**   Gave federal government authority in cases involving runaway slaves; so much more punitive and prejudiced in favor of slaveholders than the 1793 Fugitive Slave Act had been that Harriet Beecher Stowe was inspired to write *Uncle Tom's Cabin* in protest; the new law was part of the Compromise of 1850, included to appease the South over the admission of California as a free state.

**Fundamentalism**   Anti-modernist Protestant movement started in the early twentieth century that proclaimed the literal truth of the Bible; the name came from *The Fundamentals*, published by conservative leaders.

**Gadsden Purchase (1853)**   Thirty thousand square miles in present-day Arizona and New Mexico bought by Congress from Mexico primarily for the Southern Pacific Railroad's transcontinental route.

**Gentlemen's Agreement (1907)**   United States would not exclude Japanese immigrants if Japan would voluntarily limit the number of immigrants coming to the United States.

**Gettysburg, Battle of**   Fought in southern Pennsylvania, July 1–3, 1863; the Confederate defeat and the simultaneous loss at Vicksburg spelled the end of the South's chances in the Civil War.

*Gibbons* v. *Ogden* (1824)   U.S. Supreme Court decision reinforcing the "commerce clause" (the federal government's right to regulate interstate commerce) of the Constitution; Chief Justice John Marshall ruled against the State of New York's granting of steamboat monopolies.

*Gideon* v. *Wainwright* (1963)   U.S. Supreme Court decision guaranteeing legal counsel for indigent felony defendants.

***The Gilded Age***   Mark Twain and Charles Dudley Warner's 1873 novel, the title of which became the popular name for the period from the end of the Civil War to the turn of the century.

**Glass-Owen Federal Reserve Act (1913)**   Created a Federal Reserve System of regional banks and a Federal Reserve Board to stabilize the economy by regulating the supply of currency and controlling credit.

**Glass-Steagall Act (Banking Act of 1933)**  Established the Federal Deposit Insurance Corporation and included banking reforms, some designed to control speculation. A banking act of the Hoover administration, passed in 1932 and also known as the Glass-Steagall Act, was designed to expand credit.

**Good Neighbor Policy**  Proclaimed by President Franklin D. Roosevelt in his first inaugural address in 1933, it sought improved diplomatic relations between the United States and its Latin American neighbors.

**Grandfather clause**  Loophole created by southern disfranchising legislatures of the 1890s for illiterate white males whose grandfathers had been eligible to vote in 1867.

**Granger movement**  Political movement that grew out of the Patrons of Husbandry, an educational and social organization for farmers founded in 1867; the Grange had its greatest success in the Midwest of the 1870s, lobbying for government control of railroad and grain elevator rates and establishing farmers' cooperatives.

**Great Awakening**  Fervent religious revival movement in the 1720s through the 1740s that was spread throughout the colonies by ministers like New England Congregationalist Jonathan Edwards and English revivalist George Whitefield.

**Great Compromise (Connecticut Compromise)**  Mediated the differences between the New Jersey and Virginia delegations to the Constitutional Convention by providing for a bicameral legislature, the upper house of which would have equal representation and the lower house of which would be apportioned by population.

**Great Depression**  Worst economic depression in American history; it was spurred by the stock market crash of 1929 and lasted until World War II.

**Great Migration**  Large-scale migration of southern blacks during and after World War I to the North, where jobs had become available during the labor shortage of the war years.

**Great Society**  Term coined by President Lyndon B. Johnson in his 1965 State of the Union address, in which he proposed legislation to address problems of voting rights, poverty, diseases, education, immigration, and the environment.

**Greenback party**  Formed in 1876 in reaction to economic depression, the party favored issuance of unsecured paper money to help farmers repay debts; the movement for free coinage of silver took the place of the greenback movement by the 1880s.

**Habeas corpus, Writ of**  An essential component of English common law and of the U.S. Constitution that guarantees that citizens may not be imprisoned without due process of law; literally means, "you must have the body."

**Half-Breeds**  During the presidency of Rutherford B. Hayes, 1877–81, a moderate Republican party faction led by Senator James G. Blaine that favored some reforms of the civil service system and a restrained policy toward the defeated South.

**Harlem Renaissance**  African-American literary and artistic movement of the 1920s and 1930s centered in New York City's Harlem district; writers Langston Hughes, Jean Toomer, Zora Neale Hurston, and Countee Cullen were among those active in the movement.

**Harper's Ferry, Virginia**  Site of abolitionist John Brown's failed raid on the federal arsenal, October 16–17, 1859; he intended to arm the slaves, but ten of his compatriots were killed, and Brown became a martyr to his cause after his capture and execution.

**Hartford Convention**  Meeting of New England Federalists on December 15, 1814, to protest the War of 1812; proposed seven constitutional amendments (limiting embargoes and changing requirements for officeholding, declaration of war, and admission of new states), but the war ended before Congress could respond.

**Hawley-Smoot Tariff Act (1930)**  Raised tariffs to an unprecedented level and worsened the depression by raising prices and discouraging foreign trade.

**Haymarket Affair**  Riot during an anarchist protest at Haymarket Square in Chicago on May 4, 1886, over violence during the McCormick Harvester Company strike; the deaths of eleven, including seven policemen, helped hasten the demise of the Knights of Labor, even though they were not responsible for the riot.

**Hessians**  German soldiers, most from Hesse-Cassel principality (hence he name), paid to fight for the British in the Revolutionary War.

**Holding company**  Investment company that holds controlling interest in the securities of other companies.

**Homestead Act (1862)**  Authorized Congress to grant 160 acres of public land to a western settler, who had only to live on the land for five years to establish title.

**Homestead Strike**  Violent strike at the Carnegie Steel Company near Pittsburgh in 1892 that culminated in the disintegration of the Amalgamated Association of Iron and Steel Workers, the first steelworkers' union.

**House Un-American Activities Committee (HUAC)**   Formed in 1938 to investigate subversives in the government; best-known investigations were of Hollywood no tables and of former State Department official Alger Hiss, who was accused in 1948 of espionage and Communist party membership.

**Hundred Days**   Extraordinarily productive first three months of President Franklin D. Roosevelt's administration in which a special session of Congress enacted fifteen of his New Deal proposals.

**Impeachment**   Bringing charges against a public official; for example, the House of Representatives can impeach a president for "treason, bribery, or other high crimes and misdemeanors" by majority vote, and after the trial the Senate can remove the president by a vote of two-thirds.

**Implied powers**   Federal powers beyond those specifically enumerated in the U.S. Constitution; the Federalists argued that the "elastic clause" of Article I, Section 8, of the Constitution implicitly gave the federal government broad powers, while the Antifederalists held that the federal government's powers were explicitly limited by the Constitution.

**"In God We Trust"**   Phrase placed on all new U.S. currency as of 1954.

**Indentured servant**   Settler who signed on for a temporary period of servitude to a master in exchange for passage to the New World; Virginia and Pennsylvania were largely peopled in the seventeenth and eighteenth centuries by English indentured servants.

**Independent Treasury Act (1840)**   Promoted by President Martin Van Buren, the measure sought to stabilize the economy by preventing state banks from printing unsecured paper currency and establishing an independent treasury based on specie.

**Indian Peace Commission**   Established in 1867 to end the Indian wars in the West, the commission's solution was to contain the Indians in a system of reservations.

**Indian Removal Act (1830)**   Signed by President Andrew Jackson, the law permitted the negotiation of treaties to obtain the Indians' lands in exchange for their relocation to what would become Oklahoma.

**Industrial Workers of the World**   Radical union organized in Chicago in 1905 and nicknamed the Wobblies; its opposition to World War I led to its destruction by the federal government under the Espionage Act.

**Internal improvements**   In the early national period the phrase referred to road building and the development of water transportation.

**Interstate Commerce Commission**   Reacting to the U.S. Supreme Court's ruling in *Wabash Railroad* v. *Illinois* (1886), Congress established the ICC to curb abuses in the railroad industry by regulating rates.

**Iran-Contra affair**   Scandal of the second Reagan administration involving sale of arms to Iran in partial exchange for release of hostages in Lebanon and use of the arms money to aid the Contras in Nicaragua, which had been expressly forbidden by Congress.

**Iron Curtain**   Term coined by Winston Churchill to describe the cold war divide between western Europe and the Soviet Union's eastern European satellites.

**Irreconcilables**   Group of isolationist U.S. senators who fought ratification of the Treaty of Versailles, 1919–20, because of their opposition to American membership in the League of Nations.

**Jamestown, Virginia**   Site in 1607 of the first permanent English settlement in the New World.

**Jay's Treaty**   Treaty with Britain negotiated in 1794 by Chief Justice John Jay; Britain agreed to vacate forts in the Northwest Territories, and festering disagreements (border with Canada, prewar debts, shipping claims) would be settled by commission.

**Jim Crow**   Minstrel show character whose name became synonymous with post-Reconstruction laws revoking civil rights for freedmen and with racial segregation generally.

**Judiciary Act of 1801**   Enacted by the lame duck Congress to allow the Federalists, the losing party in the presidential election, to reorganize the judiciary and fill the open judgeships with Federalists.

**Kansas-Nebraska Act (1854)**   Law sponsored by Illinois senator Stephen A. Douglas to allow settlers in newly organized territories north of the Missouri border to decide the slavery issue for themselves; fury over the resulting nullification of the Missouri Compromise of 1820 led to violence in Kansas and to the formation of the Republican party.

**Kellogg-Briand Pact**   Representatives of sixty-two nations in 1928 signed the pact (also called the Pact of Paris) to outlaw war.

**Kentucky and Virginia Resolutions (1798–99)**   Passed in response to the Alien and Sedition Acts, the resolutions advanced the state-compact theory that held states could nullify an act of Congress if they deemed it unconstitutional.

**King William's War (War of the League of Augsburg)**   First (1689–97) of four colonial wars between England and France.

**King's Mountain, Battle of**   Upcountry South Carolina irregulars defeated British troops under Patrick Ferguson on October 7, 1780, in what proved to be the turning point of the Revolutionary War in the South.

**Knights of Labor**   Founded in 1869, the first national union picked up many members after the disastrous 1877 railroad strike but lasted, under the leadership of Terence V. Powderly, only into the 1890s; supplanted by the American Federation of Labor.

**Know-Nothing (American) party**   Nativist, anti-Catholic third party organized in 1854 in reaction to large-scale German and Irish immigration; the party's only presidential candidate was Millard Fillmore in 1856.

**Korean War**   Conflict touched off in 1950 when Communist North Korea invaded South Korea, which had been under U.S. control since the end of World War II; fighting largely by U.S. forces continued until 1953.

**Ku Klux Klan**   Organized in Pulaski, Tennessee, in 1866 to terrorize former slaves who voted and held political offices during Reconstruction; a revived organization in the 1910s and 1920s stressed white, Anglo-Saxon, fundamentalist Protestant supremacy; the Klan revived a third time to fight the civil rights movement of the 1950s and 1960s in the South.

**Land Ordinance of 1785**   Directed surveying of the Northwest Territory into townships of thirty-six sections (square miles) each, the sale of the sixteenth section of which was to be used to finance public education.

**League of Nations**   Organization of nations to mediate disputes and avoid war established after World War I as part of the Treaty of Versailles; President Woodrow Wilson's "Fourteen Points" speech to Congress in 1918 proposed the formation of the league.

**Lecompton Constitution**   Controversial constitution drawn up in 1857 by proslavery Kansas delegates seeking statehood; rejected in 1858 by an overwhelmingly antislavery electorate.

**Legal Tender Act (1862)**   Helped the U.S. government pay for the Civil War by authorizing the printing of paper currency.

**Lend-Lease Act (1941)**   Permitted the United States to lend or lease arms and other supplies to the Allies, signifying increasing likelihood of American involvement in World War II.

**Levittown**   Low-cost, mass-produced development of suburban tract housing built by William Levitt on Long Island in 1947.

**Lexington and Concord, Battle of**   The first shots fired in the Revolutionary War, on April 19, 1775, near Boston; approximately 100 minutemen and 250 British soldiers were killed.

**Leyte Gulf, Battle of**   Largest sea battle in history, fought on October 25, 1944, and won by the United States off the Philippine island of Leyte; Japanese losses were so great that they could not rebound.

**Liberty party**   Abolitionist political party that nominated James G. Birney for president in 1840 and 1844; merged with the Free Soil party in 1848.

**Lincoln-Douglas debates**   Series of senatorial campaign debates in 1858 focusing on the issue of slavery in the territories; held in Illinois between Republican Abraham Lincoln, who made a national reputation for himself, and incumbent Democratic senator Stephen A. Douglas, who managed to hold onto his seat.

**Little Bighorn, Battle of**   Most famous battle of the Great Sioux War took place in 1876 in the Montana Territory; combined Sioux and Cheyenne warriors massacred a vastly outnumbered U.S. Cavalry commanded by Lieutenant Colonel George Armstrong Custer.

**Lost Colony**   English expedition of 117 settlers, including Virginia Dare, the first English child born in the New World; colony disappeared from Roanoke Island in the Outer Banks sometime between 1587 and 1590.

**Louisiana Purchase**  President Thomas Jefferson's 1803 purchase from France of the important port of New Orleans and 828,000 square miles west of the Mississippi River to the Rocky Mountains; it more than doubled the territory of the United States at a cost of only $15 million.

*Lusitania*  British passenger liner sunk by a German U-boat, May 7, 1915, creating a diplomatic crisis and public outrage at the loss of 128 Americans (roughly 10 percent of the total aboard); Germany agreed to pay reparations, and the United States waited two more years to enter World War I.

**Lyceum movement**  Founded in 1826, the movement promoted adult public education through lectures and performances.

**Maize**  Indian corn, native to the New World.

**Manhattan Project**  Secret American plan during World War II to develop an atomic bomb; J. Robert Oppenheimer led the team of physicists at Los Alamos, New Mexico.

**Manifest Destiny**  Imperialist phrase first used in 1845 to urge annexation of Texas; used thereafter to encourage American settlement of European colonial and Indian lands in the Great Plains and Far West.

*Marbury* v. *Madison* (**1803**)  First U.S. Supreme Court decision to declare a federal law—the Judiciary Act of 1801—unconstitutional; President John Adams's "midnight appointment" of Federalist judges prompted the suit.

**March on Washington**  Civil rights demonstration on August 28, 1963, where the Reverend Martin Luther King, Jr., gave his "I Have a Dream" speech on the steps of the Lincoln Memorial.

**Marshall Plan**  U.S. program for the reconstruction of post–World War II Europe through massive aid to former enemy nations as well as allies; proposed by General George C. Marshall in 1947.

**Massive resistance**  In reaction to the *Brown* decision of 1954, U.S. senator Harry Byrd encouraged southern states to defy federally mandated school integration.

**Maya**  Pre-Columbian society in Mesoamerica before about A.D. 900.

**Mayflower Compact**  Signed in 1620 aboard the *Mayflower* before the Pilgrims landed at Plymouth, the document committed the group to majority-rule government; remained in effect until 1691.

**Maysville Road**  Bill Federal funding for a Kentucky road, vetoed by President Andrew Jackson in 1830.

**McCarran Internal Security Act (1950)**  Passed over President Harry S. Truman's veto, the law required registration of American Communist party members, denied them passports, and allowed them to be detained as suspected subversives.

*McCulloch* v. *Maryland* (**1819**)  U.S. Supreme Court decision in which Chief Justice John Marshall, holding that Maryland could not tax the Second Bank of the United States, supported the authority of the federal government versus the states.

**McNary-Haugen Bill**  Vetoed by President Calvin Coolidge in 1927 and 1928, the bill to aid farmers would have artificially raised agricultural prices by selling surpluses overseas for low prices and selling the reduced supply in the United States for higher prices.

**Meat Inspection Act (1906)**  Passed largely in reaction to Upton Sinclair's *The Jungle*, the law set strict standards of cleanliness in the meat-packing industry.

**Mercantilism**  Limitation and exploitation of colonial trade by an imperial power.

**Mestizo**  Person of mixed Native American and European ancestry.

**Mexican War**  Controversial war with Mexico for control of California and New Mexico, 1846–48; the Treaty of Guadalupe Hidalgo fixed the border at the Rio Grande and extended the United States to the Pacific coast, annexing more than a half-million square miles of potential slave territory.

**Midway, Battle of**  Decisive American victory near Midway Island in the South Pacific on June 4, 1942; the Japanese navy never recovered its superiority over the U.S. navy.

**Military Reconstruction Act (1867)**  Established military governments in ten Confederate states—excepting Tennessee—and required that the states ratify the Fourteenth Amendment and permit freedmen to vote.

**Minstrel show**  Blackface vaudeville entertainment popular in the decades surrounding the Civil War.

*Miranda* v. *Arizona* (**1966**)  U.S. Supreme Court decision required police to advise persons in custody of their rights to legal counsel and against self-incrimination.

**Missouri Compromise**  Deal proposed by Kentucky senator Henry Clay to resolve the slave/free imbalance in Congress that would result from Missouri's admission as a slave state; in the compromise of March 20, 1820, Maine's admission as a free state offset Missouri, and slavery was prohibited in the remainder of the Louisiana Territory north of the southern border of Missouri.

**Molly Maguires**  Secret organization of Irish coal miners that used violence to intimidate mine officials in the 1870s.

***Monitor* and *Merrimack* Battle of the**  First engagement between ironclad ships; fought at Hampton Roads, Virginia, on March 9, 1862.

**Monroe Doctrine**  President James Monroe's declaration to Congress on December 2, 1823, that the American continents would be thenceforth closed to colonization but that the United States would honor existing colonies of European nations.

**Moral Majority**  Televangelist Jerry Falwell's political lobbying organization, the name of which became synonymous with the religious right—conservative evangelical Protestants who helped ensure President Ronald Reagan's 1980 victory.

**Mormons**  Founded in 1830 by Joseph Smith, the sect (officially, the Church of Jesus Christ of Latter-Day Saints) was a product of the intense revivalism of the "Burned-Over District" of New York; Smith's successor Brigham Young led 15,000 followers to Utah in 1847 to escape persecution.

**Montgomery bus boycott**  Sparked by Rosa Parks's arrest on December 1, 1955, a successful year-long boycott protesting segregation on city buses; led by the Reverend Martin Luther King.

**Muckrakers**  Writers who exposed corruption and abuses in politics, business, meat-packing, child labor, and more, primarily in the first decade of the twentieth century; their popular books and magazine articles spurred public interest in progressive reform.

**Mugwumps**  Reform wing of the Republican party which supported Democrat Grover Cleveland for president in 1884 over Republican James G. Blaine, whose influence peddling had been revealed in the Mulligan letters of 1876.

***Munn v. Illinois*** **(1877)**  U.S. Supreme Court ruling that upheld a Granger law allowing the state to regulate grain elevators.

**NAFTA**  Approved in 1993, the North American Free Trade Agreement with Canada and Mexico allowed goods to travel across their borders free of tariffs; critics argued that American workers would lose their jobs to cheaper Mexican labor.

**National Aeronautics and Space Administration (NASA)**  In response to the Soviet Union's launching of *Sputnik*, Congress created this federal agency in 1957 to coordinate research and administer the space program.

**National Association for the Advancement of Colored People (NAACP)**  Founded in 1910, this civil rights organization brought lawsuits against discriminatory practices and published *The Crisis*, a journal edited by African-American scholar W. E. B. Du Bois.

**National Defense Education Act (1958)**  Passed in reaction to America's perceived inferiority in the space race, the appropriation encouraged education in science and modern languages through student loans, university research grants, and aid to public schools.

**National Industrial Recovery Act (1933)**  Passed on the last of the Hundred Days, it created public-works jobs through the Federal Emergency Relief Administration and established a system of self-regulation for industry through the National Recovery Administration, which was ruled unconstitutional in 1935.

**National Organization for Women**  Founded in 1966 by writer Betty Friedan and other feminists, NOW pushed for abortion rights and nondiscrimination in the workplace, but within a decade it became radicalized and lost much of its constituency.

**National Road**  First federal interstate road, built between 1811 and 1838 and stretching from Cumberland, Maryland, to Vandalia, Illinois.

**National Security Act (1947)**  Authorized the reorganization of government to coordinate military branches and security agencies; created the National Security Council, the Central Intelligence Agency, and the National Military Establishment (later renamed the Department of Defense).

**National Youth Administration**  Created in 1935 as part of the Works Progress Administration, it employed millions of youths who had left school.

**Nativism**  Anti-immigrant and anti-Catholic feeling in the 1830s through the 1850s; the largest group was New York's Order of the Star-Spangled Banner, which expanded into the American, or Know-Nothing, party in 1854.

**Naval stores**    Tar, pitch, and turpentine made from pine resin and used in shipbuilding; an important industry in the southern colonies, especially North Carolina.

**Navigation Acts**    Passed by the English Parliament to control colonial trade and bolster the mercantile system, 1650–1775; enforcement of the acts led to growing resentment by colonists.

**Neutrality Acts**    Series of laws passed between 1935 and 1939 to keep the United States from becoming involved in war by prohibiting American trade and travel to warring nations.

**New Deal**    Franklin D. Roosevelt's campaign promise, in his speech to the Democratic National Convention of 1932, to combat the Great Depression with a "new deal for the American people"; the phrase became a catchword for his ambitious plan of economic programs.

**New England Anti-Slavery Society**    Abolitionist organization founded in 1832 by William Lloyd Garrison of Massachusetts, publisher of the *Liberator*.

**New Freedom**    Democrat Woodrow Wilson's political slogan in the presidential campaign of 1912; Wilson wanted to improve the banking system, lower tariffs, and, by breaking up monopolies, give small businesses freedom to compete.

**New Frontier**    John F. Kennedy's program, stymied by a Republican Congress and his abbreviated term; his successor Lyndon B. Johnson had greater success with many of the same concepts.

**New Harmony**    Founded in Indiana by British industrialist Robert Owen in 1825, the short-lived New Harmony Community of Equality was one of the few nineteenth-century communal experiments not based on religious ideology.

**New Left**    Radical youth protest movement of the 1960s, named by leader Tom Hayden to distinguish it from the Old (Marxist-Leninist) Left of the 1930s.

**New Nationalism**    Platform of the Progressive party and slogan of former president Theodore Roosevelt in the presidential campaign of 1912; stressed government activism, including regulation of trusts, conservation, and recall of state court decisions that had nullified progressive programs.

**New Orleans, Battle of**    Last battle of the War of 1812, fought on January 8, 1815, weeks after the peace treaty was signed but prior to its ratification; General Andrew Jackson led the victorious American troops.

**New South**    *Atlanta Constitution* editor Henry W. Grady's 1886 term for the prosperous post–Civil War South he envisioned: democratic, industrial, urban, and free of nostalgia for the defeated plantation South.

**Nineteenth Amendment (1920)**    Granted women the right to vote.

**Nisei**    Japanese Americans; literally, "second generation."

**Normalcy**    Word coined by future president Warren G. Harding as part of a 1920 campaign speech—"not nostrums, but normalcy"—signifying his awareness that the public was tired of progressivism, war, and sacrifice.

**North Atlantic Treaty Organization (NATO)**    Defensive alliance founded in 1949 by ten western European nations, the United States, and Canada to deter Soviet expansion in Europe.

**Northwest Ordinance of 1787**    Created the Northwest Territory (area north of the Ohio River and west of Pennsylvania), established conditions for self-government and statehood, included a Bill of Rights, and permanently prohibited slavery.

**Nullification**    Concept of invalidation of a federal law within the borders of a state; first expounded in the Kentucky and Virginia Resolutions (1798), cited by South Carolina in its Ordinance of Nullification (1832) of the Tariff of Abominations, used by southern states to explain their secession from the Union (1861), and cited again by southern states to oppose the *Brown* v. *Board of Education* decision (1954).

**Nullification**    Proclamation President Andrew Jackson's strong criticism of South Carolina's Ordinance of Nullification (1832) as disunionist and potentially treasonous.

**Office of Price Administration**    Created in 1941 to control wartime inflation and price fixing resulting from shortages of many consumer goods, the OPA imposed wage and price freezes and administered a rationing system.

**Okies**    Displaced farm families from the Oklahoma dust bowl who migrated to California during the 1930s in search of jobs.

**Old Southwest**    In the antebellum period, the states of Alabama, Mississippi, Louisiana, Texas, Arkansas, and parts of Tennessee, Kentucky, and Florida.

**Oneida Community**   Utopian community founded in 1848; the Perfectionist religious group practiced universal marriage until leader John Humphrey Noyes, fearing prosecution, escaped to Canada in 1879.

**OPEC**   Organization of Petroleum Exporting Countries.

**Open Door Policy**   In hopes of protecting the Chinese market for U.S. exports, Secretary of State John Hay unilaterally announced in 1899 that Chinese trade would be open to all nations.

**Operation Desert Storm**   Multinational allied force that defeated Iraq in the Gulf War of January 1991.

**Operation Dixie**   CIO's largely ineffective post–World War II campaign to unionize southern workers.

**Oregon fever**   Enthusiasm for emigration to the Oregon Country in the late 1830s and early 1840s.

**Ostend Manifesto**   Memorandum written in 1854 from Ostend, Belgium, by the U.S. ministers to England, France, and Spain recommending purchase or seizure of Cuba in order to increase the United States' slaveholding territory.

**Overland (Oregon) Trail**   Route of wagon trains bearing settlers from Independence, Missouri, to the Oregon Country in the 1840s through the 1860s.

**Overseer**   Manager of slave labor on a plantation.

**Panic of 1819**   Financial collapse brought on by sharply falling cotton prices, declining demand for American exports, and reckless western land speculation.

**Panic of 1837**   Major economic depression lasting about six years; touched off by a British financial crisis and made worse by falling cotton prices, credit and currency problems, and speculation in land, canals, and railroads.

**Panic of 1857**   Economic depression lasting about two years and brought on by falling grain prices and a weak financial system; the South was largely protected by international demand for its cotton.

**Panic of 1873**   Severe six-year depression marked by bank failures and railroad and insurance bankruptcies.

**Peace of Paris**   Signed on September 3, 1783, the treaty ending the Revolutionary War and recognizing American independence from Britain also established the border between Canada and the United States, fixed the western border at the Mississippi River, and ceded Florida to Spain.

**Pendleton Civil Service Act (1883)**   Established the Civil Service Commission and marked the end of the spoils system.

**Pentagon Papers**   Informal name for the Defense Department's secret history of the Vietnam conflict; leaked to the press by former official Daniel Ellsberg and published in the *New York Times* in 1971.

**Pequot War**   Massacre in 1637 and subsequent dissolution of the Pequot Nation by Puritan settlers, who seized the Indians' lands.

**Personal Responsibility and Work Opportunity Act (1996)**   Welfare reform measure that mandated state administration of federal aid to the poor.

**Philippine Sea, Battle of the**   Costly Japanese defeat of June 19–20, 1944; led to the resignation of Premier Tojo and his cabinet.

**Pilgrims Puritan**   Separatists who broke completely with the Church of England and sailed to the New World aboard the *Mayflower*, founding Plymouth Colony on Cape Cod in 1620.

**Pinckney's Treaty**   Treaty with Spain negotiated by Thomas Pinckney in 1795; established United States boundaries at the Mississippi River and the thirty-first parallel and allowed open transportation on the Mississippi.

**Planter**   In the antebellum South, the owner of a large farm worked by twenty or more slaves.

**Platt Amendment (1901)**   Reserved the United States' right to intervene in Cuban affairs and forced newly independent Cuba to host American naval bases on the island.

*Plessy* **v.** *Ferguson* **(1896)**   U.S. Supreme Court decision supporting the legality of Jim Crow laws that permitted or required "separate but equal" facilities for blacks and whites.

**Poll tax**   Tax that must be paid in order to be eligible to vote; used as an effective means of disenfranchising black citizens after Reconstruction, since they often could not afford even a modest fee.

**Popular sovereignty**   Allowed settlers in a disputed territory to decide the slavery issue for themselves.

**Populist party**   Political success of Farmers' Alliance candidates encouraged the formation in 1892 of the National People's party (later renamed the Populist party); active until 1912, it advocated a variety of reform issues, including free coinage of silver, income tax, postal savings, regulation of railroads, and direct election of U.S. senators.

**Pottawatomie Massacre** Murder of five proslavery settlers in eastern Kansas led by abolitionist John Brown on May 24–25, 1856.

**Potsdam Conference** Last meeting of the major Allied powers, the conference took place outside Berlin from July 17 to August 2, 1945; United States president Harry Truman, Soviet dictator Joseph Stalin, and British prime minister Clement Atlee finalized plans begun at Yalta.

**Proclamation of Amnesty and Reconstruction** President Lincoln's plan for reconstruction, issued in 1863, allowed southern states to rejoin the Union if 10 percent of the 1860 electorate signed loyalty pledges, accepted emancipation, and had received presidential pardons.

**Proclamation of 1763** Royal directive issued after the French and Indian War prohibiting settlement, surveys, and land grants west of the Appalachian Mountains; although it was soon overridden by treaties, colonists continued to harbor resentment.

**Progressive party** Created when former president Theodore Roosevelt broke away from the Republican party to run for president again in 1912; the party supported progressive reforms similar to the Democrats but stopped short of seeking to eliminate trusts.

**Progressivism** Broad-based reform movement, 1900–17, that sought overnmental help in solving problems in many areas of American life, including education, public health, the economy, the environment, labor, transportation, and politics.

**Protestant Reformation** Reform movement that resulted in the establishment of Protestant denominations; begun by German monk Martin Luther when he posted his "Ninety-five Theses" (complaints of abuses in the Catholic church) in 1517.

**Pullman Strike** Strike against the Pullman Palace Car Company in the company town of Pullman, Illinois, on May 11, 1894, by the American Railway Union under Eugene V. Debs; the strike was crushed by court injunctions and federal troops two months later.

**Pure Food and Drug Act (1906)** First law to regulate manufacturing of food and medicines; prohibited dangerous additives and inaccurate labeling.

**Puritans** English religious group that sought to purify the Church of England; founded the Massachusetts Bay Colony under John Winthrop in 1630.

**Quartering Act (1765)** Parliamentary act requiring colonies to house and provision British troops.

**Radical Republicans** Senators and congressmen who, strictly identifying the Civil War with the abolitionist cause, sought swift emancipation of the slaves, punishment of the rebels, and tight controls over the former Confederate states after the war.

**Railroad Strike of 1877** Violent but ultimately unsuccessful interstate strike, which resulted in extensive property damage and many deaths.

**Reaganomics** Popular name for President Ronald Reagan's philosophy of "supply side" economics, which combined tax cuts, less government spending, and a balanced budget with an unregulated marketplace.

**Reconstruction Finance Corporation** Federal program established in 1932 under President Herbert Hoover to loan money to banks and other institutions to help them avert bankruptcy.

**Red Scare** Fear among many Americans after World War I of Communists in particular and noncitizens in general, a reaction to the Russian Revolution, mail bombs, strikes, and riots.

**Redcoats** Nickname for British soldiers, after their red uniform jackets.

**Redeemers/Bourbons** Conservative white Democrats, many of whom had been planters or businessmen before the Civil War, who reclaimed control of the South following the end of Reconstruction.

**Regulators** Groups of backcountry Carolina settlers who protested colonial policies; North Carolina royal governor William Tryon retaliated at the Battle of Alamance on May 17, 1771.

**Report on Manufactures** First secretary of the treasury Alexander Hamilton's 1791 analysis that accurately foretold the future of American industry and proposed tariffs and subsidies to promote it.

**Republican party** Organized in 1854 by antislavery Whigs, Democrats, and Free Soilers in response to the passage of the Kansas-Nebraska Act; nominated John C. Frémont for president in 1856 and Abraham Lincoln in 1860.

**Republicans** Political faction that succeeded the Antifederalists after ratification of the Constitution; led by Thomas

Jefferson and James Madison, it soon developed into the Democratic-Republican party.

**Reservationists**   Group of U.S. senators led by Majority Leader Henry Cabot Lodge who would only agree to ratification of the Treaty of Versailles subject to certain reservations, most notably the removal of Article X of the League of Nations Covenant.

**Revolution of 1800**   First time that an American political party surrendered power to the opposition party; Jefferson, a Democratic-Republican, had defeated incumbent Adams, a Federalist, for president.

**Right-to-work**   State laws enacted to prevent imposition of the closed shop; any worker, whether or not a union member, could be hired.

*Roe* v. *Wade* (1973)   U.S. Supreme Court decision requiring states to permit first-trimester abortions.

**Roosevelt Corollary (1904)**   President Theodore Roosevelt announced in what was essentially a corollary to the Monroe Doctrine that the United States could intervene militarily to prevent interference from European powers in the Western Hemisphere.

**Romanticism**   Philosophical, literary, and artistic movement of the nineteenth century that was largely a reaction to the rationalism of the previous century; romantics valued emotion, mysticism, and individualism.

**Rough Riders**   The 1st U.S. Volunteer Cavalry, led in battle in the Spanish-American War by Theodore Roosevelt; they were victorious in their only battle near Santiago, Cuba, and Roosevelt used the notoriety to aid his political career.

**Santa Fe Trail**   Beginning in the 1820s, a major trade route from St. Louis, Missouri, to Santa Fe, New Mexico Territory.

**Saratoga, Battle of**   Major defeat of British general John Burgoyne and more than 5,000 British troops at Saratoga, New York, on October 17, 1777.

**Scalawags**   Southern white Republicans—some former Unionists—who served in Reconstruction governments.

*Schenck* v. *U.S.* (1919)   U.S. Supreme Court decision upholding the wartime Espionage and Sedition Acts; in the opinion he wrote for the case, Justice Oliver Wendell Holmes set the now-familiar "clear and present danger" standard.

**Scientific management**   Analysis of worker efficiency using measurements like "time and motion" studies to achieve greater productivity; introduced by Frederick Winslow Taylor in 1911.

**Scottsboro case (1931)**   In overturning verdicts against nine black youths accused of raping two white women, the U.S. Supreme Court established precedents in *Powell* v. *Alabama* (1932), that adequate counsel must be appointed in capital cases, and in *Norris* v. *Alabama* (1935), that African Americans cannot be excluded from juries.

**Second Great Awakening**   Religious revival movement of the early decades of the nineteenth century, in reaction to the growth of secularism and rationalist religion; began the predominance of the Baptist and Methodist churches.

**Second Red Scare**   Post–World War II Red Scare focused on the fear of Communists in U.S. government positions; peaked during the Korean War and declined soon thereafter, when the U.S. Senate censured Joseph McCarthy, who had been a major instigator of the hysteria.

**Seneca Falls Convention**   First women's rights meeting and the genesis of the women's suffrage movement; held in July 1848 in a church in Seneca Falls, New York, by Elizabeth Cady Stanton and Lucretia Coffin Mott.

**"Separate but equal"**   Principle underlying legal racial segregation, which was upheld in *Plessy* v. *Ferguson* (1896) and struck down in *Brown* v. *Board of Education* (1954).

**Servicemen's Readjustment Act (1944)**   The "GI Bill of Rights" provided money for education and other benefits to military personnel returning from World War II.

**Settlement houses**   Product of the late nineteenth-century movement to offer a broad array of social services in urban immigrant neighborhoods; Chicago's Hull House was one of hundreds of settlement houses that operated by the early twentieth century.

**Seventeenth Amendment (1913)**   Progressive reform that required U.S. senators to be elected directly by voters; previously, senators were chosen by state legislatures.

**Seward's Folly**   Secretary of State William H. Seward's negotiation of the purchase of Alaska from Russia in 1867.

**Shakers**   Founded by Mother Ann Lee Stanley in England, the United Society of Believers in Christ's Second Appearing settled in Watervliet, New York, in 1774 and subsequently established eighteen additional communes in the Northeast, Indiana, and Kentucky.

**Sharecropping** Type of farm tenancy that developed after the Civil War in which landless workers—often former slaves—farmed land in exchange for farm supplies and a share of the crop; differed from tenancy in that the terms were generally less favorable.

**Shays's Rebellion** Massachusetts farmer Daniel Shays and 1,200 compatriots, seeking debt relief through issuance of paper currency and lower taxes, stormed the federal arsenal at Springfield in the winter of 1787 but were quickly repulsed.

**Sherman Anti-Trust Act (1890)** First law to restrict monopolistic trusts and business combinations; extended by the Clayton Anti-Trust Act of 1914.

**Sherman Silver Purchase Act (1890)** In replacing and extending the provisions of the Bland-Allison Act of 1878, it increased the amount of silver periodically bought for coinage.

**Shiloh, Battle of** At the time it was fought (April 6–7, 1862), Shiloh, in western Tennessee, was the bloodiest battle in American history; afterward, General Ulysses S. Grant was temporarily removed from command.

**Single tax** Concept of taxing only landowners as a remedy for poverty, promulgated by Henry George in *Progress and Poverty* (1879).

**Sixteenth Amendment (1913)** Legalized the federal income tax.

**Smith-Connally War Labor Disputes Act (1943)** Outlawed labor strikes in wartime and allowed the president to take over industries threatened by labor disputes.

***Smith v. Allwright* (1944)** U.S. Supreme Court decision that outlawed all-white Democratic party primaries in Texas.

**Social Darwinism** Application of Charles Darwin's theory of natural selection to society; used the concept of the "survival of the fittest" to justify class distinctions and to explain poverty.

**Social gospel** Preached by liberal Protestant clergymen in the late nineteenth and early twentieth centuries; advocated the application of Christian principles to social problems generated by industrialization.

**Social Security Act (1935)** Created the Social Security system with provisions for a retirement pension, unemployment insurance, disability insurance, and public assistance (welfare).

**Sons of Liberty** Secret organizations formed by Samuel Adams, John Hancock, and other radicals in response to the Stamp Act; they impeded British officials and planned such harassments as the Boston Tea Party.

***South Carolina Exposition and Protest*** Written in 1828 by Vice-President John C. Calhoun of South Carolina to protest the so-called Tariff of Abominations, which seemed to favor northern industry; introduced the concept of state interposition and became the basis for South Carolina's Nullification Doctrine of 1833.

**Southeast Asia Treaty Organization (SEATO)** Pact among mostly western nations signed in 1954; designed to deter Communist expansion and cited as a justification for U.S. involvement in Vietnam.

**Southern Christian Leadership Conference (SCLC)** Civil rights organization founded in 1957 by the Reverend Martin Luther King, Jr., and other civil rights leaders.

**Southern renaissance** Literary movement of the 1920s and 1930s that included such writers as William Faulkner, Thomas Wolfe, and Robert Penn Warren.

**Spanish flu** Unprecedentedly lethal influenza epidemic of 1918 that killed more than 22 million people worldwide.

**Spoils system** The term—meaning the filling of federal government jobs with persons loyal to the party of the president—originated in Andrew Jackson's first term; the system was replaced in the Progressive Era by civil service.

***Sputnik*** First artificial satellite to orbit the earth; launched October 4, 1957, by the Soviet Union.

**Stalwarts** Conservative Republican party faction during the presidency of Rutherford B. Hayes, 1877–81; led by Senator Roscoe B. Conkling of New York, Stalwarts opposed civil service reform and favored a third term for President Ulysses S. Grant.

**Stamp Act (1765)** Parliament required that revenue stamps be affixed to all colonial printed matter, documents, dice, and playing cards; the Stamp Act Congress met to formulate a response, and the act was repealed the following year.

**Standard Oil Company** Founded in 1870 by John D. Rockefeller in Cleveland, Ohio, it soon grew into the nation's first industry-dominating trust; the Sherman Anti-Trust Act (1890) was enacted in part to combat abuses by Standard Oil.

**Staple crop** Important cash crop, for example, cotton or tobacco.

**Steamboats** Paddlewheelers that could travel both up- and down-river in deep or shallow waters; they became commercially viable early in the nineteenth century and soon developed into America's first inland freight and passenger service network.

**Stimson Doctrine** In reaction to Japan's 1932 occupation of Manchuria, Secretary of State Henry Stimson declared that the United States would not recognize territories acquired by force.

**Strategic Defense Initiative ("Star Wars")** Defense Department's plan during the Reagan administration to build a system to destroy incoming missiles in space.

**Student Non-violent Coordinating Committee** Founded in 1960 to coordinate civil rights sit-ins and other forms of grassroots protest.

**Students for a Democratic Society (SDS)** Major organization of the New Left, founded at the University of Michigan in 1960 by Tom Hayden and A1 Haber.

**Sugar Act (Revenue Act of 1764)** Parliament's tax on refined sugar and many other colonial products; the first tax designed solely to raise revenue for Britain.

**Taft-Hartley Act (1947)** Passed over President Harry Truman's veto, the law contained a number of provisions to control labor unions, including the banning of closed shops.

**Tariff** Federal tax on imported goods.

**Tariff of Abominations (Tariff of 1828)** Taxed imported goods at a very high rate; the South hated the tariff because it feared it would provoke Britain to reject American cotton.

**Tariff of 1816** First true protective tariff, intended strictly to protect American goods against foreign competition.

**Tax Reform Act (1986)** Lowered federal income tax rates to 1920s levels and eliminated many loopholes.

**Teapot Dome** Harding administration scandal in which Secretary of the Interior Albert B. Fall profited from secret leasing to private oil companies of government oil reserves at Teapot Dome, Wyoming, and Elk Hills, California.

**Tenancy** Renting of farmland by workers who owned their own equipment; tenant farmers kept a larger percentage of the crop than did sharecroppers.

**Tennessee Valley Authority** Created in 1933 to control flooding in the Tennessee River Valley, provide work for the region's unemployed, and produce inexpensive electric power for the region.

**Tenure of Office Act (1867)** Required the president to obtain Senate approval to remove any official whose appointment had also required Senate approval; President Andrew Johnson's violation of the law by firing Secretary of War Edwin Stanton led to the Radical Republicans retaliating with Johnson's impeachment.

**Tertium Quid** Literally, the "third something": states' rights and strict constructionist Republicans under John Randolph who broke with President Thomas Jefferson but never managed to form a third political party.

**Tet Offensive** Surprise attack by the Viet Cong and North Vietnamese during the Vietnamese New Year of 1968; turned American public opinion strongly against the war in Vietnam.

**Tippecanoe, Battle of** On November 7, 1811, Indiana governor William Henry Harrison (later president) defeated the Shawnee Indians at the Tippecanoe River in northern Indiana; victory fomented war fever against the British, who were believed to be aiding the Indians.

**Title IX** Part of the Educational Amendments Act of 1972 that required colleges to engage in "affirmative action" for women.

**Tonkin Gulf Resolution (1964)** Passed by Congress in reaction to supposedly unprovoked attacks on American warships off the coast of North Vietnam; it gave the president unlimited authority to defend U.S. forces and members of SEATO.

**Tories** Term used by Patriots to refer to Loyalists, or colonists who supported the Crown after the Declaration of Independence.

**Townshend Acts (1767)** Parliamentary measures (named for the chancellor of the exchequer) that punished the New York Assembly for failing to house British soldiers, taxed tea and other commodities, and established a Board of Customs Commissioners and colonial vice- admiralty courts.

**Trail of Tears** Cherokees' own term for their forced march, 1838–39, from the southern Appalachians to Indian lands (later Oklahoma); of 15,000 forced to march, 4,000 died on the way.

**Transcendentalism** Philosophy of a small group of mid-nineteenth-century New England writers and thinkers, including Ralph Waldo Emerson, Henry David Thoreau, and Margaret Fuller; they stressed "plain living and high thinking."

**Transcontinental railroad** First line across the continent from Omaha, Nebraska, to Sacramento, California, established in 1869 with the linkage of the Union Pacific and Central Pacific railroads at Promontory, Utah.

**Truman Doctrine** President Harry S. Truman's program of post–World War II aid to European countries—particularly Greece and Turkey—in danger of being undermined by communism.

**Trust** Companies combined to control competition.

**Twenty-first Amendment (1933)** Repealed prohibition on the manufacture, sale, and transportation of alcoholic beverages, effectively nullifying the Eighteenth Amendment.

**Twenty-second Amendment (1951)** Limited presidents to two full terms of office or two terms plus two years of an assumed term; passed in reaction to President Franklin D. Roosevelt's unprecedented four elected terms.

**Twenty-sixth Amendment (1971)** Lowered the voting age from twenty-one to eighteen.

**U.S.S. _Maine_** Battleship that exploded in Havana Harbor on February 15, 1898, resulting in 266 deaths; the American public, assuming that the Spanish had mined the ship, clamored for war, and the Spanish-American War was declared two months later.

**_Uncle Tom's Cabin_** Harriet Beecher Stowe's 1852 antislavery novel popularized the abolitionist position.

**Underground Railroad** Operating in the decades before the Civil War, the "railroad" was a clandestine system of routes and safehouses through which slaves were led to freedom in the North.

**Understanding clause** Added to state constitutions in the late nineteenth century, it allowed illiterate whites to circumvent literacy tests for voting by demonstrating that they understood a passage in the Constitution; black citizens would be judged by white registrars to have failed.

**Underwood-Simmons Tariff (1913)** In addition to lowering and even eliminating some tariffs, it included provisions for the first federal income tax, made legal the same year by the ratification of the Sixteenth Amendment.

**Unitarianism** Late eighteenth-century liberal offshoot of the New England Congregationalist church; rejecting the Trinity, Unitarianism professed the oneness of God and the goodness of rational man.

**United Farm Workers** Union for the predominantly Mexican-American migrant laborers of the Southwest, organized by César Chavez in 1962.

**United Nations** Organization of nations to maintain world peace, established in 1945 and headquartered in New York.

**Universal Negro Improvement Association** Black nationalist movement active in the United States from 1916 to 1923, when its leader Marcus Garvey went to prison for mail fraud.

**Universalism** Similar to Unitarianism, but putting more stress on the importance of social action, Universalism also originated in Massachusetts in the late eighteenth century.

**V-E Day** May 8, 1945, the day World War II officially ended in Europe.

**Vertical integration** Company's avoidance of middlemen by producing its own supplies and providing for distribution of its product.

**Veto** President's constitutional power to reject legislation passed by Congress; a two-thirds vote in both houses of Congress can override a veto.

**Vicksburg, Battle of** The fall of Vicksburg, Mississippi, to General Ulysses S. Grant's army on July 4, 1863, after two months of siege was a turning point in the war because it gave the Union control of the Mississippi River.

**Virginia and New Jersey Plans** Differing opinions of delegations to the Constitutional Convention: New Jersey wanted one legislative body with equal representation for each state; Virginia's plan called for a strong central government and a two-house legislature apportioned by population.

**Volstead Act (1919)** Enforced the prohibition amendment, beginning January 1920.

**Voting Rights Act of 1965** Passed in the wake of Martin Luther King's Selma to Montgomery March, it authorized federal protection of the right to vote and permitted federal enforcement of minority voting rights in individual counties, mostly in the South.

*Wabash Railroad* **v.** *Illinois* **(1886)**   Reversing the U.S. Supreme Court's ruling in *Munn* v. *Illinois,* the decision disallowed state regulation of interstate commerce.

**Wade-Davis Bill (1864)**   Radical Republicans' plan for reconstruction that required loyalty oaths, abolition of slavery, repudiation of war debts, and denial of political rights to high-ranking Confederate officials; President Lincoln refused to sign the bill.

**Wagner Act (National Labor Relations Act of 1935)**   Established the National Labor Relations Board and facilitated unionization by regulating employment and bargaining practices.

**War Industries Board**   Run by financier Bernard Baruch, the board planned production and allocation of war materiel, supervised purchasing, and fixed prices, 1917–19.

**War of 1812**   Fought with Britain, 1812–14, over lingering conflicts that included impressment of American sailors, interference with shipping, and collusion with Northwest Territory Indians; settled by the Treaty of Ghent in 1814.

**War on Poverty**   Announced by President Lyndon B. Johnson in his 1964 State of the Union address; under the Economic Opportunity Bill signed later that year, Head Start, VISTA, and the Jobs Corps were created, and grants and loans were extended to students, farmers, and businesses in efforts to eliminate poverty.

**War Production Board**   Created in 1942 to coordinate industrial efforts in World War II; similar to the War Industries Board in World War I.

**War Relocation Camps**   Internment camps where Japanese Americans were held against their will from 1942 to 1945.

**Warren Court**   The U.S. Supreme Court under Chief Justice Earl Warren, 1953–69, decided such landmark cases as *Brown* v. *Board of Education* (school desegregation), *Baker* v. *Carr* (legislative redistricting), and *Gideon* v. *Wainwright* and *Miranda* v. *Arizona* (rights of criminal defendants).

**Washington Armaments Conference**   Leaders of nine world powers met in 1921–22 to discuss the naval race; resulting treaties limited to a specific ratio the carrier and battleship tonnage of each nation (Five-Power Naval Treaty), formally ratified the Open Door to China (Nine–Power Treaty), and agreed to respect each other's Pacific territories (Four-Power Treaty).

**Watergate**   Washington office and apartment complex that lent its name to the 1972–74 scandal of the Nixon administration; when his knowledge of the break-in at the Watergate and subsequent coverup was revealed, Nixon resigned the presidency under threat of impeachment.

**Webster-Ashburton Treaty**   Settlement in 1842 of U.S.-Canadian border disputes in Maine, New York, Vermont, and in the Wisconsin Territory (now northern Minnesota).

**Webster-Hayne debate**   U.S. Senate debate of January 1830 between Daniel Webster of Massachusetts and Robert Hayne of South Carolina over nullification and states' rights.

**Whig Party**   Founded in 1834 to unite factions opposed to President Andrew Jackson, the party favored federal responsibility for internal improvements; the party ceased to exist by the late 1850s, when party members divided over the slavery issue.

**Whigs**   Another name for revolutionary Patriots.

**Whiskey Rebellion**   Violent protest by western Pennsylvania farmers against the federal excise tax on corn whiskey, 1794.

**Whitewater Development Corporation**   Failed Arkansas real estate investment that kept President Bill Clinton and his wife Hillary under investigation by Independent Counsel Kenneth Starr throughout the Clinton presidency; no charges were ever brought against either of the Clintons.

**Wilderness, Battle of the**   Second battle fought in the thickly wooded Wilderness area near Chancellorsville, Virginia; in the battle of May 5–6, 1864, no clear victor emerged, but the battle served to deplete the Army of Northern Virginia.

**Wilderness Road**   Originally an Indian path through the Cumberland Gap, it was used by over 300,000 settlers who migrated westward to Kentucky in the last quarter of the eighteenth century.

**Wilmot Proviso**   Proposal to prohibit slavery in any land acquired in the Mexican War, but southern senators, led by John C. Calhoun of South Carolina, defeated the measure in 1846 and 1847.

**Works Progress Administration (WPA)**   Part of the Second New Deal, it provided jobs for millions of the unemployed on construction and arts projects.

**Wounded Knee, Battle of**   Last incident of the Indians Wars took place in 1890 in the Dakota Territory, where the U.S. Cavalry killed over 200 Sioux men, women, and children who were in the process of surrender.

**Writs of assistance**   One of the colonies' main complaints against Britain, the writs allowed unlimited search warrants without cause to look for evidence of smuggling.

**XYZ Affair**   French foreign minister Tallyrand's three anonymous agents demanded payments to stop French plundering of American ships in 1797; refusal to pay the bribe led to two years of sea war with France (1798–1800).

**Yalta Conference**   Meeting of Franklin D. Roosevelt, Winston Churchill, and Joseph Stalin at a Crimean resort to discuss the postwar world on February 4–11, 1945; Soviet leader Joseph Stalin claimed large areas in eastern Europe for Soviet domination.

**Yazoo Fraud**   Illegal sale of the Yazoo lands (much of present-day Alabama and Mississippi) by Georgia legislators; by 1802 it had become a tangle of conflicting claims that the U.S. Supreme Court settled in *Fletcher* v. *Peck* (1810).

**Yellow journalism**   Sensationalism in newspaper publishing that reached a peak in the circulation war between Joseph Pulitzer's *New York World* and William Randolph Hearst's *New York Journal* in the 1890s; the papers' accounts of events in Havana Harbor in 1898 led directly to the Spanish-American War.

**Yeoman farmers**   Small landowners (the majority of white families in the South) who farmed their own land and usually did not own slaves.

**Yorktown, Battle of**   Last battle of the Revolutionary War; General Lord Charles Cornwallis along with over 7,000 British troops surrendered at Yorktown, Virginia, on October 17, 1781.

**Zimmermann telegram**   From the German foreign secretary to the German minister in Mexico, February 1917, instructing him to offer to recover Texas, New Mexico, and Arizona for Mexico if it would fight the United States to divert attention from Germany in case of war.

# THE DECLARATION OF INDEPENDENCE

When in the course of human events, it becomes necessary for one people to dissolve the political bands which have connected them with another, and to assume among the Powers of the earth, the separate and equal station to which the Laws of Nature and of Nature's God entitle them, a decent respect to the opinions of mankind requires that they should declare the causes which impel them to the separation.

We hold these truths to be self-evident, that all men are created equal, that they are endowed by their Creator with certain unalienable rights, that among these are Life, Liberty, and the pursuit of Happiness. That to secure these rights, Governments are instituted among Men, deriving their just powers from the consent of the governed. That whenever any Form of Government becomes destructive of these ends, it is the Right of the People to alter or to abolish it, and to institute new Government, laying its foundation on such principles and organizing its powers in such form, as to them shall seem most likely to effect their Safety and Happiness. Prudence, indeed, will dictate that Governments long established should not be changed for light and transient causes; and accordingly all experience hath shown, that mankind are more disposed to suffer, while evils are sufferable, than to right themselves by abolishing the forms to which they are accustomed. But when a long train of abuses and usurpations, pursuing invariably the same Object evinces a design to reduce them under absolute Despotism, it is their right, it is their duty, to throw off such Government, and to provide new Guards for their future security.—Such has been the patient sufferance of these Colonies; and such is now the necessity which constrains them to alter their former Systems of Government. The history of the present King of Great Britain is a history of repeated injuries and usurpations, all having in direct object the establishment of an absolute Tyranny over these States. To prove this, let Facts be submitted to a candid world.

He has refused his Assent to Laws, the most wholesome and necessary for the public good.

He has forbidden his Governors to pass Laws of immediate and pressing importance, unless suspended in their operation till his Assent should be obtained; and when so suspended, he has utterly neglected to attend to them.

He has refused to pass other Laws for the accommodation of large districts of people, unless those people would relinquish the right of Representation in the Legislature, a right inestimable to them and formidable to tyrants only.

He has called together legislative bodies at places unusual, uncomfortable, and distant from the depository of their public Records, for the sole purpose of fatiguing them into compliance with his measures.

He has dissolved Representative Houses repeatedly, for opposing with manly firmness his invasions on the rights of the people.

He has refused for a long time, after such dissolutions, to cause others to be elected; whereby the Legislative powers, incapable of Annihilation, have returned to the People at large for their exercise; the State remaining in the mean time exposed to all dangers of invasion from without, and convulsions within.

He has endeavoured to prevent the population of these States; for that purpose obstructing the Laws of Naturalization of Foreigners; refusing to pass others to encourage their migrations hither, and raising the conditions of new Appropriations of Lands.

He has obstructed the Administration of Justice, by refusing his Assent to Laws for establishing Judiciary powers.

He has made Judges dependent on his Will alone, for the tenure of their offices, and the amount and payment of their salaries.

He has erected a multitude of New Offices, and sent hither swarms of Officers to harass our People, and eat out their substance.

He has kept among us, in times of peace, Standing Armies without the Consent of our legislatures.

He has affected to render the Military independent of and superior to the Civil Power.

He has combined with others to subject us to a jurisdiction foreign to our constitution, and unacknowledged by our laws; giving his Assent to their Acts of pretended Legislation:

For quartering large bodies of armed troops among us:

For protecting them, by a mock Trial, from Punishment for any Murders which they should commit on the Inhabitants of these States:

For cutting off our Trade with all parts of the world:

For imposing taxes on us without our Consent:

For depriving us of many cases, of the benefits of Trial by jury:

For transporting us beyond Seas to be tried for pretended offences:

For abolishing the free System of English Laws in a neighbouring Province, establishing therein an Arbitrary government, and enlarging its Boundaries so as to render it at once an example and fit instrument for introducing the same absolute rule into these Colonies:

For taking away our Charters, abolishing our most valuable Laws, and altering fundamentally the Forms of our Governments:

For suspending our own Legislatures, and declaring themselves invested with Power to legislate for us in all cases whatsoever.

He has abdicated Government here, by declaring us out of his Protection and waging War against us.

He has plundered our seas, ravaged our Coasts, burnt our towns, and destroyed the lives of our people.

He is at this time transporting large armies of foreign mercenaries to compleat the works of death, desolation, and tyranny, already begun with circumstances of Cruelty & perfidy scarcely paralleled in the most barbarous ages, and totally unworthy the Head of a civilized nation.

He has constrained our fellow Citizens taken Captive on the high Seas to bear Arms against their Country, to become the executioners of their friends and Brethren, or to fall themselves by their Hands.

He has excited domestic insurrections amongst us, and has endeavoured to bring on the inhabitants of our frontiers, the merciless Indian Savages, whose known rule of warfare, is an undistinguished destruction of all ages, sexes, and conditions.

In every stage of these Oppressions We have Petitioned for Redress in the most humble terms: Our repeated Petitions have been answered only by repeated injury. A Prince, whose character is thus marked by every act which may define a Tyrant, is unfit to be the ruler of a free people.

Nor have We been wanting in attention to our British brethren. We have warned them from time to time of attempts by their legislature to extend an unwarrantable jurisdiction over us. We have reminded them of the circumstances of our emigration and settlement here. We have appealed to their native justice and magnanimity, and we have conjured them by the ties of our common kindred to disavow these usurpations, which, would inevitably interrupt our connections and correspondence. They too must have been deaf to the voice of justice and of consanguinity. We must, therefore, acquiesce in the necessity, which denounces our Separation, and hold them, as we hold the rest of mankind, Enemies in War, in Peace Friends.

WE, THEREFORE, the Representatives of the UNITED STATES OF AMERICA, in General Congress, Assembled, appealing to the Supreme Judge of the world for the rectitude of our intentions, do, in the Name, and by Authority of the good People of these Colonies, solemnly publish and declare, That these United Colonies are, and of Right ought to be FREE AND INDEPENDENT STATES; that they are Absolved from all Allegiance to the British Crown, and that all political connection between them and the State of Great Britain,

is and ought to be totally dissolved; and that as Free and Independent States, they have full Power to levy War, conclude Peace, contract Alliances, establish Commerce, and to do all other Acts and Things which Independent States may of right do. And for the support of this Declaration, with a firm reliance on the Protection of Divine Providence, we mutually pledge to each other our Lives, our Fortunes, and our sacred Honor.

The foregoing Declaration was, by order of Congress, engrossed, and signed by the following members:

*John Hancock*

NEW HAMPSHIRE
*Josiah Bartlett*
*William Whipple*
*Matthew Thornton*

MASSACHUSETTS BAY
*Samuel Adams*
*John Adams*
*Robert Treat Paine*
*Elbridge Gerry*

RHODE ISLAND
*Stephen Hopkins*
*William Ellery*

CONNECTICUT
*Roger Sherman*
*Samuel Huntington*
*William Williams*
*Oliver Wolcott*

NEW YORK
*William Floyd*
*Philip Livingston*
*Francis Lewis*
*Lewis Morris*

NEW JERSEY
*Richard Stockton*
*John Witherspoon*
*Francis Hopkinson*
*John Hart*
*Abraham Clark*

PENNSYLVANIA
*Robert Morris*
*Benjamin Rush*
*Benjamin Franklin*
*John Morton*
*George Clymer*
*James Smith*
*George Taylor*
*James Wilson*
*George Ross*

DELAWARE
*Caesar Rodney*
*George Read*
*Thomas M'Kean*

MARYLAND
*Samuel Chase*
*William Paca*
*Thomas Stone*
*Charles Carroll,*
  *of Carrollton*

VIRGINIA
*George Wythe*
*Richard Henry Lee*
*Thomas Jefferson*
*Benjamin Harrison*
*Thomas Nelson, Jr.*
*Francis Lightfoot Lee*
*Carter Braxton*

NORTH CAROLINA
*William Hooper*
*Joseph Hewes*
*John Penn*

SOUTH CAROLINA
*Edward Rutledge*
*Thomas Heyward, Jr.*
*Thomas Lynch, Jr.*
*Arthur Middleton*

GEORGIA
*Button Gwinnett*
*Lyman Hall*
*George Walton*

*Resolved,* That copies of the Declaration be sent to the several assemblies, conventions, and committees, or councils of safety, and to the several commanding officers of the continental troops; that it be proclaimed in each of the United States, at the head of the army.

# ARTICLES OF CONFEDERATION

To all to whom these Presents shall come, we the undersigned Delegates of the States affixed to our Names send greeting.

Whereas the Delegates of the United States of America in Congress assembled did on the fifteenth day of November in the Year of our Lord One Thousand Seven Hundred and Seventy-seven, and in the Second Year of the Independence of America agree to certain articles of Confederation and perpetual Union between the States of Newhampshire, Massachusetts-bay, Rhodeisland and Providence Plantations, Connecticut, New York, New Jersey, Pennsylvania, Delaware, Maryland, Virginia, North-Carolina, South-Carolina and Georgia in the Words following, viz.

Articles of Confederation and perpetual Union between the States of Newhampshire, Massachusetts-bay, Rhodeisland and Providence Plantations, Connecticut, New-York, New-Jersey, Pennsylvania, Delaware, Maryland, Virginia, North-Carolina, South-Carolina and Georgia.

ARTICLE I. The stile of this confederacy shall be "The United States of America."

ARTICLE II. Each State retains its sovereignty, freedom and independence, and every power, jurisdiction and right, which is not by this confederation expressly delegated to the United States, in Congress assembled.

ARTICLE III. The said States hereby severally enter into a firm league of friendship with each other, for their common defence, the security of their liberties, and their mutual and general welfare, binding themselves to assist each other, against all force offered to, or attacks made upon them, or any of them, on account of religion, sovereignty, trade or any other pretence whatever.

ARTICLE IV. The better to secure and perpetuate mutual friendship and intercourse among the people of the different States in this Union, the free inhabitants of each of these States, paupers, vagabonds and fugitives from justice excepted, shall be entitled to all privileges and immunities of free citizens in the several States; and the people of each State shall have free ingress and regress to and from any other State, and shall enjoy therein all the privileges of trade and commerce, subject to the same duties, impositions and restrictions as the inhabitants thereof respectively, provided that such restrictions shall not extend so far as to prevent the removal of property imported into any State, to any other State of which the owner is an inhabitant; provided also that no imposition, duties or restriction shall be laid by any State, on the property of the United States, or either of them.

If any person guilty of, or charged with treason, felony, or other high misdemeanor in any State, shall flee from justice, and be found in any of the United States, he shall upon demand of the Governor or Executive power, of the State from which he fled, be delivered up and removed to the State having jurisdiction of his offence.

Full faith and credit shall be given in each of these States to the records, acts and judicial proceedings of the courts and magistrates of every other State.

ARTICLE V. For the more convenient management of the general interests of the United States, delegates shall be annually appointed in such manner as the legislature of each State shall direct, to meet in Congress on the first Monday in November, in every year, with a power reserved to each State, to recall its delegates, or any of them, at any time within the year, and to send others in their stead, for the remainder of the year.

No State shall be represented in Congress by less than two, nor by more than seven members; and no person shall be capable of being a delegate for more than three years in any term of six years; nor shall any person, being a delegate, be capable of holding any office under the United States, for which he, or another for his benefit receives any salary, fees or emolument of any kind.

Each State shall maintain its own delegates in a meeting of the States, and while they act as members of the committee of the States.

In determining questions in the United States, in Congress assembled, each State shall have one vote.

Freedom of speech and debate in Congress shall not be impeached or questioned in any court, or place out of Congress, and the members of Congress shall be protected in their persons from arrests and imprisonments, during the time of their going to and from, and attendance on Congress, except for treason, felony, or breach of the peace.

ARTICLE VI. No State without the consent of the United States in Congress assembled, shall send any embassy to, or receive any embassy from, or enter into any conference, agreement, alliance or treaty with any king, prince or state; nor shall any person holding any office of profit or trust under the United States, or any of them, accept of any present, emolument, office or title of any kind whatever from any king, prince or foreign state; nor shall the United States in Congress assembled, or any of them, grant any title of nobility.

No two or more States shall enter into any treaty, confederation or alliance whatever between them, without the consent of the

United States in Congress assembled, specifying accurately the purposes for which the same is to be entered into, and how long it shall continue.

No State shall lay any imposts or duties, which may interfere with any stipulations in treaties, entered into by the United States in Congress assembled, with any king, prince or state, in pursuance of any treaties already proposed by Congress, to the courts of France and Spain.

No vessels of war shall be kept up in time of peace by any State, except such number only, as shall be deemed necessary by the United States in Congress assembled, for the defence of such State, or its trade; nor shall any body of forces be kept up by any State, in time of peace, except such number only, as in the judgment of the United States, in Congress assembled, shall be deemed requisite to garrison the forts necessary for the defence of such State; but every State shall always keep up a well regulated and disciplined militia, sufficiently armed and accoutred, and shall provide and constantly have ready for use, in public stores, a due number of field pieces and tents, and a proper quantity of arms, ammunition and camp equipage.

No State shall engage in any war without the consent of the United States in Congress assembled, unless such State be actually invaded by enemies, or shall have received certain advice of a resolution being formed by some nation of Indians to invade such State, and the danger is so imminent as not to admit of a delay, till the United States in Congress assembled can be consulted: nor shall any State grant commissions to any ships or vessels of war, nor letters of marque or reprisal, except it be after a declaration of war by the United States in Congress assembled, and then only against the kingdom or state and the subjects thereof, against which war has been so declared, and under such regulations as shall be established by the United States in Congress assembled, unless such State be infested by pirates, in which case vessels of war may be fitted out for that occasion, and kept so long as the danger shall continue, or until the United States in Congress assembled shall determine otherwise.

ARTICLE VII. When land-forces are raised by any State of the common defence, all officers of or under the rank of colonel, shall be appointed by the Legislature of each State respectively by whom such forces shall be raised, or in such manner as such State shall direct, and all vacancies shall be filled up by the State which first made the appointment.

ARTICLE VIII. All charges of war, and all other expenses that shall be incurred for the common defence or general welfare, and allowed by the United States in Congress assembled, shall be defrayed out of a common treasury, which shall be supplied by the several States, in proportion to the value of all land within each State, granted to or surveyed for any person, as such land and the buildings and improvements thereon shall be estimated according to such mode as the United States in Congress assembled, shall from time to time direct and appoint.

The taxes for paying that proportion shall be laid and levied by the authority and direction of the Legislatures of the several States within the time agreed upon by the United States in Congress assembled.

ARTICLE IX. The United States in Congress assembled, shall have the sole and exclusive right and power of determining on peace and war, except in the cases mentioned in the sixth article—of sending and receiving ambassadors—entering into treaties and alliances, provided that no treaty of commerce shall be made whereby the legislative power of the respective States shall be restrained from imposing such imposts and duties on foreigners, as their own people are subjected to, or from prohibiting the exportation or importation of and species of goods or commodities whatsoever—of establishing rules for deciding in all cases, what captures on land or water shall be legal, and in what manner prizes taken by land or naval forces in the service of the United States shall be divided or appropriated—of granting letters of marque and reprisal in times of peace—appointing courts for the trial of piracies and felonies committed on the high seas and establishing courts for receiving and determining finally appeals in all cases of captures, provided that no member of Congress shall be appointed a judge of any of the said courts.

The United States in Congress assembled shall also be the last resort on appeal in all disputes and differences now subsisting or that hereafter may arise between two or more States concerning boundary, jurisdiction or any other cause whatever; which authority shall always be exercised in the manner following. Whenever the legislative or executive authority or lawful agent of any State in controversy with another shall present a petition to Congress, stating the matter in question and praying for a hearing, notice thereof shall be given by order of Congress to the legislative or executive authority of the other State in controversy, and a day assigned for the appearance of the parties by their lawful agents, who shall then be directed to appoint by joint consent, commissioners or judges to constitute a court for hearing and determining the matter in question: but if they cannot agree, Congress shall name three persons out of each of the United States, and from the list of such persons each party shall alternately strike out one, the petitioners beginning, until the number shall be reduced to thirteen; and from that number not less than seven, nor more than nine names as Congress shall direct, shall in the presence of Congress be drawn out by lot, and the persons whose names shall be so drawn or any five of them, shall be commissioners or judges, to hear and finally determine the controversy, so always as a major part of the judges who shall hear the cause shall agree in the determination: and if either party shall neglect to attend at the day appointed, without reasons, which Congress shall judge sufficient, or being present shall refuse to strike, the Congress shall proceed to nominate three persons out of each State, and the Secretary of Congress shall strike in behalf of such party absent or refusing; and the judgment and sentence of the court to be appointed, in the manner before prescribed, shall be final and conclusive; and if any of the parties shall refuse to submit to the authority of such court, or to appear or defend their claim or cause, the court shall nevertheless proceed to pronounce sentence, or judgment, which shall in like manner be final and decisive, the judgment or sentence and other proceedings being in either case transmitted to Congress, and lodged among the acts of Congress for the security of the parties concerned: provided that every commissioner, before he sits in judgment, shall take an oath to be administered by one of the judges of the supreme or superior court of the State where the case shall be tried, "well and truly to hear and determine the matter in question, according to the best of his judgment, without favour, affection or hope of reward:" provided also that no State shall be deprived of territory for the benefit of the United States.

All controversies concerning the private right of soil claimed under different grants of two or more States, whose jurisdiction as they may respect such lands, and the states which passed such grants are adjusted, the said grants or either of them being at the same time claimed to have originated antecedent to such settlement of jurisdiction, shall on the petition of either party to the Congress of the United States, be finally determined as near as may be in the same manner as is before prescribed for deciding disputes respecting territorial jurisdiction between different States.

The United States in Congress assembled shall also have the sole and exclusive right and power of regulating the alloy and value of coin struck by their own authority, or by that of the respective States—fixing the standard of weights and measures throughout the United States—regulating the trade and managing all affairs with the Indians, not members of any of the States, provided that the legislative right of any State within its own limits be not infringed or violated—establishing and regulating post-offices from one State to another, throughout all of the United States, and exacting such postage on the papers passing thro' the same as may be requisite to defray the expenses of the said office—appointing all officers of the land forces, in the service of the United States, excepting regimental officers—appointing all the officers of the naval forces, and commissioning all officers whatever in the service of the United States—making rules for the government and regulation of the said land and naval forces, and directing their operations.

The United States in Congress assembled shall have authority to appoint a committee, to sit in the recess of Congress, to be denominated "a Committee of the States," and to consist of one delegate from each State; and to appoint such other committees and civil officers as may be necessary for managing the general affairs of the United States under their direction—to appoint one of their number to preside, provided that no person be allowed to serve in the office of president more than one year in any term of three years; to

ascertain the necessary sums of money to be raised for the service of the United States, and to appropriate and apply the same for defraying the public expenses—to borrow money, or emit bills on the credit of the United States, transmitting every half year to the respective States an account of the sums of money so borrowed or emitted,—to build and equip a navy—to agree upon the number of land forces, and to make requisitions from each State for its quota, in proportion to the number of white inhabitants in such State; which requisition shall be binding, and thereupon the Legislature of each State shall appoint the regimental officers, raise the men and cloath, arm and equip them in a soldier like manner, at the expense of the United States; and the officers and men so cloathed, armed and equipped shall march to the place appointed, and within the time agreed on by the United States in Congress assembled: but if the United States in Congress assembled shall, on consideration of circumstances judge proper that any State should not raise men, or should raise a smaller number of men than the quota thereof, such extra number shall be raised, officered, cloathed, armed and equipped in the same manner as the quota of such State, unless the legislature of such State shall judge that such extra number cannot be safely spared out of the same, in which case they shall raise officer, cloath, arm and equip as many of such extra number as they judge can be safely spared. And the officers and men so cloathed, armed and equipped, shall march to the place appointed, and within the time agreed on by the United States in Congress assembled.

The United States in Congress assembled shall never engage in a war, nor grant letters of marque and reprisal in time of peace, nor enter into any treaties or alliances, nor coin money, nor regulate the value thereof, nor ascertain the sums and expenses necessary for the defence and welfare of the United States, or any of them, nor emit bills, nor borrow money on the credit of the United States, nor appropriate money, nor agree upon the number of vessels to be built or purchased, or the number of land or sea forces to be raised, nor appoint a commander in chief of the army or navy, unless nine States assent to the same: nor shall a question on any other point, except for adjourning from day to day be determined, unless by the votes of a majority of the United States in Congress assembled.

The Congress of the United States shall have power to adjourn to any time within the year, and to any place within the United States, so that no period of adjournment be for a longer duration than the space of six months, and shall publish the journal of their proceedings monthly, except such parts thereof relating to treaties, alliances or military operations, as in their judgment require secrecy; and the yeas and nays of the delegates of each State on any question shall be entered on the Journal, when it is desired by any delegate; and the delegates of a State, or any of them, at his or their request shall be furnished with a transcript of the said journal, except such parts as are above excepted, to lay before the Legislatures of the several States.

ARTICLE X. The committee of the States, or any nine of them, shall be authorized to execute, in the recess of Congress, such of the powers of Congress as the United States in Congress assembled, by the consent of nine States, shall from time to time think expedient to vest them with; provided that no power be delegated to the said committee, for the exercise of which, by the articles of confederation, the voice of nine States in the Congress of the United States assembled is requisite.

ARTICLE XI. Canada acceding to this confederation, and joining in the measures of the United States, shall be admitted into, and entitled to all the advantages of this Union: but no other colony shall be admitted into the same, unless such admission be agreed to by nine States.

ARTICLE XII. All bills of credit emitted, monies borrowed and debts contracted by, or under the authority of Congress, before the assembling of the United States, in pursuance of the present confederation, shall be deemed and considered as a charge against the United States, for payment and satisfaction whereof the said United States, and the public faith are hereby solemnly pledged.

ARTICLE XIII. Every State shall abide by the determinations of the United States in Congress assembled, on all questions which by this confederation are submitted to them. And the articles of this confederation shall be inviolably observed by every State, and the Union shall be perpetual; nor shall any alteration at any time hereafter be made in any of them; unless such alteration be agreed to in a Congress of the United States, and be afterwards confirmed by the Legislatures of every State.

And whereas it has pleased the Great Governor of the world to incline the hearts of the Legislatures we respectively represent in Congress, to approve of, and to authorize us to ratify the said articles of confederation and perpetual union. Know ye that we the undersigned delegates, by virtue of the power and authority to us given for that purpose, do by these presents, in the name and in behalf of our respective constituents, fully and entirely ratify and confirm each and every of the said articles of confederation and perpetual union, and all and singular the matters and things therein contained: and we do further solemnly plight and engage the faith of our respective constituents, that they shall abide by the determinations of the United States in Congress assembled, on all questions, which by the said confederation are submitted to them. And that the articles thereof shall be inviolably observed by the States we respectively represent, and that the Union shall be perpetual.

In witness thereof we have hereunto set our hands in Congress. Done at Philadelphia in the State of Pennsylvania the ninth day of July in the year of our Lord one thousand seven hundred and seventy-eight, and in the third year of the independence of America.

# THE CONSTITUTION OF THE UNITED STATES

We the People of the United States, in order to form a more perfect Union, establish Justice, insure domestic Tranquility, provide for the common defence, promote the general Welfare, and secure the Blessings of Liberty to ourselves and our Posterity, do ordain and establish this Constitution for the United States of America.

ARTICLE. I.

*Section. 1.* All legislative Powers herein granted shall be vested in a Congress of the United States, which shall consist of a Senate and House of Representatives.

*Section. 2.* The House of Representatives shall be composed of Members chosen every second Year by the People of the several States, and the Electors in each State shall have the Qualifications requisite for Electors of the most numerous Branch of the State Legislature.

No Person shall be a Representative who shall not have attained to the Age of twenty five Years, and been seven Years a Citizen of the United States, and who shall not, when elected, be an Inhabitant of that State in which he shall be chosen.

Representatives and direct Taxes shall be apportioned among the several States which may be included within this Union, according to their respective Numbers, which shall be determined by adding to the whole Number of free Persons, including those bound to Service for a Term of Years, and excluding Indians not taxed, three fifths of all other Persons. The actual Enumeration shall be made within three Years after the first Meeting of the Congress of the United States, and within every subsequent Term of ten Years, in such Manner as they shall by Law direct. The Number of Representatives shall not exceed one for every thirty Thousand, but each State shall have at Least one Representative; and until such enumeration shall be made, the State of New Hampshire shall be entitled to chuse three, Massachusetts eight, Rhode-Island and Providence Plantations one, Connecticut five, New York six, New Jersey four, Pennsylvania eight, Delaware one, Maryland six, Virginia ten, North Carolina five, South Carolina five, and Georgia three.

When vacancies happen in the Representation from any state, the Executive Authority thereof shall issue Writs of Election to fill such Vacancies.

The House of Representatives shall chuse their Speaker and other Officers; and shall have the sole Power of Impeachment.

*Section. 3.* The Senate of the United States shall be composed of two Senators from each State, chosen by the legislature thereof, for six Years; and each Senator shall have one Vote.

Immediately after they shall be assembled in Consequence of the first Election, they shall be divided as equally as may be into three Classes. The Seats of the Senators of the first Class shall be vacated at the Expiration of the second Year, of the second Class at the Expiration of the fourth Year, and of the third Class at the Expiration of the sixth Year, so that one third maybe chosen every second Year; and if Vacancies happen by Resignation, or otherwise, during the Recess of the Legislature of any State, the Executive thereof may make temporary Appointments until the next Meeting of the Legislature, which shall then fill such Vacancies.

No Person shall be a Senator who shall not have attained to the Age of thirty Years, and been nine Years a Citizen of the United States, and who shall not, when elected, be an Inhabitant of that State for which he shall be chosen.

The Vice President of the United States shall be President of the Senate, but shall have no Vote, unless they be equally divided.

The Senate shall chuse their other Officers, and also a President pro tempore, in the Absence of the Vice President, or when he shall exercise the Office of President of the United States.

The Senate shall have the sole Power to try all Impeachments. When sitting for that Purpose, they shall be on Oath or Affirmation. When the President of the United States is tried, the Chief Justice shall preside: And no Person shall be convicted without the Concurrence of two thirds of the Members present.

Judgment in Cases of Impeachment shall not extend further than to removal from Office, and disqualification to hold and enjoy any Office of honor, Trust or Profit under the United States: but the Party convicted shall nevertheless be liable and subject to Indictment, Trial, Judgment and Punishment, according to Law.

*Section. 4.* The Times, Places and Manner of holding Elections for Senators and Representatives, shall be prescribed in each State by the Legislature thereof; but the Congress may at any time by Law make or alter such Regulations, except as to the Places of chusing Senators.

The Congress shall assemble at least once in every Year, and such Meeting shall be on the first Monday in December, unless they shall by Law appoint a different Day.

*Section. 5.* Each House shall be the Judge of the Elections, Returns and Qualifications of its own Members, and a Majority of each shall constitute a Quorum to do Business; but a smaller Number may adjourn from day to day, and may be authorized to compel the Attendance of absent Members, in such Manner, and under such Penalties as each House may provide.

Each House may determine the Rules of its Proceedings, punish its Members for disorderly Behaviour, and, with the Concurrence of two thirds, expel a Member.

Each House shall keep a Journal of its Proceedings, and from time to time publish the same, excepting such Parts as may in their

Judgment require Secrecy; and the Yeas and Nays of the Members of either House on any question shall, at the Desire of one fifth of those Present, be entered on the Journal.

Neither House, during the Session of Congress, shall, without the Consent of the other, adjourn for more than three days, not to any other Place than that in which the two Houses shall be sitting.

*Section. 6.* The Senators and Representatives shall receive a Compensation for their Services, to be ascertained by Law, and paid out of the Treasury of the United States. They shall in all Cases, except Treason, Felony and Breach of the Peace, be privileged from Arrest during their Attendance at the Session of their respective Houses, and in going to and returning from the same; and for any Speech or Debate in either House, they shall not be questioned in any other Place.

No Senator or Representative shall, during the Time for which he was elected, be appointed to any civil Office under the Authority of the United States, which shall have been created, or the Emoluments whereof shall have been encreased during such time; and no Person holding any Office under the United States, shall be a Member of either House during his Continuance in Office.

*Section. 7.* All Bills for raising Revenue shall originate in the House of Representatives; but the Senate may propose or concur with Amendments as on other Bills.

Every Bill which shall have passed the House of Representatives and the Senate shall, before it become a Law, be presented to the President of the United States; If he approve he shall sign it, but if not he shall return it, with his Objections to that House in which it shall have originated, who shall enter the Objections at large on their Journal, and proceed to reconsider it. If after such Reconsideration two thirds of that House shall agree to pass the Bill, it shall be sent, together with the Objections, to the other House, by which it shall likewise be reconsidered, and if approved by two thirds of that House, it shall become a Law. But in all such Cases the Votes of both Houses shall be determined by Yeas and Nays, and the Names of the Persons voting for and against the Bill shall be entered on the Journal of each House respectively. If any Bill shall not be returned by the President within ten Days (Sundays excepted) after it shall have been presented to him, the Same shall be a Law, in like Manner as if he had signed it, unless the Congress by their Adjournment prevent its Return, in which Case it shall not be a Law.

Every Order, Resolution, or Vote to which the Concurrence of the Senate and House of Representatives may be necessary (except on a question of Adjournment) shall be presented to the President of the United States; and before the Same shall take Effect, shall be approved by him, or being disapproved by him, shall be repassed by two thirds of the Senate and House of Representatives, according to the Rules and Limitations prescribed in the Case of a Bill.

*Section. 8.* The Congress shall have Power To lay and collect Taxes, Duties, Imposts and Excises, to pay the Debts and provide for the common Defence and general Welfare of the United States; but all Duties, Imposts and Excises shall be uniform throughout the United States;

To borrow Money on the credit of the United States;

To regulate Commerce with foreign Nations, and among the several States, and with the Indian Tribes;

To establish an uniform Rule of Naturalization, and uniform Laws on the subject of Bankruptcies throughout the United States;

To coin Money, regulate the Value thereof, and of foreign Coin, and fix the Standard of Weights and Measures;

To provide for the Punishment of counterfeiting the Securities and current Coin of the United States;

To establish Post Offices and Post Roads;

To promote the Progress of Science and useful Arts, by securing for limited Times to Authors and Inventors the exclusive Right to their respective Writings and Discoveries;

To constitute Tribunals inferior to the supreme Court;

To define and punish Piracies and Felonies committed on the high Seas, and Offences against the Law of Nations;

To declare War, grant Letters of Marque and Reprisal, and make Rules concerning Captures on Land and Water;

To raise and support Armies, but no Appropriation of Money to that Use shall be for a longer Term than two Years;

To provide and maintain a Navy;

To make Rules for the Government and Regulation of the land and naval Forces;

To provide for calling forth the Militia to execute the Laws of the Union, suppress Insurrections and repel Invasions;

To provide for organizing, arming, and disciplining, the Militia, and for governing such Part of them as may be employed in the Service of the United States, reserving to the States respectively, the Appointment of the Officers, and the Authority of training the Militia according to the discipline prescribed by Congress;

To exercise exclusive Legislation in all Cases whatsoever, over such District (not exceeding ten Miles square) as may, by Cession of Particular States, and the Acceptance of Congress, become the Seat of the Government of the United States, and to exercise like Authority over all Places purchased by the Consent of the Legislature of the State in which the Same shall be, for the Erection of Forts, Magazines, Arsenals, dock-Yards, and other needful Buildings;— And

To make all Laws which shall be necessary and proper for carrying into Execution the foregoing Powers, and all other Powers vested by this Constitution in the Government of the United States, or in any Department or Officer thereof.

*Section. 9.* The Migration or Importation of such Persons as any of the States now existing shall think proper to admit, shall not be prohibited by the Congress prior to the Year one thousand eight hundred and eight, but a Tax or duty may be imposed on such Importation, not exceeding ten dollars for each Person.

The Privilege of the Writ of Habeas Corpus shall not be suspended, unless when in Cases of Rebellion or Invasion the public Safety may require it.

No Bill of Attainder or ex post facto Law shall be passed.

No Capitation, or other direct, Tax shall be laid, unless in Proportion to the Census or Enumeration herein before directed to be taken.

No Tax or Duty shall be laid on Articles exported from any State.

No Preference shall be given by any Regulation of Commerce or Revenue to the Ports of one State over those of another: nor shall Vessels bound to, or from, one State, be obliged to enter, clear, or pay Duties in another.

No Money shall be drawn from the Treasury, but in Consequence of Appropriations made by Law; and a regular Statement and Account of the Receipts and Expenditures of all public Money shall be published from time to time.

No Title of Nobility shall be granted by the United States: And no Person holding any Office of Profit or Trust under them, shall, without the Consent of the Congress, accept of any present, Emolument, Office, or Title, of any kind whatever, from any King, Prince, or foreign State.

*Section. 10.* No State shall enter into any Treaty, Alliance, or Confederation; grant Letters of Marque and Reprisal; coin Money; emit Bills of Credit; make any Thing but gold and silver Coin a Tender in Payment of Debts; pass any Bill of Attainder, ex post facto Law, or Law impairing the Obligation of Contracts, or grant any Title of Nobility.

No State shall, without the Consent of the Congress, lay any Imposts or Duties on Imports or Exports, except what may be absolutely necessary for executing its inspection Laws: and the net Produce of all Duties and Imposts, laid by any State on Imports or Exports, shall be for the Use of the Treasury of the United States; and all such Laws shall be subject to the Revision and Controul of the Congress.

No State shall, without the Consent of Congress, lay any Duty of Tonnage, keep Troops, or Ships of War in time of Peace, enter into any Agreement or Compact with another State, or with a foreign Power, or engage in War, unless actually invaded, or in such imminent Danger as will not admit of delay.

ARTICLE. II.

*Section. 1.* The executive Power shall be vested in a President of the United States of America. He shall hold his Office during the term of four Years, and, together with the Vice President, chosen for the same Term, be elected, as follows:

Each State shall appoint, in such Manner as the Legislature thereof may direct, a Number of Electors, equal to the whole Number of Senators and Representatives to which the State may be entitled in the Congress: but no Senator or Representative, or Person holding an Office of Trust or Profit under the United States, shall be appointed an Elector.

The Electors shall meet in their respective States, and vote by Ballot for two Persons, of whom one at least shall not be an Inhabitant of the same State with themselves. And they shall make a List of all the Persons voted for, and of the Number of Votes for each; which List they shall sign and certify, and transmit sealed to the Seat of the Government of the United States, directed to the President of the Senate. The President of the Senate shall, in the Presence of the Senate and House of Representatives, open all the Certificates, and the Votes shall then be counted. The Person having the greatest Number of Votes shall be the President, if such Number be a Majority of the whole Number of Electors appointed; and if there be more than one who have such Majority, and have an equal Number of Votes, then the House of Representatives shall immediately chuse by Ballot one of them for President; and if no Person have a Majority, then from the five highest on the List the said House shall in like Manner chuse the President. But in chusing the President, the Votes shall be taken by States, the Representation from each State having one Vote; A quorum for this Purpose shall consist of a Member or Members from two thirds of the States, and a Majority of all the States shall be necessary to a Choice. In every Case, after the Choice of the President, the Person having the greatest Number of Votes of the Electors shall be the Vice President. But if there should remain two or more who have equal Votes, the Senate shall chuse from them by Ballot the Vice President.

The Congress may determine the Time of chusing the Electors, and the Day on which they shall give their Votes; which Day shall be the same throughout the United States.

No Person except a natural born Citizen, or a Citizen of the United States, at the time of the Adoption of this Constitution, shall be eligible to the Office of President; neither shall any Person be eligible to that Office who shall not have attained to the Age of thirty five Years, and been fourteen Years a Resident within the United States.

In Case of the Removal of the President from Office, or of his Death, Resignation, or Inability to discharge the Powers and Duties of the said Office, the Same shall devolve on the Vice President, and the Congress may by Law provide for the Case of Removal, Death, Resignation or Inability, both of the President and Vice President, declaring what Officer shall then act as President, and such Officer shall act accordingly, until the Disability be removed, or a President shall be elected.

The President shall, at stated Times, receive for his Services, a Compensation, which shall neither be encreased or diminished during the Period for which he shall have been elected, and he shall not

A-9

receive within that Period any other Emolument from the United States, or any of them.

Before he enters on the Execution of his Office, he shall take the following Oath or Affirmation:—"I do solemnly swear (or affirm) that I will faithfully execute the Office of President of the United States, and will to the best of my Ability, preserve, protect and defend the Constitution of the United States."

*Section. 2.* The President shall be Commander in Chief of the Army and Navy of the United States, and of the Militia of the several States, when called into the actual Service of the United States; he may require the Opinion, in writing, of the principal Officer in each of the executive Departments, upon any Subject relating to the Duties of their respective Offices, and he shall have Power to grant Reprieves and Pardons for Offences against the United States, except in Cases of Impeachment.

He shall have Power, by and with the Advice and Consent of the Senate, to make Treaties, provided two thirds of the Senators present concur; and he shall nominate, and by and with the Advice and Consent of the Senate, shall appoint Ambassadors, other public Ministers and Consuls, Judges of the supreme Court, and all other Officers of the United States, whose Appointments are not herein otherwise provided for, and which shall be established by Law; but the Congress may by Law vest the Appointment of such inferior Officers, as they think proper, in the President alone, in the Courts of Law, or in the Heads of Departments.

The President shall have Power to fill up all Vacancies that may happen during the Recess of the Senate, by granting Commissions which shall expire at the End of their next Session.

*Section. 3.* He shall from time to time give to the Congress Information of the State of the Union, and recommend to their Consideration such Measures as he shall judge necessary and expedient; he may, on extraordinary Occasions, convene both Houses, or either of them, and in Case of Disagreement between them, with Respect to the Time of Adjournment, he may adjourn them to such Time as he shall think proper; he shall receive Ambassadors and other public Ministers; he shall take Care that the Laws be faithfully executed, and shall Commission all the Officers of the United States.

*Section. 4.* The President, Vice President and all civil Officers of the United States, shall be removed from Office on Impeachment for, and Conviction of, Treason, Bribery, or other high Crimes and Misdemeanors.

ARTICLE. III.

*Section. 1.* The judicial Power of the United States, shall be vested in one supreme Court, and in such inferior Courts as the Congress may from time to time ordain and establish. The Judges, both of the supreme and inferior Courts, shall hold their Offices during good Behavior, and shall, at stated Times, receive for their Services, a Compensation, which shall not be diminished during their Continuance in Office.

*Section. 2.* The judicial Power shall extend to all Cases, in Law and Equity, arising under this Constitution, the Laws of the United States, and Treaties made, or which shall be made, under their Authority;—to all Cases affecting Ambassadors, other public Ministers and Consuls;—to all Cases of admiralty and maritime Jurisdiction;—the Controversies to which the United States shall be a Party;—to Controversies between two or more States;—between a State and Citizens of another State;—between Citizens of different States;—between Citizens of the same State claiming Lands under Grants of different States, and between a State, or the Citizens thereof, and foreign States, Citizens or Subjects.

In all cases affecting Ambassadors, other public Ministers and Consuls, and those in which a State shall be Party, the supreme Court shall have original Jurisdiction. In all the other Cases before mentioned, the supreme Court shall have appellate Jurisdiction, both as to Law and Fact, with such Exceptions, and under such Regulations as the Congress shall make.

The Trial of all Crimes, except in Cases of Impeachment, shall be by Jury; and such Trial shall be held in the State where the said Crimes shall have been committed; but when not committed within any State, the Trial shall be at such Place or Places as the Congress may by Law have directed.

*Section. 3.* Treason against the United States, shall consist only in levying War against them, or in adhering to their Enemies, giving them Aid and Comfort. No Person shall be convicted of Treason unless on the Testimony of two Witnesses to the same overt Act, or on Confession in open Court.

The Congress shall have Power to declare the Punishment of Treason, but no Attainder of Treason shall work Corruption of Blood, or Forfeiture except during the Life of the Person attainted.

ARTICLE. IV.

*Section. 1.* Full Faith and Credit shall be given in each State to the public Acts, Records, and judicial Proceedings of every other State. And the Congress may by general Laws prescribe the Manner in which such Acts, Records and Proceedings shall be proved, and the Effect thereof.

*Section. 2.* The Citizens of each State shall be entitled to all Privileges and Immunities of Citizens in the several States.

A Person charged in any State with Treason, Felony, or other Crime, who shall flee from Justice, and be found in another State, shall on Demand of the executive Authority of the State from which he fled, be delivered up, to be removed to the State having Jurisdiction of the Crime.

No Person held to Service or Labour in one State, under the Laws thereof, escaping into another, shall, in Consequence of any Law or Regulation therein, be discharged from such Service or Labour, but shall be delivered up on Claim of the Party to whom such Service or Labour may be due.

*Section. 3.* New States may be admitted by the Congress into this Union; but no new State shall be formed or erected within the Jurisdiction of any other State; nor any State be formed by the Junction of two or more States, or Parts of States, without the consent of the Legislatures of the States concerned as well as of the Congress.

The Congress shall have Power to dispose of and make all needful Rules and Regulations respecting the Territory or other Property belonging to the United States; and nothing in this Constitution shall be so construed as to Prejudice any Claims of the United States, or of any particular States.

*Section. 4.* The United States shall guarantee to every State in this Union a Republican Form of Government, and shall protect each of them against Invasion; and on Application of the Legislature, or of the Executive (when the Legislature cannot be convened) against domestic Violence.

ARTICLE. V.

The Congress, whenever two thirds of both Houses shall deem it necessary, shall propose Amendments to this Constitution, or, on the Application of the Legislatures of two thirds of the several States, shall call a Convention for proposing Amendments, which, in either Case, shall be valid to all Intents and Purposes, as Part of this Constitution, when ratified by the Legislatures of three fourths of the several States, or by Conventions in three fourths thereof, as the one or the other Mode of Ratification may be proposed by the Congress; Provided that no Amendment which may be made prior to the Year One thousand eight hundred and eight shall in any Manner affect the first and fourth Clauses in the Ninth Section of the first Article; and that no State, without its Consent, shall be deprived of its equal Suffrage in the Senate.

ARTICLE. VI.

All Debts contracted and Engagements entered into, before the Adoption of this Constitution, shall be as valid against the United States under this Constitution, as under the Confederation.

This Constitution, and the Laws of the United States which shall be made in Pursuance thereof; and all Treaties made, or which shall be made, under the Authority of the United States, shall be the supreme Law of the Land; and the Judges in every State shall be bound thereby, any Thing in the Constitution or Laws of any State to the Contrary notwithstanding.

The Senators and Representatives before mentioned, and the Members of the several State Legislatures, and all executive and judicial Officers, both of the United States and of the several States, shall be bound by Oath or Affirmation, to support this Constitution; but no religious Test shall ever be required as a Qualification to any Office or public Trust under the United States.

ARTICLE. VII.

The Ratification of the Conventions of nine States, shall be sufficient for the Establishment of this Constitution between the States so ratifying the Same.

Done in Convention by the Unanimous Consent of the States present the Seventeenth Day of September in the Year of our Lord one thousand seven hundred and Eighty seven and of the Independence of the United States of America the Twelfth. In witness thereof We have hereunto subscribed our Names,

*G°. WASHINGTON*—Presd[t].
and deputy from Virginia.

NEW HAMPSHIRE
*John Langdon*
*Nicholas Gilman*

MASSACHUSETTS
*Nathaniel Gorham*
*Rufus King*

CONNECTICUT
*W[m] Sam[l] Johnson*
*Roger Sherman*

NEW YORK
*Alexander Hamilton*

NEW JERSEY
*Wil: Livingston*
*David A. Brearley*
*W[m] Paterson*
*Jona: Dayton*

PENNSYLVANIA
*B Franklin*
*Thomas Mifflin*
*Rob[t] Morris*
*Geo. Clymer*
*Tho[s] FitzSimons*
*Jared Ingersoll*
*James Wilson*
*Gouv Morris*

DELAWARE
*Geo: Read*
*Gunning Bedford jun*
*John Dickinson*
*Richard Bassett*
*Jaco: Broom*

MARYLAND
*James M[c]Henry*
*Dan of S[t] Tho[s] Jenifer*
*Dan[l] Carroll*

VIRGINIA
*John Blair—*
*James Madison Jr.*

NORTH CAROLINA
*W[m] Blount*
*Rich[d] Dobbs Spaight*
*Hu Williamson*

SOUTH CAROLINA
*J. Rutledge*
*Charles Cotesworth*
*  Pinckney*
*Charles Pinckney*
*Pierce Butler*

GEORGIA
*William Few*
*Abr Baldwin*

## *Amendments to the Constitution*

Articles in addition to, and Amendment of the Constitution of the United States of America, proposed by Congress, and ratified by the Legislatures of the several States, pursuant to the fifth Article of the original Constitution.

AMENDMENT I.

Congress shall make no law respecting an establishment of religion, or prohibiting the free exercise thereof; or abridging the freedom of speech, or of the press; or the right of the people peaceably to assemble, and to petition the Government for a redress of grievances.

AMENDMENT II.

A well regulated Militia, being necessary to the security of a free State, the right of the people to keep and bear Arms, shall not be infringed.

AMENDMENT III.

No Soldier shall, in time of peace be quartered in any house, without the consent of the Owner, nor in time of war, but in a manner to be prescribed by law.

AMENDMENT IV.

The right of the people to be secure in their persons, houses, papers, and effects, against unreasonable searches and seizures, shall not be violated, and no Warrants shall issue, but upon probable cause, supported by Oath or affirmation, and particularly describing the place to be searched, and the persons or things to be seized.

AMENDMENT V.

No person shall be held to answer for a capital, or otherwise infamous crime, unless on a presentment or indictment of a Grand Jury, except in cases arising in the land or naval forces, or in the Militia, when in actual service in time of War or public danger; nor shall any person be subject for the same offence to be twice put in jeopardy of life or limb; nor shall be compelled in any criminal case to be a witness against himself, nor be deprived of life, liberty, or property, without due process of law; nor shall private property be taken for public use, without just compensation.

AMENDMENT VI.

In all criminal prosecutions, the accused shall enjoy the right to a speedy and public trial, by an impartial jury of the State and district wherein the crime shall have been committed, which district shall have been previously ascertained by law, and to be informed of the nature and cause of the accusation; to be confronted with the witnesses against him; to have compulsory process for obtaining witnesses in his favor, and to have the Assistance of Counsel for his defence.

AMENDMENT VII.

In Suits at common law, where the value in controversy shall exceed twenty dollars, the right of trial by jury shall be preserved, and no fact tried by a jury, shall be otherwise re-examined in any Court of the United States, than according to the rules of the common law.

AMENDMENT VIII.

Excessive bail shall not be required, nor excessive fines imposed, nor cruel and unusual punishments inflicted.

AMENDMENT IX.

The enumeration in the Constitution, of certain rights, shall not be construed to deny or disparage others retained by the people.

AMENDMENT X.

The powers not delegated to the United States by the Constitution, nor prohibited by it to the States, are reserved to the States respectively, or to the people. [The first ten amendments went into effect December 15, 1791.]

AMENDMENT XI.

The Judicial power of the United States shall not be construed to extend to any suit in law or equity, commenced or prosecuted against one of the United States by Citizens of another State, or by Citizens or Subjects of any Foreign State. [January 8, 1798]

AMENDMENT XII.

The Electors shall meet in their respective states, and vote by ballot for President and Vice-President, one of whom, at least, shall not be an inhabitant of the same state with themselves; they shall name in their ballots the person voted for as President, and in distinct ballots the person voted for as Vice-President, and they shall make distinct lists of all persons voted for as President, and of all persons voted for as Vice President, and of the number of votes for each, which lists they shall sign and certify, and transmit sealed to the seat of the government of the United States, directed to the President of the Senate;—The President of the Senate shall, in the presence of the Senate and House of Representatives, open all the certificates and the votes shall then be counted;—The person having the greatest number of votes for President, shall be the President, if such number be a majority of the whole number of Electors appointed; and if no person have such majority, then from the persons having the highest numbers not exceeding three on the list of those voted for as President, the House of Representatives shall choose immediately, by ballot, the President. But in choosing the President, the votes shall be taken by states, the representation from each state having one vote; a quorum for this purpose shall consist of a member or members from two-thirds of the states, and a majority of all the states shall be necessary to a choice. And if the House of Representatives shall not choose a President whenever the right of choice shall devolve upon them, before the fourth day of March next following, then the Vice-President shall act as President, as in the case of the death or other constitutional disability of the President.—The person having the greatest number of votes as Vice-President, shall be the Vice-President, if such number be a majority of the whole number of Electors appointed, and if no person have a majority, then from the two highest numbers on the list, the Senate shall choose the Vice-President; a quorum for the purpose shall consist of two-thirds of the whole number of Senators, and a majority of the whole number shall be necessary to a choice. But no person constitutionally ineligible to the office of President shall be eligible to that of Vice-President of the United States. [September 25, 1804]

AMENDMENT XIII.

*Section 1.* Neither slavery nor involuntary servitude, except as a punishment for crime whereof the party shall have been duly convicted, shall exist within the United States, or any place subject to their jurisdiction.

*Section 2.* Congress shall have power to enforce this article by appropriate legislation. [December 18, 1865]

AMENDMENT XIV.

*Section 1.* All persons born or naturalized in the United States, and subject to the jurisdiction thereof, are citizens of the United States and of the State wherein they reside. No State shall make or enforce any law which shall abridge the privileges or immunities of citizens of the United States; nor shall any State deprive any person of life, liberty, or property, without due process of law; nor deny to any person within its jurisdiction the equal protection of the laws.

*Section 2.* Representatives shall be apportioned among the several States according to their respective numbers, counting the whole number of persons in each State, excluding Indians not taxed. But when the right to vote at any election for the choice of electors for President and Vice President of the United States, Representatives in Congress, the Executive and Judicial officers of a State, or the members of the Legislature thereof, is denied to any of the male inhabitants of such State, being twenty-one years of age, and citizens of the United States, or in any way abridged, except for participation in rebellion, or other crime, the basis of representation therein shall be reduced in the proportion which the number of such male citizens shall bear to the whole number of male citizens twenty-one years of age in such State.

*Section 3.* No person shall be a Senator or Representative in Congress, or elector of President and Vice President, or hold any office, civil or military, under the United States, or under any State, who, having previously taken an oath, as a member of Congress, or as an officer of the United States, or as a member of any State legislature, or as an executive or judicial officer of any State, to support the Constitution of the United States, shall have engaged in insurrection or rebellion against the same, or given aid or comfort to the enemies thereof. But Congress may by a vote of two-thirds of each House, remove such disability.

*Section 4.* The validity of the public debt of the United States, authorized by law, including debts incurred for payment of pensions and bounties for services in suppressing insurrection or rebellion, shall not be questioned. But neither the United States nor any State shall assume or pay any debt or obligation incurred in aid of insurrection or rebellion against the United States, or any claim for the loss or emancipation of any slave; but all such debts, obligations and claims shall be held illegal and void.

*Section 5.* The Congress shall have power to enforce, by appropriate legislation, the provisions of this article. [July 28, 1868]

AMENDMENT XV.

*Section 1.* The right of citizens of the United States to vote shall not be denied or abridged by the United States or by any State on account of race, color, or previous condition of servitude—

*Section 2.* The Congress shall have power to enforce this article by appropriate legislation. [March 30, 1870]

AMENDMENT XVI.

The Congress shall have power to lay and collect taxes on incomes, from whatever source derived, without apportionment among the several States, and without regard to any census or enumeration. [February 25, 1913]

AMENDMENT XVII.

The Senate of the United States shall be composed of two senators from each State, elected by the people thereof, for six years; and each Senator shall have one vote. The electors in each State shall have the qualifications requisite for electors of the most numerous branch of the State legislatures.

When vacancies happen in the representation of any State in the Senate, the executive authority of such State shall issue writs of election to fill such vacancies: *Provided*, That the legislature of any State may empower the executive thereof to make temporary appointments until the people fill the vacancies by election as the legislature may direct.

This amendment shall not be so construed as to affect the election or term of any senator chosen before it becomes valid as part of the Constitution. [May 31, 1913]

AMENDMENT XVIII.

After one year from the ratification of this article, the manufacture, sale, or transportation of intoxicating liquors within, the importation thereof into, or the exportation thereof from the United States and all territory subject to the jurisdiction thereof for beverage purposes is hereby prohibited.

The Congress and the several States shall have concurrent power to enforce this article by appropriate legislation.

This article shall be inoperative unless it shall have been ratified as an amendment to the Constitution by the legislatures of the several States, as provided in the Constitution, within seven years from the date of the submission thereof to the States by Congress. [January 29, 1919]

AMENDMENT XIX.

The right of citizens of the United States to vote shall not be denied or abridged by the United States or by any State on account of sex.

The Congress shall have power by appropriate legislation to enforce the provisions of this article. [August 26, 1920]

AMENDMENT XX.

*Section 1.* The terms of the President and Vice-President shall end at noon on the twentieth day of January, and the terms of Senators and Representatives at noon on the third day of January, of the years in which such terms would have ended if this article had not been ratified; and the terms of their successors shall then begin.

*Section 2.* The Congress shall assemble at least once in every year, and such meeting shall begin at noon on the third day of January, unless they shall by law appoint a different day.

*Section 3.* If, at the time fixed for the beginning of the term of the President, the President-elect shall have died, the Vice-President-elect shall become President. If a President shall not have been chosen before the time fixed for the beginning of his term, or if the President-elect shall have failed to qualify, then the Vice-President-elect shall act as President until a President shall have qualified; and the Congress may by law provide for the case wherein neither a President-elect nor a Vice-President-elect shall have qualified, declaring who shall then act as President, or the manner in which one who is to act shall be selected, and such person shall act accordingly until a President or Vice-President shall have qualified.

*Section 4.* The Congress may by law provide for the case of the death of any of the persons from whom the House of Representatives may choose a President whenever the right of choice shall have devolved upon them, and for the case of the death of any of the persons from whom the Senate may choose a Vice-President whenever the right of choice shall have devolved upon them.

*Section 5.* Sections 1 and 2 shall take effect on the 15th day of October following the ratification of this article.

*Section 6.* This article shall be inoperative unless it shall have been ratified as an amendment to the Constitution by the legislatures of three-fourths of the several States within seven years from the date of its submission. [February 6, 1933]

AMENDMENT XXI.

*Section 1.* The eighteenth article of amendment to the Constitution of the United States is hereby repealed.

*Section 2.* The transportation or importation into any State, Territory or possession of the United States for delivery or use therein of intoxicating liquors, in violation of the laws thereof, is hereby prohibited.

*Section 3.* This article shall be inoperative unless it shall have been ratified as an amendment to the Constitution by convention in the several States, as provided in the Constitution, within seven years from the date of the submission thereof to the States by the Congress. [December 5, 1933]

AMENDMENT XXII.

*Section 1.* No person shall be elected to the office of the President more than twice, and no person who has held the office of President, or acted as President, for more than two years of a term to which some other person was elected President shall be elected to the office of the President more than once. But this Article shall not apply to any person holding the office of President when this Article was proposed by the Congress, and shall not prevent any person who may be holding the office of President, or acting as President, during the term within which this Article becomes operative from holding the office of President or acting as President during the remainder of such term.

*Section 2.* This article shall be inoperative unless it shall have been ratified as an amendment to the Constitution by the legislatures of three-fourths of the several states within seven years from the date of its submission to the States by the Congress. [February 27, 1951]

AMENDMENT XXIII.

*Section 1.* The District constituting the seat of government of the United States shall appoint in such manner as the Congress may direct:

A number of electors of President and Vice-President equal to the whole number of Senators and Representatives in Congress to which the District would be entitled if it were a State, but in no event more than the least populous State; they shall be in addition to those appointed by the States, but they shall be considered, for the purposes of the election of President and Vice-President, to be electors appointed by a State; and they shall meet in the District and perform such duties as provided by the twelfth article of amendment.

*Section 2.* The Congress shall have the power to enforce this article by appropriate legislation. [March 29, 1961]

AMENDMENT XXIV.

*Section 1.* The right of citizens of the United States to vote in any primary or other election for President or Vice President, for electors for President or Vice President, or for Senator or Representative in Congress, shall not be denied or abridged by the United States or any State by reason of failure to pay any poll tax or other tax.

*Section 2.* The Congress shall have power to enforce this article by appropriate legislation. [January 23, 1964]

AMENDMENT XXV.

*Section 1.* In case of the removal of the President from office or of his death or resignation, the Vice President shall become President.

*Section 2.* Whenever there is a vacancy in the office of Vice President, the President shall nominate a Vice President who shall take office upon confirmation by a majority vote of both Houses of Congress.

*Section 3.* Whenever the President transmits to the President pro tempore of the Senate and the Speaker of the House of Representatives his written declaration that he is unable to discharge the powers and duties of his office, and until he transmits to them a written declaration to the contrary, such powers and duties shall be discharged by the Vice President as Acting President.

*Section 4.* Whenever the Vice President and a majority of either the principal officers of the executive departments or of such other body as Congress may by law provide, transmit to the President pro tempore of the Senate and the Speaker of the House of Representatives their written declaration that the President is unable to discharge the powers and duties of his office, the Vice President shall immediately assume the powers and duties of the office as Acting President.

Thereafter, when the President transmits to the President pro tempore of the Senate and the Speaker of the House of Representatives his written declaration that no inability exists, he shall resume the powers and duties of his office unless the Vice President and a majority of either the principal officers of the executive departments or of such other body as Congress may by law provide, transmit within four days to the President pro tempore of the Senate and the Speaker of the House of Representatives their written declaration that the President is unable to discharge the powers and duties of his office. Thereupon Congress shall decide the issue, assembling within forty-eight hours for that purpose if not in session. If the Congress, within twenty-one days after receipt of the latter written declaration, or, if Congress is not in session, within twenty-one days after Congress is required to assemble, determines by two-thirds vote of both Houses that the President is unable to discharge the powers and duties of his office, the Vice President shall continue to discharge the same as Acting President; otherwise, the President shall resume the powers and duties of his office. [February 10, 1967]

AMENDMENT XXVI.

*Section 1.* The right of citizens of the United States, who are eighteen years of age or older, to vote shall not be denied or abridged by the United States or by any State on account of age.

*Section 2.* The Congress shall have power to enforce this article by appropriate legislation. [June 30, 1971]

AMENDMENT XXVII.

No law, varying the compensation for the services of the Senators and Representatives shall take effect, until an election of Representatives shall have intervened. [May 8, 1992]

# PRESIDENTIAL ELECTIONS

| Year | Number of States | Candidates | Parties | Popular Vote | % of Popular Vote | Electoral Vote | % Voter Participation |
|---|---|---|---|---|---|---|---|
| 1789 | 11 | **GEORGE WASHINGTON** | NO PARTY DESIGNATIONS | | | 69 | |
| | | John Adams | | | | 34 | |
| | | Other candidates | | | | 35 | |
| 1792 | 15 | **GEORGE WASHINGTON** | NO PARTY DESIGNATIONS | | | 132 | |
| | | John Adams | | | | 77 | |
| | | George Clinton | | | | 50 | |
| | | Other candidates | | | | 5 | |
| 1796 | 16 | **JOHN ADAMS** | FEDERALIST | | | 71 | |
| | | Thomas Jefferson | Democratic-Republican | | | 68 | |
| | | Thomas Pinckney | Federalist | | | 59 | |
| | | Aaron Burr | Democratic-Republican | | | 30 | |
| | | Other candidates | | | | 48 | |
| 1800 | 16 | **THOMAS JEFFERSON** | DEMOCRATIC-REPUBLICAN | | | 73 | |
| | | Aaron Burr | Democratic-Republican | | | 73 | |
| | | John Adams | Federalist | | | 65 | |
| | | Charles C. Pinckney | Federalist | | | 64 | |
| | | John Jay | Federalist | | | 1 | |
| 1804 | 17 | **THOMAS JEFFERSON** | DEMOCRATIC-REPUBLICAN | | | 162 | |
| | | Charles C. Pinckney | Federalist | | | 14 | |
| 1808 | 17 | **JAMES MADISON** | DEMOCRATIC-REPUBLICAN | | | 122 | |
| | | Charles C. Pinckney | Federalist | | | 47 | |
| | | George Clinton | Democratic-Republican | | | 6 | |
| 1812 | 18 | **JAMES MADISON** | DEMOCRATIC-REPUBLICAN | | | 128 | |
| | | DeWitt Clinton | Federalist | | | 89 | |
| 1816 | 19 | **JAMES MONROE** | DEMOCRATIC-REPUBLICAN | | | 183 | |
| | | Rufus King | Federalist | | | 34 | |
| 1820 | 24 | **JAMES MONROE** | DEMOCRATIC-REPUBLICAN | | | 231 | |
| | | John Quincy Adams | Independent | | | 1 | |
| 1824 | 24 | **JOHN QUINCY ADAMS** | DEMOCRATIC-REPUBLICAN | 108,740 | 30.5 | 84 | 26.9 |
| | | Andrew Jackson | Democratic-Republican | 153,544 | 43.1 | 99 | |
| | | Henry Clay | Democratic-Republican | 47,136 | 13.2 | 37 | |
| | | William H. Crawford | Democratic-Republican | 46,618 | 13.1 | 41 | |
| 1828 | 24 | **ANDREW JACKSON** | DEMOCRATIC | 647,286 | 56.0 | 178 | 57.6 |
| | | John Quincy Adams | National Republican | 508,064 | 44.0 | 83 | |
| 1832 | 24 | **ANDREW JACKSON** | DEMOCRATIC | 688,242 | 54.5 | 219 | 55.4 |
| | | Henry Clay | National Republican | 473,462 | 37.5 | 49 | |
| | | William Wirt | Anti-Masonic | 101,051 | 8.0 | 7 | |
| | | John Floyd | Democratic | | | 11 | |

| Year | Number of States | Candidates | Parties | Popular Vote | % of Popular Vote | Electoral Vote | % Voter Participation |
|------|-----------------|------------|---------|--------------|-------------------|----------------|----------------------|
| 1836 | 26 | **MARTIN VAN BUREN** | DEMOCRATIC | 765,483 | 50.9 | 170 | 57.8 |
|      |    | William H. Harrison | Whig | | | 73 | |
|      |    | Hugh L. White | Whig | 739,795 | 49.1 | 26 | |
|      |    | Daniel Webster | Whig | | | 14 | |
|      |    | W. P. Mangum | Whig | | | 11 | |
| 1840 | 26 | **WILLIAM H. HARRISON** | WHIG | 1,274,624 | 53.1 | 234 | 80.2 |
|      |    | Martin Van Buren | Democratic | 1,127,781 | 46.9 | 60 | |
| 1844 | 26 | **JAMES K. POLK** | DEMOCRATIC | 1,338,464 | 49.6 | 170 | 78.9 |
|      |    | Henry Clay | Whig | 1,300,097 | 48.1 | 105 | |
|      |    | James G. Birney | Liberty | 62,300 | 2.3 | | |
| 1848 | 30 | **ZACHARY TAYLOR** | WHIG | 1,360,967 | 47.4 | 163 | 72.7 |
|      |    | Lewis Cass | Democratic | 1,222,342 | 42.5 | 127 | |
|      |    | Martin Van Buren | Free Soil | 291,263 | 10.1 | | |
| 1852 | 31 | **FRANKLIN PIERCE** | DEMOCRATIC | 1,601,117 | 50.9 | 254 | 69.6 |
|      |    | Winfield Scott | Whig | 1,385,453 | 44.1 | 42 | |
|      |    | John P. Hale | Free Soil | 155,825 | 5.0 | | |
| 1856 | 31 | **JAMES BUCHANAN** | DEMOCRATIC | 1,832,955 | 45.3 | 174 | 78.9 |
|      |    | John C. Frémont | Republican | 1,339,932 | 33.1 | 114 | |
|      |    | Millard Fillmore | American | 871,731 | 21.6 | 8 | |
| 1860 | 33 | **ABRAHAM LINCOLN** | REPUBLICAN | 1,865,593 | 39.8 | 180 | 81.2 |
|      |    | Stephen A. Douglas | Democratic | 1,382,713 | 29.5 | 12 | |
|      |    | John C. Breckinridge | Democratic | 848,356 | 18.1 | 72 | |
|      |    | John Bell | Constitutional Union | 592,906 | 12.6 | 39 | |
| 1864 | 36 | **ABRAHAM LINCOLN** | REPUBLICAN | 2,206,938 | 55.0 | 212 | 73.8 |
|      |    | George B. McClellan | Democratic | 1,803,787 | 45.0 | 21 | |
| 1868 | 37 | **ULYSSES S. GRANT** | REPUBLICAN | 3,013,421 | 52.7 | 214 | 78.1 |
|      |    | Horatio Seymour | Democratic | 2,706,829 | 47.3 | 80 | |
| 1872 | 37 | **ULYSSES S. GRANT** | REPUBLICAN | 3,596,745 | 55.6 | 286 | 71.3 |
|      |    | Horace Greeley | Democratic | 2,843,446 | 43.9 | 66 | |
| 1876 | 38 | **RUTHERFORD B. HAYES** | REPUBLICAN | 4,036,572 | 48.0 | 185 | 81.8 |
|      |    | Samuel J. Tilden | Democratic | 4,284,020 | 51.0 | 184 | |
| 1880 | 38 | **JAMES A. GARFIELD** | REPUBLICAN | 4,453,295 | 48.5 | 214 | 79.4 |
|      |    | Winfield S. Hancock | Democratic | 4,414,082 | 48.1 | 155 | |
|      |    | James B. Weaver | Greenback-Labor | 308,578 | 3.4 | | |
| 1884 | 38 | **GROVER CLEVELAND** | DEMOCRATIC | 4,879,507 | 48.5 | 219 | 77.5 |
|      |    | James G. Blaine | Republican | 4,850,293 | 48.2 | 182 | |
|      |    | Benjamin F. Butler | Greenback-Labor | 175,370 | 1.8 | | |
|      |    | John P. St. John | Prohibition | 150,369 | 1.5 | | |
| 1888 | 38 | **BENJAMIN HARRISON** | REPUBLICAN | 5,477,129 | 47.9 | 233 | 79.3 |
|      |    | Grover Cleveland | Democratic | 5,537,857 | 48.6 | 168 | |
|      |    | Clinton B. Fisk | Prohibition | 249,506 | 2.2 | | |
|      |    | Anson J. Streeter | Union Labor | 146,935 | 1.3 | | |

| Year | Number of States | Candidates | Parties | Popular Vote | % of Popular Vote | Electoral Vote | % Voter Participation |
|------|------------------|------------|---------|--------------|-------------------|----------------|-----------------------|
| 1892 | 44 | **GROVER CLEVELAND** | DEMOCRATIC | 5,555,426 | 46.1 | 277 | 74.7 |
|      |    | Benjamin Harrison | Republican | 5,182,690 | 43.0 | 145 | |
|      |    | James B. Weaver | People's | 1,029,846 | 8.5 | 22 | |
|      |    | John Bidwell | Prohibition | 264,133 | 2.2 | | |
| 1896 | 45 | **WILLIAM McKINLEY** | REPUBLICAN | 7,102,246 | 51.1 | 271 | 79.3 |
|      |    | William J. Bryan | Democratic | 6,492,559 | 47.7 | 176 | |
| 1900 | 45 | **WILLIAM McKINLEY** | REPUBLICAN | 7,218,491 | 51.7 | 292 | 73.2 |
|      |    | William J. Bryan | Democratic; Populist | 6,356,734 | 45.5 | 155 | |
|      |    | John C. Wooley | Prohibition | 208,914 | 1.5 | | |
| 1904 | 45 | **THEODORE ROOSEVELT** | REPUBLICAN | 7,628,461 | 57.4 | 336 | 65.2 |
|      |    | Alton B. Parker | Democratic | 5,084,223 | 37.6 | 140 | |
|      |    | Eugene V. Debs | Socialist | 402,283 | 3.0 | | |
|      |    | Silas C. Swallow | Prohibition | 258,536 | 1.9 | | |
| 1908 | 46 | **WILLIAM H. TAFT** | REPUBLICAN | 7,675,320 | 51.6 | 321 | 65.4 |
|      |    | William J. Bryan | Democratic | 6,412,294 | 43.1 | 162 | |
|      |    | Eugene V. Debs | Socialist | 420,793 | 2.8 | | |
|      |    | Eugene W. Chafin | Prohibition | 253,840 | 1.7 | | |
| 1912 | 48 | **WOODROW WILSON** | DEMOCRATIC | 6,296,547 | 41.9 | 435 | 58.8 |
|      |    | Theodore Roosevelt | Progressive | 4,118,571 | 27.4 | 88 | |
|      |    | William H. Taft | Republican | 3,486,720 | 23.2 | 8 | |
|      |    | Eugene V. Debs | Socialist | 900,672 | 6.0 | | |
|      |    | Eugene W. Chafin | Prohibition | 206,275 | 1.4 | | |
| 1916 | 48 | **WOODROW WILSON** | DEMOCRATIC | 9,127,695 | 49.4 | 277 | 61.6 |
|      |    | Charles E. Hughes | Republican | 8,533,507 | 46.2 | 254 | |
|      |    | A. L. Benson | Socialist | 585,113 | 3.2 | | |
|      |    | J. Frank Hanly | Prohibition | 220,506 | 1.2 | | |
| 1920 | 48 | **WARREN G. HARDING** | REPUBLICAN | 16,143,407 | 60.4 | 404 | 49.2 |
|      |    | James M. Cox | Democratic | 9,130,328 | 34.2 | 127 | |
|      |    | Eugene V. Debs | Socialist | 919,799 | 3.4 | | |
|      |    | P. P. Christensen | Farmer-Labor | 265,411 | 1.0 | | |
| 1924 | 48 | **CALVIN COOLIDGE** | REPUBLICAN | 15,718,211 | 54.0 | 382 | 48.9 |
|      |    | John W. Davis | Democratic | 8,385,283 | 28.8 | 136 | |
|      |    | Robert M. La Follette | Progressive | 4,831,289 | 16.6 | 13 | |
| 1928 | 48 | **HERBERT C. HOOVER** | REPUBLICAN | 21,391,993 | 58.2 | 444 | 56.9 |
|      |    | Alfred E. Smith | Democratic | 15,016,169 | 40.9 | 87 | |
| 1932 | 48 | **FRANKLIN D. ROOSEVELT** | DEMOCRATIC | 22,809,638 | 57.4 | 472 | 56.9 |
|      |    | Herbert C. Hoover | Republican | 15,758,901 | 39.7 | 59 | |
|      |    | Norman Thomas | Socialist | 881,951 | 2.2 | | |
| 1936 | 48 | **FRANKLIN D. ROOSEVELT** | DEMOCRATIC | 27,752,869 | 60.8 | 523 | 61.0 |
|      |    | Alfred M. Landon | Republican | 16,674,665 | 36.5 | 8 | |
|      |    | William Lemke | Union | 882,479 | 1.9 | | |
| 1940 | 48 | **FRANKLIN D. ROOSEVELT** | DEMOCRATIC | 27,307,819 | 54.8 | 449 | 62.5 |
|      |    | Wendell L. Willkie | Republican | 22,321,018 | 44.8 | 82 | |

| Year | Number of States | Candidates | Parties | Popular Vote | % of Popular Vote | Electoral Vote | % Voter Participation |
|---|---|---|---|---|---|---|---|
| 1944 | 48 | **FRANKLIN D. ROOSEVELT** | DEMOCRATIC | 25,606,585 | 53.5 | 432 | 55.9 |
| | | Thomas E. Dewey | Republican | 22,014,745 | 46.0 | 99 | |
| 1948 | 48 | **HARRY S. TRUMAN** | DEMOCRATIC | 24,179,345 | 49.6 | 303 | 53.0 |
| | | Thomas E. Dewey | Republican | 21,991,291 | 45.1 | 189 | |
| | | J. Strom Thurmond | States' Rights | 1,176,125 | 2.4 | 39 | |
| | | Henry A. Wallace | Progressive | 1,157,326 | 2.4 | | |
| 1952 | 48 | **DWIGHT D. EISENHOWER** | REPUBLICAN | 33,936,234 | 55.1 | 442 | 63.3 |
| | | Adlai E. Stevenson | Democratic | 27,314,992 | 44.4 | 89 | |
| 1956 | 48 | **DWIGHT D. EISENHOWER** | REPUBLICAN | 35,590,472 | 57.6 | 457 | 60.6 |
| | | Adlai E. Stevenson | Democratic | 26,022,752 | 42.1 | 73 | |
| 1960 | 50 | **JOHN F. KENNEDY** | DEMOCRATIC | 34,226,731 | 49.7 | 303 | 62.8 |
| | | Richard M. Nixon | Republican | 34,108,157 | 49.5 | 219 | |
| 1964 | 50 | **LYNDON B. JOHNSON** | DEMOCRATIC | 43,129,566 | 61.1 | 486 | 61.9 |
| | | Barry M. Goldwater | Republican | 27,178,188 | 38.5 | 52 | |
| 1968 | 50 | **RICHARD M. NIXON** | REPUBLICAN | 31,785,480 | 43.4 | 301 | 60.9 |
| | | Hubert H. Humphrey | Democratic | 31,275,166 | 42.7 | 191 | |
| | | George C. Wallace | American Independent | 9,906,473 | 13.5 | 46 | |
| 1972 | 50 | **RICHARD M. NIXON** | REPUBLICAN | 47,169,911 | 60.7 | 520 | 55.2 |
| | | George S. McGovern | Democratic | 29,170,383 | 37.5 | 17 | |
| | | John G. Schmitz | American | 1,099,482 | 1.4 | | |
| 1976 | 50 | **JIMMY CARTER** | DEMOCRATIC | 40,830,763 | 50.1 | 297 | 53.5 |
| | | Gerald R. Ford | Republican | 39,147,793 | 48.0 | 240 | |
| 1980 | 50 | **RONALD REAGAN** | REPUBLICAN | 43,901,812 | 50.7 | 489 | 52.6 |
| | | Jimmy Carter | Democratic | 35,483,820 | 41.0 | 49 | |
| | | John B. Anderson | Independent | 5,719,437 | 6.6 | | |
| | | Ed Clark | Libertarian | 921,188 | 1.1 | | |
| 1984 | 50 | **RONALD REAGAN** | REPUBLICAN | 54,451,521 | 58.8 | 525 | 53.1 |
| | | Walter F. Mondale | Democratic | 37,565,334 | 40.6 | 13 | |
| 1988 | 50 | **GEORGE H. BUSH** | REPUBLICAN | 47,917,341 | 53.4 | 426 | 50.1 |
| | | Michael Dukakis | Democratic | 41,013,030 | 45.6 | 111 | |
| 1992 | 50 | **BILL CLINTON** | DEMOCRATIC | 44,908,254 | 43.0 | 370 | 55.0 |
| | | George H. Bush | Republican | 39,102,343 | 37.4 | 168 | |
| | | H. Ross Perot | Independent | 19,741,065 | 18.9 | 0 | |
| 1996 | 50 | **BILL CLINTON** | DEMOCRATIC | 47,401,185 | 49.0 | 379 | 49.0 |
| | | Bob Dole | Republican | 39,197,469 | 41.0 | 159 | |
| | | H. Ross Perot | Independent | 8,085,295 | 8.0 | 0 | |
| 2000 | 50 | **GEORGE W. BUSH** | REPUBLICAN | 50,455,156 | 47.9 | 271 | 50.4 |
| | | Albert Gore | Democratic | 50,997,335 | 48.4 | 266 | |
| | | Ralph Nader | Green Party | 2,882,897 | 2.7 | 0 | |
| 2004 | 50 | **GEORGE W. BUSH** | REPUBLICAN | 62,040,610 | 50.8 | 286 | 60.0 |
| | | John F. Kerry | Democratic | 59,028,111 | 48.3 | 252 | |

Candidates receiving less than 1 percent of the popular vote have been omitted. Thus, the percentage of popular vote given for any election year may not total 100 percent. Before the passage of the Twelfth Amendment in 1804, the electoral college voted for two presidential candidates; the runner-up became vice-president.

# ADMISSION OF STATES

| Order of Admission | State | Date of Admission | Order of Admission | State | Date of Admission |
|---|---|---|---|---|---|
| 1 | Delaware | December 7, 1787 | 26 | Michigan | January 26, 1837 |
| 2 | Pennsylvania | December 12, 1787 | 27 | Florida | March 3, 1845 |
| 3 | New Jersey | December 18, 1787 | 28 | Texas | December 29, 1845 |
| 4 | Georgia | January 2, 1788 | 29 | Iowa | December 28, 1846 |
| 5 | Connecticut | January 9, 1788 | 30 | Wisconsin | May 29, 1848 |
| 6 | Massachusetts | February 7, 1788 | 31 | California | September 9, 1850 |
| 7 | Maryland | April 28, 1788 | 32 | Minnesota | May 11, 1858 |
| 8 | South Carolina | May 23, 1788 | 33 | Oregon | February 14, 1859 |
| 9 | New Hampshire | June 21, 1788 | 34 | Kansas | January 29, 1861 |
| 10 | Virginia | June 25, 1788 | 35 | West Virginia | June 30, 1863 |
| 11 | New York | July 26, 1788 | 36 | Nevada | October 31, 1864 |
| 12 | North Carolina | November 21, 1789 | 37 | Nebraska | March 1, 1867 |
| 13 | Rhode Island | May 29, 1790 | 38 | Colorado | August 1, 1876 |
| 14 | Vermont | March 4, 1791 | 39 | North Dakota | November 2, 1889 |
| 15 | Kentucky | June 1, 1792 | 40 | South Dakota | November 2, 1889 |
| 16 | Tennessee | June 1, 1796 | 41 | Montana | November 8, 1889 |
| 17 | Ohio | March 1, 1803 | 42 | Washington | November 11, 1889 |
| 18 | Louisiana | April 30, 1812 | 43 | Idaho | July 3, 1890 |
| 19 | Indiana | December 11, 1816 | 44 | Wyoming | July 10, 1890 |
| 20 | Mississippi | December 10, 1817 | 45 | Utah | January 4, 1896 |
| 21 | Illinois | December 3, 1818 | 46 | Oklahoma | November 16, 1907 |
| 22 | Alabama | December 14, 1819 | 47 | New Mexico | January 6, 1912 |
| 23 | Maine | March 15, 1820 | 48 | Arizona | February 14, 1912 |
| 24 | Missouri | August 10, 1821 | 49 | Alaska | January 3, 1959 |
| 25 | Arkansas | June 15, 1836 | 50 | Hawaii | August 21, 1959 |

## POPULATION OF THE UNITED STATES

| Year | Number of States | Population | % Increase | Population per Square Mile |
|------|------------------|------------|------------|----------------------------|
| 1790 | 13 | 3,929,214 | | 4.5 |
| 1800 | 16 | 5,308,483 | 35.1 | 6.1 |
| 1810 | 17 | 7,239,881 | 36.4 | 4.3 |
| 1820 | 23 | 9,638,453 | 33.1 | 5.5 |
| 1830 | 24 | 12,866,020 | 33.5 | 7.4 |
| 1840 | 26 | 17,069,453 | 32.7 | 9.8 |
| 1850 | 31 | 23,191,876 | 35.9 | 7.9 |
| 1860 | 33 | 31,443,321 | 35.6 | 10.6 |
| 1870 | 37 | 39,818,449 | 26.6 | 13.4 |
| 1880 | 38 | 50,155,783 | 26.0 | 16.9 |
| 1890 | 44 | 62,947,714 | 25.5 | 21.1 |
| 1900 | 45 | 75,994,575 | 20.7 | 25.6 |
| 1910 | 46 | 91,972,266 | 21.0 | 31.0 |
| 1920 | 48 | 105,710,620 | 14.9 | 35.6 |
| 1930 | 48 | 122,775,046 | 16.1 | 41.2 |
| 1940 | 48 | 131,669,275 | 7.2 | 44.2 |
| 1950 | 48 | 150,697,361 | 14.5 | 50.7 |
| 1960 | 50 | 179,323,175 | 19.0 | 50.6 |
| 1970 | 50 | 203,235,298 | 13.3 | 57.5 |
| 1980 | 50 | 226,504,825 | 11.4 | 64.0 |
| 1985 | 50 | 237,839,000 | 5.0 | 67.2 |
| 1990 | 50 | 250,122,000 | 5.2 | 70.6 |
| 1995 | 50 | 263,411,707 | 5.3 | 74.4 |
| 2000 | 50 | 281,421,906 | 6.8 | 77.0 |
| *2005 | 50 | 296,659,351 | 5.0 | 81.5 |

*The 2005 statistics are short term projections based on the 2000 census.

## IMMIGRATION TO THE UNITED STATES (1820–2004)

| Year | Number | Year | Number | Year | Number | Year | Number |
|---|---|---|---|---|---|---|---|
| **1820–1998** | **64,599,082** | | | | | | |
| 1820 | 8,385 | | | | | | |
| **1821–30** | **143,439** | **1871–80** | **2,812,191** | **1921–30** | **4,107,209** | **1971–80** | **4,493,314** |
| 1821 | 9,127 | 1871 | 321,350 | 1921 | 805,228 | 1971 | 370,478 |
| 1822 | 6,911 | 1872 | 404,806 | 1922 | 309,556 | 1972 | 384,685 |
| 1823 | 6,354 | 1873 | 459,803 | 1923 | 522,919 | 1973 | 400,063 |
| 1824 | 7,912 | 1874 | 313,339 | 1924 | 706,896 | 1974 | 394,861 |
| 1825 | 10,199 | 1875 | 227,498 | 1925 | 294,314 | 1975 | 386,194 |
| 1826 | 10,837 | 1876 | 169,986 | 1926 | 304,488 | 1976 | 398,613 |
| 1827 | 18,875 | 1877 | 141,857 | 1927 | 335,175 | 1976, TQ[1] | 103,676 |
| 1828 | 27,382 | 1878 | 138,469 | 1928 | 307,255 | 1977 | 462,315 |
| 1829 | 22,520 | 1879 | 177,826 | 1929 | 279,678 | 1978 | 601,442 |
| 1830 | 23,322 | 1880 | 457,257 | 1930 | 241,700 | 1979 | 460,348 |
| | | | | | | 1980 | 530,639 |
| **1831–40** | **599,125** | **1881–90** | **5,246,613** | **1931–40** | **528,431** | | |
| 1831 | 22,633 | 1881 | 669,431 | 1931 | 97,139 | **1981–90** | **7,338,062** |
| 1832 | 60,482 | 1822 | 788,992 | 1932 | 35,576 | 1981 | 596,600 |
| 1833 | 58,640 | 1883 | 603,322 | 1933 | 23,068 | 1982 | 594,131 |
| 1834 | 65,365 | 1884 | 518,592 | 1934 | 29,470 | 1983 | 559,763 |
| 1835 | 45,374 | 1885 | 395,346 | 1935 | 34,956 | 1984 | 543,903 |
| 1836 | 76,242 | 1886 | 334,203 | 1936 | 36,329 | 1985 | 570,009 |
| 1837 | 79,340 | 1887 | 490,109 | 1937 | 50,244 | 1986 | 601,708 |
| 1838 | 38,914 | 1888 | 546,889 | 1938 | 67,895 | 1987 | 601,516 |
| 1839 | 68,069 | 1889 | 444,427 | 1939 | 82,998 | 1988 | 643,025 |
| 1840 | 84,066 | 1890 | 455,302 | 1940 | 70,756 | 1989 | 1,090,924 |
| | | | | | | 1990 | 1,536,483 |
| **1841–50** | **1,713,251** | **1891–1900** | **3,687,564** | **1941–50** | **1,035,039** | | |
| 1841 | 80,289 | 1891 | 560,319 | 1941 | 51,776 | **1991–98** | **7,605,068** |
| 1842 | 104,565 | 1892 | 579,663 | 1942 | 28,781 | 1991 | 1,827,167 |
| 1843 | 52,496 | 1893 | 439,730 | 1943 | 23,725 | 1992 | 973,977 |
| 1844 | 78,615 | 1894 | 285,631 | 1944 | 28,551 | 1993 | 904,292 |
| 1845 | 114,371 | 1895 | 258,536 | 1945 | 38,119 | 1994 | 804,416 |
| 1846 | 154,416 | 1896 | 343,267 | 1946 | 108,721 | 1995 | 720,461 |
| 1847 | 234,968 | 1897 | 230,832 | 1947 | 147,292 | 1996 | 915,900 |
| 1848 | 226,527 | 1898 | 229,299 | 1948 | 170,570 | 1997 | 798,378 |
| 1849 | 297,024 | 1899 | 311,715 | 1949 | 188,317 | 1998 | 654,451 |
| 1850 | 369,980 | 1900 | 448,572 | 1950 | 249,187 | 1999 | 646,568 |
| | | | | | | 2000 | 849,807 |
| **1851–60** | **2,598,214** | **1901–10** | **8,795,386** | **1951–60** | **2,515,479** | | |
| 1851 | 379,466 | 1901 | 487,918 | 1951 | 205,717 | 2001 | 1,064,318 |
| 1852 | 371,603 | 1902 | 648,743 | 1952 | 265,520 | 2002 | 1,063,732 |
| 1853 | 368,645 | 1903 | 857,046 | 1953 | 170,434 | 2003 | 705,827 |
| 1854 | 427,833 | 1904 | 812,870 | 1954 | 208,177 | 2004 | 946,142 |
| 1855 | 200,877 | 1905 | 1,026,499 | 1955 | 237,790 | | |
| 1856 | 200,436 | 1906 | 1,100,735 | 1956 | 321,625 | | |
| 1857 | 251,306 | 1907 | 1,285,349 | 1957 | 326,867 | | |
| 1858 | 123,126 | 1908 | 782,870 | 1958 | 253,265 | | |
| 1859 | 121,282 | 1909 | 751,786 | 1959 | 260,686 | | |
| 1860 | 153,640 | 1910 | 1,041,570 | 1960 | 265,398 | | |
| **1861–70** | **2,314,824** | **1911–20** | **5,735,811** | **1961–70** | **3,321,677** | | |
| 1861 | 91,918 | 1911 | 878,587 | 1961 | 271,344 | | |
| 1862 | 91,985 | 1912 | 838,172 | 1962 | 283,763 | | |
| 1863 | 176,282 | 1913 | 1,197,892 | 1963 | 306,260 | | |
| 1864 | 193,418 | 1914 | 1,218,480 | 1964 | 292,248 | | |
| 1865 | 248,120 | 1915 | 326,700 | 1965 | 296,697 | | |
| 1866 | 318,568 | 1916 | 298,826 | 1966 | 323,040 | | |
| 1867 | 315,722 | 1917 | 295,403 | 1967 | 361,972 | | |
| 1868 | 138,840 | 1918 | 110,618 | 1968 | 454,448 | | |
| 1869 | 352,768 | 1919 | 141,132 | 1969 | 358,579 | | |
| 1870 | 387,203 | 1920 | 430,001 | 1970 | 373,326 | | |

[1] Transition quarter, July 1 through September 30, 1976.

NOTE: The numbers shown are as follows: from 1820 to 1867, figures represent alien passengers arrived at seaports; from 1868 to 1892 and 1895 to 1897, immigrant aliens arrived; from 1892 to 1894 and 1898 to 1998, immigrant aliens admitted for permanent residence. From 1892 to 1903, aliens entering by cabin class were not counted as immigrants. Land arrivals were not completely enumerated until 1908.

## PRESIDENTS, VICE-PRESIDENTS, AND SECRETARIES OF STATE

| President | Vice-President | Secretary of State |
|---|---|---|
| 1. George Washington, Federalist 1789 | John Adams, Federalist 1789 | Thomas Jefferson 1789<br>Edmund Randolph 1794<br>Timothy Pickering 1795 |
| 2. John Adams, Federalist 1797 | Thomas Jefferson, Democratic-Republican 1797 | Timothy Pickering 1797<br>John Marshall 1800 |
| 3. Thomas Jefferson, Democratic-Republican 1801 | Aaron Burr, Democratic-Republican 1801<br>George Clinton, Democratic-Republican 1805 | James Madison 1801 |
| 4. James Madison, Democratic-Republican 1809 | George Clinton, Democratic-Republican 1809<br>Elbridge Gerry, Democratic-Republican 1813 | Robert Smith 1809<br>James Monroe 1811 |
| 5. James Monroe, Democratic-Republican 1817 | Daniel D. Tompkins, Democratic-Republican 1817 | John Q. Adams 1817 |
| 6. John Quincy Adams, Democratic-Republican 1825 | John C. Calhoun, Democratic-Republican 1825 | Henry Clay 1825 |
| 7. Andrew Jackson, Democratic 1829 | John C. Calhoun, Democratic 1829<br>Martin Van Buren, Democratic 1833 | Martin Van Buren 1829<br>Edward Livingston 1831<br>Louis McLane 1833<br>John Forsyth 1834 |
| 8. Martin Van Buren, Democratic 1837 | Richard M. Johnson, Democratic 1837 | John Forsyth 1837 |
| 9. William H. Harrison, Whig 1841 | John Tyler, Whig 1841 | Daniel Webster 1841 |
| 10. John Tyler, Whig and Democratic 1841 | None | Daniel Webster 1841<br>Hugh S. Legaré 1843<br>Abel P. Upshur 1843<br>John C. Calhoun 1844 |
| 11. James K. Polk, Democratic 1845 | George M. Dallas, Democratic 1845 | James Buchanan 1845 |
| 12. Zachary Taylor, Whig 1849 | Millard Fillmore, Whig 1849 | John M. Clayton 1849 |
| 13. Millard Fillmore, Whig 1850 | None | Daniel Webster 1850<br>Edward Everett 1852 |
| 14. Franklin Pierce, Democratic 1853 | William R. King, Democratic 1853 | William L. Marcy 1853 |
| 15. James Buchanan, Democratic 1857 | John C. Breckinridge, Democratic 1857 | Lewis Cass 1857<br>Jeremiah S. Black 1860 |
| 16. Abraham Lincoln, Republican 1861 | Hannibal Hamlin, Republican 1861<br>Andrew Johnson, Unionist 1865 | William H. Seward 1861 |
| 17. Andrew Johnson, Unionist 1865 | None | William H. Seward 1865 |

| President | Vice-President | Secretary of State |
|---|---|---|
| 18. Ulysses S. Grant, Republican 1869 | Schuyler Colfax, Republican 1869<br>Henry Wilson, Republican 1873 | Elihu B. Washburne 1869<br>Hamilton Fish 1869 |
| 19. Rutherford B. Hayes, Republican 1877 | William A. Wheeler, Republican 1877 | William M. Evarts 1877 |
| 20. James A. Garfield, Republican 1881 | Chester A. Arthur, Republican 1881 | James G. Blaine 1881 |
| 21. Chester A. Arthur, Republican 1881 | None | Frederick T. Frelinghuysen 1881 |
| 22. Grover Cleveland, Democratic 1885 | Thomas A. Hendricks, Democratic 1885 | Thomas F. Bayard 1885 |
| 23. Benjamin Harrison, Republican 1889 | Levi P. Morton, Republican 1889 | James G. Blaine 1889<br>John W. Foster 1892 |
| 24. Grover Cleveland, Democratic 1893 | Adlai E. Stevenson, Democratic 1893 | Walter Q. Gresham 1893<br>Richard Olney 1895 |
| 25. William McKinley, Republican 1897 | Garret A. Hobart, Republican 1897<br>Theodore Roosevelt, Republican 1901 | John Sherman 1897<br>William R. Day 1898<br>John Hay, 1898 |
| 26. Theodore Roosevelt, Republican 1901 | Charles Fairbanks, Republican 1905 | John Hay 1901<br>Elihu Root 1905<br>Robert Bacon 1909 |
| 27. William H. Taft, Republican 1909 | James S. Sherman, Republican 1909 | Philander C. Knox 1909 |
| 28. Woodrow Wilson, Democratic 1913 | Thomas R. Marshall, Democratic 1913 | William J. Bryan 1913<br>Robert Lansing 1915<br>Bainbridge Colby 1920 |
| 29. Warren G. Harding, Republican 1921 | Calvin Coolidge, Republican 1921 | Charles E. Hughes 1921 |
| 30. Calvin Coolidge, Republican 1923 | Charles G. Dawes, Republican 1925 | Charles E. Hughes 1923<br>Frank B. Kellogg 1925 |
| 31. Herbert Hoover, Republican 1929 | Charles Curtis, Republican 1929 | Henry L. Stimson 1929 |
| 32. Franklin D. Roosevelt, Democratic 1933 | John Nance Garner, Democratic 1933<br>Henry A. Wallace, Democratic 1941<br>Harry S. Truman, Democratic 1945 | Cordell Hull 1933<br>Edward R. Stettinius Jr. 1944 |
| 33. Harry S. Truman, Democratic 1945 | Alben W. Barkley, Democratic 1949 | Edward R. Stettinius Jr. 1945<br>James F. Byrnes 1945<br>George C. Marshall 1947<br>Dean G. Acheson 1949 |
| 34. Dwight D. Eisenhower, Republican 1953 | Richard M. Nixon, Republican 1953 | John F. Dulles 1953<br>Christian A. Herter 1959 |

| President | Vice-President | Secretary of State |
|---|---|---|
| 35. John F. Kennedy, Democratic 1961 | Lyndon B. Johnson, Democratic 1961 | Dean Rusk 1961 |
| 36. Lyndon B. Johnson, Democratic 1963 | Hubert H. Humphrey, Democratic 1965 | Dean Rusk 1963 |
| 37. Richard M. Nixon, Republican 1969 | Spiro T. Agnew, Republican 1969<br>Gerald R. Ford, Republican 1973 | William P. Rogers 1969<br>Henry Kissinger 1973 |
| 38. Gerald R. Ford, Republican 1974 | Nelson Rockefeller, Republican 1974 | Henry Kissinger 1974 |
| 39. Jimmy Carter, Democratic 1977 | Walter Mondale, Democratic 1977 | Cyrus Vance 1977<br>Edmund Muskie 1980 |
| 40. Ronald Reagan, Republican 1981 | George Bush, Republican 1981 | Alexander Haig 1981<br>George Shultz 1982 |
| 41. George Bush, Republican 1989 | J. Danforth Quayle, Republican 1989 | James A. Baker 1989<br>Lawrence Eagleburger 1992 |
| 42. William J. Clinton, Democratic 1993 | Albert Gore Jr., Democratic 1993 | Warren Christopher 1993<br>Madeleine Albright 1997 |
| 43. George W. Bush, Republican 2001 | Richard B. Cheney, Republican 2001 | Colin L. Powell 2001<br>Condoleeza Rice 2005 |

## Chapter 1

**pp. 2–3:** Bridgeman Art Library; **p. 5:** Granger Collection; **p. 7:** British Library; **p. 10:** Bettmann/Corbis; **p. 12:** North Wind Picture Archives; **p. 13:** Ohio Historical Society; **p. 14:** David Muench/Corbis; **p. 15:** From the Henry Whelpley Memorial Collection at the Saint Louis Science Center; **p. 16:** Bridgeman-Giraudon/Art Resource, NY; **p. 17:** The British Museum; **p. 19:** The Metropolitan Museum of Art, Gift of J. Pierpont Morgan, 1900 (00.18.2) Photograph © 1979 The Metropolitan Museum of Art; **p. 20:** Granger Collection; **p. 24:** Library of Congress; **p. 25:** Biblioteca Apostolica Vaticana; **p. 27:** Scala/Art Resource, NY; **p. 29:** Courtesy of James Q. Jacobs; **p. 30:** Granger Collection; **p. 32:** Bildarchiv Preussischer Kulturbesitz/Art Resource, NY; **p. 33:** Library of Congress.

## Chapter 2

**p. 36:** The British Museum; **p. 38: (left)** Bettmann/Corbis; **(right):** H. Henry Meeter Center, Michigan; **p. 39:** Courtesy of the National Portrait Gallery, London; **p. 40:** National Maritime Museum, London; **p. 43:** Granger Collection; **p. 46:** Collection of the New-York Historical Society; **p. 47:** The New York Public Library: Astor, Lenox and Tilden Foundations, I.N. Phelps Stokes Collection; **p. 49:** Courtesy Ashmolean Museum, University of Oxford; **p. 50:** The British Museum; **p. 51:** Bettmann/Corbis; **p. 52:** Corbis; **p. 53:** The Library of Virginia; **p. 55:** Private Collection, © Philip Mould, Historical Portraits Ltd, London/Bridgeman Art Library; **p. 57:** Worcester Art Museum, Worcester, Massachusetts. Gift of Mr. and Mrs. Albert W. Rice; **p. 58:** Courtesy, American Antiquarian Society; **p. 63:** Warder Collection; **p. 66:** The Library Company of Philadelphia; **p. 67:** Yale Collection of Western Americana, Beinecke Rare Book and Manuscript Library; **p. 68:** Jeffrey Howe; **p. 69:** Smithsonian Institution, National Museum of American History, Behring Center. Photography by Michael Freeman.

## Chapter 3

**p. 73:** The Pennsylvania Academy of Fine Arts, Philadelphia. Gift of Mrs. Sarah Harrison (The Joseph Harrison, Jr. Collection); **p. 75:** Ham House, Surrey, The Stapleton Collection/Bridgeman Art Library; **p. 77:** Courtesy, Museum of Fine Arts, Boston, Bequest of Maxim Karolik; **p. 78:** The Historical Society of Pennsylvania; **p. 79:** The Library Company of Philadelphia; **p. 80:** Haffenreffer Museum of Anthropology, Brown University; **p. 84:** Granger Collection; **p. 86:** Colonial Williamsburg Foundation, Abby Aldrich Rockefeller Folk Art Museum, Williamsburg, VA; **p. 91:** Library and Archives Canada; **p. 92:** Courtesy, Newberry Library, Chicago; **p. 93:** North Wind Picture Archives; **p. 94:** Corbis; **p. 97:** Courtesy, American Antiquarian Society; **p. 98:** Lambeth Palace Library.

## Chapter 4

**p. 103:** Courtesy of the Harvard University Portrait Collection, Bequest of Dr. John Collins Warren, 1856, H47. Photo credit: Katya Kallsen; Image copyright: © 2004 President and Fellows of Harvard College; **p. 106:** Courtesy of the Longmeadow Historical Society; **p. 109:** Langden H. Brown, Conestoga Wagon, Index of American Design. Photograph © 2001 Board of Trustees, National Gallery of Art, Washington, DC; **p. 112:** Courtesy, American Antiquarian Society; **p. 113:** National Maritime Museum, London; **p. 114:** Colonial Williamsburg Foundation, Abby Aldrich Rockefeller Folk Art Museum, Williamsburg, VA; **p. 115:** Charleston Library Society, Charleston, SC; **p. 116:** Schomburg Center for Research in Black Culture, Photographs and Prints Division, New York Public Library; **p. 117:** Library of Congress; **p. 119: (left)** From a 1912 postcard. Courtesy, Jeffrey Howe; **(right)** Wadsworth Athenaeum, Hartford, CT; **p. 120:** Collection of the Library of the Earl of Derby, Knowsley, Prescot, Lancashire, England; **p. 123:** Bettmann/Corbis; **p. 124:** The Royal Collection © 2001. Her Majesty Queen Elizabeth II; **p. 126:** The Burndy Library, Dibner Institute for the History of Science and Technology, Massachusetts Institute of Technology; **p. 128:** Courtesy of the Bostonian Society/Old State House; **p. 129:** Courtesy of the National Portrait Gallery, London; **p. 131:** Courtesy of the National Portrait Gallery, London; **p. 133:** Washington and Lee University, Lexington, VA; **p. 135:** National Gallery of Canada, Ottawa; **p. 136:** Library of Congress.

## Chapter 5

**pp. 138–139:** Courtesy, Winterthur Museum; **p. 141:** Granger Collection; **p. 145:** Granger Collection; **p. 147:** The New York

New York Public Library; **p. 500:** Granger Collection; **p. 501:** Granger Collection; **p. 502:** Granger Collection; **p. 503:** (**both**) North Wind Picture Archives; **p. 504:** Granger Collection; **p. 506:** Granger Collection.

## Chapters 18

**pp. 510–511:** George Bellows, *Cliff Dwellers* (1913). Oil on canvas. Los Angeles County Museum of Art, Los Angeles County Fund. Photograph © 2003 Museum Associates/LACMA; **p. 513:** Granger Collection; **p. 515:** (**left**) Culver Pictures; (**right**) North Wind Picture Archive; **p. 516:** Granger Collection; **p. 518:** Granger Collection; **p. 520:** Granger Collection; **p. 522:** Granger Collection; **p. 524:** Granger Collection; **p. 525:** Granger Collection; **p. 526:** Granger Collection; **p. 528:** Granger Collection; **p. 529:** Granger Collection; **p. 531:** Corbis; **p. 532:** Granger Collection; **p. 533:** Granger Collection; **p. 534:** Granger Collection; **p. 535:** Granger Collection; **p. 538:** Library of Congress.

## Chapter 19

**p. 540:** Granger Collection; **p. 542:** Corbis; **p. 543:** Granger Collection; **p. 544:** Schomberg Center for Research in Black Culture: Photographs & Prints Division; The New York Public Library; **p. 546:** Culver Pictures; **p. 547:** North Wind Picture Archives; **p. 548:** Granger Collection; **p. 549:** Granger Collection; **p. 550:** Granger Collection; **p. 554:** Culver Pictures; **p. 555:** Granger Collection; **p. 558:** Granger Collection; **p. 560:** Granger Collection; **p. 561:** Granger Collection; **p. 562:** Corbis; **p. 566:** Jefferson Medical College, Thomas Jefferson University, Philadelphia.

## Chapter 20

**p. 569:** Granger Collection; **p. 571:** Library of Congress; **p. 573:** Bettmann/Corbis; **p. 576:** Granger Collection; **p. 577:** Bettmann/Corbis; **p. 578:** (**left**) Library of Congress; (**right**) Corbis; **p. 579:** Granger Collection; **p. 580:** (**both**) Granger Collection; **p. 581:** Granger Collection; **p. 584:** Granger Collection; **p. 585:** Granger Collection; **p. 587:** SuperStock; **p. 589:** Granger Collection; **p. 590:** (**left**) Granger Collection; (**right**) Center for Pacific Northwest Studies, Western Washington University, Bellingham WA, 98225-9123; **p. 591:** Source unknown. Reprint from p. 275 of *Story of America in Pictures* by Allan C. Collins. Doubleday, New York: 1953; **p. 592:** Granger Collection; **p. 595:** North Wind Picture Archives.

## Chapter 21

**p. 598:** Granger Collection; **p. 601:** Getty Images; **p. 603:** Granger Collection; **p. 604:** Bettmann/Corbis; **p. 605:** Getty Images; **p. 606:** Corbis; **p. 607:** Granger Collection; **p.608:** Granger Collection; **p.**

610: Granger Collection; **p. 612:** Granger Collection; **p. 613:** Granger Collection; **p. 615:** Granger Collection; **p. 616:** (**both**) Corbis; **p. 619:** Bettmann/Corbis; **p. 621:** Granger Collection.

## Chapter 22

**pp. 624–625:** Thomas Hart Benton. *Changing West* from *America Today*, 1930. Distemper and egg tempera on gessoed linen with oil glaze 92 x 160 in. Collection, AXA Financial, Inc.; **p. 627:** North Wind Picture Archive; **p. 629:** Corbis; **p. 630:** Minnesota Historical Society/Corbis; **p. 631:** Schenectady Museum; Hall of Electrical History Foundation/Corbis; **p. 632:** Granger Collection; **p. 633:** Getty Images; **p. 635:** North Wind Picture Archive; **p. 636:** Library of Congress; **p. 637:** (**left**) Granger Collection; (**right**) Westerville Public Library; **p. 638:** North Wind Picture Archive; **p. 640:** (**top**) Getty Images; (**bottom**) Granger Collection; **p. 641:** Granger Collection; **p. 642:** Library of Congress; **p. 643:** Granger Collection; **p. 644:** Underwood & Underwood/Corbis; **p. 645:** Granger Collection; **p. 648:** Corbis; **p. 652:** Bettmann/Corbis; **p. 654:** Granger Collection.

## Chapter 23

**p. 657:** Granger Collection; **p. 660:** Granger Collection; **p. 661:** Granger Collection; **p. 662:** Library of Congress; **p. 664:** Granger Collection; **p. 667:** Corbis; **p. 668:** Granger Collection; **p. 669:** Corbis; **p. 672:** Granger Collection; **p. 673:** Bettmann/Corbis.

## Chapter 24

**p.676:** Chicago Historical Society; **p. 678:** Bettmann/Corbis; **p. 679:** AP/Wide World Photos; **p. 680:** Getty Images; **p. 682:** Mississippi River Flood of 1927 Album, Ms.4373, Louisiana and Lower Mississippi Valley Collections, LSU Libraries, Baton Rouge, LA.; **p. 684:** (**top**) 2002 General Motors Corporation. Used with permission of GM Media Archives; (bottom) The New York Public Library: Astor, Lenox, and Tilden Foundations; **p. 685:** George H. Clark "Radionana" Collection, Archives Center, National Museum of American History, Smithsonian Institution; **p. 687:** Bettmann/Corbis; **p. 688:** Bettmann/Corbis; **p. 689:** AP/ Wide World Photos; **p. 690:** "Fitter Families Exhibit and Examination Building, Kansas State Free Fair, Topeka" American Eugenics Society Records, American Philosophical Society; **p. 692:** Getty Images; **p. 693:** Underwood & Underwood/Corbis; **p. 695:** Bettmann/Corbis; **p. 696:** Bettmann/Corbis; **p. 697:** Granger Collection.

## Chapter 25

**p. 700:** Library of Congress; **p. 702:** Granger Collection; **p. 705:** Getty Images; **p. 706:** Granger Collection; **p. 709:** Getty Images;

p. 710: Granger Collection; p. 713: Bettmann/Corbis; p. 714: Granger Collection; p. 715: Getty Images; p. 717: Corbis; p. 718: Library of Congress; p. 719: Granger Collection; p. 720: Library of Congress; p. 722: Bettmann/Corbis; p. 723: Bettmann/Corbis; p. 725: Granger Collection; p. 726: Bettmann/Corbis; p. 729: TRH Pictures; p. 730: Corbis; p. 731: Granger Collection.

**Chapter 26**

pp. 734–735: Time Life Pictures/Getty Images; p. 737: © 2005 Artist Rights Society (ARS), New York/ADAGP, Paris. Private Collection/Art Resource, NY. © 2005; p. 739: (left) Bettmann/Corbis; (right) Granger Collection; p. 744: Hulton Deutsch Collection/Corbis; p. 746: (both) Mary Evans Picture Library; p. 748: Granger Collection; p. 749: Hulton-Deutsch Collection/Corbis; p. 751: Time Life Pictures/Getty Images; p. 752: Granger Collection; p. 753: Granger Collection; p. 754: Granger Collection; p. 755: Granger Collection; p. 757: Bettmann/Corbis.

**Chapter 27**

p. 759: Granger Collection; p. 761: Corbis; p. 762: Granger Collection; p. 763: Granger Collection; p. 764: Time Life Pictures/Getty Images; p. 766: Bettmann/Corbis; p. 767: Granger Collection; p. 769: Corbis; p. 770: TRH Pictures/USMC; p. 771: Courtesy of The Bancroft Library, University of California, Berkeley; p. 775: Photos12.com - Keystone Pressedienst; p. 779: © 1945 by Bill Mauldin. Reprinted courtesy of the William Mauldin Estate. Image provided by 45th Division Museum; p. 781: Getty Images; p. 782: TRH Pictures/US Army; p. 783: National Archives; p. 785: Granger Collection; p. 786: TRH Pictures/US Air Force; p. 787: Bettmann/Corbis; p. 788: Getty Images.

**Chapter 28**

p. 790: National Motor Museum/Topham-HIP/The Image Works; p. 792: Getty Images; p. 793: Bettmann/Corbis; p. 794: Time Life Pictures/Getty Images; p. 795: The New York Public Library: Astor, Lenox, and Tilden Foundations; p. 797: Corbis; p. 798: Time Life Pictures/Getty Images; p. 799: Bettmann/Corbis; p. 800: SuperStock; p. 801: Anthony Potter Collection/Hulton Archive/Getty Images; p. 802: Bettmann/Corbis; p. 803: Bettmann/Corbis; p. 805: Bettmann/Corbis; p. 807: Baldwin H. Ward & Kathryn C. Ward/Corbis; p. 809: Bettmann/Corbis; p. 811: Getty Images; p. 813: Corbis; p. 814: Time Life Pictures/Getty Images.

**Chapter 29**

p. 818: Getty Images; p. 820: Bettmann/Corbis; p. 821: SuperStock; p. 822: Getty Images; p. 823: Hulton-Deutsch Collection/Corbis; p. 826: Sovfoto/Eastfoto; p. 828: Warder Collection; p. 829: Edwin Levick/Getty Images; p. 830: SuperStock; p. 831: Time Life Pictures/Getty Images; p. 832: Time Life Pictures/Getty Images; p. 834: Library of Congress; p. 835: Bettmann/Corbis; p. 837: Time Life Pictures/Getty Images; p. 838: Time Life Pictures/Getty Images; p. 839: Time Life Pictures/Getty Images; p. 840: SuperStock; p. 841: SuperStock; p. 842: Bettmann/Corbis; p. 846: Bettmann/Corbis; p. 847: Bettmann/Corbis; p. 848: Sovfoto/Eastfoto.

**Chapter 30**

p. 852: Wally McNamee/Corbis; p. 854: Getty Images; p. 856: Getty Images; p. 857: TRH Pictures; p. 858: Library of Congress; p. 859: RCA/Thomson; p. 861: Getty Images; p. 862: Time Life Pictures/Getty Images; p. 863: Saatchi Collection, London/SuperStock; p. 864: AP/Wide World Photos; p. 865: Getty Images; p. 868: David J. & Janice L. Frent Collection/Corbis; p. 869: Getty Images; p. 870: AP/Wide World Photos; p. 872: Getty Images; p. 875: TRH Pictures; p. 876: Getty Images; p. 877: Time Life Pictures/Getty Images; p. 879: Dan McCoy/The Image Works; p. 880: Benyas Kaufman/Stockphoto; p. 881: Bettmann/Corbis; p. 882: Bettmann/Corbis; p. 884: Getty Images; p. 885: Corbis.

**Chapter 31**

p. 888: RR # 70.014 Robert Rauschenberg *Signs* 1970. Silkscreen Print 43″ x 34″ Published by Castelli Graphics, printed by Styria Studio, Photo by Dorothy Zeidman. Art © Robert Rauschenberg. Licensed by VAGA, New York, NY; p. 891: Bettmann/Corbis; p. 893: Getty Images; p. 894: Time Life Pictures/Getty Images; p. 897: Warder Collection; p. 898: NASA/Science Source/Photo Researchers, Inc.; p. 899: Getty Images; p. 902: Bettmann/Corbis; p. 903: Bettmann/Corbis; p. 905: AP/Wide World Photos; p. 907: SuperStock; p. 909: (both) AP/Wide World Photos; p. 911: Charles E. Rotkin/Corbis; p. 912: AP/Wide World Photos; p. 913: AP/Wide World Photos; p. 914: Bettye Lane; p. 915: Bettmann/Corbis; p. 916: AP/Wide World Photos; p. 917: Wally McNamee/Corbis.

**Chapter 32**

p. 921: Getty Images; p. 924: Warder Collection; p. 925: SuperStock; p. 928: Bettmann/Corbis; p. 929: Geoff Hook; p. 931: Warder Collection; p. 934: Photofest; p. 935: Bettmann/Corbis; p. 937: Owen Franken/Corbis; p. 938: Peter Turnley/Corbis; p. 940: Time Life Pictures/Getty Images; p. 941: Photograph by Bill Bamberger; p. 942: Time Life Pictures/Getty Images.

## Chapter 33

**p. 945:** Time Life Pictures/Getty Images; **p. 947:** Courtesy of Microsoft Archives; **p. 949:** Ed Kashi/Corbis; **p. 950:** A. Barrington Brown/Photo Researchers, Inc.; **p. 952:** www.cartoonstock.com; **p. 954:** Lee Snider/Corbis; **p. 956:** Viviane Moos/Corbis; **p. 957:** Time Life Pictures/Getty Images; **p. 958:** Vanessa Vick/Photo Researchers, Inc.; **p. 959:** CWS/Cartoon Arts International (www .cartoonweb.com); **p. 960:** Ed Eckstein/Corbis; **p. 961:** (**both**) Time Life Pictures/Getty Images; **p. 961:** Time Life Pictures/ Getty Images; **p. 962:** Camilo Jose Vergara; **p. 963:** AP/Wide World Photos; **p. 964:** Getty Images; **p. 966:** AP/Wide World Photos; **p. 969:** Najlah Feanny-Hicks/Corbis.

## Chapter 34

**p. 972:** Trippett/Sipa; **p. 974:** Jeffrey Markowitz/Corbis Sygma; **p. 977:** Time Life Pictures/Getty Images; **p. 979:** DILBERT: © Scott Adams/Dist. by United Feature Syndicate, Inc.; **p. 980:** CWS/Cartoon Arts International (www.cartoonweb.com); **p. 983:** Wally McNamee/Corbis; **p. 985:** Reuters/Corbis; **p. 986:** Corbis; **p. 988:** AP/Wide World Photos; **p. 990:** © 2001, Nick Anderson. Distributed by The Washington Post Writers Group. Reprinted with Permission; **p. 992:** AP/Wide World Photos.

## Chapter 35

**p. 994:** James Nielsen/AFP/Getty Images; **p. 996:** Reuters New Media Inc./Corbis; **p. 997:** Reuters/New Media Inc./Corbis; **p. 1004:** Faleh Kheiber/Reuters/Corbis; **p. 1006:** Sebastian Scheiner/Reuters/Corbis; **p. 1010:** Polaris; **p. 1013:** AP/Wide World Photos.

p. 103; Courtesy of the Harvard University Portrait Collection, Bequest of Dr. John Collins Warren, 1856.

Volume 1 cover: Oakland Museum of California, Gift of the Women's Board.